THE CAMBRIDGE GAZETTEER OF THE UNITED STATES AND CANADA

THE CAMBRIDGE GAZETTEER OF THE UNITED STATES AND CANADA

A Dictionary of Places

Edited by

ARCHIE HOBSON

CAMBRIDGE
UNIVERSITY PRESS

Published by the Press Syndicate of the University of Cambridge
The Pitt Building, Trumpington Street, Cambridge CB2 1RP
40 West 20th Street, New York, NY 10011-4211, USA
10 Stamford Road, Oakleigh, Melbourne 3166, Australia

First published 1995

Printed in the United States of America

Library of Congress Cataloging-in-Publication Data

The Cambridge gazetteer of the United States and Canada : a dictionary of places / edited by Archie Hobson.

p. cm.

ISBN 0-521-41579-9

1. United States – Gazetteers. 2. Canada – Gazetteers. I. Hobson, Archie, 1946–
E154.C36 1995

917.3′003 – dc20 95-8898
CIP

A catalog record for this book is available from the British Library.

ISBN 0-521-41579-9 Hardback

CONTENTS

ACKNOWLEDGMENTS

Along with the editor, writers who contributed to the Gazetteer are: Carl Arnold, Patricia Chao, Jerilyn Famighetti, Sally Freeman, Lora Goldman, Douglas Jacobs, Susan Lacerte, Susan R. Norton, Patricia Olmstead, Zipporah Portugal, Phyllis Smith, and Kleo P. Xiros. Peter Brydges, Helen Chumbley, and Lora Goldman contributed to the editing process.

In addition to all the above, who were the central actors in turning out this book, I am grateful to many members of the Cambridge University Press staff: in particular, to Mike Agnes, who initiated the project; to Ken Greenhall, who encouraged me in the seemingly interminable middle stages; to Sophia Prybylski, who shepherded copy through the various steps to print; to Lisa Lincoln, who managed production; to Alan Harvey and Sheaver Woodfaulk, who got me through some of the computer challenges I encountered along the way; to Nancy Feldman, who made any number of small problems disappear; and especially to Sidney Landau, the North American Branch's reference director, who handled what I think is the unenviable task of dealing with the obsessions and delusions of a freelance editor.

To judge from current books and periodicals, proofreaders are an endangered species. It is a pleasure to report that the Gazetteer benefited throughout from the good work of W. M. Havighurst, who will notice that I did not follow *all* of his very sensible suggestions.

As a copyeditor, I have long been amazed at the ability of compositors to make sense of what we send them. The Gazetteer is filled with (often heavily edited) detail; somehow the people at Huron Valley Graphics rendered this, month after month, into strikingly clean and accurate text.

In the last phases of the book, Steve Davies and the folks at Mapping Specialists entered the picture. I had mentally pigeonholed any kind of illustration as at most an unfortunate necessity in a work I thought of as composed entirely of words. It was in fact fun, a pleasant kind of wrap-up, to work with them on the maps presented here.

I hope that my family, friends, and colleagues who offered material and psychological support throughout the project will forgive me if I do not mention them all by name, and that they will believe me when I say that they are entered in my private pantheon. I do want to mention a few special contributions. James Raimes of the Columbia University Press generously made the project a long loan (close to two years) of Columbia's set of the WPA American Guide series. Beverly

Lacerte donated a complete set of the last 40 years of the *National Geographic,* along with various other books and maps. Staff members of the Brooklyn (in my case) and other (in the case of some of the other writers and editors) public libraries did what we pay them to do but often forget to appreciate: make a vast range of information available to anyone who wants to use it. Finally, and most important, Susan Lacerte not only wrote entries for the Gazetteer; she also lived closest to it in every way, and she knows that I would not have gotten through it without her support.

INTRODUCTION AND GUIDE TO USING THE GAZETTEER

A gazetteer is a geographical reference book that has some of the characteristics of a dictionary, some of an encyclopedia. As a dictionary, a gazetteer puts emphasis on the name of a place, perhaps on the name's pronunciation and origin, and provides in addition some essential, but limited, information about the place. The gazetteer that accompanies the maps in many modern atlases, the kind probably most familiar to readers, is essentially the dictionary type, keyed to and distinctly secondary to its maps.

The Cambridge Gazetteer of the United States and Canada is primarily of the encyclopedic variety. Its aim is to provide varied and more extensive information on the places listed—information that could, of course, be expanded indefinitely, but that has here been selected to fit into a single, reasonably sized volume. On one hand the book is an exercise in compression. On the other, it is written to be read; it avoids telegraphic prose, employs a minimum of abbreviations and technical language, and is self-contained, not requiring continual reference to indexes or appendices. It is intended to serve anyone wishing to learn about the history, development, and present condition of the United States and Canada.

WHAT IS IN THE GAZETTEER?

With the exception of glossary terms, all entries in this book are for places in (or surrounding, possessed by, or otherwise affiliated with) the United States or Canada. The definition of *place* adopted here is broad; some entries, for example, answer the question whether a familiar name is that of an officially recognized locality, or belongs instead to an entity that has acquired some other kind of "reality" (as, for example, that of **Dogpatch**) in the general culture.

In designing and compiling this work, we have been driven by two aims: that it be inclusive and that our method be inductive. The two are of course interrelated: the more deductive planning is, the less inclusive the result will be. If the entries in a geographical reference book are limited to incorporated municipalities, it will exclude many of the places for which the reader may be looking; it will then be useful only within a narrow limitation. If, on the other hand, the book has been designed with its starting point the question *What might the reader be looking for?,* the task of selecting entries will be more complex, but the place sought will more likely be found.

Having said this, we admit that about one-third of the entries in the Gazetteer were selected deductively. We have included all states, provinces, and territories; their capitals; and all incorporated municipalities with a population over 10,000 in the United States or 8000 in Canada. Beyond these categories, however, everything in the book has been chosen for inclusion on our prediction, based on preliminary scans of a wide variety of sources, that it is something that will be looked for. It may be a place likely to appear in the news in coming years; it may be a place that figures in some period or aspect of our history; it may be important in any of a number of cultural contexts; its name may have acquired generic or metaphorical importance; it may be encountered in travel; and so on.

Here are examples of the kinds of entries included in this book that would have been omitted if we had hewed more closely to official designations and the scope of earlier gazetteers: neighborhoods and other features of major cities; municipalities that have ceased to exist officially or that have become parts of others; regional names of varying degrees of popular currency; active and historic military sites; industrial sites (like nuclear power plants); national forests and other reserves; legendary or never clearly identified places. While obviously we cannot pretend to have considered every possible source of users' interests, we will say that the effort we put into the first stage of the work, identifying the reasons why a place should be included, has produced a book we think will be useful to a wide range of readers.

Using the Gazetteer

Entry structure Typically, an entry first gives the name of a place, and defines it (as a city, neighborhood, region, historical site, etc.). Its size (in terms of population or physical extent, or both) is given, and the entry tells where it is (for instance, in what county or sector of what state or province, and how far from some familiar point of reference, like the state's major city). The rest of the entry is designed to respond to two related questions: *What is the essence of this place?* and *Why is this place of enough interest to merit inclusion in this book?*

Glossary Glossary entries comprise a mix of geological, other physical, historical, and governmental terms that are used throughout the text and that in our opinion warrant definition. Glossary entries are dispersed among and alphabetized along with place-name entries; a separate list of those included also appears on pages xii–xiii.

Maps The map section (at the end of the book) is intended to supplement the text. Illustrating selected metropolitan areas, physiographic provinces, and historical themes, the maps are intended to suggest patterns of relationship among entries—for instance, municipalities and neighborhoods in a metropolitan area, or entries germane to an historical category (like the Civil War). Although the location of every place in the book is described in its entry, the maps can often help to provide a visual reference to site one place in the context of others.

Cross-referencing Cross-referencing, indicated by the use of small capitals (BOSTON, the SOUTH, WESTCHESTER Co., etc.), refers the reader to related entries likely to be useful in further defining or characterizing the place or thing described in the primary entry. Cross-references appear within as well as at the end of entries. Thus, in the following entry for **Whiting,** the reader is referred to HAMMOND, EAST CHICAGO, and the CALUMET region.

> **Whiting** city, pop. 5155, Lake Co., extreme NW Indiana, adjacent (N) to HAMMOND (W) and EAST CHICAGO (E), on L. Michigan. In the highly industrialized CALUMET area, just SE of Chicago, it has large oil refineries, and manufactures chemicals and soap.

Some of the longer entries (such as those for major cities) are followed by cross-reference lists indicating places within them. Major city entries often also contain shorter lists referring to metropolitan county entries. Brief entries headed **United States of America** and **Canada** list the constituent parts of the two nations, as well as the US possessions and affiliated entities also included in the book.

Sources Sources for this book include general and specialized reference works; government statistics and other official information; travel literature; material from regional and local governments and chambers of commerce; a variety of maps and atlases; information collected from newspapers and other periodicals and news sources; and a wide range of histories, cultural studies, scientific works, and specialized handbooks. Official (government) names and figures have been used where available; with all other information, we have used our best judgment, choosing where necessary among differing sources. Population figures are drawn, except where otherwise indicated, from the 1990 US and 1991 Canadian censuses. Distances, heights, areas, and volumes are converted from English to metric figures for US places and from metric to English figures for Canadian places, and both are given in every appearance.

Terminology *Large* in this book refers to physical size; when population size is meant, *populous* is used. *1900s* refers to the period 1900–09, not the entire 20th century. In describing area sectors (but not compass direction), *C* (for "central") is used, as well as *N, S, W,* and *E.*

Archie Hobson

GLOSSARY ENTRIES

The following terms are defined in entries that appear in the main text of the Gazetteer:

alluvial
Amtrak
Anasazi
aquifer
Army Corps of Engineers
arroyo
atoll
badlands
bald
bank: *see* continental shelf
barrier beach (and barrier island)
barrio
base line
batholith
bayou
beltway
bluff
bore, tidal
borough
box canyon
Bureau of Land Management: *see* public lands
butte
caldera
canyon
caprock: *see* plateau
Carolina bay
census designated place: *see* unincorporated community
chaparral
cirque
city
colonia: *see* barrio
colony
commonwealth
company town
comunidad: *see* zona urbana
Confederation
continental divide
continental shelf
cordillera
coteau
coulee
county
coureurs de bois
creek
crown lands
cuesta
Dene
dissected plateau: *see* plateau
distributary
district
division point
Dominion: *see* Confederation
drift: *see* moraine
edge city
esker
exurb
factory: *see* Hudson's Bay Company
fall line
fault
fjord
flyway
free trade zone
frontier
fumarole
gentrification
geyser
ghetto
ghost town
greenbelt
hamlet
homestead
Hudson's Bay Company
hundred

independent city
Indian reservation or reserve
infrastructure
inner city
interurban
Inuit
kame
kill
lagoon
landfill
land-grant
levee
light rail
loess
Loyalists (United Empire Loyalists)
maquiladora
mesa
Métis
metropolitan area
metropolitan government
mill village: *see* company town
mint
mission
moraine
Mound Builders
municipality
municipio
muskeg
national forest
national grassland
national park (and related entities)
North West Company
outport
oxbow
parish
pass
patriotes
patroonship
permafrost
petroglyph
pictograph: *see* petroglyph
placer
plantation
plat
plate, tectonic
plateau
playa
portage
post road
prairie
presidio
province
public lands
pueblo
ranchería
rancho
red-light district
region
resaca
ribbon farm: *see* seigneurie
run
rural
salt dome
scablands
seigneurie
sierra
sink
sinkhole
skid road or skidway
state
streetcar suburb
subbarrio: *see* barrio
suburb
Superfund site
Tennessee Valley Authority
territory
theme park
till: *see* moraine
town
township
tribal jurisdiction statistical area
trunk line
tundra
turnpike
unincorporated community
urban
urban homesteading: *see* homestead
urban renewal
VIA (Rail Canada)
village
ville
voyageurs: *see* coureurs de bois
wetlands
white flight
wilderness area
wildlife refuge
wild, scenic, and recreational rivers
WPA
zona urbana

ABBREVIATIONS

State, province, and territory names are not abbreviated (except for *District of Columbia* in "Washington, D.C.").

ac	acre or acres
Ave.	Avenue
Blvd.	Boulevard
C	central or central part
C.F.B.	Canadian Forces Base
cm	centimeter or centimeters
CMSA	consolidated metropolitan statistical area
Co.	County (Note: *Company* is not abbreviated)
cu	cubic (in measures of volume, as *cu yd*)
E	east or eastern
esp.	especially
est.	established
ft	foot or feet
ha	hectare or hectares
I	Interstate (in highway names, as *I-80*)
I.	Island or Île
in	inch or inches
Is.	Islands or Îles (in group names only, as *Thousand Is.*)
km	kilometer or kilometers
L.	Lake or Lac (names)
Ls.	Lakes or Lacs (in group names only, as *Kawartha Ls.*)
m	meter or meters
mi	mile or miles
MSA	metropolitan statistical area
Mt.	Mount, Mountain, or Mont
Mts.	Mountains or Monts (in group names only)
N	north or northern
NASA	National Aeronautics and Space Administration
pop.	population
R.	River, Rivière, or Río
Rte.	Route
S	south or southern
sq	square (in measures of area, as *sq mi*)
St.	Saint (preceding a name) or Street (Note: *State* is not abbreviated)
Ste.	Sainte
Univ.	University
US	United States of America; also used in some highway names (e.g., *US 1*)
W	west or western
yd	yard or yards

THE CAMBRIDGE GAZETTEER OF THE UNITED STATES AND CANADA

Abbeville **1.** city, pop. 11,187, seat of Vermilion Parish, S Louisiana, on the Vermilion R., 17 mi/27 km SSW of Lafayette and 16 mi/26 km N of Vermilion Bay, in the Gulf of Mexico. Founded by a Capuchin missionary in 1843, it was settled by Acadians and Mediterranean immigrants, and is in the heart of CAJUN COUNTRY. Originally La Chapelle, and modeled after a provincial French village, it was built around a chapel destroyed by fire in 1854. It is a market center for farms producing rice, sugar cane, and other crops, and a service center amid natural gas fields. Dairy goods, seafood, and beef are also produced locally. **2.** city, pop. 5778, seat of Abbeville Co. (pop. 23,862), NW South Carolina, 13 mi/21 km W of Greenwood. A trade and processing center, it produces cotton textiles, cottonseed oil, and grain. John C. Calhoun was born (1782) near here and practiced law in Abbeville. The city is known as the Birthplace (or Cradle) of the Confederacy, and can be considered the scene of its death as well; the first Secession meeting took place here (Nov. 22, 1860), as did Jefferson Davis's last Confederate cabinet meeting (May 2, 1865). Abbeville's Opera House (1908) was once a famous vaudeville theater.

Abbotsford district municipality, pop. 18,864, Central Fraser Valley Regional District, SW British Columbia, S of the Fraser R., 42 mi/68 km ESE of Vancouver and 6 mi/10 km N of the Washington border. A railway and road junction, it has traditionally engaged in dairying, clay quarrying, brickmaking, and the production of strawberries, hops, and raspberries, but is increasingly industrial and suburban. The Abbotsford International Air Show is held in MATSQUI (W) in Aug.

Abegweit Micmac (Algonquian) name for PRINCE EDWARD ISLAND, usually translated as "cradled in the waves." The Micmac traditionally summered on the island, living on fish and shellfish, then returned to the New Brunswick–Nova Scotia mainland for the winter.

Aberdeen **1.** town, pop. 13,087, Harford Co., NE Maryland, at the head of Chesapeake Bay, 29 mi/47 km ENE of Baltimore. Settled around 1800, it is a primarily residential town with some light industry, including vegetable canning and the manufacture of concrete pipe, paint remover, refrigerated display cases, and rubber products. The **Aberdeen Proving Ground,** an Army ordnance test center (pop. 5267) is just S, along the bay; with adjoining (SW) EDGEWOOD Arsenal it occupies 87,000 ac/35,235 ha, and is the area's major employer. **2.** city, pop. 6837, seat of Monroe Co., NE Mississippi, 23 mi/37 km NNW of Columbus, on the East Fork of the TOMBIGBEE R. Once the river's head of navigation, it is now a port on the Tennessee-Tombigbee Waterway. A cotton market since before the Civil War, it now also processes timber and dairy goods. **3.** city, pop. 24,927, seat of Brown Co., NE South Dakota, on the James R., 75 mi/121 km NNW of Huron. Founded in 1881, it is the hub of a multimillion-dollar dairy industry, and dairy processing plants are a major basis of its economy. Set in a rich agricultural area, it is also a wholesale and retail marketing center for livestock and cereals. Automotive tools, oxygen and acetylene gas, wood products, computer parts, and farm implements are among the city's manufactures. It is the seat of Northern State College (1901) and Presentation College (1951). **4.** city, pop. 16,565, Grays Harbor Co., W Washington, at the spot where the Chehalis R. empties into GRAYS HARBOR, 37 mi/60 km W of Olympia. The twin city of HOQUIAM (immediately W), it is a port of entry and an important lumbering and fishing center. Other industries include dairying and canning. Grays Harbor College (1930) is here.

Abert Rim highest known exposed geologic FAULT in North America, extending generally N–S for 30 mi/50 km and rising over 2000 ft/610 m above the E shore of saline L. Abert, in S Oregon, 80 mi/130 km ENE of Klamath Falls. The Rim extends S into the FREMONT NATIONAL FOREST.

Abilene **1.** city, pop. 6242, seat of Dickinson Co., EC Kansas, on the Smoky Hill R., 22 mi/35 km NE of Salina. Settled in 1858, it became the first railhead of the Union Pacific Railroad at the N terminus of the CHISHOLM TRAIL from Texas (1867–71), a leading distribution point for cattle from the SW. It was also a stopping point on the Smoky Hill Trail to the W. One of the most famous of the wide-open cow towns, it was "cleaned up" by Wild Bill Hickok, who became its marshal in 1871. Today the city remains a leading shipping point for livestock, as well as for grain, melons, and dairy products; greyhounds are raised and raced in Abilene. Tourists are drawn to the city's 19th-century sites and to Dwight D. Eisenhower's boyhood home, presidential library, and grave. **2.** city, pop. 106,654, seat of Taylor Co., also in Jones Co., NC Texas, near the Clear Fork of the Brazos R., 137 mi/220 km WSW of Fort Worth, on the Osage Plains. Founded in 1881 as a railhead of the Texas and Pacific Railway for cattle drives, it took its name from Abilene, Kansas, a prior railhead. At the center of an oil and natural gas producing region, it now has many oil company offices. Ranching and farming are also important, producing cotton, peanuts, wheat, feed, grain, pecans, and beef cattle. The West Texas

Fair and other cattle shows and rodeos are held here. Manufactures include clothing, aerospace equipment, concrete, structural steel, electrical appliances, processed food, and musical instruments. The city is the seat of Hardin-Simmons University (1891), Abilene Christian University (1906), and McMurry College (1923). Dyess Air Force Base is adjacent (W). Old Abilene Town is a reconstruction of a frontier community, and Buffalo Gap frontier village is nearby.

Abingdon **1.** village in Harford Co., NE Maryland, 21 mi/34 km ENE of Baltimore, near the Bush R. and the ABERDEEN Proving Ground. The settlement was founded in 1779 by William Paca, signer of the Declaration of Independence. Cokesbury College, the first Methodist college in the Western Hemisphere, was here 1785–95. **2.** town, pop. 7003, seat of Washington Co., SW Virginia, 15 mi/24 km NE of BRISTOL, near the Tennessee line. In a farming and dairying region of the Great Appalachian Valley, it is a trade center for tobacco and grain growers. Black's Fort (1776) was attacked by Indians in the 18th century, and the town was burned by Union troops in 1864. Barter Theater (1933) is well known. Virginia Highlands Community College (1967) is here.

Abington township, pop. 56,322, Montgomery Co., SE Pennsylvania, 12 mi/19 km NNE of Philadelphia, just S of the Pennsylvania Turnpike. An aggregation of residential and commercial suburbs, it includes Ardsley, Abington, Meadowbrook, part of GLENSIDE, and other communities. Penn State University's Ogontz campus (1950) is here.

Abiquiu hamlet in Rio Arriba Co., N New Mexico, in the N foothills of the Valle Grande Mts., on the Rio Chama, 40 mi/64 km NNW of Sante Fe. This ranching community built on Tewa pueblo ruins was formerly a stop on the Spanish Trail to Los Angeles. It is best known as the home of the painter Georgia O'Keeffe (1887–1986).

Abitibi, Lake in NE Ontario and W Québec, 175 mi/280 km S of James Bay, in the CLAY BELT. Comprising two irregularly shaped lakes joined by a narrows, it covers 360 sq mi/930 sq km. Its forested shores support regional pulp and paper industries, esp. at Iroquois Falls, Ontario (town, pop. 5999, Cochran District), just W. Fur trading (from the late 17th century) and gold mining (in the 20th century) have been important in the area. Tourism and outdoor recreation are now key. The **Abitibi R.,** 340 mi/550 km long, issues from the lake and flows W past Iroquois Falls, then generally N through Ontario to the MOOSE R. just S of James Bay. In Québec, E of the lake, are the mining, farming, and foresting regions of **Abitibi** (pop. 25,334), centered on AMOS, and **Abitibi-Ouest,** on the Ontario border, centered on La Sarre (city, pop. 8513).

Abraham Lincoln Birthplace National Historic Site 3 mi/5 km S of the city of Hodgenville (pop. 2721), now in Larue Co., C Kentucky, on the Nolin R., 45 mi/72 km S of Louisville. In Dec. 1808, the Lincolns moved from ELIZABETHTOWN to Sinking Springs Farm, just S of Hodgens Mill (now Hodgenville); Abraham was born here on Feb. 12, 1809. The family moved two years later to Knob Creek Farm, 7 mi/11 km E of Hodgenville. A title dispute caused them to move again, to SPENCER Co., Indiana, in 1816. Lincoln Homestead State Park, in Frederickstown, Washington Co., 42 mi/68 km SW of Lexington, has a replica of the 1782 cabin in which Thomas Lincoln, Abraham's father, was raised. On the same site is Berry Cabin, original home of his mother, Nancy Hanks.

Absaroka-Beartooth Wilderness Area 944,000 ac/382,000 ha (1475 sq mi/3820 sq km), in SW Montana, with a small section in N Wyoming. Largely N and NE of YELLOWSTONE NATIONAL PARK, it is noted for its peaks in the Absaroka and BEARTOOTH ranges, for lakes, and for its wildlife.

Absaroka Range also, **Absaroka Mountains** 170 mi/274 km long and 50 mi/80 km wide, in the N Rocky Mts. of NW Wyoming and SC Montana. It runs mostly NW–SE, and has eight peaks over 12,000 ft/3660 m. At its SE end, in Wyoming, is Franks (also, Francs) Peak, the highest point in the range, at 13,140 ft/4008 m. In the Beartooth Range, a NE spur of the Absarokas, is GRANITE PEAK, the highest point in Montana.

Absecon Inlet inlet of the Atlantic Ocean into Absecon Channel and island-filled, 2.5 mi/4 km–long **Absecon Bay,** just NW of Atlantic City, in Atlantic Co., SE New Jersey. A break in the barrier beach lining the New Jersey coast, it marks the NE end of Absecon I., on which lie Atlantic City and other resorts. The resort city of **Absecon** (pop. 7298) lies on the NW shore of the bay.

Acadia French, **Acadie** historic territory, encompassing modern Nova Scotia, New Brunswick, and Prince Edward Island and parts of Maine, settled by the French in the 17th century. The source of the name is disputed, but may lie in Giovanni da Verrazzano's 1520s use of *Arcadie* (referring to the idyllic plain of classical Greece) for a larger coastal expanse. Acadia is usually considered as separate from NEW FRANCE. Jacques Cartier saw the area (which was inhabited by the Passamaquoddy, Micmac, and Malecite) in the 1530s, but the first attempt at settlement was at St. Croix (Dochet) I., in the SAINT CROIX R. between modern New Brunswick and Maine, in 1604. Harsh conditions there caused a move the next year to PORT-ROYAL, on the Annapolis R. in Nova Scotia. From there settlement spread to the MINAS BASIN and beyond; colonists were brought from Poitou and neighboring areas in W France, many of whom imported marshland farming techniques, including diking. The British, meanwhile, laid claim to the area, in 1621 naming much of it Nova Scotia; struggles between the two colonial powers continued for 150 years. In 1755, the British expelled the Acadians, although they had declared neutrality, from Nova Scotia. Their forced departure from GRAND PRÉ is the source of the *Evangeline* legend. Acadian deportees were scattered through New England and the West Indies, or returned to Europe. One group later migrated into W Louisiana, to the area now known as CAJUN COUNTRY, where they developed a distinctive culture and today constitute a large part of the pop. Acadians who avoided deportation fled to the Îles de la MADELEINE, to Québec's NORTH SHORE, and to other areas around the Gulf of St. Lawrence, but esp. to what is now N New Brunswick, where they settled in the MADAWASKA area and along the NORTH SHORE. In the late 18th century, Acadians began to return to Nova Scotia, where they concentrated chiefly on the FRENCH SHORE, along the Bay of Fundy, but also on Cape Breton I. Today the largest Acadian community in Canada is in New Brunswick, where francophones make up close to 40% of the pop. and have considerable political power. Not all of these have actual Acadian roots, but the term has come over time to include all French-speaking Maritimers.

Acadia National Park 41,400 ac/16,760 ha, in Hancock and Knox counties, SE Maine. It occupies a rugged, forested area, mostly on MOUNT DESERT Island, partly on the SCHOODIC Peninsula, and on half of ISLE AU HAUT, 25 mi/40 km SW of Mt. Desert. Established as Sieur de Monts National Monument in 1916, it was the first national park E of the Mississippi R. Hulls Cove, near Bar Harbor on Mt. Desert I., is headquarters. The park is dominated by CADILLAC Mt., and noted for its seaside beauty and abundant bird and flower species. A 1947 forest fire damaged much of the area.

Accomac town, pop. 466, seat of **Accomack County** (476 sq mi/1233 sq km, pop. 31,703), E Virginia, on the EASTERN SHORE. In a relatively undeveloped part of the state noted for its beaches and wildlife, it was the refuge of Governor William Berkeley during Bacon's Rebellion (1675–76).

Ackia also, **Chickasaw Village** battle site: see under TUPELO, Mississippi.

Ácoma also, **Sky City** PUEBLO (within Ácoma Pueblo and Trust Lands, pop. 2590), Cibola Co., NW New Mexico, 55 mi/89 km WSW of Albuquerque. On a 357 ft/109 m–high MESA, this pre-Columbian Keresan community, consisting of three-story stone and adobe buildings, is one of the oldest continuously occupied settlements in America. Seen in 1540 by one of Coronado's captains, it became a Spanish MISSION in 1598. In 1680, it joined the Pueblo Revolt. Today it draws many visitors.

Acton 1. town, pop. 17,872, Middlesex Co., E Massachusetts, 21 mi/34 km WNW of Boston. Settled about 1680, it was industrial in the 19th century, but is now essentially an affluent suburb of Boston. **2.** see under HALTON HILLS, Ontario.

Ada 1. township, pop. 7576, Kent Co., SW Michigan, at the confluence of the Thornapple and Grand rivers, 9 mi/14 km E of Grand Rapids. It is known for its covered bridge over the Thornapple and for its turn-of-the-century architecture. Situated on the Grand Trunk Railway, Ada is home to Amway's world corporate headquarters, which include a museum, research and development areas, and Michigan's largest commercial printshop. **2.** village, pop. 5413, Hardin Co., NW Ohio, 15 mi/24 km NE of Lima. Trading center for an agricultural district, it is the seat of Ohio Northern University (1871). **3.** city, pop. 15,820, seat of Pontotoc Co., SC Oklahoma, 65 mi/104 km SE of Oklahoma City. It is a market and shipping point for corn, cotton, dairy items, and livestock and for oil, which is refined here. Manufactures include cement, glass, mobile homes, and bricks. East Central University (1909) is here.

Ada County 1052 sq mi/2725 sq km, pop. 205,775, in SW Idaho, bounded by the Snake R. (SW). BOISE is the seat of this, the state's most populous county. Boise's metropolitan area and many industries dominate the N part of the county. An irrigated agricultural area in the Boise R. valley, Ada Co. produces dairy goods, sugar beets, hay, fruit, truck garden crops, alfalfa, and wine. The Snake River Birds of Prey Area is in the SE.

Adair County 570 sq mi/1476 sq km, pop. 8409, in SW Iowa. Its seat is Greenfield. The county is mostly agricultural, with corn and soybeans the main crops. Political leader Henry A. Wallace was born here (1888).

Adak Island one of the ANDREANOF Is., in the C ALEUTIAN Is., SW Alaska. Thirty mi/50 km N–S and 3–20 mi/5–32 km E–W, the mountainous, fogbound island is the site of the Adak Naval Station, established in 1942, after the Japanese attack on the W Aleutians. The antisubmarine patrol base is one of the largest settlements (pop. 4633) in the islands. The principal harbor on Adak is Sweeper Cove; the highest point is 3924-ft/1196-m Mt. Moffett.

Adams 1. town, pop. 9445, Berkshire Co., NW Massachusetts. At the foot of Mt. Greylock (W), on the Hoosic R., it is 13 mi/21 km NNE of Pittsfield. Settled in the 1760s, it was a Quaker center. The early economy was based on marble and limestone quarries, later on textile and paper factories powered by the Hoosic. Nearby forests, parks, and ski resorts provide a tourist base. The birthplace (1820) of suffrage leader Susan B. Anthony is in the town. **2.** town, pop. 4977, Jefferson Co., NC New York, 13 mi/21 km SW of Watertown. Situated in a dairying region, it has diversified light industry, chiefly in the village of Adams, on Sandy Creek. Library innovator Melvil Dewey (1851–1931) was born in Adams Center.

Adams, Mount 1. peak (5798 ft/1768 m) in the N section of the PRESIDENTIAL RANGE of the White Mountains, NC New Hampshire. The second-highest mountain of the Whites and in New England, it has several minor peaks, including John Quincy Adams (5470 ft/1668 m) and Sam Adams (5585 ft/1703 m). **2.** 12,276 ft/3742 m, in SW Yakima Co., SW Washington, a snow-capped extinct volcano in the Gifford Pinchot National Forest and in the CASCADE RANGE, 45 mi/72 km SSE of Mt. Rainier. It is Washington's second-highest peak.

Adams County 1235 sq mi/3199 sq km, pop. 265,038, in NC Colorado, traversed in the W by the South Platte R. BRIGHTON is its seat. Its SW corner is occupied by Denver suburbs, including Northglenn, Thornton, Westminster, Federal Heights, Commerce City, and Western Hills. The Rocky Mountain Arsenal is also in the SW, near Denver. The balance of the county is primarily farm and ranchland, producing sugar beets, beans, and livestock.

Adams-Morgan commercial and residential section of NW Washington, D.C., on rising ground just N of DUPONT CIRCLE and S of MOUNT PLEASANT. It is one of the District's most mixed neighborhoods, with a range of ethnic communities and businesses, and attracts tourists.

Adams National Historic Site see under QUINCY, Massachusetts.

Addison 1. village, pop. 32,058, Du Page Co., NE Illinois, on Salt Creek, 18 mi/29 km NW of Chicago. Although largely a bedroom community, it contains some foundries and a factory producing industrial heating equipment. O'Hare International Airport is 6 mi/10 km to the NE. **2.** city, pop. 8783, Dallas Co., NE Texas, 12 mi/19 km N of downtown Dallas, a growing residential suburb also known for its municipal airport.

Adelanto city, pop. 8517, San Bernardino Co., S California, in the Victor Valley, on US 395, 31 mi/50 km N of San Bernardino. In a desert region irrigated for agriculture by the Mojave R., it is site of George Air Force Base, a fighter facility closed in 1992, and is at the outer edge of the Los Angeles commuting area.

Adelphi unincorporated residential suburb, pop. 13,524, Prince George's Co., C Maryland, on the Northwest Branch of the ANACOSTIA R., 12 mi/19 km NNE of Washington, D.C., and just NW of the University of Maryland campus in COLLEGE PARK.

Adena estate, now a state memorial, just NW of CHILLICOTHE, Ross Co., SC Ohio. In 1807 Governor Thomas Worthington built a mansion here, giving it a name coined from the Greek word for "satisfaction." The estate in turn gave its name to a major period (c.1000 B.C.–A.D. 200) of Mound Builder culture, one of whose principal remains is here. Adena culture sites, chiefly in the Ohio Valley, include the SERPENT MOUND and MIAMISBURG.

Adirondack Mountains folded metamorphic group in NE New York. Covering an area of c.12,000 sq mi/31,000 sq km, they are bordered on the E by the L. CHAMPLAIN-L. GEORGE region; they extend from foothills near the Québec line to the Mohawk Valley (S). In the NW, they gradually descend to the St. Lawrence valley. In the SW the Black R. valley separates them from the Tug Hill plateau, a similarly infertile area that extends another 30 mi/50 km W to near the shores of Lake Ontario. The Adirondacks are geologically a S extension of the LAURENTIAN PLATEAU, and not part of the Appalachians. The range is oriented generally NE–SW; the highest peak is Mt. MARCY, 5344 ft/1630 m, 12 mi/19 km SSE of LAKE PLACID. Other well-known summits include ALGONQUIN PEAK, Mt. SKYLIGHT, and Mt. Haystack, 4959 ft/1512 m, near Mt. Marcy; WHITEFACE Mt., NE of Lake Placid; and GORE Mt., in Warren Co. There are 46 peaks over 4000 ft/1220 m. The area is noted for its dense forests and numerous glacial lakes, including George, Placid, SARANAC, Tupper, Long, and Raquette lakes and the Fulton Chain. From the Adirondacks flow the Hudson, Au Sable (to L. Champlain) and Black (to L. Ontario) rivers, and tributaries to the St. Lawrence. The region has many summer and winter resorts and sports centers. Much of the range is part of the ADIRONDACK PARK. Historic sites in the area include FORT TICONDEROGA, L. GEORGE, and PLATTSBURGH. Lumbering and mining, once major industries, have been restricted by the state. The Adirondacks were named after a local tribe, described as "tree eaters."

Adirondack Northway also, **Northway** designation for Interstate 87 from N of Albany, New York, to the Québec border. It traverses over 100 mi/160 km of the E part of the Adirondack Mts. Among the larger communities along its route are Saratoga Springs, Glens Falls, and Plattsburgh. It joins Route 15 in Québec, just NW of Rouses Point.

Adirondack Park almost 6 million ac/2.43 million ha, in the Adirondack Mts. of NE New York. The area, once inhabited by Algonquian and Iroquoian tribes, was used for hunting and logging in the 18th and early 19th century, and as a wilderness retreat for the wealthy in the late 19th and early 20th century. The park evolved from a forest preserve established in 1892, and is now the largest in the Lower 48. It includes both state and private lands, about half in wilderness; 42 mountains over 4000 ft/1220 m high (the tallest 5344-ft/1630-m Mt. MARCY); rolling uplands; meadows; and swamps. It also contains about 2800 lakes and ponds, notably L. GEORGE (SE), and numerous brooks and streams. The Adirondack Park functions to conserve forests and water resources, as well as offering a variety of year-round recreational activities. Well-known centers within the park include BLUE MOUNTAIN LAKE, SARANAC LAKE, and LAKE PLACID.

Admiralty Inlet **1.** see under BAFFIN I., Northwest Territories. **2.** 4 mi/6 km–wide N end of PUGET SOUND, in NW Washington, connecting it with the JUAN DE FUCA STRAIT (NW). It lies between WHIDBEY I. (E) and the mainland (W), where PORT TOWNSEND is at the N end of the Quimper Peninsula.

Admiralty Island National Monument occupying nearly all of 1664–sq mi/4310–sq km Admiralty I., in the ALEXANDER ARCHIPELAGO and Tongass National Forest of extreme SE Alaska. This Tlingit homeland is largely covered by the Kootznahoo ("bear fortress") Wilderness. Angoon (city, pop. 638), on the SW, is a salmon canning and trade center. Some mining and logging have been done on the island.

Adobe Walls battle site in Hutchinson Co., extreme N Texas, 61 mi/98 km NE of Amarillo and 22 mi/35 WNW of Stinnett, on the South Canadian R. and the High Plains, in the Panhandle. Two battles between whites and Indians were fought around this abandoned trading post. In 1864 Kit Carson (in his last fight) nearly lost to 3000 Kiowa and Comanche who had been attacking wagon trains and settlers. In June 1874 Lone Wolf and Quanah Parker led a dawn surprise attack against a buffalo hunters' camp near the site of the first battle, but the well-armed whites drove off the much larger attacking force with heavy losses.

Adrian city, pop. 22,097, seat of Lenawee Co., SE Michigan, on the Raisin R., 30 mi/48 km NW of Toledo, Ohio. It was founded in 1825 by Addison Comstock, who was instrumental in building (1833) the Erie and Kalamazoo Railroad, the first west of New York State. The city has a large historic district, with buildings from the 1830s to the post–Civil War period, notably the Croswell Opera House (1866). Now a trading center for wheat, corn, and livestock, it also manufactures auto and aircraft parts, paper, metals, chemicals, and dairy products. It is the seat of Adrian College (1859) and Siena Heights College (1919).

Affton unincorporated community, pop. 21,106, St. Louis Co., EC Missouri, a largely residential suburb 9 mi/14 km SW of downtown St. Louis, on Gravois Creek, inside the city's beltway (I-270). The 1850s farm of Ulysses S. Grant, now a park, is just W, near Grantwood Village.

Agana unincorporated community, pop. 1139, territorial capital of GUAM, on the island's W coast, on the Philippine Sea. With **Agana Heights** (pop. 3347), **Agana Station** (pop. 2263), APRA HARBOR (SW), and industrial TAMUNING (E), it forms Guam's urban core. A 17th-century Spanish city, long the island's main community, it was destroyed in a battle between occupying Japanese and invading US forces in July 1944, but was rebuilt after the war.

Agassiz, Lake postglacial body that covered most of Manitoba and large parts of E Saskatchewan, NE North Dakota, NW Minnesota, and W Ontario c.10,000 years ago. Formed by melting glaciers, it was larger than all of today's Great Lakes combined, and drained, at various times, S via a predecessor of the Minnesota R. and via the RED RIVER OF THE NORTH (now N-flowing); E toward L. Superior; and finally, N to Hudson Bay. Its remnants, including Lakes WINNIPEG, WINNIPEGOSIS, and MANITOBA, continue to drain N. Agassiz's sediments make the Red R. valley a rich wheat producing area.

Agassiz Peak see under SAN FRANCISCO PEAKS, Arizona.

Agate Fossil Beds 3055-ac/1237-ha NATIONAL MONUMENT, in Sioux Co., NW Nebraska, on the NIOBRARA R., 36 mi/58 km N of Scottsbluff and 13 mi/21 km E of the Wyoming line. Established in 1965, near agate-filled rock formations, it has sedimentary rocks containing well-preserved specimens of

Miocene mammal fossils. First excavated in 1904, the extensive quarries underlie a grassy, hilly landscape.

Agawam in Massachusetts: **a.** town, pop. 27,323, Hamden Co., across the Connecticut R. (SW) from Springfield, of which it is partly a residential suburb, and on the Connecticut border. The Westfield (formerly Agawam) R. flows along the N of the town to meet the Connecticut. Formerly an industrial community with the included agricultural village of Feeding Hills, Agawam has been a producer of woolen and metal products. **b.** also, **Aggawam** see under IPSWICH.

Agoura Hills city, pop. 20,390, Los Angeles Co., SW California, in the Santa Monica Mts., 29 mi/47 km WNW of Los Angeles, on the Ventura Freeway. It is an affluent residential suburb. The comedian Bob Hope owns much local land.

Aguadilla unincorporated community (ZONA URBANA), pop. 18,347, Aguadilla Municipio (pop. 59,335), extreme NW Puerto Rico, on the Bahía de Aguadilla (Aguadilla Bay) and the MONA PASSAGE (W) and the Atlantic Ocean (N), 17 mi/27 km N of Mayagüez. Founded in 1775, it is a port and a trade and shipping center for producers of fruit, sugar, coffee, and other agricultural goods. Fine lace and wicker hats are made, and there is some tourist trade.

Aiea unincorporated community, pop. 8906, Honolulu Co., S Oahu, Hawaii. On the NE shore of Pearl Harbor, this residential suburb 7 mi/11 km NW of Honolulu has shopping centers and housing developments. Many residents are employed by nearby Fort Shafter and Tripler Army Hospital. Aiea is a sugar cane refining center.

Aiken city, pop. 19,872, seat of Aiken Co. (pop. 120,940), WC South Carolina, 17 mi/27 km ENE of Augusta, Georgia, in the SANDHILLS. It was laid out in 1834 on the Charleston-Hamburg Railroad, and was a cotton mill town, site of a Feb. 1865 Civil War skirmish. By the 1880s it was becoming a wealthy resort, and has been known since as a center for horseracing and polo. The 1950s opening of the Savannah R. nuclear site, 12 mi/19 km S, brought an influx of population and industry. Aiken now produces textiles, electrical equipment, fertilizer, and fiberglass. Kaolin is mined nearby. A University of South Carolina branch (1961) and Aiken Technical College (1972) are here.

Ajax town, pop. 57,350, Durham Regional Municipality, S Ontario, on L. Ontario, 24 mi/39 km NE of Toronto. The site of a World War II munitions factory, it was developed in the 1950s as a model industrial center, and has grown recently, its pop. increasing 57% in 1986–91. Manufactures include metal and wood products, textiles, and chemicals.

Ajo unincorporated community, pop. 2919, Pima Co., SW Arizona, 106 mi/171 km W of Tucson, and just N of the Organ Pipe Cactus National Monument, in the Sonoran Desert. Copper, from deposits long known to the Papago (Tohono O'odham), was extracted commercially here from the 1910s, until dropping prices closed the mines in the 1980s. An open pit mine 1.5 mi/2.4 km across is just S. The New Cornelia Tailings Dam, composed of wastes piled so as to prevent the metal-heavy water washed from the mines from clogging streams, is variously described as the world's largest (in volume) dam or largest mine waste dump.

Aklavik see under INUVIK, Northwest Territories.

Akron city, pop. 223,019, seat of Summit Co., NE Ohio, on the Little Cuyahoga R., 30 mi/48 km SE of Cleveland. Founded in 1825, it grew rapidly, fostered by waterpower and the transportation furnished by the Ohio and Erie Canal (1827) and Pennsylvania and Ohio Canal (1840). Benjamin F. Goodrich established a small rubber factory here in 1870; by the early 20th century the city was known as the "rubber capital of the world," supplying tires and other rubber products for the growing automobile industry. Goodyear, General Tire, and Firestone still have their headquarters in the city, and there are many laboratories conducting research in rubber and plastics. However, tires have not been produced here since the recession of the early 1980s, and in recent years some manufacturing plants and major stores have closed. Akron has also been a center for the manufacture and launching of dirigibles and other lighter-than-air craft. Current manufactures include a variety of rubber, metal, and plastic products, farm machinery, aluminum siding, and transportation equipment. Akron is an important distribution point between the eastern seaboard and the Midwest. It was the site of the original Quaker Oats mills, now the Quaker Square hotel and shopping complex. The World Series of Golf, Firestone bowling championship, and Soap Box Derby are annual events. Educational and cultural institutions include the University of Akron (1870), the Akron Art Institute, and the American Indian Art Hall of Fame.

Akwesasne Iroquois reservation, 34 sq mi/89 sq km, on the St. Lawrence R. at the mouth of the SAINT REGIS R., in Québec, Ontario, and New York, just SE of CORNWALL, Ontario. In New York it is called the Saint Regis Mohawk Reservation (pop. 1978); its Canadian sections had a 1981 pop. of c.2100. The Handsome Lake religion is practiced here; agriculture, handicrafts, and commerce are central to the economy. The name means "where the partridge drums."

Alabama state of the SE US, generally considered part of the Deep SOUTH (and by the Census Bureau as in the East South Central region); 1990 pop. 4,040,587 (103.8% of 1980; rank: 22nd); area 52,423 sq mi/135,776 sq km (rank: 30th); admitted to Union 1819 (22nd). Capital: Montgomery. Most populous cities: BIRMINGHAM, MOBILE, MONTGOMERY, HUNTSVILLE. Alabama is bordered E by Georgia, with the CHATTAHOOCHEE R. forming the lower half of the boundary; N by Tennessee; and W by Mississippi, with the TENNESSEE R. forming a small part of the boundary in the NW. On the S is the Florida PANHANDLE (E and C, extending W to the PERDIDO R.), and a 60 mi/100 km–long coast on the Gulf of MEXICO, bisected by MOBILE BAY. Alabama's N is dominated by the S end of the APPALACHIAN Mts. Running from NE to SE here are (E–W) part of the PIEDMONT region; the TALLADEGA Mts. (with CHEAHA Mt., at 2407 ft/734 m, the state's high point); the Great Appalachian Valley, with long ridges including LOOKOUT Mt. and SAND Mt.; and the CUMBERLAND PLATEAU. The Tennessee R. enters the state in the NE, in the valley, and crosses NW through the Cumberland Plateau. The COOSA and TALLAPOOSA rivers, flowing SW from the Appalachians, join in SC Alabama to form the ALABAMA R., continuing SW to Mobile Bay. The BLACK WARRIOR R. flows SSW from the valley, joining the TOMBIGBEE R. near the Mississippi line. The Tombigbee, flowing from NE Mississippi, also empties into Mobile Bay. A canal in NE Mississippi created (1985) the Tennessee-Tombigbee Waterway, an alternative to the lower Mississippi R. for barge traffic from the Tennessee R. system. Most of S and W Alabama is part of the Gulf COASTAL PLAIN. The region includes the famous cotton producing BLACK BELT, across the state's C, and the WIREGRASS (SE), now a peanut producing area. South Alabama is subtropical, the Appalachian uplands temperate. Home to the Creek (including the Alibamu, who gave their name to the river and then the state), Choctaw, and Chickasaw, with the Cherokee in the NE, the area was explored by the Spanish from the 16th century, and settled (by the French, at Mobile) in 1702. Indian resistance to white expansion continued until 1814, when the defeat at HORSESHOE BEND led to the exile of the "Civilized Tribes," esp. along the 1830s TRAIL OF TEARS. Alabama became a leading PLANTATION state, with slaves forming almost half its pop. at the time of the Civil War. In the N, however, Appalachian hill people created a small-farming society, and in places (see WINSTON Co.) opposed the Confederacy. This regional division has continued to influence the state's life. After the Civil War (in which the 1864 battle of Mobile Bay was the major local action), tenant farming replaced slavery, and cotton culture continued. At the same time, railroads spurred the development of industry, esp. steelmaking, in Birmingham, BESSEMER, and other centers, and of lumbering in the S. Alabama has since that period developed along two lines, agricultural (since 1915 and the boll weevil focused less and less on cotton, more on cattle, soybeans, peanuts, and various other crops) and industrial. During World War I steel, shipbuilding (at Mobile), and creation of a nitrates plant at MUSCLE SHOALS were among industrial developments. After the war, the Muscle Shoals plant became central in the creation of the TENNESSEE VALLEY AUTHORITY, whose dams and power generation transformed the life of N Alabama. In World War II, the Redstone Arsenal was established at Huntsville, beginning the growth of that city into the aerospace giant it is today. Other modern industrial centers include DOTHAN (SE), TUSCALOOSA (WC), and GADSDEN and ANNISTON (NE). Alabama's large black minority (35% in 1940, 25% in 1990) has always had great potential political power, and in 1955, with a black boycott of segregated city buses, Montgomery, once a Confederate capital, became the flashpoint of the modern civil rights movement; in the 1960s, Selma, Anniston, and Birmingham were among scenes of demonstrations and violence. The University of Alabama is in Tuscaloosa; other noted academic centers are AUBURN and TUSKEGEE. The Alabama Gulf Coast has popular beaches, esp. at GULF SHORES, and Mobile is a commercial fishing center. There is oil and natural gas production in the S, and SYLACAUGA (EC) is a noted marble producing center. Dothan (near FORT RUCKER) and Anniston, along with Huntsville, are cities that have benefited from military spending.

Alabama Hills see under LONE PINE, California.

Alabama International Motor Speedway old name for the Talladega Superspeedway, TALLADEGA, Alabama.

Alabama River 315 mi/507 km long, in S Alabama, formed by the confluence of the COOSA and TALLAPOOSA rivers just NNE of Montgomery. It winds W and SW across the Gulf Coastal Plain past SELMA and CAHABA (where the Cahaba R. joins it). It joins the TOMBIGBEE R. some 40 mi/64 km above Mobile, forming the MOBILE R. Its valley was home to Creek tribes, one of which, the Alibamu or Alabama, gave its name to the river and eventually to the state. The first Europeans to see the river were De Soto's 1540 expedition. In the 18th century the French and British used it in the fur trade, and in the 19th century it carried cotton from the BLACK BELT to Mobile. The Coosa-Alabama system's many locks and dams have contributed greatly to the 20th-century economic development of the state.

Alabaster city, pop. 14,732, Shelby Co., C Alabama, 19 mi/31 km S of Birmingham. Formerly a small agricultural and limestone shipping community, it has grown quickly since the 1970s as a Birmingham suburb.

Alamance County 433 sq mi/1121 sq km, pop. 108,213, in NC North Carolina, in the Piedmont. Its seat is GRAHAM. The county is crossed by the Haw R. Its farms produce primarily tobacco and corn. Industry is focused in the textile center of BURLINGTON. The **Alamance Battleground,** 7 mi/11 km SW of Burlington, is the site of the battle of Alamance Creek (May 16, 1771), in which Governor William Tryon put an end to the insurrectionary Regulator Movement.

Alameda city, pop. 76,459, Alameda Co., NC California, mainly on two islands on the E side of San Francisco Bay, across Oakland Harbor just SW of Oakland. San Leandro Bay lies SE. Settled in the 1850s on part of Rancho San Antonio, it became an island city after harbor channelization was completed in 1902. Its larger island, 6.5 mi/10 km long, is the site of Alameda Naval Air station, a major carrier base ordered closed in 1993, and of the College of Alameda (1970), and has extensive Victorian and modern residential neighborhoods. Waterfront industries include shipbuilding, lumber milling, steel fabrication, and the handling of fishing and cargo vessels. The smaller Coast Guard (or Government) I. is a training center and service community. Alameda has popular parks, municipal beaches, and facilities for boating and fishing.

Alameda County 736 sq mi/1906 sq km, pop. 1,279,182, in NC California. Its seat is OAKLAND. It extends from the E shore of San Francisco Bay, over the San Leandro and other hills, E to the edge of the San Joaquin R. Valley. Oakland, Alameda, Berkeley, San Leandro, Hayward, Fremont, and other seaport, industrial, and suburban cities lie on or near the bay; to the E are the wine producing Livermore Valley and other agricultural and quarrying areas.

Alamo, the historic MISSION in downtown San Antonio, Texas, popularly known as the "Cradle of Texas Liberty." The familiar building is actually the chapel (1744) of the Franciscan Misión San Antonio de Valero (1718). Secularized toward the end of the 18th century, it became a partial ruin, and Spanish troops used the grounds occasionally after 1801. When the Texas Revolution began in 1835, a group of volunteers occupied it. When Texas leaders advocated abandoning San Antonio, the volunteers refused to leave the Alamo, and were joined by a small number of others answering their call to arms. The Mexican general Santa Anna arrived on Feb. 23, 1836, and besieged the mission. The defenders, commanded by William Travis and James Bowie, and numbering about 185, including Davy Crockett, a dozen Hispanics, and two slaves, held out for 13 days, but were overwhelmed when the attackers breached an outer wall; all died in the fighting or were killed afterward. Lost time and heavy casualties, however, delayed Santa Anna, contributing to the ultimately successful defense of Texas.

Ala Moana neighborhood W of Waikiki, in downtown HONOLULU, Hawaii. Its commercial area has a tri-level mall, reputed to be the world's largest open-air shopping center. Ala Moana Park, on the waterfront, was originally swampland and includes a popular beach between the peninsular

Aina Moana Recreation Area (formerly Magic Island) and a protective coral reef.

Alamodome see under HEMISFAIR PLAZA, San Antonio, Texas.

Alamogordo city, pop. 27,596, seat of Otero Co., S New Mexico, 155 mi/250 km SSE of Albuquerque. In the Tularosa Basin, at the W edge of the Sacramento Mts., it is a ranching and farming center founded in 1898. Aerospace industries and Holloman Air Force Base also contribute to the city's economy. The first nuclear explosion took place in July 1945 about 55 mi/89 km NNW at WHITE SANDS. The Space Center, including the International Space Hall of Fame, is NE. New Mexico State University at Alamogordo (1958) is here.

Alamo Heights city, pop. 6502, Bexar Co., SC Texas, 5 mi/8 km N of downtown San Antonio, and surrounded by the larger city. It is residential and largely affluent. Incarnate Word College (1881) is on its S Boundary.

Alamosa city, pop. 7579, seat of Alamosa Co., S Colorado, in the San Luis Valley, on the Rio Grande, 90 mi/145 km SW of Pueblo. Seat of Adams State College (1921), it developed with the arrival of the Denver and Rio Grande Railroad (1878), and was a railhead for precious metals mined in the San Juan Mts. (W). It is now the valley's industrial and retail hub. Economic activities include railroad repair, flour milling, oil refining, and stockyards. It is an agricultural shipping center, distributing potatoes, lettuce, barley, dairy and meat products, and beverages. Gateway to the Great Sand Dunes National Monument, 20 mi/32 km to the NE, it is 20 mi/32 km E of the Rio Grande National Forest and 20 mi/32 km SW of Blanca Peak (14,345 ft/4375 m).

Alaska largest and northernmost US state, on the extreme NW of North America; 1990 pop. 550,403 (136.9% of 1980; rank: 49th); area 656,424 sq mi/1,700,138 sq km (rank: 1st); admitted to Union 1959 (49th). Capital: JUNEAU. Most populous cities: ANCHORAGE, FAIRBANKS, Juneau, COLLEGE (unincorporated), SITKA. Alaska is bordered E by the Yukon Territory, and SE, along its PANHANDLE, by the Yukon Territory (N) and British Columbia (S). On the N it lies on the BEAUFORT SEA, part of the Arctic Ocean. On the NW is the CHUKCHI SEA, narrowing to c.50 mi/80 km at the BERING Strait, which separates the SEWARD PENINSULA (Alaska) from Russian East Asia; in the strait, on both sides of the International Date Line and US-Russian boundary, lie the DIOMEDE Is. To the S of the Bering Strait is the BERING SEA, in which lie SAINT LAWRENCE, the PRIBILOFS, NUNIVAK, and other islands. The Bering Sea is bounded (S) by Alaska's long ALEUTIAN Island chain, extending in an E–W arc across the North Pacific Ocean from the ALASKA PENINSULA. To the peninsula's E is the Gulf of ALASKA, lying along the state's S; KODIAK I. is the largest here, and the KENAI PENINSULA extends S from the Anchorage area, with PRINCE WILLIAM SOUND on its E. In the SE, most of the narrow Panhandle lies inside (E of) the thousands of islands of the ALEXANDER ARCHIPELAGO. Alaska's southeasternmost point is over 400 mi/640 km NW of the nearest point in the LOWER 48. The state is reached primarily by boat via the INSIDE PASSAGE and ALASKA MARINE HIGHWAY, by road over the ALASKA HIGHWAY (through the Yukon Territory), or by air; its position on the Great Circle route from the Lower 48 to Asia brings it substantial regular air service. Alaska comprises a NW continuation of major geologic regions of W North America. Across its N stands the BROOKS RANGE, an E–W extension of the Rocky Mts; to the N, on the Beaufort Sea, the vast NORTH SLOPE is analogous to the Great Plains farther S. The state's interior, through which the YUKON R. and its tributaries drain W to the Bering Sea, represents the INTERMONTANE REGION of the West. Along the S lie elements of two parallel mountain chains. The more northern of these is an extension of the COAST Mts., which farther SE include the Sierra Nevada and Cascade Range. Here its elements include the ALASKA RANGE, arcing across the state's SC, and the ALEUTIAN Range, continuing through the islands; Alaska's and North America's high point is Mt. MCKINLEY (Denali), 20,320 ft/6194 m high, N of Anchorage. The southern chain is part of the COAST RANGES, which farther to the SE lie W of the Coast Mts. The SAINT ELIAS Mts., along the Alaska-Yukon border, include Mt. LOGAN, at 19,524 ft/5951 m Canada's highest; the range rises higher from a seacoast than any other in the world, and is filled with glaciers and icefields. To the NW of the Saint Eliases, the Coast Ranges in Alaska include the CHUGACH and KENAI ranges, and end (W) with Kodiak I. Anchorage, the state's pop. center, and the MATANUSKA VALLEY, its only notable agricultural area, lie in the trough between the two chains. Although the Panhandle and Alexander Archipelago (SE) receive heavy rains and have winters kept relatively mild by ocean currents, the rest of Alaska has extremely cold winters, continental in the interior (as at Fairbanks) or Arctic on the North Slope. The state's N third, above the ARCTIC CIRCLE, also experiences complete darkness for long parts of the winter. Sparsely peopled in modern times, Alaska was the first part of North America to see human activity, as the Asian peoples whose descendants would be known as American Indians crossed the Bering Strait during glacial periods some 30,000 years ago. In historical times, the Russians who explored the region in the 18th century found Aleuts living in the islands (whose term for the mainland gave the state its name) and Tlingit and other peoples in the Alexander Archipelago. Along the W coast they encountered the INUIT, who also inhabit the North Slope. Becoming part of RUSSIAN AMERICA, Alaska had early settlements at Kodiak I., Sitka, and in other sites before the Russians lost interest in their colonial project and sold it (1867) to the US. Because secretary of state William Seward negotiated the $7 million purchase, skeptics called the acquisition "Seward's Folly" or "Seward's Icebox." Little development occurred before the 1897 Klondike gold rush, when SKAGWAY became a center of activity. Gold was soon found in Alaska itself, at NOME (1898), in PLACER deposits at the site of Fairbanks (1902), and along the IDITAROD and Yellow rivers (1900s). Alaska gained territorial status in 1912, and the ALASKA RAILROAD, from SEWARD (S) to Fairbanks, began in the 1910s to open the interior. During the 1930s Depression, a government experiment in farm settlement created PALMER and other communities in the Matanuska Valley. When World War II began, Alaska's strategic situation came to the fore. Japanese forces occupied ATTU and KISKA and bombed Dutch Harbor (see UNALASKA) in the Aleutians. The ALASKA HIGHWAY and NORTHWEST STAGING ROUTE were created to bring troops, supplies, and planes into position to aid the Soviet Union and prepare for the assault on Japan. With the war's end, the DEW LINE and air bases remained key in Cold War thinking, and development of remote as well as urban parts of Alaska continued. After statehood the business of allotting Alaska's land (which remains almost 68% Federal) continued, with legislation assigning large areas to the Inuit, Aleuts, and tribes (1971) and to NATIONAL PARKS and preserves (1980). Huge oil and gas strikes on the North Slope

(1968–) led to development there of the PRUDHOE BAY complex and the building in the 1970s of the TRANS-ALASKA PIPELINE to VALDEZ. Oil production and transportation have produced great wealth for the state, along with a 1989 tanker spill in Prince William Sound that devastated local fisheries. Tourism has become another major source of revenue. The state's eight national parks—DENALI, LAKE CLARK, WRANGELL–SAINT ELIAS, KATMAI, Gates of the Arctic (see under BROOKS RANGE), Kobuk Valley, GLACIER BAY, and Kenai Fjords—offer a range of glacial, volcanic, island, coastal, rain forest, Arctic, and mountain scenery, along with major WILDERNESS AREAS. Visitors are also drawn to Inuit settlements like BARROW, the northernmost US community, to summer's "midnight sun," and to events like the Iditarod dogsled race. In addition to oil and natural gas, Alaska still produces gold and silver. Its fisheries and timber industries provide the raw materials for much of the state's small manufacturing sector. Alaska's people are today almost 16% Inuit, Aleut, or Indian. More recently arrived groups give the state a diverse pop. of fishing, mining, oil industry, lumbering, and other industrial workers; Federal (including military) employees; and others including a number of wilderness seekers on the "last FRONTIER."

Alaska, Gulf of large (some 800 mi/1300 km E–W) inlet of the N Pacific Ocean, S of the Alaska mainland and bordered by the ALEXANDER ARCHIPELAGO on the E and the ALASKA PENINSULA on the W. The gulf is filled with islands (KODIAK is the largest) and peninsulas, creating many straits and inlets, including the N portion of the INSIDE PASSAGE, PRINCE WILLIAM SOUND, and COOK INLET. Heavily fished, and crossed by oil tankers and cruise ships, the gulf has its chief ports at SITKA, JUNEAU, VALDEZ, SEWARD, and ANCHORAGE.

Alaska Highway 1520 mi/2450 km long, between DAWSON CREEK, British Columbia, and FAIRBANKS, Alaska. Formerly known as the Alaska Canada Military Highway, the Alcan Highway, and the Alaskan International Highway, it was built in 1942 after the bombing of Pearl Harbor, to provide a protected route to Alaska. Rough terrain, including the N Rocky Mts., and freezing weather made its construction an arduous task for the thousands of soldiers who built it. The Alaska Highway is open all year, and is now paved for all but 25 mi/40 km of its course; it is used by many tourists.

Alaska Marine Highway system of ferries that provides access to much of the Panhandle and ALEXANDER ARCHIPELAGO (via the INSIDE PASSAGE and extensions), the KENAI and ALASKA peninsulas, and KODIAK and other islands in S Alaska. Established by the new state in 1959 with Seattle, Washington, as its S terminus, it is said to be the largest such system in the world. Bellingham, Washington, became the S terminus in 1987.

Alaska Peninsula mountainous expanse between Bristol Bay and the Bering Sea (N) and Shelikof Strait and the N Pacific Ocean (S), in SW Alaska. Some 480 mi/775 km NE–SW and 10–120 mi/16–190 km wide, the cool, foggy peninsula contains several volcanic peaks in the ALEUTIAN RANGE, which runs its entire length and continues, partially submerged, as the Aleutian Is. KATMAI NATIONAL PARK AND PRESERVE is at the N end of the peninsula. Moose, bear, waterfowl, and seals abound on and around the peninsula, which has few roads but is dotted with native communities.

Alaska Railroad constructed 1915–23 from SEWARD, on the Kenai Peninsula, N to Fairbanks, by way of Anchorage and Nenana, building on the precedent of a failed 1902 project to reach the MATANUSKA VALLEY's coalfields. Anchorage was founded as a rail camp in 1914. The main line is 470 mi/760 km long, and there are a number of short branches. Important to Matanuska agriculture, the railroad is now also a major tourist attraction.

Alaska Range mountain chain variously described as extending for from 400 to 600 mi (650–1000 km) in an E–W arc S of Fairbanks and N of Anchorage, from the Alaska Peninsula (W) to the Yukon border, in S Alaska. A continuation of the COAST Mts., it forms a barrier between Alaska's coastal and interior regions and includes the granitic Mt. MCKINLEY (also known as Denali; 20,320 ft/6194 m), the highest peak in North America. Older parts of the jagged range are composed of sedimentary rocks carved by erosion. Other summits include Mt. Foraker (17,400 ft/5304 m), from which the Herron Glacier originates; Mt. Hunter (14,573 ft/4442 m); Mt. Brown (14,530 ft/4429 m); Mt. Hayes (13,832 ft/4216 m), site of the Susitna Glacier; Mt. Silverthrone (13,220/4029 m); and the Cathedral Spires (8985 ft/2739 m) in the SW. Mt. Spurr (11,070 ft/3374 m), a volcano 80 mi/130 km W of Anchorage, erupted in 1992 after 39 years of dormancy.

Alava, Cape coastal promontory on the OLYMPIC PENINSULA, in Clallam Co., extreme NW Washington. Fourteen mi/23 km S of Cape Flattery, and the westernmost mainland point in the US Lower 48, at 124° 44′ W, it is in the coastal unit of OLYMPIC National Park,

Albany **1.** city, pop. 16,327, Alameda Co., NC California. On the E shore of San Francisco Bay, it adjoins (N) Berkeley. Chiefly residential, it also has several research facilities. **2.** city, pop. 78,122, seat of Dougherty Co., SW Georgia, at the head of navigation on the Flint R., 75 mi/120 km SE of Columbus. Founded in 1836, it was an important cotton market from the start. Once a railroad connection with Macon was built in 1857, it quickly became a transportation hub. Today, it is the trade center for an agricultural area producing cotton, corn, peanuts, pecans, and livestock. Aircraft, chemicals, and farm tools are manufactured. Traditionally black Albany State College (1903) and Darton College (1963) are here, as is the Albany Naval Air Station. Tourists are drawn to Radium Springs, a resort 4 mi/6 km S, featuring Georgia's largest natural spring. **3.** city, pop. 101,082, state capital and seat of Albany Co., EC New York, on the W bank of the Hudson R., at the N terminus of the deepwater Hudson R. Channel, 145 mi/233 km N of New York City. Henry Hudson arrived at the site in 1609; Fort Nassau, a trading post for the United Netherlands Company, was built five years later. The first permanent settlement, Beverwyck, was established following the building of Fort Orange in 1624. From 1629 to 1652, it was part of Rensselaerwyck (see RENSSELAER), then regained independent status. When Fort Orange was captured by the British in 1664, Beverwyck was renamed to honor the Duke of York and Albany. It became a leading city because of its strategic location, and was the central fur market of the English colonies. Known as the "Cradle of the Union," it was the site of the first intercolonial convention (1689) and of the adoption of Benjamin Franklin's "Plan of Union" by the Albany Congress (1765). The Continental Congress met here in 1774. Albany served as a major outfitting point for westbound wagon trains from the 1780s, and was made New York's capital in 1797. The opening of the Champlain Canal (1822) and the ERIE CANAL (1825), and the arrival of the railroad (1831), further strengthened its market economy. Industrialization and immigration were stimulated after the Civil War by the establishment of large manufacturing plants. In 1919, one of the first US commercial airports was built; the Port of Albany was opened in 1932. Albany is now the center of a metropolitan area including Schenectady and Troy. Government dominates the city's economy, but manufacturing and shipping are also significant; leading industries produce paper, machine tools, felt, brake linings, cement, steel products, electrical equipment, and chemicals. The Port of Albany is a petroleum storage and shipping center, handling river and ocean vessels. Albany is home to the State University of New York at Albany (1844), Albany Law School (1851), and several other institutions. **4.** city, pop. 29,462, seat of Linn Co., also in Benton Co., on the Willamette R., NW Oregon, 10 mi/16 km ENE of Corvallis. A wholesale and shipping center for local dairy and agricultural products, it has long processed and traded lumber and timber products. Founded in 1848, it boomed with the arrival of the railroad in 1870. Wood, paper, leather and food-processing industries developed, and continue to contribute to today's economy. New high-tech industries have grown from the processing of titanium and other rare metals extracted nearby. Albany hosts the annual World Championship Timber Carnival.

Albany County 524 sq mi/1357 sq km, pop. 292,594, in E New York, bounded by the Hudson R. (E) and the Mohawk R. and New York State Barge Canal (N). It includes the Helderberg Mts. and foothills of the Catskill Mts. Its seat and largest city is Albany, the state capital, which dominates much of the county with its governmental apparatus, industries, and port facilities. It also contains numerous residential and industrial suburbs. Filled with small towns and villages, the balance of the county is largely agricultural, and is active in dairy, fruit, livestock, and vegetable farming.

Albany Park residential neighborhood in Chicago, Illinois, on the far North Side, 7 mi/11 km NW of the Loop, on the North Branch of the Chicago R. Formerly largely Jewish, it has become since the 1970s one of the city's most important Asian districts, with a sizable Korean community.

Albany River 600 mi/1000 km long, in NC Ontario. It issues from L. St. Joseph and flows generally ENE to James Bay at Kashechewan and Fort Albany, an Indian reserve (pop. 1199). The HUDSON'S BAY COMPANY established the fort in the 1680s, and it was long important in the fur trade; the river and PORTAGES over low divides were part of a waterway system leading W to L. WINNIPEG.

Albemarle city, pop. 14,939, seat of Stanly Co., SC North Carolina, 37 mi/60 km ENE of Charlotte. An agricultural trade center, it produces lumber, textiles, brick, and cottonseed oil, and processes poultry.

Albemarle County 725 sq mi/1878 sq km, pop. 68,040, in NC Virginia. Its seat is CHARLOTTESVILLE. Mountainous and semirural in character, looking toward the BLUE RIDGE Mts. (W), it has attracted many affluent residents; Charlottesville, an educational, financial, and industrial center, is among the most expensive residential areas in Virginia. The county is rich in historic associations, particularly with Thomas Jefferson, whose home, MONTICELLO, is SE of Charlottesville.

Albemarle Sound protected inlet of the Atlantic Ocean, joined by the estuaries of the Chowan, Perquimans, Little, Pasquotank, and North rivers (N) and the Roanoke, Scuppernong, and Alligator rivers (S), in NE North Carolina. Fifty-five mi/89 km E–W and 4–13 mi/6–21 km wide, the sound is separated from the ocean by Bodie I., part of the OUTER BANKS. It connects with CURRITUCK SOUND on the N, and with PAMLICO SOUND via Croatan and Roanoke sounds on the S, and is part of the ATLANTIC INTRACOASTAL WATERWAY. ELIZABETH CITY, on the Pasquotank, is the sound's chief port. EDENTON, on the NW shore, is one of the oldest cities in North Carolina, and ROANOKE I., at the SE entrance, is the site of the first European settlement in the state. In an area of pine and hardwood forests, marshes, and swampland, the sound is bordered by several wildlife refuges.

Alberta province of W Canada, the westernmost PRAIRIE PROVINCE; 1991 pop. 2,545,553 (107.6% of 1986; rank: 4th of 12); land area 246,422 sq mi/638,233 sq km (rank: 5th); entered Confederation 1905. Capital: EDMONTON. Most populous cities: CALGARY, Edmonton, LETHBRIDGE, RED DEER, MEDICINE HAT. Alberta is bordered E by Saskatchewan; S by Montana, along the FORTY-NINTH PARALLEL; W by British Columbia, with the CONTINENTAL DIVIDE in the Canadian ROCKY Mts. forming much of the boundary; and N by the Northwest Territories, along the SIXTIETH PARALLEL. Most of the province lies in the N GREAT PLAINS, with High Plains areas along the Rocky Mt. front (SW). The Rockies here rise to 12,294 ft/3747 m at Mt. COLUMBIA, and contain numerous other high peaks, icefields, and glaciers; the BANFF, JASPER, and WATERTON LAKES (part of Waterton-Glacier International) national, and several provincial, parks; and the (S–N) CROWSNEST, KICKING HORSE, and YELLOWHEAD passes, critical in the development of the Canadian West. The famed resorts of Banff and LAKE LOUISE are in the mountains. Alberta's rivers flow from the Rockies: In the N, the HAY, PEACE, and ATHABASCA rivers flow NE, toward the Mackenzie R. system and the Arctic Ocean. To the S, the North SASKATCHEWAN, RED DEER, BOW, and South Saskatchewan rivers are all part of the Saskatchewan R.–L. Winnipeg–Nelson R. system, draining E to Hudson Bay. In the extreme S, the MILK R. is the northwesternmost headwater of the Missouri–Mississippi R. system, draining SE and S to the Gulf of Mexico. The extreme NE corner of the province, around L. ATHABASCA, lies on part of the CANADIAN SHIELD; along the Shield's edge is the huge WOOD BUFFALO NATIONAL PARK, extending into the Northwest Territories. The Peace R. valley, in the NW, is the northernmost major grain producing region in North America. Across the province's C, between Edmonton and Calgary, lie the PARKLANDS, a belt of mixed grassland and aspen-dominated groves. In the S, the rain shadow of the Rockies leaves the area around Lethbridge and Medicine Hat and the Red Deer R. valley (where there are noted BADLANDS) very dry; close to the Rockies is the CHINOOK BELT, where warm, dry Pacific winds spilling over the mountains can suddenly raise winter temperatures tens of degrees, melting snow and leaving the ground bare. The SE is part of PALLISER'S TRIANGLE, an area in the 19th century thought unlikely to ever be of much agricultural use, but subsequently much altered by irrigation; stock raising and the production of sugar beets and other ground crops are important here. Inhabited by the Cree, Assiniboine, Blackfoot, and various Athapascan peoples, the region of Alberta was largely within RUPERT'S LAND, granted in 1670 to the HUDSON'S BAY COMPANY. In the 18th century French traders from Montréal also operated here; organized by the NORTH WEST COMPANY from the 1780s, they clashed with HBC operatives until the two companies merged in 1821. ROCKY MOUNTAIN HOUSE, Edmonton, and FORT CHIPEWYAN were among fur trade centers. In 1870, the HBC sold its claims to the new Dominion of Canada, and Alberta became part of the Northwest Territories. The 1880s construction of the CANADIAN PACIFIC RAILWAY through Medicine Hat, Calgary, and the Kicking Horse Pass spurred rapid settlement of the S; in the 1890s the CPR built another line, through Lethbridge and the Crowsnest Pass. In 1905, with activity throughout the area stimulated by the 1890s Klondike gold rush, Alberta became a province (named for a daughter of Queen Victoria). At first primarily agricultural, with cattle and lumber as important products, it suffered during the 1930s Depression and drought. The building of what became CANADIAN NATIONAL RAILWAY lines through Edmonton and the Yellowhead Pass in the 1910s, and military aviation and related activities during World War II, helped the economy through difficult years. Then, in 1947, the LEDUC oilfield, S of Edmonton, was discovered. Subsequently, Alberta has become an energy giant. Additional oil, sulfur, and gas finds, including vast tar sands along the Athabasca R. near FORT MCMURRAY (NE), have spawned refineries at Edmonton and Calgary, pipelines to E Canada, and large secondary and support industries. Mineral wealth has placed Edmonton and Calgary among the nation's most populous and affluent cities, with financial, commercial, and cultural importance far beyond what their early life suggested. Today, outside their orbit, Alberta engages in coal mining, stock raising and dairy production, irrigated farming, lumbering, fishing (esp. at LESSER SLAVE L.), and the resort and tourist trade. The Rockies and Calgary's annual "Stampede" are the best-known visitor attractions. Alberta's people, primarily of English and North European background, include numerous distinct groups including Mormons (at CARDSTON) and MÉTIS.

Alberta, Mount peak (11,874 ft/3619 m) in W Alberta, in the Rocky Mts., 166 mi/267 km NW of Calgary and 50 mi/80 km SE of Jasper, in JASPER NATIONAL PARK.

Albert Lea city, pop. 18,310, seat of Freeborn Co., S Minnesota, on Albert Lea and Fountain lakes, 18 mi/29 km W of Austin. Situated at the hub of a regional transportation complex, it is a wholesale distribution center for local agricultural and dairy products. Meatpacking is important; clothing, farm equipment, and electrical goods are produced. Nearby lakes and Helmer Myre State Park, 2 mi/3 km E, are summer tourist attractions.

Albertson village, pop. 5166, in North Hempstead town, Nassau Co., SE New York, on the North Shore of Long Island, 2 mi/3 km N of Mineola. It is a residential suburb with some light industry.

Albertville city, pop. 14,507, Marshall Co., NE Alabama, on Sand Mt., 20 mi/32 km NW of Gadsden. It is an agricultural market and processing hub, the center of Alabama's poultry industry, with plants processing, grading, and packing chickens and eggs. Textiles and furniture are manufactured.

Albina neighborhood in North PORTLAND, Oregon, N of Downtown and the Willamette R., along Albina Ave. Before 1891 an independent city, it has long been an entry point for immigrants. One of Portland's most ethnically and racially diverse areas, it has much of the city's black pop. A target of URBAN RENEWAL programs including highway and hospital construction with accompanying residential displacement, Albina experienced unrest in the 1960s. Today, a comprehensive planning effort is underway to restore and revive the neighborhood.

Albion **1.** city, pop. 2116, seat of Edwards Co., SE Illinois, 45 mi/72 km E of Mount Vernon and 4 mi/6 km W of the Indiana border. It was founded in 1818 by the English utopians Morris Birkbeck and George Flower. Birkbeck and his community were influential in preventing slavery in Illinois. **2.** agricultural town, pop. 1736, Kennebec Co., SC Maine. Albion is 10 mi/16 km E of Waterville. It is the birthplace of abolitionist martyr Elijah Lovejoy (1802–37) and his brother Owen (1811–64). **3.** city, pop. 10,066, Calhoun Co., SC Michigan, on the Kalamazoo R., 15 mi/24 km W of Jackson. Settled in 1831, this industrial center makes iron castings, liquid gas, electrical products, wire, machine tools, and trucks. It is the site of Albion College (1835) and the Whitehouse Nature Center. **4.** town, pop. 8178, seat of Orleans Co., W New York, on the Erie Canal, 32 mi/52 km W of Rochester and 10 mi/16 km S of L. Ontario. Settled in 1811, it is a trade, storage, processing, and distribution hub for locally grown fruits and vegetables. Albion is also a summer resort with some light industry and a state reformatory.

Albuquerque city, pop. 384,736, seat of BERNALILLO Co., NC New Mexico, on the Rio Grande near a pass (E) between the Sandia and Manzano mountains. It is New Mexico's largest city and its business and industrial center. Coronado's expedition (see QUIVIRA) crossed the Rio Grande here in 1540. Old Town, the original Spanish community, founded in 1706 and named for the Duke of Alburquerque, viceroy of New Spain (Mexico), was built around San Felipe de Neri church, and is now a much-visited museum and tourist district. It developed as a trade center on the Chihuahua Trail to Mexico, and after the 1840s was an important US military outpost. The arrival of the Santa Fe Railroad in 1880 spurred development, and the city, growing all around Old Town, was incorporated in 1890. The University of New Mexico (1889) and the medical industry, which boomed with the establishment of 1920s tuberculosis sanitariums, were important elements in its economy, as was its position at the junction of ROUTE 66 with the state's major N–S transportation corridor. After World War II, the Sandia military reservation and Kirtland Air Force Base became major factors. The Sandia National Laboratory, making weapons and researching solar energy and laser technology, has been among the Southwest's largest employers since 1956. The city is today a trade center for livestock producers, and a tourist center. Banking, railroad repair shops, and the manufacture of aerospace components, building materials, and electronic products are important. Albuquerque International Airport is a major regional facility. An international hot-air balloon festival is held annually.

Alcan Highway see ALASKA HIGHWAY.

Alcatraz Island familiarly, **the Rock** 12-ac/5-ha unit of the GOLDEN GATE NATIONAL RECREATION AREA, with sheer, rocky cliffs, in the Golden Gate, 1.2 mi/1.9 km N of San Francisco, California. Once a Spanish military post, later the site of a US military prison, it was a Federal maximum security prison in 1934–63. Its walls and the strait's swift currents were considered to make escape impossible; the fate of a few who tried is unknown. In the 1960s, the island was occupied for a time by Indian activists. It is now a popular tourist site.

Alcoa see under MARYVILLE, Tennessee.

Alderson town, pop. 1152, Monroe and Greenbrier counties,

SE West Virginia, on the Greenbrier R., 12 mi/19 km SW of Lewisburg. Settled (1777) in what became an agricultural and quarrying area, it has a Federal women's reformatory (1926), and was home to Alderson Baptist Academy (1901), now part of Alderson-Broaddus College in PHILIPPI.

Alderwood Manor–Bothell North unincorporated community, pop. 22,945, Snohomish Co., WC Washington, adjacent (E) to Lynnwood and 14 mi/23 km N of Seattle. It is a largely residential suburb.

Aldine unincorporated residential and commercial community, pop. 11,133, Harris Co., SE Texas, 12 mi/19 km N of downtown Houston and just SW of Houston Intercontinental Airport.

Alert see under ELLESMERE I., Northwest Territories.

Aleutian Current also, **Subarctic Current** see under CALIFORNIA CURRENT.

Aleutian Islands archipelago of over 150 rugged volcanic islands stretching 1150 mi/1850 km SW from the Alaska Peninsula to within 200 mi/320 km of the Komandorski Is. of E Siberia, with which they separate the Bering Sea (N) from the N Pacific Ocean. The main groups (E–W) are the FOX, ANDREANOF, RAT, and NEAR islands. The treeless, grassy islands are a partially submerged extension of the ALEUTIAN RANGE (Coast Mts.). Their climate is relatively mild, but rain, constant fog, high winds, and strong currents keep them dreary and isolated. The Aleuts, for whom they are named, engage in fishing, hunting, fox farming, and sheep and reindeer herding. In 1741, the Danish explorer Vitus Bering, in Russian employ, was the first European to encounter the Aleutians. Russian fur traders followed, seeking seals, sea otters, and sea lions. By the beginning of the 19th century, the marine mammal population had been severely depleted, and many Aleuts enslaved or killed. The Aleutians passed to the US in 1867; the government now controls sealing, fishing, and fur trapping. Since World War II, when the Japanese bombed a naval base at Dutch Harbor (UNALASKA) and occupied ATTU and KISKA, the islands have been of great strategic importance; over half their pop. of 11,942 is involved in some way with the military. Most of the islands are now part of the Aleutian Islands National Wildlife Refuge.

Aleutian Range extension of the COAST Mts. SW for c.600 mi/1000 km from the W end of the ALASKA RANGE along the ALASKA PENINSULA, in SW Alaska. It is composed primarily of semiactive volcanic mountains, most notably (N–S) Redoubt (10,197 ft/3108 m) and Iliamna (10,016 ft/3053 m) in the Chigmit Mts. subrange; Katmai (6715 ft/2047 m); ANIAKCHAK CRATER (4450 ft/1356 m); VENIAMINOF (8825 ft/2690 m); and Pavlof (8215 ft/2504 m). The range continues SW as the Aleutian Is. The Shishaldin Volcano (9372 ft/2857 m) on Unimak I. is noted for its symmetrical cone and as the site of a glacier. Katmai, the Valley of Ten Thousand Smokes, Novarupta Volcano, and Mt. Douglas (7064 ft/2153 m) are within KATMAI NATIONAL PARK AND PRESERVE on the peninsula. Redoubt and Iliamna are within LAKE CLARK NATIONAL PARK AND PRESERVE, at the range's N end.

Alexander Archipelago group of some 1100 offshore islands in SE Alaska which, together with a narrow mainland coastal region, forms the Alaska Panhandle, bordering British Columbia (E) and the Gulf of Alaska (W). DIXON ENTRANCE lies S of the islands, separating them from the QUEEN CHARLOTTE Is. of British Columbia. The main islands are (N–S) Chichagof, Admiralty, Baranof, Kupreanof, Kuiu, Mitkof, Wrangell, Prince of Wales, and Revillagigedo. Many deep, narrow straits run between the mountainous islands, including the N stretch of the INSIDE PASSAGE. The chief settlements are SITKA, on Baranof I., PETERSBURG, on Mitkof I., WRANGELL, on Wrangell I., and KETCHIKAN, on Revillagigedo I. Fishing, fish processing, lumbering, and trapping are the main industries. Long inhabited by the Tlingit, the islands were first explored by Europeans (Russians) in 1741. Most are now part of the TONGASS NATIONAL FOREST.

Alexander City city, pop. 14,917, Tallapoosa Co., EC Alabama, 43 mi/70 km NE of Montgomery. Settled in 1835, it is primarily industrial, manufacturing textiles, cast iron, and lumber products. HORSESHOE BEND is 10 mi/16 km ENE.

Alexandria **1.** city, pop. 49,188, seat of Rapides Parish, C Louisiana, on the Red R., opposite PINEVILLE. Settled in 1785, it was laid out 25 years later at the rapids of the Red R., then the head of navigation. The shipping of crops and cattle sustained it before the Civil War, during which it was twice occupied, in May 1863 and March 1864. It was burned when Union troops withdrew in May 1864. Railroad expansion and the exploitation of regional forests after the war helped to rebuild the city, which is now the commercial center of an extensive forest and farming area. Cotton, sugar cane, and livestock are processed in and shipped from Alexandria. The city's industries include oil refining and the manufacture of concrete, brick and tile roofing, naval stores, valves, pipe fittings, and road machinery. Alexandria is home to an undergraduate branch of Louisiana State University (1960). England Air Force Base is 6 mi/10 km NW, and FORT POLK is 29 mi/47 km SW. **2.** city, pop. 7838, seat of Douglas Co., WC Minnesota, 30 mi/48 km SE of Fergus Falls. It occupies the site of Ojibwa and Sioux camping grounds. Center of an agricultural and lake resort area, it is known for its KENSINGTON Runestone Museum, which houses purported Viking relics including the controversial Runestone, found nearby in 1898. Sculptor Duane Hansen was born here (1925). **3.** independent city, pop. 111,183, in N Virginia, on the Potomac R., 6 mi/10 km S of Washington, D.C. It is primarily a residential suburb, although it also manufactures fertilizers, machinery, furniture, and chemicals, and is home to many business, financial, and national association offices, publishing and media headquarters, and electronics and scientific research centers. It is also a rail and water transportation center, and has some Federal offices. The city developed pursuant to a 1748 Virginia act, but became part of the DISTRICT OF COLUMBIA in 1791. It was returned to Virginia in 1846. A thriving port in the 18th century, Alexandria was overshadowed by both Washington and Baltimore in later years. Its Old Port section has many old homes, and the city has numerous historic sites. The 333-ft/102-m National Masonic Memorial (1932), designed to resemble the ancient lighthouse of Alexandria, Egypt, dominates the skyline. The *Alexandria Gazette,* begun in 1784, is one of the oldest continuously published newspapers in the US.

Alfred town, pop. 5791, Allegany Co., SW New York. Largely rural, it is home to Alfred University (1836).

Algiers district of NEW ORLEANS, Louisiana, the only part of the city on the W (S) bank of the Mississippi R. It contains naval facilities, dockyards, warehouses, and part of the Gulf Intracoastal Waterway, as well as residential neighborhoods like Aurora Gardens. The district was almost completely rebuilt after an 1895 fire.

Algodones Dunes see SAND HILLS, California.

Algoma District 19,771 sq mi/51,207 sq km, pop. 127,269, in C Ontario, on the E of L. Superior and N of the St. Marys R. and the North Channel of L. Huron. Its seat is SAULT STE. MARIE; other communities include ELLIOT LAKE and WAWA. Extending N into the CANADIAN SHIELD, the Algoma region has been an important iron and steel producer since before 1900, the industry centering on Sault Ste. Marie (the Soo) and drawing on resources in the N. The **Algoma Central Railway** (1899) connected the Soo with Wawa, later with HEARST, 290 mi/470 km N. There was a 1950s uranium boom at Elliot Lake, and pulp, lumber, and some agriculture (esp. along L. Huron) have been important.

Algonquin village, pop. 11,663, McHenry and Kane counties, NE Illinois, on the Fox R., 40 mi/64 km NW of Chicago. Situated at the outer edge of the Chicago metropolitan area, it has witnessed great residential growth in recent years, and has moved away from its traditional reliance on local agriculture. Hampers and caskets are among the goods produced here.

Algonquin Hotel on 44th Street, in the TIMES SQUARE area, Manhattan, New York City. Opened in 1902 as the Puritan Hotel, it became famous in the 1920s when its Oak Room hosted the witty luncheon set called the "Round Table," among them Alexander Woollcott, Robert Benchley, and Dorothy Parker. The *New Yorker* magazine was born out of discussions at the Algonquin.

Algonquin Peak 5114 ft/1560 m, in the MacIntyre Mts. of the Adirondack Mts., in Essex Co., NE New York, 3.5 mi/6 km NW of Mt. MARCY.

Algonquin Provincial Park c.1.9 million ac/765,900 ha (3000 sq mi/7600 sq km), in SC Ontario, 130 mi/210 km NNE of Toronto, on the watershed between the Ottawa R. (N) and Georgian Bay (S). The oldest Ontario provincial park (1893), in a former logging region, it lies in the S of the CANADIAN SHIELD, and is dotted with lakes and bogs. Well known as a wildlife preserve and recreational area, it was the subject of much of the painting of Tom Thomson (1877–1917), who died mysteriously on one of its lakes.

Alhambra city, pop. 82,106, Los Angeles Co., SW California, 5 mi/8 km NE of Los Angeles, of which it is an industrial and residential suburb. Founded in 1881, it has diverse manufactures including aircraft and electronic components, other machinery, and appliances. It has attracted many Chinese immigrants in recent decades, and has a lively Chinese commercial community.

Alibates Flint Quarries National Monument 1371-ac/555-ha site on the SE side of L. MEREDITH (the Canadian R.), in the N Texas Panhandle, 29 mi/47 km NNE of Amarillo and just SW of Fritch. Agatized dolomite was mined here for perhaps 10,000 years, into the 19th century, for tools and weapons that have been found widely across the Great Plains.

Alice city, pop. 19,788, seat of Jim Wells Co., S Texas, 37 mi/61 km W of Corpus Christi. Founded in the 1880s as a cattle shipping railroad town and named for Alice Kleberg, a daughter of the nearby (SE) KING RANCH's founder, it is now the commercial and service center of a rich oil and natural gas producing and ranching region. Oil refining, metalworking, meatpacking, and cottonseed oil and dairy processing are important. The area is noted for its hunting.

Alice's Restaurant see under STOCKBRIDGE, Massachusetts.

Alief residential section of Houston, Texas, SW of the Memorial Villages and 14 mi/23 km WSW of Downtown, on the Harris–Fort Bend county line. A farming community (rice, cotton, dairying) from the 1890s, the area was annexed in the 1970s, and is now occupied by suburban housing, shopping centers, and research facilities.

Aliquippa borough, pop. 13,374, Beaver Co., SW Pennsylvania, 20 mi/32 km NW of Pittsburgh. Founded in 1750 as a trading post on the Ohio R., it was later named in honor of "Queen" Al, a local Seneca. Early industries included saw and grist milling. Aliquippa grew dramatically with expansion of the steel industry around Pittsburgh in the early 20th century, and is a center of steel production. It merged with the adjacent borough of Woodlawn in 1928.

Allagash River 80 mi/129 km long, rising in Allagash L., in Piscataquis Co., N Maine. It flows NE, through wilderness and several other lakes, and into the SAINT JOHN R. at Allagash, in Aroostook Co. The state-administered **Allagash Wilderness Waterway** is one of America's most popular canoe routes. There are extensive logging operations in the surrounding forests, which are owned primarily by paper companies.

All-American Canal 80 mi/130 km–long irrigation conduit, diverting water from the COLORADO R. at the Imperial Dam (1938), 15 mi/24 km N of Yuma, Arizona. The canal, 200 ft/61 m wide and 22 ft/7 m deep, leads across California, just N of the Mexican border, to CALEXICO, where it feeds into a network of channels watering the IMPERIAL VALLEY. Halfway along its length, the 123 mi/198 km–long Coachella Main Canal (1948) diverts part of its flow N and W to the Coachella Valley (see COLORADO DESERT).

Allatoona Dam and Lake see under ETOWAH R., Georgia.

Allegan County 832 sq mi/2155 sq km, pop. 90,509, in SW Michigan, bounded (W) by L. Michigan, drained by the Rabbit and Kalamazoo rivers. Its seat is Allegan. The county has a number of lakeshore resorts and is the site of the large Allegan State Game Area. It is a fruit growing, dairying, and agricultural area producing grains and onions. There is some manufacturing at Allegan and Plainwell.

Allegany County **1.** 421 sq mi/1090 sq km, pop. 74,946, in NW Maryland. CUMBERLAND is its seat. The area is bounded N by Pennsylvania and S by the POTOMAC R. and its North Branch (forming the West Virginia border). It is in the Appalachian Mts., with the Allegheny Mts. W. The county includes Cumberland Narrows and Green Ridge State Forest. Industries include coal mining, limestone and clay extraction, lumbering, agriculture, and some manufacturing at Cumberland. **2.** 1032 sq mi/2673 sq km, pop. 50,470, in SW New York, along the Pennsylvania line (S). Its seat is Belmont. Its S section has long been an oil and natural gas producing region; there is also some manufacturing. Local farms produce vegetables, fruit, maple syrup, and poultry.

Allegany Indian Reservation see under CATTARAUGUS Co., New York.

Allegheny former city in SW Pennsylvania, part of the NORTH SIDE of Pittsburgh since the cities' consolidation in 1907. An industrial power in its own right, it was directly opposite Pittsburgh on the N side of the Allegheny and Ohio rivers.

Allegheny Center mixed-use development in the Allegheny section of Pittsburgh, Pennsylvania's NORTH SIDE, 0.5 mi/0.8 km N of the GOLDEN TRIANGLE. The old center of Allegheny was cleared in the 1960s for commercial and residential buildings. The subsidized Allegheny Commons East complex is here, as are the Old Post Office Museum, Buhl Planetarium, and the Institute of Popular Science. WEST PARK lies immediately W.

Allegheny County 727 sq mi/1883 sq km, pop. 1,336,449, in SW Pennsylvania. Its seat is PITTSBURGH. Allegheny Co. is in the heart of a rich coal mining and steel producing area. Corporate headquarters, research and development facilities, and heavy industry are concentrated in Pittsburgh, and there is substantial suburban development.

Allegheny Courthouse and Jail municipal building in the GOLDEN TRIANGLE, in Pittsburgh, Pennsylvania, on Grant St., between Fifth and Forbes avenues. A major achievement of architect Henry Hobson Richardson, it was completed in 1888, and was one of the first US buildings to use electricity.

Allegheny Front steep escarpment in the E US, composed of Allegheny Mt. (the westernmost ridge of the Appalachian Valley and Ridge Province) and the E edge of the Allegheny Plateau, which is the N section of the Appalachian Plateau (see APPALACHIAN Mts.). The Front, which overlooks the Great Valley, marks the place where rock strata turn abruptly upward. It is known by a variety of local names: the Helderbergs in New York, the Allegheny Front in Pennsylvania, DANS Mt. in Maryland, the Allegheny Front again in N West Virginia, and Allegheny Mt. along the Virginia–West Virginia border. The escarpment continues along the edge of the CUMBERLAND PLATEAU, the S section of the Appalachian Plateau, where it is also known by a variety of local names, including Cumberland Front or Mt. in Kentucky and Tennessee, WALDEN RIDGE in Tennessee, and SAND Mt. in Alabama.

Allegheny Mountain in Virginia and West Virginia: see under ALLEGHENY FRONT.

Allegheny Mountains also, **the Alleghenies** mountainous area of the E US, extending SW for c.500 mi/800 km from NC Pennsylvania through W Maryland and E West Virginia, to SW Virginia. The Alleghenies lie within the two westernmost bands of the APPALACHIAN Mt. system. Allegheny Mt., along the West Virginia–Virginia border, is the westernmost ridge of the Valley and Ridge Province, and is part of the ALLEGHENY FRONT. The balance of the Alleghenies lies across the E edge of the **Allegheny Plateau,** the N section of the Appalachian Plateau. The Allegheny Plateau, covering a large area reaching from S of the Mohawk R. in New York to S West Virginia and into Ohio and Kentucky, also includes the CATSKILL and POCONO mountains. The steep E escarpment of the Alleghenies marks the place where the rock strata turn up abruptly. The Alleghenies are generally lowest in Pennsylvania, but nonetheless still include that state's highest point (3213 ft/980 m) at Mt. DAVIS. The Alleghenies' highest point is at SPRUCE KNOB (4862 ft/1483 m), also the highest point in West Virginia. Laurel Hill, Chestnut Ridge, Laurel Ridge, and Rich, Cheat, Shavers, and Negro mountains are some of the generally NE–SW ridges of the Allegheny Mts. Both the North Branch of the Potomac R. and the New R. cut through the heavily forested mountains. The Alleghenies are rich in hardwood timber and bituminous coal, and also contain iron ore, natural gas, clay, and petroleum. They created a significant barrier to westward migration. Today, they are much used recreationally, especially in MONONGAHELA NATIONAL FOREST in West Virginia. Allegheny National Forest, headquartered at Warren, Pennsylvania, is on the Allegheny Plateau. *Allegany* is an older spelling of the word. Nonmountainous areas of the Allegheny Plateau are sometimes also referred to as "the Alleghenies."

Allegheny River 325 mi/523 km long, in Pennsylvania and New York. One of the main tributaries of the Ohio R., it rises at an altitude of 2250 ft/686 m in the Allegheny Plateau region of Potter Co., Pennsylvania. It flows NW into New York, where it turns abruptly SW, subsequently reentering Pennsylvania and passing Warren, Oil City, and Franklin before continuing SE to pass Kittanning. The Allegheny finally meets the MONONGAHELA R. to form the Ohio R., near Pittsburgh. Considered one of the most beautiful river junctions in North America, this confluence is often called the GOLDEN TRIANGLE. Before the coming of railroads, the river was an important commercial channel. It is still used to transport bulk cargo, and some navigational locks and dams remain above Pittsburgh.

Allegheny West residential neighborhood in the Allegheny section of Pittsburgh, Pennsylvania, immediately W of WEST PARK and MEXICAN WAR STREETS. Featuring some of the best-preserved Victorian townhouses on the NORTH SIDE, it is the birthplace of writers Gertrude Stein and Mary Roberts Rinehart. A community college campus is here.

Allen city, pop. 18,309, Collin Co., NE Texas, 24 mi/39 km NNE of downtown Dallas, on Interstate 75. A largely residential suburb, it more than doubled in population in the 1980s.

Allen County **1.** 659 sq mi/1707 sq km, pop. 300,836, in NE Indiana. Its seat is FORT WAYNE, which with its suburbs forms an industrial concentration at the county's center. Bounded (E) by Ohio, and traversed by the Maumee, St. Joseph, Little Wabash, Eel, and St. Mary's rivers, it has diverse agriculture, producing grains, corn, soybeans, livestock, and dairy items. **2.** 405 sq mi/1049 sq km, pop. 109,755, in NW Ohio, intersected by the Ottawa and Auglaize rivers. Its seat and largest city is LIMA, a manufacturing center. Diversified farming, including grain, poultry, soybeans, and livestock, is important. Limestone is quarried.

Allendale unincorporated community, pop. 6950, in Allendale township, Ottawa Co., SW Michigan, 12 mi/19 km W of Grand Rapids, and just W of the Grand R. It is the seat of Grand Valley State University (1960).

Allen Park city, pop. 31,092, Wayne Co., SE Michigan, a residential suburb 10 mi/16 km SW of Detroit.

Allens Landing site in Harris Co., SE Texas, on the BUFFALO BAYOU, where brothers John and Augustus Allen in 1836 established the land project that became the city of HOUSTON. In the heart of the modern city, it was redeveloped in the late 1960s as a small historical park.

Allentown city, pop. 105,090, seat of Lehigh Co., E Pennsylvania, on the Lehigh R., 40 mi/64 km NW of Philadelphia. It is the leading commercial and industrial center of the Lehigh Valley. Located in the fertile Pennsylvania Dutch farming region, it serves as a retail and wholesale trading center for local potatoes, orchard fruits, corn, and wheat. A major producer of cement, it also manufactures Mack trucks, electronic equipment, appliances, machinery, tools, textiles, and other products. It has, however, suffered substantial industrial decline in recent decades. The city was founded (1762) by Pennsylvania chief justice William Allen. Trout Hall (1770), now a historical museum, was erected by his son James. The Liberty Bell Shrine in Zion's Reformed Church commemorates the hiding of the Liberty Bell in an old church on the site during the Revolution. The construction of a bridge across the Lehigh R. (1812) and of the Lehigh Canal (1829) led to rapid industrial development. Iron production began in 1847, and the first cement plant opened in 1850. Allentown is home to Cedar Crest College (1867), Muhlenberg College (1848), and several other institutions. Nearby Trexler Memorial Park has a large wildlife refuge.

Allenwood prison: see under WILLIAMSPORT, Pennsylvania.

Alliance **1.** city, pop. 9765, seat of Box Butte Co., NW Nebraska, 45 mi/72 km NE of Scottsbluff. It is a trading center for vegetables (especially potatoes), grain, beef, poultry, and dairy products. Carhenge, a 1987 construction modeled after England's Stonehenge, is here. **2.** city, pop. 23,393, Stark and Mahoning counties, NE Ohio, 50 mi/80 km SE of Cleveland. The first white settlers, Quakers from Virginia, arrived in 1805, and later a station of the Underground Railroad was located here. Today steel products, electrical machinery, paint, boats, boilers, and plastics are among local manufactures. A brick and tile industry is based on nearby sources of shale and clay. Alliance is the seat of Mount Union College (1846).

Alligator Alley also, **Everglades Parkway** toll road (State Route 84), 74 mi/119 km long, running E–W through S Florida. It extends between Andytown, W of Fort Lauderdale (E), and Golden Gate, just E of Naples (W), traversing the N Everglades. Two lanes wide when built, it is now being widened as part of I-75.

Alliston town, pop. (with Beeton, Tecumseth, and Tottenham) 20,239, Simcoe Co., S Ontario, 40 mi/64 km NW of Toronto, on the Boyne R. Frederick Banting, codiscoverer of insulin, was born in 1891 in what was then an agricultural community. Today a Honda auto plant is the major employer, and potatoes are the major crop.

Allouez village, pop. 14,431, Brown Co., EC Wisconsin, on the Fox R., just S of GREEN BAY. It is named after the Jesuit missionary Claude Jean Allouez.

Allston-Brighton residential neighborhood in Boston, Massachusetts. Lying N and W of Brookline, it is a primarily commercial and residential district housing young professionals who commute to jobs in central Boston, and Boston College and Boston University students. The Massachusetts Turnpike cuts through the area; there are pockets of industry, as well as a number of hospitals. Harvard Stadium is N, near the Charles R.

Allumettes, Île aux English, **Allumette Island** 70 sq mi/181 sq km, in L. Allumette, an expansion of the OTTAWA R. in SW Québec, 66 mi/106 km NW of Ottawa. A 17th-century Algonquin base, it is directly opposite PEMBROKE, Ontario (SW). Today residential and agricultural, it contains Chapeau (village, pop. 445) and a township (pop. 985), both in the Pontiac census division.

alluvial of or relating to **alluvium,** silt, sand, and other material carried by a river and deposited in any of several ways. A **delta** is formed by alluvial matter reaching the end of a river and being continuously deposited in the ocean or another large body of water. An **alluvial fan** marks the emergence of alluvium from a narrow channel into a more open space, as when a river passes through a ridge and onto a plain. An **alluvial plain,** or flood plain, is a generally level area through which a river winds, created by periodic flooding depositing layers of sediment. Although alluvium includes gravel and heavier material, what is generally called **alluvial soil** is finer material (clay, silt, organic material), forming a rich medium for agriculture.

Alma **1.** city, pop. 9034, Gratiot Co., C Michigan, on the Pine R., 50 mi/80 km N of Lansing. Founded in 1853, it is a commercial and industrial city with oil and beet-sugar refineries and food processing plants. It also manufactures auto parts, metal and plastic products, trailers, and furniture. The city is the seat of Alma College (1886) and the Michigan Masonic Home. Alma is well known for its annual Scottish Highland Festival and Games. **2.** city, pop. 25,910, Lac-Saint-Jean-Est Co., SC Québec, at the head of the SAGUENAY R., on the E of L. SAINT-JEAN, 125 mi/200 km N of Québec City. It includes five former municipalities—Alma, Riverbend, Isle-Maligne, Naudville, and the parish of Alma—consolidated in 1962. The area was primarily a foresting and agricultural center until construction (1920s) of the Isle-Maligne hydroelectric station on the Grand Décharge R., which powers the aluminum plant and paper mills that are now Alma's major industries. Lake recreation and tourism are important.

Almanor, Lake on the North Fork of the FEATHER R., 50 mi/80 km NE of Chico, in Plumas Co., NE California. A popular resort, created by the hydroelectric L. Almanor Dam, it covers 52 sq mi/135 sq km, and is fringed with pine forests and vacation estates.

Almonte town, pop. 4382, Lanark Co., SE Ontario, on the Mississippi R., 28 mi/45 km SW of Ottawa. A mill town in the early 1800s, it became a woolen textile center. Today agricultural goods and supplies and electronics products are manufactured. The surgeon and sculptor Robert Tait McKenzie (1867) and James Naismith, inventor of basketball (1861), were born here.

Aloha unincorporated community, pop. 34,284, Washington Co., NW Oregon, a residential suburb 10 mi/16 km W of Portland, at the W edge of the city's metropolitan area.

Alondra Park unincorporated residential community, pop. 12,215, Los Angeles Co., SW California, 11 mi/18 km SSW of downtown Los Angeles and immediately W of Gardena.

Alpena city, pop. 11,354, seat of Alpena Co., NE Lower Peninsula, Michigan, a port at the mouth of Thunder Bay of L. Huron, 62 mi/100 km SE of Cheboygan. The original trading post (1835) became a major sawmilling center in the late 1800s. When limestone quarrying began (1903) the cement works became the largest employer. Cement remains an important industry; other manufactures include paper products, auto trim, machinery, hydraulic cylinders, and beverages. Alpena is a year-round resort with an annual winter carnival. Alpena Community College (1952) is here. The city's Sportsmen's Island has a wildlife sanctuary, and Thunder Bay Underwater Preserve (1981), in L. Huron just outside Alpena, contains some 80 shipwrecks.

Alphabet City also, **Alphabetland** or **Alphabetville** popular name for a section of the EAST VILLAGE, Manhattan, New York City, along Avenues A, B, C, and D. A mix of high-rise apartment buildings and dilapidated older housing, the area in the 1990s suffered from poverty and drug traffic.

Alpharetta city, pop. 13,002, Fulton Co., NC Georgia, 22 mi/35 km NNE of Atlanta. A residential suburb with large business parks, it grew over 300% in population during the 1980s.

Alpine city, pop. 5637, seat of Brewster Co. (6169 sq mi/15,978 sq km, pop. 8681), W Texas, 190 mi/306 km SE of El

Paso, between the GLASS (SE) and DAVIS (NW) mountains. In the largest Texas county (larger than Connecticut), it was founded in 1882 when the railroad arrived, becoming a cattle and sheep raising center, and developed later into a resort (the nearby mountains are referred to as the "Texas Alps") with ghost towns and dude ranches. It remains a trade center, with some light manufactures. Sul Ross State University (1917) is here. Alpine is the gateway for the BIG BEND area, 80 mi/128 km SSE.

Alsip village, pop. 18,227, Cook Co., NE Illinois, a residential suburb adjoining the SW corner of Chicago, on the Calumet Sag Channel, 15 mi/24 km SW of Chicago's Loop.

Alta town, pop. 397, Salt Lake Co., NC Utah, 17 mi/27 km SE of Salt Lake City, in the WASATCH RANGE and Wasatch-Cache National Forest. Set amid peaks over 11,000 ft/3350 m, it has been a major ski center since 1937. Snowbird, immediately W, is a noted year-round resort. Alta was originally (1865–73) a silver boom town.

Alta California Spanish (later Mexican) province incorporating lands in modern California and parts of adjoining states. It was the upper counterpart to Baja (lower) California, part of what had in the 16th century been thought an island; Eusebio Kino's 1701 expedition (see PIMERIA ALTA) showed that Alta California was mainland, Baja California a peninsula. In 1825 Alta California formally became a Mexican territory, remaining so until 1848.

Altadena unincorporated community, pop. 42,658, Los Angeles Co., SW California, immediately N of Pasadena, on the lower S slopes of the San Gabriel Mts. In an orange and avocado growing area, it was established in 1887, and is home chiefly to Pasadena and Los Angeles commuters. Altadena is known for Christmas Tree Lane, part of Santa Rosa Ave., where giant deodars (Asian cedars) are decorated with lights during the holiday season.

Altamaha River 137 mi/221 km long, in SE Georgia. It is formed by the confluence of the OCONEE and OCMULGEE rivers 7 mi/11 km NNE of Hazlehurst, and flows SE to the Atlantic Ocean at **Altamaha Sound** (2 mi/3 km wide), just N of St. Simons I. With the Oconee and Ocmulgee, it drains much of C Georgia.

Altamont 1. hamlet in Alameda Co., NC California, 7 mi/11 km NE of Livermore, near the summit of Altamont Pass, site of a windpower complex involving thousands of electricity-generating propellers. At a notorious 1969 rock concert here featuring the Rolling Stones, a spectator was murdered by Hell's Angels. **2.** unincorporated community, pop. 18,591, Klamath Co., SW Oregon, a residential suburb immediately SE of Klamath Falls.

Altamonte Springs city, pop. 34,879, Seminole Co., C Florida, a residential suburb 6 mi/10 km N of Orlando.

Alton city, pop. 32,905, Madison Co., SW Illinois, on the Mississippi R. and the Missouri border, 6 mi/10 km N of the mouth of the Missouri R., and 20 mi/32 km N of St. Louis. Along with oil refineries and shipping facilities, this highly industrialized port city has factories producing glass, paper, plastic, ammunition, hardware, steel products, boats, and clothing. Limestone and building stone are quarried in the vicinity. Settled in the late 18th century, Alton emerged as a fur trading post and an important river port by the 1830s. Discoveries of local iron ore, lead, and zinc deposits encouraged mining and industrial growth. It was a center of the slavery controversy and a stop on the Underground Railroad. Rioters killed abolitionist editor Elijah P. Lovejoy here in 1837, and in 1858 Alton was the site of the final Lincoln-Douglas debate. The first Illinois State Prison (for Confederate prisoners) was established here. In Alton is a campus of Southern Illinois University.

Altoona city, pop. 51,881, Blair Co., SC Pennsylvania, on the E slopes of the Allegheny Mts., 85 mi/137 km E of Pittsburgh. It was founded in 1849 by the Pennsylvania Railroad as a locomotive switching point and facility for engines hauling freight over the mountains. In 1864 the country's first steel rails were laid between Altoona and Pittsburgh; the first steel passenger car was built here in 1902. Still a railroad and diversified transportation hub, the city is a business center for the area's agricultural products and produces silk, apparel, food, and other manufactures. Altoona is the seat of a campus of Pennsylvania State University. To the NW are Prince Gallitzin State Park and Wopsononock Mt. (2580 ft/787 m), which offers views of six counties. Horseshoe Curve (2375 ft/724 m long), on the main line of the Pennsylvania Railroad W of Altoona, is an engineering feat that rises at 91 ft/mi (17.5 m/km) and has a central curve of more than 200°. East of Altoona is a reconstruction of Fort Roberdeau, where lead for Revolutionary troops was mined.

Alturas city, pop. 3231, seat of Modoc Co. (pop. 9678), extreme NE California, on the MODOC PLATEAU, 210 mi/340 km NNE of Sacramento. On the PIT R. at the head of a broad valley, it is the trade center for a beef and sheep raising, potato and alfalfa farming, and lumbering area; headquarters to the Modoc National Forest; and a recreational service town. Founded in 1869, it was near the center of the 1870s Modoc War.

Altus city, pop. 21,910, seat of Jackson Co., SW Oklahoma, 52 mi/83 km W of Lawton. It was founded after an 1891 flood sent the residents of the town of Fraiser to higher ground, which they renamed in Latin "high place." In an irrigation district, the city processes and distributes cotton, cottonseed, alfalfa seed, wheat, and cattle. Altus Air Force Base (NE), a major training facility, is an important employer. Western Oklahoma State College (1926) is here.

Aluminum City see KITIMAT, British Columbia.

Alva city, pop. 5495, seat of Woods Co., NW Oklahoma, 50 mi/80 km NW of Enid and 13 mi/21 km S of the Kansas border. A land-office town, it played an important part in the opening of the CHEROKEE STRIP (1893). Today it is a commercial hub for a wheat farming and cattle ranching region, and produces such items as flour, feed, and dairy goods. Northwestern Oklahoma State University (1897) is here.

Alvin city, pop. 19,220, Brazoria Co., SE Texas, 25 mi/40 km SSE of Houston. A trade center for regional nurseries, truck and dairy farms, and sulfur and oil producers, it now also has space-related industries. Alvin Community College (1948) is here.

Alvin C. York State Historic Site in Pall Mall, Fentress Co., NE Tennessee, 5 mi/8 km S of the Kentucky border, and E of Dale Hollow L. Sergeant York gained international fame as one of the most decorated soldiers of World War I. The York family farm and gristmill are on Wolf R.

Alyeska resort: see under ANCHORAGE, Alaska.

Amagansett village in EAST HAMPTON town, Suffolk Co., SE New York, 14 mi/22 km ENE of Southampton. On the SOUTH FORK of Long Island's East End, it is a resort that attracts celebrities and the wealthy, and a popular second-home community for New York City residents. In the 19th century, many Amagansett men worked as whalers out of neighboring towns; fishing remains an element in the economy.

Amana Colonies seven unincorporated villages in Iowa Co., EC Iowa, on the Iowa R., some 18 mi/29 km SW of Cedar Rapids. Consisting of East Amana, West Amana, High Amana, Middle Amana, South Amana, Amana, and Homestead, these closely tied communities were founded by German Pietists in the mid 1850s. They are known for their kitchen and laundry appliances, heating and cooling systems, furniture, woolen goods, and agricultural products, and have a lively tourist industry. The villages are still managed communally.

Amargosa Range mountain group in EC California and SW Nevada, dividing DEATH VALLEY (W) from the Amargosa Desert (E). Extending 110 mi/180 km from Grapevine Peak (8737 ft/2663 m), just over the Nevada border, SSE to the Amargosa R., it includes the Grapevine Mts., the Funeral Mts., and the Black Mts. The high point of the Funerals is Pyramid Peak (6703 ft/2043 m). The Blacks include the lookout Dante's View. The range is filled with abandoned mines.

Amarillo city, pop. 157,615, seat of Potter Co., also in Randall Co., NW Texas, in the heart of the PANHANDLE, on Interstate 40. Coronado reached this area in 1541 searching for seven mythical cities of gold (see CIBOLA). Settlement began in 1887 with a railroad construction camp, which became a major cattle shipping center. Cotton became an important local product. In the 1920s industry developed with the discovery of gas and oil. Now the industrial and business center for the Panhandle and parts of Oklahoma and New Mexico, Amarillo produces beef, cement, leather, clothing, ordnance (the PANTEX plant is just NE), and helicopters. Oil, gas, zinc, copper, helium (the city claims to be the world's largest producer), and carbon black are processed. Irrigation of the High Plains area from underground water supports wheat and other crops. The city is the headquarters of the American Quarter Horse Association, and home to Amarillo College (1929) and several technical schools. Cadillac Ranch, a noted sculptural grouping of half-buried automobiles, is just W on I-40.

Ambassador Bridge 2 mi/3 km long, with a main span of 1850 ft/564 m, across the Detroit R., between Detroit, Michigan, and Windsor, Ontario, opened in 1929.

Ambler borough, pop. 6609, Montgomery Co., SE Pennsylvania, 10 mi/16 km NW of Philadelphia. It has large nurseries and produces asbestos, chemicals, pharmaceuticals, and sheet metal products. Ambler is the seat of a campus of Temple University. An early grain and milling hub settled in the 1720s, it was a major supply center during the bitter winter of 1777–78, when George Washington's army camped at VALLEY FORGE.

Amboy 1. see PERTH AMBOY and SOUTH AMBOY, New Jersey. **2. Amboy Street** see under BROWNSVILLE, New York.

Ambridge borough, pop. 8133, Beaver Co., W Pennsylvania, on the Ohio R., 17 mi/27 km NW of Pittsburgh. It is on the site of the utopian community ECONOMY (1825–1905); remains of the original village have been restored. Modern Ambridge is named for the American Bridge Co., which was headquartered here, and developed as a steelmaking center.

Ambrose Channel dredged deepwater channel across Sandy Hook Bar at the entrance to Lower New York Bay, SE New York. The 40 ft/12 m–deep channel continues through the NARROWS and into Upper New York Bay, where it becomes Anchorage Channel, with a width of 2000 ft/600 m. It also connects with a deepwater channel in RARITAN BAY. The Federally maintained channel was long marked by the **Ambrose Lightship** (now replaced by an automatic tower), 10 mi/16 km E of Sandy Hook in the Atlantic Ocean.

Amchitka Island one of the RAT Is., in the W ALEUTIAN Is., SW Alaska. Forty mi/65 km NW–SE and 2–5 mi/3–8 km wide, the treeless island was occupied by US forces during World War II and developed into an air base from which to attack the Japanese occupying ATTU and KISKA. In the 1960s and early 1970s, Amchitka was used for the underground testing of nuclear weapons. **Amchitka Pass,** a strait (E) between the Bering Sea and the N Pacific Ocean, separates the Rat Is. from the ANDREANOF Is.

Amelia County 357 sq mi/925 sq km, pop. 8787, in SC Virginia. Its seat is Amelia Courthouse. In an area of rolling hills, it is rural, with no large towns. Sailor's (or Sayler's) Creek Battlefield, in its SW corner, is the site of a battle (April 6, 1865) that immediately preceded the Confederate surrender at APPOMATTOX, 33 mi/53 km W.

Amelia Island one of the SEA ISLANDS, 13 mi/21 km N–S and up to 2 mi/3 km wide, in Nassau Co., extreme NE Florida, on the Atlantic Ocean (E), just NE of Jacksonville. Explored by the Spanish in the 16th century, it was a haven for pirates early in the 19th century. It was the site of the "Amelia Island Affair" (1817), in which an independent government was established on the island. Captured by Union troops in 1862, it introduced Northerners to Florida and spurred subsequent tourism. A popular resort, it includes the communities of FERNANDINA BEACH and Amelia City. Its N tip is occupied by 1085-ac/440-ha Fort Clinch State Park, set around an uncompleted 1847 fort.

Amenia town, pop. 5195, Dutchess Co., SE New York, 47 mi/76 km NE of Poughkeepsie and adjacent (W) to Sharon, Connecticut. A late-18th-century furnace and foundry here used local ore to manufacture iron and steel products for American forces in the Revolution. The mystical Brotherhood of the New Life, led by Thomas Lake Harris, had its headquarters here 1863–67. Today there is some light manufacturing, dairying, and truck farming.

America name: see under UNITED STATES OF AMERICA.

American Falls see under NIAGARA R.

American Fork city, pop. 15,696, Utah Co., NC Utah, 28 mi/45 km S of Salt Lake City, on the American Fork R., just N of UTAH L. It was a fur trapping center before settlement (1850). A trade center for an area that produces sugar beets and poultry, the city is also a tourist base and headquarters for TIMPANOGOS CAVE NATIONAL MONUMENT, 7 mi/11 km E. **American Fork Canyon,** between the city and Timpanogos Mt., has been an important mining district.

American Quarter section of UPTOWN New Orleans, Louisiana, across CANAL St. SW from the VIEUX CARRÉ (French Quarter). It flourished largely after the 1815 Battle of New Orleans, when Americans poured into the area, and for a period (1835–50) had its own government, parallel with that of the older French city. Today's business district, the GARDEN DISTRICT, and the IRISH CHANNEL are parts of the American Quarter.

American River 30 mi/48 km long, in NC California. Its North and South forks flow from the Sierra Nevada NE of FOLSOM, where the Folsom Dam (1955) impounds Folsom L. The river then flows SW to the SACRAMENTO R. at Sacramento. The South Fork was the scene, in Jan. 1848, of the discovery of gold at Sutter's Mill (COLOMA), setting off the California gold rush. At Auburn, 15 mi/24 km NNE of Folsom, a dam 680 ft/207 m high, to impound the North and Middle forks, was to have been completed in 1978; a 1975 earthquake halted construction.

American Samoa unincorporated US territory, pop. 46,773, in the S Pacific Ocean, some 2500 mi/4000 km SSW of Hawaii and 1000 mi/1600 km S of the Equator. The southernmost US territory, it is part of the Samoa Islands chain, which also includes Western Samoa, an independent nation. American Samoa includes (W–E) the chain's smaller islands, E of 171° W: Tutuila and Aunuu (52 sq mi/135 sq km, pop. 45,043); the Manu'a Islands (Ta'u, Olosega, and Ofu; 22 sq mi/57 sq km, pop. 1714); and tiny, uninhabited Sand and Rose. SWAIN'S ISLAND, not part of the chain, is also part of the territory, whose total land area is 76 sq mi/197 sq km. The capital is PAGO PAGO, on Tutuila. Samoa, an ancient Polynesian homeland, was discovered by Europeans in 1722. Missionaries and traders did not arrive in numbers until the 19th century. In 1900, after a failed effort by Germany, Great Britain, and the US to create a neutral zone, the islands were divided between Germany and the US. American Samoa, under US Navy control 1900–51, is now administered by the Department of the Interior; its residents are US citizens but do not vote in Federal elections. The territory has (since 1978) an elected governor and a bicameral legislature. Its leading export is canned tuna. There is a large tourist industry; Pago Pago is a popular cruise ship port of call. The thin, rocky soil of the volcanic islands limits agriculture to coastal areas, and agricultural products to copra, cocoa, and some fruits and root crops, coffee, and tobacco. The territory's pop. has grown over 70% since 1970, although sustained emigration has led to a large majority of all American Samoans living in Hawaii or on the US West Coast.

Americus city, pop. 16,512, seat of Sumter Co., SW Georgia on Muckalee Creek, 47 mi/76 km SE of Columbus. Founded in 1832, it is a trade and processing center for regional livestock, timber, and agricultural products. Kaolin and bauxite are mined nearby. Other industries include shirtmaking and mobile home construction. Americus has many associations with President Jimmy Carter, who was born in nearby PLAINS; Georgia Southwestern College (1906) is home to the Carter Library, and the volunteer organization Habitat for Humanity was founded here in 1976.

Ames city, pop. 47,198, Story Co., C Iowa, on the Squaw and Skunk rivers, 20 mi/32 km N of Des Moines. Iowa State University was founded here in 1858, and has dominated the local economy. The school's college of veterinary medicine is the country's oldest. Related facilities include the National Animal Disease Laboratory and the Institute for Atomic Research. Industries here produce equipment for water analysis and treatment.

Amesbury town, pop. 14,997, Essex Co., extreme NE Massachusetts, on the N shore of the Merrimack R. at the New Hampshire border, 43 mi/69 km N of Boston. Settled in 1642 as part of Salisbury, it was a shipbuilding port and early textile and hat manufacturing center, and is now an auto accessories manufacturer. An historic site is the home (1836–76) of John Greenleaf Whittier, many of whose poems describe the community and surrounding countryside. Amesbury's position at the junction of Routes 495 and 95 has spurred commercial development since the 1960s.

Amherst **1.** town, pop. 35,228, Hampshire Co., WC Massachusetts, in the Pioneer Valley, 22 mi/35 km NE of Springfield. Settled in 1703, and agricultural before the Revolution, the town had various industries including hat, textile, and carriage making in the 19th century. Now it is primarily an educational center, site of Amherst College (1821), the University of Massachusetts (1863), and Hampshire College (1965). These three institutions, along with Smith College (in NORTHAMPTON) and Mt. Holyoke College (in SOUTH HADLEY), have given the Amherst vicinity the nickname "the Five College Area." Commerce has grown with the prestige of the educational cluster. Literary landmarks include the home of Emily Dickinson. **2.** town, pop. 9068, Hillsborough Co., S New Hampshire. Amherst is on Beaver Brook and the Souhegan R., 11 mi/18 km SW of Manchester and adjoining Merrimack (E). Built around the "Big Common," the town center has retained much of its 18th–19th-century character, with many Colonial, Federal, and Greek Revival buildings. Horace Greeley was born here (1811). **3.** town, pop. 111,711, Erie Co., W New York, adjacent (NE) to Buffalo. It is a largely residential suburb of Buffalo, and the new home of the State University of New York College at Buffalo. Interstate 90 and Buffalo's beltway (Route 290) meet in the town. **4.** town, pop. 9742, seat of Cumberland Co., NW Nova Scotia, on the Cumberland Basin, 2 mi/3 km E of the New Brunswick border, in the CHIGNECTO isthmus. A 17th-century Acadian settlement, Les Planches, on high ground near the huge Tantramar Marshes, it was renamed in 1760. A 19th-century textile and shoemaking center, it boomed around World War I making railway cars and other engineered products, and now has varied manufactures. Today the town is a gateway to Nova Scotia, in an agricultural area known for its blueberries. Fort Beauséjour is just NW, in New Brunswick, and the government experimental farm at Nappan is 5 mi/8 km SSW. **5.** city, pop. 10,332, Lorain Co., N Ohio, 25 mi/40 km SW of Cleveland. It is situated in a sandstone quarrying and fruit growing area.

Amherstburg town, pop. 8921, Essex Co., extreme S Ontario, 14 mi/23 km S of Windsor, on the Detroit R. near L. Erie. In 1796 the British built Fort Malden here following their evacuation from Detroit, 16 mi/26 km N. It served as their frontier base in the War of 1812 and subsequently as a garrison in the rebellion of 1837–38. With its strategic site on a narrowing of the Detroit R. it also was an escape point for fugitive slaves on the UNDERGROUND RAILROAD. In a rich agricultural region, the town today manufactures chemicals and auto parts and is involved in marine salvage.

Amish Country **1.** area of rolling farmland in NE Ohio, including parts of Stark, Wayne, Coshocton, Tuscarawas, and especially Holmes counties, where Amish migrated from Pennsylvania in the early 1800s. Today agriculture remains the economic mainstay for these self-sufficient communities; cheese is manufactured and sold to the "outside." Major centers include Berlin, Millersburg, and Wilmot. **2.** region in and around Lancaster Co., SE Pennsylvania, where a number of Amish, members of a sect of Mennonites, have lived since the early 18th century. The Amish live separate from the modern world and adhere to a lifestyle closer to that of the 18th century than the 20th. Highly productive farmers, they settled around Lancaster, where they continue to maintain their independent and tradition-rich community life. The rolling land is dotted with small family farms, where engine-powered machinery is forbidden. On its roads, now clogged with tourists, modern traffic mingles with horse-drawn Amish buggies.

Amistad Reservoir international project of the US and Mexico on the RIO GRANDE, 8 mi/13 km NW of DEL RIO, Texas. Amistad Dam stands between Del Rio and the confluence of the Rio Grande and Devils rivers. The Texas share of the reservoir is 64,900 ac/26,300 ha, or 56%; over half of the 1000-mi/1600-km shoreline is on the US side. The Amistad National Recreation Area is popular for water sports, scuba diving, fishing, and hunting. The river canyons here contain ancient pictographs now visible only from the water.

Amityville village, pop. 9286, in the town of Babylon, Suffolk Co., SE New York, on Long Island's South Shore, 32 mi/52 km ESE of Manhattan. On the Great South Bay, it is a residential and resort village on the dividing line between Suffolk and Nassau counties.

Amory city, pop. 7093, Monroe Co., NE Mississippi, 19 mi/31 km SE of Tupelo, near the East Fork of the TOMBIGBEE R. A railroad town founded in 1887 at the W edge of the Black Prairie (see BLACK BELT), it is near the site of Cotton Gin Port (1816), on the Tombigbee. With the opening of the Tennessee-Tombigbee Waterway (1985), it has become a port itself. Timber and dairy products, in addition to cotton, are produced in the area, which also went through a brief 1920s natural gas boom.

Amos city, pop. 13,783, Abitibi Co., NW Québec, 240 mi/390 km NW of Ottawa, near the head (S) of the Harricana R., in the rich farmland of the E CLAY BELT. Established in 1914 on the Canadian Northern (Canadian National) Railway, it grew on agriculture and lumbering, and has a number of large saw and paper mills.

Amoskeag Falls see under MANCHESTER, New Hampshire.

Ampersand Lake roughly 1 mi/1.6 km in diameter, in Harrietstown, Franklin Co., in the Adirondack Mts., NE New York, 9 mi/15 km SSW of Saranac Lake. Once the site of the Adirondack Club, popularly known as the Philosophers' Camp, it was in 1858 the scene of a wilderness outing organized by journalist and artist William J. Stillman (1828–1901), attended by such members of the Boston intelligentsia as Ralph Waldo Emerson, James Russell Lowell, and Louis Agassiz.

Amsterdam city, pop. 20,714, Montgomery Co., EC New York, on the New York State Barge Canal and the Mohawk R., 30 mi/48 km NW of Albany. It was settled in 1783 as Veedersburg, taking its present name in 1804. Situated on the MOHAWK TRAIL, it developed quickly, especially following completion of the Erie Canal in 1825. By 1838, textile mills had been built along the Chuctanunda Creek, which flows into the Mohawk R., and Amsterdam became a textile and carpeting center. Modern diversified industries include the manufacture of electronic games and fiberglass. Fort Johnson (1749) and the Guy Park Manor (1766) are maintained as museums.

Amtrak promotional name for the US **National Railroad Passenger Corporation,** authorized in 1970 and operational since May 1, 1971. It is a quasi-governmental body created, in reaction to the post–World War II decline or collapse of almost all American railroads, to manage long-distance passenger rail service throughout the country. Its 1971 routes were so limited that surviving US passenger runs were, in effect, cut by 50% the day it began operation. Amtrak at first managed service, using equipment and tracks belonging to various railroads. Subsequently it has built its own rolling stock, purchased some trackage, and expanded service in some areas, although total coverage remains at a small fraction of early-20th-century standards. In Canada, VIA has played an analogous role since 1978.

Anacapa Island one of the SANTA BARBARA (or Channel) Is., in the Pacific Ocean, 11 mi/18 km off the coast of Ventura Co., SW California. Actually a group of three small, rocky islets totaling 5 mi/8 km E–W, Anacapa is part of the Channel Islands National Park.

Anaconda city, pop. 10,278, seat of, and coextensive with, Deer Lodge Co., SW Montana, on Warm Springs Creek, 22 mi/35 km NW of Butte. Founded in a mineral-rich mountainous region as Copperopolis in 1883, it grew rapidly after a water powered copper smelter was built the following year. The enterprise became one of the world's largest nonferrous metal works, ultimately producing copper, gold, silver, lead, zinc, and arsenic. Smelting and phosphate production were the economic mainstays until Atlantic Richfield closed the smelter in 1980, causing severe economic hardship. The smelter's 585-ft/178-m smokestack dominates the city.

Anacortes city, pop. 11,451, Skagit Co., NW Washington, on Fidalgo I. in Puget Sound, 17 mi/27 km SSW of Bellingham. A deepwater shipping center, it is a busy port of call along the INSIDE PASSAGE. Settled in the 1850s, it was unsuccessful at attracting railroads in the late 19th century, but nonetheless became a thriving city. Its economy relies on lumbering, canning, oil refining, commercial fishing, shipbuilding, the manufacture of wood products and processed foods, and tourism. Ferries leave here for Sidney in British Columbia and the San Juan Is. There is also a bridge to WHIDBEY I. (S).

Anacostia largely residential section of Washington, D.C., in the extreme SE, across the Anacostia R. from the rest of the District, and sometimes called Trans-Anacostia. A hilly area, it first developed as an 1850s suburb, housing workers at Washington's navy yard, and remained lightly populated and isolated until after World War II. When urban renewal (chiefly highway) projects in SOUTHWEST and other District sections displaced poorer residents in the 1950s and 1960s, they began to find housing here, and in the 1960s Anacostia's older, middle-class white population fled for the suburbs. The area, which with Congress Heights (S) makes up the District's Ward 8, is now densely populated and economically marginal. The opening of subway service to Downtown in 1992 was looked to as a hopeful development. The home (1877–95) of antislavery leader and diplomat Frederick Douglass is a National Historic Site.

Anacostia River 12 mi/19 km long, in Maryland and the District of Columbia. It is formed by several branches near Hyattsville, Maryland, and flows SW past Bladensburg and through SE Washington, D.C. to the Potomac R. Military installations at its mouth in Washington include Bolling Air Force Base (S) and Fort McNair (N); the Washington Navy Yard is just NE. The National Arboretum and other parklands lie upstream.

Anadarko city, pop. 6586, seat of Caddo Co., WC Oklahoma, on the Washita R., 50 mi/80 km SW of Oklahoma City. It was founded in 1901 on lands long hunted by the Kiowa, Comanche, and Wichita. Oil was discovered nearby in 1920, and the industry remains important. The city is a commercial center for producers of cotton and cottonseed oil, peanuts, corn, livestock, poultry, and dairy goods. Light industries include rug manufacturing, and there is substantial tourism. The city has a large Indian population and is the seat of the Riverside Indian School and a Bureau of Indian Affairs Office that serves W Oklahoma and portions of Kansas. The American Indian Exposition is held here annually, and there are several museums and re-creations of tribal life.

Anaheim city, pop. 266,406, Orange Co., SW California, 25 mi/40 km SE of Los Angeles, in the Santa Ana Valley. An 1857 communal settlement its German founders named their home (*heim*) on the Santa *Ana* R., it was a small citrus and strawberry growing center until the 1950s. The prototype amusement park Disneyland opened in 1955, and the city, whose population in 1950 had been 15,000, grew rapidly. Other theme and amusement parks followed. Anaheim Stadium (1966) is home to the California Angels (baseball) and Los Angeles Rams (football). The city is now a major residential suburb; tourism dominates its economy, but it is also industrial; electronics equipment is a major manufacture.

Anahuac see under TRINITY BAY, Texas.

Anaktuvuk Pass in the Endicott Mts. of the BROOKS RANGE, NC Alaska, W of the Trans-Alaska Pipeline, and 145 mi/233 km NNW of Fairbanks. Now within the GATES OF THE ARCTIC National Park, it is said to have been an important passageway for early migration from Asia to North America. **Anaktuvuk Pass** city (pop. 259, North Slope Borough) is home to the few remaining Nunamint Eskimos.

Anamosa city, pop. 5100, seat of Jones Co., SE Iowa, 22 mi/35 km ENE of Cedar Rapids, on the Wapsipinicon R. where it is joined by Buffalo Creek. An agricultural trade center, with limestone and concrete industries and a state reformatory, it is the birthplace (1892) of the painter Grant Wood, whose work drew on local and regional themes. Stone City, 4 mi/6 km W on the Wapsipinicon, was an 1880s limestone boom town. In the early 1930s, Wood painted there and conducted an arts colony.

Anasazi general term for the people living, from as long as 4000 years ago until about 500 years ago, on the plateaus and mesas and in the canyons of N Arizona and New Mexico and S Colorado and Utah, the ancestors of today's PUEBLO Indians (the Hopi, the Zuñi, and others). Known also as the Basketmakers or the Cliff Dwellers, the Anasazi lived in stone-lined, adobe-floored pit houses, then in large communal dwellings as at MESA VERDE. Apparently nomadic at first, they became agriculturalists, farming the valley floors below their dwelling places. They are noted for their underground ritual chambers, called *kivas*.

Ancaster town, pop. 21,988, Hamilton-Wentworth Regional Municipality, S Ontario, a largely residential suburb 7 mi/11 km SW of HAMILTON.

Anchorage city, pop. 226,338, coterminous with Anchorage Borough (1732 sq mi/4486 sq km), S Alaska, 260 mi/419 km SSW of Fairbanks, at the head of COOK INLET, E of the Alaska Range and SW of the Chugach Mts. Captain James Cook arrived in the area in 1778, followed by Russian settlers. In the late 1800s gold prospectors passed through. In 1915 the city was founded as the headquarters of the ALASKA RAILROAD to Fairbanks. It grew to be the most important commercial center in the state, serving the farming, oil producing, and mining areas of the MATANUSKA VALLEY (NE) and KENAI PENINSULA (S). Oil drilled from platforms on Cook Inlet has become increasingly important to the city's economy in recent years, and is shipped year-round from the ice-free port. Anchorage has been a vital aviation and defense center since the 1940s, and Ft. Richardson and Elmendorf Air Force Base, built during World War II, continue to be major employers. The international airport is one of the busiest in the US. Tourism is an important industry; winter sports facilities include the Alyeska ski area, the state's largest, 38 mi/61 km SE. The IDITAROD race is an important annual event, as is the Fur Rendezvous, a fur buyers' market. Alaska Pacific University (1957) and a campus (1976) of the University of Alaska are here. In March 1964, a severe earthquake heavily damaged the city, but reconstruction took place quickly.

Anchor Bay see under L. SAINT CLAIR, Michigan.

Ancienne-Lorette see L'ANCIENNE-LORETTE, Québec.

Ancient Bristlecone Pine Forest see under WHITE Mts., California.

Andalusia city, pop. 9269, seat of Covington Co., S Alabama, near the Conecuh R. Settled in the 1830s, it developed after the 1899 arrival of two railroads. The city processes cotton, peanuts, and meat, and makes wood products. It is home to Lurleen B. Wallace State Junior College (1969).

Anderson **1.** city, pop. 59,459, seat of Madison Co., EC Indiana, on the West Fork of the White R., 34 mi/55 km NE of Indianapolis. It was founded on the site of a Delaware Indian village in 1823, but industrial growth did not begin until the discovery of natural gas nearby in 1887. The auto parts industry was established locally in 1901. Today the city's manufactures also include firefighting vehicles, tile, bedding, paperboard and cardboard, industrial machinery, castings, glass, and tools. Of historic interest are the restored Victorian homes of its West Eighth St. district. Anderson University (1917) is here. The prehistoric earthworks of Mounds State Park are 3 mi/5 km E. **2.** city, pop. 26,184, seat of Anderson Co. (pop. 145,196), NW South Carolina, 28 mi/45 km SW of Greenville, in the Blue Ridge foothills. It was founded (1827) on former Cherokee land, in an Up Country area settled largely by Scotch-Irish migrants from Virginia and Pennsylvania, and was a trade and Civil War munitions producing center. Its textile industry was boosted by early (1890s) hydroelectricity from the nearby Seneca R. Today it manufactures fiberglass, metals, textile machinery, clothing, fertilizer, and glass, and is an agricultural shipping center. Anderson College (1911) is here.

Andersonville **1.** village, pop. 277, Sumter Co., SW Georgia, 10 mi/16 km NNE of Americus, site (1863–65) of the Confederate prison Camp Sumter. Designed for 10,000, the camp housed as many as 33,000 men at once. Close to 14,000 died because of overcrowding, exposure, lack of food and medication, and unsanitary conditions. The camp's superintendent was hanged in Nov. 1865. Andersonville National Historic Site includes a national cemetery, where 13,741 Union soldiers are buried, a museum, and several state monuments. **2.** residential neighborhood on the North Side of Chicago, Illinois. A stable, middle-class area of Swedish immigrants dating to the 1920s, today it is home to their descendants as well as to Japanese, Koreans, and Christian Arabs.

Andover **1.** town, pop. 29,151, Essex Co., NE Massachusetts, 25 mi/40 km NE of Boston. It is the seat of Phillips Academy, popularly referred to as Andover School, one of the oldest (1778) US private boys' schools (merged with all-girls Abbott Academy in 1973). The Andover Theological Seminary, here 1808–1908, is now part of Andover Newton Theological School, in NEWTON. Situated just inside Interstate 495, Andover has some light manufacturing, biotech research, and electronics and weapons research and production. **2.** city, pop. 15,216, Anoka Co., SE Minnesota, 20 mi/32 km N of Minneapolis, a fast-growing outer-ring suburb of the Twin Cities.

Andreanof Islands group in the C ALEUTIAN Is., between the Bering Sea (N) and the N Pacific Ocean, in SW Alaska. Some 275 mi/445 km E–W, they are flanked by the Is. of the Four Mountains (E) and the RAT Is. (W). Principal islands in the group include (E–W) Amlia, Atka, ADAK, Kanaga, and Tanaga. They are treeless but covered with grasses and sedges; their Aleut pop. engages in fishing, hunting, sheep ranching, and fox farming. During World War II, US troops built several military bases here, some later enlarged and made permanent.

Andrews city, pop. 10,678, seat of Andrews Co., W Texas, 35 mi/56 km NNW of Odessa. A trade hub on the S LLANO ESTACADO, it is in the center of one of the richest US oil and gas producing regions. Long a cattle town, it grew in mid-century after regional oil began to be extracted.

Andrews Air Force Base military airport (locality pop. 10,228) in Prince George's Co., C Maryland, 10 mi/16 km SE of Washington, D.C. Established in 1942, it is home base for presidential and other governmental aircraft, and an arrival point for visiting dignitaries.

Androscoggin County 477 sq mi/1235 sq km, pop. 105,259, in SW Maine. An agricultural, dairying, and industrial region, the county includes the twin cities of Lewiston and Auburn, which form Maine's historic textile-manufacturing, and one of the major US footwear-producing, centers. Auburn is the county seat. Other industries include paper and wood production, linoleum manufacture, corn and egg farming, and hydroelectric production from the Androscoggin and Little Androscoggin rivers.

Androscoggin River 175 mi/280 km long, rising at Umbagog L., N New Hampshire, on the Maine border, and flowing through SW Maine. It joins the Kennebec to form Merrymeeting Bay just NE of Brunswick. The Androscoggin was a major industrial river in the 19th century; its flow provided power for mills and factories, some still operative, at Berlin, New Hampshire, and Bethel, Rumford, Livermore Falls, Lewiston-Auburn, Lisbon Falls, and Brunswick-Topsham in Maine.

Angeles National Forest c.693,000 ac/281,000 ha, incorporating most of the SAN GABRIEL Mts., in SW California. Mounts SAN ANTONIO, LOWE, WILSON, and Baden-Powell are in the forest, which is traversed by the **Angeles Crest Highway** (Route 2). Wildernesses, lakes, and ski areas provide recreational opportunities for Los Angeles–area residents.

Angelina River 200 mi/320 km long, in E Texas. It rises near TYLER, flowing from dam-created L. Tyler generally SE, into 115,000-ac/46,000-ha Sam Rayburn (McGee Bend) Reservoir (completed 1965). The reservoir, the largest entirely within Texas, is surrounded by 153,000-ac/61,900-ha **Angelina National Forest,** a recreational asset in the once (early 20th century) cut-over PINEY WOODS. From the reservoir the Angelina flows S to join the NECHES R., 12 mi/19 km W of Jasper.

Angelino Heights architectural preservation district in the ECHO PARK section of Los Angeles, California, along Carroll Ave., 2 mi/3 km NW of Downtown. An area of restored Victorian homes built during the real estate boom of the 1880s, it was the first of the city's many STREETCAR SUBURBS.

Angel Island 740 ac/300 ha, in San Francisco Bay, off the S coast of Marin Co., NC California, just S of Tiburon. The bay's largest island, originally a home of the Coast Miwok, it became an Army camp during the Civil War. As San Francisco's Quarantine and Immigration Station, it held immigrants, including some 200,000 Chinese, in 1910–40, then served during World War II as an internment camp for enemy aliens. Since 1966 it has been a state park. It is sometimes called the "Ellis Island of the West."

Angel Mounds see under EVANSVILLE, Indiana.

Angels Camp officially, **Angels** city, pop. 2409, Calaveras Co., NC California, in the Sierra Nevada foothills, 67 mi/108 km SE of Sacramento. It was named for the man who found gold on a creek here in 1848. A lumbering, quarrying, and ranching center after the gold boom died, it is now primarily a tourist magnet. According to legend, Mark Twain heard the basis of his 1864 story "The Jumping Frog of Calaveras County" in a local bar; the event is commemorated each May in the Jumping Frog Jubilee held just S, at Frogtown. Other local sites associated with mining days, with Twain, or with the stories of Bret Harte, include Carson Hill, Cherokee Flat (later Altaville, now part of Angels), Copperopolis, and Jackass Hill. The area now has a number of vineyards. The NEW MELONES L., on the Stanislaus R., is just S.

Angleton city, pop. 17,140, seat of BRAZORIA Co., SE Texas, 42 mi/68 km S of Houston, in the Coastal Plain. It is the trade and processing center for an area that produces fruit, vegetables, cotton, livestock, rice, oil, and gas. Banking and seafood processing are also important.

Angola **1.** city, pop. 5824, seat of Steuben Co., extreme NE Indiana, 10 mi/16 km S of the Michigan border, 10 mi/16 km W of the Ohio border, and 40 mi/64 km NNE of Fort Wayne. Once an Indian hunting ground, it was settled as a trading station in the mid 1800s. In a hilly, lake-filled region, it is a popular vacation center. Local agricultural products are processed, and there is some light industry. Angola is the seat of Tri-State University (1884). **2.** locality in West Feliciana Parish, SE Louisiana, 42 mi/68 km NW of Baton Rouge, between the Mississippi R. (W and S) and the Mississippi state line (N), site of the Louisiana State Penitentiary. **3.** village, pop. 2231, in Evans township, Erie Co., NW New York, just E of L. Erie and 19 mi/31 km SW of Buffalo. Its light manufactures include plastic products and canned goods. Air conditioning pioneer W.H. Carrier was born here in 1876.

Angoon see under ADMIRALTY ISLAND NATIONAL MONUMENT, Alaska.

Angwin unincorporated community, pop. 3503, Napa Co., NC California, 22 mi/35 km NW of Napa, in a vineyard and fruit growing region just E of the Napa Valley. Pacific Union College (1882) is here.

Aniakchak Crater 4450 ft/1356 m high, in the ALEUTIAN RANGE, 40 mi/64 km N of Chignik on the ALASKA PENINSULA, in SW Alaska. One of the largest known CALDERAS, the

Aniakchak was thought to be extinct until it erupted in 1931. Covering about 30 sq mi/78 sq km, the crater contains Surprise L., source of the Aniakchak R., which emerges from a break in the wall. It lies within the Aniakchak National Monument and Preserve (602,800 ac/244,125 ha).

Animas Mountains extension of Mexico's Sierra Madre in the SW corner of New Mexico, rising to 8519 ft/2597 m at Animas Peak.

Anjou city, pop. 37,210, a largely residential, French-speaking part of the MONTRÉAL URBAN COMMUNITY, S Québec, adjacent (NE) to Montréal.

Ankeny city, pop. 18,482, Polk Co., C Iowa, a residential suburb 8 mi/13 km N of Des Moines. It has experienced recent residential and commercial growth. Faith Baptist Bible College and Theological Seminary (1921) is here, as is a large John Deere farm machinery plant.

Ann, Cape peninsula, Essex Co., NE Massachusetts, part of the NORTH SHORE, 30 mi/49 km NE of Boston. Extending 14 mi/22 km past Gloucester Harbor into the Atlantic Ocean, it has a rocky, rugged terrain dotted with fishing villages and ports. On Cape Ann are the city of GLOUCESTER and the town of ROCKPORT. The cape is popular with artists and tourists for its charm and beauty.

Anna village, pop. 1164, Shelby Co., W Ohio, 8 mi/13 km N of Sidney. Situated in a farming area, it is the site of a Honda engine factory.

Anna, Lake see under NORTH ANNA R., Virginia.

Annandale unincorporated community, pop. 50,975, Fairfax Co., N Virginia, 7 mi/11 km W of Alexandria, just inside the BELTWAY. It is a largely residential suburb of Washington, D.C., which is 10 mi/16 km to the NE.

Annandale-on-Hudson village in rural Red Hook township, Dutchess Co., SE New York, on the E bank of the Hudson R., 21 mi/34 km N of Poughkeepsie. It is home to Bard College (1860).

Annapolis city, pop. 33,187, state capital and seat of Anne Arundel Co., C Maryland, on the S bank of the Severn R., near its mouth on Chesapeake Bay, 25 mi/40 km SSE of Baltimore. Settled as Providence in 1649, the site has been known as Town of Proctors, Town at the Severn, and Anne Arundel Town. Its present name, honoring Princess (later Queen) Anne, was chosen in 1695, a year after the provincial capital had been moved here from SAINT MARYS CITY. Annapolis is a market and shipping center for agricultural and marine products; it has research and development firms, but few industries. Housing has replaced local truck and tobacco farms. The city's extensive historic district includes the State House (1772–74), the oldest state capitol still in legislative use. The Continental Congress convened here 1783–84, receiving Washington's resignation as commander-in-chief of the Continental Army, and ratifying the Treaty of Paris. The US Naval Academy was built around Old Fort Severn in 1845. St. John's College, established in 1784, replaced King William's School (1696). An oceanographic laboratory is maintained jointly by the state government, the Naval Academy, and Johns Hopkins University.

Annapolis River 75 mi/120 km long, in W Nova Scotia. It rises SW of Kentville and flows generally WSW past Middleton and Bridgetown, through a glacial lowland, to the tidal **Annapolis Basin** at Annapolis Royal. Its fertile valley is famous for its apples. Marshland at its lower end is protected by dikes begun by 17th-century Acadian settlers; at Annapolis Royal is a pioneer (1984) tidal power generating station. The basin, an inlet of the Bay of FUNDY, extends 16 mi/26 km ENE–WSW to Digby, and connects with the bay via the narrow, cliff-bordered Digby Gut.

Annapolis Royal town, pop. 633, seat of Annapolis Co. (pop. 23,641), SW Nova Scotia, at the head of the Annapolis Basin, on the Annapolis R., 95 mi/153 km W of Halifax and 14 mi/23 km NE of Digby. PORT-ROYAL (1605) is across the river, and the town's history begins with a 1630s French fort, replaced in the 1680s by Fort Anne. Forts and the settlement changed hands several times between the French and British (and New Englanders) until ceded to Britain by the 1713 Treaty of Utrecht. A market town in an apple region, Annapolis Royal now draws visitors to the Fort Anne National Historic Park and historic gardens and dikelands.

Ann Arbor city, pop. 109,592, Washtenaw Co., SE Michigan, on the Huron R., 36 mi/58 km W of Detroit. Settled in 1823 and named for the grape arbors of Ann Allen and Ann Rumsey, wives of the settlers, it grew when the University of Michigan moved here from Detroit in 1837. The arrival (1839) of the Michigan Central and Ann Arbor railroads also made it an agricultural trading center. Today the university is one of the country's major institutions of higher learning, and the main factor in Ann Arbor's economy. Its Institute of Science and Technology has made the city a center for aerospace, metallurgical, chemical, and nuclear research, complete with a 110-ac/45-ha industrial and research park. It is also a medical center; besides the university medical school, there are several large hospitals. Local manufactures include ball bearings, coil springs, machinery, tools, cameras, and scientific instruments. Ann Arbor is surrounded by lakes and is also a summer resort. It is the seat of Washtenaw Community College (1965) and Concordia Lutheran College (1962).

Anne Arundel County 418 sq mi/1083 sq km, pop. 427,239, in C Maryland, bounded W by the Deep R., E by Chesapeake Bay, and N and NE by the Patapsco R. Its seat is ANNAPOLIS, the state capital. The county lies primarily in the coastal plain. It is more densely populated in the N where it borders on Baltimore; the shore remains relatively rural. Regional farms produce tobacco, corn, grain, and soybeans. Tourism is also important. The county includes residential suburbs of both Annapolis and Baltimore, FORT MEADE, and BALTIMORE-WASHINGTON INTERNATIONAL AIRPORT.

Annex, the affluent residential section of NC TORONTO, Ontario, immediately W of YORKVILLE, N of BLOOR St. and the University of Toronto, noted for its late-19th-century houses. It was annexed to the city in 1887.

Annisquam see under GLOUCESTER, Massachusetts.

Anniston city, pop. 26,623, seat of Calhoun Co., NE Alabama, in the foothills of the Appalachian Mts., 58 mi/93 km ENE of Birmingham. Ironworks built here in 1863 to supply the Confederate army were destroyed by Union forces in 1865. A private industrial village was created in 1872; it was incorporated as a town in 1883. Anniston is in an iron mining and cotton growing area, and produces appliances, pipe, chemicals, machine parts, industrial castings, yarn, and clothing. The city is also a military service center; the Anniston Army Depot, 10 mi/16 km W, is a major ordnance facility, and Fort McClellan (1917), with units NE and NW, is the headquarters of the Army's military police and its Chemical Corps.

Annville township, pop. 4294, Lebanon Co., SE Pennsylvania, on Quitapahilla Creek, 4 mi/6 km W of Lebanon. The seat of Lebanon Valley College (1866), it produces shoes and hosiery and engages in limestone quarrying and dairying.

Anoka city, pop. 17,192, seat of Anoka Co., SE Minnesota, on the Mississippi R., where it is joined by the Rum R., a suburb 18 mi/29 km NW of Minneapolis. Formerly a trading center for an agricultural region, it has experienced a boom in residential and commercial development over recent decades, lying in the Twin Cities–St. Cloud corridor.

Anoka County 430 sq mi/1114 sq km, pop. 243,641, in EC Minnesota, bordered by the Mississippi R. (SW). The city of ANOKA, its seat, and the communities of Ham Lake, Ramsey, and Coon Rapids are among the many Twin Cities suburbs that make up the S part this county, which is situated to the N of Minneapolis and St. Paul. The balance is largely agricultural, raising grain, dairy cattle, and other livestock. The Carlos Avery Wildlife Area is in the NE corner.

Ansley Park residential neighborhood in Atlanta, Georgia, 2.5 mi/4 km N of FIVE POINTS. Just NW of Piedmont Park, it is an affluent district of single-family homes. The Atlanta Memorial Arts Center lies in the S.

Ansonia city and coterminous township, pop. 18,403, New Haven Co., SW Connecticut, on the Naugatuck R., 16 mi/26 km NE of Bridgeport. Settled in 1651, it had a brass and copper mill by 1853, and became a major producer of metal products. Its industries, heavily tied to defense contracting, were in depression at the beginning of the 1990s.

Antelope Valley area in the far N of Los Angeles Co., SW California, 50 mi/80 km N of Los Angeles, at the W end of the MOJAVE DESERT. LANCASTER and PALMDALE are its major cities. The Antelope Valley is a rich fruit growing area; its wild poppies are famous. EDWARDS AIR FORCE BASE lies immediately N.

Anthracite Belt in Pennsylvania, areas of the VALLEY AND RIDGE PROVINCE where geologic forces produced veins of hard coal, as distinct from the soft (bituminous) coal of the Pittsburgh area. The Anthracite Belt is in NE Pennsylvania, around SCRANTON (the Lackawanna Valley) and Wilkes-Barre (the WYOMING VALLEY). Another center was Mauch Chunk (now JIM THORPE). The coal seams have been so depleted that the area is no longer central, as it once was, to heavy industry.

Anticosti, L'Île-d' English, **Anticosti Island** 3059 sq mi/7923 sq km, pop. 264, in the Gulf of SAINT LAWRENCE at the mouth of the St. Lawrence R., 50 mi/80 km NE of the Gaspé Peninsula and 375 mi/600 km NE of Québec City, in E Québec. Heavily forested, with many small rivers, canyons, and a bog, it extends 135 mi/220 km WNW–ESE, and rises to 625 ft/191 m in the N. Wildlife is abundant; there are hunting reserves. Jacques Cartier landed here in 1534. In 1680 the island was granted to Louis Jolliet; ceded to Britain in 1763, it became part of Québec in 1774. It has never supported a viable community for any length of time, but has been a hunting reserve, vacation retreat, and logging center; in 1926, it was taken over by paper interests. Port-Menier, near the W tip, is its only settlement; there are scattered campsites.

Antietam National Battlefield, 3244 ac/1314 ha, in Washington Co., NW Maryland, on the banks of Antietam Creek, just SE of SHARPSBURG, and 3 mi/5 km NW of Antietam village. Antietam National Cemetery is nearby. Antietam is the site of the bloodiest day of fighting in the Civil War (Sept. 17, 1862), on which George McClellan's Union forces repelled R.E. Lee's first invasion of the North. The Cornfield and the Bloody Lane are among parts of the Antietam battlefield that entered the national consciousness.

Antigo city, pop. 8276, seat of Langlade Co., NC Wisconsin, 26 mi/42 km NE of Wausau, on headwaters of the Eau Claire R. It is a gateway to N Wisconsin forest and lake resorts, produces processed cheese and other dairy goods, and distributes area potatoes and maple syrup.

Antigonish town, pop. 4924, seat of Antigonish Co. (pop. 19,226), NC Nova Scotia, 100 mi/160 km ENE of Halifax, near St. Georges Bay. A trade center, it is home to St. Francis Xavier University (1853; here since 1855), progenitor (1928) of the Antigonish (cooperative) Movement, which transformed the lives of Acadian fishermen.

Antioch city, pop. 62,195, Contra Costa Co., NC California, on the San Joaquin R. just S of where it joins the Sacramento R., 27 mi/43 km NE of Oakland. Founded in 1849 by New Englanders, it has chemical, paper, glass, and other industries, power plants, and facilities for packing and shipping agricultural products of the fertile San Joaquin–Sacramento delta region. Its pop. increased by over 120% in the period 1970–90.

Anvil Range see under FARO, Yukon Territory.

ANWR also, "**Anwar**" see ARCTIC NATIONAL WILDLIFE REFUGE, Alaska.

Anza Borrego Desert State Park c.600,000 ac/243,000 ha (940 sq mi/2430 sq km) in S California, in the SW of the COLORADO DESERT, from near the Salton Sea (N) to near the Baja California (Mexico) border (S). A region of arroyos, canyons, and badlands, it includes naval reservations and the Ocotillo Wells Vehicular Recreation Area, an off-road mecca. Borrego Springs (unincorporated, pop. 2244, San Diego Co.), near the N end, is the main settlement. The Coyote, Jacumba, and Tierra Blanca mountains lie on the W.

Apache Junction city, pop. 18,100, Pinal and Maricopa counties, SC Arizona, a suburb 26 mi/42 km SE of Phoenix. Originally a travelers' rest stop, the community is a recreational center and gateway to the Salt R. Canyon and Tonto National Forest. It is at the junction of the **Apache Trail** (Route 88), once an Apache trade route, later (1905) a construction road to the Theodore Roosevelt Dam, with Interstate 60, on the E edge of the built-up PHOENIX area. The SUPERSTITION Mts. are just E.

Apache Mountains NW–SE range in W Texas, between the PECOS R. (E) and the RIO GRANDE (W), near Van Horn. The rugged crests rise to a high of 5696 ft/1737 m at **Apache Peak.** During the 1960s small quantities of barite were intermittently mined from open pits in the Seven Heart Gap area. Some zinc has been produced from the Buck Prospect.

Apache Pass see under CHIRICAHUA Mts., Arizona.

Apache-Sitgreaves National Forest c.2 million ac/810,000 ha (3140 sq mi/8130 sq km), in EC Arizona, along the S rim of the COLORADO PLATEAU and N and E of the WHITE Mt. (Fort Apache) Indian Reservation. Springerville is its headquarters; it contains largely coniferous woodlands.

Apalachee Bay broad reach of the Gulf of MEXICO 30 mi/48 km S of Tallahassee, NW Florida. Forty mi/64 km E–W, it receives the Econfina, Aucilla, St. Marks, and Ochlockonee rivers. The 65,000-ac/26,325-ha St. Marks National Wildlife Refuge is an area of saltmarshes, tidal flats, and hardwood swamps bordering the bay.

Apalachicola Bay protected arm of the Gulf of MEXICO in Franklin Co., NW Florida. Thirteen mi/21 km E–W and 8 mi/13 km wide, it merges with St. George Sound (E) and St. Vincent Sound (W). St. George and St. Vincent islands separate it from the gulf. It receives the Apalachicola R. and is part of the GULF INTRACOASTAL WATERWAY. Before the Civil War, the bay was a cotton shipping center.

Apalachicola River Florida: see under CHATTAHOOCHEE R., Georgia.

Apalachin unincorporated rural community, pop. 1208, in Owego township, Tioga Co., SC New York, 14 mi/23 km W of Binghamton, on the Susquehanna R. It was the site of a 1957 organized-crime meeting at which mobsters from all over the country were surprised by state police.

Apollo Theatre on West 125th Street, in HARLEM, New York City. Opened in 1913 as a burlesque theater, it became famous in the 1930s for its revues and talent competitions, which introduced numerous black artists and entertainers to a large local, and eventually national, audience. Despite financial difficulties, it remained in operation in the 1990s.

Apopka city, pop. 13,512, Orange Co., C Florida, 12 mi/19 km NW of Orlando. Settled in 1856 on the site of a Seminole village, it is an agricultural center, shipping local citrus fruits and houseplants, and has become a bedroom and retirement community.

Apostle Islands also, **Twelve Apostles** about 20 islands in Ashland Co., in L. Superior, N Wisconsin. The largest is MADELINE, 39 sq mi/101 sq km, reached by ferry from Bayfield. They were named by early French missionaries who thought there were 12 in the group. A tourist attraction in summer, the islands abound with wild game. The Apostle Islands National Lakeshore contains all of the Apostles except Madeline; Stockton I. is the largest in the Lakeshore.

Appalachian Mountains also, **the Appalachians** the dominant topographic feature of E North America, considered under variously narrow or broad definitions. Most commonly, the term refers to a band of mountains, ridges, and valleys largely paralleling the East Coast and extending NE–SW for more than 1600 mi/2570 km, from the island of Newfoundland and Québec's GASPÉ PENINSULA to C Alabama, but it is sometimes restricted to the higher ridges in the section from Pennsylvania to Alabama. In its broadest sense, the **Appalachian System** includes most of the landforms E of the Mississippi R., plus some to the W, representing the highly eroded stumps of once much higher mountains. It is thought that the system, with fragments as far W as the ARBUCKLE, OZARK, and OUACHITA mountains in Missouri, Arkansas, and Oklahoma and in the MARATHON region of W Texas, may also have a N continuation in Western Europe and S continuation in Central America. This massive, geologically complex system, which includes most ranges in the E US except the Adirondacks, largely formed the SE border of the LAURENTIAN SHIELD in the Paleozoic Era, but older Precambrian rocks are also present, notably in the BLUE RIDGE and GREEN Mts. Through a long process of uplift, folding, erosion, intrusion, burial by later deposits, and, in the N, glaciation, the Appalachians attained their current relief. They are often divided according to one of two different schemes, based on geologic and topographic features.

The first of these divides the system into two, or sometimes three, longitudinal areas. The more strongly folded and faulted E Appalachians (often called the **Older Appalachians**), with the foothills area known as the PIEDMONT to the E, contain more highly metamorphosed rocks, including a greater proportion of gneisses, schists, and granitic rocks, such as are found in the White Mts. and the Blue Ridge. Just W lie the younger or **Folded Appalachians,** which with the Great Appalachian Valley, or Great Valley, are referred to more broadly as the **Valley and Ridge Province.** This area is characterized by a series of ridges, composed of more erosion-resistant sandstones and shales, rising above valleys created from the erosion of softer limestones. Folding is more evident in the N, with the degree of faulting increasing toward the S, so that few visibly unbroken folds remain. Although the term Great Valley is often restricted to the 5–10 mi/8–16 km lowland band extending from the Walkill Valley in New York to the valley of the COOSA R. in Georgia and Alabama, the term is sometimes used for what is considered the unifying feature of the entire Appalachian System—the nearly continuous linkage of fertile lowlands from those of the St. Lawrence and Richelieu rivers in Québec (N) to those of L. Champlain, the Hudson R., the Kittatinny, LEHIGH, Lebanon, Cumberland, and SHENANDOAH valleys, and the valleys of the Tennessee and Coosa rivers. The rich farmland of this area, along with the iron, anthracite coal, petroleum, and natural gas obtained from the long, parallel ridges to the W, make the Valley and Ridge Province extremely important economically. Industrial cities here include Bethlehem, Pennsylvania; Roanoke, Virginia; Chattanooga, Tennessee; and Birmingham, Alabama. Yet farther W is the greatly dissected **Appalachian Plateau,** which is known regionally by various names: the Allegheny Plateau (including the Allegheny, Catskill, and Pocono mountains) in the N, the CUMBERLAND PLATEAU (including the Cumberland Mts.) in the S, and the Kanawha Plateau in West Virginia. The plateau, known for its sedimentary rocks and softer (bituminous) coal deposits, blends with lowlands and the Ohio Valley farther W. PITTSBURGH is on the Appalachian Plateau.

The second scheme divides the Appalachians into N, S, and sometimes C sections. The generally older N section includes the TACONIC Mts. E of the Hudson R., the BERKSHIRE HILLS in Massachusetts, the GREEN Mts. in Vermont, the WHITE Mts. in New Hampshire, the NOTRE DAME and SHICKSHOCK mountains in Québec, and the LONG RANGE Mts. in Newfoundland. The C section includes the CATSKILL Mts., the N part of the BLUE RIDGE, and the Alleghenies. The S section includes numerous ridges; most of the Blue Ridge, including the BLACK, UNAKA, and GREAT SMOKY mountains; and the Cumberland Plateau. Mt. MITCHELL (6684 ft/2039 m), in the Black Mts., is the highest point in the S section and in the entire system.

Glaciers once extended as far S as the Susquehanna R., and were of great significance in sculpting much of the Appalachians. The topography of the system, with its steep mountains, NE–SW trending ridges, and deep valleys, created a major barrier to westward travel, and thus had a tremendous impact on early US settlement and trade patterns. The most famous passages through the Appalachians are the CUMBERLAND GAP, through which the WILDERNESS ROAD ran, in the S; Nemacolin's Path, and its expansion into the NATIONAL ROAD, in the C; and, in the N, the Hudson-Mohawk river route and the ERIE CANAL, which passed through the gap S of the Adirondacks.

The Appalachians' terrain also isolated populations, and distinct cultural patterns developed, especially in the region generally known as **Appalachia.** Roughly between SW Pennsylvania and NE Alabama, this mountainous area was settled largely by Scotch-Irish, English, and Germans, and is to this day noted for its linguistic archaism and distinctive customs, music, and crafts. The difficulties of economic life in the mountains led to a general identification of Appalachia with poverty, and migration of its inhabitants to cities, where their speech and customs stood out, reinforced a sense of mountain people as "other," an impression that has begun to fade with the increasing homogenization of American culture.

Appalachian Trail 2050 mi/3300 km–long footpath between Georgia and Maine, established 1925–37 and designated the first National Scenic Trail in 1968. The dream of Benton MacKaye (1877–1976), Massachusetts writer and outdoorsman, it follows Appalachian ridges and existing roadways, crossing farmland and residential areas as well as deep woods, and has regularly spaced shelters. It does not follow the trails of Indians, which tend to be in valleys. Usually thought of (and most often walked) from S to N, it starts at SPRINGER Mt., Georgia, and ends atop Mt. KATAHDIN, in Maine. Along the way it passes through, along, or near Mt. OGLETHORPE, Georgia (originally the S terminus); the North Carolina–Tennessee border; Damascus and Roanoke, Virginia; Harpers Ferry, West Virginia (headquarters); Frederick, Maryland; Carlisle and the Delaware Water Gap, Pennsylvania; High Point, New Jersey; Bear Mt., New York; Kent, Connecticut, and the Taconics; Great Barrington, the Berkshires, and Williamstown, Massachusetts; Bennington and Pico Peak, Vermont; Hanover and Mt. Washington, New Hampshire; and the Mahoosuc Range and Baxter State Park, Maine. In Vermont the LONG TRAIL runs with it in the S, diverging at Pico Peak.

Appaloosa see the PALOUSE, Washington.

Apple, the see BIG APPLE.

Appledore see under ISLES OF SHOALS, Maine and New Hampshire.

Appleton city, pop. 65,695, seat of Outagamie Co., also in Calumet and Winnebago counties, EC Wisconsin, on the Fox R., 17 mi/27 km NNE of Oshkosh. Founded c.1833, it is in a rich dairying and farming region. Development was spurred by the establishment (1847) of Lawrence College, now Lawrence University. Also here are the Lawrence Conservatory of Music and the Institute of Paper Chemistry. The swift-flowing Fox R. falls 33 ft/10 m within the city limits, and provided power for the first hydroelectric plant in the world, established in 1882. Waterpower, which today generates electricity for the city and its surrounding area, was a major factor in Appleton's industrialization; in the 19th century it made the city a sawmill center. Paper, pulp, paper and wood products, canned goods, beer, and building materials are among Appleton's current manufactures. Harry Houdini was born here (1874).

Apple Valley **1.** town, pop. 46,079, San Bernardino Co., SW California, on the N of the San Bernardino Mts., in the Apple Valley, a SW extension of the Mojave Desert, 26 mi/42 km NNE of San Bernardino. It is essentially a booming Los Angeles–area residential suburb, having grown from a pop. of under 7000 in 1970. **2.** city, pop. 34,598, Dakota Co., SE Minnesota, a suburb 12 mi/19 km S of Minneapolis. The site of the Minnesota Zoo, it has experienced both residential and commercial growth since the 1960s.

Appomattox County 336 sq mi/870 sq km, pop. 12,298, in C Virginia. Its seat is Appomattox (pop. 1707). In an apple and peach growing region, the county is rural. The 1325-ac/537-ha **Appomattox Court House** National Park (est. 1954), 2 mi/3 km NE of the county seat, includes the courthouse where Robert E. Lee surrendered more than 26,000 men to Ulysses S. Grant on April 9, 1865, effectively ending the Civil War. It also includes the farmhouse of Wilmer McClean, where Lee and Grant signed the terms of surrender.

Appomattox River 137 mi/221 km long, in Virginia. It rises in Appomattox Co., and flows generally E to PETERSBURG, its head of navigation, then joins the James R. at HOPEWELL. Appomattox Court House is immediately E of the river's headwaters.

Apra Harbor unincorporated community, pop. 7956, W GUAM, 5 mi/8 km WSW of AGANA, on the Philippine Sea. A Spanish port from the mid 16th century, it is today the major US military port in the W Pacific. Its large protected harbor is also the center of Guam's maritime commerce.

Aquarius Mountains see under HUALAPAI Mts., Arizona.

Aqueduct, the locally, **the Big A** horse-racing facility in South Ozone Park, Queens, New York. Situated along the Ridgewood Aqueduct, part of Long Island's water system, it opened in 1894 and was renovated in 1959. The track's future was in doubt in the early 1990s.

Aquidneck Island see RHODE I., Rhode Island.

aquifer geologic formation comprising a stratum or strata of permeable material (e.g., gravel, sand, or limestone) underlain by an impermeable layer (e.g., clay), so that a body of ground water collects and may be tapped or rises in springs. The largest US, and perhaps world, example is the **Ogallala Aquifer,** whose center lies under the Great Plains at a distance of some 150 mi/240 km E of the Rocky Mt. Front Range, from South Dakota (N) to SC Texas and E New Mexico (S). Formed of material washed down over millions of years from the once much higher Rockies, it is over 1000 ft/300 m thick in places, and has made intensive irrigated agriculture possible on much of the Plains. Since the 1940s, however, increasing use has progressively lowered the water table throughout the region; some experts predict exhaustion of the resource by early in the 21st century.

Arabi unincorporated community, pop. 8787, St. Bernard Parish, SE Louisiana, on the E (N) bank of the Mississippi R., adjacent (E) to the city of New Orleans. It is an overwhelmingly white industrial and residential suburb. CHALMETTE is just SE.

Aransas National Wildlife Refuge see under REFUGIO, Texas.

Arapahoe County 800 sq mi/2072 sq km, pop. 391,511, in NC Colorado, bounded (NW) by the city and county of Denver. Its seat is LITTLETON. Its W portion is occupied by industrial and residential suburbs of Denver, including AURORA, ENGLEWOOD, Sheridan, and Littleton. The balance of the county is sparsely populated and agricultural, primarily producing dairy products and wheat.

Arapaho National Forest over 1 million ac/400,000 ha (1562 sq mi/4050 sq km), in NC Colorado, incorporating much high mountain territory (esp. in Summit Co.) W of the Continental Divide, in the GORE RANGE. The huge Eagles Nest Wilderness occupies most of it, and there are other wilderness areas, ghost towns, and ski resorts. Mt. EVANS is here.

Arbuckle Mountains low hills rising to 1450 ft/442 m from the OSAGE PLAINS, along the Washita R., in SC Oklahoma, NNW of Ardmore. These worn-down bluffs are noted for formations created by differential erosion of limestone, sandstone, shale, and granite; the Turner Falls, 77 ft/23 m high, cascade over limestone cliffs. The Chickasaw National Recreation Area is in the foothills; its 9521 ac/3856 ha include the 2300-ac/932-ha **Lake of the Arbuckles,** created by Arbuckle Dam, and a number of sulfur, iron, bromide, and fresh water springs.

Arbutus unincorporated village, pop. 19,750, Baltimore Co., C Maryland, just SW of the Baltimore city line and Interstate 695. It is an older Baltimore suburb consisting of row and single-family houses and apartments, with some recent developments and several small industries. The University of Maryland Baltimore Co. campus (1963) is W.

Arcade see under ARDEN-ARCADE, California.

Arcadia city, pop. 48,290, Los Angeles Co., SW California, 16 mi/26 km NE of Los Angeles, at the S foot of the San Gabriel Mts., just E of Pasadena. The city grew up in the 1880s around the Santa Anita Ranch; the Santa Anita Racetrack, one of the best-known US horseracing facilities, opened in 1934 on the ranch's site. Also in Arcadia is the Los Angeles State and County Arboretum. While mainly residential, the city has a variety of high-tech manufactures.

Arcata city, pop. 15,197, Humboldt Co., NW California, on the NE of Arcata (Humboldt) Bay, 6 mi/10 km NE of Eureka and 54 mi/88 km S of the Oregon border. Founded in 1850, it was a meeting point for mule trains carrying mining supplies over mountain trails; Bret Harte lived and wrote here later in the decade. Humboldt State University (1913) now dominates the city's life. Tourists are drawn to local marshes, the bay, and the city's many Victorian homes.

Arches National Park 73,379 ac/29,718 ha of wind- and water-eroded arches, pinnacles, windows, and balanced rocks just N of MOAB, on the Colorado R. in SE Utah. Within the park are 85 natural red sandstone arches, the largest concentration in the world. Landscape Arch, with a span of 291 ft/89 m, is the longest arch in the world, while Delicate Arch overlooks a natural amphitheater.

Arcosanti arts and residential community just N of Cordes Junction, in Yavapai Co., C Arizona, 65 mi/105 km N of Phoenix. Established in the 1970s by architect Paolo Soleri, founder of the Cosanti Foundation in SCOTTSDALE, it is intended to wed architecture and ecology (as "arcology") in a community of 5000 inhabiting and working in prototype structures.

Arctic, the region of the far North, generally defined in either of two ways. In one version, it is everything N of the **Arctic Circle.** This imaginary line around the earth, at about 66° 31′ N, connects the northernmost points at which the sun may be seen for any time at all on the shortest day of the year (the Winter Solstice, around Dec. 22). In North America, the Arctic Circle passes (W–E) through KOTZEBUE Sound and near Fort Yukon (on the YUKON R.), Alaska; across the N Yukon Territory; and, in the Northwest Territories, across the top of the GREAT BEAR L., past Repulse Bay on Hudson Bay, and across BAFFIN I. (through L. Nettilling). In the second definition, the Arctic is the region in which the average temperature in the hottest month of the year (July) is not above 50°F/10°C. As this line lies generally near the northernmost limit of tree growth, the Arctic is often popularly equated with the TUNDRA. See also HIGH ARCTIC.

Arctic Archipelago thousands of islands lying N of mainland Canada and the Arctic Circle and W of Greenland. Covering an area of some 500,000 sq mi/1.3 million sq km, they all lie within the Northwest Territories, and most will be within NUNAVUT. North of the Parry Channel, an ocean trench at about 74° N, lie the QUEEN ELIZABETH Is. (ELLESMERE I., DEVON I., the PARRY Is., the SVERDRUP Is., and others), made up of largely sedimentary material folded into mountains reaching over 8000 ft/2430 m in the far N; this group is remote, largely ice-covered and icebound, and with little human (a handful of INUIT settlements and government stations), animal, or plant life. South of the Parry Channel, major islands include (W–E) BANKS, VICTORIA, Prince of Wales, KING WILLIAM, Somerset, and BAFFIN (the largest by far). Except for their N edges, these islands are part of the older CANADIAN SHIELD, and are relatively flat. They have a number of Inuit settlements, as well as government stations, and are used in places by trappers, hunters, fishermen, whalers, sealers, and mining operations. The largest community in the entire archipelago, IQALUIT, is on SE Baffin I. The NORTHWEST PASSAGE takes routes through the Parry Channel and the S tier of islands.

Arctic National Wildlife Refuge also, **ANWR** ("Anwar") 1.5 million ac/600,000 ha, in extreme NE Alaska, on the NORTH SLOPE, the Yukon border (E), and the Beaufort Sea (N). This TUNDRA and coastal area has been a recent focus of debate over whether to allow commercial oil drilling; oil has been found just offshore, but environmental concerns have caused the Federal government to withhold permission to exploit deposits.

Arctic Slope see NORTH SLOPE, Alaska.

Arden village, pop. 477, New Castle Co., N Delaware, 1.5 mi/2 km S of the Pennsylvania line, and 6 mi/10 km NE of Wilmington, on Naamans Creek. The community was founded in 1900 as a Single Tax colony by a group of artists and artisans opposed to private land ownership. It is now primarily residential.

Arden-Arcade unincorporated community, pop. 92,040, Sacramento Co., NC California, a combination of two largely residential suburbs on the E side of Sacramento.

Arden Hills city, pop. 9199, Ramsey Co., EC Minnesota, a suburb 5 mi/8 km N of St. Paul. A residential community, it is surrounded by many resort lakes.

Ardmore **1.** city, pop. 23,079, seat of Carter Co., S Oklahoma, 90 mi/144 km SSE of Oklahoma City. Originally ranchland, it was selected as a townsite by the Santa Fe Railroad in 1887. A 1913 oil strike in the local Redbeds made it an industry center. Today it is a processing and shipping point for cotton and other agricultural goods, dairy products, and livestock. Its manufactures include building materials, plastics, electronic components, and leather goods. A Federal school for Indians is here. L. Murray is adjacent to the city, and the ARBUCKLE Mts. are N. **2.** unincorporated village, pop. 12,646, in LOWER MERION township, Montgomery Co., SE Pennsylvania. Settled c.1800, it is named after a town in Ireland. Part of Philadelphia's MAIN LINE, it is an affluent residential community.

Ardsley village, pop. 4272, in Greenburgh township, Westchester Co., SE New York, 21 mi/34 km N of New York City. It is an affluent residential suburb.

Arecibo unincorporated community (ZONA URBANA), pop. 49,545, Arecibo Municipio (pop. 93,385), NW Puerto Rico, on the Atlantic Ocean at the mouth of the Arecibo R., 48 mi/77 km W of San Juan. This colonial center was settled in the mid 16th century. A port with some light manufactures and site of a college of the University of Puerto Rico, it is also a trade, processing, and distribution hub for an agricultural region producing sugarcane, coffee, fruit, and tobacco. Rum and pharmaceutical industries are important. Twelve mi/19 km S is Cornell University's Arecibo Observatory, with a radio telescope bowl said (at 1300 ft/400 m in diameter) to be the world's largest. The Cueva del Indio caves and Rio Camuy Cave Park are also nearby.

Arena, Point rocky promontory overlooking the Pacific Ocean in Mendocino Co., NW California, 100 mi/160 km NW of San Francisco. Its 115 ft/35 m–high white concrete lighthouse replaces an 1870 brick one destroyed in the 1906 San Francisco earthquake. The N land end of the SAN ANDREAS FAULT is here. The city of **Point Arena** (pop. 407) thrives on tourism, including whale watching.

Argentia community in SE Newfoundland, on the W coast of the SW arm of the AVALON PENINSULA, on Placentia Bay, just NNW of Placentia and 63 mi/102 km WSW of St. John's. Named for silver deposits mined around 1900, it had been the fishing OUTPORT of Little Placentia (Petit Plaisance) since the 17th century. It became the site in 1941 of a US air and naval base; that same year, on the USS *Augusta,* offshore, the Atlantic Charter was signed by Franklin D. Roosevelt and Winston Churchill. The naval station was closed in the mid 1970s. Argentia has ferry connections to NORTH SYDNEY, Nova Scotia.

Argonne National Laboratory multipurpose research center, in Du Page Co., NE Illinois, on the Des Plaines R., 20 mi/32 km SW of Chicago. In 1946 the US government established this 1700-ac/688-ha facility, which is dedicated to atomic research and alternative energy sources. The University of Chicago and the Argonne Universities Association run the lab jointly.

Arguello, Point coastal prominence on the Pacific Ocean in Santa Barbara Co., SW California, 11 mi/18 km SW of Lompoc, within VANDENBERG AIR FORCE BASE. Oil is drilled offshore.

Argus Range N–S mountains in EC California, W of the Slate Range and the PANAMINT Valley, and N of the Trona Pinnacles (see RIDGECREST). Maturango Peak (8839 ft/2696 m) is the high point. The range has perennial springs and streams, and includes Darwin Falls. A luxuriant Joshua tree forest is on its W slope. Some mining and quarrying has been done in this area, now on the E of the China Lake Naval Weapons Center. The Coso Range lies W.

Argyle Street see under EDGEWATER, Chicago, Illinois.

Arizona state of the SW US, variously considered part of the SOUTHWEST or Far WEST; 1990 pop. 3,665,228 (134.8% of 1980; rank: 24th); area 114,006 sq mi/295,276 sq km (rank: 6th); admitted to Union 1912 (48th). Capital and most populous city: PHOENIX. Other leading cities: TUCSON, MESA, GLENDALE, TEMPE, SCOTTSDALE. Arizona is bordered E by New Mexico; S by the Mexican state of Sonora; W by the Mexican state of Baja California and the state of California (S, with the COLORADO R. forming the boundary) and by Nevada (NW, with the Colorado forming most of the boundary); and N by Utah. In the NE, at the FOUR CORNERS, it also touches on Colorado. The C of the state is crossed (WNW–ESE) by the MOGOLLON RIM, an escarpment that separates two distinct topographic zones. On the N is the COLORADO PLATEAU, a high, arid land of plateaus cut through by canyons. The BLACK MESA, in the NE corner, is home to the HOPI INDIAN RESERVATION and much of the surrounding NAVAJO INDIAN RESERVATION. Sheep and cattle ranching are important activities in this area, and some uranium and other mining is done. In the NE, near the Four Corners, are MONUMENT VALLEY, the CANYON DE CHELLY National Monument, and WINDOW ROCK. The PAINTED DESERT and PETRIFIED FOREST are on the Black Mesa's S, where the LITTLE COLORADO R. flows NW along its base. The Colorado R. enters the state on the NW of the Black Mesa, where the Glen Canyon Dam backs L. POWELL into Utah. Below the dam, the river, proceeding SW, cuts the MARBLE CANYON and the famous GRAND CANYON into the sedimentary rock of N Arizona; leaving the Grand Canyon it enters L. MEAD, backed up by the Hoover Dam, near Las Vegas, Nevada (W). North of the Grand Canyon is the remote ARIZONA STRIP country, including the KAIBAB, KANAB, and other plateaus. South of the Canyon is the COCONINO PLATEAU and, near Flagstaff (NC), the SAN FRANCISCO PEAKS, including HUMPHREYS PEAK, at 12,633 ft/3851 m the state's high point. South of the Mogollon Rim is a highland section (the Mexican Highlands) of the BASIN AND RANGE PROVINCE, the site of PRESCOTT, PAYSON, and other mining and resort communities. The S third of Arizona lies in the SONORAN DESERT, and is drained to the SW by the GILA R. and its tributaries, including the SALT R. The desert's many mountain ranges include the HARCUVARS, KOFAS, CASTLE DOMES, CABEZA PRIETAS, AJOS, and BABOQUIVARIS. Although this is inherently unpromising land for human settlement, irrigation and transport of water from the Colorado R. has made it home to most of Arizona's pop., in the VALLEY OF THE SUN around Phoenix and in the Tucson area. Along the SW border are the large PAPAGO INDIAN RESERVATION, the ORGAN PIPE CACTUS National Monument, and units of the BARRY M. GOLDWATER Military Range. The state's name is the Spanish version of a Papago place name, "small spring," actually referring to a locality over the Mexican border. Arizona, which has been inhabited for thousands of years, by cultures including the Cochise and ANASAZI, was home to numerous tribes when whites first saw it. The Pima, Papago (Tohono O'odham), Yuma, Maricopa, and others lived in the S, and had developed irrigated agriculture in what became the Phoenix area. In the N, the sedentary Hopi were in the process of being pushed from their land by the nomadic Navajo, who with their relatives the Apache had arrived from the N Great Plains shortly before whites. The Havasupai and Hualapai lived near and in the Grand Canyon. Spanish gold seekers, including the Coronado CIBOLA expedition, saw the area in the 1530s–40s. Colonizing activity did not start until the late 17th century, however; the MISSION at SAN XAVIER DEL BAC, near Tucson, dates from 1700. In the 1750s TUBAC became the site of a PRESIDIO, moved in 1776 to Tucson. TUMACACORI was another early mission site. Little settlement was done in Arizona before the US gained control (1848) over the area N of the Gila R. in the Mexican War, and added (1853) the GADSDEN PURCHASE, setting the current boundaries. Mining had begun in the S before the Civil War, in which PICACHO Pass saw an 1862 skirmish, Arizona became a separate territory in 1863, and conflict with the Apache continued (to end in the 1880s). In the late 19th century mining was the predominant economic activity, with noted sources of gold at TOMBSTONE and copper at widespread sites including BISBEE, MORENCI, and JEROME. By the early 20th century irrigated agriculture had become important; the 1911 completion of the THEODORE ROOSEVELT Dam, E of Phoenix on the Salt R., was a leading step in the development of S Arizona farming. Before World War II, the state was said to rely on the "four Cs"—cattle, cotton, copper, and climate. The war brought industry—both an expansion of mining and processing and the introduction of aircraft and other manufacturing, increased pop. and awareness of Arizona, and greatly increased stress on water resources. In the decades since 1945, Colorado R. water has increasingly been diverted to the growing Phoenix and Tucson areas. The state's pop. has almost tripled since 1960, and irrigation and air conditioning have created communities like SUN CITY and other Phoenix suburbs. Aerospace, electronic, and other high-tech manufacturers, along with various other businesses, have been attracted to the dry, warm (in winter) climate and laws restricting labor organization. At first a retirement and recreation center of the SUNBELT, Arizona has become one of its industrial hubs as well. While they account for only 5.5% of residents, Indians occupy much of the state's land, their reservations including the Navajo, Hopi, Papago, FORT APACHE and SAN CARLOS APACHE, HAVASUPAI, Hualapai, and others. Indian crafts and folkways are one of the foundations of Arizona tourism. The Grand Canyon and the state's many natural wonders are a second. A third is the development in recent decades of a riverside recreation zone along the lower Colorado, where LAKE HAVASU CITY (with the relocated London Bridge), BULLHEAD CITY, and other resorts are within easy reach of Southern California. Wild West settings including Tombstone and YUMA, the scenery and New Age attractions of SEDONA, and scattered sights like the METEOR CRATER and the WALNUT CREEK and other cliff dweller ruins are also important attractions. ARCOSANTI, Taliesin West (at Scottsdale), and Biosphere 2 (in the SANTA CATALINA Mts.) are among well-known architectural and scientific sites. The University of Arizona is at Tucson, Arizona State University at Tempe. In 1990 Arizonans were almost 19% Hispanic and 3% black.

Arizona Strip area N of the GRAND CANYON and W of the Colorado R., in the NW corner of Arizona, comprising some 14,000 sq mi/36,000 sq km. Isolated from the rest of the state by the river and canyon, it is bound also by the Virgin Mts. and GRAND WASH CLIFFS (W), and the Vermillion Cliffs along the Utah border (N). The Shivwits, Uinkaret, Kanab, and Kaibab plateaus (W to E) are in the Arizona Strip. Ancestral land to several bands of Paiutes, the area contains historic Pipe Spring, the most reliable water source in this dry, rugged corner of Arizona, now the site of a national monument situated, along with the community of Moccasin, within the Kaibab Indian Reservation (pop. 165). Fredonia, Colorado City (formerly Short Creek), and Littlefield were originally settled (1860s–70s) by Mormons from Utah. The Navajo Bridge spans the Colorado R. near Lees Ferry, providing access to the Strip from the E.

Arkadelphia city, pop. 10,014, seat of Clark Co., SC Arkansas, 25 mi/40 km S of Hot Springs, on the Ouachita R. Founded in 1839 near an earlier (1811) salt works settlement, it now has an agricultural and light industrial economy, producing flour, lumber, cotton, and feed. It is the seat of Henderson State University (1890) and Ouachita Baptist University (1886). DeGray Dam is NW, on the Laddo R.

Arkansas state of the SC US, variously considered part of the Deep SOUTH or of the SOUTHWEST; 1990 pop. 2,350,725 (102.8% of 1980; rank: 33rd); area 53,182 sq mi/137,741 sq km (rank: 29th); admitted to Union 1836 (25th). Capital and most populous city: LITTLE ROCK. Other leading cities: FORT SMITH, NORTH LITTLE ROCK, PINE BLUFF. Arkansas is bordered S by Louisiana. Its SW corner is indented by NE Texas, in part across the RED R. On the W is Oklahoma, on the N Missouri, whose Bootheel Region indents Arkansas's NE corner, with the SAINT FRANCIS R. forming part of the boundary. On the E, Arkansas faces Tennessee (N) and Mississippi (S) across the MISSISSIPPI R. The E part of the state lies in the Mississippi ALLUVIAL plain, including the DELTA area (NE), between CROWLEY'S RIDGE and the Mississippi; the Saint Francis R. runs through this bottomland area, where cotton and rice are grown. In the S, the alluvial plain merges into the Gulf COASTAL PLAIN. In NC and NW Arkansas is the OZARK PLATEAU, extending S from Missouri in the form of the Salem Plateau (E) and Springfield Plateau (W). The E–W trending BOSTON Mts. run along the S of this section, and along their S the ARKANSAS R. bisects the state, running from NC to SE. On its S is MAGAZINE Mt., at 2753 ft/840 m the state's high point, in the OUACHITA Mts., an extension of the Ozarks that continues W into Oklahoma. The major rivers of Arkansas all drain toward the Mississippi. In addition to the Arkansas, they include the Red, crossing the SW corner; the OUACHITA and SALINE, flowing SE from the Ouachita Mts.; the WHITE, which rises in the NW and circles N through the Ozarks into Missouri and back into Arkansas; and the Saint Francis, flowing S from Missouri. The Arkansas R. is part of an important transportation corridor. Its (and the state's) name derive from a tribe encountered here by 1670s French explorers (the French plural spelling, rather than the equivalent *Arkansaw,* has survived). The state's major cities, Little Rock, Pine Bluff, and Fort Smith, developed along it; in 1971 the McClellan-Kerr Arkansas Navigation System, a massive Federal project, opened the river for oceangoing vessels all the way to Tulsa, Oklahoma, in the process making the Arkansas cities true ports. ARKANSAS POST, the state's oldest white settlement, is near its mouth. The Ouachitas and Ozarks are both recreational and tourist areas. In the Ouachitas, the old spa of HOT SPRINGS is now part of a NATIONAL PARK. Ozarks centers include MOUNTAIN HOME and EUREKA SPRINGS; the BUFFALO R. (a designated National WILD AND SCENIC RIVER) and DOGPATCH are other attractions. In the state's NW corner, FAYETTEVILLE (seat of the University of Arkansas), SPRINGDALE, ROGERS, and BENTONVILLE are centers of a region thriving on poultry raising, light manufactures, and transportation businesses. The E Ouachitas, near Little Rock, have mines producing bauxite and various minerals. In the SW, esp. around EL DORADO and SMACKOVER, are major oil, natural gas, and bromine sources, part of the OIL PATCH. Much of S Arkansas is pine-wooded and has important forest industries; TEXARKANA, on the Texas border, is a regional industrial center. Coal is mined at sites throughout the Arkansas R. valley. Seen by De Soto in his 1540s expedition, the region was home to the Quapaw, Caddo, and Osage when the French arrived in the late 17th century. Part of the LOUISIANA PURCHASE, it passed to the US in 1803, and became a territory in 1819. Cotton PLANTATIONS spread in the S and E, but the Ozarks were settled by APPALACHIAN hill people who had little connection with slavery; in the Civil War, in which sympathies were divided, there were actions at Prairie Grove (see FAYETTEVILLE) and PEA RIDGE (NW) and at Mark's Mill, near KINGSLAND, and Poison Spring, near CAMDEN (SC). After Union forces occupied much of the state, Washington (SW, near HOPE) became (1865) the capital-in-exile. From the end of the Civil War, Arkansas subsisted for decades on a largely one-crop (cotton) economy; not until the mid 20th century did modern industries become dominant. Today, food processing, lumber, oil and gas extraction, and other resource-based industries remain key, but there are also electronics and other manufacturing, as well as financial and commercial, sectors. Military sites include the inactive FORT CHAFFEE, near Fort Smith, and the large Pine Bluff arsenal, a longtime biological-weapon facility. Arkansans remain largely the descendants of the Southern and Appalachian settlers of the early 19th century; 16% are black. In 1957, the state became the center of international attention during the integration of Little Rock's Central High School, an event seen by many as having "brought Arkansas into the 20th century."

Arkansas City city, pop. 12,762, Cowley Co., SC Kansas, at the junction of the Arkansas and Walnut rivers, 45 mi/72 km SE of Wichita and 3 mi/5 km N of the Oklahoma border. It was the staging point for the opening of Oklahoma lands in 1893, when tens of thousands of homesteaders rushed into that territory to stake free land claims; the nearby CHEROKEE STRIP Land Rush Museum chronicles this history. The processing and rail hub for a grain-rich cattle raising region, the city also has oil refineries and petroleum-related industries. Cowley County Community College (1922) is here.

Arkansas Nuclear One power plant, operational since 1974, along the Arkansas R. at RUSSELLVILLE, NW Arkansas.

Arkansas Post historic site in SE Arkansas, 40 mi/64 km ESE of Pine Bluff and 22 mi/35 km NW of the Arkansas River's mouth on the Mississippi. A fort established here in 1686 was the first permanent French post in the lower Mississippi Valley. The settlement struggled through the 18th century; in 1765–1800 Spain held it. In 1819–21 it was the first territorial capital of Arkansas, and after losing that role to Little Rock, remained an important riverboat port. In Jan. 1863, Union forces captured it, holding it through the rest of the Civil War. Since 1960 the **Arkansas Post National Memorial** has commemorated this history.

Arkansas River 1450 mi/2335 km long, in Colorado, Kansas, Oklahoma, and Arkansas. The second-longest (after the Missouri R.) tributary of the Mississippi, it rises near Leadville, Colorado, on the E of the Continental Divide, and drops quickly SSE past Salida and ESE to Canon City, where it has created the ROYAL GORGE. Continuing ESE into the High Plains, it passes Pueblo, La Junta, and Bent's Fort; at Las Animas it is joined by the Purgatoire, from the SW. It then flows E and ESE through the John Martin Reservoir, past Lamar, and across the Kansas border, to Garden City and Dodge City. Turning NE, it passes Pawnee Rock and Great Bend, then flows SE to Hutchinson and Wichita, and SSE to Arkansas City and the Oklahoma border. In Oklahoma it broadens and winds SSE and SE, through Kaw and Long lakes (E of Ponca City), to its junction with the **Salt Fork** (from the W), S of Ponca City; to Tulsa (where it is joined by the Cimarron, from the W); to Muskogee (where it is joined by the Verdigris, from the N, and the Neosho, from the NE); and to the Robert S. Kerr Reservoir (where it is joined by the Canadian, from the SW). It then flows E across the Arkansas border, to Fort Smith, and winds E and ESE between the Ozark Plateau (N) and the Ouachita Mts. (S), to Dardanelle and Little Rock. Continuing SSE from Little Rock, it reaches Pine Bluff and turns SE, past Arkansas Post, to the Mississippi R. just below (and across from) Rosedale, Mississippi. Near its mouth a cutoff channel has connected it with the White R. as the latter approaches the Mississippi. A major westward transportation route in the 19th century, the Arkansas is now dammed in two dozen places in its middle course. This has both eliminated serious flooding and provided irrigation for vast wheat growing areas, to the degree that in Kansas and Oklahoma the river is in some seasons no more than a trickle. In 1971 the **McClellan-Kerr Arkansas Navigation System,** one of the most expensive Federal engineering projects ever undertaken, opened the river to oceangoing traffic all the way (via the lower stretch of the VERDIGRIS R.) to Catoosa (the port of Tulsa, Oklahoma), 446 mi/718 km upstream.

Arlington **1.** town, pop. 44,630, including East Arlington and Arlington Heights villages, in Middlesex Co., E Massachusetts, 6 mi/10 km NW of Boston. Settled in 1630 as part of Cambridge, which lies SE across Alewife Brook, it is the site of the Jason Russell House, where 12 Minutemen were killed in an April 19, 1775 skirmish with the British. The early economic base was truck farming, ice shipping, and the manufacture of textile cards; Arlington is now a largely residential suburb with active commerce and some light industry. Until 1732 it was known as Menotomy. **2.** unincorporated village, pop. 11,948, Dutchess Co., SE New York, adjoining (E) POUGHKEEPSIE. It is the seat of Vassar College (1861). **3.** city, pop. 261,721, Tarrant Co., NE Texas, between Fort Worth and Dallas, on the Trinity R. An agricultural center on the railroad since the 1870s, it developed quickly after 1954, when General Motors opened a large auto plant. The city now makes cars, trailers, steel and iron, aerospace equipment, chemicals, rubber and paper products, cans, and machinery. The University of Texas at Arlington began as a state college in 1895, and Arlington Baptist College was established in 1939. Arlington Stadium, on the NE side, was the home of the Texas Rangers (baseball), until 1994 when the 50,000-seat The Ballpark opened. Near it is Six Flags Over Texas, a huge theme park that was the progenitor of others around the US. Arlington's population almost tripled between 1970 and 1990. **4.** town, pop. 2299, Bennington Co., SW Vermont, on the Batten Kill and Warm Brook, along the New York border, 14 mi/23 km N of Bennington. In an area of country estates and summer homes, it produces furniture and wood products. Once called Tory Hollow because many Tory sympathizers lived here, it was home to Ethan Allen. The view from the site of Thomas Chittenden's home is depicted on the state seal. Dorothy Canfield Fisher (1879–1958), one of Vermont's best-known writers, lived here.

Arlington County popularly, **Arlington** 26 sq mi/67 sq km, pop. 170,936, in N Virginia, across the Potomac R. from Washington, D.C., and adjoining (N) Alexandria. Ceded by Virginia (1789) to form part of the DISTRICT OF COLUMBIA, the area was returned to Virginia in 1846. Approximately 20% of its land is owned by the Federal government, whose facilities include Arlington National Cemetery, Washington

National Airport, FORT MYER, and the PENTAGON. Arlington is a busy residential community with clusters of modern high-rise buildings like CRYSTAL CITY and some light manufacturing (electrical components, scientific instruments, machinery). It is the seat of Strayer College (1892) and of Marymount University (1950).

Arlington Heights village, pop. 75,460, Cook Co., NE Illinois, 25 mi/40 km NW of Chicago. Founded in 1836, it was once an area of dairy and truck farms, and is now largely occupied by suburban residential subdivisions. There are also research facilities and light industries. Arlington International Racecourse is here. O'Hare International Airport is 5 mi/8 km to the SW.

Armijo residential suburb of ALBUQUERQUE, New Mexico. On the W bank of the Rio Grande, just SW of Old Town, it is on the site of an Indian pueblo and was formerly a farming village.

Armonk village, pop. 2745, in North Castle township, Westchester Co., SE New York, 7 mi/11 km NNE of White Plains. Primarily residential, it is also home to the international headquarters of IBM.

Armory, the officially, **69th Regiment Armory** National Guard facility on Lexington Ave., lower Midtown Manhattan, New York City, that was the scene of the 1913 "Armory Show," which introduced modern, particularly cubist, art to the American public.

Army Corps of Engineers branch of the US Army that has both military and civil engineering functions. It is responsible for procurement, management, research and development, and construction on Army, Air Force, atomic energy, and National Aeronautics and Space Administration sites. But it is also charged with similar responsibilities in regard to major civil works. Since 1824, at the peak of the period of US water transport (esp. canal) development, the Corps has been responsible for the maintenance and improvement of US harbors and navigable waterways. In the 1930s it was also assigned responsibility for flood control efforts in American river basins. Employing a largely civilian labor force, the Corps is today engaged in works including LEVEE maintenance, harbor and river channel dredging, construction and maintenance of dams and locks, disaster response including rescue work, preservation of WETLANDS, and aspects of highway and railroad development.

Arnold **1.** unincorporated community, pop. 20,261, Anne Arundel Co., C Maryland, 5 mi/8 km N of Annapolis. It is largely residential. **2.** city, pop. 18,828, Jefferson Co., EC Missouri, 17 mi/27 km SSW of St. Louis, where the Meramec R. joins the Mississippi R. It is primarily residential.

Arnold Arboretum in the JAMAICA PLAIN section of Boston, Massachusetts. A 265-ac/107-ha garden, it was donated to the city in 1872 by James Arnold of New Bedford, and is now run by Harvard University.

Arnold Engineering Development Center see under TULLAHOMA, Tennessee.

Aroostook County 6721 sq mi/17,407 sq km, pop. 86,936, in N Maine. Houlton is the county seat. The state's largest county, and the northernmost part of the eastern US, Aroostook borders Canada on the N, W, and E. Its eastern section is a rich agricultural area, one of the nation's major producers of potatoes. Drained by the Allagash, Aroostook, Fish, Little Madawaska, Machias, Mattawamkeag, Meduxnekeag, and St. John rivers, which flow chiefly N and E from the mountainous west, Aroostook includes large tracts of wilderness surrounding lakes and rivers, including the Allagash Wilderness Waterway. Settled largely during the bloodless Aroostook War (1838–39) with Canada, it is noted for its hunting, fishing, canoeing, and lumbering. Industries include the manufacture of paper, wood products, fertilizer, and farm machinery.

Arrowhead, Lake on the Little Wichita R. in NE Texas, 13 mi/21 km SE of Wichita Falls. It covers 13,500 ac/5500 ha of a former oilfield; derricks were left standing in the middle. Along its 106-mi/171-km shoreline is L. Arrowhead State Park.

Arrowhead Region name given in 1924 to a 16,000–sq mi/41,400–sq km area in NE Minnesota, said to resemble an arrowhead in shape. The region, largely in the SUPERIOR HIGHLANDS section of the CANADIAN SHIELD, is bounded by Ontario (N) and the N shore of L. Superior (E), extending from International Falls (NW) S to the MILLE LACS area. This important recreational area includes the 3 million ac/1.2 million ha of Superior National Forest, with over 2000 lakes; VOYAGEURS NATIONAL PARK; and, in the extreme NE, Grand Portage National Monument, site of a famed 9-mi/14-km portage used by Indians, explorers, missionaries, and fur traders to avoid falls and rapids on the Pigeon R. The BOUNDARY WATERS CANOE AREA stretches 150 mi/240 km along the Ontario border. Logging has been important in this forested and lake-filled area, which also is the site of important mining operations, most notably in the MESABI RANGE. Duluth and Two Harbors, important ore shipping points, and EAGLE Mt., the highest point in the state (2301 ft/701 m), are also in the Arrowhead.

Arrowhead Stadium see under HARRY S TRUMAN SPORTS COMPLEX, Kansas City, Missouri.

Arrow Lakes in SE British Columbia, two expansions of the COLUMBIA R. between the SELKIRK (E) and MONASHEE (W) mountains, between REVELSTOKE (N) and CASTLEGAR, near the Washington border. Upper Arrow L. is 47 mi/76 km long, Lower Arrow L. 53 mi/85 km long. Noted for their scenery, they are popular with canoeists, trout fishermen, and vacationers at beaches and campgrounds. The region was settled during a mining boom in the 1890s–1900s. Steamboats long served farming, mining, and lumber industries along the lakes. Tourism increased with the opening (1960s) of the TRANS-CANADA HIGHWAY through Revelstoke.

Arrowwood National Wildlife Refuge see under JAMESTOWN, North Dakota.

arroyo Spanish for rivulet, brook, or gutter. In the SW US, a small watercourse, usually with steep sides, dry much of the year, through which flash floods may run after heavy rain.

Arroyo Grande city, pop. 14,378, San Luis Obispo Co., SW California, on Arroyo Grande Creek, 10 mi/16 km SSE of San Luis Obispo. Founded in 1877, it is in a truck farming area.

Arroyo Seco former intermittent watercourse, now an 8-mi/13-km portion of the Pasadena Freeway, between downtown LOS ANGELES and PASADENA, California. The Arroyo Seco Parkway was completed in 1940, the first link in Los Angeles's freeway network; its construction led to a surge in Pasadena land values, establishing a pattern for development throughout the region. The road passes through CHAVEZ RAVINE and ELYSIAN PARK.

Artesia **1.** city, pop. 15,464, Los Angeles Co., SW California, 16 mi/26 km SE of Los Angeles. Founded in 1875, it derived its name from the many wells in the area, used to maintain local agriculture. Though now mostly residential, the city also has a variety of light industries. **2.** city, pop. 10,610, Eddy Co., SE New Mexico, 4 mi/6 km W of the Pecos R. and 37 mi/60 km SSE of Roswell. Named for the artesian wells that irrigate the area's farms and ranches, it is (since 1923) an oil drilling center and manufactures petroleum products. The city, in an area that also yields potash and natural gas, has light industries and some tourism.

Arthur Kill narrow estuary running N–S for 14 mi/23 km between Staten Island, New York, and the New Jersey cities of Perth Amboy, Woodbridge, Carteret, Linden, and Elizabeth. Newark Bay is at its N end, Raritan Bay S. It has been heavily industrialized since the Civil War, especially on the New Jersey side. The Rahway R. in New Jersey and FRESH KILLS on Staten I. extend from it. The GOETHALS BRIDGE and Outerbridge Crossing span it. The Arthur Kill is heavily polluted, but restoration efforts are under way. Prall's Island (88 ac/36 ha), toward the N end, is a New York City heron sanctuary.

Art Museum District also, **Fairmount** residential neighborhood in CENTER CITY, Philadelphia, Pennsylvania, N of BENJAMIN FRANKLIN PARKWAY and E of FAIRMOUNT PARK. This working-class section of Ukrainians, blacks, and Puerto Ricans has become popular with affluent young professionals in recent decades.

Arundel in Maine: **a.** former name (to 1821) for KENNEBUNKPORT, summer home of novelist Kenneth Roberts (1885–1957), who used Arundel as a setting for his trilogy about Maine; the first novel, a chronicle of Benedict Arnold's march to Québec through the Maine wilderness, was titled *Arundel.* **b.** largely rural town, pop. 2669, formerly North Kennebunkport, York Co., which took its name from Roberts's novel (1930).

Arvada city, pop. 89,235, Jefferson and Adams counties, NC Colorado, at the E foot of the Front Range of the Rocky Mts., a residential suburb of Denver, 8 mi/14 km NW of Downtown. Settled around 1860 by miners who later turned to more profitable truck farming, it was an early 20th-century agricultural center. Since the 1950s, its population has increased dramatically. It is also a commercial and manufacturing center, making steel products and aerospace parts and fuels.

Arverne see under the ROCKAWAYS, New York.

Arvida former city, in 1976 amalgamated into JONQUIÈRE, S Québec, a COMPANY TOWN founded (1925) around an Alcan aluminum plant, with one of the largest smelters in the world.

Arvon, Mount 1979 ft/604 m high, the highest point in Michigan. It is located in the HURON Mts. in Baraga Co., in the NW Upper Peninsula.

Asbestos city, pop. 6487, Richmond Co., S Québec, 26 mi/42 km N of Sherbrooke, in the EASTERN TOWNSHIPS. Its economy centers around the mining of asbestos; the huge Jeffrey open-pit mine (1905) is here; a 1949 miners' strike is a key date in Québec labor history. Copper, iron, and slate are mined in the area as well; local manufactures include electrical equipment and wood products.

Asbury Park city, pop. 16,799, Monmouth Co., EC New Jersey, on the Atlantic Ocean, 5 mi/8 km SW of Long Branch. Established in 1871 as a resort area for temperance advocates in nearby (S) Ocean Grove, it became a preeminent summer resort in the 1930s and 1940s. The city declined during the 1960s, but began redevelopment in the early 1990s. Asbury Park is noted for the blue-collar rock music (of Bruce Springsteen and others) that developed from the 1960s in its clubs. Notable here are the beach, boardwalk, and Convention Hall, off which the burning liner *Morro Castle* grounded in Sept. 1934.

Ascutney, Mount monadnock (3144 ft/959 m), SE Vermont, in the Connecticut Valley, in Windsor and West Windsor townships. Glacial marks can be found on its summit, and rocks from Ascutney have been found almost as far SE as Worcester, Massachusetts, providing insights into glacial movements. Although of limited marketability, Ascutney granite and syenite have been mined in four different quarries. Mt. Ascutney State Park has trails and scenic lookouts; the Mt. Ascutney ski area is in the village of Brownsville, on the mountain's NW.

Asheboro city, pop. 16,362, seat of Randolph Co., C North Carolina, in the Uwharrie Mts. Founded on the site of a prehistoric Keyauwee settlement in 1779, it developed as a trade center. In 1889, it was linked to HIGH POINT, 20 mi/32 km NW, by railroad. Industrialization followed, beginning with lumber plants. Asheboro now houses large hosiery and knitwear mills; other manufactures include wood products and upholstery.

Asheville city, pop. 61,607, seat of Buncombe Co., W North Carolina, in the Blue Ridge Mts., at the junction of the French Broad and Swannanoa rivers. Settled in the 1790s on Cherokee hunting grounds, as Morristown, it was renamed in 1797 to honor Governor Samuel Ashe. It was a summer resort for coastal plain dwellers, and a tobacco warehouse center, until the arrival of the Western North Carolina Railroad in 1880, when industry flourished; the city now manufactures furniture, paper products, textiles, and clothing. But it is best known as a vacation and retirement center, headquarters for the Pisgah and Nantahala national forests, and the E gateway to Great Smoky Mountains National Park. The BLUE RIDGE PARKWAY passes just E. A branch of the University of North Carolina is one of several institutions here, and the city is known as a center for mountain music and culture. George Vanderbilt's Biltmore estate, with its chateau-style house (completed 1895, with more than 250 rooms, and said to be the largest US private home) and 8000 ac/3240 ha of grounds (originally 125,000 ac/50,625 ha), one of the South's most visited sites, lies S of the city center. Thomas Wolfe (1900–38), born and buried here, wrote of Asheville in *Look Homeward, Angel* and other works.

Ashfield town, pop. 1715, Franklin Co., W Massachusetts, 10 mi/16 km WSW of Greenfield. It is the seat of Sanderson Academy.

Ashland **1.** unincorporated community, pop. 16,590, Alameda Co., NC California, a primarily residential suburb just SE of San Leandro. **2.** in Kentucky: **a.** city, pop. 23,622, Boyd Co., in the extreme NE, on the Ohio R., 12 mi/19 km WNW of Huntington, West Virginia. Called Poage Settlement when established in 1815, the "Steel Buckle of the Coal Belt" is in a region rich in coal, clay, oil, limestone, and natural gas. When laid out as a town in 1850, it was renamed in honor of Henry Clay, after his home in Lexington. It manufactures iron and steel, firebrick, chemicals, oil products, coke, mining equipment, and leather, and has a community college and a Federal prison. The city is built around Central Park, noted for its Indian mounds. **b.** see under LEXINGTON, Fayette Co. **3.** city, pop. 20,079, seat of Ashland Co., NC Ohio, 13 mi/21 km NE of Mansfield. It was platted in 1815, when it was on a major stagecoach line from New England. In addition to agriculture, the economy is centered around printing and the manufacture of rubber goods, machinery, metal products, paper boxes, and medicines. The city is the seat of Ashland College (1878). **4.** city, pop. 16,234, Jackson Co., SW Oregon, in the Rogue River Valley, in the foothills of the Siskiyou Mts., 12 mi/19 km SE of Medford. Settled during a gold rush in 1852, it is best known as the site of the Oregon Shakespeare Festival, established in 1935, one of the oldest in the US. Lumber is milled and flour processed here. A resort, the city also has lithia water mineral springs. It is the seat of Southern Oregon State College (1926). **Mt. Ashland** (7533 ft/2298 m), in Rogue River National Forest, is SW of the city. **5.** town, pop. 5864, Hanover Co., EC Virginia, 15 mi/24 km N of Richmond, on US 1. In a dairying and truck farming region, it was founded as a health resort (1848), and became the seat of Randolph-Macon College (1830) when it relocated here in 1868. Ashland produces flour and lumber. Scotchtown, the home of Patrick Henry and later of Dolley Madison, is 8 mi/13 km NW. **6.** city, pop. 8695, seat of Ashland Co., N Wisconsin, 60 mi/97 km SE of Superior. It is a port on CHEQUAMEGON BAY of L. Superior and a railroad center for the surrounding lumbering, iron mining, and granite quarrying region. Manufactures include paper, wood and iron products, and tile. A French mission was established near the site in 1665. Settlement began in 1854, and iron and lumber were the foundations of the city's early growth. Ashland is the site of Northland College (1892).

Ash Lawn historic site 3 mi/5 km SE of Charlottesville, Albemarle Co., C Virginia, the home of President James Monroe, built (1799) along Carters Mountain so as to look across at MONTICELLO, the home of Monroe's friend, Thomas Jefferson, 2 mi/3 km NE. Ash Lawn covers 535 ac/217 ha.

Ashley National Forest over 1.38 million ac/560,000 ha (2160 sq mi/5585 sq km), in NE Utah. Its larger unit encompasses much of the C and S UINTA Mts., and parts of the High Uintas Wilderness and FLAMING GORGE National Recreation Area (Red Canyon). The smaller unit lies S of the Uinta and Ouray Indian Reservation, on the West Tavaputs Plateau. Established in 1908, this is one of the oldest US national forests.

Ashley River 40 mi/64 km long, in SE South Carolina. It rises in Berkeley Co., near Ridgeville, and flows SE to CHARLESTON, where it joins the COOPER R. (to its E) to form Charleston Harbor. It is estuarial in the city.

Ashokan Reservoir largest unit of the system bringing water from the CATSKILL Mts. to New York City, SE New York. Completed in 1912 and covering some 8200 ac/3320 ha, it is 12 mi/19 km E–W, and impounds waters of Esopus Creek. Kingston is 7 mi/11 km SE.

Ashtabula city, pop. 21,633, Ashtabula Co., NE Ohio, 55 mi/89 km NE of Cleveland. It was founded c.1801 on L. Erie at the mouth of the Ashtabula R., and was a vital stop on the Underground Railroad in the 1850s. Ashtabula is a trading center for the L. Erie resort area, and has long been a major port. Particularly important in the interstate transport of iron and coal, it also handles international shipping. Local manufactures include automobile, truck, and tractor parts, chemicals, farm and garden tools, fiberglass, and reinforced plastics.

Ashtabula, Lake see under VALLEY CITY, North Dakota.

Ashtabula County 703 sq mi/1821 sq km, pop. 99,821, in extreme NE Ohio, bounded by L. Erie (N) and Pennsylvania (E), and intersected by the Ashtabula and Grand rivers. The PYMATUNING RESERVOIR lies partially in the county. Its seat is Jefferson. There is manufacturing at Ashtabula and Conneaut, and the rest of the county is largely agricultural (dairy, fruit, grain, hay, livestock, and truck). There are apiaries, greenhouses, and wineries.

Ashwaubenon village, pop. 16,376, Brown Co., EC Wisconsin, on the Fox R., a residential suburb 3 mi/5 km SW of GREEN BAY.

Asilomar see under PACIFIC GROVE, California.

Aspen city, pop. 5049, seat of Pitkin Co., WC Colorado, at 7850 ft/2394 m above sea level, on the Roaring Fork R. It lies at the W edge of the White River National Forest, just W of the Sawatch Mts., and 30 mi/48 km W of Leadville. A silver boom town in the 1880s, Aspen declined with the collapse of silver prices in the 1890s. It was an agrarian community until the 1930s when the exploitation of snow-covered slopes transformed it into a recreational center. It is now a world-famous resort, known as much for its exclusivity, affluence, and the celebrity of many of its residents as for its ski areas, including those at Snowmass, Aspen Mt., Aspen Highlands, and Buttermilk Mt. It is also a cultural and New Age mecca, housing such institutions as the Aspen Music Festival, Institute for Humanistic Studies, Ballet West, DanceAspen, and Aspen Theater Institute.

Aspen Hill unincorporated residential community, pop. 45,494, Montgomery Co., WC Maryland, just E of Rock Creek Park and Rockville, 12 mi/19 km NNW of Washington, D.C.

Aspen Parkland see the PARKLANDS.

Assabet River 30 mi/48 km long, in E Massachusetts. It rises in Worcester Co., then flows NE past Hudson and Maynard. It joins the Sudbury R. to form the Concord R. in Concord.

Assateague Island barrier island, 37 mi/60 km long, along the Atlantic Coast in Worcester Co., Maryland, and Accomack Co., Virginia. Connected by highway and bridge with CHINCOTEAGUE I. (S) and the EASTERN SHORE, Assateague is an area of undeveloped beach, since 1965 the Assateague Island National Seashore, known for its herds of wild ponies; each summer some of them are rounded up on Chincoteague and auctioned.

Assawoman Bay protected inlet of the Atlantic Ocean just S of the Delaware border, in Worcester Co., SE Maryland, on the DELMARVA PENINSULA. Seven mi/11 km N–S and 2–4 mi/3–6 km wide, it is bounded E by the barrier beach on which OCEAN CITY sits.

Assawompsett Pond in Plymouth Co., SE Massachusetts, 10 mi/16 km SE of Taunton and 7 mi/11 km NNE of New Bedford. It is 3 mi/5 km long and lies in a lake region, connected by streams to Long Pond (SW) and Great Quittacus Pond (SE).

Assiniboia after the Assiniboine (or "Stoney") Indians: **1.** the district of Assiniboia (1811–69), formal name for the Red River Colony (see RED RIVER OF THE NORTH). **2.** provisional name (1870) for the MÉTIS-controlled parts of the same area, changed by Louis Riel to "Manitoba." **3.** name (1882–1905) for part of the Northwest Territories, now in Alberta and S Saskatchewan. **4.** town, pop. 2774, S Saskatchewan, 80 mi/130 km SW of Regina, an agricultural service center founded in 1912 on the Canadian Pacific Railway.

Assiniboine, Mount peak (11,870 ft/3618 m) of the Rocky Mts., 69 mi/111 km W of Calgary and 22 mi/35 km S of Banff, along the Alberta–British Columbia border. Named for the tribe, it is the center of Mount Assiniboine Provincial Park.

Assiniboine River 590 mi/950 km long, in E Saskatchewan and S Manitoba. It rises some 75 mi/120 km NW of KAMSACK, Saskatchewan, and flows SE into Manitoba, S and SE to Brandon, and generally E to WINNIPEG, where it joins the RED RIVER OF THE NORTH. Its main tributaries are the QU'APPELLE and Souris rivers, which join it from the S in SW Manitoba. The three rivers have cut wide valleys through the prairies, and the system was a major route of 19th-century settlement westward from the Red R. Today it is a major grain producing area.

Aston township, pop. 15,080, Delaware Co., SE Pennsylvania, 12 mi/19 km SW of Philadelphia. Largely residential, it is the seat of Neumann College (1965).

Astoria **1.** northwesternmost section of Queens, New York, on the Hell Gate (East R.), W of LaGuardia Airport and Steinway, and N of Long Island City. It was first called Hallett's Cove, after a 1654 settler, then incorporated as Astoria in 1839. The Triborough and Hell Gate bridges cross between Ward's Island and Astoria, and a huge gas and electric plant is on the river. Astoria has been the site of lumberyards and factories. Since World War II it has become home to perhaps the largest Greek community outside Athens, and the center of Greek-American cultural and political activities. **2.** city, pop. 10,069, seat of Clatsop Co., NW Oregon, on the Columbia R., 8 mi/13 km SE of its mouth at the Pacific Ocean, across the river from the state of Washington and 70 mi/113 km NW of Portland. An important port, it is also a trade center for a farming, fishing, and lumbering region. It has a significant fishing industry, with salmon and tuna canneries, and tourism is also vital to its economy. Site of the first permanent settlement in Oregon, it was founded by John Jacob Astor as a fur trading post in 1811, and was held by the British from 1813 to 1818. In the 1840s American settlers turned the town into the trading center of the lower Columbia Valley. Salmon canning, sawmills, dairy processing, and shipping all fueled its 19th- and early-20th-century prosperity. Astoria is the seat of Clatsop Community College (1858). A noted local sight is the 125 ft/38 m–tall Astor Column on Coxcomb Hill. Six mi/10 km SW is Fort Clatsop National Memorial, a reconstruction of the fort in which Lewis and Clark spent the winter of 1805–06.

Astrodome officially, **Harris County Domed Stadium** arena in SC Houston, Texas, near Interstate Loop 610, 7 mi/11 km SW of Downtown. Opened in 1965, it is home to the Astros (baseball) and the Oilers (football), and also hosts the Houston Livestock Show and Rodeo. The dome, 642 ft/196 m across and 218 ft/66 m high, encloses a playing field of nylon Astroturf (introduced 1966). Nearby is the Astroworld amusement park; the entire complex is called the Astrodomain.

Atascadero city, pop. 23,138, San Luis Obispo Co., SW California, 14 mi/23 km N of San Luis Obispo. A residential community and agricultural trade center, it was founded in 1913 as a model small-farm community, which soon failed. It is now the county's second-largest city.

Atchafalaya River 170 mi/275 km long, in SC Louisiana. A DISTRIBUTARY of the Red R., it also serves to control flooding on the lower Mississippi R. It flows generally SSE from near Simmesport, in Avoyelles Parish, and enters the Gulf of Mexico at Atchafalaya Bay, 20 mi/32 km S of Morgan City. The **Atchafalaya Basin,** extending from the Bayou Teche (W) to the Mississippi and the Bayou Lafourche (E), was a rich swampland that developed a farming, then a fishing and foresting economy in the 19th century. After the 1927 Mississippi flood, levees and other engineering measures brought environmental changes that continue to be debated.

Atchison city, pop. 10,656, seat of Atchison Co., NE Kansas, on the Missouri R., 40 mi/64 km NW of Kansas City. Founded in 1854 as a proslavery settlement, it grew rapidly as a wagon-train staging site, river port, and railroad terminus; the Atchison, Topeka & Santa Fe Railroad was chartered here in 1859. In a grain, fruit, and livestock producing area, the city has railroad shops and manufactures industrial alcohol, tools, textiles, and leather goods. The aviator Amelia Earhart was born here (1898). It is the seat of Benedictine College (1858).

Atchison, Topeka & Santa Fe see SANTA FE RAILROAD.

Athabasca, Lake crescent-shaped, ENE–WSW oriented body, c.200 mi/320 km long and 5–36 mi/8–58 km wide, in extreme NE Alberta and NW Saskatchewan, at the S edge of the CANADIAN SHIELD. The fourth-largest lake entirely within Canada, at 3120 sq mi/8080 sq km, it is fed by the Athabasca R. from the S, and drains N via the Slave R. into Great Slave L. and thence into the Mackenzie R. WOOD BUFFALO NATIONAL PARK is at its W end. The lake was key to early fur trading; canoe routes E via REINDEER L. and the CHURCHILL R. allowed traders from HUDSON BAY to reach the lake and return within a summer. FORT CHIPEWYAN, Alberta, was established here in 1788 by the North West Company. In the 1930s gold, in the 1940s uranium were found on the NE shore, around neighboring Beaverlodge L. The mining communities of Uranium City and Eldorado, Saskatchewan, flourished in the 1950s; by the 1980s, with mining ended, they virtually disappeared.

Athabasca, Mount see under Mt. COLUMBIA, Alberta.

Athabasca River also, **Athabaska** 765 mi/1231 km long, in Alberta. It rises in the Columbia Icefield, in the Rocky Mts., near Mt. Columbia and the British Columbia border, and flows N through Jasper National Park, then generally NE across the N plains of Alberta, past Hinton, Whitecourt, Athabasca, and Fort McMurray, to L. Athabasca, in the NE corner. It is the southernmost tributary of the MACKENZIE R. Extensive oil deposits lie in the **Athabasca Tar Sands,** along a stretch of the river near FORT MCMURRAY. The **Athabasca Pass,** an 1810s fur trade route, crosses the Rockies at 5735 ft/1748 m, near the river's headwaters; both the upper reaches of the river and the area around L. Athabasca were called **Athabasca** in the early 19th century.

Athens **1.** city, pop. 16,901, seat of Limestone Co., N Alabama, 19 mi/31 km WNW of Huntsville. Founded in 1816, it was a commercial center for a timber and cotton producing region. During the Civil War, the city was occupied by Union troops from 1862 to 1864. Athens was the first Alabama city to use TENNESSEE VALLEY AUTHORITY power, in 1934; it subsequently developed diverse industries. Today it houses cotton gins, stockyards, grist and lumber mills, and garment factories. Athens State College (1822) is here. **2.** city, pop. 45,734, seat of Clarke Co., NE Georgia, on the Oconee R., 60 mi/100 km ENE of Atlanta. It was founded in 1801 as the site for the University of Georgia (chartered 1785). The Georgia Museum of Art and State Botanical Gardens are here. A trading center for the region's poultry and cattle, the city also manufactures textiles, clothing, cottonseed products, clocks, and electrical equipment. **3.** city, pop. 21,265, seat of Athens Co., SE Ohio, on the Hocking R., 35 mi/56 km W of Marietta. It lies in a mainly agricultural region. Founded in 1800, it has many manufactures including business machines, tire molds, tools, trucks, and printed materials. Ohio University (1804) has played a prominent role in the life of the city, and was the first college established in the NORTHWEST TERRITORY. **4.** city, pop. 12,054, seat of McMinn Co., SE Tennessee, midway between Chattanooga (SW) and Knoxville (NE), in the Tennessee Valley, W of the Great Smoky Mts. Founded in 1821, it was long an agricultural center, handling tobacco, meat, and dairy cattle. Now primarily industrial, it produces furniture, electric motors, chemicals, paper, textiles, farm machinery, and animal feeds. Tennessee Wesleyan College (1857) is here. **5.** city, pop. 10,967, seat of Henderson Co., NE Texas, 65 mi/105 km SE of Dallas. Settled in 1848, it has oil and gas works and food, cotton, and meat processing plants. It has long been noted for its black-eyed pea production, and claims to be the birthplace of the hamburger. The city produces TV sets, tile and pottery, brick, glass, lumber, furniture, boats, medical equipment, and clothing. Trinity Valley Community College (1946) is here. **6.** town, pop. 741, Mercer Co., S West Virginia, 18 mi/29 km NE of Bluefield, Virginia, in a coal mining and agricultural region at the E edge of the Appalachian Plateau. Concord College (1872) is here.

Athens of America, the nickname used for Boston, Massachusetts, since the early 19th century, reflecting an estimation of the city's importance in national culture.

Athens of the South, the see NASHVILLE, Tennessee.

Athens of the West, the see LEXINGTON, Kentucky.

Atherton town, pop. 7163, San Mateo Co., NC California, between Menlo Park (SE) and Redwood City (NW), 22 mi/35 km SE of San Francisco. It is a largely residential suburb, established in 1860 with the laying out of Faxon Atherton's large estate. Menlo College (1927) is here.

Athol town, pop. 11,451, Worcester Co., NC Massachusetts, on the Millers R. It was a 19th-century industrial center with paper and cotton mills and tanneries. On the Mohawk Trail, 8 mi/13 km NE of Quabbin Reservoir and surrounded by state parks, Athol is now center of a tourist area. Industries have also included the manufacture of toys and tools.

Atikokan township, pop. 4047, Rainy River District, W Ontario, on the TRANS-CANADA HIGHWAY (Route 11), 112 mi/180 km WNW of Thunder Bay. In the 1940s it was the center of an iron ore boom around Steep Rock L. Today there is some light industry, but Atikokan is primarily an outfitting base for QUETICO PROVINCIAL PARK (S).

Atlanta city, pop. 394,017, state capital and seat of Fulton Co., also in De Kalb Co., NW Georgia, in the foothills of the Appalachian Mts., on the Chattahoochee R. (W) and Peachtree Creek. The Atlanta metropolitan area (MSA) encompasses 18 counties, including CLAYTON, COBB, DE KALB, FULTON, and GWINNETT, with a pop. of 2,833,511. Developed in the 1840s around the SE terminus of the Western & Atlantic Railroad (established 1837), the settlement, known briefly as Terminus, then as Marthasville, rapidly became a major railroad center. During the Civil War it was besieged and occupied (Sept.–Nov. 1864) by W. T. Sherman's Federal forces, who then burned a large part of the city and began their MARCH TO THE SEA. Atlanta recovered quickly following the Civil War, regaining its central role in regional trade (esp. cotton) and transportation, and becoming an important state and Federal administrative center. Chosen as the state capital in 1877, it celebrated its role as the capital of the New South (see under the SOUTH) as the site of three important expositions, the last and largest the Cotton States and International, in 1895. Georgia's largest city, Atlanta is a service, manufacturing, and shipping center, and has been the commercial and financial hub of the Southeast through the 20th century, although in the 1980s it lost regional banking preeminence to CHARLOTTE, North Carolina. Local industries manufacture metals, machinery, automobiles and transportation equipment, textiles, apparel, and food products. The city is headquarters to Coca-Cola, Georgia-Pacific (lumber and diversified products), Simmons (bedding), Delta Air Lines, and many other corporations, and to dozens of research facilities. Federal institutions in the area include the CENTERS FOR DISEASE CONTROL AND PREVENTION (in EMORY), regional Federal Reserve headquarters, Dobbins Air Force Base (see MARIETTA), and Fort McPherson, on the city's S. Hartsfield International Airport, 8 mi/13 km SSW of Downtown, is one of the busiest in the US. The city's educational and cultural institutions include the ATLANTA UNIVERSITY CENTER, Oglethorpe (1835), and Georgia State (1913) universities, and the Georgia Institute of Technology (1885). The Robert W. Woodruff (Atlanta Memorial) Arts Center and adjacent High Museum of Art are world-famous. The city also houses the headquarters of the Cable News Network. Atlanta has since the Civil War been a center of black political, business, and cultural life. Its importance is seen both in the role of the Atlanta University Center, longtime base to W.E.B. DuBois and other leaders, and in the history of Auburn Ave., where the Martin Luther King, Jr. National Historic Site is located. The city's population grew through the 1960s, and has declined from 495,039 in 1970. Much of the loss has been in white flight to suburbs. South and C Atlanta are today largely black (the city is 67% black), while more lightly populated districts in the N are largely white. Staging of the 1996 Olympic Games in the city is expected to spur redevelopment. See also: ANSLEY PARK; ATLANTA–FULTON COUNTY STADIUM; ATLANTA UNIVERSITY CENTER; AUBURN AVENUE (Sweet Auburn); BUCKHEAD; CABBAGETOWN; CASCADE HEIGHTS; CASTLEBERRY HILL; DECATUR STREET; DRUID HILLS; FAIRLIE-POPLAR; FIVE POINTS (and Zero Mile Post); GEORGIA DOME; GRANT PARK (and Cyclorama); HARTSFIELD INTERNATIONAL AIRPORT; INMAN PARK (and Little Five Points); MARTIN LUTHER KING, JR. NATIONAL HISTORIC SITE; MIDTOWN; OMNI COLISEUM; PEACHTREE CENTER; PEACHTREE CREEK (and Standing Peachtree); PEACHTREE STREET; PERIMETER HIGHWAY; PIEDMONT PARK; TECHWOOD; UNDERGROUND ATLANTA; VINE CITY; VIRGINIA-HIGHLAND; WEST END (and Ezra Church).

Atlanta–Fulton County Stadium in downtown Atlanta, Georgia, 1 mi/1.6 km S of FIVE POINTS. Opened in 1965 and seating 52,000, it is home to the Atlanta Braves (baseball). The Summerhill neighborhood lies E.

Atlanta University Center assembly of historically black institutions affiliated with Atlanta University (1867), including Morehouse (1867), Clark (1877), Morris Brown (1881), and Spelman (1881) colleges and the Interdenominational Theological Center, located just W of FIVE POINTS, in Atlanta, Georgia.

Atlantic Beach **1.** city, pop. 11,636, DUVAL Co., NE Florida, 15 mi/24 km E of downtown Jacksonville. Situated on the Atlantic Ocean 5 mi/8 km S of the mouth of the St. Johns R., it is adjacent (N) to another resort community, Neptune Beach. The N end of a 45 mi/72 km–long stretch of beachfront resorts, it has long been a popular vacation site. **2.** village, pop. 1933, in Hempstead town, Nassau Co., SE New York, on a barrier island (Long Beach I.) off the S shore of Long Island, across Rockaway Channel from Far Rockaway, Queens. A residential community, it has a number of beach clubs along its waterfront. **3.** see under BOGUE SOUND, North Carolina.

Atlantic City city, pop. 37,986, Atlantic Co., SE New Jersey, on the Atlantic Ocean, 60 mi/97 km SE of Philadelphia. Settled in the late 18th century, it was an Absecon I. fishing village until the arrival of the Camden & Atlantic Railroad (1854). It quickly became a beachfront resort, receiving its first boardwalk (1870) and first pier (1882). Atlantic City developed into one of the East Coast's most noted resorts, with a 7 mi/11 km–long boardwalk, amusement piers including the famous Steel Pier, rides (the first Ferris wheel was built here in 1869), hotels, and convention centers. After World War II, the city declined, and was seedy and dilapidated by the early 1970s. In 1976 New Jersey legalized gambling; the first casino opened in 1978, others followed, and Atlantic City became a boom town. While gambling revenues and tourism slackened in the 1990s, the city remains one of the country's most important resort and casino centers. It has many recreational and convention facilities, and presents the annual Miss America Pageant (established 1921). A local manufacture is saltwater taffy (invented here), and the distribution of seafood is important. Street names in Atlantic City and adjacent (SW) VENTNOR CITY are familiar around the world because of their use in the board game "Monopoly."

Atlantic Coastal Plain see under COASTAL PLAIN.

Atlantic County 568 sq mi/1471 sq km, pop. 224,327, in SE New Jersey, along the Atlantic Ocean (SE). Its seat is Mays Landing, on the Great Egg Harbor R., which bisects the county N–S. The E part is the site of many seaside resort communities, the most important ATLANTIC CITY. The interior has many truck and berry farms, produces dairy products and poultry, and has a number of light manufactures, including glass, building materials, textiles, and wood products.

Atlantic Fleet Weapons Training Facility see ROOSEVELT ROADS, Puerto Rico.

Atlantic Flyway bird migration route (used also by some insects) along the E coast of North America. It is traveled between wintering grounds in Central and South America and the West Indies and points as far N as Greenland and ELLESMERE I. Some species, esp. waterfowl, navigate along the coastline, swinging around Newfoundland if they nest farther N. Others, like many hawks, follow the Appalachian system, employing wind currents to aid movement.

Atlantic Intracoastal Waterway 1900 mi/3100 km–long route providing sheltered passage for commercial and pleasure craft between Boston, Massachusetts, and Key West, Florida. The toll-free system utilizes rivers, bays, sounds, and marshes, as well as important artificial waterways. It incorporates (N–S) the Cape Cod Canal; Long Island Sound; Delaware Bay; the Chesapeake and Delaware Canal; Chesapeake Bay; the Chesapeake and Albemarle Canal; Albemarle and Pamlico sounds; the marshes of the Sea Islands; and the lagoons of Florida's E coast. It is also connected to several inland waterways, including the New York State Barge Canal System and the Hudson R. Much of the waterway can accommodate deep-draft vessels; the shallowest section, only 6 ft/2 m deep, is in the Dismal Swamp of Virginia and North Carolina. Major ports include Boston; New York; Philadelphia; Baltimore; Norfolk; Beaufort, North Carolina; Charleston, South Carolina; Savannah; Jacksonville, Florida; and Miami. During World War II, the waterway was used extensively for shipping as a means of avoiding submarines in open seas. The Intracoastal Waterway was originally planned as one system extending from the Northeast to Texas; there is still a break between the Atlantic and Gulf sections because a necessary canal in S Florida was never completed, for environmental reasons. The Army Corps of Engineers administers and maintains the entire waterway.

Atlantic Provinces the Maritime Provinces (Nova Scotia, New Brunswick, and Prince Edward Island) plus Newfoundland (which did not become a province until 1949).

Atmore city, pop. 8046, Escambia Co., SW Alabama, just N of the Florida line and 43 mi/69 km NE of Mobile. A processing and shipping center in a truck and cotton farming and lumbering area, it is also home to the Alabama men's (Holman) prison.

atoll oceanic structure consisting of a coral reef or number of islets, which remain above water at least at low tide, surrounding one or more central lagoons. Found esp. in the W Pacific Ocean, atolls are thought to have formed over sunken islands or underwater volcanoes, taking essentially circular forms as coral grew upward and outward and coral skeletons and other matter accreted.

A Train subway train that connects Washington Heights, Manhattan, New York City, with Far Rockaway, Queens, by way of Manhattan and Brooklyn. First operated in part in 1932, by 1936 it connected New York's two largest black communities, Harlem and Bedford-Stuyvesant.

Attica town, pop. 7383, Wyoming Co., W New York, 12 mi/19 km SW of Batavia. Settled in 1804, it now has a variety of light manufactures and dairy farms. Attica State Prison (1931) is here; in 1971 it was the scene of a prisoner uprising and bloody police counterattack.

Attleboro city, pop. 38,383, Bristol Co., SE Massachusetts, 10 mi/16 km NE of Providence, Rhode Island. Settled in 1634, it developed after the Boston-Providence railroad was opened in 1836. A noted center of the jewelry industry, established in 1780, Attleboro also manufactures plaques and other presentation items, as well as machine tools, electronics, and plastics.

Attu Island largest of the NEAR Is., in the W ALEUTIAN Is., SW Alaska. Thirty mi/50 km E–W and 8–15 mi/13–24 km N–S, it is the westernmost island in the Aleutians, lying 430 mi/690 km from the Kamchatka Peninsula of E Siberia. Cape Wrangell, at 172° 27′ E, is the westernmost US point. Rocky and treeless, the island rises to 3100 ft/945 m. In 1942, Japanese forces occupied Attu (along with KISKA I.) and evacuated its 40-odd inhabitants to Japan. American troops landed at Holtz Bay and Massacre Bay in 1943, and following three weeks of intense fighting, recaptured the island and established an air base, since enlarged. Residents were repatriated in 1945. Attu is noted for its seabirds.

Atwater city, pop. 22,282, Merced Co., C California, 7 mi/11 km NW of Merced, in the San Joaquin Valley. It is a processing and trade center for an irrigated region producing fruits and dairy products. Castle Air Force Base is just NE.

Auau Channel see under LAHAINA, Hawaii.

Auburn **1.** city, pop. 33,830, Lee Co., E Alabama, 50 mi/80 km ENE of Montgomery. It is primarily a university town. East Alabama Male College (1856), a state institution since 1872, is now Auburn University, the largest in Alabama. There are also cotton and lumber industries. **2.** city, pop. 10,592, seat of Placer Co., NE California, on the American R., 32 mi/52 km NE of Sacramento. A gold rush town, founded in 1848, it is now a fruit growing, farming, and tourist center, with publishing and other light industries. Suburban sprawl from Sacramento is approaching it. Construction of the controversial Auburn Dam, which would be one of California's largest, was halted after a 1975 earthquake. **3.** city, pop. 9379, seat of De Kalb Co., NE Indiana, 20 mi/32 km NNE of Fort Wayne. Founded in 1836, it is a trade center in an area in which livestock, dairy items, soybeans, and grain are produced. The city was an early automobile manufacturer, home (1900–37) to the Auburn and the Cord. Today, its manufactures include auto parts, foundry products, rubber items, oil burners, and stationery. **4.** city, pop. 24,309, seat of Androscoggin Co., SW Maine, on the Androscoggin R. on hilly ground opposite Lewiston; part of the Lewiston-Auburn metropolitan area, it is 30 mi/48 km N of Portland. Settled in the 1790s, it became one of Maine's largest manufacturing centers, noted especially for producing shoes. Nearby L. Auburn, Taylor Pond, and Lost Valley ski area provide a tourist base. Auburn also has technical and bible colleges and a regional airport. **5.** town, pop. 15,005, Worcester Co., SC Massachusetts, 5 mi/8 km SW of Worcester. Robert Hutchings Goddard fired the first liquid-fuel rocket here in 1926. Industries have included warehousing and the production of electronic equipment, motors, cement, musical instruments, and plastics, but Auburn is today chiefly a residential suburb of Worcester, with commerce concentrated near the junction of the Massachusetts Turnpike with Interstate 290/395. **6.** city, pop. 31,258, seat of Cayuga Co., WC New York, at the N outlet of Owasco L., in the FINGER LAKES, 23 mi/37 km SW of Syracuse. Originally known as Hardenberg's Corners, it was founded in 1793 on the site of the Cayuga village of Wasco. The city developed around Auburn State Prison (1816) and the Auburn Theological Seminary (1822). Abundant waterpower and cheap prison labor attracted early industries. Auburn now manufactures shoes, rope, plastics, diesel engines, electronic equipment, air conditioners, and rugs, and serves as the market center of an agricultural region. The home of antislavery leader Harriet Tubman is preserved. Auburn is the seat of Cayuga Co. Community College (1953). **7.** city, pop. 33,102, King Co., WC Washington, 12 mi/19 km ENE of Tacoma. Settled in 1887, it became an important agricultural trade center when the Northern Pacific Railroad established a division point here. Today, the city manufactures aircraft parts, metal products, lumber, ceramics, and cabinetry. The Federal Aviation Administration's NW headquarters has been here since 1962. The Muckleshoot Indian Reservation (pop. 1379) lies 2 mi/3 km SE. Green River Community College (1965) is here.

Auburn Avenue popularly, **Sweet Auburn** E–W commercial and residential thoroughfare and neighborhood in downtown Atlanta, Georgia, just E of FIVE POINTS. The historic center of black enterprise in the city (and in the Southeast), it was home to the influential Atlanta Life Insurance Company, the *Atlanta Daily World* (the first black daily), and many other undertakings. The MARTIN LUTHER KING, JR. NATIONAL HISTORIC SITE is here. Many of the properties here were bought by ex-slaves after the Civil War, and the area, noted for its Queen Anne architecture, remained home to Atlanta's black elite into the 1960s. Since then it has suffered economic decline.

Auburn Hills city, pop. 17,076, Oakland Co., SE Michigan, 3 mi/5 km E of Pontiac. Situated on I-75, 25 mi/40 km NE of downtown Detroit, it has recently emerged as an important corporate office center; Chrysler moved its headquarters here in the early 1990s. It is also the site of the Palace of Auburn Hills (1988), home of the Detroit Pistons (basketball).

Audubon borough, pop. 9205, Camden Co., WC New Jersey, 4 mi/6 km SE of Camden. It is a largely residential suburb of Camden and of Philadelphia, with some light industry.

Audubon Ballroom see under WASHINGTON HEIGHTS, New York.

Audubon Park **1.** 280 ac/113 ha, in UPTOWN New Orleans, Louisiana, just NE of the Mississippi R., 2 mi/3 km W of the GARDEN DISTRICT. The site of the 1884 Cotton Centennial Exposition, it now has a noted zoo. The Tulane University campus adjoins (NE). **2.** 373 ac/151 ha, in EC Memphis, Tennessee, 8 mi/13 km ESE of Downtown. It is home to the Memphis Botanic Garden. Memphis State University's campus is just NW.

Auglaize River 100 mi/160 km long, in NW Ohio. It rises W of Wapakoneta and flows generally N, joining the Maumee R. at Defiance. Its main tributaries are the Ottawa and Blanchard rivers (E) and the Little Auglaize (W).

Augusta **1.** city, pop. 44,639, seat of Richmond Co., E Georgia, in the SANDHILLS, on the Savannah R. at the Fall Line, across from North Augusta, South Carolina. The second-oldest city in Georgia, it was founded in 1735 by James Oglethorpe as a fur trading post, and was the state capital 1786–95. An important antebellum commercial center, it boasted one of the largest inland cotton markets in the South. Brick, clay, and tile industries developed around local kaolin deposits; textile manufacturing also became important. During the Civil War the city produced Confederate munitions. After the war, industry expanded, and Augusta also became a leading resort. Its popularity with golfers continues today, with the Masters tournament being held at the **Augusta National** course, NW of Downtown. Paine College (1882), Augusta College (1925), and the Medical College of Georgia (1828) are here. **2.** city, pop. 21,325, capital of Maine and seat of Kennebec Co., SW Maine, on both sides of the Kennebec R., 50 mi/80 km NE of Portland and 39 mi/63 km from the Atlantic Ocean. In addition to its governmental importance, it is a trade center for surrounding farms and resorts, and has some light industry. Established (1628) as a trading post on an Abnaki site called Cushnoc, the settlement did not become a town and take its present name until 1797. Fort Western (1754), from which Benedict Arnold set out to capture Québec in 1775, is now a historical monument and museum. The capitol (1829) was designed by Charles Bulfinch.

Augustine, Mount see under KATMAI NATIONAL PARK AND PRESERVE, Alaska.

Auraria one of the settlements that in 1860 became DENVER, Colorado. On CHERRY CREEK across (SW) from Larimer Square and the modern Downtown, Auraria was settled by 1858–59 gold seekers and competed with the nascent Denver for a year before consolidation. Today the area is an educational center, site of a University of Colorado facility, Metropolitan State College, and Denver Community College.

Auriesville rural village in Glen township, Montgomery Co., EC New York, on the Mohawk R., 7 mi/11 km W of Amsterdam, on the site of the Mohawk village of Ossernenon. Situated here is the Roman Catholic Shrine of Our Lady of Martyrs (begun 1884), a memorial to French Jesuit missionaries Isaac Jogues, René Goupil, and Jean de Lalande and five mission priests, all killed by Indians near here during the 1640s. Auriesville is also the birthplace of Kateri Tekakwitha (1656–80), a Mohawk Christian who is being canonized; a grotto adjoining the shrine honors her.

Aurora **1.** city, pop. 222,103, Adams, Arapahoe, and Douglas counties, NC Colorado, a residential suburb 6 mi/10 km E of Denver. Founded in 1891 during the silver boom, it was a mining center until 1893, when the silver market collapsed. Now one of the largest cities in Colorado, it has some light industry, including the manufacture of sporting goods, electronic and electrical equipment, luggage, aviation parts, and precision instruments. Long a military center, it is the site of the Buckley Air National Guard Base and Fitzsimmons Army Medical Center, and nearby is LOWRY AIR FORCE BASE. Stapleton International Airport is just NE. **2.** city, pop. 99,581, Kane and Du Page counties, NE Illinois, on the Fox R., 36 mi/58 km WSW of Chicago. An important regional economic center, it manufactures and distributes such products as auto parts, office furniture and equipment, electrical and pneumatic tools, clothing, pumps, toys, tractors, and road paving machinery. Aurora was founded in 1834 as McCarty's Mills, a fur trading post and sawmill near a Potawatomi village. An important stagecoach stop on the road leading W from Chicago, it boomed when the Chicago, Burlington and Quincy Railroad built its construction and repair yards here in the 1850s. Local institutions include Aurora University (1893) and the Bellarmine School of Theology of Loyola University. There has been much recent industrial and commercial growth along I-88, on the NE edge of the city, along the ILLINOIS RESEARCH AND DEVELOPMENT CORRIDOR. **3.** city, pop. 3825, Dearborn Co., extreme SE Indiana, just SW of Lawrenceburg and 20 mi/32 km SW of Cincinnati, Ohio, on hills along the Ohio R. Founded in 1819, it has manufactured furniture, coffins, and cement vaults. **4.** GHOST TOWN, Mineral Co., WC Nevada, 20 mi/32 km SW of Hawthorne and just E of the California line. It grew when gold was discovered in the S Wassuk Mts. (1861), and until 1863 it was claimed by both Nevada and California. Its pop. was c.10,000 by 1864, and it reputedly produced $20–$30 million over seven years. Mark Twain lived here briefly during Aurora's heyday. Most of the deserted town was dismantled after World War II. It is within TOIYABE NATIONAL FOREST. **5.** village, pop. 687, in Ledyard township, Cayuga Co., WC New York, in the Finger Lakes, on the E shore of L. Cayuga, 14 mi/23 km SW of Auburn. Settled in 1789, it is the seat of Wells College (1868). **6.** village, pop. 9192, Portage Co., NE Ohio, on a branch of the Chagrin R., 22 mi/35 km SE of Cleveland. There is a sandstone quarry in the area. Primarily a residential community, Aurora is also the site of a group of "factory outlet" shops. A large amusement park and Sea World are nearby. **7.** town, pop. 29,454, York Regional Municipality, S Ontario, 22 mi/35 km N of Toronto. An agricultural community, it prospered after the 1853 arrival of the railroad. Today this residential suburb has some light industry and a number of religious educational institutions. **8.** city, pop. 567, Marion Co., NW Oregon, on the Pudding R., 18 mi/29 km SSW of Portland. The Aurora Colony was established in 1856 as a communal Christian settlement. In 1877, its property was privatized and the colony disbanded. Today Aurora constitutes a National Landmark Historic District and is the site of a five-building museum.

Au Sable River **1.** 80 mi/129 km long, in NE Michigan. It is formed by several branches near Grayling, in Crawford Co. It flows E past Mio and McKinley, turning S in Alcona Co., then E again in Iosco Co., where it flows through several ponds before entering L. Huron at Au Sable. There are several power dams in its lower course, including Mio, Alcona, Loud, Cooke, and Foote, all of which impound lakes. The main river flows through Huron National Forest. Its chief tributaries are the 30 mi/48 km–long North Branch, the 33 mi/53 km–long Middle Branch, and the 37 mi/60 km–long South Branch. **2.** also, **Ausable River** 20 mi/32 km long, in NE New York. It is formed by the confluence of the West Branch (25 mi/40 km long), which rises near Lake Placid, and the East Branch (30 mi/48 km long), which rises near Mt. Marcy, in the Adirondacks. They both flow generally NE to their junction at the town of Au Sable Forks. The Au Sable then flows NE through **Au Sable Chasm** to L. Champlain, 10 mi/16 km S of Plattsburgh.

Austerlitz town, pop. 1456, Columbia Co., SE New York. Settled c.1750 by New Englanders, it was named by Martin Van Buren, an admirer of Napoleon, for the site of the great Napoleonic victory. In rolling farm country, it is the site of Steepletop, the home (1925–50) of poet Edna St. Vincent Millay, now an artists' and writers' retreat.

Austin **1.** residential neighborhood on the far West Side of Chicago, Illinois, along the city boundary adjacent (E) to OAK PARK. A middle-class, largely Irish, community in the 1920s, it was home to the "Austin High Gang," the first important group of Northern white jazz musicians. By the 1940s most of its residents had left for suburbs, and Austin today is a struggling, almost entirely black, community. **2.** city, pop. 21,907, seat of Mower Co., SE Minnesota, on the Cedar R., 12 mi/19 km N of the Iowa border and 35 mi/56 km SW of Rochester. Originally a trading center for an agricultural hinterland, it is best known today for the George A. Hormel meatpacking and food processing plant, which is the pillar of its economy. Other industries include the manufacture of cartons, concrete products, and truck bodies, as well as printing. The Hormel Institute is affiliated with the University of Minnesota. **3.** city, pop. 465,622, state capital and seat of Travis Co., also in Williamson Co., SC Texas, 75 mi/121 km NE of San Antonio and 150 mi/240 km WNW of Houston, where the Colorado R. crosses the BALCONES ESCARPMENT. Spanish missions established here in the 1730s were short-lived. Settled in 1838 as Waterloo, the site was chosen in 1839 (and renamed) as the capital of Texas. Government moved to Houston 1842–45, but returned here when Texas became a state. The CHISHOLM TRAIL crossed the Colorado here, and arrival of the railroad in 1871 made Austin a shipping and trade center. In 1883 it became the seat of the University of Texas, which, with state government, dominated the city's economy into the 1960s, and now has some 50,000 students. Other city institutions include Huston-Tillotson College (1876), St. Edwards University (1885), and Concordia Lutheran College (1926). Building on the University of Texas's wealth and human resources, high-tech industry moved into Austin in the 1960s. The city is now a major computer, aerospace, and defense contracting center. Its other industries include brick, tile, steel, and concrete manufactures and chemicals. Its new industry, hilly surroundings, proximity to the HILL COUNTRY and the Colorado's Highland Lakes area, and university-centered amenities have made Austin an increasingly attractive residential community, and it has grown by over 33% each decade since 1950. City landmarks include the 1888 capitol, the largest in the US; the writer O. Henry's 1885–95 home; the Lyndon B. Johnson Library and Museum, established (1971) on the University campus; and the revived Sixth St. entertainment area. In recent decades Austin has become a prominent showcase for country and western music, and it is a convention center as well. Bergstrom Air Force Base, opened in World War II, is adjacent (SE).

Austintown unincorporated village, pop. 32,419, in Austintown township, Mahoning Co., NE Ohio, a residential suburb 5 mi/8 km E of Youngstown.

Austinville hamlet in Wythe Co., SW Virginia, on the New R., 10 mi/16 km SE of Wytheville. In a lead- and zinc-mining region, it is the birthplace (1793) of Texas statesman Stephen F. Austin.

Auyuittuq National Park 8300 sq mi/21,500 sq km, on the Cumberland Peninsula, E BAFFIN I., in the E Northwest Territories. Established in 1972 as the first Canadian national park N of the Arctic Circle, it is a mountain, fjord, and tundra area 25% covered by the Penny Ice Cap. Despite its sparse vegetation and harsh climate, the area has been lived in for some 2500 years. The park, reached chiefly via PANGNIRTUNG (S), is noted for 60 mi/97 km–long Pangnirtung Pass, a hiking route through a trough with sides almost 1300 ft/400 m high.

Avalon see under SANTA CATALINA I., California.

Avalon Peninsula H-shaped region, up to 110 mi/175 km NNE–SSW and 60 mi/100 km wide, in extreme SE Newfoundland. It is the most densely populated area of the island, to the rest of which it is connected by an isthmus, as little as 3 mi/5 km wide, between Placentia (S) and Trinity (N) bays. Its four constituent peninsulas are divided by Conception (N) and St. Mary's (S) bays. Visited by John Cabot in 1497, it was named and partially settled in 1623 by Sir George Calvert. Chief communities include SAINT JOHN'S (the capital; NE); its modern suburbs; and many former fishing OUTPORTS. Cape SPEAR, SE of St. John's, is Canada's easternmost point. The GRAND BANKS lie off the coast.

Avawatz Mountains range in SE California, SE of Death Valley National Park and NW of the hamlet of Baker. Extending for c.10 mi/16 km NW–SE, the rugged mountains have colorful eroded slopes and steep-walled canyons, and ascend to 6154 ft/1877 m on Avawatz Peak. The dry bed of Silurian L. is E and the SODA Mts. S. Part of the range is within the Fort Irwin Military Reservation.

Avenal city, pop. 9770, Kings Co., WC California, 53 mi/85 km SW of Fresno in the Kettleman Plain, just W of the KETTLEMAN HILLS. It is an oilfield supply center and home to oil and agricultural workers.

Avenel unincorporated community, pop. 15,504, in Woodbridge township, Middlesex Co., C New Jersey, 2 mi/3 km S of Rahway. It has many homes, office buildings, small businesses, and some light industry.

Avenues, the see under RICHMOND DISTRICT, San Francisco, California.

Averasboro hamlet in Harnett Co., C North Carolina, on the Cape Fear R., 4 mi/6 km W of DUNN. It is the site of one of the Civil War's last battles, on March 16, 1865, in which Union forces under W. T. Sherman pushed Confederates under Joseph Johnston back toward BENTONVILLE, 18 mi/29 km E.

Avery Island in Iberia Parish, S Louisiana, 9 mi/14 km SW of New Iberia. A 200 ft/60 m–high SALT DOME, 2 mi/3 km across, and surrounded by swamp, it has been mined since 1791, and was of great importance to the Confederate economy. It also houses a bird sanctuary. Tabasco (cayenne pepper) sauce has been produced here by the McIlhenny Company since the 1860s.

Avery Point see under GROTON, Connecticut.

Avon **1.** town, pop. 13,937, Hartford Co., NC Connecticut, on the Farmington R., 10 mi/16 km W of Hartford. An affluent suburb, long farmland, it has an active advertising and financial sector, and some light manufactures. Avon Old Farms School is here. **2.** town, pop. 4558, Norfolk Co., E Massachusetts, 4 mi/6 km N of Brockton. It is a residential suburb of Brockton; headquarters of the Child World toy store chain are here. **3.** city, pop. 576, Bon Homme Co., SE South Dakota, 32 mi/52 km NW of Yankton. It is situated in an area in which dairy products, livestock, poultry, corn, and wheat are produced. Avon is the birthplace (1922) of George McGovern.

Avondale **1.** city, pop. 16,169, Maricopa Co., SC Arizona, a residential suburb 15 mi/24 km W of downtown Phoenix. Long the commercial and service center of an irrigated region producing cotton, grain, and other crops, it has grown rapidly since the 1970s. Luke Air Force Base is just NW. **2.** residential and commercial section of the West Side of Chicago, Illinois, along Milwaukee Ave., 5 mi/8 km NW of the Loop. Just NW of POLONIA, it is another of Chicago's Polish heartlands; its older residents are descendants of turn-of-the-century arrivals. Since the 1970s they have been joined by Mexican and Puerto Rican immigrants moving N along Milwaukee Ave.

Avon Lake city, pop. 15,066, Lorain Co., NE Ohio, on L. Erie, 18 mi/29 km W of Cleveland. The beaches on the lakefront are a major attraction to visitors. A Ford minivan plant is situated here. Other local factories produce plastics and aluminum castings.

Avonlea see under GREEN GABLES, Prince Edward Island.

Avon Park city, pop. 8042, Highlands Co., C Florida, 40 mi/64 km SE of Lakeland. Settled in the mid 19th century, it is situated amid lakes, forests, and citrus groves, and is a resort and a market and distribution center. The city is the seat of South Florida Community College (1965). The Air Force's large **Avon Park Bombing and Gunnery Range** is just E.

Ayer town, pop. 6871, Middlesex Co., EC Massachusetts, 9 mi/14 km ENE of Leominster and 29 mi/47 km WNW of Boston. Settled in the 1670s, it is a longtime agricultural and light manufacturing center. In the 20th century its economy has largely depended on Fort Devens, just SW, an Army training facility established in 1917, important in World War II, and more recently an Intelligence center. The closing of the base in the 1990s led to efforts to attract diversified industry into the area, which is just outside Route 495, Boston's outer BELTWAY.

Aylmer city, pop. 32,244, OUTAOUAIS URBAN COMMUNITY, SW Québec, in the NATIONAL CAPITAL REGION, adjacent (SW) to HULL. On L. Deschênes in the Ottawa R., it was created (1975) by merging Aylmer, Lucerne, and Deschênes, and is a residential suburb noted for its golf courses.

Aztalan historic site: see under LAKE MILLS, Wisconsin.

Aztec city, pop. 5479, seat of San Juan Co., NW New Mexico, in the foothills of the Rocky Mts. On the Animas R., in the San Juan R. Basin, it is 12 mi/19 km S of the Colorado border and 14 mi/23 km NE of Farmington. It is a trade center for producers of fruit, vegetables, and grain. The settlement was named for 12th-century Anasazi ruins (preserved as the **Aztec Ruins National Monument** and containing the reconstructed Great Kiva) that were formerly thought to have been part of the Aztec empire.

Aztlán legendary place of origin of the Aztec, in Nahuatl the "place of the heron," where the people emerged from a cave. Although it may have been in the NW of modern Mexico, linguistic evidence suggests that Aztlán was somewhere in the US Southwest. The term has been used in describing Mexican immigration into Southern California as a "return to Aztlán."

Azusa city, pop. 41,333, Los Angeles Co., SW California, 20 mi/32 km NE of Los Angeles. Founded in 1887, just S of San Gabriel Canyon, on the San Gabriel R., it is a gateway to recreational facilities in the San Gabriel Mts. Once a citrus and avocado handling center, it now manufactures a wide range of aerospace, chemical, consumer, and other products. Azusa Pacific University (1899) is in the city, which grew rapidly in the 1980s.

B

Babine Lake in C British Columbia, on the W of the interior plateaus, 110 mi/180 km WNW of Prince George. The largest natural lake in the province, it is 95 mi/150 km NW–SE, and 1–6 mi/1–10 km wide. It drains NW via the 60 mi/100 km–long **Babine R.,** which then curves S into the SKEENA R. Homeland to the Babine (Carrier), an Athabaskan group, the lake is an important spawning ground for salmon, and a sport fishing magnet. The village of Granisle (pop. 803, Bulkley-Nechako Regional District), on the NW shore, has since the 1960s been an important center for copper mining operations, carried out on the shore and on an island in the lake. The **Babine Mts.** run NW–SE for some 100 mi/160 km W of the lake and E of the Bulkley R. and the YELLOWHEAD HIGHWAY, rising to 7828 ft/2386 m at Cronin Mt.

Baboquivari Mountains N–S trending range in S Arizona, extending for 30 mi/50 km along the SE border of the Papago (Tohono O'odham) Indian Reservation. The mountains rise to a high at Baboquivari Peak (7734 ft/2357 m), 45 mi/72 km NW of Nogales, which is topped by a 1000-ft/300-m felsite spire that forms a distinctive landmark. The range, longest and highest in the area, is sacred to the Tohono O'odham. The Quinlan Mts., including KITT PEAK, are its N terminus, with the Coyote Mts. forming an E extension.

Babson Park unincorporated community, pop. 1125, Polk Co., C Florida, 17 mi/27 km SE of Winter Haven, the seat of Webber College (1927).

Babylon in New York: **a.** village, pop. 12,249, in Babylon town, Suffolk Co., on the South Shore of Long Island, on Great South Bay. Primarily a residential community, it is also a fishing and boating center with a public beach. **b.** town, pop. 202,889, including the village and other communities including AMITYVILLE, DEER PARK, WYANDANCH, and part of JONES BEACH and FIRE ISLAND.

Bachelor, Mount also, **Bachelor Butte** elevation (9065 ft/2763 m) of the S CASCADE RANGE, in Deschutes National Forest, 22 mi/35 km SW of Bend, in WC Oregon. In the center of an extensive ski-resort area, it has been the site of a training camp for the US Olympic ski team for over 25 years.

Back Bay commercial and residential district in N Boston, Massachusetts, along the Charles R. It has some of Boston's most sophisticated restaurants and shopping, particularly along Newbury St. The Back Bay is also home to the PRUDENTIAL CENTER, COPLEY SQUARE, FENWAY PARK, and luxury hotels. Boston University is located in its NW corner. Plans to fill in the bay that separated the original Boston (the SHAWMUT PENINSULA) from ROXBURY and DORCHESTER existed as early as 1813, and the landfill was completed by the 1880s. The streets and avenues laid out along the new ground became fashionable after the Civil War for the building of row houses, establishing a pattern for Boston and other American cities.

Backbone Mountain ridge containing the highest point (3360 ft/1025 m) in Maryland, 14 mi/22 km S of Oakland, in the Allegheny Mts., in the extreme W of the state. The ridge extends SW for c.35 mi/56 km from the Savage R. W of Westernport, Maryland, into MONONGAHELA NATIONAL FOREST in N West Virginia. Big Savage Mt. continues the ridge N of the Savage R., into SW Pennsylvania; Maryland's Savage R. State Forest parallels it to the NW.

Backbone Ranges see under MACKENZIE Mts., Northwest Territories.

Back of the Yards residential neighborhood on the South Side of Chicago, Illinois. Immediately S of the old UNION STOCKYARDS, it was an Irish immigrant area shortly after the Civil War. The harsh conditions here inspired Upton Sinclair's *The Jungle* and Bertold Brecht's *Saint Joan of the Stockyards.* Today it is home to mainly working-class Polish and Hispanic families.

Bacon's Castle historic site 6 mi/10 km SE of Surry, Surry Co., SE Virginia, in the TIDEWATER. It is the oldest documented brick house in British North America. Built c.1655 as the Arthur Allen House, it gained its popular name when seized (1676) during Bacon's Rebellion. It presents elements of Jacobean baroque styling.

Bad Axe historic site in Vernon Co., SW Wisconsin, on the Mississippi R., near Victory and the Bad Axe R. It was here, on Aug. 3, 1832, that a band of fleeing Sauk and Fox under Black Hawk were attacked and killed by white settlers, in effect ending the Black Hawk War.

Baddeck resort, pop. 965, seat of Victoria Co. (pop. 8708), NE Nova Scotia, in C Cape Breton I., on the N of BRAS D'OR L., on the Cabot Trail, 25 mi/40 km W of Sydney. A 19th-century shipbuilding center, it is known as the home of inventor Alexander Graham Bell (1847–1922), who conducted many experiments, died, and is buried here. In Feb. 1909, J. A. D. McCurdy, inspired by Bell, made the first airplane flight in the British Empire here.

Baden-Powell, Mount see under SAN GABRIEL Mts., California.

badlands expanse of barren lands that have been eroded by short, sharp rains, taking on extreme shapes including deep gullies cut between ridges and pinnacles. Badlands form, usually in arid or semiarid areas, where unconsolidated sedimentary rock, clay, and soil are easily and repeatedly washed away, and there is little chance for deep-rooted vegetation to take hold. They may have originated in interglacial periods of heavy rain (compare SCABLANDS). In addition to the South Dakota area originally given the name, North America has extensive badlands in S Alberta and SW Saskatchewan.

Badlands also, **Big Badlands** or **White River Badlands** section of the Missouri Plateau of SW South Dakota, E of the Black Hills, sometimes described as extending S of the Black Hills into NW Nebraska and E Wyoming. Often approximated at 120 mi/193 km long and 25–50 mi/40–80 km wide, this area inspired the generic term "badlands." Its soft shales, clays, and limestones have been shaped by wind and infrequent, but often torrential, rain into mesas, sharp spires, saw-toothed ridges, steep gorges, and other weird shapes. The white to deep pink and orange structures present an eerie, baked, moonlike landscape, which is difficult to traverse; this may have inspired both Indians and early French traders and trappers to call the land "bad." A great number of fossils, including those of an especially rich array of Oligocene mammals, have been unearthed here. The **Badlands National Park** (243,244 ac/98,514 ha), in part located between the White and Bad rivers, was created in 1939 as a National Monument. Headquartered at Cedar Pass, it is home to a herd of bison, reintroduced to the area in 1963. Part of the PINE RIDGE Indian Reservation is in the S unit of the park. Kadoka has been an important outfitting point for journeys into the Badlands, one of the state's most popular scenic areas. The Pinnacles, in the NC section, are 3255 ft/993 m high. There is also a Badlands section of SW North Dakota, along the Little Missouri R.

Bad River 140 mi/225 km long, in South Dakota. It rises in the SW, near the Badlands National Park, and flows NE, passing Philip and other small towns before joining the Missouri R. at Fort Pierre.

Badwater see under DEATH VALLEY, California.

Baffin Bay large, deep, NW–SE oriented inlet of the N Atlantic Ocean, between Greenland (E) and (S–N) Baffin, Bylot, Devon, and Ellesmere islands, in the E Northwest Territories. It joins the Atlantic (S) via DAVIS STRAIT and the LABRADOR SEA, and the Arctic Ocean (N) via Nares Strait; Lancaster and Jones sounds (W) lead to channels through the ARCTIC ARCHIPELAGO. Some 800 mi/1300 km long and 70–400 mi/115–650 km wide, the bay reaches depths of 9000 ft/2740 m, and is ice-covered most of the year; the Labrador Current flows S from it, carrying icebergs. The first Europeans to encounter the bay were the English navigators Robert Bylot (1615) and William Baffin (1616). Whales, seals, walrus, and a variety of fish live in the bay, while many birds as well as caribou, Arctic foxes, and polar bears inhabit its shores.

Baffin Island Canada's largest and the world's fifth-largest island (195,928 sq mi/507,454 sq km), some 950 mi/1530 km NW–SE, and up to 500 mi/800 km wide, on the SE of the ARCTIC ARCHIPELAGO, in the E Northwest Territories. It is separated from Greenland (N) by Baffin Bay, and from the UNGAVA Peninsula (S) by Hudson Strait. The FOXE BASIN lies SW. The island has been home to Inuit groups for some 1500 years. It was probably visited by 11th-century Norse (see VINLAND), but the first recorded sighting was by the Englishman Martin Frobisher, in 1576. Abortive mining attempts and the search for the NORTHWEST PASSAGE brought expeditions in the 16th–18th centuries; whalers came in the 19th century. The coast is indented by FJORDS, including Frobisher Bay and Cumberland Sound (SE) and Admiralty Inlet (extreme NW), perhaps the world's largest, some 150 mi/240 km N–S. Ice-capped mountains, the source of major Ice Age glaciers, run along the E, at the E extremity of the CANADIAN SHIELD. To the N and S is plateau, on the WC coast lowland. IQALUIT, on Frobisher Bay (SE), is the largest of a half-dozen communities populated largely by Inuit who fish and hunt land and sea mammals, including white foxes and whales. Mines at Nanisivik (settlement, pop. 294) in the extreme N, off Admiralty Inlet, produce silver, lead, and zinc; iron is mined elsewhere on the island. AUYUITTUQ NATIONAL PARK is on the SE coast.

Bagotville see under LA BAIE, Québec.

Baie-Comeau city, pop. 26,012, Manicouagan census division, SE Québec, 217 mi/350 km NE of Québec City. On the N bank of the St. Lawrence R., at the mouth of the MANICOUAGAN R., it was founded around a paper mill in 1936 at the instigation of Robert McCormick, publisher of the Chicago *Tribune*. It now also has a major aluminum plant, also drawing on waterpower; the Manic 2 dam, a unit of Hydro-Québec's huge Manic-Outardes power complex, is 14 mi/23 km NW. Baie-Comeau is also a deepwater port, a transshipment point for grain.

Baie-Saint-Paul city, pop. 3733, Charlevoix census division, SE Québec, 54 mi/87 km NE of Québec City, on the St. Lawrence R. at the mouth of the Gouffre R., opposite the Île aux Coudres. The Gouffre valley has been farmed since 1678; hunting, fishing, and lumbering are also now important, and iron is mined in the area, but Baie-Saint-Paul is best-known as a summer resort and artists' colony.

Baileys Crossroads unincorporated suburban community, pop. 19,507, Fairfax Co., N Virginia, 5 mi/8 km NW of Alexandria.

Bainbridge 1. city, pop. 10,712, seat of Decatur Co., extreme SW Georgia, on the Flint R. above L. Seminole. Originally an Indian trading post, it grew from the 1820s to become a lumbering town and river port. Today, it has textile and varied light industries, is Georgia's main inland barge port, and is a gateway to the L. Seminole recreation area. Bainbridge College (1973) is here. **2.** naval training center: see under PORT DEPOSIT, Maryland.

Bainbridge Island 26 sq mi/67 sq km, in Kitsap Co., W Washington, in Puget Sound, 8 mi/13 km W of downtown Seattle. Once a Kitsap homeland, Bainbridge in the mid and late 19th century was a seaport and sawmilling and shipbuilding center. It has a naval reservation, the Bloedel (botanical) Reserve, and a noted winery, but is largely an affluent residential area, home to many professionals who commute by ferry to Seattle. Winslow (city, pop. 3081), on the E shore, is the largest community.

Baker 1. agricultural and suburban city, pop. 13,233, East Baton Rouge Parish, SE Louisiana, 10 mi/16 km N of Baton Rouge. **2.** also, **Baker City,** city, pop. 9140, seat of Baker Co., NE Oregon, on the Powder R., 47 mi/76 km SSE of La Grande. Trading center for the region's grain, dairy products, cattle, and poultry, it was just W of the OREGON TRAIL. It was the site of a gold rush in the early 1860s. Silver, lead, and copper were later discovered in the area, and Baker flourished for many decades, especially with the coming of the railroad and industry. There are still several mines operating around the city. The Oregon Trail Regional Museum, Baker College (1957), and the headquarters of the Wallowa-Whitman National Forest are here.

Baker, Mount 10,778 ft/3285 m, in Whatcom Co., extreme NW Washington, the state's third-highest peak, on the W slopes of the N CASCADE RANGE, in Mt. Baker–Snoqualmie National Forest, 30 mi/48 km E of Bellingham and 16 mi/26 km S of the British Columbia border. The northernmost Cascade volcano, it last erupted in 1843; in 1975 it released steam. Baker L. (SE) and ski slopes to the NE are popular resorts.

Baker Beach part of the GOLDEN GATE NATIONAL RECREATION AREA, along the NW edge of SAN FRANCISCO, California, just W of the PRESIDIO and SW of the Golden Gate Bridge. It is the city's most popular beach, although cove-enclosed China Beach, to the SW, is safer for swimmers. Overlooking the S end is Sea Cliff, a promontory with many elegant homes.

Baker Island c.1.4 sq mi/3.6 sq km, in the C Pacific Ocean, just N of the Equator, some 1650 mi/2700 km SW of Honolulu, Hawaii, and 40 mi/64 km SSE of HOWLAND I. Uninhabited, it was claimed by the US in 1857 and was a guano source in the late 19th century. American colonists were settled here (Meyerton) in 1935, then removed in 1942, after which an airstrip was created and used against the Japanese. Since World War II it has been deserted, and is a wildlife refuge, under the administration of the Department of the Interior.

Baker Lake hamlet, pop. 1186, Keewatin Region, E mainland Northwest Territories, on the TUNDRA at the mouth of the THELON R. and the NW end of Baker L., 375 mi/600 km NNW of Churchill, Manitoba, and 310 mi/500 km S of the Arctic Circle. Its Inuit people, the only inland group in the Territories, live on caribou and freshwater fish. Today handicrafts are important, and Baker Lake is the terminus for canoe trips on several nearby rivers. Government and scientific stations are also employers. Uranium was found nearby in the 1980s. Baker L., 70 mi/115 km E–W and 7–18 mi/11–29 km wide, is at the head (W) of CHESTERFIELD INLET, which reaches Hudson Bay 150 mi/240 km E of the hamlet.

Bakersfield city, pop. 174,820, seat of Kern Co., SC California, on the Kern R., at the S end of the San Joaquin Valley, 95 mi/153 km NNW of Los Angeles. Laid out in 1869, it developed after gold was discovered nearby in 1885, and oil in 1899. It is the industrial, commercial, and trade center for an oil and natural gas producing and agricultural region. Oil refining is the leading industry. Others include agricultural processing and the manufacture of oil industry equipment, chemicals, paints, and electronic components. The area has deposits of silver, gold, and borax. Bakersfield College (1913) and a branch of California State University (1965) are here. The city boomed (its pop. grew 65%) as a residential center in the 1980s.

Bala-Cynwyd unincorporated village in LOWER MERION township, Montgomery Co., SE Pennsylvania. Situated directly W of Philadelphia, it is an affluent MAIN LINE suburb.

Balanced Rock in parts of North America reached by glaciers, this and similar names commonly designate erratic boulders left atop other rocks or rock formations. There are Balanced Rocks in such places as Columbia, Connecticut; Andover, New Hampshire; and near Mount WACHUSETT, in Massachusetts. Precarious situations have given names to such phenomena as Hanging Rock, in Salisbury, Connecticut; Tipping Rocks, in Goffstown, New Hampshire; and various Cradle Rocks. Balanced Rock State Park, 25 mi/40 km WNW of Twin Falls, Idaho, is named for a boulder "balanced" atop a column formed by erosion of the substrata. The name "Hanging" also commonly refers to apparently overhanging rocks, as at Hanging Mt., a cliff on the Farmington R. near New Boston, SE Berkshire Co., Massachusetts.

Balboa see under NEWPORT BEACH, California.

Balboa Park municipal park, 1400 ac/567 ha, in SAN DIEGO, California, immediately NE of Downtown. Purchased in 1868 and developed after 1910, it contains the San Diego Museum of Art, the Natural History and other museums, gardens, and the 200-ft/61-m California Tower, along with the renowned San Diego Zoo. The Panama-California Expositions of 1915–16 and 1935–36 were held here.

Balch Springs city, pop. 17,406, Dallas Co., NE Texas, a residential suburb adjacent (E) to Dallas, on the beltway (Route 635), 10 mi/16 km ESE of Downtown.

Balcones Escarpment also, **Balcones Fault Zone** natural boundary between the Coastal Plains of E Texas and uplands to the W. Running some 200 mi/320 km from the Rio Grande near Del Rio (SW), it passes N of San Antonio, then swings N to run just W of Austin up to Waco and beyond. Rising to 1000 ft/300 m in the SW, it is 300 ft/90 m high at Austin, and N of Waco dwindles into visual insignificance. The BLACKLANDS belt lies E all along it. To the W lie the EDWARDS PLATEAU (SW), the HILL COUNTRY (C), and the Grand Prairie (NW).

Balcones Heights see under SAN ANTONIO, Texas.

bald in the SE US, a bare-topped mountain. The term appears in such place names as BRASSTOWN BALD and RABUN BALD.

Bald Eagle Mountain ridge, running 85 mi/140 km from near WILLIAMSPORT (NE) to SW of STATE COLLEGE, in C Pennsylvania, part of the Allegheny Front. Rising to 2000 ft/600 m, it is heavily forested.

Bald Mountains subrange of the W Appalachian chain, sometimes considered part of the UNAKA RANGE, along the North Carolina–Tennessee border, between the Nolichucky (NE) and Pigeon (SW) rivers. The mountains reach their highest elevation (5616 ft/1681 m) at Big Bald, 7 mi/11 km W of Ramseytown, North Carolina, and include Max Patch Mt. (4629 ft/1412 m), along the Appalachian Trail in the SW section, 25 mi/40 km NW of Asheville.

Baldwin **1.** unincorporated village, pop. 22,719, in Hempstead town, Nassau Co., SE New York, 28 mi/45 km E of Manhattan. Situated on the South Shore of Long Island, and settled by the Dutch in the 1640s, it is primarily a bedroom community, with some light manufacturing and a boating and fishing industry. **2.** borough, pop. 21,923, Allegheny Co., SW Pennsylvania. A suburb S of Pittsburgh, it is situated on the Monongahela R. in a coal mining region.

Baldwin City city, pop. 2961, Douglas Co., EC Kansas, 13 mi/21 km SSE of Lawrence. Laid out in 1855, it was the site of bloody clashes between pro- and antislavery factions before the Civil War. Today it is a distribution center for livestock, grain, and dairy products as well as for oil and gas from nearby wells. It is the seat of Baker University (1858).

Baldwin Hills residential section of Los Angeles, California, 6 mi/10 km SW of Downtown, and W of CRENSHAW. Built in the 1940s and 1950s as a large-scale planned development in an area that had produced oil in the 1920s, it is today an affluent black community.

Baldwin Park city, pop. 69,330, Los Angeles Co., SW California, 18 mi/29 km E of Los Angeles, of which it is a growing commuter suburb. In an agricultural area on the San Gabriel R., it raises poultry, vegetables, berries, and citrus fruits. Settled in 1870, it now has a wide variety of aerospace and other manufactures.

Baldy Mountain highest point (2727 ft/832 m) in Manitoba, 44 mi/71 km NW of DAUPHIN. The highest point in the DUCK Mt. Range, and part of the MANITOBA ESCARPMENT, it is at the SE corner of Duck Mt. Provincial Park.

Baldy Peak also, **Old Baldy** or **White Mt.** see under WHITE Mts., Arizona.

Baleine, Grande Rivière de la see GREAT WHALE R., Québec.

Bal Harbour village, pop. 3045, Dade Co., SE Florida, on the Atlantic Ocean, at the N end of the barrier island containing MIAMI BEACH. It is an affluent community known for its luxurious hotels, exclusive private beaches, and elegant shops.

Ballard residential and commercial section of NW SEATTLE, Washington, 5 mi/8 km NW of Downtown, N of the Lake Washington Ship Canal and E of Shilshole Bay (Puget Sound). A Scandinavian and Finnish community at the end of the 19th century, it was noted for its boatworks. Annexed in 1907, it now has a historic district and is a popular shopping area. Shilshole Bay has a large marina, and the Hiram M. Chittenden Locks (1917), on the canal, are noted for their fish ladder.

Balls Bluff locality in Loudoun Co., NE Virginia, on the Potomac R., 33 mi/53 km NW of Washington, D.C., and just NE of LEESBURG, the site of a battle fought on Oct. 21, 1861, in which Confederate troops defeated Union forces. A national cemetery is here.

Ballston Spa village, pop. 4937, seat of Saratoga Co., E New York, 7 mi/11 km SW of Saratoga Springs. Founded in the late 18th century, it has abundant natural springs and became a fashionable early- and mid-19th-century watering place. It was the site of knitting mills and tanneries in the late 19th century and early to mid 20th centuries. Ballston Spa now has a variety of light industries and is largely residential in character.

Ballwin city, pop. 21,816, St. Louis Co., EC Missouri, 17 mi/27 km WSW of St. Louis. Settled (1803) as Ballshow, it was renamed in 1837. Mainly a bedroom community for St. Louis, it also has some light industry.

Balsam Cone see under BLACK Mts., North Carolina.

Baltimore city, pop. 736,014, within but administratively independent of Baltimore Co., NC Maryland, at the head of the PATAPSCO R. estuary, 15 mi/24 km above Chesapeake Bay, 210 mi/340 km from the Atlantic Ocean, and 35 mi/56 km NE of Washington, D.C. With six surrounding counties (ANNE ARUNDEL, Baltimore, CARROLL, HARFORD, HOWARD, and Queen Anne's) it forms a metropolitan area (MSA) with a pop. of 2,382,172. Baltimore was founded in 1729 as a tobacco port; by the American Revolution it had become a major seaport and shipbuilding center, trading with Europe and the Caribbean. The USS *Constellation,* launched here in 1797, remains moored in the harbor. In Dec. 1776–March 1777, the Continental Congress met in Baltimore, having fled occupied Philadelphia. In the War of 1812 the British, recognizing Baltimore as a privateering and naval supply center, attacked, but were repulsed in a battle (Sept. 13–14, 1814) centered on FORT MCHENRY. Through the early 19th century, Baltimore competed with New York as a port and as a gateway to America's interior. Development of the NATIONAL ROAD after 1806 was important to the city. The Baltimore and Ohio Railroad, which eventually connected the city with areas beyond the Appalachians, became the first US public railroad when it began service from Mount Clare Station to ELLICOTT CITY in 1830. Prosperity and industrial growth had made Baltimore the second most populous (169,054) US city by 1850. Predominantly Southern in sentiment at the beginning of the Civil War, it was occupied by Federal troops in 1861. After the war, growth continued. In Feb. 1904, fire destroyed most of Downtown, but recovery was quick, and the modernized city acquired its famous brick row houses. Baltimore's industrial development intensified in World War I, as steel plants and oil refineries rose to meet war demands. In World War II, ships, aircraft, and clothing were among leading manufactures. The city's pop. peaked (at 949,708) in 1950; more recently, it has lost heavy industry and residents. Once heavily German and Irish, it is now predominantly black. A large Jewish community lives in the NW and adjacent suburbs. It remains one of the nation's most important ports. Exports include coal, coke, steel products, refined copper, grain, and feed; imports include ore, petroleum, sulfur, gypsum, and molasses. The city's industries today include ship building and repair and the manufacture of steel, chemicals, aerospace equipment, processed foods and sugar, and refined oil and copper. High-tech industries like biotechnology are growing. The city and metropolitan area house such Federal installations as Social Security Administration offices, military bases, and research and development institutions, providing much employment. Redevelopment (since the 1970s) of the INNER HARBOR led in building a thriving tourism and convention industry. Educational and cultural institutions include a University of Maryland branch (1807), the Maryland Institute College of Art (1826), Loyola College (1852), Morgan State University (1867), the Peabody Conservatory of Music (1868), the College of Notre Dame of Maryland (1873), Johns Hopkins University (1876), and Coppin State College (1900). Noted sites include the Basilica of the Assumption of the Blessed Virgin Mary (1821, designed by Benjamin Latrobe), the oldest US cathedral; the longtime home of writer H. L. Mencken; and the birthplace of Babe Ruth. See also: BOLTON HILL; BROOKLYN; CAMDEN YARDS; CHARLES CENTER; DRUID HILL PARK; EAST BALTIMORE; FEDERAL HILL; FELLS POINT; FORT MCHENRY; HARBORPLACE; INNER HARBOR; LEXINGTON MARKET; MOUNT VERNON PLACE; OTTERBEIN; PENNSYLVANIA Ave.; PIMLICO; ROLAND PARK; SOUTH BALTIMORE; UNION SQUARE.

Baltimore and Ohio Railroad the first US rail carrier, chartered in 1827, designed to bring back through Baltimore westbound traffic that had been lost to New York's new ERIE CANAL. Construction began in 1828, and in 1830 service opened to Ellicott's Mills (ELLICOTT CITY), 13 mi/21 km W; horses pulled the first trains, but were quickly replaced by the *Tom Thumb,* the first engine to operate regularly in the US. Slowed by 1830s financial difficulties, the B&O finally reached the Ohio R. (at WHEELING, then in Virginia) in 1852, by way of Cumberland, Maryland. It had earlier established a branch to Washington, D.C. (along which, in 1844, the first US telegraph line had been strung). By the end of the 1850s, the B&O had connected with Cincinnati and St. Louis; after the Civil War (in which it was an important Union carrier, protected by the keeping of what became West Virginia's Eastern PANHANDLE under Northern control), it reached Philadelphia, Chicago, and New York City. In the 1960s the B&O was taken over by the Chesapeake & Ohio (1868), a regional line noted chiefly as a coal carrier; the two roads became part of the extensive Chessie System. In 1980 this merged with the Seaboard Coast Line and other southeastern carriers (including the 1850 Louisville & Nashville) to form the even larger CSX system.

Baltimore County 598 sq mi/1549 sq km, pop. 692,134, in NC Maryland, bounded N by Pennsylvania, SE by Chesapeake Bay and the Gunpowder R., and S and SW by the Patapsco R. Baltimore Co. does not include the city of Baltimore; its seat is TOWSON. It lies primarily in the PIEDMONT region, with some of its SE in the coastal plain. Among its manufactures are communications equipment, scientific instruments, and electric tools. Agriculture and tourism are also important. The county includes Loch Raven and Prettyboy reservoirs, and many suburbs of Baltimore.

Baltimore Highlands residential neighborhood in LANSDOWNE, Baltimore Co., Maryland, 4 mi/6 km S of downtown Baltimore. It developed around a station on the Baltimore and Annapolis Railroad, and is just N of Interstate 895 (the Harbor Tunnel Thruway).

Baltimore-Washington International Airport also, **BWI** in Ferndale, Anne Arundel Co., C Maryland, 30 mi/48 km NE of Washington, D.C., and 8 mi/13 km SSW of downtown Baltimore.

Bancroft village, pop. 2383, Hastings Co., SE Ontario, on the York R., 58 mi/93 km NNE of Peterborough. In hilly country on the CANADIAN SHIELD, the site is rich in rare and other minerals, with 80% of all types found in Canada represented, including uranium. An annual Gemboree attracts rockhounds. The economy depends also on lumbering, woolen milling, dairying, and outdoor vacations.

Bandelier National Monument 32,737-ac/13,258-ha reserve on NC New Mexico's PAJARITO PLATEAU, W of the Rio Grande and 20 mi/32 km WNW of Santa Fe, protecting 12th–16th century PUEBLO dwellings, largely in the Frijoles and other canyons. WILDERNESS AREAS in the adjacent Santa Fe National Forest provide further protection.

Bandon city, pop. 2215, Coos Co., SW Oregon, on the Pacific coast, at the mouth of the Coquille R., 20 mi/32 km SSW of Coos Bay. Its major industry is the export of cranberries, grown in bogs N and S of the city. Bandon also exports cheese and other dairy products. In addition, it is a popular seaside resort community and artists' colony.

Banff town, pop. 5688, SW Alberta, in the Rocky Mts., on the Bow R., in Banff National Park, 69 mi/111 km W of Calgary. One of Alberta's most renowned vacation spots, it serves as the gateway to nearby LAKE LOUISE. Originally known as Siding 29, a proposed tunnel site (1883) for the Canadian Pacific Railway, it was soon renamed and moved 2 mi/3 km to its present location. Banff Hot Springs Reserve (1885) surrounds the popular springs. Banff Centre for Continuing Education (1933) and the Banff Springs Hotel (1888) are here.

Bangor **1.** city, pop. 33,181, seat of Penobscot Co., EC Maine, a port on the Penobscot R. where it is joined by the Kenduskeag R., opposite Brewer, 23 mi/37 km from the sea, and 60 mi/97 km NE of Augusta. Beginning in the 1770s as Kenduskeag Plantation, it was after 1830 a leading lumber port (shipping world-famous Maine pine) and shipbuilding center. It now manufactures footwear, paper, and sports and logging equipment. Bangor is home to Bangor Theological Seminary, Beal College, Husson College, and Eastern Maine Vocational and Technical Institute. Bangor International Airport lies W of the city center. **2.** city, pop. 1922, Van Buren Co., SW Michigan, on the South Branch of the Black R., 27 mi/43 km W of Kalamazoo. In a farm and apple orchard region, it was settled c.1837, manufactures valves and spray guns, and has fruit-packing facilities. It is also the site of an historic and still operating toy-train factory, housed in the restored Chesapeake and Ohio depot. **3.** naval base: see under BREMERTON, Washington.

bank ocean area: see under CONTINENTAL SHELF.

Bankers' Hill also, **Pill Hill** residential neighborhood in SAN DIEGO, California, S of HILLCREST and 1 mi/1.6 km N of Downtown. The renovated Victorian homes in this upper-middle-class area originally housed many of the city's bankers and doctors.

Bankhead National Forest 180,000 ac/73,000 ha, in NW Alabama, some 40 mi/64 km NW of Birmingham, on NW headwaters of the Black Warrior R. This hardwood forest, filled with streams and lakes, was formerly called Black Warrior National Forest. Its Natural Bridge, 80 ft/24 m long, is one of the largest in the E US. Headquarters are at Double Springs.

Banks Island westernmost ARCTIC ARCHIPELAGO island, 27,038 sq mi/70,028 sq km, c.250 mi/400 km NNE–SSW, in the W Northwest Territories. Northwest of VICTORIA I., and separated from the mainland (S) by the 85 mi/137 km–wide Amundsen Gulf, it is largely a hilly Arctic plateau with high cliffs on several shores, and rises to 2400 ft/730 m. Arctic fox, caribou, bears, wolves, other fur animals, and many bird species abound; there are two bird sanctuaries. The island was formerly inhabited by Inuit; today, at Sachs Harbour (hamlet, pop. 125) on the SW coast, servicing an airfield, oil exploration, and trapping are the main occupations.

Bannack ghost town in Beaverhead Co., SW Montana, on Grasshopper Creek, 18 mi/29 km W of Dillon. One of the oldest towns in the state and the first territorial capital (1864–65), it sprang up overnight after Montana's first major gold strike, in 1862. In a year the population numbered 10,000, but declined when miners decamped for the richer VIRGINIA CITY lode. Surrounded by parts of Beaverhead National Forest, it is now a State Historic Park.

Banner Elk town, pop. 933, Avery Co., NW North Carolina, on the Elk R. A Blue Ridge mountain resort, it is also the seat of Lees-McRae College (1900).

Banner Hill see under ERWIN, Tennessee.

Banning city, pop. 20,570, Riverside Co., SW California, 27 mi/43 km ESE of Riverside, on Interstate 10 in the San Gorgonio Pass between the San Bernardino (N) and San Jacinto (S) mountains. Founded in the 1880s, it has been a resort for sufferers from asthma and arthritis. It has some light manufactures and has grown as a residential community in recent decades. The Morongo Indian Reservation (pop. 1072) lies just NE.

Baraboo city, pop. 9203, seat of Sauk Co., SC Wisconsin, 28 mi/45 km NW of Madison, on the Baraboo R. A trade center in an agricultural area, with some light manufactures and a branch of the University of Wisconsin, it is noted as the birthplace (1882) and longtime winter headquarters of the Ringling Brothers Circus. A complex of circus buildings draws visitors. The Badger Army Ammunition Plant, established in World War II, is 8 mi/13 km S. The city is situated in the **Baraboo Range,** low, forested hills named, like it, for Jean Baribault, an early French trader. The quartzite mountains are on the NE edge of the DRIFTLESS AREA and at the SE of the SAND COUNTIES. Devil's Lake State Park, 3.5 mi/6 km S of the city, is a unit of the developing ICE AGE NATIONAL SCIENTIFIC RESERVE.

Barataria Bay inlet of the Gulf of Mexico 40 mi/64 km S of New Orleans, in SE Louisiana. Twenty mi/32 km NE–SW and 12 mi/19 km wide, the shallow, island-filled bay joins the gulf via Barataria Pass, which runs between GRAND ISLE (W) and Grand Terre I. (E). The main channel of the Mississippi R. passes to the E, through its delta, and the bay is connected by a channel to the Gulf Intracoastal Waterway. Barataria is a center for shrimping, crabbing, and muskrat trapping, and contains oil, natural gas, and sulfur deposits. In the early 19th century, a group of privateers led by Jean and Pierre Lafitte operated a smuggling operation in the bay and surrounding bayous, attacking ships in the Gulf and disposing of their cargoes in New Orleans. Lafitte (pop. 1507), N of the bay, is said to be the site of their original settlement.

Barbary Coast historic commercial and entertainment district of SAN FRANCISCO, California, in the area of today's JACKSON SQUARE, on the E of the Financial District. After 1849 a notorious RED-LIGHT DISTRICT centered on Pacific ("Terrific") St. (now Ave.), it was the scene of the "shanghaiing" of many a drugged sailor. By the 20th century it was a tourist attraction, and it had a 1930s bohemian phase. Today it is almost completely redeveloped.

Barbeau, Mount see under ELLESMERE I., Northwest Territories.

Barbers Point also, **Kalaeloa Point** cape at the SW corner of OAHU, Hawaii, 8 mi/13 km SW of Pearl Harbor, site of Barbers Point Naval Air Station.

Barberton city, pop. 27,623, Summit Co., NE Ohio, on the Tuscarawas R., 6 mi/10 km SW of Akron, of which it is a residential and industrial suburb. Founded c.1890, it was named for Ohio Columbus Barber, president of the Diamond Match Company, who moved his firm's Akron branch here. Local manufactures include rubber products, aluminum, chemicals, boilers, and insulators. The site, originally home to Delaware Indians, includes L. Anna, in the center of the city.

Barbourville city, pop. 3658, seat of Knox Co., SE Kentucky, in the Cumberland Mts., 90 mi/140 km SSE of Lexington. This agricultural trading center (tobacco, vegetables, sorghum, strawberries, timber) is a gateway to the DANIEL BOONE NATIONAL FOREST. Founded in 1800, on the Wilderness Road, it has light manufactures including wood and concrete products, and the area produces coal. Union College (1879) is here. The Dr. Thomas Walker State Historic Site (6 mi/10 km S) has a replica of Walker's 1750 house, the first white home in Kentucky.

Bardstown city, pop. 6801, seat of Nelson Co., C Kentucky, 30 mi/48 km SSE of Louisville, on the Beech R. It was laid out (1785) by William Bard. The area has since the 1770s been the center of Kentucky bourbon production, and the city has distilleries and a whiskey museum. Federal Hill Manor (built 1795–1818) is said to have inspired Stephen Foster's "My Old Kentucky Home." Old Talbott Tavern (late 1700s) is said to be the oldest stagecoach stop in the US and the oldest inn in continuous use W of the Alleghenies.

Bar Harbor town, pop. 4443, Hancock Co., SE Maine. Bar Harbor is on MOUNT DESERT ISLAND, facing Frenchman Bay on the Atlantic Ocean, 15 mi/24 km SE of Ellsworth. The town is the commercial and service center for Mt. Desert I. and Acadia National Park, with ferry service to Nova Scotia. Rosco B. Jackson Memorial Laboratory, a biological facility noted for its mice used in genetic research, and the College of the Atlantic (1969) are here. Early in the 20th century, Bar Harbor was one of America's most fashionable resorts. Much of the area was destroyed by a 1947 fire.

Barilla Mountains see under DAVIS Mts., Texas.

Barkerville ghost town, center of a provincial historic park, EC British Columbia, in the W foothills of the CARIBOO Mts., 15 mi/24 km W of Bowron L. Provincial Park and 42 mi/68 km E of Quesnel. Named for a prospector who made an important gold strike nearby in 1862, it was a gold and silver mining center during the Cariboo gold rush, and the N terminus of the 400-mi/640-km Cariboo Road, a wagon route from YALE, on the lower Fraser R. By 1900 it had declined, and by 1950 was deserted; since 1959 it has been restored.

Barksdale Air Force Base see under BOSSIER CITY, Louisiana.

Barnegat Bay tidal lagoon 30 mi/48 km NE of Atlantic City, in Ocean Co., SE New Jersey. Thirty-two mi/52 km N–S and 2–4 mi/3–6 km wide, it lies within Island Beach and the N part of Long Beach I., with outlets through the Bayhead-Manasquan Canal (N), through Little Egg Harbor (S), and directly to the Atlantic through Barnegat Inlet. The bay is part of the ATLANTIC INTRACOASTAL WATERWAY. Barnegat Lighthouse, built in 1855 and replaced in 1930 by an offshore lightship, is at Barnegat Inlet, the N tip of Long Beach I. The borough of **Barnegat Light** (pop. 681) lies just S of the lighthouse, while the township of **Barnegat** (pop. 12,226) lies opposite, on the mainland. Barnegat (Edward B. Forsythe) National Wildlife Refuge, mostly W of the bay, comprises 7580 ac/3070 ha of coastal marsh, and lies on the ATLANTIC FLYWAY.

Barnes Foundation see under MERION, Pennsylvania.

Barnesville village, pop. 4326, Belmont Co., SE Ohio, 38 mi/61 km SW of Steubenville. Local industries include the manufacture of machinery, mine cars, glass, paper, textiles, and dairy products. There are coal and natural gas deposits nearby. Inventor Elisha Gray was born here (1835).

Barnstable town, pop. 40,949, seat of Barnstable Co., SE Massachusetts, on Cape Cod. It includes the villages of Barnstable (pop. 2790), Cummaquid, West Barnstable, HYANNIS, Hyannis Port, West Hyannis Port, Craigville, Centerville, Osterville, Wiano, Marston Mills, Santuit, Cotuit Heights, and Cotuit. The area is primarily a summer resort, its winter population soaring during the summer months. There is extensive waterfront both on Cape Cod Bay (N) and on Nantucket Sound (S). Economic activity includes fishing, oyster culture, and cranberry raising and canning. Hyannis is the commercial center, with an airport. Cape Cod Community College (1961) is in West Barnstable.

Barnstable County 400 sq mi/1036 sq km, pop. 186,605, SE

Massachusetts, coextensive with Cape Cod. The county seat is Barnstable. The county is a resort area, with fine beaches and numerous villages. Hyannis, Falmouth, and Provincetown are important commercial centers. In the 19th century, local industries included whaling, shipbuilding, and shipping; today, in addition to tourism, the economy is based on oystering, fishing, and cranberry cultivation.

Barnwell County 558 sq mi/1445 sq km, pop. 20,293, in SW South Carolina, bordered by the Savannah R. and the Georgia state line (SW). It is largely swamp and pine forest. Its seat is the city of Barnwell (pop. 5255). About one-third of the county, in its W, is occupied by the US Department of Energy's SAVANNAH R. Nuclear Site (which it shares with neighboring Aiken Co.); in operation since the 1950s, this now includes the East's major nuclear waste disposal site, generally known simply as Barnwell. The county is otherwise mainly agricultural, with timber and naval stores produced.

Barranquitas unincorporated community (ZONA URBANA), pop. 2786, Barranquitas Municipio (pop. 25,605), C Puerto Rico, in the Cordillera Central, 22 mi/35 km SW of San Juan. A resort, it is the birthplace of nationalist leader Luis Muñoz Rivera (1858–1916), and has a museum tracing his career. Muñoz Rivera and his son, political leader Luis Muñoz Marín (1898–1980), are buried here.

Barre city, pop. 9482, Washington Co., C Vermont. It is on the Stevens and other Winooski R. branches, about 8 mi/13 km SE of Montpelier. East Barre, Websterville, and Graniteville villages are part of surrounding Barre township (pop. 7411). Barre became the leading US granite center after the War of 1812. Through the 19th century its quarries attracted a European and French-Canadian work force, making the city unusual in Vermont for its diversity. Other industries include dairy farming and the manufacturing of tools, machines, and wood products.

Barren Lands also, **Barren Ground** or **Barrens** name long used for TUNDRA areas of N Canada, esp. in the Northwest Territories, where their S boundary extends from the Mackenzie R. delta (NW) to Hudson Bay at the Manitoba line (SE). This is the traditional homeland of the Caribou INUIT, many now relocated into the ARCTIC ARCHIPELAGO. The border with the taiga (northern woodland) homeland of the DENE (SW), some of whom have lived on the Barren Lands, is not clearly defined, and there has long been friction between the two peoples.

Barren River 130 mi/210 km long, in Kentucky, formed by several small streams in Monroe Co., near the Tennessee border. It flows generally NW through Barren River L. (impounded by a dam near Finney), and past BOWLING GREEN, to join the Green R. just E of Woodbury. The Gasper R. joins it NW of Bowling Green.

Barrhead town, pop. 4160, C Alberta, in the Paddle R. Valley, 56 mi/90 km NW of Edmonton. Situated in an agricultural region, it processes lumber, grain, and dairy goods. An historic fur trading trail (1825) is here.

Barrie city, pop. 62,728, seat of Simcoe Co., S Ontario, on Kempenfelt Bay of L. SIMCOE, 50 mi/80 km NNW of Toronto. During the War of 1812, it was the starting point of a supply route to the upper Great Lakes. The area was permanently settled in 1828. Today it is a year-round resort in an agricultural and dairying region. Industries include tanneries, machine shops, varied light manufacturing plants, and breweries. CAMP BORDEN is 12 mi/19 km SW.

barrier beach ridge of sand or heavier material pushed by wave action into a position roughly parallel to a shoreline, and remaining above the level of high tide. If several such ridges combine, forming a wider body, it may be called a **barrier island.** The generally shallow body of water behind a barrier beach or island, now somewhat protected from waves, is a lagoon. Wind and wave continue to affect a barrier beach or island, constantly changing its shape and tending to move it along or toward the shore, depending on prevailing currents.

Barrington **1.** village, pop. 9504, Cook and Lake counties, NE Illinois, on Bakers L., 32 mi/52 km NW of Chicago. Primarily a residential suburb, it has plants processing coffee and tea and producing tableware. **2.** town, pop. 15,849, Bristol Co., E Rhode Island, on the NE shore of Narragansett Bay, adjoining (SE) East Providence. It occupies two peninsulas separated by the estuarial Barrington R. Settled in the 1670s by Colonists who left Rehoboth, Massachusetts, because of religious differences, it became part of Rhode Island in 1746. Barrington is a suburb and resort with some light industry.

barrio originally, a division of a Spanish *ciudad* (city) or PUEBLO, incorporating rural as well as urban territory. The term is now used of Hispanic sections, or of the Hispanic community taken as an entity, in any of various US cities. It is more inclusive than *vecindad* (neighborhood) and less specific than *colonia* (used of a group from a particular place of origin who form a cohesive community within a city, or, formerly, of a *barrio* on the periphery of a city.) In the Southwest barrios are essentially Mexican; in New York's EAST HARLEM, El Barrio is essentially Puerto Rican. In Puerto Rico, the barrio is one of the two types of legal subdivisions (minor civil divisions) of a MUNICIPIO. The other is the *barrio-pueblo;* a *subbarrio* is a further division of either.

Barrio Logan also, **Logan Heights** residential and commercial section of SAN DIEGO, California, on San Diego Bay, just SE of Downtown. The city's largest Mexican neighborhood was reduced in size by the construction of the San Diego–Coronado Bridge (1964). Part of the space below the bridge was reclaimed as Chicano Park.

Barrow city, pop. 3469, seat of North Slope Borough, NC Alaska, on the Arctic Ocean, 510 mi/820 km NNW of Fairbanks. The northernmost US city, it is 11 mi/18 km SW of the northernmost point in the US, **Point Barrow** (71° 23′ N). The city is the trading center for the NORTH SLOPE Borough. Its primarily Inuit pop. is engaged in whaling, trapping, crafts, government work, and the oil industry, some at PRUDHOE BAY, 200 mi/322 km to the ESE. A US meteorological station and naval and air bases are nearby. Originally an Inuit whaling village on a promontory overlooking the ocean, its earliest name was Utkiakvik ("high place for viewing"). Barrow and Point Barrow have long been jumping-off points for Arctic and North Pole aviation and exploration. A monument to the humorist Will Rogers and the bush pilot Wiley Post, who died here in a 1935 plane crash, is 13 mi/21 km SSW.

Barry M. Goldwater Range 4100–sq mi/10,620–sq km military area in the SW corner of Arizona. Extending N from the Mexican border to near the Gila R. and E from the Yuma Desert to the PAPAGO (Tohono O'odham) Indian Reservation, the area has been used as a bombing range since 1941. Most of it comprises the Luke Air Force Bombing and

Gunnery Range (Luke Air Force Base is NE, near PEORIA). There is also a Marine section. A number of NW–SE trending Great Basin ranges are here, including (roughly W–E) the Gila Mts., reaching 3156 ft/962 m at Sheep Mt.; the Tinajas Altas Mts. (noted for their "high tanks" or desert waterholes); the Copper Mts.; the Mohawk Mts.; the Granite Mts.; the Growler Mts.; the Sauceda Mts.; and the Sand Tank Mts., rising to 4084 ft/1245 m at Maricopa Peak. The area includes the "Lost City," thought to be a Hohokam site, evidence of the ancient Sand Papago people, and part of the historic EL CAMINO DEL DIABLO. The CABEZA PRIETA National Wildlife Refuge is within the range.

Barstow city, pop. 21,472, San Bernardino Co., SC California, 78 mi/126 km NE of Los Angeles, on the intermittent Mojave R. and Interstate 15 (formerly ROUTE 66), in the Mojave Desert. Founded in the 1880s, it was a mining town in the 1890s (the Calico Mts. lie E). It is a division point on rail lines into Los Angeles, and maintenance shops of the Santa Fe Railroad are here. It is now mainly a residential and military community; Marine Corps supply centers are nearby, and the Army's Fort Irwin and the Goldstone Communications Complex are 40 mi/64 km NE. Solar One, a large experimental solar energy plant, is 6 mi/10 km E. Barstow College (1959) is in the city, which is also a gateway to Death Valley and a growing residential center.

Bartholomew see BAYOU BARTHOLOMEW, Arkansas and Louisiana.

Bartlesville city, pop. 34,256, seat of Washington Co., also in Osage Co., NE Oklahoma, on the Caney R., 40 mi/64 km N of Tulsa. The site of Oklahoma's first commercially important oil well (1897), it lies in an oil-rich region, and is widely known as the home of the Phillips Petroleum Company. In addition to oil and related industries, natural gas and zinc have been important to the city, which also serves as a distribution center for livestock and agricultural products. The Frank Lloyd Wright–designed Price Tower (1955), an oil industry office building, is here. The city is the seat of Bartlesville Wesleyan College (1910).

Bartlett **1.** village, pop. 19,373, Cook, Du Page, and Kane counties, NE Illinois, a suburb 28 mi/45 km NW of Chicago. It is mainly a residential community, with some light industry producing hardware, electrical equipment, and vacuum cleaners. The nearby Villa Olivia Ski Area attracts local vacationers. **2.** town, pop. 26,989, Shelby Co., SW Tennessee, 8 mi/13 km NE of downtown Memphis, across the Wolf R. A fast-growing residential suburb, it also has manufactures including typewriters.

Bartow city, pop. 14,716, seat of Polk Co., C Florida, 11 mi/18 km SE of Lakeland, just S of L. Hancock and near the Peace R. Settled in 1851 on the site of a Seminole War fort, it is a shipping center for phosphates and citrus fruits. It also houses fruit canneries, cigar factories, fertilizer plants, and packing houses.

base line any of thousands of precisely determined latitudinal (E–W) lines measured by surveyors, beginning in 1796, from Ohio westward, as the bases for the division of the essentially flat US Midwest into square units (TOWNSHIPS of 36 sq mi/93 sq km, made up of *sections* of 1 sq mi/2.59 sq km). Corresponding N–S lines were called principal meridians.

Base Line Road see under EIGHT MILE ROAD, Michigan.

Basin, the the central district of CINCINNATI, Ohio, on level ground N of the Ohio R., and within the arc of higher ground—the "seven hills"—on which the city's more affluent residential neighborhoods developed. FOUNTAIN SQUARE is at the C of the Basin, in which both business and residential blocks have been extensively renovated or rebuilt since the 1950s.

Basin and Range Province major physiographic component of the INTERMONTANE REGION, covering (within the US) over 300,000 sq mi/777,000 sq km between the Columbia Plateau (N), the Wasatch Range and Colorado Plateau (E), and the Cascade Range and Sierra Nevada (W), and extending SE into Texas and S into the Mexican states of Sonora and Chihuahua. Occupying most of Nevada and parts of Utah, Oregon, Idaho, California, Arizona, New Mexico, and Texas, it is named for its chief structural characteristic, the alternation of mountain ranges with the valleys or depressions known as basins. The ranges are the result of the tilting of fault blocks, sections of the earth's crust turned upward by large PLATE movements; they are generally east-facing, with gradual westward slopes. The basins largely result from the corresponding lowering of crustal sections; some, most famously California's DEATH VALLEY, are now well below sea level. Drainage in the province is mostly internal, within individual basins or from one to another. The province is sometimes identified with the GREAT BASIN, its largest (over 60% of its area) constituent. In the larger sense, though, it also includes the lower SONORAN DESERT and Salton Trough (site of California's IMPERIAL VALLEY and SALTON SEA), as well as higher areas extending through SE New Mexico and to the GREAT BEND region of Texas. Within the province, the Colorado R. and its tributaries drain to the Gulf of California (the Pacific Ocean), and the Rio Grande, with the Pecos R. and other tributaries, to the Gulf of Mexico (the Atlantic Ocean); but except for a few other peripheral streams, regional water is otherwise channeled into PLAYAS, salt lakes, and SINKS, some of them vestiges of the huge glacial Lakes BONNEVILLE and LAHONTAN. The Basin and Range Province is largely arid, lying in the rain shadow (E) of California's mountains. Lack of usable water and harsh terrain have kept it for the most part uninhabited. Today mining, stock raising, military uses, and residential, resort, and agricultural development where large-scale irrigation has been undertaken are important.

Basin Street commercial and residential thoroughfare in DOWNTOWN New Orleans, Louisiana, just outside (NW) the VIEUX CARRÉ, 0.5 mi/1 km W of Jackson Square. It formed the S boundary (1898–1917) of STORYVILLE.

Basking Ridge unincorporated community in Bernards Township (pop. 17,199), Somerset Co., NC New Jersey, 7 mi/11 km SW of Morristown. It was settled in the early 1700s. White's Tavern here was the site of the British capture of Gen. Charles Lee in 1776. Today Basking Ridge is an affluent residential suburb, just E of Interstate 287 and just W the GREAT SWAMP National Wildlife Refuge. It has a financial services industry.

Bass Islands group of three resort islands in W L. Erie, Ottawa Co., NC Ohio, 35 mi/56 km E of Toledo. The largest, South Bass I. (3.5 mi/5.6 km long), lies 7 mi/11 km N of the mainland. Its harbor, Put-in-Bay, was the starting point of Oliver H. Perry's victory in the Battle of Lake Erie (Sept. 10, 1813), which is commemorated by a national peace monument here. North Bass I. (1.25 mi/2 km long) and Middle Bass I. (3 mi/4.8 km long) make up the rest of the group, which is noted for winemaking, caves, and lake hatcheries and fisheries.

Bastrop city, pop. 13,916, seat of Morehouse Parish, NE Louisiana, 20 mi/32 km NNE of Monroe. Founded in 1845, it experienced its greatest growth when the Monroe natural gas field was discovered in 1916. Manufactures include paper and wood products, printing inks, varnish, carbon black, and other chemicals. The region produces corn, cotton, soybeans, rice, and peaches; truck farming and the raising of cattle are also significant.

Batavia **1.** city, pop. 17,076, Kane Co., NE Illinois, on the Fox R., 35 mi/56 km W of Chicago. Settled in 1833 by Dutch immigrants, it was a major center of American windmill manufacture through the early 20th century. Today, it has iron and brass foundries and factories manufacturing farm machinery, electric switches, truck bodies, castings, and television tubes. There are limestone deposits nearby. Fermi National Accelerator Laboratory (Fermilab), one of the largest particle physics research centers in the US, is immediately E of the city. **2.** city, pop. 16,310, seat of Genesee Co., NW New York, on Tonawanda Creek, 36 mi/58 km E of Buffalo and 33 mi/53 km WSW of Rochester. Named for the Batavian Republic (Netherlands), it was the center of the Holland Land Company Purchase of 1793. The city is now the market and shipping center of a farming region, and has a mixed industrial sector that makes processed foods, machinery, and home products. Batavia houses a New York state school for the visually impaired (1868) and Genesee Community College (1966). The Tonawanda (Seneca) reservation is 13 mi/21 km NW.

Batesville **1.** city, pop. 9187, seat of Independence Co., NE Arkansas, 80 mi/129 km NNE of Little Rock, on the White R., in the foothills of the Ozark Plateau. It is a processing center for fruit, cotton, corn, hay, livestock, poultry, and dairy items. Among its industries are cotton ginning and grist and saw milling. It has bottling works and manufactures wood products and shoes. Limestone, manganese, and black marble are mined nearby. Arkansas College (1872) is here. **2.** city, pop. 6403, co-seat (with Sardis) of Panola Co., NW Mississippi, 36 mi/58 km ENE of Clarksdale. Founded in 1855, it acquired the population of nearby (N) Panola when the railroad came here. It trades and processes local cotton, corn, and timber. On Interstate 55, it is also an Amtrak stop.

Bath **1.** city, pop. 9799, seat of Sagadahoc Co., on the Kennebec R. in SW Maine, 36 mi/58 km NE of Portland. Sixteen mi/26 km N of POPHAM BEACH, where the *Virginia,* New England's first ship, was launched in 1607, Bath has been a shipbuilding center since 1762. Bath Iron Works, founded in 1833, is famous for its destroyers and other navy vessels, ship machinery, and marine equipment; in the late 20th century it was Maine's largest private employer. **2.** town, pop. 154, Beaufort Co., E North Carolina, on Bath Creek of the Pamlico R. estuary, 14 mi/23 km ESE of Washington. Founded in 1690 on the site of an Indian village, it is North Carolina's oldest (1705) incorporated municipality, and a former provincial capital. It was attacked (1711) during the Tuscarora War, and was later headquarters for pirate Edward Teach (Blackbeard). In a commercial fishing and agricultural area, it is now largely a tourist center. **3.** see BERKELEY SPRINGS, West Virginia.

Bath Beach seaside neighborhood in SW Brooklyn, New York, on Gravesend Bay and S of Bensonhurst, of which it is sometimes considered part. In the 1870s Bath Beach was designed to rival Coney Island as a resort. It is today a lower-middle-class district of small home lots, somewhat isolated from the water by the Shore Parkway.

batholith (Greek for "deep rock") dome-shaped mass of igneous rock, often granite, created by intrusion upward into strata that may later be eroded away, leaving some part of the batholith on the surface. The origins of batholiths are poorly understood, but they are known or assumed to underlie large parts of the US, including the Sierra Nevada, and Canada. The continent's most extensive may lie under British Columbia's coastal regions. In the US, the largest is the **Idaho Batholith,** some 250 mi/400 km N–S, with over 16,000 sq mi/41,440 sq km exposed; it lies across the state's center, forming, among other features, the Clearwater and Salmon River ranges in the North Rocky Mts. Montana's **Boulder Batholith** centers on Boulder, between Butte (SW) and Helena (NE). Both these batholiths have given rise to mining centers, the COEUR D'ALENE district lying on the N of the Idaho Batholith, the copper-rich BUTTE district lying on the Boulder Batholith.

Bathurst city, pop. 14,409, seat of Gloucester Co., N New Brunswick, on the Nepisiguit R. at its entrance (Nepisiguit Bay) into CHALEUR Bay. In the midst of a major lead, zinc, copper, and silver mining area, exploited since the 1950s, it also produces lumber, wood pulp, and paper. Nearby beaches and salmon fishing bring visitors. The pop. is predominantly francophone, with origins dating from the early 17th century.

Bathurst Island one of the PARRY Is., in the QUEEN ELIZABETH Is., N Northwest Territories, in the Arctic Ocean between Cornwallis (E) and Melville (W) islands. Its 6194 sq mi/16,042 sq km includes many nearby islets; ice cover concealed its dimensions until 1940s aerial reconnaissance. The NORTH MAGNETIC POLE now lies off its deeply indented N coast.

Batoche National Historic Site in C Saskatchewan, 40 mi/64 km SW of Prince Albert, on the E bank of the South Saskatchewan R. A settlement here was the scene of the four-day last stand of the MÉTIS in the Riel Rebellion, in May 1885. Today, the village church and rectory and remains of the Métis rifle pits and the government encampment still stand. In the nearby cemetery lie the bodies of Gabriél Dumont and other Métis leaders. DUCK LAKE and Fort Carlton, two other rebellion sites, are in the area.

Baton Rouge city, pop. 219,531, state capital and seat of East Baton Rouge Parish, SE Louisiana, on the E bank of the Mississippi R. Named ("red stick") for a cypress post once used to mark a border between tribal hunting grounds, it began life as a French fort in 1719. In 1763, the French ceded the area to Britain. Spain seized control during the American Revolution, in the first battle of Baton Rouge (Sept. 21, 1779), and, after governing Louisiana for twenty years, ceded the area back to France in 1800. At the time of the LOUISIANA PURCHASE (1803), Spain reclaimed Baton Rouge, along with WEST FLORIDA. Americans who had settled here rebelled, and in the second battle of Baton Rouge, on Sept. 23, 1810, a West Florida Republic was established; the US annexed it three months later. Baton Rouge, incorporated in 1817, became capital of Louisiana in 1849. In May 1862, the city was captured, and was occupied by Union forces until the end of the Civil War, during which other Louisiana cities served as capital. Baton Rouge became capital again in 1882, when a new statehouse (now the Old Capitol) was built. Its New Capitol (1932) was the scene of the 1935 assassination of former governor Huey Long. Through the 19th century, Baton Rouge was a port and commercial center, in addition to its governmental role. In 1909, the Standard Oil Company built a large refinery here, spurring the growth of industries based on regional oil and natural gas fields. The city is now a major oil and petrochemical processing center, with what is said to be the world's largest and most diversified refinery. It also produces rubber, plastics, concrete products, tile, computer components, and paper. Its port, a major river barge terminus and the Gulf of Mexico deepwater port the farthest inland, lies at the N end of a highly industrialized riverfront stretching along the RIVER ROAD from New Orleans. Baton Rouge is home to the main campus of Louisiana State University (1855), on its SW edge, and to historically black Southern University (1880), in its formerly independent Scotlandville district, on the city's N edge. Its suburbs, chiefly in EAST BATON ROUGE PARISH, are largely unincorporated. To the W, across the river, lie refineries and sugar cane plantations.

Batsto see under PINE BARRENS, New Jersey.

Batten Kill river, 55 mi/89 km long, rising in Dorset, Bennington Co., SW Vermont, and flowing S past Manchester and Arlington. It then flows W into New York, to Greenwich, where it joins the Hudson R. opposite Schuylerville.

Battery, the **1.** area at the S tip of Manhattan I., New York City. The name, from a gun emplacement erected by the British in 1693, now refers particularly to a 20-ac/8-ha park, largely on subsequently reclaimed land. CASTLE CLINTON National Monument is located here, and boats leave the Battery for Liberty Island and other New York Harbor destinations. The area has long been popular with workers taking breaks from offices in the nearby FINANCIAL DISTRICT, and is now also a tourist focus. **2.** see under CHARLESTON, South Carolina.

Battery Park City upscale neighborhood created on 92 ac/37 ha of landfill on Manhattan's lower West Side, New York City. Following a 1979 master plan, it incorporates the World Financial Center, which combines a series of skyscrapers just W of the WORLD TRADE CENTER with lower buildings including the Winter Garden, a "crystal palace"; other commercial establishments; housing for some 25,000 residents; and a 1.2-mi/2-km esplanade on the Hudson R.

Battle Creek city, pop. 53,540, Calhoun Co., S Michigan, at the confluence of Battle Creek and the Kalamazoo R., 19 mi/31 km E of Kalamazoo. Founded in 1831 and named for a skirmish between Indians and a surveying party (1825), it became a flour and wool milling center. Seventh-Day Adventists built a sanitarium here in 1866. One of its directors, John Kellogg (1876–1943), experimented with foods, leading to the production of ready-to-eat cereals, which became the city's biggest industry. This enterprise turned international after W.K. Kellogg (his younger brother) and C.W. Post marketed the ideas and products on a wider scale. Auto parts, farm equipment, paper products, and trucks are also made here. A station on the Underground Railroad, it was home to Sojourner Truth, who is buried in Oak Hill Cemetery. Battle Creek has a symphony, theater, and art center, as well as Kellogg Community College (1956).

Battleford town, pop. 4107, surrounded by rolling country in W Saskatchewan, 84 mi/132 km NW of Saskatoon, at the confluence of the North Saskatchewan and Battle rivers. It was the capital of the Northwest Territories (1876–83) and a North West Mounted Police post. The capital was relocated to Regina in 1883 when the Canadian Pacific Railway was routed through the S Saskatchewan plains. Battleford was then looted and burned by the MÉTIS in the 1885 Riel Rebellion, and in 1905, the Canadian National Railway bypassed it, creating NORTH BATTLEFORD across the North Saskatchewan R. Today, the twin cities constitute a service center for the surrounding region, which depends on mixed farming, oil and gas wells, some light manufacturing, fishing, and tourism. Battleford has flour mills and mineral water works. Fort Battleford National Historic Park commemorates the old capital.

Battle Ground town, pop. 806, Tippecanoe Co., WC Indiana, 7 mi/11 km NNE of LAFAYETTE, in an agricultural area. The Battle of Tippecanoe was fought here on Nov. 7, 1811. Shawnee forces camped 3 mi/5 km NE, near the junction of the Tippecanoe and Wabash rivers, in Prophetstown (named for their leader Tenskwatawa, "the Shawnee Prophet"), attacked American troops commanded by William Henry Harrison, and were repelled, after which Prophetstown was destroyed. Harrison's reputation as the "Hero of Tippecanoe" was a major factor in his successful 1840 quest for the presidency. The battle site is now a state memorial park.

Baxley city, pop. 3841, Appling Co., SE Georgia, 37 mi/60 km N of Waycross. On US 1, it is an agricultural market center known for its tobacco auctions. The Edwin I. Hatch nuclear power plant (1974) is 12 mi/19 km N, along the Altamaha R.

Baxter Peak see under Mt. KATAHDIN, Maine.

Baxter State Park 201,000 ac/81,400 ha, 15 mi/24 km NW of Millinocket, in Piscataquis Co., N Maine. Named for Gov. Percival Baxter, a wealthy industrialist who donated the land to the state, the park is a wilderness area with varied wildlife and forest and alpine vegetation. Baxter Peak (5267 ft/1606 m) on Mt. KATAHDIN is the state's highest point, and the N terminus of the APPALACHIAN TRAIL. Other mountains in the park include Traveler (3541 ft/1080 m) and North Brother (4143 ft/1264 m). Grand L. Matagamon and Nesowadnehunk L., 10 mi/16 km of the Appalachian Trail, and 65 mi/105 km of other trails are also here.

Bay, the French, **La Baie** in Canada, HUDSON BAY; also, the HUDSON'S BAY COMPANY.

Bayamón unincorporated community (ZONA URBANA), pop. 202,103, Bayamón Municipio (pop. 220,262), NE Puerto Rico, on the Bayamón R., 5 mi/8 km SW of San Juan. Settled by the Spanish early in the 16th century, it is a largely residential and industrial suburb, and an agricultural trade center; sugar, tobacco, and alcohol are processed. Manufactures include iron products, machinery, tools, and clothing. Having quadrupled in pop. since 1950, Bayamón has modern civic buildings, hotels, shopping malls, and public parks.

Bay Area in California, the communities around SAN FRANCISCO BAY. The E side, including industrial Oakland and Richmond, academic Berkeley, and their suburbs, is known as the East Bay. The South Bay, around San Jose, is better known as SILICON VALLEY.

Bay Bridge, the see SAN FRANCISCO–OAKLAND BAY BRIDGE, California.

Baychester commercial and residential section, NE Bronx, New York. It lies on partly reclaimed land E of Bronx Park and W of Pelham Bay Park; Williamsbridge lies N. CO-OP

CITY, which is E of Interstate 95, is usually considered to be in Baychester.

Bay City **1.** city, pop. 38,936, seat of Bay Co., E Michigan, on the Saginaw R. near its mouth, 13 mi/21 km N of Saginaw and 4 mi/6 km SW of L. Huron. It is a major deep-water port for Great Lakes and oceangoing ships. It was settled in 1831 by whites who came to teach farming to Chippewas in treaty-guaranteed payment for the ceding of territory. Michigan's lumber boom (1850–90) made the city "Lumber Queen of the World" until the forests were depleted. The city revived with coal mining, fishing, and beet-sugar refining. The present economy depends on shipping and commerce. Industries include shipbuilding and the manufacture of iron, magnesium castings, petrochemicals, auto and aircraft equipment, and processed foods. Bay City State Park is 5 mi/8 km to the N. **2.** city, pop. 18,170, seat of Matagorda Co., SE Texas, on the Colorado R., 25 mi/40 km N of the Gulf of Mexico and 68 mi/110 km SW of Houston. It is a shipping center for an area that produces rice, corn, pecans, cotton, figs, poultry, and cattle. Nearby are large sulfur and oil deposits. The city has oil refineries and meatpacking, rice milling, and welding and sheet metal working plants, and makes petrochemicals. Commercial fishing is important. The South Texas nuclear power plant (1988) is 20 mi/32 km SW.

Bay County 447 sq mi/1158 sq km, pop. 111,723, in E Michigan, bordered by Saginaw Bay of L. Huron (E and NE) and drained by the Saginaw and Kawkawlin rivers. Its seat and largest city is BAY CITY. It became prosperous during the Michigan lumber boom (1850–90), then developed soft-coal mining, commercial fishing, and beet-sugar refining. Agricultural products include beans, chicory, sugar beets, and dairy products. There is manufacturing in Bay City and Essexville. Fishing and hunting resorts dot the county.

Bayfront Park municipal park created in 1924 on 40 ac/16 ha of landfill, on BISCAYNE BAY in downtown Miami, Florida. Biscayne Boulevard (US 1) runs along it, and Flagler St. ends at it. In Feb. 1933 its Amphitheater was the scene of an assassination attempt on President-elect Franklin Roosevelt, in which Chicago mayor Anton Cermak was killed; there is a memorial to Cermak.

Bay Minette city, pop. 7168, seat of Baldwin Co., SW Alabama, 22 mi/35 km NE of Mobile. An industrial and agricultural trade center, it produces furniture and clothing.

Bayonet Point unincorporated community, pop. 21,860, Pasco Co., WC Florida, 28 mi/45 km NW of Tampa. It lies in the N part of the Gulf Coast area particularly popular with winter vacationers and retirees.

Bayonne city, pop. 61,444, Hudson Co., NE New Jersey, on a peninsula between Upper New York Bay (E) and Newark Bay (W), separated from Staten I. by the Kill van Kull, adjacent (S) to Jersey City. Settled by Dutch traders in the mid-1600s, it was known as Konstable's Hoeck, then as Constable Hook, for its SE section. Bayonne's port has a 9 mi/14 km–long waterfront, with a Navy supply depot and Military Ocean Terminal as well as many docks and shipyards. The E terminus of various oil pipelines from the SW, with a refinery industry that dates back to 1875, the city is a major oil processing and exporting center. Bayonne also manufactures such products as heavy machinery, chemicals, pharmaceuticals, electric motors and generators, textiles, paint, and foods.

Bayonne Bridge steel-arch vehicular bridge over the KILL VAN KULL between NW Staten Island, New York, and Bayonne, New Jersey. Before the opening of the Verrazano-Narrows Bridge (1964), it offered the quickest access to Manhattan and Long I. from Staten I. and parts of New Jersey, by way of the HOLLAND TUNNEL. Completed in 1931, it was the longest such bridge in the world, with a main span of 1675 ft/511 m (overall length 8100 ft/2470 m), until West Virginia's New River Gorge Bridge opened in 1977.

bayou in Louisiana and neighboring states, a sluggish or stationary body of water that may have been formed in any of several ways. Some are OXBOWS; others are cut off from rivers by human engineering. The expansion of the DELTA OF THE MISSISSIPPI RIVER has created thousands by closing off waterways through siltation. The term, applied to everything from ditches to larger bodies like the Bayou Teche, is a French adaptation of a Choctaw word, *bayuk*.

Bayou Bartholomew river, 300 mi/480 km long, in SE Arkansas and NE Louisiana. It rises just W of PINE BLUFF, and flows generally SE and S across the Louisiana line to join the OUACHITA R. W of Bastrop.

Bayou Cane unincorporated community, pop. 15,876, Terrebonne Parish, SE Louisiana, 4 mi/6 km NW of Houma, in an area noted for its fishing and bayou-country tourist trade.

Bayou La Batre city, pop. 2456, Mobile Co., SW Alabama, just N of the Gulf of Mexico and 20 mi/32 km SSW of Mobile. First settled in 1796, it was a steamer port between Mobile and New Orleans, and is now both a resort and a commercial fishing, canning, boatyard, and oil industry service center.

Bayou Lafourche 107 mi/172 km long, in SE Louisiana. Formerly a DISTRIBUTARY of the Mississippi R., flowing from near Donaldsonville, it is now cut off from the larger river by dams and levees. It flows generally SE to the Gulf of Mexico through an almost continuous stretch (85 mi/137 km) of small waterside communities sometimes called "the longest street in America." Along the way are sugar plantations, oilfields, and, near the S end, fishing ports.

Bayou Teche popularly, **the Teche** waterway, formed by smaller bayous in St. Landry Parish, SC Louisiana, and winding 125 mi/200 km SE to join the ATCHAFALAYA R. 11 mi/18 km NW of Morgan City. The area is noted for its sugar cane production, and as the heart of CAJUN COUNTRY. Communities along the Teche include (NW to SE) Arnaudville (town, pop. 1444, St. Landry and St. Martin parishes), Breaux Bridge (city, pop. 6515, St. Martin Parish), SAINT MARTINVILLE, NEW IBERIA, Jeanerette (city, pop. 6205, Iberia Parish), and FRANKLIN. The "Teche Country" is particularly associated with the legend of Evangeline (see SAINT MARTINVILLE).

Bay Ridge southwesternmost section of Brooklyn, New York. Its ridge is part of the terminal moraine that forms much of Brooklyn. Fort Hamilton, on its S, was established in 1825 on one site of the 1776 Battle of Long Island, and is still active. The Verrazano-Narrows Bridge (1964) from Staten Island comes ashore in Brooklyn just to the W of Fort Hamilton. Bay Ridge was rural until the 1890s, when it became a seaside home for Manhattan businessmen. Arrival of the subway in 1915 brought a boom. The area has been home to many Scandinavian, especially Norwegian, immigrants since the late 19th century, and their civic activities still focus on Leif Ericson Park. Today Bay Ridge is a mixed, largely middle-class community.

Bay Saint Louis city, pop. 8063, seat of Hancock Co., S Mississippi, on St. Louis Bay (N) and MISSISSIPPI SOUND, 48 mi/77 km NE of New Orleans, Louisiana. Part of the 1789 Spanish land grant, it had by 1812 become a coastal retreat for Natchez planters. The New Orleans, Mobile, and Chattanooga Railroad (1869) brought substantial resort trade, which remains the city's economic base. There are also lumber and bottling industries.

Bay Shore unincorporated village, pop. 21,279, in Islip town, Suffolk Co., SE New York, on Long Island's South Shore, 5 mi/8 km E of Babylon. It is situated at the widest point of GREAT SOUTH BAY, and is a fishing and boating center. Ferries from Bay Shore cross the bay to FIRE ISLAND.

Bayside residential section of N Queens, New York, on Little Neck Bay (Long Island Sound), NE of Flushing. It was developed along a railroad line in the early 20th century, then boomed after World War II. Fort Totten (established 1857 on Willett's Point, and named in 1898) is just to the N, and the Throgs Neck Bridge to the NW. Bayside is essentially a middle-class suburb, but has some light industry.

Bay Street N–S thoroughfare in the financial district of downtown TORONTO, Ontario, the site, esp. around the intersection with King St., of Canada's major concentration of banking and other financial establishments, including the Toronto Stock Exchange. It parallels (W) YONGE St.

Bayswater see under the ROCKAWAYS, New York.

Baytown city, pop. 63,850, Harris and Chambers counties, SE Texas, 22 mi/35 km E of downtown Houston, across San Jacinto Bay. Part of the vast Houston port area, in a rich oil and sulfur producing region, it was formed when Pelly, Goose Creek, and Baytown merged and incorporated as a city in 1948. Its petrochemical products include synthetic rubber, carbon black, and ink, and it has oil refineries. Lee College (1934) is here.

Bay View residential neighborhood on the SOUTH SIDE of Milwaukee, Wisconsin, on L. Michigan, immediately S of Downtown and E of the HISTORIC SOUTH SIDE. A 19th-century steel producing suburb, it was known for its labor unrest. Eastern and Southern European immigrants have long lived here, and Hispanic and Asian groups have joined them in recent decades. Young professionals priced out of the EAST SIDE have also moved into the area.

Bayview see under HUNTER'S POINT, San Francisco, California.

Bay Village city, pop. 17,000, Cuyahoga Co., NE Ohio, a residential suburb on L. Erie, 12 mi/19 km W of Cleveland. Situated here is the 116-ac/47-ha Cahoon Park, named for the Vermont family who settled the area (1810). Several wildlife preserves are nearby.

Bayway see under LINDEN, New Jersey.

Beach, the also, **the Beaches** residential and resort section of E TORONTO, Ontario, along L. Ontario, 5 mi/8 km E of Downtown, W of the SCARBOROUGH line, at the E end of Queen St. This villagelike community was a 19th-century resort; Toronto's original Woodbine (now Greenwood) Racetrack was here; the new Woodbine is in ETOBICOKE. The Beach is noted for its boardwalk and boutiques.

Beach Park village, pop. 9513, Lake Co., extreme N Illinois, adjoining (NW) Zion, and 3 mi/5 km S of the Wisconsin line. It is a largely residential community at the N extreme of the Chicago metropolitan area, 42 mi/64 km NNW of the LOOP.

Beachwood city, pop. 10,677, Cuyahoga Co., NE Ohio, a residential suburb 10 mi/16 km E of Cleveland.

Beacon city, pop. 13,243, Dutchess Co., SE New York, 60 mi/97 km N of New York City, at the foot of Mt. Beacon, on the E bank of the Hudson R., across from NEWBURGH. It was created in 1913 from the union of Matteawan and Fishkill Landing, two 17th-century villages at the junction of Fishkill Creek and the Hudson. Industries manufacture clothing, fans, rubber products, and aluminum. Mt. Beacon is a resort area. The Fishkill Correctional Facility is NE.

Beacon Hill **1.** see under VICTORIA, British Columbia. **2.** historic residential neighborhood in downtown Boston, Massachusetts. One of the oldest parts of the city, on the SHAWMUT PENINSULA, Beacon Hill is one of Boston's most exclusive areas. Its 18th- and 19th-century town houses are extensively restored, with cobblestone streets and gaslights adding atmosphere. The name derives from a beacon erected in 1634 to be set afire to warn of enemy attack. The gold-domed Massachusetts State House (1798) is on Beacon Hill's SE corner, facing the BOSTON COMMON. LOUISBURG SQUARE is on the hill's W. Beacon Hill was much higher when first settled than today; 19th-century excavations led to much of it being used as landfill in the BACK BAY and other Boston districts.

Beaconsfield city, pop. 19,616, MONTRÉAL URBAN COMMUNITY, S Québec, on the W of the I. de Montréal, 15 mi/24 km SW of downtown Montréal and adjacent (SW) to Pointe-Claire, on the L. St.-Louis (the St. Lawrence R.). It is an affluent, largely anglophone residential suburb.

Beacon Street residential and commercial thoroughfare in Boston, Brookline, Chestnut Hill, and Newton, Massachusetts. It runs along the N side of Boston Common through the BACK BAY to the Allston-Brighton area; and then into the suburbs. It passes Boston College in Chestnut Hill. The Boston Marathon route follows Beacon St. through Newton and into the Back Bay.

Beale Air Force Base see under MARYSVILLE, California.

Beale Street commercial thoroughfare and entertainment district in downtown Memphis, Tennessee, now a National Historic District. In its heyday, from about 1900 through the 1920s, it was a strip of saloons, night clubs, theaters, and gambling dens, the Mid-South's center of black commerce and entertainment, especially associated with the blues and with composer W. C. Handy, whose home is here. Largely closed down in the 1950s, it has been resuscitated as a tourist attraction.

Bean Creek in Michigan: see under TIFFIN R.

Beantown nickname for Boston, Massachusetts, reflecting the belief that its residents habitually do, or that a visitor may have to, consume Boston baked beans.

Bear Butte solitary, dome-shaped mountain, 4422 ft/1349 m high and rising 1200 ft/366 m above the surrounding plain, an outlier of the BLACK HILLS, WC South Dakota, 5 mi/8 km NE of Sturgis. An excellent example of a laccolith, a volcano that never erupted, it is sacred to several tribes and was a landmark for fur traders, pioneers, and gold prospectors. It was the site of an 1857 Indian conference called to discuss the encroachment of whites into the region. It stands in 1845-ac/747-ha Bear Butte State Park, a national Natural Landmark, which includes Bear Butte L.

Bear Mountain **1.** 2355 ft/718 m, in the Taconic Mts. in Salisbury, NW Connecticut, near the Massachusetts border. The Appalachian Trail traverses it. It is the highest mountain entirely within Connecticut; nearby Mt. FRISSELL, largely in Massachusetts, reaches 2380 ft/726 m in Connecticut. **2.** 1305 ft/398 m, on the Hudson R. across from Peekskill, in Bear Mountain Park, a section of Palisades Interstate Park, in Rockland Co., SE New York. It is a popular recreational site, with hiking trails and other facilities. Bear Mountain Bridge crosses the Hudson here.

Bear River 350 mi/560 km long, in Utah, Wyoming, and Idaho. It rises in the Uinta Mts. E of Salt Lake City, in NE Utah, flows generally N along the Utah-Wyoming border, and turns NW into SE Idaho. Passing around the N end of the WASATCH RANGE, it turns S into Utah again, to the GREAT SALT L., W of Brigham City. The river drains Bear L., on the Utah-Idaho line.

Bear Run small stream, a tributary of the Youghiogheny R., in Fayette Co., SW Pennsylvania, 12 mi/19 km N of the Maryland border. Just S of the stream are Bear Run Nature Reserve and Fallingwater (1936–37), one of Frank Lloyd Wright's most famous private houses, which is cantilevered over a waterfall. Both are owned by the Western Pennsylvania Conservancy.

Beartooth Range SW–NE trending mountains, projecting NE from the ABSAROKA Range, in S Montana, from the Wyoming border. Unlike the Absarokas, they are noted for their jaggedness, with peaks over 12,000 ft/3660 m, including GRANITE PEAK (12,799 ft/3901 m), Montana's highest. Much of the range is in the ABSAROKA-BEARTOOTH WILDERNESS AREA.

Beatrice city, pop. 12,354, seat of Gage Co., SE Nebraska, on the Big Blue R., 37 mi/59 km S of Lincoln. It was established as an OREGON TRAIL stop in 1857. The 195-ac/79-ha Homestead National Monument, 4 mi/6 km W, is the site of the first American land-claim HOMESTEAD (1862). The city trades and ships grain and dairy products and manufactures farm machinery, irrigation equipment, and hardware.

Beaufort **1.** town, pop. 3808, Carteret Co., E North Carolina, on a peninsula across (E) from MOREHEAD CITY, and 10 mi/16 km NW of Cape LOOKOUT. Established in 1722, it is a fishing and resort community, the site of the North Carolina Maritime Museum. **2.** city, pop. 9576, seat of Beaufort Co., S South Carolina, on the ATLANTIC INTRACOASTAL WATERWAY and the estuarial Beaufort R., on Port Royal Island, 50 mi/80 km SW of Charleston. In an area explored by the Spanish (1520), it was founded by the English in 1711. Tourism is now its main industry; it is also a commercial fishing and shellfishing port and a processing and distribution hub for locally produced vegetables and timber. The city has many noted 18th-century and antebellum structures, Fort Frederick (1732), and a National Cemetery (1863). A Marine Air Base lies just N, and PARRIS ISLAND is 4 mi/6 km S.

Beaufort Sea large section of the Arctic Ocean N of Alaska, the Yukon Territory, and the Arctic Archipelago of the Northwest Territories. Part of the Arctic Basin, it reaches depths of 12,000 ft/3660 m. Large oil and natural gas fields lie beneath the ice-packed sea, which is navigable only two to three months of the year.

Beauharnois city, pop. 6449, Beauharnois-Salaberry census division, S Québec, 22 mi/35 km SW of Montréal, on the S shore of L. Saint-Louis (the St. Lawrence R.), at the mouth of the R. Saint-Louis, and on the E outlet of the 16 mi/25 km–long **Beauharnois Canal** (1932), which bypasses rapids on the St. Lawrence. At those rapids, W of the city, a huge hydroelectric station supplies power for much of the province as well as for nearby aluminum, metal alloy, chemical, furniture, printing, steel, and paper industries.

Beaumont city, pop. 114,323, seat of Jefferson Co. (pop. 239,397), extreme SE Texas, on the Neches R. (the Sabine-Neches Waterway), 85 mi/137 km ENE of Houston. A deepwater channel connects it with the Gulf Intracoastal Waterway and the Gulf of Mexico. Settled in 1825, it was laid out in 1835, and became a river port and rice and lumber producing center. By the 1890s five railroads converged here. In 1901 the first Texas oil well, the Anthony F. Lucas gusher, blew in at nearby (SE) Spindletop (Gladys City), inaugurating the region's main industry. The city manufactures chemicals, oilfield equipment, rubber, fabrics, metal, paper, and plywood. Salt and sulfur mining, shipbuilding, and rice milling are important. Lamar University (1923), the South Texas State Fairgrounds, and the home of renowned athlete Mildred "Babe" Didrikson Zaharias (1914–56) are here.

Beauport city, pop. 69,158, QUÉBEC urban community, SE Québec, on the N bank of the St. Lawrence R., 7 mi/11 km NNE of downtown Québec City. One of the earliest European settlements in Canada was established here in 1634 by Robert Giffard. The modern city is an amalgamation of Beauport with the surrounding Courville, Giffard, MONTMORENCY, Saint-Michel-Archange, Sainte-Thérèse-de-Lisieux, and Villeneuve. Although principally a residential suburb, it has some light industry.

Beaupré see under SAINTE-ANNE-DE-BEAUPRÉ, Québec.

Beauregard Square in DOWNTOWN New Orleans, Louisiana, just NW of Rampart St. and the VIEUX CARRÉ, between St. Ann and St. Peter streets. It was renamed after the Civil War, for the Confederate general P.G.T. Beauregard. Earlier, it had been the site of Fort St. Ferdinand, a Spanish structure. After the fort's destruction around 1803, it became known as the Place Congo, or Congo Square. Here the city's slaves were allowed on Sundays to dance the African *bamboula* and to use drums (otherwise outlawed). Congo Square is regarded as critical in the development of African-American music. Today, Beauregard Square is part of Louis Armstrong Park (designated 1980).

Beauvoir plantation house (1853) in BILOXI, Mississippi, overlooking the Gulf of Mexico, that was the last (1877–89) home of Confederate President Jefferson Davis and his wife. After the Civil War, Davis wrote *The Rise and Fall of the Confederate Government* here. The structure became a Confederate soldiers' home after his death, and has been a museum since 1940. The cemetery here is the site of the Confederate Tomb of the Unknown Soldier.

Beaver Archipelago island group in Charlevoix Co., in N Michigan, 35 mi/56 km NW of Charlevoix, between the Upper and Lower Peninsulas. The archipelago, c.68 mi/109 km long, includes the Manitou and Fox islands and Beaver I., the largest (13 mi/21 km long and up to 6 mi/10 km wide). French explorers called the latter Île du Castor; their settlement, one of the earliest in the area, was abandoned in 1603. James Jesse Strang established a "kingdom" on the island (1847) with his Mormon followers, and crowned himself king. His tyranny ended in assassination (1856), and the last Mormons decamped in 1895. The small Beaver I. population is now augmented by hunters, fishermen, and boaters.

Beaver Brook see under NEWCASTLE, New Brunswick.

Beaver County 436 sq mi/1129 sq km, pop. 186,093, in SW Pennsylvania, NW of Pittsburgh on the Ohio and West Virginia borders. Its seat is Beaver; its major city is BEAVER

FALLS. The county contains a number of industrial suburbs of Pittsburgh, including ALIQUIPPA.

Beavercreek city, pop. 33,626, Greene Co., SW Ohio, a suburb 6 mi/10 km SE of Dayton.

Beaver Dam city, pop. 14,196, Dodge Co., SC Wisconsin, on Beaver Dam L. and the Beaver Dam R., 30 mi/48 km SW of Fond du Lac. It is a trading center for the region's agricultural and dairy products. Manufactures include stoves, shoes, cement blocks, metal products, outboard motors, and cheese; peas, corn, and beans are canned. Beaver Dam was settled in 1841. The Horicon Marsh Wildlife Area and Horicon National Wildlife Refuge are 10 mi/16 km E.

Beaver Dam Creek see under MECHANICSVILLE, Virginia.

Beaver Dams battle site: see under THOROLD, Ontario.

Beaver Falls city, pop. 10,687, Beaver Co., W Pennsylvania, on the falls of the Beaver R. near its junction with the Ohio R., 25 mi/40 km NW of Pittsburgh. Situated on an Indian trail later used by pioneers, it was settled in 1793. In a region of coal mines and natural gas deposits, the city developed as a steel manufacturing center and now also has a diversity of other manufactures. It is home to Geneva College (1848).

Beaverhead National Forest 2.15 million ac/870,000 ha (3355 sq mi/8690 sq km), in seven units in SW Montana, in the Beaverhead, Bitterroot, Anaconda, and other ranges. Hilgard Peak (11,316 ft/3449 m), in the Madison Range, is its high point. Headwaters of the Madison R. are here. On the Continental Divide is Lemhi Pass (7373 ft/2247 m), in the Beaverheads, over which Sacajawea (or Sakakawea), the Shoshone scout, led Lewis and Clark's expedition in 1805; the Sacajawea Historic Area is here. **Beaverhead Rock,** a landmark S of the pass, gave its name to the range and forest.

Beaverhead River see under JEFFERSON R., Montana.

Beaver Island see under BEAVER ARCHIPELAGO, Michigan.

Beaverlodge Lake c.8 sq mi/21 sq km, in the NW corner of Saskatchewan, immediately N of L. ATHABASCA. Fur trading and gold mining supported the area until important uranium deposits were discovered in the 1940s; in 1952 URANIUM CITY was founded. Since 1982, when mining operations ended, the region has experienced economic decline and depopulation.

Beaver River **1.** 50 mi/80 km long, in NC New York. It rises in small lakes in Hamilton Co., and flows W into Stillwater Reservoir, then generally W through the town of Croghan, past Beaver Falls, to the Black R., 7 mi/11 km N of Lowville. **2.** see NORTH CANADIAN R., New Mexico and Oklahoma. **3.** 21 mi/32 km long, in W Pennsylvania. Formed by the confluence of the Mahoning and Shenango rivers at NEW CASTLE, it flows S past BEAVER FALLS and Brighton to join the Ohio R. between Rochester (E) and Beaver (W). The Connoquenessing Creek joins it from the E at Ellwood City.

Beaverton city, pop. 53,310, Washington Co., NW Oregon, a residential and industrial suburb 8 mi/13 km W of Portland. Founded in 1868, it was a shipping point on the Oregon Central Railroad, and has long been a trade and distribution center for the agricultural products of the Tualatin Valley. Now often called Silicon Forest, the city has grown rapidly and includes many research facilities and industries making high-tech items. Athletic shoes and other consumer goods are also manufactured in Beaverton. There are many vineyards and wineries in the immediate area.

Bécancour city, pop. 10,911, Nicolet Co., S Québec, across from TROIS-RIVIÈRES on the S bank of the St. Lawrence R., where the Bécancour R. joins it. Settled in 1702, and traditionally agricultural, Bécancour today has heavy industry, including a large aluminum plant. In 1965, eleven rural muncipalities merged to create the present city. The GENTILLY nuclear power plant is here.

Becket town, pop. 1481, Berkshire Co., SW Massachusetts, 12 mi/19 km SE of Pittsfield. It is in a summer resort area of the BERKSHIRE HILLS. Becket is home to the Jacob's Pillow Dance Festival (1941), established by Ted Shawn.

Beckley city, pop. 18,296, seat of Raleigh Co., S West Virginia. Settled in 1838 in a fertile valley 50 mi/80 km SE of Charleston, it expanded after 1890, when "smokeless"coal was first shipped, and grew rapidly when the Winding Gulf coalfield opened in 1907. The city is now a commercial center for the S West Virginia region. Industries produce mining machinery and electronic devices, processed foods, and lumber. Beckley College (1933) is here.

Beckwourth Pass railroad and highway passage (now traversed by Route 70) through the N Sierra Nevada at 5212 ft/1590 m, 25 mi/40 km NW of Reno, Nevada, in NE California. Along an important 1850s trail leading to the goldfields, it was named for Jim Beckwourth, the noted black mountaineer. The Diamond Mts. lie N, the Bald Mt. Range S.

Bedford **1.** city, pop. 13,817, seat of Lawrence Co., SC Indiana, 20 mi/32 km S of Bloomington. It is a major limestone quarrying and stone milling center. There are also industries manufacturing aluminum products, tools, refrigerators, and furniture. Nearby are a state fish hatchery, Bluespring Caverns (with a navigable underground river), and HOOSIER NATIONAL FOREST. **2.** town, pop. 12,996, Middlesex Co., NE Massachusetts, 14 mi/23 km NW of Boston. Developed around a 17th-century Indian trading post, it is a residential and industrial suburb lying just outside of ROUTE 128. Its economy is largely based on such industries as electronic and systems research and software production. A veterans' hospital and Middlesex Community College (1969) are in the town, as is a large part of Hanscom Air Force Base, which straddles the town's borders with Concord, Lincoln, and Lexington, in the S. **3.** town, pop. 12,563, Hillsborough Co., S New Hampshire. It is 3 mi/5 km SW of Manchester. Like neighboring Amherst (SW) settled 1733 as a grant to Narraganset War (1675) veterans, and primarily agricultural in its history, it is now an expanding Manchester suburb. **4.** town, pop. 16,906, Westchester Co., SE New York, 33 mi/53 km NNE of New York City. MOUNT KISCO, Bedford village, Bedford Center, Bedford Hills, and KATONAH are parts of this affluent exurban community. The estate of John Jay, the Caramoor Center (arts and music), and the Bedford Hills Correctional Facility (for women) are in the town. **5.** town, pop. 11,618, Halifax Co., S Nova Scotia, at the head (NW) of **Bedford Basin,** the inner section of Halifax Harbour. It is a rapidly growing suburb 6 mi/10 km NNW of downtown Halifax. A former base for Indians and European fishermen, later a paper milling center, it was a resort in the late 19th century, and is now chiefly a bedroom community. **6.** city, pop. 14,822, Cuyahoga Co., NE Ohio, 11 mi/18 km SE of Cleveland, of which it is a residential suburb. It was founded c.1813 on the site of an earlier (1786) Moravian settlement. The diverse items manufactured here include office furniture, rubber goods, machine tools, and aircraft parts. **7.** city, pop. 43,762, Tarrant Co., NE Texas, 12 mi/19 km NE of Fort Worth. A suburb in the Dallas–Fort Worth METROPLEX, it doubled in population in the 1980s. Dallas–Fort Worth International Airport is 5 mi/8 km NE.

Bedford Heights city, pop. 12,131, Cuyahoga Co., NE Ohio, a residential suburb 10 mi/16 km SE of Cleveland. The area was first settled in 1810.

Bedford-Stuyvesant section of N Brooklyn, New York, considered the second-largest US black community, after Chicago's SOUTH SIDE. The name was first used in the early 1930s to link Bedford, which lies in the N and W (bordering Clinton Hill, Williamsburg, and Bushwick), with Stuyvesant Heights (in the S and E, bordering Bushwick and Crown Heights). Bedford was at the time absorbing heavy black immigration, while Stuyvesant Heights remained a white enclave. Bedford had been a farming community in Dutch days, and had expanded NE as Brooklyn grew after the opening of the Brooklyn Bridge in 1883. Stuyvesant Heights developed as an upper-middle-class community in the 1890s. By the 1950s the combined neighborhood had become known as a ghetto, but in the 1960s restoration efforts began, bringing manufacturing and commercial establishments back into the area. Today, Bedford-Stuyvesant is largely a middle-class and working-class community, although there are pockets of serious poverty in slums in the NE. Churches, including Concord Baptist Church, with the largest US black congregation (12,000), are key to community cohesion.

Bedloe Island also, **Bedloe's Island** former name of LIBERTY I., in New York Harbor.

Bedminster township, pop. 7086, Somerset Co., NC New Jersey, 30 mi/48 km NW of Newark. A wealthy exurb until the 1960s, it is now the site of the junction of Interstates 287 and 78, and of AT&T corporate headquarters and other business development. The WATCHUNG Mts. are E.

Beecher Island battle site in the Arikaree R., Yuma Co., NE Colorado, 15 mi/24 km S of the city of Wray and 7 mi/11 km W of the Kansas border. In 1868 it was the scene of a punishing battle between Cheyenne, Arapahoe, and Sioux and US troops led by George A. Forsythe and Fred Beecher. Continuing for more than a week, it ended in Indian defeat, breaking the power of the Plains tribes. The island was obliterated when the course of the river changed in 1934.

Beechey Island see under DEVON I., Northwest Territories.

Beech Grove city, pop. 13,383, Marion Co., C Indiana, a suburb of Indianapolis, 8 mi/13 km SE of its center, on Route 465 (the city's beltway). It has railroad shops and industries producing electrical and machine tool parts, and is also residential.

Beeville city, pop. 13,547, seat of Bee Co., S Texas, 45 mi/72 km NNW of Corpus Christi. Settled in the 1830s, it was long a typical cow town, raising cotton and cattle. Today its main economic base is oil. Leather goods, meat, brooms, soft drinks, oilfield equipment, and roofing are produced. Bee County College (1965) is here. Chase Naval Air Station is just SE.

Bel Air **1.** residential section of LOS ANGELES, California, immediately W of BEVERLY HILLS, in the S foothills of the Santa Monica Mts., and 11 mi/18 km WNW of Downtown. Enormous, secluded villas, built from the 1920s, characterize one of the nation's wealthiest communities. BRENTWOOD is just S. **2.** town, pop. 8860, seat of Harford Co., Maryland, 25 mi/40 km NE of Baltimore. A market center, it was known, until chosen as the county seat in 1787, as Aquila Scott's Old Field. Harford Community College (1957) is here. The rich horse-raising area around the town is becoming heavily suburbanized, and now includes the unincorporated communities of **Bel Air North** (pop. 14,880) and **Bel Air South** (pop. 26,421).

Belau see Republic of PALAU.

Belcher Islands see under HUDSON BAY, Northwest Territories.

Belchertown town, pop. 10,579, Hampshire Co., C Massachusetts, 20 mi/32 km NE of Springfield. Located in an apple growing and dairy farming area W of QUABBIN RESERVOIR, Belchertown was home until 1992 to Belchertown State School, an institution for the retarded.

Belgrade Lakes chain of stream-linked lakes in SC Maine, 20 mi/32 km NW of Augusta, in NW Kennebec Co. They include Messalonskee L. (10 km/16 km long, 1 mi/2 km wide), Great Pond (6 mi/10 km long, 2–4 mi/3–6 km wide), Long Pond (7 mi/11 km long, 1 mi/2 km wide), and the smaller East, North, Ellis, and McGrath ponds.

Bell city, pop. 34,365, Los Angeles Co., SW California, 5 mi/8 km SE of Los Angeles. A predominantly Hispanic business and light manufacturing center on the Los Angeles R., just W of Bell Gardens, it experienced substantial residential growth in the 1980s.

Bellaire city, pop. 13,842, Harris Co., SE Texas. Completely surrounded by Houston's SW side, it is a residential suburb with several oil research company headquarters.

Bell Buckle town, pop. 326, Bedford Co., SC Tennessee, 17 mi/29 km S of Murfreesboro. Named for an enigmatic marking found on a tree by its 1853 settlers, it is known as the home of the Webb School, located here in 1870, one of the few nonmilitary prep schools in the South.

Bellefontaine city, pop. 12,142, seat of Logan Co., WC Ohio, 46 mi/74 km NW of Columbus. Settled in the early 19th century on the site of a Shawnee village, it was named for the many natural springs in the area. Today its chief manufactures include electric motors, circuit breakers, and aluminum extrusions. Set in a fertile area that raises wheat, soybeans, and livestock, Bellefontaine is a regional trade and rail center. The first concrete street in the US was laid here in 1891. CAMPBELL HILL is just E.

Bellefontaine Neighbors city, pop. 10,922, St. Louis Co., EC Missouri, a residential suburb adjacent (N) to St. Louis.

Belle Fourche city, pop. 4335, seat of Butte Co., SW South Dakota, 13 mi/21 km N of Spearfish, on the N edge of the Black Hills, and 10 mi/16 km E of the Wyoming border. Settled in 1878 at the confluence (the *belle fourche*) of Redwater Creek and the Belle Fourche R., it became the railhead and trade center for a three-state (including SE Montana) area producing cattle, sugar beets, wool, and bentonite. Its annual (July) Black Hills Roundup draws visitors.

Belle Fourche River 290 mi/467 km long, in Wyoming and South Dakota. It rises in Campbell Co., in NE Wyoming, and flows generally NE into Crook Co., through the Keyhole Reservoir and past DEVILS TOWER, before turning SE and entering South Dakota. There, it flows generally E past Belle Fourche and then through a sparsely populated region to the Cheyenne R. in Haakon Co. The **Belle Fourche Reservoir,** 10 mi/16 km long and 3 mi/5 wide, impounded by the Belle Fourche Dam (1911), is on Owl Creek, a tributary of the Belle Fourche that drains the N part of the BLACK HILLS and irrigates an area of 75,000 sq mi/194,250 sq km.

Belle Glade city, pop. 16,177, Palm Beach Co., SE Florida, 36 mi/58 km W of West Palm Beach and just SE of L. Okeechobee. Dating from the early 1920s, it was devastated by a hurricane in 1928, then rebuilt and incorporated that year. The hub of the largest US sugar cane–producing area, it is also a processing center for vegetables and cattle. Home to numerous migrant workers, many Caribbean, its work camps swell the population during sugar and harvesting season. There is also a state prison.

Belle Harbor see under the ROCKAWAYS, New York.

Belle Isle river island, 2 mi/3 km long and 1 mi/1.6 km wide, in Wayne Co., SE Michigan, in the Detroit R., between Detroit and Windsor, Ontario, connected to Detroit by bridge. One of the largest urban island parks in the US, it is a 1000-ac/405-ha recreational area.

Belle Isle, Strait of some 60 mi/100 km NE–SW and as little as 11 mi/17 km wide, at the NE entrance to the Gulf of St. Lawrence, between Newfoundland's GREAT NORTHERN PENINSULA (SE) and S Labrador (NW). Its strong currents include part of the southward Labrador Current, which brings icebergs S from the Labrador Sea. It takes its name from 10 mi/16 km–long Belle Isle, just NE.

Bellerive village, pop. 238, St. Louis Co., EC Missouri, 9 mi/14 km NW of downtown St. Louis. The University of Missouri at St. Louis campus, with more than 12,000 students, is here.

Bellerose residential section in extreme E Queens, New York. It is an essentially suburban middle-class community much like those just across the Nassau Co. line. New York State's huge (360 ac/146 ha) Creedmoor Psychiatric Center lies just W, between Bellerose and adjacent Queens Village.

Belleville **1.** city, pop. 42,785, seat of St. Clair Co., SW Illinois, 9 mi/15 km SE of East St. Louis. The center of a coal mining region, it manufactures beverages, stoves and heating equipment, stencil machines, beer, bricks, caskets, and clothing. Founded c.1810, it was an agricultural center until the discovery of coal in the area in 1828, which brought many German miners here. Scott Air Force Base is 6 mi/10 km to the E; the National Shrine of Our Lady of the Snows is 5 mi/8 km to the NE. **2.** township, pop. 34,213, Essex Co., NE New Jersey, on the Passaic R., 4 mi/6 km N of Newark. It was settled by the Dutch in the 17th century. A section of Newark called Second River in its early years, it became a separate municipality in 1839. Once a steam engine–building site, it now manufactures electrical equipment, tools, food products, fire extinguishers, and precision instruments. **3.** city, pop. 37,243, seat of Hastings Co., SE Ontario, on the Moira R. and the Bay of Quinte, off L. Ontario, 11 mi/18 km ENE of Trenton and 45 mi/72 km W of Kingston. On a site important to earlier fur traders, it was settled in the 1790s by LOYALISTS. The river and railroad (1850s) made it a major sawmill site to late in the 19th century. It has subsequently made cheese, whiskey, optical and electrical equipment, auto accessories, and a variety of other light manufactures. It is also a yachting port and vacation area gateway. Albert College (1857) is here.

Bellevue **1.** city, pop. 30,982, Sarpy Co., E Nebraska, on the Missouri R., 8 mi/13 km S of Omaha. The oldest municipality in Nebraska, it was established as a fur trading post about 1823, became the site of an 1840s Indian mission, and served as the territorial seat. The city grew rapidly from the 1960s to the 1980s because of OFFUTT AIR FORCE BASE, headquarters of the Strategic Air Command (SAC). Major military reductions in the 1990s have had a strong impact on the economy of the city, which is shifting to light industries. **2.** municipal hospital complex, between First Ave. and the East River, lower Midtown Manhattan, New York City. The successor to institutions dating to the 1730s, it is regarded as the oldest general hospital in North America. Bellevue was a pioneer in many areas, including ambulance service, scientific laboratories, and the training of nurses, and is now affiliated with New York University. Despite its many achievements, it is often popularly associated with stories of incarceration in its psychiatric wards. **3.** borough, pop. 9126, Allegheny Co., SW Pennsylvania, on the Ohio R. Founded in 1802, it is a residential suburb SW of Pittsburgh. **4.** city, pop. 86,874, King Co., WC Washington, on the E shore of L. WASHINGTON, across the lake and 6 mi/10 km E of Seattle. Settled in the 1880s, it has gradually changed from a bedroom community for Seattle to an urban center in its own right. The city has become an important center for high-tech products such as control systems and electrical and electronic components. Candy and prefabricated houses are manufactured here, too, while printing, binding, and engraving also contribute to the economy. Bellevue's development was stimulated by the opening of two floating bridges, the Lacey V. Murrow (1939) and the Evergreen Point (1963), both crossing L. Washington from Seattle. Evergreen Point, at 1.4 mi/2.3 km, is the longest such bridge in the world. Bellevue Community College (1966) is here.

Bellflower city, pop. 61,815, Los Angeles Co., SW California, 14 mi/23 km SE of Los Angeles, on the San Gabriel R. Founded in 1906 by Dutch settlers, it was long a truck farming community, and grew rapidly as a residential and retailing center in the 1950s. It now has a variety of aerospace, high-tech, and other light manufactures.

Bell Gardens unincorporated community, pop. 42,355, Los Angeles Co., SW California, 8 mi/13 km E of Los Angeles, of which it is a commuter suburb. At the confluence of the Los Angeles R. and the Rio Hondo Channel, it adjoins the cities of BELL (W) and DOWNEY (SE). Bell Gardens has experienced rapid population growth since World War II. Auto and aircraft parts and paints are manufactured.

Bellingham **1.** town, pop. 14,877, Norfolk Co., SE Massachusetts, at the Rhode Island border, 5 mi/8 km NE of Woonsocket. Founded in 1713, the traditionally agricultural town has since the 1970s experienced suburban development along Route 495, Boston's outer beltway. **2.** city, pop. 52,179, seat of Whatcom Co., NW Washington, on Bellingham Bay, 33 mi/53 km SE of Vancouver, British Columbia. It was settled in 1852, and was the site of an early lumber mill (1853–73). Coal mining was important here until 1951. With one of the largest natural harbors in the area, this port of entry is a shipping and processing center for lumber and wood products, paper and pulp, processed foods, and various agricultural products from the region. The city is also a major supply point for salmon canneries. It is the seat of Western Washington University (1893). Bellingham is a tourist center for the nearby SAN JUAN ISLANDS, the Chuckanut Mt. Trail, Mt. Baker–Snoqualmie National Forest (35 mi/56 km NE), and Lummi Island Indian Reservation (5 mi/8 km NW). The Alaska Marine Highway Ferry docks here.

Bell Island in CONCEPTION BAY, 12 mi/20 km W of St. John's, Newfoundland. Six mi/9 km NE–SW and up to 2.5 mi/4 km wide, it had an iron-ore mining industry centered around Wabana (pop. 3608), its largest town, from the 1890s until the mid 1960s. Mineshafts ran underwater from the island. In 1942, German submarines sank two ore boats here, in the first action of World War II in Newfoundland. Lance Cove, on the S, was the first settlement on the island.

Bellmawr borough, pop. 12,603, Camden Co., SW New Jersey, on Big Timber Creek, 5 mi/8 km S of Camden. A largely residential suburb, it was built on the site of the draft horse–breeding Bell Farm.

Bellmore unincorporated village, pop. 16,438, in Hempstead town, Nassau Co., SE New York, on the South Shore of Long Island, 25 mi/40 km SE of Manhattan. Situated on East Bay, it has some diversified light industry and businesses serving recreational boaters and fishermen, but is basically residential.

Bellows Falls village, pop. 3313, in Rockingham township, Windham Co., SE Vermont. It is on the Connecticut R. and Interstate 91, 18 mi/29 km NNE of Brattleboro. Built on terraces, the village is divided into three sections: an island, center of industry; a central commercial section; and an upper residential section. An important producer of paper from 1802, it has also been a railroad center; it ships dairy products and manufactures farm machines and wood products.

Bellwood village, pop. 20,241, Cook Co., NE Illinois, a residential suburb 12 mi/19 km W of Chicago. Originally an agricultural community founded toward the end of the 19th century, it now manufactures electrical components, ink, hardware, iron castings, and trucks. Since 1950 the community has experienced rapid residential growth.

Belmar borough, pop. 5877, Monmouth Co., EC New Jersey, 3 mi/5 km WSW of Asbury Park, between the Shark R. (W) and the Atlantic Ocean (E). A summering place for the Lenni Lenape and later the Dutch, it is now one of the Jersey Shore's leading resorts, with a summer population of c.50,000. South Belmar (borough, pop. 1482) and West Belmar (unincorporated, pop. 2519) are adjacent.

Belmont **1.** city, pop. 24,127, San Mateo Co., NC California, on the San Mateo Peninsula, in hills above San Francisco Bay (E), 19 mi/31 km SE of San Francisco. Founded in the 1850s, it developed as a residential suburb after 1950. Its industries make precision instruments, electrical and electronic components, and various other products. There are a number of mental and medical institutions. Ralston Hall, converted by William C. Ralston from a hillside villa to an 80-room Victorian mansion in 1866, is now the main building of the College of Notre Dame (1851; women). **2.** town, pop. 24,720, Middlesex Co., E Massachusetts. It is a largely residential suburb 7 mi/11 km NW of Boston, on high ground just W of Cambridge. McLean Hospital, a noted psychiatric institution, is in the town. **3.** hamlet in Mississippi Co., SE Missouri, on the Mississippi R. and the Kentucky line, 44 mi/71 km SE of Cape Girardeau, the scene of a Civil War battle (Nov. 1861) in which Confederate troops under Leonidas Polk repulsed an attacking force led by U.S. Grant, who was based in CAIRO, Illinois, 17 mi/27 km N. **4.** city, pop. 8434, Gaston Co., SW North Carolina, 10 mi/16 km W of Charlotte, on the Catawba R. Its manufactures include yarn, hosiery, and dyes. Belmont Abbey College (1876) is one of several Roman Catholic institutions in the city.

Belmont County 537 sq mi/1391 sq km, pop. 71,074, in E Ohio, bounded by the Ohio R. at the West Virginia line (E). Its seat is St. Clairsville. Bellaire, Bridgeport, and Martins Ferry are manufacturing centers. The rest of the county is largely rural, with coal mining, limestone quarrying, and diversified agriculture (dairy, fruit, grain, tobacco, and truck).

Belmont-Cragin also, **Cragin** residential neighborhood on the NW side of Chicago, Illinois, 6 mi/10 km WNW of the Loop. Part of the BUNGALOW BELT, it is a middle-class, largely Italian community, with many Irish residents also. It was one of the targets of 1960s open housing marches.

Belmont Park racetrack: see under ELMONT, New York.

Beloeil city, pop. 18,516, Verchères Co., S Québec, 15 mi/25 km E of Montréal, on the Richelieu R., founded in 1735 and now largely residential.

Beloit city, pop. 35,573, Rock Co., SE Wisconsin, on the Rock R. and the Illinois border, 65 mi/105 km SW of Milwaukee. In 1824 a post was established here for trade with the Winnebago. Settlers arrived from New England in 1837. Residents provided money, land, and labor for the establishment (1846) of Beloit College, now the oldest college in the state and an important factor in the city's economy. Today, Beloit's industries include the manufacture of papermaking and woodworking machinery, diesel engines, electric motors and generators, pumps, and tools. The city is also a commercial center for the fertile farming and dairying area that surrounds it.

Belton **1.** city, pop. 18,150, Cass Co., WC Missouri, 12 mi/19 km S of Kansas City and 4 mi/6 km E of the Kansas border. A residential suburb and agricultural trade center, it was the home for some years of temperance agitator Carry Nation (1846–1911). **2.** city, pop. 12,476, seat of Bell Co., C Texas, 9 mi/14 km W of Temple. Founded in 1850, it is historically a farm and ranch trade center. The city manufactures furniture, farm implements, and insulation materials. It is the seat of the University of Mary Hardin-Baylor, founded in 1845. **Belton L.**, a 12,300-ac/5000-ha recreational asset, is 3 mi/5 km N; FORT HOOD is NW.

Beltsville unincorporated village, pop. 14,476, Prince George's Co., C Maryland, 12 mi/19 km NE of Washington, D.C., just outside the BELTWAY. The primary research center of the US Department of Agriculture and the Patuxent Wildlife Research Center of the Department of the Interior are here.

beltway shortening of **belt highway** term for a limited-access road or combination of roads encircling an urban center, with the aim of reducing congestion inside by keeping through traffic outside. Previously, major highways like US 1 had passed through downtown areas. ROUTE 128, around Boston, was the first (planned 1948, completed in the 1950s) US example. Since the 1950s beltways have been built around many cities as parts of the Interstate Highway System.

Beltway, the also **Capital Beltway** highway, part I-495 and part I-95, that circles Washington, D.C., at an average radius of c.10 mi/16 km from the White House, in Maryland and Virginia. It has come to be regarded as symbolic of national government, which is said to view the nation and the world from a limited, "inside the Beltway" viewpoint. Besides all of the District of Columbia, areas inside the Beltway include ARLINGTON Co. and ALEXANDRIA, Virginia, and such other government-dominated localities as LANGLEY and MCLEAN, Virginia, and LANDOVER and BETHESDA, Maryland.

Belvedere Park unincorporated community, pop. 18,089, De

Kalb Co., NW Georgia, 8 mi/13 km E of downtown Atlanta, and just E of Decatur. It is a residential suburb.

Belvidere city, pop. 15,958, seat of Boone Co., NC Illinois, on the Kishwaukee R., 12 mi/19 km E of Rockford. It was settled in 1836 and soon became an important stop on the Chicago–Galena stagecoach route. It also served as an agricultural trading center and a shipping point for Chicago-bound milk and grain. The main contributor to the local economy is a large Chrysler auto assembly plant. The Pettit Chapel, designed (1907) by Frank Lloyd Wright, is in the Belvidere Cemetery.

Belvoir see under FORT BELVOIR, Virginia.

Belzoni city, pop. 2536, seat of Humphreys Co., EC Mississippi, in the S DELTA, just W of the Yazoo R. and 33 mi/53 km ESE of Greenville. Laid out in 1827, it was named for an Italian archaeologist who was a friend of its founder. A longtime cotton and lumber processor, it is now a leading US catfish farming center.

Bemidji city, pop. 11,245, seat of Beltrami Co., NW Minnesota, on the Mississippi R., where it flows through L. Bemidji, 140 mi/225 km NW of Duluth. Settled in 1866, it began as a trading post and became a major 1890s lumbering center. Today, the city is a trading center for the region's wood and dairy products. Manufactures include boats, pipes, and building materials. Tourists are attracted by nearby lakes and the Mississippi Headwaters, Buena Vista, Blackduck, and Paul Bunyan state forests. Bemidji State University (1919) is here.

Bemis Heights village in Stillwater township, Saratoga Co., E New York, on the W bank of the Hudson R., 11 mi/18 km SE of Saratoga Springs. It was the headquarters of American General Horatio Gates during the Saratoga Campaign; two decisive battles, resulting in American victories that proved the Revolutionary War's turning point, took place in and around the village in Sept. and Oct. 1777. They are commemorated by the Saratoga National Historical Park, 3 mi/5 km N.

Benbrook city, pop. 19,564, Tarrant Co., NE Texas, 10 mi/16 km SW of downtown Fort Worth, on Marys Creek and the Clear Fork of the Trinity R. It is a residential suburb on 3800-ac/1530-ha **Benbrook L.**, an important Fort Worth–area recreational asset.

Bend city, pop. 20,469, seat of Deschutes Co., C Oregon, on the Deschutes R., in the E foothills of the Cascade Mts., 88 mi/142 km E of Eugene. It was originally named Farewell Bend by pioneers who forded the river here. Lumbering and tourism are central to its economy. The city is the gateway to the Mount Bachelor ski resort, 22 mi/35 km to its W, and headquarters of the Deschutes National Forest. Central Oregon Community College is here. NEWBERRY CRATER is 25 mi/40 km S.

Benicia city, pop. 24,437, Solano Co., NC California, 24 mi/39 km ENE of San Francisco, on the N shore of Carquinez Strait, between Suisun and San Pablo bays. Founded in 1846, it was capital of California for 13 months in 1853–54; its old capitol is now an historical museum. Its industrial park, on the site of a major 1840s US arsenal, has housed an oil company, a wharf for oceangoing vessels, and the manufacture of dredges, steel plates, and machinery. The city now relies substantially on tourism, and has an arts community.

Benjamin Franklin Bridge suspension bridge over the Delaware R., with a central span of 1750 ft/534 m, between Camden, New Jersey, and Philadelphia, Pennsylvania. Completed in 1926, it links the two downtown areas.

Benjamin Franklin Parkway grand boulevard, 1 mi/1.6 km long, between FAIRMOUNT PARK and PENN CENTER in CENTER CITY, Philadelphia, Pennsylvania. Inspired by Paris's Champs-Elysées, it represents the ideals promoted by the turn-of-the-century City Beautiful movement. Decorated with trees, statues, and flags, it is lined with apartment buildings, hotels, and cultural institutions, all built under strict setback requirements. The boulevard passes through LOGAN CIRCLE.

Bennettsville city, pop. 9345, seat of Marlboro Co., NE South Carolina, 30 mi/48 km NNE of Florence and 9 mi/14 km SW of the North Carolina border. Laid out in 1818, the trade center of a fertile agricultural region, it now also manufactures textiles and wood products.

Bennington town, pop. 16,451, including Bennington village (pop. 9532), North Bennington, and Old Bennington, seat of Bennington Co., SW Vermont. It is on the Walloomsac R., 34 mi/55 km NE of Albany, New York. Local products include fruit, dairy, plastic and wood items, textiles, paper, clothing, ceramics, batteries, and mill machinery. The settlement was headquarters for the Green Mountain Boys, organized in 1770 under Ethan Allen. A marker in Old Bennington commemorates the site of Catamount Tavern, where the revolutionists met with Massachusetts and Connecticut agents to plan the capture of Fort Ticonderoga. In the 1777 Battle of Bennington, which took place just W, in Rensselaer Co., New York, General Burgoyne was defeated by militia under Colonel John Stark. Bennington College (1925) is in North Bennington. Southern Vermont College (1926) is SW of the town center.

Bennion see TAYLORSVILLE-BENNION, Utah.

Bensenville village, pop. 17,767, Cook and Du Page counties, NE Illinois, 18 mi/29 km NW of Chicago. Settled by German immigrants in the 19th century, it contains a mix of residential and manufacturing areas. Situated here are railroad shops, factories producing apparel and fluid control machinery, and distribution facilities. O'Hare International Airport lies immediately N.

Benson city, pop. 3824, Cochise Co., SE Arizona, 40 mi/64 km SE of Tucson. On Interstate 10, and originally a stage stop, it developed after the 1880 arrival of the railroad. Local industries include livestock and poultry raising, dairying, and explosives manufacture. Copper mines in the DRAGOON Mts. (SE) provide some employment.

Bensonhurst largely residential section of SW Brooklyn, New York. Bath Beach lies between it and Lower New York Bay. Bay Ridge is to the W, and Borough Park to the N. The area is named for a mid-19th-century farm family. In the 1870s Bensonhurst was promoted as an alternative to Coney Island; in the 1890s a middle-class residential district developed. The opening of rapid-transit service in 1915 brought Jewish and Italian families from lower Manhattan. Bensonhurst today remains a largely Italian lower-middle-class neighborhood. Commercial activity rivals that in Manhattan's Little Italy, with which there remain strong ties, as there are with Italy itself. Bensonhurst was the setting for the 1950s television series *The Honeymooners*.

Benton city, pop. 18,177, seat of Saline Co., C Arkansas, 20 mi/32 km SW of Little Rock, near the Saline R. Originally settled in 1815 on the Missouri–Texas Military Road (present-day

Interstate 30), the city was involved in salt mining, pottery making, and logging. Light industry since World War II has included aluminum production based on local bauxite (the richest US deposits).

Benton Harbor city, pop. 12,818, Berrien Co., SW Michigan, on L. Michigan at the mouth of the St. Joseph R., opposite St. Joseph and 46 mi/74 km SW of Kalamazoo. A market and shipping center for a rich fruit growing area, it packs and cans produce. The headquarters of the Whirlpool Corporation is in the city, which also manufactures boats, wood and paper products, hardware, furniture, and welding equipment. It has long been the hub of a tourist region that features abundant beaches and mineral springs. The city is the seat of Lake Michigan College (1946).

Bentonville **1.** city, pop. 11,257, seat of Benton Co., extreme NW Arkansas, 22 mi/35 km N of Fayetteville, in the Ozark Plateau. It was established in 1837 and named for Missouri Senator Thomas Hart Benton (1782–1858). It gained an economic rival in 1881 with the founding of ROGERS, just SE. It cans fruits and vegetables, mills lumber, and is a distribution center for dairy products, grapes, apples, berries, and poultry. Sam Walton, founder of the Wal-Mart drug and discount chain, was born here (1918). **2.** hamlet in Johnston Co., C North Carolina, 17 mi/27 km WSW of Goldsboro. A monument here commemorates the largest Civil War battle in North Carolina, on March 19, 1865. Three days after AVERASBORO, W. T. Sherman's Union forces defeated Joseph Johnston's Army of Tennessee, on Sherman's march N from Savannah.

Bent's Fort historic site on the Arkansas R., 8 mi/13 km NE of LA JUNTA, in EC Colorado. A fortified trading post established here in 1833 by Charles and William Bent and Ceran St. Vrain became the most important stop on the SANTA FE TRAIL between Independence, Missouri (E), and Santa Fe, New Mexico (SW). Its role diminished by the late 1840s. Today, as the **Bent's Old Fort National Historical Site** (William Bent in 1853 built a second fort along the river, since disappeared), it is a tourist attraction based on a 1960 reconstruction.

Berea **1.** city, pop. 9126, Madison Co., C Kentucky, in the Cumberland Mts., 36 mi/58 km SSE of Lexington. It was built around Berea College (1855), founded by leaders of the Southern antislavery movement, and was the first integrated college in the region. The college and city are noted as a center of folk arts and crafts, especially handweaving. **2.** city, pop. 19,051, Cuyahoga Co., NE Ohio, 15 mi/24 km SW of Cleveland. Founded in 1809, it was famous for its sandstone quarries, which once produced most of the grindstones in the US, but were depleted in the 1930s. Metal, plastic, and paper products are manufactured. The city is also a commuter suburb, and a packing and shipping center for vegetables. Berea is the site of Baldwin-Wallace College (1845). **3.** unincorporated community, pop. 13,535, Greenville Co., NW South Carolina, 5 mi/8 km NW of downtown GREENVILLE, of which it is a residential suburb.

Bergen see under JERSEY CITY, New Jersey.

Bergen Beach see under FLATLANDS, New York.

Bergen County 237 sq mi/614 sq km, pop. 825,380, in extreme NE New Jersey, on the Hudson R. (E) and the New York border (N). Its seat is Hackensack. Largely residential, it contains the homes of many commuters to the New York City-N New Jersey area; such suburban municipalities as Paramus, Teaneck, and Englewood are here. The county also has numerous light industries and corporate office facilities.

Bergenfield borough, pop. 24,458, Bergen Co., NE New Jersey, adjacent (N) to Teaneck. Primarily a residential suburb, it also has industries making machinery and medical instruments and various business office facilities.

Bergstrom Air Force Base see under AUSTIN, Texas.

Bering Sea section of the Pacific Ocean N of the Aleutian Is., between Siberia and Alaska. Some 880,000 sq mi/2.28 million sq km, it connects with the Chukchi Sea (N) via the **Bering Strait,** 54 mi/87 km E–W, between the Chukchi Peninsula of Siberia and the SEWARD PENINSULA of Alaska. Norton Sound, Kuskokwim Bay, and Bristol Bay are Alaskan inlets; the huge YUKON R. delta empties into the sea. Alaskan ports include NOME and BETHEL. The PRIBILOF Is. contain the most extensive northern fur seal breeding grounds in the world. Vitus Bering's explorations of the sea for Russia in 1728 and 1741 revealed the density of the fur seal and sea otter populations, paving the way for Russian traders who were to lay claim to Alaska and the Aleutian Is. Following its purchase of Alaska in 1867, the US maintained a seal hunting monopoly throughout the area, leading to a controversy of 1886, in which Great Britain challenged US control of open-sea (pelagic) sealing. In 1893 it was decided that the US could not prevent pelagic hunting by other countries, and a 1911 treaty signed by the US, Great Britain, Japan, and Russia prohibited pelagic sealing in the area altogether. More than 30,000 years ago, in glacial times, Alaska and Siberia were connected by a land bridge where the Bering Strait is now; the ancestors of American Indians are believed to have migrated to the Western Hemisphere over it.

Berkeley **1.** city, pop. 102,724, Alameda Co., NC California, on the NE shore of San Francisco Bay, adjacent (N) to Oakland and 8 mi/13 km E of San Francisco. On part of an 1820 Spanish RANCHO occupied by American squatters during the 1850s gold rush, it was selected as a home for what became in 1868 the University of California. Its 1232-ac/499-ha campus is the focus of much of the city's life, and parts of it are world-famous. The Lawrence Berkeley (Lawrence Radiation) Laboratory gave birth to the cyclotron in the 1930s. In the 1960s and 1970s, civil rights, antiwar, and counterculture activities characterized Sproul Plaza (hub of the 1964 Free Speech Movement), which is flanked by the 1909 Sather Gate. The 307-ft/94-m Sproul Tower ("the Campanile") dominates the campus. Off campus, Telegraph Ave. and nearby People's Park have also been hotbeds of political activity. Berkeley's population grew quickly with refugees after the 1906 San Francisco earthquake, and with the 1930s opening of bridges to San Francisco. The city's industries, largely along the waterfront, include book and software publishing and the manufacture of pharmaceuticals, printing inks, soap, toiletries, bakery products, and structural aluminum. Divinity and other schools, tourism, and boating and fishing are all important to the economy. **2.** city, pop. 12,450, St. Louis Co., EC Missouri, 12 mi/19 km NW of St. Louis. An industrial and residential suburb of St. Louis, it manufactures aircraft and truck and automobile parts. The country's first international aviation meet was held here (1910). The Lambert–St. Louis International Airport is just W. **3.** plantation in Charles City Co., SE Virginia, on the N bank of the James R., 7 mi/11 km ENE of

Hopewell. Built in 1726, it is the birthplace of Benjamin Harrison, a signer of the Declaration of Independence, and of his son William Henry Harrison. The first American Thanksgiving had been celebrated on the site in 1619. In 1862 the Union army wintered here; one of the soldiers composed "Taps" during the encampment.

Berkeley Heights township, pop. 11,980, Union Co., NE New Jersey, on the Passaic R., in the WATCHUNG Mts., 14 mi/23 km W of Newark. A middle-class suburban residential community, it has some light industry and a number of office buildings.

Berkeley Springs officially, town of **Bath,** pop. 735, seat of Morgan Co., in the Eastern Panhandle of West Virginia, on Warm Springs Run, near the Potomac R., and 18 mi/29 km NW of Martinsburg. It has been a health resort since before Europeans came. During the Revolution, Virginia soldiers bathed their wounds in its warm mineral waters. George Washington and his family came here, and in the 19th century the spa, with a large hotel, was an important social center. The site of Berkeley Springs State Park, the town also has sandpits and canning and bottling plants.

Berkley city, pop. 16,960, Oakland Co., SE Michigan, 10 mi/16 km NW of Detroit, a residential suburb of Detroit.

Berks County 861 sq mi/2230 sq km, pop. 336,523, in SE Pennsylvania, in the Piedmont Plateau. Its seat is READING. First settled by Swedish immigrants, it is now an agricultural and industrial area, with manufacturing centered around the city of Reading. In the fertile Pennsylvania Dutch region, the county is one of Pennsylvania's most important farming centers.

Berkshire County 929 sq mi/2406 sq km, pop. 139,352, in extreme W Massachusetts. Its seat is Pittsfield. Taking in most of the BERKSHIRE HILLS, it is a resort area. Mt. GREYLOCK (3491 ft/1065 m) is the highest point in Massachusetts. The county has many popular attractions, including the Tanglewood Music Festival at Lenox and Jacob's Pillow Dance Festival at Becket. Industry is concentrated chiefly at PITTSFIELD and NORTH ADAMS. The Hoosic, Williams, Housatonic, and numerous smaller rivers drain the area.

Berkshire Hills also, **Berkshires** highland region in W Massachusetts, from the Vermont (N) to the Connecticut (S) border. Actually an eroded peneplain, the Berkshires are experienced as hills by residents and travelers in their valleys. They are geologically related to the GREEN and TACONIC mountains, and are considered to include the HOOSAC RANGE as well as Connecticut's Litchfield Hills. Mount Greylock (3491 ft/1065 m) is the highest point. The Housatonic R., HOOSAC TUNNEL, the Massachusetts Turnpike, and MOHAWK TRAIL (Route 2) go through the Berkshires. Originally agricultural, the area is now known for resorts including Lenox, Stockbridge, and Tanglewood. Pittsfield, North Adams, and Great Barrington are among the larger centers.

Berlin **1.** town, pop. 16,787, Hartford Co., NC Connecticut, 11 mi/18 km SSW of Hartford. It is an industrial suburb, producing tools, metal products, and lacquers. It was in Berlin that tinware was first made in America, in 1740. The Berlin Turnpike (Route 15) connects the cities of Meriden and Hartford. **2.** and **Berlin Ichthyosaur State Park** see under SHOSHONE Mts., Nevada. **3.** city, pop. 11,824, Coos Co., N New Hampshire. On the N edge of the White Mts., 10 mi/16 km SE of Milan Hill State Park and 5 mi/8 km NE of Moosebrook State Park, it has one of America's highest (181.5 ft/55 m) steel-tower ski jumps. The city is located at falls of the Androscoggin R., which power pulp and paper mills, the main industry. **4.** see under KITCHENER, Ontario.

Bermuda Hundred battle site in Chesterfield Co., SE Virginia, at the confluence of the James and Appomattox rivers, 15 mi/24 km SE of Richmond, and just N of Hopewell. A neck of land settled by Jamestown colonists in 1613, it was in May 1864 the site of an abortive assault by Union forces under Benjamin Butler, who were trying to cut supply lines to Richmond, but who were frustrated by P.G.T. Beauregard's troops.

Bermuda Triangle also, **Devil's Triangle** roughly triangular area of the Atlantic Ocean with South Florida (W), the British colony of Bermuda (NE), and Puerto Rico (SE) as its corners, in which a large number of ships and aircraft have disappeared under peculiar circumstances, as when the weather was apparently good, or no distress signal was received, or no trace of wreckage was found. On occasion, rescue missions have vanished as well. Although the area has unpredictable weather patterns and violent storms, some have attributed these disappearances to such agents as UFOs, underwater volcanoes, or force fields from the legendary Atlantis.

Bernalillo County 1169 sq mi/3028 sq km, pop. 480,577, in NC New Mexico. ALBUQUERQUE is its seat. The county is drained by the Rio Grande. Its S section is a Pueblo Indian area, while its E portion has part of Cibola National Forest, the Manzano Mts., and the Sandia Mts. Livestock grazing, farming, coal mining, and tourism are its main industries.

Bernardsville borough, pop. 6597, Somerset Co., NC New Jersey, 7 mi/11 km SW of Morristown. Settled in the early 18th century, it was known as Vealtown until 1840. Today Bernardsville is an affluent suburb in the New York City metropolitan area, with a variety of luxurious homes, estates, and private clubs. It also has a crushed-stone plant. The Scherman-Hoffman Wildlife Sanctuary, a birdwatching mecca, is here.

Berrien County 576 sq mi/1492 sq km, pop. 161,378, in extreme SW Michigan, bounded by L. Michigan (W) and Indiana (S), and drained by the Paw Paw, St. Joseph, and Galien rivers. Its seat is St. Joseph. In addition to commercial fishing and manufacturing at St. Joseph, Niles, and Benton Harbor, the county produces fruit, grain, vegetables, and dairy products, and raises livestock. It has several state parks and is the site of the Donald C. Cook nuclear power plant (1975), near Rosemary Beach. There are a number of health and lake resorts.

Berrien Springs village, pop. 1927, Berrien Co., SW Michigan, on the St. Joseph R., 47 mi/76 km SW of Kalamazoo. Founded in 1830, it is situated in a fruit growing, winemaking, and dairying area. Baskets, brooms, auto parts, and tools are manufactured. There are medicinal springs and attendant resorts in the city and region. Berrien Springs is home to Andrews University (1874) and Emmanuel Missionary College.

Berryessa, Lake in Napa Co., NC California, created by the construction (1957) of the Monticello Dam on Putah Creek. About 40 mi/64 km W of Sacramento and 25 mi/40 km NE of Santa Rosa, and 13 mi/21 km NW–SE, it is ringed by resorts and oak-covered foothills. The area was once the land grant of a Spanish family named Berryessa.

Berwick borough, pop. 10,976, Columbia Co., EC Pennsylvania, on the Susquehanna R., 15 mi/24 km NW of Hazleton. In a farming region, it was founded in 1786 as a Quaker refuge, but developed as an industrial center, now producing heavy equipment, clothing, metal parts, mobile homes, and other goods. The Susquehanna Nuclear Plant (1982; 1984) is just E in Luzerne Co.; adjacent to it is the 1400-ac/567-ha Riverlands recreation area.

Berwyn city, pop. 45,426, Cook Co., NE Illinois, a suburb 10 mi/16 km W of Chicago. It was planned as a residential community in 1891, and was among the earliest such ventures among railroad suburbs.

Bessemer city, pop. 33,497, Jefferson Co., NC Alabama, 10 mi/16 km SW of Birmingham, on a branch of the Black Warrior R. Founded as a steel center in 1887, it now also manufactures railroad cars, building materials, pipe, chemicals, and explosives. The city and its dominant company were named for Sir Henry Bessemer, developer of the mass steel-production process.

Bethany **1.** city, pop. 20,075, Oklahoma Co., C Oklahoma, 7 mi/11 km W of downtown Oklahoma City. Settled (1906) by Nazarene church members, it is the site of two church-affiliated colleges. A residential suburb enclosed by the larger city, it also has a variety of light industries. **2.** town, pop. 1139, Brooke Co., in West Virginia's Northern Panhandle, just NE of WEST LIBERTY and 12 mi/19 km NE of Wheeling. It is the seat of Bethany College (1840).

Bethany Beach town, pop. 326, Sussex Co., SE Delaware, on the Atlantic coast, 7 mi/11 km N of Ocean City, Maryland. Founded in 1901 as a camp meeting site, it is still church oriented. Tourism and commercial fishing are the main industries.

Bethel **1.** locality in CANAAN where Abraham built his first altar, having been promised the land by God (Genesis 12). In America, the name of numerous Protestant churches and, by extension, localities, villages, or towns, especially in New England. **2.** city, pop. 4674, in the Bethel Census Area (pop. 13,656), SW Alaska, at the mouth of the Kuskokwim R. on Kuskokwim Bay, 400 mi/644 km W of Anchorage. It is a center for fishing, trapping, and hunting, and was long a supply point for prospectors. Flooding and erosion are problematic on the low, marshy river, esp. at ice breakup in the spring. Originally an Inuit village, Bethel is the site of a Moravian mission founded in 1885. **3.** town, pop. 17,541, Fairfield Co., SW Connecticut, 5 mi/8 km SE of Danbury. Founded in 1700, it is a suburb of Danbury, with some light manufacturing, including the production of chemicals. In recent years there has also been an increase in corporate headquarters development. Bethel was once, like Danbury, a hatmaking center. **4.** town, pop. 117, Shelby Co., NE Missouri, on the North R., 35 mi/56 km SE of Kirksville. In an agricultural region, it was founded as a religious commune in 1844 by Germans from Pennsylvania and Ohio led by Wilhelm Keil. The colony was extant until 1879; over 30 of the original buildings remain. **5.** town, pop. 3693, Sullivan Co., SE New York, 8 mi/13 km WNW of Monticello. Once a Catskill Mt. resort, it is agricultural. This was the actual site of the 1969 Woodstock concert; when local restrictions in Woodstock, 45 mi/72 km to the NE, prevented performance there, promoters rented the Max Yasgur farm in Bethel.

Bethel Park borough, pop. 33,823, Allegheny Co., SW Pennsylvania, 9 mi/13 km S of downtown Pittsburgh. It is a residential suburb.

Bethesda unincorporated community, pop. 62,936, Montgomery Co., C Maryland, 7 mi/11 km NW of Washington, D.C. It is primarily an affluent residential suburb. The community takes its name from a Presbyterian church built in 1820. From 1935, Bethesda has developed as a major research center, home to the National Cancer Institute, the NATIONAL INSTITUTES OF HEALTH (1939), the National Naval Medical Center (1942), and the National Library of Medicine (1963). Private research institutes augment those sponsored by the US government.

Bethlehem city, pop. 71,428, in Northampton and Lehigh counties, E Pennsylvania, on the Lehigh R., 46 mi/74 km NNW of Philadelphia. With Allentown and Easton, it forms an industrial triangle; Bethlehem Steel has its main plant here, producing iron, steel, coke, and coke byproducts. Other manufactures include chemicals, machine parts, food products, cement, electrical equipment, metal goods, and pharmaceuticals. Bethlehem was founded in 1741 by a group of Moravian Brethren, whose traditions are reflected in a number of early stone buildings, the Moravian Cemetery, a restored 18th-century industrial area, and the city's annual Christmas observances. During the Revolution, Bethlehem provided hospital services for Continental soldiers. It grew as a steel town after the construction of the Lehigh Canal (1829). The city is home to the Bach Choir (1898), which offers a noted annual Bach Festival. Lehigh University (1865), Moravian College (1742), and Northampton Community College (1966) are here.

Bethpage unincorporated village, pop. 15,761, in Oyster Bay town, Nassau Co., SE New York. Largely residential, it is home to Grumman, a major defense contractor, and Grumman Bethpage Airfield. Adjacent (NE) is the village of Old Bethpage (pop. 5610), noted for Old Bethpage Village, a re-creation of an 1850s farming community.

Bettendorf city, pop. 28,132, Scott Co., SE Iowa, on the Mississippi R., immediately E of Davenport, across from Moline and East Moline, Illinois. It is one of the QUAD CITIES. Settled as Lilienthal in the 1840s, it was renamed for an industrialist who set up his railroad car and furniture plant here in 1902. Besides having one of the world's largest sheet aluminum plants, Bettendorf also manufactures oil burners, foundry products, machine tools, farm machinery, and dairy products.

Beulah city, pop. 3363, Mercer Co., WC North Dakota, on the Knife R., 60 mi/97 km NW of Bismarck. The main city of North Dakota's coal country, it is the home of the nation's first coal gasification plant, situated just N of the city, which converts locally mined lignite to gas. Beulah trades in the region's wheat, corn, poultry, and livestock, and produces dairy goods.

B. Everett Jordan Dam and Lake see under HAW R., North Carolina.

Beverly city, pop. 38,195, a resort, commercial, and manufacturing center in Essex Co., NE Massachusetts, across the Danvers R. from Salem, 18 mi/29 km NE of Boston. Once a thriving seafaring center, Beverly has one of the nation's largest shoe machinery factories, and is also an electronics center. New England's first successful cotton mill (1798) was built here. Endicott College for Women (1939) and North Shore Community College (1965) are in the town. Beverly numbers among its villages the summer and estate communities of Beverly Farms and Prides Crossing.

Beverly-Fairfax see under FAIRFAX DISTRICT, Los Angeles, California.

Beverly Hills **1.** city, pop. 31,971, Los Angeles Co., SW California, 10 mi/16 km NW of downtown Los Angeles, and extending up the slopes of the Santa Monica Mts. (N). It is entirely surrounded by Los Angeles. Once a Spanish land grant known as El Rancho Rodeo de las Aguas, it today has luxurious homes and shops lining its curving streets and canyons. In 1919, Douglas Fairbanks and Mary Pickford built their mansion Pickfair here, leading a wave of entertainment celebrities who made Beverly Hills famous. The city is a tourist attraction, with maps sold showing the location of movie stars' homes. There is some light manufacturing, chiefly of electronic equipment, and a number of corporate and financial offices. Rodeo Drive, N of Wilshire Blvd., is one of the most expensive and famous shopping streets. **2.** residential neighborhood on the SW side of Chicago, Illinois, immediately N of Blue Island and Calumet Park. Along with the adjoining community of Morgan Park, it is one of the wealthiest and most prestigious areas in Chicago. Its location on the highest point in Cook Co. allowed its late-19th-century developer free rein with such suburban innovations as the curvilinear street plan and large lot sizes. An affluent bedroom community until annexation in 1889, it is now mainly Irish Catholic, with some black residents. **3.** village, pop. 10,610, Oakland Co., SE Michigan, a residential suburb 12 mi/19 km NW of Detroit. New York and New England settlers first farmed the area c.1830, but agriculture has gradually disappeared since World War II. Incorporated as Westwood Village in 1958, it was renamed the following year.

Beverwyck see under ALBANY, New York.

Bexar County 1248 sq mi/3232 sq km, pop. 1,185,394, in SC Texas. Its seat is SAN ANTONIO. It is crossed by the BALCONES ESCARPMENT, which forms hills in the NW. The rest is prairie. Drained by the San Antonio and Medina rivers, the area has long grown peanuts, vegetables, grains, sorghum, corn, and potatoes, produced wool and mohair, and raised bees, poultry, and beef and dairy cattle. It is, however, increasingly urban, and has major military bases. There are deposits of oil, natural gas, limestone, clay, and gravel.

Bexley city, pop. 13,088, Franklin Co., C Ohio. Although surrounded by the E side of COLUMBUS, this residential suburb functions as a politically independent entity. Bexley is the home of Capital University (1830). A monument here commemorates the site of the Spanish-American War's Camp Bushnell.

Bible Belt term coined in 1925 by H. L. Mencken for parts of the US in which fundamentalist Christianity dominates local culture and politics. Mencken, who was reporting on the trial of John T. Scopes for teaching evolutionary theory in DAYTON, Tennessee, regarded the rural and small-town South as the Bible Belt, and once called Jackson, Mississippi, its "buckle." Later observers have expanded it to include parts of the Middle West and Southwest.

Biddeford city, pop. 20,710, York Co., SW Maine, at the falls of the Saco R., opposite Saco, 5 mi/8 km from the Atlantic Ocean, 16 mi/26 km SW of Portland. The Saco R. powers lumber and textile mills; other industries make footwear, machines, tools, and lumber products. The University of New England (1939) is in Biddeford. **Biddeford Pool,** a noted 19th-century summer resort, comprises a peninsula and enclosed cove just S of the Saco's mouth.

Big Allis see under LONG ISLAND CITY, New York.

Big Apple, the popular nickname for New York City, originating among jazz musicians, but quasi-official by the 1970s, when publicists used an apple as a symbol for the city. Also, "the Apple."

Big Bald see under BALD Mts., North Carolina.

Big Baldy see under LITTLE BELT Mts., Montana.

Big Bear Lake reservoir (created 1911 on the site of an earlier lake) in the San Bernardino Mts., S California, 80 mi/130 km ENE of Los Angeles, a popular winter and summer sports center. It is 7 mi/11 km long, and lies at an altitude of 6750 ft/2060 m. **Big Bear Lake** (city, pop. 5351, San Bernardino Co.) lies on the S shore; **Big Bear City** (unincorporated, pop. 4920) lies E.

Big Bend **1.** desert region in Brewster Co., SW Texas, 250 mi/400 km SE of El Paso, on a bend in the RIO GRANDE, across from Coahuila (SE) and Chihuahua (SW) states, Mexico. This remote area, with almost no habitation, is now the site of **Big Bend National Park** (803,000 ac/325,000 ha), known especially for its deep canyons. Most of the park is Chihuahuan desert; there are also the SIERRA DEL CARMEN and CHISOS mountains. The Chisos are wooded, and the desert is arid but rich in plants and wildlife. Recreational activities have been compromised in recent years by drug smugglers using the wilderness as an entry into the US. **2.** region in EC Washington, within the Columbia R. where the river swings W around the COLUMBIA PLATEAU. An area of some 12,000 sq mi/31,000 sq km, rugged, dry, and largely treeless, it is the site of the GRAND COULEE DAM and MOSES LAKE. **3.** village, pop. 1299, Waukesha Co., SE Wisconsin, 20 mi/32 km SW of Milwaukee, of which it is an outer suburb, in a lake-filled agricultural area.

Big Bend Tunnel built in 1872–73 by the Chesapeake and Ohio Railroad, through Big Bend Mt., in Summers Co., SE West Virginia, 24 mi/39 km ESE of Beckley, near Talcott. It was here that the legendary black steeldriver John Henry won a contest with a new steam drill, and died in his triumph. The John Henry statue stands near the entrance to the 6500-ft/2000-m tunnel. A second tube was opened in 1934.

Big Black Mountain see BLACK Mt., Kentucky.

Big Black River 330 mi/530 km long, in Mississippi. Rising in Webster Co., N of Mathiston, it flows SW across the Gulf Coastal Plain to the Mississippi R., just N of GRAND GULF and 17 mi/27 km SW of Vicksburg.

Big Blue River **1.** stream that flows NNE from just SW of KANSAS CITY, Missouri, through the city, entering the Missouri R. just NE, in INDEPENDENCE. Most of its route is parkland, paralleled by parkways. Part of the battle of WESTPORT was fought along it in Oct. 1864. The river winds from the city's more suburban SW through SWOPE PARK, then through the NE. Brush Creek, which rises in Kansas City, Kansas, and joins it from the W, is also lined by park. The **Little Blue R.** roughly parallels the Big Blue, some 5 mi/8 km E; it is dammed in GRANDVIEW (S) to form the Longview Reservoir, passes through the far SE corner of Kansas City, and continues into Independence. **2.** 250 mi/400 km long, in SE Nebraska and NE Kansas. It rises E of Grand Island and just E of the Platte R., and flows ENE, then SE, joined S of Milford by a West Fork, past BEATRICE, and into Kansas, where it flows through dam-created Tuttle Creek L. before entering the Kansas R. E of MANHATTAN. It receives the **Little Blue R.** (206 mi/330 km long) near Blue Rapids, Kansas, N of the lake. The Little Blue rises SW of Hastings, Nebraska, and follows a generally SW course into Kansas.

Big Bone Lick see under BOONE Co., Kentucky.

Big Cypress Seminole Indian Reservation see under BROWARD Co., Florida.

Big Fork River 160 mi/258 km long, in N Minnesota. It is formed by the confluence of several rivers in Itasca Co., at the N edge of the Chippewa National Forest, and flows generally N past Big Falls to join the Rainy R. at the Ontario border, 16 mi/26 km WSW of International Falls. From its source to its mouth the river's banks are lined with pine, spruce, and fragrant balsam. On the upper reaches are fields of wild rice. A wild river enjoyed by canoeists, it was a major water route for Indians and later fur traders.

Big Hole National Battlefield 656 ac/266 ha, in Beaverhead Co., SW Montana, in the BITTERROOT RANGE, 60 mi/97 km SW of Butte, near the headwaters of the Big Hole R. Established in 1910, it commemorates the battle of August 9–10, 1877 in which troops under John Gibbon fought a band of Nez Perce led by Chief Joseph, who had arrived here after refusing to be confined to a reservation in Idaho. After both sides had sustained heavy losses, the Nez Perce fled E, but were forced to surrender in the Bear Paw Mts. two months later (see NEZ PERCE TRAIL).

Big Hole River 140 mi/225 km long, in SW Montana. It rises in several branches in the Beaverhead National Forest in the BITTERROOT RANGE, just E of the Idaho border, and flows N to Deer Lodge Co. There it veers SE, passes Melrose and Glen, then turns NE and joins the Jefferson R., just N of Twin Bridges.

Bighorn Mountains also, **Big Horn** range of the Middle ROCKY Mts., in S Montana and NW Wyoming. Trending generally N–S, it extends some 120 mi/190 km in an arc around the E of the Bighorn Basin. Its streams feed into the Bighorn R., which flows along its W, and into the Powder R., along its E. Cloud Peak (13,175 ft/4016 m), in Wyoming, is its high point. In the N it ends within the CROW INDIAN RESERVATION.

Bighorn National Forest 1.1 million ac/0.45 million ha, in Bighorn and Sheridan counties, NC Wyoming, bordering Montana (N). The area includes Cloud (the forest's and the Bighorn Mountains' tallest, at 13,165 ft/4015 m), Mather (12,410 ft/3785 m), and Hazelton (10,545 ft/3216 m) peaks. Within the forest is the 189,000-ac/76,545-ha Cloud Peak Wilderness Area, with more than 200 lakes. Also here are the prehistoric Medicine Wheel, on Medicine Mt., thought to have had religious and astronomical significance; the scenic Shell Canyon and Falls; Powder River Pass; Ten Sleep Canyon; and the virtually undisturbed wilderness area around the Bighorn Mts.

Bighorn River 340 mi/550 km long, in N Wyoming and S Montana. A continuation of the WIND R. N of the Wind River Canyon and the Owl Creek Mts., in WC Wyoming, it flows N, on the W of the Bighorn Mts., into Montana. The Yellowtail Dam (1968; 525 ft/160 m high), near Fort Smith, in Montana's CROW INDIAN RESERVATION, has formed 71 mi/114 km–long **Bighorn L.** (or Yellowtail Reservoir), which backs into Wyoming. Surrounding the lake is the **Bighorn Canyon National Recreation Area,** noted for spectacular limestone walls largely viewable only by boat. Below (N of) the dam, the Bighorn is now a popular trout fishing area. The LITTLE BIGHORN R. joins it from the SE, at the reservation's N boundary. The Shoshone R. joins it in Wyoming, entering Bighorn L. from the SW.

Big Island popular name for the island of HAWAII.

Big Mound battle site in Kidder Co., SC North Dakota, 60 mi/97 km ENE of Bismarck. A July 1863 battle here between the Sioux and US troops under Henry Sibley ended in the defeat and retreat of the Indians.

Big Muddy **1.** nickname for the MISSOURI R., which transports huge amounts of Great Plains sediment, and whose brown waters mix fully with those of the bluer, clearer Mississippi only some 100 mi/160 km downstream from their junction. **2. Big Muddy Creek** 190 mi/310 km long, in Saskatchewan and Montana, one of the Missouri's northernmost tributaries, which joins it W of Culbertson, Montana, after flowing S along the E edge of the Fort Peck Indian Reservation. **3. Big Muddy River** 135 mi/220 km long, in S Illinois, flowing generally SSW from Jefferson Co. into the Mississippi, 18 mi/29 km N of Cape Girardeau, Missouri.

Big Rapids city, pop. 12,603, seat of Mecosta Co., WC Michigan, on the Muskegon R., 47 mi/76 km N of Grand Rapids. It was settled (1853) on the site of a main rest stop on the Mackinaw Trail. Lumbering was the dominant industry during the boom and decline of the latter 1800s. Present manufactures include furniture and tools. The city is also a shipping point for locally grown potatoes, fruit, grain, and dairy products. It is the seat of Ferris State University (1884). Rogers Dam (7 mi/11 km S) impounds a lake used for fishing and boating.

Big Rock Candy Mountain landmark in SC Utah, just off I-70, on the E edge of a unit of the Fishlake National Forest, 160 mi/265 km SSW of Salt Lake City and 33 mi/53 km S of Fillmore. Known for its many colors, it has mineral springs, and is a resort site; its water is said to taste lemony. Aluminum, potash, and gold have been mined locally.

Big Rock Point promontory on L. Michigan, in Charlevoix Co., Lower Peninsula, NC Michigan, 4 mi/6 km NE of Charlevoix. Less than a mile east of the point and also on the lakeshore is the Big Rock Point nuclear power plant, commissioned in 1962.

Big Sandy River 27 mi/43 km long, forming (with its tributary the Tug Fork) the West Virginia–Kentucky border. It is formed at LOUISA, Kentucky, by the confluence of the Tug Fork and the Levisa Fork, and flows N to CATLETTSBURG, Kentucky, to join the Ohio R. at the three-state corner with Ohio. The **Tug Fork,** 155 mi/250 km long, rises in McDowell Co., extreme S West Virginia, and flows NW, briefly forming the Virginia–West Virginia border, then the West Virginia–Kentucky border. The **Levisa Fork,** 165 mi/266 km long, rises in Buchanan Co., SW Virginia, and flows through Pike Co., Kentucky, to Louisa. The **Russell Fork,** a tributary of the Levisa Fork, flows from Virginia into Pike Co., Kentucky; at the Virginia-Kentucky border it passes through the Breaks of Sandy, a 5 mi/8 km–long gorge with unusual sandstone formations, a popular tourist destination.

Big Savage Mountain see under BACKBONE Mt., Maryland.

Big Sioux River 420 mi/680 km long, in South Dakota and Iowa. It rises in NE South Dakota, N of WATERTOWN, and flows generally SSE to SIOUX FALLS, then winds S, forming the South Dakota–Iowa border, before emptying into the

Missouri R. at the extreme SE corner of South Dakota, between North Sioux City and SIOUX CITY, Iowa.

Big Sky resort in Gallatin Co., SW Montana, surrounded by Gallatin National Forest and the Spanish Peaks Wilderness region, near Lone Mt., 30 mi/48 km SW of Bozeman. One of Montana's largest ski resorts, built by newscaster Chet Huntley, who was born (1911) and raised nearby, it is popular for year-round recreation. Situated 18 mi/29 km N of Yellowstone National Park, Big Sky features fishing, hunting, and white-water rafting.

Big South Fork also, **South Fork of the Cumberland River** in N Tennessee and S Kentucky. Formed by several headstreams in Scott Co., Tennessee, it runs 77 mi/124 km through mountain forest N into McCreary Co., Kentucky, and joins the Cumberland at Burnside, on the W edge of the Daniel Boone National Forest. The **Big South Fork National River and Recreation Area** is a 123,000-ac/49,800-ha wilderness set aside for hiking, camping, fishing, and white-water rafting.

Big Spring city, pop. 23,093, seat of Howard Co., W Texas, 37 mi/60 km ENE of Midland. White settlement began in 1881 when the Texas and Pacific Railway established a division point here. Rapid growth occurred after oil was discovered in the area in the 1920s. Oil refining is the biggest industry, with production of gas, chemicals, and carbon black, though crops and livestock still thrive on the surrounding plains. Big Spring has a Veterans Administration hospital and rehabilitation center and several private hospitals. Howard College (1945) is here.

Big Spruce Knob see under GAULEY Mt., West Virginia.

Big Stone Gap town, pop. 4748, Wise Co., extreme SW Virginia, in the Cumberland Mts. at the head of the Powell R., where it cuts a gap through Stone Mt., 26 mi/42 km NW of Kingsport, Tennessee. A coal mining town from the 1890s, when the railroad arrived, it is also a mountain resort center. Mountain Empire Community College (1970) is here. The area is the setting for John Fox, Jr.'s *Trail of the Lonesome Pine* (1908).

Big Sunflower River see SUNFLOWER R., Mississippi.

Big Sur see under Point SUR, California.

Big Thicket forest area of E Texas, in the PINEY WOODS, N of Beaumont. Once some 3 million ac/1.2 million ha of hardwood, pine, vine, and shrub growth, so dense that settlement passed largely around it, it has shrunk to perhaps 300,000 ac/122,000 ha, chiefly in Hardin and Tyler counties. The **Big Thicket National Preserve** (1974), covering 86,000 ac/34,700 ha, preserves some of what is variously called "the biological crossroads of America" or "America's Ark," a region of tremendous plant and animal diversity. In the Civil War and later, the Big Thicket harbored fugitives. Today its residents include the Alabama-Coushatta, who have a reservation along the Neches R.

Big Two-Hearted River see TWO-HEARTED RIVER.

Billerica town, pop. 37,609, Middlesex Co., NE Massachusetts, on the Shawsheen and Concord rivers, 7 mi/11 km S of Lowell. Settled in the 1630s as Shawsheen, one of the Praying Indian towns (set aside for tribes friendly to the Colonists), and long chiefly agricultural, Billerica, situated between Routes 128 and 495, Boston's two beltways, now has some light manufacturing and high-tech industry.

Billings city, pop. 81,151, seat of Yellowstone Co., SC Montana, on the Yellowstone R., 180 mi/290 km SE of Helena. Montana's largest city, it was founded by the Northern Pacific Railroad in 1882. It prospered as a trade center for livestock and the agricultural bounty of the irrigated Yellowstone Valley. The city remains an important trading and shipping point, the hub of Montana's "Midland Empire." Also key to its economy are oil refining, farm implement and electrical equipment manufacture, sugar beet and dairy processing, and meatpacking. Home to Eastern Mountain College (1927) and Rocky Mountain College (1878), Billings is also headquarters for the Custer National Forest. Pictograph Cave State Monument is 7 mi/11 km SE of the city.

Bill Williams Mountain isolated peak rising to 9341 ft/2847 m in NC Arizona, W of Flagstaff and overlooking the city of Williams (E; pop. 2532, Coconino Co.), a tourist center. The area is popular for skiing, hiking, and horseback riding. Named for an early-19th-century mountain man, the peak is distinct from the **Bill Williams Mts.,** a low range rising to 2700 ft/825 m SE of L. HAVASU, in W Arizona.

Biloxi city, pop. 46,319, Harrison Co., SE Mississippi, situated on a narrow peninsula between Biloxi Bay (N and E) and MISSISSIPPI SOUND (S), adjacent (E) to Gulfport. The first white settlement in the lower Mississippi valley, established in 1699 by French colonists across the bay at Fort Maurepas (now in OCEAN SPRINGS), is called Old Biloxi. Moved to the peninsula in 1719, Biloxi was the capital of French Louisiana until 1722, and was later also under the flags of Spain, England, WEST FLORIDA, and the Confederacy. It became important as a resort before the Civil War. Jefferson Davis's Beauvoir is here. The city's chief industry, fishing and seafood (especially shrimp) processing, has now melded with tourism, so that the annual Blessing of the Fleet (Biloxi is predominantly Catholic) draws many visitors. Other industries include boatbuilding, fertilizer production, and various light manufactures. Keesler Air Force Base and a large Veterans Administration medical center are here.

Biltmore see under ASHEVILLE, North Carolina.

Bingham also, **Bingham Canyon** former mining town in Salt Lake Co., NC Utah, in the Oquirrh Mts., 22 mi/35 km SSW of Salt Lake City. Gold, silver, lead, and other minerals were mined here after 1863, and the town was famous for being one street wide and 7 mi/11 km long. Copper became dominant in the early 20th century. During the 1950s, Bingham was gradually consumed by mining operations, which completely overwhelmed the town by 1961. It is now the site of Kennecott Copper's huge Bingham Canyon Copper Mine (1906), the world's oldest and largest open pit copper mine.

Binghamton city, pop. 53,008, seat of Broome Co., SC New York, at the confluence of the Chenango and Susquehanna rivers, near the Pennsylvania border. It was settled on the site of the Iroquois village of Ochenang in 1787, as Chenango Point, and later renamed for landowner William Bingham. Following the linking of the Erie and Chenango canals (1837) and the arrival of the Erie Railroad (1848), industrialization intensified. Binghamton is now the focus of a metropolitan area that includes Endicott and Johnson City, known as the Tri-Cities. Industries manufacture shoes, textiles, aviation training equipment, machinery, photo supplies, and computers. Agriculture, primarily the raising of poultry, livestock, and dairy cattle, and the production of poultry and dairy products, lumber, and pulpwood, is important in the surrounding region. Binghamton was the site of the first US farm bureau, in 1911. Broome County Community College is in Dickinson, just N. The State University of New York at Binghamton is in suburban Vestal, just SW.

Biosphere see under Île SAINTE-HÉLÈNE, Montréal, Québec.

Biosphere 2 see under SANTA CATALINA Mts., Arizona.

Birch Coulee historic site in Renville Co., SE Minnesota, 1 mi/2 km N of Morton. It is the site of an 1862 battle between whites and Sioux.

Birmingham **1.** city, pop. 265,968, seat of Jefferson Co., NC Alabama, along the NW of RED Mt., at the SW end of the Appalachian chain. The state's largest city, it is the hub of a metropolitan area that includes JEFFERSON and Shelby counties, including the industrial cities of BESSEMER, HUEYTOWN, and FAIRFIELD and numerous residential suburbs. Founded at the junction of E–W and N–S railroads in 1871, the city quickly became the industrial center (the "Pittsburgh") of the South, drawing on local deposits of iron ore, dolomite, coal, and limestone to create a major steel industry. Graphite, marble, barites, bauxite, pyrite, quartz, millstone, cement rock, clays, sand, and gravel are also abundant in the area. Significant natural gas deposits to the N, in Walker Co., were first developed in the 1970s. Birmingham boomed from the 1870s through World War II, then lost much of its importance to overseas steel centers. It has since diversified its economy. Heavy steel-based industry has been joined by publishing, technology, financial, and service industries, including health care and education. The city is home to the University of Alabama at Birmingham (1969), Birmingham-Southern College (1856), Samford University (1841), and several other institutions. Birmingham's industrial past is symbolized by its huge Sloss Furnaces and by the statue of the Roman god of fire and metalworking, Vulcan, that has stood atop Red Mt., S of Downtown, since 1937. The city's role in the civil rights struggles of the 1960s is memorialized in its Civil Rights Institute, opened across from the 16th St. Baptist Church, scene of a 1963 bombing, in 1992. **2.** city, pop. 19,997, Oakland Co., SE Michigan, on the R. Rouge, 15 mi/24 km N of Detroit. Founded in 1819, this mostly residential suburb between Detroit and Pontiac has some light manufacturing. **3.** neighborhood on the S side of Pittsburgh, Pennsylvania, across the Monongahela R. from Downtown, immediately E of the MOUNT WASHINGTON area. Laid out in 1811, the Birmingham waterfront was one of the nation's foremost glassmaking complexes. Today, the community is divided between working-class East Europeans in brick row houses on the flats and more prosperous Germans in cottages on the Mt. Washington slopes.

Bisbee city, pop. 6288, seat of Cochise Co., extreme SE Arizona, 80 mi/130 km SE of Tucson and 5 mi/8 km N of the Mexican border. In the center of what was one of the nation's richest copper regions, at its peak in the 1880s it was the world's largest copper mining town. In 1917, 1000 strikers at the Copper Queen Mine were herded into boxcars at gunpoint and shipped out of state. The 1974 closing of the Lavender Pit mine ended copper mining here, but some processing is still done. Visitors are drawn to mining-related sites and to arts events and crafts shops. There are dude ranches as well as gold, silver, and lead mines in the vicinity.

Biscayne Bay inlet of the Atlantic Ocean, 40 mi/64 km N–S, in Dade Co., SE Florida, largely between the mainland (W) and several barrier islands. This shallow body is bordered by the cities of Miami and Coral Gables (NW) and by Miami Beach and Key Biscayne (NE). On the Atlantic Intracoastal Waterway, it is a well-known resort area. **Biscayne National Park,** embracing its S end, covers 173,000 ac/70,000 ha, 97% of it water. It is noted for its coral reefs.

Bismarck city, pop. 49,256, state capital and seat of Burleigh Co., SC North Dakota, on the E bank of the Missouri R., across from Mandan. Founded in 1873, it was named after the German chancellor to attract railroad investment by his countrymen. Becoming important as a river port and rail terminus, it flourished after gold was discovered (1874) in the BLACK HILLS. It served as a supply point for the goldfields and for nearby Fort Abraham Lincoln (now restored), home base of George A. Custer, as well a gateway to the Far West. Bismarck was capital of the Dakota Territory (1883–89), then became capital of the new state. Lying in a rich oil, gas, and coal region, it is the headquarters of several energy companies, and has refineries. The city also has several industries, principally farm machinery and grain processing, related to abundant regional agriculture, and it is a trading and shipping hub for agricultural products. Notable here are the Camp Hancock Historic Site, North Dakota Heritage Center, Art Deco capitol building, and Dakota Zoo. It is the seat of Bismarck State College (1939), the University of Mary (1959), and United Tribes Technical College.

Bitterroot National Forest over 1.6 million ac/650,000 ha (2500 sq mi/6500 sq km), in W Montana and NE Idaho, NW of the Continental Divide and S of Missoula. The Bitterroot R. flows W out of it. One of the oldest national forests, it has peaks rising to 10,157 ft/3096 m at Trapper Peak. Part of the SELWAY-BITTERROOT WILDERNESS is here.

Bitterroot Range also, **Bitterroot** (or **Bitter Root**) **Mountains** extending 365 mi/588 km along the Idaho-Montana border, in the N Rocky Mts. It is in several national forests, and its S crest forms part of the CONTINENTAL DIVIDE. The highest point in the range is Scott Peak in Idaho (11,393 ft/3475 m), under which runs the almost 2 mi/3 km–long **Bitterroot Tunnel.** The Bitterroots' forbidding E face caused Lewis and Clark to detour over 100 mi/160 km N in 1805 before finding the Lolo Pass route to the Pacific Northwest.

Bitterroot River 120 mi/193 km long, in W Montana. It is formed by two forks in Ravalli Co., and flows N past Darby, Corvallis, and Stevensville, between the BITTERROOT RANGE and the Sapphire Mts., to the Clark Fork R. just W of Missoula. The river irrigates a fertile agricultural area.

Bixby town, pop. 9502, Tulsa and Wagoner counties, NE Oklahoma, on the Arkansas R., 15 mi/24 km S of downtown Tulsa. Founded in 1893, it is a business center for producers of oil from nearby wells as well as of grain, vegetables, and pecans. Food processing and tourism are also important.

Black Belt **1.** band of fertile land in the Deep South, c.300 mi/480 km long and c.25–30 mi/40–48 km wide, stretching across C Alabama and into Mississippi, where it is known as the **Black Prairie.** Named for its dark, limestone-enriched, clayey soil, it is an area of rolling prairie N of the Gulf Coastal Plain. Before the Civil War, the Black Belt was the South's chief agricultural, and the nation's most important cotton producing, region. The use of slave labor on its plantations led to the misconception that "black" referred to its population. The arrival of the boll weevil, soil erosion and depletion, and various other economic factors encouraged an increase in crop diversity by the early 20th century. Today cotton is still grown, but other products such as soybeans, peanuts, vegetables, and livestock are of greater importance.

2. in Chicago, Illinois, term for the formerly concentrated, now somewhat dispersed, black community of the SOUTH SIDE. Beginning around 1900, blacks occupied a narrow "Belt" along State St., Michigan Ave., and Cottage Grove Ave., from about 30th St. S to about 50th St. As the community boomed during and after World War I, the Belt's boundaries expanded, chiefly to the S, E, and W; it was often referred to as Bronzeville. After World War II, dispersal into suburbs of the CALUMET area and, eventually, into such West Side neighborhoods as EAST GARFIELD PARK and AUSTIN, was spurred both by urban renewal projects in the old Belt and by white flight from outer districts.

Black Bottom see under PARADISE VALLEY, Detroit, Michigan.

Black Canyon of the Gunnison see under GUNNISON R., Colorado.

Blackcomb Mountain see under WHISTLER, British Columbia.

Black Diamond see under TURNER VALLEY, Alberta.

Blackfeet Indian Reservation 2371 sq mi/6142 sq km, pop. 8549 (82% Indian), in NW Montana, adjacent (E) to Glacier National Park, along the Alberta (N) border. BROWNING is its headquarters; CUT BANK is just E. The Algonquian-speaking Blackfeet, a combination of Piegan, Blood, and Siksikan groups, once controlled a vast area between the Saskatchewan (N) and Yellowstone (S) rivers. In this lake-dotted prairie area, they have benefited from oil and gas extraction.

Blackfoot city, pop. 9646, seat of Bingham Co., SE Idaho, on the Snake R. at the Blackfoot R. junction, 24 mi/39 km NNE of Pocatello. The city is a trade center for an agricultural region producing mainly potatoes. The IDAHO NATIONAL ENGINEERING LABORATORY, 35 mi/56 km NW, stimulated the city's growth. Phosphates are mined on the FORT HALL Indian Reservation, just SE.

Black Hawk County 573 sq mi/1484 sq km, pop. 123,798, in NE Iowa. The Cedar R. crosses the county from the NW to the SE. Its seat is WATERLOO, which, with adjoining CEDAR FALLS, dominates the economy. Outside the cities, it is largely agricultural, with some recent industrial and residential growth in the SE.

Black Hawk Monument 50 ft/15 m–tall statue, in Ogle Co., NC Illinois, situated in Lowden State Park, overlooking the Rock R., just N of the city of OREGON. This memorial to the Sauk and Fox chief was sculpted by Lorado Taft in 1911.

Black Hills mountainous region about 100 mi/160 km N–S and 60 mi/100 km wide in W South Dakota and NE Wyoming. Rising to 7242 ft/2209 m at HARNEY PEAK, the ancient Black Hills are enclosed by the Belle Fourche R. (N) and the South Branch of the Cheyenne R. (S). They are known for their concentric bands of differently colored granite, shale, and limestone, exposed by weathering; their cathedral-like spires, most notably at the Needles; and numerous ridges, hogbacks, and steep canyons. The area contains a number of caves, the best-known at JEWEL CAVE NATIONAL MONUMENT and WIND CAVE NATIONAL PARK. The densely forested ridges, which appear black at a distance, are largely within the Black Hills National Forest (1.5 million ac/607,500 ha). The Black Hills Gold Rush of 1874, which brought the first significant wave of white settlers to the area, created tension with the Sioux, who were eventually driven from their sacred lands. Notable gold-mining towns include DEADWOOD, Custer, and Lead, site of the famous HOMESTAKE MINE, 3 mi/5 km NE of TERRY PEAK. Rapid City is the largest city in the mountains. Silver, tin, precious stones, mica, feldspar, lithium, clays, petroleum, and uranium are among the resources obtained from the Black Hills. Farming, dairying, and grazing are also important. Popular tourist areas include Mt. RUSHMORE and Fossil Cycad national monuments and Spearfish Creek and Canyon. DEVILS TOWER in Wyoming and the Bear Lodge Mts. are within the Black Hills.

Black Lake unincorporated village in Cheboygan Co., at the extreme N of the Lower Peninsula of Michigan, 19 mi/31 km SE of Cheboygan. This small community on the S shore of Black L. is surrounded by Mackinaw State Forest, and is 2 mi/3 km W of Onaway State Park. It is the site of the United Auto Workers Family Education Center.

Blacklands also, **Blacklands Prairies** soil zone in E Texas, running along the E side of the BALCONES ESCARPMENT from the Red R. (N) to the Rio Grande (S). It ranges from 15 mi/24 km to 70 mi/113 km in width, and covers some 12 million ac/4.9 million ha. This fertile band was settled in the 19th century and was heavily agricultural, growing cotton and other crops, into the mid 20th century, since which industrial and residential development has spread around its major cities, Dallas, Waco, Austin, and San Antonio. In the NW, the **Grand Prairie** zone, similar in its soils and covering 6.3 million ac/2.6 million ha, lies around Fort Worth, extending from the Red R. (N) to the Colorado R. (S).

Blacklick Estates unincorporated residential suburb, pop. 10,080, Franklin Co., C Ohio, 10 mi/16 km ENE of Columbus, on Blacklick Creek.

Black Mesa **1.** tableland, c.7000 ft/2135 m in elevation, in NE Arizona, reaching 8075 ft/2461 m at Yale Point. It is within the NAVAJO INDIAN RESERVATION. Projecting S from it are (E–W) First, Second, and Third mesas, site of the Hopi Indian Reservation and many abandoned and occupied PUEBLOS, including Walpi, Shipaulovi, and ORAIBI. **2.** lava-capped sandstone plateau, including the highest point (4973 ft/1516 m) in Oklahoma, in the extreme NW of the PANHANDLE. The mesa extends for nearly 45 mi/72 km into New Mexico and Colorado, where it reaches 6600 ft/2013 m. Beds of dinosaur bones and PETROGLYPHS are found here.

Black Mountain **1.** also, **Big Black Mountain** 4145 ft/1263 m, in the Big Black Mts. of the Cumberland Plateau, SE Kentucky, near Lynch, in HARLAN Co. Close to the Virginia border, it is the highest point in the state. **2.** town, pop. 5418, Buncombe Co., W North Carolina, 11 mi/18 km E of Asheville, in the BLACK Mts. A resort center, it also has hosiery and lumber mills. Montreat-Anderson College (1916) is in Montreat (town, pop. 693), just N, and religious assembly areas are nearby. The town is best known as the site of Black Mt. College (1933–57), an experimental school that became a center for 1950s avant-garde poets as well as for painters and other artists; the college was on L. Eden, W of the town.

Black Mountains range containing the highest peaks of the Appalachian system, including Mt. MITCHELL (6684 ft/2039 m), within PISGAH NATIONAL FOREST, in W North Carolina. A spur of the BLUE RIDGE Mts., the Black Mts. extend for c.20 mi/32 km roughly between the town of BLACK MOUNTAIN (S) and Burnsville (N), and include Balsam Cone (6645 ft/2028 m).

Black Patch loosely applied term for the dark tobacco-producing counties of W Kentucky, in which farmers, angered at low prices, engaged in a 1906–08 "war," involving threats and demonstrations, with big growers. The state militia was called out to end the conflict.

Black Prairie in Mississippi: see under BLACK BELT, Alabama.

Black Range N–S trending mountain crest, W of Truth or Consequences, in SW New Mexico. Largely within Gila National Forest, the range includes Reeds Peak (10,011 ft/3051 m). Kingston and Hillsboro, just E, were once noted for copper production. Silver mining, logging, and grazing have also been done in the area.

Black River **1.** 300 mi/480 km long, in SE Missouri and NE Arkansas. It rises in Reynolds Co., Missouri, near TAUM SAUK Mt., in the Mark Twain National Forest, and flows generally SE past Poplar Bluff, then SW to the WHITE R., near Newport, Arkansas. Its course marks the E edge of the OZARK Plateau. **2.** see under OUACHITA R., in Louisiana. **3.** 120 mi/193 km long, in New York. It rises in SW Herkimer Co. in small lakes of the Adirondacks, then flows generally NW through Lewis Co., between Adirondack Park (E) and Tug Hill (W), past BOONVILLE, Lowville, and Carthage, then turns W through WATERTOWN to Black River Bay, an inlet of L. Ontario. The Black River Canal, abandoned in 1926, connected it to the Erie Canal at Rome after 1836. Falls along the river's course provide power to paper mills and other industries. Its main tributaries are the Moose and Beaver rivers. SACKETS HARBOR lies S of its mouth.

Black Rock see under BRIDGEPORT, Connecticut.

Black Rock Desert stretching 65 mi/105 km NE from Gerlach, in Humboldt Co., NW Nevada. The arid alkali flats cover over 1 million ac/400,000 ha (1560 sq mi/4050 sq km), and with Smoke Creek Desert, a 40-mi/65-km extension on the S, are part of the dry bed of ancient L. Lahontan, which covered much of the W Great Basin 50,000 years ago. Just N is the N–S **Black Rock Range;** Pahute Peak (8618 ft/2627 m) is its high point.

Blacksburg town, pop. 34,590, Montgomery Co., SW Virginia, 28 mi/45 km WSW of Roanoke, in the Appalachian Mts. It is the seat of Virginia Polytechnic Institute and State University (1872). Smithfield Plantation, a 120,000-ac/49,000-ha 1740s land grant, was centered just SW of the town.

Blackstone River 50 mi/80 km long, in Massachusetts and Rhode Island. It rises in Worcester Co., Massachusetts, and flows generally SSE through Worcester, Millbury, and Northbridge, then through Woonsocket, Rhode Island, and between Central Falls and Pawtucket, where the Pawtucket Falls furnish power for industry. Below Pawtucket it is called the Seekonk R., and passes between Providence and East Providence, into the Providence R., an estuary at head of Narragansett Bay (Providence Harbor). The river is named after William Blackstone, who was the first white settler in the area (1634), having left Boston's SHAWMUT PENINSULA. The Blackstone has been one of New England's most economically important rivers, a center of the textile industry.

Black Tom see under JERSEY CITY, New Jersey.

Black Warrior National Forest see BANKHEAD NATIONAL FOREST, Alabama.

Black Warrior River 178 mi/287 km long, in Alabama. It rises in the S Appalachian Mts., in several forks NW of SAND Mt., and flows SW across Jefferson Co. into Bankhead L., then into L. Tuscaloosa, above Tuscaloosa, and joins the TOMBIGBEE R. near Demopolis, in L. Demopolis. The Tombigbee's main tributary, it provides water access to the Birmingham industrial area through its system of locks and dam-created lakes. At its NW headwaters the Lewis Smith Dam, NE of Jasper, impounds the Sipsey and East forks, creating 21,000-ac/8600-ha Lewis Smith L., in the BANKHEAD NATIONAL FOREST. The river's name is a translation of "Tuscaloosa."

Blackwell's Island former name of ROOSEVELT I., in the East R., New York City.

Bladensburg town, pop. 8064, Prince George's Co., SC Maryland, on the Anacostia R., 7 mi/11 km NE of Washington, D.C. The settlement was a busy port, shipping tobacco and flour until 1800. Today it is a largely residential suburb. On Aug. 24, 1814, American forces were routed here by British forces, who then burned most of Washington's public buildings. In 1820, on Bladensburg's outskirts, James Barron killed Stephen Decatur in a duel.

Blaine city, pop. 38,975, Anoka and Ramsey counties, SE Minnesota, 16 mi/26 km N of Minneapolis. Settled in the 1840s, it became a trading center for surrounding dairy, poultry, and wheat farms. Today, the city is largely a blue-collar residential suburb of the Twin Cities that has experienced much recent commercial development. It is known for its velodrome and a soccer stadium.

Blainville city, pop. 22,679, 20 mi/32 km NW of Montréal, in the lower Laurentians, S Québec. Incorporated in 1968, this fast-growing residential suburb E of the MIRABEL airport is noted as a center for equestrian sports.

Blair city, pop. 6860, seat of Washington Co., EC Nebraska, 22 mi/35 km NW of Omaha. Founded in 1869, it is a processing center for a grain growing and livestock raising region. It is the headquarters of Nebraska's first cooperative soil building organization. The Black Elk–Neihardt Park here houses the Tower of the Four Winds, a memorial to the visionary Black Elk and his friend, the poet John Neihardt. The city is the seat of Dana College (1884).

Blair County 527 sq mi/1365 sq km, pop. 130,542, in SC Pennsylvania, in the Allegheny Mts. Its seat is Hollidaysburg. It is in an agricultural and coal mining region. ALTOONA is its commercial and industrial center.

Blair House see under WHITE HOUSE, Washington, D.C.

Blair Mountain Appalachian ridge, near the communities of Blair and Ethel, in Logan Co., extreme SW West Virginia, scene of a weeklong battle in Aug. 1921 between coal company agents and miners, said to be the most serious armed labor conflict in US history. In the 1990s, plans to strip-mine the mountain were protested by locals who regard it as a monument.

Blanca Peak see under SANGRE DE CRISTO Mts., Colorado.

Blanco, Cape promontory on the Pacific coast in Curry Co., SW Oregon, 8 mi/13 km NNW of PORT ORFORD. The westernmost point in Oregon, it was named (1603) by Spanish sailors for its chalk-white appearance.

Blanc-Sablon municipality, pop. 1211, extreme E Québec, at its boundary with Labrador, on Blanc-Sablon Bay and the NW of the Strait of Belle-Isle, 705 mi/1135 km NE of Québec City. In an area with well-known salmon rivers, where both ancient hunters' and 16th-century Basque sealing and whaling parties' artifacts are found, it is reached by ferry from N Newfoundland and from Havre-St.-Pierre, Québec (280 mi/460 km WSW), and is the starting point for a road that proceeds a short way up the Labrador coast (E).

Blauvelt village, pop. 4838, in Orangetown, Rockland Co., SE New York, 2 mi/3 km W of the Hudson R. It is a residential suburb just N of Orangeburg. The Blauvelt section of the Palisades Interstate Park is here.

Blennerhasset Island 500 ac/200 ha, in Wood Co., NW West Virginia, in the Ohio R., 2.5 mi/4 km S of PARKERSBURG. A state park on property here owned by the Du Pont Company features a reconstruction of Harman Blennerhasset's 1800–11 mansion. In 1806, the wealthy Blennerhasset conspired with Aaron Burr to set up a Southwestern empire, with a capital at New Orleans. The plot was discovered, and both were charged with treason, but acquitted. The island was later farmed, and part of it was made an historical park in the 1870s.

Blind River town, pop. 3355, ALGOMA District, C Ontario, on the North Channel of L. Huron, at the mouth of the Mississiggi R., 78 mi/126 km ESE of Sault Ste. Marie. A fur trading site before the mid 19th century, it was subsequently a lumbering center, and today is a resort and has uranium mines that produce 40% of the national output. ELLIOT LAKE is 7 mi/11 km NE.

BLM see under PUBLIC LANDS.

Block Island 11 sq mi/28 sq km, pop. 821, in the Atlantic Ocean at the E entrance to Long Island Sound. Block Island Sound lies W. The island is part of Washington Co., Rhode Island, 10 mi/16 km SSW of Point Judith, and coextensive with the town of New Shoreham. Explored by the Dutch navigator Adriaen Block in 1614, it was settled in 1661. It boasts two good harbors, two lighthouses, over 300 ponds, and the chalk cliffs of Mohegan Bluffs on gently rolling terrain. The economy depends principally on tourism; fishing is also important.

Block Island Sound inlet of the Atlantic Ocean between the mainland of SW Rhode Island and SE Connecticut (N) and BLOCK I., Rhode Island (E) and the E tips of LONG I., New York (S). Forty mi/64 km E–W, it connects Long Island Sound (W) with the ocean, and is bordered E by Rhode Island Sound. FISHERS I., New York, lies in the sound. On the ATLANTIC INTRACOASTAL WATERWAY, the sound has heavy ferry and recreational traffic, especially in summer.

Blood Indian Reserve see under PORCUPINE HILLS, Alberta.

Blood Mountain peak (4458 ft/1360 m) in N Georgia, just NW of Robertstown, in the Chattahoochee National Forest. The name memorializes a legendary Indian battle fought on its slopes. According to Cherokee myth, a cave now known as the Rock House allowed entry for "little folk" whose music could be heard on the mountain's slopes.

Bloody Angle, the see under SPOTSYLVANIA Co., Virginia.

Bloody Falls see under COPPERMINE, Northwest Territories.

Bloody Lane, the see under ANTIETAM, Maryland.

Bloody Marsh see under SAINT SIMONS I., Georgia.

Bloomfield **1.** town, pop. 19,483, Hartford Co., NC Connecticut, adjacent (NW) to Hartford. It is a primarily residential suburb with some industrial parks and a large insurance sector, once a tobacco-growing town. **2.** see under BLOOMFIELD HILLS, Michigan. **3.** township, pop. 45,061, Essex Co., NE New Jersey, 2 mi/3 km N of Newark. Settled in the 17th century and a supply center during the Revolution, it was originally part of Newark. Named for a Revolutionary general, it became a separate township in 1812, and was a commercial hub throughout the 19th century. Now a suburb of New York City and Newark, it has such manufactures as pharmaceuticals, porcelain, and electrical appliances, and contains many office buildings. Bloomfield College (1868) is here. **4.** residential section of Pittsburgh, Pennsylvania, between Lawrenceville and East Liberty, 2.5 mi/4 km NE of the GOLDEN TRIANGLE. Bloomfield has been a largely Italian neighborhood since the 1880s. The area also includes the villages of FRIENDSHIP and GARFIELD.

Bloomfield Hills city, pop. 4288, in Bloomfield township (pop. 42,473), Oakland Co., SE Michigan, 5 mi/8 km SE of Pontiac. A wealthy residential suburb NW of Detroit, it was settled in 1819. It was primarily agricultural until c.1900, when affluent Detroit residents began to build estates. The Cranbrook estate became the highly respected Cranbrook Educational Community, which includes private schools, an art academy and museum, and a science institute. The original mansion and gardens are open to the public. Bloomfield Hills is also home to a number of businesses, notably advertising agencies.

Bloomingdale **1.** village, pop. 16,614, Du Page Co., NE Illinois, a residential suburb 27 mi/43 km NW of Chicago. **2.** Dutch, **Bloemendael** former district of upper W Manhattan I., New York, fertile lands between what is now W Midtown and MANHATTANVILLE, on the Hudson R. at 125th Street. Flower growing was an important industry. The name was long used of parts of the Upper West Side. **3.** unincorporated community, pop. 10,953, Sullivan Co., extreme NE Tennessee, a suburb 4 mi/6 km NE of Kingsport, on the Virginia border.

Blooming Grove formerly, **Corsica** village in North Bloomfield township, Morrow Co., C Ohio, 10 mi/16 km SW of Mansfield. President Warren G. Harding was born here (1865).

Bloomington **1.** unincorporated community, pop. 15,116, San Bernardino Co., S California, on the San Bernardino Freeway (I-10), 6 mi/10 km SW of San Bernardino. Citrus groves, vegetable farms, and railyards characterize this otherwise residential suburb. **2.** city, pop. 51,972, seat of McLean Co., C Illinois, on Sugar Creek, immediately S of Normal. It is the commercial center for the region's corn, livestock, and dairy products. Among the businesses headquartered here is a large insurance company. Local manufactures include agricultural items such as hybrid seed corn and farm machinery, along with builders' supplies, electronic tubes, heating and ventilating equipment, vacuum cleaners, and candy. The area was settled in 1822, and the present site was laid out in 1831. Abraham Lincoln delivered his "Lost Speech" before the convention that established the state Republican Party here in 1856. Bloomington is the seat of Illinois Wesleyan University (1850). The Mackinaw River State Fish and Wildlife Area is 18 mi/29 km NW of the city; the Moraine View State Park is 13 mi/21 km SE. **3.** city, pop. 60,633, seat of Monroe Co., SC Indiana, 45 mi/72 km SW of Indianapolis. Settled in 1815, it became the seat of Indiana University in 1820; with its 1850-ac/750-ha campus, its institutions, and its large student population, the university is a prime contributor to Bloomington's atmosphere and economy. Also of great economic importance is the cutting and processing of limestone from nearby quarries. Among the city's manufactures are machinery, television equipment, and electrical appliances; it also trades, processes, and ships products from the surrounding agricultural region. **4.** city, pop. 86,335, Hennepin Co., SE Minnesota, on the Minnesota R. and Long Meadow L., 10 mi/16 km S of Minneapolis. Long a residential community for Twin Cities commuters, it has increasingly become home to commercial and light industrial enterprises, including major electronics, computer, and photocopying firms, as well as manufacturers of farm equipment. The two main corridors of development are along I-494 in the NW and I-35W, which slices the city in half from N to S. Its location immediately SW of Minneapolis–St. Paul International Airport prompted developers to choose Bloomington as the location of the 78-ac/32-ha, four-floor Mall of America (1992), the largest fully enclosed shopping center in the world. The megamall occupies the site of the former Metropolitan Stadium, in the NE corner of the city.

Bloomsburg town, pop. 12,439, seat of Columbia Co., E Pennsylvania, on the Susquehanna R., 35 mi/56 km SW of Wilkes-Barre. It was settled in 1772 and laid out in 1802. In the 1870s, Bloomsburg was the site of murder trials growing out of violence in nearby coal mines by the Molly Maguires, an Irish miners' association. Modern industries produce such goods as clothing and electronic equipment. Bloomsburg University (1839) is here.

Bloor Street major E–W thoroughfare in TORONTO, Ontario. Some 2.5 mi/4 km N of L. Ontario, it is c.1.25 mi/2 km N of QUEEN St., and represents the early-19th-century city's second expansion northward; today it is regarded as the line between Downtown (S) and Midtown (N). Along it in the W is High Park, Toronto's largest public park. Fashionable YORKVILLE lies just N of Bloor, which at the Yonge St. intersection is central to the city's high-end shopping. To the W are many insurance offices. Across the Don R. viaduct, to the E, Bloor becomes Danforth Ave.; in the East End, the area called the Danforth is Toronto's popular Greektown.

Blue Ash city, pop. 11,860, Hamilton Co., SW Ohio, 5 mi/8 km NE of Cincinnati, of which it is a commuter suburb. A campus of the University of Cincinnati is situated here, and there is an airport.

Blue Bell unincorporated village, pop. 6091, in Whitpain township, Montgomery Co., SE Pennsylvania, 17 mi/27 km NW of Philadelphia. A residential and commercial suburb, Blue Bell is home to Unisys, US Healthcare, Castle Energy, and other corporations.

Blue Earth city, pop. 3745, seat of Faribault Co., S Minnesota, on the Blue Earth R., 9 mi/14 km N of the Iowa line and 28 mi/45 km W of Albert Lea. Established in 1856 in an agricultural and dairying area, it was named for the clay Indians dug along the river.

Bluefield **1.** town, pop. 5363, Tazewell Co., SW Virginia, 75 mi/120 km W of Roanoke, in the Appalachian Mts. It is contiguous with the larger Bluefield, West Virginia. Together, their economy is based on the coal, iron, limestone, and silica mines in the area; manufactures include mining equipment and textiles. There are also some lumber mills. Bluefield is the seat of Bluefield College (1920). **2.** city, pop, 12,756, Mercer Co., extreme S West Virginia, at the foot of East River Mt. (S), adjacent (E) to Bluefield, Virginia. The community expanded with the opening of the huge Pocahontas coalfield (1889) to service by the Norfolk and Western Railway. The economy is still based on coal and railroading. Bluefield State College (1895) is here.

Bluegrass Region also, **the Bluegrass** area in NC Kentucky, bounded NW, N, and NE by the Ohio R., and by the U-shaped KNOBS REGION on the other sides. It extends roughly from Louisville (NW) to Danville (S) to Maysville (NE), with Lexington its cultural and geographic center. Covering about 8000 sq mi/20,700 sq km, the gently rolling plateau (c.800–1000 ft/240–300 m high), with exceptionally rich phosphatic limestone soil, is extensively cultivated and used for grazing. It is especially known for its thoroughbred horse and tobacco farms, but cattle, other livestock, and forage and grain crops are also produced. The region takes its name from the plant Kentucky Bluegrass (*Poa pratensis*), probably a native of SE Europe, and introduced by early colonists; it grows abundantly, producing a bluish appearance when in bud. Once home to frontiersman Daniel Boone, the Bluegrass gave its name to a musical style and to the "Bluegrass State."

Blue Hill town, pop. 1941, Hancock Co., SE Maine. Incorporating villages including East Blue Hill and Blue Hill Falls, it lies at the head of Blue Hill Bay, 13 mi/21 km SW of Ellsworth. An early shipbuilding, seafaring, agricultural, and yarn milling center named for a 940-ft/287-m hill lying just N, it is a resort and craft center noted for its pottery. Copper and zinc mines were important in the town's early years. Author Mary Ellen Chase, born here in 1887, immortalized the town in *A Goodly Heritage* and other books.

Blue Hills range of low wooded hills S of Boston, Massachusetts. The Blue Hills Reservation lies chiefly in Quincy, Milton, Randolph, and Canton. The Blue Hills Meteorological Observatory on Great Blue Hill (635 ft/194 m) is owned by Harvard University. Uses of the hills include hiking and skiing. The name *Massachusetts* means "at the big hills," a reference to the Blue Hills.

Blue Island city, pop. 21,203, Cook Co., NE Illinois, on the Calumet Sag Channel, a residential and industrial suburb of Chicago, 15 mi/24 km SW of the Loop. Settled in 1835, it has long served as an important railroad terminal. The local economy is largely based on train yards and repair shops. Manufactures include iron and steel products, wire, tile, brick, lumber, and barrels.

Blue Licks Spring on the Robertson-Nicholas county line, in NE Kentucky, 36 mi/58 km NE of Lexington, on the Licking R. Prehistoric animals were attracted by the salt springs, which later became a focal point of Indian life. The road to it, now US 68, was called the Buffalo Trace. **Blue Licks Battlefield State Park** commemorates the last Revolutionary War battle (Aug. 19, 1782) fought in Kentucky.

Blue Mound see under FORT WORTH, Texas.

Blue Mounds village, pop. 446, Dane Co., S Wisconsin, in the DRIFTLESS AREA, 23 mi/37 km WSW of Madison. The two Blue Mounds, rising to 1716 ft/523 m, are the highest points in S Wisconsin. In the early 1830s they were a boom lead mining area. Blue Mound State Park and Little Norway, a reconstruction of an 1850s homestead, just E, now draw visitors.

Blue Mountain **1.** peak (2623 ft/800 m) in W Arkansas, in the OUACHITA Mts., 13 m/21 km NE of MENA, one of the highest points in the state. **2.** town, pop. 667, Tippah Co., N Mississippi, 30 mi/48 km SW of Corinth, seat of Blue Mountain College (1873). **3.** see under COLLINGWOOD, Ontario. **4.** range in SE Pennsylvania, part of the Appalachian Plateau, running SW–NE for 150 mi/240 km and joining KITTATINNY Mt. at its NE end. Blue Mountain is one of a series of ridges, separated by long, narrow valleys, that run through the EC section of the state.

Blue Mountain Lake 2.5 mi/4 km E–W and 1 mi/1.6 km wide, in Indian Lake township, Hamilton Co., NE New York, in the C Adirondack Mts. Blue Mt. (3782 ft/1146 m) stands above it (E). The resort village of Blue Mountain Lake is the site of the Adirondack Museum.

Blue Mountains NNE–SSW oriented range extending over 150 mi/240 km from near John Day, in NE Oregon, up to the Snake R. in SE Washington. A W offshoot of the Northern Rocky Mts., this rolling range includes all of the mountains of NE Oregon except those of the rugged WALLOWA range (E). The Blues are generally c.6500 ft/1980 m high, with the highest elevation at Rock Creek Butte (9106 ft/2776 m) in the Elkhorn Ridge or Range, 13 mi/21 km W of Baker. The Strawberry Mts., near the S end, an 1860s gold rush site, rise to 9038 ft/2755 m at Strawberry Mt., SE of John Day. The OCHOCO Mts., a SW spur of the Blues, reach E–W across C Oregon to near BEND.

Blue Point unincorporated village, pop. 4230, in Brookhaven town, Suffolk Co., SE New York, on GREAT SOUTH BAY and Long Island's South Shore, just SW of Patchogue. It gave its name to a variety of oyster. Blue Point is a boating center.

Blue Ridge also, **Blue Ridge Mts.** or **Blue Ridge Province** prominent E part of the APPALACHIAN System of E North America, variously defined. Most narrowly, the Blue Ridge (often, the Blue Ridge Mts.) is limited to the steep escarpment between the PIEDMONT (E) and the Great Appalachian Valley (W), extending SW from near Harpers Ferry, West Virginia, through W Virginia, W North Carolina, and NW South Carolina to Mt. OGLETHORPE in NW Georgia. Some of the other ranges usually considered as comprising the Blue Ridge (which has many spurs and extensions) include the BLACK Mts., rising to 6684 ft/2039 m at Mt. MITCHELL, the highest elevation in the E US; the GREAT SMOKY Mts.; and the UNAKA Mts. More broadly, the Blue Ridge (generally 10–15 mi/16–24 km wide, but reaching 75 mi/120 km across in North Carolina) is said to extend N through Maryland and into Pennsylvania, where it is known as SOUTH Mt., for a total length of c.650 mi/1050 km. Still another definition has the Blue Ridge extending nearly 2000 mi/3200 km, parallel to the Atlantic coast and incorporating the GREEN Mts. in Vermont and the LONG RANGE in Newfoundland. The **Blue Ridge Province** includes the area covered by the latter definition plus the Piedmont in the S and related structures in the N. The geologically complex Blue Ridge, which includes some of the oldest (Precambrian) rocks of the Appalachian System, comprises largely metamorphic rocks, with igneous intrusions, and is known esp. for its hard granites and gneisses. In the S it is cut by the James, Potomac, and Roanoke rivers. The area is noted for its resorts, stands of hardwood, and isolated settlements, and is the subject of many songs and legends. Lumbering and tourism are major economic activities. Shenandoah National Park and the Blue Ridge Parkway run along the Blue Ridge, and parts of the George Washington and Jefferson national forests, the Mount Rogers National Recreation Area, and the Appalachian Trail are here.

Blue Ridge Parkway 470 mi/760 km long, in W Virginia and W North Carolina. Begun in 1933, it runs along crests of the Blue Ridge Mts. from Rockfish Gap, near Waynesboro, Virginia (NE), where it connects with SKYLINE DRIVE, to near Ravensford, Swain Co., North Carolina (SW), on the edge of the Qualla (Cherokee) reservation. Administered by the National Park Service, it connects Shenandoah and Great Smoky Mountains national parks. Virginia's PEAKS OF OTTER and North Carolina's Mt. PISGAH are among the many prominences along the route, which varies from a low of about 650 ft/200 m to over 6050 ft/1845 m in elevation.

Blue Springs **1.** city, pop. 40,153, Jackson Co., WC Missouri, 18 mi/29 km E of Kansas City. In a traditionally agricultural region, it is a growing residential suburb on Interstate 70 just outside Route 470, Kansas City's beltway. Blue Springs L. and Lake Jacomo Park are SW. **2.** see under HALTON HILLS, Ontario.

Bluestem Belt see FLINT HILLS, Kansas.

Bluestone Lake see under NEW R., West Virginia and Virginia.

bluff a steep slope, where a river has cut to (or under) the base of a hill, at the edge of an alluvial plain; probably from a Dutch word (*blaf,* "broad, flat") perhaps suggesting the horizontal aspect of such a slope, viewed from a distance. In a river valley, such as that of the Mississippi, bluffs mark former as well as present river edges, indicating the farthest point ever reached by the current in a particular direction. Bluffs have been central to the siting of cities including Memphis, Tennessee, and Vicksburg, Mississippi.

Bluff, the neighborhood in Pittsburgh, Pennsylvania, on a plateau overlooking the Monongahela R., immediately E of the GOLDEN TRIANGLE and S of UPTOWN. Laid out c.1830, it is home to Duquesne University (1878).

Bluffton **1.** city, pop. 9020, seat of Wells Co., NE Indiana, 25 mi/40 km S of Fort Wayne, on the Wabash R. Settled in 1829, it is in a farming and dairying region, with limestone quarries nearby. Farm implements and wood items are among light manufactures. **2.** village, pop. 3391, Allen and Hancock counties, NW Ohio, 15 mi/24 km NE of Lima. This railway junction serves as a distribution point for the crushed stone and lime developed from limestone quarried in the area. Local manufactures include electrical appliances, clothing, and food and dairy products. It is the seat of Bluffton College (1899), a Mennonite institution.

Blytheville city, pop. 22,906, co-seat (with OSCEOLA) of Mississippi Co., extreme NE Arkansas, 6 mi/10 km S of the Missouri border, and 8 mi/13 km W of the Mississippi R. Laid out in 1880, it had a lumber-based economy until drainage of the alluvial soil led to widespread cotton production. It is also a distribution center for wheat, hay, livestock, and corn. Manufactures include farm equipment and ambulances. The Blytheville (Eaker) Air Force Base was included within the city's limits in 1962. Mississippi County Community College (1974) is here. The Big Lake National Wildlife Refuge is to the W.

Boalsburg see under STATE COLLEGE, Pennsylvania.

Boathouse Row collection of boathouses in FAIRMOUNT PARK, Philadelphia, Pennsylvania, on the E side of the Schuylkill R., 1.5 mi/2.4 km NW of City Hall. The 11 buildings, home to rowing clubs, were constructed in the late 19th century.

Boaz city, pop. 6928, Marshall and Etowah counties, NE Alabama, 17 mi/27 km NW of Gadsden. An agricultural trade center with related industries, it is home to Snead State Junior College (1898; state-operated since 1935).

Boblo Island see under BOIS BLANC I., Ontario.

Bob Marshall Wilderness see under FLATHEAD NATIONAL FOREST, Montana.

Boca Chica see under KEY WEST, Florida.

Boca Raton city, pop. 61,492, Palm Beach Co., SE Florida, on the Atlantic Coast, 17 mi/27 km N of Fort Lauderdale. A luxury spa since 1925, it remains one of the most fashionable Florida winter resorts. It also has convention facilities and luxurious resort/retirement communities crossed by waterways. A manufacturing city since the 1960s, it produces computers, plastics, electrical equipment, printed matter, and other goods in a special zoned area. Venture capital and other financial and commercial operations located in the city in large numbers in the 1970s and 1980s. Florida Atlantic University (1961), the College of Boca Raton (1962), and an Air Force radar training center are here.

Bodie ghost town in Mono Co., EC California, 10 mi/16 km N of Mono L. and 75 mi/120 km SSE of Carson City, Nevada. In the Bodie Hills on the E of the Sierra Nevada, it was in the late 1870s a wild gold town, with a pop. of c.10,000 and a reputation epitomized in the phrase "bad man from Bodie." Today it is a State Historic Park.

Boeing assembly plant: see under EVERETT, Washington.

Boeing Field 5 mi/8 km SSE of downtown SEATTLE, Washington, along the Duwamish R. (W). The original home of the aircraft manufacturer (whose main facility is now in EVERETT), it is today the King Co. International Airport (used chiefly by private and charter flights). The old Boeing building, which turned out World War II's B-17 bomber, is now the Museum of Flight. The industrial and residential Georgetown neighborhood is just NW.

Boerum Hill residential section of NW Brooklyn, New York. Lying E of Cobble Hill and N of Park Slope, it is one of the brownstone neighborhoods closest to commercial downtown Brooklyn, and became increasingly popular after the 1970s.

Bogalusa city, pop. 14,280, Washington Parish, SE Louisiana, at the junction of the Bogue Lusa Creek and the Pearl R., 57 mi/92 km NNE of New Orleans. It was settled in 1906 by the Great Southern Lumber Company, and developed as a pine logging and sawmilling center. The forest industries still dominate the economy today; major reforestation programs sustain them. Paper and tung oil are manufactured and dairy and beef cattle are raised in the area as well, and the city has other light manufactures. Bogalusa is home to the Louisiana State University forestry school and to state and Federal agricultural experiment stations.

Bogue Sound sheltered inlet of the Atlantic Ocean, 25 mi/40 km E of Jacksonville, in Carteret Co., SE North Carolina. Twenty-five mi/40 km E–W and 1–2.5 mi/1–4 km wide, the sound is separated from ONSLOW BAY (S) by the **Bogue Banks** barrier island, and connects with the ocean via Beaufort Inlet (E) and Bogue Inlet (W). A bridge crosses the E end of the sound between MOREHEAD CITY on the mainland and Atlantic Beach (town, pop. 1938) on the island, and another crosses the W end between Cape Carteret, on the mainland, and the island. The sound and island are noted for fishing, and the Theodore Roosevelt State Natural Area protects osprey, snowy egrets, and marine life. Croatan National Forest is N on the mainland.

Bohemian Grove see under MONTE RIO, California.

Boiling Springs town, pop. 2445, Cleveland Co., S North Carolina, 7 mi/11 km SW of SHELBY. It is the seat of Gardner-Webb College (1905).

Bois Blanc Island **1** 35 sq mi/ 91 sq km, pop. 59, in Mackinac Co., N Michigan, 6 mi/10 km N of Cheboygan. In the Straits of Mackinac, NW L. Huron, Bois Blanc ("white wood" in French) is 12 mi/19 km long and 4 mi/6 km wide. Very sparsely inhabited, it is used mostly as a resort, and much of it is covered by Mackinaw State Forest, which includes several lakes and marshes. A lighthouse is located at the tip of a narrow NE peninsula. **2** also, **Boblo Island** 1.5 mi/2.4 km long, in Essex Co., W Ontario, in the DETROIT R., 1 mi/1.6 km NW of Amherstburg. The island is occupied by a 272-ac/110-ha amusement park. It is accessible by ferry from Amherstburg and from Gibraltar and Detroit, Michigan.

Boisbriand city, pop. 21,124, Thérèse-De Blainville census division, S Québec, on the R. des Mille Îles, across (NW) from the I. Jésus (Laval) and 15 mi/24 km NW of Montréal, on the Laurentian Autoroute. It is a fast-growing industrial (with a General Motors plant) and residential suburb.

Boise also, **Boise City** city, pop. 125,738, state capital and seat of Ada Co., SW Idaho, on the Boise R. Situated on the OREGON TRAIL, it was founded in 1863 after the Boise Basin gold rush, when the US Army built Fort Boise. The settlement was at first a service center for nearby mines. Later the economy expanded to include agriculture and lumbering. Boise became territorial capital in 1864 and capital of the new state in 1890. The railroad arrived in 1925, commercial aviation a year later, and the city is now a major transportation hub. Surrounded by a large metropolitan area, Boise is by far the most populous city in Idaho, with a population growth of 25% between 1980 and 1990. The state and Federal governments are now major employers. The city is also a trade center for a large area of farms in SW Idaho and E Oregon producing fruit, sugar beets, dairy products, and livestock. Other industries include lumber milling, food processing, and the manufacture of electronic equipment, mobile homes, wood and steel products, and farm machinery. In recent years, Boise has become a headquarters city for both national and international businesses. The city is also the seat of Boise State University (1932).

Boise City town, pop. 1509, seat of CIMARRON Co., extreme NW Oklahoma, in the PANHANDLE's high plains, 26 mi/42 km E of the New Mexico border and 17 mi/27 km N of the Texas line. A highway junction near the old SANTA FE TRAIL, it lies in a unique geologic zone filled with rugged mesas, SE of BLACK MESA, the highest point in the state. In an agricultural and oil producing area, it stores grain and makes dairy products.

Boise National Forest 2.65 million ac/1.1 million ha (4138 sq mi/10,718 sq km), in SW Idaho, E and NE of Boise, on the W of the SAWTOOTH RANGE. It has many peaks over 9000 ft/2740 m, and headwaters of the Salmon, Boise, and other rivers. The Sawtooth (E), Challis (NE), and Payette (N) national forests adjoin.

Boise River 95 mi/153 km long, in SW Idaho. Formed by the confluence of the Middle and North forks, flowing from the Sawtooth Range, 12 mi/19 km SE of Idaho City, it continues W through Arrowrock and Lucky Peak reservoirs, past Boise, across the COLUMBIA PLATEAU's Payette section, to join the Snake R. at the Oregon border. The river's South Fork, 100 mi/160 km long, flows WNW into the Arrowrock Reservoir. The Boise's irrigation projects serve SW Idaho and neighboring E Oregon; grain, fruit, and vegetable (esp. sugar beet) farming are important; Basque sheepherders are also prominent in the area. Farmed since the 1860s, the Boise Valley was also the scene of an 1862 gold rush.

Boissevain town, pop. 1484, SW Manitoba, 45 mi/72 km S of Brandon, in a wheat producing area. It is a gateway to the INTERNATIONAL PEACE GARDEN, 15 mi/24 km S (straddling the

North Dakota border), and the nearby Turtle Mountain Provincial Park. Every July, Boissevain hosts the Canadian Turtle Derby.

Boley town, pop. 908, Okfuskee Co., EC Oklahoma, 25 mi/40 km NE of Shawnee. Established in 1903 as an all-black community similar to LANGSTON, it was set along a railway line near Creek land grants. In an agricultural region, the town has maintained a largely black population, and holds an annual black rodeo.

Bolingbrook village, pop. 40,843, Will and Du Page counties, NE Illinois, a residential suburb 25 mi/40 km SW of Chicago, at the edge of the metropolitan area. ARGONNE NATIONAL LABORATORY is 4 mi/6 km E.

Bolivar **1.** city, pop. 6845, seat of Polk Co., SW Missouri. On the Ozark Plateau, 28 mi/45 km N of Springfield. In a region producing grain and dairy products, it has bottling plants, flour mills, and other agriculture-related industries. It is the seat of Southwest Baptist University (1878). **2.** city, pop. 5969, seat of Hardeman Co., SW Tennessee, near the Hatchie R., 67 mi/108 km E of Memphis. Founded in 1824, it handles local cotton and timber. The Little Courthouse (1824) is the oldest in W Tennessee. **3.** see under HARPERS FERRY, West Virginia.

Boll Weevil Monument see under ENTERPRISE, Alabama.

Bolton see under CALEDON, Ontario.

Bolton Hill preservation district in the N midtown section of Baltimore, Maryland, consisting of several blocks of three-story 19th-century town houses restored under Baltimore's Urban Renewal and Housing Agency. Many of the buildings had been divided into apartments in the 1950s when intensified industrialization brought more workers into the city.

Bombay Hook National Wildlife Refuge at the NW end of Delaware Bay, 10 mi/16 km NE of Dover, in Kent Co., E Delaware. Consisting of 16,280 ac/6594 ha of marshes, it is the winter home of 25,000 migratory waterfowl. Over 300 species nest at Bombay Hook year round.

Bomoseen, Lake resort lake in Rutland Co., WC Vermont, 10 mi/16 km W of Rutland. The largest natural body of water entirely within Vermont, it is 8 mi/13 km long and 1–5 mi/1.6–8 km wide. Slate was once quarried from cliffs on the W shore. In the center of the lake is 10-ac/4-ha Neshobe Island; in the 1930s this was the summer home of Alexander Woollcott, who welcomed frequent theatrical and literary guests.

Bon Air unincorporated residential suburb, pop. 16,413, Chesterfield Co., EC Virginia, 5 mi/8 km SW of Richmond.

Bonanza Creek 20 mi/32 km long, in the WC Yukon Territory, flowing NNW to the Klondike R. just S of DAWSON. On Aug. 17, 1896, George Washington Carmack and two Indian partners, Skookum Jim and Tagish Charlie, discovered PLACER gold here on what was then known as Rabbit Creek, touching off the 1897–1900s KLONDIKE gold rush.

Bonavista town, pop. 4597, E Newfoundland, at the tip of the Bonavista Peninsula, on the SE shore of Bonavista Bay, 79 mi/126 km NNW of St. John's. **Cape Bonavista,** immediately N, is the reputed site of John Cabot's first landing in 1497. The cape also marked the E extension of the FRENCH SHORE from 1713 to 1783. The town was established SW of the cape and became a major fishing center. Today the leading industries are cod and salmon fishing and processing.

Bonham city, pop. 6686, seat of Fannin Co., NE Texas, 65 mi/105 km NE of Dallas and 14 mi/23 km S of the Red R. (the Oklahoma line). It is a trade and manufacturing center in a prairie area raising cotton, vegetables, and beef cattle. Gasoline pumps, lawnmowers, cheese, cables, and mattresses are manufactured. Sam Rayburn (d. here 1961), former speaker of the US House of Representatives, is honored by his hometown with a memorial library.

Bonner unincorporated village, pop. 1669, Missoula Co., W Montana, on the Clark Fork R., 7 mi/11 km SE of Missoula. It was long known for what was reputedly the world's largest sawmill, built in 1885. The mill's products included timber used in mines.

Bonneville Dam built 1933–37 on the COLUMBIA R., midway between THE DALLES (E) and PORTLAND (W), Oregon. The dam lowest on the river, it is a hydroelectric generating site with navigation locks, and is noted for its fish ladders, allowing salmon to travel upstream to spawn.

Bonneville Salt Flats section of the GREAT SALT LAKE Desert in NW Utah, 100 mi/160 km W of Salt Lake City, near the Nevada border. One of the remnants of glacial L. Bonneville (others are Great Salt, SEVIER, and UTAH lakes), it is an area of some 70 sq mi/170 sq km, characterized by flat white sands that are covered by shallow water in winter and spring, dry in summer and fall. Since 1914 the flats have been used for auto speed runs, and numerous world records have been set on them; Speed Week (Aug.) is the focus of activity. Just W is Wendover (city, pop. 1127, Tooele Co.), headquarters in World War II for a vast air training center, whose test ranges (SE and NE) are now used by aircraft from Hill Air Force Base. On I-80, Wendover is adjacent to West Wendover, Nevada (unincorporated, pop. 2007, Elko Co.). The two communities constitute a road service and tourist center.

Book Cliffs escarpment, extending 130 mi/210 km NE–SW, in Carbon, Emery, and Grand counties, E Utah, and Garfield and Mesa counties, W Colorado. The rugged sandstone cliffs rise to 9000 ft/2740 m in the S, with upper elevations receiving up to 200 in/508 cm of snow a year. Together with the Roan Cliffs, which parallel them (N), they extend over 200 mi/320 km, and are part of the S Uinta Basin of the Colorado Plateau, forming the S boundary of the East and West Tavaputs plateaus. The Colorado R. runs SW along them.

Booker T. Washington National Monument see under FRANKLIN Co., Virginia.

Boone **1.** city, pop. 12,392, seat of Boone Co., C Iowa, on the Des Moines R., 12 mi/19 km W of Ames. An 1860s railroad town, it expanded as an agricultural processing and industrial center. Machinery, steel fabrications, and plastic signs are among the products manufactured here. Many children's summer camps are located in the vicinity; nearby recreation areas include Ledges State Park, 6 mi/10 km SW, and the Iowa Arboretum, 8 mi/13 km SE. **2.** town, pop. 12,915, seat of Watauga Co., NW North Carolina, in the Blue Ridge Mts, just N of the headwaters of the Watauga R., and on the headwaters of the South Fork of the New R. Daniel Boone lived in the area in the 1760s; in the 1770s the WATAUGA Association organized local settlements. Boone is now a mountain resort and lumbering center. It is the seat of Appalachian State University (1899).

Boone County **1.** 282 sq mi/679 sq km, pop. 30,806, in NC Illinois, on the Kishwaukee R. Wisconsin borders the county on the N. Outside of BELVIDERE, the county seat, dairy farms and cornfields predominate. Some commercial and residential development has occurred along I-90 between Rockford

(W) and Belvidere. **2.** 246 sq mi/637 sq km, pop. 57,589, in N Kentucky. Its seat is Burlington, its N and W boundary the Ohio R. It grows corn, burley tobacco, and fruit, raises livestock, and produces dairy goods, but is increasingly within the Cincinnati suburban area. Big Bone Lick State Park is a site where mastodon, mammoth, primitive horse, and sloth skeletons have been found in salt spring mud. The Greater Cincinnati International Airport is in the NE.

Boonesboro unincorporated resort village in Clark Co., EC Kentucky, 16 mi/26 km SE of Lexington, on the Kentucky R. The state's second settlement, Fort Boonesboro, was built (1775) by a company of North Carolina men, led by Daniel Boone, who had just opened Boone's Trace through the Cumberland Gap. It was to be the capital of TRANSYLVANIA. Under continual attack, it was abandoned (1778) after a Shawnee raid. Fort Boonesborough State Park is just NE of the village.

Boone's Lick historic site in Howard Co., NC Missouri, 12 mi/19 km NW of BOONVILLE. In 1806 Daniel Boone's sons came here from DEFIANCE to initiate a business supplying salt to the St. Louis area by keelboat. Travel over the route here from E Missouri contributed to later settlement of the fertile Missouri Valley, and to establishment of the SANTA FE TRAIL.

Boone's Trace see under WILDERNESS ROAD.

Booneville city, pop. 7955, seat of Prentiss Co., NE Mississippi, 18 mi/29 km SSW of Corinth. Settled in 1859, it was the scene of a victory for Union troops led by Philip Sheridan on July 1, 1862, as Confederates retreated from CORINTH. In an agricultural and timbering region, it is a center for cotton ginning, lumber milling, and the manufacture of footwear, and the seat of Northeast Mississippi Community College (1948).

Boonton town, pop. 8343, Morris Co., NC New Jersey, on the Rockaway R., Route 287, and the Parsippany Reservoir, 8 mi/13 km NE of Morristown. Settled in the 18th century, it became a hub of the ironmaking industry during the mid 19th century. Boonton was also the site of many factories, including the first plant to make bakelite. Today the town has an oil refinery, and produces such goods as railway fuses, electronic equipment, batteries, pharmaceuticals, metal powder, and plastics.

Boonville **1.** city, pop. 7095, seat of Cooper Co., C Missouri, on the Missouri R., 23 mi/37 km W of Columbia. Settled in 1810, it was a major early river port and an important provisioning point for wagon trains heading SW on the SANTA FE TRAIL. It was the site of Missouri's first Civil War battle (June 17, 1861), a victory for Union troops under Nathaniel Lyon. Today livestock, grain, and dairy goods are produced, and there are other light industries. The city's historic districts include the oldest surviving theater W of the Allegheny Mts. Boone's Lick State Historic Site is N. **2.** town, pop. 4246, Oneida Co., C New York, 30 mi/48 km N of Utica. Founded on property owned by the Holland Land Company in the late 18th century, it was named for the company's agent, Garret Boon. Growth was spurred by the BLACK R. canal and railroad in the mid 19th century. It is now a trade hub for a dairy farming region. Novelist Walter D. Edmonds (*Drums Along the Mohawk*) was born here in 1903.

Boothbay Harbor town, pop. 2347, Lincoln Co., SW Maine. It is on the Atlantic Ocean, 12 mi/19 km SE of Brunswick. Originally part of Boothbay, from which it separated in 1889, the town is a popular resort, artists' retreat, and yachting and excursion-boat center. Southport, Squirrel, Capitol, and other resort islands are nearby. An early trading and shipping center and seaport, Boothbay Harbor is now supported mainly by tourism, lobstering, and fishing.

Bootheel Region southeasternmost corner of Missouri, along the Mississippi R., created in 1818 when plantation owner John Walker managed to get the proposed new state's S boundary extended from 36° 30′ N to 36° N between the SAINT FRANCIS R. (W) and the Mississippi, an area today comprising Pemiscot and Dunklin counties and the S part of New Madrid Co. KENNETT is today the largest city. Caruthersville (pop. 7389, Pemiscot Co.) was founded in 1857 on Walker's land. The alluvial area is noted for its cotton, corn, and melon production and Southern character.

Boothia Peninsula northernmost part of mainland North America, up to 120 mi/190 km wide, and extending 170 mi/275 km N into the Arctic Ocean from the area of Spence Bay, in the Kitikmeot Region, C Northwest Territories, between the Gulf of Boothia (E) and Larsen Sound (W). The 1 mi/2 km–wide Bellot Strait separates it, at 71° 58′ N, from Somerset I. (N). Discovered in 1829 by John Ross, it was at that time the estimated location of the NORTH MAGNETIC POLE. Part of the CANADIAN SHIELD, rugged Boothia is settled only on the S, at Spence Bay (hamlet, pop. 580), an INUIT community.

Boot Hill popular name for the cemetery of a cowboy town, particularly those in DODGE CITY, Kansas, TOMBSTONE, Arizona, and DEADWOOD, South Dakota.

Borah Peak 12,662 ft/3859 m, in Custer Co., SC Idaho, the highest point in the state, in the Lost River Range, in the Challis National Forest, 37 mi/60 km NE of Sun Valley. Named for Senator William E. Borah, the mountain rises from a high tableland and is crested with limestone.

Bordentown city, pop. 4341, Burlington Co., WC New Jersey, on the Delaware R., 5 mi/8 km SE of Trenton. Settled in 1682 by English Quakers, it was bombarded and partially destroyed by the British during the Revolution. Bordentown became a major 19th-century canal and railroad center. Its Historic District contains such structures as Clara Barton's school, America's first free public school, and Thomas Paine's house. Bordentown was also home (1816–39) to Joseph Bonaparte, part of whose estate remains as Bonaparte Park. Today Bordentown is residential, and manufactures bricks, wine, and printing machinery. It is the seat of Bordentown Military Institute (1881). Bordentown township (pop. 3566) is home to a reformatory and a center for the retarded.

Border States or **the Border South** see under the SOUTH.

bore also, **tidal bore** body of tidal water that moves rapidly inland, its front resembling a wall, sometimes as much as 3 ft/1 m high. Bores occur chiefly at new or full moons, when tides move into narrow, tapering, shallow estuaries or other channels, and are held up by outflowing (e.g., river) water.

Borger city, pop. 15,675, Hutchinson Co., NW Texas, in the PANHANDLE, near the Canadian R., 45 mi/72 km NE of Amarillo. It boomed suddenly in 1926 when the Panhandle oilfield was opened, and had 40,000 residents at one time. Today it makes chemicals, ink, synthetic rubber, and carbon black, and the area raises cattle. Frank Phillips College (1948) is here. The Alibates Flint Quarries National Monument is 19 mi/31 km WSW.

Borgne, Lake SW reach of MISSISSIPPI SOUND, E of New Orleans, in SE Louisiana. Twenty-five mi/40 km NE–SW and 8–15 mi/13–24 km wide, it connects L. PONTCHARTRAIN (W) with the Gulf of Mexico via the sound. It is linked with the Mississippi R. via the Lake Borgne Canal.

Borinquén also, **Boriquén** Taino (Arawakan) name for the island of Puerto Rico. It has been translated as "island of the brave lord," and gave rise to the Puerto Rican anthem, "La Borinqueña."

Boron unincorporated community, pop. 2101, Kern Co., SC California, in the MOJAVE DESERT, 70 mi/110 km NE of Los Angeles and just NE of EDWARDS AIR FORCE BASE. In an area that produces most of the world's borax, it is the site of enormous open-pit mines and of the Twenty Mule Team Museum.

borough 1. in Alaska, an administrative division, organized or unorganized; the former is essentially the equivalent of a COUNTY, the latter is administered directly by the state. Some Alaska cities (e.g., Anchorage, Juneau) are coextensive with boroughs. **2.** one of the five divisions (the Bronx, Brooklyn, Manhattan, Queens, Staten Island) of New York City, each also a county. **3.** in some US states (esp. New Jersey), an incorporated municipality, generally but not necessarily smaller than a city, and essentially the same in governance; the term derives from specially chartered, fortified towns of medieval Britain. Canada has a single borough, EAST YORK, which is of this type.

Borough Park residential and commercial section of WC Brooklyn, New York. It was part of the old township of NEW UTRECHT. Real estate development began in the 1880s, but it was in the 1920s that large numbers of Orthodox Jews moved here from crowded WILLIAMSBURG, with which Borough Park retains many links. The area is noted for its hundreds of synagogues and Jewish sales and manufacturing (especially food) establishments. Kensington, which lies to the E, is similar but ethnically more diverse.

Borrego Springs see under ANZA BORREGO DESERT STATE PARK, California.

Borscht Belt region in the CATSKILL Mts. of SE New York, mainly in Sullivan Co., 75–90 mi/120–145 km NW of New York City. Jewish (and some Italian) immigrants in New York began to use the area for summer vacations in the late 19th century. During the 1920s and 1930s, when the automobile made the area easily accessible, it became an extremely popular resort center, nicknamed for the Russian beet soup consumed at its overflowing dining tables. At centers like Monticello, Kiamesha Lake, Ellenville, and Liberty, visitors found hotels with generous menus, luxurious grounds, sports, sunshine, and entertainments (many noted mid-20th-century comedians began here). By the 1950s there were over 300 hotels in the region, but it declined rapidly from the 1960s. By the 1990s, fewer than a dozen of the old-fashioned hotels remained, but some facilities were being revived as ashrams, New Age camps, and special-interest centers.

Boscawen town, pop. 3586, Merrimack Co., SC New Hampshire. It is on high ground along the Merrimack R. above its junction with the Contoocook R., 7 mi/11 km NW of Concord. Daniel Webster established his first law office here in 1805, and Senator William Pitt Fessenden (1806–69) was born in the village. The town remains primarily residential.

Boscobel city, pop. 2706, Grant Co., SW Wisconsin, on the Wisconsin R., 23 mi/37 km NE of Prairie du Chien. It is a trade center in a dairying and farming area. Beer, lumber, garage equipment, and metal products are manufactured. Gideons, International, the bible society, was founded here (1898).

Bossier City city, pop. 52,721, Bossier Parish, NW Louisiana, across the Red R. (NE) from SHREVEPORT. Settled in 1835 as Cane's Landing, it forms, with Shreveport, one of the largest US oil and gas producing centers. It has refineries and railroad shops, and manufactures chemicals, fertilizers, cottonseed oil, playground equipment, mattresses, and candy. The ruins of the Confederate Fort Smith, built for the defense of Shreveport, lie within the city. Barksdale Air Force Base, a major Cold War facility, is just SE.

Boston city, pop. 574,283, state capital and seat of SUFFOLK Co., E Massachusetts, at the mouths of the Charles and Mystic rivers and the head of MASSACHUSETTS BAY. The most populous city in New England, it is the center of a five-county (Suffolk, ESSEX, MIDDLESEX, NORFOLK, and PLYMOUTH) metropolitan area with a pop. of 3,783,817. It was founded in 1630 by a group of colonists who had just arrived at CHARLESTOWN and were invited to share the "Trimountaine" peninsula (called by Indians Shawmut) by its solitary settler, William Blackstone (Blaxton). Its harbor soon made it central to the Puritan settlements of New England; through the 17th century it was the scene of pioneering educational, governmental, and economic undertakings. In the 18th century it became the focal point for moves toward American independence. After British troops, in response to unrest, occupied the city in 1768, the Boston Massacre (1770), the Boston Tea Party (1773), and the start of Paul Revere's ride (April 1775) to rouse Colonial forces occurred here. After an abortive attempt at BUNKER HILL (June 1775), American troops succeeded in driving the British from the city in March 1776. Following the Revolution, Boston prospered on commerce, esp. the China trade. A center of Federalism, it opposed the War of 1812, in which port activity ground to a halt. In the postwar period, industry began (aided by railroads, from the 1830s) to replace the port as the key to the economy. As the city grew with manufacturing and with new manpower brought esp. by 1840s–50s Irish immigrants, it also, drawing on its Puritan past and status as an educational and cultural center, became the center of American antislavery activism. Booming through the Civil War period, it began to expand by reclaiming the BACK BAY and by annexing ROXBURY and other neighboring towns. By 1900 it had a pop. of 560,892, fifth in the US. In the 20th century Boston has been an industrial, commercial, and institutional center. Its pop. peaked in 1950 at 801,444; since then, it has lost people and businesses to its suburbs (esp. to those on its BELTWAYS—on ROUTE 128 in the 1950s–60s, on the outer Route 495 since the 1960s) and to more distant locations. Urban renewal projects from the 1950s created such new focal points as the PRUDENTIAL CENTER and GOVERNMENT CENTER, but at the same time stripped older neighborhoods of much housing. In the 1970s high-rise construction transformed the old Downtown (the Shawmut Peninsula); the city of today has a small older core with narrow, heavily traveled streets, and less crowded residential areas developed in the late 19th century. Boston remains a major fishing port, and imports fuels, raw materials, and such manufactures as automobiles; its varied exports are led by high-tech products of the region (including

Route 128). The city makes machinery, printed materials, metal products, clothing, specialized equipment, and a variety of other goods. It is a major financial center, with a large insurance sector, and remains the commercial HUB of New England. It is perhaps best known today, however, as an educational, cultural, medical, and research center. Boston University (1839), Suffolk University (1906), a number of smaller colleges, and a University of Massachusetts branch (1964) are in the city, and institutions in such neighboring cities as CAMBRIDGE, MEDFORD, and NEWTON (many of which have medical and other professional schools in the city) combine with Boston to form a famous educational cluster. The New England Conservatory, Boston Conservatory, and Berklee College are leaders in music education. There are also noted art schools, seminaries, and other specialized schools. Massachusetts General Hospital and Peter Bent Brigham Hospital are among well-known medical centers. The Museum of Fine Arts and Isabella Stewart Gardner Museum are perhaps the best known of Boston's museums. The Athenaeum (1807) is a pioneering private library and intellectual gathering place. All these institutions draw on a tradition stretching back to America's first public school (the Latin School, 1635), and including along the way the birth and growth of such movements as Unitarianism, transcendentalism, and Christian Science. Modern Boston, having seen its industrial base shrink (high-tech manufacturing has retarded this trend), has an economy centered on education, finance, commerce, research, and Federal and state government. Tourists, drawn to the city's historic sites and older residential neighborhoods, provide much income. Well-known sports venues include FENWAY Park, home to the Red Sox (baseball), and **Boston Garden,** home to the Celtics (basketball) and Bruins (hockey), which is on the W edge of the NORTH END. The city extends from its much altered waterfront into hills in the SW. The Irish are its largest ethnic group, and it has substantial Italian, Jewish, and black communities. See also: ALLSTON-BRIGHTON; ARNOLD ARBORETUM; ATHENS OF AMERICA; BACK BAY; BEACON HILL; BEACON St.; BEANTOWN; BOSTON COMMON; BOSTON HARBOR; BREED'S HILL; BUNKER HILL; CASTLE ISLAND; CHARLES R.; CHARLESTOWN; CHINATOWN; COCOANUT GROVE; COMBAT ZONE; COPLEY SQUARE; COPPS HILL; DEER ISLAND; DORCHESTER; EAST BOSTON; FANEUIL HALL; FENWAY; FRANKLIN PARK; GOVERNMENT CENTER; HAYMARKET SQUARE; the HUB; HYDE PARK; JAMAICA PLAIN; KENMORE SQUARE; LOGAN INTERNATIONAL AIRPORT; LOUISBURG SQUARE; MATTAPAN; MYSTIC R.; NEPONSET R.; NORTH END; OLD NORTH CHURCH; OLD SOUTH MEETING HOUSE; PARKER HOUSE; PRUDENTIAL CENTER; QUINCY MARKET; ROSLINDALE; ROXBURY; SCOLLAY SQUARE; SHAWMUT PENINSULA; SOUTH BOSTON; SOUTH END; SOUTH STATION; WEST END; WEST ROXBURY.

Boston Common public park, 48 ac/19 ha, in Boston, Massachusetts, bounded by Beacon (along BEACON HILL), Park, Tremont, Boylston, and Charles (separating it from the Public Garden) streets. The oldest public park in America, it was acquired from William Blackstone, the Shawmut Peninsula's first white inhabitant, in 1634, to provide pasturage for livestock. It was used as a training ground during the Revolution. Modern Boston Common is used for public events; it is popular with political protesters, picknickers, and street performers. The Common's most famous monument is Saint-Gaudens's memorial (1897) to the 54th Massachusetts Regiment, a black Civil War force, often called the Shaw Memorial after its leader, Robert Gould Shaw; it stands at the NE corner, opposite the Massachusetts State House.

Boston-Edison residential section of C Detroit, Michigan, NW of NEW CENTER and SE of HIGHLAND PARK, on both sides of Woodward Ave. In the period after World War I, when the auto industry flourished, it became one of the areas outside of GRAND BOULEVARD that was home to executives and other affluent Detroiters who had previously lived closer to Downtown.

Boston Harbor in Boston, Massachusetts. One of the finest natural harbors in the world, and New England's leading port, with approximately 25 mi/40 km of docking space, it can accommodate the largest passenger and cargo ships. The US Navy has several facilities on the harbor. The CHARLES and MYSTIC rivers flow into Boston Harbor. Most dockage is in the inner harbor, in downtown Boston, South Boston, Charlestown, and East Boston. In the outer harbor are small islands, including Georges, Thompson, Long, and PEDDOCKS, some of which are open for recreational use.

Boston Mountains section of the S OZARK Plateau, extending from the Illinois R. in E Oklahoma to the White R. in EC Arkansas, N of the Arkansas R. Some 200 mi/320 km E–W and 35 mi/56 km wide, it rises to more than 2300 ft/715 m NW of Fort Smith, and is mostly in the Ozark National Forest. Devil's Den State Park is noted for deep (500–1400 ft/150–425 m) gorges and caves. The Bostons have long been noted for their ruggedness and rural isolation.

Boston Post Road postal route, later a highway, established in the 1670s by riders from the S tip of Manhattan, New York, to Boston. In modern terms it roughly followed the course of BROADWAY from the Battery to City Hall Park, then the BOWERY north toward Harlem, crossed the Harlem R. at Spuyten Duyvil, traversed the Bronx, and joined what became US 1, continuing through Connecticut to the E. In places it is known as the Post Road, Old Post Road, or Boston-New York Post Road.

Boston States see under NEW ENGLAND.

Bothell city, pop. 12,345, King and Snohomish counties, WC Washington, on the Sammamish R., a residential and commercial suburb 12 mi/19 km NE of downtown Seattle. Founded in 1884 by logger David Bothell, who laid it out and sold lots to settlers, the city manufactures medical equipment, computer software, and concrete products, and processes the products of nearby farms.

Boucherville city, pop. 33,796, Chambly Co., S Québec, on the SE bank of the St. Lawrence R., 9 mi/14 km NE of Montréal, to which it is linked by the LaFontaine Bridge-Tunnel. Founded in 1668, it was long a center for market gardening, food canning, and clothing manufacture. Since 1965, when the bridge-tunnel opened, it has grown as a residential suburb, with some industry. The Îles de Boucherville, a chain of islands, form a recreational area in the river.

Boulder city, pop. 83,312, seat of Boulder Co., NC Colorado, on Boulder Creek, at the base of the Flatiron Range of the Rocky Mts., 25 mi/40 km NW of Denver. Founded (1858) by gold miners, it was an early mining and agricultural center. The arrival of the railroad (1873) and the University of Colorado (1876) fostered economic growth. Since the 1950s, Boulder has been a center of scientific and environmental research. Now situated here are the National Center for Atmospheric Research, the National Bureau of

Standards, a branch of the World Data Center of Solar Activity, the Joint Institute for Laboratory Astrophysics, and a number of large corporate research facilities. The city is also a tourist and New Age center and a mecca for such sports as skiing; mountain, ice, and rock climbing; skydiving; hot-air ballooning; and kayaking. Visitors are also drawn to the University's annual Shakespeare Festival. Local manufactures include aircraft, business machines, pharmaceuticals, and chemicals.

Boulder Batholith in Montana: see under BATHOLITH.

Boulder City also, **Boulder** city, pop. 12,567, Clark Co., SE Nevada, 22 mi/35 km SE of Las Vegas and 8 mi/13 km W of the Arizona border. Named for the Boulder Canyon Project, it was established by the US government (1931) as a residential community for workers building the HOOVER DAM (just E) and other local projects. It was made self-governing in 1958. The city is headquarters for the US Water and Power Resource Service and the Lake MEAD National Recreational Area. Tourism is central to its economy.

Boulder County 742 sq mi/1922 sq km, pop. 225,339, in NC Colorado. Boulder is its seat. LONGMONT (NE) is the other large city. With its W border the Continental Divide (the FRONT RANGE), the county occupies Rocky Mt. foothills NW of Denver. The St. Vrain Creek (N) and Boulder Creek (S) drain it to the E. A diversified farming area with some mining and manufacturing, as well as Boulder's educational complex, it is also a collection of growing residential suburbs; the county's pop. has almost doubled since 1970.

Boulder Dam former (1933–47) name of Hoover Dam. See L. MEAD, Arizona and Nevada.

Boulevard of the Allies commercial thoroughfare, 2.5 mi/4 km long, between the GOLDEN TRIANGLE and SQUIRREL HILL sections of Pittsburgh, Pennsylvania. Designed by Frederick Law Olmsted, Jr., and built 1922–27, it passes through the BLUFF and OAKLAND.

Boundary Peak 13,143 ft/4006 m, in Esmeralda Co., SW Nevada, 65 mi/105 km WSW of Tonopah. In the TOIYABE NATIONAL FOREST, this northernmost peak of the WHITE Mts. is the highest point in Nevada and is just NE of the California-Nevada border.

Boundary Waters Canoe Area 975,000-ac/395,000-ha recreational and conservational wilderness in St. Louis, Iron, and Cook counties, in the ARROWHEAD REGION of NE Minnesota, stretching 150 mi/240 km along the Ontario border. On the RAINY and other rivers, with thousands of lakes, it is a popular summer retreat for Midwesterners, and the only US lake wilderness whose water area is larger than its land area. VOYAGEURS NATIONAL PARK is just NW, and Ontario's Quetico Provincial Park adjoins (N). ELY is a center of area activities.

Bound Brook borough, pop. 9487, Somerset Co., NC New Jersey, on the Raritan R., 7 mi/11 km NW of New Brunswick. It was settled in 1681 on land purchased from the Raritan Indians. American troops were defeated by the forces of Cornwallis here in April 1777. The borough's manufactures include chemicals, roofing materials, plastics, textiles, clothing, and metal products. Bound Brook is also known for its greenhouses, which produce and ship orchids and gardenias.

Bountiful city, pop. 36,659, Davis Co., N Utah, a largely residential suburb 8 mi/13 km N of Salt Lake City, and just SE of Great Salt L. Named for its abundant harvests, it is the state's second-oldest (1847) Mormon settlement. It trades and processes fruit (esp. cherries) and poultry, and has nurseries.

Bourbon County 292 sq mi/756 sq km, pop. 19,236, in NC Kentucky. Its seat is PARIS. Drained by the South Fork of the Licking R., in the BLUEGRASS REGION, it produces burley tobacco, livestock, and poultry, makes dairy products, and quarries limestone. There is some manufacturing at Paris. The first still making the whiskey named for the county was built by Baptist minister Elijah Craig in Georgetown, in 1789. Bottling almost half of US whiskey, Kentucky produces 87% of the world's bourbon, partly because of the purity of local spring water.

Bourbonnais village, pop. 13,934, Kankakee Co., NE Illinois, a residential suburb 2 mi/3 km NW of Kankakee. Originally a French-Canadian trading post settled in 1832, it was bypassed by the Illinois Central Railroad because of a land-promoting scheme in what became Kankakee. Bourbonnais is the seat of Olivet Nazarene University (1907). Kankakee River State Park is 5 mi/8 km NW.

Bourbon Street commercial thoroughfare in the VIEUX CARRÉ of NEW ORLEANS, Louisiana, three blocks NW of Jackson Square. It is noted for its nightclubs, strip joints, and bars.

Bourne town, pop. 16,064, Barnstable Co., SE Massachusetts. The westernmost community on Cape Cod, it serves as a commercial gateway to the region. The CAPE COD CANAL crosses the town between Buzzards Bay (SW) and Cape Cod Bay (NE). The Massachusetts Maritime Academy is in Buzzards Bay village, N of the canal. Agriculture, including cranberry growing, is important. Otis Air Force Base and Camp Edwards military reservations occupy much of the township.

Bow town, pop. 5500, Merrimack Co., SC New Hampshire. It is on the Merrimack R., adjoining and S of Concord. Christian Science founder Mary Baker Eddy was born here in 1821. Nearby Bow Mills village is the site of New Hampshire's oldest sawmill, established around 1800.

Bowersville village, pop. 242, Greene Co., SW Ohio, 27 mi/43 km ESE of Dayton. Situated in an agricultural region, it is the birthplace (1898) of Norman Vincent Peale.

Bowery, the street and area of lower Manhattan, New York City. A road laid out in mid 17th century from New Amsterdam to the farm (*bouwerij*) of Peter Stuyvesant was later, in the mid 19th century, New York's theatrical district. Shortly after, it fell into decline. The area has been known since the 1870s as a scene of dereliction and corruption, its flophouses, bars, and missions proverbial. Despite rehabilitation efforts, the Bowery retains some of this character.

Bowie town, pop. 37,589, Prince George's Co., WC Maryland, 15 mi/24 km NE of Washington, D.C. It is largely residential. Bowie State College, founded here in 1865, was originally a black institution. Bowie Race Track (established 1914) was formerly a leading regional horse track.

Bowling Green **1.** city, pop. 40,641, seat of Warren Co., WC Kentucky, on the Barren R., 65 mi/105 km NE of Nashville, Tennessee. Settled in 1780, it was by the mid 1800s a rail and river transportation center. It was the Confederate state capital until 1862, when Union forces took control. An important market for tobacco, tomatoes, corn, and livestock, it also has meatpacking, apparel, auto parts and assembly, and other industries. Western Kentucky University (1906) is here. **2.** oldest park in New York City, in lower Manhattan, just N of the BATTERY. The Dutch and later the English bowled on the spot, which is at the S end of Broadway, and in the 1730s an oval was leased to a private group, and fenced off. Tradition holds it as the site of Peter Minuit's trade with natives that obtained Manhattan in exchange for trinkets. **3.** city, pop. 28,176, seat of Wood Co., NW Ohio, 20 mi/32 km SSW of Toledo. Settled in 1832, it experienced brief but rapid industrial growth after a gusher oil well was struck in 1886. Meat packing and light manufacturing industries are currently important. A trading center for the surrounding dairy, livestock, and vegetable farming area, the city is also the seat of Bowling Green State University (1910).

Bowmanville see under NEWCASTLE, Ontario.

Bow River 315 mi/507 km long, in Alberta. It rises in the Rocky Mts. N of KICKING HORSE PASS, and flows SE through BANFF NATIONAL PARK, past Lake Louise and Banff. It then continues E to CALGARY, where the Elbow R. joins it from the S. From Calgary it winds SE to its confluence with the Oldman R., 45 mi/72 km WSW of Medicine Hat, forming the South SASKATCHEWAN R. To the SE of Calgary it is dammed in several places for irrigation and hydroelectric power, as at Horseshoe Bend (Bassano). The CANADIAN PACIFIC RAILWAY and TRANS-CANADA HIGHWAY follow the Bow Valley W from Calgary to Kicking Horse Pass.

Boxborough town, pop. 3343, Middlesex Co., NC Massachusetts, 27 mi/43 km NW of Boston. Settled in 1680, it has remained agricultural through its history; its situation at the junction of Routes 2 and 495 has, however, since the 1970s, attracted technological industry and suburban growth.

box canyon in the Southwest, an esp. steep-walled canyon that ends (at its head) with a vertical cliff.

Boxford town, pop. 6266, Essex Co., NE Massachusetts, 20 mi/32 km NNE of Boston. Just W of Interstate 95, it is a wooded and traditionally agricultural community in the process of becoming an outer Boston suburb.

Boyer River 140 mi/225 km long, in W Iowa. It rises W of the city of Storm Lake, in Buena Vista Co., and flows S, then SW, passing Denison and Missouri Valley before emptying into the Missouri R. 13 mi/21 km N of Council Bluffs.

Boyle Heights residential section of LOS ANGELES, California, E of the Los Angeles R. and Downtown, on the W edge of EAST LOS ANGELES. Since the late 1920s it has been home to a large working- and middle-class Mexican population.

Boyne City see under CHARLEVOIX, Michigan.

Boynton Beach city, pop. 46,194, Palm Beach Co., SE Florida, 15 mi/24 km S of West Palm Beach. Incorporated in 1920, it is a popular winter resort, connected by bridge to the barrier-island town of Ocean Ridge (pop. 1570), earlier also called Boynton Beach, on the Atlantic.

Boys Town village, pop. 794, Douglas Co., EC Nebraska, 8 mi/13 km W of Omaha. It was founded (1917) as a community for troubled and homeless boys by Father Edward J. Flanagan, and incorporated as a village in 1936. It is now a coeducational (since 1979), Catholic-run nonsectarian community, governed by the resident young people. Boys Town has several branches throughout the US and is largely supported by private charitable contributions.

Bozeman city, pop. 22,660, seat of Gallatin Co., SW Montana, 70 mi/113 km SE of Butte. Founded in 1864 and named for John Bozeman, who guided the first settlers to the Gallatin Valley, it is a trade and manufacturing center for wheat, livestock, and lumber. Montana State University (1893) is a mainstay of its economy and cultural life. A US Fish Technology Center is 2 mi/3 km E, an Agricultural Research Center is 3 mi/5 km NW, and Bozeman Hot Springs are 10 mi/16 km SW.

Bozeman Trail historic route in Wyoming and Montana. It was developed in 1862–63 by John Bozeman as an approach to SW Montana's goldfields that eliminated arduous Rocky Mt. crossings or a long upstream Missouri R. journey. From the vicinity of modern Douglas, E Wyoming, on I-25, it proceeded NW across the edge of the Missouri Plateau, crossing the upper POWDER R., proceeding along the E of the BIGHORN Mts., entering Montana near modern Decker, crossing the Bighorn R., and proceeding W along the YELLOWSTONE R. valley. The trail infringed on the lands of the Sioux, and soon came under attack; a number of famous forts and battle sites are along the route, which was abandoned by 1868. These include Fort Reno, 8 mi/13 km NNE of Sussex, Wyoming, on the Powder R.; Fort Phil Kearny, 2 mi/3 km SE of Story, Wyoming, and just W of I-90/87, on Little Piney Creek; and Fort C.F. Smith, which was within what is now the Bighorn Canyon National Recreation Area, in Montana. Near Fort Phil Kearny is the site (just NNW) of the 1866 Fetterman Massacre, in which a company of troops were annihilated. Near Story, NW of the fort, is the site of the 1867 Wagon Box Fight, in which a small group of troops inflicted heavy losses on attacking Sioux. At Ranchester, on I-90, is the Connor Battlefield, site of an 1865 battle in which troops killed dozens of Indian men, women, and children. When the forts were abandoned, the Sioux destroyed them; but historical markers are at all sites.

Bracebridge town, pop. 12,308, seat of Muskoka District Municipality, SC Ontario, on the Muskoka R., 5 mi/8 km E of L. Muskoka, 95 mi/153 km N of Toronto. It is a summer resort. The town harnessed local waterpower and had a number of industries toward the end of the 19th century. Today tanneries, lumber mills, boatworks, and brickworks continue. Furniture, textiles, rope, and auto parts are also manufactured.

Brackenridge Park major public park in San Antonio, Texas, 2 mi/3 km NNE of Downtown, at the headwaters of the San Antonio R. and just W of FORT SAM HOUSTON. The fashionable residential cities of ALAMO HEIGHTS and OLMOS PARK are just N. The park, acquired by the city in 1899, and built on former quarry land, contains lagoons, a variety of sunken and other gardens, a natural history museum, and San Antonio's well-known zoo. Some of the city's most affluent residential districts adjoin.

Braddock borough, pop. 4682, Allegheny Co., SW Pennsylvania, an industrial suburb of Pittsburgh on the Monongahela R., 7 mi/11 km SE of Downtown. The site of Edward Braddock's defeat in the French and Indian War (1755), it grew up in the 1870s around Andrew Carnegie's Edgar Thompson Steel Works, where the Bessemer process was introduced and perfected. Although still a steel town, it has declined economically in recent decades, losing most of its population. Documentary filmmaker Tony Buba features the community in his work.

Bradenton city, pop. 43,779, Manatee Co., SW Florida, 10 mi/16 km NNW of Sarasota, on the S end of Tampa Bay and the Braden and Manatee rivers. The site, reputed to be the 1539 landing place of Hernando De Soto, now the De Soto National Memorial, is just NW, at the Manatee's mouth. The area was settled in the 1850s by Joseph Braden; the ruins of his castlelike home are a tourist attraction. A popular winter resort, Bradenton is noted for its sport fishing. It has shipping facilities for local citrus and vegetables, and is the base of Tropicana, juicemakers. Travertine quarries are nearby, and the city has stoneworks.

Bradford **1.** officially, **Bradford West Gwillimbury** town, pop. 17,702, Simcoe Co., S Ontario, on the Schomberg R., 33 mi/53 km NNW of Toronto. A stop on the Toronto–L. Simcoe railroad in the 1850s, it has traditionally engaged in flour milling and diversified agriculture, and is now experiencing rapid suburban growth. **2.** city, pop. 9625, McKean Co., NW Pennsylvania, 4 mi/6 km S of the New York line. Settled in 1823, it grew into a booming 19th-century city after the discovery of oil in the 1870s. Refining became a major industry; by 1881 local oil production totaled 40% of the world's output. Today Bradford also has such manufactures as cutlery and electronic parts. The city is home to a branch of the University of Pittsburgh. Two large parks, Allegheny National Forest in Pennsylvania and Allegany State Park in New York, are nearby.

Bradley **1.** village, pop. 10,792, Kankakee Co., NE Illinois, a residential suburb immediately N of Kankakee. **2.** unincorporated community, pop. 2144, Raleigh Co., SW West Virginia, 3 mi/5 km N of Beckley. Appalachian Bible College (1950) is here.

Bradley International Airport see under WINDSOR LOCKS, Connecticut.

Braidwood city, pop. 3584, Will Co., NE Illinois, 25 mi/40 km NW of Kankakee. Before the Civil War, it was the busiest coal mining center in Illinois, a place where many labor organizers worked and tried out new strategies. A nuclear power plant opened here in 1987.

Brainerd city, pop. 12,353, seat of Crow Wing Co., C Minnesota, on the Mississippi R., 55 mi/89 km N of St. Cloud. Originally a lumber camp created by the Northern Pacific Railroad (1871), it is the heart of the region associated with Paul Bunyan tales. The Paul Bunyan Center here is a lumbering museum, and Lumbertown USA, a replica of an early logging camp, is 12 mi/19 km NW. Important industries include paper, sportswear, railroad shops, and dairy products. It is the seat of Brainerd Community College (1938). Brainerd is gateway to such recreational areas as Pillsbury and Crow Wing state forests and MILLE LACS L., and the Cuyuna Iron Range. Camp Ripley Military Reservation is 23 mi/37 km SW.

Braintree town, pop. 32,836, a suburb of Boston and Quincy, on the Weymouth Fore R. (an inlet of Hingham Bay) and Route 128, in Norfolk Co., E Massachusetts, 10 mi/16 km SSE of Boston. QUINCY and RANDOLPH were once parts of Braintree. The town has had diversified manufacturing plants since the mid 19th century, and is also largely residential. South Braintree village was the site of the 1920 robbery and murder that led to the Sacco-Vanzetti case.

Brampton city, pop. 234,445, seat of Peel Regional Municipality, S Ontario, on Etobicoke Creek, 20 mi/32 km W of Toronto. Settled in 1830, it developed as a flower center in the 1860s; nurseries remain important. Other industries include tanning and the manufacture of optical instruments, communications equipment, automobiles (Chrysler has a plant in the **Bramalea** section), furniture, paper, knit goods, soap, and shoes. In an important dairying and livestock raising area, the city is an expanding industrial and residental suburb.

Brandon **1.** unincorporated community, pop. 57,985, Hillsborough Co., WC Florida, 8 mi/13 km SE of Tampa, of which it is a growing residential suburb. **2.** second-largest city in Manitoba, pop. 38,567, in the province's SW, 130 mi/210 km W of Winnipeg, on the Assiniboine R., in a rich agricultural region. Founded in the early 1880s by the CANADIAN PACIFIC RAILWAY, it was named after Brandon House, an early Hudson's Bay Company post situated nearby. It is the distribution center for a fertile wheat producing area, and home to government experimental farms. The city's industries include oil refining and meat, poultry, and dairy processing. Chemicals, pharmaceuticals, fertilizers, agricultural machinery, textiles, boats, and furniture are manufactured as well, and three major annual provincial fairs are held. Brandon University (1899) and Assiniboine Community College, a residential Indian school, are here. **3.** city, pop. 11,077, seat of Rankin Co., SC Mississippi, 11 mi/18 km ESE of Jackson. In an area that produces cotton, corn, other vegetables, timber, and oil, it has various light industries and is also a residential suburb of Jackson. **4.** town, pop. 4223, including Brandon village and Forestdale, in Rutland Co., W Vermont. It is on Otter Creek and the Neshobe R., 15 mi/24 km NNW of Rutland, and just W of Green Mountain National Forest. Brandon Swamp, a wildlife preserve, is in the W. In a resort area, Brandon produces wood and dairy products, marble, and poultry, and has a state school for the retarded. After bog iron was discovered here in 1810, John Conant manufactured the first stoves in Vermont, contributing to the town's economic development. Stephen A. Douglas, senator and orator, was born in the village in 1813.

Brandy Station locality in Culpeper Co., E Virginia, near the Rappahannock R., 6 mi/10 km ENE of CULPEPER, the site (June 9, 1863) of the largest cavalry engagement of the Civil War, a Confederate victory. Fleetwood Hill, nearby, was successfully defended by Wade Hampton, and the entire battle is sometimes called Fleetwood Hill.

Brandywine Creek 20 mi/32 km long, rising in two branches in Chester Co., Pennsylvania, which join 10 mi/16 km SE of Coatesville, at Wawaset. It flows SE past CHADDS FORD, then through N Delaware, to its confluence with the Christina R. just above the Delaware R., at WILMINGTON. The Brandywine was once a famous fish spawning site, and with few changes in seasonal flow was one of the first rivers in America developed for waterpower. Milling and transporting of flour and gunpowder were major industries. On Sept. 11, 1777, Lord Howe defeated Washington's forces in the Battle of the Brandywine, at Chadds Ford.

Branford town, pop. 27,603, New Haven Co., SC Connecticut, on Long Island Sound, 6 mi/10 km ESE of New Haven. It is a growing residential suburb that also produces iron fittings, automotive parts, and other manufactures. Settled in 1644 by planters from Wethersfield, it was long a fishing, oystering, and shipping center. The town includes the coastal resort communities of Indian Neck, Pine Orchard, Stony Creek, and Short Beach.

Branson city, pop. 3706, Taney Co., SW Missouri, on the Ozark Plateau, on L. Taneycomo, 38 mi/61 km S of Springfield and 10 mi/16 km N of the Arkansas border. Settled at the turn of the 20th century, it was a lakeside resort. It was depicted in Harold Bell Wright's best-selling novel *The Shep-*

herd of the Hills. Branson is now a country music center and a leading resort, visited by millions annually. Developing from concerts by local bands in 1960, by the early 1990s the city had some 30 theaters lining a neon-lit STRIP, offering performances by most of the best-known country entertainers, some of whom own establishments. Nearby are several theme parks, Table Rock Dam (1959, impounding the White R.), and Table Rock State Park. Point Lookout, 2 mi/3 km S, is home to the College of the Ozarks (1906).

Brantford city, pop. 81,997, seat of Brant Co., S Ontario, on the Grand R., 60 mi/96 km SW of Toronto. Land was granted here in 1784 to the Mohawk leader Joseph Brant for the settlement of Iroquois who had fought with the British in the American Revolution. White settlement began in 1805, and in 1830 a community by the name of Brant's Ford had been established. It became an industrial, agricultural, and transportation center. It has recently witnessed many plant and business closings; surviving enterprises include various auto parts manufacturers. Brantford remains the headquarters of the Six Nations (see IROQUOIS CONFEDERACY). Alexander Graham Bell made pioneering telephone experiments here in the 1870s, and his homestead is just S, in the suburb of Tutela Heights.

Bras d'Or Lake NE–SW oriented tidal body, covering 360 sq mi/930 sq km, in C Cape Breton I., NE Nova Scotia. Surrounded by hills and deeply indented by several bays, it connects with the Atlantic Ocean by means of a canal at St. Peters (S), and via Great Bras d'Or and Little Bras d'Or channels (NE). The lake, a onetime LOYALIST center, later a shipbuilding area, and now ringed by resorts, is an important bald eagle breeding ground. BADDECK is on the N shore.

Brasstown hamlet in Clay Co., far SW North Carolina, in the Nantahala National Forest, 80 mi/130 km SW of Asheville, and 4 mi/6 km N of the Georgia border. It is known as the site of the John C. Campbell Folk School, since 1925 an instruction center in traditional crafts, music, and dance.

Brasstown Bald also, **Mount Enotah** peak (4784 ft/1459 m) just E of Blairsville, in extreme N Georgia, in the Chattahoochee National Forest. Part of the BLUE RIDGE Mts., it is the highest point in the state, with views of several states, a visitor center, and an observation tower. Cherokee myth calls it the place where flood survivors moored their giant canoe.

Brattleboro historic town, pop. 12,241, including Brattleboro village (pop. 8612) and West Brattleboro, in Windham Co., SE Vermont. It is on Interstate 91 along the Connecticut R. where the West R. joins it, 17 mi/27 km N of Greenfield, Massachusetts. Foothills of the Green Mts., to the W, and Wantastiquet Mt., across the river to the E, in New Hampshire, enclose Brattleboro's center. In an apple, maple, and dairy area, the town is a commercial and winter sports center. Vermont's first English settlement, as Fort Dummer (1724), it was named Brattleboro in 1753. Estey organs were manufactured here from 1846. Industries include printing, feed and flour milling, and the manufacture of wood products, textiles, optical goods, precision equipment, paints, and granite monuments and tombstones. From 1845, mineral springs attracted health seekers. "Naulakha," N of the village, was the home (1892–96) of Rudyard Kipling, who married a Brattleboro resident.

Brawley city, pop. 18,923, Imperial Co., S California, 10 mi/16 km S of the Salton Sea, in the IMPERIAL VALLEY. It is the trade and shipping center for an extensively irrigated agricultural area in which cattle, grain, cantaloupes, lettuce, and cotton are raised. The Imperial Valley Rodeo and Brawley Cattle Call (Nov.) is an important local event.

Brazil city, pop. 7640, seat of Clay Co., W Indiana, 15 mi/24 km ENE of Terre Haute, on Birch Creek and Interstate 40. It developed as a railroad and trade center in a region that raises grain and livestock and has claypits and strip mines producing a type of bituminous coal called Brazil coal. Brazil's manufactures have included floor wax, sewer pipes, brick, tile, and cigars. Labor leader Jimmy Hoffa was born here (1913).

Brazoria County 1407 sq mi/3644 sq km, pop. 191,707, in S Texas, in the Coastal Plain, on the Gulf of Mexico. It is drained by the Brazos and San Bernard rivers. Its seat is ANGLETON. Oil, natural gas, salt, and magnesium are among the products of its large chemical industry. Grains, vegetables, fruit, cotton, dairy cattle, and livestock are raised. The BRAZOSPORT industrial area is in the S, HOUSTON suburbs are in the N. The coast has beaches and the San Bernard National Wildlife Refuge.

Brazosport cluster of nine municipalities in SE Texas, at the mouth of the Brazos R., some 55 mi/89 km S of Houston, the site of a huge petrochemical and chemical complex. FREEPORT (including the former VELASCO) and LAKE JACKSON are the largest cities. The smaller communities are Clute, Richwood, Brazoria, Jones Creek, Oyster Creek, Surfside Beach, and Quintana. The GULF INTRACOASTAL WATERWAY passes along the S. Fishing and tourism are also important to the area's economy.

Brazos River 840 mi/1350 km long, in Texas. Its Salt and Double Mt. forks rise SE of Lubbock, on the LLANO ESTACADO, and flow ESE to meet in Stonewall Co., 60 mi/96 km NNW of Abilene. The **Clear Fork,** 220 mi/350 km long, rises N of Sweetwater, and joins the river in Young Co., SW of Graham. The **Salt Fork** is 100 mi/160 km long, the **Double Mt. Fork** 270 mi/435 km long. Just SE of the Clear Fork's confluence with the main river, the Brazos passes through 17,700-ac/7200-ha Possum Kingdom L. It then flows SE, to the W of Fort Worth. Near Whitney, it flows through 23,600-ac/9600-ha L. Whitney, at the BALCONES ESCARPMENT. It then passes WACO and continues SE into the Gulf Costal Plain, passing W of Houston into the Brazosport area on the Gulf of Mexico.

Brea city, pop. 32,873, Orange Co., S California, 23 mi/37 km ESE of Los Angeles and just NE of Fullerton. Area wells played a prominent role in the California oil boom of the early 1900s, spurring the city's growth. A trade center, Brea also manufactures oilfield supplies, metal castings, boilers, freezers, and rubber products. It has grown rapidly since the 1960s as a residential suburb.

Bread Loaf Mountain see under MIDDLEBURY, Vermont.

Breakers, the **1.** see under PALM BEACH, Florida. **2.** see under CLIFF WALK, Newport, Rhode Island.

Breaks of Sandy see under BIG SANDY R., Virginia and Kentucky.

Breckenridge town, pop. 1285, seat of Summit Co., C Colorado, 21 mi/34 km NE of Leadville and just SE of the GORE RANGE. In the Blue R. valley, it was an 1860s mining boom town, and has a large Victorian historic district. Today it is a trade center and resort, set amid several ski mountains.

Breckenridge Hills village, pop. 5404, St. Louis Co., EC

Missouri, a residential suburb 10 mi/16 km NW of downtown St. Louis.

Brecksville city, pop. 11,818, Cuyahoga Co., NE Ohio, 10 mi/16 km SSE of Cleveland, of which it is a commuter suburb. Settlement of the area began c.1811. Brecksville is the site of the B. F. Goodrich Research Center, a research facility for rubber, plastics, and textiles.

Breed's Hill historic site in the CHARLESTOWN section of Boston, Massachusetts. It was the scene of a battle between British troops and Boston militia on June 16, 1775, in which the Americans, although defeated, fought valiantly to defend their position atop the hill; it took three assaults to overcome their resistance. The battle, which became known as the battle of BUNKER HILL, established that Americans could fight respectably against British regulars, and inspired them in the fight for independence.

Breezewood road junction in East Providence township, Bedford Co., SC Pennsylvania, 36 mi/58 km NW of Hagerstown, Maryland. At the intersection of the E–W Pennsylvania Turnpike and Interstate 70, a major N–S route through the Allegheny Mts., it has a commercial strip well known to long-haul drivers.

Bremerton city, pop. 38,142, Kitsap Co., WC Washington, on Port Washington Narrows and Sinclair Inlet (both arms of Puget Sound), 15 mi/24 km W of Seattle. The economic hub of the Kitsap Peninsula, it has been dominated since 1891 by the Puget Sound Naval Shipyard, among the largest US Navy repair yards and the N home of the Pacific Fleet for much of this century. The Bangor submarine base is 12 mi/19 km NW. Other important industries include the processing of lumber and dairy products, and tourism. Its many ferries connect Bremerton with resort islands in Puget Sound. The city is home to the Bremerton Naval Museum and Olympic College (1946). The World War II battleship *Missouri* is docked here.

Brenham city, pop. 11,952, seat of Washington Co., SE Texas, 70 mi/113 km NW of Houston. With creameries (it is noted for its ice cream) and cotton mills, it is a trade and shipping center for Brazos R. valley produce. It also manufactures springs, mattresses, furniture, and brooms, and oilfields are nearby. Settled in 1844, it became heavily German in the 1860s. It was partly burned during disturbances in the Reconstruction era. Blinn College was founded in 1883.

Brentwood **1.** in California: **a.** city, pop. 7563, Contra Costa Co., on the S of the San Joaquin Delta, 11 mi/18 km SE of Pittsburg and 21 mi/34 km WSW of Stockton. A small agricultural community set among orchards, it boomed in the early 1990s as a new residential suburb. **b.** residential section of the WESTSIDE of Los Angeles, California, immediately N of Santa Monica and 13 mi/21 km W of Downtown, a wealthy community popular among young professionals. **2.** city, pop. 8150, St. Louis Co., EC Missouri, 9 mi/14 km W of downtown St. Louis. It is primarily a bedroom community. **3.** unincorporated village, pop. 45,218, in Islip town, Suffolk Co., SE New York, in C Long Island, 40 mi/64 km E of Manhattan. A residential suburb with some electronics and other light industries, it is the seat of the Pilgrim Psychiatric Center. **4.** borough, pop. 10,823, Allegheny Co., W Pennsylvania, a residential suburb 6 mi/10 km SE of downtown Pittsburgh. **5.** city, pop. 16,392, Williamson Co., C Tennessee, on the Little Harpeth R., a largely residential suburb 9 mi/14 km S of Nashville.

Breton Sound inlet of the Gulf of Mexico, N of the main channel of the Mississippi R. in its delta, and 40 mi/64 km SE of New Orleans, in SE Louisiana. It joins Chandeleur Sound on the N; the CHANDELEUR ISLANDS lie NE, and are mostly within the Breton National Wildlife Refuge.

Bretton Woods resort in the town of Carroll, Coos Co., NC New Hampshire. Bretton Woods is in the White Mts., on the Lower Ammonoosuc R., 8 mi/13 km W of Mt. Washington. The Mt. Washington Hotel (1902), a fashionable resort, was site of the United Nations Monetary and Financial Conference (July 1944), at which plans were made to establish a world bank with the US dollar as the international medium of exchange.

Brevard city, pop. 5388, seat of Transylvania Co., W North Carolina, in the Blue Ridge Mts., 27 mi/43 km SSW of Asheville, at the entrance to Pisgah National Forest. Incorporated in 1867, it is a resort center surrounded by forests and waterfalls, with a summer music festival and an increasingly popular retirement community. Brevard College (1853) is here.

Brevard County 995 sq mi/2577 sq km, pop. 398,978, in EC Florida, on the Atlantic Ocean (E). Its seat is TITUSVILLE. It is bordered on the E by barrier beaches that enclose the INDIAN R. and Banana R. lagoons and MERRITT I. Its beachfront resorts include Cocoa Beach, Melbourne, and Palm Bay. The site of Cape CANAVERAL and the John F. Kennedy Space Center, Brevard Co. is the home of Florida's space industry. The Indian R. region is particularly noted for its citrus fruits.

Brevard Zone see under PIEDMONT.

Brewer city, pop. 9021, Penobscot Co., EC Maine. It is on US 1 and the Penobscot R., across from Bangor. A former shipbuilding and pulp and paper milling center, Brewer now has light industry and distribution facilities. The house of Civil War General Joshua Chamberlain is here.

Brewster village, pop. 1566, in Southeast township, Putnam Co., SE New York, 35 mi/56 km NNE of New York City. It is a trade center for a vegetable and dairy farming area, with some light industry. Long a summer resort, it has vacation homes and recreational facilities. Situated at the junction of Interstate 84 with Route 684, and at the end of one of New York's commuter train lines, Brewster now also has corporate office buildings, and has become an affluent suburb.

Brewster County see under ALPINE, Texas.

Brewton city, pop. 5885, seat of Escambia Co., S Alabama, 67 mi/108 km ENE of Mobile, on the Murder Creek across from East Brewton (pop. 2579), just N of the Conecuh R. This agricultural, lumbering, and oil center is home to Jefferson Davis State Junior College (1965).

Briarcliff Manor village, pop. 7070, in Ossining town, Westchester Co., SE New York, 30 mi/48 km N of New York City. Founded in 1896 as a planned community for the wealthy, it remains an affluent suburb. Briarcliff Junior College and King's College were formerly here.

Brices Cross Roads battle site in Union Co., NE Mississippi, 6 mi/10 km W of Baldwyn and 17 mi/27 km N of Tupelo, along Tishomingo Creek. In a daylong battle here on June 10, 1864, Confederate troops under Nathan Bedford Forrest defeated a larger Union force led by Samuel Sturgis, driving it back (NW) toward Memphis.

Bricktown commercial and entertainment section of Detroit, Michigan, just N of the RENAISSANCE CENTER. The restored brick buildings here provide a setting for downtown nightlife.

Brick Township township, pop. 66,473, Ocean Co., EC New Jersey, 12 mi/19 km SW of Asbury Park, on the Garden State Parkway and the N end of Barnegat Bay. Named for a 19th-century ironmaster in neighboring LAKEWOOD (once Bricksburg), it is one of the Jersey Shore's residential and resort boom communities, including a half dozen villages.

Brickyard, the see under SPEEDWAY, Indiana.

Bridgeport 1. city, pop. 141,686, Fairfield Co., SW Connecticut, 60 mi/96 km NE of New York City, on Long Island Sound. Its excellent harbor spurred its shift from a 17th-century agrarian to an 18th-century mercantile economy. In the 19th century it became Connecticut's chief manufacturing city. Among the products Bridgeport is known for are valves, machine tools, turbines, hardware, firearms, electrical and transportation equipment, plastics, and auto parts; Elias Howe produced the first sewing machines here in the 1840s. The showman P. T. Barnum was mayor of Bridgeport (1875–76), and the city was winter headquarters for his circus; the Barnum Museum has a collection of circus memorabilia. The city's many parks include Frederick Law Olmsted's Seaside Park and Beardsley Park. After years of economic decline, Bridgeport began an ambitious urban renewal program in the 1970s, but recovery stalled, and in the 1990s the city flirted with bankruptcy, having lost much of its industrial and commercial base to its suburbs and to other parts of the country. The University of Bridgeport (1927) suffered severe enrollment decline. While the city's neighborhoods include exclusive Black Rock, along the water in the SW, inner city districts struggled with unemployment and related problems. **2.** residential neighborhood on the SOUTH SIDE of Chicago, Illinois, 4 mi/6 km S of the Loop. The home of five 20th-century Chicago mayors, it has been deeply enmeshed in the city's political machine for decades. Originally settled in the 1840s by Irish immigrants brought in to dig the Illinois and Michigan Canal, it is now a working-class Irish neighborhood with some Eastern European and black residents. COMISKEY PARK is here.

Bridger-Teton National Forest 3.4 million ac/1.38 million ha, in Teton and Lincoln counties, W Wyoming. It is adjacent (S) to YELLOWSTONE NATIONAL PARK and (E and S) to GRAND TETON NATIONAL PARK. Included within the forest are parts of the Gros Ventre, Teton, Wind River, Salt River, and Wyoming Mts., as well as a number of glaciers, more than 1300 lakes, the huge Gros Ventre landslide (1925), and Wyoming's highest point, GANNETT PEAK. It is traversed by the Salt R. and Fontenelle Creek. Cut by the Continental Divide, the forest contains three wilderness areas, Bridger (428,169 ac/173,408 ha), Teton (585,468 ac/237,114 ha), and Gros Ventre (287,000 ac/116,235 ha).

Bridges Creek see under WAKEFIELD, Virginia.

Bridgeton 1. city, pop. 17,779, St. Louis Co., EC Missouri, 12 mi/19 km NW of St. Louis. An industrial suburb, it has a variety of manufactures including vending machines. **2.** city, pop. 18,942, seat of Cumberland Co., SW New Jersey, on the Cohansey R., 16 mi/26 km S of Camden. Settled by Quakers in 1686, it became a 19th-century manufacturing center with a woolen mill, nail factory, and ironworks. Over 2000 Colonial, Federal, and Victorian buildings are preserved, forming New Jersey's largest historic district. In a rich truck farming region, the city is a distribution hub for agricultural products. Manufacturing remains vital; the city produces such goods as glass, processed foods (particularly local tomatoes), textiles, and fertilizer. Tourism is also important.

Bridgetown North unincorporated residential suburb, pop. 11,748, Hamilton Co., SW Ohio, 7 mi/11 km NW of Cincinnati, on the fringe of the most heavily developed part of the Cincinnati area.

Bridgeview village, pop. 14,402, Cook Co., NE Illinois, a residential suburb 12 mi/19 km SW of Chicago's Loop.

Bridgewater 1. town, pop. 21,249, Plymouth Co., SE Massachusetts, 27 mi/43 km S of Boston. Bridgewater has an iron industry dating back to Colonial times, and some light manufacturing. The town was originally called Titicut; Frederick Wiseman's controversial 1967 documentary *Titicut Follies* was filmed here in the state prison for the criminally insane. Bridgewater State College was founded in 1840. BROCKTON, 6 mi/10 km NW, was part of Bridgewater (and called North Bridgewater) until 1821. **2.** township, pop. 32,509, Somerset Co., C New Jersey, 27 mi/43 km WSW of Newark. On Interstate 287 and other highways, it is a growing residential, commercial, and industrial suburb at the outer edge of the New York metropolitan area. **3.** town, pop. 7248, Lunenburg Co., S Nova Scotia, on the La Have R., 50 mi/80 km WSW of Halifax. An agricultural and service center, it grows Christmas trees and has a tire plant. The river is noted for its salmon fishing. **4.** town, pop. 3918, Rockingham Co., NW Virginia, on the North R., 7 mi/11 km SW of Harrisonburg, in the Shenandoah Valley. The seat of Bridgewater College (1880), it produces furniture, clothing, and textiles.

Brigantine city, pop. 11,354, Atlantic Co., SE New Jersey, on Brigantine I. and the Atlantic Ocean, across ABSECON INLET (NE) from Atlantic City. Tourists are drawn by its beaches. Its Sea Life Museum/Marine Mammal Stranding Center is a rehabilitation center for injured porpoises and other marine creatures. The Edwin B. Forsythe National Wildlife Refuge covers 37,000 ac/15,000 ha on islands and mainland N of the city.

Brigham City city, pop. 15,644, seat of Box Elder Co., N Utah, on the NE shore of the Great Salt L., 52 mi/84 km NNW of Salt Lake City. It processes and distributes local peaches and other fruits, sugar beets, grain, and alfalfa, and has storage facilities, canning plants, and woolen mills. Manufactures include rocket boosters and propellants. Founded (1851) as Box Elder, it was renamed (1856) for Mormon leader Brigham Young, who gave his last speech here (1877). Its 1876 tabernacle and pioneer museum draw visitors. The city is headquarters for the Golden Spike National Historical Site, 30 mi/48 km W (see PROMONTORY Mts.).

Brighton 1. city, pop. 14,203, seat of Adams Co., also in Weld Co., NC Colorado, on the South Platte R., 20 mi/32 km NE of Denver. Founded in 1889, it is surrounded by sugar beet farms and is a center for the processing and shipping of beet sugar. **2.** see under ALLSTON-BRIGHTON, Massachusetts. **3.** town, pop. 34,455, Monroe Co., W New York, adjacent (S) to Rochester. Settled in the 18th century, it predates Rochester, of which it has long been a suburb. Routes 390 and 590 meet in this industrial and residential town, which is also on the Erie Canal and the Genesee R. Monroe Community College (1961) is here.

Brighton Beach residential section of S Brooklyn, New York, E of Coney Island. Sheepshead Bay lies to the N. Brighton Beach has been a resort since the late 1870s, and year-round residences multiplied by the 1930s. Its Jewish culture has been celebrated by Neil Simon, Woody Allen, and others. In the 1970s, changes in Soviet emigration law brought a wave of immigrants from Russia and the Ukraine, and Brighton Beach became popularly known as Little Odessa. It now contains perhaps the largest Russian population outside the former Soviet Union and Israel. Rapid immigration has brought both vibrant ethnic culture and social problems.

Brighton Park residential, formerly industrial, district on the South Side of Chicago, Illinois, S of the Chicago Sanitary and Ship Canal, 4 mi/6 km SW of the Loop. An Irish-German working-class neighborhood at the turn of the century, it has included since the 1920s a Lithuanian enclave. The UNION STOCKYARDS were just E.

Brilliant village, pop. 1672, Jefferson Co., E Ohio, on the Ohio R., 7 mi/11 km S of Steubenville. An experimental electric station is situated here on the site of a retired coal plant.

Brimfield town, pop. 3001, Hampden Co., S Massachusetts, 19 mi/31 km E of Springfield. This small agricultural center, settled in the 1700s, is now well known as the site of huge outdoor antiques markets, held annually in May, July, and Sept.

Bristol **1.** city and coterminous township, pop. 60,640, Hartford Co., WC Connecticut, on the Pequabuck R., 15 mi/24 km SW of Hartford. It was a hotbed of Tory activity during the Revolution; the name Tory's Den was given to a cave on Chippens Hill. Bristol has been a clockmaking center since the 1790s, and in the 19th and early 20th century turned out a wide range of metal products and machinery. Today, in addition to clocks, the city makes brass products, electronic devices, automotive bearings, tools, and industrial timers. The American Clock and Watch Museum is here. The township includes Edgewood and Forestville, a manufacturing village. **2.** in Pennsylvania: **a.** borough, pop. 10,405, Bucks Co., 13 mi/21 km NE of Philadelphia. Situated on the Delaware R. opposite Burlington, New Jersey, it was founded in the late 17th century. American troops were quartered here during the Revolution. Bristol was once a bustling river port and shipbuilding center as well as a spa popular with Philadelphians. Its diverse contemporary manufactures include metal products, plastics, and chemicals. A re-creation of William Penn's country manor is located 5 mi/8 km NE. **b.** township, pop. 57,129, including Bristol borough and the village of LEVITTOWN. **3.** town, pop. 21,625, including Beach Terrace and Bristol villages, seat of Bristol Co., E Rhode Island, 13 mi/21 km SW of Providence. It is situated on the Mount Hope peninsula in Narragansett Bay, with Mount Hope Bay E. A yachting center where several America's Cup defenders were built, it is a suburb with rubber and other industries. Bristol was the focus of early action in King Philip's War (1675–76), and was subsequently a maritime and slave-trading hub. Settled in 1669 as a PLYMOUTH COLONY outpost, it did not become part of Rhode Island until 1746. Roger Williams College (1948) and the Blithewold Estate (gardens) are here. **4.** city, pop. 23,421, Sullivan Co., extreme NE Tennessee, 20 mi/32 km NNE of Johnson City, and adjoining Bristol, Virginia. Settled in 1749, the two Bristols are a trade and industrial center and transportation hub, manufacturing structural steel, missile components, mining equipment, lumber, textiles, and pharmaceuticals. The area raises beef and dairy cattle, poultry, tobacco, and grain. Nearby Tennessee Valley Authority dams and lakes provide power, jobs, recreation, and tourist trade. King College (1867) and Bristol University (1895) are in the Tennessee city. **5.** city, pop. 18,426, Washington Co., SW Virginia, a dual city with BRISTOL, Tennessee. A 200-year-old boundary dispute was resolved in 1903 by having the state line run down the middle of State St. Virginia Intermont College (1884) is here.

Bristol Bay large inlet of the Bering Sea, bordered by the Ahklun Mts. and the Nushagak Peninsula (N) and the ALASKA PENINSULA (S), in SW Alaska. Some 200 mi/320 km wide at its mouth, the shallow bay is a major center for salmon fishing and canning (DILLINGHAM is an important center). It receives the Kvichak, Nushagak, and Togiak rivers. The bay was explored and named by the English navigator James Cook in 1778.

Bristol County 557 sq mi/1443 sq km, pop. 506,325, in SE Massachusetts, on Buzzards Bay and the Rhode Island border. Its seat is Taunton. The county's early industries included shipping and whaling. In the mid 19th century, the area became a center of textile manufacturing, with many mills concentrated in FALL RIVER and NEW BEDFORD. As that industry declined in the 20th century, Bristol's economy deteriorated; the county experienced high unemployment in the 1990s.

British Columbia French, **Colombie-Britannique** westernmost, and only Pacific, province of Canada; 1991 pop. 3,282,061 (113.8% of 1986; rank: 3rd of 12); land area 344,663 sq mi/892,677 sq km (rank: 4th); entered Confederation 1871. Capital: VICTORIA. Most populous cities: VANCOUVER, RICHMOND, KELOWNA, Victoria, PRINCE GEORGE, KAMLOOPS, NANAIMO. British Columbia is bordered E by Alberta, with the CONTINENTAL DIVIDE in the ROCKY Mts. forming the SE boundary; S by (E–W) Montana, Idaho, and Washington, along the FORTY-NINTH PARALLEL; N, along the SIXTIETH PARALLEL, by (E–W) the Northwest Territories and Yukon Territory; and NW, for about half its length, by the PANHANDLE of Alaska. On the SW, on the Pacific Ocean, the province has thousands of islands; the largest of these, VANCOUVER I., dips below the Forty-ninth Parallel, being separated from Washington's Olympic Peninsula by the JUAN DE FUCA Strait. Three major mountain chains form British Columbia's backbone. In the E, the Canadian Rocky Mts. run SSE–NNW, along the Alberta border (S) and then across the NE of the province. In the S they include the COLUMBIA Mts., a subgrouping incorporating the MONASHEES, SELKIRKS, and PURCELLS. The headwaters of major rivers, including the COLUMBIA, FRASER, PEACE, and KOOTENAY, flow through the Rocky Mountain and other trenches between the Rockies' high ridges, which include Mt. ROBSON (12,972 ft/3954 m), the highest point in the Canadian Rockies. Paralleling the Rockies in the W, the COAST MOUNTAINS are a N extension of the system that includes the Cascades and the Sierra Nevada. They stand above (E of) the Pacific coast, and reach 13,104 ft/3994 m at Mt. WADDINGTON. To their W are the discontinuous COAST RANGES, represented in British Columbia by Vancouver I. (where the GOLDEN HINDE rises to 7219 ft/2200 m), the QUEEN CHARLOTTE Is., and, in the far NW corner where the province meets the Yukon Territory and Alaska, the SAINT ELIAS Mts., including Mt. FAIRWEATHER (15,300 ft/4663 m). Between these three mountain chains lie two lower areas that are the pop. centers of the province. On the W, in the trough between the Coast Mts. and Coast Ranges, is a narrow coastal zone (the "Lower Mainland") in which Vancouver and other cities developed. Much of this trough is water surface, including the Strait of GEORGIA (S) and

HECATE Strait (N); the INSIDE PASSAGE runs through it. In British Columbia's interior, E of the Coast Mts., is an expanse of plateaus and lower ranges, part of the INTERMONTANE REGION. Here major rivers provide waterpower and irrigation for orcharding and other agriculture, and for lumber and extractive industries. Kelowna, Kamloops, and Prince George are major cities of the interior. Among British Columbia's rivers are the upper Columbia, which loops through the SE, and the Fraser, which rises near the Alberta border and flows SW across the province to a large delta in the Vancouver area; the Fraser's early (late-18th-century) promise as a route to the Pacific was illusory, as it is too rough for commercial navigation. The misconception that it was the Columbia, however, spurred early exploration. In the NC, the Finlay and the Parsnip meet on the E of the Continental Divide to form the Peace R., which then flows E from the Rockies into N Alberta; the junction now occurs within WILLISTON L., formed by the huge W.A.C. Bennett Dam. To the N of the Peace R., in British Columbia's NE corner, is a region of High Plains sloping N to wetlands in the Arctic Ocean (Mackenzie R.) watershed. Home to numerous small Salishan and Wakashan groups, chiefly along the coast, the region now British Columbia was first seen by the Spanish and English in the 1770s, and after some conflict around NOOTKA Sound, came under British control by a 1790 convention. Operatives of both the NORTH WEST COMPANY (including Alexander Mackenzie and Simon Fraser) and HUDSON'S BAY COMPANY were soon exploring rivers and coast; in 1821 they combined under the HBC banner. As part of the large OREGON Country, the lower coast was the object of disputes with US interests until the 1846 treaty setting the Forty-ninth Parallel as its S boundary. Vancouver I. became a colony, with Victoria its capital, in 1849. In 1858 the CARIBOO gold rush brought an influx to the mainland, and with the Queen Charlotte Is. it became a second colony, briefly called NEW CALEDONIA. In 1866 Vancouver I. and the mainland colony were united; NEW WESTMINSTER was the capital, then (1868) Victoria. In 1871, the HBC having relinquished its rights, British Columbia entered the Confederation. Canada, eager to reinforce its sovereignty in the face of possible US interest, had stipulated that it would build an intercontinental railroad to connect the province with the East. In 1885 the "last spike" was driven at CRAIGELLACHIE on the CANADIAN PACIFIC RAILWAY's line through KICKING HORSE PASS. This at first terminated at PORT MOODY, but was quickly extended to the infant city of Vancouver, a lumbering settlement that immediately boomed, becoming Canada's, and by the mid 20th century North America's, chief Pacific port. The CPR subsequently opened a second, southern line through CROWSNEST PASS, an important coalmining district. In 1915 lines that became part of the CANADIAN NATIONAL RAILWAY system opened through YELLOWHEAD PASS, continuing to Prince George and to the N coast port of PRINCE RUPERT. British Columbia now had connections that allowed it to ship local and Prairie Province wheat and other products, and to send its own fruits, fish, and minerals E. The opening of the Panama Canal (also in 1915) enhanced the role of Pacific ports. The CPR developed steamship lines that made Vancouver a leader in East Asian trade; this and demand (from the 1850s) for labor for the province's mines account for much of the size and importance of British Columbia's Asian community. Today, the province produces copper, gold, lead, zinc, silver, tungsten, and other metals from mines chiefly in the Columbia Mts. (SE) and along the Coast Mts. chain. TRAIL and KIMBERLEY are important refining and smelting centers. KITIMAT, SE of Prince Rupert, developed as a second such center by a different route, employing its port and nearby waterpower to import and process Caribbean bauxite. Lumbering remains important throughout the province, and many local manufactures are wood-based. Vancouver and Victoria have important fishing fleets, and salmon are caught in several rivers. Vancouver has acquired the commercial, financial, educational, and cultural importance of a metropolis, while Victoria's life revolves around government and tourism. British Columbia's scenery, esp. as experienced in YOHO, GLACIER, KOOTENAY, MOUNT REVELSTOKE, and PACIFIC RIM national parks; in TWEEDSMUIR, STRATHCONA, GARIBALDI, and Wells Gray provincial parks; in the Queen Charlotte Is.; and elsewhere along the coast, is a major visitor attraction. Others include the different styles of Vancouver and Victoria; skiing at WHISTLER and other resorts; gold rush reminders at BARKERVILLE and elsewhere in the Cariboo district; and lake resorts in the interior. While the people of British Columbia are heavily British in background (Victoria is famously English), they also represent a wide range of national, religious, and ethnic groups, including Russian Doukhobors, Sikhs, Chinese, 20th-century European immigrants, and descendants of the coastal peoples first encountered by 18th-century sailors.

British Mountains NW–SE trending range, rising to 5900 ft/1800 m, in the extreme NW Yukon Territory and NE Alaska. The Porcupine Plateau is to the S, the Arctic Slope to the N. The mountains, on the Continental Divide, dominate the inland (S) portion of the Northern Yukon National Park (3927 sq mi/10,170 sq km), a primarily TUNDRA wilderness area, in which the Malcolm, Firth, and Babbage rivers all run N to the BEAUFORT SEA. The park is noted for its wildlife, including one of the world's largest caribou herds.

British North America term usually designating the colonies and territories remaining under British control in North America after the 1783 treaty recognizing American independence. These comprised Québec (which then included much of modern Ontario), Nova Scotia (including modern New Brunswick), St. John's (now Prince Edward) Island, Newfoundland, the territories administered by the Hudson's Bay Company (see RUPERT'S LAND), and other CROWN LANDS, chiefly in the N. British North America was bounded S by the new American CONFEDERATION and S and W by Spanish territories. The British North America Act (1867) established the DOMINION of Canada, of which Newfoundland was the last (1949) province to become a part.

Broad River 140 mi/210 km long, in North Carolina and South Carolina. It rises E of the Blue Ridge, about 7 mi/11 km SSE of Black Mountain. As the **Rocky Broad,** it flows over Hickory Nut Falls and past CHIMNEY ROCK. It then winds SE, through L. Lure, and into South Carolina's UP COUNTRY, to Columbia, where it joins the SALUDA R. to form the CONGAREE R. It is an important source of hydroelectric power. Near Jenkinsville, 20 mi/32 km NW of Columbia, is the Summer nuclear power plant (1982).

Broad Street commercial thoroughfare, 12 mi/19 km long, in Philadelphia, Pennsylvania, between the US Naval Base on the Delaware R. and the Philadelphia-CHELTENHAM line. The city's widest N–S street and its longest straight one, it forms one of the main axes of Philadelphia, bisecting MARKET STREET at City Hall. A subway line runs beneath this corridor. Broad Street passes through the neighborhoods of Oak Lane, Fern Rock, OLNEY, LOGAN, NORTH PHILADELPHIA, CENTER CITY, and SOUTH PHILADELPHIA. Many of the city's financial and cultural establishments are located along it immediately S of City Hall.

Broadview village, pop. 8713, Cook Co., NE Illinois, a residential suburb adjacent (S) to MAYWOOD, and 11 mi/18 km WSW of Chicago's LOOP.

Broadview Heights city, pop. 12,219, Cuyahoga Co., NE Ohio, 11 mi/18 km S of Cleveland, of which it is a residential suburb. It is the site of a US veterans' hospital.

Broadway **1.** in California: **a.** commercial thoroughfare, 14 mi/23 km long, between downtown LOS ANGELES (N) and Carson (S). A major shopping strip for the Mexican community, it passes through SOUTH-CENTRAL. Before World War II, the downtown portion was the city's main retail and entertainment center. **b.** commercial thoroughfare in SAN DIEGO, between Downtown (W) and LEMON GROVE (E). The city's main street for over a century, it has recently been the site of intense commercial development in the blocks toward the waterfront. **2.** thoroughfare, said to be America's longest street. It begins at the BATTERY, Manhattan, New York City, and proceeds N through Manhattan and the Bronx into Westchester Co., and, according to some calculations, all the way to Albany. Originally the High Street of New Amsterdam, it followed Indian paths. Along its route it traverses Manhattan's Garment District and Theater District, where, in the Times Square area, it is known as the Great White Way for its nighttime brightness and activity. After passing through Columbus Circle, Manhattan's Upper West Side, and the Bronx, it continues as New York Route 9 in Westchester. From Putnam Co. N it is also called the New York-Albany Post Road. **3.** and **Broadway Limited** see under PENNSYLVANIA RAILROAD.

Brockport village, pop. 8749, in Sweden township, Monroe Co., W New York, 17 mi/27 km W of Rochester. It was an Erie Canal trade center, and remains a commercial hub for nearby truck and dairy farms. Brockport has nurseries, canneries, and other light industry; many residents commute to work in Rochester. The State University of New York at Brockport (1867) is here.

Brockton industrial city, pop. 92,788, Plymouth Co., SE Massachusetts, 20 mi/32 km S of Boston. Its land was purchased from local tribes in 1649 by Miles Standish and John Alden. An early farming community, then called North Bridgewater, it has been a leading shoe manufacturing center since 1750. The shoe and boot industry boomed in response to the Civil War, facilitated by the invention of a machine to stitch uppers and soles. Other industries include printing and the manufacture of clothing, metal products, electronics, machine tools, and plastics. Brockton, named in 1874, was a pioneer in electric street lighting, electric streetcars, and inland sewage disposal. Massasoit Community College (1966) is here.

Brockville city, pop. 21,582, seat of Leeds and Grenville United Counties, SE Ontario, on the St. Lawrence R., 57 mi/91 km S of Ottawa, opposite Morristown, New York. Settled in the late 18th century, it took its present name to honor War of 1812 hero Sir Isaac Brock. Today it manufactures hardware, food products, electrical and telephone equipment, pharmaceuticals, and metal goods. It is a departure point for boat trips to the THOUSAND ISLANDS.

Brocton village, pop. 1387, in Portland township, Chautauqua Co., W New York, just S of L. Erie, 25 mi/40 km NNW of Jamestown. It was the headquarters (1867–83) of Thomas Lake Harris's mystical Brotherhood of the New Life, which moved here from AMENIA. Brocton lies in a grape growing, wine producing region, and is an agricultural trade and processing center.

Broken Arrow city, pop. 58,043, Tulsa and Wagoner counties, NE Oklahoma, 10 mi/16 km SE of downtown Tulsa. In a mineral-rich, agriculturally fertile area in which livestock and quarter horses are raised, it is in part a commercial center and in part a growing residential suburb. Its industries include cotton ginning, fruit canning, flour and feed milling, oil refining, and coal processing.

Bronx, the fourth-largest (42 sq mi/109 sq km) and fourth most populous (1,203,789) of the five boroughs of NEW YORK CITY, coextensive with **Bronx Co.** The city's only mainland borough, directly N of Manhattan, it occupies the S part of a peninsula between the HUDSON and HARLEM rivers (W) and the EAST R. and LONG ISLAND SOUND (E). On the N it is bounded (W–E) by WESTCHESTER County's Yonkers, Mount Vernon, and Pelham Manor. Its topography is dominated by three parallel NE–SW ridges. The westernmost reaches through Riverdale, along the Hudson, to Spuyten Duyvil. The middle ridge extends from Van Cortlandt Park (N) to the vicinity of Yankee Stadium, on the Harlem R.; the Grand Concourse follows it. The easternmost ridge lies on the E of the Bronx R. Some of the Bronx's densest residential communities lie between these ridges. Jonas Bronck, a Dane connected with the Dutch West India Company, settled in 1641 on what became known as Bronck's River, which gave its name to the area. In the 1640s New England religious dissenters settled in the NE, including Anne Hutchinson and her followers, along the HUTCHINSON R., who were soon killed by local Indians. In the late 17th century, the Fordham, Pelham, and Morris families created large estates. Until the mid 19th century, the Bronx was essentially agricultural, English, and lightly populated; the 1850 pop. was 8032. Thereafter European immigrants began moving N from Manhattan, and the area acquired German, Irish, and Italian communities; the arrival of rail lines in the 1870s–80s accelerated this process. In 1874 New York City began to annex sections of the Bronx; in 1898 it was merged entirely into Greater New York. In the first half of the 20th century, the Bronx was a magnet for city dwellers seeking less crowded neighborhoods. After midcentury, aging of housing stock and departure of middle-class residents left the borough in a decline that reached crisis proportions by the 1970s. Today conditions range from the affluence of Riverdale (NW) to the poverty and housing displacement of Mott Haven (S). There are industrial and warehousing zones along the Harlem and East rivers, and the latter is the scene of large landfill areas, one of which holds the huge Hunt's Point market. The TRIBOROUGH, BRONX-WHITESTONE, THROGS NECK, and other bridges connect the borough with the rest of the city. RIKERS and the Brother Islands, in the East R., and CITY and HART islands, in Long Island Sound, are part of the Bronx. Educational and cultural institutions include Fordham University (1841), Manhattan College (1853), Lehman College (1931), and Bronx (1957) and Hostos (1970) community colleges, along with the New York Botanical Garden and Bronx Zoo, both in Bronx Park on the Bronx R.

Pelham Bay and Van Cortlandt parks are two of the largest in the city system. Today largely a bedroom and service community for New York's working classes, the Bronx is seen by many outsiders only as they pass through it on one of several major highways carrying traffic through the New York area. See also: BAYCHESTER; BOSTON POST Rd.; CITY I.; CO-OP CITY; EASTCHESTER; FORDHAM; GRAND CONCOURSE; HART I.; HUNT'S POINT; KINGSBRIDGE; MELROSE; MORRISANIA; MORRIS HEIGHTS; MOSHOLU; MOTT HAVEN; PELHAM BAY PARK; RIKERS I.; RIVERDALE; SOUTH BRONX; SPUYTEN DUYVIL; THROGS NECK; TREMONT; VAN CORTLANDT PARK; WAKEFIELD; WILLIAMSBRIDGE; WOODLAWN; YANKEE STADIUM.

Bronx River 20 mi/32 km long, flowing from the KENSICO RESERVOIR, Westchester Co., SW through the Bronx, New York, where it enters the East R. at HUNT'S POINT. It is paralleled for much of its course by the Bronx River Parkway, an early New York restricted-access highway. In the C Bronx it flows through Bronx Park, a 700-ac/284-ha preserve within which are the New York Zoological Gardens (popularly, the Bronx Zoo), established in 1895, and the New York Botanical Garden (1891). Below the park, in the last 2 mi/3 km of its length, the river is navigable and heavily industrial, except where Sound View Park occupies its E bank near its mouth.

Bronxville village, pop. 6028, in Eastchester town, Westchester Co., SE New York, 17 mi/27 km NNE of New York City. It is an affluent suburb; in the early 20th century, it attracted many artists and writers. Sarah Lawrence College (1926) and Concordia College (1881) are located here.

Bronx-Whitestone Bridge also, **Whitestone Bridge** automobile suspension bridge between Ferry Point, Throgs Neck, the Bronx, and Whitestone, Queens, New York, over the East R. It has a 2300-ft/700-m main span. The bridge and connecting roadways were built 1939–40 as part of preparations for the New York World's Fair, and fostered development of NE Queens.

Bronzeville see under BLACK BELT, Chicago, Illinois.

Brook Farm see under WEST ROXBURY, Massachusetts.

Brookfield **1.** village, pop. 18,876, Cook Co., NE Illinois, a Chicago suburb 12 mi/19 km SW of the Loop. Founded as Grossdale at the end of the 19th century, it is a bedroom community. The 204-ac/83-ha Chicago Zoological Park, commonly known as the Brookfield Zoo, was opened here in 1934. **2.** town, pop. 2968, Worcester Co., SC Massachusetts, 15 mi/24 km W of Worcester. It has some light manufacturing, a dairy industry, and a resort area on Quaboag Pond. **3.** city, pop. 35,184, Waukesha Co., SE Wisconsin, 10 mi/16 km W of Milwaukee, of which it is a residential suburb. It has some light industry.

Brookgreen Gardens see under GRAND STRAND, South Carolina.

Brookhaven **1.** city, pop. 10,243, seat of Lincoln Co., SW Mississippi, 50 mi/80 km SSW of Jackson, in a dairying, lumbering, livestock raising, and oil and gas producing area. A trade and manufacturing center, it makes mobile homes, thermometers, lawnmowers, and apparel. **2.** town, pop. 407,779, Suffolk Co., SE New York. It incorporates many suburban villages on Long Island's North and South shores, including Mastic, Patchogue, Stony Brook, Port Jefferson, and Brookhaven village (pop. 3318). The town is the site of the Brookhaven National Laboratory for Nuclear Research.

Brookings city, pop. 16,270, seat of Brookings Co., EC South Dakota, on the Big Sioux R., 50 mi/80 km N of Sioux Falls. Founded in 1879, it is a trade center for the surrounding livestock farming, dairying, and grain producing region. Medical and dental equipment, aluminum windows, doors, awnings, concrete products, and fabricated steel are manufactured. It is the seat of South Dakota State University (1881).

Brookland largely residential section of upper NORTHEAST Washington, D.C., 4 mi/6 km NE of the White House, near the Maryland line. It is a largely black middle-class area with a mixture of row house and bungalow construction. Catholic University of America (1887), Trinity College (1897), the National Shrine of the Immaculate Conception, and other Catholic institutions are here.

Brookline **1.** town, pop. 54,718, Norfolk Co., E Massachusetts, a suburb of Boston, which surrounds it to the E, S, and N. Originally a pastoral neighbor of Boston known as Muddy River, the town includes Brookline village, Longwood, Beaconsfield, and part of Chestnut Hill. An early marketing center, Brookline still bases its economy on retail and wholesale trading; furnituremaking, printing, and publishing are also important. The birthplace of President John F. Kennedy and Fairstead, the home of Frederick Law Olmsted, are National Historic Sites. The Longwood Cricket Club is famed for its tennis tournaments. Early in the 20th century, Brookline was noted for the wealth of some of its inhabitants, especially in its S and W sections; the population today is solidly middle-class, including many students and elderly persons. Several colleges are in the town. **2.** residential neighborhood on the S side of Pittsburgh, Pennsylvania, on the S slope of Mt. Washington, 3.5 mi/6 km S of the GOLDEN TRIANGLE, N of MOUNT LEBANON and DORMONT. Named for Brookline, Massachusetts, it was developed in 1910, but middle-class homes did not sell until the 1920s.

Brooklyn **1.** residential section of Baltimore, Maryland, on the S bank of the Patapsco R., S of the Harbor Tunnel Thruway (Interstate 895). The area was laid out in lots by the Patapsco Company in 1853, and annexed by the city of Baltimore in 1918. Unincorporated Brooklyn Park (pop. 10,987), adjacent (S) in Anne Arundel Co., is similar in character. **2.** village, pop. 1027, Jackson Co., SC Michigan, 13 mi/21 km S of Jackson. It is situated in an area of rolling hills and many lakes with recreational facilities. Brooklyn is home to the 2-mi/3-km Michigan International Speedway, site of the Marlboro 500 and other auto racing events. **3.** second-largest (70 sq mi/183 sq km) and most populous (2,300,664) of the five boroughs of NEW YORK CITY, coextensive with Kings Co., on the SW tip of Long Island, bordered N, NE, and E by Queens. Manhattan lies NW, across the East R. Upper NEW YORK BAY lies W; the whole E side of New York Harbor is along the Brooklyn waterfront. The Narrows lie SW, Lower New York Bay is S, and the ROCKAWAY Channel and JAMAICA BAY are on the SE. While largely residential, Brooklyn also has much and varied industry, in addition to its shipping and warehousing sector and a commercial Downtown. Home to the Canarsie Indians, it was settled beginning in the 1630s by the Dutch, who developed five towns: Nieuw Amersfoort (Flatlands), Midwout or 't Vlackbos (Flatbush), Breuckelen, Nieuw Utrecht, and Boswijck (Bushwick). In 1643 the religious dissenter Lady Deborah Moody established the first English settlement, Gravesend. The English controlled the area from 1664, establishing Kings Co. in 1683. Before 1776, some industry and commerce developed along the N waterfront, while the interior remained largely agricultural. In Aug. 1776, the British attacked New York through Brooklyn in the Battle of Long Island, fought in what is now Prospect Park, Gowanus, and Brooklyn Heights, and occupied the county for the rest of the Revolutionary War. In 1816, the village of Brooklyn was incorporated; in 1834, it became a city, and through the 19th century annexed other Kings Co. communities; by 1860, it was the third most populous US city, and when it was absorbed into Greater New York in 1898, becoming a borough, it had over 1 million inhabitants. The greatest change in Brooklyn's character came after the 1883 opening of the Brooklyn Bridge, when the direct link with Manhattan began to make it a residential annex of the central city. In the early 20th century the Williamsburg (1903) and Manhattan (1909) bridges and expansion of the New York rapid transit system brought waves of immigrants into Brooklyn; the process has continued to the present, with one community establishing itself as an earlier one departs for Long Island or other suburbs; Brooklyn's pop. has thus remained roughly stable for decades, despite continuous residential change. Today the "borough of churches" or "borough of homes" is a region of many distinct neighborhoods; its three- and four-story brownstone houses are emblematic of the borough, which also, however, has high-rise apartments and large areas of single-family housing. Some sense of competition with Manhattan (referred to locally as "New York") has survived, and Brooklyn is widely regarded as having its own distinctive dialect and culture. Among others, the borough has the largest New York black community, what is sometimes called the world's largest Jewish community, and major Irish, Italian, and Hispanic communities. Brooklyn's educational institutions include Polytechnic University (1854), Pratt Institute (1887), Long Island University (1926), Brooklyn College (1930), and a number of city and private colleges. The Academy of Music, Museum, Public Library, and Botanic Garden form a noted cultural cluster. The New York Aquarium is one of the attractions of world-famous Coney Island. See also: BATH BEACH; BAY RIDGE; BEDFORD-STUYVESANT; BENSONHURST; BOERUM HILL; BOROUGH PARK; BRIGHTON BEACH ("Little Odessa"); BROOKLYN HEIGHTS; BROWNSVILLE; BUSHWICK; CANARSIE; CARROLL GARDENS; CLINTON HILL; COBBLE HILL; CONEY ISLAND; CROWN HEIGHTS; EAST NEW YORK; EBBETS FIELD; FLATBUSH; FLATLANDS; FLOYD BENNETT FIELD; FORT GREENE; GOWANUS; GRAVESEND; GREENPOINT; GREEN-WOOD CEMETERY; MIDWOOD; NEW UTRECHT; PARK SLOPE; PROSPECT PARK; RED HOOK; SHEEPSHEAD BAY; SOUTH BROOKLYN; SUNSET PARK; WALLABOUT BAY; WEEKSVILLE; WILLIAMSBURG. **4.** city, pop. 11,706, Cuyahoga Co., NE Ohio, a residential suburb 5 mi/8 km SW of Cleveland. **5.** residential neighborhood in Southeast PORTLAND, Oregon, on the Willamette R., just SE of Downtown. One of the earliest Portland settlements E of the river, it attracted Italian farmers and workers in nearby railyards; today it is a middle-class community.

Brooklyn Army Terminal see under SUNSET PARK, New York.

Brooklyn-Battery Tunnel longest US vehicular tunnel, under the S end of the EAST R., from the Battery, Manhattan, to South Brooklyn, New York, where it connects with the Brooklyn-Queens and Gowanus expressways. Opened in 1950, it has a length of 9117 ft/2780 m. Its octagonal ventilation tower, on GOVERNORS I., is a singular New York Harbor sight.

Brooklyn Bridge suspension bridge between lower Manhattan and Brooklyn Heights, New York. Built 1869–83 by John A. and Washington A. Roebling, it was the world's longest suspension bridge at the time, the first to use steel wire in its cables. Not only the first bridge across the East R., it was a major 19th-century engineering feat, and became a symbol of New York and America to the world. Its opening brought the independent cities of New York and Brooklyn together, and in 1898 they merged. The bridge has two largely granite towers and a central span 1596 ft/487 m long. Formerly it carried trains and streetcars; today it carries motor traffic and pedestrians. Brooklyn Bridge is immortalized in the poetry of Whitman and Hart Crane, in the paintings of Joseph Stella and others, and in folklore.

Brooklyn Center city, pop. 28,867, Hennepin Co., SE Minnesota, on the Mississippi R., a residential suburb immediately N of Minneapolis. Settled in the 1840s, it was an agricultural trading center until the postwar suburban boom. There has been a steady influx of low-income residents over the past few years. The 1980s witnessed much commercial development, particularly along the I-94 corridor.

Brooklyn Ferry see under BROOKLYN HEIGHTS, New York.

Brooklyn Heights residential and commercial section of NW Brooklyn, New York, across the East R. from lower Manhattan. A lightly settled bluff used as Washington's headquarters during the battle of Long Island (1776), it became what some call America's first suburb after Robert Fulton obtained a license to run ferries from Manhattan in 1814; business leaders sought its combined isolation from and closeness to Manhattan. By the mid 19th century Brooklyn Heights was noted for its residences and churches, among them Henry Ward Beecher's Plymouth Church of the Pilgrims (1849), an abolitionist stronghold and Underground Railroad center. The opening of the Brooklyn Bridge (1883) and subway service (1908) brought changes. The neighborhood's elite character gave way in part to bohemianism; hotels were built among the brownstone residences, and many of the rich moved away. Since the 1920s the Heights have gone in and out of fashion; in the 1980s a new generation of young professionals brought an active boutique economy. Brooklyn Heights is home to the world headquarters and printing facilities of the Jehovah's Witnesses. Its Esplanade (locally, the Promenade), built above the Brooklyn-Queens Expressway when that road cut through the dockland below the Heights in the 1930s, affords noted views of Manhattan. Brooklyn Borough Hall and the downtown business district lie to the E. The Fulton Ferry district, now the area at the base of the Brooklyn Bridge, was celebrated by local resident Walt Whitman, who also called it Brooklyn Ferry.

Brooklyn Park **1.** see under BROOKLYN, Maryland. **2.** city, pop. 56,381, Hennepin Co., SE Minnesota, on the Mississippi R., a residential community 9 mi/14 km N of Minneapolis. Settled in the 1840s, it was a village surrounded by truck and dairy farms. Suburbanization occurred after World War II and accelerated during the 1980s. Today, commercial strip development characterizes much of the SE and SW areas of the city.

Brookmont see under CABIN JOHN, Maryland.

Brook Park village, pop. 22,865, Cuyahoga Co., NE Ohio, 6 mi/10 km SW of Cleveland. Most residents commute to jobs within the greater Cleveland area. It is the site of NASA's Lewis Research Center, and of Cleveland's Hopkins International Airport, one of the largest in the US.

Brooks town, pop. 9433, SE Alberta, 115 mi/185 km SE of Calgary. It is situated in an area of irrigated farm and ranch land. Agricultural products are traded and processed here, as is natural gas. Settlement began when the Canadian Pacific Railway built (1914) an irrigation dam nearby. Several horticultural and wildlife research centers, including a pheasant hatchery, are here. Also nearby are Kinbrook I. Provincial Park (S) and DINOSAUR PROVINCIAL PARK (NE).

Brooks Air Force Base in SE San Antonio, Texas, 6 mi/10 km SE of Downtown. Founded in 1917, it was the site of the world's first mass paratroop drop (1929). It is now home to the Air Force Aerospace Medical Division.

Brookside also, **Brookside Park** unincorporated community, pop. 15,307, New Castle Co., N Delaware, just SE of Newark. It is primarily residential, part of the Wilmington suburban area.

Brookside Park 2000-ac/800-ha park in Cleveland, Ohio, along Big Creek, 5 mi/8 km SW of Downtown and adjacent to suburban BROOKLYN. The Cleveland Metropark Zoo is here.

Brooks Range farthest NW extension of the ROCKY Mt. chain, comprising a number of smaller ranges extending for c.600 mi/1000 km across N Alaska from near POINT HOPE on the Chukchi Sea (W) to just over the Yukon border. Some 150 mi/240 km wide, it forms a significant barrier, esp. in the E, to travel between the NORTH SLOPE (N) and the YUKON R. basin (S). Subranges include two W arms, the DeLong and Baird mountains, and, continuing to the E, the Endicott, Philip Smith, Franklin, Romanzof, and Davidson mountains. The range is highest in the E, reaching 9060 ft/2761 m at Mt. Isto in the Romanzofs. The DALTON HIGHWAY and TRANS-ALASKA PIPELINE go through Atigun Pass (4752 ft/1448 m). The 7.5 million–ac/3.05 million–ha Gates of the Arctic National Park and Preserve contains Anaktuvuk Pass, much of the Endicotts, and Walker L., a registered Natural Landmark. Named in honor of the geologist A.H. Brooks, the mountains were formerly called the Endicott or Brooks-Endicott Range.

Brookville **1.** town, pop. 2529, seat of Franklin Co., E Indiana, 30 mi/48 km SSW of Richmond, between the East and West forks of the Whitewater R. Founded in 1804, it is a trade center in an area in which corn, grain, and tobacco are grown. Whitewater State Park is 12 mi/19 km NNE, at the upper end of 15 mi/24 km–long Brookville L. **2.** village, pop. 3716, in Oyster Bay town, Nassau Co., SE New York, on Long Island, 5 mi/8 km SE of Glen Cove. On the North Shore, it is an affluent suburb with large estates. OLD BROOKVILLE is just NW.

Broomall unincorporated village, pop. 10,930, in Marple township, Delaware Co., SE Pennsylvania, a residential suburb 8 mi/13 km W of Philadelphia.

Broome County 712 sq mi/1844 sq km, pop. 212,160, in SC New York, along the Pennsylvania line. Its seat and largest city is BINGHAMTON, situated along the Susquehanna R. with JOHNSON CITY and ENDICOTT. The Tri-Cities dominate the county's economy with their shoe manufacturing and other diversified industries. Farms raise poultry and beef and dairy cattle, and produce vegetables, maple syrup, lumber, and dairy and wood products. There is some resort development in the N, particularly around the Whitney Point Reservoir.

Broomfield city, pop. 24,638, Adams, Boulder, Jefferson, and Weld counties, NC Colorado, a suburb 15 mi/24 km NE of Denver. Surrounded by farms, it was originally a marketing and service center, but is now primarily residential and commercial, with some light manufacturing and agriculture.

Brossard city, pop. 64,793, Laprairie Co., S. Québec, across the Champlain Bridge (E) from Montréal, a growing residential and commercial suburb on the St. Lawrence R.

Broward County 1211 sq mi/3136 sq km, pop. 1,255,488, in SE Florida, on the Atlantic Ocean (E). Its seat and largest city is FORT LAUDERDALE; Hollywood, its other major city, lies just S. The populous E is lined with beachfront resorts, including Deerfield Beach, Pompano Beach, and Lighthouse Point. Just inland are a variety of residential suburbs like Coral Springs, Tamarac, and Plantation. In addition to tourism and retirees, the E part of the county has office complexes, diversified light industry, truck farms, and citrus producers. The sparsely populated balance, most of the county's area, is part of the EVERGLADES, and is cut by only one major roadway, ALLIGATOR ALLEY. The Big Cypress Seminole Indian Reservation (pop. 484) occupies the W segment of Broward, and parts of adjacent Palm Beach and Hendry counties.

Brown County 524 sq mi/1357 sq km, pop. 194,594, in E Wisconsin, bounded by L. Michigan's GREEN BAY (N). Its seat is the city of GREEN BAY. It is partly on the base of the DOOR PENINSULA, and is traversed by the Fox R. Dairying and lumbering are its primary economic activities. The county's main manufacturing centers are along the Fox R., principally at Green Bay and DE PERE.

Brown Deer village, pop. 12,236, Milwaukee Co., SE Wisconsin, 5 mi/8 km N of Milwaukee, of which it is a commuter suburb. Its chief industry is the manufacture of meters.

Brownfield city, pop. 9560, seat of Terry Co., W Texas, 38 mi/61 km SW of Lubbock. It is a trade and processing center in a rich irrigated area that grows grains, peanuts, and cotton and raises cattle. It also is an oilfield service center.

Browning town, pop. 1170, Glacier Co., NW Montana, 40 mi/64 km WSW of Cut Bank. Founded in 1895, it is the headquarters of the 1.5 million-ac/607,500-ha Blackfeet Indian Reservation and a trade center for the agricultural products of the region. With GLACIER NATIONAL PARK 18 mi/29 km to the E, Browning is also a resort town, and tourism is important to its economy.

Browns Ferry nuclear power plant on the N side of Wheeler L. (the Tennessee R.), 10 mi/16 km SW of Athens and 33 mi/53 km E of Florence, in Limestone Co., N Alabama. In operation since 1973, it is one of the world's largest nuclear plants.

Browns Mills unincorporated village, pop. 11,429, in Pemberton township, Burlington Co., C New Jersey, on Rancocas Creek, 11 mi/18 km E of Mount Holly. Long known as a health spa, it is just off Mirror L., S of FORT DIX and N of Lebanon State Forest. It is primarily residental.

Brownsville **1.** unincorporated community, pop. 15,607, Dade Co., SE Florida, a black suburb just N of Miami and E of Hialeah. **2.** residential and commercial section of E Brooklyn, New York. It is E of Crown Heights, SE of Bedford-Stuyvesant, and W of East New York. Brownsville was semirural and agricultural until the 1889 extension of the elevated railway opened it to Jews leaving Manhattan's LOWER EAST SIDE. It soon became the "Jerusalem of America," known for its Pitkin Ave. commercial life and radical politics, and celebrated in the writing of residents Henry Roth, Alfred Kazin, and Irving Shulman (whose *Amboy Dukes* took its title from a local street). Margaret Sanger opened America's first birth control clinic in Brownsville in 1916. In the 1930s an estimated 200,000 persons lived in slightly over 2 sq mi/5 sq km, making Brownsville New York's densest neighborhood. The N part, called Ocean Hill, became heavily Italian in the 1930s. After World War II, blacks began to move in as whites left for CANARSIE and areas outside the city. In 1968 a struggle over control of local schools in Ocean Hill-Brownsville focused national attention on racial issues. **3.** city, pop. 10,019, Haywood Co., W Tennessee, 24 mi/39 km W of Jackson. It is a trade center in an area producing lumber, cotton, and fruit. **4.** city, pop. 98,962, seat of Cameron Co., extreme S Texas, on the Rio Grande opposite the much larger Matamoros, Mexico, 21 mi/32 km W of the Gulf of Mexico. The Mexican War battles (May 1846) of PALO ALTO and RESACA DE LA PALMA were fought here, and Fort Brown was named after an American who died in the fighting. During the Civil War Brownsville and Matamoros were used by Confederate blockade runners, providing a major cotton outlet. On May 12–13, 1865, the last Civil War land battle was fought at Palmito Hill, E along the river. The modern city developed after 1904, when the Gulf Coast Lines Railway arrived. The "Brownsville Affair" of 1906 involved 167 black soldiers dishonorably discharged after a shooting, and not exonerated until 1972. The deepwater port, opened in 1936, is the SW terminus of the GULF INTRACOASTAL WATERWAY. The city is now an international rail, air, and highway hub, and a trade center for a large ranching, farming, and citrus growing area of the Lower Rio Grande Valley. Brownsville forms a port and industrial complex with HARLINGEN and SAN BENITO (NW) and has a large shrimping fleet; it repairs aircraft and makes processed foods, petrochemicals, and electronic equipment. A gateway to Mexico, it is thoroughly bicultural, with many Mexican residents and much business tied to MAQUILADORA plants S of the Rio Grande. Texas Southmost University (1926) is here.

Brownwood city, pop. 18,387, seat of Brown Co., C Texas, on Pecan Bayou, 64 mi/103 km SE of Abilene, in the Central Hills. It processes area pecans, cotton, grain, peanuts, and livestock. An industrial and retail center, it also has oil and natural gas wells and rail shops, and manufactures chemicals, glass, brick, and various other products. The city is home to Howard Payne University (1889), with its Douglas MacArthur Academy of Freedom.

Bruce Nuclear Power Development see under KINCARDINE, Ontario.

Bruce Peninsula 60 mi/100 km long, extending NNW from S Ontario into L. Huron, separating SW GEORGIAN BAY (E) from the lake's main body. Part of the NIAGARA ESCARPMENT forms its backbone. Lightly populated, it is noted for the cliffs and inlets on the Georgian Bay side. Tobermory, at its N tip, is a ferry port for MANITOULIN I. (NW) and the site of the Fathom Five National Marine Park, which incorporates 19 islands and surrounding waters popular with divers. OWEN SOUND is the peninsula's S gateway. The **Bruce Trail,** a footpath, follows the Niagara Escarpment for some 450 mi/720 km, through (SE–NW) the Niagara Peninsula, Hamilton, valleys SW of Toronto, the Caledon Hills, the Beaver R. valley, Owen Sound, and the Bruce Peninsula, ending at Tobermory.

Bruinsburg historic site and former town in Claiborne Co., SW Mississippi, on the Mississippi R., c.30 mi/48 km SSW of Vicksburg, just SW of PORT GIBSON, at the mouth of Bayou Pierre. During the VICKSBURG Campaign, on April 30, 1863, Union troops under U.S. Grant crossed the river from Hard Times Landing, Louisiana, to here, meeting a Northern fleet that had come downriver past Vicksburg by night. From Bruinsburg, the Northern troops began their march back toward eventual victory at Vicksburg.

Brunswick 1. city, pop. 16,433, seat of Glynn Co., SE Georgia, on the estuarial Turtle R. and Brunswick R. (W and S) and St. Simons Sound and the Atlantic Intracoastal Waterway (E), 63 mi/101 km SSW of Savannah. The second major port of Georgia, it was laid out in 1771. It is an important center for seafood (especially shrimp and crab) processing, also handling naval stores and wood and pulp products. The city is also the gateway to the coastal resorts of JEKYLL and SAINT SIMONS islands. The city's marshy E part inspired the well-known poem "The Marshes of Glynn," written in the 1870s by Sidney Lanier. **2.** town, pop. 20,906, Cumberland Co., SW Maine, at the falls of the Androscoggin R. opposite Topsham, 26 mi/42 km NE of Portland. Originally a trading post, Brunswick later manufactured paper and textiles, clothing, wood products, paper, and shoes. The town is best known for Bowdoin College (1794), alma mater of Longfellow, Hawthorne, President Franklin Pierce, and Arctic explorers Robert Peary and Donald MacMillan, whose careers are depicted in a campus museum. Stowe House, where Harriet Beecher Stowe wrote *Uncle Tom's Cabin,* is near the campus. **Brunswick Naval Air Station,** E of Brunswick Center at Cook's Corners, has been a major base for antisubmarine aircraft. **3.** nuclear power plant: see under SOUTHPORT, North Carolina. **4.** city, pop. 28,230, Medina Co., NE Ohio, 20 mi/32 km SW of Cleveland. It is largely residential. Dairy, fruit, and truck farming are carried out nearby.

Brunswick County 563 sq mi/1458 sq km, pop. 15,987, in S Virginia, on the North Carolina border. Its seat is LAWRENCEVILLE. Rural in character, the county gave its name in the mid 19th century to Brunswick stew, said to have been invented by local hunters.

Bryan 1. city, pop. 8348, seat of Williams Co., extreme NW Ohio, 16 mi/26 km NW of Defiance. Its early development was based around artesian wells reputed to be of medicinal value. Today the city is a trade center for a farming and dairying area. The economy also is supported by diversified manufacturing; products include airplane parts, truck bodies, lubricating equipment, furnaces, and furniture. **2.** city, pop. 55,002, seat of Brazos Co., EC Texas, 88 mi/142 km NW of Houston. In a region that produces cattle, sorghums, poultry, cotton, and other crops, Bryan processes agricultural goods and makes chemicals, concrete, electronic equipment, furniture, and various other products. The educational complex at COLLEGE STATION, 7 mi/11 km SE, strongly affects the city's life and economy; Texas A & M University operates a nuclear research center on the former Bryan Air Force Base. Settled in the 1820s by followers of Stephen F. Austin, Bryan was long a center of large cotton plantations.

Bryce Canyon National Park 35,835 ac/14,513 ha of limestone BADLANDS and canyons at the E end of the Paunsaugunt Plateau, in SC Utah, 47 mi/76 km E of Cedar City. The canyon is filled with pinnacles, tunnels, and natural amphitheaters formed by erosion and uplifting of the earth's crust. The floor is 6600 ft/2012 m above sea level, and the highest elevation in the park, at Rainbow Point, is 9105 ft/2775 m. Exceptionally clear air allows vistas of up to 200 mi/320 km from the canyon rim.

Bryn Athyn borough, pop. 1081, Montgomery Co., SE Pennsylvania, 12 mi/19 km NE of Philadelphia. It is the site of Bryn Athyn Cathedral (1914), the center of Swedenborgianism in the US, and home to the Academy of the New Church (1876), an independent college affiliated with the Church of the New Jerusalem, the Swedenborgian church.

Bryn Mawr unincorporated village, pop. 3271, in Lower Merion township, Montgomery Co., SE Pennsylvania, 10 mi/16 km NW of Philadelphia. An affluent MAIN LINE suburb, it is the seat of Bryn Mawr College (1885) and of Harcum Junior College (1915). In the early 1900s it was a summer resort.

Bryn Mawr–Skyway unincorporated community, pop. 12,514, King Co., WC Washington, on the S end of L. Washington, adjacent to Renton (E), a suburb 8 mi/13 km S of downtown Seattle. An area that combines residential and industrial features, it has sawmills and a cement factory, and is just NW of RENTON.

Buchanan town, pop. 1222, Botetourt Co., WC Virginia, in the Blue Ridge Mts., on the upper James R. It is the birthplace (1870) of Mary Johnston, whose novels drew on Virginia's Colonial and Civil War history.

Buchanan, Lake 23,060 ac/9339 ha, in SC Texas, on the Colorado R., 50 mi/80 km NW of Austin. Created by the Buchanan Dam (1938), it is the largest of the Highland Lakes, created by dams above Austin designed to prevent the serious flooding that had characterized the Colorado. Below L. Buchanan are the smaller Inks L., L. Lyndon B. Johnson (formerly Granite Shoals L.), and L. Marble Falls. Lake Travis, formed by the Mansfield Dam, covers 18,930 ac/7667 ha, and is 13 mi/21 km NNW of the city. The older L. Austin, formed by the Tom Miller Dam, lies partly within the city (as does Town L., formed by the Longhorn Dam, in Austin's Downtown). The Highland Lakes are a major recreational resource.

Buchans town, pop. 1164, WC Newfoundland, just N of Red Indian L., and 50 mi/80 km ESE of Corner Brook, established in the 1920s as a lead, zinc, copper, gold, and silver mining center.

Buckhannon city, pop. 5909, seat of Upshur Co., NC West Virginia, on the Buckhannon R., 21 mi/34 km SSE of Clarksburg. In an agricultural region, it is the seat of West Virginia Wesleyan College (1890). Local industries include coal mining, lumbering, and production of natural gas and building materials.

Buckhead commercial and residential section of Atlanta, Georgia, 6 mi/10 km N of Downtown. Taking its name from an 1840s trading post at a trail junction, it is now an elite area of upscale shopping centers (including the 1958 Lenox Square, a noted early mall), galleries, and mansions, the most prestigious neighborhood in the city. The Governor's Mansion and the Atlanta Historical Society are here.

Buckingham city, pop. 10,548, OUTAOUAIS URBAN COMMUNITY, SW Québec, 17 mi/27 km NE of Ottawa, on the Lièvre R. Founded in the early 1800s, it is today the service center for a mining (phosphates, graphite, and mica), lumbering, and dairying area, and has pulp and paper mills and chemical plants. Buckingham is also the gateway to a hunting and fishing region.

Buck Island Reef National Monument encompassing 880 ac/356 ha of coral reef and waters 2 mi/3 km off the NE coast of SAINT CROIX, in the US Virgin Islands. It is a noted snorkelers' resort, with marked underwater trails, and nesting grounds to frigate birds, pelicans, and sea turtles.

Bucks County 610 sq mi/1580 sq km, pop. 541,174, in SE Pennsylvania, N of Philadelphia, bordered by the Delaware R. (NE and SE). Its seat is Doylestown. Once inhabited by Lenape Indians, its towns were founded by English Quakers and its farms settled by German Mennonites in the 17th and 18th centuries. Containing many affluent Philadelphia suburbs and exurbs, it has experienced rapid growth in recent decades. The artists' colony of NEW HOPE and the planned community of LEVITTOWN are here.

Bucyrus city, pop. 13,496, seat of Crawford Co., NC Ohio, on the Sandusky R., 18 mi/29 km NE of Marion. Founded in 1818, it was named for its beauty ("Bu") and for the surveyor's personal hero, Cyrus, founder of the ancient Persian Empire. The surrounding area is agricultural. Bucyrus produces road and farm machinery, roller bearings, steel and iron stampings, copper utensils, fluorescent lamps, and rubber hose.

Buena Park city, pop. 68,784, Orange Co., S California, 20 mi/32 km SE of Los Angeles. The city is the site of Knott's Berry Farm, an internationally known "Old West" theme park, of the Los Alamitos harness-racing track, and of several other museums and theme parks that combine to draw tourists. Buena Park is also a wholesale and retail distribution center and a residential suburb.

Buena Vista independent city, pop. 6406, within Rockbridge Co., WC Virginia, 6 mi/10 km SE of LEXINGTON, at the S end of the Shenandoah Valley, on the W slope of the Blue Ridge Mts. It boomed in the 1890s, producing paper, and has also made silk, brick, and leather, rubber, and plastic products. Southern Seminary College (1867), for women, is here.

Buena Vista Lake see under KERN R., California.

Buffalo city, pop. 328,123, seat of Erie Co., W New York, at the E end of L. Erie and the W end of the New York State Barge Canal. It is New York's second-largest city. Its metropolitan area spans Erie and Niagara counties, and includes Niagara Falls, Lackawanna, Lockport, Tonawanda, and North Tonawanda. The area was settled by Senecas under British protection in 1780. In 1790, the Holland Land Company bought land near the mouth of Buffalo Creek, where Joseph Ellicott laid out the town of New Amsterdam, popularly called Buffalo, in 1803. During the War of 1812, Buffalo was headquarters for American military operations on the Niagara Frontier. It was burned by the British in 1813, and rebuilt in 1816. The completion of the Erie Canal in 1825 established it as a major port. Following the development of the first steam-powered grain elevator, created by Joseph Dart in 1843, Buffalo became the largest US grain handler, a status it still holds. During the Civil War railroads expanded, and industries, including shipyards, meat packing plants, and flour mills, flourished. The 20th century brought a transformation from a primarily commercial to a primarily industrial economy. Hydroelectricity from Niagara Falls powered iron, steel, automotive, and chemical industries. Manufactures now include automotive components, fabricated metals, industrial machinery, computers, chemicals, medical instruments, dyes, plastics, paints, abrasives, and food products, and Buffalo is one of the world's leading flour milling centers. The Port of Buffalo handles limestone, coal, iron ore, lumber, petroleum, and automobiles. Greater Buffalo International Airport is in CHEEKTOWAGA, 10 mi/16 km ENE of downtown.

Following World War II, many workers left the area as automation replaced heavy industry. Buffalo now houses several aerospace, electronic, and nuclear research centers. Service industries and wholesale and retail trade have experienced some growth since the 1970s. The city's diverse population includes large communities of Poles, Italians, and Irish in the E, W, and S sectors respectively, and a large black community in the inner city. A rapid shift of mostly white upper- and middle-class families to the suburbs caused the city's population to drop over the past few decades. Urban renewal projects have included the private rebuilding of the downtown business district, and the development of an extensive expressway serving the metropolitan area.

Buffalo Bayou watercourse, 45 mi/72 km long, on which the city of Houston, Texas, was established in the 1830s. It rises in creeks E of the Brazos R. and flows E through the modern metropolis to join the San Jacinto R. and enter Galveston Bay. The Port of Houston, with its Turning Basin, is 4 mi/6 km E of Downtown; below it the bayou has become part of the HOUSTON SHIP CHANNEL. A half-dozen smaller bayous join the Buffalo in the metropolitan area, including Brays Bayou (SW), at whose confluence with the Buffalo, SE of Downtown, the town of HARRISBURG was settled before Houston was created; others are Sims (S), White Oak (NW), Hunting (N), Green (NE), and Carpenter (NE) bayous.

Buffalo Bill Dam and Reservoir see under CODY, Wyoming.

Buffalo Grove village, pop. 36,427, Cook and Lake counties, NE Illinois, a suburb 25 mi/40 km NW of Chicago. It is named for buffalo bones found in the area. Largely a bedroom community, it has some light industry, including computer manufacture.

Buffalo River 132 mi/213 km long, in NW Arkansas. It rises in Newton Co., on the N of the BOSTON Mts. in the OZARK Plateau, and flows ENE into the WHITE R. at Buffalo City, 12 mi/19 km SSW of Mountain Home. In 1972 its course was declared the **Buffalo National River,** a 94,218-ac/38,158-ha preserve with footpaths along its bluffs, springs and sinkholes, and varied boating opportunities. The Buffalo is undammed and relatively unpolluted.

Buffalo Trace see under BLUE LICKS SPRING, Kentucky.

Buford city, pop. 8771, Gwinnett Co., NC Georgia, 33 mi/53 km NE of Atlanta. A farm trade center, it has made leather and concrete products. The Buford Dam, which forms L. Sidney Lanier on the CHATTAHOOCHEE R., is 5 mi/8 km NW.

Bugaboo Spires see under PURCELL Mts., British Columbia.

Buggs Island Lake see JOHN H. KERR RESERVOIR.

Buies Creek unincorporated community, pop. 2085, Harnett Co., C North Carolina, near the Cape Fear R., 9 mi/14 km NW of DUNN. It is the seat of Campbell University (1887), one of the largest US Baptist schools.

Bullhead City city, pop. 21,951, Mohave Co., NW Arizona, on the Colorado R. across from LAUGHLIN, Nevada, and 70 mi/110 km SSW of Las Vegas. Founded in 1945 as a construction camp for the Davis Dam, just upstream, by the early 1990s it was the fastest-growing city in Arizona, with a large second home and retiree pop.; many residents moved here from California. Bullhead City is also a resort base for fishing enthusiasts, boaters, and gamblers who frequent Laughlin's casinos.

Bull Run stream, 20 mi/32 km long, in NE Virginia. It rises in Loudoun Co. and runs SE, forming the boundary between Loudoun and Fairfax (NE) and Prince William (SW) counties, to pass E of MANASSAS, the scene of two Civil War battles, on July 21, 1861, and on Aug. 29–30, 1862. Occoquan Creek, formed by Bull Run and Cedar Creek 5 mi/8 km SE of Manassas, flows 20 mi/32 km SE to Occoquan Bay, an inlet of the Potomac R., at Woodbridge.

Buncombe County 659 sq mi/1707 sq km, pop. 174,821, in W North Carolina, in the Blue Ridge Mts., drained by the French Broad and Swannanoa rivers. Its seat is ASHEVILLE. Farming, lumbering, and tourism are important. Industries, focused in Asheville, manufacture textiles, furniture, and paper products. The county includes sections of the Pisgah National Forest in the E and SW. It gave its name to a popular term, now usually *bunkum* or *bunk,* when its congressman, Felix Walker, made a long, pointless House speech, c.1820. Asked what he had meant, he said that he had felt it his duty to speak "for Buncombe."

Bungalow Belt in Chicago, Illinois, term for scattered sections of the city and near suburbs where, especially in the 1920s, bungalow housing was constructed for new working- and middle-class homeowners moving outward from the city's central neighborhoods. Many parts of the Belt were served by streetcar lines into the LOOP. MARQUETTE PARK (SW), CHATHAM (S), and BELMONT-CRAGIN (WNW) are representative.

Bunker Hill **1.** residential and commercial section of LOS ANGELES, California, immediately NW of Downtown. In the 1880s a fashionable neighborhood, it fell into decline by the 1920s, and has since the 1960s been entirely transformed by urban renewal, much of the hill having been removed, into a cluster of high-rise apartment buildings and office blocks. The MUSIC CENTER occupies part of the area. **2.** in the CHARLESTOWN section of Boston, Massachusetts. When the American militia attempted to rout the British from Boston in 1775, one of their goals was to capture it. Patriot troops built a fortification on nearby BREED'S HILL, which was then attacked. The British eventually succeeded in dislodging the Americans, but at great cost; the "Battle of Bunker Hill" came to be seen as proof that the Colonials could stand up to the British. The Bunker Hill Monument, on Breed's Hill, is an obelisk 220 ft/67 m high; its cornerstone was laid by the Marquis de Lafayette in 1825, and it was completed in 1843. **3.** see under MARTINSBURG, West Virginia.

Bunker Hill Village see under HUNTERS CREEK VILLAGE, Texas.

Burbank **1.** city, pop. 93,643, Los Angeles Co., SW California, 10 mi/16 km N of Los Angeles, in the E San Fernando Valley. The VERDUGO Mts. lie NE. In 1887, Dr. David Burbank bought the land on which the city was built. By the 1930s it was a movie industry center. Its aircraft industry and the city itself underwent rapid growth during World War II. Today it is both a residential suburb and a center of the entertainment and aerospace inudstries; Walt Disney Productions, Warner, Columbia, and NBC have offices and studios here, along with a division of Lockheed Aircraft. Plastics and cosmetics are also produced. **2.** city, pop. 27,600, Cook Co., NE Illinois, a residential suburb immediately SW of Chicago and 10 mi/16 km SW of the Loop. The Chicago Midway Airport lies a few miles N.

Burchard village, pop. 105, Pawnee Co., SE Nebraska, 50 mi/80 km SSE of Lincoln. The early film comedian Harold Lloyd (1893–1971) was born here.

Bureau of Land Management (BLM) see under PUBLIC LANDS.

Burgess Shale see under YOHO NATIONAL PARK, British Columbia.

Burien unincorporated community, pop. 25,089, King Co., WC Washington, a residential suburb 10 mi/16 km S of downtown Seattle. Airlines and their customers constitute an important part of Burien's economy, as it is immediately NW of the Seattle-Tacoma International Airport. The community is also a retail center for other nearby suburbs. Settled in the 1860s by a German pioneer, it developed from a lumbering to a farming community, until it was overtaken by postwar suburbanization. More recently, commercial development has characterized much of the area's growth.

Burin Peninsula some 80 mi/130 km NE–SW and up to 21 mi/34 km wide, in S Newfoundland, between Placentia (E) and Fortune (W) bays. The French islands of SAINT-PIERRE ET MIQUELON are off its tip. A desolate upland area, the peninsula is fringed with OUTPORTS, including Marystown, Burin, and Grand Bank, fishing settlements and processing centers.

Burkburnett city, pop. 10,145, Wichita Co., N Texas, 15 mi/24 km NNW of Wichita Falls and just S of the Red R. and the Oklahoma line. A livestock and produce shipping center, it was settled in 1907 and, with the discovery of oil, was a boomtown of 30,000 by 1918. Today the city refines gasoline and manufactures fiberglass pipe.

Burke unincorporated community, pop. 57,734, Fairfax Co., N Virginia, 12 mi/19 km W of Alexandria, on Pohick Creek. It is a largely residential suburb of Washington, D.C.

Burleson city, pop. 16,113, Johnson and Tarrant counties, NE Texas, 14 mi/22 km S of Fort Worth. An agricultural trade center, it is experiencing suburban growth along Interstate 35W.

Burley city, pop. 8702, Cassia and Minidoka counties, SC Idaho, on the Snake R., 35 mi/56 km E of Twin Falls. It is a shipping and processing point for an agricultural and dairying area. Burley has brickyards, refines sugar beets, and mills alfalfa meal and potato flour. National speedboat racing championships are held here annually. The Minidoka National Wildlife Refuge is 20 mi/32 km NE and the City of Rocks National Reserve is 32 mi/52 km S.

Burlingame city, pop. 26,801, San Mateo Co., NC California, on the W shore of San Francisco Bay, 15 mi/24 km S of San Francisco, of which it is a suburb. Founded in 1868, it grew up around the 1893 Burlingame Country Club, becoming a fancy bayside community. Light industries today include flower growing and some high-tech manufacturing and marketing.

Burlington **1.** city, pop. 27,208, seat of Des Moines Co., SE Iowa, on the Mississippi R., 55 mi/89 km SW of Davenport. The site of an Indian village, it originated as an 1805 fort. A fur trading post and later a steamboat grain and pork shipping port, it was territorial capital in 1838–46. The founding of the Burlington and Missouri River Railroad in 1856 made it a major rail hub, and the economy passed from lumbering to manufacturing. Today, there are railroad shops, and electrical and electronic equipment, boilers, steam turbines, and furniture are among goods produced. **2.** town, pop. 23,302, Middlesex Co., NE Massachusetts, 13 mi/21 km NW of Boston. Settled in 1641 as part of Woburn, it was incorporated as a separate town in 1799. Surrounded by farming areas, it has a pre-Revolutionary meeting house. On ROUTE 128, Burlington is a residential suburb with the large Burlington Mall and other retail areas and a variety of computer and electronics operations. **3.** city, pop. 9835, Burlington Co., W New Jersey, on the Delaware R. opposite Bristol, Pennsylvania, 11 mi/18 km SW of Trenton. Settled by Quakers (1677), it became an important Colonial city. Capital (1681–1701) of WEST JERSEY, it alternated with Perth Amboy as New Jersey capital until 1790. During the Revolution it was taken by Hessians (1776) and bombarded by the British (1778). Today it is a busy manufacturing and shipping community, distributing vegetables, dairy products, and fruit from local farms. Its industries produce such goods as cast iron pipe, clothing, aircraft parts, chemicals, and medical devices. Historic buildings include the Revell House (1685), St. Mary's Church (1703), the James Lawrence and James Fenimore Cooper (1780) birthplaces, and Friends Meeting House (1784). **4.** city, pop. 39,498, Alamance Co., NC North Carolina, on the upper Piedmont plateau, 20 mi/32 km E of Greensboro. Originally called Company Shops, it was the site of North Carolina Railroad shops 1866–96. In the 1890s, hosiery and other textile plants were established, and the city became a major textile center. It now houses diverse industries, also manufacturing coffins, electronic equipment, furniture, and chemicals. The ALAMANCE Battleground is 7 mi/11 km SW. Burlington has a technical college. **5.** city, pop. 129,575, Halton Regional Municipality, S Ontario, at the W end of L. Ontario, 8 mi/13 km NNE of Hamilton, from which it is separated by Hamilton Harbour (Burlington Bay). The Mohawk Loyalist leader Joseph Brant was granted land here in 1798. In the 19th century the city was a water and rail shipping center; in the 1890s the growing of fruits and vegetables became a major focus. Today it is a residential suburb of Hamilton, with which the Burlington Bay Skyway, completed in 1958, connects it. There is also some light industry here; manufactures include furniture, chemicals, and metal tubing goods. Burlington houses the Brant Museum of Indian Exhibits. **6.** Vermont's largest city, pop. 39,127, seat of Chittenden Co. and a port and industrial center on the E side of L. CHAMPLAIN, in NW Vermont, 35 mi/56 km NW of Montpelier. An early lumber and shipbuilding center and military post settled in 1773 on terraces above Champlain, it was organized as a town in 1797, and was a critical location in the War of 1812. The Winooski R., which forms the city's N boundary, provided power for the growth of industry. The University of Vermont (1791) has been central to the life of the "Queen City"; other institutions include Champlain College (1878), Trinity College (1925), and Burlington College (1972). Burlington's industries have turned out armaments, steel and concrete products, and computer and other electronics products. Burlington International Airport is in adjoining SOUTH BURLINGTON. **7.** city, pop. 8855, Racine Co., SE Wisconsin, on the Fox and White rivers, 25 mi/40 km WSW of Racine. Settled by Vermonters in the 1830s, it was in the 1840s home to a breakaway Mormon community led by Jesse Strang, who is buried here.

In a farm and resort area, the city has various manufactures and produces chocolate and dairy and other foods.

Burlington County 808 sq mi/2093 sq km, pop. 395,066, in SC New Jersey, bounded (W) by the Delaware R, the largest county in the state. Its seat is MOUNT HOLLY. The NW part contains residential suburbs of both Trenton (N) and Camden (S); important municipalities include WILLINGBORO, BURLINGTON, and BORDENTOWN. The sparsely populated, heavily wooded, partially agricultural C and S sections contain large parts of the Wharton, Lebanon, Penn, and Bass River state forests. McGuire Air Force Base and a portion of FORT DIX are in the NE.

Burlington Northern major US rail system, formed in 1970 with the merger of the NORTHERN PACIFIC RAILROAD, GREAT NORTHERN RAILWAY, **Chicago, Burlington, and Quincy Railroad,** and other lines; it has since acquired additional lines, and in the 1990s was engaged in attempts to purchase the SANTA FE RAILROAD. The Chicago and Burlington, the oldest (1850) line in Illinois, expanded continually through the late 19th century, absorbing other Midwestern carriers and acquiring a reputation as the "Granger Road" for its haulage of farm products. In the 20th century it also became a leader in commuter transportation. Its *Zephyrs,* introduced in 1934, were pioneer long-haul (Chicago–Denver) diesel-powered passenger trains. The Burlington Northern today has lines from the Pacific Northwest E to the Great Lakes and S to the Texas coast.

Burnaby district municipality, pop. 158,858, Greater Vancouver Regional District, SW British Columbia, between Burrard Inlet (N) and the Fraser R. (S), adjacent (N) to New Westminster and (E) to Vancouver. A commercial, industrial, and residential center, it has varied industries including trucking facilities, lumber and paper mills, and manufacture of steel and telecommunications equipment. Simon Fraser University (1963) is here.

Burning River in CLEVELAND, Ohio, sardonic nickname for the CUYAHOGA R., which here flows through the FLATS, site of much of the city's heavy industry, including oil refineries and chemical and steel plants. In June 1969, the Cuyahoga, filled with industrial effluents, caught fire, damaging nearby structures. Pollution levels have subsequently been reduced.

Burns city, pop. 2913, seat of Harney Co., EC Oregon, on the NE of the HARNEY DESERT, 235 mi/378 km SE of Portland. A 19th-century cattle ranch hub, it is now a road and rail center for an extensive high desert area. The Burns Indian Reservation (Paiute, pop. 163) is here. Malheur and Harney lakes, 20 mi/32 km S, are major waterfowl stops on the PACIFIC FLYWAY; the Malheur Lake National Wildlife Refuge (185,000 ac/75,000 ha, or 289 sq mi/749 sq km) is a noted birdwatching area.

Burns Harbor town, pop. 788, Porter Co., extreme NW Indiana, on L. Michigan, adjacent (E) to PORTAGE, in which Indiana's Burns International Harbor is situated. A large Bethlehem Steel plant is here. The INDIANA DUNES NATIONAL LAKESHORE begins just E.

Burnsville city, pop. 51,288, Dakota Co., SE Minnesota, on the Minnesota R., a residential and industrial suburb 14 mi/23 km S of Minneapolis. It was an agricultural trading village until after World War II, when it became a bedroom community. Burnsville is now one of the fastest-growing places in the area, with a large amount of commercial development along I-35E and I-35W.

Burrard Inlet arm of the Strait of GEORGIA, in SW British Columbia, forming the N waterfront of VANCOUVER. It extends 19 mi/31 km E to PORT MOODY; near its E end Indian Arm extends 11 mi/18 km NE. The inlet is 4 mi/6 km wide at its mouth; English Bay is on its S, from E of POINT GREY along KITSILANO Beach, connecting with FALSE CREEK, near Downtown. The N-extending peninsula ending in STANLEY PARK encloses the inlet's First Narrows, crossed by the Lions Gate Bridge (1938); E of this is Vancouver Harbour. The Second Narrows is another 5 mi/8 km E.

Burrillville town, pop. 16,230, Providence Co, extreme NW Rhode Island, 17 mi/27 km NW of Providence, on the Branch R. and the Massachusetts and Connecticut borders. It includes the villages of Bridgeton, Glendale, Mapleville, Masonville, Mt. Pleasant, Oakland, and Pascoag. Its administrative center is Harrisville. There are textile mills, dairy farms, apple orchards, granite quarries, and resorts.

Burro Mountains also, **Big Burro Mountains** N–S trending range in SW New Mexico, SW of Silver City. In a section of the Gila National Forest, it rises to 8081 ft/2463 m at Burro Peak, 6 mi/10 km SW of Tyrone. The **Little Burro Mts.** are an extension to the NE. Turquoise, copper, zinc, and lead have been mined here.

Burton city, pop. 27,617, Genesee Co., SE Michigan, on Thread Creek, a residential suburb 2 mi/3 km S of Flint.

Busch Gardens chain of THEME PARKS including The Dark Continent (1959), in Tampa, Florida, which has a 19th-century African motif, and The Old Country (1975), in Williamsburg, Virginia, which has a 17th-century European motif.

Busch Memorial Stadium in the Civic Center in downtown SAINT LOUIS, Missouri, 0.4 mi/0.6 km W of the Gateway Arch, near the Mississippi R. Completed in 1966, it seats over 56,000, and is home to the baseball Cardinals.

Bushwick residential section of N Brooklyn, New York, on Newtown Creek and the Queens border. Established as the Dutch Boswijck (Town of the Woods) in 1664, it was agricultural before heavy 1840s German immigration made it famous for its Brewer's Row, one of America's great beer-producing complexes, where a dozen establishments produced such well-known brands as Rheingold and Schaefer. It was at the same time a theater district, Brooklyn's answer to Broadway. Prohibition and the Depression brought decline. After World War II Bushwick became largely Italian, then suffered white flight. During the 1977 New York blackout, rioters destroyed much of what business remained. In the 1990s Bushwick suffered heavily from poverty and the drug trade. The E part, on the Queens line, incorporates the old English settlement of Ridgewood.

Butler **1.** city, pop. 15,714, seat of Butler Co., W Pennsylvania, 30 mi/48 km NE of Pittsburgh. A blue-collar suburb in an area rich in coal, natural gas, oil, and limestone, and a stop on the Baltimore and Ohio Railroad, it has long also been a manufacturing center. Today's products include railroad cars and parts, metals, chemicals, and electronic equipment. It is home to Butler County Community College (1965). **2.** village, pop. 2079, Waukesha Co., SE Wisconsin, on the Menomonee R., a suburb 5 mi/8 km NW of Milwaukee.

Butler County **1.** 470 sq mi/1217 sq km, pop. 291,479, in extreme SW Ohio, bounded by Indiana (W), and intersected by the Great Miami R. Its seat is HAMILTON. Middletown and Hamilton are manufacturing cities, and the rest of the county is heavily agricultural (dairy, grain, livestock, poultry, and tobacco). Limestone quarrying is also important. **2.** 789 sq mi/2044 sq km, pop. 152,013, in W Pennsylvania, on the Allegheny Plateau. Its seat and largest city is Butler. An industrial and coal mining area, the county produces steel, gas, limestone, and chemicals.

Butler Island one of the SEA ISLANDS, in the Atlantic Ocean at the mouth of the Altamaha R., 15 mi/24 km NNE of Brunswick, E Georgia. The island was once the cotton and rice plantation of Pierce Butler, whose wife, the English actress Fanny Kemble, wrote *Journal of a Residence on a Georgian Plantation in 1838–1839,* describing her life there and the degradation of black slaves. Published in 1863, after her divorce from Butler, the work is an important source on the institution of slavery.

butte a small, steep-sided, usually flat-topped hill. The term, from the French, is used of isolated hills in the Great Plains, but also, in the Southwest and West, of small former sections of MESAS or PLATEAUS, left alone as erosion caused the edge of the larger body to retreat.

Butte city, pop. 33,336, seat of Silver Bow Co., SW Montana, on the W slope of the Continental Divide, 45 mi/72 km SW of Helena. Gold was discovered here in 1864, and Butte was laid out two years later. Known for its abundant mineral wealth, primarily copper, but also silver, lead, zinc, and manganese, it by 1900 accounted for half the copper output in the US. Butte's high-grade copper ore was largely depleted by 1955; an open pit mine now extracts low-grade ore. Light industry and the trade, processing, and shipping of livestock supplement mining in today's economy. Butte is the seat of Montana College of Mineral Science and Technology (1893). The city is surrounded by Deerlodge and Beaverhead national forests; nearby are facilities for skiing and other recreational activities.

Butte des Mortes, Lake resort lake in Winnebago Co., EC Wisconsin. It is 6 mi/10 km long and 2 mi/3 km wide, and is an expansion of the FOX R. just W of L. Winnebago. OSHKOSH lies on the Fox R. and both lakes.

Butterfield Southern Route also, **Butterfield Trail** see under OVERLAND ROUTE.

Buzzards Bay inlet of the Atlantic Ocean between the lower end of CAPE COD (E), the ELIZABETH ISLANDS (SE), and the mainland of SE Massachusetts (W). Thirty mi/48 km NE–SW and 5–10 mi/8–16 km wide, it connects with Cape Cod Bay (N) via the CAPE COD CANAL. New Bedford, on the W, a major whaling center from the mid 18th to the mid 19th centuries, is still the largest port on the bay. Woods Hole, with its Oceanographic Institute, is on the E shore; Bourne lies N, at the head of the bay. Buzzards Bay is part of the ATLANTIC INTRACOASTAL WATERWAY.

Byfield village in the town of NEWBURY, Essex Co., NE Massachusetts, just off Interstate 95, 31 mi/50 km NE of Boston.

Byron city, pop. 2284, Ogle Co., NW Illinois, on the Rock R., 15 mi/24 km SW of Rockford. A nuclear power plant was opened here in 1985. The village of Stillman Valley (pop. 848), 3.5 mi/6 km ESE, was the site of an Indian victory in the Black Hawk War (1832). Byron was active in the Underground Railroad.

Bytown see under OTTAWA, Ontario.

C

Cabbagetown **1.** generally derisive 19th-century name for a neighborhood occupied by working-class Irish, referring to their supposed penchant for growing cabbage in their yards. **2.** residential neighborhood in Atlanta, Georgia, 1 mi/1.5 km ESE of FIVE POINTS and adjacent to Oakland Cemetery. An area of row houses on narrow streets, it housed Appalachian migrants who worked now-abandoned textile mills beginning in the 1880s; the last mill closed in 1980, and the area has seen some redevelopment. **3.** in Chicago, Illinois, name for 19th-century Irish neighborhoods (including BRIDGEPORT) along the Illinois and Michigan Canal, on the South Side, where canal workers lived in crowded, hastily constructed dwellings. **4.** largely residential Victorian neighborhood in E TORONTO, Ontario, W of the Don River Parkway, between Bloor (N) and Dundas (S) streets. Named when it was a large late-19th-century English and Irish slum, it has now undergone GENTRIFICATION, and is a tourist attraction. Regent Park, less affluent, lies to the S.

Cabell County 282 sq mi/730 sq km, pop. 96,827, in SW West Virginia. HUNTINGTON is its seat and largest city. On the Appalachian Plateau, it is drained by the Guyandot and Mud rivers, and bounded NW by the Ohio R. In a mining and agricultural area, it has manufacturing centers at Huntington, Milton, and Barboursville.

Cabeza Prieta National Wildlife Refuge 860,000 ac/348,300 ha (14,333 sq mi/37,125 sq km), in the SONORAN DESERT of SW Arizona, between Yuma (W) and Ajo (E), along the Mexican border. Established in 1939, it protects desert bighorn sheep and the endangered Sonoran pronghorn. Several NW–SE trending ranges are wholly or partly within the refuge, including the **Cabeza Prieta Mts.,** rising to 2830 ft/863 m; the Sierra Pinta and Granite mountains; and the Growler Mts., which extend SE into the ORGAN PIPE CACTUS NATIONAL MONUMENT. Part of the historic EL CAMINO DEL DIABLO traverses the refuge. Headquarters are in Ajo. The refuge is also part of the Barry M. Goldwater (military) Range.

Cabildo see under JACKSON SQUARE, New Orleans, Louisiana.

Cabinet Mountains in the N Rocky Mts. of NW Montana and NE Idaho. Running 65 mi/105 km N–S from a point W of Libby along the Clark Fork R. to Thompson Falls, they are in part of the Kootenai National Forest. The Cabinets contain a number of lead and silver mines. The **Cabinet Mountains Wilderness** (94,300 ac/38,200 ha) features rock climbing, hiking, fishing, and wildlife viewing. The highest point in the Cabinets is Snowshoe Peak, at 8712 ft/2657 m, SSW of Libby.

Cabin John unincorporated village, pop. (with Brookmont, to the SE) 5341, Montgomery Co., C Maryland. It is a suburb on the Potomac R., just SW of Bethesda, 10 mi/16 km NW of Washington, D.C. Cabin John Creek Regional Park extends N to ROCKVILLE. Cabin John Bridge carries the Capital BELTWAY over the river.

Cabo Rojo unincorporated community (ZONA URBANA), pop. 10,131, Cabo Rojo Municipio (pop. 38,521), SW Puerto Rico, 8 mi/13 km S of Mayagüez. It is named for the red cliffs at C. Rojo, 11 mi/18 km SSW, at Puerto Rico's SW corner. An early smuggling, later an agricultural (sugarcane, tobacco, coffee) center, the MUNICIPIO also draws visitors to its varied coastline.

Cabot Strait channel connecting the Gulf of St. Lawrence with the Atlantic Ocean, between Cape Ray, SW Newfoundland, and Cape North, Cape Breton I., Nova Scotia. Sixty-five mi/105 km wide, it is the principal route of entry for oceangoing vessels to the Great Lakes–St. Lawrence system.

Cabrillo National Monument see under Point LOMA, California.

Cabrini-Green 91-building public housing project on the Near North Side of Chicago, Illinois. Built to house the residents of a notorious North Side slum, the high-rise development, riddled with crime and gang violence, has become a symbol of housing design and policy failure. The television program *Good Times* was based on a family living here.

Cadboro Bay inlet of the Haro Strait, extreme SW British Columbia, in OAK BAY, just E of VICTORIA. It is noted as the "home" of "Caddie," the "Cadborosaurus," a purported marine creature, similar to Scotland's Loch Ness Monster, that has also been reported in various inland lakes, where it is thought to live on migrating salmon. At L. OKANAGAN it is called "Ogopogo."

Caddo Lake the only natural lake of size in Texas, in Harrison and Marion counties. One-third of it lies in Caddo Parish, NW Louisiana. Indian legend describes the formation of this lake in the night by spirits angry at a Caddo chief; it may have been created by the NEW MADRID earthquake in 1811. Its size was increased to 25,400 ac/10,300 ha by the construction of a dam on Cypress Creek, near MOORINGSPORT, Louisiana. The lake, with its lush scenery, is a favorite with canoeists; 42 mi/68 km of channels have been marked as "boat roads."

Cadillac city, pop. 10,104, Wexford Co., WC Michigan, on Lakes Cadillac and Mitchell, 37 mi/60 km SE of Traverse City. Originally called Clam Lake by lumbermen who settled here in the 1860s, it was renamed (1877) for Detroit's founder, Antoine de la Mothe Cadillac. Cadillac is headquarters for Manistee and Huron national forests; boating, fishing, and winter sports make it a popular year-round resort. It is a distribution center for a region producing vegetables, livestock, grains, and dairy products. Manufactures include auto tires, truck parts, and leather and wood products.

Cadillac Mountain 1532 ft/467 m, highest of the glaciated granitic peaks on MOUNT DESERT ISLAND, SE Maine, in Acadia National Park, just S of Bar Harbor. Visible far at sea, Cadillac is the highest point on the US eastern seaboard.

Cadillac Ranch see under AMARILLO, Texas.

Cadillac Square public square in downtown Detroit, Michigan, just E of Woodward Ave. where it intersects with Michigan Blvd., and just N of JEFFERSON Ave. Detroit's old city hall was built here in 1835, and until 1893 the square functioned as the city's central market. In the 20th century it was the scene of frequent rallies. Part of it is now Cadillac Square Park, and the rest has been incorporated into city streets.

Cadiz village, pop. 3439, seat of Harrison Co., EC Ohio, 20 mi/32 km WSW of Steubenville, in a rich agricultural, stock raising, and coal mining area. Situated at the junction of US Routes 250 and 22, it serves as the trade and distribution center for the district.

Caesars Head also, **Caesar's** peak (3218 ft/981 m) of the Blue Ridge Mts., 20 mi/32 km NNW of Greenville, South Carolina, near the North Carolina border. Rising above a summer resort of the same name, it has vertical gneiss cliffs with a protrusion said to resemble a head, 1200 ft/370 m above the Saluda R. valley.

Caguas unincorporated community (ZONA URBANA), pop. 92,429, Caguas Municipio (pop. 133,447), EC Puerto Rico, 16 mi/26 km SSE of San Juan. This Spanish colonial settlement is now the largest urban center in Puerto Rico's interior, a hub for sugar and alcohol refining and for varied manufacturing, including the making of clothing, electronic devices, and furniture. On the San Juan–Ponce highway and the railroad, it is also the trade and distribution center for the fertile Turabo Valley, which produces sugarcane, tobacco, fruit, and livestock.

Cahaba also, **Cahawba** or **Old Cahawba** historic village in Dallas Co., WC Alabama, at the confluence of the Cahaba and Alabama rivers, 9 mi/14 km SW of Selma. On the site of a French trading post, it was Alabama's state capital, and the center of the state's industry and culture, in 1819–26. Recurrent floods caused leaders to move the capital to Tuscaloosa. Cahaba regained importance in 1840–60. During the Civil War an important prison was located here. Flooding continued and eventually Cahaba was reduced to ruins. It is now a State Historic Site.

Cahaba River 200 mi/320 km long, in C Alabama. It rises in St. Clair Co., NE of Birmingham, and flows SW on the city's SE side, and through the Talladega National Forest's Oakmulgee section, before joining the Alabama R. at Cahaba, SW of Selma.

Cahokia village, pop. 17,550, St. Clair Co., SW Illinois, on the Mississippi R. opposite St. Louis, Missouri, a residential suburb 4 mi/6 km SW of East St. Louis. One of the first permanent European settlements in Illinois, it was founded by French missionaries in 1699. It was the center of French influence in the Upper Mississippi Valley until Britain took over in 1765. A British trader bribed a Peoria warrior to murder the Ottawa chief Pontiac here in 1769. George Rogers Clark captured Cahokia for the US in 1778. Among its historic sites are the Cahokia Courthouse (1740), one of the Midwest's oldest extant buildings; the Holy Family Catholic Church (1799), a National Historic Landmark; and the Jarrot Mansion (1799–1806), probably the oldest brick structure in the region. Cahokia is 7 mi/11 km SW of the Cahokia Mounds State Historic Park (see COLLINSVILLE).

Cahuenga Pass at the E end of the Santa Monica Mts. (the Hollywood Hills) in SW California, between HOLLYWOOD (S) and UNIVERSAL CITY (N), 8 mi/12 km NW of downtown Los Angeles. The Hollywood Freeway passes through, linking Hollywood and Downtown with North Hollywood and the SAN FERNANDO VALLEY.

Cairo **1.** city, pop. 9035, seat of Grady Co., SW Georgia, 28 mi/45 km N of Tallahassee, Florida. Settled in the 1820s, it processes local agricultural products, notably collard greens. Baseball great Jackie Robinson was born here in 1919. **2.** city, pop. 4846, seat of Alexander Co., SC Illinois, at the southernmost tip of the state, on a peninsula at the point where the Ohio R. empties into the Mississippi R., on the Missouri and Kentucky borders. An agricultural and transportation center, it was settled in 1818. During the Civil War, Cairo served for a time as Ulysses S. Grant's headquarters and the base for assaults against Forts Henry and Donelson. Charles Dickens renamed it "Eden" in his novel *Martin Chuzzlewit.* Fort Defiance State Park is immediately S, and the Horseshoe Lake State Conservation Area is 13 mi/21 km NW. The region around Cairo has been known as EGYPT. **3.** town, pop. 5418, Green Co., SE New York, in the Catskill Mts., adjacent (NW) to Catskill, on Catskill Creek. In an apple growing region, it attracts visitors to a large game farm and a commercial re-creation of an Old West town. Journalist and politician Thurlow Weed (1797–1882) was born here.

Cajon Pass through Cajon Canyon, between the E end of the SAN GABRIEL Mts. and the NW end of the SAN BERNARDINO Mts., in SW California, 15 mi/24 km NW of San Bernardino. An important passageway for western travel since 1831, it links the MOJAVE DESERT (N) with the Los Angeles Basin; the completion of Santa Fe Railroad tracks through it in 1885 brought service from the E to Los Angeles. The San Andreas Fault runs NW–SE through the pass.

Cajun Country nickname and promotional term for parts of S Louisiana inhabited by exiles from ACADIA, who settled here beginning about 1765, and their descendants (Cajuns). At its broadest, the term incorporates areas from LAKE CHARLES (W) to the BAYOU LAFOURCHE (E) and N to ALEXANDRIA. The ATCHAFALAYA R. basin and BAYOU TECHE are in its heart; important centers include Lafayette, Opelousas, Eunice, Saint Martinville, Thibodaux, Abbeville, Houma, and New Iberia.

Calabasas SW SAN FERNANDO VALLEY section of LOS ANGELES, California, on the Ventura Freeway and the Arroyo Calabasas (a tributary to the Los Angeles R.), 24 mi/39 km WNW of Downtown. Woodland Hills is immediately E. An 1840s cowboy town, Calabasas is now residential and an aerospace and telecommunications manufacturing center.

Calabogie resort community in SE Ontario, 50 mi/80 km WSW of Ottawa, on the Madawaska R. and Calabogie L. Calabogie Peaks is a well-known ski area.

Calais city, pop. 3963, Washington Co., extreme E Maine. It lies along the S bank of the St. Croix R., opposite St. Stephen, New Brunswick, about 15 mi/24 km upriver from PASSAMAQUODDY BAY. It includes the villages of Milltown, Whitlocks Mill, and Red Beach. The city is a port of entry and has reciprocal arrangements with St. Stephen with regard to ambulance, fire, and water service. It was an early agricultural, lumber, and shipbuilding center. Leading industries produce wood products and shirts. Moosehorn National Wildlife Refuge is just SW.

Calamus River and Reservoir see under LOUP R., Nebraska.

Calaveras County 1021 sq mi/2644 sq km, pop. 31,998, in EC California. San Andreas (unincorporated, pop. 2115) is its seat. In the Sierra Nevada, along the MOTHER LODE and partly in the Stanislaus National Forest, Calaveras is bounded by the Mokelumne R. (N) and by the Stanislaus R. (S). The Calaveras R. rises in the county. Immortalized by Mark Twain, who wrote of events in ANGELS CAMP, the county includes old goldmining towns, Calaveras Big Trees State Park, and several lakes. Tourism, winter sports, hunting, fishing, lumbering, livestock raising, and cement production are important.

Calcasieu River 200 mi/320 km long, in SW Louisiana. It rises in Vernon Parish, N of Fort Polk, and flows E and S, widening into L. Charles at LAKE CHARLES, before flowing into Calcasieu L. (c.15 mi/24 km N–S and up to 11 mi/18 km wide), then through a narrow pass past CAMERON to the Gulf of Mexico. Just above Calcasieu L. the river is intersected by the GULF INTRACOASTAL WATERWAY, which links it with the Sabine-Neches Waterway. Calcasieu L. is surrounded by marshes, largely within the Sabine National Wildlife Refuge.

caldera large craterlike depression left by the explosion of the top of a volcano or by the collapse of a volcanic cone due to the escape of lava from inside. KILAUEA, Hawaii, and CRATER LAKE, Oregon, are examples.

Caldwell **1.** city, pop. 18,400, seat of Canyon Co., SW Idaho, on the Boise R., 24 mi/39 km W of Boise and 15 mi/24 km E of the Oregon border. In an agricultural area, the city is a processing and shipping point, with creameries, meat and poultry packing plants, stockyards, fruit packing and dehydrating plants, and a winery. A chief manufacture is mobile homes. It is the seat of the College of Idaho (1891). **2.** officially, **Caldwell Borough** township, pop. 7549, Essex Co., NE New Jersey, 9 mi/14 km NW of Newark. It is a bedroom community with a substantial office-building component, and manufactures including pharmaceuticals, plastics, clothing, and airplane parts. Grover Cleveland's birthplace (1837) is a State Historic Site. The township is the seat of Caldwell College (1939). North Caldwell (unincorporated; pop. 6706) and WEST CALDWELL adjoin.

Caledon town, pop. 34,965, Peel Regional Municipality, S Ontario, 25 mi/40 km NW of Toronto and adjacent (NW) to Brampton, on the upper Humber and Credit rivers. Chiefly residential, it was created in 1974, including the old milling, now resort, center of Bolton, as well as Caledon East and Albion. The **Caledon Hills** are noted as a fall color and skiing center.

Caledonia see under HALDIMAND, Ontario.

Calendar Islands see under CASCO BAY, Maine.

Calexico city, pop. 18,633, Imperial Co., S California, at the Mexican border, 9 mi/14 km SSE of El Centro. It is a port of entry from its sister city, the much larger Mexicali (Baja California), Mexico, and a trade center for the fruit, cotton, and vegetable producers of the S IMPERIAL VALLEY. It has a reputation for raucous night life.

Calgary city, pop. 710,677, SW Alberta, between the western prairies (E) and Rocky Mt. foothills, at the confluence of the Bow and Elbow rivers, 180 mi/290 km S of Edmonton. Alberta's largest city, it is a major oil and natural gas industry center, the financial capital of W Canada, and home to an historically important livestock industry. It is also a distribution point for the region's agriculture, and the seat of many corporate headquarters. The city has oil refineries and petrochemical complexes, meatpacking plants, flour mills, breweries, lumber, plywood, and pulp plants, and a variety of manufacturers. It is situated on the TRANS-CANADA HIGHWAY and two transcontinental rail lines. Explorers for the North West Company wintered here before 1800. Buffalo hunters from the US, engaged in illegal trading, set up a network of posts in the area in the late 1860s. In response to this, the North West Mounted Police built (1875) Fort Calgary. The Canadian Pacific Railway arrived (1883) and laid out the site for the first town in Alberta, which the railroad made a hub for the region's cattle industry and crop producers. Oil was discovered (1914) at nearby TURNER VALLEY, and two refineries were built during the following decade. The 1947 oil strike at LEDUC created a boom in Alberta, and Calgary developed rapidly. The Petroleum and Natural Gas Conservation Board is based here, and the University of Calgary (1946), Mt. Royal Community College, Southern Alberta Institute of Technology, Alberta Vocational Centre, and Alberta College of Art are all here. Besides Glenbow Museum, tourists flock to the annual (July) Calgary Stampede, the oldest such event in the country. Fish Creek Provincial Park, to the S, is one of the world's largest urban parks, and the Sarcee Indian Reserve adjoins Calgary on the SW. The Olympic Saddledome, built for the 1988 Olympic Winter Games, is home to the Calgary Flames (hockey). The Calgary Stampeders (football) play at McMahon Stadium.

Calhoun city, pop. 7135, seat of Gordon Co., NW Georgia, 61 mi/98 km NW of Atlanta, near the Oostanaula R. It is 4 mi/6 km SW of the site of New Echota, the last Cherokee capital in Georgia (1819–38). Sequoyah, creator of the Cherokee syllabary, lived in the area. The Cherokee were forced onto the TRAIL OF TEARS in 1838. Originally called Oothcaloga, Calhoun was renamed in 1850, then almost completely destroyed by Sherman's troops in 1864. Rebuilt, it continued its life as a textile center, producing sheets, bedspreads, and other home products.

Calhoun County 712 sq mi/1844 sq km, pop. 135,982, in SC Michigan, drained by the Kalamazoo and St. Joseph rivers and Battle Creek. Its seat is Marshall. With manufacturing at Battle Creek (where there is suburban development), Albion, and Marshall, it is mostly an agricultural region that raises livestock, grain, and fruit, and makes dairy products.

California state of the SW US, part of the Far WEST; 1990 pop. 29,760,021 (125.7% of 1980; rank: 1st); area 163,707 sq mi/424,001 sq km (rank: 3rd); admitted to Union 1850 (31st). Capital: SACRAMENTO. Cities over 200,000 pop.: LOS ANGELES, SAN DIEGO, SAN JOSE, SAN FRANCISCO, LONG BEACH, OAKLAND, Sacramento, FRESNO, SANTA ANA, ANAHEIM, RIVERSIDE, STOCKTON; 34 others over 100,000. California is bordered S by the Mexican state of Baja California; E by Arizona (S, across the COLORADO R.) and Nevada (N); and N by Oregon. On the W it lies on the Pacific Ocean. Formed largely by the collision of the North American and Pacific tectonic PLATES, the state is dominated by two parallel mountain systems and the intervening CENTRAL VALLEY, all oriented NW–SE. On the E, along part of the Nevada border, is the SIERRA NEVADA, the highest range in the Lower 48 (reaching 14,494 ft/4421 m at Mt. WHITNEY). Merging with it in the NW is the S CASCADE Range, in which LASSEN PEAK and Mt. SHASTA are prominent. In the W, along the Pacific, are the COAST RANGES, extending from Cape MENDOCINO (NW) to Pt. CONCEPTION, near Los Angeles. In the Coast Ranges are the SANTA CRUZ, SANTA LUCIA, DIABLO, SAN RAFAEL, and other mountains; between the ranges lie fertile valleys including the NAPA and SONOMA (N of San Francisco) and SALINAS (S of Monterey). The SAN ANDREAS FAULT, passing along the Coast Ranges, is the best-known of many in a seismically active region. At the SE end of the Coast Ranges, the TRANSVERSE RANGES, esp. the TEHACHAPI Mts., cut across the state, meeting the S end of the Sierra Nevada, while the PENINSULAR Ranges continue SE to the Mexican border. Among the mountains in the Los Angeles area and S are the SAN GABRIELS, SAN BERNARDINOS, and SANTA ANAS. The Central Valley, lying between the two major systems, extends from S of SHASTA L., in the N, to the Tehachapis in the S. Its two major rivers, the SACRAMENTO (N of SAN FRANCISCO BAY) and SAN JOAQUIN (S) give their names to sections of the valley; at the S end is the irrigated TULARE lakebed, also considered part of the Central Valley, and the oil center of BAKERSFIELD. In extreme N California, the KLAMATH Mts. occupy the W; in the NE corner, E of the Cascades, is part of the GREAT BASIN. South of the Transverse Ranges and E of the Peninsular Ranges, in SE California, are the MOJAVE DESERT, part of the BASIN AND RANGE PROVINCE, and the SALTON SEA. To the N of the Mojave is another Great Basin section, in which DEATH VALLEY, at 282 ft/86 m below sea level, the lowest point in the US, lies between the PANAMINT and AMARGOSA ranges. California's major offshore islands are the SANTA BARBARA (Channel) Is., in the S; off San Francisco Bay are the FARALLON IS. The bay, extending E to a rich delta region at the mouths of the Sacramento and San Joaquin rivers, is home to the state's major port complex, and the site of ALCATRAZ, ANGEL, and other noted islands. California, over 770 mi/1240 km in length, has a wide range of climatic and topographic zones; generally, winters are wet and summers dry; in the S mild winters make this a major component of the SUNBELT. As almost all rivers of size are in the Sacramento–San Joaquin system, flowing into San Francisco Bay, heavily developed SOUTHERN CALIFORNIA has resorted to extensive irrigation and water transportation projects (including the CALIFORNIA AQUEDUCT, Central Valley Project, ALL-AMERICAN CANAL, and LOS ANGELES AQUEDUCT) to service its pop. and agriculture. Before whites arrived, California was home to numerous small Indian tribes; natural barriers in the region probably hindered mass organization, and today the state's INDIAN RESERVATIONS are not large, many of them small RANCHERIAS. Based in Mexico, Spanish sailors first landed here in the 1540s. The English captain Francis Drake saw the N coast in 1579. There was no settlement, however, until an overland expedition from Mexico established a MISSION (1769) at San Diego and a PRESIDIO (1770) at MONTEREY. By this time a name from a 16th-century Spanish romance, designating an island inhabited by Amazon warriors and rich with gold, had been applied to the Mexican peninsula of Baja California (then thought to be an island), and extended N to include what came to be called ALTA CALIFORNIA. Until the 1820s, there was little further development. A system of missions and presidios was established between San Diego and San Francisco Bay, and in the N, FORT ROSS became (1812) the southernmost outpost of RUSSIAN AMERICA. In 1821 Mexico freed itself from Spain, and California's missions were secularized, their lands given to cattle raisers as RANCHOS. Soon after, Americans, attracted by reports from fur and hide traders and others, began to filter into the area from the E. With the start of the Mexican War (1846) the US occupied C California, where Americans had already declared (at SONOMA) the "Bear Flag Republic." In 1848, Mexico ceded the entire territory. At almost the same moment, gold was discovered on the AMERICAN R., in the Sierra foothills, and the Gold Rush was on. Americans (and soon Mexicans, Chinese, Australians, Chileans, Europeans, and others) poured in so quickly that in 1850 California became a state. Mining activities fostered the development of support industries, agriculture, and commerce, and although the state's gold production dropped by the mid 1850s, Nevada's COMSTOCK LODE (1859) started the boom again, and made San Francisco a financial hub. In 1869 the CENTRAL PACIFIC (later SOUTHERN PACIFIC) Railroad completed a transcontinental rail link, reducing California's relative isolation from the rest of the US. In 1887 the SANTA FE Railroad reached Los Angeles, opening Southern California to urban and agricultural growth. Railroad promotions in this period were important in launching the state's tourism and recreation industry. In the 1900s, Los Angeles became California's leading city; heavy immigration from the Middle West, oil finds (the first in 1892), and the beginnings of the HOLLYWOOD movie industry all contributed to its rise. San Francisco rebuilt quickly after its 1906 earthquake, but the main flow of people and development had shifted to Southern California. During the 1930s Depression, California agriculture suffered, but the state still attracted migrants from other parts of the country, esp. the DUST BOWL states, looking for a better life. World War II brought a tremendous industrial boom. The aircraft industry in the Los Angeles area, ports in the BAY AREA, the harbor of San Diego, and many other manufacturing and military sites expanded rapidly. After the war, many who had been stationed in the state were among a new, and continuing, wave of immigrants. California's pop. has more than quadrupled since 1940, and almost doubled in 1970–90. By the 1980s, cuts in military spending and other economic factors had begun to cause some emigration from California, but the effect has been slight. Today, the state is cosmopolitan, with a Hispanic minority of c.26%; almost 10% of Californians are Asian, over 7% black. Leading industries include aerospace, ship, and motor vehicle construction; electric and electronic development and manufacturing (esp. in the SILICON VALLEY area); the processing of all kinds of foods; entertainment (movie and television studios); diverse manufacturing; oil, boron, natural gas, asbestos, and other mineral extraction and refining; lumbering (esp. from redwood stands on the NW coast); tuna and other fishing (esp. from SAN PEDRO, Bay Area ports, and San Diego); commerce; finance; and various services. California agriculture produces a vast array of fruits, nuts, vegetables, rice, wheat and other grains, wine and juices, cattle, poultry and eggs, and other goods. The irrigated IMPERIAL and Central valleys are the most important farm zones. Tourists are drawn to DISNEYLAND and other film industry–related amusements; to YOSEMITE, KINGS CANYON, and SEQUOIA (in the Sierra Nevada), LASSEN VOLCANIC (in the Cascades), REDWOOD (on the NW coast), CHANNEL ISLANDS (in the Santa Barbara Is.), Death Valley, and JOSHUA TREE (in the Mojave Desert) NATIONAL PARKS; to the missions and other sites of the Spanish period; to San Francisco, Monterey, MENDOCINO, and other coastal cities and resorts; and to a variety of other natural, historic, and recreational attractions. Military sites and facilities include EDWARDS, VANDENBERG and other Air Force bases, the TWENTYNINE PALMS Marine Corps Training Center, Camp Pendleton (see OCEANSIDE), and a number of desert or coastal bases. The state's highly regarded educational system includes the main University of California campus at BERKELEY and dozens of other state universities and colleges.

California borough, pop. 5748, Washington Co., SW Pennsylvania, on the Monongahela R., 15 mi/24 km NW of Uniontown. Situated in a coal mining region, it was named by 19th-century adventurers on their way to the California gold fields. It is the seat of California University (1852).

California Aqueduct main carrier of the **California State Water Project,** initiated in the 1960s to bring water from C and N California to the SAN JOAQUIN Valley and the Los Angeles and San Diego areas. It proceeds from the San Joaquin–Sacramento delta, NW of Tracy, along the W side of the Central Valley, and passes along the N of the San Gabriel Mts., N of Los Angeles, to San Bernardino. From there the San Diego Aqueduct carries water almost to the Mexican border. Among other Water Project units supplying it is the OROVILLE Dam.

California Current cool current of the North Pacific Ocean, passing SE off the W coast of North America, from about 48° N (the latitude of Washington state) to about 23° N (near the Tropic of Cancer; the latitude of S Baja California, Mexico). It is a continuation of the E-flowing Aleutian (or Subarctic) Current, which passes S of the ALEUTIAN Is.; another part of the Aleutian Current turns N into the Gulf of ALASKA and circles back (as the Alaska Current) to the mainstream.

California Emigrant Trail see EMIGRANT TRAIL.

California Trail offshoot from the OREGON TRAIL taken by gold seekers bound for California from 1849. Most left the Oregon Trail somewhere W of FORT HALL, Idaho, turning SW, past CITY OF ROCKS, into NE Nevada, where they followed the HUMBOLDT R. across the desert to the Sierra Nevada, using the DONNER PASS to reach the goldfields. There were many variations in route, however, some passing S of L. Tahoe.

Calistoga city, pop. 4468, Napa Co., NW California, near the head (NW) of the Napa Valley, on the Silverado Trail, 13 mi/21 km NE of Santa Rosa. Established in the 1860s as a health resort with mudbaths, geysers, and hot springs, it was named in reference to Sara*toga* Springs, New York. In 1880, Robert Louis Stevenson honeymooned at the former Silverado Mine, at 4343-ft/1325-m Mt. St. Helena, about 8 mi/13 km N; the Robert Louis Stevenson State Park commemorates the stay, about which Stevenson wrote. The Old Faithful Geyser of California is just NW of the city. Calistoga is noted for its vineyards and wineries, also produces prunes and walnuts, and is a tourist center.

Callaway city, pop. 12,253, Bay Co., NW Florida, 7 mi/11 km SE of Panama City, of which it is a suburb.

Callaway County 842 sq mi/2181 sq km, pop. 32,809, in EC Missouri, bounded by the Missouri R. (S). Its seat and only large city is FULTON. During the Civil War, it seceded from the Union and, signing a treaty with the state militia, became the "Kingdom of Callaway." Then, as now, the county was primarily agricultural. Today livestock continues to be raised, and the county is particularly noted for its horses and mules; its agricultural products include corn, wheat, and oats. In addition, coal and stone are mined and lumber is cut, mainly in the W section. The Callaway nuclear power plant, operational in 1984, is also a factor in the county's economy. A unit of the Mark Twain National Forest is in the W.

Callaway Gardens see under PINE MOUNTAIN, Georgia.

Calle Ocho see under LITTLE HAVANA, Miami, Florida.

Caloosahatchee River 75 mi/120 km long, in SW Florida. It flows WSW from L. Hicpochee, just SW of L. Okeechobee, past Fort Myers and Cape Coral into the Gulf of Mexico through San Carlos Bay, inside SANIBEL I. It is connected to L. Okeechobee by the Caloosahatchee Canal, which runs through L. Hicpochee.

Calumet, the see under CALUMET R., Indiana and Illinois.

Calumet City city, pop. 37,840, Cook Co., NE Illinois, on the Little Calumet and Grand Calumet rivers, on the Indiana border immediately W of HAMMOND. It is an industrial suburb of Chicago 19 mi/31 km SE of the Loop. Originally called West Hammond and a center for heavy industry, the city grew up around its meat-packing and chemical plants. An oil refinery and steelworks also contribute to the local economy. Over the past few decades, Calumet City has become increasingly residential. L. Calumet lies 4 mi/6 km NW; the Sand Ridge Nature Center is adjacent (SW).

Calumet Farm horse farm in Fayette Co., C Kentucky, 6 mi/10 km W of downtown LEXINGTON. A thoroughbred breeding and training stable that produced Whirlaway, Citation, and other champions for over 60 years, it went bankrupt in 1991 and was auctioned in 1992. Many other Bluegrass farms had serious financial problems or were up for sale.

Calumet Park village, pop. 8418, Cook Co., NE Illinois, a residential suburb on the N side of the Calumet Sag Channel and Little Calumet R., adjoining (E) BLUE ISLAND, and 16 mi/26 km SSW of Chicago's LOOP.

Calumet River 8 mi/13 km long, formed just SE of L. Calumet, on the SE border of Chicago, Illinois, by the Little Calumet and Grand Calumet rivers. It flows N and NE through a dredged and dock-lined channel to L. Michigan at Calumet Harbor. The **Little Calumet River** rises near GARY, Indiana, and flows generally W into Illinois, to BLUE ISLAND, where it turns E again toward its junction with the Grand Calumet. Just after this turn, it is joined by the **Calumet Sag Channel,** which connects with the Chicago Sanitary and Ship Canal (see ILLINOIS WATERWAY) near Sag Bridge, 15 mi/24 km WNW. The **Grand Calumet River** also flows E from the Gary area, passing though EAST CHICAGO and HAMMOND on its way to the junction. In East Chicago it is connected directly with Indiana Harbor, on L. Michigan, by a ship canal. The Calumet area, including the Illinois communities of CALUMET CITY and southern parts of Chicago, as well as Gary, Hammond, East Chicago, WHITING, and other Indiana municipalities, is one of America's most heavily industrialized regions, and one in which natural waterways have been most thoroughly altered.

Calvert County 213 sq mi/552 sq km, pop. 51,372, in C Maryland. Prince Frederick is its seat. A peninsula bounded

E by Chesapeake Bay and S and W by the Patuxent R., it is a fishing and agricultural county producing crabs, oysters, fish, tobacco, and other crops. Maryland's smallest county, it has 165 mi/266 km of shoreline. The **Calvert Cliffs** nuclear plant (operative since 1974) is near Lusby, in the SE.

Calverton **1.** unincorporated residential suburb, pop. 12,046, in Montgomery and Prince George's counties, C Maryland, on Interstate 95, 13 mi/21 km NE of Washington, D.C. **2.** unincorporated village, pop. 4759, in Riverhead town, Suffolk Co., SE New York, in EC Long I. It is the site of Calverton National Cemetery (opened 1978), a 900-ac/365-ha facility in the PINE BARRENS. The government plans to close the cemetery to further burials in 2020, at which time Calverton will be the largest National Cemetery.

Camarillo city, pop. 52,303, Ventura Co., SW California, 57 mi/92 km WNW of Los Angeles, on the Ventura Freeway. It is a commercial center in the Pleasant Valley; a wide range of fruit, truck crops, nuts, and flowers are grown, processed, and shipped in the area. Camarillo has electronics and aerospace industries, and manufactures magnetic tape. A state psychiatric facility, Camarillo State Hospital, is in the city, as is St. John's Seminary College (1939).

Cambria County 691 sq mi/1790 sq km, pop. 163,029, in WC Pennsylvania, in the Allegheny Mts. Its seat is Ebensburg. It is a coal mining area, with some manufacturing and agriculture. The iron and steel producing center of JOHNSTOWN is its largest city.

Cambria Heights see under SAINT ALBANS, New York.

Cambridge **1.** city, pop. 11,514, seat of Dorchester Co., SE Maryland, on the S bank of the Choptank R., on the EASTERN SHORE. Founded in 1684, it developed as a plantation port, and handled small fishing and pleasure craft until the addition of deepwater facilities in 1964. Now Maryland's second-largest port, the city manufactures textiles, electronic equipment, and fertilizer; lumbering, printing, shipbuilding, and food processing and canning are also important. The Blackwater National Wildlife Refuge is 10 mi/16 km S of the city. **2.** city, pop. 95,802, co-seat (with Lowell) of Middlesex Co., E Massachusetts, on the N bank of the Charles R. opposite Boston. Cambridge has been an educational and cultural center since Harvard College was established in 1636. In 1639, Stephen Daye set up the first printing press in the Colonies here. Printing and publishing continue to be important, along with scientific and industrial research and diverse manufacturing. Harvard and the Massachusetts Institute of Technology (MIT, 1861) are the largest employers. The city is also the seat of Radcliffe and Lesley colleges and the Episcopal Divinity School, and headquarters for the Smithsonian Astrophysical Observatory. Important cultural institutions include Harvard's Peabody Museum (archaeology and ethnology) and the Carpenter Center for Visual Arts, the only building in the US designed by Le Corbusier. In the area around Harvard Square general synods of New England churches met in 1637 and 1647; George Washington assumed leadership of the Continental Army in 1775; and the first Revolutionary army camped. Technology Square and Kendall Square, near MIT, are centers for new high-tech and biotech businesses. East Cambridge, NE of the MIT area, is a commercial and working-class residential area, traditionally Irish and Italian. **Cambridgeport,** the southernmost part of the city (along the Charles opposite Back Bay, Boston), and North Cambridge are largely residential. **3.** city, pop. 11,748, seat of Guernsey Co., EC Ohio, 24 mi/39 km NE of Zanesville. It was founded in 1806 by immigrants from the island of Guernsey. Deposits of clay and natural gas in the vicinity have fostered its industrial growth. The city is particularly known for its glass industry. Other manufactures include furniture, pottery, steel, plastics, and clothing. Cambridge is also a trade center for the adjacent agricultural area. Salt Fork State Park is 5 mi/8 km NE. **4.** city, pop. 92,772, Waterloo Regional Municipality, S Ontario, on the Grand and Speed rivers, 53 mi/85 km WSW of Toronto. In 1973 the city of Galt, the towns of Hespeler and Preston, and parts of the townships of North Dunfries and WATERLOO were consolidated to form the city of Cambridge. These communities, all settled in the early 19th century, had initially developed as flour, lumber, and textile milling centers, and had more recently undergone accelerated industrialization. Metalworking and textile manufacturing are among the city's chief industries. Electronic, nuclear, generating, plumbing, and construction equipment is also produced in this constituent of the CANADIAN TECHNOLOGY TRIANGLE. A campus of Conestoga College of Applied Arts and Technology is here.

Cambridge Bay hamlet, pop. 1116, Kitikmeot Region, C Northwest Territories, on SE Victoria I., on Cambridge Bay of Dease Strait, 500 mi/800 km NNE of Yellowknife. A tiny INUIT community before the 1940s, it became a navigational and DEW LINE post, and is now an administrative center with a fish packing plant and scientific and government facilities.

Cambridge Springs borough, pop. 1837, Crawford Co., NW Pennsylvania, 11 mi/18 km NE of Meadville. A popular spa since the discovery of its mineral spring in 1884, it is a dairy center and the seat of Alliance College (1912).

Camden **1.** city, pop. 14,380, seat of Ouachita Co., SC Arkansas, 28 mi/45 km NNW of El Dorado, on a bluff overlooking the Ouachita R. Originally an Indian trail crossing, it was likely the site of a 1541 De Soto encampment. Settled in 1783, it was known as Écore à Fabre (Fabre's Bluff) until its incorporation in 1844. The Civil War battle of Poison Spring (or Springs) was fought 10 mi/16 km WNW in April 1864. This port city became a railway center during the Civil War, but boat trade was revived in 1926 when the river channel was deepened by locks and dams. It is presently a shipping center for timber, pulpwood, and paper producers. Oil and industries exploiting clay, lignite, sand, and gravel also contribute to the economy, and the city has produced missiles. Southern Arkansas University–Technical Branch (1967) is here. **2.** town, pop. 5060, Knox Co., SC Maine. It is on West Penobscot Bay, on US 1 at the foot of the Camden Hills, 8 mi/13 km NNE of Rockland. The town is a summer resort and winter sports center. The **Camden Hills,** chiefly N and W, include several of the highest prominences on the US Atlantic Coast, including Mt. Megunticook (1380 ft/421 m), Ragged Mt. (1300 ft/396 m), Bald Mt. (1272 ft/388 m), and Mt. Battie (800 ft/244 m). Known to mariners since the early 17th century, they dominate the town and nearby coast. Long known as an affluent artists' retreat, Camden in the 1990s became home to a renowned computer-imaging center. **3.** city, pop. 87,492, seat of Camden Co., SW New Jersey, on the Delaware R., across from Philadelphia, Pennsylvania, 26 mi/42 km SW of Trenton. On a site seen by the Dutch (1631), where a Swedish settlement was located (1638), it was established as a ferrying point by Quaker

William Cooper (1681), and grew supplying vegetables and other goods to Philadelphia. Industrial development began with the arrival of the Camden & Amboy Railroad (1834); numerous factories and warehouses sprang up along the river. Several American companies originated here, notably Esterbook (pens; 1858) and Campbell (soups; 1869). Still a manufacturing city, Camden produces television equipment, communications systems, pharmaceuticals, chemicals, auto parts, electrical appliances, processed food, leather, and paints, but is struggling economically. The new (1992) New Jersey State Aquarium is looked to as a revitalizing force. Camden was a shipbuilding center during both world wars, and the industry continues to be important. The city was home (1873–92) to Walt Whitman, whose house is a State Historic Site. Rutgers University has a campus here. **4.** village, pop. 2210, Preble Co., W Ohio, on Sevenmile Creek, 25 mi/40 km WSW of Dayton. Local manufactures include machinery and food products. The writer Sherwood Anderson was born here (1876). **5.** city, pop. 6696, seat of Kershaw Co., NC South Carolina, in the Sandhills, 30 mi/48 km NE of Columbia. Settled in the 1730s, it is the state's oldest inland city. During the Revolutionary War it was a British base and the site of American defeats in the battles of Camden (Aug. 16, 1780) and Hobkirk Hill (just N; April 25, 1781); it was burned before the British evacuation. During the Civil War, it held Confederate stores and hospitals until it was again put to the torch, this time by Sherman's army (Feb. 24, 1865). Among the city's many manufactures are textiles, wood veneer, cottonseed oil, and metals. A well-known winter resort, it has facilities for steeplechase and flat racing, polo, and recreational horseback riding.

Camden County 223 sq mi/578 sq km, pop. 502,824, in SW New Jersey, on the Delaware R. Its seat is CAMDEN. This industrial city and many residential suburbs, such as CHERRY HILL and HADDONFIELD, occupy the NW part of the county. Major muncipalities in its C are Marlton and Lindenwold. Dotted with small towns, much of the SE is agricultural.

Camden Yards section of downtown Baltimore, Maryland, just W of the INNER HARBOR. Oriole Park at Camden Yards, a 48,000-seat baseball stadium built in retro style, on the site of former Baltimore and Ohio Railroad yards, was opened here in April 1992. The Camden St. station, opened in 1852, was once considered the largest in the world. A 1000 ft/300 m–long B&O warehouse stands behind the new stadium's right field. Babe Ruth was born (1895) just W of Camden Yards, and his father operated a saloon in the area that is now center field.

Camelback Mountain see under PHOENIX Mts., Arizona.

Camels Hump peak (4083 ft/1245 m) in the Green Mts., SW of Waterbury, Vermont. It exhibits a variety of habitats including an alpine tundra community. The distinctive peak and 9000-ac/3645-ha Camels Hump State Park and Forest Preserve are popular with hikers.

Cameron unincorporated community, pop. 2041, seat of Cameron Parish, SW Louisiana, 30 mi/48 km SSW of Lake Charles, near the mouth of the Calcasieu R. on the Gulf of Mexico. It is an offshore oil industry service town and one of the busiest US seafood handling ports.

Cameron County 906 sq mi/2347 sq km, pop. 260,120, in extreme S Texas. It is bounded (S) by the RIO GRANDE, across which is the Mexican state of Tamaulipas, and (E) by the Gulf of Mexico. BROWNSVILLE, the county seat, and Port Isabel are ocean ports; HARLINGEN and SAN BENITO are industrial centers. Livestock are raised, citrus, vegetables, and cotton are grown, clay is mined, and natural gas and oil are produced and refined in the county. Tourism is important because of year-round warm weather, Gulf beaches, and proximity to Mexico.

Camino Real see EL CAMINO REAL.

Campbell **1.** city, pop. 36,048, Santa Clara Co., WC California, 5 mi/8 km SW of San Jose, in SILICON VALLEY, on Los Gatos Creek. It is an electronics and scientific research center. Industries include the manufacture of computer components, electrical supplies, furniture, aluminum products, and tools. Older industries include lumberyards and fruit canning and poultry processing plants. **2.** city, pop. 10,038, Mahoning Co., NE Ohio, on the Mahoning R. Called East Youngstown until 1926, it adjoins Youngstown on the SE, and is known for its extensive iron and steel works. Wood panels, sashes, and storm windows are also manufactured.

Campbell Highway 370 mi/600 km long, in the S Yukon Territory, named for and following the route of the HUDSON'S BAY COMPANY's Robert Campbell, who explored the area in the 1840s and set up trading posts from the SE to Alaska. From WATSON LAKE (SE) it swings NW to Ross River and FARO, in the heart of the Yukon's mining country, then to the KLONDIKE HIGHWAY near CARMACKS.

Campbell Hill in Logan Co., WC Ohio, just E of Bellefontaine. It is the state's highest point, 1550 ft/473 m.

Campbell River district municipality, pop. 21,175, Comox-Strathcona Regional District, SW British Columbia, at the mouth of Campbell R., on the E coast of Vancouver I., 145 mi/233 km NW of Victoria. In Kwakiutl homelands, it became before 1900 a logging settlement, and today is a lumber and paper milling center, also noted for its salmon fishing. It is also a tourist and commercial hub.

Campbells Island see under EAST MOLINE, Illinois.

Campbellsville city, pop. 9577, Taylor Co., C Kentucky, 70 mi/113 km SSE of Louisville. Incorporated in 1817, it developed as a market for livestock, tobacco, and other crops. There are limestone quarries, and textiles, fruit, dairy products, and clothing are produced. The city is home to Campbellsville College (1906).

Campbellton city, pop. 8699, seat of Restigouche Co., N New Brunswick, at the head of ocean navigation on the Restigouche R., off CHALEUR Bay, at the Québec border. It was settled by Acadians in the 1750s, then by Scots in the 1820s, when it was a shipbuilding and fishing center. Lumber became important later in the century, and pulp in the 1920s. Today Campbellton is largely a tourist center, servicing the Restigouche's salmon fishery. The Sugarloaf (984 ft/300 m) dominates the city.

Camp Borden also, **Canadian Forces Base** (or **C.F.B.**) **Borden** 33 sq mi/85 sq km, in SC Ontario, 50 mi/80 km NNW of Toronto, and 10 mi/16 km SW of BARRIE. Established in 1916, it trained soldiers and fliers in World Wars I and II. Today it is a military and civilian support center with armored and infantry schools.

Camp Bullis see under FORT SAM HOUSTON, San Antonio, Texas.

Camp David 200-ac/81-ha retreat in CATOCTIN Mountain Park, Frederick Co., NW Maryland, just W of Thurmont and 70 mi/110 km NW of Washington, D.C. Established by Franklin D. Roosevelt (who called it Shangri-La) in 1942, made an official presidential retreat by Harry S. Truman in 1945, and named for Dwight D. Eisenhower's grandson in 1953, it has been the scene of conferences, including one in 1979 that led to Israeli-Egyptian accords.

Camp Hill borough, pop. 7831, Cumberland Co., S Pennsylvania, across the Susquehanna R. 5 mi/8 km WSW of Harrisburg. Founded in 1756, it is primarily a residential suburb with some corporate development, and houses a large military contractor.

Camp Lejeune US Marine Corps base, established at the beginning of World War II along the New R. estuary in Onslow Co., SE North Carolina, just S of JACKSONVILLE. With the adjoining (N) New River Air Station, it covers some 110,000 ac/45,000 ha, and is a main Marine training center, and home to various combat units. In 1990, Lejeune had a pop. of 36,716, New River Station 9732.

Camp Logan see under MEMORIAL PARK, Houston, Texas.

Campobello Island 15 sq mi/39 sq km, pop. 1317, in Charlotte Co., SW New Brunswick, at the entrance to PASSAMAQUODDY BAY and the Bay of FUNDY, off the E tip of Maine. Linked to LUBEC, Maine, by bridge since 1962, it is a summer resort and home to fishermen. The Roosevelt Campobello International Park (2720 ac/1100 ha, est. 1964) includes, on the W side, at Welshpool, Franklin D. Roosevelt's childhood summer home, where he was stricken with polio in 1921. The park is administered by a joint US-Canadian commission.

Camp Pendleton see under OCEANSIDE, California.

Camp Roberts see under PASO ROBLES, California.

Camp Springs unincorporated suburban community, pop. 16,392, Prince George's Co., C Maryland, 10 mi/16 km SE of Washington, D.C., and just W of ANDREWS AIR FORCE BASE.

Camp Sumter see under ANDERSONVILLE, Georgia.

Camp Verde town, pop. 6243, Yavapai Co., C Arizona, 35 mi/56 km E of Prescott and 40 mi/64 km S of Flagstaff, on the Verde R. A fort established here in the 1860s (active until 1891) to protect farmers is now a state historic park. Nearby (NNE) is Montezuma Castle National Monument, with a well-preserved, 5-story cliff dwelling, built by the Sinagua in the 12th century; its name reflects the once common belief that Southwestern PUEBLOS had been built by Mexico's Aztecs.

Camp Wolters see under MINERAL WELLS, Texas.

Camp X see under WHITBY, Ontario.

Camrose city, pop. 13,420, C Alberta, on Camrose Creek and Mirror L., 48 mi/77 km SE of Edmonton. It is the distribution, industrial, and administrative center of an agricultural and coal and oil producing region. Grain, flour, and meat are processed here. Founded in 1905 by a Belgian missionary, Camrose was settled largely by Scandinavians. Camrose Lutheran College (1911) is here. One of the country's first ski clubs was founded (1911) in the city.

Canaan **1.** the land (roughly, Palestine) promised Abraham and his descendants by God (Genesis 12). To Puritan settlers, New England itself was Canaan; its native inhabitants were, like the biblical Canaanites, to be subdued or destroyed. The name Canaan (or New Canaan) was given to various New England and Western settlements. **2.** town, pop. 1057, Litchfield Co., extreme NW Connecticut, on the Housatonic and Hollenbeck rivers, 17 mi/27 km NW of Torrington. It includes the villages of South Canaan, Huntsville, Lower City, and Falls Village. The village of Canaan, in the adjoining town of North Canaan, pop. 3284, is a trade center for a resort area that attracts exurbanites from New York City.

Canada officially, **Dominion of Canada** federated state, combining in its governmental structure elements of the federal republic (of the US style) and limited monarchy (of the British style). The Dominion came into being with CONFEDERATION, on July 1, 1867, and has grown with the entry of new PROVINCES (the last, Newfoundland and Labrador, in 1949). The British North America Act, which created the Confederation, made Canada a constituent part of the British Empire (later of the Commonwealth of Nations). In 1982 the Act was "patriated," or returned to Canada, so that Canada no longer must submit constitutional changes for British approval. Nonetheless, the British monarch remains formally the head of state, and an appointed governor general represents the Crown in Canada. The nation has a bicameral Parliament, with an elected House of Commons and an appointed Senate; the prime minister is the head of government, which sits in OTTAWA, Ontario. Canada today comprises ten provinces—ALBERTA, BRITISH COLUMBIA, MANITOBA, NEW BRUNSWICK, NEWFOUNDLAND AND LABRADOR, NOVA SCOTIA, ONTARIO, PRINCE EDWARD ISLAND, QUÉBEC, and SASKATCHEWAN—and two partially self-governing territories, the NORTHWEST TERRITORIES and YUKON TERRITORY. Canada, the world's second-largest nation (land area 3,553,363 sq mi/9,203,210 sq km) after Russia, had a 1991 pop. of 27,296,859 (107.9% of 1986). It holds no overseas territories. Within its own boundaries, SAINT-PIERRE ET MIQUELON, an island group off Newfoundland's S coast, and an overseas part of France, is the only foreign territory. Canada's only land border is that with the US, much of it along the FORTY-NINTH PARALLEL. The nation's name is derived from a local term for the village of STADACONA, found in the 1530s on the site of modern Québec City. This was gradually applied to a larger and larger territory, and in 1791, with the Constitutional (or Canada) Act, was first given officially to Upper and LOWER CANADA.

Canada East see under LOWER CANADA; PROVINCE OF CANADA.

Canada West see under UPPER CANADA; PROVINCE OF CANADA.

Canadian Falls see under NIAGARA R.

Canadian Forces Base (C.F.B.) see CAMP.

Canadian National Railway government corporation that since the 1920s has combined over 200 smaller railroads in Canada and the NE US. It operates throughout Canada, from Newfoundland's narrow-gauge lines to the Northwest Territories' Great Slave Lake Railway and to docks in Churchill, Manitoba, and Vancouver and Prince Rupert, British Columbia. The CN's predecessors include some of Canada's most historic railroads: The Champlain & St. Lawrence, running between SAINT-JEAN-SUR-RICHELIEU and LA PRAIRIE, SE of Montréal, opened a 14-mi/23-km line, Canada's first, in July 1836. The Grand Trunk Railway, established in the 1850s, quickly built or took over lines from the Québec City area to Montréal (where it built the VICTORIA BRIDGE), W to Ontario, S to Portland, Maine, and E to the Maritimes. Throughout the 19th century, the Grand Trunk absorbed smaller lines. Until an 1882 merger, it competed chiefly with the Great Western Railway (1845); both systems afforded an alternate route in Ontario for US lines wanting to extend service to Detroit and Chicago. The Canadian National itself was created at the end of World War I, when several Canadian lines proposing or building elements of a transcontinental alternative to the CANADIAN PACIFIC encountered financial difficulties. These included the **Canadian Northern,** which in 1915 had completed a line from Manitoba (connecting E with L. Superior at what is now Thunder Bay) to Edmonton, Alberta, then through the YELLOWHEAD PASS and down the Fraser R. to Vancouver, British Columbia. The Grand Trunk Pacific, meanwhile, had built across the prairies parallel to the Canadian Northern and through Yellowhead Pass, then NW to PRINCE RUPERT, British Columbia. In the East, the Grand Trunk itself, operating with government backing as the National Transcontinental Railroad, had built from Moncton, New Brunswick, via Québec City (where the Québec Bridge was completed 1905–17 despite two disastrous collapses) and across the CANADIAN SHIELD in Québec and Ontario, to Winnipeg. The partly redundant system thus created was completely absorbed by the CN in 1919–23. Today, in addition to Grand Trunk Western routes into Michigan, Ohio, Indiana, and Illinois, the Canadian National system includes tracks of the Vermont Central, and other spurs in Maine and Minnesota. In Canada, it serves the Maritimes and N and C areas of Québec, Ontario, and the Prairie Provinces, as well as the SW Northwest Territories and many parts of British Columbia.

Canadian Pacific Railway today, **CP Rail** privately organized carrier that crossed W Canada in the 1870s–80s to fulfill a condition of the entry (1871) of British Columbia into Confederation—that the province be linked with the rest of Canada. The CP gradually developed into a major transportation organization, known for its steamships and resort hotels as well as for its rail service; it also has branch lines into several US states. Initial construction (1875–80) connected Fort William (now part of Thunder Bay), Ontario, on the W end of L. Superior, with Winnipeg, in the new province of Manitoba. After a period of financial uncertainty, work began again in 1881, W from Winnipeg and E from BURRARD INLET, British Columbia. A route via Moose Jaw (Saskatchewan), Calgary (Alberta), and KICKING HORSE PASS (on the Continental Divide) was chosen, after a more northerly Edmonton–YELLOWHEAD PASS route was rejected. Eastbound construction in British Columbia proceeded via part of the CARIBOO TRAIL and Kamloops. On Nov. 11, 1885, a ceremonial last spike was driven at CRAIGELLACHIE, in Eagle Pass through the Monashee Mts., W of Revelstoke, completing a continuous main line from Montréal, Québec, to PORT MOODY, on Burrard Inlet (the W terminus was extended the following year to the new city of Vancouver). Trains on this route offered the only no-change transcontinental service in either Canada or the US until the 1993 extension of the SOUTHERN PACIFIC's *Sunset Limited* to Florida. Construction of the CP line had to overcome problems posed by the rugged CANADIAN SHIELD N of the Great Lakes. The most famous obstacles to completion, though, were in the Northern Rocky Mt. ranges. Just W of Kicking Horse Pass, the line ran some 4 mi/6.4 km on a precipitous 4.5% grade. The two Spiral Tunnels (1909) under the Cathedral Mts. reduced this to an easier 2.2%, taking trains through a 3255-ft/992-m, 291° turn and a second of 2992 ft/912 m at 217°. To the W, at Rogers Pass in the SELKIRK Mts., another steep grade, sharp curves, and the need for miles of snowsheds (roofing to keep track clear in winter) were eliminated by the 1916 Connaught Tunnel, extending 4.25 mi/6.8 km through Mt. Macdonald. In the 1890s the CP built another, more southerly route through CROWSNEST PASS; the approach from the E involved constructing Alberta's Lethbridge Viaduct, at 5328 ft/1624 m and 314 ft/96 m Canada's longest and highest. In the late 19th and early 20th centuries, the Canadian Pacific played a major role in settling the Canadian West. It also developed a steamship system, connecting Vancouver with Asia, and built a chain of luxurious hotels—including Québec City's CHÂTEAU FRONTENAC and others in Lake Louise, Alberta; Ottawa; and Saint Andrews, New Brunswick. Its Soo Line subsidiary owns US trackage in Wisconsin, Minnesota, and the Dakotas. The TRANS-CANADA HIGHWAY follows the CP route much of its way, including through the Rockies. By the 1930s, the CP was cooperating on routes with its government-owned competitor, the CANADIAN NATIONAL RAILWAY; since 1978, VIA, a government corporation, has managed all Canadian passenger service.

Canadian River also, **South Canadian R.** 906 mi/1459 km long, in New Mexico, Texas, and Oklahoma. It is formed E of the Sangre de Cristo Mts. in Colfax Co., New Mexico, partly by headstreams flowing from Colorado. It flows SSE into the dam-created Conchas Reservoir, then E, into the Texas Panhandle. There it winds ENE through L. MEREDITH and into Oklahoma, where it continues E almost the width of the state. Along the way it flows through SW Oklahoma City, N of Ada, and into dam-created Eufaula L., near the city of Eufaula (pop. 2652, McIntosh Co.), where it is joined by the NORTH CANADIAN R. (also known as the Beaver R.). It then continues ENE to join the ARKANSAS R., 25 mi/40 km SE of MUSKOGEE. The Canadian, whose name is probably a corruption of a Caddoan word for "red stream," is not navigable, but is an important irrigation source.

Canadian Shield also, **Laurentian Plateau** or **Shield, Precambrian Shield,** or **Laurentia** vast plateau, called a shield for its slightly convex (upward) shape, that is the oldest and largest (c.1.9 million sq mi/5 million sq km) structural element of North America. It covers about half of Canada and most of Greenland, and underlies much of Canada's shallower northern waters (including Hudson Bay); in the S, it extends as New York's Adirondack Mts. and as the Superior Highlands, in NW Michigan, N Wisconsin, and NE Minnesota. It was formed in the Precambrian Era, from some 3.75 billion to 570 million years ago; its rocks were in that period folded and thrust upward in many places. Since the end of the Precambrian, however, it has undergone little internal change, and has remained essentially above sea level, so that ocean-produced erosion and deposition of sediments have been minimal. It has, however, been heavily glaciated; the ice reduced heights and left behind a myriad of lakes. Drainage is generally poor, although some major rivers flow across and from the Shield. In the N the Shield is largely TUNDRA, in the S forest. Its predominantly metamorphic rocks, chiefly gneisses, granites, and schists, with some lava flows, constitute the largest expanse of exposed rock of such an age on the earth's surface. In Canada, the Shield occupies Labrador; Québec N of the St. Lawrence Valley; almost all of the mainland Northwest Territories and much of the Arctic Archipelago; most of Ontario (excepting the southernmost portions); and parts of N Manitoba and NE Saskatchewan. Along its S it is fringed by (E–W) the St. Lawrence R. valley, the Great Lakes, Lake of the Woods, L. Winnipeg, L. Athabaska, Great Slave and Great Bear lakes, and the Mackenzie R. valley. The Torngat and

Laurentian mountains, in Québec, are actually upturned escarpments on its edges. Because very little of it is arable (the CLAY BELT is an exception), the Shield's presence retarded westward settlement of Canada, forcing rural expansion routes southward into the United States; development of the rich Prairie Provinces, and their ability to trade with E Canada, had to await 1860s–80s railroad development. From the earliest days of European exploration, however, the Shield has been a rich ground for the fur trade. In the late 19th century it became central to the lumber and pulp business. At the beginning of the 20th its immense deposits of metals and other minerals began to be exploited. Finally, after the mid 20th century, it became the site of huge hydroelectric projects. It remains very lightly inhabited, with scattered paper, mining (as at SUDBURY, Ontario), and other industrial settlements. In the N the INUIT live on its coasts; farther S, the DENE and Cree still hunt its forests. Today it is also dotted with lake, ski, hunting, and other resorts.

Canadian Technology Triangle popular and promotional term for the region of S Ontario bounded by the cities of WATERLOO and KITCHENER (SW), GUELPH (NE), and CAMBRIDGE (SE), lying on the W of the GOLDEN HORSESHOE and SW of Toronto. An area also noted for varied industry, it has since the 1970s, drawing on the knowledge base of the cities' universities, become home to hundreds of high-tech firms.

Canajoharie village, pop. 2278, in Canajoharie township, Montgomery Co., E New York, on the Mohawk R. and the New York State Barge Canal, 14 mi/23 km SW of Johnstown. Its Iroquoian name means "washing pot," a reference to a large pothole in Canajoharie Creek Gorge. It was settled c.1730 by Dutch and German farmers, and its Fort Rensselaer was a Revolutionary troop-gathering spot. Its light industries include food processing.

Canal Street **1.** central thoroughfare in New Orleans, Louisiana. It parallels the original boundary between the VIEUX CARRÉ (the French Quarter, N) and the first suburb of New Orleans, the Faubourg Ste. Marie, which became part of the AMERICAN QUARTER. It was set aside as a divider between the two settlements; a canal planned for the 170 ft/52 m–wide corridor was never built, leaving a wide double roadway with "neutral ground" in its center. Canal St. runs from the Mississippi R. (SE) to a cluster of cemeteries on the city's NW side; it is the site of many of the city's older shops and hotels. It marks the boundary between DOWNTOWN (N) and UPTOWN (S). Mardi Gras parades pass along it. **2.** commercial thoroughfare across lower Manhattan, New York, between the Hudson R. (where it feeds into the HOLLAND TUNNEL) and the Lower East Side (where it leads to the Manhattan Bridge, to Brooklyn). It takes its name from a stream that formerly ran along its route. Canal St. divides CHINATOWN from LITTLE ITALY, and provides the N boundary of TRIBECA. It is famous for its street markets and discount houses.

Canandaigua city, pop. 10,725, seat of Ontario Co., W New York, at the N end of Canandaigua L., 25 mi/40 km SE of Rochester. It is a manufacturing center set in a resort area; leading industries produce typewriter ribbon, labels, plastics, clothing, fishing tackle, furniture, and wine. The Pickering Treaty with the Six Nations of the Iroquois was signed here in 1794. Canandaigua is home to the Community College of the Finger Lakes (1965).

Canarsie residential section of SE Brooklyn, New York, developed on flat, swampy land on Jamaica Bay, S of East New York and Brownsville, and E of Flatbush and Flatlands. Canarsie is Brooklyn's "newest" neighborhood, settled in the 1950s by whites moving from East New York, Brownsville, and other districts. Sold to Europeans by the Canarsie tribe in the 17th century, the area long remained a rural part of Flatlands township. Early in the 20th century it was a seaside resort, before pollution in Jamaica Bay caused decline. In the 1980s and 1990s, black, Hispanic, and Asian New Yorkers began moving into Canarsie, raising the possibility of further white flight. In 1990 Canarsie was about 75% white.

Canastota village, pop. 4673, in Lenox township, Madison Co., C New York, on the New York State Barge Canal, 20 mi/32 km E of Syracuse. Settled in 1806, it was an early-20th-century center for the production of handmade crystal. It now has a variety of light industries. Situated in an agricultural area, it has canning and dairy processing facilities, and serves as a distribution point for locally grown onions and other produce.

Canaveral, Cape E extension of the Canaveral Peninsula, on the Atlantic Ocean 50 mi/80 km E of Orlando, in Orange Co., EC Florida. The Banana R. lagoon separates the peninsula from MERRITT I. (W). The John F. Kennedy Space Center, with its launching pads and space shuttle landing strip, extends over the cape, peninsula, and island. From here were launched the first US satellite in 1958, the first manned lunar probe in 1969, and many other missions. From 1963 to 1973 the cape was called Cape Kennedy. The 57,000-ac/23,100-ha **Canaveral National Seashore** is adjacent (N).

Candiac city, pop. 11,064, Roussillon census division, S Québec, on the Bassin de Laprairie (the St. Lawrence R.), 8 mi/13 km SSE of Montréal, and adjacent (SW) to La Prairie. It is an industrial (glass, other manufactures) and residential suburb.

Candler-McAfee unincorporated community, pop. 29,491, De Kalb Co., NW Georgia, a residential suburb 4 mi/6 km E of downtown Atlanta.

Candlestick Park 60,000-seat football and baseball stadium in the Candlestick Point State Recreation Area in SE SAN FRANCISCO, California, on San Francisco Bay, S of HUNTER'S POINT and 5 mi/8 km S of Downtown. Built in 1960, it is famous for its cold winds.

Candlewood Lake 6000 ac/2430 ha, in Litchfield and Fairfield counties, Connecticut, N of Danbury and near the New York border, formed in 1926 by a dam on the Rocky R. It is a popular summer resort 15 mi/24 km long, with a 65-mi/105-km shoreline.

Caneel Bay see under SAINT JOHN, US Virgin Islands.

Cane Ridge religious site: see under PARIS, Kentucky.

Caney Fork River 144 mi/232 km long, in C Tennessee. It rises in W Cumberland Co., on the CUMBERLAND PLATEAU, and flows S, W, and NW to the Cumberland R. at CARTHAGE. Center Hill Dam, which forms 15 mi/24 km–long Center Hill L., a major recreational asset, and Great Falls Dam are both units of the TENNESSEE VALLEY AUTHORITY.

Canfield Historic District residential neighborhood in the Wayne State University area of Detroit, Michigan, 2 mi/3 km N of Downtown. Victorian homes have been restored in this community of young professionals, artists, and students.

Caniapiscau, Rivière also, **Kaniapiskau** see under R. KOKSOAK, Québec.

Canisteo River 55 mi/89 km long, in SW New York. It rises near Arkport in W Steuben Co., and flows generally SE past Hornell, Canisteo, and Addison, into the Tioga R., 5 mi/8 km SW of CORNING.

Cannery Row see under MONTEREY, California.

Cannon Air Force Base see under CLOVIS, New Mexico.

Cannonball River 295 mi/475 km long, in North Dakota. It rises in the Badlands of SW North Dakota, and flows ESE past New England and across the SW part of the state to the SE border of Grant Co., where it receives CEDAR CREEK. It then continues NE to form the NE border of Sioux Co. and the STANDING ROCK INDIAN RESERVATION. The river finally enters L. OAHE on the Missouri R. at the hamlet of Cannon Ball.

Cannon Mountain see under FRANCONIA NOTCH, New Hampshire.

Cannon River 100 mi/161 km long, in SE Minnesota. It rises in the lake region of Le Sueur Co., and flows generally NE, passing Cannon Falls before joining the Mississippi R. N of Red Wing.

Canoga Park W SAN FERNANDO VALLEY section of LOS ANGELES, California, 22 mi/35 km WNW of Downtown. A residential and retail center, it also has had agricultural businesses, and has been home since the 1960s to aerospace and other high-tech manufacturers.

Canol Road see under SELWYN Mts., Yukon Territory.

Canon City city, pop. 12,687, seat of Fremont Co., SC Colorado, on the Arkansas R. at the E end of the ROYAL GORGE, 34 mi/55 km NW of Pueblo. Settled in 1859, it was an early distributing center for local gold mines. The railroad arrived in 1874 and Canon City became a shipping hub for agricultural products, livestock, and minerals, and, later, made bricks, concrete, tools, conveyors, and ore concentrates. Its economy is now largely based on livestock, agriculture, mining (oil, coal, marble, and other stone), and tourism. The state penitentary is on its outskirts, and the Colorado Territorial Prison Museum and Park is in the city.

Canonsburg borough, pop. 9200, Washington Co., W. Pennsylvania, 20 mi/32 km SSW of Pittsburgh. Settled c.1772, it was a center of the Whiskey Rebellion (1794). Long a coal mining hub, and once a leading radium manufacturer, it produces gas and oil, and has some light manufacturing.

Canso, Strait of also, **Canso Gut** deep channel between CAPE BRETON I. and the mainland of NE Nova Scotia. Fifteen mi/24 km NW–SE and 2 mi/3 km wide, it formerly provided an open waterway between the NORTHUMBERLAND STRAIT, via St. Georges Bay (NW), and the Atlantic Ocean, via Chedabucto Bay (SE). Now the Canso Causeway, completed in 1955 for rail and highway travel, bisects it. Towns along the strait include Auld Cove and Mulgrave on the mainland, and Port Hastings and Port Hawkesbury on Cape Breton I.

Canterbury town, pop. 1687, Merrimack Co., C New Hampshire, adjacent (N) to Concord. This largely rural town is known for its Shaker community, established in 1792, whose life ended in 1992 with the death of the last member. The Shaker village, in the E part of the town, is now a museum.

Canton 1. city, pop. 13,922, Fulton Co., WC Illinois, in the Illinois R. Valley, 25 mi/40 km SW of Peoria. A trading center for an area producing corn, wheat, and livestock, it was a base for the International Harvester Company, whose tillage implement factory was one of the largest in the Midwest until it closed in 1983. Bituminous coal and clay are mined in the vicinity, while manufactures include dairy products, concrete, kitchen cabinets, and overalls. Canton was founded in 1825. Spoon River College (1959) is located here. The Rice Lake and Banner Marsh wildlife areas are both 10 mi/16 km SE. **2.** town, pop. 18,530, Norfolk Co., E Massachusetts, on the S bank of the Neponset R and along ROUTE 128, 14 mi/23 km S of Boston. Originally part of STOUGHTON, it was the site of several of Paul Revere's enterprises including the gunpowder factory he operated during the Revolution and the first (1808) copper-rolling mill and brassworks in the US. Much of the BLUE HILLS Reservation is in the town. Other industries make textiles, rubber goods, and technical apparatus. **3.** city, pop. 10,062, seat of Madison Co., C Mississippi, on a low divide between the Pearl (SE) and Big Black (NW) rivers, 24 mi/39 km NNE of Jackson, just off the NATCHEZ TRACE. Incorporated in 1836, it was long a cotton center; 20th-century diversification brought truck farming, livestock raising, and the manufacture of wood products and textiles. **4.** city, pop. 2623, Lewis Co., NE Missouri, on the Mississippi R. (the Illinois border), 30 mi/48 km NNW of Hannibal. In an agricultural region where grain and poultry are raised and fisheries are important, it is a trade and distribution center, and has some light industry. It is the seat of Culver-Stockton College (1853). A large dam on the Mississippi is just N of the city. **5.** town, pop. 11,120, seat of St. Lawrence Co., N New York, 11 mi/18 km SW of Potsdam, on the Grass R. It was settled by Vermonters in the early 19th century, and was the birthplace (1861) of Western artist Frederic Remington. In an agricultural region, it is the seat of St. Lawrence University (1856) and the State University of New York Agricultural and Technical College (1907). **6.** city, pop. 84,161, seat of Stark Co., NE Ohio, 20 mi/32 km SE of Akron. Founded in 1805, it soon industrialized, spurred by nearby deposits of clay, coal, natural gas, and limestone. The city is now a major producer of metal alloys and steel. Other manufactures include metalworking presses, roller bearings, brick, and rubber gloves. It is also a trade center for the surrounding dairy and poultry farming region. President William McKinley and his wife, who lived here, are buried in Monument Park, next to the 23-ac/9-ha McKinley National Memorial. The Professional Football Hall of Fame is here, and Canton is the seat of Malone College (1892) and Walsh College (1958). **7.** city, pop. 2787, seat of Lincoln Co., SE South Dakota, on the Big Sioux R. and the Iowa line, 20 mi/32 km SE of Sioux Falls. It is a shipping center for the surrounding agricultural area, in which dairy goods, livestock, poultry, and grain are produced. Blocks, tiles, and road machinery are manufactured.

Cantons de l'Est see EASTERN TOWNSHIPS, Québec.

canyon from Spanish, *cañon,* a deep, narrow valley or ravine, cut by a stream in soft rock or soil formations in arid or semiarid areas, where other forms of erosion do not reduce the entire formation at similar speed. A *gulch* is essentially the same, although the term may be used more where there is no longer a stream (hence, "dry gulch"). See also BOX CANYON.

Canyon city, pop. 11,365, seat of Randall Co., NW Texas, in the Panhandle, 16 mi/26 km SSW of Amarillo, on the Prairie Dog Town Fork of the Red R. The last great Indian battle in Texas, fought here in 1874, was a cavalry victory over an encampment of Comanches. Once a ranch headquarters, the city is now a trade center for a farming and cattle raising area. Its largest employer is West Texas State University (1909), home to the Panhandle-Plains Historical Museum. PALO DURO Canyon State Park is just E, and Buffalo Lake National Wildlife Refuge is 12 mi/19 km SW.

Canyon de Chelly National Monument 83,840 ac/33,955 ha, in NE Arizona, within the NAVAJO INDIAN RESERVATION, 53 mi/85 km SSW of FOUR CORNERS. Set here along 26 mi/42 km of Chinle Wash are cliff dwellings and other ruins from five periods, C.A.D. 350–1300, created by the Anasazi. The Hopi lived in the area c.1300–1700; since then it has been dominated by the Navajo, who use the canyon today for summer grazing and farming, and allow limited tourism. The US Army destroyed permanent settlements here in the 1860s. The Navajo community of Chinle (unincorporated, pop. 5059, Apache Co.) lies just W.

Canyonlands National Park 337,570 ac/136,716 ha (527 sq mi/1366 sq km) of rocks, spires, and mesas rising to more than 7800 ft/2377 m, on the Colorado R., 35 mi/56 km SW of MOAB, in SE Utah. The park's features include Island in the Sky (N), a 6000-ft/1830-m mesa; the junction and canyons of the Colorado and Green rivers; the Needles (S), an area of 300 ft/91 m–high pinnacles; and the remote Maze District, W of the rivers. Horseshoe Canyon, W of the Green R., has a large collection of pictographs painted by the ANASAZI over 1000 years ago.

Cap-de-la-Madeleine city, pop. 33,716, Champlain Co., S Québec, on the N shore of the St. Lawrence R. at the mouth of the R. Saint-Maurice, across which (W) is TROIS-RIVIÈRES. Cap-de-la-Madeleine was settled in the 1630s but did not develop significantly until the 20th century, when saw and pulp mills, and then aluminum foil, clothing, abrasive, and chemical plants opened. The Sanctuaire Notre-Dame-du-Cap has been a pilgrimage site since the 1880s.

Cap-Diamant see under QUÉBEC CITY, Québec.

Cape for capes whose names begin with this word, see under the other name element, as **Mendocino, Cape.**

Cape Breton Highlands National Park 370–sq mi/960–sq km preserve of mixed forests, heath, MUSKEG, and ponds, noted for its wildlife and campgrounds, on a plateau 40 mi/65 km NW of Sydney, on N Cape Breton I., Nova Scotia. The park borders both the Gulf of St. Lawrence (W) and the Atlantic Ocean (E), and is traversed by the Cabot Trail scenic highway. Cliffs on the Atlantic side rise 985 ft/300 m, and the highest point in the province, White Hill, stands at 1747 ft/532 m in the center of the park.

Cape Breton Island 3970 sq mi/10,282 sq km, pop. 161,686, surrounded by the Atlantic Ocean and Gulf of St. Lawrence, in NE Nova Scotia. Mountainous and forested, it is separated from the mainland peninsula by the Strait of CANSO (bridged by a causeway since 1955), and bisected by the large BRAS D'OR L. It was known to European fishermen from the 15th century. From 1623 it was controlled by France and settled by Acadians. After the 1713 Treaty of Utrecht granted the Nova Scotia peninsula to Britain, the French fortress at LOUISBOURG was built, and the island called Île Royale. In 1763 it became part of Nova Scotia, following the British conquest of Canada. From 1784 until 1820, it was a separate colony, established for LOYALISTS. Sydney, its capital, became in the 1830s a coal mining center, later manufacturing steel and other products. Although mining and manufactures have slumped since the mid 20th century, **Cape Breton Co.** (pop. 120,098), in the SE, remains an industrial center. Fishing and tourism are also important. Many islanders are descended from 18th- and 19th-century Scottish immigrants, and Highlands and Gaelic, as well as elements of the earlier Acadian, folk culture remain vital.

Cape Cod peninsula, Barnstable Co., SE Massachusetts, extending 65 mi/105 km into the Atlantic Ocean. Cape Cod is a hook-shaped landmass, extending E and then N. It is bordered W by Cape Cod Bay, S by Nantucket Sound, E by the Atlantic Ocean, and SW by Buzzards Bay and Vineyard Sound. The Cape, as it is popularly known, is a resort and vacation region of sandy beaches and rolling dunes; it was created by intersecting glacial moraines. The commercial center is at HYANNIS; PROVINCETOWN, at the N end of the hook, is known as a gathering place for artists and theater people. Cape Cod National Seashore runs along the E shore from the entrance to Provincetown Harbor S to Nauset Beach, near CHATHAM, a distance of 40 mi/64 km. The ELIZABETH ISLANDS extend SW from the Cape across the mouth of Buzzards Bay. The CAPE COD CANAL separates the Cape from the rest of Massachusetts.

Cape Cod Canal ship channel largely in Bourne township, Barnstable Co., SE Massachusetts. It crosses Cape Cod at its base, connecting Buzzards and Cape Cod bays. Completed in 1914, it measures 17.5 mi/28 km long, 500 ft/150 m wide, and 32 ft/10 m deep, and is bridged at Bourne and Sagamore. The canal is part of the ATLANTIC INTRACOASTAL WATERWAY, and enables seagoing vessels to pass inside Cape Cod.

Cape Coral city, pop. 74,991, Lee Co., SW Florida, N of the mouth of the Caloosahatchee R., near the Gulf Coast, 8 mi/13 km SW of Fort Myers. A booming resort and retirement community, it more than doubled in population in the 1980s.

Cape Dorset hamlet, pop. 961, on Dorset I., just off the Foxe Peninsula of SW BAFFIN I., Baffin Region, Northwest Territories. Once a HUDSON'S BAY COMPANY post, it is now a center for INUIT artists and printmakers; sealing is also important. Archaeological remains in the area have given a name to the Dorset culture of 500–2500 years ago.

Cape Elizabeth town, pop. 8854, Cumberland Co., SW Maine. It is on the W side of Casco Bay, adjoining South Portland and 4 mi/6 km S of Portland, of which it is an affluent suburb. Portland Head Light, the oldest (1791) and best-known Maine lighthouse, is in the N part of Cape Elizabeth. Crescent Beach and Two Lights state parks are at its SE extremity, at the cape that gives the town its name.

Cape Fear River 200 mi/320 km long, in E North Carolina. It is formed in the Piedmont by the confluence of the Deep and Haw rivers, 25 mi/40 km SW of Raleigh, in Chatham Co., and winds generally S to FAYETTEVILLE, its head of navigation. It continues SE through the Coastal Plain to its estuary at WILMINGTON, where several other swampy lowland rivers join it. FORT FISHER stands 7 mi/11 km NNE of where the river enters the Atlantic, at Cape FEAR. An important early shipping route for lumber, naval stores, and agricultural produce, the river is also known for the flooding that has occurred in its lower reaches.

Cape Girardeau city, pop. 34,438, Cape Girardeau Co., SE Missouri, on bluffs overlooking the Mississippi R., 100 mi/160 km SE of St. Louis. On the site of an early-18th-century trading post established by Jean Baptiste Girardot, it was founded in 1793 and settled by Spanish immigrants. Its proximity to the Mississippi-Ohio river confluence made it a flourishing antebellum trade and shipping center. Occupied by Union forces during the Civil War (remains of fortifications still exist), it declined after the conflict but was revived with the railroad's arrival in 1881. Now SE Missouri's commercial hub, it also makes furniture, paper products, cement, and electrical equipment. Southeast Missouri State University (1873) is here. Trail of Tears State Park is N.

Cape May city, pop. 4668, Cape May Co., at the S tip of New Jersey, on Cape May Peninsula, the Atlantic Ocean, and Cape May Harbor, 40 mi/64 km SW of Atlantic City. Settled c.1664 and originally known as Cape Island, it was a major whaling port in the early 18th century. One of the nation's oldest seaside resorts, situated as far S as Washington, D.C., Cape May rivaled Newport as a fashionable summer retreat during the early 19th century. Known as the "President's Playground" later in the century, it was a vacation spot for Buchanan, Lincoln, Grant, Hayes, Arthur, and Harrison. Many Victorian buildings are preserved. The city remains a popular resort, noted for its beach, boardwalk, and boating and fishing. Cape May Point State Park (SW) contains Cape May Point Lighthouse (1859). Located on the ATLANTIC FLYWAY, the area's dunes are a birdwatching hub, site of the World Series of Birding. **West Cape May** borough (pop. 1033) and **Cape May Point** borough (pop. 241) are separate municipalities.

Cape May Court House unincorporated village, pop. 4426, seat of Cape May Co., S New Jersey, on Cape May Peninsula, 30 mi/48 km SW of Atlantic City, and 12 mi/19 km NNE of CAPE MAY. It is a resort community with a winery, gardens, a museum outlining the area's 18th-century whaling activities, and a number of 18th- and 19th-century buildings. The area has dairy and poultry farms.

Capistrano see SAN JUAN CAPISTRANO, California.

Capitan Mountains NE–SW trending range WNW of Roswell, in SE New Mexico, in the Lincoln National Forest. A NE extension of the SACRAMENTO Mts., it rises to 10,230 ft/3118 m and includes **Capitan Peak** (10,083 ft/3073 m). These mountains are the birthplace of Smokey the Bear, the world-famous symbol of forest fire prevention, found here as a cub after a May 1950 fire; on his death (1976) he was buried in Smokey Bear Historical State Park, in the village of Capitan.

Capitola city, pop. 10,171, Santa Cruz Co., WC California, on the N shore of Monterey Bay, 5 mi/8 km E of Santa Cruz. Flower growing (esp. begonias) is important in this old seaside resort, established in the 1850s as Soquel Landing.

Capitol Heights town, pop. 3633, Prince George's Co., SC Maryland, adjacent (E) to SE Washington, D.C. It is a residential suburb.

Capitol Hill **1.** section of C DENVER, Colorado, immediately SE of Downtown, on the NE, E, and SE of the state capitol (in use since 1896, completed in 1908). From the 1880s the area acquired the mansions of Denver's powerful; one survivor of the period is the house of "the Unsinkable" Molly Brown. Neighborhoods here have passed through decline and restoration. The June People's Fair is a noted event. CHEESMAN PARK is just E, the CIVIC CENTER just W. **2.** the immediate vicinity of the US Capitol, Washington, D.C., and residential and commercial neighborhoods to its E. The area developed after the Civil War, then declined as the NORTHWEST developed in the 1920s. Since the 1950s it has undergone gentrification that has left it socially mixed, with upscale housing alongside abandoned buildings. At its W end, government buildings include the Capitol, the Supreme Court, and the Library of Congress's Jefferson Building. In reference to government, the area is often called simply "the Hill." Capitol Hill's neighborhoods include Lincoln Park, 1 mi/1.5 km E, and the area of the old Eastern Market, to the S along PENNSYLVANIA Ave., an important commercial corridor. **Capitol East** is a term used for the larger area, extending to the Anacostia R. **3.** residential and commercial district of SEATTLE, Washington, 2 mi/3 km NE of Downtown. The site of one of the city's early wealthy communities, it declined through the mid 20th century and has now been rejuvenated, largely by gay residents. It is a popular shopping and restaurant zone.

Capitol Reef National Park 241,904-ac/97,901-ha (378–sq mi/979–sq km) reserve noted for fossils, petrified trees, unusual geological formations, and cliff dwellings, 10 mi/16 km E of Torrey, in SC Utah. Buttes of the WATERPOCKET FOLD form a 90-mi/145-km wall of colorful sedimentary rock. **Capitol Dome** is an outcrop topped by white sandstone. Fruita, an early Mormon agricultural settlement, lies within the park.

caprock see under PLATEAU.

Caprock Escarpment natural break between the LLANO ESTACADO (W) and the rolling plains (prairies) of N Texas (E). Created by the differential erosion of two sedimentary structures, it stands at about 2000 ft/600 m at its base, from which it rises as high as 1000 ft/300 m in places. It runs in a jagged line from the NE PANHANDLE to the EDWARDS PLATEAU (SW). "The Caprock" is a term used in Texas for the Llano Estacado itself. PALO DURO CANYON (on the Prairie Dog Town Fork of the Red R.) and breaks caused by the Canadian R. lie along the escarpment.

Cap-Rouge city, pop. 14,105, QUÉBEC Urban Community, S Québec, on the N shore of the St. Lawrence R., at the mouth of the R. du Cap-Rouge, 7 mi/11 km SW of downtown Québec City, at the SW end of the city's Cap-Diamant. It was here, in 1541, that Jacques Cartier attempted to establish the colony of Charlesbourg-Royal; local quartz, mistakenly thought to be diamonds, was a motivator. Since the 1950s, Cap-Rouge has become a residential and commercial suburb.

Captain Cook see under KONA COAST, Hawaii.

Captiva Island slender, sandy barrier island, 7 mi/11 km long, in SW Florida, on the Gulf of Mexico (W) and Pine Island Sound (E), just N of SANIBEL I., to which it is connected by causeway, and 18 mi/29 km SSW of Fort Myers. Like Sanibel, it was an 18th-century refuge for pirates. The village of Captiva, once a sleepy fishing community, is its only settlement. The island is now a popular resort, with many private homes and tourist accommodations.

Capulin Mountain symmetrical cinder cone rising more than 1000 ft/300 m from the plain, to c.8200 ft/2500 m, 27 mi/43 km ESE of Raton, in NE New Mexico. It is a representative of the last stages (some 10,000 years ago) of a period of great volcanic activity in North America. Its crater, 415 ft/126 m deep, is within the Capulin Volcano National Monument. Sierra Grande, the highest peak in this area of lava flows, reaches 8720 ft/2658 m, and is 10 mi/16 km SE of Capulin.

Caramoor see under KATONAH, New York.

Caraquet town, pop. 4556, Gloucester Co., NE New Brunswick, on the Baie de Caraquet, on the S of CHALEUR BAY, 29 mi/47 km ENE of Bathurst and 117 mi/188 km NNW of Moncton, near the mouth of the Caraquet R. Settled from the 1750s by Acadians, Bretons, and Québec fishermen, on what is popularly called the Acadian Peninsula, it today claims to be the cultural capital of Acadia; the Acadian Historical Village is 6 mi/10 km W. A fishing company based on the island of Jersey ruled its economy for over a century before World War II. Today tourism, fishing, and boatbuilding are important.

Carbondale **1.** city, pop. 27,033, Jackson Co., SC Illinois, at the N edge of the Illinois Ozarks, 33 mi/53 km NE of Cape Girardeau, Missouri. Named for local coalfields, it has been a mining and rail center since the Illinois Central Railroad founded the city in 1852 and established division headquarters here. In addition to trading local produce and repairing trains, it also manufactures apparel, dairy foods, concrete, treated wood, and plastic tape. Southern Illinois University (1869) is here. The Shawnee National Forest lies SW, and the Crab Orchard National Wildlife Refuge is on 9 mi/14 km–long Crab Orchard L., 3 mi/5 km to the E. **2.** city, pop. 10,664, Lackawanna Co., NE Pennsylvania, on the Lackawanna R., 16 mi/26 km NE of Scranton. It is named for the extensive open-pit coal mining activities in the area, which led to the building of the Delaware and Hudson Canal (1825) and of a gravity railroad from Carbondale to HONESDALE (1829). It was the site of the world's first underground anthracite mine (1831). Still a coal mining center, the city also manufactures metal products, chemicals, textiles, and other goods.

Carcross settlement, pop. 183, SW Yukon Territory, on the Klondike Highway at the N end of Bennett L., 40 mi/65 km SSE of Whitehorse. The name is an abbreviation of "*car*ibou *cross*ing." During the KLONDIKE gold rush (1897–1900s), the White Pass and Yukon Railway made this a stop, and it has figured in supplying subsequent mining operations in the area.

Cardiff hamlet in Lafayette township, Onondaga Co., NC New York, 10 mi/16 km S of Syracuse. It became famous in 1869 when a 10.5 ft/3.2 m–high human figure was unearthed by workers digging a well on a nearby farm. Dubbed the "Cardiff Giant," the figure was certified as the petrified remains of a man by various experts. The "Giant," bought and sold for increasingly large amounts and put on exhibition, was eventually discovered to be a hoax, carved of Midwestern gypsum and buried at the wellsite. It had several imitators.

Cardiff-by-the-Sea also, **Cardiff** beachside resort and residential district in San Diego Co., SW California, 20 mi/32 km NNW of downtown San Diego, on the Pacific Ocean, noted for its restaurants.

Cardigan, Mount peak (3121 ft/952 m), WC New Hampshire, in Orange and Alexandria townships. Its N spur, Firescrew, was named for the spiral of fire and smoke that rose from it during a great fire in 1855. A steep-sided rock dome also known as "Old Baldy," it is mostly in Cardigan State Park, a reservation of over 5000 ac/2025 ha with many trails.

Cardston town, pop. 3480, SW Alberta, on Lee Creek, near the St. Mary R., 15 mi/24 km N of Port of Piegan, Montana, and 42 mi/68 km SW of Lethbridge. A trade center for local ranches and farms, it also engages in dairying, banking, cabinetmaking, and commercial printing. Charles Ora Card, Brigham Young's son-in-law, led a band of Mormons here from Utah in 1887 and later built the first irrigation works on the St. Mary. Cooperatives, including a sawmill and cheese factory, have thrived here ever since. The Mormon Temple (1923) is the only such structure in Canada. The Blood Indian Reserve (pop. 4013) is to the N.

Caribbean National Forest also, **Luquillo Experimental Forest** reserve established in 1903 in the Sierra de Luquillo, 25 mi/40 km ESE of San Juan, in NE Puerto Rico. It now covers some 28,000 ac/11,350 ha of dense, cool forest receiving up to 240 in/600 cm of rainfall yearly. Popular for its footpaths and waterfalls, it is known as El Yunque, after a prominent 3494-ft/1065-m peak. The forest's wildlife includes many birds and the tiny tree frog (*el coquí*) that is a Puerto Rican icon.

Cariboo Mountains NW–SE trending range, some 200 mi/320 km long, in EC British Columbia. Part of the Columbia Mts. section of the Rocky Mts., they lie between the Fraser R. and the Rocky Mt. Trench (E) and the province's interior plateaus (W), and rise to 11,750 ft/3505 m at Mt. Sir Wilfrid Laurier (S), W of YELLOWHEAD PASS. Wells Gray and Bowron Lake provincial parks are on their W slopes. The Cariboos' W foothills were the scene of an early-1860s gold rush that centered around BARKERVILLE, and that brought fortune seekers from many directions, some via the Cariboo Road; as strikes expanded through the Fraser R. valley, the name **the Cariboo** came to embrace areas as far S as Lillooet, 110 mi/180 km NNW of Vancouver.

Cariboo Road see under BARKERVILLE, British Columbia.

Caribou city, pop. 9415, Aroostook Co., NE Maine. It is 20 mi/32 km from the New Brunswick border, on the Aroostook R. and US 1, 13 mi/21 km N of Presque Isle. Named for the animal plentiful in the area at one time, it is a shipping center for the Aroostook potato region and a gateway to the Allagash and other recreation areas. Industries include potato and sugar beet processing, fertilizer manufacture, and steam and diesel generation.

Caribou National Forest 1.2 million ac/490,000 ha (1890 sq mi/4900 sq km), in extreme SE Idaho, extreme W Wyoming, and extreme NE Utah. Named for a prospector, its area was the scene of a late-19th-century gold rush. The forest's scattered units enclose rugged peaks, grassland, lakes and reservoirs, ghost towns, and part of the OREGON TRAIL.

Carle Place unincorporated village, pop. 5107, in North Hempstead town, Nassau Co., SE New York, on Long Island, just E of Mineola. It is largely residential, but on its S and W borders is a heavily developed commercial area, with shopping malls serving Long Island and Queens residents.

Carleton, Mount 2690 ft/820 m, in Restigouche Co., N New Brunswick. Highest point in New Brunswick and in all the Maritime Provinces, it rises above the surrounding Miramichi Highlands, part of the Appalachian system. Focus of a 70–sq mi/182–sq km provincial park, it is 70 mi/110 km E of Edmundston.

Carlin see under ELKO, Nevada.

Carlinville city, pop. 5416, seat of Macoupin Co., WC Illinois, 37 mi/60 km SSW of Springfield. It is a trading center for the region's corn, soybeans, apples, and, especially, livestock. Manufactures include steel pipe fittings, agricultural implements, gloves, and dairy products. There are coal mining and oil drilling in the vicinity. The first white settlement, on Black Hawk hunting grounds, was established in 1815. Blackburn College (1837) is here. Beaver Dam State Park is 5 mi/8 km SW.

Carlisle borough, pop. 18,419, seat of Cumberland Co., S Pennsylvania, 18 mi/29 km SW of Harrisburg. Laid out in

1751, it saw the signing of several Indian treaties. Carlisle was the site of a provincial fort during the French and Indian War. A supply point during the Revolution, it was the home of Molly Pitcher, who is buried here. It also served as military headquarters during the Whiskey Rebellion (1794). An active station on the Underground Railroad, Carlisle was occupied briefly by Confederate troops in 1863. Today its economy is based on a wide variety of light manufacturing. It was the site of a noted Indian school (1879–1918) attended by Jim Thorpe, has long been the seat of Dickinson College (1773), and is home to the US Army War College, which moved here in 1951.

Carlsbad 1. city, pop. 63,126, San Diego Co., SW California, 32 mi/51 km N of San Diego, on the Pacific Ocean. It was settled and named after the Bohemian resort in 1880 when water from local springs was found to have a mineral content similar to that of one of the European spa's wells. It became a beach and health resort, with commercial flower growing and fruit and vegetable industries. Carlsbad Beach State park is just S, and the US Grand Prix of Motocross is held here annually. The city has more than quadrupled in pop. since 1970, and now also has a sizable electronics industry. **2.** city, pop. 24,952, seat of Eddy Co., SE New Mexico, on the Pecos R., 30 mi/48 km N of the Texas border. In a potash mining region, it is also at the center of a large irrigation district. Cotton, alfalfa, wool, oil, and livestock are shipped. CARLSBAD CAVERNS is 19 mi/30 km SW. New Mexico State University has a branch (1950) here.

Carlsbad Caverns one of the largest known networks of underground caves, in 47,000-ac/18,900-ha Carlsbad Caverns National Park, in the foothills of the GUADALUPE Mts., 19 mi/30 km SW of Carlsbad, in SE New Mexico. The chambers, up to at least 1100 ft/335 m below the surface, were created by water intruding into and dissolving portions of a vast Permian limestone reef; one covers nearly 14 ac/5.7 ha, reaching over 250 ft/76 m in height and containing ornate stalactites, stalagmites, draperies, and other formations. Bat Cave, a natural entrance to the caverns "discovered" in the 1880s, and famous for its huge bat pop., contains ancient pictographs, and was in the early 20th century the site of a guano mining operation. Recently discovered Lechuguilla Caverns, 4 mi/6 km W, is thought to be the deepest cave in the US. The controversial Federal Waste Isolation Pilot Plant (WIPP) has proposed burying nuclear waste in underground salt beds nearby.

Carlstadt borough, pop. 5510, Bergen Co., NE New Jersey, 3 mi/5 km SE of Passaic, on the Hackensack R. In the late 19th century, it was a cooperative, purchased from its original settlers by exiled German liberals. Today Carlstadt is a highly industrialized municipality, manufacturing such products as surgical supplies, chemicals, clothing, textiles, and processed food.

Carmacks village, pop. 243, SW Yukon Territory, on the KLONDIKE HIGHWAY, at the confluence of the Nordenskiold R. with the Yukon R., 85 mi/137 km NNW of Whitehorse. Named for one of the discoverers of BONANZA CREEK (Klondike) gold, it is a former coal mining settlement and riverboat stop, now primarily a highway service community.

Carmel 1. or, **Mount Carmel** name given numerous American churches, communities, and localities. It recalls a verdant ridge in N Israel, known for its vineyards and groves, and the refuge of early Christian hermits. It is associated particularly with the prophet Elijah's challenge (I Kings 18) to the prophets of Baal: After repairing an altar with 12 stones, representing Israel's tribes, Elijah saw his offering consumed by heavenly fire; Baal's prophets were thereafter killed en masse. **2.** city, pop. 25,380, Hamilton Co., C Indiana, 15 mi/24 km N of downtown Indianapolis. Formerly an agricultural trade center, it is now a fast-growing residential and commercial suburb just outside Route 465, the Indianapolis beltway. **3.** town, pop. 28,816, seat of Putnam Co., SE New York, 21 mi/34 km SE of Newburgh. In a lake- and reservoir-dotted region, it has long been a summer resort area, and is now home to many commuting to New York City, 35 mi/56 km to the S. Railroad magnate Daniel Drew (1797–1879) was born here. L. Mahopac is in Carmel; the village of Lake Carmel is in Kent township (N).

Carmel-by-the-Sea also, **Carmel** city, pop. 4239, Monterey Co., WC California, at the S of the MONTEREY PENINSULA, on the Carmel R. and Carmel Bay, 3 mi/5 km SSW of Monterey. Until the 1900s, when it became a popular artists' and writers' retreat, Carmel was a village in a cattle grazing area. After World War II, it became increasingly a tourist magnet, and is now home to the wealthy and prominent. Its noted residents have included poet Robinson Jeffers, whose Tor House, with the stone tower he built and wrote in, is S of the city center; photographers Ansel Adams and Edward Weston; and actor Clint Eastwood, who was elected mayor in 1986. Franciscan missionary Junípero Serra is buried at San Carlos Borromeo del Río Carmelo Mission (1771). PEBBLE BEACH is just NW, Point LOBOS just S.

Carmichael unincorporated community, pop. 48,702, Sacramento Co., NC California, 7 mi/11 km ENE of downtown Sacramento. Founded in 1910, it was named for its developer, who created a residential and agricultural community. Many residents work in local aircraft plants.

Carnegie borough, pop. 9278, Allegheny Co., in the Chartiers Valley of SW Pennsylvania, 7 mi/11 km SW of Pittsburgh. Named for steel magnate Andrew Carnegie, it is a center of steel and steel byproduct manufacture. Its industries also produce a number of other goods.

Carnegie Hall complex of concert halls and studios at 57th St. and 7th Ave., Manhattan, New York City, opened in 1891 and traditionally the goal of any musician, especially a classical performer. Its main hall (almost 2800 seats) and the smaller Weil Recital Hall were renovated in the mid 1980s.

Carney unincorporated village, pop. 25,578, Baltimore Co., N Maryland, 8 mi/13 km NE of Baltimore. Once at the end of a city streetcar line, it is a primarily residential suburb.

Carnifex Ferry see under SUMMERSVILLE, West Virginia.

Carnot-Moon unincorporated community, pop. 10,187, in Moon township, Allegheny Co., SW Pennsylvania, comprising adjacent residential suburbs, 8 mi/13 km W of Pittsburgh. Greater Pittsburgh International Airport is just SW.

Carol City unincorporated community, pop. 53,331, Dade Co., SE Florida, 5 mi/8 km NNE of Hialeah, part of the Miami suburban area. Joe Robbie Stadium is just NE.

Carolina unincorporated community (ZONA URBANA), pop. 162,404, Carolina Municipio (pop. 177,806), NE Puerto Rico, immediately E of San Juan, on the Atlantic Ocean (N). Essentially a residential and commercial suburb, it is a center for the processing of sugar and tobacco and for textile manufacturing. The San Juan (Luis Muñoz Marín) International Airport is in the Isla Verde section, near the ocean.

Carolina has been developed largely since the 1950s. It is the birthplace of baseball great Roberto Clemente (1934–72).

Carolina bay any of thousands of oval, NW–SE oriented depressions found in sedimentary formations along the SE US coastline, esp. in North Carolina. Typically some 50 mi/80 km inland, they range from a few acres to several square miles, and may be lakes, swamps, or both. They are associated with rich, forested soil. The origin of Carolina bays is unclear.

Carolina Slate Belt see under the PIEDMONT.

Caroline County 535 sq mi/1386 sq km, pop. 19,217, in E Virginia. Its seat is Bowling Green. Caroline Co. is largely rural; the Fort A.P. Hill Military Reservation occupies much of its N, along the Rappahannock R.

Carol Stream village, pop. 31,716, Du Page Co., NE Illinois, a residential suburb 27 mi/43 km W of Chicago. It and the adjacent (S) community of WHEATON have been called the "Protestant Vatican of the Midwest" because of the many Evangelical Christians who live and study here.

Carondelet former municipality in what is now the southernmost part of SAINT LOUIS, Missouri. The first successful US public kindergarten was established here in 1873 by educational pioneer Susan Blow. The largely residential area, on the R. des Peres (SW) and the Mississippi R. (SE), is dominated by Carondelet Park.

Carpentersville village, pop. 23,049, Kane Co., NE Illinois, on the Fox R., a suburb 3 mi/5 km N of ELGIN and 38 mi/61 km NW of Chicago. Originally a community of dairy and grain farms, it later came to produce plowshares and steel specialties. The village has recently become increasingly residential.

Carpinteria city, pop. 13,747, Santa Barbara Co., SW California, 12 mi/19 km SE of Santa Barbara, on the Santa Barbara Channel of the Pacific Ocean. It was founded in 1863 on the site of an Indian village and asphalt pits. The city ships citrus fruit, beans, olives, and walnuts. Carpinteria State Beach is well known.

Carrboro town, pop. 11,553, Orange Co., NC North Carolina, adjacent (SW) to Chapel Hill. Wool and lumber mills have been important here, and the town is also a residential suburb.

Carrick residential neighborhood on the S side of Pittsburgh, Pennsylvania, on the S slope of Mt. Washington, 3.5 mi/6 km S of the GOLDEN TRIANGLE. Around the turn of the century, this middle-class area housed some of the city's elite.

Carrizo Plain NW–SE oriented basin, about 8 mi/13 km wide and 50 mi/80 km long, lying along the W of the SAN ANDREAS FAULT, in San Luis Obispo Co., WC California. The Temblor Range and the San Joaquin Valley lie E, the La Panza and Caliente ranges W. A largely unvegetated area sacred to the Chumash, and subject to frequent earthquakes, it has the seasonal Soda L. in its C. The Nature Conservancy has bought large parts of the plain, which is a refuge for sandhill cranes, bald eagles, and many other species.

Carroll **1.** city, pop. 9579, seat of Carroll Co., WC Iowa. It is an agricultural trade and processing center that also manufactures farm machinery. **2.** village, pop. 545, Fairfield Co., C Ohio, 19 mi/31 km SE of Columbus, in an agricultural district. Tool manufacture is a local industry. World heavyweight boxing champion James A. Jeffries was born here (1875).

Carroll County 452 sq mi/1171 sq km, pop. 123,372, in NC Maryland, bounded NW by the MONOCACY R. and N by Pennsylvania, and drained by branches of the PATAPSCO R. Its seat is WESTMINSTER. Dairy, poultry, and livestock farming are important in this PIEDMONT county; agricultural products include corn, wheat, barley, and hay. Baltimore's NW suburbs reach into SE Carroll Co.

Carroll Gardens residential section, NW Brooklyn, New York. Part of old South Brooklyn or Red Hook, it owes its name, adopted in the 1960s, to the gardens in deep-front house lots established by an 1840s planner, Richard Butts, and to Charles Carroll and Maryland troops who fought in nearby GOWANUS in 1776. The area is largely Italian, with a smattering of artists and other professionals.

Carrollton **1.** city, pop. 16,029, seat of Carroll Co., NW Georgia, 38 mi/61 km WSW of Atlanta. Settled in the 1820s, it has always been a trade and processing center for the region's agriculture. Local industries turn out textiles, wire and metal products, and sound recordings. West Georgia College (1933) is here. **2.** largely residential section of SW (UPTOWN) New Orleans, Louisiana, along the Mississippi R., 3 mi/5 km W of Jackson Square. Settled after the War of 1812, it was connected with New Orleans by rail in 1835, and in 1874 became part of the city. Tulane and Loyola universities and AUDUBON PARK lie in the S, Xavier University just N. **3.** also, **Carrollton Manor** 18th-century estate near FREDERICK, Maryland, established by Charles Carroll, land agent to Lord Baltimore. Its name was used by his grandson, Charles Carroll of Carrollton (1737–1832), signer of the Declaration of Independence, and reappears in various Maryland sites. **4.** city, pop. 82, 169, Denton and Dallas counties, NE Texas, 15 mi/24 km NNW of downtown Dallas. Established in 1872 on the Missouri, Kansas & Texas Railroad, after an 1844 founding slightly SE, it was chiefly agricultural until the 1960s, but has doubled in population as a residential suburb each decade since.

Carson city, pop. 83,995, Los Angeles Co., SW California, 13 mi/21 km S of downtown Los Angeles. Oil refining is the chief industry of this industrial suburb; fabricated metals and paper products are manufactured. Carson is the seat of a major branch of California State University (Dominguez Hills, 1960).

Carson City independent city and state capital, pop. 40,443, W Nevada, on the E of L. TAHOE, 30 mi/48 km S of Reno. Named for frontiersman Kit Carson, it was founded as Eagle Station (1858), a trading post for California goldfield prospectors, and prospered after the 1859 COMSTOCK LODE silver strike, 15 mi/24 km NE. It became a terminus for the Virginia and Truckee Railroad, and was named state capital in 1864. It was the site of a US MINT branch (1870–93), now occupied by the State Museum. The city has become a year-round resort. In addition to government, gambling, tourism, some local mining, and the trading of livestock, the products of the surrounding irrigated farming region are now economically important.

Carson National Forest 1.4 million ac/567,000 ha (2190 sq mi/5670 sq km), in N New Mexico. Its three separate sections flank the upper Rio Grande, and include parts of the Sangre de Cristo (E) and San Juan (W) mountains. The forest contains ski resorts around TAOS (its headquarters), where its namesake Kit Carson lived in the mid 19th century. WHEELER PEAK, New Mexico's high point, is here.

Carson River c.170 mi/275 km long, in NE California and W

Nevada. Its East and West forks rise on the E of the Carson Range of the Sierra Nevada, in Toiyabe National Forest, flow N into Nevada's Carson Valley, and meet E of L. Tahoe, near GENOA. The Carson then flows NNE past Carson City, and turns ENE. Fifteen mi/24 km W of Fallon it is impounded by the Lahontan Dam (1915), which creates 23 mi/37 km–long Lahontan Reservoir. The dam is named for the glacial L. Lahontan, which covered much of NW Nevada and NE California, and whose remnants include the BLACK ROCK DESERT and PYRAMID and WALKER lakes. Northeast of Fallon, the river disappears into the shallow, marshy S end of the **Carson Sink,** another remnant. Intermittently dry, the SINK is c.20 mi/32 km NE–SW and 15 mi/24 km wide. Between the Stillwater Range (E) and Trinity Range (W), it was a formidable barrier to California-bound travelers on the Emigrant Trail. Since its damming, the Carson has been central to NW Nevada agriculture.

Carswell Air Force Base see under FORT WORTH, Texas.

Carteret borough, pop. 19,025, Middlesex Co., NE New Jersey, on the Arthur Kill and the Rahway R., opposite Staten I., New York. This highly industrialized community refines oil and smelts copper, has boiler shops and steel mills, and manufactures chemicals, fertilizer, paints and varnishes, textiles, and tobacco products.

Carter's Grove historic site just NW of WILLIAMSBURG, York Co., SE Virginia, an 18th-century plantation on land purchased by Robert "King" Carter, one of the most powerful of Colonial planters. Its 1750 manor house was built by his grandson, Carter Burwell. Also on the site are the remains of Wolstenholme Towne, a settlement founded in 1619 by colonists from JAMESTOWN, and destroyed in an Indian uprising on March 22, 1622.

Cartersville city, pop. 12,035, seat of Bartow Co., NW Georgia, on the Etowah R., 35 mi/56 km NW of Atlanta. It is known as the location (6 mi/10 km S) of the Etowah Mounds, a Mississippian (Temple Mound) site dating to A.D. 1000. Local iron ore and mineral deposits stimulated an industry that produced ammunition during the Civil War. Textiles are an important base for the modern economy.

Carterville city, pop. 3630, Williamson Co., S Illinois, 3 mi/5 km SW of HERRIN and just N of Crab Orchard L., in an area heavily strip-mined for bituminous coal. It is the seat of John A. Logan College (1967).

Carthage **1.** city, pop. 2657, seat of Hancock Co., WC Illinois, 14 mi/23 km E of Keokuk, Iowa. An agricultural trading center, it was laid out in 1833. In Old Carthage, now open to the public, Mormon founder Joseph Smith and his brother were murdered by a mob (June 17, 1844). **2.** city, pop. 10,747, seat of Jasper Co., SW Missouri, on the Spring R., 14 mi/23 km NE of Joplin. Site of a Civil War battle (July 5, 1861), it was virtually destroyed during the conflict and rebuilt afterward. The city is known for its quarries, which produce a fine gray marble that has been used in major buildings throughout the US, including Macy's department store in New York City. In an agriculturally rich livestock raising and lead and zinc mining region, it manufactures food products and is a commercial and shipping center. **3.** town, pop. 2386, seat of Smith Co., NC Tennessee, on the Cumberland R. where the Caney Fork R. joins it, 45 mi/72 km E of Nashville. This tobacco market town, founded in 1804, also makes cheese, and is known as the home of Albert Gore, Jr., US vice-president. The Cordell Hull Dam, which forms Cordell Hull L. on the Cumberland, is 2 mi/3 km N.

Carthay Circle see under WILSHIRE Blvd., Los Angeles, California.

Cary town, pop. 43,858, Wake Co., EC North Carolina, 8 mi/13 km WSW of Raleigh, on US 1. This technological boom town, which doubled in size in the decade 1980–90, has laboratories and plants developing computer systems and software. It also produces chemicals and tobacco goods.

Casa de Oro–Mount Helix unincorporated community, pop. 30,727, San Diego Co., SW California, 2 mi/3 km S of El Cajon and adjacent (N) to Spring Valley. It is a growing suburb 12 mi/19 km E of downtown San Diego.

Casa Grande city, pop. 19,082, Pinal Co., SC Arizona, 45 mi/72 km SSE of Phoenix. A health resort and trade center, it is surrounded by irrigated farms and ranches producing cotton, alfalfa, grain, and livestock. The settlement was named for an excavated 14th-century Hohokam PUEBLO in the **Casa Grande Ruins National Monument,** 20 mi/32 km NE. Copper, gold, and silver mines are nearby.

Casa Loma 98-room mansion on Davenport Ridge, 4 mi/6 km NNW of downtown TORONTO, Ontario. Built (1911–14) as Sir Henry Pellatt's private residence, it has since the 1930s been a popular museum and public resort.

Cascade-Fairwood unincorporated community, pop. 30,107, King Co., WC Washington, a residential and commercial suburb 13 mi/21 km SE of downtown Seattle, adjacent (SE) to Renton.

Cascade Heights residential section of Atlanta, Georgia, 3 mi/5 km SW of FIVE POINTS and just SW of the West End, an affluent, largely black community.

Cascade Range over 700 mi/1100 km N–S and 30–120 mi/50–190 km wide, extending N from Lassen Peak in California, (or, in other definitions, from the FEATHER R. area) through Oregon and Washington, to the Fraser R. in S British Columbia, where it is continued N by the COAST Mts. Running parallel to and about 100–150 mi/160–240 km E of the Pacific Ocean, the Cascades block moist coastal winds from reaching the interior. Between them and the ocean or elements of the Coast Ranges (W) lie Oregon's WILLAMETTE Valley and Washington's PUGET SOUND. The Columbia R. is the only major river to have cut through the Cascades. The range is heavily wooded. Mts. RAINIER, SAINT HELENS, SHASTA, ADAMS, HOOD, JEFFERSON, Saint Helena, and others are volcanic. LASSEN PEAK (1914–21) and Mt. St. Helens (1980) have erupted recently; Mt. BAKER steamed heavily in 1975. Mt. Rainier (14,410 ft/4392 m) is the highest point in the range; Mt. Hood (11,235 ft/3424 m) is the highest point in Oregon.

Casco Bay 200 sq mi/518 sq km, in the Gulf of Maine, running 20 mi/32 km from Cape Elizabeth (SW) to Bald Head on Cape Small (NE). Casco Bay has fine protected deepwater anchorage, which led to Portland's maritime importance. It also has ledges, shoals, knobs, and 222 islands, several heavily wooded, some with tall cliffs, many uninhabited. The larger islands have summer colonies, hotels, and some year-round residential communities. Peaks I., a residential Portland neighborhood reached by ferry, was a major playground for the 19th-century elite. Cliff I. was once home to the smuggler and pirate Capt. Keiff. Great Diamond, Hog, and House islands have abandoned forts. Ragged I. was a summer home of Edna St. Vincent Millay. Eagle I. was the summer home of Admiral Robert E. Peary. Other islands include Bailey and ORRS, in Harpswell town, and Great Chebeague, in Cumberland town. In addition to Peaks, Cliff, and Great Diamond, several other islands, including Cushing and Jewell, are parts of the city of Portland. Long I., pop. 160, seceded from Portland and became a town in 1993. The Casco Bay islands have long been popularly known as the "Calendar Islands," from the mistaken belief there are 365.

Casey Jones Museum State Park see under VAUGHAN, Mississippi.

Casper city, pop. 46,742, seat of Natrona Co., EC Wyoming, on the North Platte R., 145 mi/233 km NW of Cheyenne, the only other large city in the state. It originated as a ferry site (1847) operated by Mormons on the OREGON TRAIL. A fort was erected to protect westward-bound travelers (1863), and the arrival of the North Western Railroad (1888) sparked official founding of the town (1889). The community has been in the oil business since the enormous Salt Creek Oilfield opened in the 1890s. The nearby TEAPOT DOME oilfield was the center of a national scandal in the early 1920s. Oil and natural gas refining continue to be Casper's main industries. Others include shipping and wholesaling livestock and agricultural products, and servicing the local mining of uranium, coal, and bentonite. The city is also a financial and medical center. Casper College (1945) and the Tate Earth Science and Mineralogical Museum are here.

Cass Corridor commercial and residential area in Detroit, Michigan, along Cass Ave., which runs NNW from COBO HALL, between Downtown and the Wayne State University area (N). Home to the addicted and the unemployed, along with artists and the university community, Cass Corridor contains everything from restored Victorian homes to flophouses.

Cass County 1767 sq mi/4577 sq km, pop. 102,874, in E North Dakota, bordered by the Red R. of the North and the Minnesota line, and drained by the Sheyenne, Rush, and Maple rivers. Its seat is FARGO, which influences the economy of the state's most populous county. Most of Cass Co. is a rich agricultural area.

Casselberry city, pop. 18,911, Seminole Co., C Florida, 8 mi/13 km NE of Orlando, a residential suburb and retirement community set among lakes.

Cassiar Mountains NW–SE trending range on NW British Columbia's interior plateau, paralleling (W) the Rocky Mts. The Stikine Ranges (to 9055 ft/2760 m) run along the W. To the SE, the Omineca Mts. continue along the W of Williston L. The area is a Tahltan homeland, site of fur trading with whites since the 1830s, and of an 1870s gold rush. Some mining, hunting, trapping, and logging continues here today.

Cass Lake see under CHIPPEWA NATIONAL FOREST, Minnesota.

Cass River 80 mi/128 km long, in EC Michigan. It is formed near Cass City in Tuscola Co. by headstreams rising in Sanilac and Huron counties, and flows W and SW past Caro, Vassar, and Frankenmuth to the Saginaw R. S of Saginaw. The river is named after Lewis Cass (1782–1866), governor of the Michigan Territory and secretary of war under Andrew Jackson.

Castillo de San Marcos see under SAINT AUGUSTINE, Florida.

Castine town, pop. 1161, Hancock Co., SC Maine. It lies on a peninsula between the Bagaduce and Penobscot rivers, at the head of Penobscot Bay, 28 mi/45 km S of Bangor. On the site was a 1629 British trading post called Pentagoet, which was attacked by the French in 1631 and 1635. A French Capuchin mission was established by the 1640s. Pentagoet was later regained by the British, seized by the French, and held by Dutch pirates. The Baron de St. Castin controlled it, with Indian help, from 1673 to 1701. In 1779 the British took Castine, and held it to 1783, fending off an attack led by Paul Revere. The town was occupied by the British one more time, during the War of 1812. Forts George and Madison are here, as is the Maine Maritime Academy (1941). Inhabitants include retirees, fishermen, and commuters to Bangor and Bucksport.

Castle Air Force Base see under ATWATER, California.

Castleberry Hill commercial and residential district of downtown Atlanta, Georgia, just W of FIVE POINTS, along railroad tracks. A mid-19th-century warehousing (esp. cotton) center, it has recently become a loft district, housing artists and other redevelopers. The OMNI and the GEORGIA DOME lie just N.

Castle Clinton historic structure at the Battery, Manhattan, New York City. A fort built 1808–11, it became Castle Garden, a popular recreational site, in 1824. From 1855 to 1890, New York State operated its main immigrant landing facility at Castle Garden, welcoming about 8 million aliens. After 1892, immigrants landed at the federal ELLIS I. Castle Garden is now the Castle Clinton National Monument.

Castle Dome Mountains range in SW Arizona, extending NW–SE for c.30 mi/50 km, reaching 3788 ft/1155 m at Castle Dome Peak, 40 mi/64 km NE of Yuma. This dry, rugged volcanic range, SW of the KOFA Mts., is largely within the Kofa National Wildlife Refuge.

Castlegar city, pop. 6579, Central Kootenay Regional District, SE British Columbia, on the Columbia R., near the mouth of the Kootenay R., 248 mi/399 km E of Vancouver and 21 mi/34 km N of the Washington border. A trade center in a lumbering and mining region, is noted for its Doukhobor Heritage Village, which commemorates the Russian sect's settlement here (1908–24).

Castle Garden see under CASTLE CLINTON, New York.

Castle Hills city, pop. 4198, Bexar Co., SC Texas, a residential enclave on Route 410 (the beltway), entirely surrounded by NC SAN ANTONIO.

Castle Island peninsular park at the E extreme of City Point, SOUTH BOSTON, Massachusetts. Its site was once of strategic importance in the protection of BOSTON HARBOR; remains of Fort Independence (1801–80) may be seen.

Castle Pinckney see under CHARLESTON, South Carolina.

Castle Rock city, pop. 8708, seat of Douglas Co. (pop. 60,391), NC Colorado, 25 mi/40 km SSE of Denver. Named for a landmark eroded formation now visible along I-25, it is an agricultural service center becoming the hub of a fast-growing suburban area halfway between Denver and Colorado Springs (S).

Castle Rock Butte 3741 ft/1141 m, in Butte Co., WC South Dakota, just N of the community of Castle Rock and very near the geographical center of the US.

Castle Rock Lake also, **Castle Rock Flowage** in Adams and Juneau counties, SC Wisconsin. It is 12 mi/19 km long and 4 mi/6 km wide, with a 5 mi/8 km–long thumb on its W side. It was created by a hydroelectric dam on the Wisconsin R., 17 mi/27 km N of the DELLS.

Castle Shannon borough, pop. 9135, Allegheny Co., SW

Pennsylvania, a residential suburb 6 mi/10 km S of downtown Pittsburgh.

Castleton town, pop. 4278, Rutland Co., WC Vermont. It is on L. Bomoseen, 10 mi/16 km W of Rutland. The town has fine examples of 19th-century architecture, and is home to Castleton State College, which began as a grammar school in 1787. Industries produce slate, lumber, and fruit.

Castro, the residential and commercial section of C SAN FRANCISCO, California, E of Twin Peaks, at the SW end of Market St. and NW of the Mission District. Formerly known as Eureka Valley, a N counterpart to NOE VALLEY, and populated by middle-class Irish families, it became in the 1970s the center of the city's gay community; the career of city supervisor Harvey Milk (assassinated in 1978), the "Mayor of Castro St.," was emblematic of the creation of a gay community and power base here.

Castro Valley unincorporated community, pop. 48,619, Alameda Co., NC California, 8 mi/13 km SE of Oakland. It is primarily a residential suburb.

Cataño unincorporated community (ZONA URBANA) and MUNICIPIO, pop. 34,587, NE Puerto Rico, on the S shore of the Bahía de San Juan (San Juan Bay) opposite Old San Juan. An industrial suburb, it is a processing center for local sugar, fruits, and corn, and the site of a large rum distillery. Tourism is also important.

Cataraqui River 70 mi/110 km long, in SE Ontario. Rising in Rideau L., it winds generally SW to L. Ontario at KINGSTON (formerly Cataraqui), forming part of the RIDEAU CANAL system.

Catawba Reservation see under ROCK HILL, South Carolina.

Catawba River c.300 mi/480 km long, in North Carolina and South Carolina. It rises in the Blue Ridge Mts. just E of the town of BLACK MOUNTAIN, North Carolina, and is joined by a North Fork just NNE of Marion, then flows through 14 mi/23 km–long, dam-created L. James. Passing MORGANTON, it enters 15 mi/24 km–long L. Rhodhiss, followed by L. Hickory (to the N of HICKORY), Lookout Shoals L., and 32,500-ac/13,200-ha L. Norman, all impounded by dams. At the S end of L. Norman, next to the Cowans Ford Dam, is the McGuire nuclear power plant (1981). The river continues S past BELMONT, W of the Charlotte area, and into L. Wylie, created by the Catawba Dam near Fort Mill, South Carolina, which extends about 20 mi/32 km back into North Carolina. In South Carolina the river flows generally S past Rock Hill, passing the site of the Catawba nuclear plant (1985), to Great Falls, below which it is known as the **Wateree R.** The Wateree continues another 75 mi/120 km generally SSE. It is dammed 8 mi/13 km NW of Camden to form 14,000-ac/5670-ha **Wateree L.,** then continues to join the CONGAREE R. 30 mi/48 km SE of Columbia, forming the SANTEE R. The Catawba takes its name from a South Carolina tribe that still lives in the Rock Hill area; Wateree is another tribal name. The Catawba-Wateree is a major source of hydroelectric power.

Catfish Row see under CHARLESTON, South Carolina.

Cathedral City city, pop. 30,085, Riverside Co., S California, 6 mi/10 km SE of Palm Springs, in the Coachella Valley, on the Whitewater R. Named for Cathedral Canyon (S), for which it was once a gateway hamlet, it is a rapidly growing desert retirement and residential community.

Cathedral Heights residential and commercial neighborhood in NW Washington, D.C., around the Washington National Cathedral (Episcopalian; completed 1990), at Massachusetts and Wisconsin avenues. The Cathedral's tower is the District's highest point. EMBASSY ROW is just SE.

Cathedral of Learning see under PITTSBURGH, Pennsylvania.

Cathedral Pines name in various localities for groves whose closeness and natural self-pruning habit perhaps led them to be regarded as having both architectural and spiritual qualities. Two noted examples are the Bowdoin or Cathedral Pines just E of the Bowdoin College campus in BRUNSWICK, Maine, and the Cathedral or Calhoun Pines 5 mi/8 km S of Cornwall, Connecticut. Contrary to popular belief, these trees are not "virgin"; pines succeed quickly in OLD FIELDS, and may grow thick and straight. The Cathedral Woods on MONHEGAN I., Maine, are an example involving spruce, and may owe their name in part to the silence in their midst.

Cathedral Range NW–SE subrange of the SIERRA NEVADA, in Yosemite National Park, along the border of Tuolumne with Mariposa and Madera counties, in EC California. **Cathedral Peak,** 15 mi/24 km WSW of Mono L., is the high point at 10,933 ft/3335 m. The RITTER RANGE continues to the SE.

Catlettsburg city, pop. 2231, seat of Boyd Co., extreme NE Kentucky, 2 mi/3 km S of Ashland. Founded as a trading post in 1808, it is an oil refining and manufacturing city situated where Ohio, Kentucky, and West Virginia meet, at the junction of the Ohio and Big Sandy rivers.

Cato town, pop. 1503, Manitowoc Co., EC Wisconsin, 10 mi/16 km W of Manitowoc. Economist and author Thorstein Veblen was born here in 1857.

Catoctin Mountain NE prong of the BLUE RIDGE, located primarily in Maryland. The elevation, which ranges in height from c.1900 ft/580 m in the N to c.500 ft/152 m in the S, extends SSW for c.37 mi/60 km from S of the Pennsylvania border near Thurmont, Maryland, to near Leesburg, in N Virginia. CAMP DAVID is within Catoctin Mt. Park (5770 ac/2340 ha). SOUTH Mt. is the NW prong of the Blue Ridge.

Catonsville unincorporated village, pop. 35,233, Baltimore Co., C Maryland, immediately SW of Baltimore. Founded by Quakers in the 1720s, the settlement was known as Johnnycake, after a local inn, until 1800. Catonsville is a primarily residential suburb, with some light industry; manufactures include electrical, chemical, and cotton duck products. The Baltimore County Campus of the University of Maryland (1963) and a community college are here. Catonsville gained national recognition when a group of Vietnam War protesters, subsequently known as the Catonsville Nine, burned records of the local draft board in 1968.

Catoosa see under TULSA, Oklahoma.

Catskill village, pop. 4690, in Catskill town, seat of Greene Co., SE New York, on the W bank of the Hudson R., where Catskill Creek joins it, across from HUDSON and 32 mi/52 km S of Albany. Settled by the Dutch in the 17th century, it was supposedly close to the site of Rip Van Winkle's long snooze. It once had tanneries, knitting mills, brickyards, and distilleries, and during Prohibition was a bootlegging center. Catskill now has small businesses and light industry, and is an agricultural trade and distribution center. The village has long been considered the gateway to the Catskill Mts. and the Catskill Forest Preserve (W).

Catskill Creek 40 mi/64 km long, in E New York. It rises in E Schoharie Co., and flows generally SE through Greene Co. to its confluence with KAATERSKILL CREEK at Cauterskill, just W of CATSKILL village, then joins the Hudson R. It is sometimes referred to as the dividing line between the Helderbergs to the NE and the Catskill Mts. to the SW.

Catskill Mountains part of the E edge of the Appalachian Highlands, in SE New York, W of the Hudson R. The heavily wooded Catskills rise to an average of 3000–4000 ft/900–1200 m. The area around Ellenville, Monticello, and Kiamesha Lake, in the SW, was the enormously popular BORSCHT BELT. The rich soil of the Catskill valleys is farmed. The highest Catskill peaks are Slide Mt. (4204 ft/1282 m) and Hunter Mt. (4040 ft/1232 m). Catskill Park and Forest Preserve covers some 650,000 ac/263,000 ha.

Cattaraugus County 1306 sq mi/3383 sq km, pop. 84,234, in SW New York, along the Pennsylvania border (S). Its seat is Little Valley. It is predominantly agricultural; there are oil wells in the S, which adjoins Pennsylvania's oilfields, as well as some industry, particularly in and around OLEAN, the biggest city. Allegany State Park is in the SC part of the county, S of the Allegheny R., which runs through the Allegany Indian Reservation. The Seneca Iroquois National Museum is in the city of Salamanca (pop. 6566), in the center of the reservation. The Cattaraugus (Seneca) Indian Reservation is in the NW part of the county, on Cattaraugus Creek.

Cattaraugus Creek 70 mi/113 km long, in W New York. It rises in S Wyoming Co., then flows SW and W through the Cattaraugus Indian Reservation, emptying into L. Erie at Sunset Bay. The reservation is home to approximately 2400 Seneca, and was established by the Pickering Treaty in 1794.

Caubvick, Mount see under TORNGAT Mts., Labrador.

Caughnawaga see KAHNAWAKE, Québec.

Cavendish see under GREEN GABLES, Prince Edward Island.

Cave Spring unincorporated community, pop. 24,053, Roanoke Co., W Virginia, adjacent (SW) to Roanoke. It is a largely residential suburb.

Cawsons see under HOPEWELL, Virginia.

Cayce **1.** hamlet in Fulton Co., extreme SW Kentucky, 85 mi/137 km WSW of Hopkinsville. The community where John Luther "Casey" Jones moved in his youth gave him his nickname. The railroad engineer was born in 1864, probably in nearby Jordan, and died in the famous 1900 crash near VAUGHAN, Mississippi. **2.** city, pop. 11,163, Lexington Co., C South Carolina, SSW of Columbia across the Congaree R. A manufacturing center, it makes cement blocks, steel, chemicals, iron and brass, plastics, wood products, and processed foods.

Cayey unincorporated community (ZONA URBANA), pop. 23,332, Cayey Municipio (pop. 46,553), SE Puerto Rico, in the Sierra de Cayey, 24 mi/39 km S of San Juan. It lies in a tobacco producing region and is a cigarmaking and sugar and alcohol processing center, and a summer resort.

Cayuga see under HALDIMAND, Ontario.

Cayuga, Lake longest of the FINGER LAKES in WC New York, lying between Seneca L. (W) and Owasco L. (E), 25 mi/40 km SW of Syracuse. It is 38 mi/61 km long N–S, 2 mi/3 km wide, and 435 ft/133 m deep. ITHACA is at the S end. It is the only Finger Lake that extends N as marshland; the Montezuma Marshes are an extensive region of bogs and ponds, under Federal protection as the Montezuma National Wildlife Refuge. Taughannock Falls, on the SW shore of Cayuga, drop 215 ft/658 m.

Cazenovia town, pop. 6514, Madison Co., C New York, at the SE corner of Cazenovia L., 15 mi/24 km SE of Syracuse. Settled in the 1790s, it was an important stop on the westward turnpike (now Route 20). Its economy relies on agriculture and tourism. Cazenovia College was founded here in 1824. The town is said to be the birthplace of IROQUOIS CONFEDERACY leader Hiawatha.

CDC see CENTERS FOR DISEASE CONTROL AND PREVENTION, Emory, Georgia.

Cecil County 360 sq mi/932 sq km, pop. 71,347, in the NE corner of Maryland. ELKTON is its seat. Cecil Co. is at the head of Chesapeake Bay, bounded S by the Sassafras R., E by Delaware, W by the Susquehanna R., and N by Pennsylvania. It has some manufacturing at Elkton, agriculture, commercial fishing, and quarrying.

Cedar Breaks National Monument 6155 ac/2493 ha, within the DIXIE NATIONAL FOREST, encompassing a gigantic natural amphitheater, 13 mi/21 km E of CEDAR CITY, in SW Utah. Variegated purple, yellow, and red rocks, some 55 million years old, form terraces leading into a deep bowl.

Cedarburg city, pop. 9895, Ozaukee Co., E Wisconsin, on Cedar Creek, 17 mi/27 km N of Milwaukee. Settled in 1842, it was a mid-19th-century textile center. Cedarburg now serves the surrounding agricultural area as a trade and processing center. Its manufactures include aluminum castings, plastics, electric motors, auto parts, wire, paper, and wood products.

Cedar City city, pop. 13,443, Iron Co., SW Utah. A tourist center 18 mi/29 km N of the ZION NATIONAL PARK entrance, it is headquarters for the DIXIE NATIONAL FOREST. Lying in a ranching and farming area, it was settled in 1851 and soon became the site of the first iron refining furnace W of the Mississippi, which processed ore from several mines to the W. Coal mines are still active in the region. Lumber mills, brickworks, creameries, and bottling, canning, and meatpacking plants all contribute to the economy. Tourism has been important since the 1920s, with visitors drawn to local parks and forests and to the Utah Shakespearean Festival, held annually. Cedar City is the seat of Southern Utah State College (1897). The Cedar Breaks National Monument is 13 mi/21 km E.

Cedar Creek **1.** 200 mi/322 km long, in SW North Dakota. It rises in Slope Co., and flows E through Bowman and Adams counties. It then forms the boundary between Sioux and Grant counties, before joining the CANNONBALL R., which continues to the Missouri R. **2.** c.20 mi/32 km long, in extreme N Virginia, a tributary flowing SE into the North Fork of the SHENANDOAH R. On it, 20 mi/32 km SW of WINCHESTER, a battle was fought Oct. 19, 1864, in which Union forces defeated Jubal Early's Confederates, who had seemed to have the advantage. Philip Sheridan's return, from a conference in Winchester, to rally his troops, became famous as Sheridan's Ride.

Cedar Falls city, pop. 34,298, Black Hawk Co., NE Iowa, on the Cedar R., immediately W of WATERLOO. Settled in the mid 19th century, it took advantage of waterpower to become a milling center for locally produced grain. The Quaker Oats Company was founded here. Later it became an important rail shipping point for the area's grain, livestock, and lumber. The city is now mainly residential, with some industry, including manufacture of pumps, farm equipment, golf supplies, humidifiers, and air conditioning and heating grilles. The University of Northern Iowa (1876) is here.

Cedar Grove township, pop. 12,053, Essex Co., NE New Jersey, 5 mi/8 km SW of Paterson. Primarily a suburban residential community, it also has numerous office buildings and some light industry. Its manufactures include precision instruments, brushes, and tools.

Cedar Hill city, pop. 19,976, Dallas and Ellis counties, NE Texas, 18 mi/29 km SW of Dallas, on L. Joe Pool (W). Formerly agricultural, it tripled in population during the 1980s as a residential suburb.

Cedarhurst see under FIVE TOWNS, Long Island, New York.

Cedar Lake **1.** town, pop. 8885, Lake Co., extreme NW Indiana, 20 mi/32 km SSW of Gary, near the Illinois line. The lake that gives the town its name was a noted 19th- and early-20th-century resort. The area is increasingly suburban. **2.** also, **Cedar Lake Reservoir** 520 sq mi/1350 sq km, in WC Manitoba, N of L. Winnipegosis. The SASKATCHEWAN R. flows into it from the NW, and drains E into L. WINNIPEG via GRAND RAPIDS, where dams and dikes (1961–64) have raised the lake level, creating a reservoir for hydroelectric power.

Cedar Mountain locality in Culpeper Co., N Virginia, 10 mi/16 km SSW of CULPEPER, the site of a battle fought on Aug. 9, 1862, two weeks after the second battle of BULL RUN. The Confederates under Stonewall Jackson won an inconclusive victory.

Cedar Rapids city, pop. 108,751, seat of Linn Co., EC Iowa, on the Cedar R., 105 mi/169 km NE of Des Moines. Settled in the 1830s by Bohemians, it grew to become the second-largest city in the state, and the leading industrial center of E Iowa. Manufactures include printing presses, avionics equipment, heavy construction machinery, earth moving equipment, milk producing machinery, radio transmitters and receivers, and plastic products. In the heart of the CORN BELT, Cedar Rapids is a distribution and shipping center for its agricultural hinterland. Quaker Oats operates a huge cereal mill here, and corn products, syrup, and popcorn are other items processed. Coe College (1851), Mount Mercy College (1928), and Kirkwood Community College (1966) are here.

Cedar River **1.** see RED CEDAR R., Michigan. **2.** also, **Red Cedar River** 300 mi/483 km long, in Minnesota and Iowa. Non-navigable, it rises in Dodge Co., in SE Minnesota, flows S past Austin, then enters Iowa 42 mi/68 km to the S. It continues generally SE through Iowa past Charles City and through Cedar Falls, Waterloo, and Cedar Rapids to join the Iowa R. at Columbus Junction, 12 mi/19 km W of the Illinois line.

Cedar-Riverside also, **West Bank** neighborhood in Minneapolis, Minnesota, on the Mississippi R., E of Downtown. This formerly working-class Scandinavian area was centered on Cedar Ave., nicknamed "Snoose Boulevard" after the tobacco-chewing habits of the locals. In the 1960s, it emerged as a countercultural and entertainment center famed for its blues bars. Much of this was due to the influence of the nearby University of Minnesota campus.

Cedar Springs city, pop. 2600, Kent Co., W Michigan, on Cedar Creek, 16 mi/26 km NNE of Grand Rapids. Founded in 1859, it is situated in a resort and agricultural area. It has produced flannel and manufactured clothing since 1939, and celebrates Red Flannel Day annually. It is the seat of Jordan College (1967).

Cedartown city, pop. 7978, seat of Polk Co., NW Georgia, 51 mi/82 km WNW of Atlanta, on Cedar Creek. It was founded in 1854 on the site of a Cherokee village. Industries manufacture tire cord fabric, cotton and woolen goods, chemicals, paper products, furniture, agricultural tools, cheese, and vitamins. High-grade iron ore is mined nearby.

Cedarville **1.** village, pop. 751, Stephenson Co., NW Illinois, 5 mi/8 km N of Freeport. An agricultural village, it is the birthplace of social reformer Jane Addams (1860). **2.** village, pop. 3205, Greene Co., SW Ohio, 11 mi/18 km S of Springfield. Growing slowly since settlement (1805), the population received a substantial boost in 1832 when the entire congregation of the Covenanter Church of Chester, South Carolina, moved here. It is the seat of Cedarville College (1887).

Celina city, pop. 9650, seat of Mercer Co., WC Ohio, 27 mi/43 km SW of Lima. It lies on the NW shore of GRAND LAKE ST. MARYS. Well known as a summer resort, Celina is noted for its fishing and hunting. Poultry, dairy cattle, and grain are raised in the area, and building stone is quarried nearby. Manufactures include sheet metal products, furniture, lawnmowers, bicycles, and food products. A campus of Wright State University is here.

Cemetery Ridge see under GETTYSBURG, Pennsylvania.

census designated place (CDP) see UNINCORPORATED COMMUNITY.

Centennial see POWELLHURST-CENTENNIAL, Oregon.

Center City downtown area of Philadelphia, Pennsylvania, between the Delaware and Schuylkill rivers and Vine and South streets. Centered around City Hall and along the axes of BROAD and MARKET streets, it includes all of the Philadelphia laid out in William Penn's 1682 town plan. The W half was not settled by Europeans until the mid 18th century. LOGAN CIRCLE and RITTENHOUSE and WASHINGTON squares are here, along with most of the sites associated with Colonial and Revolutionary history. SOCIETY HILL, OLD CITY, CHINATOWN, and PENN CENTER also form part of the area.

Centereach unincorporated village, pop. 26,720, in Brookhaven town, Suffolk Co., SE New York, on Long Island, 7 mi/11 km SW of Port Jefferson. It is primarily residential.

Center Hill Lake see under CANEY FORK R., Tennessee.

Center Line city, pop. 9026, Macomb Co., SE Michigan, a residential suburb 8 mi/13 km N of Detroit. There is a US arsenal here.

Center Moriches see under MORICHES BAY, New York.

Center Point unincorporated community, pop. 22,658, Jefferson Co., C Alabama, a residential suburb 11 mi/18 km NE of downtown Birmingham.

Centers for Disease Control and Prevention popularly, **CDC** national public health research institution, established in 1973, in EMORY, De Kalb Co., NW Georgia, 5 mi/8 km NE of downtown Atlanta. A division of the US Public Health Service, it conducts research in various areas, particularly the battle against communicable diseases. The phrase "and Prevention" was added to the centers' name in 1992.

Center Valley unincorporated village in Upper Saucon township (pop. 9775), Lehigh Co., EC Pennsylvania, 6 mi/10 km SE of Allentown. It is the seat of Allentown College of St. Francis de Sales (1964).

Centerville **1.** residential village in New Castle Co., extreme N Delaware, on the Pennsylvania border, 7 mi/11 km NW of Wilmington. At 442 ft/135 m, it is the highest point in Delaware. The Henry Francis du Pont Winterthur Museum (1951) and gardens are here. **2.** city, pop. 21,082, Gallia Co., SW Ohio, 10 mi/16 km S of Dayton, of which it is a commuter suburb. **3.** city, pop. 11,500, Davis Co., N Utah, 9 mi/14 km N of Salt Lake City. Settled in 1847, it was named for its position between Salt Lake City and Ogden. This suburb, on the W edge of the Wasatch-Cache National Forest, lies in an agricultural area noted for its cherries and grain.

Central town, pop. 2438, Pickens Co., NW South Carolina, 23 mi/37 km WSW of Greenville, the seat of Central Wesleyan College (1906).

Central Avenue commercial thoroughfare, between downtown LOS ANGELES (N) and the Dominguez Hills in CARSON (S), California. Passing through SOUTH-CENTRAL and WATTS and the city of COMPTON, it has long served as the business artery of the area's black community. In the 1940s its entertainment zone was the West Coast counterpart of Manhattan's SWING (52nd) St. Sections were devastated by riots in 1965 and 1992.

Central Bridge village in Schoharie township, Schoharie Co., EC New York, 21 mi/34 km W of Albany. Inventor George Westinghouse (1846–1914) was born here. Howe Caverns, a series of limestone caves that are a major tourist attraction, are just W.

Central City **1.** city, pop. 335, seat of Gilpin Co., NC Colorado, in the Front Range of the Rocky Mts., on Clear Creek, 30 mi/48 km NW of Denver. It prospered during the 1860s after an 1859 gold strike, its population reaching 15,000. The railroad arrived in 1871, but with depletion of precious metal resources, it was nearly deserted by the early 20th century. The 1932 restoration of its opera house (1861) marked the beginning of Central City's popularity as a tourist attraction. Among its features are an 1867 narrow gauge railway, 19th-century gold mines, and a famous frontier hotel. There has been legalized gambling here since 1991. Central City is also the site of musical events, plays, and a summer opera festival. **2.** city, pop. 2868, seat of Merrick Co., EC Nebraska, on the Platte R., 23 mi/37 km NE of Grand Island. Platted in 1864, it grew as a railroad junction. It is a processing and shipping point for dairy products and grain from the surrounding region. Formerly known as Lone Tree because it grew around a landmark in an otherwise treeless prairie region, it appears in the writing of Wright Morris, born here in 1910.

Central Experimental Farm over 1200 ac/500 ha, on the Rideau Canal (and Dows L.), 2 mi/3 km SSW of Downtown, in OTTAWA, Ontario. Established in 1886, it is the oldest and most important of five experimental farms run by Agriculture Canada (the Federal department of agriculture); the others are in Nappan, Nova Scotia; Brandon, Manitoba; Indian Head, Saskatchewan; and Agassiz, British Columbia. There are also two dozen experimental stations throughout Canada. The Ottawa facility, noted as the headquarters for William and Charles Saunders' pioneering 1900s work on Marquis wheat, key to farm development in the prairie provinces, is also the site of the Dominion Observatory and a well-known arboretum and insectarium.

Central Expressway limited-access highway in Dallas, Texas. Designated Interstate 75, it passes from the city's extreme SE through SOUTH DALLAS, just NE of Downtown, along the E of HIGHLAND PARK and UNIVERSITY PARK, then N through NORTH DALLAS and into Richardson. It was built along the former right of way of the Texas & Central Railroad.

Central Falls city, pop. 17,637, Providence Co., E Rhode Island, adjoining (NW) Pawtucket, on the Blackstone R., between Valley Falls and Pawtucket Falls. Occupying an area of only 1.27 sq mi/3.29 sq km, it claims to be the nation's smallest city. One of the lower Blackstone Valley textile mill towns that boomed in the 19th century, it has now lost most of its industrial base. A federal prison under construction in the 1990s is looked to for economic stabilization.

Central Flyway bird migration route used chiefly by species that winter in Mexico and Central and South America, flying N over the Great Plains at varying distances from the E face of the Rocky Mts., and nesting as far N as the Beaufort Sea.

Centralia **1.** city, pop. 14,274, Clinton and Marion counties, SC Illinois, 55 mi/89 km E of East St. Louis. It is the distribution point for the region's fruit and dairy products. The many oilfields in the area have made the city a center for oil production. Local manufactures include stoves, furnaces, auto parts, fiberglass products, paper, potato chips, and candy. Centralia also has railroad shops, remnants of the Illinois Central Railroad, which founded the town in 1853. Coal mining was an important part of the economy through much of the 20th century. The largest steam locomotive ever built is displayed here. Also in the city is the Centralia Carillon, one of the largest such structures in the world. Centralia is the seat of Kaskaskia College (1940). Carlyle L., a recreation area, is 15 mi/24 km NW. **2.** city, pop. 3414, Boone Co., C Missouri, 23 mi/37 km NE of Columbia. It was founded (1857) on the proposed route of the North Missouri Railroad. During the Civil War (Sept. 27, 1864), in an incident known as the Centralia Massacre, Confederate guerrillas robbed a stagecoach and train here, killing over 20 unarmed Federal soldiers, and later ambushed and destroyed a force of over 100 Union troops. Today the city is a trade center in a grain producing and coal mining region. Among its light manufactures are wood products. **3.** city, pop. 12,101, Lewis Co., SW Washington, at the junction of the Chehalis and Skookumchuck rivers, forming an economic unit with its sister city, Chehalis (S), 25 mi/40 km S of Olympia. Centralia is said to be the only city in the West to have a black founder, George Washington, a former slave, who laid it out in 1875. Midway between Portland and Seattle, it was a stopover point for stagecoaches during its first decades. In 1919, Wesley Everest of the International Workers of the World (Wobblies) was lynched here by American Legionnaires, during labor strife in the lumbering industry. Today, the economy remains largely based on lumber, along with nearby dairy, poultry, and fruit farms. The city is the seat of Centralia College (1925).

Central Islip unincorporated village, pop. 26,028, in Islip town, Suffolk Co., SE New York, in C Long Island, 5 mi/8 km NNE of Bay Shore. A largely residential suburb, it is the site of a hospital for the mentally ill most of whose grounds are under conversion to mixed industrial, commercial, educational, and residential use.

Central Pacific Railroad one of two organizations authorized by President Lincoln in 1862 to undertake construction of the "Pacific Railroad"—the line, long envisioned, that would connect the Atlantic and Pacific oceans. The Central Pacific had its beginnings with the 23 mi/37 km–long Sacramento Valley Railroad, built in the 1850s between Sacramento and Folsom, in California's goldfields. The SVR's builder, Theodore D. Judah, ardently proposed a line E through the

SIERRA NEVADA. He found backers in four Sacramento merchants—Collis P. Huntington, Leland Stanford, Mark Hopkins, and Charles Crocker—later known as the "Big Four." With the Federal promise of grants of PUBLIC LANDS along the route, and loans per mileage completed, the Central Pacific in 1863 began building E through the Sierras (by way of the DONNER PASS), while the UNION PACIFIC began building W from Omaha, Nebraska. Problems retaining workers soon led Crocker, the project's manager, to hire thousands of Chinese laborers—former gold miners, followed by many recruited directly from S China. The initial authorization called for the two railroads to meet at the California-Nevada border, but the Central Pacific in the end built 1170 mi/1885 km of track, meeting the Union Pacific at PROMONTORY, Utah, N of the Great Salt L., where a ceremonial Golden Spike was driven on May 10, 1869. Toward the end, the return-for-mileage formula led the two railroads into a construction race; on April 28, 1869, Central Pacific teams laid a record 10 mi/16 km of track (at a rate of over 80 ft/24 m per minute). Regular service over the completed transcontinental line began immediately. The Central Pacific subsequently bought several small California lines, and in the 1870s built S down the CENTRAL (San Joaquin) VALLEY and through the TEHACHAPI Mts. to Southern California; its story from this time becomes that of the SOUTHERN PACIFIC, with which it was formally merged in 1884.

Central Park urban park, Manhattan, New York City. Conceived in the 1850s and completed in 1873, it was intended to alleviate urban problems by providing open natural (although highly manipulated) space for a growing population. It stretches from 59th to 110th St., and from Fifth Ave. to Central Park West (Eighth Ave.), comprising 840 ac/340 ha. Designed by Frederick Law Olmsted and Calvert Vaux, Central Park set a standard for urban parks in North America. It contains sunken transverse roads, lakes and ponds, skating rinks, a zoo, and various open spaces, such as the Sheep Meadow and the Great Lawn, regularly used for public events. The fate of its reservoir, which covers about one-eighth of the park's area and is obsolete, is under debate. Among Central Park's best-known features are Strawberry Fields, a memorial to John Lennon, who lived nearby, and the Delacorte Theater, site of outdoor Shakespeare performances.

Central Valley **1.** also, **Great Valley, Great Central Valley,** or **California Trough** vast central lowland of California, running some 450 mi/720 km NNW–SSE, between the Sierra Nevada and the Cascade Range (E) and the Coast Ranges (W). Its two sections are also known, after their major rivers, as the **Sacramento Valley** (N) and **San Joaquin Valley** (S). The valley, 50–80 mi/80–130 km wide, is a sediment-filled, flat plain, formerly coastal swamp; the ranges on either side are newer products of California's ongoing mountain building processes. In its center, the Sacramento and San Joaquin rivers meet in a complex delta, draining W through San Francisco Bay. In the Spanish period, the valley was little used except for cattle RANCHOS. With the discovery of gold on the American R. in 1848, however, the Sacramento Valley filled rapidly with fortune seekers. After the gold rush died down, agriculture established itself along the rivers. In the 20th century, the potential of the arid S San Joaquin Valley led to the establishment (1935) of the **Central Valley Project,** which has created dozens of dams, reservoirs, and canals from Shasta L. (N) to the Bakersfield area and the Tehachapi Mts., at the valley's S end. As a result, the San Joaquin Valley has become the heartland of California agriculture, supplier to the nation of fruits, nuts, grapes, vegetables, and other produce. More recently, the CALIFORNIA AQUEDUCT and other units of the California State Water Project have brought water through the valley to Southern California's cities. Ranching remains important in places, and there are important oilfields in the far S, near Bakersfield. The valley's major cities are (S–N) Bakersfield, Fresno, Stockton, and Sacramento. **2.** unincorporated village, pop. 1929, in Woodbury township, Orange Co., SE New York, on the New York State Thruway, 12 mi/19 km SW of Newburgh. It is best known for Woodbury Common, the large shopping facility located here.

Central Ward section of downtown Newark, New Jersey. With a population almost completely black, it was the scene of riots in 1967 and 1968 that leveled neighborhoods and destroyed hundreds of businesses. The Central Ward is an area of dilapidated wood-frame houses, partially abandoned public housing complexes, small stores, and overgrown lots, with a large homeless population. It has been the target of many urban renewal plans, none of which has had significant impact.

Centre County 1106 sq mi/2865 sq km, pop. 123,786, in C Pennsylvania, in the Allegheny Mts., bordered (NW) by the West Branch of the Susquehanna R. Its seat is Bellefonte. The county is a center of agriculture, limestone quarrying, and coal mining, and there is some manufacturing. STATE COLLEGE is its most important urban locale.

Centreville **1.** city, pop. 7489, St. Clair Co., SW Illinois, a suburb 2 mi/3 km SE of East St. Louis. It is mainly residential. The area was settled around 1805. Our Lady of Snows Shrine is 3 mi/5 km E, and Frank Holten State Park is 3 mi/5 km NE. **2.** unincorporated community, pop. 26,585, Fairfax Co., NE Virginia, on Interstate 66, just W of Fairfax and 24 mi/39 km W of Washington, D.C. It is a largely residential suburb.

Century City section of W LOS ANGELES, California, immediately SW of Beverly Hills and 9 mi/14 km W of Downtown. Built in the 1970s on 180 ac/73 ha of an old 20th Century–Fox studio back lot, it is a self-contained commercial center and residential community with high-rise apartment buildings and office towers.

Ceres city, pop. 26,314, Stanislaus Co., C California, immediately SE of Modesto, in the San Joaquin Valley. Poultry farms, vineyards, and date, fig, and peach orchards provide its economic base.

Cerrillos see under SANDIA Mts., New Mexico.

Cerritos city, pop. 53,240, Los Angeles Co., SW California, 18 mi/29 km SE of downtown Los Angeles. On the Coyote Creek, just NW of Buena Park, it is a largely residential suburb that tripled in population, to its present size, in the 1970s.

Cerro de Punta peak, 4390 ft/1338 m tall, in the CORDILLERA CENTRAL, WC Puerto Rico, 11 mi/18 km NNE of Ponce. It is the highest point in Puerto Rico.

Cerro Maravilla mountain peak in the CORDILLERA CENTRAL, S Puerto Rico, 10 mi/16 km NNE of Ponce and just SE of the Cerro de Punta. It was the site, on July 25, 1978, of the killing by police of two independence activists apparently preparing to sabotage one of its many radio and television towers. The nature of the killings has been debated since; the incident has been called "Puerto Rico's Watergate."

Ceylon city, pop. 641, Martin Co., S Minnesota, 12 mi/19 km SW of Fairmont. Former Vice President Walter Mondale was born here (1928).

C.F.B. Canadian Forces Base (see CAMP).

Chaco Culture National Historical Park formerly, **Chaco Canyon National Monument** 33,974 ac/13,759 ha, on the Navajo section of the Colorado Plateau and near the head of the Chaco R., in NW New Mexico, 90 mi/145 km NW of Albuquerque. It protects thirteen major and thousands of smaller ruins in an area where ANASAZI culture flourished in the early 12th century, which was then abandoned for reasons not yet understood. Irrigation works, a large road system, and sophisticated astronomical markers are among the remains.

Chadds Ford village in Birmingham Township (pop. 3118), Delaware Co., SE Pennsylvania, on Brandywine Creek in the Brandywine Valley, 9 mi/14 km NNW of Wilmington, Delaware. It was originally named Chad's Ford, for a crossing over the Brandywine, and was the scene of a battle (Sept. 11, 1777) in which George Washington was defeated by Sir William Howe. The restored site, including Washington's headquarters, is now Brandywine Battlefield Park. The Brandywine River Museum displays works by members of the Wyeth family, notably Andrew Wyeth, who was born here and painted many local subjects.

Chadron city, pop. 5588, seat of Dawes Co., NW Nebraska, 52 mi/83 km NNW of Alliance and 12 mi/19 km S of the South Dakota line, in the N Panhandle, N of PINE RIDGE. Situated among buttes and canyons, it was founded in 1885 and was a rough cow town in the late 19th century. Today it is a center for livestock, grain, and dairy producers. It is the seat of Chadron State College (1911). A unit of the Nebraska National Forest (SW), the Oglala National Grasslands (NW), and the AGATE FOSSIL BEDS National Monument (SW) are nearby.

Chagrin Falls village, pop. 4146, Cuyahoga Co., N Ohio, 16 mi/26 km ESE of Cleveland. Situated on the Chagrin R., it developed as an industrial center producing paper and other goods, but is now primarily residential.

Chain-O-Lakes see under FOX R., Illinois.

Chaleur Bay French, **Baie des Chaleurs** inlet of the Gulf of St. Lawrence, some 90 mi/140 km E–W and generally 15–25 mi/25–40 km wide, extending between Québec's GASPÉ PENINSULA (N) and N New Brunswick (S). The submerged valley of the RESTIGOUCHE R., it also receives the Nepisiguit and other smaller rivers. Named for its warm waters by Jacques Cartier in 1534, it is noted for its mackerel, cod, herring, salmon, and scallop fisheries. Its chief settlements are New Brunswick's CAMPBELLTON (at the head of navigation), DALHOUSIE, and BATHURST, and Québec's New Richmond and New Carlisle.

Chalk River see under ROLPHTON, Ontario.

Challis National Forest 2.5 million ac/1.02 million ha (3922 sq mi/10,158 sq km), in SC Idaho. Its many mountains include much of the SAWTOOTH, Lemhi, Lost River, and SALMON RIVER ranges. Much of the forest is also in the Frank Church–River of No Return Wilderness Area. Once a mining area, it is now noted for its fish streams and hiking trails.

Chalmette unincorporated community, pop. 31,860, seat of St. Bernard Parish, extreme SE Louisiana, on the E (N) bank of the Mississippi R., just E of New Orleans. The 140-ac/57-ha Chalmette unit of the Jean Lafitte National Historical Park occupies the site where Andrew Jackson and American forces defeated the British on Jan. 8, 1815, in the Battle of New Orleans, at the end of the War of 1812. Chalmette today is an almost entirely white residential suburb, with oil, chemical, and aluminum plants and rail terminals along its riverfront.

Chambersburg borough, pop. 16,647, seat of Franklin Co., S Pennsylvania, 45 mi/72 km SW of Harrisburg. A trading center for fruit grown in the Cumberland Valley, it is also a center of light manufacturing (food processing, clothing, machinery). Chambersburg served as John Brown's headquarters while he was planning his raid on HARPERS FERRY (1859). It was raided three times by Confederate troops and was the only Northern town to be burned in the Civil War (1864). It is the seat of Wilson College (1869).

Chamblee city, pop. 7668, De Kalb Co., NW Georgia, 10 mi/16 km NNE of Atlanta. It is an industrial, warehousing, and shipping center just inside Atlanta's beltway (Route 285). Industries here manufacture farm machinery, electrical equipment, lumber, abrasives, and medical supplies.

Chambly city, pop. 15,893, La Vallée-du-Richelieu census division, S Québec, on the Bassin de Chambly, a widening of the R. RICHELIEU, 15 mi/25 km ESE of Montréal. The first (wooden) Fort Chambly was built here in 1665 to protect against Iroquois raids. The current stone fort (1709) is a national historic park. Chambly was a mill center in the 19th century. Its canal (1843), 12 mi/19 km long, carries traffic from St.-Jean-sur-Richelieu (S) to the Bassin, avoiding the river's rapids. Today the city is a growing suburb.

Chamizal district on both sides of the RIO GRANDE in El Paso, Texas, and Ciudad Juarez (Chihuahua), Mexico. In 1864, one of the Rio Grande's periodic changes of course left land that had been Mexican on the N side. A dispute that lasted until 1963 was settled by a treaty that gave some 820 ac/330 ha to Mexico. Channelization of the river, undertaken at the same time, was designed to prevent future changes. Both countries established parks on the Chamizal land; the **Chamizal National Memorial** (1966), on the US side, incorporates 55 ac/22 ha.

Champaign city, pop. 63,502, Champaign Co., EC Illinois, adjoining URBANA to the E and 40 mi/64 km NE of Decatur. It is economically dominated by the University of Illinois, whose campus has stood just SE of the city since the 1860s. Originally a trading center for the area's corn, soybeans, and livestock, Champaign today has industries producing drop forgings, alloy castings, air conditioners, bleachers, cement products, athletic equipment, and soybean oil. In the 1850s, the Illinois Central Railroad built a depot here, outside the existing town of Urbana, and founded what became Champaign. Besides Parkland College (1966), local cultural institutions include the Krannert Art Museum (part of the University of Illinois), as well as the John Philip Sousa Museum.

Champaign County 998 sq mi/2585 sq km, pop. 173,025, in EC Illinois. The Vermilion, Kaskaskia, and Embarras rivers originate here, while the Sangamon R. flows through the NW part of the county. The twin cities of Champaign and the county seat, URBANA, in the center of the county, form the main urban area. Rantoul, to the N, is the other sizable urban center in a county producing corn, soybeans, and livestock. There has been recent commercial development along Routes 72 and 74 near Champaign and Urbana.

Champion's Hill Civil War battle site, in Hinds Co., SW Mississippi, 20 mi/32 km E of Vicksburg and E of the Big Black R. On May 16, 1863, during the VICKSBURG Campaign, Union troops under U.S. Grant here defeated Confederate forces led by John C. Pemberton, forcing them toward Vicksburg.

Champlain, Lake in the NE corner of New York and NW corner of Vermont, extending into Québec. Two-thirds of the total area (172,932 ac/70,037 ha) and all the larger islands in the lake are in Vermont. Three islands at the N end, the two HERO ISLANDS and ISLE LA MOTTE, are joined to the rest of Vermont by bridges. Champlain lies in a broad valley between the Adirondacks (W) and the Green Mts. (E). It is 125 mi/200 km long, and up to 10 mi/16 km wide. Burlington, the urban and industrial center of Vermont, is on the E shore. Plattsburgh, New York, is the largest community on the W shore. Champlain, the French explorer, was the first European to see the lake, in 1609. Historically, it was an important trade and military route. At its N end, the RICHELIEU R. connects it with the St. Lawrence. In the S, it is connected with L. GEORGE and the Hudson Valley by stream and canal. For more than two centuries, it was key to the Anglo-French-American struggle during Colonial wars, the Revolutionary War, and the War of 1812, and was the site of many forts (including FORT TICONDEROGA), and numerous battles. Today, it is known for its apple orchards, scenery, and resorts.

Champlain, Mount see under ISLE AU HAUT, Maine.

Champlin city, pop. 16,849, Hennepin Co., SE Minnesota, on the Mississippi R., 20 mi/32 km NNW of Minneapolis. Situated at the outer edge of Twin Cities suburbs, it experienced some residential growth in the 1980s. Many of its residents work across the Mississippi R. in ANOKA or COON RAPIDS.

Chancellorsville crossroads locality in Spotsylvania Co., EC Virginia, 7 mi/11 km W of FREDERICKSBURG. It is the site of one of the bloodiest battles of the Civil War, fought May 1–4, 1863, a decisive defeat for Union Gen. Joseph Hooker, who allowed himself to be outmaneuvered by Robert E. Lee and Stonewall Jackson. Jackson, however, was accidentally shot by his own troops and died eight days later. Parts of the battle involved the WILDERNESS, just W, which would be the scene of a major battle a year later; Marye's Heights, on the W edge of FREDERICKSBURG, where a Union attack on May 3 dislodged Confederates from the Sunken Road; and Salem Church, where a Union advance was halted a short while later.

Chandeleur Islands 26 mi/42 km–long, crescent-shaped archipelago in the Gulf of Mexico, in extreme SE Louisiana, enclosing Chandeleur Sound (NW, extending N to MISSISSIPPI SOUND) and BRETON SOUND (SW). Long inhabited by fishermen and trappers, the group is now almost entirely within the Breton National Wildlife Refuge. The delta of the Mississippi R. lies 20 mi/32 km S.

Chandler city, pop. 90,533, Maricopa Co., SC Arizona, in the Salt R. Valley, a suburb 17 mi/27 km SE of Phoenix. Primarily residential, it is also a winter resort and processing center in an irrigated farming and ranching area. The city has grown rapidly since the 1970s, largely because of new research and technology facilities. Among its manufactures are computer components, mobile homes, and fertilizer. The sunny winter climate, the Gila Indian Reservation (W), and golf resorts attract visitors.

Chanhassen city, pop. 11,732, Carver and Hennepin counties, EC Minnesota, on the Minnesota R., 15 mi/24 km SW of Minneapolis. A suburban residential community, it is the site of the University of Minnesota Landscape Arboretum. Among many local lakes, the largest is L. Minnewashta.

Channel Islands see SANTA BARBARA Is., California.

Channel–Port aux Basques town, pop. 5644, extreme SW Newfoundland, on the Cabot Strait, 109 mi/176 km SSW of Corner Brook. A 16th-century Basque, French, and Portuguese fishing station, it is now a fishing and fish processing center. In the coastal plains, it became a trade center after railway and steamer services were established in the 1890s. In addition it is a ferry port and is on the Trans-Canada Highway. The town, incorporated 1945, amalgamated Channel, Port aux Basques, and several smaller communities.

Channelview city, pop. 25,564, Harris Co., SE Texas, 12 mi/19 km E of Houston. Plastics and petrochemicals are manufactured in this suburb on Interstate 10 and the N side of the Buffalo Bayou (the Houston Ship Channel).

Chantilly unincorporated community, pop. 29,337, Fairfax Co., N Virginia, 20 mi/32 km W of Washington, D.C. It was the scene of a battle fought Sept. 1, 1862, in which Confederate forces led by Stonewall Jackson attempted unsuccessfully to prevent a retreat by Union forces under John Pope, after the second battle of BULL RUN. Washington Dulles International Airport is NW of this residential suburb, which is also home to some high-tech industry.

Chanute city, pop. 9488, Neosho Co., SE Kansas, 45 mi/72 km SW of Fort Scott. It is a processing center for a fertile agricultural area that also produces oil, gas, limestone, and clay, and has some light manufactures. Neosho County Community College (1936) is here. A nearby mission (1824–29) is the oldest in Kansas.

Chanute Field US Air Force base and technical school, in the SE corner of the village of RANTOUL, Champaign Co., EC Illinois, 14 mi/23 km NNE of Champaign. The base was established during World War II.

chaparral vegetation (or zone) characterized by thick, scrubby, evergreen growth, esp. dwarf oaks. Found from the Great Plains to the far Southwest, it flourishes in areas less dry than deserts but without enough rain to promote forest growth. Widely used for grazing, it is sometimes virtually impenetrable. Periodic brushfires, part of its normal life cycle, threaten communities in such areas as Southern California.

Chapel Hill town, pop. 38,719, Orange and Durham counties, NC North Carolina, 10 mi/16 km SW of Durham. Founded in 1792, it was named for New Hope Chapel, which once stood at the center of the hill settlement. Chosen for its healthy elevation (over 500 ft/152 m), it is the seat of the University of North Carolina's main campus (1795), and together with adjoining CARRBORO forms a university community with scientific and technological research centers, but no heavy industry. Corn and tobacco are raised in the surrounding Piedmont. The RESEARCH TRIANGLE lies 9 mi/14 km E.

Chappaqua village in New Castle town, Westchester Co., SE New York, 5 mi/8 km E of Ossining. It is an affluent, largely rural suburb of New York City. The offices of *Reader's Digest* are here.

Chappaquiddick Island semidetached island, up to 3 mi/5 km E–W and 5 mi/8 km N–S, part of Edgartown, MARTHA'S VINEYARD, Dukes Co., Massachusetts. It is connected with the main part of Martha's Vineyard by a barrier beach, but is usually reached by ferry from Edgartown Harbor. A quiet retreat, it is most widely known as the site of a fatal 1969 accident that occurred when Senator Edward Kennedy drove a car off a bridge on the island's E side.

Charles, Cape promontory at the S end of the DELMARVA PENINSULA, between the Atlantic Ocean (E) and Chesapeake Bay (W), in Northampton Co., SE Virginia. The cape is the site of the N end of the CHESAPEAKE BAY BRIDGE-TUNNEL and a National Wildlife Refuge on the ATLANTIC FLYWAY. Cape Charles Lighthouse is on Smith I., 3 mi/5 km E of the cape.

Charlesbourg city, pop. 70,788, QUÉBEC Urban Community, S Québec. One of the largest municipalities in the Québec area, adjacent (NE) to the city, it was created in 1976 from historically agricultural Charlesbourg (Bourg-Royal, 1659) and several other municipalities, and is a largely residential suburb, with shopping centers, Québec's zoo, and some light manufacturing.

Charlesbourg-Royal see under CAP-ROUGE, Québec.

Charles Center neighborhood in downtown Baltimore, Maryland, between the financial and legal center (E), and the retail district (W), rehabilitated since 1958. It now includes One and Two Charles Center, high-rise structures containing apartments and offices; Charles Center South; Hopkins Plaza; Center Plaza; parks; and fountains.

Charles City city, pop. 7878, seat of Floyd Co., NC Iowa, on the Cedar R., 25 mi/40 km SE of Mason City. A trading center for an agricultural region, it began with a sawmill in 1851. Charles City is the birthplace of the tractor; it still manufactures farm machinery and is the home of the sprawling New Idea plant. The production of veterinary medicines and fertilizers are also important.

Charles City County 181 sq mi/469 sq km, pop. 6282, in SE Virginia. Charles City is the seat. The county is rural, largely undeveloped, and still heavily forested. Bordering the James R. (S) are a number of noted 18th- and 19th-century plantations, among them WESTOVER, SHIRLEY, Evelynton, and BERKELEY.

Charles County 452 sq mi/1171 sq km, pop. 101,154, in S Maryland, bounded SW by the Potomac R., N by Mattawoman Creek, and E by the Patuxent R. Its seat is La Plata. Primarily tidewater plain, it encompasses the region of earliest settlement in Maryland. Tobacco has long been the chief cash crop, with La Plata and Hughesville market centers. Oystering and the raising of beef and dairy cattle are also important.

Charles Mound ancient Indian burial mound in Jo Daviess Co., NW Illinois, on the Wisconsin border, a few miles N of the village of Scales Mound. At 1235 ft/377 m, its top is the highest point in the state.

Charles River 60 mi/100 km long, in E Massachusetts. It rises in SW Norfolk Co. and flows generally E and N past Newton, Watertown, Cambridge, and Boston, separating Cambridge (N) from Boston (S). It then enters BOSTON HARBOR through locks at the Charles R. Dam, between Boston and East Cambridge. The Indian name for the river was Quinobequin, or "meandering river." It is navigable for 10 mi/16 km, to Watertown. The Charles is a major recreational waterway, particularly in the Charles R. Basin, N of Boston's BACK BAY (which was until mid 19th century a tidal inlet connected with the river).

Charleston **1.** city, pop. 20,398, seat of Coles Co., EC Illinois, 10 mi/16 km E of Mattoon. The commercial center of an agricultural and dairying area, it also contains railroad shops, lumber mills, and factories producing shoes, brooms, fertilizer, business forms, and ceramics for the steel industry. Settled in 1826, Charleston was the site of Abraham Lincoln's early law practice and hosted the fourth Lincoln-Douglas debate. Lincoln's father and stepmother lived nearby. Their reconstructed home is now the Lincoln Log Cabin National Historic Site, and they are buried in Charleston's Shiloh Cemetery. Eastern Illinois University (1895) is here. Fox Ridge State Park is 4 mi/6 km S; L. Charleston is 1 mi/2 km SE. **2.** city, pop. 80,414, seat of Charleston Co. (pop. 259,039), SE South Carolina, on the ASHLEY (W) and COOPER (E) rivers and the Atlantic Ocean. It is a major seaport, one of America's most historic cities, and the center of a three-county (Charleston, Berkeley, and Dorchester) metropolitan area with a pop. of 506,875. Both the city and its suburbs, including NORTH CHARLESTON, have grown substantially since 1970, as, already industrialized, they became an increasingly popular residential area. Charleston was founded in 1670 at what is now called Charles Towne Landing, at Albemarle Point, on the W side of the Ashley. In 1680 it was reestablished on the present site on the "Neck" between the rivers, with a pop. of French Huguenots added to the original English settlers. It flourished as a trade (deerhides, rice, indigo, cotton) center, and by the mid 18th century was the leading city in the Southeast. In March 1776, defenders of Fort Sullivan (Moultrie), on nearby SULLIVAN'S I., won a battle against British forces; in 1780–83, however, the British occupied the city. After the Revolutionary War, growth continued, and although South Carolina's capital moved from here to Columbia in 1790, Charleston remained a center of political ferment. In 1832 the Ordinance of Nullification, and in 1860 the Ordinance of Secession, key steps in creation of the Confederacy, were drawn up here. On April 12–13, 1861, the attack on Union forces at FORT SUMTER, in the harbor, initiated the Civil War. The city, although blockaded and bombarded, was not surrendered until Feb. 1865, when Union troops moving N after Sherman's MARCH TO THE SEA took control of the area. After the Civil War, Charleston lost its commercial and political preeminence. Industry grew gradually, finally booming during World War II with naval construction and related activity. Today, the city manufactures wood and paper products, fertilizer, chemicals, and rubber goods. Regional agricultural produce leaves its port, and consumer goods are imported. Shipbuilding and oil refining are important. The region has come, since World War II, to rely heavily on military spending. In the 1990s, threats of closure of the Charleston Navy Base (in North Charleston) and other cutbacks raised questions about local economic health. Air Force and Army installations are also important. The city is a major tourist hub; visitors appreciate its 18th-century architecture, food, historic sites, cultural attractions, and ambience. Leading institutions include the College of Charleston (1770), the first US municipal college; the Medical University of South Carolina (1823); and the Citadel (1842; military). Despite a major earthquake (1886), the Civil War, fires, and storms including Hurricane Hugo (1989), the city retains hundreds of 18th-century buildings. Castle Pinckney (the Charles Pinckney

National Historic Site), on an island in the harbor, is the home of a Revolutionary political leader. The Dock St. Theatre (1736) was the first US building designed as a theater; near it is Cabbage (or Catfish) Row, a building and courtyard famous as the setting for Charleston native DuBose Heyward's novel *Porgy.* The Battery, at the city's S tip, has been a military site, and is now noted for the houses and gardens that surround it. Near Charleston are several well-known plantations and gardens, including Magnolia Gardens, the 1741 Middleton Place (site of the first US landscaped garden), Boone Hall, and Drayton Hall. Once a land of rice plantations and fishing villages, the city's environs are increasingly built-up, with working-class suburbs near the military installations N of the city, and beach resorts and condominiums along the coast. **3.** city, pop. 57,287, state capital and seat of Kanawha Co., WC West Virginia. On the Appalachian Plateau, at the junction of the Elk and Kanawha rivers, it is the commercial and distribution center of the Kanawha Valley, which produces coal, chemicals, steel, glass, and timber. On the site of Fort Lee (or Fort Clendenin; 1788), early Charleston attracted settlers from the Shenandoah Valley. By the 1820s, it was an important supplier of salt from local brine wells. During the Civil War the city remained in Union hands. Industrialization escalated during the 1920s, when the chemical industry boomed. Today, corporations conduct technical research and produce mine equipment, tools and implements, glass, brick and clay products, and military hardware. The Capitol (1932) is a noted design by Cass Gilbert. Charleston's suburbs include SOUTH CHARLESTON, SAINT ALBANS, DUNBAR, and INSTITUTE.

Charlestown **1.** section of N Boston, Massachusetts, across the Charles R. from the North End. Charlestown was occupied a year before the city itself was founded; the settlers crossed the river to the Shawmut Peninsula and named their new settlement Boston in 1630. Charlestown is the site of BREED'S HILL and BUNKER HILL. On its waterfront, the Navy Yard is a National Historic Site; the USS *Constitution* ("Old Ironsides," built 1797) is on display. Bunker Hill Community College is W, along Interstate 93, one of several highways that pass over or through this traditionally working-class Irish district. The Mystic R. is N. The 1980s saw gentrification of parts of Charlestown closer to downtown Boston. **2.** town, pop. 6478, Washington Co., SW Rhode Island, 32 mi/52 km SSW of Providence, on US 1 and Block Island Sound. It includes the villages of Kenyon and Quonochontaug as well as parts of Carolina and Shannock villages. In addition to tourism, the economy is supported by farming. An Indian burial ground and a wildlife sanctuary are located here. Charlestown Beach is a summer colony; behind it lies Ninigret Pond. The Narraganset tribe retains substantial holdings in the township. **3.** city, pop. 3122, seat of Jefferson Co., in the Eastern Panhandle of West Virginia, 4 mi/6 km SW of HARPERS FERRY. It was founded in 1786 by George Washington's brother Charles, and has been a horse breeding and racing center throughout its history. Agricultural trade and quarrying are carried out in the area; industry is restricted to adjacent (N) Ranson. The trial and execution (1859) of John Brown occurred here.

Charlevoix **1.** city, pop. 3116, seat of Charlevoix Co., in the NW Lower Peninsula of Michigan, on L. Michigan. Now named for an early French explorer, it was settled in the 1850s as Pine River. Originally a fishing colony, it became, after 1876 port improvements, a major lumber exporter. Today it is a resort center. BIG ROCK POINT is just NE. The city encloses small Round L., which lies between L. Michigan and **Lake Charlevoix** (SE). The latter has a 5 mi/8 km–long main arm, at the SE end of which is Boyne City (pop. 3478). Its 3.5 mi/6 km–long South Arm extends to East Jordan (pop. 2240). The area is noted for its boating and fishing. **2.** region of SC Québec, along the N side of the St. Lawrence R., extending NE from some 40 mi/65 km NE of Québec City. Settled from the 17th century, and long noted for its maritime isolation and shipbuilding tradition, it is today a popular tourists' and artists' destination. Lumbering is important. BAIE-SAINT-PAUL and LA MALBAIE are the principal cities.

Charlevoix County 421 sq mi/1090 sq km, pop. 21,468, in the N Lower Peninsula, NC Michigan, bounded by L. Michigan (NW), drained by the Boyne and Jordan rivers, and containing L. Charlevoix. Its seat is CHARLEVOIX. The county, which includes the BEAVER ARCHIPELAGO, depends on dairying, livestock, orchards, field crops, commercial fishing, and flour and lumber milling. There is some manufacturing in Charlevoix, East Jordan, and Boyne City. Cartoonist and wildlife preservationist Jay Norwood "Ding" Darling was born (1876) in the tiny L. Michigan community of Norwood.

Charlotte **1.** city, pop. 8083, seat of Eaton Co., SC Michigan, on Battle Creek, 18 mi/29 km SW of Lansing. Settled in 1835, it is a livestock market in a dairying and vegetable growing region. Charlotte is a maple-sugar distribution point, and manufactures glass, road machinery, iron, aluminum products, and furniture. A large auto parts plant closed in 1991. Just NE of town is Fitch H. Beach Airport. **2.** city, pop. 417,621 (1991), seat of Mecklenburg Co., S North Carolina, in the Piedmont, 130 mi/210 km WSW of Raleigh and 15 mi/24 km N of the South Carolina border. It was settled around 1750 by Scotch-Irish and German colonists and named for Charlotte Sophia of Mecklenburg-Strelitz, wife of England's George III. In May 1775, the Mecklenburg Declaration and Mecklenburg Resolves, signed here, cast Charlotte as a center of Revolutionary activity. Five years later, General Horatio Gates made it his headquarters. Before 1848, Charlotte was the center of gold production in the US. A branch of the MINT operated here 1837–61 and 1867–1913; it served as the Confederate naval ordnance yard during the Civil War. The final full Confederate cabinet meeting was held here on April 10, 1865. North Carolina's largest city, now the third-largest US banking center, Charlotte is much publicized as the business leader of the late-20th-century New South. Not on a major river, it has benefited from the importance of Charlotte-Douglas International Airport, 5 mi/8 km W, as well as from liberal North Carolina banking laws. It is a major manufacturing, shipping, and retailing center. Industries manufacture textiles, machinery, processed foods, paper products, chemicals, aircraft parts, electrical and computer equipment, and primary and fabricated metals. The first college in North Carolina, chartered in 1771 as Queens College in Charlotte, was rechartered in 1857 and is affiliated with the Presbyterian Church. Charlotte also is home to a branch of the University of North Carolina (1946), Johnson C. Smith University (1867), King's College (1901), and Central Piedmont Community College (1963). **3.** town, pop. 854, seat of Dickson Co., NC Tennessee, 33 mi/53 km W of Nashville on Town Branch Creek. Basketball great Oscar Robertson was born here (1938). **4.** town, pop. 3148, Chittenden Co., NW Vermont. It lies in the Champlain Valley, along the lake, 12 mi/19 km S of Burlington. In a fruit growing area, the town is home to Garden Way, supplier of gardening tools and machinery; the Vermont Wildflower Farm; and Mt. Philo State Park. Other industries include tourism and dairy processing.

Charlotte Amalie town, pop. 12,331, territorial capital and largest community of the US VIRGIN ISLANDS, on the hilly S shore of the island of SAINT THOMAS, at the head of St. Thomas Harbor. Built on three volcanic spurs, it is a deepwater port now handling chiefly cruise ships, a commercial center, and a resort. The site was a base for English privateers in their 16th-century attacks on Spanish shipping. A settlement was established (1672) by Danes, who named it for the wife of King Christian V. A Danish colonial hub, it was important as a center for the sugar and slave trades until the abolition of slavery here in 1848. Among the town's noted sites are Fort Christian (1671) and the 18th-century Government Hill community. Some of the architecture and atmosphere of the Danish period (1660s–1917) has been retained.

Charlotte Harbor inlet of the Gulf of Mexico, 40 mi/64 km SE of Sarasota, in Charlotte and Lee counties, SW Florida. Five mi/8 km wide at its mouth, it extends NE 18 mi/29 km to receive the broad mouths of the Myakka and Peace rivers. Several barrier islands, including Gasparilla, Cayo Costa, CAPTIVA, and Pine, lie at its mouth. Pine Island Sound adjoins (S), and its mouth is crossed by the GULF INTRACOASTAL WATERWAY. A dredged shipping channel extends up the harbor to PUNTA GORDA, on its NE shore. PORT CHARLOTTE is just N.

Charlottesville independent city, pop. 40,341, seat of but administratively separate from Albemarle Co., C Virginia, 66 mi/106 km NW of Richmond on the Rivanna R., in the foothills of the Blue Ridge Mts. It is best known as the seat of the University of Virginia (1819), founded, planned, and designed by Thomas Jefferson. Its economy revolves around the university, which has attracted many research and corporate facilities. Cattle and horses are raised in the surrounding countryside. MONTICELLO, Jefferson's home, and ASH LAWN, home of James Monroe, are SE of the city. Piedmont Virginia Community College (1969) is in Charlottesville. In the 1980s the area became a popular retreat for the wealthy, attracting Hollywood stars as well as industrial heirs.

Charlottetown city, pop. 15,396, capital and largest (and only) city of Prince Edward Island, at the head of HILLSBOROUGH BAY, on a peninsula between the Hillsborough (East) and Yorke (North) rivers, 110 mi/177 km NNE of Halifax, Nova Scotia. The provincial commercial center and its chief seaport, it has industries including shipbuilding; meatpacking; woodworking; fish, dairy, and wool processing; and potato exporting. Tourism is also important. The University of Prince Edward Island (1969), combining the older Prince of Wales College and St. Dunstan's University, is here, as is Holland College (1969). Settled by the British in 1768, across its harbor (N) from the French Port La Joie (1720; controlled by the British and renamed Fort Amherst in 1758), Charlottetown became the island's capital in 1769. At the Charlottetown Conference (1864), initial steps were taken toward Canadian confederation; the Confederation Chamber, in the Province House, is much visited.

Charlton town, pop. 9576, Worcester Co., SC Massachusetts, 12 mi/19 km SW of Worcester. Settled in 1735, largely rural Charlton is an agricultural trade center with an increasing suburban component.

Charny city, pop. 10,239, Les Chutes-de-la-Chaudière census division, S Québec, 7 mi/11 km SSW of Québec City, near the mouth of the R. CHAUDIÈRE on the St. Lawrence R. Long a rail junction, it is now a growing suburb of the capital. The falls of the Chaudière here are 115 ft/35 m high.

Charter Oak tree that stood until 1856 in Hartford, Connecticut, just SW of modern Bushnell Park. Supposedly 33 ft/10 m in circumference and 1000 years old, it was said to have served to hide Connecticut's liberal 1662 royal charter when New England Governor Edmund Andros demanded the document in Oct. 1687. Fifty years after a storm destroyed the tree, a monument was erected on the site, on Charter Oak Avenue.

Chaska city, pop. 11,339, seat of Carver Co., SE Minnesota, on the Minnesota R., 20 mi/32 km SW of Minneapolis. It has only recently become an outer-ring suburb of the Twin Cities. Dairy farms are giving way to residential developments, particularly in the N part of the city.

Chateau Country see under DELAWARE.

Château Frontenac massive hotel, opened in 1893 by the CANADIAN PACIFIC RAILWAY atop Cap-Diamant, in QUÉBEC CITY's Upper Town, overlooking the narrowing of the St. Lawrence R. Noted for its towers, turrets, and steep copper roofs, it is the best-known of the CPR's grand hotels, and perhaps the most familiar building in Canada. Its central tower was completed in 1925; further expansion continues today.

Châteauguay city, pop. 39,833, Châteauguay Co., S Québec, 12 mi/19 km SW of Montréal, on L. St.-Louis (the St. Lawrence R.) and the mouth of the Châteauguay R. Long an agricultural trade center, it is today a residential suburb and fruit and dairy producing center, with some light manufactures. The **R. Châteauguay** (in New York, Chateaugay R.) rises at Chateaugay L., in the Adirondack Mts., 25 mi/40 km W of Plattsburgh, and flows generally NNW into Québec, then NE toward Montréal. On Oct. 26, 1813, British and Indian troops repelled an invading US force along it, near Ormstown, some 15 mi/24 km N of the New York border.

Chatham **1.** middle-class black residential neighborhood on the South Side of Chicago, Illinois, 7 mi/11 km S of the Loop, and E of the Dan Ryan Expressway, part of the old BUNGALOW BELT. **2.** town, pop. 6579, Barnstable Co., SE Massachusetts, at the SE "elbow" of Cape Cod. A former shipbuilding and whaling port settled in 1665, it is today a fishing port and resort. MONOMOY I. extends S from the town. Pleasant Bay is N, and the S end of NAUSET Beach provides a barrier against the sea to the E. **3.** town, pop. 6544, Northumberland Co., NE New Brunswick, on the Miramichi R. estuary, 75 mi/120 km NNW of Moncton. A former shipbuilding center, dominated in the early 19th century by the Cunard family, it has lumber, pulp, and paper mills and fish and lobster processing plants. St. Thomas University, founded here in 1910, moved to FREDERICTON in 1964. A military airbase is important to the economy. **4.** borough, pop. 8007, Morris Co., NE New Jersey, on the Passaic R., 6 mi/10 km SE of Morristown. Settled in 1749, it is basically a residential suburb of the New

York metropolitan area, but has some industry (cement blocks, chemicals) and houses several commercial greenhouses. Chatham township (pop. 9361), to the SW, is home to much of the GREAT SWAMP National Wildlife Refuge. **5.** town, pop. 4413, Columbia Co., SE New York, 22 mi/35 km SE of Albany. In a rural area, it has some light industry and a variety of small businesses. Naturalist Amos Eaton (1776–1842) was born here. A former Shaker community is now a museum in Old Chatham village. **6.** city, pop. 43,557, seat of Kent Co., extreme S Ontario, on the THAMES R., 45 mi/72 km E of Detroit, Michigan. Chosen as a military site in the late 1790s, it was the scene of a skirmish during the British retreat before the Battle of the Thames (Oct. 1813). The town was not founded until 1835. It was a terminus of the UNDERGROUND RAILROAD, and was the site of a convention held by John Brown before his 1859 raid on Harpers Ferry. The city is now the commercial and industrial center of an agricultural (fruit, grain, tobacco, and dairy goods) and natural gas producing region. Textiles, lumber, auto parts, plastics, and fabricated metals are manufactured.

Chatham County 443 sq mi/1147 sq km, pop. 216,935, in E Georgia, bounded N by the Savannah R. and South Carolina, E by the Atlantic Ocean, and S by the Ogeechee R. Its seat and industrial center is SAVANNAH. It includes TYBEE, OSSABAW, WASSAW, and Skidaway islands.

Chatsworth **1.** SAN FERNANDO VALLEY section of Los Angeles, California, 23 mi/37 km NW of Downtown, in the extreme NW corner of the city, on the S of the SANTA SUSANA Mts. Aerospace and electronics industries form the backbone of the local economy. **2.** see under PINE BARRENS, New Jersey.

Chattahoochee National Forest 750,000 ac/304,000 ha, in three units in N Georgia. It borders South Carolina (NE) and North Carolina's NANTAHALA NATIONAL FOREST and Tennessee's CHEROKEE NATIONAL FOREST (N), and is chiefly in the Blue Ridge, with one unit in the Great Appalachian Valley. The Tennessee, Savannah, Chattahoochee, and other rivers rise here, and the forest incorporates BRASSTOWN BALD, RABUN BALD, the Cohutta Wilderness, and areas along the Tallulah and Chattooga rivers. The APPALACHIAN TRAIL starts at SPRINGER Mt., in the forest.

Chattahoochee River 436 mi/702 km long, in Georgia. It is formed by headstreams S of BRASSTOWN BALD, in the Chattahoochee National Forest, in the Blue Ridge Mts., and flows generally SSW into 38,000-ac/15,400-ha L. Sidney Lanier, impounded by the Buford Dam. It then flows SW across the state, forming the city of Atlanta's NW boundary for a stretch, and into 25,900-ac/10,500-ha West Point L., impounded by the West Point Dam. From West Point the river flows 200 mi/320 km S along the Alabama-Georgia border past Columbus, and joins the FLINT R. in 37,500-ac/15,200-ha L. Seminole, in Georgia's SW corner. The Jim Woodruff Dam impounds this lake; the combined waters continue as the Apalachicola R., flowing 112 mi/180 km S across Florida's PANHANDLE to APALACHICOLA BAY on the Gulf of Mexico. The Chattahoochee is navigable to Columbus, on the Fall Line. Hydroelectric dams on its lower course include Bartlett's Ferry Dam, 15 mi/24 km N of Columbus, which impounds L. Harding, and the Walter F. George Dam, just N of Fort Gaines, which impounds L. Eufaula (the Walter F. George Reservoir).

Chattanooga city, pop. 152,466, seat of Hamilton Co., SE Tennessee, on the Georgia border and Moccasin Bend of the Tennessee R., near MISSIONARY RIDGE and LOOKOUT and SIGNAL mountains. The CHICKAMAUGA DAM and Chickamauga L. are just NE. The area was once inhabited by the Chickamauga (Cherokee). Ross's Landing, settled in 1815, traded corn and cotton. Chattanooga, renamed in 1837, grew after 1850, when the Western & Atlantic Railroad gave it an outlet to the Atlantic coast. It was an important Confederate communications post until finally controlled by Union forces in Oct. 1863. An industrial center from the 1870s, it is now a major rail junction, distributing metals, textiles, chemicals, explosives, synthetic fibers, nuclear equipment, processed foods, and other products made locally. The TENNESSEE VALLEY AUTHORITY has regional offices here. Coca-Cola built a bottling plant in 1899, and there are insurance companies. A University of Tennessee branch (1886) is one of several institutions of higher learning. Chattanooga is a growing tourism center, attracting visitors to the mountains and river; the Tennessee Aquarium (1992) is the world's largest freshwater facility.

Chattooga River 40 mi/64 km long, in North Carolina, Georgia, and South Carolina. It rises at Cashiers L., in North Carolina's Nantahala National Forest, and flows SW along the Georgia–South Carolina border to Tallulah Falls, Georgia, where it joins the TALLULAH R. to form the Tugaloo R., which continues SE to the SAVANNAH R. The Chattooga is a designated National Wild and Scenic River. Especially since the movie *Deliverance* (1972), filmed in the Tallulah Falls area, it has been extremely popular with canoeists and fishermen.

Chaubunagungamaug, Lake in Worcester Co., SC Massachusetts, on the Connecticut border, near the tristate junction with Rhode Island. It is 3 mi/5 km long, and is also called L. Webster, for the mill town it is in, or L. Chargoggagoggmanchaugagoggchaubunagungamaugg. The full form of the Algonquian name (sometimes shortened to "Lake Char,") means, roughly, "You fish on your side; we fish on our side; nobody fishes in the middle." It is often cited as the longest American place name.

Chaudière, Rivière 120 mi/190 km long, in S Québec. It issues from L. Mégantic, near the Maine border, and flows NNE, then NNW, through Appalachian highlands, to the St. Lawrence R., opposite Québec City. It is lined with small agricultural communities. Its 115-ft/35-m falls are 4 mi/6 km from its mouth. Used by the Abnaki, who had a PORTAGE between its headwaters and those of Maine's Dead and KENNEBEC rivers, the Chaudière provided the means of approach for American troops under Benedict Arnold in their 1775–76 attack on Québec.

Chaudière Falls see under OTTAWA, Ontario.

Chautauqua town, pop. 4554, Chautauqua Co., extreme SW New York, on the NW shore of Chautauqua L., 18 mi/29 km NW of Jamestown. The Chautauqua Institution was established here as a summer school in 1874. It developed into a system of popular education in the arts, sciences, and humanities, spawning a nationwide movement that influenced the course of American education. The institution still offers summer educational programs and performances. Centered around its activities, the town is now a summer resort, with Victorian cottages and lake-related recreation, as well as a seasonal hub for art and education. **Chautauqua Lake,** 18 mi/29 km NW–SE and 1–3 mi/2–5 km wide, has numerous resorts along its shores. The city of JAMESTOWN is at its SE end.

Chautauqua County 1064 sq mi/2756 sq km, pop. 141,895, in the SW corner of New York, bounded by Pennsylvania (W and S) and L. Erie (N). Its seat is Mayville, in Chautauqua town. Its largest city is industrial JAMESTOWN. There is also considerable industrial development around the Lake Erie port of DUNKIRK, in the N. The county's agriculture includes orchards and vineyards as well as truck and dairy farms. Chautauqua L. and L. Erie are central to its resort economy.

Chavez Ravine in the ELYSIAN PARK section of Los Angeles, California, just N of Downtown. Formerly an area of inexpensive and substandard housing, it became home (1962) to 56,000-seat Dodger Stadium (baseball).

Cheaha Mountain peak (2407 ft/734 m) in the TALLADEGA Mts., a continuation of the Appalachian chain, in NE Alabama, 12 mi/19 km S of Anniston, the highest point in the state. Cheaha State Park (2799 ac/1134 ha) occupies its slopes. The Talladega National Forest surrounds it.

Cheat Mountain ridge in the Allegheny Mts., extending about 45 mi/72 km SSW–NNE along the Shavers Fork (W) to NE of Elkins, in Randolph Co., E West Virginia. It reaches 4830 ft/1473 m. In Sept. 1861, Union forces won a battle on Cheat Mt. that strongly influenced the adherence to the Union of what would become West Virginia.

Cheboygan city, pop. 4999, Cheboygan Co., at the N tip of Michigan's Lower Peninsula, at the mouth of the Cheboygan R., on Lake Huron's Mackinac Channel, across from BOIS BLANC I. Settled in 1857, it was a major late-19th-century lumber port, now a commercial fishing and resort center, with some wood-based industry. The city is surrounded by lakes, marshes, and Mackinaw State Forest.

Cheektowaga town, pop. 99,314, Erie Co., W New York, on Ellicott, Scajaquada, and Cayuga creeks, adjacent (E) to Buffalo. Originally part of the Holland Land Purchase and the town of AMHERST, it was settled in 1809. The Iroquoian name means "land of the crabapple." The suburban town's greatest period of development came after World War II. Part of the New York State Thruway, extensive rail yards, and Greater Buffalo International Airport are within the town limits.

Cheesequake Creek State Park 1000 ac/400 ha, in EC New Jersey, 6 mi/10 km SSE of Perth Amboy. Surrounded by a heavily industrialized area, it has forests with recreational facilities for bathing, picnicking, fishing, cross-country skiing, and camping.

Cheesman Park 80 ac/32 ha, in C DENVER, Colorado, E of CAPITOL HILL. Created in the 1890s, it is noted for the panoramic view of the FRONT RANGE (W) it affords. The Denver Botanical Garden is on the E side. After a period of decline, neighborhoods here have undergone restoration, much of it undertaken by a thriving gay community.

Chelan, Lake in Chelan Co., NC Washington. Fifty-five mi/90 km NW–SE, and 0.5–2 mi/1–3 km wide, it lies in the E CASCADE RANGE, and is paralleled (SW) by the **Chelan Mts.**, a Cascade spur. The largest glacial lake in the Cascades, it is more than 1500 ft/460 m deep in places. Passenger ferries run from **Chelan** (city, pop. 2969), on the more developed S end, through fjordlike canyons to Stehekin on the N end, which is surrounded by the 62,000-ac/25,100-ha **Lake Chelan National Recreation Area.** The lake drains into the Columbia R. at its S end via the 4 mi/6 km–long **Chelan R.**

Chelmsford town, pop. 32,383, Middlesex Co., NE Massachusetts, on the Merrimack R. and Route 495, adjacent (SW) to Lowell, 23 mi/37 km NW of Boston. Its original industry was bog-iron forging, in the 1650s, followed by production of ice, textiles, lumber, and granite through the 19th century. Chelmsford today is an industrial and suburban town engaged in varied light industry.

Chelsea **1.** city, pop. 28,710, Suffolk Co., NE Massachusetts, on upper Boston Harbor between the Mystic R. and Chelsea Creek, 3 mi/5 km N of Boston. Connected by bridges to Charlestown and East Boston, it provides storage yards for oil and coal tankers. Manufactures have included textiles, shoes, clocks, chemicals, and building supplies, but these gave way by the late 20th century to commerce, including railyards, produce terminals, and shopping malls. In the 1990s Chelsea was severely depressed, and the possibility of annexation by Boston had been raised. A large naval hospital is on the Mystic R. **2.** residential and commercial section of the West Side of Manhattan, New York City, from 14th Street to about 30th Street. It has had several distinct characters since it developed in the area of a 1750s village. In the 1840s railroads and Irish immigration made it an industrial area. In the 1880s it was a theater district. Early movies were made c.1910 in old theater buildings, and the neighborhood became noted as bohemian, a character it retains to some extent today. The Chelsea Hotel, built 1884 on 23rd Street, is noted as home to artists and writers. General Theological Seminary's campus is in Chelsea, and the novelist Edith Wharton was born here in 1862.

Cheltenham township, pop. 34,923, Montgomery Co., SE Pennsylvania, adjacent (N) to Philadelphia. This residential suburb includes the communities of ELKINS PARK, WYNCOTE, Melrose Park, Edge Hill, and Chelten Hills. It is the seat of Beaver College (1853) in GLENSIDE, and Temple University's Tyler School of Art in La Mott.

Chemung County 411 sq mi/1064 sq km, pop. 95,159, S New York, along the Pennsylvania line. Its seat and largest city is ELMIRA, a manufacturing center. This county of gently rolling hills was a center of heavy industry in the first part of the 20th century. Most of its steel, electrical, and other factories had closed by mid-century, but many were revitalized by the arrival of Japanese electronics manufacturers and various other industries after the mid 1980s. Poultry and dairy cattle are raised, and there are some sand and gravel producers.

Chenango Canal 80 mi/130 km long, between Utica and Binghamton, C New York. Built in 1836–37 as a part of the ERIE CANAL system, it was abandoned in 1878. It acted as a link between the coal mines of Pennsylvania and the Erie Canal entrance at Utica, and inaugurated an era of enormous mid-19th-century growth in the area's transportation and industry. Some of its ruins are still visible.

Chenango River 90 mi/145 km long, in C New York. It rises in C Madison Co. near Morrisville, and flows S and SW past Sherburne, Norwich, Oxford, and Greene, before joining the Susquehanna R. at Binghamton. It receives the Tioughnioga R. (70 mi/113 km long) at Chenango Forks.

Chene Park municipal park in the RIVERTOWN area of downtown Detroit, Michigan, known for its amphitheater and riverside views.

Chequamegon Bay inlet of L. Superior, 12 mi/19 km NE–SW and 2–6 mi/3–10 km wide, in Ashland and Bayfield counties, extreme N Wisconsin. It lies largely inside the barrier of Chequamegon Point and Long I., with the Bad R. Indian Reservation to the E. ASHLAND is on its S, Washburn on its N. The 850,000-ac/344,000-ha **Chequamegon National Forest** lies largely S and W.

Cheraw town, pop. 5505, Chesterfield Co., NE South Carolina, in the SANDHILLS, on the Pee Dee R., 36 mi/58 km NNW of Florence and 8 mi/13 km S of the North Carolina border. Settled by Welsh in the 1750s in an area inhabited by the Cheraw tribe, it has many historic buildings, including Old St. David's Episcopal Church (c.1770). An important port at the head of navigation on the Pee Dee, it was a supply depot during the Civil War until captured (1865) by Sherman. In an agricultural region, Cheraw trades and processes cotton; textiles and building materials are manufactured. Jazz great Dizzy Gillespie was born here in 1917.

Cherokee Flat see under ANGELS CAMP, California.

Cherokee Lake see under HOLSTON R., Tennessee.

Cherokee National Forest 624,000 ac/253,000 ha, in E Tennessee, along the border with North Carolina. It comprises two sections, divided by the GREAT SMOKY MOUNTAINS National Park. The N section, extending S from the Jefferson National Forest at the Virginia border, is traversed by the Watauga, Nolichucky, and French Broad rivers. ROAN Mt. is here. The Ocoee, Hiwasee, and Tellico rivers flow through the S section, which extends to the Georgia border, where the Chattahoochee National Forest begins. The Little Tennessee R. forms the N boundary of the S section. The APPALACHIAN TRAIL runs through the forest, which is noted for its densely wooded mountainsides and gorges.

Cherokees, Lake o' the see LAKE O' THE CHEROKEES.

Cherokee Strip also, **Cherokee Outlet** strip of land, c.12,000 sq mi/31,080 sq km, formerly part of territory belonging to the Cherokee Nation through treaties of 1828 and 1833. Now a part of N Oklahoma, on the Kansas border, in an area containing the cities of ALVA and PONCA CITY, it was purchased from the Cherokee by the US in 1891 and opened to white settlement two years later. The ensuing land run (Sept. 19, 1893) was the largest and most spectacular of several such events in Oklahoma history.

Cherry Creek 64 mi/103 km long, in NC Colorado. It rises in N El Paso Co. and flows generally N through suburban Douglas and ARAPAHOE counties, then through SE Denver, emptying into the South Platte R. in Downtown. Talk of gold here brought Denver's first settlers to the area in 1858, and the city grew around the confluence. Floods were a problem until the building (1946–50) of the Cherry Creek Dam, 140 ft/43 m high and 14,300 ft/4359 m (2.71 mi/4.36 km) long, at the city's SE corner. Its reservoir is now in a popular state recreation area. More affluent residential neighborhoods of Denver (Country Club, Cherry Hills), as well as suburbs like **Cherry Hills Village** (city, pop. 5245, Arapahoe Co.), grew up on or near the creek.

Cherry Grove see under FIRE I., New York.

Cherry Hill township, pop. 69,359, Camden Co., SW New Jersey, on the Cooper R., the New Jersey Turnpike, and Route 295, 5 mi/8 km E of Camden. It was called Delaware until 1961. A fashionable Philadelphia suburb, it has many middle- and upper-middle-class homes. During the 1980s and 1990s Cherry Hill was one of the state's fastest-growing locations for office buildings and corporate headquarters. Its manufactures include telephone and electrical equipment, building materials, and computers. Several large commercial malls are here, as is the Garden State Park horse track (1985).

Cherry Point Marine Corps Air Station: see under HAVELOCK, North Carolina.

Cherry Valley village, pop. 617, in Cherry Valley township, Otsego Co., C New York, 50 mi/80 km WNW of Albany. Settled in 1740, it was once a stop on the westward-bound Cherry Valley Turnpike, now US Route 20. It is best known as the site of a 1778 massacre, in which Tories and Indians under the command of Walter Butler and Joseph Brant razed the village and killed over 40 residents and Patriot soldiers. Cherry Valley is also known for its medicinal springs.

Chesapeake independent city, pop. 151,976, in C Virginia, on the Elizabeth R. Formed in 1963 from the city of South Norfolk and Norfolk Co., It is one of the largest US cities in area, comprising 342 sq mi/886 sq km, and the second largest (after Suffolk) in Virginia. Situated on the Elizabeth R. and the ATLANTIC INTRACOASTAL WATERWAY, between PORTSMOUTH (W), NORFOLK (N), and VIRGINIA BEACH (E), Chesapeake includes both urban and rural areas, and takes in much of the GREAT DISMAL SWAMP (SW). It has port facilities and is a major oil storage center; manufactures include steel products, cement, and fertilizer. Agricultural activities include the processing of soybean products.

Chesapeake and Ohio Canal see under POTOMAC R.

Chesapeake and Ohio Railroad see under BALTIMORE AND OHIO RAILROAD.

Chesapeake Bay 200 mi/320 km–long estuary at the mouths of the Susquehanna, Patapsco, Patuxent, Potomac, Rappahannock, York, and James rivers (W) and the Elk, Chester, Choptank, Nanticoke, and Wicomico rivers (E), in Maryland and Virginia. It broadens generally from N to S, and is 4–30 mi/6–48 km wide. Its N end is in E Maryland; from the mouth of the Potomac R. S to its juncture with the Atlantic Ocean, between Cape Charles and Cape Henry, it is in Virginia. Its EASTERN SHORE is part of the DELMARVA PENINSULA. Chesapeake Bay is a center for commercial and recreational fishing, with over 200 species of finfish, as well as oysters and Chesapeake blue crabs, which spawn in its salty mouth, then travel upstream to the bay's 150 tributaries to mature. Baltimore, Maryland, and HAMPTON ROADS, Virginia, are major ports, with excellent deepwater shipping channels. Norfolk, Virginia, is the US Atlantic naval headquarters. The US Naval Academy is at ANNAPOLIS, Maryland. The Chesapeake Bay Bridge spans the N part of the bay, from KENT I. to Sandy Point, Maryland; the Hampton Roads Bridge-Tunnel, between Hampton and Norfolk, and the CHESAPEAKE BAY BRIDGE-TUNNEL, between Cape Charles and Virginia Beach, cross its S end. The bay is connected to the Delaware R. on the N by the Chesapeake and Delaware Canal, which is an entry point for the ATLANTIC INTRACOASTAL WATERWAY; the waterway traverses the bay, connecting with the ELIZABETH R. in the S.

The island-filled bay is actually the drowned valley of the lower SUSQUEHANNA R., which filled to its present level 3000 years ago. The first English colonists arrived at Cape Henry in 1607, and the bay was explored by John Smith in 1608, after the group had settled at Jamestown, Virginia, in the TIDEWATER. In 1631 the first permanent English settlement in modern Maryland was founded at Kent I. Today, the population of the Chesapeake region is over 9 million, while more than 12 million people live in the bay's 64,000–sq mi/

166,000-sq km watershed. Runoff from urban sewage, farms, and industry is threatening many of the 2500 species of plants and animals that live in the bay. More than 800,000 migratory waterfowl winter on the bay and the 400,000 ac/162,000 ha of tidal WETLANDS bordering it.

Chesapeake Bay Bridge-Tunnel 17.6 mi/28.3 km–long series of bridges and tunnels at the mouth of CHESAPEAKE BAY, between Cape CHARLES (N) and Virginia Beach (S), in SE Virginia. Opened in 1964, it consists of three trestles, each 3–4 mi/5–7 km long, two bridges, a causeway, and two tunnels, each 1 mi/1.6 km long, beneath Thimble Shoal and Chesapeake ship channels. Four artificial islands anchor the entrances and exits to the tunnels.

Cheshire town, pop. 25,684, New Haven Co., SC Connecticut, 14 mi/23 km N of New Haven. Founded in 1700, it is a suburban residential community situated in a farming area, with some manufacturing, including machinery and brass and wood products. In the first half of the 19th century, it was a copper and barite mining center. Cheshire is also home to the Cheshire Academy, a prep school founded in 1794, and to a four-prison Connecticut correctional center.

Chester **1.** town, pop. 9138, Orange Co., SE New York, 9 mi/15 km SE of Middletown. It lies in a dairying and horse breeding region. The famous trotter Hambletonian (1849–76), progenitor of a line of American racing horses, was born and is buried in Chester. **2.** resort, pop. 1119 (in Chester municipal district, pop. 10,762), on a headland jutting into MAHONE BAY, 32 mi/52 km WSW of Halifax, in Lunenburg Co., S Nova Scotia. Colonized by New Englanders in the 1760s, it was an important port in the 19th century, and in the 20th century has been a popular resort, well known for the variety of architectural styles represented in its homes. **3.** city, pop. 41,856, Delaware Co., SE Pennsylvania, a port on the Delaware R., 14 mi/22 km SW of Philadelphia. The second-oldest community in the state, it was settled by Swedes in 1644. The Dutch gained control in 1655, the English in 1664. Chester was the first seat of government for the colony of Pennsylvania (1681), and the site of the first provincial assembly (1682). It grew rapidly after the establishment of the John Roach Co., one of the nation's first builders of iron or steel ships. Today its industry is diversified, and includes shipbuilding and the manufacture of steel, paper, and chemicals; it is also a trading center. The city has been in economic decline since the 1950s, and is beset by a variety of urban ills. Chester is the seat of Widener University (1821) and Crozer Theological Seminary (1867). **4.** unincorporated village, pop. 14,986, Chesterfield Co., EC Virginia, on US 1 and Ashton Creek, 14 mi/22 km S of Richmond. A rail junction with a lumber industry, it is also a growing residential suburb of Richmond and Petersburg (9 mi/14 km SSE).

Chester County 758 sq mi/1963 sq km, pop. 376,396, in SE Pennsylvania, bordered NE by the Schuylkill R. and S by Delaware and Maryland. Its seat is West Chester. The county is diverse; in the E are the Philadelphia MAIN LINE suburbs of PAOLI and Berwyn; in the S are KENNETT SQUARE and other mushroom producing centers. The county also produces grapes. Largely agricultural, it has undergone a suburban housing boom since the 1980s.

Chesterfield **1.** city, pop. 37,991, St. Louis Co., EC Missouri, 20 mi/32 km W of St. Louis. It is a growing residential suburb on Route 40, just S of the Missouri R. **2.** town, pop. 3112, Cheshire Co., SW New Hampshire. It lies along the Connecticut R., 11 mi/18 km WSW of Keene. A largely agricultural community, the town also benefits from tourists visiting Chesterfield Gorge, resorts on Spofford L., and Pisgah State Park.

Chesterfield County 434 sq mi/1124 sq km, pop. 209,274, in SE Virginia, between the APPOMATTOX (S) and JAMES (NE) rivers. Its seat is Chesterfield. In the E, it contains many residential suburbs of Richmond (N) and Petersburg (S). Its W is rural and wooded, with some development around Swift Creek Reservoir.

Chesterfield Inlet also, **Chesterfield** hamlet, pop. 316, Keewatin Region, E mainland Northwest Territories, on the S side of the mouth of Chesterfield Inlet, NW Hudson Bay, 210 mi/340 km S of the Arctic Circle and 160 mi/260 km ESE of BAKER LAKE. It is a trade center with various administrative and scientific facilities. The inlet, some 115 mi/185 km long and 1–10 mi/1–16 km wide, extends WNW from Hudson Bay to Baker L.

Chester River 55 mi/89 km long, in Delaware and Maryland. It rises in NW Kent Co., Delaware, and flows SW past Millington, Maryland, the head of navigation, then past Crumpton and Chestertown. In its lower third it forms a wide estuary flowing into Chesapeake Bay.

Chesterton town, pop. 9124, Porter Co., extreme NW Indiana, 5 mi/8 km S of L. Michigan and 15 mi/24 km E of Gary, in a farming area known for its poultry, fruit, and dairy products, with a growing suburban residential component. Printing supplies are manufactured. INDIANA DUNES NATIONAL LAKESHORE is just N.

Chestertown town, pop. 4005, seat of Kent Co., NE Maryland, on the Chester R. and the EASTERN SHORE of Chesapeake Bay, 30 mi/48 km ESE of Baltimore. It is the market center for an agricultural and resort region. Local produce includes tomatoes, corn, wheat, other vegetables, and fish. Manufactures include fireworks, munitions, hosiery, and chemicals. Chestertown was laid out in 1706. Washington College (1782) is here.

Chestnut Hill **1.** residential and academic community, partly in Brookline, Norfolk Co., and partly in Newton, Middlesex Co., E Massachusetts. An affluent suburb of Boston, it is home to Boston College (1863) and Pine Manor College (1911). There are some corporate headquarters. **2.** residential neighborhood in Philadelphia, Pennsylvania, 11 mi/18 km NW of CENTER CITY, immediately W of MOUNT AIRY and SPRINGFIELD township, and NW of GERMANTOWN. Annexed to the city in 1854, this isolated rural area was subdivided into a classic planned railroad suburb designed to attract Philadelphia's Anglo-Saxon elite. It remains one of the city's most affluent sections.

Chestnut Ridge 30 mi/48 km long, in the Allegheny Mts., in SW Pennsylvania and NE West Virginia. It rises from 2200 to 2700 feet (671–823 m), extending NNE from Preston Co., West Virginia, to an area just SE of Indiana, Pennsylvania, and is cut by the Youghiogheny R.

Chesuncook Lake in Piscataquis Co., NC Maine, 30 mi/48 km NW of Millinocket, on the West Branch of the Penobscot R. This 28-mi/45-km–long lake, 1–4 mi/2–6 km wide, lies in the wilderness at an altitude of 942 ft/287 m, surrounded by the Katahdin and Sourdnahunk ranges, between MOOSEHEAD L. (SW) and Baxter State Park (E). Once a shallow stream, Chesuncook became Maine's third-largest lake after construction of a series of dams built between 1840 and 1916. Its

Abnaki name means "place where many streams emptied in." The Ripogenus Dam and Gorge, at the lake's SW extremity, are on the site of major 19th-century logging runs.

Cheverly town, pop. 6023, Prince George's Co., SC Maryland. It is a residential suburb just E of the Anacostia R. and Washington, D.C.

Chevy Chase residential suburb, pop. 8559, Montgomery Co., C Maryland, on the NW boundary of Washington, D.C. On the site of an estate known as Chevy Chase (1690–1761), it includes the town of Chevy Chase (pop. 2675), and several unincorporated villages. BETHESDA is NW. The neighboring (SE) residential section of Washington is also called Chevy Chase.

Cheyenne city, pop. 50,008, state capital and seat of Laramie Co., in the SE corner of Wyoming, on Crow Creek, 8 mi/13 km N of the Colorado border. It was settled by squatters after the Union Pacific decided to place a stop here; the town was founded with the arrival of the railroad in 1867. It became territorial capital in 1869, and capital of the new state in 1890. Cheyenne has been a livestock center since the 1870s. Its colorful early history includes the exploits of cattle barons, gunmen, gamblers, cowboys, vigilantes, and all manner of Wild West eccentrics, as well as wars between sheepmen and cattlemen. It is now an industrial city and a key trade and distribution center for the Rockies. Federal and state government, railroads, and airlines are major employers. Industries include oil refining, food and fertilizer processing, and the manufacture of electronics, precision instruments, restaurant equipment, chemicals, and plastics. Tourism is also important. Laramie County Community College is here. Cheyenne's Frontier Days is one of America's oldest and biggest annual rodeos. The Francis E. Warren Air Force Base, long a large local employer, is just NW of the city.

Cheyenne Mountain 9500 ft/2900 m, in the Rocky Mt. FRONT RANGE, immediately SW of COLORADO SPRINGS, SC Colorado. The site of a ski area and zoo, it also has, at c.8000 ft/2440 m, the Shrine of the Sun Memorial, dedicated to Will Rogers. A cairn marks the original burial site (1885) of writer Helen Hunt Jackson. Beneath the mountain, some 1700 ft/520 m within its base, are the headquarters of the North American Aerospace Defense Command (NORAD), created during the Cold War.

Cheyenne River 527 mi/848 km long, in NE Wyoming and W South Dakota. It flows E out of Niobrara Co., Wyoming, then NE through South Dakota, along the S of the BLACK HILLS, into Meade Co., where the BELLE FOURCHE R. joins it from the W. Continuing ENE, it forms the S boundary of the 4265–sq mi/11,047–sq km **Cheyenne River Indian Reservation,** and enters the W arm of L. OAHE. The reservation (pop. 7743, 66% Indian), like the adjacent (N) STANDING ROCK reservation, is home to various Sioux groups; Eagle Butte (city, pop. 489, Dewey and Ziebach counties) is headquarters.

Cheyney village in Thornburg township (pop. 5056), Delaware Co., SE Pennsylvania, 24 mi/38 km W of Philadelphia. It is the seat of Cheyney University of Pennsylvania (1837).

Chibougamau city, pop. 8855, SC Québec, 125 mi/200 km NW of L. St.-Jean and 310 mi/500 km N of Montréal. With Chapais, 24 mi/38 km SW, it developed in the 1950s to exploit rich copper deposits. Gold, silver, and zinc are mined as well, and there are sawmills. The area retains a sizable Cree pop.

Chicago city, pop. 2,783,726, seat of COOK Co., NE Illinois, on the SW shore of L. Michigan and the Indiana line (SE). The most populous city of the Midwest (third in the US, after New York and Los Angeles), it is the center of a three-state, eleven-county (including KANE, DU PAGE, MCHENRY, LAKE, and WILL, in Illinois; LAKE, in Indiana; and Kenosha, in Wisconsin) metropolitan area (CMSA) with a pop. of 8,065,633. Chicago is the transportation hub of the central US, and a major industrial, financial, commercial, and cultural center. The site, home to Algonquian groups (the name refers to the strong smell of local swamp plants like skunk cabbage), was visited by Marquette, Jolliet, and other French explorers in the 1670s. In 1779 Jean-Baptiste Point DuSable, a black fur trader from New Orleans, established a post here, and others followed. Fort Dearborn (1804; destroyed 1812, rebuilt 1816) protected them. The settlement experienced its first burst of growth when a waterway connecting L. Michigan with the Mississippi R. via the Chicago R. (see ILLINOIS WATERWAY) was initiated in 1829. By the time (1848) a canal was open, railroads had developed, and the city (incorporated 1830) became the nexus of a fast-growing network, gateway to the West as well as warehousing and shipping point for Midwestern grain. Livestock fattening and slaughtering came along with grain storage, and a farm machinery industry also existed by the late 1840s. The Civil War spurred rapid growth, and the city had over 300,000 inhabitants when, on Oct. 8–9, 1871, most of it was destroyed in the fire proverbially begun when Mrs. O'Leary's cow kicked over a lantern. The fire was an unanticipated boon, however, as Chicago quickly rebuilt, replacing vast tracts of shanty housing with modern structures. In the 1880s the city came to the forefront of world architectural practice, as the "Chicago School" built the first skyscrapers, and many other buildings, for mercantile and cultural establishments. The pop. passed 1 million in 1890, 2 million by 1910. Chicago's central position in American transportation made it the hub of mail-order merchandising, which was spurred by the rural free delivery postal system (initated 1896); Sears Roebuck, Montgomery Ward, Marshall Field, and other houses dominated the industry. The manufacturing of rails, rail cars, and other equipment also boomed, among a variety of other heavy and light industries. In the 20th century, city industries flourished in both world wars; after World War II, though, industry and residents began to move into the suburbs. The city's peak pop., in 1950, was 3,620,962. Chicago is divided, by the branches of the Chicago R., into the downtown LOOP and North, West, and South sides. It has a wide range of ethnic neighborhoods. In the mid 19th century Irish and German immigrants predominated. Late in the century Slavs (esp. Poles), Italians, Scandinavians, and Jews came in great numbers. In the 20th century black Southerners, Appalachian whites, Mexicans, Puerto Ricans, and other Hispanics have dominated in-migration, while longer-established whites have moved into the suburbs, so that the city today has a nonwhite majority. The SOUTH SIDE is said to be the largest US black community. Since the 1960s Chicago, which is highly residentially segregated, has experienced periodic racial and ethnic unrest. The famous stockyards closed in 1971, symbolizing a transition away from heavy industry toward finance, commerce, and varied smaller-scale manufacturing and processing. Chicago produces fabricated metals, foods, chemicals, pharmaceuticals, electronic equipment, clothing, and a range of other goods. It is home to the major US food commodity exchanges, the Midwest Stock Exchange, and many financial instutitions. Its best-known schools include the University of Illinois's Chicago Circle campus (1965), the (private) University of Chicago (1891), Loyola (1870) and De Paul (1898) universities, and the Illinois Institute of Technology (1890). The Art Institute of Chicago and Field Museum of National History are among the many museums and galleries contributing to its cultural importance. Wrigley Field, Comiskey Park, and Soldier Field are major sports venues. Although lake shipping declined after a spurt brought on by the 1959 opening of the Saint Lawrence Seaway, and rail traffic has declined, Chicago continues to be a trucking hub, and its O'Hare International Airport is the world's busiest. See also: ALBANY PARK; ANDERSONVILLE; AUSTIN; AVONDALE; BACK OF THE YARDS; BELMONT-CRAGIN; BEVERLY HILLS; BLACK BELT; BRIDGEPORT; BRIGHTON PARK; BUNGALOW BELT; CABBAGETOWN; CABRINI-GREEN; CHATHAM; CHICAGO CIRCLE; CHICAGOLAND; CHICAGO LAWN; CHICAGO R.; CHINATOWN; COMISKEY PARK; DAN RYAN EXPRESSWAY; DE PAUL; DIVISION St.; DOUGLAS PARK; EAST GARFIELD PARK; EDGEWATER (and Argyle St.); ENGLEWOOD; FOREST GLEN; FORT DEARBORN; GOLD COAST; GRANT PARK; HAYMARKET SQUARE; HULL HOUSE; HUMBOLDT PARK; HYDE PARK; JEFFERSON PARK; JOHN HANCOCK CENTER; KENWOOD; LAKE SHORE DRIVE; LAKE VIEW; LAWNDALE; the LEVEE; LINCOLN Ave.; LINCOLN PARK; LITTLE ITALY; LITTLE VILLAGE (Pueblo Pequeño, or South Lawndale); LOGAN SQUARE; the LOOP; MCCORMICK PLACE; MAGNIFICENT MILE; MARINA CITY; MARQUETTE PARK; MAXWELL St.; MERCHANDISE MART; MICHIGAN Ave.; MIDWAY; MIDWAY PLAISANCE; MOUNT GREENWOOD; NAVY PIER; NEAR NORTH SIDE; NEAR NORTHWEST SIDE; NEAR SOUTH SIDE; NEAR WEST SIDE (Lower West Side); NEW TOWN; NORTH SHORE; NORTH SIDE; NORWOOD PARK; O'HARE INTERNATIONAL AIRPORT; OLD TOWN; PALMER HOUSE; PILL HILL; PILSEN; POLONIA; PRAIRIE Ave.; PRINTERS' ROW; PULLMAN; RAVENSWOOD; RIVER NORTH; ROBERT TAYLOR HOMES; ROGERS PARK; ROOSEVELT ROAD; ROSELAND; RUSH St.; SAUGANASH; SEARS TOWER; SECOND CITY; SOLDIER FIELD; SOUTH SHORE; SOUTH SIDE; STATE St.; TRI-STATE EXPRESSWAY; TRI-TAYLOR; UNION STOCKYARDS; UPTOWN; WEST SIDE (and Northwest Side); WEST TOWN; WINDY CITY; WOODLAWN; WRIGLEY FIELD.

Chicago Circle site of a University of Illinois campus, on the Lower West Side of Chicago, Illinois. An enormous 1960s urban renewal project displaced an old Italian neighborhood. One of the school's buildings was designed by Ludwig Mies van der Rohe.

Chicago Heights city, pop. 33,072, Cook Co., NE Illinois, just W of the Indiana line, a suburb of Chicago 27 mi/43 km S of the Loop. Though grain, soybeans, corn, and vegetables are grown in the vicinity, the local economy centers around factories producing steel, auto-body stampings, chemicals, alloys, asphalt roofing, freight cars and railroad equipment, and glass, among other items. Originally a junction of two important Indian trails, the site was settled in the 1830s. A flood of German immigrants came here in the mid 19th century. In 1890 the Chicago Heights Land Association was able to entice manufacturers to set up factories here, making it the earliest, and at first the most important, steel town in the Chicago area. Prairie State College (1957) is here.

Chicagoland popular term, now semiofficial, for Chicago, Illinois, and its near suburbs.

Chicago Lawn residential section of Chicago, Illinois, 6 mi/10 km SW of the Loop. Once part of the holdings of speculator Hetty Green (who also owned much of nearby CICERO), and developed around World War I, it has been a largely East European district, and was a target of 1960s open housing marches, along with neighboring (E) MARQUETTE PARK.

Chicago Ridge village, pop. 13,643, Cook Co., NE Illinois, a suburb of Chicago 15 mi/24 km SW of the Loop. Mainly a residential community, it also contains steel tanks and lumber mills, remnants of an earlier time when the village was more industrial. The population grew by 500% in 1950–60. Argonne Forest, a county preserve, lies 4 mi/6 km W.

Chicago River c.36 mi/58 km long, in NE Illinois. It consists of the **North Branch,** 29 mi/47 km long, originating S of Mettawa, the **South Branch,** 5 mi/8 km long, originating on Chicago's South Side, and the less than 2 mi/3 km–long section leading from their juncture to L. Michigan. This short channel formerly flowed into the lake. The flow was reversed in 1900 so that its waters run into the South Branch, and then into the Chicago Sanitary and Ship Canal, as a means of carrying Chicago's treated wastes to the Mississippi R. via the navigable ILLINOIS WATERWAY. The Canal is connected with the Des Plaines R. at Lockport, SE of Chicago. Control locks (1938) at the Chicago River's former mouth on Chicago Harbor prevent the pollution of L. Michigan, and give lake vessels access to shipping terminals and industrial plants along its branches.

Chicago Sanitary and Ship Canal see under ILLINOIS WATERWAY.

Chic-Chocs, Monts see SHICKSHOCK Mts., Québec.

Chickahominy River 90 mi/145 km long, in E Virginia. It rises NW of Richmond, and forms the N border of Henrico Co. for much of its route around the city's N and E side, flowing generally SE to join the James R., 7 mi/11 km NW of Jamestown. The river figured in much Civil War fighting, particularly the battles of MECHANICSVILLE and FAIR OAKS, in 1862. It took its name from a tribe, one member of the Powhatan Confederacy.

Chickamauga Creek in Georgia and Tennessee, a tributary of the Tennessee R. It rises in NW Georgia, flows generally NW into Hamilton Co., Tennessee, along the E side of CHATTANOOGA, and enters Chickamauga L., on the Tennessee R. On Sept. 19–20, 1863, Confederate forces under Braxton Bragg defeated Unionists under William Rosecrans in a bloody battle along the creek, 12 mi/19 km S of Chattanooga.

Chickamauga Dam 129 ft/39 m high and 5800 ft/1770 m long, on the Tennessee R., just NE of Chattanooga, Tennessee, a TENNESSEE VALLEY AUTHORITY dam completed in 1940. It impounds 30 mi/48 km–long **Chickamauga Lake** on the Tennessee. Chickamauga Creek enters the lake 4 mi/6 km above the dam. The Sequoyah nuclear power plant (1980) is on the lake's W side, 11 mi/18 km NE of the dam.

Chickasaw city, pop. 6649, Mobile Co., SW Alabama, on Chickasaw Creek just off the Mobile R. and Mobile Bay, 6 mi/10 km N of downtown Mobile. Founded as a shipbuilding center during World War I, it is today largely residential, and is a steel port. Local industries include fisheries and paper mills.

Chickasawhay River 210 mi/340 km long, in SE Mississippi. It rises near Meridian and runs generally S to join the Leaf R. near Merrill, in George Co., forming the PASCAGOULA R.

Chickasaw Village see under TUPELO, Mississippi.

Chickasha city, pop. 14,988, seat of Grady Co., C Oklahoma, on the Washita R., 40 mi/64 km SW of Oklahoma City. It is the trade and processing center for an area rich in petroleum and agriculture. It markets corn, cotton, wheat, alfalfa, livestock, oil, and natural gas and produces cottonseed oil, flour, feed, and dairy goods. Among its manufactures are farm machinery, oilfield equipment, horse trailers, and electronic components. It is the seat of the University of Science and Arts of Oklahoma (1908).

Chico city, pop. 40,079, Butte Co., N California, in the Sacramento Valley, on Big Chico Creek, 81 mi/130 km N of Sacramento. Surrounded by an agricultural region producing rice, fruits, truck crops, walnuts, and, especially, almonds, Chico is a trade hub and packing and processing center. It has a variety of light manufactures, as well as a brewery and a publishing industry. Bidwell Park, at 2400 ac/970 ha, is one of the largest US municipal parks. California State University: Chico (1887) dominates the city's culture.

Chicopee city, pop. 56,632, Hampden Co., SC Massachusetts, at the junction of the Chicopee and Connecticut rivers, N of and adjoining Springfield. The Chicopee Falls, which drop 70 ft/21 m in about 3 mi/5 km, provided power for 19th-century cotton mills. The city has numerous plants manufacturing radios, tires, rubber goods, athletic equipment, plastics, textiles, brewing equipment, and forgings. Noted bronze work is produced in Chicopee, where the doors of the US Capitol were cast. The College of Our Lady of the Elms and Hampden College of Pharmacy are here; Westover Air Force Base is in the NE part. Villages within the city include Chicopee Falls and Willimansett.

Chicopee River 18 mi/29 km long, in SW Massachusetts. It is formed at Three Rivers by the junction of the Quaboag and Ware rivers, and flows W to the Connecticut R. at Chicopee. It drops 200 ft/61 m in 16.75 mi/27 km, with 10 dams in that distance, supplying power, especially at Chicopee Falls, in the city of Chicopee.

Chicoutimi city, pop. 62,670, SE Québec, between Jonquière (W) and La Baie (E), 109 mi/175 km N of Québec City, at the head of tides on the SAGUENAY R. Founded by the French in 1676 as a trading post, it began to develop in the 1840s around sawmills. Today local industries produce lumber, pulp, paper, aluminum, furniture, wrought iron, leather goods, and textiles. Local hydroelectric projects have also contributed to the city's growth as a rail hub and regional commercial center. Chicoutimi is the seat of a branch (1969) of the Université du Québec.

Chignecto, Isthmus of neck of land joining Nova Scotia to New Brunswick, as little as 17 mi/27 km wide, between NORTHUMBERLAND STRAIT (N) and **Chignecto Bay** (S), the 40 mi/65 km–long (with the Cumberland Basin) NE arm of the Bay of FUNDY.

Childersburg city, pop. 4579, Talladega Co., E Alabama, near the Coosa R., 31 mi/49 km SE of Birmingham. A lumber, fertilizer, and gunpowder producing center, it is on the site of a Coosa capital seen by De Soto in 1540. Nearby is Kymulga Onyx Cave, a 2000-year-old burial site in De Soto Caverns Park.

Chili town, pop. 25,178, Monroe Co., W New York, adjacent (SW) to Rochester. On Black Creek, the Genesee R., and the New York State Thruway, it is an industrial and residential suburb. The North Chili section is home to Roberts Wesleyan College (1866).

Chilkoot Pass at 3500 ft/1067 m, 17 mi/27 km N of SKAGWAY, Alaska, along the border with NW British Columbia. The Chilkoot (sometimes Chilcoot) Trail, used during the KLONDIKE Gold Rush of the late 1890s, runs for 33 mi/53 km from the former village of Dyea, just NW of Skagway, through the pass to Bennett L. in British Columbia, and is now used for hiking. The importance of the Chilkoot Pass waned after the opening of a railroad through WHITE PASS (SE) in 1900.

Chillicothe **1.** city, pop. 5959, Peoria Co., C Illinois, on the Illinois R., where it forms Douglas L., 15 mi/24 km NE of Peoria. A transportation center in a lake resort area, it is across the lake from the Woodford County Conservation Area, and just S of the Marshall State Fish and Wildlife Area. **2.** city, pop. 8804, seat of Livingston Co., NW Missouri, 65 mi/104 km E of St. Joseph. Founded in 1837, it grew with the coming of the Hannibal & St. Joseph Railroad (1859). Today it is a trade and processing center for a region that grows wheat, raises beef and dairy cattle, and mines coal and limestone. There is also some light manufacturing. **3.** city, pop. 21,921, seat of Ross Co., SC Ohio, on the Scioto R., 45 mi/72 km S of Columbus. Founded in 1796, its name is Algonquian for "principal town." In 1800 it became the capital of the NORTHWEST TERRITORY, and it was later (1803–10, 1812–16) the capital of Ohio. Today it is a trade and distribution center in a fertile agricultural area. Paper, shoes, aluminum products, building materials, and steel springs are among the goods manufactured here. The *Chillicothe Gazette,* founded in 1800, is the oldest continuously published newspaper W of the Alleghenies. ADENA, an 1807 Georgian mansion designed by Benjamin Latrobe, is here, as are many notable Greek Revival structures. The MOUND CITY GROUP National Monument is 3 mi/5 km to the N.

Chilliwack district municipality, pop. 49,531, Fraser-Cheam Regional District, SW British Columbia, in the Fraser R. Valley, near the mouth of the Chilliwack R., 10 mi/16 km N of the Washington border and 55 mi/89 km E of Vancouver. The trade center for a dairying, farming, and lumbering area, it processes fruits and vegetables, and is an expanding residential community. Developed after the discovery (1858) of gold on the Fraser R., it was incorporated as a city in 1908. A Canadian Forces Base (Vedder Crossing) and the Cultus L. recreational area are nearby (S).

Chillum unincorporated residential community, pop. 31,309, Prince George's Co., C Maryland, a suburb adjacent to NE Washington, D.C.

Chilmark town, pop. 651, W MARTHA'S VINEYARD, Dukes Co., SE Massachusetts. In a rural, hilly part of the Vineyard with many vacation homes, Chilmark includes the fishing village of Menemsha and the island of NOMANS LAND.

Chimayo unincorporated community, pop. 2789, Rio Arriba and Santa Fe counties, N New Mexico, 21 mi/34 km N of Santa Fe. Formerly a Tewa pueblo, later a Spanish frontier post, it has been a noted weaving center since 1805. Its sanctuary (1813) and chapel are both much visited for their reputed healing powers. An agricultural trade center, Chimayo handles local apples, chili peppers, and grain.

Chimney Rock **1.** eroded pinnacle (4242 ft/1294 m), jutting up from a plateau of reddish sandstone in W Nebraska, on the North Platte R., near Bridgeport and 18 mi/29 km SE of Scottsbluff. Rising 500 ft/153 m above the surrounding prairie, it was a landmark on the OREGON TRAIL, serving as a guidepost for generations of travelers. It is encompassed in the 83-ac/34-ha Chimney Rock National Historic Site. **2.** in Rutherford Co., SW North Carolina, 13 mi/21 km SSE of the town of Black Mountain. This sheer landmark rises 315 ft/96 m above its base on the S side of the Rocky Broad R., just W of L. Lure. Nearby Hickory Nut Gorge, 14 mi/23 km long, contains Hickory Nut Falls, with a 404-ft/123-m drop. Well known to the Cherokee, the area is now a popular tourist attraction.

China Beach see under BAKER BEACH, San Francisco, California.

China Lake see under RIDGECREST, California.

Chinati Mountains range in SW Texas, generally paralleling the RIO GRANDE, SW of Marfa, in Presidio Co., NW of the BIG BEND region. **Chinati Peak** (7730 ft/2358 m) is the highest elevation. Small amounts of zinc have been produced here from the Chinati and Montezuma mines; perlite has been mined in the Pinto Canyon area (N). Silver has also been produced, especially in the ghost town of Shafter, which prospered before the 1930s.

Chinatown **1.** in various US and Canadian cities, a district in which Chinese immigrants or their descendants live or continue to do business, often in close association with other Asians. **2.** commercial and former residential section of N VANCOUVER, British Columbia, just S of GASTOWN and E of the modern Downtown, centered on Pender St. Chinese miners were in the province by the time of the 1858 CARIBOO gold rush, and the Vancouver district is one of North America's oldest and largest Chinatowns. It swelled in the 1880s with Canadian Pacific Railway workers; until 1947 its residents faced restrictions on living elsewhere in the city. Today old Chinatown is a tourist and business zone. Much of Vancouver's Chinese pop., now over 100,000, live in other sections, including Strathcona, in the EAST END; among recent arrivals are many emigrants from Hong Kong, who have brought wealth and other resources to the city. **3.** in California: **a.** commercial section of LOS ANGELES, at the N edge of Downtown, between EL PUEBLO DE LOS ANGELES (S) and CHAVEZ RAVINE (N). A larger Old Chinatown to the E was destroyed in the 1930s to make way for UNION STATION. Today, Vietnamese immigrants, many of Chinese descent, also live in the community. **b.** residential and commercial section of downtown SAN FRANCISCO on the E of Nob Hill, SE of North Beach and NW of the Financial District. It grew around Portsmouth Square, the site of the 1846 US takeover of the city; Grant Ave. is its main thoroughfare. America's first real Chinese community, it was created by Cantonese miners during the 1849–50 gold rush, and expanded during the 1860s–70s with thousands who came to work on the CENTRAL PACIFIC RAILROAD. White hostility in the 1870s–80s reinforced the community's separateness. Surviving vicissitudes including the 1906 earthquake, it remains the vibrant commercial heart of the Bay Area's Chinese community, although there is a **New Chinatown** in the RICHMOND DISTRICT. **4.** in NW Washington, D.C., commercial area about 1 mi/1.5 km NE of the White House, in the EAST END, near the Washington Convention Center. Chinese businesses moved here when the FEDERAL TRIANGLE was developed in the 1930s. **5.** neighborhood in downtown HONOLULU, Hawaii, E of Honolulu Harbor. A mixture of rundown storefronts, artists' galleries, and boutiques, this section is now populated mainly by Vietnamese and Filipinos. **6.** residential and commercial neighborhood on the Near South Side of Chicago, Illinois, just SW of the Loop, the center of the local Chinese community since the 1920s. **7.** commercial and residential district in downtown Boston, Massachusetts, SE of Boston Common. **8.** in lower Manhattan, New York City, commercial and residential district on the Lower East Side, traditionally bounded N by Canal Street, but expanding into LITTLE ITALY in recent years. Its main commercial streets include Mott and Mulberry. Although most of New York's Chinese immigrants and longtime residents now live in such other areas as FLUSHING and SUNSET PARK, the Manhattan neighborhood continues to be a marketing and entertainment hub. Heavy immigration from Hong Kong in the 1980s strained housing capacity. **9.** largely commercial neighborhood centered along DUNDAS St. West, in downtown TORONTO, Ontario, NW of Eaton Centre and City Hall, and extending onto N–S SPADINA Ave. Its businesses represent several East Asian cultures. **10.** mixed residential and commercial neighborhood in Northwest PORTLAND, Oregon, between Union Station (NW) and OLD TOWN (SE). **11.** commercial and residential neighborhood in CENTER CITY, Philadelphia, Pennsylvania, NE of City Hall. Centered on a few blocks N of MARKET STREET, it is home to both Chinese and Vietnamese immigrants. **12.** in MONTRÉAL, Québec, small commercial district (the *Quartier chinois*) along and near Rue de la Gauchetière, just N (officially; actually W) of VIEUX-MONTRÉAL, near the Place d'Armes. Montréal's Chinese, here since the 1860s, now mostly live elsewhere in the city. **13.** see INTERNATIONAL DISTRICT, Seattle, Washington.

Chincoteague Island 7 mi/11 km NE–SW and up to 1 mi/1.6 km wide, in Accomack Co., E Virginia, in Chincoteague Bay, inside (NW) the barrier island of ASSATEAGUE. Every July the island has a pony penning, a roundup of wild horses from Chincoteague and Assateague. In addition to tourism, shellfishing is an important local industry. Chincoteague is a town, with a pop. of 3572.

Chinle see under CANYON DE CHELLY, Arizona.

Chino city, pop. 59,682, San Bernardino Co., SW California, 34 mi/55 km E of Los Angeles and just E of the Puente Hills. Historically a trade center in a citrus producing and dairy farming area, it has grown rapidly as a Los Angeles suburb, quadrupling in population, since 1970. There are a variety of light manufactures. The California Institution for Men, a state prison, is here, and Chino Airport (SE) is a center for recreational pilots.

Chinook Belt areas immediately E of the Rocky Mts. where moist Pacific (SW) air, having precipitated in the mountains, descends as warm, dry winds called *chinooks* (after a tribe on the Oregon coast, where the winds were thought to originate). In the E foothills of the Rockies and on plains as far as 250 mi/400 km E, chinooks in winter can quickly melt snow; they are most prominent in late winter and early spring, strongly affecting Alberta's PEACE R. valley and the Calgary area. They are experienced as far S as Colorado.

Chippawa also, **Chippewa** former village, since 1973 part of the city of NIAGARA FALLS, Ontario, on the Niagara R. It was the scene of a July 5, 1814 battle in which US troops after capturing FORT ERIE defeated a British force; the Americans' northward advance stalled, however, when reinforcements did not arrive.

Chippewa, Lake in Sawyer Co., NW Wisconsin, on the Lac Courte Oreilles Indian Reservation. Measuring 10 mi/16 km long, it has an irregular shoreline, with a number of branches, and contains many small islands.

Chippewa County 1590 sq mi/4118 sq km, pop. 34,604, in the E Upper Peninsula, NE Michigan; bounded by L. Superior (NW), Whitefish Bay (N), L. George (NE), the St. Marys R. (E), and L. Huron (S). It is drained by the Tahquamenon and Munuscong rivers. Its seat is SAULT SAINTE MARIE. The rural county includes Sugar, Neebish, and Drummond islands and large tracts of Hiawatha National Forest and Lake Superior State Forest. There is lumbering, dairying, and commercial fishing; flax and potatoes are grown. Sault Ste. Marie is a port of entry and has manufacturing and shipping.

Chippewa Falls city, pop. 12,727, Chippewa Co., WC Wisconsin, on the Chippewa R., 10 mi/16 km NE of Eau Claire. In 1837, the Ojibwa gave up their rights to the site, which became a busy sawmill center. Today, it is a trading center, set in a farming and dairying region. Butter and other dairy items are produced, and meatpacking and brewing are major industries. Manufactures include computers, textiles, doors and sashes, and tools and dies. L. WISSOTA, 2 mi/3 km E of the city, is the state's largest artificial lake.

Chippewa National Forest 660,000 ac/267,300 ha, in NC Minnesota, in Cass and Itasca counties. It includes many lakes, the largest Leech L. (250 sq mi/648 sq km), Winnibigoshish L. (180 sq mi/466 sq km), and Cass L. (25 sq mi/65 sq km), and is a popular sailing and fishing area. BEMIDJI is just W, as are the headwaters of the Mississippi R. Headquarters are at the town of Cass Lake. Most of the forest is occupied by the Leech Lake Indian Reservation (Ojibwa, or Chippewa).

Chippewa River 120 mi/193 km long, in SW Minnesota. It rises in Douglas Co., near Evansville, then flows generally S, past Benson, to the Minnesota R. at Montevideo. The **East Branch** rises in a small lake E of Glenwood, in W Minnesota, and flows 60 mi/97 km S and W to the Chippewa at Benson.

Chiputneticook Lakes chain of lakes on the Maine–New Brunswick border, WSW of Fredericton, forming the international boundary for 28 mi/45 km. The source of the SAINT CROIX R., it includes North, Grand, and Spednik lakes.

Chiricahua Mountains small range in the SE corner of Arizona, a N extension of Mexico's Sierra Madre. It reaches 9795 ft/2986 m at **Chiricahua Peak,** 38 mi/61 km NNE of Douglas, and is separated from the DOS CABEZAS Mts. (NW) by Apache Pass (5115 ft/1559 m), used by 19th-century travelers on the Butterfield stage line; the Fort Bowie (active 1862–94) National Historic Site is here. Cochise Head (8109 ft/2472 m) and Massai Point (6870 ft/2094 m) commemorate Apache leaders who, along with Geronimo, dominated the area. In the Coronado National Forest, the range includes **Chiricahua National Monument** (11,985 ac/4854 ha), which protects weirdly shaped and precariously balanced volcanic formations. The Pedregosa Mts. lie S, the Swisshelm Mts. SW.

Chisholm city, pop. 5290, St. Louis Co., NE Minnesota, 6 mi/10 km NNE of Hibbing, in the MESABI RANGE. Settled in 1898, largely by Finnish miners, it is home to the Minnesota Mining Museum and other visitors' centers related to its industrial history.

Chisholm Trail former cattle trail, some 1500 mi/2400 km long, used from 1866 through the early 1880s, between S Texas and Kansas. Following old buffalo trails in places, it built on a route developed in Oklahoma and Kansas by Jesse Chisholm (d.1866). By the 1870s the trail began in the S at Brownsville, Texas, and proceeded N through Kingville, through or near San Antonio, across the Colorado R. at Austin, across the Brazos R. near Waco, across the Trinity R. at Fort Worth, and across the Red R. into Oklahoma, where it passed through Duncan, Rush Springs, and Enid. In Kansas it brought cattle to railheads at Abilene, later at Newton, Wichita, or Dodge City. Extension of rail lines farther S gradually reduced the trail's importance. Not a single fixed route, the Chisholm Trail incorporated hundreds of bypasses and feeder trails.

Chisos Mountains N–S range lying within the BIG BEND of the Rio Grande, in SW Texas. Jutting up from the desert in Big Bend National Park, they cover approximately 40 sq mi/104 sq km, are noted for their unusual geologic formations, steep cliffs and vivid coloring, and are popular with hikers. Emory Peak (7825 ft/2387 m) is the highest point. Mercury has been mined in the area.

Chittenden County 540 sq mi/1399 sq km, pop. 131,761, in NW Vermont. BURLINGTON is the county seat. L. Champlain is the W boundary; the Green Mts. are in the E. The area is drained by the Winooski, Brown, Huntington, and Lamoille rivers. Vermont's most heavily populated county, Chittenden also is the site of Mt. MANSFIELD, the highest point in the state. The economy is based on lake and mountain resorts, dairy and maple products, fruit, granite, talc, the manufacture of textiles, wood and metal products, and Burlington's commerce and electronics plants.

Chocolate Mountains NW–SE range, running c.70 mi/115 km along the E side of the SALTON SEA and the IMPERIAL VALLEY, in SE California. Mining has been important in this area, now the site of the Chocolate Mountain Aerial Gunnery Range. The Orocopia Mts. are N, the CHUCKWALLA and Palo Verde mountains E.

Chocorua, Mount granitic mountain (3475 ft/1060 m) in the SANDWICH RANGE of the S White Mts., EC New Hampshire, 6 mi/10 km W of Conway. Noted for alpine vegetation and trails, it is accessible from the KANCAMAGUS HIGHWAY, and is named for a 1720s Pequawket chief about whom there are numerous legends.

Choctaw city, pop. 8545, Oklahoma Co., C Oklahoma, a residential suburb 14 mi/23 km E of downtown Oklahoma City.

Choctawhatchee Bay protected inlet of the Gulf of Mexico, 40 mi/64 km E of Pensacola, in Okaloosa and Walton counties, NW Florida. Thirty mi/48 km E–W and 5–10 mi/8–16 km wide, it joins the gulf through East Pass, a bridged strait between the barrier beaches, and connects with Pensacola Bay (W) via Santa Rosa Sound. The Choctawhatchee R. enters it from the E. It is traversed by the GULF INTRACOASTAL WATERWAY. Eglin Air Force Base covers much of its N shore. Fort Walton Beach, Destin, and other resorts are popular.

Choctawhatchee River 140 mi/230 km long, in Alabama and Florida. Its rises in SE Alabama and flows generally SSW into Florida, where it enters Choctawhatchee Bay.

Choke Canyon Reservoir impoundment of the Frio R., midway between San Antonio (NW) and Corpus Christi (SE), in SE Texas. It covers 26,000 ac/10,530 ha in two counties, and was created for recreation and flood control on the NUECES R., into which the Frio flows. The James E. Daughtrey Wildlife Management Area surrounds the reservoir, covering 8000 ac/3240 ha.

Cholame Hills hilly area just NW of the TEMBLOR RANGE, in

WC California, along the San Andreas Fault. A monument to the actor James Dean, who died here in an auto crash in Sept. 1955, is in the hamlet of **Cholame,** 23 mi/37 km ENE of Paso Robles.

Choptank River 70 mi/110 km long, in Delaware and Maryland. It rises SW of Dover, Delaware, and flows generally SW through Delaware and the EASTERN SHORE of Maryland past Greensboro (the head of navigation), Denton, and CAMBRIDGE, to Chesapeake Bay, S of TILGHMAN. It is tidal to Denton, and its estuary, more than 4 mi/6 km wide at its mouth, has many inlets. Fishing and oystering are important industries.

Chowan River 52 mi/84 km long, in NE North Carolina. It is formed by the confluence of the Nottaway and Blackwater rivers at the Virginia line, and flows S and SE along a swampy, then estuarial, course into ALBEMARLE SOUND, 4 mi/6 km W of EDENTON.

Christiana see under CHRISTINA R., Delaware.

Christiansburg town, pop. 15,004, Montgomery Co., SW Virginia, near the W base of the Blue Ridge Mts., 27 mi/43 km SW of Roanoke. In an agricultural and coal mining region, it produces canned goods, furniture, lumber, and clothing, and has stockyards.

Christiansted town, pop. 2555, on the NE coast of the island of SAINT CROIX, in the US VIRGIN ISLANDS. The site was settled first by the French, then (1645) by the English. Christiansted was founded by the Danes (1733), and was capital of the Danish West Indies and a thriving commercial port. It retains a colonial atmosphere, with pastel-colored stone buildings and cobblestone streets. Today tourism is the leading industry. Rum and sugar are exported from the busy port. Alexander Hamilton once lived here; his house has been reconstructed. Christiansted's 18th- and 19th-century architectural core is now a National Historic Site.

Christina River 35 mi/56 km long, in Pennsylvania, Maryland, and Delaware. It rises near Kemblesville, Chester Co., SE Pennsylvania, and flows across the NE corner of Maryland. It passes NEWARK before turning NE and entering the Delaware R. at Wilmington. The Dutch called it Minquas Kill. In March 1638, the NEW SWEDEN colony established Fort Christina at the site where the river and Brandywine Creek join, S of modern Wilmington, and the river took the name of Sweden's queen. During the Colonial period this was corrupted to "Christiana," a name still held by a village along its banks near the Delaware Turnpike.

Christmas Mountains N–S range, rising to 5735 ft/1749 m, at the N edge of BIG BEND National Park, in SW Texas. Fluorspar has been mined here. To the SW is Terlingua, which flourished in World War I on the processing of mercury from cinnabar, and is now a ghost town and tourist attraction. The Chalk Mts. lie to the N.

Chrysler Building at 42nd St. and Lexington Ave., midtown Manhattan, New York City. Opened in 1930, it was for a few months (until the EMPIRE STATE BUILDING opened) the tallest building in the world, at 77 stories and 1048 ft/320 m to the top of its spire. Its stainless steel external elements and Art Deco interior spaces are famous; William Van Alen was the architect.

Chubbuck city, pop. 7791, Bannock Co., SE Idaho, a suburb just N of Pocatello, near the E edge of the American Falls Reservoir (on the Snake R.) and the SW edge of the FORT HALL Indian Reservation.

Chuckwalla Mountains desert range in SE California, NE of the CHOCOLATE Mts. and the Salton Sea. Rising to 4505 ft/1374 m at Black Butte, it includes colorful ridges, rocky spires, washes, and springs and is cut by many canyons, including Ship Creek and Corn Springs Wash. Corn Springs, an ancient campsite, has petroglyphs and other artifacts. The **Chuckwalla Bench** (S) is a transition zone between vegetation typical of the MOJAVE (N) and COLORADO (S) deserts. The mountains have been mined; hiking and rockhounding are now popular. The lower **Little Chuckwalla** Mts. continue to the SE. The chuckwalla is a kind of lizard.

Chugach Mountains one of the COAST RANGES, in S Alaska, extending mostly E–W for c.300 mi/500 km, S of the ALASKA RANGE and near the Gulf of Alaska, from the SAINT ELIAS Mts. (E) to the head of COOK INLET. Named for the Inuit people who lived in the PRINCE WILLIAM SOUND area, the Chugach rise to a high at Mt. Marcus Baker (13,176 ft/4016 m), include Mt. Steller (10,617/3236 m), and merge with the KENAI Mts. S of Anchorage; they form the city skyline's backdrop. Within the **Chugach National Forest** (5.6 million ac/2.27 million ha), second in size in the US to the TONGASS, are the NE end of the KENAI PENINSULA; the Portage Glacier, near the center of the area affected by the Good Friday earthquake of March 1964, which reshaped the land; the S end of the Columbia Glacier, the second-largest (after the Malaspina) US tidewater glacier, towering 200 ft/61 m above water; the islands of Prince William Sound; and the Sargent Icefield.

Chukchi Sea large section of the Arctic Ocean between Siberia (W) and NW Alaska (E). It borders the BEAUFORT SEA N of Alaska, and connects with the Bering Sea (S) via the Bering Strait. The International Dateline runs through it, and oilfields are believed to lie beneath. The sea is navigable four to five months of the year. KOTZEBUE is the major Alaska settlement on the sea, which is named for a Siberian people.

Chula Vista city, pop. 135,163, San Diego Co., extreme SW California, 8 mi/13 km SSE of San Diego, of which it is a suburb. It is 6 mi/10 km from Mexico, near the lower end of San Diego Bay, and houses many active and retired military personnel, brought to the area by San Diego's naval installations. Chula Vista manufactures missile and aircraft parts, as well as structural steel, generators, hardware, chemicals, and other products. The packing and shipping of area vegetables is economically important, as is retail trade stimulated in large part by cross-border Mexican shoppers. The city has doubled in population since 1970.

Chupadera Mesa tableland (6000–9000 ft/1830–2745 m high) SSE of Albuquerque, and W of Carrizozo, in C New Mexico. It includes the Sierra Oscura (Oscura Mts.) in the SW, which rise to 8732 ft/2662 m at Oscura Peak. To the W is the Trinity Site, now within the WHITE SANDS Missile Range, where the first atomic bomb was exploded.

Churchill local government district, pop. 1143, NE Manitoba, on Hudson Bay at the mouth of the Churchill R. Settled just upstream in 1688 by the Hudson's Bay Company as Fort Churchill, it is the terminus (since 1929) of the Hudson Bay Railway, and the center of wheat export via ship from the province. A subarctic seaport, open some 3 months a year, it has been dubbed the "Polar Bear Capital of the World"—the bears' seasonal movements bring them into the settlement. Their appearance and a wide variety of other wildlife—including Arctic terns, snowy owls, white beluga whales, seals, and caribou—draw visitors. Fort Prince of Wales, a 1732 Hudson's Bay Company post, now a historic park, is just NW, across the river's mouth. The Churchill Research Range has been Canada's premier rocket station, the scene of research on the aurora borealis and northern weather.

Churchill Downs see under LOUISVILLE, Kentucky.

Churchill River **1.** before 1965, **Hamilton River** 600 mi/970 km long, the longest river in Labrador. It rises as the Ashuanipi, flowing N from L. Ashuanipi, SE of WABUSH, near the Québec border, then turns SE. Here it enters the huge Smallwood Reservoir, which has grown since the 1960s to cover over 2520 sq mi/6530 sq km. The reservoir, created by dams at Churchill (formerly Grand) Falls and on other local rivers, has subsumed Lobstick, Michikamau, and other lakes here on the edge of the Labrador Plateau. At CHURCHILL FALLS the river plunges 245 ft/75 m from the edge of a tilted portion of the CANADIAN SHIELD, and powers what was the world's largest hydroelectric plant before the JAMES BAY Project. The falls are part of a stretch in which the Churchill drops more than 1000 ft/300 m within 20 mi/32 km. It continues E through glacial McLean Canyon to the HAPPY VALLEY–GOOSE BAY area, where it enters Goose Bay and L. Melville, part of the 34 mi/55 km–long Hamilton Inlet, finally emptying into the Labrador Sea. The river, known to the Montagnais-Naskapi, who feared the falls, was seen by whites in 1839, but remained unutilized, except for a Hudson's Bay Company post at Fort Smith (now North West River, on L. Melville) until the 1950s, when iron ore on the Québec-Labrador border brought rail connections and hydroelectric development to the area. **2.** 1000 mi/1600 km long, in Saskatchewan and Manitoba. It rises in Lac La Loche, in NW Saskatchewan, and flows generally ESE, then ENE, across lowlands and through a series of lakes, to reach Hudson Bay at Churchill, Manitoba. It has also been known as the Missinipi ("big river") and as the English River, because it was a main route long used by fur traders. Its mouth was discovered in 1619 by Jens Munk, but its upper reaches, where Cree and Chipewyan groups hunted, were not explored until the 1770s, when the NORTH WEST COMPANY established fur posts. The river's lakes in Saskatchewan include (W–E) Peter Pond L., named after the first white man to visit it (1774), covering 300 sq mi/777 sq km; Churchill L. (216 sq mi/559 sq km); and L. Île à la Crosse (151 sq mi/391 sq km), where the Beaver R. joins from the S. In Manitoba are Granville L.; Southern Indian L. (868 sq mi/2248 sq km); and Northern Indian L. The river has a number of hydroelectric plants, which have reduced its flow.

Churchville rural village, pop. 1731, in Riga township, Monroe Co., W New York, 15 mi/24 km SW of Rochester. Temperance leader Frances Willard (1839–98) was born and is buried here.

Chuska Mountains range in the NE corner of Arizona and NW corner of New Mexico, reaching 9808 ft/2989 m at Roof Butte and including Matthews Peak (9403 ft/2866 m), both in Arizona. The Chuskas lie within the Navajo Indian Reservation.

Cibola Spanish, **Cíbola** legendary land of riches sought by 16th-century Spanish explorers in the Southwest. The wanderer Cabeza de Vaca and the missionary Marcos de Niza recounted stories of a fabulous gold-decked Seven Cities that, conflated with the EL DORADO legend, led to a 1540–42 expedition from Mexico led by Coronado. Arriving in the vicinity of ZUÑI, the Spaniards discovered only ordinary PUEBLOS. Their search then became further complicated by stories of QUIVIRA. The lingering death of the Cibola legend led to the spread of the name to various places in the Southwest.

Cibola National Forest 1.7 million ac/690,000 ha (2660 sq mi/6880 sq km), in C New Mexico, in scattered units W and SE of Albuquerque and W of Socorro. Its desert ranges include the SANDIA Mts. The forest, headquartered in Albuquerque, also administers NE New Mexico's Kiowa National Grassland and the Black Kettle National Grassland, in W Oklahoma and NW Texas.

Cicero **1.** town, pop. 67,436, Cook Co., NE Illinois, immediately W of Chicago, 7 mi/11 km W of the Loop. It is an important industrial and residential suburb. One-fourth of Cicero's area contains one of the world's largest concentrations of industrial activity, with over 150 factories in an area of 1.75 sq mi/4.5 sq km. Communications and electronic equipment are the most important products, followed by malleable and steel castings, tool and die makers' supplies, forgings, and rubber goods. There are also some printing presses. Settled in the 1830s, Cicero grew slowly until the Chicago, Burlington and Quincy Railroad arrived in 1864. A population boom ensued, and the Hawthorne works of the Westinghouse Electric Company were established here in 1902, soon becoming the largest local employer. During the 1920s, Cicero served as Al Capone's headquarters. Two horseracing tracks, Hawthorne Racecourse-Suburban Downs and Sportsman's Park Racetrack, are here. It is also the seat of Morton College (1924). **2.** town, pop. 25,560, Onondaga Co., C New York, 7 mi/11km NE of Syracuse. From the 19th to the mid 20th century, it was a noted producer of frogs' legs; much of the town is wetland along the S of Oneida L. The SW corner is densely suburban.

Cimarron County 1842 sq mi/4471 sq km, pop. 3301, at the tip of the Oklahoma PANHANDLE, at the extreme NW of the state. It is the only US county that borders four states: Kansas and Colorado (N), New Mexico (W), and Texas (S). Its seat is BOISE CITY. Sparsely populated, it has few other municipalities. It is made up of high plains, at an average of 4000 ft/1220 m, and includes BLACK MESA, the highest point in the state. Livestock are raised here, and grain is grown. **The Territory of Cimarron** was a name for the entire Panhandle region, settled by cattlemen in the 19th century, when it belonged to no one and was also called No Man's Land. In 1887 resident ranchers attempted to protect their land claims by forming a territorial government, but it was not recognized by Congress. In 1890 the land was incorporated into the Oklahoma Territory.

Cimarron Cutoff also, **Cutoff Division** or **Cimarron Crossing Trail** see under SANTA FE TRAIL.

Cimarron River 600 mi/1000 km long, in New Mexico, Oklahoma, Colorado, and Kansas. It rises in Colfax Co., NE New Mexico, E of Raton, and flows generally E through the NW corner of the Oklahoma PANHANDLE and NE through extreme SE Colorado, then into Kansas. It continues in a generally SE direction, reentering Oklahoma briefly, then Kansas, then Oklahoma. It finally empties into the ARKANSAS R. 17 mi/27 km W of Tulsa. Nonnavigable, the river traverses largely semiarid, sparsely populated ranching country. In places it is intermittently dry.

Cincinnati city, pop. 364,040, seat of Hamilton Co., SW Ohio, a port on the Ohio R., between the mouths of the Little Miami (E) and Great Miami (W) rivers, opposite (N of) COVINGTON, Kentucky, and 15 mi/24 km E of the Indiana line. It is the center of an eight-county (including HAMILTON, BUTLER, CLERMONT, and WARREN, and Kentucky's BOONE and KENTON) metropolitan area with a pop. of 1,744,424. Long the largest city on the river below Pittsburgh, it has been the transportation and trade center for the Ohio Valley since the early 19th century, and later a distributor of coal and iron from the Appalachian hinterland. Known as the cultural capital of the region, it has the first US municipal university (the University of Cincinnati, 1819), the oldest Jewish theological school in America (Hebrew Union College, 1875), such other institutions as Xavier University (1831) and a number of seminaries, and one of the nation's oldest zoos. Cincinnati's development was due to its position as a river gateway to the Mississippi Valley and as a bridge between North and South. Laid out in 1788 as Losantiville, on flat land with a basin along the riverfront (but renamed in 1790 for the Revolutionary War officers' society), it was protected both by a ring of "seven hills" and by Ft. Washington, a base for action against the region's Indians. As the first major stop W of the Alleghenies for pioneers and traders bound into the NORTHWEST TERRITORY or the Mississippi Valley, it mushroomed, esp. after the first steamboat arrived in 1811. The Miami and Erie Canal linked it with much of Ohio in 1827, and it became a major trader with the plantation South. Its strong Southern sympathies were counterbalanced, however, by abolitionist activism, led by such figures as J. G. Birney and Lane Theological Seminary's Lyman Beecher. It became an important stop on the UNDERGROUND RAILROAD. By the 1850s, Cincinnati was one of America's leading cities. It attracted Easterners as well as Europeans, esp. (in the 1840s) German and Irish immigrants. It was a hub of services for the Union in the Civil War. Soon after, though, river trade faded as Chicago-centered rail traffic began to shift activity elsewhere in the Midwest. The city has never regained its prominence, but has become a center of varied industries. It is a leading manufacturer of soap and cosmetic products (Procter and Gamble is a dominant employer), also producing an enormous variety of items ranging from playing cards to malt liquors to jet engines. A wholesaling and banking center, it still handles heavy river barge traffic, somewhat revived since the 1960s, and is one of the nation's largest inland coal ports. Despite losing residents to the suburbs, so that it now has about 70% of its 1950 pop. of 503,998, it is considered to have a high quality of life. Many old neighborhoods, and much of the center city, have been renovated in recent decades, and tourism has become an important contributor to the economy. The Greater Cincinnati International Airport is across the Ohio R. (SW), in Boone Co., Kentucky. See also: the BASIN (and Seven Hills); EDEN PARK; FOUNTAIN SQUARE; HYDE PARK; MOUNT ADAMS; MOUNT AIRY FOREST; MOUNT AUBURN; OVER-THE-RHINE; PORKOPOLIS; RIVERFRONT STADIUM; WEST END.

Cinnaminson township, pop. 14,583, Burlington Co., SW New Jersey, 7 mi/11 km NE of Camden. It is largely residential.

Circleville city, pop. 11,709, seat of Pickaway Co., SC Ohio, 25 mi/40 km S of Columbus, on the Scioto R. in an agricultural region. Founded in 1810, it was originally laid out on the remains of a circular fortlike structure reputedly erected by Mound Builders. Today it is home to a bible college and a few light industries, including grain and stock processing.

Circus City see under PERU, Indiana.

cirque bowllike, steep-walled hollow in the side of a mountain, created by glacial action and later shaped further by the freezing and thawing of rock that cracks and falls away. Cirques are often semicircular, and may contain lakes. The meeting of two cirques' steep walls may create a knifelike ridge called an *arete*.

Cisco city, pop. 3813, Eastland Co., NC Texas, 43 mi/68 km E of Abilene. Settled in the 1850s, it was a ranching center before a 1918 oil boom. The Mobley Hotel (1916) was bought in 1919 by Conrad Hilton, becoming the first of his chain; it is now a community center. Cisco Junior College was founded in 1909.

Citadel of the Prairie see PAWNEE ROCK, Kansas.

Citronelle city, pop. 3671, Mobile Co., SW Alabama, 30 mi/48 km NNW of Mobile. Named for the oil-producing Asian citronella grass growing locally, it became in 1906 one of the first US centers producing oil from tung nuts. Livestock, truck, and cotton have also been important. In 1952 drillers discovered, at a depth below 10,000 ft/3050 m, the **Citronelle Oilfield,** one of the South's (and the world's, at that depth) largest petroleum deposits.

Citrus Heights unincorporated community, pop. 107,439, Sacramento Co., NC California, a booming, largely residential suburb 15 mi/24 km NE of downtown Sacramento, at the Placer Co. line.

city **1.** in the US: an incorporated municipality, established under provisions of the constitution or statutes of the state in which it is situated. *City* is not a size category, although most cities are more populous than most TOWNS, BOROUGHS, or VILLAGES. The affairs of American cities (to whom the states have delegated local government authority) are generally administered by a mayor and council, by a commission, or by a nonpolitical, professional city manager. Compare METROPOLITAN AREA, and see also URBAN. **2.** in Canada: a municipality incorporated under provincial law, essentially similar to a US city. In Canada, however, *city* is a size category; under varying provincial formulas, cities are larger than towns and villages. See also METROPOLITAN GOVERNMENT.

City Island 230 ac/93 ha, in Long Island Sound, just off, and part of, the NE Bronx, New York. It is connected with PELHAM BAY PARK by a causeway. In the 1760s it gained its name as a projected commercial rival to New York City. It has remained, however, an isolated maritime community, known for its seafood and for boatbuilding (the 1960s *Intrepid* and other America's Cup yachts were built here).

City Lights see under NORTH BEACH, San Francisco, California.

City Line Avenue commercial thoroughfare, 4.5 mi/7 km long, between FAIRMOUNT PARK in Philadelphia and HAVERFORD and UPPER DARBY townships, SE Pennsylvania. It forms part of the border between Philadelphia and LOWER MERION township, in Montgomery Co. The Lower Merion suburbs of BALA-CYNWYD, MERION, Wynnewood, and Penn Wynne lie immediately N, while the city neighborhoods of Wynnefield and OVERBROOK are across the street. Many businesses fleeing Philadelphia city taxes have relocated to the Lower Merion side.

City of Children see under MOOSEHEART, Illinois.

City of Industry city, pop. 631, Los Angeles Co., SW California, 17 mi/27 km E of downtown Los Angeles and just S of El Monte, on the Southern Pacific Railroad. The 1840s adobe Workman House is part of a 6-ac/2.5-ha historic site in the midst of this industrial district, which has firms in solar energy, climate control, and other high-tech areas.

City of Refuge see under KONA COAST, Hawaii.

City of Rocks National Reserve, 14,320 ac/5800 ha, in the Albion Mts. of S Idaho, 56 mi/90 km SE of Twin Falls and 8 mi/13 km N of the Utah border. A region of towering granite structures, it was a landmark on the 1840s California emigrant trail. A state park is within the (1988) Federal reserve.

City of the Dalles see THE DALLES, Oregon.

City Park 460 ac/186 ha, in NE DENVER, Colorado, 2.5 mi/4 km E of Downtown, ENE of CAPITOL HILL and NE of CHEESMAN PARK. A major city recreational asset, it is the site of Denver's Zoo and Natural History Museum.

City Point see under HOPEWELL, Virginia.

Civic Arena stadium with a retractable dome in the LOWER HILL section of Pittsburgh, Pennsylvania. Built in 1962, and known as "the Igloo," it hosts sports events (especially hockey) and concerts.

Civic Center **1.** in California: **a.** administrative center of Los Angeles, in the heart of Downtown, immediately S of EL PUEBLO DE LOS ANGELES. A six-block group largely of government buildings, it includes City Hall (1928), at 28 stories the tallest Los Angeles building before the 1958 revocation of an earthquake-prompted ban on high-rise construction. **b.** in SAN FRANCISCO, central plaza and district, N of Market St. and SW of Union Square. The 1915 Beaux-Arts City Hall is the most prominent of the public structures here. The 1932 War Memorial Opera House was the site of the 1944 signing of the United Nations charter. On the NE was the city's Tenderloin, a RED-LIGHT DISTRICT into the 20th century, still shabby, but now home to a growing Southeast Asian community. **2.** 40 ac/16 ha, in C DENVER, Colorado, immediately SSE of Downtown. Completed in 1919, it is a landscaped collection of memorials, with an amphitheater. The state capitol lies E, the US Mint and the City-County Bldg. W, and Denver's Art Museum on the S. **3.** collection of major public institutions, covering 75 ac/30 ha, in downtown Detroit, Michigan, along the Detroit R. COBO HALL, Ford Auditorium, and Hart Plaza are among the most famous landmarks here.

Clackamas County 1870 sq mi/4843 sq km, pop. 278,850, in NW Oregon, bordered by Butte Creek and the Pudding R. (W). Its NW corner consists of many Portland suburbs, such as the county seat, OREGON CITY, and Milwaukie, Lake Oswego, and Gladstone. Its E half is occupied by Mt. Hood National Forest, while the foothills in its center are primarily given over to dairy farms, cattle ranches, and fruit orchards.

Claire, Lake see under WOOD BUFFALO NATIONAL PARK, Alberta.

Clairemont affluent, largely residential section of SAN DIEGO, California, N of Mission Valley, on the W edge of KEARNY MESA, 6 mi/10 km NNW of Downtown. Mission Bay lies SW, La Jolla W, and University City N.

Clair Engle Lake see under WHISKEYTOWN-SHASTA-TRINITY NATIONAL RECREATION AREA, California.

Clairton city, pop. 9656, Allegheny Co., SW Pennsylvania, 10 mi/16 km SE of Pittsburgh. It is the site of a major steel, coke, and coal chemical plant established by USX (formerly U.S. Steel) that runs for 4.5 mi/7 km along the Monongahela R.

Claremont **1.** city, pop. 32,503, Los Angeles Co., SW California, 30 mi/48 km E of Los Angeles. It is a residential suburb and an educational center, the seat of the Claremont Colleges, which include Pomona (1887), Scripps (1926; women), Claremont McKenna (1946), Harvey Mudd (1955; engineering and science), and Pitzer (1963) colleges and the Claremont Graduate School. The city has some light industry and fruit handling facilities. **2.** city, pop. 13,902, Sullivan Co., SW New Hampshire, 45 mi/72 km NW of Concord, near the Vermont border, on the falls of the Sugar R., near its junction with the Connecticut R. The Sugar provides power for the manufacture of mining and mill machinery, textiles, shoes, and paper, and the city is in a popular resort area. The oldest Roman Catholic church in the state (1823) is here.

Claremore city, pop. 13,280, seat of Rogers Co., NE Oklahoma, 25 mi/40 km NE of Tulsa. It is a market and processing center for livestock, agricultural products, coal, oil, and gas, and its mineral springs have made it a noted resort. It is the site of the grave (1935) of the cowboy-humorist Will Rogers, born in OOLOGAH. Oklahoma Military Academy (1920) is here.

Clarendon city, pop. 2067, seat of Donley Co., N Texas, in the Panhandle, 56 mi/90 km ESE of Amarillo. Founded in 1878 as a temperance settlement, it earned the ironic name "Saints' Roost" from cowboys. Now a ranching and agricultural (cotton, peanuts) trade center, it is home to Clarendon Junior College (1898).

Clarendon Hills village, pop. 6994, Du Page Co., NE Illinois, a residential suburb 17 mi/27 km W of Chicago.

Clarinda city, pop. 5104, seat of Page Co., SW Iowa, 55 mi/89 km SW of Council Bluffs and 10 mi/16 km N of the Missouri border. Situated in an agricultural region, it processes and ships meat. Clarinda was a stop on the Underground Railroad. It is the birthplace (1904) of band leader Glenn Miller.

Clarion borough, pop. 6457, seat of Clarion Co., W Pennsylvania, on the Clarion R., 13 mi/21 km SE of Oil City. It is the seat of Clarion University of Pennsylvania (1867).

Clark **1.** city, pop. 257, Randolph Co., NC Missouri, 10 mi/16 km SE of Moberly. It is a trading center in a farming, dairying, and coal mining region. Army general Omar Bradley (1893–1981) was born here and raised in MOBERLY. **2.** residential and industrial township, pop. 14,629, Union Co., NE New Jersey, 4 mi/6 km SW of Elizabeth, on the Garden State Parkway.

Clark County **1.** 8084 sq mi/20,938 sq km, pop. 741,459, in SE Nevada, bordered by California (W) and Arizona (E), and drained by the Colorado and Virginia rivers. Its seat is LAS VEGAS. It is by far the most populous county in the state; increasing suburbanization fueled an over 60% rise in pop. in 1980–90. Though the county has magnesium and other mineral deposits and produces livestock, dairy goods, and vegetables, much of its economy is focused on Las Vegas's gambling and tourist industry. Also in Clark Co. is HOOVER DAM, which forms L. Mead in the EC portion. **2.** 398 sq mi/1031 sq km, pop. 147,548, in WC Ohio, cut by the Mad R. and numerous other rivers and streams. The sizable Clarence J. Brown Reservoir is in the county. There is manufacturing at Springfield, the county seat. Otherwise the economy depends on the exploitation of limestone, sand, and gravel as well as mixed farming (dairy, grain, and livestock). **3.** 627 sq mi/1624 sq km, pop. 238,053, in SW Washington, bordering Oregon (the Columbia R.) on the S and W. VANCOUVER is its seat. Fruit, nuts, wool, and cheese are produced here, and along the river shipping, pulp and paper milling and diversified manufactures are important. The county, part of the PORTLAND, Oregon, metropolitan area, has doubled in pop. since 1970.

Clark Fork River 360 mi/580 km long, in W Montana and N Idaho. It rises near BUTTE as Silver Bow Creek, and flows N and NW past Deer Lodge and Missoula, where it is joined from the S by the Bitterroot R., through Lolo National Forest and along the E of the BITTERROOT Range, into Idaho, where it empties into L. PEND OREILLE, and thence into the Columbia R. via the Pend Oreille R. (sometimes also called the Clark Fork). The Clark Fork drains much of W Montana into the Columbia system. The Noxon Dam and Reservoir (1959) are near the Idaho border. During the last glacial age, the river was repeatedly dammed by ice (forming glacial L. Missoula) and released, its outflowing waters forming much of W Washington's SCABLANDS.

Clark Hill Dam and Lake also, **J. Strom Thurmond Dam and Reservoir** see under SAVANNAH R., South Carolina and Georgia.

Clarksburg city, pop. 18,059, seat of Harrison Co., NC West Virginia, at the confluence of Elk Creek and the West Fork of the Monongahela R., 92 mi/148 km NE of Charleston. Settled in the 1760s, it was a trade center, and a Union supply base during the Civil War. An area oil boom in the 1890s brought quick growth. The city is today a glass producing center, with coal, gas, military instruments, and other manufactures.

Clarksdale city, pop. 19,717, seat of Coahoma Co., NW Mississippi, in the DELTA, on the Sunflower R., 70 mi/113 km SSW of Memphis, Tennessee. Settled in the 1840s, it became a cotton processing and shipping hub, surrounded by flat expanses of the crop. It is known as a center of blues music; it houses the Delta Blues Museum, and major blues figures including Muddy Waters and Robert Johnson lived in the vicinity. The composer W.C. Handy said he had first encountered blues here. Sunflower Landing, 14 mi/23 km W, is thought to be the spot where Hernando De Soto discovered the Mississippi R. in 1541. Clarksdale now has various light manufactures.

Clarkson Valley city, pop. 2508, St. Louis Co., EC Missouri, an affluent suburb, 18 mi/29 km W of downtown St. Louis.

Clarks Summit borough, pop. 5433, Lackawanna Co., NE Pennsylvania, 7 mi/11 km N of Scranton. It is the seat of Baptist Bible College (1932).

Clarksville **1.** city, pop. 5823, seat of Johnson Co., NW Arkansas, 55 mi/89 km ENE of Fort Smith, in the Arkansas Valley. Cotton, fruit, livestock, and poultry are raised in the area, which also has gas and coal deposits. The University of the Ozarks (1834) is here. **2.** town, pop. 19,833, Clark Co., extreme SE Indiana, 5 mi/8 km N of central Louisville, Kentucky, across the Ohio R. Part of the Louisville metropolitan area, it is a commercial and residential suburb. Overlooking the Falls of the Ohio is the George Rogers Clark Homesite; Clark established the settlement in 1784. **3.** city, pop. 75,494, seat of Montgomery Co., NC Tennessee, at the confluence of the Cumberland and Red rivers, 40 mi/64 km NW of Nashville. Founded in 1784, it became a river depot for tobacco, grain, and lumber. A leading market center for dark-fired tobacco, it produces rubber, flour, clothing, machine parts, and heating and cooling equipment, and processes meat. Austin Peay University (1927) is here, and FORT CAMPBELL adjoins the city (W). Dunbar Cave is just E, and 28 mi/45 km to the W is FORT DONELSON.

Claverack town, pop. 6414, Columbia Co., SE New York, 32 mi/52 km SE of Albany, on the Hudson R. It was part of the vast Rensselaerswyck (see RENSSELAER) holdings in the mid 17th century, and was at the center of the mid-19th-century anti-rent movement of small farmers. Now primarily residential and agricultural, it also has some light industry. The town includes several small hamlets, notably Philmont and Hollowville, site of the historic Smokey Hollow Schoolhouse No. 12 (1858).

Clawson city, pop. 13,874, Oakland Co., SE Michigan, 14 mi/23 km N of Detroit. First settled in 1883, this mostly residential suburb also manufactures auto parts, tools, and dies, and has machine shops. Oakland Troy Airport is just NW.

Clay, Mount see under PRESIDENTIAL RANGE, New Hampshire.

Clay Belt in SW Québec and EC Ontario, on the CANADIAN SHIELD, S of the lowlands around James Bay and N of the lowlands around L. Huron. At the end of the 19th century, this band, some 300 mi/500 km E–W, in which glacial deposition left some of the "best" soil on the Shield, was thought likely to be an agricultural producer. In 1903 railroad builders accidentally discovered silver deposits at COBALT. Since then the area has developed chiefly with the mining and forest products industries. There is some crop farming, esp. in the Québec sections E of L. ABITIBI. Another Clay Belt is in W Ontario, along the Minnesota border.

Clay County 403 sq mi/1044 sq km, pop. 153,411, in NW Missouri, bounded by the Missouri R. (S). Its seat is LIBERTY. Its SW quarter takes in much of KANSAS CITY and its metropolitan area, whose industrial and commercial activities strongly affect the county's economy. Its other sizable city is Excelsior Springs, on its E edge. In the rest of the largely agricultural county, livestock is raised, corn, wheat, and tobacco are grown, and coal deposits are mined.

Claymont unincorporated industrial suburb, pop. 9800, New Castle Co., extreme NE Delaware, on the Delaware R., 7 mi/11 km NE of Wilmington. Industries include oil refining and the manufacture of machinery, steel, chemicals, and frozen desserts.

Clayton city, pop. 13,874, seat of St. Louis Co., EC Missouri, a residential and commercial suburb, 8 mi/13 km W of downtown St. Louis.

Clayton County 148 sq mi/383 sq km, pop. 182,052, in NW Georgia, drained by the Flint R. Its seat is JONESBORO. In the agricultural Piedmont, it now includes several of Atlanta's S residential suburbs.

Clearfield city, pop. 21,435, Davis Co., N Utah, 9 mi/14 km SW of Ogden. Hill Air Force Base (1940), just NE of the city, Utah's largest such facility, and Freeport Center, one of the state's largest industrial parks, are its major employers. Clearfield also has a naval supply depot. A commercial center in an irrigated farming area on the E of the Great Salt L., it also trades and processes sugar beets, fruits, and vegetables.

Clear Lake **1.** largest natural lake wholly within California, in Lake Co., 56 mi/90 km N of San Francisco. A popular resort center, it is 20 mi/32 km NNW–SSE and 1–10 mi/1–16 km wide, and covers 45,000 ac/18,200 ha at an altitude of

1350 ft/412 m. Its basin has been occupied for 10,000 years, and has more recently been the home (on its islands) of the Pomo, known for their basket weaving. On the SW rises Mt. Konocti (or Konochti), a dormant volcano almost 4300 ft/1311 m high. The city of **Clearlake** (pop. 11,804, Lake Co.), on the lake's SE, is the area's commercial center. Anderson Marsh State Historic Park, just S, is a leading California archaeological site. On the lake's NW, Lakeport (city, pop. 4390, Lake Co.) is a fishing and boating resort. **2.** city, pop. 8183, Cerro Gordo Co., NE Iowa, on Clear L., 10 mi/16 km W of Mason City. It is largely a summer resort community. **3.** section of Houston, Texas, 20 mi/32 km SE of Downtown, along Clear Creek and Clear L. (an inlet of Galveston Bay). Lying SE of Ellington Field, a bomber training base established in 1917, the ranchland area was in 1962 annexed and designated the site of NASA's Manned Spaceflight Center (renamed the Lyndon B. Johnson Space Flight Center in 1973). The 1620-ac/660-ha facility has since the 1960s spurred the growth of a cluster of residential and research communities. These include **Clear Lake City,** a planned industrial development that is part of Houston; **Clear Lake Shores** (SE), a city, pop. 1096, Galveston Co.; Taylor Lake Village (NE), a city, pop. 3394, Harris Co.; El Lago (E), a city, pop. 3269, Harris Co.; Nassau Bay (S), a city, pop. 4320, Harris Co.; and Webster (SW), a city, pop. 4678, Harris Co. PASADENA lies N, LEAGUE CITY S. The University of Houston at Clear Lake City (1971) is here.

Clear Lake Reservoir in Modoc Co., extreme NE California, 35 mi/56 km SE of Klamath Falls, Oregon, in the Modoc National Forest. Up to 8 mi/13 km across, it lies midway between TULE L. (W) and GOOSE L. (E). All three are remnants of glacial bodies. Clear Lake Reservoir is a major migratory waterfowl refuge on the PACIFIC FLYWAY.

Clearwater **1.** city, pop. 98,784, seat of Pinellas Co., WC Florida, on the Pinellas Peninsula, Clearwater Harbor (W, a lagoon of the Gulf of Mexico), and Old Tampa Bay (E), 20 mi/32 km W of Tampa. It is connected by causeways with Clearwater Beach, on a sand key fronting the Gulf, and with Tampa. The site of 1830s orange groves, the city grew around Fort Harrison (1841). A tourist center since the 1890s, it now is a popular year-round resort, and has a sizable deep-sea fishing and sightseeing fleet. It is also a residential center with a large retiree population, and houses a number of corporate headquarters. In addition, it engages in commercial fishing and light manufacturing and packs and ships fish and citrus. It is the seat of Clearwater Christian College (1966) and a campus of St. Petersburg Junior College. **2.** see under SARNIA, Ontario.

Clearwater Mountains part of the Northern Rocky Mts., mostly in Clearwater and Idaho counties, N Idaho. Rising to c.9000 ft/2740 m in the S, near the Salmon R., they include parts of the Nez Perce, Bitterroot, and **Clearwater** (1.8 million ac/729,000 ha, or 2812 sq mi/7284 sq km) national forests. Bounded S and W by the SALMON R. and E by the BITTERROOT RANGE, the granite mountains have deposits of gold, silver, lead, and copper. The **Clearwater R.,** 90 mi/145 km long, is formed by the confluence of its Middle and South forks at Kooskia, and flows NNW past OROFINO, then W to the SNAKE R. at Lewiston. Its main tributary, the North Fork, rises in the Bitterroot Range at the Montana border and flows 120 mi/190 km W and SW to the main stream NNW of Orofino. In 1973 it was impounded c.4 mi/6 km above its mouth by the 717 ft/219 m–high Dworshak Dam, which created the 54 mi/89 km–long Dworshak Reservoir, an important recreational resource.

Cleburne city, pop. 22,205, seat of Johnson Co., NE Texas, near L. Pat Cleburne, 27 mi/43 km S of Fort Worth. Settled in the 1850s, it is a BLACKLANDS trade and shipping center for dairying, livestock, and farming operations. It has a steel foundry, extensive railroad shops, and various manufactures including appliances.

Clemson city, pop. 11,096, Pickens and Anderson counties, NW South Carolina, 28 mi/45 km WSW of Greenville, near the Blue Ridge Mts. It is the home of Clemson University, founded in 1889 and built around Fort Hill, the estate of John C. Calhoun (1782–1850). With a 1400-ac/570-ha campus and a full-time enrollment of some 14,000, the university dominates the community.

Clergy Reserves see under UPPER CANADA.

Clermont County 456 sq mi/1181 sq km, pop. 150,187, in SW Ohio, bounded by the Ohio R. at the Kentucky line (SW) and the Little Miami R. (NW). Its seat is Batavia. The county includes the East Fork of the Little Miami R. and William H. Harsha L. A number of Cincinnati's residential suburbs occupy the NW. Agriculture (corn, fruit, dairy, livestock, tobacco, and wheat) is important, and there are nurseries. Batavia, Bethel, Milford, and New Richmond have some manufacturing.

Cleveland **1.** city, pop. 15,384, co-seat (with Rosedale) of Bolivar Co., NW Mississippi, 29 mi/47 km NNE of Greenville, in the DELTA. Known for its production of cotton, rice, soybeans, and grain crops, it also manufactures ceramic tile, pharmaceuticals, and several other products. Delta State University (1924) is here. Dockery Farms, a cotton plantation operating since the 1890s, is one of a number of places in the area that have been identified as possible "birthplaces" of blues music. **2.** city, pop. 505,616, seat of Cuyahoga Co., NE Ohio, on L. Erie, at the mouth of the Cuyahoga R. An industrial, commercial, and transportation center and port, it has thrived primarily because of its location, at first as a Great Lakes port and later as a suitable industrial site midway between the iron mines of Michigan and Minnesota and Appalachian coal sources. A giant in the iron and steel industries, the city has also figured prominently in petroleum, chemicals, automobile manufacturing, and electric power. In many ways the archetypal RUST BELT city, it has lost 45% of its pop. since a 1950 high of 914,808. It is the center of a seven-county (including CUYAHOGA, PORTAGE, SUMMIT, LAKE, MEDINA, and LORAIN) metropolitan area (CMSA) with a pop. of 2,759,823. Moses Cleaveland laid out the city in 1796 in what was then Connecticut's WESTERN RESERVE. The introduction of lake steamers (1818) and opening of the ERIE (1825) and Ohio and Erie (1832) canals stimulated growth as a trade and shipping entrepot. Beginning in the 1850s, railroad connections solidified the city's status. Iron ore, coal, copper, lumber, and farm products from throughout the Midwest were processed and distributed here, while John D. Rockefeller established the modern petroleum industry in 1862 in what became America's oil capital, the home of Standard Oil. Local factories turned out products including sewing machines and telescopes; General Electric, one of the nation's first utilities, was founded in the area; and six auto manufacturers set up shop here after 1900. The 1930s Depression initiated a period in which the decline of its industrial base destroyed much of Cleveland's economic strength. Despite the opening of the St. Lawrence Seaway in 1959 and an ambitious URBAN RENEWAL program, the city suffered precipitous pop. decline due to suburbanization and because industry moved South and West. There were racial disturbances during the 1960s, and severe unemployment. In 1978, Cleveland became the first major US city since the Depression to default on its bills. In the 1980s, it recovered, with an economy based on chemical and food processing, a scaled-down steel industry, and the manufacture of electrical products and auto parts. Printing and publishing and international and Great Lakes ore shipping also figure prominently. NASA's Lewis Research Center is nearby, next to **Cleveland Hopkins International Airport,** in BROOK PARK, and Cleveland has several hundred other industrial and scientific research facilities, as well as dozens of corporate headquarters. Cultural and educational life is centered around the University Circle area; Case Western Reserve University—a merger of Western Reserve University (1826) with the Case Institute of Technology (1880)—and Cleveland State University (1964) are the city's leading schools. The Cleveland Symphony Orchestra and Karamu House (1915) and Cleveland Play House (1916) theaters are well known. The city's pre–Civil War inhabitants were primarily from Connecticut and elsewhere in New England. In the 1830s German and Irish workers, in the late 19th century South and East Europeans, and in the early 20th century black Southerners and white Appalachians, joined them. In 1967 Carl Stokes became the first black mayor of a large US city. See also: BROOKSIDE PARK; BURNING RIVER; EAST SIDE; ERIEVIEW; EUCLID Ave.; the FLATS; GLENVILLE; HOUGH; METROPARKS; MUNICIPAL STADIUM (the Mistake on the Lake; and Jacobs Field); MURRAY HILL; OHIO CITY; PUBLIC SQUARE; TERMINAL TOWER; UNIVERSITY CIRCLE; WAREHOUSE DISTRICT; WEST SIDE. **3.** city, pop. 30,354, seat of Bradley Co., SE Tennessee, 26 mi/42 km NE of Chattanooga. Established in 1836, it was a Union headquarters during the Civil War. Local industries make furniture, textiles, clothing, chemicals, and batteries. Printing and lumber milling are also important. Lee College (1918) and two other colleges are here. The city is an important center for the Church of God.

Cleveland County 529 sq mi/1370 sq km, pop. 174,253, in C Oklahoma, bounded by the Canadian R. (SW). Its seat is NORMAN. Its N half is both urban and suburban and includes residential suburbs of OKLAHOMA CITY to its N, most notably the city of MOORE. The S half, with few towns, has both farms and ranches and oil and natural gas fields. The region produces grain, cotton, livestock, poultry, and dairy goods.

Cleveland Heights city, pop. 54,052, Cuyahoga Co., NE Ohio, 6 mi/10 km NE of downtown Cleveland, of which it is a residential suburb. Just W of the city are a cluster of museums including the Cleveland Museum of Art.

Cleveland National Forest c.420,000 ac/170,000 ha, in three units in SW California, E of Santa Ana and NE and E of San Diego, in the PENINSULAR RANGES. The COLORADO DESERT lies E. Mt. PALOMAR is in the forest.

Cleveland Park affluent residential neighborhood in NW Washington, D.C., W of Connecticut Ave., on high ground NW of the National Zoo. It developed as a summer retreat from downtown Washington during Grover Cleveland's administration (1890s). It is characterized by large homes away from the commercial avenues. The University of the District of Columbia's Van Ness campus is here. In the N, Cleveland Park shades into the neighborhoods of Friendship and Chevy Chase.

Clewiston city, pop. 6085, Hendry Co., SC Florida, on the S shore of L. OKEECHOBEE, 50 mi/80 km W of West Palm Beach. In a prime sugar cane–growing muckland region, it is, like BELLE GLADE (ESE), a center for sugar milling and distribution. It is also a resort.

Cliffside Park borough, pop. 20,393, Bergen Co., NE New Jersey, on the PALISADES of the Hudson R., across from N Manhattan, and 7 mi/11 km NE of Jersey City. Primarily a residential community, with many New York commuters living in one-family homes and tall condominium towers, it also has many new office buildings and some light industry.

Cliff Walk footpath, 3 mi/5 km long, along the E edge of NEWPORT, Rhode Island. An old fisherman's path, it was preserved for public use by 19th-century protests against the desire of Newport's rich to close it off. Many mansions, including Cornelius Vanderbilt's Breakers (1894), lie along it; Salve Regina College (1934) occupies a former estate. Bailey's Beach, once an exclusive retreat, is at the S end.

Clifton city, pop. 71,742, Passaic Co., NE New Jersey, adjacent (W and NW) to PASSAIC. It was a 17th-century fur trade center. Acquiring territory from Paterson (1831) and Little Falls (1868), it was once part of Passaic, but separated in 1917. Industrialization came rapidly in the 1930s; today the city is a manufacturing hub, making steel, chemicals, electronic equipment, machinery, paper, and metal goods, plastics, textiles, and cosmetics. There are numerous office buildings and a large residential component, with many commuters to New York City.

Clifton Forge independent city, pop. 4679, within but administratively separate from Alleghany Co., W Virginia, in the Allegheny Mts., on the Jackson R., 37 mi/59 km NNE of Roanoke. In a coal mining area, with some textile milling and light manufacturing, it is an Amtrak stop. Dabney S. Lancaster Community College (1964) is here.

Climax hamlet in Lake Co., C Colorado, on Fremont Pass in the Park Range of the Rocky Mts., 10 mi/16 km NE of Leadville. It is situated at an altitude of 11,300 ft/3446 m and is the site of the Harvard Observatory solar research station. The 1903 discovery of molybdenum at nearby Bartlett Mt. made Climax one of Colorado's most prosperous mining centers. Mill tailings also yield pyrites, monazites, tin, and tungsten.

Clinch Mountain ridge in the Valley and Ridge Province of the APPALACHIAN Mts., extending SW from Burkes Garden, a valley 11 mi/18 km SSW of Bluefield, Virginia, for 145 mi/233 km, between the Holston and Clinch rivers, to W of Cherokee L., near KNOXVILLE, Tennessee. The ridge is highest (4700 ft/1430 m) in the NE. Clinch Mt. is partially in 700,000-ac/283,500-ha Jefferson National Forest, which is headquartered in Roanoke, Virginia, and includes parts of the Allegheny and Blue Ridge mountains.

Clinch River 300 mi/480 km long, in Virginia and Tennessee. It is formed by several streams in Tazewell Co., SW Virginia, and flows SW between Appalachian ridges across the Tennessee border. Its junction with the POWELL R., 21 mi/32 km NNW of Knoxville, is now within Norris L., formed by the Tennessee Valley Authority's NORRIS DAM. Below the dam the

Clinch continues SW, past OAK RIDGE, to join the Tennessee R. in what is now WATTS BAR L.

Clingmans Dome highest point (6643 ft/2025 m) in Tennessee, along the border with North Carolina, in the GREAT SMOKY Mts. The mountain road from Gatlinburg, Tennessee, that goes into Great Smoky Mts. National Park and through Newfound Gap (5046 ft/1538 m), passes NE of the peak, which is traversed by the Appalachian Trail.

Clinton **1.** town, pop. 12,767, Middlesex Co., S Connecticut, 20 mi/32 km E of New Haven, on Long Island Sound at the mouth of the Hammonasset R., on US 1 and Interstate 95. It is a residential and resort town, with some agriculture and a fishing industry. A monument honors the early years (1701–07) of the Collegiate School, later Yale University (New Haven), which began in Clinton. **2.** city, pop. 7437, seat of De Witt Co., C Illinois, 23 mi/37 km S of Bloomington. An agricultural and industrial center with rail shops and a grain terminal, it was an important administrative town in the 19th century. A nuclear power plant, opened 1987, is 7 mi/11 km E of the city on Clinton L. Weldon Springs State Park is 2 mi/3 km SE. **3.** city, pop. 29,201, seat of Clinton Co., EC Iowa, on the Mississippi R., 28 mi/45 km NE of the QUAD CITIES and across from Fulton, Illinois. The easternmost city in Iowa, it was established in the 1830s as a ferry point. A trading hub, Clinton was once the largest sawmill center in the Midwest. Manufacturing and agricultural distribution and processing, especially the handling of corn, now dominate the economy. Manufactures include cellophane, structural steel, steel tubing, apparel, and cartons and boxes. Mount St. Clare College (1895) and Clinton Community College (1946) are here. **4.** unincorporated village, pop. 19,987, Prince George's Co., C Maryland, a suburb 12 mi/19 km SE of Washington, D.C. Its Surratt House (1852) was used in the 1865 plot to assassinate President Lincoln; tavernkeeper Mary Surratt was later hanged as an accomplice. ANDREWS AIR FORCE BASE is NE. **5.** town, pop. 13,222, Worcester Co., C Massachusetts, on Wachusett Reservoir and the headwaters of the South Branch of the Nashua R., 12 mi/19 km NE of Worcester. Originally part of Lancaster (N), it grew up around two mills that produced lace for stagecoach windows, gingham, and carpets. The town is now engaged in various manufactures, and is experiencing suburban growth. **6.** city, pop. 21,847, Hinds Co., WC Mississippi, 8 mi/13 km WNW of downtown Jackson. Settled in the early 1820s on the site of an Indian agency, it has been an academic community since Mississippi College opened in 1826. A longtime sawmill and cotton processing center, it is now a growing residential suburb of Jackson. **7.** city, pop. 8703, seat of Henry Co., WC Missouri, 37 mi/59 km SW of Sedalia. Settled in 1837, it grew rapidly after 1870, when large-scale dairy and poultry farms were introduced and coal mines were opened. In addition it is a trade center for grain producers. The large Harry S. Truman Reservoir is SE, on the OSAGE R. **8.** town (pop. 2054) and adjoining township (pop. 10,816), Hunterdon Co., WC New Jersey. Long a stage stop and mill town in a hilly agricultural area, it is now a growing residential center on Interstate 78. On the South Branch of the Raritan R., the township is the site of Spruce Run and Round Valley reservoirs, created in the 1950s and 1960s. **9.** in New York: **a.** in Manhattan, late-20th-century name for the now largely residential area formerly called HELL'S KITCHEN. **b.** village in the township of Kirkland, pop. 10,153, Oneida Co., C New York, on Oriskany Creek, 9 mi/14 km SW of Utica. Settled in 1786, it was named for Governor George Clinton. In 1793 Samuel Kirkland founded the Hamilton-Oneida Academy here. Originally an Indian school, the academy was chartered as Hamilton College in 1812, and remains the focus of the village. Clinton is located in an agricultural region with truck and dairy farms. **10.** city, pop. 9298, Custer and Washita counties, W Oklahoma, on the Washita R., 80 mi/128 km W of Oklahoma City. Founded in 1903, it is an important shipping center for cattle, wheat, and cotton. Industries include cottonseed milling and poultry packing, and it manufactures steel goods and bricks. Nearby are the Clinton Dam, Foss L. (NW), and Washita National Wildlife Refuge (NW). **11.** city, pop. 7987, Laurens Co., NW South Carolina, 55 mi/89 km NW of Columbia. The area saw several Revolutionary War skirmishes, especially the Battle of Musgrove's Mill (Aug. 19, 1780), fought 10 mi/16 km NNE. Settled around 1809, the town became a shipping point for cotton when the railroad arrived in 1835. Textiles, flour, roller bearings, and plywood are among manufactures; cotton, grain, peanuts, poultry, and dairy goods are produced locally. Presbyterian College (1880) is here. **12.** town, pop. 8972, seat of Anderson Co., E Tennessee, 15 mi/24 km NW of Knoxville, on the Clinch R., 6 mi/10 km NE of OAK RIDGE. The Tennessee Valley Authority's NORRIS DAM is 9 mi/15 km NNE. The town is the trade center for a farm and timber area.

Clinton County 573 sq mi/1484 sq km, pop. 57,883, in SC Michigan, drained by the Looking Glass, Maple, and Grand rivers. Its seat is St. Johns. The county has dairying and grows peppermint, beans, fruit, grain, and sugar beets. Oil refining and some manufacturing are carried out at St. Johns and Ovid.

Clinton Hill residential section of N Brooklyn, New York. Situated between Fort Greene and Bedford-Stuyvesant, it was an elegant late-19th-century community dominated by the family of oil magnate Charles Pratt. Although the Depression brought decline, Clinton Hill is still noted for its fine buildings, among them the residence of the Catholic Bishop of Brooklyn (a former Pratt estate) and the campus of Pratt Institute (1887).

Clinton River 30 mi/48 km long, in SE Michigan. It rises in small lakes around PONTIAC, in Oakland Co., and flows E past Pontiac and Rochester to Anchor Bay of L. St. Clair, E of Mt. Clemens and N of Detroit. The river is named after De Witt Clinton (1769–1828).

Clio agricultural town, pop. 1365, Barbour Co., SE Alabama, 36 mi/58 km NNW of Dothan, the birthplace (1919) of politician George C. Wallace.

Cloisters, the see under FORT TRYON, New York.

Cloquet city, pop. 10,885, Carlton Co., NE Minnesota, on the St. Louis R., 17 mi/27 km SW of Duluth. Situated in a heavily forested region, it has long been dominated by the paper and pulp industry. The original town was largely destroyed by fire in 1918. Paper and matches are among important manufactures. There is a gas station designed by Frank Lloyd Wright here. The Fond du Lac Indian Reservation is to the W.

Cloud Peak and **Cloud Peak Wilderness Area** see under BIGHORN NATIONAL FOREST, Wyoming.

Cloverleaf unincorporated community, pop. 18,230, Harris Co., SE Texas, 11 mi/18 km E of downtown Houston, on Interstate 10 just W of Channelview. It is largely residential.

Clovis **1.** city, pop. 50,323, Fresno Co., C California, in the San Joaquin Valley, 7 mi/11 km NE of downtown Fresno. A trade and processing center for a region producing lumber, vegetables, grapes, and other fruit, it is now a booming suburb, having quadrupled in population since 1970. **2.** city, pop. 30,954, seat of Curry Co., E New Mexico, in the High Plains, 10 mi/16 km W of the Texas border and 94 mi/151 km SW of Amarillo. Settled as a railroad town in the early 1900s, it is surrounded by irrigated farms and ranches and is a livestock auction center. Cannon Air Force Base is just W. Norman Petty Recording Studios were a noted 1950s popular music center. The city gave its name to the widespread Clovis culture (before 9000 B.C.), whose artifacts were first found here.

Clyde city, pop. 5776, Sandusky Co., N Ohio, on Raccoon Creek, 7 mi/11 km ESE of Fremont. Settled in the 1820s, it is an agricultural trade and service center. Sherwood Anderson lived here 1884–96, and the city is thought to be the model for *Winesburg, Ohio* (1919).

CN Tower tapering landmark in the waterfront area of downtown TORONTO, Ontario. Built by Canadian National Railways in 1976, it is the world's tallest free-standing structure, at 1815 ft/553 m. Its indoor and outdoor observation decks and revolving restaurant (at 1122 ft/342 m, in the Sky Pod) are tourist attractions, and the building has become emblematic of Toronto. The SKYDOME is immediately SW.

Coachella city, pop. 16,896, Riverside Co., S California, 69 mi/111 km ESE of Riverside, and just SE of Indio, in the Coachella Valley. It is a trade center in an arid region irrigated by artesian wells and the Coachella Canal, a branch of the All-American Canal, in which more than 100,000 ac/40,500 ha of land grow truck crops, dates (90% of the US total), citrus fruits, and alfalfa.

Coachella Valley see under COLORADO DESERT, California.

Coalinga city, pop. 8212, Fresno Co., SC California, 50 mi/80 km SW of Fresno. In the Coalinga Oilfield, in foothills W of the San Joaquin Valley, it is a supply and refining center for an area that began oil production in 1928. Earlier, it was a Southern Pacific Railroad settlement called "*Coaling* Station *A*."

Coamo unincorporated community (ZONA URBANA), pop. 13,266, Coamo Municipio (pop. 33,837), SC Puerto Rico, on the Coamo R. in the S foothills of the Cordillera Central, 17 mi/27 km ENE of Ponce. A Spanish colonial town, it was settled in the mid 16th century. In a fertile region that grows sugarcane and tobacco, it processes both. Cattle and horses are raised in the region. As a resort, Coamo has long been known for its hot springs.

Coast, the in the US, the Pacific coast; even Californians refer to it thus. People whose lives or business keep them moving between East and West, however, are referred to as "bicoastal."

Coastal Plain general term for the coastal lowlands of the E and S US, bordering the Atlantic Ocean and the Gulf of Mexico. The Coastal Plain is conventionally divided into the Atlantic Coastal Plain and the Gulf Coastal Plain. The **Atlantic Coastal Plain** extends from New England, where the MORAINE-formed Cape Cod, Nantucket, and Martha's Vineyard are NE extensions, to Florida, including almost all of that state except the PANHANDLE. Nowhere more than about 200 mi/320 km wide, it rises gradually to the FALL LINE, marking the beginning of the PIEDMONT zone (W). Much of the plain comprises a series of sunken river valleys, where rising water levels since the last glacial age have created bays and sounds, as well as thousands of islands; this was an important factor in the largely maritime early history of the Eastern colonies. The **Gulf Coastal Plain** extends W along the Florida Panhandle and SW along the Texas coast. Like the Atlantic plain, it rises gradually toward the S Appalachians (in the E) and toward the BALCONES ESCARPMENT and the HILL COUNTRY of Texas (in the W). It also extends northward as the alluvial plain of the Mississippi R., to near CAPE GIRARDEAU, Missouri, some 550 mi/900 km from the Gulf of Mexico.

Coast Mountains NW–SE oriented range, 1000 mi/1600 km long, in British Columbia, Alaska, and the Yukon Territory. They are a N continuation of the SIERRA NEVADA and CASCADE ranges, and are continued in Alaska by the ALASKA and ALEUTIAN ranges. The Pacific Trough (including the Strait of GEORGIA and HECATE STRAIT) separates them from the geologically distinct COAST RANGES to the W. In British Columbia the mountains are largely granite; glaciation has carved Pacific FJORDS. Mt. WADDINGTON (13,104 ft/3994 m) is the highest point. GARIBALDI and TWEEDSMUIR provincial parks are in the range.

Coast Ranges discontinuous series of mountain ranges paralleling the US and Canadian Pacific coast from Alaska to S California; they are geologically distinct from the COAST Mts., which parallel them (E) in British Columbia and Alaska, and which continue in the SIERRA NEVADA and CASCADE ranges. The two systems are separated by a series of troughs or lowlands represented by the Inside Passage in British Columbia, Puget Sound in Washington, the Willamette Valley in Oregon, and the Central Valley in California. The Coast Ranges reach their highest point at Mt. LOGAN (19,524 ft/5951 m) in the Saint Elias Mts. in the Yukon Territory. From the N, the range is submerged at Kodiak I.; it continues S and E with the KENAI, CHUGACH, and SAINT ELIAS ranges. It is again represented by islands—Alaska's ALEXANDER ARCHIPELAGO and British Columbia's QUEEN CHARLOTTE and VANCOUVER islands—before reaching the OLYMPIC Mts. in Washington. The KLAMATH Mts. in S Oregon and N California separate the N and S sections of the Coast Ranges, which then continue in the DIABLO, SANTA LUCIA, SAN RAFAEL, and a number of smaller ranges. Some consider the California Coast Ranges to end with the San Rafaels, marked by Point Concepcion (W), where continuity and the distinct NW–SE trend disappears. To the S are the SAN GABRIEL, SAN BERNARDINO, and SAN JACINTO mountains and others known collectively as the PENINSULAR RANGES.

Coatesville city, pop. 11,038, Chester Co., E Pennsylvania, 30 mi/48 km W of Philadelphia. It is an industrial center whose manufactures include steel and other metals and textiles.

Cobalt town, pop. 1470, Timiskaming District, SE Ontario, on the W side of L. Timiskaming, 70 mi/113 km NNW of North Bay and 255 mi/411 km N of Toronto. The site of a strike in 1903 that revealed one of the world's richest silver deposits, it developed as a boomtime service center; the cobalt and other minerals found in the ore began to be exploited as well. This was one of the first important mineral strikes in Canada, giving impetus to further exploration of the CANADIAN SHIELD.

Cobb County 343 sq mi/888 sq km, pop. 447,745, in NW Georgia, bounded SE by the Chattahoochee R., in the Piedmont. Its seat and industrial center is MARIETTA. Cobb Co. is the site of KENNESAW MOUNTAIN National Battlefield Park and several of Atlanta's NW suburbs. Its population rose dramatically during the 1980s as a consequence of Atlanta's suburban growth.

Cobble Hill residential section of NW Brooklyn, New York. Part of old South Brooklyn, it lies between Carroll Gardens (S) and Brooklyn Heights (N). The area, which boomed after the 1950s as an extension of Brooklyn Heights, is mixed, with older European groups now joined by young professionals and substantial Syrian, Lebanese, and Yemeni communities. The Atlantic Ave. corridor, on the N edge, is noted for its Middle Eastern restaurants and shops and as an antiques market.

Cobequid Mountains E–W oriented range lying along the N of the MINAS BASIN, in C Nova Scotia. Eighty mi/130 km long, the rolling mountains rise to 1204 ft/367 m N of Truro. **Cobequid Bay** is the easternmost extension of the Minas Basin.

Cobo Hall exhibition hall and connected indoor arena in downtown Detroit, Michigan, on Washington Blvd. at Jefferson Ave., along the Detroit R. It hosts auto shows, concerts, rallies, and other events. The JOE LOUIS ARENA is immediately SW.

Cobourg town, pop. 15,079, seat of Northumberland Co., SE Ontario, on L. Ontario, 64 mi/103 km ENE of Toronto. Settled by LOYALISTS in 1798, it prospered as a harbor, and in the 1850s was the S terminus of a railroad N to PETERBOROUGH and iron mines to the NE, and attracted Pittsburgh industrialists to the area. It continued to flourish as a summer haven for the rich, and is now a boating and fishing resort with food processing and chemical plants and a rifle factory. The town was the seat of Victoria College (1835) before its 1890s relocation to Toronto.

Cobscook Bay SW arm of PASSAMAQUODDY Bay, in Washington Co., extreme E Maine. Six mi/10 km long E to W, it has a heavily indented shoreline and is enclosed by the peninsulas on which EASTPORT and LUBEC lie, as well as CAMPOBELLO I. The bay has extremely swift and high tides; its Abnaki name means "boiling tides."

Cochise Head see under CHIRICAHUA Mts., Arizona.

Cochise Stronghold see under DRAGOON Mts., Arizona.

Cochituate, Lake 3 mi/5 km N to S, largely in Natick, Middlesex Co., E Massachusetts, 16 mi/26 km W of Boston. Part of Boston's water supply system, it is also a recreational asset, lying mostly in Cochituate State Park. The Massachusetts Turnpike and other highways cross the lake on causeways. A US Army laboratory is at the S end.

Cockeysville unincorporated village, pop. 18,668, Baltimore Co., NC Maryland, 13 mi/21 km N of Baltimore. It is a largely residential suburb between Loch Raven Reservoir (E) and Interstate 83 (W), along which there are industrial and shopping malls.

Cockrell Hill city, pop. 3746, Dallas Co., NE Texas, a residential community completely within SW Dallas.

Cocoa city, pop. 17,722, Brevard Co., EC Florida, 40 mi/64 km ESE of Orlando, on the INDIAN R. across from MERRITT I. In a citrus producing area, it is a tourist hub, connected by bridge and causeway to Merritt I., Cape Canaveral, and Cocoa Beach. It is the seat of Brevard Community College (1960).

Cocoa Beach city, pop. 12,123, Brevard Co., EC Florida, 48 mi/77 km ESE of Orlando, on a barrier island between the Banana R. (W) and the Atlantic Ocean. Like nearby COCOA, it is named for the locally abundant coconut palm. Situated midway between Cape CANAVERAL (N) and the Patrick Air Force Base (S), it has developed since 1950 as a beachfront resort and a residential center for military and space program personnel.

Cocoanut Grove former nightclub, on Piedmont St. just S of the Common and Public Garden, Boston, Massachusetts, destroyed by a flash fire on the evening of November 28, 1942, with a loss of 492 lives.

Coconino Plateau section of the San Francisco Plateau (part of the COLORADO PLATEAU), a tableland c.5000–7000 ft/1500–2150 m high, S of the Colorado R. and the Grand Canyon, in C Arizona. Bordered S in part by the MOGOLLON Rim, the lava-covered Coconino contains several hundred extinct volcanoes, including the SAN FRANCISCO PEAKS. The plateau occupies much of the S part of Coconino Co., and is the site of the Havasupai Indian Reservation (N) and parts of the Kaibab National Forest. The Aubrey Cliffs are along the W. The 1.83 million–ac/740,000-ha **Coconino National Forest** extends SE, surrounding Flagstaff and Sedona.

Coconut Creek city, pop. 27,485, Broward Co., SE Florida, 7 mi/11 km NW of Fort Lauderdale. A residential (largely retirement) community, it quadrupled in population in the 1980s.

Coconut Grove area of SW Miami, Florida, on Biscayne Bay. Settled in the early 19th century, it was officially established in 1873, and was the site of S Florida's first hotel (1882). By the early 1890s it was the largest community in the area. A winter home to noted artists and writers early in the 20th century, it became a part of Miami in 1925. Some of its early buildings, such as the Barnacle (1891; a State Historical Site) were built from shipwreck lumber. Coconut Grove is a center for local arts and crafts. Also an affluent residential community and popular tourist spot, it has a noted playhouse and a plethora of trendy shops, elegant malls, luxury hotels, fashionable restaurants, and several waterside parks.

Cody city, pop. 7897, seat of Park Co., NW Wyoming, on the Shoshone R., in a mountainous area, 90 mi/145 km SSW of Billings, Montana. It is situated in a region of dude and working ranches and oilfields, irrigated by the Buffalo Bill Dam and Reservoir, 6 mi/10 km SW. The community was founded (1898) by William "Buffalo Bill" Cody, who had spent his boyhood in the area. It is the headquarters of the SHOSHONE NATIONAL FOREST, lies near Shoshone Cavern National Monument and Shoshone Canyon, and is just E of several wilderness areas. Tourism is the mainstay of Cody's economy. Other industries include oil refining and gypsum board manufacture. The Buffalo Bill Historical Center and Whitney Gallery of Western Art are here, and Cody is the site of several rodeos. Buffalo Bill State Park is 7 mi/11 km SW.

Coeur d'Alene city, pop. 24,563, seat of Kootenai Co., NW Idaho, at the N end of Coeur d'Alene L. where the Spokane R. flows from it, 32 mi/51 km E of Spokane, Washington. A trade and processing center for an agricultural, mining, and lumbering area, Coeur d'Alene was the site of the Army's

Fort Sherman (1879). It developed after lead and silver were discovered (1883) and the railroad arrived (1886). It is headquarters for Coeur d'Alene National Forest and seat of North Idaho College (1939). Tourism is now an economic mainstay of the city, where a golf resort was completed in 1992.

Coeur d'Alene River 110 mi/180 km long, in N Idaho's PANHANDLE. It rises in the **Coeur d'Alene Mts.,** along the Montana border, SE of L. PEND OREILLE, and flows SSE through the former **Coeur d'Alene National Forest,** now a unit of the Idaho Panhandle National Forest, then turns WSW to Coeur d'Alene L. Its valley, esp. around Kellogg, is a famous mining center. **Coeur d'Alene L.,** also fed by the St. Joe R., extends N–S for some 24 mi/38 km, and is 1–3 mi/1–5 km wide. A noted beauty spot, it is the source of the Spokane R., which flows W into Washington. At the lake's S, along the Washington line, is the **Coeur d'Alene Indian Reservation** (598 sq mi/1549 sq km, pop. 5800), home to the Salishan Skitswish, known as the Coeur d'Alene ("awl-heart") for their hard bargaining.

Coffeyville city, pop. 12,917, Montgomery Co., SE Kansas, on the Verdigris R., at the Oklahoma border. It grew with the railroad's arrival in 1870, and boomed when oil and natural gas were discovered nearby in 1902. It was the scene of an 1892 bank robbery shootout in which the notorious Dalton gang was almost wiped out. The city has oil, chemical, steel, mechanical equipment, flour milling, and meat processing industries. Coffeyville Community College (1923) is here.

Cohansey River also, **Cohansey Creek** 35 mi/56 km long, in SW New Jersey. It rises in SE Salem Co. and flows S past BRIDGETON and W to Cohansey Cove, in Delaware Bay. It is navigable to Bridgeton. Chief industries along it are fruit growing and seafood production.

Cohasset town, pop. 7075, Norfolk Co., E Massachusetts, on the Atlantic Ocean, 15 mi/24 km SE of Boston. It is an affluent suburb and summer resort, in its early history an important fishing community.

Cohocton River 55 mi/89 km long, in SW New York. It rises in SE Livingston Co. and flows SE through the towns of Cohocton, Avoca, and Bath, before joining the Tioga R. at CORNING to form the Chemung R.

Cohoes city, pop. 16,825, Albany Co., E New York, at the confluence of the Mohawk and Hudson rivers, 10 mi/16 km N of Albany. The site, on the Colonial military road connecting Albany and L. George, was settled in 1665. Completion of the Erie Canal in 1825, and the damming of the Great Falls of the Mohawk R. (Cohoes Falls) significantly influenced early growth. The first power-operated knitting machines were built here in 1832, establishing Cohoes as a textile center by 1840. Abundant power supplied by the 70-ft/21-m falls fostered the development of other industries as well. The city now manufactures paper, alarm systems, and small boats. The Van Schaick House (1735) served as the headquarters of Revolutionary General Horatio Gates. Van Schaick I. and smaller Simmons I. are part of the city.

Colchester town, pop. 14,731, Chittenden Co., NW Vermont. It is on L. Champlain, just N of Burlington. Formerly part of Winooski, the town is a Burlington suburb, with dairy and truck farming and a popular summer resort at Malletts Bay.

Cold Harbor locality in Hanover Co., E Virginia, N of the Chickahominy R. and 10 mi/16 km ENE of Richmond, site of a battle (June 3, 1864) between Confederate troops led by Robert E. Lee and Union soldiers commanded by U.S. Grant, in which the Northern forces were decimated as they attempted a frontal assault on the entrenched Confederates. The area is now suburban.

Cold Spring village, pop. 1998, in Philipstown, Putnam Co., SE New York, on the E bank of the Hudson R., across from WEST POINT, and 6 mi/10 km SE of Newburgh. Its large foundry, established in 1814, produced guns used during the Civil War. In a farming and dairying region, the village is a trade center with some light industry.

Cold Spring Harbor unincorporated village, pop. 4789, in Huntington town, Suffolk Co., SE New York, on Long Island's North Shore. Situated on the SE arm of Oyster Bay, it was a 19th-century whaling port. Today it is an affluent village with many old homes. The Cold Spring Harbor Laboratory, a leading biological research center, is here.

Coldwater city, pop. 9607, seat of Branch Co., S Michigan, on the Sauk R., 28 mi/45 km SSE of Battle Creek and 12 mi/19 km N of the Indiana border. This lake resort was founded in 1830 and grew as a Chicago Turnpike village. A trade center in a fruit, grain, and dairying region, it mills flour and manufactures marine engines, plastics, cement, furnaces, furniture, and clothing. Its Tibbits Opera House (1882) has long been a major Midwestern entertainment venue. Coldwater L., 7 mi/11 km to the S, is the largest of many nearby lakes.

Cole County 392 sq mi/1015 sq km, pop. 63,579, in C Missouri, on the Ozark Plateau, bounded by the Missouri R. (N) and the Osage R. (E). Situated in the extreme N is its seat and only large city, JEFFERSON CITY, also the state capital. The rest of the county is mainly agricultural, dominated by wheat, corn, and livestock, but also contains mineral deposits.

Colesville unincorporated residential village, pop. 18,819, Montgomery Co., C Maryland, a suburb 12 mi/19 km NNE of Washington, D.C.

Colgate unincorporated community in Richfield and Lisbon townships, Washington and Waukesha counties, SW Wisconsin, a suburb 16 mi/26 km NW of Milwaukee.

College unincorporated community, pop. 11,249, Fairbanks North Star Borough, C Alaska, on FAIRBANKS's W side, along the Tanana R. (S). It is home to the University of Alaska (1917).

Collegedale city, pop. 5048, Hamilton Co., SE Tennessee, 14 mi/23 km E of downtown Chattanooga. Southern College (1892; Adventist) is here.

College Hill see under PROVIDENCE, Rhode Island.

College Park **1.** city, pop. 20,457, Fulton and Clayton counties, NW Georgia, 8 mi/13 km SSW of downtown Atlanta. The original name of Manchester was changed in 1895, when now-defunct Cox College was established here. Woodward Academy, formerly the Georgia Military Academy, dates to 1900. Atlanta's Hartsfield International Airport lies SE. **2.** city, pop. 21,927, Prince George's Co., C Maryland, 9 mi/14 km NE of Washington, D.C. It developed around Maryland Agricultural College, founded here in 1856, which became Maryland State College in 1916. College Park is the seat of the main campus of the University of Maryland, which merged with Maryland State College when it was established here in 1920. The Maryland Agricultural Experiment Station (1887) is also here. The residential town of University Park (pop. 2243) is just SW.

College Place city, pop. 6308, Walla Walla Co., SE Washington, on the Walla Walla R., 3 mi/5 km N of the Oregon border and 5 mi/8 km SE of Walla Walla. An agricultural community just E of the Whitman Mission National Historic Site, it is the seat of Walla Walla College (1892).

College Station city, pop. 52,456, Brazos Co., EC Texas, 82 mi/132 km NW of Houston. It is the home of Texas Agricultural and Mechanical University (Texas A & M, 1876), which has some 40,000 students. The university is known for research in engineering, fisheries, agriculture, nuclear technology, and animal pathology. There is some high-tech manufacturing, and there are independent research operations, in the city. The area produces cattle, gas, and oil. BRYAN is 7 mi/ 11 km NW.

Collegeville **1.** unincorporated community, pop. 993, Jasper Co., NW Indiana, just S of Rensselaer and 45 mi/72 km S of Gary. It is the seat of St. Joseph's College (1889). **2.** township, pop. 1624, Stearns Co., C Minnesota, 10 mi/16 km W of St. Cloud. St. John's University (1857) is here, as is St. John's Abbey, which has a building designed by Marcel Breuer. **3.** borough, pop. 4227, Montgomery Co., SE Pennsylvania, on the Schuylkill R., 8 mi/13 km NW of Norristown. It houses a large pharmaceuticals headquarters and is the seat of Ursinus College (1869).

Collegiate Peaks see under SAWATCH RANGE, Colorado.

Colleton County 1052 sq mi/2725 sq km, pop. 34,377, in S South Carolina, bounded by St. Helena Sound of the Atlantic Ocean (SE). The Atlantic Intracoastal Waterway runs along its coast. Its seat is the city of Walterboro (pop. 5492). Earlier known as the **Colleton District,** this historic region was the birthplace of statesmen Robert Y. Hayne (1791–1839) and Francis W. Pickens (1805–69). Once one of the country's leading rice producers, the county remains rural, producing cotton, lumber, grain, and livestock. Tourism is important, particularly at Colleton State Park (N) and in the coastal section, which includes part of EDISTO I.

Colleyville city, pop. 12,724, Tarrant Co., NE Texas, 13 mi/21 km NE of Fort Worth. A largely residential suburb W of the DALLAS–FORT WORTH INTERNATIONAL AIRPORT, it doubled in population in the 1980s.

Collierville town, pop. 14,427, Shelby Co., SW Tennessee, 20 mi/32 km ESE of Memphis. Traditionally an agricultural trade center, it is experiencing suburban growth.

Collingswood borough, pop. 15,301, Camden Co., SW New Jersey, adjacent (SE) to Camden. It was settled by Quakers in 1682. A residential suburb of Philadelphia, it has many relatively new office buildings and some light industry.

Collingwood town, pop. 13,505, Simcoe Co., SC Ontario, at the S end of Georgian Bay of L. Huron, at the base of 1775-ft/541-m Blue Mt., 27 mi/43 km WNW of Barrie and 70 mi/113 km NNW of Toronto. Once the territory of the Tionantati (Tobacco Nation), the area was settled by whites in the 1830s, when the town of Hurontario Mills was established just E of the present site. Today the town is a popular ski resort and an important port with a strong shipbuilding industry. There is also fruit canning and shipping and the manufacture of lumber, flour, furniture, and Blue Mt. pottery.

Collins Bay W suburban section of the city of KINGSTON, SE Ontario, the site of a Federal penitentiary built in 1930.

Collinsville city, pop. 22,446, Madison and St. Clair counties, SW Illinois, a suburb 10 mi/16 km NE of East St. Louis. Originally a coal mining center, it now smelts zinc and produces women's clothing and canned foods. There has also been much residential growth in recent decades. The 2200-ac/891-ha Cahokia Mounds State Historic Site, a UNESCO World Heritage Site, thought to be the remnants of the largest city N of Mexico in the 12th century, is 5 mi/8 km SW. It includes 16-ac/4-ha, 100 ft/30 m–high Monk's Mound, the largest monument of the Temple Mound (Mississippian) culture. Fairmount Race Track is in the SW part of Collinsville.

Coloma historic hamlet in El Dorado Co., NE California, 34 mi/56 km ENE of Sacramento, on the South Fork of the AMERICAN R. It was here, on Jan. 24, 1848, that James Marshall, employed by Johan Sutter (see SACRAMENTO), discovered gold while seeking to establish a sawmill, setting off the California gold rush; by 1849 Coloma had a pop. of 10,000. The reconstructed Sutter's Mill is a tourist attraction, now in the 240-ac/100-ha Marshall State Historical Monument.

Colombie-Britannique see BRITISH COLUMBIA.

colonia see under BARRIO.

Colonia unincorporated community, pop. 18,238, in Woodbridge township, Middlesex Co., NE New Jersey, 8 mi/13 km SW of Elizabeth. A residential community with many New York commuters, it also has many office buildings and some light industry.

Colonial Heights independent city, pop. 16,064, EC Virginia, on the Appomattox R., across (N) from Petersburg. Part of an industrial complex, it produces boats, paint, and dairy products. In 1781, Lafayette shelled Petersburg from here. During the 1864–65 siege of Petersburg, Robert E. Lee's headquarters were located under a huge cucumber tree in front of what is now the Violet Bank Library and Museum. Colonial Heights was not incorporated as a town until 1926.

Colonial National Historical Park see under YORKTOWN, Virginia.

Colonial Park unincorporated village, pop. 13,777, in Lower Paxton township, Dauphin Co., S. Pennsylvania, a residential suburb just NE of Harrisburg.

Colonie in New York: **a.** village, pop. 8019, in Colonie town, Albany Co., 9 mi/14 km NW of downtown Albany. It is largely residential, with several large shopping centers and malls and some light industry. **b.** town, pop. 76,494, including Colonie village, Loudonville, Roessleville, and other suburbs N of Albany, between the Mohawk and Hudson rivers.

colony **1.** group from one country that settles in another country (esp. one that is lightly populated, politically unorganized, or powerless), and that remains subject to or connected with the "mother country"; also, the land settled in. Early historic settlement of what is now the US and Canada comprised colonies of the Norse (see VINLAND), Spanish, British, French, Dutch, Swedish, and other European groups. In the 18th century, the British referred to their American settlements as **the Colonies;** after the 1763 defeat of French power in North America, this included Nova Scotia, Newfoundland, St. John's (Prince Edward) Island, and Québec. Historically, however, it has come esp. to mean the **Thirteen Colonies** (later the **Thirteen Original States**): New Hampshire, Massachusetts (including the district of Maine), Rhode Island, Connecticut, New York, New Jersey, Pennsylvania, Delaware, Maryland, Virginia, North Carolina, South Carolina, and Georgia. Colonies have often been designated by other titles, including

PLANTATION. **2.** applied to various settlements or communities perceived as separate and in some way retaining connection to a "mother country" (e.g., an "Icelandic colony" in Manitoba) or to the larger society or culture (e.g., an "artists' colony" in a small coastal town).

Colorado state of the WC US, one of the MOUNTAIN STATES; 1990 pop. 3,294,394 (114% of 1980; rank: 26th); area 104,100 sq mi/269,619 sq km (rank: 8th); admitted to Union 1876 (38th, and called the Centennial State). Capital and most populous city: DENVER. Other leading cities: COLORADO SPRINGS, AURORA, LAKEWOOD, PUEBLO, ARVADA, FORT COLLINS, BOULDER. Colorado is bordered E by Kansas (S) and Nebraska (N); N by Nebraska (E) and Wyoming (W); and W by Utah. On the SW, at the FOUR CORNERS, it meets Utah, Arizona (SW), and New Mexico. New Mexico extends E along its S border, which in the SE also adjoins part of the Oklahoma Panhandle. Almost half the state, in the E, lies in the High Plains and Piedmont sections of the GREAT PLAINS, a largely flat expanse across which the SOUTH PLATTE R. (N) and ARKANSAS R. (S) flow from their sources in the Rockies. Grasslands here support a sizable cattle industry; in irrigated areas, esp. along the Arkansas, sugar beets and other crops are grown. The plains end with foothills and the E of the FRONT RANGE of the Southern ROCKY Mts. Best-known of the Front Range mountains is PIKES PEAK, long a landmark for westbound travelers. Most of Colorado's pop., and almost all its urban and industrial development, is concentrated along the foot of the Front Range, from Fort Collins (N) through the Denver metropolitan area, past Pueblo (S). The Southern Rocky Mts., of which the Front Range is the E face, run N–S through the C of the State; roughly paralleling the Front Range is a second line of mountains including the PARK RANGE (N), SAWATCH RANGE (C), and SANGRE DE CRISTO Mts. (S, extending into New Mexico). The CONTINENTAL DIVIDE largely follows this W line of mountains, although it swings into the Front Range NW of Denver. Mt. ELBERT, in the Sawatches, is the highest point (14,433 ft/4402 m) in the state and in the entire Rocky Mt. system. In SW Colorado, the Continental Divide swings W around the SAN JUAN Mts., another Rockies subsection that, oriented NW–SE, does not fit into the two-line organization of the rest of the Colorado Rockies. The San Juans are separated from the rest of the Rockies by the broad agricultural San Luis Valley, through which the upper RIO GRANDE flows. To its N, between the parallel mountains, are the "parks," broad grassy plateaus. West of the Rockies, about one-fourth of the state lies on the COLORADO PLATEAU, a high, arid portion of the INTERMONTANE Region. The COLORADO R. and its tributaries, including the GUNNISON, drain this region W toward Utah. Among the many subsections of the Colorado Plateau are the UNCOMPAHGRE and Roan plateaus, GRAND MESA, and MESA VERDE (SW), the site of famous ANASAZI ruins. Rising from c.3350 ft/1022 m along the Arkansas R. in the E, Colorado has the highest mean elevation (c.6800 ft/2100 m) of any US state, and includes within its borders two-thirds of all peaks over 14,000 ft/4267 m on the continent. That there were no obvious passes here through the Rockies caused early westward travelers to pass N through Wyoming or S through New Mexico. Spanish explorers came N from New Mexico at times in the 18th century, and claimed the area, but made no permanent settlement. The Cheyenne, Arapaho, Comanche, and Ute were almost the only inhabitants of an area parts of which were claimed also by the French and passed (1803) to the US in the LOUISIANA PURCHASE. In the 1800s, American explorers including Zebulon Pike saw the Rockies here; trappers began to operate in the mountains, and in the 1820s the SANTA FE TRAIL crossed the future state's SE corner. In 1848 Mexico surrendered what remained of the old Spanish claim, but Mexican farmers were allowed to establish themselves in the San Luis Valley. In 1858–59, gold strikes on CHERRY CREEK, where Denver came to be established, and near Pikes Peak brought rapid settlement, and throughout the late 19th century gold, silver, and lead mining established such towns as LEADVILLE, ASPEN, and CREEDE, while today's cities began to grow along the Front Range. The Colorado Territory was created in 1861. During the Civil War, most strife in Colorado, including the 1864 SAND CREEK massacre, was between whites and Indians. In the 1870s, the plains were settled as railroads extended to and along the base of the Front Range, and silver strikes in the mountains furthered the boom there. In the 1890s, though, as silver prices collapsed, the state entered a period of depression that was relieved only by demands for its metals (esp. molybdenum and tungsten) during World War I. The beginnings of real industrial and urban growth came with World War II, when military facilities and manufacturing brought rapid development. The ROCKY MOUNTAIN ARSENAL, airfields at Denver (LOWRY AIR FORCE BASE) and Colorado Springs, infantry training camps in the mountains, and aircraft, ship, and weapons plants in Denver, Boulder, and other cities were part of the expansion. After the war, the air defense center at CHEYENNE Mt., the nuclear materials processing plant at ROCKY FLATS, and other facilities continued the military-industrial surge, and Colorado Springs became home (1954) to the Air Force Academy. Uranium mining in the W (around GRAND JUNCTION, DURANGO, and other Colorado Plateau cities) and the energy boom of the 1970s contributed to growth. Today the Denver area is a center of high-tech manufacturing and operations, esp. telecommunications. It is also the metropolis of the Mountain States, the financial and business center of a vast inland region and the second-largest (after Washington, D.C.) Federal operations base. Its suburbs, including Aurora and Lakewood, have mushroomed in recent decades. Colorado Springs has varied manufactures and is noted as a center for military retirees and conservative Christians. Boulder, seat of the University of Colorado, is noted for its environmental and New Age movements. In the mountains, ski and other resorts, including media-conscious Aspen, BRECKENRIDGE, TELLURIDE, CRESTED BUTTE, VAIL, STEAMBOAT SPRINGS, CENTRAL CITY, and GEORGETOWN represent Colorado to many outsiders. Visitors are also drawn to the ROCKY MOUNTAIN NATIONAL PARK, the BLACK CANYON of the Gunnison R., Mesa Verde National Park, the DINOSAUR NATIONAL MONUMENT, Pikes Peak, the GREAT SAND DUNES National Monument, the ROYAL GORGE of the Arkansas R., and other natural and historic sites. The UTE MOUNTAIN and Southern Ute INDIAN RESERVATIONS are in the SW corner. Colorado's Hispanic residents, many in the Pueblo area, comprise about 13% of its pop. Over 34% of land within the state's borders remains Federal. Colorado takes its name (Spanish for "reddish") from the river, although the latter was long called the Grand R.

Colorado Desert low-lying region of S California, extending into N Baja California, Mexico. About 200 mi/320 km NW–SE, and up to 50 mi/80 km wide, it lies E of the Santa Ana and Laguna Mts., and W of the San Bernardino and Chocolate Mts. Its N part, the Coachella Valley, is the site of PALM SPRINGS and other resorts. In its C is the SALTON SEA, the lowest part of the former Salton Sink or Trough. In the S is the irrigated IMPERIAL VALLEY; the SAND HILLS (Algodones Dunes) lie on the SE. Formed by the collapse of part of the Coastal Ranges to the W, the Colorado (or Low) Desert is newer and lower than the MOJAVE (or High) Desert, its NE neighbor.

Colorado National Monument 20,454 ac/8284 ha, on the Colorado R. in W Colorado, immediately W of GRAND JUNCTION, on the NW of the UNCOMPAHGRE PLATEAU. Established in 1911, it is a region of red sandstone cut into deep canyons, with isolated pinnacles and other formations and many dinosaur fossils. The noted Rim Rock Drive traverses the monument.

Colorado Plateau major section of the INTERMONTANE REGION of the W US, lying W of the Southern Rocky Mts. and NE of the SONORAN DESERT, in SW Colorado, SE Utah, NW New Mexico, and N Arizona. The Colorado R., which gives it its name, flows SW across the area, a series of arid or semiarid uplands some 4000–11,000 ft/1220–3350 m high, with peaks rising to about 13,000 ft/4000 m. The Colorado Plateau is known for its volcanic features and for deep canyons cut through colorful sedimentary strata, among them Arizona's GRAND CANYON and SE Utah's Glen Canyon (now beneath L. POWELL) and CANYONLANDS. Home for centuries to the ANASAZI, the plateau, which includes the FOUR CORNERS area, is the scene of ancient ruins like MESA VERDE and of major modern INDIAN RESERVATIONS, among them the huge NAVAJO INDIAN RESERVATION. Among its national parks and monuments are CANYON DE CHELLY, CAPITOL REEF, ARCHES, and RAINBOW BRIDGE.

Colorado River **1.** 1450 mi/2335 km long, in Colorado, Utah, Arizona, Nevada, California, and Mexico. The major river of the US Southwest, it is well known for the landscapes it has created (including the GRAND CANYON), and is of critical importance as the provider (with its tributaries) of irrigation for a largely arid area of over 240,000 sq mi/622,000 sq km. It rises on the Continental Divide in Colorado's Rocky Mountain National Park, W of Estes Park. Near its head, in Grand L., some of its waters are diverted NE across the Divide into the headwaters of the Big Thompson R., which feeds the SOUTH PLATTE R. and agricultural areas on the W edge of the Great Plains below; the key unit of the Colorado–Big Thompson Project is the 13 mi/21 km–long Alva B. Adams Tunnel. From the park, the Colorado R. flows generally WSW across Colorado. At Glenwood Springs the ROARING FORK R. joins it, at Grand Junction the GUNNISON R., both from the SE. Entering Utah, it flows SW across the state's SE corner. Above the junction of the GREEN R., its major tributary, the Colorado has also been called the Grand R., and it passes through the Grand River Valley, along the S of Arches National Park, and into Canyonlands National Park (where the Green joins it from the N). It then enters the Glen Canyon National Recreation Area, where L. POWELL has since the 1960s inundated Glen Canyon, long famous as one of the river's most spectacular stretches. From Glen Canyon Dam, at Page, Arizona, the river passes SSW through MARBLE CANYON, and enters Grand Canyon National Park. Winding WSW within the park, it separates the ARIZONA STRIP (N) from the rest of the state. The LITTLE COLORADO R. joins it, from the SE, at the E end of the park. At the park's W end, the river enters the Lake MEAD National Recreation Area, within which it begins to form the Nevada-Arizona border. It turns S from the Hoover Dam, which forms L. Mead, and passes through L. Mohave, formed by the 1949 Davis Dam, on the recreation area's S boundary. Passing Laughlin, Nevada, and Bullhead City, Arizona, it begins to wind generally S, forming the California-Arizona border. The 1938 Parker Dam forms HAVASU L., on which is Lake Havasu City; the Bill Williams R. joins from the E at the dam, which is the starting point of the **Colorado River Aqueduct,** a 240-mi/390-km conduit, completed in 1939, that carries water to L. Mathews, S of Riverside, in the Los Angeles area. Near California's SE corner, the Imperial Dam (1938) diverts water westward, via the ALL-AMERICAN CANAL and its offshoots, into the IMPERIAL VALLEY and areas E of Los Angeles. Yuma, Arizona, where the GILA R. joins from the E, is situated at the former mouth of the Colorado, which has subsequently formed a large delta. The river now continues for 90 mi/145 km, between the Mexican states of Baja California Norte (W) and Sonora (E), into the top end of the Gulf of California. Former sections of the Gulf closed off by the delta's expansion include California's Salton Trough, site of the SALTON SEA and Imperial Valley. The Colorado's valley, lived in for thousands of years, was first seen by Europeans in the 1530s–40s. Because of its remoteness and difficult terrain, it was not fully explored until the 1868–71 expeditions of John Wesley Powell. In the 20th century use of the river's water has been the subject of Congressional action, compacts among the states involved, and US-Mexican treaties. **2.** 900 mi/1450 km long, in Texas. It rises in Dawson Co., in the LLANO ESTACADO, some 60 mi/100 km S of Lubbock, in intermittent streams, and flows generally SE for its entire journey across C Texas to the Gulf of Mexico. In WC Texas it passes through Colorado City (pop. 4749) and Ballinger; it then cuts through the state's central hills to AUSTIN, at the BALCONES ESCARPMENT, from which it drops across the Coastal Plain, past BAY CITY, to MATAGORDA BAY, on the Gulf. Its chief tributaries are the CONCHO, San Saba, Llano, and PEDERNALES rivers. Dams in the HILL COUNTRY have created BUCHANAN and other lakes, in the Highland Lakes area NW of Austin, and a three-part (Upper, Central, Lower) Colorado River Authority manages a series of flood-control and power developments along the river and its tributaries. A delta formed by the river extends across Matagorda Bay.

Colorado River Indian Reservation see under PARKER, Arizona.

Colorado Springs city, pop. 281,140, seat of El Paso Co., C Colorado, at the foot of PIKES PEAK, 65 mi/105 km S of Denver. The original town was founded in 1858 and was transformed into an affluent planned community in the 1870s and 1880s. It prospered after the 1890s CRIPPLE CREEK gold strikes. Named for the nearby Manitou mineral springs, it was promoted as a health resort. Today it continues to draw many vacationers. Military installations also spurred its growth and have played an important part in the economy. Peterson Field is headquarters for the North American Air Defense and Aerospace Defense commands, and the Fourth Infantry Division is based at Fort Carson, S of the city. The US Air Force Academy (1954) is immediately NNW of the city. Colorado Springs is also the seat of Colorado College (1874) and Colorado Technical College (1965). Industries include electronics and printing. Since the 1980s, the city has also been the headquarters of several evangelical Christian sects. Colorado Springs' many visitors are drawn to spectacular local scenery, notably the Garden of the Gods, a group of massive sandstone formations. Among the city's other attractions are the Colorado Fine Arts Center and the US Olympic Sports Complex.

Colton city, pop. 40,213, San Bernardino Co., SW California, 53 mi/86 km E of Los Angeles and adjacent (SW) to San Bernardino. Concrete and cement products are manufactured, and city is also a shipping center for regional fruit. Mexicans settled the site in 1838, and Americans began arriving in the 1860s. Colton was founded in 1875, when the Southern Pacific Railroad came through the area, and has large railyards.

Colts Neck township, pop. 8559, Monmouth Co., EC New Jersey, 10 mi/16 km WSW of Long Branch. It is the site of the Earle Ammunition Depot, long a key naval facility, which straddles the borders with Howell township (S) and Tinton Falls (SE). Phalanx, a "utopian" communal organization based on the principles of the French philosopher Fourier, flourished in the E of the township in 1843–54.

Columbia **1.** see under SONORA, California. **2.** city, pop. 3845, seat of Adair Co., SC Kentucky, 90 mi/140 km SW of Lexington. Founded c.1793 in an agricultural area, it has lumber and flour mills. Quilted articles and soft drinks are made. Lindsey Wilson College (1903) is here. **3.** planned residential community, pop. 75,883, Howard Co., C Maryland, 13 mi/21 km WSW of Baltimore, and 23 mi/37 km NE of Washington, D.C. When completed its nine villages will include some 30,000 homes. Construction of the last village began in 1991, 24 years after the initiation of the project, and was scheduled for completion in 10–12 years. Columbia's plans incorporate shopping, office, and warehouse zones. It houses Howard Community College (1970) and the Merriweather-Post Pavilion, summer home of the Baltimore Symphony Orchestra. **4.** city, pop. 69,101, seat of Boone Co., C Missouri, 30 mi/48 km NW of Jefferson City. Established in 1819, it later became a pioneer outfitting station along the Boone's Lick Trail to the West. It is home to a number of educational institutions, including the University of Missouri (1839), the first public university W of the Mississippi R., Stephens College (1833), and Columbia College (1851). Also vital to its economy are the insurance industry, medical institutions, agricultural products, and coal. **5.** borough, pop. 10,701, Lancaster Co., S Pennsylvania, on the Susquehanna R., 25 mi/40 km SE of Harrisburg. Settled in 1730 by Quaker John Wright, it was originally known as Wright's Ferry. The name was changed in 1790 when it was considered as a possible US capital. A terminal for the railroad from Philadelphia (1834–57), it was also an important mid-19th-century lumbering center. Before the Civil War it was an Underground Railroad station. Today Columbia is a trading and shipping center for the fertile Susquehanna River Valley and has some manufacturing. **6.** city, pop. 98,052, state capital and seat of Richland Co., C South Carolina, on the Congaree R. where it is formed by the Broad and Saluda rivers, at the FALL LINE, 100 mi/160 km NW of Charleston. To keep peace between UP COUNTRY farmers and Low Country plantation owners, the state legislature created Columbia in 1786 to replace Charleston as capital. Government is still the dominant activity, but the city is also a financial, insurance, and communications center and an important wholesale and retail market. Textiles have been important since the 1890s, and synthetics, structural steel, firearms, cameras, and aerospace and electronics products are manufactured. A transportation center during the Civil War, and the seat of many Confederate agencies, the city was occupied in Feb. 1865 by Union troops under W.T. Sherman, and virtually destroyed by fire. Columbia is home to the University of South Carolina (1801) and several other colleges. Fort Jackson (1917), a major infantry base, lies E of the city. **7.** city, pop. 28,583, seat of Maury Co., C Tennessee, on the Duck R., 42 mi/69 km SSW of Nashville. Settled in 1807, it developed as a farm trade center and mule market. President James K. Polk's residence (1816) is here, and the city was Confederate general Nathan Forrest's base. The discovery (1890) of phosphate deposits shifted the economic base, making Columbia an important mining site and manufacturer of phosphorus and carbon products. Processed foods, clothing, and fertilizer are also made here. The city has a community college.

Columbia, Cape see under ELLESMERE I., Northwest Territories.

Columbia, District of see DISTRICT OF COLUMBIA.

Columbia, Mount highest point (12,294 ft/3747 m) in Alberta, 60 mi/97 km SE of Jasper, in the Rocky Mts., along the border with British Columbia. The mountain is encompassed by the **Columbia Icefield,** the largest mass of ice in the Rockies, covering over 116 sq mi/300 sq km of the plateau between Mt. Columbia and Mt. Athabasca (11,446 ft/3491 m) with ice accumulations 325–1200 ft/100–365 m deep. The icefield straddles the Continental Divide and includes a number of glaciers, the largest being the Athabasca and the Saskatchewan. The ATHABASCA R. has its source at Mt. Columbia.

Columbia County 638 sq mi/1652 sq km, pop. 62,982, in SE New York, bounded by the Hudson R. (W) and Massachusetts (E). It is situated mainly in the rolling Taconic Hills, along the Hudson between the Catskill Mts. (W) and Berkshire Hills (E), and is cut by creeks and dotted with small lakes. Its seat is the city of HUDSON, where there is some manufacturing. The county has traditionally been agricultural, with fruit (chiefly apple) orchards, dairy farming, and horse raising predominating. There is also some suburban development, particularly in the NW, near Albany. Columbia Co., has also become a popular exurban retreat for residents of Albany and New York City.

Columbia Heights **1.** residential neighborhood in NW Washington, D.C., E of SIXTEENTH St. and MOUNT PLEASANT, 2 mi/3 km N of the White House. Its older black residents have been joined in recent years by many of Washington's growing Hispanic community. Howard University is to the E, SHAW to the SE. **2.** city, pop. 18,910, Anoka Co., SE Minnesota, on the Mississippi R., a residential suburb immediately N of Minneapolis.

Columbiana County 534 sq mi/1383 sq km, pop. 108,276, in E Ohio, bounded by Pennsylvania (E) and by the Ohio R. at the West Virginia line (SE), and intersected by Little Beaver R. Its seat is LISBON. The county is largely agricultural (dairy, fruit, grain, truck, and livestock); coal and clay are exploited as well. There is some manufacturing at East Liverpool, East Palestine, Salem, and Wellsville.

Columbia Plateau major section of the INTERMONTANE plateaus of the NW US, in E Washington, S and W Idaho, and

E Oregon. Comprising some 100,000 sq mi/260,000 sq km, it is covered with lava flows, through which older mountains (the Blues, the Wallowas) intrude in places. Sedimentary material is mixed with the lava, and LOESS is deep enough on some surfaces to provide fertile land for farming and ranching. The plateau includes lands within the BIG BEND of the Columbia R. in Washington (the Walla Walla Plateau), the BLUE Mts. of E Oregon, the SNAKE R. Plain of S Idaho, and the HARNEY DESERT of S Oregon. All areas are characterized by harsh, arid landscapes, with COULEES, SCABLANDS, and other phenomena produced by the rush of glacial waters across the surface, and scattered volcanic features. Irrigation by the Columbia Basin Project has made much of it agriculturally productive. The Cascade Range is W, the Rocky Mts. E.

Columbia Point see under DORCHESTER, Massachusetts.

Columbia River 1243 mi/2001 km long, in British Columbia, Washington, and Oregon. The major river of the Pacific Northwest, it has been central to salmon-based native cultures, to the fur trade, to 19th-century westward expansion, and to 20th-century hydroelectric, agricultural, and industrial development. It rises in Columbia L., in British Columbia's Rocky Mountain Trench, some 100 mi/160 km SW of Calgary, Alberta, and at first flows NNW, into the S arm of 130 mi/210 km–long Kinbasket L., a reservoir created in 1972 by the Mica Dam, near Mica Creek, which also impounds waters of the Wood (from the E) and Canoe (from the NW) rivers. From the dam, the Columbia turns abruptly S, flowing between the SELKIRK Mts. (E, around the top of which it has thus turned) and the MONASHEES (W). Here it passes REVELSTOKE, where it is dammed, and flows through the two ARROW LAKES, 100 mi/160 km long in total, to CASTLEGAR, where the KOOTENAI R. joins it from the E. The Columbia continues S to the Washington border, just N of which the PEND OREILLE (or Clark Fork) R. joins it from the E. Winding SSW in Washington, it enters the upper end of Franklin D. Roosevelt L., formed by the GRAND COULEE DAM, 150 mi/240 km downstream. Within the lake, it passes down the E boundary of the COLVILLE INDIAN RESERVATION; the SPOKANE R. joins it from the E at the SE corner. It then turns W along the reservation's S, passing the Grand Coulee midway. At the SW corner, the OKANOGAN R. joins it from the N. The Columbia here swings SSW to Wenatchee, then SSE through the HANFORD military reservation to the Richland-Pasco-Kennewick area. Just below the tri-cities, the SNAKE R., its major tributary, joins it from the E. The Columbia turns S again, and 14 mi/23 km downstream begins to form the Washington-Oregon border, turning WSW. It passes Umatilla and THE DALLES, where rapids long stopped upriver navigation, and where OREGON TRAIL travelers took to boats for the last leg of their westward journey. Passing through spectacular gorge country, it reaches Portland, Oregon, and the mouth of the WILLAMETTE R. (from the S). Finally, it turns NNW past Longview, Washington, and WNW to ASTORIA and its mouth in a sandbar-protected estuary inside Washington's Cape Disappointment. In C Washington, where the Columbia turns W, then S, then SSE, it encloses the BIG BEND Country, a lava flow–covered section of the COLUMBIA PLATEAU. Federal dams on the river—the Grand Coulee; the Chief Joseph, near the Colville Reservation's SW corner; the McNary, near Umatilla, Oregon; the John Day, some 35 mi/56 km E of The Dalles; The Dalles, just E of the city of The Dalles; and the BONNEVILLE, 40 mi/64 km W of The Dalles—are combined flood control/irrigation/hydroelectric generating units. Also on the river, in the S-flowing part of the Big Bend, are five hydroelectric units—the Wells, Rocky Reach, Rock Island, Wanapum, and Priest Rapids dams. Control of flow now enables large vessels to reach the mouth of the Snake, 328 mi/528 km inland. Fish ladders at dams, allowing salmon to continue their migrations, draw visitors. Irrigation of semiarid E Washington and Oregon has been organized since 1948 by the Columbia Basin Project. A 1964 treaty governs water use questions between Canada and the US. The Columbia, long the object of searchers for a route to the Pacific, and spoken of as the **Great River of the West,** was seen but not entered in 1792 by Robert Gray, a Boston captain who named it for his ship. The LEWIS AND CLARK expedition ended (1805) by traveling its lower reaches. By 1811 the NORTH WEST COMPANY's David Thompson had explored its entire length. Its use as the last section of the Oregon Trail brought settlement to Oregon's Willamette Valley. The Columbia drains an area of some 259,000 sq mi/671,000 sq km, and has a volume second, in North America, only to that of the Mississippi.

Columbine unincorporated community, pop. 23,969, Jefferson and Arapahoe counties, NC Colorado. It is a rapidly growing E suburb of Denver.

Columbus 1. city, pop. 179,278, seat of Muscogee Co., W Georgia, at the head of navigation (the Fall Line) on the Chattahoochee R., opposite Phenix City, Alabama. Founded in 1828 on the former site of Creek villages, it quickly became a major textile center and a leading inland cotton port. During the Civil War, it was an important supply depot and arsenal. A series of locks and dams on the Chattahoochee revitalized the city's port, after a period of decline which followed the 1850s advent of the railroad. Columbus is now a distribution center for SW Georgia's and E Alabama's agriculture, a commercial and financial center, and one of the South's largest textile centers. Its industries manufacture fabricated iron and steel, cotton processing machinery, concrete pipe, clothing, hosiery, processed foods, textiles, fertilizer, soft drinks, and lumber as well. It is home to Columbus College (1958). FORT BENNING lies E and S. **2.** city, pop. 31,802, seat of Bartholomew Co., SC Indiana, on the East Fork of the White R., 42 mi/68 km SSE of Indianapolis. Founded in 1820, it became a railroad center, and its status as a Union depot in the Civil War brought industry. Over the years its manufactures have included diesel engines (Cummins), auto parts, castings, metal and plastic products, appliances, and leather. Columbus is known for its over 50 buildings designed since the 1950s by such distinguished architects as I.M. Pei, the Saarinens, Kevin Roche, Cesar Pelli, and Robert Venturi. Its major golf course was created by Robert Trent Jones. Nearby is Tipton Knoll, a large prehistoric Indian mound. **3.** city, pop. 23,799, seat of Lowndes Co., NE Mississippi, on the Tombigbee and Luxapalila rivers, 8 mi/13 km W of the Alabama line. The commercial center for an area producing cotton, corn, dairy goods, livestock, and marble, it also has light manufactures including chemicals and apparel. Settled as a trading post in 1817, it is home to the Mississippi University for Women (1884), which was the first state-supported college for women in the US. Franklin Academy, founded here in 1821, was the first public school in the state. The city's Friendship Cemetery was the site, on April 25, 1866, of the first Decoration Day observance. The playwright Tennessee Williams was born

(1911) in the city. **Columbus Air Force Base,** 9 mi/14 km NNW, contributes to the economy. **4.** city, pop. 19,480, seat of Platte Co., E Nebraska, at the junction of the Loup and Platte rivers, 80 mi/128 km WNW of Omaha. It is a trade center and railroad distribution point for livestock, grain, and dairy products, and has some light industry. **5.** village, pop. 641, Luna Co., SW New Mexico, 65 mi/105 km W of El Paso, Texas, on the Chihuahua (Mexico) border. Pancho Villa State Park here is the site of the famous March 9, 1916 raid by the bandit/rebel's forces against the cavalry post of Camp Furlong, in which 18 Americans (and some 250 Mexicans) died. General "Black Jack" Pershing led retaliatory actions against Villa's forces from the camp in the following year. **6.** city, pop. 632,958, state capital and seat of Franklin Co. (also in Fairfield Co.), C Ohio, at the junction of the SCIOTO and Olentangy rivers. A commercial, industrial, research, and educational center, it has factories and wholesale markets, but state government, 55,000-student Ohio State University, and high-tech research and development institutions set Columbus apart from other Ohio urban areas. In addition, the city is a transportation hub and a distribution point for farm produce and livestock. Rickenbacker Air Force Base is just SE. The city's seven-county (including FAIRFIELD, FRANKLIN, and LICKING) metropolitan area has a pop. of 1,377,419. Early settlers offered the new state of Ohio a large tract of land E of the Scioto, accepted in 1812, for a capital. Columbus faced an older (1797) village, Franklinton, across the river; state government moved here from CHILLICOTHE in 1816. Soon a stop on the NATIONAL ROAD, with canal connections, Columbus was incorporated as a city in 1834, annexing Franklinton. During the Civil War, Union military camps, an arsenal, and the largest Northern prison for Confederates were in the area. Financial and industrial expansion characterized the postwar period, with Columbus becoming a major buggy manufacturing center in the 1880s. A new generation of industries emerged during World War II, with the construction of a large airplane assembly plant. Today, the city manufactures various kinds of machinery, fabricated metal items, auto parts, and paints. Other important industries include food processing and printing and publishing. Services, insurance, research, and finance have expanded in recent years; Battelle Memorial Institute, the largest private organization of its kind, aims to link businesses with scientific, technological, and economic research. Other educational institutions in the city include Capital (1830) and Franklin (1902) universities. In addition, the annual Ohio State Fair and many conventions are held here, and the city is the headquarters of the American Rose Society. With its diversified economy and governmental role, Columbus has weathered recent recessions, and has outgrown both CINCINNATI and CLEVELAND, becoming in the 1980s Ohio's most populous city. **7.** city, pop. 4093, Columbia and Dodge counties, SC Wisconsin, 30 mi/48 km NE of Madison. Settled c.1840, it is set in a diversified farming area. Dairy products and vegetables are processed, beer is brewed, and machinery is manufactured.

Colville city, pop. 4360, seat of Stevens Co., NE Washington, on the Colville R., 69 mi/111 km NNW of Spokane. It was the center of a mining area from the mid 1850s. In a timbering region, between units of Colville National Forest, the city now produces silver, lead, and wheat. The huge COLVILLE INDIAN RESERVATION begins 20 mi/32 km SW.

Colville Indian Reservation 2117 sq mi/5482 sq km, pop. 6957, in NE Washington, N and W of the Columbia R. It is home to Salishan groups including the Colville, Coeur d'Alene, Kalispel, Nespelim, and Sanpoil. The smaller Spokane Indian Reservation (238 sq mi/615 sq km, pop. 1502) lies SE. To the N is the 1875–sq mi/4856–sq km **Colville National Forest,** whose units are separated by Franklin D. Roosevelt L. (the Columbia R.).

Colville River major river of Alaska's NORTH SLOPE, 375 mi/605 km long, rising in streams in the BROOKS RANGE and flowing (when not frozen) generally ENE to the BEAUFORT SEA W of PRUDHOE BAY. Its tributaries include the Anaktuvuk and Killik rivers. The Inuit community of Nuiqsut (city, pop. 354) is on the W of its delta.

Colwood city, pop. 13,468, Capital Regional District, extreme S Vancouver I., SW British Columbia, 5 mi/8 km W of Victoria, of which it is a largely residential suburb, across Esquimalt Harbour. It is home to the Canadian Services College, on Royal Roads.

Comanche County 1076 sq mi/2787 sq km, pop. 111,486, in SW Oklahoma. Its seat and only large city is LAWTON. The county includes most of the WICHITA Mts. The huge FORT SILL Military Reservation occupies much of its center, and has had a great influence on its history and economy. The rest of the county has limestone, hematite, and granite mines; gravel pits; oilfields; and some cattle ranches. Its products include cotton, wheat, hay, and oats.

Comanche National Grassland see under SAN ISABEL NATIONAL FOREST, Colorado.

Combat Zone part of the entertainment district of Boston, Massachusetts, along Washington St. just SE of Boston Common, given its name in the late 1960s when pornographic theaters and other businesses attracting "undesirables" moved there from the redeveloped SCOLLAY SQUARE area.

Comb Ridge c.100 mi/160 km N–S, crossing the San Juan R., in extreme SE Utah, and continuing SW into NE Arizona. In 1923 it was the site of the last battle between settlers and Indians in the West, after a group of dispossessed Utes under Posey raided ranchers near the hamlet of Bluff (SE). Wounded, Posey died along nearby (W) Comb Wash; but the battle led to establishment of Colorado's UTE MOUNTAIN INDIAN RESERVATION (SE).

Comiskey Park baseball field in BRIDGEPORT, on the South Side of Chicago, the home of the Chicago White Sox. The stadium has a capacity of over 44,000 and was opened in 1992, adjacent to the site of the old Comiskey Park, now torn down, which was built in 1910 and was long the oldest major league stadium.

Commack unincorporated village, pop. 36,124, in Huntington town, Suffolk Co., SE New York, in C Long Island. It is a largely residential suburb of New York City.

Commerce **1.** city, pop. 12,135, Los Angeles Co., SW California, 8 mi/13 km E of Los Angeles. A rail and road transportation hub and shipping center, it also makes chemicals and telephones, and has made automobiles. Its population is predominantly Hispanic. **2.** city, pop. 6825, Hunt Co., NE Texas, 61 mi/98 km NE of Dallas. An agricultural processing and shipping center with some light manufactures, it is home to East Texas State University (1889).

Commerce City city, pop. 16,466, Adams Co., NC Colorado, 7 mi/11 km NE of Denver, of which it is a suburb. It has oil refineries, steel plants, and flour mills, and trades and ships beans and sugar beets from nearby farms.

commonwealth 1. from 17th-century British political and philosophical thinking ("government by common consent" of the governed), the formal title of four US states: Massachusetts, Pennsylvania, Virginia, and Kentucky. **2.** the accepted translation of *estado libro asociado* (literally, "free associated state"), designating the status of PUERTO RICO chosen by a July 1952 plebiscite. **3.** the designated status of the NORTHERN MARIANA ISLANDS.

Communipaw see under JERSEY CITY, New Jersey.

Como Park residential neighborhood in St. Paul, Minnesota, NW of Downtown and adjacent to suburban Falcon Heights. An affluent area, it is the site of the city's largest park, L. Como, and a zoo.

Comox town, pop. 8253, Comox-Strathcona Regional District, SW British Columbia, on EC Vancouver I., 110 mi/177 km NW of Victoria. In a Salishan homeland, it was settled by whites in the 1860s and is a port, winter sports and retirement center, and agricultural (potatoes, fruit) service center.

company town community created or developed by one business, often with a characteristic style of worker housing and some company-established social services. The mill village, such as 1820s LOWELL, Massachusetts, is an early example; it housed workers, generally from rural backgrounds, who had come to staff the new textile industry. In the 19th and early 20th centuries company towns were established, largely in the South, in the textile, coal, lumber, and other industries. They were often physically isolated, but urban examples include PULLMAN, Illinois, and KANNAPOLIS, North Carolina. Control of workers was sometimes paternalistic, but sometimes oppressive; the **company store,** at which workers had to shop and to which they grew increasingly indebted, is proverbial. Most company towns became "public" by the 1950s.

Compton city, pop. 90,454, Los Angeles Co., SW California, between Los Angeles (N) and Long Beach (S). Settled in 1867, it was primarily agricultural until World War II, when rapid industrial and residential growth began. Electronics and heating equipment, aircraft parts, pipe, felt, roofing, tools, and structural steel are among the city's manufactures. Compton Community College (1927) is in this predominantly black, working- and middle-class city.

Comstock Lode silver and gold seam on Mt. Davidson, in the Virginia Mts., W Nevada, 20 mi/32 km SSE of Reno. Discovered in 1857, and recognized for the richness of its silver ore in 1859, it is named for Henry Comstock, one of the owners of the land it was under. The lode brought a tremendous boom to VIRGINIA CITY, Silver City, Washoe, Gold Hill, and Moundhouse, strung along its 15-mi/24-km length. The Big Bonanza (1873) was the richest US silver strike. After the peak years of the 1870s, esp. after adoption of gold, not silver, as the US monetary standard, production declined sharply; the Comstock was essentially quiet by 1900. The area is today largely a tourist center.

comunidad see under ZONA URBANA, Puerto Rico.

Conanicut Island c.9 mi/14 km long and 1–2 mi/2–3 km wide, in Newport Co., S Rhode Island; one of three main islands in Narragansett Bay, and coextensive with Jamestown, pop. 4999. It lies between Newport and the mainland (W), and is connected to both by bridge. Beaver Tail Light (1856), the latest in a series dating from 1749, is at the S tip.

Conception Bay Atlantic Ocean inlet, some 34 mi/55 km long and up to 17 mi/27 km wide, on the N of the AVALON PENINSULA, in SE Newfoundland. Its shores are the earliest and most densely settled in the province; CUPIDS is on its SW. The bay has rich iron deposits, long mined from BELL I.; resorts; fishing communities; and newer suburbs of SAINT JOHN'S (E).

Conception Bay South town, pop. 17,590, SE Newfoundland, on the NE AVALON PENINSULA and the SE shore of Conception Bay, 14 mi/22 km WSW of St. John's. An amalgamation of a number of small coastal settlements, it is a resort and bedroom community for workers in the capital.

Concho River 55 mi/89 km long, in C Texas. Formed at SAN ANGELO by the confluence of the North and South Concho rivers, it flows generally E to join the Colorado R., 18 mi/29 km SE of Ballinger. The Middle Concho R. joins the South Concho in TWIN BUTTES RESERVOIR, SSW of San Angelo.

Concord 1. city, pop. 111,348, Contra Costa Co., NC California, 15 mi/24 km NE of Oakland, in the Clayton Valley, NW of Mt. Diablo and just S of Suisun Bay. It was founded in the 1840s on the Mexican Rancho Monte del Diablo, as Todos Santos, but was renamed by 1850s New England settlers. After the railroad arrived in 1912, it developed as a fruit and poultry center, and gradually acquired some industry. Between 1950 and 1960, its population increased by over 500%. The Concord Naval Weapons Station is a dominant presence in the city. The Concord Pavilion, a performing arts and art center, is well known. **2.** town, pop. 17,076, Middlesex Co., E Massachusetts, 19 mi/31 km NW of Boston, on the Concord R. where it is formed by the joining of the Assabet and Sudbury rivers. The town developed from 1635 on the site of an Indian village, Musketaquid. It was the scene of the second April 19, 1775 skirmish between Minutemen and British regulars, at the North Bridge, now in Minute Man National Historic Park. During the 19th century, Concord was home to influential literary figures including Nathaniel Hawthorne, Ralph Waldo Emerson, Louisa May Alcott, Margaret Fuller, and Henry David Thoreau (whose WALDEN POND is 1.5 mi/2.4 km SSE of the town center). Today Concord is a Boston suburb with prep schools, some light manufacturing, and high-tech industry. The Concord Reformatory is in West Concord. **3.** unincorporated community, pop. 19,859, St. Louis Co., EC Missouri, 11 mi/18 km SW of downtown St. Louis, a largely residential suburb just within Route 270, the St. Louis beltway. **4.** city, pop. 36,006, state capital and seat of Merrimack Co., SC New Hampshire, 20 mi/32 km N of Manchester. The Indian name for the 1720s settlement, Penacook, means "crooked place," referring to the winding of the Merrimack R., on whose W bank the city developed. The community was named Concord in 1765 to commemorate the peaceful settlement of a border dispute with Massachusetts, which had claimed ownership. The early economy was based on printing, carriage making, and granite quarrying. Now, in addition to state offices, light industry, insurance, and farming are important. Schools include New Hampshire Technical Institute and St. Paul's preparatory school. **5.** city, pop. 27,347, seat of Cabarrus Co., SC North Carolina, 18 mi/29 km NE of Charlotte, in the Piedmont, just SSE of Kannapolis. Founded in the 1790s, it quickly became a mining center when the Reed Gold Mine, 10 mi/16 km SE, was discovered in 1799. In the 1850s, the textile industry became dominant. Concord presently houses several hosiery mills. Manufactures include soft drinks and foundry and machine shop products.

Concordia city, pop. 6167, seat of Cloud Co., NC Kansas, on the Republican R., 50 mi/80 km N of Salina. Founded in 1870, it is a processing and shipping center for wheat, cattle, dairy products, and poultry. Cloud County Community College (1965) is here.

Concord River 15 mi/24 km long, in E Massachusetts. It is formed in CONCORD by the confluence of the Assabet and Sudbury rivers, and flows NE and N to the Merrimack R. at LOWELL. The Battle of Concord took place just downstream from the Assabet/Sudbury confluence. The Great Meadows of the Concord, described in Thoreau's writing, are now a National Wildlife Refuge, beginning just N of the center of Concord.

Condado oceanfront section of SAN JUAN, Puerto Rico (a *subbarrio,* pop. 5582, of SANTURCE), on the Laguna de Condado (S) and the Atlantic. Its luxury hotels stretch along the Avenida Ashford, extending into Ocean Park (another *subbarrio,* pop. 2034), on the SE, and the area is noted for its tourist trade and night life; esp. in Ocean Park, it is popular with gays.

Conecuh River 230 mi/370 km long, in Alabama and Florida. It rises S of Union Springs, in Bullock Co., SE Alabama, and flows SW into Florida, where it is known as the Escambia R. It empties into Pensacola Bay just N of Pensacola. The 83,000-ac/33,600-ha **Conecuh National Forest** lies in piney woods SE of the river in Covington and Escambia counties, Alabama, along the Florida border.

Conemaugh River 70 mi/113 km long, in SW Pennsylvania. It rises in the Alleghenies near Cresson as the Little Conemaugh R., joining the Stonycreek R. and several streams around Johnstown. It flows generally W past Blairsville, joining the Loyalhanna Creek at Saltsburg to form the Kiskiminetas R. The disastrous JOHNSTOWN flood (1889) occurred when the Conemaugh's earthen dam at South Fork burst. Since then flood control projects have been developed. The name is Algonquian for "otter creek."

Conestoga township, pop. 3470, Lancaster Co., SE Pennsylvania, 7 mi/11 km SSW of Lancaster. It gave its name to two American artifacts: the Conestoga wagon, developed in this area during the early 18th century and the nation's most efficient freight carrier until it was supplanted by the railroads a century later; and the stogie, a cigar made with the local leaf tobacco.

Conestoga Creek 50 mi/80 km long, in SE Pennsylvania. It rises in E Lancaster Co. and flows SW past Lancaster to the Susquehanna R. near Safe Harbor.

Conewango Creek 65 mi/105 km long, in New York and Pennsylvania. A major tributary of the Allegheny R., it rises in W Cattaraugus Co., SW New York, and flows NW, then generally S just E of Jamestown, to join the Allegheny at Warren, Pennsylvania.

Coney Island resort and residential district, extreme S Brooklyn, New York. Originally an island (Dutch *Konijn Eiland,* Rabbit Island), it became by the 1840s a peninsula partially separated from Brooklyn by Coney Island Creek, an inlet of Gravesend Bay, on the W, and by Sheepshead Bay on the E. Hotels and bathhouses appeared at Coney Island by the 1830s, but its character as a mass resort took shape in the 1880s and 1890s, and especially after 1920, when subway lines reached the area. It is most famous for three amusement facilities, Steeplechase Park (1897; closed 1964), Luna Park (1903; burned 1946), and Dreamland (1904; burned 1911). Steeplechase Park's famous Ferris wheel, brightly lit and visible far at sea, was said to be the first part of the US many immigrants saw. After the 1940s amusement parks declined, and Coney Island gradually became a rundown working-class neighborhood, although the beach (6 mi/10 km long, including neighboring BRIGHTON BEACH and Manhattan Beach) and boardwalk (opened 1921) continued to draw visitors. In the 1960s high-rise apartments were built in the W. The New York Aquarium opened 1955, and a few remnants of the great days, such as the Cyclone roller coaster, Nathan's Famous Restaurant (where the hot dog was introduced), and the disused giant Parachute Jump, remain. At the W end is the private residential community of Sea Gate.

Confederacy, the see under the SOUTH.

Confederation 1. the political union, in effect July 1, 1867, of the United Province of Canada (modern Québec and Ontario) with New Brunswick and Nova Scotia, forming the modern Dominion of Canada. It arose from a complex of economic and political considerations, including a perceived threat of US expansionism. The concept was raised at a Sept. 1, 1864 conference in CHARLOTTETOWN, Prince Edward I., called to discuss a possible Maritime Union (of the three Maritime Provinces), and was developed at a second conference, in Québec City, the following month. Charlottetown is thus known as the "Cradle of Confederation." Britain formalized Confederation in the Constitution (British North America) Act. The title *Dominion* (taken from Psalm 72: "He shall have dominion also from sea to sea/and from the river unto the ends of the Earth") was chosen in preference to "Kingdom," which was thought likely to offend Americans. RUPERT'S LAND was sold to Canada, and Manitoba and the Northwest Territories (from which Saskatchewan, Alberta, and the Yukon Territory were later formed) were created, in 1870. British Columbia became part of Canada in 1871, Prince Edward Island in 1873, and Newfoundland not until 1949. **2.** the formal status of the American states under the Articles of Confederation (1777–89).

Confederation Chamber see under CHARLOTTETOWN, Prince Edward Island.

Congaree River formed at Columbia, C South Carolina, by the confluence of the BROAD and SALUDA rivers. It flows SE to join the WATEREE R. at a point 30 mi/48 km SE of Columbia, creating the SANTEE R. The 22,200-ac/9000-ha **Congaree Swamp National Monument,** along its N bank, preserves a bottomland hardwood forest in the Low Country floodplain.

Congo Square French, **Place Congo** see under BEAUREGARD SQUARE, New Orleans, Louisiana.

Congress Heights see under ANACOSTIA, Washington, D.C.

Conklin town, pop. 6265, Broome Co., SC New York, on the Susquehanna R., adjacent (SE) to Binghamton, along the Pennsylvania border. A largely residential suburb of Binghamton, it is also the location of a General Electric aerospace center.

Conneaut city, pop. 13,241, Ashtabula Co., extreme NE Ohio, 65 mi/105 km NE of Cleveland and 2 mi/3 km W of the Pennsylvania border. Founded c.1799, it is a major port on L. Erie, shipping large quantities of iron ore, coal, steel, and limestone from extensive automated docks. Diversified industries include railroad repair shops, tanneries, and the manufacture of chemicals, plastics, and tin cans.

Connecticut northeastern US state, in SW New England; 1990 pop. 3,287,116 (105.8% of 1980; rank: 27th); area 5544 sq mi/ 14,359 sq km (rank: 48th); ratified Constitution 1788 (5th). Capital: HARTFORD. Most populous city: BRIDGEPORT. Other leading cities: NEW HAVEN, WATERBURY, STAMFORD. Connecticut is bordered N by Massachusetts; E by Rhode Island, with the PAWCATUCK R. forming part of the boundary in the S; and W and SW by New York. On the S is LONG ISLAND SOUND, across which are New York's Long and Fishers islands. The state comprises N and C uplands, from W to E, with a narrow coastal lowland across the S; it is crossed (essentially N to S) by river valleys, including those of (W to E) the HOUSATONIC, NAUGATUCK, QUINNIPIAC, CONNECTICUT (by far the broadest), and THAMES, with their tributaries. The state's name derives from that of the river's estuarial lower reaches (Algonquian, "long tidal river"). A portion of the TACONIC Mts., in the extreme NW, rises to 2380 ft/726 m at Mt. FRISSELL, the state's high point. Agriculture, although the focus of early settlements, has not been a major factor in Connecticut's history; the Connecticut R. corridor from near Hartford N, part of which has been known as the TOBACCO VALLEY, produces vegetables and other crops, and there is scattered dairy, poultry, and other small farming. Maritime commerce gave way in the late 18th century to manufacturing as an economic base. Rivers provided power, and inventors and manufacturers like Eli Whitney (the cotton gin; interchangeable-parts machinery), Seth Thomas (clocks), and Samuel Colt (firearms) stand out in Connecticut history. The "Connecticut Yankee" became known for ingenuity as well as for sharp business practices: The nickname "the Nutmeg State" is said to derive from Connecticut peddlers having sold fake (wooden) nutmegs to frontier housewives. Twentieth-century industrial centers include declining Bridgeport, once a machine-tool and metal-goods capital; Waterbury (metals); New Haven (firearms, chemicals); GROTON (submarines; pharmaceuticals); Hartford (firearms); EAST HARTFORD (aircraft engines); and many smaller cities. The state has been heavily dependent, in recent decades, on Federal military spending. Business and finance are also important, esp. in Hartford, an insurance industry center, and in Stamford and GREENWICH, which have become home to many corporate headquarters relocating from nearby New York City. New Haven is a noted educational center (Yale University); the University of Connecticut is situated at STORRS (NE). The densely populated SW, esp. the GOLD COAST of FAIRFIELD Co. (one of America's richest, although it contains severely depressed Bridgeport), is the site of many affluent New York suburbs. LITCHFIELD, SALISBURY, and other communities in the NW display a mix of rural and EXURBAN lifestyles. East of the Connecticut R. and its industrial corridor, the state is lightly populated away from the coast, but is developing residentially, and is now home to the booming Foxwoods gambling resort operated by the Mashantucket Pequot tribe at LEDYARD. The coast, although largely rocky, has a number of popular beaches and other recreational areas. Connecticut was settled from Massachusetts in the 1630s. The 1637 Pequot War, centered around MYSTIC, destroyed much of native resistance. Hartford, WETHERSFIELD, and WINDSOR, in the Connecticut Valley, were governed under the "Fundamental Orders" of 1638, regarded as a forerunner of American constitutionalism; the 1661 charter supposed to have been hidden in the famous CHARTER OAK is an historic icon. New Haven, a separate colony, was joined to Connecticut in the 1660s. The state's COUNTIES have no governmental role, and cities and towns operate with a great deal of independence. Connecticut's people, essentially British-derived Yankees before the mid 19th century, are now also Irish, German, Italian, Slavic, French-Canadian, Hispanic, black, and members of many other groups.

Connecticut Lakes four lakes in extreme N New Hampshire, in Pittsburg township, Coos Co. They are named First Connecticut Lake, Second Lake, Third Lake, and Fourth Lake, and lie in dense forest. First Connecticut L. (4 mi/6 km long) and Second L. (3 mi/5 km long) were made larger by power dams at their outlets. Third L. (1 mi/1.6 km long) lies against the Québec border at an elevation of 2191 ft/668 m. First Connecticut, Second, and Third lakes are headwaters of the CONNECTICUT R., which continues SW through L. FRANCIS to become the border between Vermont and New Hampshire. Fourth Lake, the ultimate source of the Connecticut, is a tiny pond at an elevation of 2600 ft/793 m, just NW of Third L.

Connecticut River 345 mi/555 km long, largest river in New England. It drains an area of 11,000 sq mi/28,500 sq km. It rises in the CONNECTICUT LAKES of Coos Co., extreme N New Hampshire, and flows S and SW, forming the boundary of Vermont and New Hampshire, past the towns of Colebrook, New Hampshire, and Guildhall, Vermont, before entering a reservoir formed by the Moore Dam at Littleton, New Hampshire. This is followed by a second reservoir formed by the Comerford Dam, 5 mi/8 km W. The river then continues SSW past Hanover (New Hampshire) and White River Junction, Bellows Falls, and Brattleboro (Vermont). At Vernon, Vermont, it is dammed once more before crossing into Massachusetts. Tributaries on its upper course include INDIAN STREAM and the Nulhegan, Upper Ammonoosuc, Moose, Ammonoosuc, and White rivers. In Massachusetts the Connecticut flows S and W past Northfield, Greenfield, Deerfield, and other Franklin Co. towns, then S past Northampton, Holyoke, and Springfield, and into Connecticut. This region of Massachusetts is known as the PIONEER VALLEY. In Connecticut the river flows S and SSE toward Long Island Sound, passing Windsor Locks, Hartford, Middletown, Haddam, and Essex before emptying into the Atlantic Ocean between Old Saybrook and Old Lyme. For approximately 270 mi/435 km of its upper course its banks are wooded. The lower valley is a rich agricultural region, known for its onions and as the TOBACCO VALLEY. Flood control and hydroelectric projects were started after disastrous floods in 1936; 20 dams and reservoirs were built. In Connecticut, important tributaries include the Scantic, Farmington, and Salmon rivers. See also CONNECTICUT VALLEY.

Connecticut Valley fertile lands on either side of the Connecticut R. in Massachusetts and Connecticut, some of the best farmland in New England. During the Colonial period, settlers moved N up the river as well as W from Massachusetts Bay and Plymouth, creating a society in some ways more Connecticut than Massachusetts, in towns like Deerfield, Northampton, and Hadley. In Connecticut, Hartford, Wethersfield, and Glastonbury were among the earliest settlements. In Massachusetts the valley is often called the PIONEER VALLEY.

Connecticut Yankee nuclear plant: see under HADDAM, Connecticut.

Connellsville city, pop. 9229, Fayette Co., SW Pennsylvania, on the Youghiogheny R., 10 mi/16 km NE of Uniontown. Once a coal mining and boatbuilding hub, it remains an industrial center with manufactures that include metal castings and plastics.

Connersville city, pop. 15,550, seat of Fayette Co., E Indiana, on the West Fork of the Whitewater R., 17 mi/27 km SW of Richmond. Founded in 1813, it is now a rail and manufacturing center, with factories producing furniture, refrigerators, dishwashers, air conditioners, machine tools, auto parts, and other goods.

Conover see under NEWTON, North Carolina.

Conroe city, pop. 27,610, seat of Montgomery Co., SE Texas, 38 mi/61 km N of Houston. Founded in 1881, it was a BIG THICKET lumber center before 1931, when the Conroe Oilfield (SE) was opened, causing a boom. There is still some oil production, and agricultural processing is important. Nearby recreational facilities including **L. Conroe** (21,000 ac/8500 ha, on the West Fork of the San Jacinto R., 7 mi/11 km NW) and the Sam Houston National Forest (N) contribute to Conroe's recent growth as an outer Houston suburb.

Conshohocken borough, pop. 8064, Montgomery Co., SE Pennsylvania, on the E bank of the Schuylkill R., 14 mi/22 km NW of Philadelphia. Founded after the building of the Schuylkill Canal in 1826, this industrial suburb produces steel, automobile and iron products, and tires.

Constitution Gardens see under the MALL, Washington, D.C.

continental divide imaginary line across a continental mass, determined by the division between rivers flowing in opposite directions; the boundary line between continental watersheds. In North America, the Continental Divide (historically the GREAT DIVIDE) follows the crest of the Rocky Mts. through most of its length. On its E, all rivers flow ultimately into the Atlantic Ocean, as part of the Mississippi R. system, directly into the Gulf of Mexico, or in the N by way of Hudson Bay. In the N, where the Divide swings W, some flow into the Arctic Ocean. On its W, all rivers flow to the Pacific Ocean and its arms (e.g., Mexico's Gulf of California). In the US, the Divide (from the S) winds through several ranges in SW New Mexico, and passes W of Albuquerque; in Colorado, it swings W through the San Juan Mts., then NE to the Sawatch Range and NE and NNE to Rocky Mountain National Park, W to near Steamboat Springs, and NNW into Wyoming. In SW Wyoming, it passes around both sides of the Great Divide Basin and NW along the Wind River Range to Yellowstone National Park. It defines the Montana-Idaho border in the Beaverhead and Bitterroot ranges, then swings E around Butte and N and NNW to Glacier National Park. In Canada, it forms much of the Alberta–British Columbia border, crosses N British Columbia into the Yukon Territory, forms part of the Yukon Territory–Northwest Territories border (the Logan Mts.), and finally swings W across the Yukon to Alaska, following the crest of the Brooks Range WSW, to the W tip of the Seward Peninsula.

continental shelf undersea areas at the edge of a continent, generally defined as lying less than 600 ft/183 m below sea level, and ending with a relatively steep **continental slope** to the ocean floor. The shelf is composed largely of sedimentary material carried into the ocean by river systems; it also represents in part continental land that was above water during glacial periods. In eastern North America, the shelf extends into the ocean in places for hundreds of miles. The richness of its fisheries, esp. in the relatively shallower (or higher) sections called *banks,* has made it key to the economy esp. of New England and the Atlantic Provinces; overfishing led in the 1970s to declaration of 200-mi/320-km offshore limits, which incorporate most of the shelf and which are now patrolled by the US and Canada to enforce exclusive or regulated fishing rights. Oil is particularly important in the Gulf of Mexico's shallow waters. In the West, there is little continental shelf, as the Pacific PLATE, on which it would accumulate, continues to slide beneath the North American plate.

Contoocook River 60 mi/100 km long, in S New Hampshire. It rises in SE Cheshire Co., flowing from Contoocook L., S of Jaffrey, generally NE to the Merrimack R. at Penacook, just NW of Concord. The river furnishes waterpower at Peterborough, Hillsboro, and other manufacturing towns.

Contra Costa County 730 sq mi/1891 sq km, pop. 803,732, in NC California. Its seat is MARTINEZ. Along San Francisco, San Pablo, and Suisun bays and the Carquinez Strait (N), the county has important ports, including Richmond, and industrial cities, including Pittsburg, Concord, Antioch, and Hercules. Steelworks, refineries, shipyards, and food processing plants are here. In the E, Contra Costa produces asparagus, fruit, nuts, wine, grapes, grains, sugar beets, dairy goods, and livestock. Stone, clay, sand, and gravel are also important. Suburban residential growth characterizes much of the SW.

Converse city, pop. 8887, Bexar Co., SC Texas, 14 mi/23 km NE of San Antonio, a growing suburb just SW of RANDOLPH AIR FORCE BASE.

Conway 1. city, pop. 26,481, seat of Faulkner Co., C Arkansas, 25 mi/40 km NNW of Little Rock in the Arkansas Valley. It is the seat of the University of Central Arkansas (1907), Hendrix College (formerly in Altus; 1876), and Central Baptist College (1893). Missile sites were built nearby during the Cold War. Manufactures include bus and refrigerator bodies, furniture, pianos, and shoes. L. Conway is 2 mi/3 km S. **2.** unincorporated community, pop. 13,159, Orange Co., C Florida, a suburb on the SE outskirts of Orlando. **3.** town, pop. 1529, Franklin Co., W Massachusetts, 14 mi/22 km NNW of Northampton. It is located in an agricultural region, along the Deerfield R. and adjoining (W) the town of Deerfield, of which it was once part. **4.** town, pop. 7940, Carroll Co., NC New Hampshire, S of the White Mts. In an intervale where the Swift R. joins the Saco, this 1760s agricultural settlement has become a thriving commercial and resort town. NORTH CONWAY, Intervale, Redstone, Kearsarge, and Center Conway are included villages. Center Conway, with several shopping malls, is especially popular with tax-conscious shoppers from adjacent parts of Maine. Conway L. is in the S part of the town. **5.** city, pop. 9819, seat of Horry Co., NE South Carolina, on the Waccamaw R., 91 mi/147 km NE of Charleston and 14 mi/23 km NW of Myrtle Beach. A tourist center, it also has brickworks, lumber mills, and woodworking plants, and processes poultry and other farm products. A branch of the University of South Carolina and a technical college are here.

Cooch's Bridge see under NEWARK, Delaware.

Coogan's Bluff see under POLO GROUNDS and SUGAR HILL, New York.

Cook County 958 sq mi/2481 sq km, pop. 5,105,067, in NE Illinois, on L. Michigan (E). By far the most populous and urbanized county in the state, it is dominated by Chicago (the county seat) and includes most of its inner suburbs, including Evanston, Calumet City, Harvey, Des Plaines, Schaumburg, Wilmette, and Cicero. Cook Co. extends along L. Michigan to the Indiana line (S). The Chicago, Des Plaines, and Calumet rivers flow through it, as do the Illinois and Michigan and Chicago Sanitary and Ship canals. Cook Co. is the second most populous US county, after Los Angeles Co., California.

Cookeville city, pop. 21,744, seat of Putnam Co., NC Tennessee, at the E edge of the NASHVILLE BASIN, midway between Nashville (W) and Knoxville (E). Founded in 1854, it grew as an agricultural trade center, relying also on local coal, marble, and granite. Manufactures include clothing, furniture, auto parts, sporting goods, cheese, and pottery. Tennessee Technological University (1915) is here.

Cook Inlet W reach of the Gulf of Alaska, between the KENAI PENINSULA (E) and the mainland of SC Alaska. Some 180 mi/290 km NE–SW and 10–70 mi/15–110 km wide, it extends from Knik Arm and Turnagain Arm at ANCHORAGE (N) to SHELIKOF STRAIT (S). Narrow and curved, it is the site of strong tidal BORES. The English navigator James Cook explored the inlet in 1778, during his unsuccessful search for the NORTHWEST PASSAGE; it was long thought to offer a river route to the Arctic.

Coolidge city, pop. 6927, Pinal Co., SC Arizona, 45 mi/72 km SE of Phoenix. In a diverse farming area served by the Coolidge Dam on the GILA R. (60 mi/100 km ENE), it is a tourist base 1 mi/2 km SE of the CASA GRANDE Ruins National Monument, and home to Central Arizona College (1962).

Coolidge, Mount peak (6400 ft/1952 m) in the Black Hills, Custer Co., SW South Dakota, in CUSTER STATE PARK, 3 mi/5 km SE of the city of Custer. Formerly Sheep Mt., it was renamed in the summer of 1927 in honor of President Calvin Coolidge, who had visited in order to dedicate Mt RUSHMORE.

Coon Rapids city, pop. 52,978, Anoka Co., SE Minnesota, on the Mississippi R., 14 mi/22 km N of Minneapolis. It has experienced much commercial and residential growth over the past few decades, partly because of its location on the Twin Cities–St. Cloud corridor.

Co-op City government-planned housing complex, in the BAYCHESTER section of the extreme NE Bronx, New York. Standing along the Hutchinson R. at the Westchester Co. border, it comprises 35 high-rise towers and over 200 other buildings, with 15,400 units housing about 65,000 residents. Opened in 1970, it at first was home chiefly to Jewish former residents of older Bronx neighborhoods; its population in the 1990s is about 50% white, 30% black, and 20% Hispanic.

Cooper City city, pop. 20,791, Broward Co., SE Florida, 7 mi/11 km NW of Hollywood, a residential (largely retirement) community.

Cooper River one of two rivers (the other is the ASHLEY) that join at Charleston Harbor, South Carolina. The Cooper flows S from L. Moultrie, which is connected by channel with the SANTEE River's L. Marion. Before dams created these (the Santee-Cooper) lakes in the 1930s, the Cooper was connected to the Santee by a 22-mi/35-km canal finished in 1800. The old canal's usefulness for trade had soon been eclipsed by railroads. Much of it now lies under the lake, created by the 78 ft/24 m–high, 2 mi/3 km–long Pinopolis Dam, which provides power and creates a major recreational asset.

Cooper Station nuclear power plant, operational since 1974, at Brownville (village, pop. 148), Nemaha Co., SE Nebraska, on the Missouri R., 60 mi/100 km SSE of Omaha.

Cooperstown village, pop. 2180, seat of Otsego Co., in Otsego township, C New York, at the S tip of Otsego L. and on the headwaters of the Susquehanna R., 33 mi/53 km SE of Utica. It was founded (1786) by Judge William Cooper, whose son, James Fenimore Cooper (1789–1851), set his *Leatherstocking Tales* in the region. The author is buried here. Cooperstown is home to the National Baseball Hall of Fame and Museum. Just outside Cooperstown are the Farmers' Museum, Glimmerglass Opera House, and Fenimore House. Tourism is vital to the village's economy.

Coosa River 286 mi/460 km long, in NW Georgia and EC Alabama. It is formed by the confluence of the Etowah and Oostanaula rivers at Rome, Georgia, and flows W into Alabama. The Weiss Dam, near Leesburg, forms Weiss L., which backs up into Georgia. The Coosa winds SW from the lake through GADSDEN, and SSW through a series of dam-created lakes until it joins the TALLAPOOSA R. NE of Montgomery, forming the ALABAMA R. A system of locks built with the dams makes navigation possible all the way up to Rome.

Coos Bay city, pop. 15,076, Coos Co., SW Oregon, on Coos Bay, an inlet of the Pacific Ocean, 167 mi/268 km SSW of Portland. A major lumber-shipping port known particularly for its myrtlewood, which is unique to this area, it is the largest city on the Oregon coast. Settled in 1854, it was called Marshfield until 1944. It developed from a shipbuilding center to a lumber hub to an exporting city. High local unemployment resulted from lumber plant closings in the 1980s and early 1990s. Seafood, dairy products, and poultry are processed, and tourism is a growing industry. Southwestern Oregon Community College (1961) is here. Golden and Silver Falls State Park is 24 mi/39 km NE, the Oregon Dunes National Recreation Area is just N, and a number of state parks dot the nearby shore. The Oregon Coast Music Festival is an annual event.

Coos County 1804 sq mi/4672 sq km, pop. 34,828, in extreme N New Hampshire. Lancaster is the county seat. A recreation area bordering Vermont, Québec, and Maine, New Hampshire's largest county includes part of White Mt. National Forest and the Presidential Range. It is drained by the Androscoggin, Connecticut, and Upper Ammonoosuc rivers. The Androscoggin provides water power. The CONNECTICUT LAKES region has resorts, attracting hunters and anglers. Berlin manufactures pulp, paper, and wood products. The county also produces dairy products, poultry, and potatoes.

Copiague unincorporated village, pop. 20,769, in Babylon town, Suffolk Co., SE New York, near the S shore of Long Island and immediately NE of Amityville. It is primarily residential.

Copley Square public square in the BACK BAY section of Boston, Massachusetts. On Copley Square are the John Hancock Building (Boston's tallest skyscraper at 790 ft/241 m), the Italian Renaissance–style Boston Public Library, and H. H. Richardson's Trinity Church (1877). The square is a focal point for the cultural and street life of the Back Bay.

Coppell city, pop. 16,881, Dallas and Denton counties, NE Texas, on Grapevine and Denton creeks and the Elm Fork of the Trinity R., 16 mi/26 km NW of downtown Dallas. On the NE edge of Dallas–Fort Worth International Airport, it is a growing residential suburb.

Copperas Cove city, pop. 24,079, Coryell Co., C Texas, 53 mi/85 km SW of Waco. Adjacent (SW) to FORT HOOD, in a farming area, it is now largely a service town for the base. A 19th-century stop on the way to the CHISHOLM TRAIL, it took its name from its springs, whose water was said to have a coppery taste.

Copper City, the see under ROME, New York.

Copper Cliff see under SUDBURY, Ontario.

Coppermine hamlet, pop. 1116, Kitikmeot Region, WC Northwest Territories, on lowlands at the mouth of the Coppermine R., on Coronation Gulf of the Arctic Ocean, 85 mi/140 km N of the Arctic Circle and 350 mi/560 km N of Yellowknife. It is a fishing community; tourism is important. The Copper INUIT, so called for their metal ornaments, were encountered in the area by Samuel Hearne's expedition in 1771; they and forerunners have lived here seasonally or permanently for some 3000 years. The 525-mi/845-km **Coppermine R.** empties here after winding generally NNW across the CANADIAN SHIELD from N of Great Slave L. At Bloody Falls, 10 mi/16 km from the sea, where the river drops to the coastal plain, Hearne's Chipewyan (DENE) guides massacred an Inuit party in 1771.

Copper Mountain resort in Eagle Co., NC Colorado, in the Rocky Mts., 20 mi/32 km N of Leadville. Situated at 9680 ft/2952 m above sea level, it was once a railroad junction, shipping lumber and agricultural products. In 1972, it became a year-round resort. It is especially known for its skiing facilities.

Copps Hill historic cemetery in the NORTH END of Boston, Massachusetts. Up a hill from the Old North Church, it was used as early as 1660; among Colonists buried here is Cotton Mather. During the Revolution, the British used the hill as a cannon emplacement to defend the harbor.

Coquitlam see under PORT COQUITLAM, British Columbia.

Coral Gables city, pop. 40,091, Dade Co., SE Florida, on BISCAYNE BAY, 5 mi/8 km SW of Miami. A classic planned city, it was built around his family's farm by George E. Merrick in 1925, during the Florida land boom. Part of greater Miami, it is a bedroom community and has many new office buildings housing headquarters of large Latin American corporations. It is also a resort and the site of some industry, making fiberglass boats, cosmetics, electronic equipment, furniture, and millwork. Coral Gables is the seat of the University of Miami, founded in the same year as the city, and the site of Fairchild Tropical Garden, the Tropical Park racetrack, and the US Hurricane Research Center.

Coral Springs city, pop. 79,443, Broward Co., SE Florida, 13 mi/21 km NW of Fort Lauderdale, a residential and retirement community.

Coralville city, pop. 10,347, Johnson Co., EC Iowa, on the Iowa R., a residential suburb immediately W of Iowa City. Coralville Reservoir is just N, along the river. The city was named for ancient coral formations found under it (1866).

Coram unincorporated village, pop. 30,111, in Brookhaven town, Suffolk Co., SE New York, in C Long Island, 7 mi/11 km SSE of Port Jefferson. It is primarily residential.

Coraopolis borough, pop. 6747, Allegheny Co., SW Pennsylvania, an industrial suburb on the Ohio R., 11 mi/18 km NW of Pittsburgh. Economic activities here include oil refining and iron and steel production. It is the seat of Robert Morris College (1921).

Corbin city, pop. 7419, Whitley and Knox counties, SE Kentucky, near the Laurel R., 78 mi/126 km SSE of Lexington, on the WILDERNESS ROAD. An agricultural trading and sawmilling center, it also manufactures auto parts, brick, soft drinks, and processed foods, and gave Colonel Harland Sanders, the Kentucky Fried Chicken mogul, his start. It is a rail junction with repair shops, and a shipping point for the region's bituminous coal. DANIEL BOONE NATIONAL FOREST is just W.

Corcoran city, pop. 13,364, Kings Co., SC California, 44 mi/70 km SSE of Fresno in the San Joaquin Valley, on the NE edge of dry TULARE L. Incorporated in 1914, it is an agricultural (long a cotton) center.

Cordele city, pop. 10,321, seat of Crisp Co., SC Georgia, 32 mi/51 km NE of Albany. Founded in 1888 at the junction of two railroad lines, it has cotton mills and sawmills. The region is noted for its peanut and watermelon production.

cordillera (Spanish, "little cord, string") a mountain system, esp. the chief system of a country or land mass. The North American Cordillera (in the W, and continuing the line of South America's Andes) includes the Coast Ranges, Sierra Nevada, Rocky Mts., Cascade Range, and ranges of the Basin and Range Province. The term **Cordilleran Region** is sometimes used to designate the area in which all these are found.

Cordillera Central mountain range, some 80 mi/130 km E–W, that forms the backbone of Puerto Rico, running almost the entire length of the island. It rises to 4390 ft/1338 m at the CERRO DE PUNTA, N of Ponce. The Sierra de Luquillo (NE) and Sierra de Cayey (SE) branch from it. The source of Puerto Rico's many small, fast rivers, which provide hydroelectric power, the Cordillera is subtropical and relatively cool at higher elevations; it has many summer resorts, and coffee, tobacco, and fruit are widely grown. Rain, brought by NE TRADE WINDS, falls much more heavily on the N side; S of the Cordillera is drier terrain.

Cordova city, pop. 2110, in the Valdez-Cordova Census Area (pop. 9952), SE Alaska, on PRINCE WILLIAM SOUND, surrounded by the CHUGACH NATIONAL FOREST, 150 mi/240 km ESE of Anchorage. Its harbor was explored and named by Spanish navigators in 1792, but development came after 1910, with the discovery and mining of copper to the N and NE, esp. in the Kennecott region. Cordova was the terminus of the 195 mi/314 km–long Copper R. and Northwestern Railway, until the mines and the railroad closed in 1938. It is now a fishing center, accessible only by ferry or plane. The Copper R. delta, a major spring birding site, is NE.

Corea village in Gouldsboro town, Hancock Co., SE Maine. Corea is at the outlet of Gouldsboro Bay into the Gulf of Maine, 12 mi/19 km E of Bar Harbor. It is an artists' retreat; Lewiston-born painter Marsden Hartley lived and worked here during the 1940s.

Corinth city, pop. 11,820, seat of Alcorn Co., extreme NE Mississippi, 15 mi/24 km SW of SHILOH, Tennessee. Its strategic railroad-junction site made it important both for Confederate forces, who fell back after Shiloh, in April 1862, and for Union forces who occupied it soon after. The Battle of Corinth occurred that October, when Confederates attempted, but failed, to retake the town, in the bloodiest battle fought in Mississippi. Six thousand soldiers, most unidentified, are buried in Corinth National Cemetery. Today, Corinth is an agricultural trade center with textile and other light industries.

Corktown historic neighborhood on Detroit, Michigan's lower W side, on the SW edge of Downtown, noted in the late 19th century as home to large numbers of Irish immigrants. In the 20th century it has been home to various groups, recently including Mexicans.

Corn Belt region of the US Middle West in which corn (maize) is the predominant crop and corn-fed stock (esp. hogs) a major product. Illinois, Indiana, and Iowa are the heart of this area, which extends E to Ohio, NW into Minnesota and South Dakota, and W across Missouri into NE Kansas. The Corn Belt is distinguished from the WHEAT BELT, to the W, chiefly by its more humid weather and lower elevations.

Corner Brook city, pop. 22,410, W Newfoundland, at the head of the HUMBER R. estuary, near its mouth on the Bay of Islands. In a lumbering region near the Long Range Mts., the city is a newsprint producing center, with huge pulp and paper mills operating since the 1920s. Other industries include commercial fishing, and production of cement, gypsum, iron, and furniture. Hydroelectric power is supplied by a plant at DEER LAKE (NE). Sir Wilfred Grenfell College (1975), a branch of Memorial University, is here.

Cornfield, the see under ANTIETAM, Maryland.

Corning **1.** city, pop. 1806, seat of Adams Co., SW Iowa, on the East Nodaway R., 60 mi/97 km SE of Council Bluffs. An offshoot of the French Icarian utopians set up an agricultural commune here during the latter half of the 19th century. Some left Iowa in 1883, and later settled in Cloverdale, California. The group disbanded by the end of the century; their one-room schoolhouse and other structures are preserved. **2.** city, pop. 11,938, Steuben Co., SC New York, on the Chemung R., 10 mi/16 km N of the Pennsylvania border and 15 mi/24 km NW of Elmira. Corning Glass Works, the city's largest industry, was established in 1868 as Brooklyn Flint Glass Works. A leading manufacturer of technical glass, it now produces Steuben and flat glass, tubing, bulbs, homewares, fiber optics, and aerospace equipment. The Corning Glass Center (1951) houses a collection of historic glass. Other industries manufacture foundry products and air compressors. Over 2000 buildings were destroyed in the city by floodwaters in June 1972. The town of Corning (pop. 6367) surrounds the city.

Cornish town, pop. 1659, Sullivan Co., SW New Hampshire. Cornish is along the Connecticut R., N of and adjacent to Claremont. Sculptor Augustus Saint-Gaudens lived and worked here for over 20 years (1885–1907). His home, studios, and gardens are a National Historic Site. US Chief Justice Salmon P. Chase was born here (1808), and Cornish after the 1970s gained a specialized notoriety as the home of reclusive author J. D. Salinger.

Corn Palace see under MITCHELL, South Dakota.

Cornwall **1.** city, pop. 47,137, seat of Stormont, Dundas, and Glengarry United Counties, extreme E Ontario, on the N bank of the St. Lawrence R., at the E terminus of the Cornwall Canal. MASSENA, New York, is 5 mi/8 km SW. Cornwall was founded in 1784 as Johnstown by LOYALISTS. With the completion of the canal in 1843 and the arrival of the GRAND TRUNK RAILWAY in the 1850s, it developed as a major shipping center, and is now an important port and the industrial and commercial center of a rich farming and dairying area. It produces textiles, paper, pulp, flour, chemicals, furniture, bedding, and foundry items. The city is also the headquarters of the Canadian St. Lawrence Seaway Authority, and the site of a major international hydroelectric complex. The Seaway International Bridge connects it to Rooseveltown, New York, crossing Cornwall I., part of the city. **2.** town, pop. 1101, Addison Co., WC Vermont. It is W of Otter Creek, SW of and adjoining Middlebury. In an agricultural area, the town was formerly a breeding center for Merino sheep and Morgan horses.

Cornwall-on-Hudson village, pop. 3093, in Cornwall town, Orange Co., SE New York, on the W bank of the Hudson R., at the foot of STORM KING Mt. Writer Djuna Barnes (1892–1982) and billiards wizard Willie Hoppe (1887–1959) were born here. It is the site of the Museum of the Hudson Highlands.

Corona **1.** city, pop. 76,095, Riverside Co., SW California, 42 mi/66 km ESE of Los Angeles and 9 mi/14 km SW of Riverside, on the NE of the Santa Ana Mts. Founded in the late 19th century, it thrived on deposits of clay, sand, and gravel; quarrying is still carried out, and glass and ceramics are manufactured. Orchard equipment, citrus juices, and wood items are produced, and Corona is a packing and shipping center for regional citrus fruits. The Cleveland National Forest lies SW. Noted for its circular Grand Blvd., the city doubled in pop. as a residential suburb in the 1980s. **2.** largely residential section of N Queens, New York. It is bounded E by FLUSHING MEADOWS-CORONA PARK, W by Jackson Heights. Subdivided in the 1870s, it eventually became a lower-middle-class community of two-story homes, with some light industry. Louis C. Tiffany established a glassmaking factory here in 1885. The last home (1943–71) of Louis Armstrong is in the N section.

Corona del Mar see under NEWPORT BEACH, California.

Coronado city, pop. 26,540, San Diego Co., SW California, 2 mi/3 km SW of downtown San Diego. On a peninsula between San Diego Bay (E) and the Pacific Ocean, it is connected to San Diego by the San Diego–Coronado Bridge. The NORTH ISLAND US Naval Air Station and US Naval Amphibious Base are major employers. The city's climate and its waterfront (the Silver Strand beach) make it popular with tourists. Hotel Del Coronado (1888) is a noted landmark.

Coronado Heights see under LINDSBORG, Kansas.

Coronado National Memorial 4750 ac/1924 ha, in Cochise Co., extreme S Arizona, on the border with Sonora, Mexico. In the San Pedro R. valley, the memorial marks the site where Francisco de Coronado entered what is now the US in 1540, seeking CIBOLA. The expedition failed to find riches either there or at QUIVIRA, but was the first European venture to see many Southwestern sites, including the Grand Canyon and New Mexico's PUEBLOS. The memorial is on the S of one of a dozen scattered units of the **Coronado National Forest,** which covers 1.8 million ac/730,000 ha in Arizona and adjacent New Mexico.

Corpus Christi city, pop. 257,453, seat of Nueces Co., S Texas, on Nueces and Corpus Christi bays, 123 mi/198 km SE of San Antonio. Sheltered from the Gulf of Mexico by PADRE and MUSTANG islands, the site was seen by the Spanish explorer Alonso Alvarez de Pineda on the feast day of Corpus Christi in 1519. The natural harbor was used for many years by smugglers and pirates. The modern city, begun (1838) as a trading post and soon a cotton center, experienced Mexican War (1845–46) mobilizations and Civil War (1862) blockade skirmishes. A land boom resulted from the railroad's arrival in 1881, and growth was further spurred by the discovery of natural gas (1923) and the construction of a deepwater port (1926). A commercial and shipping center, the city handles cotton, grains, beef, oil, ore, and other bulk cargoes. It also manufactures petrochemicals, glass, and aluminum, processes seafood, and refines oil. The Corpus Christi Naval Air Station (1941) and other military facilities are important, as are Gulf Coast boating and tourism. The city is the seat of Del Mar College (1935) and Corpus Christi State University (1971).

Corpus Christi, Lake see under NUECES R., Texas.

Corsica see under BLOOMING GROVE, Ohio.

Corsicana city, pop. 22,911, seat of Navarro Co., EC Texas, 50 mi/80 km SE of Dallas. The surrounding BLACKLANDS area produces wheat, grain, sorghums, cotton, and peanuts, and Corsicana, established in 1849, has processing plants. Oil, discovered accidentally in 1894, caused a boom, and a refinery was built in 1897; natural gas was also exploited early. The city manufactures oilfield equipment and various other products, including fruitcake. Navarro College (1946) is here.

Corte Madera town, pop. 8272, Marin Co., NW California, immediately NE of Mill Valley and 12 mi/19 km N of downtown San Francisco, of which it is an affluent suburb.

Cortez city, pop. 7284, seat of Montezuma Co., in the SW corner of Colorado, 40 mi/64 km W of Durango. In the 1950s, oil and tourism replaced farming and livestock ranching as the city's economic bases. Cortez nonetheless remains a trade center in a livestock, fruit, grain, dairying, and timber region. Other industries include metal, food, and animal feed processing and the manufacture of plywood, leather goods, furniture, and industrial gases. Gateway to MESA VERDE National Park 9 mi/14 km SE, it is also 35 mi/56 km NE of the FOUR CORNERS.

Cortland city, pop. 19,801, seat of Cortland Co., C New York, on the Tioughnioga R., 30 mi/48 km S of Syracuse. It is at the center of a rich agricultural area specializing in dairy cattle; regional farms also produce cabbage, potatoes, and grains. The city's industries manufacture clothing, doors, boats, and specialized textiles. The Smith Corona Corporation, a major employer, moved its typewriter manufacturing facilities to Mexico in the early 1990s. Cortland is home to the State University College at Cortland.

Cortlandt town, pop. 37,357, in extreme N Westchester Co., SE New York, on the E bank of the Hudson R., 35 mi/56 km N of New York City. Largely residential, it contains the village of CROTON-ON-HUDSON. The city of PEEKSKILL is within its borders.

Corvallis city, pop. 44,757, seat of Benton Co., W Oregon, on the Willamette R., 28 mi/45 km SSW of Salem. At the head of navigation for the river, it was the capital of the Oregon Territory in 1846–57. Today it is a lumber and agricultural processing center. Corvallis also is the seat of Oregon State University (1868), the state's oldest public institution of higher learning. This educational base has given rise to many engineering, consulting, and business machine firms. The William L. Finley National Wildlife Refuge, 20 mi/32 km to the S, and the Siuslaw National Forest, which has its headquarters here, are important tourist destinations.

Corydon town, pop. 2661, seat of Harrison Co., extreme S Indiana, 20 mi/32 km W of Louisville, Kentucky, and 15 mi/24 km N of the Ohio R. Laid out in 1808 on branches of Indian Creek, on land belonging to William Henry Harrison, it became territorial (1811) and state (1816–25) capital, and was the early home of many of Indiana's wealthy. Now largely a tourist center, it is a state historic site. In July 1863, John Hunt Morgan's Confederate raiders occupied the town after a skirmish with defenders just S, in what is considered the only Civil War action on Indiana soil.

Cosanti Foundation see under SCOTTSDALE, Arizona.

Cos Cob village in the town of GREENWICH, Fairfield Co., extreme SW Connecticut. The local Siwanoy tribe was annihilated by New York settlers in 1644. Cos Cob is an affluent suburb and resort with a well-known yachting harbor on the Mianus R. The meaning of the Algonquian name is disputed, but may be "high rock."

Coshocton city, pop. 12,193, seat of Coshocton Co., EC Ohio, 37 mi/60 km NE of Newark, at the confluence of the Walhonding and Tuscarawas rivers where they form the Muskingum R. In 1764 an expedition was led here to rescue 363 white captives from Indians. The Indian village that stood on the site was destroyed in 1781, and in 1802 Coshocton was founded. Currently, it is a center for the manufacture of cast iron pipe, stainless steel, laminated plastics, corrugated paper, and milk products. Specialty advertising is also important. A soil and water experimental station and a restored 19th-century Ohio-Erie Canal town are nearby.

Costa Mesa city, pop. 96,357, Orange Co., SW California, N of Newport Beach and the Pacific Ocean, and adjacent (S) to Santa Ana. A 19th-century truck farming area that became a residential and cultural center, it is home to Southern California College (1920), Orange Coast College (1947), and the Orange Co. Fairgrounds. Local industries include electronics, printing, and boatbuilding. Costa Mesa is noted for its cultural facilities, which include the Orange Co. Performing Arts Center and the Pacific Amphitheatre. The South Coast Plaza is a well-known, expensive mall.

coteau name given by French explorers, esp. in the N Great Plains, to an escarpment or ridge standing above lower land. In places, *coteau* has come to mean also the plateau above the escarpment. Examples are the **Coteau des Prairies,** in W Minnesota and NE South Dakota, a fertile farming and livestock raising region continuing the glacial Drift Plain or Drift Prairie of Manitoba and North Dakota; and the **Coteau du Missouri** or **Missouri Coteau,** a plateau above (E of) the Missouri R. in the Dakotas.

Côte-Nord see NORTH SHORE, Québec.

Côte-Saint-Luc city, pop. 28,700, MONTRÉAL URBAN COMMUNITY, S Québec, 7 mi/11 km SW of downtown Montréal, SW of Hampstead and NE of Lachine. It is a predominantly anglophone, largely residential suburb.

Cottage Grove city, pop. 22,935, Washington Co., SE Minnesota, on the Mississippi R., 10 mi/16 km SE of St. Paul. A growing residential suburb, it experienced a boom in construction and commercial development in the 1980s. Many light industries have sprung up in the NW part of town, along Highway 61, some manufacturing reflector products, precision parts for aircraft, and metal products.

Cotton Belt region of the S US where cotton was in the 19th century a major, or the predominant, crop. Its heart was

Georgia, Alabama, and Mississippi (esp. the BLACK BELT), with extensions to Arkansas and Texas. The PLANTATION system and slavery combined here with rich soil and a favorable climate to produce the economic basis of the Old South; after the Civil War, the sharecropping system replaced slavery with a somewhat similar labor structure, and cotton remained central to the economy until the 20th century, when the boll weevil, the attraction of other profitable crops, competition from Arizona and California, and social change in the South reduced its importance. In its heyday the Cotton Belt was also called the **Cotton Kingdom,** a term that embraces entrepots and ports like Memphis and New Orleans as well as the growing areas.

Cotton Bowl see under FAIR PARK, Dallas, Texas.

Cotton Plant city, pop. 1150, Woodruff Co., NE Arkansas, 26 mi/42 km W of Forrest City, in the Mississippi Alluvial Plain E of the White R. Laid out in 1840, it was the site of a Civil War battle on July 7, 1862. Cotton, corn, hay, and lumber are important to its economy.

Cotton Row see under FRONT St., Memphis, Tennessee.

Cottonwood and **Cottonwood Heights** and **Cottonwood West** see under HOLLADAY-COTTONWOOD, Utah.

coulee in the NW US and W Canada, a steep-sided valley, usually dry, formed by running water, esp. by the onrush in late glacial periods of masses of water released by the melting and collapse of ice "plugs" that had been impounding glacial lakes.

Council Bluffs city, pop. 54,315, seat of Pottawattamie Co., SW Iowa, on the E bank of the Missouri R., opposite Omaha, Nebraska. A trade and industrial center for a large agricultural region, it has grain elevators, railroad shops, and food processing plants. Manufactures include farm equipment, cast iron pipes, truck bodies, structural steel, electronic equipment, and furniture. Lewis and Clark met with Otoes and Missouris on bluffs overlooking the river in 1804. In 1846 Mormons arrived, settling until 1852, when they left for Utah. The city served as an outfitting post for California-bound gold-rushers. President Lincoln chose Council Bluffs as the E terminus of the Union Pacific Railroad, the first transcontinental line. The city is the seat of Iowa Western Community College (1966). Historic sites include White Catfish Camp, a site along the Lewis and Clark National Historic Trail.

Council Grove city, pop. 2228, seat of Morris Co., EC Kansas, on the Neosho R. at the edge of the FLINT HILLS, 23 mi/37 km NW of Emporia. It was the site of the 1825 meeting between US commissioners and Osage chiefs that obtained the right of way for the SANTA FE TRAIL; the "Council Oak" marks the spot. A trading post (1847), the settlement grew as an important supply point on the Trail. A distribution center for grain, cattle, and poultry, it also processes food and engages in light manufacturing. The Kaw (Kansa) Methodist Mission (1849) State Historic Site is here.

Country Club Hills city, pop. 15,431, Cook Co., NE Illinois, a residential suburb 22 mi/35 km S of Chicago.

Country Club Plaza pioneer suburban shopping center, created in 1922–23 by J. C. Nichols, 4 mi/6 km S of downtown KANSAS CITY, Missouri. Fifteen blocks of buildings in Spanish (Moorish) style, S of the heart of old WESTPORT and on the N edge of the Country Club District, it came to be surrounded by an institutional cluster including Kansas City's Art Institute and Music Conservatory, Rockhurst College and the University of Missouri at Kansas City, and the Midwest Research Institute. The affluent **Country Club District,** laid out in the 1900s, was then in the SW part of the city, which has since expanded. Farther S today are the largely residential areas of Waldo, Red Bridge, New Santa Fe, and Martin City. To the SSE are Dodson, Ruskin Heights, Vale, and Knobtown.

Country Homes unincorporated community, pop. 5126, Spokane Co., EC Washington, a suburb 6 mi/10 km NNW of downtown Spokane. Whitworth College (1890) is here.

county 1. in the US: the largest administrative subdivision of a STATE, with the exception of Louisiana, which has PARISHES, and Alaska, which has BOROUGHS. The American county is a descendant of the English *shire,* and retains some of the shire's officers (e.g., the sheriff and justice of the peace). Except for INDEPENDENT CITIES, US municipalities are established within (or coextensive with) counties. In a few states (Connecticut, Rhode Island), the county has lost almost all governmental role. In the others, it typically has responsibility for local law enforcement and court operation, the keeping of property records, maintenance of roads and other public amenities, and various health and welfare functions. See also MUNICIPIO, in Puerto Rico. **2.** in Canada: administrative subdivision of a PROVINCE. Canadian counties were established for varying purposes, and most have lost some of their roles to other administrative forms, including district municipalities and rural municipalities. Prince Edward Island, Nova Scotia, New Brunswick, and Ontario retain counties of this sort. Quebec's counties have become **regional county municipalities.** Alberta's counties have the status of municipalities.

Coupeville see under OAK HARBOR, Washington.

coureurs de bois unlicensed, roving fur traders ("woods runners") of NEW FRANCE, who operated esp. in the L. Superior area from the late 17th century. They took to the wilderness in an attempt to sidestep existing trade arrangements between merchants in Montréal and Québec City and Indian providers. Their efforts succeeding, many were in turn licensed, as wage-earning *voyageurs.* The latter term expanded to include other "regular" participants in the fur trade. Coureurs de bois and voyageurs, traveling by canoe through forests and across plains, played an important role in exploration of C Canada, and in relations with its native inhabitants; intermarriage produced many of the MÉTIS.

Courtenay city, pop. 11,652, Comox-Strathcona Regional District, in EC Vancouver I., SW British Columbia, 90 mi/140 km NW of Vancouver and just W of COMOX. The Comox lived in the area before white traders appeared in the 1850s. Courtenay is now a commercial center in an agricultural area; it has many retirees and is noted for its winter sports and summer music festivals.

Courtland see under JERUSALEM, Virginia.

Cove Neck village: see under OYSTER BAY, New York.

Coventry 1. town, pop. 10,063, Tolland Co., EC Connecticut, on the Willimantic R., 16 mi/26 km E of Hartford. Long a rural manufacturing center, producing such goods as yarn and fishline, it has some agriculture. The birthplace (1755) of Nathan Hale and Caprilands Herb Farm draw visitors. **2.** town, pop. 31,083, Kent Co., WC Rhode Island, 12 mi/19 km SW of Providence, on the Flat R. It encompasses the villages of Anthony, Arkwright, Green, and Summitt, as well as its administrative center, Washington, and extends W to the Connecticut border. It is well known for lacemaking;

textiles, chemicals, and glass are also produced. There is some farming.

Covina city, pop. 43,207, Los Angeles Co., SW California, 20 mi/32 km E of Los Angeles, in the San Gabriel Valley. A growing and shipping center for citrus fruits from the 1880s until the 1950s, it is now a commuter suburb, with some light industry. WEST COVINA is much larger.

Covington **1.** city, pop. 10,026, seat of Newton Co., NC Georgia, 32 mi/51 km ESE of Atlanta. Founded in 1822, it manufactures concrete pipe, lumber, textiles, and tools. **2.** city, pop. 43,264, Kenton Co., NC Kentucky, on the Ohio R., opposite Cincinnati, Ohio. The LICKING R. separates it (E) from NEWPORT. It was a late-18th-century ferry crossing that became a trading center with the opening of the Covington–Georgetown Turnpike (1819) and an 1830s rise in river and road traffic. Like Cincinnati, it has been home to many German immigrants. A market for tobacco, corn, and livestock, it manufactures machine tools, freight cars, stained glass, processed fruits, and other products. Covington has declined in population since mid-century. Greater Cincinnati International Airport is W of the city, in BOONE Co. **3.** city, pop. 7691, seat of St. Tammany Parish, SE Louisiana, 37 mi/61 km N of New Orleans, on the Bogue Falia, 7 mi/11 km N of L. Pontchartrain. Settled in 1769, it has been since the late 19th century a popular country retreat for New Orleanians. Farming, lumbering, fishing, and horse breeding are important in the area. **4.** independent city, pop. 6991, seat of but administratively separate from Alleghany Co., WC Virginia, on the Jackson R., 9 mi/14 km WSW of Clifton Forge, and 12 mi/19 km E of the West Virginia border. Laid out in 1819, it is surrounded by peaks of the Allegheny Mts., and developed after the 1890s as a producer of wood products, textiles, and local limestone, coal, and iron.

Cowans Ford see under CATAWBA R., North Carolina.

Cowansville city, pop. 11,982, Missisquoi Co., in the EASTERN TOWNSHIPS, S Québec, 45 mi/72 km ESE of Montréal and 13 mi/21 km N of the Vermont border, on the S fork of the R. Yamaska. The influence of its LOYALIST founders can be seen in its Victorian architecture. It is today predominantly francophone. Long agricultural, it now has diversified manufactures, a Federal penitentiary, an annual puppet festival, and access to skiing and lake resorts.

Cow Hollow commercial district in N SAN FRANCISCO, California, along Union St. between Russian Hill and Pacific Heights (S) and the Marina District, which lies just below it (N). Used in the 1860s by dairy farmers, it soon became an industrial backwater, but has been redeveloped since the 1950s and is now a fashionable shopping and club zone.

Cowichan Lake 20 mi/32 km long and 1–2 mi/2–3 km wide, in SC Vancouver I., SW British Columbia. It is drained by the 28 mi/45 km–long **Cowichan R.,** which flows E to the Strait of Georgia near the city of Duncan. The Cowichan Valley, once heavily logged, is now a popular recreational and residential area. North Cowichan (district municipality, pop. 21,373), N of the river, is the largest municipality in this growing area N of Victoria.

Cowlitz River 130 mi/210 km long, in SW Washington. It rises in the Cascade Range just SSE of Mt. RAINIER, and flows W and S to the Columbia R. just below Kelso and Longview.

Cow Palace see under DALY CITY, California.

Cowpens town, pop. 2176, Spartanburg Co., NW South Carolina, in the Piedmont, 10 mi/16 km NE of Spartanburg. It is a trade center. About 8 mi/13 km NNW of the center is 845-ac/342-ha **Cowpens National Battlefield,** scene of a decisive victory by American militiamen under Daniel Morgan over battle-hardened British troops commanded by Banastre Tarleton (Jan. 17, 1781).

Coxsackie town, pop. 7633, Greene Co., SE New York, on the E bank of the Hudson R., 20 mi/32 km S of Albany. Settled in the 17th century, it had an almost completely Dutch population from its founding into the early 19th century. The town declared its own "declaration of independence" from British rule in 1775. Its traditional industries were brickmaking and ice cutting. Situated in a farming region, it now has a variety of light industries, and is largely residential.

Crab Orchard Lake see under CARBONDALE, Illinois.

Cradle Rock see under BALANCED ROCK.

Cragin see BELMONT-CRAGIN, Chicago, Illinois.

Craig see under PRINCE OF WALES I., Alaska.

Craigellachie locality in SE British Columbia, on the Eagle R., 22 mi/35 km W of REVELSTOKE. Here, on Nov. 7, 1885, the symbolic last spike was driven, completing the CANADIAN PACIFIC RAILWAY's transcontinental line to PORT MOODY. Just E, the line comes through Eagle Pass (1800 ft/550 m), a route through the MONASHEE Mts. also traversed today by the TRANS-CANADA HIGHWAY.

Cranberry Isles island group and town, including Little Cranberry, Great Cranberry, Sutton, Baker, and Bear islands, pop. 196, Hancock Co., SE Maine. The Cranberry Isles are in the Gulf of Maine just SE of Mount Desert I. They are nesting grounds for waterfowl and have long been a summer retreat for artists and writers. Little Cranberry includes the village of Islesford. Baker I. is part of Acadia National Park.

Cranbrook **1.** city, pop. 16,447, East Kootenay Regional District, extreme SE British Columbia, in the Kootenay R. Valley, on the W of the Rocky Mt. Trench, 335 mi/539 km E of Vancouver. In an area home to the Kootenay, it developed with lumbering and the arrival (1898) of the railroad. A rail and highway junction, it is today a trade, distribution, and service center for a ranching, lead and zinc mining, lumbering, and agricultural region. Tourism is also important. **2.** see under BLOOMFIELD HILLS, Michigan.

Crane's Beach see under IPSWICH, Massachusetts.

Cranford township, pop. 22,624, Union Co., NE New Jersey, on the Rahway R., 5 mi/8 km W of Elizabeth. In a densely populated region, it is a primarily residential suburb. Cranford has many business offices and industries producing such goods as metal products, plastics, and razor blades. It is the seat of Union County College (1933).

Cranston city, pop. 76,060, Providence Co., C Rhode Island. A suburb S of Providence, it is on Interstates 95 and 295 and the Seekonk R. A center for textile production and printing in the early 19th century, Cranston grew rapidly after 1940; it continues to manufacture textiles, and produces rubber and metal products, wire, machinery, and beer. A mental hospital and several correctional institutions are here, as well as Meshanticut State Park and other recreational areas. The city has a sizable Italian population.

Crater, the see under PETERSBURG, Virginia.

Crater Lake National Park 183,224 ac/74,206 ha (286 sq mi/741 sq km), in SW Oregon. Established in 1902, it preserves the deepest lake in the US, which reaches down 1932 ft/589 m in the CALDERA of Mt. Mazama, a CASCADE RANGE volcano that exploded c.4860 B.C., spewing ash over much of the NW from Nevada to British Columbia, and subsequently collapsed. Crater L. is known for its intense blue color. The cinder cone called Wizard I. rises 700 ft/213 m above the lake's surface. Mt. Scott (8926 ft/2721 m) is the highest point in the park.

Craters of the Moon National Monument 53,545 ac/21,686 ha, in SE Idaho, 62 mi/100 km NW of Pocatello, on the N of the SNAKE R. plain. Proclaimed in 1924, it protects an expanse of lava flow–created "lunar" landscape, including many caves and cinder cones, along the 40 mi/64 km–long Great Rift. In 1970 some 80% of the Monument was designated a WILDERNESS AREA.

Crawford city, pop. 1115, Dawes Co., NW Nebraska, on the White R., 24 mi/38 km SW of Chadron, 24 mi/38 km S of the South Dakota border, and 33 mi/53 km E of the Wyoming line. Established in 1885, it was once a wide-open frontier town. It is now a trading hub for an irrigated ranching and farming area. Fort Robinson (est. 1874) is 4 mi/6 km W of Crawford, was important in Indian wars, and was the site of the killing (1877) of Crazy Horse, who had been imprisoned there. Nearby are Toadstool Park (in the Badlands), site of erosion-created formations, and Warbonnet Battlefield, scene of an 1876 skirmish between Cheyenne and cavalry accompanied by Buffalo Bill Cody.

Crawford Notch mountain pass, altitude 1773 ft/541 m, in NW Carroll Co., N New Hampshire. Named for the Crawford family, who cut the first trail to the Mt. WASHINGTON summit in the 19th century, this U-shaped defile is 5 mi/8 km long, in the heart of the White Mts. West of the Presidential Range, it is traversed by the Saco R. Crawford Notch State Park, the Mt. Washington cog railway, and Attitash Ski area are in the vicinity.

Crawfordsville city, pop. 13,584, seat of Montgomery Co., WC Indiana, on Sugar Creek, 43 mi/69 km NW of Indianapolis. The presence of Wabash College (1832) made Crawfordsville a 19th-century cultural center; the college remains important in the city's life. Today Crawfordsville is the trading and processing hub of a livestock, dairying, and grain producing region. There is also some industry, including printing, bookbinding, and the manufacture of plastics, steel, foundry equipment, and nails and wire. The Ben Hur Museum/Gen. Lew Wallace Study (1896) memorializes the writer and Civil War general, a native of BROOKVILLE, who lived here 1853–1905.

Crazy Horse Memorial huge stone carving in Custer Co., SW South Dakota, 6 mi/10 km N of Custer, in the Black Hills. A 563 ft/172 m–high statue of the Sioux leader, mounted on his horse, is being carved into granitic Thunderhead Mt. The work was begun in 1947 by sculptor Korczak Ziolkowski, who labored on it for 44 years. Since his death in 1992, his wife and several of his children have carried on the project.

Creede town, pop. 362, seat of Mineral Co., SW Colorado, in the San Juan Mts. and the Rio Grande gorge, 65 mi/105 km NW of Alamosa. It was a raucous boom town from 1890, when silver was discovered, until 1893, when prices declined and most of the mines closed. Its ore is of very high quality, and some mines are still active. Tourism is now important.

Creedmoor see under BELLEROSE, New York.

creek **1.** in the Northeast, following older British usage, a usually narrow, winding tidal inlet or estuary. **2.** in the rest of the US and Canada, a stream, generally larger than a brook and smaller than a river.

Crenshaw section of SC LOS ANGELES, California, immediately E of BALDWIN HILLS and 5 mi/8 km SW of Downtown. Crenshaw residents are mainly middle- and lower-income. The main commercial thoroughfare, Crenshaw Blvd., has come to rival CENTRAL AVENUE as the economic spine of the Los Angeles black community.

Crescent City **1.** city, pop. 1859, Putnam Co., NE Florida, on Crescent L., 28 mi/45 km NW of Daytona Beach. It is a resort and citrus trade center, and the birthplace (1889) of labor leader A. Philip Randolph. **2.** popular nickname for New Orleans, Louisiana, from the location of the VIEUX CARRÉ, its oldest section, on a sharp bend of the Mississippi R.

Crested Butte town, pop. 878, Gunnison Co., WC Colorado, on the Slate R., 25 mi/40 km NNW of Gunnison and 128 mi/206 km WSW of Denver, in the Elk Mts. An 1880s gold and coal mining center, it is now a resort, noted as a mountain bikers' mecca. **Mount Crested Butte** (town, pop. 264), just N, is a ski resort developed in the 1980s.

Crest Hill city, pop. 10,643, Will Co., NE Illinois, on the Des Plaines R., a residential suburb immediately N of Joliet. Stateville Correctional Center is located immediately N.

Creston city, pop. 7911, seat of Union Co., SW Iowa, 50 mi/80 km SW of Des Moines. An agricultural community in the heart of Iowa's bluegrass country, it trades and processes corn and livestock. Southwestern Community College (1926) is here. Creston is 3 mi/5 km W of Twelve Mile L.

Crestview city, pop. 9886, seat of Okaloosa Co., NW Florida, in the PANHANDLE, 45 mi/72 km ENE of Pensacola. It mills lumber, processes and cans fruit, and shells and packs pecans. The Blackwater River State Forest is NW, Eglin Air Force Base S.

Crestwood **1.** village, pop. 10,823, Cook Co., NE Illinois, on the Calumet Sag Channel, a residential suburb 17 mi/27 km SW of Chicago. The Illinois State Police Headquarters and Howell Airport are here. A forest preserve is adjacent (W). **2.** city, pop. 11,234, St. Louis Co., EC Missouri, 12 mi/19 km SW of downtown St. Louis. Primarily a residential suburb, it also has some light industry.

Crete city, pop. 4841, Saline Co., SE Nebraska, on the Big Blue R., 18 mi/29 km SW of Lincoln. It is a processing center for grain, dairy products, and poultry, and has some light manufacturing. Doane College (1872) is here.

Creve Coeur city, pop. 12,304, St. Louis Co., EC Missouri, 13 mi/21 km WNW of downtown St. Louis. Housing some light industry, it is essentially a residential suburb. Monsanto, the chemical company, has its headquarters here.

Cripple Creek city, pop. 584, seat of Teller Co., C Colorado, in the Rocky Mts., 20 mi/32 km WSW of Colorado Springs. Situated at the S edge of Pike National Forest at 9375 ft/2859 m, it is in what was once a major gold-producing district, where the famed El Paso Lode was discovered in 1891, and the Gold Coin, Independence, and Cresson mines were worked. Cripple Creek was a boom town with a population that reached 50,000, until deposits were largely exhausted around 1915. In 1903–04, labor disputes arising from the attempts of workers to unionize resulted in violence and death. After 1934, new veins were found and worked; since the 1970s, some mines have been rehabilitated and tourism has become an important factor in the local economy. Legalized gambling was instituted in 1990. Florissant Fossil Beds National Monument is 12 mi/19 km NW.

Crisfield city, pop. 2880, Somerset Co., at the extreme S of Maryland's EASTERN SHORE, on Tangier Sound, 23 mi/37 km SSW of Salisbury. Settled by the 1660s, it has long been one of the Chesapeake Bay's best-known fishing centers, a marketer of oysters, crabs, finfish, and terrapin, with a large fleet and local fishing-tool producers. Janes I., a 3060-ac/1240-ha state park, is immediately W, and there are ferries to SMITH I. (W) and TANGIER I., in Virginia (SSW).

Crittenden County 599 sq mi/1551 sq km, pop. 49,939, in E Arkansas, in the DELTA between the Mississippi and the St. Francis R. Its seat is Marion (pop. 4391). It produces corn, soybeans, hay, and hardwood timber. The chief urban center is WEST MEMPHIS.

Croatan National Forest see under NEUSE R., North Carolina.

Croatan Sound passage, 8 mi/13 km NNW–SSE and about 4 mi/6 km wide, between ALBEMARLE SOUND (N) and PAMLICO SOUND (S) in Dare Co., E North Carolina. ROANOKE I. lies on the E side.

Crocus see under WEYBURN, Saskatchewan.

Crofton unincorporated residential village, pop. 12,781, Anne Arundel Co., C Maryland, 18 mi/29 km NE of Washington, D.C. A planned suburb created in the 1960s, Crofton, built around a lake, includes a variety of housing styles, and is growing quickly.

Cromwell town, pop. 12,286, Middlesex Co., S Connecticut, on the Connecticut R. It produces flowers, toys, and hardware. Cromwell is the seat of Holy Apostles Seminary and College (1956). Settled in 1650, it separated from Middletown (S) in 1851.

Crookston city, pop. 8119, seat of Polk Co., NW Minnesota, on the Red Lake R., 24 mi/39 km SE of Grand Forks, North Dakota. Settled in 1872 in the fertile valley left by glacial L. AGASSIZ, it is a trade center for wheat and diversified agricultural products and livestock.

Crooksville see under ROSEVILLE, Ohio.

Cross Keys locality in Rockingham Co., NW Virginia, 6 mi/10 km SSE of Harrisonburg, and 5 mi/8 km SW of Massanutten Mt. On June 8, 1862, in Stonewall Jackson's Shenandoah Valley campaign, his troops won a victory here over a Union army led by John Frémont.

Cross Lanes in West Virginia: **a.** unincorporated community, pop. 10,878, Kanawha Co., an industrial CHARLESTON suburb, in the Kanawha Valley between INSTITUTE (SE) and NITRO (NW). It is home to a technological campus of the National Education Center (1968). **b.** see under SUMMERSVILLE, Nicholas Co.

Cross Timbers two belts of wooded land extending S into NE Texas from the Red R. The **East Cross Timbers,** only a few miles wide, runs along the E of the BALCONES ESCARPMENT, passing just W of Dallas, and divides the BLACKLANDS from the Grand Prairie. The much more extensive **West Cross Timbers** lies W of the Grand Prairie and Fort Worth, extending S all the way to the Edwards Plateau. Named for their characteristic post oak woods, these areas have been used for rangeland and fruit and vegetable farming. Urban sprawl around Dallas and Fort Worth has virtually eliminated visible distinction between the Cross Timbers and the prairies.

Croton-on-Hudson village, pop. 7018, in Cortlandt town, Westchester Co., SE New York, on the Hudson R., 34 mi/54 km N of New York City. A residential village, it has long attracted writers and artists. The Croton-Harmon train station is a major commuting point to New York City. Van Cortlandt Manor, the home of the Van Cortlandt family from 1677 until 1945, is a museum.

Croton River 60 mi/100 km long, in E New York. It is formed in Dutchess Co. by the junction of three headstreams, the West, Middle, and East branches, which flow through Putnam Co. and converge as they enter Westchester Co. The river then continues SW to the Hudson. The New Croton Dam (2168 ft/661 m long, 297 ft/91 m high) was completed in 1905 to replace an earlier structure, 3 mi/5 km above the river's mouth, and impounds L. Croton (20 mi/32 km long). The lake's waters, drawing from various sources, are brought to New York by the **Croton Aqueduct,** a tunnel 31 mi/50 km long, built in 1842 to provide water for the city.

Crow Indian Reservation 3544 sq mi/9178 sq km, pop. 6366 (74% Indian), in SE Montana, SE of Billings and along the Wyoming border. The BIGHORN and LITTLE BIGHORN rivers flow S–N through it, meeting at Hardin, on the N. **Crow Agency** (unincorporated, pop. 1446, Big Horn Co.) is the headquarters. The Siouan Crow, an offshoot of the Hidatsa, had moved to this area from Minnesota by the 1770s. They called themselves Absaroka ("children of the raven"), and were generally friendly to whites. Crow scouts assisted George A. Custer at the battle (1876) of the Little Bighorn, fought here. The reservation, established in 1868, was then much larger. Today, the Aug. Crow Fair and recreation at Bighorn Canyon draw outsiders.

Crowley city, pop. 13,983, seat of Acadia Parish, S Louisiana, 20 mi/32 km W of Lafayette, on Interstate 10. Founded in 1886, it is the trade center for a major rice growing region. Its primarily agricultural economy is augmented by the production of burlap bags, fertilizer, clothing, and machine shop and concrete products. Seafood is packed, and truck farming is also important. Crowley is home to a joint state and Federal rice experiment station, and to an annual International Rice Festival. Petroleum and gas deposits lie in the vicinity. The city is noted as a Cajun cultural center.

Crowley's Ridge extending N–S for some 180 mi/290 km from SE Missouri to W of HELENA, in NE Arkansas. A loess deposit 2–12 mi/3–19 km wide, it rises to 250 ft/76 m above the surrounding alluvial DELTA, reaching a high of over 500 ft/150 m in the N. Forrest City, Jonesboro, and Paragould are along the ridge, and the St. Francis R. runs along its E side. It was named for Benjamin Crowley, an early-19th-century settler.

Crown Center commercial complex 1.5 mi/2.4 km S of downtown KANSAS CITY, Missouri, on the NE of PENN VALLEY PARK, constructed in the 1970s largely with funding by the Hall (Hallmark greeting cards) family. HOSPITAL HILL is just NE, the developing Union Station area just NW. A complex of sleek modern buildings that replaced older blocks, the Crown Center has offices, shops, hotels (including the Hyatt, scene of a disastrous 1981 structural collapse), and condominiums. The area is now a popular entertainment district.

Crown Heights residential and commercial section of N Brooklyn, New York, S of Bedford-Stuyvesant, N of East Flatbush, and W of Brownsville. It centers on Eastern Parkway, considered the world's first urban parkway when it was designed (1866) by Frederick Law Olmsted and Calvert Vaux. Crown Heights until about 1916 was called Crow Hill. Its boundaries with Bedford-Stuyvesant and East Flatbush have been variously defined. WEEKSVILLE is on its N side, and EBBETS FIELD was in its S section. It was a suburb before the 1880s, when brownstones were built through the area. Residents of this fashionable area moved out after World War II, and Jews and Italians moved in from older neighborhoods. They were followed in the 1950s by blacks, especially West Indians. One Jewish group, members of the Lubavitcher Hasidic sect, remained after other whites left; their world headquarters is on Eastern Parkway. In the 1990s social conflict between the black and Hasidic communities flared occasionally. The Brooklyn Museum, Prospect Park, and Brooklyn Botanic Garden are just W.

crown lands in Canada, all lands belonging to the Federal or provincial governments, amounting to almost 90% of surface area. INDIAN RESERVES are technically crown lands. At times, crown lands have been sold cheaply to settlers, as in late-19th-century Ontario to attract Americans. See also PUBLIC LANDS.

Crown Point **1.** city, pop. 17,728, seat of Lake Co., NW Indiana, 12 mi/19 km S of Hammond and L. Michigan. Its industries process grain and film, and manufacture farm implements, truck parts, furniture, sports equipment, and grinders. Crown Point is also a residential suburb. **2.** town, pop. 1963, Essex Co., NE New York, in the Adirondack Mts., on L. Champlain, just W of the Vermont border, 50 mi/80 km S of Plattsburgh. Within the township is the Crown Point Peninsula, first settled (1714) as a British trading post. Located on the route from New York to Canada, it was the site of the French Fort St. Frederic (1731). During the French and Indian Wars, this was destroyed by the British under Jeffrey Amherst (1759). The British Fort Crown Point was in turn captured by the Green Mountain Boys (1775), changed hands twice, and was abandoned to the British during the Saratoga campaign (1777). Crown Point Reservation, at the tip of the peninsula, contains ruins of the forts. The town is now primarily a resort.

Crown Reserves see under UPPER CANADA.

Crowsnest Pass also, **Municipality of Crowsnest Pass** town, pop. 6679, SW Alberta, in the Rocky Mts., on the Alberta–British Columbia border, 103 mi/166 km SSW of Calgary. It is situated at one of the lower passes (4449 ft/1357 m) in the Continental Divide, discovered by whites in the 1850s. The Canadian Pacific Railway received government subsidies to construct a rail link through the pass to British Columbia in return for signing the Crow's Nest Pass Agreement (1897), promising a permanently reduced rate for shipping grain; disputes over the agreement's economic effects lasted into the 1980s. Six coal mining towns to the E were involved in the 1932 Crowsnest Pass Strike.

Crows Nest Peak 7048 ft/2148 m, in Pennington Co., in the Black Hills, WC South Dakota, 11 mi/18 km SW of Rochford and 5 mi/8 km E of the Wyoming line.

Crow Wing River 100 mi/161 km long, in C Minnesota. It rises in a chain of lakes in S Hubbard Co., and flows SE past Motley and Pillager, then continues to the Mississippi R., 8 mi/13 km SW of BRAINERD. It receives the Long Prairie (120 mi/193 km long) and Leaf (50 mi/80 km long) rivers.

Crysler's Farm War of 1812 battle site in SE Ontario, on the St. Lawrence R. near present-day MORRISBURG. Construction of the St. Lawrence Seaway left the site under water. On Nov. 11, 1813, British troops here achieved a decisive victory over a much larger invading American force. Instrumental in preventing the capture of Montréal, the battle led to subsequent American withdrawal from Canada.

Crystal city, pop. 23,788, Hennepin Co., SE Minnesota, a residential suburb 7 mi/11 km W of Minneapolis. It was originally a community of small farmers and truck gardeners. The postwar wave of suburban development brought a housing boom and one of the first shopping malls in the Twin Cities area.

Crystal Bay see under INCLINE VILLAGE, Nevada.

Crystal City **1.** city, pop. 4088, Jefferson Co., SE Missouri, 30 mi/48 km S of St. Louis and immediately SE of FESTUS, on the Mississippi R. On the site of silica deposits exploited from the 1870s, it was incorporated in 1911 as a COMPANY TOWN, and is a noted producer of plate glass. **2.** city, pop. 8263, seat of Zavala Co., S Texas, 95 mi/153 km SW of San Antonio. In Texas's WINTER GARDEN area, it took its name from its clear springs. A center for processing, packing, and shipping vegetables, especially spinach, it calls itself the "Spinach Capital of the World." A statue of a spinach-eating Popeye (1937) is in the town square. **3.** office and hotel complex in Arlington Co., NE Virginia, adjacent (W) to Washington National Airport, and just S of the PENTAGON.

Crystal Lake city, pop. 24,512, McHenry Co., NE Illinois, on Crystal L., 44 mi/71 km NW of Chicago. First settled in 1836, it was long a summer resort for Chicago residents. Today, the city is one of the outermost suburbs of the metropolitan area.

Crystal River city, pop. 4044, Citrus Co., WC Florida, 52 mi/84 km SSW of Gainesville, on the estuarial Crystal R. and Crystal Bay, an arm of the Gulf of Mexico. A longtime fishing, oystering, and lumber shipping center, it is now popular with divers. The Crystal River nuclear power plant (1977) is 7 mi/11 km NW, on the Gulf.

Crystal Springs city, pop. 5643, Copiah Co., SW Mississippi, 24 mi/39 km SSW of Jackson. A distribution center for local produce, especially tomatoes, it also has some light manufacturing. Congressman Pat Harrison (1881–1941) was born here.

Cucamonga see RANCHO CUCAMONGA, California.

Cudahy **1.** city, pop. 22,817, Los Angeles Co., SW California, a predominantly Hispanic suburb 6 mi/10 km SE of downtown Los Angeles, on the Los Angeles R. just S of Bell. **2.** city, pop. 18,659, Milwaukee Co., SE Wisconsin, on L. Michigan, 7 mi/11 km SE of Milwaukee, of which it is a residential and industrial suburb. It was founded in 1892 as a site for meatpacking, still its major industry. There are also tanneries here, and forgings, machinery, and building equipment are among its manufactures. General Mitchell Field is just W of the city.

Cuero city, pop. 6700, seat of De Witt Co., S Texas, on the Guadalupe R., 72 mi/116 km ESE of San Antonio. Founded in 1872, it was a roundup point for a branch of the CHISHOLM TRAIL. It is today a producer of dried eggs, turkey and other poultry, and dairy goods; an annual Turkeyfest publicizes the poultry industry. Cuero also manufactures saddles and concrete and metal products, processes cotton, and has natural gas wells.

cuesta (Spanish, "shoulder, slope") a ridge with one steep side (escarpment) and one gentle, sloping side, formed as erosion operates at different speeds on the two sides; the escarpment is formed at the edge of a more resistant formation.

Culebra MUNICIPIO, pop. 1542, an archipelago in which the main island is c.7 mi/11 km NW–SE and up to 4 mi/6 km wide, 20 mi/32 km off the E coast of Puerto Rico, and belonging to it, between Vieques Sound and the Caribbean Sea (S) and the Atlantic Ocean (N). The VIRGIN Is. lie E across the Virgin Passage. Reputedly discovered by Columbus (1493), Culebra became home to Taino who fled Spanish colonization of Puerto Rico. Its harbor was a base for pirates in the 17th and 18th centuries. Settled in the 1880s, it became in 1909 largely a naval reserve, its main settlement called Dewey. Until 1974, Culebra was used by the Navy for gunnery and bombing practice, in the face of growing protest. A wide variety of flora and fauna is found here, and much of the island is now administered by the US Fish and Wildlife Service. Resort trade is growing.

Cullman city, pop. 13,367, seat of Cullman Co., NC Alabama, 46 mi/74 km N of Birmingham. Founded in 1873 by a group of German immigrants, it is a market center for an agricultural area producing strawberries, sweet potatoes, cotton, timber, and corn. The raising of poultry and the manufacture of electrical appliances and metal products are now important.

Cullowhee unincorporated community, pop. 4029, Jackson Co., SW North Carolina, on the Tuckasegee R., 40 mi/64 km SW of Asheville. It is the seat of Western Carolina University (1889).

Culpeper town, pop. 8581, seat of Culpeper Co., NC Virginia, 32 mi/51 km WNW of Fredericksburg, in the PIEDMONT. It has experienced significant growth in recent years, yet retains a small-town atmosphere. Some high-tech industry has moved into the surrounding agricultural countryside, and there are tourist businesses. Area Civil War landmarks include BRANDY STATION, just NE.

Culver City city, pop. 38,793, Los Angeles Co., SW California, 6 mi/10 km W of downtown Los Angeles. MGM/United Artists, one of the top US film studios, based here, is a leading employer. Also important economically is Los Angeles International Airport, just S. Culver City's manufactures include aircraft, electronic equipment, machine tools, house trailers, plastics, rubber products, and cosmetics. It is the seat of West Los Angeles College (1968).

Cumberland **1.** city, pop. 23,706, seat of Allegany Co., NW Maryland, on the Potomac R. and Wills Creek, at a gap in the ALLEGHENY FRONT, between the borders of Pennsylvania and West Virginia. Settled in 1750, it was known as Will's Creek until 1763, when it was renamed for Fort Cumberland, built here a decade earlier. It developed as a coal transportation center, becoming the E terminus of the NATIONAL ROAD (the first section of which, to WHEELING, was called the Cumberland Road) in 1833, a Baltimore and Ohio Railroad depot in 1842, and the W terminus of the Chesapeake and Ohio Canal in 1850. Cumberland is now the industrial center of a forest, farm, and coal region. Industries manufacture sheet metal, missile components, rubber, textiles, paper products, glass, bricks, beer, and railroad equipment. Allegany Community College (1961) is here. **2.** township, pop. 40,697, Ottawa-Carleton Regional Municipality, SE Ontario, on the Ottawa R. (N), adjacent (E) to Gloucester and 10 mi/16 km ENE of Ottawa. It is a rapidly growing (51% pop. increase in 1986–91) residential area including such small communities as Navan, Cumberland, and Sarsfield. **3.** town, pop. 29,038, Providence Co., extreme NE Rhode Island, 6 mi/10 km N of Providence and adjacent (E) to Woonsocket, along the Massachusetts border. It comprises the villages of Arnold, Ashton, Berkeley, and its governmental center VALLEY FALLS, as well as parts of Albion and Lonsdale. The area is suburban and agricultural, with dairy farms and orchards. Manufactures include textiles, wire and cable, metal goods, and electrical products. Historic sites include the Ballou Meetinghouse (c.1740) and nearby Beacon Pole Hill, a relay point during the Revolutionary War. The preacher Jemima Wilkinson was born here in 1752.

Cumberland County **1.** 876 sq mi/2269 sq km, pop. 243,135, in SW Maine. The state's most heavily and densely populated county, it has both inland and coastal resorts; manufacturing and commerce in the Portland area; and truck farming and dairying in rural sections. Industries include food canning, fishing, publishing, printing, and the manufacture of paper, footwear, hardware, textiles, and wood and clay products. Rivers include the Fore and Presumpscot at Portland, and the Nonesuch, Royal, and Stroudwater. Portland is the county seat. **2.** 498 sq mi/1290 sq km, pop. 138,053, in SW New Jersey, on the Delaware R. and N Delaware Bay. Its seat is BRIDGETON. Largely agricultural and maritime, the county also contains the cities of VINELAND and MILLVILLE. **3.** 657 sq mi/1702 sq km, pop. 274,566, in SC North Carolina, in SANDHILLS, on the N edge of the Atlantic Coastal Plain, and bisected by the Cape Fear R. Its seat is FAYETTEVILLE, where its industry is concentrated. Its agricultural products include tobacco, soybeans, corn, grain, hogs, and poultry. Lumbering is also important. The E section of FORT BRAGG, including Pope Air Force Base, lies in the NW. **4.** 547 sq mi/1417 sq km, pop. 195,257, in S Pennsylvania. Its seat is CARLISLE. BLUE Mt. forms its N boundary. The Cumberland Valley was a major pioneer route to the W; today the Pennsylvania Turnpike and Interstate 81 pass through it. The county is largely agricultural, with suburbs of Harrisburg along the Susquehanna R., in the E.

Cumberland Front also, **Cumberland Mountain** see under ALLEGHENY FRONT.

Cumberland Gap passage through the Cumberland Front, in the Appalachians, between extreme SW Virginia and SE Kentucky, just N of the Tennessee line. Cut by a stream, and followed by animals and, later, local tribes, it was discovered in 1750 by Thomas Walker, who was looking for a way to reach Kentucky, which to that point had a quasilegendary status. In 1769 Daniel Boone passed through the Gap, and in 1775 it became part of his WILDERNESS ROAD. In the years before opening of the NATIONAL ROAD took the Wilderness Road's traffic away, the Cumberland Gap was the main route through the Appalachian barrier for Americans moving west. Today it is part of the three-state, 20,270-ac/8210-ha **Cumberland Gap National Historic Park.**

Cumberland Island largest of the Georgia SEA ISLANDS, in the Atlantic Ocean between the mouths of the Satilla (N) and St. Marys (S) rivers, just N of the Florida border. Twenty mi/32 km N–S and 1–5 mi/1–8 km wide, it is a national seashore, with beach dunes, saltmarshes, and forests of live oak and pine. Many bird species inhabit the island, as well as alligators, armadillos, deer, otters, and wild horses.

Cumberland National Forest see DANIEL BOONE NATIONAL FOREST.

Cumberland Plateau also, **Cumberland Mountains** tableland in the SE US, the southwesternmost division of the APPALACHIAN Mts. It extends NE–SW for c.450 mi/725 km, in a belt up to 50 mi/80 km wide, from S West Virginia (where it is a continuation of the ALLEGHENY Plateau) along the border between Kentucky and Virginia, across E Tennessee on the W of the Tennessee R., and into Alabama, N of Birmingham. The highest area, and the section to which the name "Cumberland Mts." is often limited, stretches c.150 mi/240 km along the Kentucky-Virginia line and in N Tennessee, and includes the ridges known as **Cumberland Mt.** (c.2500–3450 ft/760–1050 m high); PINE Mt.; and BLACK Mt., at 4145 ft/1263 m the highest in Kentucky and in the Cumberlands. To the SW the plateau includes WALDEN RIDGE, the Crab Orchard Mts., LOOKOUT Mt., and SAND Mt. The CUMBERLAND GAP is in SW Virginia. Streams have formed deep valleys across the plateau in many sections, causing difficult passage and leading to poverty, isolation, and the distinctive traditions of "Appalachian" culture. Coal mining is the economic focus, with lumbering in some sections.

Cumberland River 693 mi/1116 km long, in S Kentucky and N Tennessee. It is formed on the CUMBERLAND PLATEAU by the confluence of several headstreams in Harlan Co., SE Kentucky. It winds through mountains and forests in the E, and rolling highlands in the W., From its head the Cumberland flows W through PINE Mt., a W ridge of the Appalachians, then continues W, then N through the DANIEL BOONE (formerly Cumberland) NATIONAL FOREST, in which **Cumberland Falls,** 68 ft/21 m high and 125 ft/38 m wide, are noted for their "moonbow," seen at the full moon. North of the falls the Laurel R. joins the Cumberland, which then flows W into **Lake Cumberland,** formed by the Wolf Creek Dam (1951). The BIG SOUTH FORK joins it at the lake's E end. The Cumberland then turns S into Tennessee, where the Obey R. drains DALE HOLLOW L. into it. The river flows SW through dam-created Cordell Hull L., then past Carthage, and through Old Hickory L. (impounded by Old Hickory Dam) past Hendersonville, before reaching NASHVILLE. From Nashville it turns NW and flows out of the Nashville Basin and through L. Barkley, back into Kentucky and the LAND BETWEEN THE LAKES. It then continues to the OHIO R. at Smithland, 12 mi/19 km ENE of Paducah. The Cumberland's tributaries in Kentucky include the Laurel, Little, and Tradewater rivers; in Tennessee they include the Obey, Caney Fork, Stones, and Harpeth. Dams along its course and tributaries are part of the TENNESSEE VALLEY AUTHORITY system. The Cumberland is navigable for small craft throughout most of its length, in places via locks and canals. Its valley is an historic transportation route, and has also been an important mining and agricultural area.

Cumberland Road see under NATIONAL ROAD.

Cumberland Valley **1.** in Kentucky and Tennessee, the valley of the CUMBERLAND R. **2.** in Pennsylvania and Maryland, 75 mi/120 km–long northward extension of the SHENANDOAH Valley, part of the Great Appalachian Valley. It extends from the Potomac R. and the West Virginia–Maryland border (SW) to the Susquehanna R. at Harrisburg, Pennsylvania (NE). SOUTH Mt. (the Blue Ridge) flanks it to the SE; TUSCARORA Mt., Blue Mt., and other Appalachian ridges stand to the NW. Carlisle, Chambersburg, and Shippensburg are the major cities in the Pennsylvania section. Hagerstown is the chief community in the Maryland section, which is also known as the Hagerstown Valley.

Cummington town, pop. 809, Hampshire Co., WC Massachusetts, on the Westfield R., 18 mi/29 km E of Pittsfield. In a hilly rural area, it is the birthplace (1794) of poet and editor William Cullen Bryant, some of whose works draw on local scenery. The town is agricultural, with some resort trade, and attracts exurban migrants.

Cupertino city, pop. 40,263, Santa Clara Co., NC California, in SILICON VALLEY, 8 mi/13 km W of San Jose. Headquarters for Apple Computer, it has developed westward (most rapidly in the 1970s) into an area of fruit orchards and vineyards, settled in the 1850s. Cogswell Polytechnical (1887) and De Anza (1967) colleges are here.

Cupids town, pop. 868, SE Newfoundland, on the NW arm of the AVALON PENINSULA and the W of CONCEPTION BAY, 24 mi/39 km W of St. John's. At the early-17th-century Cupers Cove, John Guy established the Sea Forest plantation, the first formal British colonization attempt in Newfoundland; it failed by 1631. The community has a subsequent history as a fishing OUTPORT.

Currituck Sound protected inlet of the Atlantic Ocean in Currituck Co., NE North Carolina. Thirty mi/48 km N–S and 3–8 mi/5–13 km wide, the shallow, island-filled sound is separated from the ocean by Bodie I., part of the OUTER BANKS. On the NE, it joins Back Bay in Virginia Beach, Virginia, and a fork on the NW leads to the Chesapeake and Albemarle Canal, a part of the Atlantic Intracoastal Waterway that connects the sound to Hampton Roads and Chesapeake Bay. It joins ALBEMARLE SOUND on the S. Mackay Island and Currituck national wildlife refuges bordering the sound are winter habitats on the ATLANTIC FLYWAY.

Custer Battlefield see under LITTLE BIGHORN R., Montana.

Custer County 1559 sq mi/4038 sq km, pop. 6179, in SW South Dakota, bounded by the Wyoming border (W). It is named for General George A. Custer, who came here in 1874; its seat is Custer. Including within its boundaries Custer State Park, Jewel Cave National Monument, and Wind Cave National Park, it has a thriving tourist industry. The county produces dairy products, livestock, poultry, grain, and timber. It was the center of the South Dakota gold rush of the mid 1870s. There are mines in the area around Custer.

Custer National Forest 1.1 million ac/450,000 ha (1740 sq mi/4500 sq km), in scattered units in SE Montana and NW South Dakota. Another 1.03 million ac/420,000 ha (1610 sq km/4170 sq km) of grasslands, chiefly in SW North Dakota's Little Missouri National Grasslands, are also administered from its Billings headquarters. The forest has a wide range of terrain, from high peaks in the BEARTOOTH Range (W) to prairie (E).

Custer Peak 6794 ft/2072 m, in the BLACK HILLS, in Lawrence Co., SW South Dakota, 6 mi/10 km SE of Lead.

Custer State Park 73,000 ac/29,565 ha, in the BLACK HILLS, in Custer Co., SW South Dakota, E of the city of Custer. Sanctuary to one of world's largest herds of bison, it is also home to deer, pronghorn antelope, mountain goats, bighorn sheep, elk, wild turkeys, and burros. It includes Mt. HARNEY, Mt. COOLIDGE, and the French Creek Gorge Wilderness Area. The 14 mi/23 km–long Needles Highway winds through the Needles, a collection of granite spires near Sylvan Lake, and the Cathedral Spires, a National Landmark.

Cut Bank city, pop. 3329, seat of Glacier Co., NW Montana, on the Cut Bank Creek, 90 mi/145 km NW of Great Falls. The city experienced two spurts of growth, in the 1890s, when the Great Northern Railway arrived, and in the 1930s, when oil and gas were discovered nearby. It now trades in oil products, wool, livestock, and grain. The Blackfeet Indian Reservation lies immediately W.

Cutchogue unincorporated village, pop. 2627, in Southold town, Suffolk Co., SE New York, on Long Island's NORTH FORK, 11 mi/18 km NE of Riverhead. It is a farming and summer resort community, with several vineyards.

Cuthbert city, pop. 3730, Randolph Co., SW Georgia, 47 mi/76 km SSE of Columbus. This agricultural and lumbering center is home to Andrew College (1854), and is the birthplace (1898) of jazz bandleader and arranger Fletcher Henderson.

Cutler Ridge unincorporated community, pop. 21,268, Dade Co., SE Florida, 16 mi/26 km SSW of Miami. The Census distinguishes **Cutler** (pop. 16,201), just NE. Both are bedroom suburbs, and with HOMESTEAD (S) took the brunt of Hurricane Andrew's (Aug. 1992) destruction.

Cuttyhunk Island southwesternmost of the ELIZABETH ISLANDS, between Buzzards Bay and Vineyard Sound, SE Massachusetts. The English explorer Bartholomew Gosnold settled here briefly in 1602.

Cuyahoga County 459 sq mi/1189 sq km, pop. 1,412,140, in N Ohio, with L. Erie to the N, drained by the Cuyahoga R., which forms its extreme SE border, and the Rocky R. Its seat is Cleveland, which with its many suburbs makes up the majority of its area. Manufacturing is centered in and around Cleveland. Farming includes dairy, vegetables, and poultry. Gravel, salt, and sands are exploited. Cuyahoga Co. is famous for its parks—a total of nine, comprising 9369 ac/3794 ha.

Cuyahoga Falls city, pop. 48,950, Summit Co., NE Ohio, 5 mi/8 km NE of Akron. The Cuyahoga R. passes through the city, dropping 220 ft/67 m through a series of falls and rapids. Founded in 1812, the city is primarily a commuter suburb. However, a wide variety of products are manufactured here, including rubber goods, rubbermaking machinery, medical supplies, steel and wire machinery, and tools and dies.

Cuyahoga Heights village, pop. 682, Cuyahoga Co., NE Ohio, on the Ohio Canal just SE of downtown Cleveland, of which it is an industrial suburb.

Cuyahoga River 80 mi/129 km long, in NE Ohio. It rises in Geauga Co. around Chardon, flows SW through Portage Co. to CUYAHOGA FALLS, then turns abruptly N, flowing to L. Erie at Cleveland, where its mouth forms part of the city's harbor. In its course it passes through the East Branch Reservoir and L. Rockwell, both impounded by dams.

Cuyuna Iron Range iron mining belt extending NE–SW along the Mississippi R., N and W of Aitkin, in C Minnesota. The ore obtained from the underground mines of this relatively flat area is distinguished by the presence of manganese, important in the production of spiegeleisen and steel. Beginning in 1911, this ore, along with that already being mined elsewhere in the state, put Minnesota in the national lead in production of iron ore. Crosby, at the E end of the range, is an important mining center. The area also includes Ironton, Deerwood, and Brainerd.

Cypress city, pop. 42,655, Orange Co., SC California, 17 mi/27 km SE of downtown Los Angeles. It was developed in the 1960s, to house aircraft and other industrial workers, in what had been a truck and dairy farming area. Cypress now has house trailer and auto plants. A branch of Forest Lawn, the well-known cemetery, is here, as is Los Alamitos Race Track (harness racing).

Cypress Gardens see under WINTER HAVEN, Florida.

Cypress Hills **1.** see under EAST NEW YORK, New York. **2.** hilly area (965 sq mi/2500 sq km) in SW Saskatchewan (226 mi/364 km W of Regina) and SE Alberta, including the highest elevations (over 4787 ft/1468 m, in Alberta) in continental Canada between the Rocky Mts. and Labrador, and the highest point in Saskatchewan (4567 ft/1392 m). These rolling, moist, forested slopes were not completely covered by glaciers during the Wisconsin era. In 1873, they were the site of the massacre of a group of Assiniboine that led to the creation of the North West Mounted Police, stationed at FORT WALSH and WOOD MOUNTAIN. The area (49,580 ac/20,080 ha) in Alberta occupied by **Cypress Hills Provincial Park** has archaeological evidence of human habitation from over 7000 years ago, as well as dinosaur fossils. Today coal mining is done in the Shaunavon area in the E, and antelope and wild horses roam the hills.

Czestochowa see under DOYLESTOWN, Pennsylvania.

D

Dade County 1955 sq mi/5063 sq km, pop. 1,937,044, in SE Florida, at the SE tip of the Florida Peninsula, on the Atlantic Ocean, bordered by barrier islands (*keys*) that enclose Biscayne Bay (SE), and by part of Florida Bay (S). Its seat and metropolis is MIAMI; just E is the vacation mecca of MIAMI BEACH. The resort-filled coastal fringe of Dade is its most developed area. Around Miami are a multitude of suburban residential communities. The economy of this section relies on retirees, tourism, business, raising and processing vegetables and citrus fruit, and light industry. The interior (W) is in the EVERGLADES. Many services throughout the county are handled by Metro-Date, a METROPOLITAN GOVERNMENT body created in 1957.

Dahlonega city, pop. 3086, seat of Lumpkin Co., N Georgia, 60 mi/100 km NNE of Atlanta. It was established when gold was discovered in the area in 1829. A Federal mint operated here 1838–61. The city is now a trade center, producing lumber and processing poultry. It is also a mountain vacation gateway. North Georgia College (1873) is here.

Daisy see under SODDY-DAISY, Tennessee.

Dakota County 574 sq mi/1487 sq km, pop. 275,227, in EC Minnesota, bordered by the Minnesota R. (NW), the Mississippi R. (NE), and the Cannon R. (S). Lying immediately S of St. Paul, it contains many Twin Cities suburbs, such as Hastings (the county seat), South St. Paul, Mendota Heights, and Eagan.

Dakota River see JAMES R., North Dakota and South Dakota.

Dale City unincorporated community, pop. 47,170, Prince William Co., NE Virginia, just W of the Potomac R. and Interstate 95, 18 mi/29 km SW of Alexandria. This burgeoning residential suburb W of Woodbridge is home to Potomac Mills, a huge "factory outlet" mall claimed to be Virginia's most visited site.

Dale Hollow Lake in N Tennessee and S Kentucky, 80 mi/130 km ENE of Nashville. Formed by the 200 ft/61 m–high **Dale Hollow Dam** (1943) just E of Celina, Tennessee, on the Obey R., it impounds the waters of the Obey, Wolf, and smaller rivers, backing over 50 mi/80 km into stream valleys in both states, and covering over 52,500 ac/21,260 ha. The dam regulates the Obey's flow into the Cumberland R. at Celina, and produces power marketed through the Tennessee Valley Authority.

Dalhousie town, pop. 4775, seat of Restigouche Co., extreme N New Brunswick, at the head of CHALEUR BAY (the mouth of the Restigouche R.), 13 mi/21 km ENE of Campbellton. A fishing port with paper and chemical plants, it is also near both lead and zinc mines and resort beaches.

Dallas **1.** city, pop. 9422, seat of Polk Co., W Oregon, 15 mi/24 km W of Salem. Settled in the 1840s, it was the site of one of the earliest woolen mills in the state. Today, lumber and leather are among its products. Wineries surround the city, and the Baskett Slough National Wildlife Refuge is just NE. **2.** township, pop. 7625, Luzerne Co., NE Pennsylvania, 9 mi/14 km NNW of Wilkes-Barre. It is the seat of College Misericordia (1924). **3.** city, pop. 1,006,877, seat of Dallas Co., also in Collin, Denton, Rockwall, and Kaufman counties, NE Texas, on the Trinity R., 33 mi/53 km E of Fort Worth. The second-most populous Texas (and eighth-largest US) city, it is one of the two poles of the Dallas–Fort Worth metropolitan area (CMSA), also known as the METROPLEX, which has a pop. of 3,885,415. The city lies at the W edge of the BLACKLANDS, with the East CROSS TIMBERS running along its W border. John Neely Bryan began its history with an 1841 land claim on a bluff over the Trinity. His idea that the river, which flows 250 mi/400 km from here to the Gulf of Mexico, would be a trade corridor has never been realized, but he soon saw that the ford he had chosen would be important to developing road systems. In 1858 members of the French utopian (Fourierist) community of La Réunion, begun in 1855 across the Trinity, moved to Dallas, bringing skills and an early cosmopolitan influence. Dallas was a Confederate supply center but saw no action in the Civil War. In the 1870s railroads arrived, and the city became a major cotton market; this mercantile base has been expanded ever since. In the 1930s the opening of the EAST TEXAS OILFIELD, 110 mi/180 km E, led to Dallas's role as the financial and managerial base for the burgeoning petrochemical industry. In the 1940s the city and surrounding prairie towns (which exploded in growth) became central to the US aircraft industry. In the 1960s this technological base expanded as Dallas and its neighbors took part in the revolution in communications and computing, becoming "Silicon Prairie." Today, local industries include oil and chemicals, aircraft and automobile production, electronics, farm machinery, and foods. The city is better known as a trade center, home to Neiman-Marcus and other upscale retailers, major wholesalers, many conventions, and the Texas State Fair. While Fort Worth is held to be thoroughly Western, Dallas has always been regarded as in one sense an outpost of the cosmopolitan East. The city's institutions include Bishop College (1881), Dallas Baptist University (1898),

Southern Methodist University (in UNIVERSITY PARK; 1911), and the University of Texas at Dallas (1969), in addition to major libraries, a lively theater community, and other arts centers. Among the city's sections, its central business district, N of the Trinity, is flanked on the E by largely black South Dallas. Across the Trinity (S) is Oak Cliff, an extensive residential and commercial section on higher ground. North Dallas contains many affluent neighborhoods and several well-known malls. See also: CENTRAL EXPRESSWAY; DALLAS–FORT WORTH INTERNATIONAL AIRPORT; DEALEY PLAZA (and the Grassy Knoll); DEEP ELLUM; EAST DALLAS; FAIR PARK (and the Cotton Bowl); GALLERIA; GREENVILLE AVENUE; MOUNTAIN CREEK; NORTH DALLAS (and Preston Hollow); OAK CLIFF; REUNION TOWER (and Arena, and La Réunion); SOUTH DALLAS; SOUTHFORK RANCH; TURTLE CREEK; WEST DALLAS; WEST END; WHITE ROCK CREEK.

Dallas County 880 sq mi/2279 sq km, pop. 1,852,810, in NE Texas. Its seat is DALLAS. In the CROSS TIMBERS (W) and BLACKLANDS (E), it is drained by the Trinity R. and its tributaries. The city of Dallas and its satellites, including Garland, Mesquite, Richardson, Grand Prairie, Farmers Branch, and Irving, have expanded since the 1940s to fill much of this cotton, vegetable, grain, and livestock producing prairie area with industrial, commercial, and residential development.

Dallas–Fort Worth International Airport in Tarrant and Dallas counties, NE Texas, 18 mi/29 km NW of Dallas and a similar distance NE of Fort Worth. Opened in 1974, succeeding Love Field, in North Dallas, as that city's chief airport, it was long the world's largest airport, covering some 17,800 ac/7200 ha in Irving, Coppell, Euless, and Grapevine. With its own hotels and services including sports and business facilities, it is in effect a self-contained community.

Dalles, the **1.** see THE DALLES, Oregon. **2.** see under SAINT CROIX R., Wisconsin.

Dalton **1.** city, pop. 21,761, seat of Whitfield Co., NW Georgia, in the Cohutta Mts., 26 mi/42 km SE of Chattanooga, Tennessee. Incorporated in 1847, it was a shipping point for copper mined in the area. In 1863–64 it was a Confederate headquarters, and fell to Sherman's advance on Atlanta. Since the early 20th century, Dalton has been a center for the tufted-textile (candlewick) industry, producing a high proportion of the bedspreads and, later, carpets made in the US. It has several large carpet plants. Dalton College (1963) is here. **2.** town, pop. 7155, Berkshire Co., W Massachusetts, 5 mi/8 km ENE of Pittsfield. A resort town with some light manufacturing, it gave its name to the Dalton plan (1919), a progressive education scheme. The Crane Paper Mills (1801) make specialty papers, including currency paper.

Dalton Highway 414 mi/667 km–long road following the TRANS-ALASKA PIPELINE from PRUDHOE BAY to FAIRBANKS, in N Alaska. Begun in 1974 to aid in the construction of the pipeline, it was originally called the North Slope Haul Road. Much of it is accessible only by permit.

Daly City city, pop. 92,311, San Mateo Co., NC California, adjacent (SW) to San Francisco, along the Pacific Ocean. A dairy and truck farming area from the 1850s, it grew rapidly after World War II to become part of the continuous urban band extending S from San Francisco. Its industries include nurseries and factories making truck bodies and other iron and aluminum products, but it is still largely residential, now with a large Asian community. The 1964 Republican national convention was held here at the Cow Palace.

Damariscotta town, pop. 1811, Lincoln Co., SW Maine. It is on the E bank of the Damariscotta R., an estuary extending about 20 mi/32 km N from a point just E of Boothbay Harbor. Twin to Newcastle, across the river, Damariscotta was an early trading post site. Shipbuilding, shellfish and lobsters, and tourism are the main industries. Along the river are shell heaps left over centuries by local tribes. PEMAQUID Point is 14 mi/22 km S, at the Damariscotta River's mouth.

Damariscove Island 2 mi/3 km long, in Boothbay town, Lincoln Co., SW Maine, 5 mi/8 km SSE of Boothbay Harbor. In the early 17th century Damariscove was one of America's major ports, sheltering European fishing fleets within the small harbor at its SW end. Abandoned in the 1950s by the last of its resident lobstermen and Coast Guardsmen, it belongs to the Nature Conservancy.

Damascus unincorporated village, pop. 9817, Montgomery Co., WC Maryland, a suburb 28 mi/45 km NNW of Washington, D.C., at the headwaters of the Patuxent R.

Dana agricultural town, pop. 612, Vermillion Co., W Indiana, 25 mi/40 km NNW of Terre Haute, and just E of the Illinois border. The Ernie Pyle State Historic Site incorporates the birthplace (and home) of the World War II correspondent (1900–45).

Dana Point city, pop. 31,896, Orange Co., SW California, 50 mi/80 km SE of Los Angeles. In the early 19th century it was a major port; the sailor/writer Richard Henry Dana, here in the 1830s, described how hides were thrown from cliffs to crews waiting on the beach below. In 1924 Dana Point was named for him. It is a popular resort, yachting port, and residential community.

Danbury city and coterminous township, pop. 65,585, Fairfield Co., Connecticut, 25 mi/40 km NW of Bridgeport, along the Still R., Interstate 84, and the New York border. Founded c.1685, it was a military supply center during the Revolution; on Sept. 26, 1777, it was burned and looted by the British. A hatting industry was founded here in 1780 by Zadoc Benedict, and until the early 20th century, Danbury was a major producer of men's hats. Since then, its industrial base has diversified; in addition to manufacturing, it is home to several major corporations, including Union Carbide and a division of American Cyanamid. The Danbury Fair (1869–1981) was formerly a major attraction. Its site was occupied by the Danbury Fair Mall, which flourished as a regional commercial center while the city's downtown stagnated. CANDLEWOOD L. lies just N. Danbury is also home to Western Connecticut State University (1903) and to a Federal prison.

Dancing Rabbit Creek in Noxubee Co., EC Mississippi, SW of the hamlet of Mashulaville, the site of the signing of a treaty (Sept. 1830) in which Choctaw leaders, pressured by government agents, ceded all Choctaw land in the state in return for promises of Western land. This agreement precipitated a rush into the DELTA by white settlers, who soon created enormous cotton plantations in the area.

Dane County 1205 sq mi/3121 sq km, pop. 367,085, in S Wisconsin, bordered by the Wisconsin R. (NW). Its seat is MADISON. It is drained by the Yahara and Sugar rivers, and contains a number of lakes, of which the FOUR LAKES are the most prominent. Mainly agricultural, the county has some industry localized in Madison and Stoughton.

Danforth, the see under BLOOR St., Toronto, Ontario.

Dania city, pop. 13,024, Broward Co., SE Florida, on the N outskirts of Hollywood. Danish immigrants settled here in 1896. A winter vacation spot and a residential community, Dania also processes and ships citrus fruit and vegetables.

Daniel Boone Homestead see under READING, Pennsylvania.

Daniel Boone National Forest formerly, **Cumberland National Forest** 670,000 ac/271,000 ha, in two large units in E Kentucky. Its larger unit runs some 125 mi/200 km SSW–NNE from the Tennessee border along the E side of the BLUEGRASS REGION. The Cumberland R., joined by the Big South Fork, cuts through it in the S, the route of the WILDERNESS ROAD in its center. MOREHEAD is within the forest's N extreme; the N boundary is formed by the headwaters of the Licking R. The second unit lies SE. The forest is known for its sandstone cliffs and gorges, natural bridges, and rough wooded hillsides.

Danielson see under KILLINGLY, Connecticut.

Dan River 180 mi/290 km long, in Virginia and North Carolina. It rises on the E side of the Blue Ridge, on the Patrick-Carroll county line, in SW Virginia. The Pinnacles of Dan, where the river falls in cascades from a 2655-ft/810-m height, is the site of the Pinnacles Hydroelectric Development, opened 1938. The river flows S and SE into Stokes Co., North Carolina, and passes E of Hanging Rock State Park. It then turns NE past Madison and Eden, where the Smith R. joins it from the N, and back into Virginia to DANVILLE, where the noted Dan River Mills use its power. It dips SE into North Carolina again, then flows NE to South Boston, Virginia, 14 mi/23 km E of which it joins the Roanoke R.

Dan Ryan Expressway Federal highway, 9 mi/14 km long, between the Loop and the Southwest Side of Chicago, Illinois. Opened in the 1960s, it has provided a direct auto link to the S suburbs. A rapid transit line runs down the middle of the road.

Dans Mountain ridge extending for 15 mi/24 km NE from the North Branch of the Potomac R. E of Westernport, Allegany Co., NW Maryland. Part of the ALLEGHENY FRONT, it rises to 2898 ft/884 m at Dans Rock, c.5 mi/8 km ENE of Lonaconing, Maryland. The ridge continues NE into Pennsylvania as Wills Mt.

Dansville village, pop. 5002, in North Dansville town, Livingston Co., W New York, 45 mi/72 km S of Rochester. Settled in 1795, it houses diverse light manufacturing plants, canneries, and nurseries. A sanitorium and health spa center since 1858, it is best known as the birthplace of the American Red Cross, whose first local chapter was founded here (1881) by Clara Barton.

Dante's View see under DEATH VALLEY, California.

Danvers town, pop. 24,174, Essex Co., NE Massachusetts, 17 mi/27 km NE of Boston, on US 1, Route 128, Interstate 95, and the estuarial Danvers R. Settled in 1636 as Salem Village, it was the scene of incidents leading to the infamous Salem witchcraft trials of 1692. Early manufactures included shoes, carpets, and bricks; the town is now engaged in a mix of suburban commerce, agriculture, and light manufacturing.

Danville 1. hamlet in Morgan Co., NC Alabama, 14 mi/23 km SSW of Decatur, the birthplace (1913) of Olympic champion Jesse (James Cleveland) Owens, who grew up in nearby (NE) Oakville. **2.** city, pop. 31,306, Contra Costa Co., NC California, 12 mi/19 km ENE of Oakland, in the San Ramon Valley, just SW of Mt. Diablo. Incorporated in the 1980s, it is largely residential. Eugene O'Neill's Tao House, where the playwright lived and wrote (1937–44), is now a National Historic Site. **3.** city, pop. 33,828, seat of Vermilion Co., EC Illinois, on the Vermilion R. and L. Vermilion, 5 mi/8 km W of the Indiana border and 36 mi/58 km E of Champaign. It is the commercial and distribution center for the area's corn and soybeans and its dairy farms. Local manufactures include lift trucks, ballasts, aerosol products, welding and mining machinery, and candy. Originally a Piankeshaw village at a trail crossroads, it was settled in the 1820s by traders and others interested in local salt deposits. Later it became a major coal mining and brick producing center. Kickapoo State Park is 4 mi/6 km W, and Middle Fork State Fish and Wildlife Area is 6 mi/10 km NW. **4.** city, pop. 12,420, seat of Boyle Co., C Kentucky, in the BLUEGRASS REGION, 36 mi/58 km SSW of Lexington. Settled c.1775 on the WILDERNESS ROAD, it was the capital of Virginia's Kentucky district. Constitution Square, where the new state's constitution was drafted in 1792, is a state shrine. A market for burley tobacco, livestock, and horses, it also manufactures clothing and furniture. Centre College (1819) is here. The house of pioneer surgeon Ephraim McDowell has been restored. **5.** town, pop. 1917, including the villages of Danville, North Danville, West Danville, and Harvey, in Caledonia Co., NE Vermont. It lies along the slopes of a high plateau, adjacent (W) to St. Johnsbury. Thaddeus Stevens, antislavery leader, was born here in 1792. Long a retreat for health seekers because of its fresh air, Danville produces lumber and wood products. For over 100 years it has been a convention site and national headquarters for the American Society of Dowsers. **6.** independent city, pop. 53,056, in but administratively separate from Pittsylvania Co., S Virginia, on the Dan R., where the Sandy R. joins it, just N of the North Carolina line. It is a market and processing center for bright leaf tobacco, and is also known for its textile industry, particularly the Dan River mills, at one time the largest cotton mills in the world. Danville also produces glass, tools, tires, and insulating materials. During the Civil War, it was the site of a prison camp, hospital, and supply depot; many Union soldiers are buried in its national cemetery. For a few days after the fall of Richmond in 1865, it served as the capital of the Confederacy. It is the seat of Averett College (1859) and Danville Community College (1967).

Darby borough, pop. 11,140, Delaware Co., SE Pennsylvania, just SW of Philadelphia. A residential and industrial suburb, it was settled by Quakers in 1682.

Dardanelle city, pop. 3722, co-seat (with Danville) of Yell Co., WC Arkansas, on the Arkansas R. and L. Dardanelle, 3 mi/5 km SSW of RUSSELLVILLE. The site of a former Indian post, it was here that the Cherokee leader Black Fox signed an 1820 treaty ceding territory S of the Arkansas R. to the US. Today it is a trade center for a farming and lumbering area, and has sawmills and other light industry.

Darien 1. town, pop. 18,196, Fairfield Co., SW Connecticut, adjacent (E) to Stamford, on Long Island Sound. Settled in 1640, it was part of Stamford until 1773. Darien is an affluent suburb, many of whose residents commute to New York City; it has some corporate headquarters, and recreational facilities include boating harbors and beaches. Noroton and Noroton Heights villages are within the township. **2.** village, pop. 18,341, Du Page Co., NE Illinois, 20 mi/32 km SW of downtown Chicago. A residential community, it is immediately N of Argonne National Laboratory.

Darke County 600 sq mi/1554 sq km, pop. 53,619, in extreme W Ohio, on the Indiana border. Its seat is GREENVILLE, where there is some manufacturing. Largely rural, it is supported mainly by agriculture, including fruit, grain, livestock, tobacco, and tomato farming. Gravel and clay are natural resources.

Darlington **1.** see under NEWCASTLE, Ontario. **2.** city, pop. 7311, seat of Darlington Co., NE South Carolina, 10 mi/16 km NNW of Florence. It was settled in 1798. In a rich farming region, Darlington is a major trade and warehouse center for locally produced tobacco and cotton, and produces cotton cloth, cottonseed oil, and wood veneer. A brief local revolt (1894) against stringent antiliquor laws was dubbed the "Darlington War." The Darlington Raceway, a stock car mecca just W of the city, holds two 500-mi/800-km races annually, and a major dragway is nearby.

Dartmouth **1.** town, pop. 27,244, Bristol Co., SE Massachusetts, 6 mi/10 km SW of New Bedford, at the mouth of Buzzards Bay. A former shipbuilding center, it now has fishing and dairying industries and is a summer resort. Southeastern Massachusetts University (1895) is in the North Dartmouth section. **2.** city, pop. 67,798, Halifax Co., SC Nova Scotia, on the E side of Halifax Harbour. Through much of its history a small town providing agricultural produce for Halifax, a mile away by ferry, it had brief importance as a whaling port at the end of the 18th century. In the 19th century the development of waterpower led to the beginnings of industry. But it was not until the opening of bridges in 1955 and 1970 that Dartmouth boomed. Today it is not only home to many of Halifax's workers, but a commercial and industrial center. Manufactures include refined oil and sugar, beer, and electrical and automotive products. Burnside Industrial Park (1968) is one of the Maritimes' major such facilities. Dartmouth is also noted for its shopping malls and service industries and as a center of oceanographic research (the Bedford Institute, 1962). It is popularly called "City of Lakes," having 22 within its limits.

Daufuskie Island one of the SEA ISLANDS, c.5 mi/8 km long, in Beaufort Co., extreme S South Carolina, on the Atlantic shore at the mouth of the New R., 13 mi/21 km NE of Savannah, Georgia, and just SW of HILTON HEAD I. Once the rural home of descendants of former slaves, it is now undergoing resort development.

Dauphin town, pop. 8453, SW Manitoba, 160 mi/258 km NW of Winnipeg, and 12 mi/19 km W of the S end of L. Dauphin. Situated in the fertile lowlands of the Vermilion R., it was founded in 1741 near a French trading post. An agricultural distribution and retail center, it is involved in lumbering and fishing as well. The National Ukrainian Festival is held every August, celebrating Ukrainian settlements of the late 1890s. RIDING MOUNTAIN NATIONAL PARK is just S.

Dauphin County 528 sq mi/1367 sq km, pop. 237,813, in SE Pennsylvania, bordered (SW and W) by the Susquehanna R. Its seat is Harrisburg, also the state capital. It is divided into two sections by the BLUE Mts., which run SW across the county, separating it into a coal mining region (N) and an agricultural/industrial region (S). The county also includes suburban areas around Harrisburg.

Dauphin Island island town, c.14 mi/23 km E–W and 75 sq mi/194 sq km, pop. 824, in the Gulf of Mexico at the SW entrance to Mobile Bay, in Mobile Co., SW Alabama. It is the site of the earliest permanent European settlement (1701) in Alabama, which provided a base for further colonization in Louisiana. Passing through Spanish and British hands later in the 18th century, it was captured by the US in 1813. Fort Gaines (1822), on the E end, was occupied by the Confederacy from 1861 until the Battle of Mobile Bay in Aug. 1864. Current residential development followed the opening of a bridge from the mainland in 1954.

Davenport city, pop. 95,333, seat of Scott Co., SE Iowa, on the Mississippi R., opposite Rock Island and East Moline, Illinois. It is the largest of the QUAD CITIES, a major rail center, a shipping point for grain, and the site of a variety of industries. One of the world's largest aluminum rolling mills is here. Manufactures include airplane parts and accessories, tractor parts, wheels, and cement, wood, and flour and meat products. Settlers set up a trading post in 1808, and the treaty ending the Black Hawk War was signed here in 1832, after which Davenport was laid out. It grew rapidly, especially with the construction of the first railroad bridge across the Mississippi R. in 1856. Chiropractic was introduced here by D. D. Palmer in 1895, and Palmer College of Chiropractic is the first institution of its kind. Davenport is also the seat of St. Ambrose University (1882) and Marycrest College (1939). The state's largest historic district, 60 square blocks, is here.

David City city, pop. 2522, seat of Butler Co., E Nebraska, 19 mi/30 km SE of Columbus. It is a processing center for livestock, dairy products, and grain and has some light industry, including the production of high-quality violins.

Davidson town, pop. 4046, Mecklenburg Co., SC North Carolina, 18 mi/29 km N of Charlotte, on the E side of L. Norman (the Catawba R.). It is the seat of Davidson College (1837), affiliated with the Presbyterian Church.

Davidson, Mount **1.** highest of 40-odd peaks in SAN FRANCISCO, California, 938 ft/286 m tall, SW of Twin Peaks and SE of the Sunset District, 4 mi/6 km SW of Downtown. A 103-ft/31-m cross crowns the summit, the site of an Easter sunrise ecumenical service. **2.** see under COMSTOCK LODE and VIRGINIA Mts., Nevada.

Davidson County **1.** 548 sq mi/1419 sq km, pop. 126,677, in C North Carolina, in the Piedmont, bounded (W and S) by the Yadkin R. Its seat is LEXINGTON. Its agricultural output includes tobacco, corn, wheat, and dairy products. Textile and other industries are centered in THOMASVILLE and Lexington. **2.** see under NASHVILLE, Tennessee.

Davie town, pop. 47,217, Broward Co., SE Florida, just SW of Fort Lauderdale. A residential (largely retirement) community, it doubled in population in the 1980s.

Davis city, pop. 46,209, Yolo Co., NC California, on Putah Creek, in the Sacramento Valley, 14 mi/23 km W of Sacramento. Founded in the 1850s as a farm by Jerome C. Davis, the community is a trade center for a region producing barley, wheat, rice, alfalfa, sugar beets, beans, and tomatoes, and has food processing, biotechnical, veterinary supply, and other light industries. In 1905, the University of California established a branch campus here with an experimental farm, now its College of Agriculture. The present Davis campus, occupying 4000 ac/1620 ha, also includes the schools of Veterinary Medicine (1948), Law (1966), and Medicine (1968). The National Primate Center (1962) and D-Q (Deganawidah-Quetzalcoatl) University (1971) are also here. The city is noted for its university-based research facilities and social life.

Davis, Mount also, **Davis Mountain** 3213 ft/980 m, in Somerset Co., SW Pennsylvania, the highest point in the state, in the Negro Mt. chain, 23 mi/37 km NW of Cumberland, Maryland.

Davis-Besse nuclear power plant: see under OTTAWA Co., Ohio.

Davis-Monthan Air Force Base see under TUCSON, Arizona.

Davis Mountains small range in SW Texas, extending generally N from near Marfa, in Presidio Co. The second-highest range in the state, it rises from a plateau of 4000–5000 ft/1200–1500 m, and is topped by Mt. LIVERMORE, at 8382 ft/2557 m. Mt. LOCKE, site of the McDonald Observatory, and Black Mt. (7550 ft/2301 m) are also in the range. Because they are in the path of moisture-bearing winds, these mountains are greener than others in the TRANS-PECOS region. The range was named in the 1850s for Jefferson Davis, then US Secretary of War. A vacation area, it encompasses Davis Mts. State Park, FORT DAVIS National Historic Site, and the San Solomon Springs at the N base of the mountains. The Barilla Mts., rising to 5560 ft/1700 m, are E.

Davis Strait N arm of the Atlantic Ocean, leading to BAFFIN BAY (N), between Greenland (E) and BAFFIN I. (W), in the Northwest Territories. Some 400 mi/640 km N-S and 200–400 mi/320–640 km wide, it is navigable from July to Nov., with most of its ports on the Greenland side. The cold Labrador Current flows down its W side, carrying numerous icebergs S, while on the E side the warmer West Greenland Current flows N. The strait was named for the English navigator John Davis, who explored it in 1585–87.

Davy Crockett Birthplace State Park 10 mi/16 km ENE of GREENEVILLE, in Greene Co., E Tennessee, on the Nolichucky R. A replica of the log cabin in which Crockett was born in 1786 is here. There are other Tennessee Crockett sites: Near MORRISTOWN is a reproduction of his boyhood home and the tavern built by father John Crockett. In Rutherford, Gibson Co., in the NW, is the reconstruction, with logs from the original, of a cabin Davy built. Just W of LAWRENCEBURG is David Crockett State Park; Davy lived here (1817–22) while in the Tennessee legislature, and a reconstruction of the gristmill he operated is near the original Shoal Creek site.

Davy Crockett Lake see under NOLICHUCKY R., Tennessee.

Davy Crockett National Forest 162,000 ac/65,600 ha, in the PINEY WOODS of E Texas, on the Neches R. (E). It is one of four national forests in the area devoted to mixed recreational and forest industry use.

Dawson also, **Dawson City** town, pop. 972, WC Yukon Territory, at the mouth of the KLONDIKE R. on the Yukon R., 50 mi/80 km E of the Alaska border, 250 mi/400 km ESE of Fairbanks, and 165 mi/265 km S of the Arctic Circle. Established in 1896, it developed rapidly after the BONANZA CREEK gold strike of 1896, just SE, and became briefly the largest W Canadian city, with a pop. as high as 25,000. From 1898 to 1953, it was the Yukon Territory's administrative center, but changes in mining technology and the gold market caused gradual decline; some gold dredging continued until 1966. Dawson is now a tourist and local trade center, with sites associated with the gold rushers and with writers Jack London and Robert W. Service.

Dawson Creek city, pop. 10,981, Peace River Regional District, NE British Columbia, on Dawson Creek, near the Alberta border, 166 mi/267 km NE of Prince George. It is the terminus of the British Columbia Railway and the S entrance to the ALASKA HIGHWAY. In an oil, coal, and gas producing and hunting and fishing area, it refines oil, has trucking facilities, and produces lumber, livestock, and grains. The highway brings tourism, and hydroelectric projects on the Peace R. have also contributed to the economy.

Dayton 1. see under SOUTH BRUNSWICK, New Jersey. **2.** city, pop. 182,044, seat of Montgomery Co., SW Ohio, 45 mi/72 km NNE of Cincinnati, at the junction of the Great Miami R. and three smaller tributaries, the Stillwater and Mad rivers and Wolf Creek. The area was originally a Shawnee hunting ground. Settlement dates from 1796; Dayton was incorporated as a city in 1841. Early growth was based on the shipment of agricultural products along the Miami Canal, and trade with the South assumed great importance. Later, the Civil War spurred Dayton's industrial development. A vital trading center for the surrounding agricultural area, today's city depends largely on extremely diversified light manufacturing for its economic well-being. Office and electrical equipment (National Cash Register was long the dominant company), automotive parts, and paper products are among items produced. Dayton has long been prominent in aviation; the Wright brothers owned a bicycle shop here where they conducted their first flight experiments. Wright-Patterson Air Force Base, just NE, is a leading employer. The Air Force Institute of Technology and Air Force Museum are in the city. Among Dayton's cultural institutions are the Art Institute and Museum of Natural History. Its institutions of higher learning include the University of Dayton (1850), Sinclair Community College (1887), and Wright State University (1964). **3.** city, pop. 5671, seat of Rhea Co., SE Tennessee, 36 mi/58 km NE of Chattanooga, on Richland Creek, just NW of Chickamauga L. Smith's Crossroads (1820) was renamed in 1895 for Dayton, Ohio. It is best known for the "Monkey Trial" of biology teacher John Scopes, accused of teaching evolution, held at the county courthouse July 10–21, 1925, which attracted worldwide attention, augmented by live radio coverage, because of the subject and because it involved two of the most famous personalities of the time: William Jennings Bryan aided the prosecution, and Clarence Darrow was the lead defense attorney. Five days after winning the case Bryan died. William Jennings Bryan College was founded here in 1930 as a memorial. The courthouse has a museum on the trial. Dayton, a trade center, also attracts tourists.

Daytona Beach city, pop. 61,921, Volusia Co., NE Florida, on both sides of the Halifax R. (a lagoon) and the Atlantic Coast, 50 mi/80 km SSE of St. Augustine. Settled in the 1870s, the present city was formed from the consolidation of three municipalities in 1926. Its hard white-sand beaches, 23 mi/37 km long and 500 ft/150 m wide at low tide, were the site of automobile trials that set many speed records in 1902–35. The beach is now central to the city's role (succeeding FORT LAUDERDALE) as the spring break mecca for college students. The city remains a racing center, with its Daytona International Speedway (just SW). Mainstays of its economy are tourism, the processing and packing of citrus and vegetables from local farms, boatbuilding, and the aerospace industry. The city is the seat of Bethune-Cookman College (1904) and Daytona Beach Community College (1958).

Deadwood city, pop. 1830, seat of Lawrence Co., W South Dakota, 27 mi/43 km NW of Rapid City, in the Black Hills.

Much of the city clings to steep canyon walls. Founded during the gold rush (1876), it was a frontier boom town that became emblematic of the Old WEST. The graves of Wild Bill Hickock, Calamity Jane, and Deadwood Dick are in Mt. Moriah Cemetery, also known as Boot Hill. Today the city has a thriving tourist industry. Buildings have been restored, and the entire downtown is a National Landmark. Gambling is legal, and there are historical museums, street "gunfights," a steam-powered railroad, and gold mine tours. A "Days of 76" celebration featuring rodeos and parades is held annually. Deadwood is also a trading center for the surrounding mining and cattle ranching area. Jewelry, gold, quartz, and cyanide are produced. The city took its name from Deadwood Gulch, which had been burned over.

Dealey Plaza in downtown Dallas, Texas, in the W end of the business district. It is the open area in which President John F. Kennedy was assassinated on Nov. 22, 1963, as his motorcade approached an underpass to the plaza's W. On the plaza's NE corner is the former Texas School Book Depository Building, from which shots were fired that day; at the top of the plaza, W of the Book Depository, is the Grassy Knoll, from which, according to some witnesses, shots were also fired.

Dearborn city, pop. 89,286, Wayne Co., SE Michigan, on the R. Rouge, adjoining Detroit on the SW. It was founded in 1795 as a stage stop on the Sauk (Chicago) Trail between Chicago and Detroit. It had several names before becoming Dearborn in honor of Revolutionary general Henry Dearborn. The birthplace (1863) of Henry Ford, it became the site of his huge River Rouge automobile assembly plant (1917), which brought over 200 other enterprises to the city. Dearborn is headquarters for the Ford Motor Co. and the location of much of its research, engineering, and manufacturing activity. The first contract for an air mail service originated here, as did the Ford Trimotor, America's first all-metal multiengine commercial airliner. In addition to automobiles, Dearborn has corporate headquarters and manufactures including plated metals, aircraft parts, computers, and tools and dies. Ford's Greenfield Village features more than 80 American buildings, including Buckminster Fuller's Dymaxion House (1948), and the Henry Ford Museum spotlights US social history and technology. Fair Lane, the Ford estate, is also here. Dearborn is the site of Henry Ford Community College (1938) and a branch of the University of Michigan (1959).

Dearborn Heights city, pop. 60,838, Wayne Co., SE Michigan, a residential suburb 8 mi/13 km W of Detroit.

Death Valley National Park, c.3.4 million ac/1.377 million ha (5312 sq mi/13,760 sq km), created in 1994, enlarging a national monument, proclaimed in 1933, covering 2.068 million ac/837,400 ha (3231 sq mi/8368 sq km) in the MOJAVE DESERT, in SE California. Called by local tribes Tomesha ("ground afire"), it gained its English name from 1849 goldseekers. Some 120 mi/190 km N–S, and 4–16 mi/6–26 km wide, it was formed by the breaking of the earth's crust into blocks, and sank while surrounding mountains rose. The PANAMINT RANGE forms its W wall, the AMARGOSA RANGE the E. The valley falls to −282 ft/−86 m at Badwater (the lowest point in the Western Hemisphere), while TELESCOPE PEAK (11,049 ft/3368 m) stands above it. Inhabited by some 900 plant and animal species, it is visited largely in winter, as summer daytime temperatures have reached 134° F/57° C. Some gold mining was done here in the 19th century, but the valley's chief product has been borax, taken in the 1880s by mule team to Mojave, on the railroad 165 mi/266 km SW. Furnace Creek (EC) is the area's visitor center; Stovepipe Wells (NC) is another roadside settlement. Just SW of Furnace Creek are the noted lookouts Zabriskie Point (710 ft/216 m) and Dante's View (5000 ft/1525 m). In the far N are the huge Ubehebe Crater (volcanic) and Scotty's Castle, an elaborate 1920s home once inhabited by the mysterious Death Valley Scotty.

Decatur **1.** city, pop. 48,761, seat of Morgan Co., N Alabama, on the S bank of the Tennessee R. (Wheeler L.), 23 mi/37 km SW of Huntsville. Founded in 1820, it became in 1832 the terminus of Alabama's first railroad, from TUSCUMBIA. The city was nearly destroyed during the Civil War, when it was occupied by both Confederate and Union troops. In 1927 it consolidated with neighboring Albany. Diverse industries developed, stimulated by TENNESSEE VALLEY AUTHORITY power. Decatur is a market and shipping center for local farms, a manufacturer of hosiery, metal products, textiles, tires, barges, air conditioning equipment, and chemicals, and the home of John C. Calhoun State Community College (1963). **2.** city, pop. 17,336, seat of De Kalb Co., NW Georgia, adjacent (E) to Atlanta. Incorporated in 1823, it was a prosperous agricultural trade center, and refused to allow the Western & Atlantic Railroad to come within its limits. The railroad then built its tracks to Terminus, now Atlanta. Decatur became a suburb. Agnes Scott College (1889) and Columbia Theological Seminary are here. **3.** city, pop. 83,885, seat of Macon Co., C Illinois, in the geographic center of the state, on the Sangamon R. where it is dammed to form L. Decatur, 36 mi/58 km E of Springfield. Its central location makes it an important communications, railway, and distribution center. The city has many processing mills for the soybeans and corn grown in the area. Decatur also manufactures iron, steel, and brass products as well as auto parts, tractors, tires, electronic components, and clothing. The Republican State Convention formally endorsed Abraham Lincoln as a presidential candidate in Decatur in 1860. Six years later, the Grand Army of the Republic, a Civil War veterans' organization, was founded here. Millikin University (1901) is here. The Lincoln Trail Homestead State Park and Memorial is 7 mi/11 km SW and the 1323-ac/536-ac Rock Springs Center for Environmental Discovery is 3 mi/5 km SW. **4.** city, pop. 8644, seat of Adams Co., E Indiana, 20 mi/32 km SE of Fort Wayne, on the St. Mary's R. Settled in 1837, it developed as a trade center for an agricultural and lumbering area. Cheese, beet sugar, soybean oil, and timber are processed, and tile and cement products manufactured.

Decatur Street commercial thoroughfare in Atlanta, Georgia. It proceeds SE and E from FIVE POINTS, paralleling railroad tracks, and joins De Kalb Ave. before passing into DECATUR. In Downtown it is home to Georgia State University (1913) and was in the early 20th century the East Side's leading entertainment zone.

Decorah city, pop. 8063, seat of Winneshiek Co., NE Iowa, on the Upper Iowa R., 63 mi/101 km NE of Waterloo and 15 mi/24 km S of the Minnesota border. Settled by Norwegians in 1849, it is a processing and shipping center for grain, dairy cattle, hogs, and poultry. There is also a variety of light industries. Nearby are limestone quarries and fish hatcheries. Luther College (1861) is here, as is the Vesterheim/Norwegian-American Museum. A Nordic Fest is held every July. Fort Atkinson State Park is 13 mi/21 km SW.

Dedham town, pop. 23,782, seat of Norfolk Co., E Massachusetts, on the Neponset and Charles rivers, 8 mi/13 km SW of Boston. Founded in 1635, it is one of the oldest inland settlements of the MASSACHUSETTS BAY COLONY. Fairbanks House is believed to be the oldest (1636) existing frame dwelling in the US. The Sacco-Vanzetti murder trial took place here in 1921. Dedham today is a residential suburb of Boston with several commercial strips and some light manufacturing.

Deep Creek Range 35 mi/60 km NNE–SSW, just E of the Nevada border and SW of the Great Salt Lake Desert, in WC Utah. The highest in W Utah, it has glacial CIRQUES and granite peaks, and reaches 12,087 ft/3684 m at Ibapah Peak and 12,020 ft/3664 m at Haystack Peak. The range is snow-covered in winter, its runoff creating trout streams on the E slope. The mountains have been mined for gold, silver, copper, lead, uranium, and zinc.

Deep Ellum commercial district in DALLAS, Texas, along Elm St., 0.6 mi/1 km NE of Downtown. The area was settled after the Civil War by ex-slaves, and called Freedman's Town. In the early 20th century, it was a famous black shopping and entertainment strip; construction of the CENTRAL EXPRESSWAY and World War II ended its heyday, but it has recently revived as a restaurant, gallery, and nightclub district.

Deephaven see under L. MINNETONKA, Minnesota.

Deep South, the see under the SOUTH.

Deerfield 1. village, pop. 17,327, Cook and Lake counties, NE Illinois, on the North Branch of the Chicago R., 25 mi/40 km NW of Chicago. It is a largely residential suburb, with some industries producing earth-moving equipment and pharmaceutical and hospital supplies. The Kitchens of Sara Lee baking plant is also headquartered here. Settled in 1835 as Cadwell's Corners, Deerfield was the site of an unsuccessful attempt at integrating a public housing project in the late 1950s; Harry and David Rosen describe the effort in *But Not Next Door.* Trinity College (1897) is here. **2.** town, pop. 5018, Franklin Co., NW Massachusetts, on the Connecticut and Deerfield rivers, 35 mi/56 km N of Springfield. Founded in the 1660s, it retains a Colonial flavor today; the town has carefully preserved its period architecture and tone. Deerfield was the target of repeated attacks during King Philip's War (1675), including the Bloody Brook massacre; during an Indian raid of 1704, 49 were killed, more than 100 taken prisoner, and the village was burned. After peace resumed, the town prospered as an agricultural community. The Deerfield Academy (1797), a noted preparatory school, is here.

Deerfield Beach city, pop. 46,325, Broward Co., SE Florida, 15 mi/24 km N of Fort Lauderdale, on the Atlantic Coast. A popular beachfront vacation community, it is also a processing and shipping center for numerous nearby truck farms.

Deer Island peninsula, part of the city of Boston, Massachusetts, but attached to the town of WINTHROP. It is on the N side of BOSTON HARBOR, 1 mi/1.5 km E of Logan International Airport, and has been the site of harbor fortifications, cemeteries, and Boston's jail.

Deer Isle 11 mi/18 km long, up to 8 mi/13 km wide, in Hancock Co., SC Maine. It is in Penobscot Bay, separated from the Blue Hill peninsula by the famous sailing passage Eggemoggin Reach. The main settlement is the town of Stonington, pop. 1252, at the S end. Deer Isle was an active 18th-century port, and once had a customs house, sawmill, and gristmill. It was home to sea captains who prospered from slave running, smuggling, and the China and East India trade. Fishing, sardine packing, and boat building are now important industries. The area is known for its pink granite, used for New York's Triborough Bridge. The Haystack Mt. School of Crafts is at Sunshine, at Deer Isle's E extremity. The town of Deer Isle, pop. 1829, incorporates numerous smaller islands.

Deer Lake town, pop. 4327, W Newfoundland, on the Humber R., at the N end of Deer L., 29 mi/47 km NE of CORNER BROOK, on the Trans-Canada Highway. It is a lumbering and sawmilling center. A hydroelectric plant here powers Corner Brook's mills.

Deer Lodge city, pop. 3378, seat of Powell Co., WC Montana, on the Clark Fork R., 30 mi/48 km NNW of Butte. Situated just E of the Flint Creek Range, it has silver and lead mining, a lumber mill, and railroad repair shops. It also markets agricultural products. Called La Barge when founded (1862), Deer Lodge was a gold-mining center and an important stop on the Mullan Wagon Road, an immigrant route. The Montana Territorial Prison (1871), the first such institution in the West, is now a law enforcement museum. The Grant-Kohrs Ranch National Historic Site, established in 1853 and a large and early ranching operation, is 3 mi/5 km N.

Deer Lodge County see ANACONDA, Montana.

Deerlodge National Forest 1.2 million ac/480,000 ha (1870 sq mi/4835 sq km), in W Montana, in two units roughly surrounding BUTTE. Mt. Evans (10,635 ft/3242 m), in the Pintlar Range, is the highest of its many peaks. The forest has many open (grassy) and timbered slopes, as well as alpine scenery.

Deer Park 1. unincorporated village, pop. 28,840, in Babylon town, Suffolk Co., SE New York, in C Long Island. It is a residential community with some light industry. **2.** city, pop. 27,652, Harris Co., SE Texas, on the S side of the Houston Ship Channel (Buffalo Bayou), 15 mi/24 km ESE of downtown Houston. It is a largely industrial suburb of Houston that grew quickly in the 1960s and 1970s. Refrigerators, plastics, and chemicals are manufactured here, and there are shipping-related industries. SAN JACINTO is immediately NE.

Defiance 1. hamlet in St. Charles Co., EC Missouri, on the Missouri R., just S of Femme Osage Creek and 30 mi/48 km W of downtown St. Louis. Frontiersman Daniel Boone settled here in 1799, having been awarded the judgeship of the Femme Osage District by Spanish authorities. His sons established a salt production center at BOONE'S LICK, 120 mi/190 km WNW, supplying the growing St. Louis area. Boone died here in 1820; his home draws visitors. **2.** city, pop. 16,768, seat of Defiance Co., NW Ohio, 60 mi/97 km SW of Toledo, at the junction of the Auglaize and Maumee rivers. It grew up around the Indian-fighting Fort Defiance, built in 1794 by General Anthony Wayne, and still visible as earthworks in the city park. The great Ottawa chief Pontiac is thought to have been born here. Some of the largest stands of trees planted by Johnny Appleseed are found in the area. Today Defiance is a trading and shipping center for a region of diverse agriculture. Local manufactures include metals, automotive parts, food products, and radio and TV capacitors. Defiance College (1850) is here.

De Forest, Lake see under HACKENSACK R.

De Kalb city, pop. 34,925, De Kalb Co., NC Illinois, on the South Branch of the Kishwaukee R., 30 mi/48 km SE of Rockford. Barbed wire was perfected and first manufactured here. Today, local manufactures include wire and cable, fencing, truck bodies, asphalt paving equipment, and appliance motors. Hybrid seed corn and chickens are processed, and truck gardening is important in the area. Founded in 1838 as Buena Vista, De Kalb is also the location of Northern Illinois University (1895). The American Farm Bureau was founded here in 1912.

De Kalb County **1.** 270 sq mi/699 sq km, pop. 545,837, in NW Georgia. Its seat is DECATUR. It contains STONE Mt. and many of adjacent ATLANTA's E residential and industrial suburbs. **2.** 634 sq mi/1642 sq km, pop. 77,932, in NC Illinois. Its seat is Sycamore. Most of the county is agricultural, raising sweet corn and poultry. There is manufacturing at DE KALB and Sycamore. The South Branch of the Kishwaukee R. flows through De Kalb; Shabbona Lake State Park is in the SW.

De Land also, **Deland** city, pop. 16,491, seat of Volusia Co., NE Florida, 20 mi/32 km SW of Daytona Beach. Founded in 1876, it was the site, during the 1880s, of Chinese immigrant Lue Gim Gong's development of important strains of oranges and grapefruit. These and other fruits are grown nearby, and De Land serves as a packing and shipping center. The city also has lumber mills, and manufactures electrical and electronic parts, medical equipment, and clothing. It is now a popular winter resort. Stetson University (1883) is here.

Delano city, pop. 22,762, Kern Co., SC California, 30 mi/48 km NNW of Bakersfield, in the San Joaquin Valley. It is a trade center for an area noted for the production of table grapes and wine; cotton and potatoes are also raised in the region, and there is some light industry. Delano is widely known as the birthplace of the United Farm Workers, first organized here in 1962 by Cesar Chavez.

Delano Peak see under TUSHAR Mts., Utah.

Delaware state of the NE US, in the Middle Atlantic region; 1990 pop. 666,168 (112.1% of 1980; rank: 46th); area 2489 sq mi/6447 sq km (rank: 49th); ratified Constitution 1787 (1st, from which it is popularly called "the First State"). Capital: DOVER. Most populous city: WILMINGTON. Delaware is bordered N by Pennsylvania, and W and S by Maryland, with which it shares the upper part of the DELMARVA PENINSULA. On the E are (N–S) the mouth of the Delaware R., Delaware Bay, and the Atlantic Ocean. The entire state lies in the Atlantic COASTAL PLAIN, with the exception of a small PIEDMONT area in the extreme N, where the land of NEW CASTLE Co. rises to 442 ft/135 m. Outside the Wilmington area, the state is largely rural and agricultural, with scattered small industrial centers and fishing communities. Barrier beaches below Cape HENLOPEN (SE) are the site of several resorts, esp. REHOBOTH BEACH, which is popular with vacationers from Washington, D.C. The Lenni Lenape lived here when Europeans first arrived; the river, bay, Indians, and eventually the state, all acquired the name "Delaware" after the first Colonial governor of Virginia, Lord de la Warr. The Dutch settled in the area (at LEWES) in the 1630s; NEW SWEDEN later incorporated part of it; and the British took control in 1674. The LOWER COUNTIES, as Delaware was then called, separated from the governance of Pennsylvania in 1704. Through the 18th century Delaware was a rural backwater. In 1802, E. I. DuPont established, on the BRANDYWINE CREEK just N of downtown Wilmington, a gunpowder mill that began an industrial empire. While the state has more diversified industry today, the DuPont firm's production of munitions and, in the 20th century, of all sorts of chemicals and synthetics, has dominated its economy. The DuPont family has also long dominated Delaware politics and culture. The other great source of Delaware wealth has been the enactment of liberal corporation (in the early 20th century) and banking (in the 1980s) laws, leading to the location here of many corporate and financial headquarters. A slaveholding BORDER STATE, Delaware remained in the Union during the Civil War; its character in all but the Wilmington area, however, remains markedly Southern. (The Census Bureau designates the state "South Atlantic.") Poultry and truck farming, fishing and shellfishing are important. The University of Delaware is near Wilmington, at NEWARK. The northernmost part of the state, site of the large estates of DuPonts and others, is popularly called the Chateau Country.

Delaware city, pop. 20,030, seat of Delaware Co., C Ohio, on the Olentangy R., 25 mi/40 km N of Columbus. Center of a fertile farming area, it was founded in 1808. Delaware is the birthplace of President Rutherford B. Hayes (1822) and the seat of Ohio Wesleyan University (1842). Local manufactures include air conditioners, gas ranges, truck bodies, valves, machine screws, and wood products.

Delaware Bay broad estuary at the mouth of the DELAWARE R., between E Delaware and SW New Jersey. Fifty-two mi/84 km NW–SE and 12 mi/19 km wide at its entrance, the bay enters the Atlantic Ocean between CAPE MAY, New Jersey, and Cape HENLOPEN, Delaware. The Chesapeake and Delaware Canal links the bay and river with CHESAPEAKE BAY.

Delaware County **1.** 1440 sq mi/3730 sq km, pop. 47,225, S New York, in the W part of the Catskill Mts., bounded by the Delaware R. (SW). Its seat is Delhi. There are numerous mountain and ski resorts in the county, which is otherwise largely agricultural, with dairying predominant. **2.** 184 sq mi/477 sq km, pop. 547,651, in SE Pennsylvania, bordered (S) by the Delaware R. and the Delaware state line. Its seat is Media. The county contains several suburbs of Philadelphia, including CHESTER and UPPER DARBY.

Delaware Mountains barren, rugged range in SW Texas, extending NW–SE for nearly 40 mi/64 km between the Guadalupe Mts. (NW) and the Apache Mts. (SE). The Delawares reach to 5870 ft/1790 m, forming part of the E border of the DIABLO BOLSON.

Delaware River 315 mi/507 km long, in New York, Pennsylvania, New Jersey, and Delaware. It is formed at Hancock, Delaware Co., New York, by the confluence of the 75-mi/120-km **East Branch** (the PEPACTON) and the 90-mi/145-km **West Branch,** both of which flow from the SW Catskill Mts. From Hancock the river flows generally SE, forming the New York-Pennsylvania border, to PORT JERVIS, New York. There it curves SW and becomes the Pennsylvania-New Jersey boundary. Some 33 mi/53 km SW, it creates the **Delaware Water Gap,** turning SE through KITTATINNY Mt. Continuing SSE, then SW, it receives the LEHIGH R. at Easton, and turns SE again, to Trenton, New Jersey, the head of navigation, on the FALL LINE. From Trenton it flows SW between Philadelphia and Camden, then between New Jersey and Delaware, into Delaware Bay and the Atlantic Ocean. The river is an important source of hydroelectric power for the Northeast. Its chief tributaries are the Neversink, Musconetcong, Lackawaxen, Schuylkill, and Lehigh rivers. It was explored by Henry Hudson in 1609, and its first European settlements were Dutch and Swedish. The river's name, from Lord de la Warr, governor of Virginia in 1610, came also to be applied to the area's native inhabitants, the Lenni Lenape (or Delaware).

Del City city, pop. 23,928, Oklahoma Co., C Oklahoma, a residential suburb 6 mi/10 km SE of downtown Oklahoma City. It was combined with the village of Midway in 1963.

Delhi Hills unincorporated community in Delhi township, Hamilton Co., extreme SW Ohio, a NW suburb of Cincinnati, on the Ohio R. just N of the Kentucky border.

Dells of the Wisconsin also, **the Dells** gorge in the Wisconsin R., in Adams, Juneau, Sauk, and Columbia counties, SC Wisconsin. Measuring 8 mi/13 km long and reaching a depth of 150 ft/46 m, they are a series of sandstone bluffs, ravines, and unusual rock formations carved out by the river over a period of 30,000 years. Recreational facilities are centered in the village of Wisconsin Dells, and the Dells are a very popular tourist attraction.

Dellwood city, pop. 5245, St. Louis Co., EC Missouri, 10 mi/16 km NNW of downtown St. Louis, a residential suburb.

Del Mar city, pop. 4860, San Diego Co., SW California, on the Pacific Ocean, 17 mi/27 km NNW of downtown San Diego. SOLANA BEACH is just N, the TORREY PINES just S. An affluent resort, it is noted for its beaches and for the Del Mar Racetrack, at the county fairgrounds, a horse facility frequented since the 1930s by Hollywood and other notables.

Delmarva Peninsula containing parts of Delaware, Maryland, and Virginia, and bordered by CHESAPEAKE BAY (W), Delaware Bay (NE), and the Atlantic Ocean (E). Approximately 180 mi/290 km N–S, it is connected to the Virginia mainland (S) by the Chesapeake Bay Bridge-Tunnel. The peninsula is low and sandy, with an irregular coast; a number of barrier islands, including ASSATEAGUE and CHINCOTEAGUE, are to the E. Its W side is often referred to as the EASTERN SHORE region of Maryland and Virginia. The peninsula has a large fishing industry, some poultry and truck farming, and many popular resort areas.

Del Norte Mountains see under SANTIAGO MTS., Texas.

Delran township, pop. 13,178, Burlington Co., W New Jersey, 10 mi/16 km NE of Camden. On the Delaware R. and Rancocas Creek, it is a largely residential suburb of Philadelphia.

Delray residential neighborhood of Detroit, Michigan, 5 mi/8 km SW of Downtown, near the confluence of the R. Rouge and the Detroit R. A Hungarian immigrant community from c.1900, it now also houses middle-class blacks.

Delray Beach city, pop. 47,181, Palm Beach Co., SE Florida, on the Atlantic Ocean, 20 mi/32 km NNE of Fort Lauderdale. Essentially a resort and residential community, it has some business and light industry. It is also a center for citrus, vegetable, chrysanthemum, and gladiolus production. The Morikami Museum reflects the traditions of the many Japanese who settled in the area early in the 20th century. The 145,000-ac/59,000-ha Loxahatchee National Wildlife Refuge is W of the city.

Del Rio city, pop. 30,705, seat of Val Verde Co., SW Texas, on the Rio Grande opposite Ciudad Acuña (Coahuila), Mexico, 145 mi/236 km W of San Antonio. It is a port of entry and the market center for a ranching area producing wool, mohair, and lamb. The name derives from a Spanish mission, San Felipe del Rio, here c.1675. The present community dates from 1868, when San Felipe Springs was used to irrigate farms. Just E is Laughlin Air Force Base, and the AMISTAD Reservoir and National Recreation Area are just NW. Del Rio was famous in the 1930s as the home of XERA, the best-known of the powerful "border" radio stations that broadcast from transmitters in Mexico.

Delta **1.** district municipality, pop. 88,978, Greater Vancouver Regional District, SW British Columbia, on a peninsula between the Fraser R. (N) and Boundary Bay (S), 12 mi/19 km SSE of downtown Vancouver. A residential suburb expanding into an agricultural area, it has truck gardens and dairy farms. Industries include fish canning, food processing, and paper milling. Ferries to Vancouver I., the Gulf Is., and other points leave from Tsawwassen terminal. The S part of the peninsula, Point Roberts, S of the 49TH PARALLEL, is part of the state of Washington, and is unconnected to other US territory. **2.** city, pop. 2998, Millard Co., WC Utah, 30 mi/48 km NW of Fillmore and 104 mi/167 km SSW of Salt Lake City, near the SEVIER R. in the Pahvant Valley, on the E edge of the GREAT BASIN. From 1905 it was developed as an irrigated farming center, producing esp. alfalfa seed. A large beryllium processing plant is here. Topaz, some 15 mi/24 km NW, is the site of a camp where over 8000 Americans of Japanese descent were interned in 1942–45.

Delta, the **1.** in E Arkansas, alluvial areas along the Mississippi R. opposite the upper part of Mississippi's "Delta." CROWLEY'S RIDGE and the St. Francis R. run N–S through the area, in which HELENA and WEST HELENA are commercial centers. The cotton plantation economy and culture of NW Mississippi extended into this area in the late 19th century. **2.** also, **Yazoo Delta, Yazoo Basin,** or **Mississippi Delta** area of NW Mississippi, consisting of the fertile flood plain (part of the Mississippi Alluvial Plain), lying largely between the Mississippi (W) and Yazoo (E) rivers. It extends almost 200 mi/320 km from Memphis, Tennessee (N), to VICKSBURG (S), and is cut by many streams, dotted with small lakes and ponds, and protected by natural and constructed LEVEES. Lightly settled until after the Civil War, the rich alluvial land has long been used for cotton growing, and now also produces soybeans, rice, and other crops, as well as livestock and catfish. Its chief cities include GREENWOOD, GREENVILLE, CLARKSDALE, and YAZOO CITY. The DELTA NATIONAL FOREST is in its S. Depicted in the writing of William Faulkner and others, the Delta is also noted for its folk culture, particularly as the home of perhaps the earliest blues music. See also DELTA OF THE MISSISSIPPI RIVER.

Delta National Forest 60,000 ac/24,300 ha, in WC Mississippi, in Sharkey and Issaquena counties, W of Yazoo City. It is unique in the US as a hardwood (ash, oak, sweet gum) bottomland national forest. Headquarters are at ROLLING FORK, just NW.

Delta of the Mississippi River the 200-mi/320-km course of the lower Mississippi R., from its confluence with the RED R., 48 mi/74 km N of Baton Rouge, Louisiana, to its mouth in the Gulf of Mexico, 90 mi/145 km SE of New Orleans. A number of DISTRIBUTARIES carry or can carry much of the discharge of the river, chief among them the ATCHAFALAYA R., diverging 53 mi/86 km NW of Baton Rouge, which may eventually become the mainstream because of the buildup of sediment at the current mouth, which continues to spread into the Gulf at the rate of .05 mi/.08 km per year. The BAYOU LAFOURCHE, diverging at Donaldsonville, below Baton Rouge, is another important distributary, and above New Orleans a floodway can divert high water E to L. PONTCHARTRAIN. Flowing SE through rich ALLUVIAL lowlands, wooded swamplands, and salt marshes, the mainstream of the river divides into several channels (passes) 73 mi/117 km below New Orleans—Main Pass, South Pass, Southwest Pass, and Pass à Loutre. The present birdsfoot structure was probably preceded by three or more earlier ones, as alluvial deposits and coastal shifts changed the course of the river. The delta is important to the Louisiana economy, from its freshwater lakes to its brackish bayous and saltwater mouth. It is navigable for oceangoing vessels to Baton Rouge. It is teeming with mullet, redfish, sea trout, and tarpon; such swamp animals as opossum, alligators, and nutria; and shellfish, chiefly crayfish, oysters, and shrimp. Sugar cane is raised in the area, and sulfur, oil, and natural gas are extracted. At the SE tip is the Delta National Wildlife Refuge. The area is crossed by the Gulf Intracoastal Waterway, which is connected to the Mississippi at New Orleans by a series of locks. Among the myriad inlets in the delta is historic BARATARIA BAY, S of New Orleans. See also the DELTA, in Mississippi.

Deltona unincorporated residential community, pop. 50,828, Volusia Co., EC Florida, on L. Monroe and many smaller lakes, midway between Orlando (SW) and Daytona Beach (NE).

Deming city, pop. 10,970, seat of Luna Co., SW New Mexico, 60 mi/96 km W of Las Cruces. An underground section of the Mimbres R. irrigates surrounding farms and ranches producing livestock, grain, poultry, fruit, beans, and cotton. A railway junction and trading center, the city has drawn retirees in recent years. Mining was formerly central to the area's economy.

Demopolis city, pop. 7512, Marengo Co., WC Alabama, at the confluence of the Tombigbee and Black Warrior rivers, just S of L. Demopolis. Noted for its antebellum mansions, dating to its heyday as a river port, it is today a center for the distribution and processing of beef cattle, dairy products, soybeans, and lumber. Manufactures include paperboard, pulp, cement, and chemicals. Napoleonic exiles founded the city in 1817, attempting unsuccessfully to grow olives and grapes in the region.

Demorest town, pop. 1088, Habersham Co., NE Georgia, 42 mi/68 km NNW of Athens, home to Piedmont College (1897).

Dempster Highway 450 mi/725 km long, in the N Yukon Territory and extreme NW Northwest Territories. It extends from the KLONDIKE HIGHWAY ESE of DAWSON to INUVIK in the MACKENZIE R. delta of the Northwest Territories. Begun to service northern oilfields in 1959, and opened in 1979, it is the only Canadian highway to cross the Arctic Circle, traversing also the Ogilvie Mts., Eagle Plain, Richardson Mts., and Peel R. It is open year-round.

Denali National Park and Preserve 4.72 million ac/1.91 million ha (7370 sq mi/19,088 sq km), in S Alaska, some 240 mi/390 km ENE of Anchorage. It is named for Denali (Mt. MCKINLEY), North America's tallest mountain. This ALASKA RANGE area is noted for its wildlife, esp. grizzly bears, timber wolves, moose, and caribou. Since 1972, when highway access was improved, pressure on the park's ecosystem has led to traffic and camping restrictions.

Dene people of the subarctic taiga (northern forest) in Alaska and the Yukon and Northwest territories. Speakers of Na-Dene (Athapascan) languages, they are traditionally hunters and fishers, and their frontier with the INUIT (to the N, on the TUNDRA) has long been a zone of conflict. Today white society and economic development have altered their way of life, and many live and work in YELLOWKNIFE or HAY RIVER. The establishment of the Inuit NUNAVUT raises the question of similar Dene sovereignty.

Denendah see under NUNAVUT.

Denham Springs city, pop. 8381, Livingston Parish, SE Louisiana, on the Amite R., 14 mi/23 km E of Baton Rouge. Settled around mineral springs in the early 19th century, it is today a livestock raising center, with some light industry.

Denison city, pop. 21,505, Grayson Co., NE Texas, on the Red R. near L. TEXOMA (impounded by the Denison Dam), 11 mi/18 km NNE of Sherman. A railroad, industrial, and meatpacking center, the city, on the site of a stage stop, was established by the Missouri, Kansas & Texas Railroad as a division point in 1872. It processes food and makes various wood and metal products. The Eisenhower Birthplace State Historic Site includes the house in which Dwight D. Eisenhower was born in 1890. Grayson County College (1965) is just SW. L. Texoma draws vacationers. Hagerman National Wildlife Refuge (11,300 ac/4580 ha), a major migratory bird site, is 11 mi/18 km W.

Denmark city, pop. 3762, Bamberg Co., SC South Carolina, 21 mi/32 km SW of Orangeburg. It is a road and rail junction and telecommunications center. Settled in 1896, it is home to Voorhees College (1897).

Dennis town, pop. 13,864, Barnstable Co., Cape Cod, SE Massachusetts, 6 mi/10 km ENE of Barnstable. It is a summer resort, and cranberries are cultivated. The town includes the villages of Dennis Port, East Dennis, South Dennis, and West Dennis, with waterfront on both the N and S of the Cape.

Denton city, pop. 66,270, seat of Denton Co. (pop. 273,525), NE Texas, 38 mi/61 km NW of Dallas. Founded in the 1850s, it has been an agricultural trade center, and its varied manufactures include plastics, processed food, clothing, brick, and business forms; but it is best known as an educational center. The University of North Texas (1890) and Texas Woman's University (1901) are here. The Denton State School (1960) for the retarded is one of a number of medical institutions. The city is also headquarters for a five-state Federal regional emergency center.

Dentsville unincorporated community, pop. 11,839, Richland Co., C South Carolina, 6 mi/10 km NE of downtown Columbia and just W of the Army's Fort Jackson. It is a primarily residential community for those working in Columbia and for military personnel.

Denver city, pop. 467,610, coextensive with Denver Co. (111 sq mi/287 sq km), in NC Colorado, on the South Platte R., at the W end of the Great Plains and the E foot of the Rocky Mt. FRONT RANGE. At 5280 ft/1610 m, Denver is called the Mile High City. It is the state capital and the major city of the US Rocky Mt. area. The Denver-Boulder metropolitan area (CMSA), including ADAMS, ARAPAHOE, Denver, Douglas, JEFFERSON, and BOULDER counties, has a pop. of 1,848,319. Denver is a transportation hub, an agricultural market, a manufacturing center, and the site of the greatest concentration of Federal agencies and installations outside Washington, D.C. It began life when rumors of gold on Cherry Creek, which here joins the South Platte, attracted 1858–59 Pikes Peak gold rushers. The disappointment of these hopes did not prevent it from growing, and it became Colorado's capital in 1867. The dry climate and mountain setting soon drew health seekers, and in the 1880s a huge Rocky Mt. silver boom brought wealth and rapid growth. Although off the major western emigration routes, the city had established rail connections in the 1870s, and it survived the 1893 crash of the silver economy as an agricultural and mining service and regional government and financial center. Until World War II it had little manufacturing, but acquired numerous Federal operations. The war brought both more government (esp. military) activity and heavy industry, a trend that has continued to the present. Postwar development of Colorado oilfields added impetus to growth, esp. in the 1970s and early 1980s. The city and region produce weaponry (see esp. ROCKY FLATS), electronic and communications equipment, chemicals, tools and precision equipment, machinery, rubber and textile goods, and a variety of other manufactures. A highway, rail, and air nexus, and a jumping-off point for mountain recreation, Denver also has large tourist and convention businesses. The University of Denver (1864) and a number of private, religious, and state and community colleges are here. Since the 1950s extensive suburbanization has occurred, both W and NW into the foothills and S and E onto the high plains. While the city itself has lost pop. in recent decades, the metropolitan area has continued to expand; AURORA, adjacent on the E, is the largest suburb. See also: AURARIA; CAPITOL HILL; CHEESMAN PARK; CHERRY CREEK; CITY PARK; CIVIC CENTER; DENVER MOUNTAIN PARK SYSTEM; LARIMER St.; LOWER DOWNTOWN (LoDo); LOWRY AIR FORCE BASE; MILE HIGH STADIUM; ROCKY MOUNTAIN ARSENAL; SEVENTEENTH St.; SIXTEENTH St.; STAPLETON INTERNATIONAL AIRPORT (and Denver International Airport); United States MINT; UNIVERSITY PARK.

Denver Harbor industrial and residential section of Houston, Texas, 3.5 mi/6 km E of Downtown, on the N of the Houston Ship Channel and on the E of the FIFTH WARD. It is one of Houston's major Mexican BARRIOS, and also has a substantial white population. On its W lie the Southern Pacific Railroad's huge Englewood Yards, used both for switching trains and for treating crossties; its chemical activity has earned the vicinity the nickname El Crisol (the crucible) or El Creosote.

Denver Mountain Park System collection of park areas scattered in the foothills of the FRONT RANGE, W and SW of Denver, Colorado. Initiated in 1912, it is one of the largest such systems of municipal parks outside city limits in America. Particularly well-known are Lookout Mt. (7374 ft/2248 m), with the tomb of "Buffalo Bill" Cody, and Red Rocks, with a 10,000-seat sandstone amphitheater.

Denville township, pop. 13,812, Morris Co., NC New Jersey, 6 mi/10 km N of Morristown. Situated on Interstate 80 in a lake-filled area, it is primarily residential.

DePaul mixed residential and commercial neighborhood on the Near North Side of Chicago, Illinois, centered around DePaul University. A collection of small detached 19th-century homes, it was a counterculture center during the 1950s and 1960s. It has since become a stylish, affluent area. The most famous landmark here is the Biograph Theatre, where John Dillinger was shot in 1934.

De Pere city, pop. 16,569, Brown Co., E Wisconsin, on the Fox R., 4 mi/6 km SW of GREEN BAY. The French explorer Jean Nicolet described the large numbers of Indians he saw here (1634). In 1669, Jesuits established Wisconsin's first mission on the site. Currently, paper and papermaking machinery, boats, pharmaceuticals, and machine parts are leading manufactures. De Pere is the seat of St. Norbert College (1898).

Depew village, pop, 17,673, Erie Co., W New York, 9 mi/15 km E of Buffalo. It grew around railroad shops established here in 1893, and is now an industrial suburb of Buffalo, manufacturing textiles, steel castings, and food products.

Derby **1.** city and coterminous township, pop. 12,199, New Haven Co., S Connecticut, at the junction of the Housatonic and Naugatuck rivers, 8 mi/13 km W of New Haven. Established as a trading post in 1642, it was for 200 years a shipbuilding, fishing, and overseas trading center. Gradual obstruction of the rivers by bridges and dams in the 19th century effectively put an end to these industries, and Derby turned to manufactures that have included brass, copper, and bronze products; hardware; shoe machinery; auto and airplane parts; chemicals; and textiles. **2.** city, pop. 14,699, Sedgwick Co., SC Kansas, on the Arkansas R. near its junction with the Wichita flood control canal, 10 mi/16 km SSE of central Wichita. Its name was changed from El Paso in 1930. Primarily a residential suburb, it also processes wheat.

De Ridder city, pop. 9868, seat of Beauregard Parish, also in Vernon Parish, SW Louisiana, 43 mi/70 km NNW of Lake Charles. It is the market and processing center of a region producing corn, grains, oranges, soybeans, pine lumber, turpentine, and wool.

Derry town, pop. 29,603, Rockingham Co., SE New Hampshire. It is on Beaver Brook, its waterpower source, 10 mi/16 km SE of Manchester. In an agricultural and resort area, it was set off from Londonderry (W) in 1827, and manufactured boots and shoes. Robert Frost's farm, where the poet lived (1900–09) while teaching at local Pinkerton Academy, is here. West-Running Brook, which gave its name to one of Frost's best-known poems, flows from near the farm into Beaver Brook.

Deschutes River 240 mi/390 km long, in Oregon. It rises in the CASCADE RANGE in WC Oregon, in the 1.6 million-ac/650,000-ha (2500–sq mi/6500–sq km) **Deschutes National Forest,** a popular forest and rock-climbing retreat. It flows NNE past BEND, then along the E of the WARM SPRINGS Indian Reservation, to join the COLUMBIA R. 12 mi/19 km E of THE DALLES. Its waters are dammed in several places for power and irrigation.

Deseret name given the short-lived (1849–51) state proclaimed by Mormon settlers based in Salt Lake City. It incorporated modern Utah and Nevada and parts of neighboring states between the Rocky Mt. crest (E) and the Pacific. The US government refused to recognize it, and in 1850 legislated instead the Utah Territory, which, much reduced, became (1896) Utah. The name Deseret ("honeybee," a symbol of industry, in the *Book of Mormon*) appears in various places in Utah, notably at **Deseret Peak** (11,031 ft/3362 m), W of Tooele and S of Great Salt L., in the Stansbury Mts.

Desert Hot Springs city, pop. 11,668, Riverside Co., S California, 9 mi/14 km N of Palm Springs, in the Coachella Valley. Its natural hot springs have made it a popular health resort and vacation area; it has doubled in pop. each decade since 1960.

Desert National Wildlife Range 1.6 million ac/643,000 ha (2482 sq mi/6430 sq km), N of Las Vegas in Lincoln Co., S Nevada. The largest US wildlife refuge outside of Alaska, it encompasses six life zones, ranging from desert floor to peaks almost 10,000 ft/3050 m high. The desert bighorn sheep, Nevada's state animal, which the refuge was created to protect in 1936, usually grazes near springs at higher elevations. A wide range of other animals, birds, and vegetation is found here. Only the E half of the refuge, in the vicinity of the SHEEP RANGE, is open to the public; the NELLIS Air Force Range adjoins (W).

Desire Street thoroughfare in DOWNTOWN New Orleans, Louisiana. It runs N from about 1 mi/1.5 km E of JACKSON SQUARE, through a largely industrial and commercial area near the Inner Harbor Navigation Canal. Tennessee Williams's 1947 play *A Streetcar Named Desire* popularized New Orleans trolleys. The Desire line has long since been discontinued; today the only streetcar running in the city is along St. Charles St., in UPTOWN.

Des Lacs River also, **Riviere des Lacs** 42 mi/68 km long, in N North Dakota. It rises in Des Lacs L. near Kenmare, and flows SE to the Souris (Mouse) R., 6 mi/10 km NW of Minot.

De Smet city, pop. 1172, seat of Kingsbury Co., E South Dakota, 36 mi/58 km W of Brookings. Founded when the railroad reached this area (1880), it is situated in a dairying region and named for a Jesuit missionary, whose statue stands in a park here. It was the home of writer Laura Ingalls Wilder, who based some of her *Little House on the Prairie* books on De Smet. The Ingalls home is preserved, and a yearly pageant is based on her tales.

Des Moines **1.** city, pop. 193,187, state capital and seat of Polk Co., C Iowa, at the confluence of the Raccoon and Des Moines rivers. The state's largest city, situated at the heart of the Corn Belt and a coal mining region, it is an important industrial, commercial, and transportation center. A major insurance and printing and publishing city, it also has meatpacking houses, chemical works, dairies, and flour mills. Some 400 local factories produce such goods as agricultural implements, plastics, outdoor clothing, auto accessories, and tires. By the time Fort Des Moines was completed in the 1840s, the local Sauk and Fox peoples under its protection had been removed farther W. Founded in 1851, the city was incorporated and became Iowa's capital in 1857. Coal mining loomed large in the economy between 1910 and the Depression. Important institutions include the Capitol, a modern Civic Center, the Des Moines Art Center, the Science Center of Iowa, and the State Historical Memorial and Art Building. It is the seat of Drake University (1881), Grand View College (1896), and Open Bible College (1931). The Iowa State Fair is held here every August. **2.** city, pop. 17,283, King Co., WC Washington, on Puget Sound, a residential suburb 13 mi/21 km S of Seattle and 10 mi/16 km NE of Tacoma. Lying just S of the Seattle-Tacoma International Airport, it has experienced rapid growth in recent years.

Des Moines River 535 mi/861 km long, in Iowa and Minnesota. It rises in forks NE of Pipestone, in SW Minnesota, and flows generally SSE into Iowa, where the forks converge S of Dakota City, in Humboldt Co. The river continues SE and S past Fort Dodge, through the Saylorville Reservoir, Des Moines, and the Red Rock Reservoir, past Ottumwa and along the Missouri line to join the Mississippi R. near Keokuk. A chief tributary is the **East Des Moines** or **East Fork** R., which is 120 mi/193 km long and rises in Martin Co., in SW Minnesota. It flows SE and S into Iowa to join the main river near Humboldt. The Boone and Raccoon rivers are other important tributaries.

Desolation Wilderness see under ELDORADO NATIONAL FOREST, California.

DeSoto city, pop. 30,544, Dallas Co., NE Texas, 13 mi/21 km SSW of downtown Dallas, on Interstate 35E. It is a residential and light industrial suburb on the Dallas city limits, just outside the beltway (I-20).

De Soto County 483 sq mi/1251 sq km, pop. 67,910, in extreme NW Mississippi, on the Mississippi R. (W) and the Tennessee line (N). Its seat is Hernando (pop. 3125). Its NW portion is adjacent to Memphis, and contains the large suburb of SOUTHAVEN. The balance of the county is agricultural, the northernmost part of the DELTA, producing cotton, grain, beef, and dairy cattle and goods.

De Soto National Forest 500,000 ac/202,500 ha, in two units in SE Mississippi. Its smaller unit is SE of Laurel, the larger SSE of Hattiesburg and extending to just N of Biloxi. In the PINEY WOODS, it is noted for its Black Creek and Leaf R. wilderness areas. Headquarters are at Laurel, Wiggins, and McHenry.

De Soto National Memorial see under BRADENTON, Florida.

De Soto Park in downtown Memphis, Tennessee, overlooking the Mississippi R. Formerly (1887–1913) known as Jackson Mound Park, for one of several ancient mounds here, it is one of the sites (Sunflower Landing, W of CLARKSDALE, Mississippi, is another) where Hernando de Soto is thought to have first seen the Mississippi, in May 1541.

Des Peres city, pop. 8395, St. Louis Co., EC Missouri, 14 mi/23 km W of downtown St. Louis, a primarily residential suburb.

Des Plaines city, pop. 53,223, Cook Co., NE Illinois, on the Des Plaines R., 20 mi/32 km NW of Chicago. It developed as a postwar bedroom community, undergoing dramatic population growth during the 1950s. It has since developed a substantial industrial area largely due to the presence of O'Hare International Airport immediately to the S. Manufactures include electrical equipment, cement blocks, radio parts, and greenhouse specialties. Founded in 1835 as Rand, the city now constitutes one of the largest suburbs in the Chicago area. De Lourdes College (1951) is here. The 1980s witnessed a great deal of industrial and commercial growth along the I-90 corridor near the airport, along the S edge of the city. McDonald's Museum, a reconstruction of the first restaurant in the famous fast-food chain, is situated on its NE edge. Glenview Naval Air Station is 3 mi/5km NE.

Des Plaines River 110 mi/177 km long, in Wisconsin and Illinois. It rises in SE Wisconsin and flows S into Lake Co., Illinois, running through the N suburbs of Chicago to Forest View. There it heads SW to join the Kankakee R. in NE Grundy Co., thus forming the Illinois R. Below Lockport, the Des Plaines is joined by the Chicago Sanitary and Ship Canal, and is part of the ILLINOIS WATERWAY.

Destrehan unincorporated community, pop. 8031, St. Charles Parish, SE Louisiana, 16 mi/26 km W of New Orleans, along the RIVER ROAD. Named for the owner of a late-18th-century plantation (who was also the founder of GRETNA), it is noted for a 1787 building thought to be the oldest European habitation in the lower Mississippi valley. Long agricultural, it is now also industrial and suburban, and tripled in population in the 1980s.

Detroit city, pop. 1,027,974, seat of WAYNE Co., SE Michigan, on the Detroit R. at the mouth of the River ROUGE, between L. Erie (S) and L. St. Clair (NE), and across from Windsor, Ontario (S). It is the center of an eight-county (Lapeer, LIVINGSTON, MACOMB, MONROE, OAKLAND, SAINT CLAIR, WASHTENAW, and Wayne) metropolitan area (CMSA) with a pop. of 4,665,236. A fur post established here (1701) by Antoine de la Mothe Cadillac became the Ville d'etroit, the "city of the strait." A key to Canada's northwestern trade, it passed to the British in 1763, survived a five-month siege by forces of the Ottawa leader Pontiac, and remained largely French in character until Americans took over in 1796. In 1805 it became the capital of the new Michigan Territory, burned, and was rebuilt. After the War of 1812, in which it was held by both British and US forces, it became a trade and administrative center as settlers poured into the territory; the ERIE CANAL and introduction of steam power on the Great Lakes accelerated its growth. In 1837–47 it was capital of the new state of Michigan. Before the Civil War it was an UNDERGROUND RAILROAD hub, with its easy access to Canada. The war and rail and lake transportation began to change it into a manufacturing center in the 1860s; soon, metal goods, furniture, and esp. carriages and other vehicles were being produced. This industrial base made Detroit a logical site for development of the nascent automobile industry around 1900, when its pop. had reached 285,704. Henry Ford and others began operations here, and by 1930 the city had quadrupled in size. After hard times and labor strife during the 1930s Depression, World War II caused a second boom, with ship, truck, tank, airplane, and other vehicle construction. During this period, a city largely Irish, Polish, and East European became home to tens of thousands of Appalachian white and Southern black workers. Rapid growth caused stresses, followed, at war's end, by the beginnings of rapid depopulation. From a peak of 1,849,568 in 1950, Detroit has lost 45% of its residents, chiefly older white groups, first to its suburbs (where many plants began to move in the 1940s), later to the SUNBELT and elsewhere. Much of its largely single-family housing stock has fallen victim to abandonment. URBAN RENEWAL and race riots in 1943 and 1967 accentuated white flight, and the city is now 76% black. Redevelopment efforts since the 1970s, like the RENAISSANCE CENTER, have had limited success. Detroit's chief industries are automaking and its ancillaries; they include metal fabrication, chemical production, and tool and hardware making. The mining of salt from beneath the city began in the late 19th century. In addition, shipping (boosted by the 1959 opening of the SAINT LAWRENCE SEAWAY), other commerce, research, and conventions bring income. Wayne State University (1868), the University of Detroit (1877), and the Detroit Institute of the Arts (1885) are leading cultural and educational institutions. Tiger Field and Joe Louis Arena host professional sports (the football Lions play at PONTIAC's Silverdome). The Detroit Metropolitan Wayne Co. Airport is 20 mi/32 km SW of Downtown, near ROMULUS. See also: AMBASSADOR BRIDGE; BOSTON-EDISON; BRICKTOWN; CADILLAC SQUARE; CANFIELD HISTORIC DISTRICT; CASS CORRIDOR; CHENE PARK; CIVIC CENTER; COBO HALL; CORKTOWN; DELRAY; DOWNRIVER; EASTERN MARKET; EIGHT MILE Rd.; FORT WAYNE; GRAND BOULEVARD; GRAND CIRCUS PARK; GREEKTOWN; INDIAN VILLAGE; JEFFERSON Ave.; JEFFERSON-CHALMERS; JOE LOUIS ARENA; LOWER EAST SIDE; MEDICAL CENTER; MOTOR CITY (Motown); NEW CENTER; OUTER DRIVE; PALMER PARK; PARADISE VALLEY (Black Bottom); POLETOWN; RENAISSANCE CENTER; River ROUGE; RIVERTOWN (and Warehouse District); TIGER STADIUM; TRAPPERS ALLEY; WOODWARD Ave.

Detroit Lakes city, pop. 6635, seat of Becker Co., W Minnesota. Situated amid hundreds of lakes, it is the center of a summer resort and fishing area. Since 1983, the city's outskirts have been the site of a huge annual country-and-western music festival. Ancient Indian mounds and purported Viking remains are found in the region.

Detroit River 30 mi/48 km–long outlet of L. SAINT CLAIR, just E of Detroit, SE Michigan, flowing generally W and S into the W end of L. Erie. It is crossed by tunnels and bridges between Detroit and Windsor, Ontario, and forms part of the US-Canada border. It is an important shipping channel between lakes Huron and Erie, and in recent years has been severely polluted by industrial waste and sewage from neighboring municipalities. Fort Detroit, the first European settlement on the river, was begun by the French explorer Antoine de la Mothe, sieur de Cadillac, in 1601.

Deux-Montagnes city, pop. 13,035, S Québec, 17 mi/28 km WNW of Montréal, at the entry into the R. des Mille Îles from the L. des Deux Montagnes (the Ottawa R.), across (W) from the SW end of the I. Jésus (LAVAL). It is a growing residential suburb.

Devil's Backbone in Iowa: **a.** narrow limestone ridge, with elevations of 80–140 ft/24–43 m, above the Maquoketa R., SW of Strawberry Point, in the E. Situated here is Backbone State Park (1800 ac/729 ha), which features unusual rock formations, bluffs, caverns, and springs. **b.** limestone ridge rising 100 ft/30 m, on the Middle R., near Winterset. It is the site of Pammel State Park (280 ac/113 ha), named for Louis Pammel, a botanist and early conservationist.

Devils Canyon see under TALKEETNA Mts., Alaska.

Devil's Courthouse see under WHITESIDE Mt., North Carolina.

Devils Lake 1. city, pop. 7782, seat of Ramsey Co., NE North Dakota, 90 mi/145 km W of Grand Forks. Settled on Devils L. in 1881, it was headquarters for steamboat navigation on the lake until it receded from the city and navigation ceased (1909). The city is a trade center for grain, livestock, and dairy products. Its manufactures include liquid fertilizer, sheet-metal products, farm equipment, and flour. Devils Lake is the seat of Lake Region Junior College (1941). Now several miles S of the city, the lake is a popular recreational site. Fort Totten (1868), 15 mi/24 km SW across the lake, is a well-preserved relic of the Indian Wars. Also in the area is the Devils Lake Indian Reservation (Sioux). **2.** see under BARABOO, Wisconsin.

Devil's Millhopper see under GAINESVILLE, Florida.

Devil's Playground see under EAST MOJAVE NATIONAL SCENIC AREA (Mojave National Preserve), California.

Devils Postpile National Monument on the John Muir (Pacific Crest) Trail in Inyo National Forest, EC California, 7 mi/11 km WSW of Mammoth Lakes, at 7600 ft/2316 m. Proclaimed in 1911, it has 800 ac/323 ha preserving columnar basalt formations resembling a huge pipe organ. Rainbow Falls, on the Middle Fork of the San Joaquin R., is nearby.

Devils Tower 865 ft/264 m–high columnar monolith, in Devils

Tower National Monument (1347 ac/546 ha), in Crook Co., NE Wyoming, rising above the Belle Fourche R., 43 mi/69 km NE of Gillette. The centerpiece of America's first (1906) national monument, it is a flat-topped rock column, probably formed by molten volcanic material pressing upward against a hard rock layer, and exposed by erosion, that resembles a gigantic tree stump. The tower is partly covered with lichen and crowned by sagebrush, moss, and grass. This formation is the central image in the film *Close Encounters of the Third Kind* (1977).

Devil's Triangle see BERMUDA TRIANGLE.

Devon Island c.21,000 sq mi/54,000 sq km, the second-largest and southeasternmost of the QUEEN ELIZABETH Is., in the Northwest Territories' Arctic Archipelago. It lies on the N of Parry Sound (the Barrow Strait on the SW, Lancaster Sound S and SE). Its E lies under deep icecap; in the C, W, and NW (the Grinnell Peninsula) is tundra-covered plateau with limited wildlife (muskoxen, lemmings, seabirds, etc.) and plant life. Off its SW is small, high (800-ft/245-m) Beechey I., a landmark for explorers of the NORTHWEST PASSAGE. Sir John Franklin's expedition wintered here 1845–46, and some members are buried on Beechey; search expeditions looking for the Franklin party later met here also.

De Witt town, pop. 25,148, Onondaga Co., C New York, immediately E of Syracuse. Interstate 90 and Route 481 pass through this residential and industrial suburb, which also contains most of Syracuse Hancock International Airport.

DEW Line (for *D*istant *E*arly *W*arning) 5000 mi/8000 km–long line of radar stations and airbases, across the Arctic from N Alaska to BAFFIN I., Northwest Territories, and E to Greenland. Established 1954–57 in response to a perceived threat from Soviet bombers, it extended the coverage of the earlier Pine Tree Line (from Vancouver, British Columbia, E to Labrador). The Mid-Canada Line or McGill Fence (at 55° N) was built entirely by the Canadians; the DEW Line was a joint effort. At the end of the Cold War, the North Warning System had extended to posts as far N as ALERT, on Ellesmere I.

Diablo Bolson also, **Diablo Plateau** or **Basin** region of far W Texas, in the BASIN AND RANGE PROVINCE, largely in Hudspeth Co. Ringed by mountains (the GUADALUPE and DELAWARE mountains E, the SIERRA DIABLO E and S, the FINLAY Mts. SW and W, the HUECO Mts. W), it has no external drainage. Large salt flats in its NE have been commercially important, and a bloody "Salt War," peaking in 1877, was fought over their control.

Diablo Canyon locality on the Pacific coast in San Luis Obispo Co., SW California, 11 mi/18 km SW of San Luis Obispo, site of a highly controversial nuclear power plant operational since 1984, which was built close to an undersea FAULT.

Diablo Range one of the COAST RANGES of C California, extending SE for some 180 mi/290 km from the isolated peak of **Mt. Diablo** (3849 ft/1174 m), E of Oakland, along the W of the CENTRAL VALLEY to the N end of the TEMBLOR RANGE. Generally 3000–4000 ft/900–1200 m in height, it reaches a high point at San Benito Mt. (5241 ft/1599 m), 20 mi/32 km NW of Coalinga, and includes Mt. HAMILTON, site of the Lick Observatory.

Diamond town, pop. 775, Newton Co., SW Missouri, 12 mi/19 km SE of Joplin. George Washington Carver (1864?–1943), the noted scientist long associated with Alabama's TUSKEGEE Institute, was born here. His home, just SW, is now part of the George Washington Carver National Monument.

Diamond Bar city, pop. 53,672, Los Angeles Co., SW California, 27 mi/43 km E of Los Angeles. Incorporated in the 1980s, it has quintupled in pop. since 1970 as a residential suburb near the junction of the Pomona and Orange freeways.

Diamond District commercial area centered on West 47th St., Manhattan, New York City, noted for the wholesaling, retailing, and repair of diamonds, gold, and other gems and jewelry. Many of its merchants are Orthodox Jews.

Diamond Head headland with a crater, a dormant volcano 760 ft/232 m high, in HONOLULU, Hawaii, E of Waikiki, a National Natural Landmark. The crater was named by sailors who mistook crystals on its surface for diamonds. Its floor was a military staging area from World War II through the Vietnam War, and is now used by the Hawaii National Guard. The ocean side of the headland is the beginning of Kahala (E), Honolulu's most expensive and exclusive area. Below the headland is Diamond Head Beach Park and Lighthouse. Fort Ruger Military Reservation lies N.

D'Iberville city, pop. 6566, Harrison Co., SE Mississippi, on the N side of BILOXI's Back Bay, at the mouth of the Biloxi R., opposite (N) Biloxi, of which it is a largely residential suburb.

Dickinson **1.** city, pop. 16,097, seat of Stark Co., SW North Dakota, 100 mi/160 km W of Bismarck. Founded in 1882 by the railroad as a forwarding point for the BLACK HILLS goldfields, it is now a trading center for a large agricultural area, specializing in livestock, wheat, and dairy goods. Other local products are lignite briquettes and pottery. Dickinson State University (1918) is here. **2.** city, pop. 9497, Galveston Co., SE Texas, on Dickinson Bayou, 20 mi/32 km NW of Galveston and 28 mi/45 km SE of downtown Houston. Texas City adjoins (SE). The city is a port in an oil producing and industrial area.

Dickson Mounds ancient Indian burial mound and National Historic Site, in Fulton Co., WC Illinois, just N of the Spoon R. and the community of Sepo. Dickson Mounds are believed to have been constructed by the Mississippian Culture between A.D. 1150 and 1350.

Dieppe town, pop. 10,463, Westmorland Co., E New Brunswick, a suburb immediately E of Moncton. Named in 1946 to honor Canadian soldiers who died in the 1942 raid on German-held Dieppe, France, it has large shopping malls and a racetrack.

Digby town, pop. 2311, seat of Digby Co. (pop. 21,250), W Nova Scotia, on the Annapolis Basin off the Bay of Fundy, 100 mi/160 km W of Halifax. The 40 mi/65 km–long **Digby Neck** peninsula extends SW, separating St. Mary's Bay (S) from the Bay of Fundy. The town is the terminus of a ferry from St. John, New Brunswick, and a port and service center. It has one of the largest scallop fishing fleets in the world, and produces other seafood, esp. smoked herring. There are local pulpwood and lumber industries, and tourism is central to the economy.

Dillingham city, pop. 2017, in the Dillingham Census Area (pop. 4012), SW Alaska, on Nushagak Bay, an arm of BRISTOL BAY in the BERING SEA, 330 mi/530 km SW of Anchorage. A center for salmon fishing and processing since the opening of a cannery in 1886, it is also a supply point for trappers along the Nushagak R.

Dillon **1.** city, pop. 3991, seat of Beaverhead Co., SW Montana, on the Beaverhead R., 55 mi/89 km S of Butte. Founded in 1880 as Terminus when the Utah and Northern Railroad arrived, it was renamed (1881) for the president of the Union Pacific Railroad, which completed the line to Butte. Dillon grew as a wool-shipping point, and now relies on cattle ranching, hay producing, mining, and tourism. Montana's first teachers' college was founded here (1893); it later became Western Montana College of the University of Montana. The Beaverhead National Forest is headquartered here. **2.** city, pop. 6829, seat of Dillon Co., NE South Carolina, 25 mi/40 km NE of Florence and 6 mi/10 km from the North Carolina line. Founded in 1887, it is now a trade, processing, and shipping hub for an agricultural, poultry, and timber producing region; manufactures include textiles, flour, lumber, and cured tobacco.

Dinkytown student neighborhood in Minneapolis, Minnesota, SE of Downtown and adjacent to the University of Minnesota campus.

Dinosaur National Monument 211,000 ac/85,500 ha (330 sq mi/854 sq km), along the Yampa and Green rivers, at their junction in extreme NW Colorado and NE Utah. In the Utah section, established in 1915, is one of the richest known deposits of dinosaur remains, the source of bones in many of the world's museums. In the Colorado section, added in 1938, are deep gorges cut through folded sandstone.

Dinosaur Provincial Park 14,681 ac/5946 ha, in SE Alberta, 110 mi/177 km E of Calgary. Situated in Canada's largest BADLANDS area and along the Red Deer R., it has a variety of sandstone and other fossil beds containing many dinosaur skeletons, and has been designated a United Nations World Heritage Site.

Dinuba city, pop. 12,743, Tulare Co., SC California, 25 mi/40 km SE of Fresno, in the San Joaquin Valley. A service and trade center in an irrigated region in which raisins, figs, grapes, and peaches are grown, it has canneries, packing houses, and wineries.

Diomede Islands two rocky islands in the Bering Strait, 25 mi/40 km NW of Cape PRINCE OF WALES (the SEWARD PENINSULA), NW Alaska, and 30 mi/48 km SE of Cape Dezhnov, E Siberia. The islands are divided by the International Date Line and the US–Russian border. Ratmanova, or **Big Diomede,** is 3–5 mi/5–8 km N–S and 1 mi/2 km E–W, and is part of Siberia. **Little Diomede,** 4.5 mi/7 km to the E, is 2 mi/3 km N–S and 1 mi/2 km E–W, and is part of Alaska. Both islands have a small pop. of Chukchi Eskimos (the city of Diomede, pop. 178, is in the Nome Census Area), and were visited by the explorer Vitus Bering on St. Diomede's Day in 1728.

Dismal Swamp also, **Great Dismal Swamp** marshland, about 600 sq mi/1550 sq km, in SE Virginia and NE North Carolina. The swamp was much larger (about 2000 sq mi/5200 sq km) before the arrival of Europeans, but beginning in the 18th century it was systematically drained; some of the first work was done by George Washington's slaves after Washington surveyed the site in 1763. The swamp was long a refuge for runaway slaves and other fugitives, who established stable communities within it. In its center is L. Drummond, roughly 2.5 mi/4 km in diameter, connected by ditch to the 22-mi/35-km **Dismal Swamp Canal,** which links CHESAPEAKE BAY and ALBEMARLE SOUND; the canal was completed in 1828, and is now part of the ATLANTIC INTRACOASTAL WATERWAY.

Disneyland see under ANAHEIM, California.

Disney World see LAKE BUENA VISTA, Florida.

dissected plateau see under PLATEAU.

distributary a channel of a river that flows away from the main stream, reducing the latter's flow, and does not rejoin it. Distributaries are found most often in deltas, where they may have been created by a shifting of the river's main flow from one channel to another; they may represent former main streams.

district 1. a division of a political entity for any of a number of purposes (as, a school district, water and sewer district, judicial district, electoral district, the District of Columbia). **2.** in Canada: any of various administrative divisions (roughly analogous to COUNTIES) of a province or territory, esp. districts in N Ontario and **regional districts** in British Columbia. **3. district municipality a.** in Ontario: a single administrative division (Muskoka). **b.** in British Columbia: any of 48 rural municipalities (roughly analogous to TOWNSHIPS). **4. local government district** in Manitoba: a municipal form (roughly analogous to a township). **5.** designation for various divisions of the territory controlled by the HUDSON'S BAY COMPANY (later the Northwest Territories), also called *departments*.

District of Columbia popularly, **D.C.** or **the District** 68 sq mi/176 sq km, pop. 606,900, coextensive (since 1895) with the city of WASHINGTON, the Federal capital of the United States. Created in 1790, pursuant to a provision of the Constitution, as a zone 10 mi/16 km square, it embraced the Maryland tobacco port of GEORGETOWN, the Virginia city of ALEXANDRIA, and newly created Washington. Its location resulted from a compromise between Northern and Southern interests; in 1800 the Federal government began operations here, having moved from Philadelphia. In its early years the District was ruled directly by Congress, then had various forms of self-government. In 1846 Virginia successfully agitated for the return of Alexandria (Alexandria Co. became ARLINGTON Co.), leaving the District its present size. After the Civil War, Congress, alarmed over political developments in the District, revoked its charter and from 1874 appointed commissioners to oversee it. It was not until 1967 that a form of "home rule" was restored. A new charter approved in 1974 gave the District an elective mayor and council; ultimate control, however, remained in the hand of Congressional committees that have veto power over budget and other legislation. In addition, citizens of the District vote in presidential elections but have only a nonvoting delegate to Congress. Discontent with this status has led to a movement for statehood; in the 1980s District voters approved a constitution and petitioned Congress for admission to the Union, but no favorable action has been taken.

division point in early railroading, point at which a TRUNK LINE was split into separately managed divisions, each responsible for operation within its territory. Typically, through trains changed locomotives and crews at division points, and there were service and repair yards.

Division Street E–W thoroughfare on the North Side of Chicago, Illinois. It extends from the S tip of Lincoln Park to suburban Oak Park. Known for the night life at its E end, it also passes near CABRINI-GREEN and through working-class neighborhoods farther W.

Dix Hills unincorporated village, pop. 25,849, in Huntington town, Suffolk Co., SE New York, in C Long Island. It is primarily residential.

Dixie also, **Dixieland** popular name for the US SOUTH, that is, the Old South of the Confederacy ("the land of cotton"), taken from an 1859 song by minstrel-show entertainer Dan Emmett. The song became popular in the Civil War with both Northern and Southern soldiers; for the latter, it was often a battle song. The source of the word *Dixie* may be either *dix,* popular name for a ten-dollar bill issued by a New Orleans bank, or the MASON-DIXON LINE.

Dixie National Forest over 1.9 million ac/770,000 ha (2970 sq mi/7690 sq km), in SW Utah. In an area called "Dixie" by early Mormon settlers for its warm climate, it has four units, noted esp. for their colorful canyons, along the divide between the Great Basin (NW) and Colorado Plateau (SE). MOUNTAIN MEADOWS is in its SW unit.

Dixon 1. city, pop. 10,401, Solano Co., NC California, in the Sacramento Valley, 20 mi/32 km WSW of Sacramento. It is a trade center in a diversified farming region. **2.** city, pop. 15,144, seat of Lee Co., NW Illinois, on the Rock R., 36 mi/58 km SW of Rockford. It is the commercial center of an agricultural area, and cement and electrical equipment are produced. It was here that John Dixon began a ferry service and tavern in 1830, along the Peoria–Galena mail route. Two years later, Fort Dixon was built as a base during the Black Hawk War; the Lincoln Monument State Memorial now marks its site. Ronald Reagan's boyhood home here has been restored and is open to the public. White Pines State Forest is 8 mi/13 km N.

Dixon Entrance strait of the N Pacific Ocean between the ALEXANDER ARCHIPELAGO of Alaska (N) and the QUEEN CHARLOTTE Is. of British Columbia (S). Sixty mi/100 km E–W and 45 mi/72 km N–S, it connects Hecate Strait (S) and the INSIDE PASSAGE with the Pacific. Prince Rupert, British Columbia, is at its E end.

Dixville Notch mountain pass, altitude 1871 ft/571 m, in Coos Co., extreme N New Hampshire. Dixville Notch is about 2 mi/3 km long, between Colebrook and Errol, in outlying ranges of the White Mts. Dixville township, pop. 50, which votes first in the nation (at midnight Election Day) in presidential elections, is the site of resorts, including the Balsams, a 19th-century hotel complex on Gloriette L.

Dobbins Air Force Base see under MARIETTA, Georgia.

Dobbs Ferry village, pop. 9940, Westchester Co., SE New York, between the Hudson R. (W) and Saw Mill R. (E), 20 mi/32 km N of New York City. It is named for a ferry operated by William Dobbs in the 18th century. Today it is a residential suburb of New York City.

Dochet Island also, **Saint Croix I.** see under SAINT CROIX R., Maine.

Dodge City city, pop. 21,129, seat of Ford Co., SW Kansas, on the Arkansas R., 150 mi/240 km W of Wichita. It was established in 1872 near Fort Dodge, an (1864) army outpost on the SANTA FE TRAIL. A railroad terminus and wide-open cow town in the late 1800s, it was famous for its saloons, gambling dens, and brothels frequented by cowboys and outlaws and policed by such lawmen as Wyatt Earp and Bat Masterson. The city remains a rail center for a rich livestock and wheat growing region. Farm equipment and supplies are major manufactures. Boot Hill cemetery and other sites evoking the city's past attract tourism. Dodge City Community College (1935) and St. Mary of the Plains College (1952) are here.

Dodger Stadium see under CHAVEZ RAVINE, Los Angeles, California.

Dogpatch fictional OZARKS home of "Li'l Abner" and other characters in the well-known comic strip by Al Capp (1909–79). Dogpatch, U.S.A., a THEME PARK 7 mi/11 km S of HARRISON, in NW Arkansas's Buffalo R. region, capitalizes on the strip's popularity.

Dogtown see under GLOUCESTER, Massachusetts.

Dollard-des-Ormeaux city, pop. 46,922, MONTRÉAL URBAN COMMUNITY, S Québec, 10 mi/16 km WSW of downtown Montréal, NW of Dorval, E of Pierrefonds, and N of Pointe-Claire. It is a largely anglophone residential suburb that grew rapidly in the 1970s.

Dollarton waterfront community now in NORTH VANCOUVER Regional District, SW British Columbia, on the North Shore of Burrard Inlet, across (WNW) from downtown Vancouver, noted as the site of the shack home (1940–54) of British novelist Malcolm Lowry, much of whose later work was set in the region.

Dolores River 250 mi/400 km long, in SW Colorado and E Utah. Its headstreams are in the NW SAN JUAN Mts., SW of TELLURIDE. It flows SW to Dolores, just NNE of Cortez, then turns NW and enters McPhee Reservoir (1987), then winds NNW, crossing the Utah border NE of Moab, to enter the COLORADO R. With its tributaries it drains much of SW Colorado's Canyon Lands.

Dolton village, pop. 23,930, Cook Co., NE Illinois, on the Little Calumet R., a Chicago suburb, 18 mi/29 km S of the Loop and 3 mi/5 km W of Hammond, Indiana. First settled in 1832, it has contained both industrial and residential sections for many decades. Factories here produce steel, chairs, and paper bags.

Dominguez Hills see under CARSON, California.

Dominion in Canadian government: see under CONFEDERATION.

Dominion Square see Square DORCHESTER, Montréal, Québec.

Donald C. Cook nuclear power plant: see under BERRIEN CO., Michigan.

Donaldsonville city, pop. 7949, seat of Ascension Parish, SE Louisiana, on the W (S) bank of the Mississippi R., at the head of BAYOU LAFOURCHE, 22 mi/35 km SSE of Baton Rouge. Founded in 1806 as a trading post, it served briefly as the state capital in 1830–31. It is now a trade center in the industrialized (oil and gas producing) and agricultural (sugar cane, rice) RIVER ROAD corridor.

Don Mills planned community in SE NORTH YORK, Ontario, on the Don R., 12 mi/19 km NE of downtown Toronto, created in the late 1940s. It has four discrete neighborhoods centered around a school, and distinguishes commercial zones from residential. One of Canada's first mall-type shopping centers was built here, and Don Mills has a wide variety of light industry and corporate headquarters.

Donna city, pop. 12,652, Hidalgo Co., extreme S Texas, in the Lower Rio Grande Valley, 12 mi/19 km E of McAllen. A processing and shipping center in a rich irrigated farming area, it has dehydrating plants and canneries. Lamb and sheep are also raised in this city founded in 1906 as a stop on the St. Louis, Brownsville & Mexico Railroad, and it is a winter resort.

Donner Pass at 7135 ft/2176 m in the SIERRA NEVADA, in NE California, 8 mi/13 km W of Truckee, 35 mi/56 km WSW of Reno, Nevada, and 2 mi/3 km S of Interstate 80. On the California Emigrant Trail, it was heavily used from 1844, and is named for the Donner Party, who, trapped on its E side by snow in Oct. 1846, resorted to cannibalism; Donner Memorial State Park, on Donner L., 2 mi/3 km E, where many died, recalls the incident. The 1849 gold rush brought heavy traffic, and in 1867–68 the Central Pacific Railroad laid tracks through the pass, connecting Sacramento with Nevada and the East. Today, the area is popular with skiers and summer visitors.

Donora borough, pop. 5928, Washington Co., SW Pennsylvania, on the Monongahela R., 20 mi/32 km SSW of Pittsburgh. Founded in 1900, Donora produces wire, steel, and appliances; there is also some agriculture. It is the birthplace (1920) of baseball great Stan Musial. On Oct. 30–31, 1948, Donora was covered by a poisonous smog that killed 20 people and sickened 5000.

Don River one of two short rivers (the HUMBER is the other) crucial to the development of TORONTO, Ontario. The Don enters L. Ontario at Toronto Harbour, where its outflow, carrying material from the Scarborough Bluffs (E), formed the peninsula that is now the Toronto Is. A source of timber, later pulp and waterpower, the river is formed in modern EAST YORK by East and West branches, between which (just N, in North York) is the post–World War II planned community of DON MILLS. The West Branch flows from VAUGHAN, the East Branch from MARKHAM, into North York. The Don Valley Parkway, a major traffic artery into Toronto, parallels the river's lower course. Much of metropolitan Toronto's parkland is along the river.

Door Peninsula 80 mi/129 km NE–SW and 30 mi/48 km wide at its base, in Door, Brown, and Kewanee counties, NE Wisconsin, with Green Bay on its W and L. Michigan on its E. At Sturgeon Bay, a 9 mi/14 km–long canal bisects it, connecting Green Bay and L. Michigan. The French explored the peninsula in the 17th century. It was settled by Moravian and Scandinavian immigrants in the 19th century, and became a popular resort location in the early 20th century. It has many towns and small cities, and is the site of Potowatomi State Park and Whitefish Dunes State Park. Tourism and cherry growing are the main economic activities. The Kewaunee nuclear power plant (1974) is at the extreme S of the peninsula, 8 mi/13 km S of Kewaunee, along L. Michigan, and 3.5 mi/5.6 km N of the POINT BEACH plant.

Doraville city, pop. 7626, De Kalb Co., NW Georgia, 13 mi/21 km NNE of downtown Atlanta. Just NE of the I-85/285 interchange, it is home to a General Motors assembly plant that is one of Georgia's largest industrial facilities.

Dorchester district in S Boston, Massachusetts. It was settled before the 1630 founding of Boston, and was a prosperous fishing port and shipbuilding community before becoming part of the city in 1874. It is now a mixed working- and middle-class residential area. The John F. Kennedy Library, Massachusetts State Archives, and University of Massachusetts at Boston (1964) are at Columbia Point, on Dorchester Bay (E). FRANKLIN PARK marks Dorchester's W boundary. ROXBURY is N, MATTAPAN S. The Battle of **Dorchester Heights** (March 16, 1776), which led to the evacuation of the British from Boston, involved the placement of American batteries on heights in what is now Thomas Park, SOUTH BOSTON.

Dorchester, Square formerly (to 1988), **Dominion Square** open space in downtown MONTRÉAL, Québec, often considered the city's central point. An 1830s cemetery, it became part of the city in 1855. The Basilique-Cathèdrale Marie-Reine-du-Monde (1870–94), on its S (officially; actually E) side, represented a move by the francophone Roman Catholic Church into a previously solidly anglophone, Protestant area; St. George's Church (Anglican) is on the W. In the early 20th century the square acquired two noted Beaux-Arts commercial centers, the Sun Life Bldg. (1913) and the Dominion Square Bldg. (1929). Place du Canada, on the S, now has high-rise office buildings. Dorchester Blvd., running along the S, became Blvd. René-Levesque in the 1980s. The fashionable Rue Peel runs along the W; Place Ville-Marie, first center of the UNDERGROUND CITY, is on the E.

Dormont borough, pop. 9772, Allegheny Co., SW Pennsylvania, 4 mi/6 km S of Pittsburgh. Settled c.1790, it is a largely residential community across the Monongahela R. from Pittsburgh's business district.

Dorval city, pop. 17,249, MONTRÉAL URBAN COMMUNITY, 7 mi/11 km W of downtown Montréal and adjacent (W) to Lachine, on L. Saint-Louis (the St. Lawrence R.). The site of Montréal's older (1960) international airport, which handles North American flights, it is a predominantly anglophone residential and commercial suburb.

Dos Cabezas Mountains small range in SE Arizona, NW of the CHIRICAHUA Mts. and separated from them by Apache Pass. The range reaches 8354 ft/2546 m at Dos Cabezas Peaks, "two heads" of nearly equal height. A copper GHOST TOWN of the same name is nearby.

Dothan city, pop. 53,589, seat of Houston Co., extreme SE Alabama, 15 mi/24 km N of the Florida line, in the WIREGRASS region. A lumbering and turpentine producing center in piney woods, it was incorporated in 1885. After the woods were cut it became a market and shipping center for a large agricultural and livestock producing area. Industries include food packing and processing, and the manufacture of hosiery, clothing, furniture, fertilizer, cigars, and toys. Dothan is home to a branch of Troy State University and to a community college. The Joseph M. Farley nuclear power plant (1977) is 16 mi/26 km ENE, near the Chattahoochee R.

Douglas **1.** city, pop. 12,822, Cochise Co., extreme SE Arizona, 23 mi/37 km SE of Bisbee and across the border from Agua Prieta (Sonora), Mexico. It is the trade center of a ranching and copper mining area. Among the the city's manufactures are gypsum products, furniture, clothing, bricks, and electronic parts. Early settlement developed around a copper smelter in 1900. Gypsum, tungsten, and limestone deposits are found in the vicinity. **2.** city, pop. 10,464, seat of Coffee Co., SC Georgia, 75 mi/120 km E of Albany. An agricultural trade center for the region, it has one of the state's major tobacco markets. Livestock (poultry and hogs) also feature in the economy, along with clothing and mobile home manufacturing. South Georgia College (1906) is here.

Douglas County 333 sq mi/862 sq km, pop. 416,444, in EC Nebraska, bounded by the Missouri R. and the Iowa state line (E) and the Platte R. (W). The seat of by far the most populous county in the state is OMAHA, which, with its suburbs and outlying areas, occupies the county's SE and dominates the economy. In the rest of the region grain and livestock production predominate.

Douglas Dam and Lake see under FRENCH BROAD R., Tennessee.

Douglas Park residential neighborhood on the West Side of Chicago, Illinois, due W of the Loop. Originally a Bohemian and Jewish community, it experienced rapid and debilitating housing turnover in recent decades; today it suffers from disinvestment and abandonment.

Douglaston residential section of NE QUEENS, New York, on the E of Little Neck Bay, near the Nassau Co. line, 12 mi/19 km E of downtown Manhattan. One of the city's most affluent neighborhoods, hilly and tree-covered, it has late-19th-century houses and 1920s apartment buildings, tennis and yacht clubs, and an atmosphere like that of the NORTH SHORE to the E.

Douglasville city, pop. 11,635, seat of Douglas Co., NW Georgia, 20 mi/32 km W of Atlanta. It has textile, asphalt, and other industries.

Dover **1.** city, pop. 27,630, state capital and seat of Kent Co., C Delaware, on the St. Jones Creek, 40 mi/64 km S of Wilmington. It was settled in 1683. Long an agricultural trade center, it is now a hub of government operations, commerce, and industry. Manufactures include gelatin, aerospace equipment, synthetic polymers, adhesives, latex, chemicals, and resins. **Dover Air Force Base,** just SE of the city, is a military cargo facility. Delaware State College (1891) and Wesley College (1873) are here. **2.** town, pop. 4915, Norfolk Co., E Massachusetts, on the Charles R., 14 mi/22 km SW of Boston. It is an affluent residential suburb, lightly populated given its proximity to the city. **3.** industrial city, pop. 25,042, seat of Strafford Co., SE New Hampshire, on the Cocheco, Bellamy, and Piscataqua rivers, 11 mi/18 km NW of Portsmouth. Founded in 1623, Dover was the first permanent New Hampshire settlement, and scene of the 1689 Cocheco Massacre of English settlers by local tribes. A 19th- and early-20th-century textile center, Dover produces electronic devices, motors, printing presses, cash registers, auto parts, shoes, and wood and aluminum products. **4.** town, pop, 15,115, Morris Co., NC New Jersey, on the Rockaway R., 7 mi/11 km NW of Morristown. The site was settled in 1722, and iron ore was soon found in the area. On the old Morris Canal (1831–1924), Dover developed as an iron manufacturing and stone processing port and shipping hub. The production of explosives at the government's Picatinny Arsenal (just N), which continues today, brought additional growth in the 1940s. Dover's manufactures include metal and food products and clothing. The town is in a mountainous, lake-filled resort area. **5.** city, pop. 11,329, Tuscarawas Co., NE Ohio, on the Tuscarawas R., 20 mi/32 km S of Canton. Founded in 1807, it is situated in a farming, coal mining, and fireclay area. Steel, electrical equipment, chemicals, clothing, garbage cans, vacuum cleaners, flooring, and other diverse items are manufactured in this industrial center.

Dowagiac city, pop. 6409, Cass Co., SW Michigan, on Dowagiac Creek, 20 mi/32 km NNE of South Bend, Indiana. A summer and winter resort, it also manufactures air-conditioning equipment, furnaces, sporting goods, and auto parts. Celery, wheat, and corn are grown in the area, and flour is milled here. Dowagiac is home to Southwestern Michigan College (1964).

Down East downwind, propelled by the prevailing SW wind. This sailing term is used variously as a name for E New England, Maine, or the Maritimes. It may also be applied within any of these areas; thus, to some in Maine, the real Down East begins at SCHOODIC Point.

Downers Grove village, pop. 46,858, Du Page Co., NE Illinois, 20 mi/32 km W of Chicago. It is a mainly residential community, with some factories. Situated at the E end of the ILLINOIS RESEARCH AND DEVELOPMENT CORRIDOR, it has grown as a high-tech and corporate headquarters center. Pierce Downers camped here in 1832 at a junction of Indian trails. George Williams College moved here from Chicago in 1967. The Morton Arboretum lies immediately NW.

Downey city, pop. 91,444, Los Angeles Co., SW California, 10 mi/16 km SE of Los Angeles and 10 mi/16 km NNE of Long Beach. A suburb of both cities, incorporated in 1957, it has aerospace-related industries including the manufacture of aircraft and missile components. Metal products, textiles, agricultural machinery, brass fittings, and rubber goods are also made. California Governor (1860–62) John Gately Downey bought the land around the site in 1873, and sold parcels of it.

Downington borough, pop. 7749, Chester Co., SE Pennsylvania, on the East Branch of Brandywine Creek, 28 mi/45 km W of Philadelphia. It produces paper and paper mill machinery.

Downriver group of blue-collar suburban communities in Wayne Co., SE Michigan, SW of Detroit, along the Detroit R. Downriver cities and towns include, among others, Allen Park, Ecorse, Lincoln Park, Melvindale, River Rouge, Southgate, Taylor, Trenton, and Wyandotte. The decline in manufacturing jobs here over the past few decades has caused employment and population loss throughout the area.

Downstate **1.** term applied to all of Illinois outside the Chicago metropolitan area, which is in the NE part of the state. The label may contain some conservative and rural connotations, but often simply refers to the state government, especially during political battles with its largest city. **2.** see under UPSTATE, New York.

Downsview suburb, now part of the city of NORTH YORK, Ontario. Twelve mi/19 km N of downtown Toronto, it is the site of a Canadian Forces Base and airport surrounded by residential areas (E and W) and a large mixed industrial zone (N).

Downtown **1.** in many US and Canadian cities, the central business district, often so called because on lower ground (as along a river) than residential neighborhoods. **2.** in New Orleans, Louisiana, section downriver from CANAL St., and E and NE of UPTOWN. Settled in the 18th century by French and Spanish, it includes the VIEUX CARRÉ, (French Quarter), BEAUREGARD SQUARE, the site of STORYVILLE, MARIGNY, the INNER HARBOR, and other, newer areas of the city. **3.** in Manhattan, New York City, the area below 14th St., or below 34th St., depending on one's definition of MIDTOWN. Downtown may be "down" because it is to the S, or because it is "down" the Hudson and East rivers. Its residential neighborhoods include GREENWICH VILLAGE and the LOWER EAST SIDE, and WALL STREET is its best-known business district. SOHO and TRIBECA are sections that mix older industrial and newer residential uses. Below Washington Square, Downtown is distinctive because its streets predate Manhattan's grid pattern.

Doylestown township, pop. 14,510, seat of Bucks Co., SE Pennsylvania, 23 mi/37 km N of Philadelphia. Settled in 1735, it is primarily residential but has some manufacturing and agriculture. The James A. Michener Art Museum, named for the author, who grew up here, is in Doylestown. Also here is Font Hill, home of archaeologist and antiquarian Henry C. Mercer; on the grounds is the Moravian Pottery and Tile Works, which produces tiles based on

Mercer's designs. The Mercer Museum maintains a well-known collection of early tools and machines. Doylestown is the seat of the Delaware Valley College of Science and Agriculture (1896), which has notable gardens. The Polish-American National Shrine of Our Lady of Czestochowa is nearby.

Dracut town, pop. 25,594, Middlesex Co., NE Massachusetts, on the Merrimack R. and the New Hampshire line, N of and adjoining Lowell. Once an Indian center, it was settled in the 1660s. Dracut's historic landmarks include the Stephen Russel House (1680), the Cutter Homestead (1720), and the Old Yellow Meeting House (1794). Commercial and suburban, the town also manufactures textiles, chemical products, and missile systems.

Dragoon Mountains small range SW of WILCOX, in SE Arizona, rising to 7512 ft/2290 m at Mt. Glenn. Within a section of the Colorado National Forest, it includes Cochise Stronghold, a natural rock fortress once used by the Apache leader. The mountains are named for US cavalry troops, until c.1860 known as dragoons. Copper has been mined in the **Little Dragoon Mts.,** a N extension rising to 6726 ft/2050 m.

Drakes Bay crescent-shaped inlet of the Pacific Ocean, 8 mi/13 km E–W, in Marin Co., NW California, 28 mi/45 km NW of San Francisco. The bluffs of the Point REYES peninsula shelter the bay, where the English navigator Francis Drake anchored his ship the *Golden Hinde* for several weeks in 1579. A brass tablet left by Drake and claiming the land for Queen Elizabeth I was found just E of the bay in 1933.

Drayton Plains unincorporated village in Oakland Co., SE Michigan, a suburban community on Loon L., 5 mi/8 km NW of Pontiac.

Dresden 1. nuclear power plant: see under MORRIS, Illinois. **2.** rural village, pop. 339, in Torrey township, Yates Co., WC New York, on L. Seneca, 48 mi/77 km SE of Rochester. It is the birthplace of orator Robert G. Ingersoll (1833–99). **3.** town, pop. 2646, Kent Co., extreme S Ontario,13 mi/21 km N of Chatham and 50 mi/80 km ENE of Detroit, Michigan, on the Sydenham R. The area was settled in the early 19th century by escaped US slaves, the best-known of whom was the Rev. Josiah Henson, who established a refuge and vocational school for fugitives; his life was the model for Harriet Beecher Stowe's *Uncle Tom's Cabin.* Henson's home is part of the Uncle Tom's Cabin Historic Site. Today the town has light industries including food processing and natural gas production. A harness racing track draws visitors.

Drewry's Bluff also, **Drury's Bluff** height on the W bank of the James R., 5 mi/8 km S of Richmond, Virginia. On May 15, 1862, Confederate batteries here repelled a Union gunboat attack. In the 1864 Union drive on Richmond, P.G.T. Beauregard and his troops here stopped (May 16) a Union advance led by Benjamin Butler.

Drexel Hill also, **Drexel Park** unincorporated village, pop. 29,744, in Upper Darby township, Delaware Co., SE Pennsylvania. Drexel Hill is a residential suburb of Philadelphia, 5 mi/8 km W of the city's downtown.

drift see under MORAINE.

Driftless Area 13,000 sq mi/33,700 sq km, largely in SW Wisconsin, also in neighboring areas of SE Minnesota, NE Iowa, and NW Illinois. An upland area, it is generally assumed to have been untouched by glaciers, leaving a rougher, craggier landscape than in areas surrounding it. In the early 19th century its hills were major lead producers, and the government forestalled settlement by farmers until the 1840s. Wisconsin's SAND COUNTIES are on its NE. The ICE AGE NATIONAL SCIENTIFIC RESERVE lies along its edge across Wisconsin.

Driskill Mountain the highest point (535 ft/163 m) in Louisiana, in the NW part of the state, NE of Bienville, along the Saline Bayou.

Droop Mountain battle site, an Allegheny ridge reaching 3060 ft/933 m, in Pocahontas Co., SE West Virginia, 22 mi/35 km NNE of White Sulphur Springs, near Droop, where on Nov. 6, 1863, Union forces under W.W. Averell broke the last serious Confederate stand in the new state.

Druid Hill Park 674 ac/273 ha, in WC Baltimore, Maryland. Acquired by the city of Baltimore in 1860, it contains several lakes, a natural history museum and conservatory, and the Baltimore Zoo.

Druid Hills in Georgia: **a.** residential neighborhood of Atlanta, 3 mi/5 km NE of Downtown, developed in the 1890s as a STREETCAR SUBURB designed by Frederick Law Olmsted, and noted for its dogwood-dominated landscaping. **b.** unincorporated community, pop. 12,174, De Kalb Co., adjacent to the Atlanta neighborhood, and similar in character. EMORY is just NE.

Drumheller city, pop. 6277, S Alberta, on the Red Deer R., 69 mi/111 km NE of Calgary. A shipping point for the area's grains, it is surrounded by coal mines, wheat fields, and oil and gas wells. First settled (1897) by ranchers, the site was purchased by Samuel Drumheller in 1910, and his coal mines supported the economy for the next half-century. A violent strike here in 1925 led to the creation of the Mine Workers' Union of Canada. The Tyrrell Museum of Paleontology and the Drumheller Dinosaur Fossil Museum and Prehistoric Park are here. The nearby Dinosaur Trail through the Red Deer Valley Badlands ends at the city.

Drummond Island 20 mi/32 km long and 11 mi/18 km wide, in Chippewa Co., extreme NE Michigan, off the E tip of the Upper Peninsula. In northern L. Huron, at the mouth of the St. Marys R., it is the only island of the Manitoulin chain that belongs to the US. It became an American possession in 1828 when it was taken over from the British, who had occupied it in 1815 and built a fort. The island is a hunting, boating, and fishing resort, and also has stone quarries and lumber resources. Much of it is covered by Lake Superior State Forest. **Drummond,** pop. 835, on Potagannissing Bay, is the only village. The island is accessible by car ferry from the mainland.

Drummondville city, pop. 35,462, seat of Drummond Co., S Québec, 58 mi/94 km ENE of Montréal, on the R. Saint-François. Founded as a British military post in 1815, it is a center of the textile industry, makes a variety of other products, and is a road transport hub.

Dryden town, pop. 6505, Kenora District, NW Ontario, on L. Wabigoon, 210 mi/338 km NW of Thunder Bay and 175 mi/280 km E of Winnipeg, Manitoba. On the railroad and Trans-Canada Highway, it is the distribution hub for its region. The local economy is centered on pulp, paper, and lumber milling as well as printing. An 1890s provincial experimental farm brought agricultural settlers into the area, which is now popular also for camping, hunting, and fishing.

Dry Tortugas also, **Tortugas** or **Tortugas Keys** group of seven islands in Monroe Co., SW Florida, lying at the entrance to the Gulf of Mexico, 67 mi/108 km W of Key West. Loggerhead Key, less than 1 mi/1.6 km long, is the largest of the islands, which are known for their marine life and migratory birds. They were discovered by Ponce de León (1513), and named by him for the many tortoises he saw. They once harbored pirates, and many shipwrecks occurred on their shoals. Fort Jefferson, the largest all-masonry fort in the Western Hemisphere, was built (1846–66) on Garden Key and used as a Union prison during the Civil War. Since 1935 the Dry Tortugas have constituted the Fort Jefferson National Monument.

Duarte city, pop. 20,688, Los Angeles Co., SW California, 19 mi/31 km NE of Los Angeles, on the San Gabriel R., just S of the San Gabriel Mts. On former orange growing land, it has some light industry. The renowned City of Hope National Medical Center is here.

Dubawnt River see under THELON R., Northwest Territories.

Dublin **1.** city, pop. 23,229, Alameda Co., NC California, in Dublin Canyon and the San Ramos Valley, 16 mi/26 km SE of Oakland. Its industries make photographic, communications, and security equipment and industrial materials. **2.** city, pop. 16,312, seat of Laurens Co., C Georgia, on the Oconee R., 47 mi/76 km ESE of Macon. Incorporated in 1812, it was a major river shipping center before railroads took its business away in the mid 19th century. Lumber and textile mills have since been the city's economic mainstay. **3.** town, pop. 1474, Cheshire Co., S New Hampshire, 12 mi/19 km ESE of Keene. One of the state's highest towns, at 1485 ft/453 m, it is just NE of Mt. Monadnock. The *Old Farmer's Almanac,* America's oldest periodical, has been published here since 1792. Dublin Pond and several other resorts are important in the local economy. **4.** city, pop. 16,371, Franklin and Delaware counties, C Ohio, on the Scioto R., 11 mi/18 km NW of Columbus. This suburban city has grown rapidly in recent years and now houses the corporate headquarters of Wendy's and other restaurant chains and of medical and pharmaceutical distributors.

Dubuque city, pop. 57,546, seat of Dubuque Co., NE Iowa, on the Mississippi R. at the Wisconsin and Illinois state lines. The oldest city in Iowa, it is named for French miner Julien Dubuque, who came to the area in search of lead in 1788. A permanent townsite dates from 1833, when the Black Hawk Treaty opened the area to settlement. The booming mining town gave way to a lumbering center, from which log rafts were floated down the Mississippi. Today, the city is a distribution and processing center for the region's agriculture and dairies, while railroad shops, shipyards, meatpacking plants, and a brewery are prominent in the economy. Factories produce cast iron and sheet metal products, chemicals, and agricultural machinery. Educational institutions include the University of Dubuque (1852), Clarke College (1843), and Loras College (1839).

Duck Lake town, pop. 661, C Saskatchewan, 32 mi/52 km SW of Prince Albert, just W of the South Saskatchewan R. It is a farming community. Just W, on March 26, 1885, MÉTIS forces from BATOCHE (SE) clashed with North West Mounted Police from Fort Carlton (13 mi/21 km WNW, on the North Saskatchewan R.), killing several of them. This skirmish set a military resolution of the North-West Rebellion in motion. Fort Carlton, an 1810 HUDSON'S BAY COMPANY post, had been garrisoned by the NWMP to face the rebellion; it was abandoned and burned, but is now a (partially restored) National Historic Park.

Duck Mountain rolling, forested upland, part of the MANITOBA ESCARPMENT, extending for 50 mi/80 km along the border of SW Manitoba and into E Saskatchewan. It includes BALDY Mt. (2727 ft/832 m), the highest point in Manitoba. Duck Mt. Provincial Park is NW of Dauphin.

Duck River 250 mi/400 km long, in Tennessee. It is formed by headstreams N of Manchester, in Coffee Co., and flows W into Normandy L., formed by Normandy Dam, just N of Tullahoma. It then flows generally W and WNW across the S of the NASHVILLE BASIN, through Shelbyville and Columbia, and winds into Kentucky L. (the Tennessee R.) SE of Camden. The Buffalo R. joins it from the S near its mouth on the lake.

Duck Valley Indian Reservation 506 sq mi/1310 sq km, straddling the Idaho-Nevada border. Established in 1877 for Shoshonean groups, it has a pop. of 1101 (93% Indian).

Due West town, pop. 1220, Abbeville Co., NW South Carolina, 12 mi/19 km N of Abbeville, home to Erskine College (1839).

Dugway unincorporated community, pop. 1761, Tooele Co., NW Utah, in the Great Salt L. Desert, 36 mi/58 km SW of TOOELE and 62 mi/100 km SW of Salt Lake City. It is situated at the E edge of the large **Dugway Proving Grounds,** an Army installation used to test chemical and biological weapons. In 1968, the base was alleged to have released nerve gas, killing 6500 sheep on neighboring ranches. The Army denied the charge, but compensated ranchers. *Dugway* is a term Mormon settlers used for a wagon road created by digging ruts into the side of a mountain.

Dukes County 102 sq mi/264 sq km, pop. 11,639, in SE Massachusetts. It comprises the island of Martha's Vineyard, the Elizabeth Islands, and other islands off Cape Cod. Its seat is Edgartown. Dukes depends on tourism and summer residents for its economic well-being; it consists primarily of summer resorts and beach communities.

Dulles Airport see WASHINGTON DULLES INTERNATIONAL AIRPORT.

Duluth **1.** city, pop. 9029, Gwinnett Co., NC Georgia, 25 mi/40 km NE of downtown Atlanta, on the Chattahoochee R. It is a growing residential suburb, with business parks. **2.** city, pop. 85,493, seat of St. Louis Co., NE Minnesota. It is situated at the W end of L. Superior, at the mouth of the St. Louis R., on St. Louis Bay across from SUPERIOR, Wisconsin (S). The W terminus of the St. Lawrence Seaway, Duluth is one of the world's largest freshwater ports, shipping iron ore, coal, grain, oil, and other products from throughout the Midwest. Industries include iron and steel making, cement production, oil refining, and meatpacking, along with the manufacture of electronics, frozen foods, and wood products. Although diversified and active, the local economy has been declining steadily for decades. The city is the site of the College of St. Scholastica (1912) and a campus of the University of Minnesota (1947). Headquarters of Superior National Forest, Duluth is also the gateway to the skiing areas of Spirit Mt., Mont du Lac, and Chester Bowl. A US Air Force Base and Coast Guard Station are here. The site was visited by French explorers in the late 17th century. Duluth developed from a fur trading post (established 1792) to an iron mining and lumbering center, becoming a transportation and shipping hub by the 1870s.

Dumas city, pop. 12,871, seat of Moore Co., NW Texas, in the PANHANDLE, 45 mi/72 km NNW of Amarillo. Founded in

1892, it is in the center of an irrigated area producing sorghum, castor beans, vegetables, wheat, and cattle. Natural gas fields in the vicinity are the major US helium producer. The city has a zinc smelter and oil refineries. Nitrates, carbon black, and fertilizer are manufactured. L. MEREDITH National Recreation Area is 20 mi/32 km SE.

Dumbarton Oaks estate and gardens in GEORGETOWN, NW Washington, D.C. Donated to Harvard University in 1940, it now houses the Center for Byzantine Studies and a 27-ac/11-ha park. It was the site, in 1944, of a conference at which the US, Britain, China, and the Soviet Union drew up proposals for the creation of the United Nations.

Dumfries town, pop. 4282, Prince William Co., NE Virginia, on Interstate 95 and Quantico Creek, 22 mi/35 km SW of Alexandria. An important 18th-century trading center, it lost importance when the creek silted up. Mason Locke ("Parson") Weems, fanciful biographer of George Washington, kept a bookshop here, now a museum. The town is a suburb with many mobile-home parks.

Dumont borough, pop. 17,187, Bergen Co., NE New Jersey, 4 mi/6 km NE of Hackensack. Settled by the Dutch in the late 17th century, it is a largely residential New York suburb, with some office buildings and light industry.

Dunbar city, pop. 8697, Kanawha Co., W West Virginia, 7 mi/11 km WNW of Charleston, on the Kanawha R. It is a part of the Kanawha Valley industrial complex, producing oil, glass, and various manufactures.

Dunbar Heights also, **Dunbar** largely residential section of W VANCOUVER, British Columbia, on high ground E of POINT GREY's University of British Columbia campus, and SW of KITSILANO. Largely developed from the 1930s, it is upper-middle-class.

Duncan city, pop. 21,732, seat of Stephens Co., SC Oklahoma, 25 mi/40 km ESE of Lawton. On the CHISHOLM TRAIL in Indian Territory, it was a stop for late-19th-century cattle drives. The city is a trade hub for cotton, grain, and livestock producers. A supply point for oil and gas fields discovered nearby in 1921, it produces oilfield machinery and asphalt and is a refining center.

Duncanville city, pop. 35,748, Dallas Co., NE Texas, 12 mi/19 km SW of downtown Dallas. It is a residential and light industrial suburb on the SW boundary of Dallas, along the beltway (Interstate 20).

Dundalk unincorporated community, pop. 65,800, Baltimore Co., NC Maryland, on the Patapsco R. and Bear Creek, immediately SE of Baltimore. It is a largely residential suburb, but also home to a large marine terminal. Dundalk Community College (1970) is here. SPARROWS POINT is just SE.

Dundas town, pop. 21,868, Hamilton-Wentworth Regional Municipality, S Ontario, 3 mi/5 km W of Hamilton. Laid out in 1801 at the head of the Desjardins Canal, it was an important lake port before the arrival of the railroad in the 1850s. It is now an industrial and residential suburb of Hamilton, and a retail and shipping center. Manufactures include furniture, textiles, and machine tools.

Dundas Street thoroughfare and historic route in S Ontario. Begun, like YONGE St., from York (Toronto) in the 1790s, it was planned as an E–W military road to LONDON, created inland from L. Ontario in case of American attack. It runs from Toronto's East End through Downtown. Joined by BLOOR St., it leaves Etobicoke as Highway 5, passes through Mississauga and Flamborough, and proceeds to Woodstock before entering London as Highway 2. Along it in Toronto are (E–W) the EATON CENTRE, City Hall, and Chinatown, among important sites.

Dunedin city, pop. 34,012, Pinellas Co., W Florida, on St. Joseph Sound of the Gulf of Mexico, 20 mi/32 km W of Tampa. Settled in the 1850s, it was an important port, but is now a winter resort and fishing center. Caladesi Island State Park lies W. The city is also active in the processing and shipping of citrus fruits and the manufacture of electrical parts, machinery, and cattle feed.

Dunellen borough, pop. 6528, Middlesex Co., NE New Jersey, 7 mi/11 km N of New Brunswick. Largely residential, it has some light industry and commercial greenhouses.

Dungeness hamlet in Clallam Co., NW Washington, on the Dungeness R., Dungeness Bay, and the Juan de Fuca Strait, at the NE end of the OLYMPIC PENINSULA, 22 mi/35 km across the Strait (SE) from Victoria, British Columbia. Dungeness crabs, found in the area's waters, were named for this village. **Dungeness Spit,** off the coast, 5.5 mi/9 km long, has a lighthouse and encloses Dungeness Bay.

Dunkirk city, pop. 13,989, Chautauqua Co., SW New York, on L. Erie, 40 mi/64 km SW of Buffalo. Settled in 1805, it was originally known as Chadwick's Bay. Following completion of the Erie Canal (1825) and arrival of the Erie Railroad (1851), Dunkirk developed as a fishing center and distribution point for its agricultural region. Local vineyards produce Concord grapes. Industries manufacture stainless steel, oil refining machinery, marine motors, radiators, boilers, valves, and tools. Dunkirk is home to Holy Cross and St. Columba's seminaries and the Conference Grounds of the Evangelical and Reformed Church. There are several beach resorts in the vicinity.

Dunmore borough, pop. 15,403, Lackawanna Co., NE Pennsylvania, 3 mi/5 km E of Scranton. Settled in 1783, it is situated in an anthracite mining and apple growing region. Dunmore is both residential and industrial, with manufactures including textiles, processed foods, and metal products.

Dunn city, pop. 8336, Harnett Co., EC North Carolina, on Interstate 95, 23 mi/37 km NE of Fayetteville. It is an agricultural trade center with some light industry.

Dunnville town, pop. 12,131, Haldimand-Norfolk Regional Municipality, S Ontario, on the Grand R., 5 mi/8 km N of L. Erie and 27 mi/43 km SSE of Hamilton. The site was chosen in 1827 for the terminus of a feeder to the Welland Canal. The town now manufactures tapestries, draperies, knitted goods, wire fencing, chemicals, boats, and doors.

Dunseith city, pop. 723, Rolette Co., N North Dakota, 75 mi/121 km NW of Devils Lake. It lies at the S edge of the TURTLE Mts., and is 12 mi/19 km S of the Manitoba border and the INTERNATIONAL PEACE GARDEN. Dunseith originated as a gristmill in 1887. The Turtle Mountain Indian Reservation is 7 mi/11 km E.

Dunstable town, pop. 2236, Middlesex Co., NE Massachusetts, 8 mi/13 km WNW of Lowell, on the New Hampshire border.

Dunwoody unincorporated community, pop. 26,302, De Kalb Co., NW Georgia, 13 mi/21 km NNE of downtown Atlanta. It is a residential suburb.

Du Page County 337 sq mi/873 sq km, pop. 781,666, in NE Illinois. Wheaton is its seat. Although there is still some truck farming in the W, Du Page Co. has become a sea of

Chicago suburbs. Downers Grove, Lisle, and Naperville are on the ILLINOIS RESEARCH AND DEVELOPMENT CORRIDOR, which follows I-88. The ARGONNE NATIONAL LABORATORY and Fermi National Accelerator Laboratory are here, as is part of O'Hare International Airport.

Du Page River 30 mi/48 km long, in NE Illinois. It rises in several branches W of Chicago and flows SW from their junction, S of Naperville, to the Des Plaines R. just above its confluence with the Kankakee R. Its **West Branch** is 30 mi/48 km long, and flows generally S through Naperville. The **East Branch** is 20 mi/32 km long; it rises W of Addison, and flows S and SW before it joins the West Branch.

Dupont Circle commercial neighborhood in NW Washington, D.C., 1 mi/1.5 km NW of the White House and just E of Rock Creek Park, at the intersection of Massachusetts and Connecticut avenues and other streets. Since the 1960s it has been one of the District's most popular boutique and entertainment districts, with an active street community. ADAMS-MORGAN is just N, GEORGETOWN just W.

Duquesne city, pop. 8525, Allegheny Co., SW Pennsylvania, on the Monongahela R., 10 mi/16 km SE of Pittsburgh. Laid out in 1885 by the Duquesne Steel Co. and soon (1890) taken over by Andrew Carnegie, Duquesne long had one of the largest steel plants in the US.

Du Quoin city, pop. 6697, Perry Co., SW Illinois, 20 mi/32 km N of Carbondale. It is a manufacturing center, producing electronic equipment, processed meats, and bottled beverages. A state fair is held annually on Labor Day.

Durand city, pop. 4283, Shiawassee Co., SC Michigan, 15 mi/24 km WSW of Flint, on Threemile Creek. Settled in the 1870s, it became a major junction for the Grand Western Trunk Railroad, famous for its large Union Station. It remains an Amtrak stop, and has railroad repair shops. Situated in an agricultural area, it has grain elevators and manufactures machinery.

Durango city, pop. 12,430, seat of La Plata Co., SW Colorado, on the Animas R., in the foothills of the La Plata Mts., 15 mi/24 km N of the New Mexico border. Settled in 1880, it was once a gold and silver mining and smelting center. Tourism is now central to its economy, with visitors drawn to its Purgatory Ski Area, one of the nation's last narrow-gauge railways, and other attractions. Durango also ships produce, livestock, timber, oil, and minerals. There is some light manufacturing. The city is headquarters for the San Juan National Forest and the seat of Fort Lewis College (1911).

Durant **1.** city, pop. 2838, Holmes Co., WC Mississippi, on the Big Black R., 56 mi/90 km NNE of Jackson. Founded in 1858 on the Illinois Central Railroad, it is an agricultural trade center. **2.** city, pop. 12,823, seat of Bryan Co., SE Oklahoma, in the Red R. valley, 43 mi/69 km ESE of Ardmore and 12 mi/19 km N of the Texas border. It is a trade and processing hub for cotton, peanut, grain, livestock, and oil producers. The city also manufactures truck bodies, cement, and clothing. It is the seat of Southeastern Oklahoma State University (1909). L. TEXOMA lies to the W.

Durham **1.** town, pop. 11,818, Strafford Co., SE New Hampshire. It is on the Oyster and Lamprey rivers, 15 mi/24 km NW of Portsmouth. Originally a parish of Dover, the town was the scene of Indian massacres in 1675, 1694, and 1704. During the Revolutionary War, gunpowder and weapons seized from the British at New Castle, near Portsmouth, were hidden in Durham Meetinghouse and supposedly later used at Bunker Hill. The town is best known as the seat of the University of New Hampshire, founded in 1866 as part of Dartmouth College and moved here in 1893. Durham is largely rural and agricultural. **2.** city, pop. 136,611, seat of Durham Co. (pop. 181,835), NC North Carolina, 20 mi/32 km NW of Raleigh. The site of Prattsburg, 2 mi/3 km E, was settled by Scotch-Irish and English during the 1750s. A century later, landholder William Pratt denied right of way for the railroad, and a second village developed on land donated by Dr. Bartlett Durham. Known as Durham Station and Durhamville, it developed into a manufacturing center, primarily as a consequence of the tobacco industry. Washington Duke and his sons began making tobacco products here after the Civil War. In the 1880s, they mechanized the industry, making Durham the leading US cigarette producer, and accumulating tremendous wealth. The city's other manufactures have included cotton textiles, hosiery, machinery, lumber and lumber products, building materials, chemicals, and feed. Durham is home to Duke University (originally Trinity College, renamed in 1924), North Carolina Central University (1909), Durham College (1947), and Durham Technical Institute (1961). The city has also become a medical center, relying largely on tobacco money. Bennett Place State Historical Park, 3 mi/5 km NW, was the site, on April 26, 1865, of Joseph Johnston's surrender of the last Confederate force active in the East. The RESEARCH TRIANGLE is 5 mi/8 km S.

Dust Bowl area of the GREAT PLAINS where in the 1930s topsoil loosened by erosion blew away in huge clouds or storms, covering areas to the N and E in layers of varying depths and types of "dust." During World War I, food demands from the European battlefront led to greatly expanded planting of wheat in former grazing areas. The turning of once sod-protected soil, and the subsequent return of large herds of cattle, who pulverized it, were followed, after 1932, by drought. In 1934 the first of the major dust storms occurred, carrying soil from the Kansas-Colorado border. In May 1934, the most famous of the storms dumped fine soil all over the E US, and carried some up to 300 mi/480 km into the Atlantic Ocean. The Texas Panhandle, W Oklahoma and Kansas, and E New Mexico and Colorado were the source of most of the "dust," which continued to blow until damper weather returned in the late 1930s. The Dust Bowl is associated with the migration of "Okies" from Oklahoma (and other states) toward the more promising agricultural lands of California; many of these were impelled not by dust storms themselves but by generally hard conditions in the Depression. Government efforts to alter the conditions leading to the Dust Bowl included planting of windbreaks, promotion of contour plowing and other changes in farming techniques, and establishment of what became NATIONAL GRASSLANDS. See also PALLISER'S TRIANGLE, W Canada.

Dutchess County 804 sq mi/2082 sq km, pop. 259,462, in SE New York, bordered by the Hudson R. (W) and the Connecticut line (E). The upper part is in the Taconic Mts. Its seat is POUGHKEEPSIE. Manufacturing and corporate office development are centered at Poughkeepsie and Beacon. Almost completely agricultural until the 1970s, the county still has many working farms (about a quarter of its area) producing dairy products, fruit, and vegetables. From the area around FISHKILL to its S boundary, it is now a residential center for New York City commuters. The N part, notably such communities as Rhinecliff and Millbrook, has many summer and weekend homes. Historic sites, such as Hyde Park, attract tourists.

Dutch Harbor see under UNALASKA I., Alaska.

Dutchtown neighborhood on the NORTH SIDE of Pittsburgh, Pennsylvania, on the Allegheny R. opposite the GOLDEN TRIANGLE, immediately E of ALLEGHENY. Home to German and Croatian immigrants who worked in the now-closed tanneries, packing houses, and breweries, Dutchtown is still dominated by H. J. Heinz Co. plants. Young professionals have begun restoring the century-old brick and wooden row houses.

Duval County 776 sq mi/2010 sq km, pop. 672,971, in NE Florida, on the Atlantic Ocean (E), coterminous since 1968 with its seat, the city of JACKSONVILLE. It also includes the municipalities of ATLANTIC BEACH, Baldwin (town, pop. 1450), JACKSONVILLE BEACH, and Neptune Beach (city, pop. 6816).

Duxbury town, pop. 13,895, Plymouth Co., SE Massachusetts, on Plymouth Bay, 30 mi/48 km SE of Boston. It was founded in 1624 by Colonists from Plymouth, including Miles Standish, William Brewster, and John Alden, whose house still stands. Formerly a shipbuilding center, it is now primarily a summer resort.

Dwight village, pop. 4230, Livingston Co., EC Illinois, 17 mi/27 km NE of Pontiac. An old commercial and rail center, it is known today for its Correctional Center.

Dworshak Dam and Reservoir see under CLEARWATER Mts., Idaho.

Dyer town, pop 10,923, Lake Co., extreme NW Indiana, 10 mi/16 km S of Hammond, along the Illinois border. A former dairying center, it is now a suburb of Chicago and the CALUMET area.

Dyersburg city, pop. 16,317, seat of Dyer Co., extreme NW Tennessee, on the North Fork of the Forked Deer R., 77 mi/127 km NNE of Memphis. Founded in the 1820s, this industrial and trade center manufactures rubber and electrical products, textiles, and cottonseed oil, mills lumber, and processes vegetables, soybeans, cotton, corn, and dairy goods. There is a community college.

Dyess Air Force Base see under ABILENE, Texas.

Dymaxion House see under DEARBORN, Michigan.

E

Eads Bridge pioneering steel-truss span across the Mississippi R. in downtown SAINT LOUIS, Missouri, just N of the Gateway Arch and Jefferson National Expansion Memorial. Built (1867–74) by James B. Eads, it is 6220 ft/1896 m in overall length; the central, and longest, of its three overwater spans is 530 ft/162 m long and 55 ft/17 m above river level. The bridge carries rail and auto traffic. Its construction, which caused 14 deaths from caisson disease (bends), foreshadowed that of the Brooklyn Bridge and other major US spans. Six later bridges cross the Mississippi at St. Louis.

Eagan city, pop. 47,409, Dakota Co., SE Minnesota, on the Minnesota R., a suburb 9 mi/14 km S of St. Paul. Just SE of Minneapolis–St. Paul International Airport, it is one of the fastest-growing communities in the area. The corridors along I-35E and Highway 13 have experienced substantial commercial development. A part of Fort Snelling State Park is here.

Eagle Bridge hamlet in Hoosick township, Rensselaer Co., E New York, 23 mi/37 km NE of Troy and 7 mi/11 km W of the Vermont line. The longtime home of the painter "Grandma" Moses (1860–1961), Eagle Bridge and its environs served as inspiration for many of her town scenes and landscapes.

Eagle Lake in Lassen Co., NE California, 12 mi/19 km NW of Susanville. Thirteen mi/21 km SE–NW and 2–6 mi/3–10 km wide, it is on the E edge of the Lassen National Forest. California's second-largest natural lake is popular for camping and boating; its shoreline is mostly privately owned.

Eagle Mountain highest point (2301 ft/701 m) in Minnesota, in Cook Co., in the NE ARROWHEAD REGION, 10 mi/16 km S of the Ontario border, c.106 mi/172 km NE of Duluth. The Misquah Hills, rising to 2230 ft/680 m, are to the NE.

Eagle Mountain Lake see under TRINITY R., Texas.

Eagle Nest Butte 3410 ft/1040 m, in Jackson Co., SC South Dakota, S of the White R. near Wanblee.

Eagle Pass **1.** see under CRAIGELLACHIE, British Columbia. **2.** city, pop. 20,651, seat of MAVERICK Co., SW Texas, on the Rio Grande opposite Piedras Negras (Coahuila), Mexico, 130 mi/210 km SW of San Antonio. The settlement began as Camp California, on a major Gold Rush route, near a crossing on the Rio Grande called El Paso de Agüila. The town grew around Fort Duncan (1849), which protected the westbound emigrants. It was active during Indian wars, and in the Civil War Confederate goods blockaded elsewhere were shipped from here. The military post remained active into the 20th century. A port of entry, the city relies heavily on international trade and tourism (fishing and hunting are popular). Natural gas and oil production and farming and ranching are important in the area, along with mineral (fluorite, barite) extraction.

Eagle Peak 7510 ft/2291 m, in Hudspeth Co., far SW Texas, near the Rio Grande, SW of Van Horn. It is the highest point in the **Eagle Mts.,** a small NW–SE range (c.15 mi/24 km long). Fluorspar production reached a peak in the area in the 1940s.

Eaker Air Force Base see under BLYTHEVILLE, Arkansas.

Earle Ammunition Depot see under COLTS NECK, New Jersey.

Easley city, pop. 15,195, Pickens Co., NW South Carolina, 13 mi/21 km W of Greenville, in the Blue Ridge foothills. A cotton milling center in a diversified farming area, it produces flour, feed, clothing, cottonseed oil, and textile and building supplies.

East, the variously defined region of the US. Historically, it often refers to lands inhabited during the first 150 years of European settlement, which occurred almost entirely E of the Allegheny Mts. (the great barrier to development of the "West"). This area includes NEW ENGLAND and the MIDDLE ATLANTIC region; from Virginia S it is more likely to be considered part of the SOUTH. A much more expansive East includes everything E of the Mississippi R. (or E of the Mississippi and N of the Ohio R., again so as to separate South from East); this East includes most of the MIDDLE WEST.

East Aurora village, pop. 6647, in Aurora township, Erie Co., W New York, 16 mi/26 km SE of Buffalo. From 1895 to 1939 it was the center of the Roycroft artists' colony and of the Roycroft Press, established by author and publisher Elbert Hubbard (1856–1915) to stimulate fine handcraftsmanship. This Buffalo suburb now has a variety of light industries, including the manufacture of metal and wood products.

East Baltimore in BALTIMORE, Maryland, anything E of Charles St., but esp. the white ethnic neighborhoods E of Downtown and the INNER HARBOR. Greektown and largely Polish Highlandtown are among these. The working- and middle-class area, which also has more racially mixed pockets closer to Downtown, is noted for its streets of brick row houses.

East Bank see SOUTHEAST, Minneapolis, Minnesota.

East Baton Rouge Parish 458 sq mi/1186 sq km, pop. 380,105, in SE Louisiana, bounded W by the Mississippi R., E by the Amite R., and S by Bayou Manchac. Its seat is BATON ROUGE. East Baton Rouge Parish is home to the vast majority of the capital area's inhabitants, who reside in the cities of BAKER and ZACHARY and in a number of unincorporated suburbs, including Shenandoah (pop. 13,429) and Merrydale (pop. 10,395). West Baton Rouge Parish, across the river, has only 19,419 inhabitants, and consists largely of huge sugar plantations, with riverfront oil-industry installations. The city of Port Allen (pop. 6277), across from Baton Rouge, is its seat.

East Bay see under BAY AREA, California.

Eastborough city, pop. 896, Sedgwick Co., S Kansas, an affluent enclave within Wichita, just E of Downtown. Now almost wholly residential, it was once a center of the petroleum industry, after oil was discovered here (1930).

East Boston section of Boston, Massachusetts, across Boston Harbor from the downtown. Part of the city since 1637, it was essentially unsettled until 1833. An industrial area with shipyards and miles of docks, it is now predominantly Italian. LOGAN INTERNATIONAL AIRPORT occupies the SE part, on largely reclaimed land.

East Brainerd unincorporated community, pop. 11,594, Hamilton Co., SE Tennessee, a suburb on the SE side of Chattanooga, 8 mi/13 km ESE of Downtown.

East Brookfield town, pop. 2033, Worcester Co., SC Massachusetts, 12 mi/19 km WSW of Worcester. It is the birthplace (1862) of baseball legend Connie Mack, and was set off from Brookfield in 1920.

East Brunswick township, pop. 43,548, Middlesex Co., C New Jersey, adjacent (SE) to New Brunswick. It is a growing suburb along the New Jersey Turnpike.

East Cambridge see under CAMBRIDGE, Massachusetts.

Eastchester in New York: **a.** commercial and residential section, extreme NE Bronx. It consists of those parts of the village of Eastchester (established in the 1660s by New Englanders) E of the Bronx R. that became part of the Bronx in 1895. Pelham Bay Park and the Hutchinson R. lie E, Baychester S, and Wakefield NW. Other parts of Eastchester village are today in MOUNT VERNON and Pelham Manor, Westchester Co. Eastchester's economy revolves around Route 1 (the Boston Post Road) and Interstate 95, which pass through it. The Vincent-Halsey House served as the US executive mansion for two months in 1797 when President John Adams, escaping a yellow fever epidemic in Philadelphia, lived here. Eastchester Bay, at the mouth of the Hutchinson R., lies SE, in Pelham Bay Park. **b.** town, pop. 30,867, in Westchester Co., adjacent (N) to Mount Vernon. Primarily residential, it includes BRONXVILLE, TUCKAHOE, and several other affluent villages whose residents are primarily New York City commuters.

East Chicago city, pop. 33,892, Lake Co., extreme NW Indiana, on L. Michigan, 18 mi/29 km SE of Chicago, Illinois. It is a major port, its dock-filled Indiana Harbor jutting out into L. Michigan. In the highly industrialized CALUMET region, it is adjacent to GARY, HAMMOND, and WHITING. East Chicago receives such raw materials as iron ore, coal, limestone, and oil at its port, and processes these and other materials into a variety of products at its refineries, foundries, chemical plants, steel mills, and smelters. It has railroad shops, and manufactures industrial equipment and clothing. East Chicago has suffered economic reversals in recent decades; its population is little more than half what it was at mid-century.

East Cleveland city, pop. 33,096, Cuyahoga Co., NE Ohio, a residential suburb of Cleveland, which it adjoins. Founded in 1801, it is today the site of the Warner-Swasey Observatory of Case Western Reserve University. Local manufactures include machine tools, trucks, and electrical parts, and there are electrical research laboratories here. A noted public recreational area, Forest Hill Park, was once the site of John D. Rockefeller's summer estate.

East Dallas largely residential section of Dallas, Texas, lying N of Interstate 30 and E of the CENTRAL EXPRESSWAY. WHITE ROCK L. is in this area of middle-class and more affluent housing. Dallas Bible College is here. Garland borders on the NE, Mesquite on the E.

East Detroit city, pop. 35,283, Macomb Co., SE Michigan, 10 mi/16 km NE of Detroit. The settlement originated in 1827 on the military road between Fort Gratiot (now Port Huron) and Fort Wayne (now Detroit). Exactly between Mt. Clemens and Detroit, it was called Halfway Village, but was renamed in 1929 when it was incorporated as a city. A largely residential suburb of Detroit, it also manufactures such products as marine and auto parts, structural steel, and tools. In 1991 it was renamed Eastpointe.

East Egg see under GREAT NECK, New York.

East End **1.** in VANCOUVER, British Columbia, sections of the city E of Downtown and the N–S Cambie St., including some of the city's poorer neighborhoods, as well as LITTLE ITALY and Japanese and other ethnic enclaves. Strathcona is a neighborhood that resisted 1950s URBAN RENEWAL plans, has been largely rehabilitated, and is now home to much of the city's Chinese pop. **2.** section of NW Washington, D.C., between the White House (W) and Capitol Hill (E), N of Pennsylvania Ave. CHINATOWN is in this commercial district, and the presence of many courts and Federal agencies in the Judiciary Square area has led to relocation by law firms since the 1980s, providing some renewal for a district that had lost many of its older businesses to areas farther W. **3.** region of Long Island, New York, including RIVERHEAD and the NORTH FORK and SOUTH FORK. Largely agricultural, it also attracts vacationers and exurbanites, particularly to the South Fork's HAMPTONS. **4.** group of neighborhoods in Pittsburgh, Pennsylvania. The district contains the city's wealthiest areas: HIGHLAND PARK, SHADYSIDE, POINT BREEZE, and SQUIRREL HILL.

Eastern Cherokee Indian Reservation also, **Qualla Boundary Reservation** 81 sq mi/210 sq km, pop. 6527 (83% Indian), on the SE edge of the Great Smoky Mountains Park, in far W North Carolina. It is home to the Eastern Band of Cherokees, who retired into the area when most of the nation were forced westward on the TRAIL OF TEARS in 1838. Arts and crafts and the historical drama "Unto These Hills" (presented outdoors during the summer) draw visitors.

Eastern Market **1.** see under CAPITOL HILL, Washington, D.C. **2.** also, **Eastern Municipal Market** or **Eastern Farmers' Market** open-air market in Detroit, Michigan, just NE of Downtown, opened in 1892 and claimed to be the largest such facility in the US. Its wall murals and shops celebrate Detroit's ethnic diversity.

Eastern Parkway see under CROWN HEIGHTS, New York.

Eastern Shore **1.** in Maryland, the region E of CHESAPEAKE BAY, on the W shore of the DELMARVA PENINSULA. Largely agricultural and maritime, it has long been regarded, or has regarded itself, as socially and culturally distinct from the rest of the state, the "Western Shore." **2.** in Nova Scotia, the Atlantic coast from Halifax E to the tip of Cape Breton I. **3.** in Virginia, the S extension of the Maryland area, comprising lightly populated Accomack and Northampton counties. The Virginia section is about 60 mi/100 km NNE–SSW. Onancock (town, pop. 1434, in Accomack Co.) and Cape Charles (town, pop. 1398, in Northampton Co.) are the largest communities.

Eastern Townships French, **Cantons de l'Est** historic region of SE Québec, between the St. Lawrence R. (NW) and the US border (S), S of Québec City and E of Montréal, with GRANBY at its W end and L. Mégantic to the E. The area includes several low mountain ranges (see NOTRE DAME Mts.), and its rivers empty into the St. Lawrence. This former Abenaki territory has its center at SHERBROOKE. After the American Revolution, LOYALISTS moved into the area and were granted tracts in the form of TOWNSHIPS. Many Irish followed in the 1840s. A major wave of French colonization occurred with industrial growth in the mid 19th century, and today the area is over 90% francophone. The region has mining (esp. at ASBESTOS and THETFORD MINES), textile, pulp and paper, and newer high-tech manufacturing industries. Tourism is important, focusing on lakes, rivers, and ski slopes. In the 1940s the name *Estrie* ("kingdom of the east") was coined for the region.

East Flatbush see under FLATBUSH, New York.

East Florida see under WEST FLORIDA.

East Garfield Park residential neighborhood on the West Side of Chicago, Illinois. The site of open housing demonstrations in the 1960s, it today has a largely black population.

East Glenville unincorporated village, pop. 6518, in Glenville township, Schenectady Co., E New York, 6 mi/10 km N of Schenectady.

East Grand Forks city, pop. 8558, Polk Co., NW Minnesota, on the Red R. of the North, opposite GRAND FORKS, North Dakota. The site of an 18th-century trading post, it now processes sugar beets.

East Grand Rapids city, pop. 10,807, Kent Co., SW Michigan, a residential suburb adjacent to Grand Rapids.

East Greenwich town, pop. 11,865, seat of Kent Co., E Rhode Island, on Narragansett Bay, 12 mi/19 km S of Providence. Formerly a farming, fishing, shipbuilding, and textile center, it now produces machinery, textiles, chemicals, and jewelry.

East Gwillimbury town, pop. 18,367, York Regional Municipality, S Ontario, just S of L. Simcoe and 33 mi/53 km N of Toronto. Sharon, its center, was settled in the 1810s by David Willson's Children of Peace, an offshoot of the Quakers, and has religious sites and artifacts from the period. East Gwillimbury is growing rapidly as a Toronto suburb and resort.

East Haddam see under HADDAM, Connecticut.

East Hampton town, pop. 16,132, Suffolk Co., SE New York, 20 mi/32 km SW of Montauk Point, on Long Island's SOUTH FORK. It is a chic summer resort for affluent New Yorkers, attracting writers, artists, and other celebrities. The village of AMAGANSETT is on the S shore, just E of East Hampton village (pop. 1402). SAG HARBOR is in the NW.

Easthampton town, pop. 15,537, Hampshire Co., WC Massachusetts, 12 mi/19 km NW of Springfield, on the Manhan R. Mt. TOM lies immediately E, between Easthampton and the Connecticut R. The town is famous for its button and elastics industries; printing and the making of rubber goods, metal doors, brushes, casting, and household chemicals have also been important. Williston Academy, a prep school, is here.

East Hanover township, pop. 9926, Morris Co., N New Jersey, on the Passaic R. and Route 280, 6 mi/10 km E of Morristown. Largely residential, it is also home to a number of corporate headquarters, notably of pharmaceutical and food companies.

East Harlem section of HARLEM, New York City, generally in its SE corner, with an ethnic history distinctive from that of Central, or black, Harlem. Italian Harlem, a tenement district along the East R. across from Randall's and Ward's islands, was densely populated around 1890–1914, when it was the largest Italian community in the US. Most Italian residents moved away around World War I. Spanish Harlem extends from East 96th Street N to about 120th Street, where it has largely absorbed Italian Harlem. Although some of its residents belong to other Latin-American groups, Spanish Harlem is predominantly Puerto Rican, its residents having arrived after World War I and established a working-class community popularly referred to as El Barrio.

East Hartford town, pop. 50,452, Hartford Co., C Connecticut, on the Hockanum R. and across the Connecticut R. from Hartford. Originally called Podunk by local tribes, it was settled in 1639. It separated from Hartford in 1783, by which time it was already producing iron, gunpowder, and hats. East Hartford, which includes the villages of Hockanum and Burnside, is heavily industrial; manufactures include firearms, steel, paper, stamp and die plates, and candy. Pratt & Whitney, maker of jet engines, based here, was in the 1990s cutting back its operations.

East Haven town, pop. 26,144, New Haven Co., SC Connecticut, adjacent (SE) to New Haven. It has a mixture of truck gardening, industry (oil refining), commerce, coastal resorts, and residences. Its villages include Foxon (N) and Momauguin, a resort on Long Island Sound. Tweed-New Haven Airport lies along the border with New Haven, and L. Saltonstall forms much of the town's E boundary.

East Helena see under HELENA, Montana.

East Highland Park unincorporated community, pop. 11,850, Henrico Co., EC Virginia, 4 mi/7 km NE of Richmond. It is a largely residential suburb.

East Hill–Meridian unincorporated community, pop. 42,696, King Co., WC Washington, a rapidly expanding suburban residential area 15 mi/24 km SE of Seattle and 15 mi/24 km NE of Tacoma.

East Islip unincorporated village, pop. 14,325, in Islip town, Suffolk Co., SE New York, on Long Island, 7 mi/11 km E of Bay Shore. It is a largely residential community on Long Island's South Shore. Heckscher State Park is S.

East Jersey half of the division of what is now New Jersey from 1686 to 1702, consisting of lands E of a line drawn from Little Egg Harbor (SE) to the Delaware Water Gap (NW); PERTH AMBOY was its capital. East Jersey was always under the influence of New York. West Jersey, with its capital at BURLINGTON, was within Pennsylvania's sphere of influence, and had many Quaker settlements. Aspects of the cultural division remain evident.

East Jordan see under CHARLEVOIX, Michigan.

Eastlake city, pop. 21,161, Lake Co., NE Ohio, on L. Erie and the Chagrin R., a residential suburb 16 mi/26 km NE of downtown Cleveland. Some light manufacturing industries are located here.

East Lansing city, pop. 50,677, Ingham Co., SC Michigan, on the Red Cedar R., adjacent to Lansing. The site was settled in 1849, but it remained relatively isolated until Michigan Agricultural College was founded here in 1855. The first state agricultural college in the US, it later became Michigan State University. City life continues to center on the university. Livestock, grain, and sugar beets are raised in the area.

East Las Vegas unincorporated community, pop. 11,087, Clark Co., S Nevada, a largely residential suburb 8 mi/13 km SE of downtown Las Vegas and just NW of Henderson, along I-93/95.

East Liberty section of Pittsburgh, Pennsylvania, between BLOOMFIELD and POINT BREEZE, 5 mi/8 km NE of the GOLDEN TRIANGLE. A turnpike town on what is now PENN AVENUE, it was laid out in 1810. It was developed by the Mellon family into a trolley hub and then an early auto center, featuring the first drive-in gas station. Despite massive urban renewal efforts during the 1960s, it steadily lost businesses and population between World War II and the 1980s.

East Liverpool city, pop. 13,654, Columbiana Co., E Ohio, on the Ohio R., 33 mi/53 km S of Youngstown. It was founded in 1795 by Thomas Fawcett, an Irish Quaker. Extensive local clay deposits made the city a ceramics center by 1839. Although the industry declined in the 1930s, the manufacture of ceramic products remains East Liverpool's economic mainstay. Siting here of a hazardous-waste incinerator stirred 1990s controversy.

East Longmeadow town, pop. 13,367, Hampden Co., SW Massachusetts, adjoining (S) Springfield, on the Connecticut border. Settled in 1740 and incorporated in 1894, East Longmeadow, which long exported brownstone and marketed garden crops, is a residential suburb with some light industry.

East Los Angeles unincorporated community, pop. 126,379, Los Angeles Co., SW California, adjacent (E) to Los Angeles, across the Los Angeles R. One of the largest BARRIOS in the US, it has been overwhelmingly Hispanic since the 1910s, its original migrants from Downtown joined over the years by immigrants from Mexico and Central America. The area is noted for its murals depicting Mexican history and Chicano life; the Plaza de la Raza has a performing arts center and cultural museum. In 1943, East Los Angeles was the scene of the "zoot suit riots" involving white servicemen and Mexican youths. Further rioting occurred in the 1970s, since which time a growing Hispanic community has expanded through BOYLE HEIGHTS and adjacent Los Angeles sections, SW into SOUTH-CENTRAL, and E into MONTEBELLO, PICO RIVERA, and other cities.

East Lyme town, pop. 15,340, New London Co., SE Connecticut, 5 mi/8 km W of New London, on Long Island Sound. Among its several coastal resort communities is Niantic (pop. 3048), on the estuarial Niantic R., a former scalloping and shipbuilding, now a yachting, center.

Eastmain River 470 mi/760 km long, in WC Québec. It rises in the Monts OTISH, and flows W to James Bay. NOUVEAU-QUÉBEC lies to its N. The Opinaca R. joins it as it enters the bay. The surrounding area, and by extension the whole E side of HUDSON BAY, was called the "Eastmain" in fur-trade days. **Eastmain** (pop. 444), near the river's mouth, site of a 1685 HUDSON'S BAY COMPANY post, is a Cree community. In the 1980s, diversion of most of the Eastmain's flow N into the LA GRANDE R., as part of the massive JAMES BAY Project, left only limited flow at its mouth.

East Meadow unincorporated village, pop. 36,909, in Hempstead town, Nassau Co., SE New York, in C Long Island, 23 mi/37 km E of Manhattan. It is primarily residential.

East Mojave National Scenic Area c.1.4 million ac/567,000 ha (2200 sq mi/5700 sq km), in the E MOJAVE DESERT, in SE California, along the Nevada border, between I-40 (S) and I-15 (N). It incorporates the Providence and New York mountains and the Piute Range, and is noted for its mesas, volcanic spires, dunes, cinder cones, and ancient petroglyphs. The Devil's Playground, noted for its sand formations, is in its W. The area was the first so designated (1980) by the Federal government. In 1994 it became the Mojave National Preserve.

East Moline city, pop. 20,147, Rock Island Co., NW Illinois, on the Mississippi R., a suburb immediately E of Moline, across from Bettendorf and Riverdale, Iowa, in the QUAD CITIES area. It is known for the large International Harvester plant located here. East Moline was settled in 1895 and soon began to produce farm implements and machinery. Quad-City Downs (for horse racing) and East Moline Speedway (for stock-car racing) are here. Campbells Island State Memorial Park, 2 mi/3km to the N, was the site of an 1814 battle between American soldiers and Indians under Black Hawk.

Eastmoreland residential neighborhood in Southeast PORTLAND, Oregon, 3 mi/5 km SE of Downtown. Built in 1912 as an exclusive development, it remains prestigious. Reed College is here.

East Naples see under NAPLES, Florida.

East New York section of extreme E Brooklyn, New York, E of BROWNSVILLE, on the Queens border, next to Woodhaven and Ozone Park. Part of the 1670s community of New Lots, established by Dutch settlers moving E from Flatbush, the village of East New York was first systematically developed in 1835–37 by John Pitkin. In 1852 New Lots separated from Flatbush, and in 1886 it was absorbed by the city of Brooklyn. The population of East New York grew after the Williamsburg Bridge (1903) opened E Brooklyn to migrants from the LOWER EAST SIDE of Manhattan, and the district became heavily Jewish and Italian. Parts remained semirural until the 1950s, when continued movement from older Brooklyn neighborhoods began to bring black and Hispanic migrants, and white flight followed. East New York is today one of New York City's poorest neighborhoods, suffering from drug traffic and high gun homicide rates. In its S section, the self-contained, government-sponsored Starett City development houses some 15,000 tenants in large 1970s apartment blocks; but most of East New York consists of dilapidated tenement and factory buildings. The NE section, variously called Cypress Hills or Highland Park, is predominantly Hispanic.

East Norriton township, pop. 13,324, Montgomery Co., SE Pennsylvania, a residential suburb 12 mi/19 km NW of Philadelphia, along the Germantown Pike.

East Northport unincorporated village, pop. 20,411, in Huntington town, Suffolk Co., SE New York, on Long Island's North Shore, 40 mi/64 km E of Manhattan. It is primarily residential.

Easton **1.** town, pop. 9372, seat of Talbot Co., Maryland, on the EASTERN SHORE, 28 mi/45 km SE of Annapolis. An agricultural trade center, it also has light manufacturing and commercial businesses, and has long been surrounded by summer homes. Its Quaker meetinghouse dates from 1683.

The county courthouse gave birth to the Talbot Resolves (1765), protesting the British Stamp Act. Black writer and statesman Frederick Douglass was born nearby in 1817. **2.** town, pop. 19,807, Bristol Co., SE Massachusetts, SW of and adjoining Brockton. Settled in the 1690s, it has been a manufacturing center, drawing originally on local (bog) iron, and part of an industrial district including Brockton and TAUNTON (S). The village of North Easton is home to Stonehill College (1948), and to H. H. Richardson's noted Ames Library (1877). **3.** city, pop. 26,276, seat of Northampton Co., E Pennsylvania, at the confluence of the Delaware and Lehigh rivers, 48 mi/77 km N of Philadelphia. Now part of the Lehigh Valley industrial complex that also includes ALLENTOWN and Wilson, it is situated on land previously owned by the Delaware Indians that was part of the infamous WALKING PURCHASE (1737) and was laid out at the direction of Thomas Penn (1750). It was the site of several peace councils during the French and Indian War, and was a Revolutionary War center. Situated in a rich farming area, Easton has diversified manufactures that include machinery, textiles, and electrical, paper, and chemical products. The city is home to Lafayette College (1826).

East Orange city, pop. 73,552, Essex Co., NE New Jersey, adjacent (NW) to Newark. Settled in 1678, it was originally part of ORANGE, from which it separated in 1863. It is a largely residential working-class suburb of New York and Newark. Many East Orange office buildings are occupied by the dozens of insurance companies located here. The city is also industrialized, with manufactures that include electric motors, hydrants, plastics, and audio-visual equipment. East Orange is the seat of Upsala College (1893) and a large veterans' hospital.

East Palo Alto industrial and residential city, pop. 23,451, San Mateo Co., NC California, on the W shore of San Francisco Bay, adjacent (N) to Palo Alto.

East Patchogue unincorporated village, pop. 20,195, in Brookhaven town, Suffolk Co., SE New York, on Long Island's South Shore. On Great South Bay and the Swan R., it is primarily residential.

East Peoria city, pop. 21,378, Tazewell Co., NC Illinois, on the Illinois R., across from Peoria. The economy of this industrial suburb is dominated by its Caterpillar tractor plant. It is the seat of Illinois Central College (1966). Just SW along the river is Fort Crevecoeur State Park, where, in 1680, La Salle built the first French fort in Illinois.

East Point city, pop. 34,402, Fulton Co., NW Georgia, 7 mi/11 km SSW of downtown Atlanta. Founded in 1853 as the E terminus for the Atlanta & West Point Railroad, it was important in the 1864 defense of Atlanta. Today, major industries make textiles, fertilizer, and metal products. The city is largely residential. Atlanta Christian College (1937) is here.

Eastpointe see EAST DETROIT, Michigan.

Eastport city, pop. 1965, Washington Co., Maine. The easternmost US city, it is on Moose I., in Passamaquoddy Bay. Cobscook Bay lies W, Lubec S, and Campobello I. SE. The main industries are fishing, sardine canning, and the manufacture of fishmeal and pearl essence (made from scales). The city also attracts a number of artists. Eastport prospered from smuggling after the 1807 Embargo Act, and was held by the British 1814–18. Boundary disputes continued until 1842. Fort Sullivan (1808) and the Old Sow, one of the world's largest whirlpools, are here; tides average 18 ft/6 m, and have reached 40 ft/12 m.

East Providence city, pop. 50,380, Providence Co., E Rhode Island, on the E shore of the Seekonk R. and the estuarial Providence R., opposite Providence. Founded in 1636 by Roger Williams, it was part of Rehoboth, Massachusetts, until 1812, when it became part of Seekonk. West Seekonk was set off and became the Rhode Island town of East Providence in 1862. It was incorporated as a city in 1958. East Providence has petroleum storage facilities, trucking terminals, and a printing industry, and manufactures chemicals, jewelry, machinery, fabricated metals, electronics, and plastics. The city includes the former village of Rumford, where Roger Williams settled in 1636, and which was noted for its production of chemicals including baking powder.

East Renton Highlands unincorporated community, pop. 13,218, King Co., WC Washington, a residential suburb NE of RENTON and 9 mi/14 km SE of downtown Seattle.

East Ridge city, pop. 21,101, Hamilton Co., SE Tennessee, adjacent (SE) to Chattanooga. Incorporated in 1921, it is a residential suburb on the Georgia border.

East River tidal strait between Manhattan and Long Island and between Long Island and the Bronx, New York. Its total length is about 16 mi/26 km. From its S end at Governors I. and the Battery, it passes between downtown Manhattan and Brooklyn, where the indentation of WALLABOUT BAY became the site of the Brooklyn Navy Yard. Newtown Creek, an inlet, divides the Brooklyn and Queens waterfronts. Roosevelt I. lies between Midtown Manhattan and Queens. At the HELL GATE, the East R. is joined by the Harlem R. Passing Ward's and Randall's islands, it widens, and in its upper half is the site, on its S side, of Riker's Island, the two smaller Brother islands, LaGuardia airport, and another inlet, Flushing Bay. On its N side, the Bronx R. enters it. The East R. passes into Long Island Sound at Throgs Neck. The BROOKLYN BRIDGE was the first to span it; later bridges include the Manhattan, Williamsburg, Queensborough, Triborough, Hell Gate (railroad), Bronx-Whitestone, and Throgs Neck. The United Nations lies on the East R. in TURTLE BAY, Manhattan.

East Riverdale unincorporated suburban village, pop. 14,187, Prince George's Co., C Maryland, 8 mi/13 km NE of Washington, D.C.

East Rockaway village, pop. 10,152, in Hempstead town, Nassau Co., SE New York, 20 mi/32 km ESE of Manhattan. Now a residential suburb and resort, it was founded in the 1680s near a grist mill, which is now a museum featuring Indian and shipping memorabilia.

East Rutherford borough, pop. 7902, Bergen Co., NE New Jersey, across railroad tracks from RUTHERFORD (SW), in the Hackensack R. meadows, on the New Jersey Turnpike. An industrial borough long engaged in producing textiles, chemicals, and medical products, it is now known as the site of the MEADOWLANDS sports and entertainment complex.

East Saint Louis city, pop. 40,944, St. Clair Co., SW Illinois, on the Mississippi R., opposite St. Louis, Missouri. A livestock center and distribution point for local farm products, it has traditionally had meatpacking plants, smelters, oil refineries, and many heavy industries. The city's roots as a transportation hub extend back to 1797, when James Piggott set up a ferry service on the river. Rail service arrived in 1855, and the building of the EADS BRIDGE across the Mississippi (1874) confirmed its importance in the national transport network. National Stock Yards opened in National City (to the N) in 1873. East St. Louis was the scene of bloody antiblack rioting on July 2, 1917. By the 1970s, most meatpackers had closed, taking other plants with them, and East St. Louis had started on a disastrous economic slide. Its population dropped by about one-half in 1960–90, with most white residents leaving the city. Today it is plagued by a variety of social and economic ills.

East San Diego largely residential section of SAN DIEGO, California, 6 mi/10 km NE of Downtown, E of Mission Valley. Its neighborhoods began largely as suburbs developed in the 1920s. UNIVERSITY HEIGHTS lies along its N.

East Setauket see under SETAUKET, New York.

East Side **1.** collection of neighborhoods in St. Paul, Minnesota, E of Downtown. Originally a middle-class area of European immigrants, it today contains mainly poor and working-class white households. **2.** of Manhattan, New York City, generally, any part E of Fifth Ave., but used chiefly of those neighborhoods above 14th St. (below which are the EAST VILLAGE and the LOWER EAST SIDE) and below 96th St. (above which is EAST HARLEM). The East Side incorporates several of the city's wealthiest neighborhoods, including Gramercy Park, Murray Hill, and Turtle Bay, and streets, including Beekman Place and Sutton Place. Above 59th St. it is largely residential and is called the Upper East Side. **3.** in CLEVELAND, Ohio, districts E of Ontario Ave., from Downtown to the suburbs. The UNIVERSITY CIRCLE cultural cluster is here; closer to Downtown are neighborhoods housing most of the city's black residents, as well as older white ethnic enclaves. EUCLID Ave. runs through the East Side. **4.** commercial and residential area of SAN ANTONIO, Texas, E of Downtown, that has historically been home to the city's black population. Houston and East Commerce streets are major thoroughfares; the latter, long the backbone of black commerce, includes Saint Paul Square, an entertainment hub and now a National Historic District. **5.** collection of neighborhoods in Milwaukee, Wisconsin, on L. Michigan, E of the Milwaukee R. and NE of Downtown. The more affluent and gentrified part of the city, it is the site of the University of Wisconsin at Milwaukee campus and PROSPECT AVENUE. Juneau, McKinley, and Lake parks are on the waterfront.

East Stroudsburg borough, pop. 8781, Monroe Co., E Pennsylvania, on the Delaware Water Gap, 32 mi/52 km NNE of Allentown. It is the seat of East Stroudsburg University (1893).

East Tavaputs Plateau NW–SE oriented tableland in Grand and Uintah counties, E Utah. Part of the Colorado Plateau, it is separated from the **West Tavaputs Plateau,** in Carbon and Duchesne counties, by the Green R. Bruin Peak rises to 10,285 ft/3135 m, in the W. The two plateaus are bounded on the S by the BOOK and Roan cliffs, and join the Roan Plateau of W Colorado on the E.

East Texas Oilfield in extreme NE Texas, centered near KILGORE, in Rusk Co., and also largely in Gregg Co. (N). Discovered by wildcat oilman "Dad" Joiner in Oct. 1930, it caused a production boom that depressed the price of oil and led to the imposition of martial law (Aug. 1931) to halt drilling. The field has had tens of thousands of working wells at one time, and has produced some 4.5 billion barrels since opening. LONGVIEW is the other major center.

East Tremont see under TREMONT, New York.

East Village residential and commercial section of lower Manhattan, New York City. Located between 14th and Houston streets E of the Bowery, it was part of the LOWER EAST SIDE; "East Village" came into general use in the 1950s and 1960s. Peter Stuyvesant's 17th-century farm extended into the vicinity, and he is buried in the churchyard of St.-Mark's-in-the-Bowery. The area has seen waves of population. A 19th-century German and Irish neighborhood sometimes called Little Germany, it came after 1900 to house East European Jews, in the 1940s Poles, Ukrainians, and Puerto Ricans. By the 1950s its residents included artists spilling over from GREENWICH VILLAGE, and it was known as a beatnik and hippie quarter, home to such culture figures as Allen Ginsberg and Ed Sanders. Gentrification set in by the 1980s, but the East Village remains synonymous with the counterculture in various forms, from punk musicians to NYU art and theater students to activists and the homeless living in Tompkins Square Park. On its E fringe is ALPHABET CITY, otherwise LOISAIDA. Cooper Union (1859) is in the Astor Square area, on the W edge.

East Windsor **1.** town, pop. 10,081, Hartford Co., NC Connecticut, on the Connecticut and Scantic rivers, 10 mi/16 km NNE of Hartford. Situated in the TOBACCO VALLEY, and now largely residential, it includes the villages of Scantic, Warehouse Point, Windsorville, and Broad Brook. Jonathan Edwards, whose preaching sparked the Great Awakening of the 1730s, was born here in 1703. **2.** township, pop. 22,353, Mercer Co., WC New Jersey, 16 mi/26 km SW of New Brunswick, along the New Jersey Turnpike. Long agricultural, it is becoming a residential suburb, with corporate office development.

East York borough, pop. 102,696, TORONTO Metropolitan Municipality, S Ontario, on the Don R., bordered by Toronto (S and W), North York (N), and Scarborough (E). Created with the consolidation (1967) of the township of East York and the town of Leaside, it is largely residential, with industrial zones along its N boundaries, esp. in Leaside (NW), and parks along the Don and its tributaries.

Eaton Centre commercial complex in downtown TORONTO, Ontario, bounded by QUEEN (S), YONGE (E), and DUNDAS (N) streets. On the site where Timothy Eaton in 1869 founded a mail-order merchandise empire, the modern Eaton's and some 300 other establishments occupy a four-level, glass-and-steel 1970s development modeled, like some other US and Canadian complexes of the same period, on Milan, Italy's Galleria.

Eatonton city, pop. 4737, seat of Putnam Co., NC Georgia, 65 mi/105 km ESE of Atlanta. Writers Joel Chandler Harris (1848) and Alice Walker (1944) were both born in this agricultural and lumbering center.

Eatontown borough, pop. 13,800, Monmouth Co., EC New Jersey, 3 mi/5 km S of Red Bank. It was settled in 1670 by Thomas Eaton, who ran a grist mill, still preserved. Primarily residential and in a truck farming region, Eatontown has an economy that is largely dependent on the US Army base at Fort Monmouth, located here, and on light manufacturing.

Eatonville town, pop. 2170, Orange Co., C Florida, 3 mi/5 km N of Orlando. Incorporated in 1886, it is one of the oldest black-established US communities. Writer Zora Neale Hurston was born here (1901), and many of her writings reflect life in the area.

Eau Claire city, pop. 58,856, seat of Eau Claire Co., also in

Chippewa Co., WC Wisconsin, at the junction of the Eau Claire and Chippewa rivers, 70 mi/113 km N of La Crosse. The trading center for a dairying region, it manufactures tires, piston rings, machine shop products, paper, and beer. Other industries include printing, electronics, and meat-packing. An early stopping point for French traders and trappers, the city was settled in the 1840s, growing with the local logging industry. Manufacturing and food processing came to dominate the economy at the turn of the century. The University of Wisconsin at Eau Claire (1916) is here.

Ebbets Field former baseball stadium, in CROWN HEIGHTS (although popularly thought of as having been in FLATBUSH), Brooklyn, New York. Built in 1912 and seating about 35,000, it was the home of the Brooklyn Dodgers. When the team moved to Los Angeles after the 1957 season, Ebbets Field was demolished to make way for a housing complex.

Echo Bay see under GREAT BEAR L., Northwest Territories.

Echo Cliffs NW–SE trending sandstone formation extending for c.50 mi/80 km along the W escarpment of the Kaibito Plateau, E of the Colorado R., in N Arizona. The cliffs reach 6654 ft/2028 m at Red Point, and include the Echo Peaks, rising to 5567 ft/1697 m, in the N. MARBLE CANYON, on the Colorado, is W, the PAINTED DESERT S.

Echo Park residential section and park in Los Angeles, California, SE of SILVER LAKE and SW of ELYSIAN PARK, 1 mi/1.6 km NW of Downtown. One of the city's first planned suburbs, it was developed mostly during the 1920s–30s; its ANGELINO HEIGHTS district dates from the 1880s. Echo Park's bungalows and small apartment complexes now house working-class Hispanics and Asians; some GENTRIFICATION has occurred recently. The Aimee Semple McPherson Angelus Temple (1923) is at the NW edge of the park.

Economy historic site in Beaver Co., W Pennsylvania, on the Ohio R., 17 mi/27 km NW of Pittsburgh. A utopian settlement, it was founded in 1825 by members of George Rapp's Harmony Society. This German group, which came to America seeking religious freedom, advocated an austere, celibate lifestyle, and settled at HARMONY before moving here. Economy prospered, but by 1906 the society's membership had dwindled to extinction. The modern borough of AMBRIDGE is on the site of Economy; 17 buildings from the original settlement are open to the public.

Ecorse city, pop. 12,180, Wayne Co., SE Michigan, on the Detroit R., 7 mi/11 km SW of Detroit. The site was originally an Indian camp and burial ground. Founded in 1812, it is named for the Rivière aux Écorces ("tree-bark river"), a small stream bordered by trees from which Indians made canoes. Growth came with the development of the Ford complex in Dearborn, 5 mi/8 km to the NW. A steel plant was built in 1930; other manufactures include chemicals, auto parts, and tools.

Eddy, Mount see under KLAMATH Mts., California.

Eden city, pop. 15,238, Rockingham Co., N North Carolina, 26 mi/42 km N of Greensboro, at the Smith R.–Dan R. junction, just S of the Virginia line. It is an agricultural trade center with a struggling textile (blankets) plant and a brewery.

Eden Park 185-ac/75-ha city park in Cincinnati, Ohio, just E of Downtown. One of the city's largest open spaces, it is the site of the Cincinnati Art Museum and the Eden Park Conservatory. The MOUNT ADAMS neighborhood is nearby.

Eden Prairie city, pop. 39,311, Hennepin Co., SE Minnesota, on the Minnesota R., a residential suburb 10 mi/16 km SW of Minneapolis. Most of the recent commercial growth here has been concentrated in the NE corner, along the I-494 corridor.

Edenton town, pop. 5268, seat of Chowan Co., NE North Carolina, on Albemarle Sound near the mouth of the Chowan R., 28 mi/45 km SW of Elizabeth City. A tourist destination and the business center of an agricultural and maritime area, it has some industries, including peanut processing. Settled before 1660, Edenton flourished shipping plantation products, lumber, and fish. The anti-British Edenton Tea Party of Oct., 1774, is believed to be the first political action organized by American women.

Edgartown town, pop. 3062, the easternmost town on Martha's Vineyard and seat of Dukes Co., SE Massachusetts, on Nantucket Sound. It includes CHAPPAQUIDDICK I. A summer resort and yachting center, Edgartown was once a whaling port and had a sperm-oil candle factory. Today its art galleries, shops, inns, and restaurants thrive on a mix of summer and year-round residents and tourists.

edge city term introduced by the writer Joel Garreau, and elaborated in his book *Edge City* (1991), for new concentrations of commerce and industry away from the old centers of major cities. According to Garreau, edge cities will gradually develop their own community and culture. They typically will not conform to existing political boundaries; will involve a lower building density than traditional cities; and will develop at transportation nodes like the intersections of BELTWAYS with interstate highways. Examples include TYSONS CORNER, Virginia; KING OF PRUSSIA, Pennsylvania; the GALLERIA areas of Dallas and Houston, Texas; PARSIPPANY–TROY HILLS, New Jersey; and IRVINE, California.

Edgefield County 490 sq mi/1269 sq km, pop. 18,375, in W South Carolina, bounded by the Savannah R. and Georgia (SW). Its seat is the town of **Edgefield** (pop. 2563). Its W quarter is occupied by part of the Sumter National Forest. Earlier part of the larger **Edgefield District,** this historic area was home to ten South Carolina governors and the birthplace of Texas Revolutionary hero William B. Travis (1809–36), Confederate general James Longstreet (1821–1904), and political leader Benjamin R. Tillman (1847–1918). It is noted for its pottery and as the site of some of the state's earliest textile mills. The rural modern county produces cotton, peaches, asparagus, and timber. Its light industries manufacture lumber, textiles, and food products.

Edgemere **1.** unincorporated residential community, pop. 9226, Baltimore Co., NC Maryland, just SE of Baltimore and E and NE of SPARROWS POINT, on the estuarial Back R. (N) and Old Road Bay (S). The area has many marinas and boatyards. **2.** see under the ROCKAWAYS, New York.

Edgewater **1.** city, pop. 4613, Jefferson Co., NC Colorado, a residential suburb 4 mi/6 km W of Denver. **2.** city, pop. 15,337, Volusia Co., NE Florida, at the head of the INDIAN R. lagoon near the Atlantic Ocean, 17 mi/27 km SE of Daytona Beach. It is a growing residential community. **3.** residential and commercial neighborhood on the far North Side of Chicago, Illinois, along L. Michigan and 7 mi/11 km NNW of the Loop. An area of single-family homes and apartment buildings, it houses a diverse community. The Argyle St. district, on its S, is a thriving Asian commercial and residential community, an outgrowth of Chicago's older CHINATOWN. UPTOWN is just S. **4.** borough, pop. 5001, Bergen Co., NE New Jersey, at the foot of the PALISADES of the Hudson R., across from New York City. An industrial district noted for its textiles, it has recently become known as the site of Yaohan Plaza, the East Coast's leading Japanese shopping mall.

Edgewood **1.** city, pop. 8143, Kenton Co., N Kentucky, 8 mi/13 km SSW of Cincinnati, Ohio, of which it is a largely residential suburb just S of I-275. **2.** unincorporated community, pop. 23,903, Harford Co., NE Maryland, 18 mi/29 km NE of Baltimore. **Edgewood Arsenal,** established here in 1917 along the Gunpowder and Bush rivers and Chesapeake Bay, now includes the Army Chemical Center and Chemical Corps School. ABERDEEN Proving Ground is adjacent.

Edina city, pop. 46,070, Hennepin Co., SE Minnesota, a suburb 8 mi/13 km SW of Minneapolis. It was mainly an upper-income residential suburb until the 1970s, when commercial development boomed along the I-494 corridor in the SE corner. Southdale, the world's first fully enclosed shopping mall, designed by Victor Gruen, opened here in 1956.

Edinboro borough, pop. 7736, Erie Co., NW Pennsylvania, on Edinboro L., 15 mi/24 km S of Erie. Edinboro University (1857) is here.

Edinburg city, pop. 29,885, seat of Hidalgo Co., extreme S Texas, in the Lower Rio Grande Valley, 48 mi/77 km WNW of Brownsville. Established as Chapin (1907), it was renamed in 1911. It developed as a cotton growing center, and is now one of the largest citrus and vegetable shippers in the state. Part of an urban complex with PHARR and MCALLEN, it benefits from nearby oil and natural gas fields. Situated here are the University of Texas: Pan American (1927) and the Tropical Texas Center for Mental Health and Mental Retardation (1967).

Edison township, pop. 88,680, Middlesex Co., EC New Jersey, 15 mi/24 km SW of Elizabeth. Originally called Raritan, it was renamed in 1954. Edison is the seat of Middlesex County College (1964). On Routes 95 and 287 and US 1, it has in recent decades become a major corporate office center, hosting businesses relocating from older urban centers. MENLO PARK is within the township, which also surrounds the borough of METUCHEN.

Edisto Island c.100 sq mi/260 sq km, in Colleton Co., S South Carolina, one of the SEA ISLANDS, on the Atlantic Ocean between the estuarial North and South Edisto rivers, 25 mi/40 km SW of Charleston. The hamlet of Edisto Island is approximately in its center and the town of **Edisto Beach** (pop. 340) is close to its S tip. Settled in 1690, it was once a center for the cultivation of Sea Island cotton. Largely developed, it is now primarily a resort.

Edith Cavell, Mount peak (11,033 ft/3363 m) of the Rocky Mts., 15 mi/24 km S of Jasper, in JASPER NATIONAL PARK, WC Alberta. Once a landmark for VOYAGEURS, it is today noted as a rock climbing site (its N face). Formerly Montagne de la Grande Traverse, it was renamed for the British Red Cross heroine in 1916.

Edmond city, pop. 52,315, Oklahoma Co., C Oklahoma, 13 mi/21 km N of downtown Oklahoma City, and just outside its limits. On the edge of the West Edmond Field, one of the largest oil and natural gas deposits in the world, it is a residential suburb, petroleum production and trade center, agricultural and commercial hub, and manufacturer of building products and oilfield equipment. Central State University (1890) is here.

Edmonds city, pop. 30,744, Snohomish Co., WC Washington, on Puget Sound, 15 mi/24 km N of Seattle. A growing residential suburb founded in 1890, it also has an oil refinery and fruit processing plants. Based here is a ferry to Kingston, on the Kitsap Peninsula, across Puget Sound. Its beaches, marina, and fishing pier make the city popular with tourists. Edmonds Underwater Park, located under downtown waterfront docks, is a well-known scuba diving site. The city is home to Edmonds Community College (1967).

Edmonton city, pop. 616,741, provincial capital, in C Alberta, on the North Saskatchewan R., 180 mi/290 km N of Calgary. It is the center of a metropolitan area (CMA) with a pop. of 839,924. A government center, it is also the trade, transportation, and industrial hub of C and N Alberta and of a large area of NW Canada. Its economy is based heavily on oil exploration, extraction, refining, and distribution; the area also produces coal, grains, oilseed, cattle and hogs, poultry, dairy goods, wood items, and pulp. Fort Augustus (1794; the NORTH WEST COMPANY) and Fort Edmonton (1795; the HUDSON'S BAY COMPANY) competed here (until the companies' 1821 amalgamation) for fur trade in Cree and Blackfoot territory. In the 1870s settlement began in what is now (Old) Strathcona, a popular residential and cafe district S of the river. Although the Canadian Pacific Railway in the 1880s chose Calgary and Kicking Horse Pass for its route, rather than Edmonton and YELLOWHEAD PASS, the 1890s Klondike gold rush showed Edmonton's potential as a travel hub. Railroad (1915) and bush pilot (1920s) activities developed this role. In the meantime (1905), the city had become capital of the new province. In World War II both ALASKA HIGHWAY construction and the NORTHWEST STAGING ROUTE (aircraft) jumped off from Edmonton. In 1947, the LEDUC oilfield opened, leading to rapid pop. growth and preeminence in the Canadian petroleum industry. The city's Refinery Row is actually in SHERWOOD PARK (Strathcona Co.), E of the river. Edmonton's stern north plains climate has led to extensive development of enclosed and underground facilities; the huge WEST EDMONTON MALL is an example. The city is today an educational and cultural center, home to the University of Alberta (1906), Concordia College (1921), and other institutions; to the July Klondike Days, a competitor to Calgary's annual Stampede; and to noted theater and music festivals. The Northlands Coliseum is home to the Oilers (hockey), Commonwealth Stadium to the Eskimos (football).

Edmundston city, pop. 10,835, seat of Madawaska Co., NW New Brunswick, on the E (N) bank of the St. John R., opposite Madawaska, Maine. The MADAWASKA R. bisects it before meeting the St. John. Settled in the 1790s as Petit-Sault (Little Falls), it was renamed in 1848. Pulp milling is now its major industry. Skiing, hunting, fishing, and whitewater canoeing are popular in the area. A fancophone center, it has long been thought of as the capital of the "Republic of MADAWASKA," and is the seat of the Collège St.-Louis, a branch of the Université de MONCTON.

Edwards Air Force Base military installation, covering more than 300,000 ac/120,000 ha in Kern, San Bernardino, and Los Angeles counties, SC California. It lies in ANTELOPE VALLEY and the Rosamond Hills, incorporating the dry Rogers and Rosamond lakes, at the W end of the MOJAVE DESERT, some 65 mi/105 km NNE of Los Angeles. The base was established in 1933 as Muroc Field. In 1947 Chuck Yeager broke the sound barrier here. The base is now a space shuttle landing site and includes the NASA Ames-Dryden Flight Research Facility. Its main runway, at 7.5 mi/12 km, is said to be the world's longest.

Edwards Plateau in SW Texas, the southernmost extension of the GREAT PLAINS, lying S and SE of the LLANO ESTACADO, at altitudes ranging from 750 ft/230 m to over 2500 ft/765 m. Its E boundary is the BALCONES ESCARPMENT. Covering some 25 million ac/10 million ha of alternately rolling and hilly country between the Rio Grande (S) and the Colorado R. and the Osage Plains (N), it has a limestone-based soil and characteristic brushy groundcover that makes it ideal grazing land; its goat, sheep, and cattle ranches are extensive, and it is also noted for its hunting. In the E it includes the HILL COUNTRY, and in the SW the similar Stockton Plateau extends beyond the BIG BEND toward El Paso. The Colorado, Concho, Nueces, Guadalupe, and other rivers rise on the Edwards Plateau and flow E.

Edwardsville city, pop. 14,579, seat of Madison Co., SW Illinois, by Dunlap L., 17 mi/27 km NE of East St. Louis. Founded in 1805, it is a trade and distribution center in an area of coal mines and dairy and truck farms. Brass goods and radiators are manufactured. A branch of Southern Illinois University is located immediately W of the city.

Edwin B. Forsythe National Wildlife Refuge see under BRIGANTINE, New Jersey.

Edwin I. Hatch nuclear power plant: see under BAXLEY, Georgia.

Eel River 200 mi/320 km long, in NW California. It rises in E Mendocino Co., in the Mendocino National Forest, and flows SE and W into dam-created L. Pillsbury, then turns W and NW along the W of the Coast Ranges, reaching the Pacific Ocean 12 mi/19 km SSW of Eureka. Its NW-flowing South Fork joins it N of Weott, in Humboldt Redwoods State Park. Its Middle Fork, flowing SE from the YOLLA BOLLY–Middle Eel Wilderness, joins it S of the Round Valley Indian Reservation.

Effigy Mounds National Monument 1481 ac/600 ha, near Marquette, in Clayton Co., NE Iowa, across the Mississippi R. (NW) from PRAIRIE DU CHIEN, Wisconsin. Its mound builder remains include earthworks in the shape of bears and birds.

Effingham city, pop. 11,851, seat of Effingham Co., EC Illinois, 56 mi/90 km SE of Decatur. Its manufactures include electrical and gas appliances, lumber, and wood products. Printing is also an important industry, and agricultural and dairy products from the surrounding region are processed and traded. Westward-bound pioneers traveled on the NATIONAL ROAD through the area from the 1830s, but Effingham itself dates to 1854, when the Illinois Central Railroad established a settlement here. The Lake Sara recreational area is 5mi/8 km NW.

Egan Range N–S trending mountains, 120 mi/190 km long, in EC Nevada. They have long been mined for gold and silver, but are best known for copper; W of ELY, at Ruth, is the famous Kennecott open-pit mine. The range reaches 10,936 ft/3169 m at Ward Mt., 10 mi/16 km S of Ely.

Eggemoggin Reach see under DEER ISLE, Maine.

Egypt also, **Little Egypt** name given to the southernmost portion of Illinois, between the Wabash and Mississippi rivers, N of the Ohio R. and centered around CAIRO, by an early-19th-century St. Louis merchant who thought the region resembled the Nile Delta. Long an economic backwater, Egypt has suffered high unemployment and population loss in recent decades.

Eielson Air Force Base see under FAIRBANKS, Alaska.

Eighteenth and Vine historic district 1 mi/1.5 km SE of downtown KANSAS CITY, Missouri. In the 1920s–30s 18th St. E of Troost Ave. (a few blocks W) was the business heart of black Kansas City. The 18th and Vine area was home to dozens of nightclubs and restaurants, one of the most important centers in the history of jazz music; the "Kansas City style" developed here, esp. in nightlong jam sessions. Today the Mutual Musicians Foundation, a famous gathering place, is one of few remaining sites of the era. The Black Archives of Mid-America is just S; Lincoln High School, alma mater of many musicians, is just SE.

Eight Mile Road also, **Base Line** or **Baseline Road** or **Base Line Highway** discontinuous road that extends some 160 mi/260 km across S Michigan from Harper Woods (E), near Detroit, to just N of South Haven, on L. Michigan. It follows surveyors' divisions between two tiers of counties. In the Detroit area, Eight Mile Rd. divides the city's N reaches from residential communities of Macomb and Oakland counties, and is seen as a racial barrier between black city dwellers (S) and white suburbanites (N).

Eisenhower, Mount see under PRESIDENTIAL RANGE, New Hampshire.

Eisenhower Tunnel see under FRONT RANGE, Colorado.

Elba village, pop. 196, Howard Co., EC Nebraska, on the North Loup R., 28 mi/45 km NW of Grand Island. Baseball great Grover Cleveland Alexander (1887–1950) was born here.

El Barrio see under EAST HARLEM, New York.

Elberon residential community in the city of LONG BRANCH, Monmouth Co., E New Jersey, on the Atlantic Ocean. Noted for its excellent fishing and its sprawling estates, it was the site of the summer home of President James Garfield, who died here in 1881.

Elbert, Mount peak, 14,433 ft/4399 m, in C Colorado, in the SAWATCH RANGE of the Rocky Mts., 12 mi/19 km SW of Leadville. The highest point in Colorado and in the Rockies, it is a popular hiking destination.

El Cajon city, pop. 88,693, San Diego Co., SW California, 12 mi/19 km E of San Diego, of which it is a largely residential suburb. Surrounded on all four sides by hills and mountains, it is almost entirely cut off from Pacific Ocean breezes; temperatures are generally 10–20 degrees higher than in San Diego. The site, part of the Mexican Rancho El Cajon, was sold to Americans in 1868. In 1878, it had a hotel and saloon serving stagecoach passengers traveling between San Diego and Yuma, Arizona; today, the Knox Hotel, in Judson Park, houses the local historical society. Grossman Community (1961), Christian Heritage (1970), and Cuyamaca (1978) colleges are here. Avocados, grapes, citrus fruits, and vegetables are grown in the surrounding region. The city's manufactures include aerospace and electronic components.

El Camino del Diablo historic E–W route extending some 120 mi/190 km from the border community of Sonoita (Sonora), Mexico, across the SW corner of Arizona, to Yuma (the Colorado R.). The "Way of the Devil" was used by Spaniards, Mexicans, and gold prospectors, and probably much earlier by the Sand Papago. This extremely dry route weaves between a number of Great Basin ranges and through the Yuma Desert, in areas now within the ORGAN PIPE CACTUS NATIONAL MONUMENT, CABEZA PRIETA NATIONAL WILDLIFE REFUGE, and Barry M. Goldwater (military) Range.

El Camino Real **1.** in California, the route N from Baja

California (Mexico) to San Francisco Bay, along which, from 1769, MISSIONS, PRESIDIOS, and PUEBLOS were established. It is also called the Mission Trail. Today, the name El Camino Real is applied chiefly to the stretch N of Los Angeles, through Santa Barbara, Santa Maria, San Luis Obispo, Paso Robles, and the Salinas Valley. Route 101 follows it. **2.** military road ("the King's Highway"), c.135 mi/220 km long, between NEW MADRID and St. Louis, Missouri, laid out in 1789, during the period of Spanish control of the Louisiana territory (see LOUISIANA PURCHASE), along an old Indian path. Probably little more than a trail itself, it ran through present-day Sikeston, Cape Girardeau, and Ste. Genevieve. Interstate 55 now roughly follows it. **3.** 16th-century Spanish trade route, extending N from Vera Cruz, on Mexico's Gulf Coast, to SANTA FE, New Mexico. It crossed into what is now US territory at El Paso, Texas, and followed the Rio Grande N to Socorro and Albuquerque, then turned NE along the SANDIA Mts. and into the Sangre de Cristo foothills to Santa Fe. Today I-25 flanks (at higher elevations) most of its route in the US. Opening of the SANTA FE TRAIL in the 1820s oriented New Mexico toward the US, and El Camino Real faded in importance; it came later to be thought of as the Old Chihuahua Trail, a S extension of the Santa Fe Trail. **4.** in Texas, Spanish colonial road between the Rio Grande (at Eagle Pass, SW) and settlements on the Sabine R. (E). Covering some 540 mi/890 km, it was established in 1691 to provide communication between Mexico and E Texas missions. It passed through or near the sites of San Antonio, Houston, and Nacogdoches, and is today followed for the most part by Texas Route 21. It is known in some areas as the Old San Antonio Road.

El Campo city, pop. 10,511, Wharton Co., SE Texas, 64 mi/103 km SW of Houston. Founded in 1884, it was a cattle center, and now processes and markets rice, pecans, cotton, oil, and sulfur. El Campo also produces aluminum, plastic, and styrofoam products.

El Capitan 1. peak (7569 ft/2309 m) of the Sierra Nevada in YOSEMITE NATIONAL PARK, EC California. A massive granite monolith with walls rising nearly vertically for over 3000 ft/1000 m above the valley floor, it is well known to photographers and rock climbers. **2.** 8085 ft/2466 m, S terminus of the GUADALUPE Mts. and the lower twin mountain to GUADALUPE PEAK, in SW Texas, S of Carlsbad, New Mexico. Because of perspective from the plain below, it was long thought to be the highest mountain in Texas. Its sheer, 1500-ft/460-m cliff is a distinctive landmark, a signpost for generations of travelers.

El Centro city, pop. 31,384, seat of Imperial Co., extreme S California, 88 mi/142 km E of San Diego. Its name refers to its central location in the IMPERIAL VALLEY. Melons, lettuce, tomatoes, sugar beets, other fruits and vegetables, grain, livestock, and cotton are produced in this highly canalized area. Founded in 1907, at 53 ft/16 m below sea level, El Centro is the valley's major shipping point. Imperial Valley College is in Imperial (city, pop. 4113), 4 mi/6 km N. The El Centro Naval Air Station, 6 mi/10 km NW, is home to the Navy's Blue Angels precision flying team.

El Cerrito city, pop. 22,869, Contra Costa Co., NC California, on San Francisco Bay, 4 mi/6 km NE of Berkeley, on the N of El Cerrito Creek, the boundary between Contra Costa and Alameda counties. The Berkeley Hills rise to the E, and Richmond is N. El Cerrito is essentially a residential suburb.

El Dorado 1. legendary land of riches, more specifically the legendary chief of a land thought to be in modern Colombia, South America, who was ceremonially covered with gold or gold dust, thus becoming *el dorado* ("the gilded man"). Stories of El Dorado contributed to the credence Spanish explorers gave the North American legends of CIBOLA and QUIVIRA. **2.** city, pop. 23,146, seat of Union Co., S Arkansas, 10 mi/16 km from the Louisiana border. Since the discovery of oil in 1921, the city has been the center of the state's oil industry. It is also a trade and processing center for lumber, cotton, sweet potato, corn, peanut, and fertilizer producers. A branch (1975) of Southern Arkansas University is here. **3.** city, pop. 11,504, seat of Butler Co., SE Kansas, on the Walnut R., 27 mi/43 km NE of Wichita. It processes and ships grain and livestock. Since oil was discovered nearby in 1915, it has been active in refining and shipping petroleum and manufacturing oil-related products. It is the seat of Butler County Community Junior College (1927).

Eldorado National Forest c.680,000 ac/275,000 ha (1062 sq mi/2752 sq km) in EC California, S and SW of L. Tahoe, on the W slope of the SIERRA NEVADA. In a noted winter sports area, it contains the popular Desolation Wilderness (63,500 ac/25,700 ha) and part of the Mokelumne Wilderness. The TAHOE NATIONAL FOREST lies N, the Stanislaus National Forest S.

Elephant Mound prehistoric earthwork in Grant Co., SW Wisconsin, on the Mississippi R., 4 mi/6 km S of Wyalusing, probably intended to represent a bear, and much eroded, an artifact of the same culture period that produced Iowa's EFFIGY MOUNDS, across the river just to the NW.

Elfers unincorporated residential community, pop. 12,356, Pasco Co., WC Florida, 23 mi/37 km NW of Tampa and just S of New Port Richey.

Elfreth's Alley historic residential street in the OLD CITY, Philadelphia, Pennsylvania. A short distance E of Independence National Historic Park, it is the oldest continuously occupied residential street in the US; its oldest house dates to 1702.

Elgin city, pop. 77,010, Cook and Kane counties, NE Illinois, on the Fox R., 36 mi/58 km W of Chicago. Situated at the edge of the Chicago metropolitan area, it is also the center of a dairying region. Local manufactures include machine tools, hobby supplies, caskets, street sweepers, electrical products, precision instruments, and belting. Elgin is also a center for the printing of religious publications. The Elgin Watch Company figured prominently in the economy for a century, until it left the state in 1970. Shortly after the city was founded (1835), a millrace and dam were constructed here, stimulating an industrial boom based on flour and saw mills. Judson College (1963) is here.

Elizabeth city, pop. 110,002, seat of Union Co., NE New Jersey, on Newark Bay and the Arthur Kill, connected to Staten I. by the GOETHALS BRIDGE, and adjacent (S) to Newark. Settled in an area purchased from the Delaware Indians (1664) and called Elizabethtown until 1740, it was New Jersey's first Colonial capital and meeting place of the Colonial assembly (1668–82). The College of New Jersey, which would become Princeton University, was founded here (1747). Elizabeth became an important seaport and a center for tanning and brewing. It was repeatedly attacked and partially destroyed during the Revolution. Railroads and proximity to New York City spurred Elizabeth's rapid industrialization in the late 19th century. Today it is a major port and transportation center, with one of the world's largest containerized docks at Port Elizabeth (in the NE). Newark International Airport (N) is partly in the city. Elizabeth also has shipyards, oil refineries, foundries, and steel mills, and manufactures machinery, chemicals, office supplies, and foods. The city is also a residential suburb of New York; its population includes a high proportion of Hispanic and European immigrants. A campus of Union College is here.

Elizabeth City city, pop. 14,292, seat of Pasquotank Co., extreme NE North Carolina, on the Pasquotank R. estuary, a N arm of ALBEMARLE SOUND, and part of the ATLANTIC INTRACOASTAL WATERWAY. It was settled in the mid 17th century. Following the completion of the Dismal Swamp Canal in 1790, trade with the West Indies flourished. Elizabeth City is now a busy maritime city, with diversified industries, including lumber and shipyards. A large Coast Guard base and airfield are just SE. It is home to Elizabeth City State University (1891), the College of Albemarle (1960), and Roanoke Bible College.

Elizabeth Islands chain with a total area of 14 sq mi/36 sq km, constituting the town of Gosnold, pop. 98, Dukes Co., SE Massachusetts. The 16 islands run SW for 15 mi/24 km from the SW tip of Cape Cod, with Buzzards Bay to the N and Vineyard Sound to the S. Their population consists mostly of summer residents. The two largest islands are NAUSHON and Nashawena. There is a coast guard station on CUTTYHUNK, the outermost island.

Elizabeth River in Virginia, short, branching estuarial river entering HAMPTON ROADS between the cities of NORFOLK (E) and PORTSMOUTH (W). Its Southern and Eastern branches are dredged channels. The Southern Branch is a link between Hampton Roads and ALBEMARLE SOUND, North Carolina, via two branches of the ATLANTIC INTRACOASTAL WATERWAY: the DISMAL SWAMP Canal, which also leads to L. Drummond, and the Albemarle and Chesapeake Canal. The Elizabeth is heavily industrial in Norfolk, Portsmouth, and CHESAPEAKE.

Elizabethton city, pop. 11,931, seat of Carter Co., extreme E Tennessee, in Happy Valley on the Watauga and Doe rivers, 8 mi/13 km ENE of Johnson City. It is among the first permanent white settlements in Tennessee. An independent, democratic government, the WATAUGA ASSOCIATION, was organized here in 1772. Just W of the settlement, at Sycamore Shoals, the site of Fort Watauga, in March 1775, Cherokees by treaty granted land for the establishment of TRANSYLVANIA. Modern Elizabethon makes rayon and aluminum products, chemicals, and piano strings. There are manganese deposits, and the river and nearby Watauga and Boone lakes, formed by Tennessee Valley Authority dams, provide recreational facilities.

Elizabethtown **1.** city, pop. 18,167, seat of Hardin Co., C Kentucky, 48 mi/77 km SSW of Louisville. Settled in 1780, it developed as a trading center for burley tobacco and other crops. It now makes magnets, processed foods, bottled drinks, and audio products, and has a community college. **2.** see under ELIZABETH, New Jersey. **3.** borough, pop. 9952, seat of Lancaster Co., SE Pennsylvania, 18 mi/29 km NW of Lancaster. It is the seat of Elizabethtown College (1899). The Masonic Homes, a retirement community that houses a noted arboretum, is here.

Elk City city, pop. 10,428, Beckham Co., W Oklahoma, on Elk Creek, 110 mi/185 km W of Oklahoma City. In the late 19th century, it was a resting spot for cattle drives from Texas to Kansas. It thrived with the discovery of oil (1947), and when reserves were depleted in the late 1960s, refocused on natural gas. The city is also a commercial center for agricultural and dairy producers. Its manufactures include furniture.

Elk Grove Village village, pop. 33,429, Cook and Du Page counties, NE Illinois, a suburb 25 mi/40 km NW of Chicago. It is a planned community with space set aside for a 2250-ac/911-ha industrial park. O'Hare International Airport lies immediately SE. Busse L. and the Ned Brown Forest Preserve are just NW.

Elkhart city, pop. 43,627, Elkhart Co., N Indiana, at the confluence of the Elkhart and St. Joseph rivers, 15 mi/24 km E of South Bend, and just S of the Michigan border. It grew from a crossroads of several Indian trails into a major mid-19th-century railroad junction; today a large Penn Central classification yard is on its outskirts. The manufacture of band instruments, begun by Charles Conn in 1875, continues to be important; a large proportion of all brass instruments produced in the US are made here. Other manufactures include pharmaceuticals (Miles), automotive products, plastics, mechanical rubber, furniture, window casings, recreational vehicles, and mobile homes.

Elkhart County 466 sq mi/1207 sq km, pop. 156,198, in N Indiana. Its seat is GOSHEN. It borders Michigan on the N, and is drained by the Elkhart and St. Joseph rivers. Largely agricultural, the county produces wheat, oats, vegetables, and timber. ELKHART and Goshen are manufacturing centers.

Elkhart Lake village, pop. 1019, Sheboygan Co., E Wisconsin, on Elkhart L., 15 mi/24 km NW of Sheboygan. Tourists are attracted to the area's water sports and camping facilities. An early sports car racing track was located here. The surrounding region is agricultural, producing dairy items and grain.

Elk Hills low range in Kern Co., SC California, some 19 mi/31 km SW of Bakersfield, on the W side of the Central Valley, just E of the Temblor Range. It is the site of a naval oil reserve created in World War I and fraudulently leased in 1921 by Albert B. Fall, secretary of the interior, to oilman Edward I. Doheny. Part of the scandal centering around Wyoming's TEAPOT DOME, the reserve was returned to government control in 1927.

Elkhorn ghost town in Jefferson Co., SW Montana, in Helena National Forest, 20 mi/32 km S of Helena. Established in 1872, this frontier mining camp flourished until the collapse of the international silver market in the 1890s. The town had many saloons, dance halls, and other establishments catering to miners. Still standing are many examples of frontier architecture.

Elkhorn River 333 mi/533 km long, in NE Nebraska. It rises in Rock Co., E of Bassett, and flows generally ESE from the High Plains into lowlands W of the Missouri R., passing S of Norfolk, to the Platte R., W of Omaha.

Elkhorn Tavern see PEA RIDGE, Arkansas.

Elkins city, pop. 7420, seat of Randolph Co., NE West Virginia, on the Tygart R., 35 mi/56 km SE of Clarksburg. It is the trade center for a lumbering, agricultural, and coal mining area, is headquarters for the Monongahela National Forest, and produces various light manufactures. Davis and Elkins College (1904) is here.

Elkins Park unincorporated village in CHELTENHAM township,

Montgomery Co., SE Pennsylvania. A suburb of Philadelphia, 4 mi/6 km NW of the city, Elkins Park is noted for its Quaker meetinghouse (1682) and Beth Sholom Synagogue (1959), designed by Frank Lloyd Wright.

Elko city, pop. 14,736, seat of Elko Co., NE Nevada, on the Humboldt R. and Interstate 80. Originating in 1868 as a construction camp for the Central Pacific Railroad, it served as a supply point for westward-bound settlers. It is now a trade and distribution center for a cattle and sheep raising area. Local mining and tourism are also important to its economy. Elko is headquarters for the HUMBOLDT NATIONAL FOREST, and is known for its annual Cowboy Poetry Gathering and National Basque Festival. Its prosperity has recently been influenced by its proximity to Carlin, site of a flourishing gold mine, 20 mi/32 km WSW.

Elk River **1.** city, pop. 11,143, seat of Sherburne Co., EC Minnesota, on the Mississippi R. where the Elk R. (dammed in the city to form Orono L.) joins it, 27 mi/43 km NNW of Minneapolis. A fur trading post in the 1840s, it was a lumbering town (as Orono) in the 1880s, then became a dairying and farm trade center and maker of concrete products. Its residential sector grew quickly in the 1980s. **2.** 172 mi/277 km long, in C West Virginia. It rises on the W slope of the Allegheny Mts. in Pocahontas Co., near the Snowshoe ski area, and flows generally NW past Webster Springs and Sutton, then generally SW to the Kanawha R. at CHARLESTON.

Elkton **1.** city, pop. 1789, seat of Todd Co., SW Kentucky, 18 mi/29 km ESE of Hopkinsville. The area grows grain, fruit, and tobacco, and has stone quarries and timber. On US 68, the city has various agriculturally related manufactures. **2.** town, pop. 9073, seat of Cecil Co., NE Maryland, at the head of navigation on the Elk R., 19 mi/31 km SW of Wilmington, Delaware. It is a commercial town with sand and gravel pits, and manufactures toys, fireworks, spark plugs, and radios. Elk Neck State Forest and the W terminus of the Chesapeake and Delaware Canal are nearby on the river. Until the 1940s Elkton was known as the goal of out-of-state couples who wished to marry quickly, and had a famous row of wedding chapels. **3.** town, pop. 1935, Rockingham Co., W Virginia, on the South Fork of the Shenandoah R., 13 mi/21 km ESE of HARRISONBURG. It is home to a Coors beer bottling plant.

Ellensburg city, pop. 12,361, seat of Kittitas Co., C Washington, on the Yakima R., 25 mi/40 km N of Yakima. It is a commercial center for surrounding coal mining towns and, since the Yakima Reclamation Project, an important trading and processing hub for cattle and the agricultural products of its irrigated river valley. Lumbering is also important. Ellensburg is the seat of Central Washington University (1891). Its annual rodeo is one of the largest in the country. Ginkgo Petrified Forest and State Park, sources of "Ellensburg Blue" agate, are 25 mi/40 km E.

Ellenville village, pop. 4243, in Wawarsing township, Ulster Co., SE New York, in the Shawangunk Mts., 27 mi/43 km W of Poughkeepsie. A sizable resort complex, typical of the BORSCHT BELT genre that has largely disappeared from the region, is still here.

Ellesmere Island third-largest (75,767 sq mi/196,236 sq km) and most northerly island in Canada, in the ARCTIC ARCHIPELAGO, Northwest Territories. Largest of the QUEEN ELIZABETH Is., some 450 mi/720 km N–S and up to 270 mi/430 km wide, it lies in the Arctic Ocean off NW Greenland, from which it is separated by the Kane Basin and Robeson and Kennedy (as little as 18 mi/30 km wide in places) channels. It is the archipelago's most rugged island, its Grant Land Mts. rising to 8583 ft/2616 m at Mt. Barbeau, in the N, the highest point in E North America. It has extensive icefields and coasts ringed with icefields and indented with FJORDS, including the 200 mi/320 km–long Nansen Sound–Greely Fiord system (NW). The N coast culminates at Cape Columbia, Canada's (and North America's) most northerly point, at 83° 07′ N. Some 70 mi/110 km SE is the radar and weather station at Alert, the world's most northerly (82° 31′ N) outpost, c.400 mi/640 km from the North Pole. Much of the N is within the **Ellesmere I. National Park Reserve,** which protects geologic features; a wide array of plant life, esp. around 50 mi/80 km–long L. Hazen; and some of the island's scattered, up to 4000-year-old INUIT sites. There is another radar station at Eureka (NW). Grise Fiord (hamlet, pop. 130), an Inuit community in the extreme S, is said to be (at 76° 25′) the continent's northernmost settlement. First sighted by Europeans in 1616, Ellesmere has seen little human activity other than Inuit hunting, but scientific and military operations, oil and gas exploration (since the 1970s), and some tourism are now part of its life.

Ellicott City unincorporated community, pop. 41,396, seat of Howard Co., NC Maryland, on the Patapsco R., 12 mi/19 km W of Baltimore. It developed from Ellicott's Mills, a small town built around the gristmill of three Quaker brothers in the late 1700s. In 1830, the first section of the Baltimore and Ohio railroad, from Baltimore, was opened, and the community became a residential and business suburb. It is now primarily residential, with a number of preserved Colonial homes.

Elliot Lake city, pop. 14,089, Algoma District, C Ontario, on Elliot L., 83 mi/134 km ESE of Sault Ste. Marie. It was established in 1954 as a planned community, following the discovery of uranium ore in the area. One of the world's largest uranium producing districts, it has experienced cycles of expansion and contraction tied to fluctuating demand. In an area with some 170 lakes, it is also a resort.

Elliott Bay inlet of PUGET SOUND at the mouth of the Duwamish R., forming the harbor of SEATTLE, Washington. The bay is 6 mi/10 km N–S at its entrance between West Point (N) and Alki Point (S), and 4 mi/6 km E–W. The Downtown area, on the E, was settled in 1852, one year after the initial settlement at Alki Point.

Elliott Knob peak, 4463 ft/1360 m, in the Appalachian Mts., 13 mi/21 km W of STAUNTON, N Virginia, overlooking the Shenandoah Valley (SE).

Ellipse, the see under WHITE HOUSE, Washington, D.C.

Ellis Island historic island in Upper New York Bay, about 1 mi/1.5 km SW of the Battery, New York City, and just off the waterfront of Jersey City, New Jersey. A 3-ac/1.2-ha body called Oyster I. in Colonial days, it was renamed for an early owner. From 1892 to 1954 it was the chief US immigration station. Expanded to 27 ac/11 ha by landfill, it received about 12 million arriving aliens. It was also used as a quarantine and detention station. Today it is a unit of the Statue of Liberty National Monument. Its main hall and some other refurbished buildings are heavily visited. The fate of numerous smaller buildings is under debate; a conference center has been proposed for the island's S part.

Ellis Island of the West see ANGEL I., California.

Ellisville city, pop. 7545, St. Louis Co., EC Missouri, 22 mi/35 km W of downtown St. Louis. Settled in 1836, it is now a primarily residential suburb.

Ellsworth city, pop. 5975, seat of Hancock Co., SE Maine. It is at the falls of the Union R., just above Union River Bay of the Atlantic Ocean, 25 mi/40 km SE of Bangor. It is the retail center and gateway to Acadia National Park and the Mount Desert region. The leading manufactures are wood products, boats, and woolen goods. Much of the business district was rebuilt after a 1933 fire.

Ellsworth Air Force Base military installation in Pennington Co., SW South Dakota, 11 mi/18 km E of Rapid City. It is the home of the Air Force's 44th Strategic Missile Wing and the 28th Bombardment Wing. Minuteman missiles controlled by the base were removed from silos in the surrounding countryside in 1992.

El Malpais National Monument 114,716 ac/46,460 ha, in WC New Mexico, between the ÁCOMA (E) and ZUÑI (W) reservations, S of Grants and 67 mi/108 km WSW of Albuquerque. In an area covered by lava flows some 1000 years ago, it protects ice caves; La Ventana ("the window"), a large natural arch; and volcanic formations. There are ANASAZI ruins, and the area has been sacred to more modern peoples. A National Conservation Area surrounds the monument.

Elmendorf Air Force Base see under ANCHORAGE, Alaska.

Elmhurst 1. city, pop. 42,029, Du Page Co., NE Illinois, 14 mi/22 km W of Chicago. A mainly residential community, with a 600-ac/243-ha light industrial park, it was founded in 1836. The coming of the railroad (1849) brought an influx of German loggers. Today local quarries supply limestone for cut stone and cement block industries. Elmhurst College (1871) is here, as is the Lizzardro Museum of Lapidary Arts. **2.** residential and commercial section of C Queens, New York. It was part of the former township of Newtown. An area of low-rise detached and apartment houses opened to large-scale development in the 1930s, Elmhurst is now perhaps New York City's most diverse neighborhood, with an estimated 114 immigrant groups represented. The Long Island Expressway passes through it. Two big gas storage tanks, the Newtown Holders (1910 and 1921) dominated the skyline until 1993. Jackson Heights is to the N.

Elmira city, pop. 33,724, seat of Chemung Co., S New York, on the Chemung R. and Newtown Creek, 5 mi/8 km from the Pennsylvania border and 45 mi/72 km W of Binghamton. Founded in 1788 as Newtown, it took its present name, for the daughter of a settler, in 1828, and grew following the completion of the Chemung Canal to Seneca L. (1832) and the arrival of the Erie Railroad (1849). Elmira's industries now manufacture office machines, electric pumps, electron tubes, glass bottles, fabricated steel, valves, hydrants, fire engines, machine tools, airplanes, and processed foods. The Elmira State Correctional Facility (Elmira Reformatory, established 1876) and Elmira College, one of the earliest US educational institutions for women (1855; now coeducational) are here. The Battle of Newtown was fought on Aug. 29, 1779, 5 mi/8 km to the SE. Mark Twain spent much of his later life at Quarry Farm; he was buried in Woodlawn Cemetery in 1910, and his study moved to Elmira College. In June 1972, floodwaters severly damaged Elmira.

Elmont unincorporated village, pop. 28,612, in Hempstead town, Nassau Co., SE New York, on W Long Island adjacent (E) to Cambria Heights, Queens, and 5 mi/8 km SW of Garden City. Residential and commercial, it is the site of Belmont Park Race Track (1905).

El Monte city, pop. 106,209, Los Angeles Co., SW California, 14 mi/23 km E of Los Angeles, on Interstate 10 and the San Gabriel R. (E). It was settled in 1852 at the terminus of the SANTA FE TRAIL, and was long a truck and dairy farming and fruit and walnut growing center. El Monte's annexation of nearby communities in 1961 tripled its population. It is now a residential suburb with manufactures including electronic and aircraft components and mobile homes.

El Morro 1. also, **Inscription Rock** sandstone formation covering 12 ac/5 ha and rising 200 ft/61 m above the surrounding valley, 30 mi/48 km WSW of Grants, in WC New Mexico. Hundreds of inscriptions in its soft yellow walls include ancient petroglyphs as well as carvings by Spaniards (Oñate's dates from 1605) and pioneers. Protected as El Morro National Monument in 1906, the area includes ruins of ancient PUEBLOS. **2.** also, **Morro Castle** in full, **El Castillo de San Felipe del Morro** fortress at the tip of the SAN JUAN Peninsula (the Punta del Morro) and of Old San Juan, overlooking San Juan Bay (S) and the Atlantic Ocean (N), in NE Puerto Rico. Built by the Spanish, it dates from 1539, and was fully completed in 1589. It was instrumental in thwarting Sir Francis Drake's invasion (1595), although the British held it for three months in 1598. Set on a rocky promontory, it has six stories of gun emplacements and massive 140 ft/43 m–high stone walls. Its architecture and the views it commands make it a tourist attraction. It is sometimes confused with the late-16th-century fortresses in Havana and Santiago, Cuba, each also known as Morro Castle.

Elmwood Park 1. village, pop. 23,206, Cook Co., NE Illinois, bordering NW Chicago, 9 mi/14 km from the Loop. Although largely a residential suburb, it contains tool-and-die shops and other industries. **2.** borough, pop. 17,623, Bergen Co., NE New Jersey, on the Passaic R., across (E) from Paterson. Formerly known as East Paterson, it has a wide variety of manufactures, and is also residential.

El Norte from the perspective of Mexicans and some Central Americans, the United States as a land of opportunity or place of refuge. The term is used specifically in reference to such goals of migrants as Los Angeles, California, and San Antonio, Texas.

Elon College town, pop. 4394, Alamance Co., NC North Carolina, 4 mi/6 km W of Burlington, the home Elon College (1889).

El Paso 1. city, pop. 2499, Woodford Co., C Illinois, 14 mi/23 km N of Normal. A grain shipping center, it is the birthplace (1895) of broadcast priest Fulton J. Sheen. **2.** city, pop. 515,342, seat of El Paso Co. (pop. 591,610), extreme W Texas, on the Rio Grande, opposite the larger Ciudad Juarez (Chihuahua), Mexico. The state of New Mexico lies W and N. El Paso forms a "V" around the FRANKLIN Mts., a S spur of the Rockies. Midway between E Texas and the California coast, it is the largest US city on the Mexican border. The Chihuahuan Desert lies to the S. The site was seen by Spanish explorers as early as the 1530s, and was named (El Paso del Norte, "the North Pass") by Juan de Oñate in 1598, as he established colonization routes N into New Mexico. A mission was founded in 1659 on the Mexican side. In 1681, Tiwa refugees from ISLETA, New Mexico, where the Pueblo Revolt had just occurred, established Ysleta del Sur, then on the river's S side, but now on the N, within El Paso's SE. Here the Tigua (the Spanish spelling) inhabit a reservation (pop. 292) that is the oldest community in Texas. In 1780 a Spanish outpost, San Elizario, was established near Ysleta; SOCORRO, outside the city limits, is the third old settlement now on the US side. Americans arrived in the area and began settlement N of the Rio Grande in 1827. FORT BLISS was established in 1848, the same year the treaty of Guadalupe Hidalgo separated El Paso (N) from Juarez (S), and the California Gold Rush of 1849 brought E–W traffic through what had long been a S–N conduit. In the Civil War El Paso was seized by Union troops from California in Aug. 1862. It was incorporated in 1873. The arrival of the Southern Pacific Railroad in 1881 brought development; ranching and the processing of ore from states to the N became important. Large-scale irrigation, begun around World War I, made the area a major producer of chili peppers, onions, beans, other vegetables, and cotton. The city now has smelters handling copper and other metals, oil and gas refineries, canneries, and meatpacking, food processing, and various manufacturing plants. Its proximity to Mexico has made it a tourist center since Prohibition. The military has also been a major factor in the economy. Border traffic and the growth of the MAQUILADORA system have been increasingly important in recent decades. El Paso's close relations with Mexico are symbolized by the international CHAMIZAL area on the river. The city is home to the University of Texas at El Paso (formerly Texas Western; 1913), whose campus incorporates the Sun Bowl, scene of a college football bowl game.

El Paso de Robles see PASO ROBLES, California.

El Pueblo de Los Angeles State Historic Park, 44 ac/18 ha, in downtown Los Angeles, California, between the CIVIC CENTER (S) and CHINATOWN (N). The 27 buildings grouped here, occupying the area where the PUEBLO was founded in 1781, include the city's oldest existing house, its first theater, and its oldest firehouse. Olvera St., a reconstructed (1930s) Mexican market street, runs NE from the Old Plaza here.

El Reno city, pop. 15,414, seat of Canadian Co., C Oklahoma, near the North Canadian R., 25 mi/40 km W of Oklahoma City. It grew with the Rock Island Railroad's arrival in 1889, and today is a processing and shipping center for wheat, cotton, oats, alfalfa, dairy goods, and livestock. There are railroad shops, flour mills, and other industries. Nearby are the remains of the cavalry outpost Fort Reno (1874), and a Federal prison.

Elsah village, pop. 2499, Jersey Co., SW Illinois, on the Mississippi R., across from Missouri, and 10 mi/16 km NW of Alton. It was an important 19th-century steamboat stopping point, and is the seat of Principia College (1898). Pere Marquette State Park is 10 mi/16 km W.

El Segundo city, pop. 15,223, Los Angeles Co., SW California, 10 mi/16 km SW of downtown Los Angeles, on Santa Monica Bay. It was founded by the Standard Oil Company in 1911 as the site for an oil refinery, the second (*el segundo*) in S California; the beachside area was accessible to tankers. Today, El Segundo remains an important refining center. It has electronics and computer industries and corporate headquarters. It has also been, since the height of the Cold War, an aerospace center, manufacturing aircraft and space vehicles. An Air Force missile station is here, and Los Angeles International Airport is adjacent (N).

Elsinore see LAKE ELSINORE, California.

El Toro unincorporated community, pop. 62,685, Orange Co., SW California, 13 mi/21 km SE of Santa Ana and 45 mi/72 km SE of Los Angeles. Founded in the 1890s as a farming community, it is now a rapidly expanding suburb. Its economy has long been tied to the El Toro Marine Corps Air Station (just NW), which was ordered closed in 1991.

Elwood **1.** city, pop. 9494, Madison Co., C Indiana, 38 mi/61 km NE of Indianapolis. Its growth was precipitated by a natural gas boom in 1887 and the introduction of sheet metal and window glass industries. Today's manufactures include specialty glass items, machine tools, wire and cable, and electronic components. In a tomato growing area, Elwood also has major canning facilities. In the city is a memorial to native son Wendell Wilkie (b. 1892). **2.** unincorporated village, pop. 10,916, in Huntington town, Suffolk Co., SE New York, on Long Island. It is primarily residential.

Ely **1.** city, pop. 3968, St. Louis Co., NE Minnesota. Settled (1885) at the E end of the VERMILION IRON RANGE, it was an important mining center and railhead. Set among lakes in the Superior National Forest and the Boundary Waters Canoe Area, it is now also a resort center, and home to Vermilion Community College (1922). **2.** city, pop. 4756, seat of White Pine Co., EC Nevada, 125 mi/200 km SSE of Elko and 46 mi/74 km W of the Utah line. Founded (1868) as a gold and silver mining camp, it grew after the beginning of large-scale copper mining in the early 1900s. Greater development came with the arrival of the Nevada Northern Railway in 1906. The well-known Kennecott Copper Liberty Pit operated near here, at Ruth (NW), until the late 1970s. The 1970s and early 1980s saw a decline in local mining operations. Ely is also the center of a ranching area, and is popular with tourists who visit nearby GHOST TOWNS, the Humboldt National Forest, and Great Basin National Park, 40 mi/64 km SE. **3.** village in Fairlee township, Orange Co., EC Vermont, on the Connecticut R. A former railroad depot for the nearby Ely Copper Mines, Ely was in 1883 the site of a miners' insurrection called the "Ely War," which was put down by the National Guard.

Elyria city, pop. 56,746, seat of Lorain Co., N Ohio, on the Black R., 23 mi/36 km W of Cleveland, and 8 mi/13 km S of L. Erie. Founded in 1817, it was a milling center and the site of the first secondary school W of the Allegheny Mts. (1830). Automotive parts, chromium hardware, and heating and air-conditioning equipment are among local manufactures. Cascade Park here is noted for its caves, waterfalls, and rock formations.

Elysian Fields see under HOBOKEN, New Jersey.

Elysian Park municipal park, 575 ac/233 ha, almost completely surrounding CHAVEZ RAVINE, in Los Angeles, California, just W of the Los Angeles R. and N of Downtown. The ARROYO SECO passes through, the Los Angeles Police Academy is here, and freeways surround the park.

El Yunque see under CARIBBEAN NATIONAL FOREST, Puerto Rico.

Emancipation Oak see under HAMPTON, Virginia.

Embarcadero in California: **a.** waterfront walkway in downtown SAN DIEGO, on San Diego Bay, site of the Maritime Museum. **b.** bayfront commercial area in SAN FRANCISCO, lined with piers, along the city's NE edge from FISHERMAN'S WHARF (N) to the China Basin (S). The elevated **Embarcadero Freeway** (I-480), built in 1959 along the waterfront, was severely damaged in the Oct. 1989 earthquake, and the city chose to demolish it.

Embassy Row area in NW Washington, D.C., a stretch of Massachusetts Ave., chiefly NW of DUPONT CIRCLE and SE of CATHEDRAL HEIGHTS, where many foreign embassies and legations are located. It is also a very affluent residential area.

Emerald Necklace see under the FENWAY, Massachusetts.

Emeryville city, pop. 5740, Alameda Co., NC California, on San Francisco Bay, adjacent to Berkeley (NE) and Oakland (SE). A waterfront community incorporated in 1896, it has had stockyards and a variety of heavy industries, and now also has research and biotechnology facilities and high-rise apartment buildings.

Emigrant Peak 10,960 ft/3343 m, in Park Co., SC Montana, in the N Rocky Mts., between the Yellowstone R. and Gallatin National Forest, 17 mi/27 km N of Yellowstone National Park and 30 mi/48 km S of Livingston.

Emigrant Trail also, **California Emigrant Trail** variously applied name for routes used by travelers to California in the 1840s–50s, esp. by gold rushers. The best-known Emigrant Trail, also called the Humboldt Trail, crossed N Nevada along the Humboldt R.; later, the CENTRAL PACIFIC RAILROAD, the Victory Highway (US 40), and I-80 all chose this route. Approaches to the Humboldt Trail were several, including one that ran S of the Great Salt L. and past Pilot Peak, on the Utah-Nevada border. The CALIFORNIA TRAIL, a S offshoot of the Oregon Trail, joined from the N in NC Nevada. In California, Emigrant Gap is on the Emigrant Trail route (and now on I-80), W of the DONNER PASS.

Emmaus borough, pop. 11,157, Lehigh Co., E Pennsylvania, 5 mi/8 km S of Allentown. Founded by Moravians c.1740, it was closed to members of other denominations from 1758 to 1836. The home of Rodale Press and site of the nonprofit Rodale Institute and its experimental organic farm, Emmaus is primarily residential but has some light industry.

Emmitsburg town, pop. 1688, Frederick Co., N Maryland, 20 mi/32 km N of Frederick, near the Pennsylvania line. It is home to Mount St. Mary's College and Seminary (1808), the oldest independent Catholic college in the US. Elizabeth Bayley Seton, founder of the Roman Catholic Sisters of Charity and the first US woman saint, is buried in the Chapel of St. Joseph's College (1809), also in the town.

Emory **1.** locality in De Kalb Co., NW Georgia, 4 mi/6 km NE of downtown Atlanta, home to Emory University (1836) and to the CENTERS FOR DISEASE CONTROL AND PREVENTION. **2.** unincorporated community in Washington Co., SW Virginia, 8 mi/13 km NE of Abingdon. In a rural valley near the Middle Branch of the Holston R., it is the seat of Emory and Henry College (1838). With neighboring (SW) Meadowview, it has a pop. of 2248.

Emory Peak see under CHISOS Mts., Texas.

Empire State Building skyscraper, on Fifth Ave. at 34th St., Manhattan, New York City. Opened in 1931, it stands 1454 ft/443 m tall including its radio/TV mast, and has 102 floors housing offices in the textile, publishing, and other industries and agencies. Its observatories on the 86th and 102nd floors are popular tourist attractions, and the building itself is a well-known symbol of New York. Until the completion of the WORLD TRADE CENTER in 1971, it was the tallest occupied building in the world.

Emporia **1.** city, pop. 25,512, seat of Lyon Co., EC Kansas, in the Flint Hills, 50 mi/80 km SW of Topeka. It is a rail and truck hub for grain and livestock, and processes such food products as flour, meat, and cheese. Manufactures include printing equipment and glass bottles. William Allen White published the nationally renowned Emporia *Gazette* here from 1895 to 1944. The city is the seat of Emporia State University (1863). **2.** independent city, pop. 5306, seat of but administratively separate from Greensville Co., SE Virginia, on Interstate 95 and the Meherrin R. (dammed just W), 10 mi/16 km N of the North Carolina line. It processes and ships peanuts and other agricultural products, and has a lumber industry. A Civil War skirmish occurred here on Dec. 10, 1864.

Encinitas city, pop. 55,386, San Diego Co., SW California, 23 mi/37 km NNW of San Diego, on the Pacific Ocean. This affluent suburb is one of the fastest-growing Southern California communities. Its pop. more than quintupled in the 1980s as it expanded from its beaches back into what has been a fruit growing area. CARDIFF-BY-THE-SEA is just S.

Encino S SAN FERNANDO VALLEY section of Los Angeles, California, 17 mi/27 km NW of Downtown, just N of the Santa Monica Mts. and S of the upper Los Angeles R. Unlike other Valley communities, affluent Encino boasts many early-19th-century homes, now mainly in Los Encinos State Historic Park. The community takes its name ("oak") from an early name for the Valley itself.

Endicott village, pop. 13,531, Broome Co., S New York, on the Susquehanna R., 8 mi/13 km W of Binghamton. Founded by George F. Johnson, it was settled around the first Endicott-Johnson Shoe Corporation factory in 1901, near the older village of Union, with which it was later consolidated. Together with Binghamton and JOHNSON CITY, Endicott forms the metropolitan area known as the Tri-Cities. The shoe industry remains important; business machines and foundry products are other manufactures.

Endicott Mountains see under BROOKS RANGE, Alaska.

Endwell village, pop. 12,602, in Union township, Broome Co., SC New York, on the Susquehanna R., between ENDICOTT and Johnson City. It is largely residential.

Enfield **1.** town, pop. 45,532, Hartford Co., NC Connecticut, 18 mi/28 km N of Hartford, on the E bank of the Connecticut R., Interstate 91, and the Massachusetts line. It includes the industrial subdivisions of Thompsonville (pop. 8458) and Hazardville (pop. 5179), and in the 19th century produced carpeting and gunpowder. Today, many residents commute to jobs in Hartford or in Springfield; local products include plastics, greeting cards, tools, and gauges. A monument marks the site of a famous 1741 Jonathan Edwards sermon. **2.** town in Hampshire Co., WC Massachusetts, settled 1742, inundated when the Swift R. was dammed to create QUABBIN RESERVOIR (1937).

England Air Force Base see under ALEXANDRIA, Louisiana.

Englewood **1.** city, pop. 29,387, Arapahoe Co., NC Colorado, on the South Platte R., adjoining the S boundary of Denver. Largely residential, the city is also a financial and trading center and a leading carnation grower. Industries produce published materials, steel items, electronic equipment, cellular telephones, and building construction materials. **2.** unincorporated resort community, pop. 15,025, Sarasota and Charlotte counties, SW Florida, 28 mi/45 km SSE of Sarasota, on Lemon Bay, separated by the barrier island of Manasota Key from the Gulf of Mexico. **3.** residential neighborhood on the SOUTH SIDE of Chicago, Illinois. A community of poor and working-class blacks, it is the terminus for Chicago's major N–S rapid transit line. **4.** city, pop. 24,850, Bergen Co., NE New Jersey, 13 mi/21 km NE of Jersey City. It was settled by the Dutch in the late 17th century. Primarily a middle-class New York suburb, it has many relatively new office buildings and various light industries. **5.** city, pop. 11,432, Montgomery Co., W Ohio, on the Stillwater R., 10 mi/16 km NW of Dayton. Machine tools and farming implements are made in the city. The Englewood Dam was built here (1922) to improve flood control. **6.** see under DENVER HARBOR, Houston, Texas.

Englewood Cliffs borough, pop. 5634, Bergen Co., NE New Jersey, on the PALISADES of the Hudson R., across from the Bronx, adjacent (E) to Englewood. The location of numerous one-family homes and riverfront condominiums with sweeping views of New York City, it is a primarily residential suburban community with some corporate (publishing, foods) headquarters.

English Bay see under BURRARD INLET, Vancouver, British Columbia.

Enid city, pop. 45,309, seat of Garfield Co., NC Oklahoma, 65 mi/104 km NNW of Oklahoma City. Near the CHEROKEE STRIP, it was settled in the land rush of 1893. A rail junction, it is a processing and shipping hub for wheat, dairy, poultry, and petroleum producers, and manufactures farm equipment. The city is home to Vance Air Force Base and is the seat of Phillips University (1906).

Ennis city, pop. 13,883, Ellis Co., NE Texas, 32 mi/51 km SSE of Dallas. An agricultural trade center, it also has railroad shops and some light manufacturing (oilfield equipment, paper goods, auto parts, bedsprings). The city holds an annual polka festival.

Enotah, Mount see BRASSTOWN BALD, Georgia.

Enterprise city, pop. 20,123, Coffee Co., SE Alabama, 28 mi/45 km WNW of Dothan. It was primarily a cotton producing center from the 1840s until 1915, when the Mexican boll weevil destroyed the crop. Quickly, local agriculture diversified to include peanut, potato, and sugar cane farming and the raising of livestock. In 1918 Enterprise erected its noted Boll Weevil Monument, thanking the weevil for forcing diversification on local farmers. The city now has various light industries, and is a service center for FORT RUCKER, 8 mi/13 km NE. Enterprise State Junior College (1963) is here.

Epcot Center see under LAKE BUENA VISTA, Florida.

Ephrata **1.** borough, pop. 12,133, Lancaster Co., SE Pennsylvania, on Cocalico Creek, 17 mi/27 km SW of Reading. It was founded in 1732 by Johann Conrad Beissel and a group of German Seventh Day Baptists as a monastic community. In the mid 18th century the group built the medieval-style Ephrata Cloister and established mills, a school, and the Cloister Press, one of the most important and prolific in the Colonies. The Ephrata community was also noted for its crafts, especially weaving, pottery, and fraktur. Ten of its original buildings have been restored. It is now a trading center for produce and livestock grown in the area; there is also some light manufacturing. **2.** city, pop. 5349, seat of Grant Co., EC Washington, at the S end of the Grand Coulee Valley, 18 mi/29 km NW of Moses Lake. Rich in springs, it was originally an Indian, later a military, campground. After the Great Northern Railroad arrived (1892), it became a cattle and sheep ranching center. In 1906 it was the scene of the state's last great wild horse roundup. Later, it became a fruit growing and commercial center. The headquarters of the Columbia Basin Reclamation Project is here.

Epworth city, pop. 1297, Dubuque Co., NE Iowa, 16 mi/26 km SW of Dubuque. Divine Word College (1912) is here.

Equinox Mountain in the Taconic Range, in SW Vermont, W of Manchester. Big Equinox (3816 ft/1164 m), the tallest peak in the Taconics and second-tallest in the state, is accompanied by Little Equinox (3320 ft/1013 m).

Erie city, pop. 108,718, seat of Erie Co., in the NW corner of Pennsylvania, on L. Erie, 43 mi/69 km W of Jamestown, New York. The third-largest city in Pennsylvania and its only port on the Great Lakes, Erie has an excellent natural harbor. It became accessible to oceangoing vessels after the completion of the SAINT LAWRENCE SEAWAY (1959), and is an important shipping point for a variety of goods. It is also a major industrial center whose products include paper and paper products, plastics, rubber, locomotives, electrical and railroad equipment, and construction machinery. It was settled by the French in 1753 and laid out by the English in 1795 on the site of the abandoned Fort Presque Isle. Shipyards here built most of the fleet led by Oliver Hazard Perry in the War of 1812. The city developed economically after the construction of the ERIE CANAL (1820s) and the Pennsylvania Railroad (1850s). Erie is the seat of Gannon University (1933), Mercyhurst College (1926), Villa Maria College (1925), and a campus of Pennsylvania State University. A reproduction of the blockhouse where Gen. "Mad" Anthony Wayne died (1796) stands on the old fort grounds. Presque Isle State Park is nearby; Perry's salvaged flagship, the *Niagara,* can be seen at the public dock.

Erie, Lake fourth-largest and shallowest of the GREAT LAKES, between Ontario (N), New York (E), Pennsylvania and Ohio (S), and Michigan (W). Some 250 mi/400 km NE–SW and 30–57 mi/48–92 km wide, it covers 9920 sq mi/25,695 sq km, with a maximum depth of 210 ft/64 m. Its surface lies 568 ft/173 m above sea level. It drains L. Huron (N) via the St. Clair R., L. St. Clair, and the Detroit R., and at its E end empties via the Niagara R. (the WELLAND CANAL avoids Niagara Falls) into L. Ontario. Long Point Peninsula, on the NE, forms Ontario's Long Point Bay; PUT-IN-BAY, formed by Bass I. and South Bass I., and peninsula-enclosed Sandusky Bay are on the SW, in Ohio. PELÉE I., the largest in the lake, is on the W, just S of POINT PELÉE National Park, in Ontario; Middle I., just off Pelée I., is Canada's southernmost point. Major ports and industrial centers on L. Erie include Buffalo and Lackawanna, New York; Erie, Pennsylvania; and Ashtabula, Cleveland, Lorain, Sandusky, and Toledo, Ohio. Detroit, Michigan, and Windsor, Ontario, are at its W end. French and English outposts dotted the lake from the 17th century; Britain controlled it from 1763 until Sept. 1813, when an American fleet under Oliver Perry won the Battle of Lake Erie (at Put-in-Bay). Later in the 19th century, Erie's position near Pennsylvania coalfields and lakeboat connections with western iron producing regions brought on heavy industrial development, which slowed only after the 1950s. In the 1960s, following years of chemical dumping around its cities, the lake was virtually dead; by the 1980s, however, US and Canadian pollution controls had begun to reverse this condition, improving the outlook for commercial fisheries and recreational use.

Erie Canal historic waterway, 365 mi/588 km long, in New York, extending from Albany and the Hudson R. (E) to

TONAWANDA and the Niagara R. (W). Construction was authorized by the state in 1817; the canal was opened in 1825, and enlarged several times thereafter. In order to cope with the 575-ft/175-m difference between the levels of L. Erie and the Hudson, it was equipped with numerous locks. This water route between the Atlantic Coast and the Great Lakes carried immigrants and manufactured goods toward the Midwest, and brought farm products from the interior to the Eastern Seaboard and New York City via the Hudson. In its heyday, many settlements and cities sprang up along its course. Unable to compete with railroads by the mid 19th century, the canal declined and fell into disuse. Improvements were undertaken in the early 20th century, and the 70 ft/21 m–wide, 7 ft/2 m–deep canal again became an important inland waterway. As part of the New York State Barge Canal system, it now follows much of its old course, and has become an important recreational resource.

Erie County **1.** 1046 sq mi/2709 sq km, pop. 968,532, in W New York, bounded NW by the Niagara R. and drained by Cattaraugus, Tonawanda, Buffalo, and Cayuga creeks. Its seat is Buffalo. It includes much of Buffalo's metropolitan area, notably the residential suburbs of Amherst and Lancaster, the town of Cheektowaga, the industrial city of Lackawanna, and the communities of Hamburg and West Seneca. **2.** 804 sq mi/2082 sq km, pop. 275,572, in extreme NW Pennsylvania, bordered by L. Erie (NW), Ohio (W), and New York (E and NE). Its seat is Erie, one of the state's leading ports and a manufacturing center. Outside Erie, the county is largely agricultural, known especially for its grapes, apples, and cherries.

Erie Railroad incorporated in 1832 as the New York & Erie Railroad, to connect the New York City area with the Great Lakes. The first US railroad conceived as a trunk line (a long-distance main line, rather than a collection of short lines), it ran through New York's SOUTHERN TIER, to provide an alternative to the Erie Canal as well as to service an overlooked part of the state. By 1851 it was completed to DUNKIRK, on L. Erie, a distance of 460 mi/740 km across much difficult terrain. The costs of construction, the decision to use unorthodox (6 ft/1.83 m–gauge) track that later had to be replaced, and the location of the Erie's E terminus at Piermont, a Rockland Co. village some distance (18 mi/29 km N of midtown Manhattan) by boat from New York City, caused continuous financial problems; nevertheless, the Erie was called the "Work of the Age," for such achievements as the 1200-ft/366-m Starrucca Viaduct (near Susquehanna, Pennsylvania). It eventually extended from Piermont S to Hoboken, New Jersey, for New York service, and from Dunkirk N to Buffalo, and built a line to Hammond City, Indiana (for Chicago service) by way of MARION, Ohio. After the Civil War made the Erie profitable, it became the object of protracted financial battles involving Jay Gould and other speculators. In 1960 it merged with the (largely coal-carrying) Delaware, Lackawanna & Western, becoming the **Erie, Lackawanna.** In 1975 the government-created Conrail took over its operations.

Erieview 163-ac/66-ha mixed-use development in Cleveland, Ohio, on L. Erie, immediately E of Downtown. An urban renewal project completed in 1973, Erieview reversed the economic decline of the Downtown area, stimulating the growth of a new financial district.

Erindale see under MISSISSAUGA, Ontario.

Erlanger city, pop. 15,979, Kenton Co., N Kentucky, 8 mi/13 km SW of Covington. A largely residential suburb in which Interstates 275 and 75 meet, it has some light industry. Greater Cincinnati International Airport is just W.

Erwin city, pop. 5015, seat of Unicoi Co., NE Tennessee, on the Nolichucky R. and Rock Creek, 13 mi/21 km SSW of Johnson City. With the adjoining community of Banner Hill (unincorporated, pop. 1717), between Rich and Buffalo mountains and the Bald Mts., it is in the Cherokee National Forest, near the Unaka Mt. Wilderness and its recreation areas. Settled in 1775, Erwin makes clothing, wood products, and pottery, has a nuclear services industry, and is home to a National Fish Hatchery.

Esalen Institute see under Point SUR, California.

Escambia County 660 sq mi/1709 sq km, pop. 262,798, in NW Florida, the westernmost county in the state, in the PANHANDLE, bounded S by the Gulf of Mexico and W and N by Alabama. Its seat is PENSACOLA. The lowlands of its S are dominated by Pensacola's naval activities and Gulf Coast tourism. The rest of the county, in rolling hills, is largely rural and agricultural, with dairy, peanut, cotton, and truck farms and some timber production.

Escambia River Florida: see under CONECUH R., Alabama.

Escanaba city, pop. 13,659, seat of Delta Co., NW Michigan, on the Upper Peninsula, on Little Bay de Noc of L. Michigan. A storage and distribution center for coal and oil products and an important Great Lakes port, it ships coal, lumber, iron ore, and other freight. There are commercial fishing and timber-based industries, and Escanaba manufactures chemicals, furniture, paper, and concrete. The site of ancient Indian villages, it developed as a lumbering center in the early 1800s and flourished when the first iron-ore dock was built by the Chicago and North Western Railway Company in 1863. It hosts the annual Upper Peninsula State Fair, is headquarters for Hiawatha National Forest, and is the seat of Bay de Noc Community College (1962).

Escanaba River 40 mi/64 km long, in the C Upper Peninsula of Michigan. It is formed by the confluence of two branches and several creeks in SE Marquette Co., and flows SE to Little Bay de Noc, 12 mi/19 km N of ESCANABA.

Escondido city, pop. 108,635, San Diego Co., SW California, 30 mi/48 km N of San Diego, on Escondido Creek. It lies in a fertile valley surrounded, or hidden (*escondido*), by rolling hills. It is the processing and trade center for a fruit and avocado growing area. The production of wine in California began here with 18th-century Spanish missionaries, and there are still local wineries. The city has a variety of light manufactures, but is primarily a booming residential community. The San Pasqual Battlefield State Historic park, 5 mi/8 km E, is the site of a battle (Dec. 6, 1846) between US troops under Stephen Kearny and Californians of Spanish ancestry under Andrés Pico, in which the American forces were outmatched until Kit Carson managed to bring reinforcements from San Diego.

esker a narrow, winding ridge, formed of sand and gravel deposited by a stream flowing under or within a glacier or ice sheet. Eskers are often of some length, and are sometimes mistaken for artificial earthworks.

Eskimo see INUIT.

Esopus town, pop. 8860, Ulster Co., SE New York, on the W bank of the Hudson R., just S of Kingston. Settled by the Dutch in the 17th century, it became a town in 1811. Esopus is the site of the Wiltwyck School for Boys, a detention facility. Naturalist John Burroughs (1837–1921) cultivated fruit trees and wrote on a farm near here. Villages in the town include Port Ewen, Ulster Park, and West Park. There are several commercial vineyards.

Espanola **1.** city, pop. 8389, Rio Arriba and Santa Fe counties, N New Mexico, on the Rio Grande, 20 mi/32 km NNW of Santa Fe. In the Santa Clara Pueblo land grant, this ranching and farming community produces chilies and vegetables, timber, fruit, livestock, and wool. The nearby LOS ALAMOS National Laboratory provides employment. Northern New Mexico Community College (1909) is here. Bandelier National Monument (SW), the Puye Cliff Dwellings (W), and the Pojoaque (SW), Nambé (SW), San Ildefonso (S), San Juan (NE), and Santa Clara (S) PUEBLOS are nearby. **2.** town, pop. 5527, Sudbury District, C Ontario, on the Spanish R., just N of L. Huron and 42 mi/68 km WSW of Sudbury. It is essentially a COMPANY TOWN for a pulp and paper milling concern that began operations in 1899. During World War II it served as a prisoner-of-war camp. Today it is the gateway to the MANITOULIN I. tourist area, and the region produces nickel, copper, and gold.

Esperance unincorporated community, pop. 11,236, Snohomish Co., WC Washington. It is a middle-income residential suburb, formerly in the city of Edmonds, on the King Co. line, 11 mi/18 km N of downtown Seattle.

Esquimalt district municipality, pop. 16,192, Capital Regional District, extreme SW British Columbia, a seaport on the Juan de Fuca Strait, at the SE end of Vancouver I., adjacent (W) to Victoria, of which it is a residential suburb. It was settled in the 1840s, and grew during the 1850s gold rush and after the building of naval drydocks in the 1880s. Its Canadian Forces naval base remains important, as is tourism.

Essex **1.** town, pop. 5904, Middlesex Co., SC Connecticut, on the W bank of the Connecticut R., 5 mi/8 km from Long Island Sound. An 18th- and 19th-century shipbuilding and mercantile center, it is now noted for its yacht harbors and old sea captains' houses. Local industries have included shad fishing, the making of piano keys (in the village of Ivoryton), and the distilling of witch hazel essence, still profitable. **2.** unincorporated community, pop. 40,872, Baltimore Co., C Maryland, 7 mi/11 km E of Baltimore, on the estuarial Back R. It is a residential and commercial suburb, with several industrial parks. Essex Community College (1957) is here. **3.** town, pop. 16,498, including the village of Essex Junction (pop. 8396), in Chittenden Co., NW Vermont. It is on the Winooski R., just E of Burlington. The town is a busy industrial center, site of an IBM plant, and manufactures bricks, concrete, and cinder block. Other industries include poultry farming and maple sugar processing. The Champlain Valley Fair is held here. Fort Ethan Allen, active through two world wars, now an inactive air base, and Camp Johnson, a Vermont National Guard facility, are in Essex and in neighboring (W) Colchester.

Essex County **1.** 495 sq mi/1282 sq km, pop. 670,080, in extreme NE Massachusetts. Its seat is Salem. The county has a long nautical tradition, maintained today in Gloucester, Newburyport, Marblehead, and other working and recreational ports. The Cape ANN area is a popular summer resort. Lawrence, Methuen, Haverhill, and other industrial cities make the lower MERRIMACK Valley one of the most important manufacturing centers in US history. SALEM and other towns are rich in historical and literary associations. Home to the post-Revolutionary "Essex Junto," ardent Federalists, the county has historically been a center of conservative merchants and industrialists. **2.** 127 sq mi/329 sq km, pop. 778,206, in NE New Jersey, bounded by the Passaic R. (E, N, and W) and Newark Bay (SE). Its seat is NEWARK. In the New York metropolitan area, the county contains residential suburbs, industry, and shipping and business offices. Some of its larger municipalities are EAST ORANGE, MONTCLAIR, and BLOOMFIELD. **3.** 1806 sq mi/4678 sq km, pop. 37,152, in NE New York, in the Adirondack Mts., bordered by L. Champlain and the Vermont line (E). Its seat is Elizabethtown. It is a resort, logging, and agricultural region, filled with peaks over 4000 ft/1220 m, and sprinkled with lakes, including L. Placid, Schroon L., and the N tip of L. George. There are several historic sites scattered along L. Champlain, among them FORT TICONDEROGA and CROWN POINT. **4.** 666 sq mi/1725 sq km, pop. 6405, on the Québec border (N) and Connecticut R. (E), extreme NE Vermont, in the NORTHEAST KINGDOM. Guildhall is the county seat. The county is drained by the Moose, Coaticook, Nulhegan, and Clyde rivers. The main industries are agriculture, particularly dairying, and lumbering. Hunting and fishing are major recreational businesses.

Essex Fells township, pop. 2140, Essex Co., NE New Jersey, 9 mi/14 km NW of Newark. It is primarily residential.

Essex Junction see under ESSEX, Vermont.

Essington see under TINICUM I., Pennsylvania.

Esterhazy town, pop. 2896, SE Saskatchewan, 115 mi/185 km E of Regina and 44 mi/71 km SE of Yorkton, in the Qu'Appelle R. valley. Named for Count Paul Esterhazy, who founded (1886) a community of Hungarians just S, it developed as the center for a mixed farming region. In the 1950s one of the largest potash mines in North America opened here. Dairying and grain storage and processing remain important industries also.

Estes Park town, pop. 3184, Larimer Co., NC Colorado, on the Big Thompson R. and L. Estes, in the Rocky Mt. Front Range, 26 mi/42 km NNW of Boulder. It was settled c.1860, its first lodge built in the 1870s. Estes Park adjoins Roosevelt National Forest and is the E entrance and headquarters for Rocky Mountain National Park. A tourist center noted for its spectacular scenery, it is also headquarters for the Colorado–Big Thompson project, with two dams and power plants. The town is near Hidden Valley Ski Area and Horseshoe Falls.

Estevan city, pop. 10,240, extreme SE Saskatchewan, 125 mi/201 km SE of Regina and 10 mi/16 km N of the North Dakota border, on the Souris R. An oil and lignite coal center, it was the site of a bloody miners' strike in 1931. Other local products include clay, natural gas, and sodium sulfite. Estevan is also the trading point for an agricultural region engaged in mixed farming, dairying, and flour milling. Coal briquettes, brick, and tile are manufactured here.

Estherville city, pop. 6720, seat of Emmett Co., NW Iowa, 7 mi/11 km S of the Minnesota border, and 15 mi/24 km E of Spirit Lake. It was settled in 1857. Fort Defiance (1862) is SW of the city. A regional trade center, with meatpacking and other agriculturally based industries, it is home to Iowa Lakes Community College (1967). Sections of an 1879 meteorite that fell here are displayed in museums in Europe and America.

Estrie see under EASTERN TOWNSHIPS, Québec.

Etobicoke city, pop. 309,993, TORONTO Metropolitan Municipality, S Ontario, on L. Ontario, bounded by Vaughan (N); Brampton (NW); Etobicoke Creek and Mississauga (W); and the Humber R., forming the boundaries of North York, York, and Toronto (E). Etobicoke was created by the consolidation, in 1967, of the township of Etobicoke with the lakeside towns of Mimico and New Toronto and village of Long Branch. The city houses diversified industries, including a large rubber and tire plant, largely on the W side. The Mimico Creek and the Humber, with its West Branch, both have substantial parkland along them. The Woodbine Race Track is in the NW. Largely residential districts include Islington (SC), Rexdale (NC), and Thistletown (NE).

Etowah Mounds see under CARTERSVILLE, Georgia.

Etowah River 141 mi/227 km long, in Georgia. It rises in the Blue Ridge Mts. NW of Dahlonega, and flows S and SW into 12,000-ac/4900-ha Allatoona L., formed by the Allatoona Dam, E of Cartersville. It continues to Rome, where it unites with the Oostanaula R. to form the COOSA R.

Ettrick unincorporated community, pop. 5290, Chesterfield Co., EC Virginia, on the Appomattox R. across from PETERSBURG and just W of Colonial Heights. It is home to traditionally black Virginia State University (1882).

Euclid city, pop. 54,875, Cuyahoga Co., NE Ohio, 12 mi/19 km NE of Cleveland. Founded in 1798, it is a residential center that also manufactures such products as multigraphing and road machinery, airplane parts, and office machines.

Euclid Avenue commercial thoroughfare on the EAST SIDE of CLEVELAND, Ohio, running E from PUBLIC SQUARE to the UNIVERSITY CIRCLE area, then NE into the suburbs, including Euclid. In the 19th century it was one of the most prestigious US residential streets.

Eufaula city, pop. 13,220, Barbour Co., SE Alabama, on the Chattahoochee R. (L. Eufaula), 43 mi/70 km SSW of Columbus, Georgia. It is an agricultural and light manufacturing center. On the site of a Eufaula (Creek) village, it was founded in 1820. It processes cotton, peanuts, lumber, and livestock.

Eufaula Lake also, **Eufaula Reservoir** see under CANADIAN R., Oklahoma.

Eugene city, pop. 112,669, seat of Lane Co., WC Oregon, on the Willamette R., 100 mi/160 km SSW of Portland. Oregon's second-largest city, it is a major educational center, home to the University of Oregon (1872). Northwest Christian College (1895) and Lane Community College (1965) are also here. It is W Oregon's leading industrial and marketing center, processing and shipping lumber and plywood and food products. Settled in 1846, Eugene grew substantially with the arrival of the railroad in 1870. Tourists are drawn to such city attractions as the Hult Center for the Performing Arts, the University Museum of Art, and the Museum of National History, as well as many parks. Eugene is also known for its annual Oregon Bach Festival. Siuslaw (to the W) and Willamette (to the E) national forests are headquartered here.

Eugene O'Neill National Historic Site see under DANVILLE, California.

Euless city, pop. 38,149, Tarrant Co., NE Texas, 16 mi/26 km NE of downtown Fort Worth. A largely residential suburb adjacent (SW) to DALLAS–FORT WORTH INTERNATIONAL AIRPORT, it has grown from a small village since the 1960s.

Eunice city, pop. 11,162, St. Landry and Acadia parishes, SC Louisiana, 30 mi/48 km NW of Lafayette. The market center of a region that produces cotton, soybeans, and rice, it also services the regional petroleum and gas industries. An undergraduate campus of Louisiana State University is here.

Eureka **1.** city, pop. 27,025, seat of Humboldt Co., NW California, on HUMBOLDT BAY, 225 mi/362 km NNW of San Francisco. A port of entry, it has been since the 1850s one of California's chief lumbering centers, drawing especially on redwoods from nearby forests. It is also a center for commercial fishing, shipping, tourism, and commerce. Ft. Humboldt (1853), where U.S. Grant once served as captain, is now a State Historic Park. Indian I., in the bay, was the scene of a massacre of Indian women and children in 1860. In 1885, Chinese residents were driven from the city. Eureka is headquarters for Six Rivers National Forest, and home to the College of the Redwoods (1964). Its well-known Victorian buildings include the 1885 Carson Mansion. The decommissioned Humboldt Bay Nuclear Power Plant (1963–76) is SW of the city center. **2.** city, pop. 4435, seat of Woodford Co., NC Illinois, 17 mi/27 km E of Peoria. It is a trade and distribution center for locally produced pumpkins and livestock. Eureka College (1855) is here.

Eureka Springs city, pop. 1900, seat of Carroll Co., NW Arkansas, 32 mi/51 km NE of Fayetteville, near the Missouri border, on the Springfield Plateau section of the Ozarks. Used earlier by Indians, the mineral springs here gave rise in the 1870s to a well-known spa, today also a tourist center drawing visitors interested in regional folklife and crafts. The huge "Christ of the Ozarks" statue is on nearby Magnetic Mt.

Eureka Valley see under the CASTRO, San Francisco, California.

Eustis city, pop. 12,967, Lake Co., C Florida, 28 mi/45 km NW of Orlando. On the E shore of L. Eustis, it is a popular resort. It also packs and ships local citrus fruits and vegetables.

Eutaw Springs locality on Eutaw Creek, a tributary of the Santee R., near L. Marion in Orangeburg Co., SE South Carolina, 45 mi/72 km NNW of Charleston. It was the scene of the last important Revolutionary War battle in South Carolina, a British victory, on Sept. 8, 1781. The modern mill town of **Eutawville** (pop. 350) is here.

Evangeline Oak see under SAINT MARTINVILLE, Louisiana.

Evans unincorporated community, pop. 13,713, Columbia Co., E Georgia, a residential suburb 8 mi/13 km NW of downtown Augusta.

Evans, Mount **1.** 14,264 ft/4348 m, in the FRONT RANGE of the Rocky Mts., 35 mi/56 km WSW of Denver, in NC Colorado. The painter Albert Bierstadt climbed the mountain and painted it in the 1860s. A highway to its summit is said to be the highest paved US road. **2.** see under DEERLODGE NATIONAL FOREST, Montana.

Evanston **1.** city, pop. 73,233, Cook Co., NE Illinois, on L. Michigan, a suburb immediately N of Chicago and 15 mi/24 km N of the Loop. Pere Marquette landed here in 1674. The community was established as Ridgeville in 1826. When a group of Chicago businessmen bought property here for a school in 1851, Evanston became intertwined with Northwestern University, the city's largest employer. It is a lake port with manufactures that include steel products, hospital and dairy supplies, textbooks, foodstuffs, paint, chemicals, and radio and TV equipment. Evanston serves as the headquarter city for the American Academy of Pediatrics, National School Boards Association, National Merit Scholarship Corporation, Woman's Christian Temperance Union, and Rotary International; both of the latter were founded here. Its institutions of higher education include the Ecumenical Institute, National-Louis College (1886), Kendall College (1934), Seabury-Western Theological Seminary, and Garrett Biblical Institute. Also in Evanston are the Evanston Art Center, Kendall College's Mitchell Indian Museum, and Northwestern's Block Gallery. **2.** city, pop. 10,903, seat of Uinta Co., extreme SW Wyoming, on the Bear R., 50 mi/80 km E of Ogden, Utah. It developed when the railroad arrived in the late 19th century. Evanston is a railroad division point and trade center for the coal-, iron-, and petroleum-rich Overthrust Belt and for a farming and dairy area.

Evansville city, pop. 126,272, seat of Vanderburgh Co, extreme SW Indiana, on the Ohio R. across from Kentucky, and 100 mi/160 km WSW of Louisville. Settled in the early 1800s, it has been a bustling river port since the days of the steamboat. The city retains many of its 19th-century buildings, together with an Old South atmosphere. Also a railroad center, it trades, processes and ships products of the surrounding farms, oil wells, and coal mines. Among its manufactures are chemicals, aluminum products, furniture, refrigerators, and plastics. Educational institutions include the University of Evansville (1854), University of Southern Indiana (1965), and a campus of Indiana State University. The 103-ac/42-ha Angel Mounds State Historic Site, a major Mississippian culture site, is just SE, on the river.

Eveleth city, pop. 4064, St. Louis Co., NE Minnesota, 54 mi/87 km NNW of Duluth, in the MESABI RANGE. Settled in 1892, it has been since 1900 a shipper of iron ore, and also handles regional dairy products. The US Hockey Hall of Fame is here.

Evendale village, pop. 3175, Hamilton Co., SW Ohio, 5 mi/8 km NNE of downtown Cincinnati. Among its industries is a General Electric jet engine plant.

Evening Shade town, pop. 328, Sharp Co., NE Arkansas, 60 mi/100 km WNW of Jonesboro, an agricultural trade center on the Salem Plateau (the E Ozark Plateau).

Everett **1.** city, pop. 35,701, Middlesex Co., NE Massachusetts, across the Mystic R. just N of Charlestown, Boston. Settled in 1630, and part of Malden to 1870, it has been a major coal, oil, and gas depot, although some of the shoreline involved is legally part of Boston. Today it is a center for weapons research and development, a wholesale and retail market, and a manufacturer of metal items, transportation equipment, paper and petroleum products, and paints. **2.** city, pop. 69,961, seat of Snohomish Co., NW Washington, at the mouth of the Snohomish R., on Possession Sound, 25 mi/40 km NNE of Seattle. Settled in 1862, the city was laid out (1890) as the W terminus of the Northern Pacific Railroad. A major cargo and commercial fishing port, it is on Port Gardner Bay, one of the best landlocked harbors on the West Coast. Today, its manufactures include finished lumber, plywood, and pulp and paper products, much of these made by a huge Weyerhaeuser mill. The Boeing aircraft assembly plant here (1968) is often cited as the largest building in the world, at 200 million cu ft/6 million cu m. The city contains foundries, machine shops, and boatbuilding yards. Other industries include salmon canning, poultry and frozen food packaging, and the processing of dairy products. Everett Community College (1941) is here.

Everett, Mount peak (2624 ft/800 m) in the SW corner of Massachusetts, in the BERKSHIRE HILLS, near Great Barrington. Surrounding the peak is 1000-ac/400-ha Mt. Everett State Reservation. The Appalachian Trail traverses the summit. Guilder Pond, at 2042 ft/623 m, is the highest natural body of water in the state.

Everglades low-lying subtropical swampland covering much of Florida S of L. OKEECHOBEE and W of the Atlantic Coast. The 4500–sq mi/11,655–sq km area includes vast prairies of saw grass, as well as hardwood hummocks, mangroves, and saltwater marshes. Rainfall (mostly in summer) averages 60 in/150 cm a year; other water sources include L. Okeechobee and Big Cypress Swamp. In no place more than a few feet above sea level, the whole area rests on a dense mat of peat underlain by limestone, with poor drainage throughout. Canals and dikes, primarily in the Okeechobee area, have "reclaimed" large tracts for cultivation of vegetables and sugar cane. The **Everglades National Park** incorporates 1.4 million ac/567,000 ha in Dade and Monroe counties below the TAMIAMI TRAIL, including much of the TEN THOUSAND Is., FLORIDA BAY, and the upper FLORIDA KEYS. Wildlife abounds in the Everglades. There is a large winter population of migratory birds, as well native egrets, herons, ibises, kites, osprey, and spoonbills. Alligators, manatees, and wild orchids are observable from the canoe and foot trails in the park. The Florida panther is rarely seen. Inhabited by various Indian tribes, the area was explored by several Spanish expeditions in the 1500s, and was the scene of battles during the Seminole War in the late 1830s. Although most of the Indians were then removed to Oklahoma, a Seminole reservation still exists in the N of the Everglades.

Everglades Parkway see ALLIGATOR ALLEY, Florida.

Evergreen city, pop. 3911, seat of Conecuh Co., SW Alabama, about halfway between Birmingham (NE) and Mobile (SW). It is known for its agricultural experiment station, which develops and ships plants, especially holly and mistletoe.

Evergreen Park village, pop. 20,874, Cook Co., NE Illinois, a residential suburb 12 mi/19 km SW of Chicago's LOOP.

Evergreen Point Floating Bridge see under BELLEVUE, Washington.

Everman see under FORT WORTH, Texas.

Ewa Beach unincorporated community, pop. 14,315, Honolulu Co., S Oahu, Hawaii, on Mamala Bay, W of the mouth of PEARL HARBOR and 10 mi/16 km W of Honolulu. Ewa Beach Park and Honolulu Observatory are here.

Ewing township, pop. 34,185, Mercer Co., WC New Jersey, adjacent (NW) to Trenton. A residential and commercial suburb, it is also the site of a large GM auto parts plant closed in 1993. Trenton State College (1855) is here.

Excelsior see under L. MINNETONKA, Minnesota.

Excelsior Springs city, pop. 10,354, Clay and Ray counties, NW Missouri, 25 mi/40 km NE of Kansas City. Founded in 1880, it became known for its many natural mineral water springs and remains a well-known spa. Largely residential, it is also a marketing center in a corn, oats, and wheat growing area that produces coal and manufactures plastics as well. The outlaw Jesse James was born (1847) near here.

Exeter **1.** historic town, pop. 12,481, seat of Rockingham Co., SE New Hampshire. It is on the Exeter R., which is called the Squamscott after it goes over Exeter's falls, 12 mi/

19 km WSW of Portsmouth. Originally a commonwealth independent from the British colonies (1638–43), Exeter was New Hampshire's capital in the 1770s. It developed as a shipbuilding center, and now manufactures textiles, leather goods, and electronic equipment. Phillips Academy (1781), widely known as the Exeter School, is here, as are the birthplaces of Constitution signer Nicholas Gilman, statesman Lewis Cass, and sculptor Daniel Chester French. **2.** town, pop. 5461, Washington Co., SC Rhode Island, 20 mi/32 km SSW of Providence, on the Queen R. Its economy depends on poultry and dairy farming.

Exhibition Park on the waterfront of SW TORONTO, Ontario, W of the HARBOURFRONT area and 2 mi/3 km WSW of Downtown. Fort Rouille, a 1750s French outpost, was in the area; Fort York, built 1793, destroyed by American forces in 1813, and re-created as an historic site, is just E, across the Gardiner Expressway. Exhibition Park has been home since the 1870s to industrial fairs, and since 1904 to the Canadian National Exhibition, said to be the world's largest such event. **Exhibition Stadium,** superseded by the SKYDOME, is here. ONTARIO PLACE extends S into the lake.

Exploits River 153 mi/246 km long, the longest river in Newfoundland. It rises in headstreams in the LONG RANGE Mts. in the SW, which flow NE into Red Indian L. The Exploits then flows ENE past GRAND FALLS–WINDSOR to the Bay of Exploits, an inlet of NOTRE DAME BAY, at Botwood. The river has several hydroelectric dams. The 40 mi/65 km–long Red Indian L. is named for the Beothuk (who painted themselves with red pigment), who lived here into the 19th century.

Exposition Park 114-ac/46-ha municipal park in Los Angeles, California, 2 mi/3 km SW of Downtown. Opened in 1910, and the main venue of the 1932 and 1984 Olympic Games, it is home to the 92,000-seat Los Angeles Memorial Coliseum (1923) and to the 15,000-seat Los Angeles Memorial Sports Arena (1959), as well as to museums and gardens.

Exton unincorporated village, pop. 2550, in West Whiteland township, Chester Co., SE Pennsylvania, 23 mi/37 km W of Philadelphia. Situated along Route 30, it is an Amtrak stop and has a chemicals industry.

exurb rural or small-town area beyond the suburban orbit of a city, which has become home to affluent former residents of the city or to those who do not need to commute regularly.

Ezra Church battle site: see under WEST END, Atlanta, Georgia.

F

factory in Canadian place names: see under HUDSON'S BAY COMPANY.

Factoryville borough, pop. 1310, Wyoming Co., NE Pennsylvania, 12 mi/19 km NNE of Scranton. It was named for a long-defunct cotton mill. Factoryville is the birthplace of baseball great Christy Mathewson (1878–1925).

Fagatogo also, **Fangatongo** see under PAGO PAGO, American Samoa.

Fairbanks city, pop. 30,843, Fairbanks North Star Borough (pop. 77,720), C Alaska, on the Chena R. near its confluence with the Tanana R., 255 mi/411 km NNE of Anchorage. The city was founded by prospectors in 1902, and PLACER gold in the area spurred its initial growth. As mining decreased, the construction of the Alaska Railroad contributed to its economy. A second boom occurred during World War II, when it became the W terminus of the ALASKA HIGHWAY and a defense center, with Fort Wainwright adjacent (E) and Eielson Air Force Base 22 mi/35 km SE. In 1958 the establishment of a missile and radar site at Clear, 55 mi/86 km SW, was a boon to the economy, as was 1970s construction of the TRANS-ALASKA PIPELINE. The city is a trade center for the interior region and is the N terminus of the RICHARDSON HIGHWAY and the ALASKA RAILROAD. Fur trapping and gold, silver, and coal mining continue, and industries include smelting, saw milling, and the production of sand, gravel, and industrial chemicals, as well as tourism. The main campus of the University of Alaska (1917) is W of Downtown, in COLLEGE.

Fairborn city, pop. 31,300, Greene Co., SW Ohio, 10 mi/16 km NE of Dayton. Settlement began c.1799, but the city was not incorporated until 1950, when the villages of Osborn and Fairfield were united. It lies in a farming area in which wheat and livestock are major products. Cement, tools, and dies are among manufactures. Wright-Patterson Air Force Base, headquarters of the Logistics Command, Aeronautical Systems Division, and Institute of Technology, is adjacent; many local residents are employees.

Fairbury city, pop. 3643, Livingston Co., EC Illinois, 11 mi/18 km SE of Pontiac. It is a coal mining center. Physician and social reformer Francis E. Townsend was born here (1867).

Fairchild Air Force Base see under SPOKANE, Washington.

Fairfax **1.** town, pop. 1749, Osage Co., NE Oklahoma, 22 mi/35 km SE of Ponca City. A petroleum industry center, with wells and refineries, it also has agriculture-related manufactures. There is a large Indian population; the ballerina Maria Tallchief, who is of Osage descent, was born here (1925). **2.** independent city, pop. 19,622, seat of but administratively separate from Fairfax Co., N Virginia, 16 mi/26 km WSW of Washington, D.C. It is a primarily residential community with some light manufacturing, including the production of optical lenses, instruments, and prefabricated buildings. It has a rich history and many old buildings, including its courthouse (1799). George Mason University (1957) is just outside the city limits (S).

Fairfax County 394 sq mi/1020 sq km, pop. 818,584, in NE Virginia, just W of Washington, D.C., bounded by the Potomac R. (E) and BULL RUN and Occoquan Creek (SW). It is a heavily developed suburban and urban area that primarily houses Federal employees and those in some way connected to the government. It contains shopping and office complexes and professional centers, wealthy suburbs, boom areas like TYSONS CORNERS, and the planned community of RESTON. Also in Fairfax are older suburbs and historic sites like MOUNT VERNON.

Fairfax District commercial and residential section of Los Angeles, California, S of West Hollywood and 7 mi/11 km W of Downtown. Fairfax Ave., between Melrose Ave. (N) and Wilshire Blvd. (S), is home to a cluster of Jewish dwellings and businesses, and the area is noted for its bungalows. BEVERLY HILLS lies SW, and the name Beverly-Fairfax is applied to the environs.

Fairfield **1.** city, pop. 12,200, Jefferson Co., NC Alabama, adjacent (SW) to Birmingham. Planned and laid out by the US Steel Corporation in 1910, it is an industrial suburb of Birmingham, producing steel, iron, chemical products, bricks, and bedding. It is the seat of Miles College (1905). Baseball great Willie Mays was born here (1931). **2.** city, pop. 77,211, seat of Solano Co., NC California, just N of arms of Suisun Bay, and 40 mi/64 km SW of Sacramento. It was founded in 1859 by Robert Waterman, a Connecticut ship captain. With its sister city, SUISUN CITY (S), it is a trade and processing center for an agricultural area producing grains, fruit, and dairy products. Local industries include winemaking, brewing, and the manufacture of sporting goods, textiles, explosives, and boats. Travis Air Force Base lies just E. **3.** town, pop. 53,418, Fairfield Co., SW Connecticut, adjacent (SW) to Bridgeport, on Long Island Sound. It is predominantly residential, and is noted for its yacht harbor (Southport Harbor). Settled in 1639, it was burned by the British in 1779. The township, which includes the villages of Southport and Greenfield Hill, has some industry, including metallurgy and chemical and machinery production. Fairfield University (1942) is here. The Great Swamp Fight of July, 1637, ending the Pequot War, took place along Fairfield's W boundary. **4.** city, pop. 9768, seat of Jefferson Co., SE Iowa, 25 mi/40 km E of Ottumwa. It is a trading center for the area's dairy products and grain, and produces washing machines, farm equipment, plastics, conveyors, and aluminum and iron castings. Settled in 1839, it hosted the first Iowa State Fair in 1854. Maharishi International University (1971) is here. **5.** city, pop. 39,729, Butler Co., SW Ohio, 17 mi/27 km N of Cincinnati, established as township in 1803. In the fertile Miami R. valley, it trades livestock, fruit, grain, and hay and manufactures such goods as auto bodies, metal products, steel abrasives, ammunition, and chemicals. **6.** town, pop. 1680, Franklin Co., NW Vermont. It is on Black Creek, 7 mi/11 km E of St. Albans. A major maple sugar production center, the town also produces dairy and wood products, lumber, and poultry. President Chester A. Arthur was born here in 1830.

Fairfield County **1.** 632 sq mi/1637 sq km, pop. 827,645, in SE Connecticut, on Long Island Sound at the New York border. It is the wealthiest county in Connecticut, and one of the wealthiest in the US. A number of its communities are home to corporate executives, professionals, and entertainment figures, many of whom commute to New York; some of its villages, in rolling countryside, are dotted with large estates and horse farms. But Fairfield also has pockets of poverty, notably in the city of Bridgeport and in parts of Stamford. In recent decades, Fairfield has become a corporate center in its own right, with offices or headquarters of major corporations locating especially in Greenwich, Stamford, and the Danbury area. **2.** 506 sq mi/1310 sq km, pop. 103,461, in C Ohio; it includes the Hocking R. and part of Buckeye L., a major recreational area in its NE corner. Its seat and only major city is LANCASTER. Dairying as well as the cultivation of fruit, grain, and livestock are important. There is some manufacturing at Bremen and Lancaster. Other county industries include timber and the exploitation of sand and gravel.

Fairhaven town, pop. 16,132, Bristol Co., SE Massachusetts, on Buzzards Bay, at the mouth of the Acushnet R., across from New Bedford. A former whaling center, it is now a suburb, resort, and fishing and boatbuilding town, also manufacturing nails and staples.

Fairhope city, pop. 8485, Baldwin Co., SW Alabama, across Mobile Bay (SE) from Mobile. Founded in 1894 by a group of Iowan followers of single-tax advocate Henry George, it is today a prosperous resort noted as a yachting, seafood, and crafts center.

Fair Lane see under DEARBORN, Michigan.

Fair Lawn borough, pop. 30,548, Bergen Co., NE New Jersey, across the Passaic R. (NE) from Paterson. Its manufactures include aircraft, textiles, dyes, and building materials, and it is a corporate base to various retailers.

Fairless Hills unincorporated village, pop. 9026, in Falls township, Bucks Co., SE Pennsylvania, a largely residential suburb 15 mi/24 km NE of downtown Philadelphia.

Fairlie-Poplar commercial district of downtown Atlanta, Georgia, immediately N of FIVE POINTS and W of PEACHTREE St., that has undergone substantial redevelopment in recent decades in an attempt to attract small business back into the area.

Fairmont **1.** city, pop. 11,265, seat of Martin Co., SW Minnesota, 53 mi/85 km W of Albert Lea and 10 mi/16 km N of the Iowa border. Originally a trading center for the area's agricultural products, it was the site of Fort Fairmont (1862), erected to protect settlers from Dakota Indians. The city has various products including railway maintenance equipment, polyethylene film, frozen and canned foods, and cement blocks. It also serves as the gateway to many recreational lakes in the vicinity. **2.** city, pop. 20,210, seat of Marion Co., N West Virginia, 19 mi/30 km SW of Morgantown, where the Tygart and West Fork rivers join to form the Monongahela R. After the Baltimore and Ohio Railroad arrived in 1852, the area's bituminous coalfield became key to the economy; coal production remains the chief industry. Mining machinery, glass, aluminum and steel products, and fluorescent lamps are made. Fairmont College (1865) is here; Prickett's Fort and Valley Falls state parks are nearby.

Fairmount **1.** town, pop. 3130, Grant Co., NC Indiana, 10 mi/16 km S of Marion. In an agricultural area from which natural gas and oil have been extracted, it has some light industries. Local institutions recall the actor James Dean, born here in 1931. **2.** unincorporated village, pop. 12,266, in Camillus township, Onondaga Co., C New York, 5 mi/8 km W of Syracuse. It is a largely residential suburb. **3.** see under ART MUSEUM DISTRICT, Philadelphia, Pennsylvania.

Fairmount Heights town, pop. 1238, Prince George's Co., C Maryland, adjacent (N) to extreme E Washington, D.C. It is a residential suburb. SEAT PLEASANT is adjacent (SE).

Fairmount Park municipal park comprising 4000 ac/1620 ha within the city of Philadelphia, Pennsylvania, along the Schuylkill R. and Wissahickon Creek, and W of the ART MUSEUM DISTRICT. It has bicycle and hiking trails, a Japanese garden, America's oldest zoo, boating, and 15 restored Colonial mansions, including Mount Pleasant, the home of Benedict Arnold. It was the site of the US Centennial Exposition (1876).

Fair Oaks **1.** unincorporated community, pop. 26,867, Sacramento Co., NC California, on the American R., 12 mi/19 km ENE of downtown Sacramento, of which it is a growing residential suburb set on former farmland. **2.** locality just S of HIGHLAND SPRINGS and 9 mi/14 km ESE of RICHMOND, Virginia, the site of a battle (May 31–June 1, 1862) in which Union forces who had crossed the Chickahominy R. fell back slightly but repelled Confederates under Gen. Joseph Johnston. The Union left had reached Seven Pines, just SE, and the battle is also known by that name. Richmond International Airport is just S.

Fair Park also, **State Fair Park** 270 ac/110 ha, in Dallas, Texas, 2 mi/3 km E of Downtown. The site of the Texas Centennial Exposition (1936), which emphasized Dallas's leading role in the Southwest's commerce, it is also home to the Texas State Fair (held in Oct.), the largest US fair. Dallas's aquarium, several museums and concert halls, and the Coliseum, used for various events, are also here, as is the 72,000-seat Cotton Bowl, site since 1937 of a New Year's Day college football bowl game, and "neutral" home to the annual game between the universities of Texas and Oklahoma. Residential areas around the park, which is on the N of SOUTH DALLAS, face many economic and social problems.

Fairview **1.** older residential and commercial section of VANCOUVER, British Columbia, immediately S of FALSE CREEK and Downtown. Its wooden row houses, largely built in the

1920s, have been home to a middle- and working-class community. **2.** city, pop. 119, Todd and Christian counties, SW Kentucky, 10 mi/16 km E of Hopkinsville. Jefferson Davis, president of the Confederacy, was born here in 1808. His adversary, Abraham Lincoln, was born less than 100 mi/160 km to the NE near Hodgenville, the following year. The 350-ft/107-m Jefferson Davis Monument is in a memorial park on US 68. **3.** borough, pop. 10,733, Bergen Co., NE New Jersey, 6 mi/10 km NE of Jersey City. On the PALISADES of the Hudson R., it was settled in 1860. Fairview's industries produce furniture and other wood products and chemicals; it is also a commercial and residential suburb. **4.** unincorporated village, pop. 4811, Dutchess Co., SE New York, adjacent (N) to Poughkeepsie. It is home to Marist College (1929).

Fairview Heights city, pop. 14,351, St. Clair Co., SW Illinois, a residential suburb 10 mi/16 km E of St. Louis, Missouri.

Fairview Park city, pop. 18,028, Cuyahoga Co., NE Ohio, 3 mi/5 km S of L. Erie and 10 mi/16 km W of Cleveland, of which it is a suburb. By law, land use here is restricted to home and apartment house development.

Fairweather, Mount 15,300 ft/4663 m, part of the Fairweather Range of the St. Elias Mts. (the Coast Ranges), on the British Columbia–Alaska border, partly in GLACIER BAY National Park. It is the highest point in British Columbia.

Fairwood see CASCADE-FAIRWOOD, Washington.

Fajardo unincorporated community (ZONA URBANA), pop. 31,659, Fajardo Municipio (pop. 36,882), extreme NE Puerto Rico, 30 mi/48 km ESE of San Juan. It developed in the 1700s as an agricultural and fishing village, and was a pirate supply port in the late 18th century. In a sugarcane growing region, it is a trade and processing center. Furniture, clothing, and cigars are among diverse light manufactures.

Falcon Heights city, pop. 5380, Ramsey Co., EC Minnesota, a suburb immediately NW of St. Paul. A residential community, it is the site of the University of Minnesota Agricultural College and the Minnesota State Fair Grounds.

Falcon Reservoir 87,200 ac/35,320 ha, on the US-Mexico border, in Starr and Zapata counties, SE Texas, and the state of Tamaulipas, Mexico. The Falcon Dam, jointly owned by the US and Mexico, was built in 1953 across the Rio Grande to supply flood control, irrigation, recreational opportunities, and hydroelectric power.

Fallbrook unincorporated community, pop. 22,095, San Diego Co., SW California, 15 mi/24 km NE of Oceanside, on the E edge of CAMP PENDLETON. It is a growing residential center in a military and fruit growing area.

Fallen Timbers battle site in Lucas Co., N Ohio, 12 mi/19 km SW of Toledo, on the Maumee R. On Aug. 20, 1794, Anthony Wayne achieved a decisive victory over the Northwest Indian Confederation here, opening up the surrounding area for American settlement.

Fallingwater see under BEAR RUN, Pennsylvania.

fall line transition, imagined as a line, between more resistant rocks that remain to form an upland and softer rocks that erode, leaving a lowland; rivers crossing the line are marked by falls. The line is a natural site for the development of water and hydroelectric power, and where the lowland is coastal usually marks the head of river navigation.

Fall Line imaginary line extending along the E border of the PIEDMONT, in the E US, where rapids and waterfalls mark the transition between the hard crystalline rocks of the Appalachian foothills and the softer deposits of the coastal plain. Industrial cities along the Fall Line include Trenton, New Jersey; Philadelphia; Baltimore; Richmond, Virginia; Raleigh, North Carolina; Columbia, South Carolina; and Augusta, Macon, and Columbus, Georgia. The Fall Line is particularly dominant in South Carolina, where it bisects the state and defines culturally distinct areas known as the UP COUNTRY and Low Country. The Carolina SANDHILLS are along the Fall Line. The line is sometimes said to curve W and N through Alabama, ending near where Kentucky, Tennessee, Missouri, and Arkansas join.

Fallon city, pop. 6438, seat of Churchill Co., W Nevada, on the Carson R., 55 mi/89 km E of Reno. A trade and processing center for livestock, dairy, and agricultural (mainly alfalfa and cantaloupe) producers, it developed when the Newlands reclamation project (1903–08) and the Lahontan Dam (1914) brought irrigation and fertile farmland to an arid region. The Fallon Indian Reservation is 5 mi/8 km NE, the Fallon Naval Air Station, which trains fighter pilots, 3 mi/5 km SE. Several small lakes and reservoirs surround the city, and the CARSON Sink is nearby (NE).

Fall River city, pop. 92,703, Bristol Co., SE Massachusetts. At the mouth of the Taunton R., on the E shore of Mt. Hope Bay, and on Watuppa and Stafford ponds, Fall River is 50 mi/80 km S of Boston. It was settled in 1656. Power from its falls stimulated textile production, and from the 1870s through the 1920s, the city was the world's leading textile manufacturer, before many mills moved south. Textiles and clothing are still major industries. The city's population is heavily French-Canadian and Portuguese in origin. Navy vessels displayed in Battleship Cove include the World War II battleship USS *Massachusetts.* Fall River's place in American culture is intertwined with that of Lizzie Borden, the local resident acquitted of hacking her father and stepmother to death in 1892.

Falls Church independent city, pop. 9578, between FAIRFAX Co. (N, W, and S) and ARLINGTON Co. (E), N Virginia, 8 mi/13 km W of Washington, D.C. It is a residential suburb. The area was settled in the 18th century; the Falls Church was built in 1734 on the road to the nearby (N) Little Falls on the Potomac R. A second church on the site, constructed 1767–69, still stands.

Falmouth **1.** town, pop. 7610, Cumberland Co., SW Maine. It is on Casco Bay, NE of and adjoining Portland, of which it is a largely residential suburb. Settled in the 1630s on land including modern Portland, Falmouth was incorporated in 1718, and includes the villages of West Falmouth and Falmouth Foreside, a fashionable waterfront community. Portland separated from Falmouth in 1786. **2.** town, pop. 27,960, Barnstable Co., SE Massachusetts, on the SW tip of Cape Cod, on Buzzards Bay (W) and Nantucket Sound (E). Formerly a whaling and shipbuilding center, it is a summer resort with some truck farming and cranberry culture. In Falmouth is the ocean sciences center at WOODS HOLE. Ferries leave for the islands of Nantucket and Martha's Vineyard. Otis Air Force Base and Camp Edwards are N.

False Creek inlet in NC VANCOUVER, British Columbia, extending SE from English Bay (BURRARD INLET), between the WEST END and Downtown (N) and FAIRVIEW (S). It has been much shortened since the 1870s, when it was the scene of early industry, including sawmilling and shipbuilding; it originally was connected at high tide with Vancouver Harbour, N across the downtown peninsula. Bridged since the 1870s, and with the Canadian Pacific Railway's yards on the N since 1887, it has been the site of much of Vancouver's commercial life. Granville I., a landfill-enlarged peninsula on the S, is now a popular gallery, market, and restaurant zone. Expo 86, Vancouver's world's fair, was based on the N side of False Creek, an area since redeveloped for commerce and residences; BC Place, a 60,000-seat, inflated-dome stadium, is there.

Faneuil Hall historic site in NE Boston, Massachusetts. Built in 1742 by merchant Peter Faneuil as a market and assembly hall, it was dubbed "the cradle of liberty" because of the pro-independence activity that took place here. Burnt in 1761, it was quickly rebuilt. In 1765, Bostonians gathered to protest the Stamp Act; in 1773, the movement began that led to the Boston Tea Party. The building was enlarged in 1805 by Charles Bulfinch, and in the 19th century antislavery orators spoke here. Faneuil Hall was part of a major 1970s restoration project that included the three QUINCY MARKET buildings behind it; today it is a tourist attraction.

Farallon Islands also, **Farallones** cluster of small islands in the Pacific Ocean, 30 mi/48 km W of San Francisco, California. Rocky and waterless, they are uninhabited except for Coast Guard personnel. The waters around them are rich in marine life, however, and as one of the Pacific's major seabird nesting grounds, they constitute the Farallon National Wildlife Refuge. Lying in a NW–SE chain c.10 mi/16 km in length, they are the above-water portion of an escarpment paralleling the coast NW of the Golden Gate. Part of San Francisco, they can be seen from the city in clear weather.

Fargo city, pop. 74,111, seat of Cass Co., SE North Dakota, on the Red R. of the North, opposite Moorhead, Minnesota, with which it has close economic and cultural relations. It was founded by the NORTHERN PACIFIC RAILROAD in 1871 as an outfitting post for settlers, and grew to be the state's largest city. It is now a trading, processing, and shipping center for wheat, meat, and dairy products. Industries manufacture farm implements, building and foundry materials, and computer software. Fargo is also a regional financial, medical, and tourism hub.

Far Hills borough, pop. 671, Somerset Co., NC New Jersey, on the North Branch of the Raritan R., 7 mi/11 km N of Somerville. Set amid rolling hills, it is an extremely affluent community, with a variety of one-family homes and estates. The US Golf Association's Golf House museum and the Leonard J. Buck Garden are here.

Faribault city, pop. 17,085, seat of Rice Co., SE Minnesota, at the junction of the Cannon and Straight rivers, 35 mi/56 km NE of Mankato. The site of an 1826 post established by French fur trader Alexander Faribault, it now manufactures heating and air-conditioning equipment, ice cube makers, woolens, plastics, office machines, and computer parts. The Minnesota State Braille and Sight-Saving School and Minnesota State Academy for the Deaf are here.

Farmers Branch city, pop. 24,250, Dallas Co., NE Texas, adjacent (NW) to Dallas and 11 mi/18 km from Downtown. This residential suburb is on part of the Peters Colony, settled in 1841; the first church and school in Dallas Co. were built here, and in the 1840s, advertisements in Europe attracted colonists to its rich farmland. The modern community dates from the 1950s. Brookhaven College (1965) is here, as are dozens of corporate offices and some light manufacturing facilities.

Farmer's Market commercial complex in WESTSIDE Los Angeles, California, 6 mi/10 km WNW of Downtown, and just N of WILSHIRE Boulevard's Miracle Mile. On part of the 1900s Salt Lake oilfield, it has been a working market since the 1930s, and is one of the metropolitan area's most visited sites.

Farmington **1.** town, pop. 20,608, Hartford Co., WC Connecticut, on the Farmington R. An affluent suburb 7 mi/11 km WSW of Hartford, it includes the village of Farmington and the industrial center of Unionville, and is now home to a number of corporate headquarters and offices. Miss Porter's School for girls is here. **2.** town, pop. 7436, seat of Franklin Co., WC Maine. It is on the Sandy R., 25 mi/40 km NW of Waterville. Farmington is the trade center of the Sandy R. valley, and a gateway to the Sugarloaf and Saddleback mountain and Rangeley Lakes region. It produces apples, maple syrup, and canned goods. Wood products and footwear have been produced. An early education center, it is home to a campus of the University of Maine. The Lillian Nordica Homestead and Museum is the singer's (1859) birthplace. **3.** city, pop. 10,132, Oakland Co., SE Michigan, on the Upper R. Rouge, 19 mi/31 km NW of Detroit. Founded in 1824, it is mainly a residential community, with some light manufacturing. **Farmington Hills,** a city, pop. 74,652, adjacent on the NE, is a larger residential suburb. It is the seat of William Tyndale College (1945) and Oakland Community Junior College. **4.** city, pop. 11,598, seat of St. Francois Co., SE Missouri, in the St. Francois Mts., 60 mi/96 km S of St. Louis. Settled in 1799, it was once the center of a busy lead mining district. Still mining and processing some lead, it also handles locally grown grain. **5.** city, pop. 33,997, San Juan Co., NW New Mexico, at the junction of the Animas and San Juan rivers, 48 mi/77 km ESE of FOUR CORNERS. Since the 1950s coal, oil, and natural gas have been central to its economy; it supplies the huge coal-fueled Four Corners power plant. Irrigated farms are also important. The city is also a trade center for the Ute Mt. and Navajo reservations. San Juan College (1956) is here. The Aztec Ruins National Monument (NE), Salmon (Pueblo) Ruins (SE), SHIPROCK (W), and Bisti Badlands (S) are nearby. **6.** city, pop. 9028, seat of Davis Co., N Utah, on the Great Salt L., 15 mi/ 24 km N of Salt Lake City. Settled by Mormons in 1848, it is a suburb and a trade center in an agricultural area. Utah State University's Botanical Gardens are here.

Farmington River 30 mi/48 km long, in Connecticut. It is formed in N Connecticut at New Hartford by the junction of the West Branch (30 mi/ 48 km long) and the East Branch (14 mi/23 km long), both of which rise in S Massachusetts. It flows SE to Farmington, thence N through Avon and Simsbury, and SE to the Connecticut R. at Windsor, above Hartford. Both its upper branches have been dammed to provide water for the Hartford area, the West Branch in Hartland and the East Branch at Barkhamsted.

Farmingville unincorporated village, pop. 14,842, in Brookhaven town, Suffolk Co., SE New York, in C Long Island. A largely residential suburb on the Long Island Expressway, it is 7 mi/11 km N of Patchogue.

Farmville town, pop. 6046, seat of Prince Edward Co., and partly in Cumberland Co., SC Virginia, 42 mi/66 km E of Lynchburg, on the Appomattox R. The seat of Longwood

College (1839), it also has tobacco storage facilities and lumber mills.

Faro town, pop. 1121, SC Yukon Territory, on the Pelly R. and the Campbell Highway, 120 mi/190 km NNE of Whitehorse. On the S of the Anvil Range, it was established in 1968 along with the open-pit Anvil Dynasty lead and zinc mine. Gold is also extracted in this center of the territory's mining operations.

Farragut town, pop. 12,793, Knox Co., E Tennessee, 13 mi/21 km SW of downtown Knoxville, a residential suburb on Fort Loudon L. (the Tennessee R.).

Far Rockaway see under the ROCKAWAYS, New York.

Fathom Five National Marine Park see under BRUCE PENINSULA, Ontario.

fault discontinuity or break in a rock or series of rocks, along which there has been movement, either lateral or vertical. Such movement is the cause of earthquakes. Faults represent the movement of different segments of the earth's crust, as at the juncture of two tectonic PLATES.

Fauquier County 651 sq mi/1686 sq km, pop. 48,741, in N Virginia. Its seat is WARRENTON. In the C Piedmont, the county is known for horse raising. Wheat, corn, and wine grapes are grown, and there is dairying.

Fayette **1.** city, pop. 1317, Fayette Co., NE Iowa, on the Volga R., 36 mi/58 km NE of Waterloo. It is home to Upper Iowa University (1857). **2.** city, pop. 1853, seat of Jefferson Co., SW Mississippi, 22 mi/35 km NE of Natchez, just E of the Natchez Trace. This almost entirely black cotton and lumber trade center gained national notice after civil rights leader Charles Evers became mayor in 1969. **3.** city, pop. 2888, seat of Howard Co., NC Missouri, 23 mi/37 km NW of Columbia. Founded in 1823, it is a trade hub in an agricultural region. Central Methodist College (1854) is here. **4.** town, pop. 3636, Seneca Co., WC New York, in the FINGER LAKES, near Cayuga L. and 15 mi/24 km SW of Auburn. Religious leader Joseph Smith (1805–44) established the first Church of Jesus Christ of Latter-Day Saints (Mormons) here in 1830, and soon sent out his first missionaries. Fayette, a rural town in a vineyard region, is just N of the Seneca Army Depot.

Fayette County **1.** 285 sq mi/738 sq km, pop. 225,366, in C Kentucky. Its seat is LEXINGTON, with which it is coextensive. Its S boundary is the Kentucky R., and it is drained by several creeks, especially Elkhorn Creek and its North Branch. In the heart of the BLUEGRASS REGION, it raises cattle, sheep, tobacco, bluegrass seed, and grain. The county is famous for its thoroughbred race and saddle horse farms, among them CALUMET FARM. There are limestone quarries, and manufacturing at Lexington. **2.** 794 sq mi/2056 sq km, pop. 145,351, in SW Pennsylvania, bordered by the Monongahela R. (W) and West Virginia and Maryland (S). Its seat is UNIONTOWN. The N part of the county touches on Pittsburgh's S suburbs. There is coal mining and dairying here, with manufacturing at Uniontown.

Fayetteville **1.** city, pop. 42,099, seat of Washington Co., NW Arkansas, 50 mi/80 km NNE of Fort Smith, in the Ozark Plateau, on the White R., 18 mi/29 km E of the Oklahoma border. On the Overland Mail Route, it was chosen as the county seat in 1828. The Civil War battle of Prairie Grove was fought nearby (SW) on Dec. 7, 1862. The city was occupied by the Federal Army from April 18, 1863, until the end of the war. Today it is an agricultural trade center, whose principal industries include poultry processing, canning, and the manufacture of farm implements and wood products. An early educational center, it was the home of Sophia Sawyer's Fayetteville Female Seminary (1838) and Arkansas College (1852), which was destroyed during the Civil War. The state's first degree-granting college (1871), now the University of Arkansas, is here. Some high-tech industry has grown around the university. **2.** city, pop. 75,695, seat of Cumberland Co., SC North Carolina, at the head of navigation on the Cape Fear R., 53 mi/85 km SSW of Raleigh. Combining the settlements of Campbelltown (1739) and Cross Creek (1746), it was incorporated in 1783 and renamed for the Marquis de Lafayette. The city served (1789–93) as the state's capital. Over 700 buildings were destroyed by fire in 1831. Through most of its history, Fayetteville was an agricultural and industrial center. Regional farms produce tobacco, soybeans, grain, corn, and livestock, especially poultry, and industries have manufactured textiles, wood products, machinery, auto filters, tires, and power tools. Since World War I, FORT BRAGG and, later, Pope Air Force Base have come to dominate the economy. The city is home to Fayetteville State University (1867), Methodist College (1956), and a technical college.

Fear, Cape sandy headland at the SE tip of Smith I., in the Atlantic Ocean 26 mi/42 km S of Wilmington, in Brunswick Co., SE North Carolina. At the mouth of the CAPE FEAR R., it marks the S tip of the OUTER BANKS barrier islands. The treacherous Frying Pan Shoals extend 20 mi/32 km S and E of the cape. Bald Head Lighthouse, built in 1817 and no longer operational, overlooks the river on the W of the island, while Oak Island Lighthouse, built to replace "Old Baldy" in 1958, stands NW across the river's mouth. FORT FISHER is 8 mi/13 km NNE of the cape.

Feather River 80 mi/130 km long, in NC California. It is formed by three forks that meet NE of OROVILLE, in the foothills of the Sierra Nevada, in dam-created L. Oroville. The 80 mi/130 km–long Middle Fork flows E from near BECKWOURTH PASS, almost on the Nevada border; on its passage through the Sierra Nevada it has been designated the Middle Fork Feather Wild and Scenic River. Just NE of L. Oroville is the 640-ft/195-m **Feather Falls,** one of the highest in the US. The South Fork, 40 mi/64 km long, rises on the Sierras' W. The North Fork, 90 mi/145 km long, rises SE of LASSEN PEAK, and flows SE to dam-created L. ALMANOR, then SW to L. Oroville; the stretch above the lake is the **Feather River Canyon,** famous for its scenery. South of Oroville, the Feather flows past YUBA CITY and MARYSVILLE (the head of navigation) to the SACRAMENTO R., 17 mi/27 km NNW of Sacramento. The river, scene of heavy gold dredging in the late 19th century, is today both a recreational magnet and a source of water and power for California's cities.

Federal Hill historic neighborhood, SC Baltimore, Maryland, on the S side of the INNER HARBOR. It developed in the 18th and early 19th century around Cross St. Market, and now has restored row houses, narrow streets, and brick sidewalks overlooking the harbor. The hill from which it takes its name was the site (1795–1895) of an observation tower; ships entering the harbor were monitored and signaled.

Federal Triangle section of NW Washington, D.C., N of the MALL and S of Pennsylvania Ave., between the White House (W) and 4th St., NW (E). Formerly part of Washington's business district, it is now occupied by government buildings, including those of the Justice Dept., Commerce Dept., Internal Revenue Service, and the National Archives. The EAST END is N across Pennsylvania Ave.

Federal Way city, pop. 67,554, King Co., WC Washington, a large residential suburb 20 mi/32 km S of Seattle and just NE of Tacoma. Incorporated in the early 1990s, it has grown rapidly as newly constructed homes have replaced many of the trees on its wooded ridges. It was named for the Federal highway built in this area in 1929. The corporate headquarters of Weyerhaeuser and of several other companies are here, and there are numerous shopping malls. Federal Way is known for its Rhododendron Species Foundation Garden and its two amusement parks.

Fells Point historic waterfront district W of the INNER HARBOR, Baltimore, Maryland. It was laid out as a separate town in 1763 by William Fell, and incorporated into the city in 1773. The area, which surrounds Market Square, where Broadway meets the harbor, flourished as a shipbuilding center 1750–1830. When plans for an expressway threatened to destroy Fells Point, the district achieved recognition by preservationists, and now is a residential and commercial area with many restored Colonial houses.

Femme Osage District see under DEFIANCE, Missouri.

Fenway, the urban park district in W Boston, Massachusetts, dominated by the Back Bay Fens (117 ac/47 ha), a strip of woodland, stream, and meadow that runs SW from the Charles R. to Jamaica Pond, in JAMAICA PLAIN. **Fenway Park** (1912), the home of the Boston Red Sox, is near the N end of the Fenway. The Back Bay Fens are part of Boston's "Emerald Necklace," a system of parks, waterways, malls, and parkways that includes the ARNOLD ARBORETUM, FRANKLIN PARK, and the Public Garden; landscape architect Frederick Law Olmsted created the overall design in the 1880s, laying out the Fens along the path of the Muddy R. "Fenway" was originally the name of a parkway E of the Fens.

Fergus Falls city, pop. 12,362, seat of Otter Tail Co., WC Minnesota, on the Otter Tail R., 50 mi/80 km SE of Moorhead and 25 mi/40 km E of the North Dakota border. Mainly a trading center for its agricultural region, it contains flour mills and a cooperative creamery. Industries include food processing, meatpacking, and farm machinery and garment manufacturing, as well as the production of electric power. It is also a lake resort. The Church of the Lutheran Brethren maintains its headquarters here, along with a religious academy and seminary. The city is also the site of Fergus Falls Community College (1960).

Ferguson city, pop. 22,286, St. Louis Co., EC Missouri, 11 mi/18 km NW of downtown St. Louis. It is a residential suburb that also has electrical and other industries.

Fermi nuclear power plant: see under MONROE Co., Michigan.

Fermi National Accelerator Laboratory see under BATAVIA, Illinois.

Fernald unincorporated village in Hamilton Co., SW Ohio, 14 mi/22 km NW of Cincinnati. It was the site of a uranium-producing nuclear weapons plant, and has been contaminated by nuclear waste.

Fernandina Beach formerly, **Fernandina** city, pop. 8765, seat of Nassau Co., extreme NE Florida, on AMELIA I., at the mouth of the St. Marys R., 20 mi/32 km N of Jacksonville. Settled by the Spanish in the 1680s, and a haven for pirates and smugglers in the early 19th century, it later developed shrimp fishing and packing and wood pulp industries. An early (late-19th-century) beach resort, it has many Victorian buildings.

Fern Creek unincorporated community, pop. 16,406, Jefferson Co., N Kentucky, a residential suburb 10 mi/16 km SE of downtown Louisville, just inside the city's outer beltway (I-265).

Ferndale **1.** unincorporated village, pop. 16,355, Anne Arundel Co., C Maryland, 8 mi/13 km S of downtown Baltimore. It is a suburb just E of Baltimore-Washington International Airport. **2.** city, pop. 25,084, Oakland Co., SE Michigan, 8 mi/13 km NW of Detroit. WOODWARD AVENUE, the main street of this primarily residential community, follows part of the historic Saginaw Trail, which led from Detroit to Saginaw. The city has factories that make chemicals, steel, castings and forgings, paint, and synthetic resins.

Ferrum unincorporated community, pop. 1514, Franklin Co., SW Virginia, 35 mi/56 km S of Roanoke. The seat of Ferrum College (1913), it is in a hilly, rural area.

Ferryland community, pop. 717, SE Newfoundland, on the SE AVALON PENINSULA, on the Atlantic Ocean, 39 mi/63 km SSW of St. John's. Its protected harbor was used by the French in the early 1500s. In 1621 George Calvert, Lord Baltimore, made it the capital of his province of Avalon (Newfoundland); by 1629, however, difficult conditions here had driven him S to initiate the establishment of MARYLAND. In 1637–51, Ferryland was the headquarters of Governor David Kirke. Today it is a fishing and service center, with no remains of the 17th-century buildings. The name probably comes from the French *forillon,* for an isolated headland.

Festus city, pop. 8105, Jefferson Co., EC Missouri, on the Mississippi R. (the Illinois border), 30 mi/48 km S of St. Louis. A residential community, it also mills flour and produces textiles and footwear.

Fetterman battle site: see under BOZEMAN TRAIL, Wyoming.

Fiddletown hamlet in Amador Co., EC California, 15 mi/24 km S of Placerville, immortalized as an 1850s gold mining town by Bret Harte in his story, "An Episode of Fiddletown."

Fifth Avenue **1.** commercial and residential thoroughfare, Manhattan, New York City. Beginning at Washington Square, it proceeds north, dividing Manhattan into EAST SIDE and WEST SIDE, and ends at the Harlem R. After the Civil War, New York's wealthy moved their residences gradually up Fifth Ave.; in the early 1900s mansions were built as far N as 96th St. Today the avenue is home to upscale shops as far N as 59th St.; it then fronts Central Park, and its E side is lined with museums and apartment houses. In Midtown, Fifth Ave. passes the Empire State Building, the New York Public Library, and Rockefeller Center. The area in front of St. Patrick's Cathedral is the site of the city's Easter "parade." North of 110th St., Fifth Ave. divides Harlem and East Harlem. **2.** commercial thoroughfare, 5 mi/8 km long, between the GOLDEN TRIANGLE and POINT BREEZE sections of Pittsburgh, Pennsylvania. An important 19th-century route for omnibus, horsecar, steam cablecar, and, finally, electric trolley service, Fifth Avenue became a growth corridor stimulating the development of the HILL, UPTOWN, SHADYSIDE, OAKLAND, SQUIRREL HILL, and Point Breeze.

Fifth Ward inner-city section of Houston, Texas, 2 mi/3 km NE of Downtown, across Buffalo Bayou. It has long been industrial, the site of railyards, lumber mills, and waterfront plants, and as a residential area has been somewhat isolated from the rest of the city. It had a black majority after the Civil War, and does so today. The Frenchtown neighborhood, in the N, was home after the 1927 Mississippi R. floods to blacks from Louisiana, who created a subculture; zydeco music was born here. Frenchtown has since lost much of its distinctiveness. On the E of the ward are the Southern Pacific's Englewood yards and DENVER HARBOR. Much housing in the Fifth, characteristically one-story "shotgun" houses, is run-down, and the district is economically depressed.

Fillmore **1.** city, pop. 11,992, Ventura Co., SW California, 42 mi/64 km NW of Los Angeles, on the Santa Clara R. Set in a fruit growing and oil producing region, it has recently experienced some residential growth. **2.** city, pop. 1956, seat of Millard Co., WC Utah, 126 mi/203 km SSW of Salt Lake City, just W of the PAHVANT RANGE, on the E edge of the Great Basin. In 1851 it was selected as capital of the Utah Territory. Its Territorial Statehouse (partial; 1855) was the site of only brief activity before government was returned to Salt Lake City. The city is now a trade center for a ranching region.

Fillmore, the see under WESTERN ADDITION, San Francisco, California.

Filoli see under WOODSIDE, California.

Financial District **1.** commercial section of SAN FRANCISCO, California, N of Market St. and E of Chinatown. Jackson Square (the old BARBARY COAST) is immediately N. Montgomery St., in the mid 19th century at the city's waterfront (Yerba Buena Cove), became the "Wall Street of the West," home to the Bank of America and other major institutions. The Financial District today contains most of San Francisco's high-rise office buildings, including the 853-ft/260-m Transamerica Pyramid, since 1972 the tapered symbol of the city's skyline. **2.** in Manhattan, New York City, extends roughly from City Hall Park S to the Battery, including at its center WALL STREET. Its narrow, angled streets reflect its past as the heart of 17th-century New Amsterdam, but skyscraper booms c.1900–31 and in the 1970s and 1980s have created a mountainlike mass of tall buildings, among them the WORLD TRADE CENTER towers. Bowling Green and Fraunces Tavern, the site of Washington's 1783 Farewell Address, are in the area.

Findlay city, pop. 35,675, seat of Hancock Co., NW Ohio, 45 mi/72 km S of Toledo, on the Blanchard R. It grew up around Fort Findlay, established during the War of 1812. It was a stop on the Underground Railroad, and its *Jeffersonian* newspaper published the letters of "Petroleum V. Nasby." After the discovery of local deposits of oil and natural gas, it underwent an industrial boom (1886–1910). Today petroleum products, rubber tires, and tiles are among items manufactured here, and Findlay is a trade center for the surrounding agricultural region.

Finger Lakes region in C New York, roughly between GENESEO (W) and SYRACUSE (E), that includes 11 finger-shaped lakes nearly parallel and oriented in a N–S direction. The four small western lakes, Conesus, Hemlock, Canadice, and Honeoye, drain W to the Genesee R. and N through Rochester, emptying into L. Ontario. The seven eastern lakes, Canandaigua, Keuka, Seneca, Cayuga, Owasco, Skaneateles, and Otisco, drain to the Seneca R., then N into L. Ontario. The lakes resemble fjords with their steep walls, many waterfalls and glens, rugged rock formations, and grottoes. Once preglacial stream valleys, they were deepened and widened by glacial gouging. The region is well suited for growing grapes because of the angle of the slopes, and many lakeshores are home to vineyards, orchards, and vegetable farms. Many resorts and 13 state parks are in the region.

Finlay Mountains NW–SE trending range in far SW Texas, extending for c.25 mi/40 km NW of the community of Sierra Blanca. The range rises to 5650 ft/723 m, and forms the SW border of the DIABLO BOLSON.

Finneytown unincorporated residential suburb, pop. 13,096, Hamilton Co., SW Ohio, 7 mi/11 km NNW of downtown Cincinnati, just outside the city limits and just E of College Hill.

Finn Hill see INGLEWOOD–FINN HILL, Washington.

fiord see FJORD.

Fire Island barrier island, Suffolk Co., SE New York, between GREAT SOUTH BAY (N) and the Atlantic Ocean, 30 mi/48 km long and up to 0.5 mi/1 km wide. A popular summer resort, it includes a number of small communities catering to different clienteles; among them are (from W to E) Kismet, Saltaire, Fair Harbor, Dunewood, Atlantique, Ocean Beach, Seaview, Point o' Woods, Cherry Grove, Fire Island Pines, and Davis Park. Cherry Grove and Fire Island Pines are noted gay resorts. At the W end is Robert Moses State Park, reached by causeway from West Bay Shore; Fire Island is otherwise accessible by ferry. The E half of the island consists of protected dune areas and beaches, parts of the 19,600-ac/8000-ha Fire Island National Seashore (which embraces the entire island except for the state park).

Firelands, the see under WESTERN RESERVE and under NORWALK, Connecticut and Ohio.

Firstside commercial district in the GOLDEN TRIANGLE, Pittsburgh, Pennsylvania, on the Monongahela R., S of the BOULEVARD OF THE ALLIES and PPG PLACE. Including four of the city blocks dating to the 1764 town plan, Firstside mainly consists of late-19th-century buildings.

Fisherman's Wharf commercial district on San Francisco Bay in NE SAN FRANCISCO, California, extending from Aquatic Park (W) to the EMBARCADERO (E), just N of NORTH BEACH. Set aside early in the 20th century for the city's mostly Italian fishermen, it is now an extremely popular tourist destination.

Fishers Hill locality in Shenandoah Co., N Virginia, just W of Strasburg and 8 mi/13 km NNE of WOODSTOCK, the site of a battle fought Sept. 22, 1864, in which Philip Sheridan's troops defeated Confederates under Jubal Early, effectively taking the N Shenandoah Valley for the Union.

Fishers Island in Southold town, Suffolk Co., SE New York, 11 mi/18 km off the NORTH FORK of Long Island, and 3 mi/5 km S of GROTON, Connecticut. About 8 mi/13 km long and 1 mi/1.6 km wide, it is an affluent summer resort and residential island with its own airfield.

Fishkill town, pop. 17,655, Dutchess Co., SE New York, 25 mi/40 km S of Poughkeepsie, on Fishkill Creek and the E bank of the Hudson R. It was settled by the Dutch in the early 17th century. During the late 1980s and early 1990s Fishkill experienced extensive residential expansion, as communities were developed for commuters to New York City, 65 mi/105 km to the S. Fishkill village (pop. 1957) has many historic buildings, among them the First Reformed (Dutch) Church and the Van Wyck Homestead (1732). The city of BEACON is almost enclosed by Fishkill. A state prison is in the town.

Fishlake National Forest c.1.5 million ac/610,000 ha (2345 sq mi/6070 sq km), in SC Utah. Its four NNE–SSW oriented sections are separated by valleys including that of the upper

SEVIER R. The forest is named for 6 mi/10 km–long **Fish L.,** a noted trout fishing resort in its E unit. The high peaks of the PAHVANT and TUSHAR ranges are in the W unit.

Fitchburg **1.** city, pop. 41,194, Worcester Co., NC Massachusetts, on the Mohawk Trail and the North Branch of the Nashua R., 45 mi/72 km NW of Boston. A manufacturing center since early in the 19th century, Fitchburg is also a trading, shopping, and financial center surrounded by dairy farms and orchards, and the site of Fitchburg State College (1894). The city's products have included firearms, bicycles, machinery, paper, and metal, plastic, and leather goods. **2.** city, pop. 15,648, Dane Co., SC Wisconsin, immediately S of Madison. This mainly residential community borders on the University of Wisconsin Arboretum.

Fitzgerald city, pop. 8612, seat of Ben Hill Co., SC Georgia, 51 mi/82 km ENE of Albany. In an effort to heal the wounds of the Civil War, the city was founded in 1896 by the American Soldiers Colony Association to house aging Union veterans. Today, it is an agricultural marketing center, and processes cotton, tobacco, and peanuts. Local industries make textiles and steel products.

Five College Area see under AMHERST, Massachusetts.

Five Forks locality in Dinwiddie Co., SE Virginia, just SW of PETERSBURG. On April 1, 1865, a Union army led by Philip Sheridan won a battle here, clearing the way for U.S. Grant's assault on Petersburg and Richmond. It is one of numerous Virginia localities called Five Forks.

Five Islands in S Louisiana, five SALT DOMES standing in the marshes of Iberia and St. Mary parishes. AVERY I. is the best-known. The others are Belle Isle, Cote Blanche I., Jefferson I., and Weeks I.

Five Points **1.** locality name, usually referring to the meeting of five streets, and usually popularly attached to an urban district. **2.** center point of downtown Atlanta, Georgia, from which the city's four quadrants (NE, NW, SW, SE) radiate. The original site of Terminus, later Atlanta, is just SE, at the Zero Mile Post, at Wall St. and Central Ave. Five major streets—PEACHTREE, Marietta, DECATUR, Edgewood, and Whitehall—meet at Five Points. Long Atlanta's business heart, the area has recently lost much trade to MIDTOWN, BUCKHEAD, and the suburbs. **3.** residential suburban district W of downtown ALBUQUERQUE, New Mexico, on the W bank of the Rio Grande. **4.** 19th-century slum district on the LOWER EAST SIDE, Manhattan, New York City. Between about 1820 and 1900 it was notorious as an overcrowded, crime-ridden neighborhood populated largely by poor Irish and German immigrants. It was one of the first symbols of the "evils" of big cities, and the target of reform drives around 1900.

Five Towns cluster of suburban communities on Long Island, New York's SOUTH SHORE, just SE of John F. Kennedy International Airport and 16 mi/26 km ESE of downtown Manhattan. LONG BEACH is just SE. Noted through much of the 20th century as home to the newly affluent, the "towns," all within the town of HEMPSTEAD (Nassau Co.) are WOODMERE, HEWLETT, Cedarhurst (village, pop. 5716), Lawrence (village, pop. 6513), and Inwood (unincorporated, pop. 7767). Such other nearby communities as Long Beach and MALVERNE have at times been considered part of the Five Towns.

fjord also, **fiord** deep valley, scoured by glacial ice and then occupied by the sea when the ice cover retreated. Fjords are characterized by high, steep sides, and often contain water deeper than that just outside their mouths, which may contain a bar or threshold of material left as the glacier began to retreat. Alaska, British Columbia, and some eastern localities are noted for fjords.

Flagstaff city, pop. 45,857, seat of Coconino Co., NC Arizona, at the S foot of the SAN FRANCISCO PEAKS, 115 mi/185 km NNE of Phoenix. Settled in 1876, it is a center of lumbering, tourism, and astronomical research. Lowell Observatory (1894), site of the discovery of the planet Pluto, is here. Flagstaff is also the site of Northern Arizona University (1899), the NASA library and laboratory, and the Museum of Northern Arizona. The ruins of many ancient PUEBLOs dot the area. Also nearby are the Sunset Crater Volcano (NE) and Walnut Canyon (E) national monuments and the Navajo Army Depot (W).

Flagstaff Lake artificial lake in Somerset Co., NW Maine, formed on a plantation (Flagstaff) that was inundated when the Long Falls Dam was constructed on the Dead R. in 1949–50. Branches of the Dead R. converge at Stratton to form this 20 mi/32 km–long lake, sometimes called the Dead R. Flowage.

Flamborough town, pop. 29,616, Hamilton-Wentworth Regional Municipality, S Ontario, 4 mi/6 km WNW of Hamilton and L. Ontario. It includes a dozen earlier municipalities, including Waterdown, Carlisle, and Millgrove, and is largely residential, with various light industries.

Flaming Gorge Reservoir 91 mi/147 km long, on the Green R., in SW Wyoming and NE Utah. Extending through the **Flaming Gorge National Recreation Area,** it was created in 1964 by the 504 ft/154 m–high **Flaming Gorge Dam** in Utah. The reservoir provides irrigation, hydroelectric power, and recreation to the surrounding area.

Flatbush historic section of C Brooklyn, New York. Settled in the 1630s, it was part of MIDWOOD before its establishment as 't Vlacke Bos (the Wooded Plain) in 1652. The name refers to the almost perfectly flat glacial plain of S Brooklyn. New Lots separated from Flatbush in 1852, and Flatbush became part of Brooklyn in 1894. Railroads brought development in the 1880s, and by 1900 Flatbush was an affluent suburb. Subway extension in the 1920s brought residents from older neighborhoods, creating a largely Jewish lower-middle-class community. Today Flatbush is a mixed community experiencing social tensions as populations shift. East Flatbush, which lies to the S of Crown Heights, contains a major Caribbean community, with newer Asian immigrants moving in since the 1980s. Flatbush Ave., which runs through the center, is one of Brooklyn's chief thoroughfares, extending from the Manhattan Bridge on the East R. SE to the Marine Parkway Bridge at Rockaway Inlet, a distance of over 10 mi/16 km. Erasmus Hall Academy (1786; a public high school since 1896), in central Flatbush, has schooled New Yorkers from the days of Alexander Hamilton to Barbra Streisand.

Flathead Indian Reservation 1938 sq mi/5020 sq km, pop. 21,259 (24% Indian), in W Montana, N of Missoula. Flathead L. is on its N, the Mission Range on its E; the Salish Mts. extend NNW from it. The Confederated Salish and Kootenai, called Flatheads by other tribes, have lived here by treaty since the 1850s. The 1910 division of the reservation into individual allotments led to the sale of much land to whites.

Flathead National Forest 2.3 million ac/945,000 ha (3640 sq mi/9430 sq km), in extreme NW Montana, bordering British Columbia (N) and Glacier National Park (E and N). In the N Rocky Mts., just W of the Continental Divide, it has high peaks, glaciers, waterfalls, lakes, and hundreds of miles of rivers and streams. The 950,000-ac/385,000-ha (1485–sq mi/3845–sq km) Bob Marshall Wilderness, here and in Lewis and Clark National Forest (E), is one of the most popular US WILDERNESS AREAS. The HUNGRY HORSE DAM is in the forest.

Flathead Range mountain system in the N Rocky Mts. of NW Montana. Covering much of Flathead and Lewis and Clark national forests, it is named for the Flathead Indians, and extends NW to SE from L. McDonald in Glacier National Park along the Hungry Horse Reservoir and the South Fork of the Flathead R. to an area N of the Blackfoot R. in Powell Co. Its highest elevation is Swan Peak, 9255 ft/2823 m.

Flathead River 240 mi/386 km long, in British Columbia and Montana. It rises as the **North Fork** in SE British Columbia, and flows S into NW Montana, just E of the Whitefish Range. It then forms the border between Glacier National Park (E) and the Flathead National Forest (W). Flowing SE, it receives its Middle Fork N of Coram. Continuing SW, it receives its South Fork and then flows through **Flathead Lake,** which with an area of 189 sq mi/490 sq km is the largest lake in Montana, before joining the Clark Fork R. just NE of Dixon. The **South Fork** of the Flathead rises in the S end of Flathead National Forest and continues N through the Hungry Horse Reservoir, which is impounded by the HUNGRY HORSE DAM. The river continues N to join the main river just SW of Coram. The **Middle Fork** rises near the Continental Divide and flows NW to join the main stream. All the branches of the Flathead flow through wilderness and are enjoyed by boaters and campers.

Flatiron Building office skyscraper, at MADISON SQUARE, where Fifth Ave. and Broadway cross, lower midtown Manhattan, New York City. At its completion (1902) it was the world's tallest building (21 stories), and its distinctive triangular shape made it a well-known emblem of New York. Today it is the lone survivor of Madison Square's heyday. It was originally named the Fuller Building. The **Flatiron District,** the area around the building, became popular in the 1980s for upscale shopping, entertainment, and apartments.

Flatlands residential section of SC Brooklyn, New York. The Dutch town of Nieuw Amersfoort, on the flat, marshy outwash plain of S Brooklyn, was established here in 1636 by settlers reminded of Holland. The town of Flatlands was established in 1666, including parts of modern MIDWOOD, to the W, and CANARSIE, to the E. The area was one of the last parts of Brooklyn to be developed, and is suburban in character. Marine Park, at 1822 ac/738 ha Brooklyn's largest park, lies S, and FLOYD BENNETT FIELD SE, projecting into Jamaica Bay. The relatively isolated residential communities of Mill Basin and Bergen Beach are to the E.

Flat Rock **1.** city, pop. 7290, Wayne Co., SE Michigan, 22 mi/35 km SSW of Detroit, on the Huron R. Settled in 1824, this factory town makes paper products and auto parts, and has railroad shops and oil refineries. A large Mazda assembly plant opened here in 1987. **2.** see under HENDERSONVILLE, North Carolina.

Flats, the neighborhood in Cleveland, Ohio, W of Downtown, on either side of the Cuyahoga R. A poor area as early as the 1830s, the Flats housed new immigrants for a century thereafter. Mills, factories, and warehouses contributed heavily to river pollution. Eventually both immigrants and industries left, replaced by artists and young people seeking cheap and convenient gallery and residential space during the 1960s. Today, the Flats is a popular retail and entertainment center known for its galleries, restaurants, and night clubs.

Flattery, Cape promontory on the NW of the OLYMPIC PENINSULA, overlooking Juan de Fuca Strait, in extreme NW Washington. A national wildlife refuge and the reservation (pop. 593) of the seafaring Makah are here. Cape Flattery Light sits on rocky Tatoosh I., just offshore. Neah Bay (unincorporated, pop. 916, Clallam Co.) is 3 mi/5 km E. The cape was named by Capt. James Cook in 1778, because it (misleadingly) "flattered" his crew with hopes of an anchorage.

Fleetwood see under MOUNT VERNON, New York.

Fleetwood Hill see under BRANDY STATION, Virginia.

Flemington borough, pop. 4047, seat of Hunterdon Co., WC New Jersey, 15 mi/24 km N of Princeton. Settled in the early 18th century, it prospered as a distribution point for local agricultural products. In 1935, its county courthouse was the scene of the sensational Lindbergh kidnapping trial. Throughout the first half of the 20th century, Flemington was a noted manufacturer of pottery and cut glass. Today, one glass factory remains, and the borough also produces rubber goods and electronic equipment. It is best known, however, for the many retail and "factory outlet" stores located here. Tourism is also important, and the borough is at the center of a fast-growing residential area.

Fleurimont see under SHERBROOKE, Québec.

Flin Flon city, W Manitoba, (pop. 7119) and E Saskatchewan (pop. 330), 72 mi/116 km N of The Pas and 400 mi/644 km NW of Winnipeg. Established in the 1930s with the help of the Hudson Bay Mining and Smelting Company, it took its name from Josiah *Flin*tabbetey *Flon*atin, a character in an old popular novel. The mining of copper, zinc, gold, and silver, along with lumbering and fishing, are major local industries.

Flint city, pop. 140,761, seat of Genesee Co., SE Michigan, on the Flint R., 58 mi/93 km NW of Detroit. Until plant closings in the 1980s and 1990s, it was second only to Detroit as a center for manufacturing automobiles, the site of several General Motors companies. Other factories produce auto accessories, textiles, chemicals, structural steel, cement blocks, and paints and varnishes. The city has suffered severe economic hardships, losing almost 20,000 residents from 1980 to 1990. Settled in 1819, it was originally a fur-trading post. The lumber industry, which supplanted trapping later in the century, required carts and wagons. These were manufactured in Flint, and in the late 1800s carriagemaking came to dominate the economy. One of the most important of these enterprises was the Durant-Dort Carriage Company (1886). Body, spring, and wheel manufacturers became the first suppliers for the Buick Motor Company, the city's first automobile company, organized (1903) by W.C. Durant, who consolidated Flint's manufacturing resources into General Motors in 1908. The Charles Stuart Mott Foundation here is a major educational and cultural philanthropy. Cultural institutions include the Sloan Museum of Transportation, DeWaters Art Center, and Longway Planetarium. Flint is the seat of the Michigan school for the Deaf (1848), the General Motors Institute of Technology, a branch of the University of Michigan (1954), and Mott Community College (1923). The 4322-

ac/757-ha Genesee Recreation Area runs along the river just NE of the city.

Flint Hills low hilly region in E Kansas, extending N–S for c.200 mi/320 km, from near the Nebraska boundary (N) into N Oklahoma (S), with elevations rising 100–500 ft/30–150 m above the surrounding plain. Named for the chert or flint that covers a limestone base, this is a major native prairie zone and an important grazing area. The region is sometimes known as the Bluestem Belt, for the bluestem grasses that grow here.

Flintridge see LA CANADA FLINTRIDGE, California.

Flint River 330 mi/530 km long, in W Georgia. It rises S of Atlanta, and flows S to Albany, its head of navigation, then SW past Bainbridge into L. Seminole, where it joins the CHATTAHOOCHEE R. to form the Apalachicola at the Florida border. A dam near Warwick, 20 mi/32 km NNE of Albany, impounds L. Blackshear.

Floral Park village, pop. 15,947, in Hempstead town, Nassau Co., SE New York, on W Long Island, adjacent (SE) to Bellerose, Queens. It is a residential suburb of New York City, with a commercial flower industry.

Florence **1.** city, pop. 36,426, seat of Lauderdale Co., in the NW corner of Alabama, on the Tennessee R., just E of the WILSON DAM, and 62 mi/100 km WNW of Huntsville. The largest of Alabama's Quad Cities (with SHEFFIELD, TUSCUMBIA, and MUSCLE SHOALS), it is a market and service center for parts of Tennessee, Mississippi, and Alabama. Local farms produce cotton, corn, soybeans, grain, and livestock. The site was laid out in 1818 at the Tennessee's Muscle Shoals. Industries, fostered by the construction of the Wilson Dam in World War I, manufacture tile, building materials, aluminum products, lumber products, and fertilizer. The city is home to the University of North Alabama (1872). The birthplace (1873) of composer W. C. Handy is a museum. **2.** town, pop. 7510, seat of Pinal Co., SE Arizona, 50 mi/80 km SE of Phoenix, on the upper Gila R. Settled in 1866, it was a stage stop and trade center in an agricultural and copper mining area. In 1909 the state prison was built here, replacing the territorial prison in Yuma. Tom Mix Wash, 17 mi/27 km SE on Route 89, is the site of the 1940 auto crash that killed the film cowboy. **3.** city, pop. 2990, Fremont Co., SC Colorado, 35 mi/56 km SSW of Colorado Springs, on the Arkansas R. just NE of the Wet Mts. Incorporated in 1887, it is in a coal and oil producing area, and has engaged in diverse agriculture. Like CAÑON CITY (6 mi/10 km NW), it has an economy now heavily dependent on prison operation; in 1994 the "Super Max," the Federal government's new maximum-security facility for hardened offenders, opened here, taking the role in the Federal system formerly held by the prison in MARION, Illinois. **4.** city, pop. 18,624, Boone Co., N Kentucky, 15 mi/24 km SW of Cincinnati, Ohio. It is a largely residential community on the N edge of the BLUEGRASS REGION and the SW edge of the Cincinnati metropolitan area. **5.** town, pop. 1831, Rankin Co., C Mississippi, 9 mi/14 km SSE of downtown Jackson, the home of Wesley College (1972). **6.** city, pop. 29,813, seat of Florence Co. (pop. 114,344), NE South Carolina, 75 mi/120 km ENE of Columbia and 10 mi/16 km W of the Pee Dee R. It was established in 1853 as a rail junction, repair center, and transfer point, and is now also a major road junction. During the Civil War it had a major prison camp, and now has a national cemetery. It is a distribution center for local crops (mainly tobacco and cotton), and manufactures steel, furniture, textiles, paper, and dental and electronic equipment. Francis Marion College (1970) and a technical college are here.

Florence-Graham unincorporated community, pop. 57,147, Los Angeles Co., SW California, immediately N of the Watts neighborhood of Los Angeles, and SW of Huntington Park, a residential and light industrial district.

Florham Park borough, pop. 8521, Morris Co., N New Jersey, 5 mi/8 km E of Morristown. It was settled in 1655. In addition to homes, Florham Park has office buildings and corporate headquarters that date mainly from the 1980s and 1990s.

Florida southeasternmost US state, in the Census Bureau's South Atlantic region; 1990 pop. 12,937,926 (132.7% of 1980; rank: 4th); area: 65,758 sq mi/170,313 sq km (rank: 22nd); admitted to Union 1845 (27th). Capital: TALLAHASSEE. Most populous cities: JACKSONVILLE, MIAMI, TAMPA, SAINT PETERSBURG, HIALEAH, ORLANDO, FORT LAUDERDALE. Florida is bordered N by Georgia (on the E, with the SAINT MARYS R. forming part of the boundary) and by Alabama (W), which also faces it on the extreme NW across the PERDIDO R. The state consists of a 400 mi/640 km–long NNW–SSE peninsula, with a 240 mi/390 km–long E–W PANHANDLE on the (mainland) NW. At the peninsula's S end, the 135 mi/220 km–long chain of FLORIDA KEYS extends to the SW. The island nation of the Bahamas lies as close as 60 mi/100 km off Florida's SE coast, and Cuba is c.90 mi/145 km S of KEY WEST, the southernmost city in the Keys (and in the continental US). On Florida's W is the Gulf of MEXICO, on the S the Straits of Florida, through which the FLORIDA CURRENT flows NE, continuing N along the E coast to merge into the GULF STREAM. South Florida is the only tropical part of the continental US; the rest of the state is subtropical. It is entirely within the Atlantic (the peninsula) and Gulf (the Panhandle) COASTAL PLAINS, rising to only 345 ft/105 mi in the NW and 325 ft/99 m at Iron Mt. (at LAKE WALES), in the peninsula's C highlands. The peninsula's C is dotted with shallow lakes. In the SC is L. OKEECHOBEE, one of the largest in the US; its waters drain largely S through the EVERGLADES, one of the largest US wetlands. Home to much distinctive wildlife, the Everglades are threatened by rapid development and growing demands on their water; agricultural ditching and other engineering have already affected their delicate ecology. The S tip of Florida is low and swampy; on the SW are the TEN THOUSAND Is., largely mangrove thicket. Because the state has little elevation, there are few rivers of size in Florida. The SAINT JOHNS R., which flows NNW from the Orlando area to Jacksonville and the Atlantic, is the most important in the peninsula. The Panhandle is crossed by rivers from Georgia to the Gulf of Mexico, including the SUWANEE and the APALACHICOLA (draining the CHATTAHOOCHEE and FLINT). In the S, in HURRICANE ALLEY, low-lying Florida is esp. prone to storm damage, and occasional frosts are a hazard to the citrus industry. The peninsula is home to the Seminole, descendants of those who remained here after the 1835–42 war in which they resisted deportation to Oklahoma; tribal centers are in the Everglades (Big Cypress)–Okeechobee area. In 1512, Caribs in Puerto Rico told Ponce de Léon of a FOUNTAIN OF YOUTH to be found on an island to the NW, and the next spring, seeking it, he landed at the site of SAINT AUGUSTINE, naming the "island" he had discovered for the Feast of Flowers (Easter). In 1565 the Spanish established there the first European city in what is now the US. PENSACOLA, in the Panhandle, was the second early Spanish center. For two centuries the Spanish contested control of Florida with the French and esp. with the English. In 1763 the English purchased Spanish claims and established East and WEST FLORIDA, colonies that continued to change hands until the US finally gained control over the whole by an 1819 treaty with Spain. Agricultural settlement, esp. in the N, peopled the state before the Civil War, in which it had little role. In the 1880s, Northern railroad and hotel developers led by Henry Flagler and Henry Plant recognized the potential of the nascent winter vacation industry, and Florida's first boom was on. PALM BEACH (center of the GOLD COAST), Tampa, and other coastal cities were soon playgrounds for the wealthy. The citrus industry, based at first in LAKELAND and other C highland centers, spread rapidly; the KISSIMMEE Prairies became home to a thriving cattle industry. By 1912, railroad lines had extended all the way to Key West. A second boom, in the 1920s, ended in 1926, when inflated real-estate values suddenly plummeted. After World War II, however, rapid development began again. Airlines and improved highways now brought vacationers to Florida from all over North America; Miami and other East Coast resorts came to be thought of as extensions of New York and the Northeast, while the Gulf Coast had more Middle Western (and later Canadian) visitors. The Panhandle remained the only Florida area that could still be considered part of the Deep SOUTH, tied to the agricultural economy of S Georgia and Alabama; Jacksonville, on the E, belongs more to that world than to the world of C and S Florida. The state now has almost three times its 1960 pop. Its people include so many Northern retirees and other SUNBELT seekers that some have considered it not a Southern state at all. In addition, since the 1959 Cuban revolution, Miami and environs have become a major exile community. The city, long a gateway to the Caribbean and South America, is today a financial, business, and cultural hub for Latin America. DADE Co., with which it is merged, is a fast-growing mix of wealthy and middle-class Cubans, Haitian refugees, other Latin Americans, longer-established American white and black communities, and recently arrived "Sunbirds"; its social tensions pull in many directions. On the GULF COAST, Tampa, an industrial and port center, is neighbor to Saint Petersburg, prominent since the 1920s as a sunny retirement haven, now also with many manufactures. Florida's phosphate extraction industry (established in the 1880s) is centered near Lakeland and Tampa Bay; farther S, the Fort Myers–Naples area is the current frontier of rapid residential development. In the NC part of the peninsula, Orlando and vicinity have boomed with residential and tourist development since the 1971 opening of Walt Disney World (see LAKE BUENA VISTA); here citrus groves and lakeside retreats are quickly giving way to residential and commercial sprawl. To Orlando's E, the aerospace complex around CAPE CANAVERAL is a tourist magnet, and DAYTONA BEACH (NE) has long been popular. The state's people in 1990 were about 83% white and 14% black; over 12% were Hispanic (white or black). Tourism, recreation, and residential construction are major Florida industries. In Miami, Tampa, Jacksonville, and other cities, chemical, furniture, food processing, apparel, and other manufacturing industries are important employers. Citrus, vegetable, cattle, sugar cane, and other farm products make the state a US agricultural leader. Phosphate mining and commercial fishing remain important. The Miami and Orlando areas have attracted many corporate offices. The University of Florida is in GAINESVILLE (N), Florida State and Florida A&M universities in Tallahassee.

Florida **1.** town, pop. 758, Berkshire Co., NW Massachusetts, 21 mi/34 km NNE of Pittsfield, on the MOHAWK TRAIL and the Deerfield R. In a mountainous wooded area, it includes the E entrance to the HOOSAC TUNNEL. **2.** village, pop. 2, Monroe Co., NE Missouri, on Mark Twain L. (formed by the damming of the Salt R.), 25 mi/40 km SW of HANNIBAL. Samuel L. Clemens (Mark Twain; 1835–1910) was born here, and four years later moved to Hannibal. Mark Twain State Park, which adjoins (SW) the village, preserves the cabin (moved here from the village in 1930) in which the author was born. **3.** village, pop. 2497, in Warwick township, Orange Co., SE New York, 10 mi/16 km SE of Middletown, in an onion growing area. A monument commemorates statesman William H. Seward (1801–72), who was born here. Glenmere L. is just E.

Florida Bay body of water off the S tip of the Florida Peninsula, between the mainland (N) and the FLORIDA KEYS (S). Most of this shallow bay is part of the Everglades National Park. Florida Bay is connected with BISCAYNE BAY (NE, via several intermediate sounds) and the Gulf of Mexico (W).

Florida Current warm current in the North Atlantic Ocean, the initial part of the GULF STREAM system. Formed from a combination of the Equatorial and Antilles currents, which mingle in the Gulf of Mexico, it flows from the Gulf as a deep blue current, c.80° F/27° C in temperature. Some 50 mi/80 km wide and 2000 ft/600 m deep, it passes through the Straits of Florida and flows N along the SE coast of the US to Cape HATTERAS, where it becomes the Gulf Stream proper.

Florida Keys chain of low-lying islands (Spanish, *cayos*), mainly in Monroe Co. and a few in Dade Co., S Florida, c.150 mi/240 km long, curving from the waters off the tip of the Florida Peninsula into the Gulf of Mexico. They extend from Virginia Key, S of Miami Beach, to KEY WEST, site of the southernmost US city outside Hawaii. The Marquesas Keys and the DRY TORTUGAS lie farther W. The Keys are composed of coral and limestone, with a series of offshore reefs, and are covered with low-growing plants and mangrove swamps. Best known are Key Largo and Key West. Others include Upper and Lower Matecumbe keys, Looe Key, Long Key, Vaca Key, Big Pine Key, and Sugarloaf Key. Commercial fishing, once the economic mainstay of the Keys, continues to be important, but tourism is now the main industry. The Keys are linked by the 113 mi/182 km–long Overseas Highway, which traces the path of a railway built 1904–12 and destroyed by hurricane in 1935. First completed in 1938, the highway was reconstructed in 1983. Greater access to the keys, largely in the 1980s, has resulted in expanded population and development, which have increased business income but led to the endangering of native flora and fauna and of the coral reefs.

Florin unincorporated community, pop. 24,330, Sacramento Co., NE California, 6 mi/10 km SSE of downtown Sacramento, and just S of the Sacramento Army Depot. It is largely residential.

Florissant city, pop. 51,206, St. Louis Co., EC Missouri, 14 mi/23 km NW of downtown St. Louis. It was founded (1786) by the Spanish, who called it St. Ferdinand, but was renamed (officially not until 1939) for its flowering (*fleurissant*) valley by French farmers and trappers who settled here in the 1780s. It was an early Jesuit missionary center, and today vestiges of this residential suburb's Gallic past draw a sizable tourist trade. The Old St. Ferdinand Shrine (1821) is believed to be the oldest Catholic church between the Mississippi R. and the Rocky Mts. The city is the seat of St. Louis Christian College (1956).

Florissant Fossil Beds National Monument 6000 ac/2430 ha, in the Rocky Mt. FRONT RANGE of SC Colorado, 25 mi/40 km W of Colorado Springs. The site of a lake that was covered with volcanic ash over 25 million years ago, it is a rich source of insect, leaf, and seed fossils and giant sequoia stumps.

Flossmoor village, pop. 8651, Cook Co., NE Illinois, a residential suburb adjacent (SW) to HOMEWOOD, and 23 mi/37 km SSW of Chicago's LOOP.

Flour City, the also, the **Flower City** see under ROCHESTER, New York.

Flower Mound town, pop. 15,527, Denton Co., NE Texas, 23 mi/37 km NW of Dallas, on the N side of Grapevine L., just W of Interstate 35E. A residential suburb, it tripled in population in the 1980s. The Dallas–Fort Worth International Airport is just S.

Floyd Bennett Field abandoned airfield, once the first New York City airport, in S Brooklyn, on Jamaica Bay. Opened in 1931, it never succeeded as a commercial field, but became famous for the individual aviators who flew from it, including Wiley Post, Amelia Earhart, Howard Hughes, and Douglas (Wrong Way) Corrigan. Since 1972 it has been part of the GATEWAY NATIONAL RECREATION AREA.

Floyd Collins Crystal Cave in Barren Co., S Kentucky, 30 mi/48 km ENE of Bowling Green. In MAMMOTH CAVE NATIONAL PARK near Cave City, the SE gateway to the park, it was discovered (1917) by Floyd Collins while checking traps. It has delicate formations of crystal gypsum and onyx resembling many different multicolored flowers. Collins's death (1925) while looking for a new entrance was a national media event. He is buried in Grand Canyon Avenue (200 ft/60 m high, 110 ft/34 m wide, and 700 ft/214 m long). Nearby are Great Onyx Cave and Diamond Caverns.

Floyd River 92 mi/148 km long, in Iowa. It rises N of Sanborn in O'Brien Co., and flows SW past Sheldon and Le Mars to join the Missouri R. at Sioux City. Its main tributary, the West Branch, rises in Sioux Co. and flows S, emptying into the main river at Merrill.

Flushing **1.** city, pop. 8542, Genesee Co., SE Michigan, on the Flint R., 10 mi/16 km W of Flint. It produces dies, has flour milling, and makes dairy products. There are Indian mounds nearby. **2.** commercial and residential section of N Queens, New York, on Flushing Creek, which leads into Flushing Bay, an inlet of the East R. FLUSHING MEADOWS-CORONA PARK lies W. The Dutch town of Vlissingen in the 1640s, it became in the 1650s a center for Quakers fleeing New England. The Bowne House (1661) is the oldest house surviving in Queens, and the Friends Meeting House dates to 1694. The first US nursery was established here in 1737, and Flushing was largely rural and agricultural until the 1930s. The BRONX-WHITESTONE BRIDGE, opened 1939 for the World's Fair in Flushing Meadows, brought rapid development. Since the 1970s Flushing has become a polyglot community, with one of the largest US Chinese and Korean concentrations. Retailing and banking have boomed in the area, which in addition to its growing population has easy access to New York's airports. The Queens Botanical Garden is here.

Flushing Meadows–Corona Park urban park, 1275 ac/516 ha, in N Queens, New York. It was created for the 1939–40 New York World's Fair on the site of the Corona Dumps, a wasteland; marshes along the Flushing R. were filled, creating lakes and parkland. Shea Stadium and the National Tennis Center (1978) are at its N extreme. The New York City Building from the 1939 fair survives; in 1946–49 it housed the UN General Assembly, and today it is home to the Queens Museum. Structures surviving from the second World's Fair on the site, in 1964–65, include the Unisphere (140 ft/43 m tall).

flyway any of the routes along which migrating birds (and some insects, like monarch butterflies) move between wintering grounds and summer (breeding) grounds. Their location is determined by factors including coastlines, major rivers, and other landmarks; available surface water along the way; and wind currents affected by the orientation of mountain ranges. North America's four major flyways are the ATLANTIC FLYWAY, the MISSISSIPPI FLYWAY, the CENTRAL FLYWAY, and the PACIFIC FLYWAY.

FM-1960 rapidly developing residential and commercial area on the edge of Houston, Texas, 19 mi/31 km NNW of Downtown. Taking its name from state farm-to-market (FM) road 1960, which crosses Interstate 75 here, it grew in the 1970s after the opening of the HOUSTON INTERCONTINENTAL AIRPORT, just E.

Foggy Bottom section of NW Washington, D.C., W of the White House and S of Pennsylvania Ave. One of the lowest parts of the District, bordered (W) by the Potomac R. and Rock Creek, it once was characterized by haze from riverfront industries. It now is home to apartment houses, to George Washington University (1821), and to the State Department; US foreign policy is often referred to as emanating from Foggy Bottom. The WATERGATE and the JOHN F. KENNEDY CENTER are W, along the river.

Fogo Island see under NOTRE DAME BAY, Newfoundland.

Folly Island 6 mi/10 km long, in Charleston Co., SE South Carolina. One of the SEA ISLANDS, it is on the Atlantic Ocean just S of JAMES I., and 12 mi/19 km S of Charleston. The resort city of **Folly Beach** (pop. 1398) is widely known.

Folsom **1.** city, pop. 29,802, Sacramento Co., NC California, on the American R. and Folsom L., 20 mi/32 km NE of Sacramento. In an area producing livestock, citrus fruits, and other crops, it is a rapidly growing suburb. In the 1840s it was on the road to the goldfields. In 1856, the first railroad in California reached here from Sacramento, and in 1860 the settlement was a PONY EXPRESS stop. Damming of the river began in 1866. Folsom State Prison was built in 1880. A hydroelectric plant, California's first, was operational in 1895. **Folsom L.,** now the third-largest lake in the California state park system, is impounded by a 1955 dam. Part of the 18,000-ac/7300-ha Folsom State Recreation Area, it has 75 mi/120 km of shoreline. One of California's most popular recreational sites, it is fed by the North and South forks of the American R. **2.** ranching village, pop. 71, Union Co., NE New Mexico, 10 mi/16 km S of the Colorado border, and 29 mi/46 km ESE of Raton. It gives its name to the widespread Folsom culture, dating from c.11,000 B.C., whose flint spear points were found here in 1925.

Fond du Lac city, pop. 37,757, seat of Fond du Lac Co., SE Wisconsin, 18 mi/29 km SSE of Oshkosh, at the S tip of L. Winnebago (thus its name, French for "end of the lake") and the mouth of the Fond du Lac R. American pioneers began settling the area in 1838, though French explorers and missionaries had been here c.1670, and a French trading post had been established here in 1785. Lumbering and milling formed the early basis of its economy. As the supply of timber declined, farming and manufacturing grew in importance. Today the city is in a dairy farming region, which it serves as a trading center. Fond du Lac's major industries include the processing of cheese and other dairy products, the production of animal feed, and the manufacture of machinery and machine tools, outboard motors, and snowmobiles.

Fontana city, pop. 87,535, San Bernardino Co., SW California, 45 mi/72 km E of Los Angeles, and 7 mi/11 km W of San Bernardino. The city's economy was agricultural until World War II, when a huge Kaiser steel plant was established. The manufacture of steel and steel products is its major industry; ammunition, electronic equipment, and industrial gases are also made. In the 1980s the city's population more than doubled.

Fontana Dam and Lake see under LITTLE TENNESSEE R.

Foraker, Mount see under ALASKA RANGE, Alaska.

Forbes, Mount peak (11,852 ft/3612 m) of the Rocky Mts., in SW Alberta, 75 mi/121 km NW of Banff, in Banff National Park.

Fordham residential and academic district, C Bronx, New York. Established 1671 as the manor of Fordham, its name referring to a ford on the nearby Spuyten Duyvil Creek, it became in 1841 home to St. John's College, which in 1905 adopted the locality's name as its own. Fordham University's campus is called Rose Hill, after a manor house of 1838. Fordham is bounded S by Tremont and N by Bedford Park. The Bronx R. is in the E part, running through Bronx Park, home to the 250-ac/101-ha New York Botanical Garden (1891) and the Bronx Zoo (1895).

Fords unincorporated village, pop. 14,392, in Woodbridge township, Middlesex Co., NE New Jersey, 2 mi/3 km W of Perth Amboy, near the intersection of the Garden State Parkway and the New Jersey Turnpike. Its manufactures include chemicals, plastics, building materials, metal products, and clothing.

Ford's Theatre historic building in NW Washington, D.C., 0.5 mi/1 km E of the White House, in the EAST END. It was the scene, on April 14, 1865, of the assassination of Abraham Lincoln. With the Peterson House, across 10th St., where the president died, it is a National Historic Site.

Fore River 5 mi/8 km–long tidal inlet of Casco Bay, SW Maine, between Portland and South Portland, forming an inner harbor and S boundary of Portland. It receives the Stroudwater R. A large tanker facility is on the South Portland side, as is the Portland International Jetport.

Forest Glen **1.** residential neighborhood on the Northwest Side of Chicago, Illinois, on the North Branch of the Chicago R., between Skokie and Niles. One of the most prestigious areas of Chicago, it is home to some of the city's wealthiest residents. **2.** unincorporated village, Montgomery Co., C Maryland, a residential suburb on Rock Creek, just NW of extreme N Washington, D.C. A unit of Walter Reed Army Medical Center is here.

Forest Grove city, pop. 15,559, Washington Co., NW Oregon, an outer residential suburb 22 mi/35 km W of Portland. Pacific University, one of the oldest colleges in the West, was founded here in 1849. There are many wineries in the area.

Forest Heights town, pop. 2859, Prince George's Co., SC Maryland, a residential suburb on Indian Head Highway, near the Potomac R., 6 mi/10 km SSE of Washington, D.C.

Forest Hill **1.** affluent residential neighborhood, N of St. Clair Ave. and W of YONGE St., 3 mi/5 km N of downtown TORONTO, Ontario. **2.** city, pop. 11,482, Tarrant Co., NE Texas, 6 mi/10 km SE of downtown Fort Worth. It is a residential suburb almost completely surrounded by SE Fort Worth.

Forest Hills residential and commercial section of C Queens, New York. It was part of the township of NEWTOWN. Kew Gardens lies SE, and Flushing Meadows-Corona Park to the E. The area's wooded heights were settled 1652. Forest Hills Gardens, originally conceived as low-income housing, became exclusive in the 1920s. The West Side Tennis Club's facility (1923) was the site until 1978 of the US Open, played here on grass. Forest Hills today is a mix of low-rise housing, office towers, and highway junctions.

Forest Lawn see under GLENDALE, California.

Forest Park **1.** city, pop. 16,925, Clayton Co., NW Georgia, 11 mi/18 km S of Atlanta. It is a largely residential suburb outside the city's beltway (Route 285), with some industry, including a metal plant. **2.** village, pop. 14,918, Cook Co., NE Illinois, on the Des Plaines R., a suburb 9 mi/14 km W of Chicago. A chiefly residential community, it has some light industries, manufacturing filing cabinets, casters, venetian blinds, containers, and ballpoint pens, among other items. Originally settled as Harlem (1856) by German immigrants, the town was renamed (1907) by combining the names of adjacent (and prestigious) River Forest and Oak Park. **3.** 1380-ac/559-ha public park in the West End of SAINT LOUIS, Missouri, 4 mi/6 km W of Downtown. Created in 1875, it was the main site of the 1904 Louisiana Purchase Exposition (the St. Louis World's Fair). One of the largest US urban parks, it is home to the city's zoo, public art museum, and municipal opera. The St. Louis Arena (1929), on its S side, is home to the Blues (hockey). Washington University is on the park's W, its medical center on the E. Areas N and E of the park have recently undergone renovation or GENTRIFICATION. **4.** city, pop. 18,609, Hamilton Co., SW Ohio, a residential suburb 9 mi/14 km N of Cincinnati. **5.** on the NE slope of the Tualatin Mts., in the NORTHWEST section of PORTLAND, Oregon. At 5000 ac/2025 ha, it is the largest park completely within the boundaries of a US city, and is noted for its miles of trails.

Forestville unincorporated community, pop. 16,731, Prince George's Co., SC Maryland, a residential suburb on Interstate 95, 10 mi/16 km SE of Washington, D.C., and just N of Andrews Air Force Base.

Forillon National Park 59,305 ac/24,019 ha, at the E tip of the GASPÉ PENINSULA, on the Gulf of St. Lawrence, in SE Québec. Established in 1970, this former Micmac hunting ground is famed for the spectacularly eroded limestone cliffs on its N and S shores; there, in its varied interior, and in surrounding waters, abundant wildlife may be seen. The city of GASPÉ is just S, across Gaspé Bay.

Forked Deer River 10 mi/16 km long, in W Tennessee. It is formed SW of DYERSBURG, where its North and South forks join, and flows SW to join the OBION R., at Moss I., on the Mississippi R. Its **South Fork** rises in McNairy Co. and flows 100 mi/160 km NW past Jackson, where it joins a short North Fork flowing W from Henderson Co. The longer **North Fork,** 50 mi/80 km long, rises near Milan, Gibson Co., and flows W past Trenton and Dyersburg. The **Middle Fork,** 60 mi/100 km long, rises in S Carroll Co., and flows generally W and NW, passing S of HUMBOLDT, to join the North Fork 10 mi/16 km E of Dyersburg. All forks of the river have been channelized in places, and near its mouth on the Mississippi the Forked Deer has abandoned its old bed, leaving bends and oxbow lakes in the Chickasaw National Wildlife Refuge.

Forrest City city, pop. 13,364, seat of St. Francis Co., EC Arkansas, 80 mi/129 km ENE of Little Rock, on the W slope of CROWLEY'S RIDGE, between the L'Anguille and St. Francis rivers. In a hardwood forest and diversified farming region, it was originally a railroad camp; former Confederate General Nathan Bedford Forrest contracted with the Memphis and Little Rock Railroad (1866) to build a line nearby over the ridge. The city now serves as a commercial center for corn, cotton, peach, rice, and sweet potato producers. It also manufactures farm machinery and electrical equipment. East Arkansas Community College (1973) is here.

Forsyth city, pop. 4268, seat of Monroe Co., C Georgia, 22 mi/35 km NW of Macon. An early (1834) railroad town, it has been a center for cotton ginning, lumber milling, and textile manufactures. Tift College (1847) is here.

Forsyth County 412 sq mi/1067 sq km, pop. 265,878, in NC North Carolina, in the Piedmont, bounded (W) by the Yadkin R. Its seat is WINSTON-SALEM, one of the world's leading tobacco markets and manufacturers of cigarettes and tobacco products, with a wide range of other industries.

Fort Albany see under ALBANY R., Ontario.

Fort Ancient prehistoric earthwork in Warren Co., SW Ohio, 6 mi/10 km SE of Lebanon. Situated on a headland on the E bank of the Little Miami R., it contains burial mounds and village sites and has been dated to the Hopewell Period (A.D. 900–1200). Subsequently (c.1400–1600), the area was occupied by the Fort Ancient peoples. An earth wall encloses about 100 ac/40 ha, divided into the Old and New forts.

Fort Apache see under WHITE Mts., Arizona.

Fort Atkinson city, pop. 10,227, Jefferson Co., SE Wisconsin, 30 mi/48 km SE of Madison. Set on both banks of the Rock R., it serves the surrounding dairy and truck farming region as a trade and shipping center. Industries include food processing, beermaking, and the manufacture of farm equipment, electrical fixtures, and hosiery. The city lies in an area where prehistoric Indian mounds are plentiful; the Panther Intaglio mound is on its W outskirts. L. Koshkonong is 3 mi/5 km SW.

Fort Augusta see under SUNBURY, Pennsylvania.

Fort Beauséjour see under SACKVILLE, New Brunswick.

Fort Belknap Indian Reservation 969 sq mi/2510 sq km, pop. 2508 (93% Indian), in NC Montana. The Milk R. is its N boundary; the Bears Paw battlefield (see NEZ PERCE TRAIL) is just W. Harlem (city, pop. 882, Blaine Co.), just N, is its headquarters. Established in 1887, N of the Little Rocky Mts., it is home to Gros Ventre and Assiniboine-Sioux groups.

Fort Belvoir military post, pop. 8590, in Fairfax Co., N Virginia, on the Potomac R., 9 mi/14 km SW of Alexandria. Formerly Camp Humphreys (1915), it has an engineering school. Belvoir, the mansion of William Fairfax, was built here in 1741, and burned in 1783.

Fort Bend County 876 sq mi/2269 sq km, pop. 225,421, in SE Texas, drained by the Brazos R. Its seat is RICHMOND. On the SW side (and containing part) of HOUSTON, the county has produced oil, natural gas, sulfur, goats, sheep, cattle, horses, hogs, poultry, rice, pecans, fruit, vegetables, cotton, and corn. It is increasingly suburban and industrial.

Fort Benjamin Harrison see under LAWRENCE, Indiana.

Fort Benning military reservation in Muscogee Co., W Georgia, E and S of Columbus. Set on 189,000 ac/76,500 ha, it is the largest infantry post in the US. Built during World War I, it is the site of the Army Infantry School and an airborne training center.

Fort Benton city, pop. 1660, seat of Chouteau Co., NC Montana, at the historical head of navigation on the MISSOURI R., 34 mi/56 km NE of Great Falls. The oldest white community in Montana, it had an 1846 fur trade fort, and by 1859 was the starting point for the Mullan Road, which crossed the Continental Divide to Walla Walla, Washington, linking the Missouri and Columbia river systems. The Whoop-up Trail was used by illegal whiskey traders going N to Alberta (see FORT WHOOP-UP). From 1859 to 1887, Fort Benton was a busy steamboat port, landing immigrants, prospectors, traders, and cattlemen. The town has monuments to Lewis and Clark's 1805 passage and to other early history.

Fort Berthold Indian reservation, pop. 5395, in McKenzie, Dunn, Mercer, McLean, Ward, and Mountrail counties, WC North Dakota, crossed by L. Sakakawea. Originally a trading post established in 1845 by the Tyrolean Bartholemew Berthold, it became a military facility 20 years later. The reservation was formed in 1870 with more than 2 million ac/810,000 ha; it is now about a quarter of that size. Though the E area is arable, most of it consists of rugged, broken badlands best suited for grazing. It is occupied by remnants of the Arikara, Mandan, and Hidatsa, three agricultural tribes that inhabited the Missouri R. Valley. The reservation headquarters is in the city of New Town, pop. 1388, created by the Army Corps of Engineers (1952) after floods inundated various Indian communities.

Fort Bliss military reservation, c.1.2 million ac/486,000 ha, in El Paso and Hudspeth counties, extreme W Texas, adjacent (NE) to El Paso, and extending into Doña Ana and Otero counties, New Mexico. It was established in 1848 to protect the frontier and wagon trains on their way to California goldfields, and was later SW headquarters for the Confederacy. Now it is home to the US Army Air Defense Artillery Center, specializing in anti-aircraft artillery training and the development and testing of guided missiles, as well as to medical units. The WHITE SANDS Missile Range is just NW, in New Mexico.

Fort Bowie National Historic Site see under CHIRICAHUA Mts., Arizona.

Fort Bragg **1.** city, pop. 6078, Mendocino Co., NW California, 136 mi/220 km NNW of San Francisco, on the Pacific coast. Named for an 1857 Army post, it engages in redwood lumber milling and fishing, ships regional farm produce, has an artists' colony, and is a popular tourist destination. **2.** military reservation, pop. 34,744, in Hoke and Cumberland counties, C North Carolina, just NW and W of FAYETTEVILLE. The 200–sq mi/520–sq km installation was established in 1918, and became an important training center in World War II and after, home in the Vietnam era to the Green Berets. The area includes Pope Air Force Base, center for troop carrier aircraft. The 82nd Airborne Division is among units based here. Fort Bragg dominates the economies and culture of Fayetteville, SOUTHERN PINES (W), and other nearby communities.

Fort Bridger historic site in extreme SW Wyoming, on the Blacks Fork R., just S of I-80, 32 mi/54 km E of Evanston and 88 mi/142 km ENE of Salt Lake City, Utah. The fur trader and scout Jim Bridger built a supply post here on the Oregon and Mormon trails in 1843. After Mormons bought it from his partner Luis Vasquez in 1855 and destroyed it, Bridger sold the site to the Army, who built another fort operational 1858–90, which was a post on the Pony Express and Overland Stage routes. Reconstructed by the state in 1920, it is a tourist site.

Fort Calhoun nuclear power plant, operational since 1973, at Fort Calhoun (city, pop. 648), Washington Co., E Nebraska, on the Missouri R., 14 mi/23 km N of downtown Omaha.

Fort Campbell military reservation along the state line in NW Tennessee and SW Kentucky, 17 mi/27 km S of Hopkinsville, Kentucky, and 7 mi/11 km NW of Clarksville, Tennessee. Its Army Air Field is in Kentucky, but most of the area is in Tennessee. Home to the 101st Airborne, it was a major basic training facility during the Vietnam War. **Fort Campbell North** (unincorporated, in Kentucky) had a 1990 pop. of 18,861.

Fort Carlton see under DUCK LAKE, Saskatchewan.

Fort Caroline see under JACKSONVILLE, Florida.

Fort Carson military reservation immediately S of COLORADO SPRINGS, in SC Colorado, at the S end of the Front Range. Established in World War II, it is a major infantry center.

Fort Chaffee World War II–era army training post, now inactive, on the SE outskirts of FORT SMITH, Arkansas.

Fort Chimo see KUUJJUAQ, Québec.

Fort Chipewyan historic trading post in NE Alberta, on the SW shore of L. Athabasca, at the SE border of WOOD BUFFALO NATIONAL PARK. Originally established (1788) some 20 mi/32 km SE of its present location, it was the starting point for the explorations of Alexander Mackenzie to the Arctic (1789) and Pacific (1792) oceans. Abandoned in 1804 and rebuilt at its present site in 1821, it served as a fur trading center and later as a North West Mounted Police post.

Fort Christina see under CHRISTINA R., Delaware.

Fort Clatsop see under ASTORIA, Oregon.

Fort Clinton Revolutionary War fort, originally Fort Arnold, located at BEAR Mt. on the W bank of the Hudson R., SE New York, S of West Point. General George Clinton stretched a huge wrought-iron chain from it across the river to block British traffic on the Hudson. In Oct. 1777, the British destroyed the chain. The ruins of the fort are now in Bear Mountain State Park.

Fort Collins city, pop. 87,758, seat of Larimer Co., NC Colorado, on the Cache la Poudre R., in the E foothills of the FRONT RANGE, 60 mi/97 km N of Denver. It was founded as a military outpost guarding the OVERLAND TRAIL. The arrival of the railroad and development of irrigation spurred its growth. The city has traditionally been a commercial and transportation center for livestock, sugar beets, barley, and other farm products. In recent years, it has also become a center for high-tech manufactures such as computers and electronic products. Manufactures include beer, combustion engines, arc welders, prefabricated buildings, cement, film, dental equipment, and plastics. Tourism is also important. Fort Collins is headquarters for the Roosevelt National Forest. Colorado State University (1879) is here.

Fort Crailo see under RENSSELAER, New York.

Fort Crevecoeur see under EAST PEORIA, Illinois.

Fort Davis historic settlement, pop. 900, the seat of Jeff Davis Co., in the TRANS-PECOS region of W Texas. Established in 1854 on the road between San Antonio (E) and El Paso (W), the fort operated until 1891 to protect settlers and stage routes. In the DAVIS Mts., 22 mi/35 km NW of Alpine and 173 mi/278 km SE of El Paso, the community is now a tourist center.

Fort Dearborn name of two historic forts in what is now Chicago, Illinois, at the site of the present Michigan Ave. Bridge over the Chicago R. The first, built in 1804 on the S bank of the river, was destroyed by Winnebago warriors after they massacred departing inhabitants during the War of 1812. The second was constructed on the N bank in 1816, and served as a base for operations during the Black Hawk War. It was demolished in 1856.

Fort Delaware see under PEA PATCH I., Delaware.

Fort Detrick see under FREDERICK, Maryland.

Fort Devens see under AYER, Massachusetts.

Fort Dix military complex, established 1917 as Camp Dix, in Burlington Co., SC New Jersey, 15 mi/24 km SE of Trenton, on the N edge of the PINE BARRENS. Covering over 30,000 ac/12,000 ha, it was the largest US training center in World War II. McGuire Air Force Base, in the NW part, is one of the major US military airfields. Lakehurst Naval Air Station adjoins to the E. Active-duty training at Fort Dix ended in 1992, and plans to convert units of the base for use by the FBI, Coast Guard, and as the largest federal prison were aired. The borough of Wrightstown (pop. 3843), a commercial center on the NW, and Pemberton township (pop. 31,342), S of the base and including BROWNS MILLS, were heavily affected by the base closing. In 1990, Fort Dix's population was 10,205, McGuire's 7580.

Fort Dodge city, pop. 25,894, seat of Webster Co., NW Iowa, on the Des Moines R., 70 mi/113 km NW of Des Moines. A trading and processing center for surrounding farms, it produces feeds, fertilizers, soybean products, and farm implements. Meatpacking is also important. The city and its environs lie over some of the world's largest gypsum deposits, which are mined; gypsum products are manufactured in Fort Dodge. Fort Clarke was built here in 1850, but abandoned in 1853; the present city grew from the settlement established one year later. Iowa Central Community College (1966) is here.

Fort Donelson Confederate fortification, established 1861 on the Cumberland R., just NW of Dover, Tennessee, and 27 mi/43 km WSW of Clarksville, in an attempt to deny Union forces access to the river and to the Nashville Basin. Following the fall of FORT HENRY, U.S. Grant marched his troops here and, supported by gunboats, attacked on Feb. 12, 1862. The fort's fall on Feb. 16 was the first major Union victory of the war, and laid C Tennessee open to Union advance. The 537-ac/217-ha Fort Donelson National Battlefield was established in 1928; there is also a national cemetery. The fort is now along L. Barkley, in the LAND BETWEEN THE LAKES.

Fort Douglas former military installation in E SALT LAKE CITY, Utah, just E of the University of Utah. Founded in 1862, it officially served as a protection for mail routes and a guard against hostile Indians; it also was a point from which a suspicious Federal government could observe the activities of Mormon settlers. It is now a museum.

Fort Drum 109,000-ac/44,000-ha Army reservation in Jefferson Co., N New York, c.0.5 mi/1 km NE of WATERTOWN. Mainly a training facility for Army National Guard and Reserve units, it is also home to the Army's Tenth Mountain Division, which was central in the humanitarian mission to Somalia begun in late 1992.

Fort Duquesne see under PITTSBURGH, Pennsylvania.

Fort Edward town, pop. 6330, Washington Co., E New York, on the E bank of the Hudson R., 5 mi/8 km SE of Glens Falls. Situated in the strategic area between the Hudson R. and L. Champlain, Fort Edward village (pop. 3561) grew up around a fort built in 1755. American forces withdrew from the fort in July 1777, before the advance of Burgoyne, who briefly occupied it. Fort Edward's mills were vital to its economy from the settlement's beginnings; it was also a pottery manufacturing center. Mills continue to be important, with pulp and paper among the village's diversified manufactures.

Fort Erie town, pop. 26,006, Niagara Regional Municipality, extreme S Ontario, on L. Erie and the Niagara R., opposite Buffalo, New York. A British military post was built here in 1764. American troops seized, held, and later destroyed it during the War of 1812. The town of Fort Erie was established in 1932 with the consolidation of the village of Fort Erie, which had developed near the fort, and the town of Bridgeburg. The fort was reconstructed in the late 1930s. Today the town manufactures steel, paint, auto accessories, pharmaceuticals, and aircraft, and is visited for its Crystal Beach (S) and its horse track. The PEACE and International Railway bridges connect it with Buffalo.

Fort Ethan Allen see under ESSEX, Vermont.

Fort Eustis military reservation in York Co., SE Virginia, on the N bank of the James R., 8 mi/13 km NW of Newport News. The site of the Army Transportation Center, it has a transportation museum.

Fort Fisher Confederate fortification, built 1862 near the mouth of the CAPE FEAR R., SE North Carolina. It was designed to protect Wilmington, 18 mi/29 km N, the South's major blockade-running port. After an abortive Dec. 1864 attack, Union forces captured it on Jan. 15, 1865. Just S of the resort of Kure Beach, the fort is now an historic site.

Fort Frances town, pop. 8891, seat of Rainy River District, W Ontario, on Rainy L. and the Rainy R., opposite International Falls, Minnesota, and 210 mi/338 km WNW of Thunder Bay. Fort St. Pierre, a fur trading post, was established here in 1731; it took its present name in 1830. Its location on trade and westward migration routes and the 1870s building of a canal to circumvent the river's falls established the town as a commercial and lumbering center. Mills continue to produce wood and pulp products, and tourism and outdoor recreation are now also major employers.

Fort Frederica see under SAINT SIMONS I., Georgia.

Fort Frontenac see under KINGSTON, Ontario.

Fort Garry see under WINNIPEG, Manitoba.

Fort George 1. see under PRINCE GEORGE, British Columbia. 2. see under NIAGARA-ON-THE-LAKE, Ontario.

Fort George River see LA GRANDE R., Québec.

Fort Gordon US Army reservation, a training center in Columbia, Jefferson, McDuffie, and Richmond counties, E Georgia, 11 mi/18 km SW of Augusta. The Signal Corps Museum is here.

Fort Greene residential section of N Brooklyn, New York, between Clinton Hill (E) and the commercial downtown (W), with WALLABOUT BAY and WILLIAMSBURG to the N. The area developed as a suburban alternative to BROOKLYN HEIGHTS through the 19th century, and has many impressive brownstone buildings. In the 1840s its free black community was an Underground Railroad center. Fort Putnam, a Colonial position of 1776, was renamed Fort Greene in 1812. In 1867 its site was chosen for a monument to Americans who had died in British prison ships in Wallabout Bay; a 145-ft/44-m Doric column now stands in Fort Greene Park. The Brooklyn Academy of Music and Long Island University are nearby. In the 1990s Fort Greene is a highly integrated neighborhood, home among others to black musicians and artists like filmmaker Spike Lee.

Fort Halifax see under WATERVILLE, Maine.

Fort Hall Indian Reservation 815 sq mi/2111 sq km, pop. 5114, in SE Idaho, N and W of Pocatello, along the Snake R. In the area of an 1830s trading post, it was established in 1869; in 1900 its lands were reduced, and whites poured into the area. The Bannock, most of whom live here now, left the reservation and fought briefly (1878) during the Nez Perce War. Other Shoshoneans now share the reservation. **Fort Hall** (unincorporated, pop. 2681) is the trade center.

Fort Hamilton see under BAY RIDGE, New York.

Fort Henry 1. see under KINGSTON, Ontario. 2. Confederate fortification, established 1861 on the Tennessee R., 13 mi/21 km NW of Dover, Tennessee, in an attempt to deny Union forces access to the river. Set low on the riverbank, it fell almost immediately when engaged in Feb. 1862, as much from the threat of rising water as from the attackers' actions. Having taken it, U.S. Grant marched his troops E to FORT DONELSON. The site of Fort Henry is now below the surface of Kentucky L., on the W side of the LAND BETWEEN THE LAKES. Some outworks remain in the adjoining woods.

Fort Hood military reservation, covering some 160,000 ac/65,000 ha in Bell and Coryell counties, C Texas, adjacent (N) to KILLEEN. Established in 1942 as Camp Hood, it was a major World War II training center, housing almost 100,000 personnel at one point. Renamed in 1946, it now is home to the 1st Cavalry and 2nd Armored divisions, and had a 1990 pop. of 35,580. GATESVILLE (N), TEMPLE (ESE), and COPPERAS COVE (SW) are other cities around its perimeter.

Fort Huachuca military reservation in the Huachuca Mts. of Cochise Co., SE Arizona, 50 mi/80 km SE of Tucson. Established in 1877 to control the Apache, it is the oldest US cavalry post; since 1954 it has been an electronics and communications headquarters. Its museum honors the Buffalo Soldiers, black cavalrymen of the 1880s. SIERRA VISTA (E) and **Huachuca City** (town, pop. 1782, just N) are among its satellite communities.

Fort Hunter Liggett see under JOLON, California.

Fort Irwin military reservation in the MOJAVE DESERT, SE California, S of Death Valley and 40 mi/64 km NE of Barstow. A major Army combat training center, it incorporates parts of the AVAWATZ Mts. and smaller ranges. The dry Bicycle L. is in its C. The Goldstone Communications Complex adjoins (W), and part of the China L. Naval Weapons Center (see RIDGECREST) is on the NW.

Fort Jackson see under COLUMBIA, South Carolina.

Fort Jefferson see under DRY TORTUGAS, Florida.

Fort Kent town, pop. 4268, Aroostook Co., extreme N Maine. Fort Kent is the N terminus of US 1, on the St. John R., opposite Clair, New Brunswick. Named for an existing fort built (1839) to protect lumber interests, the community was settled about ten years earlier by Acadians. It is a retail and service center for a potato and lumber region in Maine and Canada. A gateway to the Allagash wilderness, Fort Kent is a supply point for canoeists, hunters, and anglers. A University of Maine campus is here.

Fort Keogh see under MILES CITY, Montana.

Fort Knox Army post in Hardin, Meade, and Bullitt counties, C Kentucky, 35 mi/56 km SSW of Louisville, best known as the site of the Treasury Department's Gold Depository, also known as the Gold Vault, constructed in 1936 adjacent to the post. The original Camp Knox, established in 1917, now includes the Armor Center and School. Fort Knox had a 1990 pop. of 21,495. RADCLIFF, just SW, is a service town for the area.

Fort Laramie town, pop. 243, Goshen Co., SE Wyoming, a trade center on US 26 and the NORTH PLATTE R., where it is joined by the Laramie R., in the high plains, 82 mi/130 km NE of Laramie. Three mi/5 km SW is the site of Fort Laramie, an 1834–49 fur post purchased and operated (1849–90) by the government as a major stopover for westbound migrants on the OREGON TRAIL and routes to California. The first Wyoming military post, it was also the site of numerous parleys with regional tribes.

Fort Lauderdale city, pop. 149,377, seat of Broward Co., SE Florida, on the New R. and the Atlantic Ocean, 23 mi/37 km N of Miami. It occupies the site of a Seminole War military post (1837) commanded by William Lauderdale, around which a civilian settlement evolved. Its growth into a major city was spurred by the Florida land boom of the 1920s and the influx of new residents after World War II. Fort Lauderdale is crossed by over 270 mi/435 km of natural and artificial waterways that account for 10% of its area, turning the city into a mass of small islands, and it is connected with L. Okeechobee by canal. It possesses numerous yacht basins and marinas, and is known for its wide sandy beaches, particularly its 5 mi/8 km–long public beach, long the favorite of collegians on spring break. Retirement homes fill its residential neighborhoods. The city's economy is largely dependent on tourism, but there is a recent concentration of financial, consulting, and corporate headquarters operations. It has electronic and aerospace industries and some manufacturing, including plastic and cement products, boats, and marine supplies. It is also a trade and distribution center for citrus fruits, vegetables, and dairy products. It is the seat of Fort Lauderdale College (1940), Broward Community College (1959), and Nova University (1964). The city has a large medical center and shares an international airport with the city of HOLLYWOOD. Port Everglades, just S, is an artificial deepwater port of entry that handles a large amount of commercial and passenger traffic.

Fort Leavenworth see under LEAVENWORTH, Kansas.

Fort Lee borough, pop. 31,997, Bergen Co., NE New Jersey, on the PALISADES of the Hudson R., connected to New York City by the GEORGE WASHINGTON BRIDGE. Settled c.1700, it was the site of a Revolutionary fort defending the Hudson and West Point and abandoned after the fall of FORT WASHINGTON on the opposite shore (1776). Fort Lee was an early-20th-century center of the motion picture industry; film is still processed here. Today it is a flourishing commercial hub, with American and international businesses occupying numerous office buildings. It also has many one-family homes, apartment buildings, and high-rise condominiums, and some light industry.

Fort Leonard Wood US army post, 71,000 ac/28,755 ha, in Pulaski Co., SC Missouri, 70 mi/112 km NE of Springfield, in the Ozark foothills. Established in 1940, it is a major training center and the headquarters of the Army Engineer School. It had a 1990 pop. of 15,863.

Fort Lewis unincorporated community, pop. 22,224, Pierce Co., WC Washington, 13 mi/21 km SSW of Tacoma and just SW of Lakewood. It is a residential suburb and service town for 200–sq mi/520–sq km Ft. Lewis, established (1917) as an infantry training center, the West Coast's largest army base. McChord Air Force Base is to the NE.

Fort Loudoun Dam and Lake see under LENOIR CITY, Tennessee.

Fort Macleod see under PORCUPINE HILLS, Alberta.

Fort Madison city, pop. 11,618, co-seat (with KEOKUK) of Lee Co., SE Iowa, on the Mississippi R., across from Niota, Illinois, 14 mi/23 km SW of Burlington. Headquarters of the Sheaffer Pen Company, it also produces paper, fertilizer, cement, paints, industrial brushes, and corrugated board and containers. There are railroad shops and petrochemical plants. The first fort W of the Mississippi R. stood here from 1808 to 1813, when Black Hawk destroyed it. The modern city dates from 1833; it soon became an important river port and commercial center. The first Iowa State Penitentiary was built here (1839), and the Santa Fe Railroad made the city a division point (1879). The Lee Co. Courthouse is the oldest such structure still in use W of the Mississippi.

Fort Malden see under AMHERSTBURG, Ontario.

Fort Massachusetts see under SHIP I., Mississippi.

Fort Matanzas see under SAINT AUGUSTINE, Florida.

Fort Maurepas see under OCEAN SPRINGS, Mississippi.

Fort McClellan see under ANNISTON, Alabama.

Fort McDowell see under MCDOWELL Mts., Arizona.

Fort McHenry National Monument in Baltimore, Maryland. On the Patapsco R. at the INNER HARBOR's entrance, it was built in the 1790s, and restored in 1933. On the night of Sept. 13–14, 1812, Baltimore attorney Francis Scott Key, detained on a British ship, watched as the British bombarded the fort preparatory to attacking the city. In the morning the fort's flag still flew; Key later commemorated the event in "The Star Spangled Banner."

Fort McKinley unincorporated village, pop. 9740, in Harrison township, Montgomery Co., SW Ohio, a residential suburb 6 mi/10 km NW of Dayton.

Fort McMurray city, pop. 34,706, NE Alberta, at the confluence of the Clearwater and Athabasca rivers, 53 mi/85 km W of the Saskatchewan border and 223 mi/359 km NNE of Edmonton. The Great Canadian Oil Sands (GCOS) plant here extracts oil from the Athabasca Tar Sands, providing the mainstay for the economy. The North West Company set up (1790) a fur trading post, Fort of the Forks, nearby.

Rebuilt and renamed in 1875, Ft. McMurray saw little growth until the 1920s, when fish plants and salt extraction developed. The modern town dates to 1964, with the construction of the GCOS plant. Keyano College is here.

Fort McPherson see under ATLANTA, Georgia.

Fort Meade officially, **Fort George G. Meade** military installation, 13,500 ac/5468 ha, in Anne Arundel Co., C Maryland. Established in 1917, this Army training camp extends SE of Maryland City (unincorporated, pop. 6813), 16 mi/26 km SSW of Baltimore. The base has a pop. of 12,509.

Fort Meigs site of a former fort in Fort Meigs State Park, on the Maumee R., NW Ohio, just W of Perrysburg and 8 mi/13 km SW of Toledo. General William Henry Harrison successfully defended the newly built fort against British attack in 1813. A granite shaft commemorates the fort, whose blockhouse, stockade, and cemetery remain here and are part of an historic restoration.

Fort Miami see under MAUMEE, Ohio.

Fort Mill town, pop. 4930, York Co., N South Carolina, 7 mi/11 km NE of Rock Hill, and 13 mi/21 km SSW of Charlotte, North Carolina. Just N of the Catawba R., it is a factory center and now corporate headquarters for the Springs textile company. In 1977 television evangelists Jim and Tammy Faye Bakker opened here the 2300-ac/932-ha Heritage USA, said to be the world's largest religious theme park, complete with an amphitheater, condominiums, and waterslides.

Fort Mims historic site in Baldwin Co., SW Alabama, on L. Tensaw, near the junction of the Alabama and Tombigbee rivers, 35 mi/56 km NNE of Mobile. Around the home of settler Samuel Mims, a stockade took in soldiers and refugees from native attacks during the Creek War (1813–14). On Aug. 30, 1813, a Creek band attacked and killed hundreds, burning the fort. In response, Andrew Jackson undertook the campaign that led to the treaty of HORSESHOE BEND.

Fort Mitchell city, pop. 7438, Kenton Co., N Kentucky, a largely residential suburb just inside I-275, 5 mi/8 km SSW of downtown Cincinnati, Ohio, and just SSW of Covington.

Fort Monmouth see under EATONTOWN, New Jersey.

Fort Monroe military installation in HAMPTON, SE Virginia, at Old Point Comfort, on the N side of HAMPTON ROADS, built 1819–34 on the site of earlier (1609) English fortifications. The fort, the only one in the US surrounded by a moat, was held by Union forces throughout the Civil War, and was the prison (1865–67) of Jefferson Davis. Before 1946, it housed a coastal artillery school; in the late 1960s it was the headquarters of the Continental Army Command. Old Point Comfort was a popular 19th-century resort.

Fort Morgan city, pop. 9068, seat of Morgan Co., NE Colorado, on a plateau overlooking the South Platte R., 70 mi/113 km NE of Denver. A former military outpost (1864) on the Overland Trail, the community developed as an agricultural shipping point. It is a trade center, refines beet sugar, cans vegetables, and manufactures tools, auto parts, pipe, and concrete products. Morgan Community College is here. Pawnee National Grassland is 12 mi/19 km N.

Fort Moultrie see under SULLIVAN'S I., South Carolina.

Fort Myer military installation in Arlington Co., NE Virginia, adjacent (W) to Arlington National Cemetery. It houses communications and other commands.

Fort Myers city, pop. 45,206, seat of Lee Co., SW Florida, on the Caloosahatchee R., 65 mi/105 km SE of Sarasota and 15 mi/24 km from the Gulf of Mexico. The city grew around a fort built c.1841 during the Seminole War, which Union forces held during the Civil War. Thomas A. Edison had his longtime (1886–1931) winter home and laboratory here; it is now open to the public. Fort Myers grew rapidly as a resort during the 1920s. Still a popular tourist city, it also ships local citrus, flowers (mainly gladioli), vegetables, and seafood; manufactures electronic equipment and cigars; and processes lumber. It is known for its lush flora, in particular many varieties of palm tree. Edison Community College (1961) is here. In a pattern common in the area, the city is 32% black, while its satellites CAPE CORAL, North Fort Myers (unincorporated, pop. 30,027), **Fort Myers Beach** (unincorporated, pop. 9284), and **Fort Myers Shores** (unincorporated, pop. 5460) are almost exclusively white.

Fort Nassau **1.** see under GLOUCESTER CITY, New Jersey. **2.** see under ALBANY, New York.

Fort Necessity see under UNIONTOWN, Pennsylvania.

Fort Niagara see under NIAGARA R.

Fort Nonsense see under MORRISTOWN, New Jersey.

Fort Norman see under NORMAN WELLS, Northwest Territories.

Fort Orange see under ALBANY, New York.

Fort Ord military reservation in Monterey Co., WC California, 5 mi/8 km E of MONTEREY. Established in 1917, it became headquarters for the 7th Infantry Division, and was a major staging area in World War II. It is now a 28,000-ac/11,500-ha training center. SEASIDE (SW) and MARINA (N) are adjoining service communities.

Fort Payne city, pop. 11,838, seat of De Kalb Co., NE Alabama, on a branch of the Coosa R., 34 mi/54 km NE of Gadsden. It developed during a mining boom in the 1880s, and is now a center for farming, lumbering, light industry, and tourism. The city was named for John Payne, a government agent involved in the forced relocation westward of the Cherokees, who had established nearby Will's Town (or Willston), where Sequoyah lived and developed a Cherokee form of writing.

Fort Peck Dam in Valley Co., NE Montana, 17 mi/27 km SE of Glasgow. Constructed on the Missouri R. to provide hydroelectric power, flood control, irrigation, and better navigation, this Public Works Administration project was completed by 1940. One of the largest hydraulic earth-filled dams in the world, it is 21,432 ft/6537 m long and 249 ft/76 m high. The dam forms 90 mi/140 km–long **Fort Peck Lake,** the largest Montana reservoir and the second-largest in the US. The town of **Fort Peck,** pop. 325, was built by the Federal government in the early 1930s to house dam workers. Just NE of the dam is the **Fort Peck Indian Reservation,** pop. 10,595, home to the Assiniboine tribe.

Fort Peck Indian Reservation 3289 sq mi/8519 sq km, pop. 10,595 (55% Indian), in extreme NE Montana, N of the Missouri R. and NE of the Fort Peck Dam. Poplar (city, pop. 881, Roosevelt Co.) is its headquarters; WOLF POINT is in the S. Established in 1888, it is home to Yanktonai Sioux and Assiniboine groups.

Fort Phil Kearny see under BOZEMAN TRAIL, Wyoming.

Fort Pickens see under PENSACOLA, Florida.

Fort Pierce city, pop. 36,830, seat of St. Lucie Co., EC Florida, on the INDIAN R. at Fort Pierce Inlet, 100 mi/160 km SE of Orlando. It grew around fortifications built in 1838 as protection against the Seminoles. A Federally maintained port and excellent rail facilities make it a distribution center for local beef, citrus, tomatoes, and vegetables. The city is also active in commercial fishing, fertilizer manufacture, lumber production, and fruit canning. It is connected by bridges to oceanfront beaches and parks, and tourism is also an important industry. Indian River Community College (1960) is here. The St. Lucie nuclear power plant (1976) is on Hutchinsons I., the barrier island, 9 mi/14 km SSE of the city.

Fort Pillow historic site in Lauderdale Co., extreme W Tennessee, 40 mi/64 km NNE of Memphis, on the Mississippi R. near the mouth of the Hatchie R. In April 1864, Nathan Forrest's Confederate troops attacked this fort (built 1861), which was defended by Tennessee Unionists and black troops. A Federal investigation revealed that, after surrender, many of the blacks, including wounded men, had been slaughtered. "Remember Fort Pillow!" became a rallying cry for black soldiers going into battle. The incident is commemorated in 1650-ac/667-ha Fort Pillow State Park.

Fort Polk military training center in SW Louisiana, 30 mi/48 km SW of Alexandria and 5 mi/8 km SE of Leesville. Established in 1941 as Camp Polk, it covers some 148,000 ac/60,000 ha, overlapping with part of the KISATCHIE NATIONAL FOREST. Chosen for its topography and climate, it was a major infantry training base during the Vietnam War.

Fort Prince of Wales see under CHURCHILL, Manitoba.

Fort Pulaski see under SAVANNAH, Georgia.

Fort Raleigh see under ROANOKE I., North Carolina.

Fort Randall historic fort in Charles Mix Co., SE South Dakota, on the Missouri R., just S of Pickstown and N of the Nebraska border. Established in 1856 to protect settlers against hostile Sioux, the fort served as a prison for Sitting Bull in 1882, and was abandoned a decade later. Vandalized in the years after its closing, it now stands in protected ruins just below the Fort Randall Dam.

Fort Reno see under BOZEMAN TRAIL, Wyoming.

Fort Riley military reservation, 101,000 ac/40,905 ha, in Riley and Geary counties, on the Kansas R., NE Kansas, just N of Junction City. It was established (1852) on the SANTA FE TRAIL to protect westward-bound pioneers from hostile Indians, and became a cavalry post in 1855. When the Kansas Pacific Railroad was built after the Civil War, the fort was a command center for operations against Indian uprisings. It is now the headquarters of the First Infantry Division. A cavalry museum is located here. Fort Riley North (unincorporated) had a 1990 pop. of 12,848.

Fort Robinson **1.** see under CRAWFORD, Nebraska. **2.** see under KINGSPORT, Tennessee.

Fort Rock volcanic remnant (4695 ft/1431 m high), in SC Oregon, creating a crescent-shaped "fortress" with walls rising 325 ft/99 m above the surrounding Harney Desert, near the hamlet of Fort Rock, 50 mi/80 km SSE of Bend. Nearby is Fort Rock Cave, where artifacts over 13,000 years old have been found. Just NW is Hole-in-the-Ground, a depression of volcanic origin, almost 1 mi/1.5 km wide and 425 ft/130 m deep.

Fort Ross historic site in SONOMA Co., NW California, 65 mi/105 km NW of San Francisco and 6 mi/10 km NW of the mouth of the Russian R., on the Pacific coast. An 1812 settlement of the Russian-American Fur Company, and the chief California base of RUSSIAN AMERICA, it functioned as a trade and shipbuilding center until 1841, when the property was sold to Johan Sutter, the founder of New Helvetia (see SACRAMENTO). Today Fort Ross (whose name is an old poetic form of "Russia") is a State Historical Park.

Fort Rucker military training installation in Coffee and Dale counties, SE Alabama, 8 mi/13 km NE of ENTERPRISE. The Army Aviation Training Center and School here dates to the late 1940s. DOTHAN (SE) and OZARK (NE) have also benefited economically from the base, which had a 1990 pop. of 7593.

Fort Saint James village, pop. 2058, Bulkley-Nechako Regional District, NC British Columbia, on the SE shore of Stuart L., at the confluence of the Stuart and Necoslie rivers, 70 mi/113 km NW of Prince George. Established (1806) as a NORTH WEST COMPANY trading post, it was the capital of NEW CALEDONIA from 1821 to 1857. The oldest white community in British Columbia, it is now a rail stop in a lumbering, mining, and livestock raising area. A Carrier Indian reserve is nearby, and Fort St. James National Historic Park is here.

Fort Saint John city, pop. 14,156, Peace River Regional District, NE British Columbia, near the Alberta border, on the ALASKA HIGHWAY, 180 mi/290 km NNE of Prince George and 41 mi/65 km NW of Dawson Creek. Established (1805) as a NORTH WEST COMPANY fort, it was destroyed (1823) by Indians, rebuilt (1860), and moved several times. The community expanded with the completion (1942) of the highway; the discovery (1955) of oil and gas nearby at Taylor (10 mi/16 km SE), now a refining center, boosted the economy. Other local industries include lumbering and coalmining.

Fort Sam Houston military installation in EC San Antonio, Texas, just E of Brackenridge Park and 2 mi/3 km NE of Downtown. It was formally established in 1890, although parts of its 3300 ac/1340 ha had been in use since the 1870s. In 1898, the Rough Riders trained at "Fort Sam" under Teddy Roosevelt for the Spanish-American War. When Lt. Benjamin Foulois flew a Wright biplane here in 1910, he initiated US military aviation. The fort, known for its heavily constructed Quadrangle (1879), is now home to Brooke Army Medical Center and to the Institute for Surgical Research, famous as the "Burn Center." It is also headquarters for the Fifth Army, and controls training at 28,000-ac/11,275-ha Camp Bullis, 14 mi/23 km to the NW, outside San Antonio's limits. Bullis, in addition to its governmental activities, is a grazing area and wildlife refuge.

Fort Saskatchewan city, pop. 12,078, C Alberta, on the North Saskatchewan R., 10 mi/16 km NE of Edmonton. A center of the petrochemical industry, it has a fertilizer plant and the Sheritt Mint, which produces coins and medallions. French-Canadian farmers came here in 1872, establishing one of Alberta's oldest settlements. The North West Mounted Police set up Sturgeon Creek Post in 1875, and the Canadian National Railway arrived in 1905. Sheritt Gordon Mines built a nickel refinery here in 1952.

Fort Scott city, pop. 8362, seat of Bourbon Co., SE Kansas, 30 mi/48 km N of Pittsburg. It grew up around a military post established in 1842, abandoned, and then reestablished during the Civil War. Fort Scott National Historic Site is here. Some 5 mi/8 km W of the Missouri border, the city was a center of conflict between pro- and antislavery factions in the 1850s. Today nearby coal mines and quarries are important to the city's economy. It is the seat of Fort Scott Community College (1919).

Fort Sill military reservation, 95,000 ac/38,475 ha, in COMANCHE Co., SW Oklahoma, 4 mi/6 km N of Lawton. It is the headquarters and training center of the US Army Field

Artillery. The fort was established as a cavalry base in 1869 by Philip Sheridan. Created to control local tribes and to maintain order in the area, it formed the base for many campaigns against the Indians, and was the scene of the surrender of the Comanche and Kiowa in the mid 1870s. Such tribes as the Wichita, Kiowa, and Comanche were housed here and were taught white farming techniques. The Apache leader Geronimo, who was imprisoned here, is buried on the reservation. By the turn of the 20th century, the facility was in decline, but it gained new prominence when the field artillery school was established in 1911. The reservation had a 1990 pop. of 12,107.

Fort Sisseton historic military outpost in Marshall Co., NE South Dakota, 20 mi/32 km W of the city of Sisseton. Established in 1864, it is now the site of Fort Sisseton State Park. An annual Indian festival is held here.

Fort Smith **1.** city, pop. 72,798, co-seat (with Greenwood) of Sebastian Co., W Arkansas, on the Arkansas R., at the mouth of the Poteau R., just E of the Oklahoma line. The state's second-largest city, it has part of its METROPOLITAN AREA (pop. 175,911) in Oklahoma. It served as an Army post from 1817 to 1871. Industry was sustained by the arrival of the railroad in 1876 and by the discovery of coal and natural gas in nearby fields in 1900. In 1969 the Federal Arkansas R. navigation project enabled barges to reach the city. In a rich agricultural and timbering region, the city is home to hundreds of diverse industries. Westark Community College (1928) is here. FORT CHAFFEE is just SE. **2.** town, pop. 2480, Fort Smith Region, S Northwest Territories, on the SLAVE R. and the Alberta border, midway between L. Athabasca (SE) and Great Slave L. (NW), 185 mi/300 km SSE of Yellowknife. Settled in 1874 as a HUDSON'S BAY COMPANY trading post, at a PORTAGE hub, it was the territorial administrative center 1911–67. Now a regional government center, the town is also headquarters for nearby (SW) WOOD BUFFALO NATIONAL PARK; tourism and trapping are important.

Fort Snelling historic site and former military post, in Hennepin Co., EC Minnesota, immediately S of the Twin Cities, at the confluence of the Mississippi and Minnesota rivers. When built by Josiah Snelling c.1819, the fort (originally Fort St. Anthony) was farther NW than any other US army post; it was the only one in Minnesota before mid-century. Explorers, travelers, and settlers gathered here, the latter establishing the state's first school and forming the nucleus of the city of St. Paul. The slave Dred Scott lived here in 1836–38. The administrative center of the Territory of Minnesota, Fort Snelling later declined in importance, serving as a supply depot and Civil War training camp. Today, the fort has been restored, and is a State Historic Site.

Fort Stanwix at ROME, C New York. Originally a French trading post on the route from the Hudson R. to L. Ontario, the site was fortified by the British from 1725. Fort Stanwix was built during the French and Indian War (1756) and rebuilt by British Gen. John Stanwix (1758). It fell into disrepair, but was restored and garrisoned by Americans early in the Revolution, and called Fort Schuyler. During the Saratoga Campaign (1777), it withstood a three-week siege by British and Tory forces. Treaties with the Iroquois were signed here in 1768 and 1784. It has been a National Monument since 1935.

Fort Stewart US Army reservation, an infantry facility in Bryan, Evans, Liberty, Long, and Tattnall counties, SE Georgia, 10 mi/16 km W of Savannah.

Fort Story see under VIRGINIA BEACH, Virginia.

Fort Sumter historic brick fortification, now a National Monument, on a small sandbar at the entrance to the harbor of CHARLESTON, South Carolina, 3.5 mi/5.6 km SE of Charleston's Battery and 0.5 mi/1 km W of Fort Moultrie, which is on SULLIVAN'S I. Constructed 1829–60, it was the scene of the Civil War's first engagement (April 12–13, 1861), when it was besieged and captured by Confederate forces. Despite Union blockade and bombardment, it was not returned to Federal control until Feb. 17, 1865.

Fort Thomas city, pop. 16,032, Campbell Co., N Kentucky, along the Ohio R., 5 mi/8 km SE of Cincinnati, Ohio. This residential suburb, founded in 1867 as Highlands, was renamed (1914) in honor of George Thomas, a Union commander. It has various light industries. The Fort Thomas military reservation was established in 1887.

Fort Ticonderoga near TICONDEROGA, at the S end of L. Champlain, in E New York. Originally called Fort Carillon, it was built by the French (1755) to control traffic between Canada and the American colonies. It was successfully defended against British attack by French forces under Montcalm in 1758, but a year later fell to Jeffrey Amherst, who rebuilt and renamed it. In 1775 it was taken in a surprise attack by Ethan Allen and his Green Mountain Boys. The following year an American fleet was assembled here by Benedict Arnold. It again fell to the British in 1777, but was abandoned later that year. Briefly reoccupied in 1780, but never again garrisoned, it was restored and became a museum in 1909.

Fort Tilden see under the ROCKAWAYS, New York.

Fort Totten **1.** see under BAYSIDE, New York. **2.** see under DEVILS LAKE, North Dakota.

Fort Tryon Revolutionary fortification, built 1776 and captured by Hessian soldiers that fall, in NW Manhattan, New York City. Its site was developed in the 1930s as Fort Tryon Park (62 ac/25 ha), and in it was constructed (1934–38) the Cloisters, a branch of the Metropolitan Museum of Art comprising four complete and one partial medieval French and Spanish cloisters, along with numerous art works. Fort Tryon Park marks the transition from Washington Heights (S) to Inwood (N).

Fortune Bay Atlantic Ocean inlet, some 80 mi/130 km NE–SW and 34 mi/55 km wide at its entrance, in S Newfoundland. It is largely enclosed by the BURIN PENINSULA (SE). SAINT-PIERRE ET MIQUELON lies just SW. An historic OUTPORT fishing area with canneries onshore, it is ringed with small communities, of which the towns of Grand Bank (pop. 3528) and **Fortune** (pop. 2177), near its mouth (S) on the peninsula, are the largest.

Fort Union **1.** National Monument in NE New Mexico, 20 mi/32 km NNE of LAS VEGAS and 6 mi/10 km N of the point where the main (Mountain) division of the SANTA FE TRAIL met with the shorter Cimarron Cutoff (from the NE), near modern Watrous. Established in 1851 in grasslands just E of the Sangre de Cristo Mts., the fort protected the trail as headquarters for the Ninth Military Dept., supplying some 50 forts in the region, until decommissioned in 1891, after the Santa Fe Railroad had ended the trail's usefulness. **2.** former trading post in Williams Co., NW North Dakota, on the Missouri R., 17 mi/27 km SW of Williston and just E of the Montana line. The largest such post on the Upper Missouri, it was built in 1828 by John Jacob Astor's American Fur Company. The fort was sold to the US Army in 1867 and dismantled to provide building materials for Fort Buford, constructed in a nearby spot deemed more useful in controlling the Indians. Fort Union, reconstructed on its foundations, is a National Historic Site.

Fort Valley city, pop. 8198, seat of Peach Co., C Georgia, 20 mi/32 km SSW of Macon. Ft. Valley State College (1895) is in this peach and camellia growing center, which also produces truck bodies and chemicals.

Fort Vancouver see under VANCOUVER, Washington.

Fort Walsh National Historic Park in the CYPRESS HILLS, SW Saskatchewan, near the Alberta border, 246 mi/396 km SW of Regina. The fort was constructed (1875) as the first North West Mounted Police post, in response to the Cypress Hills massacre, in which a number of Assiniboine were slaughtered by US and Canadian wolf hunters. The post (1878–92) played a key part in settling the Canadian West, helped control Sitting Bull's Sioux followers, and was later used as a breeding ranch for police horses. Today, a replica can be seen on its original site. Farwell's Trading Post, which re-creates the "Wild West" of pre–Mounted Police days, is here.

Fort Walton Beach city, pop. 21,471, Okaloosa Co., in the PANHANDLE of NW Florida, on the Gulf of Mexico just off Choctawhatchee Bay, 40 mi/64 km E of Pensacola. In the 1830s it was a Seminole War fort, later a fishing village, and evolved into a yachting center in the 1920s. A year-round resort, it has white-sand beaches, dunes, and sport fishing. The city has grown rapidly since 1941, when Eglin Air Force Base was expanded. Manufactures include electronic equipment, lumber, concrete, and boats. Indian Temple Mound and Museum, memorializing the area's pre-Columbian cultures, is here.

Fort Washington **1.** unincorporated residential community, pop. 24,032, Prince George's Co., SC Maryland, 12 mi/19 km SSE of Washington, D.C., and just E of the Potomac R. In the area of Warburton Manor (1661) and a 19th-century fort built on the river to protect the capital, it is an area of rapidly developing housing estates, among them some of Washington's most affluent black suburbs. **2.** former fortification, upper Manhattan, New York City. It was held by George Washington's troops following the battle of HARLEM HEIGHTS, until surrounded and captured by the British in Nov. 1776. The area around the site, at about 183rd St. and Fort Washington Ave., retains the name. Riverside Park above 158th St. is called Fort Washington Park, and the neighborhood is called WASHINGTON HEIGHTS. **3.** unincorporated village, pop. 3699, in Upper Dublin township, Montgomery Co., SE Pennsylvania, a suburb of Philadelphia 13 mi/21 km N of the city. Situated here are a Revolutionary War battlefield and Hope Lodge, a 1740s Georgian mansion used as a Revolutionary field headquarters. Situated on the Pennsylvania Turnpike and Route 309, Fort Washington contains commercial strips and an industrial park.

Fort Wayne **1.** city, pop. 173,072, seat of Allen Co., NE Indiana, at the point where the St. Joseph and St. Mary's rivers meet to form the Maumee R., 100 mi/160 km NE of Indianapolis. It occupies the site of the Miami Indians' chief village, where the French established a fur trading post (c.1680) and fort (1697). Captured by the British (1760) and held by Indians during Pontiac's Rebellion (1763), it became an American fort under Anthony Wayne (1794). The settlement's growth and prosperity date from the mid 1800s, when canals and the railroad arrived. Today it is the state's second-largest city, a commercial, financial, medical, and railroad hub. Its industries produce such products as gasoline pumps, electrical equipment, electronic and auto parts (one plant gave a name in the 1940s to the Fort Wayne, now Detroit, Pistons basketball team), cranes and dredges, and processed foods. Fort Wayne is the seat of Indiana Institute of Technology (1930), St. Francis College (1890), and several other institutions of higher education. The grave of Johnny Appleseed is in a city park. **2.** former military installation in Detroit, Michigan, on high ground along the Detroit R., SW of Downtown, in the DELRAY section. Completed in 1851, it never saw action. The 83-ac/34-ha complex is today a museum with barracks and tunnels, and home to the National Tuskegee Airmen Museum, which celebrates the World War II black air unit.

Fort Wellington see under PRESCOTT, Ontario.

Fort Western see under AUGUSTA, Maine.

Fort Whoop-up historic trading post in S Alberta, near LETHBRIDGE. The most important of a number of illegal liquor forts in S Alberta and Saskatchewan during the early 1870s, it was founded (1869) by individuals from Fort Benton, Montana, who traded whiskey to local tribes for buffalo skins and other furs. The North West Mounted Police, stationed at nearby Ft. Macleod, arrived here in 1874 but found the fort deserted. The reconstructed post now stands in Indian Battle Park in LETHBRIDGE.

Fort William see under THUNDER BAY, Ontario.

Fort William Henry Colonial outpost, at the S end of L. GEORGE, in NE New York. Built by the British during the French and Indian Wars (1756), it protected the portage between the lake and the Hudson R. Successfully defended against French attack early in 1757, it fell to Montcalm later that year. Much of the garrison was massacred or carried into captivity by Indians whom Montcalm had failed to control. Thereafter, the fort was razed by the French. It was rebuilt in 1953 and is now a museum in the village of Lake George.

Fort Worth city, pop. 447,619, seat of Tarrant Co., NE Texas, at the confluence of the Clear and West forks of the Trinity R., 30 mi/48 km W of Dallas. The Grand Prairie lies to the E, higher rolling plains to the W. Camp Worth, established here in 1849, was briefly important. In the late 1860s cattle drives on the CHISHOLM TRAIL forded the Trinity here, and a "Wild West" atmosphere prevailed in Hell's Half Acre, now at the heart of Downtown. The arrival of the Texas & Pacific Railroad in 1876 led to the creation of Fort Worth's 250-ac/100-ha stockyards, and meatpacking became a major industry. Oilfields opened N and W around World War I made the city an industry center. It boomed again in the 1940s and 1950s, as defense industries were established. Today it is a high-tech aerospace, defense, and consumer products manufacturer, building computers, aircraft, and helicopters. It also makes paper currency and has a variety of other manufactures. It is a pipeline hub and headquarters to many oil industry (as well as other business) firms, and an important grain storage center. It draws substantial trade to the 14-block Tarrant Co. Convention Center. Through Fort Worth's history, wealthy individuals and corporations have established institutions or funded municipal improvements; the Amon Carter Museum of Western Art is well known, as is the Kimbell Museum of Art. Tandy, the electronics manufacturer, owns the city's subway, and the Bass family has provided a downtown security force. The stockyards, N of Downtown, are a major tourist attraction, as are the downtown Water Gardens and the museums. Carswell Air Force Base lies 6 mi/10 km W of Downtown, within the city, and Meacham Field, an older airport 5 mi/8 km NW of Downtown, is under redevelopment. Fort Worth's growth has enveloped a number of small residential cities, including WHITE SETTLEMENT on the W; River Oaks (pop. 6580) on the WNW; Sansom Park (pop. 3928), Lake Worth (pop. 4591), and Saginaw (pop. 8551) on the NW; Blue Mound (pop. 2133) on the N; and FOREST HILL and Everman (pop. 5672) on the SE. The city is home to Texas Christian University (1873), Texas Wesleyan College (1891), and several other institutions, and is noted as a theater and music center.

Fort Yates city, pop. 183, Sioux Co., S North Dakota, almost surrounded by L. OAHE (E, on the Missouri R.), and 50 mi/80 km S of Bismarck. The fort, built in 1877, was abandoned in 1895 for Fort Lincoln (Bismarck). Fort Yates is headquarters for the STANDING ROCK INDIAN RESERVATION; Standing Rock College (1971) is here. Sitting Bull was buried here in 1890; his body was moved to MOBRIDGE, South Dakota, in 1953.

Forty-ninth Parallel boundary between Canada and the United States from LAKE OF THE WOODS W to the Pacific, as determined by 1818 and 1846 agreements. Its E extreme is a line S from Minnesota's NORTHWEST ANGLE to 49° N. The border, actually a series of lines between astronomically determined points, is the line of origin for the series of surveyors' BASE LINES employed in settling Canada's Prairie Provinces. It reaches the Pacific at DELTA, British Columbia, where the Point Roberts Peninsula, unconnected to the US mainland, is part of the state of Washington. It is in places marked by open ditches, in places by cuts through stands of timber. Most Canadians actually live S of the 49th Parallel (in Ontario, Québec, and the Maritimes).

Fort York see under EXHIBITION PARK, Toronto, Ontario.

Forum, the **1.** see under INGLEWOOD, California. **2.** arena in MONTRÉAL, Québec, on the SW edge of Downtown, on the rue Ste.-Catherine and Ave. Atwater, home since 1924 to the Canadiens (hockey). Renovated in 1968, it seats 16,500 for hockey, and houses various other events.

Foster town, pop. 4316, Providence Co., NW Rhode Island, 16 mi/26 km W of Providence, along the Connecticut line, on the Moosup and Ponagansett rivers. This rural town includes Jerimoth Hill (812 ft/248 m), the highest point in the state. Timber, granite, and gravel are important resources. Foster Center, Moosup Valley, and Vernon are included villages.

Foster City city, pop. 28,176, San Mateo Co., NC California, on San Francisco Bay at the W end of the San Mateo Bridge and adjacent (E) to San Mateo. A waterfront residential community, it is largely on Brewer I.

Fostoria city, pop. 14,979, Seneca, Hancock, and Wood counties, NW Ohio, 35 mi/56 km S of Toledo. It is a trade and shipping center for the surrounding livestock and farming area. Soybean processing, meatpacking, and grain milling are leading industries. Local manufactures include lighting fixtures, automobile and electrical equipment, steel wire, machine tools, and cement blocks.

Fountain city, pop. 9984, El Paso Co., EC Colorado, on Fountain Creek, 11 mi/18 km SE of Colorado Springs. Surrounded by irrigated farms and ranches, it ships sugar beets, alfalfa, and livestock, and manufactures computer parts.

Fountain City agricultural town, pop. 766, Wayne Co., E Indiana, 10 mi/16 km N of Richmond. Called Newport at first, it was settled by Quakers in the 1820s. They later played a prominent role in the UNDERGROUND RAILROAD. A local resident, Levi Coffin, personally aided over 2000 escaping slaves; his house was so vital a link on the "railroad" that it has been called its "Grand Central Station." Indiana's highest point (1257 ft/383 m) is 2.5 mi/4 km NE, near Bethel.

Fountain Hills town, pop. 10,030, Maricopa Co., SC Arizona, 20 mi/32 km NE of Phoenix, in the MCDOWELL Mts., on the edge of the Fort McDowell (NE) and Salt R. (S) Indian reservations. This residential and resort community is noted for a 560-ft/171-m fountain, said to be the world's tallest, operated intermittently from a local lake.

Fountain of Youth legendary spring for which Juan Ponce de Léon was said to be looking when he discovered Florida on April 2, 1513. Having been told the previous year by Carib Indians in Borinquén (Puerto Rico) that the fountain, and an island rich with gold, lay somewhere NW of "Bimini" (in the Bahamas), he made landfall at the site of the later SAINT AUGUSTINE, and because it was the Feast of Flowers (Easter season) named the "island" Florida. Fountain of Youth Park, in St. Augustine, with a spring in a grotto and a variety of other historical attractions, capitalizes on the legend.

Fountain Square central point of downtown Cincinnati, Ohio. The highest point in the city, it serves as Cincinnati's focal point. Major civic buildings and department stores are nearby.

Fountain Valley city, pop. 53,691, Orange Co., SW California, 28 mi/45 km SE of Los Angeles. While primarily residential, it has laboratory and medical equipment industries and makes tools, aerospace fittings, and various other products. A Naval Reserve helicopter facility is in the city.

Four Corners **1.** locality, unique in the US, where four states—Colorado (NE), New Mexico (SE), Utah (NW), and Arizona (SW)—come together. It is surrounded on three sides by the NAVAJO INDIAN RESERVATION, and in Colorado by the Ute Mt. reservation. A monument in the ground at the meeting point is much visited. The San Juan R. flows just NE, and CORTEZ, Colorado, is 33 mi/53 km NE. FARMINGTON, New Mexico, 49 mi/79 mi ESE, is the site of the huge Four Corners coal-fueled power plant. SHIPROCK, New Mexico, is 35 mi/56 km SE. The Four Corners area is sacred to the Navajo, and is also a uranium mining district. **2.** unincorporated community, pop. 12,156, Marion Co., NW Oregon, a residential suburb immediately E of Salem.

Four Lakes group of lakes (MENDOTA, MONONA, WAUBESA, and KEGONSA) in Dane Co., SC Wisconsin, connected by the Yahara R. Madison is partially situated on an isthmus between lakes Mendota and Monona.

Fourteenth Street thoroughfare in NW Washington, D.C., running N from the Potomac R., passing just E of the White House, just W of SHAW, through COLUMBIA HEIGHTS, and through the Northwest to near the Maryland line. Heavily impacted by 1968 riots, it has not fully recovered, and remains in places depressed and severely affected by crime.

Fourth Ward one of the original (1839–40) quadrants of Houston, Texas, extending SW from Downtown. Predominantly black since the 1880s, it has now been occupied in its E half by office buildings, as the city's central business district has expanded. It was the black economic center of the city until the 1930s, after which it was succeeded by the THIRD WARD.

Foxborough also, **Foxboro** town, pop. 14,637, Norfolk Co., E Massachusetts, 12 mi/19 km W of Brockton and 23 mi/37 km SW of Boston. Foxborough has been a manufacturing center since a foundry was established in the 1780s, and is now a growing suburb on Interstate 95. Foxborough Stadium, home of the New England Patriots (football), is here; it is also known as Shaeffer Stadium.

Foxe Basin roughly circular extension of the Atlantic Ocean, up to 300 mi/500 km across, in the E Northwest Territories, between BAFFIN I. (E and N), the Melville Peninsula (W), and Southampton and other islands (S, separating it from HUDSON BAY). Named for Luke Fox(e), British navigator who explored it in 1631, it is a shallow depression on the CANADIAN SHIELD; of its several islands, Prince Charles is the largest. In the NW it is connected with the Gulf of Boothia by narrow Fury and Hecla Strait. The S end is connected with the Hudson Strait (SE) and Hudson Bay (S) by 200 mi/320 km–long Foxe Channel. The basin is usually choked with ice, and is not part of the NORTHWEST PASSAGE.

Foxhall see under SPRING VALLEY, Washington, D.C.

Fox Islands group in the E ALEUTIAN Is., between the Bering Sea (N) and the N Pacific Ocean, in SW Alaska. Some 280 mi/450 km E–W, they are flanked by the ALASKA PENINSULA (E) and Samalga Pass, which separates them from the Is. of the Four Mountains (W). The largest islands in the group are Unimak, Umnak, and UNALASKA, site of the largest settlements. Windy and fogbound, they are the site of several military bases established during World War II. Fishing, canning, sheep ranching, and fox farming are the chief occupations of the Aleut pop.

Fox Islands Thorofare see under VINALHAVEN ISLAND, Maine.

Fox Point village, pop. 7238, Milwaukee Co., SE Wisconsin, on L. Michigan, 7 mi/11 km N of Milwaukee. Settled by the Dutch c.1846, it is now primarily a residential suburb.

Fox River **1.** 185 mi/298 km long, in SE Wisconsin and N Illinois. Rising in Waukesha Co., Wisconsin, it flows generally SSW past Waukesha and Burlington. Entering Illinois, it continues SSW, past Elgin and Aurora, to join the Illinois R. at Ottawa. It connects and drains the Chain-O-Lakes in Lake and McHenry counties, N Illinois, which include L. Marie, Grass L., Fox L., and Pistakee L. **2.** 175 mi/282 km long, in Wisconsin. It rises in the lakes region of SC Wisconsin and flows SW past PORTAGE, where a canal connects it to the Wisconsin R. Leaving Portage, the Fox flows NE to Oshkosh, where it enters L. Winnebago. This section is known as the **Lower Fox** R. It exits the lake at Neenah and Menasha and continues NE past Appleton, Kaukana, and De Pere to Green Bay, an arm of L. Michigan, which it enters at the city of Green Bay. Rapids in the **Upper Fox** R., above L. Winnebago, produce hydroelectricity for paper mills and factories. The Fox's chief tributary is the Wolf R. Early explorers established forts along the river, and missions and trading posts dotted its valley. The discovery of the upper Mississippi R. by Jacques Marquette and Louis Jolliet in 1673 was accomplished by way of Green Bay and the Fox and Wisconsin rivers and their portage, which provided an all-water route from the Great Lakes to the Mississippi.

Foxwoods see under LEDYARD, Connecticut.

Framingham town, pop. 64,994, Middlesex Co., E Massachusetts, along the Massachusetts Turnpike and the Sudbury R., 21 mi/34 km SW of Boston. Framingham has manufactured textiles and carpets since the early 19th century; paper products have been an economic mainstay, and a General Motors plant was here until the 1980s. A commercial center, the town is the site of Shopper's World, New England's first planned suburban shopping complex; Framingham State College (1859); and the state women's prison. Long the most populous town in Massachusetts, Framingham is both a residential suburb and a center of the kind of high-tech industry associated with ROUTE 128, which runs 10 mi/16 km E of its center.

Francis, Lake large recreational reservoir in NE New Hampshire, created by a dam built in 1937. It lies S of the four CONNECTICUT LAKES at an altitude of 1380 ft/421 m, close to the village of Pittsburg. The Connecticut R. flows W from L. Francis to form the New Hampshire/Vermont border.

Francis E. Warren Air Force Base see under CHEYENNE, Wyoming.

Francis Marion National Forest 250,000 ac/101,250 ha, in SE South Carolina, NE of Charleston. It consists of coastal flatlands, with blackwater swamps, a mixture of pine, oak, and cypress, and CAROLINA BAYS. The Cape Romain National Wildlife Refuge adjoins to the SE, along the coast, and the Santee R. runs along the forest's N on its way to the ocean. Francis Marion (1732?–95), the Revolutionary guerrilla leader called the "Swamp Fox," was born near GEORGETOWN (just NE), and at times hid his forces in the area.

Franconia **1.** resort town, pop. 825, Grafton Co., N New Hampshire. Franconia is on the headwaters of the Gale R., 6 mi/10 km SE of Littleton. Robert Frost Place, where the poet lived 1915–20, is here. SE of the town center is FRANCONIA NOTCH. **2.** unincorporated community, pop. 19,882, Fairfax Co., NE Virginia, just SW of Alexandria and outside the BELTWAY. It is largely residential.

Franconia Notch glacial valley in the White Mts. of New Hampshire, flanked W by Cannon Mt. and the Kinsman Range and E by the **Franconia Mts.,** which include Mt. Garfield (4488 ft/1369 m); Mt. LAFAYETTE (5249 ft/1601 m), highest in the range; Mt. Lincoln (5108 ft/1558 m); and Mt. Liberty (4460 ft/1360 m). From Franconia through the town of Lincoln, this mountain pass through which the Pemigewasset R. flows is 8 mi/13 km long. Franconia Notch State Park (6000 ac/2430 ha), surrounded by the White Mountain National Forest, extends from the Flume in the S to Echo Lake in the N, and contains many well-known natural features, including New Hampshire's symbol, the Old Man of the Mountain (also known as the Profile or Great Stone Face), the granite "face" of Cannon Mt. (4077 ft/1243 m) that looks down on Profile Lake; the Flume, a gorge with moss- and fern-covered walls extending 800 ft/244 m along Mt. Liberty, terminating at 25-ft/7.6-m Avalanche Falls; and the Basin, a glacial pothole 20 ft/6.1 m in diameter.

Frank Church–River of No Return Wilderness Area see under SALMON R., Idaho.

Frankenmuth city, pop. 4408, Saginaw Co., SC Michigan, on the Cass R., 12 mi/19 km SE of Saginaw. Settled in 1845 by Germans, it was a flour milling center, and is noted for its beer and wine production; G. Heileman's brewery was founded here in 1900. It has a June Bavarian festival, with much attention to crafts.

Frankford residential RIVER WARDS neighborhood in NORTH-

EAST PHILADELPHIA, Pennsylvania, between Bridesburg and OLNEY, 6 mi/10 km NE of CENTER CITY. It originally encompassed all of what is now the Northeast. Frankford eventually became a working-class community of Irish and East European immigrants, and now also has a growing Hispanic population.

Frankfort **1.** city, pop. 14,754, seat of Clinton Co., WC Indiana, 42 mi/68 km NW of Indianapolis. Founded in 1830, it is a trade and food processing center for the surrounding agricultural area; livestock feed and dairy items are produced. The city's manufactures include plumbing fixtures, electronic equipment, auto parts, porcelain products, aluminum windows, and mobile homes. **2.** city, pop. 25,968, state capital and seat of Franklin Co., NC Kentucky, on the Kentucky R., 21 mi/32 km NW of Lexington. In addition to its government functions, it is a trading center (tobacco, corn, cattle) for the BLUEGRASS REGION. It was originally (1786) Frank's Ford, named for a frontiersman killed in an Indian skirmish. Made here are whiskey, electrical equipment, textiles, fruit, candy, and machinery. The Old Capitol (1827) houses the Kentucky Historical Society; the new Capitol was occupied in 1910. Kentucky State University was established in 1886 for blacks.

Franklin **1.** city, pop. 12,907, seat of Johnson Co., C Indiana, 20 mi/32 km S of Indianapolis. A trading and shipping center for an agricultural region, it processes food and lumber and manufactures such products as auto parts, electrical components, appliances, tools and dies, textiles, furniture, metal goods, and glue. Franklin College (1834) is here. **2.** city, pop. 9004, seat of St. Mary Parish, S Louisiana, on the Bayou Teche, 44 mi/70 km SE of Lafayette. Founded in 1800 by Pennsylvanians, it is set in a rice producing area, and processes salt, sugar, and petroleum byproducts. **3.** town, pop. 22,095, Norfolk Co., E Massachusetts, 27 mi/43 km SW of Boston, on Route 495. Situated in a dairying, poultry farming, and fruit growing region, it also has some light manufacturing. There is a memorial to the educator Horace Mann, who was born here in 1796. Dean Junior College (1865) is in the town. **4.** city, pop. 8304, Merrimack Co., SC New Hampshire. Franklin is at the junction of the Winnipesaukee and Pemigewasset rivers, where they form the Merrimack R., 17 mi/27 km NW of Concord. The early settlement was on the site of a former Abnaki village. Waterpower stimulated industrial growth, and paper, textile, hosiery, machinery, and metal mills were established. The birthplace (1742) of Daniel Webster is in a SW section originally part of Salisbury. Webster L. resort is NW of the city center. **5.** borough, pop. 4977, Sussex Co., NW New Jersey, on the Wallkill R., 16 mi/26 km N of Dover. Some 300 minerals are found in Franklin and its hilly, lake-filled environs, including the zinc ores of franklinite and willemite. The discovery of zinc was the main spur to Franklin's development; the main ore body was depleted in the 1950s. **6.** city, pop. 11,026, Warren Co., SW Ohio, on the Great Miami R., 15 mi/24 km SSW of Dayton. Founded in 1795, it was a thriving port in the mid 19th century. Paper and metal products, roofing materials, electrical goods, clothing, and porcelain are among items manufactured here. **7.** city, pop. 7329, Venango Co., NW Pennsylvania, at the junction of French Creek with the Allegheny R., 7 mi/11 km WSW of Oil City. On the site of a series of 1750s–60s French and British forts, it became an oil producer in 1860. Gas and bituminous coal are also found in the area. The city produces oilfield machinery and equipment. **8.** city, pop. 20,098, seat of Williamson Co., C Tennessee, on the Harpeth R., 17 mi/27 km SSW of Nashville. A traditional farm trade (corn, tobacco, wheat, cheese) center, in an area with phosphate mining and timber milling, it has light industries and is a growing residential suburb. An especially bloody Civil War battle was fought here on Nov. 30, 1864; the dead included six Confederate generals. **9.** independent city, pop. 7864, SE Virginia, on the Blackwater R., 9 mi/14 km N of the North Carolina line and 40 mi/64 km SW of Norfolk. It is a milling and peanut and grain processing and marketing center. **10.** city, pop. 21,855, Milwaukee Co., SE Wisconsin, 10 mi/16 km SW of Milwaukee, of which it is a commuter suburb.

Franklin, Mount see under PRESIDENTIAL RANGE, New Hampshire.

Franklin, State of unrecognized state formed in 1784, when North Carolina ceded to the Federal government westward lands it held by charter. Settlers in modern Washington, Sullivan, and Greene counties, extreme NE Tennessee, created a constitution and established their capital at GREENEVILLE. Congress refused to admit Franklin, and in 1788 control reverted to North Carolina; in 1796 the area became part of Tennessee.

Franklin County **1.** 543 sq mi/1406 sq km, pop. 961,437, in C Ohio, intersected by the Olentangy and Scioto rivers. Its seat is COLUMBUS, which, along with its suburbs, makes up much of the county's area. The diversified manufacturing at Columbus dominates its economy. Fruit, dairy, grain, livestock, and truck farming are also pursued, and limestone, sand, and gravel are exploited. **2.** 774 sq mi/2005 sq km, pop. 121,082, in SC Pennsylvania, bordered (S) by Maryland. Its seat is CHAMBERSBURG. The county has marble and limestone quarries, and is also agricultural. It was the scene of many Indian massacres in the years before the Revolution. **3.** 649 sq km/1681 sq km, pop. 39,980, on L. Champlain and the Québec border, extreme NW Vermont. St. Albans is the county seat. The area is drained by the Missisquoi and Lamoille rivers, and rises to the Green Mts. (E). Farm machinery, textile equipment, medicines, maple sugar, granite, lime, and paper, dairy, and wood products are produced. **4.** 683 sq mi/1769 sq km, pop. 39,549, in SC Virginia. Its seat is ROCKY MOUNT. At the W edge of the PIEDMONT and along the BLUE RIDGE Mts. (NW), it is largely agricultural, although there is some manufacturing, especially around Rocky Mount. Black educator Booker T. Washington was born (1856) on the James Burroughs plantation, 13 mi/21 km SE of Roanoke; the site is now the 224-ac/91-ha Booker T. Washington National Monument.

Franklin District see under NORTHWEST TERRITORIES.

Franklin D. Roosevelt Lake see under GRAND COULEE DAM, Washington.

Franklin Lakes borough, pop. 9873, Bergen Co., NW New Jersey, 8 mi/13 km NW of Paterson. In a lake-filled resort region, it is primarily a residential suburb, with some light industry.

Franklin Mountains **1.** NW–SE trending range in the W Northwest Territories, its main body extending for 300 mi/500 km along the E of the MACKENZIE R., between Great Bear L. (E) and the MACKENZIE Mts. (W), of which it is often considered an E outlier. This N extension of the Rocky Mts. reaches 5174 ft/1577 m at Cap Mt., near Wrigley (S). In the 1960s lead and zinc were found in the Franklins, and in 1972 a large natural gas pocket was found in Pointed Mt., in the S. **2.** range extending N of El Paso, extreme W Texas, into New Mexico, and reaching a high point of 7192 ft/2194 m at North Franklin Mt. (or Peak). The mass protrudes into El Paso, with Comanche Peak near its S tip. Ranger Peak is the site of an aerial tramway. Some tin mining was done here early in the 20th century.

Franklin Park **1.** village, pop. 18,485, Cook Co., NE Illinois, a suburb bordering Chicago, 13 mi/21 km NW of the Loop. Its location, immediately S of O'Hare International Airport, has precipitated substantial industrial development in recent decades, particularly along the Tri-State Tollway (I-294) in the W part of the village. Manufactures include electronics, steel and aluminum products, and rivet-setting equipment. Food processing and metal stamping also feature in the local economy. **2.** urban park, 527 ac/213 ha, between the Jamaica Plain and Dorchester sections of Boston, Massachusetts. Home to a municipal zoo, golf course, and other features, it is the largest park in the city, part of the 1880s plan that included the FENWAY.

Franklin Square unincorporated village, pop. 28,205, in Hempstead town, Nassau Co., SE New York, on W Long Island. It is a largely residential suburb.

Franks Peak also, **Francs Peak** see under ABSAROKA RANGE, Wyoming.

Fraser city, pop. 13,899, Macomb Co., SE Michigan, a residential suburb 15 mi/24 km NE of Detroit.

Fraser River 850 mi/1370 km long, the longest river in British Columbia. It rises S of YELLOWHEAD PASS, in Mt. Robson Provincial Park, just W of the Continental Divide, and flows generally NW some 220 mi/340 km, along the N of the Cariboo Mts., to PRINCE GEORGE, where the NECHAKO R. joins it from the W. It then flows S across the interior plateau through Quesnel, Williams Lake, Lillooet, and Yale to Hope, where it turns SW and W past Chilliwack into the Vancouver area, forming a delta as it enters the Strait of Georgia. Simon Fraser of the NORTH WEST COMPANY, thinking it was the Columbia R., descended it in 1808. Fur posts were established in the 1820s, but it was not until the 1850s–60s gold rush that its valley was heavily traveled, with creation of the Cariboo Road (see BARKERVILLE). The Thompson R., which rises (as the North Thompson) near the Fraser's headwaters, flows some 300 mi/480 km generally SW, via KAMLOOPS (where the South Thompson joins it) to meet the Fraser at Lytton, below which is the **Fraser Canyon,** with strong currents and walls in places 3300 ft/1000 m high. The Canadian Pacific Railway follows the Thompson–Fraser valleys from E of Kamloops. The Fraser and its tributaries are noted salmon spawning grounds.

Frayser residential and commercial section of Memphis, Tennessee, N of the Wolf R. and 5 mi/8 km NNE of Downtown.

Frayser's Farm battle site in Henrico Co., SE Virginia, 12 mi/19 km ESE of Richmond. The battle at Frayser's Farm, also called Glendale (June 30, 1862), took place S of White Oak Swamp, at the end of the Confederates' Seven Days' Campaign. Retreating Union forces fell back to MALVERN HILL.

Frederick city, pop. 40,148, seat of Frederick Co., N Maryland, 45 mi/72 km WNW of Baltimore. It is the market, shipping, and processing center of a rich PIEDMONT agricultural area, and has a variety of light manufacturing, financial, and high-tech enterprises. Settled in 1745 by Palatinate Germans, the city includes an extensive historical district of 33 blocks. On the N side is Fort Detrick, an Army installation that has been involved in both germ warfare and epidemiological research. In the city are the National Cancer Research Center, Hood College (1893), and Frederick Community College (1957). A grain and transportation center during the Civil War, Frederick saw much military activity; an 1862 Confederate occupation gave rise to the legend of Barbara Frietchie, supposed to have defiantly flown the Union flag. MONOCACY National Battlefield lies nearby (N) along the Monocacy R.

Frederick County 663 sq mi/1717 sq km, pop. 150,208, in N Maryland, bounded N by Pennsylvania, NE by the Monocacy R., and SW by the Potomac R. and Virginia. Its seat is FREDERICK. The county lies primarily in the PIEDMONT, with its extreme W in the Blue Ridge Mts. and Middletown Valley. It includes a rich agricultural area that produces wheat, corn, hay, apples, peaches, dairy products, livestock, and poultry. Frederick is its market, shipping, and industrial center.

Fredericksburg **1.** city, pop. 6934, seat of Gillespie Co., C Texas, 68 mi/109 mi W of Austin, in the HILL COUNTRY, in the PEDERNALES R. Valley. Settled by Germans led by J.O. Meusebach in 1846, it remains largely German in character. Tourism, winemaking, light manufactures, and food processing are central to its economy. The city is noted for its small "Sunday houses," built in its early days by farmers who came in to market and remained for the Sabbath. **2.** independent city, pop. 19,027, in but administratively separate from Spotsylvania Co., NE Virginia, on the Rappahannock R., 50 mi/80 km SSW of Washington, D.C. It is the commercial center of an agricultural region (dairy and beef cattle), and has some light manufacturing. Settled by the early 1700s, it developed as a Colonial port, and was a major battleground during the Civil War because of its strategic location midway between Richmond and Washington. On Dec. 13, 1862, Confederates, their forces dug in largely at Marye's Heights, W of the city, handed Union forces a major defeat. The Fredericksburg and Spotsylvania National Military Park has a cemetery and a museum. The city's historic buildings include the home and grave of Mary Ball Washington, George Washington's mother; the law office of James Monroe; and the Rising Sun Tavern, built by George Washington's brother, Charles. Mary Washington College (1908) and Germanna Community College (1970) are here.

Fredericton city, pop. 46,466, capital of New Brunswick and seat of York Co., at the junction of the Nashwaaksis R. with the Saint John R., 60 mi/100 km NW of Saint John. It was established in the 1780s for LOYALISTS fleeing the American Revolution, on the site of an earlier Acadian settlement (Ste. Anne). The N side of the river (Marysville) became industrial during the late-19th-century lumber boom, but the S side has remained essentially governmental, cultural, and educational. The University of New Brunswick (1785) is here, with affiliated St. Thomas University (1910; moved from CHATHAM in 1964).

Frederiksted town, pop. 1064, on the W coast of the island of SAINT CROIX, in the US VIRGIN ISLANDS, 11 mi/18 km WSW of CHRISTIANSTED. Columbus anchored at the Salt R. here in 1493. Founded (1751) by the Danish, the town was largely destroyed by a tidal wave (1867) and fire (1878). Today it is a port, exporting sugar and rum, and a tourist center.

Fredonia village, pop. 10,436, in Pomfret township, Chautauqua Co., SW New York, on Canadaway Creek, 5 mi/8 km E of L. Erie and adjacent (S) to DUNKIRK. Settled in 1804, it became, in 1821, the first US community to employ natural gas for illumination. The name Fredonia ("place of freedom") was originally proposed for the Union. The first chapter of the National Grange, a fraternity of farmers, was established here in 1868, and the Women's Christian Temperance Union was founded here in 1873. The village's economy depends primarily on the cultivation of Concord grapes in the surrounding area. Light manufacturing, the production of wine, and the processing of foods are important. Fredonia is home to the State University of New York College at Fredonia (1866).

Fredonia, Republic of see under NACOGDOCHES, Texas.

Freehold in New Jersey: **a.** borough, pop. 10,742, seat of Monmouth Co., 18 mi/29 km S of Perth Amboy. Settled by Scots in the mid 1600s, it was long called Monmouth Courthouse (1715–1801). Its manufactures include chemicals, rubber goods, magnetic tapes, glass, and food products, and it is also a commercial center. In Freehold are a performing arts center and Freehold Raceway, a harness-racing track. **b.** township, pop. 24,710, surrounding the borough and including the unincorporated communities of **East Freehold** (pop. 3842) and **West Freehold** (pop. 11,166). The Battle of Monmouth (1778), fought in the W, is commemorated by a state park. In the S is Turkey Swamp Park.

Freeport **1.** city, pop. 25,840, seat of Stephenson Co., NW Illinois, on the Pecatonica R., 13 mi/21 km S of the Wisconsin border and 28 mi/45 km W of Rockford. It is a trading and shipping point for local dairy and agricultural products. Manufactures include medicines, batteries, switches, paper products, steel tanks, shop and farm machinery, tires, and toys. Many insurance companies are headquartered here. Freeport was settled (1835) on the site of a Winnebago village by people dissatisfied with working conditions in the nearby Galena lead mines. Railroads arrived in the 1850s, stimulating economic development. The Freeport Doctrine, stipulating that local legislation could counteract the effects of the Supreme Court's slavery-affirming Dred Scott decision, was set forth by Stephen Douglas in the second Lincoln-Douglas debate, held here August 27, 1858. **2.** town, pop. 6905, Cumberland Co., SW Maine. Including the villages of Porter Landing and South Freeport, it is on Casco Bay and US 1, 15 mi/24 km NE of Portland. A former shipbuilding center where the final papers establishing Maine as an independent state were signed in 1820, Freeport is best known as the home of the L.L. Bean retail and mail order company. In the 1980s Bean was joined by numerous other "factory outlets" and discount stores, making the town a shopping mecca. A yachting harbor, on the Harraseeket R., and crab fishing and packing are also important. The Desert of Maine, an area of glacial sand dunes once one of the state's best-known curiosities, is in the NW. **3.** village, pop. 39,894, in Hempstead town, Nassau Co., SE New York, 25 mi/40 km ESE of Manhattan, on Long Island's South Shore. It has a well-developed commercial waterfront area, and is a center for boating and fishing, with access to the Atlantic Ocean through the Jones Inlet; it is also a gateway to JONES BEACH, and a regional shopping hub. **4.** city, pop. 11,389, Brazoria Co., SE Texas, at the mouth of the Brazos R., 55 mi/88 km S of Houston. Founded in 1912 by exploiters of local sulfur deposits, it is in an area also producing salt, oil, and gas. A deepwater port with a commercial shrimp fleet, it is the center of the BRAZOSPORT complex. The city processes and exports gasoline and chemicals, and a big desalinization plant is nearby.

Free State of Jones see under LAUREL, Mississippi.

free trade zone also, **foreign trade zone** an updating of the medieval concept of the *free port;* an area, as within an airport or city, where goods traveling between countries may be unloaded, stored, handled in various ways (e.g., repackaged), and reshipped, without payment of duties or tariffs as long as they are not imported into the country within which the zone is situated. A **free trade area** is any area within which duties or tariffs are abolished by mutual agreement, as among the US, Canada, and Mexico by a 1990s accord (NAFTA).

Fremont **1.** city, pop 173,339, Alameda Co., NC California, 20 mi/32 km S of Oakland, just SE of San Francisco Bay, on Alameda Creek and the Hetch Hetchy Aqueduct. It was incorporated in 1956, with the merger of the largely agricultural villages of Irvington, Warm Springs, Niles, Centerville, and Mission San Jose, and developed as a residential and industrial suburb. Automobile and truck manufacture became its main industry in the 1960s; earlier, the economy had centered on quarrying, salt extraction, and the production of champagne, wine, fruits, poultry, and furniture. By the 1980s, the SILICON VALLEY boom had spread N to Fremont, which now produces software, lasers, and computer equipment. Two two-year colleges are here, along with the reconstructed Dominican Mission San Jose (1809). **2.** city, pop. 3875, Newaygo Co., WC Michigan, on Fremont L., 23 mi/37 km NE of Muskegon. Best known as headquarters for the Gerber Company, with its baby-food processing plant, it is in a fruit growing, dairy, and poultry area. Nearby are several lakes and Indian village sites and mounds. **3.** city, pop. 23,680, seat of Dodge Co., E Nebraska, on the Platte R., 33 mi/53 km NW of Omaha. Established in 1856, it grew with the 1866 arrival of the Union Pacific Railroad. It is a processing and distribution center for grain, livestock, and dairy products. Midland Lutheran College (1883) is here. **4.** city, pop. 17,648, seat of Sandusky Co., N Ohio, on the Sandusky R. in rich agricultural country, 21 mi/34 km WSW of Sandusky. Birchard Library Park is on the site of Fort Stephenson, successfully defended by George Croghan's troops against the British and Indians in 1813. The home and 25-ac/10-ha grounds of Rutherford B. Hayes, Spiegel Grove, is now the Hayes Presidential Center. Fremont's economy centers around sugar beets and canneries as well as the manufacture of such goods as automobile parts, electrical products, and clothing. **5.** commercial and residential district of N SEATTLE, Washington, N of the L. Washington Ship Canal, W of the UNIVERSITY DISTRICT, and SW of Wallingford. A countercultural center of the 1960s, it is now noted for its small shops and street art. Gasworks Park is on the S.

Fremont National Forest 1.2 million ac/486,000 ha (1875 sq mi/4856 sq km), in SC Oregon, on the E of the CASCADE RANGE and SE of CRATER L. The explorer John C. Frémont was snowbound here on Winter Ridge in 1843. The volcanic dome Gearhart Mt. (8364 ft/2549 m) is here, and the S part of the ABERT RIM is in the SE.

Fremont Peak **1.** see under SAN FRANCISCO PEAKS, Arizona. **2.** see under GANNETT PEAK, Wyoming.

French Broad River 200 mi/320 km long, in North Carolina and Tennessee. Formed by the confluence of headstreams in the Blue Ridge Mts. in W North Carolina, near the South

Carolina border, it flows NE through BREVARD to ASHEVILLE, then NW into Tennessee. The NOLICHUCKY R. joins it at the NE end of 40 mi/64 km–long Douglas L., formed by the 202 ft/62 m–high Douglas Dam (Tennessee Valley Authority, 1943). From the dam, the French Broad winds W to Knoxville, where it joins the Holston R. to form the Tennessee R.

French Creek 140 mi/225 km long, in New York and Pennsylvania. It rises in SW Chautauqua Co., New York, and flows SW and S past Meadville, Pennsylvania, widening and continuing SE to join the Allegheny R. at Franklin. Many early French settlers used the stream as part of the supply route to their forts along the Ohio R. Pioneers used French Creek as a route from the Great Lakes to the interior.

French Lick **1.** town, pop. 2087, Orange Co., S Indiana, 45 mi/72 km NW of New Albany. Its mineral springs have made it a popular resort since the mid 19th century. An 18th-century French trading post and local salt lick gave the settlement its name. Fruit, livestock, and poultry are raised, and timber is harvested in the surrounding area, which also has bituminous coal mines and stone quarries. The HOOSIER NATIONAL FOREST almost surrounds the town. **2.** see under NASHVILLE, Tennessee.

Frenchman Bay inlet of the Atlantic Ocean between the mainland and Mount Desert I. in Hancock Co., SE Maine. Thirteen mi/21 km N–S and 4–9 mi/6–14 km wide, the bay is the center of a popular summer resort area, with Acadia National Park flanking it on the island to the W and on the Schoodic Peninsula to the E. Winter Harbor, Sorrento, and Lamoine Beach State Park are among much-visited locales on the bay.

French Quarter see VIEUX CARRÉ, New Orleans, Louisiana.

French Shore **1.** historic fishing territory of France on the coast of Newfoundland. From the 16th century, France and England vied for control of the GRAND BANKS and vicinity. Following the Treaty of Utrecht (1713), France gave up all claims to Newfoundland except the right to catch and dry fish in an area extending from Cape BONAVISTA (NE), around the GREAT NORTHERN PENINSULA, to Point Riche, near Port au Choix on the NW. After the Treaty of Paris of 1783, the boundaries were shifted W, with the E boundary at Cape St. John on the Baie Verte Peninsula (N), and the W boundary at Cape Ray (SW), on Cabot Strait, near modern Channel–Port aux Basques. From the 1880s on, disputes arose as Newfoundland developed its own fisheries and commerce in the area, and in 1904 France gave up all fishing rights, although it retains SAINT-PIERRE ET MIQUELON. **2.** the SW shore of Nova Scotia, between Digby (N) and Yarmouth (S); many of its francophone inhabitants resettled long after the 1755 deportations from ACADIA.

Frenchtown **1.** in various northern US cities, esp. in New England, locality name for a neighborhood housing French-Canadians. Although migration between the two countries has occurred through their history, economic crisis between 1870 and 1900 drove as many as 2 million Canadians south; many of these were Québecois who went to work in the textile and other New England industries, often drawn by recruiters aiming to undercut nascent labor organization with imported labor. French-Canadians remain an important element in the life of Maine, New Hampshire, Massachusetts, and neighboring states. **2.** see under FIFTH WARD, Houston, Texas.

Fresh Kills estuary that, with its arms Richmond Creek and Main Creek, extends into WC Staten Island, New York, from the ARTHUR KILL. The area was originally swampy pine forest, the waters a source of shellfish. In the 19th century truck farming was important. Today Fresh Kills is known as the site of the world's largest dump, a New York City landfill four times the size of Central Park and up to 200 ft/61 m tall in the early 1990s. Residential and shopping areas adjoin, and complaints about toxic effects are common, although landscaping and safety programs are ongoing, and the landfill, located on the ATLANTIC FLYWAY, attracts millions of birds. The larger area is heavily industrial: Carteret, New Jersey, lies across the Arthur Kill, and the Staten Island area just N of the estuary's mouth is known as Linoleumville, from a plant there into the 1920s. The Staten Island GREENBELT lies just E, however, and some claim that Fresh Kills will some day also be parkland.

Fresh Meadows middle-class residential and educational section, NC Queens, New York. It lies N of Jamaica and the Grand Central Parkway, SE of Flushing. A garden-city housing development was built here in the late 1940s, and the area is home to St. John's University. UTOPIA is in the NW corner.

Fresno city, pop. 354,202, seat of Fresno Co., C California, in the heart of the San Joaquin Valley, on the S side of the San Joaquin R. It is the financial, commercial, and processing center of the valley, which produces raisin grapes, wine, citrus fruit, almonds, figs, cotton, grain, poultry, and dairy goods. Founded in 1872 as a grain shipping depot by the Central Pacific Railroad, it became after the 1880s the center of an irrigated district laid out for the raisin industry. Most of its early inhabitants had moved from Millerton, a colony on the San Joaquin R. at today's Millerton L., 17 mi/27 km NE, to settle along the new railroad. The city was incorporated in 1885. It is a rail, road, and air traffic hub, and a gateway to Yosemite, Sequoia, and Kings Canyon national parks (to the E in the Sierra Nevada) and other fishing, boating, camping, and ski areas. A California State University branch (1911), Fresno City College (1910), Fresno Pacific College (1944), and West Coast Christian College (1949) are here. The city is often associated with William Saroyan, who wrote of it and of its Armenian community. The Fresno Convention Center (1966), a three-building complex, includes a theater, exhibition hall, and sports arena with seating for 15,000. One of the world's largest raisin processing plants is here, along with a major winemaker. Manufactures include glass, chemicals, machinery, fertilizers, ceramics, plastics, and wood and paper products.

Fresno County 5978 sq mi/15,483 sq km, pop. 667,490, in C California, drained by the San Joaquin R. It occupies much of the San Joaquin Valley (W) and parts of the Sierra Nevada (E). Its seat is FRESNO. The most productive US agricultural county, it turns out most of the nation's raisins as well as figs and other crops suited to a hot, dry climate. Oil and natural gas fields are worked around Coalinga, in the SW. Kings Canyon National Park and parts of Sierra and Sequoia national forests are in the E.

Friars Point town, pop. 1334, Coahoma Co., NW Mississippi, in the DELTA, 12 mi/19 km NNW of Clarksdale, on the Mississippi R. Founded in the 1830s, it was long an important river port, shipping cotton, corn, and timber, with a ferry to Helena, Arkansas (12 mi/19 km NNE).

Frick Park municipal park, between the SQUIRREL HILL and

Regent Square neighborhoods in Pittsburgh, Pennsylvania, 5 mi/8 km E of the GOLDEN TRIANGLE. This forested tract originally formed part of the estate of coke baron Henry Clay Frick.

Fridley city, pop. 28,335, Anoka Co., SE Minnesota, on the Mississippi R., 8 mi/13 km N of Minneapolis. Founded by an agent for the Hudson's Bay Company in 1847, it was an agricultural area until the 1940s, when it became a bedroom community for its urban neighbor. There has been much commercial development along Route 65 in the NE part.

Friendship village in the BLOOMFIELD section of Pittsburgh, Pennsylvania, immediately W of EAST LIBERTY. Home to upwardly mobile white-collar workers around the turn of the century, it is a largely German-American community of single-family houses. Mansions abound at the E edge.

Friendswood city, pop. 22,814, Galveston and Harris counties, SE Texas, 20 mi/32 km SE of downtown Houston, on Clear Creek. It is a largely residential suburb.

Fripp Island one of the SEA ISLANDS, c.9 sq mi/23 sq km, in Beaufort Co., SC South Carolina, on the Atlantic Ocean, 14 mi/23 km SE of Beaufort. The whole island has been developed into an exclusive resort and residential community, and is reached by private road from the adjacent Hunting I. (E).

Frissell, Mount highest point (2380 ft/725 m) in Connecticut, in SALISBURY, in the state's NW corner. Part of the Taconic Range, it is actually the S slope of a mountain largely in Mount Washington township, Massachusetts. BEAR Mt. is the highest mountain entirely within Connecticut.

Frobisher Bay inlet of the Atlantic Ocean in extreme SE BAFFIN I., E Northwest Territories. Some 160 mi/265 km NW–SE and 20–50 mi/30–80 km wide, the bay separates the Hall Peninsula (NE) from the Meta Incognita Peninsula (SW). It was explored by Sir Martin Frobisher in 1576. The town of IQALUIT (formerly Frobisher Bay) lies at its head (NW) near Qaummaarviit Historic Park, the site of a 700-year-old INUIT fishing camp.

Frogmore see under SAINT HELENA SOUND, South Carolina.

Frontenac city, pop. 3374, St. Louis Co., EC Missouri, 12 mi/19 km W of downtown St. Louis. It is an affluent bedroom community.

frontier in American usage, that part of the country at the fringe of (non-Indian) settlement, where pioneers are in the process of establishing civilization; an area essentially ungoverned (and therefore "lawless"), which calls on individual strengths and self-reliance in its inhabitants, and which creates a democratic, egalitarian society. The "Frontier Thesis" (1893) of F. J. Turner suggested that the frontier had been central in molding the character of Americans and their nation, and that it had now closed (the country had been thoroughly settled). Alaska and N Canada are today sometimes called "the last frontier."

Front Range NNW–SSE trending mountains, some 300 mi/480 km long, the easternmost face of the S ROCKY Mts. They extend from S Wyoming, where the MEDICINE BOW (W) and LARAMIE (E) mountains run parallel, into Colorado, where a single massif runs through ROCKY MOUNTAIN NATIONAL PARK and forms part of the Continental Divide. Passing W of Denver, they continue S to near Colorado Springs, where their best-known summit, PIKES PEAK, commands the Great Plains to the E. To the S, the WET Mts. and the SANGRE DE CRISTO Mts., extending into New Mexico, are considered to be extensions of the Front Range; but the range itself stops N of the Arkansas R. Grays Peak (14,270 ft/4349 m) is the highest Front Range peak. Mt. EVANS and LONGS PEAK are also particularly well known. In the 19th century westbound travelers passed around the range when possible. Today US 40 and I-70 go through it; the Berthoud (11,315 ft/3449 m) and Loveland (11,990 ft/3655 m) passes, W of Georgetown, were long key to this route; since 1973 the Eisenhower Tunnel, just SW of the Loveland Pass, has carried most traffic through the area.

Front Royal town, pop. 11,880, seat of Warren Co., N Virginia, 20 mi/32 km S of Winchester and 60 mi/97 km W of Washington, D.C. On the South Fork of the Shenandoah R., in an apple growing region, it has a fruit packing industry and produces rayon and chemicals. It was settled in the 1780s. On May 23, 1862, Confederate forces under Stonewall Jackson took the town. Front Royal, the seat of Randolph-Macon Academy, is the N terminus of the SKYLINE DRIVE.

Front Street commercial thoroughfare in downtown Memphis, Tennessee, atop the city's bluff (Chickasaw Bluff), on the Mississippi R. In the mid 19th century this was "Cotton Row," home to Memphis's major cotton merchants and warehouses. By the end of the century, MUD I. had grown to close off what had been Wolf Harbor (the mouth of the WOLF R.), and commerce moved elsewhere.

Frost Belt or **Frostbelt** also, **Snowbelt** the opposite of the SUNBELT, from a climatic standpoint; northern parts of the US. The term's implications are slightly different from those of RUST BELT.

Frostburg city, pop. 8075, Allegany Co., NW Maryland, 9 mi/14 km W of Cumberland, on Georges Creek, just E of Big Savage Mt. Frostburg State University (1898) is here.

Fruitlands utopian commune near HARVARD, Massachusetts, founded 1844 by Bronson Alcott and others and abandoned the next year. It is now a museum.

Fullerton city, pop. 114,144, Orange Co., SW California, 20 mi/32 km SE of Los Angeles. Once part of a Spanish RANCHO, it was founded in 1887, as railroads reached the area. Oil was first drilled here in the 1890s, and the area was also a major citrus, walnut, avocado, and field crop producer. In the 1950s the Santa Ana Freeway brought large-scale development. Today Fullerton makes aerospace and electronic equipment and a variety of other products, and is also a commercial and residential center. A California State University campus (1957) is here, along with Pacific Christian College (1928) and several other institutions.

Fulton **1.** city, pop. 10,033, seat of CALLAWAY Co., C Missouri, 22 mi/35 km ESE of Columbia. During the Civil War it was the center of the "Kingdom of Callaway," formed when the county seceded from the US. In a rich grain growing region that also produces clay and coal, it is a trade and processing center. Among its manufactures are firebrick, farm and industrial machinery, shoes, and processed foods. Winston Churchill's March 5, 1946 "Iron Curtain" speech was delivered here at Westminster College (1851). On the campus is the Winston Churchill Memorial and Library, which includes Sir Christopher Wren's Church of St. Mary Aldermanbury, an 18th-century London structure largely destroyed during the 1940 blitz, then brought here and reconstructed as a tribute to Churchill. Fulton is also home to William Woods College (1870). **2.** city, pop. 12,929, Oswego Co., C New York, on the Oswego R., 25 mi/40 km NW of Syracuse and 11 mi/18 km S of L. Ontario. The area surrounding the Oswego R. Falls, now the center of the city, was an important strategic point during both the French and Indian Wars and the Revolution. Intense growth followed the opening of the Oswego Canal, which connected the Erie Canal with L. Ontario in the 1820s. Fulton is primarily a manufacturing city, producing frozen foods, candy, cork, plastic, waxed cardboard, bottles, and paper-mill machinery.

Fulton County 534 sq mi/1383 sq km, pop. 684,951, in NW Georgia, bounded NW by the Chattahoochee R. and including ATLANTA, its seat, and many of the city's suburbs.

Fulton Ferry see under BROOKLYN HEIGHTS, New York.

fumarole small vent in the earth that emits chiefly steam, sometimes other gases. Fumaroles are associated with volcanic areas that are dormant or returning to quietude, as at the Valley of Ten Thousand Smokes, in Alaska's KATMAI NATIONAL PARK.

Fundy, Bay of Atlantic Ocean inlet, extending NE some 200 mi/320 km inland from the Gulf of MAINE, between NE Maine and S New Brunswick (N) and SW Nova Scotia (S). PASSAMAQUODDY BAY is an inlet on its NW, near its entrance. In the NE it divides into Chignecto Bay (N) and the MINAS BASIN (S). Fundy's fast-running tides, rising up to 53 ft/16 m, are the highest in the world; the bay's orientation, shape, and shallowness (it is on the CONTINENTAL SHELF) are contributing factors. Their hydroelectric potential remains untapped except by an experimental station at ANNAPOLIS ROYAL, Nova Scotia. The rising tide creates "reversing falls" at the mouth of the SAINT JOHN R., and the surge up the Petitcodiac R. creates a tidal BORE at Moncton, New Brunswick. The bay is a rich fishing ground. Major harbors include New Brunswick's SAINT JOHN and SAINT ANDREWS and Nova Scotia's DIGBY.

Fundy National Park 80 sq mi/206 sq km, on the N of the Bay of Fundy, at the entrance to Chignecto Bay, 35 mi/56 km SSW of Moncton, New Brunswick. It contains 50 mi/80 km of hiking trails. Tides average 29 ft/9 m in the park area. Wildlife includes moose, bobcat, black bear, and large numbers of migrating birds. Alma (village, pop. 308, Albert Co.), on the SE, is park headquarters.

Funeral Mountains see under AMARGOSA RANGE, California.

Furnace Creek see under DEATH VALLEY, California.

Furnas County 721 sq mi/1867 sq km, pop. 5553, in SC Nebraska, on the Kansas line (S). Its seat is Beaver City (pop. 707). The county was the political base of Senator George W. Norris (1861–1944), who began his career here in the 1880s. It is a grain and livestock producing area on the S edge of the High Plains.

Fur Seal Islands see PRIBILOF Is., Alaska.

G

Gabilan Range one of the COAST RANGES of WC California, running SE for c.35 mi/56 km from the vicinity of San Juan Bautista, NNE of Salinas, between the San Benito R. and the SAN ANDREAS FAULT (E) and the SALINAS Valley (W). It rises to 3171 ft/967 m at Frémont Peak, formerly Gabilan Peak, 11 mi/18 km S of San Juan Bautista. Pinnacles National Monument, in the S part of the range, is the 16,300-ac/6600-ha site of an ancient volcano carved into colorful pinnacles and crags rising 500–1200 ft/150–400 m above their surroundings.

Gadsden city, pop. 42,523, seat of Etowah Co., NE Alabama, 60 mi/97 km NE of Birmingham, on the Coosa R., in the Appalachian foothills at the SW end of LOOKOUT Mt. Settled in the 1830s, it is in an agricultural region also rich in manganese, iron ore, coal, limestone, and timber. Local industries, fostered by the development of hydropower, include food processing and the production of steel, nails, fencing, pipe, electronic and farm equipment, and tires. Gadsden State Community College (1965) is here.

Gadsden Purchase area of c.30,000 sq mi/77,700 sq km, bought from Mexico in 1854, to resolve border questions left by the 1848 treaty ending the Mexican War, and under pressure from Southern politicians aiming to assure a S route for the proposed transcontinental railroad. James Gadsden, US minister to Mexico, was the negotiator. The land, all of Arizona S of the Gila R. and adjacent parts of S New Mexico, is largely desert, and later became an important mining area. Tucson, Arizona, is its most important city.

Gaffney city, pop. 13,145, seat of Cherokee Co., N South Carolina, 18 mi/29 km NE of Spartanburg, in the Piedmont. Originally called Gaffney's Old Field, for an Irish settler who arrived in 1803, it began as a resort for Low Country plantation owners who sought its mineral springs. A market center for cotton and other crops, it grew when the Southern Railway came in the 1870s. There are limestone quarries and textile plants. Limestone College (1845) is here.

Gagetown see under OROMOCTO, New Brunswick.

Gahanna city, pop. 27,791, Franklin Co., C Ohio, a residential suburb 8 mi/13 km SE of Columbus. Situated in a previously agricultural area, it has grown rapidly in recent decades.

Gaines's Mill locality in Hanover Co., EC Virginia, 10 mi/16 km ENE of Richmond. On June 27, 1862, in part of the Confederates' Seven Days' Campaign that ended the Union's Peninsular Campaign against Richmond, Union forces under Fitz-John Porter were defeated at Gaines's Mill by Confederate troops under Robert E. Lee. The battle took place just S of the hamlet of New Cold Harbor, near the site of the 1864 battle of COLD HARBOR.

Gainesville **1.** city, pop. 84,770, seat of Alachua Co., NC Florida, in an area of small lakes, 62 mi/100 km SW of Jacksonville. On the site of an 1830 trading post, it is now an educational center; much of its activity and economy revolve around the University of Florida (1853). It also packs fruits and meat, mills lumber, and manufactures wood products and electronic equipment. Tourism is important. Among numerous local environmental sites are the San Felasco Hammock State Preserve and the Devil's Millhopper State Geological Site (where an enormous sinkhole is located). The city is also home to Santa Fe Community College (1965). **2.** city, pop. 17,885, seat of Hall Co., N Georgia, on L. Sidney Lanier (the CHATTAHOOCHEE R.), in the foothills of the Blue Ridge Mts., 51 mi/82 km NE of Atlanta. A center of the poultry processing industry, it also has textile mills and furniture factories. Brenau College (1878) a junior college, and several private schools are here. The lake is a popular resort area. **3.** town, pop. 2288, Wyoming Co., W New York, 25 mi/40 km S of Batavia, in a potato growing region. It was the birthplace of biologist and educator David Starr Jordan (1851–1931). **4.** city, pop. 14,256, seat of Cooke Co., N Texas, on the Elm Fork of the Trinity R., 61 mi/98 km NNW of Dallas. Founded in 1850 on the trail to the California goldfields, it is a trade and shipping center for an agricultural and timber and oil producing region. There are refineries and railroad shops, and the city manufactures oilfield equipment, aircraft, paint, and shoes. A gateway to N Texas, 7 mi/11 km S of the Red R. (the Oklahoma border), it is also the seat of Cooke County College (1924).

Gaithersburg city, pop. 39,542, Montgomery Co., C Maryland, 20 mi/32 km NW of Washington, D.C. It is a residential and commercial suburb on Interstate 270, home to the US Bureau of Standards and to a number of corporate facilities.

Galax independent city, pop. 6670, on the Carroll-Grayson county line, SW Virginia, 21 mi/34 km SSE of Wytheville. Founded in 1903, it grew as a Norfolk and Western Railroad spur, which made shipment of local wood, glass, textile, and dairy products feasible. But it is most identified with the mountain evergreen, used in wreaths and other decorations, that gives the city its name, and with country music.

Galena city, pop. 3647, seat of Jo Daviess Co., NW Illinois, on the Galena R., 3 mi/5 km E of the Mississippi R., 15 mi/24 km SE of Dubuque, Iowa, and 9 mi/14 km S of Hazel Green, Wisconsin. Its lead sulfide and zinc deposits and its location midway between St. Paul, Minnesota, and Rock Island, Illinois, made Galena a boom town; between 1840 and 1860 it was the wealthiest city in Illinois. Ulysses S. Grant was born here in 1822.

Galena Park city, pop. 10,033, Harris Co., SE Texas, adjacent (E) to Houston, and 9 mi/14 km from Downtown, on the Houston Ship Channel. Though this E suburb of Houston is partly residential, it also has oil refineries and steel, chemical, and gypsum plants.

Galesburg city, pop. 33,530, seat of Knox Co., WC Illinois. It serves as a trading center for the region's livestock and grain. Coal mining, once very important, still contributes to the economy. Mowers, marine paints and accessories, electrical appliances, doors and gates, and fencing are some of the goods manufactured here. Presbyterian minister George Washington Gale chose this site for what became Knox College (1837). Galesburg served as an Underground Railroad station, and a Lincoln-Douglas debate on slavery was held on the college campus in 1858. Carl Sandburg was born here (1878); his birthplace is now a State Historic Site.

Galion city, pop. 11,859, Crawford Co., NC Ohio, 15 mi/24 km SW of Mansfield. It was founded by German Lutherans in 1831, and lies in a diversified agricultural area. Manufactures include telephone equipment, brick and tilemaking machinery, and munitions parts.

Gallatin city, pop. 18,794, seat of Sumner Co., NC Tennessee, just N of the Cumberland R., and 25 mi/40 km NE of Nashville. A burley tobacco and livestock market, with various light industries, it was founded in 1802. The Tennessee Valley Authority's Gallatin Steam Plant, 6 mi/10 km SSE, is a major employer for the area. Old Hickory L., on the Cumberland, is an important recreational area.

Gallatin National Forest 1.73 million ac/700,000 ha (2710 sq mi/7020 sq km), in S Montana, in scattered units N and S of the Yellowstone R. Its rugged ranges include the Crazy Mts., sacred to the Crow, and the Absarokas and Beartooths, site of GRANITE PEAK, Montana's highest; part of the ABSAROKA-BEARTOOTH WILDERNESS is here.

Galleria in Texas: **a.** commercial development in NORTH DALLAS, at the intersection of the Lyndon B. Johnson Freeway (the city's beltway) and the Dallas Tollway, 10 mi/16 km NNW of Downtown. A mixed-use mall, it is noted for its futuristic glass-steel-and-concrete landscape. **b.** booming commercial and residential area of Houston, 7 mi/11 km WSW of Downtown, on Interstate Loop 610 just N of the intersection with US Route 59. The Houston Galleria, an upscale mall built in the late 1960s on the model of Milan, Italy's 19th-century mixed-use *galleria,* was the initial anchor for this huge commercial conglomeration; its success spawned dozens of satellites.

Gallipolis city, pop. 4831, seat of Gallia Co., S Ohio, on the Ohio R. and the West Virginia border, 58 mi/93 km SW of Marietta. One of the earliest settlements in the state, it was founded by French colonists in 1790. Its manufactures include electric motors, marine engines, powdered metals, and furniture.

Gallup city, pop. 19,154, seat of McKinley Co., NW New Mexico, on the Puerco R., 18 mi/29 km E of the Arizona border. Situated between Navajo (N) and Zuñi (S) lands, it is a center for Indian culture and trade, esp. in arts and crafts. Once a stagecoach stop, later a construction center for the Santa Fe Railroad, it also prospered from coal exploration and as a stop on ROUTE 66 (now I-40). The city is a shipping point for cattle, hides, and wool, and is engaged in uranium mining and light manufacturing. The annual Inter-Tribal Indian Ceremonial is a major event. A branch of the University of New Mexico (1968) is here.

Galveston city, pop. 59,070, seat of Galveston Co., SE Texas, 47 mi/76 km SE of Houston, on 30 mi/48 km–long **Galveston I.**, between West Bay and the Gulf of Mexico (SE). Part of the city is on Pelican I., just NW. The Spanish wanderer Cabeza de Vaca was shipwrecked somewhere in the area in 1528. Inhabited by the Karankawa tribe, the site was visited in 1686 by the French explorer La Salle. It was the headquarters of privateer Jean Lafitte in 1817–21, then was taken over by Americans. Laid out in 1834 by Michel Menard, it housed the Texas navy during the 1835–36 revolt against Mexico, and was briefly capital of the Texas republic. The first railroad arrived in 1858, and Galveston was a major Confederate port in the Civil War. The June 19, 1865, proclamation here by Union occupation commander Gordon Granger that all Texas slaves were free is celebrated each year throughout the state as "Juneteenth." Galveston lost its commercial dominance as competitive ports (like Houston) developed, and the hurricane of Sept. 8, 1900, killed more than 5000 and destroyed much of the city. The huge seawall erected afterward has afforded protection from subsequent storms. One of the largest dry cargo (now container) ports in the US, the "Oleander City" exports grain, sulfur, cotton, flour, chemicals, and fertilizer, and imports bananas, tea, and sugar. It has shipbuilding and repair yards, oil refineries, and food processing plants. The University of Texas Medical Branch (1881) and several other hospitals and medical institutions are here, as well as a branch of Texas A & M University (1962) and Galveston College (1967). Galveston's fishing piers, 30 mi/48 km of beaches, annual blessing of the shrimp fleet, and historic residential and commercial districts draw tourists.

Galveston County 399 sq mi/1033 sq km, pop. 217,399, in SE Texas. It is bounded E and N by Galveston Bay, S by the Gulf of Mexico. GALVESTON is its seat. TEXAS CITY and LEAGUE CITY are among other municipalities. Including the Bolivar Peninsula and Galveston I., it is a major industrial and port area, with oil and natural gas fields, refineries, and chemical and sulfur plants. Shipbuilding and agricultural processing are also important, along with commercial fishing, especially shrimping. The coast has numerous resorts, and tourists are also drawn to Galveston's historic sites.

Gambier village, pop. 2073, Knox Co., C Ohio, 5 mi/8 km SE of Mount Vernon, on a plateau overlooking the Kokosing R. It is primarily known as the seat of Kenyon College (1824), set on 350 ac/142 ha, whose Gothic buildings are modeled after those of Oxford University.

Gananoque town, pop. 5209, Leeds and Grenville United Counties, SE Ontario, at the confluence of the Gananoque and St. Lawrence rivers, 18 mi/29 km ENE of Kingston. Since the early 19th century its economy has depended on metal (copper and steel) works. Today auto parts manufacturing and dairying are important as well, but Gananoque is primarily a gateway to the nearby THOUSAND ISLANDS.

Gander town, pop. 10,339, NE Newfoundland, on the N shore of Gander L., 136 mi/215 km NW of St. John's. An airfield for experimental flights was opened in 1936 in this virtually fog-free location, and was completed in 1939.

Expanded during World War II, it became a major Allied base. Until the 1960s, it was an important stop for transatlantic flights. The town is also a trade center for a hunting and fishing area.

Gannett Peak highest point in Wyoming (13,804 ft/4207 m), in the WIND RIVER Range, on the Continental Divide, 59 mi/95 km ESE of Jackson. Largely surrounded by the Dinwoody Glacier, with the Bridger-Teton (W) and Shoshone (E) national forests on its two sides, it is a noted climbers' challenge. Fremont Peak (13,745 ft/4189 m), Wyoming's third-highest, is just SE.

Gantt unincorporated community, pop. 13,891, Greenville Co., NW South Carolina, near the junction of Routes 85 and 185, 4 mi/6 km SSE of downtown GREENVILLE, of which it is a predominantly black, largely residential suburb.

Gardena city, pop. 49,847, Los Angeles Co., SW California, 10 mi/16 km S of downtown Los Angeles, in an area W of Compton that was agricultural well into the 20th century. It has nurseries, and manufactures aircraft and electronic components and a range of industrial and consumer items. Gambling casinos draw visitors.

Garden City **1.** city, pop. 7410, Chatham Co., SE Georgia, 4 mi/6 km NW of Savannah, of which it is a suburb. **2.** city, pop. 24,097, seat of Finney Co., SW Kansas, on the Arkansas R. In a region made fertile by irrigation, the city processes wheat, alfalfa, sugar beets, and corn. Cattle are also central to its economy, and agricultural and building products are manufactured here. The city is the seat of Garden City Community College (1919). **3.** city, pop. 31,846, Wayne Co., SE Michigan, a residential suburb 15 mi/24 km W of Detroit. **4.** village, pop. 21,686, in Hempstead town, Nassau Co., SE New York, 18 mi/29 km E of Manhattan, in W Long Island. It is an affluent community noted for its upscale shopping district, and is home to publishing and financial services firms. The first planned community in the US, it was founded in 1869 by Alexander T. Stewart, a New York merchant. Mitchel Field, formerly the East Coast's largest military airfield, and a major Grumman aircraft producer in World War II, and Roosevelt Field, from which Charles Lindbergh took off on his historic 1927 flight to Paris, have recently become homes to shopping malls. Adelphi University and Nassau Community College are in Garden City. **5.** see under GRAND STRAND, South Carolina.

Gardendale city, pop. 9251, Jefferson Co., C Alabama, 10 mi/16 km N of Birmingham, of which it is a largely white residential suburb.

Garden District residential district in UPTOWN New Orleans, Louisiana, 2 mi/3 km SW of Jackson Square and just N of the Mississippi R. Developed during the early 19th century, after the LOUISIANA PURCHASE brought New Orleans into the Union, it was the fanciest part of the AMERICAN QUARTER. On land formerly a plantation, then the Faubourg Livaudais, then (1833–52) part of the city of Lafayette, it was annexed to New Orleans in 1852. Antebellum homes and gardens distinguish it from the Spanish and French VIEUX CARRÉ. The historic district lies between Jackson Ave. (NE) and Louisiana Ave. (SW), and between St. Charles Ave. (NW) and Magazine St. (SE), although the name is now applied to a much broader area.

Garden Grove city, pop. 143,050, Orange Co., SW California, on the Santa Ana R., 25 mi/40 km SE of Los Angeles and adjoining (SW) Anaheim. It is a middle- and working-class residential and industrial suburb with diverse manufactures. Aerospace and electronics plants in the vicinity employ many residents, as do Orange Co. tourist attractions. Once part of a large RANCHO, Garden Grove developed in the late 19th century as a trade and processing center in a region in which citrus fruit, truck crops, and walnuts were grown; some processing is still done. A thriving Vietnamese community here is locally called Little Saigon. Televangelist Robert Schuller's Philip Johnson–designed Crystal Cathedral is a well-known landmark.

Garden Island see under KINGSTON, Ontario.

Garden Isle see KAUAI, Hawaii.

Garden of the Gods see under COLORADO SPRINGS, Colorado.

Gardiner **1.** city, pop. 6746, Kennebec Co., SW Maine. It is on the Kennebec R., 6 mi/10 km S of Augusta. The city was a mid-19th-century industrial center with large wharves and saw, grist, and lumber mills; it engaged in fishing and ice cutting, shipping ice and fish. It now manufactures footwear, paper, and wood products. The poet Edwin Arlington Robinson, born in 1869 in Head Tide, a hamlet 10 mi/16 km SE, in Alna town, made Gardiner, his boyhood home, the "Tilbury Town" of his poems. **2.** see under PARADISE VALLEY, Montana. **3.** town, pop. 4278, Ulster Co., SE New York, in the Shawangunk Mts., 18 mi/29 km SW of Kingston. Settled in the 17th century, it contains the remains of a gristmill from this period. Once part of the network of BORSCHT BELT resort sites, Gardiner is now home to the largest skydiving center in the Northeast.

Gardiners Island in East Hampton town, Suffolk Co., SE New York, in Gardiners Bay, between Long Island's NORTH FORK and SOUTH FORK. Comprising approximately 3000 ac/1200 ha, it was acquired in 1639 by Lion Gardiner, making it the first permanent English settlement in New York. The island, a wildlife preserve, is still owned by his descendants. The pirate Captain Kidd is said to have buried treasure here.

Gardner city, pop. 20,125, Worcester Co., NC Massachusetts, on Crystal L., 10 mi/16 km W of FITCHBURG. It has been an important chairmaking center since the early 19th century. Manufactures include other wood products, paper goods, and time systems. Gardner is the site of Mount Wachusett Community College (1963).

Garfield **1.** city, pop. 26,727, Bergen Co., NE New Jersey, at the junction of the Passaic and Saddle rivers, 4 mi/6 km SE of Paterson. The railroad arrived here in the mid 19th century, spurring Garfield's development as an industrial center; its numerous industries still produce such goods as rubber and paper products, printing machinery, foods, pharmaceuticals, chemicals, and clothing. **2.** village in the BLOOMFIELD section of Pittsburgh, Pennsylvania, immediately N of FRIENDSHIP. Laid out in 1881, it is a black middle-class community with brick cottages on the high ground overlooking humbler row houses.

Garfield Heights city, pop. 31,739, Cuyahoga Co., NE Ohio, 8 mi/13 km SE of Cleveland, of which it is a residential and industrial suburb. Chemicals, chain hoists, and building supplies are manufactured here.

Garibaldi Provincial Park 753 sq mi/1950 sq km, in the Coast Mts. of SW British Columbia, 40 mi/64 km N of Vancouver. Established in 1927, this wilderness area surrounds Mt. Garibaldi (8787 ft/2680 m), named (1860) for the Italian patriot. Wedge Mt. (9484 ft/2893 m) and Mt. Weart (9300 ft/2837 m) are also in the park, which is noted for its hiking trails. SQUAMISH is just SW, the ski resorts of WHISTLER just NW, and Golden Ears Provincial Park adjacent (SE).

Garland city, pop. 180,650, Dallas, Collin, and Rockwall counties, NE Texas, adjacent to NE Dallas, on L. Ray Hubbard (E). This residential and industrial satellite of Dallas was a small town until the 1950s. A market center for crops from the BLACKLANDS, it also makes scientific instruments, chemicals, electronic and oilfield equipment, missiles and aircraft, paints and varnishes, and clothing (especially hats). It is home to a branch of Abilene Christian University and to Amber University (1971).

Garment Center also, **Garment District** section of Midtown Manhattan, New York City, dominated since early in the 20th century by the men's and women's apparel industries. Seventh Ave. (renamed "Fashion Avenue" in one stretch) between roughly 26th and 42nd streets is its main thoroughfare. The Fashion Institute of Technology is here.

Garment District section of LOS ANGELES, California, at the S edge of Downtown. This expanding center for clothing manufacturers and buyers currently occupies around six blocks.

Garner town, pop. 14,967, Wake Co., EC North Carolina, 5 mi/8 km SSE of Raleigh, of which it is a growing residential suburb.

Garnett city, pop. 3210, seat of Anderson Co., E Kansas, 22 mi/35 km S of Ottawa. Founded in 1856, it is a processing and shipping center for flour, livestock, dairy products, and oil. The poet Edgar Lee Masters was born here (1869).

Garrett city, pop. 5349, De Kalb Co., NE Indiana, 20 mi/32 km N of Fort Wayne. It is a railroad town and agricultural trading center, with various light manufactures.

Garrett Park town, pop. 884, Montgomery Co., C Maryland, on Rock Creek, 10 mi/16 km NW of Washington, D.C. It is an affluent residential suburb.

Garrettsville village, pop. 2014, Portage Co., NE Ohio, 25 mi/40 km ENE of Akron. There are farm- and lumber-based manufactures. The poet Hart Crane was born here (1899).

Garrison unincorporated residential suburb, pop. 5045, Baltimore Co., N Maryland, 11 mi/18 km NW of Baltimore. Fort Garrison, the oldest standing fort in Maryland, was erected in 1695 as a refuge against Indian attacks. Once surrounded by wilderness, the fort now stands amid suburban housing developments, just outside Route 695, Baltimore's beltway.

Garrison Dam completed 1956 on the MISSOURI R., 10 mi/16 km S of Garrison, in WC North Dakota. Part of the Missouri River Basin Project, the dam created Garrison Reservoir, later renamed **L. Sakakawea** (one form of the name of Sacajawea, Lewis and Clark's Shoshone guide). The dam, 210 ft/64 m high and 12,000 ft/3660 m long, is one of the world's largest earthfill structures. L. Sakakawea extends upstream for some 178 mi/286 km, to near the Montana border, with a shoreline of some 1600 mi/2600 km, much of it within the FORT BERTHOLD INDIAN RESERVATION.

Gary city, pop. 116,646, Lake Co., extreme NW Indiana, on L. Michigan and the CALUMET R., 25 mi/40 km SE of downtown Chicago, Illinois, in the highly industrialized Calumet region. A port with excellent rail and road transport, situated between the huge iron ore beds of the Northwest and the coal resources of the East and Southeast, Gary is ideally placed for steel production. The site was purchased by U.S. Steel (now the USX Corporation) in 1905, and laid out the following year. It eventually contained numerous coke plants, blast furnaces, open-hearth furnaces, steel mills, and other facilities for making such products as sheet metal, tin plate, and bridge parts. Although it has some other manufactures, Gary is essentially a one-industry city, and has suffered enormously with the decline of American steel in the 1970s and 1980s. Its work force was cut by over 75% between the early 1970s and the 1990s. The city's population has shrunk by more than 60,000, much of the middle class moving to suburbs, and the downtown business section has been decimated. Efforts to diversify industry and rebuild with Model Cities and other funds are under way. Indiana University Northwest (1922) is here.

Gasconade River 265 mi/430 km long, in Missouri. It rises on the OZARK Plateau in Wright Co., E of Springfield, and flows generally NNE to join the Missouri R. at Gasconade, 32 mi/51 km ENE of Jefferson City.

Gaslamp Quarter National Historic District, 38 ac/15 ha, in downtown San Diego, California, at the center of Alonzo Horton's 1867 NEW TOWN. Falling into decay as commercial activity moved E later in the 19th century, it became notorious as the Stingaree, a RED-LIGHT DISTRICT. It has been undergoing renovation and gentrification since the 1960s, and is now a tourist attraction. HORTON PLAZA is here.

Gaslight Square redevelopment-created entertainment district that flourished in the 1960s–70s on the North Side of Saint Louis, Missouri, 3 mi/5 km NW of Downtown, and E of Fountain Park. A complex of several dozen nightclubs and restaurants clustered in a three-block area with carefully crafted early-1900s atmosphere, it had by the 1980s lost its drawing power as WHITE FLIGHT continued to empty the city. Today, entertainment is concentrated in the LACLEDE'S LANDING and SOULARD zones.

Gasoline Alley **1.** generic for a street or area, often regarded as unsightly or otherwise undesirable, characterized by auto repair shops and similar establishments. **2.** the pit row, opposite the finish line and the main grandstand, at the Indianapolis Motor Speedway, SPEEDWAY, Indiana. Ironically, Indy cars have long run on alcohol mixtures rather than on gasoline.

Gaspé city, pop. 16,402, at the E end of the Gaspé Peninsula, SE Québec, 345 mi/555 km ENE of Québec City, at the mouth of the York R. on Gaspé Bay, an inlet of the Gulf of St. Lawrence. Here, in Micmac territory, Jacques Cartier took possession of the land in the name of the king of France, on July 24, 1534. A fishing port and supply base for New France in the 16th–18th centuries, Gaspé was the object of intermittent struggles between the French and the British. American LOYALISTS settled here following the Revolution, and the community has remained largely anglophone. The city, a 1970 amalgamation of twelve localities, is the administrative and industrial center of the peninsula, and a deepwater port. Fishing (esp. for cod and salmon) is important. Lumbering, trade, and tourism also support the economy.

Gaspee Point Revolutionary War site, originally Namquit Point, in Warwick, Kent Co., E Rhode Island, 7 mi/11 km S of Providence, on the Providence R. On this Narragansett Bay promontory the British revenue cutter *Gaspee* ran aground in 1772. A party of Providence patriots set it on fire, in the first open act of rebellion against British authority.

Gaspé Peninsula also, **Gaspésie** region in SE Québec, between CHALEUR BAY and New Brunswick (S) and the mouth of the St. Lawrence R. (N). It extends ENE from the Matapédia R. for some 140 mi/225 km, and is up to 85 mi/137 km wide. Named perhaps from a Micmac word for "land's end," it is densely wooded, with many small lakes and rivers. The SHICKSHOCK (Chic-chocs) Mts. rise to 4160 ft/1286 m at Mt. Jacques Cartier. Population is concentrated along the coast (the exception is the copper city of MURDOCHVILLE), at Gaspé, MATANE, PERCÉ, and Chandler, and in smaller villages. Traditionally a cod and salmon fishing region, the Gaspé in the 20th century saw exploitation of forest and mineral resources. Tourism and recreation are also important; the peninsula includes the Gaspésie Provincial Park and wildlife areas in the interior and FORILLON NATIONAL PARK at the E tip. Many of its inhabitants are English-speaking descendants of LOYALISTS.

Gastonia city, pop. 54,732, seat of Gaston Co., SW North Carolina, in the C Piedmont, 18 mi/29 km WNW of CHARLOTTE. Since the construction in 1848 of a cotton mill, Gastonia has been a leading US textile manufacturing center. In 1929, several persons were killed during a bitter strike at the Loray Mills; organizers were convicted of conspiracy to murder the police chief. Today, other manufactures include machinery, oil filters, corrugated boxes, plastics, and electronic equipment.

Gastown original settlement, now a historic commercial zone, in downtown VANCOUVER, British Columbia, on Burrard Inlet. It was named for "Gassy Jack" Deighton, who established a saloon here in 1867 and was central in the life of what was officially Granville after 1870. In 1886 it became Vancouver. In the 1960s the original center of the old lumbering and gold rush town was restored as a tourist attraction.

Gates town, pop. 28,583, Monroe Co., W New York, adjacent (W) to ROCHESTER. It is an industrial and residential suburb on the New York State Barge Canal and Routes 490 and 390.

Gates of the Arctic National Park and Preserve see under BROOKS RANGE, Alaska.

Gates of the Mountains see under HELENA NATIONAL FOREST, Montana.

Gatesville city, pop. 11,492, seat of Coryell Co., C Texas, 37 mi/60 km W of Waco, on the Leon R. Fort Gates (1849), 6 mi/10 km SE, was on the site of FORT HOOD. The city has varied manufactures and four state prison units.

Gateway Arch 630 ft/192 m–high stainless steel structure that dominates the 191-ac/77-ha Jefferson National Expansion Memorial (1935) in downtown SAINT LOUIS, Missouri. Designed by Eero Saarinen and completed in 1965, it has become emblematic of the city; elevators carry visitors to its top. On the Mississippi R. waterfront, the arch commemorates the city's 19th-century role (following the LOUISIANA PURCHASE) as the gateway to the West for many thousands of pioneers.

Gateway Center commercial high-rise development in the GOLDEN TRIANGLE of Pittsburgh, Pennsylvania, immediately E of the POINT. Groups of office towers cluster around Gateway and Equitable plazas, built 1950–68. The project stimulated postwar reinvestment in downtown Pittsburgh.

Gateway National Recreation Area 26,172-ac/10,600-ha protected area centering around Lower New York Bay, in SE New York and NE New Jersey. Established in 1972, it includes the marshes and islands of JAMAICA BAY and beaches along SE Staten I., both in New York City, and SANDY HOOK Peninsula in Monmouth Co., New Jersey. Park headquarters are at Jamaica Bay, which is also a wildlife refuge, particularly for migrating birds on the ATLANTIC FLYWAY.

Gatineau city, pop. 92,284, OUTAOUAIS URBAN COMMUNITY, SW Québec, at the confluence of the Gatineau and the Ottawa rivers, across the former (NE) from HULL and the latter (N) from OTTAWA. This French-speaking municipality in the NATIONAL CAPITAL REGION is a 1975 amalgamation of seven entities, including Touraine and Templeton. Cement and chemicals are manufactured in this growing, largely residential and commercial suburb.

Gatineau Park 88,000 ac/35,640 ha (137 sq mi/355 sq km), in the NATIONAL CAPITAL REGION, SW Québec, between the Gatineau R. (NE) and the Ottawa R. (SW). A wildlife preserve and recreational center that extends NW from HULL through hilly terrain, it also has governmental facilities. Kingswood (1903) and Moorside (1924), homes of prime minister W.L. Mackenzie King, are here. On Harrington L. (L. Mousseau) is the official summer residence of the prime minister. A conference center on Meech L. is the site of an abortive 1987 constitutional accord on Québec's status.

Gatineau River 230 mi/370 km long, in SW Québec. It rises on the CANADIAN SHIELD and flows SSE through L. Baskatong, then S to join the Ottawa R. Its flow was important to the industrial development of HULL, at its mouth; today it is a source of hydroelectric power.

Gatlinburg city, pop. 3417, Sevier Co., E Tennessee, 29 mi/47 km SE of Knoxville, along the Little Pigeon R. It is a gateway to the Great Smoky Mountains National Park, and has developed a sizable tourist industry, focusing on crafts. Mt. Le Conte, 6 mi/10 km SE, is, at 6593 ft/2011 m, one of the highest peaks in the Appalachian system.

Gator Bowl football stadium along the St. Johns R. in downtown Jacksonville, Florida. Part of the Jacksonville Sports Complex, which includes a baseball park, it has been the site since 1946 of a New Year's Day college bowl game of the same name.

Gauley Mountain Allegheny Mt. ridge, 14 mi/23 km NE–SW, in Pocahontas Co., E West Virginia. It includes Big Spruce Knob (4695 ft/1432 m), not to be confused with SPRUCE KNOB.

Gautier city, pop. 10,088, Jackson Co., extreme SE Mississippi, on the Gulf of Mexico W of the mouth of the Pascagoula R., 4 mi/6 km W of Pascagoula and 13 mi/21 km W of the Alabama line. Largely a resort and retirement city, it has a community college.

Gay Head headland on Martha's Vineyard, Dukes Co., SE Massachusetts. At the W end of the island, it has dramatic, multicolored clay cliffs overlooking Vineyard Sound. The town of Gay Head, pop. 200, which includes the cliffs, is a summer resort engaged also in cranberry culture, pottery making, and fishing. Many of its inhabitants are Mashpee (Wampanoag) Indians, whose ancestral claim to the area was recognized by whites in the early 18th century.

Gearhart Mountain see under FREMONT NATIONAL FOREST, Oregon.

Geddes town, Pop. 16,677, Onondaga Co., C New York, adjacent (SW) to Syracuse, along Onondaga L. Like SALINA, across the lake, it was a 1790s salt-producing settlement. It is now a residential and industrial Syracuse suburb. The village of Solvay (pop. 6717) is in the town.

General Grant Tree see under KINGS CANYON NATIONAL PARK, California.

General Sherman Tree see under SEQUOIA NATIONAL PARK, California.

Genesee County 642 sq mi/1663 sq km, pop. 430,459, in SE

Michigan, drained by the Shiawassee and Flint rivers. Its seat is FLINT. It is an agricultural and industrial region, with heavy manufacturing at Flint, in the center of the county. Fruit, vegetables, livestock, poultry, grain, beans, and sugar beets are raised.

Genesee River 144 mi/232 km long, in NW Pennsylvania and W New York. It rises near Ulysses, in Potter Co., Pennsylvania, and flows NNW into New York. Turning NNE at HOUGHTON, it continues through a noted deep gorge, largely within Letchworth State Park, then passes Geneseo, and empties into L. Ontario at ROCHESTER, where its falls have been industrially important. The Genesee Valley is agriculturally rich and draws tourists.

Geneseo town, pop. 9178, seat of Livingston Co., WC New York, on the Genesee R., 26 mi/42 km SW of Rochester. In an agricultural region, it is home to the State University of New York College at Geneseo (1867).

Geneva **1.** city, pop. 12,617, seat of Kane Co., NE Illinois, on the Fox R., a suburb 36 mi/58 km W of Chicago. It was founded in the 1830s and served as a trading center for settlers arriving in Illinois or headed farther W. Farm machinery, electronic parts, auto equipment and batteries, and foundry products are among the goods manufactured here. The Fermi National Accelerator Laboratory is 4 mi/6 km SE. **2.** town, pop. 1280, Adams Co., NE Indiana, 33 mi/53 km SSE of Fort Wayne, near the Ohio border. On the upper reaches of the Wabash R., it was the center of the Limberlost region, celebrated in the writing of Gene Stratton-Porter, who lived here 1895–1913. Her *Girl of the Limberlost* (1909) and other books depict life and characters in the swampy, forested area, which was drained and lumbered in 1913. **3.** city, pop. 14,143, Ontario Co., WC New York, at the N end of Seneca L., 40 mi/64 km SE of Rochester. It was settled in 1785 on the site of an Indian village. Hobart College for men and William Smith College for women were founded here in 1822. Elizabeth Blackwell, the first woman doctor in the modern Western tradition, graduated from Geneva Medical College in 1849. The city is the market and processing center of an agricultural region. Industries manufacture machinery, steel castings, corrugated cartons, and electronic components.

Geneva, Lake see under LAKE GENEVA, Wisconsin.

Genoa historic hamlet in Douglas Co., W Nevada, between the Carson Range (W) and the CARSON R. (E), 12 mi/19 km SSW of Carson City. Settled c.1849, it was abandoned by its original Mormon inhabitants when they returned to Utah a few years later, and taken over by traders who changed its name from Mormon Station. The seat of Carson, later of Douglas Co., it gradually lost importance to Gardnerville (SE), and is now chiefly a tourist magnet, as Nevada's oldest permanent settlement.

Gentilly **1.** largely residential section of New Orleans, Louisiana, E of the Bayou St. John and some 4 mi/6 km N and NE of the VIEUX CARRÉ, near the L. Pontchartrain shore. This large area includes such neighborhoods as Gentilly Terrace (S of MILNEBURG) and Gentilly Woods (along the Inner Harbor Navigation Canal). Newer sections of New Orleans extend E along the lake. **2.** locality, part of BÉCANCOUR, S Québec, 14 mi/23 km ENE of TROIS-RIVIÈRES, site of a Hydro-Québec nuclear power station (operational 1983) on the S bank of the St. Lawrence R.

gentrification process in which middle- and upper-income families and individuals move into an INNER CITY neighborhood, often buying housing that has been rented by poorer residents. The newcomers' motivation may be the neighborhood's proximity to Downtown and its advantages, as well as the opportunity to obtain cheaply and rehabilitate attractive older housing. The result (in addition to some amount of actual displacement of renters) may be a rise in property values, taxes, etc., forcing former residents and small businesses that serve them from the area.

George, Lake alpine lake in NE New York, 50 mi/80 km NNE of Albany, near the Vermont border. It is 33 mi/53 km long and 1–3 mi/2–5 km wide, lies in the foothills of the Adirondack Mts. S of L. Champlain, and empties into Champlain through a short outlet, near which is FORT TICONDEROGA. At its S end is **Lake George** village (pop. 933) a popular resort. The lake was named in honor of King George II by General William Johnson in 1755. The French and English waged many battles and established forts (including FORT WILLIAM HENRY) here until 1759, when the French were finally defeated. In the 20th century the lake has been popular with artists, and is an increasingly heavily used middle-class resort.

George Hill elevation (3004 ft/916 m) of the Allegheny Mts., in far NW Maryland, E of Accident. Deep Creek L. is S.

George Junior Republic former community near the village of Freeville, Dryden township, Tompkins Co., C New York, 9 mi/14 km NE of Ithaca. Founded by William Reuben "Daddy" George in 1895, it was inhabited and governed by delinquent or neglected young people aged 12 to 21 and was intended as a training ground for citizenship and practical trades. It is now a residential treatment center and school.

Georges Bank underwater Atlantic Ocean plateau, c.175 mi/280 km E–W, at the edge of the CONTINENTAL SHELF, off Nova Scotia (NE) and Cape Cod, Massachusetts (W). The mixing of tidal currents from the Bay of FUNDY and the Gulf of MAINE (N) with predominant E–W currents creates a zone rich in nutrients, one of the most productive fishing grounds in the world, esp. for cod, haddock, herring, and scallops. Traditionally fished by US and Canadian fleets, it was in the mid 20th century overfished by Soviet, Eastern European, and Japanese trawlers, severely depleting stocks. However, imposition of 200-mi/320-km offshore fishing control zones in 1977 once more limited fishing to the US and Canada. In 1984, the World Court awarded control of the eastern sixth to Canada, the rest to the US. The bank is also undergoing exploratory drilling for gas and oil.

Georgetown **1.** town, pop. 891, seat of Clear Creek Co., NC Colorado, on Clear Creek and I-70, 36 mi/58 km W of Denver. An 1859–61 gold and 1864–78 silver boom town, it has some 200 buildings of the period, as well as the refurbished Georgetown Loop Railroad, a technical marvel of 1884, now a tourist attraction. **2.** town, pop. 3732, seat of Sussex Co., S Delaware. In the center of the county, it is home to its courthouse (1839) and various small agriculturally related businesses. Although only 10 mi/16 km W of popular REHOBOTH BEACH, Georgetown has remained essentially a quiet Southern town. **3.** residential and commercial section of NW Washington, D.C., along the Potomac R., W of Rock Creek. One of the District of Columbia's original three towns, it was settled (as part of Maryland) in the 1660s and became a river port, handling tobacco and other products. Incorporated in 1789, it became part of the District the next year, and in 1895 was made part of the city of Washington. The S terminus of the Chesapeake and Ohio Canal and the site of most of the District's limited industry, it has been home to Georgetown University since 1789, and in the 20th century evolved into an affluent residential district, well-known home to Washington's powerful. It is today a vibrant tourist, shopping, and student district as well. Georgetown's residential cachet extends to such areas as Burleith and Glover Park, just NW, and Foxhall, just W. **4.** city, pop. 11,414, seat of Scott Co., NC Kentucky, on the North Branch of Elkhorn Creek, 12 mi/19 km N of Lexington. It was settled in 1776 as McClelland's Station. The site of a Toyota auto plant, it also has printshops and distilleries, makes tools and pencils, and processes flour and dairy products; limestone quarries are nearby. Georgetown College (1829) is here. **5.** village, pop. 3627, seat of Brown Co., SW Ohio, 35 mi/56 km SE of Cincinnati. It is the trade and distribution center for an agricultural district, particularly known for its tobacco. Shoes, monuments, and flour are produced locally. The boyhood home of Ulysses S. Grant and the schoolhouse he attended are popular attractions. **6.** see under HALTON HILLS, Ontario. **7.** city, pop. 9517, seat of Georgetown Co., E South Carolina, at the head of Winyah Bay, 55 mi/89 km NE of Charleston. Settled in the 1730s where four rivers (the Pee Dee, Waccamaw, Black, and Sampit) meet, it is a shipping and yachting port and a trade center. Paper products are made, and fishing, dairying, and cotton contribute to the economy. The city long exported rice and indigo to Great Britain and the West Indies. A Spanish attempt to settle the site in the 1520s failed because of climate and disease. **8.** city, pop. 14,842, seat of Williamson Co., C Texas, at the junction of the North and South forks of the San Gabriel R., 21 mi/34 km N of Austin. Founded in 1848, it is a market and processing center for wool and mohair, dairy products, poultry, cotton, and grain. Nearby are limestone quarries, mineral springs, and the popular Inner Space Cavern. Southwestern University, established here in 1873, combines four earlier schools. **9.** see under BOEING FIELD, Seattle, Washington.

George Washington Birthplace National Monument see under WAKEFIELD, Virginia.

George Washington Bridge steel suspension bridge spanning the Hudson R. between Fort Washington, New York City, and Fort Lee, New Jersey. It was completed in 1931 with a center span of 3500 ft/1067 m, making it briefly the longest such bridge in the world. In 1962 a second, lower deck was opened. Interstate 95 and US 1 cross the bridge.

George Washington Carver National Monument see under DIAMOND, Missouri.

Georgia state of the SE US, considered part of the Deep SOUTH (and by the Census Bureau as in the South Atlantic region); 1990 pop. 6,478,216 (118.6% of 1980; rank: 11th); area 59,441 sq mi/153,952 sq km (rank: 24th); ratified Constitution 1788 (4th). Capital and most populous city: ATLANTA. Other leading cities: COLUMBUS, SAVANNAH, MACON, ALBANY. Georgia is bordered NE by South Carolina (across the SAVANNAH and, in the extreme N, the CHATTOOGA, rivers); N by North Carolina (E) and Tennessee (W); W by Alabama, with the CHATTAHOOCHEE R. forming the S half of the boundary; and S by Florida, with the Chattahoochee (far W) and SAINT MARYS (far E) rivers forming parts of the boundary. On the SE, Georgia has a coastline some 90 mi/145 km long, off which are many of the SEA ISLANDS (known long ago as the GOLDEN ISLES). In the far N the state embraces part of the S APPALACHIAN system, including segments of the CUMBERLAND PLATEAU (extreme NW) and Great Appalachian Valley (to its E). On the NE is the S end of the BLUE RIDGE, rising to 4784 ft/1459 m at BRASSTOWN BALD, Georgia's high point. The upper Chattahoochee R. flows SW along the base of the Appalachians here. The state's NC section is part of the PIEDMONT, in which Atlanta and its suburbs form the Southeast's major metropolitan complex. ATHENS, home of the University of Georgia, is also here (EC). This RED CLAY region is the source of the major rivers that flow SE and SW across Georgia: the OGEECHEE and the OCONEE and OCMULGEE (which farther S form the ALTAMAHA), flowing to the Atlantic; and the FLINT, a tributary of the Chattahoochee, flowing ultimately to the Gulf of Mexico. AUGUSTA (on the Savannah), Macon (on the Ocmulgee), and Columbus (on the Chattahoochee) are FALL LINE industrial cities. Below them lies South Georgia, comprising parts of the Gulf (SW) and Atlantic (SE) COASTAL PLAINS, a sandy, low-lying zone covering more than half of Georgia. A pine-wooded and peanut, corn, vegetable, and peach producing area, the Coastal Plains have a number of regional centers, including Albany (SW), VALDOSTA (S), WAYCROSS (SE), and Savannah (NE). The OKEFENOKEE Swamp straddles the Florida border. Along the Atlantic coast, BRUNSWICK is second to Savannah as a port and shipbuilder; KINGS BAY (S) is a major submarine base; and larger Sea Islands include (N–S) WASSAW, OSSABAW, SAPELO, SAINT SIMONS, JEKYLL, and Cumberland. With important MOUND BUILDER sites including Etowah (see CARTERSVILLE), and home to the Creek (SW) and Cherokee (NW, with their last center at New Echota, near CALHOUN, before they were forced onto the 1830s TRAIL OF TEARS), Georgia (named for George II) was founded in 1733 (at Savannah) by James Oglethorpe, whose settlers, many of them English debtors, were supposed to establish a buffer between the Colonies to the N and Spanish-controlled Florida to the S. An agricultural colony, it was the scene (1793) of Eli Whitney's invention of the cotton gin, and quickly became a major producer; cotton's dominance in the economy did not end until the early 20th century, when the boll weevil forced diversification on farmers. In the 1850s, its advantageous river crossing site made the town of Terminus, soon called Atlanta (the Western & Atlantic Railroad connected it with Chattanooga, Tennessee) a transportation and trade hub. In the Civil War, when Union forces moved SE from Tennessee, this new importance cost Atlanta and C Georgia dearly; after the 1864 battles of KENNESAW Mountain and RESACA, W. T. Sherman captured and burned the city, then moved SE on the MARCH TO THE SEA, his troops and followers devastating everything in their path. In the postwar period, Georgia was the first home to the concept of the New (industrial, socially reorganized) South; textilemaking DALTON (NW) and WEST POINT (W), ROME, and the Fall Line cities are among centers of manufacturing that has grown since then. Georgia is today a major producer of fabrics, esp. for carpets, bedding, and similar uses. The forest products industries (turpentine, pulp, lumber) remain important; TOCCOA is a furniture and toolmaking center. Marble and other minerals and stone are mined in the N mountains. Chemicals, aircraft (MARIETTA), clothing, and processed foods are among other leading Georgia products.

Tobacco, like cotton, has faded in agricultural importance, as poultry, peanuts, cattle, and other farm produce have risen. The Atlanta area is now regarded by many as the "capital" of the South. It is a financial and commercial center; an educational, research, and cultural hub (the CENTERS FOR DISEASE CONTROL AND PREVENTION; Georgia Institute of Technology; Emory University; the ATLANTA UNIVERSITY CENTER); and a transportation nexus (railroads, highways, and the HARTSFIELD INTERNATIONAL AIRPORT). Its fast-growing suburbs (including DE KALB and COBB counties, home to many whites who have left the city in recent decades, as well as to new arrivals to the area) have become a major residential zone. Savannah balances modern industry and its old city center, the first planned community in America, and draws many visitors. The military is important to Georgia, esp. at the huge FORT BENNING, near Columbus. Tourism and recreation focus on historic sites including STONE Mt., the Confederate memorial E of Atlanta; the MARTIN LUTHER KING, JR. NATIONAL HISTORIC SITE, in Atlanta; and Civil War sites; and on seacoast, river (including the TALLULAH Gorge), and mountain (including the APPALACHIAN TRAIL, whose S terminus is at SPRINGER Mt.) locales. Georgia's people include many descendants of the 18th-century settlers, but the pop. has recently become more diverse. Some 27% of Georgians are black, and Atlanta in particular has been the scene of black political and social advances.

Georgia, Strait of 150 mi/240 km–long NW–SE oriented channel between SE VANCOUVER I. (W) and mainland British Columbia and Washington (E). It connects in the N with the Johnstone and QUEEN CHARLOTTE straits, on the S with the Haro and JUAN DE FUCA straits. All of these bodies are part of the coastal trough between the COAST MOUNTAINS (E) and COAST RANGES (W). Averaging 30 mi/50 km wide, the Strait of Georgia has heavily indented coastlines and is filled with islands, including TEXADA I. and the GULF Is. An important fishing ground, it also forms part of the INSIDE PASSAGE to Alaska. Formerly known as the **Gulf of Georgia,** it is still referred to locally as the Gulf.

Georgia Avenue commercial thoroughfare in NW Washington, D.C. Beginning at Florida Ave., in SHAW, it passes N in front of Howard University, in Le Droit Park, and through residential neighborhoods to the Maryland line at Silver Spring. It is often regarded as the business spine of black Washington.

Georgia Dome enclosed arena in downtown Atlanta, Georgia, 0.6 mi/1 km WNW of FIVE POINTS and just W of the OMNI. Seating 70,000 and opened in 1993, it is home to the Atlanta Falcons (football) and will be host to 1996 Olympic events.

Georgian Bay NE extension of L. HURON, in SC Ontario. Some 125 mi/200 km NW–SE and 55 mi/90 km wide, it is separated from the lake by the BRUCE PENINSULA (SW) and MANITOULIN I. (NW), two parts of the NIAGARA ESCARPMENT, between which 15 mi/25 km–wide Main Channel connects bay and lake. Killarney Provincial Park is at the N end of the bay, while the Thirty Thousand Is. lie along the E shore, where PARRY SOUND is the recreational hub. Nottawasaga Bay, at Georgian Bay's S extremity, is lined with beach resorts and the port of COLLINGWOOD. In the SE corner, where the TRENT CANAL system enters the bay, are Midland and Penetanguishene. OWEN SOUND is on the SW.

Georgia Sea Islands see SEA ISLANDS.

Georgina town, pop. 29,746, York Regional Municipality, S Ontario, on the S side of L. SIMCOE, 37 mi/60 km N of Toronto. An agricultural and resort community, now experiencing rapid residential growth, it has a number of waterfront villages. Sutton (or Sutton West), on the Black R., is an 1820s mill town noted for its 1870s St. George's Church, burial site of writers Stephen Leacock and Mazo de la Roche.

Germanna locality on the Rapidan R., 13 mi/21 km SE of Culpeper, Virginia, that was important in two Civil War campaigns. In May 1863, Federal troops crossed Germanna Ford bound for CHANCELLORSVILLE, 9 mi/14 km SE. In May 1864, they crossed again on their way to the WILDERNESS battle, 5 mi/8 km SE. Germanna Community College (1969) is nearby.

Germantown **1.** unincorporated suburban community, pop. 41,145, Montgomery Co., WC Maryland, 10 mi/16 km NW of Rockville, and 22 mi/35 km NW of Washington, D.C. A bedroom community on Interstate 270, it also has US Department of Energy and corporate technology facilities and a community college. **2.** section of NW Philadelphia, Pennsylvania. First settled in 1683 by a group of Germans, by 1750 it was a well-established community. It was the site of a defeat for Washington's army during the Revolution (Oct. 4, 1777). Consolidated with Philadelphia in 1854, Germantown became a favorite summer residence of wealthy city dwellers, who built large estates here. Some of these, such as Cliveden and Grumblethorpe, have been restored. Germantown is now an affluent residential area. **3.** city, pop. 32,893, Shelby Co., SW Tennessee, 14 mi/23 km ESE of downtown Memphis, a booming residential suburb just S of the Wolf R. **4.** village, pop. 13,658, Washington Co., SE Wisconsin, a residential suburb 15 mi/24 km NW of Milwaukee. Dairy products and vegetables are processed here.

German Village neighborhood of Columbus, Ohio, immediately S of Downtown. Originally the home of wealthy German merchants, who built large houses here, it has become a popular enclave of young professionals.

Gettysburg borough, pop. 7025, seat of Adams Co., SC Pennsylvania, 35 mi/56 km SW of Harrisburg, in the E foothills of the Allegheny Mts. It was laid out in the 1780s. Gettysburg was the site of one of the most important battles of the Civil War (July 1–3, 1863), in which Union troops commanded by George Meade halted the northward invasion of Confederate forces under Robert E. Lee. The names of parts of the battlefield, such as Cemetery Ridge, Seminary Ridge, and Little Round Top, became legendary. Four months after the battle, at dedicatory ceremonies (Nov. 19, 1863), Abraham Lincoln delivered the Gettysburg Address here. Today Gettysburg is the center of a fruit growing and processing area; there is also some light industry. In addition to the Gettysburg National Cemetery and National Military Park, other notable sites include President Dwight Eisenhower's farm and a number of Civil War museums. Gettysburg College (1832) and Gettysburg Lutheran Theological Seminary (1826) are here.

geyser (from the Icelandic) a hot spring in volcanic or postvolcanic areas that intermittently or regularly emits hot water, steam, and other material, throwing it sometimes high into the air. It is driven by the expansion of water heated below the surface, which at intervals acquires the force necessary to violently expel water lying above it. See also FUMAROLE.

ghetto (from the name of a part of medieval Venice, Italy, where Jews were required to live) a residential area, usually in the INNER CITY, inhabited primarily by members of a minority group. Although choice may play some part in a ghetto's formation, discrimination and economic hardship, trapping residents in a declining district, are more important; ghettos may be created by the departure of middle-class residents, as in WHITE FLIGHT, from what had been a healthy community.

ghost town a once-flourishing settlement, now completely abandoned or housing few residents amid remains of former days. The term came into use after mid-19th-century gold rushes left California and Nevada, in particular, with many empty towns that had thrived a few years earlier; it is now used also of such deserted settlements as former military base towns. Some ghost towns flourish as tourist attractions, in effect as THEME PARKS.

Gibbsville fictional locale: see under POTTSVILLE, Pennsylvania.

Gifford Pinchot National Forest 2143 sq mi/5551 sq km, in the CASCADE RANGE, SW Washington, extending S from the Mt. Rainier area to the Columbia R. Mt. St. Helens and Mt. Adams are here. The topographically varied forest includes seven wilderness areas.

Gila Bend town, pop. 1747, Maricopa Co., SW Arizona, just S of a bend in the Gila R., and 60 mi/100 km SW of Phoenix. The Gila Bend Indian Reservation and Painted Rock Reservoir lie N. Originally a Maricopa village, and the site of farms established (1699) by the Jesuit missionary Eusebio Kino, it is now an agricultural center and road junction.

Gila Desert see under SONORAN DESERT.

Gila Mountains in Arizona: **a.** see under BARRY M. GOLDWATER RANGE. **b.** NW–SE trending range paralleling the upper Gila R., NW of Safford. Rising to 7298 ft/2224 m at Bryce Mt., it lies along part of the S boundary of the SAN CARLOS Indian Reservation.

Gila National Forest 3.3 million ac/1.34 million ha (5160 sq mi/13,355 sq km), in SW New Mexico. In rugged mountain terrain along the Arizona border (W), it includes the MOGOLLON and MIMBRES mountains and the BLACK RANGE, as well as the Gila R. headwaters. Silver City, just S, is headquarters. The **Gila Cliff Dwellings National Monument,** preserving 13th-century ruins, is here. The **Gila Wilderness,** established 1924 by the Forest Service in the Mogollons, on the urging of naturalist Aldo Leopold, was the progenitor of all US WILDERNESS AREAS.

Gila River 650 mi/1045 km long, in SW New Mexico and S Arizona. It rises in the BLACK RANGE, in the Gila National Forest, near the Gila Cliff Dwellings National Monument, in Catron Co., New Mexico, and flows SW to the Arizona line, then generally W across Arizona, joining the COLORADO R., of which it is the major tributary, at YUMA. The Gila's tributaries include the San Simon, San Pedro, and Santa Cruz, which join it from the S in Arizona; and the SALT, Agua Fria, and Hassayampa, which join it from the N. In an arid area, it is with its tributaries the source of irrigation water used for over 1000 years, since the Hohokam developed a canal system on the site of modern PHOENIX. Today the Gila, Salt, and other rivers in the system have been dammed, and both the mainstream and tributaries flow intermittently. Cotton and fruits are among local agricultural products. In SE Arizona, the Gila passes through SAFFORD, the SAN CARLOS APACHE INDIAN RESERVATION (site of the Coolidge Dam), and FLORENCE. Passing between the CASA GRANDE (S) and Phoenix (N) areas, it proceeds W, then sharply S to Gila Bend. From the latter it winds WSW, with the harsh desert of the BARRY M. GOLDWATER Range on its S, to Yuma. Before 1854 the Gila formed the Mexican-American boundary; the GADSDEN PURCHASE then transferred to the US lands to the S, in an area still heavily Mexican, Apache, Pima, and Tohono o'Odham (Papago) in influence.

Gilbert town, pop. 29,188, Maricopa Co., SC Arizona, a booming suburb 18 mi/29 km SE of Phoenix. Largely residential, it is in an area long noted for cotton, alfalfa, and flax production.

Gillette city, pop. 17,635, seat of Campbell Co., NE Wyoming, on I-90 and the Missouri Plateau, 80 mi/128 km ESE of Sheridan. Established in 1891 with the arrival of the railroad, it was a livestock and mining center until 1967, when local oil strikes brought on a sudden boom. Large deposits of low-sulfur coal in the area (WYODAK is just E) have maintained its prosperity.

Gillette Castle see under LYME, Connecticut.

Gilmore unincorporated village in Tuscarawas Co., E Ohio, 12 mi/19 km S of New Philadelphia. Baseball great Cy Young was born here (1867).

Gilroy city, pop. 31,487, Santa Clara Co., WC California, in the Santa Clara Valley, 30 mi/48 km SSE of San Jose. It is widely known as the "Garlic Capital of the World"; although the herb is now chiefly grown elsewhere in California, Gilroy processes most of the crop, and holds a huge Garlic Festival in July. Fruit, vegetables, cattle, and poultry are also raised, and the area is noted for its wineries and vineyards. Manufactures include farm equipment, paint, fiberglass, and paper products. Gavilan Community College (1919) is here. The city's residential sector is growing rapidly.

Gimli town, pop. 1579, S Manitoba, on the SW shore of L. WINNIPEG, 50 mi/80 km N of Winnipeg. Founded in the 1870s by Icelanders, it spawned several other smaller colonies nearby. It is the largest Icelandic community outside of Iceland. The economy is supported by fishing, farming, and a Seagram distillery. The annual Islendingadagurinn (Icelandic Festival), held in August, and nearby HECLA I. draw visitors.

Ginna nuclear power plant, operational since 1969, in Ontario township, Wayne Co., NW New York, on L. Ontario, 16 mi/26 km NE of Rochester.

Girard city, pop. 11,304, Trumbull Co., NE Ohio, on the Mahoning R., 5 mi/8 km NW of Youngstown. It is situated in the heart of a steel manufacturing region, and the glow of deposits dumped from smelting furnaces can be seen at night. In the years after the area's settlement (c.1800) coal was mined here. The Ohio and Erie Canal (1837) cut through Girard and fostered its industrial growth, remaining important to the city's economy until 1867, when a railroad line was established. The first iron works (1866) is still in operation. Aluminum, plastics, tools and dies, and leather are also produced.

Gitch(e) Gumee see under HIAWATHA NATIONAL FOREST, Michigan.

Gjoa Haven see under NORTHWEST PASSAGE.

Glace Bay town, pop. 19,501, Cape Breton Co., extreme E Nova Scotia. On the E coast of CAPE BRETON I., it was once a famous coal producer. At first its cliffs were mined; in the

1890s coal was taken from under sea as well as land for the steel industry in nearby SYDNEY. By the 1960s Glace Bay was depressed; a Federal heavy water plant built on the outskirts failed to provide a new economic base. The town now lives largely on fishing and on visitors to its Miners' Museum and other attractions. At Table Head, Marconi sent the first transatlantic wireless message (Dec. 1902).

Glacier Bay National Park and Preserve 3.2 million ac/1.3 million ha (5000 sq mi/13,000 sq km), in the Panhandle of SE Alaska, NW of the Alexander Archipelago and WNW of Juneau. What the first white observers saw in the 1790s as the face of one massive glacier had become by the 1870s, when the ice had retreated over 30 mi/50 km, a deep bay into which some 18 tidewater glaciers discharge. The ice has continued to retreat, allowing the land to rise slowly. Rain forests and the Fairweather Range, peaking at Mt. FAIRWEATHER (15,300 ft/4663 m) surround the bay, whose FJORDS are seen only from boat or floatplane.

Glacier National Park **1.** 521 sq mi/1350 sq km, in the Columbia Mts. section of the Rocky Mts., in SE British Columbia. The Selkirk and Purcell ranges meet here, and Rogers Pass (see SELKIRK Mts.) is within the park. Mt. Dawson (11,122 ft/3390 m) is the high point in an area with over 400 glaciers and heavy snowfall that has led to extensive, innovative avalanche control programs. **2.** 1.014 million ac/411,000 ha (1584 sq mi/4104 sq km), in NW Montana, along the border with Alberta and British Columbia. In the N Rocky Mts., on the Continental Divide, it is noted for its peaks over 10,000 ft/3050 m, its glacial lakes, and its over 50 active glaciers. The mountains, primarily in the Lewis Range, are an overthrust structure, made of sedimentary material overlying newer igneous rock. The Going-to-the-Sun Road (1933) crosses the park SW–NE. Established in 1910, the park in 1932 joined WATERTON LAKES NATIONAL PARK, adjacent in Alberta, as the Waterton-Glacier International Peace Park; the two reserves are, however, separately administered.

Glacier Peak 10,541 ft/3213 m, in Snohomish Co., extreme NW Washington, in the CASCADE RANGE, 50 mi/80 km ENE of Everett, in the Wenatchee National Forest.

Gladstone **1.** city, pop. 26,243, Clay Co., NW Missouri, just N of downtown Kansas City and entirely surrounded by the city. It is a residential and manufacturing suburb. **2.** see PEAPACK AND GLADSTONE, New Jersey. **3.** city, pop. 10,152, Clackamas Co., NW Oregon, at the point where the Clackamas R. empties into the Willamette R., a residential suburb 11 mi/18 km SSE of Portland.

Glasgow **1.** city, pop. 12,351, seat of Barren Co., S Kentucky, 29 mi/45 km E of Bowling Green. Settled in the 1790s, it became an important road junction in the 1830s. It is the trading center for an oil and gas producing region that also grows timber, tobacco, and grains. It makes auto and electrical parts, roller bearings, clothing, explosives, and fertilizer. **2.** city, pop. 3572, seat of Valley Co., NE Montana, on the Milk R., 140 mi/225 km ESE of Havre. One of the oldest communities in E Montana, it was established in 1887 for the construction of the Great Northern Railway. Situated in an irrigated agricultural region, it is a trading and shipping point for livestock, spring wheat, and poultry, makes flour and beverages, and processes bentonite. In the mid 1930s, the city became a boom town with the construction of the FORT PECK DAM, 17 mi/27 km SE.

Glassboro borough, pop. 15,614, Gloucester Co., SW New Jersey, 16 mi/26 km S of Camden. It was settled in 1775 by Germans, who founded a still-active glassmaking industry four years later. A trading center for a truck farming and fruit growing region, Glassboro also has canneries and manufactures bottle caps. It is the seat of Glassboro State College (1923), the scene of meetings between President Johnson and Soviet Premier Kosygin in 1967; the college was renamed Rowan College in 1992 to honor a donor.

Glass Buttes volcanic elevation (6385 ft/1946 m), 50 mi/80 km W of BURNS, in the HARNEY DESERT of C Oregon. Rising 2000 ft/610 m above the surrounding terrain, they are among the largest obsidian outcroppings in the world, known especially for their colored streakings and iridescence, and long valued by Indians from a wide area for use in implements and points. Today, with the Stinking Water Mountains, 30 mi/50 km E of Burns, they are popular with rockhounds.

Glassmanor see under OXON HILL, Maryland.

Glass Mountains NE–SW range extending for c.25 mi/40 km and forming the N boundary of the MARATHON BASIN, in SW Texas. Rising over 6500 ft/1980 m and tilting northward, it is composed largely of Permian rocks lying atop older Paleozoic strata.

Glastonbury town, pop. 27,901, Hartford Co., C Connecticut, 6 mi/10 km SE of Hartford, on the Connecticut R. An historic town first settled in 1650 as part of neighboring (W) Wethersfield, it has many Colonial homes. Part of the TOBACCO VALLEY, it has fruit and poultry farms, financial and other commercial operations, and light manufactures including tools, soap, plastics, chemicals, and textiles.

Glen Abbey see under OAKVILLE, Ontario.

Glen Burnie unincorporated residential suburb, pop. 37,305, Anne Arundel Co., C Maryland, 10 mi/16 km S of Baltimore, and just E of Baltimore-Washington International Airport.

Glen Canyon and Glen Canyon Dam and National Recreation Area: see under L. POWELL, Utah and Arizona.

Glencoe village, pop. 8499, Cook Co., NE Illinois, on L. Michigan, a residential suburb 23 mi/37 km NW of Chicago. The 300-ac/122-ha Chicago Botanic Garden is situated here. The poet Archibald MacLeish was born (1892) in Glencoe.

Glen Cove city, pop. 24,149, Nassau Co., SE New York, on the North Shore of Long Island, E of the entrance to Hempstead Harbor, 22 mi/35 km ENE of New York City. Although chiefly residential, it has some light industry, including the manufacture of office supplies, hardware, and clothing. It is home to the Webb Institute of Naval Architecture, Garvies Point Preserve, and Welwyn Preserve, the former estate of industrialist Charles Pratt and now a conference and nature center.

Glendale **1.** city, pop. 148,134, Maricopa Co., SC Arizona, in the Salt R. Valley, adjacent (NW) to Phoenix. This residential suburb is one of the fastest-growing cities in the US. It is also a trade and transportation center for farms producing fruit, vegetables, and cotton, and has agricultural processing facilities. Glendale Community College (1965) is here. Luke Air Force Base, which trains jet fighter pilots, is 12 mi/19 km W. **2.** city, pop. 180,038, Los Angeles Co., SW California, 8 mi/12 km N of downtown Los Angeles, at the SE end of the San Fernando Valley, adjacent (SE) to Burbank. Many residents commute to Los Angeles or to the Valley's manufacturing plants. The city is a commercial, financial, and distribution center, with some corporate headquarters and light manufacturing. It was founded in 1886, on land that had been part of the 1784 Rancho San Rafael. The Casa Adobe de San Rafael (1864–72), once part of the RANCHO, is in a city park. The Pacific Electric Railroad connected Glendale to Los Angeles in 1904, fostering residential development. Among the city's institutions are Glendale Community College (1927) and the Brand Library and Art Center, housed in a 1904 Moorish mansion. The 300-ac/120-ha Forest Lawn Memorial Park, last resting place of many Hollywood stars, is here. **3.** city, pop. 2453, Arapahoe Co., NC Colorado. It is a largely residential community, about 1 sq mi/2.6 sq km, completely surrounded by the city of Denver. **4.** city, pop. 5945, St. Louis Co., EC Missouri, 11 mi/18 km WSW of downtown St. Louis, a residential suburb. **5.** see under FRAYSER'S FARM, Virginia. **6.** city, pop. 14,088, Milwaukee Co., SE Wisconsin, on the Milwaukee R., immediately N of Milwaukee. L. Michigan is a few miles E of this residential suburb.

Glendale Heights village, pop. 27,973, Du Page Co., NE Illinois, a residential suburb 22 mi/35 km W of Chicago.

Glendive city, pop. 4802, seat of Dawson Co., E Montana, on the Yellowstone R., 72 mi/116 km NE of Miles City and 30 mi/48 km W of the North Dakota border. Originating as Fort Canby, which protected Northern Pacific Railway workers, it became a railhead (1881) for shipping cattle and farm products. Gas, oil, and coal discoveries in the 1950s made it a supply center for Williston Basin industries. Frontier Gateway Museum is 1 mi/2 km E, and Makoshika State Park, with rugged badlands, 3 mi/5 km S.

Glendora city, pop. 47,828, Los Angeles Co., SW California, at the S base of the San Gabriel Mts., 25 mi/40 km ENE of Los Angeles, of which it is a commuter suburb. Founded in 1887, it was in the early 20th century an important citrus center, known for its orange and lemon groves. Following World War II, a housing boom largely displaced the growers. Citrus College (1915) is here, and there are some light manufactures.

Glen Echo town, pop. 234, Montgomery Co., C Maryland, on the Potomac R. 2 mi/3 km NW of the Washington, D.C. line. Glen Echo Park, an amusement park originally (1890s) reached by streetcar from Washington, is now an arts center. Clara Barton's last home (1891), once American Red Cross headquarters, is here.

Glen Ellen unincorporated community, pop. 1191, Sonoma Co., NW California, in the Valley of the Moon, in the Sonoma Mts., 40 mi/64 km NNE of San Francisco. A noted winery center, it was the home (1905–16) of Jack London, who died here having immortalized the area in his 1913 novel *The Valley of the Moon.* In 800-ac/325-ha Jack London State Historic Park, The House of Happy Walls, built by his widow, is now a museum housing the writer's memorabilia.

Glen Ellyn village, pop. 24,944, Du Page Co., NE Illinois, on the East Branch of the Du Page R., a residential suburb 26 mi/42 km W of Chicago. It was settled in 1833. Local educational institutions include Maryknoll College, College of Du Page (1966), and a campus of Lewis University College of Law.

Glen Island park in Long Island Sound, part of the city of NEW ROCHELLE, Westchester Co., New York. It was one of the most famous amusement parks in the world from 1885 to 1914. Built on five separate islands connected by bridges, it attracted visitors by steamboat from New York City. After World War I, Westchester Co. filled in the water between the islands, making them into one large island. In the 1930s, the Glen Island Casino featured the biggest of the "Big Bands." The park today has a restaurant and a public beach.

Glenmont see under WHEATON, Maryland.

Glen Ridge borough, pop. 7076, Essex Co., N New Jersey, 4 mi/6 km NW of Newark. It is an affluent commuter suburb with some light industry.

Glen Rock borough, pop. 10,883, Bergen Co., NE New Jersey, 4 mi/6 km N of Paterson. Settled in the early 18th century, it occupies an area that was a camping ground for Washington's troops during the Revolution. Today it has numerous manufactures, many office buildings, and a large residential segment.

Glens Falls city, pop. 15,023, Warren Co., E New York, at the falls of the Hudson R., 45 mi/72 km NNE of Albany and 7 mi/11 km S of L. GEORGE. The site was settled as Wing's Falls in the 1760s. It was renamed for Colonel Johannes Glen, financer of several mills, in 1788. Glens Falls developed as a lumbering and textile center, and now produces paper, paper mill machinery, cement, clothing, and pigments. The city also is a market center for the surrounding area, including the E Adirondack Mts. Glens Falls is home to the Hyde Collection (art) and to Adirondack Community College (1960).

Glenshaw village in SHALER TOWNSHIP, Allegheny Co., SW Pennsylvania, a residential suburb 5 mi/8 km N of downtown Pittsburgh.

Glenside unincorporated village, pop. 8704, in the urban townships of Cheltenham and Abington, Montgomery Co., SE Pennsylvania. A residential suburb 8 mi/13 km NNW of Philadelphia, it has some light manufacturing. Glenside is home to Beaver College (1853).

Glenvar Heights unincorporated residential community, pop. 14,823, Dade Co., SE Florida, 10 mi/16 km SW of Miami.

Glenview village, pop. 37,093, Cook Co., NE Illinois, on the North Branch of the Chicago R., a suburb 18 mi/28 km NW of Chicago. A residential community, it grew in population with the establishment of the adjacent Glenview Naval Air Station (NW) in 1940. Glenview has some manufactures including bricks and tools, and is the site of several corporate headquarters. It was founded in the 1830s as the farming settlement of Hutchings. Located here is Peacock Prairie, one of the state's few pristine black-soil prairies, which serves as a botanical research station for the University of Illinois.

Glenville **1.** residential neighborhood in Cleveland, Ohio, on L. Erie, NE of Downtown and adjacent to suburban East Cleveland. A middle-class black area of detached single-family homes, it achieved notoriety as the site of a shootout between community activists and police in 1968 that sparked two days of rioting in the city. **2.** town, pop. 1923, seat of Gilmer Co., C West Virginia, on the Little Kanawha R., 38 mi/64 km SW of Clarksburg. Glenville State College (1872) is here.

Glenwood village, pop. 9289, Cook Co., NE Illinois, on Thorn Creek, a residential suburb 21 mi/34 km S of Chicago. Forest preserves lie just N and SW of the village.

Glimmerglass see under OTSEGO L., New York.

Glitter Gulch see the STRIP, Las Vegas, Nevada.

Globe city, pop. 6062, seat of Gila Co., EC Arizona, 70 mi/113 km ESE of Phoenix. It is in a mountainous mining and ranching area, with nearby deposits of copper, silver, gold, asbestos, manganese, vanadium, and tungsten. An 1870s silver center, it later developed as one of the nation's largest copper producers; the yield declined after 1918, but some local mines are still active. Globe is on a prehistoric PUEBLO site; the 600-year-old Besh-ba-gowah cliff dwellings are 1 mi/2 km S. The huge San Carlos Apache Indian Reservation lies to the E; Globe serves as its trade center.

Glorieta Pass at 7400 ft/2260 m, in the S SANGRE DE CRISTO Mts., 10 mi/16 km SE of Santa Fe, New Mexico. It was the final pass on the SANTA FE TRAIL, and is today on I-25. In March 1862, Confederate forces, having won a skirmish at Valverde, near San Marcial, S of Socorro, advanced through Albuquerque and Santa Fe, and here, in Apache Canyon, W of the pass, were met by Union forces proceeding S from Las Vegas. The Confederates were forced to fall back after their supply train was destroyed, beginning a retreat that ensured Union control of New Mexico.

Gloucester **1.** city, pop. 28,716, Essex Co., NE Massachusetts, on Cape Ann, 30 mi/48 km NE of Boston. A maritime and fishing center since its founding in 1623, Gloucester has inspired artistic and literary works. Economic life centers on Gloucester Harbor, on the S side of the peninsula. The Fisherman's Memorial, facing the harbor, honors residents lost at sea. At present, the chief industry is processing imported frozen fish. Offshore just to the SW is the reef called Norman's Woe, key in Longfellow's ballad "The Wreck of the *Hesperus.*" Outside of the fishing port, Gloucester includes a number of resort villages, including East Gloucester and Beauport to the SE, and Annisquam, on the peninsula's N, on Ipswich Bay. The town of ROCKPORT lies E. Dogtown, an area of heath and scattered glacial boulders, with remains of 17th-century cellars, an area that has long fascinated folklorists and artists, lies S of Annisquam. **2.** city, pop. 101,677, Ottawa-Carleton Regional Municipality, SE Ontario, adjacent (E and S) to Ottawa, of which it is a residential, commercial, and industrial suburb. Part of Ottawa's International Airport and several large government complexes are here.

Gloucester City city, pop. 12,649, Camden Co., SW New Jersey, on the Delaware R. opposite S Philadelphia, Pennsylvania, and on Newton Creek, 3 mi/5 km S of Camden. Built on the site of the Dutch Fort Nassau (1623), it was settled by Irish Quakers in 1682 and witnessed several Revolutionary War clashes. Today it is a manufacturing center, producing such goods as chemicals, cork, paper products, floor coverings, roofing, and clothing.

Gloucester County **1.** 327 sq mi/847 sq km, pop. 230,082, in SW New Jersey, bordered by the Delaware R. (NW). Its seat is WOODBURY. There is substantial suburban residential and industrial development in its NE corner, particularly around its seat, an area close to Philadelphia and Camden. Industries include canning and the manufacture of clothing, building materials, electrical parts, chemicals, and glassware. In addition, there are many truck, dairy, and fruit farms throughout the county. **2.** 225 sq mi/583 sq km, pop. 30,131, in SE Virginia. Its seat is Gloucester (Gloucester Courthouse, pop. 2118). In the TIDEWATER, on the N shore of the York R., Gloucester Co. is largely agricultural, and has some fisheries. **Gloucester Point** (unincorporated; pop. 8509), across the James R. (N) from YORKSTOWN, is the largest community.

Gloversville city, pop. 16,656, Fulton Co., EC New York, on Cayadutta Creek, between the Mohawk R. and the Adirondack Mts., 12 mi/19 km NW of Amsterdam. It was established as Kingsboro in 1760, a group of glovemakers from Perthshire, Scotland, arriving to make thick gloves and mittens for regional farmers. Tanning and glovemaking remain the leading industries of Gloversville (renamed in 1832). The city also manufactures clothing, shoes, and other leather goods. Regional farms produce apples and potatoes. Gloversville is the S gateway to the lakes of the Adirondacks.

Glynn, Marshes of see under BRUNSWICK, Georgia.

Gnadenhutten village, pop. 1226, Tuscarawas Co., EC Ohio, on the Tuscarawas R., 8 mi/13 km S of NEW PHILADELPHIA. A 9-ac/3.6-ha state historical park recalls the 1782 massacre here at a Moravian mission of 96 Christian Delaware Indians by American militiamen.

Goderich town, pop. 7452, seat of Huron Co., SW Ontario, on a bluff overlooking L. Huron where it is joined by the Maitland R., 113 mi/182 km NE of Detroit, Michigan. It has a natural harbor and was founded in 1828 as a transshipment point for the Canada Company's Huron Tract development, but failed to become a thriving trade center. The discovery of rock salt in the 1860s gave a boost to the economy, and its manufacture continues. Other industries include lumbering, grain storage, and tourism.

Godfrey unincorporated community, pop. 5436, Madison Co., SW Illinois, 4 mi/6 km NNW of ALTON. It is the seat of Lewis & Clark Community College (1970).

Goethals Bridge cantilevered highway bridge over the Arthur Kill between Staten I., New York, and Elizabeth, New Jersey. With a 672-ft/205-m main span and 8600-ft/2623-m total length, it was opened 1928 and named to honor the Panama Canal's chief engineer. When the VERRAZANO-NARROWS BRIDGE opened (1964), the Goethals became a major conduit for traffic between Long Island and New Jersey.

Goffstown town, pop. 14,621, Hillsborough Co., S New Hampshire. Goffstown is on the Piscataquog R., 6 mi/10 km WNW of the center of Manchester. It is a Manchester suburb and summer resort, and produces poultry, fruit, and wood products. PINARDVILLE is in the E part.

Gogebic County 1105 sq mi/2862 sq km, pop. 18,052, in the NW Upper Peninsula of Michigan. It is drained by the Ontonagon, Presque Isle, and Montreal rivers and bounded NW by L. Superior and S and W by Wisconsin. Its seat is Bessemer. The county has many small lakes and waterfalls and abundant hunting and fishing. Resorts are numerous, particularly at L. Gogebic. Ottawa National Forest covers much of the county, which depends on lumbering and the raising of fruit, livestock, and vegetables. Manufacturing at Ironwood and Bessemer is largely due to vast iron ore deposits in the **Gogebic Range,** which is 0.5–1 mi/0.8–1.6 km wide and 80 mi/129 km long. It extends west from Wakefield, in E Gogebic Co., into Wisconsin's Iron, Ashland, and Bayfield counties. Ore was first discovered here in 1848. Main extraction centers are Ironwood and Hurley, Wisconsin. The westernmost section is sometimes called the Penokee Range.

Golconda hamlet in Humboldt Co., N Nevada, on the Humboldt R. and I-80, 13 mi/21 km ENE of Winnemucca. Named for a fabulously wealthy ancient city in India, it was first known for its hot springs. It has been a mining community for many years. There was a gold strike 20 mi/32 km N in the 1930s, and tungsten deposits were exploited during World War II. Some old mines are still worked, and there were new gold strikes in the 1980s.

Gold Coast **1.** wealthy residential district, usually along a shore, as in Chicago; around Palm Beach, Florida; along the Connecticut shore in Fairfield County; or along the NORTH SHORE of Long Island, New York. The name has also been applied to affluent neighborhoods alongside parks, as along Central Park on New York's Upper East Side. **2.** also, **Platinum Coast** see under SIXTEENTH St., Washington, D.C. **3.** in Florida, the section of the Atlantic coastline around Palm Beach and S to the Miami area, the focus of late-19th-century and early-20th-century development of exclusive resorts. **4.** see KONA COAST, Hawaii. **5.** elite residential neighborhood along L. Michigan, on the Near North Side of Chicago, Illinois, just N of the LOOP. It is a three-block-wide strip of luxury high-rise apartment buildings. The area was christened when entrepreneur Potter Palmer moved from PRAIRIE AVENUE to what was then an area of town houses and mansions in 1882, and was followed by the rest of high society.The replacement of existing structures with apartment buildings after World War I did little to diminish the prestige of the area. **6.** in Michigan, the wealthy suburbs NE of Detroit along L. SAINT CLAIR, especially the five GROSSE POINTE communities (the Pointes).

Golden city, pop. 13,116, seat of Jefferson Co., NC Colorado, on Clear Creek, at the foot of Lookout Mt., 10 mi/16 km NW of Denver. Settled as a mining town in 1859, it was capital of the Colorado Territory in 1862–67. In a mining and agricultural region producing coal, clay, gold, wheat, and sugar beets, Golden manufactures beer (Coors), porcelain, cans, bottles, firebrick, and cement blocks. It is the seat of the Colorado School of Mines (1874) and houses several technological research facilities. Nearby Lookout Mt. is the burial place of Col. William Cody and the site of the Buffalo Bill Museum; the city celebrates annual Buffalo Bill Days.

Golden Gate strait between the Pacific Ocean and San Francisco Bay, in NC California. Extending 4.5 mi/7 km E–W and 1–2 mi/2–3 km across, it reaches a depth of 400 ft/120 m, and is bordered N by the Marin Headlands and S by the San Francisco Peninsula. ALCATRAZ I. is at its E end. The first European to discover the strait was the English explorer Sir Francis Drake, in 1579. The name was used before the 1840s California gold rush, but became even more popular after. The strait is noted for its fierce currents, which reach 60 mi/100 km per hour. The **Golden Gate Bridge,** opened in May 1937, stretches 8981 ft/2739 m between San Francisco's PRESIDIO and the Marin Peninsula. Its 4200-ft/1281-m main span (the world's longest before New York's VERRAZANO-NARROWS BRIDGE opened); its twin towers, 746 ft/228 m above water; and its distinctive red-orange color contribute to its fame as an emblem of San Francisco and California.

Golden Gate National Recreation Area c.73,000 ac/29,600 ha, in San Francisco, San Mateo, and Marin counties, NC California. Established in 1972, its units include the Muir Woods National Monument and Mt. TAMALPAIS in Marin Co., ALCATRAZ I., and coastline in San Francisco from Aquatic Park, near FISHERMAN'S WHARF (N), to Fort Funston (SW). Within the city section are Fort Mason, the PRESIDIO (as of 1994), BAKER BEACH, Sea Cliff, Lands End, Point Lobos, the Cliff House, and Ocean Beach.

Golden Gate Park over 1000 ac/400 ha, in SAN FRANCISCO, California, extending from the Pacific coast (W) 4 mi/6 km into the city's heart. The RICHMOND DISTRICT lies N, the SUNSET DISTRICT S, and HAIGHT-ASHBURY E. Sand hill and scrub, the area was transformed from 1870 through the efforts of William H. Hall and John McLaren (in charge 1887–1943). It now has lakes, gardens, scenic drives and trails, museums, a planetarium, the nation's oldest (1894) Japanese garden, a bandshell, and other recreational facilities.

Golden Glades unincorporated residential community, pop. 25,474, Dade Co., SE Florida, 9 mi/14 km N of Miami.

Golden Hinde peak, 7218 ft/2200 m, of the Coast Ranges, on C Vancouver I., SW British Columbia. The highest point in STRATHCONA PROVINCIAL PARK, and on the island, it is 30 mi/48 km W of Courtenay, and was named for the ship of Sir Francis Drake, who may have seen it in the 1570s.

Golden Horseshoe popular name for the area in S Ontario extending around the W end of L. Ontario, from OSHAWA (NE) through metropolitan TORONTO to HAMILTON (SW) and then E to SAINT CATHARINES, containing much of the nation's industry and over 20% of its pop.

Golden Isles popular name, from a Spanish term of the 16th century, for several of Georgia's SEA ISLANDS, notably SAINT SIMONS, JEKYLL, and SEA islands.

Golden Mile see under HATO REY, San Juan, Puerto Rico.

Golden Mountain name given by 19th-century Chinese immigrants to California, and by extension, America.

Golden Pond see under SQUAM L., New Hampshire.

Goldenrod unincorporated residential community, pop. 12,362, Seminole and Orange counties, C Florida, 4 mi/6 km NE of Orlando.

Golden Spike National Historic Site see under PROMONTORY Mts., Utah.

Golden Square Mile also, **the Square Mile** see under Rue SHERBROOKE, Montréal, Québec.

Golden Triangle **1.** largely residential section of SAN DIEGO, California, 11 mi/18 km NNW of Downtown, NNE of La Jolla and N of the University of California: San Diego campus, along I-5. It is a rapidly developing, affluent area E of the TORREY PINES. **2.** land between the Allegheny and Monongahela rivers where they join to form the Ohio R.; the heart of downtown Pittsburgh, Pennsylvania. The area had become a deteriorated agglomeration of factories, office buildings, and slums when it was revitalized by a major urban renewal effort in the 1950s. This remade it into a bustling, modern district of corporate offices, retail establishments, and entertainment facilities. Among the projects that transformed the Golden Triangle are GATEWAY CENTER, Point State Park, and a civic center.

Golden Valley city, pop. 20,971, Hennepin Co., SE Minnesota, immediately W of Minneapolis. Although largely residential, it contains some sophisticated light industry. Manufactures include guided missile controls, thermostats, X-ray equipment, and floor scrubbers and sanders.

Goldfield hamlet, seat of Esmeralda Co. (pop. 1344), SW Nevada, 25 mi/40 km S of Tonopah. A 1902 strike brought on a gold rush and enormous prosperity. At its peak this was Nevada's largest city, with a pop. over 40,000. A bitter strike brought Federal troops here in 1907–08. Some landmark buildings remain from Goldfield's glory days. The Nellis Air Force Range is 8 mi/13 km E.

Gold Hill hamlet in Boulder Co., NC Colorado, in the E

foothills of the FRONT RANGE, 7 mi/11 km NW of Boulder. Near the Alamakee and Slide mines, the settlement was the county's first mining camp (1859) and the site of the gold-rich Horsfal Lode. Some of the Gold Hill Mining District's early regulations established principles for mining law. It is a tourist stop.

Goldsboro city, pop. 40,709, seat of Wayne Co., E North Carolina, on the Atlantic Coastal Plain, near the Neuse R., 45 mi/72 km SE of Raleigh. Settled after the 1840 establishment of a railroad, it developed as a market and distribution center for regional farms, and still has an agricultural economy, with some light manufacturing. Local farms produce corn, potatoes, soybeans, truck crops, dairy goods, poultry, and livestock. Tobacco, however, is the principal cash crop; the city is in the heart of the NEW BRIGHT BELT. Seymour Johnson Air Force Base is just SE. Wayne Community College (1957) is in the city, which also has several health facilities.

Goleta see under SANTA BARBARA, California.

Goliad city, pop. 1946, seat of Goliad Co., S Texas, near the San Antonio R., 85 mi/137 km SE of San Antonio. On the site of an Aranama Indian village, the Spanish built (1749) a MISSION and a fort (PRESIDIO) to protect it; together they were called La Bahía. The presidio was occupied for a short time by Texans in 1812 and by Mississippians in 1821. During the Texas Revolution (1835–36), control of the presidio alternated between Texas and Mexico. When Texan troops eventually surrendered, they were executed in the "Goliad Massacre," making "Remember Goliad!" as important a battle cry as "Remember the Alamo!" Now a farming and ranching center, Goliad produces some oil and gas. Goliad State Historic Park preserves the mission and presidio.

Gonzales **1.** city, pop. 7003, Ascension Parish, SE Louisiana, 20 mi/32 km SE of Baton Rouge. Oil wells and sugar and truck farming sustain its economy. **2.** city, pop. 6527, seat of Gonzales Co., SE Texas, on the Guadalupe R., 61 mi/98 km E of San Antonio. Settled in 1825, it was the scene, on Oct. 2, 1835, of the first fighting in the Texas Revolution, when residents and supporters drove off a small Mexican force. It later contributed "32 immortals" to the defense of the ALAMO. It is today an agricultural trade center with some light manufactures.

Goodfellow Air Force Base see under SAN ANGELO, Texas.

Goodhue County 763 sq mi/1976 sq km, pop. 40,690, in SE Minnesota, bordering the Mississippi R. and the Wisconsin state line (NE). Red Wing is the seat of this agricultural county, where dairy farms and corn and wheat fields predominate. The Richard J. Dorer Memorial Hardwood State Forest occupies most of the N part. Prairie I. Indian Reservation is on an island in the Mississippi R., in the NW, and the Prairie Island nuclear power plant (1973) is here. Congressman and Prohibition sponsor Andrew Volstead was born here (1860).

Goodings Grove unincorporated community, pop. 14,054, Will Co., NE Illinois, a residential suburb on the edge of the Chicago metropolitan area, 22 mi/35 km SW of the LOOP.

Goodland city, pop. 4983, seat of Sherman Co., NW Kansas, 105 mi/169 km NNW of Garden City and 20 mi/32 km E of the Colorado border. In the late 19th century it was headquarters for several rainmaking companies, and grew with the coming of the Rock Island Railroad. It is now a distribution center for wheat and livestock. Nearby (NE) is the site of the Indian massacre of a cavalry squad led by Lyman Kidder (1867).

Goodlettsville city, pop. 11,219, Davidson and Sumner counties, NC Tennessee, a growing residential suburb 12 mi/19 km NNE of downtown Nashville.

Goodman agricultural town, pop. 1256, Holmes Co., C Mississippi, on the Big Black R., 48 mi/77 km NNE of Jackson, seat of Holmes Community College (1925) and birthplace of folklorist John Lomax (1867) and Civil War historian David Donald (1920).

Goodwell town, pop. 1065, Texas Co., extreme NW Oklahoma, in the high plains of the PANHANDLE, 9 mi/14 km SW of Guymon and 7 mi/11 km N of the Texas border. In an area that raises wheat and livestock, it is the seat of Oklahoma Panhandle State University (1909).

Goose Bay see HAPPY VALLEY–GOOSE BAY, Labrador.

Goose Creek city, pop. 24,692, Berkeley Co., SE South Carolina, 15 mi/24 km N of Charleston, a growing, largely residential suburb.

Goose Lake on the MODOC PLATEAU, in Modoc Co., extreme NE California and Lake Co., S Oregon. A remnant of a much larger ice age lake, and a major migratory waterfowl refuge, it is 28 mi/45 km N–S and up to 9 mi/14 km wide, and is a noted fish and game source. The PIT R. flows S from its S end.

Gopher Prairie see under SAUK CENTRE, Minnesota.

Gore see under WINCHESTER, Virginia.

Gore Mountain 3595 ft/1096 m, in Johnsburg township, Warren Co., in the Adirondack Mts. of NE New York. It is a popular ski resort.

Gore Range NNW–SSE trending mountains, c.75 mi/120 km long, part of the W prong of C Colorado's Rocky Mts. and of the PARK RANGE, extending from near Steamboat Springs in the N to just SW of Copper Mt. and Breckenridge (S). Mt. Powell (13,534 ft/4125 m) is their high point. The Williams Fork Mts. parallel them (E) at the S end.

Gorham town, pop. 11,856, Cumberland Co., SE Maine, on the Presumpscot R., 8 mi/13 km W of Portland. Founded in 1728 as a grant to Narraganset War (1675) veterans and heirs, the town developed industries including brickmaking and metal plating and anodizing. Site of a 19th-century Shaker community, Gorham is home to the University of Southern Maine, and is a growing Portland suburb.

Goshen **1.** city, pop. 23,797, seat of Elkhart Co., N Indiana, 10 mi/16 km SE of ELKHART. Livestock, dairy products, poultry, grain, soybeans, and timber from the area are traded in the city. Among its manufactures have been bags, rubber goods, hydraulic presses, wood and metal products, boats, and mobile homes. The city has a large Mennonite population, and the Mennonite-sponsored Goshen College (1894) is here. **2.** village, pop. 5255, in Goshen township, seat of Orange Co., SE New York, 5 mi/8 km SE of Middletown. Settled in the early 18th century, it is the site of one of the world's oldest harness racing tracks, former scene (until 1956) of the Hambletonian race. The village remains a harness racing center, and, situated in a lake-dotted region, relies on tourism also. The Hall of Fame of the Trotter is here. J. Hector St. John de Crèvecoeur lived about 5 mi/8 km SE of the village before the Revolution, and his *Letters from an American Farmer* is based on his time here.

Gosnold see under ELIZABETH ISLANDS, Massachusetts.

Gospel Hump Wilderness see under NEZ PERCE NATIONAL FOREST, Idaho.

Gotham jocular nickname for New York City, introduced in 1807 by Washington Irving and others in the *Salmagundi* essays. It refers to the "wise men of Gotham," residents of an English village who in the 13th century were noted for their idiotic (or intentionally idiotic-seeming) behavior. Irving and his fellow writers used it to satirize the pomposity of New York society of their time.

Government Center administrative center and urban showcase in downtown Boston, Massachusetts. Created from 1958 through the 1960s, it eliminated notorious SCOLLAY SQUARE and surrounding streets, replacing them with a plaza, Boston's new City Hall (1968), two 26-story federal buildings, and other monuments to civic efficiency and rectitude. Faneuil Hall and the Quincy Market are just E.

Governors Island 173 ac/70 ha, in Upper New York Bay, at the S entrance to the East R., and about 1500 ft/460 m S of the Battery, Manhattan. The onetime home of Colonial governors, it has been a military site since about 1800, and is now the East Coast headquarters for the Coast Guard. Its structures include Fort Williams ("the Cheesebox") and Fort Jay.

Gowanus industrial and residential area of NW Brooklyn, New York, between Park Slope (E) and South Brooklyn (W). It bears the name of a local sachem who sold land to Dutch settlers in 1636. The district extends on both sides of the Gowanus Canal, a heavily industrial 1-mi/1.5-km inlet of Upper New York Bay. The canal, notorious for its pollution by ink and other chemical plants since the 19th century, is bridged by various structures including an elevated railway viaduct that dominates the neighborhood. Gowanus was the scene of the heaviest fighting in the Battle of Long Island (1776).

Graceland shrine in SW Memphis, Tennessee, in the N of the WHITEHAVEN district. The home and burial place (1977) of Elvis Presley, it is a museum and memorial to the singer, and one of the South's most heavily visited tourist sites.

Gracie Mansion see under YORKVILLE, New York.

Grafton village, pop. 9340, Ozaukee Co., E Wisconsin, 17 mi/27 km N of Milwaukee, in an agricultural area. Iron castings, saws, stoves, and yarn are manufactured here.

Graham **1.** see FLORENCE-GRAHAM, California. **2.** city, pop. 10,426, seat of Alamance Co., NC North Carolina, adjacent (SE) to Burlington. Established in 1849, it is a longtime textile and furniture making center. **3.** city, pop. 8986, seat of Young Co., NC Texas, 77 mi/124 km WNW of Fort Worth. Founded in 1872 just below L. Graham, on a tributary to the Brazos R., it is a commercial, processing, and service center for the wheat, cattle, and oil industries, makes aluminum, computer, leather, and other goods, and has a resort trade.

Graham, Mount see under PINALENO Mts., Arizona.

Grambling town, pop. 5484, Lincoln Parish, N Louisiana, 5 mi/8 km W of Ruston, home to historically black Grambling State University (1901).

Gramercy Park exclusive urban park, lower Midtown Manhattan, New York City. Created 1831 on the site of a "crooked little marsh" (Dutch, *krum marisje*), it is perhaps the last American example of a London-style park open only to area residents with keys. Its name is used to give cachet to businesses and residences in nearby neighborhoods.

Granada Hills largely residential N SAN FERNANDO VALLEY section of LOS ANGELES, California, 21 mi/34 km NW of Downtown, N of Northridge, and E of Chatsworth.

Granby **1.** town, pop. 966, Grand Co., NC Colorado, on the Fraser R., just SE of its junction with the Colorado R., 36 mi/58 km NW of Boulder. It originated as a railroad distribution point for local livestock and timber. Now a tourist center for numerous dude ranches, Granby is an Amtrak stop and serves as the W gateway to the Arapahoe National Forest. L. Granby, 4 mi/6 km to the NE, is part of the Colorado–Big Thompson project and irrigates the E slope of the Continental Divide. **2.** see under TOBACCO VALLEY, Connecticut. **3.** city, pop. 1945, Newton Co., SW Missouri, on the Ozark Plateau, 18 mi/29 km SE of Joplin. A boom town was created when lead was discovered here in 1853. Zinc deposits brought renewed prosperity during World War I. Today Granby is an agricultural and mining trade center. **4.** city, pop. 42,804, Shefford Co., in the EASTERN TOWNSHIPS of S Québec, 42 mi/68 km E of Montréal and 25 mi/40 km N of the Vermont border, on the R. Yamaska Nord. Long an agricultural (esp. dairying) center, it industrialized after World War II, and has a wide variety of manufactures, including high-tech products. Tourism and provincial offices are also important.

Grand Avenue commercial thoroughfare in St. Paul, Minnesota, running E–W through the SW part of the city. Parallel to SUMMIT Ave., Grand Ave. emerged in the 1980s as a popular entertainment strip noted for its night life.

Grand Avenue Mall commercial center in downtown Milwaukee, Wisconsin, between South Fourth St. and the Milwaukee R., immediately S of Wisconsin Ave. Four blocks long, the mall is linked by a network of skywalks.

Grand Banks famed fishing ground, a section of the CONTINENTAL SHELF, extending SE and S from Newfoundland into the Atlantic Ocean, and covering some 110,000 sq mi/285,000 sq km in which depths are under c. 600 ft/185 m. It is composed of several separate banks, including Grand, Green, and St. Pierre. The meeting here of the S-flowing LABRADOR current and the E-flowing GULF STREAM produces heavy fogs and severe storms, but also stirs up plankton, which feed cod, haddock, various flatfish, herring, and mackerel. First reported in Europe by John Cabot in 1498, the Grand Banks became almost immediately one of the world's major fishing zones. Struggles for control embroiled England and France for centuries; much of Newfoundland's history has been determined by them. The Banks were seriously overfished in the mid 20th century, and in 1977 Canada enforced a 200-mi/320-km limit (incorporating the vast majority of the Banks) inside which it restricted foreign fishing. By the 1990s a further drop in fish stocks led to greater restriction, and to economic distress in Newfoundland. Exploratory drilling for gas and oil began in the area in the 1970s; although icebergs and storms posed hazards, this new undertaking was looked to as a possible economic savior.

Grand Boulevard inner of two ring roads now within the city of Detroit, Michigan. Constructed in the 1880s at an average distance of 3 mi/5 km from central Downtown, it reaches the Detroit R. near the AMBASSADOR BRIDGE (SW) and at the MacArthur Bridge to BELLE ISLE (NE). Once on the city's edge, it now passes through Detroit's midsection. The city's main radial avenues, Michigan (W), Grand River (NW), Woodward (N), Gratiot (NE), and Jefferson, cross it. The second ring was formed by OUTER DRIVE.

Grand Canyon National Park 1.22 million ac/0.49 million ha (1904 sq mi/4931 sq km), along 277 mi/446 km of the COLORADO R., in NW Arizona. It is bounded by the GLEN CANYON (E) and Lake MEAD (W) national recreation areas. The canyon is 1.1 mile/1.8 km deep and up to 10 mi/16 km wide; within it, the Colorado drops 2200 ft/670 m through dozens of rapids. Geologically new, the canyon has been formed in the past 6–8 million years by the river cutting through gradually rising, generally sedimentary strata; but it reveals some of the oldest rock on the earth's surface, over 2 billion years old, at the bottom of hundreds of layers of sandstone, shale, travertine, schist, granite, and other rocks. Lived in for hundreds of years by various tribes, the area has over 500 ruin sites. Members of Coronado's 1540 expedition were the first Europeans to view it; John Wesley Powell's 1869 boat expedition through it was the first thorough exploration by whites. Protected since 1893, accessible by rail since 1901, and a national park since 1919, the Grand Canyon is now one of the most famous tourist sites in the world; visitation concentrates on its South Rim; the North Rim, closed in winter, is generally 1000–1500 ft/300–500 m higher, and accessible only from the remote ARIZONA STRIP. MARBLE CANYON, on the NE, is now part of the park. The COCONINO PLATEAU lies S, the KAIBAB and other plateaus N. Havasu Canyon, on the Havasu Creek, enters from the S near the canyon's W end; this is home to the Havasupai, whose reservation, now also including lands on the plateau above, covers 188,000 ac/76,170 ha, with a pop. of 423.

Grand Canyon of the Arkansas see ROYAL GORGE, Colorado.

Grand Canyon of the Pacific see WAIMEA CANYON, Hawaii.

Grand Canyon of the Snake see HELLS CANYON, Idaho and Oregon.

Grand Central Terminal also, **Grand Central Station** see under NEW YORK CENTRAL RAILROAD.

Grand Chute town, pop. 14,490, Outagamie Co., EC Wisconsin, a residential suburb immediately N of Appleton. Senator Joseph R. McCarthy was born here (1909).

Grand Circus Park semicircular park in downtown Detroit, Michigan, eight blocks NW of Jefferson Ave. and the RENAISSANCE CENTER. Bisected by WOODWARD Ave., it is a survivor of the 1806 plan that established Detroit's radial-and-circular street pattern.

Grand Concourse commercial and residential thoroughfare, Bronx, New York. Laid out (1892) as the Speedway Concourse, now officially the Grand Boulevard and Concourse, it runs 4.5 mi/7 km from Mott Haven (S) to the Mosholu Parkway (N). Designed to provide access to parks, it became in the 1920s a premier residential street, lined with large apartment buildings. It originally had separate lanes for horses, bicycles, and pedestrians, and is 180 ft/55 m wide.

Grand Coulee Dam gravity dam on the COLUMBIA R. in EC Washington, 80 mi/130 km WNW of Spokane. Built in 1933–42 as part of the Columbia Basin Project, it is 550 ft/168 m high and 4173 ft/1272 m along. One of the world's largest hydroelectric generating units, it also aids in flood control and creates 150 mi/240 km–long Franklin D. Roosevelt L., which backs up all the way to the British Columbia border, and which is a major recreational asset. The **Grand Coulee** itself extends some 40 mi/64 km SW of the dam. A dry former channel of the Columbia, it is now used as a (pump-filled) reservoir for irrigation of the surrounding COLUMBIA PLATEAU region.

Grand Detour locality in Grand Detour township, Ogle Co., NC Illinois, on the Rock R., 6 mi/10 km NE of Dixon. It was here in 1837 that blacksmith John Deere developed a plow with an iron landside and steel share, strong enough to cut Illinois prairie grass. The state's first plow factory was established here in 1843. The John Deere Historic Site is in Grand Detour.

Grande Prairie city, pop. 28,271, NW Alberta, on the Bear R., near the Rocky Mountains Forest Reserve, 234 mi/377 km NW of Edmonton. A commercial and transportation center for the PEACE R. region, it has an economy based on agriculture, forestry, petroleum, and tourism. Settled as a Hudson's Bay Company post in the 1880s, it began around 1910 to attract farmers. Growth followed the arrival (1916) of the railroad, and the town became a wheat trade center. Grande Prairie Regional College is here and Saskatoon I. Provincial Park is to the W.

Grand Falls see under CHURCHILL R., Labrador.

Grand Falls–Windsor town, pop. 14,693, C Newfoundland, on the Exploits R., 168 mi/270 km NW of St. John's. On the site of Beothuk villages, it flourished in the 1900s as a pulp and paper mill town and today is a major newsprint producing center. Its rail and shipping connections have also made it a regional commercial hub, and it has a hydroelectric plant. Windsor, just W of Grand Falls, was formerly the service town of Grand Falls Station.

Grandfather Mountain peak (5964 ft/1818 m) of the BLUE RIDGE Mts., 16 mi/26 km SW of Boone, in NW North Carolina. The shape of its N side is said to resemble that of an old man's profile, and it is known for the suspension bridge near its summit. Nearby Grandmother Mt. (S) rises to 4686 ft/1429 m.

Grand Forks city, pop. 49,425, seat of Grand Forks Co., NE North Dakota, at the confluence of the Red R. of the North and the Red Lake R., opposite East Grand Forks, Minnesota, and 75 mi/121 km NNE of Fargo. Established by French fur traders in 1801, it was settled in 1871. Its future was assured when the Great Northern Railway transformed it into a transportation hub. It is now the trade and processing center for the potatoes, sugar beets, wheat, and livestock of the fertile Red River Valley. Grand Forks is the seat of the state's oldest institution of higher learning, the University of North Dakota (1883). Also here are Grand Forks Air Force Base, site of a huge Cold War missile field; a Bureau of Mines coal research laboratory; and a Federal weather station.

Grand Gulf former town in Claiborne Co., SW Mississippi, on the Mississippi R. at the mouth of the BIG BLACK R., 7 mi/11 km NW of PORT GIBSON. During U.S. Grant's Vicksburg Campaign, on April 16, 1863, Union gunboats attacked Grand Gulf but were repelled by Confederates under John Bowen; the Northern fleet later landed successfully at BRUINSBURG. After the Confederate defeat at Port Gibson (May 1), Grant seized Grand Gulf's batteries and used the town as a base. The Grand Gulf Military Monument Park (400 ac/160 ha) includes Fort Wade, the Grand Gulf Cemetery, and a museum. The Grand Gulf nuclear power plant (1984) is also here.

Grand Haven city, pop. 11,951, seat of Ottawa Co., W Michigan, at the mouth of the Grand R., on L. Michigan, 12 mi/19 km S of Muskegon. Originally settled c.1834 on the site of a fur-trading post built c.1821, it is now a deepwater port and a popular resort with sandy beaches, wooded hills, and a 2.5 mi/4 km–long boardwalk. Its population more than doubles in the summer. The city also has oil refineries and manufactures pianos, pneumatic tools, refrigerators, auto parts, electrical and printing equipment, and leather. It ships grapes, potatoes, and celery from the region. There are also fishing and marine engine manufacture and repair. Hoffmaster State Park and the Gillette Nature Center are 5 mi/8 km N.

Grand Island **1.** 13,000 ac/5265 ha, pop. 21, in Alger Co., in the NC Upper Peninsula, N Michigan, in L. Superior, 3 mi/5 km N of Munising. The island is a mostly wooded game refuge. **2.** city, pop. 39,386, seat of Hall Co., SC Nebraska, 90 mi/144 km WNW of Lincoln. Established on the banks of the Platte R. in the 1850s, it was moved slightly N when the Union Pacific Railroad arrived in 1866. Still a railroad hub, it has packing houses, flour mills, and dairies, and ships livestock, meat, and fruit as well as farm, dairy, and poultry products. Manufactures include farm machinery and appliances. A mule trading center since the 19th century, it also buys and sells horses and cattle. **3.** 7.5 mi/12 km long and 1–6.5 mi/1.5–10.5 km wide, in the upper Niagara R., in Erie Co., immediately NW of Buffalo, New York. The suburban town of **Grand Island** (pop. 17,561) includes this and several other small islands. Grand I. is linked by bridges to Ontario and New York. Buckhorn State Park is on its N shore and on neighboring Buckhorn I. Beaver Island State Park is on its S shore and on neighboring Beaver I.

Grand Isle **1.** island town, pop. 1455, Jefferson Parish, SE Louisiana, at the S of BARATARIA (NE) and Caminada (NW) bays, 50 mi/80 km S of New Orleans. Seven mi/11 km NE–SW and up to 1.5 mi/2 km wide, it is wooded and has a noted beach. Its inhabitants fish and maintain truck farms, and tourism is important. In the early 19th century it was a headquarters of Jean Lafitte's smuggling operations. **2.** see under HERO ISLANDS, Vermont.

Grand Junction city, pop. 29,034, seat of Mesa Co., W Colorado, at the confluence of the Colorado (originally called the Grand) and Gunnison rivers, in Grand Valley, 30 mi/48 km E of the Utah border. The original settlement was christened Ute in commemoration of the natives removed to Utah (1880) just before white settlement began. Its importance as a distribution center began with the arrival of the Denver and Rio Grande Railroad (1887). Grand Junction remains a shipping point for surrounding farms, which produce grains, sugar beets, fruits, and vegetables, and for local oil, natural gas, vanadium, and gilsonite. Since the 1950s, uranium production has been important. The city also manufactures electronics and cans fruits and vegetables. It is the seat of Mesa College (1925). The COLORADO NATIONAL MONUMENT is 10 mi/16 km W.

Grand Lake Saint Marys also, **Lake Saint Marys, Grand Lake,** or **Grand Reservoir** in Auglaize and Mercer counties, W Ohio. One of the state's largest lakes (9 mi/14 km long, 3 mi/5 km wide, with 33 mi/53 km of shoreline), it was formed in 1845 by damming the Wabash R. Today it is the site of a state park and is known for sport fishing and duck hunting.

Grand Manan Island 60 sq mi/155 sq km, pop. 2649, some 15 mi/24 km NNE–SSW and up to 7 mi/11 km wide, off the SW coast of New Brunswick. The largest of the Fundy Isles (which include Deer and CAMPOBELLO islands), it lies at the Bay of FUNDY entrance, S of Passamaquoddy Bay and separated from the Maine coast by 8 mi/13 km–wide Grand Manan Channel, 23 mi/37 km SSE of St. Andrews and 12 mi/19 km SE of Eastport, Maine. Settled in the 1780s by LOYALISTS, after having been a French possession, it was the focus of a US-Canadian territorial dispute until it became part of New Brunswick in 1817. North Head (pop. 711) is the chief village. Fishing and dulse (seaweed) harvesting are the main industries. The island is an artists' and writers' retreat, noted for its cliffs and its variety of migratory birds.

Grand-Mère also, **Grand'Mère** city, pop. 14,287, Champlain Co., SC Québec, 21 mi/35 km N of Trois-Rivières, on the R. Saint-Maurice. Founded in the 1890s around a hydroelectric plant, it became a paper and pulp production center. Lumber, textile, clothing and shoe, and service industries have also been important. The city's name comes from a rock in the shape of an old woman's profile, found in the falls and since relocated to a city park.

Grand Mesa National Forest 360,000 ac/146,000 ha (562 sq mi/1457 sq km), in WC Colorado, on the 10,000-ft/3050-m **Grand Mesa,** a lava flow–topped mesa sometimes called the world's largest flat-topped mountain, E of GRAND JUNCTION and the GRAND VALLEY.

Grand Portage historic settlement (unorganized, pop. 321, Cook Co.) in extreme NE Minnesota, at the E tip of the ARROWHEAD REGION, on L. Superior. It is the start of a 9-mi/14-km PORTAGE that avoids the falls of the lower Pigeon R., on the Ontario border. Long used by Indians, this trail became in the 18th century key to the NORTH WEST COMPANY's fur operations, the crucial connection between the Great Lakes and Montréal (E) and the rivers and lakes of NW Canada. The earliest settlement in Minnesota, it saw heavy traffic from the 1770s until 1802, when the NWC moved operations N to the Kaministiquia R. at Fort William (now THUNDER BAY), Ontario, to keep the trade route within British territory. Today Grand Portage is a National Historic Site, with a reconstructed NWC post.

Grand Prairie city, pop. 99,616, Dallas, Tarrant, and Ellis counties, NE Texas, between Dallas and Fort Worth. Established at the end of the Civil War as a stop on the Texas & Pacific Railroad, it is on the West Fork of the Trinity R. An industrial suburb, it grew from a small agricultural community on the Grand Prairie (see under BLACKLANDS) when World War II–era defense plants were built. It has a bottling plant, and heavy industries that produce steel, tanks, air and spacecraft, pipe, mobile homes, plastics, and electronic equipment. The Dallas Naval Air Station is here.

Grand Pré historic locality in Kings Co., WC Nova Scotia, on the S shore of the MINAS BASIN, just W of the Avon R., 3 mi/5 km ENE of Wolfville and 46 mi/74 km NW of Halifax. An early (1670s) Acadian village, named for the "great meadows" created by diking, it was the main setting for Henry Wadsworth Longfellow's *Evangeline;* although the Acadian community was neutral during British-French struggles over possession of Nova Scotia, they were expelled by British authorities in 1755. The Grand Pré National Historic Site draws visitors. Vineyarding is the other chief industry in the area.

Grand Rapids **1.** local government district, pop. 506, WC Manitoba, on the NW shore of L. Winnipeg, 236 mi/380 km NNW of Winnipeg. The Grand Rapids hydroelectric generating station (1968), at the mouth of the SASKATCHEWAN R., and an Indian Reserve (pop. 374) are here. **2.** city, pop. 189,126, seat of Kent Co., SW Michigan, on rapids of the GRAND R., 60 mi/97 km SW of Lansing. A Baptist mission was built here in 1825 over several layers of Indian habitation (known from Ottawa, Chippewa, and Potawatomi burial mound relics). Two years later, Louis Campau built a trading post on the site. The settlement became a lumbering center and the city developed with the exploitation of massive waterfall power and the use of locally abundant soft and hard wood. Cabinetmakers thrived here during the last half of the 19th century, and the city continues to be known for its high-quality furniture. Other manufactures include auto bodies and parts, electrical products, hardware, tools and dies, tires, extruded metals, and clothing. There is gypsum mining nearby and wallboard production in the city. It is also a large wholesale market for peaches, flower bulbs, apples, celery, and onions. Its convention facilities are important to the economy. Grand Rapids is home to Calvin College (1876), Aquinas College (1922), and a branch of the University of Michigan.

Grand River **1.** former name for part of the COLORADO R. See GRAND VALLEY. **2.** 260 mi/419 km long, in S Michigan. Its source is only 100 mi/161 km from L. Michigan, but because of its winding course, its length is more than twice that distance. The river rises in Jackson Co., and flows N to Lansing, then NW and W past Portland, Ionia, and Grand Rapids, to Grand Haven, where it empties into L. Michigan. It is navigable for about 40 mi/64 km from its mouth to Grand Rapids. Above Grand Rapids a precipitous drop in level has allowed the river to be harnessed for hydroelectric power at several locations, facilitating the growth of local industry. **3.** 75 mi/121 km long, in Ohio. It rises in SE Geauga Co., flows NE past West Farmington, then turns N for 25 mi/40 km and veers W near Austinburg. It passes Painesville and flows into L. Erie at Fairport Harbor, NE of Cleveland. **4.** in Oklahoma, name for the NEOSHO R. **5.** in Ontario: **a.** former name for the OTTAWA R. **b.** 165 mi/266 km long, in S Ontario. It rises NNW of ORANGEVILLE and flows generally S past Waterloo, Kitchener, and Cambridge to Brantford, then SE through Haldimand and Dunnville, to enter L. Erie at Port Maitland. **6.** 210 mi/338 km long, in South Dakota. It is formed by the confluence of the North and South forks at the Shadehill Reservoir in Perkins Co., and flows ESE across the STANDING ROCK Reservation to the Missouri R. near Mobridge.

Grand Strand resort area of the NE South Carolina shore, in Horry and Georgetown counties, along the Atlantic Ocean from the North Carolina border (NE) to GEORGETOWN on Winyah Bay (SW), some 60 mi/100 km. Its focal point is MYRTLE BEACH, with the communities of North Myrtle Beach (city, pop. 8636) and Little River (unincorporated, pop. 3470) N of it and Garden City (unincorporated, pop. 6305), Murrells Inlet (unincorporated, pop. 3334), and Pawleys Island (town, pop. 176) S of it. Litchfield Beach, Surfside Beach, and Atlantic Beach are among the smaller resorts. Bathing and fishing in GULF STREAM waters, golf, and a variety of amusement parks are major attractions. Brookgreen Gardens, a 300-ac/122-ha sculpture garden, is on the grounds of a former rice plantation 3 mi/5 km S of Murrells Inlet. Four mi/6 km–long Pawleys I., 10 mi/16 km NE of Georgetown, is known for its handmade hammocks. The ATLANTIC INTRACOASTAL WATERWAY runs SW–NE behind the Grand Strand, in part following the Pee Dee R. The Grand Strand is a growing retirement area, and parts are especially popular with Canadian vacationers.

Grand Terrace city, pop. 10,946, San Bernardino Co., SW California, a largely residential suburb adjacent (NE) to Riverside.

Grand Teton National Park 310,000 ac/125,550 ha (484 sq mi/1255 sq km), in NW Wyoming, immediately S of Yellowstone National Park, surrounding Jackson L. and the valley of JACKSON HOLE. It includes much of the 40 mi/64 km–long, N–S trending Teton Range, the youngest mountains in the Rockies, noted for their sheer sides, triangular forms, and bare blue-gray peaks. **Grand Teton** (13,770 ft/4197 m) is Wyoming's second-highest point. The upper Snake R. runs through the park, which was established in 1929.

Grand Trunk Railway see under CANADIAN NATIONAL RAILWAY.

Grand Valley also, **Grand River Valley** fertile region along a 70-mi/115-km stretch of the COLORADO R., from Mesa Co., WC Colorado, SW into Grant Co., EC Utah. It is irrigated by a 55-mi/90-km diversion of the river below a dam near GRAND JUNCTION, Colorado, which is a processing and shipping center for fruit, mainly peaches. "Grand River" is a former name of the Colorado from its source in NC Colorado to its confluence with the GREEN R. in E Utah.

Grandview city, pop. 24,967, Jackson Co., W Missouri, 16 mi/26 km SSE of downtown Kansas City and almost surrounded by the city. A longtime trade hub for a farming region producing grain, apples, and dairy products, it also manufactures hardware and electrical goods. The Richards-Gebaur Air Force Base is just S.

Grandview Heights city, pop. 7010, Franklin Co., C Ohio, on the Scioto R., 6 mi/10 km NW of Columbus, of which it is a suburb.

Grandville city, pop. 15,624, Kent Co., SW Michigan, on the Grand R., 5 mi/8 km SW of Grand Rapids. In an area that grows peaches, grain, and celery, it is a residential suburb and manufactures plaster, stucco, and refrigerator parts.

Grand Wash Cliffs in NW Arizona, forming the SW edge of the Colorado Plateau. Paralleling the border with Nevada in the N, they form a W barrier of the ARIZONA STRIP. To the W of the Grand Canyon, they extend N from near Music Mt. (6677 ft/2035 m), NE of Kingman, to the W escarpment of the Shivwits Plateau NE of L. Mead. The Colorado R. cuts through them.

Granger unincorporated community, pop. 20,241, St. Joseph Co., N Indiana, 8 mi/13 km NE of South Bend, just S of the Michigan border and N of the Indiana Toll Road. It is largely residential.

Granite City city, pop. 32,862, Madison Co., SW Illinois, on the Mississippi R., across the Chain of Rocks Canal from Gabaret I., 6 mi/10 km N of East St. Louis. A graniteware factory, manufacturing enameled porcelain, was established here in 1891. The steelmaking industry followed two years later, and Granite City's economic importance was established. A large shipping point that includes a US Army Supply Depot, the city remains an industrial center. Local manufactures include iron and steel, flat rolled steel products, railroad equipment, starch, chemicals, corn products, auto frames, fire brick, and tile and coal tar products. Horseshoe Lake State Park is just SE.

Granite Peak 12,799 ft/3904 m, in Park Co., SC Montana, 80 mi/129 km SW of Billings and 10 mi/16 km N of the Wyoming border. In the Beartooth Range, in the Absaroka-Beartooth Wilderness, it is the highest point in Montana.

Graniteville historic village in Aiken Co., W South Carolina, 5 mi/8 km WNW of Aiken and 12 mi/19 km NE of Augusta, Georgia. Beginning in 1845 William Gregg (1800–67), regarded as the father of the Southern textile industry, established cotton mills and a mill village here in the Horse Creek Valley, in what was the EDGEFIELD District. Gregg's scheme, and his employment of poor whites instead of slave labor, set a pattern for regional development.

Gran Quivira see QUIVIRA.

Grantham unincorporated community in Upper Allen township (pop. 13,347), Cumberland Co., S Pennsylvania, 10 mi/16 km SW of Harrisburg. A residential suburb, it is the seat of Messiah College (1909).

Grant Park **1.** 144 ac/58 ha, in SE Atlanta, Georgia, 1.7 mi/2.8 km SE of FIVE POINTS. Fort Walker, a Confederate battery, was here in 1864. The park is noted as home to the Cyclorama, a 360-degree painting of the battle of Atlanta that is 400 ft/120 m in circumference. Other Civil War mementos and the Atlanta Zoo are also here. The historically black neighborhood around the park has been revitalized in recent years. **2.** 300-ac/121-ha public park along L. Michigan in Chicago, Illinois, immediately E of the LOOP. Designed by Daniel Burnham in his 1909 Chicago Plan, it includes Buckingham Fountain, a popular gathering place and concert site. The bandshell here features an annual Blues and Jazz Festival. Field Museum of Natural History,Shedd Aquarium, and Adler Planetarium are immediately to the S. Violent clashes took place in the park at antiwar rallies during the Democratic National Convention of 1968.

Grants city, pop. 8626, Cibola Co., WC New Mexico, on I-40 and the San Jose R., 65 mi/105 km W of Albuquerque. Founded as a Santa Fe Railroad town, it was a livestock and agricultural trade center. With the discovery of uranium in the area in 1950, the city became a mining center for several decades. New Mexico State University has a branch (1968) here. Nearby are parts of the Cibola National Forest (W and NE), the ÁCOMA (SE) and LAGUNA (E) reservations, and EL MALPAIS (S) and EL MORRO (SW) national monuments.

Grant's Farm see under AFFTON, Missouri.

Grants Pass city, pop. 17,488, seat of Josephine Co., SW Oregon, on the Rogue R., in the Klamath Mts., 24 mi/39 km WNW of Medford. From a stop on the stagecoach route to California, it grew into an important regional trading center after the arrival of the railroad in 1883. The city's economy is based on the manufacture of plywood and wood products and the shipment of locally produced horticultural bulbs. Also important is the processing of the area's fruit, dairy products, and metals. Grants Pass serves as gateway to the Siskiyou National Forest (W, SW), Rogue River National Forest (S, SE), and Oregon Caves National Monument (25 mi/40 km S).

Grant's Tomb officially, **General Grant National Memorial** mausoleum, on Riverside Drive at 122nd St., Morningside Heights, Manhattan, New York City. Completed in 1897, it contains historical displays and the sarcophagi of General and Mrs. Ulysses S. Grant.

Granville **1.** see under GASTOWN, Vancouver, British Columbia. **2.** village, pop. 4315, Licking Co., C Ohio, 6 mi/10 km W of Newark. Situated in a diversified farming district, it was settled in the early 19th century by pioneers from Massachusetts. It is the seat of Denison University, founded in 1831 as the Granville Literary and Theological Institute.

Granville Island see under FALSE CREEK, Vancouver, British Columbia.

Grapevine city, pop. 29,202, Tarrant and Dallas counties, NE Texas, 20 mi/32 km NE of Fort Worth, on Grapevine L. (N) and adjacent (N) to Dallas–Fort Worth International Airport. Established in 1854, it is an agricultural trade center becoming a residential and industrial suburb; its population more than doubled in the 1980s. The city has various light manufactures. **Grapevine L.**, 7400 ac/3000 ha, is a Dallas water source and site of the Grapevine Recreational Area.

Grass Lake village, pop. 903, Jackson Co., S Michigan, on Grass L., 10 mi/16 km E of Jackson. Situated in a dairy and field crop area, it manufactures auto parts and other products. The Phyllis Haennle Memorial Sanctuary, a large staging area for the sandhill crane, is 5 mi/8 km NW.

Grasslands National Park 64,000 ac/25,920 ha, in SW Saskatchewan, near Val Marie, on the Montana border. One of Canada's newest national parks, this Great Plains preserve was originally inhabited by nomadic tribes, but became a ranching area. Its rolling landscape features indigenous mixed-grass prairie and badlands and is home to a variety of rare flora and fauna, including the prairie falcon and Canada's only concentration of black-tailed prairie dogs.

Grass Valley city, pop. 9048, Nevada Co., NE California, on the W slope of the Sierra Nevada, 50 mi/80 km NE of Sacramento and 4 mi/6 km SW of NEVADA CITY. Center of a goldmining area that produced from 1850 through the 1950s, it is now known for its Empire Mine State Historic Park; the home of dancer/adventurer Lola Montez, which survived an 1855 fire that leveled most of the town; and other sites associated with the gold period. Today tourism, fruit growing, and some light manufactures are the city's economic base.

Grassy Knoll, the see under DEALEY PLAZA, Dallas, Texas.

Gravenhurst town, pop. 9988, Muskoka District Municipality, SC Ontario, on the S end of L. Muskoka, 87 mi/140 km N of Toronto. In the late 19th century it was the site of steamboat departures into the scenic MUSKOKA LAKES, and has remained a popular tourist destination. The birthplace (1890) of physician and political activist Norman Bethune is preserved.

Gravesend former township in S Brooklyn, New York. Patented 1645 by Lady Deborah Moody and a group of Anabaptists who had fled persecution in England and New England, it was annexed by the city of Brooklyn in 1894. A residential section of Brooklyn N of Coney Island and SE of Bensonhurst still carries the name. **Gravesend Bay,** between the NARROWS and Coney Island on the E side of Lower New York Bay, includes the waterfronts of Fort Hamilton, Bath Beach, and Bensonhurst, extending to the W end of Coney Island.

Graveyard of the Atlantic **1.** see under Cape HATTERAS, North Carolina. **2.** see SABLE I., Nova Scotia.

Grays Harbor inlet of the Pacific Ocean (up to 16 mi/26 km E–W and 13 mi/21 km N–S), in Grays Harbor Co., W Washington. At the mouth of the Chehalis R., it forms the SW boundary of the OLYMPIC PENINSULA. HOQUIAM and ABERDEEN are on its NE shore. Many streams from the Olympic Mts. feed into the harbor, which is a fishing and lumbering center.

Grayslake village, pop. 7388, Lake Co., extreme N Illinois,

10 mi/16 km W of Waukegan. In a lake-filled resort area, it is the seat of the College of Lake County (1967).

Grayson town, pop. 3510, seat of Carter Co., NE Kentucky, on the Little Sandy R., 20 mi/32 km WSW of Ashland. Near the Carter and Cascade limestone caves, it has feed and lumber mills, iron and coal mining, clay pits, and brickworks. Also here is Kentucky Christian College (1919).

Grays Peak 14,270 ft/4349 m, the highest in the FRONT RANGE of the Rocky Mts., 45 mi/72 km WSW of Denver and 10 mi/16 km WNW of Mt. EVANS, in NC Colorado.

Graystone Ballroom also, **Greystone** former dancing venue on Woodward Ave., 2 mi/3 km N of downtown Detroit, Michigan. Built in the 1920s by the bandleader Jean Goldkette, near what is now the CANFIELD HISTORIC DISTRICT, the Graystone, with its enormous revolving mirrored chandelier, catered to dancers in the Big Band era. It was torn down in 1980.

Gray Summit unincorporated community, pop. 2505, Franklin Co., EC Missouri, 32 mi/51 km SW of downtown St. Louis. It is the site of the 2400-ac/972-ha Shaw Arboretum of the Missouri Botanical Garden.

Great American Desert see under GREAT PLAINS.

Great American Pyramid 32-story steel and glass building in Memphis, Tennessee, just N of Downtown, opened in 1991. Housing a 22,000-seat arena used for basketball games and other events, it also has exhibition halls and shops.

Great Appalachian Valley also, **Great Valley** see under APPALACHIAN Mts.

Great Barrington town, pop. 7725, Berkshire Co., extreme SW Massachusetts, on the Housatonic and Williams rivers, 18 mi/29 km SSW of Pittsfield. It is the commercial center of a year-round resort area, and has some light manufacturing, dairying, and poultry farming. Simon's Rock College (1964) is in the town. Villages within Great Barrington include Housatonic, Van Deusenville, and Seekonk. The town was the birthplace (1868) of black writer W.E.B. DuBois.

Great Basin also, **Great Basin Desert** largest section of the BASIN AND RANGE PROVINCE, covering some 190,000 sq mi/492,000 sq km, between the Cascade Range and the Sierra Nevada (W), the COLUMBIA PLATEAU (N), and the COLORADO PLATEAU and Wasatch Mts. (E). On its S are the MOJAVE, COLORADO, and SONORAN deserts. The Basin's many subdivisions include DEATH VALLEY and the GREAT SALT LAKE Desert. An arid or semiarid area that covers most of Nevada and parts of Oregon, Utah, Idaho, and California, it has over 100 N–S trending mountain ranges, 50–120 mi/80–190 km long and 3–15 mi/5–24 km wide, rising generally to 7000–10,000 ft/2135–3050 m; these separate broad, mostly desert valleys lying at elevations of c.4000–6000 ft/1220–1830 m. The largest lakes in the Basin include Pyramid, Great Salt, Winnemucca, and Walker; these are remnants of the giant glacial lakes LAHONTAN (W) and BONNEVILLE (E), which covered much of the area. The Basin's few streams (including Nevada's HUMBOLDT and CARSON and Utah's SEVIER rivers) all end in internal salt lakes or SINKS; none reach the sea. Sagebrush is the characteristic vegetation. The region's mineral riches (which include gold, silver, copper, gemstones, barite, and uranium) drew prospectors and settlers from the mid 19th century, despite harsh conditions that had earlier impeded expansion into the area. Cattle and sheep foraging also became important. In the 20th century many remote sections acquired military importance, as at the NEVADA TEST SITE. The entire Basin and Range Province is sometimes called the Great Basin.

Great Basin National Park see under SNAKE RANGE, Nevada.

Great Bear Lake five-armed body, the largest (12,096 sq mi/31,330 sq km) lake entirely in Canada, and the fourth-largest in North America. About 200 mi/320 km at its longest, 25–110 mi/40–180 km wide, and reaching a depth of 1356 ft/413 m, it lies on the Arctic Circle, on the W edge of the CANADIAN SHIELD and in the Mackenzie R. lowlands, in the W Northwest Territories. It is drained (SW) by the Great Bear R., leading to the MACKENZIE R. Icebound for eight months of the year, it abounds in fish, but is not commercially fished. Fort Franklin (hamlet, pop. 551, Inuvik Region), a DENE community and 19th-century fur trading center on Keith Arm in the SW, is its major settlement. Port Radium, a mining center created in 1933 on McTavish Arm (E) to exploit local pitchblende for radium and uranium, is now deserted; it has also been called Echo Bay. Silver has been mined here also.

Great Bend city, pop. 15,427, seat of Barton Co., C Kansas. Deriving its name from its location on a sweeping curve of the Arkansas R., it was established in 1871 close to the site of the abandoned Fort Zarah, on the SANTA FE TRAIL. The following year it became a boisterous cow town after the railroad's arrival. It is now a shipping center for oil and wheat. Barton County Community College (1965) is here. PAWNEE ROCK (SW), the Cheyenne Bottoms marsh (NE; a major migratory waterfowl stop), and the Quivira National Wildlife Refuge (SE) are nearby.

Great Bridge historic site in CHESAPEAKE, SE Virginia. On Dec. 9, 1775, an American force led by William Woodford defeated British troops under John Murray, Earl of Dunmore, in a battle that lasted less than 25 minutes; American troops then occupied Norfolk. Great Bridge is just S of the Southern Branch of the ELIZABETH R., 7 mi/11 km E of the DISMAL SWAMP.

Great Central Valley see CENTRAL VALLEY, California.

Great Dismal Swamp see DISMAL SWAMP, Virginia.

Great Divide common (esp. 19th-century) name for the CONTINENTAL DIVIDE, used to refer not so much to the division of watersheds as to the barrier to migration posed by the Rocky Mts.; "across the Great Divide" meant over this barrier, into the promised lands of the West. Just S of Wyoming's SOUTH PASS, the most popular route over the Divide, is the **Great Divide Basin,** the only place in North America where the Continental Divide bifurcates, leaving in the middle an area with no drainage to either watershed. The basin, some 100 mi/160 km E–W and 65 mi/105 km N–S, and largely in Sweetwater Co., is occupied in its S by the RED DESERT. Travelers along the Union Pacific Railroad and I-80 routes, which traverse it on the S, between Rawlins (E) and Rock Springs (W), must, in effect, cross the Divide twice.

Great Egg Harbor River 50 mi/80 km long, in S New Jersey. It is sometimes called the Great Egg R. It rises SE of Camden and flows SE past Mays Landing (the head of navigation) to the head of Great Egg Harbor Bay, near SOMERS POINT. **Great Egg Harbor Inlet** is a narrow strait between Ocean City, Cape May Co. (S) and Longport, Atlantic Co. (N), leading from the Atlantic Ocean into Great Egg Harbor Bay.

Greater New York unofficial name for New York City as reorganized January 1, 1898, with the city as it had existed divided into the boroughs of Manhattan and the Bronx and enlarged by the annexation to the city of Brooklyn, Queens Co., and Staten Island.

Great Falls **1.** city, pop. 55,097, seat of Cascade Co., NC Montana, on the Missouri R., 74 mi/119 km NE of Helena. It is 12 mi/19 km WSW of the falls for which it is named, first seen by Lewis and Clark in 1805. In 1855 treaties were signed with the Blackfeet Indians that made area settlement possible, but Great Falls was not platted until the 1880s. It is now the state's second-largest city, a center of finance, manufacturing, and distribution for the abundant minerals and agricultural products of a large area of N Montana. It also has food processing facilities, plants for copper smelting and aluminum rolling, and oil refineries. Other manufactures include metal wire, building materials, and glass. Great Falls holds an annual state fair and rodeo. It is the seat of the College of Great Falls (1932). Great Springs, one of the world's largest freshwater springs, is 3 mi/5 km NE. Malmstrom Air Force Base, a major Cold War missile facility, is E of the city. **2.** see under SOMERSWORTH, New Hampshire.

Great Gorge see under VERNON, New Jersey.

Great Kills residential and recreational district of E Staten Island, New York, on Lower New York Bay, S of New Dorp. Great Kills Park, formerly Marine Park, incorporates Great Kills Harbor, and is the site of the Richmond Yacht Club, and boatbuilding has been important. Residential development of the area has accelerated since the 1960s.

Great Lakes group of five lakes, together forming the largest body of fresh water in the world, in C North America, along the S of the CANADIAN SHIELD, between Ontario (N) and (W–E) Minnesota, Wisconsin, Michigan, Illinois, Indiana, Ohio, Pennsylvania, and New York. Some 95,000 sq mi/246,000 sq km in area, and 1160 mi/1870 km W–E, they include Lakes SUPERIOR (largest, deepest, and northernmost), HURON, MICHIGAN, ERIE, and ONTARIO (which drains all of the lakes NE into the SAINT LAWRENCE R.) The international border passes through all but L. Michigan. With the completion of the St. Lawrence Seaway in 1959, the GREAT LAKES–ST. LAWRENCE WATERWAY forms a transportation network allowing deep-draft vessels access to ports as far W as Duluth, Minnesota, 2400 mi/3800 km from the Atlantic Ocean. The lakes are also connected to the Hudson R. via the NEW YORK STATE BARGE CANAL System, to the Mississippi R. via the ILLINOIS WATERWAY, and via shorter canal systems to other Middle Western and Canadian cities. The Great Lakes themselves are linked by the St. Marys R. and the SAULT STE. MARIE canals, between Superior and Huron; by the Straits of Mackinac, between Michigan and Huron (which are geologically one lake, with the same—577 ft/176 m—elevation); by the St. Clair R., Lake St. Clair, and the Detroit R., between Huron and Erie; and by the Niagara R. (bypassed by the WELLAND CANAL) between Erie and Ontario. In spite of severe winter storms and a navigation season of only about eight months, shipping is the most important economic activity on the lakes; grains, iron ore, coal and other fuels, limestone, copper, wood products, and manufactured goods are leading freights. The chief ports are Duluth, Minnesota; Superior and Milwaukee, Wisconsin; Chicago, Illinois; Gary, Indiana; Detroit, Michigan; Thunder Bay, Windsor, Hamilton, Toronto, and Kingston, Ontario; Toledo and Cleveland, Ohio; Erie, Pennsylvania; and Buffalo and Rochester, New York. Commercial fisheries, seriously undermined by the 1960s by overfishing, by pollution, and by an invasion of sea lampreys, began rebounding in the 1980s, with increased international environmental regulation. Tourism and recreational use are important throughout the region. The lakes' basins, which in many places extend barely beyond their shores, so that few rivers of any size flow into them, were scoured out some 10,000 years ago by glaciers, then filled with meltwater. Inhabited for thousands of years, the region was seen in the 1600s by French explorers, fur traders, and missionaries. In the 19th century lumbering was central to lake industry. Development after midcentury of iron deposits in Minnesota and Appalachian coal sources turned much of the lakeshore into the manufacturing complex it is today.

Great Lakes Naval Training Station see under NORTH CHICAGO, Illinois.

Great Lakes–Saint Lawrence Waterway also, **Saint Lawrence Seaway–Great Lakes Waterway** international waterway between the W end of the Great Lakes (thus, grain and iron producing regions of the Middle West) and the Atlantic Ocean, via the SAINT LAWRENCE R. The entire system is popularly thought of as the **Saint Lawrence Seaway,** although that is properly the name for the dam and lock–altered section of the St. Lawrence between Montréal, Québec and L. Ontario; the entire waterway was complete in April 1959, when this section was opened to commercial traffic. From the mouth of the St. Lawrence (at Anticosti I. on the Gulf of St. Lawrence) to Duluth, Minnesota, the waterway covers almost 2400 mi/3800 km. Canals and locks have been built in places along its route since 1780s attempts to bypass Montréal's LACHINE Rapids. Other major elements are the canals at SAULT STE. MARIE (Michigan and Ontario) and the WELLAND CANAL (bypassing the Niagara Falls). By early in the 20th century, boats of 14-ft/4.3-m draft could navigate the waterway's entire length. Improvement of the Saint Lawrence Seaway section made it possible for vessels up to 26 ft/8 m in draft, 730 ft/223 m long, and 76 ft/23 m wide to pass between the lakes and ocean. Long urged by Canada, the project was agreed to by the US in 1954. Major elements in waterway traffic are grains, coal, and petroleum products moving E, and iron ore from Labrador moving W to Canadian plants. The waterway is generally open from mid-April to mid-Dec. International agreements govern navigation, power generation, and water quality along it.

Great Meadows see under CONCORD R., Massachusetts.

Great Miami River also, **Miami River** 160 mi/258 km long, in Ohio. It rises at Indian L. in Logan Co., and flows generally SW past Sidney, Piqua, Troy, Dayton, and Hamilton to the Ohio R. in the extreme SW corner of Ohio, W of Cincinnati. Its chief tributaries are the Stillwater, Mad, and Whitewater rivers.

Great Neck village, pop. 8745, in North Hempstead town, Nassau Co., SE New York, on Long Island's North Shore at the New York City line. Set on a peninsula jutting out into Long Island Sound, it is primarily residential. In the 1920s, Great Neck was home to many film celebrities, and was the model for East Egg in F. Scott Fitzgerald's *The Great Gatsby;* Fitzgerald lived here for a time. KINGS POINT lies N.

Great Northern Peninsula 164 mi/265 km NNE–SSW, in N Newfoundland, separated from Labrador (NW) by the Gulf of St. Lawrence and the Strait of BELLE ISLE. The LONG RANGE Mts. form its backbone. Coastal settlements, some part of the historic FRENCH SHORE, include Port au Choix (W) and

SAINT ANTHONY (N). GROS MORNE National Park is in the SW, L'ANSE AUX MEADOWS at the extreme N.

Great Northern Railway northernmost US railway crossing the Rocky Mts. to the Pacific. On the basis of the abortive 1850s Minnesota and Pacific, the St. Paul and Pacific began in the 1870s to build across NW Minnesota into North Dakota. By 1887 it had reached Great Falls, Montana, by way of Grand Forks and Minot, North Dakota, and Havre, Montana. Renamed the Great Northern in 1890, it continued through the MARIAS PASS to Whitefish, Montana; the railroad has been strongly involved in the promotion of GLACIER NATIONAL PARK. In 1893, having extended through Spokane, Washington, and tunneled the Cascade Range, it reached Seattle. Since 1970, the Great Northern has been part of the huge BURLINGTON NORTHERN system.

Great Pee Dee River see PEE DEE R.

Great Plains vast grassland area of C North America, extending E from the Rocky Mts. for distances varying from c.400 mi/640 km to c.600 mi/1000 km, from N Alberta to S Texas. It comprises generally level or rolling land that rises gradually, from 1500–2000 ft/460–610 m in the E to over 4000 ft/1220 m near the Rockies. The E boundary of the Plains is usually defined as lying at roughly 100° W longitude, or in some definitions 98° W; this is substantially the same line accepted as the beginning of the American WEST. It approximates the transition from tall-grass PRAIRIE in the E to short-grass prairie, and from moister areas in the E to semiarid lands that lie in the rain shadow of the Rockies and are popularly associated with the grazing of cattle amid sparse vegetation. The Plains, however, are actually fertile agricultural land; their LOESS soils, lying atop other sedimentary strata that include the huge Ogallala AQUIFER, produce wheat and a variety of other crops. The plowing of the short-grass prairie, accelerated in response to European food shortages during World War I, led to DUST BOWL conditions in the 1930s. Later developments in farming technique and irrigation have kept that disaster from recurring, but depletion of the ground water supply now threatens. Before the arrival of the Spanish (beginning in the 16th century), the Plains had few human inhabitants; the scattered groups here lived chiefly in the bottomlands of major rivers. The arrival of the horse, however, gave birth to a new culture; peoples from elsewhere, like the Sioux (who were pushed SW from Minnesota) became "Plains Indians," expanding their buffalo hunts across wide open spaces. By the time white settlement intensified, in the mid 19th century, dozens of tribes were here to defend their homelands against the newcomers; most of the Indian wars of the period 1850–1900 occurred on the Great Plains. In the same period, the HOMESTEAD Act of 1862 and promotional efforts by the transcontinental railroads (esp. the UNION PACIFIC and the SANTA FE) brought waves of settlers, among them Europeans who introduced winter wheat and other agricultural innovations. The rate of settlement slowed by the early 20th century, as the FRONTIER closed. Depopulation of rural areas, extensive in the 1930s Depression, continues today, as large-scale agribusiness gradually eliminates opportunities for the prosperity of the family farm. The Great Plains embrace large parts of Alberta (from the PEACE R. valley southward), Saskatchewan, W Manitoba, E and C Montana, W North Dakota, NE Wyoming, W South Dakota, W Nebraska, E Colorado, W Kansas, E New Mexico, W and C Oklahoma, and the PANHANDLE, NC, and WC (Pecos R. valley) sections of Texas. Its varied terrains include the Dakota BADLANDS, Canada's PALLISER'S TRIANGLE, Texas's EDWARDS PLATEAU, the LLANO ESTACADO (Staked Plain) of Texas and New Mexico, and Nebraska's SAND HILLS. The BLACK HILLS of South Dakota are the most prominent of several scattered mountain and hill areas. In the W, from the Dakotas to Texas (where the Llano Estacado is an extension), are the **High Plains.** The highest part of the Plains, extending into the Rocky Mt. foothills, this area, dry, almost without trees, and windswept, is the heart of the **Great American Desert,** as the Plains were conceived of in the early 19th century—an expanse thought to be inhospitable to any but nomadic Indians and the occasional cattle grazer. The Great Plains are crossed from W to E by almost all the major W tributaries of the Mississippi R., chief among them (S–N) rivers in the RED, ARKANSAS, PLATTE, and MISSOURI systems; their beds provided routes for the trails, and later railroads, that both led through them and, later, led homesteaders to them.

Great Raft, the see under RED R.; SHREVEPORT, Louisiana.

Great Sacandaga Lake also, **Great Sacandaga Reservoir,** formed by the damming (1930) of the Sacandaga R. at Conklingville, 5 mi/8 km W of Lake Luzerne, Warren Co., NE New York. Now 25 mi/40 km NE–SW, and 42 sq mi/109 sq km in area, it is an increasingly popular resort at the S extreme of the Adirondacks, and functions to regulate the flow of the upper Hudson R., into which it empties.

Great Salt Lake saline body in the Great Basin, NW of Salt Lake City, in NW Utah. Up to 80 mi/130 km NW–SE and 20–45 mi/30–75 km wide, it has a 20%–25% salinity, several times that of the oceans. It has no outlets, and the S and E sectors, which receive the BEAR, Jordan, and Weber rivers, are less salty than the NW. The lake is shallow, with a maximum depth of 35 ft/11 m, and its size varies greatly, from an average of 1850 sq mi/4800 sq km to only 1078 sq mi/2792 sq km in 1940, the lowest year on record. Bacteria and algae grow in profusion in the lake, turning sections of it shades of red, orange, or blue-green. The only other life forms are brine shrimp and brine flies, although migratory birds flock to surrounding freshwater marshes, including the Bear River Migratory Bird Refuge, on the NE. The lake has eight islands, the largest of which, Antelope (SE), is a 36–sq mi/93–sq km state park. A long peninsula, its spine the PROMONTORY Mts., reaches 35 mi/56 km into the lake from the N; a rail causeway, the Lucin Cutoff (1904), crosses it between OGDEN (E) and the W, by way of Promontory Point, at the peninsula's S. The Great Salt L. is a remnant of ancient L. Bonneville, which covered close to 20,000 sq mi/52,000 sq km; to the W and SW lies the **Great Salt Lake Desert,** some 120 mi/190 km N–S and 50 mi/80 km wide. The Newfoundland Evaporation Basin, a W extension of the lake, lies here, W of the Newfoundland Mts. At its W edge, near the Nevada border, is the BONNEVILLE SALT FLATS, famed site of auto speed tests. Large sections of the desert have been used since World War II by the military, from bases at Wendover (W) and DUGWAY (SE), and from Hill Air Force Base, near CLEARFIELD.

Great Saltpeter Caves in Rockcastle Co., EC Kentucky, 32 mi/52 km SE of Danville. Near Mount Vernon on the WILDERNESS ROAD, they are in an area of lime and sandstone quarries. A main ingredient of gunpowder, saltpeter made them strategically important during the Civil War.

Great Sand Dunes National Monument 38,662 ac/15,658 ha, at the W foot of the SANGRE DE CRISTO Mts., in S Colorado's San Luis Valley, 85 mi/137 km SW of Colorado Springs. Formed of material eroded over thousands of years by the upper Rio Grande, the dunes are up to 700 ft/213 m high, and constantly shift slightly, although the material is too heavy to blow over the 14,000-ft/4270-m Sangre de Cristos.

Great Serpent Mound see SERPENT MOUND, Ohio.

Great Slave Lake chiefly WSW–ENE oriented body, North America's fifth-largest (11,031 sq mi/28,570 sq km) and deepest (to 2014 ft/614 m) lake, in the SW Northwest Territories, 56 mi/90 km N of the Alberta border. Fed by the Slave (SE) and other rivers, it drains W into the Mackenzie R., and thus into the Beaufort Sea. Its NE on the CANADIAN SHIELD, its W in the Mackenzie lowlands, the lake, frozen most of the year, has trout and whitefish fisheries, and was long a Chipewyan (DENE) fur trapping center. Since the 1930s, gold, then lead and zinc, have been mined on its shores. YELLOWKNIFE (N) and HAY RIVER (SW) are the major settlements on its shores.

Great Smoky Mountains also, **Smoky Mountains** or **Smokies** part of the Appalachian Mts., sometimes considered a subrange of the UNAKA RANGE, along the border between W North Carolina and E Tennessee. Site of some of the loftiest peaks in the E US, the Smokies rise to 6643 ft/2025 m at CLINGMANS DOME, the highest point in Tennessee, and include Mt. Le Conte (6593 ft/2010 m, near GATLINBURG, Tennessee), and Mt. Guyot (6621 ft/2018 m), 14 mi/23 km E, on the state line. Named for the deep smokelike haze that sometimes hangs over them, they merge with the BLUE RIDGE escarpment to the E, and are sometimes considered part of it. The area is the meeting point of northern and southern flora and fauna. Most of the main 5000 ft/1525 m–high crest, which is traversed by the APPALACHIAN TRAIL, has been preserved in **Great Smoky Mts. National Park** (520,269 ac/210,709 ha), famous for its dense forests, large stands of rhododendron, mountain laurel, and wildflowers, treeless mountain tops known as "balds," varied wildlife, over 800 mi/1300 km of hiking trails, and fishing streams, and as the S end of the BLUE RIDGE PARKWAY. The park extends for 54 mi/89 km between the Little Tennessee R. (SW) and the Pigeon R. (NE), and is headquartered at Gatlinburg. The area also includes Sugarland Valley; Alum Cave Bluff, site of a 19th-century alum mine; Newfound Gap (see under CLINGMANS DOME); Cades Cove, site of historic buildings; and, just NW of the park, Tuckaleechee Caverns, a large cave containing onyx formations. The Cherokee Indian Reservation lies S of the park.

Great South Bay inlet of the Atlantic Ocean between the South Shore of Long Island and its barrier islands. The bay extends 45 mi/72 km from ATLANTIC BEACH (W) to Moriches Bay (E). On the barrier islands are LONG BEACH, JONES BEACH, and the FIRE ISLAND resorts. Massapequa, Bay Shore, and Patchogue are among the communities on the bay.

Great Swamp **1.** see under FAIRFIELD, Connecticut. **2.** wetland in Morris Co., N New Jersey, a National Wildlife Refuge in parts of Chatham, Harding, Long Hill (formerly Passaic), and Bernards townships. The remnants of glacial L. Passaic, which built up on the Passaic R. NW of the WATCHUNG Mts. during the last ice age, before the river found its current bed, the swamp now covers at least 7000 ac/2835 ha, and is a migratory bird center. **3.** see under SOUTH KINGSTOWN, Rhode Island.

Great Valley **1.** see under APPALACHIAN Mts. **2.** see CENTRAL VALLEY, California.

Great Western Railway see under CANADIAN NATIONAL RAILWAY.

Great Whale River French, **Grande Rivière de la Baleine** 365 mi/590 km long, in NW Québec. It flows generally W from L. Bienville, reaching Hudson Bay at the village (pop. 605) known officially as Kuujjuarapik (its Inuit name), also as Whapmagoostui (its Cree name) or Poste-de-la-Baleine. In the 1990s the Great Whale was the focus of intense controversy over JAMES BAY Project power development, which the Cree and environmental groups opposed as destructive of wildlife, ecological balance, and the native way of life.

Great White Way see under BROADWAY, New York City.

Greece town, pop. 90,106, Monroe Co., W New York, adjacent (W) to ROCHESTER, along L. Ontario (N) and the Erie Canal (S). It is an industrial and residential suburb, heavily urban in its E, with open land and wetlands W and N.

Greektown **1.** neighborhood in downtown Detroit, Michigan, N of the RENAISSANCE CENTER. Ethnic restaurants and shops in this restoration district attract tourists. TRAPPERS ALLEY is in Greektown. **2.** see under BLOOR St., Toronto, Ontario.

Greeley city, pop. 60,536, seat of Weld Co., NC Colorado, near the confluence of the Cache la Poudre and South Platte rivers, 50 mi/80 km N of Denver. Originally called Union Colony, it was founded by New Englanders (1870) as an agricultural cooperative, formed by New York *Tribune* agriculture editor Nathan Meeker and journalist Horace Greeley. Agriculture is still central to its economy. The city is surrounded by irrigated farms producing sugar beets and other crops, and has agriculture-based industries including food processing, bottling and canning, cattle feed lots, and stockyards. It is the seat of the University of Northern Colorado (1889) and Aims Community College (1967).

Greenacres City city, pop. 18,683, Palm Beach Co., SE Florida, a residential community 8 mi/13 km SW of West Palm Beach.

Green Bank also, **Greenbank** locality in Pocahontas Co., E West Virginia, in Deer Creek Valley of the Allegheny Mts., between the Virginia border (E) and the Greenbrier R. (W), 45 mi/72 km WNW of Staunton, Virginia. The headquarters of the National Radio Astronomy Observatory (1956) is here, with a complex of six large telescopes.

Green Bay **1.** NW arm of L. Michigan, S of Michigan's Upper Peninsula and indenting E Wisconsin at the mouth of the Fox R. Measuring 115 mi/185 km NE–SW and 5–18 mi/8–29 km wide, the bay is separated from the lake by the Garden Peninsula of Michigan, which creates its N reach, Big Bay de Noc, and the DOOR PENINSULA in Wisconsin, with a canal between bay and lake at Sturgeon Bay. The bay also receives the Escanaba R. in Michigan and the Menominee R. at the Michigan-Wisconsin border. Fishing, shipping, and tourism are important to the bay, which can accommodate ocean freighters. The city of GREEN BAY, at its head, is the bay's largest port; MARINETTE, Wisconsin, and MENOMINEE, Michigan, lie on its W shore. The bay connects L. Michigan with the Mississippi R. via the Fox and Wisconsin rivers. In an area long inhabited by the Winnebago and Potawatomi, the French explorer Jean Nicolet was the first European (1634). **2.** city, pop. 96,466, Brown Co., NE Wisconsin, at the place where the Fox R. empties into Green Bay, 43 mi/69 km NE of Oshkosh. The French explorer Jean Nicolet visited the site in 1634; a trading post was established in 1665 and a mission a few years later. A fort, built here in 1717, became the center of a small French fur trading settlement. It subsequently fell under British control. The US took permanent possession of the area in 1816. With the decline of the fur trade, lumbering and agriculture became prominent. After the opening of the Erie Canal, Green Bay became a major Great Lakes port; shipping and distributing businesses remain vital to its economy. The manufacture of wood and paper products, transportation equipment, iron and steel, and auto parts, as well as cheese processing and canning, are leading industries. A campus of the University of Wisconsin (1965) is here. Other educational and cultural institutions include Northeast Wisconsin Technical Institute (1913) and the National Railroad Museum. Since 1919, the city has been home to the Green Bay Packers (football), who play their home games at Lambeau Field (1957).

greenbelt ring of open (park or farm) land, originally conceived as placing a limit on a city's outward growth. Greenbelts failed to prevent urban sprawl, as suburbs simply leapfrogged them; but they generally preserved or raised housing values near them, and they serve as amenities in many cities. The term is also used of strips of open land, not necessarily complete rings.

Greenbelt **1.** city, pop. 21,096, Prince George's Co., C Maryland, 11 mi/18 km NE of Washington, D.C. A residential suburb, it was built 1935–38 by the Federal Resettlement Administration, to provide housing for families of moderate income. Some of the parklands that surrounded it were set aside for development as Greenbelt Regional Park. Greenbelt is on the Capital BELTWAY, just E of COLLEGE PARK. **2.** in C Staten Island, New York, chain of parks, including Willowbrook, High Rock, and La Tourette, chiefly atop the spine of hills of which TODT HILL is the highest. It remains largely forested in the midst of rapid development since the 1960s. Planners intend FRESH KILLS to function as part of the Greenbelt.

Greenbrier River 170 mi/274 km long, in SE West Virginia. It rises in two headstreams just N of GREEN BANK in Pocahontas Co., and flows generally SSW past Marlinton and Alderson to the NEW R., just S of Hinton and just N of the Bluestone Dam.

Greencastle city, pop. 8984, seat of Putnam Co., WC Indiana, 30 mi/48 km NE of Terre Haute. A trade and shipping center for local livestock, grain, dairy products, lumber, and limestone, it also produces crushed stone and cement. Greencastle is the seat of DePauw University (1837).

Green Chamber, the see under PARLIAMENT HILL, Ottawa, Ontario.

Greendale village, pop. 15,128, Milwaukee Co., SE Wisconsin, on the Root R., 10 mi/16 km SW of Milwaukee. It was one of three "garden cities" built by the US government in the 1930s as an experiment in city planning, with intentionally low-cost housing. It is now a suburban residential community that also produces auto and machine parts.

Greene County **1.** 677 sq mi/1753 sq km, pop. 207,949, in SW Missouri, on the Ozark Plateau. Its seat and only large city is SPRINGFIELD, whose many industries strongly affect its economy. In the rest of the county livestock is raised and a variety of crops, including grain, fruits, and vegetables, are grown. There are also deposits of iron, lead, and limestone. **2.** 648 sq mi/1678 sq km, pop. 44,739, in SE New York, along the Hudson R. (E). Its SW section is in the Catskill Mts., much of it in the Catskill State Park. Its seat is CATSKILL, where there is some manufacturing. Ski resorts, such as Hunter and Windham, and summer vacation areas abound, with many small lakes. The county also produces such agricultural goods as vegetables, fruit, and dairy products. **3.** 416 sq mi/1077 sq km, pop. 136,763, in SW Ohio, intersected by the Little Miami and Mad rivers. Its seat is XENIA. Residential suburbs of Dayton occupy much of its W section. Otherwise, its economy depends primarily on agriculture, including grain, livestock, poultry, and truck farming. There is manufacturing at Fairborn, Xenia, and Yellow Springs. Gravel and sand are natural resources, and the area is noted for its mineral springs.

Greeneville town, pop. 13,532, seat of Greene Co., NE Tennessee, near Davy Crockett L. (the Nolichucky R.), just W of the Blue Ridge, 63 mi/101 km ENE of Knoxville. Settled by Scots-Irish Covenanters in 1780, it was the capital (1785–88) of the State of FRANKLIN. The home of President Andrew Johnson, it is a center for the curing and sale of burley tobacco. It also produces electronic equipment, furniture, dairy products, and paper, and is a gateway for Cherokee National Forest, 14 mi/23 km E.

Greenfield **1.** city, pop. 11,657, seat of Hancock Co., C Indiana, on Brandywine Creek and US 40, 20 mi/32 km E of Indianapolis. It trades local agricultural products, cans tomatoes, and engages in other light industry. James Whitcomb Riley, the "Hoosier Poet,"was born here in 1849. His birthplace, a museum, is on Main St. **2.** town, pop. 18,666, seat of Franklin Co., NW Massachusetts, at the junction of the Connecticut and Green rivers, 36 mi/58 km N of Springfield, on Interstate 91 and the Mohawk Trail. Founded in 1686 as part of Deerfield, and separated from it in 1753, Greenfield was an important silverware manufacturing center in the early 19th century, together with the industrial village of Turners Falls, across the Connecticut. Modern industries include the production of tools, paper, and electrical components, tourism, and farming. Greenfield Community College (1962) is here. **3.** city, pop. 33,403, Milwaukee Co., SE Wisconsin, on the Root R., immediately SW of Milwaukee and 12 mi/19 km SW of Downtown. It is a residential suburb.

Greenfield Park city, pop. 17,652, Champlain census division, S Québec, 5 mi/8 km E of Montréal and adjacent (N) to Brossard and (S) to Saint-Lambert. It is a largely residential suburb.

Greenfield Village see under DEARBORN, Michigan.

Green Gables home of the fictional character Anne of Green Gables, created by Lucy Maud Montgomery (1874–1942), in Prince Edward Island. Her series of six novels follows the adventures of a young orphan, its locales inspired by the hamlet of Cavendish ("Avonlea"), Montgomery's childhood home, on the Gulf of St. Lawrence, 21 mi/32 km NW of Charlottetown, and by Park Corner, her uncle's home, 9 mi/14 km NNW of Cavendish. The reconstructed Green Gables house, in PRINCE EDWARD ISLAND NATIONAL PARK, and New London, Montgomery's birthplace (7 mi/11 km SW of Cavendish), are major tourist attractions.

Green Haven locality in Beekman township, Dutchess Co., SE New York, 13 mi/21 km SE of Poughkeepsie, site of New York's Green Haven Correctional Facility.

Greenhills village, pop. 4393, Hamilton Co., in the SW

corner of Ohio. A N suburb of Cincinnati, it was completed in 1938 by the Resettlement Administration as a model low-cost housing community for 1000 families. It covers 6000 ac/2430 ha, and is based on the "garden city" plan—residential areas surrounding a core of public buildings and workplaces.

Green Lake resort lake in Green Lake Co., EC Wisconsin, 25 mi/40 km W of Fond du Lac. Eight mi/13 km long, it lies in an area of dairy farms and summer homes, and is the deepest lake in Wisconsin.

Greenlawn unincorporated village, pop. 13,208, in Huntington town, Suffolk Co., SE New York, on Long Island's North Shore. It is primarily residential.

Green Mountains northerly range of the APPALACHIAN mountains, creating a N–S backbone through the center of Vermont from Québec to Massachusetts, where in the NW they continue as the HOOSAC Mts. and in the SW as the eastern border of the BERKSHIRE HILLS. In Vermont they are traversed by three major valleys, those of the Missisquoi, Lamoille, and Winooski rivers. They provide important drainage areas for L. Champlain and the upper Connecticut R. Among the oldest of mountains in New England, they have a low (generally 2000–3000 ft/610–915 m), rolling look, having been shaped by glaciers and erosion. The LONG TRAIL traverses many of the higher peaks, which include Mt. Mansfield (4393 ft/1340 m), Killington Peak (4241 ft/1294 m), Lincoln Mountain (4013 ft/1224 m), and Camels Hump (4083 ft/1245 m). The **Green Mountain National Forest** (363,000 ac/147,000 ha) was created in 1932 and is headquartered in Rutland. Marble, granite, talc, and asbestos have been mined in the Green Mts., which (*verts monts*) gave Vermont (the Green Mountain State) its name.

Greenpoint industrial and residential district, N Brooklyn, New York, on the East R. and Newtown Creek, which separates it from Queens. Williamsburg lies directly S. Once agricultural, Greenpoint in mid 19th century became Brooklyn's industrial center. It produced, among other vessels, the Federal ironclad *Monitor* (1862); glass, ceramics, iron, printing, and the refining of sugar and oil were major industries. In the early 20th century most industry moved away, seeking more space elsewhere. Greenpoint remains the home of descendants of 19th-century workers, particularly Poles and other Slavs, as well as of later immigrants. While not ethnically uniform, it is thought of as a center of Polish-American life. In the 1980s artists and others seeking industrial lofts began to move into the area.

Greenport see under NORTH FORK, Long I., New York.

Green River **1.** 370 mi/600 km long, in C Kentucky. It rises SSE of Danville, and flows SW into Green River L., formed by a dam just E of Greensburg, then W through Greensburg, Munfordville, and Mammoth Cave National Park. Turning NW near Woodbury, in Butler Co., it passes W of Owensboro to the Ohio R. The most important of its many tributaries, the BARREN R., joins it from the S at Woodbury. **2.** 730 mi/1175 km long, in Wyoming, Colorado, and Utah. It rises in the WIND RIVER Range in W Wyoming, then flows S through Fontenelle Reservoir and generally SSE past Green River and through FLAMING GORGE Reservoir, where it crosses into Utah before turning E and entering NW Colorado. Here it turns S through DINOSAUR NATIONAL MONUMENT, then SW, back into Utah. Passing SW below the Uinta Mts., it cuts Desolation Canyon through the Tavaputs Plateau. Continuing S through Gray Canyon and Stillwater Canyon, it enters the Colorado R. within CANYONLANDS NATIONAL PARK. The river drains much of W Wyoming and E Utah, cutting across much of the Colorado Plateau. Its tributaries include the YAMPA in Colorado and the Duchesne and San Rafael in Utah. **3.** city, pop. 12,711, seat of Sweetwater Co., SW Wyoming, on the Green R., 13 mi/21 km W of Rock Springs. Originally a meeting place for trappers and a stop on the OVERLAND TRAIL, it developed after the Union Pacific Railroad arrived in 1868. The N gateway to Flaming Gorge National Recreation Area, 25 mi/40 km to the SE, with Ashley National Forest immediately S, it is now a railroad division point and a trade and shipping center for a ranching, agricultural, and forestry region. Much of America's soda ash comes from local trona mines.

Greensboro **1.** see under HALE Co., Alabama. **2.** city, pop. 183,521, seat of Guilford Co., NC North Carolina, 68 mi/110 km WNW of Raleigh. Settled in 1749, it became the county seat in 1808, and was named for Nathanael Greene, commander of the American forces during the March 15, 1781 Battle of Guilford Courthouse, just NW. Greensboro is best known as a textile center, home to Burlington Industries. It now serves as a distribution and market center, the largest city of the Piedmont Triad, which includes High Point and Winston-Salem. Other manufactures include pumping equipment, tobacco products, furniture, brick, chemicals, and pharmaceutical products, and the city has sizable financial, insurance, and advertising sectors. It is home to Guilford College (1837), Greensboro College (1838), Bennett College (1873), the University of North Carolina at Greensboro (1891), and the North Carolina Agricultural and Technical State University (1891). Students at the latter initiated the civil rights movement's sit-in demonstrations at a downtown Woolworth's lunch counter in Feb., 1960.

Greensburg **1.** city, pop. 9286, seat of Decatur Co., SE Indiana, 45 mi/72 km SE of Indianapolis. Settled in 1822, it is a trade center for an agricultural and oil and gas producing area. There are stone quarries nearby. Food products, fencing, hardware, shirts, fertilizer, cement blocks, auto accessories, and brooms have been manufactured here. **2.** city, pop. 16,318, seat of Westmoreland Co., SW Pennsylvania, 27 mi/43 km ESE of Pittsburgh. It was founded in the late 18th century by Revolutionary General Arthur St. Clair, later president of the Continental Congress and first governor of the NORTHWEST TERRITORY, who is buried here. Situated in a bituminous coal region, it is primarily a light-manufacturing center, producing glass, metal, machinery, and many other goods. The city is home to Seton Hill College (1883).

Green Valley unincorporated community, pop. 13,231, Pima Co., S Arizona, on the Santa Cruz R. and I-19, 23 mi/37 km S of Tucson. This retirement community, in a copper producing area, is the site of a former Titan intercontinental missile complex, now a museum.

Greenville **1.** city, pop. 7492, seat of Butler Co., SC Alabama, 45 mi/72 km SSW of Montgomery. Settled in 1819, it is a cotton trading center and shipping point for pecans. **2.** unincorporated residential community in New Castle Co., N Delaware, 4 mi/6 km NW of Wilmington. The Mt. Cuba Center gardens are just NW. **3.** city, pop. 4806, seat of Bond Co., SW Illinois, 30 mi/48 km NW of Centralia. It trades and distributes alfalfa grown in the area. Greenville College (1892) is here. Carlyle L., a popular recreational site, is 13 mi/21 km SE. **4.** city, pop. 45,226, seat of Washington Co., NW Mississippi, on L. Ferguson (an OXBOW open to the Mississippi R.), 90 mi/140 km NW of Jackson, and the largest city in the DELTA. Old Greenville, just SW, was destroyed by floods and by an 1863 Federal bombardment; the present city was established in 1870. Its site makes Greenville a distribution and retail hub for a three-state area that includes SE Arkansas and NE Louisiana; engineering measures have reduced the threat of floods, one of which devastated the city in 1927. Long essentially a cotton center, Greenville by the late 20th century had acquired various industries, including the manufacture of concrete, auto parts, bicycles, and metal products. It is noted as the long-time home of journalist Hodding Carter (former editor of its *Delta Democrat-Times*) and of writers Shelby Foote and Walker Percy. **5.** town, pop. 3135, Greene Co., SE New York, in the foothills of the Catskill Mts., 27 mi/43 km NW of Catskill. It is the birthplace of pioneer oil driller Edwin L. Drake (1819–80). **6.** city, pop. 44,972, seat of Pitt Co., E North Carolina, on the Tar R., 70 mi/110 km ESE of Raleigh. It was founded in 1786, and has long been one of the leading world markets for bright leaf tobacco. Pharmaceutical and other industries are also significant. The city is home to East Carolina University (1907) and Pitt Community College (1961). During the Cold War it became the center of the Voice of America's national and international radio operations. **7.** city, pop. 12,863, seat of Drake Co., WC Ohio, on Greenville Creek, 52 mi/84 km SW of Lima and 9 mi/14 km E of the Indiana border. Fort Greenville was built here (1793) during a campaign against the Indians, and formed part of a fortified line between Cincinnati and L. Erie. Shortly thereafter, the tribes signed a treaty at the fort that yielded substantial NORTHWEST TERRITORY land. It was also the site of a Shawnee village, the home of Tecumseh. When the Shawnee were forced W in the early 19th century, white settlement began. Today Greenville is a trade center for an agricultural area that grows corn, wheat, tomatoes, and tobacco. Among its industries are meatpacking and the manufacture of electrical appliances, stoves, machinery, tile, plastics, glass, and knit goods. **8.** borough, pop. 6734, Mercer Co., NW Pennsylvania, on the Shenango R., 27 mi/43 km N of New Castle. Situated in a farming area, it produces railroad cars, aluminum and dairy products, and other goods. Greenville is the seat of Thiel College (1866). **9.** city, pop. 58,282, seat of Greenville Co. (pop. 320,167), NW South Carolina, on the Reedy R., 100 mi/160 km NW of Columbia, in the foothills of the Blue Ridge Mts. One of the largest manufacturing concentrations in the Southeast and an important communications center, it was first settled in the 1760s and was a summer resort until the Civil War. Industrialization began in the 1830s. As the W terminus (after 1853) for the Greenville and Columbia Railroad, it became a commercial center for the Piedmont, and grew even more after the Civil War, utilizing power from the Reedy's falls. While textile mills have dominated, chemicals, plastics, machinery, electronics, tires and auto accessories, and aircraft are also produced. Local agriculture produces eggs, dairy goods, beef, and peaches. Furman University (1826) and Bob Jones University (1927) are among local institutions. **10.** city, pop. 23,071, seat of Hunt Co., NE Texas, on the Sabine R., 42 mi/68 km NE of Dallas. When railroads converged here in the 1880s, it developed as a shipping point and cotton center. The rich BLACKLANDS around the city also produce livestock, poultry, and various field crops. In the 1950s an aircraft plant opened, and the city became industrial; its varied manufactures include military electronics, trailers, and oilfield equipment.

Greenville Avenue commercial thoroughfare in N Dallas, Texas, extending from Downtown to I-635 (the Lyndon B. Johnson Freeway). Paralleling (E) the CENTRAL EXPRESSWAY, it is well known as an entertainment area, progressing from smaller, more bohemian establishments near Downtown to expensive restaurants and singles bars in NORTH DALLAS.

Greenwich **1.** town, pop. 58,441, Fairfield Co., extreme SW Connecticut, on Long Island Sound at the New York border. It is primarily a group of residential communities with large homes and estates set in rolling countryside or along the shore. Although many residents commute to New York City, it has some light industry and a growing service and corporate sector, including offices of major corporations. Purchased from local tribes in 1640 by settlers from New Haven, Greenwich was plundered during the Revolutionary War. It remained agricultural, with some shipping trade, before becoming suburban by the 20th century. The town includes the villages of Banksville, Byram, COS COB, Glenville, Mianus, Old Greenwich, Quaker Ridge, Riverside, Round Hill, and Stanwich. **2.** town in the Swift R. valley, Hampshire Co., WC Massachusetts, inundated during creation of the QUABBIN RESERVOIR (1937).

Greenwich Village familiarly, **the Village** historic residential section of lower Manhattan, New York City. It has been widely known since the 1920s as a home to artistic and political countercultures. Settled in 1696 as the village of Greenwich, on the site of an Indian town, Sapokanican, and later Dutch farms, it became by the 1730s a fashionable country retreat for wealthy inhabitants of New York, then farther S. In the early 19th century town houses were built in the area, following the leveling of its hills in 1811. Mid-19th-century immigration brought Irish, Germans, and Italians, and Greenwich Village gradually became a tenement district. Around World War I the now heavily Italian neighborhood was invaded by artists, writers, actors, and political oppositionists, in search of cheap housing. The Village peaked through the 1920s, when such figures as John Reed, Edna St. Vincent Millay, Eugene O'Neill, Joe Gould, and John Sloan flourished, and the ambitious arrived from all over America to take part in what was perceived as a rebellion against national materialism. Today the area is more fashionable than bohemian, but its reputation draws tourists from all over the world. Washington Square is considered the heart of the Village, although on its E edge. New York University, housed around the square, heavily influences Village life. Fourteenth St. is generally accepted as Greenwich Village's N border, Houston St. as the southern. The 17th-century village was actually located largely in what is now called the West Village, W of Sixth Avenue, a slightly more residential section known as a center of gay life and culture, centering around Christopher St. and Sheridan Square. The West Village is home to the New School for Social Research and to St. Vincent's Hospital. The South Village, a less heavily traveled section that remained working-class and Italian after fashion had transformed much of the rest of Greenwich Village, lies to the SW. To the E of Washington Square, the Astor Place district provides a transition to the EAST VILLAGE. SOHO lies directly S.

Greenwood **1.** city, pop. 26,265, Johnson Co., C Indiana, 10 mi/16 km S of central Indianapolis. Just outside the Indianapolis/ Marion Co. boundary, it is a primarily residential suburb. Such products as auto accessories and canned goods are manufactured. **2.** city, pop. 18,906, seat of Leflore Co., NW Mississippi, on the Yazoo R. at the E edge of the DELTA, 84 mi/135 km N of Jackson. It has thrived as a cotton market since the Choctaw were dispossessed in the 1830s, its trade interrupted only by the Civil War. Today its economy is also based on light manufacturing, food processing, and meatpacking. **3.** see under TULSA, Oklahoma. **4.** city, pop. 20,807, seat of Greenwood Co., NW South Carolina, 66 mi/106 km WNW of Columbia. Settled in 1824, it grew after arrival of the Greenville and Columbia Railroad in 1852; railroads eventually made it a center for cotton and synthetic fiber mills, as well as food processing and meatpacking plants. It is home to Lander College (1872) and to a technical college.

Green-Wood Cemetery between Park Slope and Sunset Park, WC Brooklyn, New York. Covering 478 ac/194 ha of morainal hills, including the highest point (219 ft/67 m) in Brooklyn, it was opened in 1840, and quickly became a popular retreat for pre–Central Park New Yorkers. The premier burial ground for New York's middle and upper classes through the 19th century, it is still in use, and houses the remains of some 500,000, famous and obscure.

Greenwood Lake in Orange Co., SE New York, and Passaic Co., N New Jersey, 20 mi/32 km NW of Paterson. Nine mi/14 km NE–SW, it is a summer resort. The village of **Greenwood Lake,** New York (pop. 3208) is at its NE end.

Greer city, pop. 10,322, Greenville and Spartanburg counties, NW South Carolina, 12 mi/19 km ENE of Greenville. Traditionally a farming and textile-mill center, it is now near Interstate 85 and the Greenville-Spartanburg Jetport, and faces a residential and industrial land boom spurred by the 1990s location of a BMW auto plant just SE.

Grenada city, pop. 10,864, seat of Grenada Co., NC Mississippi, on the Yalobusha R. at the E edge of the DELTA, 27 mi/43 km NE of Greenwood. Formed in 1836 by the merger of Tulahoma and Pittsburg, two villages established by rival speculators, it was Confederate General J. C. Pemberton's headquarters in the defense of Vicksburg in 1862. A long-time cotton market, it remains a center of agricultural (cotton, corn, livestock, dairy) trade. The Grenada Dam and Lake are just NE.

Grenville village, pop. 1362, Argenteuil census division, S Québec, on the Ottawa R., opposite Hawkesbury, Ontario (S), 52 mi/83 km WNW of Montréal and 12 mi/19 km W of Lachute. A canal built here in 1819–34 was part of a plan, centered on the RIDEAU CANAL, to provide an all-Canadian alternative to the Great Lakes as a route W from Montréal into the interior. Grenville has a mining history and is today a recreational center. It gives its name to the **Grenville Province,** a band of Precambrian (about 1 billion to 1.5 billion years old) rocks that constitute the newest and southeasternmost part of the CANADIAN SHIELD and that extend NE–SW from Labrador through the SE US and into Mexico. Roughly underlying the Appalachian system, Grenville rocks, which for the most part are today far below the surface, also extend W beyond L. Erie; the **Grenville Front,** extending NE from L. Huron's NE shore to Labrador, represents the boundary between them and older Shield rocks. The Grenville Province is thought to represent a collision of continental PLATES over 1 billion years ago; the high mountains raised by that event have long since been eroded away; various low hills throughout the Appalachian region represent their mere roots.

Gresham city, pop. 68,235, Multnomah Co., NW Oregon, 11 mi/18 km E of Portland. Founded in 1852, it is the center of a fruit growing region, and the gateway to the recreational areas of Mt. Hood and the Columbia River Gorge, to the E. Recently, the city has become more of a residential suburb of Portland, and is now linked to its larger neighbor by the Metropolitan Area Express (MAX) light-rail line. Gresham is the seat of Mount Hood Community College (1965).

Gretna city, pop. 17,208, seat of Jefferson Parish, SE Louisiana, on the W (S) bank of the Mississippi R., opposite New Orleans. Founded in the early 1800s as Mechanicsham, it merged with McDonoghville and was incorporated as Gretna in 1913; in the 19th century the settlement had served, in the tradition of Gretna Green, Scotland, as a place where couples could marry quickly. Gretna developed as an agricultural shipping center, and is now a residential and industrial suburb of New Orleans. Manufactures include cottonseed oil, asbestos roofing, fertilizer, barrels, petroleum products, molasses, and commercial alcohol.

Greylock, Mount 3491 ft/1065 m, in the BERKSHIRE HILLS of NW Massachusetts, in the town of Adams. It is the center of Mt. Greylock Reservation (8660 ac/3507 ha), which includes Mts. Fitch, Williams, Prospect, and Saddle Ball. The Appalachian Trail crosses the summit, highest point in the Commonwealth, where there is a tower dedicated to soldiers and sailors of Massachusetts.

Griffin city, pop. 21,347, seat of Spalding Co., WC Georgia, 35 mi/56 km SSE of Atlanta. Textile and clothing plants dominate the economy. The city is a processing center for regional fruit (pimento peppers are a major crop) and dairy farms.

Griffiss Air Force Base see under ROME, New York.

Griffith city, pop. 17,916, Lake Co., extreme NW Indiana, adjacent (SW) to GARY, in the highly industrialized CALUMET area, just S of L. Michigan. It produces metal products, castings, photographic supplies, and paper products, and is a residential suburb for such cities as EAST CHICAGO, HAMMOND, and Gary.

Griffith Park municipal park, 4063 ac/1645 ha, in LOS ANGELES, California, immediately N of Hollywood and W of Glendale, and 5 mi/8 km NW of Downtown. The largest park in Los Angeles, donated to the city in 1896, it comprises mostly CHAPARRAL-covered, arid hills at the E extreme of the Santa Monica Mts. The Los Angeles Zoo, Griffith Observatory and Planetarium, and Hall of Science are here.

Grimsby town, pop. 18,520, Niagara Regional Municipality, S Ontario, on L. Ontario (N), 12 mi/19 km ESE of Hamilton and 25 mi/40 km W of Niagara Falls. Settled in the 1780s by LOYALISTS in what became a major fruit growing region, it has had various light industries, and is a residential and resort town.

Grinnell city, pop. 8902, Poweshiek Co., C Iowa, 14 mi/23 km E of Newton. It is a trading center for the surrounding agricultural area, distributing and processing corn, dairy cattle, and poultry and manufacturing farm implements. Sporting goods, fertilizers, and gloves are also produced.

The abolitionist, clergyman, and railroad promoter Josiah Grinnell founded the city in 1854. Grinnell College (1846; originally Iowa College) was moved here from Davenport in 1859, and has since played an important role in the community. Rock Creek State Park is 6 mi/10 km NW.

Grise Fiord see under ELLESMERE I., Northwest Territories.

Grissom Air Force Base see under KOKOMO, Indiana.

Gros Morne mountain, 2644 ft/806 m, in the LONG RANGE, W Newfoundland, 47 mi/75 km NNE of Corner Brook, the high point of 750–sq mi/1942–sq km **Gros Morne National Park** (1970), noted for its glacial and coastal scenery.

Grosse Ile island township, pop. 9781, Wayne Co., SE Michigan, in the Detroit R., 14 mi/23 km SSW of downtown Detroit. It is bridged to TRENTON and RIVERVIEW (W). Amherstburg, Ontario, lies E. Eight mi/13 km N–S and up to 1.7 mi/2.7 km wide, it is the largest Detroit R. island. The Sieur de Cadillac owned it until 1711; it is a residential community, with an airport at its S end.

Grosse Pointe city, pop. 5681, Wayne Co., SE Michigan, 7 mi/11 km NE of Detroit, on L. St. Clair, between Grosse Pointe Park (SW) and Grosse Pointe Farms (NE). It is the smallest of the five Grosse Pointes (the Pointes), which began with ribbon farms extending back from the lake; Grosse Pointe's lakefront is only 0.75 mi/1.2 km in width. Popular summer resorts for wealthy Detroiters from the 1840s, the Pointes became exclusive residential suburbs around World War I.

Grosse Pointe Farms city, pop. 10,092, Wayne Co., SE Michigan, on L. St. Clair, 10 mi/16 km E of Detroit. A wealthy residential suburb of Detroit, it is the seat of Alger House, a branch of the Detroit Institute of the Arts.

Grosse Pointe Park city, pop. 12,857, Wayne Co., SE Michigan, on L. St. Clair, an affluent suburb 9 mi/14 km E of Detroit.

Grosse Pointe Shores village, pop. 2955, in Wayne and Macomb counties, SE Michigan, 11 mi/18 km NE of Detroit along L. Saint Clair, just NE of Grosse Pointe Woods. Incorporated in 1911, it is the outermost of the Pointes.

Grosse Pointe Woods city, pop. 17,715, Wayne Co., SE Michigan, 11 mi/18 km NE of Detroit. Originally incorporated (1926) as Lochmoor, this affluent residential suburb was renamed in 1939.

Groton **1.** town, pop. 45,144, including Groton city, pop. 9837, New London Co., SE Connecticut, 45 mi/72 km E of New Haven, on the E bank of the Thames R., opposite New London, and extending to the Mystic R. (E). It was settled in 1649. Its economy has been dominated by shipbuilding since the 18th century; Groton is home to the Navy's largest submarine base and to Electric Boat, part of General Dynamics and the township's economic cornerstone. The first US diesel-powered submarine (1912) and first nuclear-powered submarine (the *Nautilus,* 1954) were built here. The city's other major business is a Pfizer chemical complex. There is a branch of the University of Connecticut at Avery Point, on the Thames. A monument in Fort Griswold State Park commemorates the 1781 massacre of Revolutionary militia by British troops. Villages within Groton township include West Mystic, Noank, Groton Long Point, and Poquonnock Bridge. **2.** town, pop. 7511, Middlesex Co., NE Massachusetts, 14 mi/22 km WSW of Lowell. Settled in 1655, it was destroyed during King Philip's War (1675–76) and later rebuilt. It has ski areas, some light manufacturing, and some agriculture. The Groton School, a prep school (1884), is here.

Grove City **1.** city, pop. 19,653, Franklin Co., C Ohio, 7 mi/11 km SW of Columbus, in a fertile agricultural region. The local economy is based on horse racing at Beulah Park and some light manufacturing. **2.** borough, pop. 8240, Mercer Co., W Pennsylvania, 60 mi/96 km N of Pittsburgh. The city's manufactures include gas and diesel engines and iron castings. It is the seat of Grove City College (1876).

Grover City city, pop. 11,656, San Luis Obispo Co., SW California, on the Pacific Ocean, just E of Pismo Beach and 11 mi/18 km SSE of San Luis Obispo. It is largely residential.

Grover's Corners fictional New Hampshire setting of Thornton Wilder's *Our Town* (1938). The playwright, who had spent time writing at the MacDowell Colony and at L. SUNAPEE, felt that PETERBOROUGH, New London, and Keene could all be said to have contributed to his conception.

Groves city, pop. 16,513, Jefferson Co., extreme E Texas, adjadent (NE) to Port Arthur, near Sabine L. Originally called Pecan Grove when laid out in 1916, it is a residential suburb.

Groveton unincorporated community, pop. 19,997, Fairfax Co., N Virginia, 3 mi/5 km S of Alexandria, and just W of the Potomac R. Part of the Second Battle of BULL RUN (Aug. 29–30, 1862) was fought in the area, which is now a largely residential suburb.

Guadalupe town, pop. 5458, Maricopa Co., SC Arizona, a suburb 10 mi/16 km S of Phoenix. It is primarily an Indian and Mexican community.

Guadalupe Mountains NW–SE trending range, considered a subrange of the SACRAMENTO Mts., in S New Mexico and W Texas. Guadalupe Peak (8749 ft/2668 m) is the highest point in the range and in Texas; El Capitan (8085 ft/2464 m) is at the S terminus. The range is best known for its extensive network of caves, most notably CARLSBAD CAVERNS and nearby Lechuguilla Caverns.

Guadalupe Peak tallest mountain (8749 ft/2668 m) in Texas and in the GUADALUPE Mts., c.100 mi/160 km E of El Paso and S of Carlsbad, New Mexico. It is the taller twin peak to EL CAPITAN.

Guadalupe River 250 mi/400 km long, in SE Texas. It rises on the Edwards Plateau, crosses the Balcones Escarpment, and flows SE past Kerrville, New Braunfels, Seguin, Gonzalez, Cuero, and Victoria to enter San Antonio Bay of the Gulf of Mexico near Seadrift. The SAN ANTONIO R. joins it just above its mouth.

Guam unincorporated US territory, pop. 133,152, southernmost of the Mariana Is., between the Philippine Sea (W) and the SW Pacific Ocean, some 1400 mi/2300 km E of the Philippines, 4000 mi/6400 km WSW of Hawaii, and 1725 mi/2780 km SSE of Tokyo, Japan. It is some 960 mi/1540 km N of the Equator. Its capital is AGANA. A major American military asset, Guam is 30 mi/50 km NE–SW and 4–8 mi/6–13 km wide, totaling 209 sq mi/541 sq km. It is largely limestone plateau in the N and volcanic in the S, and has much jungle. The first European to see the Marianas was Ferdinand Magellan, who landed on Guam in 1521; the island was ruled by Spain, which used it primarily as a commercial port, until 1989, when it was ceded to the US after the Spanish-American War. Some development took place before the Japanese occupied Guam from Dec. 1941 to 1944. The July 1944 battle in which Americans recaptured the island caused the destruction of Agana and heavy damage elsewhere. Guam's economy since 1944 has depended on its military importance. Andersen Air Force Base, in the NE, was a major Strategic Air Command site from 1954 through the 1980s; during the Vietnam War it was the center of an island boom. The navy maintains an air station at Agana and a large base at APRA HARBOR, and there are other military installations, as well as World War II vestiges, throughout. In the 1990s, with the Cold War ending, the economy began to tilt toward tourism, esp. from Japan. Guamanians, most of whom are Chamorros, a people of mixed Micronesian-Filipino-European lineage, elect a governor and local legislature. They are US citizens and send a nonvoting delegate to the House of Representatives, but do not vote in Federal elections.

Guánica unincorporated community (ZONA URBANA), pop. 9263, Guánica Municipio (pop. 19,984), SW Puerto Rico, 18 mi/29 km WSW of Ponce, on the Bahía de Guánica and the Caribbean Sea. Settled in the 16th century around its natural harbor, it was the scene, on July 25, 1898, of the unopposed landing that led to US occupation of Puerto Rico. It has long been a sugar industry center.

Guayama unincorporated community (ZONA URBANA), pop. 21,692, Guayama Municipio (pop. 41,588), SE Puerto Rico, near the Caribbean coast and 32 mi/52 km E of Ponce. Founded in 1736, it has many Spanish colonial buildings. In an area that produces sugarcane, tobacco, coffee, fruit, and cattle, it is a trade and processing center, with harbor facilities at nearby (SE) Arroyo.

Guaynabo unincorporated community (ZONA URBANA), pop. 73,385, Guaynabo Municipio (pop. 92,886), NE Puerto Rico, 6 mi/10 km S of San Juan. Essentially a suburb of the capital, and within its urban area, it processes sugarcane and dairy goods, and has diverse manufactures.

Guelph city, pop. 87,976, seat of Wellington Co., S Ontario, on the Speed R., 47 mi/76 km WSW of Toronto. Founded in 1827 by John Galt, Scottish superintendent of the Canada Company, which dealt in immigration and land settlement, it is an agricultural, educational, and industrial center whose manufactures include rubber, iron, steel, cigarettes, and textiles. The University of Guelph (1964), incorporating Ontario Agricultural College (1874) and Ontario Veterinary College (1862), is here, as is a large correctional center and the birthplace (1872) of World War I poet-physician John McCrae. The city's academic base has since the 1980s made it part of the CANADIAN TECHNOLOGY TRIANGLE.

Guilford town, pop. 19,848, New Haven Co., S Connecticut, on Long Island Sound 13 mi/21 km E of New Haven. Primarily residential, it is also a resort, with some agriculture and a fishing industry. The town includes a number of seaside communities, including Sachem Head, Leete's Island, and Guilford and North Guilford villages.

Guilford County 651 sq mi/1686 sq km, pop. 347,420, in NC North Carolina, in the Piedmont, drained by the Deep and Haw rivers. Its seat is GREENSBORO. Industry, centered in Greensboro and HIGH POINT, two-thirds of the PIEDMONT TRIAD, is dominated by textile and furniture production. Other manufactures include chemical and pharmaceutical products, brick, clay, tobacco, and electronic equipment. **Guilford Courthouse** National Military Park, just NW of Greensboro, is the site of a battle of March 15, 1781, in which the British Commander Cornwallis won a Pyrrhic victory, which led the way to his eventual surrender at Yorktown, Virginia.

Gulf, the see Strait of GEORGIA, British Columbia.

Gulf Coast in Florida, the W coast, particularly the area between Tampa–St. Petersburg (N) and Naples (S), which developed as a resort center separately from the Eastern GOLD COAST, remains less New York–oriented in its resort and tourist trade and less Hispanic in population, and is noted for attracting Midwesterners, Canadians, and others.

Gulf Coastal Plain see under COASTAL PLAIN.

Gulf Intracoastal Waterway 1200 mi/1900 km–long portion of the Intracoastal Waterway, providing protected passage along the Gulf of Mexico from Carrabelle, W of APALACHEE BAY, in NW Florida (E), to Brownsville, S Texas (W). A minimum of 12 ft/3.7 m deep and 125 ft/38 m wide throughout, it travels along bays, rivers, bayous, and canals, including (E–W) Apalachicola Bay, Mobile Bay, Mississippi Sound, Galveston Bay and the Houston Ship Channel, San Antonio and Corpus Christi bays, and Laguna Madre. Locks at New Orleans connect it with the Mississippi R. and its inland ports. The waterway is a transportation route for crude oil and petroleum products, seafood, agricultural products, manufactured goods, chemicals, and building materials, and is also recreational. Formerly known as the Intracoastal Canal, it was completed in 1949. See also ATLANTIC INTRACOASTAL WATERWAY.

Gulf Islands group of 225 Canadian islands in the Strait of GEORGIA, between SE Vancouver I. and the mainland of SW British Columbia and NW Washington. Saltspring I. (16 mi/26 km N–S and 2–7 mi/3–11 km wide) is the largest and most populous; Ganges, on its E coast, is the largest settlement in the islands. Many Indian groups have long used the islands for food gathering, but the first permanent settlers on Saltspring were a group of black Americans, who began an agricultural community in the 1850s. Farming, as well as timbering, dairying, and sheep ranching, are still important in the islands. In recent years, the mild climate and improved ferry service have attracted many tourists and retirees. The glaciated terrain attracts hikers and naturalists. Bruce Peak (2310 ft/704 m), on the W coast of Saltspring, is the highest point.

Gulf Islands National Seashore 140,000 ac/57,000 ha of offshore islands and coastline bordering the Gulf of Mexico, from Choctawhatchee Bay, E of Pensacola, Florida (E), to Gulfport, Mississippi (W). The seashore includes white-sand beaches near Pensacola, and Fort Massachusetts on SHIP I. near Gulfport, as well as Horn and Petit Bois islands. Headquarters are in Ocean Springs, Mississippi.

Gulfport **1.** city, pop. 11,727, Pinellas Co., WC Florida, on the Pinellas Peninsula and Boca Ciega Bay, adjacent (SW) to St. Petersburg. Across the bay from Treasure Island and Long Key (W), it is a residential suburb. **2.** city, pop. 40,775, seat of Harrison Co., S Mississippi, on Mississippi Sound (the Gulf of Mexico), 66 mi/106 km NE of New Orleans, Louisiana, and adjacent (W) to Biloxi. An 1890s railroad terminus, it opened a commercial harbor in 1902, and boomed exporting cotton and lumber and importing fruit. In the 1920s the city developed as a seaside resort, utilizing its miles of beach. Gulfport was in the path of Hurricane Camille in 1969, and suffered severe damage. Shipbuilding and seafood handling are other important local industries.

Gulf Shores city, pop. 3261, Baldwin Co., SW Alabama, on the Gulf of Mexico, near the SE corner of Mobile Bay and 37 mi/60 km SE of Mobile. It is the largest resort community on Alabama's Gulf Coast, drawing millions of visitors annually to its barrier beaches, fishing pier, and other attractions.

Gulf Stream oceanic warm current along the E coast of North America. It is formed when the FLORIDA CURRENT reaches Cape HATTERAS, North Carolina, and continues NE to about 40° N, SE of Newfoundland, where it merges into the North Atlantic Current or Drift, which continues E toward Europe. The deep blue, saline, 80° F/27° C water of the Florida Current gradually cools as it moves N in the Gulf Stream, and slows from 4 mi/6 km per hour, broadening into a fanlike flow by the time it encounters the cool southward LABRADOR Current over the GRAND BANKS, an area noted for its dense fogs. The Gulf Stream was first described (1513) by Ponce de León. The entire Florida Current–Gulf Stream–North Atlantic Current system is also sometimes called "the Gulf Stream."

Gunks, the see SHAWANGUNK Mts.

Gunnison city, pop. 4636, seat of Gunnison Co., WC Colorado, on the Gunnison R., 140 mi/225 km SW of Denver, SW of the Elk Mts., W of the Sawatch Range, and N of the San Juan Mts. Established in 1874, it was a mining and ranching center. Today it is primarily a gateway to area forests, ski resorts, and river recreation, and home to Western State College (1911).

Gunnison National Forest 1.7 million ac/690,000 ha (2656 sq mi/6880 sq km), on the W slope of the Rocky Mts., in WC Colorado. Administered with the GRAND MESA National Forest (NW), it has many high peaks and alpine lakes in the West Elk and other ranges.

Gunnison River 180 mi/290 km long, in WC Colorado. Its headstreams drain the W slopes of the SAWATCH RANGE, and converge near Gunnison. The Gunnison then flows W, through Blue Mesa Reservoir, within the Curecanti National Recreation Area. It then enters the 21,000-ac/8400-ha **Black Canyon of the Gunnison National Monument,** noted for its 2000 ft/610 m–deep, heavily shaded canyons. The river then flows NW to the Colorado R. at Grand Junction; along the way it drains much of the UNCOMPAHGRE PLATEAU (SW).

Gunston Hall plantation SE of LORTON, Fairfax Co., NE Virginia, on Mason Neck, on the W bank of the Potomac R., 12 mi/19 km SW of Alexandria. Built 1755, it was the seat of George Mason, a principal architect of the Bill of Rights and Virginia's constitution.

Gunter Air Force Base see under MONTGOMERY, Alabama.

Guntersville city, pop. 7038, seat of Marshall Co., NE Alabama, on a peninsula in the Tennessee R. (Guntersville L.), 34 mi/55 km SE of Huntsville. A Cherokee village until 1837 and a river port since the 18th century, it developed rapidly with the construction (1935–39) of the Tennessee Valley Authority's Guntersville Dam, 7 mi/11 km NW. **Guntersville L.,** 68,000 ac/27,500 ha, is now a major recreation area. Local industries include the manufacture of electronic equipment, textiles, clothing, animal feed, and precision tools.

Gurnee village, pop. 13,701, Lake Co., NE Illinois, on the Du Page R., a suburb immediately W of Waukegan and 35 mi/56 km NNW of Chicago. Originally settled along the Chicago, Milwaukee and St. Paul Railroad, it is now a residential community. Gurnee Mills is one of the world's largest outlet malls. There is also a SIX FLAGS theme park.

Guthrie **1.** city, pop. 1504, Todd Co., SW Kentucky, 23 mi/37 km SE of Hopkinsville, on the Tennessee border. This rail junction in an agricultural area is the birthplace (1905) of novelist and poet Robert Penn Warren. **2.** city, pop. 10,518, seat of Logan Co., C Oklahoma, 28 mi/45 km N of Oklahoma City, near the Cimarron R. The center of the 1889 Oklahoma land rush, it was settled in one day. It was territorial capital (1890–1907) and state capital (1907–10), losing the latter role to Oklahoma City by vote. Most of the city's original buildings remain intact, forming one of the nation's largest historic districts. A commercial center in an agricultural and oil producing region, the city has machine and railroad shops and manufactures building products, steel, furniture, and oilfield equipment.

Guttenberg town, pop. 8268, Hudson Co., NE New Jersey, on and below the PALISADES of the Hudson R., across from Manhattan, New York, and 9 mi/14 km NE of Newark. It is residential and industrial. West New York adjoins (S).

Guymon city, pop. 7803, seat of Texas Co., extreme NW Oklahoma, in the PANHANDLE's high plains. It has oil and gas wells and is a trade hub for livestock, wheat, and dairy producers.

Guyot, Mount see under GREAT SMOKY Mts.

Gwillimbury see BRADFORD (West Gwillimbury) and EAST GWILLIMBURY, Ontario.

Gwinnett County 435 sq mi/1127 sq km, pop. 352,910, in N Georgia. LAWRENCEVILLE is its seat. The Chattahoochee R. and L. Sidney Lanier form its NW boundary. At the NE edge of the Atlanta metropolitan area, the county contains suburbs and exurbs, mostly in its SW, and poultry and dairy farms in the E and N.

Gwynedd Valley unincorporated community in Lower Gwynedd township (pop. 9958), Montgomery Co., SE Pennsylvania, 16 mi/26 km NW of Philadelphia. A residential suburb, it is the seat of Gwynedd-Mercy College (1948).

H

Habitat housing complex designed by architect Moshe Safdie for Expo 67, the 1967 World's Fair in MONTRÉAL, Québec. On the Cité du Havre peninsula, which encloses Montréal's harbor, E of Downtown, it is noted for its modular design of irregularly stacked concrete apartment blocks.

Hacienda Heights unincorporated community, pop. 52,354, Los Angeles Co., SW California, a residential suburb on the Pomona Freeway, in the Puente Hills, 18 mi/29 km E of downtown Los Angeles.

Hackensack city, pop. 37,049, seat of Bergen Co., NE New Jersey, on the Hackensack R., 6 mi/10 km E of Paterson. Settled by the Dutch (1639) and English (1668), it was the site of Washington's headquarters (1776) and a number of Revolutionary War skirmishes. Until 1921 it was officially New Barbadoes. By the early 1900s it was a trade and distribution center. Today it is a commercial, industrial, and residential suburb, with many one-family homes, garden apartments, and condominium towers that overlook the New York City skyline some 15 mi/24 km SW. Hackensack houses offices of banks, brokers, insurance companies, and other businesses. Its manufactures include chemicals, furniture, and food and foundry products.

Hackensack River 45 mi/72 km long, in SE New York and N New Jersey. It rises in Rockland Co., New York, and flows into 4 mi/6 km–long L. De Forest, N of West Nyack. It then flows S into L. Tappan, on the New York-New Jersey border. From there it continues S to ORADELL, New Jersey, where it is dammed a third time to form the Oradell Reservoir. It then flows through the **Hackensack Meadows,** also called the Jersey Meadows, which cover an area of 50 sq mi/130 sq km, and passes W of the PALISADES, to enter Newark Bay on the W side of Jersey City. The river is tidal and navigable (for barges) to Hackensack. Its lower third is heavily industrial and polluted.

Hackettstown town, pop. 8120, Warren Co., NW New Jersey, in the Musconetcong R. valley, 14 mi/23 km W of Dover. It has such light manufactures as leather, silk products, and other clothing, and is the trading, storage, and distribution point for local vegetables and dairy products, as well as the corporate home to the Mars candy company. Near L. HOPATCONG and Allamuchy Mt., it is also a resort center. Centenary College (1867) is here.

Haddam town, pop. 6769, Middlesex Co., SC Connecticut, on the Connecticut and Salmon rivers, 24 mi/39 km NE of New Haven. It is a summer resort, with some agriculture and light manufacturing. It was formerly a shipbuilding and shad and salmon fishing center. The Connecticut Yankee nuclear plant at **Haddam Neck,** E of the Connecticut R., went into operation in 1967. Villages in Haddam include Tylerville, Shailerville, Ponset, and Higganum. The Goodspeed Opera House, popular since the 19th century, is in adjoining East Haddam (pop. 6676).

Haddonfield borough, pop. 11,628, Camden Co., SW New Jersey, 5 mi/8 km SE of Camden. The area was settled in 1682; the town was founded (c.1710) by the English Quaker Elizabeth Haddon. Haddonfield was the site of a number of Revolutionary War clashes, and a campground for British and Hessian forces. Essentially a residential suburb of Camden and Philadelphia, it also has some corporate office parks. Historically noteworthy is the Indian King Tavern (1750), meeting place of the first state legislature (1777).

Hadley town, pop. 4231, Hampshire Co., W Massachusetts, on the Connecticut R., 18 mi/29 km N of Springfield. It was settled in the mid 17th century by Colonists from Connecticut. The English soldiers Edmund Whalley and William Goffe, supporters of Oliver Cromwell who had both signed the death warrant for Charles I, hid in Hadley after the accession (1660) of Charles II, and both died here. The town, largely agricultural and residential, lies between AMHERST and NORTHAMPTON, and includes the villages of Hadley, North Hadley, Russellville, and Hockanum. SOUTH HADLEY lies S. Mt. HOLYOKE is in Hadley.

Hagerman Fossil Beds National Monument, 4394 ac/1780 ha, on cliffs along the SNAKE R. in S Idaho, 25 mi/40 km WNW of Twin Falls. Proclaimed a National Landmark in 1975, a National Monument in 1988, it was the scene of 1920s SMITHSONIAN INSTITUTION excavations, and is noted for its fossils of ancient (some over 3 million years old) horses.

Hagerstown city, pop. 35,445, seat of Washington Co., NW Maryland, in the CUMBERLAND VALLEY, on US 40 (the NATIONAL ROAD) and Antietam Creek, between the Blue Ridge and Allegheny Mts. It was laid out by landowner Jonathan Hager in 1762. Hagerstown was occupied by both sides during the Civil War. Following the battles of ANTIETAM and SOUTH MOUNTAIN, fought 11 mi/18 km to the S, 5000 Confederate soldiers were buried in Rose Hill Cemetery. The city developed as an agricultural shipping center following the construction, in 1867, of a spur of the Baltimore and Ohio Railroad. Agriculture remains important today, augmented by industries whose manufactures have included truck engines and transmissions, aircraft, missiles, pipe organs, furniture, and blast cleaning and dust control equipment. Hagerstown is home to a junior college (1946), and to the Washington County Free Library, the second-oldest (1901) US county library.

Hagerstown Valley see under CUMBERLAND VALLEY, Maryland.

Haight-Ashbury familiarly, **the Haight** largely residential section in C SAN FRANCISCO, California, immediately E of (and encompassing the E "panhandle" of) GOLDEN GATE PARK, and 2 mi/3 km WSW of Downtown. An area of Victorian housing, mostly built 1879–1906, it declined gradually through the 1950s, then became famous as the refuge of hippies during the 1967 "Summer of Love." It has since the 1980s undergone considerable GENTRIFICATION.

Hailey city, pop. 3687, seat of Blaine Co., SC Idaho, on the Big Wood R. and the Sawtooth Scenic Route, 15 mi/24 km SSE of Ketchum. Founded in 1881, it was the thriving center of a rich gold, silver, and lead mining region. Idaho's first telephone exchange and electric light plant were inaugurated in Hailey. It is now a summer resort, headquarters for the Sawtooth National Forest, and a trade center for a livestock and timber producing and mining area. The poet Ezra Pound was born here in 1885.

Haines City city, pop. 11,683, Polk Co., C Florida, 18 mi/29 km ENE of Lakeland. At the heart of a citrus producing belt, it processes and ships these fruits. Settled in the 1870s in a lake-filled area, it has various vacation accommodations. Fertilizers, pipe castings, and electronic components are manufactured.

Halawa unincorporated community, pop. 13,408, Honolulu Co., Hawaii, a residential and commercial suburb 7 mi/11 km NW of Honolulu and just E of Pearl Harbor, in C Oahu.

Haldimand town, pop. 20,573, Haldimand-Norfolk Regional Municipality, extreme S Ontario, on L. Erie (S) and the Grand R., 22 mi/35 km S of Hamilton. Created in 1974, it includes a number of mid-19th-century settlements on land that had belonged to the Six Nations (Iroquois). Caledonia (N), on the Grand, and Cayuga (C), farther down the river and now the town center, both engaged in dairying and extraction industries (gypsum, natural gas, sandstone, and limestone). Today Haldimand is largely residential, with resorts along the lake.

Haleakala massive dormant volcano, reaching 10,023 ft/3055 m at Puu'ulaula (Red Hill), that forms the larger E portion of the island of MAUI, Hawaii. A road to its summit is noted esp. for the views it affords of sunrises. An ancient spiritual center and source of material for traditional implements (adzes), Haleakala is today revered by New Agers, who consider its size (another 20,000 ft/6100 m is below sea level), volcanic density, and pyramidal shape indicative that it is a focus of magnetic and related powers. In the C is 28,655-ac/11,605-ha **Haleakala National Park,** which includes a large area of erosional "crater" and the Kipahalu Valley, which runs E to the sea.

Hale County 661 sq mi/1712 sq km, pop. 15,498, in WC Alabama. Its seat is Greensboro (pop. 3047). The Black Warrior R. forms its W line, and the Talladega National Forest is in the NE. This rural BLACK BELT–hill country county was the site of a 1936 sojourn by writer James Agee and photographer Walker Evans that led to *Let Us Now Praise Famous Men,* their noted account of sharecropper life.

Hales Corners village, pop. 7623, Milwaukee Co., SE Wisconsin, 10 mi/16 km SW of Milwaukee, of which it is a suburb.

Halethorpe residential suburb in Baltimore Co., C Maryland, 2 mi/3 km SW of Baltimore, just outside the Beltway (I-695) and SE of Arbutus. It has an industrial park on the Patapsco R.

Half Dome mountain (8842 ft/2697 m) of the Sierra Nevada, in YOSEMITE NATIONAL PARK, EC California. Its rounded granitic form appears to have been half carved away. The sheer N face soars upward for more than 1700 ft/520 m.

Half Moon Bay crescent-shaped inlet of the Pacific Ocean in San Mateo Co., NC California, 18 mi/29 km SW of San Francisco. Pillar Point marks its N end. The resort and growing residential city of **Half Moon Bay** (pop. 8886) is on one of its many beaches. Fishing and the growing and canning of artichokes are important in the region.

Haliburton Highlands resort region in Haliburton Co., SE Ontario, just S of ALGONQUIN PROVINCIAL PARK and some 110 mi/180 km NNE of Toronto. This rocky, hilly area on the S edge of the CANADIAN SHIELD is strewn with over 600 interconnecting lakes, making it a haven for canoeists. Autumn color, fishing, and snowmobiling are also popular. Minden and Haliburton are regional centers.

Halifax **1.** town, pop. 327, seat of Halifax Co., N North Carolina, 9 mi/14 km SSE of Roanoke Rapids, on the Roanoke R. Settled before 1760, it gave its name to the Halifax Resolves, a 1776 statement urging separation from Britain. A number of 1760s buildings draw visitors to this small agricultural market center. **2.** city, pop. 114,455, provincial capital and seat of Halifax Co. (pop. 330,846), SC Nova Scotia, on Halifax Harbour, an Atlantic Ocean inlet, 4 mi/7 km from open water. The largest city in the Maritimes, it is a governmental, military, transportation, and cultural center. It was established by the British in 1749 as a strategic counterweight to LOUISBOURG, on the site (Chebucto) of earlier Micmac and French settlements, and was a major base for the British navy and privateers in 18th- and 19th-century wars. Apart from shipbuilding and repair it has never been an important industrial center. In the world wars it was a critical convoy port. Bedford Basin, a 5–sq mi/12–sq km deepwater cove, is N of the city center. In Dec. 1917 a French ammunition ship exploded here, killing close to 2000 and leveling the North End, but Halifax's hills shielded much of the rest of the city. The city now has containerports linked by rail with the rest of Canada. It is dominated by its Citadel, which with the restored harborfront, Public Garden, and downtown shopping streets, draws visitors. The Maritime Museum of the Atlantic, Dalhousie Univ. (1818), and St. Mary's Univ. (1841) are among local institutions. DARTMOUTH (E), BEDFORD (N), and the SACKVILLES (N) are leading suburbs. **3.** town, pop. 606, including the villages of West Halifax and Halifax, in Windham Co., SE Vermont. It is on the Massachusetts border, 11 mi/18 km SW of Brattleboro. Lumbering is the main industry. Elisha G. Otis, inventor of the elevator, was born here in 1811.

Halifax County 816 sq mi/2113 sq km, pop. 29,033, in S Virginia, on the North Carolina border (S) and the Roanoke (Staunton) R. (E). Its seat is Halifax. SOUTH BOSTON, on the Dan R., is its largest community. Rural Halifax Co. is a major producer of tobacco, as well as of corn and wheat.

Hallandale city, pop. 30,996, Broward Co., SE Florida, just S of Hollywood and 13 mi/21 km N of Miami. Settled by Scandinavian farmers in the 1890s, it was hit by disastrous hurricanes in 1906, 1910, and 1926. On the Atlantic Intracoastal Waterway, it has grown since 1960 as a popular beachfront and boating resort. Recreational facilities include the Gulfstream Race Track and a greyhound track. The city is also a residential (retirement) center. Its industries process fruits and vegetables and manufacture chemicals and furniture.

Hallowell city, pop. 2534, Kennebec Co., SW Maine. It is on the Kennebec R., in a natural amphitheater formed by hills, about 2 mi/3 km S of Augusta, of which it is a suburb. The settlement, along with Gardiner, was originally part of the 100,000-ac/40,500-ha Kennebec Purchase (1754). It was an important 19th-century industrial, commercial, agricultural, and social center. There are many examples of Federal, Greek Revival, and Victorian architecture.

Halls also, **Halls Crossroads** unincorporated community, pop. 6450, Knox Co., E Tennessee, 7 mi/11 km N of downtown Knoxville. It is an affluent residential suburb.

Haltom City city, pop. 32,856, Tarrant Co., NE Texas, adjacent (NE) to Fort Worth, on the city's beltway (Route 820). A largely residential suburb, it also has aircraft and other industries.

Halton Hills town, pop. 36,816, Halton Regional Municipality, S Ontario, 27 mi/43 km W of Toronto. It was created in 1974, joining Acton and Georgetown with Esquising township. Acton, an 1820s tannery center, has subsequently made a wide range of farm and other machinery and leather and agricultural goods. The Blue Springs golf club here is home to the Canadian Professional Golf Association. Georgetown, now the town center, was settled by LOYALISTS, and became a wool and paper miller and producer of a variety of light manufactures. Halton Hills, a dairying and quarrying region, is increasingly residential.

Hamburg **1.** town, pop. 53,735, Erie Co., W New York, 12 mi/19 km S of Buffalo. It manufactures metal and wood products and automobile components. Hamburg village (pop. 10,442) was settled in 1808 by German immigrants. Hilbert College was founded here in 1928. The town has several villages along L. Erie (NW), including Athol Springs, Locksley Park, Wanakah, Pinehurst, and Highland-on-the-Lake. The Buffalo Raceway (harness racing) is just N of the village. **2.** hamlet in Aiken Co., SW South Carolina, across the Savannah R. from Augusta, Georgia. In 1836 it became the W terminus of the South Carolina Railroad's 136 mi/219 km–long line to Charleston, the longest in the world at the time. The line was designed to recapture Charleston's cotton-shipping business from Savannah. Hamburg is now little more than a roadside locality on the outskirts of NORTH AUGUSTA.

Hamden **1.** town, pop. 52,434, New Haven Co., S Connecticut, adjoining (N) New Haven, on the Quinnipiac R. Settled in the 1660s and separated from New Haven in 1786, it includes the villages of Whitneyville, Spring Glen, and Mount Carmel. Primarily residential, it has some industry, including the manufacture of machine tools, firearms, and insulated wire, and is home to Quinnipiac College (1929). Sleeping Giant State Park is N. A tablet near L. Whitney Dam, on the Mill R., a Quinnipiac tributary, marks the location of a factory established here in 1798 by Eli Whitney that pioneered in the use of interchangeable machine parts and led to the development of the Winchester arms company. **2.** town, pop. 1144, Delaware Co., S New York, on the Delaware R., in the Catskill Mts., 50 mi/80 km E of Binghamton. It is the birthplace of educator James E. Russell (1864–1945).

Hamilton **1.** township, pop. 86,553, Mercer Co., WC New Jersey, adjoining (SE) Trenton. Since the 1950s it has been the primary site of Trenton's suburbanization, as residences, commercial activity, and various industries have moved into this formerly agricultural area. Communities in the township include its old center **Hamilton Square,** which with MERCERVILLE has a population of 26,873; White Horse (pop. 9397); and Yardville-Groveville (pop. 9248). Mercer Co. Community College (1966) is in Hamilton. **2.** town, pop. 6221, Madison Co., C New York, 26 mi/42 km SW of Utica. It is the seat of Colgate University (1819). **3.** city, pop. 61,368, seat of Butler Co., SW Ohio, on the Great Miami R., 20 mi/32 km N of Cincinnati. Pioneer settlement took place around Fort Hamilton (1791), one of a series of forts intended to protect homesteaders in the NORTHWEST TERRITORY from Indian attacks. Linked to the Miami and Erie Canal in the 1820s, it became a prosperous 19th-century industrial center based on waterpower. Among the city's contemporary manufactures are paper, steel, iron products, paper mill machinery, safes, diesel engines, automobile bodies, and woolens. Hamilton is also home to insurance companies and other businesses, and it is an important trading hub for the surrounding agricultural area, in which livestock farming predominates. **4.** city, pop. 318,499, seat of Hamilton-Wentworth Regional Municipality, S Ontario, at the W end of L. Ontario, 40 mi/64 km SW of Toronto. Visited by French explorers in the early 17th century, the area was not settled by Europeans until the arrival of LOYALISTS from the former American colonies in 1778. The community grew on the S shore of then landlocked Burlington Bay (now Hamilton Harbour), with the NIAGARA ESCARPMENT behind it. It grew rapidly after 1830, following the opening of the Burlington Canal, into an important rail and shipping center. Its iron and steel industry, initiated in the 1890s, now turns out much of Canada's national output. Chemicals, rubber, automobiles, electrical and agricultural equipment, and clothing are also produced. The city is also the financial and commercial center of an extensive agricultural region, and houses Canada's largest open-air market. McMaster University, founded in Toronto in 1887, has had its seat here since 1930; it is noted for its nuclear research facilities. The city is also home to several smaller institutions, to the Canadian Football Hall of Fame, and to the football Tiger-Cats, who play at Ivor Wynne Stadium.

Hamilton, Mount peak (4213 ft/1285 m) in the Mt. Hamilton Range, a N section of the DIABLO RANGE, 15 mi/24 km E of San Jose, in WC California. It is the site of the University of California's Lick Observatory, operational since 1888.

Hamilton Air Force Base see under NOVATO, California.

Hamilton County **1.** 412 sq mi/1067 sq km, pop. 866,228, in extreme SW Ohio, bounded by the Indiana line (W), the Ohio R. (S), and the Great Miami R. (NE). The Little Miami and Whitewater rivers run through the W part. Most of the county lies within the metropolitan area of Cincinnati, which is its seat. There is diversified industry, varied commercial activity, and substantial suburban development here. Farming includes dairy, poultry, livestock, and truck, and there are gravel pits. **2.** 539 sq mi/1396 sq km, pop. 285,536, in SE Tennessee. Its seat is CHATTANOOGA. Bounded (S) by Georgia, it is crossed (NE–SW) by the Tennessee R. WALDEN RIDGE forms its NW boundary. In the S are the Chickamauga and Chattanooga National Military Park and parts of LOOKOUT Mt. Chattanooga and its suburbs and Chickamauga L. now occupy much of this historically agricultural area, which also has coal and iron mines.

Hamilton Heights residential and institutional section of upper W Manhattan, New York City, named for Alexander Hamilton, a former resident. Extending from about 135th to 158th streets, it lies between WASHINGTON HEIGHTS (N) and Morningside Heights and Manhattanville (S), and looks over Harlem (SE). The City College of New York campus is in the Heights, along with the National Institute of Arts and Letters and Museum of the American Indian. SUGAR HILL is on its E edge.

Hamilton River and **Hamilton Inlet** see CHURCHILL R., Labrador.

Ham Lake city, pop. 8924, Anoka Co., SE Minnesota, 15 mi/24 km N of Minneapolis. An outer suburb of the Twin Cities, it has seen much residential growth in recent years. Carlos Avery Wildlife Area is 5 mi/8 km to the E.

hamlet **1.** a small rural settlement, in this book distinguished from an (incorporated) VILLAGE; *hamlet* is not a US Census category. **2.** in Canada: official designation of certain small Indian settlements in the Northwest Territories and Yukon Territory; Saskatchewan has 14 **northern hamlets.**

Hamlet city, pop. 6196, Richmond Co., S North Carolina, 44 mi/71 km WSW of Fayetteville and 5 mi/8 km N of the South Carolina border. A former railroad-shop and fruit shipping center, it is home to a National Railroad Museum. Its industries now include poultry processing and plastics manufacture. A Sept. 1991 fire that killed 25 poultry workers here focused attention on plant safety. Jazz giant John Coltrane was born here (1927).

Hamline student neighborhood in St. Paul, Minnesota, NW of Downtown. Hamline University (1854) is situated here.

Hammonasset River 20 mi/32 km long, in S Connecticut. It rises S of Middletown and flows SSE to Clinton Harbor in Long Island Sound, just E of Hammonasset Point and Hammonasset State Park.

Hammond **1.** city, pop. 84,236, Lake Co., extreme NW Indiana, bounded by L. Michigan (N), the Little CALUMET R. (S), and the Illinois border (E), traversed by the Grand Calumet R., and adjoining (E) Gary. Part of the Calumet region, it is connected to EAST CHICAGO's Indiana Harbor by a ship canal. Settled in 1851, it was first named Hohman, then State Line, and, finally, Hammond, after the owner of a large slaughterhouse and meatpacking house that was the city's chief industry from 1869 until its destruction by fire in 1901. Highly industrialized, with extensive rail and trucking connections, Hammond has about 200 relatively small industries manufacturing such products as railroad equipment, steel, valves, medical supplies, farm implements, soaps, books, and foodstuffs. A campus of Purdue University is here. **2.** city, pop. 15,871, Tangipahoa Parish, SE Louisiana, 40 mi/64 km ENE of Baton Rouge. Settled in the 1850s, it developed as an agricultural center, noted for its strawberry crops. Truck, dairy, poultry, and alligator farming are also important. Manufactures include clothing, brick, steel, and communications and electronic equipment. The city is the seat of Southeastern Louisiana University (1925).

Hammondsport village, pop. 929, in Urbana township, Steuben Co., SC New York, in the FINGER LAKES, at the S tip of Keuka L., 19 mi/31 km W of Watkins Glen. It is the state's most important grape growing and wine and champagne making center. Tourism is important to the local economy; there is also some light manufacturing. Hammondsport was the birthplace of aviator and inventor Glenn H. Curtiss (1878–1939), and the village was an important early aviation center, sometimes called the "Cradle of American Aviation."

Hammonton town, pop. 12,208, Atlantic Co., SE New Jersey, 27 mi/43 km SE of Camden. It was settled in the mid 1800s. Hammonton is a market and shipping center for local fruits and vegetables, and has canning and clothing industries. There is an annual blueberry festival. The 109,300-ac/44,100-ha Wharton State Forest, in the PINE BARRENS, is NE.

Hampden town, pop. 5974, Penobscot Co., SC Maine. It is on the Penobscot R., 5 mi/8 km SW and downstream of Bangor. In an agricultural area yet just outside Bangor, the town has both suburban housing and apple orchards. Dorothea Lynde Dix Memorial Park is on the site where the reformer was born in 1802.

Hampden County 618 sq mi/1601 sq km, pop. 456,310, in SW Massachusetts, in the Connecticut Valley, along the Connecticut border. Its seat is Springfield. At its center is the industrial agglomeration including Springfield, Chicopee, and Holyoke. To the E and W are largely rural areas. It is drained by the Westfield, Chicopee, and other rivers flowing into the Connecticut R.

Hampden Sydney unincorporated village, pop. 1240, Prince Edward Co., SC Virginia, 5 mi/8 km SW of Farmville and 58 mi/92 km SW of Richmond. In a rural area, it is the seat of all-male Hampden-Sydney College (1776).

Hampshire County 528 sq mi/1368 sq km, pop. 146,568. Its seat is Northampton. Situated in the Connecticut R. valley, it is well known as home to the cluster of colleges and universities in the Amherst-Northampton area. There is some long-established industry in Northampton and Easthampton. The county is otherwise largely rural and agricultural, with growth occurring in residential areas and in university-related research and business.

Hampstead city, pop. 8645, MONTRÉAL URBAN COMMUNITY, S Québec, a predominantly anglophone residential community just W of WESTMOUNT and 4 mi/6 km WSW of Downtown.

Hampton **1.** town, pop. 12,278, Rockingham Co., SE New Hampshire. It is on US 1 and the Atlantic Ocean, 10 mi/16 km S of Portsmouth. It includes Hampton village, and formerly included North Hampton (N) and Hampton Falls (W), now separate towns. Originally an outpost of the Massachusetts Bay Colony, Hampton has various light manufactures and produces fruit, dairy products, and truck garden crops. **Hampton Beach,** a resort along the Atlantic, draws large numbers of summer visitors, chiefly from S New Hampshire and the Boston area, providing much of the economic base, as well as famous weekend traffic jams. **2.** independent city, pop. 133,793, in SE Virginia, at the mouth of the James R., opposite Norfolk and adjacent (SE) to NEWPORT NEWS, on the N side of HAMPTON ROADS. It is a largely residential community, also a beach resort, whose economy depends on military installations at Langley Air Force Base (Langley Field; 1916), NASA's Langley Research Center, and FORT MONROE. Founded (1610) by colonists from Jamestown, Hampton is the oldest continuously occupied settlement of English origin in the US. The site of a 1775 battle, it was burned by the British during the War of 1812 and by Confederates during the Civil War. After the Civil War, it developed major fishing and seafood processing industries. The city is the seat of Hampton University, organized as Hampton Institute (1868) to educate former slaves; its first classes were held during the Civil War, under the famous Emancipation Oak.

Hampton Roads roadstead at the mouths of the James, Nansemond, and Elizabeth rivers, through which they flow into CHESAPEAKE BAY, in SE Virginia. Four mi/6 km long and 40 ft/12 m deep, it provides a natural deep-draft harbor for Newport News, Hampton, Portsmouth, and Norfolk. The Port of Hampton Roads, established in 1926 by the State Port Authority of Virginia, is one of the busiest in the US, and a center for shipbuilding and repair. It is also used by the US Navy, with Atlantic Fleet Headquarters at Norfolk and the Norfolk Naval Shipyard at Portsmouth. The **Hampton Roads Bridge-Tunnel,** which crosses between Hampton and Norfolk, is 7479 ft/2281 m long. The waterway has been important commercially and militarily since Colonial times, and in 1862 was the site of the battle between the ironclad *Monitor* and *Merrimack.*

Hamptons, the resort area, Suffolk Co., SE New York, on Long Island's South Fork. It comprises a group of resort villages in Southampton and East Hampton towns, running from Westhampton (W) to AMAGANSETT (E), and including QUOGUE, SOUTHAMPTON, Bridgehampton, and EAST HAMPTON. Formerly agricultural and maritime, they attract affluent summer residents, including artists and celebrities.

Hamtramck city, pop. 18,372, Wayne Co., SE Michigan, entirely surrounded by Detroit. It is named for Colonel George Hamtramck, a Franco-German hero of the Revolution and the first American commander of Fort Detroit. The automobile industry became important here early in the 20th century. There has been a large Polish community in Hamtramck since 1910. After World War II, many other Slavs found homes here. Automobile production remains its predominant industry. Among its other manufactures are machinery, electrical supplies, roofing, and auto bodies and parts, paints, and varnish.

Hanahan city, pop. 13,176, Berkeley Co., SE South Carolina, 10 mi/16 km N of downtown Charleston and just N of North Charleston. It is a largely residential community near the Charleston International Airport (W) and Charleston Naval Base (S). The Cooper R. is just E.

Hancock **1.** town, pop. 598, Berkshire Co., W Massachusetts, adjoining (W) Pittsfield. Primarily a resort community, in the Berkshire Hills, it is the site of Hancock Shaker Village, a community active from the 1790s to 1960, and known for its round barn; it is now a museum. The Jiminy Peak ski area and most of Pittsfield State Forest are in this rural town. **2.** city, pop. 4547, Houghton Co., in the NW Upper Peninsula of Michigan, on the Keweenaw Portage Canal, opposite Houghton, 70 mi/113 km NW of Marquette. Founded in 1859 during the copper boom, it relies largely on waterway trade and tourism. Hancock also makes mining machinery and wood, iron, and brass products. There is commercial fishing and lumber milling. Hancock is home to Suomi College, founded by Finns in 1896. Photographer Edward Steichen spent his boyhood here.

Hancock Park municipal park and residential neighborhood in Los Angeles, California, 7 mi/11 km W of Downtown. An affluent residential quarter laid out from 1910 in an oil-rich area, it lies adjacent to Wilshire Boulevard's "Miracle Mile." The area is more middle-class S of the park, where the Los Angeles Co. Museum of Art and the LA BREA TAR PITS draw visitors.

Hanford **1.** city, pop. 30,897, seat of Kings Co., SC California, 30 mi/48 km S of Fresno. It is a trade and shipping center for the S San Joaquin Valley, where grain, fruit, cotton, livestock, and dairy items are produced, and has food processing and oil refining industries. First settled in 1871, the city is known for its Courthouse Square and as the site of a once-thriving CHINATOWN. **2.** nuclear reservation: see under RICHLAND, Washington.

Hanging Rock **1.** also, **Hanging Mountain** see under BALANCED ROCK. **2.** see under PILOT Mt., North Carolina.

Hangtown see under PLACERVILLE, California.

Hannibal city, pop. 18,004, Marion and Ralls counties, NE Missouri, on bluffs overlooking the Mississippi R., across from Illinois and 98 mi/157 km NW of St. Louis. A river port and railroad center in a productive grain and dairy farming area, it is a trading and distribution hub. Manufactures include stoves, railroad wheels, cement, lumber, fertilizer, and metal products, and there are publishing and printing industries. Tourism is also important, largely because of Hannibal's fame as the boyhood home of Mark Twain. He used as settings in his best-known works such spots as Cardiff (or Holliday) Hill, with its cave, and Pearl (or Jackson's) Island, on the Illinois side of the river. Hannibal-LaGrange College (1858) is here.

Hanover **1.** town, pop. 3610, Jefferson Co., SE Indiana, close to the Ohio R. and the Kentucky border, and 5 mi/8 km W of MADISON. In an agricultural area, it is the seat of Hanover College (1827). **2.** town, pop. 9212, Grafton Co., WC New Hampshire. It is along the Connecticut R., 5 mi/8 km NNW of Lebanon. The town includes Hanover village (in the SW), home of Dartmouth College (1769) and a popular winter carnival. **3.** borough, pop. 14,399, York Co., S Pennsylvania, 16 mi/26 km SW of York and 5 mi/8 km N of the Maryland border. Laid out in 1763, it was nicknamed Rogue's Rest because of its reputation for lax law enforcement during an early Pennsylvania-Maryland boundary dispute. It was the site of the first Civil War battle fought N of the Mason-Dixon line (June 30, 1863). Situated in the fertile Conewago Valley, it is a trade center for agricultural products and has a variety of light manufactures. Hanover and its surrounding area are particularly known for their standardbred horses, notably the trotters and pacers raised by the 4000-ac/1620-ha Hanover Shoe Farms (1926).

Hanover County 467 sq mi/1210 sq km, pop. 63,306, in EC Virginia, between the Chickahominy (S) and North Anna and Pamunkey (N) rivers. Its seat is Hanover. Its W section is in the PIEDMONT, its E in the coastal plain. Hanover County is primarily agricultural, with some suburban development near Richmond (S). The area saw much military action during the Civil War.

Hanover Park village, pop. 32,895, Cook and Du Page counties, NE Illinois, a residential suburb 27 mi/43 km W of Chicago.

Hanscom Air Force Base see under BEDFORD, Massachusetts.

Hapeville city, pop. 5483, Fulton Co., NW Georgia, 7 mi/11 km S of downtown Atlanta, a residential and industrial suburb on Interstates 75 and 85, with a Ford assembly plant. Part of Atlanta's Hartsfield International Airport lies within the city's limits.

Happy Valley–Goose Bay town, pop. 8610, SC Labrador, on Goose Bay at the head of L. Melville (Hamilton Inlet) and the mouth of the CHURCHILL R. Goose Bay developed as a huge military airfield and seaplane base for the Royal Canadian Air Force during World War II, while Happy Valley was established as a residential community. The two were amalgamated in 1974. Today the base is used primarily to train fighter pilots. The town is a fishing and tourist center with steamer connections with St. John's, Newfoundland. It serves as a distribution center for Labrador coastal communities, and houses regional government offices.

Harahan city, pop. 9927, Jefferson Parish, SE Louisiana, on the E (N) bank of the Mississippi R., 10 mi/16 km W of New Orleans. Founded in 1920, it is a warehousing center, and developed on what had been farmland because of its accessibility to New Orleans's port and its railroad facilities. Industries process mahogany veneer and make soft drinks and glass.

Harbor Beach city, pop. 2089, Huron Co., EC Michigan, on L. Huron, 28 mi/45 km NE of Sandusky, Ohio. This summer resort, which also has commercial fishing, is in a dairy, corn, and wheat growing area. It is known as the birthplace (1890) of politician and jurist Frank Murphy.

Harbor City low- and middle-income residential and commercial section of Los Angeles, California, on Harbor L., just N of San Pedro. The **Harbor Freeway** (I-110), connecting Downtown with San Pedro, passes through; it is noted for its traffic.

Harbor Island 1 mi/1.6 km–long artificial island in N San Diego Bay, in SAN DIEGO, California. Connected to the mainland by a narrow strip of landfill, it lies immediately S of San Diego International Airport, and has much recent hotel construction.

Harborplace redeveloped waterfront on the INNER HARBOR, downtown Baltimore, Maryland. Harborplace was developed as a market when the Urban Renewal and Housing Agency of Baltimore initiated rehabilitation of the Inner Harbor. Opened in 1980, it comprises a group of shops and restaurants housed in two-story glass buildings.

Harbourfront redeveloped waterfront, 2.5 mi/4 km long, on L. Ontario, in Toronto Harbour, downtown TORONTO, Ontario, W of the foot of Yonge St. Residential developments, restaurants, cafes, marinas, galleries, shops, theaters, and a promenade transformed a dingy dock area here in the 1980s. The CN TOWER and SKYDOME are immediately N.

Harbour Grace town, pop. 3419, SE Newfoundland, on the N coast of the AVALON PENINSULA and the W shore of CONCEPTION BAY, 26 mi/42 km WNW of St. John's. It was headquarters for pirate and folk hero Peter Easton around 1610, and was settled soon after, long remaining one of the island's larger communities. During the early days of aviation, it was a starting point for transatlantic flights, including Amelia Earhart's first female solo in 1932. Today main industries are fish processing and footwear manufacture.

Harcuvar Mountains range in WC Arizona, W of Wickenburg, rising to 5242 ft/1598 m at Smith Peak (E), and separated by Cunningham Pass (2560 ft/780 m) from a W section that rises to 4618 ft/1408 m at Harcuvar Peak. The name may be from Mohave (Hokan) meaning "little water." To the SE are the Harquahala Mts., which rise to 5681 ft/1732 m, and whose name may mean "high water," referring to a spring at high elevation.

Hardware City see under NEW BRITAIN, Connecticut.

Hardwick town, pop. 2964, including Hardwick and East Hardwick villages, in Caledonia Co., NC Vermont. It is on the Lamoille R. and Hardwick L., 20 mi/32 km NNE of Montpelier. After the 1868 discovery of granite, the community became the site of the Woodbury Granite Company, once the largest construction-granite concern in the world. Other local industries turn out wood and dairy products.

Harford County 448 sq mi/1160 sq km, pop. 182,132, in NE Maryland, bounded N by Pennsylvania, NE by the Susquehanna R., and S and SE by Chesapeake Bay. Its seat is BEL AIR. The PIEDMONT agricultural region in the N produces vegetables, fruits, grains, poultry, and dairy products; Bel Air is its market center. The S section, in the coastal plain, has Federal reservations including the ABERDEEN Proving Ground and EDGEWOOD Arsenal. Light industry, centered in Aberdeen, is diverse.

Harker Heights city, pop. 12,841, Bell Co., C Texas, just E of KILLEEN and FORT HOOD. It is residential and commercial.

Harlan County 468 sq mi/1212 sq km, pop. 36,574, in SE Kentucky, in the Cumberland Mts., on the Virginia border. Its seat is the city of **Harlan** (pop. 2686). It was for years the leading county in the state for bituminous and cannel coal mining. From 1916 through the 1930s, bitter conflict flared between miners and operators, earning the county the title "Bloody Harlan." Strife has been less regular since the 1940s, but continues. Harlan also has timber and some farming. BLACK Mt., the highest point in Kentucky, is near Lynch.

Harlem **1.** see under FORT BELKNAP INDIAN RESERVATION, Montana. **2.** section of upper Manhattan, New York City, the most prominent US black community. Its boundaries are indefinite, but it generally is held to incorporate neighborhoods N of Central Park, E of the escarpment that forms MORNINGSIDE HEIGHTS (itself sometimes considered part of Harlem), W of the Harlem R., and S of about 168th St. WASHINGTON HEIGHTS has been considered part of Harlem in the past, but is today generally regarded as separate, although the valley (along West 125th St.) that cuts between the two Heights is regarded as part of Harlem. EAST HARLEM includes neighborhoods on Harlem's SE corner. The town of Nieuw Haarlem, established 1658 by governor Peter Stuyvesant, lay about 10 mi/16 km N of New Amsterdam. It retained the name "Harlem" despite the English conquest of 1664. In the early 19th century, country homes stood on the heights to Harlem's W, and in the Harlem Valley James Roosevelt (F.D. Roosevelt's great-grandfather) operated a farm. The New York & Harlem Railroad (1837) spurred development, and extension of elevated lines in 1879 and subways in 1904 accelerated growth. A key event in Harlem's history was the establishment of Philip Payton's Afro-American Realty Company in 1904. Taking advantage of a glut of new housing, Payton moved blacks from SAN JUAN HILL and other downtown neighborhoods into Harlem. White residents fled. By the 1920s Harlem was the "black capital" of the US. The Harlem Renaissance of the 1920s brought attention to the district; whites who would not live in Harlem regarded it as their playground. At the same time, Harlem was seriously overcrowded, with as many as 500,000 living in about 3 sq mi/8 sq km. The Depression hit Harlem hard, and since World War II it has lost population and much of its housing stock. High-rise apartments have replaced many tenements, but serious unemployment and associated problems continue. Harlem's neighborhoods range from the poorer "valley" blocks to fashionable SUGAR HILL. Notable sites include the Schomburg Center for Research in Black Culture; the APOLLO THEATRE; the Hotel Theresa, once America's largest black hotel and now an office building; Mount Morris (since 1973 Marcus Garvey Memorial) Park; and the Abyssinian Baptist Church. Major thoroughfares include 125th St., Adam Clayton Powell, Jr., Blvd. (Seventh Ave.), and Lenox Ave.

Harlem Heights section of upper W Manhattan, New York City, roughly equivalent to MORNINGSIDE HEIGHTS. It was the site of a battle between the British and troops led by George Washington on Sept. 16, 1776.

Harlem River tidal channel, 8 mi/13 km long, that separates Manhattan and the Bronx, New York. It connects the Hudson R., which it enters between Inwood, Manhattan, and Spuyten Duyvil, the Bronx, with the East R., which it enters at Ward's and Randall islands. Heavily industrial, the Harlem R. became a useful shipping route after a canal was cut in 1895 to eliminate a narrow section, the Spuyten Duyvil Creek, that had wound around the Marble Hill section of Manhattan.

Harlingen city, pop. 48,735, Cameron Co., extreme S Texas, 21 mi/34 km NW of Brownsville, on the (channelized) Arroyo Colorado. In the rich Lower Rio Grande Valley fruit and vegetable growing region, it is a financial and trade hub. Port Harlingen, a barge port, has chemical plants and oil refineries. The city also has vegetable and juice canneries and shrimp processing facilities. It was established in 1904, partly on land bought from the KING RANCH, as a railroad stop. It is home to several medical institutions, a technical school, and the Marine Military Academy (1963). It is a center for Confederate Air Force (see MIDLAND) activities.

Harmon Air Force Base also, **Harmon Field** see under STEPHENVILLE, Newfoundland.

Harmony borough, pop. 1054, Butler Co., W Pennsylvania, 25 mi/40 km N of Pittsburgh, on Connoquenessing Creek. It is next to Zelienople (borough, pop. 4158), whose proprietor, Baron Dettmar Basse, sold a tract to George Rapp, who organized at Harmony (1805) the first of his American collectivist religious communities. The Rappites moved on to NEW HARMONY, Indiana, leaving a cemetery and "Father Rapp's Seat," a hilltop rock the leader had used for meditative purposes. Zelienople and Harmony are in a clay and coal producing area that also is noted for resorts.

Harney Desert also, **Harney Basin** dry, largely barren expanse in SC Oregon, some 200 mi/320 km E–W and 40 mi/65 km N–S, on the N edge of the GREAT BASIN and S edge of the COLUMBIA PLATEAU, chiefly in Harney (10,185 sq mi/26,379 sq km, pop. 7060) and Lake counties. At about 4000 ft/1220 m, it has sagebrush barrens, grasslands, sand dunes, and assorted landforms including the GLASS BUTTES (NW) and STEENS Mt. and the Alvord Desert (on the S). The Cascade Range (W) shields it from moist Pacific winds. BURNS is the chief settlement.

Harney Peak granitic mountain (7242 ft/2209 m) in the Black Hills, in Pennington Co., SW South Dakota, 10 mi/16 km NE of Custer. Situated just N of Custer State Park, it is the highest point in the state and in the US E of the Rockies. It was named for General William S. Harney, who led a small force through the area in 1857.

Harpers Ferry town, pop. 308, Jefferson Co., extreme NE West Virginia, in the Eastern PANHANDLE, atthe meeting point of West Virginia, Virginia, and Maryland and the confluence of the Shenandoah and Potomac rivers, in the Blue Ridge Mts., 55 mi/89 km NW of Washington, D.C. Founded in 1734 by Robert Harper, who established a gristmill and ferry service, it developed after a Federal arsenal was established in 1796, followed by a rifle plant. The Baltimore and Ohio Railroad and the Chesapeake and Ohio Canal both arrived in the 1830s, making Harpers Ferry a transportation hub. The Oct. 16, 1859 assault onthe arsenal by armed abolitionists led by John Brown was one of the major incidents presaging the Civil War. The town was a strategic point in Washington's defense during the war, the site of several battles. It is now a residential community and resort, headquarters of the three-state, 2240-ac/907-ha **Harpers Ferry National Historical Park.** The town of Bolivar (pop. 1013), adjacent to the W, shares in Harpers Ferry's resort business.

Harper Woods city, pop. 14,903, Wayne Co., SE Michigan, a residential suburb 10 mi/16 km NE of Detroit.

Harquahala Mountains see under HARCUVAR Mts., Arizona.

Harriman city, pop. 7119, Roane Co., E Tennessee, 35 mi/56 km W of Knoxville, on the Emory R. where it cuts through WALDEN RIDGE. It is a trade and shipping center for lumber, farm, and quarry products. Just S is the N end of Watts Bar L. The OAK RIDGE complex is 10 mi/16 km E.

Harris nuclear power plant in Wake Co., C North Carolina, on the Harris Reservoir, just S of US 1 and 24 mi/38 km SSW of Durham, operational since 1987.

Harrisburg 1. city, pop. 9289, seat of Saline Co., SE Illinois, 20 mi/32 km E of Marion. The center of a coal mining and farming region, it manufactures building materials and fabricated metals. Laid out in 1853, the settlement emerged as an important barge port when the nearby Saline R. was channelized. It is the seat of Southeastern Illinois College (1960). The headquarters of the Shawnee National Forest, 7 mi/11 km to the S, is here. **2.** city, pop. 52,376, seat of Dauphin Co. and state capital, in SC Pennsylvania, on the E bank of the Susquehanna R., 100 mi/160 km W of Philadelphia. It has excellent transportation facilities and is a wholesaling, retailing, warehousing, and distribution center. Situated in a region rich in coal and iron ore, Harrisburg has huge steel mills and a variety of smaller manufacturing firms. Industries include printing and publishing, meat packing, textiles, and railroad shops. Founded as a trading post in 1710, it became state capital in 1812. It was the scene of several early political conventions, notably in 1788, 1828, and 1839. During the Civil War, Camp Curtin was an important training center. Harrisburg has an impressive Capitol building (1906), a park along the Susquehanna with a noted sunken garden, and many historical sites, such as Fort Hunter Mansion (1787). The Pennsylvania National Horse Show and other expositions are held at the huge Pennsylvania Farm Show building. Institutions of higher learning include a campus of Pennsylvania State University, a community college, and the Milton S. Hershey Medical Center. The THREE MILE ISLAND nuclear facility is 10 mi/16 km SE of the city, near MIDDLETOWN. **3.** former town in Harris Co., SE Texas, established 1823 by John Harris, one of Stephen F. Austin's Texas colonists, at the confluence of Brays and Buffalo bayous, 6 mi/10 km SE of downtown modern Houston. Briefly in 1836 the capital of Texas, it was burned (April

14, 1836) as the Mexican general Santa Anna approached. After Texas independence, efforts to reestablish Harrisburg failed in the face of the growth of Houston, established just upstream at ALLENS LANDING.

Harris County 1734 sq mi/4491 sq km, pop. 2,818,199, in SE Texas. On the Gulf Coastal Plain, it is drained by the Buffalo Bayou, the San Jacinto R., and tributaries. HOUSTON, the largest city in Texas, is its seat. The city and its industrial, commercial, and residential suburbs now occupy most of what was a rice, cotton, vegetable, timber, and cattle producing area. Oil, gas, and sulfur are major local products. Tourism and Gulf Coast fishing and shipping are important.

Harrison **1.** city, pop. 9922, seat of Boone Co., NW Arkansas, in the Ozark Plateau, on Crooked Creek. Laid out in 1860, it became a commercial center following the arrival of the Missouri and North Arkansas Railway in 1900. It ships fruit, timber, and livestock and manufactures wood products, cheese, flour, and clothing. Local lead, zinc, marble, dolomite, limestone, and silicon have contributed to its economy. North Arkansas Community College (1974) is here. **2.** town, pop. 13,425, Hudson Co., NE New Jersey, on the Passaic R. opposite Newark. In a highly industrialized area, it has steel mills and foundries, and manufactures such products as elevators, pumps, electronic and refrigeration devices, and processed foods. **3.** town, pop. 23,308, Westchester Co., SE New York, 25 mi/40 km NE of New York City. It is mainly residential, but some parts, like the village of PURCHASE, have extensive corporate development. The Westchester Co. Airport is in the N, along the Connecticut border.

Harrisonburg independent city, pop. 30,707, seat of but administratively separate from Rockingham Co., N Virginia, 23 mi/37 km NNE of Staunton, in the Shenandoah Valley. It is a shipping center for agricultural products (poultry, fruit, livestock, dairy) and produces shoes, rayon, auto parts, heating and cooling systems, and poultry raising equipment. It is the seat of James Madison University (1908) and Eastern Mennonite College (1917).

Harrison County 400 sq mi/1036 sq km, pop. 16,085, in E Ohio; it includes Conotton Creek and Stillwater Creek as well as Clendening and Tappan lakes. The seat of this largely rural county is CADIZ. Coal mining is important, and there is some manufacturing at Cadiz and Scio. Agriculture includes livestock, grain, and dairy. Limestone is quarried.

Harrison Lake in SW British Columbia, 60 mi/100 km ENE of Vancouver. Forty mi/64 km N–S and 1–5 mi/1–8 km wide, it receives the Lillooet R. in the NW and drains S into the Fraser R. It is a popular vacation spot, esp. at the S end, where the well-known resort and convention center of **Harrison Hot Springs** lies.

Harrodsburg city, pop. 7335, seat of Mercer Co., C Kentucky, 30 mi/48 SW of Lexington, near the Salt R. The oldest Kentucky settlement (1774) and the oldest English settlement W of the Alleghenies was built on the WILDERNESS ROAD by a group under James Harrod. A replica of its fort (1775) is in Old Fort Harrod State Park. The town has many restored buildings from several periods. It is an agricultural trade center, and is a noted crafts and tourist center. Nearby are mineral springs and a restored early-19th-century Shaker town, Pleasant Hill.

Harrogate unincorporated community, pop. (with neighboring Shawanee) 2657, Claiborne Co., NE Tennessee, 48 mi/77 km NNE of Knoxville. This former summer resort, near the Kentucky and Virginia borders, 2 mi/3 km SSE of the CUMBERLAND GAP, is the seat of Lincoln Memorial University (1897).

Harry S Truman National Historic Site see under INDEPENDENCE, Missouri.

Harry S Truman Sports Complex developed in the 1970s, 6 mi/10 km SE of downtown KANSAS CITY, Missouri, on Interstates 70 and 435, near the INDEPENDENCE line. It is the site of Arrowhead Stadium (1972; seats 78,000), home to the football Chiefs, and of Royals Stadium (1973; seats 41,000), home to the baseball Royals.

Hartford **1.** city and coterminous township, seat of Hartford Co. and state capital, pop. 139,739, C Connecticut. It lies at the head of navigation on the Connecticut R., 38 mi/61 km N of Long Island Sound. The second-largest city in the state, it is a major industrial and commercial center, noted particularly for its insurance industry, which began with the issuance of a fire insurance policy on Feb. 8, 1774; today more than 25 companies, the largest Aetna, are headquartered here. Other industries include the manufacture of office machines, firearms (Colt), and machine tools and gauges. Settled in 1635 by Massachusetts Colonists who in 1639 drafted Connecticut's Fundamental Orders, regarded as a prototype of constitutions, Hartford was a Federalist stronghold during the War of 1812, and the home of the Hartford Wits, a group of satirical poets in the years after the Revolution. The Wadsworth Atheneum (1842) was the first free public art museum in the United States; the Hartford *Courant* (1764) is among the nation's oldest newspapers. The city's institutions include Trinity College (1823), the Hartford Seminary Foundation (1834), the Morse School of Business (1860), Hartford College for Women (1939), and a branch of the University of Connecticut. Downtown focuses include Constitution Plaza and the Hartford Civic Center, in addition to Bushnell Park, where the Capitol (1872) is situated. Hartford has in recent years suffered the loss of much of its commerce, along with much of its middle-class population, to nearby suburbs. **2.** town, pop. 1989, Washington Co., E New York, 13 mi/21 km NE of Glens Falls, near the Vermont border. Mormon apostle Orson Pratt (1811–81) was born in this hilly rural town. **3.** town, pop. 9404, Windsor Co., EC Vermont. It is on the Connecticut R. at the mouth of the White R. The town includes the industrial and transportation center WHITE RIVER JUNCTION, gateway to resort areas. Quechee Gorge, a 165-ft/50-m gorge on the Ottauquechee R. in the S part of the town, is a well-known attraction.

Hartford County 739 sq mi/1914 sq km, pop. 851,783, in NC Connecticut, on the Massachusetts border, bisected by the Connecticut R. It is dominated by Hartford, the state capital and its commercial and financial center. Outside of Hartford are corporate installations as well as agricultural and suburban residential areas; manufacturing centers including Bristol and New Britain; and areas that remain rural.

Hart Island also, **Hart's Island** about 1 mi/1.5 km long, in Long Island Sound, just NE of City I. and E of Orchard Beach, Pelham Bay Park, extreme NE Bronx, New York. It has been owned by the City of New York since 1869, and has served as a reformatory extension of RIKERS ISLAND. It is New York's potter's field, ultimate repository of more than half a million bodies.

Hart Mountain 7710 ft/2350 m, within the **Hart Mt. National**

Antelope Refuge (241,104 ac/97,647 ha), in E Lake Co., S Oregon, 115 mi/185 km E of Klamath Falls. Warner Peak rises to 8017 ft/2444 m, the highest point in the refuge. A series of lakes and PLAYAS, the Warner Lakes, lie along the W of this pronghorn reserve in the Warner Valley.

Hartsdale unincorporated village, pop. 9587, in Greenburgh town, Westchester Co., SE New York, on the Bronx R., immediately W of White Plains. It is a residential and commercial suburb with corporate offices and a retail district that serves much of lower Westchester.

Hartselle city, pop. 10,795, Morgan Co., NC Alabama, 11 mi/18 km SSE of Decatur. Incorporated in 1875, it ships lumber and cotton.

Hartsfield International Airport officially, **William B. Hartsfield Atlanta International Airport** 8 mi/13 km SSW of downtown Atlanta, Georgia. Opened in 1980, it is the leading commercial aviation center of the SE US.

Hartsville city, pop. 8372, Darlington Co., NE South Carolina, 21 mi/32 km NW of Florence. Settled in 1760, it grew around Thomas Edward Hart's plantation. James Coker established a crossroads store (1866), built a railroad connection to the Atlantic Coast Line, and later (1908) founded Coker College. The city produces textiles, paper products, plastic, and bricks, and is an agricultural trade center. The Coker Experimental Seed Farms, noted for developing varieties of cotton and other crops, is an historic landmark. The H.B. Robinson nuclear power plant (1970) is just NW, on L. Robinson.

Harvard town, pop. 12,329, Worcester Co., NC Massachusetts, 12 mi/19 km ESE of Fitchburg. The Harvard Astronomical Observatory is here. The town was the site of FRUITLANDS, a short-lived Utopian community founded in 1844. A Shaker community established here in 1791 became the first US Shaker museum in 1922. Always essentially agricultural, Harvard has experienced some residential and commercial growth since Route 495 opened to the E in the 1960s.

Harvard, Mount see under SAWATCH RANGE, Colorado.

Harvard Yard enclosed center of the campus of Harvard University, just NE of Harvard Square, W CAMBRIDGE, Middlesex Co., E Massachusetts. Its S end is dominated by Widener Library (1914), the world's largest university library. Noted buildings include Massachusetts Hall (1720), Hollis Hall (1763), Harvard Hall (1766), and H. H. Richardson's Sever Hall (1880).

Harvey **1.** city, pop. 29,771, Cook Co., NE Illinois, a suburb 13 mi/21 km S of Chicago. Local industries produce diesel engines, castings and forgings, railroad equipment, and highway and other machinery. The city is also a center for petroleum research and development. Laid out as South Lawn in 1873, Harvey was renamed for a lumber baron who bought the land and organized a land association to attract residential and industrial development. During the 1890s, machine-shop and metalworking industries were established. **2.** unincorporated community, pop. 21,222, Jefferson Parish, SE Louisiana, on the W (S) bank of the Mississippi R., opposite New Orleans and just SW of GRETNA. The Harvey Canal connects the Mississippi R. to the GULF INTRACOASTAL WATERWAY here. Harvey is largely residential, with a variety of riverfront and canalside docks and industries making chemicals, machinery, and food products.

Harwood Heights village, pop. 7680, Cook Co., NE Illinois, a suburb 11 mi/18 km NE of Chicago's LOOP. Almost completely surrounded by the city's Northwest Side, it is a few miles E of O'Hare International Airport.

Hasbrouck Heights borough, pop. 11,488, Bergen Co., NE New Jersey, 2 mi/3 km SW of Hackensack. Settled in the late 17th century, it is essentially a residential suburb of New York, with commercial offices and light industry. Teterboro Airport is SE.

Hastings **1.** city, pop. 15,445, seat of Dakota Co., SE Minnesota, on the Mississippi R. at the mouth of the Vermillion R., just W of the Wisconsin border and 20 mi/32 km SE of St. Paul. It was founded as the trading post of Buckhorn in 1833, and the first flour mills in the state were set up here. Today, besides flour, products include sprayers, dusters, office equipment, bricks and tile, lumber, and toys. **2.** city, pop. 22,837, seat of Adams Co., SC Nebraska, on the West Fork of the Big Blue R., 23 mi/37 km S of Grand Island. It grew up around a railroad depot and today is the processing and shipping center for a wheat growing region. Its industries pursue agricultural research and manufacture building materials, farm implements, and irrigation equipment. Hastings College (1882) is here.

Hastings-on-Hudson village, pop. 8000, in Greenburgh town, Westchester Co., SE New York, on the Hudson R. opposite the Palisades. It is a primarily residential suburb of New York City, with chemical and other industries located along the river.

Hatch village, pop. 1136, Dona Ana Co., SW New Mexico, on the Rio Grande and I-25, 30 mi/48 km NNW of Las Cruces. In an irrigated area some 20 mi/32 km downstream from the Caballo Reservoir, it is known as the "Chile Capital of the World" for its chili pepper production; the Hatch Valley is becoming residentially fashionable.

Hatchie River 175 mi/280 km long, in N Mississippi and W Tennessee. It rises along the Union-Tippah county line in Mississippi and winds N into Tennessee, where its complex of channels creates marshy **Hatchie Bottom;** it passes BOLIVAR, swinging NW. The Hatchie National Wildlife Refuge lies along it here. Forming the Tipton-Lauderdale county line, it winds WNW, then WSW, to the Mississippi, just SW of the FORT PILLOW historic site.

Hatfield town, pop. 3184, Hampshire Co., W Massachusetts, on the Connecticut R., 18 mi/29 km N of Springfield and adjoining (N) Northampton. A 1661 CONNECTICUT VALLEY settlement, it was the target of Indian attacks in 1675 and 1677. The town was the birthplace of prominent 18th- and 19th-century educators Sophia Smith, founder of Smith College; Col. Ephraim Williams, founder of Williams College; Jonathan Dickinson, first president of Princeton University; and Elisha Williams, president of Yale University. Rich riverine soils made Hatfield for years a major producer of onions and tobacco; the latter has been replaced by other vegetables.

Hato Rey commercial district of SAN JUAN, Puerto Rico, comprising three BARRIOS (Hato Rey Norte, Central, and Sur, with a total pop. of 51,421), on the mainland S of SANTURCE. Under the impetus of the Federal Operation Bootstrap, Hato Rey grew from a relatively small residential and industrial suburb of the 1960s to the business and financial center it had become by the 1990s. It now houses a variety of modern office buildings, including the headquarters of many Caribbean banks and other major businesses, esp. along its "Golden Mile" section of Rte. 1. A large contemporary mall is here, as are two sports stadiums, the Estadios Hiram Bithorn and Roberto Clemente.

Hatteras, Cape sandy peninsula in the Atlantic Ocean at the SE corner of 43 mi/69 km–long Hatteras I. (part of the OUTER BANKS) in Dare Co., E North Carolina. The open waters E of the cape, including Diamond Shoals, are treacherous and subject to severe storms; colder northern waters and the GULF STREAM meet here, creating turbulence and earning this area the nickname "Graveyard of the Atlantic." The Cape Hatteras Lighthouse is the tallest in the US at 208 ft/63 m. Both the cape and lighthouse are threatened by erosion and rising sea levels, which have reduced beachfront at the light from 1500 ft/458 m when it was built in 1870 to less than 100 ft/30 m today. **Cape Hatteras National Seashore,** the country's first, established in 1953, covers 80 mi/130 km of barrier beach from NAGS HEAD on Bodie I. (N) to the S tip of OCRACOKE I. (S). Inside lie PAMLICO SOUND and ROANOKE I. The Union ironclad *Monitor,* which foundered in Dec. 1862, lies off the cape.

Hattiesburg city, pop. 41,882, seat of Forrest Co., also in Lamar Co., SE Mississippi, on the Leaf R., 85 mi/137 km SE of Jackson. The arrival of railroads in 1884 and 1897 stimulated the infant community's lumber and naval stores industries, but in the 20th century, as regional timber resources dwindled, the city turned to the manufacture of textiles (especially silk), chemicals, and metal products. It is also an agricultural trade center, and home to the University of Southern Mississippi (1910), with the state's second-largest enrollment, and to William Carey College (1906).

Hauppauge unincorporated village, pop. 19,750, in Smithtown, Suffolk Co., SE New York, in C Long Island. It is the location of federal, state, and county government offices, although the county seat is at Riverhead. It also has a publishing industry, various corporate offices, and other commercial development.

Havasu, Lake on the COLORADO R., on the border between W Arizona and SE California. Forty-six mi/74 km long and 3 mi/5 km wide, it is a popular recreational center and reservoir formed when the Parker Dam was built in 1938. Through the Colorado River Aqueduct, it supplies water and power to S California. The lake lies within the 44,400-ac/ 18,000-ha **Havasu National Wildlife Refuge.** Toprock Gorge, 8 mi/13 km N of the lake, is known for its scenery and PETROGLYPHS. LAKE HAVASU CITY is on the lake's Arizona side.

Havasu Canyon and **Havasupai Indian Reservation** see under GRAND CANYON NATIONAL PARK, Arizona.

Havelock city, pop. 20,268, Craven Co., SE North Carolina, 32 mi/52 km E of Jacksonville, on East Creek, an estuarial S arm of the Neuse R. Long a small agricultural trade center, during Prohibition a bootlegging hub, it is now largely a service center for the Cherry Point Marine Air Station, just NE.

Haverford in SE Pennsylvania: **a.** township, pop. 49,848, in Delaware Co. **b.** residential community, mainly in Lower Merion township, Montgomery Co., with the balance in Haverford township. Situated some 10 mi/16 km W of Philadelphia, it is an affluent suburb and the seat of Haverford College (1833).

Haverhill city, pop. 51,418, Essex Co., NE Massachusetts, on the Merrimack R., 33 mi/53 km N of Boston, and along the New Hampshire border. Settled in 1640, it began building ships in 1697. In the 19th century Haverhill became a major manufacturer of shoes, hats, and combs. Its great industrial period created a city of distinct ethnic neighborhoods. The last shoe factory closed in 1992. Other manufactures have included electrical products, machinery, paperboard, tools, electronics, paints, chemicals, and plastics. Home of Bradford College (1803), it is also the birthplace (1807) of John Greenleaf Whittier, some of whose early poetry describes life in the area.

Haverstraw town, pop. 32,712, Rockland Co., SE New York, on the W bank of the Hudson R., 12 mi/19 km S of West Point. A cooperative community was established here in 1825 by followers of the British social reformer Robert Owen. A system for manufacturing brick and cement was invented in Haverstraw, where these industries remain important. There are also quarries and such manufactures as leather products, clothing, and hardware. Letchworth Village, a facility for the mentally retarded, and several RAMAPO Mt. resorts are in the town.

Havertown unincorporated community in HAVERFORD township, Delaware Co., SE Pennsylvania, an affluent suburb immediately W of Philadelphia.

Haviland city, pop. 624, Kiowa Co., S Kansas, 50 mi/80 km ESE of Dodge City. In a grain and livestock producing area, it is the seat of Barclay College (1917).

Havre city, pop. 10,201, seat of Hill Co., NC Montana, on the Milk R., 102 mi/164 km NE of Great Falls. Founded in 1879 and named for Le Havre, France, home of the original settlers, it was at first 5 mi/8 km SW, near Fort Assiniboine, then was relocated to become a railroad division point. The city remains a shipping center for local livestock and crops. It is home to Northern Montana College (1929). Rocky Boy Indian Reservation, pop. 1954, is 15 mi/24 km S.

Havre de Grace city, pop. 8952, Harford Co., NE Maryland, on Chesapeake Bay, at the mouth of the Susquehanna R., 33 mi/53 km NE of Baltimore. Settled in 1658 and a trade center since the mid 19th century, it has granite quarries, canneries, and commercial fisheries, and was formerly the terminus of a canal on the lower 45 mi/72 km of the Susquehanna. Although burned by the British in the War of 1812, it has many earlier buildings. The area contains resorts and waterfront estates.

Hawaii southernmost and westernmost state of the US, in the mid Pacific Ocean; 1990 pop. 1,108,229 (114.9% of 1980; rank: 41st); area 10,932 sq mi/28,314 sq km (rank: 43rd); admitted to Union 1959 (50th). Capital and largest community: HONOLULU. Other leading communities: HILO, KAILUA, KANEOHE. The only state not part of North America, Hawaii, variously described as part of Oceania or Polynesia, comprises a WNW–ESE oriented island chain 1700 mi/2700 km in length, the E end of which lies some 2100 mi/3400 km SW of California. The Tropic of Cancer passes through the islands. The chain was formed from W to E by volcanic forces that continue to be active on the southeasternmost island, HAWAII (the "Big Island"). From E to W, the other seven main islands are MAUI, KAHOOLAWE, LANAI, MOLOKAI, OAHU, KAUAI, and NIIHAU. To their WNW are the many small islands, shoals, and banks now within the **Hawaiian Islands National Wildlife Refuge,** including Nihoa, Necker I., the French Frigate Shoals, Tern I. and La Perouse Pinnacle, the Gardner Pinnacles, Laysan I., and Lisianski I. To their NW are the group formed by the Pearl and Hermes Reef, Kittery

I., and North and Southeast islands. At the NW end of the Hawaiian chain is Kure I., site of a Coast Guard station. Between Kure and the rest of the chain lies the MIDWAY I. group, administered by the US Navy and not included when the state was admitted in 1959. MAUNA KEA, an extinct volcano on Hawaii, is the state's high point, at 13,796 ft/4205 m, and rises over 32,000 ft/9754 m from the sea floor, the highest such rise in the world. Nearby MAUNA LOA (13,680 ft/4170 m) and KILAUEA remain active; they are now within the HAWAII VOLCANOES NATIONAL PARK. KA LAE (South Cape) is the southernmost US point. Maui, the second-largest island, is noted for HALEAKALA, the world's largest extinct volcanic crater, also within a national park. Kahoolawe, to the SW, was until 1994 a navy bombing and gunnery range, and is now undergoing a cleanup period. Molokai, the fifth-largest island, has plantations and resorts, and is noted for its KALAUPAPA PENINSULA, site of a famed leper colony. Lanai, S of Molokai, is famed for pineapple production. To the W of Molokai is Oahu, the state's third-largest island and its population, institutional, military, and industrial center, the site of Honolulu and WAIKIKI, PEARL HARBOR and surrounding bases and airfields, and the parallel (NW–SE) KOOLAU and WAIANAE ranges. Farther W is Kauai, the "Garden Island," fourth-largest and the site of the WAIMEA CANYON, Na Pali Coast, and other famed scenery. WAIALEALE, on the NE facing the TRADE WINDS, is the world's wettest spot. Niihau, to Kauai's W, is privately owned and restricted to native Hawaiians; it is popularly known as the "Forbidden Island." Hawaii (the name appears to derive from that of a legendary Polynesian homeland) has been inhabited for over 1200 years by seafaring Polynesian peoples. The first whites known to have seen it were the crew of Captain James Cook, who arrived here in 1778 and named the chain the SANDWICH Is. At that period the islands were undergoing consolidation; Kamehameha I, king of the island of Hawaii, gained control of the entire group in the 1790s. Throughout the 19th century, Europeans and Americans gradually infiltrated the islands, beginning with 1820s missionaries. Lumber operations, sugar and pineapple plantations, and whaling and commercial ports sprang up. By the end of the 19th century, Americans had become dominant. In 1894, the Hawaiian monarchy was overthrown, and a republic headed by pineapple magnate Sanford Dole was established. In 1898 the US annexed it, making Hawaii a territory in 1900. In the early 20th century intensive plantation agriculture, staffed largely by Japanese and Filipino laborers, developed side by side with military construction. Pearl Harbor, HICKAM FIELD, and BARBERS POINT were among facilities operating here in 1941, when on Dec. 7 Japanese forces attacked, bringing the US into World War II. The war greatly expanded the Federal presence; afterwards, soldiers and sailors who had been stationed here were among many who thought of Hawaii as a place to visit or to live. Tourism has since become the islands' major industry, followed by military and related activities. Hawaiian agriculture produces sugar, pineapples and other fruit, macadamia nuts, coffee (esp. on the island of Hawaii's KONA COAST), livestock, orchids, dairy goods, poultry, and other products. Tuna are the primary catch of island fisheries. Hawaii has no incorporated municipalities; the COUNTY is the only level of local government. The University of Hawaii is at Honolulu, which is also home to most of the state's limited manufacturing; Hilo is the second leading industrial center. In 1990, Hawaii's people were 62% Asian or Pacific Islander, chiefly Japanese, Chinese, or Filipino; native Hawaiians were a minority. Another 33% of residents were white.

Hawaii roughly triangular volcanic mid-Pacific island, at 4021 sq mi/10,414 sq km the largest of the Hawaiian Is., popularly called the Big Island. Coextensive with Hawaii Co., it has a pop. of 120,317. The southeasternmost island of the archipelago, it is also geologically the youngest. Its chief population center is HILO. Formed from five volcanoes that are linked by lava ridges, it has an extremely varied topography and climate, ranging from the glacial peak of MAUNA KEA to lava deserts, bamboo and fern forests, sea cliffs, and tropical coastal areas. The active MAUNA LOA and KILAUEA are in HAWAII VOLCANOES NATIONAL PARK, in the SE. The N Kona district, on the W coast, is known for its coffee, and sugar is cultivated on the Kohala Peninsula (N) and on the E coast. Cattle ranching, the raising of orchids and macadamia nuts, and fishing are also important. Tourism is a key industry, esp. on the KONA (SW) Coast. KA LAE (South Cape) is the southernmost US point.

Hawaiian Gardens residential city, pop. 13,639, Los Angeles Co., SW California, 16 mi/26 km SE of downtown Los Angeles and just SE of Lakewood, on Coyote Creek.

Hawaii County 4021 sq mi/10,414 sq km, pop. 120,317, in SE Hawaii. It is coextensive with HAWAII, the southernmost island in the archipelago. HILO, on the E coast, is its seat.

Hawaii Volcanoes National Park 229,177 ac/92,817 ha, on SE Hawaii island, Hawaii, SW of Hilo. Established in 1916, it demonstrates evidence of a number of recent lava flows and is the setting for Hawaii's only active volcanoes, MAUNA LOA and KILAUEA. Topography and climate within the area vary dramatically; the park includes the arid Kau desert with its unusual lava formations, a tropical rain forest, and a bird sanctuary.

Hawkesbury town, pop. 9706, Prescott and Russell United Counties, extreme E Ontario, on the Ottawa R., 50 mi/80 km WNW of Montreal and 55 mi/89 km ENE of Ottawa. Founded in 1798, it has been a milling, more recently a hydroelectric, center. Diverse industries now contribute to an economy once dominated by lumber and related products.

Hawkins city, pop. 1309, Wood Co., NE Texas, 17 mi/27 km N of Tyler, in an oil producing area near the Sabine R. It is the seat of Jarvis Christian College (1912).

Hawk Mountain peak on the Blue Mt. ridge, near Hamburg, Berks Co., EC Pennsylvania, 28 mi/45 km W of Allentown. The 1300-ft/396-m prominence is known for its 2200-ac/891-ha bird sanctuary. Situated close to the Appalachian Trail, on a major flyway, it has been a nature refuge since 1934.

Haw Knob see under UNICOI Mts., North Carolina.

Hawksbill Mountain peak (4050 ft/1235 m) of the Blue Ridge Mts., 12 mi/19 km ENE of Shenandoah, Virginia. The highest point in SHENANDOAH NATIONAL PARK, it is crossed by the APPALACHIAN TRAIL.

Haw River 130 mi/210 km long, in C North Carolina. It rises on the Forsyth-Guilford county line, just NE of Kernersville, and flows E to the N of Greensboro, then SSE past Burlington and across the Piedmont. Twenty-five mi/40 km SW of Raleigh, the B. Everett Jordan Dam creates 47,000-ac/19,000-ha B. Everett Jordan L. Four mi/6 km below the dam, the Haw joins the Deep R. to form the CAPE FEAR R.

Hawthorne **1.** city, pop. 71,349, Los Angeles Co., SW California, 9 mi/14 km SSW of downtown Los Angeles. Incorporated in 1922 in an oil and natural gas producing area, it has a variety of aerospace and defense-related manufactures, and also makes other machinery. **2.** unincorporated community, pop. 4162, seat of Mineral Co., W Nevada, SE of WALKER L. and 77 mi/124 km SE of Carson City. Originally (1880s) a supply center for the gold and silver mines of the area, it became a military post, and in the 1930s–40s grew into a major munitions depot. Tourism is important to the economy. AURORA is 25 mi/40 km SW. **3.** borough, pop. 17,084, Passaic Co., NE New Jersey, on the Passaic R. N of Paterson. Settled in 1850, it is primarily a New York–area bedroom community. Hawthorne also has numerous office buildings and a wide variety of industries producing such goods as television parts, metal products, tiles, dyed textiles, paint, glass, chemicals, hosiery, and plastics. **4.** unincorporated village, pop. 4764, in Mount Pleasant town, Westchester Co., SE New York, 6 mi/10 km N of White Plains. It is a residential community with some light industry.

Hawthorne Waterworks Western Electric facility in the town of Cicero, NE Illinois. The psychological phenomenon known as the "Hawthorne effect" was first observed here during experiments in the late 1920s.

Hayes River 300 mi/480 km long, in EC Manitoba. It flows from L. Molson, NE of L. Winnipeg, through Oxford and several smaller lakes, to enter the HUDSON BAY at YORK FACTORY. Like the NELSON R., whose mouth on the Bay is just NW, it was a major fur trade route to L. Winnipeg, often preferred because less turbulent.

Haymarket Square **1.** former intersection on the Near West Side of Chicago, Illinois, just W of the Loop. Bombs killed and wounded policemen during a workers' demonstration here in 1886. The subsequent trial of a group of anarchists seized national and international attention, and the event inspired the construction of Ft. Sheridan on the NORTH SHORE. **2.** created 1808 in Boston, Massachusetts, and long important in the city's commercial life. It was eliminated in the 1960s in the building of the new GOVERNMENT CENTER. Haymarket Square was located just N of Faneuil Hall. A "Haymarket" continues to be held in nearby Blackstone St.

Hayneville see under LOWNDES Co., Alabama.

Hay River town, pop. 3206, Fort Smith Region, S Northwest Territories, at the mouth of the 350 mi/560 km–long **Hay R.,** on the SW shore of GREAT SLAVE L., 60 mi/96 km N of the Alberta line. It was the home of the Slavey (DENE), and a fur trading center before arrival of the Mackenzie Highway (1949) and the railway (1964) made it a commercial fishing and regional transshipment center, with a port active five months of the year. The lead and zinc mines of Pine Point are 45 mi/72 km E. The Alexandra Falls and Louise Falls, on the river SW of Enterprise (21 mi/34 km SSW), are noted sights.

Hays city, pop. 17,767, seat of Ellis Co., WC Kansas, on Big Creek, 90 mi/144 km W of Salina. It was established in 1867 near Fort Hays, a military post on the SMOKY HILL TRAIL. The city is now a rail center for an oil, cattle, and grain producing area, and has some manufacturing. Fort Hays State University (1902) is here.

Haystack, Mount see under ADIRONDACK Mts.

Haysville city, pop. 8364, Sedgwick Co., S Kansas, a suburb 7 mi/11 km SSW of downtown Wichita.

Hayward city, pop. 111,498, Alameda Co., NC California, 14 mi/23 km S of Oakland, at the E terminus of the San Mateo Bridge, on the SE of San Francisco Bay. Laid out in the 1850s on Guillermo Castro's RANCHO, it became a livestock (esp. poultry) and agricultural center, and is today a manufacturing and distribution center. Food processing and the manufacture of auto and aircraft parts, electronic equipment, containers, plastics, and chemicals are among its industries. A California State University campus (1957) and Chabot College (1961) are here.

Hazardville see under ENFIELD, Connecticut.

Hazel Crest village, pop. 13,334, Cook Co., NE Illinois, a residential suburb 20 mi/32 km S of Chicago.

Hazel Park city, pop. 20,051, Oakland Co., SE Michigan, 8 mi/13 km N of Detroit. This residential suburb has several small industries and a harness racetrack.

Hazelton Peak see under BIGHORN NATIONAL FOREST, Wyoming.

Hazelwood city, pop. 15,324, St. Louis Co., EC Missouri, 14 mi/23 km NW of downtown St. Louis. An industrial suburb, it manufactures such products as aircraft and auto parts, furniture, and a variety of processed foods. It lies just N of the Lambert–St. Louis International Airport.

Hazlehurst city, pop. 4221, seat of Copiah Co., SW Mississippi, 30 mi/48 km SSW of Jackson. Founded in 1857, it lies in a farming and timbering region, for which it is a trade center. The city is on both Interstate 55 and Amtrak's Memphis–New Orleans line.

Hazlet township, pop. 21,976, Monmouth Co., EC New Jersey, 8 mi/13 km SE of Perth Amboy, on the Garden State Parkway. It is primarily residential.

Hazleton city, pop. 24,730, Luzerne Co., EC Pennsylvania, 20 mi/32 km SSW of Wilkes-Barre. Situated atop Spring Mt. at an elevation of 1886 ft/575 m, it has the highest elevation of any city in the state. It was founded in the early 19th century as a coal mining center. With the decline of that industry, the city sought to diversify its economy. Manufactures now include clothing, iron and steel products, electronic equipment, and plastics. Hazleton has a two-year campus of Pennsylvania State University.

H. B. Robinson nuclear power plant: see under HARTSVILLE, South Carolina.

Head House Square mall and open-air marketplace, in the SOCIETY HILL section of Philadelphia, Pennsylvania. Site of the oldest public market buildings in the nation (now demolished), it still contains a mall that was the scene of 19th-century citizens' meetings.

Head of the Lake see LAKEHEAD, Ontario.

Head-Smashed-In Buffalo Jump see under PORCUPINE HILLS, Alberta.

Head Tide see under GARDINER, Maine.

Healdsburg city, pop. 9469, Sonoma Co., NW California, on the RUSSIAN R., 14 mi/23 km NW of Santa Rosa and 62 mi/100 km NNW of San Francisco. Settled in 1852, it is the center of a longtime fruit (apples, prunes, pears, peaches) growing area, and now the hub of the Russian R. wine industry. It is also noted for its pottery and as a resort.

Hearst town, pop. 6079, Cochrane District, EC Ontario, on the Mattawishkwia R., 217 mi/350 km NNE of Sault Ste. Marie. It was settled at the time of the construction of the National Transcontinental (Canadian National) Railway (completed 1913), and was reached in 1914 by the ALGOMA Central. Since 1939 it has been a Catholic bisophric, and has a predominantly French-speaking pop.; the Collège de Hearst (1953) is here. The economy is centered on lumbering, pulp and paper manufacture, and farming. Moose hunting and canoeing draw visitors.

Hearst Castle see under SAN SIMEON, California.

Heartbreak Hill see under NEWTON, Massachusetts.

Heart Mountain 8123 ft/2476 m, in NW Wyoming, just N of CODY. On its E side, in the Shoshone R. valley, was the **Heart Mountain Relocation Center,** where some 11,000 Japanese-Americans were interned in 1942–45. The area is today farmland along Highway 14A.

Heart River 180 mi/290 km long, in North Dakota. It rises in the SW, and flows NE and E past Gladstone, where it is joined by the Green R. It flows farther E through sparsely populated farmland and joins the Missouri R. at MANDAN.

Heart's Content town, pop. 567, SE Newfoundland, on an inlet on the NW arm of the AVALON PENINSULA, on the E side of TRINITY BAY, 37 mi/60 km NW of St. John's. Settled by English fishermen in the 17th century, it became in 1866 the W terminus of the first successful transatlantic submarine telegraph cable, from Valentia, Ireland, landed here by the huge steamship *Great Eastern.* Connected with a cable from New York City, Heart's Content thus was made one of the world's busiest communications stations. New technology led to the station's closing in 1965; it is now a museum.

Heavener see under POTEAU Mt., Oklahoma.

Heavenly Valley see under SOUTH LAKE TAHOE, California.

Heber Springs city, pop. 5628, seat of Cleburne Co., NC Arkansas, on Greers Ferry L., in the Ozark Plateau, 55 mi/89 km NNE of Little Rock. Laid out in 1881, it has long been known for its mineral springs. In a lumbering and stone quarrying area, it is a popular tourist spot.

Hecate Strait 160 mi/260 km NNW–SSE, between the QUEEN CHARLOTTE Is. (W) and the C British Columbia mainland. Part of the trough between the Coast Ranges (W) and Coast Mts. (E), it is 30–90 mi/50–140 km wide, and shallow. Noted for its severe weather and rich fisheries, it was long controlled by the Haida, and was named for an 1860s British survey vessel. PRINCE RUPERT is on its NE.

Hecla Island largest of the islands in Hecla Provincial Park, on L. Winnipeg, SE Manitoba, 86 mi/139 km NNE of Winnipeg. Like GIMLI, this present-day resort community was founded in the 1870s by Icelandic immigrants. It is connected to the mainland by a causeway. A 110-year-old restored fishing village is situated on the N end, and nearby is Gull Harbor Resort. Wooded and surrounded by marsh, Hecla I. has wildlife preserves containing deer, elk, moose, and rare birds.

Hector, Mount peak (11,146 ft/3400 m) of the Rocky Mts., in SW Alberta, NW of LAKE LOUISE in Banff National Park, 110 mi/177 km NW of Calgary. KICKING HORSE PASS is nearby.

Hedwig Village see under HUNTERS CREEK VILLAGE, Texas.

Heinz Hall concert hall in the GOLDEN TRIANGLE on Penn Avenue, in Pittsburgh, Pennsylvania. This 1926 vaudeville and movie theater closed down in the 1960s. Restored in 1971, it reinvigorated the arts throughout the city. The Pittsburgh Symphony performs here.

Helena 1. city, pop. 7491, seat of Phillips Co., E Arkansas, 24 mi/39 km N of Clarksdale, Mississippi, on the Mississippi R. A rail center and river port, it processes and ships lumber, cotton, and food products. Manufactures include wood products, hosiery, and fertilizer. In the Civil War, a battle here (July 4, 1863) was won by Union forces. The city is a well-known blues broadcasting center, long the home of station KFFA's "King Biscuit Hour." The Delta Cultural Center and Phillips Co. Community College (1965) are here. The St. Francis National Forest is NW. **2.** city, pop. 24,569, state capital and seat of Lewis and Clark Co., WC Montana, 48 mi/77 km NE of Butte. Founded in 1864 when gold was discovered in Last Chance Gulch, now the city's main street, it became the capital of the Montana Territory in 1875 and the state capital in 1889. Helena's prosperity came in cycles with gold, silver, lead, zinc, and copper mining; the building of a ferry and dams on the nearby Missouri R.; and the discovery of natural gas. It is now a trading and distribution hub for livestock and agricultural products. Manufactures include machinery, ceramics, and paints and varnishes. Helena is home to the Montana Historical Society Museum, Library, and Archives and Carroll College (1909). The town of East Helena, pop. 1538, is adjacent and has smelting and refining works. The Helena National Forest lies just SE.

Helena National Forest 975,000 ac/395,000 ha (1525 sq mi/3945 sq km), in W Montana, in scattered units around Helena and the headwaters of the Missouri R. On the Continental Divide, it includes parts of the Big Belt and Elkhorn mountains, ghost towns, and glaciated valleys. The nearby Gates of the Mountains, named by Meriwether Lewis in 1805, are the place (20 mi/32 km N of Helena) where the Missouri passes (under 2000-ft/610-m limestone walls) through the Big Belts; now in a WILDERNESS AREA, they are a popular rafting locale. MANN GULCH is immediately E.

Heliograph Peak see under PINALENO Mts., Arizona.

Hell Gate passage in the EAST R., New York, between Ward's I. and Astoria, Queens. As narrow as 200 ft/61 m, it is famous for its difficult currents and underwater obstacles (now removed). Contrary to popular belief, its name is from the Dutch *Hellegat,* "beautiful passage." Hell Gate is spanned by the Triborough Bridge and the Hell Gate railroad bridge (officially, the East River Arch Bridge).

Hells Canyon 125 mi/200 km-long, NNE-SSW oriented gorge along the SNAKE R. between Oregon's WALLOWA Mts. (W) and Idaho's SEVEN DEVILS Mts. (E). Also called the Grand Canyon of the Snake, it averages 5500 ft/1676 m deep for over 40 mi/65 km, and reaches 7900 ft/2408 m from the top of He Devil Mt. In 1975 the 653,000-ac/264,000-ha (1020–sq mi/2645–sq km) **Hells Canyon National Recreation Area** was created, preserving the gorge after a decade-long dispute over dam projects. In parts of three national forests in the two states, and one-third wilderness area, the recreation area is a hiking and canoeing mecca.

Hell's Hundred Acres see under SOHO, New York.

Hell's Kitchen former waterfront neighborhood, W Midtown Manhattan, New York City. It is variously defined as having extended from the 20s or low 30s up to 59th St., W of Seventh or Eighth Ave. After the Civil War, the area became known for the gangsterism that flourished amid its slaughterhouses, railroad yards, and tenements. The name appears to have come from that of one of the gangs involved. Events that gradually erased Hell's Kitchen included the development of the Times Square area in the 1890s, the building of the Pennsylvania Railroad's trans-Hudson tunnel and station (1904–10), and the opening of the Lincoln Tunnel with its approaches in the 1930s. A small black community at the area's N extreme, and that of neighboring SAN JUAN HILL, moved to Harlem around World War I. The Hell's Kitchen area remains a transportation hub; Times Square has inherited some of its reputation. Residential redevelopment since the 1970s has been accompanied by attempts to attach the name Clinton to the area.

Helluland see under VINLAND.

Hemet city, pop. 36,094, Riverside Co., S California, 30 mi/48 km SE of Riverside, in the San Jacinto Valley. Incorporated in 1910, it is a trade center for an area in which fruit, olives, walnuts, and potatoes are grown, and has various light manufactures. It has tripled in pop. since 1970 as an affluent retirement community. The annual (since 1923) Ramona Pageant, based on the 1884 Helen Hunt Jackson novel, is staged in the outdoor Ramona Bowl by residents of Hemet and its sister city (N), SAN JACINTO. Maze Stone County Park, just NW, contains a noted 15,000-year-old petrograph in the shape of a maze.

HemisFair Plaza commercial redevelopment and public space in San Antonio, Texas, immediately SE of Downtown and just E of the San Antonio R. It was created for the 1968 San Antonio World's Fair (HemisFair) by removing 92 ac/37 ha of substandard housing. Its elements include the Henry B. Gonzalez Convention Center, the Institute of Texan Cultures, the Mexican Cultural Institute (connected with the University of Mexico), and the 750-ft/230-m Tower of the Americas, a needlelike structure that dominates the city's skyline. A water park surrounds the tower. The Alamodome, an enclosed arena seating 65,000 for sports and other events, joined these in 1993.

Hempstead in New York: **a.** village, pop. 49,453, in Nassau Co., on Long Island, 22 mi/35 km E of Manhattan. Primarily residential, it is also the terminus of many bus lines and a retail center, although its importance as a shopping district has declined as malls have been built in other Long Island areas. Hempstead was founded in 1643 by settlers from Connecticut seeking religious freedom; it was part of QUEENS Co. until 1899, when Nassau Co. was formed. It is the seat of Hofstra University. **b.** town, pop. 725,639, including Hempstead village, Rockville Centre, Freeport, Levittown, and numerous other New York suburbs, extending from the Queens Co. line (W) to Oyster Bay town, almost at the Suffolk Co. line (E).

Henderson **1.** city, pop. 25,945, seat of Henderson Co., NW Kentucky, on bluffs S of the Ohio R., 7 mi/11 km SSW of Evansville, Indiana. It was founded in 1797 by the TRANSYLVANIA Co. Its economy depends on corn, soybeans, livestock, and tobacco as well as oil, coal, plastics, and chemicals. Thoroughbred and harness racing occurs at Ellis Park and Riverside Downs. John James Audubon operated a general store here (1810–19), in the period of his first bird drawings. John James Audubon State Park, just NE, memorializes him. **2.** city, pop. 64,942, Clark Co., SE Nevada, a suburb 11 mi/18 km SE of Las Vegas. Nevada's chief industrial center, it was established during World War II to house employees at a huge government magnesium plant. In 1951 the plant was converted to titanium production. Other products made here include various commercial and defense chemicals, such as chlorine, hydrogen, and ammonium perchlorate. Insecticides and jet and rocket fuels are also produced. Henderson benefits from tourism in the nearby Lake MEAD National Recreational Area and also has a large residential component. **3.** town, pop. 1268, Jefferson Co., N New York, 58 mi/93 km N of Syracuse. Railroad magnate Mark Hopkins (1813) and George W. Peck, the creator of "Peck's bad boy" (1840) were born here. In the village of **Henderson Harbor,** on a sheltered bay of L. Ontario, American gunners during the War of 1812 tried to pin down British troops on Horse I., off SACKETS HARBOR. The area is known for its sport and commercial fishing and lakeside state parks. **4.** city, pop. 15,655, seat of Vance Co., N North Carolina, 36 mi/58 km NE of Durham. In the bright leaf tobacco belt, it has manufactured tobacco and cotton products, fertilizer, flour, and trucks, and is home to a regional discount store chain. **5.** city, pop. 4760, seat of Chester Co., SW Tennessee, 16 mi/26 km SE of Jackson, near the South Fork of the Forked Deer R. Freed-Hardeman College was established in 1908 in this agricultural trade center. **6.** city, pop. 11,139, seat of Rusk Co., E Texas, 31 mi/50 km ESE of Tyler. Settled in 1844, it is in a cattle, cotton, and oil producing area. It has some light industry and is the seat of the Texas Baptist Institute.

Hendersonville **1.** city, pop. 7284, seat of Henderson Co., SW North Carolina, in the Blue Ridge Mts., 20 mi/32 km SSE of Asheville. A resort and retirement community in an agricultural area noted for its apples, it is surrounded by small lakes and streams. It has a variety of light industries. Flat Rock, 3 mi/5 km SSE, is another resort community, noted for its playhouse and as the home (1945–67) of Carl Sandburg. **2.** city, pop. 32,188, Sumner Co., NC Tennessee, a growing, largely residential suburb 13 mi/21 km NE of downtown Nashville, on Old Hickory L. (the Cumberland R.).

Henlopen, Cape promontory at the S side of the entrance to DELAWARE BAY, overlooking the Atlantic Ocean in Sussex Co., SE Delaware. Breakwaters protect the harbors W of the cape and a ferry crosses the bay from LEWES, just SW, to Cape May, New Jersey. The 3037-ac/1230-ha **Cape Henlopen State Park** is noted for its sand dunes.

Hennepin County 541 sq mi/1401 sq km, pop. 1,032,431, in EC Minnesota, bordered by the Mississippi R. (E), the Crow R. (NW), and the Minnesota R. (SE). The most populous county in the state, it includes Minneapolis, its seat, along with the mostly affluent suburbs W of the city. Bloomington, Eden Prairie, Edina, St. Louis Park, and Minnetonka are among the many communities here. L. Minnetonka is in the W. The county includes Minneapolis–St. Paul International Airport and FORT SNELLING.

Henniker town, pop. 4151, Merrimack Co., SC New Hampshire. It is on the Contoocook R., 15 mi/24 km W of Concord. New England College (1946) is here; Pat's Peak Ski Area is just S of the center. The town is also a summer resort, and produces dairy products, poultry, lumber, paper, wood products, and yarn. The composer Mrs. H.H.A. Beach (1867–1944) was born in Henniker.

Henning town, pop. 802, Lauderdale Co., W Tennessee, 47 mi/76 km NE of Memphis. This cotton-country community was home to Alex Haley, author of *Roots,* much of which was set in the vicinity. The bungalow on Haley St. where he was raised by his grandparents is now the Alex Haley House Museum.

Henrico County 238 sq mi/616 sq km, pop. 217,881, in EC Virginia, between the Chickahominy (N) and James (S) rivers. Its seat is RICHMOND, the state capital. In a rich tobacco and livestock raising area, the county is now largely occupied by suburbs. There are numerous Civil War sites.

Henry, Cape promontory overlooking the Atlantic Ocean S of the entrance to CHESAPEAKE BAY, in Virginia Beach, SE Virginia. Fort Story military installation is located on the cape, and the Cape Henry Memorial commemorates the first landing (April 26, 1607) of the Jamestown settlers.

Henry County 824 sq mi/2134 sq km, pop. 51,159, in WC Illinois, bordered by the Rock R. (NW). Cambridge is its seat. The Green R. and Hennepin Canal flow through the N section, emptying into the Rock R. Kewanee and Geneseo are the largest cities. There has been a great deal of suburban growth in the NW, just beyond the cities of Moline and E. Moline. Most of the county is agricultural, with hogs and corn the main products. Johnson Sauk Trail State Park is NE of Kewanee, and Bishop Hill Historic Site is in the S.

Hercules city, pop. 16,829, Contra Costa Co., NC California, just S of San Pablo Bay, 15 mi/24 km NNE of Oakland. Founded in 1869 to make dynamite for California's mines, it has grown rapidly as a residential suburb since 1970.

Hereford city, pop. 14,745, seat of Deaf Smith Co., NW Texas, in the PANHANDLE, 42 mi/68 km SW of Amarillo. A cattle feedlot center on the LLANO ESTACADO, it also manufactures bricks and fertilizer, and has meatpacking and printing plants and a beet-sugar refinery. Buffalo L. National Wildlife Refuge is 17 mi/27 km NE.

Heritage USA see under FORT MILL, South Carolina.

Herkimer town, pop. 10,401, seat of Herkimer Co., NC New York, on the Mohawk R., 13 mi/21 km SE of Utica. Settled by German Palatines c.1725, it was attacked repeatedly during the French and Indian Wars. Later, Revolutionary troops under Gen. Nicholas Herkimer, garrisoned at its Fort Dayton, were ambushed at Oriskany (1777). In the 19th century Herkimer boomed as a knitting and paper mill center, and was the site of the development of wood pulp paper (1865). A trial here was the inspiration for Theodore Dreiser's *An American Tragedy* (1925). Today Herkimer forms an economic unit with neighboring Mohawk, Ilion, and Frankfort, producing such goods as clothing, metal products, and office furniture.

Herkimer County 1416 sq mi/3667 sq km, pop. 65,797, in NC New York, extending from the Mohawk Valley (S) to the Adirondack Mts. (N). Its seat is Herkimer. The WC portion is close to the Utica city limits, and has had some suburban development. There is industry in municipalities along the Mohawk R., which cuts the county from E to W, principally in Frankfort, Ilion, Herkimer, and Mohawk. The fertile Mohawk Valley produces many crops and dairy cattle. The N portion contains a number of mountain and lake resorts.

Herlong locality in Plumas Co., NE California, just E of the Sierra Nevada and 45 mi/72 km NNW of Reno, Nevada. The Sierra Army Depot, embracing 13 mi/21 km–wide Honey L., is here.

Hermann Park municipal park in Houston, Texas, 3.5 mi/6 km SW of Downtown, along Main St. (NW) and Brays Bayou (S). Begun with land donated by George Hermann in 1914, it now covers 545 ac/221 ha, is home to Houston's zoo, and is the city's most important public park. The TEXAS MEDICAL CENTER adjoins (SW), and Rice University is W across Main St.

Hermiston city, pop. 10,040, Umatilla Co., NE Oregon, 28 mi/45 km WNW of Pendleton. It is part of a fertile farming area created by the Umatilla Irrigation Project. Hermiston is now particularly known for its watermelons and honey. It is also a center for recreational activity on the Columbia R., 5 mi/8 km to the N. Cold Springs National Wildlife Refuge and Reservoir lie 4 mi/6 km to the E.

Hermitage city, pop. 15,300, Mercer Co., NW Pennsylvania, 2 mi/3 km E of Sharon and 4 mi/6 km E of the Ohio border. Its Hillcrest Memorial Park houses the Avenue of 444 Flags, a commemoration of the American hostages in Tehran of 1979–81, and the American Freedom Museum.

Hermitage, the historic estate in Davidson Co., C Tennessee, 12 mi/19 km NE of downtown Nashville, between the Cumberland R. and Stoners Creek. It was the home (after 1804) of President Andrew Jackson. The Greek Revival house (rebuilt in 1836 after a fire) and formal gardens (1819) are part of a 660-ac/267-ha estate, one of the South's leading tourist attractions.

Hermosa Beach city, pop. 18,219, Los Angeles Co., SW California, 12 mi/19 km SW of downtown Los Angeles, in the SOUTH BAY, on the Pacific Ocean. Its 2 mi/3 km of sandy beach are popular with swimmers, surfers, and fishermen, and jazz and rock clubs draw visitors. The city has some light manufactures.

Herndon town, pop. 16,139, Fairfax Co., N Virginia, 20 mi/32 km WNW of Washington, D.C. In a formerly agricultural area, it is a growing residential suburb with high-tech and other businesses, many involved with Washington Dulles International Airport, just SW.

Hero Islands in L. Champlain, extreme NW Vermont. With ISLE LA MOTTE and mainland Alburg, they comprise Grand Isle Co., Vermont's smallest (89 sq mi/231 sq km, pop. 5318). North Hero, 12 mi/19 km N–S, is the county seat. South Hero, equal in length but up to 5 mi/8 km wide, includes the towns of Grand Isle and South Hero. Isle la Motte lies NW of North Hero. Ethan Allen died accidentally after an evening in his brother Ebenezer's tavern on what was then Grand Isle, in 1789; subsequently Grand Isle was renamed South Hero, and Isle Longue North Hero, to honor Ethan and Ira Allen. The islands are rural in character, with farms and summer camps. Some residents commute to Burlington.

Herrin city, pop. 10,857, Williamson Co., SC Illinois, 5 mi/8 km NW of Marion. It was a coal mining center from 1895 until after World War II. Today, manufactures include major appliances, containers, upholstery, and clothing. Settled in 1818, the city was the scene of the 1922 Herrin Massacre, where striking miners killed more than 20 nonunion workers. Crab Orchard National Wildlife Refuge is 4 mi/6 km S.

Herr's Island island in the Allegheny R., at the foot of TROY HILL, opposite the STRIP, in Pittsburgh, Pennsylvania. Stockyards and slaughterhouses occupied it for almost a century; cattle were held here en route from Chicago to New York. Today, Herr's I. is a heap of abandoned buildings awaiting redevelopment.

Hershey unincorporated village, pop. 11,860, Dauphin Co., SE Pennsylvania, 15 mi/24 km E of Harrisburg. Founded in 1903, it was developed privately as a workers' community by Hershey Foods, which remains its main employer. In addition to manufacturing chocolate and cocoa products, the company runs Hersheypark, a theme park and zoo. Tourists, who flock to the village, are also attracted by the Hershey Museum, which displays Pennsylvania Dutch artifacts and other materials of local interest.

Hesperia city, pop. 50,418, San Bernardino Co., S California, just N of the San Bernardino Mts., 20 mi/32 km N of San

Bernardino. It is a fast-growing residential suburb SW of Apple Valley.

Hetch Hetchy Reservoir 7 mi/11 km long, in YOSEMITE NATIONAL PARK, EC California. San Francisco draws 85% of its water from Hetch Hetchy, which was impounded by the O'Shaughnessy (or Hetch Hetchy) Dam (1913–38) on the TUOLUMNE R. The 430 ft/131 m–high dam inundated much of the famed Grand Canyon of the Tuolumne, amid controversy. The name Hetch Hetchy comes from a Miwok word for an edible local plant. The 156 mi/251 km–long **Hetch Hetchy Aqueduct** carries the reservoir's water to San Francisco, via Modesto and Fremont.

Hewitt city, pop. 8983, McLennan Co., EC Texas, 9 mi/14 km SSW of Waco, on Interstate 35. It is a light manufacturing and commercial center.

Hewlett unincorporated village, pop. 6620, in Hempstead town, Nassau Co., SE New York, in SW Long Island, just E of the borough of Queens and 7 mi/11 km W of Freeport. It is essentially a residential suburb, one of the FIVE TOWNS.

Hialeah city, pop. 188,004, Dade Co., SE Florida, 5 mi/8 km NW of Miami. It was settled in 1922, at the beginning of the Florida land boom. It has a variety of light manufactures, including clothing, aluminum and electronic products, furniture, plastic goods, building supplies, appliances, transportation equipment, and chemicals. Hialeah's population, which grew rapidly in the 1970s and 1980s, is almost 90% Hispanic, and consists mainly of working-class Cuban immigrants and their families. The city is best known as the home of the gardenlike Hialeah Park Race Track (1931) with its flamingo-filled lake. Just S of Hialeah is the Miami International Airport and just N is Opa-Locka Airport.

Hiawatha National Forest 880,000 ac/356,400 ha, in two sections in the UPPER PENINSULA of Michigan. The E section, N of the Straits of MACKINAC, borders on Whitefish Bay of L. Superior (N). The W section, some 100 mi/160 km distant, extends from L. Superior to L. Michigan (S). The forest owes its name to Longfellow's "Song of Hiawatha" (1855), in which L. Superior is "Gitche Gumee," the "big sea water."

Hibbing city, pop. 18,046, St. Louis Co., NE Minnesota, in the MESABI RANGE, 55 mi/89 km NW of Duluth. Established as a lumber camp (1893), it was found to be situated directly over an iron ore deposit, and the entire town was moved 2 mi/3 km S in 1919–21. The original site became the Hull-Rust Mine, the world's largest open-pit iron ore mine and now a National Historic Landmark. With the exhaustion of the original high-grade hematite deposits, the city continues to mine and process iron-rich taconite. The Greyhound Bus Line was established here to carry miners between Old and New Hibbing during the 1920s. Hibbing also manufactures rubber products, automatic doors, radiators, and other products.

Hickam Air Force Base formerly, **Hickam Field** just SE of PEARL HARBOR and 7 mi/11 km NW of Honolulu, Hawaii. Completed in 1935, it was bombed by Japanese forces on Dec. 7, 1941. It had a 1990 pop. of 6553.

Hickory city, pop. 28,301, Catawba and Burke counties, WC North Carolina, in the Piedmont, near the foothills of the Blue Ridge Mts., on the Catawba R. (dammed 10 mi/16 km NE to create Hickory L.), and 45 mi/72 km NW of Charlotte. Founded in 1874, it began to industrialize in 1880 with the establishment of a wagon factory. In 1930, the city annexed West Hickory and Highland. Today, manufactures include furniture as well as textiles, cordage, and electronic components. Hickory is home to Lenoir-Rhyne College (1891) and to a community college.

Hickory Hills village, pop. 13,021, Cook Co., NE Illinois, a residential suburb 15 mi/24 km SW of Chicago. A large slough-filled forest preserve lies directly W.

Hickory Nut Falls see under CHIMNEY ROCK, North Carolina.

Hicksville unincorporated village, pop. 40,174, in Oyster Bay town, Nassau Co., SE New York, in C Long Island, 6 mi/10 km ENE of Mineola and 25 mi/40 km E of Manhattan. It is a retailing and transportation hub for Long Island, with some light manufacturing (electronic devices, paper products, and photographic equipment) and advertising and other businesses. Hicksville developed in the second half of the 19th century after Valentine Hicks arranged to have the Long Island Rail Road pass through the area; it remained largely agricultural until the suburban boom that followed World War II.

Hidalgo County 1569 sq mi/4064 sq km, pop. 383,545, in extreme S Texas, on the Rio Grande (S). This winter resort and farming area produces a large percentage of the state's citrus crop. Vegetable and cotton farming and livestock ranching are also significant, as is the processing of regional crops and stock. There are gas and oil refineries, clay mines, and brick and tile works. The county seat is EDINBURG. Other important municipalities include MCALLEN, MISSION, PHARR, and MERCEDES.

Hidden Hills see under SAN FERNANDO VALLEY, California.

High Arctic term loosely used for the ARCTIC ARCHIPELAGO of the Northwest Territories, as opposed to the mainland or Low Arctic. It is an area characterized by little precipitation and a very short growing season, its vegetation chiefly mosses, lichens, and severely dwarfed plant species. Muskoxen, caribou, smaller mammals, and waterfowl dominate animal life. The term may owe something to the idea of high (over about 70° N) latitudes.

High Bridge oldest surviving bridge between Manhattan I., New York, and any other part of the city. It was built 1837–48 as part of the Croton Aqueduct system, over the Harlem R. between what is now the High Bridge (or Highbridge) section of the Bronx, and Washington Heights, Manhattan. It passes above High Bridge Park, along Manhattan's E shoreline. Its original stone arches were replaced by a steel span in 1923 to allow ships to pass through the Harlem R.

High Desert **1.** California term for the MOJAVE DESERT, N and E of Los Angeles, as distinguished from the COLORADO, or Low, Desert to the SE. **2.** also, **High Desert Country** arid region, much of EC and SE Oregon, S of the BLUE Mts. and covering large parts of Baker, Crook, Grant, Harney, Lake, and Malheur counties. With its many craters, the terrain is said to resemble a moonscape.

Highland **1.** city, pop. 34,439, San Bernardino Co., S California, in the foothills of the San Bernardino Mts., just E of San Bernardino, of which it is a growing, largely residential suburb. **2.** town, pop. 23,696, Lake Co., extreme NW Indiana, in the industrial CALUMET area, on the Little Calumet R., near Chicago and the Illinois border, 7 mi/11 km S of L. Michigan. Settled in 1848 on a Potawatomi trail, it is a primarily residential community of one-family homes. Among the products made by its factories are metal goods and cement blocks.

Highland Heights city, pop. 4223, Campbell Co., N Kentucky, 8 mi/13 km SSE of Cincinnati, Ohio. Northern Kentucky University (1968) is in this residential suburb.

Highland Lakes see under L. BUCHANAN, Texas.

Highland Park **1.** section of Los Angeles, California, between Elysian Park (SW) and South Pasadena (E), 3 mi/5 km NE of Downtown. Founded during the 1880s real estate boom, it became the first area annexed to the city of Los Angeles. Today, it is an ethnically diverse middle-class community. The Southwest Museum, Heritage Square, and Occidental College (1887) are here. **2.** city, pop. 30,575, Lake Co., NE Illinois, on L. Michigan, a residential suburb 25 mi/40 km N of Chicago. The Ravinia Music Festival, summer home of the Chicago Symphony Orchestra, is a 36-ac/15-ha facility originally created (1905) as an amusement park. Settled in 1834, Highland Park was established as a wealthy suburb by the turn of the 20th century. **3.** city, pop. 20,121, Wayne Co., SE Michigan, a residential and industrial suburb surrounded by Detroit. It was the site of Henry Ford's original Model T mass-production plant (1910). Production ended when the model was discontinued, and most operations moved to DEARBORN. There is still a Ford tractor plant here. It was the headquarters of the Chrysler Corporation from 1925 until its move to AUBURN HILLS in the early 1990s. This move and the general decline in the US automobile industry caused the city severe economic distress in the 1980s and 1990s. Highland Park Community College (1918) is here. **4.** residential neighborhood in St. Paul, Minnesota, SW of Downtown, MACALASTER-GROVELAND, and Summit Ave. This affluent community sits on a bluff overlooking the Mississippi R. **5.** borough, pop. 13,279, Middlesex Co., EC New Jersey, across the Raritan R. (NE) from New Brunswick. It was settled (1667) on the site of an Indian village. A Revolutionary War skirmish between the troops of Washington and Cornwallis took place here. Primarily residential, Highland Park has a printing plant and manufactures metal products and candy. **6.** see under EAST NEW YORK, New York. **7.** 360-ac/146-ha municipal park and adjacent residential neighborhood in the EAST END of Pittsburgh, Pennsylvania, 5.5 mi/9 km NE of the GOLDEN TRIANGLE and immediately N of East Liberty. An affluent residential community cut off from other areas on three sides, it was named for the Chicago suburb. The Pittsburgh Zoo is located in the park, N of the neighborhood. **8.** town, pop. 8739, Dallas Co., NE Texas. Adjacent (S) to UNIVERSITY PARK, this affluent residential community, 4 mi/6 km N of downtown Dallas, is otherwise bounded on all sides by the city.

Highland Rim see under NASHVILLE BASIN, Tennessee.

Highlands, the exclusive residential community 10 mi/16 km NNW of downtown SEATTLE, Washington, just outside the city line, on Puget Sound (W). It has private roads, private schools, and the private Seattle Golf Club.

Highland Springs unincorporated village, pop. 13,823, Henrico Co., EC Virginia, 6 mi/10 km E of Richmond. It is a residential suburb, set in an area much fought over in the Civil War; FAIR OAKS is just SE.

High Park see under BLOOR St., Toronto, Ontario.

High Plains see under GREAT PLAINS.

High Point **1.** highest elevation in New Jersey (1803 ft/550 m), on KITTATINNY Mt., in Sussex Co., 4 mi/6 km SE of Port Jervis, New York. Situated in High Point State Park, it has views of three states, and is the site of the New Jersey War Memorial, a 225-ft/69-m stone tower. **2.** city, pop. 69,496, Guilford Co. (also in Davidson, Randolph, and Forsyth counties), NC North Carolina. Settled around 1750 by Quakers, it was an agricultural (chiefly tobacco) center until the 1880s, when furniture production became the focus of its economy. Part of the Piedmont Triad, with Greensboro and Winston-Salem, it remains one of the world's leading furniture manufacturing centers. It also makes hosiery, paint, chemicals, and machinery. High Point College (1924) is here.

High River town, pop. 6269, SW Alberta, on the Highwood R., 34 mi/55 km S of Calgary. Surrounded by cattle ranches and wheat fields, it has always been an agricultural center. Founded in the 1880s by ranchers, it emerged as a shipping point for cattle after the arrival (1892) of the Canadian Pacific Railway.

High Rock Lake see under YADKIN R., North Carolina.

High Sierra see under SIERRA NEVADA, California.

Hightstown borough, pop. 5126, Mercer Co., WC New Jersey, 11 mi/18 km NE of Trenton, and just W of the New Jersey Turnpike. Settled in 1721, it is a trade center for local truck farms, the site of some light industry, and the seat of Peddie School (1864).

Highway see also entries at US and ROUTE.

Highway 61 major S–N highway, now replaced in sections by superhighways, that runs along the Mississippi R. from New Orleans, Louisiana, through Baton Rouge; Natchez, Mississippi; Memphis, Tennessee; St. Louis, Missouri; Davenport and Dubuque, Iowa; Minneapolis and Duluth, Minnesota; and N along L. Superior into Ontario. It is best known as the route from the Mississippi Delta into Memphis, where it becomes Third St., and then N in the direction of Chicago.

Hi-Line shortgrass prairie region, NC to NW Montana. The GREAT NORTHERN RAILWAY developed the area, named it for the state's northernmost line, and competed with the Union Pacific by enticing immigrants to free farmland here to keep its trains filled. The Hi-Line extends from Glacier National park to E of the Fort Belknap Indian Reservation, and from the Sun and Missouri rivers to Canada. This region of windswept, glaciated plains and shallow valleys is traversed by US Route 2. Its largest city is HAVRE.

Hill, the **1.** see under CAPITOL HILL, Washington, D.C. **2.** largely residential section S of I-44 and W of TOWER GROVE PARK, in C SAINT LOUIS, Missouri, 1 mi/1.5 km WSW of Downtown, home since the late 19th century to many of the city's Italian inhabitants, and now a popular restaurant district. **3.** see PARLIAMENT HILL, Ottawa, Ontario. **4.** group of residential neighborhoods on a plateau in Pittsburgh, Pennsylvania, between the GOLDEN TRIANGLE and OAKLAND. Divided into the LOWER HILL, MIDDLE HILL, and UPPER HILL, the area has long been a point of entry for those arriving in the area. The city's original black community was located here in the 1700s, while Scotch-Irish and Germans predominated for most of the following century. Starting in the 1880s, Jewish Central and Eastern Europeans arrived, followed by Southern blacks in World War II. Wylie Ave. is one of the Hill's major commercial streets.

Hill Air Force Base see under CLEARFIELD, Utah.

Hillandale unincorporated residential suburb, pop. 10,318, Montgomery and Prince George's counties, C Maryland, 9 mi/14 km NNE of Washington, D.C., just outside the BELTWAY. The Naval Surface Weapons Test Center adjoins (N).

Hill Country variously defined region of SC Texas, NW of the

BALCONES ESCARPMENT and drained by the Colorado and Guadalupe rivers and their tributaries. To the NW of San Antonio, it includes FREDERICKSBURG, KERRVILLE, the PEDERNALES R., and the LBJ Ranch. Recreational areas include a number of caverns and major springs. This rugged SE part of the EDWARDS PLATEAU was settled largely by Germans, Czechs, and other Central Europeans in the mid 19th century; its economy has centered on raising sheep, goats, and cattle. Today, tourism is increasingly important.

Hillcrest residential and commercial section of San Diego, California, 1.5 mi/2 km N of Downtown. One of the city's original suburbs, it is today the center of its gay community. The UPTOWN district is at its E edge.

Hillcrest Heights unincorporated residential suburb, pop. 17,136, Prince George's Co., SC Maryland, 6 mi/10 km SE of Washington, D.C., just inside the BELTWAY. It is an area of housing developments and shopping malls just S of Suitland-Silver Hills.

Hill Cumorah see under PALMYRA, New York.

Hilliard city, pop. 11,796, Franklin Co., C Ohio, a residential suburb 10 mi/16 km NW of Columbus, in an agricultural region. Grain, vegetables, and livestock long formed the basis of the local economy.

Hillsboro **1.** city, pop. 2704, Marion Co., EC Kansas, 40 mi/64 km S of Abilene. It was settled in the late 1870s by German Mennonite farmers emigrating from Russia and Poland. The city is now a trade hub in a wheat, corn, and livestock producing area. Tabor College (1908) is here. The Marion L. reservoir and dam are nearby (NE). **2.** residential town, pop. 4498, Hillsborough Co., S New Hampshire. The town, which includes Hillsboro village, is on the Contoocook R., 20 mi/32 km WSW of Concord. Hillsboro is a small commercial and agricultural center producing textiles, clothing, lumber, dairy products, poultry, and livestock. US President Franklin Pierce was born (1804) in Hillsboro. The Pierce Homestead, his childhood home, is between Upper and Lower Hillsboro villages, near Franklin Pierce L. **3.** city, pop. 6235, seat of Highland Co., SW Ohio, 54 mi/87 km E of Cincinnati and 32 mi/52 km WSW of Chillicothe, on a high plateau. The Women's Temperance Crusade was founded here in 1873. Today Hillsboro is a highway junction and trade center for the surrounding region, which depends on dairy, grain, and tobacco farming. Local manufactures include foundry products, farm machinery, and clothing. Limestone is quarried in the area. Several mound builder forts are nearby. Rocky Fork State Park at Rocky Fork L. is 4 mi/6 km SE. **4.** city, pop. 37,520, seat of Washington Co., NW Oregon, 13 mi/21 km W of Portland. Settled in 1841, it is the processing, packaging, and shipping center of a rich farming region known for its filberts, apples, wheat, and dairy products. High-tech industries are also based in the city. Wineries are numerous in the surrounding area.

Hillsborough **1.** town, pop. 10,667, San Mateo Co., NC California, adjacent (NW) to San Mateo and 14 mi/23 km S of San Francisco. It is a residential suburb on the E side of the SAN ANDREAS FAULT. **2.** also, **Hillsboro** town, pop. 4263, seat of Orange Co., NC North Carolina, on the Eno R., 11 mi/18 km WNW of Durham. Laid out in 1754 on the site of various prehistoric settlements, it was a 1768 center of the Regulator uprising against British authority. During the Revolution, the provincial assembly met here, and in 1781, Cornwallis occupied the town before the battle of Guilford Courthouse. Hillsborough today draws on its past to attract tourism. It also has furniture and other industries.

Hillsborough Bay **1.** see under TAMPA BAY, Florida. **2.** up to 12 mi/20 km E–W, and 9 mi/14 km wide, in SE Prince Edward Island. The **Hillsborough R.,** 30 mi/48 km long, rises in Kings Co. and flows 17 mi/27 km SW to CHARLOTTETOWN, where, known as the East R., it joins the North (Yorke) and West (Eliot) rivers to form Charlottetown Harbour. All three are estuarial, and connect (SE) with the bay, which contains St. Peters, Governors, and smaller islands. Rice Point marks its W edge, and Point Prim, on the E, has a lighthouse. The Fort Amherst/Port La Joye National Historic Site, on the NW shore, across from Charlottetown, marks the first European settlement on Prince Edward Island, established by the French in 1720 and captured by the British in 1758. Pownal and Orwell bays, on the E, are Hillsborough Bay's largest inlets.

Hillsborough County **1.** 1053 sq mi/2727 sq km, pop. 834,054, in WC Florida, on Hillsborough, Old Tampa, and Tampa bays (W). Its seat and largest city is TAMPA. Its W section is dominated by the city and the bays, with port activities, some industry and business, tourism, fishing, and shrimping all sharing in importance. The balance of the county, including its only other large municipality, PLANT CITY (NE) is largely agricultural. Citrus fruits, berries and vegetables, dairy goods, and poultry are produced throughout the lake-filled county. There is some forestry and phosphate mining, particularly in the N. **2.** 876 sq mi/2269 sq km, pop. 336,073, in S New Hampshire. Manchester is the county seat. A leading industrial county, Hillsborough produces shoes, textiles, wood products, paper, tools, and machinery. It has granite quarries, lumbering operations, resorts, and dairy, poultry, and livestock farms. The Contoocook, Piscataquog, Souhegan, Merrimack, and Nashua rivers provide waterpower. Hillsborough is New Hampshire's most populous county, home to almost a third of the state's residents.

Hillsdale **1.** city, pop. 8170, seat of Hillsdale Co., S Michigan, on Baw Beese L. and the St. Joseph R., 25 mi/40 km SSW of Jackson. This trade and manufacturing center, founded in 1834, makes auto and airplane parts, food products, and brooms. It is a center for year-round recreation on the surrounding 350 lakes, and the seat of Hillsdale College (1844). Indian mounds are nearby. **2.** borough, pop. 9750, Bergen Co., NE New Jersey, 9 mi/14 km N of Hackensack, on Pascack Brook. Primarily residential, it is also an agricultural trade center.

Hillside township, pop. 21,044, Union Co., NE New Jersey, adjacent (W and NW) to Elizabeth and Newark. Its many manufactures include metal castings, tools, paper and cork products, processed foods, and insulated wire. It is also a residential suburb.

Hilltop city, pop. 749, Anoka Co., SE Minnesota, 5 mi/8 km N of downtown Minneapolis. It is an affluent residential community.

Hilo unincorporated community, pop. 37,808, seat of Hawaii Co., Hawaii, on the NE coast of the island of Hawaii, on Hilo Bay, 200 mi/322 km SE of Honolulu. A former whaling port on a deepwater harbor, it is the island's shipping and service center and principal seaport. It is also a tourist base for HAWAII VOLCANOES NATIONAL PARK (SW). The rainy, tropical climate fosters a thriving orchid and anthurium industry.

Hilo has bulk sugar loading facilities, and exports also include macadamia nuts and cattle. A branch (1970) of the University of Hawaii is here.

Hilshire Village see under HUNTERS CREEK VILLAGE, Texas.

Hilton Head Island 42 sq mi/109 sq km, one of the SEA ISLANDS, in Beaufort Co., extreme S South Carolina, on the Atlantic Ocean (SE), the Atlantic Intracoastal Waterway (W) and Port Royal Sound (NE), 20 mi/32 km NE of Savannah, Georgia. It is a town with a pop. of 23,694. European settlements were attempted by the Spanish (1526), French, and English, but all were deterred by hostile natives and local pirates. Chartered by William Hilton (1663), it became an 18th-century center for English indigo, rice, and Sea Island (long-staple) cotton plantations. During the Civil War, the island was a Union base for blockading nearby Confederate ports. After the war, it was largely occupied by freed slaves, who developed their distinctive Gullah culture. A bridge to the mainland was built in 1956, and recreational development followed. Today there are four main resort communities, many smaller ones, and major facilities for golf, tennis, boating, and other activities. During the peak season, the population swells with over 50,000 tourists. Wildlife preserves here include the Sea Pines Forest Preserve and Audubon Newhall Preserve.

Hinckley Reservation 2288 ac/927 ha, in Hinckley township, Medina Co., NE Ohio, 30 mi/48 km S of Cleveland. The rocky, heavily forested reserve is the southernmost of Cleveland's Metroparks and the only one not in Cuyahoga Co. The reservation, which includes Hinckley L., is best known for the migratory turkey buzzards that summer here. The birds return in late March, and their arrival is celebrated in an annual Buzzard Sunday, attended by thousands of visitors.

Hinds County 875 sq mi/2266 sq km, pop. 254,441, in WC Mississippi, bordered by the Pearl R. (E) and the Big Black R. (NW). It is by far the most populous county in the state, with dual seats at JACKSON (the state capital) and RAYMOND. Jackson, Mississippi's largest city, is in the NE, with a metropolitan area that stretches W and S; its many industries and commercial activities dominate the county's economy. There are extensive timber resources in the rest of the county, and cotton, vegetables, cattle, and poultry are produced, processed, and shipped.

Hinesville city, pop. 21,603, seat of Liberty Co., SE Georgia, just S of Fort Stewart and 30 mi/48 km ESE of Savannah. The area produces timber and tobacco.

Hingham town, pop. 19,821, Plymouth Co., E Massachusetts, on Hingham Bay, 19 mi/31 km SE of Boston. It was settled in the 1630s. HULL lies N, between Hingham and the Atlantic. A thriving center of fishing, boatbuilding, and manufacturing until after the Civil War, Hingham has some light industry but is primarily a residential suburb, with a high proportion of parkland. Old Ship Church (1681) is considered the only church remaining from the Puritan period in Massachusetts.

Hinsdale village, pop. 16,029, Cook and Du Page counties, NE Illinois, 15 mi/24 km SW of Chicago. It is a residential community, settled in 1840.

Hinton town, pop. 9046, WC Alberta, in the Rocky Mt. foothills, near the Athabasca R., 168 mi/270 km W of Edmonton. Originally a coal center, it still has three mines. The first pulp mill in the province is here. Hinton serves as the N gateway to Jasper National Park (14 mi/23 km W).

Hiram village, pop. 1329, Portage Co., NE Ohio, 23 mi/37 km NE of Akron. Situated in hilly dairy land and orchard country, it is the seat of Hiram College (1850).

Historic South Side residential neighborhood on the SOUTH SIDE of Milwaukee, Wisconsin, 2 mi/3 km S of Downtown and immediately S of WALKER'S POINT. It forms the heart of the original community of Polish immigrants who settled here around the turn of the century. Today, the area is home to Italians, Hispanics, blacks, and others. The KINNICKINNIC PARKWAY runs through the SW corner of the area.

Hobart city, pop. 21,822, Lake Co., extreme NW Indiana, in the highly industrialized CALUMET area, near L. Michigan and adjoining (SE) GARY. It is largely a residential community for those working in surrounding cities. Its industries produce diversified goods including aluminum products, welding equipment, tools, and castings. Located within Hobart, 3 mi/5 km–long L. George is a recreational hub.

Hobbs city, pop. 29,115, Lea Co., SE New Mexico, in the High Plains, 2 mi/3 km W of the Texas border and 80 mi/130 km NW of Midland. Surrounded by irrigated farms and ranches, the city grew dramatically after the 1928 discovery here of oil and natural gas. It is the state's petroleum center. There are also potash deposits to the SW. The College of the Southwest (1956) and New Mexico Junior College (1965) are here.

Hobby Field see WILLIAM P. HOBBY AIRPORT, Houston, Texas.

Hobe Sound unincorporated community, pop. 11,507, Martin Co., SE Florida, just off the Atlantic Ocean, 20 mi/32 km NNW of West Palm Beach. It is an affluent resort community. The 1000-ac/400-ha Hobe Sound National Wildlife Refuge lies just NW along JUPITER I., the barrier island enclosing Hobe Sound.

Hobkirk Hill also, **Hobkirk's** battle site: see under CAMDEN, South Carolina.

Hoboken city, pop. 33,397, Hudson Co., New Jersey, on the Hudson R. opposite downtown Manhattan, and adjoining (NE) Jersey City. It is in an area called Hobocan Hackingh ("tobacco-pipe-land") by the Lenni Lenape (Delaware), from whom it was purchased (1630) by the Dutch. The land changed hands often before it was acquired (1784) by inventor John Stevens, who laid out the town (1804). Stevens initiated a steam ferry between Hoboken and New York in 1811, and the town soon became an amusement center for New Yorkers. The first organized baseball game was held here (1846) at Elysian Fields. Later in the century, the city developed as a trading and manufacturing hub. With its large waterfront, it became a major port, but fell into disrepair after the 1950s; redevelopment began in the 1990s. Hoboken is also an important rail terminal and office center. Its manufactures include machinery, electronic parts, chemicals, processed foods, and precision instruments. The city's restored brownstones, apartment houses, and riverfront condominium towers house many New York commuters. Stevens Institute of Technology (1870) is here.

Hochelaga palisaded Iroquoian village visited by Jacques Cartier in 1535 at the E foot of Mount ROYAL, in what is now MONTRÉAL, Québec. By the early 17th century, when French explorers returned, it had disappeared. Its site was roughly where McGill University is today. The islands here at the confluence of the St. Lawrence and Ottawa rivers, the largest the I. de Montréal and I. Jésus (see LAVAL), are called collectively the **Hochelaga Archipelago.** The former village of Hochelaga, E of Blvd. SAINT-LAURENT, was the first (1883) of numerous small communities annexed by the city at the end of the 19th century.

Hocking County 423 sq mi/1096 sq km, pop. 25,533, in SC Ohio; it is intersected by the Hocking R. Its seat is Logan, where there is some manufacturing. The rest of the county is largely woodland with some farming (dairy, grain, and livestock) as well as coal mining. Clay, gravel, and sand are also exploited.

Hocking River 100 mi/160 km long, in Ohio. It rises in Fairfield Co., then flows SE past Lancaster, Logan, Nelsonville, and Athens to join the Ohio R. in Athens Co., 13 mi/21 km SW of Parkersburg, West Virginia.

Hodgenville see under ABRAHAM LINCOLN BIRTHPLACE NATIONAL HISTORIC SITE, Kentucky.

Hodgkins village, pop. 1963, Cook Co., NE Illinois, on the Des Plaines R., a suburb 8 mi/13 km W of Chicago.

Hoffman Estates village, pop. 46,561, Cook Co., NE Illinois, a suburb 25 mi/40 km NW of Chicago. This residential community was founded in 1959. During the 1980s, there was a boom in commercial development along I-90, the Northwest Tollway, which runs through the N half of the village. The outdoor Poplar Creek Music Theatre is here.

Hogback Mountain peak (3226 ft/984 m) of the Blue Ridge Mts., 6 mi/10 km W of Landrum, Spartanburg Co., South Carolina, near the North Carolina border.

Hogtown see under TORONTO, Ontario.

Holbrook **1.** city, pop. 4686, seat of Navajo Co., NE Arizona, on Interstate 40 and the Little Colorado R., 90 mi/145 km ESE of Flagstaff. The town is a trade center and gateway to the PAINTED DESERT and PETRIFIED FOREST. The Hopi and Navajo reservations lie N. The surrounding area produces livestock, poultry, and dairy goods. A helium field is nearby. Holbrook was founded (1881) with the coming of the Atlantic and Pacific Railroad. **2.** town, pop. 11,041, Norfolk Co., E Massachusetts, a residential suburb 15 mi/24 km SSE of Boston. Originally part of Braintree, it was a 19th-century shoe industry center. BROCKTON lies directly S. **3.** unincorporated village, pop. 25,273, in Islip town, Suffolk Co., SE New York, on Long Island, immediately E of Long Island MacArthur Airport, 5 mi/8 km N of Sayville. It is primarily residential, with some high-tech industry.

Hole in the Mountain Peak see under RUBY Mts., Nevada.

Hole-in-the-Wall locality in Johnson Co., EC Wyoming, 15 mi/24 km SW of Kaycee and 80 mi/128 km SW of Gillette, along the Middle Fork of the POWDER R., in a remote ranching area. A valley with red rock walls, it was an 1880s hideout for the outlaw Wild Bunch, including Butch Cassidy and the SUNDANCE Kid.

Holiday unincorporated community, pop. 19,360, Pasco Co., WC Florida, 20 mi/32 km NW of Tampa, a Gulf Coast resort community.

Holladay-Cottonwood unincorporated community, pop. 14,095, Salt Lake Co., NC Utah, a residential suburb 8 mi/13 km SE of downtown Salt Lake City. Cottonwood Heights (unincorporated, pop. 28,766), immediately S, and Cottonwood West (unincorporated, pop. 17,476) are other parts of the suburban zone E of I-15 and W of the WASATCH RANGE.

Holland city, pop. 30,745, Ottawa and Allegan counties, SW Michigan, on L. Macatawa just off L. Michigan, 25 mi/40 km SW of Grand Rapids. Religious secessionists from the Netherlands settled the site in 1847. It became a magnet for more Dutch immigrants, who first worked at lumbering, then with field crops and poultry. Though it makes furnaces, motors, and boats, Holland is best known for its tulips, tulip bulbs, and annual tulip festival. The Netherlands Museum has exhibits that explore the city's Dutch heritage, celebrated as well at Windmill Island Park and the Dutch Village. Also here are two Dutch Reformed colleges, Hope College (1862) and Western Theological Seminary (1869).

Holland Tunnel automobile tunnel, 1.75 mi/2.8 km long, between Jersey City, New Jersey, and lower Manhattan, New York City. Built 1910–27, it is named for its chief engineer.

Hollins unincorporated community, pop. 13,305, Roanoke and Botetourt counties, SW Virginia, adjacent (N) to ROANOKE. A largely residential suburb, it is the seat of all-female Hollins College (1842).

Hollis residential section, EC Queens, New York, E of Jamaica. It was established in 1884, named for the town of Hollis, New Hampshire, and developed largely in the 1920s.

Hollister city, pop. 19,212, seat of San Benito Co., WC California, in the San Benito Valley, 41 mi/66 km S of San Jose. Its industries include fruit, vegetable, and dairy processing, winemaking, and flower growing. There is a junior college, and the county rodeo, held here since 1907, is well known.

Holliston town, pop. 12,926, Middlesex Co., E Massachusetts, 5 mi/8 km S of Framingham. Founded in 1659 and incorporated in 1724, it is a traditionally agricultural community now increasingly suburban.

Holloman Air Force Base see under ALAMOGORDO, New Mexico.

Holly Hill city, pop. 11,141, Volusia Co., NE Florida, a suburb immediately N of Daytona Beach, on the Halifax R., a lagoon separated from the Atlantic Ocean by a barrier island.

Holly Springs city, pop. 7261, seat of Marshall Co., N Mississippi, 51 mi/82 km SSW of CORINTH and 38 mi/61 km SE of Memphis, Tennessee. It was founded during the 1830s cotton boom, and also had an early iron industry. Holly Springs was strategically important during the Civil War. In 1862 U.S. Grant established a supply depot here for the VICKSBURG campaign; the town was soon retaken by Confederates under Earl Van Dorn. Hotly contested, it was raided 62 times during the war. Although the cotton economy declined later in the 19th century, the city remains an agricultural trade center. Some 90 antebellum homes are preserved here. The city is the seat of Rust College (1866), one of the oldest black liberal arts schools in the US. E.H. Crump (1876–1954), longtime political boss of Memphis, was born nearby.

Holly Springs National Forest 152,000 ac/61,600 ha, in N Mississippi, extending from the Tennessee line SW to near Oxford. Embracing Choctaw sacred ground, it is an oak, pine, and beech forest. Holly Springs, its headquarters, is just NW.

Hollywood **1.** commercial and entertainment district of Los Angeles, California, 6 mi/10 km NW of Downtown and just S of the **Hollywood Hills,** the E extreme of the Santa Monica Mts. and the site of the world-famous HOLLYWOOD (formerly HOLLYWOODLAND) sign. SILVER LAKE lies E. From the 1920s the center of the US film, later of the television, industry, Hollywood still boasts large film company headquarters and such entertainment-related businesses as advertising, talent promotion, cosmetics, and fashion, along with music recording (see TIN PAN ALLEY). Tourism is also important; such attractions as Mann's (formerly Grauman's) Chinese Theatre and the Hollywood Studio Museum in WHITLEY HEIGHTS attract visitors. Laid out in 1887 by prohibitionist Horace Wilcox, the community was annexed to Los Angeles in 1910. The first movie studio was set up one year later; the mild climate, constant sunlight, varied terrain, and abundant labor brought on a heyday that lasted until World War II, after which studios began moving to cheaper areas to the N. Television took over by the 1960s; many of those studios have also left what is now an ethnically and racially diverse section of the city. The renowned **Hollywood Bowl,** an 18,000-seat amphitheater in the hills near CAHUENGA PASS, has hosted outdoor concerts since 1922. Hollywood's contributions to America's fantasy life have earned it the nickname Tinseltown. **2.** city, pop. 121,697, Broward Co., SE Florida, on the Atlantic Ocean, 16 mi/26 km NNE of Miami. It was developed as a resort by a California speculator (hence its name) during the Florida land boom of the 1920s. Its palm-lined beaches, sport fishing, and other recreational activities continue to attract vacationers, and tourism is a major factor in its economy. The city and its environs are also the site of many planned retirement communities. It has such light manufactures as electronic equipment and building materials. Port Everglades, the deepest Atlantic Coast harbor S of Norfolk, Virginia, lies on the boundary with Fort Lauderdale (N), and has extensive docking and warehousing facilities within Hollywood's limits. The city also shares an international airport with Fort Lauderdale.

Hollywood Park see under INGLEWOOD, California.

Holman prison: see under ATMORE, Alabama.

Holmdel township, pop. 11,532, Monmouth Co., EC New Jersey, 15 mi/24 km SE of New Brunswick. Settled in the 1630s, and called Freehold before that name attached to the current borough, it was an orchard and vineyard center. It is now a growing suburb along the Garden State Parkway. AT&T Bell Laboratories, a major communications research facility, is here, as is the Garden State Arts Center, with a 5300-seat amphitheater.

Holmes County 424 sq mi/1098 sq km, pop. 32,849, in EC Ohio, intersected by Killbuck Creek and the Walhonding R. Its seat is Millersburg, where there is some manufacturing. The county is largely rural, with the farming of dairy, grain, and livestock. Natural resources include coal, gravel, and sandstone.

Holston Mountain ridge of the Appalachian Mts., extending SW from Damascus, extreme SW Virginia, into NE Tennessee near ELIZABETHTON. Sometimes considered a subrange of the UNAKA RANGE, it reaches over 4200 ft/1280 m NE of Elizabethton, at a point sometimes referred to as Holston High Knob. The South Fork of the Holston R. lies NW.

Holston River 115 mi/185 km long, in NE Tennessee. It is formed by the confluence of the North Fork and the South Fork just W of KINGSPORT. The **North Fork** (120 mi/190 km long) rises along Brushy Mt. in Bland Co., near Sharon Springs, SW Virginia, and flows SW through Washington and Scott counties into NE Tennessee. The **South Fork** (110 m/180 km long) rises just N of Mt. ROGERS, in S Smyth Co., Virginia, and flows SW into Tennessee. There it is dammed near Emmett, Sullivan Co., to form 14 mi/23 km–long South Holston L., which backs up into Virginia. It continues through Boone L., formed by a dam at Spurgeon. The South Fork receives the **Middle Fork** in S Washington Co., Virginia, at the head of the lake. From Kingsport, the Holston flows SW into 28 mi/45 km–long Cherokee L., formed by the Cherokee Dam, just N of JEFFERSON CITY. It continues SW, to join the FRENCH BROAD R. just above Knoxville, forming the Tennessee R.

Holt unincorporated village, pop. 11,744, Ingham Co., SC Michigan, a residential suburb 6 mi/10 km S of Lansing. The community lies in an agricultural area that produces poultry, grain, livestock, and dairy products.

Holtsville unincorporated village, pop. 14,972, in Brookhaven town, Suffolk Co., SE New York, in C Long Island, 5 mi/8 km N of Patchogue. Primarily residential, it has a processing center for the Internal Revenue Service.

Holy Cross, Mount of the see MOUNT OF THE HOLY CROSS, Colorado.

Holyoke city, pop. 43,704, Hampden Co., WC Massachusetts, on the W bank of the Connecticut R., 8 mi/13 km NW of Springfield. After the completion of the first of several dams in 1829, it developed rapidly. Nicknamed the "Paper City," Holyoke has been a leading producer of paper goods, especially fine stationery; printing, publishing, textiles, and metals have also been important. Holyoke Community College (1966) and the Mt. TOM ski area are in Holyoke; Mt. HOLYOKE, in HADLEY, and Mt. Holyoke College, in SOUTH HADLEY, are both across the Connecticut (E).

Holyoke, Mount 878 ft/268 m, in the town of HADLEY, Hampshire Co., W Massachusetts, at the W end of the Holyoke Range, which extends E–W for c. 8 mi/13 km just E of the Connecticut R. The range is topped by Mt. Norwottock (1106 ft/337 m). Mt. Holyoke College is in SOUTH HADLEY.

Homer **1.** city, pop. 3660, Kenai Peninsula Borough, S Alaska, on Kachemak Bay, an arm of lower COOK INLET, on the SW KENAI PENINSULA, 125 mi/201 km SSW of Anchorage. Established by a prospecting party under Homer Pennock (1896), this ice-free deepwater fishing port developed after neither gold nor coal deposits of any great size were found. Fishing and fish processing are its main industries; it is also a commercial center for a farming area, as well as a tourist center. **2.** town, pop. 6508, Cortland Co., C New York, 3 mi/5 km N of Cortland. Settled in 1791, it contains many historic houses. Homer served as the locale ("Homeville") for Edward Noyes Westcott's novel *David Harum* (1898). Situated in a dairying region, it has gravel pits and a number of small industries, including food canneries. **3.** unincorporated village in Burlington township, Licking Co., C Ohio, 10 mi/16 km S of Mount Vernon. It is the birthplace of the prominent feminist Victoria Claflin Woodhull (1838).

Homestake Mine historic gold mine in the city of Lead (pop. 3632), Lawrence Co., W South Dakota, in the Black Hills, 30 mi/48 km NW of Rapid City. Gold was discovered here during the Black Hills gold rush (1876). Operating almost continuously since its founding, and long the largest US gold mine, with miles of underground tunnels reaching a maximum depth of 8000 ft/2440 m, as well as a myriad of surface mining operations, it is now also a tourist attraction.

homestead part of US PUBLIC LANDS occupied under provisions of the 1862 Homestead Act and subsequent laws. A homesteader, who was an adult head of family, was empowered by the act to occupy 160 ac/65 ha (a quarter section) of land and farm it. A nominal fee was paid; the land was to be farmed for five years, and a home built on it. It would then belong to the homesteader (who could also, after six months, buy it for $1.25/ac, or $3.09/ha). In 1909 320-ac/130-ha tracts in semiarid areas were opened to homesteading, and under the 1916 Stock Raising Homestead Act, a full 640 ac/260 ha could be claimed in marginal areas for ranching. While there were abuses of the system, and much land passed quickly to speculators, the homestead system drew some 1 million claimants, mostly after 1900, and settled large areas of the West. The act had originally been thought likely to draw pioneers from growing Eastern cities (and thus reinforce the Jeffersonian "yeomanry" ideal), but many claimants were Europeans attracted by publicity. In Canada the **Dominion Lands Act** of 1872 was modeled on the US legislation. Both governments, responding to economic change and to perceived abuses of the system, began by World War I to restrict homestead access, turning to forms of leasing and (in Canada) to provincial, rather than Federal, control of lands. Since the 1970s, US laws have encouraged "urban homesteading" by making older existing city housing stock available, at nominal prices, to those who agree to occupy and repair it.

Homestead **1.** city, pop. 26,866, Dade Co., SE Florida, 28 mi/45 km SW of Miami. It lies in Florida's fertile Redlands district, well known for its many fruits (notably citrus and avocados) and vegetables, and is a shipping center for these products. It also manufactures rocket fuel and pharmaceuticals. It is the site of several tropical gardens, and is a gateway to Everglades National Park and to the Florida Keys. The city is a service center for **Homestead Air Force Base** (1942), 4 mi/6 km to the E. Both city and base, which was slated to close shortly, suffered catastrophic damage from Hurricane Andrew in Aug. 1992. **2.** borough, pop. 4179, Allegheny Co., SW Pennsylvania, on the Monongahela R., an industrial suburb 6 mi/10 km SE of Pittsburgh. Bessemer Steel built blast furnaces and a mill in Homestead in 1881, creating a company town at the heart of a regional steelmaking complex. The columns and beams used in the EMPIRE STATE BUILDING were produced at the plant. An unsuccessful 1892 strike by the steelworkers' union and attack by management-hired Pinkerton agents resulted in 72 deaths. The area of the plant is now part of neighboring (SE) MUNHALL.

Homestead National Monument see under BEATRICE, Nebraska.

Homeville see under HOMER, New York.

Homewood **1.** city, pop. 22,922, Jefferson Co., C Alabama, 2 mi/3 km SSE of downtown Birmingham, of which it is a primarily residential suburb. **2.** village, pop. 19,278, Cook Co., NE Illinois, a suburb 23 mi/37 km S of Chicago. A residential community, it also has some book publishing operations. The village was laid out in 1852. **3.** residential neighborhood in Pittsburgh, Pennsylvania, N of Wilkinsburg and 6 mi/10 km NE of the GOLDEN TRIANGLE. Home to Irish immigrants and blacks in the 19th century, it underwent severe social and economic dislocation following World War II. Relocating that displaced LOWER HILL residents during the 1950s contributed to overcrowding here, leading to eventual population loss, housing abandonment, and widespread demolition. However, rehabilitation and new construction projects have been under way in recent years. The community is central to the writings of John Edgar Wideman.

Homochitto National Forest 189,000 ac/76,500 ha, in six counties in the SW corner of Mississippi. Loblolly pines predominate in this area in the watershed of the 90 mi/140 km–long **Homochitto R.,** which rises in Copiah Co. and flows generally SW to the Mississippi.

Hondo city, pop. 6018, seat of Medina Co., SC Texas, 36 mi/58 km W of San Antonio, on Hondo Creek. Settled largely by Germans in the mid 19th century and incorporated in the 1890s, then dissolved and reincorporated in the 1940s, it is a ranch trade center with some manufacturing, and the site of a World War II air base.

Honeoye Falls see under MENDON, New York.

Honesdale borough, pop. 4972, Wayne Co., NE Pennsylvania, 24 mi/39 km NE of Scranton. It was founded in 1826 as a barge canal terminal and named for Philip Hone, president of the coal-shipping Delaware and Hudson Canal Company. The first steam locomotive in the US, the *Stourbridge Lion,* was brought to Honesdale from England in 1829 for a trial run hauling coal, but proved to be too heavy for existing rails. A replica of the engine is on display here. Today Honesdale's manufactures include textiles and apparels.

Honey Lake see under HERLONG, California.

Honolulu unincorporated community, pop. 365,272, state capital and seat of Honolulu Co., SE OAHU, Hawaii. Its metropolitan area, coextensive with Honolulu Co., contains over 75% (836,231) of the state's pop. Honolulu extends over 10 mi/16 km along Oahu's SE shore, from the foothills of the KOOLAU RANGE (N) to beachfront neighborhoods. Hawaii's chief port (often called the "Crossroads of the Pacific") and commercial, cultural, and industrial center, it is also a tourist magnet, and draws much of its income from a complex of nearby military bases, including PEARL HARBOR, 8 mi/13 km WNW. A small village before the 19th century, it then became the residence of Hawaiian monarchs (Iolani Palace is the only royal palace within the US), and developed as a base for European traders, whalers, and navies; at times the Russians, British, and French occupied it. Trade connections with the US grew steadily through the late 19th century, and after US annexation of Hawaii, Honolulu became territorial (1898) and state (1959) capital. A sugar exporting port with an embryonic tourist industry, it began to feel the effects of local military development in the early 20th century, and received some damage in the Japanese attack on Pearl Harbor (Dec. 7, 1941). A huge wartime buildup and the familiarity with the area gained by soldiers and sailors stationed here led to prosperity, fueled mainly by government outlays and by tourism, in the years after 1945; the Cold War and Korean and Vietnam wars did much to keep Honolulu busy. Today the long-established processing of sugar, pineapples, macadamia nuts, fish, and other island products has been joined by diverse manufacturing (metal fabrication, apparel, pharmaceuticals, optical and high-tech products) among local industries. The University of Hawaii at Manoa (1907) and Chaminade University (1955) are among local institutions. Tourism, which has led to extensive luxury hotel and condominium construction, remains central to the economy of Honolulu, which is known for its beaches, for its equable year-round climate, and as the most truly multicultural (peopled by native Hawaiians, Japanese, Chinese, Filipinos, white Americans, and others) of US urban centers. See also: ALA MOANA; CHINATOWN; DIAMOND HEAD; IWILEI; KAKAAKO; MANOA; NUUANU; PACIFIC PALISADES; the PUNCHBOWL; WAIKIKI.

Honolulu County 596 sq mi/1544 sq km, pop. 836,231, in NC

Hawaii. It includes the island of OAHU, the commercial, cultural, governmental, and population center of the state, as well as small outlying islands (NW) such as Kaula, Kure, French Frigate Shoal, Gardner Pinnacles, and Necker. The county seat is HONOLULU.

Hood, Mount highest elevation (11,239 ft/3426 m) in Oregon, in the CASCADE RANGE, 47 mi/76 km ESE of Portland and 21 mi/34 km S of the Columbia River. Vapors still emerge from FUMAROLES of this ancient glacier-capped volcano, which last erupted in 1907. The 1.1 million–ac/450,000-ha (1720–sq mi/ 4450–sq km) **Mt. Hood National Forest** surrounds it. The mountain has long been famed—in Indian legend, as marking the last leg of the journey for pioneers heading to the WILLAMETTE VALLEY, and today as a magnet for climbers and other outdoor enthusiasts. The famed WPA-sponsored Timberline Lodge is on its S flank. The area is also known for its orchards and timber.

Hood Canal see under PUGET SOUND, Washington.

Hoopa Valley Indian Reservation see under SIX RIVERS NATIONAL FOREST, California.

Hoosac Range N–S range in NW Massachusetts, a continuation of the Green Mts. of Vermont. Part of the E border of the Berkshire Hills, and E of the HOOSIC R., they are penetrated by the HOOSAC TUNNEL.

Hoosac Tunnel in the town of Florida, Berkshire Co., NW Massachusetts. A railroad tunnel about 4.75 mi/7.65 km long through the HOOSAC RANGE, it was a major 19th-century engineering feat, completed in 1875 after 24 years; nearly 200 workers died in the process.

Hoosic River 70 mi/113 km long, in Massachusetts, Vermont, and New York. It rises in the HOOSAC RANGE in NW Massachusetts, flowing N, NW, and W through North Adams and Williamstown, across the SW corner of Vermont, and continuing to Hoosick Falls in New York. It finally joins the Hudson R. in Schaghticoke, 14 mi/23 km N of Troy.

Hoosier Dome sports and event facility in downtown Indianapolis, Indiana, an air-supported dome built 1983, with a seating capacity of over 60,000. It is home to the Indianapolis Colts (football) and is noted as a basketball venue.

Hoosier National Forest 188,000 ac/76,140 ha, in two major units in S Indiana, extending to the Ohio R. near TELL CITY (S). Crossed by the Patoka, Lost, and White rivers, it has its headquarters at BEDFORD. Tell City and Brownstown are other gateways, and French Lick is just outside the park (NE).

Hoover city, pop. 39,788, Jefferson and Shelby counties, C Alabama, 8 mi/13 km S of Birmingham. A residential suburb, it has boomed since 1970, when it had a pop. of 688.

Hoover Dam see under L. MEAD, Arizona and Nevada.

Hooverville sarcastic term, in "honor" of President Herbert Hoover, for shack and tent communities of the unemployed and transient in the early Depression years. Hoovervilles were usually at the edges of cities, as along riverbanks or near railroad yards, and sometimes in parks, as in New York City's Central Park.

Hopatcong borough, pop. 15,586, Sussex Co., N New Jersey, on L. Hopatcong, 14 mi/23 km NW of Morristown. This lakeside residential and resort community has facilities for such summertime activities as swimming, boating, and fishing.

Hopatcong, Lake in NC New Jersey, 25 mi/40 km W of Paterson. It is the largest lake wholly within the state (7 mi/ 11 km NNE–SSW), and a popular year-round resort area with more than 60 mi/100 km of shoreline, beaches, and marinas. Hopatcong State Park covers 113 ac/46 ha.

Hope **1.** city, pop. 9643, seat of Hempstead Co., SW Arkansas, 30 mi/48 km NE of Texarkana. Founded in 1852 as a station on the Cairo and Fulton Railroad, it developed as a commercial and shipping center for agricultural and lumber producers; local watermelons are well known. A University of Arkansas agricultural experiment station is nearby, and Washington, site of the Confederate State Capital (1863–65), is 8 mi/13 km NW. The city is the birthplace (1946) of President Bill Clinton, who grew up in HOT SPRINGS. **2.** town, pop. 3147, Fraser-Cheam Regional District, SW British Columbia, in the Coast Mts., at the confluence of the Coquihalla and Fraser rivers, 80 mi/130 km E of Vancouver. On the site of an 1840s HUDSON'S BAY COMPANY post, the town was established (1858) during the Fraser gold rush. It is now a highway and rail junction and the S entrance to the Fraser R. valley. Nickel and copper mining, lumbering, agriculture, and the manufacture of bricks and tiles have all been important. **3.** hamlet in Pilot township, Vermilion Co, EC Illinois, 17 mi/27 km NW of Danville. It is a farming community and the birthplace (1885 and 1894) of writers Carl and Mark Van Doren.

Hope, Point see POINT HOPE, Alaska.

Hope Creek nuclear power plant: see under SALEM, New Jersey.

Hopewell **1.** township, pop. 11,590, Mercer Co., WC New Jersey, adjacent (NW) to Princeton. It was settled in the 17th century. Washington's army camped here before the Battle of Monmouth (1778). Charles Lindbergh's estate in Hopewell was the site of the kidnapping of his baby in 1932, and was deeded to the state of New Jersey in 1941. Hopewell is residential, with a commercial district in the borough (pop. 1968). **2.** in Ohio, the name of a person rather than a place. MOUND BUILDER remains excavated on the 1890s property of a farmer named Hopewell, near CHILLICOTHE in Ross Co., led to the labeling of a culture period that lasted C.A.D. 300–700 as "Hopewell." Sites are much more widely spread than ADENA sites, but the best-known are in the Ohio Valley, including those at FORT ANCIENT, the MOUND CITY GROUP, and NEWARK, Ohio. **3.** city, pop. 23,101, in but administratively separate from Prince George Co., SE Virginia, at the confluence of the James and Appomattox rivers, 8 mi/13 km NE of Petersburg. It is a port and an industrial center, making synthetic textiles, pottery, chemicals, and paper products; it flourished as a DuPont explosives center during World War I. Its oldest part, City Point (settled 1613), was a major base for the Union army during the siege of Petersburg (1864–65); it was annexed by the new (1913) city of Hopewell in 1923. Merchants Hope Church (1657), 6 mi/10 km SE, is the oldest Protestant church in America. Cawsons, the birthplace (1773) of statesman John Randolph of Roanoke, is within the city.

Hopewell Furnace see under POTTSTOWN, Pennsylvania.

Hopi Indian Reservation c.1.5 million ac/607,500 ha (2340 sq mi/6070 sq km), pop. 7360, in NE Arizona. Entirely surrounded by the NAVAJO INDIAN RESERVATION, it occupies three mesas extending S from BLACK MESA, as well as lands at their feet. In the 1880s the government gave 2.4 million ac/0.97 million ha (3750 sq mi/9712 sq km) jointly to the sedentary Hopi and the seminomadic Navajo. Land disputes set off by this arrangement continued in the 1990s, when it was proposed to relocate some dispossessed Hopi on off-reservation Federal lands in C Arizona. The Hopi, descendants of the Anasazi, have lived in the area 2000 years. They are noted for their ceremonies and for their stone PUEBLOS: Walpi, on First Mesa; Shipaulovi, on Second Mesa; and ORAIBI, on Third Mesa, are well known. Modern communities lie at the mesas' bases; Kykotsmovi (pop. 773) is tribal headquarters and a trade center. The SAN FRANCISCO PEAKS, to the SW, are sacred to the Hopi.

Hopkins city, pop. 16,534, Hennepin Co., SE Minnesota, a suburb 7 mi/11 km W of Minneapolis. It was settled in the 1850s, and became the city of West Minneapolis. Originally a center for truck farming, Hopkins is now a residential community with some manufacturing. Local industries produce farm machinery, computer and recycling equipment, and munitions. Food wholesalers are also important.

Hopkins, Mount see under SANTA RITA Mts., Arizona.

Hopkins International Airport see under BROOK PARK, Ohio.

Hopkinsville city, pop. 29,809, seat of Christian Co., SW Kentucky, 54 mi/87 km WSW of Bowling Green. A farming and livestock center in the S PENNYROYAL and a leading tobacco market, it was settled in 1797 as Elizabethtown, but was renamed to honor War of 1812 soldier Samuel Hopkins. There is some light manufacturing. FORT CAMPBELL and Campbell Air Force Base are 12 mi/19 km SW, straddling the Tennessee border.

Hopkinton **1.** town, pop. 9191, Middlesex Co., EC Massachusetts, 26 mi/42 km WSW of Boston. It is widely familiar as the starting point of the Boston Marathon. To history it is known as the birthplace of Daniel Shays, leader of a 1786–87 rebellion of debt-ridden farmers. Hopkinton, always essentially rural, with some early-19th-century shoe production, has experienced suburban growth since the 1960s, when Route 495 opened through the town. **2.** town, pop. 6873, Washington Co., SW Rhode Island, on the Connecticut border. It includes the villages of Ashaway, Canonchet, Hope Valley, Hopkinton, and Rockville, as well as part of Potter Hill. Agriculture and the manufacture of textiles and wood products are important. The town is on Interstate 95. The 1992 opening of a casino in nearby LEDYARD, Connecticut, was expected to spur resort development.

Hoquiam city, pop. 8972, Grays Harbor Co., W Washington, on Grays Harbor at the mouth of the Hoquiam R., adjacent (W) to ABERDEEN. Formerly the site of the Pacific Northwest's greatest stand of Douglas firs, it was a 19th- and early-20th-century sawmilling, lumber, shipbuilding, and cattle raising center. Also a shipbuilding hub during World War II, Hoquiam is now surrounded by areas of clearcut logging. It manufactures lumber products and has salmon and tuna fisheries and fish and oyster canneries.

Horicon Marsh see under ICE AGE NATIONAL SCIENTIFIC RESERVE, Wisconsin.

Hornell city, pop. 9877, Steuben Co., SW New York, on the Canisteo R., 56 mi/90 km S of Rochester. Settled in 1790 as Upper Canisteo, it was renamed (1820) for early settler George Hornell. Following the arrival of the Erie Railroad in 1850, Hornell experienced its greatest growth. City industries now include textile and hosiery mills and railroad shops. Ball bearings, glass, dresses, gloves, and wood trimming are manufactured as well.

Horn Island uninhabited, narrow barrier island, c.14 mi/23 km E–W, between Mississippi Sound (N) and the Gulf of Mexico (S), in S Mississippi, part of the GULF ISLANDS NATIONAL SEASHORE.

Horry County 1143 sq mi/2960 sq km, pop. 144,053, extreme E South Carolina, bounded by North Carolina (NE), the Atlantic Ocean (SE), and the Little Pee Dee R. (W). Its seat is CONWAY. Honeycombed by rivers and swamps, the county was virtually cut off from the rest of South Carolina during its early history. It developed a reputation for the independence of its farmers and foresters, and was called "**The Independent Republic of Horry.**" It now contains the vacation mecca of MYRTLE BEACH and much of the GRAND STRAND. Commercial and sport fishing, hunting, lumber, and agriculture are important to the economy; crops include tobacco, melons, fruit, corn, and vegetables.

Horseheads town, pop. 19,926, Chemung Co., SC New York, adjacent (N) to Elmira, on Newtown Creek. Settled in 1789 as Fairport, it was renamed in the 1840s to recall American troops' slaughter of their horses for food here during the Revolution. The town has contributed to the Elmira area's production of optical goods, brick, and other manufactures. It is the site of a huge (1.3 million sq ft, or 29.8 ac/12.1 ha) A&P food processing plant opened in 1964 and closed since 1973.

Horse Heaven Hills E–W oriented range in S Washington, extending some 70 mi/115 km along the S of the Yakima R., within a bend of the Columbia R., SW of Kennewick and N of the Oregon line. The area gained its name as a grazing area for wild horses.

Horseshoe Bend historic site in Tallapoosa Co., EC Alabama, on the TALLAPOOSA R., 10 mi/16 km E of Alexander City. It was here, on March 27, 1814, that Andrew Jackson decisively defeated the Creek, forcing on them a treaty that led to their removal from Alabama. Jackson emerged as an American hero, and the region was opened to white settlement. The Horseshoe Bend National Military Park covers 2040 ac/826 ha.

Horseshoe Curve see under ALTOONA, Pennsylvania.

Horseshoe Falls see under NIAGARA R.

Horsham township, pop. 21,896, Montgomery Co., SE Pennsylvania, a residential suburb 15 mi/24 km NNE of downtown Philadelphia. WILLOW GROVE is within it.

Horsimus see under JERSEY CITY, New Jersey.

Horton Plaza shopping center in the GASLAMP QUARTER in SAN DIEGO, California. A self-contained retail and entertainment complex built in 1985, it is a magnet for downtown trade.

Horton's Addition see NEW TOWN, San Diego, California.

Hospital Hill district of KANSAS CITY, Missouri, 1.5 mi/2.4 km S of Downtown, just NE of the CROWN CENTER. It has been home, since the 1880s, on high ground overlooking the business district (N), to public and private hospitals and medical teaching facilities.

Hot Springs **1.** city, pop. 32,462, seat of Garland Co., C Arkansas, 50 mi/80 km SW of Little Rock, N of the Ouachita R., at the E edge of the Ouachita Mts. and among lakes. The site, including 47 thermal springs, was set aside in 1832 as a public reserve. By the 1870s, when the railroad arrived, it had become very fashionable. In 1921 it became the focus of the now 5839-ac/2365-ha **Hot Springs National Park,** almost all of which lies within the city limits. The springs had long been used by local tribes for their apparent healing properties. The city is now a health and tourist resort with some 20 hydrotherapeutic institutions. Its economy is augmented by light manufacturing. It was the childhood home of President Bill Clinton, who was born in HOPE. Garland Co. Community College (1973) is here. **2.** see TRUTH OR CONSEQUENCES, New Mexico.

Hough residential neighborhood in Cleveland, Ohio, E of Downtown. A middle-class immigrant area before World War II, it thereafter experienced rapid racial turnover and severe commercial disinvestment, becoming one of the nation's most devastated black ghetto communities. Overcrowding, unemployment, and municipal neglect spawned rioting here in 1966. Today much of Hough continues to house poor families.

Houghton unincorporated village, pop. 1740, in Caneadea township, Allegany Co., SW New York, on the Genesee R., 52 mi/83 km SE of Buffalo. Houghton College (1883) is here.

Houghton Lake in Roscommon Co., NC Michigan, in a state forest area. The largest inland lake in the state, it is 16 mi/26 km long and 7 mi/11 km wide, and is the source of the Muskegon River. The unincorporated village of **Houghton Lake,** pop. 3353, is a year-round resort on the SW shore.

Houlton town, pop. 6613, seat of Aroostook Co., N Maine. It is on US 1 and the Meduxnekeag R., between wooded ridges, along the New Brunswick border. An early lumber center and military station, Houlton was central to the 1839 Aroostook War, a border dispute. The arrival of railroads in 1862 and 1894 stimulated development. The town is now commercial center of a potato-growing area, and gateway to hunting, fishing, and recreational regions. Industries include potato shipping and warehousing, flour milling, and the production of potato starch, fertilizer, and wood products.

Houma city, pop. 30,495, seat of Terrebonne Parish, SE Louisiana, 46 mi/74 km SW of New Orleans, on the Bayou Terrebonne and the Gulf Intracoastal Waterway, in the ATCHAFALAYA Basin. Founded in the 1830s and named for a local tribe, it developed as a trapping, fishing, and shrimping center. The canning and distribution of seafood and the trading of furs remain important. Houma is now also a center for regional oil and gas fields, sulfur mines, and sugar plantations. Many antebellum homes survive, including the Southdown Plantation (1850). A US sugar experiment station is nearby. Tourism is important in this bayou-dominated CAJUN COUNTRY community.

Housatonic River 130 mi/210 km long, in Massachusetts and Connecticut. It drains an area of 1930 sq mi/5000 sq km. Rising in the BERKSHIRE HILLS in NW Massachusetts, it continues S past Pittsfield, Stockbridge, and Great Barrington. In N Connecticut it is a narrow, fast-running recreational river, passing Canaan, Cornwall, and Kent. After widening below New Milford, it is joined by one of its main tributaries, the Naugatuck, at Derby. It then flows SE and S to empty into Long Island Sound between Stratford and Milford, E of Bridgeport. The Housatonic's many falls led to the large number of industrial settlements along its length. The river is navigable to Shelton and Derby.

Housetop Mountain see under JACKSON HOLE, Wyoming.

Houston city, pop. 1,630,553, seat of Harris Co., also in Fort Bend and Montgomery counties, SE Texas, 51 mi/82 km NW of Galveston, on the Buffalo Bayou, which becomes the HOUSTON SHIP CHANNEL in the city. Houston is the most populous city in Texas and the fourth in the US. Its metropolitan area (the Houston-Galveston-Brazoria CMSA) has a pop. of 3,711,043. Settlement of HARRISBURG, on the Buffalo Bayou, commenced in 1826, but that town, destroyed in the 1836 Texas Revolution, gave way to the nascent Houston, established the same year by the Allen brothers, land speculators from New York. Work to improve the navigability of the bayou began almost immediately, and the settlement developed as a port for local cotton and rice farmers. A Confederate port, it later in the 19th century became a railroad center as well. The opening of the Spindletop oilfield in BEAUMONT (1901), followed by strikes at HUMBLE (1904) and elsewhere nearby, made Houston central to the US oil industry, a position it retains today. The Ship Channel and surrounding area is now home to one of the world's largest oil and petrochemical complexes; so many pipelines run through the area that it is popularly called the "Spaghetti Bowl." In World War I Houston's Ellington Field and Camp Logan were important training sites. By 1930 it had become the state's largest city, and it boomed in the 1940s and 1950s, expanding across the area's flat, swampy land, unregulated by any zoning ordinance. In 1962 NASA's Manned Space Flight Center at Clear Lake was established, and Houston, known earlier as the Bayou City or Magnolia City, became the Space City. Booms in the oil and space industries, accompanied by financial, commercial, and medical industry growth, spurred continued expansion in the 1960s and 1970s, abetted by the area's new prominence as part of the SUNBELT. By the 1980s the city's population was relatively stable. Houston now covers some 557 sq mi/1443 sq km, having grown from its original four wards, annexing large parts of Harris Co. to become one of the largest US cities in area. Interstate Loop 610, encircling Downtown at a radius of about 6 mi/10 km, encloses only the inner part of a vast urban sprawl. Central business development in the 1960s and 1970s produced a cluster of tall office buildings including I.M Pei's 998-ft/304-m Texas Commerce Tower and Philip Johnson's well-known two-trapezoid Pennzoil Place, but large buildings appear also far from Downtown, in such areas as the Galleria. Houston is home to Rice University (formerly Rice Institute; 1891), the University of Houston (1927), Texas Southern University (1947), and the University of St. Thomas (1947), with its noted Rothko Chapel. Other well-known city institutions include its Alley Theatre and Grand Opera, as well as numerous art galleries and museums. See also: ALIEF; ALLENS LANDING; ASTRODOME; BUFFALO BAYOU; CLEAR LAKE (and Ellington Field and Lyndon B. Johnson Space Flight Center); DENVER HARBOR; FIFTH WARD; FM-1960; FOURTH WARD; GALLERIA; HERMANN PARK; HOUSTON HEIGHTS (the Heights); HOUSTON INTERCONTINENTAL AIRPORT; HOUSTON SHIP CHANNEL; MAGNOLIA; MEMORIAL PARK (and Camp Logan); MONTROSE; RIVER OAKS; SAN JACINTO RIVER; SECOND WARD; SHARPSTOWN; SUMMIT; TANGLEWOOD; TEXAS MEDICAL CENTER; THIRD WARD; WILLIAM P. HOBBY AIRPORT.

Houston Heights also, **the Heights** residential and commercial section of Houston, Texas, across the Buffalo Bayou 3 mi/5 km NW of Downtown. An exclusive 1890s suburb, it had a substantial Mexican population by the 1910s, and was annexed in 1918. Today it is one of Houston's older neighborhoods, undergoing restoration and becoming an entertainment area.

Houston Intercontinental Airport in Harris Co., SE Texas, 14 mi/23 km NNE of downtown Houston, and just W of US Route 59 and HUMBLE. Opened in 1969, it covers some 8000 ac/3240 ha, and has spurred residential and commercial development on Houston's N edge.

Houston Ship Channel 50 mi/80 km long, in SE Texas. It connects Houston with the Gulf Intracoastal Waterway and the Gulf of Mexico via the BUFFALO BAYOU, the mouth of the San Jacinto R., and Galveston Bay. Since the Buffalo Bayou was first improved in the 1840s, the waterway has been continually widened, and deepened to accommodate ocean-going ships. The modern channel opened in 1914. It has no locks (Houston is only 50 ft/15 m above sea level), and is at least 300 ft/90 m wide and 36 ft/11 m deep.

Howard village, pop. 9874, Brown Co., E Wisconsin, a residential suburb 5 mi/8 km NW of the city of GREEN BAY.

Howard Beach residential and commercial neighborhood along both sides of Shell Bank Basin and the Cross Bay Boulevard to the Rockaways, S Queens, New York. It is separated from Jamaica Bay by Spring Creek Park, and lies just W of John F. Kennedy International Airport. Fast-food and similar establishments are its chief businesses, with small houses in a grid pattern back from the boulevard.

Howard County 251 sq mi/650 sq km, pop. 187,328, in C Maryland, bounded NE by the Patapsco R., and W and SW by the Patuxent R. Its seat is ELLICOTT CITY. Primarily in the PIEDMONT, with a small SE section in the coastal plain, it was, until recently, almost entirely farmland, with several large estates. Following the development of COLUMBIA, now the largest community in the county, several residential and commercial centers have been constructed around older estates. The county includes many SW Baltimore suburbs.

Howe Caverns extensive limestone cavern system, to 200 ft/61 m underground, in Cobleskill town, Schoharie Co., EC New York, 32 mi/52 km W of Albany. A noted tourist attraction, they include an underground stream and lake.

Howland Hook see under MARINER'S HARBOR, New York.

Howland Island 0.7 sq mi/1.9 sq km, in the C Pacific Ocean, just N of the Equator, some 1620 mi/2610 km SW of Honolulu, Hawaii, and 40 mi/64 km NNW of BAKER I. Uninhabited, it was discovered by American traders in 1842, claimed by the US in 1857, and worked for guano until 1890 by both the US and Great Britain, which also claimed it. Americans, seeking to reinforce the US claim, colonized it (as Itascatown) in 1935; in 1936 it was placed under the jurisdiction of the Department of the Interior. Amelia Earhart was flying from New Guinea to Howland's new airfield when she disappeared in 1937. The Japanese attacked the island in 1941, and it was evacuated. Today it is a wildlife refuge.

Hualalai dormant volcano, 8271 ft/2523 m high, on W Hawaii island, Hawaii, just NE of Kailua-Kona, in the North Kona district. The third-highest point on the island, it last erupted in 1801, but is thought to be heating toward a new eruption.

Hualapai Mountains range extending SE for c.50 mi/80 km from KINGMAN, in W Arizona, rising to 8417 ft/2566 m at Hualapai Peak. Hualapai means "pine tree folk," and is a Hokan tribal name. The Aquarius Mts., rising to 6236 ft/1901 m, lie parallel to the E.

Hub, the nickname for Boston, Massachusetts. It is often taken to refer to the city's central position in New England's geography, commerce, and history. In its fuller form, "hub of the universe," however, it has been used proudly or ironically, depending on the speaker, to indicate Bostonians' feeling for their city.

Hubbardton town, pop. 576, at the N end of L. BOMOSEEN, in Rutland Co., WC Vermont. A hilly resort community, it was the site of the only battle of the Revolution fought in Vermont. On July 7, 1777, Americans under Seth Warner were defeated by the British under Simon Fraser.

Huber Heights city, pop. 38,716, Montgomery and Miami counties, SW Ohio, 7 mi/11 km NE of Dayton. A large residential suburb, it has grown significantly during recent decades.

Hudson **1.** town, pop. 17,233, Middlesex Co., EC Massachusetts, on the Assabet R., 14 mi/23 km NE of Worcester, and adjoining (N) Marlborough. It was a shoe manufacturing center from 1816 until the mid 20th century; modern industries produce tools, plastics, chemicals, and electronic equipment. Route 495 passes W of the town. **2.** town, pop. 19,530, Hillsborough Co., S New Hampshire. It is on the Merrimack R. opposite Nashua, near the Massachusetts border. Originally an agricultural community, it is now one of New Hampshire's fastest-growing suburban towns, attracting many former Boston-area residents, among others. **3.** city, pop. 8034, seat of Columbia Co., NE New York, on the E bank of the Hudson R., 30 mi/48 km S of Albany. The first permanent settlement was established by New Englanders in 1783. In the early 19th century Hudson was a bustling schooner port for whaling, sealing, and the West Indian trade. The city has numerous old buildings, many restored, from the Federal through the Victorian periods. There is some manufacturing, including cement, machinery, and processed foods and grain. A stop on the Amtrak line, Hudson has also become a center for the antiques business.

Hudson Bay vast inland sea between the Atlantic (E) and Arctic (W) oceans, bordered by the Northwest Territories (N and NW), Québec (E and SE), Ontario (S), and Manitoba (SW). Some 950 mi/1530 km N–S, including JAMES BAY, a large SE arm, and up to 600 mi/1000 km wide, it has a surface area of 320,000 sq mi/830,000 sq km. Occupying a glacial depression on the CANADIAN SHIELD, the bay is generally shallow, averaging c.450 ft/140 m. On the N, it joins the Atlantic via the HUDSON STRAIT, navigable most of the year, and the Arctic via the FOXE BASIN, almost permanently covered by ice. The bay itself is navigable from mid-July to Oct. It receives many rivers, including (E–W) the Great Whale, Eastmain, Nottaway, Moose, Abitibi, Albany, Attawapiskat, Severn, Nelson (with the Saskatchewan), Churchill, and Thelon and tributaries (via Chesterfield Inlet). They drain an area extending W to the Rocky Mts. and S to the St. Lawrence and Mississippi river watersheds. The W shore is basically flat, allowing river access to the interior. Islands, almost entirely along the E, include the Belchers (SE), home to the southernmost Inuit community, Sanikiluaq (hamlet, pop. 526); and Akimiski, in James Bay. All of them are in the Northwest Territories. Whales, seals, and walrus, along with many kinds of fish, live in the bay, and polar bears are fall visitors, stalking ringed seals on the ice. The shores are summer home to hundreds of bird species. In the summer, grain is exported from the port of CHURCHILL, Manitoba, the bay's largest community. The INUIT, here for thousands of years, live primarily by hunting caribou and beluga whales and fishing for cod and salmon. The first European to enter the bay was the English navigator Henry Hudson, in 1610, followed by Sir Thomas Button in 1612, William Baffin in 1615, Jens Munck in 1619, and Luke Fox and Thomas James in 1631. In 1662 Pierre-Esprit

Radisson reached the bay overland, and in 1668 Médart Chouart des Groseilliers built the first fur trading post, at the S of James Bay, on the mouth of the Rupert R. (Fort Rupert, Québec). The French and English vied for control of the bay until 1713, when the Treaty of Utrecht turned over all French posts in the region to England. In 1670 Charles II had chartered the HUDSON'S BAY COMPANY, which now monopolized the fur trade in the entire watershed, from Labrador to the Rocky Mts. YORK FACTORY, on the SW shore, was the center of operations until 1870, when all of RUPERT'S LAND was ceded to the new Dominion of Canada. The Hudson Bay Railway, from Winnipeg to Churchill, was completed in 1929, the Temiskaming and Northern Ontario Railway, from North Bay to MOOSONEE, on James Bay, in 1932. The lowlands surrounding the bay are characterized by bogs, marshes, and ponds underlain by PERMAFROST. The bay is subject to heavy fog in summer and high winds in autumn and winter.

Hudson City see under JERSEY CITY, New Jersey.

Hudson County 46 sq mi/119 sq km, pop. 553,099, in NE New Jersey, bounded by the Passaic R. and Newark Bay (W) and the Hudson R. and Upper New York Bay (E). Its seat is JERSEY CITY. The smallest and most densely settled county in the state, it is highly industrialized. Containing BAYONNE, HOBOKEN, UNION CITY, and WEST NEW YORK, the county has major ports as well as important railroad and trucking facilities. Oil is refined, and there is a wide variety of heavy and light industry.

Hudson Highlands mountainous region, c.1000 ft/300 m high, a part of the APPALACHIAN Mt. system, along both banks of the Hudson R., SE New York, extending S of Newburgh 15 mi/24 km to an area around Peekskill. Heavily forested, this region of rugged cliffs includes a deep, scenic gorge through which the river runs, and which is overlooked at WEST POINT by the US Military Academy. Hudson Highlands State Park on the river's E bank and BEAR MOUNTAIN State Park on its W bank are located here. The Hudson R., which narrows in the Highlands, is traversed near the region's S end by the Bear Mountain Bridge.

Hudson River 310 mi/500 km long, in E New York and NE New Jersey. It drains an area of 13,370 sq mi/34,630 sq km. Rising in L. Tear of the Clouds, in the Adirondack Mts., W of Mt. MARCY, the highest point in the state (5344 ft/1630 m), it runs generally S into Upper NEW YORK BAY, then into the Atlantic Ocean. The first European to navigate its waters was Giovanni da Verrazano, who sailed up the river for a short distance in 1524. It is named, however, for Henry Hudson, who sailed to the site of ALBANY, looking for a route to China, in 1609. Settlement began in the 1620s. In the 17th and 18th centuries the river, as the link with Albany, Kingston, and other inland ports, was key to the fur trade and to the movement of farm produce. In the 19th century its traffic flourished and expanded after the opening of the Erie Canal (1825) and canals to the Delaware and L. CHAMPLAIN, developments that spurred New York City's growth. By mid-century, however, railroads had taken the leading role from river and canal. The Hudson is noted for its early-19th-century "school" of landscape painting, typified by Asher Durand and Thomas Cole; major writers such as Washington Irving and William Cullen Bryant wrote about its valley.

In its beginning the river meanders through Essex, Warren, and Saratoga counties. From Hudson Falls, at the N end of the Hudson Valley, it runs almost due S, past Cohoes, Troy, Albany, Catskill, Kingston, Poughkeepsie, Newburgh, West Point, Peekskill, Ossining, and S through the Tappan Zee to New York Bay. Below New York City, the Hudson continues for another 200 mi/320 km SE as a submarine channel, the **Hudson Canyon,** which drops to the Atlantic Ocean floor. The river is tidal as far up as Troy, and varies in width from 0.75 mi/1.2 km to 3 mi/5 km (at Haverstraw Bay). It is a transportation route for business, industry, and outdoor recreation. The Hudson's most important tributary is the MOHAWK R.; the gentle gradient of the two rivers has allowed them to be a key route through the Appalachian Mts. for centuries. Other major tributaries include the North Creek, Sacandaga, Schroon, BATTEN KILL, Fish Creek, and Hoosic rivers. Its W banks in Ulster and Greene counties are lined by the CATSKILL Mts. The Hudson is connected with the Great Lakes, L. Champlain, and the St. Lawrence R. by the New York State Barge Canal system, of which the Mohawk is part. The Upper Hudson Falls, at Glens Falls and Hudson Falls, provide hydroelectric power. Bridges spanning the river include the Rip Van Winkle (1935) at Catskill; Kingston-Rhinecliff (1957); Mid-Hudson (1930), at Poughkeepsie; Bear Mountain (1924), at Peekskill; Tappan Zee (1956), at Tarrytown; GEORGE WASHINGTON in New York City; and VERRAZANO-NARROWS, in New York Harbor. In the New York City area, the Hudson is still sometimes called the NORTH R., a name surviving from the 17th century.

Hudson's Bay Company corporation, based in London, England, chartered 1670 by Charles II, at the urging of his cousin Prince Rupert, who became its first governor, and of French explorers Pierre-Esprit Radisson and the Sieur des Groseillers (who had failed to interest the French crown in the idea). Its purposes were to develop the fur trade around HUDSON BAY and to search for the NORTHWEST PASSAGE. It was granted all lands in the watershed of rivers flowing into Hudson Bay (from E, S, or W), the area that came to be called RUPERT'S LAND. The HBC established posts at the mouths of various rivers, run by traders called factors; the word *factory* thus became a part of various Canadian place names. Generally satisfied to wait for Indians to bring furs to these posts, and showing little interest in the Northwest Passage, the company was long criticized as "sleeping beside the frozen sea." After 1760, when the British conquered Canada, Scots merchants in Montréal created the NORTH WEST COMPANY, whose aggressive policies threatened the HBC empire. Strife between the competitors occurred in the Prairie Provinces, esp. along the RED. R., until 1821, when they were amalgamated, leading to a period (1820s–60s) in which the HBC, now focusing on landholding and development, briefly controlled the VANCOUVER I. colony and departments including the Northwest and Yukon territories. With the creation of the Dominion of Canada (1867), the HBC was forced to sell its lands in return for cash and smaller holdings, esp. around its posts. In the late 19th century it continued its evolution into a real-estate and commercial empire, and is known today chiefly as a major retailer (popularly, "The Bay"). In 1972 its headquarters were moved to Winnipeg, but most offices are in Toronto.

Hudson Strait arm of the Atlantic Ocean leading into HUDSON BAY (SW) and FOXE BASIN (NW), between BAFFIN I., Northwest Territories (N), and the UNGAVA Peninsula of Québec (S). Some 450 mi/720 km NW–SE and 70–250 mi/110–400 km wide, including Ungava Bay, a S arm, the strait is ice-free from mid-July to Oct. but navigable most of the year through the use of icebreakers. Fogbound Resolution I. lies in the E mouth of the strait, at the entrance to Frobisher Bay (S Baffin I.). INUIT communities on the strait include Cape Dorset and Lake Harbour on Baffin I., and Salluit, Kangiqsujuaq, Quaqtaq, and Ivujivik (extreme SW) on the Ungava Peninsula. The strait was probably entered by Sebastian Cabot in 1498. Its E end was explored by Martin Frobisher in 1576–78, and its entire length was navigated by Henry Hudson in 1610, on his way into Hudson Bay.

Hueco Mountains range extending N–S for c.55 mi/90 km, into far SW Texas, E of El Paso, from S New Mexico, reaching 6717 ft/2049 m at Cerro Alto Peak. The **Hueco Tanks,** natural basins created by erosion, trapped water used by generations of travelers. This jumbled mass of rocks, with numerous shallow caves, also created a natural fortress, and abounds with ancient pictographs. The Tanks today are popular with rock climbers. The range forms the W boundary of the DIABLO BOLSON.

Hueytown city, pop. 15,280, Jefferson Co., C Alabama, just NW of Bessemer and 13 mi/21 km SW of Birmingham, in the heart of a coal and methane producing area.

Hull **1.** town, pop. 10,466, Plymouth Co., EC Massachusetts, 10 mi/16 km ESE of Boston. It comprises a 6 mi/10 km–long, hooked peninsula, with Hull and Hingham bays W, Boston Harbor N, and Massachusetts Bay E. The resort of NANTASKET BEACH extends along the E side. Hull is a summer resort and residential community made up of several villages, among them Pemberton, Windemere, Allerton, and Kenberma. Point Allerton (NE) is the legendary burial site (1004) of Thorwald, son of Eric the Red. **2.** city, pop. 60,707, OUTAOUAIS URBAN COMMUNITY, SW Québec, on the N bank of the Ottawa R., opposite Ottawa, Ontario. The GATINEAU R. forms its E boundary. Founded in 1800 by the LOYALIST lumberman Philemon Wright, it has a long industrial history, drawing first on local timber and waterpower from the Ottawa's Chaudière Falls. Its industries are now highly diversified. Part of the NATIONAL CAPITAL REGION, Hull is today a business and administrative center, its largest employer the Canadian government. It has a number of Federal office complexes. The Canadian Museum of Civilization, a branch of the Université du Québec, and a music conservatory are among its many institutions.

Hull House former settlement house just W of CHICAGO CIRCLE, near the University of Illinois campus on the Near West Side of Chicago, Illinois. It was founded by social welfare advocate and Nobel Peace Prize winner Jane Addams in 1889 as a center for the education and acclimatization of immigrants, and was the first such establishment in the US; two original buildings remain as a museum.

Humacao unincorporated community (ZONA URBANA), pop. 21,306, Humacao Municipio (pop. 55,203), E Puerto Rico, on the Humacao R., 27 mi/43 km SE of San Juan. Founded in 1790, it is a port with harbor facilities in coastal Playa de Humacao. In a valley that grows sugarcane and tobacco, it is also a trade and processing center. Its light manufactures include textiles, pharmaceuticals, and cigars. Humacao is also a resort, with beachfront facilities on Vieques Sound.

Humber River **1.** 75 mi/120 km long, in W Newfoundland. It rises near the head of White Bay, on the N coast, and flows SSW along the E of the LONG RANGE Mts., through Deer L., then turns W through the range, past CORNER BROOK to the Bay of Islands in the Gulf of St. Lawrence. It is noted for its salmon fishing. **2.** one of two short rivers (the DON is the other) crucial to the development of TORONTO, Ontario. It enters Humber Bay (L. Ontario) 5 mi/8 km WSW of the modern Downtown, at the site (Toronto Carrying Place) where Indian river-and-portage routes, adopted by white traders, connected L. Ontario with L. Huron and the West. The river forms the modern boundaries between Toronto, York, and North York (E) and Etobicoke (W). It enters metropolitan Toronto from Vaughan (N) and Caledon (NW). Noted for the scenery of its headwaters, it is also lined by much of the metropolitan area's parkland.

Humble city, pop. 12,060, Harris Co., SE Texas, 16 mi/26 km NNE of downtown Houston, on the West Fork of the San Jacinto R. Founded in 1888 in what turned out in 1904 to be the huge Humble Oilfield, it has many natural gas and oil wells, and makes oilfield equipment. The Houston International Airport is just W. Several local businessmen founded (1909) the Humble Oil and Refining Company, now Exxon.

Humboldt **1.** city, pop. 2178, Allen Co., SE Kansas, on the Neosho R., 40 mi/64 km W of Fort Scott. Laid out in 1857, it is a grain and oil distribution center, and has varied light manufactures. Baseball great Walter Johnson was born here (1887). **2.** city, pop. 9651, Gibson Co., W Tennessee, 13 mi/21 km NNW of Jackson. A shipping and trade center for an area producing cotton, corn, fruits, and vegetables, it also has marble and granite works and manufactures fertilizer.

Humboldt Bay inlet of the Pacific Ocean in Humboldt Co., NW California. Thirteen mi/21 km NNE–SSW and 1–4 mi/1–6 km wide, it is sheltered on the W by two sandy barrier peninsulas, and was named for the German naturalist Alexander von Humboldt. EUREKA is on the bay's E, ARCATA just NE. The best natural harbor between SAN FRANCISCO BAY (S) and PUGET SOUND (N), the bay has been a major lumbering center since the 1850s. It is also an important fishing area. The **Humboldt Bay National Wildlife Refuge,** with marshes along the upper bay (Arcata Bay), is an important stop for migrating waterfowl.

Humboldt National Forest over 2.5 million ac/1 million ha (3900 sq mi/10,100 sq km), in scattered units in EC, NE, and NC Nevada. It has a wide range of desert, hill, lake, and high mountain terrains. Parts of the RUBY and SNAKE ranges are within the forest, and the GREAT BASIN NATIONAL PARK is almost enclosed by its southernmost unit.

Humboldt Park residential and commercial neighborhood on the NEAR NORTHWEST SIDE of Chicago, Illinois, 4 mi/6 km NW of the Loop. A formerly German neighborhood situated around the 207-ac/84-ha park named for the explorer, it is now noted as one of the centers of Chicago's Puerto Rican community.

Humboldt River c.300 mi/480 km long, in N Nevada. It is formed by East and North forks in Humboldt National Forest, in Elko Co., and flows generally WSW past Elko, Battle Mountain, Winnemucca, and Lovelock, then drains into the **Humboldt Sink,** in Churchill Co., just N of the CARSON Sink. For westward-bound 19th-century emigrants, it provided a main route from Salt Lake City, Utah, to California. The transcontinental railroad (1860s) and highways (I-80 today) followed it. In the 20th century, it has been the site of irrigation works; the Rye Patch Dam (1936) forms Rye Patch Reservoir, NNE of Lovelock.

Humboldt Trail see EMIGRANT TRAIL.

Humphreys, Mount peak (13,986 ft/4266 m) of the Sierra Nevada, 17 mi/27 km WSW of Bishop, California. On the border of the INYO (E) and SIERRA (W) national forests, it is a noted climbers' challenge.

Humphreys Peak highest point (12,633 ft/3851 m) in Arizona, one of the SAN FRANCISCO PEAKS, 10 mi/16 km N of Flagstaff, on the COCONINO PLATEAU.

hundred in Pennsylvania, Delaware, and Virginia, following British custom, an historic subdivision of a county, with its own court; seen in such place names as BERMUDA HUNDRED.

Hungry Horse Dam on the South Fork of the Flathead R., in Flathead Co., NW Montana, 16 mi/26 km NE of Kalispell. Finished in 1952, 12 mi/19 km S of Glacier National Park, the concrete, arch-gravity dam is 564 ft/172 m high and 2115 ft/645 m long. A major component of Columbia River Basin development, it impounds the 34 mi/55 km–long **Hungry Horse Reservoir,** used for irrigation, hydropower, and flood control.

Hunt, Mount see under JACKSON HOLE, Wyoming.

Hunterdon County 426 sq mi/1103 sq km, pop. 107,776, in NW New Jersey, bounded (W) by the Delaware R. Its seat and commercial center is FLEMINGTON. It is traditionally agricultural, producing vegetables, fruit, poultry, and dairy products. Attracted by its rural setting, corporations have in recent years located headquarters here, and the county is a growing residential suburb. Clustered in its center are Voorhees, Spruce Run, and Round Valley state parks.

Hunter Mountain 4040 ft/1232 m, in the Catskill Mts., Greene Co., SE New York. The second-highest peak in the Catskills, it is a popular ski resort.

Hunters Creek Village city, pop. 3954, Harris Co., SE Texas. This suburb is the largest of a cluster of six small, affluent residential cities on or near Interstate 90, on the W side of Houston, some 15 mi/24 km from Downtown. Spread along West Memorial Drive, they are known collectively as the Memorial Villages. The other cities are Spring Valley (pop. 3392), Bunker Hill Village (pop. 3391), Piney Point Village (pop. 3197), Hedwig Village (pop. 2616), and Hilshire Village (pop. 665).

Hunter's Point **1.** section of SE SAN FRANCISCO, California, on San Francisco Bay, E of US 101. It is one of the city's few heavy industrial zones. Drydocks and shipyards have been here since the 1860s. A huge Navy repair base was created during World War II, and part of the area has remained a Naval Reservation. With the Bayview neighborhood (S), Hunter's Point is today a largely depressed region characterized by deteriorating public housing. CANDLESTICK PARK is here. **2.** industrial subsection, extreme W Queens, New York, on the East R. across from Turtle Bay, Manhattan, and at the mouth of Newtown Creek. It became part of Long Island City in 1870. Its waterfront is noted among Manhattanites for the huge Pepsi-Cola sign across from the United Nations.

Huntingdon borough, pop. 6843, seat of Huntingdon Co., SC Pennsylvania, 20 mi/32 km W of Altoona. Founded c.1755, it is a manufacturing area; products include machinery, pipes, and radiators. It is the site of Juniata College (1876). RAYSTOWN LAKE and the Lincoln Caverns are nearby.

Hunting Island one of the SEA ISLANDS, 5 mi/8 km long, in Beaufort Co., SW South Carolina, on the Atlantic Ocean, 14 mi/23 km E of Beaufort. Once a hunting grounds for deer, raccoon, and waterfowl, it is now the site of the 5000-ac/2025-ha Hunting Island State Park. Hunting Island lighthouse (1859; closed 1933) is now a tourist attraction. The island is connected to FRIPP and St. Helena islands by bridges.

Huntington **1.** city, pop. 16,389, seat of Huntington Co., NE Indiana, at the junction of the Wabash and Little Wabash rivers, 24 mi/39 km SW of Fort Wayne. The forks of the Wabash were an Indian meeting place where many treaties were signed. Founded in 1831, Huntington is a trading and storage center for a farming and limestone quarrying district. It has grain elevators, meatpacking plants, dairies, and printing plants, and manufactures including auto and electronic parts, machinery, canning equipment, and rubber products. The city is the seat of Huntington College (1897). Huntington L. and a state recreational area are 3 mi/5 km SE. **2.** in New York: **a.** unincorporated village, pop. 18,243, in Huntington town, Suffolk Co., on Long Island's North Shore, 35 mi/56 km E of Manhattan, on Huntington Harbor, an inlet of Long Island Sound. Primarily residential, it has numerous boatyards; electrical equipment and boats are manufactured. Huntington is a major retailing center for the area. Settled in the 1650s, it has several preserved 18th-century homes. **b.** town, pop. 191,474, NW Suffolk Co., on the Nassau Co. line and Long Island Sound. It includes numerous affluent residential and high-tech communities, among them COLD SPRING HARBOR, Northport, and COMMACK. The local newspaper, the *Long Islander,* was edited by the poet Walt Whitman, who was born (1819) in the West Hills section (pop. 5849). **3.** city, pop. 54,844, seat of Cabell Co. and in Wayne Co., extreme W West Virginia, in the lowlands along the Ohio R. where the Guyandotte R. enters it, 45 mi/72 km W of Charleston and 12 mi/19 km ESE of Ashland, Kentucky. The metropolis of the Ohio/Kentucky/West Virginia industrial region, it is a river and rail transfer point and coal shipping center. Surrounded by fields of bituminous coal, oil, and natural gas, it has a nickel rolling mill, railroad shops, and factories producing railroad equipment, glass and stone products, chemicals, optical goods, and household appliances. Marshall University (1837) is here. After suffering repeated damage by floods, the city is now protected by a wall 11 mi/18 km long.

Huntington Beach city, pop. 181,519, Orange Co., SW California, 25 mi/40 km SE of Los Angeles, on the Pacific Ocean. Oil discovered in the area in 1920 spurred the city's growth and the industrial development of Southern California. Today local and offshore wells are among the most active in the state; petroleum and natural gas production remains the city's major industry. There is a wide variety of light manufacturing as well. The city's 8 mi/13 km of beaches are considered by some the surfing capital of California.

Huntington Park city, pop. 56,065, Los Angeles Co., SW California, 5 mi/8 km SE of downtown Los Angeles, and just E of SOUTH-CENTRAL. Founded in 1856, it was formerly a center for the production of automobiles, steel, aircraft parts, oil-well equipment, and hardware, but is now a largely residential and commercial community, whose pop. is 90% Hispanic.

Huntington Station unincorporated village, pop. 28,247, in Huntington town, Suffolk Co., SE New York, 35 mi/56 km E of Manhattan and immediately S of Huntington, on the North Shore of Long Island. Primarily residential, it is also a major retailing center for E Nassau Co. and W Suffolk Co., with a large regional mall. It also has some light manufacturing.

Huntington Woods city, pop. 6419, Oakland Co., SE Michigan, a residential suburb of Detroit, 11 mi/18 km N of Downtown.

Hunt's Point industrial section, on a low, marshy peninsula in the East R., at the mouth of the Bronx R., S Bronx, New York. Cut off from the rest of the Bronx by railroad lines and the Bruckner Expressway, it formerly housed a money-printing plant among its industries, and is now known chiefly for the New York Terminal Market (1965) and Meat Market (1976), locus of much of New York City's food wholesaling.

Huntsville **1.** city, pop. 159,789, seat of Madison Co., N Alabama, 85 mi/137 km NNE of Birmingham, between the Tennessee R. (S) and the Tennessee line. Settled by 1805, it was granted Alabama's first city charter in 1811. It was the site of Alabama's constitutional convention, and was briefly (1819) the new state's capital. Long a commercial center for local cotton, corn, and tobacco farms, it has also been a textile producer since its early years. It was occupied by Union troops in 1862. In World War II it produced munitions, and from the 1950s it developed as a world center of missile research and development, after Wernher von Braun and a group of German engineers were brought to the US. Cotton fields were replaced by housing developments as the city experienced rapid growth, which peaked in the 1960s. The city also makes automobiles (Chrysler) and computer systems. Huntsville is home to the Redstone Arsenal Complex (39,000 ac/15,000 ha, SW of Downtown), including NASA's George C. Marshall Space Flight Center (1960). The University of Alabama at Huntsville (1951), Oakwood College (1896), and Alabama Agricultural and Mechanical University (1875, in NORMAL) are also here. **2.** town, pop. 14,997, Muskoka District Municipality, S Ontario, 112 mi/180 km N of Toronto. Tourism is central to its economy. The L. of Bays resort area is SE, the MUSKOKA LAKES SW, and ALGONQUIN PROVINCIAL PARK NE. **3.** city, pop. 27,925, seat of Walker Co., E Texas, 72 mi/115 km N of Houston. Founded in 1836, it had early importance as a Texas cultural and social center. Its wooded area produces varied crops, livestock, stone, pine and hardwood lumber, and oil and gas. Buried in Oakwood Cemetery is the first president of the Republic of Texas, Sam Houston. On the grounds of Sam Houston State University (1879), two of his homes are preserved. The Texas state penitentiary and Criminal Justice department headquarters are here. The city is a gateway for the SAM HOUSTON NATIONAL FOREST.

Hurley city, pop. 1782, seat of Iron Co., N Wisconsin, in the GOGEBIC Range, across the Montreal R. from IRONWOOD, Michigan. In the 1880s it was notorious as the sin city of the range, which boomed until just before World War I; it was the setting for Edna Ferber's 1936 novel *Come and Get It.*

Huron city, pop. 12,448, seat of Beadle Co., EC South Dakota, on the James R., 45 mi/72 km N of Mitchell. It has meatpacking and lumbering industries and is a shipping and trade center for the surrounding livestock and grain farming area. Beverages, feed, and dairy products are produced. A number of Federal and state agencies have offices here. Huron University (1883) is in the city. The South Dakota State Fair is held here annually.

Huron, Lake second-largest of the GREAT LAKES, between Ontario (N and E) and Michigan (W and S). Some 210 mi/340 km N–S and up to 185 mi/300 km wide, including GEORGIAN BAY, its NE arm, it covers 23,000 sq mi/59,600 sq km, with a maximum depth of 750 ft/229 m. Its surface is 577 ft/176 m above sea level. Saginaw Bay, in the WC, indents Michigan's Lower Peninsula, and forms its "thumb." On the N, the BRUCE PENINSULA and MANITOULIN I., in Ontario, and Michigan's Drummond I., all parts of the NIAGARA ESCARPMENT, separate Georgian Bay (E) and Huron's North Channel (W) from the main body of the lake. Mackinac I. is a popular resort just E of the strait that connects Huron with L. Michigan (W); the Georgian Bay area is a Canadian vacation center. Huron drains L. Superior via the St. Marys R. (NW); it lies at the same elevation as L. Michigan. Its waters flow into L. Erie (S) via the Saint Clair R., L. Saint Clair, and the Detroit R. Major ports on the lake include Sault Ste. Marie, Ontario (at its NW entrance), and Cheboygan and Bay City, Michigan. Sarnia, Ontario, and Port Huron, Michigan, lie at its S extreme. Lumbering has been important around the lake, and commercial fishing is returning to importance following years of pollution problems. Named for the Huron, who lived here when whites first arrived, the lake was seen in 1615 by the French explorer Champlain.

Huronia area on the SE corner of GEORGIAN BAY (L. Huron), Ontario, occupied by a Huron tribe when first seen by the French c.1610, now a popular resort and tourist area with historic settlements at PENETANGUISHENE and MIDLAND.

Huron Mountains 1500–1600 ft/457–488 m high, a granitic range in Baraga and Marquette counties, in the NW Upper Peninsula of Michigan. They extend about 20 mi/32 km NW–SE near the S shore of L. Superior. The heavily forested wilderness area is noted for its hunting and fishing. There are several lakes in the area, including Independence, Ives, Mountain, and Michigamme.

Huron River 100 mi/161 km long, in SE Michigan. It rises from several lakes in Livingston and Washtenaw counties and flows generally SE past Dexter, Ann Arbor, Belleville, and Flat Rock, to L. Erie SE of Rockwood.

Hurricane Alley inexactly applied term for areas esp. vulnerable to hurricanes. In the SE US, the storms tend to take two main paths. Most Atlantic Ocean hurricanes are born off W Africa, cross the ocean (where warm water feeds them power), pass through the West Indies, and approach the S of Florida. They then may turn N along the East Coast, losing energy when they cross over land or when they finally turn NE into the cooler parts of the North Atlantic. Alternatively, they may pass S of or over Florida, entering the Gulf of Mexico. There they may continue W to the Texas coast, or may turn N and NE to the Gulf Coast of Louisiana, Mississippi, and Alabama. Occasionally, hurricanes are born in the Gulf of Mexico and proceed NE to the Gulf Coast. The Florida–Gulf Coast path is most justly called "Hurricane Alley."

Hurst city, pop. 33,574, Tarrant Co., NE Texas, on Fort Worth's NE boundary, 10 mi/16 km NE of Downtown, just outside the beltway (Route 820). Incorporated in 1952, it is a residential and industrial suburb; a Bell helicopter plant is among its manufacturing facilities.

Hutchins city, pop. 2719, Dallas Co., NE Texas, on the Trinity R. adjacent to SE Dallas. Just outside the junction of the beltway (Interstate 20) and Interstate 45, it has varied industries.

Hutchinson **1.** city, pop. 39,308, seat of Reno Co., SC Kansas, on the Arkansas R., 40 mi/64 km NW of Wichita. Established in 1871, the city grew in 1887 with the discovery of salt, which is still processed from mines beneath it and nearby; exhausted mines have been converted into space for maximum-security storage of business records and the like. Wheat, oil, cattle, and related products and light manufactures also contribute to the city's economy. The Kansas State Fair is held here. The city is the seat of Hutchinson Community College (1928). **2.** city, pop. 11,523, McLeod Co., SE Minnesota, 56 mi/90 km W of Minneapolis. It was founded (1855) by three abolitionist brothers named Hutchinson. Several encounters of the Sioux Uprising (1862) were centered here. Now the center of a dairy farming region, it is also the site of several high-tech industries.

Hutchinson River 6 mi/10 km long, flowing from Scarsdale, New York, into Eastchester Bay, Long Island Sound. It was named for the religious dissenter Anne Hutchinson, who settled along it after fleeing Massachusetts in the 1640s. Co-op City and Pelham Bay Park are at its S end. The **Hutchinson River Parkway,** one of the New York City area's early (1939) motor highways, runs along the river for much of its length on its way from the Bronx-Whitestone Bridge to the Connecticut border, where it joins the Merritt Parkway.

Hyannis village, pop. 14,120, in the town of Barnstable, Barnstable Co., SE Massachusetts, on Cape Cod. It is the commercial center for the Cape, and has an airport. The village of **Hyannis Port** (S) contains the summer home of the family of John F. Kennedy.

Hyattsville city, pop. 13,864, Prince George's Co., SC Maryland, at the head of the Anacostia R., 6 mi/10 km NE of Washington, D.C. It is a largely residential suburb, a banking and commercial center, and home to some light industry.

Hybla Valley unincorporated community, pop. 15,491, Fairfax Co., N Virginia, 4 mi/6 km S of Alexandria, a largely residential suburb of Washington, D.C., on US 1.

Hyde Park **1.** largely residential section of Los Angeles, California, between CRENSHAW and INGLEWOOD, 6 mi/10 km SW of Downtown, a middle-class black community. **2.** residential neighborhood on the South Side of Chicago, Illinois, including the University of Chicago campus, between Washington and Jackson Parks. Although never as prestigious as the GOLD COAST or PRAIRIE AVENUE, it has long been one of Chicago's mostcosmopolitan neighborhoods and features high-density apartment buildings. The Museum of Science and Industry,DuSable Museum of African-American History, Oriental Institute, and Frank Lloyd Wright's Robie House are all here. **3.** residential neighborhood in extreme S Boston, Massachusetts. Situated on Mother Brook and the Neponset R., at a distance from central Boston, it is with neighboring Readville (S) a working-middle-class enclave. **4.** town, pop. 21,230, Dutchess Co., SE New York, on the E bank of the Hudson R., adjacent (N) to Poughkeepsie. Settled by the Dutch in 1741, it was the site of a number of 19th-century riverfront mansions belonging to wealthy and powerful families, including the Roosevelts and the Vanderbilts. It is best known as the home of President Franklin D. Roosevelt, who was born and is buried here. The Roosevelt Library (1941) and Museum and a number of preserved estates are now open to the public as National Historic Sites. These include the 200-ac/80-ha home of the president (1826), Eleanor Roosevelt's Val-Kill cottage, and the Vanderbilt Mansion (1898). Also in Hyde Park is the Culinary Institute of America. **5.** neighborhood of Cincinnati, Ohio, E of Downtown. It was originally home to some of the city's wealthiest residents, who built mansions here a century ago. Today many of these homes have been restored by young professionals.

I

Iao Valley see under WAILUKU, Hawaii.

Iberville city, pop. 9352, Le Haut-Richelieu Co., S Québec, on the E bank of the R. Richelieu, 23 mi/37 km SE of Montréal. It is a primarily residential suburb of SAINT-JEAN-SUR-RICHELIEU, which it faces across the river. Local industries include dairying and a variety of light manufactures.

Ice Age National Scientific Reserve developing system of natural areas in Wisconsin, along the S limit of the Wisconsin Glacier (and thus along the NE edge of the DRIFTLESS AREA). It is jointly administered by the National Park Service and the state, and incorporates several Wisconsin state parks. Its differing terrains are intended to illustrate a variety of glacial effects. Units include the Kettle Moraine State Forest–Northern Unit, 27,500 ac/11,138 ha, near KEWASKUM; Devil's Lake (see BARABOO); Horicon Marsh, a 21,000-ac/8500-ha cattail marsh SE of WAUPUN; and Interstate State Park, along the Saint Croix R. and Minnesota border. The **Ice Age National Scenic Trail,** authorized in 1980, will eventually link the units with a 1000-mi/1600-km hiking trail.

Idaho state of the NW US, one of the MOUNTAIN STATES; 1990 pop. 1,006,749 (106.7% of 1980; rank: 42nd); area 83,574 sq mi/216,457 sq km (rank: 14th); admitted to Union 1890 (43rd). Capital and most populous city: BOISE. Other leading cities: POCATELLO, IDAHO FALLS, NAMPA, LEWISTON. Idaho is bordered E by Montana (N, with the CONTINENTAL DIVIDE, in the BITTERROOT Mts., forming part of the boundary) and Wyoming; S by Utah (E) and Nevada; W by Oregon (S, with the SNAKE R. forming much of the boundary) and Washington; and N by British Columbia. The Snake R. flows E–W in a large arc across S Idaho, through the Snake River Plain section of the COLUMBIA PLATEAU. To the N are the Northern ROCKY Mts., a jumble of NNW–SSE and otherwise trending ranges including the Bitterroots, SAWTOOTHS, SALMON RIVERS, CLEARWATERS, COEUR D'ALENES, and Lost Rivers (including BORAH PEAK, at 12,662 ft/3862 m Idaho's high point). This N part of the state is largely underlain by the massive Idaho BATHOLITH, and contains several rich mining districts. In its SE corner, Idaho includes a N part of the Middle Rocky Mts., and just to the W, a N portion of the GREAT BASIN. Home to the Shoshone, Nez Perce, and Coeur d'Alene, the region is first known to have been seen by whites when LEWIS AND CLARK crossed through Lemhi Pass from what is now Montana, turned N, crossed the Bitterroots at LOLO Pass, and found the Lochsa R., a headwater of the CLEARWATER, on their way to the Pacific. In succeeding decades trapping was the key white activity; the NORTH WEST COMPANY established a post in the far N on L. PEND OREILLE, and both British and Americans operated in what was part of the OREGON country, all of which came under US control in 1846. By this time, westward migrants were pouring through the S over the OREGON TRAIL, which utilized the Snake R. valley, and after 1848 the CALIFORNIA TRAIL branched from this. Before 1860 there were a few missions, trade posts, and Mormon settlements within modern Idaho; in that year, gold was found at OROFINO, the first of numerous strikes during the decade. In 1863 the Idaho Territory (including Montana and much of Wyoming) was formed; its name was borrowed from a location near Pikes Peak, Colorado, and appears originally to have been a Great Plains tribal name, although it came to be translated as "gem of the mountains" (giving the nickname "the Gem State"). By 1868 Idaho had its modern boundaries. Ranching flourished along with mining, and in the 1870s conflict with local tribes was resolved in the Bannock War and the pursuit along the NEZ PERCE TRAIL. In the late 19th century mining was Idaho's cheif activity, and the 1890–1900s saw violent labor disputes. Railroads and the development of irrigation on the Snake R. brought growth to cities in the S; the 1930s creation of the SUN VALLEY resort by the UNION PACIFIC RAILROAD put Idaho on the vacation and recreation map. World War II was an economic boon to the state; L. Pend Oreille became a major submarine training site, and metal mining was important. After the war, what is now the IDAHO NATIONAL ENGINEERING LABORATORY got its start in a harsh, remote part of the Snake River Plain. By the 1970s, Idaho's scenery and quality of life had begun to attract residents and business from other states, particularly California; Boise has in recent decades become a corporate and high-tech manufacturing center. Much of the state is still devoted to agriculture, to stock raising and dairy production and, in the irrigated Snake R. valley, potato and wheat production. Mining is esp. important in the N, in the COEUR D'ALENE district; silver, zinc, lead, and gold are among leading products. Many of the state's manufactures utilize the pine and other woods of Idaho's forests. Tourism and recreation are major income sources. Pend Oreille, Coeur d'Alene, Priest, and other lakes in the N PANHANDLE; mountain-and-river terrain including that of the Frank Church–River of No Return Wilderness Area (see under SALMON R.), Sawtooth National Recreation Area, and HELLS CANYON National Recreation Area; and desert sites like the CRATERS OF THE MOON National Monument, draw visitors. The FORT HALL Indian Reservation surrounds the historic junction of the Oregon Trail with the Snake R., and in the S, the CITY OF ROCKS is an important site on the California Trail. The University of Idaho is at MOSCOW, Idaho State University at Pocatello. Over 60% of Idaho's land remains Federal, most of it in NATIONAL FORESTS. Its people are overwhelmingly Northern European in background; there is a Hispanic minority of about 5%.

Idaho Batholith see under BATHOLITH.

Idaho Falls city, pop. 43,929, seat of Bonneville Co., SE Idaho, on the upper Snake R., 55 mi/89 km NE of Pocatello. It was established c.1860 as a fording site and developed as a railroad division point. Since the early 20th century it has been the trade and shipping center of a farming region producing russet potatoes as the main crop, along with sugar beets, livestock, fruits, and grain. The IDAHO NATIONAL ENGINEERING LABORATORY, 40 mi/64 km W, provides considerable local employment; tourism is also important. The city's manufactures include potato products, beet sugar, concrete, stone products, farm implements, steel products, and campers.

Idaho National Engineering Laboratory 572,000-ac/232,000-ha (891-sq mi/2307-sq km) Federal reserve on the N of the SNAKE R. plain, in SC Idaho, at the SE foot of the Lost River and Lemhi ranges, 24 mi/39 km WNW of IDAHO FALLS. In 1947 this remote, desolate area was chosen for the National Reactor Testing Station, where in 1951 the first electricity-generating reactor was developed. Nuclear submarine power plants were among other 1950s innovations. Today, over 50 reactors operate at the Laboratory, most of whose workers live in Idaho Falls.

Idaho Panhandle National Forests see under PANHANDLE, Idaho.

Iditarod River in W Alaska, rising near Russian Mt. and flowing in an arc some 150 mi/240 km to the Innoko R. Gold was discovered at the now-deserted mining town of Iditarod, on the river, in 1908. The town is on the route of, and gives its name to, the famous 1160 mi/1868 km-long Iditarod dogsled race from Anchorage to Nome, inaugurated in 1973. Following an old mail route, the race commemorates a 1925 medical mission to Nome during a diphtheria epidemic. Traversing the ALASKA RANGE and running along the Yukon R. and Bering Sea coast, it begins in March and draws some 50 drivers and teams. The winner usually takes 10–11 days to complete the course.

Idlewild see under JOHN F. KENNEDY INTERNATIONAL AIRPORT, New York.

Igloo, the see under CIVIC ARENA, Pittsburgh, Pennsylvania.

Île-aux-Noix see NOIX, Île aux, Québec.

Iliamna Volcano see under LAKE CLARK NATIONAL PARK AND PRESERVE, Alaska.

Ilion village, pop. 8888, in German Flatts township, Herkimer Co., EC New York, on the Mohawk R., 10 mi/16 km SE of Utica. Prospering with the growth of the ERIE CANAL (1820s), it declined with the waterway later in the century, but was reenergized by the opening of the Remington firearms company, and still produces guns and ammunition. In a dairy and truck farming region, it is now part of a larger community that includes the neighboring municipalities of Mohawk, Herkimer, and Frankfort. Among its other manufactures are office equipment and machinery.

Illinois state of the NC US, in the MIDDLE WEST, also in the Great Lakes region; 1990 pop. 11,430,602 (100.0% of 1980; rank: 6th); area 57,918 sq mi/150,008 sq km (rank: 25th); admitted to Union 1818 (21st). Capital: SPRINGFIELD. Most populous cities: CHICAGO, ROCKFORD, PEORIA, Springfield, AURORA. Illinois is bordered E by Indiana, with the WABASH R. forming the S half of the boundary. On the SE it faces Kentucky across the OHIO R. Its entire W boundary is formed by the MISSISSIPPI R., across which are Missouri (S) and Iowa (N). On the N it is bordered by Wisconsin. On the NE, it has a shore of c.60 mi/100 km on L. MICHIGAN; Chicago and its N suburbs occupy this strip. Almost the entire state is part of the vast glaciated, TILL-covered C lowlands of the US. In the extreme NW is a small portion of the unglaciated Wisconsin DRIFTLESS AREA; here CHARLES MOUND (1235 ft/377 m), a MOUND BUILDER structure, is the state's high point. In the extreme S, between the Ohio and Mississippi rivers, is a complex district comprising the Illinois Ozarks, a low outrider of the OZARK PLATEAU to the SW, and, in the area long called EGYPT for its floodplain landscape, extreme N segments of the Gulf COASTAL PLAIN and Mississippi R. ALLUVIAL plain; the shore of the Mississippi, at 279 ft/85 m, is the state's low point. Most Illinois rivers flow W or SW into the Mississippi; chief among them are (N–S) the ROCK, ILLINOIS, and KASKASKIA. Except in the extreme S, where there are forest areas, Illinois has an open, sometimes rolling, terrain, and did when first seen by whites; it is called the Prairie State, although PRAIRIE has given way to the plowed soil of the CORN BELT. There are important coalfields in the C and in the S, where some oil is also extracted. Fluorspar is mined near the Ohio R. Illinois has many Mound Builder sites. When French explorers first saw the area, in the late 17th century, the Algonquian Illinois inhabited it, along with Kickapoo, Sac and Fox, Potawatomi, and other groups. The French established posts along the Mississippi (CAHOKIA, KASKASKIA) and Illinois (Fort Crevecoeur, at Peoria) rivers. In 1763 the British took control. Following the American Revolution Illinois became (1787) part of the NORTHWEST TERRITORY. Early settlement occurred largely in the wooded S, but esp. after 1825, when the ERIE CANAL increased travel on the Great Lakes, the portage at the head of the Illinois–DES PLAINES river system, using the short CHICAGO R. to reach L. Michigan, loomed as key to the state's development. Creation of the ILLINOIS WATERWAY in the 1840s was followed almost immediately by an explosion in railroad building; between the two, Chicago rapidly became the chief city of the Middle West, the hub from which transportation systems reached across America, and to which the country's products (esp. grain and cattle) were brought for processing. The NE lakefront has since the 1850s dominated state and region; almost everywhere in Illinois outside the Chicago area has come to be known as DOWNSTATE, and the "country" has often chafed at the city's hegemony. Much of the state, which had experienced a late outbreak of Indian resistance in the 1832 Black Hawk War, was settled after the ILLINOIS CENTRAL RAILROAD extended from N to S (1856); large areas were then opened to farming, in many lowland sections protected by LEVEES along the Mississippi. Industry outside Chicago developed chiefly along two rivers. On the Illinois–Des Plaines system are JOLIET (various metal and other products), Peoria (farm machinery), and a number of smaller manufacturing and processing centers. On the Rock R., in the NW, are Rockford (foundry products, tools), and at its mouth, MOLINE (farm machinery) and ROCK ISLAND (munitions), two of the Illinois-Iowa Quad Cities. In the SW, EAST SAINT LOUIS, a key industrial suburb of Saint Louis, Missouri, is in severe economic distress. A belt of industrial cities across Illinois's midsection, including DANVILLE (EC), DECATUR (C), and Springfield, are healthier, although the economy of the last now revolves around state government. URBANA and neighboring CHAMPAIGN (EC) are dominated by the University of Illinois and the research and other operations clustered around it. Other educational centers, in addition to Chicago, include CARBONDALE (S) and EVANSTON (in the N Chicago suburbs). In Chicago and its suburbs, meatpacking and heavy industry are gradually giving way to a wide range of light industries and research, as along the ILLINOIS RESEARCH AND DEVELOPMENT CORRIDOR. The METROPOLITAN AREA, the nation's third most populous, remains the commercial and cultural "capital" of the central US. Most of Illinois, however, is farm country. Soybeans, corn, and wheat are all important crops, and hogs and cattle major income sources. While Chicago has been ethnically diverse since the late 19th century, much of Downstate is populated largely by the descendants of 19th-century Eastern and Southern pioneers, with a mixture of later German, Scandinavian, and Slavic immigrants.

Illinois Central Railroad originally completed in 1856 between extreme N Illinois (with a branch to Chicago that soon became the main line) and Cairo, in the state's extreme S, on the Ohio and Mississippi rivers. Extending over 700 mi/1125 km, it was regarded as one of the engineering marvels of its day, esp. as it traversed uninhabited PRAIRIES, which it quickly helped populate. By the 1890s it had reached New Orleans, Louisiana, and its connections shifted much trade from the Mississippi R. valley to the East. From the 1850s it was also an important Chicago-area commuter line; in the 20th century it was a major route N for Southern blacks.

Illinois Research and Development Corridor recent promotional name for environs of the East–West Tollway (I-88) for some 50 mi/80 km W of Chicago, Illinois, especially in DU PAGE and KANE counties. It is perceived as developing along the lines of Boston's ROUTE 128 or California's SILICON VALLEY. Area scientific institutions providing impetus are the ARGONNE NATIONAL LABORATORY, 7 mi/11 km SSE of the Tollway, and BATAVIA's Fermi National Accelerator Laboratory, just N of the road. Technological and other corporations have located nearby, and have been joined by other businesses in such suburbs as Downers Grove, Lisle, and Lombard.

Illinois River 273 mi/440 km long, in Illinois. It is formed by the confluence of the Des Plaines and Kankakee rivers just W of the boundary of Grundy and Will counties, near Dresden, in NE Illinois, and drains 28,000 sq mi/72,520 sq km. It initially flows W past Morris, Seneca, Marseilles, and Ottawa, where it is joined by the Fox R. Turning SW near Depue, it then passes Chillicothe, Peoria, East Peoria, Creve Coeur, Pekin, Havana, and Hardin before joining the Mississippi R., 25 mi/40 km above St. Louis, Missouri. The Illinois River Valley was formed by the flow of water emanating from a retreating ice sheet. The lower course has many meanders, which have formed numerous oxbow lakes and bayous that attract various kinds of wildlife. The first Europeans to explore the Illinois were the Frenchmen Louis Jolliet and Jacques Marquette, who traveled up the river in 1673. Principal occupants of the valley at that time were the Kaskakia, Sac, and Fox tribes. The area was heavily settled in the 1820s. The river's main tributaries are the Vermilion, Spoon, Sangamon, La Moine, Macoupin, and Mackinaw rivers. See also ILLINOIS WATERWAY.

Illinois Waterway historic route, 327 mi/526 km long, that connected L. Michigan with the Mississippi R. and ensured Chicago's central role in the development of the Midwest. It was created by construction (finished 1848) of the 96 mi/155 km–long **Illinois and Michigan Canal,** which connected the South Branch of the CHICAGO R. with LA SALLE, near the head of navigation on the Illinois R. The canal bypassed navigational obstructions on the Des Plaines R. In 1900, the Chicago Sanitary and Ship Canal replaced the old canal in the stretch (30 mi/48 km) between Chicago and LOCKPORT, and engineers at the same time reversed the flow of the Chicago R. by closing its outlet on L. Michigan, causing it to flow into the Waterway. The Des Plaines R. was improved below Lockport to its junction with the Kankakee R. (forming the Illinois R.) at Dresden, and the old canal sank into disuse. The Waterway, which took traffic from the Mississippi at Grafton, Illinois, only 38 mi/62 km above St. Louis, made Chicago, rather than St. Louis or other older river ports like Cincinnati, the key to Midwestern development. Railroads gradually reduced its importance, and it is today largely recreational; much of the shipping that would still use it moves by way of the SAINT LAWRENCE SEAWAY.

Immaculata unincorporated community in East Whiteland township (pop. 8398), Chester Co., SE Pennsylvania, a residential suburb 25 mi/40 km W of Philadelphia. It is the seat of Immaculata College (1920).

Immokalee unincorporated community, pop. 14,120, Collier Co., SC Florida, 31 mi/50 km SE of Fort Myers. It is a trade center for local farms raising tomatoes and other truck. During the growing season it provides housing for a large number of migrant laborers, many Mexican. It lies on the N edge of the Big Cypress Swamp.

Imperial see under EL CENTRO, California.

Imperial Beach city, pop. 26,512, San Diego Co., extreme SW California, 9 mi/14 km S of San Diego, and just S of San Diego Bay, on the Pacific Ocean, 3 mi/5 km N of the border of Baja California, Mexico. It is the most southwesterly city in the continental US. Many residents are employed at its Naval Air Station. Its 4 mi/6 km of public beaches attract tourists, as does local fishing, and there are many expensive beach houses.

Imperial Valley COLORADO DESERT area in Imperial Co., extreme SE California. In the Salton Sink, E of the Peninsular Ranges, it extends from slightly S of the Baja California (Mexico) border some 60 mi/100 km NNW to the SALTON SEA, and is bordered E by the Sand Hills (Algodones Dunes) and CHOCOLATE Mts. Formerly covered by the Gulf of California (S), it is largely below sea level, dropping to −235 ft/−72 m at the Salton Sea. The area's agricultural potential (rich alluvial soils; almost no frost; the possibility of bringing water downhill from the COLORADO R.) was recognized late in the 19th century, and the valley was named, promoted, and largely irrigated and settled in 1900–10. Today the ALL-AMERICAN and hundreds of subsidiary canals irrigate about 1 million ac/400,000 ha devoted to vegetables, citrus fruits, grains, sugar beets, dates, and cotton. The valley's major communities are (N to S) BRAWLEY, EL CENTRO, and CALEXICO.

Incline Village unincorporated community, pop. (with Crystal Bay, just W) 7119, Washoe Co., W Nevada, 10 mi/16 km NW of Carson City, on the N of L. TAHOE and the California line (W). Named for Incline Mt., down which an 1870s tramway brought timbers for the COMSTOCK LODE mines, it was reborn in the 1960s as a lakeside and mountain-region resort, and has mansions, condominiums, and a casino.

Independence **1.** ghost town, Pitkin Co., WC Colorado, on the Roaring Fork R., 20 mi/32 km SW of Leadville. Once a flourishing 19th-century mining settlement, it is just W of Independence Pass and N of Independence Mt. **2.** city, pop. 9942, seat of Montgomery Co., SE Kansas, on the Verdigris R., 57 mi/91 km WSW of Pittsburg. It was founded in 1869 on former Osage land. With the discovery of gas (1881) and oil (1903) it became a refining and distribution center, but now also processes corn, wheat, beef, and dairy products and engages in diversified manufacturing. Independence Community College (1925) is here. **3.** city, pop. 10,444, seat of Kenton Co., N Kentucky, 9 mi/14 km S of Covington. It is a largely residential Cincinnati-area suburb. **4.** city, pop. 112,301, seat of JACKSON Co., NW Missouri, 11 mi/18 km ESE of downtown Kansas City. Settled in the 1820s, it marked the starting point of three major pioneer routes to the West during the mid 19th century: the SANTA FE, OREGON, and CALIFORNIA trails. An important 1830s Mormon settlement, it is now headquarters of the Reorganized Church of Jesus Christ of Latter-day Saints. During the Civil War, it saw the early part of the Battle of WESTPORT (Oct. 21, 1864), and was occupied by Union and, briefly, Confederate troops. Best known as the hometown of President Harry S. Truman (who was born in LAMAR), it is the site of his house, the Truman Library and Museum (1957), and various other locations associated with his life. The city was also the home of frontier artist George Caleb Bingham (1811–79). Today Independence is primarily a residential suburb. Tourism is important to its economy, which is also supported by oil refining and such manufactures as chemicals, machinery, crushed stone, processed foods, and electrical components.

Independence, Mount hill in WC Vermont, in Orwell township, overlooking L. Champlain. Opposite Fort TICONDEROGA, it has remains of a Revolutionary fort and stockade.

Independence Hall historic building, part of 45-ac/18-ha **Independence National Historic Park,** in C Philadelphia, Pennsylvania. Begun in 1732, the Georgian structure served as Pennsylvania's provincial capitol until the Second Continental Congress (1775–76), which drafted and approved the Declaration of Independence here. Both the Articles of Confederation (1778) and the US Constitution (1787) were also drawn up here. With the adjacent Congress Hall, it was the headquarters of the Federal government from 1790 to 1800.

Independence Rock in Wyoming: see under OREGON TRAIL.

independent city in Maryland, Missouri, Nevada, and esp. Virginia, a city administratively independent of any COUNTY.

Indiana state of the NC US, in the MIDDLE WEST (also one of the Great Lakes states); 1990 pop. 5,544,159 (101% of 1980; rank: 14th); area 36,420 sq mi/94,328 sq km (rank: 38th); admitted to Union 1816 (19th).Capital and most populous city: INDIANAPOLIS. Other leading cities: FORT WAYNE, EVANSVILLE, GARY, SOUTH BEND. Indiana is bordered NE by Michigan; E by Ohio; SE and S by Kentucky, across the OHIO R.; and W by Illinois, with the WABASH R. forming the S half of the boundary. In the NW, Indiana has a shoreline of c.45 mi/72 km on L. MICHIGAN, site of the INDIANA DUNES (E) and of the heavily industrialized CALUMET region, in the suburbs of Chicago, Illinois (W). The entire state lies within the vast C lowlands of the US, descending gradually toward the W; it rises to only 1257 ft/383 m, in the E, near Fountain City; the Ohio R., at 320 ft/98 m, is its low point. The state's major rivers flow generally NE–SW, toward the Mississippi Valley; they include (N–S) the KANKAKEE; the WABASH with its tributaries, including the TIPPECANOE; and the WHITE with its forks and tributaries. Indiana was glaciated in the N; to the S of the Wabash, some two-thirds of the state, are rolling plains, fertile agricultural land. The Eastern woodlands give way in Indiana to the PRAIRIES of the C US. The state has MOUND BUILDER sites; when French explorers and fur traders first arrived in the late 17th century, the Miami, Delaware (Lenni Lenape) and other peoples lived here. River trade brought the earliest European settlements, at VINCENNES on the Wabash and along the Ohio R. Controlled by the British after 1763, the area became part of the NORTHWEST TERRITORY of the new US in 1787. Indiana became a separate territory in 1800, but it was not until the battle of Tippecanoe (see BATTLE GROUND), in 1811, that Indian resistance to white inroads ended. Indiana was settled in the N by New Englanders and other Easterners, many moving W along the NATIONAL ROAD, and in the S by Virginians and Kentuckians; this led to serious divisions at the time of the Civil War, when Copperheads (pro-South Democrats) were prominent in the state, which still retains many Southern influences. At the same time, early settlers included many Quakers, who made the state important in the UNDERGROUND RAILROAD; Newport (now FOUNTAIN CITY) was called the "Grand Central Station" of the fugitive-slave network. Quaker RICHMOND and Robert Owen's NEW HARMONY were among other early religious communities. Canal and railroad systems had developed by the Civil War, and after its end, industrialization began to spread. Indiana's manufacturing centers are scattered in all corners of the state. Indianapolis, in the C, is the largest. The Calumet region (NW), however, is the state's heavy-industry hub. Here Gary, HAMMOND, and EAST CHICAGO are home to massive steel plants, part of the Great Lakes coal-and-iron complex; in the late 20th century the Calumet has suffered serious decline. To the E are South Bend and ELKHART, farther SE Fort Wayne, all centers of diverse manufacturing. MUNCIE (EC), a famous glassmaking center, is the "Middletown" of a noted 1920s study in which it represented a typical American city. ANDERSON, COLUMBUS, KOKOMO, and other C Indiana cities have all, like Indianapolis, Fort Wayne, and South Bend, been heavily involved in the automobile and machinery industries. Evansville and NEW ALBANY, on the Ohio, are leading S Indiana manufacturing centers. Much coal, and some oil, is produced in the S, and Indiana is noted for its limestone production, esp. at BLOOMINGTON (also the seat of Indiana University). In the CORN BELT, the state raises crops largely to feed its cattle and hogs; the small-farming pattern of the 19th century has gradually given way to large agribusiness holdings. Indiana's losses in RUST BELT plants are to some degree offset by diversified industry and business, esp. in the Indianapolis area. The most important visitor draw is the annual Indianapolis 500 auto race, at SPEEDWAY. In addition to Bloomington, academic centers include NOTRE DAME, near South Bend, and WEST LAFAYETTE, home to Purdue University. While the late 20th century has brought increased diversity to urban areas, Indiana's people remain largely descendants of the 19th-century Easterners and Appalachians, who came to be known as "Hoosiers," a name whose origins and meaning are in dispute.

Indiana borough, pop. 15,174, seat of Indiana Co., WC Pennsylvania, 45 mi/72 km NE of Pittsburgh. Founded in 1805, it was an important station on the Underground Railroad. Indiana is a major shipping and manufacturing center for a bituminous coal mining region in the Allegheny Mts. Among its manufactures are rubber tires, leather goods, clay products, and scientific instruments. It is also a major supplier of Christmas trees. The borough is the seat of Indiana University of Pennsylvania (1875).

Indiana County 829 sq mi/2147 sq km, pop. 89,994, in WC Pennsylvania, bounded (S) by the Conemaugh R. Its seat is INDIANA. A coal mining and stone quarrying area, it also has some agriculture and manufacturing, particularly in the county seat.

Indiana Dunes National Lakeshore 13,000-ac/5200-ha tract of dunes (rising to 180 ft/55 m), swamps, and marshes at the S end of L. Michigan, 15 mi/24 km E of Gary, Indiana. On a bird migration route, the dunes encompass a wide range of vegetation, including orchids, cactuses, ferns, and mosses. The ravines, lagoons, and bogs, formed by a glacier, are a popular recreational area for the nearby urban population. In 1896–97, Octave Chanute conducted important glider experiments in the dunes.

Indiana Harbor see under EAST CHICAGO, Indiana.

Indianapolis city, pop. 741,952, state capital and seat of MARION Co., C Indiana, on the West Fork of the White R., 160 mi/255 km SE of Chicago, Illinois. It is a transportation hub, agricultural market, and manufacturing and government center. Chosen in 1820 for its central location, it became Indiana's capital in 1825, succeeding CORYDON. Although not on a navigable waterway, it was shortly (1830s) on the NATIONAL ROAD and (1847) on the railroad, and is today the nexus of dozens of highways, railways, and air routes. Grain and livestock markets and meatpacking houses were soon important. By the end of the 19th century manufacturing, spurred in part by discovery nearby of natural gas deposits, was developing. Indianapolis became a center of the new automobile industry; since 1911, this role has been symbolized by the annual 500-mi/805-km Memorial Day auto race (held in SPEEDWAY), one of the world's best-known sports events, in which technological advances have been tested through their use in "Indy" cars. The city is also a center of pharmaceutical (Eli Lilly and other firms), communications equipment, electronics, rubber goods, and other industries. It is laid out around central Monument Circle, with its 285-ft/87-m Soldiers and Sailors Monument. In 1969 Indianapolis and Marion Co. were united in Unigov, a METROPOLITAN GOVERNMENT compact that greatly enlarged the city's size and pop. Four small cities, LAWRENCE, Speedway, BEECH GROVE, and Southport (pop. 1969), remain separate within Unigov. The University of Indiana–Purdue University at Indianapolis (1969, with professional schools), Butler University (1855), several other colleges, a noted children's museum, the national headquarters of the American Legion, and the state capitol (completed 1888) are here. In recent years the city has made an effort to establish itself as a sports mecca, with the large HOOSIERDOME, the Market Square Arena, and other buildings hosting major football, basketball, hockey, tennis, swimming, bicycle racing, and other events.

Indian Creek hamlet in Brown Co., C Texas, 70 mi/113 km SE of Abilene. Just S of BROWNWOOD on County Road 586, in rolling farm country, it is the birthplace (1890) of writer Katherine Anne Porter.

Indian Head town, pop. 1827, SE Saskatchewan, 41 mi/66 km E of Regina, and S of the Qu'Appelle R. valley. Named for a range of hills just S, it was settled in 1882 in an excellent wheat growing area, and remains an agricultural center, with grain elevators and flour mills. An Agriculture Canada experimental farm (1887) as well as a tree nursery are here.

Indian Island see under OLD TOWN, Maine.

Indianola **1.** city, pop. 11,340, seat of Warren Co., SC Iowa, 15 mi/24 km S of Des Moines. It has grain elevators and feed mills and manufactures brooms and metal products. Simpson College (1860) is here. The city is known for the US National Hot Air Balloon Championships held here every August, and is the site of the National Balloon Museum. Lake Ahquabi State Park is 5 mi/8 km S. **2.** city, pop. 11,809, seat of Sunflower Co., WC Mississippi, in the heart of the DELTA, on the Sunflower R., 22 mi/35 km ENE of Greenville. Settled before the Civil War, it is a cotton-country market town, with processing plants. There are also catfish farms and a vineyard and winery. **3.** see under PORT LAVACA, Texas.

Indian Point nuclear power complex in the village of Buchanan, in Cortlandt township, Westchester Co., SE New York, on the E bank of the Hudson R., 2 mi/3 km SW of Peekskill. Its reactors have been operational since 1973 and 1976.

Indian reservation **1.** in the US: land held in trust by the Federal or a state government for a specified group (*tribe*) of Indians. While all US-born Indians, as individuals, are citizens, they are, as members of a tribe and if resident on a reservation, subject to Federal and tribal, but not generally to state, laws. The sovereignty of tribes is complex; Federal law limits their self-government in various ways determined by treaty or legislation, and they do not, as states do under the US Constitution, retain all powers not specifically delegated to the Federal government. Broadly, they have the power to control membership and land use, raise local taxes, and administer their own legal systems (subject to Federal supremacy in regard to some criminal matters). US reservations range in size from a few acres to the huge NAVAJO INDIAN RESERVATION. Social and economic conditions also vary widely; while poverty and dependence on the Federal government has afflicted many, others have prospered from on-reservation businesses including logging, mining, oil and gas extraction, tax-free retailing, tourism and recreational development, and, most recently, operation of gambling establishments. There are over 300 Federal reservations (including PUEBLOS, RANCHERIAS, and a small number of entities otherwise designated) in the US, chiefly in the West, along with some 20 state reservations (chiefly in the East). Many reservations are adjoined by additional **trust lands.** Another 200 small communities in Alaska are designated **Alaskan villages;** they do not have formal boundaries. See also TRIBAL JURISDICTION STATISTICAL AREAS, in Oklahoma. **2. Indian reserve** in Canada: analogous to a reservation in the US, and occupied by a *band* rather than a tribe. Canadian reserves are maintained for the use of "status Indians" (who have not assimilated into majority society), under various treaties and Federal laws. There are some 1000 variously designated reserves, about half in British Columbia, and 500 bands (some of whom do not have reserves). Generally, reserves are much smaller than US reservations; they remain technically CROWN LANDS (owned outright by the central government).

Indian River shallow, 115 mi/185 km–long lagoon, following the coastline and protected from the Atlantic Ocean by barrier beaches, in Brevard, Indian River, St. Lucie, and Martin counties, EC Florida. One to 5.5 mi/1–9 km wide, it joins Mosquito Lagoon (by channel) on the N and enters the ocean at St. Lucie Inlet on the S. It merges with the Banana R. lagoon (E) near Satellite Beach. Much of the S section is an aquatic reserve. Communities bordering the lagoon include (N to S) Titusville, Cocoa, Melbourne, Vero Beach, and Fort Pierce.

Indian Springs unincorporated community, pop. 1164, Clark Co., SE Nevada, 40 mi/64 km NW of Las Vegas. It is the gateway to the Air Force's **Indian Springs Gunnery Range,** part of S Nevada's huge military and nuclear test complex.

Indian Stream 25 mi/40 km long, in N New Hampshire. It rises near the Québec line and flows generally SW to the Connecticut R. in SW Pittsburg township. From 1832 to 1835, settlers in the area, which was claimed by both the US and Britain (Lower Canada), established themselves as the independent **Indian Stream Republic.** The area was subsequently occupied by the state militia and awarded to New Hampshire by the 1842 Webster-Ashburton Treaty.

Indian Territory lands reserved, pursuant to the Indian Removal Act of 1830 and Indian Trade and Intercourse Act of 1834, for a "permanent" home for the "Five Civilized Tribes" (see TRAIL OF TEARS) and others. It originally comprised all land W of the borders of the states of Arkansas, Missouri, and Iowa, N of the Red R. and S of the Missouri R., extending to 100° W, then the W boundary of the organized US. The pressure of westward white expansion was constant on the Territory. In 1854, the Kansas and Nebraska territories were organized in the N part, leaving only Oklahoma E of the PANHANDLE in Indian Territory. Meanwhile, tribes from as far as Oregon (the Modoc) were relocated here. The Federal government seized on the Five Civilized Tribes' alliance with the Confederacy to strip them of lands in the W in 1866. By the 1880s "Boomers" were squatting in various areas. The 1887 General Allotment (Dawes) Act mandated breakup of collective ownership and replacement by individual ownership; most of the "allotments" thus created were soon sold to whites by impoverished Indians. In April 1889 the "Unassigned Lands" at Oklahoma's center were thrown open in the famous "Land Run" that created OKLAHOMA CITY. The 1898 Curtis Act dissolved tribal governments altogether, and in 1907 Oklahoma became a state, finally dissolving the Indian Territory. Today, the Osage reservation (see OSAGE Co.) is Oklahoma's only INDIAN RESERVATION. Other lands that once belonged to the various peoples are classified by the Census Bureau as TRIBAL JURSIDICTION STATISTICAL AREAS (formerly "Historic Areas").

Indian Village residential neighborhood in Detroit, Michigan, E of Downtown. A collection of single-family turn-of-the-century homes built for the city's elite, it has maintained its social cohesion and architectural character largely through the efforts of the Indian Village Association.

Indio city, pop. 36,793, Riverside Co., S California, in the desert of the Coachella Valley, 18 mi/29 km SE of Palm Springs. It is a trade center for a region irrigated by the Coachella Main Canal (the All-American Canal), which produces dates, citrus fruit, and other crops. Established in 1876 as a railroad town, Indio is now a growing residential community.

Industry see CITY OF INDUSTRY, California.

infrastructure elements thought of as underlying the life of municipalities or states, especially physical structures like roads, bridges, dams, and telephone systems, but also such entities as schools, which are part physical, part intangible.

Ingersoll town, pop. 9378, Oxford Co., S Ontario, on the Thames R., 18 mi/29 km ENE of London. It is named for Thomas Ingersoll, father of War of 1812 heroine Laura Secord, who arrived here in 1793. Site of Canada's first (1864) cheese factory, it is the commercial center of an extensive dairying region; local manufactures include furniture, fertilizers, lumber, and hardware.

Ingham County 560 sq mi/1450 sq km, pop. 281,912, in SC Michigan, drained by the Grand and Red Cedar rivers. Its seat is Mason. The NE portion of the county is dominated by Lansing, the state capital, and its suburbs, where there is manufacturing. Coal and clay deposits are found in this largely agricultural region, which turns out grain, fruit, vegetables, sugar beets, livestock, and dairy products.

Inglewood city, pop. 109,602, Los Angeles Co., SW California, 8 mi/13 km S of downtown Los Angeles, and 5 mi/8 km E of the Pacific Ocean. Los Angeles International Airport is just W. Founded in 1873, the city was formed from parts of two Spanish RANCHOS. The area produces oil, and aircraft and aircraft parts, furniture, metal products, cosmetics, and enamelware have been manufactured in the city. The Forum, the Los Angeles area's leading sports arena, is here. Seating 18,000, it is home to the Lakers (basketball) and Kings (hockey), and hosts other sports and entertainments. Thoroughbred and harness racing takes place at Hollywood Park. Northrop University (1942) is here.

Inglewood–Finn Hill unincorporated community, pop. 29,132, King Co., WC Washington, on the E side of L. Sammamish, 13 mi/21 km E of Seattle. It is an upper-income residential suburb.

Inkster city, pop. 30,772, Wayne Co., SE Michigan, on the R. Rouge, 13 mi/21 km W of Detroit. A residential suburb of Detroit founded in 1825, it also manufactures tools and dies.

Inland Empire **1.** mid-20th-century promotional name for an area of SAN BERNARDINO and RIVERSIDE counties, SW California, W of the San Gabriel Valley and S of the San Bernardino Mts. Ontario, San Bernardino, and Riverside are its largest cities. **2.** vast plateau area of E Washington, extending into NW Idaho and N Oregon. Bounded W by the Cascade Range, which shields it from moist Pacific winds, it is a largely dry farming zone, noted esp. for wheat production. Its terrain is varied, ranging from SCABLANDS to rangeland to sagebrush desert to wooded hills. Irrigation projects have since the 1930s made much of it amenable to a wider range of agriculture. The BIG BEND occupies much of the region.

Inland Passage see INSIDE PASSAGE.

Inman Park residential and commercial section of NE Atlanta, Georgia, 2 mi/3 km ENE of FIVE POINTS. An 1890s streetcar suburb, it is now undergoing renovation of its Victorian housing stock. Little Five Points, just NE along

Euclid Ave., is noted for its entertainments and bohemian street life.

inner city older sections of a city close to DOWNTOWN, esp. when suffering economic and social distress, accompanied by deterioration of INFRASTRUCTURE. Inner city conditions are usually created by the departure of former residents for suburbs or outer city neighborhoods, followed by the departure of commerce and capital. Location in the inner city of industries (e.g., slaughterhouses) detrimental to living conditions may be a cause. The older area is then inhabited by those who cannot afford, or are otherwise unable, to live farther from the city center, typically the elderly or poor. Racial segregation may cause the inner city to become a GHETTO. URBAN RENEWAL programs have since the 1950s attacked inner city conditions.

Inner Harbor **1.** industrial and commercial area of DOWNTOWN New Orleans, Louisiana, 1.5 mi/2 km E of the VIEUX CARRÉ, along the Inner Harbor Navigation Canal, which connects the Mississippi R. (S) with L. Pontchartrain (N). MARIGNY is just W. **2.** redeveloped district surrounding the N section of the Port of Baltimore, in downtown Baltimore, Maryland. Formerly a scene of rotting piers and abandoned warehouses and markets, it was redeveloped in the 1970s and 1980s. Existing structures were replaced by 55 ac/22 ha of parks, a 33-story world trade center, a new marina, apartment complexes, a convention center, a new hotel, a new home for the Maryland Academy of Science, and 600,000 sq ft/55,800 sq m of office space in buildings connecting the harbor to CHARLES CENTER. Port activity was relocated to the lower and middle sections of the harbor. HARBORPLACE is in the NW corner.

Inscription Rock see EL MORRO, New Mexico.

Inside, the see under the NORTH, in Canada.

Inside Passage also, **Inland Passage** natural water route from SEATTLE, Washington, to SKAGWAY, Alaska, passing through Puget Sound, past Vancouver I. and the islands of Hecate Strait, and through the ALEXANDER ARCHIPELAGO off SE Alaska, to Lynn Canal. The many islands, straits, and inlets in the 1000 mi/1600 km–long passage offer shelter from open Pacific seas, and it is deep enough for most vessels. Both cargo and passenger ships traveling between the Pacific Northwest and Alaska generally use this route, with its views of FJORDS, conifer forests, glacial waterfalls, and snow-covered mountains. Ports along the route include Victoria, Vancouver, and Prince Rupert, British Columbia; and Ketchikan, Wrangell, and Juneau, Alaska. An alternate route at the N end leads through Cross Sound to the Gulf of Alaska. Navigators from Spain, England, Russia, and the US explored the route and named many of its islands and straits.

Institute locality in Kanawha Co., WC West Virginia, on the Kanawha R., 8 mi/13 km W of CHARLESTON. West Virginia State College, founded for black students in 1891, and a large Union Carbide chemical plant are here.

Interlochen unincorporated village in Grand Traverse Co., in the NW Lower Peninsula of Michigan, near Duck and Green lakes, 12 mi/19 km SSW of Traverse City. It is named for a town in Switzerland. It is the site of the Interlochen Center for the Arts, which includes an internationally renowned Arts Camp. Founded in 1927, the camp provides eighth-grade through college instruction during the summer for more than 1500 students in music, theater, visual arts, and dance. A popular Arts Festival is held annually. The village is situated in Pere Marquette State Forest just N of Interlochen State Park, in a fruit growing area.

Intermontane Region also, **Intermontane Plateaus** or **Intermountain Region** general term for the geologically complex region between the Rocky Mts. (on the E) and the Pacific coastal mountains (Coast Ranges and Coast Mts., on the W). In the US, it is a belt 400–600 mi/640–1000 km wide, including the mountains and depressions of the BASIN AND RANGE PROVINCE, along with the COLORADO PLATEAU (SE) and COLUMBIA PLATEAU (N). In Canada, it narrows toward the N, extending through the Interior Plateaus of British Columbia and the Yukon Territory. In Alaska, where the great mountain chains turn W, the Interior is an E–W extension of the Intermontane Region.

International District commercial and residential district of SEATTLE, Washington, immediately SE (across Yesler Way) of Downtown. Home to Chinese who have been here since the 1870s, it has been called Chinatown, but its residents also include many Filipinos, Vietnamese, Cambodians, Japanese, and Pacific Islanders. King St. is a main thoroughfare.

International Falls city, pop. 8325, seat of Koochiching Co., extreme N Minnesota, a port of entry on the RAINY R., across from Fort Frances, Ontario. In a farming and timbering region, it has an extensive paper industry. A summer tourism center, it serves as the entry point for Voyageurs National Park. The French established the trading post of St. Pierre in 1731; the town was settled 150 years later.

International Peace Garden 2330 ac/944 ha, along the North Dakota–Manitoba line. It was established in 1931 as a monument to peaceful US-Canadian relations. DUNSEITH, North Dakota, is 14 mi/23 km S; BOISSEVAIN, Manitoba, is 15 mi/24 km N. It incorporates formal gardens, a 120-ft/37-m Peace Tower, a chapel, and various other visitor facilities. An International Music Camp operates in the summer. Turtle Mt. Provincial Park is just W on the Manitoba side.

International Rapids see under SAINT LAWRENCE R.

Interstate Highway System network of US highways built and maintained under various acts establishing US-state funding mechanisms and Federally imposed engineering standards. The coast-to-coast LINCOLN HIGHWAY (begun 1913) was a forerunner of the 1916 Federal Aid Highway Act, which initiated Federal funding, and the 1921 Highway Aid Act, which initiated the designating of "primary" and other routes. Numbering of US highways (US 1, etc.) began in 1925. During the Depression, roadbuilding was a major form of government job creation. The types and number of roads falling under Federal stewardship continued to expand, and the 1956 Interstate Highway Act, creating today's interstate system, has been called the largest public works program ever; it paralleled or replaced older US highways in most places, so that, e.g., US 40 in the West has now been largely replaced by Interstate 80 (I-80). **Interstate and Defense Highways,** covering some 42,500 mi/68,500 km, are funded on a 90% Federal/10% state basis, another 800,000 mi/1.3 million km of primary, secondary, and urban roads at a 75%/25% ratio. The system is financed largely by excise (esp. gasoline) taxes.

interurban type of electric rail system that came into existence in the 1880s and shaped city life until shortly after World War I, when the private automobile caused its rapid decline and disappearance. Augmenting city trolley systems, and often paralleling existing rail lines, interurbans were a major force in the creation of STREETCAR SUBURBS.

Intracoastal Waterway see ATLANTIC INTRACOASTAL WATERWAY; GULF INTRACOASTAL WATERWAY.

Inuit indigenous peoples of the N edge of North America, from Alaska to Greenland, thought to have emigrated from Asia within the last 6000 years. They (and related Siberian groups) are also called **Eskimos;** this book adopts the prevailing (and official) Canadian, and growing American, usage, *Inuit.* The Aleuts of the ALEUTIAN Is. are related.

Inuvik town, pop. 3206, Inuvik Region, extreme NW Northwest Territories, within the Reindeer Grazing Reserve and the MACKENZIE R. delta, 70 mi/115 km E of the Yukon border and 120 mi/190 km N of the Arctic Circle. Planned in the 1950s, it is the regional administration center, the commercial and transportation center for the Mackenzie delta region (at the NE end of the DEMPSTER HIGHWAY), and a supply base for BEAUFORT SEA gas and oil exploration. The region's Inuit, who also live in the older Aklavik (hamlet, pop. 801, 31 mi/50 km W) and Tuktoyaktuk (hamlet, pop. 918, 70 mi/113 km NNE), produce crafts and clothing and are trappers, sealers, and walrus hunters.

Inver Grove Heights city, pop. 22,477, Dakota Co., SE Minnesota, on the Mississippi R., a suburb 8 mi/13 km SE of St. Paul. It has been the site of substantial recent commercial and residential development, especially along the I-494 corridor in the N.

Inwood in New York: **a.** see under FIVE TOWNS, Long Island. **b.** largely residential section, the northernmost part of Manhattan I., New York City, on the Hudson (W) and Harlem (N and E) rivers. The Inwood Valley was the site of Indian settlements, and in the 1680s was noted for its agriculture. The Dyckman House (1783) is Manhattan's only remaining 18th-century farmhouse. Much of Inwood is parkland. Inwood Hill Park (167 ac/68 ha) is on high ground along the Hudson; a bridge on the Henry Hudson Parkway passes overhead to Spuyten Duyvil, the Bronx. Columbia University's Baker Field is NE. Fort Tryon Park is SW, between Inwood and Washington Heights. Inwood, a longtime Irish neighborhood, is in transition, with a growing Dominican population.

Inyo Mountains range in EC California, extending SSE from the WHITE Mts. for c.70 mi/110 km along the E side of the OWENS Valley. It reaches its highest elevation at Waucoba Mt. (11,123 ft/3390 m), and includes **Mt. Inyo** (11,107 ft/3385 m) in the S, 10 mi/16 km NNE of LONE PINE. The range's Shoshonean name probably refers to Paiute sacred sites. **Inyo National Forest,** over 1.9 million ac/770,000 ha, is in two sections, on the E and W of the Owens Valley. The E section includes much of the Inyo and White ranges. The W includes parts of the Ansel Adams, Hoover, and John Muir wilderness areas and Mt. WHITNEY (14,495 ft/4418 m), highest point in the coterminous US.

Iola city, pop. 6351, seat of Allen Co., SE Kansas, on the Neosho R., 17 mi/27 km NNE of Chanute. It was founded in 1859. Its economy was based on natural gas from its discovery (1893) till its depletion (1920s), but today grain, livestock, dairy products, and light manufactures are central. The city is the seat of Allen County Community College (1923).

Ionia city, pop. 5935, seat of Ionia Co., SC Michigan, on the Grand R., 28 mi/45 km E of Grand Rapids. It trades in locally grown fruit, livestock, grain, and beans, and mills flour. Manufactures include auto parts, processed food, and furniture. Two districts of historic architecture are preserved.

Iowa state of the NC US, in the Upper MIDDLE WEST; 1990 pop. 2,776,755 (95.3% of 1980; rank: 30th); area 56,276 sq mi/145,755 sq km (rank: 26th); admitted to Union 1846 (29th). Capital and most populous city: DES MOINES. Other leading cities: CEDAR RAPIDS, DAVENPORT, SIOUX CITY, WATERLOO. Iowa is bordered S by Missouri, with the DES MOINES R. forming a short part of the SE boundary; W by Nebraska (across the MISSOURI R.) and by South Dakota (NW, across the BIG SIOUX R.); and N by Minnesota. Its entire E boundary is the MISSISSIPPI R., across which are Wisconsin (N) and Illinois (S). The state lies entirely within the vast C lowlands of the US, rising from under 500 ft/150 m along the Mississippi (E) to a high of 1670 ft/509 m at OCHEYEDAN MOUND, in the NW corner. In the NE corner is a small extension of Wisconsin's DRIFTLESS AREA; the rest of the state was glaciated, and consists of till- and drift-covered (see under MORAINE) plains, constituting rolling, fertile PRAIRIE. Tributaries of the Mississippi flow NW–SE across most of the state, including the MAQUOKETA, WAPSIPINICON, CEDAR, IOWA, SKUNK, and Des Moines rivers. In the SW, shorter tributaries of the Missouri flow NNE–SSW. A major consituent of the CORN BELT, Iowa also grows wheat, soybeans, and other grasses and grains, much going to feed cattle and hogs, the source of much of the state's income. Dairy and poultry farming are also important. Coal (SC), gypsum, and stone are mined in various locations. Its fertility and resources have kept Iowa from losing farmers as quickly as some of its neighbors, but in recent decades there has been drift toward cities. Agriculture-related industries have been basic in DUBUQUE, Waterloo, Cedar Rapids, and other centers, but diversification is now the rule in Iowa's urban centers. Des Moines, in particular, has financial and insurance sectors and high-tech manufactures. Davenport (with BETTENDORF part of the Illinois-Iowa QUAD CITIES) and Sioux City make various kinds of machinery. Smaller communities, like the AMANA COLONIES (refrigeration equipment), NEWTON (washing machines), and FORT MADISON (pens) contribute to the state's manufacturing income. The Mississippi R. cities, esp. (S–N) KEOKUK, BURLINGTON, Davenport, CLINTON, and Dubuque, have long prospered from river trade. Iowa has numerous MOUND BUILDER sites, including the EFFIGY MOUNDS (NE, across the Mississippi from Prairie du Chien, Wisconsin). The Siouan people who gave the state its name were here, along with the Sac and Fox and other groups, when French explorers and traders arrived in the late 17th century. The region passed to the US with the 1803 LOUISIANA PURCHASE. After the Black Hawk War (in neighboring Illinois and Wisconsin) in 1832, area tribes were forced westward, and settlers from the East poured in. An 1857 massacre by Sioux at SPIRIT LAKE (NW) was a late outbreak of resistance against the white advance. In the 1860s, COUNCIL BLUFFS, formerly on the MORMON TRAIL, was the point from which the transcontinental (UNION PACIFIC) railroad jumped off, via neighboring Omaha, Nebraska, across the Missouri and toward the West. Since the end of the Civil War, Iowa's history has been substantially the history of good and bad times in American agriculture, with the gradual development in the late 20th century of agribusiness, replacing the family farm. Iowans (popularly, Hawkeyes) remain mostly the descendants of the mid-19th-century Easterners and Southerners who began intensive settlement, and of the Germans, Scandinavians, and other Europeans who joined them later in the century. The University of Iowa is at IOWA CITY, Iowa State University at AMES; GRINNELL is another noted academic center. The birthplace of Herbert Hoover at WEST BRANCH (SE) is a popular visitor site.

Iowa City city, pop. 59,738, seat of Johnson Co., SE Iowa, on the Iowa R., 22 mi/35 km S of Cedar Rapids. An important agricultural trading and processing center, it also manufactures foam rubber, animal feed, pharmaceuticals, and coated paper. It is the seat of the University of Iowa (1847), the main pillar of the local economy and cultural life. The Iowa Writers' Workshop and Iowa Center for the Arts are among institutions connected with the school. The Iowa Health Center is one of the world's largest university-owned teaching hospitals. The Iowa State Historical Society and State Geological Survey have their headquarters here. Iowa City was established as the first seat of government in the Iowa Territory (1839), and served as capital (1846–57). Rail service arrived in the 1850s, making the city an outfitting point for westward-bound wagon trains. A thriving city, it grew by one-sixth in the 1980s.

Iowa Falls city, pop. 5424, Hardin Co., EC Iowa, on the Iowa R., 42 mi/68 km W of Waterloo. Settled in the 1850s, it has produced limestone, concrete, and processed foods. The river passes through a gorge with 70 ft/21 m–high walls here. Ellsworth Community College (1890) is here, and the city has long been a Baptist convention center.

Iowa Great Lakes resort area in Dickinson Co., NW Iowa, immediately S of the Minnesota line, centered around four lakes and the city of Spirit Lake (pop. 3871), site of an 1857 Sioux massacre. The four lakes are Spirit, East Okoboji, West Okoboji, and Silver.

Iowa River 330 mi/531 km long, in C and SE Iowa. It is formed by the confluence of several branches just S of Belmond, and flows generally SE past Iowa Falls, Marshalltown, and Iowa City, continuing to the Mississippi R. at the Illinois border, 20 mi/32 km S of Muscatine.

Ipswich town, pop. 11,873, Essex Co., NE Massachusetts, on the Ipswich R. and Ipswich Bay of the Atlantic Ocean, 30 mi/48 km N of Boston. Known for its clams, Ipswich is a summer resort with the 5-mi/8-km Crane's Beach. The town, first known as Agawam (or Aggawam), has preserved a number of Colonial homes. There is some light manufacturing. Part of PLUM I., NE across the bay, is in Ipswich.

Iqaluit town, pop. 3552, Baffin Region, E Northwest Territories, at the SE extreme of BAFFIN I., on FROBISHER BAY, 1250 mi/2000 km N of Montréal, Québec. Before 1987 called Frobisher Bay, the town is a regional government and service center, and a tourist base linked by air to major Canadian cities and to other Territories communities. It was a World War II airbase and station on the DEW LINE. In the 1950s many Inuit families were relocated here by the government; fishing, sealing, and handicraft production are economically important. Qaummaarviit Historic Park, site of a 700-year-old Inuit fishing camp, is on an island 8 mi/13 km W.

Irish Channel waterfront section of NEW ORLEANS, Louisiana, on the Mississippi R., opposite Marrero, immediately S and E of the GARDEN DISTRICT and 2 mi/3 km SSW of Jackson Square. A tough 19th-century dockside area named after an 1840s influx of Irish immigrants, it now has a mix of commercial and residential structures. Its E end was developed as part of the 1984 Louisiana World Exposition site.

Irmo town, pop. 11,280, Richland and Lexington counties, C South Carolina, 9 mi/14 km NW of Columbia, near L. Murray (the Saluda R.), a booming residential suburb of the capital.

Ironbound, the residential and commercial neighborhood on the SE side of the city of Newark, New Jersey. It is inhabited by one of the largest concentrations of Portuguese immigrants in the US. Situated in a heavily industrial zone, it has been the scene of recent toxic-waste controversies.

Irondale city, pop. 9454, Jefferson Co., C Alabama, immediately E of Birmingham, of which it is an industrial (iron producing) and growing residential suburb.

Irondequoit town, pop. 52,377, Monroe Co., W New York, on L. Ontario (N) and Irondequoit Bay (E), and almost surrounded (N, W, and S) by ROCHESTER. It is a largely residential suburb.

Iron Mountain **1.** elevation: see under LAKE WALES, Florida. **2.** city, pop. 8525, seat of Dickinson Co., in the SW Upper Peninsula of Michigan, 52 mi/84 km W of Escanaba and 2 mi/3 km E of the Wisconsin border. It was founded in 1879 and named for iron layers in nearby bluffs. Iron mining was the main activity until extraction became uneconomical in the 1930s–40s. Tourism, especially for winter sports, is now the economic mainstay. There are now tours of inoperative mines here, as well as a mining and a historical museum. Pine Mountain Ski Jump, one of the world's highest, is just N of the city. It remains a farming and trade center, and manufactures such items as mining equipment, dairy products, chemicals, tools and castings, and wood products. Early documentary filmmaker Robert Flaherty was born here (1884).

Iron Mountains ridge in the Great Appalachian Valley of the Appalachian Mts., in SW Virginia and NE Tennessee, extending for approximately 80 mi/130 km to the New R. (NE), and rising generally to about 3940 ft/1200 m. Mt. ROGERS (5729 ft/1746 m) is on a spur of the Iron Mts.

Iron Range Region area of NE Minnesota where, from S to N, the Cuyuna, Mesabi, and Vermilion iron ranges are located. Remnants of ridges worn down by glaciation, the ranges are not mountains but rock folds interlaced with iron deposits. Mining shipments began in the area in 1884, and at one time it was the source of almost all of the country's iron ore used for manufacturing. With the depletion of ore, taconite became the primary product of the area in the mid 20th century. The region includes the national historic sites at Calumet, site of the famous Hill Annex Mine, and HIBBING, site of the Hull-Rust Mine, the largest open-pit mine. The largest taconite plant in the world today is the Minntac Taconite Plant near VIRGINIA.

Ironton city, pop. 12,751, seat of Lawrence Co., SC Ohio, on the Ohio R. at the Kentucky border, 22 mi/35 km SE of Portsmouth. Once the center of the pig iron industry of S Ohio, it was founded in 1848 by furnace operators as a manufacturing and shipping center. Currently its principal manufactures are metal castings, fabricated metals, coke, industrial chemicals, and plastic.

Ironwood city, pop. 6849, Gogebic Co., at the extreme W of Michigan's Upper Peninsula, on the Montreal R., across from HURLEY, Wisconsin. It was the center of the Gogebic Range iron boom. From 1885, ore was shipped from Ironwood's mines to ESCANABA, thence to industrial centers. Dug into tilted sedimentary belts, the mines were among the world's deepest, and the city suffered subsidence of large surface areas. It is today a regional trade center, and home to Gogebic Community College (1932).

Iroquois Confederacy also, **Iroquois League** or **League of the Five** (or **Six**) **Nations** confederation (c.1570–c.1775) of Iroquoian tribes occupying C New York from the Hudson R. (E) to the W Finger Lakes, and expanding its domain at times as far E as Maine, N into Canada, and far S and W. Its constituents (E to W) were the Mohawk, Oneida, Cayuga, Onondaga, and Seneca; the Tuscarora became the sixth nation in the 1720s. The confederacy was conceived as a Long House (metaphorically adopting the tribes' characteristic dwelling), with the Mohawk as the E doorkeepers, the Seneca at the W. Founded around 1570 by Deganawidah and Hiawatha, the confederacy was hostile to the French, and allied with the British; when the Revolutionary War began, this loyalty caused its destruction. The Cayuga departed for Ontario. Many of the Mohawk moved into Ontario and Québec, and today they are centered along the SAINT REGIS R. The Oneida, Onondaga, Tuscarora (around LEWISTON), and Seneca (in CATTARAUGUS Co.) remain headquartered in New York.

Iroquois Falls see under L. ABITIBI, Ontario.

Irvine city, pop. 110,330, Orange Co., SW California, 40 mi/64 km SE of Los Angeles. It was created in the 1970s as a planned community, occupying a large part of the former Irvine Ranch, a major area RANCHO. The University of California at Irvine (1964) was an anchor for development, which now includes industrial and office complexes in the aerospace, biotech, financial, electronics, automotive research, fashion, and other sectors. Christ College Irvine (1972) is also here. Irvine continues to expand rapidly. The outdoor Irvine Meadows Amphitheatre seats 15,000 people for concerts and other events.

Irving city, pop. 155,037, Dallas Co., NE Texas, 9 mi/14 km NW of downtown Dallas, adjoining the larger city's NW side. It also adjoins the easternmost part of Fort Worth. A small agricultural community until the mid 20th century (its 1950 pop. was under 2600), it is now one of the largest industrial, commercial, and residential communities in the METROPLEX area. It has food processing, concrete and asphalt, aluminum, chemical, ink, graphite, wallboard, insecticide, and paint industries. Its 12,000-ac/4900-ha Las Colinas business complex houses some of its many financial, advertising, and corporate offices. The city is home to the University of Dallas (1956) and North Lake College (1977). The Dallas–Fort Worth International Airport lies NW, and Texas Stadium (1971), the 65,000-seat home of the Dallas Cowboys (football), is here.

Irvington **1.** township, pop. 61,010, Essex Co., NE New Jersey, adjacent (W) to Newark. Settled in 1692, it was called Camptown until 1852. Irvington's industrial sector has foundries and tanneries, and manufactures a wide variety of goods including metal castings, chemicals, tools and dies, insulators, cutlery, photographic equipment, paints, building supplies, and paper and plastic products. The town also has a large residential component. **2.** also, **Irvington-on-Hudson** village, pop. 6348, in Greenburgh town, Westchester Co., SE New York, on the Hudson R., 22 mi/35 km N of New York City. It is an affluent residential and commercial suburb. Irvington's noted estates include the Octagon House (1860) and Villa Lewaro (1916–18), former home of hair-care magnate Mme. C. J. Walker. The village has been home to Hamiltons, Morgans, and other New York plutocrats.

Isabela unincorporated community (ZONA URBANA), pop. 13,515, Isabela Municipio (pop. 39,147), NW Puerto Rico, on the Atlantic coast, 18 mi/29 km W of Arecibo. A resort, it is known for its whitewashed houses and surf-pounded beaches. It also has industries producing footwear and textiles, and is a trade center for producers of sugarcane, tobacco, coffee, fruits, and vegetables; horses are raised in the S of the MUNICIPIO.

Iselin unincorporated community, pop. 16,141, in Woodbridge township, Middlesex Co., NE New Jersey, 9 mi/14 km SW of Elizabeth. Primarily a residential suburb, it also has office space and some light industry.

Ishi Wilderness 41,840 ac/16,945 ha, within the Lassen National Forest, in NE California, 25 mi/40 km SE of Red Bluff and 30 mi/50 km SW of Mt. Lassen. On the upper Mill Creek (N) and Deer Creek (S), it was the homeland of the Yahi, and is named for Ishi, the "last wild Indian," who emerged from it and wandered into OROVILLE, 40 mi/64 km SE, in Aug. 1911.

Ishpatina Ridge high point (2274 ft/693 m) in Ontario, on the CANADIAN SHIELD, 63 mi/102 km N of Sudbury and 52 mi/84 km WSW of New Liskeard, in Lady Evelyn-Smoothwater Provincial Park.

Ishpeming city, pop. 7200, Marquette Co., in the N Upper Peninsula, N Michigan, in a lake-filled region of the Marquette Iron Range, 13 mi/21 km SW of Marquette. An iron-mining center founded in 1844, it is named "high ground" in Ojibway. It also quarries marble, mills lumber, and manufactures explosives. A ski resort since the 1880s, Ishpeming hosts an annual international ski jumping tournament and is home to the National Ski Hall of Fame. Physicist Glenn Seaborg was born here (1912).

Island Beach State Park the lower 8 mi/13 km of a barrier island 35 mi/56 km NE of Atlantic City, in Ocean Co., E New Jersey. The 2700-ac/1094-ha park is the largest stretch of undeveloped barrier beach in New Jersey, with dunes, forests, saltmarshes, and freshwater ponds; it contrasts with resort towns farther N on the island. It is bordered by Barnegat Bay (W) and the Atlantic Ocean (E); Barnegat Inlet is S.

Island Flats battle site: see under KINGSPORT, Tennessee.

Island Number 10 formerly in the Mississippi R., just S of NEW MADRID, Missouri. Fortified by the Confederacy at the Civil War's start, it blocked Union passage downriver after the fall of FORT DONELSON. On April 7, 1862, it surrendered after Union gunboats had run past it and attained a commanding position behind its guns. Part of Tennessee territory, it later disappeared because of changes in the river.

Island Pond village, pop. 1222, in Brighton township, Essex Co., extreme NE Vermont. Named for a pond at the S end of the village with a 22-ac/9-ha island in its center, it is on the Pherrins and Clyde rivers, 14 mi/23 km S of the Québec border. In the heart of the NORTHEAST KINGDOM, it is a division headquarters of the Canadian National Railway, with furniture and woodworking factories, and produces garden crops, lumber, animal feed, and dairy products.

Isla Verde see under CAROLINA, Puerto Rico.

Isla Vista unincorporated community, pop. 20,395, Santa Barbara Co., SW California, on the Santa Barbara Channel of the Pacific Ocean, 8 mi/13 km W of SANTA BARBARA, of which it is a residential suburb. It houses many students of the University of California at Santa Barbara, in neighboring (NE) Goleta.

Isle au Haut island township, pop. 40, Knox Co., SC Maine. Isle au Haut is in the Atlantic Ocean, 6 mi/10 km S of Stonington, Deer Isle. The township consists of three large and a number of smaller islands, with a total area of about 12 sq mi/32 sq km, sighted and named by Champlain in 1604. About half the area is in Acadia National Park. The main industries are lobstering, fishing, and tourism. Mt. Champlain, the high point, stands 543 ft/166 m above the water.

Isle La Motte island in L. CHAMPLAIN, 13 mi/21 km NW of St. Albans, in Grand Isle Co., extreme NW Vermont. About 5.5 mi/9 km long N–S and 2 mi/3 km wide, it is bridged to South Alburg, thence to the HERO ISLANDS. The French established the first European settlement in Vermont here, at Fort Ste. Anne, in 1665. It was latter abandoned, but in the late 18th century the town of Isle La Motte (pop. 408) was established.

Isle of Palms island city, 5 mi/8 km long, pop. 3680, Charleston Co., SE South Carolina, one of the SEA ISLANDS, on the Atlantic Ocean (S) and the Atlantic Intracoastal Waterway (N), 10 mi/16 km E of Charleston. It is particularly susceptible to frequent changes in shoreline due to tidal erosion and redepositing of sand. Extensive resort and residential development began in the 1970s, and there are now rural cottages, elegant condominiums, and multimillion-dollar homes here. The island is reached by bridge from SULLIVAN'S I. to the SW.

Isle of Wight County 319 sq mi/826 sq km, pop. 25,053, in SE Virginia. Its seat is Isle of Wight. In the TIDEWATER, S of the James R., the county is known for its SMITHFIELD hams, and raises such other products as peanuts and corn.

Isle Royale largest (210 sq mi/544 sq km) island in L. Superior, part of Michigan although offshore from GRAND PORTAGE, Minnesota (W), and 60 mi/100 km SE of Thunder Bay, Ontario. It is today part of 572,000-ac/232,000-ha (893–sq mi/2314–sq km) **Isle Royale National Park,** which includes nearby islets and surrounding waters. Some 45 mi/72 km ENE–WSW, and up to 9 mi/14 km across, the rugged, glaciated island is noted for its moose and wolves, both 20th-century arrivals from the mainland across the open (moose) or frozen (wolves) lake. It has 165 mi/266 km of trails. Copper mining was carried on here in the 19th century, and the island was a resort before becoming a park in 1931. It is reached by ferry from Houghton and Copper Harbor, Michigan, or from Grand Portage.

Isles of Shoals island group, partly in Rockingham Co., New Hampshire, partly in York Co., Maine. The Isles of Shoals are in the Atlantic 10 mi/16 km SE of Portsmouth. They were seen by Capt. John Smith in 1614. Star, Lunging, White, and Seavey are part of New Hampshire; Duck, Appledore, Malaga, Smuttynose, and Cedar are part of Maine. At low tide, White and Seavey are one island. Appledore, the largest island (400 ac/162 ha), was home to the poet Celia Thaxter. The Appledore Hotel, owned by her father, was a summer retreat for major literary figures and artists, until it burned in 1914; Childe Hassam painted the island. Shoals Marine Laboratory is on Appledore. Star Island has a resort hotel. The area has seen occasional boundary disputes between Maine and New Hampshire fishermen.

Isleta Pueblo pop. 2915, in Bernalillo and Valencia counties, C New Mexico, on the Rio Grande, 13 mi/21 km S of Albuquerque. Comprising several small settlements, it is one of New Mexico's oldest PUEBLOS, and the largest Tiwa-speaking community. A village on the site, seen in 1540 by the Spanish, was abandoned during the 1680 Pueblo Revolt; refugees later established Ysleta del Sur (see EL PASO) in Texas.

Islington see under ETOBICOKE, Ontario.

Islip in New York: **a.** unincorporated village, pop. 18,924, in Islip town, Suffolk Co., on the South Shore of Long Island, on Great South Bay. It is one of the oldest villages on Long Island, settled in the late 1600s by natives of Islip, England. Primarily residential, it has a clamming and fishing industry and a summer population drawn by beaches and nearby (SE) Heckscher State Park. **b.** town, pop. 299,587, Suffolk Co., including the village of Islip and numerous other South Shore communities, among them BAY SHORE, BRENTWOOD, and CENTRAL ISLIP. Long Island MacArthur Airport is in the NE part.

Issaquah city, pop. 7786, King Co., WC Washington, on Issaquah Creek, 2 mi/3 km SE of L. Sammamish and 15 mi/24 km SE of Seattle. It became a coal mining boom town after the arrival of the Seattle Pacific and Lakeshore Railroad in the 1880s. Lumbering has been significant since about 1900, and agriculture has been an economic factor since hops were first raised in 1885. A mill and dairy center, it is now also a trading hub for the valley, and has a candy factory and a salmon hatchery. Situated at the foot of the Cascade Range, it is a resort city as well.

Isto, Mount see under BROOKS RANGE, Alaska.

Italian Harlem see under EAST HARLEM, New York.

Italian Market open-air market in SOUTH PHILADELPHIA, Pennsylvania, 1 mi/1.6 km SE of City Hall. The market stretches for four blocks along Ninth St.

Itasca, Lake Y-shaped body in NC Minnesota, 190 mi/306 km NNW of Minneapolis and 23 mi/37 km SW of Bemidji, that was determined in 1832 to be the true head ("ver*itas ca*put") of the Mississippi R. It sits at an elevation of about 1470 ft/448 m, in a divide area where the Otter Tail R., a headwater of the N-flowing RED RIVER OF THE NORTH, also rises (just W). Today local streams flowing into Itasca are considered the Mississippi's ultimate source.

Ithaca city, pop. 29,541, seat of Tompkins Co., C New York, in the Finger Lakes, at the S end of CAYUGA L. and the S terminus of the New York State Barge Canal, 50 mi/80 km SW of Syracuse. It was founded in 1789 by the surveyor general of New York, Simeon DeWitt, and developed as an agricultural and lumber center. Cornell University (1865) and Ithaca College (1892) stimulated further development. Ithaca remains an important agricultural center, housing the state Veterinary College and the College of Agriculture, farm cooperative organizations, and a US plant and soil laboratory. Industries manufacture salt, chain drives, research instruments, heat-resistant materials, and dairy products. Ithaca is also home to Tompkins-Cortland Community College. Several gorges, carved by creeks, run through the city. Buttermilk Falls, Taughannock Falls, and Robert T. Treman state parks are nearby. Ithaca township (pop. 17,797) surrounds the city E, S, and W.

Itta Bena city, pop. 2377, Leflore Co., WC Mississippi, in the DELTA, 9 mi/14 km WSW of Greenwood. Its Choctaw name may mean "home in the woods," but it has stood amid flat cotton fields since the mid 19th century, trading, processing, and shipping the crop. It is also home to historically black

Mississippi Valley State University (1946), threatened with closure under a state reorganization plan announced in 1992.

Iuka city, pop. 3122, seat of Tishomingo Co., extreme NE Mississippi, 22 mi/35 km SE of CORINTH, 4 mi/6 km W of the Alabama line and Pickwick L. (the Tennessee R.), and 13 mi/21 km S of the Tennessee line. It was the scene of a battle (Sept. 19–20, 1862) in which Union soldiers commanded by William S. Rosecrans defeated attacking Confederate forces led by Sterling Price. In a forested region, the town mills pine lumber and produces building materials. There are many antebellum homes in the town. Near J. P. Coleman and Tishomingo state parks, WOODALL Mt., and the Tennessee, Iuka is also a resort.

Ives Estates unincorporated community, pop. 13,531, Dade Co., SE Florida, 10 mi/16 km NNE of Miami, a residential suburb just SW of Hallandale.

Ivujivik INUIT village, pop. 263, Québec's northernmost community, at the meeting of HUDSON BAY (SW) with the HUDSON STRAIT (NE), on the N tip of the UNGAVA Peninsula, 1200 mi/1900 km NNW of Montréal.

Iwilei neighborhood in WC HONOLULU, Hawaii, NNW of Honolulu Harbor. This former RED-LIGHT DISTRICT later processed pineapples. Dole Cannery Square and the Gentry Pacific Center, with shops and restaurants in an old pineapple factory, draw visitors. Honolulu Community College lies N, harbor docks S.

J

Jacinto City city, pop. 9343, Harris Co., SE Texas, 7 mi/11 km E of downtown Houston, on Interstate 10. It is a largely residential suburb.

Jackass Hill see under ANGELS CAMP, California.

Jack London State Historic Park see under GLEN ELLEN, California.

Jack Murphy Stadium see under MISSION VALLEY, San Diego, California.

Jacks Mountain Appalachian ridge, c.2000 ft/610 m high, in SC Pennsylvania. It extends 70 mi/113 km from C Huntingdon Co. (SW) to N Snyder Co. (NE). The Juniata R. crosses it at Mount Union.

Jackson **1.** town, pop. 3891, East Feliciana Parish, SE Louisiana, 27 mi/45 km N of Baton Rouge, site of a well-known state mental hospital. **2.** city, pop. 37,446, seat of Jackson Co., SC Michigan, on the Grand R., 34 mi/65 km W of Ann Arbor. It was founded in 1829 at the meeting point of several Indian trails. After meetings at RIPON, Wisconsin, a convention here officially founded the Republican Party (1854). An early auto production center, it now manufactures such products as auto parts and tires, plastics, steel, and machine tools, and is a hub for transportation services. Jackson is the site of the Michigan Space Center, housed at Jackson Community College (1928), and a 465-ac/188-ha park that features illuminated waterfalls. The Southern Michigan State Prison is just NE. **3.** city, pop. 196,637, state capital and coseat (with RAYMOND) of Hinds Co., also in Madison Co., WC Mississippi, on the Pearl R. and the NATCHEZ TRACE. Settled as a trading post in the late 18th century, it was known as LeFleur's Bluff. In 1820 the Treaty of Doak's Stand opened the territory to white settlement, and the site was selected for the state capital. During the Civil War's VICKSBURG Campaign, on May 14, 1863, Union troops forced the city's defenders to evacuate. When the Federal forces moved on to Vicksburg, Confederates reestablished themselves, only to have the city recaptured by W.T. Sherman in July. Burned, Jackson gained the nickname "Chimneyville." Its recovery was slow until the arrival of new railroads in the 1880s. The discovery of nearby natural gas fields in the 1930s stimulated industrial growth. Jackson in the 20th century has become an important railroad, shipping, telecommunications, industrial, and educational center. Its manufactures include metal and glass products, processed foods, gas and oil, and lumber. The Pearl River Flood and Drainage Project (constructed in the 1960s, impounding 30,000-ac/12,200-ha Ross Barnett Reservoir, just NE) has contributed to local farming, industry, and recreation. The city is home to Jackson State University (1877), Belhaven College (1883), Millsaps College (1890), and Tougaloo College (1867; see TOUGALOO), and to the University of Mississippi Medical Center (1955). **4.** city, pop. 9256, seat of Cape Girardeau Co., SE Missouri, 10 mi/16 km NW of Cape Girardeau. A lumbering, agricultural, and trade center, it is also a growing residential suburb. **5.** city, pop. 48,949, seat of Madison Co., W Tennessee, on the South Fork of the Forked Deer R., 74 mi/119 km NE of Memphis. A trade and distribution point for lumber, livestock, cotton, truck crops, and fruit, and a financial and medical center, it was settled in 1819. A river port and cotton depot, later a railroad junction, it was occupied by both sides during the Civil War. Growth was spurred by three religious institutions: Union University (1823, Southern Baptist), Lambuth College (1843, United Methodist), and Lane College (1882, Christian Methodist Episcopal). Jackson produces textiles, power tools, printing equipment, and aluminum foil. The home of John Luther "Casey" Jones (see CAYCE, Kentucky) is here. **6.** town, pop. 4472, seat of Teton Co., W Wyoming, at the S end of JACKSON HOLE, in the Snake R. valley. At the S entrance to GRAND TETON NATIONAL PARK, and surrounded on three sides by mountains, it is a booming tourist, vacation home, and winter sports center.

Jackson, Mount see under PRESIDENTIAL RANGE, New Hampshire.

Jackson County **1.** 705 sq mi/1826 sq km, pop. 149,756, in SC Michigan, drained by the Raisin and Grand rivers. Its seat is JACKSON. This mostly agricultural area makes dairy products and raises livestock, poultry, corn, grain, and fruit. There is manufacturing and trade in Jackson, the county's only large city. Numerous local lakes offer recreation. **2.** 611 sq mi/1582 sq km, pop. 633,232, in W Missouri, on the Ozark Plateau, bounded by the Missouri R. (N) and the Kansas line (W). Its seat is INDEPENDENCE. The W two-thirds of the county is urban and consists of part of Kansas City and S and E suburbs, including Independence, RAYTOWN, BLUE SPRINGS, GRANDVIEW, and LEE'S SUMMIT. Its industries engage in food processing, packing, and shipping, and it also contains a number of largely residential communities. The balance of the county is agricultural, producing livestock and grain.

Jackson Heights residential and commercial section, NC Queens, New York. Largely semirural before World War I, it developed rapidly after elevated service arrived in 1917, with a mixture of garden apartments and single homes. Today it is a vibrant, heterogeneous community, noted for its large Colombian and Korean populations and for its Indian commercial zone. Elmhurst is to the SE, Woodside to the W, and LaGuardia Airport just N.

Jackson Hole mountain-rimmed valley on the Snake R., 48 mi/77 km long and 6–8 mi/10–13 km wide, at an elevation of 6000–7000 ft/1830–2135 m, in Teton Co., NW Wyoming. Part of Jackson Hole is in GRAND TETON NATIONAL PARK. The valley extends from the town of JACKSON, between the Teton Range and the Continental Divide N to Jackson L. In the 19th century Jackson Hole was a hunting, trapping, and grazing area; the scene of battles between sheep and cattle ranchers; and an outlaw hideout. It is now a popular year-round resort and a major ski area, with an aerial tramway. Nearby are Housetop Mt. (10,537 ft/3214 m) and Mt. Hunt (10,783 ft/3289 m). Jackson Hole is also a mecca for hikers, campers, and rock climbers. The area serves as the winter feeding ground of the largest elk herd in the US.

Jackson Lake also, **Jackson Lake Reservoir** 40 sq mi/104 sq km, at the N end of Jackson Hole, in GRAND TETON NATIONAL PARK, NW Wyoming. The second-largest lake in Wyoming, it is 18 mi/29 km long and has an average width of 4 mi/6 km. Part of the Minidoka Irrigation Project, it was created by the **Jackson Lake Dam** (1911; 78 ft/24 m high) across the South Fork of the Snake, the river that feeds and drains it.

Jackson Park lakefront park on the South Side of Chicago, Illinois, 6 mi/10 km SSE of the Loop, the southernmost of a band of waterside parks including GRANT PARK (N) and Burnham Park (C). With lagoons and various public facilities, it is an important recreational resource. In 1893 it contained the "White City," the grouping of neoclassical and Beaux-Arts buildings and grounds created for the World's Columbian Exposition. Following an overall design by Frederick Law Olmsted, many of the most prominent architects and artists in America constructed here a monumental setting that inspired the City Beautiful movement. Exposition buildings and exhibits extended W along the MIDWAY PLAISANCE, which links Jackson Park with Washington Park. Some minor Exposition elements remain in Jackson Park, and some buildings were dismantled and reassembled elsewhere. The University of Chicago, in HYDE PARK, is adjacent (W), and middle-class black neighborhoods are to the S.

Jackson Purchase also, **the Purchase** name in Kentucky for the extreme W part of the state, W of the Tennessee R. Covering some 2570 sq mi/6660 sq km, it is part of the Gulf Coastal Plain, the lowest part of the state, a largely clayey agricultural plain. Andrew Jackson was one of the commissioners who negotiated an 1818 treaty essentially forcing the Chickasaw to relinquish the area. The adjacent, similar part of Tennessee, covering close to 6000 sq mi/15,540 sq km, was also part of the "Purchase," but is generally known simply as West Tennessee.

Jackson Square **1.** commercial district in NE SAN FRANCISCO, California. Just N of the Financial District, it has many of the city's oldest buildings, survivors of the 1906 earthquake and fire, including the Hotaling Distillery. Once the notorious BARBARY COAST, the area is now a design and retailing center, with many professional offices and a designated historic district. **2.** focal point of the VIEUX CARRÉ in New Orleans, Louisiana. It was the Place d'Armes of the old (1718) French city, later the Plaza de Armas under Spanish rule, and the Public Square following the LOUISIANA PURCHASE. It took its present name in 1851, honoring Andrew Jackson, the victor in the 1815 Battle of New Orleans. A large equestrian statue of Jackson faces St. Louis Cathedral (1794, rebuilt 1851). Flanking the cathedral are the Presbytère (1795) and the Cabildo (1795), former government buildings now preserved as museums. The Louisiana Purchase is said to have been formalized in the Cabildo. On either side of the square are the Pontalba Apartments, built 1849–51, noted for their inner courts and wrought-iron gating. The square was rehabilitated in the 1920s after experiencing a decline at the beginning of the 20th century.

Jacksonville **1.** city, pop. 10,283, Calhoun Co., NE Alabama, in the foothills of the Choccolocco Range, SW of the Blue Ridge and 13 mi/21 km NNE of Anniston. Settled in 1822, it was long a cotton trade center, but now has diversified industries. TALLADEGA NATIONAL FOREST is E and SE, and Ft. McClellan is 5 mi/8 km S. Jacksonville State University (1883) is here. **2.** city, pop. 29,101, Pulaski Co., C Arkansas, 13 mi/21 km NE of Little Rock. Settled before the Civil War, in the 1860s it became a railroad depot and later an agricultural shipping center. The city manufactures lumber, furniture, motors, metal cabinets, and pesticides and other chemicals. Little Rock Air Force Base is here. **3.** city, pop. 635,230, NE Florida, on the St. Johns R. It is the most populous city in the state. Since 1968, Jacksonville has been united with Duval Co. under one charter; its area (776 sq mi/2010 sq km) makes it one of the nation's largest cities. The region near the mouth of the SAINT JOHNS R. was explored and colonized by the French; the Fort Caroline National Memorial marks the site of the original Huguenot settlement (1564). The Spanish soon followed, and the area came under English control in 1763. Settled by Americans in 1816, it became US territory in 1822, the year the city was founded. It was originally laid out on the N bank of the river; called Cowford, it was renamed for territorial governor Andrew Jackson and incorporated in 1832. A base for Confederate blockade runners early in the Civil War, it was occupied by Union troops and largely destroyed. Its location and climate made it popular, however, and by the 1870s it had rebuilt and become a leading manufacturing and tourist city. A yellow fever epidemic (1888) and destructive fire (1902) slowed its growth, but it again rebuilt and prospered. The city is an important deepwater port of entry, with numerous shipyards. Chief among its many imports are automobiles, oil and petroleum products, and coffee. Major exports include naval stores, chemicals, phosphates, and lumber. A transportation hub, it has extensive rail, highway, and air facilities, including an international airport. Its manufactures include lumber, paper, chemicals, processed foods, beer, machinery, and cigars. It is home to a variety of major banking and insurance institutions, as well as printing, publishing, and other businesses. Naval installations are also a factor in the economy. Its large sports complex including the GATOR BOWL and facilities for golf, dog racing, swimming, boating, and fishing, draw visitors. Jacksonville's educational institutions include Edward Waters College (1866), Jones College (1918), Jacksonville University (1934), Florida Community College (1963), and the University of North Florida (1965). **4.** city, pop. 19,324, seat of Morgan Co., WC Illinois, on Mauvaise Terre Creek, 40 mi/64 km W of Springfield. It is an agricultural trading center and the home of such industries as bookbinding, food processing, and the manufacture of ferris wheels and polyethylene film. Platted in

1825, the city was an early cultural and educational center and an important station on the Underground Railroad. It is the seat of Illinois College (1829), which graduated the first college class in the state and had its first medical school, and MacMurray College (1846). The Illinois School for the Deaf and the Illinois School for the Visually Impaired are also here. L. Jacksonville is 3 mi/5 km SE. **5.** city, pop. 30,013, seat of Onslow Co., SE North Carolina, on the estuarial New R., 100 mi/160 km SE of Raleigh. Settled in 1757 as Wantland's Ferry, it was the rural county's business hub and a hunting and fishing resort until the World War II opening of the CAMP LEJEUNE and New River military bases just to the S. Today it is a military service community, water sports center, and home to Coastal Carolina Community College (1965). **6.** see under MEDFORD, Oregon. **7.** city, pop. 12,765, Cherokee Co., E Texas, 27 mi/43 km S of Tyler. Established in 1847, it moved in 1872 to its present site on the railroad. It is a shipping center in a rich truck (especially tomato) farming region. It has canneries, sawmills, nurseries, and various light manufactures. Lon Morris College (1873), Jacksonville College (1899), and a Baptist Seminary are here. Area lakes draw visitors.

Jacksonville Beach city, pop. 17,839, Duval Co., NE Florida, on the Atlantic Ocean. Governed under the Jacksonville–DUVAL Co. charter, it is a beachfront resort 12 mi/19 km ESE of downtown Jacksonville.

Jacob's Pillow see under BECKET, Massachusetts.

Jaffrey resort town, pop. 5361, Cheshire Co., SW New Hampshire. Jaffrey is on Contoocook L. and the Contoocook R., 15 mi/24 km SE of Keene. It includes Jaffrey Village, East Jaffrey, and Mt. MONADNOCK, in the town's NW corner. The main industries are tourism and the manufacture of boxes, wood products, nails, and matches.

Jalna imaginary country estate in Ontario, created by Mazo de la Roche in a romantic novel (1927) of the same name, the first in the vastly popular saga of the Whiteoak family. It is set in the OAKVILLE area.

Jamaica commercial and residential section, C Queens, New York. Settled in the 1650s, the old town of Jamaica included also modern Ozone Park, Richmond Hill, Woodhaven, St. Albans, and Queens Village. It was incorporated 1683 as the first seat of Queens Co., and became a ward of Queens borough in 1898. Long noted as the market town for Long Island truck farms, Jamaica, which is a highway hub and the major transfer point for the Long Island Rail Road, became in the early 20th century a commercial center. The first US supermarket opened here in 1930. Jamaica lost much of its importance when shopping malls opened after the 1960s in nearby Nassau Co., and in the 1990s is struggling to regain trade. A new campus (1986) of York College (City University of New York) and Social Security Administration regional headquarters (1989) are among recent developments. Jamaica's name is a corruption of that of a local Indian tribe. South Jamaica, S of the LIRR tracks, is a generally poorer subsection.

Jamaica Bay protected inlet of the Atlantic Ocean at the SW end of Long I., in BROOKLYN and QUEENS, New York. Seven mi/11 km E–W and 4.5 mi/7 km wide, the marshy, island-filled bay is bordered on the S by the Rockaway Peninsula, and enters the ocean at Rockaway Inlet, which is bridged. The bay is also spanned by a causeway between HOWARD BEACH (N) and the ROCKAWAYS (S), by way of Broad Channel. John F. Kennedy International Airport extends into the NE of the bay, while the rest of the bay and its islands are part of Gateway National Recreation Area, with park headquarters at FLOYD BENNETT FIELD, on the SW shore. Much of the bay is also a wildlife refuge, home or a stopping point for large numbers of migratory waterfowl and shorebirds.

Jamaica Plain residential section of SW Boston, Massachusetts, 3 mi/5 km from downtown. It is home to the ARNOLD ARBORETUM, Jamaica Pond, and part of FRANKLIN PARK, all components of the "Emerald Necklace" that winds through the city. A traditionally Irish middle-class area, it now has a more diverse population including many students.

James Bay shallow SE arm of HUDSON BAY, between WC Québec (E) and NE Ontario (W). Some 275 mi/445 km N–S and 140 mi/230 km wide, it receives the La Grande, Eastmain, Rupert, Nottaway, Harricanaw, Moose, Abitibi, Albany, and Attawapiskat rivers. Akimiski, Charlton, and Twin islands, bird sanctuaries, lie in the bay. MOOSONEE, Ontario, is its largest community; most of the others began as HUDSON'S BAY COMPANY trading posts and are now inhabited mainly by Cree. The **James Bay Project** of Hydro-Québec, begun in 1979, has dammed the tremendous waterpower of the La Grande and other nearby rivers to provide power for Québec and New England.

James City County 153 sq mi/385 sq km, pop. 34,859, in SE Virginia. Its seat is WILLIAMSBURG. Along the James R. (S), in the TIDEWATER, the county is largely agricultural, and is home to two of Virginia's major tourist attractions, Williamsburg and JAMESTOWN, the first successful English settlement in North America.

James Island 9 mi/14 km long, one of South Carolina's SEA ISLANDS, on CHARLESTON Harbor (N), Elliotts Cut Creek (N), and the Stono R. (W), connected to the mainland (N) and FOLLY I. (S), just SW of downtown Charleston. Once the site of a quarantine station, it is now a largely suburban residential and resort community. FORT SUMTER is just off its E point.

James River **1.** also, **Dakota River** 710 mi/1143 km long, non-navigable river in North and South Dakota. It rises in C North Dakota, then flows SSE past Jamestown and La Mour and across the border into South Dakota. There the James traverses the entire state N to S, flowing past Huron and Mitchell to the Missouri R. at YANKTON. **2.** 340 mi/550 km long, in Virginia. It is formed by the confluence of the Jackson and Cowpasture rivers 3 mi/5 km SE of CLIFTON FORGE, in Botetourt Co. It flows generally SSE to BUCHANAN, then turns NE to Glasgow, then SE again, crossing the BLUE RIDGE Mts. by cutting a deep gorge and spilling over Balcony Falls and three series of rapids. It flows SE to LYNCHBURG, then winds its way generally NE and E across the PIEDMONT to RICHMOND, on the FALL LINE, the head of navigation for deep-draft vessels. Rapids above the city provide hydroelectric power. The James then winds SE, forming a wide estuary after the APPOMATTOX R. joins it at HOPEWELL, and empties into HAMPTON ROADS between Newport News and Portsmouth. The estuary has great historic significance, being the site of JAMESTOWN and other early English settlements. During the Civil War, Union forces attacked up the river repeatedly in attempts on Richmond. The James's chief tributaries are the Appomattox and Chickahominy rivers.

Jamestown **1.** city, pop. 34,681, Chautauqua Co., SW New York, at the S end of L. Chautauqua, 60 mi/100 km SSW of Buffalo. It developed initially (after 1806) as a furniture and textile center. Industrialization intensified following the opening of the Erie Canal (1825), an 1840s influx of skilled workers from Sweden, and the arrival of the Erie Railroad (1850s). Jamestown now manufactures washing machines, dryers, tools, bearings, auto parts, office furniture, kitchen equipment, and voting machines. The surrounding area contains orchards, vineyards, and truck and dairy farms. Jamestown is a base for the resort areas of L. Chautauqua and the Allegheny Mts., and home to Jamestown Community College (1950). **2.** city, pop. 15,571, seat of Stutsman Co., SC North Dakota, at the confluence of the James and Pipestem rivers, 90 mi/145 km W of Fargo. Settled near the 19th-century Fort Seward, it is primarily an agricultural center, trading and distributing wheat, livestock, poultry, and dairy products. There are also cement and concrete works. The 15,934-ac/6453-ha Arrowwood National Wildlife Refuge is 20 mi/32 km to the N. **3.** see under CONANICUT I., Rhode Island. **4.** historic site in James City Co., SE Virginia, on a peninsula (Jamestown Island) on the N side of the James R. It is the setting of the first successful English settlement in North America (1607), the capital of Virginia 1607–98, and the meeting place of the first Colonial legislative assembly (1619). Destroyed in Bacon's Rebellion (1676), it was rebuilt, but declined after the capital was relocated to WILLIAMSBURG. The site is now a national historical park. Nearby is the state-run Jamestown Settlement, a re-creation of the original James Fort, along with a re-created 17th-century Indian village.

Janes Island see under CRISFIELD, Maryland.

Janesville city, pop. 52,133, seat of Rock Co., S Wisconsin, on the Rock R., 30 mi/48 km SE of Madison. It was founded in 1835. General Motors automobiles and auto bodies, organs, padding and insulation, and electrical equipment are among items produced here. In operation since 1892, the Parker Pen Company is also a leading manufacturer. Janesville is a commercial center for the surrounding dairy, grain, and tobacco farming area. Tallman House, once a station for the UNDERGROUND RAILROAD and visited by Abraham Lincoln (1859), is preserved as the Lincoln Tallman Museum.

Japantown see under WESTERN ADDITION, San Francisco, California.

Jarvis Island 1.7 sq mi/4.5 sq km, in the C Pacific Ocean, in the LINE Is., just S of the Equator and some 1540 mi/2480 km SSW of Honolulu, Hawaii. Discovered in 1821, it was claimed by the US in 1857 and worked for guano until 1879. In 1889 it was annexed by Great Britain. In 1935 Americans colonized it (as Millerville) from Hawaii, and it has been administered by the US Department of the Interior since 1936. It has had weather and radio stations, and is now a wildlife refuge.

Jasmine Estates unincorporated community, pop. 17,136, Pasco Co., WC Florida, in a resort and retirement area on the Gulf of Mexico, 28 mi/45 km NW of Tampa.

Jasper **1.** city, pop. 13,553, seat of Walker Co., NW Alabama, 35 mi/56 km NW of Birmingham. Settled in 1815, it has an economy largely based on coal mining and the raising of poultry. Food processing and the manufacture of furniture, clothing, mattresses, and golf bags are also significant. Walker College (1938) is here. **2.** city, pop. 2099, seat of Hamilton Co., N Florida, 72 mi/116 km NW of Gainesville and 7 mi/11 km S of the Georgia line. Settled early in the 19th century, it is a lumbering, agricultural, and mining (phosphates) trade center. It was the birthplace (1897) of writer Lillian Smith. **3.** city, pop. 1772, seat of Pickens Co., NW Georgia, 48 mi/77 km N of Atlanta. An industrial community in the foothills of the Blue Ridge Mts., it has been a marble producing center since the 1830s. **4.** city, pop. 10,030, seat of Dubois Co., SW Indiana, 45 mi/72 km NE of Evansville, in a mainly agricultural district. Strawberries and grain are major local crops. There are bituminous coal mines nearby, and timber is harvested. Manufactures include wood products, veneer, and canned goods. Founded in 1818, the city was dominated by German Catholics for over a century after 1838.

Jasper National Park in WC Alberta, in the Rocky Mts., 193 mi/311 km W of Edmonton. A tourist center and railway divisional point, the unincorporated settlement of Jasper was originally a supply depot for traders crossing Athabasca Pass. Jasper Hawes of the North West Company established the post on nearby Jasper L. in the early 1800s, naming it Fitzhugh. The park was established in 1907 and tourism emerged with the arrival of two railroads (1911; 1912), the construction of two hotels (1921; 1922), and a road link to Edmonton (1936). In the park (4200 sq mi/10,878 sq km) are Athabasca Falls, the Miette Hot Springs, and the Columbia Icefield (see Mt. COLUMBIA).

Jay Peak also, **Big Jay Peak** 3861 ft/1178 m, in N Vermont, 14 mi/22 km W of Newport and 6 mi/10 km S of the Québec line. Near the N terminus of the LONG TRAIL and the headwaters of the Missisquoi R., it is a popular ski resort, especially with visitors from Québec.

Jeannette city, pop. 11,221, Westmoreland Co., SW Pennsylvania, 22 mi/35 km SE of Pittsburgh. It is situated in an agricultural and coal mining region rich in natural gas. Among its many manufactures are power plant equipment, turbines and motors, plastics, glass, and lighting fixtures. Jeannette is sometimes known as the "Glass City" because of a well-known glassworks built here (1889) by a group that included H. S. McKee, for whose wife it is named.

Jefferson **1.** city, pop. 4292, seat of Greene Co., WC Iowa, 36 mi/58 km W of Ames. It is an agricultural center, producing farm machinery and processing soybeans. Statistician George Gallup was born here (1901). **2.** also, **Jefferson Heights** unincorporated community, pop. 14,521, Jefferson Parish, SE Louisiana, on the E (N) bank of the Mississippi R., 5 mi/8 km W of New Orleans, of which it is a primarily residential suburb. METAIRIE is just NE. **3.** unincorporated community, pop. 25,782, Fairfax Co., N Virginia, between FALLS CHURCH (NE) and the BELTWAY (W). It is a largely residential suburb of Washington, D.C.

Jefferson, Mount **1.** peak (5715 ft/1743 m) in the N section of the PRESIDENTIAL RANGE of the White Mts., NC New Hampshire, just N of Mt. Washington. South of the peak is Monticello Lawn, a smooth, grassy plateau. **2.** peak (10,497 ft/3199 m) of the CASCADE RANGE, in NW Oregon, 63 mi/101 km SE of Salem, on the NE boundary of the Willamette National Forest, at the SW corner of the WARM SPRINGS INDIAN RESERVATION. This volcanic cone, second-highest elevation in the state, is the site of several small glaciers. The PACIFIC CREST TRAIL passes on its W.

Jefferson, State of see under YREKA, California.

Jefferson Avenue major riverside thoroughfare, 14 mi/23 km long, in Detroit, Michigan, following the Detroit R., between TRENTON (SW) and GROSSE POINTE PARK (NE). Jefferson Ave. passes through Delray, Downtown, Indian Village, and Jefferson-Chalmers. The Civic Center and Renaissance Center are located along the avenue. It is the site, 5 mi/8 km E of Downtown, of "Old Jeff," the auto plant, opened 1907, that became Chrysler's main plant. In 1992 Chrysler opened its new Jefferson Ave. North plant on the same spot, in an attempt to revitalize Detroit's East Side.

Jefferson Barracks historic Army post just outside SAINT LOUIS, Missouri, on the Mississippi R., 9 mi/14 km SSW of Downtown and just E of MEHLVILLE. Established in 1826, it was the center of military operations in the West in the period when the city was the gateway for US expansion. Closed after World War II training use, it is now a park with a cluster of 1850s buildings. A major national cemetery is also here, and a Veterans Administration medical center.

Jefferson-Chalmers neighborhood in SE Detroit, Michigan, along the Detroit R. and JEFFERSON Ave., SW of GROSSE POINTE PARK. Long dominated by three auto assembly plants, Jefferson-Chalmers has been hit hard by plant closings since the 1970s. Abandonment and demolition affected much of the W end of the community, but the 1980s witnessed new construction and neighborhood revitalization efforts.

Jefferson City **1.** city, pop. 35,481, state capital and seat of Cole Co., also in Callaway Co., C Missouri, on the Missouri R., 27 mi/43 km SSE of Columbia. A river port, it was named the state capital in 1821 and became seat of the legislature in 1826. It was occupied by Union troops during the Civil War. State government is the city's economic mainstay. A rail and river shipping hub, it is also an important trading, processing, and distribution center for grain and dairy producers. It has railroad shops; printing, publishing, and bookbinding facilities; and industries manufacturing such products as clothing, shoes, cosmetics, and electrical appliances. The CARTHAGE marble Capitol Building (1917) has murals by Thomas Hart Benton and N.C. Wyeth. Lincoln University (1866) is here. **2.** city, pop. 5494, Jefferson Co., E Tennessee, 26 mi/42 km NE of Knoxville, near the Cherokee Dam, at the SW end of Cherokee L. (on the Holston R.). Carson-Newman College (1851) is central to the life of this community, which also has some light manufacturing.

Jefferson County **1.** 1119 sq mi/2898 sq km, pop. 651,525, in NC Alabama. Bankhead L., on the BLACK WARRIOR R., forms part of the W boundary. Alabama's most populous county is dominated by BIRMINGHAM, its seat, whose suburbs occupy much of the E half. The region's wealth rests on the combination of iron ore in the mineral belt in the S and coal mines in the N. **2.** 768 sq mi/1989 sq km, pop. 438,430, in C Colorado, bounded by the South Platte R. (SE). GOLDEN is its seat. The rapidly growing NE section of the county contains such Denver suburbs as ARVADA, LAKEWOOD, and WHEAT RIDGE. The agricultural portions of the county produce sugar beets, beans, and livestock. Its W area includes parts of Arapahoe, Pike, and Roosevelt national forests, and part of the Front Range of the Rocky Mts., where there is some coal mining. **3.** 386 sq mi/1000 sq km, pop. 664,937, in NC Kentucky, bounded NW by the Ohio R. and Indiana. Its seat is LOUISVILLE, Kentucky's largest city. The metropolitan area is the site of residential suburbs and much of the state's manufacturing. Outer parts of the county raise onions, potatoes, burley tobacco, grain, fruit, and livestock. **4.** 661 sq mi/1712 sq km, pop. 171,380, in EC Missouri, bounded by the Mississippi R. (the Illinois border, E). Its seat is Hillsboro (pop. 1625). The NE section, just S of St. Louis, contains a number of residential suburbs, which have grown enormously since the 1970s. A considerable amount of manufacturing is carried on here, particularly close to the Mississippi, in cities such as FESTUS. The county also produces livestock and grains and contains lead and zinc deposits in the S. **5.** 1273 sq mi/3297 sq km, pop. 110,943, in N New York, bounded by L. Ontario (W) and the St. Lawrence R. and Canadian border (NW). It includes a number of the THOUSAND ISLANDS in the Gulf of St. Lawrence. Its seat is Watertown, a major industrial center. FORT DRUM occupies the NE portion. Jefferson Co. has many lakeside resorts and state parks; it is also the site of many dairy farms, and fishing is important. Iron, limestone, and talc are mined. **6.** 410 sq mi/1062 sq km, pop. 80,298, in E Ohio, bounded by the Ohio R. at the West Virginia line (E). Its seat and major city is STEUBENVILLE, a manufacturing center, particularly known for its steel and other metals. Coal mining is important here. There is also diversified farming (dairy, fruit, livestock, and truck).

Jefferson Davis Monument see under FAIRVIEW, Kentucky.

Jefferson Memorial see under TIDAL BASIN, Washington, D.C.

Jefferson National Expansion Memorial see under GATEWAY ARCH, St. Louis, Missouri.

Jefferson Parish 348 sq mi/901 sq km, pop. 448,306, in SE Louisiana, in the delta of the Mississippi R., bounded N by L. PONTCHARTRAIN, S by the Gulf of Mexico, and adjoining (W and S) New Orleans. Its seat is GRETNA. It includes many residential and industrial suburbs of New Orleans like METAIRIE, KENNER, and GRETNA, as well as the New Orleans International Airport. BARATARIA BAY is at its S extreme.

Jefferson Park residential neighborhood on the far Northwest Side of Chicago, Illinois. For much of the 20th century, it was a low-density community of blue-collar Poles and Ukrainians. With the building of O'Hare International Airport to the NW, the area emerged as a transit hub. It has since attracted denser commercial development and undergone some gentrification.

Jefferson Proving Ground see under MADISON, Indiana.

Jefferson River 207 mi/333 km long, in Montana. Known at its origin as the Red Rock R., it rises in the Gravelly Range of SW Montana. It flows through the Red Rock lakes, then swings N at Lima, passing Dillon, where it becomes the Beaverhead R. It is joined some 25 mi/40 km downstream by the Big Hole and Ruby rivers at Twin Bridges. It continues NE for the remainder of its course as the Jefferson R. until it meets with the Madison and Gallatin rivers just NE of THREE FORKS to form the Missouri R.

Jeffersontown city, pop. 23,221, Jefferson Co., NC Kentucky, 12 mi/19 km E of Louisville. It is a fast-growing residential suburb, formerly a farm, orchard, and nursery center.

Jefferson Valley unincorporated village in Yorktown, N Westchester Co., SE New York, just S of the Putnam Co. line. It is a residential community.

Jeffersonville city, pop. 21,841, seat of Clark Co., SE Indiana, across the Ohio R. (NE) from Louisville, Kentucky. Founded (1802) on the site of Fort Steuben by veterans of the George Rogers Clark expedition to the Northwest, it was planned by Thomas Jefferson and served (1813–16) as territorial capital. A river port and railroad center, it has also been a shipbuilding center since the 19th century. Louisville Slugger (Hillerich & Bradsby) baseball bats are manufactured here. Other industries refine oil and produce wood products, chemicals, machinery, and sporting goods. A US army quartermaster depot is located here. Also in the city is a campus of Indiana University Southeast.

Jekyll Island one of the SEA ISLANDS, in the Atlantic Ocean 5 mi/8 km SE of Brunswick, in Glynn Co., SE Georgia. Seven mi/11 km N–S and 1–2 mi/1–3 km wide, it is connected to the mainland by a causeway. Like many of the Sea Islands, it was a slave port in the 18th and 19th centuries, receiving one of the last such cargoes in 1858. It has been a winter resort since the 1880s, when a group of wealthy Northern industrialists built homes on the island, calling themselves the Jekyll Island club. After World War II it became less exclusive.

Jemez Mountains range NW of Santa Fe in N New Mexico, rising to 11,950 ft/3642 m at Chicoma Peak, and including Redondo Peak (11,254 ft/3430 m). In its center is Valle Grande, one of the largest CALDERAS in the world, covering 176 sq mi/456 sq km, with walls rising 500 ft/152 m from floor to rim. The elevations around the caldera, which was once thought to be simply a valley, are sometimes referred to as the Valle Grande Mts. The range is partly within the Santa Fe National Forest.

Jemez Pueblo pop. 1750, Sandoval Co., NC New Mexico, 37 mi/60 km N of Albuquerque, in the foothills of the Jemez Mts., on the Jemez R. and the Rio Grande. It is known for its pottery, weaving, and basketmaking.

Jenison unincorporated community, pop. 17,882, Ottawa Co., SW Michigan, on the Grand R., a residential suburb 7 mi/11 km W of Grand Rapids.

Jenkin's Ferry hamlet in Grant Co., SC Arkansas, 30 mi/48 km W of Pine Bluff, on the SALINE R. On April 30, 1864, this river crossing was the scene of a bloody, indecisive battle in which Union troops retreating from an advance on Camden (S) repelled a Confederate attack.

Jenkintown borough, pop. 4574, Montgomery Co., SE Pennsylvania, a residential suburb 10 mi/16 km NE of Philadelphia. It also produces steel and paper products and is the seat of Manor Junior College (1947).

Jennings **1.** city, pop. 11,305, seat of Jefferson Davis Parish, SW Louisiana, 31 mi/50 km E of Lake Charles. It is the market and processing center of an area that produces huge amounts of rice, as well as some truck crops. The first oil strike in Louisiana (1901) occurred 5 mi/8 km NE, and oil remains the second basis of the local economy. **2.** city, pop. 15,905, St. Louis Co., EC Missouri, 8 mi/13 km NNW of downtown St. Louis, a residential suburb.

Jenny Jump Mountain Appalachian ridge in Warren Co., NW New Jersey, NE of Belvidere, c.1100 ft/336 m high. The Delaware Water Gap is NE. Jenny Jump State Forest covers 1220 ac/494 ha in several separate units.

Jericho unincorporated village, pop. 13,141, in Oyster Bay town, Nassau Co., SE New York, in C Long Island, just N of Hicksville. Formerly agricultural, it developed as a residential suburb in the 1950s and 1960s.

Jerimoth Hill (812 ft/248 m) highest point in Rhode Island, in the town of Foster, near the Connecticut border.

Jerome town, pop. 403, Yavapai Co., WC Arizona, 38 mi/61 km SW of Flagstaff, in the Black Hills. From the 1880s through the 1920s it was a wild copper boom town, with a peak pop. of 15,000. After the 1950s closing of local mines, it became an arts and tourist center.

Jersey City city, pop. 228,537, seat of Hudson Co., NE New Jersey, on a peninsula between the Hackensack R. and Newark Bay (W) and the Hudson R. and Upper New York Bay (E), opposite downtown Manhattan, to which it is connected by the HOLLAND TUNNEL, subway, and ferry. The area was purchased from the Indians by the Dutch c.1630, and was part of PAVONIA. Dutch trading posts were established at Communipaw, Paulus Hook, and Horsimus, all in the modern city. The British ruled after 1664, and a town was chartered in 1668. Paulus Hook Fort was captured (1779) by American forces. Jersey City was incorporated in 1820, and later consolidated with the early settlements of Bergen and Hudson City. The city's development was stimulated by the arrival of railroads and the Morris Canal (1830s) and the building of railroad tunnels to New York City (1910). Today Jersey City is a busy port (part of the Port of New York) with 11 mi/18 km of waterfront and an enormous computerized shipping terminal. Its transportation complex, warehouses, and railheads make it a major assembling and shipping point. Its importance as a military port was emphasized when German agents blew up the Black Tom ammunition facility in Communipaw in July 1916. The city has railroad shops, oil refineries, and some 600 diversified industries manufacturing products including chemicals, processed foods, toiletries, pencils, electronic equipment, clothing, and paper and rubber goods. It is also residential, with several rehabilitated neighborhoods. Jersey City has a large medical center with medical and dental colleges, and is the seat of St. Peter's College (1872) and Jersey City State College (1927). Liberty State Park (1114 ac/451 ha) is on Upper New York Bay facing ELLIS I. and LIBERTY I.

Jersey Meadows see under HACKENSACK R.

Jersey Shore Atlantic coastal region of E New Jersey, running 127 mi/204 km from Sandy Hook (NNE) to Cape May (SSW), in Monmouth, Atlantic, Ocean, and Cape May counties. An area of tidal marshes, sandy beaches, dunes, and estuaries fringed with barrier islands, it was used by whalers and fishermen during the 18th century. Various communities along the shore became summer resorts, reached by rail, during the 19th century; its lower end is as far S as Baltimore and Washington. Accessible throughout its length by means of the Garden State Parkway, it now serves as a warm-weather recreational site for residents of the New York and Philadelphia areas. The region includes such popular sites as Long Branch, Asbury Park, Atlantic City, Ocean City, Wildwood, and Cape May. Among its larger barrier islands are LONG BEACH and Absecon islands. The SANDY HOOK portion of the GATEWAY NATIONAL RECREATION AREA is at its N tip, and ISLAND BEACH STATE PARK is in its C portion.

Jerusalem **1.** rural town, pop. 3784, Yates Co., on the NW shore of Keuka L., in the Finger Lakes, W New York, 25 mi/40 km SW of Auburn. Located here was a community founded in the late 1780s and inhabited by the mystic celibate sect that followed religious leader Jemima Wilkinson (1752–1819), who claimed to have been returned from the dead and called herself the "Public Universal Friend." The community dispersed after her death, but her clapboard home remains. **2.** former town in SOUTHAMPTON Co., SE Virginia, 8 mi/13 km WNW of Franklin, and 27 mi/43 km W of SUFFOLK. The county seat, it was the objective of the slave rebellion leader Nat Turner, in Aug. 1831, and later the site of his trial and execution. Today, as Courtland (pop. 819), it remains the county seat.

Jerusalem of America see under BROWNSVILLE, New York.

Jesup city, pop. 8958, seat of Wayne Co., SE Georgia, 38 mi/61 km NW of Brunswick. Its industries make textiles and furniture, and the area produces timber and tobacco.

Jésus, Île English, **Jesus Island** see under LAVAL, Québec.

Jewel Cave National Monument park (1274 ac/516 ha) in the BLACK HILLS of South Dakota, in Custer Co., 13 mi/21 km W of the city of Custer. A cave with many chambers lined with colorful calcite crystals, in limestone cliffs on the E side of Hell Canyon, is the focus of the park. Discovered by prospectors in 1900, it was established as a National Monument in 1908. Thought to be one of the longest cave systems in the US, it contains more than 80 mi/129 km of mapped passageways.

Jicarilla Mountains N–S trending range, a N extension of the SACRAMENTO Mts., in a section of Lincoln National Forest in SC New Mexico. Jicarilla Mt. reaches 8200 ft/2500 m. The name refers to the basketry drinking cups made by the group of Apache whose 722,000-ac/292,000-ha **Jicarilla Apache Reservation** (pop. 2617) is in N New Mexico, NW of Santa Fe and extending to the Colorado border.

Jimmy Carter National Historic Site see under PLAINS, Georgia.

Jim Thorpe borough, pop. 5048, seat of Carbon Co., E Pennsylvania, on the Lehigh R., in the W Poconos, 23 mi/37 km NW of Allentown. Founded in 1815 as Mauch Chunk, in 1954 it was merged with East Mauch Chunk and renamed Jim Thorpe, after the renowned American athlete, whose tomb was relocated here. Once a busy railroad and manufacturing hub, it still has a number of industries, but relies largely on coal mining and tourism.

Jockey Hollow see under MORRISTOWN, New Jersey.

Joe Louis Arena sports venue opened in 1979 in downtown Detroit, Michigan, on Jefferson Ave., W of the CIVIC CENTER. Seating 19,000, it features hockey and boxing events, along with concerts and conventions.

Joe Robbie Stadium sports facility in Dade Co., SE Florida, just NE of Carol City and 12 mi/19 km NNW of downtown Miami. The 75,500-seat stadium is home to the Miami Dolphins (football), and, beginning in 1993, to the Florida Marlins (baseball). Many other sporting events and concerts are held here. The Calder Race Course, a thoroughbred facility, is just NW.

John Day Fossil Beds National Monument 14,014 ac/5676 ha, comprising three separate sites on or near the John Day R., in NC Oregon. In its Sheep Rock and Clarno units it preserves fossils, including those of saber-toothed tigers, dog-sized horses, ferns, and flowers, dating back some 55 million years, from the Eocene to the Pleistocene epochs. The Painted Hills Unit, 8 mi/13 km NW of Mitchell, is known for its rounded, colorfully banded hills.

John Day River 280 mi/450 km long, in NC Oregon. It rises near the peak of the Strawberry Mts., SE of Canyon City, and winds N and W past the trading and ranching city of **John Day** (pop. 1836), eventually joining the Columbia R. 28 mi/45 km ENE of THE DALLES. River and city were named for an 1810s frontiersman.

John F. Kennedy Center for the Performing Arts in NW Washington, D.C., along the Potomac R. at the W edge of FOGGY BOTTOM, just S of the WATERGATE. Designed by Edward Durrell Stone and opened in 1971, it has six halls of varying size in which performances of all sorts are held.

John F. Kennedy International Airport one of the New York City area's three major airports (with LAGUARDIA and Newark), in SE Queens, New York, on Jamaica Bay. Opened in 1948, it was known officially as New York International Airport and unofficially as Idlewild until it was renamed after the death of President Kennedy. Covering almost 5000 ac/2025 ha, it handles primarily overseas and transcontinental traffic.

John F. Kennedy Space Center see under Cape CANAVERAL, Florida.

John Hancock Center 100-story residential and commercial skyscraper on N Michigan Ave., on the MAGNIFICENT MILE of the Near North Side of Chicago, Illinois. Noted for its tapering shape, bold crisscross external members, and twin communications masts, it dominates the city's lakefront, standing 1127 ft/344 m.

John Henry statue see under BIG BEND TUNNEL, West Virginia.

John H. Kerr Reservoir also, **Buggs Island Lake** in Mecklenburg Co., S Virginia, and Vance and Warren counties, North Carolina, covering 76 sq mi/197 sq km, formed by a dam across the Roanoke R. near Buggs I. and Castle Heights.

John Muir National Historic Site see under MARTINEZ, California.

Johns Island one of the SEA ISLANDS, 5 mi/8 km WSW of Charleston, South Carolina. With Wadmalaw I. (SW, separated by a narrow tidal channel) it is c.16 mi/26 km NE–SW and up to 8 mi/13 km wide. The STONO R. passes behind it (N) and between it and James I. (E). KIAWAH and Seabrook islands lie S along the ocean.

Johnson town, pop. 3156, Lamoille Co., NC Vermont. It is on the flats of the Lamoille R. at its junction with the Gihon R., 10 mi/16 km NE of Mt. Mansfield. Industries include the production of lumber, textiles, clothing, machinery, talc, and woolens. Johnson State College (1828) is here, and the town is an artists' colony.

Johnson City **1.** village, pop. 16,890, in Union township, Broome Co., S New York, on the Susquehanna R., adjacent (NW) to Binghamton and 5 mi/8 km E of Endicott. Together with Binghamton and Endicott, it forms the industrial metropolitan area known as the Tri-Cities, and was home to the Endicott-Johnson shoe company. **2.** city, pop. 49,381, Washington Co., also in Carter and Sullivan counties, extreme NE Tennessee, in the Great Appalachian Valley, on Brush Creek, 90 mi/145 km NE of Knoxville. The region was first settled in the 1760s by farmers and ironmakers. With the arrival in 1857 of the Eastern Tennessee & Virginia Railroad, a settlement grew around the water tank called Johnson's Depot; it was incorporated as Johnson City in 1869. The area has farms and limestone quarries. The city produces textiles, clothing, chemicals, tools, plastics, and hospital supplies, and has a burley tobacco market. A large Veterans Administration center is here. East Tennessee State University (1911) is in the city; the unincorporated academic community of Milligan College (college founded 1866) is 4 mi/6 km SE. Johnson City is the largest of the Tri-Cities, which include BRISTOL, 23 mi/37 km NE, and KINGSPORT, 22 mi/35 km NW. **3.** city, pop. 932, seat of Blanco Co., C Texas, on the Pedernales R., 39 mi/63 km W of Austin, in the HILL COUNTRY. It was settled in 1856, and ancestors of Lyndon B. Johnson had a ranch here in the 1860s. Johnson, born nearby near Stonewall, spent his childhood here; the Lyndon B. Johnson National Historic Park incorporates ranch and home.

Johnson County 478 sq mi/1238 sq km, pop. 355,054, in NE Kansas, on the Kansas R. (N). Its seat is OLATHE; its other major city is OVERLAND PARK. The county's NE section is largely occupied by affluent residential suburbs of Kansas City. The balance is agricultural, with livestock, grain, dairy products, oil, and natural gas contributing to the economy.

Johnson Space Flight Center see under CLEAR LAKE, Houston, Texas.

Johnston town, pop. 26,542, Providence Co., NC Rhode Island, adjacent to Providence (E) and Cranston (S). It was an agricultural community before 19th-century textile mills were established. The modern economy has been based on insurance and the manufacture of worsted yarns, machinery, jewelry, fabricated metals, and textiles.

Johnston Atoll land area 1.1 sq mi/2.8 sq km, in the C Pacific Ocean, some 700 mi/1120 km WSW of Honolulu, Hawaii. The ATOLL, some 10 mi/16 km across, encloses four islands—Johnston, Sand, Akau, and Hikina. Most of Johnston, the largest, is an airstrip. First landed on by a British captain in 1807, the atoll was claimed by the US and by Hawaii in the 1850s. Guano was collected in the late 19th century. The US Navy took over in 1934. After World War II nuclear weapons were tested here. Johnston today is run by the Department of Defense; it has become a site for the incineration of US chemical weapons, with over 1000 military and civilian personnel.

Johnstown **1.** city, pop. 9058, seat of Fulton Co., EC New York, 40 mi/64 km NW of Albany. It was founded (1762) by William Johnson, a British general. The last battle of the Revolutionary War was fought nearby on Oct. 25, 1781; the battlefield has been preserved. Johnstown has been a center for leather tanning and glovemaking since the 18th century. Among its other products are textiles, wood products, blankets, and hosiery. It is the seat of Fulton-Montgomery Community College (1963). Women's rights activist Elizabeth Cady Stanton (1815–1902) was born here. **2.** city, pop. 28,134, Cambria Co., SW Pennsylvania, at the confluence of the Conemaugh and Stonycreek rivers, 60 mi/97 km SE of Pittsburgh. Founded in 1800, it became important as the W terminus of the Allegheny Portage Railroad. Johnstown had the nation's first steel blooming mill and first domestic steel rails; by 1873 it was a leading steel center. The city continues to produce iron and steel, and has a number of other industries. Johnstown was the site of a disastrous flood on May 31, 1889, when the South Fork Dam across the Conemaugh R., 12 mi/19 km above the city, burst after heavy rains; 2200 people were killed. Another major flood occurred in 1936. Although a flood control program was instituted by US Army engineers, another severe flood occurred in 1977, claiming 68 lives. A flood museum is here, as is a branch of the University of Pittsburgh. The Johnstown Flood National Memorial is nearby. **3.** town, pop. 850, Rock Co., S Wisconsin, 11 mi/18 km E of Janesville. Poet Ella Wheeler Wilcox was born here (1850).

John Wayne Airport also, **Orange County Airport** facility between IRVINE (E), SANTA ANA (N), and COSTA MESA (W), in SW California, 29 mi/48 km SE of downtown Los Angeles. It is one of the metropolitan area's major airports.

Joliet city, pop. 76,836, seat of Will Co., NE Illinois, on the Des Plaines R. and the Chicago Sanitary and Ship Canal, 35 mi/56 km SW of Chicago. An important transportation hub on the Illinois Waterway, it is the headquarters of many interstate barge lines. The city manufactures electric components, earth-moving and road equipment, steel rods, nails, wire, steel tanks, chemicals, and insulation, among many other items. Printing, publishing, meat processing, and oil refining are also important industries. The College of St. Francis (1920) and Joliet Junior College (1901) are here. The city is well known for its penal institutions. Stateville Correctional Center is 5 mi/8 km N, and the Joliet Correctional Center and Illinois Crime Laboratory are in the NE part of the city. Louis Jolliet visited the site in 1673, and American settlement dates to the 1830s. Joliet grew with the opening of the Illinois and Michigan Canal (1848), which created the first navigable route between L. Michigan and the Mississippi R. The Rock Island Railroad arrived in 1852, followed by the Chicago Sanitary and Ship Canal in 1900. Joliet was long known as "The Stone City" because limestone quarried in the vicinity was used for the Illinois State House and Springfield's Lincoln Monument.

Joliette city, pop. 17,396, seat of Joliette Co., S Québec, 37 mi/60 km NE of Montréal, in a rich farming region near the Laurentians, on the R. L'Assomption. Founded in the 1820s, it has varied manufactures, including foods and beverages, clothing, textiles, tires, and building materials. Joliette is also a cultural and service center for the region, with a noted summer music festival.

Jollyville unincorporated community, pop. 15,206, Williamson Co., C Texas, just NNW of Austin, 13 mi/21 km from Downtown. It is primarily residential.

Jolon hamlet in Monterey Co., EC California, in a valley between the Diablo Range (E) and the Santa Lucia Mts. (W), 35 mi/56 km NW of Paso Robles. It was the site, in 1771, of the establishment of the third California MISSION, San Antonio de Padua. Today it is surrounded by Fort Hunter Liggett, a military reservation.

Jones Beach state park, Nassau Co., SE New York, on a barrier island, S of Long Island, between the Atlantic Ocean and GREAT SOUTH BAY. Covering 2413 ac/965 ha, it is connected to the mainland by two causeways. Its facilities include a boardwalk and a marine theater. Jones Beach is one of the New York area's most popular summer resorts.

Jonesboro **1.** city, pop. 46,535, co-seat (with Lake City) of Craighead Co., NE Arkansas, 65 mi/105 km NW of Memphis, Tennessee, on CROWLEY'S RIDGE, in the Mississippi Valley. A sawmilling town until 1910, it became an agricultural processing center, handling rice, soybeans, and cotton. Manufactures include electric motors, shoes, machinery, and plumbing fixtures. It is the seat of Arkansas State University (1909). **2.** city, pop. 3635, seat of Clayton Co., N Georgia, 20 mi/32 km S of downtown Atlanta. This commercial and manufacturing center was seized by Union forces on Sept. 1, 1864, cutting off Atlanta's last outside rail connection and forcing Confederates to abandon the city to W.T. Sherman that night. TARA, in Margaret Mitchell's *Gone with the Wind,* is set in the area.

Jonquière city, pop. 57,993, Chicoutimi Co., S Québec, 5 mi/8 km W of CHICOUTIMI and 109 mi/175 km N of Québec City, on the SAGUENAY R. and the R. aux Sables. With Chicoutimi, it forms the industrial hub of the Saguenay–Lac-Saint-Jean area. Founded in 1847, it was a farming community before about 1900, when it became a lumber and pulp milling center. In the 1920s neighboring (E) ARVIDA was established as an Alcan (aluminum) COMPANY TOWN. In 1976 Jonquière absorbed Arvida and Kénogami. Pulp and paper manufacture and aluminum smelting still form the base of the economy. The Collège de Jonquière (1967) is here. The experimental Pont d'Aluminum (Aluminum Bridge, 1948) and the Shipshaw Dam attract visitors.

Joplin city, pop. 40,961, Jasper and Newton counties, SW Missouri, on a high prairie at the edge of the Ozark Plateau, 70 mi/112 km WSW of Springfield and just E of the Kansas border. Lead was discovered here in 1849 and zinc in 1860, and Joplin lies atop water-filled abandoned mines. It was established when two competing post–Civil War mining towns were united in 1873. Shortly thereafter, the railroad arrived, spurring growth. Today the city continues as a lead and zinc smelting center and the trading and shipping hub for grain, livestock, dairy, and fruit. Its manufactures include alcohol, fertilizer, aircraft parts, typesetting equipment, chemicals, and leather goods. It is the seat of Missouri Southern State College (1937) and Ozark Christian College (1942).

Joppatowne unincorporated village, pop. 11,084, Harford Co., NE Maryland, 17 mi/27 km NE of Baltimore. The site of the seat (1712–68) of old Baltimore Co., it is on the Gunpowder R. Joppatowne is a residential suburb.

Jornada del Muerto arid region of desert, dunes, and lava beds extending N–S for some 100 mi/160 km between the SAN ANDRES Mts. (E) and the RIO GRANDE (W), in S New Mexico. Nearly waterless, it presented the most difficult section (the "journey of death") of New Mexico's E–W EL CAMINO REAL crossed by early Spanish travelers. The Trinity Site, where the first atomic bomb was exploded on July 16, 1945, is on the NE, in the WHITE SANDS Missile Range.

Joseph M. Farley nuclear power plant: see under DOTHAN, Alabama.

Joshua Tree National Monument 560,000 ac/227,000 ha, in San Bernardino and Riverside counties, S California, on the S edge of the Mojave Desert, some 150 mi/240 km ESE of Los Angeles. Established in 1936, it ranges from 1000–6000 ft/300–1800 m, incorporating the Little San Bernardino Mts.; its varied flora and fauna include, in addition to the yucca it is named for, the creosote bush, ocotillo, chuckwalla, and foxes. TWENTYNINE PALMS is headquarters. In 1994 the monument attained NATIONAL PARK status, with enlarged boundaries.

J. Strom Thurmond Dam and Reservoir also, **Clark Hill Dam and Lake** see under SAVANNAH R., South Carolina and Georgia.

Juan de Fuca Strait 100 mi/160 km–long, WNW–ESE oriented channel between S VANCOUVER I., British Columbia, and the OLYMPIC PENINSULA of NW Washington. It connects the Strait of GEORGIA (via Haro Strait) and Puget Sound (via Admiralty Inlet) with the Pacific Ocean. The strait is named for a Spanish sailor who reputedly was the first European to discover it, in 1592. The name is also given to the **Juan de Fuca Plate,** a major undersea tectonic PLATE W of Vancouver I. that is moving under the North American continent.

Juanita unincorporated community, pop. 17,232, King Co., WC Washington, on Juanita Bay, at the N end of L. Washington, a suburb 8 mi/13 km NE of downtown Seattle. The community, which grew up around a shingle mill, is a residential area with a popular lakeside park.

Judith, Point promontory in Narragansett town, Washington Co., Rhode Island, SW of the entrance to Narragansett Bay. It is the site of Sprague Memorial Park, a lighthouse, a Coast Guard station, and Pt. Judith Pond, an inlet that provides a sheltered harbor.

Julesburg town, pop. 1295, seat of Sedgwick Co., in the NE corner of Colorado, on the South Platte R., 3 mi/5 km E of the Nebraska border and 55 mi/89 km NE of Sterling. Founded in 1881 as a railroad division point, it remains a major agricultural shipping station. It is also a trade center for a sugar beet region, mills flour, and has a fish hatchery. Julesburg is the fourth town by that name in this area. The original settlement, an Overland Stage and Pony Express station and a notorious outlaw center, was completely destroyed in an 1865 Indian raid.

Jumbo statue see under SAINT THOMAS, Ontario.

Junction City city, pop. 20,604, seat of Geary Co., NE Kansas, at the confluence of the Smoky Hill and Republican rivers, 18 mi/29 km SW of Manhattan. Founded in 1858, it was primarily a supply station for nearby FORT RILEY (N), on the SANTA FE TRAIL. In a limestone quarrying area, it is also a rail hub, with repair shops, and a distribution center for livestock, grain, and dairy products.

Junction Hollow residential neighborhood in Pittsburgh, Pennsylvania, between SCHENLEY PARK and OAKLAND. It is a middle-class Italian community.

Juneau city, pop. 26,751, state capital, coterminous with Juneau Borough (2626 sq mi/6801 sq km), SE Alaska, 570 mi/918 km ESE of Anchorage. Situated between Gastineau Channel and Mt. Juneau and Mt. Roberts, the city center lies on a narrow strip of land that borders British Columbia (NE) and is connected by bridge to Douglas I. (SW). Because of the relative lack of level land, Downtown is long and narrow, with most cross streets on a steep incline. In 1880, Joe Juneau, Richard Harris, and three Tlingit Indians discovered gold near the site, beginning the first Alaska gold rush. A mining town quickly sprang up and in 1900 replaced SITKA as the capital of the Alaska Territory. (Recent attempts to relocate the capital at WILLOW have stalled.) Today the city, with its ice-free harbor, is a trade center for the Alaska PANHANDLE. Although gold mines stopped operating in the 1940s, lumbering and silver mining continue in the area. Fishing for salmon and halibut remains important to the economy, despite its decline in the 1970s because of overfishing. State government and the tourist industry are prominent employers. The University of Alaska Southeast (1972) is here.

Juneau Park municipal park on the EAST SIDE of Milwaukee, Wisconsin, on L. Michigan, immediately E of Downtown. One of the city's most historic open spaces, Juneau Park is the site of the War Memorial Building and Art Museum, Wisconsin Conservatory of Music, and McKinley Marina. Lincoln Memorial Drive runs through the park.

Juniata River 95 mi/153 km long, in SC Pennsylvania. It is formed just NW of HUNTINGDON by the junction of the Little Juniata R. and the Frankstown Branch of the Juniata. It flows generally E, past Huntingdon, Mount Union, and Lewistown, joining the Susquehanna R. just above Duncannon. The 105 mi/169 km–long **Raystown Branch** of the Juniata rises in the Allegheny Mts. in E Somerset Co., and winds E past Bedford for 12 mi/19 km before turning NNE and snaking through RAYSTOWN L. to join the Juniata R. just below Huntingdon. The Juniata is a focus of the writing of Malcolm Cowley.

Jupiter town, pop. 24,986, Palm Beach Co., SE Florida, on Jupiter Inlet at the mouth of the Loxahatchee R., near the S end of JUPITER I., 15 mi/24 km NNW of West Palm Beach. With sandy beaches on the Atlantic Coast and small pastel-tinted buildings, Jupiter, unlike other tourist locales, has retained the atmosphere of a small town. Once the railroad hub of SE Florida, it now has various recreational facilities and some light industry; tomatoes grown nearby are processed.

Jupiter Island narrow barrier island in the Atlantic Ocean bordering Martin and Palm Beach counties, SE Florida. Sixteen mi/26 km long, it runs from St. Lucie Inlet E of Stuart (N) to Jupiter Inlet, at the mouth of the Loxahatchee R. (S), and is bordered by Hobe Sound on the W. Its N is occupied by the Hobe Sound National Wildlife Refuge, its S by exclusive homes and private beaches.

Justice village, pop. 11,137, Cook Co., NE Illinois, on the Chicago Sanitary and Ship Canal, a residential suburb 14 mi/23 km SW of Chicago.

K

Kaaterskill Creek 20 mi/32 km long, in SE New York. It rises in a marsh in the Catskills, near Haines Falls, in Hunter township, Greene Co., where it flows over double falls 160 ft/49 m high, highest in the NE US, at the head of Kaaterskill Clove, a gorge. The creek continues along a meandering course filled with rapids and falls, into the NE corner of Ulster Co., then turns NE to empty into the CATSKILL CREEK at Cauterskill, just W of Catskill.

Kahnawake also, **Caughnawaga** Indian reserve, pop. (1981) 5218, S Québec, just S of Montréal and opposite LACHINE on the Lac St.-Louis (the St. Lawrence R.). Founded in the 1660s as a refuge for Christian Iroquois, in LA PRAIRIE, it relocated here shortly after. Kateri Tekakwitha, born near AURIESVILLE, New York, lived here 1677–80. In 1980 she became the first American Indian beatified by the Roman Catholic church. A shrine contains her tomb and relics. In the 1880s, jobs building a nearby railroad bridge introduced residents to high steel construction, in which they became world-famous.

Kahoolawe eighth-largest (45 sq mi/117 sq km) of the Hawaiian Is., part of Maui Co., 6 mi/10 km SW of Maui, from which the Alalakeiki Channel separates it. Formerly privately owned, it was used by the US Navy as a bombing and gunnery target area from the 1940s through 1994. Control was then turned over to the state; a cleanup of military debris now under way may take until 2003.

Kahului unincorporated community, pop. 16,889, Maui Co., EC Hawaii, on the NW coast of Maui I., in the Maui isthmus, just E of Wailuku. Its airport is central to Maui tourism. Kahului was an important port from the 1880s, exporting sugar and pineapples. Maui Community College and shopping facilities are here, along with a museum of the sugar industry.

Kaibab Plateau tableland, c.9000 ft/2740 m high, part of the COLORADO PLATEAU, extending N of Arizona's GRAND CANYON into S Utah. The lower (c.6000 ft/1830 m) Kanab Plateau lies W, across Kanab Creek. The North Rim entry to the Grand Canyon and part of the ARIZONA STRIP are on the plateau, which was called Buckskin Mt. by 19th-century Mormon settlers. The **Kaibab National Forest** (1.56 million ac/630,000 ha), with units N and S of the canyon, is home to the rare Kaibab squirrel.

Kailua unincorporated community, pop. 36,818, Honolulu Co., SE Oahu, Hawaii, on Kailua Bay, 10 mi/16 km NE of Honolulu. The name means "two currents in the sea," a reference to offshore Pacific currents. Oahu's medieval kings lived on this community's windward white beach, using the Kawainui swamplands (W) as fishponds. There are numerous temple ruins in the vicinity. Kailua Bay Beach and Park and some of the University of Hawaii's agricultural research stations are here.

Kailua-Kona also, **Kailua** see under KONA COAST, Hawaii.

Kaiparowits Plateau tableland, 55 mi/90 km NW–SE, lying W of the Escalante R. and N of L. POWELL, in SC Utah. Dry, and at an elevation of 7000–8000 ft/2135–2440 m, with steep ridges and valleys supporting scrubby vegetation, it is suitable for sheep and cattle grazing. The Straight Cliffs (E) rise 1000 ft/305 m above the plateau to Fiftymile Mountain, an area noted for fossils, cliff dwellings, and dinosaur tracks.

Kakaako commercial and light industrial district on the waterfront of HONOLULU, Hawaii. Resisting development and high rents, it lies between Downtown and Waikiki Beach (E).

Ka Lae also, **South Cape** or **South Point** cape on the S extremity of the island of HAWAII, at 18° 56′ N the southernmost point in the United States.

Kalaeloa Point see BARBERS POINT, Hawaii.

Kalamazoo city, pop. 80,277, seat of Kalamazoo Co., SW Michigan, on the Kalamazoo R., 50 mi/80 km S of Grand Rapids. A fur-trading post occupied this spot (1823), and a settlement was founded in 1829. Its name is from the Algonquian "Kee-Kalamazoo," meaning either "boiling pot" or "it smokes," and referring to the river springs. Growth came with the arrival of the Michigan Central Railroad (1846) and a government land office. Dutch farmers were prominent among those who migrated here in the mid 1800s. Kalamazoo was an Underground Railway stop. The city produces nursery plants and trades locally produced fruits and vegetables. It manufactures paper, aircraft and missile components, clothing, musical instruments, pharmaceuticals, and chemicals. Many wholesale companies are headquartered here. Kalamazoo's cultural institutions include a symphony, an arts institute, and an aviation museum. Among its educational institutions are Kalamazoo College (1833), Western Michigan University (1903), Nazareth College (1924), and Kalamazoo Valley Community College (1966).

Kalamazoo County 562 sq mi/1456 sq km, pop. 223,411, in SW Michigan, drained by the Portage and Kalamazoo rivers. Its seat is Kalamazoo, which dominates the county's economy with its educational institutions and industry. It is a region of many small lakes, and a rich farming area that raises peppermint, fruit, grain, livestock, and dairy cattle.

Kalaupapa Peninsula also, **Makanalua Peninsula** on the N coast of the island of MOLOKAI, Hawaii. This 10–sq mi/26–sq km plateau is isolated from the rest of the island by dramatic cliffs rising as high as 2000 ft/600 m. The village in the SW is the site of a former leper colony established by King Kamehameha V in 1866; the martyr Father Damien (1840–89) worked (from 1873) and died here. The colony was disestablished in 1969; older residents were allowed to remain. In 1980 nearly 11,000 ac/4455 ha were set aside as a national historic park.

Kalihi neighborhood in N HONOLULU, Hawaii, NW of IWILEI, E of the Army's Fort Shafter, and near the Lunalilo Expressway. It is the site of the noted Bernice Pauahi Bishop Museum, a study center displaying artifacts and relics of Hawaii and the Pacific.

Kalispell city, pop. 11,917, seat of Flathead Co., NW Montana, 95 mi/153 km N of Missoula. Named for the Kalispel Indians when the Great Northern Railway arrived and the town was established in 1891, it is a market center for lumber, Christmas trees, and crops, especially seed potatoes, sweet cherries, and apples. Its industries produce plywood, logging equipment, concrete products, and trailers. Kalispell is headquarters for the Flathead National Forest. Tourism is significant due to its location in Flathead Valley, surrounded by mountains, between Glacier National Park (NE) and Flathead L. (SE).

kame any of various small rounded hills or elongated ridges, usually isolated and with steep sides, formed by deposition of gravel, sand, etc., through melting glacial ice. They are most often found near the farthest edge of an ice sheet (thus, near terminal MORAINES), as in Ohio.

Kamloops city, pop. 67,057, Thompson-Nicola Regional District, SC British Columbia, at the confluence of the North and South Thompson rivers, 160 mi/260 km NE of Vancouver. The administrative headquarters for the province's S interior, it is a division point for the Canadian Pacific and Canadian National railways, a highway junction, and the service and processing center for an agricultural, ranching, mining, and lumbering region. Founded (1812) in Shuswap (Salishan) territory as a fur trading post, the settlement grew during the 1850s gold rush, and continued developing, especially with the arrival of the CPR (1885). In 1967, it merged with North Kamloops to form the present city. Kamloops has mills and a smelter, and tourism is also important. Kamloops Indian reserve (pop. 799) and the Highland Valley Copper Mines are nearby. Cariboo Community College is here.

Kamsack town, pop. 2323, SC Saskatchewan, 40 mi/64 km NE of Yorkton and 167 mi/268 km NE of Regina, just W of the Manitoba border, at the confluence of the Assiniboine and Whitesand rivers. It is a service center for regional grain and mixed farming, stock raising, and lumbering. Local industries include oil refining and dairying. Kamsack was originally a fur trading center. Doukhobors, including a radical nonconformist group called the Sons of Freedom, settled here in the late 1890s, having escaped religious persecution in Russia. The village of Veregin (pop. 126), named after their leader, is just W.

Kanab Plateau see under KAIBAB PLATEAU, Arizona.

Kanata city, pop. 37,344, Ottawa-Carleton Regional Municipality, SE Ontario, on the Ottawa R. (N), 12 mi/19 km W of downtown Ottawa. A planned community initiated in 1964 with villages around a city center, it has become a center of semiconductor, laser, and other high-tech industries, and continues to grow rapidly as a residential suburb.

Kanawha County 901 sq mi/2334 sq km, pop. 207,619, in WC West Virginia. CHARLESTON is its seat. The Elk and Kanawha rivers meet in the industrial and governmental complex around Charleston, in what is by far West Virginia's most populous county.

Kanawha Plateau see under APPALACHIAN Mts.

Kanawha River also, **Great Kanawha** 97 mi/156 km long, in WC West Virginia. It is formed at Gauley Bridge by the confluence of the NEW and Gauley rivers, and flows NW through the CHARLESTON area to join the Ohio R. at POINT PLEASANT. The river has extensive hydroelectric, navigational, and flood control works on its tributaries. The **Kanawha Valley** is noted for its coal, natural gas, and brine, key to the industrial importance of the Charleston area. The **Little Kanawha River** rises in Upshur Co. and flows 160 mi/260 km W and NW to join the Ohio R. at Parkersburg. Both rivers drain the Kanawha Plateau.

Kancamagus Highway 33 mi/53 km long, between Conway (E) and North Woodstock (W), in the S White Mts., NC New Hampshire. Named for a 17th-century Penacook chief, the highway follows the Swift R. and the Hancock Branch of the Pemigewasset R., reaching 2890 ft/881 m at Kancamagus Pass. It is famous for fall foliage.

Kane County 524 sq mi/1357 sq km, pop. 317,471, in NE Illinois, traversed in the E by the Fox R. Most of the population lives in a number of communities clustered in the E part of the county, many of which are old industrial river ports. These include GENEVA (the county seat), Aurora, Elgin, Batavia, and St. Charles. The rest of Kane Co. is mainly agricultural, producing corn, fruits, and vegetables.

Kaneohe unincorporated community, pop. 35,448, Honolulu Co., E Oahu, Hawaii. It extends from the foothills of the Koolau Range to Kaneohe Bay and is 9 mi/14 km NNE of Honolulu, where many residents are employed. This windward community was once the residence of Oahu's early kings. Kaneohe Bay Marine Corps Air Station is nearby. The University of Hawaii's Marine Laboratory is on Moku o'Loe (Coconut I.), one of the few coral islands in the bay. Hawaii Loa (1963) and Windward Community (1972) colleges are here.

Kaniapiskau River see under R. KOKSOAK, Québec.

Kankakee city, pop. 27,575, seat of Kankakee Co., NE Illinois, on the Kankakee R., 55 mi/89 km SSW of Chicago. A retail, processing, and shipping center for a rich soybean and corn producing area, it is also an industrial center, with manufactures that include home appliances, furniture, foundry products, brick, tile, paint, farm implements, and pharmaceuticals. It was founded by the Illinois Central Railroad in the 1850s, when the site was chosen over nearby BOURBONNAIS. The city is the seat of Olivet Nazarene University (1907) and Kankakee Community College (1966). Kankakee State Park is to the NW.

Kankakee County 679 sq mi/1759 sq km, pop. 96,255, in NE Illinois, drained by the Iroquois and Kankakee rivers. The E border is the Indiana state line. The county is dominated economically by the county seat of Kankakee and its two suburbs, Bradley and Bourbonnais. The rest of Kankakee Co. lies within a rich corn belt, with soybeans the other important crop.

Kankakee River 135 mi/217 km long, in Indiana and Illinois.

It rises near South Bend in N Indiana, and flows SW, then W to be joined by the Iroquois R. 2 mi/3 km SE of Kankakee, where it turns NW for 32 mi/52 km before joining the Des Plaines R. to form the Illinois R., SW of Joliet.

Kannapolis city, pop. 29,696, Cabarrus and Rowan counties, WC North Carolina, 25 mi/40 km NNE of Charlotte. Established in 1877, Cannon Mills (now Fieldcrest Cannon), one of the world's leading household textile manufacturers, built the town around its mills in 1906. For decades it was an unincorporated company town. Principal manufactures include towels, blankets, sheets, and pillowcases.

Kansas state of the C US, considered both part of the MIDDLE WEST and a GREAT PLAINS state; 1990 pop. 2,477,574 (104.8% of 1980; rank: 32nd); area 82,282 sq mi/213,110 sq km (rank: 15th); admitted to Union 1861 (34th). Capital: TOPEKA. Most populous cities: WICHITA, KANSAS CITY, Topeka, OVERLAND PARK. Kansas is bordered S by Oklahoma; W by Colorado; N by Nebraska; and E by Missouri. In the NE corner it faces Missouri across the MISSOURI R. The state's E third lies on the W edge of the vast C lowland of the US. Near the E border, elevations are around 1000 ft/300 m. Much of the SE is in the OSAGE PLAINS. Beyond the low FLINT HILLS (EC) Kansas rises gradually into the Great Plains. The SMOKY HILLS and other low ranges across the state's C rise to about 2000–2300 ft/610–700 m. In the High Plains of the W, Mt. SUNFLOWER, on the Colorado border, is the state's high point, at 4039 ft/1231 m, only slightly above the surrounding terrain. Two major river systems cross Kansas from W to E. The SMOKY HILL R., flowing across the NC, joins the REPUBLICAN R. (flowing SE from Nebraska) at JUNCTION CITY, forming the KANSAS (or Kaw) R., which meets the Missouri R. on the Missouri border, at Kansas City. The SALINE and Solomon rivers, tributaries of the Smoky Hill, parallel it (N) across much of the state. In the SW, the ARKANSAS R. enters Kansas from Colorado. After turning NE to GREAT BEND, it turns SE through HUTCHINSON, Wichita, and ARKANSAS CITY, continuing into Oklahoma. In Kansas's SE, the VERDIGRIS and NEOSHO rivers flow SE to meet the Arkansas in Oklahoma. From EC Kansas, the MARAIS DES CYGNES R. flows E into Missouri, where it joins the Osage R. and eventually the Missouri R. Kansas is characterized by extensive fields of wheat, corn, sorghum, sunflowers, and other crops; on the High Plains, esp., irrigation, including wells into the Ogallala AQUIFER, are critical to farming. Beef and dairy cattle are major sources of income. Natural gas, oil, and salt are extracted, particularly in the SW and C; the state leads the US in helium production. Coal is mined in the SE corner, around PITTSBURG, in an area that has also produced much lead and zinc. Kansas City and Topeka (NE) have agriculture-related industries. The former, its meatpacking and railroading heyday passed, has benefited from its position as part of a major METROPOLITAN AREA to attract auto assembly, high-tech, and other industries. Topeka has state government and a number of manufactures. Wichita (SC), once essentially a cattle town on the CHISHOLM TRAIL, has been since World War II a major aircraft and aerospace manufacturer. The state takes its name from the Kansa (or Kaw), one of a number of peoples living here when Europeans arrived. The Osage, Pawnee, Kiowa, Arapaho, and other plains peoples formerly roamed the region; the villages of the (then) sedentary Wichita in the Great Bend region proved, in 1541, to be the legendary QUIVIRA for which the Spanish adventurer Coronado was looking. Kansas was still little-known when it passed to the US in the 1803 LOUISIANA PURCHASE. The opening (1821) of the SANTA FE TRAIL brought increasing traffic across the plains, but the region was regarded as essentially Indian territory until the passage of the Kansas-Nebraska Act (1854) opened it to white settlement, and to competition for control between pro- and antislavery pioneers. It rapidly became "Bleeding Kansas," in which precursors to the bloodshed of the Civil War occurred at Lawrence, at OSAWATOMIE, on the Marais des Cygnes, and in many other places. Some communities, like Lawrence, were established by Northerners, others, like LEAVENWORTH and ATCHISON, by Southerners. In 1861, Kansas entered the Union as a Free State. After the Civil War, travel on the OREGON TRAIL and through the Smoky Hill valley increased. In the 1860s, the SANTA FE, UNION PACIFIC, and other railroads extended across the state, and cattle towns like ABILENE and the notorious DODGE CITY sprang up. Recruited by the Santa Fe, German Mennonite farmers from Russia introduced winter wheat brought from Europe; the use of expanses of previously unplowed PRAIRIE to meet World War I wheat demands left much of the W vulnerable, in the dry 1930s, to DUST BOWL conditions, alleviated eventually by irrigation and improved farming techniques. Kansas today remains a primarily agricultural state, with a few major industrial centers. FORT RILEY, at Junction City, and Fort Leavenworth are major military installations. Particularly well-known among its communities are Abilene, the boyhood home of Dwight Eisenhower, and site of his presidential library; EMPORIA, home to newspaperman William Allen White and his *Gazette;* and Topeka, for its Menninger (psychiatric) Foundation. The University of Kansas is in Lawrence, Kansas State University at MANHATTAN. The state's people remain largely descendants of the Northern ("Jayhawker") and Southern settlers of the 1850s, along with those of late-19th-century German and other European immigrants.

Kansas City **1.** second most populous (149,767) city in Kansas, seat of Wyandotte Co., in the NE, on the S bank of the Missouri R. across from Kansas City, Missouri, and on the Kansas R. at its junction with the Missouri. Settled by Wyandot Indians in 1843, the site was sold to the Federal government (1855) and settled by whites (1857) as Wyandotte. The first Kansas constitution (1859) was drawn up here. Wyandotte grew as a shipping point for livestock and grain. When it was consolidated (1886) with Old Kansas City (S of the Kansas R.) and Armourdale, the unified communities became known as Kansas City. Today it is an agricultural market with stockyards, meatpacking plants, grain elevators, and flour mills. Other industries include oil refining, auto assembly, and the manufacture of aircraft engines, furniture, clothing, steel and aluminum products, chemicals, soap, and farm machinery. Among educational institutions are the University of Kansas Medical Center, Kansas City Kansas Community College (1923), and Donnelly College (1949). **2.** city, pop. 435,146, JACKSON, CLAY, PLATTE, and Cass counties, NW Missouri, at the confluence of the Missouri and Kansas (Kaw) rivers, on both banks of the former and across State Line Rd. from Kansas City, Kansas (W). The most populous Missouri city, it is the center of a ten-county (also including JOHNSON and WYANDOTTE in Kansas) metropolitan area with a pop. of 1,566,280. A fur trading post was established by François Chouteau at the river junction in 1821. Called Westport Landing, this developed into the town

(1838) and city (1853) of Kansas—Kansas City after 1889. Near the point where the SANTA FE and OREGON trails diverged, the settlement, in both Missouri and Kansas, grew with the nation's westward expansion. Development was hastened by the arrival of the Missouri Pacific Railroad (1865), linking the region with markets in Chicago and the East; eight more lines soon joined it. Kansas City, already a staging area for the West and a flourishing inland port, became a major supplier of wheat and livestock. From the post–Civil War era into the 20th century, its economy was almost entirely based on regional agriculture. After 1900, diverse industries and commercial enterprises broadened the city's economic base. A transportation hub and agribusiness center, it today has railroad shops, livestock and wheat exchanges, stockyards, grain elevators, meatpacking plants, flour mills, and farm equipment makers. Other industries include auto and truck assembly, oil refining, steel and aluminum fabrication, printing and publishing, and the manufacture of aerospace equipment and chemicals. Limestone caves beneath the city store a variety of foreign goods (in a unique FREE TRADE ZONE) and domestic foodstuffs. Regional Federal offices, wholesale and retail industries, and service organizations are among major employers. Kansas City has a long urban planning history. Poorer residential areas have been subject to URBAN RENEWAL undertakings since the 1970s. Among its suburbs, those in Johnson Co., Kansas (SW), are esp. affluent. The city's extensive park system, developed largely around 1900, includes well-known SWOPE PARK and PENN VALLEY PARK; the PASEO is one of numerous parkways. Sports are centered at the 1970s HARRY S TRUMAN SPORTS COMPLEX and KEMPER ARENA, cultural and business events at the CROWN CENTER complex. The city's museums and historic sites include the Nelson-Atkins Museum of Art, the Thomas Hart Benton Home and Studio, and EIGHTEENTH AND VINE, early-20th-century hub of Southwestern black culture. Educational institutions include the Kansas City Art Institute (1885), Rockhurst College (1910), Avila College (1916), and the University of Missouri at Kansas City (1929). The city has expanded through a series of annexations, including that of WESTPORT in 1897, more recently the 1950s–60s enlargements N of the Missouri R. that included land in Platte Co. on which the huge Kansas City International Airport, 16 mi/26 km NW of Downtown, was completed in the 1970s. The most affluent residential areas of the city are in the SW, along the Kansas line S of COUNTRY CLUB PLAZA. See also: BIG BLUE R.; COUNTRY CLUB PLAZA (and District, and S Kansas City neighborhoods); CROWN CENTER; EIGHTEENTH AND VINE; HARRY S TRUMAN SPORTS COMPLEX (and Arrowhead and Royals stadiums); HOSPITAL HILL; KEMPER ARENA (and the West Bottoms); NORTHEAST; the PASEO (and Troost Ave.); PENN VALLEY PARK; SWOPE PARK; WESTPORT (and Westport Landing).

Kansas Pyramids see MONUMENT ROCKS, Kansas.

Kansas River 170 mi/275 km long, in E Kansas. It is formed at JUNCTION CITY by the confluence of the SMOKY HILL and REPUBLICAN rivers, and flows E past Manhattan (where the BIG BLUE R. joins it from the N), Topeka, and Lawrence, to join the Missouri R. at Kansas City. Named for the Kansa (or Kaw, an alternate name for the river also), a Siouan people, the river in turn gave its name to the state. Since the 1950s its tributaries have been dammed in several places to prevent periodic flooding.

Kapuskasing town, pop. 10,344, Cochrane District, C Ontario, on the Trans-Canada Highway (Route 11) and the Kapuskasing R., 240 mi/386 km NNE of Sault Ste. Marie. It became the site of an agricultural experiment station in 1913 and a transcontinental railroad depot in 1914. During World War I, the town housed a large prisoner of war camp. In 1922 it became the site of the Spruce Falls Power and Paper plant, which harnessed the power of Smokey Falls, 50 mi/80 km N; Kapuskasing has been a major newsprint producer since then.

Karnack hamlet in Harrison Co., NE Texas, 14 mi/23 km NE of Marshall and just S of CADDO L. Claudia Alta Taylor (Lady Bird Johnson) was born here in 1912. The wife of President Lyndon B. Johnson, she was later an influential advocate of roadside and countryside beautification. In a tourist area, Karnack now also makes rocket fuel.

Kaskaskia village, pop. 32, Randolph Co., SW Illinois, on the W (Missouri) bank of the Mississippi R., across from Chester, Illinois. Kaskaska I., the only part of Illinois W of the Mississippi, was formerly on the E bank; traces of the river's old course remain along the state line. One of the oldest European settlements in the West, Fort Kaskaskia was built by the French (1733) near a 1703 Jesuit mission. Kaskaskia soon became one of the largest and most important French communities in the Mississippi Valley. Capital of the Territory of Illinois from 1809, it served as the first state capital in 1818–20. The first newspaper in Illinois was published here in 1814. Old Kaskaskia was destroyed by floods in 1844, 1881, and thereafter. Now all that remains are a few structures in the Fort Kaskaskia Historic Site, near Ellis Grove, and the Kaskaskia Bell memorial, a State Historic Site in the village. July, 1993 floods caused heavy damage here.

Kaskaskia River 320 mi/510 km long, in Illinois. It rises near Urbana and winds in a generally SW direction across the state, entering the Mississippi R. just NW of Kaskaskia and 46 mi/74 km SSE of East St. Louis. Draining much of SW Illinois, it flows through dam-created L. Shelbyville, past the old capital of Vandalia, and through dam-created Carlyle L. The river is named for an Illinoisan tribe.

Katahdin, Mount also, **Ktaadn** granitic peak, 5267 ft/1606 m, highest in the Katahdin Range (46 ridges and peaks), in Baxter State Park, NC Maine. The highest mountain in Maine, Katahdin is the N terminus of the Appalachian Trail. Its dominance over its surroundings made it prominent in Indian legend as in the work of later writers and painters. Among its features are the Great Basin, a huge cirque, and the Knife Edge, a precipitous ridge. The mountain's high point is also known as Baxter Peak.

Katmai National Park and Preserve 4.09 million ac/1.66 million ha (6391 sq mi/16,552 sq km), comprising a large part of the ALASKA PENINSULA, in SW Alaska. The area contains a wide assortment of lakes, rivers important for red salmon, wildlife including the Alaska brown bear, and a number of volcanoes. **Mt. Katmai** (6715 ft/2047 m) and the Novarupta Volcano (4860 ft/1481 m) together were part of a violent eruption in 1912; it is thought that lava from Katmai helped feed an explosion of Novarupta that spread steam and ash over a large area. The explosion created the Valley of Ten Thousand Smokes, which extends for 32 mi/52 km and covers 70 sq mi/181 sq km; it was named for countless FUMAROLES that emerged through the ash, only a few of which are active today. Recent area volcanic activity has been seen at the Trident Volcano (1968) and at 4025-ft/1227-m Mt. Augustine, on Augustine I. in COOK INLET, just NE (1987). Naknek L. and the Alganak Wild & Scenic R. are within the park.

Katonah village in BEDFORD township, Westchester Co., SE New York, 16 mi/26 km N of White Plains, on the Croton R. (New Croton Reservoir). It is an affluent residential suburb. Caramoor, a mansion become a concert center, and the John Jay Homestead are here.

Katy city, pop. 8005, Harris, Waller, and Fort Bend counties, SE Texas, 30 mi/48 km W of Houston. A manufacturing and commercial center, it has recently undergone some suburban growth.

Kauai fourth-largest island of Hawaii, 551 sq mi/1427 sq km, in Kauai Co., 72 mi/116 km NW of Oahu. Popularly referred to as the Garden Isle, it is the northernmost, and geologically the oldest, large island of the archipelago. The first to be settled by Polynesians, it was also the first visited by Captain James Cook, in 1778. LIHUE, on the E coast, is its chief community, and its principal harbors are Nawiliwili, Hanalei, and Hanapepe. The highest points on the island, in its C, are the peaks of KAWAIKINI (5243 ft/1598 m) and WAIALEALE (5100 ft/1530 m); the latter drops off dramatically into WAIMEA Canyon. To the NW are the cliffs of the Na Pali Coast; the S and the E coasts constitute a fertile plain for sugar, rice, and pineapple cultivation. The island receives heavy rainfall and is susceptible to Pacific hurricanes. Cattle ranching and tourism are important as well.

Kauai County 620 sq mi/1606 sq km, pop. 51,177, in NW Hawaii, containing Kauai, the privately owned NIIHAU island, and two uninhabited islets, Lehua and Kaula, which lie N and S of Niihau. The county seat is LIHUE, on the E coast of Kauai; Kapaa (E coast) and Hanapepe (W coast) are other major communities. Sugar, rice, and pineapple cultivation; diversified light manufacturing; the tourist industry; and cattle ranching are important.

Kaukauna city, pop. 11,982, Outagamie Co., EC Wisconsin, on the Fox R., 6 mi/10 km NE of Appleton. Its manufactures include precision tools, paper, and cheese and other dairy products. The site of an early portage around waterfalls on the Fox R., it was settled by the French in 1793. The state's first gristmill and sawmill were here. The Wisconsin International Raceway is just S of the city.

Kawaikini volcanic mountain in C KAUAI, Hawaii. Its peak, at 5243 ft/1598 m, is the highest point on the island. WAIALEALE, another major mountain, is just N.

Kawartha Lakes series of interconnected bodies in SE Ontario, centered c.70 mi/110 km NE of Toronto and just NW of Peterborough. The TRENT CANAL system runs through most of the Kawarthas, which include (roughly E–W) Katchewanooka, Clear, Stony, Lower Buckhorn, Chemong, Buckhorn, Pigeon, Sturgeon, Scugog (alone, some 25 mi/40 km to the SW), Cameron, Balsam, Mitchell, and artificial Canal. The last connects via the Talbot R. with L. SIMCOE (W). On the E, the chain connects via the Otonabee R. with RICE L., thence via the Trent R. with the Bay of Quinte (L. Ontario). In glacial terrain just S of the Canadian Shield, the Kawarthas are a boating and fishing mecca.

Kaweah, Mount also, **Big Kaweah** highest (13,816 ft/4211 m) of four mountains of the Kaweah Peaks Ridge in SEQUOIA NATIONAL PARK, EC California. West of the Kern R. Canyon, the ridge includes Red Kaweah (13,754 ft/4192 m), Black Kaweah (13,752 ft/4192 m), and Gray Kaweah (13,728 ft/4184 m).

Kaw River see KANSAS R.

Kayak Island in the Gulf of ALASKA, 60 mi/100 km SE of Cordova, in SC Alaska. Twenty mi/32 km NE–SW and 2 mi/3 km wide, it lies within the Chugach National Forest. Cape St. Elias is at its S end. In 1741 Vitus Bering, a Danish officer in the Russian navy, anchored at the island, calling it St. Elias. It is said to be the first place in Alaska on which Europeans set foot.

Kayenta unincorporated community, pop. 4372, Navajo Co., NE Arizona, S of MONUMENT VALLEY and 16 mi/26 km S of the Utah border. In an arid valley, on the site of prehistoric lakes, it is an important Navajo center. Founded as a trading post in 1910, it is now also a tourist base. Local uranium deposits are also important to its economy.

Kaysville city, pop. 13,961, Davis Co., N Utah, on the GREAT SALT L., midway between Salt Lake City (S) and Ogden (N). In an irrigated truck farming area, it has flour mills and food processing plants, and is a growing residential suburb.

Kealakekua Bay inlet on the W coast of the island of HAWAII (Kona District). In 1779, on his second visit to Hawaii, Captain James Cook was killed here in a dispute with the natives; a monument stands on the shore.

Keansburg borough, pop. 11,069, Monmouth Co., EC New Jersey, on Raritan Bay, 9 mi/14 km SE of Perth Amboy. Situated on Point Comfort, which extends into the bay, it is a popular summer resort community with an amusement park, and a busy port for commercial and pleasure craft.

Kearney city, pop. 24,396, seat of Buffalo Co., SC Nebraska, on the Platte R., 43 mi/69 km SW of Grand Island. It is a processing and rail center for grain and livestock producers. Among its many manufactures are farm and irrigation equipment. Nearby (S) Fort Kearney (est. here 1848, after two years near the site of NEBRASKA CITY) once protected OREGON TRAIL pioneers. A University of Nebraska campus (1903) and Kearney State College (1905) are here.

Kearns unincorporated community, pop. 28,374, Salt Lake Co., N Utah, a residential suburb 9 mi/14 km SW of Salt Lake City. There are dairy and sugar beet farms in the area.

Kearny town, pop. 34,874, Hudson Co., NE New Jersey, on the Passaic (W) and Hackensack (E) rivers, at the head of Newark Bay, between Newark (W and S) and Jersey City (E). It was separated from HARRISON (SW) in 1867. Long known for its drydocks and bustling shipyards, which flourished during World War II, it still supports some shipbuilding; has oil, gold, and platinum refineries; and is a manufacturing center, producing communications equipment, chemicals, plastics, truck bodies, paints and varnishes, brick, tile, processed foods, and textiles.

Kearny Mesa highland area of SAN DIEGO, California, lying N of Mission Valley. MIRAMAR and its Naval Air Station occupy much of the mesa, which is also the site of major aerospace manufacturing facilities. CLAIREMONT and Linda Vista lie on the W. Camp Kearny (1917) was a major World War I Army training center.

Kearsarge, Mount monadnock (2937 ft/896 m) between Wilmot and Warner townships, SC New Hampshire. Winslow State Park extends from its N slope, Rollins State Park from the S. The peak is not to be confused with Mt. **Kearsarge North** (3268 ft/997 m) in Bartlett and Chatham townships, 65 mi/105 km NE, which was called Pequawket from 1915 to 1957.

Keene **1.** city, pop. 22,430, seat of Cheshire Co., SW New Hampshire, on the Ashuelot R., 10 mi/16 km NW of Mt. Monadnock. The Boston and Maine Railroad stimulated industrial development after 1840. Manufactures now include optical instruments, furniture, textiles, and shoes. The city is a center for the Monadnock region's commerce and winter sports. Keene's toboggan slides are among the best-known in the Northeast. Keene State College (1909) is here. **2.** city, pop. 3944, Johnson Co., NC Texas, 23 mi/37 km S of Fort Worth. In an agricultural area, it developed around a Seventh Day Adventist Academy (1893), now Southwestern Adventist College.

Keeneland see under LEXINGTON, Kentucky.

Keesler Air Force Base see under BILOXI, Mississippi.

Keewatin administrative region (formerly district) of the SE NORTHWEST TERRITORIES. The name, from an Ojibwa (Algonquian) name for the North Wind, was once also proposed for Manitoba.

Kegonsa, Lake in Dane Co., SC Wisconsin. Three mi/5 km long and 2.5 mi/4 km wide, it is the southernmost of the FOUR LAKES group connected by the Yahara R.

Keizer unincorporated community, pop. 21,884, Marion Co., NW Oregon, on the Willamette R., a rapidly expanding residential suburb 4 mi/6 km N of Salem.

Kejimkujik National Park 150–sq mi/385–sq km preserve of hemlock stands, bogs, lakes, and marshes, 50 mi/80 km NE of Yarmouth, in SW Nova Scotia. Early Micmac inhabitants left numerous PETROGLYPHS in the area, and lakes and streams are popular with canoeists. The Tobeatic Wildlife Management Area lies on the S.

Keller city, pop. 13,683, Tarrant Co., NE Texas, 14 mi/23 km NNE of Fort Worth. A residential suburb in a prairie agricultural area, it tripled in population in the 1980s.

Kelleys Island island and summer resort village, pop. 159, Erie Co., N Ohio, in L. Erie off the NE coast of Ottawa Co., 10 mi/16 km N of Sandusky and 4 mi/6 km S of the Ontario border. This shield-shaped island of 2888 ac/1170 ha measures 7 mi/11 km across at its widest point and has 18 mi/29 km of rocky, irregular shoreline. It is noted for its limestone deposits. Winemaking, truck gardening, fishing, and tourism are also important. Local attractions include Glacial Grooves and Kelleys Island state parks and Inscription Rock, an example of prehistoric petroglyphs.

Kelly Air Force Base in San Antonio, Texas, 5 mi/8 km SW of Downtown. Adjacent (E) to LACKLAND AIR FORCE BASE, it houses the San Antonio Material Area, responsible for logistics and maintenance operations, including the Air Force Electronic Security Command. Established in May 1917, Kelly quickly became the world's largest air training center; for two decades virtually all US military aviators trained here.

Kelowna city, pop. 75,950, Central Okanagan Regional District, S British Columbia, on the E shore of OKANAGAN L., 170 mi/275 km ENE of Vancouver. The settlement was founded (1859) by Oblate missionaries who planted the area's first fruit trees here. The trade center of a large fruit growing and winemaking region, Kelowna cans and packs apples, grapes, and vegetables, and produces lumber and dairy goods. Tourism and year-round lake and mountain recreation are also important. Okanagan College (1963) is here, and the summer Kelowna Regatta has been held since 1906. Okanagan L. is crossed here by a 4600-ft/1400-m floating (pontoon) bridge.

Kelso city, pop. 11,820, seat of Cowlitz Co., SW Washington, on the Cowlitz R. near its junction with the Columbia R., 38 mi/61 km S of Centralia and immediately NE of LONGVIEW. Used as early as the 1840s by Hudson's Bay Company traders as a shipping point, it was settled in 1847. It became an important 19th-century logging, milling, and fishing town and a steamboat port. Today its economy centers on fishing (smelt, steelhead, sturgeon) and fish canning. The city also packs meat and processes local agricultural and dairy products.

Kemano see under KITIMAT, British Columbia.

Kemper Arena multiuse facility, completed 1975, in the West Bottoms area of NW KANSAS CITY, Missouri, on the Kansas line and near the Kansas R., just S of its junction with the Missouri R. The arena occupies part of the grounds of the extensive Kansas City stockyards, which declined after a 1940s peak in which they were briefly the nation's busiest. Professional hockey and soccer and college basketball are among sports events held in the 16,000-seat Kemper, which has also seen political conventions and is home to the annual (Nov.) American Royal Livestock and Horse Show, one of the city's major events.

Kenai Peninsula projection into the Gulf of Alaska, between COOK INLET (NW) and Prince William Sound (NE), in S Alaska. The 150 mi/240 km–long peninsula is separated from Anchorage (N) by Turnagain Arm. The glacier-filled **Kenai Mts.,** part of the COAST RANGES, run the length of the peninsula, rising to nearly 7000 ft/2134 m. Farming and fishing are important in the mild coastal areas; the NE part lies within the CHUGACH National Forest. The main communities are SEWARD (SE); **Kenai** (city, pop. 6327), site of the oldest Russian Orthodox church in Alaska (NW); and HOMER (SW). **Kenai Peninsula Borough** has an area of 16,056 sq mi/41,585 sq km and a pop. of 40,802.

Ken Caryl unincorporated community, pop. 24,391, Jefferson Co., NC Colorado, a residential suburb of DENVER, 10 mi/16 km SSW of Downtown, and just W of Littleton.

Kendall unincorporated community, pop. 87,271, Dade Co., SE Florida, 10 mi/16 km SW of Miami. A booming suburb since the 1960s, it now houses a burgeoning population of new homeowners, many Hispanic, moving out from central Miami.

Kendall County 322 sq mi/834 sq km, pop. 39,413, in NE Illinois. Yorkville is the seat of this corn and livestock producing area. The Fox R. runs through the N part of the county, where some Chicago exurban development occurred during the 1980s, especially in the NE township of Oswego.

Kenilworth borough, pop. 7574, Union Co., NE New Jersey, 5 mi/8 km W of Elizabeth. It is a largely residential suburb with a variety of light manufactures and laboratories.

Kenmore village, pop. 17,180, in the township of Tonawanda, Erie Co., W New York, adjacent (N) to Buffalo. A residential suburb, it is home to the Sulpician Seminary of the Northwest.

Kenmore Square intersection and commercial district in the BACK BAY, Boston, Massachusetts, just W of the N end of the FENWAY. Commonwealth Avenue and BEACON STREET cross at the square. Fenway Park is just S. Kenmore Square is a focus of the student area around Boston University.

Kennebec County 876 sq mi/2269 sq km, pop. 115,904, in SW Maine. AUGUSTA is the county seat. The Sebasticook and Kennebec rivers provide waterpower; the Belgrade and Kennebec lake regions are popular resorts. Manufacturing operations at Hallowell, Waterville, Augusta, and Gardiner produce shoes, textiles, paper, wood and pulp products, dairy products, and agricultural products.

Kennebec River 150 mi/242 km long, flowing generally S from Moosehead L. in WC Maine to the Atlantic Ocean. It receives the ANDROSCOGGIN R. to form Merrymeeting Bay about 25 mi/40 km below Augusta, then flows past Bath to Popham Beach and the Gulf of Maine. The Kennebec furnishes waterpower at Bingham, Skowhegan, Waterville, Augusta, and Gardiner, but its industrial role is today much reduced. Champlain explored the river in 1606. In the 18th century the Kennebec became an important timber source, providing in particular mast pines for the British navy. In 1775, Benedict Arnold made his famous trek up the river in an ill-fated attempt to capture Québec.

Kennebunk town, pop. 8004, York Co., SW Maine. Kennebunk is on the Kennebunk and Mousam rivers and US 1, 4 mi/6 km N of the Atlantic coast, 9 mi/ 14 km SW of Biddeford. An early shipbuilding, trade, and industrial center, the town has many fine examples of period architecture, including the jigsaw-Gothic Wedding Cake House. It is the birthplace of author Kenneth Roberts (1885–1957), and gained note in the 1980s as the headquarters of Tom's of Maine, producers of natural toiletries. **Kennebunkport,** pop. 3356, is just below Kennebunk, at the mouth of the Kennebunk R., and includes the villages of Cape Porpoise, Arundel, and Goose Rocks Beach. Until 1821, Kennebunkport was known as Arundel, and appeared as such in the works of Kenneth Roberts, who summered here, along with other literary notables. The Kennebunk Playhouse is here. The vacation home of President George Bush, at Walkers Point, attracted much attention during his time in office.

Kennecott Copper Mine **1.** see under ELY, Nevada. **2.** see under BINGHAM, Utah.

Kennedale city, pop. 4096, Tarrant Co., Texas. A largely residential suburb 9 mi/14 km SE of downtown Fort Worth, on the city limits at the junction of Routes 20 and 820, it has some light manufactures.

Kennedy see JOHN F. KENNEDY.

Kennedy, Cape see under Cape CANAVERAL, Florida.

Kenner city, pop. 72,033, Jefferson Parish, SE Louisiana, on the Mississippi R. (S) and L. PONTCHARTRAIN (N), 10 mi/16 km W of New Orleans. Founded in 1885, it was laid out on the sugar plantation of William Kenner. In what had been an agricultural and lumbering region, it has oil and gas industries and manufactures various wood-based products, but is essentially a bedroom community. The New Orleans International Airport is in its SE. Kenner grew most rapidly in the 1970s.

Kennesaw city, pop. 8936, Cobb Co., NW Georgia, 20 mi/32 km NNW of Atlanta, of which it is a growing outer suburb. **Kennesaw** (also, **Kenesaw**) **Mountain,** an isolated mountain with two summits, Big Kennesaw (1809 ft/552 m) and Little Kennesaw (1550 ft/473 m), just S, was the scene of a Union victory (June–July 1864) in W.T. Sherman's advance on Atlanta. The site is part of Kennesaw Mountain National Battlefield Park.

Kennett city, pop. 10,941, seat of Dunklin Co., extreme SE Missouri, in the state's BOOTHEEL, 40 mi/64 km SSE of Poplar Bluff and close to the Arkansas border (W). Essentially a Southern city in a cotton farming region, it gins cotton and processes various other agricultural and forest products.

Kennett Square borough, pop. 5218, Chester Co., SE Pennsylvania, 33 mi/53 km WSW of Philadelphia and 3 mi/5 km N of the Maryland border. It is a major producer of mushrooms and has some light industry. It has a significant population of Mexican immigrants, most of whom are pickers in local mushroom houses. The 350-ac/142-ha Longwood Gardens is just NE.

Kennewick city, pop. 42,155, Benton Co., SE Washington, on the Columbia R. 3 mi/5 km W of its junction with the Snake R., opposite PASCO (N) and 7 mi/11 km SE of RICHLAND. The largest of these Tri-Cities, it is both a blue-collar residential community for workers at the nearby Hanford nuclear weapons plant and the site of chemical and agricultural (grapes, fruit, corn, soybeans, alfalfa, sugar beets, dairy products) processing industries. The beginning of irrigation projects in the area near Kennewick around 1900 stimulated local agricultural development. This was followed by the damming of the Columbia R., which provided hydroelectric power for the region.

Kenora town, pop. 9782, seat of Kenora District, W Ontario, on the N end of the LAKE OF THE WOODS, 285 mi/459 km WNW of Thunder Bay and 30 mi/50 km E of the Manitoba border. A fur trade point from the 18th century, it later developed as a lumbering center, and had an 1890s gold mining boom. It was incorporated as Rat Portage, Manitoba, in 1882, when the Canadian Pacific Railway was building in the area, became an Ontario township in 1892, and was renamed in 1904. It has pulp, paper, and flour mills, fish processing plants, and boatyards, but depends heavily on vacationers and tourists.

Kenosha city, pop. 80,352, seat of Kenosha Co., SE Wisconsin, on L. Michigan, 35 mi/56 km S of Milwaukee. Its name is derived from an Algonquian word for pike or pickerel. It was founded by New Englanders in 1835, and the state's first public school was established here in 1849. Wisconsin's southernmost L. Michigan port and an important trading center for a truck farming district, it produces cranberry and dairy items, commercial fertilizer, automobile engines, tools, furniture, clothing, and metal products. The city has developed extensive L. Michigan frontage as parks. Carthage College (1846, moved here 1964) and the University of Wisconsin–Parkside (1965) are in Kenosha.

Kensico Reservoir in Westchester Co., SE New York, 3 mi/5 km N of White Plains. Impounded by the Kensico Dam, a stone-veneered structure, built in 1915 across the Bronx R., it is part of New York City's water supply system. It serves as a holding pond for water from the ASHOKAN RESERVOIR in the Catskills, 77 mi/124 km to the NNW.

Kensington **1.** town, pop. 1713, Montgomery Co., C Maryland, on Rock Creek, 8 mi/13 km NW of Washington, D.C. An affluent residential suburb just outside the BELTWAY, it is home to the largest Mormon temple in the Northeast. **South Kensington** (unincorporated, pop. 8777) is similar. **2.** city, pop. 295, Douglas Co., WC Minnesota, 36 mi/58 km W of Sauk Centre. It was here that the Kensington Runestone, alleged to be of Viking origin, was found in 1898. **3.** see under BOROUGH PARK, New York. **4.** neighborhood in NE Philadelphia, Pennsylvania, one of the RIVER WARDS. It is a working- and middle-class residential area.

Kensington Market see under SPADINA Ave., Toronto, Ontario.

Kent **1.** town, pop. 2918, Litchfield Co., NW Connecticut, on the Housatonic R. at the New York line, 19 mi/30 km WSW of Torrington. Situated in the LITCHFIELD HILLS, it is an arts colony and resort, with summer camps and vacation homes. Some dairy farming remains. Kent has three state parks, and L. Waramaug is to the SE; the Schaghticoke tribal reservation is in the SW corner. **2.** city, pop. 28,835, Portage Co., NE Ohio, on the Cuyahoga R., 11 mi/18 km NE of Akron. It is the seat of Kent State University (1910), which came into national prominence in 1970 when four students were killed by National Guard troops during anti–Vietnam War protests. Castings, rubber, plastic goods, highway maintenance vehicles, and food products are among the many locally manufactured items. **3.** city, pop. 37,960, King Co., WC Washington, 18 mi/29 km S of Seattle. It is a growing bedroom community in the Seattle-Tacoma area, and has also become an industrial center in its own right. Electronics manufacturing, fruit and vegetable canning, frozen-food preparation, cold storage plants, and greenhouses are the main pillars of its economy. Its manufactures include furniture, clothing, lumber, crates, and plastics. Dairy and fruit and vegetable farming are common in the surrounding area.

Kent County **1.** 862 sq mi/2233 sq km, pop. 500,631, in WC Michigan, drained by the Thornapple, Rogue, and Flat rivers and crossed by the Grand R. The furniture-manufacturing city of GRAND RAPIDS is its seat; with its suburbs, which occupy much of the county's W section, it also dominates the economy. The area has gypsum and gravel deposits, orchards, and dairy and truck farms. Also in the county are a state fish hatchery and numerous lake resorts. **2.** 172 sq mi/445 sq km, pop. 161,135, in C Rhode Island, bounded E by Narragansett Bay and W by the Connecticut line, and intersected by the Flat, Moosup, Pawtuxet, and Wood rivers. Its seat is East Greenwich. It is known for its coastal resorts. Local agriculture includes corn, dairy, fruit, mushroom, potato, poultry, and truck farming; textiles and textile machinery, tools and metal products, and chemicals are produced. There are fishing and lumbering in the area, and a number of state parks and forests.

Kent Island in Queen Anne's Co., C Maryland, the largest island in Chesapeake Bay, 14 mi/23 km NNE–SSW and up to 5 mi/8 km wide. Settled in 1631, it did not become part of Maryland until 1657, but is the oldest European settlement now in the state (SAINT MARYS CITY, settled in 1634, has been in Maryland all along). Traditionally a trading post and fishing center, Kent I. is becoming more residential. It is 8 mi/13 km E of Annapolis, and is connected with the Western Shore by the Preston Lane (Chesapeake Bay) Bridge. Chester and Stevensville are among its villages.

Kenton County 163 sq mi/422 sq km, pop. 142,031, in extreme N Kentucky. Its seat is INDEPENDENCE. It is bounded (N) by the Ohio R. and Ohio. Rolling farmland in the N BLUEGRASS REGION, it is increasingly industrial and residential, part of the Cincinnati, Ohio, metropolitan area.

Kentucky officially, **Commonwealth of Kentucky** state of the EC US, one of the Border States of the Upper SOUTH (designated East South Central by the Census Bureau); 1990 pop. 3,685,296 (100.7% of 1980; rank: 23rd); area 40,411 sq mi/104,644 sq km (rank: 37th); admitted to Union 1792 (15th). Capital: FRANKFORT. Most populous cities: LOUISVILLE, LEXINGTON. Extending over 400 mi/640 km E–W, Kentucky has the OHIO R. along its entire N boundary; across the river are (E–W) Ohio, Indiana, and Illinois. On the E, the Tug Fork and BIG SANDY rivers separate it from West Virginia. On the SE, it is bordered by Virginia, with the CUMBERLAND GAP at the extreme S. From there along its entire S boundary, to the MISSISSIPPI R., it is bordered by Tennessee. Across a small stretch of the Mississippi, on the W, it faces the NEW MADRID area of Missouri. Kentucky's E third is part of the CUMBERLAND PLATEAU section of the APPALACHIAN system, a region of secluded valleys and hills and mountains rising to 4145 ft/1264 m at BLACK (Big Black) Mt., on the Virginia border. Kentucky's major internal rivers, the CUMBERLAND, KENTUCKY, and LICKING, flow W or NW across the state from this upland region. On the NW of the Cumberland Plateau, and extending NE–SW across the state, is a belt of lower plateaus. This contains, in the NE, the famous BLUEGRASS, a phosphate-rich region known for its pasturage and horses, and now undergoing urban development esp. in Lexington and surrounding Fayette Co. (C), as well as around Louisville (NW) and COVINGTON and other suburbs of Cincinnati, Ohio (N). To the SW of the Bluegrass is the PENNYROYAL (or Pennyrile), where water drains so quickly through underlying limestone that agriculture is more difficult, although still important. MAMMOTH CAVE is the largest of numerous caverns in this area, in which BOWLING GREEN is the largest city. Northwest of the Pennyroyal, along the Ohio R., is an area of coalfields, in which OWENSBORO is the major city. The plateaus of C Kentucky are crossed by scattered hills called the KNOBS, and ringed by an escarpment known as the Highland Rim (which continues S to encircle Tennessee's NASHVILLE BASIN). On the E this runs along the W edge of the Cumberland Plateau. On the W, it divides the plateaus from the valley of the Cumberland (E) and TENNESSEE (W) rivers, where side by side they cut N across Kentucky to meet the Ohio R. Between the rivers is the LAND BETWEEN THE LAKES, developed by the TENNESSEE VALLEY AUTHORITY. West of the rivers is lowland W Kentucky, the most Southern part of the state in economy and culture, at the extreme N of the Gulf COASTAL PLAIN and Mississippi alluvial plain. The once crucial Ohio R. port of PADUCAH is the largest city in W Kentucky. The Shawnee, Cherokee (in the S), and other peoples inhabited Kentucky's E and C regions, whose salt licks attracted much game, when whites began to penetrate from Virginia in the mid 18th century. Daniel Boone's WILDERNESS ROAD opened the way to settlement at HARRODSBURG and elsewhere in the abortive colony of TRANSYLVANIA. Kentucky (from an Iroquoian term for "prairie") remained Virginia territory until it became (1792) the first state W of the Appalachians. It boomed through the early 19th century, drawing Easterners to what was reputed to be an agrarian paradise. In 1818 W Kentucky was added to the state, as part of the JACKSON PURCHASE, lands here and in adjacent (S) Tennessee obtained from the Chickasaw. A typically Southern culture grew up in the Bluegrass and in the Purchase, while in the E mountains, independent farmers lived a very different life. This dichotomy resulted in severe splits when the Civil War began; a state of virtually fratricidal warfare ensued, with members of families joining opposing armies, and raiding was endemic in Kentucky. That both Confederate president Jefferson Davis and US president

Abraham Lincoln were natives was emblematic of the conflicts, which continued long after the war in feuding, political enmities, and social divisions of various sorts. Soon after the war, coal became central to the state's economy, and has remained so. Today both the W coalfields and the E mountains rise and fall economically with fluctuations in the demand for the fuel; coal's history in Kentucky has been a violent one, strife in HARLAN Co. (SE) the best-known example. In the Bluegrass, horse breeding has declined slightly, but Lexington's CHURCHILL DOWNS and regional farms still draw visitors and money to the region. BOURBON Co. remains a whiskey producer. Tobacco is grown in all parts of the state, and has had its own periods of strife, as in the 1900s BLACK PATCH "War." ASHLAND (NE, on the Ohio R.) is an oil center, and the Cincinnati suburbs (N) have gained much business from the city. Tourism focuses on Churchill Downs, Mammoth Cave, Cumberland and Tennessee river recreational areas, historic sites in the Bluegrass, and the folkways of the Appalachian region, fostered esp. at BEREA. The state's people remain largely of British (esp. Scotch-Irish) background, with a large black minority. Periods of economic adversity have long driven many to seek work in Detroit, Cincinnati, Cleveland, and other Northern cities. FORT KNOX (NC), the US MINT's gold bullion depository, and FORT CAMPBELL (SW, extending into Tennessee), a major training facility, are important Federal installations. The University of Kentucky is at Lexington.

Kentucky Dam TENNESSEE VALLEY AUTHORITY project on the Tennessee R., 22 mi/35 km above its mouth on the Ohio R., and now at the NW corner of the LAND BETWEEN THE LAKES. Completed in 1944, at 206 ft/63 m high and 8422 ft/2567 m long, the concrete and earthfill structure is the largest dam on the river. It impounds 184 mi/296 km–long **Kentucky L.,** which extends S through W Tennessee, with an area of 250 sq mi/649 sq km.

Kentucky River 260 mi/420 km long, in Kentucky. It is formed by the junction of its North and Middle forks, 4 mi/6 km ENE of Beattyville, and is joined at Beattyville by its South Fork. It then flows NW through the Daniel Boone National Forest and W past Boonesboro, then NW around Lexington's suburbs and past Frankfort to the Ohio R. at Carrollton. It is navigable for its entire course by means of locks. Its **North Fork,** 168 mi/270 km long, rises in the Cumberlands in Letcher Co., near the Virginia border, and flows generally NW past Hazard and Jackson. The **Middle Fork,** 97 mi/156 km long, rises in the Cumberlands in Leslie Co., and flows generally N, past Hyden and through Buckhorn L. The **South Fork** is formed by the confluence of the Red Bird R. and Goose Creek, in the E unit of the Daniel Boone National Forest, and flows generally N to Beattyville.

Kentville town, pop. 5506, seat of Kings Co., WC Nova Scotia, on the Cornwallis R., 52 mi/84 km NW of Halifax. It was settled in 1760 by New Englanders, following the 1755 expulsion of Acadians from nearby lands, and is now a commercial center for the fruit and dairy producing Cornwallis and Annapolis R. valleys, and a popular tourist destination.

Kentwood city, pop. 37,826, Kent Co., WC Michigan, 8 mi/13 km SE of Grand Rapids. Since it was settled in 1833, this largely residential suburb of Grand Rapids has developed a varied industrial base, including publishing, printing, and the manufacture of electronics, auto parts, and office furniture.

Kenvil see under SUCCASUNNA, New Jersey.

Kenwood **1.** residential neighborhood just N of HYDE PARK, on the South Side of Chicago, Illinois. An area of mansions dating to shortly after the Civil War, it has long been home to wealthy Jewish, Irish, and black families. The headquarters of Jesse Jackson's Operation PUSH and the Nation of Islam in the West (Black Muslims) are situated here. **2.** residential neighborhood in Minneapolis, Minnesota, SW of Downtown. Part of the LAKES DISTRICT, it has imposing single-family homes built for the local elite during the early 20th century. **3.** unincorporated residential suburb, pop. 7469, Hamilton Co., SW Ohio, 6 mi/10 km NE of downtown Cincinnati.

Keokuk city, pop. 12,451, co-seat (with FORT MADISON) of Lee Co., extreme SE Iowa, on the Mississippi R., at the foot of the Des Moines R. rapids, across from Hamilton, Illinois, and 2 mi/3 km NE of the Missouri border. It is a processing and distribution center for such local farm products as corn and soybeans. Manufactures include sponge rubber goods, corrugated cartons, and various metals and metal products. The huge Keokuk Dam (1910–13) impounds the waters of the Mississippi R. for hydroelectric power, navigation, and flood control, creating L. Keokuk. The first settlers arrived in 1820, and the American Fur Company established a post in 1829, around which the modern city grew. Mississippi steamboat traffic halted at the rapids in the 19th century, and Keokuk served as an important gateway to points in Iowa and farther W and N; a canal was built around the rapids in 1877.

Keosauqua city, pop. 1020, seat of Van Buren Co., extreme SE Iowa, on a bend in the Des Moines R. Settled in 1836 at Ely's Ford, it was an early Mormon center. Its 1842 courthouse is the oldest in use in Iowa. Keosauqua was the center of the 1839–49 "Honey War" with Missouri, a boundary dispute involving 12 mi/19 km of riverbank lined with "bee trees." In 1849 the Supreme Court decided in favor of Iowa. Phil Stong, best known for his novel *State Fair* (1932), was born here (1899).

Kern County 8130 sq mi/21,057 sq km, pop. 543,477, in SC California. BAKERSFIELD is its seat. A rich agricultural and oil producing area, it is bordered S by the Tehachapi Mts., at the S end of the San Joaquin Valley; E by the Sierra Nevada; and W by the Coast Ranges. It also includes part of the Mojave Desert (SE).

Kernersville town, pop. 10,836, Forsyth Co., N North Carolina, 7 mi/11 km E of Winston-Salem. A mill town settled by Germans before 1770, it is now also suburban.

Kern River 155 mi/250 km long, in SC California. Its headstreams are in the S Sierra Nevada, in Sequoia National Park, 10 mi/16 km NW of Mt. WHITNEY. It flows S through the Kern Canyon, into dam-created Isabella L., then SW through BAKERSFIELD and another 18 mi/29 km SW into the now largely dry L. Buena Vista. The Kern's waters are distributed via canal to various parts of the San Joaquin Valley (the S CENTRAL VALLEY), including the TULARE L. area. The upper Kern is famous for its deep canyon and its trout.

Kerrisdale largely residential section of SC VANCOUVER, British Columbia, developed in the early 20th century S of the site of Queen Elizabeth Park, and SE of SHAUGHNESSY, along INTERURBAN lines to Lulu I. (RICHMOND). Its large houses are home to an upper-middle-class community.

Kerrville city, pop. 17,384, seat of Kerr Co., SC Texas, on the

Guadalupe R., 55 mi/88 km NW of San Antonio. Founded in 1847, it is a resort center in the HILL COUNTRY. Spas, dude ranches, religious camps, and hunting and fishing draw visitors to the area. The city ships furs, poultry, and dairy goods, builds aircraft, and is a wool and mohair market. Schreiner College was founded here in 1923, and there are several hospitals.

Kerry Patch former Irish residential section of the North Side of SAINT LOUIS, Missouri, 1 mi/1.5 km N of Downtown. The area, heavily populated with immigrants and their descendants from the 1840s until the 1960s, has now been thoroughly changed by URBAN RENEWAL. The Cervantes Convention Center is on the S. Cass Ave., on the N, was a Polish immigrant center.

Ketchikan city, pop. 8263, Ketchikan Gateway Borough (pop. 13,828), on Revillagigedo I., in the ALEXANDER ARCHIPELAGO, extreme SE Alaska. Situated 230 mi/370 km SE of Juneau, it is a port on the INSIDE PASSAGE and a major salmon fishing center. Lumbering, pulp milling, and mining are also important. The city developed as a supply stop for prospectors heading north during the 1890s gold rush, and is now a trade center for the region. The area is known for its Tlingit and Haida totems and other carvings.

Ketchum city, pop. 2523, Blaine Co., C Idaho, on the Big Wood R., 80 mi/129 km N of Twin Falls. It was a late-19th-century center for the smelting and shipping of ores from surrounding mines. Situated 2 mi/3 km SW of SUN VALLEY, it is the gateway to the resort area and headquarters of the Sawtooth National Recreation Area. Ernest Hemingway, who had a home in Ketchum, died and was buried here in 1961. The Hemingway Memorial is nearby.

Kettering city, pop. 60,569, Montgomery Co., SW Ohio, 10 mi/16 km SE of Dayton. Late-18th-century settlers came here to work the large stone quarries nearby. It is today primarily a commuter suburb, but electric motors and generators, precision tools, automotive and aircraft parts, electronic components, and other goods are produced here. First called Van Buren township, it was renamed in 1952 after inventor Charles Franklin Kettering.

Kettleman Hills low range (c.1300 ft/400 m) in C California, running c.20 mi/32 km NNW–SSE along the W side of the San Joaquin Valley. Oil and natural gas are extracted here; **Kettleman City** (unincorporated, pop. 1411, Kings Co.), 20 mi/32 km SE of COALINGA, on the E, and AVENAL, on the W, are area centers.

Kettle Moraine see under ICE AGE NATIONAL SCIENTIFIC RESERVE, Wisconsin.

Keuka Lake one of the FINGER LAKES in WC New York, 45 mi/72 km SE of Rochester; also known as Crooked L. It is the only Finger Lake that branches into two arms. Eighteen mi/29 km long and 1.5–2 mi/2–3 km wide, with a 7 mi/11 km–long NW arm, it lies in a grape growing, winemaking resort region. HAMMONDSPORT at the S end and PENN YAN at the N end are trade centers of this region. The lake drains NE through Penn Yan to Seneca L., 5 mi/8 km E and 270 ft/82 m lower.

Kewanee city, pop. 12,969, Henry Co., NW Illinois, 30 mi/48 km NE of Galesburg. Its economy is partially dependent on the slaughter and shipment of locally raised hogs. Manufactures include heating equipment, farm and mining implements, and work clothes. Settlement began in 1854, after the arrival of the Chicago, Burlington and Quincy Railroad. Johnson-Sauk Trail State Park is 4 mi/6 km NNE, and Black Hawk College-East Campus is 4 mi/6 km S.

Kewaskum agricultural town, pop. 2515, Washington and Fond du Lac counties, SE Wisconsin, on the Milwaukee R., 8 mi/13 km N of West Bend. Author Glenway Wescott was born here (1901), and drew on the area in his writing.

Kewaunee nuclear power plant: see under DOOR PENINSULA, Wisconsin.

Keweenaw Peninsula including all of Keweenaw Co. and part of Houghton Co., in the extreme NW of the Upper Peninsula, N Michigan, jutting into L. Superior; the Copper Range runs its entire length. It was a camp area for early explorers, trappers, and missionaries, and is now a summer resort region, especially known for its fishing. The **Keweenaw Waterway** is a shipping shortcut that crosses the peninsula, cutting through Portage L. There is some industry at HANCOCK and HOUGHTON, the largest communities. Also here are several state parks and parts of Copper Country State Forest. At the SE end is the L'Anse Indian Reservation; at the N tip is Keweenaw Point, off of which lies tiny Manitou I.

Kew Gardens residential community, C Queens, New York. One of a series of planned pre–World War I "villages," it is similar in character to Forest Hills, to the W. Nearby parks and cemeteries add to the suburban feel created by rolling terrain, Tudor architecture, and masses of trees.

Keya Paha River 100 mi/160 km long, in South Dakota and Nebraska. It rises in Todd Co., SC South Dakota, and flows ESE to the NIOBRARA R. SW of Butte, Nebraska.

Key Biscayne island, 4 mi/6 km N–S and up to 1 mi/1.6 km wide, pop. 8854, in Dade Co., SE Florida, between the Atlantic Ocean (E) and Biscayne Bay (W), 5 mi/8 km SE of Miami, to which it is connected by the Rickenbacker Causeway (via VIRGINIA KEY). The 900-ac/365-ha Bill Baggs Cape Florida State Recreation Area, at its S end, includes the Cape Florida Lighthouse (1825; now a museum). There are waterfront estates, marinas, and a variety of recreational facilities on the island.

Key Largo island, 30 mi/48 km N–S and less than 2 mi/3 km wide, pop. 11,336, the longest and closest to the mainland of the FLORIDA KEYS, in Monroe Co., between Florida Bay, Blackwater, Barnes, and Card sounds (W) and the Atlantic Ocean (E), 30 mi/48 km S of Miami. It is linked by bridge to the mainland by the Overseas Highway to Key West, part of US 1. The low-lying island is composed mainly of coral and mangroves. Key Largo is a center for water recreation, with many marinas and fishing and diving facilities. The John Pennekamp Coral Reef State Park is here.

Keystone resort, Summit Co., NC Colorado, 30 mi/48 km NE of Leadville. A self-contained center, noted especially for its skiing, it is surrounded by mountains and has runs on Outback Mt., North Peak, Keystone Mt., and the Arapahoe Basin. Also here are a conference center and ski school.

Key West city, pop. 24,832, seat of Monroe Co., on the island of Key West in the FLORIDA KEYS, the southernmost US city outside Hawaii, 150 mi/240 km SW of Miami and 90 mi/140 km N of Cuba. Once a pirate base, then settled in the 1820s, it is filled with small Caribbean-style houses and lush tropical vegetation, and surrounded by sand and coral beaches and rocky promontories. In the mid 19th century it was a center for ship salvaging, sponge gathering, turtle hunting, cigarmaking, shrimping, and fishing. The latter three remain important, but tourism is the modern city's primary industry.

Its economy is also based on numerous US naval installations, including an air station on neighboring (E) Boca Chica Key. Key West was the terminus of the Florida East Coast Railroad (1912) connecting the Keys; largely destroyed by a hurricane in 1935, this was replaced by the Overseas Highway (1938). Cuban cigarmakers, fishermen, and political exiles have given the community a distinct Latin flavor since the 1840s. An earlier group, the English-speaking Conchs, settled here from the Bahamas in the 1820s, and have retained distinct speech and social patterns. Long known as an artists' colony, the city was home to John James Audubon, whose home and gardens are maintained, and to Ernest Hemingway, whose house is now a museum. It also has two civil war forts, several tropical gardens, the Tennessee Williams Fine Arts Center, and Florida Keys Community College (1965).

Kiamichi River 165 mi/264 km long, in SE Oklahoma. It rises near the Arkansas border in the OUACHITA Mts., and flows SW and S around the N of the **Kiamichi Mts.** subrange, to Antlers, then SE to the Red R., SE of Hugo. Dam-created Hugo L. is 7 mi/11 km NE of Hugo, which is not itself on the river. Sardis L., N of Clayton, on a short tributary of the Kiamichi, also contributes to Red R. basin flood control.

Kiawah Island island town, pop. 718, 7 mi/11 km long, one of the SEA ISLANDS, in Charleston Co., SC South Carolina, on the Atlantic Ocean (S), 15 mi/24 km SW of Charleston. It has several affluent resort developments and is reached by bridge from Seabrook I. (W).

Kicking Horse Pass at 5338 ft/1627 m, on the Continental Divide in the Rocky Mts., between Alberta (E) and British Columbia, just W of LAKE LOUISE. It was explored in 1858 by a party whose leader, James Hector, was kicked unconscious by one of his packhorses. The CANADIAN PACIFIC RAILWAY chose it as its route through the Rockies, completed in 1884. The 4.5% downgrades on the British Columbia side led to construction of the two Spiral Tunnels (1909), now a famous tourist attraction. The TRANS-CANADA HIGHWAY also runs through the pass.

Kilauea in Hawaii: **a.** active volcanic crater on the SE slope of MAUNA LOA, in HAWAII VOLCANOES NATIONAL PARK, SC Hawaii island. At 4090 ft/1250 m, its cone has collapsed to form a CALDERA of about 4 sq mi/10 sq km, surrounded by volcanic rock. Its enormous central fire pit, with a diameter of 3000 ft/900 m, and 470 ft/143 m deep, is known as Halemaumau. The first recorded eruption of Kilauea was in 1790. Today it is observed on a constant basis by the Hawaiian Volcano Observatory, situated on its rim. **b.** unincorporated community, pop. 1685, Kauai Co., a former sugar plantation town, now a tourist center, on the NE shore of Kauai.

Kilgore city, pop. 11,066, Gregg and Rusk counties, E Texas, 112 mi/180 km ESE of Dallas. In the middle of the EAST TEXAS OILFIELD, it is a refining and distribution center. At one time over 1200 derricks were within city limits. Cotton and lumber are also important, and the city manufactures ceramics and oilfield and plumbing supplies. Settled in 1872 as a railroad stop in what had been plantation country, it boomed after the 1930 discovery of the oilfield. It is home to Kilgore College (1935) and a large rehabilitation hospital.

kill element in place names in New York and neighboring parts of the former NEW NETHERLAND. From the Dutch *kil,* it denotes a body of water, and appears in the names of tidal channels like the KILL VAN KULL, rivers like the BATTEN KILL, and cities like PEEKSKILL.

Killbuck Creek 75 mi/121 km long, in NE Ohio. It rises in Medina Co., W of Akron, and flows S past Wooster and Millersburg, joining the Walhonding R. 5 mi/8 km NW of Coshocton.

Killdeer Mountains in Dunn Co., W North Dakota. Running SW–NE and towering 600 ft/189 m above the surrounding landscape, to 3140 ft/958 m, this series of buttes is 10 mi/16 km long. Medicine Hole, a depression in one of the cliffs, figured largely in Indian legends, and a battle between the Sioux and US troops was fought in the mountains in July 1864.

Kill Devil Hills see under KITTY HAWK, North Carolina.

Killeen city, pop. 63,535, Bell Co., EC Texas, 56 mi/90 km N of Austin. Settled on the Santa Fe Railroad in 1882, it was a small ranching and farming town until Camp Hood (see FORT HOOD) was established in 1942. It developed into a military service center, and has only a little industry; it is also an agricultural trade center. Central Texas College was founded here in 1965 and the University of Central Texas in 1973.

Killingly town, pop. 15,889, Windham Co., NE Connecticut, on the Quinebaug R. and the Rhode Island border, 18 mi/29 km NE of Willimantic. It includes the industrial borough of Danielson (pop. 4441) and the villages of East Killingly, Dayville, Attawaugan, Ballouville, and South Killingly. Once a major cotton milling center, it still produces some textiles.

Killington Peak mountain (4241 ft/1294 m) in SC Vermont, E of Rutland. One of the highest elevations of the Green Mts., it is a popular summer and winter recreation area; the LONG TRAIL passes near the peak, and the Killington Ski Area is one of New England's most popular, with a 3175-ft/968-m vertical drop.

Kill van Kull tidal strait, 4 mi/6 km long and 0.5 mi/1 km wide, between Bayonne, New Jersey, and N Staten Island, New York. It connects Upper New York Bay with Newark Bay, and is the main entry for shipping into Ports Newark and Elizabeth. It is badly polluted by local industry and by recurrent chemical spills from vessels moving through. The BAYONNE BRIDGE is at its W end.

Kimberley city, pop. 6531, East Kootenay Regional District, SE British Columbia, on Sullivan and North Star hills (in the PURCELL Mts.), near the St. Mary R., 16 mi/26 km NNW of CRANBROOK and 320 mi/520 km E of Vancouver. The Sullivan Mine, one of the world's largest lead and zinc mines, is here. The city, at 3662 ft/1117 m said to be Canada's highest, has since the 1970s become a Bavarian-theme tourist center. It has for much longer been a winter sports hub.

Kinbasket Lake in British Columbia: see under COLUMBIA R.

Kincardine town, pop. 6585, Bruce Co., S Ontario, on the E shore of L. Huron, 120 mi/193 km WNW of Toronto. One of the oldest (1840s) settlements in the area, it was a furnituremaking center until the 1960s. Today it is best known for its harbor and beaches. The Bruce Nuclear Power Development, 15 mi/24 km N, near Tiverton, is a major employer. Other industries include commercial fishing, dairying, and livestock raising.

Kinderhook town, pop. 8112, Columbia Co., SE New York, 20 mi/32 km SE of Albany. It was settled by the Dutch in the mid 18th century. Kinderhook was the birthplace of Martin Van Buren, who is also buried here. Lindenwald, Van Buren's home 1841–62, is now a National Historic Site. Kinderhook is now residential and agricultural.

Kindersley town, pop. 4572, SW Saskatchewan, 154 mi/248 km SW of Saskatoon and 40 mi/65 km E of the Alberta border. Since 1909, when the Canadian National Railway built tracks through the town, it has been a service center for an agricultural region. Oil and natural gas are developed as well.

Kineo, Mount 1806 ft/551 m, on Kineo Peninsula, which juts W into MOOSEHEAD LAKE, WC Maine, at its narrowest point. Known to natives for its rhyolite, from which arrowheads were made, Kineo became in the 19th century home to a succession of vacation hotels, the last demolished 1938. Its cliff dominates the lake.

King County 2128 sq mi/5512 sq km, pop. 1,507,319, in WC Washington, bordered by Puget Sound (W). SEATTLE is its seat. By far the state's most populous county, it is dominated by Seattle, its suburbs, and its satellite cities such as BELLEVUE, RENTON, and AUBURN, which occupy its W portion. Also in the W are Vashon and Maury islands, in Puget Sound. The county also includes part of Snoqualmie National Forest and the Snoqualmie R., which rises in the E, in the Cascade Range. Seattle's many industries are economic mainstays of King Co. Its other chief economic activities include lumbering, coalmining, truck gardening, and livestock and dairy ranching.

Kingdome enclosed stadium in SEATTLE, Washington, just S of Downtown. Built in 1976, and seating over 60,000, it is home to the Mariners (baseball) and Seahawks (football), and hosts a variety of entertainment and commercial events.

Kingfisher city, pop. 4095, seat of Kingfisher Co., C Oklahoma, 40 mi/64 km NW of Oklahoma City. Founded during the 1889 land rush, it was a stagecoach station and a stop on the CHISHOLM TRAIL (a route now followed by US 81). In a grain and livestock producing region, it has an enormous wheat market. Agricultural goods are processed and oil is refined here.

Kingman city, pop. 12,722, seat of Mohave Co., NW Arizona, in the NW foothills of the Hualapai Mts., 30 mi/48 km ENE of the point on the Colorado R. where Arizona faces the California-Nevada border. Since its founding in 1880, on the Santa Fe Railroad, it has been a shipping and trade center for NW Arizona; ROUTE 66 (now I-40) later came through it. Principal industries include copper mining, ranching, and tourism. Ghost towns and old gold mines dot the area.

Kingman Reef ATOLL and islet in the C Pacific Ocean, northwesternmost of the LINE Is., 35 mi/56 km NW of PALMYRA and 920 mi/1480 km SSW of Honolulu, Hawaii. Discovered in 1798 and claimed by the US in 1922, it was used briefly in the 1930s as a stopover for Honolulu–Samoa seaplane flights, but is now abandoned.

King of Prussia unincorporated village, pop. 18,406, in Upper Merion township, Montgomery Co., SE Pennsylvania, a suburb 15 mi/24 km NW of downtown Philadelphia. This affluent residential community is also a major retailing center, with a number of large shopping malls.

King Ranch c.825,000 ac/334,000 ha, in Kleberg, Nueces, Kenedy, and Willacy counties, SE Texas, SSW of Corpus Christi. Headquarters are at KINGSVILLE. The largest US ranch was begun in 1853 by Richard King, a New York steamboat captain, who bought the Santa Gertrudis land grant. The ranch has controlled as much as 1.25 million ac/506,000 ha. It bred race and quarter horses, and developed the Santa Gertrudis beef breed (part Shorthorn, part Brahman). Irrigated agriculture and oil and gas (1940s) provided further income. Members of the King and Kleberg families still own the ranch.

Kings Bay locality in Camden Co., SE Georgia, inside (W of) CUMBERLAND I., and 28 mi/45 km NNE of Jacksonville, Florida, site of the Naval Submarine Support Base, a major Atlantic military port, with a 1990 pop. of 3463.

Kingsbridge residential and commercial section, NW Bronx, New York. It takes its name from King's Bridge (1693), which formerly crossed the Spuyten Duyvil from Marble Hill, Manhattan. The area around the bridge was the scene of fighting between Washington's retreating troops and the British after HARLEM HEIGHTS (Sept. 1776). Kingsbridge Heights, to the E, slopes upward to Van Cortlandt Park. Jerome Park Reservoir, a unit of the New York City system, lies to the E.

Kings Canyon National Park 462,000 ac/187,000 ha (722 sq mi/1869 sq km), in the Sierra Nevada, EC California, adjacent (N) to SEQUOIA NATIONAL PARK. It is named for the deep, granite-walled canyons of the Middle and South forks of the Kings R. Established in 1890 as General Grant National Park (it took its current name in 1940), it contains the Grant Grove, with giant sequoias including the 267 ft/81 m–tall, 107 ft/33 m–around General Grant Tree, the world's second-largest after Sequoia National Park's General Sherman.

Kings County coextensive with the New York City borough of BROOKLYN. Organized in the 17th century, it included areas that gradually became part of the city of Brooklyn; city and county became coterminous in 1896, two years before Brooklyn became a borough of Greater New York.

Kingsgate unincorporated community, pop. 14,259, King Co., WC Washington, just E of L. Washington, a residential and industrial suburb 10 mi/16 km NE of Seattle.

King's Highway **1.** see EL CAMINO REAL. **2.** see under US 1.

Kingsland city, pop. 395, Cleveland Co., SC Arkansas, 30 mi/48 km SSW of Pine Bluff. The Civil War battle of Marks' Mill took place nearby on April 25, 1864. Today the city is an agricultural shipping center. Famed football coach Bear Bryant (1913–83) was born here.

Kings Mountain **1.** city, pop. 8763, Cleveland and Gaston counties, SW North Carolina, 28 mi/45 km W of Charlotte, near the South Carolina line. It manufactures textiles. Kings Mountain National Military Park is 7 mi/11 km S, in South Carolina. **2.** lone ridge (1040 ft/320 m), crossing the South Carolina–North Carolina border SW of Gastonia, North Carolina. Interstate 85 runs NW of it. **Kings Mountain National Military Park,** 15 mi/24 km NE of Gaffney, South Carolina, was the site of an important defeat of the British on Oct. 7, 1780, said by some to have marked the turning point in the Revolutionary War. The Overmountain Victory Trail, along a Revolutionary War route from ABINGDON, Virginia, ends here. The park is headquartered in Kings Mountain, North Carolina.

Kings Park unincorporated village, pop. 17,773, in Smithtown, Suffolk Co., SE New York, on the North Shore of Long Island. It is a residential suburb. Kings Park State Hospital for the mentally ill is here; Sunken Meadow State Park is immediately N.

Kings Peak 13,528 ft/4123 m, the highest point in Utah, in the UINTA Mts., 80 mi/130 km E of Salt Lake City. It is in the High Uintas Wilderness Area of Ashley National Forest.

Kings Point village, pop. 4843, in North Hempstead town,

Nassau Co., SE New York, on Manhasset Bay at the tip of the Great Neck peninsula, on Long Island's North Shore, just E of the New York City line. It is an affluent suburb with a number of large estates. The US Merchant Marine Academy (1942) is located here, on the former estate of industrialist Walter Chrysler. The peninsula was the model for "West Egg" in F. Scott Fitzgerald's *The Great Gatsby.*

Kingsport city, pop. 36,365, Sullivan and Hawkins counties, NE Tennessee, on the Holston R., 81 mi/130 km NE of Knoxville. Originally called Island Flats, it was after 1750 an important ford, and became a key point on the WILDERNESS ROAD. A 1776 victory over the Cherokee ensured settlement where Fort Robinson (1761) and Fort Patrick Henry (1775) had been built. Iron, nails, tobacco, limestone, grain, and cattle were early products, and the city was an important shipping point. Arrival of the railroad (1909) and World War I brought accelerated industrial growth. Kingsport now produces synthetics, adhesives, explosives, textiles, machinery, paper, and leather. One of the largest US book plants is here. With JOHNSON CITY and BRISTOL, Kingsport is one of Tennessee's Tri-Cities.

Kings River 125 mi/200 km long, in SC California. Its Middle and South forks flow W from the Sierra Nevada through KINGS CANYON NATIONAL PARK, join W of its boundary, and receive the North Fork, then descend (generally SW) into the San Joaquin Valley by way of Pine Flat Reservoir, created by the 440-ft/134-m Pine Flat Dam (1954), a unit of the CENTRAL VALLEY project. The river continues to the SW, passing E of Sanger and W of Reedley, before disappearing into the TULARE lakebed; its waters are drawn off by canals to irrigate the valley's agriculture.

Kingston **1.** city, pop. 23,095, seat of Ulster Co., SE New York, on the W bank of the Hudson R., at the mouth of Rondout Creek, 15 mi/24 km NNW of Poughkeepsie. A Dutch trading post was established here in 1610. The area was settled as Esopus in 1652, and renamed Wiltwyck in 1661. The British gained control in 1667, and renamed the settlement Kingston. In 1777 it was chosen as New York's first capital, and was the site of the state's first governmental meetings. In October of the same year, it was burned by British troops. The settlement was rebuilt and eventually absorbed the adjacent villages of Rondout, Wiltwyck, and Wilbur. Completion of the Delaware and Hudson Canal (1828) and the arrival of the railroad (1860s) contributed significantly to its growth. Early industries included boatbuilding, limestone quarrying, and cement production. Kingston now manufactures electronic components, computers, bricks, clothing, and furniture. Apples, grapes, and corn are produced in the surrounding area. The city is a gateway to the Catskill Mts. Ashokan Reservoir, an important source of New York City's water, is 5 mi/8 km NW. **2.** city, pop. 56,597, seat of Frontenac Co., SE Ontario, at the NE end of L. Ontario where it joins the St. Lawrence R. and is joined by the Cataraqui R., at the S entrance to the RIDEAU CANAL, 90 mi/144 km SSW of Ottawa. In 1673, the French Fort Frontenac was erected here on the site of a Cataraqui settlement, to challenge Iroquois control of L. Ontario. Destroyed by the Iroquois, it was rebuilt in 1695, and again destroyed, by the British, in 1758. In the early 18th century Kingston was an important base on the Great Lakes for MONTRÉAL traders. The area was resettled in 1783 by LOYALISTS, and soon became the chief British naval base on L. Ontario. Fort Henry, built during the War of 1812, is now a museum. Today the city is an important transshipment port. It manufactures ships, aluminum products, mining and diesel equipment, synthetic fibers, ceramics, and food products. Also an educational center, it is home to Queen's University (1841), the Royal Military College of Canada (1876), and several other schools. The COLLINS BAY section is home to a Federal prison. Garden I., just SE in the St. Lawrence, was a noted 19th-century lumbering and shipbuilding center. **3.** borough, pop. 14,507, Luzerne Co., NE Pennsylvania, on the Susquehanna R. opposite Wilkes-Barre. Founded in 1769, it manufactures various products including cigars and synthetic fabrics, and has railroad shops. Kingston was heavily damaged by a 1972 flood. Nearby is the site of the Battle of Wyoming (1778), in which settlers were massacred by British troops and Iroquois Indians. **4.** village, pop. 6504, part of SOUTH KINGSTOWN township, Washington Co., S Rhode Island, 17 mi/27 km NE of Westerly and 24 mi/39 km S of Providence, in an agricultural area. Known as Little Rest until 1885, it boasts a number of well-preserved 18th- and 19th-century houses. It was the county seat from 1752 to 1900. The University of Rhode Island (1892) is here.

Kingstree town, pop. 3858, seat of Williamsburg Co., E South Carolina, 32 mi/52 km SE of Sumter. It was settled by Irish Calvinists in 1732 on the Black R. In a fertile farm and timbering area, it is a trade and processing center for tobacco, vegetables, dairy products, and lumber. With hunting and fishing in the area, it is also a winter resort.

Kingsville city, pop. 25,276, seat of Kleberg Co., S Texas, 34 mi/55 km SW of Corpus Christi. Seat of the famed KING RANCH, in which it was established (1903) as a railroad stop, it is a commercial center and has some light manufacturing. The economy also depends on the Kingsville Naval Air Station. Dates, olives, citrus fruit, and dairy and beef cattle are produced locally, and there are also natural gas processing and petrochemical plants. Texas A & I University (1925) is here.

King William District historic residential district in San Antonio, Texas, on the E bank of the San Antonio R., just S of Downtown and immediately W of HEMISFAIR PLAZA and S of LA VILLITA. The mid-19th-century home to German merchants who invigorated the city's commercial life, it fell into decline by the early 20th century, but has been renovated and gentrified, and now draws visitors with its Victorian architecture and ambience.

King William Island over 5000 sq mi/13,000 sq km, in the Arctic Archipelago, Northwest Territories, SW of the Boothia Peninsula, SE of Victoria I., and in places only a few miles from the mainland (the Adelaide Peninsula). Long an INUIT hunting ground, it was seen in 1830 by John Ross, and in 1847–48 Sir John Franklin and members of his expedition disappeared on the W side; traces of the ill-fated party have been found in various places. In 1903–04 and 1904–05, Roald Amundsen used what is now called Gjoa Haven, on the SE, as his winter headquarters, in the course of conquering the NORTHWEST PASSAGE.

Kingwood unincorporated community, pop. 37,397, Harris and Montgomery counties, SE Texas, 22 mi/35 km NNE of downtown Houston, and N of L. Houston. It is primarily residential.

Kinnickinnic Parkway scenic drive, 2 mi/3 km, on the SOUTH SIDE of Milwaukee, Wisconsin. It runs between South Tenth and South 43rd streets and follows the Kinnickinnic R.

Kinsman unincorporated village in Kinsman township, Trumbull Co., NE Ohio, 18 mi/29 km NE of Warren, and just W of the Pennsylvania border. Lumber, brass goods, and feed are produced locally. Essentially New England in character, Kinsman is the birthplace (1857) of the lawyer Clarence Darrow, and was portrayed in his novel *Farmington.*

Kinston city, pop. 25,295, seat of Lenoir Co., E North Carolina, at the head of navigation on the Neuse R., 70 mi/110 km SE of Raleigh. Incorporated in 1762 as Kingston, in honor of George III, it was reincorporated in 1784, the *g* having been dropped to avoid the royal word. Kinston is an important bright leaf tobacco market and processing center, and the trade center for the surrounding agricultural region. Manufactures include textiles, chemicals, lumber, paper boxes, molded concrete, and processed foods. It is home to Lenoir Community College (1958).

Kinzua Creek in NW Pennsylvania, rising in McKean Co., and flowing generally NW through the Allegheny National Forest past Westline to the Allegheny R. E of Warren. Its Algonquian name means "turkey stream"; many of the native birds were found along its banks. **Kinzua Dam,** also called the Allegheny Dam, is just W of the mouth of the Kinzua, on the Allegheny. It is 234 ft/71 m high, was completed in 1965, and forms the 27 mi/43 km–long Allegheny Reservoir, which extends into S New York.

Kips Bay section of lower Midtown Manhattan, New York City, along the East R. from 23rd to 34th streets. Named for Jacobus Kip, who had a 1650s farm here, the area is partly landfill. In Sept. 1776 it was the site of a bombardment by British warships that forced Americans into retreat to HARLEM HEIGHTS. Kips Bay is a mixed residential neighborhood, formerly industrial, dominated by BELLEVUE and other hospitals and large apartment blocks.

Kirkland **1.** city, pop. 17,495, MONTRÉAL URBAN COMMUNITY, S Québec, a growing residential suburb near the W end of the I. de Montréal, adjacent (N) to Beaconsfield and 15 mi/24 km SW of Downtown. **2.** city, pop. 40,052, King Co., WC Washington, on the E shore of L. Washington, a residential suburb 7 mi/11 km NE of Seattle. The city's population more than doubled from 1980 to 1990 as part of the expanding Seattle-Tacoma metropolitan area. It is the headquarters of a major cellular telephone company and other businesses. Kirkland's manufactures include wood, agricultural, and chemical products as well as furniture and paint. It is the seat of the Northwest College of the Assemblies of God (1934).

Kirkland Lake town, pop. 10,440, Timiskaming District, E Ontario, on Kirkland L., 75 mi/121 km ESE of Timmins and 125 mi/200 km NNE of Sudbury, near the Québec border. One of Canada's leading gold mining centers since discoveries in the area during construction of the Ontario Northland Railway in 1911, it thrived until the 1950s, but has since then seen fluctuations in the market affect its prosperity. Iron mining has also become a leading industry, and tourism is important.

Kirksville city, pop. 17,152, seat of Adair Co., NE Missouri, 72 mi/115 km NW of Hannibal. The largest city in this sparsely populated part of the state, it is a manufacturing and processing center in an agricultural, dairy farming, and coal mining area. Its industries produce shoes, electrical appliances, clothing, and hospital equipment. An educational center, it is the seat of Northeast Missouri State University (1867) and Kirksville College of Osteopathic Medicine (1892), established as the world's first college of osteopathy by the founder of osteopathy, Dr. Andrew Taylor Still.

Kirkwood city, pop. 27,291, St. Louis Co., EC Missouri, 13 mi/21 km WSW of downtown St. Louis. It was founded in 1853 after the arrival of the Missouri Pacific Railroad. A residential suburb, it also manufactures cement, lime, lumber products, fabrics, and processed foods. Located here is Meramec Community College.

Kirtland village, pop. 5881, Lake Co., NE Ohio, 20 mi/32 km NE of Cleveland. Settled 1808–09, it was a Mormon center in the 1830s; its temple (1836) was constructed by Joseph Smith and his followers. Today it is an affluent residential suburb. The Holden Arboretum is 5 mi/8 km NE.

Kirtland Air Force Base see under ALBUQUERQUE, New Mexico.

Kiryas Joel village, pop. 7437, in Monroe town, Orange Co., SE New York, 40 mi/64 km NNW of New York City. This residential community, established in 1977 by Orthodox (Satmar) Jews from Brooklyn, was in the national spotlight in the early 1990s as courts considered the legality of state support for religious school systems.

Kisatchie National Forest 600,000 ac/243,000 ha, in six units in C Louisiana. The state's only national forest, it ranges from hilly pine woods to hardwood swamp. Established in 1930, it has recovered much cut-over timberland. Headquarters are at Pineville, ranger offices at Natchitoches, Homer, Winnfield, Pollock, Leesville, and Alexandria.

K.I. Sawyer Air Force Base in Marquette Co., in the C Upper Peninsula, N Michigan, on Silver Lead Creek, 16 mi/26 km SE of Ishpeming. Tourist exhibits on this former Strategic Air Command base include B-52 bombers and other aircraft. It is also a training area for military dogs.

Kiska Island largest of the RAT Is. in the W ALEUTIAN Is. chain, SW Alaska. Twenty mi/32 km NE–SW and 2–7 mi/3–11 km wide, it rises to 4004 ft/1220 m at Kiska Volcano. Kiska Harbor is on the E coast. The island, along with ATTU to the W, was occupied by Japanese forces in 1942; they evacuated it in 1943, following heavy bombing and the recapture of Attu by US forces. Since then, Kiska has been the site of air and naval facilities.

Kissimmee city, pop. 30,050, seat of Osceola Co., C Florida, on the N shore of L. Tohopekaliga, 16 mi/26 km S of Orlando. The city grew around an early trading post, sugar plantation, and lumber camp, beginning its major development in the early 1880s. It quickly evolved into the trade center for the cattle producing **Kissimmee Prairies** and for neighboring citrus groves. These activities remain important to the economy, supplemented by boatbuilding and plastics manufacturing. The city retains much of its historic flavor, with many older structures preserved. Tourism is its major industry, driven by the proximity of Orlando and of Epcot Center and Walt Disney World (10 mi/16 km NW), and by its own lakefront and other amusements.

Kissimmee River 140 mi/225 km long, in SC Florida. It rises at an elevation of only 16 ft/5 m in L. Tohopekaliga, S of Kissimmee, and flows generally S through other small lakes into 55–sq mi/142–sq km **L. Kissimmee,** then SSE into L. OKEECHOBEE.

Kitchener city, pop. 168,282, seat of Waterloo Regional Municipality, S Ontario, on the Grand R., adjoining (S) WATERLOO and 57 mi/91 km WSW of Toronto. In the early 1800s Germans from Pennsylvania settled the area. By 1833 the community was known as Berlin, and it was incorporated as a town (1871) and city (1912). In 1916 its present name was chosen, in response to anti-German sentiment. Kitchener is now an industrial, shipping, and financial center, with meatpacking, brewing, distilling, and tanning plants; it makes auto accessories, rubber products, textiles, furniture, shoes, and appliances. The Conestoga College of Applied Arts and Technology and St. Jerome's College, federated with the University of Waterloo, are here. The boyhood home of former prime minister William Lyon Mackenzie King (1874–1950) is preserved in Woodside National Historic Park.

Kitikmeot Region see under NORTHWEST TERRITORIES.

Kitimat district municipality, pop. 11,305, Kitimat-Stikine Regional District, WC British Columbia, at the head of Douglas Channel, 70 mi/110 km SE of Prince Rupert. A seaport named for a local tribe who traded here in the 1830s with the Hudson's Bay Company, it was founded (1954) as the site of a huge aluminum smelter, accessible to vessels bringing ore from the Caribbean. It receives hydroelectric power from a huge plant at Kemano, 45 mi/72 km SSE. Although called the "Aluminum City," Kitimat now also makes paper, methanol, and other products.

Kitsap County 393 sq mi/1018 sq km, pop. 189,731, in W Washington, on a peninsula between the Hood Canal (W) and Puget Sound (E). Port Orchard (pop. 4984) is its seat, BREMERTON its largest city. The county also includes BAINBRIDGE ISLAND in Puget Sound and W Seattle suburbs. The Port Madison and Port Gamble Indian reservations are at the N tip of the peninsula. Leading industries include fishing, dairying, and truck farming. There is manufacturing in and around Bremerton, and tourism is important.

Kitsilano largely residential section of NW VANCOUVER, British Columbia, fronting Kitsilano Beach, on English Bay (BURRARD INLET), 2 mi/3 km SW of Downtown. Presettlement Squamish villages, public parks and beaches, and wartime military encampments have lined its N. In the early 20th century rows of wood-frame houses were built here; affluent then, Kitsilano lost some of its cachet before the 1960s, when it became a hippie neighborhood. It is now a popular, youthful district.

Kittatinny Mountain Appalachian range running NW–SE in NE Pennsylvania and NW New Jersey, cut through at the DELAWARE WATER GAP and rising to a height of 1803 ft/550 m at HIGH POINT, in extreme N New Jersey. It continues NE into New York as the SHAWANGUNK Mts.

Kittery town, pop. 9372, York Co., extreme S Maine. It is on the Atlantic coast at the mouth of the Piscataqua R., across from Portsmouth, New Hampshire. Despite its name, Portsmouth Naval Shipyard (1806) is here, spread over several islands in the river. Kittery produced John Paul Jones's *Ranger,* the Civil War *Kearsarge,* submarines for both world wars, the first atomic-powered ship, and the first Polaris missile–launching submarine. A US naval prison is here. The ISLES OF SHOALS lie offshore. Kittery also produces pleasure boats and wood products.

Kitt Peak highest point (6880 ft/2097 m) of the Quinlan Mts., which extend from the N end of the BABOQUIVARI Mts. in S Arizona. Fifty mi/80 km SW of Tucson, within the Papago (Tohono O'odham) Indian Reservation, the peak, sacred to ancient tribes, gained fame in 1965 with the opening of Kitt Peak Observatory, administered by a consortium including the University of Arizona, and a unit of the National Radio Astronomy Laboratory.

Kitty Hawk resort town, pop. 1937, Dare Co., NE North Carolina, on Bodie I., an OUTER BANKS barrier island, between Kitty Hawk Bay, an inlet of ALBEMARLE SOUND (W), and the Atlantic Ocean (E). Just SE is Kill Devil Hills (town, pop. 4238), where the Wright brothers conducted glider experiments in 1901–03 and made the first sustained airplane flight on Dec. 17, 1903. The Wright Brothers National Memorial is here. NAGS HEAD is just SE on the island. ROANOKE I. is 7 mi/11 km SSW in the sound.

Klamath Falls city, pop. 17,737, seat of Klamath Co., SW Oregon, at the S end of Upper Klamath L., at the source of the Klamath R., in the E foothills of the Cascade Mts., 15 mi/24 km N of the California border. Settled in 1867, it is the major marketing and distribution center of S Oregon. Its industries include lumber milling, plywood making, shipbuilding, and the processing of livestock, grain, and potatoes. The Oregon Institute of Technology (1947) is here. The city is a gateway to Lower Klamath National Wildlife Refuge (12 mi/19 km S), Crater Lake National Park (40 mi/64 km NNW), and Winema National Forest (NE and NW).

Klamath Mountains region in NW California, extending into SW Oregon, made up of a number of subranges oriented in different directions, including (roughly N–S) the Rouge River, SISKIYOU, MARBLE, Scott, and SALMON mountains; the South Fork Range; and the TRINITY and YOLLA BOLLY mountains. The granitic Klamaths, usually considered part of the COAST RANGES, extend for c.250 mi/400 km from foothills S of the WILLAMETTE VALLEY in SW Oregon, joining with the CASCADE RANGE to form the N boundary of the Sacramento Valley; they then continue S along the W side of the valley. They rise to a high at Mt. Eddy (9038 ft/2755 m), SW of Mt. Shasta, and include small glaciers and areas of volcanic formation. Castle Crags, S of Shasta, has noted castlelike granite spires. Named for the Klamath people, the mountains, with ample (over 100 in/254 cm) rainfall and often densely wooded, embrace a network of national forests, wilderness and natural refuge areas, and private property; the **Klamath Basin National Wildlife Refuge,** an important spot on the PACIFIC FLYWAY, is known as a winter home to bald eagles. The Klamaths are dissected by the Klamath, Rogue, and many other rivers, including headwaters of the Sacramento R. Their clear streams are important spawning grounds for salmon and steelhead. Primary economic activities include lumbering, dairying, fruit growing, and servicing anglers, hunters, and hikers.

Klamath National Forest c.1.7 million ac/700,000 ha (2697 sq mi/6985 sq km), in extreme N California, with a small segment in S Oregon. In the COAST RANGES, it includes the Marble Mt. and Trinity Alps wildernesses, and is noted for its dense foxtail pines and other conifers.

Klamath River 250 mi/400 km long, in S Oregon and N California. It is fed by the waters of 20 mi/32 km–long **Upper Klamath L.,** at Klamath Falls, Oregon, and flows S and W into California, where it winds through the Klamath Mts., receiving the Shasta R. (N of Yreka), the Scott R. (at Hamburg), and the Salmon R. (at Somes Bar), all from the SE. Near Weitchpec, in the Hoopa Valley Indian Reservation, it is joined by the TRINITY R., from the S. It then flows to the Pacific Ocean at Requa. The Klamath's course in California takes it through high, heavily forested mountains, where it cuts a deep valley. The upper reaches, in Oregon, flow through more open country. **Lower Klamath L.,** in California, 13 mi/21 km below Klamath Falls, connected with the river by canals, is the center of a two-state National Wildlife Refuge, the first (1908) designated waterfowl refuge, on the PACIFIC FLYWAY.

Kleinburg see under VAUGHAN, Ontario.

Klickitat River 85 mi/137 km long, in SW Washington. Rising in the NW corner of the YAKIMA INDIAN RESERVATION, in the E Cascade Range, it flows generally S, entering the Columbia R. at Lyle. The river winds through a high plateau in which it has cut a deep gorge, producing canyons up to 1000 ft/305 m deep.

Klondike region in the NW Yukon Territory, named for the 100 mi/160 km–long **Klondike R.,** which enters the Yukon R. from the E at DAWSON, the area's main settlement. The discovery (1897) of PLACER gold on BONANZA CREEK, a small tributary just SE of Dawson, started a gold rush that brought thousands of prospectors from the S Alaska coast, via the CHILKOOT and WHITE passes, then (N) down the Yukon; from Alaska (W) up the Yukon; or along the "back door" or "all Canadian" route from the SE, using the LIARD R. and valleys now on the CAMPBELL HIGHWAY to approach from NE British Columbia. After a boom decade, the Klondike grew quiet again; gold dredging operations continued into the 1960s, and other metals have also been mined. Fluctuations in the gold market, as in the late 1970s, have caused spurts of activity. The area now draws tourists.

Klondike Gold Rush National Historical Park see under SKAGWAY, Alaska; PIONEER SQUARE, Seattle, Washington.

Klondike Highway also, **Klondike Loop** 445 mi/716 km long, from WHITEHORSE (S) to DAWSON (NW) in the Yukon Territory, with a S extension to SKAGWAY, Alaska. From a junction with the ALASKA HIGHWAY N of Whitehorse, it roughly follows overland 1890s gold rush routes to the KLONDIKE. The CAMPBELL HIGHWAY meets it N of Carmacks; the Silver Trail, to the MAYO area, branches off N of Stewart Crossing. The DEMPSTER HIGHWAY branches off E of Dawson on its way to the Mackenzie R. delta. Built in 1950–55, the highway acquired its Skagway extension in the 1980s.

Kluane National Park in the SW corner of the Yukon Territory, on the Alaska (W, S) and British Columbia (S) borders. Established in 1972, it encompasses 8500 sq mi/22,000 sq km, and includes Mt. LOGAN (19,524 ft/5951 m), the highest point in Canada and second-highest in North America, in the SAINT ELIAS Mts. The park contains what is said to be the largest concentration of glaciers and icefields in the world outside polar regions, including the Steele and Kaskawulsh glaciers, and extending (W) into Alaska's WRANGELL–ST. ELIAS National Park. Kluane, with its alpine meadows, tundra, and forests and abundant wildlife, was the hunting and fishing ground of many ancient peoples. The Alaska and Haines highways run along the NE border, N of the Kluane Ranges; entry into the park is by hiking trails. Headquarters is at Haines Junction.

Knightstown town, pop. 2048, Henry Co., EC Indiana, 35 mi/56 km E of Indianapolis, on US 40 and the Big Blue R. Settled in 1825, it is situated in a livestock and grain producing district, and has various light manufactures. Historian Charles A. Beard was born here (1874).

Knobs Region also, **the Knobs** U-shaped area encircling Kentucky's BLUEGRASS REGION on the W, S, and E, and bounded by the PENNYROYAL (W) and mountains and coal fields (E). Covering c.2200 sq mi/5700 sq km, it is an irregular plain from which many dome-shaped hills, erosional remnants locally called "knobs," emerge. The larger part of the DANIEL BOONE NATIONAL FOREST lies in the E Knobs. Louisville is at the NW edge of the Knobs, which continue N into the area of NEW ALBANY, Indiana, across the Ohio R.

Knott's Berry Farm see under BUENA PARK, California.

Knox County 506 sq mi/1311 sq km, pop. 335,749, in E Tennessee. Its seat is KNOXVILLE, which with its industry and suburbs dominates the county. In the Great Appalachian Valley, it has produced dairy goods, livestock, tobacco, fruit, corn, hay, marble, bituminous coal, and zinc. The FRENCH BROAD and HOLSTON rivers meet here to form the Tennessee R.

Knoxville **1.** city, pop. 8232, seat of Marion Co., SE Iowa, 33 mi/53 km SE of Des Moines. Settled in 1845, in an area that has produced coal, limestone, and livestock, it has a large Veterans Administration hospital. Red Rock Reservoir, on the Des Moines R., is 6 mi/10 km NE. **2.** city, pop. 165,121, seat of Knox Co., E Tennessee, on the Tennessee R., just below the confluence of the Holston and French Broad rivers, 100 mi/160 km NE of Chattanooga. White's Fort was established after a 1785 treaty with the Cherokee opened the region to settlers; it was renamed in 1791. A river port and later a railroad center, it was a commercial hub in the 19th century, and Tennessee's capital during most of the period 1796–1818. It was a Unionist stronghold in the Civil War. In the 1930s, the TENNESSEE VALLEY AUTHORITY, headquartered here, spurred industrial (textiles, clothing, chemicals) growth, augmenting the area's quarrying and tobacco and livestock agriculture. A second growth spurt was due to the construction of OAK RIDGE, 20 mi/32 km WNW, in the 1940s. The TVA and the University of Tennessee (1794) are the largest employers. Tourism is also significant.

Kodiak Island in the Gulf of Alaska, SW Alaska. Some 100 mi/160 km NE–SW and 10–60 mi/16–100 km wide, the state's largest island (3670 sq mi/9505 sq km) is separated from the Alaska Peninsula (NW) by Shelikof Strait. Afognak I. and the Kenai Peninsula lie NE. Kodiak has a heavily indented coastline with many good harbors, hills and forests in the N, and good grazing land in the S. Fishing, trapping, dairying, and sheep and cattle ranching are important industries. The Kodiak (Alaska brown) bear and Kodiak king crab are native. The largest city is **Kodiak** (pop. 6365), on the NE coast, a seafood processing and Coast Guard center. Russian fur traders settled the island, beginning in 1763. In 1784, Gregory Shelekhov founded the first permanent Russian settlement in Alaska at Three Saints Bay, on the SE; Aleksander Baranof moved it to Kodiak in 1792. The village remained the center of Russian activities in Alaska until 1804, when Baranof moved his Russian-American Company to SITKA. Most of Kodiak I. is now a national wildlife refuge.

Kofa Mountains NNE–SSW trending range extending for c.20 mi/32 km in the SW corner of Arizona, NE of Yuma, reaching 4877 ft/1487 m at Signal Peak, a massive W-facing block that rises more than 3000 ft/914 m above the desert. The volcanic range is extremely rugged, with many cliffs, gorges, box canyons, and pinnacles. The Kofa and CASTLE DOME mountains together comprise the **Kofa National Wild-**

life Refuge, a 664,000-ac/269,000-ha sanctuary for desert bighorn sheep. Gold was discovered here in 1896; some mining continues today. The name is from "K of A," for the King of Arizona Mine.

Kohler village, pop. 1817, Sheboygan Co., E Wisconsin, 5 mi/8 km W of Sheboygan. The manufacture of plumbing fixtures is the major basis of this planned community's economy. The Kohler fixture plant here has been the site of some of the longest and most acrimonious labor disputes in US history. Kohler also manufactures leisure products, engines, and generators.

Kokomo city, pop. 44,962, seat of Howard Co., NC Indiana, on Wildcat Creek, 50 mi/80 km N of Indianapolis. Founded in the 1840s and named for a Miami chief, it boomed after the discovery of natural gas (1886). The highly industrialized city manufactures auto parts, electrical machinery, plastics, steel and metal products, glass, and canned goods. Kokomo is also a commercial hub for local livestock, grain, and vegetables. Elwood Haynes built the first commercial automobile here in 1894; a museum displays many of his inventions. A regional campus of Indiana University (1945) is here. Grissom Air Force Base is 15 mi/24 km N.

Koksoak, Rivière 90 mi/140 km long, in N Québec. Formed by the confluence of the Larch R. (R. aux Mélèzes) and the R. Caniapiscau, it flows NE into UNGAVA Bay, passing KUUJJUAQ (formerly Fort Chimo). The 270 mi/430 km–long Larch flows generally NE from lakes near Hudson Bay, crossing the Canadian Shield through numerous rapids. The Caniapiscau (or Kaniapiskau), 450 mi/720 km long, flows NE, then NNW, from L. Caniapiscau, in NC Québec. Damming on the river has tripled the size of the lake, which is on the Hudson Bay–Saint Lawrence watershed; its waters are now largely diverted, as part of the JAMES BAY Project, to the LA GRANDE R.

Kona Coast section of the SW coast of the island of HAWAII, between Keahole Point (N) and KA LAE (South Cape; S), comprising two divisions (North Kona and South Kona) of Hawaii Co. On the dry W side of MAUNA LOA and MAUNA KEA, it is noted for its sunny weather, ranches, sports fishing, and production of coffee (and, more recently, cacao), and is sometimes called the Gold Coast. Kailua-Kona (or Kailua, unincorporated, pop. 9126) is the chief settlement of North Kona; Kailua Bay was the site of the first landing (1820) of missionaries in Hawaii. South Kona stretches S from Captain Cook (unincorporated, pop. 2595), near which is KEALAKEKUA BAY, where the explorer was killed in 1779. Just S is Pu'uhonua O Honaunau (City of Refuge) National Historical Park, best-known of a number of localities in the Hawaiian Is. where outcasts, esp. breakers of taboos, could traditionally escape vengeance.

Koocanusa, Lake formed by the LIBBY DAM (1972) on the KOOTENAI R. in extreme NW Montana, and backing up 90 mi/145 km into British Columbia. Its name is a combination of *Koo*tenai, *Can*ada, and *USA*.

Koolau Range NW–SE volcanic group running the length of the NE coast of OAHU, Hawaii. Rising to 3105 ft/947 m at Konahuanui peak, NNE of Honolulu, the chain parallels the WAIANAE Mts. to the SW, from which it is separated by Oahu's fertile central plain. Two passes—Waimanalo Pali and Nuuanu Pali—are at the head of the Nuuanu Valley at the SE end, near Honolulu. At the NUUANU Pali Lookout, in 1795, Kamehameha the Great, after invading the island, is said to have trapped Oahu warriors and forced them over the cliff to their death on the rocks below.

Kootenai National Forest 2.25 million ac/910,000 ha (3520 sq mi/9105 sq km), in the NW corner of Montana and N Idaho. In the Cabinet, Purcell, and Whitefish ranges, on the Kootenai R., it is noted for its wilderness areas, elk herds, and lakes and streams.

Kootenai River also, **Kootenay** 448 mi/721 km long, in British Columbia, Montana, and Idaho. It rises in SE British Columbia, flows through Kootenay National Park and S into NW Montana, NW of Eureka. Flowing through L. KOOCANUSA, the waters of the river are impounded by the LIBBY DAM. The river turns W and runs past LIBBY before continuing NW into Idaho. Cutting NW across the N tip of the state, it re-enters British Columbia at the S end of L. Kootenay. It then flows out of the W arm of the lake past NELSON, and joins the Columbia R., 20 mi/32 km SW of Nelson.

Kootenay Lake in SE British Columbia, covering 157 sq mi/407 sq km. A widening of the Kootenai R., it is 64 mi/103 km N–S and 1–4 mi/1–6 km wide, and lies between the SELKIRK (W) and PURCELL (E) mountains. Its West Arm extends 22 mi/35 km SW to NELSON, and the Kootenai R. then continues SW to the COLUMBIA R. S of the Arrow Lakes. Fur traders, loggers, and miners have all used Kootenay L., which is today also noted as a waterfowl and osprey sanctuary and resort.

Koreatown residential and commercial section of LOS ANGELES, California, 3 mi/5 km W of Downtown, between WILSHIRE Blvd. (N) and the SANTA MONICA FREEWAY (S). The center since the early 1970s of Los Angeles's growing Korean immigrant community, it suffered extensive damage during 1992 rioting.

Koror see under Republic of PALAU.

Kosciusko city, pop. 6986, seat of Attala Co., C Mississippi, on the NATCHEZ TRACE, near the Yockanookany R., 63 mi/101 km NE of Jackson. A station on the Trace from about 1811, it later became an agricultural market center and developed lumber, textile, furniture, and other industries.

Kotzebue city, pop. 2751, Northwest Arctic Borough (pop. 6113), NW Alaska, at the tip of Baldwin Peninsula in Kotzebue Sound, 180 mi/290 km NE of Nome. Set on TUNDRA near the Arctic Circle, it was founded in the 18th century as a trading post for Arctic Alaska and part of Siberia, and is one of the largest Inuit settlements in Alaska. It is a trade center for the surrounding area; tourism is also important. There is mining for zinc and lead N of the city.

Kotzebue Sound inlet of the Chukchi Sea between the Baldwin Peninsula (NE) and Seward Peninsula (S and W), in NW Alaska. Some 80 mi/130 km E–W and 65 mi/105 km N–S, it has the city of Kotzebue NE of its entrance. It was explored by the Russian naval officer Otto von Kotzebue, searching for the NORTHWEST PASSAGE, in 1816.

Kouchibouguac National Park see under NORTHUMBERLAND STRAIT, New Brunswick.

Krusenstern, Cape see under POINT HOPE, Alaska.

Ktaadn see Mount KATAHDIN, Maine.

Kuskokwim Mountains range extending NE–SW for c.300 mi/500 km from C to SW Alaska, W of the Alaska Range. Von Frank Mt. (4508 ft/1374 m) is the high point. The 600 mi/1000 km–long **Kuskokwim R.** is formed by four branches in the Alaska Range, and flows NW through the Kuskokwims, then generally SW, through 110 mi/180 km–wide **Kuskokwim Bay,**

to the Bering Sea. PLACER gold has been obtained along it. BETHEL, near the bay's head, is the river's most important community.

Kutztown borough, pop. 4704, Berks Co., SE Pennsylvania, 15 mi/24 km NE of Reading. Settled by Germans in 1771, it produces shoes and clothing. It is the seat of Kutztown University (1866).

Kuujjuaq formerly, **Fort Chimo** INUIT village, pop. 1405, N Québec, on the Koksoak R., 30 mi/50 km S of its mouth on UNGAVA BAY, and 790 mi/1270 km NNE of Québec City. This former HUDSON'S BAY COMPANY post is now noted for its handicraft cooperative.

Kyle unincorporated community, pop. 914, Shannon Co., SW South Dakota, 65 mi/105 km SE of Rapid City. Within the PINE RIDGE Sioux Reservation, near Badlands National Park, it is the seat of Oglala Lakota College (1971).

L

La Baie city, pop. 20,995, S Québec, 6 mi/10 km SE of Chicoutimi and 105 mi/170 km NNE of Québec City, on the Baie des Ha! Ha! (Ha! Ha! Bay), an inlet at the head of navigation on the SAGUENAY R. A 1976 amalgamation of Bagotville, Port-Alfred, and the parishes of Grand-Baie and Bagotville, 1830s–40s lumbering communities, it overlooks a deepwater harbor. Paper milling, bauxite importation and aluminum smelting, port installations, and a military base (at Bagotville) are central to the economy. *Haha* is an old French word for "dead end."

Labrador see under NEWFOUNDLAND AND LABRADOR.

Labrador City town, pop. 9061, SW Labrador, near the Québec border, 270 mi/435 km W of Happy Valley–Goose Bay. It was founded in the 1950s as a planned community for the Carol Lake mining region. The surrounding mining area, which includes WABUSH, is one of the world's largest producers of iron ore concentrates, which are shipped S by rail to SEPT-ÎLES, Québec. The town, in a ski area, is also a training center for the Canadian cross-country team.

Labrador Sea NW section of the Atlantic Ocean, some 550 mi/900 km wide, between Labrador (SW) and S Greenland (NE). It connects with BAFFIN BAY (N) via the DAVIS STRAIT, and with Hudson Bay and Foxe Basin (W) via the HUDSON STRAIT. The cold **Labrador Current** flows S through it along the coast of Labrador, while the warmer West Greenland Current flows N along the Greenland coast. The sea is navigable from mid-summer to late fall; cod fishing is the major industry. Shipping is hindered by the generation of many icebergs, esp. in the W. Some of these, traveling the Current, enter the open Atlantic, as did the one that in April 1912 sank the *Titanic*.

La Brea Tar Pits paleontological site in HANCOCK PARK, Los Angeles, California, 6 mi/10 km W of Downtown, along WILSHIRE Blvd. Pitch springs formed 12,000 years ago trapped animals whose fossilized remains are on display here at the George C. Page Museum. The Gabrielinos later used the "tar" to roof their dwellings.

La Canada Flintridge residential city, pop. 19,378, Los Angeles Co., SW California, in the San Gabriel Mt. foothills, 5 mi/8 km NW of Pasadena. Its Descanso Gardens are noted for their roses and camellias.

Lacey city, pop. 19,279, Thurston Co., WC Washington, 3 mi/5 km E of Olympia. Livestock is still raised here and there is some dairy farming, despite recent suburban residential growth. Nisqually National Wildlife Refuge is 5 mi/8 km NE. St. Martin's College (1895) is here.

Lachenaie city, pop. 15,074, Les Moulins census division, S Québec, 13 mi/21 km N of Montréal, on the R. des Prairies, across from the N end of the I. de Montréal and just SW of REPENTIGNY, part of a complex of rapidly growing residential suburbs.

Lachine city, pop. 35,266, MONTRÉAL URBAN COMMUNITY, S Québec, on the St. Lawrence R., 7 mi/11 km SW of downtown Montréal. The area was granted in the 1670s to the explorer La Salle, and acquired its name ("China") in sardonic reference to his constant, unsuccessful search for a route W to Asia. French settlers were massacred here by Iroquois in a raid in Aug. 1689. Overlooking the **Lachine Rapids** of the St. Lawrence, which prevented travel between the L. St.-Louis, the Ottawa R., and the interior (W) and the lower river, Montréal, and the Atlantic (E), Lachine became a hub for the fur trade. In the 1820s, the **Lachine Canal** was built NE from Lachine, across the I. de Montréal, to Montréal's harbor. Railroad connections followed in the 1840s. Lachine industrialized and now makes steel, appliances, electronic and other machinery, and construction components. The canal, superseded by the Saint Lawrence Seaway in 1959, is now recreational.

Lachute city, pop. 11,730, Argenteuil Co., S Québec, 40 mi/64 km WNW of Montréal, on the R. du Nord (North R.). Settled in the 1790s, it developed in the 19th century as a grain milling, later a paper and textile making, center, employing power from the falls for which it is named. Today it has diversified industries.

Lackawanna city, pop. 20,585, Erie Co., W New York, on L. Erie, adjoining (S) Buffalo. Originally part of an Indian reservation, it was settled as part of West Seneca in 1850. Known as Limestone Hill, it was primarily agricultural until the arrival of the Lackawanna Steel Corporation in 1899, then became one of the leading US steel manufacturers, taking its present name in 1909. In 1977, the steel facilities, owned by Bethlehem Steel, were considerably reduced. Steel production, however, remains Lackawanna's primary industry, augmented by bridgeworks, shipyards, and the manufacture of cement, concrete, and, abrasives. There are extensive railyards.

Lackawanna County 461 sq mi/1194 sq km, pop. 219,039, in NE Pennsylvania. Its seat and major city is SCRANTON. The county is heavily industrialized and urbanized, and its economic life has depended on its proximity to vast beds of anthracite coal. Impacted by the decline in the state's mining activities, much of the county has endured high unemployment and depressed income since the 1970s.

Lackland Air Force Base in San Antonio, Texas, 8 mi/13 km SW of Downtown, with an Annex on the city's SW edge. The "Gateway to the Air Force," a training base, originally established in 1941 as the San Antonio Aviation Cadet Center, it is the largest of San Antonio's air bases, at over 6800 ac/2775 ha. KELLY AIR FORCE BASE adjoins (E).

Laclede city, pop. 410, Linn Co., N Missouri, 20 mi/32 km E of Chillicothe. Army general John J. Pershing (1860–1948) was born nearby; his boyhood home here is now a State Historical Site.

Laclede's Landing redeveloped waterfront district of downtown SAINT LOUIS, Missouri, just N of the EADS BRIDGE. It is the site of the original establishment of the city, on Feb. 14, 1764, by 13-year-old René Auguste Chouteau, acting for his stepfather and employer Pierre Laclède. Long a warehouse zone, it has since the 1970s been turned into a nine-block historic district with shops, restaurants, nightclubs, and some offices.

Lacolle village, pop. 1392, Le Haut-Richelieu census division, S Québec, 9 mi/14 km N of Rouses Point, New York, and just W of the R. RICHELIEU, site of a March 30, 1814 battle in which invading American troops were defeated by the British.

Lacombe town, pop. 6934, SC Alberta, 76 mi/122 km S of Edmonton and 14 mi/23 km N of Red Deer. In an agricultural region, it processes dairy products and has grain elevators and flour, grist, and lumber mills. Settlement began in the early 1880s, and increased with the arrival of the railroad in the 1890s. Lacombe is a summer resort with a number of lakes and provincial parks nearby. A government experimental farm (1908) is here.

Laconia city, pop. 15,743, seat of Belknap Co., C New Hampshire. Laconia lies on a peninsula between Lakes Winnisquam and Winnipesaukee, and to the SE across Paugus and Opechee bays, two smaller bodies between the lakes, 22 mi/35 km N of Concord, in the foothills of the White Mts. Settled in the 1770s, it is the manufacturing and trade center of an agricultural and year-round resort region. Laconia was a railway car construction center through the late 19th century and early 20th century. Modern industries produce boots, skis, textiles, textile machinery, metal products, and leather goods.

Lac Qui Parle River 70 mi/113 km long, in South Dakota and Minnesota. It rises in L. Hendricks in Deuel Co., E South Dakota, enters SW Minnesota near the city of Hendricks, and flows NE past Dawson to the Minnesota R., at the SE end of Lac qui Parle L.

La Crescenta–Montrose unincorporated community, pop. 16,968, Los Angeles Co., SW California, a residential suburb in the San Gabriel Mt. foothills, 12 mi/19 km NNE of downtown Los Angeles.

La Crosse city, pop. 51,003, seat of La Crosse Co., W Wisconsin, on the Mississippi R, at the mouths of the Black and La Crosse rivers, at the Minnesota border. An agricultural trading and shipping center, it also manufactures such items as farm implements, rubber footwear, sheet metal, lumber, beer, and air-conditioning systems. French explorers observed Indians playing lacrosse here and named the site "Prairie La Crosse." A trading post was established in 1841, and the town grew as a river port and later as a center for sawmills and gristmills. Railroads arrived in 1858, and a bridge was built over the Mississippi (1876), stimulating the city's further growth as a transportation hub. Brewing and diverse manufacturing emerged around the turn of the century with the decline of the lumber industry. The University of Wisconsin–La Crosse (1909) is here, as is Western Wisconsin Technical Institute (1912). The annual Oktoberfest draws large crowds.

Ladd Addition residential neighborhood in Southeast PORTLAND, Oregon, 1.5 mi/2.4 km SE of Downtown. An early-20th-century development, it has middle-class Victorian homes and a radial street pattern unique in the city.

Ladson unincorporated community, pop. 13,540, Berkeley and Charleston counties, EC South Carolina, 17 mi/27 km NNW of Charleston. Just off Interstate 26 some 5 mi/8 km from North Charleston, it is a primarily residential suburb.

Ladue city, pop. 8847, St. Louis Co., EC Missouri, 10 mi/16 km WNW of downtown St. Louis. It became a city in 1936 as a result of the consolidation of the towns of Ladue, Deer Creek, and McKnight. Today it is primarily an affluent suburb.

Ladysmith city, pop. 3938, seat of Rusk Co., N Wisconsin, on the Flambeau R., 50 mi/80 km NE of Eau Claire. In a lake resort and farming area, it processes dairy products. Canned vegetables, paper, and wooden items are also produced. Ladysmith is the seat of Mount Senario College (1962).

Lafayette **1.** city, pop. 3151, seat of Chambers Co., EC Alabama, 38 mi/61 km NW of Columbus, Georgia. An industrial center, with pulpwood mills and clothing factories, it is noted as the birthplace (1914) of boxing champion Joe Louis. **2.** city, pop. 23,501, Contra Costa Co., NC California, 8 mi/13 km NE of Oakland. Walnut and fruit growing and horse raising have been important in what is now essentially a residential suburb. **3.** city, pop. 14,548, Boulder Co., NC Colorado, a largely residential suburb, 20 mi/32 km N of Denver. **4.** city, pop. 43,764, seat of Tippecanoe Co., NW Indiana, on the Wabash R., 60 mi/100 km NW of Indianapolis. Founded in 1830, it is a market, processing, and shipping hub for local grain, cattle, and hogs. Its many manufactures include pharmaceuticals, prefabricated houses, automobiles and auto and electronic parts, wire, chemicals, and rubber and aluminum products. BATTLE GROUND, the site of the 1811 Battle of Tippecanoe, is 7 mi/11 km NE, and WEST LAFAYETTE, home of Purdue University, adjoins the city. **5.** city, pop. 94,440, seat of Lafayette Parish (pop. 164,762), S Louisiana, on the Vermilion R., 50 mi/80 km WSW of Baton Rouge. It is the center of the area settled during the late 18th century by Acadians exiled from Nova Scotia. Vermilionville, settled in the 1770s and renamed Lafayette in 1884, was the earliest village. It was long primarily an agricultural trade center, handling sugar cane, cotton, rice, and corn. After the mid 20th century it became an operations and processing center for much of Louisiana's oil and gas industry, particularly offshore producers. Heymann Oil Center, in the city, houses several major oil and gas companies. Despite the city's industrialization, elements of the Cajun culture survive. The Camellia Show and Mardi Gras and the Festivals Acadiens are celebrated annually. Lafayette is home to a Carmelite monastery and to the University of Southwestern Louisiana (1898).

Lafayette, Mount highest peak (5249 ft/1601 m) in the Franconia Range of the White Mts., NC New Hampshire. Previously known as Great Haystack, it was renamed for the French hero of the American Revolution when he visited in

1825. The Appalachian Mountain Club's Greenleaf Hut, at 4200 ft/1281 m, overlooks Eagle Lake.

Lafayette County 669 sq mi/1733 sq km, pop. 31,826, in NC Mississippi, in the NE DELTA, bounded by the Tallahatchie R. (NE). A section of the Holly Springs National Forest occupies its NE corner. The county seat is OXFORD, whose university and industries strongly influence the economy. Otherwise it is largely agricultural, producing cotton, corn, dairy goods, and poultry. Pine and hardwood timber are cut. Lafayette is generally recognized as the model for William Faulkner's YOKNAPATAWPHA Co.

Lafayette Square see under WHITE HOUSE, Washington, D.C.

Lafitte see under BARATARIA BAY, Louisiana.

La Follette city, pop. 7192, Campbell Co., NE Tennessee, 30 mi/48 km NNW of Knoxville, along the SE foot of Cumberland Mt. A coal mining center incorporated in 1897 along Big Creek, in the Powell Valley, it is now almost on the NW shore of Norris L.

Lafourche see under BAYOU LAFOURCHE, Louisiana.

lagoon **1.** see under BARRIER BEACH. **2.** the body of water inside an ATOLL.

La Grande city, pop. 11,766, seat of Union Co., NE Oregon, on the Grande Ronde R., in the E foothills of the Blue Mts., 40 mi/64 km SE of Pendleton. Settled in 1861, it lies in the Grande Ronde Valley and is a trading center for cattle, lumber, and wheat producers. Since the early 1990s wild mushrooms from the Blue Mts. have become an important source of income. La Grande's manufactures include particle board, trailers, and chemical products. It is the seat of Eastern Oregon State College (1929). The Wallowa-Whitman National Forest lies to the E and W.

La Grande Rivière also, **Fort George** or **Big River** 500 mi/800 km long, in C Québec, flowing from L. Nichicun W to James Bay. Since the 1980s construction of units of the JAMES BAY Project, the La Grande has received waters diverted from the R. Caniapiscau (see under R. KOKSOAK), and its flow has doubled. Works on the river now include a huge multitiered spillway and, at La Grande 2, the largest underground powerhouse in the world. The Cree settlement of Chisasibi (formerly Fort George), at the river's mouth, has been moved upstream; the Cree gave up land claims in the area in 1975, but disputes over the Project's effects on their hunting and fishing grounds continue, esp. in relation to further development on the GREAT WHALE R. (N).

La Grange **1.** city, pop. 25,597, seat of Troup Co., W Georgia, 41 mi/66 km N of Columbus. Incorporated in 1828, it is a textile center, home to Callaway Mills (1900), and has other diversified industries. Tourists are drawn to its old houses and to nearby West Point L. La Grange College dates to 1831. **2.** village, pop. 15,362, Cook Co., NE Illinois, 15 mi/24 km W of Chicago. Although mainly a residential suburb, it also manufactures aluminum products.

La Grange Park village, pop. 12,861, Cook Co., NE Illinois, on Salt Creek, a residential suburb 13 mi/21 km W of Chicago.

LaGuardia Airport one of three major airports in the New York City area (the others are John F. Kennedy and Newark), on Flushing Bay and the East R., in N Queens, New York. Opened in 1939 and originally known as North Beach Airport, it was renamed LaGuardia Municipal Field in honor of New York Mayor Fiorello H. LaGuardia (d. 1946). It handles primarily domestic traffic.

Laguna Beach city, pop. 23,170, Orange Co., SW California, on the Pacific Ocean, 6 mi/10 km SW of Laguna Hills and 43 mi/69 km SE of Los Angeles. Its coves, headlands, and relative seclusion made it an artists' colony by the early 20th century. Its beaches have long been popular, and the city is now a growing residential center.

Laguna Hills unincorporated community, pop. 46,731, Orange Co., SW California, in the San Joaquin Hills, 12 mi/19 km SE of Santa Ana. It is a growing residential and commercial center NE of LAGUNA BEACH, SW of EL TORO, and SE of IRVINE.

Laguna Mountains wooded range in extreme S California, E of San Diego, extending for c.35 mi/56 km NW from the Mexican border and the N end of the Sierra Juárez. Garnet Peak (5909 ft/1801 m), Garnet Mt. (5665 ft/1727 m), and Mt. Laguna, also known as Stephenson Peak, are in the range. Mount Laguna Air Force Station, a radar site, and the uninhabited Cuyapaipe Indian Reservation are in the E part.

Laguna Niguel city, pop. 44,400, Orange Co., SW California, just SE of Laguna Beach and 45 mi/72 km SE of Los Angeles. Settled largely since the 1970s around Niguel Hill, it is one of the fastest-growing middle-class exurbs in S California.

Laguna Pueblo pop. 3731, in Cibola Co., WC New Mexico, just E of ÁCOMA and 42 mi/68 km W of Albuquerque. On the San Jose R., the Keresan pueblo, formed in the late 1690s by groups from Santo Domingo and Cochiti pueblos, has six villages. Many members left in the late 1800s when Americans brought pressure against traditional culture. One of the world's richest uranium mines, now closed, was here.

La Habra city, pop. 51,266, Orange Co., SW California, 20 mi/32 km ESE of downtown Los Angeles. Named for a local pass (*abra*) in the hills, it was settled in the 1860s, and became a trade center for a citrus fruit and avocado growing area. The arrival of the Pacific Electric Railroad (1908) and the discovery of oil in the Coyote Hills (1912) spurred growth. Oil and agriculture have been joined by electronics and other manufacturing in the city's economy. La Habra grew most quickly in the 1950s and 1960s. **La Habra Heights** (city, pop. 6226), adjacent (N), is in Los Angeles Co.

Lahaina unincorporated community, pop. 9073, Maui Co., Hawaii, on the W coast of Maui and the Auau Channel (the Lahaina Roadstead.) Formerly the residence of Hawaiian royalty, Lahaina was the first white settlement in the area and a whaling port in the 19th century, serving briefly as the seat of the islands. More recently, it has been an anchorage for the US Pacific Fleet. Today the economy depends on tourism and on sugarcane and pineapple cultivation. The Lahainaluna (missionary) School (1831) is here.

Lahontan, Lake body that occupied some 8500 sq mi/22,000 sq km, and was almost 900 ft/275 m deep, in NW Nevada and NE California, late in the last glacial age. It disappeared gradually from about 15,000 years ago; today, its largest vestiges include PYRAMID, WALKER, and Winnemucca lakes and the CARSON Sink. The Carson, Humboldt, and Truckee rivers and the BLACK ROCK DESERT are in the area. The irregularly shaped lake, which occupied what are now basins and made islands of what are now mountain ranges, was filled by rains generated by the presence (immediately N) of the glacial front. It extended N to near the Idaho-Nevada border, S to just below Walker L., and W to the Sierra Nevada. Archaeological sites along its former shoreline, testifying to human presence as long as 10,000 years ago, include those at Lovelock Cave. Lake Bonneville, to the E (see BONNEVILLE SALT FLATS), was more than twice as large.

Lahontan Dam and Reservoir see under CARSON R., Nevada.

Laie unincorporated community, pop. 5577, Honolulu Co., NE Oahu, Hawaii, on Laie Bay, 25 mi/40 km NW of Honolulu. The Polynesian Cultural Center, with seven re-created historical villages, is a central tourist attraction. Mormon Temple (1919) and a branch (1955) of Brigham Young University are here.

Lair Hill residential neighborhood and historic district in Southwest PORTLAND, Oregon, S of Downtown. An area of Victorian frame houses threatened by URBAN RENEWAL in the late 1960s, it was one of the first Portland communities to successfully challenge city government's plans.

La Jolla seaside resort, residential, and academic section of SAN DIEGO, California, 10 mi/16 km NNW of Downtown. Known for its rocky bluffs, caves, and cliffs on the Pacific, it was first developed as a resort in the 1880s. Its scenery and hotels, art galleries, and fine stores attract tourists, and it has much of San Diego's most expensive housing. The Museum of Contemporary Art (1941) and the University of California, San Diego (1959) are here. The Scripps Institute of Oceanography (1903) and the Salk Institute (1960; biomedicine) are world-famous research facilities. The TORREY PINES lie immediately N.

La Junta city, pop. 7637, seat of Otero Co., SE Colorado, on the Arkansas R., 60 mi/97 km ESE of Pueblo. Originally at the site of the Bent's Fort fur-trading post, now a National Historic Site 8 mi/13 km NE, it was moved with the arrival of the Santa Fe Railroad in 1875. It is still an important trade and railroad center for cattle and produce. Also here are canneries and meatpacking plants, railroad repair shops, and cattle auction facilities. La Junta is the seat of Otero Junior College (1941) and the birthplace (1935) of novelist Ken Kesey. Comanche National Grassland is SW of the city.

Lake for lakes whose names begin with this word, see under the other name element, as **Superior, Lake.** Lakes whose names are phrases beginning with *Lake* appear as, for example, **Lake of the Woods.**

Lake Buena Vista city, pop. 1776, Orange Co., C Florida, 15 mi/24 km SW of Orlando. Walt Disney World, opened 1971, occupies 28,000 ac/11,300 ha along its W, in Orange and Osceola counties, and includes Epcot Center ("Experimental Prototype Community of Tomorrow"), the Magic Kingdom, other theme parks, and resort and retirement complexes. Lake Buena Vista includes additional attractions, and is the gateway to the Disney complex.

Lake Charles city, pop. 70,580, seat of Calcasieu Parish (pop. 168,134), SW Louisiana, 70 mi/113 km W of Lafayette, connected to the Gulf Intracoastal Waterway and to the Gulf of Mexico (30 mi/48 km S) via a deepwater channel in the Calcasieu R. The site was settled in 1781. It developed as a lumber center in the 1880s, exploiting pine forests to the N and W. Accompanying railroad expansion also encouraged regional agriculture, and Lake Charles soon became the largest US rice-exporting port. Exploitation of local sulfur, oil, and gas deposits has made it today one of the leading US petrochemical production centers as well. McNeese State University (1939) is in the city.

Lake City city, pop. 10,005, seat of Columbia Co., N Florida, 41 mi/68 km NNW of Gainesville. On a former Seminole site, it was founded as an 1830s military post, called Alligator until 1859. An important 19th-century farm hub, it trades local tobacco, lumber, poultry, and turpentine. On the SW edge of OSCEOLA NATIONAL FOREST, it is also a tourist destination.

Lake Clark National Park and Preserve 4.04 million ac/1.64 million ha (6319 sq mi/16,366 sq km), along the W shore of COOK INLET, in SW Alaska. It contains two active symmetrical volcanoes, Iliamna (10,016 ft/3053 m) and Redoubt (10,197 ft/3108 m). The latter, which erupted in 1989–90, and most of the NE–SW Chigmit Mts., sit atop the juncture of the North American and Pacific PLATES, the site of much volcanic and earthquake activity. The park takes its name from 40 mi/64 km–long, recreational L. Clark. The area is also known for the Chilikadrotna, Mulchatna, and Tlikakila wild rivers; glaciers in Merrill and Lake Clark passes; and caribou, bears, and Dall sheep.

Lake County **1.** 454 sq mi/1176 sq km, pop. 516,418, in NE Illinois, bordered by L. Michigan (E) and Wisconsin (N). Its seat is WAUKEGAN. The county contains a mix of affluent Chicago suburbs (such as Highland Park and Lake Forest), industrial cities (such as North Chicago and Waukegan), and summer lake resorts (such as Channel Lake and Round Lake) in the NW. Most of the population is in the urban centers of the E and S, with dairy and truck farms covering much of the rest of the county. **2.** 501 sq mi/1298 sq km, pop. 475,594, in the NW corner of Indiana. Its seat is CROWN POINT. Bordered (N) by L. Michigan and (W) by Illinois, it is crossed in the N by the Grand Calumet and Little Calumet rivers, in the extensively industrialized Calumet area, a major steel producer. In the S it is suburban and has some agriculture; soybeans, truck crops, corn, and poultry are among items produced. **3.** smallest county in Ohio, 231 sq mi/598 sq km, pop. 215,499, in the NE, bounded (N) by L. Erie, and intersected by the Chagrin and Grand rivers. Its seat is Painesville. A number of Cleveland's residential suburbs, such as Eastlake and Mentor, are situated in the W of the county. Local agriculture includes fruit growing as well as truck and poultry farming. There is manufacturing at Painesville and other locations. Commercial fishing and salt production are pursued, and the region is known for its lake resorts.

Lake Drive scenic route, 23 mi/37 km long, following the L. Michigan shoreline, between South Milwaukee and Bayside, Wisconsin. It passes through downtown Milwaukee, the city's East and South sides, and the suburbs of Cudahy, St. Francis, Shorewood, Whitefish Bay, and Fox Point. Downtown, the road becomes the Lake Freeway, passing through JUNEAU PARK as Lincoln Memorial Drive.

Lake Elsinore also, **Elsinore** city, pop. 18,285, Riverside Co., S California, 20 mi/32 km SSE of Riverside, on the N side of L. Elsinore. The lake and area mineral springs made the city, founded in 1883, a popular resort. Some quarrying is carried out in the area.

Lake Forest city, pop. 17,836, Lake Co., NE Illinois, on L. Michigan, 30 mi/48 km N of Chicago. Although first settled in 1835, it was laid out in 1856 as one of the earliest examples of the classic 19th-century railroad suburb. Today the community is one of the most affluent of Chicago's residential suburbs. There is no industrial development here. The city is the seat of Lake Forest College (1857) and Barat College (1858). Fort Sheridan is immediately S.

Lake Geneva city, pop. 5979, Walworth Co., extreme SE Wisconsin. It is on the White R. at the NE end of 7.5 mi/12 km–long L. Geneva, which in the 1870s became the resort and country home of the wealthy of Chicago, 65 mi/105 km SE. It is a year-round resort, noted for summer and ice fishing, skiing, beaches, and other amusements. WILLIAMS BAY is on the lake's NW.

Lake Grove village, pop. 9612, in Brookhaven town, Suffolk Co., SE New York, on Long Island, just N of LAKE RONKONKOMA. It is a residential suburb.

Lake Havasu City city, pop. 24,363, Mohave Co., WC Arizona, on L. HAVASU (the Colorado R.), at the California border. Designed in the 1960s, it is a recreational and retirement center with some light manufacturing, in a cattle ranching area. Havasu L. National Wildlife Refuge is immediately N and L. Havasu State Park immediately S. The city is well known as the site of the 19th-century London Bridge, moved here from England in 1971, which now spans an inlet on the Colorado R.

Lakehead in Ontario, the area at the W end of L. Superior, around THUNDER BAY. Earlier, the term (or **Head of the Lake**) was applied to the W end of L. Ontario, the area around Hamilton.

Lakehurst borough, pop. 3078, Ocean Co., EC New Jersey, 22 mi/35 km SW of Asbury Park. The US Naval Air Station established here in 1919 was the American terminal for transatlantic dirigible flights from 1924 until the deadly *Hindenburg* fire of May 6, 1937. It maintained facilities for lighter-than-air craft until 1962, and has been a Naval Air Engineering Center since 1974. FORT DIX is immediately W.

Lake Jackson city, pop. 22,776, Brazoria Co., SE Texas, on the Brazos R., 48 mi/77 km S of Houston. Part of the BRAZOSPORT complex, it was founded by the Dow Chemical Company in 1941 for defense plant workers. There are petrochemical and metalworking plants as well as fruit and dairy farms. Brazosport College (1968) is here.

Lakeland city, pop. 70,576, Polk Co., C Florida, 30 mi/48 km ENE of Tampa. Set amid citrus groves, it is a leading center for processing, packing, and shipping these fruits; growers' organizations have headquarters here. More than half the nation's phosphates are mined in the area, and the city manufactures fertilizers. There are a variety of other light industries. Tourists are attracted to the many small lakes in and near the city and to spring training baseball. Lakeland is the seat of Florida Southern College (1885), the site of a group of buildings designed by Frank Lloyd Wright, and of Southeastern College of the Assemblies of God (1935).

Lakeland North unincorporated community, pop. 14,402, King Co., WC Washington, a residential and industrial E suburb of Seattle.

Lake Louise unincorporated resort in SW Alberta, in the Rocky Mts. in BANFF NATIONAL PARK, just E of KICKING HORSE PASS and 34 mi/55 km NW of Banff. L. Louise, a world-famous resort, is a pristine, turquoise-colored body, 1.5 mi/2.5 km by 0.75 mi/1.2 km, lying at 5680 ft/1731 m. It empties via a stream into the BOW R. First settled in 1884 as a CANADIAN PACIFIC RAILWAY workers' camp, the area developed into a popular recreational spot, and is known for the landmark Chateau Lake Louise, one of the CPR's chain of grand hotels.

Lake Mills city, pop. 4143, Jefferson Co., SE Wisconsin, on Rock L., 25 mi/40 km E of Madison. Settled c.1836, it is situated in an area of poultry and dairy farms and lakes, and is a popular summer resort. A large fish hatchery is in the city. Dairy equipment, shoes, canned vegetables, and powdered milk are produced. Aztalan State Park, 3 mi/5 km to the E, along the Crawfish R., contains remains of a prehistoric Indian village; adjacent is the Aztalan Museum.

Lake of the Ozarks created on the OSAGE R. by the 1931 Bagnell Dam, in C Missouri, 50 mi/80 km SSW of Columbia. The Harry S Truman Dam and Reservoir are upstream. Some 98 mi/158 km long, with a shoreline of over 1150 mi/1850 km, the Lake of the Ozarks is a major recreational facility on the N edge of the OZARK PLATEAU. It is heavily used for motorboating, houseboating, fishing, waterskiing, and huge waterborne parties.

Lake of the Woods in SE Manitoba, W Ontario, and N Minnesota. A remnant of glacial L. AGASSIZ, it covers 1680 sq mi/4350 sq km (c.62% in Canada), and is up to 70 mi/110 km across. On the SW is Minnesota's NORTHWEST ANGLE, and the FORTY-NINTH PARALLEL extends W as the international boundary from a point in the lake's SW corner. The lake is fed by the RAINY R. from the S, and drained to the NW by the WINNIPEG R. The S shore is low and sandy. The N shore, on the S edge of the CANADIAN SHIELD, is granitic and irregular, with over 14,000 mostly wooded islands. The Aulneau Peninsula thrusts into the lake from the E. The Cree, Ojibwa, and Sioux have lived here; French explorers were in the area by 1688, and the lake was on the main fur trading route W from the Great Lakes. It is now a tourist magnet; each Aug. the Lake of the Woods Regatta, a seven-day sailboat race around the lake, is held. Fishing, hunting, and lakeside resorts bring trade.

Lake of the Woods County 1296 sq mi/3357 sq km, pop. 4076, in NC Minnesota, bordered by the Rainy R. at the Ontario border (NE) and the Lake of the Woods (NW). Baudette is the seat of an area mostly preserved as wilderness. The W half of the county is occupied by Beltrami Island State Forest; portions of the Red Lake Indian Reservation are scattered throughout the S and SE. The NORTHEAST ANGLE is part of the county. Fishing and lumbering are the chief occupations.

Lake Orion village, pop. 3057, Oakland Co., SE Michigan, on L. Orion, 11 mi/18 km NNE of Pontiac. It is a popular summer resort in an area of numerous lakes, and a trading center for local field crops and dairy products. Just to the S is Bald Mountain State Recreation Area.

Lake Oswego city, pop. 30,576, Clackamas, Multnomah, and Washington counties, NW Oregon, on L. Oswego and the Willamette R., a residential suburb 8 mi/13 km SSW of Portland. Settled in the 1850s, it was once an iron foundry center.

Lake o' the Cherokees also, **L. of the Cherokees, Grand L., Grand Lake o' the Cherokees,** or **Pensacola Reservoir** 64 sq mi/166 sq km, in the NE corner of Oklahoma, formed by the impounding (1940) of the NEOSHO (Grand) R. by the Pensacola Dam. There are numerous recreational sites along the shores of the irregularly shaped lake.

Lake Placid village, pop. 2485, in North Elba township, Essex Co., NE New York, in the Adirondack Mts., on the small Mirror L. and at the S end of the 4 mi/6 km–long, 0.5 mi/1 km–wide L. Placid, 40 mi/64 km SW of Plattsburgh. Founded in 1849, it was the site of the exclusive Lake Placid Club, established as a sports club by Melvil Dewey (1895). It is surrounded by ADIRONDACK PARK and set at an altitude of 1864 ft/569 m. A famous winter resort and the site of the

1932 and 1980 Winter Olympics, it has downhill (at nearby Whiteface Mt.) and cross-country ski trails, a bobsled run, and other sports facilities. The Olympic Center, a multipurpose site with four ice rinks built for the 1980 games, is in the village. Just SE is the Olympic Jumping Complex, the training area for American and Canadian Olympic teams and the site of international competitions. Lake Placid is also a popular summer resort. The John Brown Farm State Historic Site, 2 mi/3 km S of the village, marks the home and grave of the abolitionist.

Lakeport see under CLEAR L., California.

Lake Ridge unincorporated community, pop. 23,862, Prince William Co., NE Virginia, a residential suburb on the S side of Occoquan Reservoir (the Occoquan R.), 21 mi/34 km SW of Washington, D.C.

Lake Ronkonkoma unincorporated village, pop. 18,997, in Brookhaven town, Suffolk Co., SE New York, on Long Island, 3 mi/5 km N of Long Island MacArthur Airport and abutting L. Ronkonkoma. It is primarily residential.

Lakes District residential and recreational area of Minneapolis, Minnesota, SW of Downtown. The city's scenic lakes are here, and the district includes some of the most affluent neighborhoods in the Twin Cities, including KENWOOD and LOWRY HILL.

Lake Shore unincorporated community, pop. 13,269, Anne Arundel Co., NC Maryland, a residential suburb on the estuarial Magothy R. and the W shore of Chesapeake Bay, 14 mi/22 km SE of Baltimore.

Lake Shore Drive parkway along L. Michigan in Chicago, Illinois. Extending 18 mi/29 km from the N edge of LINCOLN PARK, through Grant and Burnham parks to Jackson Park, it features prestigious addresses, especially N of the LOOP, and excellent views of the city and L. Michigan.

Lakeside 1. unincorporated community, pop. 39,412, San Diego Co., SW California, a booming residential suburb 17 mi/27 km NE of San Diego. **2.** unincorporated community, pop. 12,081, Henrico Co., EC Virginia, adjacent (NW) to Richmond. It is a largely residential suburb.

Lake Station city, pop. 13,899, Lake Co., extreme NW Indiana, adjacent (SE) to Gary, and 5 mi/8 km S of L. Michigan. Part of the highly industrialized CALUMET area, it was formerly known as East Gary. Its manufactures include cement and processed foods.

Lake Success village, pop. 2484, in North Hempstead town, Nassau Co., SE New York, on the small L. Success, near the N shore of W Long Island, adjacent (E) to Little Neck, Queens. In an area settled by the Dutch in the 17th century, it served as the temporary site (1946–51) of the United Nations headquarters. Primarily a residential suburb, it is now also home to a number of corporate headquarters, research and development facilities, and office buildings.

Lake View also, **Lakeview** residential and commercial neighborhood on the North Side of Chicago, Illinois. It is named for Lake View House, an 1854 resort hotel that attracted summer homes of the elite. The area later housed various immigrant groups, such as Germans and Mexicans. In the 1970s and 1980s, Lake View emerged as one of the trendiest gentrified areas of the North Side, with a large community of young professionals, artists, and gays.

Lakeville city, pop. 24,854, Dakota Co., SE Minnesota, 18 mi/29 km S of Minneapolis. A fast-growing outer Twin Cities suburb, it has experienced a recent boom in residential and light industrial development. Numerous shopping centers have been built near I-35 W of the city.

Lake Wales city, pop. 9670, Polk Co., C Florida, 10 mi/16 km SE of Winter Haven. A popular winter vacation locale set amid small lakes, it has a noted museum and cultural center. It is best known as the site of Iron Mt. (325 ft/99 m, the highest point on the Florida Peninsula), home to Bok Tower Gardens, including the Singing Tower, a marble tower (1929) with a 57-bell carillon. Lake Wales is also a market, processing, and distribution center for local citrus fruit.

Lake Wobegon fictional Minnesota town, central to the work of writer and radio comedian Garrison Keillor (1942–), who was born in ANOKA and has lived in Saint Paul. In Lake Wobegon, which has been featured on the radio show *A Prairie Home Companion* since 1974, "all the women are strong, all the men are good-looking, and all the children are above average."

Lakewood 1. city, pop. 73,557, Los Angeles Co., SW California, just N of Long Beach and 13 mi/21 km SE of downtown Los Angeles. It was developed in the 1950s in a formerly agricultural and oil producing area to house workers at Long Beach aircraft plants, and remains essentially a working-middle-class suburb. **2.** city, pop. 126,481, Jefferson Co., NC Colorado, a residential and commercial suburb adjacent (W) to Denver. The Denver Federal Center is here. The community boomed in the 1960s and was incorporated in 1969. **3.** township, pop. 45,048, Ocean Co., EC New Jersey, on the Metedeconk R. and the Garden State Parkway, 14 mi/23 km SW of Asbury Park. Settled in 1800, in a pine forest among small lakes, less than 10 mi/16 km W of the Atlantic, it has long been a popular health resort. Lakewood also has numerous manufactures, including furniture, plastics, doors and windows, weather instruments, clocks, and electronic components. It is home to Georgian Court College (1908), which has a noted aboretum and garden on the former Gould estate. The former Rockefeller estate is a state reserve. **4.** city, pop. 59,718, Cuyahoga Co., NE Ohio, on L. Erie, 5 mi/8 km W of Cleveland, of which it is a mainly white, middle-class suburb. Largely residential, it also manufactures sheet metal, conveying equipment, nuts and bolts, castings, dry batteries, and other products. It has a large civic auditorium, and the Great Lakes Shakespeare Festival is held here. **5.** also, **Lakewood Center** unincorporated community, pop. 58,412, Pierce Co., WC Washington, on Steilacoom L., 6 mi/10 km SW of Tacoma. A residential suburb, it is also home to McChord Air Force Base, immediately S. FORT LEWIS is also nearby.

Lake Worth 1. city, pop. 28,564, Palm Beach Co., SE Florida, on L. Worth, a lagoon that opens into the Atlantic, 6 mi/10 km S of West Palm Beach. Settled in the 1870s, it began rapid development early in the 20th century when waterfront lots were given away to purchasers of nearby farmland. Today the city is a busy winter vacation spot with a 1000-ft/300-m municipal pier. There are some light manufacturing and processing of local farm produce. Palm Beach Community College (1933) is here. **2.** see under FORT WORTH, Texas.

Lake Zurich village, pop. 14,947, Lake Co., NE Illinois, on L. Zurich, 35 mi/56 km NW of Chicago. It has long served as a resort area for Chicago residents. Recently, residential development has brought it within the Chicago suburban belt. Concrete products and tools are manufactured here.

La Malbaie English, **Murray Bay** city, pop. 3968, Charlevoix-

Est census division, S Québec, 76 mi/122 km NE of Québec City, at the mouth of the R. Malbaie on the St. Lawrence R. Visited in 1608 by Champlain, who found it a difficult anchorage (hence the name), it was settled (as Murray Bay) by Scots after the 1760s British conquest. The area has long been renowned for its summer resorts, including Pointe-au-Pic (just SW), with its huge Manoir Richelieu (now a hotel) and Cap-à-l'Aigle (NE). It is popular with artists and performers. There is some industry in the city.

Lamar **1.** city, pop. 8343, seat of Prowers Co., SE Colorado, on the Arkansas R., 50 mi/80 km ENE of La Junta. A processing center for a livestock and grain area, it produces flour, feed, and dairy goods. Lamar Community College (1937) is here. **2.** city, pop. 4168, seat of Barton Co., SW Missouri, 32 mi/51 km NNE of Joplin. Founded in 1856, it was the E terminus of the FORT SCOTT Military Road (to Kansas). The well-known Missouri newspaper the Lamar *Democrat* was founded before the Civil War. President Harry S. Truman was born in Lamar in 1884, moving later to INDEPENDENCE. His birthplace is a State Historical Site.

La Marque city, pop. 14,120, Galveston Co., SE Texas, adjacent (SW) to Texas City, and 12 mi/19 km NW of Galveston, on Highland Bayou just above Galveston's West Bay. A mostly residential suburb with oil refineries, it also produces strawberries and vegetables.

La Mauricie see under R. SAINT-MAURICE, Québec.

Lambertville city, pop. 3927, Hunterdon Co., WC New Jersey, 14 mi/23 km NW of Trenton, across the Delaware R. from NEW HOPE, Pennsylvania. Originally Coryel's Ferry, it became an industrial center after the railroad arrived in 1851. Some light industry remains, but the city today relies heavily on commerce generated by the area's tourist traffic.

Lame Deer unincorporated village, pop. 1918, Rosebud Co., SE Montana, on Deer Creek, 90 mi/145 km ESE of Billings. Situated in a livestock raising region of rolling grassland with some forest, it is headquarters of the Northern Cheyenne Indian Reservation, pop. 3923.

La Mesa city, pop. 52,931, San Diego Co., SW California, 9 mi/14 km ENE of downtown San Diego. It is an affluent residential suburb overlooking San Diego's MISSION VALLEY, E of San Diego State University. Incorporated in 1912, the city has been a trade center for poultry, citrus, avocado, and grape producers. Coleman College (1963) is here.

Lamesa city, pop. 10,809, seat of Dawson Co., W Texas, 58 mi/93 km S of Lubbock. There are oil and lime deposits in this HIGH PLAINS area. Founded in 1903, the city is a processing and shipping center for cotton, grain, and wheat, with some light manufactures.

La Mirada city, pop. 40,452, Los Angeles Co., SW California, 19 mi/31 km SE of downtown Los Angeles, on Coyote Creek (E). Once part of a vast Spanish land grant, Rancho Los Coyotes, it became after the 1880s a center of fruit cultivation, home to the regional olive industry. The city, incorporated in 1960, is the seat of Biola University (1908), and is largely residential.

Lamoille River 72 mi/116 km long, rising S of Glover in Orleans Co., NC Vermont, and flowing S and W through the Green Mts., past Hardwick, Wolcott, and Morrisville, where a hydroelectric dam impounds L. Lamoille. The river receives the North Branch at Jeffersonville, then continues W through Fairfax and Milton, and into L. Champlain, 10 mi/16 km N of Burlington.

Lamoni city, pop. 2319, seat of Decatur Co., SC Iowa, 36 mi/58 km SE of Creston and 3 mi/5 km N of the Missouri border. Founded by Mormon leader Joseph Smith III, it was named for a king in church literature. Graceland College (1895) is here, as is Liberty Hall Historic Center, at Smith's home.

Lamy hamlet, 16 mi/26 km SSE of Santa Fe, in NC New Mexico, in the foothills of the Sangre de Cristo Mts. San Cristobal Pueblo was here from the 13th century until the 1680 Pueblo Revolt. Established as a Santa Fe Railroad depot in the 1870s, Lamy is now best known as the junction for Santa Fe, which is served by bus.

Lanai sixth-largest (140 sq mi/363 sq km) island of Hawaii, part of MAUI Co., W of Maui, S of MOLOKAI, and NW of KAHOOLAWE. It was formed by the extinct volcano Palawai, with its highest point at Lanaihale, 3370 ft/1028 m above sea level. The island was used mainly for cattle grazing before 1922, when it was purchased by the Dole corporation and developed into a pineapple plantation. The hub of the island is **Lanai City** (unincorporated, pop. 2400), situated in the C and connected by highway to Kaumalapau Harbor on the W coast. The remains of the village of Kaunolu on the S coast, once a resort of King Kamehameha I, are a local attraction.

Lancaster **1.** city, pop. 97,291, Los Angeles Co., SW California, 45 mi/72 km NNE of Los Angeles, in the ANTELOPE VALLEY, on the W edge of the Mojave Desert. Settled in the 1880s, it became a trade center for an irrigated area that has grown alfalfa, sugar beets, and grain. Its major modern industries are the manufacture and testing of aircraft and electronic equipment; EDWARDS AIR FORCE BASE is just NNE. The city, which grew rapidly through the 1970s and 1980s, is the seat of Antelope Valley College (1929). In late March, the valley's blooming poppies draw visitors. **2.** town, pop. 6661, Worcester Co., C Massachusetts, 10 mi/16 km SE of Fitchburg, on the Nashua R. Atlantic Union College (1882) is located at the village of South Lancaster. The First Church of Christ (1816–17), designed by Charles Bulfinch, is well known. Lancaster, industrial in the 19th century, is now primarily residential. **3.** town, pop. 32,181, Erie Co., W New York, 10 mi/16 km E of Buffalo. It is a primarily residential suburb on Cayuga Creek and Routes 20 and 90. **4.** city, pop. 34,507, seat of Fairfield Co., SC Ohio, 25 mi/40 km SE of Columbus, on the Hocking R. It is primarily a trade center for the rich livestock raising and dairying region that surrounds it. Glassware, fiberglass, batteries, paper, and automobile parts are manufactured. The city was founded c.1800. The home of William Tecumseh Sherman, who was born here (1820), is maintained as a museum. **5.** city, pop. 55,551, seat of Lancaster Co., SE Pennsylvania, 60 mi/97 km W of Philadelphia. Situated in the heart of the fertile Pennsylvania Dutch farming region, it has a highly diversified economy. The area's Amish and Mennonite residents, who follow centuries-old traditions, have inspired a large tourism industry. A number of farmers' markets, old homesteads, and restored villages, as well as malls filled with "factory outlets," draw visitors. The area's largest crop is tobacco; industrial products include pharmaceuticals, electrical equipment, farm machinery, candy, and other foods. Settled in 1721, Lancaster served as the nation's capital for one day (Sept. 27, 1777) when the Continental Congress held a session here after fleeing Philadelphia. From 1799 to 1812 it was the state capital. Lancaster is home to Franklin and Marshall College (1787) and Lancaster Bible College (1933).

Local landmarks include the Old City Hall (1795), Hans Herr House (1719), and Wheatland, the home of President James Buchanan. **6.** city, pop. 8914, seat of Lancaster Co., N South Carolina, 21 mi/32 km SE of Rock Hill and 7 mi/11 km S of the North Carolina border. Founded before 1800 by settlers from Lancaster, Pennsylvania, it was identified in the early 19th century with the Waxhaw Revival, part of a national religious movement. It has a textile-based economy (Springs Industries is a major factor), also producing cottonseed oil, fertilizer, and lumber. The WAXHAW settlement, Andrew Jackson's birthplace, is NNW, along the state line. **7.** city, pop. 22,117, Dallas Co., NE Texas, 10 mi/16 km S of downtown Dallas, on Interstates 20 and 35 E. One of the older communities in the area (settled 1846), it had a Civil War gun factory. It is now a commercial, warehousing, and light industrial center. Cedar Valley College (1974) is here.

Lancaster County 952 sq mi/2466 sq km, pop. 422,822, in SE Pennsylvania, bordered by the Susquehanna R. (W) and Maryland (S). Its seat is LANCASTER. The county is the heart of Pennsylvania Dutch country, with its traditional Amish and Mennonite communities, which attract legions of tourists. It is also one of the state's richest farming and livestock raising areas, producing a variety of crops, including tobacco and wheat.

L'Ancienne-Lorette city, pop. 15,242, QUÉBEC Urban Community, S Québec, 6 mi/10 km W of downtown Québec City, on the R. Lorette. The Québec airport adjoins (W) this residential suburb. LORETTEVILLE is 5 mi/8 km N.

Land Between the Lakes in Trigg and Lyon counties, SW Kentucky, and Stewart Co., NW Tennessee. Managed by the Tennessee Valley Authority as an educational and recreational park, the wooded peninsula (36 mi/58 km N–S and 7 mi/11 km wide) lies between L. Barkley on the Cumberland R. (E) and Kentucky L. on the Tennessee R. (W). It embraces waterfowl and wildlife management areas, 200 mi/320 km of trails, and a pre–Civil War living history farm. The region is rich in iron ore, and by the 1830s, Kentucky was a major pig-iron producer; furnaces are preserved at Model, Tennessee. At the SE corner of the park is FORT DONELSON.

Lander city, pop. 7023, seat of Fremont Co., WC Wyoming, on the Popo Agie R., just E of the WIND RIVER RANGE and 120 mi/190 km W of Casper. Camp Augur, a military post, was established here in 1869, and the SOUTH PASS gold rush brought brief prosperity. Lander subsequently became a ranching, farming, and mining trade center. Today it also has a large state mental institution, outdoor recreation and environmental concerns, the state winter fair, and government offices.

landfill any bulk material used to fill in low land, extend a waterfront, etc. In modern use it is often equated with **sanitary landfill,** garbage and trash buried with layers of soil as a means of dealing with a sanitation problem. In this book it also refers to soil, rock, dredged material, and the like moved to another location during the development of urban areas or deepening of harbors or channels—as in the leveling of hills and shifting of their constituent materials to extend the land area of San Francisco or Boston.

land-grant designating colleges and universities established following the 1862 Morrill Act, named for Vermont Congressman Justin S. Morrill (1810–98). The act provided Federal land on which states could create institutions dedicated to teaching agriculture, engineering, and home economics, in addition to standard academic subjects. Later enactments provided money for research facilities and extension programs, as well as for the schools' general funds. Most US state universities began as land-grant institutions.

Landover unincorporated community, pop. 5052, Prince George's Co., C Maryland, 8 mi/13 km NE of Washington, D.C. Largely residential, it also has shopping plazas and the Capital Centre (built 1973; seats 18,000), home to the Washington Bullets (basketball) and Caps (hockey) and a venue for various other events. **Landover Hills** (pop. 2074) is a separate but adjacent residential town.

Lane County 4620 sq mi/11,966 sq km, pop. 228,483, in W Oregon, extending from the Pacific coast, which forms its W border, through the Siuslaw National Forest, across the Willamette River Valley, and E to the Willamette National Forest. EUGENE, its seat, and SPRINGFIELD lie at its heart, in an area abundant in fruits, vegetables, and lumber.

Lanesboro also, **Lanesborough** town, pop. 3032, Berkshire Co., NW Massachusetts, adjoining (N) Pittsfield. It is a mountainous and residential community in the Berkshire Hills. American humorist Henry Wheeler Shaw ("Josh Billings") was born here in 1818.

Langhorne borough, pop. 1361, Bucks Co., SE Pennsylvania, a suburb 20 mi/32 km NE of downtown Philadelphia. Sesame Place, a theme park based on the popular television series *Sesame Street,* is here. Langhorne is the seat of Philadelphia College of Bible (1913). The borough of **Langhorne Manor,** pop. 807, lies just S.

Langley **1.** city (pop. 19,765) and district municipality (pop. 66,040), Greater Vancouver Regional District, SW British Columbia, between the Fraser R. and Washington border, a suburb 21 mi/34 km ESE of Vancouver. The Hudson's Bay Company's Fort Langley (1827) served briefly (1858) as the capital of the colony of British Columbia; partially restored, it is now a national historical park. Fruit and vegetable growing, dairying, and varied manufacturing and warehousing are important in the area; both city and district municipality are growing rapidly. **2.** town, pop. 526, Mayes Co., NE Oklahoma, on the L. o' the Cherokees (the Neosho R.), 50 mi/80 km NE of Tulsa. It is noted as the site of fiddling exhibitions and country music festivals. **3.** locality in Fairfax Co., NE Virginia, just inside the BELTWAY and along the Potomac R., 8 mi/13 km NW of Washington, D.C. It is home to the Central Intelligence Agency, which shares a large government reservation with the Federal Highway Administration. MCLEAN is just SW.

Langley, Mount peak (14,028 ft/4276 m) of the SIERRA NEVADA, 4 mi/6 km SSE of Mt. WHITNEY, on the E border of Sequoia National Park, in EC California.

Langley Field see under HAMPTON, Virginia.

Langley Park unincorporated community, pop. 17,474, Prince George's and Montgomery counties, C Maryland, 8 mi/13 km NNE of Washington, D.C. It is a largely residential suburb just W of COLLEGE PARK.

Langston town, pop. 1471, Logan Co., NC Oklahoma, 36 mi/58 km NNE of Oklahoma City, near the Cimarron R. Founded in 1890 as an all-black town, as was the later BOLEY, it is the seat of Oklahoma's first black agricultural and mechanical college, Langston University (1897).

Langtry hamlet in Val Verde Co., SW Texas, on the Rio Grande, 14 mi/23 km NW of where the PECOS R. joins it, and

50 mi/80 km NW of Del Rio. The original site was established (1881) when the Galveston, Harrisburg, and San Antonio Railway was being built. There Judge Roy Bean (1825?–1903) dispensed the "law west of the Pecos" from his frontier saloon/billiard hall/courtroom. The settlement was called Vinegaroon, after a species of whip scorpion, until the judge renamed it for British actress Lillie Langtry, the "Jersey Lily." Today it is a tourist attraction.

Lanham unincorporated village in Prince George's Co., C Maryland, 10 mi/16 km NE of Washington, D.C. It is a residential and commercial suburb on the Capital BELTWAY, with a major suburban Amtrak station. With neighboring (NE) Seabrook, it has a pop. of 16,792.

Lansdale borough, pop. 16,362, Montgomery Co., SE Pennsylvania, 21 mi/34 km NNE of Philadelphia. Largely residential, it also has several light industries producing electronic systems, clothing, metal products, tiles, and glue.

Lansdowne **1.** unincorporated suburb, Baltimore Co., C Maryland, 5 mi/8 km WSW of downtown Baltimore. Including the Baltimore Highlands district (E), it has a pop. of 15,509. **2.** borough, pop. 11,712, Delaware Co., SE Pennsylvania, a residential suburb 7 mi/11 km SE of Philadelphia. It produces such goods as metal products, paper, and abrasives.

L'Anse aux Meadows National Historic Park in NW Newfoundland, at the N tip of the GREAT NORTHERN PENINSULA, on the Strait of BELLE ISLE, 16 mi/26 km NNE of SAINT ANTHONY. Here, discovered in 1960, are remains of the only proven Viking settlement in North America, believed to have been colonized by Leif Ericsson around A.D. 1000, in a period when Norse explorers were probing S from Greenland. It is thought possible that this is the VINLAND of Norse literature. The locality has been part of the FRENCH SHORE (*anse* is French for "cove"), and is now a fishing settlement.

Lansing **1.** village, pop. 28,086, Cook Co., NE Illinois, on the Little Calumet R. and the Indiana border, 12 mi/19 km W of Gary and 20 mi/32 km S of Chicago. Founded in 1864, it is a mainly residential community almost surrounded by industrial cities. **2.** city, pop. 127,321, state capital, Ingham and Eaton counties, SC Michigan, at the confluence of the Grand and Red Cedar rivers, 80 mi/130 km NW of Detroit. Settled c.1840 by families from Lansing, New York, it consisted of a sawmill and log house when the Michigan legislature compromised on the undeveloped site as the new state capital to be moved from Detroit (1847). Rapid development, assured by the railroad's arrival in 1871, brought manufacturing plants, schools, hotels, and two newspapers. Lansing soon became a center for the construction of carriages, wagons, and wheels. Ransom E. Olds built two factories here c.1900 making Reos and Oldsmobiles. Today Lansing remains the headquarters of the Oldsmobile division of General Motors. It also has many associated industries: engines, trucks, and parts, as well as other manufactures. The economy also benefits significantly from state government agencies. Lansing is the site of various institutions, including a symphony, Potter Park and Zoo, the Fenner Arboretum, and various museums. It is the seat of Michigan State University (1855), Lansing Community College (1957), and the Michigan School for the Blind (1879).

La Palma city, pop. 15,392, Orange Co., SW California, 17 mi/27 km SE of downtown Los Angeles, and E of Coyote Creek. Originally called Dairyland, it was established by dairy farmers during the 1960s in an attempt to prevent urban development, but changed its name in 1965 and became primarily residential.

La Panza Mountains one of the COAST RANGES, trending NW–SE for c.30 mi/50 km in SW California, E of San Luis Obispo. It rises to 4062 ft/1238 m at Machesna Mt., within a 20,000-ac/8100-ha wilderness area of the same name. The range itself is within Los Padres National Forest.

Lapeer city, pop. 7759, seat of Lapeer Co., SE Michigan, on the South Branch of the Flint R., 20 mi/32 km E of Flint. It is a resort in a lake-dotted region also known for its orchards and its blueberry and mushroom farms. Lapeer manufactures foundry products, furniture, and aircraft parts. Just W is a state home and school for the mentally ill.

La Perla waterfront shantytown in Old SAN JUAN, Puerto Rico, just E of EL MORRO. A hillside squatter settlement, it was made famous by the anthropologist Oscar Lewis's study *La Vida* (1965), and remains the focus of much visitor attention.

La Place also, **Laplace** unincorporated community, pop. 24,194, St. John the Baptist Parish, SE Louisiana, on the E (N) bank of the Mississippi R., 25 mi/40 km WNW of New Orleans. In a longtime sugar cane and truck farming area, it experienced a 50% rise in population in the 1980s.

La Plata city, pop. 1401, Macon Co., NE Missouri, 13 mi/21 km S of Kirksville. Laid out in 1855 at the junction of the Wabash and Santa Fe railroads and now an Amtrak stop, it is also a trade center for grain, dairy, and poultry producers.

La Plata Peak see under SAWATCH RANGE, Colorado.

La Pocatière city, pop. 4648, Kamouraska census division, S Québec, 65 mi/105 km NE of Québec City, on the St. Lawrence R. Home to a pioneering (1859) agriculture school and a noted ethnology museum, it is best known for its Bombardier (transportation equipment) plant.

La Porte **1.** city, pop. 21,507, seat of La Porte Co., NW Indiana, 33 mi/53 km E of Gary. It was founded by French pioneers in 1830. The city has diversified manufactures, including boilers, radiators, steel castings, rubber goods, baby carriages, farm implements, clothing, and wine. In the vicinity of several lakes, it is also a popular year-round resort, with Soldiers Memorial Park and Ski Valley offering various recreational activities. The Kingsbury State Fish and Wildlife Area is 8 mi/13 km SE. **2.** city, pop. 27,910, Harris Co., SE Texas, on Galveston Bay, near the mouth of the Houston Ship Channel and 20 mi/32 km ESE of downtown Houston. It has insecticide and petrochemical plants and is a deepwater port, but is also residential and a beach resort center. The Houston Yacht Club is here.

La Prairie also, **Laprairie** city, pop. 14,938, Laprairie Co., S Québec, on the S bank of the St. Lawrence R. (here widened into the **Bassin de Laprairie**), 8 mi/13 km SSE of downtown Montréal. Granted as a SEIGNEURIE to Jesuits in 1647, it developed slowly; in 1691 it repelled an attack by New England forces. In 1836 the first railway in Canada ran from here to SAINT-JEAN-SUR-RICHELIEU (SE). Primarily a residential suburb today, La Prairie has some diversified industry and summer resort trade.

La Puente city, pop. 36,955, Los Angeles Co., SW California, in the Puente Hills, 18 mi/29 km E of downtown Los Angeles, of which it is a commuter suburb.

La Quinta city, pop. 11,215, Riverside Co., S California, in the Coachella Valley, 16 mi/26 km SE of Palm Springs. On the E side of the Santa Rosa Mts., it is a former stagecoach stop and ranching community, now a growing, fashionable resort noted for its tennis.

Laramie city, pop. 26,687, seat of Albany Co., SE Wyoming, on the Laramie R., 40 mi/64 km NW of Cheyenne. It is the headquarters of the surrounding Medicine Bow National Forest. The first Europeans to inhabit the area were fur trappers who arrived early in the 19th century. Laramie was settled in 1868, with the arrival of the Union Pacific Railroad. Also on the old Cherokee Trail, Overland Trail, Pony Express route, and Oregon Trail, it was a center for westward-bound travelers. Now the city is a resort as well as a trade and distribution center for the surrounding cattle and sheep ranching and mining region. It processes gold, silver, coal, and petroleum. Laramie also has railroad shops, processes forest products, and manufactures cement, brick, and tile. It is the seat of the University of Wyoming (1886).

Laramie Mountains also, **Laramie Range** part of the S Rocky Mts., an extension of Colorado's FRONT RANGE, trending N from Rocky Mountain National Park into SE Wyoming, then curving NW to just S of Casper. The **Laramie R.** rises near its S end, separating it from the MEDICINE BOW Mts. (W), flows N along it out of Colorado, and cuts E through it to the North Platte R. **Laramie Peak** (10,272 ft/3131 m), 60 mi/100 km SE of Casper, is the highest point in the 140 mi/230 km–long range.

Larchmont village, pop. 6181, in Mamaroneck town, Westchester Co., SE New York, 20 mi/32 km NE of New York City, on Long Island Sound. It is an affluent suburb with many large homes and private clubs. The Larchmont Yacht Club, founded in 1880 by Andrew Carnegie, J. P. Morgan, and William K. Vanderbilt, holds an annual regatta.

Larch River French, **Rivière aux Mélèzes** see under R. KOKSOAK, Québec.

Laredo city, pop. 122,899, seat of Webb Co., S Texas, on the Rio Grande opposite the much larger Nuevo Laredo (Tamaulipas), Mexico, 140 mi/225 km WSW of Corpus Christi. Founded in 1755 as a ferry crossing on a Spanish land grant, it has a history of conflict, from Indian and border battles to fights among adventurers bound for California goldfields. Seven flags have flown over it. After the 1835–36 Texas Revolution, it hovered between American and Mexican control until 1847. Railroads in the 1880s brought the city into commercial contact with the rest of Texas, opening Mexican markets to Americans. It is today a major inland port, and the finance and trade center for a rich irrigated farming (especially onions) and ranching area. It is an important port of entry, with travelers flowing in both directions. The MAQUILADORA system, in which US goods are assembled in Mexican border plants, is important to Laredo's economy, which also relies on natural gas, oil, fertilizer, feed, citrus, and vegetable production. Manufactures include electronic components, bricks and cement, furniture, machine tools, tile, and glass and leather products. The city is home to Laredo Junior College (1946) and Laredo State University (1969).

Lares unincorporated community (ZONA URBANA), pop. 5627, Lares Municipio (pop. 29,015), W Puerto Rico, 17 mi/27 km ENE of Mayagüez. This 19th-century coffee growing center at the W end of the Cordillera Central was the scene, on Sept. 23, 1868, of the beginning of the nationalist uprising called the *Grito de Lares* (the "Shout of Lares"), a touchstone for supporters of Puerto Rican independence. It is today also a summer resort.

La Réunion see under REUNION TOWER, Dallas, Texas.

Largo 1. city, pop. 65,674, Pinellas Co., WC Florida, on the Pinellas Peninsula, adjacent (SW) to Clearwater. In a popular beachfront tourist area, it has many recreational facilities, and holds an annual Renaissance Festival. A citrus producing center since the 1880s, it is increasingly a retirement and resort community, with some business offices. **2.** unincorporated suburb, pop. 9475, Prince George's Co., C Maryland, 12 mi/19 km E of Washington, D.C., just outside the BELTWAY. Prince George's Community College (1958) is here, as are large shopping centers and much parkland. Landover is just N.

Larimer residential neighborhood in Pittsburgh, Pennsylvania, between HIGHLAND PARK and LINCOLN, 6 mi/10 km NE of the GOLDEN TRIANGLE. This largely black working-class community also contains an Italian enclave.

Larimer Street commercial thoroughfare in Lower Downtown DENVER, Colorado. In 1858, Denver consisted of one block on CHERRY CREEK, now the site of **Larimer Square,** a restored shopping and restaurant zone. From here the street runs NE for some 20 blocks. A longtime "Wild West" scene, complete with cowboys and saloons, it was in the early 20th century the city's "Broadway" (not to be confused with the thoroughfare of that name, which crosses it). For decades before 1980s refurbishing, it was a rundown area with pawnshops and saloons, romanticized by Jack Kerouac and other writers.

Larkspur city, pop. 11,070, Marin Co., NC California, 12 mi/19 km N of San Francisco, of which it is an affluent suburb, and just NE of Mt. Tamalpais. Corte Madera adjoins (SE).

Larned city, pop. 4490, seat of Pawnee Co., SC Kansas, on the Arkansas R. where Pawnee Creek joins it (from the W). Fort Larned was established here (1859) on the SANTA FE TRAIL, figured in Indian wars, and was deactivated in 1878; its stone buildings are now a National Historic Site. The Santa Fe Railroad later came through the city, which is an agricultural trade center.

La Salle 1. city, pop. 9717, La Salle Co., NC Illinois, on the Illinois R., 13 mi/21 km W of Ottawa. Part of a three-city area that includes Peru and Oglesby, it manufactures chemicals, electrical equipment, motors, and clocks. There are also zinc and steel works here. First settled c.1830, La Salle grew with the opening of the Illinois and Michigan Canal, which was followed by the arrival of the Illinois Central and Rock Island railroads in the 1850s. The city was a coal mining center until World War II. Matthiesen and Starved Rock state parks are to the SE. **2.** also, **LaSalle** city, pop. 73,804, MONTRÉAL URBAN COMMUNITY, S Québec, on the S shore of the I. de Montréal, 7 mi/11 km SSW of downtown Montréal. Settled as part of LACHINE, it was in 1912 separately incorporated, and is today a primarily residential suburb, with diversified manufactures including chemicals and pharmaceuticals, heating and cooling equipment, food products, and beverages.

La Salle County 1139 sq mi/2950 sq km, pop. 106, 913, in NC Illinois. The Illinois R. flows E–W through the county, and is joined by the Fox R., from the N, at OTTAWA, the seat. Except for Streator (S) and Mendota (NW), all urban areas, including Peru, La Salle, Ottawa, and Marseilles, are along the Illinois. The Vermilion R. flows into the Illinois from the

SE. The county is agricultural, and has manufactures based to some degree on its coal, limestone, silica, and other minerals. The La Salle nuclear plant (1982) is 12 mi/19 km SE of Ottawa, near La Salle L.

La Sal Mountains N–S trending range, 20 mi/32 km long, E of the Colorado R. and SE of MOAB, near the Colorado border in SE Utah. In a unit of the Manti–La Sal National Forest, it is the second-highest range in Utah, rising to 12,721 ft/3877 m at Mt. Peale. The La Sals, on the Colorado Plateau, contain gold and copper deposits; many trails through them were created by early miners.

La Sarre see under L. ABITIBI, Québec.

Las Colinas business complex: see under IRVING, Texas.

Las Cruces city, pop. 62,126, seat of Dona Ana Co., S New Mexico, on the Rio Grande, 42 mi/68 km NNW of El Paso, Texas. Founded in 1848 and named for the crosses used to mark graves of a group of ambushed early settlers, it is the economic and cultural center of S New Mexico. Tourism is important; the city is surrounded by GHOST TOWNS, old forts, extinct volcanoes, and Indian communities. The JORNADA DEL MUERTO lies N, WHITE SANDS NE. Historic MESILLA is just SW. New Mexico State University (1888) is now central to the city's economy. Pecans, chilies, cotton, and other crops are grown in the vicinity, and the city has a growing manufacturing sector.

Lassen Peak also, **Mount Lassen** southernmost volcano (10,457 ft/3187 m) of the CASCADE RANGE, 50 mi/80 km ESE of Redding, in N California. Named for Peter Lassen, a Danish pioneer, it is surrounded by Lassen Volcanic National Park and Lassen National Forest. One of few historically active volcanoes in the coterminous US, it erupted intermittently in 1914–21 after 200 years of quietude. Today, steam is ejected and hot springs and mud pots are visible. Rising out of the crater left by the collapse of an older volcano, Lassen exhibits a variety of volcanic types. The area was home to four native groups, the Atsugewi, Maidu, Yana, and Yahi, and to Ishi, the "last wild Indian," who emerged from the mountain's foothills in 1911 (see ISHI WILDERNESS).

Lassen Volcanic National Park 106,372 ac/43,081 ha, within **Lassen National Forest** (1.1 million ac/450,000 ha), in N California, 40 mi/64 km ENE of Red Bluff. Countless effects of volcanic activity can be seen in the park, which encloses LASSEN PEAK and the Cinder Cone (6907 ft/2105 m), a mound of lava surrounded by multicolored cinders; both were declared national monuments in 1907. Many dangerous thermal areas exist, where only a thin crust lies over steam chambers below. Especially well known are the Sulphur Works, in the SW corner, and Bumpass Hell, named for an 1860s guide. In the NW corner are the pinkish lava plugs of Chaos Crags, where a volcano once collapsed. Manzanita and Butte lakes, Eagle Peak (9222 ft/2811 m), and the Lassen Volcanic Wilderness are in the park, which is also traversed by the PACIFIC CREST TRAIL.

Last Chance Gulch see under HELENA, Montana.

Last Mountain elevation (2275 ft/694 m) in S Saskatchewan, 50 mi/81 km N of Regina. Just E is Last Mt. Lake, a nearly 58 mi/93 km–long, narrow body of water that flows into the Qu'Appelle R. It is the site of the first bird sanctuary in North America (1887), home especially to ducks, geese, and swans.

Las Vegas **1.** city, pop. 258,295, seat of CLARK Co., S Nevada, 225 mi/362 km NE of Los Angeles, California, and 17 mi/27 km W of L. MEAD (the COLORADO R.). Its metropolitan area, coextensive with Clark Co., has a pop. of 741,459; SUNRISE MANOR, NORTH LAS VEGAS, SPRING VALLEY, and PARADISE are among its residential suburbs. The fastest-growing large US city, Las Vegas doubled in pop. in 1970–90. In a N SONORAN DESERT valley lived in for over 4000 years, most recently by the Paiute, the site was seen by Spanish travelers in the 1770s; its springs made it a stop on the Old Spanish Trail between Santa Fe, New Mexico, and S California. But its harsh climate frustrated early-19th-century Mormon settlement attempts, and at the end of the 19th century it was home chiefly to ranchers. In 1905, connections with the Union Pacific Railroad opened, and a land boom ensued. Growth was slow until the 1930s, when the construction of nearby HOOVER DAM and Nevada's legalization of gambling and easing of residency requirements for divorce and marriage began to attract visitors and in-migrants; the city's pop. was still only 8500 in 1940, however. In World War II expansion of its airport into the Las Vegas Aerial Gunnery Range (see NELLIS AIR FORCE BASE), and operation of a large magnesium plant at HENDERSON (just SE) accelerated development. By the late 1940s the city was drawing water from L. Mead, and beginning its expansion into the gambling, entertainment, and convention mecca it is today. It is famous for its STRIP, which extends SW from Downtown, along and near which are some of the world's largest, gaudiest, and best-known hotels and casinos. The city draws over 20 million visitors a year, chiefly from California, but many, via McCarran International Airport (S), from all over the US and beyond. Its winters are mild, but summers are torrid; its consumption of electricity and water, much going to air conditioning, is legend. The area's best-known institution, the University of Nevada at Las Vegas, is in PARADISE, just outside city limits. **2.** city, pop. 14,753, seat of San Miguel Co., NC New Mexico, 40 mi/64 km ESE of Santa Fe, in the E foothills of the Sangre de Cristo Mts., along the Gallinas R. Site of a military post and a trading center on the SANTA FE TRAIL, it became a stop on the Santa Fe Railroad in 1879. Surrounded by irrigated farms, it is today a shipping center for grain, wool, livestock, lumber, and dairy producers, and a base for area resort trade. New Mexico Highlands University (1893) is here.

Latham unincorporated village, pop. 10,131, in Colonie township, Albany Co., N New York, 7 mi/11 km N of downtown Albany. It is a commercial center, with many small businesses, shopping areas, and light industry, and a bedroom community for Albany.

Lathrup Village city, pop. 4329, Oakland Co., SE Michigan. It is a suburb of Detroit, 13 mi/21 km NW of the downtown area, and just W of Berkley.

Latin Quarter see under Rue SAINT-DENIS, Montréal, Québec.

Latrobe borough, pop. 9265, Westmoreland Co., SW Pennsylvania, on the Loyalhanna Creek in the foothills of the Allegheny Mts., 33 mi/53 km ESE of Pittsburgh. Situated amid rich farmlands, it has light manufacturing, making tools, plastics, and ceramics, and is the home of Rolling Rock beer. In 1946 Latrobe was recognized by the National Football League as the birthplace of professional football, in honor of a game played here Sept. 3, 1885. It is the seat of St. Vincent College (1846).

La Tuque city, pop. 10,003, Champlain Co., S Québec, 75 mi/120 km N of Trois-Rivières, on the R. SAINT-MAURICE, in a vast forest region. Founded around a pulp mill in the 1900s, it derives its name from a nearby mountain shaped like a trapper's hat called a *tuque*. The economy centers around forestry and wood-based industries. Hunting, fishing, camping, canoeing, and skiing are also important.

Lauderdale city, pop. 2700, Ramsey Co., SE Minnesota, a Twin Cities suburb immediately NE of Minneapolis and NW of St. Paul.

Lauderdale Lakes city, pop. 27,341, Broward Co., SE Florida, just NW of Fort Lauderdale. A suburb of the larger city, it boomed in the 1970s with planned communities for retirees.

Lauderhill city, pop. 49,708, Broward Co., SE Florida, 4 mi/6 km WNW of Fort Lauderdale. Like neighboring (E) Lauderdale Lakes, it is a residential suburb that grew most quickly in the 1970s.

Laughlin unincorporated community, pop. 4791, Clark Co., extreme S Nevada, on the Colorado R. across (W) from BULLHEAD CITY, Arizona. Established in the early 1970s by Don Laughlin, who had bought a bait shop here, it became by the mid 1980s one of the largest US gambling meccas. Today it has a riverfront strip of huge casinos, and more hotel rooms than inhabitants.

Laurel **1.** city, pop. 19,438, Prince George's Co., C Maryland, on the Patuxent R., 20 mi/32 km SW of Baltimore and 18 mi/29 km NE of Washington, D.C. It was settled in 1669, and had some industry, but grew as a residential center only after World War II. Laurel Race Course (horses; 1911) is here. FORT MEADE is just E. The area includes the unincorporated communities of **North Laurel** (pop. 15,008), **South Laurel** (pop. 18,591), and **West Laurel** (pop. 4151). **2.** city, pop. 18,827, co-seat (with Ellisville) of Jones Co., SE Mississippi, on Tallahala Creek, 76 mi/122 km SE of Jackson, in the PINEY WOODS. Founded in 1882 as a railroad lumber camp, and named for abundant native shrubs, it became the world's largest shipping center for yellow pine lumber by 1920. After the forests were cut over, by the end of the 1920s, the city faced economic collapse until William Mason arrived and developed Masonite, a hardboard made from sawmill waste. The Masonite Corporation remains a major industrial concern, and there are poultry and meatpacking plants. Oil companies arrived here after the 1943 discovery of a field under Jones and adjacent counties. During the Civil War, a group led by Newt Knight declared Jones Co. (the "Free State of Jones") loyal to the Union, and fought their own war against the Confederate Army. **3.** unincorporated community, pop. 13,011, Henrico Co., EC Virginia, 6 mi/10 km NW of Richmond. It is a largely residential suburb.

Laurel Canyon in the Hollywood Hills (SANTA MONICA Mts.), 8 mi/13 km NW of downtown LOS ANGELES, California, connecting Studio City (N) with West Hollywood (S). Noted for its rustic scenery and secluded homes, it has been a hideaway for 19th-century outlaws and 20th-century bohemians.

Laurel Hill **1.** ridge in the Allegheny Mts., in SW Pennsylvania. It extends 55 mi/89 km NE, from Fayette Co. SE of Uniontown to an area slightly W of Nanty Glo, and has an elevation of 2400–2900 ft/732–885 m. The Youghiogheny R. cuts through the S tip of the ridge S of Confluence, and the Conemaugh R. cuts through W of Johnstown. Known for its bituminous coal deposits, the ridge also has limestone, sandstone, and clay. **2.** also, **Laurel Ridge** see under TYGART R., West Virginia.

Laurelhurst residential neighborhood on the line between Northeast and Southeast PORTLAND, Oregon, 2 mi/3 km E of Downtown. A middle-class development designed by the Olmsted firm around a park of the same name, Laurelhurst has Eclectic-style homes built in 1910–29.

Laurence Harbor see under OLD BRIDGE, New Jersey.

Laurens city, pop. 9694, seat of Laurens Co., NW South Carolina, on the Little R., 33 mi/53 km SE of Greenville. Its varied manufactures include carpets, roller bearings, ceramics, glass, and textiles. It was settled before the Revolution by people of Scotch-Irish ancestry.

Laurentian Mountains French, **Laurentides** also, **Laurentian Hills** low range, actually the dissected S edge of the CANADIAN SHIELD (Laurentian Plateau), along the N of the St. Lawrence R. valley in S Québec. Extending from the Gatineau R. (W), above Ottawa, to L. Saint-Jean and the Saguenay R. (E), it averages c.800 ft/240 m, but rises to 3150 ft/960 m at Mont TREMBLANT. The Lièvre, Rouge, Nord, Saint-Maurice, and Montmorency are among the rivers flowing from the Laurentians into either the Ottawa or the St. Lawrence. Late-19th-century efforts, led by the churchman Antoine Labelle, to settle the Laurentians with farmers met limited success, but in the 20th century the area NW of Montréal became one of the world's leading ski resort centers. The Laurentians are now popular also for their lakes and rivers and their fall color. The Laurentian Autoroute (Autoroute des Laurentides) connects them with Montréal.

Laurentian Shield or **Plateau** also, **Laurentia** see CANADIAN SHIELD.

Laurinburg city, pop. 11,643, seat of Scotland Co., S North Carolina, 38 mi/61 km SW of Fayetteville. It is noted as the home of St. Andrew's Presbyterian College and the Laurinburg Industrial Institute, and has varied light manufactures.

Lauzon see under LÉVIS-LAUZON, Québec.

Lava Beds National Monument 46,600-ac/18,860-ha area of the MODOC PLATEAU, near the Oregon border, just S of Tule L., in NE California. Molten lava once flowed over the region, leaving formations including cinder cones, chimneys, fumaroles, basaltic cliffs, lava tubes, and caves; volcanic activity continues. The Skull Ice Cave, noted for its pronghorn and bighorn sheep skulls, and a number of other caves contain ice. There are numerous carved and painted petroglyphs in the area. The formations were used defensively by the Modoc during the Modoc War of 1872–73.

Laval city, pop. 314,398, occupying the 21 mi/34 km–long Île Jésus (95 sq mi/245 sq km), just NW of the I. de MONTRÉAL, S Québec. The R. des Mille Îles lies N, the R. des Prairies S, and the L. des Deux Montagnes (at the confluence of the Ottawa and St. Lawrence rivers) W. The island was granted in the 17th century to Jesuits, and settled slowly by farmers. The 20th century brought expansion pressure from Montréal, but by the 1940s the Île Jesus was still a predominantly agricultural community with a pop. just over 20,000. Growth accelerated rapidly thereafter. In 1965 six cities and eight towns on the island were merged to form the city of Laval, now Québec's second most populous. A residential suburb, it also has widely diversified manufacturing; research facilities; institutions including the Collège Montmorency and the St.-Vincent-de-Paul penitentiary; and a large amount of protected market gardening land.

La Vérendrye Wildlife Reserve French, **Réserve Faunique La Vérendrye** 5257 sq mi/13,615 sq km, in SW Québec, 93 mi/

150 km NNW of Ottawa. Created in 1939, on the headwaters of the Ottawa R., it has canoeing and camping facilities.

La Vergne city, pop. 7499, Rutherford Co., NC Tennessee, 15 mi/24 km SE of Nashville, on Hurricane Creek, near J. Percy Priest L. (the Stones R.). It is a residential suburb with toolmaking and other light industries.

La Verne city, pop. 30,897, Los Angeles Co., SW California, 28 mi/45 km ENE of Los Angeles and just W of Claremont. A citrus packing center, it was settled during the 1890s land boom, with the 1891 arrival of the Santa Fe Railroad. The University of La Verne (1891) is here; the Los Angeles Co. Fairgrounds are immediately S.

La Villita tourist attraction in downtown San Antonio, Texas, on the site of the earliest (1718) Spanish settlement, a squatter colony ("the little village") that grew near the ALAMO. The district, run-down and bohemian in the early 20th century, was restored in 1939 by the WPA, at the time the adjacent PASEO DEL RIO was being constructed, and now approximates its early-19th-century appearance.

La Vista city, pop. 9840, Sarpy Co., EC Nebraska, 8 mi/13 km SW of Omaha, primarily a bedroom community.

Lawndale 1. city, pop. 27,331, Los Angeles Co., SW California, 10 mi/16 km SSW of Los Angeles, and immediately S of Hawthorne. An area of cemeteries, nurseries, and small farms before World War II, it is now a residential suburb. **2.** residential neighborhood on the far West Side of Chicago, Illinois, between Douglas Park and suburban Cicero. Formerly an industrial area populated by working-class Bohemians, it is today largely a Hispanic and black community. Factory closings in recent decades have left it economically distressed.

Lawrence 1. city, pop. 26,763, Marion Co., C Indiana, on Fall Creek, 8 mi/13 km NE of downtown Indianapolis, on Route 465 (the beltway), and within the larger city's borders. Built on land purchased from the Miami Indians in 1783, it is basically a residential community. Electronic products are manufactured, and mushrooms are grown. The Army's Fort Benjamin Harrison is along the NE. **2.** city, pop. 65,608, seat of Douglas Co., NE Kansas, on the Kansas R., halfway between Kansas City (E) and Topeka (W). It was founded (1854) by the abolitionist New England Emigrant Aid Company and rapidly became the hub of Kansas Free State activities and a stop on the UNDERGROUND RAILROAD. In 1856 it was attacked by proslavery forces (in retaliation John Brown carried out the POTTAWATOMI attack), and in 1863 it was sacked and burned by William Quantrill's Confederate raiders. The rebuilt city grew as an educational and commercial center. Today it processes numerous foodstuffs and has light manufactures. The University of Kansas (1866) is here, as well as Haskell Indian Junior College (1884). Clinton L. is W. **3.** city, pop. 70,207, Essex Co., NE Massachusetts, 27 mi/43 km NW of Boston, on Route 495 and Interstate 93 near the New Hampshire border. The Merrimack R. flows through the city; Bodwell's Falls provided power for textile manufacturing, begun in 1845; by the late 19th century, Lawrence was one of the largest textile centers in the world, partly through the organizational efforts of Abbott Lawrence, for whom the city was named. A strike of 1912, which attracted international attention, and was eventually settled by a one-cent-an-hour pay increase, is commemorated in an annual Bread and Roses Festival. Contemporary industries turn out clothing, leather, paper, chemicals, machinery, plastics, rubber, fabricated metal products, and electronics. The city covers only 7 sq mi/18 sq km, and has always been densely populated with millworkers from all over the world; industrial decline by late 20th century had led to conversion of many mills to commercial and residential use. **4.** township, pop. 25,787, Mercer Co., WC New Jersey, adjacent (NE) to Trenton. It is an affluent residential suburb with numerous corporate offices and research centers, and home to Rider College (1865). Lawrenceville, (pop. 6446), settled in 1692, is its trading center and the seat of the Lawrenceville School (1810). **5.** see under FIVE TOWNS, Long Island, New York.

Lawrenceburg city, pop. 10,412, seat of Lawrence Co., S Tennessee, on Shoal Creek, 70 mi/113 km SSW of Nashville. Founded in 1815 in an agricultural area (poultry, dairy products, cotton), it has manufactured clothing, bicycles, and concrete products, and has a steel plant.

Lawrence National Laboratories 1. Lawrence Berkeley Laboratory see under BERKELEY, California. **2. Lawrence Livermore Laboratory** see under LIVERMORE, California.

Lawrenceville 1. city, pop. 16,848, seat of Gwinnett Co., N Georgia, 26 mi/42 km NE of Atlanta. Local industries manufacture aluminum products, boats, and clothing. The city doubled in population in the 1980s. **2.** see under LAWRENCE, New Jersey. **3.** section of Pittsburgh, Pennsylvania, on the Allegheny R., W of BLOOMFIELD and 3 mi/5 km NE of the GOLDEN TRIANGLE. A Delaware Indian village until the 18th century, it was laid out in 1814. The area is divided between industrial and commercial flats characterized by now-closed mills and blast furnaces, and residential higher ground. Composer Stephen Foster was born here (1826). **4.** town, pop. 1486, seat of Brunswick Co., S Virginia, 40 mi/64 km SW of Petersburg, and 15 mi/24 km N of the North Carolina line. A trade center for the area's tobacco, grain, and cotton, it is home to St. Paul's College (1888).

Lawton city, pop. 80,561, seat of Comanche Co., SW Oklahoma, on Cache Creek, 75 mi/120 km SW of Oklahoma City. It dates from 1901, when a land auction opened the area to white settlement. FORT SILL, just N, is an important factor in its economy. The city is a trade and processing center in an agricultural (mainly cotton and wheat), mining (limestone, hematite, and granite) and oilfield region. Its manufactures include cement, clothing, and mobile homes. Cameron University (1909) is here.

LAX see LOS ANGELES INTERNATIONAL AIRPORT, California.

Layton city, pop. 41,784, Davis Co., N Utah, 10 mi/16 km S of Ogden, in the irrigated agricultural Weber Basin. Its industries have processed flour, lumber, sugar beets, potatoes, and animal feed. The city experienced rapid growth during the 1970s and 1980s, and now has many office complexes, light manufacturing plants, and new housing units.

LBJ Ranch see under PEDERNALES R., Texas.

Lead see under HOMESTAKE MINE, South Dakota.

Leadville city, pop. 2629, seat of Lake Co., Colorado, in the Sawatch Range of the Rocky Mts., near the headwaters of the Arkansas R., 75 mi/121 km SW of Denver. At 10,190 ft/3108 m above sea level, it is reputed to be the highest incorporated place in the US. Founded in 1860, Leadville was one of the principal centers of 19th-century American mining, and has produced vast quantities of gold, silver, lead, zinc, copper, bismuth, manganese, and molybdenum. Among the sites that attract contemporary tourists are the

Matchless Mine, Tabor Opera House (1879), and Healy House (1878). The Timberline campus of Colorado Mountain College (1965) is here.

League City city, pop. 30,159, Galveston and Harris counties, SE Texas, just SE of Houston's CLEAR LAKE section, and 22 mi/35 km NW of Galveston, on Clear Creek. A residential suburb in an oil producing and truck farming area, it doubled in population in the 1980s.

League of the Five (or Six) Nations see under IROQUOIS CONFEDERACY.

Lealman unincorporated community, pop. 21,748, Pinellas Co., WC Florida, a residential suburb immediately N of St. Petersburg.

Leamington town, pop. 14,182, Essex Co., extreme S Ontario, on L. Erie, 30 mi/48 km SE of Windsor. Canning of tomatoes and other foods is central to the economy of what has also been a tobacco producing center. POINT PELÉE NATIONAL PARK is just SE.

Leaside see under EAST YORK, Ontario.

Leavenworth city, pop. 38,495, seat of Leavenworth Co., NE Kansas, on the Missouri R. (the Missouri border), 20 mi/32 km NW of Kansas City. The oldest city in Kansas, it was founded (1854) by proslavery Missourians. Situated S of the army post Fort Leavenworth (1827), it was a supply point for westward-bound pioneers. Prisons at or near the fort (a Federal maximum-security penitentiary and a military prison) and S of it in Lansing (the state penitentiary) are important to the city's economy. A rail hub, the city processes and ships grain and livestock and manufactures iron, steel, farm machinery, and wood products. There is also a commercial shipyard. St. Mary College (1923) is here. Fort Leavenworth (6000 ac/2430 ha) is also home to the Army Command and General Staff School.

Leawood city, pop. 19,693, Johnson Co., NE Kansas, 14 mi/23 km S of downtown Kansas City, on the Missouri border. Primarily a bedroom community, it also processes dairy products and vegetables from nearby farms.

Lebanon **1.** town, pop. 6041, New London Co., EC Connecticut, 5 mi/8 km S of Willimantic. In a farming region, it has a number of 18th-century buildings, including the Gov. Trumbull House (1740). The Trumbull family, based here, were important actors in the Revolutionary period. **2.** city, pop. 3688, St. Clair Co., SW Illinois, 20 mi/32 km E of East St. Louis. McKendree College, founded here in 1828, is the oldest college in Illinois. Scott Air Force Base is 5 mi/8 km to the SW. **3.** city, pop. 12,059, seat of Boone Co., C Indiana, 25 mi/40 km NW of Indianapolis. A trade center for dairy products and livestock from surrounding farms, it is also a manufacturing city, making tools, auto parts, and farm equipment. **4.** city, pop. 9983, seat of Laclede Co., SC Missouri, on the Ozark Plateau, 47 mi/75 km NE of Springfield. Situated on a Civil War road between St. Louis and Springfield, it was held alternately by Union and Confederate forces. Popular with outdoor vacationers, it is also a manufacturing center that produces aluminum boats, compressors, tools and dies, clothing, and cheese and other food products. In a lake-filled region popular with tourists, it is near a unit of Mark Twain National Forest (E). **5.** city, pop. 12,183, Grafton Co., WC New Hampshire. On the Mascoma R. E of its Connecticut R. junction, Lebanon is 4 mi/6 km S of Hanover. A lake resort and winter sports area, it is just S of the Appalachian Trail. Industries include printing, poultry raising, dairy production, and the manufacture of sporting goods and clothing, ball bearings, electrical equipment, and wood, leather, and metal products. **6.** city, pop. 10,453, seat of Warren Co., SW Ohio, 28 mi/45 km NE of Cincinnati, a trading center set in an agricultural area. Fabricated steel is manufactured here. A number of early-19th-century structures are preserved in Lebanon, lending the city a Colonial air rare in the Midwest. A harness racing track is situated here. A Shaker village was nearby, and a Shaker museum is now housed at the Golden Lamb Inn (1803). **7.** city, pop. 10,950, Linn Co., NW Oregon, on the Santiam R., 16 mi/26 km E of Corvallis. A center for the region's fruit and berry farms, it also has sawmills. The annual Lebanon Strawberry Festival is famous for featuring the world's largest strawberry shortcake. **8.** city, pop. 24,800, seat of Lebanon Co., SE Pennsylvania, 23 mi/37 km NE of Harrisburg. Laid out by Moravian settlers in 1756, it developed as a pre-Revolutionary iron center due to its proximity to the rich Cornwall ore mines, and grew with the completion of the Union Canal and Lebanon Valley Railroad. Lebanon is in the fertile Pennsylvania Dutch farming region and is known, in addition to manufactures such as boilers, iron and steel products, and textiles, for its Lebanon bologna, a Pennsylvania Dutch sausage. Notable nearby sites include the Edward Martin (Indiantown Gap) Military Reservation, Cornwall Iron Furnace (in use 1742–1883), and Union Canal Tunnel (opened 1827). **9.** city, pop. 15,208, seat of Wilson Co., NC Tennessee, 30 mi/48 km E of Nashville. Established in 1802 on a stagecoach route, it developed as a trade center for livestock and dairy and agricultural products, particularly tobacco. Manufactures have included bedding, leather and rubber goods, and auto parts. The city is home to Cumberland University (1842) and to a restaurant chain.

Lebanon County 363 sq mi/940 sq km, pop. 113,744, in SE Pennsylvania, in the Piedmont Plateau. Its seat and main city is LEBANON. The county contains the **Lebanon Valley,** part of the Pennsylvania Dutch region of the state and a rich farming area. It was settled by German immigrants around 1710, and their influence can still be felt in the regional culture.

Lecompton city, pop. 619, Douglas Co., NE Kansas, between Lawrence (8 mi/13 km to the SE) and Topeka (20 mi/32 km to the W). It was the capital of the Kansas Territory (1855–58). The proslavery Lecompton Constitution, written here (1857), was defeated by the electorate (1858). Now primarily a residential suburb, it has some agriculture-related commerce.

Le Conte, Mount see under GATLINBURG, Tennessee.

Leduc city, pop. 13,970, C Alberta, 19 mi/30 km S of Edmonton. Although there is some light industry here connected with oil production, Leduc has recently become a largely residential community. Founded as a telegraph station and stop on the Calgary and Edmonton Railway, it became an agricultural center named for a pioneer priest. In 1947, the Leduc No. 1 well was sunk and an enormous oilfield discovered, launching an economic boom for the city, for Edmonton, and for the province. Edmonton International Airport lies just N.

Ledyard town, pop. 14,913, New London Co., SE Connecticut, on the Thames R., 7 mi/11 km NE of New London. Largely residential, it is in a farming area. The site of Fort Decatur, built during the War of 1812, is marked. Ledyard is home to the first legal gambling casino in New England, opened Feb. 1992 on the Mashantucket Pequot reservation, in the NE corner. The casino, known as Foxwoods, promises to transform the life of Ledyard and nearby rural communities.

Lee town, pop. 5849, Berkshire Co., SW Massachusetts, 9 mi/14 km S of Pittsfield, on the Housatonic R. It is primarily a summer resort community in the Berkshire Hills, with paper mills and marble quarries.

Leech Lake see under CHIPPEWA NATIONAL FOREST, Minnesota.

Leeds city, pop. 9946, Jefferson, St. Clair, and Shelby counties, NC Alabama, 14 mi/23 km E of Birmingham. Lumber, coal, steel wire, and textiles are produced here.

Leesburg **1.** city, pop. 14,903, Lake Co., C Florida, between L. Harris (S) and L. Griffin (N), 35 mi/56 m NW of Orlando. Founded in 1856, it has long been a shipping center for local citrus fruit, watermelons, and truck, with facilities for processing and packing. Cattle raising is important, as is the manufacture of fertilizer, furniture, concrete, mobile homes, and boxes. In a hilly, lake-studded area, the city is also a popular resort. It is the site of Lake-Sumter Community College (1962). **2.** town, pop. 16,202, seat of Loudoun Co., N Virginia, 33 mi/53 km NW of Washington, D.C. Incorporated in 1758, it was the refuge of government leaders when the British occupied Washington in 1812. In 1861, the battle of BALLS BLUFF was fought just NE. Local industries include meatpacking and wheat processing, and the town is growing in popularity as a residential suburb.

Lee's Summit also, **Lees Summit** city, pop. 46,418, Jackson Co., NW Missouri, 18 mi/29 km SE of downtown Kansas City. A trucking center near major interstate highways, it manufactures and ships machinery, tools, plastics, electronic equipment, and meat and dairy products. The Richards-Gebaur Air Force Base (SW) is also important to its economy.

Leesville city, pop. 7638, seat of Vernon Parish, W Louisiana, 50 mi/80 km WSW of Alexandria. It has an agricultural and forest-based economy. FORT POLK is just SE, and units of Kisatchie National Forest are nearby.

Le Gardeur city, pop. 13,814, L'Assomption census division, S Québec, 18 mi/29 km NNE of Montréal, across the R. de l'Assomption (NW) from REPENTIGNY. It is a fast-growing, largely residential suburb.

Lehi city, pop. 8475, Utah Co., NC Utah, on Utah L., 15 mi/24 km NW of Provo. Settled in 1848, it was named for a *Book of Mormon* prophet. The city is a trade center for an irrigated agricultural area producing sugar beets, fruit, and alfalfa. It processes sugar, flour, feed, and farm produce, and manufactures clay products.

Lehigh County 348 sq mi/901 sq km, pop. 291,130, in EC Pennsylvania, bordered (NE) by the Lehigh R. Its seat is ALLENTOWN. Lehigh County is part of a highly industrial region that developed in the 19th century due to its proximity to vast anthracite deposits. The decline of coal mining has brought hard economic times to the area, which continues to endure high unemployment. Moreover, Allentown's manufacturing base in textiles, transportation, heavy machinery, and other industries has deteriorated.

Lehigh River 103 mi/166 km long, in E Pennsylvania. It rises near Pocono Springs, in extreme S Wayne Co., and flows SW, forming Luzerne County's SE border. It turns S, cutting through Appalachian ridges, past Jim Thorpe, Lehighton, and Palmerton, S of which it forms the **Lehigh Gap** in Blue Mt. The river then flows SE to Northampton and Allentown, turns sharply E past Bethlehem, and winds NE to Easton, where it joins the Delaware R. The Lehigh was the route by which coal from the ANTHRACITE BELT reached 19th-century industrial centers, beginning in about 1818 and aided by the opening (1829) of the Lehigh Canal. Its great coal period is past, but the Lehigh Valley remains industrial.

Lehman Caves see under SNAKE RANGE, Nevada.

Leimert Park largely residential section of SW LOS ANGELES, California, 6 mi/10 km SW of Downtown, E of Baldwin Hills and W of Exposition Park. A middle-class black community, it is a noted arts center.

Leisure City unincorporated community, pop. 19,379, Dade Co., SE Florida, 3 mi/5 km NE of Homestead. Just W of Homestead Air Force Base, it houses military and civilian families associated with the base and retirees. Damage from Hurricane Andrew (Aug. 1992) and the base's scheduled closing posed serious problems for Leisure City as the 1990s progressed.

Le Mars city, pop. 8454, seat of Plymouth Co., NW Iowa, on the Floyd R., 25 mi/40 km NE of Sioux City. Founded in the 1870s along the new railway to Sioux City, it has been a trading and shipping center for a dairy and farming region ever since. There is also meatpacking and dairy production. Westmar College (1900) is here.

Lemay unincorporated community, pop. 18,005, St. Louis Co., E Missouri, a largely residential suburb of St. Louis, 12 mi/19 km SW of Downtown and just outside the city's beltway (I-270). MEHLVILLE is immediately NE.

Lemhi Pass see under BEAVERHEAD NATIONAL FOREST, Montana.

Lemmon, Mount see under SANTA CATALINA Mts., Arizona.

Lemon Grove city, pop. 23,984, San Diego Co., SW California, a suburb 7 mi/11 km E of downtown San Diego. Largely agricultural well into the 20th century, it is now residential and has various light industries.

Lemont village, pop. 7348, Cook Co., NE Illinois, a suburb on the S side of the Des Plaines R., 23 mi/37 km SW of Chicago's Loop. Across the river from the Argonne National Laboratory, it is an affluent community noted for the huge Cog Hill golf course and as a Lithuanian center.

Lemoore city, pop. 13,622, Kings Co., SC California, 30 mi/48 km S of Fresno, in the San Joaquin Valley. Dairy goods, fruit, poultry, and truck crops are produced in the area. The Lemoore Naval Air Station lies W, across the Kings R.

Lenexa city, pop. 34,034, Johnson Co., NE Kansas, 13 mi/21 km SW of downtown Kansas City. Founded in the 1860s, it is now a residential and commercial suburb.

L'Enfant Plaza governmental and corporate office area of SW Washington, D.C., just S of the MALL, developed in the 1960s and 1970s on the site of part of the old SOUTHWEST. It is named for Pierre L'Enfant (1754–1825), whose monumental 1791 plan for Washington was only partly carried out but was resurrected at the end of the 19th century, since which time much of it has been realized.

Lennox unincorporated community, pop. 22,757, Los Angeles Co., SW California, 8 mi/13 km SW of downtown Los Angeles. It is bordered N and E by Inglewood, S by Hawthorne, and W by the Los Angeles International Airport. Many residents are employed at the airport or in nearby aircraft plants. Originally a farming and dairying community, Lennox is now residential and industrial.

Lennoxville city, pop. 4046, S Québec, 4 mi/6 km SSE of Sherbrooke, in the EASTERN TOWNSHIPS, on the Saint Francis

R. at its junction with the Massawippi R. Established in 1794 by LOYALISTS, it produces maple syrup, and has a Federal experimental station. Bishop's University (1843) and Bishop's College School (1836) make Lennoxville a center of English-model education.

Lenoir city, pop. 14,192, seat of Caldwell Co., W North Carolina, in the foothills of the Blue Ridge Mts., 16 mi/26 km NW of Hickory, on Lower Creek. In an agricultural and lumber producing region, it manufactures furniture, textiles, and hosiery, and is a summer resort.

Lenoir City city, pop. 6147, Loudon Co., E Tennessee, 23 mi/37 km SW of Knoxville. It was founded in 1840 at the junction of the Little Tennessee and Tennessee rivers, and has manufactured textiles, railway cars, and other goods. The city is now 1 mi/2 km downstream on the Tennessee from the Fort Loudoun Dam, one of the TENNESSEE VALLEY AUTHORITY's major units, completed in 1943 and 4190 ft/1278 m long. The dam impounds Fort Loudoun Lake, which backs up 55 mi/89 km to Knoxville. A lock here allows ships to pass up to Knoxville. In 1979 the Tellico Dam was completed at the LITTLE TENNESSEE's mouth, enhancing Lenoir City's position at the hub of a power generating complex.

Lenox town, pop. 5069, Berkshire Co., W Massachusetts, 7 mi/11 km S of Pittsfield. Lenox is the center of a popular summer resort area. Among its major attractions is the Berkshire Music Festival, held each summer at TANGLEWOOD. The summer home of writer Edith Wharton is open to the public, and the Berkshire Opera Company also performs in Lenox. The beauty of the area has long attracted visitors, among them Nathaniel Hawthorne, who wrote *The House of the Seven Gables* and *Tanglewood Tales* here. Large homes line the streets of the town; many large estates are now schools or other institutions.

Leominster city, pop. 38,145, Worcester Co., NC Massachusetts, on the Nashua R. immediately SE of Fitchburg and 38 mi/61 km NW of Boston. Originally part of Lancaster, it was settled in the 1650s, and became a separate town in 1740. An early (1770s) center for the making of combs from animal horn, Leominster now has varied light manufactures. Johnny Appleseed (John Chapman) was born here in 1774; Johnny Appleseed Day is celebrated in June.

Leon Valley city, pop. 9581, Bexar Co., SC Texas, on Route 410, 9 mi/14 km NW of downtown San Antonio and completely surrounded by the city's NW side. It is largely residential.

Lepreau, Point locality on the Bay of Fundy, 23 mi/37 km SW of Saint John, New Brunswick, site of a nuclear power plant constructed in the 1980s.

Les Cheneaux Islands popularly, from a corrupted pronunciation, **the Snows** group of about 35 islands in Mackinac Co., Michigan, along the SE shore of the Upper Peninsula, across L. Huron, 11 mi/18 km N of Bois Blanc I. Oriented NW–SE, and mostly long and thin, they are named for the channels (*cheneaux*) between them. Marquette I., the largest (6 mi/10 km long), was the site of one of the French missionary's establishments. The islands are now home to fishermen and vacationers.

Lesser Slave Lake in C Alberta, 130 mi/210 km NNW of Edmonton. Covering 451 sq mi/1168 sq km, it is 60 mi/100 km E–W and 3–12 mi/5–20 km wide. Fed by several small rivers, it empties E via the marshy Lesser Slave R. to the ATHABASCA R. It was named for the Athabaskan Slavey people. *Lesser* was added to distinguish it from GREAT SLAVE L. in the Northwest Territories. The town of SLAVE LAKE, on the SE shore, occupies a longtime gathering place for hunting and war parties; there are still several Indian reserves along the S shore. The Klondike gold rush brought 1890s settlement; the railway arrived in 1915. Oil is important in the area, as are commercial fishing and lumbering.

Lester B. Pearson International Airport also **Pearson** or **Toronto International Airport** in NE MISSISSAUGA (and partly in W Etobicoke), Ontario, 18 mi/29 km NW of downtown Toronto. Canada's busiest airport is flanked by industrial areas of MALTON (part of Mississauga) and Etobicoke.

Le Sueur city, pop. 3714, Le Sueur Co., SC Minnesota, on the Minnesota R., 20 mi/32 km NNE of Mankato. In a farming region, it is the headquarters of the Green Giant canned and frozen foods company. It was the home of physician William W. Mayo, founder of the Mayo Clinic, whose house is preserved. His son, William J. Mayo, later clinic director, was born here in 1861.

Lethbridge city, pop. 60,974, S Alberta, on the Oldman R., 100 mi/160 km SE of Calgary. It is a trade and service center for surrounding ranches and irrigated farmland. In the vicinity are coal mines and oil and sulfur wells. The local industrial park manufactures cellular telephones, farm equipment, camping trailers, and foodstuffs, among other products. In addition, Lethbridge has flour mills, beet sugar refineries, breweries, canneries, meatpacking plants, and Canadian Pacific Railway maintenance facilities. FORT WHOOP-UP, an illegal whiskey-trading post, was suppressed in 1874, and the town emerged as a mining settlement known as Coalbanks. Renamed (1885) Lethbridge, it grew with the CPR link to the mines and the railroad's operations here, early-20th-century irrigation projects, and exploitation of regional oil and natural gas deposits. The University of Lethbridge (1967) and Lethbridge Community College (1957) are here, as are a Department of Agriculture research station, the Animal Diseases Research Institute, and the provincial headquarters for the Royal Canadian Mounted Police. Nikka Yuko Centennial Garden (1967) is among the largest Japanese gardens in North America. Indian Battle Park has a reconstruction of Ft. Whoop-up.

levee a raised earthen embankment along the course of a river. In the lower Mississippi R. valley, levees are ubiquitous, protecting both farmland and cities (like New Orleans) from flooding. A levee may be natural, the result of accumulation of silt along a river that eventually leads to both banks and riverbed rising above the level of the surrounding floodplain. It may also be wholly or partly artificial. In places the levee is accompanied by *batture,* land on the riverside built up by further siltation, and in places occupied by shantytowns.

Levee, the notorious 19th-century red-light district on the NEAR SOUTH SIDE of Chicago, Illinois, along State St. and nearby streets.

Levelland city, pop. 13,986, seat of Hockley Co., W Texas, on the LLANO ESTACADO, 30 mi/48 km W of Lubbock. Cereal magnate C.W. Post laid it out in 1912 on former ranch land. Livestock and fruit are produced locally, and the city has oil and gas refineries and makes fertilizer, oilfield and irrigation equipment, and plastics. South Plains College (1957) is here.

Levels, the see under MIDDLETOWN, Delaware.

Leverett town, pop. 1785, Franklin Co., NC Massachusetts, adjoining (N) Amherst. It is rural and residential.

Levisa Fork see under BIG SANDY R., Virginia and Kentucky.

Lévis-Lauzon city, pop. 39,452, Lévis Co., S Québec, on the St. Lawrence R., directly opposite (SE of) Québec City. Lévis and industrial Lauzon developed separately and were merged in 1989. British general James Wolfe used the cliffs here for gun emplacements during the siege of Québec in 1759. Fort Number 1 at Pointe-Lévis, built to protect against US attack during the American Civil War, is a national historic site. The local economy is based on shipbuilding and ship repair, important since the early 19th century; the largest drydock in Canada is here. The Caisse Populaire (cooperative bank) is another major employer. There are also diverse manufactures. The Collège de Lévis (1853) is here.

Levittown **1.** see under WILLINGBORO, New Jersey. **2.** unincorporated village, pop. 53,286, in Hempstead town, Nassau Co., SE New York, 10 mi/16 km E of New York City. It was built by William J. Levitt in 1947-51 as a residential community for World War II veterans. A total of 17,447 homes were constructed; the community also includes schools and extensive recreational facilities. **3.** unincorporated suburb, pop. 55,362, Bucks Co., SE Pennsylvania, 19 mi/31 km NE of Philadelphia and 9 mi/14 km SW of Trenton, New Jersey. It was built as a residential community (1951–55) by Levitt and Sons, following the same mass-production formula the company had used in Long Island, New York. The first house was occupied in June 1952. Levittown comprises more than 40 coterminous communities in three townships and one borough, each with its own schools, shopping, and recreational facilities. It also has steel and chemical complexes. **4.** unincorporated community (*comunidad*), pop. 30,807, Toa Baja Municipio, NE Puerto Rico, on the Atlantic Ocean, 5 mi/8 km W of San Juan, and immediately W of Cataño. A planned 1960s development, it is home to many Puerto Ricans formerly resident on the US mainland.

Lewes city, pop. 2295, Sussex Co., SE Delaware, on Delaware Bay just W of Cape HENLOPEN. Settled by the Dutch (1631) as Swanendael or Zwaanendael, the first European settlement in Delaware, it became Lewes after 1682. It has long been Delaware's maritime center, its Pilot Town serving as home to specialists who guided ships up the Delaware R. In the 20th century it became a sport fishing center, but fish factories and mosquitoes prevented its becoming a popular tourist destination until the 1960s. Lewes has Coast Guard and marine studies facilities, and is the terminus for a ferry from Cape May, New Jersey.

Lewis and Clark National Forest 1.84 million ac/747,000 ha (2881 sq mi/7461 sq km), in WC Montana, on the Continental Divide. Its two major divisions are W (Rocky Mt.) and SE (Jefferson) of GREAT FALLS, its headquarters. The Little Belt and several other mountain ranges are here, and parts of the Bob Marshall and other major WILDERNESS AREAS.

Lewis and Clark National Historic Trail system of trails, marked highways, river routes, and selected sites, first designated in 1978, marking the route of the 1803–06 expedition led by Meriwether Lewis and William Clark, at the instigation of President Thomas Jefferson, to explore the LOUISIANA PURCHASE and routes from it to the Pacific coast. It embraces some 4500 mi/7200 km and 500 sites. The expedition's route followed the Missouri R. NW from St. Louis, Missouri, to the THREE FORKS, in W Montana; took the Jefferson R. SW to its head; crossed the Continental Divide at Lemhi Pass; crossed the Bitterroot Mts. at Lolo Pass; descended the Clearwater R. to the Snake (originally Lewis) R.; followed the Snake to the Columbia R.; and descended the Columbia to the Pacific, ending at Oregon's Fort Clatsop. On their return E, the explorers also examined the Marias and Yellowstone rivers, in Montana.

Lewisburg **1.** borough, pop. 5785, seat of Union Co., EC Pennsylvania, on the West Branch of the Susquehanna R., 20 mi/32 km SSE of Williamsport. It is the seat of Bucknell University (1846) and has a federal penitentiary. Furniture and electronic products are among the goods produced here, and there are dairy farms and limestone quarries nearby. **2.** city, pop. 9879, seat of Marshall Co., SC Tennessee, on Big Rock Creek, 49 mi/79 km S of Nashville. Settled in the 1830s, it is a trade center for a rich Nashville Basin agricultural area, and has had various light manufactures, including stoves. The city is the world headquarters of the Tennessee Walking Horse Breeders and Exhibitors Association. There is a Federal experimental dairy farm just to the S. **3.** city, pop. 3598, seat of Greenbrier Co., SE West Virginia, 7 mi/11 km W of White Sulphur Springs. The settlement developed around Camp Union, where Virginia militiamen met (1774) before the battle at POINT PLEASANT. On May 23, 1862, Union forces won a battle here. The city is now an agricultural center, and home to medical institutions including an osteopathic school.

Lewis Hills range, extending some 40 mi/64 km SSW–NNE, and rising to 2672 ft/815 m, the island's high point, in SW Newfoundland, WSW of Corner Brook. Running along the Gulf of St. Lawrence between Port au Port Bay (S) and the Bay of Islands (N), they are a W spur of the LONG RANGE Mts.

Lewisporte see under NOTRE DAME BAY, Newfoundland.

Lewis Smith Lake see under BLACK WARRIOR R., Alabama.

Lewiston **1.** city, pop. 28,082, seat of Nez Perce Co., NW Idaho, at the junction of the Snake and Clearwater rivers, adjacent to Clarkston, Washington (W). Named for explorer Meriwether Lewis, who camped here with the Lewis and Clark party in 1805 and 1806, it was the territorial capital in 1863–64. Originally a mid-19th-century gold mining community, it is now a bustling barge port, shipping wheat, paper, wood chips, and agricultural products from the area and neighboring states as far as the Pacific coast. Other industries include lumber, pulp, and paper production, food canning and freezing, and the manufacture of ammunition and concrete products. Lewis-Clark State College (1955) is here. The Nez Perce Indian Reservation is 20 mi/32 km E and the Nez Perce National Historical Park 5 mi/8 km NE. **2.** city, pop. 39,757, Androscoggin Co., SW Maine, on the Androscoggin R. opposite Auburn. In size, Lewiston is second in Maine only to Portland, 32 mi/52 km to the SW. Located at the Androscoggin's "Twenty-Mile" Falls, and a leading textile center since 1836, Lewiston also has footwear, electronic equipment, and metallurgical plants. Bates College (1855) and Memorial Armory (which has one of the state's largest auditoriums) are in the city. In the late 20th century Lewiston struggled with the decline of the textile industry. Its population is made up largely of descendants of French-Canadian millworkers. The painter Marsden Hartley (1877–1943), a native, wrote of his childhood in the city. **3.** town, pop. 15,453, Niagara Co., W New York, on the Niagara R. across from Queenston, Ontario, and just N of Niagara Falls. A hydroelectric reservoir and power station, NIAGARA UNIVERSITY, and the Tonawanda (Seneca) reservation are here.

Lewistown borough, pop. 9341, seat of Mifflin Co., C Pennsylvania, on the Juniata R., 45 mi/72 km WNW of Harrisburg. It was laid out (1790) on the site of a Shawnee Indian village. An Amtrak stop and trading hub in a farming region, it has diversified manufacturing, including the production of synthetic yarn, locomotive parts, clothing, and electronic equipment. Many Amish live in the area.

Lewisville city, pop. 46,521, Denton and Dallas counties, NE Texas, 21 mi/34 km NW of downtown Dallas, on Lewisville L. Settled in 1844, it became an agricultural trade center. Since 1960 it has doubled in population every decade, and is now a residential suburb with some manufactures, including electronics, boats, toys, and aluminum products. Adjacent (N) **Lewisville L.,** on the Elm Fork of the TRINITY R., covers 23,300 ac/9430 ha, and is an important area recreational asset.

Lexington **1.** city, pop. 225,366, coextensive with FAYETTE Co., C Kentucky, in the BLUEGRASS REGION, 24 mi/39 km SE of Frankfort. Founded in 1779, it was the first meeting place of the Kentucky legislature in 1792. It was soon called the "Athens of the West" because of its Transylvania College (1780; now Transylvania University), street lights, public library, theater, musical society, and other cultural assets. A horse racing and breeding center since the 1780s, it is headquarters for the American Thoroughbred Breeders Association, and such breeding centers as CALUMET FARM and Darby Dan Farm are world-famous. Keeneland Race Course, 6 mi/10 km W of the center, is a racing and horse sales mecca. Lexington is also an important market for beef, sheep, bluegrass seed, and looseleaf tobacco. It manufactures electrical and computer equipment, whiskey, and paper products. It is home to the University of Kentucky and Lexington Theological Seminary (both 1865) and two business colleges. Ashland, the home (1811–52) of Henry Clay, and the Mary Todd Lincoln House (1803) are here. The Lexington–Blue Grass Army Depot is E of the center, and the Federal government's main narcotics facility is here. **2.** town, pop. 28,974, a suburb 10 mi/16 km NW of Boston, in Middlesex Co., E Massachusetts. Lexington Green was the site of the first Revolutionary War battle, on April 19, 1775. The large historical district incorporates the Green, the Hancock-Clarke House (1698), where John Hancock and Samuel Adams stayed before the battle; Munroe Tavern (1695), which the British used as a hospital; and Buckman Tavern (1710), where the Minutemen met. Minute Man National Historic Park encompasses 4 mi/6 km of Battle Rd. (Route 2A), between Lexington and CONCORD, along with various sites in the latter town. Lexington is currently a center for publishing and electronic, optical, and scientific research, part of the ROUTE 128 area; it is also an affluent Boston suburb. **3.** city, pop. 4860, seat of Lafayette Co., WC Missouri, on the Missouri R., 35 mi/56 km ENE of Kansas City. Founded in the 1820s by Kentucky settlers, it grew as an important port and stop on what became the SANTA FE TRAIL. In Sept. 1861, Confederate forces under Sterling Price won a three-day battle here, attempting to break Union control of the river valley. The Wentworth Military Academy (1880) is here. The area produces coal and gravel. **4.** city, pop. 16,581, seat of Davidson Co., C North Carolina, 19 mi/31 km S of Winston-Salem. A market center for Piedmont dairy and crop farms, it also houses diverse industries, processing food and manufacturing textiles, clothing, hosiery, furniture, fences, electronic components, and mattresses. Davidson County Community College (1958) is here. **5.** independent city, pop. 6959, in but administratively separate from Rockbridge Co., WC Virginia, on the Maury R., at the S end of the Shenandoah Valley. A tourist center, it is also a market for the surrounding agricultural area. It is the seat of the Virginia Military Institute (1839). Washington and Lee University, also here, was founded as Augusta Academy in 1749, and went through several name changes; after Robert E. Lee served (1865–70) as president, it took its present name; Lee is buried on the campus. Stonewall Jackson lived in Lexington and is buried in the local cemetery. The city is also the birthplace (1793) of Sam Houston.

Lexington Market public market, in operation since the 1770s, at the E end of Lexington St., just NW of downtown BALTIMORE, Maryland. It is noted esp. for its Chesapeake Bay seafood. The University of Maryland at Baltimore and the Social Service Administration building are nearby.

Lexington Park unincorporated village, pop. 9943, St. Mary's Co., S Maryland, just W of the Patuxent Naval Air Test Center, near Chesapeake Bay. It was known as Jarboesville until 1950.

L. I. Long Island, New York, as seen in the common form of many addresses, especially in sections of Queens whose inhabitants continue to distinguish themselves from other New York City residents by designating themselves as residents of, for instance, "Maspeth, L. I." The practice is unknown in Brooklyn.

Liard River 570 mi/920 km long, in the SE Yukon Territory, N British Columbia, and SW Northwest Territories. It rises in the Yukon's PELLY Mts., and flows generally SE to Nelson Forks, British Columbia, where it is joined by the Fort Nelson R., from the E. The Liard then turns generally NNE into the Northwest Territories, passing Fort Liard, to Fort Simpson, where it joins the MACKENZIE R. The ALASKA HIGHWAY follows the Liard's course for over 100 mi/160 km in extreme N British Columbia. The Liard has carved out a gap through the Rocky Mts., near its headwaters, and has been both a 19th-century fur trade route and an approach to the KLONDIKE during the 1890s gold rush.

Libby city, pop. 2532, seat of Lincoln Co., NW Montana, in the Kootenai National Forest, on the Kootenai R., 60 mi/97 km WNW of Kalispell. Founded in the 1860s as a gold mining village, it saw the arrival of the Great Northern Railway in 1892. Today Libby is a trade center for lumber, silver, copper, and vermiculite mining, and agricultural products.

Libby Dam on the Kootenai R., in Lincoln Co., NW Montana, 13 mi/21 km E of Libby. Part of the Columbia River Basin development project, the concrete gravity-type dam was completed in 1973. It has a height of 443 ft/135 m, and forms the 90 mi/145 km–long L. KOOCANUSA. Libby Dam provides power to much of the Northwest, as well as local flood control and recreational opportunities.

Liberal city, pop. 16,573, seat of Seward Co., SW Kansas, on the Oklahoma border, 70 mi/112 km SW of Dodge City. It is a processing center for grain and livestock, and aircraft and metals are fabricated here. On the E edge of the Hugoton gas field, it also refines oil and natural gas. The city is the seat of Seward County Community College (1967). Visitors are drawn to Dorothy's House, a replica of the farmhouse in the 1939 film *The Wizard of Oz;* US Route 54 between Liberal and Wichita has been officially designated The Yellow Brick Road.

Liberty **1.** town, pop. 2051, seat of Union Co., E Indiana, 13 mi/21 km S of Richmond. Farm implements and paint are manufactured here. The surrounding area produces livestock, grain, and dairy items, and the town, settled in 1822, is a shipping point. **2.** city, pop. 20,459, seat of Clay Co., NW Missouri, 13 mi/21 km NNE of downtown Kansas City. In an agricultural area growing corn, wheat, and tobacco and raising livestock, it has grain elevators and is a commercial and railroad shipping center. In 1838–39 Mormon prophet Joseph Smith was imprisoned in its jail. In 1866 it was the site of a famous daylight bank robbery by the James gang; the bank is now a museum. The city is the seat of William Jewell College (1849).

Liberty Bowl see under MID-SOUTH FAIRGROUNDS, Memphis, Tennessee.

Liberty City predominantly black residential section of Miami, Florida, about 7 mi/11 km NW of Downtown. BROWNSVILLE lies W. Liberty Square, a segregated Federal housing project constructed along NW 14th Ave. in 1936–37, established several hundred families in the area, and the community gradually expanded, making it today the largest black neighborhood within the city.

Liberty Island historic island, 10 ac/4 ha, in Upper New York Bay, off the Jersey City, New Jersey waterfront. Having served various purposes earlier, the then Bedloe's Island became the site (1885) of the 151-ft/46-m Statue of Liberty,which was erected on a base provided by the 150-ft/46-m tall, star-shaped Fort Wood. A Federal property since about 1800, the island, renamed in 1956, is today a unit (along with ELLIS ISLAND) of the Statue of Liberty National Monument. It incorporates an immigration museum.

Liberty Place **1.** battle site in New Orleans, Louisiana, at the foot of CANAL St., near the Mississippi R. The name is given to the shifting ground of a bloody skirmish on Sept. 14, 1874, between supporters and agents of the Reconstruction government and a force of members and supporters of the White League, bent on restoring white Democratic power. The white supremacists took control of the city briefly. A monument to White League fighters stood in the area from 1891 until the city removed it in 1989. **2.** commercial high-rise development containing the tallest buildings in Center City, Philadelphia, Pennsylvania, on MARKET STREET, W of City Hall. The two towers, One and Two Liberty Place, completed in 1987 and 1989, and 960 ft/293 m and 845 ft/258 m high respectively, were the first to break the traditional rule that no building surpass City Hall (548 ft/167 m) in height.

Liberty State Park see under JERSEY CITY, New Jersey.

Libertyville village, pop. 19,174, Lake Co., NE Illinois, on the Des Plaines R., a suburb 36 mi/58 km NNW of Chicago. A residential community settled in the 1830s, it also manufactures mobile farm equipment.

Licking County 686 sq mi/1777 sq km, pop. 128,300, in C Ohio; it includes part of Buckeye L. Its seat is NEWARK, where there is diversified manufacturing. The county is primarily agricultural—chiefly grain, dairy, and livestock farming. There are sand and gravel pits. A number of mound builder sites are here.

Licking River 320 mi/515 km long, in E Kentucky. Rising in S Magoffin Co., it flows NW through Cave Run L. in the DANIEL BOONE NATIONAL FOREST, then past BLUE LICKS SPRING to the Ohio R. between COVINGTON and NEWPORT, opposite Cincinnati, Ohio. The **North Fork,** 80 mi/130 km long, rises in Fleming Co., at the Forest's N end, and flows generally WNW to join the main stream at Licking, 10 mi/16 km SE of Falmouth. The **South Fork** is formed in Bourbon Co. by the confluence of Stoner and Hinkston creeks, and flows generally N, past Cynthiana and Morgan, to join the main branch at Falmouth. The Licking was an important route for both Indians and early European settlers.

Lick Observatory see under Mt. HAMILTON, California.

Lighthouse Point city, pop. 10,378, Broward Co., SE Florida, adjacent (N) to Pompano Beach. On the Atlantic Intracoastal Waterway, just off the Atlantic coast, it is residential and has winter resort facilities.

light rail term applied in the 1970s to new types of urban rail systems. Originally it included only such technologies as MORGANTOWN, West Virginia's Personal Rapid Transit (PRT) system (1972), with single-car modular "trains." The term has come, however, to include various updates of city trolley systems and late-19th-century INTERURBAN lines.

Lihue unincorporated community, pop. 5536, seat of KAUAI Co., SE Kauai, Hawaii. Lying just N of deepwater Nawiliwili Harbor, it is the commercial and cultural center of the island. Sugar cane cultivation and processing are important. Kauai Community College (1926) is here.

Lilburn city, pop. 9301, Gwinnett Co., NC Georgia, 22 mi/35 km NE of downtown Atlanta. A residential suburb with shopping centers and industrial parks, it more than doubled in population in the 1980s.

Lily Dale resort village in Pomfret township, Chautauqua Co., extreme W New York, 8 mi/13 km S of L. Erie and 20 mi/32 km NNW of Jamestown. From the late 19th to the mid 20th century it was a spiritualist center. The Lily Dale Assembly, organized in 1879, was associated with American spiritualism's leading lights, Margaret Fox and her sisters Katherine and Leah.

Lilydale city, pop. 506, Dakota Co., SE Minnesota, on the Mississippi R., a suburb immediately S of St. Paul.

Lilypons see under SUGAR LOAF Mt., Maryland.

Lima **1.** town, pop. 4187, Livingston Co., WC New York, 18 mi/29 km S of Rochester. Largely rural, it has some light industry. It was the original seat of Genesee College, which became (1870) Syracuse University. **2.** city, pop. 45,549, seat of Allen Co., NW Ohio, on the Ottawa R. in a rich agricultural region, 64 mi/103 km N of Dayton. Formerly a major oil boom town (1885–1910), it remains an oil pipeline and refining center. Manufactured goods include cranes and power shovels, aircraft parts, automobile engines, tanks, machine tools, electric motors, neon signs, chemicals, and cigars. The processing and marketing of foodstuffs round out the economy. Local attractions include Fort Amanda State Park, the site of a fort built during the War of 1812. **3.** see under MIDDLETOWN, Pennsylvania.

Limberlost region: see under GENEVA, Indiana.

Limerick township, pop. 6691, Montgomery Co., SE Pennsylvania, site of a nuclear power plant on the E bank of the Schuylkill R., 7 mi/11 km SE of POTTSTOWN, in operation since 1985.

Lime Rock **1.** village in the town of SALISBURY, Litchfield

Co., extreme NW Connecticut. An ironmaking center during the Revolution, it is now home to the Lime Rock Raceway, a sports-car circuit. **2.** see under LINCOLN, Rhode Island.

Limestone town, pop. 9922, Aroostook Co., extreme NE Maine, on the New Brunswick border, 10 mi/16 km ENE of Caribou. In a potato growing area, the town is the site of Loring Air Force Base, which stimulated an economic boom after it was established in 1947. The base, due to close in 1994, has employed close to 10,000 workers.

Lincoln **1.** city, pop. 15,418, seat of Logan Co., C Illinois, 28 mi/45 km NE of Springfield. It was founded as Postville (1837). Abraham Lincoln practiced law here, and this is the only place named for him with his consent (1853). It is a trading center for an area rich in grain, poultry, and cattle. Manufactures include glassware, fixtures, toiletries, corrugated boxes, electrical equipment, and clothing. There are sand and gravel deposits in the vicinity. Lincoln College (1865) and Lincoln Christian College and Seminary (1944) are here. **2.** town, pop. 7666, Middlesex Co., NE Massachusetts, 13 mi/21 km NW of Boston. It is an affluent suburb of Boston, with some ROUTE 128 technological industry. Battle Rd. (Route 2A), along which the British marched on April 19, 1775, passes through Lincoln. **3.** city, pop. 191,972, state capital and seat of Lancaster Co. (pop. 213,641), SE Nebraska, on Salt Creek, 49 mi/79 km SW of Omaha. Founded by Methodist settlers in 1864 and originally called Lancaster, it became Nebraska's capital and was renamed three years later. It grew with the coming of the railroad (1870) and underwent economic and governmental reform during the 1880s. From this movement emerged William Jennings Bryan, who lived in Lincoln (1887–1916) and whose home is preserved. The city is now a governmental and educational center. It is the seat of the main campus of the University of Nebraska (1869), Nebraska Wesleyan University (1887), and Union College (1889). It is also a major processing and rail and trucking center for an area producing grain and livestock. Other key industries include the manufacture of pharmaceuticals and machinery. The city also serves as headquarters for over 30 insurance companies. Its capitol (1922–32), designed by Bertram Goodhue, is well known. The Salt Valley region is dotted with recreational lakes. **4.** town, pop. 17,149, Niagara Regional Municipality, S Ontario, on the Niagara Peninsula, 21 mi/32 km WNW of Niagara Falls. A 1970 amalgamation of Clinton, Beamsville, and Louth, it comprises a patchwork of communities, including Vineland and Jordan, and rural regions. An 18th-century agricultural settlement, the town has one of the region's oldest wineries as well as government research farms. Tourism and light industry are also important. **5.** residential section in the far NE corner of Pittsburgh, Pennsylvania, between LARIMER and PENN HILLS, 6 mi/10 km NE of the GOLDEN TRIANGLE. This hilly plateau of very low- density suburban-style homes, a middle-class black community, overlooks the Allegheny R. **6.** town, pop. 18,045, Providence Co., NE Rhode Island, 7 mi/11 km N of Providence, on the Blackstone R. It includes the villages of Lime Rock and Manville, as well as parts of Albion and Lonsdale. Lincoln Woods Reservation, a state park, is situated here. Manufactures include metals and machinery, and there are limestone quarries in the area.

Lincoln, Mount **1.** see under PARK RANGE, Colorado. **2.** see under FRANCONIA NOTCH, New Hampshire.

Lincoln Avenue major commercial thoroughfare, 11 mi/18 km long, running NW through the North Side of Chicago, Illinois, from the DEPAUL neighborhood to Lincolnwood and Skokie. Following an old Indian trail, it has been the center of the German community since the mid 19th century. Its renowned theaters have made the street a popular night spot, especially along its partially gentrified lower stretch.

Lincoln Boyhood National Memorial see under SPENCER Co., Indiana.

Lincoln Center for the Performing Arts cultural complex built 1959–72, its first buildings opened 1962, on the Upper West Side of Manhattan, New York City. Its principal elements include the Metropolitan Opera House, Avery Fisher (Philharmonic) Hall, New York State Theater, and the Juilliard School of Music.

Lincoln County 4832 sq mi/12,515 sq km, pop. 12,219, in SC New Mexico. Its seat is Carrizozo. A livestock grazing area irrigated by the Rio Hondo, it has coal mines and parts of Lincoln National Forest and the Sacramento Mts. In 1878 a rivalry between two local merchants exploded in the brief "Lincoln County War," in which combatants included Billy the Kid, who was eventually killed by county sheriff Pat Garrett.

Lincoln Highway designation (1913) for the first fully paved coast-to-coast US highway, between New York and San Francisco, by way of Philadelphia, Chicago, Omaha, and Salt Lake City. Extending 3300 mi/5300 km, it was completed by 1927. Also called the Official Transcontinental Route, it was later designated US 30 through much of its length (and has been replaced by I-80). From Salt Lake City across C Utah and C Nevada, it was designated US 50; it passes through Carson City and S of L. Tahoe, to Placerville and Sacramento, where it rejoins the I-80 route into San Francisco. The name "Lincoln Highway" still appears in various localities.

Lincoln Homestead State Park see under ABRAHAM LINCOLN BIRTHPLACE NATIONAL HISTORIC SITE, Kentucky.

Lincolnia unincorporated community, pop. 13,041, Fairfax Co., N Virginia, adjacent (W) to Alexandria. It is a residential suburb of Washington, D.C.

Lincoln Memorial at the W end of the MALL, in Washington, D.C. Completed in 1922, in a Greek temple plan by Henry Bacon, it contains a massive seated statue of Abraham Lincoln by Daniel Chester French, and is a popular site for tourists and as a backdrop for rallies.

Lincoln Mountain peak (4013 ft/1224 m) in the Green Mts., in WC Vermont, 15 mi/24 km NE of Middlebury, on the LONG TRAIL.

Lincoln National Forest 1.1 million ac/450,000 ha (1725 sq mi/4465 sq km), in three units in SC New Mexico, NE, E, and SE of Alamogordo. The MESCALERO APACHE INDIAN RESERVATION lies between the two northern units. The CAPITAN (N), SACRAMENTO (C), and GUADALUPE (S) mountains are all partly within the forest, which rises from low desert to over 11,500 ft/3530 m. The N slopes of the SIERRA BLANCA are here, in the N, near Ruidoso; in the C is the Cloudcroft ski and recreation area.

Lincoln Park **1.** see under CAPITOL HILL, Washington, D.C. **2.** municipal park and zoo on the North Side of Chicago, Illinois, along L. Michigan. Lincoln Park is also the name of the upscale residential neighborhood immediately W. **3.** city, pop. 41,832, Wayne Co., SE Michigan, on the

Ecorse R., 9 mi/14 km SW of Detroit. It is a commuter suburb of Detroit, with some small machine shops. On this site, then called Council Point, Indians held a conference (April 1763) at which the Ottawa chief Pontiac laid plans to take Detroit from the British, thus starting Pontiac's War. **4.** borough, pop. 10,978, Morris Co., N New Jersey, 7 mi/11 km W of Paterson, on the Pompton R. Once a popular summer resort, it is now essentially residential, with some light industry.

Lincoln Tunnel automobile tunnel under the Hudson R. between Weehawken, New Jersey, and Manhattan, New York City. With two tubes, opened in 1937 and 1945, it is 8215 ft/2506 m long.

Lincoln University locality in Upper Oxford township (pop. 1615), Chester Co., SE Pennsylvania, 6 mi/10 km N of the Maryland state line and 20 mi/32 km NW of Wilmington, Delaware. In a rural area, it is the seat of Lincoln University (1854).

Lincolnwood village, pop. 11,365, Cook Co., NE Illinois, adjoining (S) SKOKIE and (W) the ROGERS PARK section of Chicago, 3 mi/5 km W of L. Michigan. It is a residential suburb, known until 1935 as Tessville.

Lindbergh Field also, **San Diego International Airport** facility along the N side of San Diego Bay, only 2 mi/3 km from downtown San Diego, California. Claude Ryan established an airfield at adjacent (N) Dutch Flats in 1925. In 1927 the city voted to reclaim tidelands, and in Aug. 1928 opened an airport named for Charles Lindbergh, who in 1927 had flown one of Ryan's monoplanes across the Atlantic. San Diego's aircraft industry began just N of the airport, which today is one of the closest to Downtown in any American city.

Linden city, pop. 36,701, Union Co., NE New Jersey, adjoining (S) Elizabeth, and on the Rahway R. (S) and ARTHUR KILL (E). In an area once filled with linden trees and purchased from the Lenni Lenape (Delaware) in 1664, it was settled in the early 18th century, and was part of Elizabeth until 1861. Highly industrialized, it has oil refineries (including the huge Bayway facility) and manufactures trucks, chemicals, machine tools, paint and varnish, pharmaceuticals, and alcoholic beverages.

Lindenhurst **1.** village, pop. 8038, Lake Co., extreme N Illinois, 7 mi/11 km NW of Waukegan and 41 mi/68 km NNW of Chicago's LOOP. It is a residential and resort community in a lake-filled area just E of the Fox River's Chain-O-Lakes. **2.** village, pop. 26,879 in Babylon town, Suffolk Co., SE New York, on the South Shore of Long Island, on Great South Bay, 33 mi/53 km E of Manhattan. Among this industrial and residential community's manufactures are electrical equipment, aircraft parts, and paper products. Fishing and boating are also important to the economy.

Lindenmeier archaeological site N of Fort Collins, Larimer Co., NC Colorado. Spears and arrowheads some 10,000 years old, produced by the culture that takes its name from FOLSOM, New Mexico, were first discovered here in 1926.

Lindenwold borough, pop. 18,374, Camden Co., SW New Jersey, 12 mi/19 km SE of Camden. Settled in 1742, and once a health resort area, it is now residential and has meat packing plants and manufactures such goods as plastics and plumbing fixtures.

Lindgren Acres unincorporated residential community, pop. 22,290, Dade Co., SE Florida, 16 mi/26 km SW of Miami, on the edge of the metropolitan area.

Lindsay town, pop. 16,696, seat of Victoria Co., SE Ontario, on the Scugog R., 60 mi/96 km NE of Toronto. The town was laid out in 1825. In 1844 a lock was built on the Scugog, but it was the development of the TRENT CANAL in 1853, linking Sturgeon L. with L. Scugog, that brought real growth. Today the town is a gateway to the Kawartha Lakes recreational area, with lumbering, agriculture, and light industry also contributing to the economy.

Lindsborg city, pop. 3076, McPherson Co., C Kansas, on the Smoky Hill R., 19 mi/31 km SSW of Salina. Established by Swedes in 1868, it retains some of its founders' traditions. The city is a grain and livestock market. It is the seat of Bethany College (1881), site of an annual Messiah Festival. Nearby Coronado Heights (N) is a SMOKY HILLS butte reputed to have been one of Coronado's 1541 campsites in his search for QUIVIRA.

Line Islands also, **Equatorial Islands** NW–SE oriented group of islands, reefs, and ATOLLS in the C Pacific Ocean, some 1000 mi/1600 km S of Hawaii, and N and S of the Equator. Three of the group—JARVIS I., PALMYRA, and KINGMAN REEF—are US possessions. All other Line Is., formerly claimed by Britain and/or the US, now belong to the Republic of Kiribati.

Lino Lakes city, pop. 8807, Anoka Co., SE Minnesota, 14 mi/23 km N of St. Paul. It is largely residential; much of its area is occupied by Chain of Lakes–Rice Creek Regional Park.

Linoleumville see under FRESH KILLS, New York.

Linthicum unincorporated residential suburb, pop. 7547, Anne Arundel Co., C Maryland, 7 mi/11 km SW of downtown Baltimore. Baltimore-Washington International Airport is immediately S.

Lisbon **1.** town, pop. 9457, Androscoggin Co., SW Maine. Including Lisbon Falls (pop. 4674) and Lisbon Center villages, it is on the Androscoggin R., SE of and adjacent to Lewiston. The main industries are linoleum, textile, and gypsum product manufacture. **2.** village, pop. 3037, seat of Columbiana Co., NE Ohio, 23 mi/37 km SSW of Youngstown. It is noted for its coal, clay, and limestone. Local products include ceramics, leather goods, and electrical appliances. John Morgan's Confederate forces were defeated by Union troops near here in one of Ohio's few Civil War encounters (July 26, 1863); a monument 8 mi/13 km S of Lisbon marks the site.

Lisle village, pop. 19,512, Du Page Co., NE Illinois, on the East Branch of the Du Page R., 22 mi/35 km W of Chicago. Largely residential, it experienced substantial light industrial and commercial development during the 1980s, especially along I-88, the ILLINOIS RESEARCH AND DEVELOPMENT CORRIDOR. Settled around 1830, the village served as a stopping point on the road between Chicago and Aurora. Illinois Benedictine College (1887) is here. Lisle is also the site of the well-known, 1500-ac/600-ha Morton Arboretum (1922).

Litchfield town, pop. 8365, seat of Litchfield Co., NW Connecticut, on the Naugatuck R. in the Litchfield Hills. Settled in 1720, it is noted for its streets lined with old trees and homes. The area attracts exurbanites, many from New York City. The Tapping Reeve House is the site of the first law school in America, attended by Aaron Burr and John C. Calhoun. The town is also the birthplace of Ethan Allen, Oliver Wolcott, Henry Ward Beecher, and Harriet Beecher Stowe. Litchfield was a military depot before and during the Revolutionary War; although it had a number of industries, including iron ore mining and agriculture, its early wealth came from overseas trade. In later years, it became a summer resort, and recently an arts colony.

Litchfield County 921 sq mi/2385 sq km, pop. 174,092, in extreme NW Connecticut, at the New York and Massachusetts borders. Litchfield is its seat. It is agricultural and also has some manufacturing, especially in Torrington, Thomaston, and Winsted. There are many resorts on its lakes, along the Housatonic R., and in the Litchfield Hills; the county has a number of state parks and forests, and is a popular exurban and vacation retreat.

Litchfield Hills extension of the BERKSHIRE HILLS S through Litchfield Co., W Connecticut, between the Housatonic (W) and Naugatuck (E) rivers. MOHAWK Mt. (1680 ft/512 m) is the high point.

Lithia Springs unincorporated community, pop. 11,403, Douglas Co., NW Georgia, 14 mi/23 km NNW of downtown Atlanta. A popular late-19th-century resort called Salt Springs, it was an important Chautauqua site. It is now primarily residential.

Lititz borough, pop. 8280, Lancaster Co., SE Pennsylvania, 8 mi/13 km N of Lancaster. It was founded in the mid 18th century by Moravians; several of their early buildings have been preserved. Organs and pianos were manufactured here in the 18th century. Pretzels, which are still made in Lititz, were first baked here in 1861. The borough's products also include chocolate, clothing, and cigars. Tourism is important.

Little America travelers' center in Sweetwater Co., SW Wyoming, 20 mi/32 km W of Green River. Situated on I-80, on the former Oregon, California, Mormon, and Overland trails, it was established as a way station for gasoline-powered travelers in 1932. Today, it is a gigantic truck stop surrounded by barren countryside.

Little Belt Mountains range in C Montana. About 40 mi/64 km long, it forms a crescent in Lewis and Clark National Forest, originating S of Great Falls and pointing toward the Big Snowy Mts. The range has yielded silver, gold, lead, zinc, and sapphires. Its highest point is Big Baldy, 9191 ft/2803 m.

Little Bighorn River 90 mi/145 km long, in N Wyoming and SE Montana. Its rises in the BIGHORN Mts., and its course is almost entirely within the CROW INDIAN RESERVATION, at the N of which, at Hardin, it joins the BIGHORN R. Along it, on June 25–26, 1876, combined Cheyenne and Sioux forces led by Sitting Bull, Crazy Horse, and Gall annihilated the 7th US Cavalry of George A. Custer. The battlefield, 54 mi/89 km ESE of Billings, was called the Custer National Battlefield until 1992, when it was renamed the **Little Bighorn National Battlefield.**

Little Blue River see under BIG BLUE R.

Little Canada city, pop. 8971, Ramsey Co., SE Minnesota, a residential suburb immediately N of St. Paul.

Little Chute village, pop. 9207, Outagamie Co., E Wisconsin, on rapids of the Fox R., a residential suburb 5 mi/8 km E of Appleton. Settled in 1850, it is situated in a dairying area. Many residents are employed as papermill workers in nearby APPLETON and Kimberly.

Little Colorado River 315 mi/507 km long, in Arizona. It rises in S Apache Co., near the New Mexico border, and flows generally NW, past Holbrook and near Winslow, along the SW boundary of the Navajo Section of the COLORADO PLATEAU, with BLACK MESA and the PAINTED DESERT to its N, reaching the Colorado R. near the upper (E) end of the GRAND CANYON.

Little Compton town, pop. 3339, Newport Co., SE Rhode Island. The state's southeasternmost community, it lies between the Sakonnet R. (W) and Westport, Massachusetts (E). It has an agricultural and maritime history, and is today noted as an affluent coastal resort.

Little Creek Naval Amphibious Base: see under VIRGINIA BEACH, Virginia.

Little Current see under MANITOULIN I., Ontario.

Little Dixie see under state of MISSOURI.

Little Egypt see EGYPT, Illinois.

Little Falls township, pop. 11,294, Passaic Co., NE New Jersey, on the Passaic R., 3 mi/5 km SW of Paterson. In an area purchased from local Indians (1711), it grew with the opening of the Morris Canal (1831). Little Falls has been a resort, a freshwater pearl center, and an agricultural hub. Now largely a residential suburb, it also has laboratories and such manufactures as machinery and rugs.

Little Ferry borough, pop. 9989, Bergen Co., NE New Jersey, on the Hackensack R., 4 mi/6 km E of Passaic. Settled in 1636, it is a largely residential suburb, and produces such goods as carpets, ornamental iron and other metal products, and machinery.

Little Five Points see under INMAN PARK, Atlanta, Georgia.

Little Germany see under EAST VILLAGE, New York.

Little Haiti residential and commercial section of N Miami, Florida. In an area of some 200 square blocks, its main commercial artery is NE Second Ave. The neighborhood is largely inhabited by Haitians, most fairly recent immigrants. Filled with brightly painted buildings recalling the Caribbean, the area has Haitian markets, restaurants, and *botánicas* (specialized Caribbean pharmacies).

Little Havana residential and commercial section of S Miami, Florida, some 27 blocks long and 24 blocks wide. Cutting through the area is its main commercial street, SW Eighth St., or "Calle Ocho." Since the 1960s, when Cuban immigrants began to flood into S Florida, this area has been a thriving ethnic neighborhood. Little Havana has many Cuban cafes, open-air markets, music shops, and *botánicas,* as well as a cigar factory. Located here are two Spanish-language theaters, the Bay of Pigs Monument, and Jose Martí and Maximo Gomez parks. Carnaval Miami, a ten-day festival, is held each March.

Little India residential and commercial section of SC VANCOUVER, British Columbia, 3.5 mi/6 km SSE of Downtown, along and E of S Main St., SE of Queen Elizabeth Park. Among its residents are members of British Columbia's Sikh community, who began to arrive, as loggers, in the 1900s.

Little Italy **1.** commercial and residential district of the EAST END of Vancouver, British Columbia, along Commercial Drive, just SE of Chinatown and Gastown. **2.** see NORTH BEACH, San Francisco, California. **3.** in Chicago, Illinois, old Italian neighborhood on the NEAR WEST SIDE, just SW of the Loop. HULL HOUSE is in the area, which has been radically altered by the construction since the 1950s of CHICAGO CIRCLE, the CABRINI-GREEN houses, and expressways. Most of Chicago's Italian community now lives on the far NW side, in neighborhoods like BELMONT-CRAGIN, Montclare, and Dunning. **4.** commercial and residential section of the Lower East Side, Manhattan, New York City. Traditionally bounded by the BOWERY to the E and CANAL St. to the S, and centering on Mulberry St., it has lost much of its Italian population since the 1960s, while CHINATOWN has expanded N across Canal. It remains a popular tourist area.

Little Kanawha River see KANAWHA R., West Virginia.

Little Miami River 95 mi/153 km long, in SW Ohio. It rises just S of Springfield, in Clark Co., and flows generally SW, passing E of Yellow Springs, W of Xenia, and E of the Dayton area, then through the E suburbs of Cincinnati, to join the Ohio R. Its **East Fork** flows 80 mi/130 km from Clinton Co., to join it at Milford.

Little Missouri River **1.** 150 mi/240 km long, in SW Arkansas. It rises in the OUACHITA Mts., and flows through L. Greeson, impounded by the Narrows Dam, 7 mi/11 km NNW of Murfreesboro, then continues generally SE to join the OUACHITA R. 27 mi/43 km above (NNW of) Camden. **2.** 560 mi/900 km long, in Wyoming, Montana, South Dakota, and North Dakota. It rises NW of DEVILS TOWER, in extreme NE Wyoming, and flows NE through Montana's SE corner, then generally NNE through South Dakota and North Dakota, through the Little Missouri National Grassland (administered with the CUSTER NATIONAL FOREST), to join the MISSOURI R. at L. SAKAKAWEA. All units of the THEODORE ROOSEVELT NATIONAL PARK are along the river in North Dakota's BADLANDS.

Little Neck Bay arm of Long Island Sound at the NE corner of Queens, New York, on the Nassau Co. border. Alley Creek, in Alley Pond Park, Douglaston, connects with the bay at the S. The residential neighborhood of Little Neck is just N of Douglaston. On the bay's W are Bayside and Fort Totten; on the E, the Great Neck Peninsula. Until the 20th century, when urban pollution ended the trade, Little Neck Bay was noted as the source of Little Neck clams as well as oysters.

Little Odessa see under BRIGHTON BEACH, New York.

Little Pee Dee River 90 mi/140 km long, in E South Carolina. It rises E of Bennettsville, in E Marlboro Co., near the North Carolina border, and flows SE to a point E of Mullins, in Marion Co., where it is joined by the Lumber R., which drains swampy tracts S and E of LUMBERTON, North Carolina. The Little Pee Dee then turns S, joining the PEE DEE R. 18 mi/29 km W of MYRTLE BEACH.

Little River see under GRAND STRAND, South Carolina.

Little Rock city, pop. 175,795, state capital and seat of Pulaski Co., C Arkansas, on the S bank of the Arkansas R., opposite NORTH LITTLE ROCK. Its metropolitan area has a pop. of 513,117. Founded in 1819 on the site of a former Quapaw village, the city became the Arkansas territorial capital in 1821. It was incorporated in 1831 and became the state capital in 1836. In 1861 Confederate sympathizers seized the Federal arsenal in the city. In Sept. 1863, Federal troops retook the strongly anti-Union city. In the 1880s railway expansion made it an important shipping center. Industrial growth was further spurred by World War II and by the availability of timber, oil, coal, gas, and rich mineral deposits nearby. In 1957 the city became the focus of worldwide attention when Governor Orval Faubus ordered national guardsmen to bar the admission of nine black students to Central High School, and President Dwight Eisenhower federalized the guard and sent in US troops to enforce desegregation. Today the city is the state's transportation center, having become a river port in 1969 when a system of locks and dams was opened on the Arkansas R. It is also a retail and wholesale hub, particularly in the trade of cotton, soybeans, and other agricultural goods. Recently developed industrial parks produce goods made of fabricated metal, paper, lumber, and wood, as well as an increasing number of high-tech products. Nearby mines are the nation's chief supplier of bauxite. A campus of the University of Arkansas (1927), its medical school (1876), Philander Smith College (1877), and Arkansas Baptist College (1884) are here.

Little Rock River see under ROCK R., Minnesota and Iowa.

Little Round Top see under GETTYSBURG, Pennsylvania.

Little Sioux River 220 mi/354 km long, in Minnesota and Iowa. It rises in Jackson Co. in SW Minnesota, and enters Iowa 3 mi/5 km S of Sioux Valley. Here the river flows S past Spencer to Sioux Rapids, turning SW and flowing past Cherokee and Little Sioux, where it joins the Missouri R. at the Nebraska border. The Little Sioux irrigates a large agricultural area in NW Iowa. Its main tributaries are its 75 mi/121 km–long **West Fork** and the Maple and Ocheyedan rivers.

Little Switzerland see WALLOWA Mts., Oregon.

Little Tennessee River 135 mi/217 km long, in Georgia, North Carolina, and Tennessee. It rises near Mountain City, in the Chattahoochee National Forest, in N Georgia. It flows N through Macon Co., SW North Carolina, to Franklin, then winds NW and through 15 mi/24 km–long Fontana L., impounded by the 480 ft/146 m–high Fontana Dam, a 1945 Tennessee Valley Authority facility between the Nantahala (S) and Great Smoky (N) mountains. The lake also collects waters of the Tuckasegee R. and other creeks. The Little Tennessee then flows into Tennessee, past Chilhowee Dam and L., into 20 mi/32 km–long Tellico L. This lake is impounded by the Tellico Dam (1979), which regulates the Little Tennessee's flow into the Tennessee R., opposite LENOIR CITY. Tellico L. also collects waters of the Tellico R., which flows N out of Cherokee National Forest.

Little Tokyo commercial and residential district in downtown LOS ANGELES, California, just S of EL PUEBLO DE LOS ANGELES and SE of the CIVIC CENTER. A black neighborhood in the 1880s, it emerged in the early 20th century as an important center of Japanese immigrants and their businesses. Forcibly removed during World War II, many later returned and reestablished their community, which is today a thriving business center. The Japanese American Cultural and Community Center is here.

Littleton **1.** city, pop. 33,685, seat of Arapahoe Co., also in Douglas Co., NC Colorado, on the South Platte R., 10 mi/16 km S of Denver. Settled in the 1860s, it has been a research and development center for the computer and aerospace industries since the arrival of the Martin Marietta Corp. in the late 1950s. Manufactures include trucks, explosives, cameras, rubber products, and electronic and precision instruments. Arapahoe Community College (1965) is here. **2.** town, pop. 5827, Grafton Co., NW New Hampshire. It is on Interstate 93 and the Ammonoosuc and Connecticut rivers, 30 mi/48 km WSW of Berlin. A summer and winter resort and trade center, it produces dairy products, gloves, shoes, wood products, and pulpwood. Eleanor Hodgman Porter, author of *Pollyanna,* was born here in 1868.

Little Village Spanish, **Pueblo Pequeño** also, **South Lawndale** commercial and residential district on the NEAR WEST SIDE of Chicago, Illinois, SW of PILSEN and E of the Cicero line, 4 mi/6 km WSW of the Loop. Once a Czech neighborhood, it became after the 1940s, when wartime labor agreements brought workers north, the heartland of Chicago's large Mexican community, many of whom moved here from Pilsen as they became more affluent, and many of whom have since the 1970s moved on into the suburbs.

Little White House see under WARM SPRINGS, Georgia.

Live Oak **1.** in California: **a.** unincorporated community, pop. 15,212, Santa Cruz Co., immediately E of Santa Cruz. It is a resort and residential suburb. **b.** city, pop. 4320, Sutter Co., 50 mi/80 km N of Sacramento, in the Sacramento Valley, just W of the Feather R. It is a trade center for an area producing fruit, nuts, and truck crops. **2.** city, pop. 10,023, Bexar Co., SC Texas, a residential suburb 13 mi/21 km NE of downtown San Antonio, on Interstate 35.

Livermore city, pop. 56,741, Alameda Co., NC California, in the Livermore Valley, 25 mi/40 km ESE of Oakland. Incorporated in 1876, it has long been a noted wine producer. The Lawrence Livermore National Laboratory (1952; formerly the Lawrence Radiation Laboratory), run by the University of California, is a leading nuclear physics and weapons research center. The city is also a cattle and produce processing and shipping center, and has nurseries, extracts sand and gravel, and makes industrial glass.

Livermore, Mount also, **Mount Baldy** or **Old Baldy** 8382 ft/2557 m, highest peak of the DAVIS Mts., in far SW Texas, W of Fort Davis.

Liverpool see under SALINA, New York.

Livingston **1.** city, pop. 3530, seat of Sumter Co., WC Alabama, 58 mi/93 km SW of Tuscaloosa. An agricultural trade center, it is the seat of Livingston University (1835). **2.** city, pop. 6701, seat of Park Co., SC Montana, on the Yellowstone R., 23 mi/37 km E of Bozeman. Situated at the head of PARADISE VALLEY, between the Absaroka and Gallatin ranges, it is a trade center for an agricultural, quarrying (marble, granite), and mining (arsenic, silver, gold) area. Forty-five mi/72 km N of Yellowstone National Park, and near skiing and mountain climbing areas, it is also a popular resort. Livingston has housed a contingent of literary and other public figures, beginning with Martha Jane "Calamity Jane" Canary and Kitty "Madame Bulldog" O'Leary, who ran a dance hall/bordello here. **3.** township, pop. 26,609, Essex Co., NE New Jersey, 8 mi/13 km WNW of Newark. It was created (1813) from seven hamlets, and was a trading and distribution center for local dairy products, poultry, and vegetables. It is now mainly an upper-class commuter suburb with corporate offices and some light industry.

Livingston, Lake on the TRINITY R., 6 mi/10 km SW of Livingston and 65 mi/105 km NNE of Houston, in E Texas. Covering 82,600 ac/33,450 ha in four counties and operated by the Trinity R. Authority and the city of Houston, it was created for water supply, irrigation, and recreation. Its 452 mi/728 km of timbered shoreline include part of the SAM HOUSTON NATIONAL FOREST (SW).

Livingston County 574 sq mi/1487 sq km, pop. 115,645, in SE Michigan. Its seat is Howell. An agricultural county, with manufacturing at Howell, it grows beans, potatoes, sugar beets, and grain; raises poultry and livestock; and makes dairy products. Many of its small lakes are resort areas.

Livingston Manor in New York: **a.** land aquired in a 1686 patent by Robert R. Livingston (1654–1728), consisting of some 160,000 ac/65,000 ha on the E bank of the Hudson R., in the SE. It was one of four important semifeudal PATROONSHIPS in this area, the others being Rensselaerswyck, Van Cortlandt Manor, and Philipsburgh. The land is now in Dutchess and Columbia counties. **b.** village, pop. 1482, in Rockland township, Sullivan Co., in the Catskill Mts., 20 mi/32 km NW of Monticello and 15 mi/24 km E of the Pennsylvania border. It is one of many small resort villages in this area.

Livonia city, pop. 100,850, Wayne Co., SE Michigan, 15 mi/24 km W of Detroit. It is largely dependent on the automobile industry, and has large General Motors and Ford assembly plants, as well as factories producing auto parts. The city also manufactures paint and tools and dies. It is home to Madonna College (1947) and Schoolcraft College (1961).

Llano Estacado also, **Staked Plain** HIGH PLAINS region in the PANHANDLE of N Texas and in adjoining E New Mexico. Its S boundary is the EDWARDS PLATEAU. The W boundary is Mescalero Ridge, overlooking the PECOS R. in New Mexico. On the E, the CAPROCK ESCARPMENT separates it from C Texas prairies. Legend has it that the 1541 Coronado expedition placed wooden stakes in the ground here so it could find its way back through seemingly endless grasslands. Another theory for the name is that the Caprock resembles palisades ("stakes"). Known for severe weather (such as sandstorms and "blue northers" from the Rockies), the plains are semi-arid and broken by only occasional depressions. The fertile soil (largely alluvial material blown here) supported ranching until the 1920s, when extensive irrigation allowed grain and cotton farming. LUBBOCK and AMARILLO are the most important cities in a region that also has significant oil, natural gas, and helium deposits. The area around Lubbock, at an altitude of c.2500 ft/760 m, is usually called the **South Plains,** while to the N, around Amarillo, at c.4000 ft/1220 m, are the Panhandle Plains or High Plains.

Llewellyn Park see under WEST ORANGE, New Jersey.

Lloyd District mixed residential, commercial, and cultural development in Northeast and North PORTLAND, Oregon, on the Willamette R., across from Downtown. A 100-block area of what had been small factories, warehouses, and houses until the 1950s, it now has residential and commercial buildings, the Memorial Coliseum (sports), and the Oregon Convention Center. Private investment has followed public programs into the area.

Lloyd Harbor village, pop. 3343, in Huntington town, Suffolk Co., SE New York, on Long Island's North Shore, on a peninsula jutting into Huntington Bay, 2 mi/3 km NW of the village of Huntington. It is an exclusive residential suburb.

Lloydminster city, pop. 17,283, straddling the border between Alberta and Saskatchewan, in EC Alberta (pop. 10,042) and WC Saskatchewan (pop. 7241), 135 mi/217 km E of Edmonton. It is the commercial and industrial center for a region with abundant natural resources and agricultural products. Gas and oil wells, wheat fields, cattle ranches, and salt-extraction operations are in the area. The city itself has dairy cooperatives, oil refineries, and asphalt plants. Founded in 1903 by British religious colonists, it was divided in 1905 with the creation of Alberta and Saskatchewan; unified in 1930, it is incorporated in both provinces.

Lobos, Point rocky headland jutting into Carmel Bay, just S of CARMEL, California. The 1250-ac/506-ha Point Lobos State Reserve is home to the rare Monterey cypress, as well as to sea otters, sea lions, and harbor seals.

Lochearn unincorporated village, pop. 25,240, Baltimore Co., NC Maryland, a residential suburb 6 mi/10 km NW of central Baltimore, just inside Baltimore's Beltway (I-695).

Locke, Mount 6791 ft/2071 m, in the DAVIS Mts. in far SW Texas, NW of Fort Davis, the site of the McDonald Observatory (opened May 5, 1939), a major astronomical facility established by the Universities of Texas and Chicago.

Lockhart 1. unincorporated community, pop. 11,636, Orange Co., C Florida, a suburb of Orlando, just NW of its city limits. **2.** city, pop. 9205, seat of Caldwell Co., SC Texas, 27 mi/43 km S of Austin. Founded in 1848, it was on the CHISHOLM TRAIL in the 1870s. Just NE, in Lockhart State Park, is the site of the battle of Plum Creek (Aug. 1840), a victory by Texans over raiding Comanches. Today the city is an agricultural trade center with some light manufactures.

Lock Haven city, pop. 9230, seat of Clinton Co., NC Pennsylvania, on the West Branch of the Susquehanna R., 22 mi/35 km WSW of Williamsport. Settled (1769) on the site of Fort Reed, it was a major 19th-century lumbering center and a port on the Pennsylvania Canal. It is the seat of Lock Haven University (1870), produces light aircraft, paper, and brick, and has some agriculture.

Lockport 1. city, pop. 9401, Will Co., NE Illinois, immediately N of Joliet and 30 mi/48 km SW of Chicago. It is the site of locks that connect the Chicago Sanitary and Ship Canal with the Des Plaines R. on the ILLINOIS WATERWAY. Lockport's economy is dominated by an oil refinery, grain elevators, and the Stateville Correctional Center, to the W. Manufactures include cement and gravel products. It was founded in 1836 by the Illinois and Michigan Canal Commission as the headquarters for the building of the new canal. Some of the original locks are preserved. Lockport is now the home of Lewis College of Science and Technology (1930) and the Illinois and Michigan Canal Museum. **2.** city, pop. 24,426, seat of Niagara Co., W New York, on the New York State Barge Canal, 21 mi/33 km NE of Buffalo. Founded in 1821, it developed around a series of five double locks, for which it was named, built along the original Erie Canal. The locks, built to overcome a 66-ft/20-m difference in level between L. Erie and the Genesee R., were replaced by two modern locks when the canal system was enlarged at the turn of the century. Lockport is the center of the Niagara Frontier fruit belt, an agricultural area that produces apples, prunes, cherries, and peaches. Industries, sustained by Niagara Falls power, manufacture paper, textiles, plastics, automobile radiators and air conditioners, chemicals, and foundry products. Limestone and sandstone quarrying is also significant.

Locust Grove unincorporated village in Oyster Bay town, Nassau Co., SE New York, on Long Island, 8 mi/13 km NE of Mineola. It is primarily residential.

Locust Valley unincorporated village, pop. 3963, in Oyster Bay town, Nassau Co., SE New York, on Long Island's North Shore, 10 mi/16 km NE of the QUEENS line. It was established in the 17th century. Now primarily a residential suburb, it has some light industry and is near bayfront beaches.

Lodgepole Creek 212 mi/341 km long, in SE Wyoming, W Nebraska, and NE Colorado. It rises in E Albany Co., Wyoming, and flows generally E through rangeland and into Nebraska, just E of Pine Bluffs. There it continues E past Kimball, Sidney, and Chappell, dipping for 5 mi/8 km into extreme NE Colorado, where it joins the South Platte R. near Julesburg.

Lodi 1. city, pop. 51,874, San Joaquin Co., NC California, on the Mokelumne R., at the N end of the San Joaquin Valley, 10 mi/16 km N of Stockton. A processing center for local cereals, fruits, and vegetables, it has been noted for making Tokay and other wines since the 1880s. Its industries include the manufacture of food, metal, and rubber products, and it is growing as a residential center. **2.** borough, pop. 22,355, Bergen Co., NE New Jersey, on the Saddle R., 5 mi/8 km SE of Paterson. Its many factories produce chemicals, dyes, machinery, plastics, textiles, and clothing. There is also a large residential section. Lodi is the seat of Felician College (1942).

loess a brownish yellow soil (a type of loam) found esp. in the Great Plains, assumed to have been formed by materials carried by winds away from (in front of) glaciers, which had ground it from soft rock strata. Rich in calcium carbonate (lime), unconsolidated, fine, and easily worked and drained, it is a fertile agricultural medium.

Logan 1. residential section of Philadelphia, Pennsylvania, 5 mi/8 km N of CENTER CITY, between OLNEY and NORTH PHILADELPHIA. It is a working-class black and Hispanic area. **2.** city, pop. 32,762, seat of Cache Co., N Utah, on the Logan R. in the Cache Valley, 36 mi/58 km NNE of Ogden. Founded by Mormons in 1859 and built on terraces created by the glacial L. Bonneville, it is a marketing center for an agricultural and dairy region. Its industries produce cheese, beet sugar, canned fruit, flour, lumber, dairy goods, candy, pianos, organs, farm equipment, and clothing. Visitors are drawn to its Mormon temple (1884) and its tabernacle, which contains a well-known genealogical library. Also here is Utah State University (1888).

Logan, Mount highest point in Canada (19,524 ft/5951 m) and second-highest in North America, in KLUANE NATIONAL PARK and the SAINT ELIAS Mts. in the SW corner of the Yukon Territory, near the Alaska line. Rising steeply 13,615 ft/4150 m above the Seward Glacier (S), Logan has multiple summits, three over 19,000 ft/5790 m, projecting from a massive, primarily granitic mountain block. The first known ascents were made by a joint US-Canadian expedition in 1925. The mountain was named after Canadian geologist Sir William E. Logan (1798–1875). Research on high-altitude physiology, meteors, and glaciers has been conducted here.

Logan Circle landscaped traffic circle and park, in CENTER CITY, Philadelphia, Pennsylvania, on BENJAMIN FRANKLIN PARKWAY, NW of City Hall. One of four open spaces laid out in William Penn's original town plan, it served as common pasture, burial ground, and public execution site before undergoing monumentalization with the construction of the Parkway in the 1920s.

Logan Heights see BARRIO LOGAN, San Diego, California.

Logan International Airport in EAST BOSTON, Massachusetts, across Boston Harbor from downtown. Built largely on landfill, it is one of the nation's busiest airports, and one of those closest to the center of the city it serves.

Logan Mountains NW–SE trending range, at the SE end of the SELWYN Mts., along the border of the SE Yukon Territory and SW Northwest Territories, including Mt. Laporte (7050 ft/2149 m). The 125-mi/200-km Nahanni Range Road here follows the Hyland R. NE into the mountains from the CAMPBELL HIGHWAY to the settlement of Tungsten, Northwest Territories, site of Canada's largest (intermittently producing) tungsten mine.

Logan's Crossroads battle site: see under MILL SPRINGS, Kentucky.

Logansport city, pop. 16,812, seat of Cass Co., NC Indiana, at the junction of the Wabash and Eel rivers, 22 mi/35 km NW of Kokomo. It is a trading, processing, and shipping center for livestock and grain from local farms. Among its diversified manufactures are airplane parts, batteries, electrical components, die castings, rubber products, suspension blocks, and thermostats.

Logan Square residential and commercial neighborhood on the NEAR WEST SIDE of Chicago, Illinois, along Milwaukee Ave., 3 mi/5 km NW of the Loop and just SE of AVONDALE. It is inhabited largely by Mexican and other Hispanic residents.

Log College historic site: see under NESHAMINY CREEK, Pennsylvania.

Loisaida popular name for the Hispanic, largely Puerto Rican, community on the LOWER EAST SIDE of Manhattan, New York City; or for the Lower East Side itself, particularly ALPHABET CITY.

Lolo National Forest 2.1 million ac/850,000 ha (3280 sq mi/8500 sq km), in W Montana, surrounding Missoula and extending to the Idaho border, largely in the Swan, Rattlesnake, Sapphire, and Bitterroot ranges. Parts of the SELWAY-BITERROOT and other WILDERNESS AREAS are here. There are ski resorts, lakes, elk herds, and Montana's Smokejumper (airborne firefighting) center. The **Lolo Pass** (5187 ft/1581 m) crosses the Bitterroots SW of Missoula.

Loma, Point peninsula on the Pacific Ocean, at the entrance to San Diego Bay, S California. At its S tip is the Cabrillo National Monument, a 144-ac/58-ha park honoring the Portuguese navigator Juan Rodríguez Cabrillo, the first European to see the bay (1542). Fort Rosecrans, a Navy installation and national cemetery, is here, along with Point Loma Nazarene College (1902). The peninsula's N is the site of affluent residential neighborhoods as well as of older Portuguese fishing communities. MISSION BAY lies N.

Loma Linda city, pop. 17,400, San Bernardino Co., SW California, a residential suburb 4 mi/6 km SSE of San Bernardino, in fruit producing country.

Lombard village, pop. 39,408, Du Page Co., NE Illinois, a suburb 20 mi/32 km W of Chicago. A residential community, it also produces plastics. Local educational institutions include the National College of Chiropractic (1906), Northern Baptist Theological Seminary, and Bethany Theological Seminary. The village is known for the many varieties of lilac in its Lilacia Park, and for its annual Lilac Festival. American settlement dates to 1834.

Lomita city, pop. 19,382, Los Angeles Co., SW California, 17 mi/27 km S of downtown Los Angeles. It is a residential suburb in an oil producing and refining area just S of Torrance.

Lompoc city, pop. 37,649, Santa Barbara Co., SW California, 45 mi/72 km WNW of Santa Barbara and just NE of Point ARGUELLO. Its proximity to Vandenberg Air Force Base (W) and the Naval Missile Facility has made it a military center, and it is home to a Federal prison and minimum-security prison camp ("Club Fed"). Oil wells and truck farms are in the area, and the city is the leading US producer of flower seed. Diatomaceous earth products are mined and processed. The completely restored Mission of La Purísima Concepcion, (1787), just NE, is a California historic park.

London city, pop. 303,165, seat of Middlesex Co., extreme S Ontario, on the Thames R., 23 mi/37 km N of L. Erie and 100 mi/160 km ENE of Detroit, Michigan. The city's site was chosen in 1792 for the capital of UPPER CANADA, but settlement did not begin until 1826. The community grew rapidly during the mid 19th century, housing a British garrison (1838–53), serving as the early center of the Ontario petroleum industry, and developing as a railroad distribution center for the Great Lakes region. Today it is the commercial, financial, and distribution center of Canada's L. Erie industrial and agricultural region. Manufactures include adhesives, abrasives, diesel equipment, textiles, refrigerators, baked goods, beer, and electrical, brass, iron, steel, paper, leather, and food products. Dairying is also important. The city is home to the University of Western Ontario (1878), with its affiliate Brescia, King's, and Huron (1863) colleges.

London Bridge see under LAKE HAVASU CITY, Arizona.

Londonderry town, pop. 19,781, Rockingham Co., SE New Hampshire, 14 mi/22 km SE of Manchester. Early settlers, here since the 1720s, grew flax and potatoes and made linen. Near Merrimack and Nashua, and on Interstate 93 on the fringes of the Boston area, Londonderry is now a growing suburb, although agriculture remains important.

Lone Pine unincorporated community, pop. 1818, Inyo Co., EC California, in the OWENS Valley, 90 mi/140 km E of Fresno. It is a service town for the area, which includes the Inyo Mts. and Death Valley (E), Mt. Whitney (W), and the N–S Alabama Hills (immediately W), a favorite shooting site for westerns. Manzanar, 9 mi/14 km N, was the site of the best-known of the relocation camps in which Americans of Japanese ancestry were interned in 1942–45. At that time a community of 10,000, it is now a scattering of physical reminders.

Lone Tree see under CENTRAL CITY, Nebraska.

Long Beach **1.** city, pop. 429,433, Los Angeles Co., SW California, 19 mi/31 km SSE of downtown Los Angeles, on San Pedro Bay. Founded in the 1880s, it was a major early-20th-century beach resort. The building of docks in 1911 and the discovery of oil in 1921 contributed to rapid growth. During World War II, the world's largest dry dock and a Douglas aircraft plant spurred a population boom. Today, the Los Angeles–Long Beach Naval Station, a large naval shipyard, oil wells both underground and offshore, and deposits of natural gas contribute to the economy. Seafood, chemical, aircraft, shipbuilding, and electronics industries are important. The port is one of the busiest on the West Coast. Long Beach has over 5 mi/8 km of bathing beaches and large marinas. The famed transatlantic liner *Queen Mary,* moored here since 1967, is a tourist attraction; its companion, Howard Hughes's huge "Spruce Goose" flying boat, was moved in 1992 to MCMINNVILLE, Oregon. Remnants of Rancho Los Alamitos (1806) constitute the oldest adobe structure in Los Angeles Co. Among educational and cultural institutions are Long Beach City College (1927), the California State University at Long Beach (1949), and the Long Beach Museum of Art. The city has a large Hispanic community and is one of the leading US centers of recent Cambodian immigration. **2.** resort and residential city, pop. 15,804, Harrison Co., SE Mississippi, on Mississippi Sound, 5 mi/8 km W of Gulfport. **3.** city, pop. 33,510, Nassau Co., SE New York, on a barrier island off Long Island's South Shore, 25 mi/40 km SE of Manhattan. It is a residential community and beach resort, with a large number of facilities providing long-term care to the elderly and infirm.

Long Beach Island barrier island 20 mi/32 km N of Atlantic

City, in Ocean Co., SE New Jersey. Eighteen mi/29 km NNE–SSW, and 0.5 mi/1 km wide, it lies between Barnegat Bay and Little Egg Harbor (W) and the Atlantic Ocean (E). The Barnegat Lighthouse, on Barnegat Inlet, is at its N end, while its S tip is on Beach Haven Inlet. The main communities, N–S, are Barnegat Light, Harvey Cedars, Surf City, Ship Bottom (bridged to the mainland), Brighton, Beach Haven Gardens, and Beach Haven.

Long Branch **1.** city, pop. 28,658, Monmouth Co., EC New Jersey, on the Atlantic Ocean, 5 mi/8 km N of Asbury Park. Settled in 1740 and one of the nation's oldest seaside vacation spots, it was a fashionable leisure center from the early 19th century, and was a summer home to Presidents Grant, Hayes, Garfield, Harrison, McKinley, and Wilson. While no longer a favorite of socialites, Long Branch remains a popular summer resort, with a 2 mi/3 km–long boardwalk, beaches, surf fishing, and the oceanfront Seven Presidents Park. Boats, clothing, and electronic products are manufactured. **2.** see under ETOBICOKE, Ontario.

Longfellow Mountains name adopted 1958 for the Maine continuation of the WHITE MOUNTAINS, extending 160 mi/260 km SW to NE from the MAHOOSUC RANGE to Baxter State Park. Mt. KATAHDIN (5267 ft/1606 m) is the highest point.

Long House, the see under IROQUOIS CONFEDERACY.

Long Island 130 mi/210 km long, extending from New York Bay and the East R. (W) to Block Island Sound (E), in SE New York. On the N, it is separated from Connecticut by LONG ISLAND SOUND; the Atlantic Ocean is S. The island's maximum width is 20 mi/32 km. Its EAST END is divided into the NORTH FORK and the SOUTH FORK. Long Island contains two independent counties, Nassau and Suffolk, and at its W end two boroughs of New York City, BROOKLYN (Kings Co.) and QUEENS. Its total population is 6,861,474. The region is highly diverse. Brooklyn and Queens, although primarily residential, are congested and highly developed. Nassau is perhaps the quintessential suburban county; once agricultural, it was heavily developed after World War II, and contains many bedroom communities for New York City, with small retail districts that have suffered as regional malls grew. Suffolk is suburban in its W part, but to the E has less development and more agriculture, notably potato and truck farms and, recently, vineyards. Its East End has both agricultural and resort areas.

Long Island's industry has been heavily defense-based; the largest employer in recent years has been Grumman, in Bethpage. There are also many high-tech facilities, including the Brookhaven National Laboratory and several biotechnology installations. Recreational facilities include many town and state parks, including Jones Beach State Park, and numerous other beaches.

Long Island City industrial and residential section, NW Queens, New York. It was incorporated as a city, separating from NEWTOWN, in 1870, and became a ward of Queens borough 1898. With the East R. to the E and Newtown Creek on its S boundary, Long Island City was situated to become one of New York's industrial hubs, and by the early 19th century the first of hundreds of paint, food processing, shoemaking, stoneworking, and other establishments located here. ASTORIA and STEINWAY, similarly industrial, were NE. Today, Long Island City retains much industry, and is a rail and highway nexus. The Queensborough Bridge and Queens-Midtown Tunnel cross to Manhattan. Subsections of Long Island City include HUNTERS POINT, SUNNYSIDE, and Blissville. The area along the East R. opposite Roosevelt Island is called Ravenswood; some of its former manufacturing sites have been transformed into housing or into such cultural sites as the Isamu Noguchi Garden Museum and the Socrates Sculpture Park. Ravenswood is also the site of "Big Allis," the Consolidated Edison power plant that failed during the 1965 New York blackout, whose 450- and 500-ft (137- and 152-m) stacks dominate the skyline.

Long Island MacArthur Airport see under ISLIP, New York.

Long Island Rail Road familiarly, **LIRR** major commuter railroad serving New York City and Long Island. Created in 1834 from the Brooklyn and Jamaica Railroad (1832), it has four New York City termini, at Pennsylvania Station (Manhattan), Flatbush Ave. (Brooklyn), and Long Island City and Hunters Point (Queens); extensive yards in Sunnyside, Queens; its major transfer point at Jamaica; and nine branches, serving all parts of Long Island from Queens and Brooklyn to Montauk.

Long Island Sound arm of the Atlantic Ocean between S Connecticut and Long Island, SE New York. One hundred mi/160 km E–W and 5–20 mi/8–32 km wide, it connects with Upper New York Bay via the EAST RIVER on the W, and with Block Island Sound on the E. It is a center for commercial and sport fishing, as well as sailing, and an important section of the ATLANTIC INTRACOASTAL WATERWAY. Ports on the sound include New London, New Haven, and Bridgeport, Connecticut, and Port Jefferson, New York.

Longmeadow town, pop. 15,467, Hampden Co., SW Massachusetts, on the Connecticut R., at the Connecticut border. It is a largely residential suburb of Springfield, which it adjoins (S). Purchased from local tribes in 1636, it has many historic houses. Quarrying was formerly important.

Longmont city, pop. 51,555, Boulder Co., N Colorado, 30 mi/48 km NNW of Denver. Established in 1871, the agricultural settlement was named for the explorer Stephen H. Long. Situated in the fertile St. Vrain Valley, irrigated by the Colorado–Big Thompson project, Longmont processes and ships beet sugar, vegetables, and livestock. Manufactures include automotive filters, chemicals, truck campers, business machines, and agricultural and electronic equipment.

Long Range Mountains SSW–NNE trending range, extending over 300 mi/500 km along the entire W shore of Newfoundland. The flat-topped mountains average about 2200 ft/670 m in elevation, rising to 2672 ft/815 m in the LEWIS HILLS, a W spur, and are the NE extreme of the APPALACHIAN system. The HUMBER R. cuts W through them, passing CORNER BROOK. Their forests supply much of W Newfoundland's pulp and paper industry.

Longs Peak 14,255 ft/4345 m, the highest point in ROCKY MOUNTAIN NATIONAL PARK, in the FRONT RANGE of the Rocky Mts., in N Colorado, on the Continental Divide, 50 mi/80 km NW of Denver. Granitic and snow-capped, with a sheer NE face, it is popular with climbers and hikers.

Long Trail hiking route (265 mi/427 km) through the GREEN Mts. of Vermont, running between the Canadian border and Massachusetts. Following footpaths and logging roads, often through wilderness areas, the trail traverses (from N to S) JAY PEAK, Belvidere Mt., Mt. MANSFIELD, CAMELS HUMP, Lincoln Gap, Bread Loaf Wilderness, KILLINGTON PEAK, Clarendon Gorge, STRATTON Mt., and Glastonbury Mt. Completed in 1931, it is maintained by the Green Mountain Club.

Longueuil city, pop. 129,874, seat of Chambly Co., S Québec, on the St. Lawrence R. directly across (E) from Montréal. Settled after 1657 as the SEIGNEURIE of Charles Le Moyne, it has developed since the mid 20th century into a major residential suburb, as well as an industrial center. Manufactures include food products, furniture, clothing, aircraft parts, toys, and farm machinery; there are also iron and steel plants. Longueuil is the E terminus of the Montréal subway system, and the Jacques Cartier bridge provides access to the larger city.

Longview **1.** city, pop. 70,311, seat of Gregg Co., also in Harrison Co., E Texas, on Grace Creek near the Sabine R., 58 mi/93 km W of Shreveport, Louisiana. Settled in the early 1800s, in plantation country, it was named by Texas & Pacific Railroad surveyors in the 1870s, and became a livestock trading center. When the EAST TEXAS OILFIELD was discovered in the 1930s, it boomed, becoming the area's commercial center, with refineries and pipeline terminals. Today it manufactures aircraft components, farm and earth-moving equipment, truck beds and trailers, and a variety of other products, and has food processing plants and breweries. It is the seat of LeTourneau University (1946) and the Caddo Indian Museum. Nearby lakes draw visitors. **2.** city, pop. 31,499, Cowlitz Co., SW Washington, at the confluence of the Cowlitz and Columbia rivers and the Oregon border, 2 mi/3 km SW of Kelso. It is on the site of Monticello, where settlers convened in 1852 to petition Congress to create the Washington Territory. In 1923 timber baron R.A. Long founded it as a model city, the first planned city in the Northwest. A deepwater port, Longview has the largest such facility on the Columbia R., and is a major center of the lumber and pulp industry. Other manufactures include aluminum, paint, and processed foods.

Longwood **1.** city, pop. 13,316, Seminole Co., C Florida, 10 mi/16 km N of Orlando, a residential suburb set amid small lakes. **2.** see under BROOKLINE, Massachusetts.

Longwood Gardens see under KENNETT SQUARE, Pennsylvania.

Lookout, Cape sandy S end of 24 mi/38 km–long Core Banks, part of the OUTER BANKS, overlooking Cape Lookout Shoals, in the Atlantic Ocean 12 mi/19 km SE of BEAUFORT, E North Carolina. The **Cape Lookout National Seashore** covers 55 mi/89 km of dunes, inlets, and marshes along the lower Outer Banks on Portsmouth I. (NE), Core Banks (C), and Shackleford Banks (SW), between the ocean and Pamlico, Core, and Back sounds. Most of the area is uninhabited and accessible only by boat. The 160-ft/49-m Cape Lookout Lighthouse was built in 1859.

Lookout, Point headland at the S tip of Maryland's Western Shore, between Chesapeake Bay (E) and the Potomac R. (W). It was the site of a Union prison during the Civil War.

Lookout Mountain **1.** ridge of the CUMBERLAND PLATEAU, extending SSW for c.75 mi/120 km from S of Moccasin Bend on the Tennessee R., near CHATTANOOGA, Tennessee, across the NW corner of Georgia, to near GADSDEN, Alabama. The ridge, which attains its highest elevation (2392 ft/730 m) at its NE end, is noted as the site (near Chattanooga) of a steep incline railway; subterranean caverns containing 145-ft/44-m Ruby Falls, 1120 ft/342 m below the earth's surface; and Rock City Gardens, a 10-ac/4-ha area of sandstone formations. The site of the Nov. 24, 1863 Battle of Lookout Mt., on Chattanooga's SW side, is partially within Chickamauga and Chattanooga National Military Park (see MISSIONARY RIDGE). **2.** city, pop. 1636, Walker Co., extreme NW Georgia, just SE of LOOKOUT Mt. It is home to Covenant College (1955). **3.** see under ZUÑI Mts., New Mexico.

Loop, the central business district of Chicago, Illinois. The old core of the city, it is bordered N and W by the Chicago R. and E by GRANT PARK. It contains such city landmarks as the SEARS TOWER, Chicago Board of Trade, Marshall Field department store, and the PALMER HOUSE Hotel. Centered on the intersection of STATE and Madison streets, the Loop was named in the 1880s when the Chicago City Railway built a circular loop for its surface-level cars. The present-day elevated tracks appeared by the turn of the century.

Lorain city, pop. 71,245, Lorain Co., NC Ohio, a port on L. Erie at the mouth of the Black R., 25 mi/40 km W of Cleveland. The first permanent settlement on this site, a trading post, was established in 1807. A major harbor and shipbuilding center since the early 19th century, it is a shipping hub for coal, iron ore, and stone. Lorain is also in a popular resort area. Steel and motor vehicle assembly plants are situated here. Manufactured goods include power shovels and cranes, bearings, pumps, and building products. Its industrial sector slumped when the city suffered many plant closings and the loss of thousands of jobs during the 1980s and early 1990s. Commercial fishing is also a factor in its economy. The unusual ethnic diversity of Lorain's population, the result of labor influxes, is celebrated in an annual international festival.

Lorain County 495 sq mi/1282 sq km, pop. 271,126, in N Ohio; bounded by L. Erie (N), and intersected by the Black and Vermilion rivers. Its seat is ELYRIA. The economy is supported by dairy, fruit, grain, livestock, and poultry farming as well as sandstone quarrying. There is substantial heavy manufacturing at Elyria, the port city of Lorain, and Wellington.

Lordsburg city, pop. 2951, seat of Hidalgo Co., in the SW corner of New Mexico, on I-10, 20 mi/32 km E of the Arizona border and 115 mi/185 km W of Las Cruces. The city is in an area known for its geothermal resources, with temperatures to 246° F/119° C recorded in shallow wells to its S. The mining GHOST TOWN of Shakespeare is also S.

Lordstown village, pop. 3404, Trumbull Co., NE Ohio, 12 mi/19 km NW of Youngstown. Situated on the Baltimore and Ohio Railroad, it is an industrial center particularly known for its large General Motors automobile assembly and stamping plants.

Loretteville city, pop. 14,219, Québec Co., 7 mi/11 km WNW of Québec City, S Québec, on the R. St.-Charles, part of the QUÉBEC Urban Community. It was settled (1697) as Jeune-Lorette, when Hurons who had been living on a mission in L'ANCIENNE-LORETTE, just S, relocated here. Wendake (Village-des-Hurons) survives on the E side of the modern suburb.

Loretto borough, pop. 1072, Cambria Co., SW Pennsylvania, 11 mi/18 km W of Altoona. It is the seat of St. Francis College (1847).

Loring Air Force Base see under LIMESTONE, Maine.

Loring Park residential neighborhood of Minneapolis, Minnesota, immediately SW of Downtown. An area of high-density brick apartment buildings, it has become popular with affluent young professionals due to its proximity to the center of the city, its bohemian flavor, and the adjacent park for which it is named. There is also a large and organized gay community.

Lorman hamlet in Jefferson Co., SW Mississippi, 27 mi/43 km NE of Natchez and 9 mi/14 km SSW of Port Gibson, on the Natchez Trace. Just to the W is Alcorn State University, the oldest black land-grant college in the US. Beginning as Oakland Presbyterian College (1830), it became a state school for the higher education of blacks in 1871.

Lorraine Motel see under NATIONAL CIVIL RIGHTS MUSEUM, Memphis, Tennessee.

Lorton unincorporated community, pop. 15,385, Fairfax Co., NE Virginia, 12 mi/19 km SW of Alexandria. A residential suburb, it is the N terminus of the auto train from Florida. GUNSTON HALL, the estate of George Mason, lies SE, and Lorton Reformatory, the District of Columbia's prison, is here.

Los Alamitos city, pop. 11,676, Orange Co., SW California, 18 mi/29 km SE of downtown Los Angeles. A residential suburb, it also has a military airfield. The well-known Los Alamitos Race Track is actually in neighboring (NE) CYPRESS.

Los Alamos unincorporated community, pop. 11,455, seat of Los Alamos Co. (pop. 18,115), NC New Mexico, 23 mi/37 km NW of Santa Fe. On the PAJARITO PLATEAU, surrounded by Santa Fe National Forest, it is N of Anasazi ruins in the BANDELIER NATIONAL MONUMENT. The site of an isolated boys' school (1918) here was chosen (1942) by J. Robert Oppenheimer for the Manhattan Project laboratory that developed the first atomic bomb, and that grew into the Los Alamos National Laboratory. The community was under Federal control until 1962; the county was formed in 1969.

Los Altos city, pop. 26,303, Santa Clara Co., NC California, in the foothills of the Santa Cruz Mts., 10 mi/16 km WNW of downtown San Jose. It is a residential and technological suburb. The adjacent (W) town of **Los Altos Hills** (pop. 7514) is home to Foothill College (1958), whose Electronics Museum details the early history of SILICON VALLEY.

Los Angeles second most populous (3,485,398) US city, seat of Los Angeles Co., SW California, 350 mi/565 km SE of San Francisco. From the Los Angeles Basin, a coastal plain S of the SANTA MONICA Mts., the city sprawls N into the SAN FERNANDO VALLEY, and extends S along the narrow "Industrial Corridor" paralleling the Los Angeles R. on its course to Los Angeles Harbor. It is the largest California city in area (over 465 sq mi/1200 sq km), and the center of a metropolitan area (CMSA) with a pop. of 14,531,529. The area, inhabited by seminomadic groups including the Gabrielino, was visited by the explorer Cabrillo in 1542, but European settlement did not begin until the PUEBLO of Nuestra Señora La Reina de Los Angeles de Porciúncula was established in 1781. In the early 19th century, Los Angeles was for some time the capital of ALTA CALIFORNIA, and a hub of SOUTHERN CALIFORNIA's cattle-based RANCHO economy. The American takeover of 1847 and the Northern California gold rush (1849–50) stimulated growth of the city, which was incorporated in 1850. In 1876 the Central Pacific Railroad linked Los Angeles to the BAY AREA, and in 1885 the Santa Fe connected it with the East, setting off a real-estate boom as Midwesterners and others sought homes in the sun. Orange groves provided a springboard for agricultural prosperity, and in 1891 oil was discovered in the heart of the growing city. Between 1880 and 1910, the pop. soared from 12,000 to 320,000. In the 20th century, the industries that dominate modern Los Angeles emerged rapidly. Oil discoveries in the area continued. The beginnings of the air age brought the first of many aircraft, later aerospace, manufacturing and testing operations. By 1914, when the Panama Canal was opened and World War I began, the harbor at San Pedro had become an important commercial and naval port. Tourism flourished, and visitors traveled Henry Huntington's Pacific Electric Railway, the world's largest INTERURBAN network, both for pleasure and to explore the area's real estate potential. By 1920, Los Angeles was the largest city in the West, quadrupling in size through annexation of the San Fernando Valley and other areas during this period. Film studios sprang up in HOLLYWOOD after 1910, and Los Angeles became the movie capital of the world. With the emergence of the automobile from the 1910s, what became the world's largest urban highway network began to take shape. The auto facilitated the dispersal of the city's communities; Downtown declined as commerce and industry followed residences to the WESTSIDE and SOUTH BAY, and after World War II to the San Fernando Valley and adjacent counties. The leading manufacturing, retail, and wholesale center W of the Mississippi R., Los Angeles (with its suburbs) dominates the US entertainment industry as the capital of the electronic media. Home to the Pacific Coast Exchange, the city is also the nation's main financial center after New York. In the 1980s, however, its industrial base began to erode as aerospace and related industries cut back or relocated elsewhere. The city's SUNBELT "good life" has been challenged by inner-city poverty and rioting in Watts (1965) and South-Central (1992); by pollution, esp. automobile-generated smog; and by freeway overcrowding. These problems are added to the ever-present danger of earthquakes on the SAN ANDREAS and other faults and of fires in the surrounding CHAPARRAL. Hopeful indicators include new investment and construction Downtown and the beginnings of a 160-mi/260-km rapid transit system designed to replace the one allowed to die in the 1940s. Los Angeles is today the country's largest immigration center, esp. for Asians and Latin Americans, the latest agents in the city's history of social and cultural change. Major city institutions include the University of Southern California (1980), University of California: Los Angeles (1919), Loyola Marymount (1911) and Pepperdine (1937) universities, and a wide range of other schools, museums, and cultural centers. See also ANGELINO HEIGHTS; ARROYO SECO; BALDWIN HILLS; BEL AIR; BOYLE HEIGHTS; BRENTWOOD; BUNKER HILL; CAHUENGA PASS; CALABASAS; CANOGA PARK; CENTRAL AVENUE; CENTURY CITY; CHATSWORTH; CHAVEZ RAVINE (and Dodger Stadium); CHINATOWN; CIVIC CENTER; CRENSHAW; ECHO PARK; EL PUEBLO DE LOS ANGELES (and Olvera St.); ELYSIAN PARK; ENCINO; EXPOSITION PARK (and Los Angeles Memorial Coliseum); FAIRFAX DISTRICT; FARMER'S MARKET; GARMENT DISTRICT; GRANADA HILLS; GRIFFITH PARK; HANCOCK PARK; HARBOR CITY (and Harbor Freeway); HIGHLAND PARK; HOLLYWOOD; HYDE PARK; KOREATOWN; LA BREA TAR PITS; LAUREL CANYON; LEIMERT PARK; LITTLE TOKYO; LOS ANGELES INTERNATIONAL AIRPORT (LAX); LOS FELIZ; MACARTHUR PARK (Westlake Park); MALIBU; MELROSE AVENUE; MISSION HILLS; MULHOLLAND DRIVE; MUSIC CENTER; NORTH HOLLYWOOD; NORTHRIDGE; PACIFIC PALISADES; PACOIMA; PANORAMA CITY; PERSHING SQUARE; PICO-UNION; RESEDA; SAN FERNANDO VALLEY; SAN PEDRO; SANTA MONICA FREEWAY; SEPULVEDA; SHERMAN OAKS; SILVER LAKE; SOUTH BAY; SOUTH-CENTRAL; STUDIO CITY; SUNSET BOULEVARD (and Sunset Strip);

SYLMAR; TARZANA; TOPANGA CANYON; TUJUNGA; VAN NUYS; VENICE (and Muscle Beach); VENTURA BOULEVARD; VENTURA FREEWAY; WATTS; WEST ADAMS; WESTSIDE (and West Los Angeles); WESTWOOD; WILMINGTON; WILSHIRE BOULEVARD (and Miracle Mile); WOODLAND HILLS.

Los Angeles Aqueduct 233 mi/375 km long, in EC and S California. Built in 1908–13 following a series of questionable land transfers, it taps the OWENS R. near Aberdeen, 26 mi/42 km NNW of Lone Pine, and flows S along the E of the Sierra Nevada, then SSW across the W Mojave Desert, to the San Fernando Reservoir, N of Los Angeles. Its opening, enabling the agricultural use and settling of the SAN FERNANDO VALLEY, was a key event in Los Angeles history. At the same time, it brought on the desiccation and general abandonment of the Owens Valley. Subsequent (1940–41) connection of the Aqueduct with streams feeding MONO L. (N) led to lowered levels there and a long political struggle over water use and environmental effects.

Los Angeles County 4070 sq mi/10,541 sq km, pop. 8,863,164, in SW California, on the Pacific Ocean. One of the most urbanized US counties, it centers on the city of Los Angeles, its seat, and is the most populous county in the nation. The ANGELES NATIONAL FOREST, in the San Gabriel Mts., occupies much of the N, along with the S ANTELOPE VALLEY. Below the mountains sprawls the city, from the suburban SAN FERNANDO VALLEY across the Santa Monica Mts., through the Los Angeles Basin and down the coast along the SOUTH BAY. Santa Catalina and San Clemente islands are also part of the county. Major cities include LONG BEACH, PASADENA, SANTA MONICA, BURBANK, GLENDALE, and BEVERLY HILLS. For the first half of the 20th century, Los Angeles Co. was the richest US agricultural county; its oilfields, opened from 1891 through the 1920s, also contributed to economic growth.

Los Angeles International Airport familiarly, from its airport code, **LAX** leading facility of the Los Angeles, California area, on the Pacific Ocean, 14 mi/23 km SW of Downtown, adjacent to El Segundo (S) and Inglewood (E). One of the world's busiest airports, it was modernized in the 1950s, 1960s, and 1980s, building on an airfield established in the 1920s. Dockweiler State Beach lies along the water. Aerospace and related industries flourished in the vicinity in the 1960s.

Los Angeles Memorial Coliseum and Sports Arena see under EXPOSITION PARK, Los Angeles, California.

Los Angeles Ranges any of the mountain ranges in a large area around Los Angeles, in SW California. The PENINSULAR RANGES and TRANSVERSE RANGES, separated by the Los Angeles Basin, are sometimes considered subsets of the Los Angeles Ranges.

Los Angeles River c.50 mi/80 km long, in SW California. It is formed by several streams in the SAN FERNANDO VALLEY, flows E along the N side of the Santa Monica Mts., then turns S into downtown Los Angeles, flowing to San Pedro Bay. Its tributaries include the Pacoima R., Tujunga Wash, and the Rio Hondo, which joins it from the E at South Gate. Formerly variable, at times flowing through the *ciénagas* (marshes) of today's WESTSIDE, it has been controlled with dams and channeling. The Spanish founders of Los Angeles chose a site (1781) on what they called the Porciúncula R. because it did not dry out like other local streams. Today the river is considered a social boundary between the Westside and Hispanic areas to the E, including EAST LOS ANGELES.

Los Banos city, pop. 14,519, Merced Co., C California, in the San Joaquin Valley, 62 mi/100 km NW of Fresno. Irrigated diversified farming and dairying are its main industries.

Los Feliz residential neighborhood in Los Angeles, California, 5 mi/8 km NNW of Downtown, and NE of HOLLYWOOD. Laid out after World War I as an exclusive enclave, it was home to film stars through the 1940s. GRIFFITH PARK lies immediately N.

Los Gatos city, pop. 27,357, Santa Clara Co., NC California. in the foothills of the Santa Cruz Mts., 8 mi/13 km SW of San Jose. Named for wild cats that once roamed the area, it was a small fruit growing community until World War II. Its industries now include winemaking and electronics research and manufacture. It is also a residential suburb and health resort.

Los Padres National Forest c.1.75 million ac/710,000 ha (2734 sq mi/7082 sq km), in C and S California. It includes most of the Coast Ranges in this part of the state, including the Santa Ynez, San Rafael, Sierra Madre, and La Panza mountains, the San Rafael, Ventana, Machesna, and other wilderness areas, and condor sanctuaries. On the SE it borders the Angeles National Forest. A separate N unit borders the Big Sur area, and includes parts of the Santa Lucia Mts.

Lost Colony, the the 1587 colony on ROANOKE I., E North Carolina, which had vanished by 1591. Its members may have crossed CROATAN SOUND to the mainland, or may have perished at sea in attempting to return to England.

Lost Dutchman Mine see under SUPERSTITION Mts., Arizona.

Loudonville unincorporated village, pop. 10,822 in Colonie township, Albany Co., E New York, 3 mi/5 km N of downtown Albany. A residential and commercial suburb, it is home to Siena College (1937).

Loudoun County 521 sq mi/1349 sq km, pop. 86,129, in extreme N Virginia, bordered by the Potomac R. (NE), the BLUE RIDGE Mts. (NW), and BULL RUN (SW). Its seat is LEESBURG. The county, in the PIEDMONT, has a number of large estates. Horses and cattle are raised, and tobacco, wheat, and corn are grown. There is also some dairying. Washington Dulles International Airport is in the S, and suburban development is expanding NW from the Washington area into the county.

Louisa city, pop. 1990, seat of Lawrence Co., NE Kentucky, where the Levisa and Tug forks meet to form the Big Sandy R., across from Fort Gay, West Virginia, and 26 mi/42 km S of Ashland. It is a trade and shipping center for field crops, poultry, livestock, and dairy products. It is the birthplace (1890) of Supreme Court Chief Justice Fred Vinson.

Louisbourg town, pop. 1261, Cape Breton Co., NE Nova Scotia, on the E coast of Cape Breton I., on the Atlantic Ocean, 18 mi/29 km SE of Sydney. A fishing and fish processing community, it is adjacent (E) to the site of 18th-century Louisbourg, established in 1713 as the capital of the French colony of Île Royale (Cape Breton I.), and strongly fortified (1720s–40s) to control the entrance to the Gulf of St. Lawrence. Captured by New Englanders under Sir William Pepperell in 1745, Louisbourg was returned to France in 1748, but in 1758 was seized by the British, who destroyed the fortifications. Under reconstruction since the 1960s, the Fortress of Louisbourg National Historic Park is now Canada's largest (16,550 ac/6700 ha).

Louisburg town, pop. 3037, Franklin Co., EC North Carolina, 28 mi/45 km NE of Raleigh, on the Tar R. A tobacco, cotton, and lumber trade center settled in 1758, it is home to Louisburg College (Methodist; 1787).

Louisburg Square residential square on the W side of Beacon Hill, Boston, Massachusetts. On it is a group of meticulously maintained 1830s town houses, one of Boston's most desirable addresses. Writers who have lived on Louisburg Square include Louisa May Alcott, William Dean Howells, and Henry James.

Louisiana state of the SC US, variously considered part of the Deep SOUTH and the easternmost of the SOUTHWEST states; 1990 pop. 4,219,973 (100.3% of 1980; rank: 21st); area 51,843 sq mi/134,273 sq km (rank: 31st); admitted to Union 1812 (18th). Capital: BATON ROUGE. Most populous cities: NEW ORLEANS, Baton Rouge, SHREVEPORT, METAIRIE (unincorporated), LAFAYETTE. Louisiana is bordered N by Arkansas; W by Texas, with the SABINE R. and TOLEDO BEND RESERVOIR forming much of the boundary; and E by Mississippi, with the MISSISSIPPI and PEARL rivers forming much of the boundary. On the S, the state extends into the Gulf of MEXICO, its area expanding continuously through the accretional growth of the DELTA OF THE MISSISSIPPI RIVER; much of Louisiana consists literally of fragments of other states in the Mississippi-Missouri system. The entire state lies within the Gulf COASTAL PLAIN and intersecting Mississippi ALLUVIAL plain, rising to only 535 ft/163 m at DRISKILL Mt. (NW). The coast is a land of BAYOUS and marshes, SALT DOMES like AVERY I., islets and channels that are always changing shape, and brackish lakes like PONTCHARTRAIN and MAUREPAS. DISTRIBUTARIES of the Mississippi, like BAYOU LAFOURCHE and the ATCHAFALAYA R., pass through the delta, representing past or possible future main channels of the river, which is now, however, heavily engineered, LEVEES and floodways in place to prevent catastrophic change. Most of the land in the S, including the city of New Orleans, lies below river level. As part of HURRICANE ALLEY, it is also vulnerable to flooding from the sea. Behind the coast the land rises through a low, rich plain or prairie, and into slightly higher rolling, pine-covered land in the NW. The interior is well drained by the RED and OUACHITA rivers and their tributaries, and has important soybean, cotton, and lumber industries. Louisiana is part of the OIL PATCH, second only to Texas as a petroleum producer. There are thousands of wells along its coast and far onto the CONTINENTAL SHELF in the Gulf of Mexico. In the SW, LAKE CHARLES and Lafayette are centers of the industry, and along the SW and SC coast salt and sulfur, as well as oil and gas, are extracted in many places. The other major drilling zone extends along the N of the state, and into Arkansas; Shreveport is the industrial hub of the region. Between New Orleans and Baton Rouge, a 70-mi/115-km stretch of the Mississippi, navigable by ocean going vessels, has filled with refineries and petrochemical plants, existing side by side with older sugar plantations and small river communities. Sixteenth-century Spanish explorers found the region thinly populated by now largely disappeared tribes. In 1682 La Salle claimed the entire Mississippi R. basin for France, naming it for Louis XIV (the modern form combines the French *Louis* with a Spanish ending). The French founded New Orleans in 1718, four years after their first settlement at NATCHITOCHES (NW). Under Spanish control 1763–1800, the colony reverted to France briefly before it was sold to the US (1803) in the LOUISIANA PURCHASE. Its French/Spanish past heavily influences Louisiana's life. Inhabitants of PARISHES (counties) in the S, called Creoles, originally represented a mix of the two peoples. Cosmopolitan New Orleans developed into something closer to a multiracial society than seen elsewhere in the US, even though slavery had been introduced in the 1720s. After 1755, French expelled from ACADIA came to settle in the SW, in what is now called CAJUN COUNTRY (or Acadiana), whose original center was the BAYOU TECHE country around SAINT MARTINVILLE, but which has expanded throughout the SW. After 1803, Americans moved into Louisiana, and it came to be viewed as having a "French" S and an "American" N. Parishes in the SE (involved in an ongoing territorial dispute with WEST FLORIDA) were added in 1812. In early 1815, the last battle of the War of 1812 (fought after a peace had been signed in Europe) ended with a crushing victory over the British by Andrew Jackson's motley forces at CHALMETTE, just SE of New Orleans. In 1824 the state adopted a Civil Code based on French (Napoleonic) and Roman models, which is unique in the US. Cotton and sugar dominated agriculture in the 19th century, and New Orleans was one of America's leading ports, the outlet for the COTTON BELT. In the Civil War the Union established control of the Mississippi in 1862, but Confederate forces held parts of the W until 1865. In 1901, oil was found, and Baton Rouge became a refining center. In the 1920s, with agricultural importance shifting to lumber and industry, the "American" N became politically dominant, personified in the career of Huey Long (1893–1935), from rural WINNFIELD. In recent decades, the rise and fall of the world oil market has caused up and down cycles in the state's economy. New Orleans, Baton Rouge, and their region remain a vital refining, petrochemical, and shipping hub. Fishing, trapping, and other ancient occupations remain important along the coast and in the Delta. Tourism is a major industry, centering on New Orleans and its famous Mardi Gras and on Cajun Country. The state's peoples have continued to mix, producing one of the most richly "ethnic" of American communities. Almost 31% of Louisianans are black, a proportion second only to that in neighboring Mississippi.

Louisiana Purchase area (some 830,000 sq mi/2.15 million sq km) W of the Mississippi R., acquired by the US from France in 1803. The French colony of Louisiana came into being when the explorer La Salle, descending the Mississippi to the Gulf of Mexico, claimed (1682) the entire river basin, naming it for Louis XIV. This Louisiana was never clearly defined. It passed into Spanish hands in 1762. In 1763 the British took control of areas E of the river, most of which passed to the US after the American Revolution; in 1783 Britain gave WEST FLORIDA back to Spain. In 1800 the Spanish secretly returned Louisiana to the French. In 1803 Napoleon I, fearing the loss of the area to the British, and wanting to strengthen the US as a rival to Britain, negotiated with US emissaries, who had been instructed by President Jefferson to acquire New Orleans and West Florida; the main American interest was free commercial outlet via the Mississippi for burgeoning American settlements across the Midwest. The French, to the Americans' surprise, sold them all of Louisiana for $15 million. The Purchase doubled the size of US-controlled territory. Its outlines, which were in dispute for some time, followed the Red and Arkansas rivers W and NW to the Rocky Mts., then proceeded N along the Continental Divide. It thus included all of modern Arkansas, Missouri, Iowa, Nebraska, and South Dakota; most of North Dakota, Minnesota, Montana, Wyoming, Kansas, Oklahoma, and Louisiana; and parts of Colorado. Jefferson soon dispatched expeditions up the Red. R. and the Missouri (see LEWIS AND CLARK NATIONAL HISTORIC TRAIL) to explore the new acquisitions and strengthen American claims to them and to neighboring territory. Westward settlement continued, and treaties with the British in 1818 (establishing the FORTY-NINTH PARALLEL as a N boundary) and with the Spanish in 1819 (opening Texas and areas in the SW, and the Oregon Territory in the NW) furthered American territorial expansion.

Louisiana Superdome enclosed arena in New Orleans, Louisiana. Built in 1971–75, it seats 76,000, is home to the New Orleans Saints (football) and since 1975 to the Sugar Bowl (New Year's Eve college bowl game), and is used for conventions and trade shows as well as a wide range of sports events.

Louisville **1.** city, pop. 12,361, Boulder Co., NC Colorado, a residential suburb 16 mi/26 km NNW of Denver. Once a coal mining center, it now includes computer components and telephone systems among its manufactures. **2.** city, pop. 269,063, seat of Jefferson Co., NC Kentucky, at the Falls of the Ohio R. opposite JEFFERSONVILLE, CLARKSVILLE, and NEW ALBANY, Indiana. The "Gateway to the South," a railroad and river traffic hub, it is widely known as the site of the Kentucky Derby. George Rogers Clark settled on Corn I. (1778); after the Kentucky shore was settled, the site was named for Louis XVI of France. Populated by Pennsylvania Germans and Louisiana French, Louisville grew prosperous because it was at the non-navigable falls, the only spot on the Ohio between Pittsburgh and New Orleans where goods and passengers had to go ashore. It was later a supply center and headquarters for the Union army in the Western theater. The city manufactures whiskey, tractors, paint and varnishes, household appliances, cars and trucks (Ford; Mazda), and aluminum. The Louisville Slugger baseball bat, long made here, is now made in Jeffersonville. The city is also a financial and corporate center, and home to the Humana hospital chain. The University of Louisville (1798), Spalding University (1814), and Bellarmine College (1950) are among numerous institutions. Churchill Downs, home of the Kentucky Derby, initiated in 1875, is on Central Ave., SSW of Downtown.

Loup River 68 mi/109 km long, in EC Nebraska. It is formed by three branches that drain much of C Nebraska, flowing generally SE from the High Plains into the Platte R. valley. The **North Loup** rises in Cherry Co., and flows 212 mi/339 km to join the **Middle Loup** (which also rises in Cherry Co., and flows 221 mi/354 km), forming the mainstream some 23 mi/37 km N of Grand Island. The main Loup then continues ENE to join the PLATTE R. at COLUMBUS. The **South Loup** rises N of North Platte and flows 152 mi/243 km to join the Middle Loup E of Boelus. The 76 mi/122 km–long Calamus R. joins the North Loup near Burwell, having passed through dam-created Calamus Reservoir, one of several power and flood control projects on the Loup system.

Love Canal former canal and subdivision in the city of NIAGARA FALLS, W New York. It gave its name to one of the best-known toxic waste scandals of the 20th century. Land surrounding the canal, the site of a middle-class residential community, was polluted by dumping by a nearby chemical company. Many inhabitants experienced serious health problems; community complaints and demonstrations escalated, peaking in the late 1970s. The government declared a state of emergency; the neighborhood was evacuated, and most of its homes were destroyed. The area was subsequently cleaned up and partially rebuilt, and in the early 1990s families began to move into newly built homes in what is now called Black Creek Village.

Love Field also, **Dallas-Love Field** see under NORTH DALLAS, Texas.

Loveland **1.** city, pop. 37,352, Larimer Co., NC Colorado, on the Big Thompson R., 11 mi/18 km S of Fort Collins. It was founded in 1877 during the construction of the Colorado Central Railroad. The early settlers were unsuccessful gold prospectors who took up farming. Current industries include the trading, processing, and shipping of sugar beets, alfalfa, vegetables, grains, cherries, and livestock. Among its manufactures are electronic instruments, steel, prefabricated and mobile homes, and furniture. The city is also a tourist base for Rocky Mountain National Park, to its W. **2.** city, pop. 9930, Clermont, Warren, and Hamilton counties, SW Ohio, on the Little Miami R., 15 mi/24 km NE of Cincinnati. Founded in 1825, it is primarily a residential suburb.

Lover's Leap or, **Lovers' Leap** common locality name, given to a cliff or promontory from which one or both of a pair of star-crossed lovers are said to have jumped in despair. A noted example is a 230-ft/70-m bluff in Hannibal, Missouri. Experts have noted that while local legend often describes the lovers as Indians, the name Lover's Leap exists also in England.

Loves Park city, pop. 15,462, Winnebago Co., NC Illinois, on the Rock R., a residential suburb immediately NE of Rockford and 12 mi/19 km S of the Wisconsin border. Developed on the site of a local picnicking area in 1925, it now manufactures ready-mix concrete, machine tools, sheet metal, and potato chips. Rock Cut State Park is just to the NE.

Lovington city, pop. 9322, seat of Lea Co., SE New Mexico, 15 mi/24 km W of the Texas border, 20 mi/32 km NW of Hobbs. It is the center of a LLANO ESTACADO farming and ranching area rich in natural gas and oil.

Low Country see under UP COUNTRY, South Carolina.

Lowe, Mount 5650 ft/1722 m, in the San Gabriel Mts., SW California, immediately NW of Mt. WILSON and 4 mi/6 km N of downtown PASADENA. It was a noted early-20th-century resort, esp. for its incline (funicular) railway.

Lowell **1.** city, pop. 1224, Benton Co., NW Arkansas, in the Ozark Plateau, 13 mi/21 km N of Fayetteville. In an urbanized corridor running N along US 71 from Fayetteville through Springdale to Rogers, it is home to the J.B. Rogers trucking company. **2.** city, pop. 103,439, co-seat (with CAMBRIDGE) of Middlesex Co., NE Massachusetts, at the junction of the Concord and Merrimack rivers, 25 mi/40 km NW of Boston. From the 1650s an agricultural community, part of Chelmsford, it developed rapidly as a textile manufacturer after 1822, when associates of Francis Cabot Lowell built the first factory. The Pawtucket Falls, which drop 32 ft/10 m, augmented by the flow through a series of canals, provided abundant power, and the industry flourished until 1924, after which Southern competition closed down several plants. Electronics (Wang Laboratories is here) is now the chief industry; chemicals, leather, apparel, and publishing are also important. Prominent sites include Lowell National Historical Park, with restorations of early mills; the birthplace (1834) of James Abbott McNeill Whistler, a gallery exhibiting his etchings; and a memorial to Jack Kerouac, who was born (1922) and buried here. Lowell has been noted for the strength of its diverse ethnic communities, among them French-Canadians, English, Irish, Greeks, Poles, and, recently, Cambodians.

Lowell Observatory see under FLAGSTAFF, Arizona.

Lower Burrell city, pop. 12,251, Westmoreland Co., SW Pennsylvania, on the Allegheny R., 16 mi/26 km NE of Pittsburgh. Steel is produced here.

Lower Canada in 1791–1841, the E ("lower" on the St. Lawrence R.) part of the older British Province of Quebec, equivalent to modern Québec below what was RUPERT'S LAND, and including at times Labrador; UPPER CANADA was created as a separate province in 1791. In the 19th century, growing conflict between the interests of the francophone majority and the political and economic hegemony of the anglophone minority led to the 1837–38 PATRIOTE rebellion in Lower Canada, and in 1841 to the establishment of the United PROVINCE OF CANADA, in which Lower Canada became Canada East.

Lower Counties the three counties of Delaware (New Castle, Kent, and Sussex) considered as the S part of the 1680s grant to William Penn that created Pennsylvania. They held their first separate assembly in 1704 at NEW CASTLE.

Lower Downtown familiarly, **LoDo** redeveloping restaurant, arts, and entertainment district in the NW of Downtown, DENVER, Colorado, close to the South Platte R. Union Station and railyards are here, and LARIMER St. runs through the area. Just NE is the Curtis Park neighborhood, which has undergone substantial gentrification.

Lower East Side **1.** section of Detroit, Michigan, just NE of Downtown, home in the 20th century to successive waves of immigrants arriving to work in the auto industry. Germans and Eastern and Southern Europeans have lived here. By the 1930s thousands of Southern blacks were jammed into the PARADISE VALLEY (Black Bottom) area; from the 1940s the "Detroit Plan" broke up thisneighborhood with roadways and housing projects. Among more recent Lower East Side residents are a large number of Syrians and other Arabs. **2.** historic residential and commercial district, lower Manhattan, New York City. Chinatown and Little Italy lie to the S and SW of the area, the East R. to the E. That part of the Lower East Side lying N of Houston Street came later to be called the EAST VILLAGE. Although parts of the area were inhabited by large numbers of Irish and German immigrants in the mid 19th century, it was after the 1880s, when East European Jews moved into hundreds of six-story railroad-flat tenement buildings, that the Lower East Side took on the character it is famous for. Many noted New Yorkers were born or first lived here, moving later to neighborhoods in other parts of the city. The Lower East Side's delicatessens, street markets, bathhouses, and synagogues throbbed with Jewish culture in the period through World War I. In the district B'nai B'rith, Lillian Wald's Henry Street Settlement, and the Jewish newspaper the *Forward* were founded. The Lower East Side today retains some of its past character, as at the Orchard St. market, but its population is more mixed, including many Hispanics as well as Chinese moving north from Chinatown.

Lower Fort Garry see under SELKIRK, Manitoba.

Lower 48 from an Alaskan point of view, the contiguous (and earlier admitted) 48 US states.

Lower Hill mixed-use section of Pittsburgh, Pennsylvania, immediately E of the GOLDEN TRIANGLE. The CIVIC ARENA and high-rise apartment and office buildings here were erected as part of urban renewal projects during the 1950s and 1960s. In the process, 8000 mostly black residents and their businesses were displaced.

Lower Mainland in SW British Columbia, the coastal area around and including VANCOUVER, which faces Vancouver I. (W) across the Strait of Georgia.

Lower Merion township, pop. 58,003, Montgomery Co., SE Pennsylvania, just W of Philadelphia. Primarily an affluent residential suburb on Philadelphia's MAIN LINE, it includes such communities as ARDMORE, BALA-CYNWYD, part of BRYN MAWR, HAVERFORD, MERION, ROSEMONT, and Penn Wynne.

Lower Peninsula the mitten-shaped S portion of the state of Michigan. It is rich in forests and agriculture, which includes field crops, livestock, a large dairy industry, and many orchards. The S section is heavily populated, with several major industrial concentrations, including what has historically been the world center of auto manufacturing, in and around Detroit. It also engages in shipbuilding and commercial fishing, and trades both nationally and internationally via the Great Lakes. Michigan's UPPER PENINSULA lies just to the N and NW.

Lower Town **1.** section of OTTAWA, Ontario, E of the RIDEAU CANAL, which bisects the city, and W of the Rideau R., extending SE from the Ottawa R. The oldest part of Ottawa, it was settled (as Bytown) by soldiers and canal laborers in the 1820s, and was the city's commercial center through the 1860s. SUSSEX DRIVE winds around its W. Historically Catholic and largely French-speaking, the area is today noted for its boutiques, restaurants, bars, and night clubs, as well as the 19th-century Byward Market. **2.** French, **Basse-Ville** site of Samuel de Champlain's original (1608) settlement of QUÉBEC CITY, Québec, on the N side of the St. Lawrence R., at the foot of Cap-Diamant, extending around its base to the city's harbor and the mouth of the R. St.-Charles (N). In decline after the mid 19th century, the area has recently been rehabilitated and is a commercial, residential, and tourist district, noted for its narrow streets and old houses, many around the Place-Royale, site of Champlain's *habitation*.

Lowertown commercial neighborhood in downtown St. Paul, Minnesota, along the Mississippi R. With the conversion of its old and obsolete warehouses, it became an upscale office, residential, and shopping center during the 1980s.

Lower West Side see NEAR WEST SIDE, Chicago, Illinois.

Lowndes County 714 sq mi/1849 sq km, pop. 12,658, in SC Alabama, SW of Montgomery. At the center of the BLACK BELT, it is rich in cotton, cattle, and pecans. Hayneville (pop. 969) is its seat. The Alabama R. forms its N boundary. Lowndes's population has long been predominantly black (75% in 1990). This fact encouraged the Student Nonviolent Coordinating Committee to seek political control here after 1964, but their Lowndes Co. Freedom Organization (called the Black Panther Party, a name later used elsewhere) was ultimately unsuccessful.

Lowry Air Force Base on the E boundary of DENVER, Colorado. Established as an Air Corps technical school in 1937, it occupied nearly 65,000 ac/26,325 ha, almost all of which was a practice range for bombers. Today it has been reduced to a small administrative center, as the city and suburbs have grown around it. STAPLETON INTERNATIONAL AIRPORT is just N.

Lowry Hill upscale residential neighborhood and cultural center in Minneapolis, Minnesota, immediately SW of Downtown. It is the site of the Guthrie Theater and the Walker Arts Center.

Lowry Hill East see the WEDGE, Minneapolis, Minnesota.

Loxahatchee National Wildlife Refuge see under DELRAY BEACH, Florida.

loyalists also, **United Empire Loyalists** in Canada, American colonists who, for various reasons, remained loyal to Britain during the American Revolution (1775–83), many of whom, leaving the new United States, settled in parts of Canada. Although many had commercial, professional, or military ties to British administration, others were farmers, recent immigrants, members of religious sects, blacks, or Indians. Important concentrations included those in what are now Québec's Eastern Townships; along the Atlantic Coast, in Halifax, and on Cape Breton I. (for a time officially a loyalist colony), Nova Scotia; on St. John's (now Prince Edward) I.; in the St. John R. valley of New Brunswick; and in previously lightly settled S Ontario, where their presence prompted the 1791 establishment of UPPER CANADA.

Lubbock city, pop. 186,206, seat of Lubbock Co., W Texas, 112 mi/180 km S of Amarillo, in the heart of the South Plains section of the LLANO ESTACADO. Formed in 1891 when rival towns Monterey and old Lubbock agreed to merge in a new location, it was incorporated when the Santa Fe Railroad arrived in 1909. It began as a ranching center, but artesian wells brought mixed farming, so that the area is now a leader in production of grains and cotton. It has large cattle feedlots. The manufacturing and commercial hub of the South Plains, Lubbock produces earth moving machinery, pipe, pumps, farm equipment, electronic components, and prefabricated and mobile homes. Reese Air Force Base, 9 mi/14 km W, contributes significantly to the economy. The "Chrysanthemum Capital of the World" hosts the annual Panhandle–South Plains Fair. It is home to Texas Tech University (1923) and to Lubbock Christian College (1957).

Lubec easternmost US town, pop. 1853, Washington Co., E Maine. Lubec lies between Cobscook Bay and the Atlantic Ocean, just S of EASTPORT, of which it was originally part. It includes several villages, and WEST QUODDY HEAD, the nation's easternmost point. An international bridge connects Lubec with CAMPOBELLO I. Chaloner Tavern (1804) was a 19th-century trading point for sugar, molasses, flour, and rum smuggled from Canada. Tourism and fishing are the local economy's mainstays.

Lucas County 341 sq mi/883 sq km, pop. 462,361, in NW Ohio, bounded by Michigan (N), L. Erie (NE), and the Maumee R. (SE). Its seat is TOLEDO, which, along with its suburbs, takes up a large part of the county. The city's economy is a primary factor in the county's economy. Agriculture includes corn, fruit, livestock, soybean, vegetable, and wheat farming. FORT MEIGS and FALLEN TIMBERS State Park are here.

Ludington city, pop. 8507, seat of Mason Co., WC Michigan, on L. Michigan and Pere Marquette L., at the mouth of the Pere Marquette R., 50 mi/80 km NNW of Muskegon. It is a beach resort, with sport fishing in L. Michigan, on the river, and in nearby lakes and streams. Ludington is a manufacturing center making game boards, rail equipment, auto parts, chemicals, clothing, and furniture. It is also an important port, with commercial fishing and train, car, and passenger ferries across L. Michigan. The spot where the French missionary Père Marquette is thought to have died (1675) is marked by a large illuminated cross that overlooks the harbor.

Ludlow **1.** locality in the N section of TRINIDAD, Colorado. The Ludlow Monument marks the site of the Ludlow Massacre, where women and children died in a fire during a 1913–14 coal mining strike. **2.** town, pop. 18,820, Hampden Co., SC Massachusetts, on the Chicopee R., just NE of Springfield. Settled in 1751 as part of Springfield, it was an early mill town, and an important jute and flax processor in the early 20th century. Now it produces machinery and plastics and processes food.

Lufkin city, pop. 30,206, seat of Angelina Co., in the PINEY WOODS of E Texas, 120 mi/193 km NNE of Houston, near the Angelina R. and Sam Rayburn Reservoir. Founded in 1882 as regional railroads expanded, it became a major sawmilling center. It has woodworking, pulp, and newsprint plants, and makes mill and oilfield machinery and trailers. Deposits of oil, natural gas, and clays are important in the area. Between the Davy Crockett (W) and Angelina (E) national forests, the city has both Federal and Texas forestry facilities. Angelina College (1966) is here.

Luke Air Force Range and Base see under BARRY M. GOLDWATER RANGE, Arizona.

Lukens, Mount see under SAN GABRIEL Mts., California.

Lumberton city, pop. 18,601, seat of Robeson Co., SE North Carolina, on Interstate 95 and the Lumber R., 30 mi/48 km SSW of Fayetteville. Founded in 1787, it developed as a distribution point for lumber and naval stores. It is now a tobacco and agricultural market center with manufactures including textiles, clothing, and tobacco products. The Lumbee (Croatan) have inhabited the area since before whites arrived.

Lundy's Lane battle site in NIAGARA FALLS, S Ontario. This roadway (now Route 20, leading W) was the scene of an encounter on the evening of July 25, 1814, between British and invading American forces, in which both sides suffered their heaviest losses of the War of 1812. By midnight the Americans were retreating S toward FORT ERIE. Although less than decisive, this action effectively quelled the American invasion of Canada.

Lunenburg town, pop. 2781, seat of Lunenburg Co. (pop. 47,634), SW Nova Scotia, on a peninsula on the Atlantic Ocean, 40 mi/64 km WSW of Halifax. Once an Acadian village, it was resettled by the British in 1753 with largely German-speaking Protestants, and became an agricultural and fishing center. In the 19th century it was central to Canada's Atlantic fisheries, producing esp. dried cod. As a shipbuilder, it is best known for the fishing/racing schooner *Bluenose* (1921). Today shipyards, fish processing plants, foundries, and marine engine works are important. A tourist center, the town has an annual Fisheries Exhibition and Fishermen's Reunion, crafts and folk festivals, artists' studios, and the Fisheries Museum of the Atlantic.

Luray Caverns geologic site in Luray, Page Co., NW Virginia, on the W side of the Blue Ridge Mts., in the Shenandoah Valley. A popular tourist site, they are the largest caverns in the eastern US. Discovered in 1878, they cover approximately 65 ac/26 ha; some of the caves are nearly 300 ft/90 m high. The town of **Luray** (pop. 4587), just E, is a resort and commercial center on Hawksbill Creek, a tributary to the Shenandoah's South Fork.

Lutcher town, pop. 3907, St. James Parish, SE Louisiana, on the RIVER ROAD, 38 mi/62 km WNW of New Orleans. In an agricultural area that produces sugar cane and rice, it is noted as the world's only producer of perique tobacco, a strong black type used in making blends.

Lutherville unincorporated residential suburb, Baltimore Co., N Maryland, 9 mi/14 km N of downtown Baltimore, on the Baltimore Beltway (I-695). With Timonium (N), it has a pop. of 16,442.

Luzerne County 891 sq mi/2309 sq km, pop. 328,149, in E Pennsylvania. Its seat is WILKES-BARRE. The Susquehanna R. cuts through its N portion. Nearness to the huge deposits of anthracite coal in the WYOMING VALLEY spurred the county's development, and the decline of the coal mining industry has meant economic difficulties for workers here, particularly in highly industrialized Wilkes-Barre.

Lycoming County 1237 sq mi/3204 sq km, pop. 118,710, in NC Pennsylvania. Its seat, largest city, and main industrial center is WILLIAMSPORT. The county is in a hilly and heavily forested part of the state. The West Branch of the Susquehanna R. runs across the S of Pennsylvania's largest county.

Lyell, Mount see under YOSEMITE NATIONAL PARK, California.

Lyme town, pop. 1949, New London Co., SE Connecticut, on the Connecticut R., 12 mi/19 km WNW of New London. A resort town with some agriculture and fishing, it includes the villages of Hadlyme, North Lyme, and Hamburg, and has three state parks. Hadlyme is the site of Gillette Castle, the fanciful home (1919) of actor William Gillette, now a major tourist attraction. Lyme disease was first described here in the 1970s.

Lynbrook village, pop. 19,208, in Hempstead town, Nassau Co., SE New York, 18 mi/29 km SE of Manhattan, on Long Island's South Shore. It produces sheet metal products and furniture, but is primarily residential.

Lynchburg 1. town, pop. 4721, seat of Moore Co., S Tennessee, 16 mi/26 km SSE of Shelbyville. The Jack Daniel's whiskey distillery was established in this agricultural area in 1866, at Cave Spring, on the East Fork of Mulberry Creek. Tourism is important. **2.** city, pop. 66,049, in but administratively separate from Campbell Co., WC Virginia, on the James R., 90 mi/140 km WSW of Richmond, in the foothills of the BLUE RIDGE Mts. It is a transportation, trade, and distribution center for the Piedmont region, and an historic tobacco market. Its varied industries manufacture shoes, apparel, pharmaceuticals, cosmetics, electronic equipment, and steel products. Founded in 1757 by Quakers, Lynchburg grew rapidly after the James River and Kanawha Canal (1840) linked it with Richmond. It was a Confederate supply base during the Civil War, and was attacked unsuccessfully by Union troops in June 1864. It has many institutions of higher learning, including Randolph-Macon Woman's College (1891), Lynchburg College (1903), Central Virginia Community College (1966), and Liberty University (1971).

Lynches River 140 mi/210 km long, in S North Carolina and E South Carolina. It rises just SW of Monroe, North Carolina, crosses the state line, and flows SE through the SANDHILLS into the Low Country past Lee State Park (E of Bishopville) and Lynchburg to the PEE DEE R., 5 mi/8 km E of Johnsonville.

Lyndhurst 1. township, pop. 18,262, Bergen Co., NE New Jersey, 3 mi/5 km SE of Passaic. Primarily a residential suburb, it is also an office and manufacturing center whose products include metal goods, machinery, clothing, textiles, and processed foods. Lyndhurst is also the site of the Environmental Education Center, an urban wetlands facility, and a popular medieval-style tournament. **2.** city, pop. 15,982, Cuyahoga Co., NE Ohio, a residential suburb, 11 mi/18 km E of Cleveland.

Lyndon town, pop. 5371, Caledonia Co., NE Vermont, on the Passumpsic R., 7 mi/11 km N of St. Johnsbury. Lyndon State College (1911) is in Lyndonville village, at the town's center.

Lyndon B. Johnson National Historic Park see under JOHNSON CITY, Texas.

Lynn city, pop. 81,245, Essex Co., NE Massachusetts, on Lynn Harbor in Massachusetts Bay, 11 mi/17 km NE of Boston. It has made shoes since the 1630s, and has been a shoe manufacturing center since 1848. An iron-smelting works was established in 1643. Since 1930, when General Electric established a plant, industry has diversified; electrical instruments, generators, machinery, textiles, and clothing are produced. In 1942, the first successful US turbojet engine was designed and built here. An historical landmark is the house where Mary Baker Eddy lived and held the first Christian Science meeting (1875). The town of NAHANT extends S on a long peninsula.

Lynnfield town, pop. 11,274, Essex Co., NE Massachusetts. It is adjacent (NW) to Lynn and (W) to Peabody. Lynnfield is largely a residential suburb of these and other towns. Routes 95 and 128 and US 1 pass through the town, with commercial development along them.

Lynn Haven city, pop. 9298, Bay Co., NW Florida, on the N arm of St. Andrew Bay, 5 mi/8 km N of Panama City. Settled in 1912, it is a trade center for local lumber.

Lynnwood city, pop. 28,695, Snohomish Co., WC Washington, 15 mi/24 km N of Seattle. A growing residential and industrial suburb, it manufactures prefabricated homes and wood and agricultural products.

Lynwood city, pop. 61,945, Los Angeles Co., SW California, 10 mi/16 km S of downtown Los Angeles, and just N of Compton. Founded in 1896, it was a dairying community, and is now a residential suburb and an industrial center producing oil industry equipment, machinery, paints, and pottery.

Lyons 1 village, pop. 9828, Cook Co., NE Illinois, on the Des Plaines R., a residential suburb 10 mi/16 km SW of the Loop. Sometimes called the "Gateway to the West," Lyons is the site of the Chicago portage used by Indians and French explorers traveling between the Great Lakes and the Des Plaines R., which joins the Illinois R. and ultimately flows into the Mississippi R. **2.** city, pop. 3688, seat of Rice Co., C Kansas, 26 mi/42 km NW of Hutchinson. The area was visited by Coronado in 1541 in his search for QUIVIRA, and a settlement was laid out in 1876 on the SANTA FE TRAIL. Salt mining and processing began here in 1890, and remain important. Wheat also contributes to the city's economy. **3.** town, pop. 6315, seat of Wayne Co., W New York, on the Erie Canal, 15 mi/24 km S of L. Ontario and 32 mi/52 km SE of Rochester. It was settled in 1800. In a region filled with orchards, Lyons is a canning center; other industries produce machinery, fertilizer, and chemicals. Summer tourism is also important.

M

Mableton unincorporated community, pop. 25,725, Cobb Co., NW Georgia, 13 mi/21 km WNW of Atlanta, of which it is a residential suburb.

Macalaster-Groveland residential neighborhood in St. Paul, Minnesota, SW of Downtown. Long the wealthiest area of the city, it includes SUMMIT AVENUE and its mansions.

MacArthur Park 32-ac/13-ha municipal park on WILSHIRE Blvd. in Los Angeles, California, 1.5 mi/2 km W of Downtown. Its original name, Westlake Park, was also applied to the densely settled middle-class residential area around it.

MacDill Air Force Base see under TAMPA, Florida.

MacDowell Colony see under PETERBOROUGH, New Hampshire.

Machesna Mountain see under LA PANZA Mts., California.

Machesney Park village, pop. 19,033, Winnebago Co., NC Illinois, on the Rock R., a residential suburb 5 mi/8 km N of Rockford and 10 mi/16 km S of the Wisconsin border. Rock Cut State Park is immediately to the E.

Machias town, pop. 2569, seat of Washington Co., E Maine. Machias is on US 1 and the Machias R., at the head of Machias Bay, 25 mi/40 km SW of Eastport. Originally an English trading post, in the 1700s it became a stronghold for pirates, including Samuel Bellamy, the Robin Hood of American piracy. In 1775, the British vessel *Margaretta* was captured in Machias Bay, in one of the Revolution's first naval engagements. The settlement developed as a lumber and shipbuilding center, one of the last communities to have spring log drives on the river. In a depressed industrial area of lumber and paper mills and canneries, Machias is now engaged in tourism, timber, granite quarrying, grist and rayon milling, and farming. The University of Maine has a campus here. **Machiasport,** pop. 1166, became a separate town in 1862, and lies adjacent to the E and along the water.

Mackenzie District see under NORTHWEST TERRITORIES.

Mackenzie Mountains N range of the Rocky Mts., comprising several NW–SE trending subranges along much of the border between the Yukon Territory (W) and Northwest Territories (E). Extending for 500 mi/800 km from the British Columbia border (S) to the Peel R. valley (N), the range is abutted by the Yukon Plateau to the W. The Backbone Ranges form the main core of the Mackenzies, attaining the greatest elevation at Mt. Sir James MacBrien (9062 ft/2762 m), the highest point in the Northwest Territories. The Canyon Ranges are E of the Backbones, and the FRANKLIN Mts. (c.300 mi/500 km long) are an E outlier. The Mackenzies, with precipitation blocked by the SELWYN Mts. (W), are relatively dry, and have a low timberline. They form a watershed between tributaries of the Mackenzie (parallel to the E) and Yukon (W) rivers, and are the source for the Pelly R., a headstream of the Yukon. The peaks of the Selwyns are often considered part of the Mackenzies. Lead and zinc were found here in the 1960s.

Mackenzie River 1120 mi/1800 km long, in the Northwest Territories. Taking its most distant headstream, British Columbia's Finlay R. (via L. WILLISTON, the PEACE R., the SLAVE R., and GREAT SLAVE L.) into account, it is North America's second-longest river system (after the Mississippi-Missouri), at 2635 mi/4340 km; it drains an area of c.680,000 sq mi/1.8 million sq km, including much of the W Northwest Territories, N British Columbia, N Alberta, and extreme NW Saskatchewan. The Mackenzie proper flows from marshes at the W end of Great Slave L., and proceeds WNW to Fort Simpson, where the LIARD R. joins it from the SW. It then flows generally NW, between the Mackenzie Mts. (W) and Franklin Mts. (E), through the Mackenzie Lowlands, past Wrigley, Fort Norman (where the Great Bear R. drains GREAT BEAR L. into it from the E), the oil center of NORMAN WELLS, and Fort Good Hope, to Arctic Red River, where the river of the same name joins it from the SW and the DEMPSTER HIGHWAY crosses it. It then enters (N) a 90 mi/145 km–long, 60 mi/100 km–wide delta, where the INUIT communities of INUVIK, Aklavik, and Tuktoyaktuk lie, and empties into Mackenzie Bay (the BEAUFORT SEA). Other major headstreams include the ATHABASCA R., which flows through the Slave R. to join it, and the Hay R., which joins it at HAY RIVER, on the S of Great Slave L. The **Mackenzie Lowlands,** some 200 mi/320 km wide, are a N extension of the Great Plains, lying between the Rocky Mts. (the Mackenzies) and the W edge of the CANADIAN SHIELD. Near Fort Good Hope, the river flows through the Ramparts, 200 ft/61 m–high limestone cliffs; but most of its lower course is relatively flat, and in the N there are myriad islands and sandbars. The river's valley has long been home to Inuit on the tundra in the N and to DENE groups in the forests of the S. Alexander Mackenzie explored it in 1789 for the NORTH WEST COMPANY (it disappointed him by not flowing to the Pacific), and by the 1820s there were fur posts along it. Fur was central until gold rushes in the 1920s–30s brought prospectors to Yellowknife and the region, and World War II spurred development of the oil complex at Norman Wells. The river, lakes, and tributaries have been traveled by steamboats since the 1880s; the ice-free season is normally June through October.

Oil and gas exploration at Norman Wells and in the delta and Beaufort Sea have spurred talk of pipeline development, and in 1984 a sunken pipeline from Norman Wells to Alberta was put into service. The **Mackenzie Highway,** paralleling the river, is now open from S of Great Slave L. to Wrigley, and winter roads continue N to Fort Good Hope.

Mackinac, Straits of passageway between L. Huron (E) and L. Michigan (W), bridged by the MACKINACBRIDGE between Michigan's Lower Peninsula (S) and Upper Peninsula (N). The straits narrow to about 3.5 mi/5.6 km. MACKINAC, Round, and BOIS BLANC islands lie E. MACKINAW CITY is S, St. Ignace N.

Mackinac Bridge toll bridge, 5 mi/8 km long, over the Straits of Mackinac, joining St. Ignace on the Upper Peninsula with MACKINAW CITY on the Lower Peninsula of Michigan. Opened in 1957, it is one of the longest suspension bridges in the world. The center span is 3800 ft/1159 m long; 8344 ft/2545 m separate the main anchorages, and it has two 552-ft/168-m towers.

Mackinac Island 3 mi/5 km long and 2 mi/3 km wide, in Mackinac Co., N Michigan, in L. Huron at the E entrance of the Straits of Mackinac. A state park since 1895, the thickly forested island was an ancient burial ground, called Michilimackinac—"big turtle"—by the Ojibway. The French explorer Jean Nicolet first visited here in 1634. Its British fort (1780) was taken over by the US in 1783, and soon after the island became the headquarters of John Jacob Astor's American Fur Company. Today it is a city, with a pop. of 469, and a summer resort. Automobiles are forbidden, and there is horse and buggy and bicycle transport. On the island is the restored Fort Mackinac.

Mackinaw City village, pop. 875, Cheboygan and Emmet counties, opposite St. Ignace on the Straits of Mackinac, in the extreme N of the Lower Peninsula of Michigan. A French trading post (1673), it became Fort Michilimackinac in 1715. The British captured the fort in 1760, and it was held at various times thereafter by the French and Indians. The settlement was laid out in 1857, and its name was shortened in 1894. It is now a summer resort.

Mackinaw River 130 mi/209 km long, in Illinois. It rises near Sibley, in Ford Co., and flows W, SW, and then N to join the Illinois R. below PEKIN.

Macomb city, pop. 19,952, seat of McDonough Co., WC Illinois, on the East Fork of the La Moine R., 39 mi/63 km SW of Galesburg. It produces art pottery, porcelain products, and roller bearings, and there is some agricultural processing. Founded in 1829 as Washington, Macomb eventually became a center for farming and coal mining. It is the seat of Western Illinois University (1899). Argyle Lake State Park is 5 mi/8 km W.

Macomb County 1025 sq mi/2655 sq km, pop. 717,400, in SE Michigan, bounded by L. St. Clair's Anchor Bay (SE) and drained by the Clinton R. Its seat is Mount Clemens. It is heavily populated where it adjoins Detroit at its S end, containing such suburbs as Warren, Roseville, Sterling Heights, and St. Clair Shores. Most of the county, however, is devoted to vegetable, poultry, grain, and dairy farming. It has a US military reservation and Selfridge Air Force Base.

Macon city, pop. 106,612, seat of Bibb County, C Georgia, at the head of navigation (the Fall Line) on the Ocmulgee R., 75 mi/120 km SE of Atlanta. It is the industrial, commercial, and distribution center of a rich agricultural (fruit, truck crops, peanuts, pecans) region. Manufactures include textiles, farm machinery, pulpwood products, aircraft parts, chemicals, tile, tires, tobacco products, and brick. One of the world's largest deposits of kaolin is nearby. In 1806, the US Army established Fort Hawkins on the E side of the river; used in the War of 1812, it was abandoned in 1821, and the community took the name of Newtown. Macon was laid out in 1823 across the river, and annexed Newtown in 1829. During the Civil War, Macon was a Confederate supply depot and gold depository. World War I brought industrial growth, and in World War II Robins Air Force Base, 17 mi/27 km S in WARNER ROBINS, added further stimulus. Macon is home to Mercer University (1833), Wesleyan College (1836), and Macon College (1968). Several antebellum mansions and 19th-century cottages are preserved as museums, including the home of the poet Sidney Lanier. Ocmulgee National Monument, including temple mounds (A.D. 900–1100) is on the city's E side.

Macon County 581 sq mi/1505 sq km, pop. 117,206, in C Illinois. It is cut by the Sangamon R., which flows through the center of the county and through DECATUR, its seat. Outside the communications, distribution, and manufacturing center of Decatur, Macon Co. is agricultural, with soybeans and corn the main crops.

Macoupin River also, **Macoupin Creek** 100 mi/160 km long, in SW Illinois. It rises in NW Montgomery Co., and flows SW and W to the Illinois R., 2 mi/3 km NE of Hardin.

Madaket village in Nantucket Co., SE Massachusetts, at the SW corner of Nantucket I., noted for its beaches and harbor.

Madawaska River 30 mi/48 km long, in S Québec and NW New Brunswick. It flows from L. Temiscouata into the SAINT JOHN R. at Edmundston, New Brunswick, across from the mill center of **Madawaska,** Maine (town, pop. 4165, Aroostook Co.). New Brunswick's **Madawaska Co.** (1321 sq mi/3422 sq km; pop. 36,554), into which the river flows, became in the late 18th century home to many Acadians who had moved N following LOYALIST settlement of the Ste. Anne (Fredericton) area. The lumbering and farming district developed a fierce sense of separate identity as the "**Madawaska Republic,**" with its own flag and its capital at Edmundston; its citizens were known as *Brayons,* a name derived from an agricultural tool. Until 1842, when the "AROOSTOOK War" ended, Québec, New Brunswick, and Maine all had territorial designs on the Madawaska area. Today Madawaska remains a francophone center; its history contributes to its tourist industry.

Madeira city, pop. 9141, Hamilton Co., SW Ohio, a residential suburb on the NE edge of the most heavily developed part of the Cincinnati area.

Madeleine, Îles de la English, **Magdalen Islands** archipelago of 15 islands, pop. 13,991, in the Gulf of St. Lawrence, in extreme SE Québec, 60 mi/100 km NW of Cape Breton I., Nova Scotia, 100 mi/160 km W of Newfoundland, and 50 mi/80 km N of E Prince Edward I. Some 53 mi/85 km SW–NE, the group includes Île du Havre Aubert (Amherst), Île d'Entrée, Île du Cap aux Meules (Grindstone, the largest community), Île du Havre aux Maisons (Alright), Île aux Loups (Wolf), Île de la Grande Entrée (Coffin), Grosse Île, Île de l'Est (East), and Île Brion. Sandspits and dunes connect most of the islands. Fishing, fish processing, lobstering, sealing, and tourism are the main industries. The islands have large colonies of seabirds, and dramatically sculpted red and gray sandstone cliffs. They were probably first visited by Basque fishermen in the early 1500s, and were explored by Jacques Cartier in 1534 and Samuel de Champlain in 1609. Acadians came here in 1755 and developed communities, but after 1787, when Isaac Coffin controlled the islands, many left, to establish BLANC-SABLON and other mainland towns. In 1895 a new law encouraged many to return. Presently the islands contain both French- and English-speaking communities; Fatima (pop. 3106) and L'Étang-du-Nord (pop. 3044), both on L'Île du Cap aux Meules, are the largest.

Madeline Island 14 mi/23 km long, largest of the APOSTLE ISLANDS, in Ashland Co., NW Wisconsin, in L. Superior, N of the entrance to Chequamegon Bay. La Pointe (pop. 147), the only settlement in the Apostles, is here. The site of the earliest European trading and missionary activity in the continent's interior, Madeline I. was discovered in 1659 and became a French trading post in 1693. Reached by ferry from Bayfield, the island includes a museum, an airfield, Big Bay State Park, and the Bad River Indian Reservation.

Madera city, pop. 29,281, seat of Madera Co., C California, in the San Joaquin Valley, 20 mi/32 km NW of Fresno, on the Fresno R. The trade and processing center of an irrigated agricultural region, it has wineries, canneries, and lumber, meatpacking, and metal plants.

Madison **1.** city, pop. 14,904, Madison Co., N Alabama, 7 mi/11 km SW of downtown Huntsville and just NW of the Redstone Arsenal. Just off Interstate 565 between Huntsville and Decatur, it is a growing residential suburb. **2.** town, pop. 15,485, New Haven Co., SC Connecticut, on Long Island Sound and the Hammonasset R., 17 mi/27 km E of New Haven. Once a shipping center, now primarily residential, it has many Colonial homes. The town includes Madison village, East River village, and Hammonasset Beach State Park, at Hammonasset Point. **3.** city, pop. 12,006, seat of Jefferson Co., SE Indiana, on the Ohio R. (bridged here to Milton, Kentucky) and 40 mi/64 km NE of Louisville, Kentucky. A river port and tobacco market, with warehouses and auctions, it also has manufactures including furniture, machinery, metal and canvas products, shoes, and clothing. Settled early in the 19th century, the city is known for its many historic homes in the Federal, Greek Revival, Georgian, Gothic, and other styles. The Jefferson Proving Ground is 5 mi/8 km N of the city. **4.** borough, pop. 15,850, Morris Co., N New Jersey, 4 mi/6 km SE of Morristown. Settled in 1685, it was known as Bottle Hill until renamed for President Madison in 1834. It is primarily residential, with some industries and numerous corporate offices. The borough also has greenhouses, and is widely known for its roses. The Sayre House (1745) was headquarters for Anthony Wayne during the Revolution. Drew University (1866) and a campus of Fairleigh Dickinson University are here. **5.** village, pop. 2477, Lake Co., NE Ohio, 15 mi/24 km SW of Ashtabula, S of L. Erie and N of the Grand R. The local economy is supported by nurseries, winemaking, and the manufacture of pipe, mats, and wood products. The cartoonist Frederick B. Opper ("Happy Hooligan") was born here (1857). **6.** city, pop. 6257, seat of Lake Co., SE South Dakota, 38 mi/61 km NW of Sioux Falls. Madison L. is just S of the city, and L. Herman State Park is just to the SW. It is a trading center for the surrounding farming area, in which livestock, poultry, grain, and dairy goods are produced. Madison is the site of Dakota State University (1881). **7.** city, pop. 191,262, state capital and seat of Dane Co., SC Wisconsin, 75 mi/121 km W of Milwaukee. It is located in the FOUR LAKES district, known for its natural beauty. The center of the city is on an isthmus between L. Mendota and L. Monona; to the S are L. Kegonsa and L. Waubesa. The four are connected by the Yahara R., which flows through central Madison. The site was chosen for the capital of the newly organized Wisconsin Territory in 1836, and the city was incorporated in 1846. Its importance as a governmental center and the establishment of the University of Wisconsin here (1848) aided the city's growth. The university, today one of the largest in the US, is a leading employer and plays an enormous part in the city's life. Madison is a trade center for a rich agricultural and dairy region. Food processing and the manufacture of farm machinery, machine tools, and batteries are important industries. Major medical and scientific research institutions are here, as is the Museum of Wisconsin History, Madison Art Center, and US Forest Products Laboratory. Madison is also the site of the US Armed Forces Institute world headquarters.

Madison, Mount northernmost peak (5363 ft/1636 m) in the PRESIDENTIAL RANGE of the White Mts., NC New Hampshire. The mountain, with bedrock of micaceous schist and a steep cone made up of large talus blocks, drops sharply to the Androscoggin R. at Gorham (NE). In 1888 a stone climbers' hut, one of the first such in the US, was built by the Appalachian Mountain Club on its slopes; the present hut dates from 1940.

Madison Avenue commercial thoroughfare, Manhattan, New York City. It is popularly known as the home of America's advertising industry. Above 59th St. it is today the site of much of Manhattan's most expensive boutique and gallery shopping.

Madison County **1.** 806 sq mi/2088 sq km, pop. 238,912, in NC Alabama, N of the Tennessee R. and S of the Tennessee state line. HUNTSVILLE, the county seat, and its suburbs account for most of its population. The Redstone Arsenal and Wheeler National Wildlife Refuge occupy much of the SW corner. In the N and E, cotton and lumber are the main products, while Tennessee R. recreational areas attract tourists. **2.** 728 sq mi/1886 sq km, pop. 249,238, in SW Illinois, bordered by the Mississippi R. (W). Its SW border is across from St. Louis, and the center of its border lies at the mouth of Missouri R. Its seat is EDWARDSVILLE. Most of its population lives in the SW, part of the St. Louis industrial complex, which includes such manufacturing and mining cities as Alton, Wood River, Granite City, Collinsville, Edwardsville, and Glen Carbon. Agricultural areas in the N and E produce wheat, fruits, and vegetables.

Madison Heights **1.** city, pop. 32,196, Oakland Co., SE Michigan, a suburb 10 mi/16 km N of Detroit. The area was inhabited in the late 17th century by French Jesuit missionaries; other settlers arrived in 1818. It is now a residential, business, and industrial community, which manufactures auto parts, tools and dies, and aerospace products. **2.** unincorporated community, pop. 11,700, Amherst Co., WC Virginia, across the James R. immediately NE of LYNCHBURG, of which it is a suburb.

Madison River 185 mi/298 km long, in SW Montana and NW Wyoming. It is formed in the NW corner of Yellowstone National Park by the juncture of the Gibbon and Firehole rivers. It flows NW into SW Montana through Hebgen L., then N, running between the Madison Range and Tobacco

Root Mts., to THREE FORKS, just NE of which it joins the Gallatin and Jefferson rivers to form the Missouri R. The Madison is artificially enlarged to a width of 5 mi/8 km at Ennis L., where there is a hydroelectric power project.

Madison Square urban park, lower Midtown Manhattan, New York City. At its SW corner is the FLATIRON BUILDING. The square gave its name to **Madison Square Garden,** the first of a succession of indoor arenas famous for sports spectacles, political conventions, and other events. The first (1879–90) and second (1890–1925) Gardens were on Madison Square. The third, built 1925, was on Eighth Avenue at 50th St. In 1967 the present Garden was opened as part of the Madison Square Garden Complex, connected with Pennsylvania Station (railroad), at 32nd St. and Seventh Ave.

Madisonville **1.** city, pop. 16,200, seat of Hopkins Co., W Kentucky, 33 mi/53 km N of Hopkinsville. In a coal mining area, it is an agricultural trade center, an important looseleaf tobacco market, and a timber shipping point, with some light manufactures. **2.** town, pop. 3033, seat of Monroe Co., SE Tennessee, 38 mi/61 km SW of Knoxville. Political leader Estes Kefauver was born (1903) in this agricultural trade center.

Mad River 26 mi/42 km long, rising S of Warren, in Washington Co., C Vermont, and flowing NE through Waitsfield and Moretown to join the Winooski R. at Middlesex, 6 mi/10 km NW of Montpelier. **Mad River Glen,** near Waitsfield, is a popular downhill and cross-country skiing area. A natural bridge crosses the river at Warren.

Magazine Mountain peak (2753 ft/840 m) in the OUACHITA Mts., 12 mi/19 km NW of Havana, and 43 mi/69 km ESE of Fort Smith, in WC Arkansas. The highest point in the state, it is in the Ozark National Forest.

Magdalen Islands see Îles de la MADELEINE, Québec.

Magna unincorporated community, pop. 17,829, Salt Lake Co., N Utah, a suburb 10 mi/16 km WSW of Salt Lake City. Copper mining began here in 1906, and Kennecott maintains a huge nonferrous smelting plant. There is also an aerospace plant. The area produces grain, sugar beets, and fruit.

Magnificent Mile fashionable commercial and residential strip on North Michigan Ave. between the LOOP and the GOLD COAST, on the Near North Side of Chicago, Illinois.

Magnolia **1.** city, pop. 11,151, seat of Columbia Co., SW Arkansas, 32 mi/52 km W of El Dorado, in the W Gulf Coastal Plain. Settled in the 1850s, it developed as an agricultural trade center. Following the discovery of the Buckner oilfield in 1938, it became an important oil center as well. Industries include refining, cotton processing, lumber milling, and the manufacture of wood, steel, aluminum, and chemical products. It is the home of Southern Arkansas University (1909). **2.** industrial, commercial, and residential section of Houston, Texas, 4 mi/6 km SE of Downtown and SE of the SECOND WARD, along the Buffalo Bayou. It is Houston's oldest (since World War I) Mexican BARRIO, home to textile plant, HOUSTON SHIP CHANNEL, and other industrial workers. **3.** largely middle-class residential district of NW SEATTLE, Washington, 4.5 mi/7 km NW of Downtown, on a peninsula between the L. Washington Ship Canal (N) and ELLIOTT BAY (S). QUEEN ANNE HILL is immediately SE.

Magog city, pop. 14,034, Stanstead Co., S Québec, in the EASTERN TOWNSHIPS, 15 mi/25 km SW of Sherbrooke and 73 mi/117 km ESE of Montréal, at the N end of L. MEMPHRÉMAGOG and just S of Mt. ORFORD. Settled (1799) by LOYALISTS, it developed as a textile center, and today also has agricultural and light industrial enterprises, but is best known as a resort and for the Benedictine monastery in nearby (SW) St.-Benoît-du-Lac.

Mahone Bay Atlantic Ocean inlet, some 12 mi/19 km NE–SW and up to 9 mi/14 km deep, 30 mi/48 km WSW of Halifax, in SW Nova Scotia. Islands in the bay include Big Tancook (the largest) and legend-shrouded OAK. Local communities include LUNENBURG (SW), CHESTER, and **Mahone Bay** (town, pop. 1096). From the 18th century a shipbuilding, agricultural, and fishing center, the bay is today popular for its scenery and resorts.

Mahoning County 417 sq mi/1080 sq km, pop. 264,806, in NE Ohio; bounded by Pennsylvania (E) and intersected by the Little Beaver and Mahoning rivers. It includes L. Milton and part of Berlin L. Its seat is YOUNGSTOWN, a major industrial center surrounded by suburbs. There is dairy, fruit, grain, livestock, and poultry farming; other industries include coal mining and limestone quarrying.

Mahoning River 90 mi/140 km long, in Ohio and Pennsylvania. It rises in Columbiana Co., E Ohio, and flows NW to Alliance, then NE by way of dam-created Berlin L. and L. Milton, to Newton Falls and Warren. It then turns SE and flows through the area known as the **Mahoning Valley,** past Youngstown, and into NW Pennsylvania, to NEW CASTLE, where it joins the Shenango R. to form the Beaver R. The Mahoning Valley was an early focus of the steel industry, since regional coal and Great Lakes iron ore could be easily delivered to its plants; but by the later 19th century railroad transportation had reduced the area's advantage, and the valley entered into a long, gradual decline.

Mahoosuc Range extension of New Hampshire's White Mountains into W Maine, separated from the body of the Whites by, and N of, the Androscoggin R. Baldpate Mt. (3812 ft/1163 m), Old Speck (4180 ft/1275 m), Grafton and Mahoosuc notches, and the Sunday River ski facility are in the area.

Mahwah township, pop. 17,905, Bergen Co., N New Jersey, 12 mi/19 km N of Paterson and along the New York border, on the Ramapo R. Railroad and automobile parts are manufactured (Mahwah formerly had a Ford assembly plant), and the township has a railroad museum, Darlington County Park, and a ski center. Ramapo College (1969) is here.

Main, the see Blvd. SAINT-LAURENT, Montréal, Québec.

Maine northeasternmost US state, the largest in NEW ENGLAND; 1990 pop. 1,227,928 (109.2% of 1980; rank: 38th); area 35,387 sq mi/91,652 sq km (rank: 39th); admitted to Union 1820 (23rd). Capital: AUGUSTA. Most populous city: PORTLAND. Other leading cities: LEWISTON, BANGOR. Maine is bordered NW by Québec; N and E by New Brunswick, with the SAINT JOHN and St. Croix rivers forming parts of the border; E and S by the Atlantic Ocean (the Bay of FUNDY on the E; the Gulf of Maine on the S); and W by New Hampshire, with the Piscataqua R. forming the S part of the border. It is the sole US state contiguous with only one other state. WEST QUODDY HEAD is the easternmost US point; the state (and region) is popularly known as DOWN EAST. Maine's interior (NW and N) is upland, part of the Appalachian system; the SW–NE LONGFELLOW Mts. (an extension of New Hampshire's White Mts.) reach 5268 ft/1606 m at Mt. KATAHDIN, the state's high point. The peak, in BAXTER STATE PARK, is the N terminus of the APPALACHIAN TRAIL. To its NE lie the rich farmlands of AROOSTOOK Co., primarily a potato producing region. To the SE of the Longfellow Mts., the state's terrain slopes gradually to the Atlantic. Maine's coastline is highly indented; 228 mi/367 km in a direct line from KITTERY (SW) to EASTPORT (NE), it has a total length of about 3500 mi/5600 km. Its contours are the result of the postglacial flooding of river valleys, which turned high land into some 2000 islands, some as large or isolated as ISLE AU HAUT, MONHEGAN, and MATINICUS; created CASCO, PENOBSCOT, and other large bays; and made ridges into long peninsulas, now the site of coastal settlements far apart by road but neighbors by water. The coast is rugged, formed chiefly of granite. At MOUNT DESERT I. (in ACADIA NATIONAL PARK), CADILLAC Mt. stands 1532 ft/467 m above the water, the highest point on the US eastern seaboard. In the SW, esp. SW of Casco Bay, there are some long sand beaches, of which OLD ORCHARD BEACH is the best known. About 90% of the state is forested, and wood, along with the sea, has been a major determinant in Maine's history. Shipbuilding, utilizing towering "mast pines," among other resources, was important from the 18th century; although the big trees are gone, their successors remain central to Maine's life, as suggested in its nickname: "The Pine Tree State." Since the late 19th century, the state's huge lumber industry has evolved into what is now chiefly a pulp and paper industry; large unorganized tracts of the interior are owned by major producers. Rivers, esp. the PENOBSCOT, KENNEBEC, ANDROSCOGGIN, and SACO, have powered industry since the mid 19th century; in addition to lumber and paper milling, leather good (esp. shoe) and textile manufacturing have been key, although they are now much reduced. Shipbuilding remains important; US Navy contracts have kept the BATH Iron Works the state's single largest employer through much of the 20th century. Today there is a wide range of light manufactures, including specialized wood products, some high-tech machinery, boats, and outdoor gear. In addition to potatoes, the state produces poultry and eggs, dairy goods, apples, blueberries, and other smaller crops. Its fishing and shellfishing industries, utilizing the long shoreline and rich Gulf of Maine waters, are major employers; lobsters, clams, sardines, cod and other larger fish, and marine worms (for bait) are leading products. The coast is also home to major tourism and resort industries, and the site of thousands of summer homes. Inland, the mountains (including such ski centers as SUGARLOAF) and lakes (including MOOSEHEAD, Flagstaff, and the RANGELEY and BELGRADE groups) are year-round resort centers; the ALLAGASH, with other rivers, is a popular canoeing destination. The University of Maine, at ORONO, and Bowdoin College, at BRUNSWICK, are among academic centers. Home to the Penobscot (now centered at OLD TOWN's Indian I.) and the Passamaquoddy (in the E), Maine was first settled by the French (temporarily at Dochet I., in the SAINT CROIX R., in 1604); the boundaries of ACADIA were for a time in the area of Mt. Desert. An abortive British settlement (1607) at POPHAM BEACH (now in Phippsburg) was followed by the 1620s by numerous small coastal communities, and offshore islands like DAMARISCOVE became fishing stations. The region acquired its name ("the maine," or mainland) in this period. The MASSACHUSETTS BAY COLONY purchased Maine in 1677, but intensive settlement did not occur until the late 18th century. Estrangement from Massachusetts and its government led to separation and statehood in 1820. The border with New Brunswick was settled finally in 1842. The state's harsh winters and difficult soil have combined throughout its history to limit pop. growth; Maine has long exported people—for instance, farmers to the Middle West, or the ambitious young to Boston and other cities. Its citizenry remains largely British in background, with a substantial French-Canadian (here called "Franco-American") minority, and various other European groups. In the late 20th century, the SW has become the outer fringe of MEGALOPOLIS (the Boston–Washington region), and retirees and increasingly decentralized small business (including retailing, esp. at FREEPORT) have spurred growth along the coast. Much of the interior, however, remains thinly peopled and economically marginal.

Maine township, pop. 572, Otter Tail Co., WC Minnesota, 12 mi/19 km NE of Fergus Falls. Supreme Court Justice William O. Douglas was born in this lake-filled rural area in 1898.

Maine, Gulf of area of the Atlantic Ocean indenting the coast of North America from the mouth of the Bay of FUNDY, between NE Maine and SW Nova Scotia (NE) to Cape ANN, in NE Massachusetts (SW). It is a famous fishing ground.

Maine Yankee nuclear plant: see under WISCASSET, Maine.

Main Line series of communities just W of Philadelphia, Pennsylvania, so called because the "main line" of the old Pennsylvania Railroad linking Philadelphia and Paoli ran through them. Among the communities on the Main Line are ARDMORE, BRYN MAWR, HAVERFORD, MERION, and VILLANOVA, all affluent residential suburbs.

Main Street the primary thoroughfare in thousands of small (and some larger) American towns and cities, and as such a metaphor for the culture, economy, politics, and outlook of small-town or MIDDLE AMERICA. Sinclair Lewis satirized this culture harshly in his novel *Main Street* (1920), drawing on aspects of his home town, SAUK CENTRE ("Gopher Prairie"), Minnesota. The term is also used in suggesting the importance of a street, road, or region, as in the nicknaming of ROUTE 66 "the Main Street of America."

Maisonneuve former (1883–1918) municipality, now a district of MONTRÉAL, Québec, 3 mi/5 km E (officially; actually N) of Mt. ROYAL. Established by French-speaking developers as a counterweight to anglophone domination of the city's W end, it had varied industries and large homes, but collapsed financially around World War I. Its large **Parc Maisonneuve,** through which Rue SHERBROOKE runs, gradually became home to recreational and sporting centers. For the 1976 Olympics, the part S of Sherbrooke became Parc Olympique, home to facilities including Olympic Stadium (Stade olympique), known for its cantilevered ribs and 554-ft/169-m inclined tower. The stadium, with huge costs and mechanical problems, became known locally as the "Big O" (to some, as in "owe"). It is now the home of the Expos (baseball), who moved here in 1977 from Parc Jarry, on the N Blvd. Saint-Laurent, and is used for a wide range of events. North of Sherbrooke, Parc Maisonneuve is home to the noted Montréal Botanical Garden, the Insectarium, and various other facilities.

Malabar Farm see under MANSFIELD, Ohio.

Malaspina Glacier see under WRANGELL–ST. ELIAS NATIONAL PARK AND PRESERVE, Alaska.

Malden 1. city, pop. 53,884, Middlesex Co., E Massachusetts, on the Malden R., a branch of the Mystic R., 5 mi/8 km N of Boston. A commercial and residential suburb of Boston, it also produces footwear, electronic parts, metal cans, paints, drugs, and clothing. Landmarks include the Parsonage House (1724) and Bell Rock Memorial Park, near the site of the first (1640) settlement N of the Mystic R. **2.** suburban hamlet in Kanawha Co., WC West Virginia, about 5 mi/8 km S of Charleston, along the Kanawha R. An important mid-19th-century salt producing center, it was the childhood home of Booker T. Washington.

Malheur Lake see under BURNS, Oregon.

Malheur River 165 mi/266 km long, in E Oregon. It rises in the Strawberry Mts. (see BLUE Mts.), and flows SE, then generally ENE, to the Snake R. at ONTARIO, on the Idaho border. Warm Springs Dam (1919), NW of Riverside, impounds Warm Springs Reservoir. Surrounding the river's headstreams is the 1.46 million-ac/591,000-ha (2284–sq mi/5916–sq km) **Malheur National Forest,** which includes the Strawberry Mts. and nearby high desert areas.

Malibu residential and resort section of LOS ANGELES, California, 24 mi/39 km W of Downtown, between the Santa Monica Mts. (N) and N Santa Monica Bay. One of the area's most affluent communities, it is known for its miles of beaches and for its expensive homes, many lived in by Hollywood stars. The Chumash, who lived here, gave the area its name. In 1892 Frederick H. Rindge purchased 16,000 ac/6700 ha along the shore to create an exclusive resort. Development came in the 1920s after the Pacific Coast Highway cut through the area. The J. Paul Getty Museum, a major art collection, is here, along with Pepperdine University (1937). PACIFIC PALISADES is immediately E, and Malibu, TOPANGA, and other canyons extend N into the mountains.

Mall, the also, **National Mall** public space in Washington, D.C., reaching (with Constitution Gardens, its W extension) 2.5 mi/4 km between CAPITOL HILL (E) and the LINCOLN MEMORIAL and the Potomac R. (W). About 0.4 mi/0.6 km wide, it contains 146 ac/59 ha between the Capitol and the WASHINGTON MONUMENT. It is connected with the White House (N) by the Ellipse, and at its SW corner adjoins the TIDAL BASIN. FEDERAL TRIANGLE lies along its N side, the headquarters of the SMITHSONIAN INSTITUTION along its S. To the W of the Washington Monument are Constitution Gardens (52 ac/21 ha), with the Reflecting Pool in front of the Lincoln Memorial, and the Vietnam Veterans Memorial in the NW. FOGGY BOTTOM lies N. Potomac Park extends from the W end down the Potomac to Hains Point, where the Anacostia R. and the Potomac join.

Mall of America see under BLOOMINGTON, Minnesota.

Malmstrom Air Force Base see under GREAT FALLS, Montana.

Malpeque Bay inlet of the Gulf of St. Lawrence deeply indenting the NW shore of Prince Edward Island. Twelve mi/20 km N–S and 10 mi/16 km wide at its mouth, it is almost entirely enclosed by Hog I., a BARRIER ISLAND, with passages through Malpeque Harbour (E) and Hardy Channel (W). Several islands, Lennox being the largest, lie in the bay. Malpeque is fed by the Grand, Indian, and other estuarial rivers, and is famous for its oysters.

Malta **1.** village, pop. 865, De Kalb Co., N Illinois, 5 mi/8 km W of De Kalb. Kishwaukee College (1967) is in this rural community. **2.** city, pop. 2340, seat of Phillips Co., N Montana, on the Milk R., 55 mi/89 km NW of Glasgow. Situated in an irrigated region near L. Bowdoin, it was the center of a large 19th-century cattle raising area that stretched from Canada to the Missouri R. and from GLASGOW (E) to HAVRE (W). Today Malta is a trade center for livestock, wheat, alfalfa, and natural gas. A large buffalo-shaped boulder, revered by the Assiniboine, was moved here from a nearby location in 1934.

Malton community formerly within the township of Toronto (now in MISSISSAUGA), S Ontario. It was a 19th-century railway hamlet, and the site of an aircraft plant that built bombers during World War II. Important test flights took place here, and aerospace manufacturing continues. The LESTER B. PEARSON INTERNATIONAL AIRPORT is just S, industrial Bramalea (see BRAMPTON) just NE.

Malvern **1.** city, pop. 9256, seat of Hot Springs Co., C Arkansas, 17 mi/27 km SE of Hot Springs, near the Ouachita R. In an agricultural area that produces sweet potatoes, corn, and cotton, it manufactures wood products, brick, tile, and chemicals, and processes cotton. **2.** borough, pop. 2944, Chester Co., SE Pennsylvania, primarily a residential suburb, 22 mi/35 km W of Philadelphia. Companies specializing in pharmaceuticals and information technology are also situated here.

Malverne village, pop. 9054, in Hempstead town, Nassau Co., SE New York, on Long Island, 17 mi/27 km SE of Manhattan. It is a residential suburb of New York City.

Malvern Hill historic site on the N bank of the James R., 15 mi/24 km SE of Richmond, in Henrico Co., Virginia. On July 1, 1862, the day after FRAYSER'S FARM, Robert E. Lee, trying to drive Union forces S to the James, led Confederates in a frontal attack on a well-fortified hilltop position, and suffered heavy casualties. Malvern Hill was the last battle of the Seven Days, the Confederate campaign that ended the Union's Peninsular Campaign against Richmond.

Mamaroneck town, pop. 27,706, Westchester Co., SE New York, on Mamaroneck Harbor of Long Island Sound, 22 mi/35 km NE of New York City. Although primarily residential, it has some industry, including the manufacture of electronic components and lighting fixtures. It is noted as a boating center.

Mammoth Cave in Edmonson, Hart, and Barren counties, WC Kentucky. A vast subterranean cavern system discovered by whites around 1799, it was formed by water dissolving limestone, and boasts a variety of formations, with underground lakes, rivers, domes, and pits. A link was found (1972) between Mammoth Cave and the Flint Ridge cave system; the combined length of passages is well over 400 mi/644 km, on at least five levels, and roughly 12 mi/19 km are discovered each year. Temperature is a steady 54° F/12° C. With an estimated age of 340 million years, the system has cave crickets, blind crayfish, and unpigmented blindfish in the Echo R., which drains into the Green R. Human artifacts found here, up to 4000 years old, include mummies, pottery, wooden bowls, and sandals. Saltpeter and nitrates were mined during the War of 1812 and the Civil War. **Mammoth Cave National Park,** covering over 52,400 ac/21,200 ha, opened in 1941, and is also noted for its trails and wildlife.

Manassa town, pop. 988, Conejos Co., SC Colorado, on the North Branch of the Conejos R., 11 mi/18 km N of the New Mexico border and 22 mi/35 km SSW of Alamosa. A trade point in the San Luis Valley, it is the birthplace (1895) of heavyweight boxing champion Jack Dempsey, the "Manassa Mauler."

Manassas independent city, pop. 27,957, seat of Prince William Co., N Virginia, just SW of BULL RUN and 25 mi/40 km

WSW of Washington, D.C. Formerly a trade center for an agricultural, dairying, and livestock region, it has become largely a bedroom community for Washington, D.C., and other Virginia towns. A rail junction here connected the Shenandoah Valley and the Washington-Richmond railroads at the time of the Civil War, giving the town strategic importance. Nearby are the sites of two battles, the First Battle of Bull Run (1861) and the Second Battle of Bull Run (1862), both significant defeats for the Union; they are also referred to as the first and second battles of Manassas, and are commemorated by Manassas National Battlefield Park, 4 mi/6 km NW of the city. The city of **Manassas Park** (pop. 6734) lies between Manassas and Bull Run.

Manatí unincorporated community (ZONA URBANA), pop. 16,352, Manatí Municipio (pop. 38,692), N Puerto Rico, on the Atlantic Ocean and the Rio Grande de Manatí, 25 mi/40 km WSW of San Juan. A longtime sugar, tobacco, coffee, and fruit growing and processing center, it now also has a pharmaceutical industry.

Manayunk residential neighborhood in NW Philadelphia, Pennsylvania, across the Schuylkill R. from LOWER MERION township, W of FAIRMOUNT PARK, and 6 mi/10 km NW of City Hall. A largely Polish working-class community, it has recently attracted a significant artists' colony drawn to its hilly terrain.

Manchester **1.** town, pop. 51,618, Hartford Co., C Connecticut, on the Hockanum R., 9 mi/14 km E of Hartford. Settled in the 1670s, it had by the end of the 18th century developed an industrial base, producing glass, silk, paper, clocks, farm implements, and lumber. Today it produces plastics, electrical and heating equipment, and parachutes, and is a residential suburb with a growing commercial (mall) component. Manchester Community College (1963) is here. **2.** city, pop. 99,567, Hillsborough Co., S New Hampshire, 60 mi/96 km N of Boston. It is the largest city in the three northern New England states. On the Amoskeag Falls of the Merrimack R., with Massabesic L. about 4 mi/6 km E of the city center and the Piscataquog R. joining the Merrimack from the W, Manchester is at the center of a resort area, surrounded by mountains, forests, and lakes. Fishing was an important early industry. The Amoskeag Falls, which drop 85 ft/26 m, provided waterpower for textile manufacturing, established in 1805, and Manchester became home to one of the world's largest mill complexes. A canal built around the falls opened up the Boston market. Cotton fabric manufacture was the chief industry until the late 1930s. Manchester is now a wholesale and retail trade center for much of N New England, and manufactures textiles, shoes, leather products, automobile accessories, electronics, hardware, and paper. St. Anselm College (1889, in PINARDVILLE), Notre Dame College, Hesser College, New Hampshire College, the Manchester Institute of Arts and Sciences, the Currier Gallery of Art, and several other institutions are here. **3.** village, pop. 2211, Adams Co., S Ohio, 37 mi/60 km W of Portsmouth, on the Ohio R. at the Kentucky border. One of the earliest white settlements in the state, it was founded in 1791 by General Nathaniel Massie. In the 19th century it was an important steamboat landing between Portsmouth and Cincinnati. Today the local economy is supported by a sawmill and factories manufacturing clothing, buttons, and bakery goods. It is the birthplace (1893) of baseball great George Sisler. **4.** residential neighborhood on the NORTH SIDE of Pittsburgh, Pennsylvania, immediately NW of the MEXICAN WAR STREETS, 1.5 mi/2.4 km NW of the GOLDEN TRIANGLE. An industrial center dating to 1832, it has been declining economically since the Depression. Nearby factories closed or were cut off from the area by highway construction, further impoverishing this black community. Destructive riots occurred here during the 1960s. Today, the Manchester Citizens' Corporation has led efforts at rehabilitating old Victorian row houses and mansions without displacing lower-income residents. **5.** town, pop. 3622, Bennington Co., SW Vermont. It is on the Batten Kill, E of Mt. EQUINOX, 20 mi/32 km NE of Bennington. A former unofficial state capital, where the Vermont Council of Safety met in 1777, the town has several Colonial buildings. Seth Warner camped here with his regiment before the Battle of BENNINGTON (1777). Once industrial, Manchester became a well-known resort by the mid 19th century. Robert Todd Lincoln, who died here (1926), made his home at Hildene, a 412-ac/167-ha estate now a tourist attraction. Near Bromley, Stratton, and other ski areas, the town has summer film and art festivals. Fishing rods and tackle are the main local products.

Mandan city, pop. 15,177, seat of Morton Co., SC North Dakota, on the Missouri R. across from Bismarck. Named after local Indians ("river bank dwellers"), it was founded in 1872. It became a bustling commercial and shipping hub after the Northern Pacific built a railroad bridge here 10 years later. Mandan continues to be known for livestock auctions and as a trade center for local dairy products and grain. Plentiful lignite deposits have also encouraged iron and brass making. The Fort Lincoln State Park here contains the reconstruction of George A. Custer's last headquarters before the Battle of the LITTLE BIG HORN.

Mandeville city, pop. 7083, St. Tammany Parish, SE Louisiana, on the N side of L. PONTCHARTRAIN, 28 mi/45 km N of New Orleans. Founded in 1830, it is a resort, with boatbuilding and agricultural industries.

Mangilao unincorporated community, pop. 5608, EC GUAM, 5 mi/8 km SE of Agana, on the Pacific Ocean. It is the island's educational center, seat of the University of Guam (1952) and Guam Community College.

Manhasset unincorporated village, pop. 7718, in North Hempstead town, Nassau Co., SE New York, on the North Shore of Long Island near the head of Manhasset Bay. Originally called Cow's Neck, it was settled in the mid 17th century by 40 English families and a few Dutch settlers, who bought the land from the Matinecock tribe. The town was occupied by British soldiers for seven years during the Revolution, making it the American territory held the longest by foreign forces. Today Manhasset is an affluent suburb; its Miracle Mile, an upscale retail strip, is well known, as is North Shore University Hospital.

Manhattan **1.** city, pop. 37,712, seat of Riley Co., also in Pottawatomie Co., NE Kansas, on the Kansas R., 48 mi/77 km WNW of Topeka. A pre–Civil War Free State stronghold, it flourished after the coming of the railroad (1870), which made it an important shipping point for agricultural products and livestock. Today food is processed and farm machinery is manufactured. Kansas State University (1863, the first US LAND-GRANT institution) and Manhattan Christian College (1927) are here. The Army installation at nearby FORT RILEY (W) is also important to the city's economy. Tuttle Creek Dam and 15,000-ac/6100-ha Tuttle Creek L. are nearby (N) on the Big Blue R. **2.** smallest (28 sq mi/

74 sq km) and third most populous (1,487,536) of New York City's five boroughs. Coextensive with **New York Co.,** it is the part of the city known widely as "New York," and the center of one of the world's major financial, cultural, and commercial complexes. The island of Manhattan, 13 mi/21 km NNE–SSW and up to 2.3 mi/3.7 km across, is bounded by the HUDSON R. (W), SPUYTEN DUYVIL Creek and the HARLEM R. (N and NE), the EAST R. (E), and Upper NEW YORK BAY (S). Also part of the borough are Marble Hill, physically part of the Bronx; WARD'S and RANDALL'S islands, at the Harlem R.–East R. junction; ROOSEVELT I., in the East R.; and GOVERNORS, LIBERTY, and ELLIS islands in Upper New York Bay. Manhattan is famous for its skyscrapers, esp. prominent in the Wall Street (S) and Midtown areas, where hard schist provides a solid base for construction; during the day commuters from across the metropolitan area swell the island's pop. Almost all housing in the borough is in apartment buildings ranging from three to dozens of stories in height. New York's shipping business, once concentrated on both the Hudson and East River sides of the island, has now largely transferred to Brooklyn, PORT NEWARK, Elizabeth, and other nearby harbors, and Manhattan's manufacturing is limited to apparel, printed material, and other light industries located chiefly in small areas of Downtown. The dominant businesses of the island are banking and finance, commerce, advertising, education and culture, publishing and communications, entertainment, and tourism. Major educational institutions include Columbia (1754), New York (1831), Yeshiva (1886), and Pace (1906) universities; the City College of New York (1847), now part of the City University system; other units of the city system; Cooper Union (1859); the New School for Social Research (1919); the Juilliard (1905), Mannes (1916), and Manhattan (1917) schools of music; Union (1836) and Jewish (1886) theological seminaries; the Parsons School of Design (1896); the Fashion Institute of Technology (1944); and the Art Students League. The Metropolitan, Modern, Whitney, Guggenheim, and other art museums are famous. Carnegie Hall and Lincoln Center are best known of local concert venues. The presence of the United Nations headquarters on the East Side adds an international-politics element to the borough. The island was home to the Manhattan Indians, who sold it (proverbially for $24 in trade goods) to Peter Minuit of the Dutch West India Company in 1626. NEW AMSTERDAM, established at the S tip, was the capital of NEW NETHERLAND until the British takeover of 1664, when it was renamed New York. Settlement spread progressively N through the next two centuries, with improving roads and rail systems transforming country estates and villages into dense urban districts. In 1898 New York City, at that time comprising Manhattan and parts of the Bronx, became officially Greater New York, the five-borough city of today. The first of the boroughs to develop fully, Manhattan has today only 80% of its 1930 pop. For more than a century it has been a magnet to the ambitious from all over the US (and large parts of the world), and has seen continuous residential turnover; pop. decline has come in economic slumps (esp. in the 1930s and 1970s), during the suburban exodus of the 1950s, and through loss of older housing stock. The island rises to 268 ft/82 m in Inwood, at the N extreme. Harlem, Manhattan's black center, lies largely below (E of) a ridge along the Hudson that includes Washington Heights and Morningside Heights. South of Central Park, the island is generally flatter, and along its S shores there is a substantial amount of landfill, most recently the site of Battery Park City. See also: ALGONQUIN HOTEL; ALPHABET CITY; APOLLO THEATRE; the ARMORY; the BATTERY; BATTERY PARK CITY; BELLEVUE; BLOOMINGDALE; the BOWERY; BOWLING GREEN; BROADWAY; CANAL St.; CASTLE CLINTON (and Castle Garden); CENTRAL PARK; CHELSEA; CHINATOWN; CHRYSLER Bldg.; DIAMOND DISTRICT; DOWNTOWN; EAST HARLEM; EAST SIDE; EAST VILLAGE; EMPIRE STATE Bldg.; FIFTH Ave.; FINANCIAL DISTRICT; FIVE POINTS; FLATIRON Bldg. (and District); FORT TRYON; FORT WASHINGTON; GARMENT CENTER; GRAMERCY PARK; GRANT'S TOMB; GREENWICH VILLAGE; HAMILTON HEIGHTS; HARLEM; HARLEM HEIGHTS; HELL'S KITCHEN (Clinton); INWOOD; KIPS BAY; LINCOLN CENTER; LITTLE ITALY; LOISAIDA; LOWER EAST SIDE; MADISON Ave.; MADISON SQUARE; MANHATTANVILLE; MARBLE HILL; MIDTOWN; MORNINGSIDE HEIGHTS; MURRAY HILL; PARK Ave.; PLAZA HOTEL; POLO GROUNDS; RANDALL'S I.; RIVERSIDE DRIVE; ROCKEFELLER CENTER (and Radio City); ROOSEVELT I.; SAN JUAN HILL; SOHO; the STONEWALL; STRIVER'S ROW; SUGAR HILL; SWING St.; TAMMANY HALL; the TENDERLOIN; TIMES SQUARE; TRIBECA; TURTLE BAY; UNION SQUARE; UNITED NATIONS; UPTOWN; WALL St.; WARD'S I.; WASHINGTON HEIGHTS; WASHINGTON SQUARE; WEST SIDE; WORLD TRADE CENTER; YORKVILLE.

Manhattan Beach **1.** city, pop. 32,063, Los Angeles Co., SW California, 13 mi/21 km SW of downtown Los Angeles, on the Pacific Ocean just N of HERMOSA BEACH. A popular resort, it has an annual Surf Festival and bicycle races. Industries include oil refining and the manufacture of aerospace, electrical, sporting, and other goods. **2.** see under CONEY I., New York.

Manhattanville historic name for a section of upper W Manhattan, New York City, lying where a geologic fault and stream bed pass between Morningside Heights and Hamilton Heights to the Hudson R., along modern West 125th St. The area is today generally considered part of Harlem. The industrial village of Manhattanville grew up in the early 1800s. The Catholic Society of the Sacred Heart established Manhattanville College here in 1841; in 1952 the college moved to PURCHASE, New York. Manhattan College was also founded (1853) in the area, later moving to RIVERDALE.

Manicouagan, Rivière 283 mi/455 km long, in SC Québec, rising near the Labrador border and flowing generally S through heavy forest to the St. Lawrence R. at BAIE-COMEAU. The 270 mi/435 km–long R. Outardes, flowing from L. Plétipi, follows a roughly parallel course on its W. Since the 1960s the two rivers have been dammed by seven units of Hydro-Québec's huge **Manic-Outardes** power complex. Manic 5 (the Barrage Daniel-Johnson) is the world's largest multiple-arch dam, over 700 ft/214 m high and over 4300 ft/1310 m long; above it is the circular **Manicouagan Reservoir** (formerly two semicircular lakes), which occupies part of the depression called the **Manicouagan Crater,** a meteorite impact zone 60 mi/100 km in diameter. In the reservoir's center is the Mont de Babel, high ground rising almost 2000 ft/600 m above the lake. Manic 2, just NW of Baie-Comeau, is a 300 ft/93 m–high concrete gravity dam, also the world's largest of its type.

Manistee city, pop. 6734, seat of Manistee Co., NW Michigan, on L. Michigan and Manistee L., at the mouth of the Manistee R., 70 mi/113 km N of Muskegon. An important mid-19th-century lumber camp, it was largely destroyed by fire in 1871. When the timber was depleted a few years later, it produced salt from local deposits, and became a health resort. Situated just W of the Manistee National Forest, in an area known for its hunting and fishing, it remains a popular lakefront vacation site. It is also an important port, known particularly for its agricultural shipping. Manistee also manufactures chemicals, machinery, and wood products, and still mines and processes salt.

Manistee River 170 mi/274 km long, in the NW Lower Peninsula of Michigan. It rises in Antrim and Otsego counties, and flows generally SW to widen into Manistee L., before entering L. Michigan at MANISTEE. The Manistee flows through much of the scenic back country of Michigan, and is used for boating and trout and coho fishing.

Manistique city, pop. 3456, seat of Schoolcraft Co., in the SC Upper Peninsula of Michigan, on L. Michigan, 40 mi/64 km NE of Escanaba, at the mouth of the Manistique R. Behind the city lies 3 mi/5 km–long Indian L., a camping and fishing center. From about 1860 to 1900 Manistique was a great lumber processing and shipping center; after the industry collapsed, tanneries, iron furnaces, and other industries sprung up, and commercial fishing became important.

Manistique River in the S part of the Upper Peninsula of Michigan. It rises in and around Manistique L., in Luce, Mackinac, and Schoolcraft counties, and flows SW to L. Michigan, just below the city of Manistique. It is fed by many streams; its main tributaries are the Driggs and Fox rivers. **Manistique Lake** is in the SE Upper Peninsula, 13 mi/21 km SW of Newberry. It is 7 mi/11 km long and 3 mi/5 km wide, and is drained by the river. It is situated between the smaller South Manistique L. and North Manistique L.

Manitoba province of C Canada, the easternmost of the PRAIRIE PROVINCES; 1991 pop. 1,091,942 (102.7% of 1986; rank: 5th of 12); land area 211,469 sq mi/547,704 sq km (rank: 7th); entered Confederation 1870. Capital and most populous city: WINNIPEG. Other leading cities: BRANDON, THOMPSON, PORTAGE LA PRAIRIE. Manitoba is bordered E by Ontario and by Minnesota's NORTHWEST ANGLE (SE); S (on the FORTY-NINTH PARALLEL) by Minnesota (E) and North Dakota (W); W by Saskatchewan; and N (on the SIXTIETH PARALLEL) by the Northwest Territories. On the NE it fronts HUDSON BAY. The northern two-thirds of the province, and its E edge, lie on the CANADIAN SHIELD or on lowlands adjoining Hudson Bay. This is a largely unpopulated region, where the CHURCHILL, NELSON (draining the Saskatchewan R.–L. Winnipeg system), and HAYES rivers flow to the bay through forests (in the C) and over TUNDRA (in the NE). The mining centers of Thompson (C) and FLIN FLON (on the Saskatchewan border) are here. On Hudson Bay is CHURCHILL, a seasonal port reached by rail from THE PAS (WC). To Churchill's SE, at the mouth of the Hayes R., is YORK FACTORY, an early HUDSON'S BAY COMPANY post. At the SW edge of the Shield, lying across SC Manitoba, is a group of large lakes, including WINNIPEG, WINNIPEGOSIS, MANITOBA, and CEDAR. The RED RIVER OF THE NORTH, flowing N from Minnesota and North Dakota, enters L. Winnipeg, thence draining to Hudson Bay; it is thus the southernmost river in the Hudson Bay watershed, and a key to early Manitoba history. The ASSINIBOINE R., which joins the Red R. at Winnipeg, and the WINNIPEG R., which flows into the SE of L. Winnipeg, are also parts of this watershed. Almost all the province's arable land, and almost all its pop. centers, lie S of the lakes, on higher ground at the E edge of the GREAT PLAINS. Here Manitoba produces wheat, barley, and other grains, which are processed at Winnipeg or shipped via Churchill or by rail. Baldy Mt., SW of L. Winnipegosis, is the province's high point (2727 ft/831 m). Winnipeg, which is home to 56% of Manitoba's people, began life as a railhead and milling center; today it has diverse industrial and commercial enterprises. Brandon (which is a chemical manufacturing center) and all other cities and towns with any industry are engaged almost exclusively in processing local resources—oil, natural gas, lumber, copper, gold, other metals, or foods. Home to Assiniboine, Sioux, Cree, Ojibwa, and other peoples, the region was entered by French fur traders in the 17th century, although in 1670 it was part of the grant by the British crown to the Hudson's Bay Company establishing RUPERT'S LAND. When NEW FRANCE fell in 1763, French claims here were extinguished, but a community of MÉTIS, of mixed French and Indian heritage, had come into being. The Métis allied themselves with the Montréal-based NORTH WEST COMPANY, and a period of strife between the two fur empires ensued. The HBC-backed Red River Settlement of 1812, bringing Scottish and Irish farmers into the area where Winnipeg is today, touched off fighting that climaxed in the 1816 SEVEN OAKS massacre. In 1821, the HBC and NWC merged, seeming to end contention. In 1870, however, when the HBC sold its lands to the new Dominion of Canada, the Métis rose in a revolt led by Louis Riel, based at Fort Garry (Winnipeg). This was quickly suppressed, but Canada in response created the province of Manitoba (probably from the Algonquian *Manitou,* "great spirit"), originally comprising only a small area around the lower Red R. In 1881 and again in 1912 (establishing present boundaries), the province was enlarged with land taken from the Northwest Territories. The CANADIAN PACIFIC RAILWAY's extension through Winnipeg and across the S in the 1880s enabled large-scale farm settlement, and in the late 19th and early 20th centuries Manitoba became home to Ukrainians, German Mennonites from Russia, Icelanders, and other Europeans, in addition to American and Ontarian homesteaders. In the late 20th century, the impetus toward consolidation of small farms by agribusiness has driven many families into Winnipeg or from the province; mining, oil refining, and manufacturing have gained in prominence, but the countryside of S Manitoba remains essentially part of the WHEAT BELT. RIDING MOUNTAIN National Park, DUCK MOUNTAIN and WHITESHELL provincial parks, the INTERNATIONAL PEACE GARDEN (on the North Dakota border near Boissevain), and HECLA I. in L. Winnipeg are among scattered visitor attractions. Winnipeg, which incorporated its near suburbs within a single city government in 1972, is the educational and cultural hub of the province and of much of the Canadian prairies.

Manitoba, Lake NNW–SSE oriented body in S Manitoba, over 1800 sq mi/4660 sq km, and over 120 mi/190 km long. One of the three large lakes that occupy the lowland where glacial L. AGASSIZ covered what is now S Manitoba, it is fed by L. WINNIPEGOSIS (NW), and drains NE, via the Dauphin R., to L. WINNIPEG. The marshy S end is important to waterfowl. There is a commercial fishery, and several Indian reserves lie on the W shore.

Manitoba Escarpment series of rolling uplands in SW Manitoba, extending into E Saskatchewan. They include (N–S) the PORCUPINE, DUCK, RIDING, and PEMBINA mountains. These peaks, or hills, created by TILL deposits, are generally 1200–

2600 ft/370–790 m high, and reach their greatest elevation at BALDY Mt. (2727 ft/832 m), the highest point in Manitoba.

Manitou Beach unincorporated village, pop. 2061, Lenawee Co., S Michigan, 19 mi/31 km SSE of Jackson. It is a resort on Devils L. and Round L.

Manitoulin Island largest lake island in the world, part of Ontario, in an archipelago at the N end of L. Huron. It is separated from the Ontario mainland by the North Channel (N) and Georgian Bay (E). Some 75 mi/120 km WNW–ESE and 4–28 mi/6–45 km wide, the hilly island, whose backbone is the NIAGARA ESCARPMENT, comprises 1068 sq mi/2766 sq km, and rises to 1175 ft/358 m. It has a heavily indented coastline, numerous bays, and several large lakes. Little Current (town, pop. 1511), its largest community, is bridged to the mainland S of ESPANOLA. South Baymouth (SE) has ferry service to the BRUCE PENINSULA. Gore Bay (town, pop. 916, N) is seat of the Manitoulin District (pop. 11,192), comprising the island and others nearby, including Cockburn, Great Duck, Barrie, Birch, Lonely, and Fitzwilliam. Occupied by the Ottawa before the 17th century, Manitoulin was visited by Jesuit missionaries in 1648. In the 1830s, Indians from across N Ontario were settled here, and some remain on small reserves. Tourism and outdoor recreation and some farming, livestock raising, and commercial fishing are important.

Manitowoc city, pop. 32,520, seat of Manitowoc Co., E Wisconsin, on L. Michigan at the mouth of the Manitowoc R., 22 mi/34 km N of Sheboygan. Its name is derived from an Indian term meaning "home of the spirit." A British fur trading post existed here in 1795, but permanent settlement did not begin until 1835. It was an important port by the late 1830s. Shipbuilding has been the city's major industry since 1848. Aluminum products, major appliances, cement, and soap are also manufactured. Manitowoc is the seat of Silver Lake College (1869).

Mankato city, pop. 31,477, seat of Blue Earth Co. and also in Nicollet Co., SC Minnesota, on the Minnesota R. at the mouth of the Blue Earth R., 56 mi/90 km SW of Bloomington. A distribution center for dairy and other farms in the region, it has a number of agriculture-related industries. There are processing plants for flour and livestock feed and farm equipment is manufactured. Cans, generators, fishing reels, boats, and paper products are also produced. Limestone quarries nearby supply processing facilities in the city. "Mankato" is a Sioux term for the blue clay in local riverbeds. Settled in 1852, the city was the site of a mass hanging of 38 Sioux in the wake of their 1862 uprising and the massacre at NEW ULM. Mankato State University (1867) and Bethany Lutheran College (1927) are here.

Manlius town, pop. 30,656, Onondaga Co., C New York, 6 mi/10 km E of Syracuse. Settled in 1789, it is a residential suburb, with some light industry and a military academy established in 1869. In the E are lakes, parks, and agricultural land.

Mann Gulch ravine on the W side of the Big Belt Mts. of WC Montana, above (immediately E of) the Missouri River's Gates of the Mountains, in the HELENA NATIONAL FOREST, 20 mi/32 km NNE of Helena. In a wilderness area, it is the site of an Aug. 1949 forest fire in which 13 "Smokejumpers" (airborne firefighters) died, the subject of Norman Maclean's *Young Men and Fire* (1992).

Manoa neighborhood 5 mi/8 km E of downtown HONOLULU, Hawaii. In the Manoa Valley, it is 2 mi/3 km N of Waikiki and S of Paradise Park and Manoa Falls. The central campus of the University of Hawaii (1907), the East-West Center, and the Korean Studies Center are here.

Mansfield 1. town, pop. 21,103, Tolland Co., NE Connecticut, 20 mi/32 km E of Hartford. It is best known for the academic center of STORRS. Other villages include Mansfield Four Corners, Mansfield Center, and Mansfield Hollow, site of 450-ac/182-ha Mansfield Hollow L., an impoundment of the Natchaug R. The Willimantic R. forms the town's W boundary. **2.** city, pop. 5389, De Soto Parish, NW Louisiana, 33 mi/53 km S of Shreveport. Incorporated in 1847, it has been a trade center for a farming and lumbering area that now produces oil, and has some light manufactures. Mansfield Female College (1852–1929) pioneered in women's education. The battle of Sabine Crossroads, on April 8, 1864, in which Confederate defenders drove advancing Federals back toward Alexandria (SE), was fought 4 mi/6 km SE, at a site now memorialized as Mansfield Battle Park. **3.** city, pop. 1429, Wright Co., S Missouri, on the Ozark Plateau, 40 mi/64 km ESE of Springfield. A trade center in a farming and lead and zinc mining region, it is noted as the home (1894–1957) of Laura Ingalls Wilder, who wrote her *Little House* books after moving here from the Dakotas. Her home and grave and the grave of her daughter, Ozarks writer Rose Wilder Lane, draw visitors. **4.** city, pop. 50,627, seat of Richland Co., NC Ohio, 56 mi/90 km SW of Akron. Situated in a fertile agricultural region in the foothills of the Appalachians, it is named for Jared Mansfield, US Surveyor General, who laid out the town in 1808. During the War of 1812, John Chapman (Johnny Appleseed) raced to Mansfield to warn of an Indian attack. The city grew as an industrial center, prospering from the 1840s to the present day. It is now a principal manufacturer of electrical appliances, steel and rubber products, brass goods, automobile bodies, sports vehicles, machinery, and bathroom fixtures. Mansfield is home to a branch of Ohio State University. Malabar Farm, the home of novelist Louis Bromfield, who was born here (1896), is 12 mi/19 km SE of Mansfield, and is now an ecological center and experimental farm. **5.** borough, pop. 3538, Tioga Co., N Pennsylvania, on the Tioga R., 39 mi/62 km N of Williamsport and 14 mi/22 km S of the New York border. It is the seat of Mansfield University (1854). Local industries include coal mining, gas production, and dairy farming. **6.** city, pop. 15,607, Tarrant, Johnson, and Ellis counties, NE Texas, 17 mi/27 km SE of downtown Fort Worth. In formerly agricultural area, it is a growing residential suburb with some light manufacturing.

Mansfield, Mount 4393 ft/1340 m, highest in Vermont and the Green Mts., 20 mi/32 km NE of Burlington. The 5 mi/8 km–long, treeless summit ridge resembles the profile of a face turned upwards, and the various peaks are named after facial features, with the Chin the high point. The LONG TRAIL goes over the summit. Popular tourist attractions include Smuggler's Notch, a narrow cliff path with 1000-ft/300-m cliffs on either side. Mount Mansfield State Forest, between Stowe and Jefferson, covers over 20,000 ac/8100 ha.

Manteca city, pop. 40,773, San Joaquin Co., C California, 10 mi/16 km SSE of Stockton. In the N San Joaquin Valley, a grape, olive, and vegetable producing region, it has historically been a dairy center, and has winemaking and other agriculturally related industries.

Manti–La Sal National Forest c.1.3 million ac/530,000 ha (2030 sq mi/5260 sq km), in SE and C Utah. Its largest (Manti) division, on C Utah's Wasatch Plateau, includes most of 100 mi/160 km–long, unpaved Skyline Drive, largely above 10,000 ft/3050 m, and famous for its views W to Nevada and E to Colorado. The smaller (La Sal) division, in the SE, incorporates much of the LA SAL and Abajo ranges, and extends over the Colorado border.

Manville borough, pop. 10,567, Somerset Co., C New Jersey, 8 mi/13 km NW of New Brunswick, on the Raritan R. Its manufactures include plastics, cement blocks, and clothing, and it was formerly a major producer of asbestos insulation (Johns-Manville).

Manzanar see under LONE PINE, California.

Manzano Mountains range extending N for c.40 mi/64 km from near Mountainair in C New Mexico, in the Cibola National Forest, to some 20 mi/32 km SE of Albuquerque. It reaches 10,098 ft/3078 m at Manzano Peak, in the SW. The Salinas Pueblo Missions National Monument is to the SE.

Maple see under VAUGHAN, Ontario.

Maple Grove city, pop. 38,736, Hennepin Co., SE Minnesota, 14 mi/23 km NW of Minneapolis. A fast-growing outer suburb of the Twin Cities, it experienced a significant rise in population during the 1980s and 1990s. Commercial development concentrated along I-94 and I-494.

Maple Heights city, pop. 27,089, Cuyahoga Co., NE Ohio, 10 mi/16 km SE of Cleveland. Primarily a residential suburb, it also manufactures electrical appliances and metal products.

Maple Ridge district municipality, pop. 48,422, Dewdney-Alouette Regional District, SW British Columbia, on the Fraser R. (S), 41 mi/65 km E of Vancouver. In an agricultural and lumber milling area just E of PITT MEADOWS, it is a rapidly growing residential suburb.

Maple Shade township, pop. 19,211, Burlington Co., SW New Jersey, 5 mi/8 km E of Camden. A residential and commercial suburb, it also produces clothing and building products.

Maplewood **1.** city, pop. 30,954, Ramsey Co., SE Minnesota, a suburb 6 mi/10 km NE of St. Paul. It experienced much residential and commercial development during the 1970s and 1980s. Its numerous new shopping centers are not clustered along arterials, but are distributed throughout the community. **2.** city, pop. 9962, St. Louis Co., EC Missouri, 7 mi/11 km WSW of downtown St. Louis. A residential and industrial suburb, it has manufactures that include steel and aluminum products and tools. **3.** township, pop. 21,659, Essex Co., NE New Jersey, 5 mi/8 km W of Newark. Settled in 1866, it is a primarily residential suburb. There are some office buildings, a map publisher, and light industries making jewelry, cutlery, and precision instruments.

maquiladora Mexican term for a factory that fabricates products using materials or parts supplied from elsewhere. Maquiladora plants along the US border, especially across the Rio Grande from S Texas and in the Tijuana area S of San Diego, California, have since the 1970s caused regional booms, both on the Mexican side and in nearby US cities where transporters, warehousers, and other service industries have located. At the same time, many in the US have argued that the maquiladora system, encouraging industries to seek out cheaper Mexican labor, has damaged large parts of the US industrial base.

Maquoketa River 130 mi/209 km long, in E Iowa. It rises N of Manchester and flows SE past Monticello to Maquoketa, turning E and entering the Mississippi R. SE of Bellevue. It receives its main tributary, the **North Fork** (75 mi/121 km long), near Maquoketa.

Marais des Cygnes River 150 mi/240 km long, in E Kansas and SW Missouri. It rises N of Emporia, and flows SE and E, past OTTAWA and OSAWATOMIE, into Missouri, to join the Little Osage R., forming the OSAGE R., SE of Rich Hill. Flood control projects on the Marais des Cygnes ("swan marsh") and tributaries have created Kansas's Melvern and Pomona lakes. Just W of the Missouri border, in a wetlands area 30 mi/48 km N of Fort Scott, Kansas, is the site of the killing (the "Marais des Cygnes Massacre") of a number of antislavery settlers on May 19, 1858. Pottawatomie Creek, a tributary that joins the Marais des Cygnes from the SW at Osawatomie, had been the site of the killing ("the Pottawatomie Massacre") of five proslavery settlers by John Brown and his sons, on May 24, 1856.

Marathon unincorporated community, pop. 800, Brewster Co., far W Texas, 28 mi/45 km SE of Alpine, and just SE of the GLASS Mts. On the site of Fort Pena (1879), and reached by the railroad in 1882, it is a ranching center and a gateway to the BIG BEND region (S). The **Marathon Basin,** in which it lies, is one of the oldest sedimentary formations in the US, and is noted for its minerals.

Marble Canyon gorge, usually considered a N extension of the GRAND CANYON, and now within the Grand Canyon National Park, extending for c.60 mi/100 km along the COLORADO R., from the mouth of the LITTLE COLORADO R. (S) to the mouth of the Paria R. (N), in N Arizona. It is noted for its smooth, vertical 3000-ft/915-m walls of red sandstone and white limestone. The Navajo Bridge (1929) spans the canyon near Lees Ferry.

Marblehead town, pop. 19,971, Essex Co., NE Massachusetts, 15 mi/24 km NE of Boston. On a rocky double peninsula surrounded by Massachusetts Bay (E and S) and Salem Harbor (W), and settled in 1629, it was an early fishing and shipbuilding center, during the Revolutionary War a privateering center. Its economy is based on boatbuilding, boating, fishing, and light manufacturing. East Coast yacht owners have long made Marblehead their base or a port of call, and the town is home to many affluent suburbanites.

Marble Hill residential neighborhood, the only part of Manhattan, New York City, on the mainland. It was cut off from the rest of Manhattan by an 1895 straightening of the Harlem R., then joined to the Bronx in 1913 by landfill, but remains in Manhattan politically. Its name refers to former quarries on the site. King's Bridge, a 1693 toll bridge, formerly crossed the Spuyten Duyvil Creek between Marble Hill and the mainland. Marble Hill is now connected with the rest of Manhattan by a bridge on Broadway.

Marble Mountains subrange of the KLAMATH Mts., in NW California, rising to 6900 ft/2103 m at Buckhorn Mt. The **Marble Mountain Wilderness Area** (214,500 ac/86,900 ha) of the Klamath National Forest, encompassing parts of both the Marble and the SALMON (S) mountains, is noted for its clear lakes and popular with anglers and hikers.

Marceline city, pop. 2645, Linn and Chariton counties, NC Missouri, 32 mi/51 km ESE of Chillicothe. Once a freight division point on the Atchison, Topeka & Santa Fe Railroad, it is now an Amtrak station and shipping point for locally produced grain, livestock, and dairy products and coal from nearby mines. It was the boyhood home of Walt Disney (1901–66).

March Air Force Base see under MORENO VALLEY, California.

March to the Sea also, **Sherman's March** route taken by Union commander W.T. Sherman and troops following the 1864 fall of Atlanta, Georgia. Sherman determined to wage "total war," destroying the productivity and infrastructure of the region while advancing on Savannah and the coast. The march proceeded some 200 mi/320 km generally SE, through the Ocmulgee, Oconee, and Ogeechee river valleys, and took from Nov. 11 to Dec. 10, 1864; spreading out across a 60 mi/100 km-wide front, troops seized produce and livestock, burned buildings, and destroyed railways; their efforts were augmented by those of unofficial outriders ("bummers") and liberated slaves.

Marco Island resort island in the Gulf of Mexico, 15 mi/24 km SSE of Naples, in Collier Co., SW Florida. Seven mi/11 km NW–SE and 0.5–3.5 mi/1–6 km wide, it rises out of mangrove swamps and is connected to the mainland by two causeways. The unincorporated resort community of **Marco** (pop. 9493) is on its N end, and the fishing village of Goodland is on its SE tip. The Cape Romano–Ten Thousand Islands Aquatic Preserve lies SE.

Marcus Baker, Mount see under CHUGACH Mts., Alaska.

Marcus Hook borough, pop. 2546, Delaware Co., SE Pennsylvania, a port on the Delaware R., 18 mi/29 km WSW of Philadelphia. Settled by Swedes in the 1640s, it was a haven for pirates in the late 17th and early 18th centuries. Today it has oil refineries, shipyards, and factories producing rayon and other goods.

Marcy, Mount 5344 ft/1630 m, the highest point in New York, in the NE Adirondack Mts., in Keene township, Essex Co. It is 10 mi/16 km SSE of LAKE PLACID. The Hudson R. rises in L. Tear of the Clouds, on the W slope.

Mare Island see under VALLEJO, California.

Marfa city, pop. 2424, seat of Presidio Co., SW Texas, S of the DAVIS Mts. and 80 mi/130 km NW of the BIG BEND National Park. Founded as a railroad town in 1881, it is at 4688 ft/1429 m one of the state's highest communities, noted for the surrounding mountain scenery; as the setting for the 1956 motion picture *Giant;* as home to the Chinati Foundation, an arts center; as a mecca for hunters; and for the puzzling "Marfa Lights," seen in the area since the 19th century.

Margate city, pop. 42,985, Broward Co., SE Florida, 10 mi/16 km NW of Fort Lauderdale, a resort and retirement community that boomed especially in the 1970s.

Margate City city, pop. 8431, Atlantic Co., SE New Jersey, on Absecon I., 5 mi/8 km SW of Atlantic City. Part of the Atlantic City resort complex, it is known as the site of Lucy the Elephant (1881), a six-story pachyderm-shaped building complete with a canopied howdah on top, which has been an office, home, and tavern.

Mariana Islands see GUAM; Commonwealth of the NORTHERN MARIANA ISLANDS.

Marias River 210 mi/340 km long, in NW Montana. It flows E in several headstreams from the Lewis Range, on the Continental Divide, through the Blackfeet Indian Reservation and past Cut Bank, then through L. Elwell, formed by the 1956 Tiber Dam (a Missouri R. Basin Project unit), and SE to the Missouri, 11 mi/18 km NE of FORT BENTON. In 1804 the Lewis and Clark expedition explored the Marias as possibly the mainstream of the Missouri, but turned back. Later in the 19th century, the **Marias Pass** was discovered near its head; at 5215 ft/1590 m, the pass would have provided the route (although seasonal) through the Rockies for which they were looking.

Maricopa County 9127 sq mi/23,639 sq km, pop. 2,122,101, in SC Arizona. It is home to almost 60% of Arizona's pop. Its seat is PHOENIX, which, with its suburbs in the VALLEY OF THE SUN, including MESA, GLENDALE, and PEORIA, dominates the county's (and state's) economy. The McDowell Mts. and portions of the Mazatzal Mts. are in the NE. Along the Salt, Gila, Santa Cruz, Verde, and Agua Fria rivers, irrigated farmland produces cotton, citrus fruits, figs, alfalfa, lettuce, and truck crops. There are also ranches and resorts throughout the county.

Marietta **1.** city, pop. 44,129, seat of Cobb Co., NW Georgia, 15 mi/24 km NNW of Atlanta, in the foothills of the Blue Ridge Mts. Lockheed Aircraft, based here since 1951 near Dobbins Air Force Base, operates Georgia's largest single manufacturing site. There are also electronics and other industries. Incorporated in 1834, Marietta developed as a railway center before the Civil War. Northern and Southern soldiers lie in its National and Confederate cemeteries, casualties of the Battle of KENNESAW Mt., just W. Southern College of Technology (1948) and Kennesaw State College (1966) are here. **2.** city, pop. 15,026, seat of Washington Co., SE Ohio, at the confluence of the Ohio and Muskingum rivers, on the West Virginia border, 45 mi/72 km SE of Zanesville. The first permanent settlement of the NORTHWEST TERRITORY (originally its capital) and one of the oldest settlements in Ohio, Marietta (named after the queen of France, Marie Antoinette) was founded in 1788 and developed as a major port and a shipbuilding center. Local sites include the original land office of the Ohio Company and Mound Cemetery, with well-preserved prehistoric earthworks and the graves of a number of Revolutionary War officers. Marietta is a trade center for an agricultural region. Office equipment, alloys, and plastics are among the products manufactured locally. It is the seat of Marietta College (1835).

Marigny also, **Faubourg Marigny** commercial and residential district of DOWNTOWN New Orleans, Louisiana, just E of the VIEUX CARRÉ, along the Mississippi R. On 18th-century lands of Bernard de Marigny, it is now a fashionable and avant-garde neighborhood near the INNER HARBOR's industrial areas.

Marina city, pop. 26,436, Monterey Co., WC California, on Monterey Bay, 7 mi/11 km NE of Monterey. A residential and resort community, it has a beach popular with surfers and hang gliders, and is economically tied to the Army's FORT ORD, just S.

Marina City apartment complex on the N side of the Chicago R., in CHICAGO, Illinois, directly across from the LOOP. Its twin cylindrical 61-story towers are a well-known icon of the city. The complex has private boat berths on the river.

Marina del Rey see under VENICE, California.

Marina District waterfront residential and commercial district of N SAN FRANCISCO, California, between the Presidio (W) and Fort Mason (E). It sits on land reclaimed after the 1906 earthquake for the 1915 Panama-Pacific International Exposition, just N of Cow Hollow, and has become a popular "Mediterranean" part of the city, home both to Italian families and to young professionals. Bernard Maybeck's Palace of Fine Arts (W) is the only Exposition building remaining; it houses the noted Exploratorium science museum. The Oct. 1989 earthquake badly damaged the landfill-based Marina.

Marin County 523 sq mi/1355 sq km, pop. 230,096, in NW California, largely on the Marin Peninsula, between San Pablo and San Francisco bays (E) and the Pacific Ocean, and across the GOLDEN GATE (N) from San Francisco. SAN RAFAEL is its seat. Among its woods, hills, and beaches are many of San Francisco's most affluent suburbs, including Sausalito, Mill Valley, Tiburon, and Corte Madera. NOVATO and San Rafael are the largest cities. Mt. Tamalpais, Muir Woods National Monument, Point Reyes National Seashore, and San Quentin Prison are here. Tourism, some agriculture and light industry, and extraction of sand, clay, and stone contribute to the economy.

Marine Park see under FLATLANDS, New York.

Mariner's Harbor industrial section, NW Staten Island, New York, on Newark Bay and the Kill van Kull. An oyster producing community early in the 19th century, it became heavily industrialized, with shipyards, oil refineries, and plants of such companies as Bethlehem Steel and Procter & Gamble, whose soap gave part of the area the name Port Ivory. There are marine terminals and railyards at Howland Hook, on the W, and the Goethals Bridge crosses to Elizabeth, New Jersey. Shooter's I., just offshore, has also been the site of shipyards. Location of a New York City sewage conversion plant in Mariner's Harbor was in controversy in the 1900s. Sailor's Snug Harbor, the charitable and cultural center, is to the NE.

Marinette city, pop. 11,843, seat of Marinette Co., NE Wisconsin, on Green Bay, at the mouth of the Menominee R., across from Menominee, Michigan (N) and 43 mi/69 km NE of the city of Green Bay. It is a port of entry, trade center, summer resort, and industrial city, producing chemicals, metal castings, auto parts, and wood and paper items. A trading post was established here in 1795 by an American Fur Company agent who named it for "Queen" Marinette Chevalier, a renowned French fur trader based here. During much of the 19th century, the logging of white pine dominated the local economy. Manufacturing replaced lumbering around 1900, and now merchandising is also important.

Marion **1.** city, pop. 4211, seat of Perry Co., C Alabama, near the Cahaba R., 63 mi/101 km WNW of Montgomery. The home of Marion Military Institute (1842) and Judson College (1838), it was settled in 1817. The Talladega National Forest is 10 mi/16 km NE. **2.** city, pop. 14,545, seat of Williamson Co., SC Illinois, 16 mi/26 km E of Carbondale. Local industries make explosives and batteries, while the region has coal mines and fruit farms. The large Crab Orchard L. and the 43,000-ac/17,415-ha Crab Orchard National Wildlife Refuge are just W and SE. The Shawnee National Forest and L. of Egypt are 7 mi/11 km S. A Federal penitentiary lies 4 mi/6 km SW. **3.** city, pop. 32,618, seat of Grant Co., EC Indiana, on the Mississinewa R., 30 mi/48 km NW of Muncie. Settled in 1826 along a major Indian trail, it became a boom town with the discovery of oil and gas in the 1880s, and is now a trade, processing, and shipping center for an agricultural region. Its manufactures include auto parts, television sets, oilfield equipment, paper products, glass, plastics, and wire. The Miami Indian Historical Site here marks a final battle (1812) between settlers and natives. The city is home to Indiana Wesleyan University (1920). **4.** city, pop. 20,403, Linn Co., EC Iowa, a suburb immediately NE of Cedar Rapids. Settled in 1839, it became a rail center with repair shops and freight yards. Since 1950, residential growth has transformed it into a bedroom community. Today, home construction and mobile-home manufacture are important industries, along with feed, tools, and wood products. **5.** town, pop. 4496, Plymouth Co., SE Massachusetts, on the W side of Buzzards Bay, 9 mi/14 km ENE of New Bedford. A summer resort, it has a boatbuilding industry. **6.** city, pop. 34,075, seat of Marion Co., NC Ohio, 45 mi/72 km N of Columbus. Named after Revolutionary War leader Francis Marion, it was founded in 1820. Its manufactures include steam shovels (the first of which was produced here, 1874) tractors, road rollers, farm implements, automobile bodies, and refrigerators. The home of Warren G. Harding has been preserved as a museum. **7.** town, pop. 6630, seat of Smyth Co., SW Virginia, on the Middle Fork of the Holston R., 92 mi/148 km SW of Roanoke, in the Great Appalachian Valley, just N of the IRON Mts. A trade and vacation center with various historic manufactures drawing on local wood and limestone, it is in the midst of Jefferson National Forest. From 1924 to 1941 the writer Sherwood Anderson lived here and at Trout Dale, a locality 10 mi/16 km SE, near Mt. Rogers.

Marion, Lake see under SANTEE R., South Carolina.

Marion County **1.** 396 sq mi/1026 sq km, pop. 797,159, in C Indiana. Its seat is INDIANAPOLIS, which occupies almost the entire area. LAWRENCE, BEECH GROVE, SPEEDWAY, and several smaller municipalities are also within the county (and city). **2.** 1194 sq mi/3092 sq km, pop. 228,483, in NW Oregon, bordered by the Willamette R. (W), the North Santiam R. (S), and the Pudding R. and Butte Creek (N). The Cascade Range runs through its E section. SALEM is its seat and industrial center and, along with its suburbs, dominates the NW portion. The balance of the W, in the fertile Willamette Valley, and the C, are agricultural, producing fruit, vegetables, grain, and other goods. Lumber is another important product, and the E contains a section of the Willamette National Forest.

Mariposa see under ORILLIA, Ontario.

Maritime Provinces also, **the Maritimes** Nova Scotia, New Brunswick, and Prince Edward Island, all entirely or largely surrounded by the sea and dependent on it in their economy and development.

Market Square **1.** commercial and residential center in the GOLDEN TRIANGLE of Pittsburgh, Pennsylvania, near the Downtown end of Fifth Ave. This 20-block area served as the city's original center, with the only open space provided for in the 1784 town plan. Many of its Victorian storefronts have been restored. **2.** Spanish, **El Mercado** restored plaza in San Antonio, Texas, just W of Downtown, an 1840s center of city commerce that is now a popular Mexican entertainment and shopping area, noted for its mariachi music, fiestas, and other activities.

Market Street **1.** commercial thoroughfare running NE–SW across SAN FRANCISCO, California, from the EMBARCADERO to TWIN PEAKS, where it merges with Portola Drive. Districts N of Market historically have included the city's power centers and more affluent residential neighborhoods; along the street these include the FINANCIAL DISTRICT, UNION SQUARE, the CIVIC CENTER, and the WESTERN ADDITION. Facing them (S) are SOUTH OF MARKET (SoMa), the MISSION DISTRICT, and the CASTRO. **2.** commercial thoroughfare in Philadelphia, Pennsylvania, running 5.5 mi/8.8 km between the Delaware R. (E) and the Philadelphia-Upper Darby township line (W). Originally named High Street, it has served as the city's main street since the time of William Penn. The widest E–W avenue and one of the axes of the original 1682 plan, it bisects BROAD STREET at City Hall and passes through OLD CITY, CENTER CITY, UNIVERSITY CITY, and WEST PHILADELPHIA. A subway line runs along this corridor. Independence National H2storic Park, PENN CENTER, and the READING TERMINAL MARKET are situated along Market St.

Markham **1.** village, pop. 13,136, Cook Co., NE Illinois, a residential suburb 18 mi/29 km SW of Chicago. **2.** town, pop. 153,811, York Regional Municipality, S Ontario, on the Rouge R., 15 mi/24 km NE of downtown Toronto. An agricultural community since the early 19th century, it is now a rapidly growing (34% pop. increase in 1986–91) suburb, both residential and home to many corporate offices.

Markland see under VINLAND.

Marks' Mill battle site: see under KINGSLAND, Arkansas.

Marksville city, pop. 5526, seat of Avoyelles Parish, SC Louisiana, 27 mi/43 km ESE of Alexandria. Settled in the late 18th century on the Red R. (which later moved 5 mi/8 km N), it was the site of a battle on March 14, 1864, when Fort De Russy fell to Union forces. The area produces rice, sugar cane, cotton, yams, and other crops. The Marksville State Commemorative Area is the site of an ancient (before A.D. 400) ceremonial complex.

Mark Twain National Forest only Missouri national forest, covering some 1.5 million ac/600,000 ha (2345 sq mi/6070 sq km) in nine sections, all in the N Ozark Plateau except for one E of Columbia, on the Missouri R. FORT LEONARD WOOD is almost surrounded by a SC unit. The forest has many recreational areas.

Mark Twain National Wildlife Refuge 25,000 ac/10,125 ha, in nine units in Illinois, Missouri, and Iowa. Spread over 250 mi/400 km of the MISSISSIPPI FLYWAY, the units are along the Mississippi and Illinois rivers and on lakes; many are closed to recreational use during migration seasons. Headquarters are at Quincy, Illinois.

Marlboro town, pop. 929, Windham Co., SE Vermont, on the Molly Stark Trail (Vermont Rte. 9) just W of Brattleboro. It is known for its summer chamber music festival, held on the campus of Marlboro College (1946). Industries include the manufacture of wood products, textiles, and toys.

Marlborough city, pop. 31,813, Middlesex Co., EC Massachusetts, 27 mi/43 km W of Boston. It has been a shoe manufacturing center since 1812. Other industries include the manufacture of missile components, metal stampings, electronics, chemicals, sporting goods, computers, and paper boxes.

Marlton unincorporated village, pop. 10,228, in Evesham township, Burlington Co., W New Jersey, 10 mi/16 km E of Camden. Named for its marl pits, it has clothing and other industries, and is a residential suburb.

Maroon Bells pair of peaks 10 mi/16 km SW of ASPEN, in the Elk Mts. of WC Colorado. **Maroon Peak** (14,156 ft/4315 m) and **North Maroon Peak** (14,014 ft/4271 m) are named for their shape and for their color, which is due in part to their unusual (for the area) sedimentary composition. Seen across Maroon L., in the Maroon Bells–Snowmass Wilderness, they are one of the state's most photographed sights.

Marple township, pop. 23,123, Delaware Co., SE Pennsylvania, a residential suburb 8 mi/13 km W of Philadelphia, containing a number of communities.

Marquette city, pop. 21,977, seat of Marquette Co., in the NC part of the Upper Peninsula of Michigan, on a bluff overlooking L. Superior, 66 mi/106 km NNW of Escanaba. In 1849, Amos Harlow, the first settler, built a forge here for newly discovered iron from the Marquette Iron Range. In a mining, lumbering, and agricultural region, the community became an important shipping point for lumber and iron ore. Marquette produces mining machinery, iron ore pellets, cement blocks, and wood and foundry products. It is the seat of Northern Michigan University (1899); Marquette University is in Milwaukee, Wisconsin. Tourists are attracted by Presque Isle Park, on a forested peninsula just N of the city.

Marquette County 1821 sq mi/4716 sq km, pop. 70,887, in the NW Upper Peninsula of Michigan, on L. Superior, and drained by the Dead and Michigamme rivers and branches of Escanaba R. Its seat is MARQUETTE. The largest county in the state, it is rich in minerals; it is the site of the Marquette Iron Range, marble quarries, and gold mines. There is also lumbering throughout the densely forested county. Some field crops and livestock are raised. The city of Marquette has manufacturing and ships iron ore. There are numerous lakes, and the county has camping, hunting, and fishing resorts.

Marquette Iron Range also, **Marquette Range** in Marquette Co., in Michigan's NC Upper Peninsula, mainly W of Marquette. ISHPEMING is its chief center. In 1848 it became the first Lake Superior–area iron-exporting district, moving its ore through Marquette and, later, Escanaba.

Marquette Island see under LES CHENEAUX Is., Michigan.

Marquette Park residential neighborhood on the Southwest Side of Chicago, Illinois. A blue-collar Lithuanian area, it was the target of an open-housing march led by Martin Luther King, Jr. in 1966. Some integration occurred subsequently.

Marrero unincorporated community, pop. 36,671, Jefferson Parish, SE Louisiana, on the W (S) bank of the Mississippi R., opposite New Orleans. Largely residential, it also has riverfront and canalside industries manufacturing chemicals, paper, and other products.

Marshall **1.** city, pop. 6891, Calhoun Co., S Michigan, on the Kalamazoo R., 12 mi/19 km SE of Battle Creek. Settled in 1831, it flourished as a manufacturing center on the road between Detroit and Chicago and, later, on the Michigan Central Railroad. In the 1830s and 1840s it vied to become Michigan's capital. The arrest (1846) of slavehunters pursuing Adam Crosswhite, which was a national sensation, is memorialized by the Crosswhite Boulder. Marshall has varied light manufactures, and is noted for its mid-19th-century architecture. **2.** city, pop. 12,023, seat of Lyon Co., SW Minnesota, on the Redwood R., 60 mi/97 km SW of Willmar. It is a trading and processing center for a farming region, with an economy based on dairy products and diversified agriculture. Southwest State University (1963) is here. **3.** city, pop. 12,711, seat of Saline Co., WC Missouri, 28 mi/45 km N of Sedalia. In the heart of a farming and livestock raising region, it trades and processes these goods, producing feed, flour, dairy products, and packed meat. It is the seat of Missouri Valley College (1888). Van Meter State Park (NNW) is noted for its ancient burial mounds. **4.** city, pop. 23,682, seat of Harrison Co., NE Texas, 34 mi/55 km W of Shreveport, Louisiana. In the EAST TEXAS OILFIELD, it also has dairy, cotton, and vegetable farming. Settled in 1839 in a thickly forested region that had been home to the Caddo, it had become important by the 1860s, and provided clothing, gear, and ammunition for Southern armies. During the Civil War it was the seat of the exiled Confederate government of Missouri. In the 1930s, the oil boom invigorated the economy. The city has railway repair shops and manufactures petrochemicals, carbon, plastics, clothing, ceramics, and aluminum and steel products. Wiley College (1873) and East Texas Baptist University (1912) are here.

Marshall Space Flight Center see under HUNTSVILLE, Alabama.

Marshall State Historical Monument see under COLOMA, California.

Marshalltown city, pop. 25,178, seat of Marshall Co., C Iowa, on the Iowa R., 50 mi/80 km NE of Des Moines. Settled in the 1850s, it has long been an industrial center, producing such goods as plumbing and heating equipment, tools, furnaces, castings, agricultural equipment, and lawnmowers. The city also remains a wholesale trading center for grain and livestock from the surrounding region. It is the seat of Marshalltown Community College (1927).

Marshfield **1.** town, pop. 21,531, Plymouth Co., SE Massachusetts, 15 mi/24 km E of Brockton, on the Atlantic Ocean. A summer resort, it is also a residential suburb, and cultivates cranberries. Daniel Webster lived here for the last part of his life, and is buried here. The town contains a number of resort villages, including Ocean Bluff, Brant Rock, and Green Harbor. **2.** the name of COOS BAY, Oregon, until 1944. **3.** city, pop. 19,291, Marathon and Wood counties, C Wisconsin, 33 mi/53 km SW of Wausau. It is set in a dairy and poultry farming area. Cheese, beer, shoes, mobile homes, and wood products are among its manufactures. It is also a medical center, known for the Marshfield Medical Research Foundation and St. Joseph's Hospital. A University of Wisconsin Center (1964) is situated here. Founded c.1868, Marshfield was a railroad hub and was rebuilt after a catastrophic fire (1887).

Mars Hill town, pop. 1611, Madison Co., W North Carolina, 15 mi/24 km N of Asheville. In an agricultural area of the Blue Ridge Mts., it is home to Mars Hill College (1856).

Martha's Vineyard island, 108 sq mi/280 sq km, pop. 11,541, situated 5 mi/8 km S of CAPE COD, Massachusetts, and constituting most of DUKES COUNTY. Roughly triangular in shape, it measures 20 mi/32 km at its longest; its greatest width is 10 mi/16 km. Its population quintuples during the summer months. The island's beauty and location attract writers, artists, and celebrities. Its communities have distinct characters; the towns are EDGARTOWN (including CHAPPAQUIDDICK I.), CHILMARK, OAK BLUFFS, TISBURY (including VINEYARD HAVEN), WEST TISBURY, and GAY HEAD.

Martin city, pop. 8600, Weakley Co., NW Tennessee, 13 mi/21 km ESE of Union City, on Cane Creek. This seat of a University of Tennessee campus (1927) is in a truck farming, tobacco growing, and dairying area.

Martinez **1.** city, pop. 31,808, seat of Contra Costa Co., NC California, on the SW shore of Suisun Bay, across the Carquinez Strait from Benicia, and 18 mi/29 km NNE of Oakland. Long an industrial center, it has engaged in copper smelting, winemaking, oil refining, shipbuilding, fishing, and canning. The John Muir National Historic Site includes the naturalist's 1882 home. Traditionally a largely Italian community, Martinez was the birthplace (1914) of baseball great Joe DiMaggio. **2.** unincorporated community, pop. 33,731, Columbia and Richmond counties, E Georgia, 7 mi/11 km NW of AUGUSTA, of which it is a residential suburb.

Martin Luther King, Jr. National Historic Site on AUBURN Ave., 0.8 mi/1.4 km E of FIVE POINTS, in downtown Atlanta, Georgia. Established in 1980, the 23-ac/9-ha site includes Dr. King's 1929 birthplace; the Ebenezer Baptist Church, where he was a preacher; and his tomb, adjacent to the church. Freedom Hall, home of the Martin Luther King, Jr. Center for Nonviolent Social Change and the King Archives, is adjacent.

Martinsburg city, pop. 14,073, seat of Berkeley Co., extreme NE West Virginia, in the Eastern Panhandle, 16 mi/26 km SW of Hagerstown, Maryland. Founded in 1759, the community has many Colonial homes; Bunker Hill (1729), 10 mi/16 km SSW, is the oldest European settlement in the state. Martinsburg developed after the Baltimore and Ohio Railroad arrived in the 1840s. During the Civil War, it was occupied by both sides; troops were raised for both South and North, and the Confederate spy Belle Boyd was active here. The city is a railway center surrounded by apple and peach orchards. Industries make glassware, auto parts, and various other products, and there are county and Federal offices.

Martins Ferry city, pop. 7990, Belmont Co., extreme E Ohio, 19 mi/31 km S of Steubenville, on the Ohio R. opposite Wheeling, West Virginia. Established in the 1780s, it is one of Ohio's oldest settlements. The city is situated in a coal mining district. Local manufactures include steel and steel products, furniture, and glass. Early settlers Betty and Ebenezer Zane are buried in the Walnut Grove Cemetery. Martins Ferry is the birthplace (1837) of novelist William Dean Howells. The city figures in the works of writer Zane Grey and of poet James Wright, who was born here (1927).

Martinsville **1.** city, pop. 11,677, seat of Morgan Co., C Indiana, on the White R., 28 mi/45 km SW of Indianapolis. Settled in the 1820s around artesian springs, it became a health spa with several sanitariums. Other industries are now more important to the economy; manufactures include aircraft parts, furniture, and other wood products. The city is also an agricultural trade center, producing flour, feed, and other processed foodstuffs. **2.** city, pop. 16,162, seat of but administratively separate from Henry Co., S Virginia, in the Piedmont, SE of the Blue Ridge Mts., on the Smith R., 32 mi/51 km WNW of Danville. It is a commercial center for a timbering and agricultural (tobacco, corn, wheat) region. Among its manufactures are furniture, textiles, fiberboard, and lumber. Patrick Henry Community College (1962) is here.

Martyrs' Shrine, the see under MIDLAND, Ontario.

Marye's Heights see under FREDERICKSBURG and CHANCELLORSVILLE, Virginia.

Maryknoll locality in Westchester Co., SE New York, immediately NE of Ossining. It is the site of the headquarters of the Catholic Foreign Mission Society of America (1912), an organization that trains missionaries sent around the world.

Maryland state of the NE US, in the Middle Atlantic region (also considered a BORDER STATE, or, by the Census Bureau, part of the South Atlantic region); 1990 pop. 4,781,468 (113.4% of 1980; rank: 19th); area 12,407 sq mi/32,134 sq km (rank: 42nd); ratified Constitution 1788 (7th). Capital: AN-

NAPOLIS. Most populous city: BALTIMORE. Maryland is bordered N by Pennsylvania, along the old MASON-DIXON LINE, and E by Delaware. It shares most of the DELMARVA PENINSULA with Delaware, and at the peninsula's S end borders also on part of Virginia. Along the state's mainland S is the POTOMAC R., which (with its North Branch) forms Maryland's boundary with West Virginia (which also borders on the W) and Virginia. At the FALL LINE, where the ANACOSTIA R. joins the Potomac, is the DISTRICT OF COLUMBIA, carved out of Maryland (and Virginia) in 1790. The state's dominating physical feature, CHESAPEAKE BAY, extends almost entirely through it in the E, from S (the mouth of the Potomac) to N (the mouth of the SUSQUEHANNA R.). On the E of the bay is the largely rural, low-lying EASTERN SHORE section of the Delmarva Peninsula, reached from Delaware (N), from Virginia (S), or by the Chesapeake Bay Bridge (1952), near Annapolis. Poultry and other farming, fishing and shellfishing, tourism, boatbuilding, and some exurban and suburban housing contribute to the economy of the Eastern Shore, in which SALISBURY is the largest community, and which still bears reminders of its PLANTATION South past. In the extreme SE, Maryland reaches across the peninsula to the Atlantic, where the popular resort OCEAN CITY and the ASSATEAGUE ISLAND National Seashore draw visitors. Chesapeake Bay's marine produce (esp. crabs and oysters) is famous, and (along with tobacco) provided the livelihood of many early Marylanders, who settled at SAINT MARYS CITY and other sites along the small estuarial rivers on both sides of the bay, and on KENT, TILGHMAN, and other islands. In the W, Maryland is a land of small farms, forests, and hill communities, set among APPALACHIAN ridges and valleys. Here the BLUE RIDGE is represented by CATOCTIN Mt., the site of CAMP DAVID; in the extreme W BACKBONE Mt., at 3360 ft/1024 m the state's high point, is a ridge of the ALLEGHENY Mts. Many of the settlers in this region, in which HAGERSTOWN and CUMBERLAND are leading cities, moved S from Pennsylvania in the 18th century. Between the Eastern Shore and the W hills, in the PIEDMONT and along the W shore of Chesapeake Bay, Maryland is now a densely populated, ethnically diverse, largely suburban part of MEGALOPOLIS, its life revolving around two major cities, Baltimore and Washington, D.C. Baltimore, a great port since the early 19th century, the point from which the NATIONAL ROAD, and BALTIMORE AND OHIO RAILROAD penetrated the interior, and a major industrial center, has long been the blue collar hub of Maryland life. Since World War II, an expanding Federal government has made Washington's influence perhaps even more important. MONTGOMERY, PRINCE GEORGE'S, and other Maryland counties are now dominated by Washington residential, office, and research development. The long list of Maryland communities in the Federal orbit includes BETHESDA, CHEVY CHASE, GAITHERSBURG, ROCKVILLE, BELTSVILLE, SILVER SPRING, and other Washington suburbs within and outside the BELTWAY. Military and other government facilities are also central to the lives of ABERDEEN, EDGEWOOD, FREDERICK (Fort Detrick), and other cities across Maryland, including Baltimore itself (home to Social Security headquarters). ANDREWS AIR FORCE BASE, FORT MEADE, the PATUXENT naval air base, and the Naval Academy in Annapolis are also in the state. Within the Baltimore–Washington corridor are the University of Maryland, at COLLEGE PARK; the planned community of COLUMBIA; and many zones of rapid residential development. The Maryland colony began in 1632 with a grant from the (Protestant) British crown to Cecil Calvert, 2nd Lord Baltimore (a Catholic) of land westward from Chesapeake Bay between the Potomac (S) and a N boundary that was later adjusted with Pennsylvania. A haven for Catholics, Maryland nevertheless has never (despite large-scale immigration by such groups as the Germans and Irish) had a largely Catholic pop. It developed as a typical Southern colony, and at the start of the Civil War was deeply divided but remained with the Union, despite street fighting in Baltimore. It was the scene of major conflict both in the War of 1812 (BLADENSBURG; Baltimore's FORT MCHENRY) and in the Civil War (ANTIETAM).

Maryland City see under FORT MEADE, Maryland.

Maryland Heights city, pop. 25,407, St. Louis Co., EC Missouri, E of the Missouri R. and 16 mi/26 km WNW of downtown St. Louis. A residential suburb, it is also the site of Westport Plaza, a growing commercial/office complex on I-270, the St. Louis BELTWAY.

Mary's Peak elevation (4097 ft/1249 m) of the COAST RANGES, 13 mi/21 km SW of Corvallis, in W Oregon, in the SIUSLAW NATIONAL FOREST.

Marystown town, pop. 6739, S Newfoundland, on the E of the BURIN PENINSULA, on an inlet (Mortier Bay) of W PLACENTIA BAY, 116 mi/187 km WSW of St. John's. Fish processing and ship construction and repair are the main industries; vessels used in the GRAND BANKS fisheries have long been built here.

Marysville **1.** city, pop. 12,324, seat of Yuba Co., NC California, at the confluence of the Yuba R. with the Feather R., opposite YUBA CITY, in the Sacramento Valley, 40 mi/64 km N of Sacramento. A supply point during the 1850s gold rush, when it was the head of Feather R. navigation, it is now a trade and shipping center for a fruit growing area. Yuba College (1927) is here; Beale Air Force Base, to the E, a reconnaissance aircraft center, is a major employer. **2.** city, pop. 9656, seat of Union Co., C Ohio, 27 mi/43 km NW of Columbus. This highway junction serves as the trade center for an agricultural and stock raising district. It is the site of a large Honda automobile plant. Other local manufactures include brass products, plastics, dairy goods, and lumber. The Ohio State Reformatory for Women is here. **3.** city, pop. 10,328, Snohomish Co., NW Washington, 3 mi/5 km NNE of Everett and N of the mouth of the Snohomish R. An agricultural center settled in the 1880s, it has boatbuilding, other wood-related, and dairy industries, and is a residential suburb. To the W, on Puget Sound, is the 35–sq mi/91–sq km Tulalip Indian Reservation (pop. 7103), established in 1909.

Maryville **1.** city, pop. 10,663, seat of Nodaway Co., NW Missouri, 40 mi/64 km N of St. Joseph and 15 mi/24 km S of the Iowa border. It was settled in the mid 1840s. Its manufactures include cement blocks and tools, and it is also a trade and distribution hub for livestock, grain, and dairy producers. The city is the seat of Northwest Missouri State University (1905). **2.** city, pop. 19,208, seat of Blount Co., E Tennessee, 16 mi/26 km S of Knoxville. Fort Craig was built here in 1785, and the settlement grew around it. From 1910 nearby dams provided power for Aluminum Company of America plants, on which the economy, with that of adjoining Alcoa (pop. 6400), is largely based. Also produced are building materials, textiles, lumber, limestone, processed foods, and electronic components. Maryville College (1819) is here. It is a gateway to Great Smoky Mountains National Park.

Mascouche city, pop. 25,828, Les Moulins census division, S Québec, on the R. Mascouche, 4 mi/6 km NNE of Terrebonne and 16 mi/26 km N of Montréal. A longtime agricultural and mill town, it is now a growing residential suburb.

Mashpee town, pop. 7884, Barnstable Co., SE Massachusetts, on Cape Cod, adjacent (SW) to Barnstable. It is a summer resort, the fastest-growing town on the Cape in the 1980s, and also cultivates cranberries. The boggy, wooded area was once home to the Mashpee (Wampanoag) Indians. Otis Air Force Base lies W.

Mason city, pop. 11,460, Warren Co., SW Ohio, 20 mi/32 km NE of Cincinnati. Set in an agricultural area, it produces canned goods and metal products.

Masonboro see under WILMINGTON, North Carolina.

Mason City city, pop. 29,040, seat of Cerro Gordo Co., NC Iowa, on the Winnebago R., 63 mi/101 km NW of Waterloo. The rail, trade, and industrial center of a livestock raising and farming area, it manufactures such products as steel doors and window frames, fertilizer, feeds, and electrical and grain drying equipment. The city sits atop clay and limestone deposits, which give rise to large cement, brick, and tile industries. Founded in 1853 by Freemasons, it has several homes designed by Frank Lloyd Wright in the Rock Glen district. Mason City provided the setting ("River City") for *The Music Man,* written by resident Meredith Willson. It is the seat of North Iowa Area Community College (1918).

Mason-Dixon Line surveyed 1763–67 by Charles Mason and Jeremiah Dixon, British astronomers, to establish the boundary between Pennsylvania and Maryland. It extended W from the Delaware border, and by 1779 had been extended to demark Pennsylvania from Virginia (now West Virginia). Before the Civil War, it was regarded as the line between free (N) and slave (S) states, and was thought of as continuing along the Ohio R. and then N around Missouri. It is still popularly thought of as separating the SOUTH from the North. Its creation temporarily left Delaware's anomalous WEDGE.

Maspeth industrial and residential district, W Queens, New York, across Newtown Creek from Greenpoint, Brooklyn. It takes its name from a local Indian tribe. British troops embarked here for their 1776 assault on Manhattan. Maspeth, almost surrounded by cemeteries, is like Greenpoint a largely Polish and Lithuanian neighborhood.

Massabesic Lake in S New Hampshire, just E of Manchester, New Hampshire's largest city. This irregularly shaped lake is 4 mi/6 km long and provides municipal water and serves as a recreation center for the area.

Massachusetts officially, **Commonwealth of Massachusetts** northeastern US state, in C NEW ENGLAND; 1990 pop. 6,016,425 (104.9% of 1980; rank: 13th); area 10,555 sq mi/27,337 sq km (rank: 44th); ratified Constitution 1788 (6th). Capital and most populous city: BOSTON. Other leading cities: WORCESTER, SPRINGFIELD, LOWELL, NEW BEDFORD. Massachusetts is bordered N by Vermont (W) and New Hampshire (E); W by New York; S by Connecticut (W) and Rhode Island (E); and SE and E by the Atlantic Ocean (including, SE to NE, the inlets of BUZZARDS BAY, NANTUCKET SOUND, CAPE COD Bay, and MASSACHUSETTS BAY). From the W, the state includes part of the TACONIC Mts.; the valley of the HOUSATONIC R.; the upland known as the BERKSHIRE HILLS; a S spur of Vermont's GREEN Mts., containing Mt. GREYLOCK, at 3491 ft/1065 m the state's high point; a central upland bisected by the CONNECTICUT R.; coastal lowlands drained E by the CHARLES, MERRIMACK, and other rivers; and the northeasternmost section of the Atlantic COASTAL PLAIN, represented by the MORAINE-formed Cape Cod and ELIZABETH, NANTUCKET, and MARTHA'S VINEYARD islands. It takes its name from an Algonquian term ("big hills") for the BLUE HILLS, just S of Boston; this attached first to the bay, then to the colony and state (known as "the Bay State"). Inhabited by the Natick and other Algonquian peoples, the region was first seen (unless VINLAND was in fact here) by whites when John Cabot sailed into the area in 1498. GEORGES BANK and other local waters soon drew large European fishing fleets. In 1620 the Pilgrims' *Mayflower,* bound for Virginia, landed on Cape Cod instead, and shortly proceeded to establish the PLYMOUTH settlement. By 1630 the Massachusetts Bay Colony had also been founded (at SALEM) and extended to the SHAWMUT PENINSULA (Boston). Fishing, commerce, and shipbuilding, along with subsistence farming, maintained the coastal colonies for the next century and a half; gradually, settlement spread W to the fertile PIONEER (Connecticut R.) VALLEY, as well as N into New Hampshire and Maine (part of Massachusetts 1677–1820) and S into Rhode Island and Connecticut. Massachusetts's maritime economy made it vulnerable to the pressures of British mercantile policy, and this contributed to Boston's leading role in protest and eventually in the American Revolution. LEXINGTON, CONCORD, and BUNKER HILL are among famed area battle sites. In the 19th century, Boston lost commercial supremacy to New York and other cities, and began a transition to an industrial economy; abundant waterpower soon made other Massachusetts communities, esp. the Merrimack R. cities of Lowell, LAWRENCE, and HAVERHILL, as well as FALL RIVER (SE) and Springfield (WC), factory centers. Worcester, in the state's C, BROCKTON (SE), and closer Boston suburbs like CAMBRIDGE, SOMMERVILLE, and WALTHAM also became industrial, along with a host of smaller cities. Textiles, shoes, and clothing were the chief manufactures of this Massachusetts industrial epoch. By the early 20th century, labor troubles and the flight of manufacturers to the South began to strip the state of its factories, a process exacerbated by the 1930s Depression. In the 1950s, however, drawing on the state's academic and research base, a boom began in high-tech industries along ROUTE 128, the first Boston BELTWAY; this has continued, with cyclical variations, into the area of Route 495, the outer (1960s) beltway, which passes near Worcester. Massachusetts industry is today diversified, although electronic and other high-tech machinery, advanced weaponry, and other research products are prominent. Boston is a major financial, insurance, service industry, and commercial center, and these sectors are important in both Worcester (also a machinemaker) and Springfield (long a major military contractor). GLOUCESTER, on the North Shore (NE), and New Bedford (SE) are centers of the fishing industry, which has recently declined. Tourism and recreation are esp. important at historic and cultural sites in the Boston area; on the beaches and islands of Cape ANN, the SOUTH SHORE, and Cape Cod; and in the Berkshires. The academic base on which much of the Massachusetts economy rests began in the 1630s with Boston's Latin School and Cambridge's Harvard College. Today, the Boston region is the HUB of American higher education, if not in other senses. A second, younger educational cluster is the FIVE COLLEGE AREA around AMHERST (where the University of Massachusetts is situated) and

NORTHAMPTON. The state's intellectual activity (centered in Boston, Cambridge, and Concord) contributed not only to its Revolutionary history but to the state's leading role in abolitionism as the Civil War approached, and a strong reform tradition continues today. In its first two centuries, Massachusetts was essentially a community of British origin. The wave of immigration from potato blight-stricken Ireland that began in the 1840s transformed the state, creating a long-term social division between the older, Puritan Yankees (or Boston Brahmins) on one hand and the mostly Catholic immigrants on the other. Eastern Europeans, Italians, Portuguese, Jews, and French- Canadians are among the many groups that arrived after the Civil War, staffing industry and creating a progressively more diverse society. Today the Boston metropolitan area, at the NE end of MEGALOPOLIS, is one of America's largest. Most of Massachusetts's people live here, and the state has a relatively high pop. density; in far corners, however, there remain pockets of rural isolation.

Massachusetts Bay inlet of the Atlantic Ocean stretching from Cape Ann (N) to Cape Cod (S), off E Massachusetts. Sixty-five mi/105 km long NW–SE and 25 mi/40 km wide, its three major arms are BOSTON HARBOR, Plymouth Bay, and Cape Cod Bay. Important harbors include Gloucester, Salem, and Marblehead, a famous yachting port; fishing and lobstering are important. The Italian navigator Giovanni Verrazano was the first European known certainly to have encountered the bay, in 1524. In 1620, the Pilgrims founded the first permanent New England settlement at Plymouth, on the SW shore. The ATLANTIC INTRACOASTAL WATERWAY traverses the bay.

Massachusetts Bay Colony colonial settlement, E Massachusetts. It was established 1628 at SALEM, by John Endecott; the colony expanded in 1630 and reestablished itself at Boston, electing John Winthrop governor. Its original charter included all the land W to the Pacific Ocean between the Charles R. (S) and the headwaters of the Merrimack R. (N), and granted the settlers a large measure of self-rule, although suffrage was limited to men who were property owners and members of the Congregational Church. The colony prospered, and outlying settlements were begun; Winthrop's autocratic manner, as well as religious dissension, however, led some, including Roger Williams, to emigrate and found other communities. The Massachusetts Bay Colony retained its charter until 1684; in 1686 it became part of the Dominion of New England.

Massanutten Mountain ridge, 45 mi/72 km long, running NNE–SSW through the middle of the SHENANDOAH VALLEY, in NW Virginia. The North and South forks of the Shenandoah R. flank it, meeting at its N end, near Front Royal. Rising to 3000 ft/915 m, and hiding one side of the Valley from the other, the ridge was strategically important in the Civil War, particularly during Stonewall Jackson's 1862 Shenandoah Campaign.

Massapequa Park village, pop. 18,044, in Oyster Bay town, Nassau Co., SE New York, on the South Shore of Long Island, 30 mi/48 km SE of Manhattan. It is primarily residential, and adjacent (E) to but separate from the unincorporated residential village of **Massapequa** (pop. 22,018).

Massena town, pop. 13,826, St. Lawrence Co., extreme N New York, on the Grass, Raquette, and St. Lawrence rivers, 68 mi/110 km SW of Montréal. Named for one of Napoleon's marshals by the first (1792) European settler, it became a popular 19th-century health spa. Following the construction, in 1900, of a power canal connecting the Grasse with the St. Lawrence, industrialization took place, led by the establishment (1903) of the Aluminum Company of America. The production of aluminum remains important, along with engine blocks and automobile parts. Massena is the headquarters of the St. Lawrence Development Corporation and the center of Seaway power structures, including the Moses-Saunders Power Dam, the Massena Intake, and Eisenhower and Snell locks. Units of Robert Moses State Park are in the N. Massena is connected by bridge with CORNWALL, Ontario.

Massillon city, pop. 31,007, Stark Co., NE Ohio, on the Tuscarawas R., 25 mi/40 km S of Akron. Founded in the early 19th century, it was named in honor of Jean-Baptiste Massillon, a French cleric and author. Massillon was initially a grain marketing center on the Ohio and Erie Canal. Industrial development was triggered in 1855 when nearby deposits of coal were discovered. Today, stainless steel, roller bearings, and hospital supplies are among local manufactures. The city is also an agricultural distribution center. The National Shrine of St. Dymphna is at the Massillon Psychiatric Center. Jacob Coxey lived here at the time (1894) he led his "army" of the unemployed to Washington.

Massive, Mount see under SAWATCH RANGE, Colorado.

Mastic unincorporated village, pop. 13,778, in Brookhaven town, Suffolk Co., SE New York, on Long Island's South Shore, where the estuarial Forge R. enters Moriches Bay. It is primarily residential. The unincorporated village of **Mastic Beach** (pop. 10,293), just SW, on Narrow Bay facing Fire I., is a residential and resort community.

Matagami city, pop. 2467, SW Québec, 340 mi/550 km NW of Montréal. On the R. Bell, S of L. Matagami, it is at the center of a copper and zinc mining region.

Matagorda Bay inlet of the Gulf of Mexico, almost landlocked by the Matagorda Peninsula, 75 mi/121 km SW of Galveston, in SE Texas. Fifty-two mi/84 km NE–SW and 2–10 mi/3–16 km wide, it receives the COLORADO R. at Matagorda and joins the gulf via Cavallo Pass at Port O'Connor, on its S end. Known for its fishing and oystering, it is part of the GULF INTRACOASTAL WATERWAY. The French explorer La Salle was the first European to encounter the bay, in 1685. The South Texas nuclear power plant (see BAY CITY) is N of the bay.

Matagorda Island barrier island lying between San Antonio and Espiritu Santo bays (NW) and the Gulf of Mexico (SE), 50 mi/80 km NE of Corpus Christi, in SE Texas. Matagorda Peninsula (behind which is Matagorda Bay) lies to the NE, across Cavallo Pass. Thirty-five mi/56 km NE–SW and 0.5–3 mi/1–5 km wide, the sandy island contains conservation and wildlife areas.

Matamoras borough, pop. 1934, Pike Co., extreme NE Pennsylvania, on a tableland above the Delaware R. opposite its sister city, PORT JERVIS, New York. It was settled by the Dutch in the mid 18th century, and was a popular resort until the mid 20th century.

Matane city, pop. 12,756, Matane Co., SE Québec, on the GASPÉ PENINSULA, 53 mi/85 km NE of Rimouski, on the S bank of the St. Lawrence R., at the mouth of the R. Matane. Settled in the 1680s in Micmac territory, it developed in the 19th century around forestry. Today its main industries are wood-based. There is also some farming, and the city is a port and distribution center for the region. Shrimping and salmon fishing are important, and there is a francophone community college.

Matanuska Valley rich agricultural region extending 50 mi/80 km along the lower Matanuska R., NE of the Knik Arm of COOK INLET, in SC Alaska. Lying between the Talkeetna (N) and Chugach (S) mountains, it (along with the SUSITNA R. valley to the NW) produces grains, root vegetables, dairy goods, and oversize cabbages and strawberries grown in the long summer daylight hours. Birch, spruce, and poplar forests surround the valley, and the Matanuska Glacier is nearby (E). PALMER and Wasilla (pop. 4028, Matanuska-Susitna Borough) are the area's largest communities. In 1935, during the Depression, the Federal government provided loans and assistance for 200 farm families from the Midwest to resettle in the valley; many of their descendants remain in and around Palmer.

Matawan borough, pop. 9270, Monmouth Co., EC New Jersey, 10 mi/16 km NW of Red Bank. In a truck-farming region, it is an agricultural trading center, and manufactures ceramics and electroplating equipment.

Matewan town, pop. 619, Mingo Co., extreme SW West Virginia, on Tug Fork, at the Kentucky border, 60 mi/100 km SW of Charleston. In a bituminous coalfield, it was the scene of violent labor struggles in 1920.

Mather Air Force Base see under SACRAMENTO, California.

Mather Peak see under BIGHORN NATIONAL FOREST, Wyoming.

Matinicus Island 1 sq mi/2.6 sq km, in Knox Co., SC Maine. Largest of the islands in Matinicus Isle Plantation, pop. 63, it is in the Atlantic Ocean, 20 mi/32 km SE of Rockland. The 800-ac/324-km area is largely unspoiled and a noted nesting ground for seabirds. Fishing and lobstering are the chief occupations.

Matsqui district municipality, pop. 68,604, Central Fraser Valley Regional District, SW British Columbia, between the Fraser R. (N) and the Washington border, 40 mi/65 km ESE of Vancouver. In an alluvial agricultural area noted esp. for its raspberries, it has various light manufactures and is a rapidly growing residential suburb. ABBOTSFORD is adjacent (E).

Mattagami River see under MOOSE R., Ontario.

Mattapan section of Boston, Massachusetts, S of Dorchester, along the Neponset R. In the 19th century it was a mill center. Today it is a largely black middle-class section of Boston; Hyde Park lies SW, the town of Milton S.

Mattapoisett town, pop. 5850, Plymouth Co., SE Massachusetts, on Buzzards Bay 6 mi/10 km E of New Bedford. Formerly a shipbuilding and whaling center, it is today a resort area.

Mattaponi River 120 mi/190 km long, in E Virginia. It is formed by the confluence of several streams in Caroline Co., and flows in a winding course, generally SE, joining the PAMUNKEY R. at WEST POINT to form the YORK R. The Mattaponi (or Mattapony) tribe, for whom the river is named, have a reservation on the S bank, 10 mi/16 km NW of West Point.

Matteson village, pop. 11,378, Cook Co., NE Illinois, a residential suburb 26 mi/42 km S of Chicago.

Matthews town, pop. 13,651, Mecklenburg Co., S North Carolina. This affluent suburb 10 mi/16 km SE of central Charlotte grew in population by over 800% in the 1980s.

Mattoon city, pop. 18,441, seat of Coles Co., EC Illinois, 10 mi/16 km W of Charleston. Founded in 1854 at a junction of the Illinois Central and New York Central railroads, it developed as a transportation hub and agricultural processing center. The discovery of oil in the area in 1940 stimulated industrial expansion. Today, Mattoon's manufactures include photo lamps, brass fittings, clothing, and road building machinery. Lake Land College (1966) is 5 mi/8 km S. The Shelbyville Wildlife Management Area is 10 mi/16 km NW, and L. Mattoon is 8 mi/13 km SW.

Mattydale see under SALINA, New York.

Mauch Chunk see under JIM THORPE, Pennsylvania.

Maui volcanic mid-Pacific island, in Maui Co., Hawaii, SE of MOLOKAI, E of LANAI, and NW of the island of HAWAII. At 728 sq mi/1886 sq km, it is the second-largest island of the Hawaiian archipelago. Important communities are WAILUKU, KAHULUI, and LAHAINA. The island was formed in the E by the extinct volcano HALEAKALA and in the W by Puu Kukui; they are connected by a flat, fertile isthmus. The high point in the E is Red Hill, at 10,023 ft/3057 m; in the W the high point is 5787 ft/1765 m. The island's economy is based on livestock, pineapple, and sugarcane, and on tourism.

Maui County 1175 sq mi/3043 sq km, pop. 100,374, in SE Hawaii, comprising the islands of KAHOOLAWE, LANAI, MAUI, and MOLOKAI. Its seat is WAILUKU, on Maui's NW peninsula.

Mauldin city, pop. 11,587, Greenville Co., NW South Carolina, 6 mi/10 km SE of downtown GREENVILLE, of which it is a growing residential suburb.

Maumee city, pop. 15,561, Lucas Co., NW Ohio, on the Maumee R., 7 mi/11 km SW of Toledo. It was founded in 1817 on the site of Fort Miami (originally British but captured by the US during the War of 1812). At the site where the Ohio and Erie Canal was connected to the Maumee R., it became a bustling trade and commercial center. Today its chief industry is grain storage, and limestone is quarried in the region. Historic FALLEN TIMBERS and FORT MEIGS are nearby.

Maumee River 130 mi/209 km long, in Indiana and Ohio. It is formed at Fort Wayne, Indiana, by the St. Joseph and St. Marys rivers. It flows NE into Ohio past Defiance, Napoleon, and Toledo, where it forms Maumee Bay on L. Erie. Its main tributary is the AUGLAIZE, which joins the Maumee at Defiance.

Mauna Kea extinct volcano on the NC part of the island of HAWAII. At 13,796 ft/4208 m above sea level, its peak is the high point of the state of Hawaii; it is considered the highest island mountain in the world, some 32,000 ft/9760 m from submarine base to tip. The diameter of its dome is 30 mi/48 km. It has many cinder cones, with its W and S slopes buried in lava from the active neighboring MAUNA LOA. Despite its tropical situation, it was glaciated, and has a snow cover on which some skiing is done. Its top is home to the famous Mauna Kea Observatory Complex, including the huge Maxwell and Keck telescopes.

Mauna Loa in Hawaii: **a.** active volcano on the SC part of the island of Hawaii. In HAWAII VOLCANOES NATIONAL PARK, it is one of the largest mountain masses in the world, rising 13,678 ft/4172 m above sea level and 29,000 ft/8845 m from its submarine base, with a dome measuring up to 75 mi/120 km across. Its many craters include KILAUEA on its SE slope and its central crater, Mokuaweoweo, occupying 4 sq mi/10 sq km. Averaging one eruption every 3½ years, it is considered an effusive, rather than an explosive, volcano, with eruptions along fissures in its flank as well as in its central crater. Its total lava flow covers an area of some 2000 sq mi/5200 sq km. **b.** mountain on W MOLOKAI; its peak stands 1382 ft/422 m.

Maurepas, Lake shallow, brackish, roughly circular body up to 13 mi/21 km across, some 28 mi/45 km NW of New Orleans, in SE Louisiana. It is connected with L. PONTCHARTRAIN (E) by 6 mi/10 km–long Pass Manchac. The Tickfaw and Amite rivers flow into it.

Maurice see under ORANGE CITY, Iowa.

Maurice River 50 mi/80 km long, in S New Jersey. It rises near GLASSBORO, and flows past VINELAND and MILLVILLE, where a dam forms the 3 mi/5 km–long Union L. From there the river flows SE to Maurice R. Cove on Delaware Bay, just S of Bivalve and Port Norris. It is navigable to Millville; industries along its S reaches have included sand and gravel production, oystering, and fishing.

Mauricie see R. SAINT-MAURICE, Québec.

Maverick County 1280 sq mi/3315 sq km, pop. 36,378, in SW Texas, on the Rio Grande (SW). Its seat is EAGLE PASS. In the rich WINTER GARDEN area, it handles spinach and other crops, and there is sheep, goat, and cattle ranching. Samuel Maverick, an early landowner whose herd was (apparently accidentally) unbranded, gave his name to the county and to the general term *maverick*.

Max Patch Mountain see under BALD Mts., North Carolina.

Maxwell Air Force Base see under MONTGOMERY, Alabama.

Maxwell Street commercial street on the Lower West Side of Chicago, Illinois, S of the University of Illinois at CHICAGO CIRCLE. It was the center of the city's original Jewish community. Once full of pushcarts and stalls, the street today features an open-air flea market with jazz and blues buskers.

May, Cape see CAPE MAY, New Jersey.

Mayagüez unincorporated community (ZONA URBANA), pop. 83,010, Mayagüez Municipio (pop. 100,371), W Puerto Rico, on the Mona Passage, 70 mi/115 km WSW of San Juan. Founded c.1760, it is the hub of Puerto Rico's W coast. It has been subject to many earthquakes, the worst of which (1918) severely damaged the city. Its deep harbor is important in the export of such island products as sugar, tobacco, coffee, and fruit. Mayagüez also has an important fishing industry and is a major tuna packing center. There are alcohol distilleries and plants manufacturing pharmaceuticals, electronic components, food products, and beverages. For centuries the city has been known for its needlework and embroidery. It is home to the Department of Agriculture's Tropical Agriculture Research Station and to the University of Puerto Rico's College of Agriculture and Engineering.

Mayesville agricultural town, pop. 694, Sumter Co., C South Carolina, 9 mi/14 km NE of Sumter, best known as the birthplace of educator Mary McLeod Bethune (1875–1955).

Mayfield city, pop. 9935, seat of Graves Co., W Kentucky, on Mayfield Creek, 22 mi/35 km S of Paducah. This tobacco and mule market was settled in 1823. With the coming of the New Orleans & Ohio Railroad (1854), it grew as a market for grain, livestock, and dark-leaf tobacco. The area is noted for its clay; manufactures include brick, furniture, and snuff.

Mayfield Creek 70 mi/110 km long, in W Kentucky. It rises in SW Calloway Co., near Lynn Grove, and flows generally N past MAYFIELD and W to the Mississippi R., just S of Wickliffe.

Mayfield Heights city, pop. 19,847, Cuyahoga Co., NE Ohio, a residential suburb 12 mi/19 km E of Cleveland.

Maynard town, pop. 10,325, Middlesex Co., NE Massachusetts, 16 mi/26 km SSW of Lowell. Situated between Routes 128 and 495, just W of Concord on the Assabet R., it was an important mid-19th-century woolen mill town; today it is the home of the Digital Equipment Corporation.

Mayo village, pop. 243, C Yukon Territory, on the Stewart R., at its confluence with the Mayo R., 112 mi/180 km ESE of Dawson. The settlement developed as a river shipping point after the 1902 discovery of local gold and the 1919 discovery of silver and lead at Keno Hill (Keno City), 28 mi/45 km NE, and flourished until the 1940s. In the late 1960s, new deposits of lead, zinc, and silver were discovered; Mayo is now connected to the KLONDIKE HIGHWAY, and is a service center for an active mining district.

Mayo Clinic see under ROCHESTER, Minnesota.

Maysville city, pop. 7169, seat of Mason Co., NE Kentucky, on the Ohio R., 54 mi/87 km NE of Lexington. As Limestone, it was laid out in 1787 at the mouth of Limestone Creek. Long a river port and shipbuilding center, it is now an important burley tobacco market, and has some metal and textile industries.

Mayville city, pop. 2092, Traill Co., E North Dakota, on the Goose R., 50 mi/80 km NNW of Fargo. Situated in the rich Red R. Valley, it was settled in 1881 and became a commercial center for livestock, grain, and dairy products. It is the site of Mayville State University (1889) and the Goose River Heritage Center, a local history museum.

Maywood **1.** city, pop. 27,850, Los Angeles Co., SW California, 5 mi/8 km SE of downtown Los Angeles. A predominantly Hispanic suburb just NE of Huntington Park, it has some industry, including food processing, and furniture and other manufactures. **2.** village, pop. 27,139, Cook Co., NE Illinois, on the Des Plaines R., 11 mi/18 km W of Chicago. Primarily a residential community, it has industries producing cans, cartons, metal tubing, and surgical equipment. Chicago Lutheran Theological Seminary is situated here. Maywood Park Race Track is 1 mi/2 km N of the village. Located just S of Maywood is a group of medical institutions including Loyola University Medical Center and John J. Madden Health Center.

Mazatzal Mountains range in C Arizona, extending S c.50 mi/80 km along the E of the East Verde R. to the Salt R., NE of Phoenix. It reaches 7903 ft/2409 m at Mazatzal Peak, and includes Four Peaks (7657 ft/2334 m), a group long noted as a landmark.

McAlester city, pop. 16,370, seat of Pittsburg Co., SE Oklahoma, 75 mi/120 km SSE of Tulsa. Once the capital of the Choctaw Nation, it grew from a trading post operated by James McAlester at the crossroads of the westward California Trail and the N–S Texas Road. A coalmining center in the 1870s, it is now a trade and manufacturing center for an agricultural and coal, oil, and natural gas producing region. Aviation and marine industries are prominent. The state penitentiary is here, and a large Army Ammunition Plant is SW, near Savanna. EUFAULA L. lies N and E.

McAllen city, pop. 84,021, Hidalgo Co., extreme S Texas, in the Lower Rio Grande Valley, 48 mi/77 km WNW of Brownsville. A processing center for the region's sugar cane, grain, vegetables, cotton, and citrus fruit, it was founded in 1905 and named for the settler whose ranch became the townsite. In addition to natural gas and oil production and refining, the city has machinery and textile plants and is an important center for trade with Mexico (Reynosa, Tamaulipas, is just

S). Tourists and winter vacationers are now key to the economy; the subtropical climate, proximity to Mexico, and recreational and convention facilities make the city popular especially with Canadians and Midwesterners.

McCausland see under SCOTT Co., Iowa.

McChord Air Force Base see under LAKEWOOD, Washington.

McClellan Air Force Base see under SACRAMENTO, California.

McClellan-Kerr Arkansas Navigation System see under ARKANSAS R.

McComb city, pop. 11,591, Pike Co., S Mississippi, 58 mi/93 km ESE of Natchez and 15 mi/24 km N of the Louisiana border. Founded with the 1857 construction of the Illinois Central Railroad between Jackson and New Orleans, in an area of farms and forests, it is a trade and distribution hub for livestock, cotton, vegetables, dairy products, and timber, and has railroad shops. Lumber is milled, clothing is manufactured, and there are other light industries.

McConnell Air Force Base see under WICHITA, Kansas.

McConnelsville village, pop. 1804, seat of Morgan Co., SE Ohio, on the Muskingum R., 22 mi/35 km SSE of Zanesville. Formerly supported by river commerce, it now depends on the manufacture of such items as lumber, meat products, tools, bearings, and furniture. Natural gas and oil are developed in the area.

McCook city, pop. 8112, seat of Red Willow Co., SW Nebraska, on the Republican R., 65 mi/104 km S of North Platte and 13 mi/21 km N of the Kansas line. It was founded as Fairview in 1881. Its name was changed and the railroad arrived the following year. The city continues to be a rail and processing center for grain, livestock, and dairy producers. The home of influential Senator George W. Norris (1861–1944), who was born in Ohio and moved to this area in the 1880s, is in McCook.

McCormick Place exposition and convention center on L. Michigan and LAKE SHORE DRIVE, in Burnham Park, on the South Side of Chicago, Illinois. Rebuilt after a fire in the 1960s, it also hosts plays, concerts, and exhibitions.

McDonald Observatory see under Mt. LOCKE, Texas.

McDowell hamlet in Highland Co., N Virginia, 25 mi/40 km NW of Staunton, the site of Stonewall Jackson's first victory (May 8, 1862) in his Shenandoah Campaign. It is on the Bullpasture R. in the Appalachian Mts., W of the Shenandoah Valley.

McDowell Mountains NW–SE trending range, extending for 12 mi/19 km and rising to McDowell Peak (4116 ft/1255 m), 15 mi/24 km NE of Scottsdale, in C Arizona. The range includes Thompson Peak (3980 ft/1213 m), site of a radio facility; Tom's Thumb, a popular rock climbing location; and an important Hohokam site near Pinnacle Peak, at the N end. A fort built in 1865, the Fort McDowell Indian Reservation (Mohave and Apache; pop. 640), and a regional park in the area all bear the name of General Irvin McDowell (1818–85).

McDuffie County 256 sq mi/663 sq km, pop. 20,119, in E Georgia. On the W fringe of the AUGUSTA area. Thomson (city, pop. 6862) is its seat. Ft. GORDON is on its SE edge. Thomas Edward Watson, "the Sage of McDuffie," populist leader and US senator, was born in this agricultural county in 1856.

McFarland village, pop. 5232, Dane Co., SE Wisconsin, on L. Waubesa, a suburb 6 mi/10 km SE of Madison. Biochemist Conrad A. Elvehjem was born here (1901).

McGregor city, pop. 4683, McLennan Co., EC Texas, 18 mi/29 km WSW of Waco. It is a farm (cotton, livestock) trade center with some light manufactures.

McGuire nuclear power plant: see under CATAWBA R., North Carolina.

McGuire Air Force Base see under FORT DIX, New Jersey.

McHenry city, pop. 16,177, McHenry Co., NE Illinois, 48 mi/77 km NW of Chicago. A growing exurb, it attracts residents to its abundant lakes, and has long served as a summer resort for Chicagoans. Moraine Hills State Park is just SE, and Wonder L. is 4 mi/6 km to the NW. Pistakee L. is 3 mi/5 km to the NE.

McHenry County 606 sq mi/1570 sq km, pop. 183,241, in NE Illinois. The N border coincides with the Wisconsin line. The Fox R. flows out of Pistakee L. down through the E part of the county. It is here that Chicago exurban communities, such as Barrington Hills, Algonquin, Crystal Lake, and McHenry have been growing in recent years. Even the seat, Woodstock, in the center of the county, has become partly absorbed into the Chicago metropolitan area. Dairy and vegetable farms dominate the W.

McKeesport city, pop. 26,016, Allegheny Co., SW Pennsylvania, at the confluence of the Monongahela and Youghiogheny rivers, 10 mi/16 km SE of Pittsburgh. It was settled in 1755 by David McKee, who operated a ferry here from 1769. It was a center of the Whiskey Rebellion (1794). McKeesport grew slowly until the opening of the coalfields in the area in 1830. It had a thriving barge building industry into the 1850s, and flourished after the opening of its first iron factory (1851). Today McKeesport is part of the industrial complex around Pittsburgh. Its manufactures include steel products, auto bodies, and tools and dies. A branch of Pennsylvania State University is here.

McKees Rocks borough, pop. 7691, Allegheny Co., SW Pennsylvania, on the Ohio R., an industrial suburb 4 mi/6 km NW of Pittsburgh. It was settled c.1764 on the site of an Indian village. The borough's many products include ships, steel, railroad cars, paint, and castings.

McKenzie city, pop. 5168, Carroll, Weakley, and Henry counties, NW Tennessee, 39 mi/63 km NE of Jackson. This rail junction has various light manufactures, food processing, and extractive industries. Bethel College (1842) is here.

McKinley, Mount also, **Denali** highest peak in North America (20,320 ft/6194 m), in DENALI NATIONAL PARK, in the ALASKA RANGE, 130 mi/210 km NNW of Anchorage, Alaska. Named Denali (the "High One" or "Great One") by Athabascans, it is composed primarily of erosion-resistant granite, and remains above many other sections of the Alaska Range composed of softer sedimentary materials. Its N face rises more than 17,000 ft/5180 m above the plains at its base, the highest such rise in the world. The lower N peak (19,470 ft/5934 m) was first climbed in 1910, the higher S peak in 1913; together they have been known as the Churchill Peaks. Surrounding the mountain are the Muldrow, Kahiltna, and other glaciers. Talkeetna, SE of the summit and outside the park, is a staging ground for many climbing expeditions.

McKinney city, pop. 21,283, seat of Collin Co., NE Texas, on Interstate 75 and the East Fork of the Trinity R., 28 mi/45 km NNE of Dallas. Established in 1842 in the BLACKLANDS belt, it has raised beef and dairy cattle, cotton, corn, and grain. Agricultural processing and various other industries contribute to the economy, and there was suburban growth in the 1980s.

McLean unincorporated community, pop. 38,168, Fairfax Co., N Virginia, 9 mi/14 km NW of Washington, D.C. It is an affluent residential suburb just inside the BELTWAY, home to many upper-level Federal employees, and to the offices of numerous national associations and government-related businesses.

McLean County 1185 sq mi/3069 sq km, pop. 129,180, in C Illinois. The Mackinaw R. flows across the N. The twin cities of Normal and BLOOMINGTON, the county seat, are in the center of the county. Around them lie farms turning out corn, livestock, and dairy products.

McLoughlin, Mount volcanic peak (9495 ft/2894 m) of the S CASCADE RANGE, W of Upper Klamath L. and 30 mi/48 km ENE of Medford, in the Rouge River National Forest in SW Oregon.

McMinnville 1. city, pop. 17,894, seat of Yamhill Co., NW Oregon, 17 mi/27 km NNW of Salem. An important center for regional farm and lumber industries, it was settled in 1844. McMinnville lies in the heart of Oregon's winemaking district. The city's manufactures include mobile homes, paint, and electronic parts. It is the seat of Linfield College (1849). The *Spruce Goose,* Howard Hughes's huge flying boat, was brought here in 1992 from Long Beach, California. **2.** town, pop. 11,194, seat of Warren Co., EC Tennessee, midway between Nashville (NW) and Chattanooga (SE), on the Barren Fork, a branch of the Caney Fork R. In an agricultural area, it has had wood, extractive, and textile industries. A noted photography school flourished here c.1906–29.

McNeil Island 3 mi/5 km long, in Pierce Co., WC Washington, in Puget Sound, 8 mi/13 km WSW of Tacoma. A Federal women's penitentiary is here.

McPherson city, pop. 12,422, seat of McPherson Co., C Kansas, 25 mi/40 km NE of Hutchinson. It was founded in 1872 on the SANTA FE TRAIL. In a farming area with oilfields, it has a variety of processing plants and light manufactures. McPherson College (1887) and Central College (1884) are here.

Meacham Field see under FORT WORTH, Texas.

Mead, Lake largest-capacity US reservoir (holding 28.3 million ac-ft/34.8 billion cu m), covering 246.5 sq mi/638 sq km, 115 mi/185 km long and 1–10 mi/1.5–16 km wide, in extreme SE Nevada, 17 mi/27 km E of LAS VEGAS and along the Arizona border. BOULDER CITY and HENDERSON, Nevada, are immediately SW. L. Mead was created by the construction (completed 1936) of the Hoover (in 1933–47 the Boulder) Dam on the COLORADO R., and provides irrigation, flood control, and hydroelectric power (chiefly to Las Vegas and to the Los Angeles, California area). Hoover Dam, one of the world's tallest, stands 727 ft/222 m high and is 1282 ft/391 m across. The dam and lake are major attractions in the 1.5 million-ac/607,000-ha (2340-sq mi/6070-sq km) **Lake Mead National Recreation Area,** which extends downstream (S) to near Laughlin, Nevada, and upstream (E) to the W boundary of Arizona's GRAND CANYON NATIONAL PARK.

Meadow Lake town, pop. 4318, NW Saskatchewan, 154 mi/248 km NW of Saskatoon and 62 mi/100 km E of the Alberta border. Once a site of contention between the rival Hudson's Bay and North West companies, it subsequently developed as a farming, timbering, and ranching area. Meadow Lake Provincial Park lies just N, and an Indian Reserve (pop. 319) is here. Nearby Steele Narrows Provincial Historic Park, on Loon L. (W), marks the site of a last battle (1885) of the Riel Rebellion.

Meadowlands sports and entertainment complex opened 1976–81 in the Hackensack (Jersey) Meadows, in EAST RUTHERFORD, Bergen Co., NE New Jersey, 5 mi/8 km NW of Manhattan. It includes 77,000-seat Giants Stadium, home of the New York Giants and Jets (football) and a frequent concert and exhibition venue; 20,000-seat Byrne Meadowlands Arena, where professional and college basketball and hockey and other events are held; Meadowlands Racetrack, a thoroughbred and harness-racing facility; and a 1.2-mi/2-km auto racetrack.

Meadowview also, **Meadow View** see under EMORY, Virginia.

Meadville city, pop. 14,318, seat of Crawford Co., extreme NW Pennsylvania, on French Creek, 87 mi/140 km N of Pittsburgh. Founded in 1788, it is the oldest settlement in this part of Pennsylvania. The commercial center of a dairy farming region, it also has oil and gas deposits nearby, and manufactures zippers. Conneaut L., the state's largest natural lake (3 mi/5 km NNW–SSE), is 10 mi/16 km W of the city. Meadville is home to Allegheny College (1815).

Mechanicsburg borough, pop. 9452, Cumberland Co., SC Pennsylvania, 8 mi/13 km WSW of Harrisburg. Situated in an agricultural area, it produces clothing and metal and food products, and has a US naval supply depot.

Mechanicsville unincorporated community, pop. 22,027, Hanover Co., EC Virginia, 7 mi/11 km NE of Richmond, a largely residential suburb on the Chickahominy R. It is the site of a Civil War battle fought June 26, 1862, in which the Union army fought off a Confederate attack in the first battle of Robert E. Lee's Seven Days' Campaign, along small Beaver Dam Creek. It was followed the next day by a battle at GAINES'S MILL.

Mecklenburg County 528 sq mi/1368 sq km, pop. 511,433, in S North Carolina, in the Piedmont, bounded by the Catawba R. (W) and South Carolina (S). It is North Carolina's most populous county, and its seat, CHARLOTTE, the state's largest city. Charlotte's industry, commerce, and residential suburbs increasingly dominate this once agricultural county.

Meddybemps Lake in Washington Co., extreme E Maine, 5 mi/8 km W of the New Brunswick border. This 6 mi/10 km–long lake fed by the Dennys R. is a popular resort area. Moosehorn National Wildlife Refuge is on the E shore. The Passamaquoddy name means "plenty of alewives."

Medfield town, pop. 10,531, Norfolk Co., E Massachusetts, 17 mi/27 km SW of Boston, on the E bank of the Charles R. Founded in 1650, it was burned during King Philip's War (1675), but soon rebuilt. In the 19th century it was for a time the home and subject of the landscape painter George Inness. Long an affluent, largely rural community, it is now a growing suburb.

Medford 1. city, pop. 57,407, Middlesex Co., NE Massachusetts, on the Mystic R., 5 mi/8 km NW of Boston, of which it is a residential and industrial suburb. Somerville lies S, the Middlesex Fells Reservation N; Interstate 93 passes through the city. Medford began building ships in the 1630s. During the 19th century, the city prospered from the Triangle Trade, trading rum made locally from West Indian sugar for African slaves, who were then sold in the West Indies. Printing and the manufacture of truck parts, furniture, chemicals, and paper products have provided the more recent economic base. The city is the seat of Tufts University (1852). **2.** unincorporated village, pop. 21,274, in Brookhaven town, Suffolk Co., SE New York, in C Long Island, 5 mi/8 km NNE of Patchogue. It is primarily residential. **3.** city, pop. 46,951, seat of Jackson Co., SW Oregon, on Bear Creek, 23 mi/37 km N of the California border. It is the commercial hub of SW Oregon and an important shipping point for lumber, fruit (especially pears), and other agricultural, mine, and dairy products. Tourism is also important. In 1883, settlers paid railroad barons to bypass the older gold rush city of Jacksonville (pop. 1896; 5 mi/8 km W) and link Medford to a wider transport network. The city is the headquarters of and SW gateway to the Rogue River National Forest; it also serves as the SW gateway to Crater Lake National Park.

Media borough, pop. 5957, Delaware Co., SE Pennsylvania, 15 mi/24 km WSW of Philadelphia. A producer of plastics and pork products, it now also houses banking and insurance operations.

Medical Center hospital complex, 307 ac/124 ha, in Detroit, Michigan, 2 mi/3 km NW of Downtown. A residential community here was leveled in the 1950s, providing space for the expansion of four hospitals and the Wayne State University medical school.

Medicine Bow town, pop. 389, Carbon Co., S Wyoming, on the Medicine Bow R., 50 mi/80 km NW of Laramie. It was a Union Pacific Railroad pumping station in the 1870s, and is now a supply point in an oil and livestock region. Deposits of oil, magnesium sulfate, and bentonite are found nearby. Otherwise undistinguishable from other local towns, Medicine Bow was immortalized by Owen Wister, who rode for the Two Bar outfit here and used it and its surrounding forest as settings for his novel *The Virginian.* **Medicine Bow National Forest** includes 1.4 million ac/576,000 ha in SE Wyoming. The forest is divided into four separate sections. The Douglas District, its N portion, is in the Laramie Mts., its highest point at Laramie Peak (10,272 ft/3133 m). The Haydn District is in the Sierra Madre Mts. on the Continental Divide and W of the town of Encampment. The Pole Mt. area is E of Laramie. The fourth unit is in the Medicine Bow Mts., and reaches its greatest elevation at Medicine Bow Peak (12,013 ft/3664 m).

Medicine Bow Mountains 100 mi/160 km–long NW extension of the Rocky Mt. FRONT RANGE into SE Wyoming from N Colorado's Rocky Mountain National Park. Much of the Wyoming section is in the Medicine Bow National Forest. Medicine Bow Peak (12,013 ft/3662 m) is the highest point in the range.

Medicine Hat city, pop. 43,625, SE Alberta, on the South Saskatchewan R. and Seven Persons and Ross creeks, at the foot of the CYPRESS HILLS, 166 mi/267 km SE of Calgary and 35 mi/57 km W of the Saskatchewan border. A trade center for cattle, wheat, and vegetable producers, it also has clay and natural gas deposits. Local industries produce petrochemicals, glass, brick, tile, and pottery. The city has flour mills, canneries, breweries, and a Goodyear tire factory as well. Medicine Hat was founded (1883) as a Canadian Pacific Railway tent town and North West Mounted Police post. Medicine Hat College (1965) is affiliated with the University of Calgary.

Medicine Mountain see under BIGHORN NATIONAL FOREST, Wyoming.

Medina city, pop. 19,231, seat of Medina Co., N Ohio, 20 mi/32 km NW of Akron. The processing of food from local dairy, grain, fruit, and truck farms is an important basis of the city's economy. Metal castings and lumber are also produced. Medina is 5 mi/8 km NE of Chippewa L. resort area.

Medina County 422 sq mi/1093 sq km, pop. 122,354, in N Ohio. Its seat is MEDINA. The county is largely rural, with dairy, fruit, grain, and truck farming. There is some manufacturing at Medina, Brunswick, and Wadsworth. Chippewa L. is in the SW.

Medora city, pop. 101, seat of Billings Co., W North Dakota, 35 mi/56 km W of Dickinson. On the Little Missouri R. in the Badlands, this largely restored cattle town is a grain and livestock center. It was founded in 1883 by the Marquis de Mores, a French nobleman who began a cattle empire here, and named for his wife. The De Mores Historic Site, just SW, includes his original chateau. Theodore Roosevelt raised stock at nearby Chimney Butte Ranch, now the Theodore Roosevelt National Park. Medora is the SW entrance to the park's South Unit. Sully's Creek Primitive State Park is just S of the city.

Meech Lake see under GATINEAU PARK, Québec.

Megalopolis term (from the name of a city of ancient Greece that was intended to be the country's largest) employed by geographer Jean Gottman (d. 1994) in a 1961 study of the "Urbanized Northeastern Seaboard of the United States." Megalopolis was the 600 mi/1000 km–long, continuously urban stretch from the S suburbs of Washington, D.C., to the N suburbs of Boston, Massachusetts, which Gottman saw as the harbinger of a new form of social organization. The region subsequently acquired other names, including "the Boston–Washington Corridor" or "BoWash Corridor," and, esp. in railroading, "the Northeast Corridor." *Megalopolis* is now used generically of similarly urbanized regions.

Mégantic, Mont English, **Mount Megantic** peak (3625 ft/1105 m) of the Appalachians, in the EASTERN TOWNSHIPS of S Québec, 38 mi/62 km E of Sherbrooke. It is the site of an astronomical observatory. This area near the Maine border is sometimes referred to as the **Megantic Hills.** Six mi/10 km to the E is 10 mi/16 km–long **L. Mégantic,** with the resort center of Lac-Mégantic (pop. 5838) at its N end. The R. Chaudière flows N from the lake.

Mehlville unincorporated community, pop. 27,557, St. Louis Co., EC Missouri, 11 mi/18 km SW of downtown St. Louis, on Gravois Creek. Near the Mississippi R. (E), with origins that reach back to the 19th century, Mehlville is now a residential suburb.

Meigs County 432 sq mi/1119 sq km, pop. 22,987, in SE Ohio, bounded by the Ohio R. (E and SE) where it forms the West Virginia line. Its seat is Pomeroy. The county is primarily rural, with dairy, fruit, grain, truck, and livestock farming as well as some manufacturing at Pomeroy. Natural resources include coal, limestone, and salt.

Melbourne city, pop. 59,646, Brevard Co., EC Florida, on the INDIAN R. lagoon, 55 mi/89 km SE of Orlando. It is connected to the barrier island towns of Indialantic and Melbourne Beach by bridge, and offers a variety of recreational facilities. The city's economy once relied mainly on tourism and the shipping of locally grown citrus fruits. With the 1960s development of the nearby (N) Kennedy Space Center, Melbourne saw the growth of a number of aerospace and electronics industries. It is the seat of the Florida Institute of Technology (1958).

Mélèzes, Rivière aux English, **Larch River** see under R. KOKSOAK, Québec.

Melfort city, pop. 5628, C Saskatchewan, 53 mi/85 km SE of Prince Albert. Originally settled (1892) on Stoney Creek, the town was moved 1 mi/2 km NW to its present site in 1902. Expansion followed with the arrival of the Canadian National Railway, and today Melfort is a service center for the extremely fertile Carrot R. Valley.

Mellon Square municipal park in the GOLDEN TRIANGLE of Pittsburgh, Pennsylvania, laid out in 1955.

Melrose **1.** city, pop. 28,150, Middlesex Co., E Massachusetts. It is a largely residential suburb 7 mi/11 km N of Boston. There is some light manufacturing. **2.** commercial and residential district, S Bronx, New York. Once an industrial area, with bakeries and ironworking plants, it is today the business center of a black and Hispanic community. High Bridge lies to the W, Morrisania to the E.

Melrose Avenue commercial thoroughfare running E–W between SILVER LAKE in Los Angeles and BEVERLY HILLS, California. A popular, chic shopping, restaurant, and entertainment strip, it skirts Hollywood (N) and the Fairfax District (S).

Melrose Park village, pop. 20,859, Cook Co., NE Illinois, 12 mi/19 km W of Chicago. A residential community with some industry, it manufactures plastics, machinery, and steel and rubber products.

Melville unincorporated village, pop. 12,586, in Huntington town, Suffolk Co., SE New York, on Long Island, just S of South Huntington. Situated on the Long Island Expressway, it has had much recent commercial development, with financial and electronics firms and other corporate offices taking advantage of its central position on the Island.

Melvindale city, pop. 11,216, Wayne Co., SE Michigan, between the Ecorse R. (S) and the R. Rouge (N), a residential suburb 8 mi/13 km SW of Detroit.

Memorial Park municipal park in Houston, Texas, on the N side of Buffalo Bayou, NW of Downtown and across from River Oaks. Established in 1924 on 1500 ac/610 ha, it is home to Houston's arboretum and botanical gardens. Camp Logan, a World War I training center here, was base to black soldiers involved in Houston's Aug. 1917 race riots. West Memorial Drive passes through the park NW to the cluster of affluent independent municipalities collectively called the **Memorial Villages** (see under HUNTERS CREEK VILLAGE).

Memphis city, pop. 610,337, seat of Shelby Co., extreme SW Tennessee, at the mouths of the WOLF R. (N) and NONCONNAH CREEK (S), on the Mississippi R. Forts and a trading post were here on the Fourth Chickasaw Bluff before the end of the 18th century, but the Chickasaw controlled the area until 1818; Chucalissa Village, on the city's SW, re-creates settlements going back 1000 years, and there are numerous Indian mounds in the vicinity. Memphis was laid out in 1819, taking the name of the ancient Egyptian river city. It grew quickly as the trade hub for a plantation region. Before the Civil War it was known for its cotton warehouses and slave markets. Captured by Union forces in June 1862, it was occupied for the remainder of the war. In the 1860s and 1870s it declined; a series of yellow fever epidemics caused such havoc that in 1879 the city gave up its 1849 charter. But by the 1890s it had recovered as a cotton, lumber, mercantile, and river and rail shipping center. The city is sometimes called the "capital of the Mississippi DELTA," which extends to the S, and it is the metropolis of a tri-state region including N Mississippi and E Arkansas. It is also the hub of a region vaguely defined as the Mid-South (see the SOUTH) or Mid-Valley. It is today a transportation and retailing center, still a leading cotton and lumber market, and home to major medical care and equipment industries. It is the base of operations of Federal Express (package delivery) and headquarters for Holiday Inn, whose first facility opened here in 1952. Its manufactures include pharmaceuticals, chemicals, foods, and railroad equipment. Rhodes (formerly Southwestern; 1848), LeMoyne-Owen (1862), and Christian Brothers (1871) colleges and Memphis State University (1912) are here, as are the University of Tennessee medical schools. Beale St. is the focus of Memphis's identification with Delta blues music, and the city has a thriving popular music recording industry. Elvis Presley's Graceland is one of the leading US tourist sites, and the National Civil Rights Museum (scene of the assassination of Dr. Martin Luther King, Jr.) is a well-known shrine. See also: AUDUBON PARK; BEALE STREET; DE SOTO PARK; FRAYSER; FRONT STREET (Cotton Row); GRACELAND; GREAT AMERICAN PYRAMID; HIGHWAY 61; MID-SOUTH FAIRGROUNDS (and Liberty Bowl); MIDTOWN; MUD ISLAND; NATIONAL CIVIL RIGHTS MUSEUM (Lorraine Motel); OVERTON PARK; PARKWAY; PEABODY HOTEL; PINCH; POPLAR CORRIDOR; PRESIDENT'S ISLAND; RALEIGH; WHITEHAVEN; WHITE STATION.

Memphrémagog, Lac English, **Lake Memphremagog** N–S oriented body in N Vermont and S Québec. Thirty mi/48 km long and up to 4 mi/6 km wide, it is noted for its scenery and recreational amenities; about one-quarter lies in Vermont. NEWPORT, Vermont, and MAGOG, Québec, are trade and resort centers at its S and N end, respectively.

Menasha city, pop. 14,711, Winnebago and Calumet counties, E Wisconsin, 4 mi/6 km S of Appleton, at the place where the Fox R. flows out of L. Winnebago. Part of the city is located on Doty I., where it adjoins its sister city, NEENAH. The two cities are economically linked, and the river, which here has a fall of 12 ft/4 m, generates power for both. Permanent settlement began in the 1840s. Since the late 19th century, Menasha has been a major manufacturer of paper and paper products. Flour, machinery, wood and metal products, and textiles are also produced. L. Winnebago provides recreational opportunities; the city is also a summer resort. A plaque marks the site where Jean Nicolet, the French explorer, visited the lake outlet (c.1634).

Mendocino coastal resort community in Mendocino Co., NW California, on Mendocino Bay and the Big R., 9 mi/14 km S of Fort Bragg and 135 mi/217 km NW of San Francisco. An 1850s lumbering town, settled by New Englanders, it has been a noted artists' colony since the 1950s, and is now increasingly fashionable.

Mendocino, Cape promontory overlooking the Pacific Ocean in Humboldt Co., NW California, 28 mi/45 km SSW of Eureka. It is the extreme W point of California, at 124° 24′ W. The Cape was named (1542) by the explorer Cabrillo for Don Antonio de Mendoza, the first viceroy of New Spain (Mexico).

Mendocino National Forest c.900,000 ac/365,000 ha (1400 sq mi/3640 sq km), in NW California, in the Coast Ranges, extending from 90 mi/140 km N of San Francisco to the Six Rivers National Forest (N). The YOLLA BOLLY–Middle Eel Wilderness is at its N end, the Snow Mt. Wilderness in the S.

Mendon town, pop. 6845, Monroe Co., W New York, 13 mi/21 km SSE of Rochester. Mormon leader Brigham Young lived here from 1830 to 1832, the period when he first saw the Book of Mormon and was baptized into the church by Joseph Smith. Smith's chair factory was also located in this still largely rural, agricultural town, which includes the village of Honeoye Falls (pop. 2340).

Mendota **1.** city, pop. 7018, La Salle Co., NC Illinois, 12 mi/19 km N of Peru. A trade and canning center in a corn and livestock area, it also manufactures farm implements and building materials. Wild Bill Hickok State Memorial is 7 mi/11 km SE. **2.** city, pop. 164, Dakota Co., SE Minnesota, a Twin Cities suburb at the junction of the Mississippi and Minnesota rivers, across (N) from St. Paul. Its name is Sioux for "meeting of two waters." The first permanent European settlement in Minnesota, it was founded as St. Peter's in the 1830s, and grew around nearby FORT SNELLING. When Henry H. Sibley established the American Fur Company here in 1834, Mendota became the hub of the Red R. country fur trade and the busiest commercial center in the NW. The proclamation establishing the Territory of Minnesota was issued here. Mendota is the site of the first stone house W of the Mississippi R. (1835), now the Sibley House Museum.

Mendota, Lake 6 mi/10 km long and 4 mi/6 km wide, in Dane Co., SC Wisconsin. It is the largest of the FOUR LAKES group and is connected to L. Monona by the Yahara R. The University of Wisconsin at Madison is situated on a peninsula on the S shore of the lake, which is also a recreational site.

Mendota Heights city, pop. 9431, Dakota Co., on the Mississippi R., a residential suburb of the Twin Cities, immediately S of St. Paul and E of MENDOTA.

Menemsha see under CHILMARK, Massachusetts.

Menlo Park **1.** city, pop. 28,040, San Mateo Co., NC California, immediately NW of Palo Alto and 25 mi/40 km S of San Francisco. Settled in the 1860s, it was long a railroad suburb. It is now a residential community with industrial parks and office buildings, a publishing center with financial, insurance, medical systems, pharmaceutical, and electronics industries. The Stanford Research Institute (1946) and St. Patrick's Seminary (1898) are here; Stanford University is immediately SE. **2.** unincorporated community in EDISON township, Middlesex Co., C New Jersey, 8 mi/13 km NE of New Brunswick. It was settled in the late 17th century. Now a residential suburb, it was the site (1876–87) of the laboratory of Thomas A. Edison (the "Wizard of Menlo Park"). Edison invented the incandescent light bulb here in 1879. A Memorial Tower (1938) topped by an enormous replica of the original bulb marks the spot. Edison State Park and an Edison museum are also here, as is a large retail mall complex.

Menninger Foundation see under TOPEKA, Kansas.

Menominee city, pop. 9398, seat of Menominee Co., on Green Bay in the SC part of the Upper Peninsula of Michigan, opposite Marinette, Wisconsin (S) across the Menominee R. This southernmost city of the Upper Peninsula began as a fur-trading post in the 1790s, and became prosperous after 1832 from its sawmills. Lumbering peaked in the 1890s and ceased by 1930, but the economy by then included dairying and cheese and beet sugar production. It is now a large producer of fishing nets. Waterpower from the Menominee R. facilitates the manufacture of furniture, electrical equipment, and paper products. Menominee is also a hunting resort, and a fishing and yachting port.

Menominee River 118 mi/190 km long, in Michigan and Wisconsin. Its name is Algonquian for "wild rice," which natives gathered along its banks. It is formed by the confluence of the Brule and Michigamme rivers in SE Iron Co., Michigan. It flows SSE through an iron ore region, forming part of the Michigan-Wisconsin border, and finally flowing into Green Bay at Menominee. An important water-way in logging days, it now provides hydroelectric power.

Menomonee Falls village, pop. 26,840, Waukesha Co., SE Wisconsin, on the Menomonee R., 15 mi/24 km NW of Milwaukee. Founded in 1843, it was settled mainly by German immigrants. It is located in a dairy farming area. Dairy products, flour, iron castings, paper products, computer keyboards, and hospital and scientific equipment are produced here.

Menomonee River 25 mi/40 km long, in SE Wisconsin. It rises in Washington Co. and flows SE through Menomonee Falls. It joins the Milwaukee R. at Milwaukee, where they enter L. Michigan.

Menomonie city, pop. 13,547, seat of Dunn Co., W Wisconsin, on the Red Cedar R. and L. Menomin, 22 mi/35 km NW of Eau Claire. Settled in the 1830s, it was originally a lumber town; its ornate civic center (1890) and several mansions were built by lumber tycoons. Today, Menomonie is primarily a trade and processing center for the surrounding dairy farming region. Industries include the production of dairy items, canning, flour milling, and the manufacture of aluminumware and bricks. The University of Wisconsin Stout campus (1891) is in Menomonie.

Mentor city, pop. 47,358, Lake Co., NE Ohio, 22 mi/35 km NE of Cleveland and 5 mi/8 km S of L. Erie. Founded in 1799, it is a residential and industrial suburb. Lawnfield, James A. Garfield's farm, features a museum depicting WESTERN RESERVE history. Lakeland Community College (1967) is here. Manufactures include trucks, forklifts, computer components, electronic instruments, and air conditioners; garden nurseries also form part of the economy.

Mentor-on-the-Lake village, pop. 8271, Lake Co., NE Ohio, on L. Erie, a residential community just NW of Mentor and 21 mi/34 km NE of Cleveland.

Mequon city, pop. 18,885, Ozaukee Co., SE Wisconsin, on L. Michigan and the Milwaukee R., 10 mi/16 km N of Milwaukee, of which it is a residential suburb. Founded in 1846, it has varied light industries. Concordia Univ. (1881) is here.

Meramec River 175 mi/280 km long, in SE Missouri. It rises in Dent Co. and flows N and NE into the St. Louis suburbs, turning SE at KIRKWOOD and continuing to the Mississippi R. at ARNOLD. On its upper course it passes through the Shaw Arboretum of the Missouri Botanical Garden at GRAY SUMMIT, and past the site of TIMES BEACH.

Merced city, pop. 56,216, seat of Merced Co., C California, in the San Joaquin Valley, on Bear Creek, 55 mi/89 km NW of Fresno. It is the gateway to Yosemite National Park, 45 mi/72 km to the NE, and draws visitors to a variety of local natural attractions as well. The center of an irrigated agricultural region, the city is a processing, packing, and shipping point for corn, rice, sugar beets, vegetables, fruits, nuts, cotton, dairy goods, and figs. Other industries make metal and concrete products, carpets and drapes, and recreational vehicles. Nearby Castle Air Force Base (see ATWATER) is a major employer. Merced College (1962) is here.

Mercedes city, pop. 12,694, Hidalgo Co., extreme S Texas, in the Lower Rio Grande Valley, 30 mi/48 km WNW of Brownsville. In an oil and natural gas producing area, it processes local vegetables and citrus fruit, makes boots, and draws winter vacationers.

Merced River 150 mi/240 km long, in C California. It rises in S YOSEMITE NATIONAL PARK, near Merced Peak (11,726 ft/3574 m), and flows generally W, passing through the famed Yosemite Valley, out of the park, and into L. McClure, formed by the 490 ft/149 m–high New Exchequer Dam (1966, replacing a 1926 structure), then passes SW through **Merced Co.** (1944 sq mi/5035 sq km, pop. 178,403), to the San Joaquin R., 10 mi/16 km SW of Turlock. Along its route it was formerly dredged for gold; it now irrigates orchards and other Central Valley agriculture.

Mercer County 227 sq mi/588 sq km, pop. 325,824, in WC New Jersey, bounded (W) by the Delaware R. Its seat and largest city is TRENTON; heavy industry is concentrated in and around the city. Light manufacturing, agriculture (truck and fruit farms, poultry, dairy), and business and residential areas mark the rest of the county. The educational complex of PRINCETON is in the N part; HIGHTSTOWN is in the E.

Mercer Island city, pop. 20,816, King Co., WC Washington, on Mercer I. in L. Washington, 5 mi/8 km SE of Seattle. Situated between Seattle and Bellevue (3 mi/5 km NE), it is an upper-middle-class bedroom community. Its growth is directly related to the construction of the Lacey V. Murrow Floating Bridge (1939), the first such structure ever built, which connects the island to Seattle. The bridge sank in 1990, but was reopened in 1993.

Mercersburg borough, pop. 1640, Franklin Co., S Pennsylvania, 17 mi/27 km SW of Chambersburg. It is the seat of Mercersburg Academy (1836), and was the boyhood home of President James Buchanan. It produces industrial equipment, leather goods, hardwood lumber, and limestone.

Mercerville unincorporated village in HAMILTON township, Mercer Co., WC New Jersey, 2 mi/3 km E of Trenton. A residential and commercial Trenton suburb, it has some light industry. With neighboring (E) Hamilton Square, it has a pop. of 26,873.

Merchandise Mart wholesale clothing center immediately N of the LOOP, in Chicago, Illinois. A major center for the apparel industry in the Midwest, it is the largest such building in the world. Built by Marshall Field in the 1920s for his company, it today serves as a showcase for interior decorators and furniture wholesalers.

Meredith, Lake 16,500 ac/6685 ha, in the high plains of the N Texas PANHANDLE, 18 mi/29 km NNE of Amarillo, on the CANADIAN R. Created by the Sanford Dam (earthfill), it provides water for Amarillo, Lubbock, and nine other Panhandle cities. It is surrounded by 200 ft/60 m–deep canyons and colorful buttes. The 45,000-ac/18,225-ha Lake Meredith National Recreation Area embraces eight parks. The ALIBATES FLINT QUARRIES National Monument is on the SE shore.

Meriden city and coterminous township, pop. 59,479, New Haven Co., SC Connecticut, 18 mi/29 km S of Hartford, on the Quinnipiac R. It is noted for the manufacture of silverplate and sterling silverware, and has also produced electrical equipment, nuclear instrumentation, cabinets, jewelry, and aircraft components. Meriden was founded in 1661; in 1794, Samuel Yale started a pewter shop here, and in 1808 Ashbil Griswold began the production of britannia (a variant of pewter). In the 1990s it suffered from business loss and high unemployment.

Meridian **1.** city, pop. 9596, Ada Co., SW Idaho, 8 mi/13 km W of Boise. Situated in a fruit, grain, livestock, and poultry producing area, it packs fruit and has other agriculture-related industries. **2.** city, pop. 41,036, Lauderdale Co., E Mississippi, 88 mi/141 km E of Jackson and 17 mi/27 km W of the Alabama line. Settled in 1854 at the junction of two railway lines, it was a Confederate military center (and briefly, in 1863, Mississippi's capital) until the town was destroyed in 1864 by W.T. Sherman's troops. It recovered by the 1870s as a market center for farm produce, cattle, and timber; by the early 20th century, textiles, wood and clay products, chemicals, and machinery were being made. Meridian Community College (1937) is here, and a Naval Air Station is just NE. Country music pioneer Jimmie Rodgers (1897–1933), the "Singing Brakeman," was born in Meridian. **3.** see EAST HILL–MERIDIAN, Washington.

Merion locality in LOWER MERION township, Montgomery Co., SE Pennsylvania, immediately W of Philadelphia. Primarily a MAIN LINE residential suburb, it has some manufacturing (auto parts, textiles, clothing, clay and stone products), and is noted as home to the Barnes Foundation (1922), one of America's best-known art museums, on the former estate of Albert C. Barnes (d.1951).

Merriam city, pop. 11,821, Johnson Co., NE Kansas, 6 mi/10 km SSW of downtown Kansas City. A residential suburb (inc. 1950), it has a variety of light industries.

Merrick unincorporated village, pop. 23,042, in Hempstead town, Nassau County, SE New York, on the South Shore of Long Island, adjacent (E) to Freeport. It is primarily a residential suburb, with some manufacturing, on East Bay and the Meadowbrook State Parkway.

Merrill city, pop. 9860, seat of Lincoln Co., NC Wisconsin, at the confluence of the Wisconsin and Prairie rivers, 15 mi/24 km N of Wausau. Founded in 1847 and originally a lumbering center, it now produces paper, furniture, woolens, and beer. The surrounding area is agricultural.

Merrill Park residential neighborhood on the WEST SIDE of Milwaukee, Wisconsin, immediately W of Downtown. It is a changing community, characterized at present by racial, ethnic, and economic diversity.

Merrillville town, pop. 27,257, Lake Co., extreme NW Indiana, adjacent (S) to Gary. At the S edge of the highly industrialized CALUMET area, it is a largely residential suburb.

Merrimack town, pop. 22,156, Hillsborough Co., S New Hampshire. On the Merrimack R. where the Souhegan R. joins it, between Nashua (S) and Manchester (N), the town manufactures wood products and shoes. An Anheuser-Busch brewery is here, and Clydesdale Hamlet stables draft horses are used in the brewery's advertising. Merrimack is one of S New Hampshire's rapidly growing suburban communities.

Merrimack County 936 sq mi/2424 sq km, in SC New Hampshire. Concord is the county seat. This hilly area is drained by the Merrimack, Contoocook, Suncook, Soucook, and several smaller rivers, which furnish hydroelectric power. Industries include mica mining and granite quarrying; flour milling; dairy, poultry, and truck farming; fruit growing; and the manufacture of textiles, shoes, paper, machinery, instruments, and wood, leather, and metal products. There are a number of lake resorts in the county.

Merrimack River also, **Merrimac** 110 mi/177 km long, in New

Hampshire and Massachusetts. It is formed by the confluence of the Pemigewasset and Winnipesaukee rivers just below Franklin Falls Reservoir, in the town of Franklin, Merrimack Co., New Hampshire. It flows generally S through Concord, Manchester, and Nashua, then crosses into Massachusetts, where just above Lowell it turns to flow NE through Lawrence and Haverhill and on to the Atlantic Ocean at Newbury. This area, widely known as the **Merrimack Valley,** is one of the most industrialized regions of the US, the cradle of America's 19th-century industrial revolution, and is noted for its manufacture of shoes, hosiery, woolens, and textile products. The river is also one of New England's major sources of hydroelectric power. Its major tributaries include the Piscataquog, Nashua, and Concord rivers.

Merritt, Lake see under OAKLAND, California.

Merritt Island unincorporated community, pop. 32,886, Brevard Co., EC Florida, on Merritt I., 52 mi/84 km ESE of Orlando and 11 mi/18 km SW of Cape Canaveral. It is connected by causeway across the INDIAN R. lagoon to Cocoa, on the mainland (W), and across the Banana R. lagoon to the Cape (E). Merritt Island is a waterfront resort, also popular with visitors to the Kennedy Space Center. Its population swelled from the 1960s with residents employed in the space program and the military. The 140,000-ac/57,000-ha **Merritt Island National Wildlife Refuge** lies N on the island and lagoons.

Merritt Parkway in Connecticut, running from the New York border, where it connects with the Hutchinson River Parkway, NE to Meriden, where it joins Interstate 91. From Greenwich to Bridgeport, the parkway is known as the Merritt Parkway; at Bridgeport, it becomes the Wilbur Cross Parkway, named for a former (1931–39) governor of Connecticut. Total length is 60 mi/96 km. Completed in the 1930s, the parkway provided an inland alternative to US 1 (the Boston Post Rd.).

Merrydale see under EAST BATON ROUGE PARISH, Louisiana.

Merry Mount see under QUINCY, Massachusetts.

mesa a tableland with steep sides, formed in a dry area. Its relatively flat top is a layer of hard rock (caprock) that withstands the forces wearing away surrounding strata. A mesa is generally smaller than a PLATEAU and larger than a BUTTE, one type of which is formed by separation from the edge of a mesa.

Mesa city, pop. 288,091, Maricopa Co., SC Arizona, on the Salt R., a suburb 13 mi/21 km ESE of Phoenix. It was settled (1878) by Mormons who transformed the desert into an agricultural, esp. fruit growing, region. The city grew rapidly after World War II and has continued to expand, its pop. increasing by nearly 90% from 1980 to 1990. Its economy relies in part on food processing and retailing industries; manufactures include electronic components, fabricated metals, aircraft parts, heavy machinery, and clothing. It is also a popular winter resort. Mesa Community College (1965), a Mormon temple, a University of Arizona agricultural experiment station, and the Oakland Athletics (baseball) spring training camp are here. The Salt R. Indian Reservation is immediately S across the river.

Mesabi Range also, **Mesabi Iron Range** low range of hills containing iron ore deposits, 110 mi/175 km long, in NE Minnesota. It extends NE from Grand Rapids, in Itasca Co., to Babbitt, in St. Louis Co. When discovered in 1865, it had the world's largest concentration of iron ore deposits. Mined using enormous open pits from 1892 on, the range provided one-third of the iron ore in the world by the 1940s. Much depleted today, the mines yield only low-grade taconite. VIRGINIA and HIBBING are the main commercial centers.

Mesa Verde National Park 52,085 ac/21,094 ha, in extreme SW Colorado, just SE of Cortez. The Ute Mountain Indian Reservation adjoins (S). Established in 1906, the park is atop and in canyons of a tableland 15 mi/24 km long and 8 mi/13 km wide, rising to 8752 ft/2668 m in the N. It has over 300 PUEBLO ruins, including multistoried apartments under overhanging cliffs. Cliff Palace, in a cave, has over 200 rooms. The dwellings, dating from the 6th century, were abandoned around 1300, presumably because of drought; they constitute one of the most important ANASAZI sites.

Mescalero Apache Indian Reservation 719 sq mi/1862 sq km, pop. 2695 (93% Indian), in SC New Mexico, NE of Alamogordo and between two units of the LINCOLN NATIONAL FOREST. Mescalero (unincorporated, pop. 1159, Otero Co.) is headquarters. The Mescalero here operate several successful businesses: lumbering; cattle raising; the well-known Ski Apache resort (see SIERRA BLANCA); and other recreational and tourist operations. Their interest in storing nuclear wastes on the reservation raised controversy in the mid 1990s. RUIDOSO is immediately N, the resort center of Cloudcroft immediately S.

Mesilla town, pop. 1975, Dona Ana Co., SW New Mexico, immediately S of LAS CRUCES, on the Rio Grande, in the Mesilla Valley. It was established in the early 1850s by Mexicans moving S into what was still (after 1848) Mexican territory; in 1854, however, the GADSDEN PURCHASE brought it within the US. The Butterfield (OVERLAND) stage route came through Mesilla in the late 1850s. In 1861 Confederate forces proclaimed Mesilla the capital of a territory embracing much of the Southwest, but in Aug. 1862 Union forces took over. The Rio Grande shifted course in 1865, leaving Mesilla on the Las Cruces (E) side. The town is now visited for its history.

Mesquite city, pop. 101,484, Dallas Co., NE Texas, adjacent (E) to Dallas, on Route 635, the beltway. Established in 1872 by the Texas & Pacific Railroad, it was a small agricultural community until the 1950s, when it mushroomed as a residential and industrial suburb. Its manufactures include tools, brick, tile, pharmaceuticals, plastics, telephone equipment, and paper products, and it is a warehousing and distribution hub. Eastfield College (1970) is here. Mesquite is regional headquarters for several major utilities companies, and draws visitors to rodeos, ballooning festivals, and other events.

Metairie unincorporated community, pop. 149,428, Jefferson Parish, SE Louisiana, adjacent (NW) to New Orleans. The area was farmed in *metairies* (small plots in a sharecropping system) from early in the 18th century. Metairie today stretches from the Mississippi R. (S) to L. Pontchartrain (N); by far the largest New Orleans suburb, it is 92% white, while the city is 62% black.

Meteor Crater meteorite impact site on C Arizona's COCONINO PLATEAU, 17 mi/27 km W of Winslow and 35 mi/56 km ESE of Flagstaff. The result of an event 50,000 years ago, the crater is 4100 ft/1250 m across; from its rim, which rises 150 ft/46 m above the plateau, it is 570 ft/174 m to its floor. NASA has used the crater, which is privately owned, as a training site.

Methuen town, pop. 39,990, Essex Co., NE Massachusetts. On the Spicket and Merrimack rivers, Methuen lies between Haverhill (NE) and Lawrence (S), along the New Hampshire border. Founded in 1642 as part of Haverhill, the town manufactures shoes, electronics, textiles, apparel, paper goods, and food products, and is a residential suburb of the neighboring cities.

Métis certain groups of mixed-race (*métis*) people in W Canada. While intermarriage between Europeans and natives has occurred throughout Canada since the earliest European settlement, the Métis of the plains provinces are regarded as having acquired a distinct culture and group characteristics by the early 19th century. More French than British, and allied with Montréal's NORTH WEST COMPANY against the HUDSON'S BAY COMPANY in 1810s struggles in ASSINIBOIA (the RED R. area), they also figured in 1840s conflict and in the 1869–70 Red R. Rebellion led by Louis Riel, which contributed to the establishment of Manitoba. Having lost land allotments there, they rose again in 1885 in the abortive North-West Rebellion, after which most were settled on remote lands in NW Alberta.

Metro see under TORONTO, Ontario.

Metrodome domed sports stadium in downtown Minneapolis, Minnesota. Officially the Hubert H. Humphrey Metrodome, it has a capacity of 56,000 and was constructed in 1981. It is home to the Minnesota Twins (baseball) and Vikings (football).

Metropark large suburban Amtrak station, in Woodbridge township, Middlesex Co., New Jersey, near ISELIN. Featuring huge parking facilities, it is a much-used commuter stop near the junction of the New Jersey Turnpike and Garden State Parkway, and has become the center of a growing office-park complex.

Metroparks officially, **Cleveland Metropolitan Park System** in CLEVELAND, Ohio and its near suburbs, system of parks and parkways that roughly circles the city on the W, S, and E. Cleveland's zoo is in one unit; others include bicycle, walking, and horse paths, golf courses, and a variety of other amenities.

Metroplex popular and promotional term for the Dallas–Fort Worth metropolitan area (CMSA), NE Texas. Denton, Arlington, and Irving are other major cities in the complex, which has a pop. of 3,885,415.

Metropolis city, pop. 6734, seat of Massac Co., extreme S Illinois, on the Ohio R., 7 mi/11 km NW of Paducah, Kentucky. The French Fort Massac (1757) is now in a 1500-ac/600-ha state park. A 1796 settlement near it and Metropolis City (1839) combined to form the modern city, which is an agricultural and wood products center. It has a Superman statue and holds a June Superman Festival, capitalizing on the comic-book hero.

metropolitan area a "population nucleus" (US) or "large urban area" (Canada) along with adjacent "communities" (US) or "urban or rural areas" (Canada) that have a "high degree of economic and social integration with it" (both countries). In the US, a **metropolitan statistical area (MSA)** generally either has a central place with a pop. of 50,000 or is an urbanized area with a total pop. of at least 100,000; the outlying areas (counties, except in New England, where they may be towns) must have a certain level of commutation to the central place, as well as meet certain standards in regard to pop. density and URBAN character. A **consolidated metropolitan statistical area (CMSA)** is a metropolitan area of at least 1,000,000 pop., which may have within it **primary metropolitan statistical areas (PMSAs),** one or more "central places." In Canada, a **census metropolitan area (CMA)** has an urban core and a pop. of at least 100,000; a **consolidated CMA** is made up of two or more CMAs with a specified level of commuting interchange.

metropolitan government the URBAN form of regional government; the creation of an additional level of government, empowered to address concerns common to the various MUNICIPALITIES in an urbanized area, such as land use, transportation, policing, water and sewage systems, and public health. Experiments in metropolitan government have been more prominent in Canada than in the US; the TORONTO METROPOLITAN MUNICIPALITY and MONTRÉAL URBAN COMMUNITY are the best-known. In the US, annexation of suburbs by the central city has been the more common approach to similar concerns. Miami, Florida (Metro-Dade), Nashville, Tennessee, and Indianapolis are among the few major US cities that have undertaken forms of metropolitan government.

Metuchen borough, pop. 12,804, Middlesex Co., NE New Jersey, 6 mi/10 km NE of New Brunswick. Settled in the 17th century, it was the site of a Revolutionary War clash (1777). It is essentially residential, but has industries producing chemicals, electrical appliances, electronic parts, tools, and paper products.

Mexican War Streets residential neighborhood on the NORTH SIDE of Pittsburgh, Pennsylvania, immediately N of WEST PARK, and 1 mi/1.6 km N of the GOLDEN TRIANGLE. This 12-block area marked the first attempt at local historic preservation. The streets celebrate Mexican War sites and heroes; their row houses were built for professionals and small businessmen. Today, this integrated community is attempting to retain its older residents in the face of gentrification.

Mexico city, pop. 11,290, seat of Audrain Co., NE Missouri, on the South Fork of the Salt R., 28 mi/45 km NE of Columbia. Founded in 1836, it grew with the arrival of the railroad (1858). Since around 1900, when clay deposits were discovered beneath the city and nearby, it has been a center of the fire-clay industry, with refractories and brick factories. Horses have long been bred, and it is a commercial hub for livestock, wheat, and soybeans. The Missouri Military Academy (1889) is here.

Mexico, Gulf of arm of the Atlantic Ocean, c.700,000 sq mi/1.8 million sq km, over 1100 mi/1800 km E–W and some 800 mi/1300 km N–S, in SE North America. It is bordered by (E to W) the states of Florida, Alabama, Mississippi, Louisiana, and Texas in the US (N) and by Mexico (SW). The Gulf is connected to the Atlantic by the Straits of Florida and to the Caribbean by the Yucatan Channel. Its mainly low-lying, sandy, and marsh-lined shores receive a number of US rivers, notably the Alabama, Brazos, Mississippi, and Rio Grande. There are rich oil deposits, many tapped by offshore wells, on its wide continental shelf, part of the OIL PATCH. In addition, commercial shrimping and fishing are important. The Gulf's waters are also plied by commercial shipping. Principal US ports include Galveston, Houston, Port Arthur, and Corpus Christi, Texas; New Orleans, Louisiana; Mobile, Alabama; and Pensacola and Tampa, Florida. Havana is the preeminent port S of the Gulf, in Cuba.

Miami 1. city, pop. 358,548, seat of DADE Co., SE Florida, on Biscayne Bay, separated from the Atlantic Ocean by Miami

Beach and other islands. It is on the Intracoastal Waterway, at the mouth of the Miami R., and is connected by canal to L. Okeechobee. The second most populous city in the state (after Jacksonville), it is one of 27 municipalities in Metro-Dade, a METROPOLITAN GOVERNMENT compact that since 1957 has administered traffic, parks, health, and other services throughout the county. The Miami–Fort Lauderdale metropolitan area, embracing Dade and BROWARD counties, has a pop. of 3,192,582. Localities in Dade Co. outside the city are commonly thought of as "Miami." Settlement began here around the Seminole War Fort Dallas (1836), and Miami was founded in 1870. Its subtropical climate soon attracted railroad magnate Henry M. Flagler, who in 1896 extended his East Coast Railroad into the city, dredged its harbor, and began developing the area as a resort. The city experienced great growth during the Florida land boom of the 1920s, and became an immensely popular winter recreation center. After 1959, when Fidel Castro came to power in Cuba, thousands of affluent Cubans relocated to Miami. Immigration from the Caribbean and Latin America has continued, making the city highly cosmopolitan and establishing such ethnic neighborhoods as Little Havana and Little Haiti; in 1990, Miami was 62% Hispanic, and had become an international business capital. The city is a transportation hub and a trade and passenger gateway, with the extensive PORT OF MIAMI and an international airport. It has a free trade zone (est. 1980), and offices of hundreds of multinational corporations and international banks. Manufactures include textiles, clothing, shoes, aviation and other transportation equipment, processed foods, machinery, and wood products. Miami attracts some 10 million tourists and vacationers annually, with an array of recreational facilities, spectator sports venues, and cultural attractions. It is the seat of Florida International University (1965), Florida Memorial College (1892), Miami Christian College (1949), Miami-Dade Community College (1959), and several other institutions. The main campus of the University of Miami is in nearby (S) CORAL GABLES. The US city most directly involved in the life of the Caribbean and parts of Latin America, Miami has acquired an aura of glamour and excitement. At the same time, it continues to struggle with severe poverty in some of its neighborhoods, and with attendant social problems. See also: BAYFRONT PARK; COCONUT GROVE; JOE ROBBIE STADIUM (in Dade Co.); LIBERTY CITY; LITTLE HAITI; LITTLE HAVANA (and Calle Ocho); ORANGE BOWL; OVERTOWN; PORT OF MIAMI. **2.** city, pop. 13,142, seat of Ottawa Co., in the NE corner of Oklahoma, on the Neosho R. near Grand L., 78 mi/125 km NE of Tulsa. A railroad junction named for the Miami Indians, it is a trade and distribution center in what has been an agricultural, cattle raising, dairying, and lead and zinc mining area. Manufactures include clothing, particle board, furniture, and aluminum products. It is the seat of Northeastern Oklahoma Agricultural and Mechanical College (1919).

Miami Beach city, pop. 92,639, Dade Co., SE Florida, occupying the S end of a 7.5-sq mi/19-sq km barrier island between the Atlantic Ocean (E) and Biscayne Bay (W), across the bay from Miami and linked with it by several causeways. BAL HARBOUR and Surfside (town, pop. 4108) are at the island's N end. It was connected to the mainland by a bridge in 1913 when it was still jungle wilderness, and Miami Beach was incorporated in 1915, but real development did not come until the Florida land boom of the 1920s. Its white sand beaches are bordered by hundreds of hotels, many of them huge pastel Art Deco palaces, and by numerous condominiums. A variety of recreational facilities, such as tennis courts and golf courses, are sandwiched between the bay and ocean. Tourism is by far its largest industry, but there is also some light manufacturing and a number of corporate headquarters. The city has a large Convention Center, the Bass Museum of Art, numerous theaters, and its own symphony orchestra. South Beach, a 20-block stretch along the ocean at the city's SE, also called the Art Deco District for its older buildings, became extremely trendy in the 1980s.

Miami County 410 sq mi/1062 sq km, pop. 93,182, in W Ohio, intersected by the Great Miami and Stillwater rivers. Its seat is TROY. Corn, livestock, tobacco, and wheat are farmed, and there are nurseries throughout the region. Piqua, Tipp City, and Troy have some manufacturing. Natural resources include sand, stone, and gravel.

Miami River see GREAT MIAMI RIVER.

Miamisburg city, pop. 17,834, Montgomery Co., SW Ohio, on the Miami R., 10 mi/16 km S of Dayton. Founded in 1818 in the heart of a tobacco growing region, it has industries including the manufacture of metal and paper products and diversified agriculture. The Mound Plant, a nuclear weapons component plant, is here. A large Indian mound is located outside the city.

Miami Shores village, pop. 10,084, Dade Co., SE Florida, 6 mi/10 km NNE of downtown Miami. Originally part of Miami, it was separated from the city in 1932; it is a residential suburb. Barry University (1940) is here.

Miami Springs city, pop. 13,268, Dade Co., SE Florida, 4 mi/6 km W of downtown Miami, a residential suburb just N of Miami International Airport.

Mianus River 25 mi/40 km long, in New York and Connecticut. It rises NE of Armonk, New York, then flows generally S through Connecticut to Long Island Sound at COS COB Harbor, in Greenwich.

Michigan state of the NC US, in the MIDDLE WEST and GREAT LAKES regions; 1990 pop. 9,295,297 (100.4% of 1980; rank: 8th); area 96,810 sq mi/250,738 sq km; rank: 11th); admitted to Union 1837 (26th). Capital: LANSING. Most populous cities: DETROIT, GRAND RAPIDS, WARREN, FLINT, Lansing, STERLING HEIGHTS, ANN ARBOR, LIVONIA. Michigan comprises two major peninsulas and a number of islands. The mitten-shaped, N–S oriented **Lower Peninsula** is bordered S by Ohio (E) and Indiana (W). On the E it is bounded by (S–N) L. ERIE; the DETROIT R., L. SAINT CLAIR, and the Saint Clair R., across from all of which is SW Ontario; and L. HURON. SAGINAW BAY is a large inlet of the lake, in the EC, forming the "thumb" of the "mitten." At the N, the Lower Peninsula is separated from the Upper Peninsula by the Straits of MACKINAC; to the E of the Straits are MACKINAC and BOIS BLANC islands. To the W of the Straits is L. MICHIGAN, which forms the Lower Peninsula's W boundary. The BEAVER ARCHIPELAGO is to the NW, off Grand Traverse and Little Traverse bays, the major indentation in the Lower Peninsula's W coast. The **Upper Peninsula,** oriented E–W, is bordered W and SW by Wisconsin, with the MENOMINEE R. forming the SE third of the boundary. On the S the "U.P." is bounded by L. Michigan and (E of the Straits of Mackinac) L. Huron. On its E, where it includes DRUMMOND and several other islands, it faces WC Ontario across the SAINT MARYS R., in the SAULT SAINTE MARIE (Soo) region. Just NW of the Soo, at the entrance onto L. SUPERIOR, is Whitefish Bay. The major protrusion of the Upper Peninsula into L. Superior is the KEWEENAW PENINSULA (NW). ISLE ROYALE, site of a national park, in the lake's NW off Thunder Bay, Ontario, is also part of Michigan. The state thus divides the three largest Great Lakes, and has shoreline on all except L. Ontario; it takes its name from the Algonquian one for the lake. Heavily glaciated, Michigan lies in the C lowlands area of the US, with the exception of the NW Upper Peninsula, a copper and iron mining region that is part of the SUPERIOR HIGHLANDS, a S extension of the CANADIAN SHIELD. There, Mt. ARVON (1980 ft/604 m), in the Huron Mts., is the state's high point (nearby Mt. Curwood has about the same elevation). The NIAGARA ESCARPMENT cuts across the Upper Peninsula, which was taken from the Wisconsin Territory and became part of Michigan in return for the loss (1837) to Ohio of the TOLEDO STRIP. The U.P. is lightly populated, with MARQUETTE (NC), ESCANABA (SC), and Sault Sainte Marie (E), the largest communities; the region is noted for mining, forestry, and outdoor recreation, and has coastal fisheries. The PICTURED ROCKS National Seashore (NE) draws visitors. The opening of the MACKINAC BRIDGE (1957) greatly enhanced access to the Upper Peninsula. The Lower Peninsula has a number of short rivers, including the W-flowing MUSKEGON, GRAND, and Kalamazoo, along which industry has developed, but most of its pop. lives in the extreme SE, in the Detroit area. Fruit and bean growing, stock raising, and dairy farming are important, and in the S, Michigan blends into the CORN BELT. The N Lower Peninsula, scene of a huge lumber boom in the late 19th century, is still a productive forest area. Coal, salt (notably beneath Detroit), and oil and natural gas (esp. in the NW) are among the peninsula's resources. The Ojibwa and Ottawa were among the peoples inhabiting the area when French explorers arrived in Michigan early in the 17th century. The fur trade and lake route were central to early white interest in Michigan; Detroit became a key post by 1701. After the British took control in 1763, the future city withstood a long siege by forces of the Ottawa leader Pontiac. Part of the NORTHWEST TERRITORY after the American Revolution, Michigan became a separate territory in 1805. Parts of it were held by the British during the War of 1812, and settlement began slowly, gaining momentum after the ERIE CANAL facilitated (1825) westward movement on the Great Lakes. In the 1830s many New Englanders arrived, followed in mid-century by Europeans, among them Germans (who settled in SAGINAW, FRANKENMUTH, Ann Arbor, and other communities), Dutch (who made HOLLAND a noted center), Scandinavians (who gravitated toward the forest and mine areas of the N), and Irish. An Upper Peninsula copper boom (1840s) and the opening (1855) of canals at Sault Ste. Marie fostered development. By the end of the century, Michigan had varied and scattered industrial centers. Grand Rapids became a noted furnituremaker. Detroit built ships, machinery, and carriages. As the 20th century began, this industrial base combined with a central position between Minnesota and Upper Peninsula iron and Appalachian coal to make Detroit suddenly the center of world automobile manufacture. Through the 20th century, the motor industry and its offshoots (such as wartime tank and aircraft production) have dominated Michigan's, as well as much of the Middle West's, life. Flint, PONTIAC, YPSILANTI, Warren, DEARBORN, and other cities in the SE blossomed as satellites of, and in some cases new homes for, the great automobile plants. Machine, tool, fabricated metal, and other industries have employed thousands of Michiganders. In the late 20th century removal of plants to the SUNBELT and other cheap-labor areas, and increased competition from overseas carmakers, have brought decline in Detroit, but while the city itself has lost much of its pop., the METROPOLITAN AREA remains one of America's largest. The Lower Peninsula has substantial tourism and recreation business; thousands of lakes and small rivers, coves and beaches draw vacationers. The SLEEPING BEAR DUNES National Lakeshore (NW) is popular, along with dunes in the SW, near the Indiana border. The University of Michigan is at Ann Arbor, Michigan State University at EAST LANSING. Except for the diverse Detroit area (the city is now predominantly black), Michigan's people are largely descendants of the 19th-century Eastern and European immigrants who settled in her cities. The Wolverine State takes its nickname from a ferocious forest animal no longer found here.

Michigan, Lake third-largest of the GREAT LAKES, between Michigan (N and E), Indiana and Illinois (S), and Wisconsin (W). Some 310 mi/500 km N–S and 50–85 mi/80–137 km wide, it covers 22,350 sq mi/57,890 sq km, and lies 577 ft/176 m above sea level. Its greatest depth is 923 ft/281 m. Green Bay, a large W arm, is separated by the DOOR PENINSULA of Wisconsin, which with the parallel (N) Garden Peninsula of upper Michigan is the W extension of the NIAGARA ESCARPMENT. Grand Traverse and Little Traverse bays indent the NW corner of Michigan's Lower Peninsula. The largest island in the lake is Beaver, in Michigan's BEAVER ARCHIPELAGO. The only Great Lake lying entirely within the US, Michigan connects at its NE end with L. Huron (E), with which it is geologically one lake, via the Straits of MACKINAC. At Chicago, Illinois, at the SW corner, the Chicago R. and ILLINOIS WATERWAYconnect it with the Mississippi R. and the Gulf of Mexico. The lake's main ports and industrial centers include Escanaba, Menominee, Ludington, Muskegon, Grand Haven, and Benton Harbor, Michigan; Michigan City, Hammond, and Gary, Indiana; Chicago and Waukegan, Illinois; and Racine, Milwaukee, Sheboygan, Manitowoc, and Green Bay, Wisconsin. Car ferries cross between Michigan and Wisconsin at several points. The Hiawatha National Forest covers much of Michigan's Upper Peninsula N of the lake, and sandy beaches and dunes lie along parts of its E and S shores, which include the Sleeping Bear and Indiana Dunes national lakeshores. Wisconsin's Door Peninsula is another popular resort area. The first European to encounter the lake was the French explorer Jean Nicolet, in 1634. The lake gave its Algonquian name ("big water") to the state.

Michigan Avenue commercial and residential thoroughfare in Chicago, Illinois, running N–S from just below LINCOLN PARK on the Gold Coast, between Grant Park (E) and the Loop (W), to the South Side. It parallels (E) State St., and contains Chicago's largest upscale shopping district, including the MAGNIFICENT MILE.

Michigan City city, pop. 33,822, La Porte Co., NW Indiana, a port 25 mi/40 km ENE of Gary. On the dune-dominated S shore of L. Michigan, it is a popular summer resort and yachting harbor; fishing from private and charter boats is important. Tourists are also attracted to parks, gardens, theaters, and annual pageants. The city has such manufactures as electronic parts, steel products, cast iron boilers, railroad cars, furniture and other wood products, air compressors, and chemicals. There is a state prison. The INDIANA DUNES NATIONAL LAKESHORE is W of the city.

Michilimackinac see under MACKINAC I. and MACKINAW CITY, Michigan.

Mid-Cities popular term for cities between Dallas (E) and Fort Worth (W), NE Texas, in the METROPLEX; of these, ARLINGTON is the largest.

Middle America also, **Mid-America** the American middle class considered as representing a "place" that is neither politically nor culturally "extreme." It is not equivalent to MIDDLE WEST, but the term does manage to suggest that the "extremes" are more likely to be found on "the coasts" than in the nation's midsection.

Middle Atlantic region of the E US lying between NEW ENGLAND (NE) and the SOUTH (SW), usually taken to include New York, New Jersey, Delaware, Pennsylvania, and Maryland (the **Middle Atlantic States** or **Middle States**), as well as the District of Columbia. The Census Bureau places Delaware, Maryland, and the District of Columbia in the South Atlantic region instead.

Middleburg Heights city, pop. 14,702, Cuyahoga Co., NE Ohio, a residential suburb 8 mi/13 km SSW of Cleveland.

Middlebury town, pop. 8034, including Middlebury village, seat of Addison Co., WC Vermont. It is on the Middlebury R. and Otter Creek, 32 mi/52 km S of Burlington. In an agricultural and resort area, partly in Green Mt. National Forest, Middlebury is a former marble quarrying and milling center. Industries include fruit, poultry and cattle raising, and the manufacture of wood products, plastics, and business forms. The town is best known as the site of Middlebury College (1800). The college's Bread Loaf School of English is held in the adjoining (E) town of Ripton, and takes its name from Bread Loaf Mt. (3823 ft/1166 m).

Middle Hill neighborhood in Pittsburgh, Pennsylvania, 1 mi/1.6 km E of the GOLDEN TRIANGLE. An affluent middle-class area in the 19th century, it was eventually subdivided for Irish, Jewish, Russian, and other immigrants. Blacks arrived later, and now constitute a majority.

Middle Island **1.** unincorporated village, pop. 7848, in Brookhaven town, Suffolk Co., SE New York, on Long Island. It is a largely residential community situated just W of the Brookhaven National Laboratory, with wildlife and other open areas surrounding. **2.** see under PELÉE I., Ontario.

Middle River **1.** 105 mi/169 km long, in SC Iowa. It rises in SW Guthrie Co., and flows SE, then ENE, to join the Des Moines R. SE of Des Moines. **2.** unincorporated industrial and residential suburb, pop. 24,616, Baltimore Co., N Maryland, at the head of the estuarial Middle R., 9 mi/14 km E of downtown Baltimore. The former site of the Glenn L. Martin aircraft plant, one of the world's largest early (1920s–30s) producers, it now has boat basins, industrial parks, and the Glenn L. Martin State Airport.

Middlesborough also, **Middlesboro** city, pop. 11,328, Bell Co., extreme SE Kentucky, at the W end of the CUMBERLAND GAP, 50 mi/80 km NNE of Knoxville, Tennessee. It was developed by English investors (1889) to be an ironmaking center. The English company went bankrupt (1893), but the city recovered as the center of E Kentucky coalfields. It trades in tobacco and dairy cattle, and has tanning, plastic, mobile-home, and food processing industries. Cudjo's Cave is one of several in the vicinity that draw visitors.

Middlesex borough, pop. 13,055, Middlesex Co., NE New Jersey, 6 mi/10 km NW of New Brunswick. It has a diverse group of manufactures including chemicals, building products, and paint.

Middlesex County **1.** 373 sq mi/966 sq km, pop. 143,196, in S Connecticut, on Long Island Sound and bisected by the Connecticut R. Its diversified economy includes agriculture, fishing, tourism, manufacturing, and quarrying. The area around Middletown, the county seat, is the center of population and business activity. **2.** 822 sq mi/2129 sq km, pop. 1,398,468, in NE Massachusetts. Its co-seats are Cambridge and Lowell. The most populous Massachusetts county contains many residential and industrial suburbs of Boston, the historic towns of Lexington and Concord, most of the ROUTE 128 high-technology complex, and the industrial area around Lowell. **3.** 316 sq mi/818 sq km, pop. 671,780, in C New Jersey, on Raritan Bay and cut by the Raritan R. Its seat is NEW BRUNSWICK. Its N half is both residential (suburban) and industrial, and is the site of such municipalities as Perth Amboy, Piscataway, Metuchen, and Sayreville. The rest of the county is largely agricultural, dotted with fruit, truck, and dairy farms, although suburban development is rapidly consuming farmland.

Middleton city, pop. 13,289, Dane Co., S Wisconsin, on L. Mendota, 5 mi/8 km NW of Madison. A residential suburb in a farming region, it produces condensed milk and has other light industries.

Middletown **1.** in sociological literature: see under MUNCIE, Indiana. **2.** section of SAN DIEGO, California, 2 mi/3 km N of Downtown, and W of Balboa Park. Formerly home to aircraft plant workers and Italian fishermen, now to transients, artists, and young professionals, it retains a bohemian flavor. **3.** city and coterminous township, pop. 42,762, seat of Middlesex Co., C Connecticut, on the Connecticut R., 15 mi/24 km S of Hartford. Settled in 1650, it was a prosperous shipping port in the 18th and 19th centuries, engaged in the Triangle Trade with Africa and the West Indies. Today it manufactures automobile accessories, electronic equipment, and aircraft engines; there is also an active banking and insurance sector. Middletown is the seat of Wesleyan University (1831) and Middlesex Community College (1966). **4.** town, pop. 3834, New Castle Co., NC Delaware, on Deep Creek, 22 mi/35 km SSW of Wilmington. It was an important mid-19th-century agricultural market town, in the middle of the Levels, a basically flat expanse containing Delaware's largest farms. ODESSA is 3 mi/5 km E. **5.** township, pop. 68,183, Monmouth Co., E New Jersey, across the Navesink R. from, and adjacent (NW) to, Red Bank. Settled by the Dutch in 1665, it was the site of the first Baptist church (1668) in New Jersey. In a part of the state formerly agricultural and maritime, it is increasingly suburban in character. **6.** city, pop. 24,160, Orange Co., SE New York, in the foothills of the Shawangunk Mts., 56 mi/90 km NW of New York City. Named for its location midway along the Minisink Trail between the Delaware and Hudson rivers, it was settled in 1756. It became the headquarters of several turnpike companies, and later a center for the ERIE RAILROAD. It is the market and processing center of a dairy and fruit region. Industries include railroad shops and foundries, and manufacture clothing, leather goods, and machinery. Middletown is home to Orange County Community College (1950). **7.** city, pop. 46,029, Butler and Warren counties, SW Ohio, on the Great Miami R., 11 mi/18 km NE of Hamilton, midway (hence its name) between Cincinnati and Dayton. It flourished with the building of the Miami and Erie Canal and the arrival of several railroads. Situated in a fertile agricultural region, it is a manufacturing center for flat-rolled steel products (a rolling process mill was built in 1900) as well as paper, paperboard, and papermaking machinery. A campus of Miami University is here. A large amusement park is 5 mi/8 km S of the city. **8.** in Pennsylvania: **a.** township, pop. 43,063, Bucks Co., 5 mi/8 km NE of Philadelphia's NE boundary. It includes suburban areas along Interstate 95 adjacent (NW) to LEVITTOWN. **b.** borough, pop. 9254, Dauphin Co., on the Susquehanna R., 8 mi/13 km SE of Harrisburg, at the mouth of Swatara Creek. Home to Olmsted Air Force Base (Harrisburg International-Olmsted Field), it manufactures stoves, clothing, and shoes. **c.** township, pop. 14,130, Delaware Co., adjacent (SW) to MEDIA. It includes the residential and commercial suburbs of Franklin Center and Lima (pop. 2670), home of the Tyler Arboretum. **9.** town, pop. 19,460, Newport Co., SE Rhode Island, on Rhode I. between Narragansett Bay and the Sakonnet R. Named for its location between Newport (SW) and Portsmouth (NE), it was settled in 1639 as part of Newport, and separated in 1743. Surrounded by farmland, it bases its economy on extensive Navy facilities here and in Newport. Notable sites include Whitehall, home (1729–31) to Irish philosopher George Berkeley, and the Norman Bird Sanctuary. St. George's prep school is in Middletown.

Middle Valley unincorporated community, pop. 12,255, Hamilton Co., SE Tennessee, on Chickamauga L., 12 mi/19 km NE of downtown Chattanooga. This residential community is 4 mi/6 km WSW of the Sequoyah nuclear power plant.

Middle West also, **Midwest** variously defined region of the US. Following an historical approach, some consider it the land W of the Allegheny Mts. (the great barrier to early migration from the East) as far as the Rocky Mts., the next great barrier westward and the end of the generally level central PRAIRIES and plains. The Ohio R. and the S boundaries of Missouri and Kansas have generally been accepted as the S limits of the Middle West. The *states* in which the Alleghenies and Rockies stand (Pennsylvania; Colorado, Wyoming, and Montana) have never, however, been considered Midwestern states; the latter, therefore, are most often taken to be twelve: Ohio, Indiana, Illinois, Michigan, Wisconsin, Minnesota, North Dakota, South Dakota, Iowa, Missouri, Kansas, and Nebraska. The Census Bureau does not use the term "Middle West." Rather, it groups the twelve as **East North Central** (Ohio, Indiana, Illinois, Michigan, and Wisconsin) and **West North Central** (the other seven).

Midland 1. city, pop. 38,053, seat of Midland Co. and also in Bay Co., C Michigan, on the Tittabawassee R., 18 mi/29 km W of Bay City. Originally a lumbering community, it is renowned for its chemical industry, originally based on extensive brine deposits, and begun in 1888 by Herbert Dow. The city grew with the expansion of his company and became its world headquarters. It is also the site of Dow Corning, a leading manufacturer of silicones. Agriculture and a wide range of industries additionally contribute to the economy. Midland is the seat of Saginaw Valley University (1963) and the Northwood Institute (1959). The Midland Center for the Arts and Dow Gardens are also here. The 1000-ac/405-ha Chippewa Nature Center is 3 mi/5 km to the SW. **2.** town, pop. 13,865, Simcoe Co., S Ontario, on Severn Sound, off Georgian Bay of L. Huron, 80 mi/129 km NNW of Toronto. It was the site of an important French mission in HURONIA in the 1600s. The arrival of the railroad spurred settlement of the modern town in the 1870s. Today it is the manufacturing center of an agricultural and resort region. Industries include boatbuilding, and there are large harbor installations. Sainte-Marie among the Hurons, the reconstructed site of Jesuit mission headquarters (1639–49), is 3 mi/5 km E, along with the Martyrs' Shrine, memorial to eight 1640s missionaries. **3.** city, pop. 89,443, seat of Midland Co., SW Texas, 255 mi/411 km ENE of El Paso and 20 mi/32 km NE of its sister city, ODESSA. Named for its position approximately midway between Fort Worth and El Paso, it is the hub of a ranching region famous for its Hereford cattle. Established in 1885 on the Texas & Pacific Railroad, it developed as a cattle shipping center. Oil was discovered in the PERMIAN BASIN in 1923, and the city boomed (especially after 1950). It is the administrative center of the oilfields, and also produces chemicals, plastics, clothing, aircraft, and oilfield equipment, as well as dairy products, cotton, and livestock. It is home to Midland College (1969). Human remains found locally, dated to 20,000 B.C., are known as those of Midland Man. Midland International Airport, 10 mi/16 km SW, is the home base of the recreational Confederate Air Force.

Midlothian village, pop. 14,372, Cook Co., NE Illinois, a residential suburb 18 mi/29 km SW of Chicago.

Mid-South Fairgrounds 4 mi/6 km SE of downtown Memphis, Tennessee, near the corner of the E and S PARKWAY. Successor to Montgomery Park, an 1882–1906 horseracing resort, it is home to the Liberty Bowl Memorial Stadium, scene of a college football bowl game; the Mid South Coliseum; and Libertyland, a patriotic theme park. The Mid-South Fair is held here in Sept.

Midtown 1. commercial and cultural district in Atlanta, Georgia, 1.5 mi/2 km N of the older downtown (FIVE POINTS) area. The Georgia Institute of Technology lies W, ANSLEY PARK and PIEDMONT PARK N and NE. Midtown has long housed many of Atlanta's museums and theaters. Development since the 1980s of residential and office towers, along with retail space, is transforming it into a residential, financial, and commercial district rivaling Downtown. **2.** commercial section of Manhattan, New York City, generally defined as extending from 59th St. S to 34th St., below which skyscrapers were not built because of a change to softer subsoil. In some definitions Midtown extends as far as 14th St., with the section below 34th called Lower Midtown. **3.** in Memphis, Tennessee, commercial and middle-class residential neighborhoods to the E of Downtown, away from the Mississippi R.

Midvale city, pop. 11,886, Salt Lake Co., N Utah, on the Jordan R., a suburb 10 mi/16 km S of Salt Lake City. Surrounded by lead, copper, zinc, gold, and silver mines, the city is a smelting center. It also produces beet sugar, flour, and packaged poultry.

Midway 1. also, **Midway Islands** ATOLL, land area c.2 sq mi/5 sq km, in the NC Pacific Ocean, 1300 mi/2100 km WNW of Honolulu, Hawaii, part of the Hawaiian Is. chain, but not part of the state. Eastern and Sand islands are the center of this area administered by the US Navy, which uses it as a base. Occupied by the US in 1867 and named for its position between California and Japan, it became a submarine cable station in 1903 and a commercial air station in 1935. Naval facilities were built in 1941. The Japanese attacked unsuccessfully in 1941–42; in the Battle of Midway, June 3–6 1942, US aircraft dealt a critical blow to the Japanese navy. Eastern I. is today a wildlife refuge. **2.** cargo airport and residential neighborhood on the Southwest Side of Chicago, Illinois, NE of Bedford Park. The neighborhood is a working-class area. Once a passenger hub, the airport no longer handles major airline flights.

Midway Plaisance park now in the center of the University of Chicago, between Jackson and Washington parks, on the South Side of Chicago, Illinois, created during the 1892 World Columbian Exposition. As the locus of amusements during the Exposition, it gave its name to the generic carnival term *midway.*

Midwest see MIDDLE WEST.

Midwest City city, pop. 52,267, Oklahoma Co., C Oklahoma, 8 mi/13 km E of downtown Oklahoma City, and on its limits. It was founded in the early 1940s with the building of the adjacent Tinker Air Force Base (S), which remains important to its economy. Just off Interstate 40, this residential suburb was a planned city. Oscar Rose State College (1968) is here.

Midwood largely residential section of C Brooklyn, New York. Midwout (Middle Woods) was a Dutch town established in 1652, but much of modern Midwood was part of FLATLANDS in the 17th century. The area was largely undeveloped until the 20th century, and was an early center of the movie industry; the Vitagraph Studio (1925), located here because of the open space, was succeeded (1953) by NBC television studios, still in use. Midwood is a tree-filled area of detached houses, with apartment buildings along major avenues. Today it contains the largest Sephardic community outside of Israel, in particular some 30,000 Syrian Jews. Midwood is closely associated with Flatbush, to its N. Brooklyn College's campus is here.

Milan **1.** city, pop. 4040, Monroe and Washtenaw counties, SE Michigan, on the Saline R., 13 mi/21 km SSE of Ann Arbor. It manufactures lumber and wood products, automotive plastics and parts, and furnaces. A large Federal correctional institution is just NE of the city. **2.** village, pop. 1494, Erie and Huron counties, N Ohio, overlooking the Huron R., 12 mi/19 km SSE of Sandusky. Situated in an agricultural district, Milan owes its distinctive New England style to settlers from Connecticut. Formerly a shipbuilding center, it is now supported by light industry, including the manufacture of clay and wood products and beer. A 35-ac/14-ha bird and wildlife sanctuary and the Ohio State Soldiers and Sailors Home (1866) are here. The house where Thomas A. Edison was born (1847) is preserved. **3.** city, pop. 7512, Gibson Co., W Tennessee, 22 mi/35 km NNE of Jackson. An agricultural shipping center with various light manufactures, it also services the large Milan Arsenal, which lies SE, along with a Tennessee National Guard reservation. A University of Tennessee agricultural facility is just NE.

Mile High Stadium in WC DENVER, Colorado, just W of the South Platte R. and Downtown. Home to the football Broncos since 1960, it was built in 1948, and seats 76,000. The baseball Rockies began play here in 1992, before moving to nearby (NE) Coors Field, opened in 1995. Just S is the McNichols Arena (1975), home to the basketball Nuggets.

Milenberg see MILNEBURG, New Orleans, Louisiana.

Miles City city, pop. 8461, seat of Custer Co., SE Montana, at the junction of the Yellowstone and Tongue rivers, 135 mi/217 km NE of Billings. When established (1877) on the edge of Fort Keogh, it was named for Nelson Miles, builder of the fort. It became a sheep, wool, cattle, and crop market after the Northern Pacific Railway arrived (1881), and remains a commercial hub for the products of local farms and ranches, now supplemented by the output of nearby oilfields. The city also makes flour, dairy and meat products, saddles, and leather goods. On its W edge, Fort Keogh has been rebuilt and now houses the Range Riders Museum and a Federal livestock and range research station.

Milford **1.** city and coterminous township, pop. 49,938, New Haven Co., SW Connecticut, 10 mi/16 km W of New Haven, on the Housatonic, Oyster, Indian, and Wepamaug rivers. Settled in 1639, it has a fine natural harbor on Long Island Sound and was a major oystering center from the mid 19th century until pollution ruined the business in recent years. Milford is a residential suburb and summer resort with some light industry, including the manufacture of pens, fabricated metal parts, and marine hardware and equipment. **2.** city, pop. 6040, Kent and Sussex counties, EC Delaware, at the head of navigation on the Mispillion R., which divides the city into North and South Milford, 18 mi/29 km SSE of Dover. A 17th-century plantation, the settlement developed as a shipping and shipbuilding center. Now it is a trade, processing, and shipping point for a truck farming area, and produces dental supplies, wood products, clothing, canned goods, and bricks. Its historic buildings include the Parson Thorne Mansion (c.1785). **3.** town, pop. 25,355, Worcester Co., SE Massachusetts, on the headwaters of the Charles and Blackstone rivers, 30 mi/48 km SW of Boston. Originally part of Mendon, it is located in a farming region and has been famous for its pink granite since the mid 19th century. It has also produced tile, machine tools, ceramics, electronic equipment, textile machinery, rubber goods, shoes, truck bodies, and hats. Situated on Route 495, it is experiencing suburban growth. **4.** town, pop. 11,795, Hillsborough Co., S New Hampshire. It is on the Souhegan R., 11 mi/18 km WNW of Nashua. In an agricultural and increasingly suburban area, the town has granite quarries and apple and peach orchards, and manufactures textiles and wood products.

Milford Mill unincorporated suburb, pop. 22,547, Baltimore Co., NC Maryland, 8 mi/13 km NW of central Baltimore, on Interstate 695. Like Baltimore's NW corner, to which it is adjacent, it is a largely Jewish residential community.

Mililani Town unincorporated community, pop. 29,359, Honolulu Co., Hawaii, a residential and commercial suburb in OAHU's central valley, SE of Wheeler Air Force Base and N of PEARL HARBOR.

Military Plaza Spanish, **Plaza de las Armas** public space in downtown San Antonio, Texas, established by Canary Islanders who settled the city in 1731. The early center of political life in San Antonio, it is the site of the 1772 Governor's Palace and the 1888 City Hall. San Fernando Cathedral (1738) is also here.

Military Tract see under POMPEY, New York.

Milk River 625 mi/1000 km long, in Montana and Alberta. It rises near the Continental Divide, in NW Montana's Blackfeet Indian Reservation, and flows ENE into Alberta, across the province's S, and back (SE) into Montana, where it flows through the dam-created Fresno Reservoir, winds past Havre, forms the N boundary of the Fort Belknap Indian Reservation, passes Malta and through the dam-created Nelson Reservoir, turns SE past Glasgow, and enters the MISSOURI R. on the W edge of the Fort Peck Indian Reservation. The Milk is the main river of the northwesternmost part of the Missouri R. Basin.

Mill Basin see under FLATLANDS, New York.

Millbrae city, pop. 20,412, San Mateo Co., NC California, on the W shore of San Francisco Bay, 13 mi/21 km S of San Francisco, adjacent (SW) to San Francisco International Airport. Named for the country estate (1866) of banker/mine investor Darius Ogden Mills, it has some light industry but is largely a commuter suburb.

Millbrook village, pop. 1339, in Washington township, Dutchess Co., SE New York, 13 mi/21 km NE of Poughkeepsie. Once an artists' colony, it is surrounded by sumptuous estates, and is a favorite exurban retreat for wealthy residents of New York City, some 60 mi/100 km to the S. There is a winery outside the village, and the Mary Flagler Cary Arboretum is W.

Millburn township, pop. 18,630, Essex Co., NE New Jersey, on the Rahway R., in the WATCHUNG Mts., 6 mi/10 km W of Newark. Settled in the early 18th century, it became a 19th-century manufacturing center. Today it is primarily residential, and includes the fashionable community of SHORT HILLS within its borders. There are also corporate offices and some some light industry. Millburn is the site of the Papermill Playhouse, the official state theater of New Jersey.

Millcreek unincorporated community, pop. 32,230, Salt Lake Co., NC Utah, 6 mi/10 km S of downtown Salt Lake City, adjacent (S) to South Salt Lake. With East Millcreek (unincorporated, pop. 21,181), between it and the WASATCH RANGE, it is part of the residential suburbs of Utah's capital.

Mill Creek Valley urban renewal area of C SAINT LOUIS, Missouri, between Downtown (1.3 mi/2 km E) and the WEST END, along Market and neighboring streets. Notorious for its slums, it was bulldozed from 1959. Much of its space is now occupied by Interstate 64 and connecting roads. The new (1960s) campus of St. Louis University is on the N, railyards on the S.

Milledgeville city, pop. 17,727, seat of Baldwin Co., C Georgia, on the Oconee R. at the Fall Line, 22 mi/35 km NE of Macon. Laid out in 1803 as Georgia's capital, it remained so until 1868. It was an early stagecoach and then (1850s) railroad hub. Landmarks include the Old Governor's Mansion and the Old State Capitol. Local manufactures include building materials (made from local clays), mobile homes, pharmaceuticals, and textiles. Georgia Military College (1879) and Georgia College (1889) are here. The writer Flannery O'Connor (1925–64) lived and died in Milledgeville.

Mille Lacs Lake 197 sq mi/510 sq km, in N Minnesota, 90 mi/140 km NNW of Minneapolis. It is roughly circular and 14–18 mi/23–29 km in diameter. A famous fishing center, it has in some winters 5000 ice-fishing houses on its surface. The Mille Lacs Band of Ojibwa, who live around the lake's S side, have recently opened gambling casinos on the lake and nearby, and hunting and fishing rights under an 1837 treaty have been in dispute.

Millersville borough, pop. 8099, Lancaster Co., SE Pennsylvania, 4 mi/6 km SW of Lancaster. Millersville University of Pennsylvania (1835) is here.

Millerton **1.** see under FRESNO, California. **2.** village, pop. 884, in Northeast township, Dutchess Co., SE New York, 27 mi/43 km NE of Poughkeepsie, and just W of the Connecticut line. In a farming area, it is the birthplace of baseball great Eddie Collins (1887–1951).

Milligan College see under JOHNSON CITY, Tennessee.

Millington town, pop. 17,866, Shelby Co., SW Tennessee, 15 mi/24 km NE of Memphis. Although Memphis Naval Air Station is its biggest employer, it is a commercial center for an agricultural region, and has various light manufactures.

Millinocket town, pop. 7567, Penobscot Co., C Maine. Millinocket is on the West Branch of the Penobscot R., 55 mi/88 km N of Bangor. In 1899–1900, the Great Northern Paper Co. built a newsprint plant, established a hotel, provided homes for workers, constructed roads, opened schools, and founded a government. A settlement rapidly grew up around the mill, one of the largest of its kind in the nation. Near Black Cat ski area and 20 mi/32 km SE of Mt. Katahdin, Millinocket is now a pulp milling town and headquarters for hunters, anglers, and campers bound for BAXTER STATE PARK and nearby lake regions.

Mill Springs hamlet in Wayne Co., S Kentucky, on the Cumberland R. and L. Cumberland, 15 mi/24 km SW of Somerset. It gives its name to a battle of Jan. 19–20, 1862, in which Confederate forces advancing across the Cumberland were defeated, after which Union forces advanced into E Tennessee. The battle is also called Logan's Crossroads, for its site, 10 mi/16 km N of Mill Springs.

Millstone nuclear power plant: see under WATERFORD, Connecticut.

Millstone River 40 mi/64 km long, in C New Jersey. It rises SW of Freehold and flows NW and N of Hightstown, to Princeton, where it is dammed to form L. Carnegie. Paralleled by the Delaware and Raritan Canal, it continues N to Millstone and MANVILLE, where it joins the RARITAN R.

Milltown borough, pop. 6968, Middlesex Co., C New Jersey, 2 mi/3 km SE of New Brunswick. It was settled in the 18th century, and produces textiles, clothing, paper products, and other goods; there are sand pits nearby.

Mill Valley city, pop. 13,038, Marin Co., NW California, an affluent suburb 10 mi/16 km NW of San Francisco, at the head of Richardson Bay, an inlet of San Francisco Bay, and the SE foot of Mt. TAMALPAIS. Set in wooded hills and valleys, it has a seminary, an artists' colony, a film festival, and some corporate offices.

mill village see under COMPANY TOWN.

Millville **1.** see under NEW CASTLE, Indiana. **2.** city, pop. 25,992, Cumberland Co., S New Jersey, across the Maurice R. (S) from Vineland. At the head of navigation on the Maurice, it began early in the 18th century as a river port, and flourished as a 19th-century glass center, using local sand. Glass manufacturing (mainly bottles and other containers) remains a key industry, along with the production of such goods as clothing and aircraft parts. Millville is also a resort community, and has a large municipal airport. Wheaton Village, an 88-ac/36-ha re-creation of an 1888 glassmaking town, also includes the Museum of American Glass. The area is also known for holly tree cultivation. **3.** village, pop. 747, Butler Co., extreme SW Ohio, 5 mi/8 km W of Hamilton. It is the birthplace (1866) of Kenesaw Mountain Landis, jurist and first baseball commissioner.

Milneburg also, **Milneberg** or **Milenberg** residential area of N New Orleans, Louisiana, near L. Pontchartrain, 3 mi/5 km E of the WEST END. An early 19th-century lake port, it became the terminus of the Pontchartrain Railroad, where travelers from across the lake debarked for New Orleans, in 1831. Through the late 19th and early 20th centuries it was a lake resort, famous for its dozens of waterside eating and music clubs. Today Milneburg is inland, separated from the lake by the landfill area on which the University of New Orleans is situated.

Milpitas city, pop. 50,686, Santa Clara Co., NC California, just SE of San Francisco Bay, and 7 mi/11 km N of San Jose. Incorporated in 1954 in a farming area (the name means "little fields"), it has a large auto assembly plant, and has now become an important part of SILICON VALLEY, manufacturing computer software and chips and other high-tech products.

Milton **1.** town, pop. 25,725, Norfolk Co., E Massachusetts, across the Neponset R. from MATTAPAN, 8 mi/13 km S of downtown Boston. During the 18th century, it was a mill town and manufacturing center. Now a wealthy Boston suburb, it is home to Milton Academy and several other prep schools, two colleges, and some light industry. The Blue Hill reservation is immediately S. **2.** town, pop. 32,075, seat of Halton Regional Municipality, S Ontario, 18 mi/29 km N of Hamilton. The area was opened to white settlement with the sale of land by the Mississauga in the early 1800s. Traditionally agricultural, the town is now suburban and has some light manufacturing.

Milwaukee city, pop. 628,088, seat of Milwaukee Co., SE Wisconsin, on the W shore of L. Michigan, where the Milwaukee, Menomonee, and Kinnickinnic rivers join and flow into Milwaukee Bay. It is the center of the five-county (MILWAUKEE, Ozaukee, Washington, WAUKESHA, and RACINE) Milwaukee-Racine metropolitan area (CMSA), with a pop. of 1,607,183. Its Algonquian-derived name is variously translated as "good land" or "gathering place by the river." French missionaries and fur traders were in the area from the late 17th century, and the NORTH WEST COMPANY built a post in 1795. Permanent white settlement began in the 1830s, when three villages, Juneautown (established by Solomon Juneau, here from 1818), Kilbourntown, and Walker's Point, sprang up. After a brief period of rivalry, they were united as the city of Milwaukee, incorporated in 1846. German immigrants soon played a vital role in the city's development, esp. with wealthy and educated refugees arriving after the failed revolution of 1848. The pre–Civil War Milwaukee was primarily a trade and shipping hub for the region, in which wheat and hogs were the leading products; after the war it became a brewing, tanning, and meatpacking center. At the end of the 19th century the "German Athens" was noted for its very European culture and politics. Brewing money (Schlitz, Pabst, Blatz) poured into civic improvements, and a socialist tradition developed that elected three mayors—Emil Seidel (1910–12), Daniel W. Hoan (1916–40), and Frank P. Zeidler (1948–60)—and sent Victor Berger as the first Socialist to sit in Congress (1911). By 1900, Milwaukee was becoming a manufacturing center, and with the decline of brewing (hastened by Prohibition, 1919–33), it emerged as one of the leading US heavy industrial centers. Its manufactures now include gasoline and diesel engines, outboard motors, motorcycles, turbines, other machinery, fabricated metal products, electrical and electronic equipment, printed materials, processed foods, and beer. Its harbor, since the 1959 opening of the St. Lawrence Seaway, serves both domestic and international commerce; coal and iron lead items shipped. The city is home to Marquette University (1881; Catholic), the Milwaukee School of Engineering (1903), the University of Wisconsin–Milwaukee (1956, combining earlier schools), and a number of other colleges, conservatories, and seminaries. Its extensive park system and lakeshore provide recreational facilities and contribute to its often described "small town" feel. World War I brought the "Americanization" of much of German Milwaukee, which also has large Polish, other East and South European, and black communities. Milwaukee County Stadium (1953; seats 53,000) is home to the Brewers (baseball), and formerly (through 1994) site of half the home games of the football GREEN BAY Packers. The Bucks (basketball) play at the 19,000-seat Bradley Center (1988). The General Mitchell International Airport is on the city's S side. See also: BAY VIEW; EAST SIDE; GRAND AVENUE MALL; HISTORIC SOUTH SIDE; JUNEAU PARK; KINNICKINNICK PARKWAY; LAKE DRIVE; MERRILL PARK; MITCHELL PARK; OLD WORLD THIRD St.; PROSPECT Ave.; RIVER WEST; SHERMAN PARK; SOUTH SIDE; THIRD WARD; WALKER'S POINT; WEST SIDE; WISCONSIN Ave.

Milwaukee County 241 sq mi/624 sq km, pop. 959,275, in SW Wisconsin, bordered by L. Michigan (E) and cut by the Milwaukee R. MILWAUKEE is the seat of the most urbanized county in the state. The city has annexed most county land, but such independent suburbs as Whitefish Bay, Shorewood, Wauwatosa, West Allis, Oak Creek, and South Milwaukee are also here.

Milwaukee River 85 mi/137 km long, in SE Wisconsin. It rises in the lakes of Fond du Lac Co. and flows SE through West Bend into L. Michigan at Milwaukee. The area along the river was occupied by the Potawatomi as early as 1674, and was an important fur trading center for the French and British by the middle of the 18th century.

Milwaukee Road formally, **Chicago, Milwaukee, and Saint Paul Railroad,** later, **Chicago, Milwaukee, Saint Paul, and Pacific Railroad** former carrier that developed N and W of Chicago in the 1870s and 1880s. It joined Chicago (by way of Evanston and other N suburbs and Milwaukee) with the Twin Cities by 1884; at first connecting there with the GREAT NORTHERN, it had by 1909 constructed its own line across Montana, Idaho, and C Washington, reaching the Pacific (Puget Sound) at Tacoma. The Milwaukee was noted as the first (1913) long line to electrify major sections. In the 1970s it failed; parts were sold to the Soo Line (a CANADIAN PACIFIC subsidiary). Large sections of track from the Dakotas W were abandoned.

Milwaukie city, pop. 18,692, Clackamas Co., NW Oregon, on the Willamette R., a residential suburb 4 mi/6 km S of Portland. It is a trading and shipping hub for the fruit and other agricultural bounty of the Willamette Valley, and has extensive warehousing facilities. Its manufactures include batteries and plywood.

Mimbres Mountains range, sometimes considered a subchain of the BLACK RANGE, in SW New Mexico, WSW of Truth or Consequences. It extends N from the vicinity of Cookes Peak (8404 ft/2562 m), and is partly in the GILA NATIONAL FOREST. The Mimbres R. valley (W) was home to the pre-Columbian Mimbres and to the Mimbreño Apache. The area has gold mines and hot springs.

Mimico see under ETOBICOKE, Ontario.

Minarets, the see under RITTER RANGE, California.

Minas Basin SE extension of the Bay of FUNDY, into C Nova Scotia, 75 mi/120 km E–W and up to 25 mi/40 km wide, connecting with the bay (W) by the **Minas Channel,** and ending (E) in Cobequid Bay. Noted for some of the world's highest (to 52 ft/16 m) tides, it receives the Cornwallis, Avon, Shubenacadie, and several smaller rivers. The COBEQUID Mts. and PARRSBORO lie N. On the S, esp. in the GRAND PRÉ area, Acadian settlers employed dikes to turn marshlands into fertile farming areas.

Minden city, pop. 13,661, seat of Webster Parish, NW Louisiana, 28 mi/45 km ENE of Shreveport. Germans settled the area in the 1830s. A processing and distribution center for an agricultural region, it is also amid oil and natural gas fields.

Mine Creek battle site: see under PLEASANTON, Kansas.

Mineola village, pop. 18,994, seat of Nassau Co., in North Hempstead town, SE New York, on Long Island, 20 mi/32 km E of Manhattan. Although chiefly residential, it is also a commercial center for C Long Island, and has some light industry. It was founded in the 17th century by settlers from Connecticut.

Mineral King Valley see under SEQUOIA NATIONAL PARK, California.

Mineral Wells city, pop. 14,870, Palo Pinto and Parker counties, NC Texas, 43 mi/69 km W of Fort Worth. Livestock, gas, and oil are important in the area, but the city is nationally known for its mineral waters, which made it a prosperous resort and hospital convention center. The Crazy Well, discovered in 1885, was said to cure mental disorders. Founded in 1872, the city now has various light manufactures. Camp (later Fort) Wolters, a major World War II training facility, is just NE.

Minerva village, pop. 4374, Stark and Carroll counties, NE Ohio, on the Sandy R., 15 mi/24 km ESE of Canton. Founded during the building of the Sandy and Beaver Canal, it now depends on diversified farming and the manufacture of such products as electrical equipment and tools and dies.

Mingo County 424 sq mi/1098 sq km, pop. 33,739, in extreme SW West Virginia, separated (SW) from Kentucky and Virginia by Tug Fork. Its seat is Williamson. On the Appalachian Plateau, and rich in bituminous coal, "Bloody Mingo" was the scene of labor struggles in the 1920s. In 1920 MATEWAN exploded in violence, and the next year miners headed for Mingo fought with coal company agents at BLAIR Mt. in adjoining (NE) Logan Co. Mingo is named for the tribe that lived here into the 18th century, whose leader was Logan.

Minneapolis most populous (368,383) city in Minnesota, seat of HENNEPIN Co., in the SE, on both sides of the Falls of St. Anthony, the head of navigation on the Mississippi R., just above the mouth of the Minnesota R. and adjacent (W) to SAINT PAUL, with which it forms the Twin Cities (pop. 640,618). It is the center of an eleven-county (including ANOKA, DAKOTA, Hennepin, RAMSEY, SCOTT, and WASHINGTON) metropolitan area with a pop. of 2,464,124. An industrial, commercial, financial, educational, and cultural center, Minneapolis is the transportation hub of the upper Midwest, with air routes, barge lines, railroads, and highways converging on the largest urban area between the Great Lakes and the Pacific. In addition, the city has long been a processing and distribution point for a vast hinterland of dairy, grain, and cattle farms. French missionary Louis Hennepin visited the Falls of St. Anthony in 1680, but permanent settlement occurred only after the establishment of FORT SNELLING in 1819. East of the Falls, the village of St. Anthony had appeared by 1850, while squatters to the W laid out Minneapolis a few years later. After Minneapolis was chartered as a city in 1867, the two merged in 1872, in time to attract mostly North European immigrants to work its water-powered sawmills, flour mills, and meatpacking plants. Modern Minneapolis is a leader in manufacturing and commercial and financial services. The world's largest flour milling and trading firms are here, as is the Minneapolis Grain Exchange, also the largest in the world; such industry giants as Cargill, Pillsbury, and General Mills are based in the Twin Cities area. Electronics and high-tech firms (Honeywell, 3M) are prominent, along with food processing, publishing, and the production of textiles, machinery, and fabricated metals. The city's educational institutions include the huge University of Minnesota (1851), the Minnesota College of Art and Design (1886), and Augsburg College (1869). The renowned Tyrone Guthrie Theatre and Walker Arts Center anchor a widely-known arts cluster, The METRODOME and the 18,000-seat Target Center (1990) are among city sports venues. Local urban design innovations include Downtown's glass-enclosed, climate-controlled SKYWAY SYSTEM and one of the nation's earliest auto-free transit malls. The Metropolitan Council (1967) was established as a planning and advisory body for seven counties, to draw up areawide tax sharing and school choice programs. Minneapolis, which has lost 30% of its pop. from a 1950 peak of 521,718, is widely regarded as one of the most liveable US cities. Its 22 lakes, many along Minnehaha Creek, and 6000 ac/2430 ha of parks complement well-shaded residential neighborhoods that spread S and W from Downtown on rolling plateau terrain above the Mississippi. See also: CEDAR-RIVERSIDE (West Bank); DINKYTOWN; KENWOOD; LAKES DISTRICT; LORING PARK; LOWRY HILL; METRODOME; MINNEHAHA PARK (and Falls); NEAR NORTH SIDE; NEAR SOUTH SIDE; NICOLLET ISLAND; NICOLLET MALL; NORTHEAST; NORTH MINNEAPOLIS; PHILLIPS; PROSPECT PARK; SKYWAY SYSTEM; SOUTHEAST; UPTOWN; WAREHOUSE DISTRICT; the WEDGE; WHITTIER. See also entries listed at SAINT PAUL.

Minnedosa town, pop. 2526, SW Manitoba, in the valley of the Minnedosa R., 29 mi/47 km N of Brandon. In the late 1880s, it was a popular area for buffalo hunting, and served as a major grain supplier. Today it is a resort; local industry includes the manufacture of farm equipment and the distilling of ethyl alcohol from grain.

Minnehaha County 810 sq mi/2098 sq km, pop. 123,809, in SE South Dakota. Its seat and major city is SIOUX FALLS, which with its suburbs dominates an historically agricultural area. The county, South Dakota's most populous by far, is bounded by Minnesota (E) and Iowa (SE), and drained by the Big Sioux R.

Minnehaha Creek see under L. MINNETONKA, Minnesota.

Minnehaha Park city park and residential neighborhood, in S Minneapolis, Minnesota, along Minnehaha Creek, S of Downtown. The neighborhood is an affluent area of mostly prewar single-family homes. The park contains **Minnehaha Falls,** prominent in Henry Wadsworth Longfellow's 1855 poem, "The Song of Hiawatha."

Minnesota state of the NC US, considered part of the Upper MIDDLE WEST and a Great Lakes state; 1990 pop. 4,375,099

(107.3% of 1980; rank: 20th); area 86,943 sq mi/255,182 sq km (rank: 12th); admitted to Union 1858 (32nd). Capital: SAINT PAUL. Most populous cities: MINNEAPOLIS, Saint Paul, BLOOMINGTON, DULUTH, ROCHESTER. Minnesota is bordered S by Iowa. On its W are (S–N) South Dakota, with the MINNESOTA R. forming part of the boundary; and North Dakota, with the Bois de Sioux R. (S) and RED RIVER OF THE NORTH (N) forming most of the boundary. On the N are (W–E) Manitoba; the LAKE OF THE WOODS, in which the NORTHWEST ANGLE is the northernmost point in the Lower 48; and NW Ontario, across the RAINY R., Rainy L., and BOUNDARY WATERS–Pigeon R. system. On the NE is L. SUPERIOR, at the SW end of which is Duluth, the westernmost Great Lakes port. On the E is Wisconsin, with the SAINT CROIX (EC) and MISSISSIPPI (SE) rivers forming most of the boundary. Minnesota's NE section, the ARROWHEAD REGION, is part of the SUPERIOR HIGHLANDS, a S extension of the CANADIAN SHIELD; this is the site of the famed MESABI and VERMILION iron ranges. EAGLE Mt., the state's high point, reaches 2310 ft/702 m near the NE extreme; its lowest point, the shore of L. Superior, at 600 ft/183 m, is nearby. Outside the Arrowhead Region, the state comprises sections of the vast C lowlands of the US. In the SE corner, along the Mississippi, is a limited extension of Wisconsin's DRIFTLESS AREA. The rest of Minnesota was glaciated, and is covered with varying depths of drift or till (see under MORAINE). The state contains the beginnings of three great North American river systems: The St. Louis R., in the Arrowhead, which enters L. Superior in Duluth, is the ultimate headwater of the entire Great Lakes–Saint Lawrence R. system. In the NW, the Otter Tail R. is the head of the Red River of the North–L. WINNIPEG–NELSON R. system, which drains into HUDSON BAY. Most notable of all, though, is that L. ITASCA, lying just E of the Otter Tail's headwaters, is the ultimate source of the Mississippi R. The state's other major river, the Minnesota, swings SE and NE across the state's S, joining the Mississippi at the TWIN CITIES. The river gave its name (from Siouan words for "water" and "cloud") to the state. Minnesota is also dotted with lakes (proverbially 10,000), and is known as the "Land of Sky Blue Waters." Large and small lakes are found throughout, but esp. in the N. Among the largest are RED, Leech and Winnibigoshish (see under CHIPPEWA NATIONAL FOREST), and MILLE LACS; MINNETONKA, near the Twin Cities, is a famed residential and recreational lake. When French explorers, missionaries, and VOYAGEURS appeared in the area, in the late 17th century, the Santee Sioux occupied much of Minnesota. On their E were the Ojibwa, who soon, armed by trade with the French, began to push the Sioux SW, toward the GREAT PLAINS (a process that finally led, in 1862, to a bloody Sioux rebellion in the S, and the tribe's banishment to the West). The Ojibwa remain on a number of Minnesota reservations. The British-French rivalry that ended in 1763 with the fall of NEW FRANCE left Minnesota E of the Mississippi R. nominally in British hands, and it passed in 1783 to the US, becoming the ill-defined NW extremity of the NORTHWEST TERRITORY. The LOUISIANA PURCHASE (1803) brought most of the rest under US control; but it was not until 1818, with the establishment of the FORTY-NINTH PARALLEL as the international boundary, that modern borders were established. An important early fur trade post, at GRAND PORTAGE, was key to westward expansion in the border area. FORT SNELLING, on the site of the Twin Cities, foreshadowed (1819) agricultural and commercial settlement. The fur trade soon gave way to lumbering and (in the S) the growing of grain; from the 1840s Minneapolis developed as a regional milling center, at the head of navigation on the Mississippi. After the Civil War, the Twin Cities' location made Saint Paul a rail hub; the GREAT NORTHERN RAILWAY and other lines worked their way W from here. In the 1890s, the IRON RANGE REGION in and near the Arrowhead became the center of the US industry. All these activities generated tremendous wealth, and in the 20th century, as dominance in the primary industries began to fade, Minnesota was able to diversify into related areas (e.g., from milling to food processing and grain handling and trading; from lumber to pulp production). Today, the state has a range of industries, including the manufacturing of electronic and other high-tech machinery. Iron, corn (more than wheat), and pulp remain important, but esp. in the SE, research, finance, and corporate operations have come to the fore, drawn in part by the state's reputation for progressive government and a high quality of life. Rochester (SE) is noted esp. for the Mayo Clinic, one of America's premier medical and research complexes. Minneapolis (seat of the University of Minnesota) and Saint Paul are educational centers. Tourism and recreation are important, visitors being drawn to the lakes and rivers, the VOYAGEURS NATIONAL PARK and Boundary Waters Canoe Area, and cultural attractions of the Twin Cities. Minnesota's people remain overwhelmingly descendants of the Yankee, German, and Scandinavian settlers of the 19th century.

Minnesota River 322 mi/535 km long, in Minnesota. It flows in the wide valley carved out by a glacial river that drained the prehistoric L. Agassiz. It runs through the S part of the state, from W to E, flowing first SE, then NE in a broad "V." The river rises in Big Stone L., in Big Stone Co., W Minnesota, on the border with South Dakota. It flows SE through several lakes, including Lac qui Parle L. and continues past Montevideo and Granite Falls. Thirty mi/48 km SE, at Redwood Falls, its 19th-century head of navigation, rock steps in the river valley provide power sites. At Mankato, the river abruptly changes direction to flow NE. This area is now its head of navigation, and at this point it has two dams providing flood control. The river continues N, flowing by St. Peter, Le Sueur, and Belle Plaine, then enters the Twin Cities industrial region near Shakopee. It continues NE before emptying into the Mississippi R. at Mendota, just S of St. Paul. The Minnesota, earlier known as the St. Pierre or St. Peter, was a key artery that carried early explorers and traders. Its chief tributaries are the Lac Qui Parle, Redwood, Earth, and Cottonwood rivers.

Minnetonka city, pop. 48,370, Hennepin Co., SE Minnesota, at the E end of L. Minnetonka, a residential suburb 10 mi/16 km W of Minneapolis. Settlers in the 1850s named their village using the Siouan word for "big water." A postwar bedroom community, Minnetonka has undergone a boom in commercial and office development since the 1970s, particularly along the I-494 corridor.

Minnetonka, Lake 11 mi/18 km ENE–WSW, in Hennepin Co., SE Minnesota. Twelve mi/19 km W of downtown Minneapolis, this irregular body, with numerous arms and bays, is the site of many of the Twin Cities' most affluent suburbs, most of which were resorts in an agricultural area before acquiring a year-round residential population. The city of

MINNETONKA is E of the lake. Wayzata (city, pop. 3806) is on Wayzata Bay, at the NE extreme. Deephaven (city, pop. 3653) is also at the E end. The cities of Tonka Bay (pop. 1472), Excelsior (pop. 2367), and Shorewood (pop. 5917) are along the S side. Minnetrista (city, pop. 3439) is at the W end. On peninsulas in the lake's WC are Spring Park (city, pop. 1571) and **Minnetonka Beach** (city, pop. 573). The city of Mound (pop. 9634) is on W arms of the lake and on neighboring, smaller lakes. Orono (city, pop. 7285) is on the N shore. Minnetonka is drained by Minnehaha Creek, which flows from the E end, through Minneapolis, to the Mississippi R. at Minnehaha Falls.

Minnetrista see under L. MINNETONKA, Minnesota.

Minot city, pop. 34,544, seat of Ward Co., NC North Dakota, on the Souris (Mouse) R., 100 mi/160 km N of Bismarck. Founded in 1887 as a railroad tent city, it is now a shipping, processing, and trading center for dairy and meat products, and has railroad shops. Farm machinery, building materials, and petroleum products are manufactured here. The Minot Air Force Base also contributes to the economy. The annual state fair is held here.

mint government facility at which metallic money is produced and medals and other items containing precious metals are manufactured. Refining, assaying, and other handling of metals may also be undertaken. The **United States Mint,** a bureau of the Treasury Department, currently operates at five sites: Coins are produced at Philadelphia, Pennsylvania (the oldest facility, dating from 1792), and at Denver, Colorado (where there is also a gold depository); the main assay office is at San Francisco, California (which has an Old Mint building, opened 1874, and a 1937 facility); FORT KNOX, Kentucky, is the site of the main gold bullion depository; and West Point, New York, is the site of a silver depository. The Mint at Carson City, Nevada, in operation 1870–93, is now the Nevada State Museum. The **Royal Canadian Mint**'s main Ottawa facility (1908) now refines gold and makes numismatic coins, medals, plaques, and other items; a Winnipeg, Manitoba plant (1976) is engaged in mass production of coins.

Mint Hill town, pop. 11,567, Mecklenburg Co., S North Carolina, a booming residential suburb 10 mi/16 km ESE of Charlotte.

Minto village, pop. 3096, Queens Co., SC New Brunswick, 28 mi/45 km ENE of Fredericton, on the NW of Grand L. The first coal mined in Canada was taken from the area in 1639, and mines here have produced regularly since the 1820s. Brickmaking is also important.

Minute Man National Historical Park see under LEXINGTON, Massachusetts.

Miquelon see SAINT-PIERRE ET MIQUELON.

Mirabel city, pop. 17,971, S Québec, 24 mi/39 km NW of Montréal. Created from 14 municipalities merged in 1979, it is the site of Montréal's newer (1975) international airport, connected to the city by the Laurentian Autoroute. The economy of the region remains agricultural, while Mirabel itself is dominated by the airport and related businesses.

Miracle Mile see under WILSHIRE Blvd., Los Angeles, California.

Miramar **1.** section of N SAN DIEGO, California, 12 mi/19 km N of Downtown, on KEARNY MESA. The site of the Scripps family's Miramar Ranch in the 1890s, it is now both residential and an aerospace manufacturing site. United States International University (1952) and Miramar College (1969) are here. Miramar Naval Air Station is immediately S. **2.** city, pop. 40,663, Broward Co., SE Florida, midway between Fort Lauderdale (N) and Miami (S), 5 mi/8 km WSW of central Hollywood and 10 mi/16 km inland from the Atlantic Ocean. A residential and retirement community, it grew most quickly in the 1960s. **3.** district of SAN JUAN, Puerto Rico, a *subbarrio* (pop. 5266) of SANTURCE, S of the Laguna de Condado and E of Isla Grande and its airport. Closest to Old San Juan (NW) of the capital's newer neighborhoods, it is a hilly area of modern residences mixed with a range of businesses.

Miramichi River 135 mi/220 km long, in NC and NE New Brunswick. Its system comprises several streams that flow from the province's central highlands E into an estuary that begins at NEWCASTLE and extends 15 mi/24 km ENE past CHATHAM, to Miramichi Bay of the Gulf of St. Lawrence. The longest of these is the Southwest Miramichi. The area has many Acadian fishing settlements, and since the 1950s mining has joined lumbering in economic importance, but the Miramichi is best known as one of the world's finest salmon rivers.

Misenheimer hamlet in Stanly Co., S North Carolina, 36 mi/58 km NE of Charlotte, the seat of Pfeiffer College (1885).

Mishawaka city, pop. 42,608, St. Joseph Co., NC Indiana, on Interstate 80/90 and the St. Joseph R., adjacent (E) to SOUTH BEND. Its many industries manufacture such products as missiles, plastic and rubber goods, drop forgings, tools and dies, automobile and aircraft parts, industrial machinery, clothing, and processed foods. Mishawaka is the seat of Bethel College (1947) and the United Missionary Church School.

Mispillion River 15 mi/24 km long, in Delaware. It rises in streams W of MILFORD, then flows E and NE through Milford to Delaware Bay, 16 mi/26 km NW of Cape Henlopen. Its Algonquian name probably refers to tubers dug locally.

Missinaibi River see under MOOSE R., Ontario.

mission Spanish, **misión** in the US Southwest, any of the Spanish religious outposts established from the 16th through the 18th centuries to evangelize American tribes and further Spanish colonial expansion. Initiated chiefly by Franciscans, they were under way in New Mexico by the 1590s, in Arizona and Texas by the 1690s, and in California by 1769. They typically included chapels, other religious and administrative buildings, residences, and agricultural structures like granaries and *acequias* (irrigation systems). The chapels are now generally thought of as "missions"; in many cases the other structures have disappeared. Local tribes were encouraged to settle around them in agricultural communities known as PUEBLOS (not to be confused with the native communes also so called). A military PRESIDIO was sometimes attached. The missions gave birth to modern cities including San Antonio and San Diego; they gave their name to California's Mission Indians, who settled near them; and they also gave a name to popular architectural and furniture styles.

Mission **1.** district municipality, pop. 26,202, Dewdney-Alouette Regional District, SW British Columbia, on the N bank of the Fraser R., 40 mi/65 km E of Vancouver. Founded (1860) as an Oblate mission, it grew with the arrival of the railway (1885) and a bridge (1891). Industries include fruit and vegetable processing, lumbering, and dairying. It is experiencing suburban residential growth. **2.** city, pop.

9504, Johnson Co., NE Kansas, an affluent residential suburb 5 mi/8 km SSW of downtown Kansas City. **3.** city, pop. 28,653, Hidalgo Co., extreme S Texas, in the Lower Rio Grande Valley, adjacent (W) to McAllen. A mission built by Franciscans in 1824 eventually led to a settlement 3 mi/5 km N in 1908. The area produces oil, vegetables, and citrus. Mission's Texas Citrus Fiesta celebrates the Ruby Red grapefruit, originally planted by the monks; the city is also national headquarters for the American Poinsettia Society.

Missionary Ridge battle site, a 1000-ft/300-m NE–SW Appalachian ridge in Hamilton Co., Tennessee, and Walker Co., Georgia, along the SE of CHATTANOOGA. In Oct.–Nov. 1863, Union forces in Chattanooga were besieged by Southern troops under Braxton Bragg. When U.S. Grant took over leadership, they seized the offensive, lifting the siege by taking (Nov. 23) Orchard Knob, a prominence N of the ridge; storming (Nov. 24) LOOKOUT Mt.; and finally, on Nov. 25, taking Missionary Ridge itself. Though costly for the North, the victory forced their enemy into retreat and opened the way for Sherman's MARCH TO THE SEA the following year. The ridge (10 mi/16 km long) is partly included in the Chickamauga and Chattanooga National Military Park.

Mission Bay shallow, dredged inlet of the Pacific Ocean in SAN DIEGO, California. Lying inside the popular oceanfront **Mission Beach,** whose narrow peninsula separates it from the ocean, the bay and its shores form a 4600-ac/1860-ha park featuring sites for water sports, bike paths, and an artificial island. Sea World, on a peninsula (S) between the bay and the outlet of the San Diego R., is a 150-ac/60-ha marine life park. PACIFIC BEACH lies N of the bay.

Mission District section of SE SAN FRANCISCO, California. The area surrounding the 1776 MISSION of San Francisco de Asis (later called Mission Dolores) became home to a wide range of ethnic groups in the 19th century. It is now a low-rent community where large numbers of recent Latin American immigrants mix with Asians, lesbians, and the elderly.

Mission Hills **1.** in California: **a.** largely residential N SAN FERNANDO VALLEY section of LOS ANGELES, 19 mi/31 km NW of Downtown and just SW of SAN FERNANDO. It is the site of the 1797 Mission San Fernando Rey de Espana. Pacoima lies E, the Pacoima waterworks SE. **b.** country club in RANCHO MIRAGE, Riverside Co., noted as a venue for golf and tennis tournaments. **c.** residential section of uptown SAN DIEGO, 2 mi/3 km N of Downtown. OLD TOWN is immediately W, MIDDLETOWN S, and MISSION VALLEY N. Mansions here built for the local elite and Eastern vacationers in the late 19th century house some of the city's more affluent citizens. **2.** city, pop. 3446, Johnson Co., NE Kansas, an affluent suburb 6 mi/10 km S of downtown Kansas City.

Mission San Jose see under MISSION TRAIL, San Antonio, Texas.

Mission San Luis Rey see under OCEANSIDE, California.

Mission San Xavier del Bac on the San Xavier Reservation (pop. 1172), 9 mi/14 km SW of Tucson, Arizona. The original MISSION was founded by Jesuit priest Eusebio Kino before 1700. The present church, built in the late 18th century by Franciscans, is considered one of America's finest examples of Spanish colonial architecture. It is the only Kino mission church still active; local Tohono O'odham (Papago) worship here.

Mission Trail **1.** see under EL CAMINO REAL, California. **2.** route in S San Antonio, Texas, along the San Antonio R., that passes four of the city's five (the fifth is the ALAMO) Spanish MISSIONS. These collectively represent the hub of Spain's 18th-century colonization of Texas; some were moved here from earlier locations, encouraged by the friendly or at least neutral attitude of the local Coahuiltecans. The Misión Nuestra Señora de la Purísima Concepción de Acura (**Mission Concepción,** 1731), 2.7 mi/4.3 km S of Downtown, incorporates a 1755 stone church, the oldest unreconstructed church of its type in the US. The Misión San José y San Miguel de Aguayo (**Mission San José,** 1720), 4.5 mi/7 km S of Downtown, is noted for its Churrigueresque chapel (1760s–80s). The Misión San Juan Capistrano (**Mission San Juan,** 1691; moved here 1731) is 6.5 mi/10 km SSE of Downtown. The Misión San Francisco de la Espada (**Mission Espada,** 1690; moved here 1731) is 8 mi/12 km SSE of Downtown, at the city limits; it is noted for its early-18th-century *acequia* (irrigation) system.

Mission Valley low-density commercial area of San Diego, California, along the San Diego R., 5 mi/8 km N of Downtown. Hotels, shopping malls, and restaurants sprang up here from the 1950s. Junipero Serra's Mission Basilica San Diego de Alcala was moved here from PRESIDIO HILL in 1773, and was restored in 1931. Jack Murphy Stadium (1967; 60,000 seats), home to the city's major-league teams, is nearby, in the valley's E.

Mission Viejo city, pop. 72,820, Orange Co., SW California, 50 mi/80 km SE of Los Angeles. EL TORO is immediately NW. Originally part of Rancho Santa Margarita, it is a planned community, begun in 1965, now a rapidly growing, affluent residential city in foothills 7 mi/11 km NE of Laguna Beach and the Pacific Ocean.

Missisquoi River 96 mi/155 km long, rising near Lowell, in Orleans Co., NW Vermont, and flowing N past North Troy into Québec. From there it flows SW, back into Vermont, past East Richford, in Franklin Co., then W through Enosburg Falls and the Green Mts., forming a delta as it flows into Missisquoi Bay of L. Champlain, N of Swanton. The Missisquoi is known for its walleyed pike. In the late 1980s, disputes over aboriginal river-fishing rights arose between local Abenaki Indians and the state. The 5839-ac/2365-ha **Missisquoi National Wildlife Refuge** lies in the marshy delta, and is an important stop for migrating waterfowl.

Mississauga city, pop. 463,388, Peel Regional Municipality, S Ontario, on the Credit R. and the W end of L. Ontario, adjacent (W) to ETOBICOKE and immediately SW of metropolitan Toronto. White settlement of the area began in 1805, when it was purchased from the Mississauga (Ojibwa). It was Toronto Township from 1850 until its incorporation as the town of Mississauga in 1968, and became a city in 1974. Now a fast-growing residential and industrial suburb of Toronto, it is also an important lake port. Manufactures include chemicals, appliances, pharmaceuticals, aircraft, engines, turbines, motor vehicles, construction materials, plastics, and rubber, petroleum, and steel products, and the city has packaging, bioengineering, and research firms. It is the home of Erindale College of the University of Toronto and several smaller institutions. Toronto's LESTER B. PEARSON INTERNATIONAL AIRPORT is in its N, next to the industrial district of MALTON. Port Credit, at the river's mouth, has long been an important lake/rail nexus.

Mississippi state of the SE US, generally considered part of the Deep SOUTH (and in the Census Bureau's East South

Central region); 1990 pop. 2,573,216 (102.1% of 1980; rank: 31st); area 48,434 sq mi/125,444 sq km (rank: 32nd); admitted to Union 1817 (20th). Capital and most populous city: JACKSON. Other leading cities: BILOXI, GREENVILLE, HATTIESBURG, MERIDIAN. Mississippi is bordered E by Alabama, with the TENNESSEE R. forming part of the boundary in the extreme NE (in TISHOMINGO Co.); N by Tennessee; and W by Arkansas (in the NW, across the Mississippi R.) and by Louisiana (SW, across the Mississippi; by an E–W land border; and across the PEARL R.). On the S the state has a coast c.70 mi/115 km long on the Gulf of MEXICO, with a number of islands (part of the GULF ISLANDS NATIONAL SEASHORE) in MISSISSIPPI SOUND. The state lies entirely within the Gulf COASTAL PLAIN and Mississippi ALLUVIAL plain, with high ground in various hills and ridges including the N–S PONTOTOC RIDGE (E) and WOODALL Mt., the high point (806 ft/246 m, in the extreme NE). The PASCAGOULA (SE) and Pearl (SC) rivers flow to the Gulf. In the NE the TOMBIGBEE R. flows SSE into Alabama; at its N end it has since 1985 been linked with the Tennessee R. by the Tennessee–Tombigbee Waterway, which creates an alternative route to the Gulf (avoiding the lower Mississippi) for Tennessee R. traffic. Mississippi's other rivers flow SW from the state's C to the Mississippi R. The southernmost major river in this area is the BIG BLACK. To the N is the YAZOO (with its tributaries the YALOBUSHA, TALLAHATCHIE, and SUNFLOWER). Between the Yazoo and the Mississippi lies the famous DELTA, a flat, rich agricultural zone at the heart of the COTTON BELT. Named for the river (whose Algonquian name—"big river"—actually comes from tribes hundreds of miles to the N), Mississippi has a primarily agricultural history. The Chickasaw and Choctaw (in the N), the Natchez (in the S), and other groups lived here when the French arrived in the Biloxi area (1699). Struggles for control among the French, Spanish, and English lasted for a century; meanwhile, Americans were entering the area along the Mississippi R. and passing up the NATCHEZ TRACE. In 1795 the US took control by treaty with Spain, settling a WEST FLORIDA boundary dispute. What is now Alabama and Mississippi became the Mississippi Territory in 1798. The spurious treaty of DANCING RABBIT CREEK and other mechanisms were employed to force the Choctaw and other tribes to give up their lands, and in the 1830s heavy settlement began. Mississippi was shortly a major cotton producer, its lowlands becoming PLANTATION country, while in its hills APPALACHIAN settlers developed a small-farming economy and culture. By 1860, well over half the pop. consisted of slaves. The Civil War devastated the state, with battles at VICKSBURG, CORINTH, TUPELO, BRICES CROSSROADS, and IUKA, and the burning of Jackson and Meridian. After the war, however, the cotton economy was reconstituted, esp. in the Delta, where black tenants worked on the area's large farms in a state of virtual peonage. After the Reconstruction era ended (1875), politicians passed laws disenfranchising and otherwise disabling the black majority, and Mississippi entered a long period in which cotton and timber products (largely from the PINEY WOODS in the S) generated money but blacks and most whites struggled in poverty. By the early 20th century the Delta's workers were leaving for nearby Memphis or for Northern cities, esp. Chicago; the ILLINOIS CENTRAL RAILROAD became a major exit route. A World War I boom in cotton slowed the exodus, but by the 1940s it reached huge proportions. World War II and development policies adopted in the 1930s began at this time to bring industry into the state. PASCAGOULA became a naval shipbuilding center, and Jackson began to grow. Today there is an assortment of light industry in Jackson; Hattiesburg and LAUREL (SE, in the Piney Woods); GREENVILLE, in the Delta; Tupelo and Columbus (NE); Meridian (EC); and GULFPORT, Biloxi, and Pascagoula, on the Gulf. Oil and gas are extracted at various places across S Mississippi. Soybeans, poultry, and rice are important farm products, the forest industries remain strong, and commercial fishing and tourism are central to the Gulf cities. The US state with the highest proportion of black residents (35.6% in 1990), Mississippi was perhaps the most resistant to integration, and such incidents as the 1964 murder of three civil rights workers near PHILADELPHIA marked a difficult transition. The University of Mississippi is in OXFORD (N), also the home of William Faulkner and model for the seat of his fictional YOKNAPATAWPHA Co. Mississippi State University is in STARKVILLE (EC). The Delta is widely known as a source of blues music and other black cultural expressions, and has, in addition, a vibrant literary tradition centered in Greenville.

Mississippi Delta 1. see DELTA OF THE MISSISSIPPI RIVER. 2. also, **Yazoo Delta** or **Yazoo Basin,** in N Mississippi: see the DELTA.

Mississippi Flyway bird migration route used by species that winter in Central America and along the US Gulf Coast and follow the Mississippi R. valley N to nest in summer. Among species on this flyway, some swing E over the Great Lakes to areas E and N of Hudson Bay; others fly over the large lakes along the W of the Canadian Shield, nesting as far N as the Beaufort Sea.

Mississippi River 1. 2340 mi/3770 km long, the longest North American river. Rising at L. ITASCA in NC Minnesota, it flows generally SSE and S to the Gulf of Mexico below New Orleans, Louisiana. The Mississippi (from an Algonquian word for "big river") is generally regarded as dividing the United States into East and West (although roughly two-thirds of US land area lies to its W). Its system drains an area of 1.23 million sq mi/3.2 million sq km between the Rocky Mts. (W) and the Appalachians (E, although some headwaters flow W through them), including part or all of 31 states, Alberta, and Saskatchewan. This expanse has been called the "Great Valley" or "Central Valley" of America, and is now more often referred to as the Mississippi R. Basin; it comprises ALLUVIAL plain, PRAIRIE, the GREAT PLAINS, Rocky Mt. and Appalachian foothills, and other topographical regions of the C US. The MISSOURI R. is the Mississippi's major tributary; the combined Mississippi-Missouri extends 3710 mi/5973 km from the Continental Divide in SW Montana to the Mississippi's mouth, and is the world's third-longest river system (after the Nile and the Amazon). From L. Itasca, the Mississippi winds N, E, SE, SW, and SE again past Bemidji and across C Minnesota to Minneapolis–Saint Paul, where the Falls of St. Anthony mark its head of navigation. Just below the Twin Cities, the SAINT CROIX R. joins it from the N, at the Wisconsin border. Below this point, the Mississippi forms the border between Minnesota, Iowa, Missouri, Arkansas, and Louisiana (W) and Wisconsin, Illinois, Kentucky, Tennessee, and Mississippi (E). Only below its junction with the Red R., near Angola, Louisiana, does it flow again within the boundaries of a single state, bisecting SE Louisiana on its way to the Gulf of Mexico. Its major West Bank tributaries (N–S) include the CEDAR, IOWA, DES MOINES, MISSOURI, MERAMEC, SAINT FRANCIS, WHITE, ARKANSAS, and RED rivers. In Louisiana the

ATCHAFALAYA R. and BAYOU LAFOURCHE (both on the W) are DISTRIBUTARIES; the former in particular has been engineered to draw off floodwaters, and some scientists believe that without human intervention the lower Mississippi, which within its alluvial plain has continually changed direction, will switch its mainstream to the Atchafalaya's course. On the Mississippi's East Bank, major tributaries (N–S), in addition to the Saint Croix, include the CHIPPEWA, WISCONSIN, ROCK, ILLINOIS, OHIO, YAZOO, and BIG BLACK rivers; in Louisiana a floodway to L. PONTCHARTRAIN is designed to draw off high water. Mississippi tributary headwaters in the East extend as far as New York's ALLEGHENY, Pennsylvania's MONONGAHELA, West Virginia's and Maryland's YOUGHIOGHENY, and North Carolina's NEW, FRENCH BROAD, and LITTLE TENNESSEE rivers, all parts of the Ohio R. system. Hernando de Soto was probably the first (1541) white to see the "Father of Waters," but it was the French who first thoroughly explored it; on traveling from the Great Lakes to the Gulf of Mexico in 1682, La Salle claimed the entire basin for France, giving the area the name Loisiana (after Louis XIV). The French maintained control until their 1763 defeat in Canada by the British; they then ceded the river to the Spanish, although the British were in possession of such outposts as Natchez. Regaining control (1800) after the American Revolution, the French sold the entire river basin to the US in the LOUISIANA PURCHASE (1803). American pioneers, who had already been infiltrating foreign territory, now poured into the region, continuing W through the Arkansas and Missouri valleys, improving on flatboat and keelboat trade with the introduction (from 1811) of steam-powered riverboats, and, in the South, establishing the plantations and trade centers of the COTTON BELT. Before the Civil War, shipping of lumber and Middle Western farm products, as well as cotton and other plantation goods, made New Orleans and the Mississippi central to the US economy. The river was first bridged in 1855, by the ROCK ISLAND (Illinois) Railroad. The war (eclipsing the cotton economy) and the contemporaneous growth of railroads reduced its importance; while it has remained a major trade route, it has never regained its pre–Civil War predominance. In the late 20th century, freight carried on the Mississippi is largely fuels and chemicals, sand and gravel, and other heavy materials. Oceangoing vessels can reach BATON ROUGE, Louisiana, between which and New Orleans is a heavily industrialized port and oil refinery zone. Above Baton Rouge is an 1830-mi/2950-km navigation channel, extending to Minneapolis, with locks at Keokuk, Iowa, and at the QUAD CITIES. The ILLINOIS WATERWAY, connecting the Mississippi with Chicago and the Great Lakes, is one of numerous canals and other works contributing to traffic in the Mississippi Basin. The Tennessee-TOMBIGBEE Waterway, connecting the Gulf of Mexico with the Tennessee R., is a recent attempt to divert some traffic from the Mississippi's lower reaches. In C Minnesota, the Mississippi passes through numerous small lakes and is dammed repeatedly. Below the Twin Cities, it flows openly and more slowly through rolling prairie terrain. CAPE GIRARDEAU, Missouri marks the N end of the river's alluvial plain; below this point, and esp. below CAIRO, Illinois, where the Ohio R. joins it from the E and it broadens to about 0.85 mi/1.4 km, the Mississippi passes through lowlands lying between high BLUFFS (which generally mark the edges of the floodplain, but in places meet the river itself). In its lower reaches it is well known for its winding, swampy course, for the OXBOWS, BAYOUS, and cutoff channels that flank it, and for the LEVEES that line it (although these are also important far to the N, in the Middle West). Below Baton Rouge the DELTA OF THE MISSISSIPPI RIVER begins; this is often confused with the state of Mississippi's DELTA, which lies between the river and the Yazoo. Major cities and historic sites on the river, in addition to Minneapolis–Saint Paul, include (N–S) LA CROSSE and PRAIRIE DU CHIEN, Wisconsin; DUBUQUE, Iowa; the Iowa-Illinois QUAD CITIES; BURLINGTON and KEOKUK, Iowa; QUINCY, Illinois; HANNIBAL, SAINT LOUIS, and CAPE GIRARDEAU, Missouri; CAIRO, Illinois; NEW MADRID, Missouri; MEMPHIS, Tennessee; GREENVILLE, VICKSBURG, and NATCHEZ, Mississippi; and BATON ROUGE and NEW ORLEANS, Louisiana. The Mississippi's periodic floods have prompted levee building and other engineering measures since the 18th century. The importance of floodplain agriculture is such that major effort and expenditure continues, although questions have been raised as to their ultimate effect. In the 20th century 1927 and 1993 have seen the most disastrous periods of high water. These episodes are among the many factors that have made "Old Man River" a central figure in American culture. **2.** 110 mi/180 km long, in SE Ontario. It flows NE from a series of lakes NNW of Kingston, passing through 11 mi/18 km–long Mississippi L., to Carleton Place, then NNW through ALMONTE to Lac des Chats (the Ottawa R.), just E of Arnprior and 27 mi/43 km W of Ottawa.

Mississippi Sound N reach of the Gulf of Mexico, S of W Alabama, Mississippi, and E Louisiana. Eighty-five mi/137 km E–W, it extends from Mobile Bay (E) to L. Borgne (W). Many islands lie in the sound, which is a busy section of the Gulf Intracoastal Waterway. Seafood production is important. Gulfport, Biloxi, and Pascagoula, Mississippi, are major ports.

Missoula city, pop. 42,918, seat of Missoula Co., W Montana, on the Clark Fork R. at the mouth of Hell Gate Canyon, 90 mi/145 km NW of Butte. Lewis and Clark camped at the site in 1806, and the settlement was founded as a trading post in 1860, serving as a supply point for gold miners. Its growth was spurred by the coming of the Northern Pacific Railroad in 1883. The city became a trade and shipping center for cattle and crops, lumber and paper mills were established, and it grew rapidly. The state university, now the University of Montana, was established in 1895, and has been a major cultural and economic factor. Near the entry points of several national forests, Missoula is the regional headquarters for both the Montana and US forest services, which maintain a smoke jumper training center nearby.

Missouri state of the C US, considered part of both the MIDDLE WEST and the Border SOUTH; 1990 pop. 5,117,073 (104.1% of 1980; rank: 15th); area 69,709 sq mi/180,546 sq km (rank: 21st); admitted to Union 1821 (24th). Capital: JEFFERSON CITY. Most populous cities: KANSAS CITY, SAINT LOUIS, SPRINGFIELD, INDEPENDENCE. Missouri is bordered S by Arkansas, with the SAINT FRANCIS R. forming part of the boundary of the BOOTHEEL REGION (SE). On the W are (S–N) Oklahoma; Kansas, with the MISSOURI R. forming part of the boundary; and Nebraska, also across the Missouri. On the N is Iowa, with the DES MOINES R. forming part of the NE boundary. Along the E is the MISSISSIPPI R., across which Missouri faces Illinois and, in the extreme SE, parts of Kentucky and Tennessee. Missouri's N half is part of the vast C lowlands of the US, including a section of the OSAGE PLAINS

(W). In the S are sections of the OZARK PLATEAU, here called the Springfield Plateau (SW) and Salem Plateau (SE), with TAUM SAUK Mt., the state's high point at 1772 ft/540 m, on the E. The Bootheel and adjoining SE counties lie in the Mississippi ALLUVIAL plain, where the state's low point (230 ft/70 m) is at the mouth of the Saint Francis R. The state's development and life have been largely determined by the junction here of North America's two largest rivers, which occurs just NW of Saint Louis, where the Missouri R. flows into the Mississippi R. A tribe dwelling near the junction, encountered in the 1670s by French explorers, gave its name to the river and state. The Missouri enters the state from the NW and flows across its midsection; its major tributaries include the Grand R., from the NW, and the OSAGE R., which flows E across the Ozark Plateau to join it just E of Jefferson City (C). Several rivers in the SE, including the Saint Francis and the BLACK, flow from the E edge of the Ozark Plateau into the Mississippi alluvial plain. The plains N of the Missouri R. are, like those of neighboring Iowa, extremely fertile, yielding soybeans and other field crops, much going to feed cattle and hogs. Settled by Southerners moving upriver, the region has long been called "Little Dixie." The Ozarks, an area of secluded valleys, natural springs, dense woods, and rocky terrain, were settled by APPALACHIAN hill people; at the time of the Civil War, the region was pro-Union. Until recent decades, the Ozarks remained relatively isolated and somewhat impoverished. They are now a major tourist area, drawing visitors interested in their distinctive folkways and arts; marketing of the Ozarks has reached special heights at BRANSON. The LAKE OF THE OZARKS, on the Osage R., is a regional recreational hub. Springfield is the gateway and commercial center for the area. On the E of the Ozarks is a district noted for lead, zinc, copper, and iron mining. The Bootheel is a piece of the post-PLANTATION South, with cotton raised on large bottomland farms. Home to the Osage, Missouri, and other groups, and first visited by French explorers in the 1670s, Missouri saw several short-lived French missionary and trading posts before SAINTE GENEVIEVE, its oldest city, was established in 1732. Control of the area changed hands between the French and Spanish in the 18th century, before the LOUISIANA PURCHASE brought it (1803) under US control. Early American development had primarily to do with transportation, esp. (after 1817) steamboat travel, as St. Louis, from which LEWIS AND CLARK had set out to explore the Purchase, became the gateway to the opening West. The Missouri valley provided a route from St. Louis to the junction of the Missouri and KANSAS (Kaw) rivers, where Independence, WESTPORT, and Westport Landing became jumping-off points for the SANTA FE and OREGON trails, and Kansas City later grew as a rail, stockyard, and industrial hub. A little farther up the river, SAINT JOSEPH became another trailhead (esp. for the PONY EXPRESS), rail center, and manufacturer. From the 1840s, American settlers in Missouri were joined by an influx of Germans, who quickly impressed their culture and industry on the region. Irish, Italians, and other Europeans arrived throughout the 19th century, gravitating toward the larger cities. The Civil War found Missouri, a slave state with many antislavery citizens, badly divided. Pro-Union forces quickly took control at Camp Jackson in St. Louis, but there were battles at BELMONT, LEXINGTON, and PILOT KNOB, and extensive, vicious guerrilla action throughout the war. An arsenal for the Union, Missouri after the war continued its rapid industrial development. Saint Louis has long been one of America's premier heavy industrial centers, noted in the 20th century for auto and aerospace manufacturing. Booming during the World Wars, it has declined since 1950, losing much of its pop. and industrial base to its suburbs as well as out of state. Kansas City, developing more recently, has more diverse light industries. JOPLIN and Springfield (SW) and St. Joseph are also industrial centers. Jefferson City's life revolves almost entirely around state government, for which its central location was chosen. The University of Missouri's main campus is at COLUMBIA (C). FORT LEONARD WOOD, in the Ozarks (SC), is the largest military facility in the state. In addition to the Ozarks and the two major cities, visitors to Missouri are drawn to sites associated with Mark Twain, in HANNIBAL and FLORIDA, and with Harry S Truman, in Independence and LAMAR. In the SE, NEW MADRID is noted as the center of a huge 1811 earthquake that altered the Mississippi's course. To its N is the old river city of CAPE GIRARDEAU, at the N extreme of the Mississippi alluvial plain; below this point the Mississippi widens, beginning the pattern of loops and bends for which its lower course is well known. Missouri's nickname, the "Show Me State," is attributed to a 19th-century politician who boasted of his constituents' skepticism.

Missouri Botanical Garden **1. Shaw's Garden** see under TOWER GROVE PARK, St. Louis. **2. Shaw Arboretum** see under GRAY SUMMIT.

Missouri Breaks eroded region in Garfield Co., EC Montana, N of the Piney Buttes. This area of deep gorges was cut by the Missouri R. when it created a new bed across the prairie after the last glaciation. The Breaks are rich with ancient fossils, particularly at Hell Creek, 20 mi/32 km N of Jordan. Part of this region is in the vast Charles M. Russell National Wildlife Refuge.

Missouri City city, pop. 36,176, Fort Bend and Harris counties, SE Texas, adjacent (SW) to Houston, and 18 mi/29 km from Downtown. It is a growing residential suburb.

Missouri River popularly, **the Big Muddy** (for its brown, sediment-filled waters), 2315 mi/3727 km long, in Montana, North Dakota, South Dakota, Nebraska, Iowa, Missouri, and Kansas. The longest tributary of the (slightly longer) MISSISSIPPI R., it constitutes with the latter a system with a total length of 3710 mi/5973 km, from the Missouri's farthest (Red Rock–Beaverhead–JEFFERSON, from SW Montana's Continental Divide) headstream to the Gulf of Mexico. The Missouri itself drains some 580,000 sq mi/1.5 million sq km, including parts of S Alberta and Saskatchewan. The river is thought to have flowed N to Hudson Bay until redirected by glacial blockages in the last Ice Age; it now marks for much of its course the southernmost extent of the continental ice sheet. The Missouri is formed at THREE FORKS, Montana, by the Jefferson, Gallatin, and Madison rivers. It flows NNW through Canyon Ferry L. and to the E of Helena, to the GATES OF THE MOUNTAINS, a famous gorge where mountain and plain meet. Turning NE, it passes through a series of cataracts at GREAT FALLS and proceeds to FORT BENTON, long the head of navigation. The MARIAS R. joins it from the NW, and it then winds in a generally ESE direction across the Great Plains section of Montana. The MUSSELSHELL R. joins it from the SW before it passes through the MISSOURI BREAKS region and FORT PECK Reservoir. The MILK R. joins it from the N just E of Fort Peck Dam. Continuing E, it is joined just past the North Dakota line, near FORT UNION, by the

YELLOWSTONE R., which has crossed S Montana. In North Dakota the Missouri winds E past Williston and into L. Sakakawea, formed by the GARRISON DAM. The LITTLE MISSOURI R. joins it here (from the SW), within the Fort Berthold Indian Reservation. Below the dam it turns SSE, past Bismarck, and into the N end of L. OAHE, formed by South Dakota's Oahe Dam. Still in North Dakota, the river begins to run along the E of the Standing Rock Indian Reservation. In South Dakota it passes Mobridge and continues along the E of the Cheyenne River Indian Reservation, where the CHEYENNE R. joins it in a W arm of L. Oahe. Below the Oahe Dam it passes Pierre and winds SE, collecting the WHITE R. (from the W) before reaching the Nebraska line. Flowing ESE as the South Dakota–Nebraska border, it receives the NIOBRARA R. from the W and the JAMES R. from the N, passes Yankton, and reaches SIOUX CITY, Iowa, where it receives the BIG SIOUX R. from the N and swings SSE, forming the Nebraska-Iowa border. Passing Omaha–Council Bluffs, it receives the PLATTE R. from the W. Farther SSE, the river forms the Missouri-Kansas border, winds past St. Joseph, Missouri, and reaches KANSAS CITY, the largest metropolitan area on its course, where the KANSAS R. joins it from the W. It then winds E and ESE across Missouri, passing Lexington, Boonville, and Jefferson City, to reach the Mississippi some 17 mi/27 km upstream from St. Louis, having circled around the city's N side. In Missouri the OSAGE and GASCONADE rivers (from the SW) are its major tributaries. The Missouri was a major Indian trade route, and early Plains villages were scattered along it when Europeans first saw it. In the 18th century French and British explorers and trappers knew parts of it, but the first thorough exploration of the river was by the 1803–06 Lewis and Clark expedition, which followed it to its headwaters in order to confirm the LOUISIANA PURCHASE and find a route for westward expansion. Other expeditions followed, and in 1819 steamboats began to use the river; by the 1830s Fort Benton, Montana, had been reached. Across the state of Missouri and to the NW, the Missouri and its valley were part of the trail system used during the westward migrations of the mid 19th century. River traffic diminished after the Civil War, as railroads spread through the West; the river (and its tributaries) began to be used more for irrigation and power generation. In 1944 the **Missouri River Basin Project** was authorized, embracing existing dam and reservoir projects and initiating others. Today, the main river has 7 dams, tributaries close to 100. Sioux City, 760 mi/1235 km upstream, is the head of navigation for barge traffic. The Missouri's dams create recreational and wildlife areas, control flooding and siltation, regulate flow, irrigate dry plains land, and generate power.

Misty Fjords National Monument covering some 3600 sq mi/9275 sq km on Revillagigedo I. (in the ALEXANDER ARCHIPELAGO) and the mainland of the Panhandle, in extreme SE Alaska, along the British Columbia border. Ketchikan is the gateway to a region reached chiefly by floatplane, and noted for its dense rain forest, waterfalls, and cliff faces.

Mitchel Field see under GARDEN CITY, New York.

Mitchell city, pop. 13,798, seat of Davison Co., SE South Dakota, 62 mi/100 km W of Sioux Falls. Founded in 1879, it is a trade, distribution, and shipping center for a rich grain, dairy, and livestock area. It has meat and food packing industries. Its huge Corn Palace, built in the Moorish style in 1892, has murals of colored corn along its entire exterior, which are changed annually at a harvest festival. Also situated here are the reconstructed Prehistoric Indian Village and Museum of Pioneer Life. The city is the seat of Dakota Wesleyan University (1885) and Mitchell Vocational Technical School (1990).

Mitchell, Mount highest point (6684 ft/2039 m) in North Carolina and in the US E of South Dakota's Black Hills, in the BLACK Mts., 20 mi/32 km NE of Asheville.

Mitchell Park municipal park in Milwaukee, Wisconsin, immediately S of the Menomonee R. and 1 mi/2 km S of Downtown. It is best known for its three geodesic domes, built for the Horticultural Conservatory in 1959–67.

Moab city, pop. 3971, seat of Grand Co., EC Utah, 2 mi/3km E of the Colorado R., which it overlooks, and 25 mi/40 km W of the Colorado line. Founded by Mormon missionaries (1855) and named for a biblical nation, it was a famous Wild West locale and figured in several Zane Grey novels. Today, its picturesque quality and mountainous scenery make Moab popular with tourists, and a favorite motion picture setting. It is a trade center for an area producing livestock, fruit, and truck crops. Near uranium, vanadium, salt, and potash mines, Moab is the site of a major uranium mill. It is headquarters for the Manti–La Sal National Forest (W and S) and gateway to Canyonlands National Park (12 mi/19 km SW) and Arches National Park (2 mi/3 km N).

Moberly city, pop. 12,839, Randolph Co., NC Missouri, 34 mi/54 km NNW of Columbia. In a farm, dairying, and coal mining area, it is a trade and processing center. Its manufactures include shoes, auto parts, and paints. Moberly Area Community College (1927) is here.

Mobile city, pop. 196,278, seat of Mobile Co. (pop. 378,643), extreme SW Alabama, at the mouth of the Mobile R., on the NW shore of Mobile Bay, 30 mi/48 km from the Gulf of Mexico. Established in 1710, it was governed by France (to 1763), Britain (1763–80), and Spain (1780–1813) before being claimed by the US. The only seaport in the state, it developed as a shipping center for cotton, lumber, and farm produce, trading with Europe and the West Indies. During the Civil War it continued in this role, despite the Federal blockade, until the Battle of Mobile Bay, in Aug. 1864; the city surrendered in March 1865. Mobile recovered by the early 1900s, and became a shipbuilding center and military supply base in World War II. It now houses diverse industries, producing wood products, aircraft engines, chemical and petroleum products, computer equipment, and textiles. It is home to Spring Hill College (1830), Mobile College (1961), and the University of South Alabama (1963). A tourist center, it is noted for its Mardi Gras and for its 37-mi/60-km Azalea Trail, which leads through residential sections. Among its suburbs are CHICKASAW, PRICHARD, SARALAND, and TILLMANS CORNER.

Mobile River 40 mi/64 km long, in SW Alabama. Formed by the confluence of the Alabama and Tombigbee rivers N of Mobile, it flows, alongside the Tensaw R. (just E, which forks from the Mobile), into the Gulf of Mexico, through Mobile Bay. The river has been the last part of an extensive cotton, lumber, and farm produce transporting system. It takes its name from the Mobile or Mauvila, who lived along its banks when Europeans first arrived in the 1540s. The port of Mobile is at its mouth. **Mobile Bay,** some 30 mi/48 km N–S and up to 20 mi/32 km wide, has a long commercial and strategic history. During the Civil War it remained an active

Confederate port, protected by Forts Gaines (W of its entrance, on DAUPHIN I.) and Morgan (E, at Mobile Point) until Aug. 1864, when a Union fleet under David Farragut passed the forts and took control. Today the area at the bay's SE, around GULF SHORES, is a booming tourist center.

Mobridge city, pop. 3768, Walworth Co., NC South Dakota, on the Missouri R., 90 mi/145 km W of Aberdeen and 25 mi/40 km S of the North Dakota border. Once the site of Arikara and Sioux villages, it was founded in 1906, and is a trade and shipping hub for a ranching and farming region. West of Mobridge is the burial site of Sitting Bull, killed near here (1890) and moved to this location from FORT YATES, North Dakota, in 1953.

Modesto city, pop. 164,730, seat of STANISLAUS Co., NC California, on the Tuolumne R., in the N San Joaquin Valley, 22 mi/35 km SSE of Stockton. Founded by the Central Pacific Railroad in 1870, it developed as a shipping and trade center for an irrigated region producing peaches, apricots, almonds, melons, beans, peas, and livestock. Gallo, America's largest winery, is here. Other industries include fruit and vegetable canning and freezing and the manufacture of bottles, chemicals, electrical equipment, and wood and paper products. Modesto Junior College (1921) is here.

Modoc Plateau high, semiarid plateau, with extensive lava beds and caves, blending (W) into the CASCADE Mts., in NE California and S Oregon. The WARNER Mts. are on the E. The PIT R. is its only major natural waterway, but it has a number of lakes, ponds, reservoirs, and mineral and hot springs, and includes CLEAR LAKE RESERVOIR and GOOSE L. The area was home to the Modoc, esp. around Lower Klamath (or Modoc) and Tule lakes, and was the site of the Modoc War of 1872–73. The Modoc National Wildlife Refuge, S of ALTURAS, is an important waterfowl breeding area along the PACIFIC FLYWAY. The plateau is heavily managed and used for grazing, farming, and lumbering (esp. pine); gold, gravel, pumice, and sand are extracted. The LAVA BEDS NATIONAL MONUMENT is on the W. The 1.65 million–ac/670,000-ha **Modoc National Forest,** entirely within California, covers most of Modoc Co., and extends into Siskiyou (W) and Shasta (S) counties.

Moffat Tunnel see under WINTER PARK, Colorado.

Moffett Field Naval Air Station: see under MOUNTAIN VIEW, California.

Mogollon Mountains range E of the San Francisco R. and N of SILVER CITY, in WC New Mexico, along the SW edge of the GILA NATIONAL FOREST. Elevations include Whitewater Baldy (10,892 ft/3320 m), the high point, and Mogollon Baldy Peak (10,778 ft/3285 m). Gold and silver mining boomed here in 1912–15.

Mogollon Plateau also, **Mogollon Mesa** tableland, c.7000–8000 ft/2130–2440 m high, in EC Arizona. Its S escarpment is part of the **Mogollon Rim,** a natural barrier extending diagonally across EC Arizona, the dividing line between the COCONINO PLATEAU (the COLORADO PLATEAU) to the NE and the GREAT BASIN to the SW. The rim is sometimes referred to as the Mogollon Mts., not to be confused with the Mogollon Mts. of W New Mexico. The Mogollon, who lived in the area 2000 years ago, may have been the ancestors of the Zuñi.

Mohave see MOJAVE.

Mohawk Mountain 1680 ft/512 m, highest point in the LITCHFIELD HILLS of Connecticut, near Goshen. Mohawk State Forest and Mohawk Mountain State Park comprise 3504 ac/1419 ha. A beacon maintained by local tribes to warn of invasion by Mohawks is said to have inspired the mountain's name.

Mohawk River 140 mi/225 km long, in C New York. It drains an area of 3412 sq mi/8837 sq km. It rises in several small streams and Delta L., near Rome in Oneida Co. At Rome it begins to parallel the NEW YORK STATE BARGE CANAL, once the ERIE CANAL, and winds E across the bed of prehistoric L. Iroquois. It then continues through a steep glacial valley, flowing over falls at Utica, the largest city in the Mohawk Valley. Continuing past Herkimer, Little Falls, and Amsterdam to Schenectady, the river widens and meanders across the bed of another vanished lake, then flows E to join the HUDSON R. at COHOES. Most of the Mohawk's course is canalized as part of the New York State Barge Canal, and the use of the Hudson and Mohawk valleys for barge traffic after 1825 was instrumental in opening the West and making New York City America's economic capital. The Mohawk is paralleled by the New York State Thruway between Schenectady and Utica.

Mohawk Trail **1.** scenic highway (Route 2) in Berkshire and Franklin counties, NW Massachusetts. Running 30 mi/48 km between Greenfield (E) and North Adams (W), it follows the path of a trail established by Mohawk Indians. In the 19th century, a major rail route, for which the HOOSAC TUNNEL was built, followed the path. **2** in C New York, route from the Schenectady area (E) to Rome (W2, heavily traveled by westward migrants in the 18th and early 19th centuries. It comprised a series of turnpikes along the Mohawk R., and lost importance as the Erie Canal (1825) and railroads opened. Passing S of the Adirondacks and N of the Catskills, it was one of the easiest ways through America's eastern mountain "spine."

Mohonk 5600-ac/2270-ha nature preserve on the N shore of L. Mohonk, in Ulster Co., SE New York, in the Shawangunk Mts., 4 mi/6 km W of New Paltz. A scenic area with numerous trails, it encloses a sprawling Victorian (1870) resort, Mohonk Mountain House, still in operation.

Mojave Desert also, **Mohave** 15,000–sq mi/38,900–sq km section of the GREAT BASIN, mostly in San Bernardino, also in Kern and Los Angeles counties, S California. It borders the SONORAN DESERT on the E, at the Nevada and Arizona lines, and merges into the COLORADO DESERT (S). The Tehachapi Mts. form its W, the San Gabriel, San Bernardino, and San Jacinto mountains its SW, boundaries. The JOSHUA TREE National Park is on the S, DEATH VALLEY on the N. Sparse, hardy flora and fauna survive here on 5–7 in/13–18 cm of annual rainfall; the mountains to the W and SW form a shield from moist Pacific air. Summer temperatures rise to 125° F/52° C. The desert was once an inland sea, and is covered in part by COLORADO R. sediments. Its only large stream, the **Mojave R.,** flows N from the San Bernardinos, then E, largely underground, to Soda L., a usually dry sink 50 mi/80 km E of Barstow. Granite, gold, silver, tungsten, iron, salt, borax, and potash are extracted in various areas. The Mojave became in World War II a major military area; TWENTYNINE PALMS, EDWARDS AIR FORCE BASE, the CHOCOLATE Mts., and other sites are important today. Irrigated agriculture (alfalfa, citrus, etc.) is carried on, esp. along the SW edge. BARSTOW and VICTORVILLE, in the W, and NEEDLES, in the E, are the major older settlements; suburban growth is now moving into the desert from the Los Angeles area (SW).

Interstates 15 (from Las Vegas, Nevada) and 40 (the former ROUTE 66) cross the Mojave; railroads generally follow the Mojave R. course as they approach Los Angeles.

Mojave National Preserve see EAST MOJAVE NATIONAL SCENIC AREA, California.

Mokelumne River 140 mi/225 km long, in EC California. Its North Fork, its longest headstream, rises in the Sierra Nevada near Ebbets Pass, in Alpine Co., and flows generally WSW to LODI, then to the SAN JOAQUIN R., 20 mi/32 km NW of Stockton. The Pardee Reservoir (impounded 1929), 25 mi/40 km ENE of Lodi, provides water to cities in the E San Francisco Bay area, and the river has also been dammed for power. **Mokelumne Hill,** a hamlet 7 mi/11 km ENE of the Pardee Reservoir, was one of the wildest towns on the MOTHER LODE during the 1850s–70s gold days.

Moline city, pop. 43,202, Rock Island Co., NW Illinois, on the N bank of the Rock R. and the E bank of the Mississippi R. It is one of the QUAD CITIES. It was founded as a steamboat port in the early 1830s. After inventing an improved steel plow, John Deere set up a workshop here in 1847, and Moline developed into a major center of plow production by the late 19th century. The company Deere started is still headquartered here. Belgian immigrants also established an early lace industry in Moline. In addition to farm implements and machinery, local manufactures now include elevators and escalators, machine tools, foundry equipment, and metal products. Black Hawk College (1946) is here. The Quad City Airport is immediately S, across the Rock R.

Molokai fifth-largest (261 sq mi/676 sq km) island of HAWAII, in Maui Co., 22 mi/35 km E of Oahu, across the Kaiwi Channel. Lanai lies 10 mi/16 km S, Maui 10 mi/16 km SE. Some 38 mi/61 km E–W and up to 10 mi/16 km wide, Molokai reaches 4970 ft/1515 m in the E, at Kamakou; the NE coast is noted for its 3300-ft/1000-m sea cliffs, said to be the world's highest, and for its heavy rains, waterfalls (1750 ft/533 m at Kahiwa Falls), and deep ravines (including the Halawa Valley). In the middle of the N coast is the isolated KALAUPAPA PENINSULA, home of a famed leper colony; the peninsula is unofficially considered a separate (Kalawao, pop. 130) county. The W of Molokai is lower, an eroded plain dominated by a huge cattle ranch. Kaunakakei (unincorporated, pop. 2658), on the S coast, is the island's main settlement. Molokai, traditionally a spiritual center and refuge from other parts of Hawaii, is now largely a resort for Oahuans. Its soil has not supported large-scale agriculture, and tourism is its major industry.

Monadnock, Mount also, **Great Monadnock** isolated, barren-topped metamorphic mountain (3165 ft/965 m) in the town of Jaffrey, SW New Hampshire, popular with hikers for its panoramic views. It gave its name to the geologic term *monadnock*.

Monadnock Building historic office building constructed 1891 on W. Jackson Blvd., in the LOOP, Chicago, Illinois. Designed by Burnham & Root, it is the last of a generation of masonry skyscrapers, employing walls 15 ft/4.58 m thick at the base to support its 16 stories. Its tapered sides and "Chicago" bay windows contribute to its fame as a landmark. Steel skeleton construction, introduced at the time it was being built, became the norm for tall buildings.

Monahans city, pop. 8101, seat of Ward Co., also in Winkler Co., far W Texas, 35 mi/56 km SW of Odessa, at the SW edge of the PERMIAN BASIN. Founded in 1881 on the Texas & Pacific Railroad, it is a ranch area trade center with oil, gas, and pecan processing industries. The **Monahans Sandhills State Park** (3840 ac/1555 ha) preserves part of a natural barrier that caused hardship to westbound pioneers but in which Indians knew where to find water; the park is noted for its dwarf oak forest. The Monahans Sandhills are a small part of the Texas Sandhills region, which stretches to the N.

Mona Passage ocean body, 75 mi/120 km wide, separating Puerto Rico (E) from the Dominican Republic. Known for its treacherous currents and winds, it is a major gateway between the Atlantic Ocean (N) and the Caribbean Sea (S). The **Isla Mona,** in midpassage 48 mi/77 km WSW of Mayagüez, is noted for its 200-ft/61-m cliffs and caves. Some 25 sq mi/65 sq km in area, it is a wildlife preserve.

Monashee Mountains N–S trending range, 200 mi/320 km long, part of the Columbia Mts. section of the Rocky Mts., in SE British Columbia. They lie W of and parallel to the SELKIRK Mts. and the Columbia R., extending from near the Washington border (S) to near the SE end of the CARIBOO Mts. (N). Hallam Peak (10,560 ft/3219 m), near the N end, is the high point. The CANADIAN PACIFIC RAILWAY crossed the range at Eagle Pass (see CRAIGELLACHIE), W of Revelstoke, in 1885, and the TRANS-CANADA HIGHWAY now also follows this route. In the S copper, gold, silver, lead, and zinc have been mined.

Moncton city, pop. 57,010, Westmorland Co., SE New Brunswick, on the Petitcodiac R., 90 mi/145 km NE of Saint John. It was settled by Pennsylvania Dutch and Acadians in the 18th century, and known as The Bend, then became a largely English-speaking shipbuilding center in the mid 19th century. In the 1870s, regional railways made it their Maritimes hub, and they were a major employer until cutbacks in 1988. Today telemarketing has taken a leading role, along with oil and gas refineries, food and feed processors, various light manufactures, and fisheries. Modern Moncton is a fast-growing commercial and distribution center. Its tidal BORE, driven upstream from the Bay of Fundy, is a tourist attraction, as is Magnetic Hill, where an optical illusion makes cars seem to roll uphill. Although French speakers are in the minority, the city is regarded as an Acadian center; the francophone Université de Moncton (1963) is here.

Monessen city, pop. 9901, Westmoreland Co., SW Pennsylvania, 20 mi/32 km SSE of Pittsburgh, on the Monongahela R. An industrial city, it produces steel and tin, glass, bituminous coal, and dairy products.

Monguagon battle site: see under TRENTON, Michigan.

Monhegan Island 2.5 sq mi/6.5 sq km, in Lincoln Co., SW Maine. Monhegan Plantation, pop. 87, includes Monhegan village and neighboring Manana I., in the Gulf of Maine, 11 mi/18 km ESE of Pemaquid Point. It is believed that surrounding waters, considered one of the best fishing grounds in the world, were fished by Europeans from the time of Columbus. Captain John Smith landed here in 1614. Monhegan was a base for explorers, port of call for Europe-bound vessels, trade and shipbuilding center, and sometime pirate stronghold. In 1813, the US privateer *Enterprise* defeated the British *Boxer* in an offshore battle. Since 1878, prominent artists have painted here, including Rockwell Kent, who popularized the island as an arts colony. Cathedral Woods and 150-ft/46-m cliffs, along with the artists, draw visitors. Lobstering is the chief year-round occupation.

Monk's Mound see under COLLINSVILLE, Illinois.

Monmouth **1.** city, pop. 9489, seat of Warren Co., WC Illinois, 14 mi/23 km W of Galesburg. Its economy is based on the area's beef and corn. The city produces processed meats and pet foods, as well as pottery (manufactured here for over a century), farm implements, and boats. Settled in the 1830s, it is the seat of Monmouth College (1853). **2.** city, pop. 6288, Polk Co., NW Oregon, 11 mi/18 km SW of Salem. It is the seat of Western Oregon State College (1853), the oldest liberal arts college in the state.

Monmouth County 472 sq mi/1222 sq km, pop. 553,124, in EC New Jersey, bordered by the Atlantic Ocean (E) and Raritan and Sandy Hook bays (N). Its seat is FREEHOLD. The county has many coastal resorts, including KEANSBURG in the N and LONG BRANCH and ASBURY PARK in the E. Inland portions contain fertile farmland, where vegetables are the main product; fruit, dairy products, and poultry are also produced. There is some manufacturing, notably of processed foods, chemicals, wood products, and electronics. Suburbanization has moved through the county in recent decades.

Monmouth Courthouse see under FREEHOLD, New Jersey.

Monmouth Junction see under SOUTH BRUNSWICK, New Jersey.

Monocacy River 60 mi/100 km long, in Pennsylvania and Maryland. It is formed S of Gettyburg at the Pennsylvania/Maryland border by the confluence of several small creeks. It winds its way SSW through Maryland to the Potomac R., 6 mi/10 km SE of Point of Rocks. The battle of Monocacy, in which Union forces under Lew Wallace delayed Jubal Early's advance on Washington, was fought along it just SE of Frederick on July 9, 1864.

Mono Lake in EC California, between the Nevada border (E) and the Sierra Nevada (W), 85 mi/137 km SSE of Carson City, Nevada. Remnant of an ancient inland sea, it may be the oldest body of water in North America. At an elevation of 6425 ft/1958 m, it is roughly oval, and up to 13 mi/21 km wide. Its highly saline and alkaline water fosters large populations of brine shrimp and flies, attracting California gulls, grebes, phalaropes, and other birds. Towers of calcified rock (tufa), up to 13,000 years old, appear along the shoreline. A food source for the Paiute and other peoples, Mono is now largely recreational. Water from its feeder streams has been diverted to Los Angeles, 275 mi/445 km to the S, by aqueducts completed in 1941 and 1970, lowering the lake and causing a long battle between local residents and environmentalists and urban interests in Southern California.

Monomoy Island peninsula, at times an island, in Barnstable Co., SE Massachusetts, extending 10 mi/16 km S of the town of CHATHAM on Cape Cod. A National Wildlife Refuge here covers 2700 ac/1094 ha, and is an important migratory-bird site.

Monona city, pop. 8637, Dane Co., S Wisconsin, on L. Monona, 10 mi/16 km E of Madison. Situated in a dairy farming region, it is a suburb of Madison.

Monona, Lake 4 mi/6 km long and 3 mi/5 km wide, in Dane Co., SC Wisconsin. It is one of the FOUR LAKES chain connected by the Yahara R. MADISON lies on its W shore and the city of Monona on its E.

Monongahela National Forest 900,000 ac/365,000 ha, in E West Virginia. In the Allegheny Mts., it includes SPRUCE KNOB (4862 ft/1483 m), the highest point in West Virginia; tributaries to both the Ohio (W) and Potomac (E) rivers; ski resorts, hiking trails, caves, and rock climbing locations. The GREENBRIER R. runs through it.

Monongahela River 128 mi/206 km long, in West Virginia and Pennsylvania. It is formed by the Tygart and West Fork rivers near Fairmont, in Marion Co., West Virginia. It flows NNE past MORGANTOWN and N into Pennsylvania, where it is joined by the Cheat R. at Point Marion. It then flows a winding northerly route through W Pennsylvania, passing CALIFORNIA, MONESSEN, DONORA, and CLAIRTON. It is joined by the Youghiogheny R. at MCKEESPORT, and turns NW through the Pittsburgh area, joining the ALLEGHENY R. at the GOLDEN TRIANGLE to form the OHIO R. The Monongahela has been an important freight route.

Monroe **1.** town, pop. 16,896, Fairfield Co., SW Connecticut, on the Housatonic R., 10 mi/16 km N of Bridgeport. It includes the villages of Stepney Depot and Stevenson, where a dam across the Housatonic forms L. Zoar. The area is agricultural, with some manufacturing, but has become increasingly suburbanized with the influx of corporate offices into the county. **2.** city, pop. 9759, seat of Walton Co., NC Georgia, 40 mi/64 km ENE of Atlanta. Trade center of a cotton producing area, it also manufactures textiles. **3.** city, pop. 54,909, seat of Ouachita Parish, NE Louisiana, on the Ouachita R., between the cotton country of the Mississippi Alluvial Plain (E) and an upland timber, fruit, and cattle region (W), 69 mi/111 km WNW of Vicksburg, Mississippi. The area was settled in the early 18th century by fur trappers and traders. In 1785 a French group under Jean-Baptiste Filhiol established Fort Miró as a trading post; it was renamed in 1819. Together with WEST MONROE, across the river, it has long been the market center of agricultural NE Louisiana, where lumbering and the raising of cotton, soybeans, and cattle are dominant. The Monroe natural gas field, one of the largest in the US, was discovered in 1916, and forms the basis for chemical and carbon-black industries. Monroe also manufactures paper, furniture, and fertilizer. It is home to Northeast Louisiana University (1931). **4.** city, pop. 22,902, seat of Monroe Co., SE Michigan, on L. Erie at the mouth of the R. Raisin, 34 mi/55 km SW of Detroit. Michigan's only L. Erie port, it manufactures and ships many items, especially auto parts, paper products, furniture, and castings. It was established by French-Canadians (c.1780) as Frenchtown, a fort and trading post. In the War of 1812, Monroe was the site of the Battle of Frenchtown and the River Raisin Massacre (Jan. 1813), in which Indians allied with the British defeated US troops. It was also pivotal in the bloodless Toledo War, a boundary conflict between Michigan and Ohio. The boyhood home of George A. Custer is here. The city is the seat of Monroe County Community College (1964). Sterling State Park is just E on the lake. **5.** city, pop. 16,127, seat of Union Co., S North Carolina, 23 mi/37 km SE of Charlotte, near the South Carolina border. An agricultural market and shipping center, it processes poultry and has various light manufactures. **6.** city, pop. 10,241, seat of Green Co., S Wisconsin, 30 mi/48 km NW of Beloit. It was settled by Swiss, who established its cheese industry in 1865. Today many of its residents are of Swiss origin, and the city is one of the state's main cheese producers and distributors. A cheese fair is held annually. Other industries include brewing beer, churning butter, and manufacturing cheesemaking equipment and wood products.

Monroe County **1.** 557 sq mi/1443 sq km, pop. 133,600, in extreme SE Michigan, bounded by L. Erie (E) and Ohio (S) and drained by the R. Raisin. Its seat is MONROE. The county's agriculture emphasizes livestock, dairying, field crops, and nurseries. There are limestone and salt deposits, and manufacturing at Dundee and Monroe. The Fermi Atomic Power Plant (1963), built on the L. Erie shore 7 mi/11 km NE of Monroe, near Newport, experienced a meltdown and was shut down in 1972. It was replaced by Fermi II (1985). **2.** 663 sq mi/1717 sq km, pop. 713,968, in W New York, bounded by L. Ontario (N) and crossed by the New York State Barge Canal. Its seat and largest city is ROCHESTER, also its major industrial center. Rochester's metropolitan area occupies a sizable part of the county's NC region, where there is considerable suburban development. The balance of the county is noted for its apple orchards, and produces vegetables, grains, and dairy products. There are many resorts along L. Ontario.

Monroeville borough, pop. 29,169, Allegheny Co., W Pennsylvania, on the Pennsylvania Turnpike, 13 mi/21 km E of Pittsburgh. In the 19th century, it was a stop on the Philadelphia–Pittsburgh stagecoach run; its early growth came from its function as a transportation hub. Today Monroeville has steel, coal, and nuclear research centers and is a commercial center for the surrounding townships and boroughs. It is home to the Boyce campus of Allegheny Community College.

Monrovia city, pop. 35,761, Los Angeles Co., SW California, 15 mi/24 km NE of downtown Los Angeles, in the foothills of the San Gabriel Mts. Settled in the 1880s, it was long a packing and trade center for an area producing citrus fruit, avocados, poultry, and dairy items. It now has a wide range of manufactures, including electronic equipment, plastics, chemicals, and various machinery.

Monsey unincorporated village, pop. 13,986, in Ramapo township, Rockland Co., SE New York, 5 mi/8 km E of Suffern. It is a largely residential suburb on the New York State Thruway.

Monson town, pop. 7776, Hampden Co., SW Massachusetts, 13 mi/21 km E of Springfield. Largely rural, it produces woolens and granite, and has dairying and poultry and truck farming.

Montana state of the NW US, one of the MOUNTAIN STATES; 1990 pop. 799,065 (101.6% of 1980; rank: 44th); area 147,046 sq mi/380,849 sq km (rank: 4th); admitted to Union 1889 (41st). Capital: HELENA. Most populous cities: BILLINGS, GREAT FALLS, MISSOULA, BUTTE, Helena. Montana is bordered E by South Dakota and North Dakota; N by (E–W) Saskatchewan, Alberta, and British Columbia; W by Idaho; and S by (W–E) Idaho and Wyoming. Despite its name (proposed in the 1860s, from the Latin or Spanish), two-thirds of the state lies in the GREAT PLAINS, rising gradually from 2000–2500 ft/610–760 m in the E. In the W are NNW–SSE trending ranges of the Northern ROCKY Mts., in a band extending some 120 mi/190 km E from the Idaho line. Chief among these ranges are the BITTERROOTS; in the SW the CONTINENTAL DIVIDE follows their crest along the border. It then swings E to the Butte area, and NNW again along the crest of the Lewis Range, into Canada. Among subranges of the Northern Rockies in Montana are the CABINET and FLATHEAD mountains. Outliers (WC) include the LITTLE BELT Mts. In the extreme NW is a section of British Columbia's PURCELL Mts. To the SE of the Northern Rockies, straddling the Wyoming border, is the northernmost section of the Middle Rocky Mts., including part of the ABSAROKA and BEARTOOTH ranges. GRANITE PEAK, in the Beartooths, is (at 12,799 ft/3904 m) the high point in Montana. The MISSOURI R. rises in SW Montana; its uppermost headwater is the Red Rock R., which rises on the Idaho border W of Yellowstone National Park, and flows into the Beaverhead R., then the JEFFERSON R. The Jefferson, MADISON, and Gallatin rivers meet at THREE FORKS to form the Missouri, which flows generally N past Helena and Great Falls, NE to FORT BENTON (its head of navigation), and then generally E across the state. The Missouri's major tributary, the YELLOWSTONE R., flows from Wyoming into SW Montana, and then in a generally ENE direction across the state, meeting the Missouri at the North Dakota line, near FORT UNION. Leading cities along the Yellowstone include LIVINGSTON, Billings, MILES CITY, and GLENDIVE. Major tributaries of the Missouri in Montana include the MARIAS, MILK, and MUSSELSHELL rivers. Tributaries of the Yellowstone, flowing N from Wyoming, include the BIGHORN, ROSEBUD, and POWDER rivers. To the W of the Continental Divide, the KOOTENAI and CLARK FORK rivers are part of the Pacific-bound Columbia R. system. When first seen by whites (at some unrecorded point in the late 18th century), Montana was home to Plains tribes including the Crow, Blackfeet, and Cheyenne; in the mountains lived Flathead and Shoshone, among others. The LOUISIANA PURCHASE (1803) embraced the region as far as the Continental Divide, and was explored in 1804–06 by LEWIS AND CLARK, whose route took them to the headwaters of the Jefferson R. and then across the Continental Divide at Lemhi Pass (see under BEAVERHEAD NATIONAL FOREST). Fur trappers and explorers soon expanded knowledge of the mountains and other routes through them, and by the 1830s Missouri R. steamboats reached Fort Benton. In the 1860s, gold strikes in the SW, esp. at BANNACK and VIRGINIA CITY, brought the first real white influx, and stirred conflict with local tribes along the BOZEMAN TRAIL and elsewhere. Montana separated from the Idaho Territory in 1864. The 1877 surrender of the NEZ PERCE in the Bear Paw Mts. brought Montana's Indian wars to an end, and in the 1880s the NORTHERN PACIFIC and GREAT NORTHERN (via the HI-LINE) railroads crossed the territory, by then busy with ranching in the E and mining in the SW. The production of copper in the Butte-ANACONDA area dominated the economy through the early 20th century, a period during which the open-range cattle industry, devastated by 1886–87 blizzards, was largely replaced in the E with fenced-in HOMESTEADS. World War I wheat demands made farms boom, but at the end of the war they declined, and remained depressed until World War II. Today, Montana's extractive industries include coal mining in the SE, esp. at Colstrip, in Rosebud Co.; oil drilling esp. in the E, around Glendive, in the Williston Basin (extending into North Dakota); and production of copper, gold, lead, zinc, and other metals in the mountains of the W. Lumbering has also been important, and ranching and wheat growing remain the mainstay of the plains economy. Refining and processing of the state's raw materials dominate the small manufacturing sector. Tourism and outdoor recreation have become increasingly important: GLACIER NATIONAL PARK (NW); the high mountains and approaches to Yellowstone National Park (SW); skiing at BIG SKY and other resorts; fishing and boating on the Yellowstone and Missouri and their tributaries; and the FLATHEAD, Beaverhead, DEERLODGE, and other NATIONAL FORESTS, and WILDERNESS AREAS in the mountains, for which Helena, Missoula, and KALISPELL are major gateways, all draw visitors. The FLATHEAD, BLACKFEET,

FORT BELKNAP, FORT PECK, NORTHERN CHEYENNE, and CROW (site of the LITTLE BIGHORN National Battlefield) INDIAN RESERVATIONS, as well as sites including POMPEY'S PILLAR, Fort Union, and the Gates of the Mountains (in the HELENA NATIONAL FOREST) attract esp. the historically inclined. The increasing size of individual farms has been one factor in keeping Montana from rapid pop. growth; while the state's natural attractions and outdoor lifestyle continue to attract new residents, significant gain has occurred chiefly when (as in the 1970s) there have been booms in the energy industry. Malmstrom Air Force Base, at Great Falls, was a crucial Cold War bomber base, and the state had numerous intercontinental missile sites. The University of Montana is at Missoula. RED LODGE is a noted cultural center. Montana is officially the "Treasure State," and is popularly called "Big Sky Country."

Montauk Point E tip of Long Island, in East Hampton town, Suffolk Co., SE New York, at the end of the SOUTH FORK, 115 mi/185 km ENE of New York City. It is the easternmost point in New York. A lighthouse has existed on the point since 1745. The unincorporated resort village of **Montauk** (pop. 3001) is 5 mi/8 km SW.

Montclair **1.** city, pop. 28,434, San Bernardino Co., SW California, 32 mi/51 km E of downtown Los Angeles and immediately SSE of Claremont. Incorporated in 1956, it is a residential suburb with a lively shopping economy and some light industry. **2.** township, pop. 37,729, Essex Co., NE New Jersey, 5 mi/8 km NW of Newark. Settled in 1666, it was part of Newark until 1812, and was united with Bloomfield until 1868, when it became a separate town. Today it is a popular hillside commuter residential area, with a busy suburban business center. The UPPER MONTCLAIR section is the most affluent part of the town.

Monteagle town, pop. 1138, Grundy and Marion counties, S Tennessee, on the Cumberland Plateau, 5 mi/8 km NE of Sewanee. A summer resort and winemaking center, it is also home to Tennessee's largest Chautauqua (educational) organization.

Montebello **1.** city, pop. 59,564, Los Angeles Co., SW California, 10 mi/16 km E of downtown Los Angeles. Oil was discovered in the vicinity in 1896; the city was incorporated in 1920, and is a largely Hispanic residential and industrial suburb just SE of EAST LOS ANGELES. Its varied manufactures include machinery, plastics, and cosmetics. **2.** village, pop. 1022, Papineau census division, S Québec, on the Ottawa R., 38 mi/62 km ENE of Ottawa. Louis-Joseph Papineau, former PATRIOTE leader, made his home here in the 1840s; his manor remains, and the Château Montebello (1930) is a noted resort hotel and conference center.

Montecito see under SANTA BARBARA, California.

Monteregian Hills French, **Montérégies** series of isolated small mountains in the St. Lawrence Lowlands of S Québec, igneous plugs (volcanic intrusions) that have survived the erosion of surrounding material, and that now dominate local landscapes. Montréal's Mt. ROYAL is the best known. Others are Mont Saint-Bruno (see SAINT BRUNO-DE-MONTARVILLE); MONT SAINT-HILAIRE; Mont Saint-Gregoire (751 ft/229 m); Mont Rougemont (1201 ft/366 m); and Mont Yamaska (1348 ft/411 m).

Monterey city, pop. 31,954, Monterey Co., WC California, on the N side of the Monterey Peninsula and the S end of Monterey Bay, 85 mi/137 km SSE of San Francisco. Founded as a MISSION and PRESIDIO in 1770, it was an important port and the capital of ALTA CALIFORNIA from the 1780s to the 1840s; Americans took control in 1846. In 1849 the constitutional convention leading to California statehood met at Colton Hall. Formerly a leading fishing and whaling port, Monterey now bases its economy on tourism. Cannery Row, made famous by novelist John Steinbeck, houses the popular Monterey Bay Aquarium (1984); Fisherman's Wharf (1846) and historic sites, as well as other attractions on the peninsula and bay, draw throngs of visitors. Nearby military installations, esp. FORT ORD, are also important. Monterey Peninsula College (1947) and the Monterey Institute of International Studies (1955) are in the city, which has long been a retreat for artists and writers, and is also the site of the Monterey Jazz Festival.

Monterey Bay crescent-shaped inlet of the Pacific Ocean, 65 mi/105 km S of San Francisco, in WC California. Twenty-seven mi/43 km N–S, it is bordered on the N by the Santa Cruz Mts., on the S by the Monterey Peninsula. On it are the cities of Santa Cruz (N) and Monterey (S), many resorts, and FORT ORD. The SALINAS and Pajaro rivers empty into it.

Monterey Park city, pop. 60,738, Los Angeles Co., SW California, 6 mi/10 km E of downtown Los Angeles, and immediately NE of EAST LOS ANGELES. Primarily a residential suburb, it has some light industry, making electronic devices, air conditioners, and printed materials. East Los Angeles College (1945) is here. The city has recently attracted many Chinese immigrants, and now has an Asian majority and many Chinese-owned businesses. It also has a large Hispanic minority.

Monterey Peninsula rocky, windswept peninsula in WC California, on the Pacific Ocean between Monterey Bay (N) and Carmel Bay (S). Five mi/8 km N–S and 3 mi/5 km E–W, it is noted for the scenery along its Seventeen-Mile Drive. The cities of PACIFIC GROVE and MONTEREY, as well as Asilomar State Beach and PEBBLE BEACH, are on the peninsula; Point Pinos lighthouse is at its NW tip, and CARMEL-BY-THE-SEA is immediately S.

Monte Rio unincorporated community, pop. 1058, Sonoma Co., NW California, 56 mi/90 km NNW of San Francisco. This resort and lumbering community is home to Bohemian Grove, a 2500-ac/1000-ha retreat in the redwoods belonging to the Bohemian Club of San Francisco, which holds a July encampment. Although the club, begun in the 1870s, formerly embraced such bohemians as Jack London, it is now noted for the high jinks of its rich and powerful, and exclusively male, members.

Montevallo city, pop. 4239, Shelby Co., C Alabama, 30 mi/48 km SSW of Birmingham. Seat of the University of Montevallo (1896), it was settled in 1815.

Montezuma Castle National Monument see under CAMP VERDE, Arizona.

Montezuma Marshes see under L. CAYUGA, New York.

Montgomery **1.** city, pop. 187,106, state capital and seat of Montgomery Co. (pop. 209,805), SC Alabama, on the S bank of the Alabama R., 84 mi/136 km SSE of Birmingham. Long inhabited by Alabama tribes, the area was settled by Americans following the opening of the Territory of Alabama for sale in 1817. Montgomery was created in 1819, when the settlements of Alabama and East Alabama were consolidated. The city served as the first capital of the Confederacy, in Feb.–July 1861, and was captured by Union troops in April 1865. By 1900 the longtime cotton market center had industrialized. In Dec. 1955, black residents began a yearlong boycott of the city's buses, protesting segregation; the action catapulted the Rev. Dr. Martin Luther King, Jr., to fame, and Montgomery remained a center of the civil rights movement through the mid 1960s. Situated in the BLACK BELT, the city is a processing and shipping center for local farm and lumber products, and manufactures furniture, fertilizer, textiles, pharmaceuticals, electronics equipment, and brick. Its economy is further augmented by the presence of adjacent Gunter (NE) and Maxwell (W) Air Force bases; the latter houses the Air University, and both have various other military educational facilities. Huntingdon College (1854), Alabama State University (1874), Faulkner University (1942), and Auburn University at Montgomery (1967) are here. The Alabama Capitol (1857) and the Dexter Ave. Baptist Church, where King preached (1954–60), face each other across Dexter Ave. The Civil Rights Memorial (1989), a block away on Washington St., remembers those who died in the civil rights movement. **2.** city, pop. 9753, Hamilton Co., SW Ohio, a residential suburb 8 mi/13 km NE of Cincinnati. **3.** city, pop. 2449, Fayette and Kanawha counties, SC West Virginia, on the Kanawha R., 22 mi/35 km SE of Charleston. The seat of West Virginia Institute of Technology (1895), it is in a bituminous coal, natural gas, and oil producing area.

Montgomery County **1.** 495 sq mi/1282 sq km, pop. 757,027, in C Maryland. ROCKVILLE is its seat. The Patuxent R. is its NE, the Potomac R. its W and S, boundary. A rolling Piedmont area drained by Rock Creek, it is a traditionally agricultural county with many affluent suburbs of Washington, D.C. (S), including Chevy Chase, Bethesda, Rockville, Gaithersburg, and Takoma Park. There are many government installations. **2.** 404 sq mi/1046 sq km, pop. 51,981, in EC New York. It is cut from E to W by the Mohawk R. and the New York State Barge Canal, and lies in the Mohawk Valley. Its seat is Fonda; its largest city is AMSTERDAM. There are many farms in this fertile valley county, and dairying is an important component of its economy. **3.** 458 sq mi/1186 sq km, pop. 573,809, in SW Ohio, intersected by the Great Miami, Mad, and Stillwater rivers. Englewood Dam and the Miamisburg Mound State Memorial are here. Its seat is the industrial city of DAYTON, which, along with its suburbs, takes up its E half. Agriculture includes dairy, grain, livestock, tobacco, and truck farming. There are sand and gravel deposits, and cement is manufactured. **4.** 486 sq mi/1259 sq km, pop. 678,111, in SE Pennsylvania. Its seat is NORRISTOWN. Montgomery Co. is immediately N, NW, and W of Philadelphia, and contains suburbs including the townships of ABINGTON, CHELTENHAM, LOWER MERION, and UPPER MERION, as well as industrial centers like CONSHOHOCKEN, NORRISTOWN, and POTTSTOWN. In its NW reaches the county has rich agricultural land that is gradually giving way to suburban sprawl. **5.** 1044 sq mi/2704 sq km, pop. 182,201, in E Texas, drained by forks and tributaries of the San Jacinto R. Bisected by Interstate 45, it contains parts of the Sam Houston National Forest, and produces lumber, oil and natural gas, sweet potatoes, cotton, vegetables, peanuts, beef and dairy cattle, poultry, and hogs. In its S, especially, it is home to many Houston workers.

Montgomery Village unincorporated residential village, pop. 32,315, Montgomery Co., Maryland, 22 mi/35 km NW of Washington, D.C., and just NW of GAITHERSBURG.

Monticello **1.** city, pop. 8116, Drew Co., SE Arkansas, 45 mi/72 km SSE of Pine Bluff. In an alluvial plain area producing cotton, fruit, and truck crops, it has industries that include lumber milling, cotton processing, and textile manufacturing. It is the site of the University of Arkansas at Monticello (1909). **2.** city, pop. 4941, Wright Co., EC Minnesota, on the Mississippi R., 35 mi/56 km NE of Minneapolis. An agricultural trading center, it stands on a site originally owned by a Hungarian nobleman whose claims came to nought in the face of determined squatters. A nuclear power plant was opened here in 1971. **3.** historic site just SE of CHARLOTTESVILLE, Albemarle Co., C Virginia, the home of Thomas Jefferson. The site, on Carters Mt., overlooking plains to the E and the Blue Ridge Mts. to the W, was inherited by Jefferson in 1757. He named it Monticello (Italian, "little mountain") and began building the mansion he designed in the Classical Revival style in 1769; it was not finished until 1809.

Montmagny city, pop. 11,861, Montmagny Co., S Québec, 33 mi/53 km ENE of Québec City, on the St. Lawrence R. Founded in 1678, it is a longtime industrial center, making machinery, appliances, textiles, and a range of other products. Grosse Île, just NW, was an 1830s–1930s immigration quarantine station, now a national historic site. The Île aux Grues (NE) is a resort and wildlife sanctuary.

Montmorency former village, now part of BEAUPORT, S Québec, 6 mi/10 km NE of Québec City. It was named for the nearby **Chute Montmorency** (Montmorency Falls), where the R. Montmorency, which flows 60 mi/100 km S from the Laurentians, plunges 275 ft/84 m from the CANADIAN SHIELD into the St. Lawrence. The cliffs here were the site of a 1759 battle in which the French defeated British forces under James Wolfe. Settled in the 1780s, Montmorency became a textile center in the late 19th century, and is now largely residential.

Montour Falls village, pop. 1845, in Montour township, Schuyler Co., WC New York, on Catharine Creek, 3 mi/5 km SSE of Watkins Glen and the S tip of Seneca L. It was once the site of Catherine's Town, a Seneca settlement governed by "Queen" Catharine Montour. It is surrounded by seven scenic glens with a number of caverns, cliffs, and waterfalls, the best-known of which, Shequaga Falls, is 156 ft/48 m high. There is some manufacturing, and the village is also a summer resort.

Montpelier **1.** city, pop. 8247, state capital and seat of Washington Co., C Vermont. It is on the Winooski R. and a pass through the Green Mts., 5 mi/8 km NW of Barre. Near ski areas, the city is a government and insurance center, engages in light manufacturing, and is home to Norwich University's Vermont College and to the New England Culinary Institute. The capitol, made of Barre granite, has a gold dome noted for its beauty. Flooding by the Winooski has been a recurrent problem. In 1848, largely agricultural sections of Montpelier were set off as the town of East Montpelier (pop. 2239). **2.** historic site in Orange Co., NC Virginia, 3.5 mi/6 km SW of Orange and 21 mi/34 km NE of Charlottesville, the family estate of James Madison, fourth US president, who lived here on and off all his life, and is buried nearby.

Montréal city, pop. 1,017,666, S Québec, the most populous in Canada and in the Montréal Urban Community (pop. 1,775,871), on the 32 mi/51 km–long I. de Montréal and several small islands of the Hochelaga Archipelago, at the confluence of the St. Lawrence and Ottawa rivers, 145 mi/235 km SW of Québec City and 310 mi/500 km ENE of Toronto, Ontario. The city occupies about half the island, which is bounded by the St. Lawrence (S and E) and the R. des Prairies (N and W). Its metropolitan area (CMA) has a pop. of 3,127,242, including some 100 municipalities, of which LAVAL (just N) is the largest. The city is named for 763-ft/233-m Mt. ROYAL, around which it developed. Jacques Cartier visited the Iroquoian village of HOCHELAGA here in 1535. Paul de Chomedey, Sieur de Maisonneuve, acting for the Sulpician religious order, who had been granted a SEIGNEURIE here, established Ville-Marie in 1642, on the site of today's VIEUX-MONTRÉAL. The community became the hub of the fur trade and other commerce, being at the point (the LACHINE rapids) where direct water passage between the sea (via the St. Lawrence) and the interior was blocked. Hostilities with the Iroquois retarded development before 1701, after which Montréal grew more rapidly. It was the last (1760) city of NEW FRANCE captured by the British. After they took power, a group of Scottish merchants, through the NORTH WEST COMPANY and other instrumentalities, made it gradually the most powerful and wealthiest city in Canada. It was held briefly (1775–76) by American forces, but remained loyal, despite its French history, to the British Empire. In 1837, however, it was a center of the French PATRIOTE rebellion. For a period in the mid 19th century it had an anglophone majority, but after the 1860s, in-migration from rural districts gave it a francophone majority again, although money and power remained concentrated in British hands. Growing more industrial later in the century, Montréal also became more cosmopolitan, as Russian Jews (from the 1880s) and Italians, Greeks, Portuguese, and other groups began to arrive. In the 20th century it has been Canada's industrial center, and until the 1970s, when many anglophone-dominated firms moved headquarters to Toronto, its financial and business center as well. Today it is an industrial, commercial, educational, cultural, and governmental center. Both major railways (Canadian Pacific and Canadian National) are headquartered here, as is Air Canada, the UN's International Civil Aviation Organization, and the International Air Transport Association. The city and its suburbs have chemical, iron and steel fabricating, brewing, food processing, oil refining, transportation equipment, textile and clothing, aircraft, and various other industries. Regional banks, the Montréal Stock Exchange, and other financial institutions anchor the downtown business district, along with major retailers. Educational institutions include McGill University (1821) and Concordia University (1974), both anglophone; and the huge Université de Montréal (1876) and Université du Québec à Montréal (UQAM; 1968), both francophone. The city, which is today c.66% francophone, 11% anglophone, the rest largely speakers of other European languages, has a dual (francophone/Roman Catholic and anglophone/Protestant) public school system, and continues to be the focal point of debates over language and Québec's political future. In the 1960s, the "Quiet Revolution" brought increased power, self-awareness, and cosmopolitanism to the city's French-speakers, and Montréal today, said to be the world's third-largest French-speaking city (after Paris and Kinshasa), is a vibrant metropolis. Expo 67 (the 1967 World's Fair) and the 1976 summer Olympic Games, with attendant development, brought much physical change, including the initiation of the noted UNDERGROUND CITY. Montréal's airports are at DORVAL (on the island) and MIRABEL (NW, in the Laurentian foothills). See also: MONTRÉAL URBAN COMMUNITY; CHINATOWN; Square DORCHESTER (Dominion Square); the FORUM; HABITAT; HOCHELAGA; MAISONNEUVE (and Olympic Stadium); Île NÔTRE-DAME; PLACE DES ARTS; PLATEAU MONT-ROYAL; POINTE-AUX-TREMBLES; Mt. ROYAL; Rue SAINT-DENIS (and Latin Quarter); Rue SAINTE-CATHERINE; Île SAINTE-HÉLÈNE (and Biosphere); SAINT JAMES St. (Rue Saint-Jacques); Blvd. SAINT-LAURENT (the Main); Rue SHERBROOKE (and Golden Square Mile); UNDERGROUND CITY (and Place Ville-Marie); VICTORIA BRIDGE; VIEUX-MONTRÉAL (Ville Marie); WEST ISLAND.

Montréal-Nord city, pop. 85,516, MONTRÉAL URBAN COMMUNITY, S Québec, on the S shore of the R. des Prairies, facing Laval, and 8 mi/13 km NNW of downtown Montréal. A major francophone residential suburb, it also has some industry.

Montréal Urban Community French, **Communauté urbaine de Montréal** METROPOLITAN governmental entity (created 1970) including the city of Montréal, Québec, and 28 other municipalities, its neighbors on the I. de Montréal, the I. Bizard (off its SW) and smaller islands in the St. Lawrence R. (SE) and the R. des Prairies (NW). Its total pop. is 1,775,871, making it the second-largest entity of the kind in Canada, after the TORONTO Metropolitan Municipality. In addition to Montréal itself, other municipalities in the MUC, all of which are often thought of collectively as "Montréal," include (the most populous first) MONTRÉAL-NORD, LASALLE, SAINT-LÉONARD, SAINT-LAURENT, VERDUN, PIERREFONDS, DOLLARD-DES-ORMEAUX, ANJOU, LACHINE, CÔTE-SAINT-LUC, POINTE-CLAIRE, OUTREMONT, WESTMOUNT, BEACONSFIELD, MONT-ROYAL, KIRKLAND, DORVAL, SAINT-RAPHAËL-DE-L'ÎLE-BIZARD, HAMPSTEAD, and nine smaller communities.

Montreat see under BLACK MOUNTAIN, North Carolina.

Montrose **1.** see LACRESCENTA–MONTROSE, California. **2.** city, pop. 8854, seat of Montrose Co., W Colorado, on the Uncompahgre R., 55 mi/89 km SE of Grand Junction. An 1880s lumbering and mining community, it is now a trade and processing center for an irrigated agricultural region. With the Ute Indian Museum 4 mi/6 km S, it is also a tourist base for the Black Canyon of the Gunnison, 5 mi/8 km N, and for the Curecanti National Recreation Area and Uncompahgre and Gunnison national forests, which lie some 15 mi/24 km E of the city. **3.** residential and commercial section of Houston, Texas, just W of Downtown and E of RIVER OAKS, along the S of the Buffalo Bayou. An affluent 1910s suburb, it is now Houston's most bohemian district, with ongoing restoration of early-20th-century housing, a profusion of small shops, and a substantial community of artists and gays.

Mont-Royal city, pop. 18,212, MONTRÉAL URBAN COMMUNITY, S Québec, on the W side of Mt. ROYAL, in the C of the I. de Montréal, 6 mi/10 km W of Downtown, E of Saint-Laurent and SW of Outremont. It is a wealthy, largely anglophone residential community.

Mont-Saint-Hilaire city, pop. 12,341, La-Vallée-du-Richelieu census division, S Québec, 20 mi/32 km ENE of Montréal, on the E bank of the R. Richelieu, opposite Beloeil. An agricultural community also noted for a number of artists who have lived here, it was a PATRIOTE stronghold in 1837, after which Scots settled here. Mt. St.-Hilaire (1348 ft/411 m) is the highest of the MONTEREGIAN HILLS.

Montvale borough, pop. 6946, Bergen Co., NE New Jersey,

10 mi/16 km N of Hackensack, on the New York border. A residential suburb on the Garden State Parkway, it has a rural character that has attracted a number of corporate headquarters.

Monument Rocks also, the **Kansas Pyramids** grouping of a dozen chalk and shale bluffs, pinnacles, and pyramids rising abruptly 60 ft/18 m above the plain of the Smoky Hill R., WC Kansas, 26 mi/42 km SE of Oakley. Rich with fossils, they were sculpted by wind and water erosion from the sediment of an ancient sea. A landmark for western travelers, they are now a National Natural Landmark.

Monument Valley area in NE Arizona and SE Utah, W of FOUR CORNERS, characterized by monumentlike BUTTES of red sandstone rising up to 1000 ft/300 m from a sandy floor. Since director John Ford filmed *Stagecoach* (1939) here, it has been familar as the setting for westerns. Needlelike Agathla Peak (7100 ft/2164 m) is at the S end, just N of KAYENTA.

Moody Air Force Base see under VALDOSTA, Georgia.

Moon see under CARNOT-MOON, Pennsylvania.

Moore city, pop. 40,318, Cleveland Co., C Oklahoma, 9 mi/14 km S of downtown Oklahoma City. A bedroom community, it also has some agriculture and light industry.

Moores Creek Bridge battle site: see under WILMINGTON, North Carolina.

Moorestown township, pop. 16,116, Burlington Co., SC New Jersey, 9 mi/14 km NE of Camden. Settled by Pennsylvania Quakers (1682), it served as Hessian headquarters for a time (1776) during the Revolutionary War. A largely residential suburb of Camden and Philadelphia, it has manufactures that include chemicals, electronic equipment, and wood and metal products.

Mooresville **1.** town, pop. 5541, Morgan Co., WC Indiana, 10 mi/16 km SW of Indianapolis. Settled in 1824, in a grain, fruit, and dairy farming area, it produces paint, burial vaults, flour, and engine bearings. Early baseball star Amos Rusie ("the Hoosier Thunderbolt") was born here in 1871. **2.** town, pop. 9317, Iredell Co., WC North Carolina, 23 mi/37 km NNE of Charlotte. Cotton goods and furniture are its chief manufactures.

Moorhead **1.** city, pop. 32,295, seat of Clay Co., W Minnesota, on the Red R. of the North, opposite Fargo, North Dakota. Founded as a stop along the railroad and named for a Northern Pacific director, it became an important transportation hub at the junction of rail, road, and river. The city serves as the processing center for an agricultural region. Important industries include sugar-beet refining, dairying, and potato processing, as well as the manufacture of farm equipment and fiberglass boats. Moorhead State University (1885) and a campus of Concordia College (1891) are both here. **2.** city, pop. 2417, Sunflower Co., NW Mississippi, in the DELTA, 19 mi/31 km WSW of Greenwood. Incorporated in 1889, this cotton town is famous in song as the place where the "Southern cross the Yellow Dog" (where the Southern and the Yazoo & Mississippi Valley, or Yellow Dog, railroads crossed at right angles). It is home to Mississippi Delta Community College (1926).

Mooringsport town, pop. 873, Caddo Parish, NW Louisiana, on Caddo L., 17 mi/27 km NW of Shreveport and 4 mi/6 km E of the Texas border, in oil and farming country. The folk singer Leadbelly was born here (1888).

Moorpark city, pop. 25,494, Ventura Co., SW California, 38 mi/61 km NW of Los Angeles. In an area noted for its walnuts, apricots, tomatoes, citrus groves, and oil wells, it is a fast-growing residential suburb.

Moose Factory Indian reserve and historic site, Cochrane District, NE Ontario, on Moose Factory I. in the Moose R., 15 mi/24 km S of the S end of JAMES BAY, just E of MOOSONEE, and 325 mi/520 km N of Sudbury. Originally known as Moose Fort, it was the site of one of the HUDSON'S BAY COMPANY's earliest (1673) fur trading posts in RUPERT'S LAND, and is considered Ontario's first English settlement. Captured (1686) by the French, it was in 1713 returned to the HBC, which resumed operations. Today a Cree band inhabit the island, which draws tourists.

Moosehead Lake in Somerset and Piscataquis counties, WC Maine. About 35 mi/56 km N–S and 2–10 mi/3–16 km E–W, with an area of about 120 sq mi/311 sq km, it is the largest lake in Maine. Moosehead is the focus of a resort and lumbering area. Mt. KINEO stands on a peninsula at the lake's center, and the Squaw Mountain ski resort (Big Squaw Mt., 3196 ft/975 m) is just SW. Greenville, at the lake's S extremity, is the area's chief town. The Kennebec R. originates from the lake's W side.

Mooseheart community established by James J. Davis of the Loyal Order of Moose in 1913 as a home for orphans and other disadvantaged children. It is 4 mi/6 km N of AURORA, in Kane Co., N Illinois, on the Fox R., and incorporates a large dairy farm. Operated as a self-governing community, it was long famous for radio broadcasts from the "City of Children."

Moosehorn National Wildlife Refuge see under WASHINGTON COUNTY, Maine.

Moose Jaw city, pop. 33,593, SC Saskatchewan, 40 mi/65 km W of Regina, at the confluence of the Moose Jaw R. and Thunder Creek. The third-largest city in the province, it developed with the Canadian Pacific Railway and became the trading center for a wheat growing region. By the 1950s, the CPR became less dominant, though today much of the economy is still centered around wheat. In addition, there are stockyards, slaughterhouses, oil refineries, a sheet steel mill, and other farm-related and manufacturing industries. An air force training base, home to the flying stuntmen the Snowbirds, a community college, and a provincial technical institute are here.

Mooselookmeguntic Lake see under RANGELEY LAKES, Maine.

Moose Mountain hilly area extending E–W for 30 mi/48 km, rising to 2740 ft/835 m, and protected in Moose Mt. Provincial Park, 103 mi/166 km SE of Regina, in SE Saskatchewan. The area, with Kenosee L. its main resort, is noted for its fishing, woods, and wildlife.

Moose River 50 mi/80 km long, in NE Ontario. It is formed by the confluence of the Mattagami and Missinaibi rivers, and flows NE to its confluence with the ABITIBI R., then passes between MOOSONEE and MOOSE FACTORY on its way to JAMES BAY. The Mattagami (260 mi/420 km long), which flows from the TIMMINS area N, and the Missinaibi (265 mi/430 km long), which flows NNE from the ALGOMA DISTRICT, with their tributaries drain much of NC Ontario into Hudson Bay.

Moosonee township, pop. 1213, Cochrane District, NE Ontario, on the W bank of the Moose R. near its mouth on James Bay, directly opposite MOOSE FACTORY and 325 mi/520 km N of Sudbury. It is the N terminus of the Ontario Northland Railway, which arrived in 1932, and is Ontario's only saltwater port. Reached by the ONR's "Polar Bear

Express," from Cochrane (155 mi/250 km S), it is a jumping-off point for tourists and hunting and fishing parties, esp. those headed for Hannah Bay, at the river's mouth.

Moraga Town also, **Moraga** city, pop. 15,852, Contra Costa Co., NC California, 6 mi/10 km NE of Oakland. St. Mary's College of California (1863) is in this largely residential community.

moraine any of various landforms created by a mass of debris (rock, sand, clay, etc.) carried and deposited by a glacier or ice sheet. The mixed, unstratified material within a moraine is called *till;* the more general term *drift* is used of any material transported, esp. by ice, whether stratified or not. A **terminal moraine** marks the farthest reach of an ice sheet that then retreated.

Moraine city, pop. 5989, Montgomery Co., SW Ohio, on the Great Miami R., an industrial suburb 5 mi/8 km S of Dayton. A General Motors truck assembly plant is here.

Moraviantown battle site: see under THAMES R., Ontario.

Morden town, pop. 5273, SC Manitoba, 7 mi/11 km W of Winkler, and 64 mi/103 km SW of Winnipeg. Local industries include farming, food processing, and grain storage. The Agricultural Canada Research Station, a government experimental farm, is here. Blossom Week (spring) and the Corn and Apple Festival (Aug.) are major annual events.

Moreau River 290 mi/467 km long, in South Dakota. It is formed in Perkins Co., in the NW, by the confluence of its North and South forks, and flows E to join the Missouri R. S of MOBRIDGE. Much of its course is through the Cheyenne River Indian Reservation.

Morehead city, pop. 8357, seat of Rowan Co., NE Kentucky, in the DANIEL BOONE NATIONAL FOREST, 58 mi/93 km E of Lexington. In a timber, burley tobacco, and clay producing region, it manufactures firebrick, clay pipe, concrete and wood products, clothing, soft drinks, and lumber. Morehead State University (1923) is here.

Morehead City town, pop. 6046, Carteret Co., E North Carolina, on a peninsula between BOGUE SOUND (S) and the estuarial Newport R. (N), across (W) from BEAUFORT. Founded in 1857, it has been a beach resort and fishing port. In 1935–37, a major terminal facility constructed here with rail connections made the town North Carolina's second deepwater port (after WILMINGTON).

Morenci unincorporated community, pop. 1799, Greenlee Co., SE Arizona, 105 mi/169 km NE of Tucson. A copper center since the 1870s, it is a COMPANY TOWN with one of the world's largest open-pit mines, a huge spiral continually working its way into the earth near US Route 666.

Moreno Valley city, pop. 118,779, Riverside Co., SW California, 10 mi/16 km E of Riverside, and W of the hilly Moreno Badlands. It is just N of March Air Force Base, the oldest (1918) military airfield on the West Coast. Moreno Valley is a booming new residential community. The L. Perris Recreation area, to the SE, draws rock climbers and bird watchers.

Morgan City city, pop. 14,531, St. Mary Parish, SE Louisiana, on Berwick Bay of the ATCHAFALAYA R., and on the Gulf Intracoastal Waterway, 50 mi/80 km S of Baton Rouge. Founded in 1850 in an area formerly inhabited by the Chitimacha, and in the 18th century by Acadians, it has long been a fur trapping center and fishing, shrimping, and oystering port. An early railroad terminus, it had strategic importance during the Civil War. After oil was discovered in the Gulf of Mexico in 1947, it became the headquarters for offshore drilling companies. Local industries process seafood, build ships, and manufacture machinery, chemicals, and metal products.

Morgan Hill city, pop. 23,928, Santa Clara Co., C California, in the S Santa Clara Valley, 17 mi/27 km SE of San Jose. Its industries include winemaking, food and feed processing, fruit shipping, and some light manufactures.

Morganton city, pop. 15,085, seat of Burke Co., WC North Carolina, on the Catawba R., 60 mi/97 km NW of Charlotte. Its industries manufacture furniture and clothing, and the city is a commercial center for resorts on the dam-created lakes nearby on the river. It is home to Western Piedmont Community College (1964) and to several state health institutions.

Morgantown city, pop. 25,879, seat of Monongalia Co., N West Virginia, on the Monongahela R., 56 mi/90 km S of Pittsburgh, Pennsylvania. It was settled in 1767, and was a road and, from 1826, river traffic hub. Bituminous coal has been shipped from here since 1833; the area is also rich in oil, gas, glass sand, and limestone. The city is home to West Virginia University (1867), and is noted for its Personal Rapid Transit (PRT) system, opened in 1972, which connects campus units.

Moriah, Mount see under SNAKE RANGE, Nevada.

Moriches Bay inlet in Suffolk Co., SE New York, on S Long Island, between the mainland and the FIRE ISLAND and Westhampton Beach barrier islands. It runs 12 mi/19 km from Mastic Beach (SW) to Westhampton Beach (NE), and is up to 2.5 mi/4 km wide. The unincorporated village of Center Moriches (pop. 5987) is one of the larger communities on the bay, which is a fishing and boating center.

Mormon Trail route taken by Mormon migrants in the mid 1840s from their unsuccessful settlement at NAUVOO, Illinois, to Utah, where they established Salt Lake City. It led across S Iowa to Council Bluffs. In 1846, the first year of travel, Mormons established Winter Quarters at Florence, now a N section of Omaha, Nebraska. The trail then ran W along the N bank of the Platte R. (paralleling the OREGON TRAIL, on the S bank). Continuing up the North Platte R. into Wyoming, it ran with the Oregon Trail as far as FORT BRIDGER, in the SW, then proceeded SW into Utah, to the Great Salt L. Subsequently, Mormon migrants aiming to settle in S California (establishing an expansive DESERET) used a SW route that joined the SPANISH TRAIL to the Los Angeles area.

Morningside Heights academic and residential district of upper Manhattan, New York City, between Riverside Park (W) and an escarpment above Morningside Park (E), from 110th St. (Cathedral Parkway) to 125th St. Known as HARLEM HEIGHTS in Revolutionary times, it was also considered part of BLOOMINGDALE. The relocation of Columbia University's campus here in 1897 was key to the area's development. Morningside Heights is home also to the Cathedral of St. John the Divine (1892–1942, under construction again 1979); Riverside Church; Union Theological Seminary; Jewish Theological Seminary; and GRANT'S TOMB. The area has the feeling of an academic village high above the city.

Morris 1. city, pop. 10,270, seat of Grundy Co., NE Illinois, on the Illinois R. and the Illinois and Michigan Canal, 22 mi/35 km E of Ottawa. A grain shipping center and transportation hub, it grew with the construction of the canal. Gebhard Woods State Park is just SW, William G. Stratton State Park just S. The Heidecke L. Fish and Wildlife Area and the Goose L. Prairie Natural Area are a few miles E; the

Dresden nuclear power plant, operative since 1970, is just NE of them. A 200-year-old cottonwood 2 mi/3 km SW of the city that was the state's largest tree was toppled in a 1992 storm. **2.** city, pop. 5613, seat of Stevens Co., WC Minnesota, on the Pomme de Terre R., 45 mi/72 km SSE of Fergus Falls. It is the center of an agricultural and recreational area. A campus of the University of Minnesota is here.

Morrisania residential neighborhood and former estate, S Bronx, New York. In 1670, the Morris brothers, merchants, bought Jacob Bronk's 1639 estate. The hilly district, through which the BOSTON POST ROAD would run, was agricultural through the 18th century. Among the Morrises resident were Lewis, a Declaration of Independence signer, and Gouverneur, one of the authors of the Constitution. The Bronx grew around the village of Morrisania, which in 1874 became a ward of New York City. In the late 19th century German immigrants brought brewing and other industries to the area. Later residents included Irish, Italians, and Jews. Today Morrisania is largely black and Hispanic, densely populated despite a long period of economic decline. MOTT HAVEN, to the S, was once part of Morrisania, which has shrunk in most definitions to a neighborhood between Melrose (W) and Tremont (E).

Morrisburg village, pop. 2429, Stormont, Dundas, and Glengarry United Counties, SE Ontario, on the St. Lawrence R., 22 mi/35 km WSW of Cornwall. With the 1950s construction of the St. Lawrence Seaway, the community was forced to relocate to higher ground, but buildings from the 1860s town are preserved at Upper Canada Village, a major tourist attraction 7 mi/11 km E, in the park that also commemorates the nearby battle (1813) of CRYSLER'S FARM. Morrisburg today is a tourist and commercial center with some light industry.

Morris County 470 sq mi/1217 sq km, pop. 421,353, in NC New Jersey, bounded E and SE by the Passaic R. Its seat is MORRISTOWN. The county is largely suburban and residential. It is hilly and lake-studded, with L. HOPATCONG on its W border, and has many recreational facilities. Its agricultural activities include fruit, truck, and dairy farming. Corporate headquarters and light industry are spreading through the county, especially in areas along Interstate 80 like PARSIPPANY-Troy Hills.

Morris Heights residential section, WC Bronx, New York. Located on a ridge high above the Harlem R., it is N of High Bridge and S of University Heights. The Cross-Bronx Expressway passes through the area. Below, along the river, are Roberto Clemente State Park and the River Park Towers housing complex.

Morristown **1.** town, pop. 16,189, seat of Morris Co., N New Jersey, on the Whippany R., 16 mi/26 km NW of Newark. Settled in 1709–10, it was called West Hanover until 1740. Morristown was a Revolutionary War center, producing iron and gunpowder for the Continental Army and serving as its winter camp (1777, 1779–80). It grew as a 19th-century iron processing hub. Today it is residential and commercial, has stone quarries, corporate headquarters, and research laboratories, and produces chemicals, pharmaceuticals, clothing, and metal products. The Seeing Eye School for dogs has been here since 1929. **Morristown National Historical Park** (1671 ac/677 ha), preserves buildings and sites of the Revolutionary period. It incorporates Fort Nonsense, a 1777 earthwork on a 597-ft/182-m prominence, and Jockey Hollow, 2 mi/3 km W, where Washington's army camped. Historic Speedwell ironworks and the Frelinghuysen Arboretum are in Morristown. **Morris Township** (pop. 19,952) surrounds the borough, and **Morris Plains** borough (pop. 5219) is just N. **2.** city, pop. 21,385, seat of Hamblen Co., NE Tennessee, 40 mi/64 km NE of Knoxville, just SE of Cherokee L. (the Holston R.), in a valley between Clinch Mt. (NW) and the Great Smoky Mts. (SE). It was settled in 1783. Area agricultural products have included tobacco, corn, soybeans, poultry, and beef cattle. Local industries produce synthetic fibers, furniture, electronic equipment, and canned goods. Walters State Community College (1970) is here, as is the David Crockett Tavern and Museum.

Morrisville borough, pop. 9765, Bucks Co., SE Pennsylvania, across the Delaware R. (W) from Trenton, New Jersey. Washington had his headquarters here Dec. 8–14, 1776. Site of a large steel plant, Morrisville also produces rubber and plastic products and tile.

Morro Bay city, pop. 9664, San Luis Obispo Co., SW California, on Morro Bay, an inlet of Estero Bay (the Pacific Ocean), 12 mi/19 km WNW of San Luis Obispo. The 3.5 mi/5.6 km–long bay is guarded by **Morro Rock,** a 576-ft/176-m volcanic cone connected to the mainland by causeway. The city, a tourist destination, has a large fishing fleet and a big Pacific Gas & Electric power plant.

Morro Castle see EL MORRO, San Juan, Puerto Rico.

Morton village, pop. 13,799, Tazewell Co., C Illinois, a residential suburb 10 mi/16 km SE of Peoria. Local manufactures include tractors and washing machines. The Mackinaw R. State Fish and Wildlife Area is 8 mi/13 km SE.

Morton Arboretum see under LISLE, Illinois.

Morton Grove village, pop. 22,408, Cook Co., NE Illinois, on the North Branch of the Chicago R., a suburb 14 mi/22 km N of Chicago. Although mainly a residential community, it has some manufactures, including electric motors, pumps, cosmetics, and plastics.

Moscow city, pop. 18,519, seat of Latah Co., NW Idaho, on Paradise Creek, 22 mi/35 km N of Lewiston and 1.5 mi/2.4 km E of the Washington border. Originally called Hog Heaven, for the camas root, loved by pigs, that grew here, it was renamed for a Harrisburg, Pennsylvania suburb in 1876. The University of Idaho (1889), which houses the state Bureau of Mines and Geology, is here. The university and US Forest Service jointly sponsor Moscow's Intermountain Forest and Range Experiment Station. The city is a trade center for the fertile PALOUSE area. It is also a processing center for nearly all of America's lentils and dried and seed peas as well as for wheat and barley.

Moses Lake city, pop. 11,235, Grant Co., C Washington, on the E shore of Moses L., 54 mi/89 km ESE of Wenatchee. Settled in 1897, the city has served as a trading and shipping center for the agricultural products of the Columbia Basin. Food processing (sugar, dairy products) is important. Big Bend Community College (1962) is here. The Moses Lake State Park is 3 mi/5 km SW, the Potholes Wildlife Area is 5 mi/8 km SW, and there are many recreational facilities at Potholes Reservoir, 7 mi/11 km SW.

Mosholu Indian name for a stream in NW Bronx, New York, where today the Mosholu Parkway connects, in Van Cortlandt Park, with the Major Deegan Expressway and Henry Hudson Parkway. A residential neighborhood just W of the park is also called Mosholu.

Mosport see under NEWCASTLE, Ontario.

Mosquito Lake also, **Mosquito Creek Lake** or **Mosquito Creek Reservoir** reservoir in Trumbull Co., NE Ohio, just N of Warren, 9 mi/14 km above the mouth of Mosquito Creek. This narrow, oblong body of water stretches 9 mi/14 km N–S. A state park is at its S tip.

Moss Point city, pop. 17,837, Jackson Co., extreme SE Mississippi, 4 mi/6 km N of PASCAGOULA and the Gulf of Mexico, on the Escatawpa R. Paper, pulp, textiles, lumber, and fish meal are produced in this primarily industrial, predominantly black city.

Mother Lode, the gold-bearing quartz vein, or the area containing this vein, along the W side of the SIERRA NEVADA, in EC California. Named (*la Veta Madre*) by Mexicans who worked its S section, the Lode has been delineated in various ways. At its farthest, it is described as extending some 170 mi/275 km NNW from the vicinity of Mariposa, in Mariposa Co. Some say that only the Southern Mines, in a band 70–100 mi/110–160 km long, roughly from Mariposa (S) to PLACERVILLE, is the true Lode; others include the Northern Mines, up to NEVADA CITY or even OROVILLE. It is variously described as from 2 mi/3.2 km to 6.5 mi/10.5 km wide. PLACER gold was discovered in 1848 on the South Fork of the AMERICAN R. at Sutter's Mill (COLOMA). In the following decade, the area was inundated by gold rushers, who panned for the metal in streams and then mined it from the earth ("dry diggings"); the name derived from the belief that somewhere the "mother" of the placer gold would be found. Among well-known centers along the Lode are (S–N) SONORA, TUTTLETOWN, ANGELS CAMP, MOKELUMNE HILL, Amador City, and FIDDLETOWN. The bandits Joaquin Murrieta and Black Bart and the authors Bret Harte and Mark Twain figure in the Mother Lode's story. Today, some commercial mining and much recreational gold-panning is done, and GHOST TOWNS attract tourists. Silver, tungsten, molybdenum, and other minerals have also been obtained in the area.

Motor City 20th-century nickname for Detroit, Michigan, center of the world automobile industry. Detroit's black community altered it to **Motown,** and in the 1960s this version attached to the rhythm and blues–based popular music associated with the city. The original home of Tamla-Motown Records, on West Grand Blvd., is today a museum; the Motown company moved to Los Angeles in 1972.

Mott Haven depressed industrial and residential section, SW Bronx, New York. It is the most often discussed part of the SOUTH BRONX. Bounded W by the Harlem R., S by Bronx Kill (a passage N of Randall's I. that joins the Harlem and East rivers), and E by Hunt's Point, Mott Haven is the former site of many factories, foundries, and rail and materials yards. The district is named for J. L. Mott, inventor of coal stoves, who established his plant here in 1828. The Bruckner and Major Deegan expressways pass over and through Mott Haven; the GRAND CONCOURSE is its former commercial and residential spine. Yankee Stadium is just NW. Mott Haven is today almost entirely Hispanic and black. In the early 1990s it suffered from 50% unemployment and the aftereffects of a wave of arson in the 1970s. Its boundary with MELROSE, just N, is variously defined.

Moultrie city, pop. 14,865, seat of Colquitt Co., S Georgia, 33 mi/53 km SE of Albany. Founded in 1890, it was a lumbering center; today, textiles, fertilizer, beverage containers, and meats are produced.

Moultrie, Lake see under COOPER R., South Carolina.

Mound see under L. MINNETONKA, Minnesota.

Mound Bayou city, pop. 2222, Bolivar Co., NW Mississippi, in the Delta, 23 mi/37 km SSW of Clarksdale, on Highway 61. Named for nearby Mississippian mounds, it was founded in 1887 by blacks in cooperation with the Yazoo & Mississippi Valley Railroad, which was laying track through the area. Its founders were seeking to escape post-Reconstruction social oppression by establishing an all-black town. Today, essentially agricultural, it remains 99.6% black, and is sometimes called the largest US black municipality.

Mound Builders general name for the peoples, of pre-Columbian and early historic times, who built a wide array of ceremonial mounds, fortifications, symbolic earthworks, and other structures, most notably in the Mississippi and Ohio river valleys, in the period roughly from 1000 B.C. to the 16th century. Works of earlier parts of this period are attributed to the ADENA and HOPEWELL cultures, those in the millennium before European contact to the Mississippian culture, presumably ancestors of modern tribes in the area. The mounds at CAHOKIA, Illinois, are the most extensive works of this latter period. Mound Builder structures are found from the Gulf Coast (S) to S Ontario (N), and from W Pennsylvania and New York (E) to E Kansas and Minnesota (W).

Mound City Group National Monument (1923), in Ross Co., S Ohio, on the Scioto R., 4 mi/6 km N of Chillicothe. Covering over 60 ac/24 ha, it contains a number of conical pre-Columbian burial mounds. Exploration, which began in 1846, has uncovered jewelry, stone utensils, and other artifacts of the Hopewell culture (A.D. 500–700).

Mound Plant see under MIAMISBURG, Ohio.

Mounds View city, pop. 12,541, Ramsey Co., SE Minnesota, a residential suburb 9 mi/14 km NE of Minneapolis. The Anoka Co.–Blaine Airport is just N.

Moundsville city, pop. 10,753, seat of Marshall Co., in the Northern PANHANDLE of West Virginia, along the Ohio R., 12 mi/19 km S of Wheeling. In a coal, salt, and natural gas producing area, it has one of the nation's largest handmade glass factories. Settled in 1771, it grew up around Grave Creek Mound, one of America's largest conical Indian mounds (69 ft/21 m high, 900 ft/275 m in circumference).

Moundville town, pop. 1348, Hale and Tuscaloosa counties, WC Alabama, on the Black Warrior R., 15 mi/24 km SSW of Tuscaloosa. Numerous square and oval platform mounds from the Mississippian period (around A.D. 1000) are preserved here at 320-ac/130-ha Mound State Monument.

Mount for mountains whose names begin with this word, see under the other name element, as **Shasta, Mount.**

Mount Adams residential neighborhood in Cincinnati, Ohio, immediately E of Downtown. Named after a visit by John Quincy Adams in 1843, this area of Victorian homes originally housed middle-class German and Irish immigrants. Occupied by poorer residents for much of this century, it has recently experienced an infusion of private investment in its housing stock.

Mountain Brook city, pop. 19,810, Jefferson Co., NC Alabama, 4 mi/6 km SE of downtown Birmingham, along Shades Mt. An affluent residential suburb noted for its large homes, it is 99% white.

Mountain Creek small tributary of the Trinity R., flowing generally N along the SW boundary of Dallas, Texas. It is dammed to form Joe Pool Reservoir, 14 mi/23 km SW of

Downtown, and **Mountain Creek L.,** 10 mi/16 km WSW. The Dallas Naval Air Station is on the N side of Mountain Creek L., and Dallas Baptist College on the E side. GRAND PRAIRIE lies immediately W.

Mountain Home **1.** city, pop. 9027, seat of Baxter Co., N Arkansas, 11 mi/18 km S of the Missouri border, in the Ozark Plateau, near the White R. In an area with cattle and dairy farms, the city also depends on tourism. Norfolk L. (E), Bull Shoals L. (NW), and a unit of the Ozark National Forest (S) are nearby. **2.** city, pop. 7913, seat of Elmore Co., SW Idaho, 40 mi/64 km SE of Boise. Originally called Rattlesnake Station, the settlement was moved 10 mi/16 km to its present site in 1883. It is a wool and agricultural shipping point in a sheep, cattle, fruit, and hay producing area, near gold and copper mines and sugar beet fields. The Mountain Home Air Force Base, just SW of the city, has played an important role in its economy.

Mountain Meadows historic site in Washington Co., extreme SW Utah, c.35 mi/56 km WSW of Cedar City, W of the Pine Valley Mts. A monument marks the site, now in a unit of the DIXIE NATIONAL FOREST, where Mormons and Paiutes massacred some 120 people in a California-bound wagon train in Sept. 1857.

Mountainside borough, pop. 6657, Union Co., NE New Jersey, 11 mi/18 km SW of Newark. It is a residential suburb in the WATCHUNG Mts., home to the Watchung Reservation, a popular wildlife and recreational area.

Mountain States US states containing parts of the Rocky Mts.: Montana, Idaho, Utah, Wyoming, Colorado, and New Mexico. The Rockies extend into NE Washington and NE Oregon, but these are not generally considered among the Mountain States. Also, the **Mountain West.**

Mountain View city, pop. 67,460, Santa Clara Co., NC California, just S of San Francisco Bay, NE of the Santa Cruz Mts., and adjacent (SE) to Palo Alto. Incorporated in 1902, it became a publishing and fruit packing center. Moffet Field Naval Air Station (1929) and NASA's Ames Research Center are adjacent (NE). Mountain View is now a major SILICON VALLEY manufacturer of computer components, systems, and software; the first silicon chip, opening the way to a technological revolution, was developed here. Other prominent businesses include consulting and capital management.

Mount Airy **1.** town, pop. 3730, Carroll and Frederick counties, N Maryland, in an agricultural area, 30 mi/48 km WNW of Baltimore. Wine is produced locally. **2.** residential neighborhood in NW Philadelphia, Pennsylvania, between GERMANTOWN and CHESTNUT HILL. It is a racially integrated community of middle-class professionals, characterized by both row houses and 19th-century detached homes.

Mount Airy Forest 1476-ac/598-ha park, at the NW edge of Cincinnati, Ohio, 5 mi/8 km NW of Downtown. It is the largest park in the city.

Mount Angel city, pop. 2778, Marion Co., NW Oregon, named for a local butte (330 ft/101 m), 15 mi/24 km NE of Salem. Mt. Angel Abbey was established on the butte in 1883 by Benedictine monks from Switzerland; the community is known for its July Bach festival, Alvar Aalto–designed library, and Oktoberfest.

Mount Auburn neighborhood in Cincinnati, Ohio, NE of Downtown. Situated close to the University of Cincinnati campus, it has a residential mixture of students and professionals who occupy its many restored Victorian homes.

Mount Baker–Snoqualmie National Forest 1.724 million ac/698,000 ha (2694 sq mi/6977 sq km), on the W slopes of the CASCADE RANGE in W Washington, from the British Columbia border (N) to Mt. Rainier National Park (S), a distance of some 150 mi/240 km. Dense with Douglas fir, hemlock, and red cedar, it is noted for its primitive areas and for its heavy rain and snowfall.

Mount Berry see under ROME, Georgia.

Mount Carmel **1.** see CARMEL. **2.** city, pop. 8287, seat of Wabash Co., SE Illinois, on the Wabash R., across from the junction of the White R., and 27 mi/43 km NNW of Evansville, Indiana. An agricultural trade center with various light manufactures, it is the seat of Wabash Valley College (1960). Established in 1818, it was long noted for its freshwater mussel (shell for buttons; pearls) industry.

Mount Clemens city, pop. 18,405, seat of Macomb Co., SE Michigan, on the Clinton R., a residential suburb 20 mi/32 km NE of Detroit. It was settled in 1795 and laid out by Christian Clemens in 1818. Cooperage and glassmaking were early industries, and local sulfur springs soon brought bathers and tourists. Now noted for pottery manufacture, it also relies on fabric plants and on Selfridge Air Force Base, which is just NE, on Anchor Bay. It is the seat of Macomb Co. Community College (1954).

Mount Desert Island 42.6 sq mi/110 sq km, in Hancock Co., SE Maine. It is in the Gulf of Maine, between Blue Hill and Frenchman bays, 40 mi/64 km SE of Bangor. Somes Sound, a narrow, 6 mi/10 km–long fjord, divides the S half of the wooded, mountainous island. Most of the island is in ACADIA NATIONAL PARK. The area includes BAR HARBOR, NORTHEAST HARBOR, Southwest Harbor, CADILLAC Mt., Seal Harbor, and numerous hills, lakes, and ponds. Named L'Ile des Monts Déserts by Champlain in 1604, Mt. Desert became by the 19th century a fashionable resort. It suffered extensive damage in a 1947 forest fire. Tourism is the main industry. The CRANBERRY ISLES lie just SE.

Mount Gilead village, pop. 2896, seat of Morrow Co., C Ohio, 16 mi/26 km ESE of Marion. The economy is centered around the manufacture of hydraulic presses, pumps, electrical equipment, pottery, foundry products, and chemicals. Seed growing is also important.

Mount Greenwood residential neighborhood on the SW side of Chicago, Illinois. It is a nearly exclusively white middle-class community.

Mount Healthy city, pop. 7580, Hamilton Co., SW Ohio, 9 mi/14 km NNW of Cincinnati. Founded in 1817, it is one of the city's older suburbs, with a history both industrial and residential.

Mount Helix see CASA DE ORO–MOUNT HELIX, California.

Mount Holly township, pop. 10,639, seat of Burlington Co., SC New Jersey, on Rancocas Creek, 17 mi/27 km NE of Camden. Settled by Quakers (1676), it was occupied by British forces during the Revolution and served briefly (1779) as New Jersey's capital. It was an important abolitionist center. Today it is a commercial hub and manufacturing center, producing clothing, textiles, footwear, and leather goods. Historic buildings include the Friends' meetinghouse (1775), courthouse (1796), county prison (1810), and Victorian Smithville Mansion complex.

Mount Hope Bay NE arm of Narragansett Bay, 7 mi/11 km long and 2–3 mi/3–5 km wide, between Massachusetts and Rhode Island, just SW of Fall River; it receives the Taunton R. in the extreme NE. It runs SW into Narragansett Bay and S into the Sakonnet R., where the Mt. Hope Bridge (1929) joins Bristol and Portsmouth. Its name derives from Montaup, the Narraganset name for the peninsula on which BRISTOL was established.

Mount Kisco town, pop. 9108, Westchester Co., SE New York, 36 mi/58 km NNE of New York City. It is a largely affluent residential community with many restored Victorian homes; much of the film *Ragtime* was photographed in a Mount Kisco home. Its shopping district serves much of N Westchester.

Mountlake Terrace city, pop. 19,320, Snohomish Co., WC Washington, a residential suburb 10 mi/16 km N of Seattle.

Mount Laurel township, pop. 30,270, Burlington Co., WC New Jersey, 5 mi/8 km E of Camden. It is a largely residential suburb of Camden and Philadelphia, with some high-tech businesses along Interstate 295 and the New Jersey Turnpike.

Mount Lebanon township, pop. 33,362, Allegheny Co., SW Pennsylvania, 5 mi/8 km SW of Pittsburgh. It is a primarily residential suburb.

Mount of the Holy Cross 14,005 ft/4269 m, just SW of VAIL, in WC Colorado. In the N SAWATCH RANGE of the Rocky Mts., in White River National Forest, it is named for the "cross" formed near its summit by snow-filled crevices.

Mount Olive town, pop. 4582, Wayne Co., E North Carolina, 13 mi/21 km SSW of Goldsboro. An agricultural trade center (noted as a bean market) established with the arrival of the railroad in 1839, it is home to Mount Olive College (Baptist; 1951).

Mount Pearl city, pop. 23,689, SE Newfoundland, on the NE Avalon Peninsula, 6 mi/9 km SW of St. John's. A commercial and residential suburb of the capital, and now the island's second most populous city, it has a large industrial park (at Donovans) and a government experimental farm. Before the 1950s it was largely a resort area.

Mount Pleasant **1.** residential neighborhood in NW Washington, D.C., W of SIXTEENTH ST. and E of the National Zoo and Rock Creek Park, 2 mi/3 km N of the White House. A 19th-century hill retreat, it has become one of the District's most mixed communities, and recently has become home to many Salvadorans and other Hispanics. **2.** city, pop. 8027, seat of Henry Co., SE Iowa, 25 mi/40 km NW of Burlington. A shipping point for livestock, it also manufactures bus bodies. First settled in 1834, it had the state's first courthouse and an early wagon industry. Iowa Wesleyan College (1842) is here. The Mount Pleasant Correctional Facility and Mental Health Institute is just S of the city. **3.** city, pop. 23,285, seat of Isabella Co., C Michigan, on the Chippewa R., 26 mi/42 km W of Midland. In the 1850s it was an Indian trading post and lumber camp. It then became a farm trade center whose development was assured by the railroad's arrival (1879). It is the site of Central Michigan University (1891) and the Center for Cultural and Natural History. The discovery of oil nearby (1927) made it the state's petroleum capital, with many companies servicing that industry. The economy is now supported by agriculture and the manufacture of auto parts, gasoline, processed foods and food-service equipment, and stock and dog feeds. A Chippewa reservation is just E. **4.** village, pop. 468, Jefferson Co., E Ohio, 6 mi/10 km NW of MARTINS FERRY. Its Friends Meeting House (1814) is the oldest Quaker house of worship W of the Allegheny Mts. Early settlers included those moving W from Virginia in order to manumit slaves on Free Soil. **5.** town, pop. 30,108, Charleston Co., SE South Carolina, just E of Charleston across the Cooper R. A 1690s resort for local planters overlooking Charleston Harbor, it has grown dramatically in recent decades (over 100% in the 1980s) as a residential and commercial suburb, resort, and retirement haven. SULLIVAN'S I. and the ISLE OF PALMS lie SE across the Atlantic Intracoastal Waterway. **6.** city, pop. 12,291, seat of Titus Co., NE Texas, 108 mi/174 km ENE of Dallas. Settled in the early 1800s, it is in an area of diverse agriculture, and is a food processing and former lumbering center. It now refines and ships oil and has varied manufactures.

Mount Pocono see under POCONO Mts., Pennsylvania.

Mount Prospect village, pop. 53,170, Cook Co., NE Illinois, a suburb 23 mi/37 km NW of Chicago. Due to its proximity to O'HARE INTERNATIONAL AIRPORT, almost immediately S, the village experienced dramatic growth during the 1980s. Originally a farming community, it was founded in 1871. Business machines, housewares, and pharmaceuticals are manufactured.

Mount Rainier city, pop. 7954, Prince George's Co., SC Maryland, a residential suburb on the NE boundary of Washington, D.C.

Mount Revelstoke National Park 102 sq mi/260 sq km, in the Columbia Mts. section of the Rocky Mts., SE British Columbia, just NE of REVELSTOKE, between the Monashee Mts. and Columbia R. (W) and the Selkirk Mts. (E). Mt. Coursier (8681 ft/2646 m) is its high point; Mt. Revelstoke (6358 ft/1938 m) has a road to its summit.

Mount Vernon **1.** city, pop. 1914, seat of Montgomery Co., SC Georgia, 75 mi/120 km SE of Macon. Brewton-Parker College (1904) is here. **2.** city, pop. 16,988, seat of Jefferson Co., SC Illinois, 20 mi/32 km SE of Centralia. An agricultural, industrial, and distribution center, it manufactures shoes, furnaces, and women's clothing. Oil is produced in the area. Founded in 1819, the city is the home of the Mitchell Art Museum, and of Mount Vernon Nazarene College (1966). Rend L. is 10 mi/16 km S. **3.** city, pop. 7217, seat of Posey Co., extreme SW Indiana, 18 mi/29 km W of Evansville, on the Ohio R. Settled in 1816, it is a trade and processing center for the surrounding agricultural area. The city's industries include oil refining and the manufacture of threshing machines and stoves. **4.** city, pop. 3657, Linn Co., EC Iowa, 15 mi/24 km SE of Cedar Rapids. Produce packing is the main industry. It is the seat of Cornell College (1853). **5.** city, pop. 67,153, Westchester Co., SE New York, on the Bronx and Hutchinson rivers, adjoining (N) the BRONX. Settled in the 1660s, it became a suburban city in 1852. Today it is primarily residential, although it has industries producing pharmaceuticals, electrical components, processed foods, and machinery, as well as corporate offices. St. Paul's Church (1763) is a national historic site. The journalist John Peter Zenger, whose acquittal in 1735 of charges of seditious libel established principles of freedom of the press in America, had been arrested for printing an article involving a Mount Vernon election. The city's neighborhoods range from poorer, largely black areas along the Bronx line (S) to affluent Fleetwood, a commuter suburb in the NW. **6.** city, pop. 14,560, seat of Knox Co., C Ohio, on the Kokosing R., 25 mi/40 km NNW of Newark. John Chapman (Johnny Appleseed) was an early landowner in this rural commercial center. Oil and gas are produced in the region;

manufactured goods include diesel engines, compressors, and glass and paper products. Mount Vernon is the birthplace of Daniel Decatur Emmett, composer of "Dixie," and of Mary Ann ("Mother") Bickerdyke, a pioneering Union nurse in the Civil War. The city has a junior college. **7.** historic site in Fairfax Co., NE Virginia, on the Potomac R., 13 mi/21 km SSW of Washington, D.C., the home of George Washington from 1747 until his death in 1799. Washington enlarged the existing cottage into a Georgian mansion with a pillared portico overlooking the Potomac, and added to the attached land, which eventually reached more than 8000 ac/3240 ha. The unincorporated suburb of Mount Vernon has a pop. of 27,485. **8.** city, pop. 17,647, seat of Skagit Co., NW Washington, on the Skagit R., 60 mi/97 km N of Seattle. Founded in 1877, it is one of the country's largest flower bulb producers. The surrounding region produces a large part of the US green pea crop, which is processed here. Frozen foods, dairy goods, fruit, and vegetable seeds are also produced. Skagit Valley College was founded here in 1926.

Mount Vernon Place or **Square** in BALTIMORE, Maryland, 1 mi/1.5 km N of Downtown, on Charles St. Around the 165-ft/50-m Washington Monument, designed (1815) by Robert Mills earlier than his better-known one in Washington, D.C., noted institutions (including the Peabody Conservatory of Music and the Walters Art Gallery) are joined by well-preserved 19th-century houses.

Mount Washington neighborhood on the S side of Pittsburgh, Pennsylvania, across the Monongahela R. from Downtown. Middle-class Italians occupy most of the Victorian single-family homes. Coal was mined here during the 19th century. Chatham Village is near the summit, and STATION SQUARE lies at the river's edge.

Mouse River see SOURIS R., Saskatchewan, North Dakota, and Manitoba.

Moxie Mountain 2925 ft/892 m, in Somerset Co., WC Maine, 20 mi/32 km SW of Moosehead L. Moxie Pond (6 mi/10 km long N–S), below it to the NE, drains N into Moxie Stream, which flows 5 mi/8 km W into the Kennebec R., over Moxie Falls (90 ft/27 m). Prominent in Maine logging history, the area is now primarily recreational.

Mud Island 52-ac/21-ha park in the Mississippi R. at Memphis, Tennessee, an educational and entertainment complex that includes the Mississippi River Museum, with an outdoor scale model of the river, and a music theme park connected with the GREAT AMERICAN PYRAMID.

Mugu, Point see under OXNARD, California.

Muir, Mount peak (14,015 ft/4272 m) of the Sierra Nevada, just S of Mt. WHITNEY, in EC California. The mountain and nearby Muir Pass (11,955 ft/3644 m) were named to honor naturalist John Muir (1838–1914), one of the founders of the Sierra Club and a father of the conservation movement.

Muir Woods National Monument see under Mt. TAMALPAIS, California.

Mulberry city, pop. 2988, Polk Co., C Florida, 9 mi/14 km W of Bartow. A longtime phosphate mining center, it was noted for its wildness in the 1880s and for a violent 1919 strike, and much of its area is covered by strip mines. In 1992 the first food irradiation plant in the US opened here amid health and environmental controversies.

Mulholland Drive scenic road, 40 mi/64 km long, between HOLLYWOOD (E) and WOODLAND HILLS (W), in Los Angeles, California. Following the summit of the Santa Monica Mts., it is famous for its views of the Los Angeles Basin (SE) and SAN FERNANDO VALLEY (N). Built in 1923–24, it is named for William Mulholland, architect of the Los Angeles Aqueduct.

Mullan Road see under FORT BENTON, Montana.

Mullica River 55 mi/90 km long, in SE New Jersey. It rises near Berlin, in Camden Co., and flows generally SE, forming part of the Burlington-Atlantic county line and passing through the Wharton State Forest, in the PINE BARRENS, to empty into Great Bay N of BRIGANTINE. Its tributaries include the Batsto and Bass rivers and Tulpehocken Creek. The major Pine Barrens river, the Mullica was, in the 18th and 19th centuries, an important bog iron–producing area; today it is recreational.

Multnomah County 465 sq mi/1204 sq km, pop. 583,887, in NW Oregon, bounded by the Columbia R., forming the Washington border (N). The most urbanized and most populous county in the state, it is dominated by PORTLAND, the county seat, and many of its suburbs, which occupy most of the W part. The Willamette R. flows through Portland, emptying into the Columbia R. The balance of the county is agricultural (fruit, truck crops, grain, dairy products) or heavily wooded. Mount Hood National Forest is in the E.

Muncie city, pop. 71,035, seat of Delaware Co., EC Indiana, on the White R., 50 mi/80 km NE of Indianapolis. First occupied by the Munsee (Delaware) tribe, it was ceded to the US by treaty (1818) after white settlement had begun. An early agricultural trading center, it is now a commercial, processing, and distribution hub for dairy, livestock, grain, soybeans, and other crops. Industrial development came with the mid-19th-century arrival of the railroad and the discovery of natural gas nearby in 1886. Muncie became home to many industries, most notably Ball, producer of fruit jars. The Ball family has been widely involved in all facets of the city's life. Today the city makes aircraft, steel forgings, wire, metal products, storage batteries, power transformers, transmissions, glass, and machine tools. It is the seat of Ball State University (1918). Muncie is the quintessential American small city described in the *Middletown* sociological studies by Robert and Helen Lynd and others (1929, 1937, 1982).

Mundelein village, pop. 21,215, Lake Co., NE Illinois, on Loch Lomond and St. Mary and Diamond lakes, 34 mi/55 km N of Chicago. A residential community and religious and educational center, it was founded in 1835. The village changed names numerous times before it was named for George William Mundelein, the Archbishop of Chicago, who founded the University of St. Mary of the Lake–Mundelein Seminary here early in the 20th century.

Munfordville city, pop. 1556, seat of Hart Co., S Kentucky, on the Green R., 35 mi/56 km ENE of Bowling Green. Just NE of MAMMOTH CAVE, this agricultural and mill center is where confederate general and later Kentucky governor Simon Buckner was born (1823) and died (1914). In Sept. 1862, Braxton Bragg captured a Union garrison here.

Munhall borough, pop. 13,158, Allegheny Co., SW Pennsylvania, on hills along the Monongahela R., 7 mi/11 km ESE of Pittsburgh. It has large steel and iron works, and was the site of the famous HOMESTEAD strike (1892).

municipality term variously used for a district or settlement that is incorporated and has some form of local government. In Canada the term appears in almost a dozen official designations, ranging from the TORONTO Metropolitan Municipality in Ontario to Québec's 46 **municipalités de paroisse** (parish municipalities). In the US it is not a Census designation, and appears only rarely in place names.

Municipal Stadium built 1931 on the L. Erie front in CLEVELAND, Ohio, just NW of PUBLIC SQUARE. Seating over 80,000, it has long been home to the Browns (football). The Indians (baseball), their co-tenants, departed in 1994 for the new 42,000-seat Jacobs Field, part of the Gateway Complex, which will also, in a 21,000-seat arena, house the Cavaliers (basketball), who have been based in the Coliseum, in RICHFIELD. Municipal Stadium, regarded as cold and shabby, has long been derisively referred to as "the Mistake on the Lake."

municipio in Puerto Rico, a primary civil division (treated by the US Census as the equivalent of a COUNTY), with its own mayor and assembly. There are at present 78 *municipios*. The BARRIO and *barrio-pueblo* are legal subdivisions.

Munster town, pop. 19,949, Lake Co., extreme NW Indiana, adjacent (S) to Hammond. It is a primarily residential community, with a variety of light industries. It began as a stop for pioneers headed for Chicago, and developed first into a farming community and then into part of the industrialized CALUMET area. It is the site of Our Lady of Mount Carmel Monastery, with a number of shrines.

Murdochville city, pop. 1689, on the GASPÉ PENINSULA, SE Québec, 47 mi/75 km W of GASPÉ. The only sizable settlement in the interior of the peninsula, in the SHICKSHOCK Mts., it is a copper mining center.

Murfreesboro city, pop. 44,922, seat of Rutherford Co., C Tennessee, on the West Fork of the Stones R., 30 mi/48 km SE of Nashville. Founded in 1811 in an agricultural area, it was Tennessee's capital 1819–26. Just NW is the site of a major Civil War battle (Dec. 31, 1862–Jan. 2, 1863), in which Union forces under William Rosecrans won a bloody strategic victory over Confederates under Braxton Bragg. The battle is known as either Murfreesboro or Stones River. Murfreesboro is a marketing center, and manufactures electrical equipment, cedar products, flour, hosiery, and hospital supplies. Cattle and various types of horses are raised, especially Tennessee walking horses.

Murphysboro city, pop. 9176, seat of Jackson Co., SW Illinois, on the Big Muddy R., 7 mi/11 km NW of Carbondale. Settled in 1850, it was during the Civil War the secret headquarters of the Knights of the Golden Circle, a group of Confederate sympathizers. Feed and fertilizer are among the products manufactured here. Kinkaid L. and Lake Murphysboro State Park are to the NW.

Murray **1.** city, pop. 14,439, seat of Calloway Co., SW Kentucky, on the East Fork of the Clarks R., 37 mi/60 km SSE of Paducah. The town has flour, feed, and lumber mills, and various light manufactures. It is also a trade center and gateway to the LAND BETWEEN THE LAKES. Murray State University (1922) is here. **2.** city, pop. 31,282, Salt Lake Co., NC Utah, a residential suburb 8 mi/13 km S of Salt Lake City. It is also a retail hub and a trade center for an irrigated farming area. There is a diversity of light manufacturing, including computer technology. The county fairgrounds are here.

Murray, Lake see under SALUDA R., South Carolina.

Murray Bay see LA MALBAIE, Québec.

Murray Hill **1.** residential and commercial section, E Midtown Manhattan, New York City. The 18th-century estate of Robert Murray, at the site of modern Park Ave. and 37th St., gave the area its name. It was a popular country retreat in the early 19th century, rivaling Bloomingdale and Harlem; by the 1890s it was a stronghold of New York high society. Today it is a district of private clubs, homes, and offices close to some of New York's tallest office buildings. Kips Bay lies S, Turtle Bay N. **2.** neighborhood in Cleveland, Ohio, immediately E of UNIVERSITY CIRCLE, 6 mi/10 km E of PUBLIC SQUARE. It has long been Cleveland's main Italian neighborhood.

Murrells Inlet see under GRAND STRAND, South Carolina.

Murrysville borough, pop. 17,240, Westmoreland Co., SW Pennsylvania, 15 mi/24 km ESE of Pittsburgh, of which it is a largely residential suburb.

Muscatine city, pop. 22,881, seat of Muscatine Co., SE Iowa, on the Mississippi R., across from Illinois City, Illinois, and 25 mi/40 km SW of Davenport. A shipping and processing center for the region's corn and other farm products, it is well known for the pearl buttons produced from mussel shells found in nearby streams. Canned foods, grains, industrial alcohol, and fertilizers are also produced. Founded as a trading post in 1833, it was an important 19th-century river port and lumbering center. It is the site of Muscatine Community College (1929). Wildcat Den State Park and the Fairport National Fish Hatchery are 8 mi/13 km ENE.

Muscle Beach see under VENICE, California.

Muscle Shoals city, pop. 9611, Colbert Co., NW Alabama, on the Tennessee R., 5 mi/8 km S of Florence. It is named for the former 37 mi/60 km-long Tennessee R. rapids also known as Mussel Shoals. This stretch of the river, originally unnavigable, was harnessed by the WILSON DAM at the end of World War I. Designed to provide nitrates for munitions, the project turned to producing fertilizer and chemicals as well as hydroelectric power. The TENNESSEE VALLEY AUTHORITY took over in 1933, building the WHEELER and PICKWICK dams. In the 1960s Muscle Shoals acquired another reputation, as a recording center for soul and other popular artists. Shoals Community College (1966) is here.

Musconetcong Mountain Appalachian ridge in NW New Jersey, 800–900 ft/250–275 m high. It runs NE from the Delaware R., 7 mi/11 km S of Phillipsburg, paralleling (E) the MUSCONETCONG R., some 20 mi/32 km, and is continued NE as Schooleys Mt.

Musconetcong River 45 mi/72 km long, in WC New Jersey. It flows from L. HOPATCONG and smaller (SW) L. Musconetcong, in SE Sussex Co., SW through HACKETTSTOWN, Changewater, Hampton, and Bloomsbury, to join the Delaware R. opposite Riegelsville, Pennsylvania.

Musgrove's Mill battle site: see under CLINTON, South Carolina.

Music Center entertainment complex in downtown LOS ANGELES, California, immediately W of the Civic Center, on BUNKER HILL. Built between 1964 and 1969, the Dorothy Chandler Pavilion, Ahmanson Theater, and Mark Taper Forum were joined by the Walt Disney Music Hall in 1992.

muskeg term (from the Algonquian) for a kind of northern (chiefly subarctic, and associated with PERMAFROST) bog within which mosses and sedges are in the process of producing layers of peat. Immediately surrounding trees, mostly larches and spruces, are usually stunted. In North America, muskeg covers large areas around Hudson Bay, but is found as far E as Newfoundland and as far W as Alaska.

Muskeget Channel strait (8–14 mi/13–23 km wide) separating the islands of NANTUCKET (E) and MARTHA'S VINEYARD

(W), between Nantucket Sound and the Atlantic Ocean, in SE Massachusetts. Muskeget and Tuckernuck islands, part of Nantucket, lie in the channel.

Muskego village, pop. 16,813, Waukesha Co., SE Wisconsin, on Little Muskego L., a residential suburb 15 mi/24 km SW of Milwaukee.

Muskegon city, pop. 40,283, seat of Muskegon Co., W Michigan, on L. Michigan and Muskegon L. at the mouth of the Muskegon R., 33 mi/53 km NW of Grand Rapids. It was founded as a fur-trading post (1812) and named in Algonquian for its "marshy river." It had numerous sawmills during the late-19th-century lumber boom, and was a major lumber shipping point. When forests were depleted, Muskegon developed manufacturing, now including metals, tools and dies, chemicals, heavy machinery, and auto engines and parts. This port of entry enjoys an international trade and ships oil products, pig and scrap iron, coal, and coke. Tourism is also important to the economy. The Muskegon Business College (1885) and Muskegon Community College (1926) are here. Muskegon State Park is 5 mi/8 km NW of the city, and P.J. Hoffmaster State Park is 7 mi/11 km SW. Two large amusement parks are also nearby.

Muskegon County 507 sq mi/1313 sq km, pop. 158,983, in W Michigan, bounded by L. Michigan (W) and drained by the Muskegon and White rivers. Its seat is MUSKEGON. There are numerous state parks and recreation areas along the lakeshore, and inland are the Muskegon State Game Area and parts of Manistee National Forest. Commercial fishing and tourism are important in the W, and there is manufacturing at Muskegon. The county's agricultural output includes vegetables, fruit, beans, poultry, livestock, grain, and dairy products.

Muskegon Heights city, pop. 13,176, Muskegon Co., W Michigan, adjacent (S) to MUSKEGON. Machinery is manufactured in this largely residential suburb.

Muskegon River 227 mi/365 km long, in Michigan. It rises in HOUGHTON L., then flows SW, past Big Rapids and Newaygo, forming Muskegon L. (5 mi/8 km long and 2 mi/3 km wide), before entering L. Michigan just W of Muskegon. Hardy Dam, completed in 1932, impounds Hardy Dam Pond, SE of White Cloud.

Musketaquid see under CONCORD, Massachusetts.

Muskingum County 654 sq mi/1694 sq km, pop. 82,068, in EC Ohio, intersected by the Licking and Muskingum rivers and including Dillon L. Its seat is ZANESVILLE, the only major city in this largely rural county. Agriculture includes dairy, fruit, grain, and livestock farming, and there is some manufacturing at Roseville and Zanesville. Gravel, clay, coal, limestone, and sand are natural resources.

Muskingum River 112 mi/180 km long, in Ohio. It rises in C Ohio at the confluence of the Walhonding and Tuscarawas rivers, at Coshocton. It flows S past Dresden, the head of navigation, and Zanesville, McConnelsville, and Stockport, joining the Ohio R. at Marietta. Its main tributaries are the Licking and Zanesville rivers.

Muskogee city, pop. 37,708, seat of Muskogee Co., EC Oklahoma, on the Arkansas R. near its confluence with the Verdigris and Grand rivers, 45 mi/72 km SE of Tulsa. A fur trading center, it became in 1874 the administrative center for the Five Civilized Tribes. Today this railroad junction and port city processes and ships potatoes, cotton, and grain, and is a commercial hub for livestock and dairy producers. Oil is refined and petroleum products are shipped. Among local manufactures are iron, steel, wood products, glass, and clothing. It is the seat of Bacone College (1880).

Muskoka Lakes three interconnected bodies in SC Ontario, E of Georgian Bay, N of L. SIMCOE, and 90 mi/140 km N of Toronto. L. Muskoka (15 mi/24 km NE–SW and 5 mi/8 km wide) is connected to L. Rosseau by the Indian R. L. Rosseau is connected to L. Joseph by the St. Joseph R. After the 1875 arrival of the railroad, the area attracted wealthy summer vacationers. The Muskoka Lakes Association was formed in 1894 to prevent overdevelopment; the area now has thousands of vacation homes, chiefly of Torontonians. GRAVENHURST (S) is the primary gateway; Bracebridge (SE) and HUNTSVILLE (NE) are other centers of the larger area popularly called **the Muskokas,** which extends from ALGONQUIN PROVINCIAL PARK (E) to Georgian Bay (W) and contains hundreds of smaller lakes.

Musselshell River 292 mi/470 km long, in Montana. It rises in the Crazy Mts., and flows generally E, passing the cities of Harlowton and Roundup, then turns abruptly N at Melstone and continues to the SW shore of the huge FORT PECK L. on the Missouri R.

Mustang city, pop. 10,434, Canadian Co., C Oklahoma, 13 mi/21 km SW of Oklahoma City. Essentially a residential suburb, it has some light industry.

Mustang Island barrier island in Nueces Co., S Texas. Across the entrance to Corpus Christi Bay, it is 23 mi/37 km long and up to 4 mi/6 km wide. At the NE end is Port Aransas (pop. 2233), a fishing and ocean research center. The SW end is separated from PADRE I. by a narrow channel. The island is known as a bird habitat, and is popular for its beaches, fishing, and camping.

Myrtle Beach city, pop. 24,848, Horry Co., E South Carolina, on the Atlantic Ocean, 86 mi/138 km NE of Charleston. A year-round vacation center, now also a retirement community, it grew quickly in the 1970s and 1980s. Named for the profuse local myrtle bushes, it is the hub of the GRAND STRAND area, home to Myrtle Beach State Park, high-rise condominiums, golf courses, a convention center, a beach music culture, and other concomitants of a major coastal resort.

Myrtle Grove 1. unincorporated residential community, pop. 17,402, Escambia Co., NW Florida, in the extreme SW of the PANHANDLE, 2 mi/3 km E of Perdido Bay and the Alabama border, on the W side of Pensacola. **2.** see under WILMINGTON, North Carolina.

Mystic village, pop. 2618, in the town of STONINGTON, New London Co., extreme SE Connecticut. Situated on the estuarial Mystic R., it was a shipbuilding center by the end of the 17th century. In mid 19th century it was a whaling port and the builder of whalers and clipper ships. Today it is a tourist center known for its re-created Mystic Seaport and aquarium.

Mystic River 1. see under MYSTIC, Connecticut. **2.** 7 mi/11 km long, rising in Mystic Lakes, Winchester and Arlington, E Massachusetts, and flowing, by way of Medford, Somerville, Malden, and Everett, into Boston Harbor at Charlestown. Heavily industrial in its lower sections, it is the site of container and liquefied natural gas terminals. Above a dam at the Malden/Everett line, it has been somewhat reclaimed, and is partly lined by parks. The Mystic River (Tobin) Bridge carries traffic on US 1 between Charlestown and Chelsea, at the river's mouth.

N

Naalehu unincorporated community, pop. 1027, Hawaii Co., on the S coast of the island of HAWAII. At 19° 03′ N, it is the southernmost settlement in the United States. KA LAE (South Cape) is 12 mi/19 km SSW.

Nacogdoches city, pop. 30,872, seat of Nacogdoches Co., E Texas, near the Angelina R., 130 mi/210 km NNE of Houston. In 1716, a Spanish mission was built here near a Nacogdoche Indian village. Stephen F. Austin State University (1923) is nearby on the site of the original (1779) settlement, which began with a Spanish post now called Old Stone Fort, built on El Camino Real, a 1691 Spanish highway. Americans moved into the area around 1820; it was here that Hayden Edwards declared Texas independence in 1826; he tried to organize the Republic of Fredonia, but fled in 1827 after receiving little support. Nacogdoches published the state's first newspaper, and was active in the 1835–36 Texas Revolution. Nacogdoches University, which operated for a while after 1845, was the first nonsectarian Texas institution. The Civil War and collapse of the plantation system caused a decline, but the city rebounded as a lumber and manufacturing center. The state's first oil wells were drilled here in 1859. The area produces beef and dairy cattle and poultry, and the city has processing plants. It also makes feed, fertilizer, and various other products. Nearby Sam Rayburn Reservoir and Davy Crockett, Angelina, and Sabine national forests all add to its attractiveness to visitors. The city's name derives from the same source as that of NATCHITOCHES, Louisiana.

Nags Head town, pop. 1838, on Bodie I., between the Atlantic Ocean (E) and Roanoke Sound, just SSE of KITTY HAWK and Kill Devil Hills, in Dare Co., E North Carolina. One of the oldest OUTER BANKS resort communities, it is known for its fine beaches and excellent fishing. Jockey's Ridge State Park has the highest sand dunes on the East Coast, reaching 140 ft/43 m, and is popular with hikers, hang gliders, and kite flyers.

Nahanni National Park 1815 sq mi/4700 sq km, along the South Nahanni R. in the MACKENZIE Mts., extreme SW Northwest Territories. It was established in 1972 in an area that saw a 1900s rush of gold prospectors, some of whom disappeared mysteriously. Remote and without roads, the park draws visitors attracted to this history and to the 200 mi/320 km of the river, noted for its gorges and whitewater canoeing. Virginia Falls has a drop of 294 ft/90 m.

Nahant town, pop. 3828, Essex Co., NE Massachusetts, 9 mi/14 km ENE of Boston. It is a rocky "island" situated at the end of a long peninsula that runs from Lynn S into Massachusetts Bay. A popular summer resort as early as the 1820s, the retreat of numerous writers, painters, and wealthy Bostonians, Nahant is also a residential suburb.

Nampa city, pop. 28,365, Canyon Co., SW Idaho, 18 mi/29 km W of Boise. Founded in 1886, it was originally an agricultural hamlet, and became a railroad center in the 1890s. It remains a processing and shipping center, serving a farming region that produces fruits, vegetables, dairy products, livestock, feed, vegetable seed, and grain. Industries include frozen food, potato, and meat processing. It is the seat of Nazarene College (1913). Since 1915, Nampa has hosted the annual Snake River Stampede, one of the West's largest rodeos. The Deer Flat National Wildlife Refuge on L. Lowell is 3 mi/5 km SW.

Nanaimo city, pop. 60,129, Nanaimo Regional District (pop. 101,736), SW British Columbia, on the Strait of Georgia and SE Vancouver I., 55 mi/90 km NNW of Victoria. A seaport, it was originally a Hudson's Bay Company post (1849). The settlement developed after the discovery (1852) of coal, and the industry was central until 1953. Today Nanaimo is the center of a lumbering region and salmon and cod fisheries, and a ferry port. Shipbuilding and tourism are important. A biological research station and the preserved HBC fort (1853) are here.

Nanih Waiyah Choctaw site: see under PHILADELPHIA, Mississippi.

Nanisivik see under BAFFIN I., Northwest Territories.

Nansemond River 25 mi/40 km long, in SE Virginia. It rises in SUFFOLK city, where it is dammed to form several lakes. A Western Branch, flowing SE from Isle of Wight Co., is dammed to form Western Branch Reservoir. Below the confluence of the two branches, the river is estuarial, flowing N into HAMPTON ROADS.

Nantahala Mountains range extending S from the junction of the Nantahala and Little Tennessee rivers in W North Carolina for c.50 mi/80 km into the Chattahoochee National Forest in NE Georgia. It includes Wayah Bald (5400 ft/1647 m), 9 mi/14 km W of Franklin, North Carolina, which is noted for its wild azaleas, and is largely within 525,000-ac/213,000-ha **Nantahala National Forest,** which also includes the Cheoah, Cowee, SNOWBIRD, Tusquitee, and Valley River mountains. The forest, headquartered at Asheville, includes Standing Indian Mt. (5498 ft/1677 m); WHITESIDE Mt.; Jackrabbit Mt. Wilderness Area near Chatuge L.; Fontana L. along the border with Great Smoky Mts. National Park;

the Joyce Kilmer Memorial Forest near Santeetlah L.; L. Hiwassee; 8 mi/13 km–long Nantahala Gorge; Whitewater R. and its 411-ft/125-m falls; Glen Falls; and segments of the TRAIL OF TEARS and the APPALACHIAN TRAIL.

Nantasket Beach in Plymouth Co., E Massachusetts, on Massachusetts Bay, 10 mi/16 km SE of Boston. It is a popular resort in the town of HULL.

Nanticoke **1.** city, pop. 22,727, Haldimand-Norfolk Regional Municipality, extreme S Ontario, on L. Erie (S), 27 mi/43 km SW of Hamilton. It was created in 1974, amalgamating seven municipalities. Port Dover, on the lake, now the town center, was settled in the 1800s on a Neutral (Iroquoian) site. An agricultural service center, now also a well-known beach resort, it has what is said to be the world's largest freshwater fishing fleet. Nanticoke is also the site of a huge steel plant and of an Ontario Hydro coal-fired power station, also said to be the world's largest. **2.** city, pop. 12,267, Luzerne Co., NE Pennsylvania, on the Susquehanna R., 7 mi/11 km SW of Wilkes-Barre. Formerly an important coal center, it has diversified its economy and manufactures chemicals, clothing, shoes, and cigars.

Nanticoke River 50 mi/80 km long, in Delaware and Maryland. It is formed by the confluence of several streams in Sussex Co., Delaware, just E of SEAFORD. It flows SW, through Seaford, then into Maryland, and enters the large estuary of Tangier Sound, part of Chesapeake Bay. Its main tributary is Marshyhope Creek, formerly called the Northwest Fork of the Nanticoke.

Nantucket island, 46 sq mi/120 sq km, coterminous, with small adjacent islands, with Nantucket town and county, pop. 6012, in the Atlantic Ocean 28 mi/45 km S of Cape Cod, Massachusetts. It measures 14 mi/23 km long, and averages 3.5 mi/6 km wide. Originally part of the Plymouth Colony, then of New York, Nantucket was ceded to Massachusetts in 1692. It developed as a whaling port in the 18th century, and is today an artists' colony and summer resort known for its beaches and for Nantucket village, the main commercial center, and other small communities on the island, including SIASCONSET, Wauwinet, and MADAKET. Nantucket has many homes from the 18th and 19th centuries, and a cobblestoned main street lined with shops.

Nantucket Sound inlet of the Atlantic Ocean between Cape Cod (N), Nantucket and Martha's Vineyard islands (S), and lower Cape Cod and the Elizabeth Is. (W). Twenty-eight mi/45 km long E–W and 5–25 mi/8–40 km wide, it joins Vineyard Sound on the W. The sound is noted for its treacherous currents and other navigational challenges.

Nanuet unincorporated village, pop. 14,065, in Clarkstown, Rockland Co., SE New York, 5 mi/8 km W of Nyack. A largely residential suburb just S of the New York State thruway, it is home to the International Shrine of St. Anthony.

Napa city, pop. 61,842, seat of Napa Co. (pop. 110,765), NC California, 36 mi/58 km NE of San Francisco. Founded on part of an 1838 Spanish RANCHO, it became county seat in 1848. Its position at the head of navigation on the Napa R. made it a shipping point for cattle, lumber, and minerals. Later it developed as a market for agricultural produce, and now ships wines and fruits, and has varied light manufactures. Tourism is important, and Napa State Hospital and Napa Valley College (1940) are here. The **Napa Valley,** extending 30 mi/48 km NW from the city, is the best-known US winemaking district, with over 50 wineries in such communities as CALISTOGA and SAINT HELENA. It, and the parallel SONOMA Valley (W), are also major tourist attractions. The city of Napa houses many Napa Valley workers (it does not itself have wineries), and has recently become a popular exurban home for Bay Area residents.

Na Pali Coast see under WAIMEA CANYON, Kauai, Hawaii.

Naperville city, pop. 85,351, Du Page and Will counties, NE Illinois, on the West Branch of the Du Page R., a suburb 30 mi/48 km W of Chicago. It is mainly a residential community, but furniture, electronic switching equipment, plastic products, building blocks, and ice cream are manufactured here. Recent large-scale commercial and industrial development, particularly in high-tech fields, has clustered along I-88, the ILLINOIS RESEARCH AND DEVELOPMENT CORRIDOR, at the N edge of the city. Captain John Naper built a sawmill on the site in the early 1830s. Farming and lumbering gave way to industry with the arrival of the Chicago, Burlington and Quincy Railroad in 1864. North Central College (1861) and its affiliate Evangelical Theological Seminary are here.

Naples city, pop. 19,505, Collier Co., SW Florida, on the Gulf of Mexico, 35 mi/56 km S of Fort Myers, at the W end of the TAMIAMI TRAIL and ALLIGATOR ALLEY. Developed as a resort from the 1880s, it was long accessible only by boat from Fort Myers; its 1000-ft/300-m fishing pier dates from that era. It is an increasingly fashionable winter resort, known for its miles of beaches and its elegant Fifth Ave. shopping district. Commercial shrimping and fishing and the packing and shipping of vegetables are important. Naples is situated an area rich in wildlife and vegetation, with Rookery Bay (including the Briggs Nature Center) 5 mi/8 km S, Collier Seminole State Park 15 mi/24 km SE, and the Corkscrew Swamp Sanctuary 20 mi/32 km NE. East Naples (unincorporated, pop. 22,951) is the scene of much recent residential development.

Napoleon city, pop. 8884, Henry Co., NW Ohio, on the Maumee R., 14 mi/22 km ENE of Defiance. It is the marketing center for a fertile diversified farming area. Local manufactures include automobile parts, agricultural machinery, metal goods, brick, tile, and food products.

Nappanee city, pop. 5510, Kosciusko and Elkhart counties, N Indiana, 20 mi/32 km SE of South Bend, in an agricultural area in which grain, onions, and mint are major crops. Commercial flower growing, lumber milling, and the production of canned goods, furniture, and flour are among the city's industries. The area is heavily Amish.

Naranja see under PRINCETON, Florida.

Narraganset Fort see under SOUTH KINGSTOWN, Rhode Island.

Narragansett town, pop. 14,985, Washington Co., S Rhode Island, 27 mi/43 km S of Providence and 9 mi/14 km WSW of Newport, at the entrance of Narragansett Bay. Point JUDITH is at its S extreme. Settled in the mid 1600s, it was not made a town until 1901; it is named for the local Narraganset Indians. It developed as a resort in the late 19th century. The township includes the summer resort of Narragansett Pier and the villages of Galilee and Jerusalem, as well as a state reservation with Scarborough Beach. Fishing and agriculture are important.

Narragansett Bay island-filled arm of the Atlantic Ocean extending deep into Rhode Island. Thirty mi/48 km N–S and 2–12 mi/3–19 km wide, it has been important to shipping since Colonial times, and is now a center for summer resorts and fishing. PROVIDENCE is at the head of the bay, on the

Providence R.; MOUNT HOPE BAY, a NE branch, provides a harbor for Fall River, Massachusetts. The largest island in the bay is RHODE I., bordered by the Sakonnet R. (E) and East Passage (W), with the town of Newport on its SW side. Conanicut and Prudence islands also lie in the bay, which was originally the home of the Narraganset Indians. The Italian explorer Giovanni Verrazano was the first European known to have encountered the bay, in 1524.

Narrows, the tidal strait, 1 mi/1.5 km wide and 3 mi/5 km long, between Staten I. and Brooklyn, New York. It provides passage between Upper and Lower New York Bay. In the early 20th century a tunnel under the Narrows was discussed; the VERRAZANO-NARROWS BRIDGE finally closed the gap in 1964, carrying highway traffic between Fort Wadsworth, Staten Island, and Bay Ridge, Brooklyn.

NASA Space Flight Center see **1.** HUNTSVILLE, Alabama (George C. Marshall Space Flight Center). **2.** CLEAR LAKE, Houston, Texas (Lyndon B. Johnson Space Flight Center).

Nashoba former utopian community in Shelby Co., SW Tennessee, on the Wolf R., within modern GERMANTOWN. Frances Wright founded this settlement in 1827 to educate freed slaves for freedom; it lasted barely three years.

Nashua city, pop. 79,662, second-largest in the state and seat of Hillsborough Co., S New Hampshire. Originally a fur trading post, Nashua is on the Merrimack and Nashua rivers, 18 mi/29 km S of Manchester, just N of the Massachusetts border. It was settled in 1655 as part of Massachusetts, and successfully claimed by New Hampshire in 1741. Two settlements on opposite sides of the river, one an Indian village, were joined in 1837 and incorporated in 1853. A textile manufacturer until after World War II, Nashua now produces shoes, asbestos, electronics, chemicals, office equipment, plastics, metals, machines, glass, toys, greeting cards, and textiles. The Federal Aviation Agency Center controlling New England and upstate New York air traffic, New England Aeronautical Institute, Rivier College (1933), Daniel Webster College (1965), and a federal fish hatchery are here.

Nashville city, pop. 488,374, state capital and seat of Davidson Co., NC Tennessee, in the NASHVILLE BASIN, on the Cumberland R. It almost completely occupies the county (501 sq mi/1298 sq km; pop. 510,784), in which there are also a half-dozen small suburbs. It was founded in 1779 as part of the TRANSYLVANIA purchase from the Cherokees, at a place called French Lick; here Fort Nashborough, named for a Revolutionary general, was built on a bluff above the river. At the N end of the NATCHEZ TRACE, Nashville, incorporated in 1806, became a regional trade center and, in 1843, Tennessee's capital. The city was occupied by Union forces in 1862, and became a base of operations. Heavily fortified, it withstood a desperate attack by John Bell Hood's Confederate forces in Dec. 1864. In the 1930s, power from Tennessee Valley Authority dams allowed Nashville's economy to expand, and it is now diverse. The city is headquarters for finance and insurance companies. Its manufactures include clothing, heating and cooking equipment, tires, and auto glass. There is a large recording industry, and several Protestant denominations maintain publishing and administrative operations. Since 1925 the Grand Ole Opry has broadcast hillbilly and country and western music, and OPRYLAND and other local sites associated with the music and its stars draw tourists. The city is also a convention center and location for film and television production. The "Athens of the South" numbers among its institutions the Cumberland Museum and Science Center, Tennessee Center for Performing Arts, Fisk University (1867), Vanderbilt University (1873), Meharry Medical College (1876), and Tennessee State University (1912). Its replica of the PARTHENON is well known. President James K. Polk is buried on the grounds of the Capitol (1859), and Andrew Jackson's home, the HERMITAGE, is 12 mi/19 km NE of Downtown.

Nashville Basin region in C Tennessee, a lowland segment of the low plateaus along the W of the Appalachian system. Stretching some 120 mi/190 km E–W, it is similar to the BLUEGRASS REGION of Kentucky, to the N; its limestone underlies a fertile agricultural area, and is quarried. Phosphates and zinc are important products. The Highland Rim, an escarpment 400 ft/122 m above the Basin, lies in a semicircle (W, S, and E) around it. In the N, the Cumberland R. cuts through; the city of Nashville is in the Basin's NW.

Nassau Bay see under CLEAR LAKE, Houston, Texas.

Nassau County 287 sq mi/743 sq km, pop. 1,287,348, in SE New York, at the W end of Long Island, adjacent to QUEENS. It is often considered the prototypical suburb; it developed rapidly after World War II thanks to housing tracts such as LEVITTOWN and its imitators and to construction of a network of parkways making the region easily accessible. Today almost the entire county is heavily built up. Over 95% of Nassau's residents live in three towns, HEMPSTEAD, NORTH HEMPSTEAD, and OYSTER BAY. The North Shore, with rolling hills and large estates, is less crowded; some of its villages retain a small-town aspect. The South Shore's beaches and inlets attract swimmers, boaters, and fishers. The economy is diversified, with many high-tech companies, defense contractors, and financial, insurance, and publishing concerns.

Natchez city, pop. 19,460, seat of Adams Co., SW Mississippi, on the Mississippi R., 60 mi/97 km SW of Vicksburg. Home to the tribe that gave it its name, the site was chosen for the French Fort Rosalie in 1716. The Natchez destroyed the settlement in 1729, but were themselves exterminated in 1730. The French lost control to the British in 1763, but the Spanish took Natchez in 1779. The US took possession in 1798, and made Natchez the first capital of the territory of Mississippi. It quickly gained importance as a supply depot and river port. The S terminus of the NATCHEZ TRACE, the city experienced quick growth in the early 19th century as waves of immigrants arrived to share the prosperity of a cotton-based economy. Natchez's aristocratic community wielded cultural and political influence through the mid 19th century, until railroads took trade away from the river. Bombarded and briefly occupied by Union forces in 1863, the city has since then served as a regional trade center, and has acquired some industry, making wood, rubber, paper, and textile products. Today Natchez is a tourist mecca best known for its annual spring "pilgrimage," when its antebellum homes are open to the public and historical pageants are held.

Natchez Trace historic road, c.450 mi/720 km long, running between Natchez, Mississippi, and Nashville, Tennessee, through NW Alabama. A buffalo track heavily traveled by Chickasaws and Choctaws, and later by the French, English, and Spanish, it assumed commercial and military significance in the newly formed US. Employed as a northward route for homebound flatboatmen who had floated goods down the Mississippi R. to New Orleans, it soon became a highway for pioneers settling the Southwest. Made a post road in 1800, it remained important until the 1830s, when faster steamboat travel became common. The modern **Natchez Trace Parkway** (1938) generally follows the old road; the **Natchez Trace National Scenic Trail,** under development, will parallel the parkway.

Natchitoches city, pop. 16,609, seat of Natchitoches Parish, NW Louisiana, on Cane River L. (formerly part of the RED R.), 48 mi/77 km NW of Alexandria. Founded in 1714 as Fort St. Jean Baptiste, a French military and trading post, it was later renamed for the Natchitoches tribe, who also gave their name, in another form, to NACOGDOCHES, Texas. The oldest permanent white settlement in the LOUISIANA PURCHASE, it developed in the early 19th century as a cotton center. It declined, however, after 1832, when the Red R. changed its course, moving 5 mi/8 km to the E. Natchitoches is now primarily a processing and market center for regional farms. It has diversified light manufactures, and attracts tourists. It is home to Northwestern State University (1884).

Natick **1.** town, pop. 30,510, Middlesex Co., E Massachusetts, on L. COCHITUATE, 15 mi/24 km SW of Boston. Founded in 1650 for missionary John Eliot's Indian converts, it has a monument to Eliot and an Indian burying ground. White settlers eventually crowded out the Indians, and agriculture developed. Now a suburb of Boston, Natick has manufactured leather, paper, and food products; beer; baseballs; preserves; apparel; and chemicals. The US Army maintains a large research laboratory on L. Cochituate. **2.** see under WEST WARWICK, Rhode Island.

National Capital Region 1800 sq mi/4660 sq km, embracing OTTAWA, Ontario, Canada's capital, and neighboring communities. Established in 1958, it is administered by the National Capital Commission, which has legal control only over the Federal land (about 30%) within its boundaries, and is concerned primarily with land use planning and cultural development. Ottawa, the Québec cities of AYLMER, HULL, and GATINEAU, and other municipalities entirely or partly within the region govern themselves.

National City city, pop. 54,249, San Diego Co., SW California, 4 mi/6 km S of downtown San Diego, on San Diego Bay. Incorporated in 1887, it has been a fruit packing center; other industries have turned out processed meats and wood products. It is now largely reliant on military spending: the Navy's largest surface vessel base, the San Diego Naval Station, on the bay, is important to its economy; the mothballed Pacific Reserve Fleet is anchored nearby. The National Steel and Shipbuilding Company and other maritime corporations are major employers.

National Civil Rights Museum formerly, **Lorraine Motel** on Mulberry St. in downtown Memphis, Tennessee. The site where the Rev. Martin Luther King, Jr., was assassinated in April 1968 reopened (1991) as a museum, with exhibits on movements and individuals of the civil rights struggle.

national forest section of US PUBLIC LANDS reserved for purposes enumerated under various Federal laws, and maintained and preserved by the Forest Service, an arm of the Department of Agriculture. There are 156 national forests, 19 NATIONAL GRASSLANDS, and 15 other related designated areas in the National Forest System, covering over 190 million ac/77 million ha (close to 300,000 sq mi/773,000 sq km, or c.8.4% of all US land area) in 44 states, the Virgin Is., and Puerto Rico. Federal law prescribes two basic principles for these lands: multiple uses and a sustained yield of resources. The uses permissible include wood and paper production, recreation, livestock grazing, mining, and the maintenance of natural beauty, wildlife habitat, and watersheds. About one-sixth of national forest land is also in WILDERNESS AREAS, which may overlap with various other state and Federal reserves. A timber reserve (1891) attached to Yellowstone National Park, now in the Shoshone National Forest, was the first element in the system; national forests as such came into being in 1907. Canada does not have "national forests"; its immense forests (49% of its land area, of which only 3% is reserved for other purposes) are managed chiefly by the Dominion government (in the Yukon and Northwest territories) or by the provinces (90% of forest lands in the provinces are provincial CROWN LANDS), under various policies and guidelines. The nation is the world's leading exporter of forest products.

national grassland any of 19 separate areas administered by the US Forest Service under the same mandate as the national forests, essentially that they be open to multiple uses and be managed so as to permit a sustained yield; in the case of the grasslands, watershed conservation and grazing are key. They tend to be much less used recreationally than the forests. The vast majority are in the W Great Plains.

National Institutes of Health also, **NIH** Department of Health and Human Services agency, the largest single supporter of biomedical research in the US. Its 200-ac/81-ha campus is 8 mi/13 km NW of Washington, D.C., in BETHESDA, Maryland.

national park reserve designated and maintained by a national government, to protect and make available for public enjoyment an area regarded as having scenic, natural, scientific, historical, or other interest. **1.** in the US: any of the 50 generally largest and most varied units of the National Park System. Yellowstone National Park (1872) is the oldest of these, although Yosemite National Park, originally a state reserve, predates it. All elements of the National Park System are under the control of the Department of the Interior; they were for the most part created from PUBLIC LANDS, although since 1925 the government has been empowered to accept donations of land from other sources. The more than 300 other units of the system include **national monuments,** which are generally smaller and display less diversity than national parks, tending to focus on one site, geologic formation, or structure of historic importance. National monuments may be proclaimed by the president, while establishment of a park requires an act of Congress. **National historic sites, national memorials, national military parks, national battlefield parks, national battlefields,** and **national battlefield sites** all preserve discrete sites of varied historic importance. **National seashores, national lakeshores,** and **national rivers** have been established with greatest emphasis on conservation of the areas included (see also WILD, SCENIC, AND RECREATIONAL RIVERS). **National recreation areas** are zones near major cities or near certain engineering sites (e.g., dams) that have been reserved esp. for recreational use in densely populated areas. **National parkways** are roadways that have been preserved for their scenic value. **National scenic trails, national historic trails, national recreational trails,** and other affiliated units are elements of the National Trails System (1968), established to preserve and maintain a wide variety of public footpaths. **2.** in Canada:

any of 35 units of a system developed since the creation (1885, during the period of Pacific Railway construction) of the forerunner of Banff National Park. Recent additions to the system have included the BRUCE PENINSULA's Fathom Five National Marine Park (1987), the first of its kind, and five **national park reserves,** representing a shift in emphasis toward natural conservation.

National Radio Astronomy Observatory **1.** see under GREEN BANK, West Virginia. **2.** see under KITT PEAK, Arizona; VERY LARGE ARRAY, New Mexico; GREEN BANK, West Virginia.

National Reactor Testing Station see IDAHO NATIONAL ENGINEERING LABORATORY, Idaho.

National Road also, **National Pike** historic highway, authorized in 1806, that led W from Cumberland, Maryland, eventually reaching all the way to St. Louis, Missouri. It was the major route for trans-Appalachian migration in the early 19th century. Its first section, the Cumberland Road, was completed in 1818. This followed Nemacolin's Path, a trail blazed by the Delaware chief in 1749–50 between the Potomac and Monongahela rivers, and used during the French and Indian Wars; after reaching the junction of the Redstone Creek with the Monongahela (near modern Brownsville, Pennsylvania), the Cumberland Road proceeded to Wheeling. The route was paved with crushed stone. In the 1820s the road was extended from Wheeling through Cambridge, Zanesville, Columbus, and Springfield, Ohio, to Vandalia, Illinois, and finally to St. Louis. Individual states took over its operation. The growth of railways by the 1850s ended the National Road's central role in moving America west. Modern US 40 generally follows its route.

National Tennis Center see under FLUSHING MEADOWS-CORONA PARK, New York.

Natrona Heights village in Harrison Township, (pop. 11,763), Allegheny Co., SW Pennsylvania, 19 mi/31 km NE of Pittsburgh, on the Allegheny R. It produces chemicals, and had a major salt works as far back as 1853.

Natural Bridge **1.** see under BANKHEAD NATIONAL FOREST, Alabama. **2.** see under TALLAHASSEE, Florida. **3.** in the DANIEL BOONE NATIONAL FOREST, 5 mi/8 km SE of Slade, Powell Co., EC Kentucky, 52 mi/84 km SE of Lexington. It is 85 ft/26 m wide at the base, and clears c.65 ft/20 m. **4.** natural wonder in Rockbridge Co., WC Virginia, 12 mi/19 km SSW of Lexington and just N of the James R., a limestone span over Cedar Creek that was formed by the collapse of most of the roof of a cavern. With a span of 90 ft/27 m, it is 215 ft/66 m high and 50–100 ft/15–30 m wide. The bridge is on land once owned by Thomas Jefferson, who maintained a guest cottage nearby. Today a variety of tourist facilities are clustered around it.

Natural Bridges National Monument 7636-ac/3093-ha area of canyons and natural sandstone bridges, 30 mi/48 km W of Blanding, in San Juan Co., SE Utah. Three large bridges, named Owachomo, Sipapu, and Kachina by the Hopi, are in two adjacent canyons, and are linked by an 8-mi/13-km paved hiking loop. The ancient ANASAZI left pictographs and the remainders of cliff dwellings in the area.

Naugatuck borough and coterminous township, pop. 30,625, New Haven Co., SW Connecticut, on the Naugatuck R., adjacent (S) to Waterbury. It includes Union City and part of the Naugatuck State Forest. The area's abundant waterpower led to early industrial development; Charles Goodyear perfected the vulcanization process for rubber here in 1843. The modern diversified economy includes the manufacture of metals, plastics, chemicals, machinery, and instruments.

Naugatuck River 65 mi/105 km long, in W Connecticut. It rises in Litchfield Co. at the confluence of several small streams and flows S past several important manufacturing centers, supplying power at Torrington, Thomaston, Waterbury, Naugatuck, and Ansonia, to join the Housatonic R. at Derby. There are numerous short, steep tributaries that flow into the industrialized and deforested valley, causing extremely fast runoff, sometimes resulting in severe flooding. In Aug. 1955, a flood claimed 42 lives and caused $220 million in damage; as a result, local protection works and flood control dams have been built.

Nauset Harbor sheltered harbor on the E coast of Cape Cod, Barnstable Co., SE Massachusetts, between Eastham and Orleans. The long barrier beach extending N and S from the Nauset Inlet along the E of the Cape is called **Nauset Beach.**

Naushon Island 7 mi/11 km long, the largest of the ELIZABETH Is., Dukes Co., SE Massachusetts.

Nauvoo city, pop. 1108, Hancock Co., WC Illinois, on the Mississippi R., opposite Montrose, Iowa, 38 mi/61 km W of Macomb. Settled as Commerce in 1830, Nauvoo (from the Hebrew for "beautiful place") was renamed with the arrival of Mormons led by Joseph Smith, who made the city their headquarters. In 1838–46, the Mormon community swelled to over 12,000 people, attracting converts whose contributions and real estate purchases made it the state's wealthiest city. At its peak, Nauvoo was the state's largest city, courted by state political parties who granted the Mormons a home-rule charter and their own militia. Anti-Mormon hostilities led to Smith's murder and the departure of his followers in 1846. French disciples of utopian Étienne Cabet soon established a communistic Icarian settlement here (1849). After it was disbanded in 1858, German and Irish immigrants rebuilt the city, which today depends on tourism and the production of wine (introduced by the Icarians) and blue cheese. The homes of Brigham Young and other Mormon leaders, the Joseph Smith Historic Center, and Nauvoo State Park and Historic Site are popular tourist attractions.

Navajo Indian Reservation c.16 million ac/6.5 million ha (25,000 sq mi/65,000 sq km), pop. 148,451, in NE Arizona, SE Utah, and NW New Mexico. It surrounds the FOUR CORNERS on three sides, and extends SW across Arizona's BLACK MESA. The largest US reservation, it is home to about 70% of the largest US tribe (generally called the Navajo Nation). It surrounds Arizona's HOPI INDIAN RESERVATION; since the 1880s parts of the Hopi reservation have been jointly inhabited, and a process of relocating members of both groups continued into the 1990s. The Navajo, Athabascan nomads from W Canada, moved into the area in the 17th century, around which time they adopted sheepherding; their mobile lifestyle brought conflict with the Hopi and other sedentary local peoples. The reservation was created in 1868, and has since almost tripled in size. In the 1930s the government restricted the movement of the tribe's sheep, and promoted agriculture. Oil, gas, uranium, and various minerals have been extracted on Navajo land in recent years. WINDOW ROCK, Arizona, is the Navajo capital. SHIPROCK, New Mexico, and KAYENTA, Arizona, are other centers. Tuba City, Arizona (unincorporated, pop. 7323, Coconino Co.) is a trade center in the reservation's W. CANYON DE CHELLY is in NE Arizona; the Navajo Community College Tsaile campus is in neighboring Chinle. MONUMENT

VALLEY is in the reservation's N; the **Navajo National Monument,** protecting three Anasazi cliff dwellings (Betatakin, Keet Seal, and Inscription House), is just SW, outside Kayenta.

Navasota city, pop. 6296, Grimes Co., EC Texas, on the Navasota R. just NE of its confluence with the BRAZOS R., 63 mi/101 km NW of Houston. An important railroad junction, it ships cotton, other agricultural produce, livestock, and lumber, and has some light manufactures. Tradition has it that the French explorer La Salle was killed near here in March 1687, shot by mutineers.

Navassa Island French, **La Navase** c.2 sq mi/5 sq km, in the Caribbean Sea, 35 mi/56 km W of Haiti's southwesternmost point (Cap Carcasse), and 80 mi/130 km ENE of easternmost Jamaica. At the S of the Windward Passage, a major entry to the Caribbean, it has a lighthouse and is administered by the US Coast Guard. Haiti has also claimed the island, which was once an important guano source.

Navesink River estuary, 8 mi/13 km long, in Monmouth Co., NE New Jersey. It extends ENE from RED BANK to a junction with the Shrewsbury R. estuary, and passes N into SANDY HOOK Bay (Lower New York Bay). The Navesink Highlands lie N, Rumson and Fair Haven S.

Navy Island in the Niagara R., just SE of NIAGARA FALLS, Ontario, and NW of GRAND I., New York. Property of the Canadian government and managed by the Niagara Parks Commission, this small wilderness reserve was a British shipbuilding center in the 1760s. In 1837–38 it was occupied by William Lyon Mackenzie and his rebel followers for a short time, and subsequently had a brief life as a summer resort.

Navy Pier 3000 ft/915 m–long dock with a ballroom at its end, on L. Michigan, on the NEAR NORTH SIDE of Chicago, Illinois. Constructed in 1916 as a shipping pier, it was later the site of a University of Illinois campus. Today, the dock is the setting for events that include ChicagoFest and the International Folk Festival.

Nazareth borough, pop. 5713, Northampton Co., E Pennsylvania, 13 mi/21 km NE of Allentown. Settled (1740) by Moravians, it remained open only to members of the sect until 1865. The sect were noted for their work among the Indians and for their contributions to education. Today Nazareth is noted for the production of musical instruments, especially guitars, and as home to the auto racing Andretti family. It makes cement and paper boxes, and is surrounded by rich farm country.

Near Islands westernmost group in the ALEUTIAN Is., between the Bering Sea (N) and the N Pacific Ocean, in SW Alaska. Sixty mi/100 km E–W, the islands are 1100 mi/1800 km W of the ALASKA PENINSULA and 430 mi/700 km E of the Kamchatka Peninsula of E Siberia. The largest islands in the rocky, treeless group are uninhabited Agattu and ATTU, which was the scene of intense fighting during World War II. Shemya Air Force Base is on Shemya I. The group was named by the Russians, as nearest (of the Aleutians) to Asia.

Near North Side **1.** area of mixed residential and commercial neighborhoods immediately N of the LOOP in Chicago, Illinois. Aside from the economically distressed CABRINI-GREEN housing project, Near North includes such wealthy areas as the GOLD COAST and MAGNIFICENT MILE, along with OLD TOWN and DEPAUL. **2.** neighborhood in Minneapolis, Minnesota, immediately NW of Downtown. Originally housing immigrants, it experienced a postwar decline in population and housing quality. Recently, young professionals have discovered it, restoring many older homes and stimulating new residential construction.

Near Northside neighborhood in Columbus, Ohio, E of the Olentangy R., immediately S of the Ohio State University campus. An area of late-19th-century single-family homes, it saw its housing stock deteriorate after World War II. Since the 1970s, the nearby Battelle Memorial Institute has led efforts at restoring the older houses, displacing many poorer residents in the process. Today, it is a fashionable neighborhood of affluent homeowners.

Near Northwest Side group of neighborhoods just NW of the LOOP in Chicago, Illinois. Many of its communities were among the first stops for arriving immigrants from Eastern Europe and Latin America. Wicker Park, POLONIA, and Ukrainian Village are here.

Near South Side **1.** mixed commercial and residential area immediately S of the LOOP in Chicago, Illinois. Many abandoned warehouses and factories here have been converted into fashionable shops and apartments in such areas as PRINTERS' ROW. **2.** group of neighborhoods in Minneapolis, Minnesota, immediately S of Downtown. Areas range from the troubled PHILLIPS community to trendy LORING PARK; the WEDGE and WHITTIER combine aspects of both.

Near West Side **1.** also, **Lower West Side** collection of old ethnic neighborhoods near the University of Illinois at CHICAGO CIRCLE, SW of the LOOP, in Chicago, Illinois. HULL HOUSE, MAXWELL STREET, CHINATOWN, Old Greek Town, PILSEN, and the Italian enclave of Taylor Street are all here. **2.** see OHIO CITY, Cleveland, Ohio.

Nebo, Mount **1.** see under PISGAH. **2.** flat-topped mountain (1800 ft/549 m) in WC Arkansas, 7 mi/11 km W of DARDANELLE. A longtime resort site, it is in Mount Nebo State Park, overlooking the Arkansas River Valley. **3.** 11,877 ft/3620 m, the highest peak in the WASATCH RANGE, 30 mi/48 km S of Provo, in Juab Co., C Utah. Mount Nebo Wilderness Area of the Uinta National Forest surrounds the peak, and a scenic drive between Payson (N) and Nephi (S) traverses its alpine terrain.

Nebraska state of the C US, considered part of the MIDDLE WEST and a GREAT PLAINS state; 1990 pop. 1,578,385 (100.5% of 1980; rank: 36th); area 77,358 sq mi/200,357 sq km (rank: 16th); admitted to Union 1867 (37th). Capital: LINCOLN. Most populous cities: OMAHA, Lincoln, GRAND ISLAND. Nebraska is bordered S by Kansas and (indenting its SW to form the PANHANDLE) Colorado; W by Wyoming; N by South Dakota, with the MISSOURI R. forming part of the boundary in the E; and E (across the Missouri) by Iowa (N) and Missouri (S). Except for a band some 75 mi/120 km W from the Missouri R., which is the W edge of the vast C lowlands of the US, the entire state lies in the Great Plains, and rises gradually from about 1000 ft/300 m in the E to over 5000 ft/1500 m in the High Plains of the W, with the highest point (5426 ft/1655 m) in the SW corner (Kimball Co.). Across it flow (generally W–E) rivers in the Missouri system, including the PLATTE, formed (SC, near the city of NORTH PLATTE) by the North and South Platte rivers; the LOUP and its branches; the ELKHORN; and the NIOBRARA (N, along the S of PINE RIDGE). These are generally slow-moving and sediment-filled; the Platte's French name is a translation of the Siouan words (for "flat water") that give the state its name. Of some value for irrigation, Nebraska's rivers are best known as transportation corridors; the OREGON and MORMON trails and UNION PACIFIC RAILROAD all followed the Platte. In the state's WC is the SAND HILLS region, an extensive dune-dominated ranching area. In almost all sections soil is rich, but except in the E requires extensive irrigation; the underlying Ogallala AQUIFER has been substantially depleted. Corn, wheat, and other crops are grown, much of the output going to feed cattle and hogs; Nebraska's nickname is the Cornhusker State. The state's cities are almost all in the SE, where Omaha, Lincoln, and Grand Island all have agriculture-related industries (Omaha is a longtime stockyard and meatpacking center). In addition, Omaha is now a railroad, insurance, and telemarketing center. Lincoln, home to the University of Nebraska and to state government, also has insurance offices and other business. NORTH PLATTE (SW) is a railroad center. Oil and natural gas are extracted in various areas across the S and SW. Home to various Plains peoples including the Cheyenne, Arapaho, Omaha, Sioux, Oto, and Pawnee, Nebraska became part of the 1803 LOUISIANA PURCHASE. There were a few settlements, including BELLEVUE, early in the 19th century. In mid-century, the westward trails became important. The much larger Nebraska Territory was organized in 1854; in 1862 began the HOMESTEAD movement, celebrated here by a National Monument at BEATRICE. Later in the decade the Union Pacific moved W from Omaha, establishing towns along its route. Through the last quarter of the 19th century, German and other farmers came to populate the plains. Nebraska's rural agricultural base made it a populist stronghold in the late 19th and early 20th centuries, as reflected in the careers of native son William Jennings Bryan and Senator George Norris. In the 1930s, in one of many reform moves, it became the only state with a unicameral legislature. The Depression hit Nebraska agriculture hard, and by the mid 20th century, many farm people were moving to cities; most of the state is now sparsely populated. Sights along the Oregon Trail, at CHIMNEY ROCK and SCOTTSBLUFF (W) and Fort KEARNEY (SC) attract visitors, and a well-known Nebraska institution is BOYS TOWN, near Omaha. OFFUTT AIR FORCE BASE, S of Omaha, was noted in the Cold War as the headquarters of the Strategic Air Command. The OMAHA INDIAN RESERVATION (NE) is said to be the birthplace of the modern powwow.

Nebraska City city, pop. 6547, seat of Otoe Co., SE Nebraska, on the Missouri R. and the Iowa state line, 40 mi/64 km S of Omaha. Fort Kearney was established near here in 1846, but moved to KEARNEY two years later. Founded in 1854, the city flourished as a river port. It is a processing and shipping center for livestock and grain producers. It is also a shopping outlet center and manufactures tin cans and canned food, building materials, and clothing. The mansion and arboretum of J. Sterling Morton (1832–1902), originator of Arbor Day, and John Brown's Cave, a stop on the UNDERGROUND RAILROAD, are here.

Nechako River some 250 mi/400 km long, in C British Columbia. It rises in the Coast Mts. NW of TWEEDSMUIR PROVINCIAL PARK. The Kenney Dam (1950s) backed up the Nechako's headwaters, forming the many-armed **Nechako Reservoir;** much of its water is diverted W to power KITIMAT's aluminum smelter. From the dam the Nechako flows NE and E to join the FRASER R. at PRINCE GEORGE.

Neches River 416 mi/670 km long, in E Texas. It rises in Van Zandt Co., NW of Tyler, and flows generally SE past Beaumont to the head of Sabine L., where it joins the SABINE R. A deepwater channel (part of the Sabine-Neches Waterway) connects Beaumont and Sabine L. The ANGELINA R. joins the Neches just S of Angelina National Forest, in the PINEY WOODS.

Nederland city, pop. 16,192, Jefferson Co., SE Texas, 10 mi/16 km SE of BEAUMONT, near the Neches R. Founded by Dutch immigrants in the late 19th century in an area of rice, dairy, and truck farms, it grew markedly after discovery of the nearby Spindletop oilfield in 1901. It has a large refinery and is a rail shipping point for oil. Tourism is also important.

Needham town, pop. 27,557, Norfolk Co., E Massachusetts, a residential suburb 12 mi/19 km SW of Boston, on the Charles R. and Route 128. It was settled in 1680. Factories at Needham Heights have produced woolen and cotton goods, textiles, paper products, electronic equipment, elastic webbing, and surgical instruments.

Needles city, pop. 5191, San Bernardino Co., SE California, in the E MOJAVE DESERT, just NE of the Sacramento Mts., on I-40 and the Colorado R. (the Arizona line), 94 mi/151 km SSE of Las Vegas, Nevada. In a mining area with deposits of gold and semiprecious stones, the city, founded by the Santa Fe Railroad in 1882, is a trade center and railroad division point, named for peaks visible to the E in Arizona. Known for its very hot climate, it produces dates and other fruits and vegetables. The Fort Mohave (or Mojave) Indian Reservation lies to the E and N. Resort development along the river has increased the city's tourist trade in recent years.

Needles, the see under CUSTER STATE PARK, South Dakota.

Neenah city, pop. 23,219, Winnebago Co., E Wisconsin, where the Fox R. flows out of L. Winnebago, 10 mi/16 km NNE of Oshkosh. It is partly on Doty I., where it is joined to its sister city, MENASHA. The two function as one economically. Neenah derives its name from a Winnebago term for "running water," referring to the rapids here. It was once the site of a Winnebago village, and later of a French trading post. The first permanent settlement took place c.1835. Flour mills were vital to Neenah's early economy, and flour is still an important product. Since 1865, it has been a major manufacturer of paper and paper products. Other industries make machinery, wood and metal products, and textiles. The city is also a commercial center for the surrounding dairy farming region.

Neepawa town, pop. 3258, SW Manitoba, 35 mi/56 km NE of Brandon, on the Whitemud R. Situated on the Canadian Pacific and Canadian National railways, Neepawa ships the surrounding agricultural region's grain and livestock. Other industries include woodworking and marble processing. The Beautiful Plains County Court Building, a designated heritage site, is here. Every July, Neepawa hosts the Manitoba Holiday Festival of the Arts.

Nellis Air Force Base in Clark Co., S Nevada, 9 mi/14 km NE of downtown Las Vegas. It is headquarters for the immense **Nellis Air Force Range,** which, with the adjoining Indian Springs Gunnery Range and NEVADA TEST SITE, covers c.7500 sq mi/20,000 sq km, in Clark, Nye, and Lincoln counties, crossed by (NW–SE) the Cactus, Belted, Spotted, and Pintwater ranges. East of the range and N of the base is the DESERT NATIONAL WILDLIFE RANGE.

Nelson city, pop. 8760, Central Kootenay Regional District,

SE British Columbia, on the Kootenai R. and the W arm of Kootenay L., in the Selkirk Mts., 35 mi/55 km N of the Washington border and 266 mi/428 km E of Vancouver. It developed with the opening of a silver mine in the late 1880s and is now a rail center and service point for a lumbering, mining, and farming area. Tourism is important.

Nelson River 400 mi/640 km long, in E Manitoba. It issues from the N end of L. WINNIPEG, through Playgreen L., past NORWAY HOUSE. It continues generally NE, through Cross and Sipiwesk lakes, by way of falls and rapids, to Split L., where the Burntwood and Grass rivers join it. It then flows NE through the Hudson Bay Lowlands to Port Nelson, on the Bay, 12 mi/19 km W of the mouth of the HAYES R. at York Factory. Fur traders used this short, although often turbulent, route connecting L. Winnipeg to Hudson Bay; in 1682 the HUDSON'S BAY COMPANY established Fort (now Port) Nelson at the river's mouth. The Nelson drains not only L. Winnipeg but the Saskatchewan R. system; it thus has a huge volume, which, with its various drops along the CANADIAN SHIELD, has made it the site of numerous hydroelectric power plants.

Nemacolin's Path see under NATIONAL ROAD.

Nemaha River **1. Big Nemaha R.** 40 mi/64 km long, in SE Nebraska. It is formed by the confluence of its 95 mi/152 km–long North Fork and 68 mi/109 km–long South Fork W of Falls City, and flows E to the Missouri R. just N of the Kansas line. The **North Fork** rises 15 mi/24 km S of Lincoln and flows generally SE. The **South Fork** rises near Seneca, in NE Kansas, and flows N, then E to the junction. **2. Little Nemaha R.** 90 mi/145 km long, following a SE course roughly parallel to, and some 20 mi/32 km NE of, the Big Nemaha, entering the Missouri just SE of Nemaha, Nebraska (village, pop. 188).

Neosho city, pop. 9254, seat of Newton Co., SW Missouri, on the Ozark Plateau, 16 mi/26 km SE of Joplin. Its name is Osage for "water," referring to a spring in the city. It was the site of an ineffectual attempt at secession by a pro-Confederate convention in 1861. The artist Thomas Hart Benton was born here in 1889. In a fruit growing, dairying, and lumbering area, the city is a trade center.

Neosho River also, in Oklahoma, the **Grand R.** 460 mi/740 km long, in Kansas and Oklahoma. It rises in Morris Co., EC Kansas, and flows SE through dam-created Council Grove L. and COUNCIL GROVE, past Emporia, through the John Redmond Reservoir near Burlington, to IOLA, then S past Chanute and into NE Oklahoma. Here it continues SE past Miami and into the long, irregular LAKE O' THE CHEROKEES, in the area settled at the end of the TRAIL OF TEARS. From this lake it winds S, through the Fort Gibson Reservoir, joining the ARKANSAS R. at MUSKOGEE.

Nepean city, pop. 107,627, Ottawa-Carleton Regional Municipality, SE Ontario, on the Ottawa R., adjacent (SW) to Ottawa and (E) to Kanata, opposite Aylmer, Québec. Several large national military, communications, and agricultural research centers are here. Industries include computer technology and brewing. Residential neighborhoods are concentrated in the NE, while the Stony Swamp Conservation Area encompasses much of the W.

Neponset River 25 mi/40 km long, in E Massachusetts. It rises in Foxborough, SW Norfolk C., and flows NE past Walpole, Norwood, and Dedham, to Milton, the head of navigation. From Milton E it forms the S boundary of the city of Boston, entering Boston Harbor between the Boston section of Neponset and the city of Quincy.

Neponsit see under the ROCKAWAYS, New York.

Neptune township, pop. 28,148, Monmouth Co., EC New Jersey, on the Atlantic coast and the Shark R., just S and W of Asbury Park. It includes the unincorporated community of Ocean Grove (pop. 4818), founded (1869) as a Methodist meeting camp, and is adjoined (SE) by the borough of **Neptune City** (pop. 4997), both popular recreational sites. The resort township offers swimming, fishing, golfing, and other sports; it is largely residential, with some diversified manufacturing.

Nesconset unincorporated village, pop. 10,712, in Smithtown, Suffolk Co., SE New York, on Long Island, approximately 4 mi/6 km NE of Hauppauge. It is primarily residential.

Neshaminy Creek 50 mi/80 km long, in SE Pennsylvania. It flows generally SE from near DOYLESTOWN, by way of Newtown, to enter the Delaware R. SW of Bristol. A North Branch flows from NE of Doylestown, where it is dammed to form L. Galena, and a West Branch from Hatfield, in Montgomery Co. The Neshaminy was the W boundary of the infamous 1682/1737 WALKING PURCHASE. On **Little Neshaminy Creek,** a tributary NW of Warminster, Log College, the first Presbyterian college in America (and the fourth college in the US) was opened in 1727; it closed in 1747, to be succeeded by the College of New Jersey at Elizabethtown (today's PRINCETON University).

Neshobe Island see under L. BOMOSEEN, Vermont.

Nettiling, Lake Canada's tenth-largest (2140 sq mi/5540 sq km), in S BAFFIN I., Northwest Territories, 100 mi/160 km W of Pangnirtung. It empties (W) into Foxe Basin.

Neuse River 275 mi/443 km long, in North Carolina. The former confluence of the Flat and Eno rivers, which formed the Neuse in the Piedmont 8 mi/13 km NNE of Durham, now lies within 38,000-ac/15,500-ha Falls L., formed by a dam 10 mi/16 km NNE of Raleigh. From the dam the Neuse flows S to the E of Raleigh, then generally SE, through Smithfield, Goldsboro, and Kinston, to New Bern, at the head of its 40 mi/64 km–long estuary on PAMLICO SOUND. It is navigable to Kinston. Croatan National Forest, on the S side of the river's estuary, comprises 158,000 ac/64,000 ha of swamps and cypress and red gum forest.

Nevada state of the W US, in the INTERMONTANE Region; 1990 pop. 1,201,833 (150.1% of 1980; rank: 39th); area 110,567 sq mi/286,369 sq km (rank: 7th); admitted to Union 1864 (36th). Capital: CARSON CITY. Most populous cities: LAS VEGAS, RENO, PARADISE (unincorporated), SUNRISE MANOR (unincorporated), HENDERSON. Nevada is bordered E by Utah (N) and by Arizona (S, with the COLORADO R. forming most of the boundary); SW and W by California (with L. TAHOE forming part of the boundary); and N by Oregon (W) and Idaho (E). The state lies almost entirely in the GREAT BASIN, with a small section of the SONORAN DESERT at its S tip and a section of the COLUMBIA PLATEAU in the extreme NE. Along its W boundary lies the SIERRA NEVADA, from which it takes its name and which, blocking moist Pacific winds, makes it the driest US state. BOUNDARY PEAK, the state's high point at 13,143 ft/4006 m, is along the SW boundary. Except in the S, Nevada consists largely of basins lying at about 4000 ft/1220 m, separated by dozens of short, principally N–S trending mountain chains, among them the SHOSHONE, TOIYABE, SNAKE, EGAN, RUBY, and TUSCARORA mountains. In the extreme S, along the Colorado, the land drops to 470 ft/143 m. In the N, the HUMBOLDT R. flows ENE–WSW, ending in the Humboldt SINK. The Humboldt Valley has been a corridor for travelers since the late 18th century, and was followed by the Central OVERLAND ROUTE, CALIFORNIA TRAIL, PONY EXPRESS route, and CENTRAL PACIFIC RAILROAD; today Interstate 80 traverses it. Most of NW Nevada was covered, in glacial times, by L. LAHONTAN; remnants of the huge lake include PYRAMID, WALKER, and Winnemucca lakes, the Humboldt and CARSON sinks, and the BLACK ROCK DESERT. The short TRUCKEE, CARSON, and WALKER rivers, flowing from the Sierra Nevada near L. Tahoe, have been engineered to create an agricultural zone and to provide water for Reno, Carson City, and other communities in the area. Lake MEAD, formed in the state's S corner by the Hoover Dam on the Colorado R., lies E of the urban complex of Las Vegas, Henderson, Paradise, Sunrise Manor, and neighboring communities. Despite its aridity and harsh landscape, Nevada has been the fastest-growing US state for over three decades. In 1960 it had only 285,278 residents, but its gambling industry and a lifestyle made possible by massive Federal investment in irrigation and hydroelectric projects, have made it one of the most flourishing parts of the SUNBELT. The Shoshone, Washoe, and Paiute were among the peoples who lived in this part of Spain's North American empire when whites began to appear in the 18th century. Through the mid 1850s the area (ceded to the US in 1846) was explored by government expeditions and crossed by California-bound emigrants and (from 1849) gold seekers; a Mormon community was established at GENOA before 1850, as part of DESERET, but Mormons in the area soon returned to Utah. In 1858, though, the silver riches of the COMSTOCK LODE were recognized, VIRGINIA CITY sprang into life, and a boom was on. Nevada was rushed into territorial status (1861) and statehood (1864), its mines providing much of the financial base for the Union's Civil War effort. The 1860s extension of the Central Pacific Railroad across N Nevada spurred a grazing economy there, but through the late 19th and early 20th century, the state's fortunes rose and fell with silver and other metal markets and with changes in Federal monetary policy. In the 1900s strikes at TONOPAH and GOLDFIELD revived the economy, and ELY became a copper center. By the beginning of the 1930s Depression, however, Nevada was in dire straits, and it turned in 1931 to a legalization of gambling and liberalization of marriage and divorce laws. Both measures were designed to attract business primarily from California, but esp. with the extensive use of air conditioning, the abundant power available from the Hoover Dam made Las Vegas a national, eventually an international, resort. Reno became better known as a marriage-and-divorce capital. With the beginning of World War II, the Federal government began to use some of its remote PUBLIC LANDS here (it still holds over 80% of Nevada) for aircraft training and weapons testing. NELLIS Air Force Base and its test range and the NEVADA TEST SITE (with Yucca Flats and Yucca Mt.) are among military facilities in the state. Most US nuclear weapons tests have taken place on the Test Site, which was chosen for its seclusion and distance from pop. centers, although communities like Saint George, Utah, have documented health problems caused by being downwind. Today, Nevada has a highly urban culture; the vast majority of its people live in the Las Vegas and Reno areas. Tourism, focused on casinogoing and other entertainments, is the chief industry; L. Tahoe, L. Mead, GHOST TOWNS, and the state's BASIN AND RANGE scenery attract other visitors. Mining, spread throughout the state, produces a range of metals and other minerals, including mercury, copper, gold, tungsten, barite, and silver. Cattle and sheep grazing is important in the N. State politicians were at the center of the 1970s–80s SAGEBRUSH Rebellion, agitation to have the Federal government release public lands to the state. The University of Nevada was founded in Reno in 1864; its 1957 Las Vegas branch is now larger. The Pyramid Lake and Walker River INDIAN RESERVATIONS are home to descendants of some of the region's early inhabitants.

Nevada city, pop. 8597, seat of Vernon Co., W Missouri, 45 mi/72 km N of Carthage and 14 mi/23 km E of the Kansas line. It was founded in 1855 by settlers from Kentucky and Tennessee. During the early years of the Civil War, Nevada (the "Bushwhackers' Capital") served as a headquarters for Confederate troops and Bushwhackers, proslavery bands who fought abolitionist Kansas Jayhawker guerrillas in the Kansas-Missouri border wars. It was burned to the ground by Kansas militiamen (1863), but was soon rebuilt. For many years the city has been a wholesale hub and shipping point for wheat, corn, hay, livestock, and poultry. There is also some light manufacturing. Director and actor John Huston (1906–87) was born in Nevada. It is the seat of Cottey College (1884).

Nevada City city, pop. 2855, seat of Nevada Co., NE California, on Deer Creek, in the NW foothills of the SIERRA NEVADA, 4 mi/6 km NE of GRASS VALLEY and 55 mi/89 km NE of Sacramento. In the 1850s it was a gold boom town, the third-largest California settlement; Nevada Co. produced roughly half of all California gold. At first a PLACER camp, it became the center of hydraulic mining activity, until the method was banned in 1884. Today it is a resort and headquarters for the Tahoe National Forest, makes wine and beer, and is noted for the restoration of its Victorian houses.

Nevada Test Site 1350–sq mi/3500–sq km government reservation in SW Nevada, some 60 mi/100 km NW of Las Vegas, surrounded W, N, and E by the NELLIS Air Force Range, between the Belted (N) and Spotted (S) ranges. Beginning in 1951, it was the site of over 120 atmospheric and 550 underground nuclear detonations, many in the Yucca Flats area, a PLAYA on the E. Mercury, on US 95 (S), is the point of entry to the site. High-secret aircraft development is carried on today. YUCCA Mt., proposed high-level nuclear waste repository, is on the W.

New Albany **1.** city, pop. 36,322, seat of Floyd Co., S Indiana, on the Ohio R., just W of Clarksville and Jeffersonville and opposite Louisville, Kentucky. A 19th-century steamboat building center, it now produces such goods as plywood, furniture, machinery, stoves, glue, clothing, and fertilizer. In an area noted for its strawberries, the city processes and ships several agricultural products. Preserved here are the George Rogers Clark Homesite and numerous 19th- and early-20th-century mansions. **2.** city, pop. 6775, seat of Union Co., NE Mississippi, 23 mi/37 km NW of Tupelo. It has long been a trade hub for local farmers producing cotton, sorghum, and dairy goods. Manufactures include lumber, furniture and other wood products, auto parts, and clothing. New Albany was the birthplace (1897) of the novelist William Faulkner, who lived most of his life in OXFORD, 30 mi/48 km WSW.

New Amsterdam Dutch, **Nieuw Amsterdam** commercial settlement, established 1624 on the S tip of Manhattan I., New York, and on adjacent islands, that was the capital of the Dutch colony of NEW NETHERLAND. After its capture by the British in 1664, it was renamed New York.

New Archangel see SITKA, Alaska.

Newark **1.** city, pop. 37,861, Alameda Co., NC California, on the SE shore of San Francisco Bay, adjacent (SW) to Fremont and 22 mi/35 km SE of Oakland. Incorporated in 1955, it has engaged in salt refining and the manufacture of chemicals, and is also a residential suburb. **2.** (pronounced "new ark") city, pop. 25,098, New Castle Co., NW Delaware, on White Clay Creek, 12 mi/19 km WSW of Wilmington, just E of the Maryland border. During the 1680s it grew up around a Quaker meetinghouse. In Sept. 1777, Delaware's only Revolutionary War battle was fought at Cooch's Bridge, just S on the Christina R. In 1798, a paper mill was established on White Clay Creek. Today the city is home to the University of Delaware (1833), research laboratories, and food processing, auto parts, and auto assembly plants, and manufactures paper, vulcanized fiber, and concrete products. **3.** city, pop. 275,221, largest in the state and seat of Essex Co., NE New Jersey, on the Passaic R. and NEWARK BAY, 9 mi/14 km W of Manhattan. A part of New York City's metropolitan area, it is also the hub of NE New Jersey's immense industrial complex. Newark's first white settlers were Connecticut Puritans led by Robert Treat, who purchased land from local Indians (1666) and established a small theocratic farming community. The population was soon swelled by Dutch, Irish, Scottish, and German immigrants. Several skirmishes were fought during the Revolution. Newark was incorporated as a town in 1833 and as a city in 1836. Its pre-Revolutionary industries were mainly tanning and shoemaking. After the war, the economy grew rapidly. Jewelry manufacture was initiated in 1801, and the first insurance company established in 1810. Leather and jewelry making continue, and the city is now an important insurance center. Newark's 19th-century industrial growth was spurred by the opening of the Morris Canal (1832), the arrival of the railroad (1834), and the expansion of port facilities. With the opening of PORT NEWARK (1915), the city became a port of entry and important shipbuilding center. Today Newark is a major transportation center, served by rail lines and interstate highways, with its commercial port and Newark International Airport (1928; partly in ELIZABETH), one of the New York area's three major airports. While its manufacturing base has been declining since the 1930s, Newark is still a major industrial city, producing chemicals, plastics, electrical equipment, processed foods, beer, paints, machinery, and toys. In addition to its insurance companies, it has printing and publishing industries; headquarters of banking, retail, and commercial businesses; and offices of state and federal agencies. It is also an important educational center; included in its midtown college complex are Rutgers University's Newark campus, Seton Hall Law School, the University of Medicine and Dentistry of New Jersey (1976), New Jersey Institute of Technology (1884), and Essex County College (1968). The city is home also to the Newark Museum (1909), Symphony Hall, a noted public library (1888), the New Jersey Historical Society (1845), and Military, Washington, and Branch Brook parks. Newark's burgeoning industries drew many late-19th- and early-20th-century immigrants, principally Irish, German, Russian, Italian, and Slavic. After World War II, the city attracted many blacks, who constituted a majority by the 1960s. In 1967 the poverty-riddled CENTRAL WARD was the scene of severe rioting. Hispanic and Portuguese immigrants have recently made the city their home, many in the IRONBOUND. Largely because of middle-class movement to suburbs, Newark's population has been dropping since the 1950s, and while downtown experienced some economic revival at the end of the 20th century, the city remained burdened by underemployment and associated problems. **4.** village, pop. 9849, in Arcadia township, Wayne Co., W New York, 29 mi/47 km ESE of Rochester, on the New York State Barge Canal. An agricultural trade center, it produces roses, paper products, and various light manufactures. **5.** city, pop. 44,389, seat of Licking Co., C Ohio, at the junction of the three branches of the Licking R., 30 mi/48 km E of Columbus. Founded in 1802, it is surrounded by a rich diversified agricultural region in which oil and gas wells and coal fields are also located. It was a busy Ohio and Erie Canal and railroad hub in the 19th century. Newark is still a trade and industrial center, producing missile and electronic components, truck parts, catalytic converters, lighting fixtures, fiberglass, and plastic and aluminum goods. Several earthworks created by pre-Columbian mound builders and the sites of Moundbuilders State Memorial and the Octagon Mound State Memorial lie in the W part of Newark. The Dawes Arboretum is 5 mi/8 km to the S. **6.** see under NIAGARA-ON-THE-LAKE, Ontario.

Newark Bay 6 mi/10 km NNE–SSW, and 1 mi/1.5 km wide, in NE New Jersey. Its NE end lies at the confluence of the PASSAIC and HACKENSACK rivers. Its SW end connects with the ARTHUR KILL (SW) and the KILL VAN KULL (SE) and, through the latter, with Upper New York Bay. Newark Bay lies between Staten Island (S), Bayonne and Jersey City (E), and Newark and Elizabeth (W). On its W shores are PORT NEWARK, Port Elizabeth, and Newark International Airport.

New Barbadoes see under HACKENSACK, New Jersey.

New Bedford city, pop. 99,922, Bristol Co., SE Massachusetts, at the mouth of the Acushnet R., on the W shore of Buzzards Bay, 56 mi/90 km S of Boston and 13 mi/21 km ESE of Fall River. A fishing community since 1760, it was the world's most active whaling port from 1820 to 1860. In 1857 it was the fourth-ranking US port, and had the world's highest per capita income. During the late 19th century, after whaling's decline, it was a textile center. Now the city is a port for coastal freighters and ocean fishing boats, and a marketing center, and manufactures apparel, electrical equipment, and diverse other products. Numerous historic sites include the Whaling Museum and the Seamen's Bethel, a chapel described in Melville's *Moby Dick.* New Bedford's population is heavily French-Canadian and Portuguese. In the 1990s the city struggled with severe unemployment.

Newberg city, pop. 13,086, Yamhill Co., NW Oregon, on the Willamette R., 20 mi/32 km SW of Portland. It is a trade, processing, and shipping center for the area's lumber, fruit, nut, and paper and wood producers. Founded in 1869 by Quakers, this was the group's first settlement in the Northwest. George Fox College (1891) is here. The Hoover-Minthorn House Museum (1881) preserves Herbert Hoover's boyhood home. Champoeg State Park, 5 mi/8 km SE, marks the site of the 1843 vote by Oregon settlers to break with the Hudson's Bay Company and orient their provisional government toward the US.

New Berlin **1.** town, pop. 3046, Chenango Co., C New York, on the Unadilla R., 20 mi/32 km NW of Oneonta. In a dairy and farming region, it processes grain and mills lumber. It was the birthplace of diplomat Anson Burlingame (1820–70). **2.** city, pop. 33,592, Waukesha Co., SE Wisconsin, 10 mi/16 km SW of Milwaukee. Founded in 1840, it is primarily a residential suburb, and has some light industry.

New Bern city, pop. 17,363, seat of Craven Co., E North Carolina, at the confluence of the Neuse and Trent rivers, 30 mi/48 km W of Pamlico Sound. Settled by Swiss and Palatinate Germans in 1710, it is North Carolina's second-oldest city. It was nearly destroyed in 1711 by the Tuscarora, but survived and was incorporated in 1723. North Carolina's first printing press was founded here in 1749, and in 1764 the state's first tax-supported school was opened. New Bern served as colonial, provincial, and then state capital in 1746–92. The city prospered from its trade relations with New England and the West Indies, and was one of the region's social and cultural centers, until it was captured by Federal forces in 1862. After the Civil War, New Bern reestablished trade relations with New England. It is a now a commercial center in an agricultural (tobacco, corn, cotton, berries) and resort area. Manufactures include wood and stone products, boats, and processed foods. New Bern is a service center for the Marine air station at Cherry Point, 16 mi/26 km SE, home to Craven Community College (1965), and a growing retirement community.

Newberry town, pop. 10,542, seat of Newberry Co., WC South Carolina, in the Piedmont, 38 mi/61 km NW of Columbia. A gateway to Sumter National Forest, it markets grain, cotton, and lumber, and has granite quarries and dairy and truck farms. The town was founded in 1832, Newberry College (Presbyterian) in 1856.

Newberry Crater CALDERA, 4–5 mi/6–8 km wide, 25 mi/40 km S of BEND, in C Oregon, formed after the collapse c.10,000 years ago of the huge volcano known as Mt. Newberry. Paulina L. and East L., separated by a more recently developed cinder cone and lava flow, are in the caldera, and have hot sulfur springs. A black obsidian flow to the S of Paulina L. creates a surrealistic landscape. Paulina Peak (7985 ft/2434 m) is the highest point on the rim. On the NW slope of Newberry Crater is the 5–sq mi/13–sq km Lava Cast Forest, featuring castings or impressions formed when a lava flow engulfed an existing forest. Farther to the NW is Lava River Cave, popular with spelunkers, with a 5200-ft/1585-m main tube. Lava Butte, rising abruptly c.500 ft/152 m, is one of several hundred cinder cones that grew up on the flanks of Mt. Newberry.

New Boston agricultural town, pop. 3214, Hillsborough Co., S New Hampshire. New Boston is on the South Branch of the Piscataquog R., 12 mi/19 km W of Manchester.

New Braunfels city, pop. 27,334, seat of Comal Co., also in Guadalupe Co., SC Texas, on the Comal (entirely within city limits) and Guadalupe rivers, 30 mi/48 km NE of San Antonio. Sponsored by Prussian noblemen, it was settled in 1845, and for a short while existed as a thoroughly German community. In a ranching, dairying, limestone quarrying, and farming region, the city has various light manufactures and a number of medical facilities. Its German heritage, celebrated in various annual events, combines with nearby springs, caverns, and hill scenery to draw visitors.

New Brighton **1.** city, pop. 22,207, Ramsey Co., SE Minnesota, on Long L., 8 mi/13 km NW of St. Paul. It is a residential suburb with some light industry. The Twin Cities Army Ammunition Plant, a toxic waste site, is here. **2.** historic industrial, now largely residential section, N Staten I., New York, on the Kill van Kull, W of St. George. An early-19th-century resort, it became a shipyard and factory district with the imposing homes of business owners on its terraced hillsides. Today it has a mix of small businesses, apartment houses, and remaining mansions. SAILOR'S SNUG HARBOR Cultural Center is here. West New Brighton, more popularly known as West Brighton, just W, is similar.

New Britain **1.** city and coterminous township, pop. 75,491, Hartford Co., C Connecticut, 9 mi/14 km SW of Hartford, on Interstate 84. It is known as the Hardware City because of its importance as a producer of hardware; it is home to Stanley and other toolmakers, and also manufactures computer components, machinery, and electrical equipment. Founded in 1686 by settlers from nearby Berlin, it was by 1800 producing sleighbells for sale by itinerant peddlers. By 1832 steam was powering its lock factories. New Britain is the site of Central Connecticut State University (1849). **2.** township, pop. 9099, Bucks Co., SE Pennsylvania, 3 mi/5 km WSW of Doylestown. It is a largely residential Philadelphia suburb.

New Brunswick province of E Canada, the largest of the MARITIME PROVINCES; 1991 pop. 723,900 (102% of 1986; rank: 8th of 12); land area 27,633 sq mi/71,569 sq km (rank: 10th); entered Confederation 1867. Capital: FREDERICTON. Most populous cities: SAINT JOHN, MONCTON, Fredericton. New Brunswick is bordered SE by Nova Scotia, in the CHIGNECTO isthmus; W by Maine, with the SAINT JOHN and SAINT CROIX rivers forming parts of the boundary; and N by Québec, with the Patapédia and RESTIGOUCHE rivers forming part of the boundary. On the E lies the Gulf of SAINT LAWRENCE, with CHALEUR BAY (NE) separating the North Shore from Québec's Gaspé region, and the NORTHUMBERLAND STRAIT (SE) separating the SE region from Prince Edward I. On the S is the Bay of FUNDY, with its inlets, Chignecto Bay (NE) and PASSAMAQUODDY BAY (SW). GRAND MANAN and CAMPOBELLO islands lie on the SW, at Fundy's mouth. The province comprises APPALACHIAN upland in the W, with coastal lowlands in the E. Its rivers almost all flow from the upland to the ocean—the Saint John and Saint Croix SE into the Bay of Fundy, and the Restigouche, MIRAMICHI, and smaller rivers E into the Gulf of Saint Lawrence. Mt. CARLETON (NC) is the high point, at 2690 ft/820 m. New Brunswick is heavily forested; most of its limited agricultural land is in the Saint John Valley, where orcharding, potato growing, and dairy production dominate. Coal is mined in the MINTO area (SC), and copper, lead, and zinc near BATHURST (NE). The region was home to the Micmac and Malecite before whites appeared in the early 17th century. Dochet (Saint Croix) I., in the St. Croix R. on the Maine boundary, was the site of a short-lived French outpost in 1604, and coastal settlements of ACADIA spread through the area. After the Treaty of Utrecht (1713), British control of the area was extended only slowly, and the French Fort Beauséjour, near SACKVILLE in the Chignecto isthmus, briefly asserted French claims. In the 1750s–60s, however, the Acadians were forced to flee from the colony or retreat inland, up the Saint John Valley. After the British defeat of NEW FRANCE in 1763, New Brunswick was part of Nova Scotia until 1784, when booming LOYALIST settlements around Saint John and along the S coast were recognized in the establishment of a new colony. Saint Anne's, up the Saint John, became the new capital of Fredericton, and Acadians in the area retreated farther NW, to the MADAWASKA region, where they created a distinctive culture centered around EDMUNDSTON. Disputes with the US over the W border continued through the 1830s "AROOSTOOK War" and the 1840s Madawaska controversy. In the late 18th century, Acadians began to resettle the Chaleur Bay area, esp. around CARAQUET and SHIPPAGAN; their fishing and farming settlements gradually spread S. Throughout the 19th century, the ports and shipbuilding centers of the S, esp. Saint John and SAINT ANDREWS, flourished; fishing was also economically critical, and Moncton became the rail nexus for Maritime Canada. New Brunswick was one of the first proponents of CONFEDERATION (1867); ironically, Canadian union changed economic patterns in favor of regions to the W, bringing local decline. In the 20th century, the province has struggled with cycles in the lumber business and the decline of Atlantic fisheries and of railroading. Pulp manufacture and oil refining (at Saint John) remain important. Tourism focuses on the Bay of Fundy's extreme tides, its phenomena seen esp. at FUNDY NATIONAL PARK and Saint John's Reversing Falls. The growth and movement S of the Acadian community has made New Brunswick Canada's most linguistically balanced province, francophones forming a large minority with their own educational and cultural centers at Moncton and Caraquet. The majority anglophones are primarily descendants of Loyalists and 19th-century English and Irish immigrants. The University of New Brunswick is one of several institutions at Fredericton, a city with little industry. The Miramichi and Restigouche and their tributaries are among the world's best-known salmon fishing rivers.

New Brunswick city, pop. 41,711, seat of Middlesex Co., C New Jersey, at the head of navigation on the Raritan R., 9 mi/14 km W of Perth Amboy. Settled by British colonists (1681) and originally called Prigmore's Swamp, it became a busy ferry crossing. By the mid 18th century its excellent port and abundant waterpower had made it a flourishing shipping and milling center. During the Revolution, it was held by both British and American forces. Later it became the terminus of the Delaware and Raritan Canal. Today New Brunswick's economy is supported by industry, shipping, and higher education. It is particularly active in the health care industry, producing pharmaceuticals (Johnson & Johnson is based here) and medical/surgical supplies. Other industries manufacture automobile parts, chemicals, machinery, clothing, electrical supplies, and leather products. New Brunswick is the seat of Rutgers, The State University (1766), and of the New Brunswick Theological Seminary.

New Buffalo city, pop. 2317, Berrien Co., extreme SW Michigan, on L. Michigan, 20 mi/32 km W of Niles and 2 mi/3 km N of the Indiana border. In a farm and orchard area, it was long a center of summer camps, hotels, and cottages, frequented until the 1950s by vacationers from Chicago, Illinois, and Gary, Indiana. The area declined in popularity during the 1960s and 1970s. In 1979 the city's harbor was dredged, leading to a rejuvenation of the L. Michigan shore, including renovation of old hotels and rental cottages, and construction of new vacation homes and condominiums.

Newburg unincorporated community, pop. 21,647, Jefferson Co., N Kentucky, a largely black suburb 7 mi/11 km SE of downtown Louisville, just outside I-264, the city's inner beltway.

Newburgh **1.** town, pop. 2880, Warrick Co., SW Indiana, on the Ohio R., 9 mi/14 km E of Evansville. Settled in 1803, it has many early buildings in a noted historic district. It is the site of an aluminum plant, and has a variety of other manufactures including concrete and processed foods. **2.** city, pop. 26,454, Orange Co., SE New York, on the W bank of the Hudson R., opposite Beacon, 58 mi/93 km N of New York City. Settled in 1709 by Palatinate Germans, it took its present name following an influx of English and Scots, in 1752. Newburgh served as the final headquarters of George Washington in 1782–83; here he officially disbanded the Continental Army. Washington stayed in the Hasbrouck House, which is preserved. Newburgh developed as a whaling port in the 19th century, and as a ferry point for coal being shipped from Pennsylvania to New England. The city is now a market and distribution center for a dairy and fruit region. Industries manufacture textiles, clothing, electronic components, aluminum products, bricks, tile, plastics, and cosmetics. Stewart Field, an Air Force base, closed in 1970, is now Stewart International Airport; it is W of the city, in Newburgh township (pop. 24,058). Newburgh is home to Mount St. Mary College.

Newbury town, pop. 5623, Essex Co., NE Massachusetts, 33 mi/53 km NE of Boston, on US 1 and Interstate 95, and just S of NEWBURYPORT. Settled in 1635, it was an early shipbuilding and seafaring center on the Atlantic and on estuarial Plum Island R. At the village green in Newbury Old Town, 19th-century villagers gathered to greet ships arriving from the West Indies. Among historic buildings are the Coffin House (1653) and the Noyes Homestead (1646). Newburyport was set off from Newbury in 1764. The village of Byfield is in the town's W.

Newburyport city, pop. 16,317, Essex Co., NE Massachusetts, at the mouth of the Merrimack R., 35 mi/56 km NE of Boston. It was set off from Newbury (S) in 1764. Before the Revolutionary War, Newburyport drew its wealth from fishing, shipbuilding, whaling, and a merchant fleet. During the 1840s the shipyards built many famous clipper ships. Newburyport draws many tourists seeking its Federal-style houses and nearby resorts, and is a center for boating, fishing, and diverse manufacturing. Abolitionist leader William Lloyd Garrison was born here in 1805.

New Caledonia name given (1806) by Simon Fraser of the NORTH WEST COMPANY to interior C and EC highland parts of what is now British Columbia. The NWC's westernmost trade area (FORT SAINT JAMES was the regional headquarters), it was isolated from the Pacific coast by the difficulties of descending the Fraser R., and by the HUDSON'S BAY COMPANY's control of routes to the S. After the 1821 combination of the two companies, a route via the OKANAGAN R. to the COLUMBIA R. was developed. "New Caledonia" was only one of several names for the area, which became British Columbia when the colony was established in 1858.

New Canaan town, pop. 17,864, Fairfield Co., SW Connecticut, 7 mi/11 km NE of Stamford, on the New York border. An affluent suburb, it is also an arts center; the Silvermine Guild of Artists (1922), in Silvermine, a village along the Silvermine R. in the New Canaan-Wilton-Norwalk corner

(E), grew from one of America's first artists' colonies. New Canaan is also home to several corporate headquarters.

New Carlisle city, pop. 6049, Clark Co., WC Ohio, 14 mi/22 km NE of Dayton. Its economy depends on diversified farming and light manufactures.

New Carrollton city, pop. 12,002, Prince George's Co., SC Maryland, on the Capital BELTWAY, 10 mi/16 km NE of Washington, D.C., of which it is a residential and commercial suburb.

New Castle **1.** city, pop. 4837, New Castle Co., N Delaware, on the Delaware R., 5 mi/8 km S of Wilmington. Founded in 1651 by NEW AMSTERDAM governor Peter Stuyvesant as Fort Casimir, it was taken by the Swedes in 1654, recovered by the Dutch a year later, and claimed by William Penn in 1682. An early Dutch capital, it was seat of the LOWER COUNTIES 1704–76. It has a town green laid out by Stuyvesant, and is home to Wilmington College (1967). Industries produce rayon, steel, paint, and drugs. **2.** city, pop. 17,753, seat of Henry Co., EC Indiana, on the Big Blue R., 18 mi/29 km S of Muncie. The trading hub for a farming region, it has a financial sector and such manufactures as auto and truck parts and metal products. Roses are grown in local greenhouses. New Castle has several parks, a speedway, and the Indiana Basketball Hall of Fame; a number of prehistoric Indian mounds are also here. The Wilbur Wright State Historic Site, in Millville, 6 mi/10 km E, is the birthplace (1867) of the aviation pioneer. **3.** city, pop. 28,334, seat of Lawrence Co., extreme W Pennsylvania, at the junction of the Shenango and Neshannock rivers, in the foothills of the Allegheny Mts., 20 mi/32 km SE of Youngstown, Ohio, and 43 mi/69 km NW of Pittsburgh. On the site of a Delaware Indian capital, it was founded in 1798 by John Stewart, who built an iron furnace. New Castle became a terminus for the Erie Extension Canal (1833) and was an important station on the Underground Railroad. Its economy is based on large deposits of coal, iron ore, limestone, and fire clay in the area; it manufactures steel and allied products, pottery, chemicals, bronze castings, explosives, and machinery.

Newcastle **1.** town, pop. 5711, seat of Northumberland Co., NE New Brunswick, on the Miramichi R. estuary, 75 mi/120 km NNW of Moncton. A port with coastal trade, the town ships lumber and iron ore, and has shipyards, creosote manufacturing facilities, and pulp mills. It was the boyhood home of British financier and press mogul Max Aitken, Lord Beaverbrook (1879–1964), who took his title from Beaver Brook, a local stream. **2.** town, pop. 49,479, Durham Regional Municipality, SE Ontario, on L. Ontario, immediately NE of Oshawa and 38 mi/61 km ENE of Toronto. This rapidly growing town (45% pop. increase in 1986–91) was created in 1974, including a number of early-19th-century townships and villages. Bowmanville, on the lake, is a port with an industrial history, having made toys, auto parts, rubber goods, flour, and many other products; it is also a resort and bedroom community. Darlington, just W of Bowmanville, is the site of a four-unit nuclear power plant operational since 1992. Apple growing, dairying, and other farming remain important in Newcastle, which has also, at Mosport, 10 mi/16 km N of Bowmanville, been home since 1961 to Canada's major auto road racing track.

New Castle County 396 sq mi/1026 sq km, pop. 441,946, in N Delaware. WILMINGTON is its seat. Pennsylvania borders it N, Maryland W, the Smyrna R. S, and the Delaware R. E. The Chesapeake and Delaware Canal, Christina R., and Brandywine, Red Clay, and White Clay creeks cross it. The main industries are dairying; poultry, corn, and livestock raising; and commerce and industry in the Wilmington area.

New Center office development in Detroit, Michigan, just NW of the intersection of GRAND Blvd. and WOODWARD Ave., 3 mi/5 km NW of Downtown. Home to the Fisher Building and its theater (1928), among other landmarks, the New Center served as General Motors headquarters from 1919.

New City unincorporated village, pop. 33,673, seat of Rockland Co., SE New York, 5 mi/8 km NW of Nyack. Primarily a residential suburb, 26 mi/42 km N of Manhattan, it is part of the town of Clarkstown. DeForest L. is E.

New Concord village, pop. 2086, Muskingum Co., EC Ohio, 15 mi/24 km ENE of Zanesville. The trade center for an agricultural district, it is also the seat of Muskingum College (1837). Educator William Rainey Harper was born here (1856).

New Cornelia Tailings Dam see under AJO, Arizona.

New Dorp largely residential section, EC Staten Island, New York, on Lower New York Bay, between Todt Hill (N) and Richmondtown and Great Kills (S). The New Dorp Moravian Church (1762) is here. Area beaches, including what was called New Dorp Beach, were fashionable in the 1890s; they are now part of the GATEWAY NATIONAL RECREATIONAL AREA.

New Echota see under CALHOUN, Georgia.

New England today, the six northeasternmost US states—Maine, New Hampshire, and Vermont (Northern New England), and Massachusetts, Rhode Island, and Connecticut (Southern New England). The name began to be used in the early 17th century; John Smith is thought to have likened the region's coast to that of England. The **Council of New England** (1620–35) attempted (from Britain) to oversee the affairs of the area's new colonies. In 1643 the **New England Confederation** (the first American body of its type) allied the Massachusetts Bay, Plymouth, Connecticut, and New Haven colonies for mutual protection; it survived until 1684. After Massachusetts Bay lost its charter (1684), giving way to provincial government, the **Dominion of New England** briefly (1686–89) united New Hampshire, Massachusetts, Rhode Island, Connecticut, New York, and New Jersey. As a region New England, noted for its hard winters, short growing season, difficult soil, river-powered mill (later, factory) towns, maritime (shipbuilding, fishing, trading) centers, and (before the mid 19th century) largely British-derived people, is held to have developed a characteristic "Yankee" type. Its metropolis, Boston, exerted an influence seen in the former custom in the Maritime Provinces of referring to the region (and by extension, to the US), as the "Boston States."

Newfound Gap see under CLINGMANS DOME, Tennessee.

New Found Lake in SE Grafton Co., C New Hampshire, N of the town of Bristol. It is 6 mi/10 km long and 2.5 mi/4 km wide, and is fed by the Cockermouth R. Along its shores are numerous beaches, parks, and summer camps. The lake was called Pasquaney by Algonquian tribes who favored it for their camps.

Newfoundland and Labrador newest Canadian province, one of the ATLANTIC PROVINCES; 1991 pop. 568,474 (100.0% of 1986; rank: 9th of 12); land area 143,488 sq mi/371,635 sq km (rank: 9th); entered Confederation 1949 (10th). Capital and most populous city: SAINT JOHN'S. Other leading cities and towns: MOUNT PEARL, CORNER BROOK, CONCEPTION BAY SOUTH, GRAND FALLS–WINDSOR, GANDER. The province comprises two very different regions. The island of **Newfoundland** (French, **Terre-Neuve;** Latin, **Terra Nova**) has an area of 41,003 sq mi/106,198 sq km and a pop. of 538,099 (99.7% of 1986). It lies in the Atlantic Ocean at Canada's extreme E, with the Gulf of SAINT LAWRENCE to its W. On the N the narrow Strait of BELLE ISLE separates it from Labrador. On the SW, the CABOT STRAIT separates it from Nova Scotia's Cape Breton I. On its S coast, just off the BURIN Peninsula, lies the French overseas *département* of SAINT-PIERRE ET MIQUELON. Newfoundland sits at the NE end of the APPALACHIAN system. The LONG RANGE Mts., which form the spine of its GREAT NORTHERN PENINSULA, are Appalachian, as are the LEWIS HILLS, just SSW, which rise to the island's high point of 2672 ft/814 m. The AVALON PENINSULA, on the SE, is home to most of Newfoundland's people. The island's deeply indented coastline includes FORTUNE and PLACENTIA bays (S) and CONCEPTION, TRINITY, and NOTRE DAME bays (N). The cold LABRADOR CURRENT, from the N, and the warm GULF STREAM, from the S, meet off SE Newfoundland, creating heavy fogs and a rich mix of marine nutrients in the area of Cape RACE and the GRAND BANKS, one of the world's richest fishing grounds. Much of Newfoundland's interior is uninhabited forest and MUSKEG. Mainland **Labrador** is bounded W and S by the UNGAVA region of Québec, and has the LABRADOR SEA on its NE, the Strait of Belle Isle at its SE corner. With a pop. of only 30,375 (105.7% of 1986) in an area of 102,485 sq mi/265,437 sq km, it is a rugged E section of the CANADIAN SHIELD, with abundant surface water, esp. in what is now the Smallwood Reservoir, and crossed by the CHURCHILL R., but almost uninhabited except in small coastal INUIT and fishing settlements (including RED BAY) and in mining communities along the Québec border (SW). In the N, in the TORNGAT Mts. (actually an edge of the Shield), it rises to 5420 ft/1652 m at Mt. CAUBVICK, also on the Québec border. Labrador's mineral and hydroelectric resources are of great importance to chronically depressed Newfoundland. Both Newfoundland and Labrador have been inhabited for thousands of years by ancestors of today's Inuit, and the island was home, when Europeans arrived, to the Beothuk, the last of whom died in the 1820s. Leif Ericsson probably saw Labrador's S coast around the year 1000, calling it Markland ("land of forests"); continuing S, he wintered at what he called VINLAND, which may have been Newfoundland's L'ANSE AUX MEADOWS, the only proven Viking site in Canada or the US. In 1497 John Cabot, exploring for the English, reported the rich fisheries of the area; the Grand Banks were soon busy with English, French, Basque, Portuguese, and other fleets. The English claimed Newfoundland in 1583, and maintained a policy of discouraging settlement, using the island as a mere fishing base. In 1713 the French surrendered their competing claim, receiving the right to use the FRENCH SHORE in return; after the fall of New France in 1763, they also acquired Saint-Pierre et Miquelon, and continued to use French Shore bases until the early 1900s. English settlement of Newfoundland began late in the 17th century, and expanded through the 18th; Saint John's was long the only recognized community, but small OUTPORTS (including CUPIDS and HEART'S CONTENT) sprang up around the island. Newfoundland refused to join the new Canadian CONFEDERATION in the 1860s, remaining a crown colony. In the 1890s–1900s iron mining (esp. at BELL I.) and lumbering and pulp production (esp. at Grand Falls) created some wealth. Labrador (its name, from a Portuguese term for "landholder," has been used since the 16th century), which had never been clearly defined beyond a narrow coastal strip, became an object of contention between Québec and Newfoundland, until an English decision (1927) setting the present boundaries. The 1930s Depression devastated Newfoundland, and local government was suspended. After the economic respite afforded by World War II, in which Gander, ARGENTIA, STEPHENVILLE, and Goose Bay (now used as a training base for European air forces; see HAPPY VALLEY–GOOSE BAY) were major military sites, Newfoundland and Labrador finally voted, in 1949, to join Canada. In the 1950s mining in the LABRADOR CITY area and hydroelectric development at CHURCHILL FALLS created bright spots in an economy otherwise buffeted by the gradual decline of the Atlantic fisheries. Pulp and paper production, at Grand Falls–Windsor, Corner Brook, Stephenville, and a few other centers, has also experienced cyclical distress. Almost all commercial, institutional, and educational activity is concentrated at Saint John's. In the 1980s offshore oil exploration held out the promise of further mineral income. Tourism on Newfoundland focuses on the GROS MORNE and TERRA NOVA national parks, L'Anse aux Meadows, and coastal towns and scenery. The island is noted for its distinctive, insular culture, built on Scottish, Irish, and French antecedents; "Newfies" are widely regarded as perhaps the most distinctive of Canadians.

New France term used by late in the 16th century for lands held or claimed by the French crown in North America. Jacques Cartier's 1534 claim at GASPÉ and the 1605 settlement at Port-Royal (ANNAPOLIS ROYAL), in Acadia, were important, but the 1608 settlement of Québec City is regarded as the key date in the colony's establishment. New France flourished as a royal province under Louis XIV (after 1663), and eventually embraced lands extending from the mouth of the St. Lawrence R. through the Great Lakes and the Mississippi Valley. ACADIA is often regarded as a separate development. Control was lost to the British in 1763, at which time SAINT-PIERRE ET MIQUELON was acquired as a base for the French fishing fleet. French control of lands in the Mississippi Valley was restored briefly after the American Revolution (see LOUISIANA PURCHASE).

New Glarus village, pop. 1899, Green Co., S Wisconsin, on headwaters of the Little Sugar R., 24 mi/38 km SW of Madison. An 1845 Swiss settlement, it is now noted as a Swiss-theme tourist center, with an Historical Village and festival; it produces cheese and other dairy products and embroidery.

New Glasgow town, pop. 9905, Pictou Co., NC Nova Scotia, on the East R. of Pictou, an inlet from NORTHUMBERLAND STRAIT, 78 mi/126 km NE of Halifax. It is the center of a cluster of industrial towns including Trenton, Westville, and STELLARTON. New Glasgow was a coal, steel, and shipbuilding center in the 19th century, and built railway cars early in the 20th century. It continues to produce brick and tile, tires, furniture, pulp, and wood products, and is a regional commercial center.

Newhall see under SANTA CLARITA, California.

New Hampshire northeastern US state, in N New England; 1990 pop. 1,109,252 (120.5% of 1980; rank: 40th); area 9351 sq mi/24,219 sq km (rank: 46th); ratified Constitution 1788

(9th). Capital: CONCORD. Most populous cities: MANCHESTER, NASHUA. New Hampshire is bordered E by Maine, with the PISCATAQUA R. forming part of the border in the S; N by Québec; W by Vermont, with the CONNECTICUT R. forming the entire boundary; and S by Massachusetts. On the SE is an 18 mi/29 km–long strip of low coastal land, where HAMPTON and other beach towns and the old commercial and naval port of PORTSMOUTH are situated; the ISLES OF SHOALS, offshore, are shared with Maine. The rest of the state is upland and glaciated mountain; the SSW–NNE oriented WHITE Mts. (part of the Appalachian system) dominate the N, rising to 6288 ft/1918 m at Mt. WASHINGTON, in the PRESIDENTIAL RANGE, the highest point in the NE US. Other mountains include isolated MONADNOCK (SW, near KEENE and PETERBOROUGH) and the other high peaks of the Presidentials and the neighboring SANDWICH RANGE; openings ("notches") through the ranges, including PINKHAM NOTCH and DIXVILLE NOTCH, are resort centers. TUCKERMAN RAVINE and BRETTON WOODS are well-known White Mt. sites. New Hampshire's predominant hard rock gives it the name "the Granite State"; the Old Man of the Mountain, a natural "profile" in FRANCONIA NOTCH, is a widely known emblem. On the W the upland drops to the upper Connecticut R. valley, in which CLAREMONT, LEBANON, and the college town of HANOVER are leading communities. Through the C runs the MERRIMACK R., source of power for the state's textile industry, now much diminished from the early 20th century, when Manchester's Amoskeag Mills were the world's largest. Concord and Nashua are also on the Merrimack. In the SC are WINNIPESAUKEE, SQUAM, OSSIPEE, and the other resort lakes. In the far N the state's forest industries center in the BERLIN area. Year-round tourism and recreation, including skiing and hiking in the mountains and coastal beach trade, are important to New Hampshire, but the state has been primarily industrial from the mid 19th century. Since the 1960s it has grown rapidly as a residential, commercial, and light industrial component of the greater Boston area; much of this expansion has been fostered by the absence of state income or sales taxes, which has also attracted retail trade and vacation- and retirement-home ownership. New Hampshire was first settled, from Massachusetts, in the 1620s, and became a separate colony in 1741. Portsmouth developed as an early shipping and fishing center; another important early town in the coastal area was EXETER. Agricultural development was difficult (today the state produces dairy goods, eggs, apples, maple syrup, and some smaller crops), and it was not until 19th-century industry located along the rivers that the pop. grew appreciably, with the addition of a large French-Canadian working class to the original Yankees. The older industries (lumber, textiles, shoes) slumped in the early 20th century, but their dominant role has recently been assumed by high-tech manufacturing and other light industry in the SE, where HILLSBOROUGH and Rockingham counties are now suburbs of Boston and in a sense extensions of Massachusetts's ROUTE 128. The University of New Hampshire is at DURHAM (SE). A unique state institution is the quadrennial political bonanza created by New Hampshire's first-in-the-nation presidential primary election.

New Harmony historic town, pop. 846, Posey Co., extreme SW Indiana, 23 mi/37 km WNW of Evansville, on the Wabash R. A trading center in an agricultural area, it was made a National Historic Landmark in 1965. In an area once occupied by mound builders and later tribes, it was in the 19th century the site of two utopian communities. The first (1815–24) was founded by the Harmony Society, led by the Pennsylvania German Pietist preacher George Rapp. Hostile neighbors eventually induced the group to leave, and they returned to Pennsylvania to establish ECONOMY. They sold the site to Robert Owen, the British reformer. He attempted to build a cooperative community based on "rational thinking" and free education. Open to all comers, it apparently attracted misfits who were unwilling to work, and dissolved in 1828. The town of New Harmony survived, however, becoming a prominent intellectual and cultural center. It was the site of the first US kindergarten, the first free public school, the first free library, and the first school that provided equal education to girls and boys. The first American geological laboratory was established here in 1837; it was the headquarters for what in time became the US Geological Survey.

New Haven city, pop. 130,474, seat of New Haven Co., SC Connecticut, on the West, Mill, and Quinnipiac rivers at the head of New Haven Harbor, 4 mi/6 km from Long Island Sound and 35 mi/56 km SSW of Hartford. Known as the seat (since 1716) of Yale University, situated in the downtown, adjacent to the Green, it is also a port and manufacturing center, producing apparel, firearms, paper, chemicals, rubber, and plastics, and the largest wholesale distributing center in the state. It was founded in 1638 as a theocracy by English Puritans; absorbed by the Connecticut Colony in 1662, it served (1701–85) as joint capital, with Hartford. Modern industrial development began in 1798, when Eli Whitney started a gun factory on the Mill R., just N of New Haven in Hamden. New Haven's industrial base has been eroding since World War II; urban renewal efforts, begun in the 1950s, failed to reverse decline in such districts as the Hill (SW of the city center) and the Dixwell and Newhallville neighborhoods (NW). Physically New Haven is dominated by two cliffs, West Rock (NW) and East Rock (NE, on the Hamden line). In addition to Yale, New Haven is home to Southern Connecticut State College (1893), Albertus Magnus College (1925), and South Central Connecticut Community College (1968).

New Haven County 610 sq mi/1580 sq km, pop. 804,219, in SW Connecticut, on Long Island Sound. It is largely a manufacturing and commercial region, with some agriculture and with resort areas along the Sound. Industrial centers include New Haven (the county seat), Waterbury, Wallingford, Naugatuck, and Meriden; truck, dairy, and fruit farming and fishing are other important economic activities.

New Helvetia see under SACRAMENTO, California.

New Hope **1.** city, pop. 21,853, Hennepin Co., SE Minnesota, 7 mi/11 km NW of Minneapolis. Primarily a residential suburb, it has experienced some commercial development in recent decades. **2.** borough, pop. 1400, Bucks Co., SE Pennsylvania, 16 mi/26 km NW of Trenton, New Jersey, on the Delaware R. It is a popular artists' colony, summer theater center, and tourist attraction. The painter Joseph Pickett (1848–1918) lived here all his life. WASHINGTON CROSSING is 6 mi/10 km SE.

New Hyde Park village, pop. 9728, in North Hempstead town, Nassau Co., SE New York, adjacent (E) to Bellerose, Queens. It was part of a manor granted in 1683 to Thomas Dongan, royal governor of New York; after his death, the property was subdivided but continued to attract the wealthy.

After the Revolution, the village, then called Hyde Park, became agricultural and less gilded. By the 19th century, the name had been changed to New Hyde Park to avoid confusion with the Dutchess Co. town of HYDE PARK. Today it is a middle-class suburban residential community.

New Iberia city, pop. 31,828, seat of Iberia Parish, S Louisiana, on the BAYOU TECHE, and connected via canal with the Gulf Intracoastal Waterway, 19 mi/31 km SE of Lafayette. Settled by Acadians, who were joined by Spanish (Canary Islanders) in the 18th century, it was incorporated in 1836. In 1863, the city and local salt mines were occupied by Union troops. New Iberia developed as a processing and shipping center for regional sugar cane, rice, salt, vegetables, and, most recently, petroleum. It is one of several area cities that are now staging points for offshore oil drillers. The Louisiana Sugar Cane Festival is held here annually. AVERY ISLAND is 9 mi/14 km SW.

Newington **1.** town, pop. 994, Rockingham Co., SE New Hampshire. Newington is on Great Bay and the Piscataqua R., just W of Portsmouth. Pease Air Force Base, a 4255-ac/1723-ha military installation, was open here from 1956 to 1991; it was home to the 509th Bombardment Wing, a heavy bomber and aerial tanker unit. The closing of the base left Newington's economic future uncertain; moves to clean up hazardous waste and attract industrial development were under way. **2.** unincorporated community, pop. 17,965, Fairfax Co., NE Virginia, along Interstate 95, 7 mi/11 km SW of Alexandria, and adjacent (NW) to FORT BELVOIR. It is primarily residential.

New Jersey northeastern US state, in the Middle Atlantic region; 1990 pop. 7,730,188 (105% of 1980; rank: 9th); area 8722 sq mi/22,590 sq km (rank: 47th); ratified Constitution 1787 (3rd). Capital: TRENTON. Most populous cities: NEWARK, JERSEY CITY, PATERSON, ELIZABETH. New Jersey is bordered N by New York. It lies largely between two rivers, the HUDSON (E) and DELAWARE (W), with the Atlantic Ocean along its SE and S. New York faces it across the Hudson (Staten Island, part of New York City, is separated from New Jersey by the Arthur Kill and Kill van Kull). Pennsylvania lies W, across the Delaware; on the SW, across the river's mouth and DELAWARE BAY, is the state of Delaware. New Jersey lies largely in the Atlantic COASTAL PLAIN; in the N it rises into a narrow PIEDMONT band, and then, in the NW, into Appalachian highlands, rising to HIGH POINT (1803 ft/550 m) in the extreme N corner. Along its E are (N–S) NEWARK BAY and RARITAN BAY, as well as BARNEGAT BAY, ABSECON INLET, and other breaks in the JERSEY SHORE's line of BARRIER islands and beaches (inside which the INTRACOASTAL WATERWAY passes). The RARITAN and MULLICA are among rivers that drain E and SE to the ocean. In the NE corner, the PASSAIC and HACKENSACK rivers flow S, along the W side of the PALISADES of the Hudson, into Newark Bay. The most densely populated US state, New Jersey lies in the SUBURBAN orbits of New York City (E) and Philadelphia (W). The New Jersey Turnpike, traversing much of the zone of heaviest development, is the busiest US highway. But while the state, at the heart of MEGALOPOLIS, contains many bedroom communities and routes to elsewhere, it also has large agricultural regions (chiefly in the S) that gave it the nickname "the Garden State," a seacoast in places still lightly settled, the wilderness of the PINE BARRENS (S), hilly and lake-dotted resort areas in the N, and its own long-established industrial centers, including Newark and Paterson, which in 1791 was the first planned (by Alexander Hamilton) US manufacturing community. In the 20th century much industry, along with research centers and corporate headquarters, from the two neighboring metropolises has relocated in New Jersey, and suburban areas like CHERRY HILL, EDISON, and PARSIPPANY–TROY HILLS have grown rapidly, while Newark, Jersey City, and other older centers have lost pop. Much of New York's harbor traffic is now handled in PORT NEWARK and Elizabeth, and the state is a major importer, warehouser, and assembler of varied goods. Chemical and pharmaceutical refining and manufacturing are leading industries, but New Jersey makes a wide range of products. The financial, insurance, and service sectors are important, along with communications and other research. The state's farms are noted most for their tomatoes and other truck crops and fruits, berries, and dairy goods. Tourism focuses on the beaches and inlets of the Jersey Shore, while the MEADOWLANDS complex and ATLANTIC CITY's casinos draw many other visitors. Rutgers, the state university, is based in NEW BRUNSWICK; PRINCETON is another noted academic center. Home to the Lenni Lenape (Delaware), the area was settled by the Dutch in the 1660s, and soon taken over by the British. Its early division into Pennsylvania-oriented West Jersey and New York–oriented EAST JERSEY is reflected to a large degree in today's South Jersey/North Jersey distinctions; the West (or South) was settled largely by Quakers, and remained agricultural and lightly populated until recent decades, while the East (North) was within America's most active commercial zone, and was soon heavily developed. New Jersey was a Revolutionary War battleground, with celebrated engagements at Trenton, Princeton, and MONMOUTH. In the late 20th century, following two centuries of industrialization and later suburbanization, the state's people are highly diverse in background and lifestyle.

New Kensington city, pop. 15,894, Westmoreland Co., SW Pennsylvania, on the Allegheny R., 14 mi/23 km NE of Pittsburgh. Built on the site of a Revolutionary War fort, New Kensington was founded in 1891; in 1931, it absorbed the neighboring town of Parnassus. Since 1892, it has been one of the world's leading producers of aluminum; it also manufactures petroleum and electrical products, steel, glass, and textiles, and has industrial research and development centers nearby.

New Lebanon rural town, pop. 2379, Columbia Co., SE New York, 25 mi/40 km SE of Albany and adjacent (W) to HANCOCK, Massachusetts. In the 19th century it was a Shaker center, and the restored Mount Lebanon Shaker Village is here. New Lebanon was the birthplace of political leader Samuel J. Tilden (1814–86).

New Lenox village, pop. 9627, Will Co., NE Illinois, on the LINCOLN HIGHWAY, 6 mi/10 km ESE of JOLIET. In the Hickory Creek area, site of many Indian villages long before the first (1820s) white settlement, it became after the 1920s an area of exurban small farms, and remains chiefly residential.

New Lexington city, pop. 5117, seat of Perry Co., SE Ohio, 19 mi/31 km SSW of Zanesville. It is a trade and distribution center for the area, which is supported by coal mining and gas and oil wells. There is also some farming in the region.

New Liskeard town, pop. 5431, Timiskaming District, E Ontario, on the NW end of L. Timiskaming near the Québec border, 80 mi/130 km NNW of North Bay. Founded in the late 19th century, it developed as a service center to the fertile Little CLAY BELT after the 1905 arrival of the railroad. Today it is a hunting, fishing, and lake resort in a mining (COBALT is just S) region. Local industries include dairying, lumbering, canning, and pulp manufacture. A college of agricultural technology is here.

New London **1.** city and coterminous township, pop. 28,540, New London Co., SE Connecticut, on the W bank of the Thames R., opposite GROTON, 51 mi/82 km E of New Haven, on Long Island Sound. Founded in 1646, it was a haven for privateers during the Revolutionary War; the British attacked and burned it in Sept. 1781. Rebuilt, it became a shipping, whaling, and shipbuilding center in the 19th century. It was a base for submarine chasers during World War I, and an active port during World War II. New London is the seat of the US Coast Guard Academy (1876) and Connecticut College (1911). The annual Yale-Harvard crew races take place on the Thames. Industries include the manufacture of pharmaceuticals, diesel engines, and chemicals. **2.** town, pop. 3180, Merrimack Co., WC New Hampshire. It is 40 mi/64 km NW of Concord, at 1326 ft/404 m. Colby-Sawyer College (1837) is here. L. SUNAPEE and Little Sunapee L. are in the W. The town is a resort and winter sports center. **3.** see under GREEN GABLES, Prince Edward Island.

New London County 669 sq mi/1733 sq km, pop. 254,957, in SE Connecticut, on Long Island Sound at the Rhode Island border. Fishing, oystering, shipping, and shipbuilding have long been major industries. More recently, the area has been a major defense supplier, with Electric Boat's submarine plant in Groton the largest employer. Tourism is also an important industry; the introduction (1992) of casino gambling in Ledyard was expected to stimulate this sector.

New Lots see under EAST NEW YORK, New York.

New Madrid city, pop. 3350, seat of New Madrid Co., SE Missouri, on the Mississippi R. (the Tennessee border), 48 mi/77 km S of Cape Girardeau. The city is situated at the top of New Madrid Bend, where the Mississippi R., at one of its widest points, curves almost 360°. It was established (1783) as a French-Canadian fur trading post, and settled by American pioneers six years later. The town's development was rapid until the disastrous earthquake of 1811, which largely destroyed it and changed the surrounding landscape. Tremors continued for some two years thereafter, and many residents fled the county. The town was moved at least three times before the Civil War. During the war, New Madrid, which held a strategically important position on the Mississippi R., was occupied (1861–62) by Confederate troops under George Hollins and successfully besieged (1862) by Union forces under John Pope. In 1990 a serious quake was forecast for the area, but did not materialize. Today, as throughout its history, the city is involved in the trade and shipping of local agricultural products. The **New Madrid Fault,** a seismic zone some 120 mi/192 km long that precipitated the historic 1811 earthquake (estimated to have measured over 8 on the Richter scale) and many other smaller quakes before and since, extends from New Madrid NE to the Kentucky border near Cairo, Illinois, SE across the Mississippi R. into Tennessee, and SW to a spot near Marked Tree, Arkansas. Tiny earthquakes occur almost weekly somewhere in the zone.

New Market town, pop. 1435, Shenandoah Co., NW Virginia, 16 mi/26 km NE of Harrisonburg, the site of a battle fought May 15, 1864, in which Confederate forces under John C. Breckenridge defeated a Union army under Franz Sigel, retaining control of the Shenandoah Valley's summer grain harvest. New Market, just W of MASSANUTTEN Mt., is a tourist base for nearby Endless Caverns and Shenandoah Caverns.

Newmarket town, pop. 45,474, seat of York Regional Municipality, S Ontario, on the Holland R., 28 mi/45 km N of Toronto. An early-19th-century Quaker settlement with an agricultural (esp. dairying) history, it is now experiencing rapid suburban growth.

New Melones Dam and Lake see under STANISLAUS R., California.

New Mexico state of the SW US, considered both as part of the SOUTHWEST and as one of the MOUNTAIN STATES; 1990 pop. 1,515,069 (116.3% of 1980; rank: 37th); area 121, 598 sq mi/314,939 sq km (rank: 5th); admitted to Union 1912 (47th). Capital: SANTA FE. Most populous cities: ALBUQUERQUE, LAS CRUCES, Santa Fe, ROSWELL. New Mexico is bounded E by Texas and the Oklahoma Panhandle, and N by Colorado. On the NW, at the FOUR CORNERS, it meets Colorado, Utah, and Arizona; Arizona also lies along its W border. In the S, it is bordered (W–E) by the Mexican states of Sonora (extreme SW) and Chihuahua, and by the Trans-Pecos section of Texas. The E third of the state lies at the W extreme of the GREAT PLAINS. In this High Plains region the CANADIAN R. drains E toward the Oklahoma and Texas panhandles, and the PECOS R. drains SSE toward the Rio Grande. In the SE, the LLANO ESTACADO (Staked Plain) straddles the Texas–New Mexico border. In New Mexico's C, the Southern ROCKY Mts. extend S from Colorado, in the form of the SANGRE DE CRISTO (E) and SAN JUAN Mts., ending near Santa Fe and the headwaters of the Pecos (NC). Below this point are ranges (esp. the SACRAMENTO and GUADALUPE Mts.) sometimes considered part of the Rockies system, but sometimes considered extreme E elements of the BASIN AND RANGE PROVINCE. Running N–S through New Mexico's C is the Rio Grande, whose valley is home to most of the state's pop. In the NW are sections of the COLORADO PLATEAU, a high, dry region in which FARMINGTON and GALLUP are the leading cities. WHEELER PEAK (13,161 ft/4014 m), in the Sangre de Cristos, is New Mexico's high point; the low, on the SE border at Red Bluff Reservoir, is 2817 ft/859 m. Home to humans at least since the FOLSOM period (20,000 years ago), and 2000 years ago to the ANASAZI and other early cultures, the region was inhabited by various PUEBLO communities in the 16th century, when Spanish explorers entered it up the Rio Grande from Mexico, looking for CIBOLA. Also here were the nomadic Navajo and Apache, more recently (within several centuries) arrived from the N. The Spanish soon established MISSIONS; by 1610 Santa Fe was the regional capital. SOCORRO, MESILLA, and other settlements in the Rio Grande valley lay along EL CAMINO REAL. In 1680, the Pueblo Revolt drove the Spanish out for a dozen years, but they returned to control a colony that remained essentially isolated from the rest of what is now the US until Mexican independence (1821) brought the opening of the SANTA FE TRAIL from Missouri. American power and settlement soon spread into the Southwest, and the Mexican War, sparked (1846) by events in Texas, ended with US control of all of New Mexico except the GADSDEN PURCHASE (S), which was added in 1853. The California boom of the 1850s brought increased travel through New Mexico, esp. on the SPANISH TRAIL and the Butterfield OVERLAND ROUTE. During the Civil War, the

1862 battle of GLORIETA PASS ended a Confederate thrust during which Mesilla had been envisioned as a regional capital. The territory remained lightly populated until the late 1870s, when the SANTA FE RAILROAD reached Santa Fe (1879) and continued S to DEMING, joining the SOUTHERN PACIFIC and creating a second transcontinental rail link. By the 1890s stock raising and irrigated farming were flourishing in the SE, and gold, silver, and coal mining were rising to importance. Oil was discovered in the SE in 1909. In the 1920s, the new state drew visitors to mountain and health resorts and old Spanish and Indian communities, among them Santa Fe, TAOS, and ABIQUIU. One mountain community, LOS ALAMOS, secretly became (1943) the center of the US effort to build the first atomic bomb, which was exploded (1945) in the desert NW of ALAMOGORDO. Los Alamos continued as a major government installation after the war's end, and Albuquerque (with its Sandia Laboratory) and WHITE SANDS were also key to US weapons research. Today, New Mexico is a major producer of uranium, coal, copper, potash, and natural gas. Cattle and sheep raising and lumbering (esp. in the GILA, LINCOLN, and other NATIONAL FORESTS) are important. Crop raising remains limited by the scarceness of water, but certain areas are highly productive, like the HATCH section of the Rio Grande valley, now noted for its chili peppers. Albuquerque and environs are the industrial hub of the state, home to a large electronics industry and various light manufactures. Tourists are drawn to Santa Fe, Taos, and the pueblos, which include ÁCOMA, ZUÑI, SAN ILDEFONSO, and JEMEZ, and retirees and others seeking a place in the SUNBELT have increased the pop. of communities around the state in recent decades. Skiing is popular at sites as widespread as Taos (N), the SANDIA Mts. (C), and the SIERRA BLANCA (S). Well-known historic and natural preserves include the CARLSBAD CAVERNS (SE) and the CHACO CULTURE National Historical Park. The huge NAVAJO INDIAN RESERVATION lies partly (with its hub at SHIPROCK) in NW New Mexico, and the JICARILLA and MESCALERO APACHE reservations are here also. The University of New Mexico is at Albuquerque, New Mexico State University at Las Cruces. Reflecting its varied history, the state's people are today 38% Hispanic and almost 9% Indian, but grow increasingly cosmopolitan.

New Milford **1.** town, pop. 23,629, Litchfield Co., NW Connecticut, on the Housatonic R., 12 mi/19 km N of Danbury. Settled in 1707, and the largest Connecticut town in area, it makes metal and electrical products and silverware, is a commercial center, has some agriculture, and is exurban in parts. The township includes Gaylordsville and several other villages and part of CANDLEWOOD L. **2.** borough, pop. 15,990, Bergen Co., NE New Jersey, on the Hackensack R., 4 mi/6 km NE of Hackensack. Settled (1667) by French Huguenots, who bought the area from Tappan Indians, it was the site of Washington's crossing of the Hackensack in retreat from Fort Lee to Trenton (1776). New Milford was created from three settlements in 1922. Today it is an almost completely residential suburb.

Newnan city, pop. 12,497, seat of Coweta Co., W Georgia, 32 mi/51 km SW of Atlanta. Founded in 1828, it is a textile center, producing plastics, lumber, and peanuts as well.

New Netherland Dutch colony, formalized by charter granted to the Dutch West India Co. in 1621. It came to include Fort Orange (Albany) and other lands along the Hudson R.; NEW AMSTERDAM; and, later, lands on the lower Delaware R. New Netherland was abolished by the British conquest of 1664.

New Orleans city, pop. 496,938, coextensive with Orleans Parish, SE Louisiana, in the DELTA OF THE MISSISSIPPI RIVER, at the SE end of the RIVER ROAD, bounded N by L. PONTCHARTRAIN and E by L. Borgne, on the Gulf of Mexico. Most of the city lies between L. Pontchartrain and the E (here, N) bank of the Mississippi, in terrain slightly above or below river or sea level, and is protected by LEVEES. The six-parish (including JEFFERSON and SAINT TAMMANY) New Orleans metropolitan area (MSA) has a pop. of 1,238,816. New Orleans was founded by the Sieur de Bienville for the French in 1718, and became the capital of the colony of Louisiana in 1722. In 1763, it was ceded to Spain, rebelled briefly, and continued to trade freely despite Spanish restrictions. In 1800, it was returned to France, then sold (1803) to the US as part of the LOUISIANA PURCHASE. Its French and Spanish "Creole" pop., formed during the 18th century, and now almost disappeared as a district element, has had a dominant role in the city's culture. As New Orleans expanded, *faubourgs,* or suburbs, developed outside the VIEUX CARRÉ or French Quarter, the oldest section of city. The first of these, the Faubourg Ste. Marie, across what is now CANAL St., became part of the AMERICAN QUARTER as post-1803 arrivals from the US developed an important business and residential district. Friction between Creoles and Americans subsided gradually. During the War of 1812 the British advanced on New Orleans from the Gulf of Mexico. They were defeated on Jan. 8, 1815 by an army under Andrew Jackson (after a treaty ending the war had been signed in Europe) in nearby (E) CHALMETTE. An important cotton port in the early 19th century, New Orleans was occupied by Union forces on April 25, 1862, and held for the rest of the Civil War; it was at the time the largest city in the Confederacy. In the postwar period, the ascendance of railroads contributed to the port's slow recapture of its importance. Improvements in the river's channels (1870s) and the city's strategic location in the Spanish-American War (1898) contributed to eventual recovery, and by mid 20th century New Orleans was again the second-leading US port, after New York. Another round of port and transportation improvements took place from the 1950s through the 1970s. New Orleans is now a shipping center for OIL PATCH petroleum and natural gas, aluminum, grain, tobacco, chemicals and oils, textiles, and varied agricultural goods. A long-term project is relocating much port activity in the Inner Harbor area in order to free riverfront property for residential, commercial, and public use. Plants in New Orleans, which include NASA's Michoud rocket assembly facility and major shipyards, also manufacture petroleum, oilfield equipment, foods, stone, clay, and glass products, primary and fabricated metals, pharmaceuticals, chemicals, paint, and transportation equipment. Tourism, a major industry along with convention and business visitor trade, draws much of its strength from the city's rich ethnic and cultural history. In addition to the Creole strain, New Orleans was from the 18th century home to both slave and free black communities. Americans arrived at the beginning of the 19th century, Italians at the end. At the E fringe of CAJUN COUNTRY, the city has also absorbed much from its culture. The result is a metropolis more truly multicultural than any US city except Honolulu, noted for its distinctive foods, architecture, patois (also called "Creole"), "good times" lifestyle, and esp. music; it is widely known as the birthplace, or at least the incubator (c.1900–20), of jazz. Mardi Gras, the pre-Lenten carnival, is the city's most famous event; the annual Jazz and Heritage Festival and festivities around the New Year's Eve Sugar Bowl (football) game are also key. Educational institutions include Dillard (1869), Loyola (1912), Tulane (1834), and Xavier (1915) universities, the University of New Orleans (1956), and a number of other schools and seminaries. The city's pop. peaked at 627,575 in 1960, since when it has lost residents to METAIRIE and other suburbs. The international airport is in nearby (W) KENNER. See also: ALGIERS; AMERICAN QUARTER; AUDUBON PARK; BASIN St.; BEAUREGARD SQUARE (Congo Square); BOURBON St.; CANAL St.; CARROLLTON; CRESCENT CITY; DESIRE St.; DOWNTOWN; GARDEN DISTRICT; GENTILLY; INNER HARBOR; IRISH CHANNEL; JACKSON SQUARE (Place d'Armes; and Cabildo); LIBERTY PLACE; LOUISIANA SUPERDOME (and Sugar Bowl); MARIGNY; MILNEBURG; RAMPART St.; SPANISH FORT; STORYVILLE; TOURO; TREMÉ; UPTOWN; VIEUX CARRÉ (French Quarter; and Ursuline Convent); WAREHOUSE DISTRICT; WEST END.

New Paltz town, pop. 11,388, Ulster Co., SE New York, on the Walkill R., 10 mi/16 km WNW of Poughkeepsie and just E of the Shawangunk Mts. The State University of New York College at New Paltz (1828) is here.

New Philadelphia city, pop. 15,698, seat of Tuscarawas Co., EC Ohio, on the Tuscarawas R., 20 mi/32 km S of Canton. It is situated in an area of coal, sand, and clay deposits. A major state flood control project has its headquarters here, and the city is the site of a branch of Kent State University. Local manufactures include tools, machinery, ceramics, plastics, and construction equipment. The state's first village, SCHOENBRUNN, is just S of the city. To the N is the site of Fort Laurens, the state's only Revolutionary War fort.

Newport **1.** city, pop. 7459, seat of Jackson Co., NE Arkansas, 35 mi/56 km SW of Jonesboro, on the White R. It is a railroad and trade center for an agricultural region producing cotton, rice, pecans, and livestock. Cotton and food processing, lumber milling, and the manufacture of wood products are among its industries. Wal-Mart founder Sam Walton opened his first store here in 1945. **2.** town, pop. 1240, New Castle Co., N Delaware, on the Christina R., 4 mi/6 km SW of Wilmington. Its manufactures include paints and chemicals. **3.** in Indiana: **a.** town, pop. 627, seat of Vermillion Co., 30 mi/48 km N of Terre Haute, on the Little Vermillion R. at its junction with the Wabash R. **b.** see under FOUNTAIN CITY, Wayne Co. **4.** city, pop. 18,871, Campbell Co., extreme N Kentucky, across the Licking R. (E) from COVINGTON, and on the Ohio R. opposite (S) Cincinnati, Ohio. Settled in 1790, it is one of Cincinnati's older suburbs. A bridge to Cincinnati and an influx of German immigrants spurred growth in the 1880s–90s. Livestock, fruit, and tobacco are traded, and manufactures have included steel, clothing, beer, printed material, auto parts, and chemicals. The city has lost population in recent decades. **5.** city, pop. 8437, seat of Lincoln Co., NW Oregon, a resort on Yaquina Bay, at the mouth of the Yaquina R. on the Pacific Ocean, 55 mi/89 km SW of Salem. Developed around 1860s hotels, it is best known for its oysters, clamming, crabbing, fishing, beaches, and Victorian waterfront, more recently for its shops and galleries. It also has government oceanographic laboratories. **6.** city, pop. 28,227, seat of Newport Co., Rhode Island, at the S tip of Rhode I. in Narragansett Bay, 25 mi/40 km SE of Providence. A port of entry made wealthy by the slave trade, and important during the Revolution, it has been a popular resort since shortly after the Civil War. Until 1900 it was one of Rhode Island's two capitals. Newport has many Colonial buildings, among them the TOURO Synagogue, the nation's oldest (1763). The late 19th century saw the city's development as the playground of the rich. The Newport Casino became in the 1880s the center of American tennis, and the first amateur golf championships were held in the 1890s. Opulent mansions spread along the CLIFF WALK. Yachting and banquets characterized the life of Newport's summer elite. **7.** city, pop. 4434, seat of Orleans Co., at the mouth of the Black R., on L. Memphremagog, NC Vermont. Tourism, sawmills, dairying, and granite quarrying are the main industries. South Bay Wildlife Management Area, S of the city, contains 1559 ac/631 ha of marshlands.

Newport Beach city, pop. 66,643, Orange Co., SW California, 38 mi/61 km SE of Los Angeles, on the Balboa Peninsula, between Newport Bay and the Pacific Ocean, and on lands around the bay. The city includes several islands, including Lido and Linda isles and Balboa I. Its 5.5 mi/9 km of sandy beach and its yacht harbor have made it a popular, affluent resort. The Corona del Mar section, E of the bay, and Balboa, on the peninsula, are particularly well known. Luxury hotels and seaside villas accommodate tourists. The city's manufactures include electronic equipment, computer software, plastics, and fiberglass boats, and it has financial and insurance sectors. Newport Bay is the site of boat parades (festivals) and the starting point of the annual Newport-to-Ensenada (Mexico) race.

Newport Hills unincorporated community, pop. 14,736, King Co., WC Washington, just E of L. Washington, an affluent residential suburb 8 mi/13 km SE of Seattle.

Newport News independent city, pop. 170,045, in SE Virginia, at the mouth of the James R., on the N side of HAMPTON ROADS. With Norfolk and Portsmouth, it is part of the Port of Hampton Roads, and the seaboard terminus of the Chesapeake and Ohio Railroad system, which handles coal, tobacco, grain, ores, and other bulk goods for export. The Newport News Shipbuilding and Drydock Company (1886), one of world's largest shipyards, has built large passenger vessels like the *United States,* submarines, aircraft carriers, and nuclear-powered vessels. Although its economy is dominated by industries related to its port, the city also produces chemicals, textiles, building materials, and processed seafood. During the Civil War, Newport News was occupied by Union troops. The city was a major point of embarkation for soldiers and supplies during World Wars I and II. Newport News is the seat of Christopher Newport College (1960), a branch of the College of William and Mary. The city's name developed from "New Port Newce," after a 1620s family that owned much land here.

New Port Richey city, pop. 14,044, Pasco Co., WC Florida, on the Gulf of Mexico, 25 mi/40 km NW of Tampa, and just S of the 1880s port city of Port Richey (pop. 2523), at the mouth of the Pithlachascotee R. A popular winter vacation locale, it is also home to some light industry, processes and ships local citrus fruits, and makes concrete products.

New Providence borough, pop. 11,439, Union Co., NE New Jersey, on the Passaic R., 12 mi/19 km SW of Newark, in the Watchung Mts. It was settled in the early 18th century on a site purchased from Delaware Indians, and called Turkey Town until 1778. It has long been a horticultural center, known for its roses. Today, it is essentially residential, with some light industry, research facilities, and numerous office buildings.

New Quebec see NOUVEAU-QUÉBEC, Québec.

New River **1.** air station: see under CAMP LEJEUNE, North Carolina. **2.** 320 mi/515 km long, in North Carolina, Virginia, and West Virginia. Its **South Fork** rises near Boone, Watauga Co., NW North Carolina, in the Blue Ridge, and flows NE. Near Weavers Ford, just S of the Virginia border, it receives the **North Fork,** which flows E from the Stone Mts., on the Tennessee border. The New R. flows NE and N across Virginia, past REDFORD and through the Allegheny Mts., and enters West Virginia, where it receives the GREENBRIER and Bluestone rivers. A dam (1948) below the confluence with the Bluestone, near Hinton, impounds Bluestone L., which extends 36 mi/58 km back upriver into Virginia. Below Hinton, 52 mi/84 km of the river have been designated the **New River Gorge National River.** At its lower (N) end is the New R. Gorge Bridge, completed in 1977, near Fayetteville, with the world's longest steel arch span (1700 ft/519 m). Five mi/8 km NW of the bridge, the New R. joins the Gauley R. to form the KANAWHA R.

New Rochelle city, pop. 67,265, Westchester Co., SE New York, on Long Island Sound, 16 mi/26 km NNE of Manhattan. It is a residential and commercial suburb of New York City with some light industry, including the manufacture of chemicals, metals, and clothing. New Rochelle was settled in 1688 by French Huguenots seeking religious freedom, and city records were kept in French until 1828. Memorials to Thomas Paine, who lived here 1802–06, are maintained. Iona College (1940) and the College of New Rochelle (1904) are here. GLEN ISLAND and other resorts are on the Sound.

New Rumley unincorporated village in Rumley township, Harrison Co., EC Ohio, 21 mi/34 km WNW of Steubenville. A small trading center, it is best known as the birthplace (1839) of cavalry leader George A. Custer. A bronze statue marks the site of the Custer homestead.

New Salem see under PETERSBURG, Illinois.

New Shoreham see under BLOCK ISLAND, Rhode Island.

New Smyrna Beach formerly, **New Smyrna** city, pop. 16,543, Volusia Co., EC Florida, on both sides of the INDIAN R. lagoon, just SE of the Ponce de Leon Inlet and 13 mi/21 km SSE of Daytona Beach. One of the oldest settlements in this part of Florida, it was established (1696) as the Atocuimi Mission by Spanish Franciscans on the site of an Indian village. A shell- and artifact-filled Indian mound and ruins of the European mission remain. Recolonized as a plantation in 1767, it was named by settler Andrew Turnbull for his wife's Turkish birthplace, and he brought Greek, Italian, and Minorcan workers into the area. It was abandoned in 1776 during Revolutionary War upheaval, was resettled in the early 1800s, and flourished with the mid-19th-century arrival of the railroad. Today it is a year-round resort with 8 mi/13 km of white sand beaches. Industries include commercial fishing, seafood and citrus packing, and light manufacturing.

New Sweden colony established 1638 along the lower Delaware R. by Peter Minuit, under the aegis of the Swedish king; the settlers were Swedes and Finns. New Sweden extended from BOMBAY HOOK (S) to the SCHUYLKILL R. (N). Fort Christina, built along the Minquas Kill (the CHRISTINA R.) in what is now Wilmington, Delaware, was central to the colony. TINICUM I., Pennsylvania, became its capital in 1643. Before the New Amsterdam–based Dutch took over in 1655, New Sweden set a precedent of local self-sufficiency. Its colonists are said to have introduced the log cabin building style into North America.

Newton **1.** city, pop. 14,789, seat of Jasper Co., C Iowa, 30 mi/48 km E of Des Moines. Settled in 1846, it has been the home of Maytag, manufacturers of washing machines, since 1898. **2.** city, pop. 16,700, seat of Harvey Co., SE Kansas, 26 mi/42 km N of Wichita. German Mennonites recruited from Russia's Volga region settled here in the 1870s, bringing with them seeds for a resilient winter wheat, Turkey Red, which revolutionized Great Plains agriculture. Today the city and its environs are the nation's largest Mennonite settlement. Agriculture remains central to the economy of this railroad city, which was an 1870s CHISHOLM TRAIL railhead; it also refines oil and manufactures aircraft, mobile homes, and farm implements. The Mennonite-affiliated Bethel College (1887) is in adjacent North Newton (city, pop. 1262). **3.** city, pop. 82,585, Middlesex Co., E Massachusetts, on the Charles R., 7 mi/11 km W of downtown Boston. Settled in 1640, a city since 1873, it comprises 14 villages set on hilly terrain. The lower Charles R. falls stimulated early industrial development (iron forges and textile mills). After railway transportation opened in 1834, Newton became a major Boston suburb. Manufacturing plants make electrical components, textiles, paper, plastics, and rubber products. A nationally known center for education, Newton has first-rate public schools, the Andover-Newton Theological School, and several junior colleges. Its villages, essentially a series of railway suburbs, are Newton Center, Newton Corner, Newton Highlands, Newton Upper and Lower Falls, West Newton, Newtonville, Auburndale, CHESTNUT HILL (part of which is in BROOKLINE), Waban, Riverside, Oak Hill, Eliot, and Nonantum. Along Beacon St. in Newton Center is the infamous Heartbreak Hill, bane of Boston Marathon runners. **4.** city, pop. 9304, seat of Catawba Co., WC North Carolina, 7 mi/11 km SE of Hickory. With the adjacent (N) city of Conover (pop. 5465), it forms a textile center; furniture and fertilizer are also manufactured.

Newtonbrook see under NORTH YORK, Ontario.

New Toronto see under ETOBICOKE, Ontario.

New Town **1.** in SAN DIEGO, California, the 960-ac/390-ha area along N San Diego Bay purchased in 1867 by Alonzo Horton, who developed it as an alternative to the OLD TOWN, 3 mi/5 km NNW on the San Diego R. By the 1870s it had become the city's new center, and is today the core of Downtown. HORTON PLAZA, the GASLAMP QUARTER, and BROADWAY are in New Town, also known in its early days as Horton's Addition. **2.** residential and commercial neighborhood on the NORTH SIDE of Chicago, Illinois, between LINCOLN PARK and LAKE VIEW. **3.** see under FORT BERTHOLD, North Dakota.

Newtown **1.** town, pop. 20,779, Fairfield Co., SW Connecticut, on the Housatonic R., adjacent (E) to Danbury. An historically agricultural town with some manufacturing, it is experiencing suburban development. **2.** in New York: **a.** see under ELMIRA. **b.** former township, C Queens. It was settled around 1642. In 1683, when Queens Co. was organized, there were three towns, Flushing, Newtown, and Jamaica. Newtown was agricultural, noted for its apples, Newtown pippins, exported to Britain. LONG ISLAND CITY broke away from Newtown in 1870, and when Queens became part of New York City in 1898, Newtown became a ward of Queens.

The modern districts of Jackson Heights, Rego Park, Forest Hills, and Elmhurst were in Newtown, the name of which survives in many local addresses. **Newtown Creek** is a 4 mi/6 km-long, heavily industrial tidal inlet of the East R. that separates Brooklyn (Greenpoint and Bushwick) from Queens (Long Island City, Sunnyside, and Maspeth). **3.** township, pop. 13,685, Bucks Co., SE Pennsylvania, 21 mi/33 km NE of Philadelphia. It is largely residential and suburban. The George School, a prep school, and Bucks County Community College (1964) are here. Newtown borough (pop. 2565) is within the township.

New Ulm city, pop. 13,132, seat of Brown Co., SW Minnesota, on the Minnesota R. near the mouth of the Cottonwood R., 25 mi/40 km WNW of Mankato. Settled by German immigrants in 1854, it processes many of the area's farm products, especially beef, grain, and dairy items. It also manufactures electric equipment and plastics. Attacked twice during the Sioux uprising of 1862, most of the original village was destroyed and the inhabitants fled to Mankato until the Indians were defeated. Situated here, Dr. Martin Luther College dates to 1884. Fort Ridgely, Minnesota's third frontier military post, is in the state park of the same name, 20 mi/32 km NW.

New Utrecht former township, S Brooklyn, New York. Established in the 1650s by Dutch settlers, it was a town until annexed by the city of Brooklyn in 1894. Modern Bay Ridge, Fort Hamilton, Borough Park, Bath Beach, and parts of Bensonhurst were within New Utrecht, the name of which survives in neighborhood institutions.

New Waterford town, pop. 7695, Cape Breton Co., extreme E Nova Scotia, on Cape Breton I., near the entrance to SYDNEY Harbour. Its coal mines, which extend underwater, once made it E Canada's largest producer. It has suffered with the decline of coal since the 1960s. A coal-fired power station is here, and the town has a large fishing fleet.

New Westminster city, pop. 43,585, Greater Vancouver Regional District, SW British Columbia, on the N bank of the Fraser R., a suburb 10 mi/16 km ESE of downtown Vancouver and adjacent (SE) to Burnaby. It was established as capital (1859–66) of the British Columbia colony. An administrative and trade center, it has been an important port and industrial and marketing center, with lumber and paper, distilling, brewing, shipbuilding, oil refining, grain storage, and food processing industries. It is today increasingly residential. The Canadian Lacrosse Hall of Fame is here.

New Wilmington borough, pop. 2706, Lawrence Co., extreme NW Pennsylvania, 8 mi/13 km N of New Castle. It is the seat of Westminster College (1852).

New York northeastern US state, in the Middle Atlantic region; 1990 pop. 17,990,455 (102.5% of 1980; rank: 2nd, but in 1994 the Census Bureau estimated that Texas had replaced it in this position); area 54,475 sq mi/141,090 sq km (rank: 27th); ratified Constitution 1788 (11th). Capital: ALBANY. Most populous cities: NEW YORK CITY, BUFFALO, ROCHESTER, YONKERS. New York is bordered N by Québec (E) and Ontario (EC, across the SAINT LAWRENCE R.); E by (N–S) Vermont (largely across L. CHAMPLAIN), Massachusetts, and Connecticut; and S by (W–E) Pennsylvania and New Jersey. On the W is a strip of Pennsylvania that reaches N to L. Erie. New York has shores on both L. ERIE (W) and L. ONTARIO (WC), between which it faces part of Ontario across the NIAGARA R. In the SE it faces New Jersey (W) across the lower HUDSON R. (the KILL VAN KULL and ARTHUR KILL separate New York City's STATEN ISLAND from New Jersey). LONG ISLAND extends E from New York Bay into the Atlantic, with Connecticut and Rhode Island (in the extreme E) lying N across Long Island Sound. The state's shape was determined by two great travel and trade routes. The first runs S–N from NEW YORK BAY (the East Coast's largest harbor), up the Hudson R. past Albany, and via Lakes GEORGE and Champlain, to the St. Lawrence R. valley, where the R. Richelieu provided 17th-century water access to NEW FRANCE; this route was important in the fur trade, in general commerce, and in the struggle between England and France for control of E North America. The second (E–W) route connects the Hudson at Albany with the Great Lakes (W), via the MOHAWK R. and its valley. The largest break in the barrier of the APPALACHIAN system, the Mohawk Valley provided settlers (from the 18th century) a land route westward. In 1825 the ERIE CANAL, paralleling the river, connected New York City with the Great Lakes and the developing Middle West. The canal itself (now part of the NEW YORK STATE BARGE CANAL SYSTEM) was soon paralleled by the NEW YORK CENTRAL RAILROAD's famous "water level route." Along the river, canal, and railroad, industrial cities grew up. North of Albany and the Mohawk Valley are the rugged ADIRONDACK Mts. (rising to 5344 ft/1630 m at Mt. MARCY, the state's high point), a S extension of the CANADIAN SHIELD; this region and the lowlands along the Saint Lawrence R. and L. Ontario are known collectively as the NORTH COUNTRY. To the S of the Mohawk Valley is the SOUTHERN TIER, a region of farms and cities (BINGHAMTON is the largest) on the upper ALLEGHENY and SUSQUEHANNA rivers, and thus economically isolated from the rest of the state until the ERIE RAILROAD reached them in the 1840s. The Southern Tier and the CATSKILL Mts., to the E, are part of the massive Appalachian plateau. Along the plateau's N, on the edge of the Great Lakes lowlands, are the glacial FINGER LAKES, a resort, winemaking, and farming region. Below Albany, the Hudson R. cuts through the Appalachian front. On its W are the HUDSON HIGHLANDS and the PALISADES; on its E the TACONIC Mts. run N–S along the borders of New England. New York Bay is the sunken lower valley of the Hudson, which continues underwater as the Hudson Canyon until it drops from the edge of the CONTINENTAL SHELF. Long Island is formed largely by a pair of terminal MORAINES, part of a glacial formation extending E through Rhode Island's Block I. and Massachusetts's Cape Cod, Martha's Vineyard, and Nantucket. The state is highly urban, with the New York City METROPOLITAN AREA, the nation's most populous, encompassing WESTCHESTER and other counties along the lower Hudson and on Long Island as well as in New Jersey and Connecticut. The city's commerce, industry, and institutions have dominated regional history; within New York there has long existed a split between the City and UPSTATE. The latter has always been largely rural, despite its many industrial cities, and less cosmopolitan, its people wary (and at times resentful) of the City's economic, cultural, and political hegemony. In the late 20th century the City and its SUBURBS retain a majority of New York's pop., but suburbanites have more often shared the Upstate outlook. When whites first appeared in New York, what is now the state's center was occupied by the peoples who formed the IROQUOIS CONFEDERACY. In the SE were Algonquian groups, including the Mohegan, Canarsie, and other smaller tribes. The Hudson Valley was settled (as part of NEW NETHERLAND) in the 1620s by the Dutch, who lost power in 1664 to the British. New York's harbor soon became the commercial hub of the Colonies, and was an early focus of Revolutionary War fighting; the British controlled it in 1776, after the Battle of Long Island. To the N, the 1777 SARATOGA Campaign was also important. Soon after independence, industry began to grow; this thrived from the 1840s on wave after wave of European immigration. While New York Harbor was a gateway for many headed west, the city also became home to a huge labor pool, and diversified manufacturing, led by textiles, boomed. Manufacturing gradually spread to cities in the interior; some eventually became strongly identified with particular industries, including Rochester (photographic and optical equipment) and SCHENECTADY (electrical machinery). In the late 20th century, New York has lost much of its older industrial base, but its diversity, human resources (continuously replenished by immigration both from abroad and to New York City from across the US), and academic and research base have helped to prevent the kind of decline suffered in some states more dependent on single industries. Agriculture remains important, led by apple and wine grape production, dairying, and the raising of a wide variety of truck and other crops. Tourism and recreation, focusing esp. on New York City's sights and institutions, the Catskills and Adirondacks, the Finger Lakes, the THOUSAND ISLANDS (in the St. Lawrence R.), and NIAGARA FALLS, make a major contribution to the state's economy. New York's people, in the 17th and 18th centuries primarily British and Dutch, in the mid 19th century also largely Irish and German, now include (esp. in the New York City area) representatives of every group that has come to North America, with esp. large Italian, Jewish, Slavic, Puerto Rican, Chinese, and black communities.

New York Bay Atlantic Ocean inlet at the mouth of the Hudson R., in New York and New Jersey, site of the largest US port complex. It is divided into two sections, separated by a strait called the Narrows. **Upper New York Bay,** which is roughly 6 mi/10 km in diameter, is surrounded by New York's Manhattan (NE), Brooklyn (E), and Staten Island (SW), along with New Jersey's Bayonne (W) and Jersey City (NW); the Hudson R. enters it from the N. The KILL VAN KULL leads W from it into Newark Bay, and the EAST R. leads NE to Queens, the Bronx, and Long Island Sound. The facilities of New York Harbor lie almost entirely on the Upper Bay, which also contains LIBERTY, ELLIS, and GOVERNOR'S islands. **The Narrows,** 3 mi/5 km long and 1 mi/1.6 km wide, lie between Staten Island (W) and Brooklyn (E), and form a passage into the Upper Bay. They are crossed by the VERRAZANO-NARROWS BRIDGE. **Lower New York Bay** is bounded by Staten I. (NW and W), Brooklyn and its Gravesend Bay (NE and E), Queens's Rockaway Point and Channel (E), New Jersey's Raritan Bay (SW), and the open Atlantic (S). The AMBROSE CHANNEL leads shipping through the Bay and Narrows. Giovanni da Verrazano was the first European (1524) to enter the Bay; Henry Hudson claimed it for the Dutch in 1609.

New York Central Railroad created 1853 by the merger of a number of small lines across C New York, including the 17-mi/27-km Mohawk & Hudson (1831, between Albany and Schenectady). These lines had sprung up paralleling the ERIE CANAL, and had begun to show the efficacy of rail as an alternative to barge transport. Connecting Buffalo and Albany, the Central connected in the E with two lines S to New York City—the New York & Harlem (1831, via Chatham) and the Hudson River Railroad (1846, via Hudson, Poughkeepsie, and Peekskill); these later became divisions of its system. In the W it acquired the Lake Shore and Michigan Southern, giving it a continuous route to Chicago, known, for its easy gradients through the Hudson and Mohawk valleys and along the Great Lakes, as the "water level route." John A. Roebling's 1855 Niagara suspension bridge gave it another route W, via Canadian lines, across S Ontario. It also, in the 1850s, extended service to St. Louis, Missouri. The Central long dominated New York City rail traffic, as the PENNSYLVANIA, ERIE, and other competitors had to employ ferry service from their New Jersey termini. Its Grand Central Depot (1871) and successor Grand Central Terminal (or Station, 1913), on East 42nd St. in Midtown Manhattan, were among the world's best-known, and its crack *Twentieth-Century Limited* (1902–67), to Chicago, one of the world's most prestigious trains. Flourishing through World War II, the Central soon after began to suffer, as did all US railroads, from the competition of the growing INTERSTATE HIGHWAY and airline systems. In 1968 it merged with the Pennsylvania Railroad as the Penn Central, and in 1970 was taken over by the government-created Conrail system. Its New York commuter service is now run by the Metro-North Commuter Railroad.

New York City also, **Greater New York** most populous (7,322,564) US city, in SE New York, on the mainland and islands at the mouth of the Hudson R. on NEW YORK BAY, LONG ISLAND SOUND, and the Atlantic Ocean. Covering 309 sq mi/800 km, the city comprises five boroughs, each also a county: the BRONX (Bronx Co.), N, on the mainland; BROOKLYN (Kings Co.), on the SW end of Long I.; MANHATTAN (New York Co.), the central island on the Hudson R.; QUEENS (Queens Co.), on the NW end of Long I.; and STATEN ISLAND (Richmond Co.), to the SW, along the New Jersey shore. New York City is the center of the largest US METROPOLITAN AREA, with a pop. of 17,953,372. In addition to the five boroughs, this includes Connecticut's FAIRFIELD Co.; New York's NASSAU, ORANGE, PUTNAM, ROCKLAND, SUFFOLK, and WESTCHESTER counties; and New Jersey's BERGEN, ESSEX, HUDSON, HUNTERDON, MIDDLESEX, MONMOUTH, MORRIS, OCEAN, PASSAIC, SOMERSET, SUSSEX, and UNION counties. Home to the Manhattan, Canarsie, Rockaway, and other peoples, the area was first seen by Europeans when Verrazano (1524) and Hudson (1609) sailed into New York Bay. The Dutch settled what became NEW AMSTERDAM in 1624. In 1664 the British seized the settlement, naming it New York. The harbor and strategic location made the city an important commercial and governmental center by the mid 18th century. During the Revolution the British occupied it (1776–81). In 1789–90 New York was the first US capital. By 1790, consisting solely of Manhattan I., it was also the largest US city. The Hudson–Mohawk R. westward migration route and the opening (1825) of the ERIE CANAL, linking the city with the developing Middle West, solidified the city's commercial role; railroads, developing in the area from the 1830s, reinforced its importance. As the major US port of entry, New York Harbor received much 19th-century immigration, and the huge labor pool created by newcomers settling in the area made the city the nation's most important industrial center before 1900, with thousands of plants producing clothing and accessories, textiles, fuels and chemicals, foods, books and printed materials, machinery, and other, chiefly light, manufactures. The press of pop. growth also led New Yorkers into neighboring counties. By the 1870s part of the Bronx had been annexed, and in 1898 Brooklyn, the third most populous US city, and the other elements of the modern five boroughs combined as Greater New York. To many, Manhattan is still "New York"; the "outer boroughs" provide most of the city's workers, and have their own industrial and commercial zones, but their primary role is as bedroom communities for Manhattan's business center. The city's pop. has been basically stable, fluctuating between 7 and 8 million, since the 1930s; this, however, obscures the size of in-migration and out-migration during the period, which has seen the loss of much of the harbor's trade and much industrial base, along with the decline of overseas immigration and a rush to the suburbs by second- and third-generation immigrant groups. Where the city has lost middle-class Europeans, it has gained less affluent black Southerners and Hispanics, and now is roughly half white, half nonwhite. The loss of job (and tax) base has led to fiscal and social problems expressed most clearly in the distress of certain neighborhoods. Other parts of the city, however, continue to flourish, and New York remains a magnet, through its commerce, finance, and cultural life, for the ambitious from all over America. The city's tremendous diversity is seen in its range of ethnic neighborhoods and blocks, which contribute much to its politics and flavor. For information on New York neighborhoods and features, see the BRONX, BROOKLYN, MANHATTAN, QUEENS, and STATEN ISLAND, and additional entries listed there.

New York County coextensive since 1898 with the New York City borough of MANHATTAN. Organized in the 17th century, it before 1898 included parts of what is now Bronx Co.

New York State Barge Canal inland waterway, 525 mi/845 km long, crossing New York, connecting the Great Lakes (W) with the Hudson R. and L. Champlain (E). Begun in 1905 and completed in 1918, it resulted from the modernization and modification of the ERIE CANAL, which remains its main component. Also in the system are the Champlain, Oswego, and Seneca canals. In order to compensate for the different levels of the more than 50 cities and other municipalities it serves, the system is equipped with 57 locks. Originally intended for commercial use, it is now mainly traveled by pleasure craft.

Nez Perce Indian Reservation 1195 sq mi/3095 sq km, pop. 16,160 (12% Indian), in NW Idaho, on the S of the PANHANDLE, S of COEUR D'ALENE L. and E of Washington's PALOUSE country. Lapwai is the headquarters of this home of the Sahaptin people noted for their (Appaloosa) horses and their 1877 attempt, under Chief Joseph, to escape white control. In 1855 they ceded much of their homeland, which had included parts of Idaho, Washington, and Oregon. When a gold rush brought prospectors into Oregon's WALLOWA Valley, Chief Joseph's group went to war; remaining Nez Perce were pushed into the Lapwai area. The **Nez Perce National Historical Park** (1965) unites 24 separate sites with historical, archaeological, or scenic interest, spread over a wide area of N Idaho.

Nez Perce National Forest 2.2 million ac/900,000 ha (3466 sq mi/8976 sq km), in NC Idaho, N of the Salmon R. and S and SE of the Nez Perce Indian Reservation, in the Clearwater Mts. and extending E to the Montana border, in the Bitterroot Mts. It contains parts of several of C Idaho's well-known wilderness areas, and all of the 207,000-ac/83,835-ha Gospel Hump Wilderness, along the Salmon.

Nez Perce Trail also, **Nee-Me-Poo Trail** 1700 mi/2737 km–long route the Nez Perce (also, Percé; "pierced nose") Indians took to seek freedom. It began in their homeland, where Washington, Oregon, and Idaho meet. In 1877, unwilling to accept vastly reduced reservation lands, a band of between 700 and 800 led by Chief Joseph set out on a trail that was ultimately to have Canada as its destination. It led from NE Oregon through Idaho, into E Montana, and through Wyoming's Yellowstone National Park. All along the route, the Nez Perce were pursued by US troops. Several battles ensued, notably at Clearwater Creek, Fort Missoula, and BIG HOLE. After losing 239 people, Chief Joseph was finally forced to surrender in Montana's Bear Paw Mts., less than 40 mi/64 km from freedom in Canada. The route is now a National Historic Trail.

Niagara County 526 sq mi/1362 sq km, pop. 220,756, in W New York, bounded W by the Niagara R. and L. Erie, and N by L. Ontario, drained by Tonawanda Creek, and crossed by the New York State Barge Canal. Its seat is LOCKPORT. It contains much of Buffalo's metropolitan area and the industrial cities of Niagara Falls, Tonawanda, and North Tonawanda. Hydroelectric plants powered by the falls sustain major electrometallurgic, electrochemical, and aerospace industries. Tourism, farming, and diverse manufacturing are also important.

Niagara Escarpment ridge, the residue of glacial lake formation and shrinkage, running W from near Rochester, New York, to Wisconsin's Green Bay. The Niagara R. cut Niagara Falls through it. From the falls area it runs through Hamilton, Milton, the Caledon Hills, Collingwood, Owen Sound, the Bruce Peninsula, and Manitoulin and St. Joseph islands, in Ontario; along the S of Michigan's Upper Peninsula; and into Green Bay. Averaging about 300 ft/90 m in height, and capped by limestone (dolomite), it has provided waterpower (falls) and quarry material, but is now largely recreational. In Ontario the Bruce Trail (see BRUCE PENINSULA) follows it.

Niagara Falls **1.** waterfall: see under NIAGARA R. **2.** city, pop. 61,840, Niagara Co., W New York, at the great falls of the Niagara R., opposite Niagara Falls, Ontario, 20 mi/32 km NNW of Buffalo. The site was crucial to the French and British in their struggle for control of the Great Lakes from 1669 to 1783, when the Treaty of Paris delineated a border between British Canada and the US. The city was established over a century later, with the consolidation of the two villages of Niagara Falls and Suspension Bridge, in 1892. Niagara Falls is now one of the world's leading producers of hydroelectric power, with a major electrochemical and electrometallurgic industry. The city also manufactures abrasives, aircraft and aerospace components, lubricants, foods, and wood and paper products, and is a major tourist center. The area has over 200 hazardous waste sites, including LOVE CANAL. **3.** city, pop. 75,399, Niagara Regional Municipality, S Ontario, on the W bank of the Niagara R., just below (N of) the river's falls, opposite the New York city. It incorporates settlements as early as Drummondville (c.1800), and includes the CHIPPAWA and LUNDY'S LANE battle sites. The Ontario community's growth was spurred by the 1855 completion of the first suspension bridge across the river, and it shared in the tremendous tourist trade generated by the falls. The city was incorporated in 1904. Its area increased twelve times in 1963, when it was consolidated with the township of Stanford. In addition to tourism, the city is an industrial center. Using abundant hydroelectric power, it manufactures chemicals, silverware, abrasives, machinery, and paper, food, and other products. Its location brings it heavy cross-border retail and other trade, and many US firms have offices here. Historic NAVY I. is just SE.

Niagara Frontier see under LOCKPORT, New York.

Niagara-on-the-Lake town, pop. 12,945, Niagara Regional Municipality, S Ontario, on the S shore of L. Ontario, at the mouth of the Niagara R., opposite New York State. The site was chosen for the first (1792–96) capital of UPPER CANADA, and named Newark. Settled by LOYALISTS, it served as capital until administration moved to York (Toronto). In the War of 1812, the area saw much action. QUEENSTON, now part of the city, was the scene of a British victory in Oct. 1812. Fort George, built in the 1790s on L. Ontario, was occupied by American forces May–Dec. 1813; when they abandoned it, they burned Newark. Today Niagara-on-the-Lake is a summer resort and a canning and processing center for an extensive fruit and vegetable growing and winemaking region. Other industries include basketry and boat building.

Niagara River 35 mi/56 km long, between New York and Ontario. It issues from L. Erie between Buffalo, New York, and Fort Erie, Ontario, and flows N around GRAND I. and over **Niagara Falls,** then another 10 mi/16 km N to L. Ontario. Goat I. separates the American Falls (167 ft/51 m high and 1060 ft/323 m wide) from the Horseshoe or Canadian Falls (162 ft/49 m high and 3000 ft/915 m wide) to the SW. The falls were created during the last ice age, when the river formed to drain glacial waters from the region around L. Erie. Below the falls the river flows through a canyon 250–350 ft/76–107 m deep for 4 mi/6 km, before emerging at Queenston, Ontario. Then, flowing between NIAGARA-ON-THE-LAKE, Ontario (W), and Youngstown, New York (E), the site of Old Fort Niagara (1726), long key to British-French power struggles, and thought to be the oldest European building on the Great Lakes, it empties into L. Ontario.

The falls are famous as a honeymoon spot, and by the 19th century had become a scene of derring-do. Charles Blondin, tightrope artist, crossed them in a series (1859–60) of increasingly complex stunts. Others went over the edge in barrels and various other vehicles. The Rainbow International Bridge (1941) spans the gorge between Niagara Falls, New York, and Niagara Falls, Ontario. Another bridge across the river is the PEACE BRIDGE, at Buffalo. Dams and conduits have been built to divert water from above the falls to large power developments downstream. The flow over the falls is cut back at night and increased during the day for scenic purposes; 94% of the water is carried over the Horseshoe Falls. The river is navigable for 20 mi/32 km above the Falls, and again in its lower 7 mi/11 km from Lewiston, New York, to L. Ontario. The NEW YORK STATE BARGE CANAL enters the river at TONAWANDA, New York, above the Falls, thus connecting E New York with L. Erie and the West. In Ontario, the WELLAND SHIP CANAL carries lake freight around the Falls.

Niagara University section of LEWISTON, W New York, adjacent (N) to NIAGARA FALLS, Niagara Co. Niagara University was established here in 1856.

Niantic see under EAST LYME, Connecticut.

Niceville city, pop. 10,507, Okaloosa Co., NW Florida, on Choctawhatchee Bay, in the Panhandle, 45 mi/72 km ENE of Pensacola. Surrounded on three sides by EGLIN AIR FORCE BASE, it has an economy that is dependent upon military personnel and tourism. Okaloosa-Walton Community College (1963) is here.

Nicholasville city, pop. 13,603, seat of Jessamine Co., C Kentucky, in the BLUEGRASS REGION, 13 mi/21 km SSW of Lexington. Founded in 1798, it is an agricultural trade center.

Nichols Hills city, pop. 4020, Oklahoma Co., C Oklahoma, 4 mi/6 km N of downtown Oklahoma City and inside its limits. It is a primarily residential suburb.

Nickajack see under WINSTON Co., Alabama.

Nickel Centre town, pop. 12,332, Sudbury Regional Municipality, EC Ontario, adjacent (NE) to SUDBURY, and part of the Sudbury Basin's mining complex.

Nickel Mountain 3533 ft/1077 m, in Douglas Co., SW Oregon, 17 mi/27 km SSW of ROSEBURG, on the E of the Coast Ranges. It is the site of open-pit mining in what is thought to be the largest US nickel deposit.

Nicodemus hamlet in Graham Co., NW Kansas, in the valley of the South Fork of the Solomon R., 39 mi/63 km NNW of Hays, on US 24. It is the last of several settlements established in the late 1870s by Exodusters, farmers from the upper South who were resettled by a Nashville, Tennessee–based black organization. It is named for a legendary slave who bought his own freedom.

Nicollet Island small island in the Mississippi R., in Minneapolis, Minnesota, immediately N of Downtown. Long neglected by the city, this old shipping and warehouse area has recently been developed into a residential neighborhood with parkland.

Nicollet Mall pedestrian mall, along eight blocks of Nicollet Ave. in downtown Minneapolis, Minnesota. Created in 1967, it was the nation's first auto-free thoroughfare. Open to buses and taxicabs, it houses several major department stores.

Nieuw Amsterdam see NEW AMSTERDAM.

Niihau volcanic mid-Pacific island, 72 sq mi/181 sq km, in Kauai Co., Hawaii, SW of Kauai. It has a rocky E shore, arid lowlands, and a plateau rising 1300 ft/390 m. Since the 1860s it has been owned by the Robinson family, and is populated by native Hawaiians (about 200) only, in an effort to preserve Hawaiian culture. In a dry zone, it lives on cattle and sheep ranching and the manufacture of tourist products, esp. shellwork. The chief settlement is Puuwai, on the W coast.

Niles **1.** village, pop. 28,284, Cook Co., NE Illinois, on the North Branch of the Chicago R., a suburb adjoining NW Chicago, 14 mi/23 km NW of the Loop. It is an affluent bedroom community. **2.** city, pop. 12,458, Berrien Co., SW Michigan, on the St. Joseph R., 10 mi/16 km N of South Bend, Indiana. Settled in 1828 and named for Hezekiah Niles, editor of a Baltimore newspaper, it had earlier been a Jesuit mission (1690), and became a 19th-century stage stop between Chicago and Detroit. Niles is an agricultural center for the St. Joseph R. valley's dairy and berry farms, orchards, and vineyards. It also manufactures wire and cable, refrigeration equipment, paper products, and processed foods. Writer Ring Lardner was born here (1885). **3.** city, pop. 21,128, Trumbull Co., NE Ohio, on the Mahoning R., 8 mi/13 km NW of Youngstown, in an agricultural region also rich in coal, iron ore, and limestone. Structural steel, sheet steel products, boilers, chemicals, laths, tools and dies, and construction materials are principal local manufactures. Niles is the birthplace (1843) of President William McKinley.

Nine Mile Point nuclear plant: see under OSWEGO, New York.

Ninety Six town, pop. 2099, Greenwood Co., W South Carolina, 8 mi/13 km ESE of Greenwood. A frontier settlement built here (c.1730) on an Indian trade route was reputedly named for its distance in miles from a Cherokee village in the Blue Ridge. The Revolutionary War's first Southern land battle took place here (Nov. 1775). In May–June 1781, Continental forces under Nathanael Greene unsuccessfully besieged British troops, who subsequently abandoned their fortifications; the **Ninety Six National Historic Site,** 2 mi/3 km S of the present town, marks the spot. The town, an agricultural trade center, was moved to its present location when the railroad arrived (1855). The **(Old) Ninety Six District,** named in honor of the battle, embraced part or all of six modern counties, including Laurens, Abbeville, Greenwood, and Edgefield.

Niobrara River 431 mi/694 km long, in E Wyoming and N Nebraska. It rises in Niobrara Co., E Wyoming, and flows generally E across the border into Nebraska, where it continues almost the length of the state, emptying into the Missouri R. near Niobrara. It drains a High Plains area along the S of PINE RIDGE, close to the South Dakota border, irrigating dry ranchland. Its longest tributary, the KEYA PAHA R., joins it from the NW 50 mi/80 km WNW of its mouth.

Nipigon, Lake largest lake entirely within Ontario, covering 1870 sq mi/4840 sq km in the NW, 75 mi/120 km NNE of Thunder Bay. It drains S into L. Superior through the 40 mi/65 km–long **Nipigon R.** Water diverted S from the ALBANY R. watershed into L. Nipigon enhances the flow to hydroelectric plants on the Nipigon R. In the 18th century, the Ojibwa displaced the Cree as the area's main inhabitants. Noted for Kelvin, Shakespeare, and many other islands, the lake is a fishing, hunting, and recreational destination. Some commercial fishing and logging are carried on in the area.

Nipissing, Lake in EC Ontario, 40 mi/65 km NE of GEORGIAN BAY (L. Huron). Some 50 mi/80 km E–W, it covers 320 sq mi/830 sq km. From the 1610s, when Étienne Brulé and Champlain reached the lake, VOYAGEURS, missionaries, and others followed the Ottawa R.–L. Nipissing route, which employed the Mattawa R. (E) and Rivière des Français (W), to the upper Great Lakes. Permanent white settlement around the lake dates from the 1870s. In the late 19th century settlers, lumberjacks, railroad builders, and miners moved into the area. Today the waterway is chiefly recreational. NORTH BAY, on the NE shore, is the major lakeside city. The Ojibwa name means *little water* (compared with Georgian Bay).

Nishnabotna River 12 mi/19 km long, in SW Iowa and NW Missouri. It is formed by the junction of the **East Nishnabotna** and **West Nishnabotna** rivers, both of which rise in S Carroll Co., Iowa. They follow generally parallel SW courses, about 15 mi/24 km apart, for 100 mi/160 km, joining N of Hamburg. The main river continues S to join the Missouri R. in NW Missouri. There are flood control canals along the main stream and its tributaries.

Niskayuna town, pop. 19,048, Schenectady Co., E New York, on the Mohawk R., adjacent (E) to Schenectady. It was the site of the first upstate settlement of Mother Ann Lee and her small band of Shakers (1776). Primarily a residential suburb, it also has a variety of industries. General Electric has atomic research facilities here along the Mohawk.

Nitro city, pop. 6851, Putnam and Kanawha counties, SW West Virginia, on the Kanawha R., 12 mi/19 km WNW of Charleston. Its main industries are chemical, rayon, and pencil manufacture. In 1918, the community grew up "overnight" around a huge government explosives plant, then the world's largest, rushed into operation for World War I. A year later, the plant closed.

Nittany Mountain see under STATE COLLEGE, Pennsylvania.

Nob Hill 1. largely residential neighborhood in N SAN FRANCISCO, California, just W of Chinatown and S of Russian Hill. From the 1870s until the 1906 earthquake and fire, the 376-ft/115-m hill was the home of the railroading Big Four (see SACRAMENTO) and those who had made fortunes from the gold rush and silver boom (collectively "nabobs" or "nobs"). It is now an affluent neighborhood, the site of Grace Cathedral and fancy hotels, including the Mark Hopkins (famous for its Top of the Mark bar) and many that were originally mansions. **2.** also, **Northwest 23rd** residential and commercial district in Northwest PORTLAND, Oregon. One of the city's more affluent sections, noted for its boutiques, it is 1.5 mi/2.5 km WNW of Downtown.

Noblesville city, pop. 17,655, seat of Hamilton Co., C Indiana, 20 mi/32 km NE of Indianapolis, on the West Fork of the White R. and Morse Reservoir. It is a trading center for a livestock and grain producing area, and manufactures rubber goods, truck bodies, and processed foods. Conner Prairie, a living history museum that includes the estate (1823) of Noblesville founder William Conner, is 4 mi/6 km S.

Nodaway River 190 mi/306 km long, in Iowa and Missouri. It is formed in Montgomery Co., Iowa, by the junction of the Middle and West Nodaway rivers. It flows S past Clarinda and into Missouri past Quitman and Fillmore, to join the Missouri R. above St. Joseph. Its main tributary is the 60 mi/97 km–long **East Nodaway** R.

Noe Valley largely residential section of S SAN FRANCISCO, California, S of the CASTRO and SE of TWIN PEAKS. Named for the city's last Mexican mayor, it is a longtime middle-class area undergoing some GENTRIFICATION pressures.

Nogales city, pop. 19,489, seat of Santa Cruz Co., S Arizona, 60 mi/97 km S of Tucson, on the border opposite Nogales (Sonora), Mexico. The twin border towns were established in the 1880s when the railroad was built along an ancient trade route from the Gulf of California (S). The US community was menaced briefly by Pancho Villa's Mexican rebel forces in 1916. An international trading hub, Nogales is a commercial and shipping center for surrounding cattle ranches and mines. During the 1980s its Mexican counterpart became a MAQUILADORA center. Gold, silver, lead, molybdenum, and copper mines and vineyards are in the vicinity. To the NNW are TUBAC, Arizona's first white settlement (20 mi/32 km) and TUMACACORI (16 mi/26 km).

NoHo see under SOHO, New York.

Noix, Île aux islet in the R. RICHELIEU, S Québec, 30 mi/49 km SSE of Montréal, former site of a fort built by the French in 1759 and captured by the British in 1760. In 1775 American forces took the site and rebuilt the fort as military headquarters. In the War of 1812, after another American occupation, the British constructed Fort Lennox here (1820s).

Nolichucky River 150 mi/240 km long, in North Carolina and Tennessee. One of the earliest settlement routes into Tennessee, it is formed in the Blue Ridge, in North Carolina's Pisgah National Forest, by the junction of the North Toe and

Cane rivers, and flows NW into Tennessee through the Bald Mts. After passing Erwin it winds W and SW. The DAVY CROCKETT BIRTHPLACE is on the river SW of Limestone. The **Nolichucky Dam,** 7 mi/11 km SSW of Greeneville, forms 5 mi/8 km–long Davy Crockett L. The Nolichucky then continues W and NW to join the FRENCH BROAD R. at the NE end of Douglas L.

No Man's Land see under PANHANDLE, Oklahoma.

Nomans Land also, **No Mans Land** island in the Atlantic Ocean, 6 mi/10 km SW of Martha's Vineyard I., in Dukes Co., SE Massachusetts. Two mi/3 km long and 0.5–1 mi/0.8–1.6 km wide, it is a National Wildlife Refuge. The name is thought to derive from a Wampanoag name; its appearance as "no man's" is probably due to the island's former use as a gunnery range.

Nome city, pop. 3500, Nome Census Area (pop. 8288), WC Alaska, on the S shore of the Seward Peninsula, on the Bering Sea and Norton Sound, 520 mi/837 km W of Fairbanks. Founded after gold was discovered nearby (1898), it briefly had a pop. estimated at 20,000. Gold mining, now done by dredging, is still important. The city is a trade and distribution center for NW Alaska, and its largely Inuit pop. produces handicrafts, chiefly ivory carving and needlework. Tourism is a major industry, and there is oil and gas leasing in the area. Accessible by ship only in summer, Nome is served by airlines year-round. It is the destination of the IDITAROD race.

Nonconnah Creek 30 mi/50 km long, in extreme SW Tennessee. Rising along the Mississippi border ESE of Memphis, near Collierville, it flows along the city's S side, and enters the Mississippi just S of Riverside Park, opposite PRESIDENT'S I. WHITEHAVEN and the Memphis International Airport lie S of the creek.

Nooseneck see under WEST GREENWICH, Rhode Island.

Nootka Island 21 mi/34 km NW–SE and up to 16 mi/26 km wide, off WC VANCOUVER I., SW British Columbia, 170 mi/275 km NW of Victoria. It is a homeland of the Wakashan tribe whose name it bears, who fished salmon and whales and built long wooden houses and large totem poles. **Nootka Sound,** which lies S and E, with several arms reaching into Vancouver I., gave its name to the 1790 Nootka Convention, in which the British and Spanish resolved a territorial dispute. The convention opened the era of British settlement in the Pacific Northwest.

Noranda see under ROUYN-NORANDA, Québec.

Norco city, pop. 23,302, Riverside Co., SW California, 10 mi/16 km W of Riverside, and adjacent (N) to CORONA. On the Santa Ana R., it has a poultry and egg industry and a large naval hospital, and is residential.

Norcross city, pop. 5947, Gwinnett Co., NC Georgia, 19 mi/31 km NE of downtown Atlanta. Surrounded by technological parks, it is home to a major AT&T plant and to a packaging technology center, and grew rapidly in the 1980s.

Norfolk **1.** city, pop. 21,476, Madison Co., NE Nebraska, on the Elkhorn R., 90 mi/144 km NW of Omaha. It processes and ships grain, dairy products, and foods. One of the world's largest livestock auction centers, it ships a great quantity of cattle. The city also houses Nebraska's only steel mill. Northeast Community College (1927) is here. **2.** independent city, pop. 261,229, in SE Virginia, at the mouth of Chesapeake Bay, on the Elizabeth R. and the S side of HAMPTON ROADS, adjacent (W) to VIRGINIA BEACH. Settled in 1682, it is a port with one of the finest natural harbors on the Atlantic coast, and was the Confederacy's most important naval base. The Norfolk Naval Base and Air Station is one of the largest naval installations in the US; it is headquarters for the Atlantic Fleet and other naval commands. Although it is predominantly a navy town, Norfolk has varied industries including shipbuilding, seafood and meat packing, auto assembly, and some manufacturing. Dominion University (1930), Virginia Wesleyan College (1961), and Norfolk State University (1935) are here. The Norfolk Naval Shipyard is in neighboring (S) PORTSMOUTH.

Norfolk County 400 sq mi/1036 sq km, pop. 616,087, in E Massachusetts. Its seat is Dedham. The county lies S and W of Boston, extending to the Rhode Island border. The town of BROOKLINE is enclosed by Middlesex and Suffolk counties. Norfolk Co. is thickly populated in its NE part, which includes the industrial city of Quincy and the affluent suburbs of Brookline and Milton. To the SW it becomes increasingly rural, although post-1960s development along Route 495, Boston's outer beltway, has brought a more suburban mode of life.

Norland unincorporated residential community, pop. 22,109, Dade Co., SE Florida, in the Fort Lauderdale–Miami corridor, 5 mi/8 km SW of Hollywood.

Normal **1.** neighborhood of NE HUNTSVILLE, Alabama, 4 mi/6 km from Downtown. The Alabama Agricultural and Mechanical University (1875), established by an ex-slave, has been here since 1891. **2.** town, pop. 40,023, McLean Co., C Illinois, immediately N of Bloomington. Dominated by Illinois State University (1857), it is also a processing and trading center for the region's corn, oats, wheat, nursery stock, and livestock. Industries include a large Chrysler-Mitsubishi auto plant, canning, and tire manufacturing. Evergreen L. is 7 mi/11 km to the N.

Norman city, pop. 80,071, seat of Cleveland Co., C Oklahoma, on the South Canadian R., 17 mi/27 km S of Oklahoma City. It was founded by homesteaders (1889) when the territory was opened to white settlers. The University of Oklahoma, opened here in 1892, forms an essential part of the city's economy. Norman is a processing and distribution point for agricultural products, livestock, and oil. Manufactures include aircraft and bedding.

Norman, Lake see under CATAWBA R., North Carolina.

Normandy city, pop. 4480, St. Louis Co., EC Missouri, 8 mi/13 km NW of downtown St. Louis, a primarily residential community.

Norman's Woe see under GLOUCESTER, Massachusetts.

Norman Wells village, pop. 627, Inuvik Region, W Northwest Territories, at the W foot of the FRANKLIN Mts., on the MACKENZIE R., 395 mi/635 km NW of Yellowknife. Oil was discovered in the area in 1920, and during World War II, a refinery was connected via the American-built Canol pipeline with Whitehorse, Yukon Territory. The Canol was abandoned at war's end, but in 1984 a new pipeline to Alberta was placed in operation. Fort Norman (hamlet, pop. 375), a DENE community and early-19th-century fur post, is 41 mi/65 km SE, where the Great Bear R. meets the Mackenzie.

Noroton see under DARIEN, Connecticut.

Norridge village, pop. 14,459, Cook Co., Illinois, surrounded by NW Chicago on three sides, a residential suburb 12 mi/19 km NW of the Loop. O'Hare International Airport is 4 mi/6 km W.

Norridgewock town, pop. 3105, Somerset Co., WC Maine. It is on the Kennebec R., 13 mi/21 km NW of Waterville and adjoining SKOWHEGAN (E). On the site of an Abnaki village on the Maine–Québec trade route, the settlement was a mid-17th-century French Indian mission. The town has a monument to the Jesuit linguist Sébastian Rasles, one of the victims of a 1724 assault by British forces.

Norris Dam first major TENNESSEE VALLEY AUTHORITY dam, on the Clinch R. in E Tennessee, 20 mi/32 km NW of Knoxville. Named for Senator George W. Norris, the TVA's sponsor, it was completed in 1936, and is 265 ft/81 m high and 1860 ft/567 m long. **Norris Lake,** created by the dam, extends back up the Clinch over 70 mi/110 km. Another arm extends back up the POWELL R., which formerly met the Clinch near the dam, for over 55 mi/89 km. Other streams impounded in the lake include Cove Creek (NW) and Big Creek (N), on which LA FOLLETTE is now virtually a lakeside city.

Norristown borough, pop. 30,749, seat of Montgomery Co., SE Pennsylvania, on the N bank of the Schuylkill R., 17 mi/27 km NW of Philadelphia. It is located on a site purchased in 1704 by Isaac Norris and William Trent from the Penn family. Norristown's development as an industrial center was hastened by the canalization of the Schuylkill and Delaware rivers and the completion (1834) of a rail link to Philadelphia. Today, it is a residential suburb, but also produces clothing, chemicals, machinery, rubber, steel tubing, and plastics.

North one of the five sections of PORTLAND, Oregon, due N of Downtown and NE of the Willamette R. A largely middle-class residential area, it has the University of Portland campus in its NW, Memorial Coliseum at its extreme S (on the river). The ALBINA district is along the E.

North, the 1. also, **North Country** in Canada, variously defined region, generally the largely uninhabited (and for the most part inhospitable) lands N of the belt along the US border where most Canadians live. Much of it on the CANADIAN SHIELD, the North consists mostly of boreal (northern) forest or of TUNDRA (the BARREN LANDS). The area along the Shield's S edge, in Ontario, has been called the **Near North.** The 60th Parallel (60° N), which in the W forms the S boundary of the Northwest Territories and Yukon Territory, is often called the beginning of the **True North** ("North of 60"); to the E of Hudson Bay, this would include large parts of NOUVEAU-QUÉBEC, as well as the extreme N tip of Labrador. Its isolation and "emptiness" has led this part of Canada to be called also **the Inside** or **the Silent Places. 2.** in the US, term with various historical and geographical meanings. Before the Civil War, the MASON-DIXON LINE and its extension divided the nonslaveholding North from the slaveholding South. The 23 states that remained in the Union during the Civil War, as well as those that joined during the struggle, are another North; several of them (Delaware, Kentucky, Maryland, Missouri, and what became West Virginia) had been slave territory, and others (California, Oregon) are not thought of as "Northern" in other contexts. More recently, the North has been taken to include New England, the Middle Atlantic region N of the Mason-Dixon Line (New York, New Jersey, and Pennsylvania), and states of the Middle West as far W as the point where the concept WEST supplants "North."

North Adams city, pop. 16,797, Berkshire Co., NW Massachusetts, on the Hoosic R. at the W end of the MOHAWK TRAIL and HOOSAC TUNNEL. The Hoosic R. provided waterpower for early 19th-century manufacturing. North Adams was set off from ADAMS in 1878. The city produces electronics, textiles, paper, electrical machinery, and leather goods, but suffered severe unemployment in the 1980s and 1990s.

North Amityville unincorporated village, pop. 13,849, in Babylon town, Suffolk Co., SE New York, on Long Island's South Shore, just N of Copiague and Amityville, and 32 mi/51 km ESE of Manhattan. Primarily residential, it is immediately E of the Nassau-Suffolk border and S of Republic Airport.

Northampton 1. city, pop. 29,289, seat of Hampshire Co., WC Massachusetts, on the Connecticut R., 17 mi/27 km NW of Springfield. A center of the PIONEER VALLEY region, it is the site of Smith College (1871). It was settled in the 1650s by colonists moving N from Connecticut. An 18th-century woolen and silk manufacturing center, Northampton now produces cutlery; wood, paper, and plastic products; electronics; and optical instruments. Landmarks include two homes of Calvin Coolidge, who practiced law, served as mayor, and died here. **2.** in Pennsylvania: **a.** township, pop. 35,406, Bucks Co., 16 mi/26 km NNE of Philadelphia. Its developing residential suburbs include Richboro (pop. 5332). **b.** borough, pop. 8717, Northampton Co., E Pennsylvania, on the Lehigh R., 6 mi/10 km N of Allentown. It produces furniture, paint, and ammunition, and is the seat of Mary Immaculate Seminary.

Northampton County 376 sq mi/974 sq km, pop. 247,105, in E Pennsylvania, bordered E by the Delaware R., W by the Lehigh R., and N by Blue and Kittatinny mountains. Its seat is EASTON. It has much industry, especially in Easton, BETHLEHEM, and NAZARETH, and suburban development and agriculture outside these centers. In the N it reaches into the Pocono Mt.-Delaware Water Gap resort area.

North Andover town, pop. 22,792, Essex Co., NE Massachusetts, on the Merrimack and Shawsheen rivers, 26 mi/42 km N of Boston. Lawrence is adjacent (W). Merrimack College (1947) and the Merrimack Valley Textile Museum are here, as well as the 1660s home of Colonial poet Anne Bradstreet. North Andover produces textiles, machinery, wood products, plastics, and telephone equipment.

North Anna River 70 mi/113 km long, in C Virginia. It rises in the PIEDMONT near Gordonsville, Orange Co., and flows generally SE into 15 mi/24 km–long Lake Anna, formed by the North Anna Dam, near Partlow, Spotsylvania Co. The **North Anna Nuclear Powerplant,** opened 1978, is on the lake's S shore, in Louisa Co. The river continues SE, and is joined 5 mi/8 km NE of ASHLAND by the South Anna R., whose headstreams are very close to the North Anna's and which follows a more southerly, entirely rural course. At their confluence the two rivers form the PAMUNKEY R.

North Arlington borough, pop. 13,790, Bergen Co., NE New Jersey, on the Passaic R., 6 mi/10 km NE of Newark. It was settled in the 18th century. Both residential and industrial, it has widely diversified industries that process food, grow plants and flowers, and manufacture plastic, rubber, and metal products; cement blocks; paint; and other goods.

North Atlanta unincorporated community, pop. 27,812, De Kalb Co., NW Georgia, an affluent residential suburb, 9 mi/14 km NNE of downtown Atlanta. Oglethorpe University is here.

North Attleboro also, **North Attleborough** town, pop. 25,038,

Bristol Co., SE Massachusetts, 12 mi/19 km NNE of Providence, Rhode Island. Originally settled as part of ATTLEBORO, it includes North Attleboro Village and Attleboro Falls. It is a noted center of the jewelry industry, established in 1807. Woodcock Tavern (1670) is an historical landmark.

North Augusta city, pop. 15,351, Aiken Co., W South Carolina, on the Savannah R., across (NE) from AUGUSTA, Georgia. Settled around 1860, it is a largely residential suburb with veneer and other light industries.

North Babylon unincorporated village, pop. 18,081, in Babylon town, Suffolk Co., SE New York, on Long Island's South Shore, just N of Babylon and 37 mi/59 km ESE of Manhattan. It is a residential suburb.

North Battleford city, pop. 14,350, surrounded by rolling country in W Saskatchewan, 84 mi/132 km NW of Saskatoon, at the confluence of the Battle and North Saskatchewan rivers, on the Yellowhead Highway. North Battleford was created in 1905 with the laying of the Canadian Northern Railway on the N bank of the North Saskatchewan R. rather than on the S bank, where BATTLEFORD is situated. Today North Battleford and Battleford are a trade center for NW Saskatchewan, which depends on diversified agriculture, lumbering, and fishing.

North Bay city, pop. 55,405, seat of Nipissing District, EC Ontario, on the NE shore of L. NIPISSING, 190 mi/310 km WNW of Ottawa and 180 mi/290 km N of Toronto. The site of a rail yard (1882) for the Canadian Pacific Railway, it developed as an important distribution center and is now the S terminus and headquarters of the Ontario Northland Railway and a depot on two transcontinental lines, as well as a junction of the TRANS-CANADA HIGHWAY with other roads. The processing and marketing of fur have been important since the Nipissing traded with the French here along the river and PORTAGE route between the Ottawa R. (E) and Georgian Bay (SW), beginning in the late 17th century. The city makes wood and dairy products, mining machinery, and printed goods, and is a major wholesale and retail distribution center, as well as a tourist and outdoor activities hub. An air base and Canada's first missile base are here, and North Bay is the seat of Nipissing College (1967). The home of the Dionne quintuplets (b.1934) is a noted attraction.

North Bay Shore unincorporated village, pop. 12,799, in Islip town, Suffolk Co., SE New York, on Long Island's South Shore, immediately N of Bay Shore and 5 mi/8 km NE of Babylon. It is primarily residential.

North Bay Village city, pop. 5383, Dade Co., SE Florida, on two islands in BISCAYNE BAY between the N corner of Miami (W) and Normandy Isle, part of Miami Beach (E). It is connected by causeway to both, and is about 6 mi/10 km NNE of downtown Miami. It is residential.

North Beach residential and commercial section of N SAN FRANCISCO, California, immediately N of CHINATOWN, SW of TELEGRAPH HILL, E of RUSSIAN HILL, and S of FISHERMAN'S WHARF. Named for a beach that lay between the two hills before landfill operations, it was from the 1850s home to waves of immigrants. Italians predominated in "Little Italy" for decades before World War II. In the 1950s North Beach was a famous bohemian quarter, home to the beats, who congregated at the City Lights bookstore (1953). The area was also a center of the psychedelic subculture of the 1960s. Washington Square, where the church of St. Peter and Paul is located, is the center of a community now a mix of Italian, Chinese, and bohemian.

North Bellmore unincorporated village, pop. 19,707, in Hempstead town, Nassau Co., SE New York, on Long Island's South Shore, just NE of Merrick. It is a residential suburb.

North Bend **1.** village, pop. 550, Hamilton Co., extreme SW Ohio, 11 mi/18 km W of Cincinnati, on the Ohio R. One of the earliest white settlements in the state (1789), it is the birthplace (1833) of President Benjamin Harrison. His grandfather, President William H. Harrison, spent much of his adulthood here; his tomb lies behind the Harrison Monument in nearby William Henry Harrison State Park. **2.** city, pop. 9614, Coos Co., SW Oregon, on an inlet of the Pacific Ocean, immediately N of COOS BAY. Settled in 1853, this port city is a trade and transportation center in a fishing and lumbering area. It has sawmills, a shipyard, and fish and crab packing plants. Mining machinery and plywood are manufactured, and tourism is important. **3.** see under SNOQUALMIE R., Washington.

North Bergen township, pop. 48,414, Hudson Co., NE New Jersey, 5 mi/8 km NE of Jersey City, on the W side of the PALISADES of the Hudson R. It is a residential suburb of New York City, with industries producing such diverse goods as textiles, clothing, machinery, watches and other jewelry, electrical equipment, batteries, light bulbs, cardboard boxes, and metal products.

Northborough town, pop. 11,929, Worcester Co., C Massachusetts, 9 mi/14 km ENE of Worcester, of which it is a suburb located along Routes 290 and 20 (the Boston Post Road). Its proximity also to the Massachusetts Turnpike and to Route 495 have led to rapid growth since the 1970s.

Northbrook village, pop. 32,308, Cook Co., NE Illinois, on the West Fork of the North Branch of the Chicago R., a residential suburb 22 mi/35 km N of Chicago. Glenview Naval Air Station is just to the S.

North Brunswick township, pop. 31,287, Middlesex Co., C. New Jersey, adjacent (SW) to NEW BRUNSWICK. Situated along US 1, it is a residential and industrial extension of New Brunswick into formerly agricultural land.

North Caldwell see under CALDWELL, New Jersey.

North Canaan see under CANAAN, Connecticut.

North Canadian River also, **Beaver R.** 800 mi/1300 km long, in New Mexico, Texas, and Oklahoma. It rises in the High Plains area of Union Co., NE New Mexico, and flows generally E through the PANHANDLE of Oklahoma, dipping briefly into extreme N Texas, then turns ESE through Oklahoma, passing Woodward and El Reno, then bisecting Oklahoma City before winding E, past Shawnee, to join the CANADIAN R. in Eufaula L. It has a number of dams and reservoirs along its route and on its tributaries. The name Beaver R. has been used in the Oklahoma Panhandle and W. The river generally parallels the Canadian's course.

North Canton city, pop. 14,748, Stark Co., NE Ohio, 5 mi/8 km N of Canton, in an agricultural area. Vacuum cleaners and brick are among the products manufactured here.

North Carolina state of the SE US, variously considered to be in the Upper SOUTH or Mid-South region (or, by the Census Bureau, in the South Atlantic region); 1990 pop. 6,628,637 (112.7% of 1980; rank: 10th); area 53,821 sq mi/139,936 sq km (rank: 28th); ratified Constitution 1789 (12th). Capital: RALEIGH. Most populous cities: CHARLOTTE, Raleigh, GREENS-

BORO, WINSTON-SALEM, DURHAM. North Carolina is bordered N by Virginia, and NW and W by Tennessee, from which it is separated by the GREAT SMOKY (Unaka) Mts., part of the BLUE RIDGE. On the S it is bordered by Georgia (W) and South Carolina (S). On the E it lies on the Atlantic Ocean; its OUTER BANKS, a series of BARRIER islands, enclose ALBEMARLE and PAMLICO sounds and other narrower bodies through which the ATLANTIC INTRACOASTAL WATERWAY passes. About half the state, in the E, is in the Atlantic COASTAL PLAIN; in this Tidewater region are part of the Great DISMAL SWAMP (NE, straddling the Virginia border) and the lower reaches of the ROANOKE, NEUSE, and CAPE FEAR rivers. Cape HATTERAS ("the Graveyard of the Atlantic") and Cape LOOKOUT mark the easternmost and southernmost points of the Outer Banks. Cape FEAR, in the extreme SE, is another important coastal promontory; WILMINGTON, above it on the Cape Fear R., and the only city of size on the North Carolina coast, is the primary port. Morehead City, NW of Cape Lookout, was developed in the 1930s to handle oceanic traffic. JACKSONVILLE, on the New R. estuary, is the site of CAMP LEJEUNE, a Marine training center. The Outer Banks (NE) contain such well-known resorts as NAGS HEAD and OCRACOKE I., as well as historic KITTY HAWK. Behind the Banks, between Albemarle and Pamlico sounds, is ROANOKE I., scene of a 1580s English settlement (Walter Ralegh's Lost Colony, on Croatan Sound) that disappeared mysteriously, its members perhaps moving W to mix with the local Lumbee Indians. NEW BERN, WASHINGTON, and EDENTON are among early waterside communities on the estuaries of this area. The Tidewater is a major tobacco growing district; poultry and peanuts are other important crops. To the W is the PIEDMONT section of North Carolina. Along the FALL LINE, which separates it from the coastal plain, are FAYETTEVILLE (SC), in the SANDHILLS, service community for the large Army training center at FORT BRAGG; and ROCKY MOUNT (NC). The Piedmont is home to the bulk of the state's pop. and industry. Here, powered by many quick rivers, are thousands of textile mills and clothing and furniture plants. Major concentrations are around Charlotte-GASTONIA (SW), Winston Salem–High Point–Greensboro (the PIEDMONT TRIAD, NC), and Raleigh-Durham (NC); other centers include HICKORY (furniture) and KANNAPOLIS (textiles). In the W North Carolina rises into the Blue Ridge region of the Appalachians, here represented by the UNAKA Mts., including the well-known Great Smoky Mts. ASHEVILLE is the major mountain region city. In addition to many small industrial and agricultural towns, this W section includes part of the Great Smoky Mts. National Park, the EASTERN CHEROKEE (Qualla Boundary) INDIAN RESERVATION, resort and academic centers like BLACK MOUNTAIN, and Mt. MITCHELL, at 6684 ft/2039 m the highest point in the E US. After abortive attempts by the Spanish and French and at Roanoke I., the area that is now North Carolina was settled in the 1630s from Virginia, largely by Scotch-Irish farmers. The PLANTATION economy of South Carolina also began to extend into the area, in the SE, where rice, indigo, tobacco, and cotton were grown. Unlike Virginia and South Carolina, however, North Carolina did not develop quickly, remaining a small-farming and foresting area for two centuries. Its early naval stores (turpentine, etc.) production is somehow connected with its having come to be called the "Tarheel State"; the exact reason is subject to dispute. The 1775 MECKLENBURG Declaration was a precursor of the Declaration of Independence, but the area saw little action in the Revolutionary War, and the Civil War also saw few local fights, conflict concentrating instead to the SW and NE. In the late 19th century, North Carolina suddenly blossomed into industrial prominence, its waterpower and cheap labor attracting textile and clothing manufacturers esp. from the New England states. In the same period James B. Duke mechanized (1880s) the cigarette industry, and furnituremaking, utilizing the Piedmont's abundant hardwoods, boomed. Textile COMPANY TOWNS came into being, and the locating of manufacturing establishments in dozens of small communities left the state without a single major city, a situation that began to change only in the 1980s as Charlotte flowered as a banking and business center. The academic centers of Durham (Duke University), Raleigh (North Carolina State University), and CHAPEL HILL (the University of North Carolina) gave birth in 1958 to the RESEARCH TRIANGLE, a planned high-tech manufacturing, research, and office complex, and diversified industry is now spreading throughout North Carolina; but the long-established triad of tobacco, textiles, and furniture remains the heart of the economy. Outer Banks tourism and recreation, agriculture (including esp. hog production), and commercial fishing are important in the E, and the mountains of the W draw skiers, summer vacationers, and scenery and folklore enthusiasts. The state's people remain largely a mix of the older white (Scotch-Irish, French, German, etc.) groups that settled the Piedmont and mountain areas; a large black minority lives chiefly in the Tidewater and in Durham.

North Cascades National Park 505,000 ac/205,000 ha (790 sq mi/2044 sq km), in N Washington, in the CASCADE RANGE, along the British Columbia border (N). The Skagit R. crosses the park, which is part of a WILDERNESS AREA also including sections of the Ross L. and L. Chelan national recreation areas. The Cascades here, around Mt. Shuksan, have over 300 glaciers; the W slopes are noted for their heavy precipitation and densely vegetated valleys.

North Charleston city, pop. 70,218, Charleston and Dorchester counties, SE South Carolina, on the Ashley and Cooper rivers, adjoining (N) Charleston. It is the largest of the bedroom and commercial suburbs that surround the old city. It has some industry (fibers). The Charleston International Airport lies just N, and Air Force (N) and Navy (SE) installations adjoin. Having mushroomed since mid-century to house military personnel, base and airport employees, and former Charleston residents, North Charleston faced an uncertain future following 1990s military cutbacks.

North Chicago city, pop. 34,978, Lake Co., Illinois, on L. Michigan, immediately S of Waukegan and 40 mi/64 km N of Chicago. Part of the industrial complex centered around Waukegan, it manufactures chemicals, candy, refractory metals, electrical condensers and generators, locks, hardware, auto parts, and machinery. A 1937 labor dispute here resulted in a Supreme Court decision banning sit-down strikes. The University of Health Sciences of the Chicago Medical School is here, as is the Great Lakes Naval Training Station.

North Chili see under CHILI, New York.

North College Hill city, pop. 11,002, Hamilton Co., SW Ohio, 10 mi/16 km N of Cincinnati, of which it is a residential suburb.

North Conway unincorporated village, pop. 2032, in Conway township, Carroll Co., EC New Hampshire. North Conway is in the White Mts., on the Saco R. near the Maine border. It is an outfitting center for White Mt. hikers and skiers, and produces grain and hay. The Conway Scenic Railroad, Eastern Slope Inn, Mt. Cranmore, Cathedral Ledge lookout, and nearby Attitash, Tyrol, and Black Mt. ski areas draw visitors.

North Country in New York, region N of the Hudson-Mohawk river and canal system, where settlement and industry penetrated little in the early 19th century. Comprising the Adirondack region and the St. Lawrence Valley, it has been primarily an agricultural and lumbering region, now important for tourism and hydroelectric power production. WATERTOWN, MASSENA, and PLATTSBURGH are important centers.

North Cowichan see under COWICHAN L., British Columbia.

North Dakota state of the NC US, considered in the Upper MIDDLE WEST and as a GREAT PLAINS state; 1990 pop. 638,800 (97.9% of 1980; rank: 47th); area 70,704 sq mi/183,123 sq km (rank: 19th); admitted to Union 1889 (39th). Capital: BISMARCK. Most populous cities: FARGO, GRAND FORKS, Bismarck, MINOT. North Dakota is bordered S by South Dakota; W by Montana; and N by Saskatchewan (W) and Manitoba (E). On its E, it faces Minnesota across the RED RIVER OF THE NORTH (N) and the Bois de Sioux R. (S). The MISSOURI R. winds through the state from WC to S; the two-thirds of North Dakota that lies E and N of the river represents the W extremity of the vast C lowlands of the US. The Missouri COTEAU, flanking the river to its E, marks the W edge of this glaciated section, in which the SE-flowing JAMES R. is part of the Missouri system and other E-flowing rivers, like the SHEYENNE, are part of the Red R. system, draining N toward Hudson Bay. The TURTLE Mts. lie across the Manitoba border (NC). The Missouri R. marks the NE edge of the unglaciated Missouri Plateau, the beginning of the Great Plains. The state slopes up from an elevation of 750 ft/229 m on the Red R., in the extreme NE, to over 3000 ft/1220 m in the W, peaking at 3506 ft/1069 m at WHITE BUTTE, near Amidon (SW). In North Dakota's E are fertile black-soil PRAIRIES, in which huge crops of wheat and other grains are raised. Cities in the region, including Fargo and Grand Forks on the E border and Minot (NC), are engaged largely in agriculture-related industry and commerce. On the sparsely populated Missouri Plateau (SW), ranching is important. The SW region also has a tourist industry, drawing visitors to the BADLANDS along the LITTLE MISSOURI R., where the units of the THEODORE ROOSEVELT NATIONAL PARK are scattered. On the Missouri R., the GARRISON DAM has created extensive L. Sakakawea, much of which lies within the FORT BERTHOLD Indian Reservation. In the S is the top end of L. OAHE, created by a dam in South Dakota, with part of the STANDING ROCK Indian Reservation on its W. Between the two lakes is Bismarck, a center for varied light industries in addition to state government; oil is refined nearby. North Dakota has huge deposits of lignite coal, which is mined in the N and W, and oil is extracted in the NW, esp. in the WILLISTON area. French explorers first saw the region, home to sedentary Mandans and related groups and to nomadic Sioux (Lakota, or Dakota), in the 1730s. The LOUISIANA PURCHASE brought the Missouri R. valley under US control in 1803. Near Washburn, NNW of Bismarck, LEWIS AND CLARK, exploring the Purchase, wintered in 1804–05 at Mandan villages. In the E, the British controlled the Red R. valley, in which they made an abortive settlement attempt in 1812, before ceding it to the US in 1818. There was little settlement in the area until the 1850s. The Dakota Territory was organized in 1861, and through the 1860s the Sioux were pushed farther W or confined to reservations. In the 1870s large-scale establishment of homesteads began. The NORTHERN PACIFIC RAILROAD pushed across the S, through Fargo and Bismarck, while slightly later the GREAT NORTHERN RAILWAY took a N route, through Grand Forks and Minot, on their way to the Pacific, and farmers recruited from Russia (Germans) and Scandinavia arrived to convert the prairie to cropland. The state grew rapidly into the early 20th century, but since the 1930s Depression has been forced to diversify its farming (from an almost all-wheat regime) to remain economically healthy. The University of North Dakota is at Grand Forks, North Dakota State University at Fargo. The INTERNATIONAL PEACE GARDEN, straddling the Manitoba border near DUNSEITH (NC) gives the state one of its nicknames. The geographic C of North America has been determined to be some 30 mi/48 km S of the Garden, near RUGBY.

North Dallas extensive residential and commercial section of Dallas, Texas, N of the Trinity R., Downtown, and Interstate 30. Many of the city's most affluent neighborhoods are here, as well as prestigious HIGHLAND PARK and UNIVERSITY PARK (the independent Park Cities). Preston Hollow, NW of University Park, was independent until annexed in 1945. The upper reaches of WHITE ROCK CREEK are on the E; on the W, TURTLE CREEK has been a major avenue of development. North Dallas is noted for its shopping malls. The Lyndon B. Johnson Freeway, Dallas's beltway, here crosses the Dallas Tollway (W) and the CENTRAL EXPRESSWAY (E), both radiating from Downtown; at the intersections are the GALLERIA and other major commercial developments. Love Field (superseded as the city's major airport in 1973 by Dallas–Fort Worth International) is in the NW. The adjoining cities of Addison (NW), Plano (N), and Richardson (NE) are the site of much electronics industry development on Dallas's N side; the area is popularly called Silicon Prairie.

North Decatur unincorporated community, pop. 13,936, De Kalb Co., NW Georgia, a heavily white residential suburb 6 mi/10 km ENE of downtown Atlanta.

North Druid Hills unincorporated community, pop. 14,170, De Kalb Co., NW Georgia, 5 mi/8 km E of downtown Atlanta, adjacent to the affluent DRUID HILLS section.

Northeast **1.** second-largest quadrant of Washington, D.C., lying N and E of the Capitol. Its neighborhoods range from the struggling **Near Northeast,** which lies just NE of Union Station and the Capitol, to middle-class areas, like BROOKLAND, along the Maryland border. Outer areas of the Northeast have been less developed than the rest of the District. New York Ave., long a major approach to the District, passes through the Northeast. Gallaudet University (1857), the nation's leading higher institution for the deaf, is in the Trinidad neighborhood. **2.** collection of neighborhoods in Minneapolis, Minnesota, NE of Downtown. This working-class area primarily houses Polish immigrants and their descendants. **3.** largely residential district of KANSAS CITY, Missouri, 3 mi/5 km ENE of Downtown, from Independence Ave. N to Cliff Drive and North Terrace Park, overlooking the industrial/commercial Missouri R. bottoms area. In the early 20th century this was an exclusive housing area. The Kansas City Museum is here. **4.** one of the five sections of PORTLAND, Oregon, E of the Willamette R., and N of Burnside St. Largely residential, it includes some of the poorer areas of the city. There have been many recent public redevelopment projects here, esp. in the LLOYD DISTRICT along the river. LAURELHURST is on the S, ALBINA on the W.

Northeast, the in the US, region including NEW ENGLAND and, according to various definitions, (a) New York; (b) New York, New Jersey, and Pennsylvania—states of the MIDDLE ATLANTIC region; or, (c) all areas within the NE quadrant of the nation as a whole.

Northeast Harbor village in Mount Desert town (pop. 1899), on Mt. Desert I., Hancock Co., SE Maine. It lies between part of Acadia National Park and Somes Sound, opposite the town of Southwest Harbor, and is a popular pleasure boat and yachting harbor with summer homes and hotels.

Northeast Kingdom nickname for the N Vermont region encompassing three counties (Essex, Orleans, and Franklin) bordering Canada and New Hampshire. The area is wooded and rural, with many lakes, including Willoughby and MEMPHREMAGOG. St. Johnsbury is the southeastern gateway; ISLAND POND and NEWPORT are major centers.

North Easton see under EASTON, Massachusetts.

Northeast Philadelphia residential section, the largest geographic area of Philadelphia, Pennsylvania. Although parts were settled in the early 1700s, significant growth came only with tract development after World War II. Today the area is home to a white middle-class population, largely Jews, Poles, and Italians.

North End residential and commercial section of Boston, Massachusetts. A small, congested area on Boston Harbor, it is one of the city's oldest neighborhoods, home to generations of immigrants, beginning with Puritans who settled here in 1630 and including Irish (from the 1840s) and Jews (in the late 19th century). Today it is heavily Italian. The North End has many historic sites, including the Paul Revere house (the oldest wooden building, built ?1660s, in Boston), COPPS HILL, and the OLD NORTH CHURCH. Cut off from the rest of the city by an expressway, it is a popular tourist destination. Substantial residential development has occurred along the waterfront since the 1970s.

Northern California inexact term reflecting the historical development of California. It is often taken to mean everything N of the TEHACHAPI Mts., near Santa Barbara. A stricter definition includes only the area from San Francisco Bay N, leaving everything S to the TRANSVERSE RANGES in "Central California." Either way, the term has less historical resonance than its opposite, SOUTHERN CALIFORNIA. Northern California developed largely after the gold rush of 1849; with its major city, San Francisco, it dominated the state's economy and politics well into the 20th century, until the rise of Los Angeles.

Northern Cheyenne Indian Reservation 697 sq mi/1806 sq km, pop. 3923 (90% Indian), in SE Montana, adjacent (E) to the CROW INDIAN RESERVATION, and 68 mi/109 km ESE of Billings. LAME DEER is its headquarters. It is home to an Algonquian-speaking people who left Minnesota in the 18th century and were living to the E, in the BLACK HILLS, by 1800. In the 1870s they fled confinement on a reservation during the Black Hills gold rush, and joined the Sioux in the battle of the LITTLE BIGHORN R., just W. The ROSEBUD R., which flows S–N through the reservation, was the scene of a preliminary skirmish. The current reservation, established in 1884, sits atop huge coal deposits, development of which the Cheyenne have blocked. The Southern Cheyenne, who split off and moved to Colorado in the 1830s, now live with the Arapaho in Oklahoma.

Northern Liberties old industrial and immigrant area of Philadelphia, Pennsylvania, NE of CENTER CITY, between Broad St. and the Delaware R. Part of William Penn's original land grant but outside the Colonial city, the area was opened for development in 1741. Waterfront land attracted numerous settlers, establishing a growth pattern for early Philadelphia along the Delaware R., in contrast to the orderly westward movement envisioned by Penn. During the 19th century, the Northern Liberties served as the first stop for many East European immigrant groups, including Slovaks, Hungarians, Ukrainians, and both Jews and Christians from Poland and Russia. Today many of its abandoned warehouses and factories have become artists' lofts or popular night spots.

Northern Mariana Islands, Commonwealth of the island group in the W Pacific Ocean, some 1500 mi/2400 km E of the Philippines and 1600 mi/2600 km SSE of Japan. Lying in a N–S arc some 430 mi/700 km long, and flanked (E and S) by the **Mariana Trench,** which includes the world's greatest ocean depth (−35,839 ft/−10,924 m), the Northern Marianas comprise 14 islands, totaling 185 sq mi/478 sq km, the largest of which are SAIPAN, TINIAN, and ROTA. (GUAM, the southernmost of the Marianas, is a separate US territory.) The administrative center is Garapan, on Saipan. The pop. is 43,345. The Marianas, inhabited for at least 4000 years, were discovered by Magellan in 1521. Spain, which settled them in the 17th century, sold them, except for Guam, to Germany in 1899. They became a Japanese mandate after World War I, and were settled with Asian laborers growing sugarcane and fruits. Saipan and Tinian were seized by the US in 1944. From 1947 part of the US-administered Trust Territory of the PACIFIC ISLANDS, established by the United Nations, the Northern Marianas voted to become a US COMMONWEALTH in 1978. Residents, who are chiefly Chamorros (see GUAM), are US citizens but do not vote in Federal elections and have no representation in Congress. The economy is based on tourism (mostly from Japan), military expenditures, apparel assembly (fostered by tax incentives), and some ranching, fishing, and agriculture.

Northern Neck peninsula, comprising King George, Westmoreland, Richmond, Lancaster, and Northumberland counties, in E Virginia, bordered by the Potomac (N) and Rappahannock (S) rivers. In the TIDEWATER, it is historically agricultural, has always been rural, and is now a tourist destination, the site of WAKEFIELD, STRATFORD HALL, and other plantations. From 1669 until the Revolution, the Northern Neck was a royal proprietorship, granted by the British crown to four landowners, and held by the Fairfax family after 1689.

Northern Pacific Railroad first railroad to cross the Rocky Mts. and reach the Pacific coast to the N of the original (1869) UNION PACIFIC–CENTRAL PACIFIC line. Chartered in 1864, it was designed to connect L. Superior with Puget Sound, and in 1883 completed lines from Ashland, Wisconsin, and Duluth, Minnesota, by way of Fargo and Bismarck, North Dakota, and Billings, Montana, to Portland, Oregon, from which a branch turned N to Tacoma, Washington. Since 1970 it has been part of the huge BURLINGTON NORTHERN system.

Northern Yukon National Park see under BRITISH Mts., Yukon Territory.

Northfield **1.** town, pop. 2838, Franklin Co., NW Massachusetts, on the Connecticut R. and the Vermont and New Hampshire borders, 10 mi/16 km NE of Greenfield. It was settled in 1673. The town is the site of Northfield Seminary for girls (1879), now combined with the Mt. Hermon school for boys, in adjacent (SW) Gill, as a prep school. The evangelist Dwight L. Moody was born in 1837 in this rural town, which had a long history of producing missionaries. **2.** city, pop. 14,684, Rice and Dakota counties, SE Minnesota, on the Cannon R., 12 mi/19 km NE of Faribault. It is the commercial center for a large cattle raising region, and processes grain and poultry. Woodworking machinery, polyethylene, research balloons, and solar heating equipment are among the manufactures. The city is the seat of Carleton College (1866) and St. Olaf College (1874). Originally a flour milling center, Northfield achieved fame in 1876 when its inhabitants prevented a bank robbery by the gang associated with Jesse James. **3.** town, pop. 5610, including Northfield village, South Northfield, Northfield Falls, and Northfield Center, in Washington Co., C Vermont. It is on Interstate 89, 10 mi/16 km SSW of Montpelier. A former railroad center, the town is home to Norwich University, the oldest (1819) US military college. Industries include production of textiles and hosiery, lumbering, maple sugaring, and granite and slate quarrying.

North Fork northern peninsula of the EAST END of Long Island, in Riverhead and Southeld towns, Suffolk Co., New York, terminating at ORIENT POINT. It is a rural area with a growing wine industry, dotted with small villages, the largest Greenport (pop. 2070). Boating, fishing, and tourism are major industries.

North Fort Myers see under FORT MYERS, Florida.

Northgate commercial and residential section of N SEATTLE, Washington, 7 mi/11 km N of Downtown, along I-5. The large Northgate Mall is here, along with hospitals, a Seattle Community College campus, and cemeteries. Nearby residential neighborhoods include North Park (W), Lake City (NE), Greenwood (SW), and Green Lake (S).

Northglenn city, pop. 27,195, Adams Co., NC Colorado, a residential suburb 12 mi/19 km N of Denver.

North Great River unincorporated village, pop. 3964, in Islip town, Suffolk Co., SE New York, on Nicoll Bay of Great South Bay, 50 mi/80 km E of Manhattan. It is primarily residential.

North Haven town, pop. 22,247, New Haven Co., S Connecticut, just NE of New Haven on the Quinnipiac R. and Interstate 91. Originally part of New Haven, it became independent in 1786. Early industries included brickmaking and shipbuilding; today North Haven is a residential suburb and produces chemicals, tools, aircraft engine parts, and machinery. The town includes the villages of Montowese and Clintonville.

North Hempstead town, pop. 211,393, on Long Island's NORTH SHORE, in Nassau Co., SE New York, adjacent (NE) to Queens. It includes such suburban communities as MANHASSET, ROSLYN, GREAT NECK, and PORT WASHINGTON.

North Hero see under HERO ISLANDS, Vermont.

North Highlands unincorporated community, pop. 42,105, Sacramento Co., NC California, adjacent (NE) to Sacramento, of which it is a largely residential suburb. McClellan Air Force Base lies SW.

North Hills group of N suburbs of Pittsburgh, Pennsylvania, in Allegheny Co., N of the Allegheny R., including Sewickley Hills, Evergreen, Millvale, Etna, Sharpsburg, and Fox Chapel.

North Hollywood SAN FERNANDO VALLEY section of Los Angeles, California, N of the CAHUENGA PASS and UNIVERSAL CITY and W of BURBANK, 9 mi/14 km NW of Downtown. Some studios have moved from Hollywood to this commercial and residential area.

North Island Naval Air Station immediately W of Coronado, California, in N San Diego Bay; part of the city of San Diego. It was established in 1917 on the site of the first US aviation school. Charles Lindbergh departed from here in 1927 for New York before his pioneering transatlantic flight.

North Kansas City city, pop. 4130, Clay Co., NW Missouri, on the N side of the Missouri R., surrounded by Kansas City, Missouri, and just E of Kansas City, Kansas (across the river). Founded in 1912 by the North Kansas City Development Company as a planned community, this suburb has industries including food processing and the manufacture of metal products and paints, as well as older residences originally designed for factory workers. Kansas City Downtown Airport is immediately SW.

North Kingstown town, pop. 23,786, Washington Co., SC Rhode Island, on the W side of Narragansett Bay. Settled in 1641, it was incorporated 1674 and separated from South Kingstown in 1722. Its villages include Saunderstown, Hamilton, Allenton, WICKFORD, and Lafayette. There is heavy industry at QUONSET POINT. The economy includes commerce, light industry, fishing, and tourism.

Northlake city, pop. 12,505, Cook Co., NE Illinois, a suburb 16 mi/26 km W of Chicago. O'Hare International Airport is just to the N, stimulating commercial and industrial development along the Tri-State Tollway (I-294), in the W part of the city.

North Las Vegas city, pop. 47,707, Clark Co., SE Nevada, on the N boundary of Las Vegas. Founded in the 1920s, it is primarily a bedroom community. NELLIS AIR FORCE BASE is just E.

North Lauderdale city, pop. 26,506, Broward Co., SE Florida, 8 mi/13 km NW of Fort Lauderdale, a residential and retirement community.

North Lindenhurst unincorporated village, pop. 10,563, in Babylon town, Suffolk Co., SE New York, on Long Island's South Shore, immediately N of LINDENHURST. It is primarily residential.

North Little Rock city, pop. 61,741, Pulaski Co., C Arkansas, on the N bank of the Arkansas R., opposite LITTLE ROCK. It developed after the arrival of the railroad in 1853, later becoming home to the Missouri Pacific's freight classification yards and maintenance shops. Separating from Little Rock in 1903, and given its present name in 1917, it is commercial and industrial. Manufactures include paper and food products, textiles, clothing, machinery, chemicals, and metals. It is the home of Shorter College (1886) and military training Camp Joseph T. Robinson.

North Magnetic Pole the northern geomagnetic pole, or place to which a compass will point, as distinguished from the earth's rotational or geographic North Pole (90° N). Since 1831, when James Ross located it on KING WILLIAM I., in the Arctic Archipelago, measurement with improved instruments has combined with magnetic fluctuations, due primarily to fluid activity in the earth's core, to move the North Magnetic Pole in a generally northward line. It is now estimated to be just NW of BATHURST I., at around 77° N.

North Manchester town, pop. 6383, Wabash Co., NE Indiana, on the Eel R., 35 mi/56 km WSW of Fort Wayne. A trade hub for a region growing grain and raising livestock, it also manufactures such products as furniture, auto parts, electrical appliances, and processed food. It is the seat of Manchester College (1889).

North Mankato city, pop. 10,164, Nicollet Co., SE Minnesota, a suburb across the Minnesota R. from Mankato. The recreational area of Swan L. is 13 mi/21 km NW.

North Marysville unincorporated community, pop. 18,711, Snohomish Co., NW Washington, adjacent to MARYSVILLE, 6 mi/10 km N of Everett and 25 mi/40 km N of Seattle. It has recently grown as a residential suburb. It lies just E of the Tulalip Indian Reservation (pop. 7103). Its economy is largely based on lumbering, dairy products, and high-tech manufactures.

North Massapequa unincorporated village, pop. 19,365, in Oyster Bay town, Nassau Co., SE New York, on Long Island's South Shore, just S of Farmingdale. It is a residential suburb.

North Merrick unincorporated village, pop. 12,113, in Hempstead town, Nassau Co., SE New York, on Long Island's South Shore, 4 mi/6 km SE of Hempstead. It is primarily residential.

North Miami city, pop. 49,998, Dade Co., SE Florida, on the N end of Biscayne Bay, a largely residential suburb of Miami, on its N fringe. Fiberglass boats, aluminum products, kitchen equipment, and furniture are manufactured and local citrus is processed in the city.

North Miami Beach city, pop. 35,359, Dade Co., SE Florida, on Maule L. and the Oleta R., which connect to the N end of Biscayne Bay, 12 mi/19 km N of Miami. It was formed from the towns of Fulford and Fulford-by-the-Sea in 1931. A resort and suburban residential center, it also processes local citrus and has such light manufactures as pet food, candy, and concrete products. It is not adjacent to MIAMI BEACH.

North Minneapolis collection of neighborhoods in Minneapolis, Minnesota, NW of Downtown. It has the highest concentration of black residents in the city, both poor and middle-class, but mostly contains white middle-class homeowners. Certain sections, such as the NEAR NORTH SIDE, have experienced some gentrification in recent years.

North Myrtle Beach see under GRAND STRAND, South Carolina.

North New Hyde Park unincorporated village, pop. 14,359, in North Hempstead town, Nassau Co., SE New York, in WC Long Island, adjacent (E) to Bellerose, Queens. It is primarily residential.

North Newton see under NEWTON, Kansas.

North Ogden city, pop. 11,668, Weber Co., N Utah, immediately N of Ogden, of which it is a suburb. On the W edge of the Wasatch-Cache National Forest, it is in an area noted for fruit growing.

North Olmsted city, pop. 34,204, Cuyahoga Co., N Ohio, a residential and industrial suburb 13 mi/21 km SW of Cleveland. Machine tools are among the products made here. A large nature reserve adjoins the W part of the city.

North Palm Beach village, pop. 11,343, Palm Beach Co., SE Florida, on L. Worth (a lagoon just off the Atlantic), 7 mi/11 km N of West Palm Beach. It is a resort and residential community.

North Park largely residential section of SAN DIEGO, California, 2 mi/3 km NE of Downtown. Centered on Park Blvd. N of BALBOA PARK, it is home to a growing Asian immigrant community. Local landmarks include the Park Theatre and Egyptian Court Apartments, built in the 1920s Egyptian Revival style.

North Philadelphia residential and industrial section of Philadelphia, Pennsylvania. It is one of the city's oldest areas, and contains such historic districts as NORTHERN LIBERTIES and Spring Garden. Large sections have deteriorated badly in recent decades. The population of North Philadelphia is heavily black; institutions of importance to the black community, including Progress Plaza, Heritage House, and the offices of the Opportunities Industrialization Center, are here. Also in North Philadelphia are Temple University (1884) and the Albert Einstein Medical Center.

North Plainfield borough, pop. 18,820, Somerset Co., NE New Jersey, 9 mi/14 km N of New Brunswick. It was settled in 1736, and its growth was spurred by the opening of neighboring quarries and mills. Today it is essentially residential, with a variety of industries.

North Platte city, pop. 22,605, seat of Lincoln Co., WC Nebraska, at the confluence of the North Platte and South Platte rivers. Near the OREGON TRAIL military post Fort McPherson (SE), the city was laid out in 1866. In 1870 Buffalo Bill Cody settled here. Today the city's economy revolves around railroads, grain, livestock, and dairy products. The Union Pacific's Bailey Yards, just N, form the world's largest railroad classification complex.

North Platte River 618 mi/955 km long, in N Colorado, SE Wyoming, and W Nebraska. It rises in Jackson Co., N Colorado, W of the Medicine Bow Mts. and just E of the Continental Divide, and flows N into Wyoming, then NNW past Saratoga and through the SEMINOE RESERVOIR (1939), where the Medicine Bow R. joins it from the E. It continues N into the 1909 PATHFINDER RESERVOIR, where the Sweetwater R. joins it from the W, then curves NE through the Alcova Reservoir and to CASPER, where it turns E to Fort Fetterman and Douglas before turning SE, around the E of the Laramie Range, through the Glendo Reservoir, to FORT LARAMIE, where it is joined by the Laramie R. From SE Wyoming into W Nebraska, it continues generally ESE, irrigating a High Plains grain and stock raising area, before passing the city of NORTH PLATTE and joining the SOUTH PLATTE R. to form the PLATTE R. The North Platte is shallow, intermittent in dry seasons. The OREGON TRAIL and other westward routes follow it from the Platte junction into Wyoming.

North Port city, pop. 11,973, Sarasota Co., SW Florida, adjacent (N) to PORT CHARLOTTE. It is a retirement and residential community.

Northport city, pop. 17,366, Tuscaloosa Co., WC Alabama, on L. Tuscaloosa and the Black Warrior R., opposite (N) Tuscaloosa, of which it is a largely residential suburb.

North Providence town, pop. 32,090, Providence Co., NE Rhode Island, adjacent (NW) to Providence. Formerly an important textile manufacturing center, it still produces textiles, also jewelry, food products, chemicals, machinery, and lumber. A large portion of Rhode Island College is in this suburban town.

North Reading town, pop. 12,002, Middlesex Co., NE Massachusetts, on the Ipswich R., 15 mi/24 km N of Boston, immediately NW of Peabody and Danvers. Settled in 1651 as part of Reading, and long predominantly agricultural, it is a suburb just outside ROUTE 128.

North Richland Hills city, pop. 45,895, Tarrant Co., NE Texas, 10 mi/16 km NE of downtown Fort Worth, on the beltway (Route 820). It is a growing, primarily residential suburb. The adjacent (S), older city of Richland Hills has a pop. of 7978.

Northridge **1.** SAN FERNANDO VALLEY section of LOS ANGELES, California, 20 mi/32 km NW of Downtown. Largely residential, it is also home to electronics firms and to a California State University campus (1958). The epicenter of a destructive 1994 earthquake was under Northridge. **2.** unincorporated village, pop. 9448, in Harrison township, Montgomery Co., SW Ohio, on the Stillwater R., 4 mi/6 km NE of Dayton, of which it is a suburb.

North Ridgeville city, pop. 21,564, Lorain Co., N Ohio, a residential suburb 18 mi/29 km SW of Cleveland.

North River in 17th-century NEW NETHERLAND, the Hudson R., as distinguished from the South R., the Delaware. The name is encountered into the 20th century in reference to the part of the Hudson at New York City.

North Riverside see under RIVERSIDE, Illinois.

North Royalton city, pop. 23,197, Cuyahoga Co., N Ohio, 13 mi/21 km S of Cleveland, of which it is a residential suburb. There is also some light manufacturing here.

North Saint Paul city, pop. 12,376, Ramsey Co., SE Minnesota, a residential suburb 7 mi/11 km NE of St. Paul.

North Saskatchewan River see under SASKATCHEWAN R.

North Shore **1.** in British Columbia, the N side of the BURRARD INLET, across from the city of Vancouver, site of the affluent suburbs of WEST VANCOUVER and NORTH VANCOUVER, and of extensive recreational and wilderness areas. It is reached from the city by the Second Narrows Bridge (1925) or by the Lions Gate Bridge (1938), which crosses from STANLEY PARK, at the First Narrows. **2.** group of suburbs N of Chicago, Illinois, along L. Michigan. It includes the communities of Evanston, Wilmette, Kenilworth, Winnetka, Glencoe, Highland Park, Highwood, and Lake Forest. These suburbs are considered the wealthiest and most prestigious in the Chicago metropolitan area. **3.** coastal region of Essex Co., NE Massachusetts, N of Boston. It includes both historic towns and popular resorts. Much of the region reflects its maritime traditions; GLOUCESTER and other cities and towns continue to operate as ports. The North Shore also includes such affluent Boston suburbs as Beverly, Hamilton, and Wenham; historic SALEM; and the resorts of Cape ANN. **4.** in New Brunswick, E and N coastal areas, on (from SE to NW) Northumberland Strait, the Gulf of St. Lawrence, and Chaleur Bay. It is home, esp. in the N, to most of the province's large francophone (chiefly Acadian in origin) pop. **5.** region of Long Island, SE New York, along Long Island Sound, E from the New York City (Queens) border. The area is hilly, with numerous inlets and bays. The section from GREAT NECK (Nassau Co.) to HUNTINGTON, just over the Suffolk Co. border, is known as the GOLD COAST; once home to wealthy financiers and industrialists like the Whitneys and Vanderbilts, it now has communities of upper-middle-class professionals. Some communities, such as Old Westbury, Locust Valley, and the Brookvilles, still contain extensive estates. The towns of Suffolk Co., to the E, are more rural in feel. At Long Island's EAST END, the North Shore terminates in the NORTH FORK. **6.** waterfront development district in the ALLEGHENY section of Pittsburgh, Pennsylvania, along the Allegheny R., opposite the GOLDEN TRIANGLE. A former industrial area, it now houses THREE RIVERS STADIUM and various mixed-use projects. **7.** French, **Côte-Nord** the N shore of the St. Lawrence R. and Gulf of St. Lawrence, in S Québec, esp. the area E from the mouth of the SAGUENAY R. to the Labrador border. Once home to INUIT and Montagnais groups, it was settled largely after the mid 19th century, and in the 20th century has seen lumber and pulp, mining, and hydroelectric development. Its scattered small communities are reached chiefly by boat and by air.

North Shore Drive see under SAWTOOTH Mts., Minnesota.

North Side **1.** collection of neighborhoods N of the LOOP in Chicago, Illinois. Settled by Germans and, later, Eastern Europeans, it emerged as a fashionable part of town with the development of the GOLD COAST. **2.** also, **North Saint Louis** sections of Saint Louis, Missouri, N of Forest Park and the West End (on the W) and Downtown (on the E). The old **North End** is in the N of this area, between Fairground and O'Fallon parks. The North Side is today largely black, following the departure of Irish, German, and other white groups for the suburbs from the 1950s. It has several large URBAN RENEWAL zones. Major public housing construction included the ill-fated PRUITT-IGOE, while the Tandy (C) and Murphy (SE) sections have seen substantial rehabilitation of housing stock. The KERRY PATCH and GASLIGHT SQUARE were here. Delmar Boulevard, which runs WNW from Downtown, was long the main street of the city's black community. Martin Luther King (formerly Easton) Boulevard, which parallels it (N), runs from the city into a series of small, largely black, residential suburbs. **3.** district in Pittsburgh, Pennsylvania, N of the Allegheny and Ohio rivers. ALLEGHENY, MANCHESTER, DUTCHTOWN, Perry Hilltop, Fineview, SPRING HILL, and TROY HILL are all North Side communities.

North Slope also, **Arctic Slope** area stretching 600 mi/1000 km across N Alaska from POINT HOPE (W) to the border of the Yukon Territory. The term is used of either the high plateau (c.2500 ft/760 m) in the foothills N of the BROOKS RANGE or of the entire division extending N for 250 mi/400 km from the Brooks Range to the Arctic Ocean. Geologically it is a N extension of the GREAT PLAINS. The **North Slope Borough** (90,955 sq mi/235,575 sq km, pop. 5979) approximates the latter. Predominantly TUNDRA with little vertical relief, it is at places underlain by PERMAFROST up to 1000 ft/300 m thick, which prevents drainage, resulting in many ponds and shallow lakes. The major river is the COLVILLE; winds are strong and precipitation is light. The chief pop. center is BARROW. Other communities include Point Hope, Point Lay, Wainwright, Atqasuk, Nuiqsut, ANAKTUVUK PASS, and Kaktovik. A National Petroleum Reserve, occupying 37,000 sq mi/96,000 sq km in the C and W, was established in 1923. Although the discovery of huge petroleum and natural gas reserves in PRUDHOE BAY (NE) in 1968 has had a tremendous impact on local life, the area's Inuit still rely heavily on marine mammals, caribou, and fish. The ARCTIC NATIONAL WILDLIFE REFUGE is NE, along the Yukon border.

North Smithfield town, pop. 10,497, Providence Co., N Rhode Island, on the Massachusetts line, 13 mi/21 km NW of Providence and adjacent (W) to Woonsocket, on the Branch R. It contains the villages of Union Center, Primrose,

Branch Village, Forestdale, and Slatersville, the government center. Industries have included textile manufacturing and finishing and thread and wool processing; the area is today largely residential.

North Sydney town, pop. 7260, Cape Breton Co., extreme E Nova Scotia, on the E coast of Cape Breton I. and the W side of Sydney Harbour, 6 mi/10 km NW of Sydney. It is a port and trade center for the surrounding coal mining and industrial area. Ferries for Newfoundland leave from North Sydney, and the town is the winter base for a large fishing fleet.

North Tarrytown village, pop. 8152, in Mount Pleasant town, Westchester Co., SE New York, on the Hudson R., 26 mi/42 km NNE of New York City and immediately N of TARRYTOWN. It was the site of the capture of the British spy John Andre in 1780. North Tarrytown is now a largely residential suburb; a General Motors assembly plant along the Hudson, slated to close in 1995, has been key to the local economy.

North Tonawanda city, pop. 34,989, Niagara Co., W New York, at the junction of the Niagara R. with the W end of the New York State Barge Canal and Tonawanda Creek, 10 mi/16 km N of Buffalo. The area was settled in 1823, when construction began on the ERIE CANAL. Tonawanda Township was separated from Buffalo in 1836, and North Tonawanda incorporated in 1865. In the 1890s, hydroelectric power stimulated industrial growth. Together with Tonawanda, North Tonawanda now serves as a market and shipping center. Industries manufacture paper, paints, plastics, and musical instruments (the Wurlitzer company's plant is in Wurlitzer Park Village, in the NE).

Northumberland County 376 sq mi/974 sq km, pop. 96,771, in EC Pennsylvania, bordered (W) by the Susquehanna R. Its seat is SUNBURY. In the Appalachian Mts., it is a coal mining and agricultural county.

Northumberland Strait SW arm of the Gulf of St. Lawrence, separating Prince Edward Island from E New Brunswick and N Nova Scotia. Some 190 mi/310 km NW–SE and 9–30 mi/14–48 km wide, the shallow channel has strong tidal currents and important shellfish and lobster industries. The warmest waters in E Canada attract tourists to beaches along its shore. Kouchibouguac National Park (92 sq mi/238 sq km), in E New Brunswick, at the strait's NW end, features forests, saltmarshes, lagoons, and sand dunes; bike and hiking trails; and wild orchids and the endangered piping plover. Ferries cross the strait from Cape Tormentine, New Brunswick, to Borden, Prince Edward Island, and from Caribou, Nova Scotia, to Wood Is., Prince Edward Island. The former crossing, at the narrowest point, is the site of a bridge under construction, due to be completed in the late 1990s.

North Valley Stream unincorporated village, pop. 14,574, in Hempstead town, Nassau Co., SE New York, on Long Island's South Shore, just E of Cambria Heights, Queens. It is a residential suburb.

North Vancouver city (pop. 38,436) and district municipality (pop. 75,157), Greater Vancouver Regional District, SW British Columbia, along the N shore of Burrard Inlet, opposite Vancouver. A seaport, it ships grain, lumber, and ore. Other industries include shipbuilding and sawmilling. Tourism and outdoor recreation, in an area filled with mountains, streams, and parks, are also important. The Capilano Suspension Bridge (450 ft/137 m), one of the world's longest such pedestrian spans, is here.

North Vernon city, pop. 5311, Jennings Co., SE Indiana, 20 mi/32 km SE of Columbus. It was platted in 1854. Traditionally a railroad and trading hub, it now has an auto accessories industry and also manufactures such products as carpets and appliances. Lumber production and furniture making are also significant. Vernon (town, pop. 370), the county seat, is adjacent.

Northville city, pop. 6226, Wayne and Oakland counties, SE Michigan, 23 mi/37 km NW of Detroit. This suburban community is known for its Victorian architecture. It manufactures furnaces, furniture, glass products, and auto parts, and has a winery and cider mills. Northville Downs Race Track is here. Maybury State Park is adjacent (W).

North Wantagh unincorporated village, pop. 12,276, in Hempstead town, Nassau Co., SE New York, on Long Island, immediately N of Wantagh and 7 mi/11 km S of Hicksville. It is a residential suburb.

Northway see under ADIRONDACK NORTHWAY.

Northwest **1.** largest quadrant of Washington, D.C., lying N and W of the Capitol, bounded by the Potomac R. (W) and the Montgomery Co., Maryland line (N). It comprises virtually all of Washington known to visitors, including most Federal buildings (the WHITE HOUSE, physically at the center of the District, is in the Northwest), as well as a wide range of residential neighborhoods. WEST OF THE PARK is the affluent, heavily white Ward 3. Closer to Downtown are SHAW, ADAMS-MORGAN, and the EAST END. Farther N are MOUNT PLEASANT, COLUMBIA HEIGHTS, the Gold Coast, and neighborhoods along the Maryland line. **2.** residential and commercial section of PORTLAND, Oregon, W of the Willamette R. and N of Burnside St. The wealthiest area of the city, it encompasses an old industrial riverfront just N of Downtown; part of OLD TOWN; CHINATOWN; and farther residential neighborhoods including NOB HILL, NORTHWESTERN HILLS, and part of WEST HILLS. The main upscale shopping districts and FOREST PARK are also here.

Northwest, the **1.** in Canada, variously defined region. Historically it has meant everything W and N of Upper Canada (Ontario), or (esp. in the fur trade) W and N of L. Superior. Today it generally refers to the Yukon Territory and Northwest Territories and adjacent areas in British Columbia and the Prairie Provinces; much within this definition is alternatively considered part of the NORTH. **2.** in the US: **a.** the Old Northwest (see NORTHWEST TERRITORY). **b.** areas in the NW, esp. Washington and Oregon (the Pacific Northwest) and Idaho.

Northwest Angle 130 sq mi/337 sq km, northernmost part of the Continental US, in Lake of the Woods Co., NC Minnesota, on the NW shore of L. of the Woods, bordering Manitoba and Ontario. The Northwest Angle State Forest occupies the entire area, which includes part of the Red Lake Indian Reservation. Separated from the US by the L. of the Woods, the Northwest Angle became American territory due to a geographical error in the Treaty of 1783 with Great Britain. Its boundary was fixed in 1908 and 1925. Several offshore islands are also US territory.

North West Company combine created in Montréal, Québec, after the British conquest (1760), when newly arrived Scots entrepreneurs, employing the services of French VOYAGEURS, set up a fur trading network across S Canada and challenged the older HUDSON'S BAY COMPANY along the borders of its territories. More aggressive traders, the Northwesters (also called Canadians, to distinguish them from the British-based HBC operatives) pushed into the interior and explored the Northwest (Alexander Mackenzie's journeys to the Arctic and Pacific were under the NWC aegis). The company was wracked by internal strife, and in 1821, after the rivals had warred in the RED. R. territory, the NWC was amalgamated into the HBC, which kept its name but acquired some NWC characteristics.

Northwestern Hills affluent residential neighborhood in the Northwest section of PORTLAND, Oregon, 2 mi/3 km WNW of Downtown, on the SE of FOREST PARK.

Northwest Passage sea route around North America, long sought by Europeans seeking to reach China and India; the search led to much knowledge of the Arctic. Martin Frobisher's 1576 trip to DAVIS STRAIT (when it was already apparent that the continent presented a solid barrier) raised the possibility. From then until about 1820, it was hoped, despite repeated disappointment, that a commercially feasible route could be found. More recently, scientific and strategic interests, including Canada's aim to establish sovereignty in the ARCTIC ARCHIPELAGO, have driven exploration. The search, after 1845, for the expedition of Sir John Franklin, lost near KING WILLIAM I., also contributed greatly to knowledge of the area. The first completed trip through the archipelago occurred in 1853–54, when Robert McClure traveled much of the way (W–E) across Parry Channel, S of the QUEEN ELIZABETH Is., by dogsled, on ice and land. A sea passage first occurred in 1903–06, when the Norwegian Roald Amundsen, in his ship *Gjoa,* sailed N of Baffin I., E in the Parry Channel, and S through Peel Sound, between Prince of Wales I. (W) and Somerset I. and the BOOTHIA PENINSULA (E); wintered at Gjoa Haven (now a hamlet, pop. 783, Kitikmeot Region, an Inuit community) on KING WILLIAM I.; and proceeded W through Queen Maud and Coronation gulfs, S of VICTORIA I. In 1940–42 the Canadian police vessel *St. Roch* traveled W across the Parry Channel, S between BANKS (W) and VICTORIA (E) islands, and into the Beaufort Sea. In 1944 it returned, roughly following Amundsen's route until it turned E through Bellot Strait, at the N of the Boothia Peninsula, then N through Prince Regent Inlet, and back to Parry Channel. Icebreakers have subsequently traversed the Passage, and in 1969 they led the US tanker *Manhattan,* symbolic of new interest in possible commercial use, through.

Northwest Side in Chicago, Illinois: see under WEST SIDE.

Northwest Staging Route series of World War II airfields used to ferry aircraft from Edmonton, Alberta to Fairbanks, Alaska, en route to the Pacific or the Soviet Union. Its development was important in the growth of northwestern settlements including Grande Prairie, Alberta; Fort Saint John, British Columbia; and Watson Lake and Whitehorse, Yukon Territory.

Northwest Territories northernmost and largest governmental division of Canada, totaling 1,253,432 sq mi/3,246,389 sq km in land area, about one-third of the nation; 1991 pop. 57,649 (110.4% of 1986; rank: 11th of 12). Capital and only city: YELLOWKNIFE. Bordered W by the Yukon Territory, and S by (W–E, along the SIXTIETH PARALLEL) British Columbia, Alberta, Saskatchewan, and Manitoba, the Territories are also surrounded by the BEAUFORT SEA and Arctic Ocean (NW) and by BAFFIN BAY and straits separating them from Greenland (NE). In the SE are HUDSON BAY, JAMES BAY, and the HUDSON STRAIT, in which all islands, even those below 60° N, are in the Territories. The Northwest Territories are divided into five administrative regions. The **Fort Smith Region** (235,697 sq mi/610,456 sq km; pop. 27,553), in the SW, has its administrative center at FORT SMITH; Yellowknife, and most other pop. centers, are also here. The **Inuvik Region** (152,129 sq mi/394,015 sq km; pop. 8491), in the NW, has its center at INUVIK, in the MACKENZIE R. delta. The **Keewatin Region** (228,701 sq mi/592,335 sq km; pop. 5834), in the SC, has its center at RANKIN INLET, on the W of Hudson Bay. The **Kitikmeot Region** (243,898 sq mi/631,695 sq km; pop. 4386), on the NC mainland and in islands of the S ARCTIC ARCHIPELAGO, has its center at CAMBRIDGE BAY, on VICTORIA I. The **Baffin Region** (393,007 sq mi/1,017,889 sq km; pop. 9975), including BAFFIN I. and all the QUEEN ELIZABETH Is. in the N, has its center at IQALUIT. Formerly, the Territories were divided into three administrative districts, Mackenzie (SW), Keewatin (SE), and Franklin (N); the creation of NUNAVUT (to come into existence in 1999) is the next step in their gradual evolution. Geologically, most of the region lies on the CANADIAN SHIELD. On the SW, running SSE–NNW, are (E–W) the Shield's border, site of the huge GREAT BEAR (N) and GREAT SLAVE (S) lakes; lowlands along the Mackenzie R.; the river itself; the MACKENZIE Mts. (part of the Canadian ROCKY Mts.); and, on the SW boundary with the Yukon Territory, the SELWYN Mts. and some parts of the INTERMONTANE Region. Mount Sir James MacBrien, on the Yukon border, is the high point in the Territories at 9062 ft/2762 m. Along the S border, extending N from Alberta, is part of the High Plains section of the GREAT PLAINS. In the NE, in the Queen Elizabeth Is. (in the N of the Arctic Archipelago) are plateaus and mountains rising above the Shield and reaching 8000 ft/2430 m in the far N. Except in the SW, where the Mackenzie lowlands have large coniferous forests (boreal forest, or taiga), the Territories are covered with TUNDRA, long known as the BARREN LANDS. Thousands of small lakes, bogs, and streams characterize this terrain, which has as little precipitation as many deserts, but where PERMAFROST keeps water on or near the surface; MUSKEG is common. Caribou cross this land, and were the traditional sustenance of the INUIT, whose lives are now much altered by contact with white society. The DENE (woodland Indians speaking Athapascan tongues) live in the woods of the SW, and there is a MÉTIS community in the far SW. The three groups make up the majority of the Territories' pop. Whites live largely in the SW, around Yellowknife, and in scattered scientific and government posts as far N as Alert, at the top of ELLESMERE I.; miners and prospectors make up most of the nongovernmental white pop., and there are some fishermen on Great Slave L. and hunters and trappers working as far N as the S Arctic Archipelago. The voyage of Leif Ericsson (c.1000 A.D.), whose Helluland (see under VINLAND) was apparently the coast of Baffin I., represents the first known European appearance in the Territories. In 1570, Martin Frobisher rediscovered the island, and in 1610–11 Henry Hudson sailed into Hudson Bay. The search for the NORTHWEST PASSAGE brought expeditions into the region's waters from the early 17th century. By 1670 trapping was flourishing in the North, and in that year the HUDSON'S BAY COMPANY was chartered, with jurisdiction over RUPERT'S LAND, the entire Hudson Bay watershed. In the 1770s Samuel Hearne traveled overland from the Bay to the COPPERMINE R. From the 1780s, the Montréal-based NORTH WEST COMPANY competed with the HBC, and sent explorers through the W; in 1821, the two companies combined. After

Canadian CONFEDERATION (1867), the HBC sold Rupert's Land and areas to the W called the "North Western Territories" to the Federal government, and the Northwest Territories were born. With the exception that most of the islands of the Arctic Archipelago were added to the region in 1880, the history of the Territories since their creation has been one of diminution. Manitoba was created from a small S section in 1870, and enlarged in 1881 and 1912. Ontario received lands extending to the S of James Bay in 1874 and 1889. The Yukon Territory was separated in 1898, and Québec received lands on the SE of James Bay. Saskatchewan and Alberta were created in 1905. Finally, in 1912, in addition to Manitoba's enlargement, Ontario received more lands on Hudson Bay, and Québec received lands comprising NOUVEAU-QUÉBEC (most of UNGAVA). In addition to the traditional pursuits of the Inuit and Dene, economic life in the Northwest Territories has included trapping (now much diminished in importance); whaling (important in the early 19th century at Baffin I. and in the N of Hudson Bay); and fishing in Great Slave L. and Hudson Bay. Mining, however, has been the leading income producer. The existence here of copper, coal, and oil has been known since the end of the 18th century. Since the 1920s, oil has been extracted at NORMAN WELLS and elsewhere; World War II caused a boom in the industry, and exploration along the Beaufort Sea continues. In the 1930s the Yellowknife area became a gold rush site, and the shores of Great Bear L. were mined for pitchblende (around Port Radium). There was a nickel boom at Rankin Inlet in the 1950s. Iron is now extracted in the HIGH ARCTIC, and gold, uranium, tungsten (in the Selwyn Mts.), lead, zinc, other metals, and coal are all produced in various localities. The environmental (and social, esp. on the Inuit) effects of these undertakings have been widely discussed. Since the 1960s, tourism has grown. Traditional handicrafts are among the few manufactures in the Territories, and Inuit settlements have begun to draw tourists to observe folkways. NAHANNI (SW) and AUYUITTUQ (on Baffin I.) national parks, created in the 1970s, are among outdoors attractions; WOOD BUFFALO National Park (1922, on the Alberta border) and the THELON game sanctuary (1927, protecting muskoxen) are major wildlife preserves. Citizens of the Northwest Territories vote for a territorial assembly, and for a representative in the Federal House of Commons. The central government appoints a commissioner for the Territories, and a representative in the Federal Senate.

Northwest Territory lands between the Ohio R. (S) and the Mississippi R. (W) that became the modern states of Ohio, Indiana, Michigan, Illinois, and Wisconsin, as well as part of Minnesota. The area, known as the Old Northwest, had come under British control in 1763, at the end of long British-French struggles. After the 1783 Treaty of Paris, the United States gained control. Four of the original thirteen states (Virginia, Connecticut, Massachusetts, and New York) had claims in the Old Northwest. The other nine states argued that the entire area should be put under central control, with a mechanism for the creation of new states. A series of laws, the last the Northwest Ordinance of 1787, put this mechanism into operation. The four states had in the meantime relinquished their claims, Virginia retaining the VIRGINIA MILITARY DISTRICT, and Connecticut the WESTERN RESERVE. The battle of FALLEN TIMBERS (1794) reduced native opposition to the point that settlement could begin on a large scale. Ohio became a state in 1803, the battle of TIPPECANOE (1811) further reduced tribal opposition, and the other states entered the union between 1816 and 1848.

North Wildwood see under WILDWOOD, New Jersey.

North Wilkesboro see under WILKESBORO, North Carolina.

Northwoods city, pop. 5106, St. Louis Co., EC Missouri, 8 mi/13 km NW of downtown St. Louis, an essentially residential suburb.

North York city, pop. 562,564, TORONTO Metropolitan Municipality, S Ontario, bounded by Vaughan and Markham (N); East York, Toronto, and York (S); Scarborough (E); and Etobicoke (W). Initially part of York Township, it became a separate township in 1922, a borough in 1967, and a city in 1979. The East and West branches of the Don R. flow through the city. Largely residential sections of North York include Willowdale (EC) and Newtonbrook (NE). The planned industrial-residential community of DON MILLS is in the SE, military-industrial-residential DOWNSVIEW in the WC section. York University (1959) is on the NW boundary. The Ontario Science Centre is in the SE, in Ernest Thompson Seton Park, on the Don's West Branch.

Norton 1. town, pop. 14,265, Bristol Co., SE Massachusetts, 11 mi/18 km SW of Brockton. Essentially rural, it is the home of Wheaton College (1834), and has some light industry. **2.** city, pop. 11,483, Summit and Wayne counties, N Ohio, a residential suburb 6 mi/10 km SW of Akron. L. Dorothy is just SW of the city.

Norton Air Force Base see under SAN BERNARDINO, California.

Norton Shores city, pop. 21,755, Muskegon Co., SW Michigan, on L. Michigan and Mona L., a residential suburb 7 mi/11 km S of Muskegon. P. J. Hoffmaster State Park is 2 mi/3 km S.

Norton Sound inlet of the Bering Sea S of the SEWARD PENINSULA and N of the YUKON R. delta, in WC Alaska. It is c.100 mi/160 km N–S and 125 mi/200 km E–W. Norton Bay is at its NE end, and NOME on its NW shore. The sound is navigable May–Oct.

Norumbega name inexactly applied on 16th- and 17th-century maps in the area of Maine's PENOBSCOT R.; it also appears as *Aranbega* and in other forms, and is probably an Abnaki locality name. By the 1560s, however, fabulous stories attached to it, of a wealthy city of Norumbega, a northeastern analogue to EL DORADO or QUIVIRA or CIBOLA. In addition, the form of the name led some to see it as an "Indian" version of *Norway,* and it became confused with the mystery of VINLAND.

Norwalk 1. city, pop. 94,279, Los Angeles Co., SW California, 16 mi/26 km SE of downtown Los Angeles, E of the San Gabriel R. Incorporated in 1957, it is mainly a residential suburb, housing workers in the area's electronics, aircraft, and auto industries. There is a large state mental hospital. The city is the seat of Cerritos Community College (1955). **2.** city and coterminous township, pop. 78,331, Fairfield Co., SW Connecticut, on Long Island Sound, 14 mi/23 km E of Bridgeport. Settled in 1649, it was burned by the British in 1779; some residents accepted compensatory "fire lands" in the old NORTHWEST TERRITORY, eventually settling what is now Norwalk, Ohio. Once a popular summer resort and oystering center, it is now both a residential suburb and an industrial and research center producing electronic and optical equipment, radar equipment, hardware, automobile accessories, and signaling devices. It is home to Norwalk Community College and the Norwalk State Technical College, both founded in 1961. Norwalk includes the former city of South Norwalk, which faced economic distress in the 1990s; East Norwalk, now a "factory outlet" center; Rowayton; and several other villages. **3.** city, pop. 14,731, seat of Huron Co., NC Ohio, 15 mi/24 km SE of Sandusky. Originally part of the WESTERN RESERVE slated for Connecticut residents whose homes had been burned by Tories, Norwalk today is a trade and processing center for an agricultural area. Manufactures include furniture, iron, and steel. A number of the original settlers' houses still stand, and Norwalk is the site of the Firelands Museum.

Norway House Indian reserve, pop. 2818, C Manitoba, on Little Playgreen L. (the Nelson R.), NE of L. Winnipeg. In the 18th and 19th centuries it was a major post for the Hudson's Bay Company's fur trade with the Cree and Assiniboine. About 500 non-Indians live in this close-knit community.

Norwich **1.** city and coterminous township, pop. 37,391, seat of New London Co., at the confluence of the Yantic and Shetucket rivers, where they form the Thames R., 13 mi/21 km N of New London, SE Connecticut. Founded in 1659 on a grant from the Mohegan leader Uncas, it was an important 18th-century center for shipbuilding, shipping, and the production of cotton, nails, and paper. In the 19th century, it produced firearms and textiles. Industries today include apparel, electronic equipment, and paper and leather goods. Thames Valley State Technical College (1963) and Mohegan Community College (1970) are here. The villages of Norwichtown, Taftville, and Occum are included. **2.** city, pop. 7613, seat of Chenango Co., SC New York, on the Chenango R., 37 mi/60 km NE of Binghamton. Settled in 1788, it lies in a dairying and farming area. Among the city's manufactures are pharmaceuticals, wood products, and farm machinery. **3.** town, pop. 3093, including Pompanoosuc, Norwich, West Norwich, Lewiston, and New Boston villages, in Windsor Co., EC Vermont. It is on the Connecticut R. opposite Hanover, New Hampshire, 35 mi/56 km ENE of Rutland. In an agricultural area, the town was formerly the site of Norwich University, founded 1819, now in NORTHFIELD. Lumbering is the main industry.

Norwood **1.** town, pop. 28,700, Norfolk Co., E Massachusetts. On the Neponset R. and Interstate 95, it is a producer of electronic and computer equipment, floor coverings, roofing materials, machinery, measuring instruments, athletic footwear, and surgical and foundry products. Norwood is at the S end of the ROUTE 128 technology complex. **2.** see under YOUNG AMERICA, Minnesota. **3.** city, pop. 23,674, Hamilton Co., SW Ohio, 5 mi/8 km NE of downtown Cincinnati. Almost surrounded by the larger city, it is at once an enclave and a suburb. Norwood was founded in 1804. Local industries include printing, lithography, and the manufacture of office equipment, playing cards, machine tools, electric motors, and airplane parts. The site of its General Motors automobile assembly plant, which closed in 1987, is now a business development.

Norwood Park residential neighborhood on the far NW side of Chicago, Illinois, near NORRIDGE and PARK RIDGE. A low-density suburblike bastion of the upper middle class, it has long been primarily Irish.

Notre Dame unincorporated academic community in St. Joseph Co., N Indiana, a suburb just N of South Bend. It is the seat of the University of Notre Dame (1842), St. Mary's College (1844), and Holy Cross College (1966).

Nôtre-Dame, Île landfill island E of MONTRÉAL, Québec, in the St. Lawrence R. next to Île SAINTE-HÉLÈNE, created for Expo 67, the 1967 World's Fair, and the site of many of its pavilions. The French pavilion is now an exhibition hall, the Palais de la Civilisation. The Floralies International was held here in 1980, and a floral park has been maintained since. Recreational facilities include the rowing basin for the 1976 Olympics, which serves as a skating rink during the winter, and the Gilles Villeneuve Racetrack, on which the Grand Prix Molson du Canada is held. The St. Lawrence Seaway and SAINT-LAMBERT are immediately E.

Notre Dame Bay Atlantic Ocean inlet in N Newfoundland, 155 mi/250 km NW of St. John's. The Baie Verte Peninsula borders it (W). Some 80 mi/130 km across, it has more islands than any of Newfoundland's other bays, the largest of them Fogo I. (E), a former Beothuk summer home, since the 1500s also a European fishing center, and known for its rural life movement and folklore. The EXPLOITS R. empties into the bay; Lewisporte (town, pop. 3848), near its mouth, is a fishing and ferry port. Twillingate (town, pop. 1397), another former Beothuk home, on the Twillingate Is., is a fishing and trade center. Lobstering, sport fishing, sealing, and lumbering have all been important on the bay.

Notre Dame Mountains French, **Monts Notre-Dame** broad upland (rising to c.3500 ft/1070 m) of the Appalachian Mts., in Québec. A continuation of the GREEN Mts. of Vermont, they extend NE from the border along the S of the Saint Lawrence R. valley into the GASPÉ PENINSULA, where they include the SHICKSHOCK Mts., near the E tip. In the S, where the EASTERN TOWNSHIPS were settled by English-speakers, they are called the Sutton Mts.

Nottoway River 170 mi/275 km long, in S Virginia. It rises on the N border of Lunenburg Co., flows generally SE in a winding course, through swampy, rural country, to Courtland (JERUSALEM), and joins the Blackwater R. at the North Carolina line, to form the CHOWAN R.

Nouveau-Québec English, **New Quebec** district, c. 300,000 sq mi/780,000 sq km, of N Québec, bounded by the EASTMAIN R. (S), JAMES BAY and HUDSON BAY (W), LABRADOR (E), and the HUDSON STRAIT and UNGAVA BAY (N). Formerly part of the Northwest Territories, the region was annexed by Québec in 1912. In 1927, the Québec-Labrador boundary was established, and in 1967 what is now Nouveau-Québec became the largest and least populated political subdivision of the province. Mining along the Labrador border was the incentive for the settling of SCHEFFERVILLE. Along the N and W coasts are a number of INUIT and Cree communities. Hydroelectric development on rivers flowing into James Bay, esp. the LA GRANDE, has raised controversy over environmental effects and native rights. In the 1980s, much of the area was also designated the Inuit "sociocultural" region of Nunavik.

Nouvelle-Écosse see NOVA SCOTIA.

Novarupta Volcano see under KATMAI NATIONAL PARK AND PRESERVE, Alaska.

Nova Scotia French, **Nouvelle-Écosse** province of E Canada, one of the MARITIME PROVINCES; 1991 pop. 899,942 (103.1% of 1986; rank: 7th of 12); land area 20,402 sq mi/52,841 sq km (rank: 11th); entered Confederation 1867. Capital and most populous city: HALIFAX. Other leading cities and towns: DARTMOUTH, SYDNEY, GLACE BAY. Nova Scotia's land is a hilly outlier of the APPALACHIAN system. The province comprises a V-shaped, SW–NE oriented peninsula, joined at the CHIGNECTO isthmus to New Brunswick (W); and CAPE BRETON I. (NE), separated from the peninsula by the Strait of CANSO. On the peninsula's W is the Bay of FUNDY, whose NW (Chignecto Bay) and NE (the MINAS Channel, Minas Basin, and COBEQUID Bay) extensions indent NW Nova Scotia; the world's highest tides are found here. On the N, the NORTHUMBERLAND STRAIT separates the province from Prince Edward I. Cape Breton I. lies on the Gulf of SAINT LAWRENCE (N) and CABOT STRAIT (NE). It and the peninsula have a long, indented coastline on the Atlantic Ocean (SE). Far to the E of the peninsula, near the edge of the Continental Shelf, is SABLE I., a low, sandy spit that was the site of 16th-century settlement attempts, and that came to be known, for its many shipwrecks, as the "Graveyard of the Atlantic." Cape Breton Island's land mass surrounds BRAS D'OR LAKE, a sunken valley that is the site of BADDECK and other small ports and residential villages. The CAPE BRETON HIGHLANDS NATIONAL PARK, in the N, is the site of Nova Scotia's high point (1747 ft/532 m). Along the peninsula's Atlantic coast, Halifax Harbour and MAHONE BAY are among the many inlets that have afforded sites for fishing and commercial harbors, shipyards, and resorts. In the S interior is the wilderness of KEJIMKUJIK NATIONAL PARK. The province's most important river is the ANNAPOLIS, which runs ENE–WSW along the peninsula's NW, into the tidal Annapolis Basin; the Annapolis Valley is a noted apple producing center, and the site of some of the province's earliest settlements. A Micmac homeland, the region was seen by Cabot (for the English) in 1497, by Verrazano and Cartier (for the French) in the 1520s–30s. Both countries claimed it, but the French settled first, at PORT-ROYAL, on the Annapolis Basin, in 1605, and the peninsula became the center of ACADIA. In 1621 the British crown granted a charter for the settlement of Nova Scotia (New Scotland), in the same area. Before 1713, the colony changed hands repeatedly; then, the Treaty of Utrecht restricted French control to the Île Saint-Jean (Prince Edward I.) and Île Royale (Cape Breton I.). The French fortress at LOUISBOURG, on Cape Breton I., became the object of British (and American Colonial) assaults in the 1740s, and Halifax was founded as a military center to counter Louisbourg's presence. The Acadians remaining in Nova Scotia, although they professed neutrality, were deported in the 1750s, most famously from GRAND PRÉ. They were largely replaced with New Englanders, although many returned gradually, settling chiefly along the SW coast (the FRENCH SHORE). At the time of the American Revolution, Nova Scotian sympathies were mixed, but the colony remained out of the struggle, and received a massive influx of LOYALISTS, effectively ending any chance of its joining the new American republic. From 1784 to 1820, Cape Breton I. existed as a separate colony, and in 1784 New Brunswick also was created. The late 18th and early 19th centuries were prosperous times, with lumbering, fishing on the GRAND BANKS (NE) and GEORGES BANK (SW), the building of wooden (including clipper) ships, and Halifax's rising importance contributing to Nova Scotia's growth. In the 19th century mining became increasingly important. The Chignecto area, around AMHERST and SPRINGHILL, is a center of coal, salt, and gypsum production, and Sydney, SYDNEY MINES, Glace Bay, and neighboring communities in E Cape Breton I. have used local coal to fuel their steel industries, now in decline. NEW GLASGOW (NC) and Halifax have also been steel producers. In addition, lead and barite are mined in the province. Steel and wood pulp production made fortunes in the early 20th century, and Halifax has prospered from its strategic position esp. in both World Wars, despite a 1916 explosion that leveled much of the city. Today, oil refining and varied light manufactures contribute to the industrial base. The shipbuilding industry, with such centers as LUNENBURG and SHELBURNE, is long past its prime, but tourism has grown, with Cape Breton I. and the numerous coastal villages drawing visitors. Halifax and Dartmouth are the center of an expanding commercial complex. Halifax and WOLFVILLE are academic centers.

Novato city, pop. 47,585, Marin Co., NW California, 25 mi/40 km N of San Francisco, on Novato Creek, W of San Pablo Bay. Largely residential, it is set in a dairy farming area. Hamilton Air Force Base (1935) lies SE, on the bay. Retail distribution operations and some light manufactures are among local businesses, and the Renaissance Pleasure Faire, in the autumn, is a major tourist attraction.

Novi city, pop. 32,998, Oakland Co., SE Michigan, on Walled L., 15 mi/24 km NW of Detroit. Mostly residential, this suburban community has some light industry and large retail malls.

Nueces River 315 mi/507 km long, in S Texas. It rises, with its parallel headstream the West Nueces, in Edwards Co., on the EDWARDS PLATEAU, NE of Del Rio. It flows SSE to Crystal City, then SE and E to Three Rivers, where the Frio R., flowing from the CHOKE CANYON RESERVOIR, joins it. It then winds SE, and below Dinero enters 19,300-ac/7820-ha L. Corpus Christi, a water-supply and recreational impoundment some 35 mi/56 km upstream from the city of CORPUS CHRISTI, at which it enters Nueces Bay, an inlet of the Gulf of Mexico. The Nueces was named for the pecan nuts (Spanish, *nueces*) found along its course. Between the Texas Revolution (1836) and the treaty (1848) ending the Mexican War, it was the N boundary (the Rio Grande was the S boundary) of the disputed Mexican province of Nuevo Santander, which was finally awarded to the US.

Nuevo Santander see under NUECES R., Texas.

Nunavik see under NOUVEAU-QUÉBEC, Québec.

Nunavut meaning "our land" in a local dialect, is the proposed new Canadian territory of the INUIT, to come into being in 1999, with full governmental powers by 2008. It will comprise all of the ARCTIC ARCHIPELAGO with the exception of a western zone including BANKS I., W VICTORIA I., and much of the PARRY Is. The Belcher Is., in HUDSON BAY, site of the southernmost Inuit community, will also be included, as will mainland TUNDRA areas N and E of Great Bear L. and along the W Hudson Bay shore N of Manitoba. Negotiations with the DENE, who live to the SW and who envision a territory of their own called Denendeh, are continuing; depending on further developments, the Northwest Territories may cease to exist. Nunavut's total area will be some 772,000 sq mi/2 million sq km; of this, the Inuit will have full control of 135,000 sq mi/350,000 sq km and will retain some subsurface mineral rights, and will give up their aboriginal title to the rest.

Nunivak Island in the Bering Sea, 140 mi/230 km WSW of Bethel, in SW Alaska. Fifty-five mi/90 km E–W and 42 mi/68 km N–S, it is separated from Nelson I. and the mainland by Etolin Strait. Treeless and fogbound, it is inhabited mainly by Inuit engaged in hunting, fishing, and the herding of introduced reindeer and musk oxen. A seabird habitat, it lies within the Alaska Maritime National Wildlife Refuge.

Nutley township, pop. 27,099, Essex Co., NE New Jersey, 3 mi/5 km S of Passaic, on the Passaic R. Dutch and English settlers arrived here in the 1660s and 1670s. Successively part of Newark, Bloomfield, and Belleville, Nutley became an independent town in 1874. It was a post–Civil War mecca for artists and writers. Primarily a New York–area bedroom community, it also manufactures pharmaceuticals, electronic components, clothing, and paper products.

Nuuanu largely residential district N of downtown HONOLULU, Hawaii, along Nuuanu Stream, W and N of the PUNCHBOWL, extending into the KOOLAU RANGE. The Royal Mausoleum is here. **Nuuanu Pali Lookout,** 5 mi/8 km NE of Downtown, is the site where Kamehameha the Great is said to have driven Oahu's defenders off a cliff in 1795.

Nyack village, pop. 6558, in Orangetown, Rockland Co., SE New York, on the W bank of the Hudson R., on the TAPPAN ZEE, opposite Tarrytown, 8 mi/13 km NW of the Bronx. It was settled in the late 17th century and became a busy river landing; its still-active waterfront is home to many pleasure craft. Primarily a commuter village since the early 20th century, Nyack also has some industry, including boatbuilding and the manufacture of sewing machines. Tourism is a mainstay of the economy. The home of artist Edward Hopper (1882–1967), who was born here, is now an art gallery.

O

Oahe, Lake formed by the **Oahe Dam** (completed 1963), on the MISSOURI R., just NW of Pierre, South Dakota. A unit of the Missouri River Basin Project, the 9400 ft/2860 m–long dam, 242 ft/74 m high, is one of the world's largest earthfill structures. The lake backs up on the Missouri to near Bismarck, North Dakota, and W on the CHEYENNE R., a tributary, along the S boundary of the Cheyenne R. Indian Reservation. Mobridge, South Dakota, and the STANDING ROCK reservation are also along the Missouri section, which is some 250 mi/400 km long.

Oahu third-largest island of Hawaii, 607 sq mi/1572 sq km, in HONOLULU Co., SE of Kauai and NW of Molokai. It was formed by volcanoes now represented by two parallel NW–SE mountain groups, the KOOLAU RANGE along the NE coast (its highest point Konahuanui, at 3105 ft/947 m), and the WAIANAE Mts. along the SW coast (their highest point Kaala, at 4039 ft/1232 m). Between lies a fertile plain irrigated by water from the mountain slopes. Oahu's famous craters include DIAMOND HEAD, Koko Head, and the PUNCHBOWL. The most important Hawaiian island commercially, Oahu is also the most densely populated, and the state's cultural and educational center. It is also the focus of island tourism, its best-known resort being WAIKIKI, in the state's capital, Honolulu. The US defense hub of the Pacific, Oahu is the site of the PEARL HARBOR complex and HICKAM AIR FORCE BASE, on the S coast, and of SCHOFIELD BARRACKS, on the C plateau. Principal communities beside Honolulu include AIEA, EWA BEACH, KAILUA, KANEOHE, PEARL CITY, WAHIAWA, and WAIPAHU. Tourism; defense spending; sugarcane, pineapple, and some other crop production; and some light industry are important.

Oak Bay district municipality, pop. 17,815, Capital Regional District, SW British Columbia, at the SE tip of Vancouver I., on the Strait of Juan de Fuca, a suburb adjacent (E) to Victoria. A residential and retirement community, it is noted for its British influence, its architecture, and its annual (June) tea party.

Oak Bluffs town, pop. 2804, NE MARTHA'S VINEYARD, Dukes Co., SE Massachusetts. Settled in the 1640s, it flourished in the 1830s as a Methodist summer camp. The community has dozens of small gingerbreaded cottages surrounding a semi-enclosed Methodist tabernacle. Today Oak Bluffs is a summer resort, with tourist trade in the downtown area. The town is especially popular with black vacationers.

Oak Brook village, pop. 9178, Du Page Co., NE Illinois, 18 mi/29 km W of Chicago. It is the site of numerous corporate headquarters, and has become an important center of international business and finance. **Oakbrook Terrace,** a city, pop. 1907, just NW, also has many office facilities. Both communities are residential suburbs of Chicago.

Oak Cliff extensive residential and commercial section of Dallas, Texas, lying S of the Trinity R. and Downtown. On higher ground than the original city, it was known as Hord's Ridge in the 1840s, then was the site (1855–58) of La Réunion, the French utopian community whose members later moved to Dallas. Oak Cliff's hills and bluffs attracted residential development in the period 1890–1930; by mid 20th century its housing stock had declined, but it became home to workers in the new aircraft and related industries in the Mid-Cities between Dallas and Fort Worth. Today it has a variety of working- and middle-class neighborhoods; closer to Downtown parts have become fashionable with renovators. Bishop (SE) and Dallas Baptist and Mountain View (SW) colleges are here.

Oak Creek city, pop. 19,513, Milwaukee Co., SE Wisconsin, on L. Michigan, 10 mi/16 km S of Milwaukee, of which it is a suburb. Its manufactures include electronic components, concrete and aluminum products, and heavy machinery.

Oakdale **1.** city, pop. 11,961, Stanislaus Co., NC California, on the Stanislaus R., in the N San Joaquin Valley, 12 mi/19 km NE of Modesto. Its industries include dairy farming; fruit, vegetable and almond growing; and food processing. **2.** city, pop. 18,374, Washington Co., SE Minnesota, a residential suburb 10 mi/16 km NE of St. Paul. It has experienced recent commercial growth, particularly in its SE corner, at the junction of I-94 and I-494. **3.** unincorporated village, pop. 7875, in Islip town, Suffolk Co., SE New York, on Long Island's South Shore, just E of East Islip. It is a residential community on the Connetquot R. and Great South Bay.

Oak Forest village, pop. 26,203, Cook Co., NE Illinois, a suburb 20 mi/32 km S of Chicago. This residential community experienced substantial population growth during the 1970s and 1980s.

Oak Grove unincorporated community, pop. 12,576, Marion Co., NW Oregon, a residential suburb immediately NE of Salem. The Oregon State Fairgrounds are 1 mi/2 km W.

Oak Harbor city, pop. 17,176, Island Co., NW Washington, near the N end of Whidbey I., on a bay off Saratoga Passage in Puget Sound. It was settled by sea captains, who later gave way to Irish immigrants and to Dutch settlers, who arrived around the turn of the century. The city's annual Holland Happenings, its windmills, and its fields of flowering bulbs reflect this heritage. The entire town of Coupeville, pop. 1377, 6 mi/10 km S, is part of the Ebey's Landing National Historic Reserve, site of an 1852 pioneer community, one of the oldest in the state. Deception Pass State Park, on land sighted by George Vancouver in 1792, is 7 mi/11 km N, and Whidbey Island Naval Air Station is 3 mi/5 km NW.

Oak Island islet in MAHONE BAY, SW Nova Scotia, 4 mi/6 km SW of Chester. Captain Kidd is one of many pirates (or others) said to have buried treasure here. Plank flooring, oak chests, and other clues have been found since 1795, but even high-tech 1970s expeditions failed to prove anything.

Oakland **1.** city, pop. 372,242, seat of ALAMEDA Co., NC California. An industrial port on San Francisco Bay, 10 mi/16 km E of San Francisco, it is the largest EAST BAY community. On part of the huge 1820 Rancho San Antonio, it was settled by Americans during the 1840s gold rush, and incorporated in 1852. Ferry service to San Francisco, begun in 1851, made it a bedroom community at the same time that farmers and lumbermen were establishing themselves. In 1869 Oakland became the terminus of the first transcontinental railroad, and its harbor grew. The 1906 San Francisco earthquake sent thousands of refugees across the bay to the city; as its pop. grew, its inner harbor, between Downtown and ALAMEDA (SW), was improved. World War I brought the opening of major shipyards and the establishment of a military presence that expanded in World War II. The opening of the SAN FRANCISCO–OAKLAND BAY BRIDGE (1936) and other bridges and tunnels to neighboring communities put Oakland at the center of an industrial/residential complex. Today the city has a major container port and large ship and rail yards, in addition to Army and Navy depots. It makes chemicals, processed foods, electrical equipment and other machinery, and a variety of other products, and has headquarters of health-industry and other corporations. Mills College (women; 1852), Holy Names College (1868), and several other colleges are here. The focus of Downtown is 155-ac/63-ha L. Merritt, created (1898) from a tidal lagoon. The well-known Oakland Museum is on the lake, as is the L. Merritt Waterfowl Refuge (1878), the first US wildlife refuge. The Oakland–Alameda County Coliseum Complex is home to the Athletics (baseball) and Golden State Warriors (basketball). Jack London Square, on the waterfront where the writer worked c.1900, is a major tourist attraction. Other writers associated with the city include Joaquin Miller (the "poet of the Sierras") and Gertrude Stein. The Berkeley (or Oakland) Hills, rising to c.1200 ft/370 m E above Downtown, have many affluent neighborhoods, which suffered heavily in 1991 wildfires; several major parks and Skyline Blvd. lie E above the city. A 1989 earthquake badly damaged Downtown, collapsing part of the Nimitz Freeway (I-880). The Metropolitan Oakland International Airport lies to the S, on Bay Farm I. Oakland is noted as the birthplace of both the Hell's Angels and the Black Panther Party. **2.** borough, pop. 11,997, Bergen Co., NE New Jersey, in the Ramapo Mts. and on the Ramapo R., 10 mi/16 km NW of Paterson. Settled in the early 18th century, it is in an area filled with small lakes, near Ramapo Mountain State Forest. Primarily residential, it has a growing commercial component; Interstate 287 is under construction through the borough. **3.** educational, cultural, and medical center of Pittsburgh, Pennsylvania, between the HILL and SQUIRREL HILL, 3 mi/5 km E of the Golden Triangle. It is home to the University of Pittsburgh, Carnegie-Mellon University, Carlow College, Carnegie Institute, Carnegie Library, University Health Center, and the residential developments of SCHENLEY FARMS and OAKLAND SQUARE. A wealthy residential community annexed by Pittsburgh in 1867, Oakland served as the vehicle by which steel magnate Andrew Carnegie and developer Franklin Nicola hoped to rebuild the "Smoky City" in accordance with the principles of the City Beautiful movement. Carnegie's efforts attracted other business leaders, who built mansions and endowed institutions here. Nicola divided the center of Oakland into four quarters: residential, educational, monumental, and social.

Oakland City city, pop. 2810, Gibson Co., SW Indiana, 28 mi/45 km NE of Evansville and 12 mi/19 km ESE of Princeton. In a coal mining and grain farming area, it is the seat of Oakland City College (1885).

Oakland County 875 sq mi/2266 sq km, pop. 1,083,592, in SE Michigan, drained by the R. Rouge and the Shiawassee, Clinton, and Huron rivers. Its seat is PONTIAC. There is manufacturing at Pontiac, Royal Oak, and Ferndale. Detroit's largely affluent N suburbs and many business complexes, notably housing research and technology companies, occupy the county's SE section. Many resorts are situated on its numerous small lakes. The rural portions of the county have apple, cherry, and peach orchards, and turn out field crops, livestock, poultry, and dairy products.

Oakland Park city, pop. 26,326, Broward Co., SE Florida, a suburb on the NW side of Fort Lauderdale. A bedroom community, it also houses packing facilities for vegetables grown on local truck farms.

Oakland Square residential development in the OAKLAND section of Pittsburgh, Pennsylvania, above Junction Hollow. Two-family wooden and brick homes built here in 1885 now house a largely Italian community. Artist Andy Warhol was born here.

Oak Lawn village, pop. 56,182, Cook Co., NE Illinois, immediately SW of Chicago, 12 mi/19 km SW of the Loop. The population of this residential suburb has risen dramatically over the past few decades.

Oakmont borough, pop. 6961, Allegheny Co., SW Pennsylvania, on the Allegheny R., 8 mi/13 km NE of downtown Pittsburgh. An industrial (pharmaceuticals, metal and food products) and residential suburb, it is noted as the scene of numerous golf tournaments.

Oak Park **1.** village, pop. 53,648, Cook Co., NE Illinois, a suburb immediately W of Chicago and 9 mi/14 km W of the Loop. A middle-class residential community, it is known as the site of numerous buildings designed by Frank Lloyd Wright, who lived here for many years. These include Unity Temple, his first public building, and 24 other structures within a large architectural National Historic District. Settled in 1833, the village became an important stopping place for Chicago-bound farmers. Situated at the junction of three different train lines, Oak Park developed rapidly into a railroad suburb after the Chicago fire of 1871. Emmanuel Bible College (1941) is here. Oak Park is the birthplace of the writers Ernest Hemingway (1899) and Kenneth Fearing (1902). **2.** city, pop. 30,462, Oakland Co., SE Michigan, 9 mi/14 km NW of Detroit. Since 1950, this largely affluent residential suburb has grown rapidly. It produces tools and dies, auto parts, canvas products, abrasives, and wire.

Oak Ridge city, pop. 27,310, Anderson and Roane counties, E Tennessee, 17 mi/27 km NW of Knoxville, on the Clinch

R., just SE of WALDEN RIDGE. It was built in great secrecy by the Army Corps of Engineers in 1942 to house personnel of the Clinton Engineer Works (CLINTON is 7 mi/11 km NE), part of the atom bomb–making Manhattan Project. From 1949 the area, previously restricted, was opened for private development. The economy still depends primarily on nuclear energy research (the Oak Ridge National Laboratory) and production. Related industries produce radioactive pharmaceuticals, electronic instrumentation, and machines and tools. The laboratory's graphite reactor, the world's oldest nuclear plant, taken out of operation in 1963, is one of a number of visitor sites.

Oakton unincorporated community, pop. 24,610, Fairfax Co., N Virginia, 10 mi/16 km W of Washington, D.C., and just N of Fairfax, on Interstate 66. It is a residential suburb.

Oakville **1.** see under WATERTOWN, Connecticut. **2.** unincorporated community, pop. 31,750, St. Louis Co., EC Missouri, on the Mississippi R., 12 mi/19 km SSW of downtown St. Louis, a growing residential suburb. **3.** town, pop. 114,670, Halton Regional Municipality, S Ontario, on Bronte Creek and the W end of L. Ontario, 22 mi/35 km SW of Toronto and adjacent (SW) to Mississauga. White settlement accompanied the establishment of shipyards here in 1830. Incorporated as a town in 1857, the community was consolidated with the township of Trafalgar in 1962, and is today a fast-growing industrial port and residential suburb. One of Canada's largest (Ford) automobile plants is here; other industries make glass, chemicals, petroleum and rubber products, and electrical machinery. The Canadian Open golf championship is held at the Glen Abbey course. Mazo de la Roche's JALNA saga is set in the area.

Oberlin city, pop. 8191, Lorain Co., NC Ohio, 7 mi/11 km SW of Elyria. It is situated in a dairy, poultry, and truck farming region. The life of the city revolves around Oberlin College, founded in 1833 as the first coeducational liberal arts college in the world, and especially noted for its conservatory of music. Oberlin was an antislavery center before the Civil War and an important station on the Underground Railroad. It has also been a base for reform and religious movements, including temperance, woman suffrage, and evangelism.

Obey River see under DALE HOLLOW L., Tennessee.

Obion River 50 mi/80 km long, in W Tennessee. It is formed in Obion Co., 7 mi/11 km ENE of the town of **Obion** (pop. 1241) by the confluence of **North Fork,** 45 mi/72 km long, and **South Fork,** 55 mi/89 km long, and flows SW past Obion to the Mississippi R. at Hales Point. It receives the FORKED DEER R. at Moss I., just before entering the Mississippi. The South Fork receives the 50 mi/80 km–long **Middle Fork,** which rises near PARIS, in Henry Co., 7 mi/11 km SE of its confluence with the North Fork. Two mi/3 km E of the confluence it receives (from the S) the 50 mi/80 km–long **Rutherford Fork,** which rises near the Carroll-Henderson county line and passes NE of Milan and past Rutherford, once Davy Crockett's home.

Ocala city, pop. 42,045, seat of Marion Co., NC Florida, 35 mi/56 km SSE of Gainesville. Named for a nearby Indian village, it grew around the Seminole War post of Fort King (1827). Today it is in a thoroughbred raising, citrus producing, and truck farming region that also has phosphate mines and produces lumber. Its industries pack fruit, vegetables, nuts, tobacco, and cotton; produce fertilizer; process dairy products, limestone, and phosphate; fabricate metal; and manufacture wood products, boxes, mobile homes, fire trucks, sewer pipe, and clothing. In an area of abundant lakes and streams, with Silver Springs just E and the 383,000-ac/155,000-ha, sand pine–dominated **Ocala National Forest** some 8 mi/13 km E, Ocala is a popular year-round resort. Central Florida Community College (1957) is here.

Occoquan Creek see under BULL RUN, Virginia.

Oceana Naval Air Station: see under VIRGINIA BEACH, Virginia.

Ocean Beach oceanside section of SAN DIEGO, California, S of Mission Bay, on the Point LOMA peninsula, 5 mi/8 km WNW of Downtown. Early (1910) efforts at creating a wealthy seaside resort here collapsed with the Depression; the area's collection of bungalows and Mission-style houses became home to middle-class families, and by the 1960s this self-contained community had developed a bohemian diversity.

Ocean City **1.** town, pop. 5146, Worcester Co., SE Maryland, the E terminus of US 50, on an Atlantic barrier beach just N of ASSATEAGUE I., 28 mi/45 km E of Salisbury. Ocean City Inlet, just S, connects ASSAWOMAN and SINEPUXENT bays with the ocean. Maryland's largest ocean resort developed after the railroad reached the area in 1878. The town is a seafood shipping point, and is noted for its marlin fishing, water sports, boardwalk, and amusement district. **2.** city, pop. 15,512, Cape May Co., SE New Jersey, on the 8 mi/13 km–long Peck Beach peninsula, a barrier island between the Atlantic Ocean and Great Egg Harbor Bay, 10 mi/16 km SW of Atlantic City. Established as a summer resort by Christian ministers in 1879, it became a fashionable family beach community. Ocean City has a boardwalk with such features as the Music Pier, an entertainment center, and Wonderland Pier, with amusement facilities including a Ferris wheel.

Ocean County 641 sq mi/1660 sq km, pop. 433,203, in E New Jersey. It includes LONG BEACH ISLAND and the ISLAND BEACH peninsula, enclosing BARNEGAT BAY (N) and Little Egg Harbor (S). Its seat is TOMS RIVER. The county's long coast has some of the state's most popular resorts. Fishing and shellfishing have some economic importance. Inland sections are largely agricultural, producing truck crops, apples and other fruits, dairy products, and poultry. A portion of the county is in the PINE BARRENS. There is some manufacturing, particularly around the largest communities, Toms River, LAKEHURST, and LAKEWOOD.

Ocean Grove see under NEPTUNE, New Jersey.

Ocean Hill see under BROWNSVILLE, New York.

Ocean Park **1.** see under SANTA MONICA, California. **2.** see under CONDADO, San Juan, Puerto Rico.

Oceanside **1.** city, pop. 128,398, San Diego Co., SW California, 34 mi/55 km NNW of San Diego, on the Pacific Ocean. Primarily a fast-growing middle-class residential community, it is also a beach and fishing resort. Adjoining (N) is 125,000-ac/51,000-ha Camp Pendleton, a Marine Corps amphibious training base; Oceanside has been called "Marine Town, U.S.A," and is a trade center for the base. Pendleton contains huge mountain (the Santa Margaritas) and forest reserves and the SAN ONOFRE State Beach. Incorporated in 1888, Oceanside prospered as a hub on the Santa Fe Railroad for regional farms, and developed a thriving flower and bulb industry. Electronic and other light manufactures are now also produced. Mira Costa College (1934) is here. Mission San Luis Rey de Francia (1798) is one of the largest of 21 California MISSIONS constructed along EL CAMINO REAL under the supervision of Junipero Serra; a July fiesta draws visitors. **2.** unincorporated village, pop. 32,423, in Hempstead town, Nassau Co., SE New York, on Long Island's South Shore, 5 mi/8 km S of Hempstead. It is primarily residential but also a summer resort.

Ocean Springs city, pop. 14,658, Jackson Co., SE Mississippi, a resort on the E side of Biloxi Bay. It developed around the site of Old Biloxi, where Fort Maurepas, the first permanent European settlement in the lower Mississippi Valley, was established by the French in 1699. It was named in 1854 by Dr. George Austin, who established a sanitarium here. Primarily a fishing village until the 1880s, it then began to become a popular Gulf Coast resort. A number of noted painters have made it an artists' colony today.

Ocheyedan Mound hill, highest point in Iowa (1670 ft/509 m), in Osceola Co., in the NW part of the state, 5 mi/8 km NE of Sibley. It is a kame rising 170 ft/52 m above the surrounding flat plain. Its name is from the Siouan for "spot where they weep," because of its use as a place for mourning.

Ochlockonee River 150 mi/240 km long, in Georgia and Florida. It rises SE of Albany, in SW Georgia, and flows generally SSE into NW Florida W of Tallahassee, then through the Apalachicola National Forest and into the W end of APALACHEE BAY of the Gulf of Mexico.

Ochoco Mountains westernmost spur of the BLUE Mts., in C Oregon, trending generally E–W for 50 mi/80 km, NE of Prineville. The range is largely within 959,000-ac/388,000-ha (1500–sq mi/3880–sq km) **Ochoco National Forest.** Cinnabar was once mined in the Ochocos; the area is now used for sheep and cattle ranching, timbering, rockhounding, and outdoor recreation.

Ocmulgee National Monument see under MACON, Georgia.

Ocmulgee River 255 mi/411 km long, in C Georgia. It flows SSE from Jackson L., 40 mi/64 km SE of Atlanta. MACON is its head of navigation, at the Fall Line. Continuing S, it passes Warner Robins, then turns gradually SE, joining the OCONEE R. to form the ALTAMAHA R.

Ocoee city, pop. 12,778, Orange Co., C Florida, 10 mi/16 km W of Orlando. Close to Orlando's attractions and just E of L. Apopka, it is a resort and residential community. Local citrus fruits and vegetables are shipped from the city.

Oconee County 629 sq mi/1629 sq km, pop. 57,494, in extreme NW South Carolina, in the Blue Ridge Mts., bounded by North Carolina (N) and by the Chattooga R. (NW) and Tugaloo R. (SW), along the Georgia line. Its seat is Walhalla (town, pop. 3755). In the mid 18th century, the area was a center of the Regulator movement, which sought to bring law and order to the back country. The heavily wooded NW section is today a unit of the Sumter National Forest. Mountainous, with abundant lakes and rivers, Oconee Co. is a popular vacationing area and has a number of retirement communities. Timber, cotton, corn, and wheat are produced. The Oconee nuclear power plant (1973), along L. Keowee NE of Seneca, is also a factor in the economy.

Oconee River 280 mi/450 km long, in E Georgia. It rises NE of Gainesville and flows SSE past Athens and through the 109,000-ac/44,200-ha **Oconee National Forest.** In the forest it enters 19,000-ac/7700-ha **L. Oconee,** formed by a dam E of Eatonton, followed by 15,000-ac/6100-ha L. Sinclair, formed by a dam NNE of Milledgeville, the river's head of navigation. It then flows SSE past Dublin to its confluence with the OCMULGEE R., 7 mi/11 km NNE of Hazlehurst, forming the ALTAMAHA R.

Oconomowoc city, pop. 10,993, Waukesha Co., SE Wisconsin, on the Oconomowoc R. and Lac La Belle, 30 mi/48 km W of Milwaukee. In an area of many lakes and mineral springs, it has long been a popular resort. Honey, vegetables, cheese, and other dairy items are processed here. Among other industries are brewing and the manufacture of boats and machine tools.

Ocracoke Island OUTER BANKS barrier island in Hyde Co., E North Carolina, between Pamlico Sound (NW) and the Atlantic Ocean (SE), just SW of Cape HATTERAS. The 12 mi/19 km–long island has an area of 9 sq mi/23 sq km. The village of Ocracoke, at the SW end, was an active port before the Civil War. Fishing and tourism are important on this unit of the Cape Hatteras National Seashore. The pirate Edward Teach (Blackbeard) was killed here (1718) at Teach's Hole, near the village.

Odenton unincorporated community, pop. 12,833, Anne Arundel Co., C Maryland, 14 mi/23 km NW of Annapolis and 5 mi/8 km E of Fort Meade. It is largely residential.

Odessa **1.** town, pop. 303, New Castle Co., NC Delaware, 3 mi/5 km E of MIDDLETOWN. A toll bridge on Appoquinimink Creek gave Cantwell's Bridge, as it was known, importance in the grain trade until the 1850s, when a railroad was built through Middletown. Cantwell's Bridge was renamed after the Ukrainian grain port in a vain attempt to lure business back. Today Odessa draws on its history as an 18th-century Quaker settlement to attract tourism. **2.** city, pop. 89,699, seat of Ector Co., also in Midland Co., SW Texas, 20 mi/32 km SW of its sister city, MIDLAND. Founded in 1881 in the PERMIAN BASIN, it was a livestock shipping point on the Texas & Pacific Railroad until oil was discovered in 1926. It then expanded rapidly into a processing and distribution point, with huge petrochemical plants. It is the seat of Odessa College (1946) and the University of Texas of the Permian Basin (1969). A Shakespeare Festival is held annually. **West Odessa** (unincorporated, pop. 16,568) is a growing suburb.

O'Fallon **1.** city, pop. 16,073, St. Clair Co., SW Illinois, 15 mi/24 km E of East St. Louis. This residential suburb of St. Louis, Missouri, developed around nearby coal mines. Scott Air Force Base is 4 mi/6 km SE of the city. **2.** city, pop. 18,698, St. Charles Co., EC Missouri, 30 mi/48 km NW of downtown St. Louis. On Interstate 70, it is a trade and distribution center for a varied agricultural region.

Offutt Air Force Base military installation just outside BELLEVUE, Nebraska, some 8 mi/13 km SSE of Omaha. Established as the Army's Fort Crook (1896), it became an air facility in the early 20th century and was renamed in 1924. After World War II, it became the headquarters of the Strategic Air Command (SAC). Here SAC maintained an underground command post, controlling missiles stored in underground silos around the US and keeping bombers in the air on constant alert. An integral part of the local economy, the base had a 1990 pop. of 10,883, which has since diminished.

Ogallala city, pop. 5095, seat of Keith Co., W Nebraska, on the South Platte R., 52 mi/83 km W of North Platte. After the coming of the Union Pacific Railroad (1867), Ogallala was a major cattle shipping depot. The end of the trail for livestock drives from Texas, it developed a reputation as a rowdy cow town. It is now a processing and shipping point for agricultural producers and has some light manufacturing and tourism.

Ogallala Aquifer see under AQUIFER.

Ogden city, pop. 63,909, seat of Weber Co., N Utah, on the Weber and Ogden rivers just E of their junction, 30 mi/48 km N of Salt Lake City. The oldest continuous white community in Utah, it was a trading post before Mormon settlement in 1847. Ogden became the main Utah rail junction shortly after the transcontinental railway was completed in 1869. It remains the main rail center between the Rocky Mts. and the West Coast, served by five lines. A military supply center, it is 6 mi/10 km N of Hill Air Force Base, has the Ogden Defense Depot on its NW edge, and has other military depots and an aerospace industry, all of which are major employers. There are also stockyards and factories producing building materials, chemicals, furniture, processed food from local farms, clothing, batteries, and stone, clay, and glass items. Ogden is the seat of Weber State College (1889). Tourism is important, with visitors exploring museums, theaters, and Fort Buenaventura State Park. There are also skiing facilities to the N and E.

Ogdensburg city, pop. 13,521, St. Lawrence Co., N New York, on the St. Lawrence R., at the mouth of the Oswegatchie R., and linked to Ontario by the Ogdensburg-Prescott International Bridge. It was a fort and trading post, occupied alternately by the French and British until the 1790s and recaptured briefly by the British during the War of 1812. On Aug. 17–18, 1940, President F.D. Roosevelt and Prime Minister W.L. Mackenzie King created the Permanent Joint Board of Defense between the US and Canada in the Ogdensburg Declaration. The city is a leading distributor of coal, oil, and gas. Industries manufacture paper, wood and aluminum products, and office equipment and supplies. Ogdensburg is home to Mater Dei (1960) and Wadhams Hall (1924) colleges and the Frederic Remington Art Museum.

Ogeechee River 250 mi/400 km long, in E Georgia, it rises E of Greensboro and flows generally SE through forested coastal plain to the Atlantic Ocean at Ossabaw Sound, 15 mi/24 km S of Savannah.

Ogilvie Mountains range N of Dawson, in the NW Yukon Territory. Rising to c.7750 ft/2360 m, the mountains separate the Yukon Plateau (S) from the Porcupine Plateau (N). The DEMPSTER HIGHWAY goes through the Ogilvies at North Fork Pass (4229 ft/1289 m), 50 mi/80 km NE of Dawson.

Oglesby city, pop. 3619, La Salle Co., NC Illinois, 3 mi/5 km SE of La Salle, on the Vermilion R. A longtime river port noted as a cement shipper, it is the seat of Illinois Valley Community College (1966).

Oglethorpe, Mount 3290 ft/1003 m, at the S end of the BLUE RIDGE, in N Georgia, near Jasper. In 1929 its name was changed from Grassy Mt. as a tribute to General James E. Oglethorpe, founder of Georgia. The original S terminus of the APPALACHIAN TRAIL, it was abandoned in favor of SPRINGER Mt. because of nearby industrial development.

Ogunquit town, pop. 976, York Co., SW Maine. It is on the Gulf of Maine, 30 mi/48 km SSW of Portland. A former Abnaki campground, the settlement is a summer resort with a noted playhouse and art colony where many distinguished painters have worked.

O'Hare International Airport in Chicago, Illinois, 15 mi/24 km NW of the Loop, and immediately S of Des Plaines. The airline hub of the Midwest, it is the busiest airport in the world.

Ohio state of the NC US, a Great Lakes state and generally considered the easternmost state of the MIDDLE WEST; 1990 pop. 10,847,115 (100.5% of 1980; rank: 7th); area 44,828 sq mi/116,105 sq km (rank: 34th); admitted to Union 1803 (17th). Capital and most populous city: COLUMBUS. Other leading cities: CLEVELAND, CINCINNATI, TOLEDO, AKRON, DAYTON. Ohio is bordered E by Pennsylvania; E and SE by West Virginia, with the OHIO R. forming the boundary; SW by Kentucky, across the Ohio R.; W by Indiana; and NW by Michigan's Lower Peninsula. On the N is L. ERIE. The SE third of the state lies on the W of the APPALACHIAN (or Allegheny) Plateau. Most of this area is unglaciated, and is characterized by low but steep-sided hills and the valleys of many small rivers; the SCIOTO and the MUSKINGUM flow through it from the NW to the Ohio. The rest of the state is part of the vast central lowland area of the US. Along the N is a strip of plain along L. Erie; the MAUMEE, SANDUSKY, and CUYAHOGA rivers flow N or NE into the lake. The rest of C and SW Ohio is rolling glaciated (largely TILL-covered) plain, rising to 1550 ft/472 m at Campbell Hill (the state's high point), NW of Columbus. The Miami and Olentangy-Scioto river systems drain this area to the S. Before white settlement, Ohio was almost entirely covered by hardwood forest, the woods of which were used throughout the state's industrial development (one of the most common, the buckeye, gave the state and its people a nickname). It is today largely open farmland, thought of as the E section of the CORN BELT. Many of the best-known MOUND BUILDER remains are in the state, which has been inhabited for at least 7000 years; the ADENA, HOPEWELL, FORT ANCIENT, SERPENT MOUND, and MOUND CITY GROUP sites are esp. well known. Ohio has been a crossroads, on lake (N) and river (S and E), since before Europeans arrived; among the peoples encountered here by white explorers and settlers were the Erie, Miami, Shawnee, Ottawa, and Wyandot. From the 17th century until 1763, when NEW FRANCE fell, the British and French struggled for control in the area, forming alliances with various tribes. In the American Revolution, reacting to the incursions of American frontiersmen, most Indians sided with the British, and their opposition to US control (after 1783) did not end until after the 1794 battle of FALLEN TIMBERS. Once the British had ceded Ohio, American surveyors began to lay out settlements. In 1787 the area became part of the NORTHWEST TERRITORY; the claims of Eastern states on land here were surrendered to the new central government, although Connecticut (the WESTERN RESERVE) and Virginia (the VIRGINIA MILITARY DISTRICT) reserved lands to compensate their soldiers or those who had lost property to British action. Ohio became a separate territory in 1798; its name derives ultimately from an Iroquoian name ("fine river") for the ALLEGHENY, one of the Ohio River's headwaters (in New York). Early settlement followed the Ohio, along which MARIETTA and Cincinnati were soon prominent. By the late 1790s, the sites of Cleveland (in the Western Reserve), Dayton, and CHILLICOTHE had also been settled. During the War of 1812, important engagements occurred at FORT MEIGS, near Toledo, and PUT-IN-BAY, in L. Erie; after the war, heavy settlement ("Ohio fever") began, spurred esp. by hard conditions in New England. In the 1820s, the completion of the ERIE CANAL brought increased commerce to the Great Lakes, causing growth in Cleveland, ASHTABULA, Toledo, and other lakefront communities. In the same period extension of the NATIONAL ROAD through C Ohio, and the building of canals connecting L. Erie and the Ohio R., spurred growth throughout the state. In the 1850s the boom in railroad building further linked the state with the East and with Chicago and the growing Great Lakes region. Although settled as an essentially agricultural territory, Ohio soon after statehood began to industrialize. It has large coal deposits (esp. in the SE), along with iron, sand, clay, and other basic materials, and soon had ironmaking, glass, ceramic, and wood-based manufactures. These were important in the Civil War, but it was after the war, when the iron ranges of Minnesota and Michigan's Upper Peninsula became accessible via the lakes, and the size of the coal reserves in the Ohio-Pennsylvania region was recognized, that Ohio's position resulted in its growth into an industrial giant. YOUNGSTOWN, WARREN, and the MAHONING Valley became a key part of the steel complex around Pittsburgh. Cleveland soon followed, and in the same period also became home to the nascent American oil industry. Akron soon became the "rubber capital," and CANTON, STEUBENVILLE, and other steel, glass, and pottery producing cities in the NE became archetypal "smokestack" communities. In the SW, Dayton and HAMILTON joined the boom, although Cincinnati never recovered its pre–Civil War eminence. The growth from the 1900s of the automobile industry, based in nearby Detroit, involved Ohio deeply; the state quickly became, and has remained, a major maker of auto parts and assembler of vehicles. All this development made Ohio central to the US economy, a position it retains despite the flight of much of its heavy industrial base since World War II. It is the quintessential RUST BELT state, today struggling with pollution and the need to diversify. In recent decades the coal industry has thrived in the SE (but the amount of strip mining involved has caused controversy). That Columbus is now Ohio's largest city is suggestive; the capital's life is based on state government, Ohio State University, research facilities, corporate offices, and very little manufacturing. Ohio is also a leading agricultural state, however. Corn and other field crops, and the hogs and cattle they feed, are important, as are dairy goods. In the Ohio Valley, early farmers were famously aided by the efforts of Johnny Appleseed, and orcharding has been important. The state is noted for its educational centers, including many small-college communities like OBERLIN, YELLOW SPRINGS, WOOSTER, WILBERFORCE, and GAMBIER. Early New England settlers were joined here by Germans (esp. in Cincinnati) in the 1840s and 1850s, and by workers from all over Europe after the Civil War, as industry demanded manpower. In the 20th century, Southern blacks and Appalachian whites in large numbers joined an already diverse pop.

Ohio City also, **Near West Side** neighborhood in Cleveland, Ohio, W of Downtown, on the W side of the Cuyahoga R. Originally a separate city, it was annexed by Cleveland in 1854. Home to immigrants, especially Irish and Hungarians, it blended with the FLATS, to the E. During World War II, an influx of Puerto Ricans and Appalachian migrants replaced the earlier Europeans. More recently, Indochinese refugees have moved into the area.

Ohio River 981 mi/1579 km long, in Pennsylvania, West Virginia, Ohio, Kentucky, Indiana, and Illinois. The major E tributary of the Mississippi R., it is formed at the GOLDEN TRIANGLE, in downtown Pittsburgh, by the junction of the Allegheny and Monongahela rivers. It swings NW to a junction with the BEAVER R., S of Beaver Falls, then WSW to form the West Virginia–Ohio border, turning near East Liverpool, Ohio, to the SSW, along the W of West Virginia's PANHANDLE. In this industrial region it passes Steubenville, Ohio, and Wheeling and New Martinsville, West Virginia. It then swings SW to Marietta, Ohio, where the MUSKINGUM R. joins it from the NW; to Parkersburg, West Virginia, where the Little Kanawha R. joins from the SE; to Point Pleasant, West Virginia (across from Gallipolis, Ohio), where the KANAWHA R. joins it from the SE; and to Huntington, West Virginia. For the rest of its course, which takes it WNW, then WSW in a series of wide bends, Kentucky is on its S. The TUG FORK R. joins it from the S at the Kentucky border, and it passes Ashland, Kentucky, then Portsmouth, Ohio, where the SCIOTO R. and the 1832 **Ohio and Erie Canal,** from Cleveland, join it from the N. It continues WNW to Cincinnati, Ohio, the major city on its course below Pittsburgh, where the Great and Little MIAMI rivers join from the N and Kentucky's LICKING R. from the S. Fifteen mi/24 km W of Cincinnati, Ohio gives way to Indiana on the N bank, and the river begins its generally WSW swing, past Louisville, Fort Knox, and Owensboro, Kentucky, and Evansville, Indiana. The WABASH R. joins it from the N at the Illinois border. To the SW, the Ohio receives from the S, within a stretch of some 10 mi/16 km, the waters of its two major tributaries, the CUMBERLAND (E) and TENNESSEE (W), emptying large areas of the S Appalachians. It then passes Paducah, Kentucky, and enters the Mississippi at Cairo, Illinois. La Salle saw the river, whose basin was home to many peoples, including the ancient MOUND BUILDERS, in 1669; the area around its head (Pittsburgh) was fought over by the French and British for a century. After the 1780s, when the new US government opened the NORTHWEST TERRITORY to settlement, and Americans began also to travel to the Mississippi and down it, the Ohio became the country's major westbound artery. From the 1810s it was traveled by steamboat, supplementing flatboat and keelboat trade, and Cincinnati, Louisville (where canals bypassed its only falls in 1830), Paducah, and other cities rose to prominence. Before the Civil War the Ohio was the extension, W of the MASON-DIXON Line, of the boundary between slave states (S) and free states (N), and its booming communities were therefore the scene of continual turbulence and political activism. After the war, the rapidly spreading Midwest rail network took away much of its trade, and the era of the river's centrality in American development was over. It remains a major carrier of (Appalachian) coal, as well as sand, gravel, and other resources; in its upper reaches (Pennsylvania, West Virginia, and SE Ohio), these have also made it a heavily industrial river. Both flooding and pollution have been major problems. Flooding, which reached a disastrous peak in 1937, has been opposed with damming and other works on the river and its tributaries; pollution, considered by an eight-state Sanitation Commission since 1948, has been somewhat abated, and fishing and other recreational uses have increased.

Oil City city, pop. 11,949, Venango Co., NW Pennsylvania, on the Allegheny R. at the mouth of Oil Creek, 70 mi/113 km NNE of Pittsburgh. Founded on the site of a Seneca village, it grew dramatically after Edwin L. Drake struck oil at TITUSVILLE, 12 mi/19 km NNE, in 1859, and became a major oil producing, refining, and shipping center. It has manufactured oilfield equipment, steel, glass, metal products, paints, and gas engines, and is a financial and banking center. Oil City has a branch of Clarion State College.

Oildale unincorporated community, pop. 26,553, Kern Co., SC California, across the Kern R. (N) from Bakersfield. It is an oilfield trade center, with a large tank farm, and a residential suburb.

Oil Patch generically, an oil producing area; specifically, a popular name for areas of Louisiana, Texas, Arkansas, Oklahoma, and neighboring states that have been central to the US oil industry since the beginning of the 20th century. The Oil Patch extends along the continental shelf into the Gulf of Mexico, where in the 1990s there were almost 4000 offshore wells.

Ojai city, pop. 7613, Ventura Co., SW California, in the Ojai Valley, 11 mi/18 km N of Ventura and 60 mi/100 km NW of Los Angeles. Settled in the 1870s in an oilfield area, it is a resort with citrus and avocado groves, and an artists' colony, with a June music festival and an April tennis tournament said to be the oldest in the US. The Thacher School (1888) is a well-known preparatory institution. Ojai was "Shangri-La" in the 1937 film *Lost Horizon.*

Oka parish, pop. 1656, S Québec, 8 mi/13 km W of the I. de Montréal, on the Lac des Deux-Montagnes, at the mouth of the Ottawa R. In 1717 a Sulpician mission was established here for several Indian groups, and the Kanesatake Mohawk reserve now adjoins (W). In the 1880s the large Trappist Abbey of Notre-Dame-du-Lac was established here, and a provincial park is just E. Oka is now primarily a resort; in 1990 expansion onto Kanesatake land caused an armed confrontation and brought international attention to the cause of Québec's Indians.

Okanagan, Lake in S British Columbia, 170 mi/275 km ENE of Vancouver. Seventy mi/113 km N–S and 2–4 mi/3–6 km wide, it is the largest of a number of postglacial lakes in the fertile **Okanagan Valley** region, noted for its fruit production. Long inhabited by the Okanagan (Interior Salish), the area was entered by missionaries c.1840. The largest cities around the lake today are VERNON, at the N end; KELOWNA, on the E shore; and PENTICTON, at the S end. The dry, warm valley and numerous lake beaches have made the area popular with tourists; the lake is also noted as the reported home of "Ogopogo," a creature similar to CADBORO BAY's "Caddie." The **Okanagan R.** (**Okanogan** in the US), 118 mi/190 km long, flows S from the lake, through Skaha and Osoyoos lakes, into N Washington. After forming the W boundary of the Colville Indian Reservation, it joins the COLUMBIA R. near Brewster, 40 mi/64 km W of the Grand Coulee Dam.

Okanogan National Forest 2727 sq mi/7062 sq km, in NE Washington, largely in the E Cascade Range (the Okanagan Range). The 827–sq mi/2143–sq km Pasayten Wilderness lies in the N, extending to the British Columbia border. Smaller units of the forest lie N of the Colville Indian Reservation, extending E to the Columbia R.

O.K. Corral see under TOMBSTONE, Arizona.

Okeechobee city, pop. 4943, seat of Okeechobee Co., SC Florida, 61 mi/98 km NW of West Palm Beach. Two mi/3 km N of the N shore of L. Okeechobee, the city is a trade center for local fish, frogs' legs, and agricultural products. Tourism is also important; it has numerous facilities for lake fishing. The Brighton Seminole Indian Reservation (pop. 524) is 15 mi/24 km SW.

Okeechobee, Lake in SC Florida, at the N edge of the EVERGLADES. The second-largest freshwater lake wholly within the US (after L. Michigan), it covers 730 sq mi/1900 sq m, is roughly circular, and is nowhere more than about 20 ft/6 km deep. There are numerous small islands in the lake, and it receives the Kissimmee R. from the NW. Since the 1930s diking around the S shore has prevented overflow; drainage canals are used for light navigation to the Atlantic Ocean. The drained fertile mucklands on the S shore support major truck and sugar cane industries in such centers as BELLE GLADE and CLEWISTON. The lake is a fishing resort with some commercial fisheries.

Okefenokee Swamp wetland, c.45 mi/72 km N–S and 30 mi/48 km wide, mostly in SE Georgia and partly in NE Florida, covering some 700 sq mi/1800 sq km. One of the largest US freshwater swamps, it is drained by the SAINT MARYS R. E to the Atlantic Ocean and by the SUWANNEE R. SW across Florida to the Gulf of Mexico. A region of water, prairie, hammocks, and forests of gum and cypress trees, it is accessible only by boat or canoe. Noted for its diverse subtropical wildlife and plants, it is the habitat of heavy concentrations of deer, bears, raccoons, alligators, turtles, and lizards. It is especially important as a haven for 200 varieties of birds, including the white ibis and endangered species like the bald eagle and Florida sandhill crane. About 95% of the swamp is a National Wildlife Refuge established in 1937. Okefenokee is also famous as the home of Pogo, Walt Kelly's comic-strip character, and his neighbors. WAYCROSS (N) and Folkston (SE), Georgia, are gateways to the area.

Okemah city, pop. 3085, seat of Okfuskee Co., EC Oklahoma, 65 mi/105 km E of Oklahoma City. Settled in 1902, the city processes petroleum and agricultural products (wheat, cotton, and pecans), and has other light industries. Composer and balladeer Woody Guthrie (1912–67) was born here.

Okemo, Mount peak (3343 ft/1020 m) in the Green Mts., near Ludlow, in SC Vermont. At the heart of a popular ski area, it is in Okemo State Park.

Okemos unincorporated community, pop. 20,216, Ingham Co., SC Michigan, on the Red Cedar R., a suburb 7 mi/11 km E of downtown Lansing.

Oklahoma state of the SC US, usually considered part of the SOUTHWEST; 1990 pop. 3,145,585 (104% of 1980; rank: 28th); area 69,903 sq mi/181,049 sq km (rank: 20th); admitted to Union 1907 (46th). Capital and most populous city: OKLAHOMA CITY. Other leading cities: TULSA, LAWTON, NORMAN. Oklahoma is bordered S by Texas, with the RED R. forming the SE boundary, the Texas Panhandle the rest. On the W, at the extreme of the Oklahoma PANHANDLE, it is bordered by New Mexico. On the N it is bordered by Colorado (in the W section of the Panhandle) and Kansas. On the E are (N–S) Missouri and Arkansas. Most of the state lies in the vast C lowlands of the US, including part of the OSAGE PLAINS. In the extreme SE, dropping to 287 ft/88 m, is a swampy, humid section along the Red R., the N extreme of the Gulf COASTAL PLAIN. To its N are W sections of (S–N) the OUACHITA Mts. and OZARK PLATEAU, which extend E into Arkansas. The Panhandle (W) is part of the GREAT PLAINS, its W two-thirds in the High Plains, rising to 4973 ft/1517 m at BLACK MESA. The land rises gradually from E to W across the 450 mi/720 km–long state; except in the

Ozarks-Ouachitas section in the E, there are few hill sections of note, chiefly the WICHITA and ARBUCKLE mountains (SC). The state is crossed in a generally WNW–ESE direction by long but slow and sometimes even intermittent rivers flowing from the Rocky Mts. or the High Plains into the Mississippi R. basin, including (N–S) the SALT FORK of the Arkansas, CIMARRON, NORTH CANADIAN, CANADIAN, and WASHITA. The ARKANSAS R. itself enters the state in the NE, N of PONCA CITY, and flows SE through the Tulsa area; since 1971 it has been open to ocean shipping as far as CATOOSA, Tulsa's port. The other rivers are used primarily for irrigation, or have in recent decades been dammed to create recreational assets like Eufaula L. and L. TEXOMA. The VERDIGRIS and NEOSHO rivers, entering NE Oklahoma from Kansas and flowing to the Arkansas, have also been dammed, creating the LAKE O' THE CHEROKEES and other reservoirs, and establishing a growing recreational hub. Oklahoma is the US state most associated with Indians; its name is a Choctaw coinage meaning "red people," which in the 1880s came to designate its future capital, and later was used to name the territory and state. When Europeans (Coronado's 1540–41 QUIVIRA expedition) first saw the area, and for centuries afterward, it was inhabited by Plains peoples, including the Apache, Kiowa, and Comanche. Coming under US control in the 1803 LOUISIANA PURCHASE, it began to be crossed by users of the SANTA FE TRAIL in the 1820s; the hazardous Cimarron Cutoff crossed the Panhandle. In the same period, the US government decided to expel the Creek, Choctaw, Cherokee, Chickasaw, and Seminole from their Southeastern homes, and selected E Oklahoma for their exile, promising that they would be undisturbed there. This process, carried out in part by forcing the Cherokee along the TRAIL OF TEARS, created the INDIAN TERRITORY. Some of the tribes were slaveholders, and sympathetic with the South, and at the end of the Civil War much land was removed from them and designated for the relocation of other Indians from all over the West. In the same period, the CHISHOLM TRAIL and other cattle routes traversed C Oklahoma, and the expansion of white settlement throughout the West gradually increased pressure for the opening of the territory, esp. the "Unassigned Lands" at its C, to homesteaders. With "Boomers" just outside the borders promoting the idea, April 22, 1889 was set for what became the famous Oklahoma Land Run. (Some "Sooners" crossed the border early, obtaining choice locations.) In a single day, Oklahoma City, Norman, STILLWATER, and other towns were established. Two entities, the Oklahoma Territory (W, including the Panhandle) and the Indian Territory (E) soon existed side by side. In 1897, at BARTLESVILLE (NE), the region's first commercial oil well went into operation, initiating what would be Oklahoma's chief 20th-century industry. Before 1907, continued pressure had persuaded the tribes in Indian Territory to surrender communally held lands, accepting allotments and allowing whites to buy from individuals. Today, the only INDIAN RESERVATION in the state is that of the Osage, coextensive with OSAGE Co. Limited self-government by other tribes is recognized in TRIBAL JURISDICTION STATISTICAL AREAS; about 8% of Oklahomans are Indians. The state is a major producer and refiner of oil and gas, and raises beef and dairy cattle, along with cotton, wheat, peanuts, and other crops. Tulsa and Oklahoma City are both deeply involved in the oil business, but have also diversified into high-tech and other manufacturing and service industries. Bartlesville, PONCA CITY, ANADARKO, and ARDMORE are among other oil centers. Oil and gas wells are found in most parts of the state, and coal mining is important in the Ozark-Ouachitas area. The University of Oklahoma is central to the life of Norman; Oklahoma State University is at Stillwater. FORT SILL, near Lawton (SW), has been an important Army training center, and there is an ammunition plant near MCALESTER (SE). Tourism and recreation focus largely on rivers and lakes and on such Indian culture centers as TAHLEQUA. Will Rogers, the famous humorist born in OOLOGAH in 1879, is buried in CLAREMORE.

Oklahoma City city and state capital, pop. 444,719, seat of Oklahoma Co. (pop. 599,611), C Oklahoma, on the NORTH CANADIAN R. The state's most populous city, it is the center of a six-county (including Canadian, CLEVELAND, Logan, McClain, Oklahoma, and Pottawatomie) metropolitan area with a pop. of 958,839. It is also, since 1961 expansion, one of the largest (636 sq mi/1646 sq km) US cities, extending SW beyond the CANADIAN R., and encloses several small municipalities, including BETHANY, NICHOLS HILLS, THE VILLAGE, and WARR ACRES. The city was established in the famous "Land Rush" of 1889, when on April 22, as a site on the Red Plains in the "Unassigned Lands" of INDIAN TERRITORY, it acquired 10,000 residents by nightfall. Incorporated in 1890, it became the state capital in 1910 (succeeding GUTHRIE). It was largely a cattle and meatpacking center before 1928, when it was discovered to be sitting on an oilfield; thousands of wells sprang up, including the well-known one on the Capitol grounds. Today, still a cattle and grain market, it is also a manufacturer of aircraft and aerospace equipment, computers and other electronic equipment, foods, petroleum products, and a variety of other goods. The city is also a major medical center, with a number of noted hospitals. Tinker Air Force Base, on the SE side, has been important to the economy. A University of Oklahoma campus (1900), Oklahoma City University (1904), and Oklahoma Christian University (1950) are among local institutions. The National Cowboy Hall of Fame, National Softball Hall of Fame, Western Heritage Center, and a large zoo draw visitors, and the city has over 70 parks.

Okmulgee city, pop. 13,441, seat of Okmulgee Co., EC Oklahoma, 37 mi/59 km S of Tulsa. Capital (1868–1907) of the Creek Nation, it is the site of an annual Creek Nation Festival, and a council house (1878) still used for tribal meetings. Oil was discovered nearby in 1904, bringing on a boom. Oil and natural gas wells dot the area, and the city is a refining center. Agricultural and meat products are processed, and oilfield equipment, glass, and furniture are manufactured.

Okolona **1.** unincorporated community, pop. 18,902, Jefferson Co., N Kentucky, 8 mi/13 km SSE of Louisville, of which it is a largely residential suburb. **2.** city, pop. 3267, co-seat (with Houston) of Chickasaw Co., NE Mississippi, 17 mi/27 km S of Tupelo. This farming, lumbering, and dairying center was fought over repeatedly in the Civil War; Nathan Bedford Forrest won a victory here in Feb. 1864, but Federal troops later burned Okolona twice.

Olana mansion on the E bank of the Hudson R., just SW of the city of HUDSON, in Columbia Co., SE New York. On a peak that commands spectacular views of the river and the Catskill Mts. (W), it was built in 1870–76 by the Hudson River School painter Frederic Church (1826–1900). Modified after Church visited the Middle East, it has pointed arches, fanciful tilework, and a tall bell tower; it is now a state historic site.

Olathe city, pop. 63,352, seat of Johnson Co., NE Kansas, 20 mi/32 km SW of downtown Kansas City. It was established in the 1850s, after the Shawnee relinquished title to the land, and given the Shawnee name for "beautiful." Capital of the Kansas Territory after 1858, it was largely destroyed by William Quantrill's Confederate raiders in 1861, and was rebuilt after the Civil War. The city continues to be a processing and shipping point for produce and livestock, and also manufactures leather goods, chemicals, farm machinery, plastics, and electronics systems. Mid-America Nazarene College (1966) is here.

Old Baldy lighthouse: see under Cape FEAR, North Carolina.

Old Bethpage see under BETHPAGE, New York.

Old Bridge township, pop. 56,475, Middlesex Co., E New Jersey, 7 mi/11 km SE of New Brunswick. Established by English, Scottish, and French Huguenot settlers, it was separated from South Amboy in 1869. Its Laurence Harbor section (pop. 6361) on Raritan Bay was a popular beachfront community in the 1920s. The township had grain and lumber mills in the 19th century, and was primarily agricultural until the 1950s. Called Old Bridge since 1976, it grew rapidly in the 1980s into a middle-class residential area, with some surviving farmland. CHEESEQUAKE STATE PARK is here.

Old Brookville village, pop. 1823, in Oyster Bay town, Nassau Co., SE New York, on Long Island's North Shore, 4 mi/6 km SE of Glen Cove. The C. W. Post Center of Long Island University is here; its campus is the former estate of heiress Marjorie Merriweather Post.

Old City historic neighborhood in CENTER CITY, Philadelphia, Pennsylvania, on the Delaware R. between NORTHERN LIBERTIES and SOCIETY HILL. One of the city's first residential areas, it boasts many of its earliest houses and religious structures. ELFRETH'S ALLEY is here; the BENJAMIN FRANKLIN BRIDGE and Independence National Historic Park are nearby. Many of the brick and cast-iron buildings have been restored in what is now a wealthy residential enclave.

Old Crow see under PORCUPINE R., Yukon Territory.

Old Faithful **1.** see under CALISTOGA, California. **2.** see under YELLOWSTONE NATIONAL PARK, Wyoming.

Old Field or, **Old Fields** element in locality names, especially in the East, that often indicates land once farmed by Indians, or land on which settlers established and then abandoned farms. Indian Old Fields, in Hardy Co., West Virginia, and Old Field Point, near Stony Brook, Long Island, New York, are examples of such names.

Old Lyme town, pop. 6535, New London Co., Connecticut, at the mouth of the Connecticut R., on the E bank, 10 mi/16 km ESE of New London. A resort and exurban town noted for many old homes of architectural interest, it includes the villages of South Lyme, Laysville, and Black Hall. The town of LYME is adjacent (N).

Old Man of the Mountain see under FRANCONIA NOTCH, New Hampshire.

Old North Church historic site in the NORTH END, Boston, Massachusetts. Built in 1723, it is the oldest Boston church still in use. It is particularly famous for its steeple, from which Sexton Robert Newman hung two lanterns on April 18, 1775, alerting Paul Revere (watching from CHARLESTOWN) and others to British plans to advance on CONCORD the next day.

Old Northwest see under NORTHWEST TERRITORY.

Old Oraibi see ORAIBI, Arizona.

Old Orchard Beach town, pop. 7789, York Co., SW Maine. It is named for its beach, on the Atlantic Ocean, extending 5 mi/8 km from the Saco R. to the Scarborough R., SSW of Portland. The city of SACO adjoins to the W. Old Orchard Beach is a popular recreation and amusement area, attracting so many Canadian visitors it has been called "Québec's Riviera." Old Orchard Pier, now mostly demolished, was for many years noted for its promenade and dance hall.

Old Point Comfort see under FORT MONROE, Virginia.

Olds town, pop. 5542, SC Alberta, 55 mi/89 km N of Calgary. Situated in a fertile agricultural region, it has feed mills, grain elevators, and creameries, as well as oil and natural gas resources. It was founded (1891) after the construction of the Calgary-Edmonton railway. Olds College (1913) is here.

Old Saybrook also called **Saybrook** town, pop. 9552, Middlesex Co., SE Connecticut, on Long Island Sound and the W bank of the Connecticut R., opposite OLD LYME and 28 mi/45 km E of New Haven. A resort town, it includes Fenwick and other coastal villages. On Interstate 95 and with an Amtrak station, it is exurban and has some manufacturing and a fishing industry. Neighboring ESSEX and Deep River were formerly parts of Old Saybrook.

Old South Meeting House historic site in Boston, Massachusetts. Built in 1729 as the Third Congregational Church, it was used for religious and political meetings; here the Sons of Liberty planned the Boston Tea Party in 1773. Replaced as a place of worship by New Old South Church in the Back Bay in 1875, it is now a public monument.

Old Spanish Trail see SPANISH TRAIL.

Old Town **1.** original settlement area and State Historical Park, in SAN DIEGO, California, 3 mi/5 km NNW of the modern Downtown (see NEW TOWN). The Spanish settlement developed here from the 1770s, at the foot of PRESIDIO HILL, on the San Diego R. just SE of MISSION BAY. The 13-ac/5.3-ha park boasts 19th-century houses. The center of San Diego until the 1870s, Old Town is now a tourist magnet. **2.** residential and commercial neighborhood on the NEAR NORTH SIDE of Chicago, Illinois. Once home to those almost wealthy enough to afford the nearby GOLD COAST, in the 1950s and 1960s it became an avant-garde community of artists, beatniks, and hippies. Gentrification followed, turning the area into an expensive enclave of young professionals by the 1980s. Second City Theater improvisation originated here. **3.** city, pop. 8317, Penobscot Co., EC Maine. It is on the Penobscot R., 11 mi/18 km NNE of Bangor. Indian Island, in the river N of the city center, is the site of the Penobscot reservation. Old Town is noted for its fine canoes. Other industries include truck gardening and the manufacture of wood pulp and lumber products. **4.** see under ALBUQUERQUE, New Mexico. **5.** historic neighborhood on the line between the Northwest and Southwest sections of PORTLAND, Oregon, on the W bank of the Willamette R. Part of the 19th-century core of the city, it today boasts a restored commercial stretch of century-old buildings.

Old Westbury village, pop. 3897, in North Hempstead town, Nassau Co., SE New York, in WC Long Island, 3 mi/5 km NE of Mineola. It is an affluent New York suburb, with large estates and horse farms. New York Institute of Technology (1910) and the State University of New York College at Old

Westbury (1966) are here. Old Westbury Gardens is a popular attraction.

Old World Third Street commercial thoroughfare, 0.5 mi/0.8 km, in downtown Milwaukee, Wisconsin, between WISCONSIN AVENUE and Juneau Avenue, W of the Milwaukee R. The business center of the German immigrant community, the street has been revitalized in recent years.

Olean city, pop. 16,946, Cattaraugus Co., W New York, on the Allegheny R., at the mouth of Olean Creek, 60 mi/100 km SSE of Buffalo, near the Pennsylvania line. Settled as a lumber camp in 1804, it was named for the first European child to born here. It served as a point of departure for settlers traveling to the Ohio Valley, and, because of its proximity to Pennsylvania oilfields, developed an oil-based economy. The engineering industry has more recently become dominant. City manufactures include compressors, turbines, and electric components. In June 1972, floodwaters destroyed over 3000 homes.

Olivet city, pop. 1604, Eaton Co., SC Michigan, 16 mi/26 km NE of Battle Creek. In a farming area, it manufactures auto parts. It is home to Olivet College (1844), established by the Abolitionist minister who also founded Oberlin College.

Olivette city, pop. 7573, St. Louis Co., EC Missouri, a residential suburb 11 mi/18 km WNW of downtown St. Louis.

Olmos Park city, pop. 2161, Bexar Co., SC Texas, a residential community entirely surrounded by N SAN ANTONIO.

Olmsted Air Force Base see under MIDDLETOWN, Pennsylvania.

Olmsted County 655 sq mi/1696 sq km, pop. 106,470, in SE Minnesota. Centered around ROCHESTER, the county seat, it is largely agricultural, with dairy products, peas, and corn of prime importance.

Olmsted Falls city, pop. 6741, Cuyahoga Co., N Ohio, on Plum Creek, 14 mi/23 km SW of Cleveland. Machine tools, electrical products, and abrasives are manufactured in this industrial suburb.

Olney **1.** city, pop. 8664, seat of Richland Co., SE Illinois, on US 50, 30 mi/48 km WNW of Vincennes, Indiana. It is the trade center of an agricultural area, with some light manufactures. Olney Central College (1962) is here. The city is noted for its bird sanctuary and for its protected population of white (albino) squirrels, which draw visitors. **2.** unincorporated residential village, pop. 23,019, Montgomery Co., C Maryland, an affluent suburb 17 mi/27 km N of Washington, D.C. **3.** residential neighborhood in Philadelphia, Pennsylvania, immediately E of GERMANTOWN and 6 mi/10 km N of City Hall. It is one of the city's most racially and ethnically diverse working-class areas, housing blacks along with Hispanic and Asian immigrants.

Olustee hamlet in Baker Co., NE Florida, 13 mi/21 km E of Lake City, on the S edge of the OSCEOLA NATIONAL FOREST. About 2.5 mi/4 km E is the site of Florida's largest Civil War battle, in which forces led by Joseph Finnegan repelled an invading Union army on Feb. 20, 1864.

Olvera Street see under EL PUEBLO DE LOS ANGELES, Los Angeles, California.

Olympia city, pop. 33,840, state capital and seat of Thurston Co., WC Washington, on Budd Inlet at the S end of Puget Sound, 25 mi/40 km SW of Tacoma. A deepwater port and manufacturing city, it was settled in 1846, and became territorial capital in 1853 and state capital in 1859. Lumber, agricultural products, and Olympia oysters (found only in Puget Sound) are pillars of the economy, as is the large merchant reserve fleet in the harbor. Other manufactures include plastics, mobile homes, and beer. A salmon run takes place in local waters each fall. Six white sandstone capitol buildings (1911–35) are grouped on high ground here. Olympia is the seat of Evergreen State College (1967). Fort Lewis Military Reservation, one of the largest Army bases on the West Coast, is 13 mi/21 km NE.

Olympia Heights unincorporated community, pop. 37,792, Dade Co., SE Florida, 9 mi/14 km SW of downtown Miami. It is a predominantly Hispanic residential suburb.

Olympic Peninsula region of extreme NW Washington, bounded N by the Juan de Fuca Strait, W by the Pacific Ocean, E by PUGET SOUND, and S by GRAYS HARBOR and the Chehalis R. valley. Its narrow coastal plains are dominated by the central **Olympic Mts.,** part of the COAST RANGES, rising to 7965 ft/2428 m at **Mt. Olympus.** Much of the range, surrounded by glaciers and rain forest, is within 922,000-ac/373,000-ha (1441–sq mi/3731–sq km) **Olympic National Park,** which is almost surrounded by 632,000-ac/256,000-ha (988–sq mi/2559–sq km) **Olympic National Forest.**

Olympic Stadium French, **Stade olympique** see under MAISONNEUVE, Montréal, Québec.

Omaha city, pop. 335,795, the largest in the state and seat of Douglas Co., EC Nebraska, on the Missouri R. opposite Council Bluffs, Iowa. Originally an Omaha Indian settlement, it was the site of a westbound Mormon encampment in the winter of 1846–47. The Indians abandoned their lands after signing a treaty with the US in 1854. White settlement came swiftly, and the city served as territorial capital (1854–67) and flourished both as a river port and as a supply point for Great Plains travelers. After the transcontinental Union Pacific Railroad began its move westward from here in 1865, the city also became one of the nation's most important rail shipping points, particularly active in the distribution of livestock and grain. In a fertile lowland agricultural region, it remains a transportation center, with large stockyards, an immense livestock market, meatpacking plants, and major food processing facilities. Insurance companies have long formed the backbone of its business base, and in the 1980s the city became the leading US telecommunications and telemarketing center. Its industries also manufacture farm, railroad, and electronic equipment and petroleum products. Concerts, rodeos, and other events are held in the city's Ak-sar-ben Coliseum. President Gerald Ford's 1913 birthplace is preserved. The city is the seat of the University of Nebraska Medical Center (1869), Creighton University (1878), the University of Nebraska at Omaha (1908), the College of St. Mary (1923), Grace College of the Bible (1943), and Metropolitan Community College (1974). Rosenblatt Stadium is home to the annual college baseball World Series. BOYS TOWN (W) and OFFUTT AIR FORCE BASE (S) are nearby.

Omaha Indian Reservation 312 sq mi/808 sq km, pop. 5227 (36% Indian), in NE Nebraska, on the Missouri R. (E), 60 mi/100 km NNW of Omaha and 25 mi/40 km S of Sioux City, Iowa. Macy (unincorporated, pop. 836, Thurston Co.) is headquarters. The Omaha moved W from the Ohio area in the 18th century, arriving here around 1802. In 1865, part of their land was sold to create the adjacent (N) Winnebago Indian Reservation (173 sq mi/449 sq km, pop. 2341, 49% Indian) for part of the people whose homeland had been the Green Bay–L. Winnebago area of E Wisconsin. The Omaha,

Siouan speakers but enemies of the Sioux, began regular powwows on their land here around 1803; the custom spread to many other US reservations.

Omni Coliseum popularly, **the Omni** enclosed multiuse complex, opened 1972, in downtown Atlanta, Georgia, just NW of Five Points. It is part of the CNN (Cable News Network) center, and the home of the Atlanta Hawks (basketball).

Onalaska city, pop. 11,284, La Crosse Co., W Wisconsin, on the Black R. and L. Onalaska in the upper Mississippi R. valley, 5 mi/8 km N of La Crosse and 5 mi/8 km E of the Minnesota border. In a farming and dairying area, it processes foods, producing canned vegetables, pickles, and dairy goods. It is also a summer resort. The La Crosse Municipal Airport is just W, on French I.

Onancock see under EASTERN SHORE, Virginia.

101 Ranch also, **Miller 101 Ranch** historic former property in N Oklahoma, just S of PONCA CITY. Established in the 1870s in Osage territory by George W. Miller, it grew to over 100,000 ac/40,000 ha, and operated until 1936. The 101 was the site, after 1900, of the development of the modern rodeo. Its traveling troupe, at its peak in the period just before World War I, popularized the sport all over America, and featured the famous black "bulldogger" Bill Pickett (d. 1932), who is buried here, near the hamlet of White Eagle.

Oneida city, pop. 10,850, Madison Co., C New York, on Oneida Creek, 6 mi/10 km SE of Oneida L. and 26 mi/42 km E of Syracuse. Settled in 1834, it developed as a supply point and depot for the Utica and Syracuse Railroad. In 1848, the **Oneida Community** settled here. Marked by their belief in perfectionism, complex marriage, collective child-raising, and a nonsexist division of labor, its members flourished as farmers, loggers, and, later, as industrial entrepreneurs, manufacturing steel traps, silverware, and embroidered silks. In 1880, following hostility from the outside community, they reorganized as Oneida Community, Limited, a joint-stock company manufacturing silverware and dishes. Now the city's leading industry, it preserves some of its early cooperative elements. Other local manufactures include office furniture, plastics, paper and wood products, burial vaults, dairy equipment, castings, and bearings.

Oneida County 1219 sq mi/3157 sq km, pop. 250,836, in C New York. Its seat and largest city is UTICA. Traversed by the New York State Barge Canal and the Mohawk R., it has diversified industry, much of it centered around Utica and Rome. Its S section has many small towns, some suburban, some largely agricultural. Dairying, truck farming, and stock raising flourish in the nonindustrialized parts. There are also resorts around the E shores of Oneida L., in the W, and around the smaller Adirondack lakes of the NE. It is the location of FORT STANWIX and various other Revolutionary War sites.

Oneida Lake in C New York, 15 mi/24 km NE of Syracuse and 12 mi/19 km W of Rome. It is part of the New York State Barge Canal (Erie Canal) system, and is drained (W) by the Oneida R. Twenty mi/32 km E–W and up to 5 mi/8 km wide, it is ringed by beach resorts and wetlands.

Oneonta city, pop. 13,594, Otsego Co., C New York, on the Susquehanna R., in the foothills of the Catskill Mts., 45 mi/72 km SSE of Utica. Settled in the late 1700s, it was first known as McDonald's Bridge or Mill. The settlement took its present name (Iroquoian for "stony place") in 1832. Following the arrival of the Albany and Susquehanna Railroad in 1865, railroad shops were established. In 1883, the Brotherhood of Railroad Trainmen was founded here. The city now manufactures plastics, clothing, and electronic components, and remains a distribution point. Hartwick College (1797), the State University of New York College at Oneonta (1887), and the National Soccer Hall of Fame are here.

Onondaga County 784 sq mi/2031 sq km, pop. 468,973, in C New York, in the FINGER LAKES region. Its seat and by far its largest municipality is SYRACUSE, whose metropolitan area occupies a large part of its EC portion. The city serves as a distribution point for the dairy products, poultry, and vegetables produced in the rural sections of the county. There is considerable resort development, particularly in the SW, around Otisco and Skaneateles lakes.

Onondaga Lake see under SYRACUSE, New York.

Onslow Bay reach of the Atlantic Ocean between Cape LOOKOUT (NE) and Cape FEAR (SW), off SE North Carolina. One hundred mi/160 km NE–SW, it has many ports, including (N–S) BEAUFORT, MOREHEAD CITY, JACKSONVILLE (via the New R.), and WILMINGTON (via the Cape Fear R.).

Ontario most populous and southernmost Canadian province; 1991 pop. 10,084,885 (110.8% of 1986); land area 353,951 sq mi/916,734 sq km (rank: 3rd of 12); entered Confederation 1867. Capital and most populous city: TORONTO. Other cities with over 100,000 pop.: NORTH YORK, SCARBOROUGH, MISSISSAUGA, HAMILTON, OTTAWA, ETOBICOKE, LONDON, BRAMPTON, WINDSOR, KITCHENER, YORK, BURLINGTON, OSHAWA, SAINT CATHARINES, THUNDER BAY, VAUGHAN, NEPEAN, EAST YORK (borough), GLOUCESTER. Ontario is bordered E and NE by Québec, with the OTTAWA R. forming most of the boundary; W and NW by Manitoba; and SW by Minnesota, with the LAKE OF THE WOODS, RAINY R., BOUNDARY WATERS, and Pigeon R. forming the boundary. On the N it lies on JAMES (E) and HUDSON (W) bays. On the S it lies along, and extends into, all of the Great Lakes except L. Michigan. From the W, it fronts L. SUPERIOR; the SAINT MARYS R. and canals and rapids at SAULT STE. MARIE; L. HURON (with GEORGIAN BAY); the SAINT CLAIR R., L. Saint Clair, and the DETROIT R.; L. ERIE; the NIAGARA R.; L. ONTARIO; and the SAINT LAWRENCE R. Across from it lie (W–E) Minnesota, Wisconsin, Michigan, Ohio, Pennsylvania, and New York. Middle I. (see under PELÉE I.), in L. Erie, is Canada's southernmost point. Except in the SE and along the bays in the N, the province lies on the CANADIAN SHIELD. This forested hard-rock upland is dotted with lakes, the largest of which include NIPIGON, NIPISSING, and ABITIBI. The SEVERN, Winisk, Attawapiskat, Kenogami, MOOSE, and other rivers drain it N toward Hudson and James bays, while rivers flowing S into the Great Lakes are fewer and shorter. ISHPATINA RIDGE, WSW of NEW LISKEARD, is (at 2274 ft/693 m) the province's high point. The CLAY BELT, along the Québec border in the Abitibi region, is the only part of the Shield in Ontario that is extensively farmed. The SUDBURY Basin, ELLIOTT LAKE, TIMMINS, and the ALGOMA and KENORA districts are mining centers; the Shield contains huge deposits of nickel, iron, cobalt, copper, uranium, gold, lead, and other metals and minerals, sources of which continue to be found. Lumbering and pulp and paper production are other Shield industries; Kenora and KAPUSKASING are among leading centers. Along the Shield's S edge are ports and processing centers including Thunder Bay, Sault Ste. Marie, and NORTH BAY. Along Hudson and James bays (N) are lowland areas of newer rock; this area is largely uninhabited, except for small Cree communities; MOOSONEE–MOOSE FACTORY is one of a number of former fur trade posts. The vast majority of Ontario's people and settlements are in the lowland areas along the Great Lakes and the Saint Lawrence R., in the SE. The GOLDEN HORSESHOE, extending around the W of L. Ontario, with Toronto and Hamilton as its hubs, is Canada's largest extended urban area, home to much of the nation's industry. The land on which urban Ontario developed is for the most part rolling farm country. The NIAGARA ESCARPMENT, marking the S edge of a major glacial advance, runs from the Niagara R. (SE) across S Ontario, forming the BRUCE PENINSULA (enclosing Georgian Bay of L. Huron) and MANITOULIN I., before continuing (NW) into Michigan's Upper Peninsula. The Huron and Ottawa and other Algonquian and Iroquoian peoples inhabited the region when French explorers first arrived in the early 17th century; for the most part they allied themselves with the French, and cooperated with them in the fur trade. The Iroquois of New York, allied with the British, soon destroyed or dispersed these peoples; after the British defeat in the American Revolutionary War, they, in turn, fled to S Ontario, where the Six Nations lands at BRANTFORD now constitute Canada's largest INDIAN RESERVE. Subsequently, forest Ojibwa moved S from the Shield, occupying areas of C and W Ontario. European activity in Ontario largely followed the Ottawa R.–Mattawa R.–L. Nipissing–Georgian Bay route in the French period, as fur traders developed connections between Montréal and the Northwest. From the early 17th century, the HUDSON'S BAY COMPANY had established bases on Hudson and James bays, but the HBC did little to develop these beginnings. After the British defeat of NEW FRANCE (1763), the NORTH WEST COMPANY became increasingly busy along the lakes. The American Revolution drove thousands of LOYALISTS into the W section of the (British) Province of Quebec, and in 1791 the S part of what is now Ontario was separated from Quebec and became Upper Canada. In the War of 1812, the new capital at York (later, Toronto) was occupied and sacked by Americans, and fighting on Lakes Erie and Ontario put Upper Canada on the front lines; LUNDY'S LANE, QUEENSTON Heights, STONEY CREEK, and Beaver Dams (see under THOROLD) were all battle sites. With the end of the war, the British promoted settlement in the region, and large numbers of Scots, Irish, and English farmers and merchants began to fill the fertile S. Apprehension of continued US aggression led to the development of the RIDEAU CANAL, which with the WELLAND CANAL (W of Niagara Falls) and TRENT CANAL (between L. Ontario and Georgian Bay) provide alternatives to the natural lake-and-river routes. Dissatisfaction with oligarchic power in the province led to an abortive 1837 uprising in Toronto that, coupled with the PATRIOTE rebellion in the Montréal area, caused Britain to reunite Upper and Lower Canada; eventually, at CONFEDERATION, what had been called (1841–67) Canada West became the province of Ontario, taking its name from the Iroquoian ("fine lake") name for the lake. In 1874, 1889, and 1912, the province obtained lands from the Keewatin district of the Northwest Territories, expanding to its modern boundaries on James and Hudson bays. In the past century Ontario has grown increasingly industrial. The CANADIAN PACIFIC (along the N of L. Superior) and CANADIAN NATIONAL (through the Clay Belt and C Shield areas) railways gave local manufacturers access to resources in addition to those carried on the Great Lakes, and heavy and light industry boomed in what became the Golden Horseshoe. Today, automobiles (Oshawa, Windsor), high-tech equipment (KANATA, the CANADIAN TECHNOLOGY TRIANGLE), steel and related products (Hamilton, Sault Ste. Marie), refined oil (SARNIA), paper (Thunder Bay, Kenora), and a wide variety of other manufactures are made. Toronto, esp. since the flight of much anglophone capital from Montréal in the 1970s, has become Canada's financial and business hub. Ottawa, the Federal capital since 1867, has developed into a cultural, educational, and light industrial center as well. Toronto, London, GUELPH, WATERLOO, Hamilton, and PETERBOROUGH are other noted academic centers. Tourism and recreational visiting focus on the Shakespeare Festival at STRATFORD; the PUKASKWA, Bruce Peninsula and Fathom Five, POINT PELÉE, QUETICO, and ALGONQUIN (subject of much painting by the noted Group of Seven) parks; the cities of Toronto and Ottawa; NIAGARA FALLS; the THOUSAND Is., in the St. Lawrence; and lakes SIMCOE and Huron (esp. Georgian Bay, with its Thirty Thousand Is.). Ontario's people, once primarily English, Scottish, and American Loyalist, now include large Slavic, Italian, Greek, West Indian, and other groups; the descendants of American slaves who arrived via the UNDERGROUND RAILROAD at such "terminals" as AMHERSTBURG and DRESDEN form a notable minority. The Ottawa area and some communities in the Clay Belt are centers of francophone pop.

Ontario **1.** city, pop. 133,179, San Bernardino Co., SW California, 35 mi/56 km E of Los Angeles, and adjacent (E) to Pomona. Founded in 1882 by Canadians George and William Chaffee, it was a planned community. Irrigation, making possible the cultivation of citrus fruits and grapes, was provided by a mutually held water company, a revolutionary idea at the time. Today, the area produces fruits, vegetables, flowers, ornamental shrubs, and olives, and vineyards to the E are among the world's largest. To the S are dairy and poultry farms. The city packs fruit and olives. Its manufactures include electrical appliances, aircraft parts, clothing, plastics, tile, rubber products, and chemicals. Ontario International Airport is the Los Angeles area's second most important, and the Ontario Motor Speedway is a major attraction. **2.** city, pop. 9392, Malheur Co., E Oregon, on the Snake R. just S of its junction with the Malheur R., 4 mi/6 km SW of PAYETTE, Idaho. With the arrival of the Union Pacific Railroad in 1884, it emerged as an important regional trade and distribution center. The coming of the Owyhee and Malheur irrigation projects made Ontario a shipping point for the fruits and other products raised in this agricultural belt. Today, the processing and distribution of fruits and vegetables, along with tourism, are mainstays of the economy.

Ontario, Lake smallest and easternmost of the GREAT LAKES, lying between Ontario (N and W) and New York (E and S). Some 190 mi/306 km E–W and up to 55 mi/90 km wide, it has a surface area of 7340 sq mi/19,010 sq km. Its surface lies 245 ft/75 m above sea level, and its greatest depth is 802 ft/244 m. Ontario drains the other four Great Lakes via the NIAGARA R.; the WELLAND CANAL, bypassing Niagara Falls, links it with L. Erie (SW). At its NE end it empties into the SAINT LAWRENCE R. and Seaway. It also connects with the Hudson R. and New York City via the NEW YORK STATE BARGE CANAL system. The TRENT CANAL (to Georgian Bay of L. Huron) and RIDEAU CANAL (to the Ottawa R.) lead N from the lake. Major cities around the lake include Kingston, Belleville, Oshawa, Toronto, and Hamilton (the last three in the

GOLDEN HORSESHOE) in Ontario, and Oswego and Rochester in New York. Ontario's Prince Edward County Peninsula extends 25 mi/40 km into the lake on the NE, and is separated from the mainland by the 50 mi/80 km–long Bay of Quinté (on which Belleville and Trenton are situated). The THOUSAND Is., in Ontario and New York, are at the broad entrance (NE) to the Saint Lawrence R. The French explorers Étienne Brulé and Samuel de Champlain encountered L. Ontario, which the French called L. Frontenac, in 1615. Struggles for control of the area ended in 1763, when the British, who called it by the Algonquian name ("beautiful lake") it later gave to the province, conquered New France. During the War of 1812 British-US conflict on the lake included the American sack of York (Toronto). Industrialized from the mid 19th century, L. Ontario has suffered pollution problems; a 1972 US-Canadian pact addresses these.

Ontario County 644 sq mi/1668 sq km, pop. 95,101, in WC New York, in the FINGER LAKES. The county is partially bounded by Seneca L. (SE) and contains Canandaigua, Honeoye, and Canadice lakes. Its seat is Canandaigua, where there is some light industry. There is also industrial development in the city of Geneva. Tourism and resorts are important throughout. Fruit and vegetables are grown, and there are wineries; the county also produces poultry, grain, and dairy products.

Ontario Place 96-ac/39-ha entertainment complex on three artificial islands in L. Ontario, just S of Exhibition Park and SW of downtown TORONTO, Ontario, owned and operated by the provincial government.

Ontonagon River 22 mi/35 km long, in Michigan's NW Upper Peninsula, emptying into L. Superior at the village of **Ontonagon** (pop. 2040), the seat of Ontonagon Co. It is formed by the confluence of East, Middle, South, and West branches, which flow through the Ottawa National Forest. The Ontonagon Boulder, first seen by whites in the 1660s, was a huge block of very pure copper that led many to think the area a land of riches. Mining, begun seriously in the 1840s, did not succeed, and the Ontonagon became a lumber (particularly matchwood) producer; but the story of the boulder served to bring prospectors into the area of the Porcupine Mts. (S), which later became copper producers.

Oolitic town, pop. 1424, Lawrence Co., S Indiana, 4 mi/6 km NNW of Bedford. The limestone quarries in the area provide the town with its major industry and its name. The quarries supplied stone for New York's EMPIRE STATE BUILDING.

Oologah also, **Oolagah** town, pop. 828, Rogers Co., NE Oklahoma, 25 mi/40 km NNE of Tulsa. The nearby birthplace (1879) of cowboy-humorist Will Rogers has been preserved. **Oologah L.,** created by the damming of the Verdigris R., lies E and NE, extending into Nowata Co.

Opa-Locka city, pop. 15,283, Dade Co., SE Florida, 8 mi/13 km NNW of downtown Miami. It has a variety of light manufacturing, including foodstuffs, cardboard boxes, boats, clothing, and furniture. The Opa-Locka Airport houses a Coast Guard station, and the city is home to aviation-based industries and schools. Its castlelike city hall and other Moorish-style buildings were constructed in 1926–30 under the direction of Opa-Locka's founder, aircraft designer Glenn Curtiss, who wanted to give the city an Arabian Nights atmosphere.

Opelika city, pop. 22,122, seat of Lee Co., E Alabama, 25 mi/40 km NW of Columbus, Georgia. Settled in the 1830s, it developed into an agricultural market town, and remains a commercial center for surrounding cotton, corn, beef, and dairy farms. Local industries produce textiles, fitness equipment, fertilizer, tires, and magnetic tape.

Opelousas city, pop. 18,151, seat of St. Landry Parish, SC Louisiana, 22 mi/35 km NNW of Lafayette, in CAJUN COUNTRY. Founded in 1720 as a French post on the W border of the ATCHAFALAYA swamps, and named for the area's native inhabitants, it became in 1769 the capital of the Spanish district of Opelousas. In the early 1800s Texas hero Jim Bowie lived here. The Louisiana Supreme Court was housed here until 1819, and during the Union occupation of Baton Rouge Opelousas was briefly (1863) the capital of Louisiana. The city has an agricultural and industrial economy. Regional farms produce cotton, sweet potatoes (there is an annual Yambolee festival), rice, and cattle. Industries are based on oil and natural gas discovered at nearby (E) Port Barre in 1929, and also manufacture wood products, fertilizers, pharmaceuticals, and processed foods. The city is noted as a center of zydeco music.

Opportunity unincorporated community, pop. 22,326, Spokane Co., E Washington, a residential suburb 10 mi/16 km SE of Spokane and 9 mi/14 km W of the Idaho border.

Opryland in NE Nashville, Tennessee, on Briley Parkway and the Cumberland R., 9 mi/14 km NE of Downtown. The entertainment complex includes country music's mecca, the Grand Ole Opry House (1974), as well as the Opryland USA theme park and various music-related and other attractions. From 1943 to 1974 the Opry was housed Downtown, in Ryman Auditorium.

Oracle see under SANTA CATALINA Mts., Arizona.

Oradell borough, pop. 8024, Bergen Co., NE New Jersey, on the Hackensack R. at the SW end of the 4 mi/6 km–long **Oradell Reservoir,** 5 mi/8 km N of Hackensack. Settled by the Dutch, it is now a New York-New Jersey suburb with some light industry and office development.

Oraibi also, **Old Oraibi** PUEBLO in Navajo Co., NE Arizona, 70 mi/113 km NE of Flagstaff, on Third Mesa, in the Hopi Indian Reservation. One of America's oldest communities, it dates from about 1150, and was the site of a 17th-century Franciscan MISSION. By 1900, it was one of the largest Hopi settlements, but disputes among its residents caused many to leave.

Orange **1.** city, pop. 110,658, Orange Co., SW California, 30 mi/48 km SE of Los Angeles, and adjacent (N) to Santa Ana. Founded before 1870, it is in an irrigated area long known for its oranges; residential and business development replaced the last groves in the city in the 1960s, but the packing and shipping of fruits, nuts, and vegetables remain important. The city has a wide range of manufactures, along with wholesale and other businesses. It is the seat of Chapman College (1861). **2.** town, pop. 12,830, New Haven Co., SW Connecticut, immediately SW of New Haven and on the Housatonic R. (W). Settled in 1639 on land bought from the Paugusset Indians, it joined with part of New Haven to form the town of Orange in 1822; part seceded in 1921 to become WEST HAVEN. Orange has always been primarily residential, with some manufacturing. **3.** officially, **City of Orange** township, pop. 29,925, Essex Co., NE New Jersey, 3 mi/5 km NE of Newark. Founded as Mountain Plantations (1678), it was separated from Newark (1806) and from East, South, and

West Orange (1861–63). Orange and the latter three form the suburban complex commonly known as the Oranges. Now a primarily residential commuter suburb, Orange was long a manufacturing center; surviving industries produce office machines, pharmaceuticals, textiles, electrical supplies, and clothing. **4.** city, pop. 19,381, seat of Orange Co., extreme E Texas, on the Sabine R., at the Louisiana border, 110 mi/175 km E of Houston. Part of an oil producing triangle with BEAUMONT (W) and PORT ARTHUR (SW), it was founded in 1836. It thrived on lumber, cattle, and rice in the 19th century. Its deepwater harbor, once a haven to the privateer Jean Lafitte, also made it a shipbuilder; the Navy subsequently maintained a mothball fleet here. In addition to oil and petrochemicals, Orange manufactures fabricated steel, paper products, and cement. A branch of Lamar University opened here in 1969.

Orange Beach town, pop. 2253, Baldwin Co., SW Alabama, 40 mi/64 km SE of Mobile, on Perdido Bay (N) and the Gulf of Mexico. It is Alabama's second-largest Gulf Coast resort, after GULF SHORES, 8 mi/13 km WSW.

Orange Bowl sports facility in downtown Miami, Florida, home to the University of Miami Hurricanes (football), and the scene of a variety of sporting events and concerts. It seats 74,000. The college football bowl game to which it gives its name is to move in 1997 to JOE ROBBIE STADIUM.

Orangeburg **1.** village, pop. 3583, in Orangetown, Rockland Co., SE New York, 3 mi/5 km SW of Nyack. It has some light industry, and is home to the Dominican College of Blauvelt (1950). **2.** city, pop. 13,739, seat of Orangeburg Co., SC South Carolina, on the North Fork of the Edisto R., 38 mi/61 km SSE of Columbia. Germans, Dutch, and Swiss founded it in 1735, and it was long a cotton-country trade center. Its agricultural economy has largely been overtaken by diversified light industry, making textiles, tools, and chemicals. There are three colleges, including the historically black Claflin College (1869) and South Carolina State College (1896).

Orange City city, pop. 4940, seat of Sioux Co., NW Iowa, on the West Branch of the Floyd R., 40 mi/64 km NE of Sioux City. Founded by Dutch settlers in 1869, it hosts an annual Tulip Festival. Northwestern College (1882) is in the neighboring city of Maurice, pop. 243, 2 mi/3 km S.

Orange County **1.** 798 sq mi/2067 sq km, pop. 2,410,556, in SW California, on the Pacific Ocean, between Los Angeles Co. (NW) and San Diego Co. (SE). The Santa Ana R. bisects it. Heavily urbanized, especially in the NW, it is one of the wealthiest counties in the US, and has increased tenfold in pop. since 1950. Major cities include SANTA ANA, the county seat, and Orange, Anaheim, Fullerton, Costa Mesa, Irvine, Huntington Beach, Newport Beach, and Laguna Beach. The Cleveland National Forest occupies part of the E edge, in the Santa Ana Mts. Most of the agricultural land, once abundant with orange groves, has been developed; strawberries remain a major crop. Orange Co. has numerous military installations and coastal resorts. **2.** 910 sq mi/2357 sq km, pop. 677,491, in C Florida, bounded (E) by the St. Johns R. Its seat is ORLANDO. This city and Walt Disney World (in LAKE BUENA VISTA) dominate and give character to Orange's theme park–filled center, where tourism drives the economy. The county occupies a hilly, lake-dotted region, rich in orange groves. Agriculture remains important, particularly in the S and E. In addition to citrus fruits, local production includes vegetables, dairy goods, poultry, and lumber. **3.** 826 sq mi/2139 sq km, pop. 307,647, in SE New York, bounded by the Hudson R. (E), New Jersey (SE), and the Pennsylvania line and the Delaware R. (SW). Its varied geography includes portions of the Hudson Highlands (E), the Ramapo (SE), Shawangunk (C) and Catskill (NW) mountains, and many small lakes. Its seat is Goshen, its major industrial centers NEWBURGH and MIDDLETOWN. The SE portion, once rural and exurban, is becoming suburban. There is a great deal of resort development in the W. WEST POINT is along the Hudson, along with a number of state parks.

Orange Grove unincorporated community, pop. 15,676, Harrison Co., extreme SE Mississippi, a resort and residential suburb 7 mi/11 km NE of Pascagoula, near the Alabama line.

Orange Park town, pop. 9488, Clay Co., NE Florida, on the St. Johns R., 12 mi/19 km S of downtown Jacksonville. It is a bedroom community for Jacksonville and for the Jacksonville Naval Air Station, which lies just NE.

Oranges, the see under ORANGE, New Jersey.

Orangevale unincorporated community, pop. 26,266, Sacramento Co., NC California, 15 mi/24 km NE of Sacramento, of which it is a largely residential suburb, and across the American R. (W) from Folsom.

Orangeville town, pop. 17,921, seat of Dufferin Co., S Ontario, on the Credit R., 40 mi/64 km WNW of Toronto. An 1860s mill town, it now has diverse light industries and a tourist trade.

Orcas Island largest (57 sq mi/147 sq km) of the SAN JUAN Is., off the NW Washington coast. Hilly and deeply indented (S) by East and West sounds, it is a residential EXURB with some agriculture (sheep, hay, garlic, strawberries), resort trade, and tourism.

Orchard Beach see under PELHAM BAY PARK, New York.

Orchard Knob battle site: see under MISSIONARY RIDGE, Tennessee.

Orchard Lake Village city, pop. 2286, Oakland Co., SE Michigan, on Orchard L. and Upper Straits L., 6 mi/10 km SW of Pontiac. A suburban community, it is the seat of St. Mary's College (1885), and is in a lake resort area.

Orchard Park town, pop. 24,632, Erie Co., W New York, 10 mi/16 km SSE of Buffalo. A largely residential suburb, it was known as East Hamburg until 1934. Rich Stadium (1973), the 80,000-seat home of the Buffalo Bills (football) is here.

Oregon state of the NW US, in the PACIFIC NORTHWEST; 1990 pop. 2,842,321 (107.9% of 1980; rank: 29th); area 98,386 sq mi/254,820 sq km (rank: 9th); admitted to Union 1859 (33rd). Capital: SALEM. Most populous cities: PORTLAND, EUGENE, Salem, GRESHAM, BEAVERTON. Oregon is bounded E by Idaho, with the SNAKE R. forming the N half of the boundary; N by Washington, with the COLUMBIA R. forming most of the boundary; and S by California (W) and Nevada (E). On its W is the Pacific Ocean. The W third of the state is dominated by two N–S mountain ranges, with the broad WILLAMETTE Valley between them. The W range is a section of the COAST RANGES (rising to only c.4000 ft/1220 m), the E part of the CASCADES (in which Mt. HOOD, near Portland, is, at 11,239 ft/3428 m, the state's high point). In the S, at the top end of the Willamette Valley, the two ranges converge in the KLAMATH Mts., through which the ROGUE R. runs W to the Pacific. Along the California border, GOOSE L. and other bodies are important sites on the PACIFIC FLYWAY. Oregon's narrow coastal margin, W of the Coast Ranges, is noted for its scenery, including the OREGON DUNES; it has many small inlets, but no major harbor. The Willamette Valley, through which the Willamette R. runs N to the Columbia R., is the agricultural and urban hub of the state. To the E of the Cascades, Oregon is higher and drier. Of the state's E two-thirds, the NC section is part of the COLUMBIA PLATEAU, drained (S–N) by the DESCHUTES and JOHN DAY and (W–E) by the MALHEUR and OWYHEE rivers. In the NE are the BLUE and WALLOWA mountains, a W extension of the Northern ROCKY Mts.; this rugged and remote region ends at the Idaho boundary with the famous HELLS CANYON of the Snake R. The HARNEY DESERT (EC) is an arid S section of the Columbia Plateau, adjoining (S) the N edge of the GREAT BASIN. The state's forests, dense with Douglas fir, hemlock, and cedar in the W, dominated by pine E of the Cascades, are its most important natural resource, the basis for the leading US lumber (now esp. pulp and paper) industry. NICKEL Mt., S of ROSEBURG (SW), is the leading US source of the metal, and the state's only major mine site. When first explored by whites in the 1770s, the region was home to the Chinook and Tillamook, in the NW; to the Bannock and Nez Perce, in the NE; and to the Klamath, in the SW. The fur trade soon drew expeditions here; in 1792, the American Robert Gray and the Englishman George Vancouver both entered the Columbia R. and claimed the area for their countries. Alexander Mackenzie of the NORTH WEST COMPANY arrived overland the following year, and a period of rivalry between the NWC and the HUDSON'S BAY COMPANY ensued. In late 1805, the LEWIS AND CLARK expedition reached the coast, and wintered at Fort Clatsop (see under ASTORIA), reinforcing the American claim. In 1812 the American Fur Company founded Astoria, but during the War of 1812 the British reasserted control. In 1818 a treaty allowed both British and US interests to operate in the Oregon country, a region extending E to the Continental Divide and N into what is now Canada. Trade and missionary activities preceded the 1840s, when real American settlement began. In 1842–43 the OREGON TRAIL, leading via the LA GRANDE valley (NE) and THE DALLES (NC, on the Columbia) to the agricultural "promised land" of the Willamette Valley, began to be heavily used; settlers came primarily from New England and the Border South, and farms and sawmills flourished. OREGON CITY became the provisional capital of the region. By 1846, agitation for clarification of American claims in the area led to the treaty establishing the FORTY-NINTH PARALLEL as Oregon's N boundary; in 1848 the **Oregon Territory** was formalized, containing modern Oregon, Washington, and Idaho, Montana W of the Continental Divide, and the NW corner of Wyoming. The Washington Territory was separated in 1853, leaving Oregon within its present boundaries, and statehood followed. After the Civil War, the 1872–73 Modoc War (on the California border) and the 1877 flight of Chief Joseph and his followers on the NEZ PERCE TRAIL were final incidents in the pacification of local Indians; today, the WARM SPRINGS and UMATILLA reservations are home to some of their descendants. In the 1880s railroads crossed the state, swelling settlement, esp. in the less easily farmed E. By 1900, Oregon's lumber industry had come to prominence, and Portland was the leading city of the Northwest. The 1930s Depression hit the state's agriculture hard, but in World War II it recovered, and industry, led by Portland shipyards, gained a new prominence. In the postwar era, the BONNEVILLE DAM and other power projects spurred further industrial growth. The Portland area (the lower Willamette Valley) is today a manufacturing and business center, with fabricated metal, clothing, wood-based, and electronics industries prominent in addition to shipbuilding. Lumbering in the state has been subject recently to market swings; its importance to Oregon's economy is such that hard times affect the entire state. Wheat (on the Columbia Plateau) and fruit (esp. in the MEDFORD area and Willamette Valley) are important crops, and dairying is esp. important in TILLAMOOK Co. Major salmon and tuna industries are based in Portland. Tourism and outdoor recreation focus on Mt. Hood and the Cascades, the CRATER LAKE National Park, the Pacific coast, and Portland itself. The University of Oregon is at Eugene, Oregon State University at CORVALLIS. The state's name is thought to be the result of a misspelling for *Ouisconsink* (Wisconsin) arising on an 18th-century French map. Oregon's people today are about 4% Hispanic, 2% Asian, and less than 2% black; the overwhelming majority are descendants of the 19th-century Easterners who settled here, or of Northern Europeans who have arrived since.

Oregon city, pop. 18,334, Lucas Co., NW Ohio, 5 mi/8 km E of Toledo, of which it is a residential suburb.

Oregon Caves National Monument labyrinthine series of caverns and corridors carved in Elijah Mt. (7000 ft/2134 m) in the SISKIYOU Mts. of SW Oregon, 34 mi/55 km WSW of Medford, near the California border. Also sometimes called "The Marble Halls of Oregon," the chambers, passageways, and pillars were formed by groundwater dissolving marble bedrock.

Oregon City city, pop. 14,698, seat of Clackamas Co., NW Oregon, on the Willamette River's Willamette Falls, 10 mi/16 km S of Portland. Founded in 1828, it was the end of the OREGON TRAIL, the first incorporated city W of the Mississippi R., and the capital of Oregon Territory (1849–51). Today, it is a Portland suburb and a trade center for the region's cattle and fruit producers. Manufactures include wood pulp, paper, batteries, cutlery, and canned foods.

Oregon Dunes National Recreation Area 40 mi/64 km–long stretch of sand dunes bordering the Pacific Ocean in Lane, Douglas, and Coos counties, W Oregon. The shifting dunes run from Florence on the N to COOS BAY on the S, extending 3 mi/5 km inland, and reaching heights of 90 ft/27 m.

Oregon Trail major westward migration route of the 1840s–70s, covering some 2000 mi/3200 km from INDEPENDENCE and WESTPORT Landing (Kansas City), Missouri, to the WILLAMETTE Valley of W Oregon, with many alternate routes, connections with other trails, and varying destinations. Its use was spurred by talk of the ease of farming in Oregon (a name that, at the time, applied to a larger area than the modern state); it declined as railroads spread across the West, available land became occupied, and other destinations beckoned. The Trail was traveled by wagon train, often (esp. in early years) changing to pack mule through mountains, and by boat down the Columbia R. (W) from THE DALLES, Oregon. In drier terrain, traces of the Trail are still visible. Interstate highways parallel it in places. From Missouri, the Oregon Trail's main route ran with the SANTA FE TRAIL briefly, to Gardner, Kansas (names given here are those of modern municipalities and states), then cut NW to Lawrence and along the Kansas R., then NW across country again, along the BIG BLUE R. It crossed S Nebraska to the Platte R. near Fort KEARNEY, and ran along the S bank to North Platte, where it continued with the South Platte R. to near Julesburg, Colorado, then NW along Nebraska's Lodgepole Creek and NNW to the North Platte R. Continuing NW, it passed the great landmarks of CHIMNEY ROCK and SCOTTSBLUFF, and entered Wyoming. FORT LARAMIE was a major rest stop. The Trail then turned WNW and W with the river, and SW to 193 ft/59 m–high Independence Rock, on the Sweetwater R. just NW of today's Pathfinder Reservoir; groups who had left Missouri in the spring hoped to arrive here by July 4. Continuing WSW along the Sweetwater, the Trail crossed the Continental Divide at SOUTH PASS. It continued SW along the Big Sandy Creek and across rough, mountainous country to FORT BRIDGER, in Wyoming's SW corner, another major rest stop and the point at which the MORMON TRAIL diverged for Utah. From Fort Bridger the Oregon Trail wound NNW along the Wyoming-Utah border and into SE Idaho, through the Bear R. valley, to Soda Springs (the first of several places at which the CALIFORNIA TRAIL diverged after 1849) and to FORT HALL, on the SNAKE R. It then traversed the dry Snake R. valley in its great arc across S Idaho, reaching Fort BOISE and crossing (NW) into Oregon. Continuing NNW, it crossed through the BLUE Mts. by way of the Grande Ronde Valley past La Grande, then cut W along the Umatilla R. and across the plateau S of the Columbia R., to The Dalles, where travelers finally entered boats for the trip to the mouth of the Willamette. The entire journey took about six months.

Orem city, pop. 67,561, Utah Co., NC Utah, on Utah L., at the base of Mt. Timpanogos, just N and W of PROVO, of which it is a suburb. Situated in a productive irrigated fruit growing region, Orem more than doubled in pop. between 1970 and 1990. The city's manufactures include steel, electrical components, and ski equipment.

Orford, Mont peak (2890 ft/881 m) in the Sutton Mts. range of the Appalachian Mts., just N of MAGOG, in S Québec's EASTERN TOWNSHIPS, site of a provincial park and ski area.

Organ Mountains N–S range rising out of the desert in S New Mexico, just E of Las Cruces. Noted for its granite spires and cliffs, it includes Organ Needle (9012 ft/2747 m) and Organ Peak (8870 ft/2704 m). The White Sands Missile Range is NE, Fort Bliss SE.

Organ Pipe Cactus National Monument 331,000 ac/134,000 ha, in PIMA Co., SW Arizona, along the Mexican border. It preserves large stands of organ pipe cactus, as well as the rare senita cactus and elephant tree. Ancient human sites have been discovered in this part of the SONORAN DESERT, just W of the PAPAGO (Tohono O'odham) Indian Reservation. The crest of the NW–SE trending Ajo Range (Sierra del Ajo) forms the E boundary. EL CAMINO DEL DIABLO traversed this extremely dry land. The CABEZA PRIETA NATIONAL WILDLIFE REFUGE lies W.

Orient Point tip of Long Island's NORTH FORK, in Southold town, Suffolk Co., SE New York, between Gardiners Bay (S) and Long Island Sound (NW). It is connected by ferry to New London, Connecticut. PLUM I. is just NE.

Orillia city, pop. 25,925, Simcoe Co., S Ontario, at the junction of Ls. Simcoe (S) and Couchiching (N), 66 mi/106 km N of Toronto. A community known as The Narrows was established here in 1832, in ancient Huron, later Ojibwa, territory. In 1902 the Orillia Company built Canada's first municipally owned hydroelectric plant here. Lumbering, once the economic mainstay, has been largely replaced by tourism and by industries making machinery, wood and steel products, boats, and electrical appliances. The summer home of humorist Stephen Leacock (1869–1944), who made Orillia his "Mariposa," is preserved.

Orinda city, pop. 16,642, Contra Costa Co., NC California, 4 mi/6 km E of Berkeley, across the Berkeley Hills. John F. Kennedy University (1964) is in this largely residential suburb.

Orion township, pop. 24,076, Oakland Co., SE Michigan, near L. Orion, 10 mi/16 km NNE of Pontiac. A General Motors assembly plant is situated in this suburban township.

Oriskany village, pop. 1450, in Whitestown, Oneida Co., C New York, on the Mohawk R., 7 mi/11 km NW of downtown Utica. It was originally the Indian village of Oriska. Just NW is the site of a bloody battle during the Saratoga Campaign (Aug. 6, 1777), when Tories and Indians ambushed Revolutionary forces headed toward FORT STANWIX.

Orlando city, pop. 164,693, seat of Orange Co., EC Florida, 80 mi/130 km NE of Tampa. The settlement grew up near the Seminole War Fort Gatlin (1837) during the 1840s. Major growth occurred after the arrival of the South Florida Railroad (1880). Its mild climate made Orlando ideal for citrus growing, and by the early 20th century it was a trade, processing, and shipping center for the fruit; the industry remains important. Situated on rolling hills amid numerous small lakes (over 50 within city limits), Orlando also developed a tourist trade. After the opening of Walt Disney World (1971) in Lake Buena Vista, some 16 mi/26 km SW of Downtown, it became a vacationers' mecca, drawing some 14 million visitors by the early 1990s. Its metropolitan (including Orange, Osceola, Seminole, and Lake counties) population rose 54% in the 1970s, and Orlando is now Florida's largest inland city. Also in and around Orlando are dozens of theme and amusement parks, gardens, and other tourist attractions. Orlando has also become an important business hub, with numerous corporate office complexes, convention facilities, and electronic and aerospace industries. Its manufactures include citrus industry equipment, boats, furniture, and clothing. It has an international airport, built in 1983. The city is also the site of the Orlando Naval Training Center, a major basic-training facility (1968), and the seat of the University of Central Florida (1963) and several smaller schools.

Orland Park village, pop. 35,720, Cook Co., NE Illinois, a residential suburb 26 mi/42 km SW of Chicago.

Orléans, Île d' 73 sq mi/190 sq km, pop. 6938, in the St. Lawrence R., just downstream (NE) from Québec City, S Québec. Some 5 mi/8 km wide and 21 mi/34 km long, it is the largest island in the river between Montréal (SW) and the I. d'Anticosti (NE). Jacques Cartier (1535) called it the I. de Bacchus, because he found it covered with wild grapevines. Settled in the 1650s, it flourished, despite a 1656 massacre by the Iroquois, with the ribbon farms typical of the SEIGNEURIE. It has had shipyards, but has always been primarily agricultural, and is noted for its berries and maple syrup. Today tourism is important to the economy of the island, which has five parishes and one village.

Orleans Parish 199 sq mi/515 sq km, pop. 496,938, in SE Louisiana, coextensive with the city of NEW ORLEANS.

Ormond Beach city, pop. 29,721, Volusia Co., NE Florida, on the Halifax R. lagoon and the Atlantic Ocean, 5 mi/8 km NNW of Daytona Beach. It was founded in the early 1870s as a health resort. Wealthy Northerners wintered in estates they built here throughout the early part of the 20th century; John D. Rockefeller's last (1914–37) home, "The Casements," is now a popular attraction. Early (1900s) automobile races were held on the city's hard sand beaches. Today, it is a busy tourist city, with beaches, sport fishing, and an annual antique car festival.

Orofino city, pop. 2868, seat of Clearwater Co., N Idaho, on the Clearwater R., 37 mi/60 km E of Lewiston. A mining town during the 1860 gold rush, Orofino was moved 25 mi/40 km from its original site in 1898. The railroad's arrival in 1928 made it a timber shipping point. The city is still gateway to one of the nation's largest stands of white pine. Lumbering, lumber milling, diverse agriculture, dairying, and livestock raising all contribute to today's economy. The DWORSHAK DAM is just NW.

Oromocto town, pop. 9325, seat of Sunbury Co., SC New Brunswick, where the Oromocto R. flows N into the Saint John R., 13 mi/21 km SE of Fredericton. On the site of Malecite and Acadian settlements, it was established in 1783 by LOYALISTS, and remained a small agricultural and timber-based community until the 1950s, when C. F. B. Gagetown, Canada's largest (275,000 ac/110,000 ha) military training facility, grew on its E border. It is now primarily a service center for the base.

Orono **1.** town, pop. 10,573, Penobscot Co., EC Maine. Orono, which originally included OLD TOWN, is along the Penobscot R., 8 mi/13 km N of Bangor. The town was named for a Penobscot chief friendly to settlers. It is the seat of the main campus of the University of Maine (1862). Industries include the manufacture of textiles, wood and paper products, canvas products, oars and paddles, and concrete. **2.** in Minnesota: **a.** in Hennepin Co.: see under L. MINNETONKA. **b.** former name for ELK RIVER, Sherburne Co.

Oroville city, pop. 11,960, seat of Butte Co., NC California, at the W base of the Sierra Nevada (the MOTHER LODE), on the Feather R., 66 mi/106 km N of Sacramento. Settled in 1849, it was one of the largest of the gold rush towns, peopled by waves of miners, including Chinese who built the 1863 Temple of Assorted Deities. With many signs of its boom days still to be seen, Oroville is a tourist destination, and the processing and shipping center for an area producing citrus fruit, olives, vegetables, and lumber. It was into Oroville that Ishi, "the last wild Indian," wandered in 1911, 40 mi/64 km S of his home in the Lassen foothills (see ISHI WILDERNESS). **L. Oroville,** just NE, is a popular recreational center. Many-fingered, with a shoreline over 165 mi/266 km long, it lies at an elevation of 900 ft/274 m, and is part of the California State Water Project. **Oroville Dam,** completed 1967 and 755 ft/230 m high, impounds the Feather R. to form the lake. It is a major power generation source.

Orrs Island 4 mi/6 km long, in Cumberland Co., SW Maine. It is part of the town of Harpswell, in Casco Bay, 10 mi/16 km S of Brunswick. Pearl of Orrs Island House is believed to be the residence of the heroine of *Pearl of Orr's Island* by Harriet Beecher Stowe. Orrs is connected with Bailey I. (S) and the mainland (N) by bridges and causeways. It is both residential and recreational in character.

Orwell town, pop. 1114, Addison Co., WC Vermont. It is on L. Champlain, 21 mi/34 km NW of Rutland. A former sheep raising center, it remains primarily agricultural. Mt. INDEPENDENCE is in the W.

Osage city, pop. 3429, seat of Mitchell Co., NC Iowa, 20 mi/32 km NE of Mason City. A trading center for the region's corn and hogs, with limestone quarries, it was the boyhood home of author Hamlin Garland, and figures in some of his fiction.

Osage County 2265 sq mi/5866 sq km, pop. 41,645, in NE Oklahoma, bordered by Kansas (N) and the Arkansas R. (SW). It is the largest county in the state, with its seat at PAWHUSKA. The county is coextensive with the Osage Indian Reservation, formed in the 1870s after most Osage lands had been taken by white settlers. Since the discovery of oil beneath the reservation early in the 1920s, the tribe (most of whom live here) and county have prospered. There are also livestock raising and some diversified agriculture.

Osage Plains extensive section of the central US PRAIRIES, covering the eastern third of Kansas, S of the Kansas R., and the center of Oklahoma, and extending S into NC Texas and NE into W Missouri, to the edge of the Kansas City area. The Osage Plains lie between the GREAT PLAINS (W) and the Ozark Plateau and lower-lying prairie areas (E). They are generally 1000–2000 ft/300–600 m in elevation, with flat or rolling terrain, and lie S of the extent of Pleistocene ice sheets. The Arkansas, Cimarron, Canadian, Washita, Red, and Brazos are among rivers that drain them to the E or SE. Wichita, Oklahoma City, Tulsa (on the E edge), and Wichita Falls are among important cities. The Osage, who lived in the Ohio Valley before migrating W, gave their name to the area, living in parts of it.

Osage River 360 mi/580 km long, in Missouri. It is formed by the junction of the MARAIS DES CYGNES and Little Osage rivers SE of Rich Hill, and flows generally ENE, widening into the Harry S Truman Reservoir, formed by a dam near Warsaw, then continues into the LAKE OF THE OZARKS, impounded by the Bagnell Dam, at the head of navigation. It then winds NE to join the Missouri R., 12 mi/19 km E of Jefferson City. The Osage lived along the river's banks in the 17th century, when whites first arrived. With its tributaries the river drains parts of the Osage Plains (W) and the N OZARK PLATEAU (S).

Osawatomie city, pop. 4590, Miami Co., EC Kansas, on the Marais des Cygnes R., 47 mi/75 km SW of Kansas City. Founded by the New England Emigrant Aid Company (1855), it was a temporary home to the abolitionist John Brown, and a station on the UNDERGROUND RAILROAD before the Civil War. In 1856 it was the site of the "Battle of Osawatomie," a bloody clash between Brown and his anti-slavery forces and proslavery Kansans. Today it is a rail shipping center for grain and fruit.

Osceola city, pop. 8930, co-seat (with BLYTHEVILLE) of Mississippi Co., NE Arkansas, 15 mi/24 km S of Blytheville, on the Mississippi R. In a rich agricultural area producing cotton and alfalfa, the city is also involved in the manufacture of cottonseed oil, cotton ginning, and sawmilling.

Osceola National Forest about 180,000 ac/73,000 ha, in NE Florida, W of Jacksonville. LAKE CITY (SW) and OLUSTEE (S) are gateways. Established in 1932 as an experimental naval stores (turpentine, etc.) growing area, it is now largely recreational, and noted as a hunting site. It is characterized by flat pine woods, swamps, and ponds.

Oscoda see under WURTSMITH AIR FORCE BASE, Michigan.

Oshawa city, pop. 129,344, Durham Regional Municipality, S Ontario, on the N shore of L. Ontario, 30 mi/48 km ENE of Toronto. Founded in 1795 on the Toronto–Kingston military road, it developed as a lake port and agricultural market town, and is now a major manufacturing center. The headquarters of Canada's General Motors is here; automobiles and auto accessories, pharmaceuticals, plastics, metal, leather, and woolen goods, machinery, furniture, and glass are manufactured.

Oshkosh city, pop. 55,006, seat of Winnebago Co., EC Wisconsin, on the W shore of L. Winnebago, at the mouth of the upper Fox R., 80 mi/128 km NW of Milwaukee. Settlement of the area began c.1830, and the city became an important 19th-century lumbering center. Its name honors a Menominee chief. Industries include dairy processing, and the manufacture of transportation equipment, electronic components, wood and paper products, paints, tools, concrete blocks, and pumps. A campus of the University of Wisconsin (1871) is in the city.

Oskaloosa city, pop. 10,632, seat of Mahaska Co., SC Iowa, 22 mi/35 km NW of Ottumwa. A small fort (1835) preceded a Quaker settlement in 1843. Iowa's first coal mine was located here. Later, the city became an agricultural trading center, processing farm products and shipping livestock raised in the region. Farm equipment, feed, and clothing are among its manufactures. William Penn College (1873) is here. Lake Keomah State Park is 4 mi/6 km E.

Ossabaw Island one of the SEA ISLANDS, in the Atlantic Ocean 15 mi/24 km S of Savannah, in Chatham Co., E Georgia. Ten mi/16 km N–S and 8 mi/13 km wide, the marshy island is at the mouth of the Ogeechee R., on Ossabaw Sound.

Ossining town, pop. 34,124, Westchester Co., SE New York, on the E bank of the Hudson R., 32 mi/52 km NNE of New York City. Primarily residential, it has some light manufacturing, including the production of wire, office furniture, and medical instruments, and has electronics research facilities. The Sing Sing Correctional Facility was established here (1824) when the community was called Sing Sing, after the Sing Sing Kill, which runs through the center and is crossed by the Croton Aqueduct Arch (1838–40).

Ossipee, Lake resort lake in Freedom and Ossipee townships, Carroll Co., E New Hampshire, named for the Ossipee Indians. It is 2 mi/3 km wide and 3.5 mi/6 km long, and is a year-round sports center. The resort village of Center Ossipee is on the SW shore.

Oswego city, pop. 19,195, co-seat of Oswego Co., NC New York, on L. Ontario, at the mouth of the Oswego R., 35 mi/56 km NW of Syracuse. The site of Fort Oswego (1727) and Fort Ontario (1755), it was strategically important during the Colonial period. The first permanent settlement was established in 1796, and following the opening of the Oswego Canal in 1828, developed as an important distribution point. Railroad competition briefly interrupted Oswego's importance as a port, until it became the N terminus of the New York State Barge Canal in 1917, and, in 1959, a port on the SAINT LAWRENCE SEAWAY. Oswego now manufactures paper, marine engines, textiles, clothing, metal products, and foods, and is a leading power production center. The State University of New York College at Oswego (1861) is here. The Nine Mile Point nuclear plant in Scriba, 6 mi/10 km NE on L. Ontario, houses two reactors (1969, 1987) with a history of safety problems.

Oswego County 954 sq mi/2471 sq km, pop. 121,771, in NC New York, bounded by L. Ontario (N) and by Oneida L. and the Oneida R. (S). Its dual seats are Oswego and Pulaski. The city of Oswego is a diversified manufacturing and power-producing center, and there is industry in the city of FULTON. Largely agricultural, the county produces dairy products, fruits, and vegetables. There is a good deal of resort development, especially on the lakes.

Oswego River 23 mi/37 km long, in NC New York. It is formed by the confluence of the Oneida and Seneca rivers just S of Phoenix, and flows past Fulton to L. Ontario at Oswego, and is part of the New York State Barge Canal System.

Otay Mesa in San Diego Co., extreme SW California, 13 mi/21 km SSE of downtown San Diego, extending along the border of Baja California, Mexico. A flat, scrubby area just N of the city of Tijuana, it has been discussed as the possible site of a huge international airport.

Otish, Monts English, **Otish Mountains** range of the CANADIAN SHIELD, in C Québec, W of the Labrador border and NW of the Manicouagan Reservoir, reaching 3724 ft/1135 m at Mt. Yapeitso. It is the source of the Eastmain, Péribonca, Outardes, and other rivers flowing N or W in the Hudson Bay watershed or S in the St. Lawrence watershed.

Otsego Lake in Otsego Co., EC New York, 28 mi/45 km SE of Utica. It is 7 mi/11 km NNE–SSW and up to 1.5 mi/2 km wide, and is the primary source of the SUSQUEHANNA R. COOPERSTOWN is at the S end. Otsego L. is called "Glimmerglass" in James Fenimore Cooper's novel *The Deerslayer;* the name is used locally.

Ottawa **1.** city, pop. 17,451, seat of La Salle Co., NC Illinois, at the junction of the Fox and Illinois rivers, 40 mi/64 km S of De Kalb. Besides serving as an agricultural trade center, it manufactures glass and plastic materials; nearby are deposits of silica, sand, clay, coal, and gravel. The site was visited by early French explorers and missionaries, but permanent settlement dates from 1830. It grew with the opening of the Illinois and Michigan Canal (1848) and the arrival of the Rock Island Railroad (1853). The first Lincoln-Douglas debate was held here in 1858. Buffalo Rock State Park is 4 mi/6 km W; Illini State Park is 7 mi/11 km, and the Marseilles Wildlife Area 9 mi/14 km SE. **2.** city, pop. 10,667, seat of Franklin Co., EC Kansas, on the Marais des Cygnes R., 23 mi/37 km S of Lawrence. Settled in 1832 on land ceded by the Ottawa Indians, it grew as a pioneer village after the establishment of a Baptist mission (1837). A railroad center in an agricultural region, the city processes and ships grain, livestock, poultry, and dairy products and manufactures textiles, cement, and plastics. Ottawa University (1865) is here. **3.** city, pop. 313,987, capital of Canada and seat of the Ottawa-Carleton Regional Municipality (pop. 678,147, including GLOUCESTER, KANATA, NEPEAN, and other communities), SE Ontario, on the Ottawa R., opposite (S) HULL, Québec. It is the center of the National Capital Region and of the Ottawa-Hull Census Metropolitan Area (CMA), Canada's fourth-largest, with a pop. of 920,857. At the Chaudière Falls of the Ottawa and the mouth of the RIDEAU R., and across from the mouth of Québec's GATINEAU R., Ottawa's site was important in the movements of Algonquian and other peoples long before Europeans (Champlain, 1613) first saw it. It was little but a transportation nexus until around 1800, when Hull was settled as a timber center. The War of 1812 made the Rideau's potential as a protected route between the East (via the Ottawa) and L. Ontario (S) clear, and in 1826 the RIDEAU CANAL was initiated to develop this resource. Its engineers, under Lt. Col. John By, established what came to be known as Bytown, on the site of Ottawa's LOWER TOWN. At the same time, the area's lumber industry boomed, and Bytown grew as a military and industrial settlement. In 1855 it was given the Algonquian tribal (and the river's) name Ottawa (*Outaouais* in French), in part to attract possible selection as the capital of a newly united Province of Canada. In 1857 Queen Victoria chose Ottawa for the new capital; the neutral site (away from both Montréal and its burgeoning rival Toronto) and safe distance from the United States recommended it. Government quickly assumed primacy in Ottawa's life. Today the city has become a carefully developed world capital. Since the late-19th-century decline of the lumber industry it has not been notably industrial. A recent boom in electronics and communications technology has occurred in the city and in Kanata and other nearby communities; but Ottawa's business is basically government and related commerce, finance, research, and cultural activity. A city long roughly half British and Protestant, half French or Irish and Catholic, has acquired greater diversity. It is known for its government buildings; its parkland, including a GREENBELT and the now recreational Rideau Canal; its galleries and museums; and institutions including Carleton University (1942) and the University of Ottawa (1848). See also: CENTRAL EXPERIMENTAL FARM; LOWER TOWN; NATIONAL CAPITAL REGION; PARLIAMENT HILL (and the Peace Tower, Red Chamber, and Green Chamber); SUSSEX DRIVE; UPPER TOWN.

Ottawa County **1.** 567 sq mi/1469 sq km, pop. 187,768, in SW Michigan, bounded by L. Michigan (W) and drained by the Macatawa, Black, and Grand rivers. Its seat is Grand Haven. Along the L. Michigan shore are commercial fisheries, beach resorts, and oil refineries. There is manufacturing at Grand Haven, Holland, Jenison, and Zeeland. The county raises tulips, celery, livestock, poultry, grain, potatoes, and sugar beets, and makes dairy products. Also situated here are two state parks and the Grand Haven State Game Area. **2.** 253 sq mi/655 sq km, pop. 40,029, in N Ohio, bounded (NE) by L. Erie and (SE) by Sandusky Bay. Its seat is Port Clinton, and it includes the BASS ISLANDS. Agriculture includes dairy, fruit, grain, sugar beet, and truck farming. There is manufacturing at Genoa, Oak Harbor, and Port Clinton. Commercial fishing and limestone quarrying are also important. The Davis-Besse nuclear power plant (1977) is in the E.

Ottawa River French, **Rivière des Ontaouais** 700 mi/1100 km long, in Québec and Ontario. It rises on the Laurentian Plateau in SW Québec, E of the La Vérendrye Wildlife Reserve, and winds W through a series of lakes and reservoirs, into the N of L. Timiskaming, on the Québec-Ontario border. From the lake it emerges as a wide, powerful river, flanked by steep walls, and continues SSE to Mattawa, where the Mattawa R. connects it with L. NIPISSING (W) and thence with GEORGIAN BAY via a major early river-and-PORTAGE route. Farther downstream (SE) at Deep River, the Ottawa forces through a narrow gorge 700 ft/213 m in depth. Passing over rapids to the SE, it widens and splits into two channels, forming Allumette (near PEMBROKE) and Calumet islands before reaching the Chaudière Falls at Ottawa, where the RIDEAU CANAL and GATINEAU R. join it. Below Ottawa it widens and flows E through farmland, before splitting into DISTRIBUTARIES and joining the St. Lawrence R. just W of Montréal. Formerly called the Grand R. of the Algonquins, the Ottawa now bears the name of an Algonquian tribe. It was a major early trade and exploration route to the interior, key to the fur operations of Montréal's NORTH WEST COMPANY. As that trade declined, lumbering gained in importance, peaking in the mid 19th century. Construction (completed 1832) of the RIDEAU CANAL created a protected route to the S Great Lakes, but it was only briefly important. The Ottawa today has numerous hydroelectric plants, and is also recreationally important. Through almost its entire length below L. Timiskaming, it forms the Québec-Ontario border. It is the St. Lawrence's largest tributary.

Otter, Peaks of see PEAKS OF OTTER.

Otterbein inner-city neighborhood in SW BALTIMORE, Maryland, just E of CAMDEN YARDS and W of the INNER HARBOR. Named for Philip William Otterbein, 18th-century German pastor who founded the United Brethren in Christ while working in the area, it is a center of revival of older buildings by urban homesteaders. Baltimore's Convention Center and Federal Reserve Bank branch are here; FEDERAL HILL is just SE.

Ottumwa city, pop. 24,488, seat of Wapello Co., SC Iowa, on the Des Moines R., 73 mi/118 km SE of Des Moines. A trading center for the region's farms, it also has a major meatpacking plant, railroad shops, and factories making such goods as automotive products, electric components, and agricultural and materials-handling equipment.

Ouachita Mountains series of narrow E–W shale and sandstone ridges, considered a S continuation of the OZARK PLATEAU, extending some 220 mi/350 km in a belt 50–60 mi/80–100 km wide, from W of Little Rock, Arkansas, into E Oklahoma, where they reach 2800 ft/854 m. The Fourche Mts. are an eastern subdivision. The **Ouachita National Forest,** established in 1907 and covering more than 1.6 million ac/650,000 ha (2500 sq mi/6500 sq km), has headquarters in Hot Springs, Arkansas. Unusual for their E–W orientation, the Ouachitas contain numerous valuable minerals, including barite, mined commercially in the Magnet Cove area, SW of Little Rock. Magazine Mt. (2753 ft/840 m), in the N Ouachitas, is Arkansas's highest point.

Ouachita River formerly, **Washita** 600 mi/970 km long, in Arkansas and Louisiana. It rises near Mena, in Polk Co., W Arkansas, in the Ouachita Mts., and flows E into the Hot Springs area, where it passes through L. Ouachita (formed by the Blakey Mt. Dam, 1955); L. Hamilton (the Carpenter Dam, 1931); and L. Catherine (the Remmel Dam, 1925). Turning SSW, it is joined by the Caddo R. (from the W) and passes Arkadelphia. It then flows SSE, is joined by the Little Missouri R. (from the W), and passes Camden. Turning SE across the Mississippi alluvial plain, it reaches L. Jack Lee, formed at the Louisiana border by the Felsenthal Dam; the Saline R. (from the N) joins it here, within the lake and the Felsenthal National Wildlife Refuge. In Louisiana, the river is joined by the Bayou Bartholomew (from the E) as it winds S to Monroe. It continues SSE to Jonesville, where the Tensas R. joins it; below this point the Ouachita is known as the **Black R.** At Acme, it empties into the Red R. Navigable as far as Camden, Arkansas, the Ouachita flows through resort areas in its upper reaches, forests in its middle stretches, and cotton and ranch lands in its lower section.

Ouray city, pop. 644, seat of Ouray Co., SW Colorado, in a mountain-bounded box canyon in the San Juan Mts., on the Uncompahgre R., 52 mi/84 km NNE of Durango. Named for a Ute chief, it was originally (1875) a silver-mining town. Tourism and ranching are now economic mainstays, and the city is a health resort with hot mineral springs. After the silver crash of 1893, Ouray became known for its gold-producing Camp Bird mine. Many local mines are still in operation, yielding gold, lead, zinc, silver, uranium, and copper.

Outagamie County 642 sq mi/1663 sq km, pop. 140,510, E Wisconsin. Its seat is APPLETON. It is drained by the Wolf, Fox, and Embarrass rivers. Dairying throughout the county and papermaking in communities along the Fox R., in the SE, are the main economic activities. Some livestock, oats, and corn are produced.

Outaouais Urban Community 182 sq mi/470 sq km, pop. 201,536, comprising the five cities of AYLMER, BUCKINGHAM, GATINEAU, HULL, and Masson (pop. 5753). It includes the Québec suburbs of Ottawa, Ontario (its name is the French spelling of Ottawa); it is part of the Ottawa metropolitan area, and much of it is within the NATIONAL CAPITAL REGION.

Outardes, Rivière see under R. MANICOUAGAN, Québec.

Outer Banks narrow, sandy barrier reef stretching almost the entire length of the North Carolina coastline, and broken by inlets into a chain of islands. The main islands, N to S, are Bodie, Hatteras, OCRACOKE, Portsmouth, and Core Banks. Three prominent capes dominate the banks: Cape HATTERAS on Hatteras I., Cape LOOKOUT on Core Banks, and Cape FEAR on Smith I., all infamous for their numerous shipwrecks. Cape Lookout, however, is often considered the Banks' S boundary, and Cape Henry, in Virginia, the N limit. Lying between the islands and the irregular mainland shoreline are, N to S, CURRITUCK, ALBEMARLE, PAMLICO, Core, and BOGUE sounds. ROANOKE I. lies in a channel between Albemarle and Pamlico sounds, and is connected by bridges with the mainland on the W and Bodie I. on the E. Another link to the islands is the Wright Memorial Bridge from the mainland, farther N on Bodie I. Ferries provide access to Ocracoke I. The Banks' main settlements, N to S, are Southern Shores, KITTY HAWK, Kill Devil Hills (site of the Wright Brothers National Memorial), and NAGS HEAD on Bodie I.; Rodanthe, Salvo, Avon, Buxton, and Hatteras on Hatteras I.; and Ocracoke on Ocracoke I., once a shipping center and the haunt of Blackbeard and other pirates in the 18th century. Manteo, on Roanoke I., is the location of the Fort Raleigh National Historic Site. Cape Hatteras National Seashore includes Bodie I. S of Nags Head, and all of Hatteras and Ocracoke islands. Vegetation consists primarily of dune and marsh grasses, live oaks, red cedars, and yaupons. Pea Island National Wildlife Refuge covers over 5900 ac/2390 ha on the N end (also called Pea I.) of Hatteras I. The main industries on the Banks are commercial and sport fishing and tourism. Since the 18th century, isolation has produced distinctive cultural, particularly linguistic, patterns among the permanent inhabitants, who are known as Bankers. The Banks are frequently battered by northeasters in winter and hurricanes in summer and fall. Erosion has moved much of the shoreline westward, continually creating new inlets, islands, shoals, and sandbars.

Outer Boroughs, the to Manhattanites, the other four boroughs of New York City: the Bronx, Brooklyn, Queens, and Staten Island.

Outerbridge Crossing see under TOTTENVILLE, New York.

Outer Drive outer of two ring roads in Detroit, Michigan, contemplated as early as 1805; the inner ring was formed by GRAND BOULEVARD. Outer Drive, which circles Downtown at distances up to 10 mi/16 km, now exists as a segmented boulevard extending from the Detroit R. at Ecorse (SW) through Dearborn and River Rouge Park (W), and across the N part of Detroit, reaching L. Saint Clair at Grosse Pointe Park. Once suburban, it now passes through a variety of urban neighborhoods.

outport in Newfoundland, any coastal community other than the capital, St. John's. The term's historical resonance is owed partly to the 17th-century British policy that outlawed any settlement except at St. John's, to discourage competition with officially sanctioned fishing. Outports, which ring the island's bays, were established from the early 16th through the early 19th centuries by Basque, French, English, and other settlers; most have remained very small throughout their history.

Outremont city, pop. 22,935, MONTRÉAL URBAN COMMUNITY, S Québec, on the NE slope of Mt. Royal, "across the mountain" from Downtown. Incorporated in 1875, it is an affluent, largely francophone residential community. The Collège Jésus-Marie d'Outremont is here.

Oval Office, the see under WHITE HOUSE, Washington, D.C.

Overbrook in Pennsylvania: **a.** residential district, W Philadelphia, between FAIRMOUNT PARK (E) and the Montgomery Co. line, N of WEST PHILADELPHIA. The MAIN LINE tracks pass through Overbrook, which is also home to several institutions including St. Joseph's College (1851). **b.** residential neighborhood on the S side of Pittsburgh, on the S slope of MOUNT WASHINGTON, 4 mi/6 km S of the GOLDEN TRIANGLE, and N of Whitehall and Baldwin Township. Named for the Philadelphia district, it was built up after World War I, and filled with middle-class families during the 1920s.

Overland city, pop. 17,987, St. Louis Co., EC Missouri, 12 mi/19 km NW of downtown St. Louis. Essentially a residential suburb, it has some light industry.

Overland Park city, pop. 111,790, Johnson Co., NE Kansas, 9 mi/14 km SSW of downtown Kansas City. This relatively new (inc. 1960) city is a leading business center and the site of several national coporate headquarters. It also serves as a residential suburb. The National Collegiate Athletic Association (NCAA) headquarters are here, and it is also the seat of Johnson County Community College (1967).

Overland Route also, **Overland Trail** term variously used for mid-19th-century land routes to California. The OREGON TRAIL was one Overland Route, but the name came to refer esp. to alternates. The **Southern Overland Route,** otherwise the Butterfield Southern Route or Butterfield Trail, was used in 1858–61 by carriers for the Butterfield Stage (American Express) company. Their route, 2800 mi/4500 km long, began at Tipton, Missouri, 30 mi/48 km WSW of Jefferson City, where the PACIFIC RAILROAD had extended from St. Louis. It ran across SW Missouri, through Springfield, into NW Arkansas, through Fayetteville and the Boston Mts., to Fort Smith. Continuing through SE Oklahoma, past McAlester, it crossed the Red R. at Preston, Texas. From Denison, founded on the trail, it then cut SW across NC Texas, around the Guadalupe Mts., and W, via the Hueco Tanks, to El Paso, the halfway point. From El Paso it ran through Mesilla, Deming, and Columbus, New Mexico, and across S Arizona, via the Apache Pass, to Yuma. Finally, it crossed the Mojave Desert to Los Angeles and NW to San

Francisco. The Southern Overland Route was abandoned when the Civil War began, and Butterfield business shifted to the **Central Overland Route.** This basically followed the Oregon Trail into S Wyoming, where it diverged from the North Platte R. and ran through desert areas to Fort Bridger and SW into Utah. From the Great Salt L. it proceeded W along the route roughly followed later in the decade by the UNION PACIFIC and CENTRAL PACIFIC railroads, across N Nevada and through the Sierra Nevada (via the Carson Pass, also used by the Pony Express) to San Francisco Bay. The opening of the transcontinental railroad in 1869 wiped out the stagecoach business.

Overlea unincorporated suburb, pop. 12,137, Baltimore Co., N Maryland, 6 mi/10 km NE of downtown Baltimore, between the city line (W) and Interstate 695.

Overlook–Page Manor unincorporated community, pop. 13,242, Montgomery Co., SW Ohio, adjacent (E) to Dayton, near Wright-Patterson Air Force Base and the Mad R. It is a primarily residential suburb.

Overseas Highway see under FLORIDA KEYS.

Over-the-Rhine residential neighborhood in Cincinnati, Ohio, N of Downtown and immediately N of the Miami and Erie Canal. Its name derives from the preponderance of German residents here around the turn of the 20th century. Residents here today, a mix of Appalachian and black migrants, are largely poor and working-class families. The area has, however, experienced a great deal of private investment in home renovation in recent years.

Overton Park 355 ac/144 ha, in Memphis, Tennessee. Established in 1900 on what was then the city's extreme NE, it is at the corner of the East and North sections of the PARKWAY, 3 mi/5 km E of Downtown. The Memphis Zoo, Brooks Memorial Art Gallery, Memphis College of Art, and a golf course are among the features of the city's major park. Rhodes College lies just N.

Overtown predominantly black neighborhood just N of the Government Center in downtown Miami, Florida. Settled by railroad workers in the 1920s, it was a thriving commercial and residential district into the 1950s. Overtown Square, on NW 2nd Ave., was called "Little Broadway" or "The Great Black Way" for its entertainments. Urban renewal in the 1950s and 1960s brought displacement by freeway construction, and the area is now economically distressed. The Miami Arena, home to the Miami Heat (basketball), is here.

Oviedo city, pop. 11,114, Seminole Co., EC Florida, 12 mi/19 km NE of Orlando, just S of L. Jessup. Incorporated in 1925, it has produced citrus fruits and fertilizer, and is now a growing residential community.

Owasco Lake one of the FINGER LAKES in WC New York, 22 mi/35 km SW of Syracuse. It is 11 mi/17 km NNW–SSE and 1 mi/1.5 km wide, and lies between L. Cayuga (SW) and Skaneateles L. (NE). Its outlet runs N through AUBURN and into the Seneca R.

Owasso city, pop. 11,151, Tulsa and Rogers counties, NE Oklahoma, 10 mi/16 km NE of downtown Tulsa. A residential suburb, it also processes agricultural products.

Owatonna city, pop. 19,386, seat of Steele Co., SE Minnesota, on the Straight R., 15 mi/24 km S of Faribault. It is the trading, processing, and transportation center for the surrounding dairy and truck farming area. Cooperative creameries dominate the economy. Jewelry, tools, and farm equipment are manufactured. The city is also the headquarters of Federated Insurance. Settled in the 1850s as a trading post, Owatonna became the state's first health spa, due to its numerous mineral springs. Louis Sullivan designed its National Farmers' Bank Building (1908).

Owego village, pop. 4442, seat of Tioga Co., SC New York, on the Susquehanna R., 19 mi/31 km W of Binghamton and 7 mi/11 km N of the Pennsylvania border. It is on the site of an Iroquois village destroyed in 1779. Situated in a dairy farming area, it has light manufactures including furniture and other wood products, and depends somewhat on summer tourism.

Owego Creek 35 mi/56 km long, in SC New York. It rises in an East Branch in S Cortland Co., and a West Branch that forms the border of Tompkins and Tioga counties, and flows generally SSW, meeting with the Catatonk Creek before joining the Susquehanna R. at OWEGO.

Owensboro city, pop. 53,549, seat of Daviess Co., NW Kentucky, on the Ohio R., 38 mi/61 km SE of Evansville, Indiana. Laid out in 1816 as Rossborough, it had been Yellow Banks to early flatboatmen, because of the riverine clay. It became Owensboro only in 1866. In a rich agricultural area producing tobacco, soybeans, corn, fruit, and wheat, it is now W Kentucky's largest city. A river port and the site of a Federal encampment, it was partly burned in an 1864 Confederate attack. With abundant oil, gas, and coal deposits nearby, the city makes iron and steel products, chemicals, whiskey, cigars, plastics, and aluminum, and there is canning and meatpacking. Owensboro is home to Kentucky Wesleyan College (1858) and Brescia College (1950).

Owen Sound city, pop. 21,674, seat of Grey Co., S Ontario, on the Sydenham R. and Owen Sound of GEORGIAN BAY, L. Huron, 100 mi/160 km NW of Toronto. Settled in the 1840s, this port city now manufactures auto parts, rubber and glass products, and electrical components. Grain storage, publishing and printing, and tourism are also important; Owen Sound is a gateway to the BRUCE PENINSULA (NW) and Georgian Bay. The boyhood home of landscape painter Tom Thomson (1877–1917) is a museum.

Owens River 120 mi/190 km long, in EC California. It rises in the Sierra Nevada 15 mi/24 km SSE of MONO L., and flows generally SSE through the **Owens Valley,** between the Sierra Nevada (W) and the White and Inyo mountains (E), to **Owens L.,** just S of LONE PINE. The lake, once 18 mi/29 km long, is now a dry bed. The river's water is drained above the lake by the LOS ANGELES AQUEDUCT (1913), which taps it near Aberdeen; before the aqueduct, the valley was a fertile farm and orchard area. Lake Crowley (Long Valley Reservoir), 8 mi/13 km long, is near the Owens's source, NW of the valley.

Owings Mills unincorporated village, pop. 9474, Baltimore Co., N Maryland, 12 mi/19 km NW of downtown Baltimore. It developed around three grist mills established by Samuel Owings in the mid 18th century; his home and the upper mill still stand. An affluent residential suburb just outside the Baltimore Beltway (I-695), Owings Mills has substantial parkland, corporate facilities, and some high-tech industry.

Owl Creek stream at SHILOH, Tennessee, thought to have given its name to the story "An Occurrence at Owl Creek Bridge" by Ambrose Bierce, who fought here (April 1862), although he places the action in Alabama.

Owosso city, pop. 16,322, Shiawassee Co., SC Michigan, on the Shiawassee R., 26 mi/42 km NE of Lansing. Founded c.1835, it is a trading center for an area of truck and livestock farms. The city mills grain and manufactures a number of goods including electric motors and metal and wood products. It is the seat of John Wesley College. Politician Thomas E. Dewey was born here (1902).

Owyhee River 300 mi/480 km long, in N Nevada, SW Idaho, and SE Oregon. It rises in several forks in Elko Co., Nevada, and flows (the East Fork passing through the Duck Valley Indian Reservation) into Idaho. It crosses here through SW Owyhee Co., and is joined by more forks before crossing into Oregon. It continues NW and N through Malheur Co., being joined by the Little Owyhee R., to 48 mi/77 km–long, dam-created **L. Owyhee,** central unit of an extensive irrigation district, then NNE to meet the Snake R., 18 mi/29 km SSW of ONTARIO.

oxbow a river bend, likened to the shape of an ox yoke. As a river meanders, its flow may cause such a bend to become almost circular, at which point it may cut through the remaining neck of land. The old channel may then be closed by silt, leaving a crescent-shaped body of slack water, open at both ends, open at only one end, or closed at both ends (an **oxbow lake**). The land within such a bend is also often called an oxbow. In the lower Mississippi Valley, many BAYOUS are oxbows.

Oxford **1.** city, pop. 9362, Calhoun and Talladega counties, NE Alabama, just S of Anniston. A Civil War–era iron center, it later developed textile industries, and is now part of the industrial and commercial complex centered on Anniston. **2.** town, pop. 9984, seat of LAFAYETTE Co., NC Mississippi, 47 mi/76 km WNW of Tupelo. Settled in 1835 in an area previously inhabited by the Chickasaw, it became in 1848 the seat of the University of Mississippi, officially located in adjacent (SW) University. It is primarily an academic town. During the Civil War "Ole Miss" buildings were used as Confederate hospitals, and the town was burned by Union forces in Aug. 1864. Nonetheless, many antebellum buildings remain. Today the city is a trading center for local crops including cotton, corn, and other vegetables and for timber, poultry, and dairy products. There are sawmills, and manufactures include wood products, clothing, motors, and electrical appliances. Tourism is also important. Oxford was the longtime home of novelist William Faulkner (born 1897 in NEW ALBANY), who used it as the model for his fictional Jefferson, seat of YOKNAPATAWPHA Co.; his home, Rowan Oak (1844), is open to the public. The University is noted for its Center for the Study of Southern Culture. The campus was the scene of violent unrest in Sept. 1962 when the first black student, James Meredith, was enrolled. **3.** city, pop. 7913, seat of Granville Co., N North Carolina, 9 mi/14 km W of Henderson. It has been a tobacco marketing and processing center since the mid 19th century. **4.** city, pop. 18,937, Butler Co., SW Ohio, 12 mi/19 km NW of Hamilton. It is the seat of Miami University (1809).

Oxnard city, pop. 142,216, Ventura Co., SW California, 53 mi/85 km WNW of Los Angeles, immediately N of PORT HUENEME, on the Santa Barbara Channel of the Pacific Ocean. Incorporated in 1903, it is in an alluvial plain S of the Santa Clara R. that is one of the state's most fertile agricultural areas; lemons and vegetables are raised. The city grew rapidly in the early 1900s as an agricultural trade center, and has since diversified. Oil and natural gas are found in the area. The port serves as a shipping outlet and commercial and sport fishing base. Naval facilities at Port Hueneme and the Pacific Missile Test Center, 5 mi/8 km SE at Point Mugu, also contribute to the economy, as do visitors to beaches and other attractions. Among Oxnard's manufactures are aerospace equipment, paper products, agricultural chemicals, mobile homes, and processed foods.

Oxon Hill unincorporated suburb in Prince George's Co., C Maryland, 7 mi/11 km S of Washington, D.C. Large estates and fortifications defending the capital characterized the area in the late 18th through the 19th century. John Hanson, president of the pre-Constitution United States, died and was buried in 1783 at Oxon Hill Manor. In the 20th century the area has been a bedroom community for lower-level Washington workers. With Glassmanor (N) it has a pop. of 35,794.

Oyster Bay in New York: **a.** unincorporated village, pop. 6687, in Oyster Bay town, Nassau Co., on Oyster Bay Harbor. A quiet village on Long Island's North Shore, it is primarily residential. Theodore Roosevelt's home, Sagamore Hill, is in Cove Neck (pop. 332), just NE. **b.** town, pop. 292,657, the easternmost in Nassau Co. Stretching from the North Shore to the South Shore, it includes Oyster Bay village, Hicksville, Bethpage, Syosset, Farmingdale, Massapequa, and numerous other suburban and resort communities.

Oyster Creek 9 mi/14 km long, in Ocean Co., New Jersey, 10 mi/16 km S of TOMS RIVER. It flows E into Barnegat Bay, and is the site of a nuclear power plant, opened 1969 just E of the Garden State Parkway.

Ozark city, pop. 12,922, seat of Dale Co., SE Alabama, 5 mi/8 km E of Ft. Rucker and 22 mi/35 km NW of Dothan. An old cotton center, it today processes and ships the area's hogs, peanuts, and corn. Local growth soared with the establishment of Ft. Rucker during World War II. The Alabama Aviation and Technical College (1960) is here, and the city builds helicopters.

Ozark Plateau or **Plateaus** also, **the Ozarks** or **Ozark Mountains** eroded tableland, covering some 50,000 sq mi/130,000 sq km in S Missouri, N Arkansas, NE Oklahoma, and SE Kansas. Bounded SW by the Neosho R., S by the Arkansas R., and N by the Missouri and Osage rivers, the region is considered to end in the E at the Black R., in Arkansas and Missouri. A SW element of the APPALACHIAN System, the Ozarks, comprising igneous roots with an overlay (largely eroded away except in the W) of limestone and dolomite mixed with flints, generally reach 1200–1800 ft/370–550 m. Their "mountains" are in many places called *knobs.* The region is conventionally divided into four sections. In the NE is Missouri's Salem Plateau, which extends into NE Arkansas; in the NW, also chiefly in Missouri, is the Springfield Plateau. In the E are the SAINT FRANÇOIS Mts. of Missouri. In the SW are the rugged BOSTON Mts., the plateau's highest (over 2300 ft/710m), which extend from W Arkansas into Oklahoma. The OUACHITA Mts., S of the Arkansas R., are sometimes considered an extension of the Ozarks. The area was settled in the early 19th century, largely from Tennessee and Kentucky, by migrants accustomed to relatively isolated hill life, and has remained throughout its history a marginal farming zone (there is substantial fruit and poultry farming in NW Arkansas). Lead mining was formerly important in SE Missouri, in the area of Viburnum (the Old Lead Belt). In the 1830s Cherokees driven westward on the TRAIL OF TEARS settled areas on the E Oklahoma edges of the plateau.

Today, the lakes created in the 20th century by dams on Ozark rivers have helped to draw tourist and resort trade and retirees, altering the traditional pattern of poverty and isolation. BRANSON, Missouri, and EUREKA SPRINGS, Arkansas, are centers of this kind of development. Ozark folklore, music, and crafts now have a wide popularity. The **Ozark National Forest** (over 1 million ac/405,000 ha), with four separate units in NW Arkansas, was the scene (from 1908) of pioneering "scientific forestry" efforts. Much of Missouri's MARK TWAIN NATIONAL FOREST is in the Ozarks. The region's major rivers are the WHITE and its tributaries, including the BUFFALO, which flow W–E through the plateau; many others flow N into the Missouri. The **Ozark National Scenic Riverways** incorporates 134 mi/216 km of the Current and Jacks Fork rivers NW of Poplar Bluff, in SE Missouri.

Ozona unincorporated community, pop. 3181, seat of Crockett Co., SW Texas, 65 mi/105 km SW of San Angelo, on the Edwards Plateau. In an oil producing and ranching area, it is a wool processor and a noted hunting center.

Ozone Park residential and commercial section, SW Queens, New York. It lies W of Jamaica and NW of John F. Kennedy International Airport. Part of the old town of Jamaica, Ozone Park was developed in the early 20th century in a largely agricultural area N of Jamaica Bay; the name refers to the supposed healthy qualities of "ozone," or seaside air. Furnituremaking and other light manufactures have been pursued here, but the modern economy is geared largely to the nearby airport. South Ozone Park, the district closer to Kennedy, includes some of the area's poorer neighborhoods, as well as the AQUEDUCT race track, whose future is in doubt.

P

Pacifica city, pop. 37,670, San Mateo Co., NC California, 10 mi/16 km S of downtown San Francisco, on the Pacific Ocean. Incorporated in 1957, it merged nine small communities in a hilly coastal area formerly noted as a producer of artichokes, and is an affluent suburb.

Pacific Beach affluent oceanfront residential community in SAN DIEGO, California, between LA JOLLA (N) and Mission Beach, 8 mi/13 km NW of Downtown.

Pacific Crest Trail 2600-mi/4200-km footpath extending from the Baja California (Mexico) border c.40 mi/64 km ESE of San Diego, California, to the Washington–British Columbia border near the Skagit R. It follows or parallels crests in the PENINSULAR RANGES and SAN GABRIEL Mts., crosses the W edge of the Mojave Desert (the Antelope Valley), proceeds up the SIERRA NEVADA, skirts Mts. LASSEN and SHASTA, and continues along the CASCADES through Oregon and into Washington, ending at Manning Provincial Park, British Columbia. Initiated in 1920, it was designated a National Scenic Trail in 1968, and completed in 1993.

Pacific Flyway migration route used by birds and some insects (e.g., monarch butterflies) that winter in South or Central America or in Mexico (esp. Baja California). Many species follow the Pacific coastline, some swinging along the Aleutian Is. chain or Alaska's W coast to nest; others follow the Coast Ranges, Coast Mts., or Sierra Nevada, summering as far N as Canada's Arctic coast.

Pacific Grove city, pop. 16,117, Monterey Co., WC California, adjoining (NW) Monterey, on the S end of Monterey Bay. The city has been a meeting center since 1874, when it was founded by Methodists as a religious retreat; it was an early CHAUTAUQUA site. At Asilomar State Beach, on the W, is a well-known state conference facility. From Oct. to March, Pacific Grove is home to monarch butterflies migrating here from Canada and Alaska; there is a Butterfly Parade in Oct. Point Piños Lighthouse, the oldest (1855) working lighthouse on the US Pacific coast, and a state marine wildlife refuge are here.

Pacific Heights largely residential section of N SAN FRANCISCO, California, on high ground S of the MARINA DISTRICT, SE of the PRESIDIO, W of NOB HILL, and N of the WESTERN ADDITION. The city's most expensive neighborhood, it sprouted mansions (some of which survived the 1906 earthquake and fire) from the 1870s. Fillmore St. is its commercial spine.

Pacific Islands **1.** US possessions in the Pacific Ocean: see AMERICAN SAMOA; BAKER I.; GUAM; HOWLAND I.; JARVIS I.; JOHNSTON ATOLL; KINGMAN REEF; PALMYRA; SWAINS I. **2. Trust Territory of the Pacific Islands** US-administered trust established by the United Nations in 1947 for the Marshall, Caroline, and Northern Mariana islands, all in Micronesia, in the W Pacific Ocean. Ostensibly created to decolonize islands formerly occupied by Japan and other powers, it was a "strategic trust," allowing US military development; nuclear and missile testing and air and naval bases proliferated from the 1940s through the 1980s. Altogether, the trust comprised more than 2000 islands, of which approximately 100 are inhabited, in an area covering more than 3 million sq mi/7 million sq km. PALAU, in the W Caroline Is., was until 1994 the sole remaining trust territory. The NORTHERN MARIANAS became a US commonwealth in 1978. The Republic of the Marshall Islands and the four other island groups in the Carolines, now known as the Federated States of Micronesia, became independent in 1979, although they signed defense compacts with, and remain closely tied economically to, the US.

Pacific Northwest in the US, usually, the states of Washington and Oregon. The **Northwest** generally includes these states plus Idaho, sometimes also Montana. The Census Bureau defines California, Oregon, Washington, Alaska, and Hawaii as the **Pacific Region,** states immediately to the W the Mountain Region. The **Pacific Rim** comprises countries bordering the Pacific, including the US, Canada, Japan, China, and the Koreas.

Pacific Palisades **1.** oceanfront section of LOS ANGELES, California, on Santa Monica Bay, NW of Santa Monica and 16 mi/26 km W of Downtown. Founded in 1921 as a Methodist community, it became a writers' and artists' colony, and is now one of the wealthiest areas of the city, home to numerous Hollywood figures. **2.** residential community in HONOLULU Co., S Oahu, Hawaii, just NNE of PEARL CITY, and 9 mi/14 km NW of downtown Honolulu.

Pacific Railroad **1.** transcontinental railroad, linking the East and California, by way of the largely uninhabited (by whites) Great Plains, Rocky Mt., and Intermontane regions, contemplated from the 1830s and completed in the 1860s. The discovery (1848) of gold in, and rapid development of, California spurred planning for such a railroad. The outbreak of the Civil War, ending Congressional rivalry between North and South over choice of a route, allowed quick decision, and in July 1862, the Pacific Railroad Act authorized the UNION PACIFIC (from Nebraska) and CENTRAL PACIFIC (from California) railroads to build toward each other. The meeting of these lines at PROMONTORY, Utah, on

May 10, 1869, completed the first transcontinental railroad. East and West were subsequently joined by the meeting of the SANTA FE and SOUTHERN PACIFIC lines at Deming, New Mexico, in 1881; by the 1883 completion of the NORTHERN PACIFIC's line to Puget Sound; by the 1885 completion of the CANADIAN PACIFIC RAILWAY's main line to BURRARD INLET, British Columbia (the "**Pacific Railway**"); by the 1893 GREAT NORTHERN RAILWAY line; by the 1909 MILWAUKEE ROAD line; and by the 1915 completion of the Canadian Northern line (now part of the CANADIAN NATIONAL RAILWAY system). **2.** chartered in 1849 in Missouri, to build W from St. Louis to the Kansas border. After the Civil War it became part of the Missouri Pacific Railroad, now part of the UNION PACIFIC system.

Pacific Rim National Park 197 sq mi/510 sq km, in three units on the SW coast of VANCOUVER I., SW British Columbia, 53 mi/85 km NW of Victoria. Its 7-mi/11-km Long Beach is a noted beachcombing site. The more than 100 Broken Group Is. are in Barkley Sound. The southernmost unit includes the 48 mi/77 km–long West Coast Trail, which winds through coastal forest that receives over 120 in/300 cm of rain yearly. PORT ALBERNI is a gateway to the park, in which canoeing, kayaking, fishing, and wreck diving are popular.

Pacoima N SAN FERNANDO VALLEY section of LOS ANGELES, California, 18 mi/29 km NW of Downtown and just SE of San Fernando, on the intermittent Pacoima R. Its name is Shoshonean for "running water." Developed in the 1870s on the Southern Pacific Railroad, it has been a commercial and residential suburb, with large waterworks, one of the Valley's least affluent communities.

Padre Island Gulf of Mexico BARRIER ISLAND in five counties of S Texas. At 113 mi/183 km N–S (and up to 3 mi/5 km in width), it is the longest such island in the US, and consists mostly of beach and grassy dunes. When first seen (1519) by Europeans, it was inhabited by the Karankawa. When Father Nicholas Balli used it for ranching (around 1800), it came to be called Isla del Padre. Most of it (67.5 mi/109 km of beach; 130,400 ac/52,800 ha) became **Padre Island National Seashore** in 1962. It is known for its marine life, fishing (mackerel, sailfish, tarpon), and bird-watching. **South Padre Island** (town, Cameron Co., pop. 1677), a resort community at the S end, is the only settlement. CORPUS CHRISTI is near the N end, BROWNSVILLE the S.

Paducah city, pop. 27,256, seat of McCracken Co., W Kentucky, 66 mi/106 km WNW of Hopkinsville, on the Ohio R., just W of where the Tennessee R. joins it. It is a major river port and an important market for strawberries, soybeans, corn, timber, coal, and livestock. It was laid out (1827) by William Clark (of Lewis and Clark fame), and named for a Chickasaw chief, Paduke. In 1861, Union troops occupied it; Confederate forces under Nathan Forrest attacked in 1864, but withdrew. The river and several railroads made Paducah the leading trade center of W Kentucky into the 20th century, but it is now a smaller and quieter city than in its heyday. It has several small colleges, and attracts tourists.

Page Manor see OVERLOOK–PAGE MANOR, Ohio.

Page Valley see under SHENANDOAH R.

Pago Pago also, **Pango Pango** village, pop. 3519, capital of AMERICAN SAMOA, along expansive Pago Pago Harbor on the S coast of Tutuila I. Its business and administrative center lies next to Fagatogo (or Fangatongo, village, pop. 2323), site of a US naval station 1900–51. Modernized in the 1960s, Pago Pago is a popular tourist destination and cruise ship port of call. Matafao Peak (2142 ft/653 m) dominates the harbor, which is itself within a large CALDERA.

Pahvant Range NE–SW trending mountains, 40 mi/64 km long, W of the SEVIER R., in Fishlake National Forest, C Utah, with several peaks over 10,000 ft/3050 m. The TUSHAR Mts. are to the S, Fillmore and the Sevier Desert to the W. Interstate 70 runs along the range's E.

Painesville city, pop. 15,699, seat of Lake Co., NE Ohio, on the Grand R., 25 mi/40 km NE of Cleveland and 2 mi/3 km S of L. Erie. Founded in 1805, it is a trading center for the surrounding fruit, truck, and dairy farming area, and has had a nursery industry since the 1850s. Chemicals, rayon, machinery, and magnesium are produced here. Painesville is the seat of Lake Erie College (1856).

Painted Desert extending along the SW base of BLACK MESA and its extensions, in NE Arizona, for some 150 mi/240 km, from MARBLE CANYON (NW) to the area of the PETRIFIED FOREST (SE), along the N of the Little Colorado R. The ECHO CLIFFS rise E above the desert's N end. Effects of heat and light playing on this mineral-tinted BADLANDS produce unusual color effects; the surface is broken by ravines, columns, buttes, and other exposed and eroded sandstone formations. Wupatki National Monument, noted for ruins including the "tall house" from which it takes its name, is on the desert's SW edge, 25 mi/40 km NE of Flagstaff.

Painted Post village, pop. 1950, in Erwin Township, Steuben Co., SW New York, at the junction of the Tioga and Cohocton rivers, just NW of CORNING. An Indian memorial post once stood here, and an Iroquois village was wiped out in 1779. White settlement began in 1789, and a treaty with the Indians was signed here in 1791. Wood and metal products are manufactured.

Pajarito Plateau tableland (6000–8000 ft/1800–2450 m) W of Santa Fe, in N New Mexico, extending S from the Rio Chama for c.40 mi/65 km along the W side of the Rio Grande and on the SE edge of the JEMEZ Mts. This volcanic MESA, cut by many canyons, has been home to many different groups, including the Anasazi, since perhaps the 12th century. Its most notable ruins include those in Bandelier National Monument in Frijoles Canyon and the Puye Cliff Dwellings on the Santa Clara Indian Reservation. Many modern PUEBLOS are also in the region.

Palatine village, pop. 39,253, Cook Co., NE Illinois, a suburb 26 mi/42 km NW of Chicago. Mainly a residential community, it also has factories manufacturing auto supplies, safety glass, plastic molds, and fuses. Settled in 1833, Palatine remained a tiny agricultural trade settlement, even with the opening of the rail link to Chicago in 1853. Post–World War II suburbanization changed everything, turning the village into the large middle-class bedroom community it is today. William Rainey Harper College (1965) is here.

Palatka city, pop. 10,201, seat of Putnam Co., NE Florida, on the St. Johns R., 26 mi/42 km SW of St. Augustine. Built on the site of an Indian (Seminole, "boat-crossing") village, it was founded as a trading post in 1821. A military outpost in the Seminole War, it became a flourishing river port, railroad hub, and resort later in the century. It now ships lumber, wood products, foodstuffs, and other goods; wood and paper are milled and furniture is built. Commercial fishing is important, and local seafood, citrus, and vegetables are processed and packed. Palatka is known for its azalea gardens and for its many restored 19th-century buildings. St. Johns River Community College (1957) is here.

Palau, Republic of also, **Belau** NNE–SSW oriented group of islands, c.100 mi/160 km long, at the W end of the Caroline Is. chain, in the S Philippine Sea (at the W end of the Pacific Ocean, just N of the Equator). With over 340 islands and a land area of 192 sq mi/497 sq km (pop. 15,122), it is the last remaining district of the United Nations Trust Territory of the PACIFIC ISLANDS (TTPI), administered by the US. The government center is Koror (pop. 9018), a former Japanese settlement. In 1982, Palau and the US signed a 50-year compact of free association; further political development was long stymied by a provision in the 1979 Palauan constitution forbidding the storage of nuclear weapons on the islands, which Palauans in repeated referenda refused to overturn. In late 1994, however, Palauans voted to become a sovereign nation. Palau's economy is based on subsistence agriculture and fishing. The chief cash crop is coconuts; coconut oil and copra are the chief exports. There is some commercial tuna fishing and a tourist industry. Babeldaop (Babelthuap), at 153 sq mi/396 sq km, is by far the largest island. Six mi/10 km–long Pelelieu I., in the S, was the scene of bloody fighting when US troops invaded in Sept. 1944, seeking to dislodge Japanese defenders and establish an airbase.

Palestine city, pop. 18,042, seat of Anderson Co., E Texas, 94 mi/151 km SE of Dallas. Settled in 1846, it is in a wooded area with lignite, clay, natural gas, and oil deposits. A rail and highway junction, it has repair shops and a range of manufactures. A NASA scientific balloon base is here. **L. Palestine,** a 25,600-ac/10,350-ha impoundment on the NECHES R., is 23 mi/37 km NNE.

Palisades **1.** see under SPRING VALLEY, Washington, D.C. **2.** nuclear power plant, opened 1972, in Covert township, Van Buren Co., SW Michigan, on L. Michigan, 5 mi/9 km SSW of South Haven.

Palisades of the Hudson line of high cliffs of traprock, approximately 15 mi/24 km long, from Hoboken, New Jersey (SW) into Rockland Co., New York (NE), rising over 500 ft/150 m above the W bank of the Hudson R. The Palisades Interstate Parkway runs along the cliffs N of the GEORGE WASHINGTON BRIDGE, through Palisades Interstate Park, which covers approximately 70 sq mi/182 sq km in New York and New Jersey, including 22 mi/35 km of river frontage, as far upriver as NEWBURGH.

Palisades Park borough, pop. 14,536, Bergen Co., on Overpeck Creek and the W side of the PALISADES of the Hudson R., 4 mi/6 km SE of Hackensack. It is primarily a commuter suburb; there is some light industry. Palisades Park is best known for the once very popular large amusement park located in the borough.

Palisades Peaks also, **Palisade Range** group in the SIERRA NEVADA, W of Big Pine, in EC California. Along the E edge of KINGS CANYON NATIONAL PARK, the group includes North Palisade (14,242 ft/4341 m), Mt. Sill (14,162 ft/4317 m), Middle Palisade (14,040 ft/4279 m), and Thunderbolt and Polemonium peaks, both 14,000 ft/4267 m. The relatively unfractured, precipitous granite faces of these peaks, and the glaciers of North and Middle Palisade, make them a noted rock-climbing site.

Palliser's Triangle area, some 700 mi/1130 km WNW–ESE, in the Prairie Provinces, along the US border. Named for the head of an 1857–60 British expedition that surveyed and examined it for possible settlement, the Triangle is an area of shortgrass prairie, with sandhills and other barren areas, and little rainfall. It extends ESE from the Calgary area (W) across SE Alberta, S Saskatchewan, and into SW Manitoba, with a N apex near LLOYDMINSTER, on the Alberta-Saskatchewan line. Despite Palliser's conclusion that the area was unsuitable for agriculture, homesteading began in 1908, touching off a land rush. After a few years of (unusually, as became apparent later) good harvests during World War I, a drought began, which quickly depopulated what was called the Prairie Dry Belt, in SE Alberta and SW Saskatchewan. The general drought of the 1930s, which created the US DUST BOWL, only added to problems here, and resettlement had to wait for advances in irrigation and farming technology. Medicine Hat and Lethbridge, Alberta, and Moose Jaw and Regina, Saskatchewan, are within Palliser's Triangle.

Palm Bay city, pop. 62,632, Brevard Co., EC Florida, W of the Indian R. lagoon, 60 mi/98 km SE of Orlando. Like Melbourne, just NNE, it is a residential center that has grown rapidly since the building of the Kennedy Space Center at Cape CANAVERAL. Its population more than tripled in the 1980s.

Palm Beach town, pop. 9814, Palm Beach Co., SE Florida, on a narrow barrier beach between the Atlantic and L. Worth, directly E across this lagoon from WEST PALM BEACH. Settled during the 1870s, it was developed as a resort by railroad magnate Henry Flagler during the 1890s. For a century it has been a favorite wintering spot for the socially prominent. The town is dotted with beachfront estates, private clubs, lavish shops (especially on Worth Ave.), and luxury hotels (including the 1925 Italian Renaissance–style Breakers), and its population swells during the winter "season." Zoning laws ban manufacturing. There are an opera, several theaters, and a variety of fashionable galleries.

Palm Beach County 1993 sq mi/5162 sq km, pop. 863,518, in SE Florida, on the Atlantic Ocean (E) and L. Okeechobee (NW). Its seat is WEST PALM BEACH. Its E fringe, including barrier islands, is the site of resort and residential communities including Jupiter, Riviera Beach, Lake Worth, Delray Beach, and Boca Raton. In the NW, around Belle Glade and South Bay, it is largely agricultural (sugar cane, vegetables). The S part is very sparsely populated. The tip of the Everglades and the Loxahatchee National Wildlife Refuge are in its SE.

Palm Beach Gardens city, pop. 22,965, SE Florida, 9 mi/14 km NNW of West Palm Beach, a resort and residential community. The US Croquet Association is based here.

Palmdale city, pop. 68,842, Los Angeles Co., SW California, 35 mi/56 km NNE of Los Angeles, in the ANTELOPE VALLEY, just N of the San Andreas Fault and the San Gabriel Mts. Since the 1950s the region has been a center for aircraft testing and assembly; EDWARDS AIR FORCE BASE is 13 mi/21 km N. The city, now also a booming residential suburb, quintupled in pop. in the 1980s.

Palm Desert city, pop. 23,252, Riverside Co., S California, at the NE foot of the Santa Rosa Mts., in the Coachella Valley, 10 mi/16 km SE of Palm Springs and 114 mi/184 km ESE of Los Angeles. A wealthy desert resort, it has golf courses, a shopping mall, hotels, and The Living Desert, a 1200-ac/486-ha nature park. The College of the Desert (1958) is here.

Palmer city, pop. 2866, Matanuska-Susitna Borough (pop. 39,683), SC Alaska, on the Matanuska R., 34 mi/55 km NE of Anchorage. At the C of the MATANUSKA VALLEY, it is a trade and supply center for the vegetable, grain, and dairy farms in the region. An agricultural research center and extension service of the University of Alaska is here. It is also the site of the Alaska State Fair.

Palmer House elegant hotel on STATE STREET, in the LOOP, Chicago, Illinois, noted for its sumptuous Empire Ballroom.

Palmer Park residential neighborhood in Detroit, Michigan, near Woodward Ave., 7 mi/11 km NW of Downtown and 1 mi/1.6 km N of Highland Park. Home to immigrants, gays, and young professionals, it experienced a wave of gentrification during the 1980s.

Palmetto city, pop. 9268, Manatee Co., W Florida, on the Manatee R., across its mouth (N) from Bradenton. A resort noted for its boating and fishing, it also packs and ships local vegetables and citrus fruit and has some light manufacturing.

Palm Harbor unincorporated community, pop. 50,256, Pinellas Co., WC Florida, 20 mi/32 km WNW of Tampa, on St. Joseph Sound (the Gulf of Mexico). It grew almost tenfold in the 1980s as a retirement and resort community.

Palmito Hill battle site: see under BROWNSVILLE, Texas.

Palm Springs **1.** city, pop. 40,181, Riverside Co., S California, 105 mi/169 km ESE of Los Angeles, at the E foot of the SAN JACINTO Mts. and the W end of the Coachella Valley. This world-famous resort is protected from rain and fog by the San Jacinto and the Santa Rosa (S) Mts., and is known for its comfortable, dry climate. Though in the Colorado Desert, it has mineral springs and palm trees; the Spanish who explored the area in 1774 called it Agua Caliente ("hot water"). The Cahuilla, who then inhabited the area, still own much of the land. Palm Springs was developed as a resort in the 1920s, and soon became fashionable with movie stars. Today it is known for its golf courses and for the homes of the rich and famous. The Desert Museum, an art center; Moorten Botanical Garden, exhibiting desert flora; and an aerial tramway into the San Jacintos draw visitors. **2.** resort village, pop. 9763, Palm Beach Co., SE Florida, just NW of Lake Worth and 5 mi/8 km SW of West Palm Beach.

Palmyra **1.** borough, pop. 7056, Burlington Co., WC New Jersey, 6 mi/10 km NE of Camden. An industrial community, it is connected with NE Philadelphia, Pennsylvania, by the Tacony-Palmyra Bridge (1929). **2.** town, pop. 7690, Wayne Co., W New York, on the Erie Canal, 23 mi/37 km SE of Rochester. Religious leader Joseph Smith (1805–44) lived at a farm here from the age of 10 to 21. He had his vision (1823) of the Angel Moroni here, and claimed to have found the golden tablets of Mormon at Hill Cumorah, a local drumlin. The text was dictated by Smith to a Palmyra schoolteacher and published as the *Book of Mormon* (1830). The Smith home is now open to the public, and a 40-ft/12-m figure of Moroni stands atop the hill. Palmyra has fruit orchards and dairy and vegetable farms. **3.** US possession, an ATOLL with three lagoons near the N end of the LINE Is., some 960 mi/1550 km SSW of Honolulu, Hawaii, in the C Pacific Ocean. Its land area, some 1 sq mi/3 sq km at its discovery (1802) by the ship *Palmyra,* has been enlarged by dredging. The atoll was part of Hawaii from 1862, but was excluded when Hawaii became a state in 1959. A World War II naval airbase, Palmyra is today a yacht stopover. Largely uninhabited private property, it is undergoing development for tourism.

Palo Alto **1.** city, pop. 55,900, Santa Clara Co., NC California, on the SW shore of San Francisco Bay, 32 mi/51 km S of San Francisco. It was founded (1891) as a residential community for adjacent (W) Stanford University (in unincorporated Stanford, pop. 18,097). Stimulated by the university, Palo Alto has developed as a research center; its role in aerospace, communications, and electronics development spurred the growth of SILICON VALLEY. It is also a retail, financial, professional-services, and medical center. Its industries include electrical and computer research and production, biomedical research and pharmaceutical manufacture, printing, and publishing. The ancient landmark redwood for which the city ("tall tree") is named still stands. At the 8200-ac/3300-ha Stanford campus ("the Farm") are the Hoover Institution on War, Revolution, and Peace; the 285-ft/87-m Hoover Tower; the Stanford Medical Center; and the 2 mi/3 km–long Stanford Linear Accelerator. **2.** battle site in Cameron Co., extreme S Texas, 8 mi/13 km N of downtown Brownsville, scene of the first important encounter (May 8, 1846) of the Mexican War. Zachary Taylor's victory over a larger Mexican force here, followed the next day by that at RESACA DE LA PALMA, opened the way to an American invasion of Mexico.

Palo Duro Canyon on the Prairie Dog Town Fork of the RED R., 14 mi/23 km E of CANYON, and 18 mi/29 km SE of Amarillo, in the High Plains of the N Texas Panhandle. Palo Duro Canyon State Park is, at 16,400 ac/6640 ha, the largest in Texas; some 200 million years of geologic history may be examined. The canyon was probably explored by Coronado's expedition in 1541. In 1874, US troops fought Kiowa and Comanche forces here. Charles Goodnight drove a herd through the canyon (1876) and established a ranch; cattle are still kept in the canyon.

Palomar Range series of three mountain uplifts in SW California, NE of Escondido. Including Agua Tibia Mt.; **Mt. Palomar,** or Palomar Mt. (6140 ft/1871 m); and Aguanga Mt., the range is largely within the Cleveland National Forest. Mt. Palomar is famous as the site of an astronomical observatory with a giant (200-in/508-cm lens) telescope, one of the Hale Observatories (with Mt. WILSON). Five small Indian reservations are in the area. The Agua Tibia Primitive (or Wilderness) Area (15,934 ac/6453 ha) is popular with hikers.

Palos Heights city, pop. 11,478, Cook Co., NE Illinois, on the Calumet Sag Channel, a residential suburb 17 mi/27 km SW of Chicago. Trinity Christian College (1959) is here. PALOS HILLS is just NW.

Palos Hills city, pop. 17,803, Cook Co., NE Illinois, on the Calumet Sag Channel, 10 mi/16 km SW of Chicago. A large forest preserve lies just W of this suburban bedroom community.

Palos Verdes Estates city, pop. 13,512, Los Angeles Co., SW California, 19 mi/31 km SSW of downtown Los Angeles, an affluent suburb on the hilly Palos Verdes Peninsula, on the Pacific Ocean. ROLLING HILLS (SE) and RANCHO PALOS VERDES (S) are nearby.

Palouse, the agricultural area in E Washington. Largely in Whitman Co., and one of the world's most productive wheat-growing areas, also noted for soybeans and other crops, it extends S from Spokane to the Snake R. and E into W Idaho. Steady SW winds (*palousers*) have blown fertile loess soil into drifts here, and rich grass covers the Palouse Hills. A livestock grazing area, the Palouse is generally assumed to have give an alternate form of its name to the Appaloosa horse. The **Palouse R.,** 140 mi/230 km long, rising in Latah Co., W Idaho, flows generally W past the city of **Palouse,** Washington (pop. 915), then turns S to the Snake R., dropping 198 ft/60 m at **Palouse Falls,** 5 mi/8 km N of the confluence.

Palo Verde nuclear power plant, operational since 1985, E of the Palo Verde Hills and 50 mi/80 km W of Phoenix, Arizona. It lies 6 mi/10 km S of Interstate 10.

Pamlico River see under TAR R., North Carolina.

Pamlico Sound arm of the Atlantic Ocean sheltered by the OUTER BANKS barrier islands of Bodie, Hatteras, Ocracoke, and Portsmouth (Core Banks), in E North Carolina. Eighty mi/130 km NE–SW and 10–35 mi/16–56 km wide, the sound has numerous coves and inlets, and receives the Pungo, Pamlico, Neuse, and other rivers. It is connected to ALBEMARLE SOUND on the N via Roanoke and Croatan sounds, and joins Core Sound on the S. Outlets to the ocean are (N to S) Oregon Inlet, Hatteras Inlet, and Ocracoke Inlet. The sound is part of the Atlantic Intracoastal Waterway.

Pampa city, pop. 19,959, seat of Gray Co., NW Texas, 55 mi/88 km ENE of Amarillo. Established on the Santa Fe Railroad in 1888, it is in the PANHANDLE oil and natural gas field. It has machine shops, oilfield supply companies, and one of the world's largest producers of carbon black. Cattle and wheat raised in the region are processed and shipped.

Pamunkey River 90 mi/140 km long, in E Virginia. It is formed by the confluence of the NORTH ANNA and South Anna rivers, 18 mi/29 km NNE of Richmond, near Ashland. It flows SE in a winding, often swampy course, joining the MATTAPONI R. at WEST POINT to form the YORK R. The Pamunkey tribe, from whom it takes its name, has a reservation on the N bank 11 mi/18 km WNW of West Point.

Panama City city, pop. 34,378, seat of Bay Co., NW Florida, a deepwater port on St. Andrew Bay off the Gulf of Mexico, 90 mi/140 km ESE of Pensacola. Settled by the English in 1765, it developed into a fishing village, then into a busy port and resort center. Commercial and sport fishing, papermaking, and the manufacture of clothing, plastics, and chemicals are important. The Naval Coastal Systems Center diving school and Gulf Coast Community College (1957) are here. The bayfront resort of **Panama City Beach** (pop. 4051), the air tactical school at Tyndall Air Force Base (just SE), and the US Mine Defense Laboratory are nearby.

Panamint Range desert mountain group in EC California, between the Panamint Valley (W) and DEATH VALLEY (E). With average elevations of 6000–11,000 ft/2000–3300 m, it reaches its high point at Telescope Peak (11,049 ft/3368 m), and is noted for its great vertical relief, sheer rocky walls, and deep canyons. The Panamint Dunes, covering c.6 sq mi/16 sq km and rising up to 250 ft/76 m above the surrounding terrain, are in the barren Panamint Valley. The ghost mining towns of Panamint and Skidoo are here. The Panamint are a Shoshonean people.

Pancho Villa State Park see under COLUMBUS, New Mexico.

Pangnirtung hamlet, pop. 1135, Baffin Region, E Northwest Territories, on a FJORD in SE BAFFIN I., on the N side of Cumberland Sound, 180 mi/290 km NNE of IQALUIT. The gateway to AUYUITTUQ NATIONAL PARK, it is also a fishing, sealing, whaling, fur producing, Inuit arts, and tourism center, with a noted crafts co-op and various government stations. Kekerten Island Historic Park, 30 mi/50 km SE, in the sound, preserves an 1850s–1920s whaling station.

Pango Pango see PAGO PAGO, American Samoa.

Panhandle **1.** in the US, part of a state (or, previously, a territory) that is not a peninsula and that projects from the rest of the state like the handle of a frying pan. **2.** see under ALEXANDER ARCHIPELAGO, Alaska. **3.** in Florida, the nonpeninsular NW section, part of the GULF COASTAL PLAIN. It consists almost entirely of rolling country slightly higher than peninsular Florida, with piney woods, an agricultural (foresting, cotton) and maritime economy now augmented by military operations and growing tourism, and folkways more "Southern" than those of the peninsula, reflecting its closeness to Georgia and Alabama. Pensacola (W) and Tallahassee (E) are its major cities. **4.** N section of Idaho, bounded by British Columbia (N), Washington (W), and Montana (E), in Boundary, Bonner, Kootenai, Benewah, and Shoshone counties. An area some 140 mi/230 km N–S and 42–75 mi/68–120 km wide, it is noted for its N Rocky Mt. ranges, including the Cabinets, the Coeur d'Alenes, the Bitterroots, and the Selkirks; for its popular lakes, including Pend Oreille, Coeur d'Alene, Hayden, and Priest; and for a mining (centered around Kellogg) and lumbering economy now in transition to a tourism base. Farragut State Park, at the S end of L. Pend Oreille, was a major World War II naval base, a center for submarine training. The Idaho Panhandle National Forests, a combination of the former St. Joe, Kaniksu, and Coeur d'Alene national forests, occupy 2.5 million ac/1 million ha (3900 sq mi/10,120 sq km). **5.** the NW portion of the state of Nebraska, jutting from its basically rectangular outline, bordered by Colorado (S), Wyoming (W), and South Dakota (N). This area was traversed by pioneer wagon trains along the Mormon, Oregon, and other trails (the North Platte R. valley). Sugar beets and other crops are produced in the S, ranching is important throughout, and some oil and gas are produced. Tourists are drawn to spectacular buttes and tableland in the N, in the PINE RIDGE area. Major cities are Scottsbluff, Alliance, and Chadron. **6.** 168 mi/269 km–long, 33 mi/53 km–wide strip of land in NW Oklahoma, bordered by New Mexico (W), the Texas Panhandle (S), and Colorado and Kansas (N). It includes (W–E) CIMARRON, Texas, and Beaver counties. Before 1890 it was claimed by no state or territory, and was commonly known as No Man's Land. Some of it was settled by ranchers, who attempted to create a new territorial government, Cimarron, in 1887, but the area soon (1890) became part of the Oklahoma Territory. Sparsely populated, it has few important municipalities; these include BOISE CITY, GUYMON, GOODWELL, and Beaver. The area has oil and gas wells, and produces cattle, poultry, grain, and dairy goods. **7.** northernmost portion (c.23,000 sq mi/59,400 sq km) of Texas, bounded (N and E) by Oklahoma and (W) by New Mexico. Much of it is in the immense High Plains area of the LLANO ESTACADO; the principal city is AMARILLO. The CAPROCK ESCARPMENT, in the E, marks the High Plains' limit. The CANADIAN and RED rivers cross W to E. **8.** in West Virginia: **a. Eastern Panhandle.** about 3500 sq mi/9100 sq km, bounded E and N by the Potomac R., separating it from Maryland, and S by Virginia. In the Allegheny Mts., it includes all or part of ten counties; MARTINSBURG is the largest city. HARPERS FERRY is at the E extreme. **b. Northern Panhandle.** 584 sq mi/1513 sq km, bordered E by Pennsylvania and N and W by the Ohio R., separating it from Ohio. It includes Marshall, Ohio, Brooke, and Hancock counties. WEIRTON and WHEELING are its industrial centers. The area is rich in glass sand, clay, salt, coal, and natural gas.

Panorama City largely residential EC SAN FERNANDO VALLEY section of LOS ANGELES, California, N of Van Nuys and S of Pacoima, and 15 mi/24 km NW of Downtown. Middle-class, it now has a sizable Asian community.

Pantego town, pop. 2371, Tarrant Co., NE Texas. On the Pioneer Parkway 10 mi/16 km ESE of Fort Worth, it is a suburb surrounded by ARLINGTON and adjacent to similar Dalworthington Gardens (S; pop. 1758).

Pantex industrial site in Carson Co., N Texas, 19 mi/31 km NE of Amarillo, in the Panhandle. Covering some 9000 ac/3650 ha, it was used during the Cold War for final assembly, and is now being used for disassembly, of US nuclear weapons.

Panthersville unincorporated community, pop. 9874, De Kalb Co., 8 mi/13 km ESE of downtown Atlanta, a predominantly black residential suburb.

Paoli unincorporated village, pop. 5603, in Easttown and Tredyffrin townships, Chester Co., Pennsylvania, 18 mi/29 km WNW of Philadelphia. It is a MAIN LINE suburb; the "Paoli local" has long been one of Philadelphia's best-known commuter trains. Paoli produces cement, flour, and pharmaceuticals. It was the scene of Anthony Wayne's defeat by British troops on Sept. 20, 1777.

Papago Indian Reservation c.2.8 million ac/1.13 million ha (4375 sq mi/11,330 sq km), pop. 8730, in S Arizona, in the SONORAN DESERT. A smaller separate unit surrounds the MISSION SAN XAVIER DEL BAC near Tucson. The second-largest US reservation, after that of the Navajo, it is the longtime home of the agricultural people called Papago ("bean people") by the Spanish, who call themselves Tohono O'odham ("desert people who came from the earth"). KITT PEAK is here. Sells (unincorporated, pop. 2750, Pima Co.) is headquarters.

Papillion city, pop. 10,372, seat of Sarpy Co., EC Nebraska, 10 mi/16 km SW of Omaha. A residential suburb, it is also a center of local government and supports diversified agricultural activities.

Paradise **1.** town, pop. 25,408, Butte Co., NC California, in the W Sierra Nevada foothills, 11 mi/18 km E of Chico, and just NW of L. Oroville, along the West Branch of the Feather R. A tourist center and fruit producer, it is also an increasingly popular retirement community. **2.** unincorporated community, pop. 124,682, Clark Co., SE Nevada, a largely residential suburb on the S side of LAS VEGAS, E of the famous STRIP. Its growth (over 400% pop. gain since 1970) is part of the immense expansion of the Las Vegas area in recent years. The University of Nevada at Las Vegas (1957) is here.

Paradise Springs treaty site: see under WABASH, Indiana.

Paradise Valley **1.** town, pop. 11,671, Maricopa Co., SC Arizona, 8 mi/13 km NE of downtown Phoenix and just N of Camelback Mt. It is an affluent suburb. **2.** nickname for prewar black ghetto in Detroit, Michigan, E of Woodward Ave. and NE of Downtown. It was also known as Black Bottom. Housing almost three-fourths of the city's black population in its dilapidated units, it was notorious for its poverty and overcrowding, but also known for the entertainnment district that flourished around Hastings St. Construction of the Chrysler Freeway and other roads eliminated most of Paradise Valley. **3.** in Park Co., SW Montana, on the Yellowstone R. It is a broad NW–SE valley between the Gallatin (W) and Absaroka (E) ranges. Once inhabited by Crow Indians, the valley was the site of an 1864 gold strike, was later a coalmining region, and is now mainly occupied by cattle and sheep ranches as well as by smaller ranchettes, especially around LIVINGSTON. Within the valley is the village of Gardiner, entrance to Yellowstone National Park, 2 mi/3 km to the S. Gardiner is also the headquarters of the Church Universal and Triumphant, led by Elizabeth Claire Prophet, which owns much surrounding land. Also in the Paradise Valley are Yankee Jim Canyon, Gallatin Petrified Forest, and the ghost town of Jardine.

Paragould city, pop. 18,540, seat of Greene Co., NE Arkansas, 18 mi/29 km NNE of Jonesboro and 9 mi/14 km W of the Missouri Bootheel. Founded in 1882, it was named for railroad magnates J.W. Paramore and Jay Gould. In an agricultural area, it manufactures clothing, wood products, feed, and flour, and gins cotton. It is the home of Crowley's Ridge College (1964). Crowley's Ridge State Park is nearby.

Paramount city, pop. 47,669, Los Angeles Co., SW California, 9 mi/14 km SE of downtown Los Angeles, and across the Los Angeles R. (E) from Compton. Incorporated in 1957 in a formerly agricultural (dairying) area, it is a largely Hispanic industrial suburb, turning out metal and plastic products, auto parts, furniture, and chemicals, and refining oil.

Paramus borough, pop. 25,101, Bergen Co., NE New Jersey, 5 mi/8 km NE of Paterson. Settled by the Dutch in 1666, it was long a trading and distribution center for local farm produce. Today it is a residential and commercial suburb of the New York City–N New Jersey region, with research facilities, some manufacturing, and many corporate office buildings. Paramus is particularly known for its large retail malls. It is the seat of Bergen Community College (1965).

Parchman hamlet in Sunflower Co., NW Mississippi, 46 mi/75 km NE of Greenville, in the DELTA, the site of the Mississippi penitentiary, known as Parchman Farm. With up to 20,000 ac/8100 ha of cotton and vegetable fields, the institution has used convict labor to sustain itself. It is known through numerous blues, work songs, and ballads, among them "Midnight Special," referring to a train that passed the prison or brought visitors.

Paria Plateau tableland, c.6000 ft/1830 m high, W of the Colorado R. and NE of the KAIBAB PLATEAU, in N Arizona, along the Utah border. Once known as the Sand Hills, the dry plateau sits above the 75 mi/120 km–long **Paria R.** (NE), which joins the Colorado R. near Lees Ferry. Ancient PUEBLOS and PETROGLYPHS are found on the plateau. Hiking is popular in the colorful **Paria Canyon,** along the river, and in the extremely narrow Buckskin Gulch, on a tributary. The Vermilion Cliffs are along the plateau's E edge, above MARBLE CANYON.

Paris **1.** city, pop. 8987, seat of Edgar Co., EC Illinois, on Sugar Creek and Twin Ls., 27 mi/43 km NE of Charleston and 9 mi/14 km W of the Indiana border. Besides boasting of the world's largest broom factory, it is known as the site of two speeches by Abraham Lincoln, and as a haven for Confederate sympathizers during the Civil War. Metal and electronic products are also manufactured here. **2.** city, pop. 8730, seat of Bourbon Co., NC Kentucky, on the South Fork of the Licking R. (Stoner Creek), 17 mi/27 km NE of Lexington. Settled as Hopewell (1789), it was called Paris (1790) in gratitude for French aid to the Revolution. The whiskey named after the county has been made here since 1790. Claiborne Farm and other BLUEGRASS REGION horse farms are in the vicinity. Cane Ridge Meetinghouse (1791), 8 mi/13 km E, is the birthplace (1804) of the Disciples of Christ. In Aug. 1801 it was the scene of the huge Cane Ridge Revival, a major event in US religious history. **3.** town, pop. 4492, including the villages of Paris Hill and South Paris, seat of Oxford Co., W Maine. It is on the Little Androscoggin R. adjoining the town of Norway, 18 mi/29 km NW of Lewiston. Paris Hill, 1809 birthplace of Vice President (1861–65) Hannibal Hamlin, supplied skis and sledges to the Arctic explorers Peary and MacMillan, and has some of the state's most architecturally interesting old buildings, including Old Stonewall Jail (1828). South Paris, the town's industrial center, home of the oldest commercial US ski manufacturer, also produces textiles and leather. The Norway-South Paris area is a regional trade center. **4.** town, pop. 4414, Oneida Co., C New York, 8 mi/13 km SW of Utica. Hawaiian statesman Gerrit Judd (1803–73) and biologist Asa Gray (1810–88) were born in this rural agricultural town, the latter in the hamlet of Sauquoit. **5.** city, pop. 9332, seat of Henry Co., NW Tennessee, 80 mi/130 km WNW of Nashville. A trade center in an area producing clay, timber, livestock, and field crops, it makes building materials, clothing, cosmetics, rubber goods, and auto parts, and has pottery works and railroad shops. **6.** city, pop. 24,699, seat of Lamar Co., NE Texas, 95 mi/153 km NE of Dallas. Settled around 1840 on a ridge between the Red and Sulphur rivers, it is a trade hub for the BLACKLANDS region, which produces livestock, cotton, and grains; it has varied light manufactures and medical and corporate facilities. Here also is Paris Junior College (1924).

parish **1.** from the historic British church district (usually comprising a central village and outlying hamlets), any of various historic ecclesiastical and/or political units in E Canada. Today there are in Québec over 400 parishes (*paroisses*), a form of county subdivision. **2.** in Louisiana, a civil division, the equivalent of a COUNTY in other states. It takes its name from, and is the American successor to, an ecclesiastical division of the French-Spanish colonial period (before 1803).

Park Avenue residential and commercial thoroughfare, Manhattan, New York City. Although it was the site of railroad tracks through the 19th century, Park Ave. was by the 1920s one of New York's most prestigious residential streets, particularly in the stretch from Grand Central Terminal (42nd–46th streets) north to 96th St., where the tracks now emerge from underground. This part of the avenue is lined by large apartment houses as well as some corporate buildings of architectural importance, including Lever House (1952) and the Seagram Building (1958).

Park Cities, the HIGHLAND PARK (S) and UNIVERSITY PARK (N), adjacent cities independent of, but within, NORTH DALLAS, Texas. A third, similarly affluent suburb, Preston Hollow, just NW, was annexed by Dallas in 1945.

Park City city pop. 4468, Summit and Wasatch counties, NC Utah, 18 mi/29 km ESE of Salt Lake City, at 7000 ft/2135 m in the WASATCH RANGE. In the 1860s–70s it was a booming silver mining center; after a long decline it boomed again in the 1970s as a skiing center. The US ski team has made its headquarters here, and a film festival affiliated with the SUNDANCE Institute is held (Jan.).

Parker town, pop. 2897, seat of La Paz Co., WC Arizona, on the Colorado R. (the California border), 130 mi/210 km WNW of Phoenix. Headquarters of the Colorado R. Indian Reservation (established 1865; 269,000 ac/108,930 ha, pop. 7865), inhabited by Mohave, Chemehuevi, and members of other tribes in both Arizona and California, the town is a railroad stop and now the base for a popular riverside recreational area extending to the Parker Dam and L. HAVASU, 15 mi/24 km NE. Poston, 12 mi/19 km SW, was the World War II site of the largest single relocation camp housing Americans of Japanese ancestry who had been interned; it held as many as 18,000 persons at one time.

Parker House historic hotel in downtown Boston, Massachusetts, just E of Beacon Hill and S of Government Center. Among its many associations, it was the 1850s meeting place of the Saturday Club, including Oliver Wendell Holmes and others, who constituted Boston's literary establishment. The hotel, long a stop for the influential, also gave its name to a type of bread roll.

Parker Peak 4848 ft/1479 m, in the SW corner of South Dakota, in the BLACK HILLS, W of Hot Springs.

Parkersburg city, pop. 33,862, seat of Wood Co., NW West Virginia, on the Ohio R. where the Little Kanawha R. joins it, 11 mi/18 km SW of Marietta, Ohio. Settled in the 1770s, and industrial since the 1860s, when the Burning Springs oilfield was discovered nearby, it is also an agricultural marketing and shipping center, and has railway repair shops. Manufactures include oil well equipment, glass and porcelain products, paper, metals, plastics, synthetic rubber, rayon, and chemicals. A West Virginia University campus (1971) and Ohio Valley College (1960) are here. BLENNERHASSET I. is 2.5 mi/4 km W.

Park Forest village, pop. 24,656, Cook and Will counties, NE Illinois, a suburb 28 mi/45 km SW of Chicago. It was developed as a planned residential community by American Community Builders after World War II, and promoted to middle-income families, with a mix of owners and renters. Food processing equipment and hand tools are manufactured here. In *The Organization Man,* William H. Whyte, Jr. described the environment of Park Forest in the 1950s. UNIVERSITY PARK is 4 mi/6 km S.

Parkland unincorporated community, pop. 20,882, Pierce Co., WC Washington, 6 mi/10 km S of Tacoma. Situated in parklike terrain, it is a residential suburb and a college town, seat of Pacific Lutheran University (1890). McChord Air Force Base is just W.

Parklands, the in Manitoba, Saskatchewan, and Alberta, belt of grassy, rolling country lying between the northern forest (N) and the shortgrass prairie (S). It is sometimes called the Aspen Parkland, for its dominant tree, which appears typically in small clumps. In Alberta the parklands extend N from the Calgary area to the Edmonton area. Another, separate, parkland section is the fertile PEACE R. valley (NW). To the E the parklands narrow across Saskatchewan, where Saskatoon is in the belt, and end in S Manitoba, below the edge of the CANADIAN SHIELD.

Park Range NNW–SSE trending range, part of the W tier of the S Rocky Mts., in S Wyoming and NC Colorado. It extends some 200 mi/320 km from near Rawlins, Wyoming, to near Leadville, Colorado. In S Wyoming it is called the Sierra Madre. About half its length, in Colorado, is the GORE RANGE. At the S end is the short Mosquito Range, which includes Mt. Lincoln (14,286 ft/4354 m), its highest point. Many of Colorado's well-known resorts, including Steamboat Springs, Vail, Breckenridge, and Copper Mountain, lie along the Park Range, which takes its name from the regional term for a grassy intermontane valley.

Park Ridge city, pop. 36,175, Cook Co., NE Illinois, on the Des Plaines R., adjacent to the NW corner of Chicago, and 13 mi/21 km NW of the Loop. A residential community, it has many corporate headquarters, which benefit from its proximity to O'Hare International Airport. First settled in the 1850s by George Penny, who made bricks out of the area's red clay, it was named Pennyville, then Brickton. The arrival of the Chicago and North Western Railway spurred economic growth, and suburbanization began before the close of the 19th century.

Parkside 1. see under SUNSET DISTRICT, San Francisco, California. **2.** locality, name for a campus (1965) of the University of Wisconsin, in Kenosha Co., extreme SE Wisconsin, 4 mi/6 km NNW of the center of KENOSHA.

Park Slope locally, **the Slope** residential section, WC Brooklyn, New York. Situated on the slope W from PROSPECT PARK down toward Gowanus and South Brooklyn, it is one of New York's most prestigious neighborhoods. Developed after the Civil War on land once owned by the Litchfield family, whose villa (1857) on the W edge of the park looked downhill toward New York, Park Slope was a streetcar suburb, first of row houses, and then, around World War I, of large apartment buildings. Grand Army Plaza is at its NE corner. Prospect Heights, across Flatbush Ave. to the NE, is often regarded as an extension of Park Slope. The area S of 9th Street is locally referred to as the South Slope; farther S, around 16th Street, Park Slope merges into SUNSET PARK.

Parkville 1. unincorporated residential community, pop. 31,617, Baltimore Co., C Maryland, 6 mi/10 km NE of downtown Baltimore, between the city's NE corner and the Beltway (I-695). **2.** city, pop. 2402, Platte Co., NW Missouri, on the Missouri R., adjacent to NW Kansas City, Missouri, and across the river (N) from Kansas City, Kansas. In the 1840s, it was one of the major Missouri R. towns. In 1855, it saw a violent clash between proslavery Missourians and the abolitionist owners of the local newspaper. Now largely a residential suburb, it is the seat of Park College (1875).

Parkway double-laned, tree-lined thoroughfare in Memphis, Tennessee, which forms (with Riverside Drive, on the W) a rectangle, roughly 4 mi/6 km E–W and 2 mi/3 km N–S, around the city's center. South Parkway runs from 427-ac/173-ha Riverside Park (SW) to the MID-SOUTH FAIRGROUNDS (SE). East Parkway then runs N to near OVERTON PARK, and North Parkway W to Downtown. Riverside Drive was added after a 1926 cave-in of the city's bluffs; Tom Lee Park is below it, on the river. Many of Memphis's 20th-century residential neighborhoods developed along the Parkway.

Parkway–South Sacramento unincorporated community, pop. 31,903, Sacramento Co., NC California, a largely residential suburb on the S side of the Sacramento metropolitan area.

Parliament Hill familiarly, **the Hill** in UPPER TOWN, Ottawa, Ontario, the site of Canada's parliament. Set on a limestone bluff above the Ottawa R., it was Barracks Hill, home to British soldiers, before its purchase in 1859 for the construction (1859–65) of the three chief government buildings: the East and West blocks, housing offices, and the Centre Block, home to the Houses of Parliament. The Centre Block was rebuilt after a 1916 fire. In it are the Red Chamber, home to the Senate, and the Green Chamber, home to the House of Commons. In 1927 the Peace Tower, which stands at the Centre Block's front entrance, was added: standing 295 ft/90 m above the river, the tower contains a Memorial Chamber dedicated to Canadians who served in World War I, and a 53-bell carillon, familiar (via broadcast) throughout Canada. Parliament Hill is home to numerous other government buildings. Immediately SE is Confederation Square, site of the National War Memorial, and E across the Rideau Canal is the huge Château Laurier, a hotel built by the Grand Trunk Railway in 1908–12.

Parma city, pop. 87,876, Cuyahoga Co., NE Ohio, 7 mi/11 km S of downtown Cleveland. Founded in 1816 by New Englanders, in 1826 it was renamed after the Italian city. In 1931 a proposal for annexation to Cleveland was defeated and Parma was incorporated as a city. It is now primarily a residential suburb. A large industrial center, automotive parts factories, and tool-and-die works are located here, as well as a junior college.

Parma Heights city, pop. 21,448, Cuyahoga Co., NE Ohio, a residential suburb 9 mi/14 km S of Cleveland, near Cleveland Hopkins Airport (W). It is surrounded on three sides by the city of Parma, from which it seceded in 1912. The two cities share a school system and other facilities.

Parris Island 6 mi/10 km long, pop. 7172, in Beaufort Co., SC South Carolina. One of the SEA ISLANDS, it is on Port Royal Sound, S of Port Royal I., W of St. Helena I., NE of Hilton Head I., and 7 mi/11 km S of Beaufort. The Spanish attempted to settle here in 1526; French Huguenots led by Jean Ribaut tried in 1562, and were successful in establishing a settlement at nearby PORT ROYAL. Used militarily since the Civil War, the island became the US Marine Corps Recruit Depot, a basic training facility, in 1915.

Parrsboro town, pop. 1634, Cumberland Co., NC Nova Scotia, on the N shore of the MINAS BASIN, 30 mi/48 km S of Amherst. The largest town on the basin, it is a center for tourists who come to see the area's high tides, and to collect semiprecious zeolites. It is also a geological and paleontological research center; the area is rich in plant fossils and prehistoric animal bones. Local industries include coal and lumber shipping and fishing.

Parry Channel see under QUEEN ELIZABETH Is., Northwest Territories.

Parry Islands archipelago in the NW Northwest Territories, the southwesternmost part of the QUEEN ELIZABETH Is., in the Arctic Ocean. In a rough triangle some 375 mi/600 km E–W at the base and 250 mi/400 km on each side, they include Cornwallis and Bathurst (SE), Melville (S), Prince Patrick (SW), Borden and Mackenzie King (N), and smaller islands. The SVERDRUP Is. lie NE, DEVON I. SE. The entire Queen Elizabeth group was called the Parry Is. before 1953.

Parry Sound town, pop. 6125, Parry Sound District (pop. 38,423), SC Ontario, on an inlet of EC GEORGIAN BAY, 121 mi/195 km NNW of Toronto, and roughly halfway on the railroad and Trans-Canada Highway (Route 69) between Toronto (S) and Sudbury (N). Laid out in 1867, it was a major lumbering center until supply diminished. Still an important port, it is now the boating gateway to the bay's Thirty Thousand Is. vacation area, and is noted as a fishing, diving, and summer music festival center.

Parsippany booming residential and commercial community, part of **Parsippany-Troy Hills** township (pop. 48,478), Morris Co., N New Jersey, 5 mi/8 km NE of Morristown. Situated at the junction of Interstates 80 and 287, it has residential housing, major corporate headquarters, office towers, and retail shopping facilities.

Parsons city, pop. 11,924, Labette Co., SE Kansas, 30 mi/48 km WSW of Pittsburg. A railroad center for an agricultural region, it processes grain, livestock, wool, dairy products, and poultry. Nearby lakes attract visitors. Labette Community College (1923) is here.

Parthenon in Centennial Park, C Nashville, Tennessee, the world's only full-sized replica of the temple on the Acropolis in Athens, Greece. A temporary structure was dedicated in May 1897 for the Tennessee Centennial Exposition, and the final concrete version was completed in 1930.

Pasadena **1.** city, pop. 131,591, Los Angeles Co., SW California, 9 mi/14 km NE of downtown Los Angeles, in the S foothills of the San Gabriel Mts. Founded in 1875, it soon became a winter resort popular with Midwestern retirees. By the end of the 19th century it had begun to acquire its imposing homes. The California Institute of Technology (Caltech; 1891) and its Jet Propulsion Laboratory are widely known. Also here are Pasadena City College (1924), Pacific Oaks College (1951), and several other institutions. Mt. WILSON is just N. Pasadena's industries make a variety of high-tech products, and the city has engineering, financial, and research firms. College football's Rose Bowl, held here on New Year's Day at the 104,000-seat Rose Bowl Stadium, is part of the Tournament of Roses (first held in 1890), also famous for its parade. The satirical Doo Dah Parade (Nov.) is more recent. City cultural institutions include the Norton Simon Museum (art) and the Pacific Asia Museum. **2.** city, pop. 119,363, Harris Co., SE Texas, adjacent (E) to Houston, on the Houston Ship Channel (N). Vince's Bayou, important in the battle of SAN JACINTO, flows through. The city was incorporated in 1928, and was at first a bedroom community for oil workers. Industrial development after World War II, particularly in aerospace and petrochemicals, was responsible for rapid growth. Pasadena now has huge refineries, and petrochemical, plastics, paper, steel, and synthetic rubber plants, and is a shipping center. San Jacinto College (1960) is here, as is Texas Chiropractic College.

Pascagoula city, pop. 25,899, seat of Jackson Co., SE Mississippi, at the mouths of the Pascagoula and Escatawpa rivers on Mississippi Sound (the Gulf of Mexico), 20 mi/32 km E of Biloxi. Pascagoula grew up around the "Old Spanish Fort" built by the Frenchman Joseph Simon de la Pointe in 1718. The city has been held in turn by Britain, Spain, WEST FLORIDA, and the US. It became a summer resort in the mid 19th century and from the 1870s thrived as a lumber shipping port. Abundant SE Mississippi wood also made it a shipbuilding center, a role in which it boomed during both World Wars. Through the Cold War it continued to build destroyers and other naval vessels. Today the city also manufactures paper products, petroleum, chemicals, and clothing, is a fishing center, and remains a popular resort.

Pascagoula River 90 mi/140 km long, in SE Mississippi. It is formed by the junction of the Leaf and CHICKASAWHAY rivers near Merrill, and flows S to MISSISSIPPI SOUND between Gautier and the port of PASCAGOULA. The Pascagoula has been an important lumbering river since the 1870s. It is popularly called the Singing River because of humming or buzzing sounds it seems to emit. Local legend says that the "singing" is the death song of the Pascagoula tribe, who long ago entered its waters rather than surrender to the more powerful Biloxi.

Pasco city, pop. 20,337, seat of Franklin Co., SE Washington, in the Columbia Basin, on the Columbia R. just NW of its junction with the Snake R., across the Columbia (N) from KENNEWICK and 8 mi/13 km SE of RICHLAND. The smallest and oldest of these Tri-Cities, it was founded in the late 1800s and grew as a railroad town. Like its sister cities, it developed rapidly during World War II with the construction of the nearby Hanford nuclear facility. The Northern Pacific Railroad and four dams on the Snake R., which rendered it navigable for barges, have made Pasco a trade and transportation hub for SE Washington. The city lies in a rich agricultural area, and the Pasco Farmers' Market is the region's largest. The 3600-ac/1458-ha McNary National Wildlife Refuge is 5 mi/8 km SE, and Sacajawea State Park is 3 mi/5 km SE. There are several wineries in the city's environs.

Paseo, the urban parkway, running S from the NORTHEAST section of Kansas City, Missouri, passing E of Downtown, just W of EIGHTEENTH AND VINE, E of WESTPORT and the COUNTRY CLUB District, and ending at 79th St. The Battle of Westport (Oct. 1864) was fought near what is now the 63rd St. intersection. Laid out in the early 20th century, in a period of extensive urban planning activity, the Paseo was the grandest of the city's boulevards, but residential fashion later moved to the SW. Troost Ave., a N–S thoroughfare generally four blocks to the W of the Paseo, is the traditional divider between black (E) and white (W) Kansas City.

Paseo del Rio English, **River Walk** public way in downtown San Antonio, Texas, covering some 2.5 mi/4 km along a loop in the San Antonio R. Constructed by the WPA in 1939–41, it was reemphasized at the time of the 1968 San Antonio world's fair (HemisFair), and has become a major visitor attraction and a widely recognized symbol of San Antonio. It consists of walkways 20 ft/6 m below street level, along the river's banks, lined with hotels, shops, cafes, and galleries. Passing LA VILLITA and leading to the KING WILLIAM DISTRICT (S), it has also been extended into a lagoon in HEMISFAIR PLAZA. Visitors move along it both on foot and in boats.

Paso Robles officially, **El Paso de Robles** city, pop. 18,583, San Luis Obispo Co., WC California, 24 mi/39 km N of San Luis Obispo, on the Salinas R. and US 101 (EL CAMINO REAL). Its sulfur springs and mud baths have long attracted visitors. Wine, grapes, and almonds are major local products; tourism is important. The large Camp Roberts military reservation, an important World War II training center, lies N, near San Miguel.

Pasquia Hills region in EC Saskatchewan, 133 mi/214 km E of Prince Albert, near the Manitoba border and N of the Red Deer R. Wildcat Hill (2565 ft/782 m) and the Wildcat Wilderness Area are here.

pass **1.** in mountainous terrain, a narrow section of lower ground or of a gentler gradient, allowing passage, as for walkers, riders, roads, or railways. **2.** along coasts, esp. in the SE US, an opening in a BARRIER BEACH or reef that allows passage for vessels. **3.** a navigable channel in the delta of a river, or among many channels in an alluvial plain.

Passaconaway, Mount see under SANDWICH RANGE, New Hampshire.

Passaic city, pop. 58,041, Passaic Co., NE New Jersey, on the Passaic R., 4 mi/6 km SE of Paterson. Once an Indian camping ground, it was settled by Dutch traders (1678), and called Acquackanonk until 1854. It was occupied by both American and British troops during the Revolutionary War. In the 1850s a dam was built, and Passaic developed into a major textile manufacturing city; it was a labor union center in the early 20th century. The city's largest woolen mill was later converted into an industrial park; today Passaic has widely diverse industries manufacturing clothing, electronic components, rubber goods, plastics, and aircraft parts.

Passaic County 187 sq mi/484 sq km, pop. 453,060, in N New Jersey, bounded by the Passaic R. (E). Its seat is PATERSON. Part of the New York-New Jersey metropolitan complex, it is highly industrialized, with a diverse heavy and light manufacturing base, some of which has undergone considerable decline in the late 20th century. It also has office complexes, corporate headquarters, and suburban residences. Among its largest communities are Paterson, CLIFTON, PASSAIC, TOTOWA, and WAYNE.

Passaic River 80 mi/130 km long, in N New Jersey. It rises in Mendham, in Morris Co., and flows S through the Great Swamp National Wildlife Refuge, then generally NE on the W side of the Watchung Mts., past Little Falls, to Paterson, where its 70-ft/21-m Great Falls powered the textile industry. The river then continues S and SSW past Passaic, Clifton, and Nutley to Newark, where it joins the Hackensack R. to form NEWARK BAY.

Passamaquoddy Bay familiarly, **Quoddy Bay** inlet of the Bay of FUNDY, up to 30 mi/48 km NE–SW across its entrance, at the St. Croix R. mouth, between SW New Brunswick and NE Maine. New Brunswick's GRAND MANAN, Deer, and CAMPOBELLO islands lie between its outer and inner sections. The waters yield herring, clams, sardines, lobster, and other fish. Important coast towns include Maine's Eastport and Lubec and New Brunswick's St. Andrews. Tides average 18–25 ft/5.5–7.6 m; tidal flow is 70 billion cu ft/2 billion cu m twice daily at the change. During the 1920s, 1930s, and 1960s, the bay was investigated as a potential source of tidally generated electricity, but the projects were always suspended due to environmental, engineering, and political obstacles. WEST QUODDY HEAD, at the bay's S extremity, is the easternmost point in the US.

Pass Christian city, pop. 5557, Harrison Co., S Mississippi, 9 mi/14 km WSW of Gulfport, on the E side of the entrance to St. Louis Bay, and on Mississippi Sound. Named in 1699, it has had social and strategic importance since the 18th century. In 1812 a battle was fought just SW between British and American vessels. Early in the 19th century the settlement became a resort for wealthy planters; in 1849 the first US yacht club was established. It is now a beach resort, and processes local oysters, shrimp, and lumber.

Patapsco River 65 mi/105 km long, in Maryland. It is formed 20 mi/32 km W of Baltimore by the junction of the North Branch (c.45 mi/72 km long) and the South Branch (c.30 mi/48 km long) and flows generally SE to Chesapeake Bay. Baltimore is at the head of its estuary, which includes the lower 14 mi/23 km and is up to 3 mi/5 km wide, with a deep dredged channel. Harbor, residential, and industrial (like SPARROWS POINT) areas line its shores and inlets. **Patapsco State Park** (11,500 ac/4660 ha), along the river W of Baltimore, is an important regional recreational area. Above it the Liberty Dam, near REISTERSTOWN, forms Liberty Reservoir.

Patchogue village, pop. 11,060, in Brookhaven town, Suffolk Co., SE New York, on Long Island's South Shore, on Great South Bay, 53 mi/85 km E of Manhattan. A residential village and summer boating resort, it also has some light manufacturing.

Paterson city, pop. 140,891, seat of Passaic Co., NE New Jersey, on the Passaic R., 13 mi/21 km N of Newark and 14 mi/23 km NW of Manhattan. The 70-ft/21-m Great Falls of the Passaic had such obvious waterpower potential that Alexander Hamilton and his Society for Establishing Useful Manufactures founded Paterson (1791) to promote American economic independence. Its enormous industrial development began with the first cotton mill (1792), and the textile industry grew rapidly. In 1839 silk production started, and Paterson was soon famous as the "Silk City." At about the same time, Colt began producing revolvers here; locomotives were manufactured later in the century. Largely due to its textile workers, Paterson was a labor union center early in the 20th century. Today many of the old mills have been recycled, and while some silk, rayon, clothing, and ribbons are still produced, a variety of new industries have become prominent. These include chemicals, electronic components, television equipment, machinery, and machine tools. Throughout its 200 years of industrial history, Paterson has experienced successive booms and busts. It has a large minority and immigrant population. Paterson's past is preserved in the Great Falls Historic District.

Pathfinder Reservoir 35 sq mi/91 sq km, 23 mi/37 km long, and 1 mi/2 km wide, in Natrona and Carbon counties, SC Wyoming. Fed by the Sweetwater and North Platte rivers, it was created by the 218 ft/66 m–high, 432 ft/132 m–long granite and concrete **Pathfinder Dam** (1909) across the North Platte. The main unit in the North Platte Irrigation Project, the reservoir irrigates E Wyoming and W Nebraska. The 16,807-ac/6807-ha **Pathfinder National Wildlife Refuge** occupies numerous sections around the reservoir.

Patience Island see under PRUDENCE I., Rhode Island.

Patoka River 138 mi/222 km long, in SW Indiana. It rises in SE Orange Co., in the HOOSIER NATIONAL FOREST. It is dammed near Cuzco to form Patoka L., then flows in a winding course, generally W, past JASPER and Winslow, just N of PRINCETON, and past Patoka, to the Wabash R. at East Carmel.

Patowmack Canal see under POTOMAC R.

Patrick Air Force Base see under SATELLITE BEACH, Florida.

patriotes French-Canadian activists, variously nationalists, reformers, or protesters of various stripes, in early-19th-century LOWER CANADA. Reacting to rural poverty at a time of rising anglophone financial power and immigration, and to the British government's refusal to empower the francophone majority politically, the patriotes rose in scattered fighting in 1837–38, centered in Montréal and in the RICHELIEU valley. They were quickly defeated and harshly repressed; the rebellion, however, contributed to the creation (1840) of the United PROVINCE OF CANADA, and some of their leaders, notably Louis-Joseph Papineau, were important in later Canadian politics.

patroonship quasifeudal estate in the colony of NEW NETHERLAND, chiefly along the Hudson R. Patroons were granted stretches (usually 8 mi/13 km on both sides, or twice that distance on one side) of riverfront, and had to settle a number (usually 50) of farmers within a specified time. They could exercise local legal and administrative powers, and settlers owed them rent and some services. Patroonships were granted from the 1620s, but most, like PAVONIA, dissolved quickly. The most successful, Rensselaerswyck (see RENSSELAER, New York), lasted into the 19th century. Hangovers of the patroons' powers in the Hudson Valley brought on New York's 1839 "Antirent Wars." Compare SEIGNEURIE.

Patuxent River 100 mi/160 km long, in Maryland. It rises in NW Howard Co., and flows generally SE and S, forming the E boundaries of MONTGOMERY and PRINCE GEORGE'S counties, to Chesapeake Bay. Its estuary is c.5 mi/8 km wide at its mouth, and has deepwater anchorage. The river is navigable for c.45 m/72 km, and tidal for c.56 mi/90 km. Dams on its upper reaches form the Tridelphia and Rocky Gorge reservoirs. The Patuxent Naval Air Test Center is S of the river's mouth, near LEXINGTON PARK.

Paulus Hook see under JERSEY CITY, New Jersey.

Pavonia former estate, the 17th-century patroonship of Michael Paauw, which embraced Staten Island, New York, as well as the area of Jersey City and part of Hoboken, New Jersey. Its name was created by Latinizing Paauw.

Pawcatuck River 30 mi/48 km long, in Rhode Island and Connecticut. It rises in Worden Pond, South Kingstown, S Rhode Island, and flows generally W and SW through Charlestown and Westerly, forming part of the state border, and into Little Narragansett Bay, 13 mi/21 km E of New London.

Pawhuska city, pop. 3825, seat of OSAGE Co., NE Oklahoma, 20 mi/32 km SW of Bartlesville. It is the administrative capital of the Osage Nation (whose reservation is coextensive with Osage Co.), and was named for a 19th-century chief. The tribal council conducts government business at the Osage Agency here. The city is a trade center for oil, natural gas, livestock, and agricultural producers.

Pawleys Island also, **Pawley's** see under GRAND STRAND, South Carolina.

Pawnee city, pop. 2197, seat of Pawnee Co., NE Oklahoma, 30 mi/48 km SSE of Ponca City. Settled in an area inhabited by the Pawnee, it was a trading post and Indian agency before its 1890s founding. Many Pawnee remain here, along with members of the Otoe, Kaw (Kansa), Ponca, and Tonkawa; the Pawnee Indian Agency is here. The city has some industry and tourism and is a trade and processing center for livestock and grain producers. Just W are the mansion and ranch of Gordon W. "Pawnee Bill" Lillie, one of the original settlers and a Wild West showman.

Pawnee Rock also, **Citadel of the Prairie** huge sandstone promontory in SC Kansas, just N of Pawnee and 12 mi/19 km SW of Great Bend. A famous rendezvous on the SANTA FE TRAIL, it was the site of many skirmishes between pioneers and Indians, and is now a State Historic Site.

Pawtucket city, pop. 72,644, Providence Co., NE Rhode Island, on the Blackstone (Seekonk) R., just NE of Providence, at the head of Narragansett Bay. It was part of both Rhode Island and Massachusetts until 1862. Pawtucket was one of the first American industrial centers. Ironworks date from 1690, when Joseph Jenks Jr. began forging kitchen implements. During the Revolution, Pawtucket supplied arms and ammunition to the Revolutionary army. Cotton milling began in 1790, powered by 50-ft/15-m Pawtucket Falls, in what is now the center of the business district; Pawtucket became known as the cradle of the US textile industry. The restored Slater Mill (1793) is a National Historic Site. Today, the city produces a wide range of textile and other manufactures.

Pawtucket Falls **1.** see under LOWELL, Massachusetts. **2.** see under BLACKSTONE R. and PAWTUCKET, Rhode Island.

Payette city, pop. 5592, seat of Payette Co., SW Idaho, on the Snake R. at the Oregon border, 48 mi/77 km NW of Boise. It is a trade, processing, and shipping center for an agricultural, dairying, and poultry raising area. Among the goods made here are canned and dried fruits and vegetables. Baseball great Harmon Killebrew was born here (1936).

Payette National Forest 2.3 million ac/932,000 ha (3594 sq mi/9308 sq km), in WC Idaho, bordered by the SNAKE R. and HELLS CANYON (W) and the Salmon R. (N). A large part of the Frank Church–River of No Return Wilderness is within the forest, which has hundreds of miles of trails, fishing streams, and ski slopes. Headquarters are at McCall.

Payson **1.** town, pop. 8377, Gila Co., C Arizona, in the Tonto National Forest, 57 mi/92 km NE of Phoenix. In a wooded, lake-dotted area S of the MOGOLLON RIM, this 1880s goldmining, later ranching and lumbering, town is now a tourist center and popular summer retreat for Phoenix residents. The novelist Zane Grey lived and wrote here in the 1920s. **2.** city, pop. 9510, Utah Co., NC Utah, 15 mi/24 km SSW of Provo. Settled by Mormons in 1850, it is now a trade and processing center in an irrigated agricultural area producing sugar beets, onions, alfalfa, eggs, and fruit, and has railroad shops.

Peabody city, pop. 47,039, Essex Co., NE Massachusetts, on the Danvers R., 15 mi/24 km NE of Boston. Settled in 1633, it was incorporated as South Danvers in 1855, and in 1868 renamed after philanthropist George Peabody, born here. It was a glassmaking center from the 1630s, and its famous tanneries were established before the Revolution. A major leather processing center, Peabody also produces chemicals and fabricated metals, and makes wood products, machine tools, shoes, clothing, and electronics.

Peabody Hotel in downtown Memphis, Tennessee, two blocks N of BEALE St. Since the 1920s it has been the city's premier hotel, noted for its restaurants and entertainment. The Peabody Ducks, a group of mallards that live in a penthouse, descend in the elevator daily to enjoy the lobby's fountain. The Peabody has been called the N limit of the Mississippi Delta.

Peace Bridge international bridge between Buffalo, New York, and Fort Erie, Ontario. The 4400-ft/1340-m steel span was opened on Aug. 7, 1927 as a memorial to 100 years of peace between Canada and the United States.

Peace River **1.** town, pop. 6717, NW Alberta, at the confluence of the Peace and Smoky rivers, 240 mi/386 km NW of Edmonton. It is a trade and transportation hub, shipping Peace R. valley grain and livestock. Originally Peace River Crossing, it was the base for Alexander Mackenzie's expedition (1793) into the Northwest, and later an important ferry and rail crossing for the region. Although missions were established here from 1879, permanent settlement began only in 1913. The Rocky Mountains Forest Reserve is nearby. **2.** 1194 mi/1923 km long, in British Columbia and Alberta. Formerly created by the confluence of the Finlay and Parsnip rivers, now within WILLISTON L., in NE British Columbia, it flows E from the lake through the Rocky Mts., past FORT SAINT JOHN, into Alberta, through the **Peace River Lowland,** to the town of Peace River, then turns N to near

Fort Vermilion, and ENE, through WOOD BUFFALO NATIONAL PARK, to the Slave R. just NW of L. ATHABASCA. The Slave drains into GREAT SLAVE L., and the Peace is thus part of the MACKENZIE R. system. White traders were on the river from the 1780s, in territory of the Cree and Beaver. The railroad reached the area 1915–16, opening up the Peace River District to agriculture; it is the northernmost grain producing zone on the continent, nourished by rain-bearing Pacific winds. Oil and natural gas lie beneath the district, and have been exploited in recent years.

Peace Tower see under PARLIAMENT HILL, Ottawa, Ontario.

Peach Bottom township, pop. 3444, York Co., SE Pennsylvania, site of a nuclear power plant on the W bank of the Susquehanna R., just N of the Maryland line. Its initial unit, opened 1966, was shut down in 1974; two units opened that year are in operation.

Peachtree Center multiuse complex in downtown Atlanta, Georgia, on Peachtree St., just N of FIVE POINTS. Completed between 1967 and 1981, it incorporates office towers, a hotel, the Merchandise and Apparel marts, and the Atlanta International Museum of Art and Design. All elements are linked by skywalks and underground arcades.

Peachtree City city, pop. 19,027, Fayette Co., WC Georgia, 25 mi/40 km SSW of Atlanta. A planned residential community, it was established in 1960.

Peachtree Creek tributary of the Chattahoochee R., in N Georgia. Its **North Fork** rises S of Norcross, in Gwinnett Co., and flows SW through Atlanta's N, through the Peachtree Hills residential section. The **South Fork** rises near Tucker, in De Kalb Co., flows WSW through EMORY, and joins the North Fork in NE Atlanta. The Peachtree Trail, entering the area from Toccoa (NE), paralleled the creek to its junction with the Chattahoochee; in the late 18th century this was the site of **Standing Peachtree,** a Creek settlement, named for a tree, either a peach or a pine (pitch), atop a prominent mound. The battle of Peachtree Creek was fought along its banks on July 20, 1864, as Confederates tried in vain to break Union lines establishing a siege of the city.

Peachtree Street main commercial thoroughfare of N Atlanta, Georgia, running 6 mi/10 km N from FIVE POINTS to BUCKHEAD, where it continues NE into the suburbs as Peachtree Rd. Atlanta's oldest (1840s) street, it follows in part the earlier Peachtree Trail, and forms much of the line between the city's NW and NE quadrants. From Five Points it passes Midtown, Ansley Park, and Peachtree Hills before entering Buckhead.

Peacock Prairie see under GLENVIEW, Illinois.

Pea Island National Wildlife Refuge: see under OUTER BANKS, North Carolina.

Peaks Island see under CASCO BAY, Maine.

Peaks of Otter twin summits in the BLUE RIDGE Mts., W Virginia, 23 mi/37 km W of Lynchburg. Flat Top, to the N, rises to 4001 ft/1220 m; Sharp Top, to the S, rises to 3875 ft/1182 m.

Peapack and Gladstone borough, pop. 2097, Somerset Co., NC New Jersey, 10 mi/16 km SW of Morristown. Settled in the mid 18th century in an area of limestone quarries, it is an essentially residential community with some corporate headquarters, situated just N of the junction of Interstates 78 and 287.

Pea Patch Island 1 mi/1.5 km long, in New Castle Co., N Delaware, in the Delaware R., just NE of Delaware City. Fort Delaware (1814; 1850) was built for river and coast defense. It was used in the 1860s to house Confederate prisoners of war, many of whom died as a result of epidemics. The fort was active through World War II; the island is now a state park.

Pea Ridge city, pop. 1620, Benton Co., extreme NW Arkansas, in the Ozark Plateau, 8 mi/13 km NW of Rogers and 5 mi/8 km S of the Missouri line. The Battle of Pea Ridge (or Elkhorn Tavern), Arkansas's most important Civil War engagement, was fought here March 7–8, 1862. Union troops under Samuel Curtis defeated Confederate forces commanded by Earl Van Dorn, and secured Missouri for the Union. The 4300-ac/1742-ha Pea Ridge National Military Park preserves the battle site.

Pearl city, pop. 19,588, Rankin Co., SC Mississippi, 7 mi/11 km SE of downtown Jackson, of which it is a primarily residential suburb.

Pearland city, pop. 18,697, Brazoria and Harris counties, SE Texas, 15 mi/24 km SE of downtown Houston, on Clear Creek. A residential suburb, it also engages in oil refining, and has machine shops and chemical plants.

Pearl City unincorporated, largely residential community, pop. 30,993, Honolulu Co., S Oahu, Hawaii, on PEARL HARBOR and the Pearl R., 9 mi/14 km NW of Honolulu. It was damaged in the 1941 attack on Pearl Harbor. The main industry is sugar processing. Leeward Community College (1968) and the University of Hawaii: West Oahu (1976) are here.

Pearl Harbor inlet forming an almost entirely landlocked harbor on the S coast of Oahu, Honolulu Co., Hawaii. Connected to the Pacific Ocean by the Pearl Harbor Entrance, it has been improved to create a major US naval base, headquarters of the Pacific Fleet. From the early 1900s this, later joined by HICKAM AIR FORCE BASE (SE) and other posts on Oahu, has formed a strategic defense complex. Pearl Harbor covers 10 sq mi/26 sq km of navigable waters and more than 10,000 ac/4000 ha of land surrounded by the communities of EWA BEACH, WAIPAHU, PEARL CITY, AIEA, and HONOLULU. There are naval shipyards, a supply center, and a submarine base. Pearl Harbor was the focus of a surprise Japanese air attack on Dec. 7, 1941, bringing the US into World War II. The battleship USS *Arizona* remains as a memorial at the spot where it was sunk, entombing 1100 crewmen.

Pearl River **1.** 485 mi/781 km long, in S Mississippi and E Louisiana. It rises in the Red Hills of EC Mississippi, NE of Philadelphia, and winds generally SW through the Ross Barnett Reservoir and past JACKSON. It continues generally SSE across the Coastal Plain, through the PINEY WOODS, past Monticello, Morgantown, and Columbia, before forming the Louisiana-Mississippi border for the last 116 mi/187 km of its course. In this section the largest city is Bogalusa, Louisiana. Thirty mi/48 km from its mouth, near Picayune, Mississippi, it divides into two parallel channels. The main channel, the East Pearl, empties into L. BORGNE on the Gulf of Mexico. The West Pearl enters the Rigolets, a channel draining L. PONTCHARTRAIN. The river's name refers to the pearl oysters formerly abundant on its banks. Its tributaries include the YOCKANOOKANY R., which joins it above Jackson, at the Ross Barnett Reservoir. **2.** unincorporated village, pop. 15,314, in Orangetown, Rockland Co., SE New York, on the New Jersey line, 12 mi/19 km NE of

Paterson. It is a largely residential suburb with some corporate and research facilities.

Pearson International Airport see LESTER B. PEARSON INTERNATIONAL AIRPORT, Ontario.

Pease Air Force Base see under NEWINGTON, New Hampshire.

Pebble Beach resort on the SW of the MONTEREY PENINSULA, in WC California, along Seventeen-Mile Drive, 3 mi/5 km SW of Monterey and just NW of Carmel-by-the-Sea. A windy, cliffside area created from the Del Monte Forest by the Southern Pacific Railroad around 1900, it is widely known as the site of what is often considered the world's finest golf course (1919).

Peconic Bay inlet of the Atlantic Ocean, Suffolk Co., SE New York, SW of GARDINERS BAY, at the E end of Long Island, between the North and South forks. It is divided into Great Peconic Bay (SW) and Little Peconic Bay (NE); uninhabited Robins I., 445 ac/180 ha, sits between the two. Great Peconic Bay, 8 mi/13 km NE–SW, and up to 4 mi/6 km wide, ends at Flanders Bay (SW), where the PECONIC R. empties. It is connected by canal to SHINNECOCK BAY (S) at the village of Hampton Bays. Little Peconic Bay lies within SHELTER I., beyond which is Gardiners Bay and the open sea. Peconic Bay is a noted boating, fishing, and shellfishing area.

Peconic River 15 mi/24 km long, in E Long I., SE New York. It rises in Brookhaven, and flows generally E past Calverton and RIVERHEAD, to Flanders Bay and Great Peconic Bay. It is navigable to Riverhead.

Pecos **1.** village, pop. 1012, San Miguel Co., NC New Mexico, in the S Sangre de Cristo Mts., on the Pecos R., 16 mi/26 km ESE of Santa Fe. The **Pecos National Monument,** 2 mi/3 km S, preserves the ruins of a PUEBLO and two Franciscan MISSION churches, all abandoned by the 1830s and later a landmark on the SANTE FE TRAIL. Just NW is GLORIETA PASS. **2.** city, pop. 12,069, seat of Reeves Co., SW Texas, on the Pecos R., 72 mi/116 km SW of Odessa. Established by the Texas & Pacific Railroad in 1881, it was a cow town, and grew into an important livestock trading center. Area crops include vegetables, cotton, and cantaloupes. Sulfur, natural gas and oil deposits are exploited. Pecos calls itself the home of "the World's First Rodeo," held in 1883 and reenacted annually; tourism and hunting are important to the economy.

Pecos River 926 mi/1491 km long, in New Mexico and Texas. It rises in the Sangre de Cristo Mts. E of Santa Fe, and flows SE, then S through E New Mexico, at the W edge of the Great Plains, joined by numerous intermittent streams. On the E it is flanked by the LLANO ESTACADO. Passing E of Roswell and Artesia, the Pecos flows through several small reservoirs, and despite silting problems, provides irrigation for area agriculture. Longstanding disputes between New Mexico and Texas over water use were settled in 1949. The Pecos now swings SE in Eddy Co., past CARLSBAD. It then winds into Texas, through dam-created Red Bluff L. and SE across the Stockton Plateau to the head of the Amistad Reservoir, on the RIO GRANDE, just SE of LANGTRY. In Texas the river is regarded as the boundary between the rest of the state and the more rugged territory "West of the Pecos."

Peddocks Island 1.8 mi/2.9 km long, in BOSTON HARBOR, Massachusetts. It is part of Boston Harbor Island State Park. Politically, the partly wooded island is in HULL, Plymouth Co. Until 1992 it was home to a community of fishermen and squatters who were evicted as renovations for park use proceeded. An army fort on Peddocks was operational from the 1890s until 1947.

Pedernales River 105 mi/169 km long, in SC Texas. It rises in W Gillespie Co., on the Edwards Plateau, and flows E through the HILL COUNTRY to join the Colorado R. WNW of Austin. The Pedernales passes JOHNSON CITY, and is closely associated with President Lyndon B. Johnson; his LBJ Ranch, where he died in 1973, is near Stonewall, about 16 mi/26 km E of FREDERICKSBURG, and the Lyndon B. Johnson National Historic Park is at Johnson City.

Pee Dee River also, **Great Pee Dee** and **Pedee** in North Carolina and South Carolina. It is formed 7 mi/11 km ENE of ALBEMARLE where the Uwharrie R. joins the YADKIN R., which has flowed 200 mi/320 km from the Blue Ridge Mts. The Pee Dee continues another 230 mi/370 km SSE into South Carolina, passing Cheraw and joining the LITTLE PEE DEE R. before emptying into Winyah Bay, at GEORGETOWN. The river is named after the Pedee tribe, whose villages were located along its middle course. The entire Yadkin–Pee Dee system is sometimes called the Pee Dee.

Peekskill city, pop. 19,536, Westchester Co., SE New York, on the E bank of the Hudson R., 40 mi/64 km N of New York City. Founded by Jan Peek as a trading post in 1654, it developed as an agricultural market and river port, served as headquarters for General Israel Putnam during the Revolutionary War, and in 1777 was burned by the British. Heavily industrial in the 19th century, it is today a market center and base for the Palisades recreational region. Varied industries remain, but the city is attempting to revitalize itself as a residential and artistic community.

Peggy's Cove resort and fishing hamlet at the mouth of St. Margarets Bay on the Atlantic Ocean, 20 mi/32 km SW of Halifax, in SC Nova Scotia. With its granite ledges, sailboats, and lighthouse, it is one of the most visited and photographed spots in Canada.

Pekin city, pop. 32,254, seat of Tazewell Co., C Illinois, on the Illinois R., 10 mi/16 km S of Peoria. A river port and rail center, it is a shipping point for the region's grain, cattle, and coal. Local manufactures include corn products, alcohol and liquors, steel tanks, barrels, burial vaults, and metal castings. Pekin was settled in 1824. It is the birthplace (1896) of Everett M. Dirksen, and the Dirksen Congressional Leadership Research Library is located here. The Powerton Fish and Wildlife Area is 4 mi/6 km SW.

Pelée, Point see POINT PELÉE NATIONAL PARK, Ontario.

Pelée Island c.18 sq mi/47 sq km, in extreme S Ontario, lying in L. Erie, 15 mi/24 km SW of Pt. Pelée and 16 mi/26 km SSW of Leamington. About 9 mi/14 km N–S and 4 mi/6 km wide, it is the largest island in the lake. Three mi/5 km S is Middle I., at 41° 41′ N Canada's southernmost point. Pelée is a township (pop. 272, Essex Co.) noted for growing wine grapes and as a resort, largely for Ohioans (it is reached by ferry from Sandusky, as well as from Ontario ports). In the summer its pop. quadruples. In the fall it has a noted, brief pheasant shooting season.

Pelelieu island: see under Republic of PALAU.

Pelham **1.** city, pop. 9765, Shelby Co., C Alabama, 17 mi/27 km S of Birmingham, of which it is a growing outer suburb. **2.** town, pop. 11,903, Westchester Co., SE New York, just N of the New York City line, between New Rochelle (E) and Mount Vernon (W). **Pelham Manor,** which included the present villages of Pelham (pop. 6413) and

Pelham Manor (pop. 5443), was purchased in 1664 from the Siwanoy Indians by Thomas Pell. Today the Pelhams are residential suburbs of New York. **3.** town, pop. 13,328, Niagara Regional Municipality, S Ontario, between the Niagara Escarpment (N) and the Welland R. (S), 14 mi/23 km WSW of Niagara Falls. In the 1780s LOYALISTS chose the site, at the highest point of the Niagara Plain, for its defensibility. The area developed agriculturally, with quarrying and some light industry, and after World War II became a bedroom community for Welland, St. Catharines, and Niagara Falls.

Pelham Bay Park largest New York City park (1997 ac/809 ha), extreme NE Bronx, on Pelham Bay, Long Island Sound, and Eastchester Bay, at the mouth of the HUTCHINSON R., on both sides of which it lies. The park incorporates a peninsula called Hunters Island, the southernmost part of which is Rodman Neck; the Split Rock golf course; and Orchard Beach, a popular working-class resort. CITY I. is connected with Rodman Neck by bridge, and HART I. lies farther offshore. New York City purchased most of the area in 1888.

Pella city, pop. 9270, Marion Co., SC Iowa, 15 mi/24 km NW of Oskaloosa. Dutch settlers arriving in 1847 took the name from a biblical city of refuge. Known for its bologna, bakeries, animated musical clock, carillon, and annual Tulip Festival, Pella is a trade center for the region's farm products and livestock. It is the seat of Central College (1853). Red Rock Reservoir on the Des Moines R. is 5 mi/8 km SW.

Pell City city, pop. 8118, co-seat (with Ashville) of St. Clair Co., NE Alabama, near the Coosa R. and 31 mi/49 km E of Birmingham. It is chiefly a distribution center for the area's lumber and cotton.

Pelly Mountains NW–SE trending range, c.200 mi/320 km long, in the SC Yukon Territory. The LIARD R. flows SE from the range, which includes Fox Mt. (7886 ft/2404 m). The **Pelly R.,** 330 mi/530 km long, rises in the Mackenzie Mts. on the Northwest Territories border, and flows generally WNW along the N of the range, past Ross River and Faro, paralleling the CAMPBELL HIGHWAY, to join the Yukon R. at Fort Selkirk, W of the Klondike Highway. The Ross and Macmillan rivers (from the NE) are its chief tributaries.

Pemaquid Neck peninsula in Bristol town, Lincoln Co., SW Maine, 6 mi/10 km E of Boothbay Harbor, marking the W boundary of Muscongus Bay. By around 1600 an English fishing and trading settlement was in the area; the 1620 Plymouth settlers knew of it. Several forts have been built at Pemaquid Beach, on the W side; Fort William Henry is a replica of one there in 1692. Pemaquid Point lighthouse (1827) is at the S tip.

Pemberton see under FORT DIX, New Jersey.

Pembina Mountain also, **Pembina Hills** rolling upland in S Manitoba, extending (NW–SE) 60 mi/97 km between the Assiniboine R. (N) and the North Dakota border (S), part of the MANITOBA ESCARPMENT.

Pembina River **1.** 350 mi/560 km long, in WC Alberta. Flowing generally NE from the Rocky Mts., E of Jasper National Park, it winds along the NW of the Edmonton area to the ATHABASCA R., SE of Lesser Slave L. **2.** 275 mi/443 km long, in Manitoba and North Dakota. It rises in the Turtle Mts. and the Drift Prairie of S Manitoba, and flows generally SE into North Dakota NW of Walhalla, then E to join the Red R. of the North at the city of Pembina, on the Minnesota border.

Pembroke **1.** town, pop. 2241, Robeson Co., S North Carolina, 11 mi/18 km NW of Lumberton. The center of a Croatan (Lumbee) community, it is home to Pembroke State University, chartered in 1887 and opened to non-Indians in 1953. **2.** city, pop. 13,997, seat of Renfrew Co., SE Ontario, on Allumette L. (the Ottawa R.), 75 mi/120 km WNW of Ottawa. The Indian and Muskrat rivers meet the Ottawa here. Settled in the 1820s, Pembroke (earlier Campbellton and Miramichi) became a major lumbering center, and still makes a wide variety of wood products. It is also a gateway to ALGONQUIN PROVINCIAL PARK (W), a fishing and rafting base, and a noted migratory swallow and waterbird stopover.

Pembroke Pines city, pop. 65,452, Broward Co., SE Florida, adjacent (W) to Hollywood and 6 mi/10 km from the Atlantic. In a suburban corridor midway between Miami and Fort Lauderdale, it mainly consists of planned (especially retirement) communities of middle-class one-family homes with various recreational facilities. Its population has grown enormously since its incorporation in 1961 (320% in the years 1970–90).

Pendleton **1.** city, pop. 15,126, seat of Umatilla Co., NE Oregon, on the Umatilla R., 22 mi/35 km S of the Washington line. Once a major stop on the OREGON TRAIL, it was founded in 1869. Since its early days, it has been a commercial and distribution hub for a livestock raising and wheat growing region. Its lumber and woolen mills are also central to its economy. In addition, food processing, flour milling, canning, and leatherworking are important industries. The Pendleton Round-Up has been a renowned annual rodeo since 1910. The Umatilla Indian Reservation is 6 mi/10 km E of the city, and McKay Creek National Wildlife Refuge is 3 mi/5 km S. **2.** town, pop. 3314, Anderson Co., NW South Carolina, in the Piedmont, 14 mi/23 km NW of Anderson. The oldest settlement in the area, it was founded on land ceded (1777) by the Cherokee to South Carolina, known as the **Pendleton District.** In the early 19th century this was an affluent region, with many summer retreats as well as flourishing industries (iron and carriage making). The 6316-ac/2558-ha Pendleton Historic District, which comprises the whole town and portions of Anderson, Oconee, and Pickens counties, contains a myriad of historic locales and structures, including the Woodburn and Ashtabula plantations. Tourism is now important. The town produces textiles and cottonseed oil.

Pend Oreille River also, **Pend d'Oreille** 155 mi/250 km long, draining L. Pend Oreille, in N Idaho's Panhandle, and flowing generally W and N through NE Washington and into S British Columbia, where it joins the COLUMBIA R. near Montrose, just N of the Washington border. Silver, lead, and zinc mines brought settlers to its valley in the early 20th century. **L. Pend Oreille,** some 40 mi/64 km long, and fed primarily by Montana's CLARK FORK R., is a noted trout-fishing site. SANDPOINT is on its NW.

Penetanguishene familiarly, **Penetang** town, pop. 6643, Simcoe Co., SC Ontario, on Penetanguishene Bay, an arm of Severn Sound (GEORGIAN BAY), 82 mi/133 km WNW of Toronto. From the early 17th century French missionaries and VOYAGEURS visited the Huron, later the Ojibwa, here. After the War of 1812, the site was developed as a naval yard and military base. Later in the century it was a logging center. Today it is a tourist hub with a growing residential component.

Peninsula, the land between the James (S) and York (N)

rivers, in E Virginia, the site of the Peninsular Campaign (March–Aug. 1862), a Union effort to take RICHMOND from the SE. At the outset, the Union commander, George McClellan, laid siege to YORKTOWN, a Confederate strong point at the Peninsula's SE. The Confederates withdrew NW toward Richmond, and McClellan's inaction gave them time to organize their defenses and eventually to launch the Seven Days' Campaign, which began NE of Richmond at MECHANICSVILLE, and which finally ended the Union's offensive.

Peninsular Ranges any of a number of mountain ranges extending N from Baja California, Mexico, into S California. The Peninsular Ranges and the TRANSVERSE RANGES, which are separated by the Los Angeles Basin, are together sometimes referred to as the Los Angeles Ranges. The Imperial and Coachella valleys and the Salton Sea lie E of the Peninsular Ranges, shielded by them from moist ocean air. Largely granitic, the fault-block mountains, like the Sierra Nevada, have steep E faces with more gentle slopes toward the Pacific. With few peaks over 6000 ft/1850 m, they include the SAN JACINTO, SANTA ANA, SANTA ROSA, Coyote, and Cuyamaca mountains.

Penn Avenue commercial thoroughfare, 9 mi/14 km long, between the GOLDEN TRIANGLE in Pittsburgh and Churchill (E), Pennsylvania. Following an Indian trail on flat land, it parallels railroad tracks and a high-speed busway. The road serves the Strip, Lawrenceville, Bloomfield, Friendship, Garfield, East Liberty, Larimer, Point Breeze, and Wilkinsburg.

Penn Center **1.** office complex in C Philadelphia, Pennsylvania. Situated across from City Hall, it was part of the city's major urban renewal effort of the 1960s. It includes offices, promenades, fountains, and a skating rink. **2.** see under SAINT HELENA SOUND, South Carolina.

Penn Hills township, pop. 51,479, Allegheny Co., SW Pennsylvania. It incorporates industrial and residential suburbs NE of Pittsburgh.

Pennington County 2783 sq mi/7208 sq km, pop. 81,343, in SW South Dakota. Its seat is RAPID CITY, which is also its major manufacturing center. Traversed by the Cheyenne R. and crossed on the W by the Black Hills, it is a farming and ranching region, with substantial mineral wealth. Grain, livestock, timber, granite, and gold are produced. Pennington Co. has a thriving tourist industry; it is the site of the Mt. RUSHMORE National Memorial, and parts of both the Black Hills National Forest and Badlands National Park.

Penn-Lincoln Highway limited-access highway, running 22 mi/35 km between Pennsbury Village (W) and Monroeville (E), Pennsylvania. Passing through downtown Pittsburgh, it connects the city with the Pennsylvania Turnpike (E) and Greater Pittsburgh International Airport (W).

Pennsauken township, pop. 34,733, Camden Co., SW New Jersey, just NE of Camden, on the Delaware R. Settled in 1840, it is a largely residential suburb of Camden and Philadelphia.

Penn's Landing municipal waterfront park, 37 ac/15 ha, in Philadelphia, Pennsylvania, along the Delaware R., E of SOCIETY HILL and CENTER CITY. It was here that William Penn first set foot (1682) in his new settlement.

Pennsylvania officially, **Commonwealth of Pennsylvania** northeastern US state, in the Middle Atlantic region; 1990 pop. 11,881,643 (100.1% of 1980; rank: 5th); area 46,058 sq mi/119,290 sq km (rank: 33rd); ratified Constitution 1787 (2nd). Capital: HARRISBURG. Most populous cities: PHILADELPHIA, PITTSBURGH, ERIE, ALLENTOWN. Pennsylvania is bordered N by New York, and has a small coastal strip on L. ERIE; Ohio and the West Virginia PANHANDLE lie W; along the S, on what was the MASON-DIXON LINE, lie (W–E) West Virginia, Maryland, and Delaware; on the E is the DELAWARE R., across which is New Jersey. The state is crossed (SW–NE) by elements of the APPALACHIAN system, including (E to W) SOUTH Mt., an extension of the BLUE RIDGE; the Great Appalachian Valley; and the ALLEGHENY Mts. (rising to 3213 ft/980 m at Mt. DAVIS, in the SW, the state's high point), beyond which lies the Appalachian Plateau (which in the N extends all the way across the state to the Delaware). In the SE is part of the PIEDMONT region, the first section of Pennsylvania settled by Europeans, through which the Delaware, SCHUYLKILL, and SUSQUEHANNA rivers flow SE from the Appalachians. In the SW the YOUGHIOGHENY and MONONGAHELA rivers flow N (from Maryland and West Virginia) and the ALLEGHENY R. SW (from New York); their junction is the site of Pittsburgh, and the beginning of the OHIO R. Pennsylvania is, with New York, the only state with ports on both the Atlantic (Philadelphia) and the Great Lakes (Erie). Its W, with its coalfields, is part of the MIDDLE WEST's industrial heartland; its SE is part of the seaboard MEGALOPOLIS. The state is the site of rich anthracite coalfields (in the NE, around SCRANTON and WILKES-BARRE) that were key to the heyday of steam railroads. Its bituminous coal made the Pittsburgh area, with its easy access to the Great Lakes and their iron ore, America's steel center. The first (1859) drilled oil well was at TITUSVILLE (NW). Limestone, needed for steelmaking, and other minerals are abundant. All these made Pennsylvania the hub of American industry in the late 19th and early 20th century; today many of its heavy-industrial cities, including Pittsburgh, Scranton, Wilkes-Barre, BETHLEHEM, JOHNSTOWN, and ALTOONA, are struggling to adjust to the decline of steel and allied manufactures and of railroads. The pop. of the state has not grown appreciably in recent decades, and the cities are shrinking. Today oil refining, metal fabrication, chemical and pharmaceutical production, and food processing are important. Banking and finance, services, research, and education have replaced some of the job loss in heavy industry. Tourism and recreation are important in the POCONO Mts. (E) and in historic (Philadelphia, GETTYSBURG) or folkloric (PENNSYLVANIA DUTCH COUNTRY, AMISH COUNTRY) districts. Agriculture, the basis of the earliest European settlement (along the Delaware), is now centered on dairy goods, poultry and eggs, apples, and such specialized crops as mushrooms (in the KENNETT SQUARE area, SE). Home to the Lenni Lenape (Delaware) and other Algonquian, and to some Iroquoian, groups, the region saw 1630s–40s settlement as part of NEW SWEDEN and by the Dutch. After the 1664 British conquest of NEW NETHERLAND, the Quaker leader William Penn was granted a charter to what became "Penn's Woods." Philadelphia, the "City of Brotherly Love," was the capital of his settlement. Relations with local Indians were at first good, and Penn's policy of toleration attracted religious dissidents from England, Germany, and elsewhere in the Colonies. The prosperous agricultural settlement E of the Appalachians soon came to be regarded as the "Keystone" of the British colonies, midway between New England and the plantation South. Philadelphia's commercial importance and Penn's legacy contributed to Pennsylvania's key role in the American Revolution, when both political and military (at VALLEY FORGE, GERMANTOWN, the BRANDYWINE, and elsewhere) action centered here. After the revolution the lack of an easy pioneering or trade route W across the state diminished its importance. Attempts to develop a canal system to compete with New York's Erie Canal and Maryland's canals and railroad were only partly successful, and it was not until the PENNSYLVANIA RAILROAD crossed (1850s) the Appalachians, in the same period that Pittsburgh's coalfields were rising to importance, that the state began to enter its industrial era. In the Civil War, Pennsylvania's position on the Mason-Dixon Line, and its resources, made it a target of Southern military advances, which were stemmed at Gettysburg. Largely British and German to that point, its pop. soon embraced Slavic, Italian, and other European groups; today it is diverse, with large black communities in Philadelphia and Pittsburgh and a cosmopolitan mix esp. in the SE.

Pennsylvania Avenue **1.** thoroughfare in Washington, D.C., between GEORGETOWN (NW) and ANACOSTIA (SE). It passes in front of the WHITE HOUSE (No. 1600), makes a dogleg, and proceeds to CAPITOL HILL. Resuming again SE of the Capitol, it passes through SE Washington, where it is a major commercial street, into Prince George's Co., Maryland, where it becomes the Marlboro Pike when it crosses the BELTWAY. Pennsylvania Ave. is the route of the presidential inaugural and many other parades. **2.** commercial thoroughfare, running SE–NW, from downtown BALTIMORE, Maryland, to S of Druid Hill Park. Through most of the early 20th century this was the focal street of Baltimore's black community. In the 1970s URBAN RENEWAL did away with much of it. Areas to the W have traditionally been Baltimore's black heartland, although much of the city's 57% (1990) black pop. now lives in the more integrated NE and in parts of the NW.

Pennsylvania Dutch Country popular name for the parts of E Pennsylvania settled after 1683, esp. in the early and mid 18th century, by German (*Deutsch*) settlers coming directly from Europe or from earlier settlements in New York's Hudson R. valley. Drawn by the religious tolerance proclaimed in William Penn's colony, they included Moravians, Mennonites (including the Amish), Dunkards (members of the Church of the Brethren), Schwenkfelders, and others. The heart of Pennsylvania Dutch Country is a ring some 50 mi/80 km around Philadelphia, from the LEHIGH VALLEY (N) to the AMISH COUNTRY of Lancaster Co. (W). In this area, where names, arts and crafts, building styles, farming techniques, and local dialect reflect German influences, the major cities are Allentown, Bethlehem, Reading, and Lancaster; other communities include Nazareth, Kutztown, Ephrata, Strasburg, and Lebanon.

Pennsylvania Railroad incorporated 1846, to connect Harrisburg and Pittsburgh, by way of Altoona. Operating from 1850 over lines of the abortive 1830s canal-and-incline-railway "Main Line" (a name later used for the Pennsy's Philadelphia–Paoli commuter line and the W suburban area it served), it reached Pittsburgh by 1854, preempting a move there by the BALTIMORE and OHIO, and connected with Philadelphia. Expanding quickly, it acquired New Jersey's 1831 Camden & Amboy, one of the first US railroads, as well as various short Pennsylvania lines. An important Union carrier in the Civil War, it by the 1870s had connections with St. Louis. Purchasing the Pittsburgh, Fort Wayne & Chicago, it completed a route from New York (Jersey City, New Jersey, with ferry service across the Hudson R.) to Chicago; this was developed into a four-track (two freight, two passenger) corridor known as "Broadway," giving its name in 1902 to the *Broadway Limited,* the Pennsy's famous competitor with the NEW YORK CENTRAL'S *Twentieth-Century Limited.* From the 1850s the Pennsy used anthracite coal as fuel, and it undertook much of the development of steam locomotives. Its main shops were in ALTOONA, 5 mi/8 km W of which was the noted Horseshoe Curve, over the height of the Allegheny Mts. In 1910 the Pennsy tunneled under the Hudson and reached Manhattan, where **Pennsylvania Station** (the 1910 original by McKim, Mead & White was demolished in 1963) became the world's busiest; in addition to providing a direct link with New England (through another tunnel under the East R.), it handled the heavy commuter traffic of the LONG ISLAND RAIL ROAD, a subsidiary. It also was a major commuter line in New Jersey and in the Philadelphia suburbs, and as a freight carrier was central to the coal-and-steel economy of W Pennsylvania and E Ohio. In 1968 it merged with the New York Central to form the short-lived **Penn Central;** in 1970 this collapsed into Conrail (the government-created Consolidated Rail Corporation), which also absorbed other eastern routes. Passenger service along these lines is now handled by Amtrak.

Pennsylvania Turnpike toll highway extending 470 mi/757 km across S Pennsylvania between the Delaware R. at Bristol (E) and the Ohio border (W). The first portion was completed in 1940 between Middlesex, near Carlisle, and Irwin. The E extension opened in 1950 and the W extension in 1951. The road was joined to the New Jersey Turnpike in 1956, and later spurs connect it to Wilkes-Barre and Scranton, Philadelphia, and Pittsburgh. Constructed at an original cost of $540 million, it is considered the nation's first superhighway.

Penn Valley Park 176-ac/71-ha public park in Kansas City, Missouri, 1.5 mi/2.4 km S of Downtown, created in 1897, partly on the site of a slum area called Vinegar Hill. It inaugurated a wave of park and parkway development that transformed the early-20th-century city. The CROWN CENTER is today on the NE, HOSPITAL HILL slightly farther NE. The Scout (1917) and Pioneer Mother (1927) monuments are in the park.

Penn Yan village, pop. 5248, in Milo township, Yates Co., WC New York, 15 mi/24 km SSW of Geneva, at the N end of Keuka L. It is a tourist and boatbuilding community in a winemaking region. Its name is a compromise struck by settlers from *Penn*sylvania and *Yan*kees from New England. Jemima Wilkinson's JERUSALEM was 6 mi/10 km SW.

Pennyroyal also, **Pennyrile** or **Pennyroyal Plateau** area (c.7800 sq mi/20,200 sq km) covering much of SC and W Kentucky. Separated from the KNOBS REGION (NE) and the mountains and coalfields in the E by a 600–700 ft/180–210 m escarpment, and extending SW to the Tennessee R., the rolling, hilly region is underlain by an extensive network of subterranean passages, the most famous of which is MAMMOTH CAVE. Water sinks quickly through the porous limestone, leaving few large rivers on the surface. "Pennyrile" is the local pronunciation of pennyroyal, a mint that grows abundantly.

Penobscot Bay island-filled inlet of the Atlantic Ocean at the mouth of the Penobscot R., 25 mi/40 km SSW of Bangor, in coastal C Maine. Measuring 35 mi/56 km N–S and 5–20 mi/8–32 km E–W, the irregularly shaped bay heavily indents the rugged, granite-lined coast. Fishing, lobstering, and tourism are major industries on the bay. The main harbors, E to W, are Stonington (on DEER ISLE), CASTINE, Bucksport, Searsport, Belfast, CAMDEN, and ROCKLAND. VINALHAVEN I. lies at the mouth of the bay, and ISLE AU HAUT is 10 mi/16 km to the E. Tiny Hurricane I., 4 mi/6 km SW of Vinalhaven, is the site of an Outward Bound school. Holbrook Island Sanctuary State Park and other refuges on the islands are home to many marine birds. Camden Hills State Park borders the bay on the W.

Penobscot County 3430 sq mi/8884 sq km, pop. 146,601, in EC Maine. Bangor is the county seat. The area is drained by the Penobscot R., and includes numerous lakes. There are lumbering, hunting, and fishing in the sparsely populated N; agriculture and the manufacture of pulp, paper, wood products, textiles, and boats are important in the Bangor area, in the S.

Penobscot River about 350 mi/563 km from the head of its longest branch, formed by headstreams draining off many lakes in C and W Maine, flowing generally S and SE into Penobscot Bay. It is Maine's most extensive river, with an 8500-sq-mi/22,000-sq-km basin. The 110-mi/177-km West Branch and shorter East Branch join at Medway to run past Old Town, Orono, and Bangor. The river is a source of waterpower, and is navigable to Bangor. Explored by Champlain in 1604, it was early noted for salmon fishing. In the 19th century it became one of the world's leading lumbering rivers. The end of river logging by the mid 20th century promised a return to some of its former character.

Penokee Range see under GOGEBIC Co.

Pensacola city, pop. 58,165, seat of Escambia Co., extreme NW Florida, in the PANHANDLE, on Pensacola Bay, 10 mi/16 km E of the Alabama border (Perdido Bay). The Spanish settled the area briefly in 1559–61, then permanently in 1698. Since that date, it has flown the flags of Spain, France, England, the Confederacy, and the US, changing governments 13 times. While still Spanish, it was used as a British stronghold in the War of 1812, and was captured by Andrew Jackson in 1814 and 1818. Florida passed into American hands in 1821, and the city was chartered the following year. It was held alternately by Confederate and Union forces in the Civil War, while Fort Pickens (built 1829–34 on the Santa Rosa barrier island), was always under Federal control. Today this fort is open to the public, as is the 1830s Fort McRae and the Spanish Forts Barrancas and San Carlos. Pensacola's deep natural harbor makes it a thriving shipping port and commercial fishing center. Its naval station, established in 1914, figured prominently in the city's growth; it now houses centers for flight and cartographic training and electronic warfare. Also an industrial city, Pensacola numbers synthetic fibers, boats, chemicals, paper goods, naval stores, lumber, and cottonseed oil among its products. Tourism is important; the city has several historic districts, notably the Seville Square area, and a number of historical museums. Its annual Festival of Five Flags celebrates its heritage. The University of West Florida (1963) and Pensacola Junior College (1948) are here.

Pentagon, the government installation, a building in ARLINGTON Co., N Virginia, adjacent (SE) to Arlington National Cemetery, and just W of the Potomac R., comprising five concentric pentagonal rings, the headquarters of the Department of Defense and of US armed forces. With five stories above ground and two below, it accommodates 23,000 workers. Measuring nearly 1 mi/2 km in circumference, and covering 34 ac/14 ha, it was built in 1941–43.

Penticton city, pop. 27,258, Okanagan-Similkameen Regional District, S British Columbia, on the Okanagan R., at the S end of Okanagan L., 165 mi/265 km E of Vancouver and 34 mi/54 km N of the Washington border. It is situated in a fruit growing area; the first orchards were planted here in 1874. Industries include canning, packing, and distributing fruit; winemaking; lumber milling and wood products manufacturing; and ranching. Tourism, focusing on nearby beaches and ski slopes, is also important. An Indian reserve (pop. 908) and Okanagan College are here.

Peoria **1.** city, pop. 50,618, Maricopa Co., SC Arizona, a suburb 12 mi/19 km NW of downtown Phoenix. An agricultural trade center from the 1890s, it is now part of the VALLEY OF THE SUN's residential boom; its pop. quadrupled in the 1980s. **2.** city, pop. 113,504, seat of Peoria Co., C Illinois, on the Illinois R. where it forms Upper Peoria L. and Peoria L., 50 mi/80 km N of Springfield. It is an industrial and transportation hub, as well as the trade, processing, and distribution center of an agricultural region producing corn and livestock. The Caterpillar Tractor Company has traditionally been the city's largest employer. In addition, Hiram Walker & Sons operates one of the world's largest distilleries here, and there are other brewing and distilling facilities. A port on the ILLINOIS WATERWAY, Peoria also serves as a rail terminus and freight transfer point. Besides tractors, earth moving equipment, and farm machinery, local manufactures include diesel engines, fabricated metals, air-conditioning and heating equipment, chemicals, and electronic components. Named for a tribe in the Illinois Confederacy, the area was visited by French explorers as early as 1673. La Salle built Fort Crevecoeur in what is now EAST PEORIA in 1680. Fort St. Louis, on the W side of the Illinois R., dates to 1691. The British held the area from 1763 to 1778, when their forts were captured by George Rogers Clark. Bradley University (1897) and the Illinois College of Medicine are here, as is the United States Department of Agriculture's Northern Regional Research Laboratory.

Peoria County 621 sq mi/1608 sq km, pop. 182,827, in C Illinois, bordered E and SE by the Illinois R., which forms several lakes along its course. In the SE, Peoria and its suburbs (such as Peoria Heights and Bartonville) account for most of the population. Manufacturing and transportation are key economic activities in this portion of the county. Chillicothe, in the NE, is another important city. Corn and livestock are raised in the rest of Peoria Co.

Pepacton Reservoir 18 mi/29 km long, in SE New York. It is an artificial lake, holding water for New York City, impounded on the East (Pepacton) Branch of the DELAWARE R. by the Downsville Dam, in Colchester, Delaware Co. The dam was begun in 1947 and completed in 1955, and is 2450 ft/747 m long and 200 ft/61 m high. A 25-mi/40-km water tunnel, the Delaware Aqueduct, leads SE to the Rondout Reservoir, and from there on to New York.

Pepin village, pop. 880, Pepin Co., W Wisconsin, on the Mississippi R. and L. Pepin, at the Minnesota border, 30 mi/48 km S of Menomonie. Fishing and water sports attract tourists to the area. Dairy products are processed and agricultural implements manufactured here.

Pepper Pike city, pop. 6185, Cuyahoga Co., NE Ohio, 15 mi/

24 km E of Cleveland, of which it is a suburb. It is the seat of Ursuline College (1871).

Percé city, pop. 4028, SE Québec, at the E extreme of the GASPÉ PENINSULA, 23 mi/37 km SSE of Gaspé. Settled by missionaries in the 1670s, this small fishing community has become a well-known summer resort and a haven for artists. Local scenery includes the nearby islands of **Percé Rock** (Rocher Percé, because of an erosional arch at one end), after which the village was named, and Bonaventure, both of which are now bird sanctuaries.

Perdido River 60 mi/97 km long, in Alabama and Florida. It rises just NW of Atmore, S Alabama, and flows generally S, forming the border between Alabama and Florida, into 15 mi/24 km–long **Perdido Bay,** just W of Pensacola, Florida.

Péribonca, Rivière some 300 mi/480 km long, in SC Québec, the largest river feeding L. SAINT-JEAN. It rises in the Monts OTISH and flows S. Engineering works in the 1950s created two reservoirs, and the river is an important hydroelectric power source. Near its mouth on the lake is **Péribonka** (pop. 635), the agricultural community to which the French writer Louis Hémon (1880–1913) came in 1912, to work on a farm and gather material for *Maria Chapdelaine,* his famous romantic pastoral novel. The area is now a popular resort.

Perimeter Highway circumferential limited-access road (I-285) around Atlanta, Georgia, 65 mi/105 km long. Completed in 1985, "The Perimeter" has stimulated much low-density suburban commercial development, particularly along its N arc in COBB (especially where I-75 crosses it, near Smyrna) and FULTON counties.

permafrost perennially frozen soil in arctic and subarctic regions, associated with TUNDRA vegetation because it prevents water (melted ice, in summer) and roots from penetrating beyond its upper surface (the **permafrost table**). Typically, only the upper 3 ft/1 m or so (the **active layer**) of overlying soil melts, and is therefore waterlogged.

Permian Basin region of far W Texas, at the S edge of the LLANO ESTACADO, centered around the cities of ODESSA and MIDLAND. The floor of a sea in the Permian period (280 to 225 million years ago), it is now the source of massive oil and gas deposits, first exploited in 1921. Encompassing all or part of 17 counties, the basin is bordered (SW) by the MONAHANS Sandhills.

Perrine unincorporated community, pop. 15,576, Dade Co., SE Florida, 13 mi/21 km SW of Miami. It lies in an expanding residential, commercial, and industrial area within a traditionally citrus producing and truck farming region. Three mi/5 km E of the Miami Metrozoo and just N of Cutler Ridge, it suffered extensive damage during Hurricane Andrew (Aug. 1992).

Perris city, pop. 21,460, Riverside Co., SW California, in the Perris Valley, E of the Santa Ana Mts., 14 mi/23 km SE of Riverside. Incorporated in 1911 in an area known for its gold mines, it has been a farming community until recent residential growth; its pop. tripled in the 1980s. L. Peris, 5 mi/8 km NE, is an important reservoir and recreational center.

Perry **1.** city, pop. 9452, seat of Houston Co., C Georgia, 24 mi/38 km S of Macon. It is a center of the peach industry, produces carpets and veneer, and has a brewery. **2.** village, pop. 1012, Lake Co., NE Ohio, 6 mi/10 km NE of Painesville and 3 mi/5 km S of L. Erie. A nuclear power plant opened in 1986 is nearby.

Perry Hall unincorporated village, pop. 22,723, Baltimore Co., N Maryland, 11 mi/18 km NE of downtown Baltimore. It is primarily residential.

Perrysburg city, pop. 12,551, Wood Co., NW Ohio, on the Maumee R., 8 mi/13 km SSW of Toledo, of which it is a residential and industrial suburb. Metal stampings, chemicals, plastics, and cigars are among products manufactured here. FORT MEIGS is just SW.

Perryville city, pop. 815, Boyle Co., C Kentucky, on the Chaplin R., 36 mi/58 km SW of Lexington. The largest Civil War battle in Kentucky occurred here on Oct. 8, 1862. It was a deadly (7500 casualties) standoff between Braxton Bragg's Confederate troops and Don Carlos Buell's Union forces, and was the South's last serious attempt to gain control of Kentucky. Perryville is also the birthplace (1886) of novelist and poet Elizabeth Madox Roberts.

Pershing Square municipal park, established 1866 in downtown LOS ANGELES, California, the city's premier park in the early 20th century.

Perth Amboy city, pop. 41,967, Middlesex Co., NE New Jersey, on Raritan Bay at the mouth of the Raritan R. and the S end of the ARTHUR KILL, bridged here by the Outerbridge Crossing (1928) to Staten I., 16 mi/26 km S of Newark. Situated on a tract purchased from the Indians (1651), it was settled by Scots (1683), and served as capital (1684–1702) of EAST JERSEY. After the union of East and West Jersey, it alternated with Burlington as capital until 1790. Perth Amboy was a summer resort in the early 1800s. An important port, the city grew with the arrival of the Lehigh Valley Railroad (1876), which connected it with the W and S, and it became a distribution point for coal. It remains industrial, with oil refineries, steel mills, printing and chemical plants, and such other manufactures as electrical equipment, clothing, building materials, paints, jewelry, cosmetics, and processed foods.

Peru **1.** city, pop. 9302, La Salle Co., NC Illinois, on the Illinois R., 2 mi/3 km W of La Salle. Its manufactures have included timepieces and various metal products. **2.** city, pop. 12,843, seat of Miami Co., NC Indiana, on the Wabash R., 18 mi/29 km N of Kokomo. It was founded in the early 19th century on the site of a Miami Indian village. A trade, processing, and shipping center for local farm products, it has railroad shops and a number of manufactures, including auto parts, wood and metal products, fertilizer, furniture, electrical and heating equipment, and plastic goods. For many years, traveling circuses had their headquarters here, constituting Peru's main industry. An annual circus celebration and the Circus City Festival Museum recall these days. The songwriter Cole Porter was born (1891) and is buried here. **3.** city, pop. 1110, Nemaha Co., SE Nebraska, on the Missouri R. and the Missouri state line, 15 mi/24 km SE of Nebraska City. It is a distribution point for fruit, grain, livestock, and dairy products. Peru State College (1867) is here.

Peshtigo town, pop. 2807, Marinette Co., NE Wisconsin, 6 mi/10 km SW of Marinette, and 5 mi/8 km W of Green Bay of L. Michigan. A major 19th-century lumber center on the Peshtigo R., it is now chiefly a resort town. On Oct. 8, 1871, the same night as the great Chicago fire, Peshtigo was at the center of perhaps the worst forest fire in US history, which killed 600 and devastated the town.

Petaluma city, pop. 43,184, Sonoma Co., NW California, at the head of navigation on the Petaluma R., 32 mi/52 km N of

San Francisco. The city is a noted poultry and dairy center. Other industries include winemaking and the production of feed, fertilizers, and a wide variety of light manufactures. Settled by Mexicans in 1833, Petaluma is now also a growing residential suburb.

Petawawa village, pop. 5793, Renfrew Co., SE Ontario, 85 mi/137 km WNW of Ottawa and 10 mi/16 km NW of Pembroke, on the Petawawa R. and Allumette L. (a widening of the Ottawa R.). A summer militia camp here (1905) developed into a major staging and training base for World Wars I and II, eventually into a permanent Canadian Forces Base, home to airborne and other units.

Petenwell Lake also, **Petenwell Flowage** in Adams and Juneau counties, SC Wisconsin. Measuring 15 mi/24 km long and 2–5 mi/3–8 km wide, it is impounded by a dam in the Wisconsin R., 25 mi/40 km S of Wisconsin Rapids.

Peterborough **1.** town, pop. 5239, Hillsborough Co., S New Hampshire. It is on the Contoocook R., 16 mi/26 km SE of Keene. Tourism, apple orchards, and the manufacture of textiles and baskets are the leading industries. Miller and Greenfield state parks, with popular summer and winter resorts, and Temple and Crotched Mt. ski slopes are nearby. The town was settled in the 1740s. Here Brigham Young became Mormon church leader (1844). Peterborough is home to the MacDowell Colony, founded by Marian Nevins, widow of composer Edward MacDowell, in 1908, a retreat for composers and writers. **2.** city, pop. 68,371, seat of Peterborough Co., S Ontario, on the Otonabee R. and TRENT CANAL (which here has a famous hydraulic lift lock), 70 mi/113 km ENE of Toronto. The community developed around sawmills and gristmills established in 1821. It is now the industrial and commercial center of an extensive agricultural region. Manufactures include auto, electrical, marine, and agricultural equipment; snowmobiles; textiles; furniture; lumber; hardware; and plastic items. The city is also gateway to the Kawartha Lakes summer resort region. Sir Sandford Fleming College and Trent University are here. PETROGLYPHS PROVINCIAL PARK is 34 mi/55 km NE, and SERPENT MOUNDS PROVINCIAL PARK is 9 mi/14 km SE.

Petersburg **1.** city, pop. 3207, Wrangell-Petersburg Census Area (pop. 7042), SE Alaska, on Mitkof I., 120 mi/193 km SSE of Juneau, on the ALASKA MARINE HIGHWAY, in the ALEXANDER ARCHIPELAGO. Founded in 1897 by Norwegian fishermen, it retains its Scandinavian influence and remains a fishing center, with some fur farming and lumbering carried on in the area. **2.** city, pop. 2261, seat of Menard Co., C Illinois, on the Sangamon R., 18 mi/29 km NW of Springfield. Abraham Lincoln surveyed the site in the 1830s. Anne Rutledge and Edgar Lee Masters are buried in the local cemetery. Just S of Petersburg is the restored pioneer village of New Salem, which features reconstructed buildings associated with the years (1831–37) when Lincoln lived in this now-abandoned river port. The Edgar Lee Masters Memorial Museum is also here. **3.** independent city, pop. 38,386, in SE Virginia, on the S bank of the Appomattox R., 22 mi/35 km S of Richmond. An industrial city and trade center for the surrounding agricultural area, it is an important tobacco market, and produces cigarettes, textiles, chemicals, and furniture. Settled in the 1640s, Petersburg saw action in the Revolutionary War, and as a transportation hub was of great strategic importance during the Civil War. It was under siege from June 1864 by Union forces based chiefly at City Point (HOPEWELL). On July 30, 1864, Union forces exploded a huge mine under the Confederate earthworks, and attacked through what became known as the Crater, but were repelled. After Petersburg finally fell, on April 3, 1865, Union forces went on to take Richmond, and the war ended.

Petersham town, pop. 1131, Worcester Co., C Massachusetts, on the Swift R., 25 mi/40 km NW of Worcester. It was the site of the final battle of Shays's Rebellion (1786–87), an insurrection of farmers protesting high taxes and low prices for farm goods; their forces, led by Daniel Shays, were defeated here on Feb. 4, 1787. Harvard Forest (2100 ac/840 ha) and a bird sanctuary are here. QUABBIN RESERVOIR lies SW.

Peters Mountain ridge of the Allegheny Mts., extending NE from the New R. near Narrows, Giles Co., SW Virginia for c. 50 mi/80 km, along the West Virginia border to SW of Covington, in Alleghany Co., Virginia. It rises to just over 4000 ft/1220 m.

Petoskey city, pop. 6056, seat of Emmet Co., in the N portion of the Lower Peninsula of Michigan, on Little Traverse Bay of L. Michigan at the mouth of the Bear R., 31 mi/50 km SW of Mackinaw City. Named in Algonquian as "between two swamps," it was settled in 1852. Originally a lumber town, Petoskey now has some light manufacturing, but mainly relies on year-round tourism. The St. Francis Solanus Indian Mission (1859) still stands here. It is home to North Central Michigan College (1958). Ernest Hemingway's vacation home was on Walloon L., 4 mi/6 km to the S. The Little Traverse Historic Museum here has Hemingway memorabilia. Petoskey stones, the petrified coral that are Michigan's state stone, can be found on the lakeshore around the city. Near Petoskey, beneath Little Traverse Bay, is the Skin Divers' Shrine, a submerged statue of Christ. There are also several ski developments in the area.

Petrified Forest National Park 93,532 ac/37,880 ha, in EC Arizona, 18 mi/29 km E of HOLBROOK. Over 200 million years ago rivers brought tree trunks and other plant matter to a swamp here; the preserved material now includes agate logs, fossil plants, and some fossil animals, set in a high, dry area protected by law since 1906. The PAINTED DESERT lies N, and there are archaeological sites in the area over 1500 years old.

petroglyph a carving in rock, esp. one left, often within caves, under ledges, on cliffs, etc., by prehistoric or premodern peoples. A **pictograph** is a painting, done with red ocher or other pigments, often on harder rock surfaces like those of the CANADIAN SHIELD. Animal and human figures and various other symbols are common; their religious or social importance is unclear.

Petroglyphs Provincial Park 34 mi/55 km NE of PETERBOROUGH, Ontario, with approximately 900 carvings dating from c.900–1400.

Peyton Place fictional New Hampshire town, the setting for Grace Metalious's sensational, best-selling 1956 novel of the same name, which spawned a movie, several sequels, and a long-running television soap opera. The book was based partly on events in the agricultural and resort town of Gilmanton (pop. 2609, Belknap Co.), 15 mi/24 km NNE of Concord and just S of L. Winnipesaukee, where Metalious had lived for a time in the former mining village of Gilmanton Iron Works.

Phalanx see under COLTS NECK, New Jersey.

Pharr city, pop. 32,921, Hidalgo Co., extreme S Texas, in the

Lower Rio Grande Valley, 46 mi/74 km WNW of Brownsville and adjacent (E) to MCALLEN. Established in 1909, it grows cotton, citrus fruits, and vegetables. Natural gas and oil are produced, and leather clothing is made. Pharr is also a winter vacation center.

Phenix City city, pop. 25,312, seat of Russell Co., also in Lee Co., E Alabama, on the Chattahoochee R., opposite (W) Columbus, Georgia. Its industries include the manufacture of textiles, carpets, paperboard, brick, metal products, modular homes, and recreational equipment. The city also benefits from the proximity of Fort Benning, in Columbus. It is home to Chattahoochee Valley Community College (1974).

Philadelphia 1. city, pop. 6758, seat of Neshoba Co., EC Mississippi, 36 mi/58 km NW of Meridian. Settled in the 19th century on Choctaw land, in a timbered and now agricultural area, it is a market for cotton and lumber, with some light manufactures. Once the seat of the Choctaw Indian Agency, it is now the site of the Choctaw Museum of the Southern Indian. The Nanih Waiya Historic Site, a mound dating back c.1600 years and considered the spiritual home of the Choctaw, is 20 mi/32 km N of the city, near Noxapater. During the civil rights struggles of the 1960s, Philadelphia was the site of the murder, in the summer of 1964, of activists Andrew Goodman, James Chaney, and Michael Schwerner. **2.** popularly, **the City of Brotherly Love** or **Quaker City** city, pop. 1,585,577, coextensive with **Philadelphia Co.**, E Pennsylvania, on the Delaware R. where the Schuylkill R. joins it, across from Camden, New Jersey, 90 mi/145 km SW of New York City and 90 mi/145 km NE of Baltimore, Maryland. The fifth most populous US city, it is the center of a four-state, thirteen-county metropolitan area (Philadelphia-Wilmington-Trenton CMSA) with a pop. of 5,899,345. In the heart of the urbanized Boston–Washington Corridor (MEGALOPOLIS), the CMSA includes BUCKS, CHESTER, DELAWARE, MONTGOMERY, and Philadelphia counties, Pennsylvania; BURLINGTON, CAMDEN, GLOUCESTER, MERCER, CUMBERLAND, and Salem counties, New Jersey; NEW CASTLE Co., Delaware; and CECIL Co., Maryland. Founded in 1681 by deputies for William Penn in what had been NEW SWEDEN, Philadelphia grew rapidly, and by the middle of the 18th century was the most populous city in the American colonies (and proverbially the second most populous English-speaking city in the world). Penn's policy of religious tolerance, as well as the natural advantages of the site (esp. its large harbor) spurred growth of a commercial hub. A vibrant intellectual life fostered in large part by Benjamin Franklin, who arrived here in 1723, made the city by the 1770s a center of learning, culture, and political ferment. Despite the conservative leanings of its merchants, it took the leading role in the American Revolution: Continental Congresses met here from 1774, and the Declaration of Independence emerged in 1776. After the British held the city for nine months in 1777–78, while Washington's forces wintered at nearby (W) VALLEY FORGE, Philadelphia resumed its role: the Articles of Confederation (1778) and Constitution (1787) were both drafted here, and the city was US capital in 1790–1800, before government moved to the new District of Columbia. In the 19th century commercial preeminence also shifted away from the city, to New York, Baltimore, and other portals to westward expansion, and Philadelphia became industrial. In the post–Civil War period it received waves of European immigrants who manned its heavy and light industries. After World War II a further shift began, from manufacturing to finance and various service industries. The city today retains a sizable industrial base, although many manufacturers have moved into surrounding areas, and remains a commercial, financial, educational, cultural, and governmental center. It has about 76% of its 1950 peak pop. of 2,071,605, and is about 40% black, having shared in the 20th-century national pattern of black migration to cities and white removal to suburbs. Its major industries include shipbuilding (the Philadelphia Navy Yard has been key), oil importation and refining, printing and publishing, and the manufacture of machinery, chemicals, pharmaceuticals, electrical and electronic items, foods, textiles, and a wide variety of technical equipment. Leading educational institutions include the (private) University of Pennsylvania (1740); St. Joseph's (1851), La Salle (1863), and Temple (1884) universities; Drexel University (1891, formerly Drexel Institute of Technology); the Curtis Institute of Music (1924); and several medical schools. Philadelphia's Symphony Orchestra, Art Museum, and Fairmount Park (site of the 1876 Centennial Exposition) are esp. well known. Major sports venues include Veterans Stadium, the Spectrum, and John F. Kennedy Stadium, all in a South Philadelphia complex. See also: ART MUSEUM DISTRICT; BENJAMIN FRANKLIN BRIDGE; BENJAMIN FRANKLIN PARKWAY; BOATHOUSE ROW; BROAD St.; CENTER CITY; CHESTNUT HILL; CHINATOWN; CITY LINE Ave.; ELFRETH'S ALLEY; FAIRMOUNT PARK; FRANKFORD; GERMANTOWN; HEAD HOUSE SQUARE; INDEPENDENCE HALL; ITALIAN MARKET; KENSINGTON; LIBERTY PLACE; LOGAN; LOGAN CIRCLE; MAIN LINE; MANAYUNK; MARKET St.; MOUNT AIRY; NORTHEAST PHILADELPHIA; NORTHERN LIBERTIES; NORTH PHILADELPHIA; OLD CITY; OLNEY; OVERBROOK; PENN CENTER; PENN'S LANDING; POWELTON VILLAGE; QUEEN VILLAGE; READING TERMINAL MARKET; RITTENHOUSE SQUARE; RIVER WARDS; ROOSEVELT Blvd.; SCHUYLKILL EXPRESSWAY; SOCIETY HILL; SOUTH PHILADELPHIA; SOUTH St.; SOUTHWARK; the SPECTRUM; UNIVERSITY CITY; VETERANS STADIUM; WALT WHITMAN BRIDGE; WASHINGTON SQUARE; WEST PHILADELPHIA; YORKTOWN.

Philippi city, pop. 3132, seat of Barbour Co., NE West Virginia, on the Tygart R., 19 mi/31 km ESE of Clarksburg. The first land battle of the Civil War was supposedly fought here on June 3, 1861, when Confederate forces retreated so quickly that the battle is known as the "Philippi Races." Alderson-Broaddus College (1871) is here; Tygart L. State Park is immediately N.

Philipse Manor historic estate, Westchester Co., SE New York. In 1681 Frederick Philipse began acquiring land along the Hudson R. in Westchester, eventually owning nearly all the shore from YONKERS to OSSINING. His manor house in Yonkers, built in 1682 and added onto over the years, was for a while Yonkers City Hall, and is now a museum. The Philipse family were Loyalists during the Revolution, and their properties were confiscated after the war. A residential section just NE of North Tarrytown is today called Philipse Manor.

Phillips neighborhood of Minneapolis, Minnesota, immediately S of Downtown. Home to a large Indian population, it has suffered economic and social stress for many decades.

Phillipsburg town, pop. 15,757, Warren Co., NW New Jersey, on the Delaware R. opposite Easton, Pennsylvania, 42 mi/68 km NW of Trenton. Settled in 1739, it grew with the coming of the railroad and was an iron and steel center by the mid 19th century. Situated in an agricultural area, it produces and ships such goods as boilers, pipes, chemicals, tools, and processed food.

Philomath city, pop. 2983, Benton Co., NW Oregon, 5 mi/8 km WSW of Corvallis, in the Willamette Valley. Founded around the United Brethren Church's Philomath College (1867–1929), it is now a residential and tourist center with a July rodeo and an important electronics plant.

Phoenix city, pop. 983,403, state capital and seat of MARICOPA Co., SC Arizona, in the VALLEY OF THE SUN, on the SALT R. It is the center of a metropolitan area (MSA, pop. 2,122,101) coextensive with the county; both city and MSA are growing rapidly, and epitomize the SUNBELT. The valley, in the N SONORAN DESERT, was settled more than 2000 years ago by the Hohokam, agriculturists who established an extensive canal network; 1000 years ago Phoenix's forerunner may have been the largest community in what is now the US. After the 15th-century disappearance of the Hohokam, the Pima moved into the area. Americans who arrived in the 1860s found and restored the canals, predicting that a new city would rise phoenixlike from the ruins. Laid out in 1870, Phoenix was an Army supply point and base for miners and ranchers. It became the territorial capital in 1889 (and state capital in 1912). By the 1880s the region's climate was attracting growth; the railroad arrived in 1887. The THEODORE ROOSEVELT Dam (E), completed in 1911, further enhanced the water supply, and the city in the early 20th century was a farming (citrus, melons, cotton, vegetables) and tourism (dude ranches, winter resorts) center. World War II brought a boom in aircraft and other manufacturing industries, along with military training facilities. After the war, rapid and decentralized residential and industrial growth continued; the old Downtown declined until 1970s redevelopment, while MESA, SCOTTSDALE, TEMPE, and other suburbs burgeoned. Today, agriculture remains important on the fringes of urban development. The city manufactures aerospace, electronic, and medical equipment; various machinery; leather goods; and other products. It is a convention and resort center, and home to institutions including the Heard Museum (Southwest Indians), Phoenix College (1920), and the University of Phoenix (1976). The SOUTH Mts. and Phoenix Mts. (with Camelback Mt.) rise from the desert within the urban area, and there are ski resorts to the E.

Phoenix Mountains desert range NE of Phoenix, in C Arizona. Squaw Peak (2608 ft/795 m), 9 mi/14 km NE of Downtown, is heavily used by hikers. Camelback Mt. (2704 ft/824 m), the site of the huge Phoenician resort, is on a SE spur.

Phoenixville borough, pop. 15,066, Chester Co., SE Pennsylvania, on the Schuylkill R., 24 mi/39 km NW of Philadelphia. It was settled by German immigrants c.1720; English settlers followed later. A steel industry was established by 1785. In 1856, John Griffen, superintendent of the Phoenix Iron Works, turned out the first Griffen gun, a light cannon used during the Civil War. Industries make steel, auto parts, apparel, abrasives, rubber products, and felt. The borough is home to Valley Forge Christian College (1938). A monument marks the point of westernmost British penetration (1777) in Pennsylvania during the Revolutionary War.

Picacho Mountains N–S trending range in S Arizona, rising to 4508 ft/1374 m at Newman Peak, 24 mi/39 km SE of CASA GRANDE. Isolated **Picacho Peak** (3382 ft/1031 m), a volcanic landmark that rises abruptly from the desert, is separated from the range by **Picacho Pass,** site of the only Civil War skirmish (April 15, 1862) in Arizona. Unrelated **Picacho Butte** (7250 ft/2210 m) is in NC Arizona, 60 mi/100 km W of Flagstaff.

Picatinny Arsenal see under DOVER, New Jersey.

Picayune city, pop. 10,633, Pearl River Co., S Mississippi, 35 mi/56 km WNW of Gulfport and 4 mi/6 km E of the Pearl R. and the Louisiana line. Settled in 1885, and taking its name from a New Orleans newspaper, it is a trade hub for local lumber, livestock, and dairy producers. Tung oil is prominent among its manufactures, which also include truck parts and textiles. Thirteen mi/21 km to the S is NASA's John C. Stennis Space Center, a 13,500-ac/5460-ha installation for space, oceanographic, and environmental research.

Pickering town, pop. 68,631, Durham Regional Municipality, S Ontario, 18 mi/29 km NE of downtown Toronto, on L. Ontario. A two-unit nuclear power station is on the lake. Like AJAX (E), which has absorbed Pickering Village, this is a fast-growing residential suburb.

Pickwick Landing Dam see under SAVANNAH, Tennessee.

Pico Peak mountain (3967 ft/1210 m) in W Vermont, in the Green Mts., 7 mi/11 km NE of Rutland, noted for its ski trails.

Pico Rivera city, pop. 59,177, Los Angeles Co., SW California, 9 mi/14 km ESE of downtown Los Angeles, on the Rio Hondo and San Gabriel rivers. It was incorporated in 1958, joining Pico and Rivera. A predominantly Hispanic industrial suburb, it has made cars, trucks, hardware, electronic components, and a variety of other products.

Pico-Union residential and commercial section of LOS ANGELES, California, 2 mi/3 km WSW of the Civic Center and just NE of EXPOSITION PARK, around the intersection of Pico Blvd. and Union Ave. It is largely Hispanic.

pictograph see under PETROGLYPH.

Pictou town, pop. 4134, Pictou Co., NC Nova Scotia, on Pictou Harbour of Northumberland Strait, 7 mi/11 km NNW of New Glasgow. Modern settlement began here in 1773, with the arrival of 178 Highland Scots on the *Hector*. Pictou Academy opened in 1809, and the region remains a center of Scottish culture and architecture. Shipping, shipbuilding, fishing, lobstering, and tourism are the main industries. Pictou is the terminus for a car ferry to Wood Islands, Prince Edward Island.

Pictured Rocks National Lakeshore in Alger Co., in Michigan's NC Upper Peninsula, on L. Superior, NE of Munising. Covering 73,000 ac/29,600 ha, it was the first designated US lakeshore (1966). Its colored sandstone cliffs rise 800–1000 ft/240–400 m above the lake.

Piedmont 1. also, **Piedmont Plateau** area of the E US, between the uplands of the APPALACHIAN Mts. (W) and the FALL LINE (E), extending SW roughly from New Jersey, where it reaches 20 mi/32 km in width, along the ATLANTIC COASTAL PLAIN to Virginia and North Carolina, where it attains its maximum width at nearly 190 mi/310 km, before ending in C Alabama. The Piedmont is lowest in New Jersey, rising less than 300 ft/90 m, and highest (2000 ft/600 m) in Georgia. Often termed the "foothills" of the Appalachians, the region is not so much a plateau as an area containing rolling hills and ridges, a number of fertile valleys, dense forests, and numerous swift streams. The BLUE RIDGE forms much of its W border, with the transition area between rock types, about which there is much geological controversy, being called the Brevard Zone; it may be the leading edge of the African tectonic plate. Some sections of the Piedmont abound in crystalline rocks bearing resemblance to the Avalonian rocks of Newfoundland, and the area also includes the Carolina Slate Belt, which extends 400 mi/640 km from S Virginia across the Carolinas to C Georgia. The Piedmont is known both for its red clay and for sandy loams that support cotton, tobacco, fruit and vegetable crops, livestock, and dairy farms. The highest point (442 ft/135 m) in Delaware, in CENTERVILLE, is in the Piedmont. The UP COUNTRY of WC South Carolina comprises the Piedmont and Blue Ridge, or upland, areas of the state. The Piedmont takes its name from N Italy's Piemonte (in French, Piedmont). **2.** city, pop. 10,602, Alameda Co., NC California, surrounded by the N part of OAKLAND, of which it is an affluent residential suburb set in the Oakland Hills.

Piedmont Park 185 ac/75 ha, in NE Atlanta, Georgia, 2.5 mi/4 km NNE of FIVE POINTS. On the site of the 1895 Cotton States and International Exposition, it became a city park in 1904. ANSLEY PARK adjoins (NW), the Morningside section is E, and MIDTOWN is S and SW. The Atlanta Botanical Garden is in the park.

Piedmont Triad the industrial region in NC North Carolina anchored by Greensboro (E; textiles), High Point (S; furniture), and Winston-Salem (NW; tobacco products), and now home to increasingly diversified manufactures.

Pierce County 1675 sq mi/4338 sq km, pop. 586,203, in WC Washington, bounded by the Nisqually R. (S, SW); Puget Sound (NW); Dalco Passage on Puget Sound (NE); and the White, Greenwater, and Little Naches rivers (N and E). TACOMA is its seat and, with its suburbs, dominates the N part. The balance is a rich agricultural region producing fruit, nuts, flower bulbs, truck crops, and dairy goods. Pierce also has lumber and coal resources. The large Fort Lewis Military Reservation is in its N section. The area is drained by the White and Puyallup rivers, and includes parts of Mt. Rainier National Park and Mount Baker–Snoqualmie National Forest.

Piermont New York: see under ERIE RAILROAD.

Pierre city, pop. 12,906, state capital and seat of Hughes Co., C South Dakota, 140 mi/225 km E of Rapid City, on the E bank of the Missouri R. It is a trade and shipping center for an agricultural region primarily producing grain and livestock. The area around the city was claimed for France by Pierre Gaultier de Varennes in 1743. Before 1800, the capital of the Arikara nation was here. In 1832, Fort Pierre was built just across the river from the site of the present city, and it became the fur trading capital of the NW. Pierre was founded in 1880 as the W terminus of the Chicago and Northwestern Railway. The railroad spurred its growth as a trade center for a large district of farms, cattle ranches, and Indian reservations. It became the state capital, first on a temporary basis (1889) and then permanently, on the basis of a statewide vote. L. OAHE is 4 mi/6 km NW.

Pierrefonds city, pop. 48,735, MONTRÉAL URBAN COMMUNITY, S Québec, near the SW end of the I. de Montréal, along the R. des Prairies facing the I. Bizard, and 15 mi/24 km WSW of Downtown. During the 1980s it was one of the MUC's faster-growing residential communities.

Pike County 673 sq mi/1743 sq km, pop. 15,969, in NE Missouri, bounded by the Mississippi R. (E). Its seat is Bowling Green (pop. 2976). Other cities are Louisiana and Clarksville, both on the Mississippi. Named for Zebulon Pike (1779–1813), discoverer of Pikes Peak, the county is said to be the source of the slang term *piker,* and was the home of the heroine of the frontier ballad "Sweet Betsy from Pike." The county is mainly agricultural, with some light manufacturing.

Pike National Forest 1.1 million ac/445,000 ha (1720 sq mi/4450 sq km), in the FRONT RANGE of the Rocky Mts., including Pikes Peak as well as the Lost Creek area, named for a stream that disappears in several places into the granitic mountains. Near Denver and Colorado Springs, Pike is one of the most heavily used NATIONAL FORESTS.

Pikes Peak 14,110 ft/4301 m, in the FRONT RANGE of the Rocky Mts., 10 mi/16 km W of Colorado Springs, C Colorado, in the SE corner of Pike National Forest. The reddish granite peak is famous for its domination of the W end of the Great Plains; for thousands of 19th-century migrants, it was their first sight of the Rockies. To the Ute, it was the place where the Great Spirit created living things. Katherine Lee Bates, on visiting it in 1893, was moved to write "America the Beautiful." It is named for the Army's Zebulon Pike, whose 1806 expedition were the first whites to see it; James Long climbed it in 1820. In 1859 the gold rush in the CRIPPLE CREEK district, just SW, inspired the slogan "Pikes Peak or Bust!" Today the mountain has ski slopes, a cog railway, a foot trail to the top, and the Pikes Peak Highway, paved one-third of its length, the scene of an annual auto hill climb and annual footrace.

Pikesville unincorporated residential village, pop. 24,815, Baltimore Co., NC Maryland, adjacent to the NW corner of the city of Baltimore. Settled in the 1770s, it is now an affluent community along the Baltimore Beltway (I-695).

Pikeville city, pop. 6324, seat of Pike Co., E Kentucky, in the Cumberland Mts., 62 mi/100 km S of Ashland. A coal, gas, and timber shipping point, it has various light industries. Pikeville College (1889) is here.

Pile o' Bones see REGINA, Saskatchewan.

Pilgrim nuclear power plant: see under PLYMOUTH, Massachusetts.

Pill Hill **1.** see BANKERS' HILL, San Diego, California. **2.** residential neighborhood on the SOUTH SIDE of Chicago, Illinois. One of the city's wealthiest black neighborhoods, it has many large mansions. Its name derives from the perception that many doctors have lived here.

Pilot Knob town, pop. 783, Iron Co., SE Missouri, 16 mi/26 km SW of Farmington and near the iron-filled hill that gave it its name. Just S of town an attack by Confederate troops under Sterling Price was repulsed by a much smaller Union force (Sept. 27, 1864).

Pilot Mountain rock formation (2415 ft/737 m high) in the Piedmont, rising above the town of **Pilot Mountain** (pop. 1181, Surry Co.) 23 mi/37 km NNW of Winston-Salem, North Carolina. This quartzite monadnock, a landmark, was called "Great Guide" by Indians. Both Pilot Mt. and Hanging Rock, 13 mi/21 km ENE, are remnants of the ancient Sauratown Mts. There are a number of other peaks in North Carolina bearing the name Pilot Mt.

Pilsen residential neighborhood on the NEAR WEST SIDE of Chicago, Illinois. Formerly the largest Bohemian community outside Europe, it is now a largely Mexican neighborhood.

Pima County 9187 sq mi/23,794 sq km, pop. 666,880, in S Arizona, bordering on Sonora, Mexico. TUCSON, its seat, dominates the economy of the NE. Most of the county is in the Sonoran Desert; the Organ Pipe National Monument and the Papago (Tohono O'odham) Indian Reservation (pop. 7830) are in the W. There are several luxurious health resorts around Tucson. Along the Santa Cruz R. (E) is an irrigated area producing alfalfa, citrus fruits, truck crops, and cotton (the Egyptian-derived pima cotton takes its name from the county).

Pimeria Alta term ("upper Pima land") used by the Spanish in the 17th–18th centuries for areas now in S Arizona and N Sonora (Mexico) inhabited by the Pima. The Jesuit missionary Eusebio Kino was active here from the 1690s to his death in 1711, and Spanish travelers passed across the Colorado R. from Pimeria Alta into ALTA CALIFORNIA.

Pimlico section of NW BALTIMORE, Maryland, 5 mi/8 km from Downtown, centered around the Pimlico Race Track, home since 1873 to the Preakness, the second leg of horse racing's Triple Crown, and to the National Jockey Hall of Fame. Preakness Week, in May, has become an important civic festival. The surrounding neighborhood is largely Jewish. Cylburn Park is just E.

Pinaleno Mountains NW–SE trending range, 35 mi/56 km long, in SE Arizona, SW of Safford. Within a unit of the Coronado National Forest, it rises to 10,720 ft/3267 m at Mt. Graham, which stands almost 8000 ft/2440 m above its surroundings. Graham, home to subalpine plants and to animals including a unique red squirrel, is the announced site of a new observatory, controversial for its anticipated effects on the local ecosystem. Heliograph Peak (10,022 ft/3055 m) is named for a signal station built in 1886. To the NW are the Santa Teresa Mts., rising to 8282 ft/2524 m at Mt. Turnbull, on the San Carlos Indian Reservation. The prehistoric Cochise and Hohokam peoples lived in the area; Pinaleno, from an Apache word, means "deer people."

Pinal Mountains small, rugged range in SC Arizona, SW of GLOBE. Within the Tonto National Forest, it rises to 7848 ft/2392 m at Pinal Peak, and includes Signal Peak (7812 ft/2381 m). Silver and copper have been mined here.

Pinardville village, pop. 4654, in Goffstown, Hillsborough Co., SC New Hampshire. It is on the Piscataquog R., immediately W of Manchester. Saint Anselm College (1889) is here.

Pinch also, **Pinchgut** former residential and commercial district of Memphis, Tennessee, just N of the modern Downtown. On the N side of the early (1820s–1830s) city, near Catfish Bay (a since-disappeared lake), it was noted as an Irish quarter in the 1850s; in the early 20th century it was a Jewish neighborhood. Today the business district has absorbed it.

Pincher Creek town, pop. 3660, SW Alberta, in the foothills of the Rocky Mts., 110 mi/177 km S of Calgary. It was established (1878) as a horse farm for the mounted police based at nearby FORT MACLEOD. The town was laid out (1882) in what is now a lumbering, ranching, and coal and natural gas producing region, and has become a trade and processing hub. Kootenai Brown Historical Park is here.

Pinconning city, pop. 1291, Bay Co., E Michigan, on the Pinconning R., 2 mi/3 km W of Saginaw Bay of L. Huron, 18 mi/29 km N of Bay City. This summer resort is well known for its cheese production. A trading center for chicory, beans, sugar beets, and livestock, it also makes pickles and has an auto parts plant. The Nayanquing Point State Wildlife Area is 4 mi/6 km SSE.

Pine Barrens **1.** region, c.1000 sq mi/2600 sq km, in S New Jersey, occupying parts of Atlantic, Cumberland, Ocean, and Burlington counties. Situated in the state's coastal plain, it has sandy soils atop an enormous shallow aquifer, and is cut by meandering streams, the largest the MULLICA R., and marked by swamps and marshes. Stands of scrub and pitch pine, some oak, and occasional Atlantic white cedar mingle with cranberry bogs and blueberry fields. Both kinds of berry are commercial, and vegetables are grown. The Pine Barrens also contain unusual insectivorous plants and orchids, rare animals, and microorganisms important in producing antibiotics. The Barrens once occupied almost a quarter of the state; until the mid 19th century trees were cut for shipbuilding and charcoal production, exhausting nearly all of the first-growth forests. The region now has extensive second growth, and is the site of several state forests, among them the 109,300-ac/44,300-ha Wharton State Forest. It is very lightly populated; its inhabitants, nicknamed "Pineys," are mainly descendants of 18th- and 19th-century residents. Typical of early Pine Barren settlements, most of them now vanished, is Batsto, a village dating from 1766. It was once the site of a flourishing bog iron foundry, brickyards, glassworks, and other industries; its iron production was important to the American cause during the Revolution. Restored to its 18th-century appearance, Batsto is now a state historic site. The Pine Barrens' major settlement is now the small community of Chatsworth, in Woodland Township (pop. 2063), Burlington Co., near the region's center. **2.** also, **Central Pine Barrens** 100,000 ac/40,000 ha, in EC Long I., SE New York, in Brookhaven, Riverhead, and Southampton towns, Suffolk Co. They lie over Long Island's major aquifer, and contain many wildlife areas and wetlands. The SUNRISE HIGHWAY runs along their S. YAPHANK, CALVERTON, and the Brookhaven National Laboratory are within them. In the 1990s they were under severe development pressure.

Pine Bluff city, pop. 57,140, seat of Jefferson Co., SE Arkansas, 40 mi/64 km SSE of Little Rock, on a high bluff overlooking the Arkansas R. Originally known as Mt. Marie, the site was settled in 1819 as a trading post and renamed in 1832. A Civil War battle took place here on Oct. 25, 1863, when a Federal brigade under Powell Clayton defended the city from the Confederate forces of John S. Marmaduke. The first port city upstream on the Arkansas from the Mississippi R., it is an industrial and agricultural marketing center, making or handling cotton and cotton byproducts, farm implements, electrical transformers, lumber and wood products, textiles, and chemicals. The Pine Bluff Arsenal, with chemical and biological warfare laboratories, is here, as well as the University of Arkansas at Pine Bluff (1873).

Pine City see under SOUTHPORT, New York.

Pine Hills unincorporated community, pop. 35,322, Orange Co., C Florida, a residential suburb on the W outskirts of Orlando.

Pinehurst town, pop. 5103, Moore Co., SC North Carolina, 3 mi/5 km WSW of SOUTHERN PINES and 28 mi/45 km WNW of Fayetteville, in the SANDHILLS. Beginning in 1895 it was developed as a resort, designed in part by Frederick Law Olmsted, and is noted for its dozens of golf courses. The PGA World Golf Hall of Fame is here.

Pine Lawn city, pop. 5092, St. Louis Co., EC Missouri, 7 mi/11 km NW of downtown St. Louis. It is a working-class, largely black residential suburb.

Pinellas County 280 sq mi/725 sq km, pop. 851,659, in WC

Florida, mainly consisting of the **Pinellas Peninsula** and the barrier islands off its W shore, bounded (W) by the Gulf of Mexico and (E and S) by Tampa Bay. Its seat is CLEARWATER, and its largest city is SAINT PETERSBURG, which occupies its populous S tip. Other important municipalities include Tarpon Springs, Largo, and Safety Harbor. Tourism and retirees are major economic factors throughout, and business centers are found in the S. There is also some citrus and dairy farming, fishing, and sponge fishing.

Pinellas Park city, pop. 43,426, Pinellas Co., WC Florida, 7 mi/11 km NW of downtown St. Petersburg. A bedroom community, it also has a number of industries, manufacturing electronic and medical equipment, sailboats and yachts, plastics, air conditioners, and tools and dies.

Pine Mountain **1.** town, pop. 875, Harris Co., W Georgia, 29 mi/47 km NNE of Columbus. It takes its name from **Pine Mt.,** a 9 mi/14 km–long ridge that rises up to 400 ft/122 m above its surroundings. Callaway Gardens, a 2500-ac/1012-ha park noted for its azaleas and its butterfly center, endowed with Callaway textile money (see LA GRANGE), is S of town. Franklin D. Roosevelt State Park (10,000 ac/4050 ha) is 5 mi/8 km SE. **2.** ridge in the Cumberland Plateau, c.125 mi/200 km long, mostly in SE Kentucky, parallel with the Virginia border and extending into Tennessee. Created by erosion, it rises to above 3000 ft/915 m in the NE section, around Pound Gap, near Jenkins, Kentucky. Pine Mountain State Resort Park, Kentucky's first state park (1924), overlooks the Kentucky Ridge State Forest near Pineville, where the Cumberland R. cuts through the ridge at the Narrows.

Pine Ridge unincorporated village, pop. 2596, Shannon Co., SW South Dakota, 80 mi/129 km SE of Rapid City and 3 mi/5 km N of the Nebraska border. It is the headquarters of the **Pine Ridge Indian Reservation** (Oglala; pop. 11,385), which extends into NW Nebraska. Situated 4 mi/6 km to the W is the 1888 Red Cloud Indian School, which is still a school and also houses an Indian Heritage Center. Oglala Chief Red Cloud is buried in a cemetery adjacent to the school. WOUNDED KNEE is on the reservation. Pine Ridge, which gives the village and reservation their name, is the N limit of the HIGH PLAINS in E Wyoming, extreme S South Dakota, and N Nebraska.

Pineville **1.** city, pop. 12,251, Rapides Parish, C Louisiana, on the E bank of the Red R., opposite ALEXANDRIA. It is a distribution center for local timber, farm produce, and livestock, and has wood-based industries, fishing operations, and stoneworks. It was settled in the early 18th century, and was burned during Union operations in 1864. Louisiana College (1906) is here. **2.** town, pop. 2970, Mecklenburg Co., S North Carolina, 11 mi/18 km SSW of central Charlotte. President James K. Polk was born (1795) in this rural settlement, now lying within Charlotte's suburban area.

Piney Point Village see under HUNTERS CREEK VILLAGE, Texas.

Piney Woods **1.** loosely defined term for the S half of Mississippi, from the Jackson area S to the Gulf Coast, in the East Gulf Coastal Plain. With rolling topography and fair soils, and dominated by longleaf yellow pine, it was settled after the War of 1812 by uplanders from Georgia and the Carolinas, and was an area of small farms until the arrival of railroads in the mid 19th century opened it to extensive lumbering. When the lumber boom had passed, it reverted to farming, with cultivation of tung trees added to previous crops. LAUREL and HATTIESBURG are the area's largest cities. **2.** also, **Pine Belt** region of E Texas, covering some 16 million ac/6.5 million ha, in 43 counties along the Louisiana, Arkansas, and Oklahoma borders. The source of almost all Texas timber, it is also useful grazing and farm land, and was the first part of the state to be heavily settled. The discovery of the EAST TEXAS OILFIELD (1930) brought industry into the area. The BIG THICKET and Davy Crockett, Sam Houston, Sabine, and Angelina national forests preserve some of the area's forest. Nacogdoches, Kilgore, Longview, and Marshall are important centers.

Pinkham Notch glacial valley in the W part of the White Mts., New Hampshire, flanked W by the PRESIDENTIAL RANGE and E by the Carter-Moriah Range. Pinkham Notch Scenic Area, c. 5600 ac/2268 ha, includes TUCKERMAN and Huntington ravines, the Crystal Cascade, Hermit Lake, Glen Ellis Falls, and the Glen Boulder, a noted large glacial erratic. Named for Daniel Pinkham, who completed a road from Jackson to Randolph in 1834, the notch is also headquarters for the Appalachian Mountain Club's huts and trails system.

Pinnacles National Monument see under GABILAN RANGE, California.

Pinnacles of Dan see under DAN R., Virginia.

Pinole city, pop. 17,460, Contra Costa Co., NC California, on the SE shore of San Pablo Bay, 14 mi/23 km N of Oakland. Once a farming and livestock center, it is now a growing suburb, with high-tech and other light industries.

Pinos, Mount peak (8831 ft/2692 m) of the COAST RANGES, 40 mi/64 km SSW of Bakersfield, in SW California. It is the highest point in the Los Padres National Forest.

Piños, Point see under PACIFIC GROVE, California.

Pinto Butte mountain (3350 ft/1048 m) in SW Saskatchewan, 113 mi/182 km SE of Moose Jaw, near the Montana border.

Pioche hamlet, seat of Lincoln Co., E Nevada, 128 mi/207 km NNE of Las Vegas. During the 1870s, this silver center enjoyed a reputation as one of the West's wildest mine towns. The restored "Million Dollar Courthouse" (1871) draws visitors.

Pioneer Square 30-block historic district just S of downtown SEATTLE, Washington, on the city's waterfront, at the W end of Yesler Way (the original SKID ROAD). It is the site of the 1852 city center, which burned in 1889 and was replaced with buildings here today. During reconstruction, the use of landfill from the leveling of some of the city's hills left former lower floors beneath street level; they are now a tourist attraction as Seattle's Underground. Pioneer Square has galleries, boutiques and the 42-story Smith Tower (1914; long the tallest building in the West). Just S is the Seattle unit of the Klondike Gold Rush National Historic Park (see also SKAGWAY, Alaska), celebrating the involvement of the city in the 1897 rush.

Pioneer Valley nickname for region in C Massachusetts along the Connecticut R. An area of rolling hills and valleys, it was settled in the mid 17th century by colonists moving N up the river. It contains the historic town of DEERFIELD, the industrial area around SPRINGFIELD, and the college towns of the AMHERST-NORTHAMPTON area.

Pipe Spring National Monument see under ARIZONA STRIP, Arizona.

Pipestone National Monument 283 ac/114 ha, in SW Minnesota, 45 mi/72 km NW of Worthington. It is the site of quarries long used by Plains Indians to obtain pipestone, a red clayey stone used for making ceremonial pipes. Believing that this is where man was created and seeing the red stone as the flesh of their ancestors, various tribes long fought over this sacred area. Established in 1937, the monument is just N of the city of Pipestone, on the COTEAU DES PRAIRIES. Pipestone is also known as catlinite, after artist and author George Catlin, who first described the quarries.

Pippa Passes city, pop. 195, Knott Co., SE Kentucky, on the Cumberland Plateau, 60 mi/100 km SSW of Ashland. In a coal mining and agricultural area, it is home to Alice Lloyd College, founded in 1923 as Caney Creek Junior College. The city's unusual name comes from a Robert Browning poetic drama (1841) involving an innocent mill worker who unconsciously changes the lives of people who hear her singing.

Piqua city, pop. 20,612, Miami Co., W Ohio, on the Great Miami R., 25 mi/40 km N of Dayton. It was founded in the 1790s. Once a major port and canal center, Piqua is now chiefly a manufacturing hub, in which steel and iron, airplane and auto parts, paper, aluminum, and wood and metal items are among the goods produced. The Piqua Historical Area, 2.5 mi/4 km N of the city, was once the site of Miami and Shawnee villages, of a 1748 trading post, and of battles during the French and Indian War.

Piscataqua River 12 mi/19 km long, forming part of the Maine/New Hampshire border. It is formed by the Salmon Falls and Cocheco rivers below Dover, New Hampshire, and flows SSE past Kittery, Maine, and Portsmouth, New Hampshire, to Portsmouth Harbor.

Piscataquis River 78 mi/126 km long, in C Maine. Rising in two branches just S of Moosehead L., it flows S and E past Dover-Foxcroft, where it provides waterpower, to the Penobscot R. at Howland.

Piscataquog River 30 mi/48 km long, in S New Hampshire. Its North Branch flows from Everett L., in Weare township, generally S, and is joined by the South Branch, flowing S and E from Pleasant Pond, Francestown. The Piscataquog then flows E through Goffstown, where it is dammed, to join the Merrimack R. at Manchester.

Piscataway township, pop. 47,089, Middlesex Co., New Jersey, on the Raritan R. opposite (N) New Brunswick, on Interstate 287. Settled in the 17th century, it includes the village of the same name. Piscataway is largely residential, but also produces pharmaceuticals, health products, and packaging machinery, and is home to corporate offices and research centers. The Hutcheson Memorial Forest of Rutgers University is here.

Pisgah high ground E of the River Jordan from which the aged Moses saw the land promised the Israelites (Deuteronomy 3, 34). Its highest peak was Mount Nebo. Pisgah is a common locality name in New England and in other parts of America, often bestowed by a settler whose "promised land" was within its view.

Pisgah National Forest 498,000 ac/202,000 ha, in W North Carolina, in the S Appalachian Mts. It comprises two large segments, one largely NE of Asheville and along the Tennessee border, the other SW of Asheville. Mt. MITCHELL and GRANDFATHER Mt. are in the NE segment; 5749-ft/1753-m **Mt. Pisgah** is in the SW section. Parts of the Appalachian Trail and the Blue Ridge Parkway pass through this hardwood forest.

Pismo Beach city, pop. 7669, San Luis Obispo Co., SW California, on the Pacific Ocean and EL CAMINO REAL, 10 mi/16 km S of San Luis Obispo and adjacent (NW) to GROVER CITY. Near oil and natural gas fields, it is known for its beach and extensive nearby sand dunes. Tourism, diverse agriculture, and fishing are important. The Pismo clam, named after the beach and found along the S California coast, is now much reduced in numbers, and clamming is limited.

Pit River 200 mi/320 km long, in NE California. It flows (as the North Fork) from the S of GOOSE L., on the Oregon border, to ALTURAS, where the N-flowing South Fork joins it. It continues generally SW from the MODOC PLATEAU through the CASCADE RANGE, to SHASTA L., on the SACRAMENTO R. The Pit takes its name from a local tribe noted for their use of pitfalls to catch game.

Pitt Meadows district municipality, pop. 11,147, Dewdney-Alouette Regional District, SW British Columbia, on the Fraser R. (S) at the confluence of the Pitt R. (W), 33 mi/53 km E of Vancouver. Settled in the 1870s on lands of the Katzic, a fishing people, it has been agricultural along the Fraser, and is now a growing residential suburb.

Pittsburg **1.** city, pop. 47,564, Contra Costa Co., NC California, 23 mi/37 km NE of Oakland, at the confluence of the Sacramento and San Joaquin rivers at the E end of Suisun Bay. It was laid out in 1849 by William Tecumseh Sherman. Coal was discovered here in the 1850s, and was mined until the early 1900s. When production declined, fishing gained importance, but the community became industrial by 1911, and was renamed to indicate its role as a steel producer. It has had a range of other manufactures. Ship repair has been important, and Camp Stoneman, operating in World War II and the Korean War, was a major military embarkation point. PORT CHICAGO is just W. **2.** city, pop. 17,775, Crawford Co., SE Kansas, 143 mi/231 km ESE of Wichita and 2 mi/3 km from the Missouri line. Settled as a mining camp in the 1870s, it remains a processing center for most of the coal mined in the state as well as for zinc, lead, clay, limestone, oil, and gas. A shipping point for agricultural products, it also has railroad shops and foundries and a large industrial park. Manufactures include coal mining equipment and building supplies. Pittsburg State University (1903) is here.

Pittsburgh city, pop. 369,879, seat of Allegheny Co., W Pennsylvania, at the junction of the Allegheny and Monongahela rivers, forming the Ohio R., 250 mi/400 km W of Philadelphia, on the Appalachian Plateau. The "**Steel City**" is the hub of a five-county (BEAVER, ALLEGHENY, FAYETTE, WASHINGTON, and WESTMORELAND) metropolitan area (the Pittsburgh–Beaver Valley CMSA) with a pop. of 2,242,798. One the world's most famous heavy industrial centers, it has since the 1950s, when its pop. peaked at 676,806, been engaged in redefining itself as a home to education, research, corporate headquarters, and varied, esp. service, industries. It began life as an Indian village and fur trade post. In the 18th century the British and French, realizing its strategic importance, fought to control the site at the junction of forest paths and river highways. A British fort begun in 1754 was seized by the French and named Fort Duquesne; regaining it in 1758, the British renamed it Fort Pitt, built other enclosures nearby, and held it through the American Revolution. Under American control in the late 1780s, it became the portal to the NORTHWEST TERRITORY, reached along the Ohio R. Boatbuilding and other related industries flourished, and canal (1830s) and rail (1850s) connections accelerated development. The location of the city (chartered 1816) in W Pennsylvania's huge bituminous coalfields, and the drilling of oil, begun at TITUSVILLE (NNE) in 1859, made Pittsburgh an industrial capital. During the Civil War it was a key Union manufacturing center, and by the 1870s coke and Bessemer steel were being mass-produced. In its heyday (1870s–1940s), industrial Pittsburgh was synonymous with steel and coal, and turned out many other basic products. Peopled largely by E and S European immigrants, it was a city of ethnic neighborhoods clinging to its hills, of intense labor organization and outbreaks (as in 1877 and again in 1892 at HOMESTEAD) of industrial strife. After World War II, the general trend toward suburbanization and movement of industry away from Northern centers began to shrink Pittsburgh's job base; at the same time, efforts to clear air and other pollution began to change the city's image. Today it is developing a reputation as a more livable, if smaller and less prominent, city. Its institutions include the University of Pittsburgh (1787), with its famous 42-story "Cathedral of Learning"; Duquesne University (1878); Carnegie-Mellon University (a 1967 merger of the 1900 Carnegie Institute of Technology with the Mellon Institute for Industrial Research), several other colleges, and the Phipps Conservatory. The Carnegie Library, Pittsburgh Symphony Orchestra, and American Wind Symphony are well known. The Gateway Center and Golden Triangle redevelopment zones, along with Three Rivers Stadium and the Civic Arena, draw visitors. See also: ALLEGHENY; ALLEGHENY CENTER; ALLEGHENY COURTHOUSE AND JAIL; ALLEGHENY WEST; BIRMINGHAM; BLOOMFIELD; the BLUFF; BOULEVARD OF THE ALLIES; BROOKLINE; CARRICK; CIVIC ARENA; DUTCHTOWN; EAST END; EAST LIBERTY; FIFTH Ave.; FIRSTSIDE; FRICK PARK; FRIENDSHIP; GARFIELD; GATEWAY CENTER; GOLDEN TRIANGLE; HEINZ HALL; HERR'S ISLAND; the HILL; HOMEWOOD; JUNCTION HOLLOW; LARIMER; LAWRENCEVILLE; LINCOLN; LOWER HILL; MANCHESTER; MARKET SQUARE; MELLON SQUARE; MEXICAN WAR STREETS; MIDDLE HILL; MOUNT WASHINGTON; NORTH HILLS; NORTH SHORE; NORTH SIDE; OAKLAND; OAKLAND SQUARE; OVERBROOK; PENN Ave.; PENN-LINCOLN HIGHWAY; the POINT; POINT BREEZE; POLISH HILL; PPG PLACE; SCHENLEY FARMS; SCHENLEY PARK; SHADYSIDE; SOUTH HILLS; SPRING HILL; SQUIRREL HILL; STATION SQUARE; the STRIP; TEMPERANCEVILLE; THREE RIVERS STADIUM; TROY HILL; UPPER HILL; UPTOWN; WEST PARK.

Pittsburg Landing see under SHILOH, Tennessee.

Pittsfield city, pop. 48,622, seat of Berkshire Co., extreme W Massachusetts, on the Housatonic R., in the Berkshire Hills. Settled in 1752, it became industrialized early in the 19th century, as New England's textile business boomed. It is now a producer of electrical and electronic equipment, with a large General Electric facility, and manufactures paper, textiles, plastics, and foundry products. Long sought out as a resort for its good air (it is situated at 1028 ft/314 m above sea level), the city provides a commercial base for the Berkshire Hills. Landmarks include Arrowhead, Herman Melville's home (1850–63), where he completed *Moby Dick*. Berkshire Community College (1960) is here.

Pittsford town, pop. 24,497, Monroe Co., W New York, on the New York State Barge Canal, 6 mi/10 km SE of downtown Rochester. It is a primarily residential suburb. Nazareth College (1924) and St. John Fisher College (1948) are here.

Pittston city, pop. 9389, Luzerne Co., NE Pennsylvania, on the Susquehanna R., S of the mouth of the Lackawanna R., 8 mi/13 km NE of Wilkes-Barre. Settled in 1770 by the Susquehanna Co. of Connecticut, it produces textiles, stoves, paper, and cigars, mines coal, and has railroad shops.

Pittsylvania County 995 sq mi/2577 sq km, pop. 55,655, in S Virginia. Its seat is Chatham. It is in the PIEDMONT, bounded S by North Carolina and N by the Roanoke (Staunton) R. A rich tobacco growing area, it also produces corn and timber. The marketing and manufacturing city of DANVILLE is in but independent of the county.

Place des Arts cultural center in MONTRÉAL, Québec, developed from the 1960s just W (officially; actually S) of the Blvd. Saint-Laurent, S of Rue SHERBROOKE, and SE of McGill University. The Salle Wilfrid Pelletier is the city's largest concert hall, home to its major symphonic, ballet, and opera organizations. The Musée d'Art Contemporain moved here in 1991. The complex, regarded as the citadel of Montréal high culture, is connected with the UNDERGROUND CITY.

Placentia city, pop. 41,259, Orange Co., SW California, 25 mi/40 km SE of Los Angeles and adjacent (SW) to Yorba Linda. Incorporated in 1926, it has developed from a farming community into a residential suburb with shopping centers and some light manufacturing.

Placentia Bay NE–SW oriented Atlantic Ocean inlet, extending some 80 mi/130 km inland, and 50 mi/80 km wide at its entrance, between the BURIN (W) and AVALON (E) peninsulas, in SE Newfoundland. Its coastal fishing settlements (OUTPORTS) have lobster and fish processing plants. **Placentia** (town, pop. 1954), on the SW arm of the Avalon Peninsula and the E shore of the bay, 64 mi/103 km WSW of St. John's, was originally a Basque fishing village. It became Newfoundland's first and most important French settlement in the 1620s. It served as a fortified base for French attacks against the English until it was ceded to Britain by the Treaty of Utrecht in 1713. From the 1940s to the 1970s nearby ARGENTIA's naval station provided employment. Today fishing and tourism are the town's leading industries.

placer Southwestern term for an alluvial or glacial deposit of sand or gravel from which particles of heavy elements (e.g., gold or platinum) may be washed. A placer may be along or in a current riverbed, or it may be at some distance from water; examples of the latter during the SIERRA NEVADA gold rush were often called "dry diggings."

Placerita see under SANTA CLARITA, California.

Placerville city, pop. 8355, seat of El Dorado Co., NC California, in the W Sierra Nevada foothills, near the South Fork of the American R., 37 mi/60 km ENE of Sacramento. A boom town during the 1849 gold rush, which began just NW in COLOMA, Placerville was at first known as Dry Diggings, because ore here was found away from running water, then as Hangtown, because of numerous executions at the height of the rush. The city ships local pears and other fruit; limestone, lumber, and building materials are produced. Tourism focuses on the city-owned Gold Bug Mine and reminders of the boom days. Placerville is headquarters for the El Dorado National Forest and a gateway to Sierra resorts, as well as a growing Sacramento exurb.

Place Ville-Marie see under UNDERGROUND CITY, Montréal, Québec.

Placid, Lake see LAKE PLACID, New York.

Plainfield **1.** town, pop. 10,433, Hendricks Co., C Indiana, 14 mi/23 km WSW of central Indianapolis, on US 40. Primarily a residential suburb, it also has some light industry.

2. town, pop. 556, Hampshire Co., NW Massachusetts, 18 mi/29 km ENE of Pittsfield on the headstreams of the Westfield R. In a hilly rural area, it is the birthplace of the writer and editor Charles Dudley Warner (1829). **3.** city, pop. 46,567, Union Co., NE New Jersey, 10 mi/16 km NE of New Brunswick. Settled by Quakers as Milltown (1684), it was a center of activity during the Revolution; the Drake House (1746) was Washington's headquarters, and today's Cedar Brook Park housed a fort. Plainfield has diversified manufactures including printing equipment, electronic and automotive parts, chemicals, tools, housewares, and clothing; it is also a residential suburb with a large medical center. The city holds an annual arts festival and has a symphony orchestra. **4.** town, pop. 1302, on the Winooski R., 8 mi/13 km E of Montpelier, in Washington Co., NC Vermont. It is the site of the innovative Goddard College, founded in 1938, and an artists' community.

Plains city, pop. 716, Sumter Co., WC Georgia, 10 mi/16 km WSW of Americus. The birthplace (1924) and home of President Jimmy Carter, it is now largely within the Jimmy Carter National Historic Site. The area is noted for its peanuts.

Plainsboro township, pop. 14,213, Middlesex Co., C New Jersey, adjacent (E) to Princeton. In rolling agricultural land along US 1, it is a longtime dairying community that is growing as part of the area's technological complex. Princeton University's Forrestal research campus is here.

Plains of Abraham plateau, now the **Parc des Champs-de-Bataille,** SW of the Citadel and the UPPER TOWN of QUÉBEC CITY, site of a decisive battle in the French and Indian (Seven Years') War. The tract was named for Abraham Martin, to whom it was granted in the 1600s. On Sept. 13, 1759, a British party under James Wolfe sailed up the St. Lawrence R. and attacked Québec by scaling the cliffs leading to the Plains. Five days later, the French, who had been led by the Marquis de Montcalm, surrendered the city. Both generals were mortally wounded in the fighting. Subsequent British fortifications included Martello towers and the Citadel itself, designed to prevent any similar attack on the city's rear. The Musée du Québec is here.

Plainview 1. unincorporated village, pop. 26,207, in Oyster Bay town, Nassau Co., SE New York, in WC Long Island, 3 mi/5 km E of Hicksville. It is a primarily residential community. **2.** city, pop. 21,700, seat of Hale Co., N Texas, in the South Plains, 40 mi/64 km NNE of Lubbock. Many wells provide irrigation here for castor beans, vegetables, cotton, wheat, and sorghums. The city manufactures irrigation equipment and packs meat. Founded in 1887, it is home to Wayland Baptist University (1908), to a number of medical institutions, and to the Llano Estacado Museum, which has artifacts of Plainview Man (8000 B.C.).

Plainville town, pop. 17,392, Hartford Co., C Connecticut, on the Quinnipiac R. adjacent (W) to New Britain. An industrial town, it produces photographic equipment, ball bearings, and tools.

Plano 1. city, pop. 5104, Kendall Co., NE Illinois, near the Fox R., 18 mi/29 km SW of Aurora. An agricultural trade center settled by Norwegians, it also manufactures such products as hardware and plastic items. Plano is 1 mi/2 km NE of Maramech Hill, the site of a 1730 skirmish between Fox Indians and the French. Silver Springs State Park is just to the S of the city. **2.** city, pop. 128,713, Collin and Denton counties, NE Texas, 17 mi/27 km NNE of downtown Dallas. Adjacent to N Dallas and on Interstate 75, it manufactures communications equipment, snack foods, metals, printed materials, and brass products, and has growing medical and financial sectors. Settled in 1845, it remained agricultural for a century, growing cotton and raising cattle. After 1960 (when its pop. was 3695), it boomed with the suburbanization of Dallas.

plantation 1. historically, esp. in the US Northeast and the Maritime Provinces, a colony or settlement. The term survives in scattered designations, e.g., of MONHEGAN I., Maine, as a plantation, or in "Providence and Rhode Island Plantations," the official name of the state of Rhode Island. **2.** a large agricultural estate, staffed by workers (in the Old South, where climatic conditions were thought inimical to whites, esp. by slaves) living on it. Typically a plantation raised one or a few cash crops, and some processing was done on the property.

Plantation city, pop. 66,692, Broward Co., SE Florida, 6 mi/10 km W of downtown Fort Lauderdale. One the largest residential suburbs in the Miami–Fort Lauderdale area, it was incorporated in 1953 and grew most quickly in the 1970s. Many retirees live here, and there is some light industry.

Plant City city, pop. 22,754, Hillsborough Co., WC Florida, 20 mi/32 km ENE of Tampa. On the site of an Indian village, it developed rapidly after the arrival of the railroad in 1884. It is situated in a rich agricultural region, known formerly for cotton, now particularly for its strawberries. Processing and shipping the berries, and citrus fruits and truck, are central to its economy. Plant City also produces lumber and fertilizer. Home to a state-run farmers' market and an annual strawberry festival, it has a renovated downtown area and also draws tourists.

Plaquemine city, pop. 7186, seat of Iberville Parish, SE Louisiana, on the W bank of the Mississippi R., along the RIVER ROAD, 9 mi/14 km SSW of Baton Rouge. Before the Civil War and again in 1909–61 (thanks to locks) it was the point at which Plaquemine Bayou served as a DISTRIBUTARY for the Mississippi; Port Allen, across from Baton Rouge, has replaced it. The city processes sugar, lumber, moss, and fish, and is in an oil producing region.

Plaquemines Parish 1035 sq mi/2681 sq km, pop. 25,575, in extreme SE Louisiana. Its seat is Pointe a la Hache. It occupies most of the delta of the Mississippi R. below New Orleans, and consists largely of swampland crossed by bayous. At its S end are islands separated from the mainland by the passes of the Mississippi, through which the river finally enters the Gulf of Mexico. Plaquemines Parish is partly suburban, with mixed agriculture and fishing, along with gas, oil, and sulfur extraction. There are several wildlife areas.

plat variant of *plot* encountered in the language of land development. Platting is the process of laying out townsites, building lots, etc.

plate one of the large rigid segments of the earth's crust (lithosphere) that move across its surface, impelled by poorly understood currents in the more fluid asthenosphere below. There are considered to be six major plates underlying continents or sea floors, and some dozen smaller ones. Seismic and volcanic activity occurs chiefly where plates collide or slide along each other, as at the SAN ANDREAS FAULT between the North American and Pacific plates.

plateau extensive, generally flat tract of land standing above the level of surrounding terrain; tableland. It is bounded clearly on at least one side by steep slopes. A plateau may be formed when a relatively hard stratum (caprock), either sedimentary or a lava flow, survives erosion that lowers surrounding lands, or when previously deposited sedimentary layers are uplifted by large-scale earth movement. A plateau cut by streams is called *dissected.*

Plateau Mont-Royal also, **the Plateau** district of MONTRÉAL, Québec, on the E (officially; actually N) side of Mt. ROYAL, extending along the N of Rue Sherbrooke to Parc Lafontaine. An ethnically diverse, commercially varied, and densely residential area, it is crossed by the Blvd. SAINT-LAURENT and Rue SAINT-DENIS.

Platinum city, pop. 64, Bethel Census Area, SW Alaska, at the entrance to Goodnews Bay off Kuskokwim Bay (the Bering Sea), 125 mi/200 km SSW of Bethel. Settled after a 1927 platinum strike, it became for a time home to many miners and adventurers seeking escape from the LOWER 48 during the 1930s Depression, and remains a center for platinum and iridosmine mining.

Platte County 421 sq mi/1090 sq km, pop. 57,867, in NW Missouri, bounded by the Missouri R. (W and S). Its seat is Platte City. The NW corner of Kansas City, its International Airport, and residential suburbs such as Lake Waukomis, Platte Woods, and PARKVILLE occupy the county's SE corner. The balance is filled with small towns and is agricultural; wheat, corn, oats, and tobacco are grown.

Platte River 310 mi/500 km long, the major river of Nebraska. It is formed just E of the city of NORTH PLATTE by the junction of the NORTH PLATTE and SOUTH PLATTE rivers, and flows ESE, then ENE, in a wide arc, passing Kearney, Grand Island, and Columbus, where the LOUP R., its largest tributary, joins it from the NW. From Columbus it continues E to Fremont, then SSE and E in the outer Omaha area, to join the Missouri R. just above Plattsmouth. Its drainage area of some 90,000 sq mi/233,000 sq km includes the ELKHORN R., which joins it W of Omaha. The valley of the Platte has been a major route to the West since the early 19th century. The OREGON and MORMON trails followed it, later the Union Pacific railroad. The river was named for the very flat area surrounding it. It is too shallow and silted for navigation, but has long been used for irrigation. With the North Platte, it has a total length of 930 mi/1495 km.

Platteville city, pop. 9708, Grant Co., extreme SW Wisconsin, 60 mi/97 km SE of Madison. Founded in 1827 as a lead mining town, it is a trade center for the surrounding dairy farming region. There are still some zinc and lead mines in the area. The city processes cheese and other dairy products, and has machine shops. It is the site of a campus of the University of Wisconsin (1866).

Plattsburgh city, pop. 21,255, seat of Clinton Co., NE New York, on the W shore of L. Champlain, at the mouth of the Saranac R., 20 mi/32 km S of the Québec border. Several important battles in the Revolution and the War of 1812 were fought in the area, including a 1776 naval battle off Valcour I., 5 mi/8 km SSE. Plattsburgh developed as a lumber and paper center, utilizing the region's abundant waterpower. It is a base for the Champlain resort area and the center of a rich agricultural area, with the world's largest McIntosh apple orchards. Industries manufacture paper, pulp, and plastic products. The production of milk is also important. Plattsburgh is the home of the State University of New York College at Plattsburgh (1899) and Plattsburgh Air Force Base (1955).

playa desert basin with no external drainage that becomes a temporary lake after heavy rain, but usually has a mud, salt, or alkaline surface.

Plaza Hotel luxury hotel at the SE corner of CENTRAL PARK, Manhattan, New York City, on Fifth Ave. at Grand Army Plaza. Opened in 1907, it is noted for such amenities as its Oak Bar and Palm Court, and has many literary associations.

Pleasant, Mount peak (4071 ft/1242 m) of the BLUE RIDGE Mts., 10 mi/16 km E of Buena Vista, in Amherst Co., C Virginia, in George Washington National Forest.

Pleasant Bay protected inlet of the Atlantic Ocean between Orleans and Chatham on the SE end of Cape Cod, SE Massachusetts. Six mi/10 km long N–S and 0.5–2.5 mi/0.8–4 km wide, the bay is almost enclosed by Nauset Beach on the E. MONOMOY I. lies SW of its entrance.

Pleasant Grove **1.** city, pop. 8458, Jefferson Co., C Alabama, 9 mi/14 km W of downtown Birmingham, of which it is a largely residential suburb. **2.** city, pop. 13,476, Utah Co., NC Utah, 10 mi/16 km NNW of Provo, on Battle Creek (its original name), site of an early battle between settlers and Indians. It has canning factories and flour mills, and ships fruit and livestock. There are silver and lead mines nearby.

Pleasant Hill **1.** city, pop. 31,585, Contra Costa Co., NC California, on Walnut Creek, 14 mi/23 km NE of Oakland. Largely rural until World War II, it is a residential suburb. Diablo Valley College (1948) is here. **2.** Shaker community: see under HARRODSBURG, Kentucky.

Pleasant Hills borough, pop. 8884, Allegheny Co., SW Pennsylvania, 7 mi/11 km S of Pittsburgh, of which it is a largely residential suburb.

Pleasanton **1.** city, pop. 50,553, Alameda Co., NC California, 22 mi/35 km SE of Oakland. In a vineyarding, dairying, and quarrying area at the W end of the Livermore Valley, it has grown rapidly since the 1960s, and is home to publishing, research, and computer and other high-tech companies, shopping malls, and suburban housing. The Alameda Co. Fairgrounds are here. **2.** city, pop. 1231, Linn Co., E Kansas, near the Missouri line, just S of the Marais des Cygnes R., and 22 mi/35 km N of Fort Scott. It is a commercial center in a farm region in which lead and zinc mining has also been important. Just S is the site of the battle of Mine Creek (Oct. 25, 1864), in which Federal troops defeated Confederate raiders led by Sterling Price, in the last Civil War action in Kansas.

Pleasant Point Passamaquoddy reservation: see under WASHINGTON Co., Maine.

Pleasant Ridge city, pop. 2775, Oakland Co., SE Michigan. It is a N Detroit residential suburb, 8 mi/13 km NW of Downtown, and adjacent (S) to the Detroit Zoological Park.

Pleasantville **1.** city, pop. 16,027, Atlantic Co., SE New Jersey, just W of Atlantic City. It was settled in 1702. A popular tourist spot, it bases its economy on sport fishing and other water-based recreation, commercial deep-sea fishing, shellfishing, boat-building, and such light industry as the manufacture of stockings. **2.** village, pop. 6592, in Mount Pleasant town, Westchester Co., SE New York, 30 mi/48 km NNE of New York City. A residential community with a branch of Pace University, it is often identified with the *Reader's Digest,* headquartered in adjacent (NE) CHAPPAQUA.

Pleasure Ridge Park unincorporated community, pop. 25,131, Jefferson Co., NC Kentucky, 6 mi/10 km SW of Louisville, of which it is a largely residential suburb.

Plum borough, pop. 25,609, Allegheny Co., SW Pennsylvania, on the Allegheny R., 12 mi/19 km ENE of Pittsburgh. It is primarily residential, with some light industry.

Plumas National Forest c.1.15 million ac/470,000 ha (1800 sq mi/4655 sq km), in NE California, in the Sierra Nevada (S) and Cascade Range (N). The Tahoe National Forest adjoins (S), and L. ALMANOR is just N. BECKWOURTH PASS is at the SE corner. Headwaters of the Feather R. are in the forest.

Plum Creek battle site: see under LOCKHART, Texas.

Plum Island **1.** peninsula, in Newbury, Rowley, and Ipswich, Essex Co., NE Massachusetts, just S of the mouth of the Merrimack R. Approximately 8.5 mi/14 km long, it is the site of the Parker River National Wildlife Refuge (4700 ac/1900 ha), and has more than 6 mi/10 km of beaches. It encloses the estuarial Plum Island R. **2.** between Long Island and Block Island sounds and Gardiners Bay, at the NE tip of Long Island's NORTH FORK, SE New York. The hilly, 850-ac/344-ha island is part of the terminal moraine extending from Long I. to Watch Hill, Rhode Island, and is owned by the US Department of Agriculture, which operates an Animal Disease Laboratory. Originally inhabited by the Montauk tribe, it became a sheep ranch in the early 1800s, and by the mid 19th century was a popular resort. Plum Gut, a treacherous channel between the island and Orient Point, is marked by a lighthouse.

Plymouth **1.** city, pop. 8303, seat of Marshall Co., N Indiana, 25 mi/40 km S of South Bend. Livestock, dairy items, soybeans, and grain are produced in the surrounding area, which the city serves as a shipping and trading center; manufactures include grinding machines, auto parts, batteries, fertilizer, emery products, and plastics. The city was settled in 1834 on what once had been the site of a Potowatami village. Led by Menominee, the tribe refused to recognize an 1832 treaty ceding their land, until forced, in 1838, to leave on the 900-mi/1400-km "Trail of Death," a forced march to Kansas. A statue of Menominee, 5 mi/8 km SW of the city, marks the beginning of the Trail. **2.** town, pop. 45,608, seat of Plymouth Co., SE Massachusetts, on Plymouth Bay (an inlet of Cape Cod Bay), 37 mi/60 km SE of Boston. The base (1620) of the PLYMOUTH COLONY, the first New England settlement, it was an early seafaring town; some wharves and boatyards are still active. The modern economy is based largely on tourism, fishing, and cranberry growing, with some light manufacturing. Historic attractions include Plimoth Plantation, a recreation of the original village; Plymouth Rock; a replica of the *Mayflower;* and many restored Colonial homes. The Pilgrim nuclear power facility (1972), the state's only operating nuclear plant, is in Plymouth. **3.** city, pop. 9560, Wayne Co., SE Michigan, on the Middle R. Rouge, 22 mi/35 km W of Detroit. This suburban community manufactures air rifles, electronic appliances, furniture, and metal products. It is the site of St. John's Provincial Seminary (1949). **4.** city, pop. 50,889, Hennepin Co., SE Minnesota, on Medicine L., a residential and industrial suburb 10 mi/16 km NW of Minneapolis. Settled in the 1880s, it has grown rapidly since World War II. A bedroom community, it now also has industries manufacturing computers, air conditioners, microwave ovens, and construction equipment. Most of the recent commercial and industrial park development has been in the center of the city, along I-494, and in the SW corner, on Highway 55. **5.** town, pop. 5811, Grafton Co., C New Hampshire. It is on the Pemigewasset R. where it is joined by the Baker R., S of White Mt. National Forest, 20 mi/32 km NW of Laconia. Parts of Hebron and Campton were annexed in 1845 and 1860. A popular resort since the 19th century, the town is near Squam and New Found lakes, the Plymouth Mts., the Tenney Mt. Ski Area, and Polar Caves. In 1864, Nathaniel Hawthorne died here in the Pemigewasset House. Industries have included lumbering and the manufacture of pig iron, gloves, mattresses, and sporting goods. Plymouth State Fair is an annual event. Plymouth State College (1871) is here. **6.** town, pop. 447, including Tyson, Plymouth (or Plymouth Notch), and Plymouth Union villages, in Windsor Co., SC Vermont, 13 mi/21 km SE of Rutland. President Calvin Coolidge was born (1872) and is buried in Plymouth village. Tyson is a resort village on small Echo L.; Plymouth Union is on historic Crown Point Military Road, now Calvin Coolidge Memorial Highway. Units of Calvin Coolidge State Forest are scattered throughout the mountainous rural town.

Plymouth Colony colonial settlement in Plymouth Co., SE Massachusetts, founded in 1620 by the Pilgrims, who had set sail in the *Mayflower* from England, having first sought religious freedom and prosperity in the Netherlands. Although they were sailing for Virginia, they were blown off course, and landed at what is now PROVINCETOWN, on Cape Cod. A month later (December) they moved across Cape Cod Bay and settled at PLYMOUTH. The colony was soon dwarfed by the MASSACHUSETTS BAY COLONY, founded in 1628. In 1686, Plymouth was added to the Dominion of New England.

Plymouth County 655 sq mi/1696 sq km, pop. 435,276, in SE coastal Massachusetts. Its seat is Plymouth. The county contains the city of BROCKTON and the towns of Hingham and Hull in the N as well as, at its S end, a number of summer resorts and the historic town of PLYMOUTH. Shipbuilding and fishing have been important industries from early years.

Pocahontas town, pop. 513, Tazewell Co., SW Virginia, 5 mi/8 km NW of Bluefield, on the West Virginia border. It is in the middle of the Pocahontas coalfield, a noted source of soft coal exploited heavily after the Norfolk and Western Railroad arrived in 1882, and the town was founded. Mining ceased in the 1950s, and the site of operations now draws tourists.

Pocantico Hills hamlet in Mt. Pleasant township, Westchester Co., SE New York, 1 mi/1.5 km E of North Tarrytown. It is the site of a 600-ac/243-ha property of the Rockefeller family, including Kykuit (1908), a mansion built by John D. Rockefeller. Part of the estate will be open to the public from 1994.

Pocasset village in the town of BOURNE, Barnstable Co., SE Massachusetts, on Buzzards Bay at the W end of Cape Cod. A resort community, it also produces cranberries and marine instruments.

Pocatello city, pop. 46,080, seat of Bannock Co. and also in Power Co., SE Idaho, on the Portneuf R., 70 mi/113 km W of the Wyoming border and 60 mi/97 km N of the Utah border. The settlement was a prominent depot on the UNION PACIFIC Railroad, which arrived in 1882. It later became a processing and distribution center for an irrigated farming region. A naval ordnance plant and phosphate works spurred development in the 1940s. The city is now a commercial, industrial, and transportation hub. Its manufactures include electronics, steel, cement, machinery, food products, and chemicals. Seat of Idaho State University (1901), it is one of the state's educational centers.

Pocomoke River 65 mi/105 km long, in Delaware and Maryland. It rises in swamps in S Sussex Co., in S Delaware, and flows S into Maryland. Pocomoke State Forest flanks the river SW of Snow Hill. It then continues SW past Pocomoke City, the head of navigation, and just below Shelltown empties into **Pocomoke Sound,** an inlet of Chesapeake Bay on the Maryland/Virginia border.

Pocono Mountains range in NE Pennsylvania, some 90 mi/145 km N of Philadelphia and 70 mi/113 km WNW of Manhattan, with an average height of 1400–1800 ft/430–550 m. The Poconos constitute the S and E edge of the Pocono Plateau, part of the Alleghenies. They are heavily forested, and the region, with its streams and rolling hills, is a popular resort area, especially with lake vacationers, skiers, and honeymooners. Some of the best-known resorts are Tamiment, Mount Pocono (borough, pop. 1795, in Monroe Co.), and Pocono Manor. **Pocono International Raceway,** an automobile circuit, is near Long Pond, in Tunkhannock township, in the SW part.

Podunk since the mid 19th century, any insignificant rural locality. The original is perhaps a tribal settlement near Hartford, Connecticut, the name an Algonquian term from a word for "swamp."

Pohatcong Mountain Appalachian ridge in NW New Jersey, c. 800 ft/245 m high. It runs NE some 19 mi/31 km from a point SE of PHILLIPSBURG to the area of HACKETTSTOWN, and continues NE as Allamuchy Mt.

Point for points whose names begin with this word, see under the other name element, as **Arguello, Point.**

Point, the historic site and state park in Pittsburgh, Pennsylvania, where the Allegheny and Monongahela rivers form the Ohio R. French, British, and American forts were erected here during the 18th century. Here arose the settlement that became Pittsburgh. Fort Pitt Museum re-creates the 1758 post.

Point Beach recreational area in Manitowoc Co., EC Wisconsin, along L. Michigan, just NE of TWO RIVERS. The Point Beach State Forest is here, and another 2 mi/3 km N is the Point Beach nuclear power plant (1970).

Point Breeze residential neighborhood in the EAST END of Pittsburgh, Pennsylvania, between EAST LIBERTY and WILKINSBURG, 5 mi/8 km NE of the GOLDEN TRIANGLE. An enclave of industry barons from the 1860s through the 1920s, Point Breeze today is a racially mixed neighborhood popular with first-time home buyers. FRICK PARK is just S.

Point Comfort see under PORT LAVACA, Texas.

Pointe-aux-Trembles former city, pop. (1981) 36,720, at the N extreme of the I. de Montréal, on the St. Lawrence R., annexed in 1982 into MONTRÉAL, Québec. It is essentially French-speaking and residential.

Pointe-Clair city, pop. 27,647, MONTRÉAL URBAN COMMUNITY, S Québec, 13 mi/21 km SW of downtown Montréal, on L. St.-Louis (the St. Lawrence R.), W of Dorval, E of Beaconsfield, and S of Dollard-des-Ormeaux. It is an affluent, largely anglophone residential suburb.

Pointes, the see under GROSSE POINTE, Michigan.

Point Grey residential and academic section of W VANCOUVER, British Columbia, on Burrard Inlet (N) and the Strait of Georgia (W). In 1908–29 it was a separate municipality. One of the city's most affluent areas, it is dominated by the University of British Columbia, whose grounds (the University Endowment Area) are outside city limits and are surrounded by the Pacific Spirit Regional Park. SHAUGHNESSY and DUNBAR HEIGHTS are on the E. Several of the city's well-known beaches lie around Point Grey.

Point Hope city, pop. 639, North Slope Borough, NW Alaska, 560 mi/900 km WNW of Fairbanks and 300 mi/480 km SW of Barrow, at the W end of the BROOKS RANGE, on the Lisburne Peninsula and the Chukchi Sea. This largely Inuit sealing and fishing community is 105 mi/170 km NW of Cape Krusenstern, where the 660,000-ac/267,300-ha Cape Krusenstern National Monument preserves remains of over 100 successive beachfront communities going back some 6000 years, important evidence of early settlement in W Alaska.

Point Lookout see under BRANSON, Missouri.

Point o' Woods see under FIRE I., New York.

Point Pelée National Park 8 sq mi/20 sq km, in extreme SW Ontario, just SE of LEAMINGTON, on the tip of Pt. Pelée, at the W end of L. Erie. This resort area on the southernmost Canadian mainland point was established in 1918. It is at the convergence of two major (Atlantic and Mississippi) FLYWAYS, and over 300 species of migratory birds have been recorded in its dunes, woods, and marshlands, along with rare or unique reptiles and amphibians. PELÉE I. is 15 mi/24 km SW.

Point Pleasant **1.** borough, pop. 18,177, Ocean Co., E New Jersey, on the Jersey Shore 10 mi/16 km SSE of Asbury Park, between the estuarial Manasquan (N) and Metedeconk (S) rivers. A seaside resort, it has a boardwalk, amusement center, and state marina. Point Pleasant is also residential, and has some light industry. **Point Pleasant Beach** (borough; pop. 5112) is adjacent (NE), on the Atlantic. **2.** unincorporated village in Monroe township, Clermont Co., extreme SW Ohio, on the Ohio R., 21 mi/32 km SE of Cincinnati. It is noted as the birthplace (1822) of Ulysses S. Grant. A replica of the Grant house is a local attraction; Grant Memorial State Park is adjacent to the village. **3.** city, pop. 4996, seat of Mason Co., W West Virginia, just N of the junction of the KANAWHA R. with the Ohio R., 5 mi/8 km NE of Gallipolis, Ohio. Settled in the 1770s, it was the site of a victory (Oct. 10, 1774), by Virginia troops over Shawnee forces led by Cornstalk. This key battle in Lord Dunmore's War has been called the "first battle of the Revolution." Point Pleasant, long a river port, is increasingly popular as a resort.

Poison Spring or **Springs** battle site: see under CAMDEN, Arkansas.

Poland town, pop. 4342, Androscoggin Co., SW Maine. It is spread over seven hills, on part of the Range Ponds, 10 mi/16 km WSW of Auburn. The town includes West Poland, on Tripp L., and **Poland Spring,** widely known for its mineral water. The remains of Poland Spring House, one of the great 19th-century resort hotels, are here.

Polar Bear Express see under MOOSONEE, Ontario.

Polar Bear Provincial Park 11,233 sq mi/29,093 sq km, in far N Ontario, on subarctic Hudson Bay, 225 mi/360 km NW of Moosonee. Established in 1970, it is accessible by boat and plane only, and entry is restricted. Protected species include caribou, moose, walrus, bearded seal, red and arctic fox, polar and black bear, Canada and snow goose, and arctic loon. The Winisk R. flows through the area into the bay.

Poletown residential and industrial neighborhood largely in

HAMTRAMCK, also in adjoining Detroit, Michigan. It was the site, from 1910 until 1980, of the Dodge automobile plant (Dodge Main), one of the largest in the world. In the 1980s General Motors offered to build a new auto plant in the Detroit area if a cleared 500-ac/200-ha site were provided. Poletown was selected for this purpose as the region scrambled to retain manufacturing jobs; the new plant opened in 1985.

Polish Hill neighborhood in Pittsburgh, Pennsylvania, E of the STRIP, 2 mi/3 km NE of the GOLDEN TRIANGLE. This working-class neighborhood on the N slope of the HILL has housed Polish immigrants and their descendants since the 1880s.

Polk County **1.** 1823 sq mi/4722 sq km, pop. 405,382, in C Florida, bounded (E) by the Kissimmee R. and L. Kissimmee. Its seat is BARTOW. It is hilly, and sprinkled with hundreds of small lakes. Its economy relies largely on tourism, particularly in its C section; among the municipalities in this most populous part of the county are Lakeland, Winter Haven, and Lake Wales. The N is swampy and sparsely populated. There are many small residential communities in the S. Polk Co. is also agricultural, producing and processing citrus fruit, strawberries, and vegetables, and raising cattle and poultry. Rich in phosphates, it also produces fertilizer. **2.** 582 sq mi/1507 sq km, pop. 327,140, in C Iowa. It is drained by the Des Moines R.; the large Saylorville Reservoir lies in the NW. DES MOINES is the county seat. Polk is by far the most populous and urbanized county in the state, containing the cities of Des Moines, with its suburbs, and Ankeny. The N and E areas are agricultural.

Polk Street N–S commercial thoroughfare in N SAN FRANCISCO, California, extending from San Francisco Bay to Market St., passing W of RUSSIAN and NOB hills, and ending immediately SE of the CIVIC CENTER. It parallels Van Ness St. (one block W), the grand boulevard of pre–1906 earthquake San Francisco. Its N section has many popular restaurants; S of California St. (SW of Nob Hill) is **Polk Gulch,** the center of the city's gay community before the development of the CASTRO.

Polo Grounds former stadium, upper Manhattan, New York City. Opened in 1912 on the Harlem R. at 155th St., just to the E of a rise called Coogan's Bluff, it was the home of the baseball Giants until they left New York after the 1957 season. A housing development now stands on the spot.

Polonia residential and commercial neighborhood on the NEAR NORTHWEST SIDE of Chicago, Illinois. Centered on Noble St. and Milwaukee Ave., it became a Polish enclave after the 1860s when waves of immigrants replaced German residents here. Today, a growing portion of its population is Hispanic. AVONDALE is just NW.

Pomona **1.** city, pop. 131,723, Los Angeles Co., SW California, 25 mi/40 km E of Los Angeles, in the valley S of the San Gabriel Mts. The area was settled by Mexicans in the 1830s; Americans founded the city in 1875, naming it for the Roman goddess of fruits. Oranges and lemons, the area's main crops, have been processed and shipped from here since then. Manufactures have included guided missiles, auto and aircraft parts and equipment, electronic items, tile, and naval ordnance. A campus of California State Polytechnic University (1938) is here. Pomona College is in neighboring (NNE) CLAREMONT. Pomona is the site of the Los Angeles Co. Fair (Sept.-Oct.) **2.** unincorporated village, pop. 2624, in Galloway township, Atlantic Co., SE New Jersey, 10 mi/16 km NW of Atlantic City. It is the seat of Stockton State College (1969), which is known for its performing arts center. Atlantic City International Airport is just S.

Pompano Beach city, pop. 72,411, Broward Co., SE Florida, on the Atlantic Ocean, 8 mi/13 km NNE of Fort Lauderdale. Tourism, which developed after the arrival of the Dixie Highway in the 1920s, is its main industry. Originally on the shore, the city center was moved inland after it was devastated by a 1928 hurricane. Crossed by the Atlantic Intracoastal Waterway and by canals lined with one-family homes, Pompano Beach also has some 20 parks and a noted harness-racing track. It ships local winter vegetables, and has a variety of manufactures, such as pleasure boats, plastics, and electronic equipment.

Pompey rural town, pop. 5317, Onondaga Co., C New York, 12 mi/19 km SE of Syracuse. On a high ridge, it was one of the first settlements in the enormous Military Tract, 1.5 million ac/610,000 ha E of Seneca L., given (1789) to Revolutionary War veterans, and once marked the W end of the Great Western Turnpike from Albany. In the early 19th century it was the birthplace of many prominent Americans, including two governors and transportation entrepreneur W. G. Fargo (1818–81). It was also the site of the "Pompey Stone" hoax, the "discovery" of a supposed 1589 Spanish relic.

Pompey's Pillar huge sandstone mass, a National Historic Landmark, in Yellowstone Co., SC Montana, on the Yellowstone R., 30 mi/48 km NE of Billings. This 200 ft/61 m–high formation is named for the son of Lewis and Clark's Shoshone guide Sacajawea and her French-Indian husband Toussaint Charbonneau. Still preserved is William Clark's autograph, carved July 26, 1806, on the expedition's return leg. The rock also bears the carved names and initials of many trappers, troopers, and pioneers who passed it in their travels.

Pompton Lakes borough, pop. 10,539, Passaic Co., NE New Jersey, bounded by the Pompton, Ramapo, and Pequannock rivers, 9 mi/14 km NW of Paterson. In a lake-dotted region just NW of the New York City–N New Jersey metropolis, it has been a summer resort and is now a commuter suburb; Interstate 287 is being completed around the borough. Pompton Lakes has some manufacturing, primarily of textiles and explosives. It was settled by the Dutch in 1682.

Pompton River 8 mi/13 km long, in NE New Jersey. It is formed at POMPTON LAKES by the confluence of the Pequannock, Ramapo, and Ringwood rivers, continuing S into the Passaic R. at Fairfield.

Ponca City city, pop. 26,359, Kay Co., NC Oklahoma, 50 mi/80 km NE of Enid, near the Arkansas R. It was settled in 1893 as part of the CHEROKEE STRIP land rush. With oilfields nearby, it has an economy centered around petroleum research and products. It is also a center for processing and shipping flour, feed, meat, and other goods, and it manufactures ceramics and clothing.

Ponce unincorporated community (ZONA URBANA), pop. 159,151, Ponce Municipio (pop. 187,749), S Puerto Rico, on the Caribbean Sea, 45 mi/72 km SW of San Juan. Puerto Rico's largest urban center outside the San Juan area, and its chief Caribbean port, it was founded in 1692 by Juan Ponce de León Loaiza, grandson of explorer and conquistador Ponce de León. During the 19th century it was transformed from a sleepy provincial town into a sophisticated city by wealth from nearby sugar and coffee plantations. Its port, Playa de Ponce, is a major shipper of such products as sugar, tobacco, rum, coffee, and tropical fruits. Local industries distill rum and process sugarcane and a variety of agricultural goods, and produce cement and textiles. In addition, tourism is important. Ponce's central section has a variety of historic public buildings and Spanish colonial mansions, many restored in the 1990s, and wide, tree-shaded plazas. The Catholic University of Puerto Rico (1948) is here.

Ponchatoula city, pop. 5425, Tangipahoa Parish, SE Louisiana, 38 mi/61 km NW of New Orleans and 4 mi/6 km SSE of Hammond. Founded in 1830, it is a fruit (strawberries) and truck farming center.

Pond Inlet hamlet, pop. 974, Baffin Region, E Northwest Territories, an INUIT community on N Baffin I., on the S of Pond Inlet, opposite Bylot I.

Pontchartrain, Lake shallow, brackish body N of New Orleans and of the delta of the Mississippi R., in SE Louisiana. Some 41 mi/66 km E–W, up to 25 mi/40 km wide, and no more than 16 ft/5 m deep, it is connected with Lakes MAUREPAS (W) and BORGNE (the Gulf of Mexico, E). New Orleans and Metairie lie along most of its SE, protected by a seawall. A 10 mi/16 km–long bridge crosses the lake's E end, between New Orleans and Slidell. The **Lake Pontchartrain Causeway,** which crosses the lake's middle between Metairie (S) and Covington (N), has a double roadway; at 24 mi/39 km over water, it is the longest such bridge in the world, taking drivers out of sight of land for about 8 mi/13 km. The lake's area is about 630 sq mi/1632 sq km. It has been an important seafood source for New Orleans, and is lined with both urban and country resorts.

Pontiac **1.** city, pop. 11,428, seat of Livingston Co., NC Illinois, on the Vermilion R., 33 mi/53 km NE of Normal. Its economy depends on local agriculture and on industry. Corn and soybeans are traded and processed here. Manufactures include furniture, industrial storage equipment, lawnmowers, gloves, and shoe heels. Commercial printing is also important. Settled in the 1830s, Pontiac was named for the famed Ottawa chief. Pontiac Correctional Center, a state penitentiary, is at the city's S outskirts. **2.** city, pop. 71,166, seat of Oakland Co., SE Michigan, on the Clinton R., 25 mi/40 km NW of Detroit. Settled in 1818 on the Saginaw Trail and named for the Ottawa chief, who lived and is reputedly buried near here, it became an important wagon and carriage production center in the 1880s. It later evolved into a major manufacturing hub for autos, buses, and trucks, the home of General Motors. Pontiac also manufactures rubber, paint and varnish, boats, plastic, and dairy products. Its 80,000-seat Silverdome arena (1975) is the home of the Detroit Lions (football).

Pontotoc Ridge range of hills in NE Mississippi, running S from Tishomingo Co., in the state's NE corner, for some 150 mi/240 km. Once inhabited by the Chickasaw, it forms the line between the Mississippi R. (W) and Alabama R. (SE) watersheds, and the NW boundary of the Black Prairie (see BLACK BELT). It is now cut by a canal connecting the Tombigbee and Tennessee rivers, part of the Tennessee-Tombigbee Waterway.

Pony Express relay service established in April 1860 to carry mail from the W end of the transcontinental telegraph line (then at SAINT JOSEPH, Missouri) to California. Its route, some 2000 mi/3200 km, was covered in about 8 days by riders who changed horses at stations 10–15 mi/16–24 km apart; riders were supposed to change every 75 mi/120 km. Completion of the telegraph line to San Francisco in Oct. 1861 ended the service's usefulness. Its most famous rider was "Buffalo Bill" Cody. From St. Joseph, the Express followed the OREGON TRAIL as far as Fort Bridger, in W Wyoming, then turned SW to Salt Lake City and across the Utah and Nevada deserts, along the Central OVERLAND TRAIL, to Carson City. It crossed the Sierra Nevada through Carson Pass, near the headwaters of the West Fork of the Carson R., and ended at Sacramento.

Popham Beach village in the town of Phippsburg (pop. 1815), Sagadahoc Co., SW Maine. It is at the end of a peninsula, between the mouth of the Kennebec R. and the Atlantic Ocean, 12 mi/19 km S of Bath. Remains of the Civil War Fort Popham stand next to the beach. In 1607, Popham Beach was the site of the Popham Colony, the first attempted English settlement in the Northeast. In the severe winter of 1607–8, many died, and the colony dispersed, but not before the *Virginia,* the first American-built English vessel, was launched. Putative 11th-century Nordic runes have also been found here. Seguin Island, with one of Maine's most prominent lighthouses (1795, rebuilt 1887; 180 ft/55 m above water) is 3 mi/5 km SE.

Poplar Bluff city, pop. 16,996, seat of Butler Co., SE Missouri, 60 mi/96 km SW of Cape Girardeau. Founded in 1850, it developed a thriving lumber industry upon the completion of the Iron Mountain Railroad in 1873. Today it is a vacation center in addition to being a marketing hub for agriculturally rich SE Missouri and NE Arkansas, whose products include cotton and livestock. Manufactured here are wood and paper products, flour, plastics, electrical equipment, and concrete. Poplar Bluff is the seat of Three Rivers Community College (1966). L. Wappapello (N), on the St. Francis R., a unit of Mark Twain National Forest (N), and Mingo National Wildlife Refuge (NE) are all nearby.

Poplar Corridor in Memphis, Tennessee, affluent, largely white residential districts along Poplar Ave., which runs from the Mississippi R. opposite MUD I. (W) through Midtown, to the suburb of Germantown (E). OVERTON and AUDUBON parks are along the corridor.

Poplarville city, pop. 2561, Pearl River Co., S Mississippi, 36 mi/57 km SSW of Hattiesburg. A lumber, naval stores, and tung oil producing center, it is home to Pearl River Community College (1922). White supremacist political leader Theodore Bilbo (1877–1947) came from Poplarville.

Poquoson independent city, pop. 11,005, in SE Virginia, 9 mi/14 km NNE of Newport News, of which it is a residential suburb. Plum Tree I. National Wildlife Refuge lies E, on Chesapeake Bay.

Porciúncula River see under LOS ANGELES R., California.

Porcupine Hills **1.** hilly area of SW Alberta, extending N–S for 30 mi/48 km and rising to over 4000 ft/1220 m, NW of Lethbridge. Along with the CYPRESS HILLS, they were not completely covered by ice during the last glacial age. On their S edge is Head-Smashed-In Buffalo Jump, protected site of a 33-ft/10-m cliff over which Blackfoot hunters for thousands of years drove herded buffalo. To the SE is the Blood Indian Reserve (pop. 4013), at 552 sq mi/1429 sq km Canada's largest. Fort Macleod (town, pop. 3112), NW of the reserve and E of the jump, was an 1870s mounted police post, today a trade and tourist center. **2.** also, **Porcupine Mountain** rolling upland extending 60 mi/97 km along the border of W Manitoba and into E Saskatchewan. The hills are part of the MANITOBA ESCARPMENT, and reach their highest elevation at Hart Mt. (2700 ft/823 m), 25 mi/40 km NNW of Swan River. Porcupine Provincial Forest surrounds the area.

Porcupine River 450 mi/720 km long, in the Yukon Territory and Alaska. It rises on the Eagle Plain, W of the MACKENZIE Mts., in the Yukon, and flows N, then WSW, passing Old Crow (settlement, pop. 256), a fur trapping community of the Loucheux (Kutchin), then continues into Alaska, joining the Yukon R. at Fort Yukon, 140 mi/230 km NNE of Fairbanks. One of the Yukon's major tributaries, the Porcupine has seen some PLACER gold mining.

Porkopolis mid-19th-century nickname for CINCINNATI, Ohio, which was in the 1850s, before railroads farther W destroyed its dominance (as a river port), the leading US meatpacking center.

portage place or route where boats, esp. canoes, are carried overland between two navigable bodies of water, or from one point to another on the same waterway where an obstacle such as a rapid must be avoided. Portages were focal points in early commercial development and settlement of many parts of the US and Canada.

Portage 1. city, pop. 29,060, Porter Co., NW Indiana, on L. Michigan, adjacent (E) to Gary. On the E edge of the highly industrialized CALUMET area, it is a shipping center with Burns International Harbor, a port accommodating ocean-going vessels. Sports fishing also contributes to the economy, and the city produces steel and other products. **2.** city, pop. 41,042, Kalamazoo Co., SW Michigan, 6 mi/10 km S of Kalamazoo. A residential suburb of Kalamazoo, in an area dotted with small lakes, it has been known as a celery farming center for some 200 years. Portage manufactures mobile homes, pharmaceuticals, and paper products. **3.** city, pop. 8642, seat of Columbia Co., SC Wisconsin, on the Wisconsin and Fox rivers and the Portage Canal, 35 mi/56 km N of Madison. It was settled in 1835 around Fort Winnebago (1828). A portage between the two rivers was located here. The first Europeans to cross it were Jolliet and Marquette in 1693; it was replaced by a canal in the 1850s, and was an important 19th-century trade route. Portage is located in a diversified farming and lake area, and is a summer resort. Plastics, shoes, boats, airplane parts, beer, dairy items, and canned goods are produced here.

Portage Bay widening of the Lake Washington Ship Canal, in NE SEATTLE, Washington, 2 mi/3 km N of Downtown, the site of yacht clubs and a houseboat colony. The UNIVERSITY DISTRICT is N, the Montlake residential district SW. To the W is the larger Lake Union, with docks, restaurants, and more yacht clubs.

Portage County 493 sq mi/1277 sq km, pop. 142,585, in NE Ohio, intersected by the Cuyahoga R. and including a number of lakes. Its seat is RAVENNA; the Ravenna Arsenal occupies much of the county's NE corner. The area is primarily agricultural, with dairy, fruit, grain, livestock, and truck farming. There is manufacturing at Garrettsville, Kent, and Ravenna. Coal is mined, and there are sand and gravel pits.

Portage Lakes unincorporated community, pop. 13,373, Summit Co., NE Ohio, on the interconnected Portage Lakes, a residential suburb 4 mi/6 km SW of downtown Akron.

Portage la Prairie also, **Portage-la-Prairie** city, pop. 13,186, SC Manitoba, on the Assiniboine R., 54 mi/87 km W of Winnipeg. The site was used by early French fur traders as a crossing point or *portage* between the Assiniboine R. and L. Manitoba. Nearby is Fort La Reine, built in the 1730s as a headquarters by the explorer La Vérendrye. In a rich agricultural area, the city is a shipping point for grain and livestock as well as a railway center. Local manufactures include dairy products and other processed foods, soft drinks, machinery, concrete products, clothing, electric cables, and glassware. Island Park and Crescent L. house a wildlife sanctuary. Portage la Prairie hosts Canada's National Strawberry Festival and the Central Manitoba Trade Fair.

Portage River 33 mi/53 km long, in N Ohio. It is formed in E Wood Co. by the North, Middle, and South branches and flows NE, past Woodville and Oak Harbor, joining L. Erie at Port Clinton.

Port Alberni city, pop. 18,403, Alberni-Clayoquot Regional District, SW British Columbia, on SC Vancouver I., at the head of Alberni Inlet, 86 mi/138 km NW of Victoria. A seaport, it developed with the construction (1860) of a sawmill, and today is a lumber, pulp and paper, and plywood producer. Mining and salmon fishing are also important. Alberni (N) became part of the city in 1967.

Portales city, pop. 10,690, seat of Roosevelt Co., E New Mexico, in the High Plains, 17 mi/27 km W of the Texas border and 17 mi/27 km SSW of Clovis. Established in 1903 and surrounded by irrigated farms and ranches, it is a market center for producers of peanuts, sweet potatoes, and other agricultural goods. Eastern New Mexico University (1927) is here.

Port Allen in West Baton Rouge Parish, Louisiana: see under EAST BATON ROUGE PARISH.

Port Angeles city, pop. 17,710, seat of Clallam Co., NW Washington, on the Strait of Juan de Fuca, opposite Victoria, British Columbia, 20 mi/32 km to its NNE. Settled permanently in 1862, this port of entry has a fine sheltered harbor. It was the second city after Washington, D. C., to be planned by the Federal government. Fishing; lumbering, pulp, and paper milling; and food processing are its major industries. Port Angeles has numerous boating facilities and is the N gateway to Olympic National Park. Peninsula College (1961) is here. There is year-round ferry service to Victoria.

Port Aransas see under MUSTANG I., Texas.

Port Arthur 1. see under THUNDER BAY, Ontario. **2.** city, pop. 58,724, Jefferson Co., SE Texas, on the Neches R., Sabine L. (the Sabine R.), and the Gulf Intracoastal Waterway, 94 mi/151 km ENE of Dallas. Settled unsuccessfully in the 1830s, it was named for himself by railroad builder Arthur Stilwell, who organized the town in 1895 as a terminus for the Kansas City, Pittsburg & Gulf Railroad. A deepwater canal was opened in 1899 to connect the railroad with the Gulf of Mexico. The city developed into a major center of the oil and chemical industries after the Spindletop oilfield (see BEAUMONT) opened in 1901. Shipbuilding, refining, petrochemicals, and fabricated metals are its economic mainstays. The area also raises beef and farms rice. Lamar University at Port Arthur began as Port Arthur College in 1909. Fishing and tourism contribute to the economy. The SABINE PASS battle site is 15 mi/24 km SSE.

Port au Port Peninsula on the Gulf of St. Lawrence, between

Port au Port Bay (N) and St. George's Bay (S), in SW Newfoundland. Twenty-six mi/42 km E–W and 10 mi/15 km wide, it is connected to the mainland by a narrow isthmus W of Stephenville. Long Point is a spit of land extending 13 mi/22 km NE from the peninsula. Once part of Newfoundland's FRENCH SHORE, the peninsula still contains the province's highest proportion of francophones.

Port aux Basques see CHANNEL–PORT AUX BASQUES, Newfoundland.

Port Charlotte unincorporated community, pop. 41,535, Charlotte Co., SW Florida, 33 mi/53 km NNW of Fort Myers, on the N side of CHARLOTTE HARBOR. Once cattle grazing territory, and on land formerly owned by the Vanderbilt family, it was developed as a planned community during the 1950s. A well-known winter resort, it has hundreds of miles of artificial waterway and natural waterfront. Its annual fishing tournament and windsurfing regatta are popular attractions.

Port Chester village, pop. 24,728, in Rye town, Westchester Co., SE New York, on Long Island Sound, 25 mi/40 km NE of New York City, on the Byram R. at the Connecticut border. It is a commercial and residential suburb, with some light manufacturing. Until 1984 it was noted as home to the Life Savers candy factory.

Port Chicago industrial area on the S shore of Suisun Bay, in Contra Costa Co., NC California, 8 mi/13 km W of PITTSBURG and now within the CONCORD Naval Weapons Station. On July 17, 1944, it was the site of an ammunition ship explosion that killed more than 320.

Port Colborne city, pop. 18,766, Niagara Regional Municipality, S Ontario, on the NE shore of L. Erie, at the S end of the WELLAND CANAL, 14 mi/23 km SW of Niagara Falls. Settlement dates from 1832, when the canal, which here has a 1380 ft/420 m–long lock, was completed locally. Today the city is a shipbuilding and repair and TRANSSHIPMENT center. Leading industries produce refined nickel, iron, cement, and flour. Tourism is also important.

Port Conway hamlet in King George Co., E Virginia, on the Rappahannock R., 17 mi/27 km SE of Fredericksburg. It is the birthplace of James Madison, fourth president of the US.

Port Coquitlam city, pop. 36,773, Greater Vancouver Regional District, SW British Columbia, in the lower Fraser Valley, bordered by the Coquitlam (W), Pitt (E), and Fraser (S) rivers, 17 mi/27 km E of Vancouver. The center of a truck gardening and fruit growing region, it grew after the 1880s around the Canadian Pacific Railway's W terminus (PORT MOODY is adjacent), and has rail repair shops. Industries include boatbuilding, tungsten refining, metalworking, quarrying, and food processing. **Coquitlam** (district municipality, pop. 84,021), which lies N and W, is largely residential, with warehousing, dairy and poultry farming, quarrying, and other industries. It is undergoing rapid suburban growth.

Port Credit see under MISSISSAUGA, Ontario.

Port Deposit town, pop. 685, Cecil Co., extreme NE Maryland, on the Susquehanna R., 4 mi/6 km N of HAVRE DE GRACE. It was an important 19th-century port, shipping granite from quarries in 200-ft/60-m local cliffs that have been worked since 1808. The Navy maintained a training facility here (at Bainbridge) from 1942 to 1976.

Port Dover see under NANTICOKE, Ontario.

Porterville city, pop. 29,563, Tulare Co., SC California, 65 mi/105 km SE of Fresno, on the Tule R., on the E side of the San Joaquin Valley. Founded in 1859 on the Los Angeles–San Francisco stage route, it houses Porterville College (1927) and the headquarters of the SEQUOIA NATIONAL FOREST (E). The Tule R. Indian Reservation (pop. 798) is just E. Oranges and other fruit are shipped from the city, which also produces olive oil; granite and marble are quarried in the area.

Port Everglades see under HOLLYWOOD, Florida.

Port Gibson city, pop. 1810, seat of Claiborne Co., SW Mississippi, near the Bayou Pierre, 36 mi/58 km NE of Natchez and 5 mi/8 km E of the Mississippi R. Settled in the mid 18th century, it became a cotton plantation center. The town was the scene of a Union victory (May 1, 1863), following BRUINSBURG and preceding GRAND GULF, during the advance on Vicksburg, and was reputedly spared from destruction when U.S. Grant declared it "too beautiful to burn." Thus, antebellum homes and churches remain; many are open to the public during an annual festival. Port Gibson remains active in trading and processing local products, including cotton and lumber. To the W are the ruins of Windsor, Mississippi's largest antebellum mansion, destroyed by a fire in 1890.

Port Henry village, pop. 1263, in Moriah township, Essex Co., NE New York, on the W shore of L. Champlain, 53 mi/85 km N of Glens Falls and just NW of CROWN POINT. It is a resort community on a series of terraces above the lake.

Port Hope town, pop. 11,505, Northumberland Co., S Ontario, on L. Ontario, 60 mi/96 km ENE of Toronto. A fur trade center from 1778, it developed in the early 19th century as a manufacturing center, and still has diverse light industries. At the mouth of the Ganaraska R., it is known for its sport fishing.

Port Hudson hamlet in East Baton Rouge Parish, SE Louisiana, on the E bank of the Mississippi R., 16 mi/26 km NNW of Baton Rouge. A strong point in Confederate control of the river, it was surrendered to Union troops under Nathaniel P. Banks on July 9, 1863, just after the fall of VICKSBURG, having been besieged for six weeks.

Port Hueneme city, pop. 20,319, Ventura Co., SW California, adjacent (S) to OXNARD, and 50 mi/80 km WNW of Los Angeles, on the Pacific Ocean (the Santa Barbara Channel). It is the site of a naval construction battalion (Seabees) base that played a prominent role in World War II. Founded in 1870 as Hueneme, the city has been an important shipper of regional fruits and produce, and is known for its sport fishing facilities.

Port Huron city, pop. 33,694, seat of St. Clair Co., SE Michigan, on L. Huron at its junction with the St. Clair R., opposite Sarnia, Ontario, and 53 mi/85 km NE of Detroit. A village and Fort Gratiot were built (1814) over the French Fort St. Joseph (1686). Four villages on this site were combined to create Port Huron in 1837. One of the few natural deepwater ports on the Great Lakes, it developed into a shipbuilding, lumber, rail, and shipping center. Its manufactures include machinery, tools, auto parts, salt and cement products, and brass. Thomas Edison spent his early years here, and the Museum of Arts and History has memorabilia connected with him. St. Clair County Community College (1923) is here.

Port Isabel city, pop. 4467, Cameron Co., extreme S Texas, 21 mi/34 km NE of Brownsville, on Laguna Madre (N) and South Bay (S), across (W) from the S end of PADRE I. A resort, fishing center, and port on the GULF INTRACOASTAL WATERWAY, it is connected by ship channel to Brownsville. In

1846–48, Point Isabel, as it was then called, was Zachary Taylor's supply base in his campaign against the Mexican army.

Port Ivory see under MARINER'S HARBOR, New York.

Port Jefferson village, pop. 7455, in Brookhaven town, Suffolk Co., SE New York, on Long Island Sound, 19 mi/30 km E of Huntington. A residential village and summer resort, it has an active boating and yachting community. The downtown area has been developed as a tourist attraction. Port Jefferson is the terminus of a ferry from Bridgeport, Connecticut. The unincorporated village of **Port Jefferson Station** (pop. 7232) is just S.

Port Jervis city, pop. 9060, Orange Co., SE New York, on the Delaware R. at the mouth of the Neversink R., near the point where New York, New Jersey, and Pennsylvania meet, 13 mi/21 km SW of Middletown. It was originally the home of a band of Lenni Lenapes, who were joined by Dutch and Huguenot farmers in the late 17th century. Indians and Tories wiped out the white settlement in 1779. Port Jervis developed rapidly after the opening of the Delaware and Hudson Canal (1828) and later became an important railroad center. The city has a number of manufactures, including glass, sportswear, and cosmetics; summer tourism is also important.

Port Kent resort community in Chesterfield township, Essex Co., NE New York, on the W bank of L. Champlain, 12 mi/19 km S of Plattsburgh. It is an Amtrak stop and port for a ferry to Burlington, Vermont.

Portland **1.** town, pop. 8418, Middlesex Co., SC Connecticut, across the Connecticut R. (E) from MIDDLETOWN. Settled in 1690, it has prospered from quarrying (brownstone) and tobacco growing, and now has various light manufactures. The village of Gildersleeve was a 19th-century shipbuilding center. **2.** city, pop. 6483, seat of Jay Co., E Indiana, 27 mi/43 km NE of Muncie, on the Salamonie R. Livestock, dairy goods, soybeans, and grain are produced in the surrounding farmland, and the region contains natural gas and oil deposits. Portland produces clothing, brushes, canned goods, metal products, vehicle parts, silos, and brooms. **3.** city, pop. 64,358, seat of Cumberland Co., SW Maine, on a hilly peninsula overlooking Casco Bay. It is the largest city in Maine and the hub of Maine's largest metropolitan area. A seafaring community since its founding in 1632, Portland has an excellent deep harbor and is the US port closest to Europe. With SOUTH PORTLAND a major petroleum port at the end of a pipeline to Montréal, it is a center for foreign and coastal trade. During World Wars I and II it was a shipbuilding center; the Bath Iron Works maintains a dry dock, and shipyards are still active. Other industries are fishing, printing and publishing, the manufacture of paper and wood products, footwear, chemicals, metals and machinery, seafood processing, and textiles. The community, then called Falmouth, was raided by Indians in 1676, and bombarded and burned by British soldiers in 1775. It was renamed Portland in 1786 and was the first state capital (1820–32). Extensively damaged by fire in 1866, much of Portland has been rebuilt. Deering Oaks Park, the Cumberland County Civic Center, the Henry Wadsworth Longfellow home, and the Portland Art Museum are among the city's better-known sites, and its restored Old Port district is heavily visited. The famous Portland Head Light is just S, in the suburb of CAPE ELIZABETH. **4.** city, pop. 437,319, seat of MULTNOMAH Co., NW Oregon, on the Willamette R., at its junction with the Columbia R. An industrial, commercial, and educational center and port, it is the transportation and distribution center for farms, orchards, dairies, and forests of a large region including the Willamette Valley, parts of the Cascade Range, and SW Washington. The main West Coast livestock market is here. The city is the leader in manufacturing between PUGET SOUND (N) and SAN FRANCISCO BAY (S), turning out metal products, processed foods, furniture, lumber, and other wood and pulp items, chemicals, aircraft and electronic components, and clothing. The area, esp. SAUVIE I. (just NW), was home to the Multnomah (Chinook); Lewis and Clark saw it in 1805. The French-Canadian trader Etienne Lucier settled here in 1829, but soon departed. Asa Lovejoy (from Boston) and Francis Pettygrove (from Portland, Maine) surveyed and platted the town in 1845; Pettygrove won a coin toss to name it. In 1851, it was incorporated as a city, booming with saw and flour mills, and grew as a supply base (and steamboat port) for the military and for pioneers seeking gold and area farmland. Development of the West Coast salmon industry, arrival of rail connections, and the 1890s Alaska/Yukon gold rush all contributed to the city's growth at the beginning of the 20th century; in 1900–10 its pop. more than doubled, to 207,000. During World War II, shipbuilding emerged as a key industry. Today, Portland is the center of a five-county (Multnomah, CLACKAMAS, WASHINGTON, and Yamhill, in Oregon; CLARK, in Washington) metropolitan area (CMSA) with a pop. of 1,477,895, and a vital industrial and cultural center. The University of Portland (1901), Reed College (1910), and Portland State University (1946) are among its many institutions. The Memorial Coliseum is home to the Trail Blazers (basketball). The city is generally considered one of the most liveable in the country, in part because its use of hydroelectric power has kept its industry "clean." It boasts 140 parks within the city limits, with numerous mountains, waterways, and national forests nearby. See also: ALBINA; BROOKLYN; CHINATOWN; EASTMORELAND; FOREST PARK; LADD ADDITION; LAIR HILL; LAURELHURST; LLOYD DISTRICT; NOB HILL (Northwest 23rd); NORTH; NORTHEAST; NORTHWEST; NORTHWESTERN HILLS; OLD TOWN; PORTLAND HEIGHTS; SOUTHEAST; SOUTH PARK; SOUTHWEST; TERWILLIGER; WEST HILLS; YAMHILL HISTORIC DISTRICT. **5.** city, pop. 12,224, San Patricio and Nueces counties, S Texas, 10 mi/16 km N of Corpus Christi, on the N side of Corpus Christi Bay. It is primarily residential.

Portland Heights residential neighborhood in Southwest PORTLAND, Oregon, 2 mi/3 km SW of Downtown, part of WEST HILLS. Built in 1890 as an exclusive enclave, it was the first section of West Hills to be developed, at first linked by cable car to Downtown.

Port Lavaca city, pop. 10,886, seat of Calhoun Co., S Texas, on the S side of Lavaca Bay, 108 mi/174 km SW of Houston. It was established in 1840, after Comanches burned the earlier settlement of Linnfield, and later took its name from an earlier (1815) Spanish town and the Lavaca R. (N across the bay). The French explorer La Salle landed at Indianola, 12 mi/19 km SE, in 1685. Before hurricanes wrecked it in 1875 and 1886, Indianola was a major S Texas port; today it is a much visited ghost town. Offshore gas and oil wells and commercial fishing are now central to Port Lavaca's economy. The city processes and markets seafood, especially shrimp and oysters. In the 1960s, a huge Alcoa bauxite plant opened across a causeway (N) in Point Comfort, enlarging the area's economic base. Sport fishing, duck hunting, and beaches attract tourists.

Port Moody city, pop. 17,712, Greater Vancouver Regional District, SW British Columbia, at the head of Burrard Inlet, 12 mi/20 km E of downtown Vancouver. A longtime sawmill center, it now has oil refineries and diverse manufactures, and is a deepwater port. Chosen (1879) as the W terminus of the CANADIAN PACIFIC RAILWAY, it was soon supplanted by Vancouver, but was the site (1886) of the arrival of the first transcontinental passenger train.

Port Neches city, pop. 12,974, Jefferson Co., SE Texas, adjacent (N) to PORT ARTHUR, on the Neches R. (the Sabine-Neches Waterway). Incorporated in 1927, the city grew during World War II. It has large oil refineries and chemical plants, and ships petrochemical products.

Port Newark deepwater port in Newark, New Jersey, on NEWARK BAY. Opened in 1915, it is one of the eastern seaboard's chief ports of entry and departure. During World War I it became an important shipbuilding center. Over the years it has handled about 30% of the New York area's shipping. It has been a key importer of automobiles, as well as a leading national lumber and foodstuffs port. Operated since 1948 by the Port Authority of New York and New Jersey, which is also in charge of Newark International Airport, Port Newark has highly sophisticated computerized facilities, and is one of the world's largest container ports.

Port of Miami deepwater marine facility on BISCAYNE BAY, in S Miami, Florida. Situated on a 300-ac/120-ha landfill on a ship channel, it is connected to the mainland by the MacArthur Causeway. A major facility for the import and export of containerized cargo, it also serves as a passenger depot for cruises to and from Latin America and the Caribbean. Bases are maintained here by the National Oceanic and Atmospheric Administration and by the University of Miami's School of Marine and Atmospheric Sciences.

Portola Valley town, pop. 4194, San Mateo Co., NC California, an affluent suburb 16 mi/26 km WNW of San Jose, in the foothills of the Santa Cruz Mts.

Port Orange city, pop. 35,317, Volusia Co., NE Florida, on the Halifax R. lagoon, 5 mi/8 km SSE of Daytona Beach. Now a popular vacation site, it has since the 19th century been a center for commercial fishing, shrimping, and oystering and the processing of local citrus fruit.

Port Orford city, pop. 1025, Curry Co., SW Oregon, on the Pacific coast, 45 mi/72 km SSW of Coos Bay. It is the westernmost city in the LOWER 48 states. Perched on high bluffs overlooking the ocean, the place was first sighted by George Vancouver's ship in 1792, and was settled, despite vigorous Indian resistance, in the early 1850s. Its natural deepwater harbor was an early cedar shipping site and today serves as a center for logging and fishing industries. The Grassy Knob Wilderness is 4 mi/6 km E.

Porto Rico see PUERTO RICO.

Port Radium see under GREAT BEAR L., Northwest Territories.

Port Republic hamlet in Rockingham Co., NW Virginia, in the Shenandoah Valley, on the South Fork of the Shenandoah R., 11 mi/18 km SSE of HARRISONBURG. It is the site of a battle, fought June 9, 1862, that, with the battle of CROSS KEYS (5 mi/8 km NNW), climaxed Stonewall Jackson's Shenandoah Campaign, temporarily ending a Union drive to control the valley.

Port Richey see under NEW PORT RICHEY, Florida.

Port Royal town, pop. 2985, Beaufort Co., SC South Carolina, on Port Royal I. and the Atlantic Intracoastal Waterway, 5 mi/8 km S of Beaufort. One of the earliest settlements in the state, it was established by French Huguenots under the leadership of Jean Ribaut in 1562. The town has a fine natural harbor and by the early 1800s was a center for the trade and shipment of Sea Island cotton and local timber. A Union amphibious assault took Port Royal on Nov. 7, 1861. Later, it was important in shipping phosphates. Today, it is a popular tourist center and hub for shrimping, crabbing, and commercial and sport fishing.

Port-Royal historic settlement on the N of the Annapolis Basin, 5 mi/8 km WSW of ANNAPOLIS ROYAL, in SW Nova Scotia. In the summer of 1605, following a harsh winter at Dochet (St. Croix) I. in the St. Croix R. (between modern Maine and New Brunswick), a fortified French habitation was established here by the Sieur de Monts and Samuel de Champlain. Regarded as the first permanent European settlement N of St. Augustine, Florida, it struggled through several decades of agricultural and orcharding experimentation; it was sacked by an expedition from Virginia in 1613, and taken by the British in 1654. The Ordre de Bons Temps, established in the winter of 1606 by Champlain, is held to be the first New World social organization, and produced the first theatrical in America. Restored since 1938, the Port-Royal National Historic Site now draws visitors.

Port Royal Sound inlet of the Atlantic Ocean at the mouth of the Broad R. and other estuaries, in SE South Carolina, 25 mi/40 km NE of Savannah, Georgia. To the N are Port Royal, Parris, St. Helena, St. Phillips, and Pritchard islands; to the S are Hilton Head and Pinckney islands. The sound, on the Atlantic Intracoastal Waterway, has a deepwater channel to the port of BEAUFORT on 13 mi/21 km–long **Port Royal I.,** which lies at the head of the sound and is a tourist and fishing center connected to the mainland and other islands by bridges. The town of PORT ROYAL is at its S tip. Explored by the Spanish in the early 16th century, the sound and island were given their present name by the French Huguenot mariner Jean Ribaut, who in 1562 established a short-lived colony on PARRIS I. Early in the Civil War, the sound and nearby islands were occupied by Union forces, who used them as a shipping and repair station.

Port Saint Joe see under SAINT JOSEPH BAY, Florida.

Port Saint Lucie city, pop. 55,866, St. Lucie Co., EC Florida, on the North Fork of the St. Lucie R., 13 mi/21 km NW of the St. Lucie Inlet on the Atlantic and 10 mi/16 km S of Fort Pierce. A booming retirement and resort community (its pop. in 1970 was 330), it has miles of artificial waterways and the spring training baseball complex of the New York Mets.

Portsmouth 1. city, pop. 25,925, Rockingham Co., SE New Hampshire, a port of entry 3 mi/4.8 km up the Piscataqua R. from the Atlantic. New Hampshire's oldest settlement and only seaport, Portsmouth was also its capital until 1808. Across the Piscataqua and Portsmouth Harbor from KITTERY, Maine, it was a shipbuilding center from the 18th century. Portsmouth Naval Shipyard (in Kittery) and Pease Air Force Base (in NEWINGTON) long boosted the economy. A center for agricultural trade and tourism, Portsmouth also has light manufacturing. Strawberry Banke, which takes one of the settlement's 17th-century names, is a popular restoration area with Colonial homes and shops. The 1905 Portsmouth Treaty, ending the Russo-Japanese War, was concluded at the Portsmouth Naval Shipyard. **2.** city, pop. 22,744, Scioto Co., S Ohio, at the confluence of the Scioto R. and the Ohio R., at the Kentucky border, 86 mi/138 km S of Columbus. Founded in 1803, it grew after the opening (1832) of the Ohio Canal from Portsmouth to Cleveland. Natural resources in the area include iron ore, coal, limestone, fire clay, and shale. A uranium enrichment plant to the N underwent expansion in the 1970s. The manufacture of steel is a major industry; dairy and food items, chemicals, shoes, plastics, brick, and concrete are also produced. A branch of Ohio University and the Southern Ohio Museum and Cultural Center are situated here. Many prehistoric mounds are found in the vicinity. **3.** town, pop. 16,857, Newport Co., S Rhode Island, the northernmost town on Rhode I., 20 mi/32 km SSE of Providence, in Narragansett Bay. It was settled in 1638, and became a maritime and farming center. In Aug. 1778, the Battle of Rhode Island occurred here. In the 19th century low-grade coal was mined in the hilly township. Today Portsmouth is a residential and resort area. PRUDENCE I. is part of the town. Bridges connect with Bristol (N) and Tiverton (E). **4.** independent city, pop. 103,907, in SE Virginia, on HAMPTON ROADS, separated from NORFOLK (E) by the Elizabeth R. It is part of the great naval complex at Hampton Roads, and the site of the Norfolk Naval Shipyard, one of the world's largest. It also has a huge naval hospital and is a Coast Guard district headquarters. A major commercial shipping center, Portsmouth also produces fertilizers, plastics, and tools. Built on the site of an Indian village, the city grew after Andrew Sprowle started the Gosport naval yard (1767), which was taken over by the Federal government in 1801 and renamed the Norfolk Naval Shipyard. In 1862 the yard, seized by Confederates, rebuilt the wooden *Merrimack* as the ironclad *Virginia,* which then met the Union's *Monitor* in battle. The Old Towne Historic District has many old homes. Portsmouth is the seat of Tidewater Community College (1968).

Portsmouth Square see under CHINATOWN, San Francisco, California.

Port Townsend city, pop. 7001, seat of Jefferson Co., NW Washington, at the N tip of the Olympic Peninsula, on Admiralty Inlet at the entrance to Puget Sound, 25 mi/40 km NW of Everett. Settled in 1851, it is one of the state's oldest cities and was a bustling port of entry during the 19th century. When it was bypassed by the Union Pacific Railroad, most of the shipping went to SEATTLE and TACOMA, causing an economic slump. Later, military installations and a pulp and paper industry restored the economy. Situated 1 mi/2 km S of Fort Worden State Park and 20 mi/32 km NW of Fort Flagler State Park, the city is now a tourist center and a gateway to Olympic National Park. It trades, processes, and ships lumber, wood pulp, coal, fish, grain, paper, and dairy items.

Port Washington **1.** unincorporated village, pop. 15,387, Nassau Co., SE New York, on Long Island's North Shore, overlooking Manhasset Bay, 6 mi/10 km NW of Mineola. It is a residential suburb and yachting and boatbuilding center, with publishing and some other light industry. **2.** city, pop. 9338, seat of Ozaukee Co., E Wisconsin, on L. Michigan, 25 mi/40 km N of Milwaukee. Situated in a dairying and farming area, it is a commercial and sport fishing port with a major fish processing industry. It also produces canned vegetables, beer, diesel engines, tractors, concrete mixers, prefabricated houses, furniture, and clothing.

Possum Kingdom Lake see under BRAZOS R., Texas.

Poston see under PARKER, Arizona.

post road in the US, from the 17th century, road along which riders carried mail (and later, coaches carried passengers), changing horses and taking refreshment at regularly spaced stations. These roads, including the BOSTON POST ROAD, were the basis for the early development of the modern highway system.

Poteau Mountain timbered ridge (2579 ft/787 m) of the OUACHITA Mts., along the Oklahoma-Arkansas border. It overlooks the city of Heavener (pop. 2601, LeFlore Co.), Oklahoma. A 12 ft/4 m–high slab, purported to have been carved by Nordic explorers on Nov. 11, 1012, is within Heavener Runestone State Park. The 128 mi/206 km–long **Poteau R.** rises in Scott Co., Arkansas, and flows W into Oklahoma, S of Heavener; turning NNE it flows past Poteau, to the ARKANSAS R. at Fort Smith. The 1949 Wister Dam, W of Heavener, impounds Wister Reservoir.

Potomac unincorporated residential suburb, pop. 45,634, Montgomery Co., C Maryland, 3 mi/5 km E of the Potomac R. and 13 mi/21 km NW of Washington, D.C. **North Potomac** (unincorporated, pop. 18,456) is similar.

Potomac Mills see under DALE CITY, Virginia.

Potomac River 287 mi/462 km long, in West Virginia, Maryland, Virginia, and the District of Columbia. It rises in the Appalachian Mts., in NE West Virginia. The main river is formed by two headstreams, the **North Branch** (95 mi/153 km long) and the **South Branch** (130 mi/210 km long), which flow NE to join at a point 15 mi/24 km SE of Cumberland, Maryland. The Potomac then flows NE and SE along the Maryland-Virginia line, cutting a gorge through the Blue Ridge at Harpers Ferry, West Virginia, where the SHENANDOAH R. joins it. From Harpers Ferry it continues generally SE across the PIEDMONT, separating Virginia from Maryland, and is joined by the MONOCACY R., flowing S from Frederick, Maryland. Above Washington, D.C., the river descends from the Piedmont to the Atlantic Coastal Plain in a series of rapids and waterfalls, of which the **Great Falls,** 35 ft/11 m high and 10 mi/16 km NW of Washington, is the highest. At Washington, the ANACOSTIA R. enters the Potomac from the N. Below Washington, the river flows 70 mi/113 km S and SE to CHESAPEAKE BAY, and is navigable by large vessels. The Chesapeake and Ohio Canal, completed in 1850, runs parallel to the river from GEORGETOWN, District of Columbia, NW to Cumberland. Failing in the face of railroad competition, the canal ended its commercial life at the turn of the 20th century, but is now a popular recreational asset. The Patowmack Canal, built 1786–1802 to bypass the Great Falls, also failed financially but is today a recreational center.

Potrero Hill largely residential section of SE SAN FRANCISCO, California, on San Francisco Bay, E of the MISSION DISTRICT, N of HUNTER'S POINT, and SE of SoMa. Waterfront plants in the area have built railway equipment, and shipyards operated from the 1880s. Inland, this is a hilly working- and middle-class area of small homes and shops, undergoing some GENTRIFICATION.

Potsdam town, pop. 16,822, St. Lawrence Co., N New York, on the Raquette R., 30 mi/48 km E of Ogdensburg. It was settled in 1803 as a cooperative community, which was disbanded in 1810. The village of Potsdam (pop. 10,251) was separately incorporated in 1831. Sandstone quarrying was important until 1922. Potsdam now makes dairy products, paper, and electric power, and is home to the State University of New York College at Potsdam (1816) and Clarkson College of Technology (1896).

Pottawatomie Creek see under MARAIS DES CYGNES R., Kansas.

Pottawattamie County 953 sq mi/2468 sq km, pop. 82,628, in SW Iowa, bordered by the Missouri R. and the Nebraska line (W). Its seat and major city is COUNCIL BLUFFS in the SW corner. Most of the county is a wheat growing area.

Pottstown borough, pop. 21,831, Montgomery Co., SE Pennsylvania, on the Schuylkill R., 37 mi/59 km NW of Philadelphia. It was the site of the region's first iron forge, built in 1716; the Coventry forge here produced the first commercial steel in Pennsylvania, in 1732. Pottstown is a trading center for the farming, dairy, and industrial region around it; it also produces structural steel, auto parts, rubber and plastic products, and textiles. The Hill School (1851), a prep school, is here. Pottsgrove Mansion (1732) was used by George Washington during the winter of 1777–78; Hopewell Furnace National Historic Site, a restored 1770s ironmaking community, is 7 mi/11 km SW.

Pottsville city, pop. 16,603, seat of Schuylkill Co., EC Pennsylvania, situated where the Schuylkill R. cuts through Sharp Mt., 35 mi/56 km NNW of Reading and 91 mi/146 km NW of Philadelphia. John Pott settled here in 1806. Later arrivals established iron works, and the area boomed with the discovery of nearby coal. In the 1860s and 1870s, it was a hotbed of activity by the Molly Maguires, a secret miners' labor organization; in 1877, six members were hanged after a trial here. Pottstown was the model for Gibbsville in the fiction of John O'Hara, who was born here in 1905.

Poughkeepsie city, pop. 28,844, seat of Dutchess Co., SE New York, on the E bank of the Hudson R., 65 mi/105 km N of New York City. Settled in 1683 by Dutch colonists, it was the state capital, 1777-97; New York ratified the federal Constitution here in 1788. The city was an important port for its agricultural region until the completion of the Erie Canal (1825) brought competition from western farms. Industrialization followed, including the establishment of the Smith Brothers cough drop factory in 1850. Industries now manufacture dairy equipment, business machines, ball bearings, chemicals, electronic components, and clothing. Computer research and assembly is also important. Poughkeepsie is home to Dutchess Community College (1958). Vassar College (1861) is in adjacent (NE) ARLINGTON.

Poultney town, pop. 3498, including Poultney, East Poultney, and South Poultney villages, in Rutland Co., WC Vermont. It is on the Poultney R. and the New York line, 15 mi/24 km SW of Rutland Lake. St. Catherine State Park is in the S, on the 3 mi/5 km–long lake. Green Mt. College (1834) is in Poultney village. The town makes quarry machinery, slate, and dairy and maple products. Horace Greeley began his career in East Poultney.

Pound Ridge town, pop. 4550, Westchester Co., SE New York, on the Connecticut border. An affluent exurb and suburb of New York City, it is adjacent (N) to Stamford, Connecticut, in hilly and lake-filled terrain.

Poway city, pop. 43,516, San Diego Co., SW California, 17 mi/27 km NNE of downtown San Diego, of which it is a fast-growing residential suburb.

Powder River 485 mi/781 km long, in NE Wyoming and SE Montana. It is named for the black sand along its banks that resembles gunpowder. It rises from several forks in the BIGHORN Mt. foothills in Wyoming, and flows N through the sparsely populated cattle and sheep ranching country of Johnson and Sheridan counties before crossing into Montana. Then it runs generally NE to join the Yellowstone R. just S of Terry. The upper river valley is extremely rich in bituminous coal. The Powder River's main tributaries are the Little Powder R. in Wyoming and Montana and Crazy Woman Creek in Wyoming.

Powell, Lake second-largest (after L. MEAD, downstream) US reservoir, almost entirely in S Utah, impounded by the Glen Canyon Dam on the COLORADO R. The 186 mi/299 km–long lake is within the 1.24 million–ac/501,000-ha (1933–sq mi/5005–sq km) Glen Canyon National Recreation Area, which extends NE to the boundary of CANYONLANDS NATIONAL PARK. The dam, 710 ft/216 m high, was completed in 1964 and is near Page, Arizona, just S of the Utah border; it regulates flow and provides hydroelectric power. The meandering Colorado R. canyons now under L. Powell, as well as those on the tributary Escalante (NW) and San Juan (SE) rivers, were among the most spectacular on the Colorado's course. Still above water level are numerous inlets and caves, many with ancient PETROGLYPHS and pictographs created by the ANASAZI. L. Powell is popular with fishing enthusiasts, many of whom vacation in houseboats. Hiking trails lead to numerous canyons, as well as to Rainbow Bridge National Monument, on a tributary just E of the lower lake in San Juan Co., 5 mi/8 km N of the Arizona border. The 160-ac/65-ha monument incorporates a pink sandstone natural bridge resembling a rainbow that arches to 309 ft/94 m above Bridge Creek, making it the highest in the world. It is sacred to the Navajo, on the N edge of whose huge NAVAJO INDIAN RESERVATION it stands.

Powellhurst-Centennial unincorporated community, pop. 28,756, Multnomah Co., NW Oregon, a residential suburb immediately SE of Portland.

Powell River **1.** district municipality, pop. 12,991, Powell River Regional District (pop. 18,477), SW British Columbia, on the E side of the Strait of Georgia, 80 mi/130 km NW of Vancouver. It developed as an 1880s pulp and paper milling center, and has become one of the world's largest producers of newsprint. Other industries include tourism, mining, and fishing. Cranberry Lake Wildlife Sanctuary is here. **2.** c.150 mi/240 km long, in Virginia and Tennessee. It rises in Wise Co., SW Virginia, cuts through Stone Mt. at BIG STONE GAP, and winds SW into Tennessee, where it enters Norris L., impounded by the NORRIS DAM on the Clinch R., into which the Powell emptied before the dam was built.

Powelton Village residential neighborhood in WEST PHILADELPHIA, Pennsylvania, immediately N of UNIVERSITY CITY. An early suburb of the local elite, it today boasts many single-family Victorian homes restored and maintained by an educated, racially mixed community.

Powhatan Village see WEROWOCOMOCO, Virginia.

Pownal town, pop. 3485, including Pownal village, Pownal Center, and North Pownal, in Bennington Co., extreme SW Vermont. It is on the Hoosic R., just S of Bennington. Bounded by Massachusetts (S), New York and the TACONIC Range (W), and the Green Mts. (E), the town is home to Green Mt. Raceway, a dog track. Industries include limestone production and dairying. Pownal was the setting for Christopher Morley's *Blythe Mountain*. Railroad and financial speculator Jim Fisk was born in North Pownal in 1834.

Presidents Chester Arthur and James Garfield both taught, as young men, in Oak Grove Seminary, in Pownal Center.

Poygan, Lake in Winnebago and Waushara counties, EC Wisconsin. Ten mi/16 km long and 3 mi/5 km wide, it is a widening of the Wolf R. where it joins the Fox R., 12 mi/19 km NW of Oshkosh. Its E extension is called L. Winneconne.

PPG Place office complex in the GOLDEN TRIANGLE of Pittsburgh, Pennsylvania, between MARKET SQUARE and FIRSTSIDE. The most distinguished feature of this group of buildings around a plaza is the neo-Gothic Two PPG Place Tower, 635 ft/194 m high.

Prague city, pop. 2308, Lincoln Co., C Oklahoma, 17 mi/27 km NNE of Shawnee. Settled by Czechs in the 19th century, it has some manufacturing and is a trade and processing center for cotton, oat, and wheat producers. A significant portion of its population is Indian; the great athlete Jim Thorpe (1888–1953) was born nearby.

prairie term first applied by French explorers to vast, largely level grasslands in C North America, centered on the Mississippi R. valley, which extend from the Gulf of Mexico to C Alberta, and from W of the Appalachian system (E) into the Great Plains (W). When first seen (in the E) by whites, the prairies were characterized by unbroken, waist-high, coarse grasses. Trees were common only along rivers and streams, or in occasional depressions in the land. This prairie is now almost gone, altered by farming into the CORN BELT, much of the WHEAT BELT, and other plowed lands; its humus-rich black LOESS soils, adequate rainfall, and warm summers foster heavily productive agriculture. On the W, beginning in a band represented by W Kansas, Nebraska, and the Dakotas, is the **short-grass prairie,** occupying large parts of the GREAT PLAINS; higher, drier land here has been employed primarily for wheat production (aided by deep-well irrigation) and stock raising. The prairies were formerly the primary habitat of the American bison; other prominent species include prairie dogs, deer and antelope, grasshoppers, and a variety of prairie birds. The term *prairie* is also used generically, of similar level areas in other parts of the continent.

Prairie Avenue historic area on the SOUTH SIDE of Chicago, Illinois. During the 1870s and early 1880s the mansions and town houses of the most prominent Chicago citizens were built here. This was the most fashionable address in the city until the emergence of the GOLD COAST.

Prairie Dry Belt see under PALLISER'S TRIANGLE, Alberta and Saskatchewan.

Prairie du Chien city, pop. 5659, seat of Crawford Co., SW Wisconsin, on the Mississippi R. just N of the mouth of the Wisconsin R., across (E) from Marquette, Iowa, and the EFFIGY MOUNDS. The oldest settlement in Wisconsin after Green Bay, it was of great importance when the Fox–Wisconsin river route (via PORTAGE) was the easiest way from the Great Lakes to the Mississippi. French explorers were here as early as 1673, and British and American outposts followed, protecting and servicing the fur trade. The city is now a trade center for a farming area. Its name refers to an 18th-century Fox leader known as the Dog.

Prairie Grove battle site: see under FAYETTEVILLE, Arkansas.

Prairie Island see under GOODHUE Co., Minnesota.

Prairie View city, pop. 4004, Waller Co., SE Texas, 43 mi/69 km NW of Houston. On plantation property here deeded to the state in 1876, Prairie View Agricultural and Mechanical College was established for black youth. It is now Prairie View A & M State University.

Prairie Village city, pop. 23,186, Johnson Co., NE Kansas, on the Missouri border, 6 mi/10 km S of downtown Kansas City. Primarily a residential suburb, it developed rapidly in the 1950s and 1960s.

Prall's Island see under ARTHUR KILL, New York-New Jersey.

Prattville city, pop. 19,587, seat of Autauga Co., also in Elmore Co., C Alabama, 10 mi/16 km NW of Montgomery. Its industries include lumber milling and the production of wood products and textiles. Maxwell Air Force Base is just SE.

Precambrian Shield see CANADIAN SHIELD.

Prescott **1.** city, pop. 26,455, seat of Yavapai Co., WC Arizona, 68 mi/109 km NNW of Phoenix. Founded (1864) by gold prospectors and an early farming and ranching settlement, it was twice (1864–67; 1877–89) capital of the Arizona Territory. Situated in a mountain basin, and surrounded by cattle ranches, it has some light industry and is a mining center. Tourism is also important. The 1.25 million–ac/500,000-ha **Prescott National Forest** is headquartered here, and Prescott and Yavapai colleges (both 1966) are here. **2.** former agricultural town, in WC Massachusetts, inundated in 1937 as part of the construction of QUABBIN RESERVOIR. In the 1870s it was a bee-raising center. **3.** town, pop. 4512, Leeds and Grenville United Counties, SE Ontario, on the St. Lawrence R. opposite Ogdensburg, New York, to which it is connected by bridge, and 47 mi/76 km S of Ottawa. Settled by LOYALISTS in the early 1800s, it developed as the only deepwater port between Montréal and Kingston. Today it manufactures clothing, tools, paper and cement products, and sporting and electronic goods. Metal- and woodworking, silk milling, brewing and distilling, and dairying are important in the area. Fort Wellington, a military post originally built during the War of 1812, is now part of a National Historic Park, which also includes the structure defended by rebel followers of William Lyon Mackenzie in the Battle of the Windmill (1838).

Prescott National Forest c.1.25 million ac/506,000 ha (1950 sq mi/5060 sq km), in C Arizona, on the COCONINO PLATEAU. Its two units enclose a series of NW–SE trending mountain ranges, with a mix of grassland and conifer forest. Prescott (the headquarters), Jerome, and Camp Verde are within it. The Kaibab, Coconino, and Tonto national forests lie E.

Presidential Range chain of peaks in the Mt. Washington Range of the WHITE MTS., running NE–SW between Pinkham Notch (E) and Crawford Notch (W). The Northern Presidentials include Mt. MADISON (5363 ft/1636 m), Mt. ADAMS (5798 ft/1768 m), Mt. JEFFERSON (5715 ft/1743 m), and Mt. Clay (5532 ft/1687 m). Mt. WASHINGTON (6288 ft/1918 m) stands between them and the Southern Presidentials, which include Mt. Monroe (5385 ft/1642 m), Mt. Franklin (5004 ft/1526 m), Mt. Eisenhower (formerly Mt. Pleasant, 4761 ft/1452 m), Mt. Pierce (Mt. Clinton until 1913, 4312 ft/1315 m), Mt. Jackson (4052 ft/1236 m), and Mt. Webster (3910 ft/1193 m). The mostly rocky area above treeline is the site of the largest alpine plant zone in the E US. Krummholz, or stunted trees, occur at timberline, 4800–5200 ft/1464–1586 m. The range was shaped by mammoth continental glaciers, small ravine glaciers, streams, wind, and other natural forces. TUCKERMAN and Huntington ravines; the valley known as the Great Gulf; the Alpine Garden and Bigelow Lawn, noted for alpine flowers; and the two Lakes of the Clouds are particularly well known. The Crawford Path, first cut in 1819; the Appalachian Trail; and many other trails are popular hiking routes. Many of the mountains' names were bestowed by Secretary of State Philip Carrigain in 1820.

President's Island in the Mississippi R., 4 mi/6 km SW of downtown Memphis, Tennessee. Once the largest island in the Mississippi, it was joined to the city by a 1951 causeway, and river silting has filled much of the former gap. Long used as a cotton plantation, the 12 mi/19 km–long island was also a refuge for freed slaves at the Civil War's end. Both Andrew Jackson (in the 1820s) and Nathan Bedford Forrest (in the 1870s) owned land here. Industrial development is now increasing.

presidio in Spanish-settled parts of the West and Southwest, a military garrison established to protect the colonizing work of the MISSION and PUEBLO against external (e.g., Russian or English) or internal (native uprisings) forces. The term is often taken to mean the physical structure of such a garrison.

Presidio historic military reservation, c.1500 ac/600 ha, at the N tip of the peninsula of SAN FRANCISCO, California, on the GOLDEN GATE. Established in 1776 by the Spanish, and a Mexican garrison 1821–46, it has been a US post since then, but in 1994 was decommissioned and became part of the GOLDEN GATE NATIONAL RECREATION AREA. The fashionable residential district of Presidio Heights adjoins on the SE, next to Pacific Heights (E). BAKER BEACH is on the W.

Presidio Hill in SAN DIEGO, California's OLD TOWN, the site of the PRESIDIO and California's first MISSION (established July 16, 1769, and moved 6 mi/10 km E up the Mission Valley in 1773). In 1846 occupying Americans established Fort Stockton here. Today, Presidio Hill Park is the site of the Junipero Serra Museum.

Presque Isle **1.** city, pop. 10,550, Aroostook Co., NE Maine, on the Aroostook R. and Presque Isle Stream, 11 mi/18 km W of the New Brunswick border. Shipping point for the Aroostook Valley, Presque Isle is a major potato processing center. Hunting and winter sports are also important; there is some light manufacturing. The University of Maine has a campus, and Northern Maine Vocational and Technical Inst. is here. **2.** see under ERIE, Pennsylvania.

Preston Hollow see under NORTH DALLAS, Texas.

Pribilof Islands also, **Fur Seal Is.** group of five rocky volcanic peaks in the Bering Sea, 320 mi/520 km W of the mainland of SW Alaska. Only two, St. Paul and St. George, are inhabited; the harvesting of northern fur seals is the major occupation. The Russian explorer Gerasim Pribilof visited the islands in 1786, and Russian traders later imported Aleuts from the Aleutian Is., 275 mi/445 km to the S, to hunt the seals. The herds were nearly destroyed by the beginning of the 20th century, but international treaties controlling the catch have allowed them to flourish again. Over 1.5 million seals, 75% of the world's pop., now gather at Pribilof rookeries during the annual breeding season. The blue arctic fox is also native to the islands, and some 200 species of birds inhabit or migrate through them.

Price city, pop. 8712, seat of Carbon Co., EC Utah, on the Price R., 65 mi/105 km SE of Provo. The settlement grew after the early 1880s arrival of the railroad and the discovery of coal. In today's economy, coal mining is supplemented by flour milling and the processing and shipping of sugar beets and vegetables. Price is a road junction and gateway to canyons, mountains, and nearby ghost towns. It is the seat of the College of Eastern Utah (1937), known for its Prehistoric Museum. The Cleveland-Lloyd Dinosaur Quarry is 30 mi/48 km S.

Prichard city, pop, 34,311, Mobile Co., extreme SW Alabama, 5 mi/8 km NW of downtown Mobile. Although primarily a suburb, it houses significant industries of its own, including shipbuilding, cotton processing, meatpacking, canning, and the production of wood products and fertilizer. The area developed as a distribution center after 1879, when Cleveland Prichard purchased land on the Mobile and Ohio Railroad and began shipping farm produce to the Northeast. The city is today predominantly black.

Prides Crossing village in the city of BEVERLY, Essex Co., NE Massachusetts, just N of Salem, a summer, more recently year-round, retreat of the wealthy.

Primrose town, pop. 534, Dane Co., SE Wisconsin, 20 mi/32 km SW of Madison. Robert M. LaFollette was born here (1855).

Prince Albert city, pop. 34,181, C Saskatchewan, on the North Saskatchewan R., 82 mi/132 km N of Saskatoon, near the geographic center of the province. Founded in 1866 as a Presbyterian mission, it had been surrounded by fur trading posts a century earlier. Today it is the fourth-largest city in the province and a trading and service center for N Saskatchewan, which depends on lumbering and mining, as well as for agricultural C Saskatchewan. Local industries include pulp, paper, and flour milling, oil refining, woodworking, tanning, brewing, manufacture of dairy products, and food packaging. A Federal penitentiary (1911) is here. **Prince Albert National Park,** 30 mi/48 km NW of the city, contains the cabin and grave of the conservationist Grey Owl. The resort village of Waskesiu Lake is nearby. Covering some 960,000 ac/388,000 ha, the park lies at the transition between prairie (S) and boreal forest (N).

Prince Edward Island French, **Île du Prince-Edouard** smallest Canadian province, one of the MARITIME PROVINCES; 1991 pop. 129,765 (102.5% of 1986; rank: 10th of 12); land area 2185 sq mi/5660 sq km (rank: 12th); entered Confederation 1873. Capital and only city: CHARLOTTETOWN. A low, hilly outlier of the APPALACHIAN region, rising to just over 460 ft/140 m, the island lies in a WNW–ESE arc some 130 mi/210 km long and up to 45 mi/72 km wide, in the Gulf of SAINT LAWRENCE, separated by the narrow NORTHUMBERLAND STRAIT from New Brunswick (SW) and Nova Scotia (S and SE). HILLSBOROUGH BAY, on the S, is the site of Charlottetown and of most of the province's population and commercial activity. On the N shore MALPEQUE BAY (WC) is noted for its oysters and other seafood; just to the E are the beaches of PRINCE EDWARD ISLAND NATIONAL PARK. The island's rich red soil supports production of potatoes, other vegetables and fruits, cattle and hogs, and tobacco. The processing of these goods and of local fish and shellfish is almost the only manufacturing industry, based at Charlottetown and at SUMMERSIDE, the second-largest community (SW). The mainland Micmac summered on the island, calling it ABEGWEIT. Cartier (1534) and Champlain (1603) saw it, the latter claiming it for France and naming it the Île Saint-Jean. In the 18th century some French settlers arrived, including 1750s refugees from ACADIA. In 1763 the British took control of what they called St. Johns I. Briefly annexed to Nova Scotia, it became a separate colony in 1769, and in 1799 was renamed for Edward, Duke of Kent. Scottish and American LOYALIST settlers replaced the Acadians, and Prince Edward I. grew as a farming, lumbering, shipbuilding, and fishing colony. In 1864, the first of the conferences leading toward the establishment of modern Canada made Charlottetown the "Cradle of CONFEDERATION"; the island hesitated six years, however, before entering the Dominion. Today, Prince Edward I. retains its essentially tranquil, rural character. The bridging of the Northumberland Strait from Cape Tormentine, New Brunswick, to Borden (SW), in progress in the 1990s, promised to end the island's wintertime isolation, while at the same time threatening profound change in its nature. Tourism focuses on the N shore beaches and on Cavendish and other sites associated with Lucy Maud Montgomery's GREEN GABLES books.

Prince Edward Island National Park 25 mi/40 km–long coastal strip along the Gulf of St. Lawrence, in NC Prince Edward Island, from Tracadie Bay (E) to New London Bay (W). The park is a stretch of white sand beaches, dunes, red sandstone cliffs, saltmarshes, and coves, and is very popular for swimming and windsurfing. Its headquarters are at Cavendish. Within it is GREEN GABLES House, a museum devoted to the *Anne of Green Gables* novels and their author, Lucy Maud Montgomery.

Prince George city, pop. 69,653, Fraser–Fort George Regional District, C British Columbia, at the confluence of the Nechako and Fraser rivers, 324 mi/522 km NNE of Vancouver. A NORTH WEST COMPANY fur post, Fort George, was established here in 1807. Arrival (1913) of the railroad spurred settlement, and in the 1940s the forest products industry led development. A railway division point, the city is the transportation and distribution center for a vast lumbering, mining, and livestock raising region. It has rail repair shops, wood and pulp mills, oil refineries, breweries and bottling plants, and machine shops.

Prince George County 266 sq mi/689 sq km, pop. 27,394, in SE Virginia. Its seat is Prince George. In the TIDEWATER, it is primarily agricultural, with peanut growing, truck farming, and livestock raising. There is some manufacturing at HOPEWELL, which is within but independent of the county. Some maneuvers in the 1864–65 siege of PETERSBURG, adjacent NW, took place here.

Prince George's County also, **Prince Georges** 487 sq mi/1261 sq km, pop. 729,268, in SC Maryland. Upper Marlboro is its seat. Partly in the PIEDMONT, partly in the coastal plain, "P.G." is bounded W by the Potomac R. and Washington, D.C.; NW by Montgomery Co.; and E and NE by the Patuxent R. The county contains many Washington suburbs; although generally less affluent than Montgomery Co., it includes new, upscale development. Also here are the University of Maryland at COLLEGE PARK and ANDREWS AIR FORCE BASE and other government installations.

Prince of Wales, Cape promontory on the Bering Strait at the W end of the SEWARD PENINSULA, in NW Alaska. Some 110 mi/180 km NW of Nome and 58 mi/93 km E of Cape Dezhnev, E Siberia, it is the westernmost point on the North American continent, at 168° 05′ W.

Prince of Wales Island largest in the ALEXANDER ARCHIPELAGO, 25 mi/40 km W of Ketchikan, in SE Alaska. Some 135 mi/217 km NW–SE and 5–40 mi/8–64 km wide, the hilly island rises to 3996 ft/1218 m, and has many bays and inlets along its coast. The homeland of the Haida, it is a center for lumbering, fishing, and fish processing. Craig (city, pop. 1260), on the W coast, is a supply port for commercial fishermen.

Prince Rupert city, pop. 16,620, Skeena–Queen Charlotte Regional District, WC British Columbia, on Kaien I., N of the mouth of the Skeena R., in Chatham Sound (SE of DIXON ENTRANCE), 485 mi/780 km NNW of Vancouver and 35 mi/56 km S of Alaska's S tip. It is the NW terminus of the YELLOWHEAD HIGHWAY and a seaport on the INSIDE PASSAGE, and serves surrounding lumbering, mining, and farming areas. Fish handling and processing are important, and there are large pulp mills, cold storage plants, sawmills, and a cellulose plant.

Princess Anne town, pop. 1666, seat of Somerset Co., SE Maryland, on the EASTERN SHORE, 13 mi/21 km SW of Salisbury. It is home to the University of Maryland-Eastern Shore, formerly Princess Anne College (1886).

Princeton **1.** unincorporated community, pop. 7073, Dade Co., SE Florida, 20 mi/32 km SW of Miami. In a citrus and vegetable producing area, it is, like Naranja (pop. 5790, just SW), one of the newest developing suburbs in the Homestead area. Both suffered heavy damage from Hurricane Andrew (Aug. 1992). **2.** city, pop. 7197, seat of Bureau Co., NC Illinois, 15 mi/24 km NW of Peru. An agricultural center, it is best known as the 1840s–50s home of abolitionist minister Owen Lovejoy. **3.** city, pop. 8127, seat of Gibson Co., SW Indiana, 27 mi/43 km N of Evansville. Founded in 1814, it is situated in an agricultural and oil and coal producing area, and produces processed food items and various other light manufactures. **4.** city, pop. 6940, seat of Caldwell Co., W Kentucky, 33 mi/53 km E of Paducah. This N gateway to the LAND BETWEEN THE LAKES is a rail junction with repair shops, and a trade center for vegetables, burley tobacco, and livestock. The vicinity produces fluorspar, coal, stone, and timber. There are various light industries, including apparel manufacture. **5.** city, pop. 1021, seat of Mercer Co., N Missouri, 41 mi/66 km N of Chillicothe. Settled in the 1840s, it was the birthplace of frontier scout Calamity Jane (1852?–1903). Local livestock and grain are handled here. **6.** borough (pop. 12,016) and surrounding township (pop. 13,198), Mercer Co., WC New Jersey, 50 mi/80 km SW of New York City and 10 mi/16 km NE of Trenton, on the MILLSTONE R. (dammed 1906 to create L. Carnegie) and the Delaware & Raritan Canal. Its life has been dominated by the College of New Jersey, founded 1746 and renamed Princeton University in 1896. The Battle of Princeton (Jan. 1777) was fought just SW of the borough. The college's Nassau Hall was the seat of the Continental Congress, and thus in effect the national capital, June–Nov. 1783. The Institute for Advanced Study (1930), Westminster Choir College (1926), and the New Jersey Governor's mansion (Drumthwacket) are in Princeton. While it is in a greenbelt, without industry, and characterized by large homes and estates, Princeton has since the 1950s become increasingly surrounded by research and corporate facilities, particularly in LAWRENCE (SW) and in the US 1 corridor (E). The unincorporated community of **Princeton Junction** (pop. 2462), where local and through trains meet, is 4 mi/6 km SE, in West Windsor township. **7.** city, pop. 7043, seat of Mercer Co., extreme S West Virginia, 12 mi/19 km NE of BLUEFIELD. Settled in 1826, it was burned by Confederate forces in 1862. It is a trade center for a coal mining area, with various manufactures.

Prince William County 339 sq mi/878 sq km, pop. 215,686, in NE Virginia. Its seat is MANASSAS. It is bounded E by the Potomac R. and NE and N by Occoquan Creek and BULL RUN. The county is both suburban and rural, containing in its E such Washington suburbs as DALE CITY and WOODBRIDGE.

Prince William Sound island-filled inlet of the Gulf of Alaska, E of the Kenai Peninsula and S of the Chugach Mts., in SC Alaska. CORDOVA (SE, on Orca Inlet) and VALDEZ are major ports on the 80 mi/130 km–wide sound, which is a fishing, mining, and oil shipment (at the S terminus of the TRANS-ALASKA PIPELINE) center. Montague and Hinchinbrook are its largest islands. In March 1964 a severe earthquake damaged communities around the sound, and in March 1989 11 million gallons (42 million liters) of oil spilled into the sound when the tanker *Exxon Valdez* went aground. Commercial fishing, birds, sea mammals, and hundreds of miles of shoreline were devastated.

Printers' Row residential and commercial neighborhood on the NEAR SOUTH SIDE of Chicago, Illinois, immediately S of the LOOP. Originally a printing and warehouse district, the area became a shopping, gallery, and residential section after many of the abandoned industrial buildings were renovated during the 1980s.

Prior Lake city, pop. 11,482, Scott Co., SE Minnesota, on Prior L., 16 mi/26 km SW of Minneapolis. It is one of the outer ring of Twin City suburbs.

Promontory Mountains NNW–SSE trending range, 30 mi/48 km long, forming a peninsula extending S into the GREAT SALT L. in Box Elder Co., N Utah, some 50 mi/80 km NW of Salt Lake City. The North Promontory Range continues N into Idaho. The Golden Spike National Historic Site, at Promontory Summit, in a pass between the two parts of the range, marks the meeting of the Union Pacific and Central Pacific railroads, completing the first US transcontinental railroad, on May 10, 1869. **Promontory Point,** the S end of the mountains and peninsula, overlooks the Lucin Cutoff, a rail causeway (1904) across the lake that by the 1940s rendered the Promontory Summit route obsolete.

Prophetstown see under BATTLE GROUND, Indiana.

Prospect Avenue commercial thoroughfare, 2 mi/3 km long, on the EAST SIDE of Milwaukee, Wisconsin. At its S end, it meets WISCONSIN AVENUE, skirting JUNEAU PARK. It has long been lined with the city's most expensive high-rise apartment buildings.

Prospect Heights **1.** city, pop. 15,239, Cook Co., NE Illinois, a residential suburb 20 mi/32 km NW of Chicago. The Pal-waukee Airport is in its NE corner. **2.** see under PARK SLOPE, New York.

Prospect Park **1.** residential neighborhood in Minneapolis, Minnesota, SE of Downtown. Part of SOUTHEAST, it has middle-class homes built for University of Minnesota faculty in 1910–30. The university campus lies immediately W, and many residents work there. **2.** urban park, 526 ac/213 ha, C Brooklyn, New York. Designed by Frederick Law Olmsted and Calvert Vaux, who considered it their masterpiece, it was built 1866–74, and is noted for its Long Meadow and other naturalistic sections. Across Flatbush Ave. from the park are the Brooklyn Botanic Garden, Brooklyn Public Library, and Brooklyn Museum. Grand Army Plaza is at its N tip. PARK SLOPE is W.

Prout's Neck village in the town of Scarborough, Cumberland Co., SW Maine, on a peninsula at the Nonesuch R. mouth, on Saco Bay, 8 mi/13 km SSW of Portland. The area includes a bird sanctuary and Massacre Pond, where Richard Hunnewell and 19 others were killed by Indians in 1713. Prout's Neck is best known as the site of artist Winslow Homer's home and studio.

Providence city, pop. 160,728, state capital and seat of Providence Co., NE Rhode Island, 45 mi/72 km SW of Boston, at the head of Narragansett Bay on the Providence R. Settled in 1636 by Roger Williams as a haven from religious persecution, it played a key role in King Philip's War (1675–76) and in the Revolution. Today it is a major commercial and industrial center, as well as one of the busiest ports in New England. Banking, insurance, and medicine are major businesses. Manufactures include costume jewelry, watches, silverware, textiles, yarn, rubber and petroleum products, electronic equipment, machine tools and machinery, hardware, metal and wire products, paper, plastics, chemicals, synthetics, optical products, and paint. Printing, publishing, textile dyeing and bleaching, oil refining, and commercial fishing also contribute to the economy. Historic buildings in the city include the marble state house (1762) and the First Baptist Meeting House (1775). Providence is home to Brown University (1764), Rhode Island College (1854), Rhode Island School of Design (1877), Johnson and Wales College (1914), and Providence College (1917). Eighteenth-century College Hill, E of downtown, and the 19th-century Armory District, to the W, are noted for their architecture.

Providence County 416 sq mi/1077 sq km, pop. 596,270, in N Rhode Island, bounded W by the Connecticut line and N and NE by Massachusetts. The area is drained by a number of rivers, including the Blackstone (Seekonk), Branch, Chepachet, Moshassuck, Providence, and Wonnasquatucket. It also includes the Sales, Scituate, Smith, and Pascoag reservoirs. Its seat is Providence. Resorts, fishing, granite mining, farming, and gravel pits help support the economy outside the cities of Providence, Cranston, Pawtucket, East Providence, and Woonsocket.

Providence River see under BLACKSTONE R., Rhode Island.

province **1.** any of the ten chief, self-governing administrative divisions of Canada, either derived from former COLONIES or created (after 1870) from the Northwest Territories. The **Province of Canada** was the union (1841–67) of Canada East (now Québec) and Canada West (now Ontario). **2.** physiographic province a major geological and climatic region (e.g., the BASIN AND RANGE PROVINCE), distinguished by characteristic landforms. **3.** historic designation for certain colonies, such as 17th-century Maine.

Province of Canada also, **United Province of Canada** transitional phase (1841–67) in the government of Canada. It was created in response to the rebellions of 1837–38 in both UPPER CANADA (by reformers, against oligarchy) and LOWER CANADA (by the francophone PATRIOTES, against anglophone hegemony and economic distress), and transformed the two provinces into Canada West and Canada East, parts of a single province in which French speakers, who could no longer be denied full political participation, would be a minority, instead of the majority they would be in a separate Lower Canada (Québec). The "solution" was only temporary, however, as reformers in East and West continued their efforts. Confederation (1867) finally created the modern Dominion of Canada.

Provincetown town, pop. 3561, Barnstable Co., SE Massachusetts, at the tip of Cape Cod. RACE POINT is its W extreme. It is a summer resort and artists' colony. Founded as a fishing community in the early 18th century, it depended on its Yankee, and later, Portuguese seafarers until around 1900, when it began to attract summer visitors. The Cape Cod School of Art was founded here in 1901; the Provincetown Players theater, founded 1915, produced the first staging of any of Eugene O'Neill's works, *Bound East for Cardiff* (1916). The town has a 253-ft/77-m monument commemorating the first landfall made by the Pilgrims on Nov. 21, 1620, about one month before they moved to Plymouth. Provincetown has long been a favorite with gay vacationers.

Provo city, pop. 86,835, seat of Utah Co., NC Utah, on the Provo R. and Utah L., 38 mi/61 km SSE of Salt Lake City. Settled by Mormons in 1849, it was later named for fur trapper Étienne Provost, who had explored the Salt Lake Valley in 1825. The railroad, which arrived during the 1870s, was instrumental in Provo's development as a silver, lead, copper, and gold mining center. It is now a leading producer of iron, steel, and foundry products. It is also the commercial center of the irrigated agricultural county. Manufactures include jet fuselages, helicopters, computer software, electronic machinery, and clothing. Provo also has canning, food processing, and fertilizer plants. It is headquarters for the Uinta National Forest. The city is the seat of the huge Mormon-run Brigham Young University (1875).

Prudence Island in Narragansett Bay, 15 mi/24 km S of Providence in Portsmouth, Newport Co., SE Rhode Island. Seven mi/11 km long NW–SE and 0.5–1.5 mi/1–2 km wide, it is a resort and fishing area; Narragansett Bay Estuarine Sanctuary covers the N part. Much smaller Patience I. is just NW, and tiny Hope I. is SW.

Prudential Center commercial complex in the BACK BAY section of Boston, Massachusetts. Constructed over railyards in the 1960s, the huge complex, with a 52-story, 750-ft/229-m office tower, was intended to serve as a suburban-style mall within the city. In 1991 work began on reconstruction and expansion to make it more attractive and accessible to surrounding neighborhoods.

Prudhoe Bay inlet of the BEAUFORT SEA, 200 mi/320 km ESE of Point BARROW, in N Alaska. The 9 mi/14 km–wide bay and a small community (pop. 47) on it are at the center of immensely rich petroleum and natural gas fields discovered on the NORTH SLOPE in 1968, and estimated to contain 9.6 billion barrels of oil and 26 trillion cubic ft/0.73 trillion cubic m of natural gas. Prudhoe Bay is now the largest oilfield complex in the US, producing about 2 million barrels a day. The 800 mi/1300 km–long TRANS-ALASKA PIPELINE, completed in 1977, carries oil S from the bay to the ice-free port of VALDEZ on PRINCE WILLIAM SOUND.

Pruitt-Igoe massive multistory public housing development built with Federal funds on the NORTH SIDE of SAINT LOUIS, Missouri, in 1954, and regarded then as a model for US URBAN RENEWAL projects. By the late 1960s the crime-ridden 33-building complex, which had held up to 20,000 residents, was in a state of dilapidation and largely abandoned. In 1972 it was decided that Pruitt-Igoe was unliveable and that the only solution was to raze the buildings; their destruction was completed by 1976. Failure of the project has been considered emblematic of the need to change from high-rise public housing construction to neighborhood preservation, in St. Louis and throughout the US.

public lands in the US, Federal lands not reserved for specific (e.g., military, park, or conservation) uses, on which it was possible after 1862 to HOMESTEAD. Public land first came into being when seven of the thirteen STATES ratifying the Constitution ceded their Western land claims (with the exception of certain areas like the WESTERN RESERVE) to the new Federal government. The 1803 LOUISIANA PURCHASE and all subsequent accessions of territory (except Texas, which by its statehood compact kept its unclaimed areas as *state* public land) created more land in the public domain; much was allotted to veterans of US wars before 1861. With the 1862 Homestead Act, public land, mapped by the US Land Office Survey, was thrown open to homesteaders. Other public land has been granted to house and support LAND-GRANT institutions, to developing railroads, and directly to the states. Today, much public land is leased by mining, forest industries, and other concerns. The Bureau of Land Management (BLM), in the Department of the Interior, is responsible for "total management" of some 420,000 sq mi/1.1 million sq km of public lands, largely in the West and in Alaska; multiple use of these lands, analogous to but broader than that of NATIONAL FOREST land, is encouraged. See also CROWN LANDS, in Canada.

Public Square center of downtown Cleveland, Ohio, near the TERMINAL TOWER. The centerpiece of the Cleveland Group Plan of the early 20th century, it is near the Mall, which extends to L. Erie. The major avenues of the city all radiate from this point.

pueblo **1.** communal village or building of certain Southwestern tribes, typically constructed of stone or adobe, sometimes against a cliff face. Pueblos were constructed by the pre-Columbian Anasazi and Mogollon, as well as by the Hopi, Zuñi, and related peoples, to whose communities the Spanish applied the term. The tribes themselves came to be called Pueblo Indians or Pueblos. **2.** the modern community of a Pueblo Indian group, typically including a central village (sometimes a number of villages) and surrounding lands. **3..** in the scheme of Spanish settlement in the 16th–18th century Southwest, a civil community established near a MISSION or PRESIDIO, originally for colonial soldiers, their families, and other settlers. The RANCHO was often an outgrowth of the pueblo.

Pueblo city, pop. 98,640, seat of Pueblo Co., SC Colorado, on the Arkansas R., in the foothills of the Rocky Mts., 40 mi/64 km SSE of Colorado Springs. Settled in the 1840s as a trading post, it was devastated by a Ute raid in 1854. With the arrival of the Denver and Rio Grande (1872) and the Atchison, Topeka and Santa Fe (1876) railroads and the discovery of nearby coal, the settlement grew rapidly as a smelting and shipping center for ore from local mines, and as a producer of iron and steel. Now one of Colorado's major cities, it is a trucking, manufacturing, and commercial hub for surrounding farms and ranches. It is also headquarters for San Isabel National Forest, and a tourist base for local recreation areas. Steel and steel products are its chief manufactures. The University of Southern Colorado (1933) is here, the US Department of Transportation's High Speed Ground Test Center is 15 mi/24 km NE, and an Army ordnance depot is 13 mi/21 km E.

Pueblo Pequeño see LITTLE VILLAGE, Chicago, Illinois.

Puerto Rico officially, **Estado Libre Asociado** (free associated state) **de Puerto Rico** or **Commonwealth of Puerto Rico** island state at the E end of the Greater Antilles, between the Atlantic Ocean (N) and the Caribbean Sea (S), a possession of the US since 1898 and a commonwealth since July 25, 1952; 1990 pop. 3,522,037 (110.2% of 1980); area 3515 sq mi/ 9104 sq km. Capital and largest ZONA URBANA: SAN JUAN. Other leading urban centers: BAYAMÓN, CAROLINA, PONCE, CAGUAS, MAYAGÜEZ. Puerto Rico (formerly called by the US government **Porto Rico**) lies some 1600 mi/2600 km SE of New York City; the MONA PASSAGE (W) separates it from the Dominican Republic (the island of Hispaniola). The US VIRGIN Is. lie some 40 mi/64 km to the E. Puerto Rico's principal island is 111 mi/178 km E–W, and up to 40 mi/64 km wide; Mona I. (in the Mona Passage) and VIEQUES and CULEBRA islands (on the E), along with scattered minor islands, are also part of the commonwealth. Roughly rectangular, the main island is crossed by the CORDILLERA CENTRAL, which rises to 4389 ft/1338 m at CERRO DE PUNTA (SC, near Ponce). The mountainous interior is surrounded by a coastal plain. Most of the numerous small rivers on the island flow N from the Cordillera; they are not navigable, but have been dammed in places for hydroelectric and recreational use. The climate is tropical (within HURRICANE ALLEY), with cooler higher elevations the site of vacation homes and coffee plantations. Puerto Rico is densely populated, with some 1028 persons per sq mi (397/sq km), slightly less than the ratio in New Jersey, the densest US state. Most of the pop. lives in the San Juan area (NE), with Ponce (S) and Mayagüez (W) the other most populous districts. Columbus (1493) was the first European to see the island, which was home (called BORINQUÉN) to the Taino (Arawak). In 1508 Ponce de León began Spanish settlement; the natives were soon killed off, and Puerto Rico (named for the port at San Juan, where the fortress of EL MORRO guarded the harbor) passed over two centuries as primarily a military post, attacked periodically by the English or Dutch as key to control of the Caribbean sea lanes. Some gold mining and cattle raising were done in this period, but an agricultural economy, with African slaves raising sugar cane, tobacco, and coffee, developed in the 19th century. Agitation for independence began later in the century (an 1868 rising at LARES has great symbolic importance), slavery ended in 1873, and by the 1890s Spain had granted some self-government. In 1898 the US, at war with Spain, invaded; in 1900 the first American governor was appointed. Gradual increases in self-government followed. In 1917 Puerto Ricans gained US citizenship. In 1946 the first native governor was appointed, and popular voting for the office was initiated the following year. World War II brought some relief to a depressed agricultural economy, and in 1947 the Federal "Operation Bootstrap," using tax incentives to attract industry and business to Puerto Rico, began. Since then chemical and pharmaceutical plants have led in the development of industrial zones, esp. on the N coast. Puerto Rico's ability to retain the industry thus gained is continually threatened, however, by the availability of even cheaper labor and lower costs in other Caribbean countries. Today industry, tourism, business, and agriculture all play a role in the island's economy. Puerto Ricans at present elect their own governor and legislature (the commonwealth is divided into 78 MUNICIPIOS, analogous to counties), but have no vote in US elections or in Congress. They do not pay Federal income taxes, but are liable to military service. The debate over Puerto Rico's political status is ongoing. In the 1990s advocates of continued commonwealth status outnumbered those desiring statehood; there was also a small independence party. Since the 1940s hundreds of thousands of Puerto Ricans have moved to the US mainland (chiefly to the New York City area); their role in the island's political future is unclear. The people of Puerto Rico are predominantly of mixed Spanish and African heritage, Spanish-speaking, and Roman Catholic. Their distinctive culture is one of the foundations of the commonwealth's tourist economy. Visitors are drawn to San Juan's sights and entertainments, and to tropical beaches lined with luxury hotels. San Juan is a major cruise ship port. The CARIBBEAN NATIONAL FOREST (popularly, El Yunque) is a well-known natural preserve. ARECIBO (NW) is noted as the site of a major radio telescope facility. ROOSEVELT ROADS, on the E coast, is home to the Atlantic Fleet Weapons Training Facility, which utilizes a large area of the surrounding ocean for gunnery and other naval exercises; the use of Vieques and Culebra islands in these exercises is the focus of a long-standing dispute. The main campus of the University of Puerto Rico is at RIO PIEDRAS.

Puerto Rico Trench ocean depth, running E–W for some 450 mi/720 km, c.75 mi/120 km N of Puerto Rico. Some 100 mi/ 160 km NW of the island's NW point, it reaches 28,374 ft/ 8648 m below sea level, the deepest point in the Atlantic Ocean.

Puget Sound 100 mi/160 km–long inlet of the Pacific Ocean, joining the SE end of JUAN DE FUCA STRAIT at Admiralty Inlet and extending S into W Washington, forming on its W the OLYMPIC PENINSULA. A W arm, the 75 mi/120 km–long Hood Canal, extends S into the E side of the Olympic Peninsula, dividing from it the Kitsap Peninsula (E). Many rivers from the CASCADE RANGE (E) feed into Puget Sound, through the Puget Sound Lowland, a rich agricultural region which, since World War II, has also become an industrial and military center. Natural harbors and advantageous city sites make the area the most densely populated in the state, from PORT TOWNSEND, at its NW extreme, to BREMERTON, on the Kitsap Peninsula, to OLYMPIA, the state capital, on its S end, to TACOMA, SEATTLE, and EVERETT, on its E side. Navigable for large ships, the sound has numerous naval and commercial port facilities. Aircraft manufacture, fostered originally by plentiful spruce wood, is also important in the region. Ferries and bridges are vital to transportation throughout the sound, with its many islands, which include WHIDBEY, VASHON, and BAINBRIDGE. The sound was named (for a naval colleague) by the English captain George Vancouver, in 1792.

Pugwash hamlet at the mouth of the Pugwash R. on Northumberland Strait, 26 mi/42 km E of Amherst, in Cumberland Co., N Nova Scotia. The mining of rock salt, fishing, shipping, and tourism are the main local industries. The town was the site of the Pugwash Conferences, meetings of scientists, statesmen, and philosophers from the East and West, established in the 1950s by the industrialist Cyrus Eaton (1883–1979), a native and summer resident.

Pukaskwa National Park 467,000 ac/189,000 ha (729 sq mi/ 1888 sq km), in C Ontario, on the N shore of L. Superior, 137 mi/220 km E of Thunder Bay. Established in 1971, and the largest national park in the province, it has a dramatic rocky coastline; the interior is a CANADIAN SHIELD wilderness, accessible only on foot or by canoe, cut through by rivers, with forests of black spruce, white birch, and jack pine.

Pulaski **1.** city, pop. 7895, seat of Giles Co., SC Tennessee, 30 mi/48 km S of Columbia, on Richland Creek. This agricultural trade, processing, and shipping center is the place where the Ku Klux Klan was founded in 1865. It is also the birthplace (1888) of poet and teacher John Crowe Ransom. **2.** town, pop. 9985, seat of Pulaski Co., SW Virginia, in the Great Appalachian Valley, 12 mi/19 km WSW of Radford, and just W of Claytor L. (on the New R.). It is a rail junction and trade and industrial center in a livestock, dairying, and lumbering area. Furniture, chemical, and wood products are manufactured.

Pulaski County 767 sq mi/1987 sq km, pop. 349,660, in C Arkansas, bisected by the Arkansas R. Its seat is LITTLE ROCK, the state's capital and largest metropolitan center. Agricultural and suburban, the county produces cotton, corn, hay, truck crops, and livestock. There is substantial industry at Little Rock and NORTH LITTLE ROCK. The county's mines are the leading US source of bauxite, and there are oil and gas wells and stone quarries.

Pulaski Skyway automobile thoroughfare, 3.5 mi/6 km long, between Newark and Jersey City, New Jersey. Built in 1932 and named for the Polish general who commanded American forces in the Revolution, it is a steel and concrete viaduct that rises 145 ft/44 m, carrying US 1 over the Passaic and Hackensack rivers near Newark Bay, a pioneering effort in the control of traffic in a congested urban area.

Pullman **1.** neighborhood and Historic District in SE Chicago, Illinois. The brainchild of railcar manufacturer George Pullman, it was a planned industrial community originally outside the city limits and completely under its owner's control. A large strike by employees in 1894 against wage reductions led to Federal intervention on Pullman's behalf. **2.** city, pop. 23,478, Whitman Co., SE Washington, on the South Fork of the Palouse R., 9 mi/14 km W of Moscow, Idaho, and 60 mi/97 km SSE of Spokane. It developed as an important stop on the Northern Pacific Railroad. It is now a trading center and shipping point for wheat, peas, and dairy products from the surrounding agricultural region. Much of Pullman's E half is devoted to Washington State University (1890), one of the largest institutions of higher education in the state.

Pultneyville resort community in Williamson township, Wayne Co., W New York, on the S shore of L. Ontario, 23 mi/37 km NE of Rochester. Before the Civil War it was a station on the Underground Railroad, sending runaway slaves across the lake into Canada.

Punchbowl, the extinct volcanic crater in HONOLULU, Hawaii. Just inland, it rises 498 ft/152 m above Downtown, and is 500 ft/153 m wide. The National Memorial Cemetery of the Pacific here contains some 24,000 graves of soldiers who died in World War II or the Korean or Vietnam wars.

Punta, Cerro de see CERRO DE PUNTA, Puerto Rico.

Punta Gorda city, pop. 10,747, seat of Charlotte Co., SW Florida, on CHARLOTTE HARBOR, 20 mi/32 km from the Gulf of Mexico, near the mouth of the Peace R. and 23 mi/37 km NW of Fort Myers. It is a resort noted for its sport fishing and yachting facilities, and a shipping point for local fish, shellfish, and vegetables.

Punxsutawney borough, pop. 6782, Jefferson Co., WC Pennsylvania, 65 mi/105 km NE of Pittsburgh. Punxsutawney is best known as the home of Punxsutawney Phil, the groundhog who appears every Feb. 2 (Groundhog Day); if he sees his shadow winter will continue for an additional six weeks. Punxsutawney produces textiles and beverages; it has some coal mining and also grows potatoes.

Purcell Mountains NNW–SSE trending range, part of the Columbia Mts. section of the ROCKY Mts., in SE British Columbia, extending some 160 mi/260 km from near ROGERS PASS (N) to the vicinity of LIBBY, in NW Montana. They are paralleled (W) by the taller SELKIRK Mts. and a deep trench filled by Kootenay L., and (E) by the Rocky Mt. Trench and front ranges. The range is largely sedimentary in composition. The granitic Bugaboo Spires, in the N, are a noted rock climbing site.

Purchase locality in Harrison town, Westchester Co., SE New York. It is an area of large estates, with only two major streets and few shops. Commercial development is focused along Route 287; offices of Texaco and the headquarters of Pepsico, among others, are here. Also in Purchase are Manhattanville College and a branch of the State University of New York.

Purchase, the see JACKSON PURCHASE, Kentucky.

Purgatoire River 186 mi/299 km long, in SE Colorado. It is formed by headstreams on the E slopes of the SANGRE DE CRISTO Mts., and flows E past Trinidad, then NE through canyons to join the ARKANSAS R. just E of Las Animas, at the John Martin Reservoir.

Put-in-Bay War of 1812 battle site, in L. Erie, in Ottawa Co., N Ohio, N of Sandusky, between Middle Bass I. and South Bass I. Here Commodore Oliver H. Perry, leading a squadron from Erie, Pennsylvania, achieved a decisive victory over a British fleet on Sept. 10, 1813. The Americans thus gained control of L. Erie, allowing the invasion of Canada and the subsequent success at the Battle of the THAMES. The resort village of Put-in-Bay, pop. 132, is on Put-in-Bay Harbor, South Bass I. Its economy relies on tourism, commercial fishing, and winemaking. Perry's Victory and International Peace Memorial is at the SE corner of the village.

Putnam town, pop. 9031, Windham Co., extreme NE Connecticut, on the Quinebaug R., 20 mi/32 km NE of Willimantic. An industrial center at Cargill Falls, it produces textiles, metal products, and paper goods. There is some dairy farming, and the town's position on Interstate 395 and other roads makes it a local trade hub.

Putnam County 231 sq mi/598 sq km, pop. 83,941, SE New York, bounded by the Hudson R. (W) and Connecticut (E), in the Hudson Highlands and Taconic Mts. Its seat is Carmel; it has no large towns or cities. Its lake-filled S portion, around the county seat and such places as BREWSTER and Putnam Valley, is both a residential New York suburb and a recreational area. Also here is the N part of the Croton Reservoir system, which supplies much of New York City's drinking water. The county's agriculture has lessened in importance in the late 20th century.

Putney town, pop. 2352, Windham Co., SE Vermont, on the Connecticut R. and Interstate 91, 9 mi/14 km N of Brattleboro. It is best known as the site of Putney School (1935). Landmark College (1983) is also here. In an orchard and berry area, Putney is a retail center with a noted basket store, a nursery, and Santa's Land, a theme park. Other industries include paper milling and boxmaking.

Puyallup city, pop. 23,875, Pierce Co., WC Washington, on the Puyallup R., 8 mi/13 km SE of Tacoma. Situated in a fertile agricultural region, it processes and ships lumber, produce, and iris, daffodil, and tulip bulbs. The city is host to the large annual Western Washington State Fair.

Pymatuning Reservoir 17,200 ac/6960 ha, in NW Pennsylvania (Crawford Co.) and NE Ohio (Ashtabula Co.), 7 mi/11 km NNW of Greenville, Pennsylvania. Formed in 1932 by damming the Shenango R. for flood control, it is open for recreation. It is c.16 mi/26 km long, in a crescent shape.

Pyramid Lake in Washoe Co., W Nevada, 30 mi/48 km NNE of Reno, between the Lake Range (E) and Virginia Mts. (W). Explorer John C. Frémont named it (1844) for a huge stone rising from its E side. Fed by the TRUCKEE R., the largest natural lake in Nevada, a remnant of ancient L. Lahontan, stretches some 27 mi/43 km N–S. Known for its sandstone and tufa scenery, its cutthroat trout, and the endangered cui-ui fish, it contains Anaho I., a US wildlife refuge and white pelican breeding ground. The lake, esp. its N end, is sacred to the Paiute, whose 554–sq mi/1435–sq km **Pyramid L. Indian Reservation** (pop. 1388, 69% Indian) surrounds it.

Pyramid Mountains range extending S of LORDSBURG in SW New Mexico, including Pyramid (or North Pyramid) Peak (6008 ft/1831 m). Copper, gold, and silver have been mined in the mountains, the location of Shakespeare, now a privately owned GHOST TOWN.

Q

Qaummaarviit Historic Park: see under IQALUIT, Northwest Territories.

Quabbin Reservoir 39 sq mi/101 sq km, in Worcester, Franklin, and Hampshire counties, WC Massachusetts. Undertaken in 1937, on the SWIFT R., it required the flooding of three towns, Prescott, Enfield, and Greenwich. Dammed by Winsor Dam and Quabbin Dike, the reservoir serves the Boston area. Its waters flow E to the WACHUSETT Reservoir through Quabbin Aqueduct (25 mi/40 km). Quabbin Reservoir has 177 mi/283 km of shoreline.

Quad Cities **1.** in Alabama, FLORENCE, SHEFFIELD, and TUSCUMBIA, formerly called the Tri-Cities, along with more recently incorporated MUSCLE SHOALS. **2.** metropolitan and industrial area at the junction of the Rock and Mississippi rivers, in NW Illinois and NE Iowa. The four cities are BETTENDORF and DAVENPORT, Iowa, and ROCK ISLAND and MOLINE, Illinois. The area also includes the industrial communities of East Moline, Milan, and Silvis, Illinois. The Quad Cities nuclear power plant (1972) is on the Mississippi, 20 mi/32 km NE.

Quaker Square see under AKRON, Ohio.

Quakertown borough, pop. 8982, Bucks Co., SE Pennsylvania, 13 mi/21 km SE of Allentown. Its industries include clothing production and agriculture.

Qualla Boundary Reservation see EASTERN CHEROKEE INDIAN RESERVATION, North Carolina.

Quantico town, pop. 670, Prince William Co., NE Virginia, on the Potomac R., 30 mi/48 km SW of Washington, D.C. Adjacent is a Marine Corps station established as a naval base during the Revolution and made a permanent base in 1916. Long known as the Quantico Marine Corps Air Station, it is now the headquarters of the Combat Development Command, the Marines' educational center. Unincorporated **Quantico Station** has a pop. of 7425. Quantico is also an FBI training center.

Qu'Appelle River 270 mi/430 km long, in S Saskatchewan and SW Manitoba. It flows from Diefenbaker L. on the South SASKATCHEWAN R., NW of Moose Jaw (before creation of the lake in the 1960s it rose in the area), and winds E across Saskatchewan, N of Regina and past Fort Qu'Appelle, to join the ASSINIBOINE R. just over the Manitoba border. Its valley is agricultural, producing esp. berries. The name comes from a Cree legend, of a youth who thought he heard his name called, and responded, *Qu'appelle?* ("Who calls?"), learning later that what he had heard was the last words of his dying betrothed.

Quartz Mountains hilly area with elevations of nearly 800 ft/244 m, in SW Oklahoma, N of Altus. These red granite and quartz hills are strewn with large boulders. The area was a winter camping spot for the Kiowa and Comanche. The hills, and Quartz Mountain State Park in Lugert, are at the S end of Altus L., on the North Fork of the RED R.

Quartzsite town, pop. 1876, La Paz Co., SW Arizona, 120 mi/190 km W of Phoenix and 18 mi/29 km E of the California border (the Colorado R.), just off I-10. Established as Fort Tyson in the 1850s, and later a stage stop, it is now noted as the site of a huge midwinter rock and gem show. The Hi Jolly Memorial is the grave of Hadji Ali, an Arab camel driver imported during 1850s Army experiments with the animals, who remained in the area as a prospector.

Québec largest Canadian province, second in area among the nation's subdivisions only to the Northwest Territories; 1991 pop. 6,895,963 (105.6% of 1986; rank: 2nd of 12); land area 524,252 sq mi/1,357,812 sq km; entered Confederation 1867. Capital: QUÉBEC CITY. Most populous cities (*villes*): MONTRÉAL, LAVAL, Québec City, LONGUEUIL, GATINEAU, MONTRÉAL-NORD, SHERBROOKE, SAINT-HUBERT, SAINT-LÉONARD, SAINT-LAURENT. Québec is bordered NE by Labrador; SE by (E–W) New Brunswick (with the Patapédia and RESTIGOUCHE rivers forming part of the boundary) and Maine: S by New Hampshire, Vermont (with Lakes MEMPHRÉMAGOG and CHAMPLAIN forming parts of the boundary), and New York; and SW and W by Ontario (with the OTTAWA R. forming much of the boundary). It is also bounded W by JAMES and HUDSON bays; N by the HUDSON STRAIT and UNGAVA Bay; and SE by the Gulf of SAINT LAWRENCE, in which lie its ANTICOSTI and MADELEINE islands. Except in the SE, the province occupies part of the CANADIAN SHIELD, a domelike, largely forested expanse of hard Precambrian rock on which lie thousands of lakes, and from which flow numerous rivers. The Shield areas of N Québec have little arable land (the CLAY BELT of the SW, in the ABITIBI region, is an exception), and are lightly populated, with scattered mining towns and hydroelectric complexes, and Cree and INUIT settlements around the edges. The Nottaway, EASTMAIN, LA GRANDE, GREAT WHALE (Baleine) and other rivers drain the Shield W toward James and Hudson bays. The Caniapiscau–Mélèzes–KOKSOAK system drains N, to Ungava Bay. On the SE, the MANICOUAGAN, Outardes, SAGUENAY, and SAINT-MAURICE are among rivers that drain from the Shield into the Saint Lawrence R. valley, and, entering the populated part of the province, have cities and industrial development along them. Hydro-Québec, the provincial power authority, has developed massive dams and diversions on the La Grande, Manicouagan, and other rivers in the N. The LAURENTIAN Mts. (Laurentides), actually an edge of the Shield, are a popular resort area just NW of Montréal. In the N, where the TORNGAT Mts., on the Labrador border, comprise another edge of the Shield, Mt. D'Iberville (5210 ft/1588 m) is the province's high point. Among mining centers on the Shield are ROUYN-NORANDA and VAL-D'OR. The Ottawa R. rises on the Shield in the SW and swings around its S edge; near Montréal it joins the Saint Lawrence. The latter, the most important river in Québec's (and Canada's) history, then drains NE to the Atlantic, widening gradually into the Gulf of Saint Lawrence below (NE of) Québec City. In the St. Lawrence valley are fertile lowlands, mostly on the river's S shore. Most of Québec's cities are in this valley. The MONTEREGIAN HILLS, which rise from the lowlands near the Ottawa–Saint Lawrence junction, include MOUNT ROYAL, around which Montréal and its suburbs developed. CAP-DIAMANT, on which Québec City's UPPER TOWN is built, represents the intersection of the Shield with the St. Lawrence; this locality gave its name (Algonquian, "where the river narrows") to the province. Along the S of the St. Lawrence valley, extending through the GASPÉ PENINSULA, at the river's mouth, run a series of APPALACHIAN hills, including the NOTRE DAME and SHICKSHOCK mountains; this is a region of small farming and industrial communities (Sherbrooke is the largest city), with mining centers at ASBESTOS and THETFORD MINES, in the EASTERN TOWNSHIPS, and at MURDOCHVILLE, in the Gaspé. In the 16th century, when Europeans first arrived, Algonquian and Huron peoples who inhabited the region were at war with Iroquoians in the SW. In 1534–35, Jacques Cartier found villages at STADACONA (later Québec City) and at HOCHELAGA (later Montréal), near the LACHINE Rapids, the head of navigation on the St. Lawrence. The French first settled on CHALEUR BAY and islands of the Gulf of St. Lawrence. In 1608 NEW FRANCE was established at Québec City by Champlain, and settlement soon spread to TROIS-RIVIÈRES and Ville Marie (Montréal). Early communities centered around SEIGNEURIES, semifeudal landholdings along the St. Lawrence. Outside the agricultural settlements, the fur trade was key, sending adventurers (later called COUREURS DE BOIS and VOYAGEURS) up the St. Lawrence, Ottawa, Saguenay, and other routes to the interior. In the 18th century, French-British struggles dominated E North America, and in 1763 the British, having captured Québec's cities, took complete control. Renaming New France (which then extended to the Ohio and Mississippi rivers) the province of Quebec, they passed laws protecting many rights of the French inhabitants, but at the same time established an economic hegemony that survived until the 1970s; Montréal's NORTH WEST COMPANY, organized by Scottish merchants, was at the center of a concentration of anglophone wealth. After the American Revolution, LOYALISTS settled in the Eastern Townships and the Gaspé, as well as in the W part of the province; in 1791, their concentration N of L. Ontario led to the creation of Upper Canada (later Ontario); what remained LOWER CANADA eventually became today's province of Québec. The 1830s PATRIOTE rebellion, expressing francophone protest against anglophone control, was an element in the 1840 transformation of Upper and Lower Canada into the unified Canada East and West, and with CONFEDERATION, in 1867, Québec became one province in the new Dominion of Canada. In 1912 NOUVEAU-QUÉBEC (New Quebec), comprising a large part of the UNGAVA region, was taken from the Northwest Territories and added to Québec; delineation of the border with Labrador was not completed until a 1927 British Privy Council decision. English Quebecers, their capital at Montréal, remained dominant in the province's life until the 1960s, when the "Quiet Revolution" finally awakened French political and cultural forces. Since then, separatist or nationalist groups have several times appeared close to achieving their goal of taking Québec part or all of the way out of Canada, and esp. in the 1970s anglophone Quebecers moved in large numbers, and their businesses relocated with them, largely to Toronto. The Cree in Nouveau-Québec have at the same time expressed a desire to secede from the province. Montréal remains cosmopolitan, but about four-fifths of Quebecers are today French-speaking; outside of the metropolis, there are few anglophone concentrations. Today, Québec has, in the Montréal area, one of Canada's major commercial, institutional, and industrial complexes; transportation equipment, metals, textiles, chemicals, processed foods, and refined oil and sugar are among its products. Elsewhere in the province, pulp and paper, lumber, and metals are among leading manufactures. The OUTAOUAIS Urban Community (including HULL and Gatineau) near Ottawa, the CHICOUTIMI-JONQUIÈRE district on the Saguenay and L. SAINT-JEAN, the Trois-Rivières–SHAWINIGAN region (La Mauricie, on the R. Saint-Maurice), and the Québec City–LÉVIS-LAUZON area are the province's industrial hubs. Montréal, Québec City, Sherbrooke, and LENNOXVILLE are academic centers. Tourism and recreational visits focus on such varied sites as the shrine at SAINTE-ANNE-DE-BEAUPRÉ, distant coastal communities like BAIE-COMEAU, ski resorts like Mt. TREMBLANT (in the Laurentians), the Gaspé's FORILLON NATIONAL PARK, the provincial GATINEAU PARK, and the historic Île d'ORLÉANS, as well as on the major cities.

Québec City also, **Québec** city, pop. 167,517, set at the base of, on, and around Cap-Diamant, a rocky promontory rising over 320 ft/98 m from the N bank of the St. Lawrence R., where the R. Saint-Charles joins it, 300 mi/480 km W of the Gulf of St. Lawrence and 145 mi/235 km NE of Montréal. The area was visited by Jacques Cartier in 1534–35 (see CAP-ROUGE), and the settlement founded in 1608, as a trading post, by Samuel de Champlain, on the site of the former Iroquoian village of STADACONA. The British held it in 1629–32. In 1663 it became the capital of the province of NEW FRANCE. Following failed attempts in 1690 and 1711, the British took it again in 1759 at the PLAINS OF ABRAHAM. From 1763 to 1791, it was the capital of the British province of Québec, in 1791–1841 the capital of LOWER CANADA. Capital of the United Province of Canada in 1851–55 and 1859–65, it has been since 1867 the capital of the Canadian province of Québec. The city's political history is reflected in its fortifications, in its historic and active government buildings, and in its continuing role as a government, cultural, and service center. Almost entirely francophone, it is regarded by many as the true stronghold of French Canadian culture; it has a longstanding rivalry in this area with the larger, more cosmopolitan Montréal. At a key point on the St. Lawrence, Québec ("where the river narrows") was the early center of fur export and other trade with Europe. It held a dominant position in both French and British colonial life until the mid 19th century, when upstream dredging, along with the failure of railroads to reach the city until 1879, allowed Montréal to assume the central role. Industry to a large degree replaced trade in the late 19th century, with textiles and shoemaking, shipbuilding, and later paper and pulp production important. But the city has grown recently in its governmental and cultural roles and as a tourist center (noted esp. for its winter carnival). It is the only walled city north of Mexico, its walls largely constructed by the British after 1759. Visually, it is dominated by the CHÂTEAU FRONTENAC, which stands at the edge of the Upper Town, looking over the St. Lawrence and down on the Lower Town. To the SW, at the upstream end of Cap-Diamant, is the **Québec Bridge** (1917), the world's longest (with an 1800-ft/550-m central span) cantilever bridge. The city has numerous seminaries and other religious and educational institutions; the Université Laval (1852) is now largely in the suburb of Sainte-Foy (SW). The Nordiques (hockey) play at the 15,400-seat Colisée. The **Québec Urban Community** (1970) now comprises fifteen municipalities on the St. Lawrence's North Shore, with a pop. of 490,271, including the cities of BEAUPORT, CAP-ROUGE, CHARLESBOURG, L'ANCIENNE-LORETTE, LORETTEVILLE, SAINTE-FOY, SILLERY, VAL-BÉLAIR, and VANIER. See also: CHÂTEAU FRONTENAC; LOWER TOWN (Basse-Ville); PLAINS OF ABRAHAM; STADACONA; UPPER TOWN (Haute-Ville); VIEUX-QUÉBEC.

Quechee Gorge see under HARTFORD, Vermont.

Queen Anne Hill residential district of SEATTLE, Washington, 3 mi/5 km NNW of Downtown, on the highest ground in the city, the site of some of Seattle's older houses.

Queen Charlotte Islands NNW–SSE oriented archipelago, 170 mi/275 km long, of some 150 Pacific Ocean islands in W British Columbia. Totaling c.3700 sq mi/9600 sq km, they are surrounded by the DIXON ENTRANCE (N), HECATE STRAIT (E), and Queen Charlotte Sound (S). The homeland of the Haida, they are wooded and mountainous (their W backbone is part of the COAST RANGES), with a rain forest climate in parts and many plant and animal subspecies found only here. Graham (N), the largest (almost 2500 sq mi/6450 sq km), is the site of Masset (pop. 1476), the largest village, which has roughly half the islands' pop. Moresby I. (990 sq mi/2565 sq km), S of Graham, is occupied in part by the South Moresby National Park Reserve (est. 1988). Forest, island, and marine wildlife and Haida sites and artifacts (esp. totem poles) draw visitors to islands formerly important for logging and mining.

Queen Charlotte Sound 140 mi/230 km–long, NW–SE oriented inlet of the Pacific Ocean between the Queen Charlotte Is. (NW) and Vancouver I. (SE), in W British Columbia. The INSIDE PASSAGE winds among the many coastal islands along the mainland (E). The sound merges with Hecate Strait (N) and narrows (SE) to form 60 mi/100 km–long **Queen Charlotte Strait;** the strait continues SE, connecting, via Johnstone Strait, with the Strait of GEORGIA.

Queen Elizabeth Islands name given in 1953 to all islands in the ARCTIC ARCHIPELAGO of the Northwest Territories lying N of about 74° N, where the Parry Channel—comprising (E–W) Lancaster Sound, Barrow Strait, Viscount Melville Sound, and McClure Strait—separates them from the rest of the archipelago. The Queen Elizabeths, formerly called the Parry Is., form a rough triangle some 750 mi/1200 km SW–NE, 600 mi/1000 km N–S, and 675 mi/1100 km E–W, with a total land area of some 164,000 sq mi/475,000 sq km. About 20% permanently ice-covered, they consist of sedimentary rocks newer than the Canadian Shield, folded in the N, on ELLESMERE I., to heights over 8000 ft/2430 m. They receive little precipitation, and have limited animal and plant life. Ellesmere I. (NE) is by far the largest; DEVON I. (SE), Cornwallis I. (S), and the PARRY Is. (SW) and SVERDRUP Is. (C) are other constitutents. INUIT occupation in the Queen Elizabeths is relatively recent; Grise Fiord, on Ellesmere, and Resolute, on Cornwallis, are the main settlements. There are radar and weather stations, including ALERT, and exploration for gas and oil has increased in recent years; commercially valuable minerals are thought to be limited.

Queen Mary see under LONG BEACH, California.

Queens largest (109 sq mi/283 sq km) and second most populous (1,951,598) of NEW YORK CITY's five boroughs, coextensive with **Queens Co.,** on the NW end of Long Island, bordering Brooklyn (SW and W) and Nassau Co. (E). The EAST R. and LONG ISLAND SOUND lie on its N, JAMAICA BAY and the Atlantic Ocean on the S. It is the heartland of single- and two-family housing in the city, and is rated the most racially diverse US county. The home of the Rockaway tribe, it was first settled by the Dutch in the 1630s, in the Newtown area (W). In the 1640s, English groups settled Flushing and Jamaica (E), and religious dissenters from New England also arrived. Controlled by the British after 1664, Queens Co., which included parts of modern Nassau Co., was organized in 1683, taking its name from Catherine de Braganza, wife of Charles II. For the next two centuries, it remained largely an agricultural district, with small inland villages connected by farm-to-market roads, and some industrial and port development around the edges. After the American Revolution, many LOYALIST inhabitants left for Newfoundland. In the late 19th century, coastal resorts began to develop (N and S), and railroads began to bring new residents. In 1898, parts of the county decided not to remain with the new city borough, and joined NASSAU Co. The borough of Queens had a pop. of 152,999 in 1900. In 1900–10, Queens was linked to Manhattan by the Queensborough (59th Street) Bridge and by LONG ISLAND RAIL ROAD tunnels, and a real estate boom began. Rapid transit systems spread through the borough in the 1910s. In 1930, the pop. had reached 1,079,129, and much former farmland had disappeared beneath new housing. In the 1930s the TRIBOROUGH and BRONX-WHITESTONE (opened for the 1939 World's Fair in Flushing Meadows) bridges and Queens-Midtown Tunnel further connected Queens with the rest of the city. After World War II, there was another housing boom. The THROGS NECK Bridge, to the Bronx, was opened (1961) just before a second World's Fair (1964). Queens today is a borough of neighborhoods, a few inner-city, some quite suburban. Its tremendous diversity is seen even within such discrete areas as Flushing and Jackson Heights. Numerous highways cross the borough, connecting Long Island with the rest of the country and Long Island's SOUTH SHORE with the NORTH SHORE. Two of New York's three major airports, LA GUARDIA and JOHN F. KENNEDY, are also here, and the Jamaica facility of the Long Island Rail Road is the busiest US passenger rail junction. Saint John's University (1870), Queens College (1937), and several city and county campuses are here. The Aqueduct (horse racing), National Tennis Center, and Shea Stadium (home to the baseball New York Mets) are among sports facilities. See also: ASTORIA; BAYSIDE; BELLEROSE; CORONA; DOUGLASTON; ELMHURST; FLUSHING; FLUSHING MEADOWS–CORONA PARK; FOREST HILLS; FRESH MEAD-

OWS; HOLLIS; HOWARD BEACH; HUNTERS POINT; JACKSON HEIGHTS; JAMAICA; KEW GARDENS; LONG ISLAND CITY; MASPETH; NEWTOWN; OZONE PARK; RICHMOND HILL; ROCKAWAYS; SAINT ALBANS; SHEA STADIUM; STEINWAY; SUNNYSIDE; UTOPIA; WHITESTONE; WOODHAVEN; WOODSIDE.

Queen's Park neighborhood and park 1 mi/2 km NNW of downtown TORONTO, Ontario, just S of Yorkville. The Ontario Parliament (itself called Queen's Park by locals) and other government buildings here adjoin (S) the main campus (largely early-20th-century) of the University of Toronto and the noted Royal Ontario Museum (1914).

Queenston residential community, now part of NIAGARA-ON-THE-LAKE, Ontario, on the Niagara R., 4 mi/6 km N of Niagara Falls. At the foot of the Niagara Escarpment, it is a hydroelectric power center. On Oct. 13, 1812, the escarpment above the village, QUEENSTON HEIGHTS, was briefly seized by American troops invading Canada. The heights were retaken by the British when New York militia refused to cross the border to reinforce the salient. A monument to British general Isaac Brock, who died in the battle, is here. Queenston is also the site of the house where, in June 1813, Laura Secord overheard occupying Americans planning an attack; from here she walked through the night to Beaver Dams in THOROLD to warn British troops.

Queen Street E–W thoroughfare in TORONTO, Ontario, extending from the Scarborough city line (E) to near High Park (W), where it becomes the Queensway. As Lot St. it was York's (Toronto's) original N boundary. Today it passes many of the city's important sites, including (from the YONGE St. intersection W) the Eaton Centre, the old (1892) City Hall, Nathan Phillips Square and the new City Hall, and Osgoode Hall (19th-century law buildings). To the W is the area called **Queen St. West,** now well-known as a bohemian and fashionable "village."

Queen Village residential neighborhood in Philadelphia, Pennsylvania, immediately S of SOCIETY HILL and SOUTH STREET. One of the city's most historic areas, it was a Dutch and Swedish settlement long before the arrival of William Penn. Later home to poor immigrants, it is today an affluent enclave of young professionals.

Quesnel town, pop. 8179, Cariboo Regional District, SC British Columbia, at the confluence of the Quesnel and Fraser rivers, 262 mi/422 km NNE of Vancouver and 65 mi/105 km S of Prince George. On the CARIBOO Road, it developed during the 1860s Cariboo gold rush. Industries include plywood manufacturing, lumbering, mining, and agriculture. BARKERVILLE is 40 mi/64 km E.

Quetico Provincial Park 1837 sq mi/4758 sq km, in W Ontario, 80 mi/130 km W of Thunder Bay, N of the Rainy R. Like Minnesota's BOUNDARY WATERS CANOE AREA, adjacent to the S, it is noted for its canoe routes and hiking trails.

Quidi Vidi Lake see under SAINT JOHN'S, Newfoundland.

Quinault River 75 mi/120 km long, in W Washington, rising SE of Mt. Olympus, in Olympic National Park, and flowing SW through the 325–sq mi/842–sq km **Quinault Indian Reservation** (pop. 1216) to the Pacific Ocean. Within the park, the river valley is filled with massive old-growth trees, and is part of the Quinault Rain Forest.

Quincy 1. city, pop. 39,681, seat of Adams Co., WC Illinois, on the Mississippi R. and the Missouri border, 95 mi/153 km W of Springfield. It is the trading and distribution center for an agricultural and livestock region. Manufacturing is prominent in the local economy; important industries produce metal wheels, compressors, agricultural equipment, and truck and tractor bodies. Settled in 1822 as Bluffs, Quincy boomed as a steamboat port and as a stopping point for westbound pioneers, becoming the second-largest city in the state by 1840. Mormons found refuge here in 1838–39. The sixth Lincoln-Douglas debate was held (1858) in Quincy. Industrial development grew with the decline in steamboat traffic during the late 19th century. Many historic buildings including the Governor John Wood Mansion and riverfront estates are preserved in the city. Gem City College (1870) and Quincy College (1860) are here, as is the Quincy National Cemetery. **2.** city, pop. 84,985, Norfolk Co., E Massachusetts, on Boston Harbor across the Neponset R. from SE Boston. Quincy was originally (1625) a trading post at Mount Wollaston (now an included section), known as Merry Mount because of its perceived bacchanalian temper; its proprietor, Thomas Morton, was run out of the colony for celebrating May Day, then considered a pagan festival. Four generations of Adamses occupied what is now the Adams National Historic Site. An early commercial ironworks was in Quincy, and granite from local quarries became famous in the 1750s. In the 1880s the city became a shipbuilding center; it was a major builder of naval and other vessels until the 1980s. Current industries include printing, publishing, and the manufacture of machinery, electronics, plastics, transportation equipment, and soap products. Quincy's neighborhoods include Squantum, on a peninsula to the N; Norfolk Downs; South Quincy; Wollaston (with Merrymount Park); and Adams Shore, Houghs Neck, and Germantown, on another peninsula in the SE. Eastern Nazarene College (1900) and Quincy College (1956) are in the city.

Quincy Market group of commercial buildings just E of Government Center and Faneuil Hall, in downtown Boston, Massachusetts. Built in 1825–26 under the aegis of Mayor Josiah Quincy, they replaced the Town Dock. The 555 ft/169 m–long granite central market building is flanked by matching warehouses. The group and surroundings were renovated in the late 1970s and are now one of New England's leading tourist attractions, also called Faneuil Hall Marketplace.

Quinebaug River 80 mi/129 km long, in Massachusetts and Connecticut. It rises just N of the Connecticut-Massachusetts border in Sturbridge, and flows through Southbridge, then generally S through Connecticut, passing Putnam (Cargill Falls), Danielson, Plainfield, and Jewett City, to join the Shetucket R. at Norwich.

Quinnipiac River 50 mi/80 km long, in C Connecticut. It rises in Plainville and flows generally S through Southington, Meriden, Wallingford, and North Haven, bisecting New Haven, and entering Long Island Sound at New Haven Harbor.

Quinsigamond, Lake in C Massachusetts, forming much of the E edge of the city of Worcester. This narrow, 7 mi/11 km–long lake, lined in part with waterside homes, is a noted site for rowing races.

Quitman city, pop. 1684, seat of Wood Co., NE Texas, 75 mi/120 km E of Dallas. An agricultural and oil center (the Quitman Oilfield was opened in 1942), it was the 1870s home of James S. Hogg, who edited a newspaper in 1873 and went on to become governor (1891–95) and the head of a Texas political dynasty.

Quitman Mountains NW–SE range in far W Texas, extending from W of the community of Sierra Blanca (Hudspeth Co.) to the Rio Grande. Rising to 6687 ft/2040 m, it has been mined for sphalerite (zinc).

Quivira also, **Gran Quivira** legendary land or city sought by Francisco de Coronado in the 1540–42 expedition that had already disproved stories of CIBOLA. Sketchy accounts led the expedition E from New Mexico through the Texas Panhandle, N through Oklahoma, and into Kansas. "Quivira" was discovered to be not a wealthy city but a collection of Wichita villages along the Arkansas R. near the site of GREAT BEND. The legend did not die there, however; various other "real" Quiviras have been claimed. These include the vicinity of Glazier, near the Canadian R., 50 mi/80 km NE of Amarillo, Texas; the area around Junction City, Kansas; and the Republican R. valley in Nebraska. Salinas Pueblo Missions National Monument, in C New Mexico, was called Gran Quivira National Monument from 1909 to 1980, although without apparent connection to the legend. Quivira National Wildlife Refuge occupies some 22,000 ac/8900 ha along the Rattlesnake R. SE of Great Bend, Kansas, not far from the site of Coronado's "discovery."

Quoddy Bay see PASSAMAQUODDY BAY.

Quogue village, pop. 898, in Southampton town, Suffolk Co., SE New York, on Long Island's SOUTH FORK. It is an affluent resort community, part of the HAMPTONS.

Quonset Point peninsula in North Kingstown township, Washington Co., SC Rhode Island, on the W shore of Narragansett Bay. Once a resort area, it is the site of a naval air station, a naval construction center at which the quonset hut was developed, and a major General Dynamics facility connected with the Electric Boat shipyard in Groton, Connecticut.

R

Rabun Bald peak (4696 ft/1432 m) of the Blue Ridge Mts., E of the resort community of **Rabun Gap,** in the NE corner of Georgia, near the North Carolina border. Rabun Gap, on the Little Tennessee R., has been noted as the seat of the pioneering (1920) Nacoochee School, an adult literacy center, and more recently as the home of the student-produced *Foxfire* magazine (begun 1967) and books.

Raccoon Creek 100 mi/160 km long, in S Ohio. It rises in Hocking Co., and flows generally S, through Zaleski State Forest and other rural areas, to the Ohio R., 7 mi/11 km S of Gallipolis. The Little Raccoon is its main tributary.

Raccoon Mountains see SAND Mt., Georgia.

Raccoon River 200 mi/320 km long, in C Iowa. It rises in NE Buena Vista Co., and flows generally SE to join the Des Moines R. at Des Moines. The **South Raccoon** R. (50 mi/80 km long), rises in NW Guthrie Co., and flows SE to join the main river near VAN METER. The **Middle Raccoon** R. (75 mi/121 km long) rises in NW Carroll Co., and flows to the South Raccoon R. near Redfield.

Race, Cape headland at the SE tip of the AVALON PENINSULA, the SE extremity of Newfoundland, 65 mi/105 km SSW of St. John's. It is a traditional reference point for ocean locations.

Race Point headland at the tip of CAPE COD, in Provincetown, Barnstable Co., SE Massachusetts. Race Point Lighthouse marks the entrance to Cape Cod Bay.

Racine city, pop. 84,298, seat of Racine Co., SE Wisconsin, on L. Michigan at the mouth of the Root R., 25 mi/40 km S of Milwaukee. A trade center for the surrounding agricultural region, it was founded in 1834. A threshing machine plant, established here by Jerome I. Case in 1842, was the West's first farm machinery factory. Today, the production of agricultural machinery continues in this highly industrialized city. Racine also manufactures books, steel castings, and various auto parts and accessories. The Johnson Wax Company, which produces waxes, polishes, and other household goods, is important to the local economy; its buildings, designed by Frank Lloyd Wright, are among the architect's outstanding works.

Racine County 335 sq mi/868 sq km, pop. 175,034, in SE Wisconsin. Its seat is RACINE. Traversed by the Fox and Root rivers, it is mainly agricultural. Dairy items, livestock, vegetables, corn, and oats are produced. There is substantial manufacturing at Racine and Burlington. The county also contains a number of lake resorts.

Radburn residential community, part of FAIR LAWN, Bergen Co., NE New Jersey. It was designed (1928) by urban planners who modeled it on England's New Towns. The plan utilizes "superblocks" with parks in their centers, and a series of meandering streets, cul-de-sacs, and pathways; schools and other institutions are integrated into the community.

Radcliff city, pop. 19,772, Hardin Co., WC Kentucky, on the SW edge of the FORT KNOX military reservation, for which it is largely a service community.

Radford independent city, pop. 15,940, in but administratively separate from Montgomery Co., W Virginia, 12 mi/19 km SE of Blacksburg, on the New R. It is the seat of Radford University (1910), and has various manufactures. The Radford Army Ammunition Plant is 5 mi/8 km NNE.

Radio City see under ROCKEFELLER CENTER, New York City.

Radium Springs see under ALBANY, Georgia.

Radnor township, pop. 28,703, Delaware Co., SE Pennsylvania, 12 mi/19 km W of Philadelphia. A residential and commercial MAIN LINE suburb, it has long been corporate home to the Sun Oil Company, and is the seat of Cabrini College (1957) and Eastern College (1952), in the Saint Davids section, and of Villanova University (1842), in the VILLANOVA section. Valley Forge Military College (1938) is in Wayne, on the border with Tredyffrin township (NW).

Rahway city, pop. 25,325, Union Co., NE New Jersey, on the Rahway R., 6 mi/10 km SW of Elizabeth. Settled in the early 18th century as a part of Elizabethtown, it was the scene of several skirmishes during the Revolution. The manufacture of pharmaceuticals, one of the city's oldest industries, continues to be one of its most important; Merck headquarters are here. Other products include soap and soap dispensers, automobile parts, batteries, chemicals, and vacuum cleaners. A Revolutionary cemetery is here, and a state prison farm.

Rahway River 30 mi/50 km long, in NE New Jersey. It rises in the Oranges, Essex Co., flows S to Rahway, and continues E to the ARTHUR KILL, between Carteret (S) and Linden (N).

Rainbow Bridge National Monument see under L. POWELL, Utah.

Rainier, Mount Washington's and the CASCADE RANGE's highest peak, noted for its beauty and 14,410 ft/4392 m tall, in Pierce Co., SW Washington, 40 mi/65 km SE of Tacoma. A young, snow-capped volcano, it occupies about one-fourth of 235,400-ac/95,300-ha (368–sq mi/953–sq km) **Mt. Rainier National Park.** With 26 glaciers covering 40 sq mi/104 sq km, Rainier has one of the largest single-peak glacier systems in the US. Formed by explosions, including one that blew off its summit 2000 years ago, the mountain continues to steam. It was first climbed in 1870.

Rainy River 50 mi/80 km long, in N Minnesota and SW Ontario. It rises in Rainy L. and flows NW along the international border, passing International Falls and Baudette and emptying into the LAKE OF THE WOODS. At International Falls the river is dammed to produce power, and it is also used for logging and fishing. **Rainy Lake,** which lies partly in Koochiching and St. Louis counties, Minnesota, and partly in the Rainy River District of Ontario, is 50 mi/80 km long; 35 mi/56 km of it runs along the international line. The lake is filled with many small islands, has numerous peninsulas and bays, and borders a densely forested area. It is continuous with Namakan L. in its SE corner, and its W outlet flows into the Rainy R. The river and lake are so named because Indians said it "rained all the time," referring to the mist surrounding the waterfall where the lake empties into the river.

Raisin River also, **River Raisin** 115 mi/185 km long, in SE Michigan. It is formed by the confluence of several streams along the Jackson-Washtenaw county line, SE of Jackson, and flows generally ESE to enter L. Erie at MONROE. The battle of the River Raisin, at which US troops were massacred, occurred at Monroe in Jan. 1813.

Rajneeshpuram former religious community, in Wasco and Jefferson counties, near Antelope, 110 mi/180 km ESE of Portland, in NC Oregon, founded in 1983 by Bhagwan Shree Rajneesh, an Indian religious teacher with a multinational following. Having acquired one of the largest ranches in the region, the group encountered local hostility and antagonized community and state officials. Within a few years, Bhagwan was deported and Rajneeshpuram broke up.

Raleigh **1.** city, pop. 207,951, state capital and seat of Wake Co., EC North Carolina, 20 mi/32 km SE of Durham and 50 mi/80 km S of the Virginia line. The site was chosen in 1788, following the Revolution, when North Carolina and other states moved their capitals inland (NEW BERN was the capital until 1792). The first capitol, completed in 1794, was destroyed by fire in 1831. The second capitol (1840) is a noted example of Greek Revival architecture. On April 13, 1865, the city, which had been a Confederate troop gathering point, surrendered to William Tecumseh Sherman. Industrialization began with late-19th-century textile mills, but did not accelerate until World War II, then boomed with the development, in the 1960s, of the RESEARCH TRIANGLE just NW. Raleigh is now, in addition to its governmental role, a retail and wholesale center for E North Carolina. Its manufactures include electronic equipment, textiles, processed foods, and computers. It is home to North Carolina State University (1887), St. Mary's College (1842), Shaw University (1865), St. Augustine's College (1867), Meredith College (1891), and Peace College (1857). **2.** residential section of Memphis, Tennessee, 9 mi/14 km NE of Downtown and just W of BARTLETT. It is on the site of a former summer resort long (1850s–1920s) favored for such amenities as springs, horseracing, and swimming on the WOLF R.

Raleigh Bay bight of the Atlantic Ocean between Cape HATTERAS (NE) and Cape LOOKOUT (SW), off Hatteras, Ocracoke, Portsmouth, and Core Banks islands (the OUTER BANKS), E North Carolina. PAMLICO SOUND lies NW of the barrier islands.

Ralston **1.** see under SUFFIELD, Alberta. **2.** city, pop. 6236, Douglas Co., EC Nebraska, 5 mi/8 km SW of Omaha. An affluent suburb, it also manufactures rubber products and has agriculture-related businesses.

Ramapo Mountains Appalachian Mt. range, running NE–SW between Rockland Co., SE New York, and NE New Jersey; they reach 1164 ft/355 m. Their wooded slopes and rocky cliffs are the site of several state forests and parks; immediately SE are heavily settled outer New York suburbs. The Ramapos were an important iron producer in the 18th century.

Ramapo River 32 mi/52 km long, in New York and New Jersey. It rises N of the Ramapo Mts. in Orange Co., New York, and flows SE through the Ramapos, past Suffern, then continues SW along the SE of the range, through Oakland, into the POMPTON R. at Pompton Lakes.

Ramona Bowl see under HEMET, California.

Rampart Street thoroughfare in DOWNTOWN New Orleans, Louisiana, that marks the upper (NW) boundary of the 1718 VIEUX CARRÉ (French Quarter) and extends into UPTOWN (S) and Downtown (E).

Ramsey **1.** city, pop. 12,408, Anoka Co., SE Minnesota, on the Mississippi R., 23 mi/37 km NW of Minneapolis. One of the outermost suburbs of the Twin Cities, it lies along the Twin Cities–St. Cloud corridor. New commercial development occurred in the 1980s along Route 47 in the E part of the community. The Gateway North Industrial Airport is on its S edge. **2.** borough, pop. 13,228, Bergen Co., NE New Jersey, 10 mi/16 km N of Paterson and just S of the New York border. It was settled in the mid 19th century, and is now essentially a bedroom community for the New York metropolitan area. A skiing area, several small lakes, and dairy farms are nearby.

Ramsey County 154 sq mi/399 sq km, pop. 485,765, in EC Minnesota, E of Minneapolis and bordered by the Mississippi R. (W and S). One of the state's most urbanized counties, it consists mainly of St. Paul, its seat, and suburbs to the N, such as Roseville, Arden Hills, and White Bear Lake. There are many recreational lakes in the NE.

ranchería in California, hut settlement of any of numerous native "tribelets," which usually consisted of 100–200 people. While these groups were seminomadic, they often had a favored site; Spanish MISSIONS were established there, and the locals gradually became "Mission Indians." The term survives today in the names of numerous small reservations. In British Columbia, a **rancherie** is a hut settlement, esp. the central village of an Indian Reserve.

rancho in California, land grant of the Spanish (1769–1822) or esp. the Mexican (1822–46) period, to individuals or families generally in the cattle hide and tallow trade. Following the secularization of the MISSIONS in 1834–36, the number of these grants increased, and claimants often used them to raise former mission cattle. After the American takeover of California in 1846, and esp. during the 1849–50s gold rush, many ranchos were squatted on or bought by newcomers; while most were broken up for settlement, some large holdings have survived in transmuted form as elements in today's agribusiness. The term survives in numerous place names.

Rancho Bernardo residential and resort section of SAN DIEGO, California, 20 mi/32 km NNE of Downtown and just S of Escondido. A planned community developed from the 1960s, it is noted for its Mediterranean-style housing and its golf and tennis facilities.

Rancho Cordova unincorporated residential community, pop.

48,731, Sacramento Co., NC California, on the American R., 9 mi/14 km ENE of Sacramento. Mather Air Force Base, immediately S, is an important employer, and there are environmental engineering and other high-tech firms.

Rancho Cucamonga popularly, **Cucamonga** city, pop. 101,409, San Bernardino Co., SW California, just S of the San Gabriel Mts., 13 mi/21 km W of San Bernardino and 40 mi/64 km E of Los Angeles. **Cucamonga Peak** (8911 ft/2718 m) stands above it, 7 mi/11 km N, in the Cucamonga Wilderness. The historic center of a grape and olive growing and winemaking region, the city now has a variety of health- and defense-related industries, and is a fast-growing residential suburb. Chaffey Community College (1883) is here. The Indian name means "sandy place."

Rancho Mirage city, pop. 9778, Riverside Co., SW California, a posh residential and desert resort community in the Coachella Valley, 7 mi/11 km SE of Palm Springs.

Rancho Palos Verdes city, pop. 41,659, Los Angeles Co., SW California, on the Palos Verdes Peninsula and the Pacific Ocean, 20 mi/32 km SSW of downtown Los Angeles. It is an affluent residential community in the Palos Verdes Hills. Marymount College (1933) is here.

Rancho Santa Fe residential area of San Diego Co., SW California, on the San Dieguito R., 18 mi/29 km N of San Diego and just NE of Solana Beach. Hollywood celebrities have lived here since the 1920s, in a hilly region known for its horse farms.

Ranchos de Taos see under TAOS, New Mexico.

Rancho Seco locality in Sacramento Co., NE California, 25 mi/40 km SE of SACRAMENTO, near the W foothills of the Sierra Nevada, the site of a controversial nuclear power plant, operational 1974–89, and a recreational lake.

Rancocas Creek 30 mi/50 km long, in SW New Jersey. Its **North Branch** rises E of BROWNS MILLS; flowing through Mirror L., and continues W and NW to MOUNT HOLLY, then to the Delaware R. at Riverside. Its main tributary, the **South Branch,** 15 mi/24 km long, joins it W of Mount Holly. The Rancocas is navigable 9 mi/14 km from the Delaware.

Randall's Island 194 ac/79 ha, between the East and Harlem rivers, New York City. It is part of the borough of Manhattan. Randall's I. was originally separated from WARD's I., to its S, by the Little Hell Gate channel, but landfill has now closed the gap. The Bronx Kill separates its N shore from MOTT HAVEN, the Bronx. With Downing Stadium and other facilities, Randall's I. is today an important recreational center for the city's working class. Three sections of the TRIBOROUGH BRIDGE roadway pass over and meet above it.

Randallstown unincorporated village, pop. 26,277, Baltimore Co., C Maryland, 11 mi/18 km NW of Baltimore. It is an affluent, largely residential suburb just SW of OWINGS MILL.

Randolph **1.** town, pop. 30,093, Norfolk Co., E Massachusetts. It is an industrial, commercial, and residential suburb 14 mi/23 km S of Boston. A 19th-century shoe manufacturing center, Randolph, now just outside ROUTE 128, produces paper boxes, business machines, and rubber footwear. Mary E. Wilkins Freeman, born here in 1852, wrote many short stories set in the community. **2.** town, pop. 4764, Orange Co., C Vermont, on the White R., 24 mi/39 km S of Montpelier. It is at the center of a farming and dairying region. The Morgan horse, Vermont's state animal, was first bred in Randolph, c.1800. The town was ravaged by a series of fires in 1992. Vermont Technical College is in Randolph Center.

Randolph Air Force Base in Bexar Co., SC Texas, 15 mi/24 km NE of downtown San Antonio, adjoining CONVERSE (W) and UNIVERSAL CITY (NW). Headquarters for the Air Training Command for pilots, it opened in 1930, and was called the "West Point of the Air" in the World War II–Korean War period. Randolph also houses the Air Force Records Center.

Rangeley Lakes group of stream-linked resort lakes, W Maine, close to the New Hampshire border, including Rangeley, Mooselookmeguntic, Upper Richardson, Lower Richardson, Cupsuptic, Aziscohos, and Umbagog, which lies partly in New Hampshire. The MAHOOSUC RANGE is S of these lakes, which lie at altitudes of around 1500 ft/450 m. The area was named for Squire Rangeley, an English industrialist who arrived here in 1825, established an estate, and gave much of the land to settlers.

Rankin Inlet hamlet, pop. 1706, Keewatin Region, S Northwest Territories, on the NW shore of HUDSON BAY, 290 mi/470 km NNE of Churchill, Manitoba. An INUIT community in an area used by 19th-century whalers, it had a 1957–62 nickel-mining boom; some copper was also extracted nearby.

Rantoul village, pop. 17,212, Champaign Co., EC Illinois, 13 mi/21 km NNE of Champaign. A trading center for an agricultural region, it also manufactures electronic and motorcycle parts, bicycle helmets, doors and windows, and phone equipment. CHANUTE FIELD is one of the oldest and largest technical training centers of the US Air Force. The first American settler built a cabin in the area in 1848, but Rantoul really dates from 1854, when the ILLINOIS CENTRAL Railroad established a station here.

Rapidan River 90 mi/140 km long, in E Virginia. It rises near Big Rock Falls, in the Blue Ridge, in Madison Co., and flows S, NE, and E across the Piedmont to the area of GERMANNA, where Wilderness Run joins it from the S. It then continues E to a point 9 mi/14 km NW of Fredericksburg, where it joins the RAPPAHANNOCK R.

Rapid City city, pop. 54,523, seat of Pennington Co., SW South Dakota, in the Black Hills, 140 mi/225 km W of Pierre. Tourism is vital to the local economy. Mt. RUSHMORE is 15 mi/24 km SW of the city; also nearby are Dinosaur Park, the CRAZY HORSE MEMORIAL, CUSTER STATE PARK, and Rockerville, a rebuilt ghost town. Range Days, an annual event, is celebrated with a carnival and rodeo. The Sioux Indian and Minnilusa Pioneer museums, South Dakota School of Mines and Technology (1885), and National College (1941) are here. ELLSWORTH AIR FORCE BASE is nearby, and is an important employer. Rapid City is also a commercial, processing, and distribution center for the surrounding agricultural and livestock raising area. The manufacture of computer components, mobile homes, and cement products are among local industries. Rapid Creek flows through the city; flooding in 1972 killed more than 200 people.

Rappahannock River 212 mi/341 km long, in Virginia. It rises in the Blue Ridge Mts., 5 mi/8 km SE of Front Royal, near Chester Gap. It flows SE through the PIEDMONT, and receives the RAPIDAN R. 8 mi/13 km NW of FREDERICKSBURG, the head of navigation. South of Fredericksburg the Rappahannock forms the S boundary of the NORTHERN NECK. It widens gradually and is estuarial for its last 50 mi/80 km. Marshy and rural, it is bridged at PORT CONWAY–Port Royal, at Tappahannock, and at its mouth (the Robert O. Norris, Jr. Bridge).

In its lower reaches, in the TIDEWATER, the river valley was important in 17th-century European settlement, and earlier had been part of the homeland of the Powhatan Confederacy.

Raquette River 140 mi/225 km long, in N New York. It issues from Raquette L. in Hamilton Co., in the Adirondacks 55 mi/89 km NE of Utica. It flows NE through Forked L. and Long L., then generally NW through Franklin Co., through Tupper L., and into St. Lawrence Co. It continues NW past POTSDAM, N and NE to MASSENA, and ENE into the St. Lawrence R. at the Saint Regis Mohawk reservation.

Raritan Bay W reach of Lower NEW YORK BAY, at the mouth of the RARITAN R., in NE New Jersey and SE New York. The bay also receives the ARTHUR KILL, connecting it to Newark Bay and PORT NEWARK, on the N. Staten I., New York, lies N, and the city of PERTH AMBOY, New Jersey, lies at the W end. The triangular-shaped bay has a dredged, deepwater shipping channel.

Raritan River 35 mi/56 km long, in C New Jersey. It is formed W of Raritan, Somerset Co., by the **North Branch,** c.25 mi/40 km long, which rises in Mendham, Morris Co., and the **South Branch,** c.50 mi/80 km long, which rises at Budd L., in W Morris Co. and flows in a wide arc S, W, then E. The Raritan flows generally SE, past Somerville, Manville, Bound Brook, and Middlesex, to NEW BRUNSWICK, the head of navigation, and then between Perth Amboy and South Amboy, into RARITAN BAY. Formerly of great importance as a freight route, the river carried coal, refined metals, brick, sand, and clay products.

Rat Islands group in the W ALEUTIAN Is., between the Bering Sea (N) and the N Pacific Ocean, in SW Alaska. Some 110 mi/180 km E–W, they are flanked by the ANDREANOF Is. (E) and NEAR Is. (W). The chief islands in the group are AMCHITKA, KISKA, and Semisopochnoi. Strategically important since World War II, the Rats are the site of military bases, and have been used for underground nuclear testing. They are also important as wildlife refuges.

Raton city, pop. 7372, seat of Colfax Co., NE New Mexico, in the Raton Mts., on Interstate 25, just S of the Colorado border and 120 mi/193 km NE of Santa Fe. **Raton Pass** (7834 ft/2388 m), just N, was the most imposing physical barrier on the SANTA FE TRAIL; in 1879 the Santa Fe Railroad built through it. In the early 20th century coal mining and railroading provided the city's economic base. Now it is a resort, highway town, and trade center for grain and wood producers. Coal and molybdenum are mined nearby. CAPULIN Mt. is ESE.

Ravenna city, pop. 12,069, seat of Portage Co., NE Ohio, 15 mi/24 km NE of Akron. Situated in a lake-dotted agricultural region, it was founded in 1799. Rubber, electric, and plastic products are manufactured here. A large US arsenal is NE of the city.

Ravenswood 1. residential neighborhood on the NORTH SIDE of Chicago, Illinois. A 1920s development of modest bungalows for the middle class, it has become home to young professionals priced out of trendier areas closer to L. Michigan. **2.** see under LONG ISLAND CITY, New York. **3.** city, pop. 4189, Jackson Co., NW West Virginia, on the Ohio R., 26 mi/42 km SW of Parkersburg. In an agricultural area, it has various light industries and a large aluminum rolling mill.

Rawlins city, pop. 9380, seat of Carbon Co., SC Wyoming, on I-80 just E of the RED DESERT and the Continental Divide, 94 mi/151 km WNW of Laramie. Founded in 1868, it has been a railroad division point and ranching and mining (and rockhounding) trade center. In the 1970s–80s it had oil and coal booms. Its old (1901–81) state prison is a tourist attraction; the new state penitentiary is just S.

Ray Hubbard, Lake see under TRINITY R., Texas.

Raymond 1. town, pop. 3130, S Alberta, 18 mi/29 km SE of Lethbridge. Its economy is dominated by a beet sugar factory and the production of honey. Many residents commute to Lethbridge to work. Originally a Mormon settlement, the town also has residents of Japanese ancestry who were forcibly relocated to the area during World War II. Canada's first rodeo was held here in 1903. **2.** town, pop. 2275, co-seat (with Jackson) of Hinds Co., WC Mississippi, 13 mi/21 km WSW of downtown Jackson, on the NATCHEZ TRACE. During the 1863 Vicksburg Campaign, after Confederate defeats at PORT GIBSON and GRAND GULF, it was the scene of another victory for U.S. Grant's army (May 12). The town remains an agricultural trade center; it is also a residential suburb of Jackson. It is the seat of Hinds Community College (1917).

Raymondville city, pop. 8880, seat of Willacy Co., extreme S Texas, 43 mi/69 km NW of Brownsville. It is a trade and shipping center for irrigated Lower Rio Grande Valley crops (citrus, vegetables, onions, cotton). Tourism and oil are also important.

Rayne city, pop. 8502, Acadia Parish, S Louisiana, 6 mi/10 km W of Lafayette. Rice, cotton, sugar, and other crops are raised in the area, along with frogs, and there are oil wells.

Ray Roberts, Lake see under TRINITY R., Texas.

Rayside-Balfour see under SUDBURY, Ontario.

Raystown Lake also, **Raystown Reservoir** in SC Pennsylvania, created by damming the Raystown Branch of the Juniata R. It is approximately 25 mi/40 km in length, making it the largest lake wholly in the state. It is a popular recreational site.

Raytown city, pop. 30,601, Jackson Co., W Missouri, 9 mi/14 km SE of downtown Kansas City. In the late 19th century it was the first stopping point on the SANTA FE TRAIL leading from INDEPENDENCE to the West. Completely surrounded by the Kansas City metropolitan area, it is now a populous residential suburb. Near the Blue R. (W), Raytown is also close to Kansas City's SWOPE PARK (W).

Reading 1. town, pop. 22,539, Middlesex Co., NE Massachusetts, on the Aberjona R. and ROUTE 128, 12 mi/19 km N of Boston. In the 19th century, Reading was a center for the manufacture of clocks, shoes, and furniture. Now printing and textiles, along with athletic footwear, are the main industries. The town is largely residential. **2.** city, pop. 12,038, Hamilton Co., SW Ohio, 10 mi/16 km NNE of Cincinnati, of which it is a suburb. Founded in 1798, it is the site of varied light manufacturing industries. **3.** city, pop. 78,380, seat of Berks Co., SE Pennsylvania, on the Schuylkill R., 50 mi/80 km NW of Philadelphia, in a rich agricultural, as well as an industrial, area. Its manufactures include stainless steel, hosiery, auto parts, electronic equipment, pretzels, and textiles; factory outlets attract shoppers from several states. Reading was first settled in 1733 by members of William Penn's family. During the Revolution it was a supply depot for the Continental army; its iron foundries produced ordnance. Nineteenth-century growth was spurred by the construction of canals and railroads and the state's developing iron and steel industry. Reading's suburbs include the boroughs of Wyomissing (pop.

7332), Shillington (pop. 5062), and West Reading (pop. 4142), all SW across the Schuylkill. The Daniel Boone homestead is 7 mi/11 km SE, near Birdsboro. Albright (1856) and Alvernia (1958) colleges are in Reading.

Reading Prong SW extension of the New England Uplands, part of the older APPALACHIAN Mts., across the Hudson R., through New York and New Jersey, to the area of Reading, SE Pennsylvania. Its crystalline Paleozoic rocks are overlaid in places with sandstone. The prong was much in the news in the 1980s when fears were raised regarding high levels of radon, a naturally occurring radioactive gas, found in homes built atop it.

Reading Terminal Market indoor market in Center City, Philadelphia, on Market St., E of City Hall. In 1893, the original Farmers' Market in operation on the site relocated to the train shed of the newly built Reading Railroad terminal.

Readville see under HYDE PARK, Massachusetts.

Redan unincorporated community, pop. 24,376, De Kalb Co., NC Georgia, 18 mi/29 km E of downtown Atlanta, just SE of STONE Mt. It is a residential suburb.

Red Bank **1.** borough, pop. 10,636, Monmouth Co., E New Jersey, on the NAVESINK R., about 5 mi/8 km W of the Atlantic, and 9 mi/14 km NW of Asbury Park. Settled in the mid 17th century and once a shipping hub, it is now a yachting and fishing center, year-round resort, and residential community. It also has manufactures including boats, wood products, electrical equipment, and soft drinks. The Monmouth Arts Center/Count Basie Theater, named in honor of the Red Bank native (b. 1904), is here. **2.** city, pop. 12,322, Hamilton Co., SE Tennessee, a largely residential suburb 5 mi/8 km N of downtown Chattanooga.

Red Bay community, pop. 288, at the extreme SE corner of Labrador, on the N shore of the Strait of BELLE ISLE. It is the site of a Basque whaling colony founded in the 1540s; well-preserved remains of the whaler *San Juan* (1565) and other shipwrecks of the period have been found offshore. The community, named for its prominent red cliffs, today relies on fishing.

Red Bluff city, pop. 12,363, seat of Tehama Co., N California, on the Sacramento R., near the N end of the Sacramento Valley, 39 mi/63 km NW of Chico. It was a busy river port during the 1850s, but declined as irrigation schemes lowered the Sacramento's level in succeeding decades. It is now a market center for agricultural and livestock producers; the lumber and wood industry is also important. Red Bluff, noted for its summer heat, is also a tourist center, gateway to NE California wildernesses; Mt. LASSEN is 50 mi/80 km NE.

Red Cedar River **1.** 45 mi/72 km long, in SC Michigan. It rises SW of Howell, in Livingston Co., and flows NW past Fowlerville, Williamston, and East Lansing, to join the Grand R. at Lansing. It is sometimes called the Cedar R. **2.** see CEDAR R., Minnesota and Iowa.

Red Chamber, the see under PARLIAMENT HILL, Ottawa, Ontario.

Red Clay name variously applied to areas in the PIEDMONT or the Southeast characterized by iron oxide–rich clayey soil. Rapid erosion in hilly areas also lends streams here a reddish appearance. The Red Clay includes parts of C and NW Georgia (including the Atlanta area), Tennessee, Alabama, and Mississippi. Tennessee's **Red Clay State Historic Area,** S of Cleveland, preserves the last council ground of the Cherokee before their 1838 departure on the TRAIL OF TEARS.

Red Cloud city, pop. 1204, seat of Webster Co., S Nebraska, on the Republican R., 35 mi/56 km SSW of Hastings and 6 mi/10 km N of the Kansas border. In an area once hunted by the Omaha, Pawnee, and Oto, it was founded as a white settlement in 1870 and named for the Sioux leader. The city is a processing and shipping hub for grain, livestock, dairy goods, poultry, and produce. It became famous as the model for various communities in the work of novelist Willa Cather (1873–1947), who spent much of her youth here.

Red Deer city, pop. 58,134, C Alberta, on the Red Deer R., midway between Edmonton and Calgary. It is a center for the petroleum industry and for area farms. Manufactures include electric transformers, diamond drills, beer, and dairy and wood products. Scottish settlers came here in 1882, and settlement increased (1885) with the building of nearby Ft. Normandeau by the Canadian military. It was later moved to the Calgary-Edmonton Railway, stimulating an agricultural boom. Further growth occurred after World War II with the discovery of oil and natural gas and the construction of petrochemical plants. The Michener Centre is an institution for the mentally handicapped. Red Deer College (1964) is here.

Red Deer River 385 mi/620 km long, in Alberta. It rises in the Rocky Mts. in BANFF NATIONAL PARK, and flows NE to Red Deer, then SE to DRUMHELLER and DINOSAUR PROVINCIAL PARK, in a BADLANDS area, and E to join the South SASKATCHEWAN R. just over the Saskatchewan border.

Red Desert in the S portion of the GREAT DIVIDE BASIN, E Sweetwater Co., S Wyoming. The Red Desert is part of a break in the Continental Divide. A high, treeless, sagebrush-covered plateau, named for the bricklike color of its soil and lying N of the Delaney Rim, it has traditionally been a sheep and antelope grazing area, and is also home to wild horses and desert elk. Although the town of Red Desert is here, the area has few human inhabitants. Its name is also sometimes used to denote the whole Great Divide Basin.

Redding **1.** city, pop. 66,462, seat of Shasta Co., N California, on the Sacramento R., at the N end of the Sacramento Valley, 65 mi/105 km NNW of Chico. It is the largest California city N of Sacramento. A trade center since the 1850s gold rush, it was incorporated in 1872 when the railroad arrived, and replaced Shasta as county seat in 1888. In the 20th century, commerce, lumbering, and tourism have been central to its economy. Headquarters for the Shasta-Trinity National Forest, Redding is also the gateway to recreational and wilderness areas across N California, in the KLAMATH and CASCADE ranges. Simpson (1921) and Shasta (1948) colleges are here; Shasta, a mining ghost town, is 5 mi/8 km W. **2.** town, pop. 7927, Fairfield Co., SW Connecticut, on the Saugatuck R., 13 mi/21 km NW of Bridgeport. Formerly agricultural, it is now a residential exurb. Its library was a gift from Mark Twain, one of many writers and performers who have made summer or year-round homes here. Putnam Memorial Campground marks General Israel Putnam's campground during the winter of 1778–79.

Redford township, pop. 54,387, Wayne Co., SE Michigan, on the R. Rouge, a residential suburb 13 mi/21 km W of Detroit. It is adjacent to Ladbrokes Detroit Race Course (S).

Red Hill peak in HALEAKALA NATIONAL PARK, E Maui, Hawaii. The highest point on the island and on the extinct Haleakala, it rises to 10,023 ft/3055 m.

Red Hook waterfront section, NW Brooklyn, New York, across Buttermilk Channel from Governor's I., Upper New York Bay. The Gowanus Canal separates Red Hook from the rest of Brooklyn, but its boundaries and those of SOUTH BROOKLYN are variously defined. Red Hook (Dutch, Roode Hoeke, or Red Point) was a spit of land named in the 17th century for the color of its soil. From the 1840s the area was heavily developed, with docks and artificial basins obliterating the original shoreline; it became a major US shipping center, home to maritime unions and to a population of largely Italian dockworkers. It also developed a reputation for corruption and crime; Al Capone's early career centered here. By the 1930s government rehabilitation efforts included large-scale housing development. In an attempt to escape Red Hook's associations, parts came to be known in the 1950s and 1960s as CARROLL GARDENS and COBBLE HILL. Containerization took Red Hook's harbor business to such ports as Newark and Elizabeth, New Jersey, by the 1970s. In the 1990s, Red Hook remained depressed.

Red Indian Lake see under EXPLOITS R., Newfoundland.

Red Lake Minnesota's largest lake, covering about 430 sq mi/1114 sq km, 30 mi/48 km N of Bemidji. A remnant of glacial L. AGASSIZ, it is shallow, and is almost divided into Upper and Lower lakes; a 1.5 mi/2.4 km–wide Narrows connects the two sections. The **Red Lake Indian Reservation** (Ojibwa, pop. 3699) lies largely along its W and S. The **Red Lake River** flows from the lake's SW to THIEF RIVER FALLS, where the Thief R. joins it, then S to Red Lake Falls, SW to Crookston, and W and NW to East Grand Forks, where it enters the Red R. of the North; it is 196 mi/316 km long.

Redland unincorporated residential village, pop. 16,145, Montgomery Co., C Maryland, a suburb on Rock Creek, 18 mi/29 km NW of Washington, D.C.

Redlands city, pop. 60,394, San Bernardino Co., S California, 65 mi/105 km E of Los Angeles and 7 mi/11 km SE of San Bernardino, at the foot of the San Bernardino Mts. Founded in 1881, it became a shipping center for an irrigated citrus growing district where navel oranges were the main crop. A popular resort in the late 19th and early 20th centuries, it retains many elegant mansions from that period. The Redlands Bowl, noted for musical performances, is in Smiley Park. The city is the seat of the University of Redlands (1907). A residential community, it also has manufactures including aerospace and electrical machinery and furniture.

red-light district urban district characterized by the presence of many houses of prostitution. While many have been lawless or uncontrolled waterfront or INNER CITY areas like San Francisco's BARBARY COAST or San Diego's STINGAREE, some, like New Orleans's STORYVILLE, have been legal or officially tolerated.

Red Lion borough, pop. 6130, York Co., S Pennsylvania, 8 mi/13 km SE of York. It manufactures tobacco products and furniture.

Red Lodge city, pop. 1958, seat of Carbon Co., S Montana, 50 mi/80 km SW of Billings, on Rock Creek, E of the Beartooth Range. The 68-mi/109-km Beartooth Highway (1936) runs from here into NW Wyoming. Crow territory to the 1880s, the area was mined heavily for coal into the 1940s. The city is now a resort, noted for its music festival.

Redmond city, pop. 35,800, King Co., WC Washington, at the N end of L. Sammamish, a residential suburb 10 mi/16 km NE of Seattle. Originally a boat landing along a slough between Lakes Washington and Sammamish, it now houses the headquarters of the computer software giant Microsoft, and has various computer and electronic industries and light manufactures.

Red Mountain wooded ridge extending SW–NE from Bessemer through Birmingham and up to Gadsden, C Alabama. Rising c.1000 ft/300 m, it is mined for iron and coal, and also contains red sandstone.

Redondo Beach city, pop. 60,167, Los Angeles Co., SW California, 15 mi/24 km SSW of downtown Los Angeles and adjacent (W) to Torrance, on Santa Monica Bay (the Pacific Ocean). Incorporated in 1892, it boomed in the 1900s as a resort, and is today an affluent community with many elegant homes; its limited industry includes aerospace research and development. King Harbor is a leading private marina. The city's wide, crescent-shaped beach attracts tourists and surfers; fishing and boat tours are also important.

Redoubt Volcano see under LAKE CLARK NATIONAL PARK AND PRESERVE, Alaska.

Red River 1300 mi/2100 km long, in Texas, Oklahoma, Arkansas, and Louisiana. It rises on the LLANO ESTACADO in the N Texas PANHANDLE in several intermittent headstreams. The main headstream, the **Prairie Dog Town Fork,** is formed SW of Amarillo by Palo Duro and Tierra Blanca creeks, and flows generally SE, through PALO DURO CANYON, to where it forms the Oklahoma-Texas border. To the N of Vernon, Texas, it is joined by the **Salt Fork** and then by the **North Fork,** both of which rise in the Texas Panhandle E of Amarillo. Now called simply the Red, it continues E, passing N of Wichita Falls, where it is joined by the WICHITA R. Upstream from Denison, Texas, it flows through dam-created L. TEXOMA, where Oklahoma's WASHITA R. joins it. In SE Oklahoma the Kiamichi R. also joins it. The Red briefly forms the Arkansas-Texas border, passes N of Texarkana, then turns S near Fulton, Arkansas, and enters Louisiana. It continues S and SSE, past Shreveport, Natchitoches, and Alexandria, then winds E across alluvial plain, where the Black (OUACHITA) R. joins it. Some 50 mi/80 km NNW of Baton Rouge, near Torras, the Red forms two DISTRIBUTARIES: The ATCHAFALAYA R. flows SSE to the Gulf of Mexico; the Old River continues a short distance E to the Mississippi R. Although the Red is technically a tributary of the Mississippi, most of its water is discharged through the Atchafalaya, and the Mississippi periodically backs through the Old River into the Atchafalaya. The meeting of the rivers here illustrates the variability in course common in both the lower Mississippi and the Red, which has in places (e.g., at Natchitoches) moved away from what were riverfront settlements. Fulton, Arkansas, is the normal head of navigation, but most of the river's traffic is below Shreveport. The upper river cuts through deep canyons, but along the Texas-Oklahoma border, it flows through rich red clay ranch and farm lands. In the lower course are many OXBOWS and BAYOUS. In the 1830s the Great Raft, a natural logjam solidified with silt and debris, which extended some 160 mi/260 km upstream from near Natchitoches, was cleared, allowing upstream navigation. In April 1864, a Union expedition trying to reach Texas up the river was defeated at Sabine Crossroads, near MANSFIELD, Louisiana.

Red River Army Depot see under TEXARKANA, Texas.

Red River of the North 545 mi/877 km long, in North Dakota, Minnesota, and Manitoba. It is formed by the confluence of the Bois de Sioux and Otter Tail rivers at Wahpeton, North

Dakota/Breckenridge, Minnesota, and flows N, forming the North Dakota–Minnesota boundary, past Fargo-Moorhead and Grand Forks, into Manitoba, where it is joined at the Forks, in Winnipeg, by the ASSINIBOINE R. It then discharges (N) into L. Winnipeg. Draining part of the area of the glacial L. AGASSIZ, the Red runs through fertile prairie, now a major wheat growing area. The Sheyenne (from the W) and Red Lake (from the E) rivers join it before it reaches Manitoba. An important fur trade route in the 18th century, the river became the site, in 1812, of the **Red River Colony** (also called Assiniboia) established by the HUDSON'S BAY COMPANY'S governor, Lord Selkirk, as a separate undertaking in this corner of RUPERT'S LAND. After struggles with the NORTH WEST COMPANY and the MÉTIS, and with floods, the colony reverted to the HBC in 1836. In the 1860s, the HBC agreed to relinquish control of its lands; the Métis, fearing that their established settlement in the area would be ignored as the new, anglophone-dominated confederated Canada expanded, began the Red River Rebellion (or Resistance) of 1869–70, which, despite its military failure, led to the establishment of Manitoba.

Red Rock River see under JEFFERSON R., Montana.

Redstone Arsenal see under HUNTSVILLE, Alabama.

Red Wing city, pop. 15,134, seat of Goodhue Co., SE Minnesota, on the Mississippi R., across from Hager City, Wisconsin, and 40 mi/64 km SE of St. Paul. Settled by Scandinavians in 1849, it was named for Dakota leaders who wore the scarlet-dyed wing of a wild swan. One of the nation's largest wheat markets in the late 19th century, the city is known for the pottery and footwear that bears its name. Other products include marine engines and rubber goods. Frontenac State Park is 10 mi/16 km SE and the Richard J. Dorer Memorial Hardwood State Forest lies to the W and S.

Redwood City city, pop. 66,072, seat of San Mateo Co., NC California, on the SW shore of San Francisco. Incorporated in 1868, it was an early Bay Area port and shipbuilding center with lumber mills and tanneries; modern deepwater facilities have fostered growth. The city is a noted producer of cut flowers, especially chrysanthemums. Other industries have included salt extraction from the bay; various manufactures; and, in recent years, computer, biotech, and other technological research and development connected with the industries of SILICON VALLEY, to the S. Canada College (1968) is here.

Redwood National Park 110,000 ac/44,600 ha, along 40 mi/64 km of the NW California coast, between Crescent City (N) and Orick (S). Established in 1968, it incorporates three earlier-established state parks, saltmarshes, and beaches. Its Tall Tree Grove includes the Howard Libby Redwood, at 368 ft/113 m thought to be the world's tallest tree, and other similar coast redwoods. The area was heavily logged from the 1850s through the 1950s; in the 1960s a bitter battle was fought between environmentalists and logging interests over the park's expansion.

Reedley city, pop. 15,791, Fresno Co., C California, on the Kings R., in the San Joaquin Valley, 20 mi/32 km SE of Fresno. An agricultural center, it produces and ships fruits, olive oil, and wine. Kings River Community College (1926) is here. Kings Canyon and Sequoia national parks are 30 mi/48 km E.

Reedsburg city, pop. 5834, Sauk Co., SC Wisconsin, 25 mi/40 km W of Portage. Situated in a timber and agricultural region, it produces dairy items, lumber, and canned foods. It is the site of the Museum of Norman Rockwell Art.

Reelfoot Lake in extreme NW Tennessee, 14 mi/22 km SSE of New Madrid, Missouri. Formed in 1811–12 by shocks of the NEW MADRID Earthquake, it filled with water from the Mississippi R. The lake is roughly hook-shaped, paralleling a bend in the Mississippi (now 4 mi/6 km NE), and 10 mi/16 km SSW–NNE. Lying on the MISSISSIPPI FLYWAY, it is the site of a National Wildlife Refuge and a Wilderness Management Area. The area is popular with hunters. The lake takes its name from a Chickasaw chief of the earthquake period.

Refinery Row see under EDMONTON, Alberta.

Refugio town, pop. 3158, seat of Refugio Co., S Texas, 35 mi/56 km NNE of Corpus Christi, on the Mission R. A commercial center for an oil, cattle, cotton, and grain producing area, it also has some manufactures, and fishing and hunting are important to the economy. In 1795 the Mission Nuestra Señora del Refugio located here. The town, settled around 1830, was fought over both during the Texas Revolution and during the Mexican War. The Aransas National Wildlife Refuge, wintering ground of the endangered whooping crane, is 26 mi/42 km E, on Aransas Bay. Baseball great Nolan Ryan, born (1947) in Refugio, later lived in ALVIN.

Regent Park see under CABBAGETOWN, Toronto, Ontario.

Regina city, pop. 179,178, capital of Saskatchewan, in the S of the province, 103 mi/166 km N of the Montana border, on Wascana Creek, on the site of a frontier settlement called Pile o' Bones. Founded in 1882 on the Canadian Pacific Railway and named in honor of Queen Victoria, it was designated capital of the Northwest Territories, supplanting BATTLEFORD, and subsequently (1905) capital of the newly created province. The city served as headquarters for the Royal Canadian Mounted Police until 1920, and today is the site of its training barracks. Regina is the province's commercial and financial center. Situated in the heart of a rich wheat farming region, it is home to the Saskatchewan Wheat Pool, the world's largest wheat cooperative. Manufactures include steel, chemicals, electrical equipment, beer, leather, dairy products, paint, farm implements, and communications and construction equipment. Oil and potash are refined, and there are railroad shops and packing plants as well. Wascana Centre, built around artificial Wascana L., contains the Legislative Building (1912) and other provincial government offices. Campion College (1917), Luther College (1921), Canadian Bible College (1941), and the University of Regina (1974) are here. The QU'APPELLE R. Valley is to the N.

region any of several variously defined political or geographic divisions of nations, states, continents, etc. **Regional government** (in urban settings, METROPOLITAN GOVERNMENT) is the establishment of a new level of administration for some combination of communities that surrender some of their local government powers to it; COUNTIES may be seen as a form of regional government. In the US, the TENNESSEE VALLEY AUTHORITY is the outstanding example of large-scale regional government. The Northwest Territories, Yukon Territory, and British Columbia have a total of seven entities designated **administrative regions.** Ontario has at present 10 **regional municipalities,** embracing cities and suburban and rural areas; British Columbia has 29 analogous **regional districts.**

Rehoboth town, pop. 8656, Bristol Co., SE Massachusetts, 10 mi/16 km NNW of Fall River and 8 mi/13 km E of Providence, Rhode Island. Formerly part of the neighboring (W) town of Seekonk, Rehoboth was founded in 1636 by Congregationalists from Plymouth. The town was the scene of bloody fighting during King Philip's War (1675). An iron industry developed here in the 18th century, but Rehoboth remained essentially rural, and is now a growing residential suburb of Providence and other nearby cities.

Rehoboth Bay lagoon just SW of REHOBOTH BEACH, in Sussex Co., SE Delaware. Five mi/8 km N–S and 3 mi/5 km wide, it is separated from the Atlantic Ocean by a barrier beach, and joins Indian River Bay on the S. It is connected to DELAWARE BAY by the 15 mi/24 km–long Lewes and Rehoboth Canal, at its N end.

Rehoboth Beach city, pop. 1234, Sussex Co., SE Delaware, on the Lewes and Rehoboth Canal (W) and the Atlantic coast, 5 mi/8 km SE of Lewes. Originally a Methodist camp meeting site, the city developed as a popular resort during a 1920s real estate boom, and is now Delaware's largest summer resort, a favorite of Washington, D.C. residents.

Reidsville city, pop. 12,183, Rockingham Co., N North Carolina, 20 mi/32 km NNE of Greensboro. An important tobacco market and cigarette manufacturing center, it also makes textiles and beverages.

Reindeer Lake irregularly shaped, NNE–SSW oriented body in NE Saskatchewan and NW Manitoba. The ninth-largest lake in Canada, it covers 2470 sq mi/6400 sq km, and is 145 mi/233 km long. Deep and island-dotted, it attracts sport and commercial fishermen. It drains S via the Reindeer R. into the CHURCHILL R., thence E to Hudson Bay. At the N end is Brochet, Manitoba, at the S end Southend, Saskatchewan, both Indian reserves.

Reisterstown unincorporated village, pop. 19,314, Baltimore Co., NC Maryland, 17 mi/27 km NW of downtown Baltimore. Settled in 1758 by German colonists, it is a largely residential suburb at the end of Baltimore's Northwest Expressway (Route 795).

Renaissance Center high-rise complex in Detroit, Michigan. A renovation project on the city's downtown riverfront, it is made up of five large towers. The centerpiece, the 73-story Detroit Plaza Hotel, opened in 1977, is surrounded by four 39-story office buildings. The complex was constructed to revitalize the central business area, but as the city remains plagued by economic and social problems, the intention is yet to be fulfilled.

Renfrew town, pop. 8134, Renfrew Co., SE Ontario, on the Bonnechere R., 48 mi/77 km W of Ottawa. Founded by Scots in the 1840s in a timbering district, it is a commercial and light industrial center; milling, mining, and dairying have recently been joined by varied high-tech manufactures.

Reno city, pop. 133,850, seat of Washoe Co., W Nevada, on the Truckee R., just E of the SIERRA NEVADA, 20 mi/32 km NNE of L. TAHOE, and 180 mi/290 km ENE of San Francisco, California. Widely known as the "Biggest Little City in the World," it began in 1860 with a toll bridge over the river, became a settlement during the construction of the Central Pacific Railroad (1868), and developed into an important link with the rich gold and silver mines of VIRGINIA CITY (SSE). It is now a distribution, warehousing, and light manufacturing center. Year-round tourism here focuses on gambling, skiing, hunting, and fishing. Nevada's second-largest city is the seat of the University of Nevada (1874), and has an international airport. State laws allowing easy divorce and marriage made Reno famous from the early 1930s.

Rensselaer city, pop. 8255, Rensselaer Co., E New York, on the E bank of the Hudson R., across from Albany. Settled in the early 17th century, it was formed from several villages in the Dutch patroonship of **Rensselaerswyck,** land granted to Kiliaen Van Rensselaer by the Dutch West India Company (1630). This most successful of all patroonships lasted until 1685, when the British governor converted it into an English manor. Fort Crailo (1704), erected here to protect from hostile Indians, is now a state historic site. The city was formed from the union of the villages of East Albany, Greenbush, and Bath-on-the-Hudson (1897). It flourished as a center for the New York Central and Boston and Albany railroads as well as a lumber port, and as a manufacturing center, producing dyes, chemicals, concrete, and textiles. It is also a residential suburb of Albany.

Rensselaer County 655 sq mi/1696 sq km, pop. 154,429, E New York, bounded by the Hudson R. (W) and the Massachusetts (SE) and Vermont (NE) lines. Its seat and major manufacturing and business center is TROY. The city of Rensselaer is also an industrial and commercial hub. There are many small residential villages scattered throughout the S section. Most of the county is agricultural, with dairy, truck, and poultry farms as well as orchards. The TACONIC Mts. are SE.

Renton city, pop. 41,688, King Co., WC Washington, at the S end of L. Washington, a residential and industrial suburb 10 mi/16 km SE of Seattle. It developed as an early 20th-century clay and iron processing center. Boeing has maintained a large aircraft plant here since World War II, and there is also a railroad car plant. Other manufactures include electronic equipment and plastic products. Oceangoing ships dock at this freshwater port of entry, passing through the Ballard Locks between Puget Sound and L. Washington. Horse races are held at Longacres Race Track.

Repentigny city, pop. 49,630, Assomption Co., S Québec, 16 mi/26 km NNE of Montréal, on the St. Lawrence R., where the R. des Prairies and the R. de l'Assomption meet it, just N of the NE tip of the I. de Montréal. It is a fast-growing, primarily residential suburb.

Republican River 445 mi/716 km long, in NE Colorado, S Nebraska, and NE Kansas. It is formed by the confluence of the short North Fork and Colorado's 129 mi/206 km–long Arikaree R. at Haigler in extreme SW Nebraska, near the Kansas and Colorado lines, and flows generally E past MCCOOK and along the S edge of the High Plains, N of the Kansas line, then turns SE near Superior and across Kansas, passing CONCORDIA and Clay Center, to join the SMOKY HILL R. at JUNCTION CITY, forming the KANSAS R. Dams on the Republican, including the Harlan Dam, near Alma, Nebraska, and the Milford Dam, near Junction City, are part of the Missouri River Basin project. The Republican's tributaries, also dammed in places, include its South Fork, which joins it from the SW (Colorado and Kansas) 20 mi/32 km E of its formation, near Benkelman, Nebraska; the Frenchman R., Red Willow Creek, and Medicine Creek (from the N); and (from the SW) Beaver, Sappa, and Prairie Dog creeks. The Republican takes its name from a Pawnee tribe.

resaca in S Texas, any of a number of bodies of water, many used as reservoirs, created by the movement of riverbeds, leaving cut-off loops and bends. They are analogous to BAYOUS.

Resaca city, pop. 410, Gordon Co., NW Georgia, 65 mi/105 km NW of Atlanta. Originally called Dublin by Irish workers building the Chattanooga–Atlanta railroad, it was renamed by veterans of the 1846 Mexican War battle of Resaca de la Palma, Texas. A three-day battle for this strategic junction in May 1864 was part of W.T. Sherman's advance on Atlanta.

Resaca de la Palma battle site in Cameron Co., extreme S Texas, 4 mi/6 km N of downtown Brownsville. The battle here (May 9, 1846), at the start of the Mexican War, was won by Zachary Taylor's troops, following their victory the day before at PALO ALTO, 6 mi/10 km N. It led to the relief of Fort Taylor at Brownsville, sending Mexican forces across the Rio Grande.

Research Triangle also, **Research Triangle Park** university research center in Durham Co., C North Carolina. In a triangle formed by Duke University (in Durham, to the N), North Carolina State University (in Raleigh, SE), and the University of North Carolina (in Chapel Hill, SW), the 6000-ac/2430-ha area is 5 mi/8 km S of Durham. Established in 1958 to attract and develop new industry, the complex now houses firms doing research and manufacturing in fiber, biomedical, environmental, computer and other technological and humanities fields. The Environmental Protection Agency, National Institute for Environmental Health Sciences, IBM, and the Burroughs Wellcome (drugs) company are among organizations with operations here.

Reseda SAN FERNANDO VALLEY section of LOS ANGELES, California, 20 mi/32 km NW of Downtown, a middle-class residential area N of Tarzana and W of Van Nuys.

Reserve unincorporated community, pop. 8847, St. John the Baptist Parish, SE Louisiana, on the E (N) bank of the Mississippi R., 29 mi/47 km WNW of New Orleans, along the RIVER ROAD. It is a refining and shipping center for the region's sugar cane industry.

Resolute Bay also, **Resolute** hamlet, pop. 171, Baffin Region, N Northwest Territories, at the S of 2700–sq mi/7000–sq km Cornwallis I., in the QUEEN ELIZABETH Is., on the N of the Parry Channel. In an area long used by INUIT hunting parties, the *Resolute,* a ship involved in the search for the lost Franklin Expedition (see NORTHWEST PASSAGE), wintered here in 1850. In 1947 the Canadian government moved Inuit here from Baffin I. and N Québec, and established what is now an air transshipment center and tourist base.

Restigouche River 130 mi/210 km long, rising in NW New Brunswick and flowing generally NE. From its confluence with the Patapédia R. it forms the border between New Brunswick and Québec's GASPÉ region. After being joined by the Upsalquitch (from the S) and Matapédia (from the N) rivers, it broadens into a tidal estuary, passing Campbellton and Dalhousie, and enters CHALEUR BAY. It is famous for its salmon.

Reston planned community, pop. 48,556, Fairfax Co., N Virginia, 17 mi/27 km WNW of Washington, D.C. It was founded in 1961 as a self-contained city with industry, commercial areas, and residential sections offering a diversity of housing. The first village center, at L. Anne (formed 1965 by damming Colvin Run), has shops, offices, apartments, and town houses, clustered around the lake. Additional village centers are separated from one another by wilderness. Under Virginia law, Reston cannot incorporate; governmental functions are performed by the county and the state. Residents belong to a community association, which must adhere to the master plan for the community. Reston has attracted government workers and high-tech, commercial, and service businesses.

Reunion Tower 560-ft/170-m, 50-story building in downtown Dallas, Texas. A narrow shaft surmounted by a three-level geodesic dome, it is the best-known sight on the city's skyline. Nearby is the 17,000-seat **Reunion Arena,** home to the Dallas Mavericks (basketball), conventions, and other events. Both buildings recall in their name the French utopian (Fourierist) community of La Réunion, which flourished briefly (1855–58) in OAK CLIFF, in SW Dallas; after its failure its highly skilled members moved to Dallas and became an important element in the city's early development.

Revelstoke city, pop. 7729, Columbia-Shuswap Regional District, SE British Columbia, on the Columbia R. (S of the 574 ft/175 m–high **Revelstoke Dam**), between the Selkirk (E) and Monashee (W) mountains, 252 mi/406 km ENE of Vancouver. It developed with the arrival (1886) of the CANADIAN PACIFIC RAILWAY, and today is the trade center of a mining, lumbering, farming, and resort region. The Rogers Pass (E) and Eagle Pass (W), on the CPR line, are now also on the TRANS-CANADA HIGHWAY. Industries include brewing, sawmilling, and dairying. Hunting, fishing, and tourism are also important. MOUNT REVELSTOKE NATIONAL PARK is just NE.

Revere city, pop. 42,786, Suffolk Co., EC Massachusetts, on Broad Sound of Massachusetts Bay, the Chelsea R., and the Pines R., 4 mi/6 km NE of Boston. Settled in 1636 as part of Boston, Revere is the "Coney Island" of the area, with 3 mi/5 km of beaches, a dog track, and various other recreational facilities. There are various light manufactures.

Rexburg city, pop. 14,302, seat of Madison Co., E Idaho, on a branch of the Teton R., 27 mi/43 km NE of Idaho Falls. Founded in 1883, it is a trade center for the Teton Valley's dairy, lumber, sugar beet, potato, and livestock industries. Ricks College (1888) and a large Mormon tabernacle are here. The International Folk Dance Festival is an annual event.

Rexdale see under ETOBICOKE, Ontario.

Reyes, Point steep bluff at the SW end of a triangular peninsula in Marin Co., NW California, 36 mi/58 km NW of San Francisco. It overlooks the Pacific Ocean to the NW and DRAKES BAY to the SE. Point Reyes is one of the windiest and foggiest places on the West Coast. It is part of the 71,000-ac/28,770-ha **Point Reyes National Seashore,** which includes beaches, cliffs, lagoons, bird and sea lion colonies, and grazing land.

Reynoldsburg city, pop. 25,767, Franklin and Licking counties, C Ohio, 10 mi/16 km E of Columbus, of which it is a commuter suburb. It was founded in 1805, on lands set aside for Canadian refugees who had supported the American Revolution.

RFK Stadium officially, **Robert F. Kennedy Memorial Stadium** sports facility in E Washington, D.C., along the Anacostia R., 2 mi/3 km E of the Capitol. Completed in 1961, it seats over 56,000; it is home to the Washington Redskins (football), and was formerly home to the Senators (baseball), who had moved there from the older Griffith Stadium.

Rhinebeck town, pop. 7558, Dutchess Co., SE New York, on the E bank of the Hudson R., 4 mi/6 km E of KINGSTON. It was settled by the Dutch in the late 17th century and by German

Palatines after 1712. An affluent exurb and summer resort community, it is home to the Old Rhinebeck Aerodrome, the Dutchess Co. Fairgrounds, and many galleries, and host to a well-known annual crafts show. The riverfront hamlet of **Rhinecliff** is a commuter rail stop; the Kingston-Rhinecliff Bridge is 3.5 mi/6 km N.

Rhinelander city, pop. 7427, seat of Oneida Co., N Wisconsin, on the Wisconsin R., 47 mi/76 km NNE of Wausau. In an area producing potatoes, berries, and dairy goods, it has a large paper mill, and is a lake and winter sports resort center and the headquarters for Nicolet National Forest. An 1890s hoax involving the hodag, a forest "creature" put together from hides and various other materials, gave Rhinelander the name Hodag City, by which it is widely known.

Rhode Island officially, **Rhode Island and Providence Plantations** northeastern US state, in SE New England; 1990 pop. 1,003,464 (105.9% of 1980; rank: 43rd); area 1545 sq mi/4002 sq km (rank: 50th); ratified Constitution 1790 (13th). Capital and most populous city: PROVIDENCE. Other leading cities: WARWICK, CRANSTON. Rhode Island is bordered N and E by Massachusetts (with MOUNT HOPE BAY lying across part of the boundary); W by Connecticut, with the PAWCATUCK R. forming part of the boundary in the S; and S by the Atlantic Ocean, with Block Island Sound on the SW and Rhode Island Sound on the SE. Comprising forested, lightly populated upland in the W (reaching 812 ft/248 m at JERIMOTH HILL, in the NW) and lowland in the E, the state is deeply (to 30 mi/48 km inland) indented by NARRAGANSETT BAY, in which are RHODE (formerly Aquidneck), CONANICUT, PRUDENCE, and many smaller islands. Eight mi/13 km off the SW coast is BLOCK I., standing at the E entrance to Long Island Sound; New York's Fishers I. lies just SW of WATCH HILL, at Rhode Island's SW extreme. Most of the state's pop. lives in Providence and its industrial suburbs along the BLACKSTONE and Providence rivers, including WOONSOCKET, PAWTUCKET, and CENTRAL FALLS, or on Narragansett Bay (Warwick, BRISTOL). Rhode Island apparently takes its name from Giovanni da Verrazano's likening Rhode I. to Greece's Rhodos when he saw it in 1524; the Dutch word for "red," referring to coastal soils, may have influenced the choice. Inhabited by the Narraganset, the area became the home of Roger Williams and other religious dissenters (largely from Massachusetts) in the 1630s; although white-Indian relations were at first friendly, the colony (chartered 1644) was the scene of some of the worst fighting in King Philip's War (1675–76). Providence and NEWPORT became early centers of a community that thrived on commerce, fishing, and some agriculture before the Revolution. In 1790, the American factory system was inaugurated at Slater's Mill, in Pawtucket, and the state became a center of silver, jewelry, and other metal, along with textile and machine, manufacturing. Much industry moved to the South in the 20th century, and Providence was forced to diversify. Today, along with the metal industries, insurance, banking, electronics, and education (at Brown University and the Rhode Island School of Design, among other institutions) are important. The state's agriculture produces poultry (esp. Rhode Island red chickens), dairy goods, and vegetables, and fishing and shellfishing are important. Newport has declined as a naval center (while submarine manufacture has continued at QUONSET POINT), but remains a summer resort and tourist magnet, and Narragansett Bay is a sailing and beach mecca. KINGSTON is home to the University of Rhode Island. The state's people were essentially of British Protestant and French Huguenot origin until the mid 19th century, when Italians, French-Canadians, Poles, Portuguese, and other groups began to arrive. Today Rhode Island is the most Catholic of US states.

Rhode Island also, **Aquidneck Island** 45 sq mi/117 sq km, largest island in Narragansett Bay, in Newport Co., SE Rhode Island. Visited in 1524 by Italian explorer Giovanni da Verrazano, Rhode I. was settled at PORTSMOUTH in 1638. The Battle of Rhode Island was fought here in 1778. The city of NEWPORT is on its SW coast. It is largely rural, with fishing, farming, and some light industry; in the S, naval facilities and tourism dominate. The island gave its name to the state.

Rialto 1. city, pop. 72,388, San Bernardino Co., SW California, 4 mi/6 km W of San Bernardino, of which it is a largely residential suburb. Incorporated in 1911, it has some fruit packing and other light industries. **2.** popular name for the theater district of BROADWAY, New York City (and, less frequently, for similar districts in other cities); it refers to the Rialto Bridge, in Venice, Italy, a traditional meeting and business-transacting locale.

ribbon farm see under SEIGNEURIE.

Rib Mountain 1940 ft/592 m, just W of Wausau, in NC Wisconsin. Estimated to be a billion years old, the 3 mi/5 km–long quartzite hogback is popular with hikers and skiers for its panoramic views of the Wisconsin R. valley. The peak is in Rib Mountain State Park.

Rice Lake SE of the Kawartha Lakes, in SE Ontario, 12 mi/19 km S of Peterborough. Twenty mi/32 km NE–SW and up to 3 mi/5 km wide, it is named for the wild rice that once flourished in the area. The lake is now part of the TRENT CANAL system. SERPENT MOUNDS PROVINCIAL PARK is on the N shore.

Rice Park city park in St. Paul, Minnesota, in the heart of Downtown. It is a focal point and gathering place for the city, surrounded by such important buildings as the Hotel St. Paul, Landmark Center, and Ordway Music Center. The park is decorated with elaborate ice sculptures during the city's Winter Carnival.

Richardson city, pop. 74,840, Dallas and Collin counties, NE Texas, adjacent to NE Dallas. Settled in the 1870s when the railroad came through the area, it remained a small agricultural town until the mid 1950s, when Dallas suburbanization boomed. Though mostly residential, it has some light industry including production of radios and telecommunications, computer, and other electronic goods. The University of Texas at Dallas (1961) and Richland College (1972) are here.

Richardson Highway 370 mi/600 km long, from FAIRBANKS, in C Alaska, S to VALDEZ, on PRINCE WILLIAM SOUND. It parallels the S section of the TRANS-ALASKA PIPELINE, and joins the ALASKA HIGHWAY at Delta Junction, 75 mi/120 km SE of Fairbanks.

Richardson Mountains mostly N–S trending range, a N extension of the Rocky Mts., in the N Yukon Territory between the upper PORCUPINE R. and the lower MACKENZIE R., along the border of the Northwest Territories. The DEMPSTER HIGHWAY crosses the range NE of Eagle Plains, on its way to Fort McPherson in the Northwest Territories. The range averages 4000 ft/1220 m and reaches c.6000 ft/1830 m.

Richboro see under NORTHAMPTON, Pennsylvania.

Richburg hamlet in Forrest Co., SE Mississippi, 4 mi/6 km SSW of Hattiesburg, known as the 1889 site, in a natural amphitheater, of an illegally organized 75-round bare-knuckle (the last such US championship bout) prizefight, in which John L. Sullivan defeated Jake Kilrain.

Richelieu, Rivière 75 mi/120 km long, in S Québec. It issues from the N end of L. CHAMPLAIN and flows N past SAINT-JEAN-SUR-RICHELIEU, CHAMBLY, and BELOEIL, to join the St. Lawrence R. at SOREL. A key to the Hudson–St. Lawrence river waterway, it was discovered in 1609 by Champlain, and for two centuries figured in the struggle for control of the region among France, Britain, and the US. The historic Île aux NOIX is near its S end.

Richfield **1.** city, pop. 35,710, Hennepin Co., SE Minnesota, immediately S of Minneapolis. Its proximity to Minneapolis, Bloomington, and the Minneapolis–St. Paul International Airport has made Richfield one of the fastest-growing suburbs in the area. A string of shopping malls and office parks have been built along I-35W, in the NC part, and along the I-494 corridor, which follows the city's S border with Bloomington. Richfield was settled in the 1850s. **2.** village, pop. 3117, Summit Co., NE Ohio, 14 mi/22 km NW of Akron. The abolitionist John Brown lived in this farming center during the 1840s. Traces of prehistoric earthworks can be seen nearby. The Coliseum, former home to the Cleveland Cavaliers (basketball), is in Richfield township, 2 mi/3 km NE of the village.

Richford rural town, pop. 1153, Tioga Co., WC New York, 17 mi/27 km SE of Ithaca. It is the birthplace (1839) of John D. Rockefeller.

Richland city, pop. 32,315, Benton Co., SE Washington, on the Columbia and Yakima rivers just NW of their confluence, 10 mi/16 km NW of Kennewick and 9 mi/14 km NW of Pasco (the other two Tri-Cities). It was an agricultural hamlet, settled in 1910, until 1943–44, when the US government built the Hanford Reservation just to its N. Created as part of the project developing the atomic bomb, Hanford was headquartered in Richland, which grew rapidly. The city was managed by the Federal government until the late 1950s, and Hanford made plutonium for nuclear weapons into the 1980s. The facility has since housed a nuclear power plant (in operation 1984) and a nuclear storage facility; grave concerns were voiced in the early 1990s over the safety of its storage tanks; cleanup efforts were expected to extend well into the 21st century. There are lush irrigated farms, vineyards, and orchards in the Richland area, and produce is shipped through the city.

Richland Center city, pop. 5018, seat of Richland Co., SW Wisconsin, 52 mi/84 km NW of Madison. Settled in 1849, it is in a region of dairy and livestock farms, fruit orchards, and stands of hardwood. It is the birthplace (1869) of Frank Lloyd Wright, whose early A. D. German Warehouse is here.

Richland County **1.** 497 sq mi/1287 sq km, pop. 126,137, in NC Ohio, intersected by forks of the Mahoning R. Its seat and largest city is MANSFIELD. The economy is supported primarily by agriculture, including dairy, fruit, grain, livestock, and potato farming, as well as greenhouses. There is manufacturing at Mansfield, Plymouth, and Shelby. Natural resources include sand and gravel. **2.** 762 sq mi/1974 sq km, pop. 285,720, in WC South Carolina, in the SANDHILLS, bounded by the Congaree R. (SW) and the Wateree R. (E). Its seat, the state capital, COLUMBIA, is its industrial and commercial hub and primary employer. Many of the city's residential suburbs and the large Fort Jackson military reservation are here. The county also produces cotton, tobacco, peaches, corn, dairy products, and livestock. The Congaree Swamp National Monument is in its S part.

Richland Hills see under NORTH RICHLAND HILLS, Texas.

Richmond **1.** city, pop. 126,624, Greater Vancouver Regional District, SW British Columbia, on Lulu, Sea, and smaller islands in the Fraser R. delta and the Strait of Georgia, a suburb immediately S of Vancouver. Settled from the 1860s at the salmon fishing village of Steveston, on the W shore, and long an agricultural and fish processing center, it has grown gradually into a large residential community. The Vancouver International Airport is on Sea I. **2.** city, pop. 87,425, Contra Costa Co., NC California, on the NE shore of San Francisco Bay and SW shore of San Pablo Bay, 6 mi/10 km NNW of Berkeley and connected to Marin Co. (W) by the Richmond–San Rafael Bridge. It is one of the busiest US Pacific ports, and an oil refining center. Becoming the W terminus of the Santa Fe Railroad in 1900, it was connected by ferry with San Francisco (SW). Shipbuilding became a major activity, and during World War II the city's pop. increased by 400%. After 1945, more diversified industry expanded. Manufactures now include petroleum products, electronic and transportation equipment, housewares and plumbing fixtures, and processed foods. The city also has railroad shops and large residential and commercial components. **3.** city, pop. 38,705, seat of Wayne Co., EC Indiana, on the Whitewater R., 35 mi/56 km SE of Muncie, and just W of the Ohio border, on the NATIONAL ROAD (US 40). Settled (1806) by Quakers from North Carolina, it remains a center of Friends' activities, organizations, and publications. A renowned rose growing city, it ships some 20 million blooms annually. A longtime manufacturing center, it produces truck and bus bodies, drilling machines, fabricated metals, home insulation, electronic wire and cable, tools, and plastics. Richmond is the seat of Earlham College (Friends; 1847) and Indiana University East (1971). **4.** city, pop. 21,155, seat of Madison Co., EC Kentucky, 24 mi/39 km SSE of Lexington, in the BLUEGRASS REGION. It was settled in 1784 on the WILDERNESS ROAD. Control of the city was contested throughout the Civil War, and its courthouse (1849) was a hospital for both sides. Corn, tobacco, and livestock are important to its economy, which also relies on light manufactures. Eastern Kentucky University (1906) is here. White Hall, the abolitionist Cassius Marcellus Clay's restored 1799 home, is a state historic site 7 mi/11 km N. **5.** see STATEN ISLAND, New York. **6.** city, pop. 9801, seat of Fort Bend Co., SE Texas, 25 mi/40 km SW of Houston, on the Brazos R. The smaller sister city to ROSENBERG, it is in an area that produces oil, rice, cotton, livestock, and vegetables. It has processing plants and other light manufactures. The area was settled in 1822 by Stephen F. Austin's followers. **7.** city and state capital, pop. 203,056, seat of but independent of Henrico Co., E Virginia, at the head of navigation of the James R. It is a major financial and industrial center for the Upper South, and the hub of a metropolitan area that extends into Henrico, Chesterfield, and Hanover counties. Its manufacturing focuses on tobacco products, printing and publishing, chemicals, textiles, and pharmaceuticals; there are a number of corporate headquarters, and the city is an important insurance and financial center. Settled in 1733, it became the state capital in 1779, and was pillaged by the British in 1781. Its capitol was begun in 1785 following a design by Thomas Jefferson. Following Virginia's secession from the Union in 1861, Richmond became the capital of the Confederacy, and was a major military target during the Civil War; in 1865, much of it was burned by the evacuating Confederates. At St. John's Church (1741), Patrick Henry made his "Give me liberty . . ." speech. The Confederate White House (1818); Robert E. Lee House (1844); and Edgar Allan Poe Museum are here. The Richmond National Battlefield Park commemorates Civil War sites in and around the city. J. Sargeant Reynolds Community College (1972), Virginia Commonwealth University (1838), Virginia Union University (1865), the University of Richmond (1830), and Union Theological Seminary (1812) are all here.

Richmond County New York, coextensive with the New York City borough of STATEN ISLAND. Organized after the British conquest of New Amsterdam and named for Charles II's son, the Duke of Richmond, it shared its name with the borough, which was officially Richmond, until 1975.

Richmond District also, **the Richmond** predominantly residential section of NW SAN FRANCISCO, California, N of Golden Gate Park and SW of the Presidio. Developed largely after World War I in a foggy, sand dune–dominated area extending W to the Pacific, it is an expanse of family dwellings. A section along Clement St., in the NE, is now the city's New Chinatown. Many earlier Richmond residents were Jewish or Japanese. With the Sunset District (S across the park), the Richmond is also known as "the Avenues," for the numbered avenues that run N–S through it.

Richmond Heights **1.** city, pop. 10,448, St. Louis Co., EC Missouri, 8 mi/13 km W of downtown St. Louis. Just off Interstate 64, it is a residential community. **2.** city, pop. 9611, Cuyahoga Co., NE Ohio, 4 mi/6 km S of L. Erie, a residential suburb 7 mi/11 km NE of Cleveland. The Euclid Creek Reservation is just NW.

Richmond Highlands unincorporated community, pop. 26,037, King Co., WC Washington, a residential suburb 9 mi/14 km N of Seattle.

Richmond Hill **1.** residential section, SC Queens, New York. It lies just E of Woodhaven and W of Jamaica, with Forest Park and the Interborough Parkway N and the Atlantic Ave. commercial and industrial corridor S. The area has no prominent hill, but was named for a London suburb or for the designer, Edward Richmond, involved in the 1860s plan of development. Shingle-style houses still characterize the middle-class neighborhood. **2.** town, pop. 80,142, York Regional Municipality, S Ontario, 15 mi/24 km N of Toronto. Originally known as Mt. Pleasant, it developed in the early 19th century along YONGE St. (Route 11). Long agricultural, it is now undergoing rapid suburban growth; its pop. increased by 70% in 1986–91. The University of Toronto's David Dunlap (astronomical) Observatory is here.

Richmondtown residential and commercial section, C Staten Island, New York. Known as Cocclestown in the late 17th century, when "cockles" (probably oysters) were taken locally, it had become Richmond Town before the Revolution. In the 19th century it was Staten Island's governmental center. Richmondtown lies just E of the Staten Island GREENBELT, with La Tourette Park in the hills to the W. The Richmondtown Restoration is a collection of 18th- and 19th-century buildings illustrating local history.

Rich Mountain see under TYGART R., West Virginia.

Richton Park village, pop. 10,523, Cook Co., NE Illinois, a residential suburb 30 mi/48 km S of Chicago, at the S end of the metropolitan area.

Rideau Canal 125 mi/200 km long, in SE Ontario, linking the Ottawa R. (at Ottawa) with L. Ontario (at Kingston). Conceived as an alternate to the American-threatened St. Lawrence R. route between Montréal and L. Ontario, the canal was designed by Lt. Col. John By, who oversaw the project (1826–32). From the Ottawa R., where it bisects the city of Ottawa, it parallels or follows the **Rideau R.** SW to its source, at 406 ft/124 m, in the **Rideau Lakes,** then proceeds via the Cataraqui R. to Kingston. A 7-mi/11-km branch connects Lower Rideau L. to Perth (W). The canal has a system of 50 dams and 47 locks. Used for lumbering for some time after its completion, it is today recreational; its N end, 5 mi/8 km in Ottawa, is famous as, in winter, "the world's longest skating rink."

Ridgecrest city, pop. 27,725, Kern Co., SC California, in the Indian Wells Valley (the N Mojave Desert), 75 mi/120 km ENE of Bakersfield. China L., a PLAYA 7 mi/11 km NE, gives its name to the huge China Lake Naval Weapons Center (N and E), established in World War II. The Trona Pinnacles, 16 mi/26 km E, are a field of hundreds of calcium carbonate spires up to 100 ft/30 m tall, in a rich borate-producing area. Ridgecrest is the seat of Cerro Coso Community College (1973). It is a growing residential center.

Ridgefield **1.** town, pop. 20,919, Fairfield Co., SW Connecticut, on the New York line, 12 mi/19 km NNW of Norwalk. It is an affluent suburb with many Colonial homes. A battle was fought here April 27, 1777, between British forces led by William Tryon and Colonists trying to block their retreat from Danbury. **2.** borough, pop. 9996, Bergen Co., NE New Jersey, 8 mi/13 km NE of Jersey City, on the PALISADES of the Hudson. It is a residential suburb with a variety of corporate headquarters and small industries.

Ridgefield Park village, pop. 12,454, Bergen Co., NE New Jersey, on the Hackensack R., 9 mi/14 km N of Jersey City and across Overpeck Creek (NW) from RIDGEFIELD. It is a chiefly residential suburb, with office buildings and such industry as the manufacture of paper products.

Ridgeland city, pop. 11,714, Madison Co., WC Mississippi, a growing residential suburb 10 mi/16 km NNE of downtown Jackson, on the NATCHEZ TRACE Parkway. The Ross Barnett Reservoir (on the Pearl R.) is just E.

Ridgeway town, pop. 407, Fairfield Co., NC South Carolina, 22 mi/35 km NNE of Columbia. Settled by Scotch-Irish Presbyterians, it was for many years a lumber center. Since 1989, when a large mine began production, it has been the center of South Carolina's new gold mining industry.

Ridgewood **1.** village, pop. 24,152, Bergen Co., NE New Jersey, 6 mi/10 km NNE of Paterson. Settled by the Dutch in the early 18th century, it was called Newton (1810), Godwinville (1829), and finally Ridgewood (1866). The community was small until the railroad's arrival in 1848. It is now mainly a residential suburb. **2.** see under BUSHWICK, New York.

Riding Mountain National Park 1147 sq mi/2970 sq km, in SW Manitoba, 10 mi/16 km S of Dauphin, and 169 mi/272 km NW of Winnipeg. Established in 1929 on former Assiniboine and Cree hunting grounds, this plateau forms part of the MANITOBA ESCARPMENT, rising over 1500 ft/457 m above the surrounding prairie. It combines boreal forest, mixed deciduous woods, open grasslands, meadow, a number of lakes (of which Clear L. is the largest), a rich variety of bird and animal life, and year-round recreational facilities.

Riker's Island 400 ac/162 ha, in the East R., New York City. Although it is just off the shore of ASTORIA and LaGuardia Airport, both in Queens, it is part of the BRONX. Riker's is the site of New York City's major prison, which replaced one on Welfare (now ROOSEVELT) I. in 1935. The two small Brother Islands, North and South, are just NW.

Rimouski city, pop. 30,873, Rimouski-Neigette Co., SE Québec, 190 mi/310 km NE of Québec City, on the S shore of the St. Lawrence R. It was a 1690s SEIGNEURIE. With a deepwater port, it is a transport, service, and educational center for the region. Local industries process foods, lumber, and pulpwood, and make mattresses, carpeting, leather, and shoes. The Collège de Rimouski (1855), the Collège des Ursulines (1906), and a center for oceanographic research are among local institutions. The city was largely rebuilt after a 1950 fire.

Rindge town, pop. 4941, Cheshire Co., SW New Hampshire. It is on US 202, in a hilly lake region, 18 mi/29 km SE of Keene. Franklin Pierce College (1962) is in the NW part of the town.

Ringwood borough, pop. 12,623, Passaic Co., N New Jersey, in the Ramapo Mts., on the Wanaque R., 16 mi/26 km NW of Paterson, along the New York line. Iron was discovered near here in 1730, and the first forge built nine years later. Extensive mines and works followed, and Ringwood became a major center for the production of munitions, cannons, and chain for the Continental Army. The iron mine here continued producing until 1931. The area was given to the state (1936) and 4318-ac/1749-ha **Ringwood State Park,** which adjoins the borough (E), was created (1939). In the park are ironmaster Robert Erskine's home, Ringwood Manor (a National Historic Landmark), and the 300-ac/120-ha State Botanical Gardens at Skylands (a 1924 mansion). With the park, lakes, and WANAQUE Reservoir nearby, Ringwood is a popular tourist destination, as well as a residential suburb.

Rio Grande **1.** major river of the Southwest, 1900 mi/3100 km long, in Colorado, New Mexico, and Texas. For some 1300 mi/2100 km, it forms the border between Texas and Mexico, where it is known as the **Río Bravo del Norte.** It rises in the San Juan Mts. of SW Colorado, just ESE of Silverton, on the E of the Continental Divide, and flows ESE to Del Norte, then SE and S through the broad San Luis Valley, between the San Juan (W) and Sangre de Cristo (E) Mts., past Alamosa, into New Mexico. There it passes through the rugged **Rio Grande Gorge,** and proceeds W of Taos and Santa Fe, to Albuquerque. To the S, its valley widens, E of the edge of the Colorado Plateau; it flows SSW to Socorro and through the 1916 Elephant Butte Reservoir, just NE of Truth or Consequences. This and the 1938 Caballo Reservoir, just S, from which it turns SSE, irrigate farmlands in the HATCH Valley and S to Las Cruces and Mesilla. The Rio Grande briefly forms the Texas–New Mexico border, then enters El Paso, the largest city along its route, with its sister city of Ciudad Juarez, Chihuahua. Here it swings SE, between Texas and Chihuahua. At the BIG BEND it turns NE, with the state of Coahuila now on its S, through rugged, lightly populated terrain. Winding gradually E, it reaches LANGTRY, just SE of which is the mouth of the PECOS R., its largest tributary. Here it enters the international AMISTAD RESERVOIR (1969), heading SE past Del Rio (with its Mexican twin of Ciudad Acuña) and Eagle Pass (and Piedras Negras). The state of Nuevo Léon is briefly on its SW, then Tamaulipas. The river passes Laredo (and Nuevo Laredo) and through the 1954 FALCON RESERVOIR, then runs through the more heavily populated region generally called the **Rio Grande Valley,** with Texas's agricultural WINTER GARDEN on its N. Brownsville (its twin is Matamoras), 17 mi/27 km from the Gulf of Mexico, is its chief port. The river is navigable only this far from the sea; through most of its course it is narrow, sand- and silt-clogged, and variable, ranging from a trickle in dry seasons to a torrent in rainy periods. Its dams have now regulated the flow along much of its length. Flooding and course changes were formerly serious, leading to the long-lived CHAMIZAL border dispute in El Paso, water use disputes between the US and Mexico that were resolved in 1945, and sudden changes in condition for such settlements as MESILLA, New Mexico. The border has been the scene of much illegal immigration and smuggling activity, the various twin cities of much MAQUILADORA manufacturing. The Rio Grande Gorge stretch, 48 mi/77 km in N New Mexico, was designated a protected WILD RIVER in 1970. **2.** village, pop. 965, Gallia Co., S Ohio, 10 mi/16 km WNW of Gallipolis. Community life centers around Rio Grande College (1876).

Rio Grande National Forest 1.85 million ac/750,000 ha (2890 sq mi/7487 sq km), on the headwaters of the Rio Grande and in mountain areas around the San Luis Valley, in S Colorado. Parts of the SANGRE DE CRISTO (E) and SAN JUAN (SW) mountains are within it.

Río Piedras district of SAN JUAN, Puerto Rico, 5 mi/8 km SE of Old San Juan. Formerly a separate municipality, it was annexed by San Juan in 1951. Like adjacent HATO REY, it developed in part with the spur of the Federal Operation Bootstrap. It is best known as the seat of the University of Puerto Rico (1903) and as a center of the island's intellectual life. Several other institutions, including Puerto Rico Junior College (1949), are also here. In addition, Río Piedras is an agricultural trade and processing hub and has diverse manufactures, along with noted botanical gardens maintained by the Agricultural Experimental Station and a large open-air market.

Rio Rancho city, pop. 32,505, Sandoval Co., NC New Mexico, on a mesa 9 mi/14 km NNW of downtown Albuquerque. Begun as a residential development, Rio Rancho Estates, in 1961, this "fastest growing small US city" has expanded beyond retiree homes to house camera, medical equipment, and other manufacturers, and in the mid 1990s was acquiring a huge computer chip factory.

Ripley **1.** town, pop. 2967, Chautauqua Co., extreme W New York, on L. Erie, 28 mi/45 km NW of Jamestown, on the Pennsylvania line. Before waiting-period laws were passed, Ripley was the fast-marriage capital of the state. There are vineyards and beaches in this rural township. **2.** village, pop. 1794, Brown Co., SW Ohio, on the Ohio R. and the Kentucky border, 42 mi/68 km SE of Cincinnati. Situated at the junction of three US routes, this former steamboat center is a distribution point for tobacco. Corn and hogs are also raised in the area. Ripley is the site of the Rankin House, an UNDERGROUND RAILROAD station that has been turned into a state memorial. After the Civil War a number of freed slaves settled here.

Ripon city, pop. 7241, Fond du Lac Co., E Wisconsin, on Silver Creek, 20 mi/32 km NW of Fond du Lac. It was settled in 1844 by Fourierists; their socialistic community was disbanded in 1850. Ripon is widely regarded as the birthplace of the Republican party, which was organized at a meeting held at the Little White Schoolhouse here on March 20, 1854. A convention later that year at JACKSON, Michigan, founded the party. In an agricultural area, the city produces canned foods, flour, and home appliances. It is the seat of Ripon College (1851).

Rittenhouse Square residential neighborhood in C Philadelphia, Pennsylvania, one of the city's original five squares. In the 19th century, wealthy Philadelphians built mansions around the park; today, it is ringed by high-rise apartment buildings and condominiums, as well as town houses. The square is a popular gathering place for area residents; art exhibits and flower shows are held.

Ritter Range mountains of the SIERRA NEVADA, SE of Yosemite National Park, in EC California. Continued by the CATHEDRAL RANGE to the NW, they include the Minarets, a collection of granite spires popular for climbing that are named for their resemblance to mosque towers; Mt. Ritter (13,157 ft/4010 m); and Banner Peak (12,946 ft/3946 m). The range is in the Ansel Adams Wilderness Area (228,000 ac/ 92,340 ha).

River for rivers whose names begin with this word, see under the other name element. Thus for River Rouge, see **Rouge, River.**

River Bend nuclear power plant: see under SAINT FRANCISVILLE, Louisiana.

River City dramatic locale: see under MASON CITY, Iowa.

Riverdale **1.** city, pop. 9359, Clayton Co., NW Georgia, 13 mi/21 km S of downtown Atlanta, a residential suburb. **2.** village, pop. 13,671, Cook Co., NE Illinois, on the Little Calumet R., immediately S of Chicago, and 15 mi/24 km S of the Loop. This bedroom community was settled in the 1840s at the intersection of the river with an Indian trail. **3.** affluent residential section, extreme NW Bronx, New York. A semisuburban district of winding lanes, large estates, and schools and other institutions, it lies on a high ridge between Van Cortlandt Park (E) and the Hudson R. (W), from the Westchester line to Spuyten Duyvil in the S. A mid-19th-century country haven, Riverdale was annexed to New York City in 1874. Wave Hill, home to Theodore Roosevelt, Mark Twain, and Toscanini, now a public garden, is here, as is Mt. St. Vincent College.

River Edge borough, pop. 10,603, Bergen Co., NE New Jersey, on the Hackensack R., 4 mi/ 6 km N of Hackensack. Settled by the Dutch in the 17th century, it is now primarily a bedroom community in the New York metropolitan area. Located here is the sandstone Demarest House (1678), Bergen Co.'s oldest Colonial dwelling.

River Falls city, pop. 10,541, Pierce and St. Croix counties, NW Wisconsin, on the Kinnickinnic R., 12 mi/19 km NE of the junction of the St. Croix and Mississippi rivers and the Minnesota line. The center of an agricultural region, it has grain elevators and poultry farms. The University of Wisconsin at River Falls (1874) is here. Kinnickinnic State Park is 5 mi/8 km SW.

River Forest village, pop. 11,669, Cook Co., NE Illinois, on the Des Plaines R., 16 mi/26 km W of Chicago. A residential suburb, it was settled in 1836 as part of the community of Harlem. Local educational institutions include Rosary College (1901), Concordia University (1864), and Dominican College. Frank Lloyd Wright designed the village's Winslow House (1893) and River Forest Tennis Club (1906).

Riverfront Stadium completed 1970, now on Pete Rose Way, in downtown CINCINNATI, Ohio, on the Ohio R., just SSE of Fountain Square. Seating 60,000, it is home to the Reds (baseball) and Bengals (football). The stadium is one element of a large-scale redevelopment of the city's waterfront, now a tourist as well as shipping zone.

River Grove village, pop. 9961, Cook Co., NE Illinois, on the Des Plaines R., bordering NW Chicago, and 10 mi/16 km NW of the Loop. Triton College (1964) is in this residential suburb.

Riverhead in New York: **a.** unincorporated village, pop. 8814, seat of Suffolk Co., on Long Island on the Peconic R. near the mouth of Great Peconic Bay. It is a commercial center with some light manufacturing, and the E terminus of the Long Island Expressway, from New York City. **b.** town, pop. 23,011, containing the village and surrounding NORTH FORK communities. It has an agricultural and resort economy.

River North commercial and artists' neighborhood on the NORTH SIDE of Chicago, Illinois, immediately N of the LOOP. This area was developed and named during the 1980s, with the conversion of abandoned warehouses and factories into galleries, lofts, and shops.

River Oaks in Texas: **a.** see under FORT WORTH. **b.** elite residential section of Houston, 4 mi/6 km W of Downtown, along the Buffalo Bayou (N). Development here began in the 1920s around a country club, on land held by the powerful Hogg family. Bayou Bend, her mansion in the Homewoods neighborhood, was left to the city by Ima Hogg, in 1966, MEMORIAL PARK is NW, across the bayou.

River of No Return see SALMON R., Idaho.

River Road combination of roads paralleling both banks of the Mississippi R. between New Orleans (SE) and Baton Rouge (NW), in SE Louisiana. A stretch of about 115 mi/ 185 km, it became a leading plantation area in the 18th and 19th centuries, when communities like METAIRIE, DESTREHAN, LUTCHER, DONALDSONVILLE, and PLAQUEMINE developed. It has long been noted for producing and processing sugar cane and cotton. Since the early 20th century it has become almost continuously industrialized, as the New Orleans–Baton Rouge area became a major oil refining, chemical producing, and shipping center.

River Rouge city, pop. 11,314, Wayne Co., SE Michigan, on the Detroit and Rouge rivers, 7 mi/11 km SW of Detroit. It grew from an early French settlement. The city's water resources made it a natural industrial location, and the coming of rail lines added to its development. The opening of the Ford Motor Company's River Rouge plant in nearby DEARBORN (1917) also helped speed its growth. Today River Rouge manufactures marine engines, chemicals, auto parts, paper and gypsum products, and steel. It also has oil refineries and shipyards for building and repair. Zug I. is an industrial park in the NE corner of the city that is surrounded by the Detroit R. (SE) and a deepwater canal.

Riverside **1.** city, pop. 226,505, seat of Riverside Co., SW California, 50 mi/80 km E of Los Angeles, on the Santa Ana R. It was founded in 1870. In 1873, Eliza and Luther Tibbetts planted three Brazilian seedless orange saplings here; the navel orange revolutionalized the citrus industry, and the city remains an important center. One of the original trees still produces. Acres of groves are within the city limits, as are extensive packing plants. The Mission Inn, a resort hotel built here in 1876 after the architectural style of Spanish MISSIONS, began a revival movement in California. The city is home to the University of California at Riverside (1954), California Baptist College (1950), La Sierra University (1905), and several other institutions. Expanding rapidly in the 1950s and 1960s, it became a residential and industrial center. Aerospace motor assemblies, electronic components, and mobile homes are its chief manufactures. The Riverside International Raceway draws visitors to auto racing events, including the California 500. March Air Force Base, 7 mi/11 km SE, near MORENO VALLEY, has contributed to Riverside's economy. **2.** see under GREENWICH, Connecticut. **3.** village, pop. 8774, Cook Co., NE Illinois, adjacent (W) to BERWYN, and 10 mi/16 km WSW of Chicago's LOOP, on the Des Plaines R. It was designed in 1868 by Frederick Law Olmsted as one of his first planned towns, with curving, wooded streets, and remains an affluent residential suburb. North Riverside (village, pop. 6005) adheres more closely to the grid development pattern of other suburbs near Chicago.

Riverside County 7214 sq mi/18,684 sq km, pop. 1,170,413, in S California. RIVERSIDE is its seat. The county extends from the Arizona line (E) to ORANGE Co. and the Los Angeles area (W). In the E it includes several Indian reservations and most of the JOSHUA TREE National Monument. In the C are the Coachella Valley, with Palm Springs and other resorts, and part of the Salton Sea (S). To the W, suburbs and exurbs of the Los Angeles area have spread into the valleys between mountains of the Coast Ranges. The county produces citrus fruits, poultry, livestock, dairy products, grain, dates, nuts, and field and truck crops, and is increasingly industrial in the Riverside area, which is a growing high-tech business zone.

Riverside Drive **1.** prestigious residential boulevard on the Upper West Side from West 72nd St. to Dyckman St. (Fort Tryon Park) at Manhattan's N end, New York City. Built 1873–1910, it is paralleled for most of its length by Riverside Park, while the Henry Hudson Drive (1930s) lies below, closer to the Hudson R. Riverside Church (1930) and GRANT'S TOMB are on Riverside Drive in Morningside Heights. **2.** and **Riverside Park** see under PARKWAY, Memphis, Tennessee.

Riverton **1.** city, pop. 11,261, Salt Lake Co., NC Utah, on the Jordan R., a residential suburb 15 mi/24 km S of Salt Lake City. **2.** city, pop. 9202, Fremont Co., WC Wyoming, surrounded on all sides by the WIND RIVER INDIAN RESERVATION, and 22 mi/35 km NE of Lander. An 1830s fur post was here at the confluence of the Wind and Popo Agie rivers. After tribal land was purchased in 1904, agriculture flourished. The city is a processing and trade center for dairy, livestock, beet, potato, and other crop producers. It had a 1960s uranium boom, and now has varied light (some high-tech) manufactures. Central Wyoming College (1906) is here.

Rivertown also, **Warehouse District** restored commercial section of downtown Detroit, Michigan, NE of the RENAISSANCE CENTER, between Jefferson Ave. and the Detroit R. Recent investment has turned an abandoned area into an upscale residential and commercial showcase. CHENE PARK is here.

Riverview **1.** city, pop. 13,894, Wayne Co., SE Michigan, on the Detroit R., a residential suburb 16 mi/26 km SW of Detroit. **2.** town, pop. 16,270, Albert Co., SE New Brunswick, on the Petitcodiac R. opposite (S of) MONCTON. Although in an area rich in minerals and oil shale, it is primarily a bedroom community.

River Walk see PASEO DEL RIO, San Antonio, Texas.

River Wards collection of neighborhoods in Philadelphia, Pennsylvania, along the Delaware R., N of NORTHERN LIBERTIES. Once home to Irish and East European immigrants who worked in local factories, the area has become progressively poorer with the decline in manufacturing jobs over the past half-century. Today, KENSINGTON, Richmond, FRANKFORD, Bridesburg, and Wissinoming are home to Hispanic and other immigrants.

River West residential and commercial neighborhood on the West Side of Milwaukee, Wisconsin, 1 mi/2 km N of Downtown. With a population mixture of blacks, Hispanic immigrants, and artists, it has recently experienced a surge in investment and rehabilitation.

Riviera Beach city, pop. 27,639, Palm Beach Co., SE Florida, on the L. Worth lagoon, just N of West Palm Beach. It was settled in the 1920s by descendants of Bahamian fishermen, and remains predominantly black. It is a popular winter resort, connected by bridges to Palm Beach Shores (town, pop. 1040) on the Atlantic barrier island. Both commercial and sport fishing are important to its economy. Aerospace and electronics industries as well as high-tech research, development, and engineering facilities are located here.

Riviere des Lacs see DES LACS R., North Dakota.

Rivière-du-Loup city, pop. 14,017, Rivière-du-Loup Co., SE Québec, 100 mi/160 km NE of Québec City, on the S shore of the St. Lawrence R., at the mouth of the R. du Loup. A 1673 SEIGNEURIE that was lightly populated until the 1800s, it then grew with the expansion of forest industries. These and trade, regional administration, and tourism are important today, and the city is a ferry, rail, and highway hub, and the center of a resort area.

Roan Cliffs see under BOOK CLIFFS, Utah.

Roan Mountain elevation of the Appalachian Mts. on the border between NE Tennessee and W North Carolina, 20 mi/32 km SE of Johnson City, Tennessee, reaching 6313 ft/1925 m at Roan High Knob. It is noted for its large natural stand of rhododendrons.

Roanoke independent city, pop. 96,397, in WC Virginia, on the Roanoke (Staunton) R., at the S end of the Shenandoah Valley, between the Blue Ridge and Allegheny mountains, 140 mi/230 km WSW of Richmond. It is an industrial, trade, and transportation center for W Virginia. Among its manufactures are electrical equipment, furniture, paper goods, apparel, structural steel, chemicals, plastics, and cement. It also has some tourist trade based on its proximity to SKYLINE DRIVE and the Blue Ridge. Roanoke is headquarters for the Norfolk and Western Railroad and for the Jefferson National Forest. It remained a small town until 1882, when the Shenandoah Valley Railroad was built to connect with the Norfolk and Western Railroad; the growth of railroad shops and foundries spurred its rapid development. Western Virginia Community College (1966) and National Business College (1886) are here. Roanoke College is in neighboring (W) SALEM.

Roanoke County 251 sq mi/650 sq km, pop. 79,332, in WC Virginia. Its seat is SALEM. It lies just W of the BLUE RIDGE Mts., in a rich agricultural region. The cities of Salem and ROANOKE (which is in the county but administratively separate) are manufacturing centers.

Roanoke Island in Dare Co., E North Carolina, near the S entrance to ALBEMARLE SOUND, between Roanoke (E) and Croatan (W) sounds, 40 mi/64 km N of Cape Hatteras. It is 10 mi/16 km NW–SE, and up to 2 mi/3 km wide. Manteo (pop. 991), the seat of Dare Co., is its chief town. At the N end is Fort Raleigh National Historic Site, location of the first English settlement in North America, established here by Walter Raleigh in 1585; it lasted only 10 months. In July 1587, a second colony was organized by John White, who had been appointed governor by Raleigh. By 1591 the colonists had vanished, among them Virginia Dare, the first English child born in the Americas. Their fate has been debated ever since. The enigmatic word "Croatoan," carved on a tree, has been taken to mean that they joined the Croatan (Lumbee) tribe on the mainland.

Roanoke Rapids city, pop. 15,722, Halifax Co., NE North Carolina, on the Roanoke R., 5 mi/8 km S of the Virginia border, on Interstate 95. Founded in the 1890s, it has an economy based on textiles, lumber, and paper products.

Roanoke River 410 mi/660 km long, in Virginia and North Carolina. It rises in North and South forks in Montgomery Co., SW Virginia, W of the Blue Ridge Mts., and cuts through a gap occupied by the cities of SALEM and ROANOKE. It then cuts SE through the Blue Ridge into the PIEDMONT. It is dammed at Smith Mt. to form irregularly shaped Smith Mountain L., one of Virginia's largest bodies of water, with arms up to 10 mi/16 km long. From the lake it continues generally E in a winding course past Altavista and Brookneal, then SE to the JOHN H. KERR RESERVOIR, where it is joined by the DAN R. Above this point the Roanoke was formerly called the Staunton R. The Roanoke continues SE into North Carolina, through Gaston L. to the mill town of ROANOKE RAPIDS. It then flows SE through the coastal plain to enter Batchelor Bay of ALBEMARLE SOUND.

Roaring Fork River 70 mi/113 km long, in C Colorado. It rises just W of Mt. ELBERT, in the Sawatch Range, and flows NW through Aspen and Carbondale, joining the Colorado R. at Glenwood Springs. Passing through the White Mt. National Forest, it is a noted fishing, rafting, and kayaking site.

Robbinsdale city, pop. 14,396, Hennepin Co., SE Minnesota, immediately NW of Minneapolis. It has experienced a great deal of recent commercial growth, particularly along Route 81, its main artery.

Robert Taylor Homes public housing complex, said to be the world's largest, on the SOUTH SIDE of Chicago, Illinois, 3.5 mi/6 km S of the LOOP. Built beginning in 1962 as one of the city's major urban renewal projects, the complex replaced a large area of deteriorating housing and commercial space in the heart of the old BLACK BELT with 28 matching 16-story towers lining the E side of the DAN RYAN EXPRESSWAY. Poverty and associated problems, however, soon made the Homes themselves emblematic of conditions they had been intended to alleviate.

Roberval city, pop. 11,628, Lac St.-Jean Ouest Co., S Québec, 125 mi/200 km NNW of Québec City, on the SW shore of L. SAINT-JEAN. Founded in 1855, it is the administrative, commercial, and service center for the area. Local industries include dairying, potato growing, and salmon fishing. Roberval is also a noted lake resort; the Traversée Internationale du L.-St.-Jean, a swim marathon between Péribonka (on the lake's N) and Roberval, is held every July.

Robins Air Force Base see under WARNER ROBINS, Georgia.

Robins Island see under PECONIC BAY, New York.

Robstown city, pop. 12,849, Nueces Co., S Texas, 15 mi/24 km W of downtown Corpus Christi, a suburb in an oil, livestock, cotton, vegetable, and grain producing area.

Rochelle city, pop. 8769, Ogle Co., N Illinois, on the Kyte R., 14 mi/23 km W of DE KALB. In an agricultural area now crossed by I-88 (the East–West Tollway), it has been noted especially for canning asparagus grown locally and as a builder of small diesel engines.

Rochester **1.** see under ROCHESTER HILLS, Michigan. **2.** city, pop. 70,745, seat of Olmsted Co., SE Minnesota, on the South Fork of the Zumbro R., 70 mi/113 km SE of St. Paul. Originally a camping ground for wagon trains and settled in 1854, it is now an internationally renowned medical center. Dr. William Mayo arrived in 1863, and his two sons founded the Mayo Clinic in 1889. The Mayo Medical Center now includes extensive diagnostic, treatment, laboratory, and library facilities. The Museum of Hygiene and Medicine is part of the complex. The Mayo Foundation for Medical Education and Research, affiliated with the University of Minnesota, is also based here. Rochester has diverse manufacturing, including the production of computers, tractor cabs, phonographs, and medical supplies and instruments. Vegetables grown in the area are canned here and dairy products are processed. Rochester Community College (1915) is here. **3.** city, pop. 26,630, Strafford Co., SE New Hampshire, on the Cocheco and Salmon Falls rivers, 7 mi/11 km NE of Dover. The city includes the villages of Gonic and East Rochester. Rochester was a 19th-century industrial center, making textiles and shoes. The Rochester State (agricultural) Fair dates to 1875. Industries make fiberboard, paper, and fabricated metal products. **4.** city, pop. 231,636, seat of Monroe Co., W New York, on the Genesee R. and L. Ontario, 70 mi/113 km ENE of Buffalo. The site was settled in 1789 around a grist mill powered by the Genesee's falls, and developed into a flour milling center. Its nickname, the Flour City, changed to Flower City as the relative importance of the nursery business grew. The clothing and shoe industry flourished during the Civil War, and in the 1890s, industrialists launched the Bausch and Lomb, Eastman Kodak, and Taylor Instrument companies. Rochester is now one of the world's leading manufacturers of optical and photographic equipment, film, and scientific instruments. Other manufactures include photocopy machines, thermometers, machine tools, business machines, dental and electrical equipment, glass-lined tanks, and automotive parts. Rochester is also a processing and shipping center. Its institutions include the University of Rochester (1850) and the Rochester Institute of Technology (1829). In the 20th century the city's industries and population expanded into suburbs including BRIGHTON, IRONDEQUOIT, GREECE, and GATES.

Rochester Hills city, pop. 61,766, Oakland Co., SE Michigan, on the Clinton R., 8 mi/13 km NE of Pontiac. Local industries include electronic automobile components and pharmaceuticals. The city is the seat of Michigan Christian College (1959). The neighboring city of Rochester (N), pop. 7130, is the site of Meadow Brook Hall and Oakland University (1957). Situated in wooded hills, the two affluent residential suburbs constitute Greater Rochester.

Rockaway borough (pop. 6243) and township (pop. 19,572), Morris Co., NE New Jersey, 26 mi/42 km NW of Newark. The area has produced munitions since the Revolution, and much of Picatinny Arsenal is in the township. Among local manufactures in the 18th and 19th centuries were four-wheeled horse carriages that came to be known as rockaways. Communities in the township include the ghost town of Hibernia and Lake Telemark (unincorporated, pop. 1139). The **Rockaway River** rises in NW Morris Co. and flows generally S through the area, past Dover and Boonton, where it is dammed, to join the Passaic R. W of Caldwell.

Rockaways, the series of largely residential neighborhoods along Rockaway Peninsula, which extends 11 mi/17 km across the mouth of Jamaica Bay, S Queens, New York. The peninsula's name means "sandy place" in the Rockaway tongue. Separated from the rest of New York City, the Rockaways were long reachable by land only through Nassau Co. Far Rockaway, the southeasternmost New York City neighborhood, is their commercial hub. Bayswater, to its NW, is somewhat isolated even from Far Rockaway. Edgemere, farther W, was, along with Arverne and Hammel, a bungalow community largely razed in the 1960s for a renewal project never built. The Edgemere landfill, begun in 1938, acquired a height of 70 ft/21 m, an area of 178 ac/72 ha, and the sarcastic nickname "Mount Edgemere" before it was closed in 1991. Farther W are Seaside, Rockaway Park, and the wealthier communities of Belle Harbor and Neponsit. Jacob Riis Park and Fort Tilden, built for coastal defense in 1917, lie W of Neponsit. West of the fort site are the small communities of Roxbury, Rockaway Point, and Breezy Point. The Rockaways were resort communities in the 19th century. Year-round residents began to arrive in the 1930s, and subway service from Queens opened in 1956. Automobile bridges now connect the peninsula with FLOYD BENNETT FIELD, Brooklyn, and HOWARD BEACH, Queens.

Rockbridge County 603 sq mi/1562 sq km, pop. 18,350, in WC Virginia. Its seat is LEXINGTON. At the S end of the Shenandoah Valley, it includes part of the George Washington National Forest. Mineral springs and the NATURAL BRIDGE are among its tourist attractions. There is also livestock raising, dairying, fruit growing, and some quarrying.

Rock City area of more than 200 unusual sandstone concretions in the Smoky Hills of C Kansas, 2.5 mi/4 km SW of Minneapolis and 18 mi/29 km NNW of Salina. Erosion continues to reveal new formations in the shape of toadstools, pyramids, and spheres, and has long prompted the belief that the rocks are growing.

Rockcliffe Park also, **Rockcliffe** village, pop. 2113, Ottawa-Carleton Regional Municipality, SE Ontario, on the S bank of the Ottawa R., opposite Gatineau, Québec. A wealthy residential suburb surrounded by NE OTTAWA and adjacent (N) to VANIER, it takes its name from a popular riverside park on its SE.

Rock County 723 sq mi/1873 sq km, pop. 139,510, in S Wisconsin, bordered by the Illinois line (S). Its seat is JANESVILLE. It is bisected by the Rock R. A fertile agricultural area, it produces tobacco, dairy items, livestock, and poultry. There is diverse manufacturing at Beloit in the S, and at Janesville in the center of the county.

Rock Creek 30 mi/48 km long, in Maryland and the District of Columbia. It rises in two branches S of Laytonsville, Montgomery Co.; the branches join just NE of Rockville, and Rock Creek flows S into the District, finally joining the Potomac R. just N of the Watergate, in FOGGY BOTTOM. In the District, 1754-ac/710-ha **Rock Creek Park,** a national park, is a major recreational facility. In Maryland, Rock Creek Regional Park lies along the upper creek.

Rockefeller Center commercial building complex, Midtown Manhattan, New York City. A project of John D. Rockefeller, Jr., it was largely built 1931–39 between Fifth and Sixth avenues and 48th and 51st streets. The 70-story RCA Building (now officially the GE Building) was its centerpiece. Radio City, a complex on its W side, is known for its 6200-seat Music Hall.

Rock Falls city, pop. 9654, Whiteside Co., NW Illinois, across the Rock R. from STERLING. It is situated at the mouth of the Hennepin Feeder Canal. It has machine and tool industries.

Rockford city, pop. 139,426, seat of Winnebago Co., NC Illinois, bisected by the Rock R., 18 mi/29 km S of Beloit, Wisconsin. The state's second-largest city, it is the industrial and commercial center for a 12-county area in two states. Local manufactures include machine tools, screws and fasteners, containers, auto parts, electric motors, metalworking machinery, aviation and space instruments, and air-conditioning equipment, among many other products. It was settled (1834) by a group of New Englanders on the stage-coach route between Chicago and Galena. The Rock R. was dammed within a decade, providing waterpower for sawmills and farm machinery production. The Galena and Chicago Union Railroad arrived in 1852, bringing Swedish immigrants, many of them carpenters who stimulated the local furniture industry. Rockford's educational institutions include Rockford College (1847), Rock Valley College (1964), and the University of Illinois College of Medicine at Rockford. Rock Cut State Park is just NE.

Rock Forest city, pop. 14,551, Sherbrooke census division, S Québec, on the R. Magog. It is a largely residential suburb 6 mi/10 km SW of SHERBROOKE.

Rock Hill **1.** city, pop. 5217, St. Louis Co., EC Missouri, a residential suburb 10 mi/16 km WSW of downtown St. Louis. **2.** city, pop. 41,643, York Co., N South Carolina, 26 mi/42 km SSW of Charlotte, North Carolina. Named for a flint hill nearby, it has diverse industries producing textile and wood pulp products, printed materials, truck bodies, chemicals, and concrete. First settled in 1735, it became a railroad depot in 1851, and was a transfer point for Confederate troops and supplies in the Civil War. Cotton mills encouraged growth, and the damming of the Catawba R. N of the city (forming L. Wylie) created electric power. The Catawba Indians, whose 640-ac/260-ha reservation (pop. 174) is nearby along the river, were in the 1990s settling a claim to a much larger area embracing Rock Hill, FORT MILL, and several other communities. Rock Hill is home to Winthrop College (1886) and to a junior college.

Rockingham city, pop. 9399, seat of Richmond Co., S North Carolina, on Hitchcock Creek, just E of the Pee Dee R., 60 mi/97 km ESE of Charlotte. Settled in the 1780s in an area that produces fruit, tobacco, cotton, and lumber, it has produced textiles, paper, and other light manufactures.

Rock Island city, pop. 40,552, seat of Rock Island Co., NW Illinois, at the place where the Mississippi R. is joined by the Rock R., immediately W of Moline and across the Mississippi from Davenport, Iowa. It is one of the QUAD CITIES. Local manufactures include farm implements, aluminum products, machinery, and clothing. One of the largest employers is on nearby Rock I., a 1000-ac/405-ha limestone formation in the Mississippi R. that is the site of the world's largest manufacturing arsenal, and is now the Armament National Readiness Command Headquarters for the US Army. Originally a Sauk and Fox village, Rock Island attracted Americans for its strategic value and fertile surrounding lands, which soon became cornfields. Fort Armstrong was built on the island in 1816, while the city itself was settled in 1826. Serving as US military headquarters during the Black Hawk War, Rock Island thrived as a steamboat port. A Civil War prisoner camp was established on the island, which is also the site of a National and a Confederate cemetery. Augustana College (1860) is in the city. The Black Hawk Historic Site is just S.

Rock Island County 423 sq mi/1096 sq km, pop. 148,723, in NW Illinois, bordered by the Mississippi R. (W and N) and the Rock R. (SE). The Rock empties into the Mississippi at the industrial centers of Moline and Rock Island, the county seat, two of the QUAD CITIES. In the N and SW, the county is agricultural, specializing in corn, hogs, and dairy products.

Rockland **1.** city, pop. 7972, seat of Knox Co., SC Maine. It is on US 1 and the W shore of Penobscot Bay, 70 mi/113 km NE of Portland. Originally part of Thomaston, it was an early limestone quarrying and shipbuilding center. The clipper ship *Red Jacket* (1854) was built here. Now commercial center for the Penobscot Bay region, Rockland has significant summer tourism and an annual Seafoods Festival. It is the 1892 birthplace of poet Edna St. Vincent Millay and the site of the Farnsworth Memorial Library and Art Museum, noted for its collection of paintings by Andrew Wyeth and his family, nearby summer residents. **2.** town, pop. 16,123, Plymouth Co., SE Massachusetts, 19 mi/31 km SE of Boston. Manufactures include fiberglass boats, shoes, and sheet metal. South Weymouth Naval Air Station lies across the town's N border.

Rockland County 175 sq mi/453 sq km, pop. 265,475, in SE New York, bordered by the Hudson R. (E) and the New Jersey line (S and SW). Its seat is NEW CITY. Once primarily rural and agricultural, by the late 20th century it had become overwhelmingly suburban, with many residents commuting to work in New York City, and commercial and light manufacturing operations relocating here. Rockland Co. includes such residential communities as Nyack, Nanuet, Spring Valley, Suffern, and Haverstraw. Recreational areas include a large section of Harriman State Park and Bear Mountain State Park, on the Hudson.

Rockledge city, pop. 16,023, Brevard Co., EC Florida, immediately S of Cocoa, and often referred to as its (older) twin city, on the INDIAN R. lagoon. Its name derives from local coquina (seashell) rock ledges. Its economy relies on tourism, fruit processing, and Cape Canaveral's aerospace industry, but it is chiefly residential.

Rocklin city, pop. 19,033, Placer Co., NE California, 18 mi/29 km NE of Sacramento. Once a largely Finnish granite-quarrying community, also a fruit shipping center, it grew quickly in the 1980s as a residential suburb. Sierra College (1914) is here.

Rockport **1.** see under SPENCER Co., Indiana. **2.** town, pop. 7482, Essex Co., NE Massachusetts, 30 mi/48 km NE of Boston. A summer resort located at the tip of Cape Ann on the North Shore, it has a fishing village, artists' colony, and various tourist attractions. Bearskin Neck contains a number of restored fishermen's cottages; at its end is "Motif No. 1," a fishing shanty that with its backdrop has attracted countless painters and photographers.

Rock River **1.** 285 mi/459 km long, in Wisconsin and Illinois. It rises in lake-filled country S of Fond du Lac. It flows generally S past Watertown and Jefferson, where it is joined by the Crawfish R., and widens before passing through L. Koshkonong, N of Janesville. It occupies a broad glacial channel formed by meltwater draining from the area of L. Winnebago and Green Bay. Continuing S, it passes through Beloit and into Illinois, where it flows SW past Rockford, Dixon, Rock Falls, Erie, and Moline before entering the Mississippi R. at Rock Island. The original inhabitants of the Rock R. valley were the Winnebago in the N and the Sauk in the Illinois section. White settlers came to the valley in the 1830s. Many Swedes, Germans, and New Englanders settled the area over the next two decades. Today, larger cities and towns on the Rock R. are important manufacturing centers. **2.** 100 mi/161 km long, in Minnesota and Iowa. It is formed in Pipestone Co., in SW Minnesota, and flows S past Luverne and into NW Iowa. There it continues SW past Rock Rapids and Rock Valley to the Big Sioux R., 6 mi/10 km N of Hawarden. Its tributary, the Little Rock R., rises in Nobles Co., SW Minnesota, and flows 40 mi/64 km SW into Iowa, to the Rock R. just S of Doon.

Rock Springs city, pop. 19,050, Sweetwater Co., SW Wyoming, on Bitter Creek, 13 mi/21 km ENE of GREEN RIVER. It originated as a station on the Overland Trail in 1862 and developed as a coal mining and ranching center after the Union Pacific arrived in 1868. The community now is a trade and processing center for a livestock and mining region producing coal, soda ash, oil, and natural gas. Gateway to mountain recreation areas, Rock Springs provides a base for tourists, hunters, and anglers. Western Wyoming Community College (1959) is here.

Rockville city, pop. 44,835, seat of Montgomery Co., C Maryland, 14 mi/22 km NW of Washington, D.C. Settled during the Revolutionary War around Hungerford's Tavern, it was known as Montgomery Court House and Williamsburg before taking its present name in 1801. Rockville was raided frequently by Confederate troops during the Civil War. Commercial and research development related to government operations intensified following World War II; aerospace, computer, nuclear, and communications facilities are here. Rockville is home to both federal (FDA) and private health industry offices, and to a campus of Montgomery College (1946). Zelda and F. Scott Fitzgerald are buried in St. Mary's Cemetery.

Rockville Centre village, pop. 24,727, in Hempstead town, Nassau Co., SE New York, on Long Island's South Shore, 19 mi/31 km SE of Manhattan. Primarily residential, it is the seat of Molloy College (1955), and home to some financial and commercial operations.

Rockwall city, pop. 10,486, seat of Rockwall Co., NE Texas, 21 mi/34 km NE of Dallas, on L. Ray Hubbard (the East Fork of the TRINITY R.). In the agricultural BLACKLANDS, it has some light industries. Lakeside residential growth almost doubled its population in the 1980s.

Rocky Flats government nuclear weapons plant, opened 1952 on the Rocky Flats in the foothills of NC Colorado's Front Range, 15 mi/24 km NW of Denver and 6 mi/10 km SSE of Boulder. Long the assembly plant for plutonium bomb triggers, it has since the 1970s been the subject of disputes over its safety record, hazardous residues, and its future role or closure.

Rocky Hill **1.** town, pop. 16,554, Hartford Co., C Connecticut, on the Connecticut R. and Interstate 91. A suburb of Hartford, it was an important river port in the 18th century. Today it is home to corporate and state offices, and produces firearms, chemical coatings, and metal products. Dinosaur State Park preserves tracks found by accident in 1966 during a construction project. **2.** see under WASHINGTON'S HEADQUARTERS, New Jersey.

Rocky Mount **1.** city, pop. 48,997, Nash and Edgecombe counties, EC North Carolina, on the Tar R., near its falls, 48 mi/77 km ENE of Raleigh. The site was settled in 1818, when the Rocky Mount Cotton Mills were built by the falls. In the 1840s railroad service reached Rocky Mount, and today the tracks of the Seaboard Coast Line bisect its main street, also delineating the county border. Rocky Mount is one of the world's leading bright leaf tobacco market and processing centers. Other manufactures include textiles, clothing, furniture, fabricated metals, chemicals, electrical components, and stone, glass, and clay products. North Carolina Wesleyan College (1956) is 4 mi/6 km N. **2.** town, pop. 4098, Franklin Co., SW Virginia, 18 mi/29 km S of Roanoke, in the E foothills of the Blue Ridge Mts. It produces textiles, furniture, and plywood, and has a tobacco market. It was the longtime home of Confederate general Jubal Early.

Rocky Mountain Arsenal weapons plant and storage facility in Adams Co., immediately NE of STAPLETON INTERNATIONAL AIRPORT and DENVER, Colorado. From World War II, incendiaries and chemical weapons were manufactured or stored here; in the 1990s, leakage of toxic materials caused local concern.

Rocky Mountain House town, pop. 5461, WC Alberta, on the North Saskatchewan R., 100 mi/161 km SW of Edmonton. The local economy is based on oil, coal, lumber, some mixed farming, and tourism. The North West Company established (1799) a fur trading post here from which David Thompson set out (1807) to explore the Rocky Mts. The post was later (1875) abandoned, but European settlers and two railways arrived in the early 1900s, attracted by the farmland and the discovery of coal. Rocky Mt. House National Historic Park is nearby.

Rocky Mountain National Park 265,200 ac/107,400 ha (414 sq mi/1073 sq km), 50 mi/80 km NW of Denver, in NC Colorado. ESTES PARK is just E. The CONTINENTAL DIVIDE and the FRONT RANGE run through the park, which reaches 14,256 ft/4345 m at LONGS PEAK. The Big Thompson and Cache la Poudre rivers, tributaries of the South Platte R., flow N and E from the park; the headwaters of the SW-flowing Colorado R. are here also. The park's valleys are over 8000 ft/2440 m high. Trail Ridge Rd. runs 50 mi/80 km through it, reaching 12,183 ft/3713 m.

Rocky Mountains also, **the Rockies** major North American range, extending over 3000 mi/4800 km, from NW Alaska E to the Yukon Territory, then generally SSE to C New Mexico. Forming the E face of the continental CORDILLERA, the Rockies carry the CONTINENTAL DIVIDE along their crest through most of their length. To the E are the Great Plains (in the N the Mackenzie R. lowlands and Alaska's North Slope); to the W is the INTERMONTANE REGION. In the US, the Rockies themselves were long thought of as the GREAT DIVIDE, the barrier to westward migration. Their name may be owed to the Assiniboine ("stony" or "rocky") Indians, who lived near them in Alberta, rather than to their structure. They have also been called the Shining Mountains, for their appearance from the Plains. The Rockies are considered to be continued southward in Mexico by the Sierra Madre; but between that range and the end of New Mexico's Sangre de Cristo Mts., the generally accepted S terminus of the Rockies proper, is a SE extension of the BASIN AND RANGE PROVINCE, through which the Rio Grande flows SE to the Gulf of Mexico. Formed by various processes (but largely by the tilting of FAULT blocks) over a period ending some 60 million years ago, the Rockies differ widely in elevation and appearance. The highest US peaks are in Colorado, rising to 14,433 ft/4399 m at Mt. ELBERT; Mt. ROBSON, on the Alberta–British Columbia border, is the highest (12,972 ft/3954 m) peak in the Canadian Rockies. The chain is conventionally divided into five sections: the Southern Rockies (in New Mexico, Colorado, and Wyoming); the Middle Rockies (in Utah, Wyoming, and Idaho); the Northern Rockies (in Idaho, Montana, and Washington, extending to the Alberta and British Columbia borders); the Canadian Rockies (in British Columbia, Alberta, and the Yukon and Northwest territories); and the Alaskan Rockies (essentially the BROOKS RANGE). The **Southern Rockies** comprise two parallel N–S groups, between which lie Colorado's high basins, called "parks." On the E is Colorado's FRONT RANGE, towering over the High Plains, and extended, S of the Arkansas R., by the WET Mts; in the N, it extends into Wyoming's LARAMIE Mts. On the W are the SANGRE DE CRISTO, extending N into the SAWATCH RANGE, site of Elbert and other high peaks; on the Sangre de Cristo's W is the broad San Luis Valley, cut by the upper Rio Grande, with the SAN JUAN Mts., a largely volcanic group, to its W. The Sawatch Range extends N into the PARK RANGE and into Wyoming's Sierra Madre. Above the Southern Rockies is the Wyoming plateau, across which the North Platte and Sweetwater rivers flow, and in which SOUTH PASS offered the most important break in the Rockies for 19th-century travelers; through this area the Oregon and other trails, and later the Union Pacific Railroad, passed. The **Middle Rockies** lie across NW Wyoming, extending SW to Utah's E–W UINTA Mts. and to the WASATCH RANGE, and W into the SE corner of Idaho. In Wyoming the WIND RIVER and Teton ranges contain the highest peaks; far to the E the BIGHORN Mts. rise above the plains and extend N into S Montana. The **Northern Rockies** are separated from the Middle Rockies by the Snake River Plain section of the COLUMBIA PLATEAU. They occupy almost all of C and N Idaho, most of W Montana, and parts of Washington NE of the Okanagan R. Major components include the Lewis Range, BITTERROOTS, CLEARWATERS, SALMON RIVER Mts., and the S end of the SELKIRKS. Much of the Northern Rockies, which include dozens of variously oriented subranges, is underlain by the huge Idaho BATHOLITH. Toward the N, and extending into the Canadian Rockies, are three NNW–SSE oriented trenches, the largest the **Rocky Mountain Trench,** which extends from near Montana's Flathead L. for some 800 mi/1300 km through British Columbia on the W of the Rocky Mt. front; in it flow stretches of the Kootenay, Columbia, and Fraser rivers. The Purcell Trench, running N from the Idaho Panhandle, joins the Rocky Mt. Trench where the Columbia R. bends around the N of the PURCELL Mts. The Selkirk Trench parallels it to the W. In Canada the

Front Range of the Rockies, with the Continental Divide, runs along the Alberta–British Columbia border. To the W are the Columbia Mts., comprising the Selkirks, Purcells, MONASHEES, CARIBOOS, and other British Columbia ranges. After the Alberta border swings N, away from the Front Range, the Rockies gradually diminish as they cross N British Columbia and form the Northwest Territories–Yukon Territory border; major subranges in the N include the MACKENZIE, FRANKLIN, RICHARDSON, and Peel mountains. As they enter Alaska, the Rockies swing W, paralleling the Coast Ranges on the state's S; the Brooks Range, remote and unforested, remains less well known than the rest of the chain. The Rocky Mts. were first known to whites as a legendary, and eventually a real, barrier marking the W end of the Great Plains, standing between westward expansion and the Pacific regions already known through sailors and through Spanish colonizers from Mexico. Before the Continental Divide was understood, it was thought that one or more major rivers might cross the range to the Pacific. In the 19th century the search for routes around or through the Rockies led to discovery of the LEWIS AND CLARK route, and later to development of trails through South Pass and from Santa Fe via the SPANISH TRAIL and other southwestern routes. In the N, early exploration via the Mackenzie and Fraser rivers was followed by discovery of the KICKING HORSE, YELLOWHEAD, and CROWSNEST passes, through which Canadian railroads and highways finally linked British Columbia with the rest of the country. Parts of the Rockies were the last strongholds of various Indian tribes. From the mid 19th century, gold, silver, and lead mining brought rapid development in scattered localities; in the 20th century copper, molybdenum, and other minerals are also important. Denver, Colorado, and Calgary, Alberta, both at the E feet of the Rockies, are the region's major cities. Today the Rockies are increasingly developed for recreational and residential use; large parts of the region are reserved, however, as NATIONAL PARKS, NATIONAL FORESTS, or WILDERNESS AREAS, and in other forms.

Rocky River **1.** city, pop. 20,410, Cuyahoga Co., NE Ohio, on L. Erie at the mouth of the Rocky R., a residential suburb 8 mi/13 km W of downtown Cleveland. There is some light manufacturing. **2.** 10 mi/16 km long, in NE Ohio. It is formed by two branches at Olmsted Falls, and flows NNE, through the W suburbs of Cleveland, to L. Erie at Rocky River. The **West Branch** rises near Medina and flows 25 mi/40 km N to the junction with the **East Branch,** which is 33 mi/53 km long, and rises S of the HINCKLEY RESERVATION.

Rodeo Drive see under BEVERLY HILLS, California.

Rodman rural town, pop. 1016, Jefferson Co., NC New York, 10 mi/16 km S of Watertown. It is the birthplace of five-and-dime merchant F. W. Woolworth (1852–1919).

Roeland Park city, pop. 7706, Johnson Co., NE Kansas, a residential suburb 4 mi/6 km SSW of downtown Kansas City.

Rogers city, pop. 24,692, Benton Co., extreme NW Arkansas, 20 mi/32 km N of Fayetteville and 12 mi/19 km S of the Missouri border, in the Ozarks, near Beaver L. It developed as an agricultural market and processing center after the arrival of the railroad in 1881, and now has meatpacking, fabric production, and other plants. PEA RIDGE National Military Park lies 10 mi/16 km N.

Rogers, Mount peak, 5729 ft/1746 m, on a spur of the IRON Mts. of SW Virginia, 12 mi/19 km S of MARION, near the North Carolina border. It is the highest point in the state.

Rogers Park residential neighborhood on the NORTH SIDE of Chicago, Illinois, on L. Michigan, immediately S of Evanston. An area with a large Jewish and student population, it also houses many new immigrants from Southeast Asia and India. Loyola University (1870) is here.

Rogers Pass see under SELKIRK Mts., British Columbia.

Rogue River 200 mi/320 km long, in SW Oregon. It rises in the CASCADE RANGE W of CRATER LAKE, and flows SW, then generally W through the KLAMATH Mts., past GRANTS PASS, and winds to the Pacific Ocean at Gold Beach. The river drains the fruit growing region around MEDFORD, had an 1850s gold rush, and is noted for its salmon and trout. Its headwaters are in the larger E unit of the 629,100-ac/255,000-ha (983–sq mi/2546–sq km) **Rogue River National Forest,** whose W unit, along the California border SW of Ashland, includes Mt. Ashland (7533 ft/2296 m), in the SISKIYOU Mts.

Rohnert Park city, pop. 36,326, Sonoma Co., NW California, 38 mi/61 km NNW of San Francisco and 7 mi/11 km S of Santa Rosa, on US 101. Sonoma State University (1960) is in this growing residential suburb.

Roland Park residential neighborhood in NC Baltimore, Maryland, W of Charles St., on both sides of Cold Spring Lane. Built in the early 1900s, it is part of one of the first completely planned residential communities in the US. Loyola College (1852) is just NE.

Rolla city, pop. 14,090, seat of Phelps Co., SC Missouri, on the Ozark Plateau, 48 mi/77 km SE of Jefferson City. The city is a trading, processing, and distributing center for a farming and livestock raising region. Manufactures include pet food and machine parts. A campus of the University of Missouri (1870) and the Mid-Continent Mapping Center of the US Geological Survey are here. Rolla lies in an area of abundant springs and caves near the Gasconade R. (W), and is near units of the MARK TWAIN NATIONAL FOREST, for which it is headquarters.

Rolling Fork city, pop. 2444, seat of Sharkey Co., WC Mississippi, on Deer Creek, 33 mi/53 km SSE of Greenville and 9 mi/14 km E of the Mississippi R., in the S DELTA. Settled in the late 1820s, it is an agricultural trade center, and the birthplace (1915) of blues great Muddy Waters. Indian mounds and the Delta National Forest are nearby.

Rolling Hills city, pop. 1871, Los Angeles Co., SW California, 18 mi/29 km SSW of downtown Los Angeles. It is an affluent suburb set in the Palos Verdes Hills on the Palos Verdes Peninsula. **Rolling Hills Estates** (city, pop. 7789), immediately NNW, is similar.

Rolling Meadows city, pop. 22,591, Cook Co., NE Illinois, on Salt Creek, a residential suburb 27 mi/43 km NW of Chicago. The Ned Brown Forest Preserve and Busse L. lie immediately S.

Rolphton locality in Renfrew Co., SE Ontario, on the Ottawa R., 110 mi/180 km WNW of Ottawa. Ontario Hydro here operates a small nuclear power facility that was Canada's first (1962). Chalk River (village, pop. 874), 16 mi/26 km SE, is the site of Canada's first reactor, an experimental facility opened in 1944.

Romain, Cape headland at the S end of Cape I., in the Atlantic Ocean 8 mi/13 km SE of McClellanville and 25 mi/40 km NE of Charleston, in Charleston Co., E South Carolina. The cape, several islands, and marshy Bulls Bay (SW) are included in the 60,000-ac/24,300-ha **Cape Romain National Wildlife Refuge,** an important stop on the ATLANTIC FLYWAY.

Roman Nose Mountain peak (3140 ft/958 m) of the Allegheny Mts., in far NW Maryland, S of Deep Creek L.

Rome **1.** city, pop. 30,326, seat of Floyd Co., NW Georgia, where the Etowah and Oostanaula rivers join to form the Coosa R., 54 mi/89 km NW of Atlanta. Founded in 1834 around seven Appalachian foothills, it was an important cotton market, but developed iron and other industries by the 1850s. In 1864 it was occupied and largely destroyed by W.T. Sherman's troops. Today, it is a mining, lumbering, and manufacturing center, making carpets, textiles, foundry products, and electrical transformers. Shorter College (1873) is here; Berry College (1902) is in Mount Berry, just NW. **2.** city, pop. 44,350, Oneida Co., C New York, at an ancient portage between Wood Creek and the head of the MOHAWK R., 15 mi/24 km NW of Utica. The site was fortified by the British as early as 1725. FORT STANWIX (1758), the third fort built here, was the target of an unsuccessful British siege that led to the Battle of ORISKANY, 6 mi/10 km SE. The area was mapped and named Lynchville in 1786; its growth was fostered by a canal connecting Wood Creek and the Mohawk in 1797, and later, by construction of the ERIE CANAL, which began here in 1817. Lynchville became Rome in 1819. It is known as the Copper City because of its early and continued production of copper and brass products. City industries also produce heavy machinery, vacuum cleaners, wire, cable, precision tools, and ready-mix concrete. Rome is the site of Griffiss Air Force Base, and units of the State University of New York and Mohawk Valley Community College. **3.** township in Lawrence Co., extreme S Ohio, 7 mi/11 km NE of Huntington, West Virginia. It was here, along the Ohio R., that the Rome Beauty apple was developed in 1848.

Romeo village, pop. 3520, Macomb Co., SE Michigan, 19 mi/31 km NE of Pontiac. It was settled (1827) on a Chippewa winter campground, and grew as a center for the production of carriages, brooms, and cigars. Today Romeo is a market center for the surrounding orcharding area and has some light industry. The central village contains more than 80 19th-century homes. Ford Motor Company's Proving Ground is 4 mi/ 6 km NW.

Romeoville village, pop. 14,074, Will Co., NE Illinois, on the Des Plaines R. and Chicago Sanitary and Ship Canal, a residential suburb 8 mi/13 km N of Joliet and 27 mi/43 km SW of Chicago. Lewis University (1932) is at the S edge of the village.

Romney city, pop. 1966, seat of Hampshire Co., in West Virginia's Eastern PANHANDLE, on the South Branch of the Potomac R., 22 mi/35 km S of Cumberland, Maryland. One of the state's oldest towns, settled 1738, it developed around Fort Pearsall. Strategically located on the Baltimore and Ohio Railroad, it changed hands more than 50 times during the Civil War. Romney is an agricultural trade center.

Romulus city, pop. 22,897, Wayne Co., SE Michigan, 20 mi/32 km SW of Detroit. Its economy is based mostly on the auto industry. The city also makes industrial ovens and dental supplies and equipment. Detroit Metropolitan Wayne Co. Airport is SE.

Ronkonkoma unincorporated village, pop. 20,391, in Brookhaven town, Suffolk Co., SE New York, in C Long Island, immediately N of Long Island MacArthur Airport and S of LAKE RONKONKOMA. It is a residential community.

Rookery, the office building in the Romanesque style, built 1888 in the LOOP, Chicago, Illinois, by Burnham & Root, one of the landmarks of Chicago architecture. At La Salle and Adams streets, it is near the MONADNOCK Bldg.

Roosevelt **1.** borough, pop. 884, Monmouth Co., C New Jersey, 5 mi/8 km SE of Hightstown. Originally called Jersey Homesteads, it was built in 1935 as a project of the Federal Resettlement Administration. Constructed for needle trade workers from Philadelphia and New York City, it was an experimental cooperative that combined residential, manufacturing, and agricultural elements. When the original plans proved unworkable, the community was opened to other residents (1940); after President Roosevelt's death (1945), it was renamed in his honor. Roosevelt has long attracted artists. **2.** unincorporated village, pop. 15,030, in Hempstead town, Nassau Co., SE New York, in WC Long Island, immediately N of Freeport. It is primarily residential.

Roosevelt Boulevard main thoroughfare and longest street in Philadelphia, Pennsylvania, a section of US 1 extending 12 mi/19 km between the Schuylkill R. (SW) and the border with Bensalem township (NE). Lined with businesses and homes, it runs like a spine through NORTHEAST PHILADELPHIA.

Roosevelt Campobello International Park see under CAMPOBELLO I., New Brunswick.

Roosevelt Dam and Lake see THEODORE ROOSEVELT L., Arizona.

Roosevelt Field see under GARDEN CITY, New York.

Roosevelt Island 140 ac/57 ha, in the East R., New York City, between Midtown Manhattan and Long Island City, Queens. The 1.75 mi/2.8 km–long island was known as Blackwell's I., and long housed prisons and communicable disease hospitals. In 1921 its reputation caused its name to be changed to Welfare I. In 1935 its last prisoners were moved to RIKER's I. The island's hospitals have now been reduced to two, and Franklin D. Roosevelt I., as it was designated in 1973, is largely a quiet residential neighborhood, reached by subway and by bridge from Queens and aerial tramway from Manhattan. The Queensborough Bridge passes above the island. Roosevelt I. is part of the borough of Manhattan.

Roosevelt National Forest 790,000 ac/320,000 ha (1234 sq mi/3200 sq km), on the E slope of the Rocky Mts., in NC Colorado. Administered with the ARAPAHO National Forest (W), it has large WILDERNESS AREAS and several small glaciers. ESTES PARK is here. The Medicine Bow Mts. are on the NW, Fort Collins just E.

Roosevelt Road major E–W thoroughfare, 31 mi/50 km long, in and W of Chicago, Illinois. It runs from the NEAR SOUTH SIDE through Cicero, Oak Park, and farther suburbs to the W boundary of Du Page Co. In the city, it divides many neighborhoods in the South and West sides.

Roosevelt Roads officially, **Atlantic Fleet Weapons Training Facility** US Naval reserve based on Puerto Rico's E coast, 30 mi/48 km ESE of San Juan, and just S of Ceiba. Developed originally to protect the Panama Canal around World War I, it was greatly expanded in World War II, and now uses some 200,000 sq mi/520,000 sq km of adjacent waters for exercises. The islands of CULEBRA (until 1974) and VIEQUES, within this area, have been employed as test ranges, despite protests.

Root River 60 mi/97 km long, in SE Minnesota. It is formed by the confluence of the **North Branch** (70 mi/113 km long) and the **South Branch** (50 mi/80 km long) near Lanesboro. It flows E past Rushford and Houston to empty into the Mississippi R. across from La Crosse, Wisconsin.

Rose Bowl see under PASADENA, California.

Rosebud unincorporated village, pop. 1538, Todd Co., S South Dakota, 80 mi/129 km SW of Pierre. Located on the **Rosebud Indian Reservation** (pop. 8352), the village serves as its headquarters and is the seat of Sinte Gleska College (1970). The Sioux Indian Museum is nearby.

Rosebud Creek SSW–NNE flowing tributary of the YELLOWSTONE R., in SE Montana. Rising E of the Rosebud Mts., near the Wyoming border, it flows through the NORTHERN CHEYENNE INDIAN RESERVATION. Near its headwaters, on June 17, 1876, Sioux forces under Crazy Horse defeated George Crook's cavalry in an overture to the battle of the LITTLE BIGHORN R. (just W).

Roseburg city, pop. 17,032, seat of Douglas Co., SW Oregon, on the South Umpqua R., 60 mi/97 km SSW of Eugene. Founded in 1851 as Deer Creek, it is a processing center for area products including lumber, sheep, and cattle. Nickel mined at Nickel Mt., 17 mi/27 km SSW, is smelted here. It is the seat of Umpqua Community College (1964). There are many wineries in the area, and Roseburg is the headquarters of the Umpqua National Forest, 17 mi/27 km E.

Rosedale **1.** unincorporated residential community, pop. 18,703, Baltimore Co., NC Maryland, a suburb just E of the Baltimore city limits on Interstate 95. **2.** affluent residential section of N TORONTO, Ontario, 2 mi/3.5 km NNE of Downtown, SE of FOREST HILL and W of the East York line. Named after an 1821 estate, and settled from that period, it is noted for its mansions.

Rose Garden, the see under WHITE HOUSE, Washington, D.C.

Rose Hill **1.** see under FORDHAM, New York. **2.** unincorporated community, pop. 12,675, Fairfax Co., NE Virginia, 3 mi/5 km SW of Alexandria. It is a residential suburb of Washington, D.C.

Roseland working-class residential community on the far South Side of Chicago, Illinois, 9 mi/14 km S of the Loop, centered on S. State St. PULLMAN and L. Calumet are just SE. Close to the CALUMET area's industry, it was occupied by white workers until the 1960s, when residential integration led to rapid white flight, and is now almost entirely black.

Roselle **1.** city, pop. 20,819, Cook and Du Page counties, NE Illinois, a residential suburb 27 mi/43 km NW of Chicago. **2.** borough, pop. 20,314, Union Co., NE New Jersey, 3 mi/5 km W of Elizabeth. Separated from Linden in 1890, it was at one time the site of Thomas Edison's laboratory, and became the world's first community to be illuminated by electric street lights. Today it is a largely residential suburb. It also manufactures pumps, luggage, furniture, machinery and metal products, and has numerous warehouses.

Roselle Park borough, pop. 12,805, Union Co., NE New Jersey, just NW of ROSELLE. Founded in the early 18th century and once called North Roselle, it was the site of a communications equipment factory established by Marconi (1913). Today it is much like Roselle in its residential character, industries, and warehouse facilities. Additional manufactures include leather goods, surgical instruments, and carpets.

Rosemead city, pop. 51,638, Los Angeles Co., SW California, 10 mi/16 km E of Los Angeles, and immediately SE of San Gabriel. Incorporated in 1959, it is a largely Hispanic and Asian residential suburb.

Rosemère city, pop. 11,198, Thérèse–De Blainville census division, S Québec, on the R. des Mille Îles, across (NW) from the I. Jésus (Laval) and 15 mi/24 km NW of Montréal, between Boisbriand (SW) and Blainville (N). It is a growing residential suburb.

Rosemont **1.** unincorporated community, pop. 22,851, Sacramento Co., NE California, 6 mi/10 mi ESE of downtown Sacramento, on the S side of the American R. It is largely residential. Mather Air Force Base is just E. **2.** village, pop. 3995, Cook Co., NE Illinois, on the Des Plaines R., immediately NW of the Chicago line, and 15 mi/24 km NW of the Loop. Just E of O'Hare International Airport, it contains one of the area's largest highway interchanges, where the Northwest Tollway and JFK Expressway meet the Tri-State Tollway. There are a number of corporate headquarters and office buildings here. **3.** locality in LOWER MERION township, Montgomery Co., SE Pennsylvania, 11 mi/18 km W of Philadelphia. A MAIN LINE suburb just N of Bryn Mawr, it is the seat of Rosemont College (1921).

Rosemount city, pop. 8622, Dakota Co., SE Minnesota, 3 mi/5 km E of Apple Valley and 15 mi/24 km SSE of Minneapolis. This largely residential suburb grew quickly in the 1980s. It is home to Dakota Co. Technical College (1971).

Rosenberg city, pop. 20,183, Fort Bend Co., SE Texas, 30 mi/48 km SW of Houston, on the Brazos R. Founded in 1883 on the railroad, it forms an economic complex with RICHMOND, a trade center for cotton, rice, cattle, sulfur, natural gas, and oil producers. Rosenberg manufactures oilfield equipment, tubing, and valves.

Rosetown town, pop. 2519, SW Saskatchewan, 72 mi/116 km SW of Saskatoon, in an extremely rich wheat farming prairieland. Founded in 1904, it grew into a farm center in 1908 with the arrival of the Canadian National Railway. Today, it is a major transportation hub and service center for the region.

Roseville **1.** city, pop. 44,685, Placer Co., NE California, in the W foothills of the Sierra Nevada, 14 mi/23 km NE of Sacramento. In an area that has produced fruits, grain, poultry, livestock, and wine, it has extensive railroad yards and repair shops and various light manufactures, and is a rapidly growing residential suburb. **2.** city, pop. 51,412, Macomb Co., SE Michigan, 10 mi/16 km NE of Detroit. A post office was constructed in 1836, and the community grew rapidly with the influx of Irish and German immigrants in the 1840s. Detroit's industrial expansion after World War I further spurred the city's growth. Now a largely residential suburb, it has a sheet-metal plant and some light industry. **3.** city, pop. 33,485, Ramsey Co., SE Minnesota, immediately N of St. Paul. It was settled in 1843. Its current boom began when it became a residential suburb after World War II. Commercial development followed, and the city is now a retail, research, and truck transportation center. Manufactures include computers and aeronautical products. There has been much commercial and retail development in the W part, especially along the corridors of I-35E and Highways 36 and 51. **4.** village, pop. 1857, Muskingum and Perry counties, SC Ohio, on Moxahala Creek, 9 mi/14 km SSW of ZANESVILLE. It is the center of a district that since early in the 19th century has produced pottery. Ironspot, just NE, and Crooksville (pop. 2601), just SW, are other production centers; the potteries are now open to tourists.

Rosillos Mountains range in Brewster Co., SW Texas, rising to 5420 ft/1653 m at Rosillos Peak, partially in the BIG BEND National Park.

Roslindale residential section of Boston, Massachusetts. In the SW corner of the city, S of and between the ARNOLD ARBORETUM and Forest Hills Cemetery, it has a somewhat suburban character that increases in the direction of WEST ROXBURY (SW).

Roslyn **1.** village, pop. 1965, in North Hempstead town, Nassau Co., SE New York, on Long Island's North Shore. It is an upper-middle-class residential suburb of New York City. William Cullen Bryant, the 19th-century poet and editor, lived here, and his home, Cedarmere, still stands. In the early years of the 20th century, Roslyn attracted residents of tremendous wealth; much of the land they owned has been sold to developers. Nearby are the villages of **Roslyn Estates** (SW; pop. 1184); **Roslyn Harbor** (NE; pop. 1114); and **Roslyn Heights** (SSW; pop. 6405). **2.** locality in ABINGTON township, Montgomery Co., SE Pennsylvania, 10 mi/16 km N of Philadelphia. It is chiefly residential.

Ross township, pop. 33,482, Allegheny Co., SW Pennsylvania, adjoining the NORTH SIDE of Pittsburgh, and including suburbs in the NORTH HILLS.

Ross Barnett Reservoir see under JACKSON, Mississippi.

Ross Lake see under SKAGIT R., Washington.

Rosslyn commercial and office district of ARLINGTON Co., Virginia, just across the Potomac R. (S) from GEORGETOWN, D.C. Its high-rise buildings house many government-related operations.

Roswell **1.** city, pop. 47,923, Fulton Co., NW Georgia, 18 mi/29 km N of Atlanta, on the Chattahoochee R. Founded in 1838, when Roswell King led a group of wealthy families here from the coast, it is an affluent residential suburb. **2.** city, pop. 44,654, seat of Chaves Co., SE New Mexico, on the Rio Hondo, 160 mi/265 km SE of Albuquerque. An 1860s cattle drive stop and ranch center, it grew rapidly after extensive underground water was discovered in 1891. From the 1940s to the 1960s Walker Air Force Base was central to the economy. The city is now a road junction and a market center for producers of cotton, alfalfa, and livestock. It also processes oil and meat and has some manufactures. The outlying prairie was the site of early rocket experiments by Robert H. Goddard until his death in 1945. The New Mexico Military Institute (1891) and a branch (1958) of Eastern New Mexico University are in the city.

Rota limestone and coral–overlaid volcanic island, 33 sq mi/86 sq km, pop. 2295, in the Commonwealth of the NORTHERN MARIANA Is., in the W Pacific Ocean, 32 mi/51 km NNE of Guam. It was a Japanese base during the 1941 attack on Guam. Severely bombed by the US in 1944, it was not occupied until the end of the war. Songsong (SW) is the main settlement.

Rotterdam town, pop. 28,395, Schenectady Co, E New York, on the Mohawk R., adjacent (W) to Schenectady. Settled in the 1600s by Dutch colonists, it served as an important rail and river transfer point for Erie Canal shipments from 1833 to 1931. The town is now primarily residential. Industries include a power plant, a varnish factory, and a central market warehouse.

Rouge, River in SE Michigan. Critical in the development of Detroit, it has four branches that flow through the metropolitan area. The main branch is formed by headstreams in Bloomfield township, Oakland Co., and flows 30 mi/48 km S and SE through Birmingham, Beverly Hills, Southfield, and the far W side of Detroit, into DEARBORN, where it is joined by the other three branches. The **Upper Rouge,** 18 mi/29 km long, rises in Farmington Hills and flows SE through Livonia, Redford, and Detroit to Dearborn. The **Middle Rouge,** 20 mi/32 km long, is formed near Plymouth, in NW Wayne Co., and flows through River Rouge Park, Livonia, Westland, and Dearborn Heights to Dearborn. The **Lower Rouge** has its headstreams near Willow Run, E of Ypsilanti, Washtenaw Co., and flows E through Wayne and Inkster to Dearborn. From Dearborn, the navigable mainstream flows SE through SW Detroit to the Detroit R. at the city of RIVER ROUGE, where it flows around ZUG I. The Ford River Rouge Plant (built 1917–25, known simply as the "Rouge") is along the river in Dearborn.

Round Lake Beach village, pop. 16,434, Lake Co., NE Illinois, on Round L., 45 mi/72 km NW of Chicago. Situated in a lake-dotted region, it is a residential suburb on the NW edge of the Chicago metropolitan area.

Round Rock city, pop. 30,923, in Williamson Co., C Texas, 18 mi/30 km NNE of Austin. Named for a large boulder in Brushy Creek, it was settled in 1850. The area produces cheese, cotton, grains, broomcorn, and lime. Renowned outlaw Sam Bass was killed here in July 1878 by Texas Rangers, in a celebrated ambush. The city grew rapidly in the 1980s as an Austin suburb.

Round Top town, pop. 81, Fayette Co., EC Texas, 63 mi/101 km ESE of Austin. This prairie farming community, founded in 1835, is well known for its restored buildings and its International Music Festival-Institute.

Rouses Point village, pop. 2377, in Champlain township, Clinton Co., extreme NE New York, on L. Champlain where it empties into the Richelieu R., just S of the Québec border, 22 mi/35 km NNE of Plattsburgh, and connected by bridges with Alburg, Vermont (E). It is a port of entry and resort. Just N was Fort Blunder, abandoned in 1818 when it became apparent that it was on Canadian land, and replaced by Fort Montgomery, which now lies in ruins on a peninsula.

Route 1 see US 1.

Route 128 beltway ringing Boston, Massachusetts, at an average distance of about 10 mi/16 km from downtown. High-tech industries, particularly electronics manufacturers, computer companies, and defense contractors, located in communities along Route 128 during the 1960s, 1970s, and 1980s, taking a leading role in the so-called Massachusetts Miracle, a boom in (largely government-funded) research, development, and manufacturing. Route 128 terminates in the N at Gloucester. Route 495, Boston's outer beltway, lies an average of another 15 mi/24 km outside Route 128.

Route 66 interstate highway, some 2260 mi/3640 km long, designated in 1926, between Chicago, Illinois, and Santa Monica, California. Long called the "Main Street of America" (also called the "Will Rogers Highway of America" through efforts of Oklahoma boosters), it is familiar as the route taken by "Okie" migrants in John Steinbeck's *Grapes of Wrath* and as the subject of Bobby Troup's popular song. In Illinois its route, paralleled today by I-55, runs through Joliet, Bloomington, Normal, and Springfield. From St. Louis, Missouri, to Oklahoma City, its route is now paralleled for the most part by I-44; it runs through Rolla, Springfield, the Ozarks, and Joplin; through the extreme SE corner of Kansas; and in Oklahoma through Claremore and

Tulsa. West of Oklahoma City, its route is today roughly that of I-40 all the way to Barstow, California. Its passes through El Reno and Weatherford, Oklahoma; Amarillo and the Texas Panhandle; Tucumcari, Santa Rosa, Albuquerque, Grants, and Gallup, New Mexico; Holbrook, Flagstaff, and Kingman, Arizona; and Needles, the Mojave Desert, and Barstow, California. From Barstow it cuts SW (now paralleled by I-15) to the Cajon Pass and San Bernardino, then W (today's I-10 route) to Los Angeles and Santa Monica.

Routt National Forest 1.125 million ac/455,600 ha (1758 sq mi/4553 sq km), in NC Colorado, on both sides of the Continental Divide in the PARK RANGE, extending to the Wyoming border. It is noted for its alpine lakes, mountain grasslands, and WILDERNESS AREAS, esp. that around Mt. Zirkel.

Rouyn-Noranda city, pop. 26,448, in the Abitibi region of SW Québec, 310 mi/500 km NW of Montréal. It is an amalgamation (1986) of two municipalities established in the 1920s around the Cadillac Fault's rich copper and gold deposits. Noranda was the COMPANY TOWN of Noranda Mines, which here has one of the largest smelters in Québec. Rouyn, directly S on L. Osisko, was a mining village, and became the administrative, commercial, and industrial heart of the complex and of the surrounding mining area. Lumbering, dairying, and paper milling are also important.

Rowayton see under NORWALK, Connecticut.

Rowe rural town, pop. 364, Franklin Co., NW Massachusetts, 10 mi/16 km E of North Adams. It is the site of the Yankee Rowe nuclear power plant, the oldest (1961) US commercial reactor, located just S of the Vermont border on the Deerfield R., which was shut down in Sept. 1991 after repeated questions about its safety were raised. Rowe's other major source of income is a hydroelectric project.

Rowland Heights unincorporated residential community, pop. 42,647, Los Angeles Co., SW California, 20 mi/32 km ESE of downtown Los Angeles and just E of Hacienda Heights, on the N of the Puente Hills.

Rowlett city, pop. 23,260, Dallas and Rockwall counties, NE Texas. It is a residential and industrial suburb on L. Ray Hubbard, 17 mi/27 km NE of downtown Dallas.

Rowley town, pop. 4452, Essex Co., NE Massachusetts, 6 mi/10 km S of Newburyport, on the estuarial Plum Island R. Settled in 1638, the agricultural NORTH SHORE community had a 19th-century shipbuilding boom. Situated in the US 1–Interstate 95 corridor, it is now a largely residential suburb.

Roxboro city, pop. 7732, seat of Person Co., N North Carolina, 10 mi/16 km S of the Virginia border and 28 mi/45 km N of Durham. It is a tobacco marketing center, and manufactures cotton and aluminum products.

Roxbury **1.** town, pop. 1825, Litchfield Co., W Connecticut, on the Shepaug R., 14 mi/22 km W of Waterbury. In an agricultural area, it produces dairy products and is an exurb. In the 18th and 19th centuries, iron was mined here. Roxbury was home in the 18th century to Ethan Allen and in the 20th to artist Alexander Calder. **2.** section of SC Boston, Massachusetts. Situated on high ground, it was connected with the original Boston (the SHAWMUT PENINSULA) by a narrow "neck" of land sometimes called Roxbury Neck. Settled in 1630, and originally agricultural, it became increasingly suburban, and was annexed by Boston in 1868. Until the 20th century, Roxbury was an upper- and middle-class district. It became home to groups in transition from the inner city, among them Jews from the NORTH END. By the 1930s it had become the center of Boston's black community. It remains largely residential, with various light industries and commercial neighborhoods. **3.** town, pop. 2388, Delaware Co., S New York, in the Catskill Mts., on the East (Pepacton) Branch of the Delaware R., 37 mi/60 km W of Catskill. It lies in a popular resort area. Roxbury was the birthplace of naturalist and writer John Burroughs (1837–1921) and of railroad tycoon Jay Gould (1836–92), who together attended grammar school here.

Roy city, pop. 24,603, Weber Co., N Utah, a residential suburb 5 mi/8 km SW of Ogden, and separated from it by the Ogden Municipal Airport. Its economic base is provided by local agriculture and Hill Air Force Base, on its SE edge.

Royal, Mount 763 ft/233 m, westernmost of the MONTEREGIAN HILLS in S Québec, the dominating physical feature of the city of MONTRÉAL, and the source of its name and of those of such local municipalities as OUTREMONT and WESTMOUNT. It is occupied by two large cemeteries and a park, laid out in a naturalistic design in 1874 by Frederick Law Olmsted. McGill University, at its E foot in the modern city, occupies the site of the 16th-century HOCHELAGA. On the mountain's SW side, the Côte des Neiges, is the Oratoire St.-Joseph (completed 1967), whose dome is said to be second in size only to St. Peter's, in Rome.

Royale, Isle **1.** see ISLE ROYALE NATIONAL PARK, Michigan. **2.** **Île Royale** see under CAPE BRETON I., Nova Scotia.

Royal Gorge also, **the Grand Canyon of the Arkansas** on the upper Arkansas R., 10 mi/16 km W of CAÑON CITY, in SC Colorado. Granite walls rise steeply above the river; the gorge is crossed by a suspension bridge said, at 1053 ft/321 m, to be the world's highest. There are also an incline railway and aerial tramway, in an area heavily commercialized.

Royal Oak city, pop. 65,410, Oakland Co., SE Michigan, 13 mi/21 km NW of Detroit. It is primarily a residential suburb of Detroit. There is also considerable industry, and auto products, machine tools, abrasives, paint, mattresses, and scales are among the products manufactured. Royal Oak is the site of the 122-ac/49-ha Detroit Zoological Park, a campus of Oakland Community College, and the Troy-Oakland Airport. The reactionary "radio priest" Charles E. Coughlin, who broadcast in the 1930s, built and was pastor of the Shrine of Little Flower church here.

Royal Palm Beach village, pop. 14,589, Palm Beach Co., SE Florida, a booming inland residential suburb of West Palm Beach, which is 8 mi/13 km ENE.

Royal Roads see under COLWOOD, British Columbia.

Royals Stadium see under HARRY S TRUMAN SPORTS COMPLEX, Kansas City, Missouri.

Royalton **1.** town, pop. 7453, Niagara Co., extreme NW New York, 8 mi/13 km E of Lockport. It is the birthplace of woman suffrage leader Belva Ann Lockwood (1830–1917). **2.** town, pop. 2389, including Royalton and South Royalton villages, Windsor Co., EC Vermont. It is on the White R., along Interstate 89, 25 mi/40 km S of Barre. In an agricultural area, the town makes wood and dairy products, maple sugar, poultry, cider, and gloves. Royalton was formerly the site of Royalton Academy; the Vermont Law School (1972) is in South Royalton.

Rubidoux unincorporated residential community, pop. 24,367, Riverside Co., SW California, across the Santa Ana R. (N) from Riverside. **Mt. Rubidoux** (1337 ft/408 m), on the Riverside city line (SE), is the site of the Father Serra Cross and World Peace Tower.

Ruby Mountains in Elko and White Pine counties, NE Nevada. The "Alps of Nevada," 10 mi/16 km wide, extend SSW from the Humboldt Range, near I-80, for c.100 mi/160 km, in a section of Humboldt National Forest. The Rubies have lush alpine vegetation; they reach 11,387 ft/3471 m at **Ruby Dome,** and 11,276 ft/3437 m at Hole in the Mountain Peak, in the N, 27 mi/43 km ENE of Elko, which derives its name from a natural "window" in its side near the summit. Extending SSW from the Rubies are the Diamond Mts.

Rugby **1.** city, pop. 2909, seat of Pierce Co., NC North Dakota, 60 mi/97 km E of Minot. Settled in 1886, it is a center for local dairy products, poultry, livestock, and grain. Rugby is best known for its geographical location at what has been determined to be the center of North America. The Geographical Center Museum here explores the area's history. **2.** hamlet in Morgan Co., NE Tennessee, on the Clear Fork R., just S of the Big South Fork National River and Recreation Area. Established in 1880 as an experimental colony by Thomas Hughes, author of *Tom Brown's School Days* (set in Rugby, England), it was to be a rationally developed agricultural and industrial community peopled by both English immigrants and local families. Though the experiment failed within a decade, Rugby remains a rural community visited by those interested in its history.

Ruidoso village, pop. 4600, Lincoln Co., SC New Mexico, along the Ruidoso ("noisy") R., in the Sacramento Mts. Just E of this year-round resort community is Ruidoso Downs, a well-known horse track. Ski Apache is NW, in the Sierra Blanca Mts. The huge MESCALERO APACHE INDIAN RESERVATION lies to the S.

Ruleville city, pop. 3245, Sunflower Co., NW Mississippi, in the DELTA, E of the Sunflower R. and 9 mi/14 km ESE of Cleveland. A plantation-country trade center, processing cotton and lumber, it is noted as the longtime home of civil rights leader Fannie Lou Hamer (1917–77).

Rumford see under EAST PROVIDENCE, Rhode Island.

run in the Middle Atlantic states, esp. in Virginia and Maryland, a small stream; seen in such place names as BULL RUN.

Runnemede borough, pop. 9042, Camden Co., SW New Jersey, 6 mi/10 km S of Camden. Originally called New Hope, it was settled by Quakers in 1683. It is now a primarily residential suburb of Camden and Philadelphia.

Rupert's Land name for the lands granted by British king Charles II to the HUDSON'S BAY COMPANY in 1670 (and named for his cousin Prince Rupert, first HBC governor). They comprised all land in the watershed of rivers running into Hudson Bay—an area covering modern N Québec, Ontario N of the St. Lawrence watershed, all of Manitoba, almost all of Saskatchewan, S Alberta, and much of the Northwest Territories (with which Rupert's Land, also once called "the North-West," should not be confused), as well as parts of what are now North Dakota and Minnesota. The rivers involved, esp. the SASKATCHEWAN, allowed the HBC access to much of what is now Canada, and it established almost 100 trading posts in the area. In 1870 Rupert's Land passed to Canada, in exchange for money and land grants in the Prairie Provinces.

rural lightly populated or settled; historically, agricultural (if settled). As used by both the US and Canadian censuses, the term means the opposite of URBAN (in the US, it thus applies basically to all areas that are not part of a community with a pop. of at least 2500; in Canada, of at least 1000). In Manitoba and Saskatchewan, there are over 400 **rural municipalities,** local administrative entities.

Rushmore, Mount peak in the BLACK HILLS of SW South Dakota, 17 m/27 km SW of Rapid City. The faces of presidents George Washington, Thomas Jefferson, Abraham Lincoln, and Theodore Roosevelt have been carved into the granite side of the mountain in the 1278-ac/518-ha Mount Rushmore National Memorial, a famous attraction. Requiring both engineering and sculptural skills, creation of the colossal heads, which measure 60 ft/18 m from chin to top of the head, was begun in 1927 by sculptor Gutzon Borglum and completed by his son Lincoln (1941) after his death. Nearby Rushmore Cave is still largely unexplored. The peak and cave are named for Charles E. Rushmore, a New York attorney who visited the Black Hills in the late 1870s.

Rush Street commercial entertainment strip in OLD TOWN, on the NEAR NORTH SIDE of Chicago, Illinois.

Rushville city, pop. 3229, seat of Schuyler Co., WC Illinois, 23 mi/37 km S of Macomb. A trading center for the area's grain and fruit, it is the site of a major genealogical research institution, the Schuyler Jail Museum and Research Center.

Russell city, pop. 4781, seat of Russell Co., C Kansas, 37 mi/59 km N of Great Bend and just N of Interstate 70. Grain and oil are central to its economy. Wilson L. is 10 mi/16 km NE.

Russell Cave National Monument 310 ac/126 ha site in the NE corner of Alabama, 8 mi/13 km NW of Bridgeport, along the Tennessee line. A cavern here, discovered by amateur archaeologists in 1953, is one of the oldest known sites of human habitation in North America, containing an almost continuous record of use from at least 7000 B.C. to about A.D. 1650. The site includes a museum and trails.

Russell Fork see under BIG SANDY R., Virginia and Kentucky.

Russellville **1.** city, pop. 7812, seat of Franklin Co., NW Alabama, 21 mi/32 km SSW of Florence. An agricultural trade center, it has grain mills, cotton gins, and quarries. **2.** city, pop. 21,260, seat of Pope Co., NW Arkansas, 60 mi/100 km NW of Little Rock, near L. Dardanelle, on the Arkansas R. It grew as an agricultural shipping center in the 1870s after the arrival of the railroad, and later developed light manufacturing as well. The city is the headquarters of the OZARK NATIONAL FOREST and the home of Arkansas Tech University (1909). **3.** city, pop. 7454, seat of Logan Co., S Kentucky, 30 mi/48 km SW of Bowling Green, in the PENNYROYAL. Called Big Boiling Springs when settled in the 1780s, it was renamed in 1798. Secessionists in conference here in 1861 declared Kentucky a Confederate state. The economy depends on agriculture (tobacco, cattle), light manufacturing, and milling, and local coal and asphalt deposits.

Russian America territory held by Russia in North America between 1741 and 1867, including the ALEUTIAN Is., mainland Alaska N of 54°40′ N latitude, and settlements on the Pacific coast as far S as FORT ROSS, in N California. Beginning with the exploration of W Alaska in 1741 by Vitus Bering, a Danish navigator employed by Peter the Great, the area was seen primarily as a fur producer. The trader Gregory Shelekhov established the first permanent Russian settlement in Alaska at Three Saints Bay on KODIAK I. in 1784. New Archangel, now SITKA, in the Alexander Archipelago, was Russian America's capital from 1806 until the US purchase of Alaska in 1867. Aleksandr Baranof, governor 1790–1818, was also head of the Russian-American Company, chartered in 1799; under him, the Russians explored and settled much of W Alaska, introducing agriculture and trade, and building schools, churches, and sawmills. The virtual enslavement of native peoples led to a Tlingit uprising in 1802, in which many Russians were killed and Sitka was destroyed. Eventually depletion of the sea otter, Russia's political problems following the 1853–56 Crimean War, and the difficulty of maintaining remote settlements led to the dissolution of Russian territories in North America. Following a series of agreements with the US and Great Britain, in which possessions and hunting rights were reduced, Russia finally sold Alaska and the Aleutians to the US for $7.2 million. The Russian heritage of the area is preserved in many place names and Russian Orthodox churches throughout Alaska.

Russian Hill residential section of N SAN FRANCISCO, California, SW of NORTH BEACH and N of NOB HILL. On and around a 294-ft/90-m hill that according to legend is the burial site of a group of early-19th-century Russian sailors, it has been home to many of the city's artists and writers, and is now a mixture of bohemian and upscale. Lombard St., reputed to be the most crooked in the world, draws visitors. The San Francisco Art Institute is on the E side.

Russian River 100 mi/160 km long, in NW California. It rises in Mendocino Co. and flows SSE past UKIAH, along the W of the Coast Ranges. Above HEALDSBURG, it turns SW to the Pacific Ocean, 20 mi/32 km W of Santa Rosa and 5 mi/8 km SE of FORT ROSS. Along it are redwood groves, orchards and vineyards, and resort areas.

Rust Belt term in use since the 1970s to describe the opposite of the SUNBELT: those areas of the US North and Northeast characterized by heavy, older industry and cold weather, which have lost much of their industrial base to the South and Southwest. The term implies the centrality of the steel industry and the steel-consuming auto industry to such states as Pennsylvania, Ohio, and Michigan.

Ruston city, pop. 20,027, seat of Lincoln Parish, N Louisiana, 33 mi/53 km W of Monroe. Founded in 1884 on the Shreveport, Vicksburg, and Pacific Railroad, it is a market and processing center for farms producing cotton, corn, vegetables, peaches, poultry, and cattle, and a service town for nearby oil and gas fields. Louisiana Tech University (1894) is here. GRAMBLING is 5 mi/8 km W.

Rutherford borough, pop. 17,790, Bergen Co., NE New Jersey, 3 mi/5 km SE of Passaic. Settled in the 17th century, it was called Boiling Springs until 1875. Primarily a New York area residential suburb, it is also a center for textile dyeing. The William Carlos Williams Center is named for the poet, who was born here in 1883, practiced medicine here, and drew on the community's life for his poetry. Fairleigh Dickinson University was founded here (1942).

Rutherford Fork see under OBION R., Tennessee.

Rutland city, pop. 18,230, seat of Rutland Co., SC Vermont, on Otter Creek, at the S edge of the Green Mt. National Forest, 50 mi/80 km SW of Montpelier. Founded in 1759 as a military outpost, it was an early marble quarrying and railroad center. Stone finishing and the manufacture of stone-working machinery are now important, along with tourism and diverse manufacturing. The College of St. Joseph (1954) and Green Mt. National Forest headquarters are located in Vermont's second-largest city.

Rye city, pop. 14,936, Westchester Co., SE New York, on Long Island Sound, 24 mi/39 km N of New York City. Founded in 1660, it is primarily residential, although there are some corporate offices. In the Colonial era it was an important stop along the BOSTON POST ROAD from New York. The Square House (c.1730), a popular tavern, is now a museum. Rye Playland (a county-run amusement park), the Marshlands Conservancy (a wildlife sanctuary), and the Rye Nature Center are here. The town of Rye (pop. 39,524) includes the villages of PORT CHESTER and **Rye Brook** (pop. 7765).

S

Saanich district municipality, pop. 95,577, Capital Regional District, SW British Columbia, on the Saanich Peninsula of SE Vancouver I., adjacent (NW) to Victoria. It is a growing residential suburb of the capital, with coastal and interior parkland and beaches. **Central Saanich** (district municipality, pop. 13,684) and **North Saanich** (district municipality, pop. 9645), site of the Victoria International Airport and the Swartz Bay ferry terminal, are farther up the peninsula. Both are also growing rapidly.

Sabbathday Lake last remaining US Shaker colony, in the W part of New Gloucester town, Cumberland Co., SW Maine, 22 mi/35 km NNW of Portland and 3 mi/5 km S of Poland Spring. Established in 1793, the community, on a hill overlooking the small recreational lake of the same name, has fewer than a dozen members, who raise sheep and herbs and maintain a museum of Shaker history.

Sabine Crossroads see under MANSFIELD, Louisiana.

Sabine Pass 7 mi/11 km–long passage at the mouth of the Sabine R. on the Gulf of Mexico, between Louisiana (E) and Texas. It was the site, in April 1863, of the defeat of a Federal gunboat force attempting to begin an invasion of Texas. Sabine Pass Battleground State Park commemorates the battle and Richard Dowling's role leading Confederate defenders.

Sabine River 360 mi/580 km long, in E Texas and Louisiana. It rises about 50 mi/80 km NE of Dallas, its headstreams impounded in 36,700-ac/14,900-ha L. Tawakoni by the Iron Bridge Dam (1961). It then flows SE out of the BLACKLANDS into wooded E Texas, once the home of the Caddo. From near Logansport, Louisiana, the river forms the Louisiana-Texas border. Here it passes SSE through the TOLEDO BEND RESERVOIR, flanked (W) by the 159,000-ac/64,200-ha **Sabine National Forest,** in the PINEY WOODS. It then continues S through the oil-rich Texas-Louisiana coastal area, reaching the Gulf of Mexico at SABINE PASS. In the early 19th century, jurisdiction over the land between the Sabine and the NECHES (W) was disputed between the US and Spain. Lumbering and other wood industries, in addition to oil, dominate the economy of the lower Sabine. ORANGE is the head of deepwater navigation; a dredged channel links it with **Sabine L.** (17 mi/27 km long, 7 mi/11 km wide), from which Sabine Pass leads into the Gulf. The **Sabine-Neches Waterway** is a system of dredged, tidal channels connecting Sabine L. with the Neches R. at Beaumont and the Sabine with Calcasieu L. and the Lake Charles, Louisiana area. It forms part of the GULF INTRACOASTAL WATERWAY.

Sable, Cape **1.** swampy peninsula at the SW tip of Monroe Co., S Florida. Covered with mangroves, it almost encloses Whitewater Bay (NE). FLORIDA BAY (S) separates it from the Florida Keys. It lies within Everglades National Park. East Cape, on its S extremity, is the southernmost point on the US mainland, at 25° 08′ N. **2.** sandspit just off the S extremity of **Cape Sable I.,** 40 mi/64 km SE of Yarmouth, in SW Nova Scotia. The cape, the southernmost point of Nova Scotia, is marked by a lighthouse.

Sable Island crescent-shaped island in the Atlantic Ocean, 175 mi/285 km ESE of Halifax, Nova Scotia. Some 25 mi/40 km E–W, and 1 mi/1.5 km wide at the center, it narrows to sandspits on either end, which continue underwater as shallow bars. These and nearby shoals have caused many shipwrecks over the years, and the island has been called the graveyard of the Atlantic. It has been the scene of many unsuccessful settlement schemes. Lighthouses were established in 1873, and lifesaving stations were manned from the early 19th to the mid 20th centuries. Weather and navigation station personnel are current inhabitants. The island has ridges of dunes covered with grasses and shrubs, and a freshwater lake. A herd of 150 to 400 Sable Island horses, probably introduced in the 18th century, are now protected.

Sacajawea Historic Area see under BEAVERHEAD NATIONAL FOREST, Montana.

Sachs Harbour see under BANKS I., Northwest Territories.

Sackets Harbor resort village, pop. 1313, in Hounsfield township, Jefferson Co., N New York, on Black River Bay, an inlet on the E shore of L. Ontario, 11 mi/17 km WSW of Watertown. Settled c.1801, it was the site of one of the first battles of the War of 1812 (July 19, 1812). The battlefield, just SW of the village, is now a state historic site. Gen. Zebulon Pike (d. 1813) is buried in the village's Old Military Cemetery.

Sackville **1.** town, pop. 5494, Westmorland Co., extreme SE New Brunswick, at the head of the Bay of Fundy's Chignecto Bay (Cumberland Basin), in the CHIGNECTO isthmus, 24 mi/39 km SE of Moncton, near the Nova Scotia border. The surrounding Tantramar Marshes were diked for farming by 17th-century Acadian settlers. A 19th-century shipbuilding center, Sackville now has varied light manufactures and is noted as the home of Mt. Allison University (1839). Fort Beauséjour, 5 mi/8 km E, was built by the French in 1751, and fell to the British in 1755. It is now a National Historic Site. **2. the Sackvilles** fast-growing, unorganized suburban communities in Halifax Co., SC Nova

Scotia, in the Halifax metropolitan area, 8 mi/13 km NNW of Halifax and just N of BEDFORD. Lower Sackville, Middle Sackville, and Upper Sackville are expanding into forest land to the NW. All three are bedroom and service communities.

Saco city, pop. 15,181, York Co., SW Maine, on the Saco R. across from Biddeford, 15 mi/24 km S of Portland. Saco and Biddeford were founded as one town in 1630, and separated in 1762. Manufactures have included textiles, clothing, shoes, firearms, and rawhide products.

Saco River 105 mi/170 km long, in E New Hampshire and S Maine. Its name derives from an Indian word meaning "the outlet of the river." Rising in the White Mountains at an altitude of 1900 ft/580 m, near Crawford Notch, it flows SE to the Atlantic, 5 mi/8 km below the twin cities of Saco and Biddeford, Maine. Falls at Biddleford, the head of navigation, furnish hydroelectric power. A dam located at Union Falls, 8 mi/13 km above Saco and Biddeford, was completed in 1949. In its upper reaches the Saco is a popular canoeing river.

Sacramento city, pop. 369,365, state capital and seat of Sacramento Co. (pop. 1,041,219), NC California, in the Central (Sacramento) Valley, at the confluence of the Sacramento and American rivers, just W of the Sierra Nevada. It is the center of a metropolitan area (MSA) embracing Sacramento, El Dorado, Placer, and Yolo counties, with a pop. of 1,481,102. In traditional Maidu and Miwok territory, the Swiss visionary/entrepreneur Johann Sutter founded here (1839) New Helvetia, which was to be an agricultural empire on 50,000 ac/20,000 ha granted by the Mexican government. Remains of Sutter's Fort, his base of operations, built with furnishings from FORT ROSS, are in the city. Sutter welcomed migrants to California through the 1840s. In 1848 his carpenter John Marshall, seeking to locate a sawmill, accidentally discovered gold 40 mi/64 km NE at COLOMA. The ensuing gold rush destroyed Sutter's dreams but made Sacramento (named for the river) a bustling port and road hub. In 1854, after lobbying, it became California's capital; its position midway between the Bay Area and the goldfields was key. In 1856, Theodore D. Judah built the first railroad in the West, to FOLSOM (NE). In 1860–61, Sacramento was the W terminus of the PONY EXPRESS. In the 1860s four local merchants, Collis P. Huntington, Mark Hopkins, Charles Crocker, and Leland Stanford, bankrolled the development of the Central Pacific (later Southern Pacific) Railroad over the DONNER PASS, connecting California with the rest of the US; the "Big Four" and their railroad dominated the state's development for four decades. When the gold rush was over, Sacramento, now a major transportation hub, became a shipper of the valley's truck crops, flowers, grains, livestock, and fruit. Processing and shipping remain central to the economy; Del Monte, Libby, and other companies have plants here, and the city is associated especially with its tomatoes and camellias. Dredging of the river (1911) and completion (1963) of a deepwater channel to SUISUN BAY have enhanced Sacramento's position as a river port. In World War II, Mather (E, near RANCHO CORDOVA) and McClellan (NE, near NORTH HIGHLANDS) air force bases and the Sacramento Signal (Army) Depot spurred further development, which continued in the 1950s and after with missile and other military research and development. More recently important industries include computer and medical technology development and manufacturing. State government and communications are other major economic sectors. A California State University branch (1947) and several smaller colleges are in the city. The capitol (completed 1874) and historic sites draw visitors.

Sacramento Mountains N–S trending range, sometimes considered to be part of the ROCKY Mts., in S New Mexico, extending into W Texas. This tilted fault-block range is usually described as including the JICARILLA Mts., a N extension, and the SIERRA BLANCA, including Sierra Blanca Peak (12,003 ft/3659 m), the high point of the entire system; often, the SE-trending GUADALUPE Mts., at the S end, are included. It extends through different sections of the Lincoln National Forest and the MESCALERO APACHE INDIAN RESERVATION.

Sacramento River 380 mi/610 km long, in N California, the state's longest and the N CENTRAL VALLEY's chief river. It rises 12 mi/19 km SW of Mt. Shasta and flows S through SHASTA L., past Redding, and into the valley, where Red Bluff is the head of shallow-draft navigation. It then continues in a generally SSE direction through the agricultural **Sacramento Valley** (the Central Valley's N section), to Sacramento, S of which it is paralleled by a ship channel. From Sacramento it flows SSW into the complex delta it forms with the N-flowing SAN JOAQUIN R., emptying W into Suisun Bay, the innermost arm of San Francisco Bay, near Pittsburg and Antioch. The Sacramento's major tributaries join it from the E, and include (N to S) the PIT R. (from the Cascade Range and the Modoc Plateau, which now joins it within Shasta L.); and the FEATHER, YUBA, AMERICAN, and Cosumnes rivers, from the Sierra Nevada. After 1848 the E tributaries, on the MOTHER LODE, were the scene of frantic gold seeking activity; in the heyday of hydraulic mining (1870s–84), huge amounts of debris that washed down the Sacramento clogged the delta, raised water levels, and contributed to the diminution of San Francisco Bay. In the 20th century, the value of the Sacramento system as a source of fresh water led to establishment (1935) of the Central Valley Project, which sends its waters S to the San Joaquin Valley. The California State Water Project has also, since the 1960s, drawn on this resource, to supply the cities of Southern California.

Saddleback Mountain 4116 ft/1255 m, in Franklin Co., W Maine. Conical in form, its sides heavily wooded, Saddleback is 5 mi/8 km E of Rangeley Lakes, and is a popular ski area.

Saddle Brook township, pop. 13,296, Bergen Co., NE New Jersey, 3 mi/5 km E of Paterson, on the SADDLE R. and Interstate 80. Essentially a New York–area residential suburb, it is noted for its elegant and exclusive neighborhoods.

Saddle River 25 mi/40 km long, in New York and New Jersey. It rises in small streams in Rockland Co., SE New York, just N of the New Jersey line, and flows S in New Jersey through UPPER SADDLE RIVER, the borough of **Saddle River** (pop. 2950, in Bergen Co.), and other communities including SADDLE BROOK, to the Passaic R., opposite PASSAIC.

Safety Harbor city, pop. 15,124, Pinellas Co., WC Florida, 15 mi/24 km W of Tampa and 15 mi/24 km N of St. Petersburg, at the head of Old Tampa Bay. It draws its name from early mariners' use of its inlet as a haven from hurricanes. Settled as a plantation in the 1820s, it later became a health resort noted for its mineral springs and is now a resort and residential community.

Safford city, pop. 7359, seat of Graham Co., SE Arizona, on the Gila R., 85 mi/137 km NE of Tucson. Founded by farmers in 1874, it is now the trade center of an agricultural valley producing cotton, grain, and livestock. A Federal prison camp is 8 mi/13 km S. Safford serves as a gateway to the Coronado National Forest (SW) and to an area of hot mineral baths to its S.

Sagamore Hill see under OYSTER BAY, New York.

Sagebrush, the popular term for semiarid areas of the US West characterized by the prevalence of sagebrush (species of *Artemisia*) amid sparse vegetation, esp. in the GREAT BASIN. Nevada is known as the **Sagebrush State.** The plant, long used for a range of purposes by local tribes, has provided fuel and cattle forage to settlers since the 19th century. It grows in fertile soil, but is difficult to clear in order to farm. The Sagebrush War was a bloodless 1860s border dispute between Nevada and California. The Sagebrush Rebellion was an inconclusive early-1980s movement by politicians in Nevada, Utah, and neighboring states to gain control over millions of acres of PUBLIC LANDS; while its rhetoric was anti-Federal, critics argued that it was actually driven by commercial interests seeking privatization of government property.

Sag Harbor village, pop. 2134, in East Hampton town, Suffolk Co., SE New York, on Long Island's SOUTH FORK facing Gardiners Bay, 25 mi/40 km W of Montauk Point. It is a popular summer resort. In the mid 19th century it was a major whaling port, and many whalers' homes survive. The Long Island *Herald,* the Island's first local newspaper, was founded here in 1791.

Saginaw **1.** city, pop. 69,512, seat of Saginaw Co., EC Michigan, on the Saginaw R., 31 mi/50 km NNW of Flint. The early-19th-century fur trading post built near the present city site developed into a small community of fur traders, and was protected by Fort Saginaw (1820). The rise of the lumber industry later in the century made Saginaw one of the lumbering centers of the US. After lumbering declined with forest depletion at the turn of the century, the economy relied on extracting from major oil, coal, and salt deposits and on the processing and shipping of beans and sugar beets. It is now based on a large iron foundry and on manufactures, including auto parts, machinery, fabricated metals, paper, and graphite. Saginaw remains a trade and distribution center for local agricultural products. A large General Motors foundry closed here in 1986, eliminating 1700 jobs, a pattern typical of this entire region. **2.** see under FORT WORTH, Texas.

Saginaw Bay 50 mi/80 km NE–SW, and 25 mi/40 km wide, a SW arm of L. Huron, deeply indenting the E shore of Michigan. The bay extends from Pointe Aux Barques (SE) to Au Sable Point (NW) across its mouth, to BAY CITY (its chief port) and the mouth of the Saginaw R. at its head. Fishing and tourism are the bay's main industries.

Saginaw County 815 sq mi/2111 sq km, pop. 211,946, in C Michigan, drained by the Tittabawassee, Shiawassee, Flint, and Saginaw rivers. Its seat and only large city is SAGINAW, where there is considerable manufacturing. The county has traditionally been a source of oil, salt, and coal. Its agriculture is based on dairy products, grain, corn, beans, vegetables, sugar beets, livestock, and poultry. It includes the Shiawassee and Crow Island state game areas, and the Shiawassee National Wildlife Refuge.

Saginaw River 22 mi/35 km long, in C Michigan. It is formed by the joining of the Shiawassee and Tittabawassee rivers, just SW of SAGINAW, and flows NNE through Saginaw and Bay City to the SW end of Saginaw Bay. The Saginaw also receives the Cass R.

Saguaro National Monument 83,600 ac/33,850 ha, in two units E and W of TUCSON, in the SONORAN DESERT of S Arizona. The Rincon Mt. unit (E) has an older forest of the huge, endangered cactus, unique to the Sonoran, whose blossom is the Arizona state flower. The Tucson Mt. unit (W) contains a mix of mountain and desert floor, with younger, denser cacti.

Saguenay River 110 mi/180 km long, in S Québec. Draining L. SAINT-JEAN, it flows ESE, dropping 300 ft/91 m by the time it reaches CHICOUTIMI, where it becomes broad and tidal, continuing through the **Saguenay Fjord,** with walls rising to c.1500 ft/460 m. It flows into the St. Lawrence R. near TADOUSSAC. In its upper reaches it provides power for the industry of JONQUIÈRE and neighboring cities, now through the Shipshaw and other hydroelectric stations. To the ESE of Chicoutimi is Ha! Ha! Bay, site of LA BAIE. Below Chicoutimi the Saguenay is plied by both commercial and pleasure craft, and is much visited for its scenery. In the 16th century Cartier and other explorers were driven by stories of an opulent Kingdom of Saguenay somewhere in the interior; the name Saguenay was subsequently used of the entire region inland from the St. Lawrence to the divide between its watershed and that of Hudson Bay (NW).

Sailor's Creek also, **Sayler's Creek** see under AMELIA Co., Virginia.

Sailor's Snug Harbor charitable institution, for "aged, decrepit, and worn-out sailors," established 1801 in Manhattan, located 1833 on the N shore of Staten I., New York, on the KILL VAN KULL. Noted for its Greek Revival buildings and landscaped grounds, it became the Snug Harbor Cultural Center after the institution moved to North Carolina in 1976. MARINER'S HARBOR lies SW.

Saint Albans **1.** residential section, E Queens, New York. Lying E of Jamaica and S of Hollis, close to the Nassau Co. border, it is a semisuburban, largely black, middle-class neighborhood. Cambria Heights, just to the SE, is similar. **2.** city, pop. 7339, surrounded by St. Albans town (pop. 4606), on St. Albans Bay of L. Champlain. It is the seat of Franklin Co., extreme NW Vermont. In the Green Mt. foothills, 24 mi/39 km N of Burlington, the city is a railroad and manufacturing center and port of entry. The community was an early-19th-century smugglers' base, and a refuge for French-Canadian rebels during the 1837 Papineau War. In Oct. 1864, it was the site of a Confederate bank raid constituting the most northerly engagement of the Civil War. In 1866, St. Albans was a gathering point for Irish Fenians before an abortive invasion of Canada. Local industries make maple, dairy, metal, wood, and paper products, along with poultry and cattle feed, sugarmaking equipment, batteries, and canned goods. **3.** city, pop. 11,194, Kanawha Co., W West Virginia, at the junction of the Coal and Kanawha rivers, 12 mi/19 km W of Charleston. It is in a coal and natural gas producing and farm area; many residents work at nearby chemical plants. The Battle of Scary Creek, a Confederate victory, was fought just NW on July 17, 1861.

Saint Albert city, pop. 42,146, C Alberta, on the Sturgeon R., adjoining (NW) Edmonton, and 14 mi/23 km NW of its Downtown. An agricultural service center for farms N of Edmonton, it has experienced increasing residential development in recent decades. The community was founded (1861) by a missionary and later attracted MÉTIS settlers. The local bridge was the first in W Canada, and the original chapel still stands.

Saint Andrews **1.** also, **Saint-Andrews-by-the-Sea** town, pop. 1652, seat of Charlotte Co., SW New Brunswick, on a rocky headland in PASSAMAQUODDY BAY, 50 mi/80 km WSW of Saint John and 13 mi/21 km NNW of Eastport, Maine. The international border runs through the bay just W of the town, at the mouth of the SAINT CROIX R. Formerly important as a commercial and lumbering port, the town is now known for tourism and fishing. The Huntsman Marine Science Centre offers interpretive exhibits on the nearby Bay of Fundy, an area noted for its marine mammals and seabirds. The town was laid out in 1783 by LOYALISTS. The Algonquin Hotel (1914) is one of the well-known resorts developed by the Canadian Pacific Railway. **2.** unincorporated community, pop. 25,692, Richland Co., C South Carolina, 5 mi/8 km NW of downtown COLUMBIA. Between the Broad (E) and Saluda (W) rivers, it is a largely residential suburb of the capital. **3.** see under SEWANEE, Tennessee.

Saint Ann city, pop. 14,489, St. Louis Co., EC Missouri, 13 mi/21 km NW of downtown St. Louis. An industrial suburb, it is situated near the Lambert–St. Louis International Airport (N).

Saint Anthony town, pop. 3164, NW Newfoundland, near the N tip of the GREAT NORTHERN PENINSULA. A FRENCH SHORE fishing station, Saint-Antoine, it was resettled by Newfoundlanders in the mid 19th century, and became a key port in Newfoundland-Labrador trade. In 1900 Wilfred Grenfell established a mission hospital here, and the Grenfell Association, serving coastal fishing communities nearby and in Labrador, has been based in the town since 1912.

Saint-Antoine city, pop. 10,232, La Rivière-du-Nord census division, S Québec, 27 mi/44 km NW of Montréal and just S of Saint-Jérôme, on the Laurentian Autoroute. A residential and commercial suburb incorporated in 1967 on the R. du Nord, it is just N of the MIRABEL airport.

Saint Augustine city, pop. 11,692, seat of St. Johns Co., NE Florida, largely on a peninsula between the Matanzas and San Sebastian rivers (lagoons), partially separated from the Atlantic by Anastasia I., 35 mi/56 km SE of Jacksonville. The oldest continuously settled US city, it was founded in 1565 on the site of an Indian village by Spanish explorer Pedro Menéndez de Avilés, near the 1513 landing place of Ponce de León. Twice burned by English buccaneers (Francis Drake in 1586, John Davis in 1665), it passed to England in 1763, and was a Tory refuge during the American Revolution. It reverted to Spain in 1783, and was ceded to the US in 1821. A military post in the Seminole War, it was occupied by Union troops during the Civil War. Many historic buildings remain, and year-round tourism is key to its economy. A port with the Atlantic Intracoastal Waterway passing through it, it also relies on fishing, shrimping, and the processing and shipping of local produce and lumber. Among its best-known landmarks are two national monuments: the city's massive Castillo de San Marcos (1672), the oldest masonry fort in the US, and Fort Matanzas (1740), 13 mi/21 km SSE, both built of native coquina (calcified shells). Structures reputed to be the first of their kind in the US include a house, wooden schoolhouse, and store. There are also a restored Spanish Quarter, Huguenot cemetery, slave market, cathedral (1793–97; rebuilt 1887), city gates (1804), and a wide variety of commercial tourist attractions. Flagler College (1967) is here.

Saint-Basile-le-Grand city, pop. 10,127, La-Vallée-du-Richelieu census division, S Québec, 14 mi/23 km E of Montréal, a suburb just W of the R. Richelieu.

Saint Bonaventure unincorporated village, pop. 2397, in Allegany township, Cattaraugus Co., SW New York. The home of St. Bonaventure University (1859), it is immediately W of OLEAN.

Saint-Boniface former city, now part of WINNIPEG, Manitoba, E of the Red. R. of the North. Settled around an 1818 mission (with which Saint Boniface College was founded), it developed as a MÉTIS community and one of the leading francophone centers of the prairies. In the 20th century it became heavily industrial; in 1972 it became part of Winnipeg (Unicity). The grave of Métis leader Louis Riel and his family's home are here.

Saint Bonifacius city, pop. 1180, Hennepin Co., EC Minnesota, 23 mi/37 km W of Minneapolis. Established by a Lutheran minister, it was an early beekeeping center. It is the seat of St. Paul Bible College (1916).

Saint Bride, Mount peak (10,875 ft/3317 m) of the Rocky Mts., 30 mi/48 km NW of Banff, in Banff National Park, SW Alberta.

Saint-Bruno-de-Montarville city, pop. 23,849, La Vallée-du-Richelieu census division, S Québec, 11 mi/18 km E of Montréal. Established in 1958 in an agricultural area, it is a largely residential suburb. Mt. St.-Bruno, one of the MONTEREGIAN HILLS, rises to 699 ft/213 m.

Saint Catharines city, pop. 129,300, seat of Niagara Regional Municipality, S Ontario, 10 mi/16 km NW of Niagara Falls, on the S shore of L. Ontario, at the N entrance of the WELLAND CANAL. Founded in 1790, it was known for its mineral springs in its early years. The construction of the first canal in 1829 and the arrival of the railroad made it a shipping and manufacturing center. Today it is the largest city on the canal and the center of a fruit growing and winemaking region. Industries include shipbuilding and repair, canning, and the manufacture of auto and airplane parts, electrical equipment, textiles, and paper and wood products. Brock University (1962) is here, and the annual Royal Canadian Henley Regatta is held at Port Dalhousie Harbour, on the lake.

Saint Charles **1.** city, pop. 22,501, Kane and Du Page counties, NE Illinois, on the Fox R., a suburb 35 mi/56 km W of Chicago and 8 mi/13 km S of Elgin. At the outer edge of the Chicago metropolitan area, it contains some farmland, which is gradually giving way to residential development. Metal and plastic products are produced. Founded in 1834, it emerged as one of the string of agricultural communities trading on the Fox R. between Chicago and points W. **2.** unincorporated village, pop. 28,717, Charles Co., SW Maryland, 5 mi/8 km SW of Cedarville State Forest and 22 mi/35 km SSE of Washington, D.C. It is largely residential. **3.** city, pop. 54,555, seat of St. Charles Co., EC Missouri, on the Missouri R., 21 mi/34 km NW of downtown St. Louis. It was founded by French traders in 1769, becoming the first permanent white settlement on the Missouri R. A trading post, it was the origination point for the Boone's Lick Trail to the West. When Missouri was admitted to the Union, St. Charles became its capital (1821–26), and the capitol building is preserved. German settlers who arrived here 1832–70 were key in making it a shipping center, and today it remains a trading, processing, and distribution hub for a fertile grain farming area. It has foundries, processes coal and lumber, and manufactures metal products, engines, electronic components, and clothing. Its historic Downtown also attracts tourists. Lindenwood College (1827) is here.

Saint Charles County 558 sq mi/1445 sq km, pop. 212,907, in EC Missouri, bounded by the Missouri R. (S) and the Mississippi R. (E), which meet at the county's E tip. Its seat is St. Charles. It is one of Missouri's five original counties. From the 1970s to the 1990s suburban growth around St. Louis made it one of the fastest-growing counties in the US. The balance of the region is richly agricultural, with corn, wheat, and oats grown and livestock raised.

Saint Clair, Lake in SE Michigan and extreme S Ontario, joining L. Huron on the N, via the SAINT CLAIR R., and L. Erie on the S., via the DETROIT R. Twenty-seven mi/43 km N–S and 8–24 mi/13–39 km wide, the lake is bisected by the Canada-US border, and is an important link in Great Lakes shipping. Its N arm, Anchor Bay, is a resort area with several islands and the St. Clair Flats Wildlife Area. Detroit suburbs including Saint Clair Shores and the five GROSSE POINTE communities lie on L. Saint Clair's W shore. The lake's fishing industry was ruined by industrial and other pollution in the 20th century, but it is still an important recreational area. On its E side is some of Ontario's richest agricultural land.

Saint Clair County **1.** 672 sq mi/1740 sq km, pop. 262,852, in SW Illinois, bordered by the Mississippi R. (W), opposite St. Louis, Missouri. Its seat is BELLEVILLE. In the NW, industrial East St. Louis is the center of one of Illinois's largest urban areas outside Chicago. Nearby factory and coal-related cities include Centreville, Cahokia, O'Fallon, Belleville, and Swansea. Farther E and S, in the valleys of Silver Creek and the Kaskaskia R., truck farming is the mainstay of the economy. **2.** 734 sq mi/1901 sq km, pop. 145,607, in E Michigan, bounded by L. Huron and the St. Clair R., which form the borders with Ontario (E), and Anchor Bay of L. St. Clair (S), and drained by the Belle and Black rivers. Its seat is Port Huron. The county has commercial fishing, salt mines, and resorts, and manufacturing at Port Huron and Marysville. It makes dairy products and raises livestock, grain, vegetables, and sugar beets.

Saint Clair River 40 mi/64 km long, in SE Michigan and S Ontario. It drains L. Huron between Port Huron, Michigan (W) and Sarnia, Ontario (E), and flows S as part of the US-Canada boundary to L. St. Clair, E of Detroit. At its mouth the river forms a delta known as St. Clair Flats, a resort area with several islands, the largest of which, Walpole, in Ontario, is the site of an Indian reserve.

Saint Clair Shores city, pop. 68,107, Macomb Co., SE Michigan, on L. St. Clair, 12 mi/19 km NE of Detroit. The population of this affluent residential community has increased over 400% since 1950. Among its amenities are beaches and marinas that lie along the shore of L. St. Clair.

Saint Clairsville city, pop. 5162, seat of Belmont Co., extreme E Ohio, 10 mi/16 km W of the Ohio R. and Wheeling, West Virginia. The Union Humane Society, an antislavery organization, was founded here in 1815. It is a trading center for a dairy farming and coal mining district, where oil and natural gas are also developed.

Saint Cloud **1.** city, pop. 12,453, Osceola Co., C Florida, on East L. Tohopekaliga, 25 mi/40 km SE of Orlando. Tourism is its main industry, and it is also a trade center for the cattle industry. **2.** city, pop. 48,812, seat of Stearns Co., also in Benton and Sherburne counties, EC Minnesota, on both banks of the Mississippi R., 60 mi/97 km NW of Minneapolis. Laid out as a fur trading post in the 1850s, it emerged as a transportation hub and processing center for regional agricultural goods, especially dairy products. Nearby deposits of colored granite were discovered in 1870 and local quarries have since dominated the economy, stimulating a building stone and monument industry. In addition, St. Cloud has railroad repair shops and factories making refrigeration equipment, paper, iron and brass products, and optical goods. It is the seat of St. Cloud State University (1869). The Minnesota State Reformatory lies in the SE part. Sherburne National Wildlife Refuge and Sand Dunes State Forest are to the SE.

Saint-Constant city, pop. 18,423, Roussillon census division, S Québec, 10 mi/16 km S of Montréal, and adjacent (SE) to Kahnawake. Originally agricultural, it industrialized with railroad development in the area in the 1880s, and is today a manufacturing and residential suburb.

Saint Croix largest (80 sq mi/207 sq km) and most populous (50,139) of the US VIRGIN ISLANDS, in the Caribbean Sea, 38 mi/61 km S of Saint Thomas. Its principal towns are CHRISTIANSTED and FREDERIKSTED. St. Croix was inhabited by Caribs when it was seen by Columbus on his second voyage (1493), and was depopulated by the mid 16th century. It was settled (1641) by the Dutch, who were followed by the English, Spanish, French, and, briefly (1651–65), the Knights of Malta. In 1733 it was purchased from France by Denmark, whose planters grew sugarcane, employing slave labor until emancipation in 1848. Today, tourism is the leading industry, but sugarcane, fruits, and vegetables are grown, livestock is raised, and there is some fishing. In addition, Caribbean oil is refined; African bauxite and local sugar are processed; rum is manufactured; and all are exported. BUCK ISLAND REEF National Monument is off the NE shore.

Saint Croix River **1.** 75 mi/121 km long, in Maine and New Brunswick. It rises in the CHIPUTNETICOOK LAKES and flows SE into PASSAMAQUODDY BAY, forming the international boundary. Textile milling and hydroelectric development have been important at CALAIS, Maine–SAINT STEPHEN, New Brunswick. In 1604 Samuel de Champlain and the Sieur de Monts established the first French settlement in North America here on Dochet (Saint Croix) I., 8 mi/13 km SE of downtown Calais; after a harsh winter, the colony moved to PORT-ROYAL, in modern Nova Scotia. In 1798 a British claim that Maine's Penobscot R. was actually the Saint Croix, and the border thus well to the W, was disproved when settlement remains were found on the island, which is part of Maine. **2.** 164 mi/264 km long, in Wisconsin and Minnesota. It rises near Solon Springs, in NW Wisconsin, and flows generally SW. It is a National Scenic Riverway. The upper section is narrow and turbulent, cutting through a deep gorge known as the Dalles. The river forms part of the Minnesota-Wisconsin boundary for most of its course, and at Stillwater, Minnesota, it broadens into Lake St. Croix, and flows downstream to its merger with the Mississippi R. at Prescott. The valley was inhabited by Sioux and Chippewa, and traveled by British and French fur traders, until the mid 19th century, when logging became the major activity.

Saint Davids see under RADNOR, Pennsylvania.

Saint-Denis, Rue commercial, educational, and residential thoroughfare in MONTRÉAL, Québec, running N (officially; actually W) from the St. Lawrence R., usually seven blocks

E of Blvd. SAINT-LAURENT. Shortly after 1900 it became the site of several educational institutions, and acquired a reputation as the city's Latin Quarter (*Quartier latin*). Today it is the site of the Université du Québec à Montréal (UQAM) campus (1979), and a popular entertainment and cafe zone. North of Rue SHERBROOKE its student flavor gives way gradually to that of a boutique-and-Victorian-house neighborhood. The Square Saint-Louis here is one of the city's best known, and from its W side extends the pedestrian restaurant zone of Rue Prince-Arthur.

Sainte-Anne-de-Beaupré city, pop. 3146, La Côte-de-Beaupré census division, S Québec, 21 mi/34 km NE of Québec City, on the N shore of the St. Lawrence R. A shrine here dedicated to the patron saint of sailors has been one of the most important pilgrimage sites in Canada since the 17th century; the first chapel was erected in 1658. The present Romanesque basilica, latest in a series of replacements, was constructed in 1926. The memorial chapel (1878) and other religious sites also attract large numbers of visitors. The mill town of **Beaupré** (pop. 2676), just E, separated in 1927. The narrow coastal strip called the **Côte de Beaupré** extends from MONTMORENCY (SW) to Cap Tourmente (NE), some 25 mi/40 km, between the cliffs of the CANADIAN SHIELD and the St. Lawrence. It was named ("beautiful meadow") for its rich, if limited, bottomland.

Sainte-Anne-de-Bellevue city, pop. 4030, MONTRÉAL URBAN COMMUNITY, S Québec, at the SW end of the I. de Montréal, on L. St.-Louis. A summer resort and residential suburb, it is also the seat of the Macdonald College of Agriculture, a branch of McGill University. The Federal Arctic Biological Station is here as well.

Sainte-Anne-des-Plaines city, pop. 10,787, Thérèse–De Blainville census division, S Québec, 22 mi/35 km NW of Montréal and adjacent (NE) to Mirabel, at the SE feet of the Laurentians, an agricultural (esp. strawberries) and residential suburb.

Sainte-Catherine, Rue commercial thoroughfare in downtown MONTRÉAL, Québec, running E–W (officially; actually N–S) through the central business district, of which it was the chief street through most of the 20th century. Major department stores have been joined here since the 1970s by many boutiques.

Sainte-Foy city, pop. 71,133, QUÉBEC Urban Community, S Québec. The chief residential suburb of Québec City, it is 4 mi/6 km SW of Downtown. The village of Sainte-Foy was the site of a 1760 battle in which the French under François de Lévis defeated a British force based in Québec City but on arrival of British reinforcements were forced to retreat to Montréal. The modern suburb, which has grown largely since the 1950s, houses government-related agencies, and is home to L'Université Laval, the first (1852) francophone Roman Catholic university on the continent.

Sainte Genevieve city, pop. 4411, seat of Sainte Genevieve Co. (pop. 16,037), SE Missouri, on the Mississippi R., 45 mi/72 km SSE of Saint Louis. The oldest European settlement in the state, it was established around 1735 by the French, attracted by lead mines in the area. Farms were established along the river, and Ste. Genevieve became an important port. It has produced limestone, marble, and some light manufactures. The city has long been prone to serious flooding.

Sainte-Hélène, Île in the Saint Lawrence R., just NE of Vieux-Montréal and downtown MONTRÉAL, Québec. Once an Iroquoian stronghold, then part of the SEIGNEURIE of Longueuil, it was fortified by the British, whose Old Fort (1820) is now a museum and visitor center within the popular La Ronde amusement park. Part of the city of Montréal in the 20th century, the island was expanded as the main site for Expo 67, the 1967 World's Fair. Buckminster Fuller's Biosphere, then the largest geodesic dome in the world, was damaged by fire in 1978, and has been partially restored. The Île NÔTRE-DAME is immediately E.

Sainte-Julie city, pop. 20,632, Lajemmerais census division, S Québec, 14 mi/23 km ENE of Montréal and just E of BOUCHERVILLE, a growing residential suburb.

Saint Elias Mountains also, **Saint Elias Range** part of the COAST RANGES, in SE Alaska and SW Yukon Territory. Extending SE for more than 200 mi/320 km from the WRANGELL and CHUGACH mountains, the range includes Mt. LOGAN (19,524 ft/5951 m), the highest point in Canada; **Mount Saint Elias** (18,008 ft/5489 m); Mount Lucania (17,146 ft/5226 m), Mt. Steele (16,644 ft/5073 m), and numerous other peaks. It is one of the world's highest coastal ranges. An extensive glacial system, the largest in the world outside polar regions, extends from the Alsek R. (S) to Mt. Saint Elias (NW), and includes the Malaspina, Hubbard, and Seward glaciers; the mammoth Bering Glacier W of Cape Yakataga is sometimes considered part. The WRANGELL–ST. ELIAS NATIONAL PARK incorporates much of the Alaska part of the range, the KLUANE NATIONAL PARK much of the Yukon portion.

Sainte-Marie city, pop. 10,542, La Nouvelle-Beauce census division, S Québec, 28 mi/45 km SSE of Québec City, on the R. Chaudière. A trade center, it is noted for its baked goods and other foods, and has had textile, metal, and woodworking industries. The Maison Taschereau (1809) survives from the 18th-century SEIGNEURIE that gave rise to the community.

Sainte-Thérèse formerly, **Sainte-Thérèse-de-Blainville** city, pop. 24,158, S Québec, 18 mi/29 km NW of Montréal, on the Laurentian Autoroute. A fast-growing suburb just SE of the MIRABEL airport, it has diversified manufacturing plants.

Saint-Eustache city, pop. 37,278, Deux-Montagnes census division, S Québec, 18 mi/29 km WNW of Montréal, at the mouth of the R. du Chêne on the R. des Mille Îles, across from the I. Jésus (Laval). Settled in the 1770s, it was the site of a battle of the 1837 uprising in which British troops cornered and defeated the PATRIOTES and burned the village. In an agricultural area, the city is a growing residential and industrial suburb.

Saint Francis city, pop. 9245, Milwaukee Co., SE Wisconsin, on L. Michigan, immediately SE of Milwaukee. A residential community, it is just E of General Mitchell Air Field.

Saint Francis River 425 mi/684 km long, in SE Missouri and E Arkansas. It rises in the St. François Mts., N of TAUM SAUK Mt., the highest peak in Missouri, and flows generally SSE, through units of the Mark Twain National Forest and into L. Wappapello, impounded by the Wappapello Dam. Continuing S, it forms the boundary between NE Arkansas and Missouri's BOOTHEEL REGION for a distance of some 50 mi/80 km, then proceeds S in Arkansas, on the E of CROWLEY'S RIDGE, into the DELTA, winding past Marked Tree and Madison to join the Mississippi R. just N of HELENA. For some 40 mi/64 km, N and S of Madison, it flows in two roughly parallel channels. Near its mouth, at the S end of Crowley's Ridge, is the 21,000-ac/8500-ha **Saint Francis National Forest.**

Saint Francisville town, pop. 1700, seat of West Feliciana Parish, SC Louisiana, on the E bank of the Mississippi R., 26 mi/42 km NW of Baton Rouge. A 1785 Capuchin monastery here gave its name to this river port and trade center. In 1810 it was briefly the capital of the WEST FLORIDA republic. Cotton, sweet potatoes, and other crops are grown locally. Rosedown Plantation (1835) and other antebellum sites draw visitors. The River Bend nuclear power plant (1985) is nearby.

Saint François Mountains also, **Saint Francis Mountains** range of igneous rocks rising above the NE OZARK Plateau in SE Missouri. Topped by TAUM SAUK Mt. (1772 ft/540 m), highest in the range and the state, they are the center of a lead and zinc mining region. The odd-shaped formations in Elephant Rock State Park and Pilot Knob, near Graniteville, were sculpted by weathering.

Saint-Gaudens National Historic Site see under CORNISH, New Hampshire.

Saint George **1.** commercial and residential section, extreme N Staten I., New York. Ferries between Staten I. and Manhattan dock at St. George, a community set on the slopes of Fort Hill, which was a British post during the Revolution. In the late 19th century the area, known in part as Brighton Heights, was a waterside resort. Staten Island's borough hall and other government buildings are here. Bayonne, New Jersey, is SW across the KILL VAN KULL. **2.** city, pop. 28,502, seat of Washington Co., in the SW corner of Utah, 50 mi/80 km SW of Cedar City and 8 mi/13 km N of the Arizona border. It was settled (1861) by Mormons, who were sent to this warm area to grow cotton. A commercial and tourist center, it is a gateway to Dixie National Forest (8 mi/13 km N) and Zion National Park (15 mi/24 km NE). The city is surrounded by poultry and produce farms and gold, copper, and iron mines. Utah's first Mormon temple (1877), an 1863 tabernacle, the Jacob Hamblin Home (1863), and the Brigham Young Winter Home (1873) draw visitors to the city, which is also the seat of Dixie College (1919) and the Dixie Regional Medical Center, a major employer. Recently it has become home to many retirees from S California.

Saint-Georges city, pop. 19,583, Beauce Co., SE Québec, 53 mi/86 km SE of Québec City, on the R. CHAUDIÈRE at its confluence with the R. Famine. After the American invasion of 1775 along the Chaudière, the area was settled by the British. Its economy is based on forest industries and some dairying.

Saint George's Bay inlet of the Gulf of St. Lawrence at the mouth of the St. George's R., S of the PORT AU PORT Peninsula, on the SW coast of Newfoundland. Sixty mi/100 km NE–SW and 38 mi/62 km wide at its mouth, it is bounded by Cape St. George (N) and Cape Anguille (S). Once part of the FRENCH SHORE, the area around the bay still has a large francophone pop. STEPHENVILLE, at the head of the bay, is the area's largest town. **St. George's** (town, pop. 1678) is a port nearby on the SE shore.

Saint Helena city, pop. 4990, Napa Co., NW California, in the NC Napa Valley, 16 mi/26 km NW of Napa and 48 mi/77 km NNE of San Francisco. Incorporated in 1876, it is a major winemaking center, settled originally by Swiss, Germans, and Italians. It is now also a tourist magnet and wealthy EXURB.

Saint Helena, Mount see under CALISTOGA, California.

Saint Helena Sound inlet of the Atlantic Ocean 15 mi/24 km E of Beaufort, in S South Carolina. Eight mi/13 km wide at its mouth, the sound receives the Edisto, Ashepoo, and Combahee rivers and is crossed by the Atlantic Intracoastal Waterway. It is bordered by Edisto and other islands on the N and St. Helena, Morgan, and Hunting islands on the S. **St. Helena I.,** 20 mi/32 km N–S and 12 mi/19 km wide, is the site of Frogmore plantation and the Penn Center, site of one of the first schools for blacks in the US, founded in 1862.

Saint Helens city, pop. 7535, seat of Columbia Co., NW Oregon, on the Columbia R. and the Washington line, 24 mi/39 km NNW of Portland. A river port, it has salmon fisheries and processes and ships dairy and truck farm products. A large paper and pulp plant is also here.

Saint Helens, Mount 8363 ft/2550 m, in Skamania Co., SW Washington, a volcano on the W flank of the CASCADE RANGE, 35 mi/56 km E of Kelso, in the Gifford Pinchot National Forest. Dormant since 1857, it erupted on May 18, 1980, in an explosion that blasted away its 9677-ft/2950-m peak and buried an area 17 mi/27 km to the NE in mud and ash; 60 people were killed. Lower-level volcanic activity continued through the 1980s. The 110,000-ac/44,500-ha **Mt. St. Helens National Volcanic Monument** now surrounds the peak.

Saint-Hubert city, pop. 74,027, Chambly Co., S Québec, 7 mi/11 km E of Montréal, on the S(E) bank of the St. Lawrence R. One of the largest municipalities in the Montréal area, it is principally a residential suburb, with some industry. Its airport handles military and private aircraft.

Saint-Hyacinthe city, pop. 39,292, Les Maskoutains census division, S Québec, 31 mi/50 km ENE of Montréal, on the R. Yamaska. With rail and road connections, it is the service, commercial, and cultural center for an agricultural area, and has a variety of manufactures including machinery, textiles, and paper and food products. Its institutions include the Séminaire de Saint-Hyacinthe (1811), L'École Médicine Vétérinaire (1866), and the Collège Saint-Maurice (1935).

Saint James unincorporated village, pop. 12,703, in Smithtown, Suffolk Co., SE New York, on Long Island's North Shore, 8 mi/13 km SW of Port Jefferson. It is primarily residential.

Saint James Street French, **Rue Saint-Jacques** commercial thoroughfare in downtown MONTRÉAL, Québec, running S (officially, W) from Vieux-Montréal. The traditional center of Canadian high finance before losing much of that role to Toronto's BAY St. in the 1970s, it remains the site of the Montréal Stock Exchange and other local institutions.

Saint-Jean, Île English, **Saint Johns Island** see PRINCE EDWARD ISLAND.

Saint-Jean, Lac 521 sq mi/1350 sq km, in SC Québec, 114 mi/184 km NNW of Québec City. It receives a number of rivers, including the Ashuapmushuan, Mistassini, and PÉRIBONCA; on its E end it is drained by the SAGUENAY R. Jesuit missionaries and fur traders settled the area in the 17th century, and agriculture and forestry later became important. In the 20th century paper mills and aluminum plants formed an industrial base. Today Lac Saint-Jean is known primarily as a summer resort, with beaches, sailing, and fishing. Péribonka (N) and ROBERVAL (S) are important lakefront communities.

Saint-Jean-Chrysostome city, pop. 12,717, Les Chutes-de-la Chaudière census division, S Québec, 6 mi/10 km S of Québec City, of which it is a suburb.

Saint-Jean-Port-Joli municipality, pop. 3369, S Québec, 51 mi/82 km NE of Québec City, on the S bank of the St. Lawrence R., known as a center for traditional Québec wood sculpture and other handicrafts.

Saint-Jean-sur-Richelieu also, **Saint-Jean** city, pop. 37,607, Le Haut-Richelieu census division, S Québec; 21 mi/34 km SE of Montréal, on the R. Richelieu opposite IBERVILLE. This trade center was built on the site of Fort-Saint-Jean (1666); in 1836, the first railway built in Canada linked it with LA PRAIRIE. Its economy is based on diversified manufacturing, and it has a military college.

Saint-Jérôme city, pop. 23,384, La Rivière-du-Nord Co., S Québec, 30 mi/49 km NW of Montréal, in the lower Laurentians, on the R. du Nord. Founded in 1834, it became the center for colonization of a lumbering and farming area. Today it makes textile, paper, and other products. With ski areas and summer resorts just N, tourism is also important, and there is a community college.

Saint John **1.** city, pop. 7466, St. Louis Co., EC Missouri, a residential suburb 11 mi/18 km NW of downtown St. Louis. **2.** city, pop. 74,969, seat of Saint John Co. (pop. 81,462), SE New Brunswick, at the Saint John River's entry into the Bay of Fundy. The most populous New Brunswick city, with a metropolitan area (CMA) pop. of 124,981, it was known as the "Liverpool of America" during its 19th-century heyday. Micmac and Malecite villages on the site were succeeded by Acadian (1700s), English (1760s), and LOYALIST (1783) settlements. In 1785 Saint John became the first incorporated city in what is now Canada. It boomed in the wooden-ship period, then declined after the 1860s when steamships and Canadian CONFEDERATION caused trade to move elsewhere, and many residents emigrated to Boston and other American cities. Modern Saint John is a major ice-free port and center of paper and pulp, refined oil and sugar, drydocking, and food processing industries. A campus (1964) of the University of New Brunswick is here. The city's Reversing Falls, caused by the change of the Bay of Fundy's high tides at the river's mouth, are a noted attraction, as is nearby (S) Partridge Island, a 19th-century quarantine station. The city's suburbs, in Kings Co., include Rothesay, Quispamis (pop. 8446), and Fairvale to the NE and Grand Bay and Westfield to the NW. **3.** smallest (20 sq mi/52 sq km) and least populous (3504) of the three main islands in the US VIRGIN ISLANDS, 4 mi/6 km E of SAINT THOMAS. European discovery came with the second voyage of Columbus (1493). Settled by Danes in 1716, it had a sugarcane economy before a 1733 slave revolt, but was little developed thereafter. Purchased by the US in 1917, it is today largely a tourist center; over half of its landmass and nearby waters are within the VIRGIN ISLANDS NATIONAL PARK, established in 1956 through the efforts of Laurance Rockefeller, who also developed the well-known Caneel Bay resort, on the W coast. Cruz Bay (unincorporated, pop. 2466), on the W, is the main settlement; Coral Bay, on the SE, is a large sheltered harbor.

Saint John River 418 mi/673 km long, draining 21,000 sq mi/54,400 sq km. It rises in Somerset Co., NW Maine, flowing NE and E. It forms the border between Maine and New Brunswick for 70 mi/113 km, then flows SE to enter New Brunswick above Grand Falls, where it drops 75 ft/23 m, then E and S to the Bay of Fundy at St. John. At its mouth it narrows to a gorge 450 ft/137 m wide, 100 ft/30 m high, where there are "reversing falls"—rapids caused by the Bay of Fundy's strong tides, which when high force the river to reverse its flow. The St. John is navigable by large vessels to Fredericton, a distance of 81 mi/130 km. From Fredericton up to Grand Falls, another 65 mi/105 km, it is navigable by smaller vessels. A noted canoeing and fishing area, the St. John was seen by Sieur de Monts and Champlain in 1604. Its main tributaries are the Allagash and Aroostook rivers in Maine, the Madawaska in Québec, and the Tobique and Nashwaak in New Brunswick. There are numerous hydroelectric plants along its course.

Saint John's city and provincial capital, pop. 95,770, in SE Newfoundland, on the NE of the AVALON PENINSULA, on St. John's Bay of the Atlantic Ocean. Protected by hills, its ice-free harbor was known to European fishermen by about 1500. Colonized by the British from 1583, but occupied chiefly seasonally (by fishermen) for over a century, it was taken several times (the last in 1762) by the French. In the 19th century it became (1832) the seat of colonial government, and burned five times. After 1815, Irish immigrants swelled its pop. Until World War II, its fortunes rose and fell chiefly with the international fish market. Today, it is Newfoundland's governmental, cultural, and commercial center; its port services the international fishing fleet. Queen's College (1841) and the Memorial University of Newfoundland (1925) are here. During the world wars St. John's was an important naval and air base. Ship building and repair is the most important of its industries; since the 1980s, decline in the Atlantic fisheries and oil exploration on the GRAND BANKS have suggested a possible new direction for the city. Signal Hill (525 ft/160 m), E of the harbor, was the scene of the last (1762) French-English battle here, and in 1901 was the site at which Marconi received the first transatlantic wireless message. Quidi Vidi L., just N, is home to a regatta dating to 1818, said to be North America's oldest sporting event.

Saint Johnsbury town, pop. 7608, including St. Johnsbury village, St. Johnsbury Center, and East St. Johnsbury. It is the seat of Caledonia Co., NE Vermont. St. Johnsbury is on Interstate 91, at the confluence of the Passumpsic, Moose, and Sleeper rivers, 13 mi/21 km NW of Littleton, New Hampshire. In 1830 Thaddeus Fairbanks patented the first lever scale, spurring the community's industrial and population growth. St. Johnsbury is also a trade and maple sugar center, home to a large trucking company, and produces gourmet vegetables and herb plants and seeds.

Saint Johns Island see PRINCE EDWARD ISLAND.

Saint Johns River 285 mi/459 km long, in E Florida. It rises in swamps in Brevard Co., SW of Melbourne, at an altitude of about 20 ft/6 m, and flows N through a series of lakes including Harney, Monroe, and George. It passes Palatka, Orange Park, and Jacksonville, then turns E into the Atlantic. Its main tributary, the Oklawaha, joins it N of the Ocala National Forest. North of L. George, the St. Johns becomes estuarial, widening to 2.5 mi/4 km near Jacksonville.

Saint Joseph **1.** city, pop. 9214, seat of Berrien Co., SW Michigan, on L. Michigan at the mouth of the St. Joseph R., opposite Benton Harbor. On this site La Salle built Fort Miami (1679), from which he explored the region. The first permanent settlement (c.1830) was a fur trading post. Growth occurred with the building of improved harbor facilities and the opening of the Territorial Road from Detroit. Economic activities have long included commercial fishing and fruit processing. In addition, auto parts, rubber, machinery, castings, clothing, and paper are manufactured.

The city's beaches and mineral springs have attracted a lively tourist trade. **2.** city, pop. 3294, Stearns Co., C Minnesota, 6 mi/10 km W of St. Cloud. The College of St. Benedict (1913) is here. The large St. Benedict's Convent is 1 mi/2 km E. **3.** city, pop. 71,852, seat of Buchanan Co., NW Missouri, on the Missouri R. and the Kansas border (W), 46 mi/74 km NW of downtown Kansas City. Founded in 1826 as a fur trapping station and trading post, this river port was a focal point for 19th-century steamboat, stagecoach, and freight lines heading west. A major frontier supply depot, it also became the E end (1860) of the PONY EXPRESS, whose stables and headquarters are now museums. The city flourished commercially during the Civil War, and continued to prosper throughout the century. Today it is a grain, livestock, manufacturing, wholesale, and transportation hub. It packs meat, mills flour, processes dairy products and other foods, and has machine shops and foundries. Manufactures include electrical and firefighting equipment, metal products and wire, concrete, chemicals, and paper goods. Tourism is also a factor in its economy, and it is the site of the house where Jesse James was killed (1882) and the home of writer Eugene Field (1850–95). Missouri Western State College (1915) is here.

Saint Joseph Bay inlet of the Gulf of Mexico on the Florida PANHANDLE, 80 mi/130 km SW of Tallahassee, in Gulf Co., NW Florida. Fourteen mi/23 km N–S and 2–6 mi/3–10 km wide, it is separated from the Gulf by 17 mi/27 km–long St. Joseph Peninsula, a narrow sand spit with Cape San Blas at its S tip and St. Joseph Point at its N end. The bay forms the harbor for the lumber and paper producing and fishing city of Port St. Joe (pop. 4044), and was the site of the early settlement of **Saint Joseph,** where Florida's constitution was drawn up (1838). Saint Joseph was destroyed by yellow fever and storms in the 1840s.

Saint Joseph County 459 sq mi/1189 sq km, pop. 247,052, in N Indiana, bounded N by Michigan. Its seat is SOUTH BEND. The county is largely agricultural; grain, fruit, and mint are major crops. The S part has lake resorts. There is extensive and diversified manufacturing in the South Bend–MISHAWAKA area.

Saint-Lambert city, pop. 20,976, S Québec, on the S shore of the St. Lawrence R., opposite Montréal, with which it is linked by the VICTORIA BRIDGE. It has a diversified industrial base, its manufactures including machinery, metal and wood products, and fountain pens. L'Écluse de Saint-Lambert, the easternmost lock of the St. Lawrence Seaway, is here. The city is also a yachting center.

Saint-Laurent city, pop. 72,402, MONTRÉAL URBAN COMMUNITY, S Québec, in the center of the I. de Montréal, W of MOUNT ROYAL and N of DORVAL. First settled by 17th-century farmers, it is now a residential and industrial suburb, making aircraft, railway cars, chemicals, pharmaceuticals, textiles, electronic equipment, and a range of other products. The Collège de Saint-Laurent (1847), the Séminaire Sainte-Croix (1899), and the Collège Basile-Moreau (1929) are here.

Saint-Laurent, Boulevard familiarly, **the Main** major N–S (officially; actually E–W) thoroughfare of MONTRÉAL, Québec, proceeding from the St. Lawrence R. across the I. de Montréal to the R. des Prairies; it is entirely within the city. When Montréal was divided into E and W wards in 1792, St.-Laurent became the dividing line, and still divides E and W addresses. It is also traditionally the line between the anglophone-dominated W side (see WEST ISLAND) and the francophone E side. The boulevard itself has been since the late 19th century home to immigrants, who are said to have walked up it from the port. Russian Jews, here from the 1880s, made it a famous ethnic and cultural zone; later, Greeks, Italians, Portuguese, Eastern Europeans, and others joined them. Closer to the St. Lawrence (S of Rue SHERBROOKE), the boulevard has been the city's red-light district, but is increasingly trendy. North of the PLATEAU MONT-ROYAL, its ethnic flavor has recently been diluted by fashion, influenced in part by the proximity of affluent, francophone OUTREMONT.

Saint Lawrence, Gulf of inlet of the Atlantic Ocean at the mouth of the St. Lawrence R., bordered by the North Shore (Côte-Nord) of Québec (N), the GASPÉ PENINSULA and New Brunswick (W), Nova Scotia (S), and Newfoundland (E). Québec's Île d'ANTICOSTI lies in the gulf across the mouth of the St. Lawrence R., and its Îles de la MADELEINE are in the S, along with PRINCE EDWARD ISLAND. CHALEUR BAY is a W arm S of the Gaspé. Some 475 mi/765 km NE–SW and 275 mi/445 km wide, the gulf connects with the ocean via the Strait of BELLE ISLE on the NE, between Labrador and Newfoundland, and via CABOT STRAIT on the SE, between Newfoundland and Cape Breton I., Nova Scotia. It receives a huge volume of fresh water from the river that gives it its name. With extensive deeps and shallows, and crossed (NW–SE) by the Laurentian Channel, it is an important fishing ground. Long lived on by the Inuit (N), Micmac (S), and Beothuk (E), it was visited by Basque whalers and fishermen from about 1525, and was explored by Jacques Cartier in 1534. With the St. Lawrence R., it forms the historic entry to the settlement and development of Canada.

Saint Lawrence County 2728 sq mi/7066 sq km, pop. 111,974, in N New York, bounded N and NW by the St. Lawrence R. Its seat is Canton; POTSDAM, OGDENSBURG, and MASSENA are the largest communities. The plains of the N part are a leading dairying region, with many other kinds of farming. The S part of New York's largest county is in the Adirondack Mts. Maple sugar is produced, and zinc, lead, pyrite, and limestone are mined. The mountainous, lake-dotted SE third and the island-filled N are popular resort areas.

Saint Lawrence Island largest island in the Bering Sea, 140 mi/230 km SW of Nome, in WC Alaska. Some 92 mi/148 km E–W and 8–23 mi/13–37 km N–S, the volcanic, tundra-covered island, rising to 2070 ft/631 m at Atuk Mt., is inhabited mainly by Inuit, with settlements at Gambell (city, pop. 525) and Savoonga (city, pop. 519) on the N coast. The International Dateline passes 35 mi/56 km to the W, and the tip of Siberia's Chukchi Peninsula lies 50 mi/80 km NW. Vitus Bering encountered and named the island on St. Lawrence Day in 1728. Extensive archaeological studies of Inuit culture have been conducted here.

Saint Lawrence River 744 mi/1197 km long, flowing NE from L. Ontario, between Ontario and New York, then through Québec's Saint Lawrence Lowland, into the Gulf of Saint Lawrence; the boundary between river and gulf is conventionally defined as a line N from the GASPÉ PENINSULA, passing just W of ANTICOSTI I. The Saint Lawrence is the last link of a system extending over 2400 mi/3800 km from the head of Minnesota's Saint Louis R., through the Great Lakes (which it drains), to the Gulf of Saint Lawrence. This waterway, along with the Ottawa R., the Saint Lawrence's chief tributary, is the most important geographical factor in Canadian (earlier in NEW FRANCE's) history. The names *Québec* ("where the river narrows") and *Canada* ("settlement," referring to the site that became Québec City) both suggest the importance of the point at which the Saint Lawrence leads into the North American interior. Even after the American Revolution, when the new nation to the S threatened it at times, the river-and-lake route (augmented by the RIDEAU and TRENT canals and Ottawa R.–L. NIPISSING–Georgian Bay alternative) continued as the mainstream of Canadian development, the highway traveled by NORTH WEST COMPANY and other adventurers, traders, and pioneers. With the 1959 completion of the GREAT LAKES–SAINT LAWRENCE WATERWAY, the river is today part of an international system allowing all but the largest oceangoing vessels to reach ports as far W as Duluth, Minnesota, and Thunder Bay, Ontario. The Saint Lawrence itself is now the site of the 189 mi/304 km–long **Saint Lawrence Seaway** (a name also often applied to the entire waterway), allowing ships to bypass rapids and hydroelectric dams between Montréal, Québec, and L. Ontario (which is 223 ft/68 m higher than the river at Montréal). From L. Ontario, near Kingston, the river flows NE past the THOUSAND Is., and past Prescott, Ontario, and Ogdensburg, New York, to the Iroquois Lock, near Iroquois, Ontario. Below this is L. St. Lawrence, a 28 mi/45 km–long widening in the river created by the (US-controlled) Moses-Saunders Power Dam, and bypassed by the Eisenhower and Snell locks, near Massena, New York. At Cornwall, Ontario, just NE of the Moses-Saunders project, the river widens into L. Saint Francis, which extends to just SW of Montréal. The upper Saint Lawrence between L. Ontario and Cornwall is also known as the International Rapids Section. At the Soulanges section, SW of Montréal, the river narrows, and the two Beauharnois locks bypass another power dam. Below (NE of) these is L. Saint-Louis, the widening of the St. Lawrence at the point where the Ottawa R. joins it (from the NW, by way of the L. des Deux Montagnes). The Saint Lawrence here divides, the R. des Mille Îles passing N around the Île Jésus (LAVAL), the R. des Prairies passing between the I. Jésus and the I. de MONTRÉAL, and the main channel continuing S of the city; the three rejoin N of Montréal. The final elements of the Saint Lawrence Seaway are on the main channel; the 20 mi/33 km–long South Shore Canal and locks bypass the LACHINE Rapids, which were the original head of navigation, the natural barrier that led to Montréal's founding here. From Montréal, the Saint Lawrence runs unimpeded to the Gulf of Saint Lawrence. The R. RICHELIEU, which joins it from the S at Sorel, provided an early (and much fought over) route to L. Champlain, and from there to the Hudson R. and New York. Below the Richelieu's mouth the Saint Lawrence widens into L. St. Pierre, above (SW of) Trois-Rivières, where the R. SAINT-MAURICE joins it from the N; at this point it begins to be affected by tides. At Québec City, the high edge of the CANADIAN SHIELD (N) intersects the river, forming the famous narrows. Below (NE of) the city, the river passes around the I. D'ORLÉANS, then widens, becomes increasingly tidal, and deepens as it passes over the channel it formerly cut in what is now CONTINENTAL SHELF. At Tadoussac, where the R. SAGUENAY joins it from the NW, it is 16 mi/26 km wide. To the E of Baie-Comeau (where the R. MANICOUAGAN joins it), it widens rapidly as its remote NORTH SHORE (Côte-Nord) swings NNE toward the port of Sept-Îles. At its mouth it is 90 mi/145 km across. The Saint Lawrence is today a major shipping lane and, in its upper sections, an important power source. Tourism is a key industry throughout its valley. Jacques Cartier, who found Iroquoian villages at Stadacona (Québec City) and Hochelaga (Montréal) in 1534–35, is the first European known to have explored it.

Saint Leo town, pop. 1009, Pasco Co., WC Florida, 30 mi/48 km NE of Tampa, home to St. Leo's College (1889).

Saint-Léonard city, pop. 73,120, MONTRÉAL URBAN COMMUNITY, S Québec. One of the largest residential suburbs of Montréal, it is 6 mi/10 km NNW of Downtown.

Saint Louis city, pop. 396,685, independent of but surrounded by St. Louis Co., EC Missouri, on the W bank of the Mississippi R. across from East St. Louis, Illinois. It is the second most populous Missouri city, after Kansas City. Its metropolitan area also embraces nine counties (including Missouri's St. Louis, JEFFERSON, and SAINT CHARLES, and Illinois's MADISON and SAINT CLAIR) and has a total pop. of 2,444,099. Dozens of residential suburbs ring the city to its N, W, and S; the Illinois suburbs are more industrial. St. Louis was founded in 1764 as a fur trading post by Pierre Laclède and René Auguste Chouteau, in what was then Spanish territory. By the time of the LOUISIANA PURCHASE (1803), the settlement, 10 mi/16 km S of the Missouri River's junction with the Mississippi, was beginning to realize the benefits of its location. It was a major port in the steamboat era (from 1817), and, after 1857, a rail hub. Through the 19th century, St. Louis was a staging and supply point for travelers to the West, from the 1803–06 Lewis and Clark expedition, through trapping parties, to thousands bound for the Sante Fe, California, and Oregon trails. The city's French character was modified by the arrival from the 1830s of German, Irish, and other European immigrants. During the Civil War, residents were largely sympathetic to the Union cause. Camp Jackson, a Confederate post in the city, surrendered in 1861, and St. Louis grew as a supplier and arsenal to the Northern army. Further development was stimulated by the opening (1874) of the EADS BRIDGE, connecting the city with the industry and coal reserves of Illinois. In 1876, the city established its independence and current boundaries. In 1904, when it hosted the huge Louisiana Purchase Exposition (the St. Louis World's Fair), St. Louis was the fourth most populous (575,238) US city. Although its industries boomed in both world wars, it has gradually lost the relative importance it had in the era of Western expansion. It remains a major inland port and railroad and trucking hub, and Lambert–St. Louis Municipal Airport, 11 mi/18 km NW of Downtown, near HAZELWOOD, is important. It also has a long history as a market and processing and shipping center for regional agriculture, and as a wholesale center. Its industries, some now relocated in suburbs, include automobile, barge and boat, rail car, aircraft, and aerospace vehicle assembly and the manufacture of iron, steel, and metal products; beer; refined petroleum; electrical appliances; and chemicals. The city has a rich cultural life, with one of the nation's oldest (1880) symphony orchestras, a municipal opera, outdoor theater, and municipal art museum. The former theater district, on North Grand Blvd., is being redeveloped. Its newspapers, the *Globe-Democrat* (1852) and Joseph Pulitzer's *Post-Dispatch* (1878), are nationally known. Forest Park and Tower Grove Park, with the Missouri Botanical (Shaw's) Garden, are among the more significant US municipal parks. Sports facilities include Busch Memorial Stadium, home of the baseball Cardinals, and the St. Louis Arena, home of the hockey Blues. On the waterfront is the celebrated Gateway Arch, in the Jefferson National Expansion Memorial, and near it the renovated Laclede's Landing, at the site of the original settlement. An educational center, St. Louis is home to St. Louis University (1818), Washington University (1853, also largely in UNIVERSITY PARK), and a number of state and community colleges, seminaries, and conservatories. From a pop. peak of 856,796 in 1950, the city declined rapidly (esp. in the 1970s, when it lost over 27% of its residents) as older whites moved to suburbs, while URBAN RENEWAL projects leveled large tracts of deteriorating housing. This process appeared to slow in the 1980s, leaving a smaller, racially diverse city. See also: BUSCH MEMORIAL STADIUM; CARONDELET; EADS BRIDGE; FOREST PARK; GASLIGHT SQUARE; GATEWAY ARCH (and Jefferson National Expansion Memorial); the HILL; JEFFERSON BARRACKS (in St. Louis Co.); KERRY PATCH; LACLEDE'S LANDING; MILL CREEK VALLEY; NORTH SIDE; PRUIT-IGOE; SOULARD; SOUTH SIDE; TOWER GROVE PARK (and Missouri Botanical Garden); WAINWRIGHT BUILDING; WEST END.

Saint Louis County 506 sq mi/1311 sq km, pop. 993,529, in EC Missouri, bounded by the Mississippi R. (E), Missouri R. (NW), and Meramec R. (SE and SW). Its seat is CLAYTON. This populous county does not include the independent city of St. Louis, but lies directly to the S, W, and E of it, constitutes the largest part of its metropolitan area, and contains most of its residential suburbs. Among these are BELLEFONTAINE NEIGHBORS, NORTHWOODS, UNIVERSITY CITY, BRENTWOOD, WEBSTER GROVES, and MAPLEWOOD. The largest part of the suburban development occurred after World War II, and it peaked in the 1970s. Wheat and corn are grown and dairy cattle are raised in the few agricultural pockets that remain along the county's perimeter. There are also some manufacturing and business development. The W part of the county has a number of parks and nature preserves that maintain the bluffs and other features of the original landscape.

Saint Louis Park city, pop. 43,787, Hennepin Co., a suburb SW of Minneapolis. Settled in the 1850s, it mushroomed with the postwar suburban boom. Recently, the city has emerged as a commercial and industrial center. Warehouses and office buildings abound. Local manufactures include plastic and rubber parts, computers, precision machinery parts, paint, aluminum cookware, and window and door frames. There are also printing and graphic arts firms here. Industrial parks and shopping malls have sprung up, particularly along Highway 7 in the SW and E parts of the city.

Saint-Luc city, pop. 15,008, Le Haut-Richelieu census division, S Québec, 16 mi/26 km SE of Montréal, and E of LA PRAIRIE. It is a fast-growing suburb.

Saint Lucie nuclear power plant: see under FORT PIERCE, Florida.

Saint Marks National Wildlife Refuge see under APALACHEE BAY, Florida.

Saint Martinville city, pop. 7137, seat of St. Martin Parish, S Louisiana, on the BAYOU TECHE, 45 mi/72 km SW of Baton Rouge. Refugees from ACADIA settled the area in the 1760s, during which time the reunion of the separated lovers whose story gave rise to Longfellow's poem *Evangeline* (see GRAND PRÉ, Nova Scotia) is supposed to have taken place under the Evangeline Oak, still standing. Following the French Revolution, many royalists and other exiles arrived to join the Acadians. A river resort in the early 19th century, St. Martinville declined before the Civil War, and gradually became agricultural. Today, farming, fishing, nearby oil and gas production, some light industry, and tourism are all important. The Longfellow-Evangeline State Commemorative Area, just N along the bayou, recalls Acadian history.

Saint Mary-of-the-Woods unincorporated academic community, Vigo Co., WC Indiana, 2 mi/3 km NW of Terre Haute and 3 mi/5 km E of the Illinois border, seat of St. Mary-of-the-Woods College (1840), the oldest Roman Catholic college for women in the US.

Saint Marys also, **Saint Mary's** postal designation for the campus of St. Mary's College, in NOTRE DAME, Indiana.

Saint Marys City historic village in St. Marys Co., S Maryland. The first settlement in Maryland, it was established in 1634 on lands purchased from the Yaocomico tribe by Leonard Calvert. The village served as provincial capital from 1676 to 1694, when the government moved to Annapolis. St. Mary's College of Maryland (1839) is here. An 800-ac/324-ha historic area draws tourists.

Saint Marys River **1.** 180 mi/290 km long, in Georgia and Florida. It flows from the SE of the OKEFENOKEE SWAMP, and winds S, E, N, and E, forming the boundary between the two states, and entering the Atlantic Ocean between CUMBERLAND I., Georgia (N), and AMELIA I., Florida (S), on which Fernandina Beach is near its mouth. It is estuarial for its lower 80 mi/130 km. **2.** 63 mi/101 km long, in C Ontario and NE Michigan. It issues from the SE end of Whitefish Bay of L. Superior, and flows E to the twin cities of SAULT STE. MARIE, where the Soo Canals bypass its rapids. It then flows SE to the NW end of L. Huron, which it enters via the Detour Passage, W of Drummond I. The St. Mary's forms part of the border between the US and Canada.

Saint Mary's Street commercial thoroughfare that runs N–S through the heart of San Antonio, Texas. Its STRIP, N of Downtown and near BRACKENRIDGE PARK, is a popular entertainment zone, the site of many music and other clubs in the area between San Antonio College (S) and Trinity University (N).

Saint Matthews city, pop. 15,800, Jefferson Co., NC Kentucky, adjacent (E) to Louisville. It is a primarily residential suburb, formerly an important producer of potatoes.

Saint-Maurice, Rivière 325 mi/525 km long, in S Québec. It rises above the Réservoir Gouin, and flows SE across the Canadian Shield to LA TUQUE, then S toward the St. Lawrence Valley, where it joins the St. Lawrence R. at TROIS-RIVIÈRES. In its lower stretches, it passes GRAND-MÈRE and SHAWINIGAN, where falls have powered industry since the 19th century. Settled around Trois-Rivières in the 1630s, the lower St. Maurice was one of the earliest centers of New France. The **Forges Saint-Maurice,** within modern Trois-Rivières, was the site of Canada's first (1730s) heavy industry, ironmaking that continued into the 1880s. Pulp, aluminum, hydroelectric, and chemical plants later opened on the river. Its valley, esp. the area below La Tuque, is called **La Mauricie;** the 210–sq mi/544–sq km Parc National de la Mauricie, above Grand-Mère, preserves former forest hunting grounds.

Saint Meinrad religious community in Spencer Co., extreme S Indiana, 15 mi/24 km NNW of TELL CITY. It is the site of Saint

Meinrad Seminary, founded 1857 by German Swiss Catholics, noted for its Romanesque abbey and its history of training priests.

Saint Paul **1.** town, pop. 4881, EC Alberta, on Upper Therien L., 97 mi/156 km ENE of Edmonton. In an agricultural region, it has grain elevators and feed and flour mills, processes fruit and dairy products, and has some light industry. It is also a lake resort. Originally reserved (1895) for a MÉTIS settlement, the town later opened (1909) to others. A Canadian National Railway line arrived in 1920. Saddle Lake Indian Reserve (pop. 1893) is nearby. **2.** city, pop. 272,235, state capital and seat of RAMSEY Co., SE Minnesota, on the Mississippi R., adjacent (E) to MINNEAPOLIS, with which it forms the Twin Cities (pop. 640,618). At the river's head of navigation, it has long been a transportation hub, a barge terminus and later a railroad and motor freight center, as well as a regional market for the upper Midwest and parts of Canada. A modern financial and manufacturing city, it produces computers, electronic, medical, and research equipment, textiles and clothing, and household appliances; merchandising, printing, publishing, and food processing are important. The city was settled in 1838, near FORT SNELLING, by a French-Canadian trader, and at first called Pig's Eye. As St. Paul (from 1841), it became an important steamboat port and headquarters for the American Fur Company. In 1849, it became the capital of the Minnesota Territory, and in 1858 capital of the new state. Its Capitol (1896–1904) was designed by Cass Gilbert. An educational and cultural center, St. Paul is home to the University of Minnesota College of Agriculture; arts, historical, and science museums; Macalester College (1874); Hamline University (1854); and a number of professional schools and seminaries. The Minnesota State Fair is held here every summer, and a Winter Carnival each Jan. See also: COMO PARK; EAST SIDE; GRAND Ave.; HAMLINE; HIGHLAND PARK; LOWERTOWN; MACALASTER-GROVELAND; RICE PARK; SUMMIT Ave.; WEST SIDE. For more on the Twin Cities, see MINNEAPOLIS.

Saint Peter city, pop. 9421, seat of Nicollet Co., SC Minnesota, on the Minnesota R., 12 mi/19 km N of Mankato. An agricultural trading center founded in 1854, it grew up around its Episcopal church. The city is the site of the Old State Capitol Building, built during an unsuccessful effort at becoming Minnesota's capital city. Gustavus Adolphus College (1876) is here.

Saint Peters city, pop. 45,779, St. Charles Co., EC Missouri, 25 mi/40 km NW of downtown St. Louis. A residential suburb, it tripled in population in the 1980s.

Saint Petersburg city, pop. 238,629, Pinellas Co., WC Florida, at the S tip of the Pinellas Peninsula, on Tampa Bay (E and S), Old Tampa Bay (NE), and Boca Ciega Bay, off the Gulf of Mexico (W), 17 mi/27 km SW of Tampa. It is connected to the Tampa area by causeway and bridge over Old Tampa Bay and with the Bradenton area by the Sunshine Skyway over the mouth of Tampa Bay. Settled in the mid 1800s, it has been a favorite retirement locale since the 1880s, and has many planned adult communities. With an average of 360 sunny days annually, St. Petersburg has been dubbed the "Sunshine City," and attracts numerous tourists; boating and sport fishing are popular. The city has many parks, and there are 28 mi/45 km of beaches just to its W. Corporate offices began to locate here in the late 20th century, and newer buildings are mainly business centers and condominium towers. The city also processes and ships citrus fruits, has a commercial fishing fleet, and manufactures electronic equipment, boats and trailers, and building products. Primary among its newer landmarks is the immense Florida Suncoast Dome (1991), for sports and other events. The city is home to St. Petersburg Junior College (1927), Eckerd College (1958), and Hillsborough Community College (1968).

Saint-Pierre et Miquelon French archipelago in the Atlantic Ocean, consisting of 93 sq mi/241 sq km of small islands, 18 mi/29 km W of the BURIN PENINSULA of Newfoundland. Miquelon, the largest island, is 25 mi/40 km N–S and up to 10 mi/16 km wide; it has two sections, Grande Miquelon (N) and Petite Miquelon (S), once separate but connected by an isthmus since the mid 18th century. Saint-Pierre, a smaller island on the SE, is home to most of the pop. of some 6200. On the W of the GRAND BANKS, the islands provide a center for French fishing activities, the port of Saint-Pierre being ice-free throughout the year. The rocky islands support only scrubby vegetation, and virtually all goods must be imported. Originally settled by Basque and Norman fishermen around 1600, they were claimed by the British in 1713, then relinquished in 1763 to the French, who populated them with Acadians expelled from Canada. The British again took them during the American Revolution, but they have been in French domain since 1814, and in 1976 became a *département,* or full member of the French polity. The French hold fishing rights (defined 1992) in a narrow corridor S across the Grand Banks. During the period of Prohibition in the US, Saint-Pierre was a major bootlegging center; today, tourism is central to the economy.

Saint-Raphaël-de-l'Île-Bizard parish, pop. 11,352, MONTRÉAL URBAN COMMUNITY, S Québec, on the I. Bizard, just N of the SW end of the I. de Montréal. It is bridged to PIERREFONDS. Some 4 mi/6 km NE–SW and up to 3 mi/5 km wide, the island is an agricultural and resort community (it has large golf clubs) now being rapidly settled as a residential suburb.

Saint Regis River 80 mi/130 km long, in New York. It rises in the Adirondacks, NW of the SARANAC LAKES, and flows generally NW and N to the St. Lawrence R. NE of Hogansburg. It receives the West Branch (65 mi/105 km long) near Brasher Falls, and the East Branch (35 mi/56 km long) just above St. Regis Falls. It drains Upper and Lower St. Regis lakes, St. Regis Pond, and other mountain lakes. Named after a French Jesuit missionary, the river passes at its mouth through the **St. Regis Indian Reservation,** which straddles the New York-Québec-Ontario borders. Founded by a group separating in the 18th century from KAHNAWAKE, this part of the Mohawk lands is also called AKWESASNE.

Saint Simons Island one of the SEA ISLANDS, in the Atlantic Ocean at the mouth of the Altamaha R., 8 mi/13 km NE of Brunswick, in Glynn Co., E Georgia. Twelve mi/19 km N–S and 3–6 mi/5–8 km wide, with a pop. of 12,026, it is heavily developed with hotels, golf courses, and condominiums, and is connected to Brunswick by causeway. Fort Frederica, now a national monument, at the N end, was built by the British troops of James Oglethorpe in 1736–48. St. Simons was unsuccessfully attacked by the Spanish in 1742 at the Battle of Bloody Marsh, on the island's S, one of their last attempts to retain control of the SE US.

Saint Stephen town, pop. 4931, Charlotte Co., extreme SW New Brunswick, at the head of navigation on the SAINT CROIX R. opposite CALAIS, Maine, with which it is closely tied economically, socially, and by cooperative arrangements. Founded in the 1780s by LOYALISTS, it was a 19th-century lumbering and shipbuilding center. It amalgamated with Milltown (SW) in 1973, and today has several light industries. Its Aug. chocolate festival celebrates the creation of what is said to have been the world's first chocolate bar by a local company in 1910. Candy is still made here.

Saint Tammany Parish 873 sq mi/2261 sq km, pop. 144,508, in SE Louisiana, bounded (E) by the Pearl R. and Mississippi, and (S) by L. PONTCHARTRAIN. Its seat is COVINGTON; industry is centered in SLIDELL. The parish has two wildlife areas, a number of resorts, and a growing residential and retiree population, augmenting its older farming, lumbering, and maritime economy.

Saint Thomas **1.** city, pop. 29,990, seat of Elgin Co., extreme S Ontario, on Kettle Creek, 8 mi/13 km N of L. Erie and 14 mi/23 km S of London. Established in the 1800s on CROWN LANDS as the center of the Talbot settlement, which by the 1830s had peopled some 30 townships in this part of Ontario, it later developed as a rail and industrial center, and now manufactures auto parts, tools, construction equipment, bearings, pipe, and paper products. The Jumbo statue memorializes the famous circus elephant, killed here in 1885. **2.** second-largest (32 sq mi/83 sq km, pop. 48,166) of the US VIRGIN ISLANDS, whose capital, CHARLOTTE AMALIE, is on its S coast. It lies some 40 mi/64 km E of Puerto Rico, across the Virgin Passage, and extends c.18 mi/29 km E–W. European discovery dates from the second voyage of Columbus in 1493, when the island was inhabited by Caribs and Arawaks; it was unsuccessfully settled (1657) by the Dutch. The Danish West India & Guinea Company established Denmark's first settlement here in 1672. Slavery was important to the island's development as a sugarcane producer, until abolished in 1848. St. Thomas was acquired by the US in 1917. Tourism is today the greatest factor in the economy of the island, the most commercially important of the Virgins. It has a busy port at Charlotte Amalie's St. Thomas Harbor, and produces and exports rum and bay rum.

Saipan limestone and coral–overlaid volcanic island, 47 sq mi/123 sq km, pop. 38,896, largest and most important in the NORTHERN MARIANA Is., in the W Pacific Ocean, 150 mi/240 km NNE of Guam and 3 mi/5 km NE of TINIAN. Garapan (pop. 3904), the old Japanese capital, on the W coast, is the administrative seat of the Commonwealth of the Northern Mariana Islands. Saipan is hilly; Mt. Tapochau reaches 1551 ft/472 m. The island produces sugar, coffee, and copra, and has some mineral deposits. Its economy is dominated by Japanese tourism. Saipan is dotted with World War II remains and sites, including Banzai Cliff (N), where many Japanese leaped to their death in 1944 rather than surrender to US forces, and which is regarded as a shrine.

Sakakawea, Lake see under GARRISON DAM, North Dakota.

Sakonnet River E arm of Narragansett Bay, in Newport Co., SE Rhode Island. Thirteen mi/21 km long N–S and 2 mi/3 km wide, it separates the peninsula containing the towns of Tiverton and Little Compton (E) from Rhode I. (W). It borders Mount Hope Bay on the N and Rhode Island Sound on the S. Sakonnet Point is on the SW tip of the peninsula, with the resort village of Sakonnet, in Little Compton, just N.

Salaberry-de-Valleyfield also, **Valleyfield** city, pop. 27,598, S Québec, 32 mi/52 km SW of Montréal, on the NE end of L. Saint-François (the St. Lawrence R.), at the head of the modern (1932) Beauharnois Canal. The canal has left the city, in effect, on an island in the St. Lawrence. A SEIGNEURIE settled largely in the 1840s, when the first canal was built, it developed with saw and cotton milling, and today remains a commercial and industrial center as well as a port. Its manufactures include rubber, chemical, paper, bronze, and wood products, textiles, and foodstuffs. Its annual speedboat regatta is the largest in the world.

Salamanca see under CATTARAUGUS Co., New York.

Salamonie River 82 mi/132 km long, in E and EC Indiana. It rises near Salamonia, in SE Jay Co., and flows NW past PORTLAND and Montpelier to join the Wabash R. near Lagro, 5 mi/8 km E of Wabash, having passed through 9 mi/14 km–long Salamonie L., created by a 1966 dam. The Algonquian name refers to bloodroot, a plant found along its banks.

Salem **1.** city, pop. 7470, seat of Marion Co., SC Illinois, 13 mi/21 km NE of Centralia. An agricultural center, it is best known as the birthplace (1860) of William Jennings Bryan. **2.** city, pop. 5619, seat of Washington Co., S Indiana, 27 mi/43 km SE of Bedford. It is a trade center for the surrounding agricultural area. Limestone and timber are produced nearby, and the city has various light manufactures. Diplomat and author John Hay was born here in 1838; his home is preserved. The city was raided by John Hunt Morgan's Confederate irregulars on July 10, 1863. **3.** city, pop. 38,091, seat of Essex Co., NE Massachusetts, on the Danvers R. and Salem Harbor of Massachusetts Bay, 16 mi/26 km NE of Boston. One of the oldest New England seaports, settled in 1626, Salem was a base for privateers in the Revolution and the War of 1812, a center of the 18th–19th-century China trade, and a major shipbuilder. In the mid 19th century, losing its maritime eminence, it turned to textiles and other manufactures. The main industries now are diverse manufacturing and tourism. Heavily visited sites include Pioneer Village, a reconstruction of 1630s Salem; Nathaniel Hawthorne's "House of the Seven Gables" (1668), the Custom House (1819), where Hawthorne worked and wrote, and buildings associated with the 1692 witchcraft hearings, which followed events that took place in nearby DANVERS (then Salem Village). The Essex Institute contains materials on the witchcraft hysteria. **4.** town, pop. 25,746, Rockingham Co., SE New Hampshire. It is on the Massachusetts border, 20 mi/32 km NE of Nashua. Originally part of Haverhill, Massachusetts, Salem includes Salem Depot Village, where shoe manufacture was developed by Prescott C. Hall during the Civil War. Various light manufactures are carried on now in this growing Boston-area suburb. Canobie Lake Park, Rockingham Race Track, and America's Stonehenge (Mystery Hill), an archaeological site featuring 4000-year-old stone walls, are in the town. **5.** city, pop. 6883, seat of Salem Co., SW New Jersey, on the Salem R. above its mouth at Salem Cove on the Delaware R., 16 mi/26 km NW of Bridgeton. It was settled by English Quakers (1675) on lands of the Lenni Lenape (Delaware). A major port with a superb harbor, it was occupied by the British during the Revolution. Situated in an agricultural region, it is now a market and distribution center for SW New Jersey. Salem also produces such goods as glass products, canned foods, and linoleum; tourism is important. The Salem Oak, over 80 ft/24 m tall and 500 years old, is at the entrance of the Friends Burying Ground (1676). A nuclear power plant is at Hope Creek, 9 mi/14 km SSW, near the Delaware R. **6.** city, pop. 12,239, Columbiana Co., NE Ohio, 17 mi/27 km SW of Youngstown, in a rich coal region. Settled by New Jersey Quakers in the early 19th century, it was an early abolitionist center and an important station on the Underground Railroad. Local industries include the manufacture of machinery, tools and dies, and furniture. **7.** city, pop. 107,786, state capital and seat of Marion Co., also in Polk Co., NW Oregon, on the Willamette R., 43 mi/69 km SW of Portland. It was founded in 1840 by Methodist missionaries. Its Indian name meant "place of rest," and the biblical version of the term was chosen by the city's founders. The missionaries also established Willamette University (1842), the oldest institution of higher learning in the West, originally a manual training school for Indians. Salem became capital of the Oregon Territory in 1851 and of the new state in 1859. Today, Salem is a major commercial and distribution center for locally produced fruit, vegetables, dairy goods, and livestock. Important industries include canning, lumber and paper milling, and the manufacture of textiles, wood products, and concrete. High-tech equipment, silicon wafers, and metal goods are also manufactured. The city's Mission Mill Village contains the oldest documented buildings in the state, and is situated not far from the oldest winery in Oregon. Salem is also the seat of Chemeketa Community College (1962) and the neoclassical marble capitol (1937). **8.** independent city, pop. 23,756, seat of Roanoke Co., SW Virginia, on the Roanoke (Staunton) R., just W of the Blue Ridge Mts., adjacent (W) to ROANOKE. Laid out in 1802 and long a summer resort, it has become part of Roanoke's manufacturing complex; among its products are machinery, medicines, clothing, brick, and furniture. It is the seat of Roanoke College (1842) **9.** city, pop. 2063, Harrison Co., N West Virginia, 12 mi/19 km W of Clarksburg. It is the seat of Salem-Teikyo University, founded (1888) as Salem College.

Salem Church see under CHANCELLORSVILLE, Virginia.

Salem Plateau see under OZARK PLATEAU, Missouri.

Salida city, pop. 4737, seat of Chaffee Co., C Colorado, on the Arkansas R., 40 mi/64 km WNW of Canon City. Its river locale and the coming of the Denver and Rio Grande Railroad (1880) made Salida a distribution point for area mines. Today it ships grain, minerals, and livestock. There are railroad shops, sheet metal works, and several other industries. A tourist center, it has hot springs.

Salina **1.** city, pop. 42,303, seat of Saline Co., C Kansas, on the Smoky Hill R. just SW of its confluence with the Saline R., 80 mi/128 km NNW of Wichita. Founded in 1858 and an early antislavery center, it flourished with the coming of the railroad (1867). Now a major processing and shipping center for winter wheat, alfalfa, livestock, and dairy products, it is also in an area rich in oil and natural gas. The city contains foundries, and its manufactures include aircraft, clothing, and farm equipment. It is the site of Kansas Wesleyan University (1886) and Marymount College of Kansas (1922). **2.** town, pop. 35,145, Onondaga Co., C New York, adjacent (N) to Syracuse, on the NE shore of Onondaga L. Established in the 1790s in a salt-producing area (hence its name), it is a residential and industrial Syracuse suburb; the villages of Mattydale (unincorporated; pop. 6418) and Liverpool (pop. 2624) are within the town. **3.** town, pop. 1153, Mayes Co., NE Oklahoma, on the Neosho R., 45 mi/72 km ENE of Tulsa. On this site in the early 19th century Oklahoma's first permanent white settlement was established by the fur trader Jean Pierre Chouteau.

Salinas city, pop. 108,777, seat of Monterey Co. (pop. 355,660), WC California, near the NW end of the 100 mi/160 km–long **Salinas Valley,** on EL CAMINO REAL and the Salinas R., 85 mi/137 km SSE of San Francisco. Named for the river and its saltmarshes, it is the processing center for an exceptionally fertile area (irrigated by the largely underground river) noted for its dairy products, sugar beets, fruits, and vegetables, esp. lettuce. Settled in 1856 in cattle country, the city prospered with the arrival of the Southern Pacific railroad in 1868. John Steinbeck (1902–68), born in the city, depicted the lives of migrant workers and others in the valley in much of his writing. Hartnell College (1920) is here, and the annual California Rodeo has been held in the city since 1911.

Salinas Pueblo Missions National Monument 1077 ac/436 ha, in three units (Gran Quivira, Abó, and Quarai) near Mountainair, SE of Albuquerque, in C New Mexico. It protects three large PUEBLO villages and Franciscan MISSION churches, all abandoned by the late 17th century. The largest unit was formerly (1909–80) the Gran Quivira National Monument.

Saline River **1.** 300 mi/480 km long, in C and S Arkansas. It flows in forks from the Ouachita Mts., W of Little Rock, and winds generally SSE to join the OUACHITA R. in L. Jack Lee, 10 mi/16 km WNW of Crossett. **2.** 340 mi/550 km long, in Kansas, a N tributary that runs parallel (E–W) to the SMOKY HILL R. for much of its length, and joins it just E of Salina. It is dammed to create Wilson L., 48 mi/77 km W of Salina.

Salisbury **1.** town, pop. 4090, Litchfield Co., extreme NW Connecticut, on the Massachusetts and New York borders in the Taconic Mts. An exurban and resort town, it includes the villages of Lakeville, Salisbury, Ore Hill, Taconic (near Mt. Riga State Park), and LIME ROCK. The Housatonic R. is the town's E boundary. **2.** city, pop. 20,592, seat of Wicomico Co., SE Maryland, at the head of navigation on the Wicomico R., in the SC part of the Delmarva Peninsula, near the Delaware border. Founded in 1732, it developed as a distribution center for the peninsula, and was long the second port of Maryland. Its economy is now primarily agricultural; regional farms produce poultry, fruits, and vegetables. Industries process foods and manufacture textiles, cabinets, plastics, service station equipment, and printed computer forms. Salisbury State University (1925) is here. **3.** town, pop. 6882, Essex Co., extreme NE Massachusetts, 36 mi/58 km NNE of Boston, at the mouth of the Merrimack R. It was founded in 1638; the economy has depended on fishing, shipbuilding, and 19th-century woolen manufacture. Salisbury is now primarily residential and commercial. **4.** town, pop. 1061, Merrimack Co., SC New Hampshire, 15 mi/24 km NNW of Concord. It is a residential and agricultural community. Daniel Webster was born (1782) in a section that is now part of the town of Franklin, just E. **5.** city, pop. 23,087, seat of Rowan Co., WC North Carolina, in the Piedmont, 32 mi/51 km SW of Winston-Salem. Settled in 1753 as a road junction, it saw action in the Revolution, just before Guilford Courthouse (Feb. 1781). It was the site of one of the largest Confederate prisons during the Civil War; its National Cemetery houses the graves of 11,700 Federal soldiers. The city is an industrial center, manufacturing textiles, machinery, chemicals, furniture, paper products, glass, mobile homes, rubber hose, soft drinks, and pharmaceuticals. It is home to Catawba College (1851),

Livingston College (1879), a technical institute, and a Veterans Administration hospital.

Salmon Arm district municipality, pop. 12,115, Columbia-Shuswap Regional District, SE British Columbia, on Salmon Arm of Shuswap L., 49 mi/77 km E of Kamloops, at the N end of the OKANAGAN Valley. In a lumbering and fruit raising area, it is also a popular resort.

Salmon Mountains subrange of the KLAMATH Mts., in NW California. Extending SE from the SISKIYOU Mts., they have high peaks of about 7000–9000 ft/2130–2740 m. Parts of the range are included in the Trinity Alps and Marble Mountain wilderness areas.

Salmon River 425 mi/685 km long, in C Idaho. Rising in forks in the SAWTOOTH and Salmon River Mts., it flows NNE to N of Salmon, where it turns and flows W across the state's center. At Riggins, it turns sharply N and flows N and NW, around the SEVEN DEVILS Mts., then SW into the Snake R., 38 mi/61 km SSE of Lewiston. Its **Middle Fork,** which rises in the N SAWTOOTH RANGE and flows 100 mi/160 km NNE to the main river, is a fishing and whitewater boating mecca, largely in the Challis National Forest. The Salmon, noted for its sockeye, rainbow trout, and other fish, remains undammed; for its turbulence, it has long been called the "River of No Return," a nickname incorporated into the name of the Frank Church–River of No Return Wilderness, a 2.3 million–ac/938,000-ha (3620–sq mi/9375–sq km) wild zone (including the former Idaho Primitive Area) spreading into six national forests in Idaho and Montana. The 1.8 million-ac/730,000-ha (2812–sq mi/7284–sq km) **Salmon National Forest** lies on the Continental Divide's W side, along the Montana border, surrounding the river's turn to the W. The **Salmon River Mts.** are a W sector of the Rocky Mts., occupying the center of Idaho and bounded E and N by the Salmon R. They include sections of the Payette, Challis, Boise, and Salmon national forests, and reach 10,328 ft/3148 m at Twin Peaks. The SAWTOOTH RANGE lies S.

Salt Creek Oilfield see under CASPER, Wyoming.

salt dome domelike structure produced by the upward pressure of a body of rock salt, which has plastic properties, against relatively light overlying rock layers. In addition to providing salt mines, domes often contain oil, natural gas, or sulfur. Some are used for storage of chemicals or hazardous wastes. Louisiana's FIVE ISLANDS, including AVERY I., are examples.

Salt Fork 1. Salt Fork of the Arkansas R. 192 mi/309 km long, in S Kansas and N Oklahoma. It is formed by the confluence of headstreams near Buttermilk, in Comanche Co., S Kansas, and flows SE into Oklahoma, passing Alva and continuing E through the **Great Salt Plains L.,** a reservoir impounded by a 1948 dam, in an area long used for salt extraction, and now a wildlife refuge. From the reservoir it winds E to join the Arkansas R., 7 mi/11 km S of PONCA CITY. **2.** see RED R., in Texas and Oklahoma.

Salt Lake City city, pop. 159,936, state capital and seat of Salt Lake Co., NC Utah, on the Jordan R., near the SE end of GREAT SALT L., at the foot of the WASATCH RANGE. The state's largest city, it is also world capital of the Church of Jesus Christ of Latter Day Saints (Mormons). Its three-county (Davis, Salt Lake, and Weber) METROPOLITAN AREA (MSA) has a pop. of 1,072,227, 62% of Utah's pop. Founded in 1847 by Brigham Young, it began life as a religious refuge, intended as the center of an agricultural theocracy that soon acquired the name DESERET. During the 1849 California gold rush, the community prospered from trade with westbound prospectors. But these outsiders brought with them non-Mormon ("gentile") interests; friction between them (and the Federal government) and the Mormons led to conflict that continued into the 20th century. Local mining and transcontinental railroad connections at OGDEN established Salt Lake City as a commercial hub by the end of the 1860s. Today, it is a center for regional banking, shipping, and trade, and a processor for an irrigated agricultural area. The smelting of ore from nearby silver, lead, zinc, coal, iron, gold, and copper (esp. at BINGHAM) mines is important to the economy. Other industries include oil refining and the manufacture of computer and mining equipment, textiles, steel, aerospace machinery, medical supplies, sports gear, and electrical equipment. The city is also a telecommunications center and a tourist base for visitors to nearby mountains and ski resorts. The University of Utah (1850), Westminster College (1875), and several other institutions are in the city. Salt Lake City is home to the Mormon Tabernacle and its famous choir, Brigham Young's "Beehive House" (1877), the copper-domed Capitol (1915), and FORT DOUGLAS. The Utah Jazz (basketball) play in the 13,000-seat Salt Palace (1969).

Salt Lake County 737 sq mi/1909 sq km, pop. 725,956, in NC Utah, bounded in the SW by Great Salt L. Salt Lake City is its seat; with its suburbs, it dominates the economic life of by far the most populous of Utah's counties. A tableland drained by the Jordan R., the county has the WASATCH RANGE in the E. Outside the urban areas, there are copper, lead, silver, zinc, and gold mining; livestock ranching; truck farming; and the growing of alfalfa, sugar beets, grain, and fruit.

Salton Sea saline lake, 374 sq mi/969 sq km, in Imperial and Riverside counties, SE California, 80 mi/130 km ENE of San Diego. Oriented NW–SE, it is 38 mi/61 km long and 9–15 mi/14–24 km wide, and averages only c.20 ft/6 m deep. Its surface lies 235 ft/72 m below sea level. Before 1905, it was a salt-covered depression, part of the **Salton Sink,** a portion of the Gulf of California that had been enclosed by Colorado R. silting and had then undergone evaporation. When engineers were diverting the Colorado in 1905, in the course of creating the IMPERIAL VALLEY, it broke through canal walls and flooded the basin, creating the "sea." The Salton Sea is a popular waterskiing, swimming, and fishing resort. An 18,000-ac/7300-ha State Recreation Area is on its NE, and a naval test range on its SW. The S shore and adjoining marshlands are a refuge for migrating waterfowl.

Saluda River 200 mi/320 km long, in NW and C South Carolina. Its North and South forks rise in the Blue Ridge Mts. near the North Carolina line and join 10 mi/16 km NW of Greenville. The Saluda flows SSE across the PIEDMONT, passing Ware Shoals, into L. Greenwood, E of Greenwood, formed by the Buzzard Roost Dam (1940). It then flows SE into 50,000-ac/20,250-ha L. Murray, impounded by the **Saluda Dam,** 208 ft/63 m high and 7838 ft/2391 m long, built in 1930. From there the river flows SE, joining the BROAD R. at Columbia to form the CONGAREE R.

Sam Houston National Forest 161,000 ac/65,200 ha, in the PINEY WOODS of E Texas, just W of the Trinity R. and some 50 mi/80 km N of Houston. It is one of four national forests in the area that combine recreational and forest industry use.

Samoa see AMERICAN SAMOA.

San Rayburn Reservoir see under ANGELINA R., Texas.

Sam's Point see under SHAWANGUNK Mts.

San Andreas Fault major FAULT trending NW–SE through California, representing the interface of the North American and Pacific PLATES, which collided some 65 million years ago. With its many smaller associated faults, it is the source of most of California's earthquake activity. The San Andreas runs over 600 mi/1000 km, emerging from the Pacific near Point ARENA, reentering the ocean, passing under TOMALES BAY, E of Point REYES, crossing the mouth of San Francisco Bay, and coming ashore again in Daly City, just SW of San Francisco. It then passes down the San Francisco Peninsula along the E of the Santa Cruz Mts., and past HOLLISTER, where faults that run under the EAST BAY area join it. Continuing SE, it runs along the TEMBLOR RANGE and under the CARRIZO PLAIN to Palmdale, on the edge of the San Gabriel Mts., then through the Cajon Pass to San Bernardino, passing c.36 mi/58 km NE of downtown Los Angeles. Running well E of the San Diego area, it passes into Baja California, Mexico, and into the Gulf of California. The San Andreas was responsible for the 1906 and 1989 (Loma Prieta) San Francisco earthquakes. Its last major movement in the Los Angeles area was in 1857; although there are thousands of quakes yearly in Southern California along associated faults, the next "Big One" is awaited with apprehension. The Pacific Plate is estimated to be moving NW against the North American Plate at a rate of 2 in/5 cm a year; Los Angeles and San Diego, on the Pacific Plate, are thus moving closer to San Francisco, on the North American Plate.

San Andres Mountains N–S trending range rising to 9040 ft/2755 m at Salinas Peak, 45 mi/72 km NW of Alamogordo, in SC New Mexico. This dry, rugged range separates the JORNADA DEL MUERTO (W) from WHITE SANDS (E).

San Angelo city, pop. 84,474, seat of Tom Green Co., WC Texas, 79 mi/127 km SW of Abilene, at the junction of the North and South CONCHO rivers, on the EDWARDS PLATEAU. It was settled when Fort Concho was built in 1867, and quickly developed as a trade center for sheep, goat, and cattle ranchers. It is now a leading US market for wool and mohair. Oil and natural gas are produced in the area. Other products are glass, stone, clay, cottonseed, saddles, footwear, grain, and pecans. San Angelo is home to Goodfellow Air Force Base and to Angelo State University (1928). TWIN BUTTES RESERVOIR is just SW.

San Anselmo city, pop. 11,743, Marin Co., NW California, in the Ross Valley, 14 mi/23 km NNW of San Francisco and adjacent (W) to San Rafael. The San Francisco Theological Seminary is in this largely residential suburb.

San Antonio city, pop. 935,933, seat of Bexar Co., SC Texas, 190 mi/306 km WSW of Houston, at a point where the Hill Country of the EDWARDS PLATEAU (N) and the Coastal Plain (SE) converge, at the BALCONES ESCARPMENT. The city developed on the headwaters of the San Antonio R. and tributary creeks. The third-largest Texas and tenth-largest US city, it is the center of a three-county (Bexar, Comal, and Guadalupe) metropolitan area (MSA) with a pop. of 1,302,099. San Antonio completely surrounds the cities of ALAMO HEIGHTS (NC), CASTLE HILLS (NC), LEON VALLEY (NW), OLMOS PARK (C), Balcones Heights (NW, pop. 3022), Terrell Hills (EC, pop. 4592), and Hill Country Village (N, pop. 1038). Named by a Spanish expedition on June 13, 1691, the feast day of San Antonio de Padua, it was the site of the Coahuiltecan village of Yanaguana. The mission of San Antonio de Valero (the ALAMO) was founded here in 1718, and a settlement grew around it. Canary Islanders laid out a town in 1731, calling it San Antonio de Béjar (Béxar). With the location of four other MISSIONS here by the 1730s, San Antonio became central to Spanish colonization; EL CAMINO REAL ran through it to East Texas, and it was an important administrative center. Stephen F. Austin came here in 1821 to obtain authorization for his American colony on the Brazos R. At the beginning of the Texas Revolution, in 1835, Americans seized San Antonio, and a group of volunteers held the Alamo until the famous 1836 siege. After Texas independence, in the 1840s, Germans and other Europeans arrived, expanding the city's commercial and industrial base. In the 1860s San Antonio became a key stop on the CHISHOLM TRAIL and other cattle routes; eventually, slaughtering and packing meat became a major city industry. The beginnings of FORT SAM HOUSTON in the 1870s introduced a military presence that has been central to the city's 20th-century development. Long-established food industries have been joined by a large variety of manufactures, including furniture, aircraft, auto accessories, data processing equipment, furniture, fabricated steel, and clothing. In the late 20th century SUNBELT retirement, particularly by former military personnel, swelled the population. Through its history San Antonio has been a gateway to and from Mexico; it is the largest US city with a Hispanic majority (56%), and the US city best known throughout large parts of Mexico. Its extensive West Side community is one of the largest US BARRIOS, and the city celebrates this heritage in a variety of festivals and monuments. Among local institutions are St. Mary's (1852), Trinity (1869), and Our Lady of the Lake (1911) universities; Incarnate Word College (1881); and the University of Texas at San Antonio (1969). In addition to the Alamo, San Antonio is widely known as the site of the riverside PASEO DEL RIO and of HEMISFAIR PLAZA, scene of a 1968 world's fair celebrating the city's 250th anniversary. See also: the ALAMO; BRACKENRIDGE PARK; BROOKS AIR FORCE BASE; EAST SIDE; FORT SAM HOUSTON; HEMISFAIR PLAZA (and Tower of the Americas; and Alamodome); KELLY AIR FORCE BASE; KING WILLIAM DISTRICT; LACKLAND AIR FORCE BASE; LA VILLITA; MARKET SQUARE; MILITARY PLAZA; MISSION TRAIL; PASEO DEL RIO (River Walk); SAINT MARY'S STREET; WEST SIDE.

San Antonio, Mount also, **Old Baldy** or **San Antonio Peak** highest elevation (10,080 ft/3105 m), in the SAN GABRIEL Mts. and the Angeles National Forest, 23 mi/37 km NW of San Bernardino, in SW California. Barren and rounded, it is a popular hiking spot.

San Antonio River 180 mi/290 km long, in S Texas. It is formed by several small springs within the city of San Antonio, and flows SE to join the GUADALUPE R. near its mouth at San Antonio Bay in the Gulf of Mexico. It receives the Medina R. just S of San Antonio and Cibolo Creek 50 mi/80 km SE, near Helena. Two Texas Revolution sites, the ALAMO and GOLIAD, are along the San Antonio.

San Benito city, pop. 20,125, Cameron Co., extreme S Texas, in the Lower Rio Grande Valley, 18 mi/29 km NW of Brownsville and adjacent (SE) to HARLINGEN. Settled in the 1770s by Mexican ranchers, it was incorporated in 1911. Tourism and retirees are important to the economy, and the city packs and ships fruits and vegetables, bottles juices, and has a variety of manufactures.

San Bernardino city, pop. 164,164, seat of San Bernardino Co., S California, 60 mi/100 km E of Los Angeles, in the San Bernardino Valley, just S of the San Bernardino Mts. It is a trade and processing center for INLAND EMPIRE producers of citrus fruits, grapes, truck crops, milk, and poultry, and has a variety of manufactures including chemicals, stone and clay products, textiles, furniture, mobile homes, and plumbing supplies. A MISSION was established here on the feast day of San Bernardino of Siena (May 20, 1810) and the name given to the valley and mountains. The city was founded in 1851 by Mormons, and patterned after Salt Lake City. The Mormons were recalled to Utah by Brigham Young in 1857, but San Bernardino, on the main road to Los Angeles, and on the railroad after 1875, continued to grow. The planting of citrus groves in the 1870s also spurred development. Since 1915, the National Orange Show has been held here in March, at the end of the winter harvest. A gateway to mountains and forests, the city is the seat of a California State University campus (1962) and of San Bernardino Valley College (1926). Norton Air Force Base is on its SE.

San Bernardino County largest US county, 20,064 sq mi/51,966 sq km, pop. 1,418,380, in S California. Its seat is San Bernardino. Largely in the MOJAVE DESERT, it stretches from the KERN Co. line (W) to the Arizona (Colorado R.) and Nevada line (E). The San Bernardino Mts. are in its SW corner, in the Los Angeles area. This high desert county contains the TWENTYNINE PALMS Marine base and all or part of a number of other military and space facilities. Its pop., industry, and agriculture are concentrated in its SW corner, where Los Angeles suburban development is "reclaiming" desert; VICTORVILLE, APPLE VALLEY, and FONTANA are among its larger cities. NEEDLES and BARSTOW are the principal settlements in the desert, where characteristic features include small mountain ranges, soda lakes, and sand dunes.

San Bernardino Mountains at the junction of the COAST and TRANSVERSE ranges of S California, lying N and E of the city of San Bernardino, and extending for c.55 m/90 km SE from CAJON PASS to SAN GORGONIO PASS. The range contains Southern California's highest point, Mt. SAN GORGONIO (11,502 ft/3506 m), at the SE end, in a Wilderness Area of the same name. The mountains are largely within a division of the **San Bernardino National Forest** (818,999 ac/331,695 ha). The winding, 45-mi/72-km Rim of the World Drive eases recreational access to the mountains and leads to the resorts at L. Arrowhead and BIG BEAR L. The lower **Little San Bernardino Mts.** (c.4000–5500 ft/1220–1675 m) are a SE continuation of the main range for c.40 mi/64 km along the E side of the Coachella Valley, and are partly within the Joshua Tree National Monument.

San Bruno city, pop. 38,961, San Mateo Co., NC California, on San Francisco Bay, 10 mi/16 km S of San Francisco. A largely residential suburb, it has naval facilities and a Federal recordkeeping center. Tanforan Race Track, on the site of a modern shopping center, was an early (1910s) aviation center, and San Francisco International Airport lies SE. The city has a variety of light industries.

San Buenaventura see VENTURA, California.

San Carlos city, pop. 26,167, San Mateo Co., NC California, near the S end of San Francisco Bay, 21 mi/34 km SSE of San Francisco. A flower growing center incorporated in 1925, it has now become an electronics producer on the N fringe of SILICON VALLEY.

San Carlos Apache Indian Reservation pop. 7294, across the Salt R. (S) from the WHITE Mt. (Fort Apache) reservation, and 70 mi/115 km NE of Phoenix, Arizona. Set in a mix of forest, desert, and grassland, it is home to several different groups forced here after 19th-century US-Apache wars. **San Carlos** (unincorporated, pop. 2918, Gila Co.) is its headquarters, GLOBE (just W) a trade center.

San Clemente city, pop. 41,100, Orange Co., SW California, on the Pacific Ocean, 60 mi/100 km SE of Los Angeles and just W of Camp Pendleton. A Spanish-style house with a 25-ac/10-ha estate, La Casa Pacifica, was bought here in 1969 by President Richard Nixon, and used as his "Western White House." Tourism and retirees are important to the city's economy; its beach is well known. San Clemente was founded in 1925 during the Southern California real estate boom that followed World War I. It was named for offshore San Clemente I. Cut flowers, eggs, and strawberries are produced locally.

San Clemente Island southernmost of the SANTA BARBARA Is., in the Pacific Ocean, 70 mi/110 km WNW of San Diego, in SW California. The US Navy has a technology center on the 60–sq mi/155–sq km island.

Sand Counties also, the **Sand Area** region of C Wisconsin, chiefly in Adams, Juneau, Wood, Jackson, Marquette, and Waushara counties, characterized by poor soils containing ancient (Cambrian) sands mixed in the N part with gravel deposited by the Wisconsin Glacier. Settled in the mid 19th century, the area was cut over by loggers and then fell into decline. The naturalist Aldo Leopold moved here in 1935 and wrote extensively about the area until his death in 1948.

Sand Creek historic site in Kiowa Co., SE Colorado, 10 mi/16 km N of Chivington and W of the Kansas border. It was a Cheyenne and Arapahoe village and the S boundary of Plains Indian territory. Cheyennes, led by Black Kettle, had sued for peace and camped here near Fort Lyon. On Nov. 29, 1864, hundreds of Indian men, women, and children were murdered here by Colorado troops.

Sandersville city, pop. 6290, seat of Washington Co., C Georgia, 51 mi/83 km ENE of Macon, settled in 1796. Black Muslim leader Elijah Muhammad was born (as Elijah Poole) near this cotton, timber, and livestock producing community.

Sand Hills **1.** also, **Algodones Dunes** in SE California, 15 mi/24 km W of Yuma, Arizona, and N of Algodones, Baja California, Mexico. This dune system, one of the largest in the US, is variously described as occupying from 68,700 to 90,000 ac (27,800–36,500 ha) in a rough triangle, c.40 mi/64 km long and up to 8 mi/13 km wide, just N of the Mexican border. It includes many different types of dunes, some partly stabilized by vegetation, some migrating, with heights of up to 300 ft/90 m. The N section includes 22,000 ac/8900 ha that have been declared a National Natural Landmark. **2.** region in the High Plains of WC Nebraska, N of the North Platte R., variously described as covering 18,000–24,000 sq mi/47,000–62,000 sq km. A dune area stabilized largely by grasses, it has mostly E–W ridges up to 1 mi/2 km across and 10 mi/16 km long. Large AQUIFERS lie below; the high water table results in many lakes, ponds, marshes, and wet meadows, especially in the N and W sections. Branches of the LOUP R. drain to the SE. Excellent cattle country, the region includes an entirely planted unit (over 20,000 ac/8100 ha) of the Nebraska National Forest. Mari Sandoz (1901–66), born in the hamlet of Ellsworth, on the W, wrote of the Sand Hills in *Old Jules* and other works.

Sandhills 1. also, **Sand Hills** band of low sandy hills, 20–40 mi/30–60 km wide, extending from C North Carolina across South Carolina to C Georgia, along the inner border of the ATLANTIC COASTAL PLAIN. Remnant dunes, marking what was the coast millions of years ago, they extend diagonally across South Carolina, roughly between Cheraw (NE) and North Augusta (SW). Southern Pines and Pinehurst, North Carolina, and Aiken, Columbia, and Camden, South Carolina, are in the Sandhills, which lie along the FALL LINE. The region has been the focus of soil and plant restoration projects; peaches and other crops are grown. Carolina Sandhills National Wildlife Refuge (45,586 ac/18,462 ha), with dunes up to 500 ft/152 m high, lies SW of Cheraw. **2.** in Texas: see under MONAHANS.

Sandia Mountains range NE of Albuquerque, in C New Mexico, rising to a high point of 10,678 ft/3255 m at Sandia Crest. On the E side of this rugged range is the Turquoise Trail, a 60-mi/100-km road (NM 14) between Albuquerque and Santa Fe, passing through Cerrillos, a 19th-century gold and turquoise center, as well as GHOST TOWNS where silver, coal, and lead have been mined. The range, largely within Cibola National Forest, is noted for skiing, esp. at 10,378-ft/3163-m **Sandia Peak,** reached by one of the world's longest (2.7 mi/4.3 km) aerial tramways. **Sandia Cave,** where artifacts were found in the 1920s, is thought to have been used as much as 25,000 years ago.

Sandia National Laboratory see under ALBUQUERQUE, New Mexico.

San Diego city, pop. 1,110,549, seat of San Diego Co., extreme SW California, on San Diego, Mission, and La Jolla bays, 105 mi/170 km SSE of Los Angeles, extending to the border of Baja California, Mexico. California's second (and the US's sixth) most populous city, it is the center of a metropolitan area coextensive with San Diego Co. (pop. 2,498,016). Discovered for Europeans by Juan Rodriguez Cabrillo (1542), San Diego was not settled until 1769, when Gaspar de Portolá established a PRESIDIO here, along with Junipero Serra's first Alta California MISSION. Despite its excellent harbor, the community, established at the mouth of the San Diego R. (OLD TOWN), grew slowly; it was incorporated as an American city in 1850. After Alonzo Horton's NEW TOWN was established in 1867 on San Diego Bay, growth was steadier, but the city remained in the shadow of San Francisco and Los Angeles. The opening of the Panama Canal in 1914, however, and the subsequent Panama-California Exposition in BALBOA PARK, spurred new growth. World War I brought military activity, and the fledgling aircraft industry was nourished by war training and production. World War II wedded the city firmly to its military sector; the Pacific Fleet was headquartered here after the attack on Pearl Harbor. Postwar military spending and SUNBELT residential growth and other in-migration made San Diego one of the fastest-growing US areas in the late 20th century. Beside the military, the local economy is based on manufacturing, tourism and resort trade, agriculture, and finance. Aircraft, missiles, electronics, and other machinery are among the most important manufactures, while most of the region's farm products pass through here. A center for oceanographic research, San Diego also boasts large commercial (esp. tuna) fishing fleets. The city's institutions include San Diego State University (1897) and a number of other schools. The LA JOLLA section is home to the University of California: San Diego (1959) and to the well-known Scripps and Salk institutes. Covering some 320 sq mi/830 sq km, San Diego is a city of many, widespread residential communities. Its gentle climate, resilient economy, and recreational resources continue to attract other Americans, along with Latin American and Asian immigrants. See also: BALBOA PARK; BANKERS' HILL (Pill Hill); BARRIO LOGAN (Logan Heights); BROADWAY; CLAIREMONT; EAST SAN DIEGO; EMBARCADERO; GASLAMP QUARTER (and the Stingaree); GOLDEN TRIANGLE; HARBOR ISLAND; HILLCREST; HORTON PLAZA; KEARNY MESA; LA JOLLA; LINDBERGH FIELD (San Diego International Airport); Point LOMA; MIDDLETOWN; MIRAMAR; MISSION BAY (and Mission Beach); MISSION HILLS; MISSION VALLEY (and Jack Murphy Stadium); NEW TOWN (Horton's Addition); NORTH ISLAND; NORTH PARK; OCEAN BEACH; OLD TOWN; PACIFIC BEACH; PRESIDIO HILL; RANCHO BERNARDO; SAN DIEGO–CORONADO BRIDGE; SAN YSIDRO; SEAPORT VILLAGE; SHELTER ISLAND; UNIVERSITY CITY; UNIVERSITY HEIGHTS; UPTOWN.

San Diego–Coronado Bridge 2.2 mi/3.5 km long, crossing San Diego Bay, linking SAN DIEGO (E) and CORONADO (W), California. Opened in 1964, it rises to a height of 246 ft/75 m.

San Diego County 4212 sq mi/10,909 sq km, pop. 2,498,016, in extreme SW California, on the Pacific Ocean and the Mexican border. Citrus fruits, truck crops, and livestock are raised in its C and N, and there are wineries. Along the coast and in the PENINSULAR RANGES inland, resorts and retirement communities abound. SAN DIEGO, the county seat, dominates the western third. Other important cities include CORONADO, CHULA VISTA, EL CAJON, ESCONDIDO, and OCEANSIDE. The CLEVELAND NATIONAL FOREST occupies much of the C, and the ANZA BORREGO DESERT STATE PARK much of the E. Camp Pendleton (see OCEANSIDE) in the NW is one of many military bases, and there are Indian reservations scattered throughout.

San Dimas city, pop. 32,397, Los Angeles Co., SW California, at the S base of the San Gabriel Mts., 25 mi/40 km ENE of downtown Los Angeles and 5 mi/8 km NW of Pomona. It is a largely residential suburb in an area noted for citrus groves and nurseries. The Frank G. Bonelli Regional Park and Raging Waters theme park are popular recreational assets.

Sand Mountain also, **Raccoon Mountains** ridge, c.1800 ft/550 m high and 80 mi/130 km long, extending SW from WALDEN RIDGE near Chattanooga, Tennessee, across NW Georgia, into the NE corner of Alabama. Part of the CUMBERLAND PLATEAU, the ridge runs between and parallel to LOOKOUT Mt. (E) and the Tennessee R. (W).

Sand Point district of NE SEATTLE, Washington, on L. Washington, 7 mi/11 km NE of Downtown. Today largely residential, with a Naval support station, National Oceanic and Atmospheric Administration facility, and Warren G. Magnuson Park on the water, it was in March and Sept. 1924 the starting and finishing point for the first around-the-world airplane flight.

Sandpoint city, pop. 5203, seat of Bonner Co., N Idaho, on L. Pend Oreille, 40 mi/64 km NNE of Coeur d'Alene. It is a year-round resort and a rail center. Sandpoint is also a noted artists' community and center for affluent retirees. Industries include lumber milling and the shipment of dairy products and livestock. A large ski resort, refurbished in 1993, is 10 mi/16 km N.

Sand Springs city, pop. 15,346, Tulsa Co., NE Oklahoma, 10 mi/16 km W of Tulsa. This suburb has numerous oil and natural gas wells. Its many manufactures include textiles, glass, fiberglass, plastics, oilfield equipment, building materials, and processed foods.

Sandstone city, pop. 2057, Pine Co., NE Minnesota, on the Kettle R. The center of an agricultural and dairying area, it developed around sandstone quarries along the river. A Federal prison is situated here.

Sandusky city, pop. 29,764, seat of Erie Co., N Ohio, on Sandusky Bay of L. Erie, 60 mi/97 km W of Cleveland. Its name derives from an Iroquoian word meaning "at the pure water," referring to nearby springs. Settled in 1816, Sandusky has long been an important port of entry and a major Great Lakes shipping point, particularly for coal. Deposits of sand, gravel, and clay nearby have contributed to the growth of industries, which include the manufacture of metal and rubber goods, chemicals, plastics, paper items, boats, and machinery, as well as commercial fishing. Surrounding farmland grows fruits, which are processed in the city, and nearby vineyards supply its wineries. Located in the heart of the lake region, Sandusky is a popular vacation spot. It is the site of the Follett House (1827), a station of the Underground Railroad, now a museum. NASA's Plum Brook Research Center is situated just S of the city.

Sandusky County 409 sq mi/1059 sq km, pop. 61,963, in N Ohio, bounded (NE) by Sandusky Bay (L. Erie), and intersected by the Portage and Sandusky rivers. Its seat and largest city is FREMONT. Agriculture includes fruit, grain, sugar beet, and truck farming. Limestone is quarried, and there is some manufacturing at Clyde and Fremont.

Sandusky River 120 mi/193 km long, in Ohio. It rises in Crawford Co., where it flows generally W past Bucyrus, turning N in Wyandot Co. to continue N and NE past Upper Sandusky, Tiffin, and Fremont, to empty into Sandusky Bay of L. Erie.

Sandwich town, pop. 15,489, Barnstable Co., SE Massachusetts, on NW CAPE COD, along Cape Cod Bay. The Cape's oldest settlement, it was founded in 1637. From 1827 to 1888, it was the site of the Sandwich Glass Factory, famed for its pressed and lace glass. The Cape Cod Canal's E end is in Sandwich. An area of beaches, dunes, and cranberry bogs, the town is one of the faster-growing residential sections of the Cape.

Sandwich Islands name given (1778) by Captain James Cook to the Hawaiian Is., honoring John Montague, 4th Earl of Sandwich, then first lord of the British admiralty, Cook's superior.

Sandwich Range group of peaks in the White Mts., EC New Hampshire. Extending for c.30 mi/48 km from near Conway (E) to near Compton (W), the range includes Mt. Tripyramid (4140 ft/1263 m), the high point; Mt. Passaconaway (4060 ft/1238 m), named for a chief who ruled the Penacooks in the early 17th century; Mt. Whiteface (4015 ft/1225 m); Sandwich Mt. (3993 ft/1218 m); and Mt. CHOCORUA (3475 ft/1060 m).

Sandy city, pop. 75,058, Salt Lake Co., NC Utah, 15 mi/24 km S of Salt Lake City. A smelting and shipping center in the late 19th century, this booming residential suburb and commercial center grew by about one-third in 1980–90. The Lone Peak and Twin Peaks WILDERNESS AREAS are directly E of the city, in the WASATCH RANGE.

Sandy Hook low, narrow peninsula, about 5 mi/8 km long, in Monmouth Co., NE New Jersey, between Sandy Hook and Raritan bays (W) and the Atlantic Ocean (E). Its N tip is about 7 mi/11 km S of New York City (Coney Island, Brooklyn) and lies S of the entrance to Lower NEW YORK BAY. The area was explored by Hudson (1609), and was occupied by the British during the Revolution. Fort Hancock, at its N end, was constructed as a protection for New York Harbor. It has served as an artillery proving ground. The Sandy Hook Lighthouse (1763) is the oldest still in use in the US. Sandy Hook is part of the GATEWAY NATIONAL RECREATION AREA.

Sandy Springs unincorporated community, pop. 67,842, Fulton Co., NW Georgia, 9 mi/14 km NNE of downtown Atlanta, a residential and commercial suburb on the city's beltway (Route 285).

San Elizario see under EL PASO, Texas.

San Felipe town, pop. 618, Austin Co., SE Texas, on the Brazos R., 42 mi/68 km W of Houston. Settled in 1823 by Stephen F. Austin's colonists, and known as San Felipe de Austin, it produced the first Texas newspaper (1829) and was the site of 1830s conventions leading toward independence. It was burned (1836) in the face of the advance of Santa Anna's Mexican forces. Today it draws visitors interested in Texas history.

San Felipe Pueblo pop. 2434, in Sandoval Co., NC New Mexico, on the Rio Grande, 33 mi/53 km SW of Santa Fe. This Keresan PUEBLO is known for its Green Corn Dance and its jewelry.

San Fernando city, pop. 22,580, Los Angeles Co., SW California, in the N San Fernando Valley, 20 mi/32 km NW of downtown Los Angeles. The MISSION church and monastery of San Fernando Rey de Espana (1797) are just SW. Gold was mined here in the 1840s, and the city was founded in 1874. Since 1915 it has been surrounded by lands of the city of Los Angeles. It is just E of the San Fernando Reservoir, S terminus of the Los Angeles Aqueduct; San Fernando Pass, between the San Gabriel (NE) and Santa Susana (NW) mountains, is 6 mi/10 km NW. Citrus fruit, oil, clothing, and electronics industries have contributed to the economy.

San Fernando Valley popularly, **the Valley** basin of neighborhoods and suburbs of LOS ANGELES, California, covering 260 sq mi/670 sq km, between the Santa Monica Mts. (S), the Simi Hills (W), and the San Gabriel (NE) and Santa Susana (NW) mountains, 10 mi/16 km NW of Downtown, from which it is reached most directly through the CAHUENGA PASS. Home to one-third of the city's people, the Valley was the site of RANCHOS before the 1870s, when the arrival of the railroad spurred the founding of a number of small towns. Most of the area was annexed to Los Angeles in 1915 to gain access to municipal water from the Los Angeles Aqueduct (see OWENS R.). Truck gardens and walnut and citrus orchards predominated in the lightly populated Valley until the area became a focus for booming post–World War II residential development. Beside the separate municipalities of SAN FERNANDO, Hidden Hills (city, pop. 1729), and BURBANK, the Valley includes NORTH HOLLYWOOD, VAN NUYS, STUDIO CITY, SHERMAN OAKS, ENCINO, RESEDA, TARZANA, NORTHRIDGE, CHATSWORTH, WOODLAND HILLS, CANOGA PARK, CALABASAS, PANORAMA CITY, GRANADA HILLS, PACOIMA, SYLMAR, and UNIVERSAL CITY. Many of its communities, long regarded as low-density bastions of the white middle and upper middle class, with their own "Valley" culture, are becoming racially and economically diverse, esp. those in the central "flats," where multiunit dwellings are increasing in numbers. The entertainment and aerospace industries have been prominent in various Valley locations.

Sanford **1.** city, pop. 32,387, seat of Seminole Co., NC Florida, on L. Monroe and the St. Johns R., 20 mi/32 km NNE of Orlando. Established as a trading post near Fort Mellon in 1837, it was part of land purchased for citrus groves in the early 1870s by Henry Sanford. A center for the packing and shipping of local vegetables (notably celery) and citrus fruits, it is also a thriving tourist center. Boats, clothing, mobile homes, aluminum products, and electronic equipment are manufactured. It is the site of Seminole Community College (1965) and a naval air station. **2.** town, pop. 20,463, York Co., extreme S Maine, on the Mousam R., 35 mi/56 km SW of Portland. The town includes Sanford Center (pop. 10,296) and Springvale. Industrialized since 1867, when a carriage robe and blanket factory was built, it manufactures aircraft components, plastic, wood, textile products, electronics, and carpets. **3.** city, pop. 14,475, seat of Lee Co., C North Carolina, 38 mi/61 km SW of Raleigh. An important tobacco market, it has manufactures including brick and tile, textiles, clothing, furniture, electronic equipment, and machinery.

San Francisco city, pop. 723,959, coterminous with San Francisco Co., NC California, on the N San Francisco Peninsula, between the Pacific Ocean (W) and San Francisco Bay, 350 mi/560 km NNW of Los Angeles and 2530 mi/4075 km W of New York City. The Golden Gate lies N, San Mateo Co. S. The city includes the Farallon Is. (in the Pacific); Alcatraz I. (in the Golden Gate); and Yerba Buena and Treasure islands (in the bay). It is the center of a three-county METROPOLITAN AREA (PMSA) with a pop. of 1,603,678, and of the fourth-largest US CMSA, covering ten counties with a pop. of 6,253,311. The anchor community of the BAY AREA, it is now less populous than San Jose (SSE), and has lost much of its industry to Oakland and the East Bay (E). The city's noted Seven Hills are in reality over 40, the highest Mt. Davidson (938 ft/286 m); many are serviced by the famous cable cars. Its excellent natural harbor has been much altered by landfill operations. On the ocean side esp., San Francisco is windy and foggy, and it has cool summers and mild winters. The area was unknown to Europeans until a Spanish overland expedition led by Gaspar de Portolá first saw the bay in 1769. In 1776 a PRESIDIO and MISSION were established; but it was not until 1835 that real settlement, at Yerba Buena Cove, was begun. The 1849 gold rush brought quick change to a small port that had just (1846) come under US control; thousands of adventurers poured in from the East and from Europe, China, Australia, and other parts of the world. The city entered a boom that was sustained by, among other forces, the 1850s COMSTOCK LODE discovery and completion (1869) of the transcontinental railroad; by the 1870s it was a major US city. The April 1906 earthquake on the SAN ANDREAS FAULT, and resulting fires, destroyed large areas of the city, but it rebuilt quickly, displaying its confidence in the 1915 Panama-Pacific Exposition. (The smaller Oct. 1989 earthquake elicited a similar response.) World War II brought an industrial boom to the Bay Area, with shipyards and other plants, embarkation centers and other military installations humming with activity. The war also brought workers and soldiers from all directions, furthering the cosmopolitanism that has characterized San Francisco since the 1840s; it is a city of diverse groups, including the first large US Chinese colony, a growing Asian-Pacific population, large Hispanic and Italian sections, and one of the largest and most cohesive US gay communities. Today much less than before a manufacturing center, it still has important textile, food processing, and shipbuilding industries. Long the banking and business center of the West Coast, it has been challenged in that role by Los Angeles, but is home to many major corporations. Its port, now handling recreational as well as commercial traffic, remains central to its economy. The city is also a cultural hub, home to the University of San Francisco (1855), a University of California branch (1864), San Francisco State University (1899), numerous other educational centers, and a wide variety of well-known museums and arts institutions. Tourism is a major industry, and the city has long drawn migrants attracted by its diversity, activity, and physical beauty. See also ALCATRAZ I.; BAKER BEACH (and China Beach and Sea Cliff); BARBARY COAST; CANDLESTICK PARK; the CASTRO (and Eureka Valley); CHINATOWN (and Portsmouth Square); CIVIC CENTER (and the Tenderloin); COW HOLLOW; Mt. DAVIDSON; EMBARCADERO; FARALLON Is.; FINANCIAL DISTRICT (and Transamerica Pyramid); FISHERMAN'S WHARF; GOLDEN GATE (and Golden Gate Bridge); GOLDEN GATE NATIONAL RECREATION AREA; GOLDEN GATE PARK; HAIGHT-ASHBURY; HUNTER'S POINT (and Bayview); JACKSON SQUARE; MARINA DISTRICT; MARKET St.; MISSION DISTRICT; NOB HILL; NOE VALLEY; NORTH BEACH (Little Italy; and City Lights, Washington Square); PACIFIC HEIGHTS; POLK St. (and Polk Gulch); POTRERO HILL; PRESIDIO; RICHMOND DISTRICT; RUSSIAN HILL; SAN FRANCISCO INTERNATIONAL AIRPORT; SAN FRANCISCO–OAKLAND BAY BRIDGE; SEVEN HILLS; SOUTH OF MARKET (SoMa); SUNSET DISTRICT (and Parkside); TELEGRAPH HILL; TREASURE I.; TWIN PEAKS; UNION SQUARE, WESTERN ADDITION (the Fillmore; and Japantown); YERBA BUENA I.

San Francisco Bay crescent-shaped bay in WC California, paralleling the Pacific coast and linked to the ocean by the GOLDEN GATE between Marin Co. (N) and San Francisco. Sixty mi/100 km N–S and 3–12 mi/5–20 km wide, it is an ancient river valley in the COAST RANGE, running between the Hayward (E) and SAN ANDREAS (W) faults. With depths up to 100 ft/30 m, it is an excellent natural harbor and an active international port. Its NE arm, SAN PABLO BAY, is connected via CARQUINEZ STRAIT (E) with SUISUN BAY, and thus with the Sacramento–San Joaquin river system and California's CENTRAL VALLEY. San Francisco is the largest city on the bay. Others around it include San Mateo and Palo Alto (W); San Jose and neighboring South Bay cities; the EAST BAY cluster including Alameda, Oakland, Berkeley, and Richmond; and San Rafael (N). The computer and electronics industries of SILICON VALLEY and numerous military installations have contributed to the economy of the Bay Area. Alcatraz, Angel, Treasure, and Yerba Buena islands lie in the bay, and the Golden Gate, Richmond–San Rafael, San Francisco–Oakland Bay, and San Mateo bridges span it. Missed by various European navigators in the 16th and 17th centuries, the bay was first seen by the Spanish when an overland expedition came upon it in 1769; they began settlement in 1776. Landfilling and other human activities have reduced the bay's size by as much as 40%.

San Francisco International Airport formerly, **Mills Field** 13 mi/21 km S of Downtown, 6 mi/10 km S of the city limits, and just SE of San Bruno, California, on landfill in W San Francisco Bay.

San Francisco Mountains or **Mountain** see SAN FRANCISCO PEAKS, Arizona.

San Francisco–Oakland Bay Bridge familiarly, **the Bay Bridge** 8.25 mi/13 km long, opened Nov. 1936 over San Francisco Bay, linking San Francisco with Oakland and the EAST BAY. A two-span suspension bridge (the West Bay Crossing) extends from San Francisco to YERBA BUENA I.; a tunnel runs under the island; and a latticework bridge (the East Bay Crossing) extends to Oakland. In the Oct. 1989 earthquake, a section of the bridge collapsed, closing it briefly.

San Francisco Peaks also, **San Francisco Mts.** or **Mt.** collection of peaks in N Arizona, including HUMPHREYS (12,633 ft/3851 m), the state's highest elevation; Agassiz (12,356 ft/3766 m); and Fremont (11,969 ft/3648 m). They rise out of a 3000–sq mi/8000–sq km volcanic field, either extinct or dormant, on the San Francisco (or COCONINO) section of the Colorado Plateau, 10 mi/16 km N of Flagstaff. Formed 8–10 million years ago, probably by the explosion and collapse of one massive volcano, they were subsequently worn down by glaciers. Sacred to the Navajo, Hopi, and Havasupai, they are also popular for skiing and hiking. Among other volcanic features in the area is Sunset Crater (8029 ft/2447 m, just E), which last erupted about 700 years ago, and which is noted for the glowing colors on its edges.

San Francisquito Canyon see under SANTA CLARITA, California.

San Gabriel city, pop. 37,120, Los Angeles Co., SW California, 9 mi/14 km E of downtown Los Angeles and just E of Alhambra. The Mission San Gabriel Arcangel (1771) houses paintings and relics. For many years after its founding, the community was the gateway to the Pacific coast from the W side of the Mojave Desert; in 1781, the Spanish governor set out from here to found the PUEBLO that became Los Angeles. Largely residential, the city has some light industry.

San Gabriel Mountains at the junction of the COAST and TRANSVERSE ranges in S California, extending E–W for 63 mi/100 km from CAJON PASS, at the NW end of the San Bernardino Mts., to Newhall Pass, at the E end of the SANTA SUSANA Mts. Largely within the Angeles National Forest, the range includes the high point of Mt. SAN ANTONIO or Old Baldy (10,080 ft/3105 m); the twin peaks of North Baldy (9131 ft/2783 m) and Mt. Baden-Powell (9399 ft/2865 m); Mt. WILSON (5710 ft/1740 m), the site of an astronomical observatory; and Mt. Lukens (5074 ft/1547 m), the highest point in the city of Los Angeles. The action of the SAN ANDREAS and numerous other faults has resulted in the San Gabriels being among the most fractured ranges in California. They form a barrier from dry (NE) desert winds, but also trap Los Angeles's smog. Area history includes the discovery of gold in Placerita Canyon in 1842 (see SANTA CLARITA), construction of the Mt. LOWE Scenic Railway in the 1890s, creation here of the first forest reserve in California in 1892, opening of the Angeles Crest Highway in 1929, and the damming of the Big Tujunga Canyon (the "Big T") to control runoff into the SAN FERNANDO VALLEY. The S foothills are both residential and agricultural, being noted esp. for citrus production. Until 1927 the San Gabriels were sometime referred to as the Sierra Madre. They are much used for recreation, and include the Sheep Mountain, San Gabriel, and Cucamonga wilderness areas.

Sangamon County 866 sq mi/2243 sq km long, pop. 178,386, in C Illinois, partially bordered on the E by the Sangamon R. The river flows W through SPRINGFIELD, the county seat and state capital. Various streams feed L. Springfield, in the center of the county. Outside of industrial Springfield, Sangamon Co. is mostly farmland, with wheat and soybeans the main crops.

Sangamon River 250 mi/402 km, in C Illinois. Its source is in the morainic ridges NW of Champaign and Urbana, in EC Illinois. It flows SW, carving out a wooded valley, passing Decatur, where it is dammed to form L. Decatur, 13 mi/21 km long. It then turns W and, E of Springfield, is joined by its South Fork. The Sangamon veers NW at the state capital, and 40 mi/64 km downstream it receives the Salt Creek, then turns W for some 15 mi/24 km before joining the Illinois R. above Beardstown. The Sangamon is famous for its association with Abraham Lincoln, who in the late 1820s moved to the area from Kentucky, and lived in a log cabin on a bluff overlooking the river.

Sanger city, pop. 16,839, Fresno Co., C California, in the San Joaquin Valley, 12 mi/19 km E of Fresno, just W of the Kings R. An agricultural shipping and processing center, it handles grapes, oranges, plums, and peaches. It has some light manufactures.

San Germán unincorporated community (ZONA URBANA), pop. 11,977, San Germán Municipio (pop. 34,962), SW Puerto Rico, 10 mi/16 km SE of Mayagüez. Originally (1512) founded on the S coast, and moved to its present location in 1573, it was Puerto Rico's second city until the rise of Ponce in the 19th century. In a fertile agricultural region on the SW of the Cordillera Central, and one of the island's coffee capitals in the 19th century, it is now a trade and coffee and sugar processing center. It has a variety of historic buildings, including 19th-century haciendas. The Porta Coeli Church (1606), one of the oldest in the Americas, now houses a museum. San Germán is the seat of the Inter-American University of Puerto Rico (1912), which today dominates its life.

San Gorgonio, Mount also, **San Gorgonio Mountain** peak (11,502 ft/3506 m) in the SE of the SAN BERNARDINO Mts., in the San Gorgonio Wilderness Area, 27 mi/43 km E of San Bernardino. It is the highest point in Southern California.

San Gorgonio Pass between the SE end of the SAN BERNARDINO Mts. and the N end of the SAN JACINTO Mts., in SW California, providing a link between the San Bernardino (W) and Coachella (E) valleys, and between Los Angeles and the E. The broad (3–4 mi/ 5–7 km) floor of the pass is the site of BANNING and of extensive orchards. Surveys in 1853 led to railway construction through the gap.

Sangre de Cristo Mountains N–S trending range, some 250 mi/400 km long, extending from the Arkansas R. at SALIDA, in SC Colorado (N), to near SANTA FE, in NC New Mexico (S). It is the southernmost range of the Rocky Mts., extending Colorado's FRONT RANGE. To their W is the San Luis Valley, with the upper RIO GRANDE running through it. Blanca Peak (14,345 ft/4372 m), the range's high point, is 20 mi/32 km ENE of Alamosa, Colorado. Twelve mi/19 km to its N is the GREAT SAND DUNES NATIONAL MONUMENT. New Mexico's highest point, WHEELER PEAK (13,161 ft/4011 m), is near TAOS. The headstreams of the PECOS and CANADIAN rivers flow S and E from the range.

Sanibel Island narrow, sandy barrier island, c.10 mi/16 km E–W, in Lee Co., SW Florida, between the Gulf of Mexico (S and W) and Pine Island Sound and San Carlos Bay (N), some 20 mi/32 km SW of Fort Myers. It is connected to the mainland and to the smaller CAPTIVA I. (NW) by causeways. Sanibel (a city, pop. 5468) is a popular resort, with many hotels and beaches long a mecca for shell hunters. It was a favorite refuge of the 18th-century Spanish pirate José Gaspar. Much of the island's NC portion is occupied by the J.N. "Ding" Darling National Wildlife Refuge, a 5000-ac/2000-ha preserve noted for its over 200 species of birds and many other animals.

San Ildefonso Pueblo pop. 1499, in Santa Fe Co., NC New Mexico, on the Rio Grande, 17 mi/27 km NW of Santa Fe. This Tewa-speaking PUEBLO was one of the last to surrender in the 1680 Pueblo Revolt. During the 1920s and 1930s it was a center for the pueblo arts revival, and is known for its traditional black pottery, esp. that of Maria Martinez.

San Isabel National Forest 1.2 million ac/486,000 ha (1875 sq mi/4856 sq km), in units in the SAWATCH RANGE, the WET Mts., and the E side of the SANGRE DE CRISTO Mts., in SC Colorado. Another unit is in the Spanish Peaks area, near Trinidad. Including many of Colorado's highest peaks and the headwaters of the Arkansas R., the San Isabel has the highest average elevation of any national forest. Along with the 419,000-ac/170,000-ha (655–sq mi/1696–sq km) Comanche National Grassland, to the SE in the HIGH PLAINS, it is administered with the PIKE National Forest.

San Jacinto city, pop. 16,210, Riverside Co., S California, in the San Jacinto Valley, SW of the San Jacinto Mts. and 27 mi/43 km SE of Riverside. It is a health resort, fruit producer, and growing residential community just W of the Soboba Indian Reservation and Soboba Hot Springs.

San Jacinto Mountains in S California, at the junction of the COAST and PENINSULAR ranges. Extending for c.30 mi/50 km SSE from SAN GORGONIO PASS to the SANTA ROSA Mts., the granitic range reaches an elevation of 10,804 ft/3293 m at **San Jacinto Peak.** PALM SPRINGS is E of the peak. The San Jacintos rise abruptly from the desert, esp. in the NE, supporting a range of flora, from desert to alpine. They are largely within the S part of the San Bernardino National Forest.

San Jacinto River 85 mi/137 km long, in SE Texas, formed in Harris Co. by West and East forks, which meet in 12,240-ac/5000-ha L. Houston, impounded by the San Jacinto Dam. It then flows SSE to join Buffalo Bayou (the HOUSTON SHIP CHANNEL) and enter Galveston Bay on the Gulf of Mexico. Sam Houston's Texas volunteers defeated the Mexican army of Santa Anna on the banks of the river, on April 21, 1836, securing the independence of the Republic of Texas. The **San Jacinto Battleground State Historical Park,** on the S bank where river and ship channel meet, 16 mi/26 km E of downtown Houston, commemorates the battle; it is dominated by the San Jacinto Monument, a 570-ft/174-m obelisk.

San Joaquin County 1415 sq mi/3665 sq km, pop. 480,628, in C California. STOCKTON is its seat and largest city; LODI, TRACY, and MANTECA are the other centers of an area that extends from the Coast Ranges (SW) to the Sierra Nevada foothills (E). In the heart of the CENTRAL VALLEY, the county includes much of the San Joaquin R. delta, and is crisscrossed with natural and constructed channels, esp. in the NW. A rich agricultural region, watered by the Mokelumne, Stanislaus, and Calaveras rivers, it produces a wide variety of fruits, vegetables, nuts, grains, dairy goods, and livestock. Stockton is an inland port and a manufacturing center.

San Joaquin River 350 mi/560 km long, in SC California, the chief river in the S of the CENTRAL VALLEY. It rises in several forks in the Sierra Nevada, NE of Fresno, and flows SW into Millerton L., formed by the Friant Dam (1944), E of Madera. Continuing WSW, it crosses the valley N of Fresno, and turns NNW, up the valley's W side. By the time it reaches STOCKTON, the head of oceangoing navigation, the San Joaquin has entered a delta it shares with the SACRAMENTO R. (N); here a maze of natural ("sloughs") and artificial channels are used for transportation and irrigation. The San Joaquin enters the Sacramento just above the latter's mouth on Suisun Bay, the innermost extension of San Francisco Bay. The river's major tributaries, flowing from the Sierra Nevada (E) into the valley, are (S–N) the Fresno, Merced, Tuolumne, Stanislaus, Calaveras, and Mokelumne rivers. The **San Joaquin Valley,** however, is considered to include areas S to the TEHACHAPI Mts. (the Transverse Ranges) that are watered by the KINGS, KERN, and other rivers not tributary to the San Joaquin itself; thus, Fresno, Bakersfield, and many agricultural cities are included. Canalization, largely under the Central Valley Project, has brought water to most parts of this formerly arid district; thus, the Friant-Kern Canal runs S from the Friant Dam to Bakersfield, and the 120 mi/190 km–long Delta-Mendota Canal connects the S San Joaquin (at Mendota) with the delta (N) near Tracy, running along the valley's W side. In the 19th and early 20th centuries the valley was used to raise cattle and some crops (chiefly grains); for a period one agribusiness concern (Miller-Lux, based on old RANCHO holdings), controlled almost the entire flow of the river for its own operations. Today, the region produces a wide range of fruits, grapes, vegetables, nuts, and other crops; cattle raising is still important. In the S, from the Kettleman Hills to the Bakersfield–Elk Hills area, are major oilfields.

San Jose city, pop. 782,248, seat of SANTA CLARA Co., WC California, along Coyote Creek and the Guadalupe R., 10 mi/16 km below the S end of San Francisco Bay, and 44 mi/71 km SE of San Francisco. It is the largest city in Northern California, and the state's third-largest. In the heart of the rich Santa Clara Valley, it was the first civic settlement (PUEBLO) in California, established (1777) to supply farm produce and cattle to the Monterey and San Francisco PRESIDIOS. In 1849–51 it was California's first state capital; in 1850 it became the state's first incorporated city. In 1864, railroad connections with San Francisco were established. The Santa Clara Valley soon developed as an important producer of fruits and nuts, esp. plums, apricots, apples, cherries, almonds, peaches, and pears; vineyards joined cattle ranches and grain fields. The city's importance as a fruit processing center dates from 1871, when the first cannery opened. Until World War II, San Jose remained essentially agriculture-based. It then developed rapidly as an industrial center; aerospace, motor vehicle, and business equipment firms established plants. The city's pop. doubled in the 1950s and again in the 1960s; additional growth was spurred by the development of the Santa Clara Valley into SILICON VALLEY, the computer manufacturing center, and land was annexed at a rapid rate. San Jose is now the hub of a growing metropolitan area (PMSA, pop. 1,497,577), with fruit processing, winemaking, and nuclear and other engineering industries; its manufactures include computers, software, chemicals, aerospace and auto parts, and food processing machinery. San Jose State University (1857), San Jose City College (1921), and several other colleges are here. The Winchester Mystery House, an architectural curiosity, and the Rosicrucian Museum, headquarters of the Union of Rosicrucians, draw visitors. The city has a sizable Asian community, including many Cambodians and other recent refugees from Southeast Asia.

San Juan **1.** unincorporated community (ZONA URBANA), pop. 426,832, capital of Puerto Rico, in San Juan Municipio (pop. 437,745), in the NE, on the Bahía de San Juan (San Juan Bay) and the Atlantic Ocean. It is the island's leading port and chief industrial center. Within its metropolitan area are such MUNICIPIOS as BAYAMÓN, CAGUAS, CAROLINA, CATAÑO, GUAYNABO, and Toa Baja, which with San Juan have a combined pop. of 1,186,187, or 34% of Puerto Rico's total. **Old San Juan** (San Juan Antigua), settled in 1521, occupies an island between the Atlantic and capacious San Juan Bay (the "rich port" that gave the entire island its name), and is connected to the mainland (S) and to CONDADO (SE) by bridges and causeways. Ponce de León founded Puerto Rico's first settlement at nearby (W) Caparra in 1508. Thirteen years later, the settlement moved across the bay to its present site. Its massive EL MORRO fortress (1539) repelled various attacks, although the English (1598) and the Dutch (1625) temporarily took control. San Juan became an important port in the 18th and 19th centuries. During the Spanish-American War (1898), it passed under US control. Today it is a major port, exporting sugar, tobacco, coffee, and tropical fruits, mostly to the US mainland, and providing the world's busiest cruise ship base. Its (Muñoz Marín) international airport is in Isla Verde (CAROLINA), just E, and there is a second airport in Isla Grande (SANTURCE). Sugar and petroleum are refined, and rum is distilled. Other industries produce pharmaceuticals, cement, textiles, clothing, furniture, jewelry, and electronic equipment. Banking, metalworking, and publishing are also important. San Juan is also a tourist mecca, with a mild, constant climate, picturesque streets in Old San Juan, gambling casinos, modern hotels, and beachfront facilities. Among the old city's sites are the governor's palace, La Fortaleza (begun 1533); the San Juan Cathedral (1540), containing Ponce de León's tomb; the San José Church (c.1532); Casa Blanca (1521); El Morro; Fort San Cristóbal (1643–1783); the 17th-century City Hall and 18th-century Casa de Callejon; and the Pablo Casals Museum. See also: CONDADO (and Ocean Beach); EL MORRO; HATO REY (and the Golden Mile); LA PERLA; MIRAMAR; RÍO PIEDRAS; SANTURCE. **2.** city, pop. 10,815, Hidalgo Co., extreme S Texas, 6 mi/10 km E of McAllen, in the Lower Rio Grande Valley. It is a trade, processing, and shipping center, handling local vegetables, fruit, and cotton. There is also a large irrigation-pipe plant.

San Juan Bautista city, pop. 1570, San Benito Co., C California, on Highway 101 and the San Andreas Fault, in the E foothills of the GABILAN RANGE, 26 mi/42 km NE of Monterey. Established around a 1797 mission, with the largest mission church in California (completed 1812), it has been a ranching center, and draws tourists.

San Juan Capistrano **1.** city, pop. 26,183, Orange Co., SW California, 3 mi/5 km from the Pacific Ocean, halfway between Los Angeles (NW) and San Diego (SE). It grew around its MISSION (1776), and is today largely a residential and resort community, with some light industry. In 1812, an earthquake destroyed much of the mission's Great Stone Church, but it was partly restored, and other buildings survived. Migrating swallows arrive from South America every year on March 19, St. Joseph's Day, to nest in the ruins of the church, and leave on Oct. 23, the day of St. John's (San Juan's) death. According to legend, their arrival has been delayed only once, by a storm at sea. **2.** see under MISSION DRIVE, San Antonio, Texas.

San Juan Hill former neighborhood on the WEST SIDE of Manhattan, New York City. Around 1900 it was a center of New York's black population, and gained its name in reference to the bravery of black soldiers at San Juan Hill, near Santiago, Cuba, in July 1898. By World War I most of its residents were moving N to Harlem. San Juan Hill was just W of where LINCOLN CENTER stands today.

San Juan Islands 172-island archipelago in NW Washington, N of PUGET SOUND, S of the Strait of GEORGIA, and E of Vancouver I., British Columbia. The islands form San Juan Co. (pop. 10,035). The four largest and most populated are ORCAS (57 sq mi/147 sq km), San Juan (55 sq mi/143 sq km), Lopez (30 sq mi/76 sq km), and Shaw (8 sq mi/20 sq km). Half the county's year-round pop. lives on **San Juan I.** The islands are a year-round EXURB and a vacation hub; numbers increase greatly during the summer months. The Spanish explored the San Juans c.1790, and they became part of the US in 1872, following a boundary dispute with Great Britain.

San Juan Mountains NW–SE trending range, some 150 mi/240 km long, part of the W tier of the Rocky Mts., extending from the vicinity of Ouray and Telluride, SW Colorado, into N New Mexico. The RIO GRANDE rises in them and flows along their N, then through the agricultural **San Juan Valley,** NE of the range. Headwaters of the San Juan R. drain them to the SW. The high point is Uncompahgre Peak (14,309 ft/4361 m), at the NW end. The San Miguel Mts., a short W spur near the NW end, reach 14,246 ft/4342 m at Mt. Wilson, SW of Telluride. The San Juans have been mined for gold, silver, lead, copper, and other minerals; resorts are now important.

San Juan National Forest 1.87 million ac/757,000 ha (2922 sq mi/7568 sq km), in SW Colorado, on the SW of the San Juan Mts. and the Continental Divide. It includes the huge Weminuche Wilderness, headwaters and valleys of the Animas and other SW-flowing rivers, winter sports areas in the mountains, and the 236-mi/380-km San Juan Skyway, a noted scenic highway.

San Juan Pueblo pop. 5209, in Rio Arriba Co., N New Mexico, 27 mi/43 km NNW of Santa Fe and W of the Sangre de Cristo Mts., on the Rio Grande. In 1598 its central village was the first Spanish capital in New Mexico. In 1680, Popé, a San Juan medicine man, led the Pueblo Revolt. The pueblo is headquarters for the Northern Indian Pueblo Council. Its crafts include red pottery, wood and stone carvings, and jewelry.

San Leandro city, pop. 68,223, Alameda Co., NC California, on the E side of San Francisco Bay, adjoining (SE) Oakland and its International Airport. Originally part of Rancho San Leandro, it was settled after the 1849 gold rush, and was the county seat 1854–71. It was long a cherry growing and dairying center, with a large Portuguese community. Now part of the East Bay metropolis, it has nurseries and truck assembly, baking, and food processing plants, and manufactures paint, electronic and office equipment, chemicals, gardening supplies, and a variety of other products.

San Lorenzo unincorporated community, pop. 19,987, Alameda Co., NC California, on the E shore of San Francisco Bay, between San Leandro (N) and Hayward (S), 11 mi/18 km SE of downtown Oakland. Fruit, vegetable, and flower growing have been important in this suburb.

San Luis Obispo city, pop. 41,958, seat of San Luis Obispo Co. (pop. 217,162), WC California, on EL CAMINO REAL and San Luis Obispo Creek, in the Los Osos Valley at the base of the Santa Lucia Range, 160 mi/260 km NW of Los Angeles. In an agricultural area, the early community grew up around the Mission San Luis Obispo de Tolosa (1772). Ceramic tile developed here became the norm in regional architecture, and olive trees are said to have been introduced to North America at the mission. It became a PUEBLO (1844), then a city (1856). After 1894, it grew as a Southern Pacific Railroad DIVISION POINT, and local oil was shipped through Port San Luis, 8 mi/13 km SSW. Tourism has long been important in this highway community, home of a pioneering 1925 "motel." Government offices and various light manufactures employ residents. A California Polytechnic State University branch (1901), Cuesta College (1964), and a National Guard Reservation are here. The controversial DIABLO CANYON nuclear power plant (1984) is 11 mi/18 km SW.

San Marcos **1.** city, pop. 38,974, San Diego Co., SW California, 28 mi/45 km NNW of downtown San Diego and 6 mi/10 km W of Escondido. Palomar College (1946) and a California State University campus are in this growing residential community, which has some agriculture and light industry. **2.** city, pop. 28,743, seat of Hays Co., also in Caldwell Co., SC Texas, 30 mi/48 km SSW of Austin, on the San Marcos R. The site of earlier Spanish missions, it was settled in 1845 by Americans who developed it as a ranching and agricultural center. It now also has aircraft engine and assembly and other industries. Aquarena Springs, just NW where the river crosses the BALCONES ESCARPMENT, attracts tourists, as do other parks and caves along the river. The large Southwest Texas State University (1899), San Marcos Baptist Academy, and a number of hospitals and therapeutic centers are in the city.

San Marino city, pop. 12,959, Los Angeles Co., SW California, 9 mi/14 km NE of downtown Los Angeles and immediately SE of Pasadena. Incorporated in 1913, this wealthy suburb was founded by Henry E. Huntington, nephew of railroad baron Collis Huntington (see SACRAMENTO), whose estate includes the renowned Huntington Library, Art Gallery, and Botanical Gardens.

San Mateo city, pop. 85,486, San Mateo Co., NC California, on the W shore of San Francisco Bay, 15 mi/24 km SSE of downtown San Francisco. Although there was a mission hospice here by 1793, the community was not laid out until 1863, when wealthy San Franciscans began to build luxurious homes in a planned community. San Mateo is now a financial, commercial, and shopping center for the Bay Area, and has a substantial amount of SILICON VALLEY–related technological industry. The College of San Mateo (1922) and Bay Meadows Race Course are here. The five-span **San Mateo–Hayward Bridge** (1967), passing some 7 mi/11 km over the bay, is one of America's longest.

San Mateo County 447 sq mi/1158 sq km, pop. 649,623, in NC California, on the S of the San Francisco–San Mateo Peninsula. Its seat is REDWOOD CITY. Originally part of San Francisco Co., it includes many San Francisco suburbs along San Francisco Bay (E) and the Pacific Ocean (W) with the Santa Cruz Mts. running NW–SE through its center. Its cities include South San Francisco, San Mateo, Burlingame, Daly City, Hillsborough, San Bruno, Atherton, and Menlo Park. Its W valleys produce a major portion of the nation's artichokes; the E suburban area has truck farms, dairies, nurseries, and technological industry. In the SW are forested hillsides.

San Miguel Island northwesternmost of the SANTA BARBARA Is., in the Pacific Ocean, separated from the coast of SW California by the SANTA BARBARA CHANNEL. Eight mi/13 km E–W, it is part of the Channel Islands National Park, and is reputed to be the burial place of Juan Rodriguez Cabrillo, the group's discoverer, who died here in 1543. Many varieties of sea birds, seals, and sea lions frequent the windswept island.

San Miguel Mountains see under SAN JUAN Mts., Colorado.

San Nicolas Island one of the SANTA BARBARA Is., in the Pacific Ocean, 75 mi/120 km SW of Los Angeles, California. Ten mi/16 km long, it is a Naval reservation.

San Onofre locality on the Pacific Ocean in SW California, just SE of San Clemente and 58 mi/93 km SE of Los Angeles, within Camp Pendleton (see OCEANSIDE). It is the site of a state beach and of a nuclear power plant operational since 1967.

San Pablo city, pop. 25,158, Contra Costa Co., NC California, on San Pablo Bay, adjoining (N) Richmond and 12 mi/19 km NNE of San Francisco. One of the Bay Area's oldest (1810s) Spanish settlements, it was long agricultural, and is now a commercial and residential center with medical and seafood industries and various light manufactures. Contra Costa College (1948) is here.

San Pablo Bay N arm of SAN FRANCISCO BAY, NC California. Fourteen mi/23 km E–W, it connects with SUISUN BAY on the E via Carquinez Strait. The city of VALLEJO and Mare I. Naval Shipyard are on the E, RICHMOND and SAN PABLO on the S.

San Pasqual battle site: see under ESCONDIDO, California.

San Pedro harbor section of LOS ANGELES, California, on San Pedro Bay (E) and the Palos Verdes Peninsula (W), 22 mi/35 km S of Downtown and 6 mi/10 km WSW of Long Beach. Early in the 19th century, San Pedro was a shallow, difficult harbor. Dredging began in the 1850s, and improvements have been made periodically. A railroad link with Los Angeles was established in 1869. Incorporated as a city in 1888, San Pedro was annexed by Los Angeles in 1909. On one of the world's largest constructed harbors, it has shipyards, dry docks, fish canneries, and oil refineries. Terminal I. (E) has a Coast Guard base, a Federal prison, and various facilities for the Port of Los Angeles. WILMINGTON is just N.

San Pedro Channel strait of the Pacific Ocean between SANTA CATALINA I. and the coast of SW California. Twenty mi/32 km wide, it is crossed by ferries to the island, and entered by Los Angeles port traffic.

San Quentin locality (Point San Quentin) in Marin Co., NW California, on NW San Francisco Bay, just SE of San Rafael and 9 mi/14 km N of downtown San Francisco, site of large state prison established in 1852. The W end of the Richmond–San Rafael Bridge is close by.

San Rafael city, pop. 48,404, seat of Marin Co., NW California, on San Rafael Bay (an arm of San Francisco Bay), 13 mi/21 km NNW of San Francisco. It grew up around San Rafael Arcángel Mission (1817), and was a ranch town. The arrival of the railroad in 1884 and 20th-century bridge connections spurred suburban residential and light industrial growth. Frank Lloyd Wright's Marin Civic Center is well known. The Dominican College of San Rafael (1890) is here.

San Rafael Mountains one of the COAST RANGES, curving for c.50 mi/80 km between the SIERRA MADRE and SANTA YNEZ Mts., N of Santa Barbara, in SW California. The range reaches its greatest elevation at Big Pine Mt. (6828 ft/2081 m) and includes San Rafael Mt. (6595 ft/2010 m). The San Rafael (149,170 ac/60,414 ha) and nearby Dick Smith (64,700 ac/26,200 ha) wilderness areas are used recreationally. The mountains, within the Los Padres National Forest, contain a condor sanctuary.

San Ramon city, pop. 35,303, Contra Costa Co., NC California, in the San Ramon Valley, 15 mi/24 km E of Oakland. A residential community with some light industry, it has grown rapidly since the 1970s.

San Simeon hamlet in San Luis Obispo Co., WC California, on the Pacific Ocean, 36 mi/58 km NW of San Luis Obispo. In the 19th century it was a largely Portuguese fishing and whaling port. Around it and for 50 mi/80 km along the coast the Hearst estate, a 245,000-ac/99,000-ha property, was developed in the 1890s by the mine magnate George Hearst. On 1600-ft/490-m La Cuesta Encantada (Enchanted Hill), 3 mi/5 km back from the port, Hearst's son, publisher William Randolph Hearst (1863–1951), had architect Julia Morgan build La Casa Grande, an immense Spanish-style structure also known as the Hearst Castle, where he entertained lavishly. In 1958, 123 ac/50 ha, including the castle, became the Hearst–San Simeon State Historical Monument, now one of the West's leading tourist sites.

Santa Ana city, pop. 293,742, seat of ORANGE Co., SW California, on the Santa Ana R., at the SW base of the Santa Ana Mts., 28 mi/45 km SE of Los Angeles. It is the commercial and financial center of the irrigated Santa Ana Valley. Founded in 1869 on the Rancho Santiago de Santa Ana, it was connected to Los Angeles in 1878 by the Southern Pacific Railroad, and became a processing and market center for the valley's produce. In the 1920s, nearby oilfields brought wealth to the community. After World War II, freeway connections stimulated residential and industrial growth. Santa Ana's varied manufactures include aircraft, computer and electronic parts, plastics, sporting and rubber goods, metal products, and fiberglass. Rancho Santiago Community College (1915) is here. The city has almost doubled in pop. since 1970.

Santa Ana Mountains range in SW California, part of the COAST and PENINSULAR ranges, extending for c.25 mi/40 km SE from the Santa Ana R. along the Riverside-Orange county line. Their high point is Santiago Peak (5687 ft/1733 m), also known as Old Saddleback. Most of the range lies within the Trabuco District of the Cleveland National Forest. The Santa Anas have been mined for coal, lead, silver, and zinc, and are used recreationally. Santa Ana Canyon, at the range's NW, gives its name to the Santa Ana winds, hot, dry desert winds that funnel through this and other mountain gaps into the Los Angeles Basin.

Santa Anita see under ARCADIA, California.

Santa Barbara city, pop. 85,571, seat of Santa Barbara Co. (pop. 369,608), SW California, at the foot and on slopes of the SANTA YNEZ Mts., on the Santa Barbara Channel of the Pacific Ocean, 90 mi/145 km WNW of Los Angeles. It was settled as a PRESIDIO on EL CAMINO REAL in 1782, and its Franciscan MISSION has been in continuous use since 1786. A cattle raising center until the 1860s, it was occupied by Americans in 1846, and its commercial growth was accompanied by an 1870s real estate boom and spurred by the 1887 arrival of the Southern Pacific Railroad. By the early 20th century it was a popular resort. A 1925 earthquake destroyed much of the city, and it was rebuilt in the Spanish colonial style. The community of Montecito, on the E, became particularly well known for its wealthy habitués. Today, in addition to the resort trade and tourism, electronic and aerospace research and assembly are leading industries, along with commercial fishing. The oil industry's roots here go back to the mid 19th century, when sailors observed slicks in the channel. Petroleum and natural gas have been obtained from wells 5 mi/8 km offshore, but a huge 1969 oil spill forced industry cutbacks. The University of California at Santa Barbara (1898) is in Goleta, 7 mi/11 km W of Downtown. Santa Barbara City College (1908) and Westmont College (1940) are also here, along with the Center for the Study of Democratic Institutions and a number of museums and other cultural centers.

Santa Barbara Channel arm of the Pacific Ocean between the mainland of SW California (N) and the Santa Barbara Is. (S). In an area where the coast dips inward, the channel runs 70 mi/110 km E–W and is 20–30 mi/30–50 km wide. The cities of Santa Barbara, Ventura, and Oxnard lie along it. The channel has been the site of extensive offshore oil drilling.

Santa Barbara Island one of the SANTA BARBARA Is., in the Pacific Ocean, 50 mi/80 km SW of Los Angeles, California. Covering 640 ac/260 ha, the triangular island is part of the Channel Islands National Park, and has 5 mi/8 km of hiking trails. It is home to the Santa Barbara ice plant and the giant elephant seal.

Santa Barbara Islands also, **Channel Islands** group of eight major, and a number of minor, islands in the Pacific Ocean, 10–80 mi/16–130 km off the coast of SW California, stretching 155 mi/250 km from near Los Angeles to near San Diego. They include (NW–SE) a group of four—San Miguel, Santa Rosa, Santa Cruz, and Anacapa; a group of three—Santa Barbara, Santa Catalina, and San Nicolas; and San Clemente. The first five constitute the 250,000-ac/100,000-ha **Channel Islands National Park,** known for its distinctive animal and plant life, such as the island fox, giant yellow coreopsis, and Santa Cruz Island pine. Sea mammals abound, the California gray whale the largest. The islands are separated from the mainland on the N by the SANTA BARBARA CHANNEL, and on the E by the SAN PEDRO CHANNEL and the Gulf of SANTA CATALINA. Rising from the continental shelf, they are related to the COAST RANGES. Their highest point, on Santa Catalina, is over 2000 ft/600 km, while troughs between the islands reach depths of 6000 ft/1830 m. Santa Cruz, the largest island, has vineyards and sheep and cattle ranches; Santa Catalina, with its brisk tourist industry, is the most developed. Sport fishing is popular throughout the islands. A 1969 oil slick, caused by a leaking undersea well in the Santa Barbara Channel, caused heavy damage to the islands' marine life and beaches.

Santa Catalina, Gulf of inlet of the Pacific Ocean between

SAN CLEMENTE (S) and SANTA CATALINA (N) islands and the SW California mainland. Its N end connects with SANTA MONICA BAY via the SAN PEDRO CHANNEL, and the city of San Diego lies at its S extremity.

Santa Catalina Island resort island in the Pacific Ocean, 26 mi/42 km SSW of Los Angeles, California. Twenty-two mi/35 km NW–SE and 1–8 mi/2–13 km wide, it is one of the SANTA BARBARA Is., and was seen by the Portuguese navigator Juan Rodriguez Cabrillo in 1542. In 1919 William Wrigley bought Santa Catalina and developed an estate. Avalon (pop. 2918, Los Angeles Co.), the island's only city, has a boardwalk, golf course, casino, and ferry linking it to the mainland. The interior wilderness region has been in conservancy since 1974. The island is popular for deep-sea fishing.

Santa Catalina Mountains small range in SE Arizona, NE of Tucson. Largely within a section of the Coronado National Forest, it reaches 9157 ft/2791 m at Mt. Lemmon, noted for skiing and as the site of a University of Arizona telescope. In the N foothills, in the desert near Oracle (unincorporated, pop. 3043, Pinal Co.), is Biosphere 2, a 3-ac/1.2-ha glass-enclosed structure, scene of controversial, privately funded 1990s experiments in self-sustained living.

Santa Clara **1.** city, pop. 93,613, Santa Clara Co., NC California, in the Santa Clara (see SILICON) Valley, adjoining (W) San Jose and 40 mi/64 km SSE of San Francisco. The early settlement grew up around the Mission Santa Clara de Asís (1777). In the 1850s, building on the mission's orchards, it developed as a center of the fruit industry; the city is noted for its dried fruit, esp. prunes, and the valley remains a major canning and packing center. A small, largely agricultural community through World War II, it boomed in the 1950s, and is now at the heart of Silicon Valley. Its industries develop and manufacture electronic and electrical products, machinery, chemicals, and fiberglass. The University of Santa Clara, founded as a mission school in 1851, is one of California's oldest institutions of higher learning. The 100-ac/40-ha Great America theme park is a noted attraction. **2.** unincorporated community, pop. 12,834, Lane Co., WC Oregon, a residential suburb 5 mi/8 km NW of Eugene.

Santa Clara County 1293 sq mi/3349 sq km, pop. 1,497,577, in NC California. SAN JOSE is its seat. It extends SE from San Francisco Bay between the Diablo Range (NE) and the Santa Cruz Mts. (SW), incorporating the N Santa Clara Valley, a rich fruit growing region. Since the 1950s, technological research and manufacturing have spread through the county's N, creating what is today known as SILICON VALLEY. During this period there has been tremendous growth around the educational and industrial centers of PALO ALTO, San Jose, and SANTA CLARA and in their suburbs. In the S, winemaking, fruit production, and other agriculture remain dominant.

Santa Clara Pueblo pop. 10,193, in Rio Arriba, Sandoval, and Santa Fe counties, N New Mexico, on the Rio Grande, 21 mi/34 km NNW of Santa Fe. The Indian pop. of the pueblo is only 1246; its lands are, in effect, suburbs of Santa Fe and LOS ALAMOS (just SW). It is noted for its black pottery. The Puye Cliff Dwellings are just S.

Santa Clarita city, pop. 110,642, Los Angeles Co., SW California, in the Santa Clarita Valley, on the Santa Clara R., 30 mi/48 km NW of downtown Los Angeles, and just N of the Santa Susana Mts. The Newhall (San Fernando) Pass connects the valley with the SAN FERNANDO VALLEY (S). Created in the 1980s, Santa Clarita includes the former communities of Rancho Santa Clarita, Newhall, Saugus, and Valencia. In 1842 the first, but minor, California gold strike was made at Placerita, just SE. In 1861, oil was found in the Newhall Basin, and the state's first refinery was built here in 1876. Oil production continues, largely to the W. The Newhall Pass is a major gateway to the Los Angeles area. The Saugus Tunnel, built just N in 1876 by the Southern Pacific Railroad, connected Los Angeles with Northern California by way of the San Joaquin Valley. The CALIFORNIA AQUEDUCT brought water through it to the growing city. The dry Newhall winds blow through the pass into the San Fernando Valley. The Santa Clarita Valley itself figured in early Los Angeles water schemes, and the San Francisquito Canyon, just N, was the site of a March 1928 damburst in which hundreds died along the Santa Clara R. as a wall of water rushed W through Ventura Co. Today, the Santa Clarita area is a growing suburb. Master's College (Newhall; 1927) and the College of the Canyons (Valencia; 1967) are here, as is the large Six Flags Magic Mountain amusement park.

Santa Claus town, pop. 927, Spencer Co., SW Indiana, 35 mi/56 km ENE of Evansville. Each Christmas season, its post office marks and remails tons of packages and greeting cards. A holiday theme park draws tourists year round.

Santa Cruz city, pop. 49,040, seat of Santa Cruz Co. (pop. 229,734), WC California, on the N shore of MONTEREY BAY, 60 mi/100 km S of San Francisco. Founded in 1791 as a MISSION (destroyed by an 1859 earthquake), it became an early supply port for whalers, and by 1840 had a prosperous redwood lumbering industry. From the 1860s it was an increasingly popular resort, drawing San Franciscans to its beaches and entertainments; its famous boardwalk is still a magnet. Local industries include commercial fishing; fruit, flower, and vegetable growing; food processing; and various light manufactures. A University of California campus, opened in 1965, has brought a renaissance of cultural activity to this popular resort.

Santa Cruz Island largest of the SANTA BARBARA Is., in the Pacific Ocean, 25 mi/40 km off the coast of SW California, opposite (SSW) the city of Santa Barbara. Twenty-three mi/37 km E–W, it is part of the Channel Islands National Park. This and the other northern islands in the group are an extension of the SANTA MONICA Mts. on the mainland.

Santa Cruz Mountains one of the COAST RANGES in WC California, extending NW for c.70 mi/110 km along the W side of the Santa Clara Valley from N of the GABILAN RANGE up the San Francisco peninsula, and reaching 3806 ft/1160 m. The 30 mi/50 km–long Skyline-to-the-Sea Trail connects Big Basin Redwoods (15,000 ac/6100 ha) and Castle Rocks state park. There are also redwood groves near the resort of Ben Lomond.

Santa Fe city, pop. 55,859, state capital and seat of Santa Fe Co. (pop. 98,928), NC New Mexico, on the Santa Fe R., at the S foot of the Sangre de Cristo Mts., 53 mi/86 km NE of Albuquerque. One of the oldest European settlements in the US, it was founded by the Spanish in 1609 on the ruins of a Tiwa PUEBLO, abandoned after the 1680 Pueblo Revolt, and reclaimed in 1692. It remained a Spanish colonial capital, closed to Americans, until Mexico achieved independence from Spain in 1821; traders from the US soon arrived, and the SANTA FE TRAIL was established, spurring American expansion into the area. Santa Fe became American in 1846, after a bloodless victory during the Mexican War. In 1851, it became the capital of the New Mexico Territory, and in 1912 the capital of the new state. In 1879, it was reached (at LAMY) by the SANTA FE RAILROAD. Long a trade hub for ranchers, farmers, and Indians, Santa Fe is now an artists' colony and a cultural, tourist, and retirement center, with a large Hispanic pop. augmented by wealthy Easterners and Californians. It is noted for its adobe architecture. Built around a central plaza fronted by the Palace of the Governors (1610), it has some of the oldest churches in the US, as well as its well-known Cathedral (1869–86, built on the site of the 1610 MISSION church). An internationally recognized summer opera and several museums draw visitors. Government, commerce in Indian arts and crafts, and some light manufacturing are central to the economy. The College of Santa Fe (1947), Institute of American Indian Arts (1962), St. John's College (1964), and Santa Fe Community College (1983) are here.

Santa Fe National Forest 1.57 million ac/635,000 ha (2450 sq mi/6340 sq km), in N New Mexico, on both sides of the upper Rio Grande, in the S Sangre de Cristo (E) and Jemez (W) mountains. On both sides it is adjacent (S) to the CARSON NATIONAL FOREST, and extends S beyond Santa Fe, its headquarters. In the E are headwaters of the Pecos R., and part of the large Pecos Wilderness (shared with the Carson National Forest). The Santa Fe Basin recreation area is here.

Santa Fe Railroad formally, **Atchison, Topeka & Santa Fe** first organized in Kansas in 1863 as the Atchison & Topeka Railroad, and today a major carrier of the US Southwest. It is best known as the line that in 1880 reached Santa Fe (Lamy), New Mexico, ending the era of the Santa Fe Trail, and that later in the decade reached the Los Angeles area, bringing major development to Southern California. In the 1870s it crossed Kansas, connecting the heads of cattle trails there with Chicago; NEWTON and DODGE CITY were among the cities the Santa Fe made famous "cow towns." The line's agents in Europe attracted Mennonite farmers from Russia, who subsequently introduced winter wheat to the Great Plains. After crossing (by tunneling through the summit) the RATON Pass and reaching Santa Fe, the ATSF met the eastward-extending SOUTHERN PACIFIC at Deming, New Mexico, just W of El Paso, Texas, in 1881, forming the second transcontinental rail line; it later constructed or bought a number of lines through the Southwest. Beginning in Topeka in 1876, the Santa Fe financed construction of Fred Harvey restaurants along its lines, introducing a new standard of passenger service. In the 20th century it became well known for its Chicago–Los Angeles expresses, esp. the *Super Chief* (1935) and *El Capitan* (1938); its lines remain an important part of the AMTRAK passenger network.

Santa Fe Springs city, pop. 15,520, Los Angeles Co., SW California, 12 mi/19 km SE of downtown Los Angeles, and adjacent (E) to Downey. Established by the Santa Fe Railroad in 1886, it is an oil production center, and manufactures oilfield equipment, clay products, chemicals, and machinery.

Santa Fe Trail historic route linking the E US (via Missouri) with Santa Fe, New Mexico, after 1821, when Mexican independence eliminated Spanish trade restrictions. Much commerce of the period moved W from Saint Louis up the Missouri R. to Old Franklin, just N of modern BOONVILLE, Missouri. From here, in 1822, the first regular party continued overland along the Missouri, past Arrow Rock, Marshall, and Lexington, to INDEPENDENCE. The latter, with nearby WESTPORT (now part of Kansas City), became the chief outfitters for the Trail, and are usually thought of as its starting point. In Kansas, the Trail passed through Overland Park and Olathe to COUNCIL GROVE, at the Neosho R. crossing; this was the last opportunity to obtain supplies and marshall wagons. From Council Grove, the Trail continued WSW, reaching the Arkansas R. at Great Bend; proceeding along the N of the river past PAWNEE ROCK, Fort LARNED, and Dodge City, it reached Cimarron, where travelers were faced with a choice: The Main, or Mountain, Division continued along the Arkansas into Colorado. The **Cimarron Cutoff** (or Cutoff Division or Cimarron Crossing Trail) left the river, setting off to the SW across dry grasslands. The Mountain Division was longer but safer, with water at hand, forts along the way, and usually more fellow travelers. The Cimarron Cutoff, while shorter, passed through areas with little water, and where the Comanche posed a constant threat. In Colorado, the main route passed Lamar and reached BENT'S FORT, near La Junta. It then left the Arkansas, crossing the plains to Trinidad and crossing the Sangre de Cristo Mts. through RATON PASS, the Trail's highest point. In New Mexico it continued through Cimarron and reached Fort Union, just S of which the Cimarron Cutoff rejoined it. The unified Trail then proceeded to Las Vegas and then through the GLORIETA PASS to Santa Fe. The Cimarron Cutoff, leaving the Arkansas, continued SW to Ulysses, Kansas, and S to Wagon Bed Springs, where it crossed the Cimarron R., then followed it SW for some 75 mi/120 km (part in today's Cimarron National Grassland). Cutting through part of what is now the Oklahoma PANHANDLE, it entered NE New Mexico, crossing the North Canadian R., and proceeded WSW to near Springer, SSW to Wagon Mound, and to the junction with the main division. The Santa Fe Trail was the main trade and travel road to the Southwest for over 50 years, until the Santa Fe Railroad, built largely along its route, reached Santa Fe in 1880, rendering it obsolete. From Santa Fe the SPANISH TRAIL continued W, EL CAMINO REAL (the old Chihuahua Trail) S. Modern highways along parts of its route include US 56 and US 50 in Kansas and Colorado, and I-25 S of Trinidad, Colorado. The main route (Mountain Division) was almost 1000 mi/1600 km long; travelers on the Cimarron Cutoff shortened this to c.780 mi/1260 km. About six weeks was normal for wagon trains between Westport and Santa Fe.

Santa Gertrudis see under KING RANCH, Texas.

Santa Lucia Range one of the COAST RANGES in WC California, extending SE for c.140 mi/225 km from CARMEL Bay to the Cuyama R., paralleling the Pacific Ocean (W) and the SALINAS Valley (E). The heavily wooded mountains reach 5863 ft/1787 m in the N at Junipero Serra Peak, in the Ventana Wilderness (164,503 ac/66,624 ha), within the Los Padres National Forest. The entire natural range of the rare bristlecone or Santa Lucia fir is here. The range descends steeply to the ocean for 60 mi/100 km in the N section, where BIG SUR's coastline is famous. SAN SIMEON, Fort Hunter Liggett Military Reservation, and numerous state parks are along the range. Wineries dot its SE foothills.

Santa Maria city, pop. 61,284, Santa Barbara Co., SW California, on the Santa Maria R., in the Santa Maria Valley, 11 mi/18 km E of the Pacific Ocean and 54 mi/87 km NW of Santa

Barbara. It is the trade, processing, and shipping center for the valley, which produces flower seeds and bulbs, vegetables, beans, sugar beets, dairy goods, and grains. Founded in 1871, the community was sparsely settled until 1902, when oil began to be extracted. Industries now include refining and varied light manufactures. VANDENBERG AIR FORCE BASE, to the SW, is an important employer. Allan Hancock College (1920) and the county fairgrounds are here.

Santa Monica city, pop. 86,905, Los Angeles Co., SW California, on Santa Monica Bay, where WILSHIRE BOULEVARD and other thoroughfares meet the Pacific, 15 mi/24 km W of downtown Los Angeles, and surrounded on three sides by the larger city. Laid out in 1875, it prospered as a seaside resort, port (although it lost an 1890s competition with SAN PEDRO to become the port of Los Angeles), and railroad depot. Its pier, beaches, sidewalks, and elegant residences now attract tourists, and the city is an artists' colony, with dozens of galleries; the painter Richard Diebenkorn (1922–93) worked for years in the Ocean Park section (S). Aircraft and communications industries began to develop here after World War I, and have been joined by large retailing, electronics, and medical sectors. Santa Monica College (1929) and the J. Paul Getty Museum are here.

Santa Monica Bay crescent-shaped inlet of the Pacific Ocean in Los Angeles Co., SW California. Bordered by the Santa Monica Mts. (N) and the beach communities of Los Angeles, including the SOUTH BAY (E), it is lined with fishing piers, beaches, exclusive enclaves, and yacht harbors, but also, in places, by oilfields and industrial sites.

Santa Monica Freeway 17 mi/27 km long, between downtown LOS ANGELES (E) and SANTA MONICA (W), California. The shortest route linking Downtown and the ocean, the freeway (I-10) is one of the most heavily used in the Los Angeles network.

Santa Monica Mountains one of the TRANSVERSE RANGES in SW California, extending E–W for c.40 mi/64 km from GRIFFITH PARK in Los Angeles to Point Mugu, near OXNARD. The range, including the Beverly Hills and Hollywood Hills, largely parallels the N shore of Santa Monica Bay, with elevations mostly around 1000 ft/300 m, rising to 3111 ft/948 m at Sandstone Peak, also known as Mount Allen; it attains a maximum width of 12 mi/19 km. The **Santa Monica Mts. National Recreation Area** (150,000 ac/61,000 ha) encompasses an array of city, county, state, and Federal park areas including Will Rogers, Topanga, Malibu Creek, and Point Mugu state parks, and boasts diverse ecological areas and recreational opportunities. The 50-mi/80-km Mulholland Scenic Corridor and the Backbone Trail are two of many means of access.

Santanoni Peak 4621 ft/1409 m, in the Adirondack Mts., Essex Co., NE New York, 16 mi/26 km SW of LAKE PLACID.

Santa Paula city, pop. 25,062, Ventura Co., SW California, on the Santa Clara R., 52 mi/84 km WNW of Los Angeles. Laid out in 1875, it developed (1880s–90s) as an oil producing and refining and lemon growing center. It also packs and ships other fruits and nuts, and has some light manufactures. The Unocal (Union Oil Company) Oil Museum and Thomas Aquinas College (1971) are here.

Santa Rita Mountains NNE–SSW trending range in extreme S Arizona, rising to 9453 ft/2881 m at Mt. Wrightson, 25 mi/40 km NNE of NOGALES. Much mining has been done here, esp. for gold. The SMITHSONIAN INSTITUTION and University of Arizona's Whipple Observatory is on Mt. Hopkins (8585 ft/2617 m). Outdoor enthusiasts, esp. birdwatchers in search of the coppery-tailed trogon, visit Madera Canyon.

Santa Rosa city, pop. 113,313, seat of SONOMA Co., NW California, on the Santa Rosa R., 46 mi/74 km NNW of San Francisco. Incorporated in 1868, it has long been a fruit processing and shipping center, and was formerly a ranch hub. Drawn to its mild climate and fertile soil, horticulturist Luther Burbank lived here and developed hundreds of plant varieties in 1875–1926; he is buried in the Memorial Gardens at his home. Santa Rosa Junior College (1918) is also here. The city is growing rapidly as a residential community, and has varied agricultural, financial, and light manufacturing industries. It also is a gateway to N California natural attractions.

Santa Rosa Island one of the SANTA BARBARA Is., in the Pacific Ocean, separated from the SW California mainland by the SANTA BARBARA CHANNEL. Seventeen mi/27 km long, it is part of the Channel Islands National Park.

Santa Rosa Mountains one of the PENINSULAR RANGES of SW California, W of the Coachella Valley and Salton Sea. The rugged, boulder-strewn mountains extend for c.30 mi/50 km SE from S of the SAN JACINTO Mts., rising to 8717 ft/2657 m at Toro Peak, 22 mi/35 km S of Palm Springs. The Santa Rosa Wilderness Area of the ANZA BORREGO DESERT STATE PARK is noted for its beauty.

Santa Susana Mountains short component of the E–W TRANSVERSE RANGES, N of CHATSWORTH, in SW California. Separated from the SAN GABRIEL Mts. (E) by Newhall Pass (see SANTA CLARITA), the range lies between the SAN FERNANDO VALLEY (S) and Santa Clara R. valley (N), and rises to 3747 ft/1142 m at Oat Mt. The Santa Susanas, which contain oilfields and orchards, are rounder and taller than the Simi Hills (SW). The Santa Susana Pass, just S, connects the San Fernando Valley (E) with the Simi Valley (W).

Santa Teresa Mountains see under PINALENO Mts., Arizona.

Santa Ynez Mountains E–W range of S California, just N of SANTA BARBARA, considered to be both a COAST RANGE and the westernmost part of the TRANSVERSE RANGES. Rising 2000–4000 ft/600–1200 m, it is variously described as extending W for c.50 or c.75 mi (80 or 120 km) from the Ventura R. to Gaviota Canyon or to Point ARGUELLO, on the coast. El Camino Cielo (the Sky Road) follows much of its crest. Esp. around L. Cachuma (N) the area is popular for recreation; most of the range is within the LOS PADRES NATIONAL FOREST.

Santee city, pop. 52,902, San Diego Co., SW California, 11 mi/18 km NE of downtown San Diego, and just N of El Cajon. It is a fast-growing residential and commercial suburb.

Santee River 143 mi/230 km long, in E South Carolina. It is formed 30 mi/48 km SE of Columbia by the confluence of the CONGAREE and Wateree (see CATAWBA) rivers, and flows generally SE to the Atlantic just NE of the FRANCIS MARION NATIONAL FOREST. Before 1940, the Santee was linked with the COOPER R. by a 22-mi/35-km canal completed in 1800. Then the Santee-Cooper project was undertaken: The **Santee Dam** (1941), 45 ft/14 m high and almost 8 mi/13 km long, created L. Marion, which now backs up 40 mi/64 km to the Congaree/Wateree confluence. The Pinopolis Dam, on the Cooper, created L. Moultrie. A channel between the lakes replaced the old canal. The two lakes, known as the **Santee-Cooper Lakes,** inundated much old Low Country plantation land;

they now provide a major recreational asset. Before railroads developed (1830s–40s), the Santee–Wateree–Catawba system, with its Congaree and Cooper river connections, was the commercial lifeline of South Carolina. The system drains over half the state.

Santee Sioux Indian Reservation or **Santee Reservation** 173 sq mi/448 sq km, pop. 758 (56% Indian), in NE Nebraska, on Lewis and Clark L. (the Missouri R.) just E of the mouth of the Niobrara R. and 70 mi/113 km WNW of Sioux City, Iowa. It is home to members of the Mdewakanton (Sisseton) and Wahpeton groups of the Eastern Dakota (Sioux), who lived in Minnesota until removal following their 1862 uprising there.

Santiago Mountains range extending for c.35 mi/56 km between the Del Norte Mts. (NW) and the SIERRA DEL CARMEN (SE), SE of Alpine, in Brewster Co., in SW Texas. It attains its highest elevation at Santiago Peak (6521 ft/1989 m), and reaches along the NE of BIG BEND National Park. The Woods Hollow Mts., rising to 4661 ft/1422 m, lie just NE. The Del Norte Mts. rise to 6151 ft/1876 m.

Santo Domingo Pueblo pop. 2992, in Sandoval Co., C New Mexico, on the Rio Grande, 26 mi/42 km SW of Santa Fe. An agricultural community, this Keresan PUEBLO is known for its jewelry and pottery.

Santurce BARRIO, pop. 95,184, containing much of the modern business and governmental district of SAN JUAN, Puerto Rico, on peninsulas and the mainland, S and E of Old San Juan. HATO REY lies S. Originally a residential suburb, Santurce is now central to metropolitan San Juan's transportation network, and contains many of its offices. The waterfront communities of MIRAMAR, CONDADO, and Ocean Park are part of the *barrio,* and the Isla Grande airport is here, on San Juan Bay.

San Xavier del Bac see MISSION SAN XAVIER DEL BAC, Arizona.

San Ysidro section of SAN DIEGO, California, 12 mi/19 km SSE of Downtown, at the border with N Baja California, Mexico. A residential and commercial area with strong Mexican ties, it is the S terminus of San Diego's light rail system.

Sapelo Island one of the SEA ISLANDS, in the Atlantic Ocean 20 mi/32 km NNE of Brunswick, in McIntosh Co., E Georgia. Eleven mi/18 km N–S and 5 mi/8 km wide, it is part of the Sapelo I. National Estuarine Sanctuary, with cordgrass marshes and hardwood hummocks.

Sappington unincorporated community, pop. 10,917, St. Louis Co., EC Missouri, 12 mi/19 km SW of downtown St. Louis. Essentially a residential community, it also has some light industry. It is situated near the Mississippi (E) and Meramec (W and S) rivers and close to St. Louis's national cemetery (E).

Sapulpa city, pop. 18,074, seat of Creek Co., NE Oklahoma, 12 mi/19 km SW of Tulsa. Settled as farmland (1850), it grew with the coming of the railroad (1886). Today this suburb is a processing and shipping center for agricultural, livestock, oil, and gas producers. Important manufactures include glass, brick, pottery, tile, furnaces, tanks, and drilling equipment.

Saraland city, pop. 11,751, Mobile Co., SW Alabama, 9 mi/14 km N of downtown Mobile, of which it is a growing residential suburb.

Saranac Lakes in Franklin Co., NE New York, in the Adirondack Mts., 10 mi/16 km W of Lake Placid. These three resort lakes lie W of **Saranac Lake** village (pop. 5377), the site of the first outdoor sanatorium for tuberculosis, established here in 1876 by Dr. Edward Livingston Trudeau, and now a world-famous health resort. The lakes are (W to E) Upper Saranac L. (8 mi/13 km long), Middle Saranac L. (2 mi/3 km long), and Lower Saranac L. (5 mi/8 km long); they are linked by the **Saranac River,** which then flows through the village and generally NE for 50 mi/80 km, entering L. CHAMPLAIN at PLATTSBURGH.

Sarasota city, pop. 50,961, seat of Sarasota Co., SW Florida, on Sarasota Bay, separated by Longboat, Lido, and Siesta keys from the Gulf of Mexico, 45 mi/72 km S of Tampa. It was settled by Scots in the 1880s. From the late 1920s it was winter headquarters for the Ringling Brothers Barnum & Bailey Circus (moved to nearby VENICE in 1960). John Ringling's massive investments in the city were instrumental in its growth. The Ringling Museum, a 66-ac/27-ha complex, houses a noted art collection among its displays. Sarasota is a flourishing winter resort known for its water sports, gardens, and golf courses, a spring training baseball center, and an entertainment hub with several performing arts facilities. The city is a processing and shipping center for local citrus fruits, vegetables (notably celery), and beef. Its industries include boatbuilding, electronics research and development, and the production of mobile homes. Sarasota is the seat of New College of the University of South Florida (1960).

Saratoga **1.** city, pop. 28,061, Santa Clara Co., WC California, in the E foothills of the Santa Cruz Mts., 8 mi/13 km SW of San Jose. It is a winery and orchard center, and home to West Valley College (1963). The city is noted for a number of gardens, including those at Villa Montalva (1912). **2.** town, pop. 1969, Carbon Co., SC Wyoming, on the North Platte R., 32 mi/52 km SE of Rawlins. **Saratoga Hot Springs,** a reputedly medicinal natural hot spring with bathing facilities, is in the town. Lumber is milled and furniture manufactured here.

Saratoga County 810 sq mi/2098 sq km, pop. 181,276, E New York, bounded by the Hudson R. (E) and the Mohawk R. (S), lying partially (N) in the Adirondack Mts., and containing Saratoga L. and part of GREAT SACANDAGA L. Its seat is BALLSTON SPA. The county is known for its resorts, particularly SARATOGA SPRINGS. Largely rural, it has dairy and truck farming and stock and poultry raising. There is some suburban development in the S, in the ALBANY area, and industry in such places as South Glens Falls, Schuylerville, Mechanicville, Corinth, Waterford, Saratoga Springs, and the county seat. The 2800-ac/1134-ha Saratoga National Historical Park is along the Hudson.

Saratoga Springs city, pop. 25,001, Saratoga Co., E New York, in the foothills of the Adirondack Mts., 3 mi/5 km W of Saratoga L., and 30 mi/48 km N of Albany. The site, rich in mineral springs and an ancient Indian campground, was ceded to the Dutch in 1684. It began attracting European visitors in 1771, and became the most fashionable US resort of the 19th century. In 1863 the Saratoga Association for the Improvement of the Breed of Horses began sponsoring races, now conducted by the New York Racing Association. The state placed 83 springs under government regulation in 1909, to counteract their depletion by commercial exploitation. Saratoga Springs is the seat of Skidmore College (1911) and Empire State College (1971). Yaddo, a large private estate in the city, has served as a retreat for writers and painters since 1926. The Saratoga Spa State Park, which includes the Performing Arts Center, is the summer home of the New York City Ballet and the Philadelphia Orchestra. Industries manufacture textiles, wallpaper, electronic equipment, and mobile homes.

Sarnia officially, **Sarnia-Clearwater** city, pop. 74,376, seat of Lambton Co., S Ontario, on the St. Clair R., at the S end of L. Huron, opposite Port Huron, Michigan (reached by rail and the Bluewater Bridge). The site was visited by French explorers in the 17th century, but white settlement did not begin until 1807. The present city was founded in 1833 as The Rapids, and became Port Sarnia in 1836. Following the 1850s discovery of oil in the region, it rapidly became Canada's leading petroleum center. Today it has Ontario's largest concentration of petrochemical industries, and is the terminus for pipelines carrying Alberta crude oil. Diverse manufacturing, including auto parts production, and a busy Great Lakes port contribute to the economy.

Sarpy County 238 sq mi/616 sq km, pop. 102,583, in EC Nebraska, bounded E by the Missouri R. (the Iowa border) and S by the Platte R., which turns N at South Bend and bisects the county. Its seat is PAPILLION. Part of its NE is in the Omaha area, and contains suburban development. OFFUTT AIR FORCE BASE, just outside Bellevue, has contributed significantly to the county's economy. The balance of the region produces grain, livestock, fruit, poultry, and dairy goods.

Saskatchewan province of WC Canada, the middle PRAIRIE PROVINCE; 1991 pop. 988,928 (98% of 1986; rank: 6th of 12); land area 220,121 sq mi/570,113 sq km (rank: 6th); entered Confederation 1905. Capital: REGINA. Most populous cities: SASKATOON, Regina, PRINCE ALBERT, MOOSE JAW, YORKTON, SWIFT CURRENT. Saskatchewan is bordered E by Manitoba; S (along the FORTY-NINTH PARALLEL) by North Dakota (E) and Montana (W); W by Alberta; and N (along the SIXTIETH PARALLEL) by the Northwest Territories. Its N third lies on the CANADIAN SHIELD, a forested, rugged region dotted with lakes (including the large ATHABASCA, Wollaston, Cree, and REINDEER) and largely uninhabited except for small Indian communities and scattered mining and logging centers. In its S two-thirds, Saskatchewan rises gradually through PARKLANDS into the GREAT PLAINS region, to a high of 4567 ft/1392 m in the CYPRESS HILLS (SW). It takes its name (from a Cree word for "swift flowing") from the E-flowing SASKATCHEWAN R., long a trade artery, which is formed by the junction of the North and South Saskatchewan rivers near Prince Albert. The upper CHURCHILL R. (NC) and the QU'APPELLE (SE) also flow E into the Hudson Bay watershed. Some Shield rivers, in the far N, flow into the Arctic Ocean watershed. In the more populated S, Saskatchewan is an important component of the WHEAT BELT. Except for local agricultural and mineral processing, almost all industry is concentrated in Regina, Saskatoon, Moose Jaw, and Prince Albert. Mines on the Shield produce uranium (esp. near L. Athabasca), copper, and zinc, and natural gas, potash, coal, and oil are extracted in the prairie S. FLIN FLON, on the Manitoba border; LLOYDMINSTER, on the Alberta border; ESTEVAN, Swift Current, and WEYBURN are among mineral centers. The Assiniboine, Cree, and various Athapascan peoples lived here when French fur traders began to operate in the area in the mid 18th century. The competing HUDSON'S BAY COMPANY, which claimed the region as part of RUPERT'S LAND, established Cumberland House on the Saskatchewan, at Cumberland L. (EC), in 1774. There was intermittent trading and missionary activity before the mid 19th century, when a government expedition pronounced the S unfit for farming (see PALLISER'S TRIANGLE). Scattered MÉTIS communities developed in the 1870s in what had become (1870) part of the Northwest Territory. In the 1880s the CANADIAN PACIFIC RAILWAY crossed the region, and large-scale settlement began. An 1885 rebellion headed by the Métis leader Louis Riel was put down quickly (see BATOCHE; BATTLEFORD; DUCK LAKE), and in 1905 Saskatchewan became a province. Its people today are primarily English, German, Ukrainian, Scandinavian, and French in background; a substantial Indian pop. remains, largely on over 100 INDIAN RESERVES. Prince Albert National Park (C) and Lac la Ronge Provincial Park are important outdoor recreation areas.

Saskatchewan River major river of the Prairie Provinces, in Alberta, Saskatchewan, and NW Manitoba. The mainstream is formed by the confluence of the North and the South Saskatchewan some 50 mi/80 km E of PRINCE ALBERT, Saskatchewan, and flows to L. WINNIPEG, from which its waters are drained by the NELSON R. to Hudson Bay. The **North Saskatchewan,** 760 mi/1220 km long, rises in the Rocky Mts., on the E of the Continental Divide, in Banff National Park, near Mt. Columbia. It flows E to Rocky Mountain House, N and E to Edmonton, and then NE and E into Saskatchewan, where it flows SE to North Battleford, then SE and NE to Prince Albert. The **South Saskatchewan,** 865 mi/1393 km long, is formed by the confluence of the BOW and Oldman rivers, 43 mi/70 km W of Medicine Hat, Alberta. It flows ENE to Medicine Hat, NE into Saskatchewan (where the RED DEER R. joins it), E into dam-created Diefenbaker L., N to Saskatoon, and NNE, paralleling the North Saskatchewan, to the confluence. From the confluence, the mainstream flows ENE through Tobin L. (formed by the Squaw Rapids Dam), to Cumberland House, then E into Manitoba, to The Pas. It continues ESE into Cedar L., through which it flows SE, via Grand Rapids, into L. Winnipeg. The Bow–South Saskatchewan–Saskatchewan system totals 1200 mi/1930 km, and is the longest headstream of the Nelson. The Saskatchewan (Cree, "swift flowing") system was critical to the fur trade and to European exploration W to the Rockies. It is navigable for small craft all the way to ROCKY MOUNTAIN HOUSE, despite rapids, shallows, and heavy siltation in places. From the South Saskatchewan, river-and-portage routes SW into Wyoming were available. Since the 1880s, dams and power projects have been built along the system.

Saskatoon city, pop. 186,058, SC Saskatchewan, in rolling parklands 146 mi/235 km NW of Regina, on the South Saskatchewan R. Now the largest city in the province, it was founded in 1883 by Ontario Methodists as a temperance colony. Three separate communities combined to form the city in 1906. Saskatoon (the Cree Indian word for a local red berry) developed into the retail center of a major grain and livestock area after the railroad arrived in 1890. Today its largest employers are the University of Saskatchewan (1907) and associated religious colleges, city government, and Intercontinental Packers Ltd. Industries include food and dairy processing, flour milling, grain storage, brewing, tanning, oil refining, commercial banking, and the manufacture of clothing, road machinery, chemicals, fertilizers, and electronic equipment. The mining of potash and uranium to the N is important to the city. In the 1980s high-tech industry moved in and boosted the economy.

Sassafras Mountain highest elevation (3560 ft/1085 m) in South Carolina, in the Blue Ridge Mts., 28 mi/45 km NW of Greenville, along the North Carolina border.

Satellite Beach city, pop. 9889, Brevard Co., EC Florida, 14 mi/23 km SE of Cocoa, on a barrier island between the Atlantic (E) and the Banana R. lagoon (W). It grew with the space industry in the 1960s, and houses personnel from neighboring (N) Patrick Air Force Base and the Kennedy Space Center, 18 mi/29 km N.

Sauganash residential neighborhood on the far NW side of Chicago, Illinois, near Niles and Park Ridge. Low-density homes bordering a forest preserve make wealthy Sauganash one of the most suburban neighborhoods in Chicago. There are many Irish families in this prestigious area.

Saugatuck River 30 mi/48 km long, in SW Connecticut. It rises in Danbury, Fairfield Co., and flows SE and S to Long Island Sound at Westport.

Saugerties town, pop. 18,467, Ulster Co., SE New York, on the W bank of the Hudson R. at its confluence with Esopus Creek, at the E foot of the Catskill Mts., 11 mi/18 km N of Kingston. During the 18th and 19th centuries, its village (pop. 3915) was a bustling river port. Cement and clothing are among contemporary manufactures, and there are flagstone and limestone quarries. The village still has many Colonial and Greek Revival structures.

Saugus 1. see under SANTA CLARITA, California. **2.** town, pop. 25,549, Essex Co., E Massachusetts, at the mouth of the Saugus R. on Massachusetts Bay. It is a suburb 10 mi/16 km NE of Boston and adjoining (S) Lynn. The birthplace of the American iron and steel industry in 1646, when the settlement was called Hammersmith, Saugus Iron Works National Historic Site includes a reconstruction of the ironworks. Saugus was also one of the first communities in the nation to manufacture shoes and woolens. The town now produces various light manufactures, attracts tourists, and has extensive commerce along US 1 N of Boston.

Sauk Centre city, pop. 3581, Stearns Co., C Minnesota, on the Sauk R. at the S tip of Sauk L. An agricultural service center, it is known as the model for Gopher Prairie in *Main Street.* The novel's author, Sinclair Lewis, was born here in 1885; his restored boyhood home is a local attraction.

Sauk Village village, pop. 9926, Cook and Du Page counties, NE Illinois, a residential suburb 27 mi/43 km S of Chicago and just W of the Indiana border.

Sault Sainte Marie 1. city, pop. 14,689, seat of Chippewa Co., in the E part of the Upper Peninsula of Michigan, on the St. Mary's R., opposite its namesake in Ontario. The site was visited by French explorers in 1620, and in 1668 a Jesuit mission was built there by Father Jacques Marquette, making this the oldest permanent settlement in Michigan. It became part of the US in 1820, and Fort Brady was constructed two years later. The city is situated on the Soo Canals, which convey ships carrying enormous amounts of freight between lakes Superior and Huron. The river rapids (*saults*) supply the power used in the manufacture of lumber, concrete, pulp and paper, veneer, and other products. The John Johnson home (1796), one of the oldest in the state, was the home of Henry Schoolcraft, the 1820s Indian agent whose tales inspired Longfellow's "Song of Hiawatha." The city is the seat of Lake Superior State University (1946). **2.** city, pop. 81,476, seat of ALGOMA District, SC Ontario, opposite Sault Ste. Marie, Michigan, with which it shares an early history. Ceded by the French to the British in 1762, it became the site (1783) of a NORTH WEST COMPANY trading post, and in 1797–98 of a small lock. This lock, destroyed by US troops during the War of 1812, was later rebuilt as an historical site. A second, built 1895, and the four locks on the US side now circumvent the St. Mary's Rapids. A major Canadian port, the city has also developed as a manufacturing center, producing iron, steel, paper, tar, chemicals, and beer. It is also a gateway to N and C Ontario.

Sauquoit see under PARIS, New York.

Sausalito city, pop. 7152, Marin Co., NW California, on Richardson Bay, a W inlet of San Francisco Bay, just N of the Golden Gate Bridge and 5 mi/8 km N of downtown San Francisco. A fishing and whaling port from about 1800, it was called Saucelito (little willow). It is now a Mediterranean-looking tourist destination, a mix of the bohemian (artists; the houseboat colony at Waldo Point) and expensive residences. The Army Corps of Engineers San Francisco Bay Model, a well-known scientific display, is on the site of an important World War II shipyard.

Sauvie Island 24,000 ac/9720 ha, immediately NW of PORTLAND, Oregon, at the junction of the Willamette and Columbia rivers, on the Columbia (N) and the Multnomah Channel (S), a distributary of the Willamette. Once a seasonal home for the Multnomah, the island was visited by Lewis and Clark (1805) and had a HUDSON'S BAY COMPANY trading post in the early 19th century. Later, Canadian Laurent Sauvé set up a dairy here; today, Sauvie has farmland, a wildlife sanctuary, beaches, and other recreational attractions.

Savage city, pop. 9906, Scott Co., SE Minnesota, on the Minnesota R. where the Credit R. joins it, just SSW of Bloomington. Primarily agricultural until the 1960s, it is a growing Twin Cities suburb.

Savage's Station also, **Savage Station** historic site 9 mi/14 km ESE of Richmond, EC Virginia. In a battle fought here on June 29, 1862, part of the Confederate Seven Days' Campaign, forces led by John B. Magruder pursued the Union army as it retreated S to the James R. from Richmond. This battle was followed the next day by that of FRAYSER'S FARM.

Savanna city, pop. 3819, Carroll Co., extreme NW Illinois, on the Mississippi R. where the Plum R. joins it, 38 mi/62 km SE of Dubuque, Iowa. Settled in 1828, it has been since 1850 an important railroad town, with repair shops and yards, and the shipping point for area agriculture. The Mississippi Palisades State Park covers 2500 ac/1012 ha with cliffs along the river, and the UPPER MISSISSIPPI NATIONAL WILDLIFE AND FISH REFUGE extends in both directions along the river. The Savanna Army Depot, 10 mi/16 km NW along the river, has been a major ordnance center.

Savannah 1. city, pop. 137,560, seat of Chatham Co., E Georgia, across from South Carolina on the Savannah R., 17 mi/27 km W of its mouth on the Atlantic Ocean and 85 mi/137 km SW of Charleston, South Carolina. Founded in 1733 by James Oglethorpe, it is the first planned US city, and the oldest city in Georgia. It became the seat of government of the province of Georgia in 1754. In 1778 the city was captured by the British and held until the end of the Revolutionary War. A flourishing cotton industry and the success of the *Savannah,* the first steamboat to sail across the Atlantic (1819), were key to the city's shipping economy. Early in the Civil War it was a major Confederate supply depot. Union forces seized Fort Pulaski, at the river's mouth, on April 11,

1862, closing the port, and Savannah fell to W.T. Sherman's forces in Dec. 1864. Following the Civil War, Savannah regained its importance as a cotton exporter, and is now a major Southeastern port. Its industries, largely developed in the 20th century, include shipbuilding and the manufacture of paper, sugar, oils, paints, containers, truck bodies, aircraft, industrial gases, and petroleum and wood products. Principal exports include lumber, paper products, fertilizer, machinery, and naval stores. Oil, ores, nitrates, and raw sugar are major imports. The city is also a popular tourist center. In the 1950s 3000 historic buildings were placed on the National Register of Historic Places, and the city's original squares have been converted to parks. Savannah is home to Armstrong State College (1935), Savannah State College (1890), and several other institutions. **2.** city, pop. 6547, Hardin Co., SW Tennessee, on the Tennessee R., 40 mi/64 km SE of Jackson and 15 mi/24 km N of the Mississippi line. Settled in the 1820s, it has handled regional timber, limestone, marble, cotton, and other crops. The SHILOH battlefield is 7 mi/11 km SW, and the Pickwick Landing Dam, 11 mi/18 km S, forms Pickwick L., which backs up over 25 mi/40 km into NE Mississippi and NW Alabama.

Savannah River 314 mi/506 km long, in Georgia and South Carolina. It is formed by the Tugaloo and Seneca rivers, both impounded in Hartwell L. on the South Carolina–Georgia border, 10 mi/16 km SW of Anderson, South Carolina, and flows SE, forming the state boundary. The Richard B. Russell Dam, 17 mi/27 km SE of Elberton, Georgia, impounds Richard B. Russell L. Twenty-two mi/35 km above AUGUSTA, Georgia, the 200 ft/61 m–high, 5700 ft/1730 m–long Clark Hill Dam (also called the J. Strom Thurmond Dam) impounds the 40 mi/64 km–long Clark Hill L. (or J. Strom Thurmond Reservoir). Augusta, on the FALL LINE, is at the head of navigation, and tobacco and cotton were once shipped downriver from the city. From Augusta, the Savannah flows SE across the Atlantic coastal plain, through a broad, swampy valley, and empties into the Atlantic Ocean below the city of Savannah. Twenty mi/32 km SE of Augusta, on the South Carolina side, is the 200,000-ac/80,000-ha **Savannah River Plant,** a major US Department of Energy nuclear facility located largely in BARNWELL Co., South Carolina. Below Savannah, the river flows through a delta, once used for rice culture.

Savin Rock see under WEST HAVEN, Connecticut.

Sawatch Range NNW–SSE trending mountains, part of the W tier of the Rocky Mts. in C Colorado. They extend some 100 mi/160 km from the Eagle R. (N) to Saguache Creek (S); the Arkansas R. rises on and flows down their E side. Mt. ELBERT, the highest (14,433 ft/4399 m) point in Colorado and in the Rockies, is here. Other high peaks include Mt. Massive, the state's second-highest (14,421 ft/4369 m, 10 mi/16 km WSW of LEADVILLE); La Plata Peak (14,361 ft/4377 m), 17 mi/27 km SW of Leadville; and the Collegiate Peaks, 17 mi/27 km S of Leadville, which include Mts. Harvard, Yale, Princeton, Columbia, and Oxford, all over 14,000 ft/4267 m.

Sawtooth Mountains low range, reaching heights of about 2000 ft/610 m, paralleling the shore of L. Superior in the ARROWHEAD REGION of NE Minnesota, and including several state forests. The 150 mi/240 km–long scenic North Shore Drive, extending from Duluth to Grand Portage, runs between the glacier-scoured mountains and L. Superior.

Sawtooth Range rugged, largely NW–SE trending group in SC Idaho, part of the N Rocky Mts., covered by parts of the Boise (SW), Sawtooth (S), and Challis (N, SE) national forests. The Salmon R. rises on its E side. The 760,000-ac/308,000-ha **Sawtooth National Recreation Area,** 60 mi/100 km ENE of Boise, is a popular lake and mountain vacation site. The 2.1 million–ac/850,000-ha **Sawtooth National Forest** encloses the recreation area's S, and has smaller separate units in far S Idaho.

Saybrook see OLD SAYBROOK, Connecticut.

Sayler's Creek see AMELIA Co., Virginia.

Sayreville borough, pop. 34,986, Middlesex Co., E New Jersey, near the mouth of the Raritan R., 5 mi/8 km SE of New Brunswick. Chemicals, plastics, ceramics, photographic film and supplies, and building materials are manufactured here. Sayreville is also a fashionable residential community.

Sayville unincorporated village, pop. 16,550, in Islip town, Suffolk Co., SE New York, on Long Island's South Shore, on Great South Bay, 50 mi/80 km E of Manhattan. It is a summer resort; boating and fishing are important activities. The harvesting of oysters, clams, and scallops were long key to the local economy.

scablands generally flat-topped landscape in which glacial action has loosened volcanic (basaltic) material, leaving a thin, not very fertile soil. BADLANDS are formed by similar action over softer sedimentary rock. The major US scablands are in EC Washington, in areas SW of Spokane, where late-glacial floods also created COULEES in the Columbia Plateau, as in the PALOUSE.

Scapegoat Mountain 9185 ft/2801 m, in the N Rocky Mts., in Lewis and Clark Co., NW Montana, on the Continental Divide, 60 mi/97 km NW of Helena. It rises above the Dearborn R. valley, and is in the Scapegoat Wilderness Area.

Scarborough **1.** town, pop. 12,518, Cumberland Co., SW Maine. It is a residential suburb of Portland and Biddeford-Saco, at the mouth of the Nonesuch R., on the Atlantic coast and US 1 and the Maine Turnpike, about 8 mi/13 km S of Portland. The town incorporates several villages, including PROUT'S NECK. The Snow seafood canning company and Scarborough Downs Race Track are leading industries; others include truck farming, tourism, and the manufacture of shoes and potato chips. The estuary at the Nonesuch River's mouth is called the Scarborough R. **2.** city, pop. 524,598, Toronto Metropolitan Municipality, S Ontario, on L. Ontario, bounded by Markham (N); Pickering and the Rouge R. (E); and Toronto, East York, and North York (W). Formerly chiefly agricultural, it became the site of planned industrial and residential development after World War II. Most heavily developed in the S and W, it also has extensive parkland; the Metro Toronto Zoo is in the NE. Scarborough College of the University of Toronto (1964) is the largest of several local institutions. Scarborough is the fastest-growing city in the Toronto Metropolitan Municipality (8% pop. increase in 1986–91), but rapid expansion is now occurring chiefly in such N suburbs as VAUGHAN and RICHMOND HILL.

Scarsdale town, pop. 16,987, Westchester Co., SE New York, 20 mi/32 km N of New York City. It is an upper-middle-class residential suburb of New York City. British general Sir William Howe had his headquarters in the Griffin House here in Oct. 1776, just before the battle of White Plains.

Scary Creek see under SAINT ALBANS, West Virginia.

Schaumburg village, pop. 68,586, Cook and Du Page counties, NE Illinois, 30 mi/48 km NW of Chicago. It is a residential community that has grown rapidly since the 1960s. There is some light industry, but the main engine of the local economy is the large, multilevel Woodfield Mall. There are also a number of office buildings here. Busse L. is immediately E. Schaumburg Airport is located on the county line, at the S edge of the village.

Schefferville city, pop. 303, in the Nouveau-Québec region of NE Québec, 580 mi/935 km NNE of Québec City, on the Labrador border. It was founded as a COMPANY TOWN in the 1950s, to exploit iron ore deposits, after hydroelectricity became available and rail connections to SEPT-ÎLES and Port Cartier were established. By the 1980s the boom had passed; Schefferville today still has some mining, and is a scientific and regional service center.

Schenectady city, pop. 65,566, seat of Schenectady Co., E New York, on the Mohawk R. and New York State Barge Canal, 13 mi/21 km NW of Albany. Settled in 1661 by Dutch colonists, it took an Iroquoian name referring to local pine plains. In 1690, the settlement was nearly destroyed by Indian and French forces in a siege known as the Schenectady Massacre. English colonists arrived in the 1700s; the site was fortified and developed as a distribution center. Following the opening of the Erie Canal in 1825, shipyards began building canal and river craft. Arrival of the Mohawk and Hudson R. Railroad in 1831 fostered the development of locomotive works, which dominated local industry throughout the 1850s. In 1886, Edison Machine Works moved here from New York City, and the General Electric Company was established in 1892. Industries now manufacture electrical, atomic, and jet machinery, diesel locomotives, wire and cable equipment, chemicals, plastics, and insulating materials. Schenectady houses several industrial research centers, and is the seat of Union College and University (1795) and Schenectady County Community College (1968).

Schenectady County 206 sq mi/534 sq km, pop. 149,285, in E New York, partially in the Mohawk Valley. This small county is cut in the NE by the Mohawk R. and the New York State Barge Canal, on whose S banks lies its seat and largest city, Schenectady. This industrial giant influences the economy of the whole county with its many manufactures and its suburban sprawl, which includes the large township of ROTTERDAM. Dairying, fruit orchards, and other kinds of farming are important in the rural parts of the county.

Schenley Farms residential development in the OAKLAND section of Pittsburgh, Pennsylvania. The residential component of developer Franklin Nicola's plan for Oakland, it features 96 houses by various architects built 1906–20. Marketed to the upper middle class, the homes boasted many features that had been associated exclusively with mansions of the wealthy.

Schenley Park municipal park, 380 ac/154 ha, in Pittsburgh, Pennsylvania, between OAKLAND and SQUIRREL HILL. Phipps Conservatory and the Westinghouse Memorial are here.

Schererville town, pop. 19,926, Lake Co., extreme NW Indiana, 7 mi/11 km S of Hammond and adjacent (E) to Dyer, on the S edge of the highly industrialized CALUMET region. It is a growing residential suburb.

Schertz city, pop. 10,555, in Guadalupe, Bexar, and Comal counties, SC Texas, 19 mi/31 km NE of San Antonio, on Cibolo Creek. An agricultural town, now a growing suburb, it is just N of RANDOLPH AIR FORCE BASE.

Schiller Park village, pop. 11,189, Cook Co., NE Illinois, on the Des Plaines R., immediately NW of Chicago and 13 mi/21 km NW of the Loop. Mainly residential in character, it has such industries as food processing and packaging and the manufacture of tools, clamping devices, and electrical appliances. O'Hare International Airport is adjacent to the W. During the 1960s there was a spate of commercial development along I-294, the Tri-State Tollway, along the W edge of the village.

Schoenbrunn restored village in Tuscarawas Co., EC Ohio, on the Tuscarawas R., just S of New Philadelphia. Located in the 190-ac/77-ha Schoenbrunn State Memorial, it is a replica of the state's first white settlement, founded in 1772 by a group of Moravian missionaries from Pennsylvania led by David Zeisberger, with the aid of Christian Indians. Faced with hostility from the British and their Indian allies, the village was torn down and deserted by its citizens in 1776. Restoration began in the 1920s.

Schofield Barracks military base (1990 pop. 19,597), in Honolulu Co., C Oahu, Hawaii, 19 mi/31 km NW of Honolulu, on the island's central plateau. Wheeler Air Force Base and WAHIAWA are adjacent. With PEARL HARBOR, HICKAM AIR FORCE BASE, and a number of other posts on Oahu, it forms a major US defense complex. It was one target of the Dec. 7, 1941 Japanese attack on Pearl Harbor.

Schoharie County 624 sq mi/1616 sq km, pop. 31,589, in EC New York. Its seat is the village of Schoharie (pop. 1045). The county is overwhelmingly rural and agricultural. Dairy and truck farming, haying, fruit orchards, and poultry raising are all important. There are several noted underground caves, including HOWE CAVERNS.

Schoharie River also, **Schoharie Creek** 85 mi/137 km long, in EC New York. Its name Iroquoian for "driftwood," it rises on the NE slopes of the Catskills, in Greene Co., and flows NW to Prattsville, where it enters the **Schoharie Reservoir,** impounded by Gilboa Dam. It then passes NNE through Middleburgh to Schoharie, where it receives Cobleskill Creek from the W. Its valley is a fertile area ideal for growing vegetables. The reservoir provides water to the New York City area through the Shandaken Tunnel, which runs c.17 mi/27 km SSE to Esopus Creek, which in turn feeds into the ASHOKAN RESERVOIR. From Schoharie the river flows NE and N past Central Bridge, Esperance, and Burtonsville, to the Mohawk R. at Fort Hunter, 5 mi/8 km W of AMSTERDAM. Before reaching the Mohawk, it is crossed by an old trestle of the ERIE CANAL.

Schoodic Peninsula coastal promontory marking the E boundary of FRENCHMAN BAY, Winter Harbor town, Hancock Co., SE Maine, 8 mi/13 km SE of Bar Harbor. Schoodic Head stands 440 ft/134 m. Most of the peninsula is part of Acadia National Park. The small Schoodic I. is just SE of the peninsula; **Schoodic Point,** its SE extreme, is considered the divide between the western, more heavily traveled, and the eastern, relatively isolated, parts of the Maine coast.

Schroon Lake in NE New York, in the E Adirondack Mts., 15 mi/24 km WSW of Ticonderoga. It is 9 mi/14 km NNE–SSW, and up to 1.5 mi/2 km wide. Schroon Lake village lies at the N end.

Schuylkill County 782 sq mi/2025 sq km, pop. 152,585, in EC Pennsylvania. The Schuylkill R. flows through it from N of POTTSVILLE, the county seat and largest community. In the Allegheny Mts., the county is heavily forested; coal mining is important.

Schuylkill Expressway limited-access highway, running 21 mi/34 km between the WALT WHITMAN BRIDGE in South Philadelphia (SE) and the Pennsylvania Turnpike in KING OF PRUSSIA (NW), Pennsylvania. The expressway follows the course of the Schuylkill R., passing through West Conshohocken and Fairmount Park, and crossing City Line Ave. and Market St.

Schuylkill River 130 mi/210 km long, in E Pennsylvania. It rises at Sharp Mt., in Schuylkill Co., and flows SW to Pottsville, then generally SE past Reading, Pottstown, and Norristown, to join the Delaware R. at Philadelphia. It is navigable by canal boat as far as Port Clinton, 98 mi/158 km upstream, where it is joined from the N by the **Little Schuylkill River** (c. 35 mi/56 km long).

Scioto County 613 sq mi/1588 sq km, pop. 80,327, in S Ohio, bounded by the Ohio R. (S), and intersected by the Scioto R. Its seat is Portsmouth, where there is diversified manufacturing. Iron ore, coal, and limestone are among its resources. The county is largely woodland, with Shawnee State Forest in the SW. There is also dairy, fruit, grain, and livestock farming.

Scioto River 237 mi/382 km long, in Ohio. It rises W of Kenton in W Ohio and flows SE, turning S just W of Marion and running past Columbus and Chillicothe to join the Ohio R. at Portsmouth.

Scituate 1. town, pop. 16,786, Plymouth Co., SE Massachusetts, on the Atlantic Ocean, 21 mi/34 km SE of Boston. Long a summer resort with truck and fruit farming and maritime trades, it is now a growing suburb. The villages of North Scituate, Egypt, Shore Acres, Sand Hill, and Greenbush are included. **2.** town, pop. 9796, Providence Co., NC Rhode Island, just W of Cranston and 11 mi/18 km W of Providence, on the North Branch of the Pawtuxet R. (dammed to create the Scituate Reservoir). It includes the villages of Hope and North Scituate, the administrative center, and is largely suburban and rural.

Scollay Square former district in downtown Boston, Massachusetts, at the E foot of Beacon Hill. A fashionable mid-19th-century residential area, it had become by 1900 the resort of gamblers, prostitutes, tattoo artists, and servicemen and others looking for a good time in its burlesque theaters and other institutions. In 1958 the city began a transformation of the area into the GOVERNMENT CENTER; Scollay Square's habitués moved a short distance SW, to the COMBAT ZONE.

Scotch Plains township, pop. 21,160, Union Co., NE New Jersey, 8 mi/13 km W of Linden. It is bounded by the Watchung Reservation (N) and the Ashbrook Reservation (S). Originally a Lenni Lenape village, it was settled by Scottish dissenters and Quakers (1684). It was part of Elizabeth until 1794, of WESTFIELD (1794–1877), and of Fanwood (1877–1917), before becoming independent. Scotch Plains is now an affluent suburb.

Scotchtown see under ASHLAND, Virginia.

Scotlandville see under BATON ROUGE, Louisiana.

Scott Air Force Base see under BELLEVILLE, Illinois.

Scott County 1. 459 sq mi/1189 sq km, pop. 150,979, in EC Iowa, on the Mississippi R. across (W and N) from Illinois, and on the Wapsipinicon R. (N). The industrial cities of DAVENPORT and BETTENDORF are in the S; the agricultural N is rich in corn. Showman "Buffalo Bill" Cody was born near McCausland, in the NE, in 1846. **2.** 357 sq mi/925 sq km, pop. 57,846, in EC Minnesota, bordered by the Minnesota R. (N and W). At the SW edge of the Twin Cities metropolitan area, it ranges from outer suburbs like SHAKOPEE (its seat) and PRIOR LAKE in the N to dairy farmland in the S.

Scott Peak see under BITTERROOT RANGE, Idaho.

Scottsbluff city, pop. 13,711, Scotts Bluff Co., W Nebraska, on the North Platte R., 20 mi/32 km E of the Wyoming border, in the PANHANDLE. It is named for nearby buttes that rise steeply from the plains; these formed a major landmark for travelers along the OREGON and MORMON trails. Just SW is the **Scotts Bluff National Monument,** incorporating an 800-ft/245-m promontory. In a fertile river valley, the city is an important trade center for W Nebraska and E Wyoming. Among the products it processes and distributes are flour, beet sugar, corn, beans, dairy goods, and meats. Oil is refined, and tourism is also important. Nebraska Western College (1926) is here.

Scottsboro city, pop. 13,786, seat of Jackson Co., NE Alabama, near the Tennessee R., at the edge of the Cumberland Plateau, 35 mi/56 km ESE of Huntsville. An agricultural center, it processes cotton and lumber, and makes clothing. In 1931 it was the focus of national and international attention during the first trial of the nine "Scottsboro Boys," black youths charged with raping two white women on a train elsewhere in Alabama; subsequent trials in DECATUR, appeals, and other legal procedures followed before eight were freed in the 1940s (the last escaped to Michigan in 1948).

Scottsdale city, pop. 130,069, Maricopa Co., SC Arizona, a largely residential suburb 8 mi/13 km ENE of downtown Phoenix. It lies at the W edge of the Salt R. Indian Reservation. Settled in 1895, it is now a rapidly expanding center for resort and retirement communities. Tourism is an important industry, with visitors attracted to Taliesin West, the architectural school established (1937) by Frank Lloyd Wright; the Cosanti Foundation, an architectural and crafts complex initiated in 1956 by Paolo Soleri; and Rawhide, a replica of an 1880s Western town, among other sites. The business district features Arizona arts and crafts and retail stores. Manufactures include electronic components, clothing, and ceramics, and there is a growing financial and corporate sector.

Scotts Valley city, pop. 8615, Santa Cruz Co., WC California, on the Carbonera Creek, 5 mi/8 km N of Santa Cruz. It has some high-tech industry and is home to Bethany Bible College (1919).

Scranton city, pop. 81,805, seat of Lackawanna Co., NE Pennsylvania, on the Lackawanna R., 104 mi/167 km NNW of Philadelphia, in the ANTHRACITE BELT, and NW of the Pocono Mts. It is an industrial and trade center producing electrical machinery, electronic equipment, metal goods, textiles, clothing, and leather goods. Printing is also important. Scranton was founded in 1786 but did not really develop until George and Selden Scranton arrived in 1840 and established five iron furnaces. Their Lackawanna Iron and Steel Company moved to Buffalo in 1902, but Scranton continued to grow. As the coal industry declined after the 1920s, city leaders devised the Scranton Plan for industrial expansion, which drew national recognition. Scranton in the 1990s, however, much reduced in population, struggled against regional decline. One development looked to was Steamtown National Historic Site, devoted to the history of steam railroads, and due to open in 1994. Educational institutions in the city include the University of Scranton (1888) and Marywood College (1915).

Scugog, Lake see under KAWARTHA LAKES, Ontario.

Scuppernong River short estuarial river on the S side of Abermarle Sound, SE of Edenton, in E North Carolina. The town of Columbia (pop. 836, seat of Tyrrell Co.) is on it. The river gave its name to a type of green grape.

Seabrook **1.** see under LANHAM, Maryland. **2.** town, pop. 6503, Rockingham Co., SE New Hampshire. It is on US 1 and 95, the Atlantic Ocean, and the Massachusetts border, 13 mi/21 km SW of Portsmouth. Settled in 1638, it has been a boat and shoe manufacturing town. Seabrook is best known today as the site of a Public Service Company of New Hampshire nuclear plant, on saltmarshes in the town's NE, that opened in 1990, eleven years behind schedule, after years of protest by environmentalists and area residents.

Sea Cliff see under BAKER BEACH, San Francisco, California.

Seadrift city, pop. 1277, Calhoun Co., S Texas, on San Antonio Bay, 56 mi/89 km NE of Corpus Christi. Near the mouth of the Guadalupe R., it is a fishing and chemical production center.

Seaford **1.** city, pop. 5689, Sussex Co., SW Delaware, at the head of navigation on the NANTICOKE R., 14 mi/23 km WSW of Georgetown. Du Pont first produced nylon here in 1939, and Seaford is a nylon industry center. Other industries have included canning, oyster packing, and shipbuilding. **2.** unincorporated village, pop. 15,597, in Hempstead town, Nassau Co., SE New York, on Long Island's South Shore, 25 mi/40 km ESE of Manhattan. It is almost entirely residential. The Tackapausha Nature Preserve is here.

Sea Gate see under CONEY ISLAND, New York.

Seagoville city, pop. 8969, Dallas and Kaufman counties, NE Texas, 17 mi/27 km SE of downtown Dallas and adjacent to the larger city's SE. A suburb with corporate offices, it also has a Federal prison.

Sea Island one of Georgia's SEA ISLANDS, separated from SAINT SIMONS I. (NW) by narrow creeks. It has been noted since the late 19th century as a resort for the wealthy and powerful, with luxury hotels and golf courses.

Sea Islands group of several hundred islands in the Atlantic Ocean off the coast of South Carolina, Georgia, and N Florida, between Winyah Bay and the GRAND STRAND (N) and the mouth of the SAINT JOHNS R. (S). Some of the islands are uninhabited nature preserves, some are resorts, and some are repositories of Gullah culture, a blend of West African, Caribbean, and American influences maintained by blacks whose ancestors settled there as slaves in the 18th and 19th centuries. The main islands, N–S, are Isle of Palms, Sullivans, Folly, James, Johns, Kiawah, Wadmalaw, Edisto, St. Helena, Port Royal, Morgan, Hunting, Parris, Hilton Head, Daufuskie, and Folly in South Carolina; Tybee, Wassaw, Ossabaw, St. Catherines, Sapelo, Butler, St. Simons, Jekyll, and Cumberland in Georgia; and Amelia in Florida. CUMBERLAND I., 20 mi/32 km long, is the largest island in the chain. Hilton Head, Daufuskie, St. Simons, Sea, Jekyll, and Amelia islands are primarily resorts; Parris I. is a Marine Corps base. The islands are low and sandy, with pine and live oak forests, tidal creeks, and saltmarshes. Truck farming, oystering, fishing, and tourism are the main industries. Causeways and bridges connect many of the islands to the mainland and each other, and the Atlantic Intracoastal Waterway runs through the passages between them and the coast. Originally inhabited by the Guale and Cusabo Indians, some as early as 2500 B.C., the islands were explored and partially colonized by the Spanish in the 16th century. Black slaves were present almost from the first European settlement. By the mid 18th century, with the founding of the Georgia colony by James Oglethorpe, the English were well on their way to taking over the southern Atlantic coast and islands from the Spanish. Rice, indigo, and long-staple Sea Island cotton were grown on plantations in the early 19th century, but during the Union occupation of the Civil War and afterwards, many white owners left, as freed slaves from many parts of the South were apportioned land on the islands by the Federal government. Cotton remained the major crop until an influx of boll weevils in the 1920s destroyed the plants, and more diversified farming was introduced.

Seal Beach city, pop. 25,098, Orange Co., SW California, on the Pacific Ocean, across Coyote Creek (SE) from Long Beach. Incorporated in 1915, it has a Naval Weapons Station and a National Wildlife Refuge, along with oilfields, some corporate offices, and bathing beaches. It was largely agricultural until the 1960s.

Seaport Village shopping and entertainment complex in Downtown SAN DIEGO, California, on San Diego Bay. Initiated in 1980, it stimulated much subsequent waterfront development.

Searcy city, pop. 15,180, seat of White Co., EC Arkansas, 45 mi/72 km NE of Little Rock, near the Little Red R. A popular 19th-century spa known as Sulphur Springs, it later developed as an agricultural center. Cotton and timber production became central to the economy. Today, livestock, poultry, eggs, strawberries, and light manufacturing are important. Harding University (1924) is here.

Sears Tower office tower, the world's tallest occupied building, in the LOOP in Chicago, Illinois. Designed by architect Bruce Graham and opened in 1973, it is 1454 ft/443 m high, and has 110 stories.

Seaside **1.** city, pop. 38,901, Monterey Co., WC California, on the S shore of Monterey Bay, immediately E of Monterey. It is a growing resort, residential, commercial, and tourist center, one of the Monterey area's less affluent communities. FORT ORD adjoins (N and E). **2.** city, pop. 5359, Clatsop Co., extreme NW Oregon, on the Pacific Ocean, 74 mi/119 km NW of Portland. Thirteen mi/21 km SSW of Astoria, and just NE of Tillamook Head, it is at the end of the Lewis and Clark Trail, where the explorers wintered in 1805–06. A monument and a salt cairn, where they extracted salt from seawater, are here. In the 1870s Seaside became a major summer resort, and remains popular today.

Sea-Tac also, **Seatac** unincorporated community, pop. 22,694, King Co., WC Washington, surrounding the Seattle-Tacoma International Airport, 8 mi/13 km S of downtown Seattle. It is a commercial and residential suburb.

Seat Pleasant city, pop. 5359, Prince George's Co., SC Maryland, adjacent to the E corner of Washington, D.C., and (SE) to Fairmount Heights. It is a residential suburb.

Seattle city, pop. 516,259, seat of King Co., WC Washington, on Puget Sound (W) and L. Washington (E), which are connected by the Lake Washington Ship Canal, bisecting the city. The most populous city and the industrial and commercial center of the Pacific Northwest, it is the center of the three-county (KING, SNOHOMISH, and PIERCE) Seattle-Tacoma metropolitan area (CMSA), which has a pop. of 2,559,164. Major suburbs include EVERETT, REDMOND, BELLEVUE, and RENTON, and many commuters live on BAINBRIDGE and other Puget Sound islands. The city was first settled on Alki Point (now in WEST SEATTLE) in 1851, and moved the next year to the present site of PIONEER SQUARE, on the E of ELLIOTT BAY, where Henry Yesler's sawmill and SKID ROAD formed an early focal point. Boatbuilding was another important industry in the settlement, which was named for Sealth (or Seathl), a friendly Duwamish leader. Growth at first lagged behind that of Tacoma, 27 mi/43 km SSW. In 1889, fire destroyed the business district, which was soon rebuilt. In the 1890s the Great Northern Railway reached Seattle, and the port became more active. The Klondike-Alaska gold rush (1897) brought a sudden boom, and Seattle soon outstripped not only Tacoma but also Portland, Oregon, as the region's leading city. The opening (1914) of the Panama Canal and World War I shipbuilding furthered the prosperity of the city, which engaged in major engineering projects, building (1917) the L. Washington Ship Canal, vastly extending its port facilities, and leveling some of its many hills to provide landfill for new waterfront development. The rapid growth of industry in Seattle contributed to strains expressed in a brief 1919 general strike. Shipbuilding was again prominent in World War II, in which the Boeing company also made the area a center of aircraft production, a role it still holds today. Continuing prosperity was reflected in the Century 21 World's Fair (1962), which was not only a financial success but left the city with the SEATTLE CENTER and other new developments. Its position as the gateway to Alaska (it is at the S end of the INSIDE PASSAGE) has contributed to Seattle's importance since the 1897 gold rush; that it is the Lower 48 port closest to Japan and the rest of East Asia has also been key. Its situation between the Cascade Range (E) and the Olympic Peninsula (W), and on Puget Sound, along with its hills and varied water frontage, have made the city also a tourist and convention mecca, and have contributed to its attractiveness as a residential center. It has a large fishing fleet and extensive recreational boating facilities. It remains a major shipbuilder, and other manufactures include wood and paper products, metal goods, machinery, canned fish and other processed foods, and a range of high-tech items. Leading institutions include the University of Washington (1861), Seattle University (1891; Catholic), and Seattle Pacific University (1891; Methodist). A cultural hub, the city is noted for its cosmopolitanism and, among others, for its painters, cartoonists, and rock musicians. Seattle-Tacoma International Airport is 11 mi/18 km S of Downtown, about halfway between the two cities. See also: BALLARD; BOEING FIELD (and Georgetown); CAPITOL HILL; FREMONT; the HIGHLANDS; INTERNATIONAL DISTRICT (Chinatown); MAGNOLIA; NORTHGATE; PIONEER SQUARE (and Underground, and Klondike Gold Rush National Historic Park); PORTAGE BAY (and L. Union); QUEEN ANNE HILL; SAND POINT; SEATTLE CENTER (and the Space Needle); SKID ROAD; UNIVERSITY DISTRICT; WEST SEATTLE (and Alki Point).

Seattle Center 74-ac/30-ha multiuse complex, 1.4 mi/2.3 km NW of downtown SEATTLE, Washington. It was created for the 1962 Century 21 World's Fair, and is now a focal point of city cultural and entertainment life. The 605-ft/184-m Space Needle, with a rotating restaurant near the top, dominates the complex, which also includes the 14,000-seat Coliseum, home to the SuperSonics (basketball); the Opera House; the Pacific Science Center; and other heavily visited buildings. A monorail connects the center with the Westlake Mall, near Downtown.

Sea World any of several marine-life theme parks that are major tourist attractions in their areas. The largest, Sea World of Texas, is 15 mi/24 km NW of downtown San Antonio, Texas, outside the city limits at the edge of the Hill Country. Covering 250 ac/100 ha, it is adjoined by Fiesta Texas, another major theme park. Other Sea Worlds are in San Diego, California; Orlando, Florida; and Aurora, Ohio.

Sebago Lake resort lake, the second-largest lake in Maine, in Cumberland Co., 12 mi/19 km NW of Portland. About 12 mi/19 km long and 1–8 mi/1.6–13 km wide, it is connected by locks with neighboring Long Lake, forming a popular boating waterway on the old (1830s) Cumberland Canal system. Sebago is the primary source of Portland's water.

Sebastian city, pop. 10,205, Indian River Co., EC Florida, 11 mi/18 mi NNW of Vero Beach. It boomed in the 1980s as a resort community. Sebastian Inlet, a breach in the barrier island across the Indian R. lagoon (E), was the site of early 18th-century Spanish landings.

Sebastopol city, pop. 7004, Sonoma Co., NW California, 7 mi/11 km WSW of Santa Rosa, the center of a hillside area famous for its apples, with processing plants and a growing residential sector. Tourism is important, and there are wineries nearby.

Sebec Lake in Piscataquis Co., C Maine, 5 mi/8 km N of Dover-Foxcroft. This 6000-ac/2400-ha lake is 10 mi/16 km long, and is the source of the Sebec R. Bordered by Peaks-Kenny State Park, it is a popular resort area.

Sebring city, pop. 8900, seat of Highlands Co., SC Florida, on L. Jackson, 50 mi/80 km SE of Lakeland. In one of Florida's finest citrus and avocado growing areas, it is a fruit and beef packing and shipping center. It is best known, however, for its Grand Prix sports car race, a 12-hour endurance contest run annually since 1959. The city was established as a planned community in 1912 by pottery manufacturer George Sebring.

Secaucus town, pop. 14,061, Hudson Co., NE New Jersey, on the Hackensack R., 4 mi/6 km N of downtown Jersey City. Manufactured here are metal goods, pharmaceuticals, coffee, frozen food, and other products; there are numerous warehouses. Secaucus is the site of an enormous retail outlet complex and of the Meadowlands Convention Center.

Second City nickname for Chicago, Illinois, referring to its relationship to New York. Used since about 1900, the name may suggest a cultural role, among others; it no longer describes population size, as Los Angeles surpassed Chicago in the 1980s.

Second Ward one of the original (1839–40) quadrants of Houston, Texas, extending E and NE from Downtown, along the Buffalo Bayou. The site of Frosttown, a black post–Civil War settlement, it became by the 1920s a central part (with MAGNOLIA, SE) of Houston's Mexican BARRIO.

Security-Widefield unincorporated community, pop. 23,822, El Paso Co., C Colorado, on Fountain Creek, 7 mi/11 km SE of Colorado Springs. It is a rapidly expanding residential suburb whose population more than quadrupled in the 1980s.

Sedalia city, pop. 19,800, seat of Pettis Co., WC Missouri, 58 mi/93 km WNW of Jefferson City. It is a trading and rail shipping center for a rich agricultural region, with railroad shops, meatpacking plants, flour mills, and many industries producing such products as glass, trailers, chemicals, and foodstuffs. The city celebrates its former resident the ragtime composer Scott Joplin (1868–1917) with an annual ragtime festival. Sedalia is home to the Missouri State Fair each August, and State Fair Community College (1966) is here. Whiteman Air Force Base is W.

Sedgwick County 1007 sq mi/2608 sq km, pop. 403,662, in SC Kansas. Its seat and by far its largest city is WICHITA. DERBY, HAYSVILLE, Valley Center (pop. 3624), and Park City (pop. 5050) are other larger municipalities. This plains county engages in wheat growing and cattle raising, and there are some oil and natural gas fields. The aircraft industry in and around Wichita is important.

Sedona city, pop. 7720, Yavapai and Coconino counties, NC Arizona, 25 mi/40 km SSW of Flagstaff. An agricultural community from prehistory into the 20th century, it has since the 1970s been an art and tourist center and a resort, retirement, and spiritual mecca. "Vortexes," which adherents of New Age philosophy believe to be intense concentrations of spiritual energies, were identified here in the 1980s, attracting numbers of metaphysical believers to the red rocks and mesas surrounding Sedona. The city lies at the N end of popular Oak Creek Canyon. The Catholic Chapel of the Holy Cross, designed by Frank Lloyd Wright, is just SE.

Sedro Woolley city, pop. 6031, Skagit Co., NW Washington, on the Skagit R., 20 mi/32 km SE of Bellingham. In 1898, Sedro (from the Spanish *cedro,* for its native cedar), a supply center for miners and loggers at the head of navigation on the Skagit, merged with Woolley, a sawmill center and railroad junction. The commercial hub of an agricultural and lumbering region, the city is also an outfitting center for tourists going to North Cascades National Park (E).

Seekonk town, pop. 13,046, Bristol Co., SE Massachusetts, adjacent (E) to East Providence and Pawtucket, Rhode Island. Settled in 1636 as part of Rehoboth, it was separately incorporated in 1812; East Providence was set off from Seekonk in 1862. Seekonk is a largely residential suburb.

Seekonk River see under BLACKSTONE R., Massachusetts and Rhode Island.

Seguin city, pop. 18,853, seat of Guadalupe Co., SC Texas, 33 mi/52 km NE of San Antonio, on the Guadalupe R. Founded in 1838, it is named to honor Juan Seguin, a Texas independence hero. The city has agricultural processing and varied other industries, and is in an oil and livestock producing region. It is the seat of Texas Lutheran College (1891).

Seguin Island see under POPHAM BEACH, Maine.

seigneurie form of land ownership in NEW FRANCE between 1627 and 1854. Inspired by Norman feudal customs, the seigneurie was a grant by the royally established Compagnie des Cents-Associés (Company of the Hundred Associates), or Company of New France, to a colonist (the *seigneur*) who undertook to people the land and develop an agricultural community. The land was then subdivided and rented to *habitants,* who farmed what was usually a long, thin lot (*rang* or *concession,* later also called a ribbon farm) extending inland from the riverbank; these allowed access to transportation, and kept the community compact. The habitant's duties included paying rent and milling fees to the seigneur, performing collective labor for the seigneurie, and occasionally bearing arms. Seigneuries were granted to nobles, but also to religious institutions, military leaders, and civil administrators; over time, many habitants became seigneurs. After the British conquest (1763), seigneuries began to give away to free TOWNSHIPS. In 1854 they were abolished. Their effect on community development is seen most clearly in Québec's St. Lawrence Valley, but also as far away as Louisiana.

Selden unincorporated village, pop. 20,608, in Brookhaven town, Suffolk Co., SE New York, in C Long Island, 6 mi/10 km S of Port Jefferson. A primarily residential community, it has some light industry, and Suffolk County Community College (1959) is here.

Selfridge Air Force Base see under MOUNT CLEMENS, Michigan.

Selinsgrove borough, pop. 5384, Snyder Co., C Pennsylvania, on the Susquehanna R., 39 mi/63 km N of Harrisburg. The seat of Susquehanna University (1858), it is also the birthplace of Jacob S. Coxey, a quarry owner who led the march of "Coxey's Army" on Washington in 1894, demanding job creation through public works projects.

Selkirk town, pop. 9815, SE Manitoba, 20 mi/32 km N of Winnipeg, on the Red R., near the S end of L. Winnipeg. A Scottish settlement, it was founded (1812) in the Earl of Selkirk's RED RIVER COLONY. Lower Fort Garry, an 1830s stone structure, built by fur traders, is nearby. L. Winnipeg's chief port, Selkirk is today the service center for an agricultural region. Fish and lumber exports, boatbuilding, ship repair, and commercial fishing are major industries. It has iron and steel foundries as well. The Manitoba Highland Gathering takes place here every July.

Selkirk Mountains NW–SE trending range, in the Columbia Mts. section of the ROCKY Mts., mostly in SE British Columbia. They extend over 200 mi/320 km S from the Columbia R. bend near Mica Creek, 80 mi/130 km N of REVELSTOKE, into Idaho, and are flanked by the Columbia R. and the MONASHEE Mts. (W) and by the PURCELL Mts. and Kootenay L. (E). The highest peaks, in the N, are Mt. Sir Sandford (11,590 ft/3533 m) and Mt. Farnham (11,342 ft/3457 m). In the N section is GLACIER NATIONAL PARK. Within the park the CANADIAN PACIFIC RAILWAY follows Rogers Pass (4364 ft/1330) m), surveyed 1881. Heavy snowfall (sometimes over 700 in/1780 cm annually) led to construction of the Connaught Tunnel (1916) in the pass. In 1962 the TRANS-CANADA HIGHWAY's final section was opened through the pass. In the S, the Selkirks have been mined and logged.

Selma **1.** city, pop. 23,755, seat of Dallas Co., SC Alabama, 43 mi/70 km W of Montgomery, on the Alabama R. Settled in 1815, it served as a major Confederate arsenal, foundry, and supply depot during the Civil War, and was burned by Union troops following a battle outside the city on April 2, 1865. After the Civil War, agriculture and industry diversified. In early 1965 a black voter registration drive in the city was met with violence, and on March 7 a protest march to Montgomery was violently suppressed on the far side of the Edmund Pettus Bridge, across the Alabama. Civil rights activists then marched from Selma to Montgomery, with the Rev. Martin Luther King, Jr., on March 21–25. A shipping and market center for local farms, Selma houses cotton gins and meatpacking plants, and manufactures farm equipment, lawnmowers, brick, and cigars. It is the seat of Selma University (1878) and Concordia College (1922). **2.** city, pop. 14,757, Fresno Co., SC California, in the San Joaquin Valley, 15 mi/24 km SE of Fresno. Incorporated in 1893, it is a processing center for grapes and other local produce. **3.** town, pop. 4600, Johnston Co., C North Carolina, near the Neuse R., 28 mi/45 km SE of Raleigh. A trade and manufacturing center and rail junction, it produces textiles, fertilizer, cottonseed oil, lumber, and wine. A state prison is just NW.

Selway-Bitterroot Wilderness 1.3 million ac/530,000 ha (2030 sq mi/5260 sq km), in EC Idaho and W Montana. One of the largest US WILDERNESS AREAS, it incorporates parts of four national forests on both sides of the Continental Divide and the Bitterroot Mts. The 100 mi/160 km–long **Selway R.** runs N and W from it to join the Middle Fork of the CLEARWATER R.

Selwyn Mountains NW–SE trending range along the border of the Yukon Territory (W) and Northwest Territories (E), reaching 9751 ft/2972 m at Keele Peak, the site of a major ice field. The Selwyns were largely unexplored until after World War II, when the 513-mi/825-km Canol (Canadian Oil) Road was built to service an abortive pipeline between WHITEHORSE, Yukon Territory, and NORMAN WELLS, Northwest Territories. The LOGAN Mts. (SE) are often considered part of the Selwyns, and the Selwyns part of the MACKENZIE Mts.

Seminary Ridge see under GETTYSBURG, Pennsylvania.

Seminoe Reservoir 32 sq mi/83 sq km, in Carbon Co., SC Wyoming. Fed by the Medicine Bow and North Platte rivers, it is impounded just S of the PATHFINDER RESERVOIR by the concrete-arch **Seminoe Dam,** part of the Kendrick Irrigation Project, providing flood control, irrigation, and hydroelectric power. It was completed in 1939 and is 295 ft/90 m tall.

Seminole city, pop. 7071, Seminole Co., C Oklahoma, 15 mi/24 km SE of Shawnee. Settled in 1890, it has oil refineries and manufactures oilfield equipment. It also has creameries and produces various processed foods.

Seminole, Lake see under CHATTAHOOCHEE R., Georgia.

Seminole County 298 sq mi/772 sq km, pop. 287,529, in EC Florida, bounded N and E by the St. Johns R. Its seat is SANFORD. The county is a popular vacation site. Its SW corner is just N of Orlando, and contains such communities as Altamonte Springs and Casselberry. Agricultural activity in the county is concentrated in its E section. The region is noted for its celery, and produces vegetables, citrus fruits, corn, livestock, and poultry.

Senatobia city, pop. 4772, seat of Tate Co., NW Mississippi, in the N DELTA, on Interstate 55, 28 mi/45 km SE of Oxford. Near Senatahoba Creek, on an ancient trail from PONTOTOC RIDGE to the Mississippi R., which De Soto may have used, it was settled on the new railroad in 1856 as a cotton trade center. Union forces burned it during the Civil War. Northwest Mississippi Community College (1927) is here.

Seneca County **1.** 327 sq mi/847 sq km, pop. 33,683, in WC New York, in the heart of the FINGER LAKES, partially bounded by the two largest lakes, Seneca L. (W) and Cayuga L. (E). It has two seats, Ovid and WATERLOO. The long, narrow county is crossed in the NE by the New York State Barge Canal. It is mainly a dairying and farming region, with a number of wineries, and attracts many tourists. There is some manufacturing, particularly in SENECA FALLS and Waterloo, in the N part. The **Seneca Army Depot,** in Varick and Romulus townships (C), has been a major US nuclear weapons storage facility through the Cold War. **2.** 553 sq mi/1432 sq km, pop. 59,733, in N Ohio, intersected by the Sandusky R. and tributaries. The seat of this largely rural county is TIFFIN. The economy depends primarily on farming (dairy, grain, livestock, and poultry), and there are clay and limestone deposits. Fostoria and Tiffin have substantial manufacturing.

Seneca Falls town, pop. 9384, Seneca Co., WC New York, in the FINGER LAKES, on the Seneca R. just W of Cayuga L., 35 mi/56 km WSW of Syracuse. It was settled in 1787, and its 50-ft/15-m waterfall powered early industries including the production of fire engines. It was the home of Amelia Jenks Bloomer (1818–94), the suffragist who introduced bloomers to the world. Her colleague Elizabeth Cady Stanton (1815–1902) lived here and was a prime organizer of the first women's rights convention in the US, held here in 1848; the Women's Rights National Historical Park is here. Today Seneca Falls is a manufacturing center, producing television components, pumps, metal products, hosiery, and processed food from nearby orchards. It is the seat of Eisenhower College of the Rochester Institute of Technology (1965).

Seneca Lake largest and deepest of the FINGER LAKES in WC New York. It is 35 mi/56 km N–S, 2 mi/3 km wide, and 600 ft/183 m deep. It lies between KEUKA L. (W) and L. CAYUGA; WATKINS GLEN is at its S end. At the N end, across from GENEVA, the **Seneca River** drains the lake toward L. Cayuga. The river passes Waterloo and Seneca Falls, and flows generally ENE, 65 mi/105 km, before joining the Oneida R., 12 mi/19 km NW of Syracuse, to form the Oswego R.

Sept-Îles city, pop. 24,848, Côte-Nord (North Shore) region, SE Québec, 332 mi/534 km NE of Québec City, on the Gulf of St. Lawrence. Built on the site of a 17th-century trading post, it is the administrative and service center for the region. A group of rocky islands protects its circular bay, which is a transshipment point for ocean trade and (since the 1950s) a shipping outlet for the mineral and iron ore deposits of Nouvelle-Québec and Labrador. Salmon fishing and hunting are also important.

Sepulveda C SAN FERNANDO VALLEY section of Los Angeles, California, 17 mi/27 km NW of Downtown, S of Mission Hills and NW of Panorama City. Largely residential, it takes its name from a local RANCHO family. Sepulveda Blvd., which runs N–S through the Valley as I-405, connects San Fernando (N) with WESTSIDE Los Angeles through **Sepulveda Canyon** in the Santa Monica Mts.; S of the mountains it becomes the San Diego Freeway.

Sequatchie River 80 mi/130 km long, in E Tennessee. It rises on Brady Mt., in S Cumberland Co., and flows SSW past Pikeville, Dunlap, and Whitewell, to the Tennessee R., S of Jasper, on the Alabama border. Its NE–SW valley separates the main body of the CUMBERLAND PLATEAU (W) from WALDEN RIDGE (E).

Sequoia National Forest c.1.1 million ac/460,000 ha (1765 sq mi/4575 sq km), in SC California, S of SEQUOIA NATIONAL PARK, at the S end of the SIERRA NEVADA, with two separate units on the NW edge of the Mojave Desert. Noted for its sequoias and foxtail pines, it extends W to the San Joaquin Valley.

Sequoia National Park 402,500 ac/163,500 ha (629 sq mi/1629 sq km) in the Sierra Nevada, EC California, adjacent (S) to KINGS CANYON NATIONAL PARK. Mt. WHITNEY and the Sierra Crest are on its E border. The park encloses Mineral King Valley, an 1870s silver boom locale, and headwaters of the Kaweah and Kern rivers, but is best known for its big trees (sequoias), esp. for the Giant Forest, home to the General Sherman Tree, at 275 ft/84 m tall and with a 103-ft/

31-m girth considered the world's largest tree; it is more than 2500 years old.

Sequoyah nuclear power plant: see under CHICKAMAUGA DAM, Tennessee.

Serpent Mound also, **Great Serpent Mound** prehistoric earthwork and archaeological site, in Adams Co., S Ohio, near Locust Grove. One of the best-known of the Indian mounds, this sinuous structure resembles a serpent swallowing an egg. Measuring 1330 ft/406 m long and 1–5 ft/0.3–1.5 m high, it was probably used for religious purposes. It is situated in Serpent Mound State Park, along with adjacent mounds.

Serpent Mounds Provincial Park in S Ontario, 8 mi/13 km SE of PETERBOROUGH. The 194 ft/59 m–long earthen structure on a cliff overlooking Rice L. is Canada's only known MOUND BUILDER site, over 1800 years old.

Setauket unincorporated village, pop. (with E. Setauket) 13,634, in Brookhaven town, Suffolk Co., SE New York, on Setauket Harbor (the W arm of Port Jefferson Harbor), 2 mi/3 km W of Port Jefferson. It is a residential village with a number of Colonial homes.

Seul, Lac in NW Ontario, 30 mi/50 km N of DRYDEN. Highly irregular in shape, it covers some 640 sq mi/1658 sq km, and is drained W toward L. WINNIPEG by the English R. The Cree, before the mid 18th century, and now the Ojibwa, have lived in the area. Now an important outdoor recreation area, the lake also has some commercial fishing.

Seven Corners unincorporated community, pop. 7280, Fairfax Co., NE Virginia, a Washington suburb adjoining (SE) Falls Church and (W) Arlington Co. US 50 and other roads meet here, and there are several large shopping plazas at the intersections.

Seven Devils Mountains semicircle of peaks in W Idaho, forming part of the E wall of HELLS CANYON, on the Snake R., in a region rich in copper and other minerals. Their highest point is 9393 ft/2863 m at He Devil Mt.

Seven Hills **1.** in reference to the hills on which classical Rome was built, the hills of SAN FRANCISCO, California. Although there are more than 40 sizable hills in the city (a few have been removed for landfill), the seven most prominent are said to be Mt. DAVIDSON (the highest, at 938 ft/286 m); the TWIN PEAKS; NOB, RUSSIAN, and TELEGRAPH hills; and either Lone Mt. or Mt. Sutro. **2.** city, pop. 12,339, Cuyahoga Co., N Ohio, 10 mi/16 km S of Cleveland, of which it is a commuter suburb. Part of its city hall is a schoolhouse dating from 1861.

Seven (Lost) Cities of Cibola see CIBOLA.

Seven Oaks site of a historic massacre (1816) in the former RED RIVER COLONY, in the N of present-day Winnipeg, Manitoba. The rivalry over land domination between the North West and Hudson's Bay companies came to a head when HBC governor Robert Semple and 20 other Red River settlers were slaughtered here by North West Company agents and their allies, the mixed-race MÉTIS. The Red River leader, the Earl of Selkirk, retaliated by capturing FORT WILLIAM, the North West headquarters on L. Superior. The Seven Oaks incident is regarded as important in the growth of the Métis sense of identity that affected later Manitoba history.

Seven Pines see under FAIR OAKS, Virginia.

Seventeenth Street commercial thoroughfare in downtown DENVER, Colorado, running between Union Station (NW) and Broadway (SE), noted since the early 20th century as a financial center, the "Wall Street of the West." The "17th Street Crowd" of the period patronized the Brown Palace Hotel (1892) and other luxury establishments. Modern bank buildings line the street today.

Severn unincorporated village, pop. 24,499, Anne Arundel Co., NC Maryland, a largely residential suburb 15 mi/24 km SSW of central Baltimore.

Severna Park unincorporated village, pop. 25,879, Anne Arundel Co., C Maryland, on a peninsula of Chesapeake Bay and the estuarial Severn R., 17 mi/27 km S of Baltimore and 7 mi/11 km N of Annapolis. It is primarily residential.

Severn River **1.** estuary, 11 mi/18 km long, extending NW into Anne Arundel Co., C Maryland, from Chesapeake Bay. ANNAPOLIS is on its S bank near its mouth. Severna Park is near its head. **2.** in Ontario: **a.** 600 mi/1000 km long, in the NW, flowing through Sandy L. and generally NE to Fort Severn, a 17th-century fur trading post, now an Indian reserve (pop. 335), before emptying into HUDSON BAY. **b.** 30 mi/50 km long, the final W section of the TRENT CANAL (which is also called the Severn Waterway), entering Severn Sound of GEORGIAN BAY.

Sevier River 325 mi/525 km long, in Utah. It is formed by headstreams near Panguitch, in Garfield Co., and flows NNE past Junction, Big Rock Candy Mt., and Richfield, along the E of the PAHVANT RANGE, then turns NW around the range's N, and SW into the Sevier Desert section of the GREAT BASIN, where it passes DELTA and enters **Sevier L.,** a shrinking salt lake now some 18 mi/29 km long, and usually dry. The Sevier is dammed in several places. Near its NE apex it forms 22 mi/35 km–long **Sevier Bridge Reservoir,** a popular recreational site. In the area around Delta it irrigates alfalfa fields and farms.

Sevierville town, pop. 7178, seat of Sevier Co., E Tennessee, 22 mi/35 km SE of Knoxville, on the Little Pigeon R. Laid out in 1795, it is a trade center for a farm and timber area. To the S are the Great Smoky Mts., and 5 mi/ 8 km to the NE is Douglas L. on the French Broad R.

Sewanee unincorporated community, pop. 2128, Franklin Co., S Tennessee, 35 mi/56 km WNW of Chattanooga, on Boiling Fork Creek, near the NW edge of the Cumberland Plateau. The University of the South, founded here in 1857, dominates its life. A summer resort, it is also home to a military academy. Saint Andrews, site of the school attended by writer James Agee, is just NE.

Seward **1.** city, pop. 2699, Kenai Peninsula Borough, S Alaska, 75 mi/120 km SSE of Anchorage, on the KENAI PENINSULA at the head of Resurrection Bay, an arm of the Gulf of Alaska. In the late 18th century Russians explored the area and built a shipyard. Most of the first settlers, however, came after 1902 to build the ALASKA RAILROAD, which extends N. The city is also an important highway terminus and a key distribution center for the Alaskan interior. Its harbor is ice-free all year. Lumber, fish, and oil are the region's major products. Forests in the area are famous for hunting, and Kenai Fjords National Park is just W. **2.** city, pop. 5634, seat of Seward Co., SE Nebraska, on the Big Blue R., 22 mi/35 km WNW of Lincoln. Founded in 1865, it is a trade center for an agricultural region, and produces feed, flour, and dairy goods. Building products are also manufactured here. It is the seat of Concordia College (1894).

Seward Mountain 4404 ft/1343 m, in the Adirondack Mts., NE New York, 14 mi/23 km SW of LAKE PLACID.

Seward Peninsula extension of NW Alaska bordered by Kotzebue Sound and the Chukchi Sea (N), the Bering Strait (W), and Norton Sound (S). Some 200 mi/320 km E–W and 145 mi/235 km N–S, the tundra-covered peninsula supports a small pop. engaged mainly in mining and trapping. Rapid but temporary development followed the 1898 discovery of gold in the area around NOME, on the S coast. Cape PRINCE OF WALES, on the W tip, is the westernmost point on the North American continent. The yearly IDITAROD dogsled race from Anchorage to Nome crosses the peninsula.

Seward's Folly also, **Seward's Icebox** see under ALASKA.

Sewickley borough, pop. 4134, Allegheny Co., SW Pennsylvania, on the Ohio R., 12 mi/19 km WNW of Pittsburgh. It is a largely residential suburb.

Seymour **1.** town, pop. 14,288, New Haven Co., SW Connecticut, on the Naugatuck R., 10 mi/16 km NW of New Haven. In 1802, David Humphreys of Derby brought the first (Spanish) merino sheep to America, and started a woolen mill here; in 1880, the first mohair plush in the US was made. Other industries have included the manufacture of brass, wire, cables, and paper. Since the 1970s the brass industry has virtually disappeared. **2.** city, pop. 15,576, Jackson Co., S Indiana, 38 mi/62 km SE of Bloomington. Its many industries produce such goods as auto parts, heavy machinery, wood products, textiles, packaging materials, pharmaceuticals, appliances, fertilizer, and plastics. In an agricultural region, it also processes food and is a shipping center. Muscatatuck National Wildlife Refuge is 5 mi/8 km E.

Seymour Johnson Air Force Base see under GOLDSBORO, North Carolina.

Shade Mountain Allegheny Mt. ridge in C Pennsylvania, rising to 1800–2000 ft/550–600 m and extending about 30 mi/50 km from the Juniata R. at LEWISTOWN (SW) to near SELINSGROVE (NE). It forms part of the border between Juniata and Mifflin counties.

Shadwell plantation in Albemarle Co., C Virginia, about 5 mi/8 km E of CHARLOTTESVILLE. In what was then Goochland Co., it was the estate of Peter Jefferson and the birthplace (1743) of his son Thomas, third president of the US. The house burned in 1770, and Thomas Jefferson moved to MONTICELLO, 3 mi/5 km E.

Shadyside residential neighborhood in the EAST END of Pittsburgh, Pennsylvania, NW of SQUIRREL HILL, and 3.5 mi/5.6 km NE of the GOLDEN TRIANGLE. The original estates here were subdivided into lots varying widely in square footage, resulting in a diversity of housing types, styles, and sizes. Shadyside is nevertheless one of the most affluent parts of Pittsburgh.

Shaeffer Stadium see under FOXBOROUGH, Massachusetts.

Shafter city, pop. 8409, Kern Co., SC California, 17 mi/27 km NW of Bakersfield, in the extreme S San Joaquin Valley. An agricultural community that also produces cement, it was the site of Minter Field, a World War II air base.

Shaker Heights city, pop. 30,831, Cuyahoga Co., NE Ohio, 8 mi/13 km E of Cleveland. The Shaker religious community of North Union was established here c.1820. Its membership began to decline in the 1860s, and it was disbanded in 1889; a museum details its history. The site was sold to commercial developers who built a residential community. Since 1920, a rapid transit railroad system has linked Shaker Heights to downtown Cleveland. It is an affluent commuter suburb, with costly homes and estates, scenic parks and lakes. An ongoing plan to foster racial integration in the community resulted in a rise in the percentage of black residents here from 17% in 1960 to 30% in 1990.

Shakopee city, pop. 11,739, seat of Scott Co., SE Minnesota, on the Minnesota R., an outer suburb, 18 mi/29 km SW of Minneapolis. Named for a local Sioux chief, it was settled around 1850. Sioux burial mounds are located in its Memorial Park. Soft drinks are manufactured here. The city has a state reformatory. The Valley Fair amusement park is 2 mi/3 km E.

Shaler Township township, pop. 30,533, Allegheny Co., SW Pennsylvania. Just E of ROSS, it includes some of Pittsburgh's NORTH HILLS suburbs.

Shamokin city, pop. 9184, Northumberland Co., EC Pennsylvania, on Shamokin Creek, 12 mi/19 km ESE of Sunbury. In the ANTHRACITE BELT, it is a mining center and also produces textiles, machinery, meat products, and fertilizer. The borough of **Shamokin Dam** (pop. 1690) is in Snyder Co., across the Susquehanna R. (W) from Sunbury and the mouth of Shamokin Creek.

Shangri-La **1.** see under OJAI, California. **2.** see under CAMP DAVID, Maryland.

Sharon **1.** town, pop. 15,517, Norfolk Co., E Massachusetts, 20 mi/32 km SSW of Boston. A growing suburb just E of Interstate 95, it is largely residential, with various light industries, including the production of medical devices. **2.** see under EAST GWILLIMBURY, Ontario. **3.** city, pop. 17,493, Mercer Co., extreme NW Pennsylvania, on the Shenango R., 60 mi/97 km NNW of Pittsburgh and 14 mi/23 km NE of Youngstown, Ohio. It was founded c. 1800. The Sharon Furnace, built after the completion of the L. Erie Extension of the Pennsylvania Canal in 1844, spurred the growth of the steel industry, still important to the city, which also manufactures electrical equipment and metal products. A campus of Pennsylvania State University is here. The Shenango Dam and Reservoir are NE.

Sharonville city, pop. 13,182, Hamilton and Butler counties, SW Ohio, 15 mi/24 km NE of Cincinnati, of which it is a commuter suburb. It is also the site of a large automobile transmission plant. A restored 19th-century Ohio village is maintained within the city's Sharon Woods Park.

Sharpsburg town, pop. 659, Washington Co., NW Maryland, on the W side of Antietam Creek, 13 mi/21 km S of HAGERSTOWN. It is a trade center for an agricultural area. The ANTIETAM battlefield is just SE; the battle (Sept. 17, 1862) is often referred to as the battle of Sharpsburg.

Sharpstown residential and commercial section of Houston, Texas, 13 mi/21 km SW of Downtown, along US Route 59. The Sharpstown Mall (1961) anchored development of this growing suburban area.

Shasta ghost town: see under REDDING, California.

Shasta, Mount highest point (14,162 ft/4317 m) in the California part of the CASCADE RANGE, NE of the city of **Mount Shasta** (pop. 3460, Siskiyou Co.), and 55 mi/89 km NNE of Redding. An isolated, dormant volcano covering 17 sq mi/44 sq km, it last erupted in 1786, and shows mild activity in boiling sulfur springs near its summit. Worn down by glaciation, Shasta now has three separate vents, with Steep Rock the highest, followed by Shastina at 12,433 ft/3790 m. The nearly treeless mountain, bearing five glaciers, including the largest one in California, has a wide variety of alpine plants as well as virgin stands of the rare Shasta red fir. Shasta has been associated with the beliefs and myths both of ancient Californians and of modern occultists; beings from the Great Spirit to descendants of peoples of the lost continent of Lemuria to Bigfoot are reputed to have lived within the mountain or in the area. Hiking is popular here and at Black Butte (6325 ft/1928 m), a cinder cone N of Shasta. The summit is in the Shasta-Trinity National Forest.

Shasta Lake many-armed body in N California's Shasta-Trinity National Forest, 40 mi/64 km S of Mt. Shasta, and part of the WHISKEYTOWN-SHASTA-TRINITY NATIONAL RECREATION AREA. The largest (c.30,000 ac/12,150 ha) artificial lake in California, it is a popular water resort, called by some the "houseboat capital of the world," with a 365-mi/590-km shoreline. Shasta L. is formed by the impounded waters of the SACRAMENTO (NW), PIT (NE), and McCloud (N) rivers. The **Shasta Dam** (completed 1945; 600 ft/180 m high), a unit of the CENTRAL VALLEY Project, regulates the flow of the Sacramento and its N tributaries to aid in navigation and flood control, and produces hydroelectric power.

Shasta-Trinity National Forest over 2 million ac/810,000 ha (3125 sq mi/8100 sq km), in N California. It extends from the Coast Ranges (W) to the Modoc Plateau (NE), and includes parts of the Yolla Bolly–Middle Eel and Salmon–Trinity Alps wildernesses, Mt. Shasta, and the WHISKEYTOWN-SHASTA-TRINITY NATIONAL RECREATION AREA.

Shaughnessy also, **Shaughnessy Heights** residential section of VANCOUVER, British Columbia, 2.5 mi/4 km S of Downtown, on high ground S of FALSE CREEK. Developed in the 1910s by the Canadian Pacific Railway, it quickly acquired the nickname "CPR Heaven" for its mansions and gardens. Until 1929 it was part of POINT GREY. Some of its huge houses have become apartment buildings, but the area remains affluent.

Shaw commercial and residential section of NW Washington, D.C., 1.5 mi/2 km NNE of the White House, on the E side of the FOURTEENTH St. corridor. The longtime business and cultural center of Washington's black community, it declined in the 1960s and has been slow to recover from 1968 riot damage. The area around U St. was the site of noted theaters and music clubs. Le Droit Park, just N, is home to Howard University (1867). Completion of a subway line through the area in 1991, accompanied with increased local investment, suggested an upturn for Shaw.

Shaw Air Force Base see under SUMTER, South Carolina.

Shawangunk Mountains familiarly, **the Gunks** range, consisting mainly of a single ridge, part of the Appalachian Mts. They extend SW from Roundout Creek, near Kingston, New York, to join the Kittatinny Mt. ridge near Port Jervis, on the New Jersey border. The ridge is 45 mi/72 km long, with a maximum altitude of 2289 ft/698 m, although Sam's Point, 2255 ft/688 m, near ELLENVILLE, is the most famous peak. The Shawangunks are sometimes divided into the North and South, divided at Sam's Point. Geologically, the Northern Shawangunks are a hard sedimentary conglomerate and sandstone band around 6 mi/10 km wide. The Southern Shawangunks are only a mile across. The "Gunks" are popular with rock climbers from nearby metropolitan areas; New York is only 50 mi/80 km to the SE.

Shawano County 897 sq mi/2323 sq km, pop. 37,157, in EC Wisconsin. It is crossed by the Wolf and Embarrass rivers, and contains several lakes, of which L. Shawano in the NE is the largest. Its seat is Shawano. The county is heavily forested. Sawmilling and dairy farming are major economic activities. The Stockbridge Munsee Indian reservation is situated in the county.

Shawinigan city, pop. 19,931, in the La Mauricie region of S Québec, 17 mi/28 km NW of Trois-Rivières, on the R. SAINT-MAURICE. Its powerful falls provide hydroelectricity for Montréal as well as for local industry, which includes the manufacture of chemicals, abrasives, aluminum, pulp and paper, textiles, clothing, and plastics. A science and engineering college (1943) and the Séminaire Sainte-Marie (1947) are here. Largely residential **Shawinigan-Sud** (city, pop. 11,584) is 3 mi/5 km S, and GRAND-MÈRE is 4 mi/7 km NE.

Shawmut Peninsula hilly, open body of land, less than 800 ac/324 ha, on which the city of BOSTON, Massachusetts, was founded. The first white resident, William Blackstone (or Blaxton), settled on what is now Boston Common in 1625; in 1630, colonists led by John Winthrop arrived at CHARLESTOWN. Winthrop's group moved across the Charles R. to what Blackstone called Trimountaine, and renamed it Boston after a town in England. Blackstone's name for the peninsula reflected its three "mountains," of which BEACON HILL is the only survivor. Earth from the three hills went largely to expand Boston, which was at first connected with ROXBURY by only a narrow "neck" of land.

Shawnee **1.** city, pop. 37,993, Johnson Co., NE Kansas, 13 mi/21 km SW of downtown Kansas City. Once known as Gum Springs, it was the site of the 1830 Shawnee Indian Methodist Mission, the 1855 meeting place for the proslavery territorial legislature, and for a time the Kansas Territory's largest town. Now a residential suburb, it has some light industry. **2.** city, pop. 26,017, seat of Pottawatomie Co., C Oklahoma, on the North Canadian R., 35 mi/56 km ESE of Oklahoma City. A land-rush city, it was settled in former Indian Territory and incorporated in 1894. It boomed after the discovery of oil in 1926. Today it processes and distributes grain, dairy products, livestock, oil, and natural gas. Among diversified manufactures are aircraft parts, electronic equipment, and clothing. It is the seat of Oklahoma Baptist University (1906) and St. Gregory's College (1875).

Shawnee County 549 sq mi/1422 sq km, pop. 160,976, in NE Kansas. Its seat and only major city is TOPEKA. Outside the city and its suburbs, the county is rural, with grain, livestock, and diversified agriculture all important.

Shawnee National Forest over 263,000 ac/106,500 ha, in the 10 southernmost Illinois counties, between the Mississippi R. (W) and the Ohio R. (E and S). It is adjoined to the N, in Williamson Co., by the 43,500-ac/17,620-ha Crab Orchard National Wildlife Refuge. Forest headquarters are at Harrisburg, in Saline Co.

Shea Stadium sports facility, on Flushing Bay, Queens, New York, just SE of LaGuardia Airport. At the N end of FLUSHING MEADOWS-CORONA PARK, the stadium, completed in 1964, is the home of the New York Mets (baseball).

Sheboygan city, pop. 49,676, seat of Sheboygan Co., E Wisconsin, on L. Michigan at the mouth of the Sheboygan R., 53 mi/85 km N of Milwaukee. The first permanent settlement in the area took place in 1838. Sheboygan, adjoining a rich dairy farming region, is an agricultural trade center and one of the largest US exporters of cheese. Sausage and beer are also produced. The city is a busy port with manufactures that include plastics, clothing, furniture, stainless steel, and leather goods. It is the seat of Lakeland College (1862). Sheboygan Indian Mound Park on its S edge contains burial mounds in the shapes of panthers and deer that date from 500–750 A.D.

Sheboygan County 515 sq mi/1334 sq km, pop. 103,877, in EC Wisconsin, bordered by L. Michigan (E). Its seat is Sheboygan. Drained by the Sheboygan R., it is one of the nation's foremost dairy farming and cheese producing regions. There is diversified industry in Sheboygan, Sheboygan Falls, Kohler, and Plymouth.

Shediac town, pop. 4343, Westmorland Co., SE New Brunswick, on Shediac Bay of NORTHUMBERLAND STRAIT, 15 mi/24 km NE of Moncton. It is a seafood producing center, noted esp. for its lobster and oysters, and has an annual lobster festival. Its warm waters draw beachgoers.

Sheep Range 50 mi/80 km NE–SW, in Clark Co., SE Nevada. Within the DESERT NATIONAL WILDLIFE RANGE, it reaches 9720 ft/2963 m at **Sheep Peak,** 30 mi/48 km N of Las Vegas.

Sheepshead Bay maritime commercial and residential section, S Brooklyn, New York. Sheepshead Bay is an inlet between the neighborhood it gives its name to and the peninsula extending E of Coney I. The name derives from a once locally important food fish. In the early 19th century the area became popular as a resort; it is still known for its restaurants and its now economically threatened charter fishing fleet. A horse track opened in the 1870s became briefly (1915–19) the world's fastest auto speedway. The neighborhood is middle-class, once largely Italian and Irish, now largely Jewish.

Sheffield city, pop. 10,380, Colbert Co., NW Alabama, on the S bank of the Tennessee R., across from Florence, in the MUSCLE SHOALS region. In an iron and coal producing area, it is a metalworking center. Together with Florence, Tuscumbia, and the city of Muscle Shoals, it forms Alabama's Quad Cities. A trading post in 1815, it was later a cotton port, then developed following the construction of the WILSON DAM after World War I. The city's economy is based largely on the Tennessee Valley Authority dams, and on local deposits of iron ore, limestone, clays, asphalt, phosphates, and bauxite.

Sheffield Lake city, pop. 9825, Lorain Co., N Ohio, on L. Erie. It is a residential community 5 mi/8 km NE of Lorain.

Shelburne **1.** town, pop. 2245, seat of Shelburne Co., SW Nova Scotia, on Shelburne Harbour, off the Atlantic Ocean, 104 mi/167 km SW of Halifax. A small port, after 1783 it became home to over 10,000 LOYALISTS from New York and New England. Although most moved elsewhere within the decade, their influence lingers in the town. In the early 19th century it was a shipbuilding center; clipper ship designer Donald McKay (1810–80) from nearby (E) Jordan Falls, learned his craft here. Fishing and tourism are important in today's economy. **2.** town, pop. 5871, including Shelburne and Shelburne Falls villages, in Chittenden Co., NW Vermont. Shelburne is on the La Platte R., Shelburne Bay, and L. Champlain, 7 mi/11 km S of Burlington, of which it is a commercial and residential suburb. Shelburne Museum and Heritage Park, one of the region's leading tourist complexes, is here.

Shelby **1.** city, pop. 2763, seat of Toole Co., N Montana, 72 mi/116 km NNW of Great Falls. Founded in 1863, it was situated on the route of the Great Northern Railway and became a trade center for cowboys and sheepherders. Its development was spurred by the discovery of oil in 1921. Its nearly overnight prosperity caused local citizens to sponsor the Dempsey-Gibbons heavyweight championship bout held here in 1923. Shelby still has oil and gas wells and a refinery. It houses large grain elevators, deals in grain, livestock, poultry, and dairy products, and is an important rail shipping point. **2.** city, pop. 14,669, seat of Cleveland Co., SW North Carolina, in the Piedmont, 38 mi/61 km ENE of Charlotte. Settlement began around 1760, and the town was chartered in 1843. Arrival of the railroad in 1870 stimulated growth, and textile manufacturing became the city's chief industry. The city is now the market center of an agricultural region that produces fruit, dairy products, beef cattle, and cotton. Textiles remain important, augmented by lumbering and the manufacture of hosiery, flour, and baked goods. Shelby is home to Cleveland Community College (1965). **3.** city, pop. 9564, Richland Co., NC Ohio, 10 mi/16 km NW of Mansfield. It is surrounded by a rich farming area in which grain is a leading crop. Automobile parts are manufactured.

Shelby County 772 sq mi/1999 sq km, pop. 826,330, in extreme SW Tennessee, bounded (S) by Mississippi and (W) by the Mississippi R. and Arkansas. Drained by the Wolf and Loosahatchie rivers, it is a cotton, beef, and dairy cattle producing area increasingly dominated by the county seat, MEMPHIS, one of South's major commercial and manufacturing centers.

Shelbyville **1.** city, pop. 15,336, seat of Shelby Co., C Indiana, 25 mi/40 km SE of Indianapolis. In an area that raises corn and livestock and has many dairy farms, it is a trade, processing, and distribution hub. Among its manufactures are electrical and heating equipment, furniture, radio and television parts, fiberglass, plastics, and clothing. **2.** city, pop. 14,049, seat of Bedford Co., SC Tennessee, on the Duck R., 49 mi/79 km SSE of Nashville. It is called the "Pencil City" for its chief product. It has other light manufactures (clothing, plastics, truck transmissions), handles local grains, livestock, and poultry, and is widely known as a center for breeding and training Tennessee walking horses.

Shelikof Strait inlet of the Pacific Ocean between the Alaska Peninsula (NW) and KODIAK and Afognak islands (SE), in SW Alaska. Some 125 mi/200 km NE–SW and 30–40 mi/50–65 km wide, it joins COOK INLET and the Gulf of Alaska at its N end. The fjord-laced NW shore lies at the border of the Katmai National Monument. The strait is named for Gregory Shelekhov, fur trader and founder of the first permanent Russian settlement (on Kodiak I.) in Alaska.

Shelter Island **1.** landfill construction, 0.8 mi/1.2 km long, in San Diego Bay, in SAN DIEGO, California. Linked by causeway to Point LOMA since 1950, this resort area has become the site of hotels, boatyards, and parks, along with the San Diego Yacht Club. **2.** island town, pop. 2263, Suffolk Co., SE New York, between Little Peconic and Gardiners bays and between the North and South forks of Long Island. Shelter I. measures 7 mi/11 km long and up to 6 mi/10 km wide. Formerly (from 1652) a refuge for Quakers, it is now primarily a summer resort.

Shelton city and coterminous township, pop. 35,418, Fairfield Co., SW Connecticut, on the Housatonic R. opposite Derby, 10 mi/16 km NE of Bridgeport. Settled in the 1690s, it developed industrially after 1870, when the Derby Dam was completed. Today manufactures include foam rubber and metal products and electronic equipment.

Shenandoah **1.** city, pop. 5572, Page Co., extreme SW

Iowa, 42 mi/68 km SE of Council Bluffs, in the Nishnabotna R. valley. Founded in 1870, it has long been a nursery and seed-producing center. **2.** see under EAST BATON ROUGE PARISH, Louisiana.

Shenandoah County 512 sq mi/1326 sq km, pop. 31,636, in N Virginia. Its seat is WOODSTOCK. It embraces much of the N Shenandoah Valley, and is bounded N and NW by West Virginia and E and SE by MASSANUTTEN Mt. The county has diversified agriculture, quarrying, and livestock raising, and there are a number of resorts catering to tourists drawn by the area's scenery, its limestone caverns, and the George Washington National Forest. Strasburg and Woodstock are market centers. FISHERS HILL and NEW MARKET are Civil War sites.

Shenandoah Mountain ridge of the Appalachian Mts., extending for 80 mi/128 km NE–SW along the Virginia-West Virginia border, and rising to more than 4400 ft/1340 m.

Shenandoah National Park 195,000 ac/79,000 ha, in the Blue Ridge Mts., W Virginia. The park extends for approximately 75 mi/120 km NNE–SSW along the crest of the Blue Ridge from S of Front Royal (N) to near Waynesboro (S), where it adjoins the George Washington National Forest. The Shenandoah Valley lies W, the Virginia PIEDMONT E. The park has hiking trails and recreational facilities, and there is abundant wildlife. SKYLINE DRIVE and the APPALACHIAN TRAIL run through the park.

Shenandoah River 55 mi/90 km long, in Virginia and West Virginia. It is formed just N of FRONT ROYAL, Virginia, by the confluence of the North Fork (100 mi/160 km long) and the South Fork (95 mi/153 km long). The **North Fork** is formed at a gap in Little North Mt., Rockingham Co., and flows E to Timberville, then NE past NEW MARKET, WOODSTOCK, and Strasburg, before turning E to the confluence. The larger **South Fork** is formed by the confluence of several streams near Grottoes, and flows NE past PORT REPUBLIC, ELKTON, Shenandoah, and Luray, to the confluence. The two forks, separated by MASSANUTTEN Mt., follow parallel, sinuous paths. The main river flows NE through the N portion of the valley, across the PANHANDLE of West Virginia, to the POTOMAC R. at HARPERS FERRY. The **Shenandoah Valley,** part of the Great Appalachian Valley, is 150 mi/240 km long and 10–20 mi/15–30 km wide, and lies between the Allegheny Mts. (W) and the BLUE RIDGE Mts. (E). The portion E of Massanutten Mt. is called the Page Valley. During the Civil War the valley was a Confederate route in invading the North, and a chief supply source for the Southern army; many battles were fought in the area. The valley's cities include LEXINGTON, STAUNTON, HARRISONBURG, and WINCHESTER.

Shenango River c.60 mi/100 km long, in W Pennsylvania and NE Ohio. It rises in Crawford Co., NW Pennsylvania, and is dammed to form PYMATUNING RESERVOIR, partly in Ashtabula Co., NE Ohio. It then flows S past GREENVILLE, Pennsylvania, and through Shenango L., before reaching SHARON. It continues S to join the Mahoning R., 4 mi/6 km SW of NEW CASTLE, to form the BEAVER R.

Shepherdstown town, pop. 1287, Jefferson Co., extreme NE West Virginia, in the Eastern PANHANDLE. It is on a bluff overlooking the Potomac R., 12 mi/19 km SW of Hagerstown, Maryland, and 10 mi/16 km NW of Harpers Ferry. Settled by Pennsylvania Germans before 1730, it is one of West Virginia's oldest communities. George Washington considered locating the nation's capital here. In 1787, James Rumsey successfully ran the first steamboat on the river. Shepherd College (1871) is here.

Sheppard Air Force Base see under WICHITA FALLS, Texas.

Sherbrooke city, pop. 76,429, S Québec, in the EASTERN TOWNSHIPS, 83 mi/134 km E of Montréal, in rolling hills, at the confluence of the Magog and Saint-François rivers. Settled in the 1800s by Vermonters, it industrialized in the 1840s, and is now the commercial and industrial center of an agricultural and mining region, and a transportation hub. It developed as a textile center; today heavy machinery, pulp and paper, rubber and leather goods, clothing, and dairy goods are also produced. Most employment, however, is in commerce and service industries, including teaching, health care, and regional administration. Tourism is also important, and Sherbrooke is a resort center with lakes and mountains nearby. Institutions include the Collège du Sacre-Coeur (1945), the Séminaire de Sherbrooke (1875), the Université de Sherbrooke (1954), and the École des Sciences Domestiques (1956). Fleurimont (pop. 14,727, just E) is a residential suburb.

Sherbrooke, Rue English, **Sherbrooke Street** major commercial, institutional, and residential thoroughfare of MONTRÉAL, Québec. It extends over 20 mi/30 km from the N (officially E) end of the I. de Montréal (at POINTE-AUX-TREMBLES) to Montréal-Ouest, S of the city center. In the city's E, it passes through MAISONNEUVE, past the Parc Olympique and Botanical Garden. Just W of the Blvd. SAINT-LAURENT begins the famous Golden Square Mile (also, "the Square Mile"), between Sherbrooke and Mt. ROYAL (W), ending at the Chemin de la Côte-des-Neiges, where after the British conquest (1760) Scottish entrepreneurs built lavish hillside country homes. In this area, nurtured by the fur trade and later by brewing, railroad, and other industrial money, the greatest concentration of wealth in Canadian history developed; around 1900 it was estimated that some 100 local families controlled 70% of Canada's money. Today, most of the large homes in the Square Mile have disappeared; McGill University (1821) is on the E side. Along Sherbrooke in the area are consulates, exclusive clubs, galleries, and expensive hotels and boutiques. Anglophone wealth is still represented in nearby (SW) WESTMOUNT.

Sheridan city, pop. 13,900, seat of Sheridan Co., NC Wyoming, at the junction of Big Goose and Little Goose creeks, 13 mi/21 km S of the Montana border. Situated on the E slope of the Bighorn Mts., it is the headquarters of the BIGHORN NATIONAL FOREST. The area saw bloody battles between whites and Sioux, Cheyenne, and Arapaho from the late 1860s to the late 1870s. After the Indian Wars ended, Sheridan was founded (1882) and became the center of a cattle ranching area. The community's growth was hastened by the discovery of coal (1890) and the arrival of the railroad (1892). Sheridan's industries include ranching, truck farming, flour and lumber milling, and the processing and shipping of oil and coal. Sheridan College (1948) is here.

Sheridan's Ride see under CEDAR CREEK, Virginia.

Sherman city, pop. 31,601, seat of Grayson Co., NE Texas, 55 mi/88 km N of Dallas, near L. Texoma (the Red R.), 15 mi/24 km S of the Oklahoma line. Settled in 1846, it developed as a stage line stop in the 1850s. In the 1870s railroads arrived, and Sherman remains a freight line center. A distribution point for regional oil, crops, and livestock, it developed industrially after World War II, and has a wide range of manufactures. It also processes foods. Austin College (Presbyterian) was founded in 1849.

Sherman Oaks affluent S SAN FERNANDO VALLEY residential section of Los Angeles, California, 12 mi/19 km NW of Downtown, and just W of STUDIO CITY.

Sherman Park residential neighborhood on the WEST SIDE of Milwaukee, Wisconsin, 2.5 mi/4 km NW of Downtown. A racially integrated middle-class community, it has become a popular area for first-time home buyers.

Sherman's March see MARCH TO THE SEA.

Sherwood city, pop. 18,893, Pulaski Co., C Arkansas, a growing residential suburb 5 mi/8 km NNE of downtown Little Rock and adjacent (NE) to North Little Rock.

Sherwood Park industrial and residential community, seat of Strathcona Co. (pop. 56,573), Alberta, immediately E of the North Saskatchewan R. and EDMONTON. A suburb of Edmonton, it is centered around a large golf course 6 mi/10 km E of Downtown. On its W, along the river, is Edmonton's "Refinery Row."

Sheyenne River 325 mi/523 km long, in North Dakota. It rises in C North Dakota and flows E through Benson and Eddy cos., where it forms the S boundary of the Devils Lake Reservation. It turns sharply S, flowing through L. Ashtabula and past Valley City. Veering NE at Fort Ransom, it joins the Red R. of the North 10 mi/16 km N of Fargo.

Shickshock Mountains French, **Monts Chic-Chocs** part of the APPALACHIAN system, a continuation of the NOTRE DAME Mts. for 100 mi/160 km on the N GASPÉ PENINSULA in SE Québec. The range rises to 4160 ft/1268 m at Mt. Jacques Cartier, the second-highest point in the province, which is 70 mi/110 km W of Gaspé. A provincial park and a wildlife reserve encompass much of the Shickshocks. Copper is mined here, at MURDOCHVILLE.

Shield, the see CANADIAN SHIELD.

Shillington see under READING, Pennsylvania.

Shiloh **1.** town in Palestine where the Israelites' Ark of the Covenant rested within its tabernacle (Joshua 18). In America the name was usually given to a church, as both a consecrated and a meeting place, and by extension to some localities. **2.** unincorporated community in Harrison township, Montgomery Co., SW Ohio, on the Stillwater R., just NW of Dayton, of which it is a residential suburb. **3.** battle site in Hardin Co., SW Tennessee, 9 mi/15 km SW of the city of Savannah, at and near Pittsburg Landing, on the Tennessee R. and OWL and Snake creeks. After taking FORT HENRY and FORT DONELSON, U.S. Grant gathered his soldiers at Pittsburg Landing before advancing south. They were surprised there on April 6–7, 1862, by a strong Southern force led by Albert Sidney Johnston, which attacked first near rural Shiloh Church. There were over 10,000 casualties on each side in two days of fighting, after which Union troops essentially reoccupied their initial positions, while the Confederates withdrew to CORINTH, Mississippi, leaving W Tennessee under Union control.

Shining Mountains see ROCKY Mts.

Shinnecock Bay inlet of the Atlantic Ocean just W of SOUTHAMPTON on the South Fork of Long I., SE New York. Ten mi/16 km E–W and 1–4 mi/2–6 km wide, it is protected by barrier beaches, with entrance to the ocean at Shinnecock Inlet. It joins Great Peconic Bay on the N via the Shinnecock Canal, which is bridged. **Shinnecock Hills** (unincorporated; pop. 2847) is a popular resort village between the two bays, while the **Shinnecock Indian Reservation** (pop. 375) lies on a peninsula between Southampton and the bay.

Ship Island c.5 mi/8 km E–W, S Mississippi, in the GULF ISLANDS NATIONAL SEASHORE, one of several barrier islands between Mississippi Sound (N) and the Gulf of Mexico (S), 12 mi/19 km SSW of Biloxi. From the late 17th century until the 1720s, it served as a port for Spanish and French ships, and in the early 18th century was a base for France's exploration of the Gulf Coast. It was a British base during the War of 1812, and became an American military installation in 1847. During the Civil War, Ship I. was held alternately by Confederate and Union forces. It was a staging area for Northern troops before Farragut's attack on New Orleans (1862), and its Fort Massachusetts (1858) was used as a Union prison camp. The island became a quarantine station in 1878. Today it is accessible by ferry from Gulfport and Biloxi, and has tourist facilities.

Shippagan also, **Shippegan** or **Shippigan** town, pop. 2760, Gloucester Co., extreme NE New Brunswick, 15 mi/24 km E of CARAQUET and 120 mi/194 km N of Moncton, at the tip of the Acadian Peninsula. A Jesuit mission was here in the 1630s, and Acadians, Jerseymen, and others settled in the late 18th century. Shippagan is a fishing and tourist center and the site of a Université de Moncton campus. To its NE extend the peat bog–dominated I. Lamèque and the scenic I. Miscou.

Shippan Point see under STAMFORD, Connecticut.

Shippensburg borough, pop. 5331, Cumberland and Franklin counties, SC Pennsylvania, 40 mi/64 km SW of Harrisburg. It produces furniture, clothing, and flour, and is the seat of Shippensburg University of Pennsylvania (1871).

Shippingport hamlet in Greene township, Beaver Co., W Pennsylvania, 9 mi/14 km SW of Beaver Falls, site of a nuclear power plant opened in 1957 on the S bank of the Ohio R. Its first unit was shut down in 1982; units opened in 1976 and 1987 are in operation.

Shiprock basaltic formation (7178 ft/2188 m high), rising over 1400 ft/425 m above the desert floor in the FOUR CORNERS section of extreme NW New Mexico, in the NAVAJO INDIAN RESERVATION. An eroded volcanic neck, sacred to the Navajo and a landmark to pioneers, it is thought to resemble a huge ship at sail. The community of **Shiprock** (unincorporated, pop. 7687), 10 mi/16 km NE, is an important Navajo trade center, site of a noted tribal fair. Oil, natural gas, and uranium have been extracted in the area.

Shirley **1.** town, pop. 6118, Middlesex Co., NE Massachusetts, 7 mi/11 km ESE of Fitchburg, on the Nashua R. Hilly and rural, it has had various light manufactures, and is a residential suburb. Shirley is the former site of a Shaker community established in 1793. **2.** unincorporated village, pop. 22,936, in Brookhaven town, Suffolk Co., SE New York, on Long Island's South Shore, 4 mi/6 km W of Center Moriches. It is primarily residential. Brookhaven Airport is just N, MASTIC just NE. **3.** historic site in Charles City Co., SE Virginia, at the junction of the James and Appomattox rivers, across from BERMUDA HUNDRED. Its manor house, built in 1723, and still owned by descendants of Edward Hill III and Robert "King" Carter, Virginia's leading planter, was occupied by Union general George McClellan during the siege of PETERSBURG, 9 mi/14 km SW.

Shishaldin Volcano see under ALEUTIAN RANGE, Alaska.

Shively city, pop. 15,535, Jefferson Co., N Kentucky, adjacent

(SW) to Louisville. Known for its whiskey distilleries and tobacco storage warehouses, it is now largely residential.

Shivwits Plateau tableland, c.7000 ft/2150 m high, N of the Colorado R. and W of the Uinkaret Plateau, in N Arizona. The farthest W of the major plateaus of the ARIZONA STRIP, it includes volcanic Mt. Dellenbaugh (7072 ft/2156 m). The Hurricane Cliffs are on the E, the N section of GRAND WASH CLIFFS on the W.

Shooter's Island see under MARINER'S HARBOR, New York.

Shoreham village, pop. 540, in Brookhaven town, Suffolk Co., SE New York, 8 mi/13 km E of Port Jefferson. A residential village, it is the site of a nuclear power plant built in the 1970s and 1980s by the Long Island Lighting Co. The plant, which generated enormous cost overruns and public opposition, was eventually sold to New York State and dismantled, having never been on line.

Shoreview city, pop. 24,587, Ramsey Co., SE Minnesota, 6 mi/10 km N of St. Paul. Primarily a residential community on several small lakes, it has become home to some light industry, mainly electronics and printing. In the summer, its lakefront beaches are popular with area residents.

Shorewood **1.** see under L. MINNETONKA, Minnesota. **2.** see WHITE CENTER–SHOREWOOD, Washington. **3.** village, pop. 14,116, Milwaukee Co., SE Wisconsin, on L. Michigan, 5 mi/8 km N of Milwaukee, of which it is a commuter suburb.

Short Hills residential community in MILLBURN, Essex Co., NE New Jersey, 7 mi/11 km W of Newark. An extremely affluent suburb, it has many estates in elegantly landscaped settings, and is the site of a large and exclusive shopping mall.

Shoshone city, pop. 1249, seat of Lincoln Co., S Idaho, on the Little Wood R., 25 mi/40 km N of Twin Falls. Settled in 1882, it was originally a cattle town. A 1907 irrigation project spurred its development as a trade and shipping center for a sheep raising and agricultural region. Idaho's Mammoth Cave is 9 mi/14 km N, and the Shoshone Indian Ice Caves are 18 mi/29 km NNE.

Shoshone Lake 10 mi/16 km long and up to 4 mi/6 km wide, in YELLOWSTONE NATIONAL PARK, NW Wyoming, 6 mi/10 km W of Yellowstone L. It is one of the sources of the Snake R.

Shoshone Mountains NE–SW trending range, 100 mi/160 km long, partly in the Toiyabe National Forest, W of the Toiyabe Range, in C Nevada. They rise to 10,320 ft/3146 m at **North Shoshone Peak** and 10,065 ft/3068 m at **South Shoshone Peak.** At the S end of the range is Berlin Ichthyosaur State Park, encompassing the GHOST TOWN of Berlin and a site in Union Canyon with fossils of the giant marine reptiles that inhabited a shallow sea covering Nevada 150 million years ago. North of the Shoshone Mts. is the smaller **Shoshone Range,** which stretches 55 mi/90 km NE to Beowawe, on the Humboldt R.

Shoshone National Forest 2.47 million ac/1 million ha, E of Yellowstone National Park and the Teton National Forest, S of the Montana border, and N of the Wind River Mts., in Park and Fremont counties, W Wyoming. Established in 1891 as Yellowstone Forest Reserve, it is the oldest national forest in the US. It includes portions of the Absaroka, Beartooth, and Wind River mountains, and is drained by tributaries of the Yellowstone R. More than half of the huge forest is wilderness, including the Absaroka-Beartooth, North Absaroka, Washakie, Fitzpatrick, and Popo Agie areas. It has several glaciers, hundreds of lakes, and extremely varied topography, ranging from towering mountains to level meadows. GANNETT PEAK is in the Shoshone and BRIDGER-TETON national forests.

Shoshoni town, pop. 497, Fremont Co., C Wyoming, on Poison Creek, 95 mi/153 km NW of Casper. In the early days of the community, its general store was surrounded by a tall stockade to keep out bears. The town is now a sheep raising center, and is known for its annual fiddling contest.

Shreveport city, pop. 198,525, seat of Caddo Parish (pop. 248,253), also in Bossier Parish, NW Louisiana, on the Red R., opposite BOSSIER CITY and 14 mi/23 km E of the Texas line. Settled in 1835, it was named for Henry Shreve, who cleared the Red R. of a centuries-old, 160 mi/260 km–long driftwood jam known as the Great Raft, allowing the settlement, founded on land bought from the Caddo, to develop as a shipping center for regional cotton farms. At the end of the Civil War Shreveport was briefly Louisiana's capital and a Confederate headquarters. Union attempts to capture it were fought off in 1864. By 1900 river traffic declined, largely replaced by rail transport. In 1906, oil was discovered at Caddo L., 20 mi/32 km NW, stimulating rapid growth. Shreveport is now the commercial and processing center for petroleum, natural gas, cotton, and lumber industries in a large area of three states—Louisiana, Arkansas, and Texas. Its industries make metal products, machinery, chemicals, stone, clay, and glass products, clothing, and processed foods. The city is home to Centenary College of Louisiana (1825), a campus of Southern University (1964), and a campus of Louisiana State University (1967).

Shrewsbury town, pop. 24,146, Worcester Co., C Massachusetts. It is a largely residential suburb adjoining (E) Worcester. L. QUINSIGAMOND forms much of its W boundary. Surrounded by hilly farming areas, Shrewsbury manufactures plastics and has computer-industry offices.

Shuksan, Mount glacier-strewn peak (9127 ft/2782 m) of the CASCADE RANGE, just NE of Mt. BAKER and 40 mi/64 km ENE of Bellingham, Washington, in North Cascades National Park.

Siasconset village, extreme SE NANTUCKET I., Nantucket Co., SE Massachusetts. Familiarly known as 'Sconset, it was originally a fishing village, now a primarily summer community. The first wireless station in the US operated here 1901–18.

Sibley Provincial Park see under THUNDER BAY, Ontario.

Sidney **1.** town, pop. 10,082, Capital Regional District, extreme SE Vancouver I., SW British Columbia, 15 mi/24 km N of Victoria, on Haro Strait and adjacent (E) to North SAANICH. A commerical center for the Saanich Peninsula, it has ferry connections with Anacortes, Washington (E). The Victoria International Airport is on the W. **2.** city, pop. 18,710, seat of Shelby Co., W Ohio, on the Great Miami R., 30 mi/48 km NW of Springfield. In 1739 a trading post was established in the area, but the first permanent settlement by whites did not come until c.1820. The city is named for the Elizabethan poet and soldier, Sir Philip Sidney. Today, industries include metal finishing and fabrication, and the manufacture of lathes, compressors, road machinery, and machine tools.

Sidney Lanier, Lake see under CHATTAHOOCHEE R., Georgia.

sierra from the Spanish, a mountain range with jagged peaks that suggest the teeth of an upturned saw.

Sierra Army Depot see under HERLONG, California.

Sierra Blanca range in SC New Mexico, attaining an elevation of 12,003 ft/3659 m at **Sierra Blanca Peak,** also the high point of the more extensive SACRAMENTO Mts. The peak, important in Apache mythology, is in the MESCALERO APACHE INDIAN RESERVATION, and is the site of the Indian-owned resort Ski Apache. Iron ore, soft coal, and molybdenum deposits are in the area.

Sierra de Cristo Rey English, **Mountain of Christ the King** elevation (4576 ft/1396 m) just NW of downtown EL PASO, Texas, near the point where Texas, New Mexico, and Chihuahua (Mexico) come together. The summit, topped by a massive limestone statue of Christ on the Cross, dominates El Paso's skyline. It is noted as a Catholic pilgrimage site.

Sierra del Carmen also, **Carmen Mountains** N spur of the Sierra Madre Oriental of Mexico, extending generally NW–SE for c.80 mi/130 km, located partially in the E section of BIG BEND National Park in SW Texas. The name Carmen Mts. is sometimes used for the US section, which rises over 5000 ft/1525 m (it reaches over 9000 ft/2750 m in Mexico). The RIO GRANDE goes through the mountains at Boquillas Canyon.

Sierra Diablo largely N–S range rising over 6600 ft/2010 m in far W Texas, N of Van Horn. The S portion also extends E–W, with the Baylor Mts. on the E. The Sierra Diablo forms part of the E border of the DIABLO BOLSON.

Sierra Madre city, pop. 10,762, Los Angeles Co., SW California, in the S foothills of the San Gabriel Mts., immediately E of Pasadena and 13 mi/21 km NE of downtown Los Angeles. A residential community in an area noted for its orange groves, it has some light high-tech manufactures.

Sierra Madre Mountains **1.** in California: **a.** NW–SE oriented segment of the COAST RANGES, E of Santa Maria and N of the Santa Ynez Mts., in SC California. Situated S of the Cuyama R., the range is in Los Padres National Forest and partially within the San Rafael Wilderness Area. **b.** see under SAN GABRIEL Mts. **2.** see under PARK RANGE, Wyoming.

Sierra National Forest 1.3 million ac/525,000 ha (2025 sq mi/5245 sq km), in EC California, between Yosemite (N) and Kings Canyon (S) national parks, from the crest of the Sierra Nevada (E) to its foothills in the San Joaquin Valley (W). Including all or parts of the Ansel Adams, John Muir, and Kaiser wildernesses and headwaters of the Kings and San Joaquin rivers, it is an area noted for remote High Sierra scenery, glacial ice, and dense sequoia and pine forests.

Sierra Nevada massive N–S mountain range, along California's E boundary and projecting slightly into W Nevada, roughly paralleling the Pacific coast. Its N limit is variously described as where it meets the CASCADE RANGE just S of Mt. LASSEN, at Fredonyer Pass W of Susanville, or at the North Fork of the FEATHER R. The range runs S along the E edge of the CENTRAL VALLEY, extending for c.400 mi/640 km, in a band 50–80 mi/100–160 km wide, to (variously) WALKER PASS, the TEHACHAPI Mts., or TEJON PASS. The predominantly granitic range, with its E slope falling from its crest in some of the steepest gradients in North America, and its gentle W slopes, is thought to have formed when part of the earth's crust lifted up and tilted westward along a major FAULT. The E slope is relatively dry, while the W Sierra receives abundant precipitation, esp. in the form of snow, from moisture-bearing Pacific winds. The range generally increases in height from N to S. Few peaks exceed 8000 ft/2440 m in the N, but the crest is over 11,000 ft/3350 m in the S, rising to 14,494 ft/4418 m at Mt. WHITNEY, the highest point in the coterminous US. The southern **High Sierra** includes the greatest clustering of high peaks. Generally described as starting just N of YOSEMITE NATIONAL PARK and extending S for 150 mi/240 km in a 20 mi/32 km–wide band, it is noted for its granite domes, glacial lakes, mountain meadows, recreational areas, and minerals; other peaks over 14,000 ft/4267 m are Mt. Williamson, North Palisade, White Mt. Peak, Mt. Russell, Mt. Split, Middle Palisade, Mt. Langley, Mt. Muir, Mt. Tyndall, and Mt. Barnard. Lake TAHOE, lying E of the Sierra's main mass, is the largest of more than 1200 in the range. Major rivers that drain the Sierra (E–W) include (N–S) the FEATHER, YUBA, AMERICAN, TUOLUMNE, MERCED, KINGS, and KERN. With few E–W gaps, the Sierra presented a daunting obstacle to 19th-century travelers; passes they developed include (roughly N–S) BECKWOURTH, Yuba, DONNER, Luther, Carson, Monitor, Ebbetts, SONORA, and TIOGA. The California Trail through the Donner Pass, the route most used by emigrants, was followed closely by the later LINCOLN HIGHWAY, now by Interstate 80. Gold, discovered at Sutter's Fort in COLOMA in 1848, led to the 1849–50s gold rush; the promise of wealth from the MOTHER LODE and from other mines to the N, and later from the COMSTOCK LODE on the E, was of major importance in Western settlement; many GHOST TOWNS exist in the Sierra. The famed giant sequoia or big tree, *Sequoiadendron giganteum,* native to the W slopes, are now largely protected in YOSEMITE, SEQUOIA, and KINGS CANYON national parks and Calaveras Big Tree State Park. The PACIFIC CREST TRAIL traverses the Sierra. Wilderness areas include those named for the naturalist John Muir and the photographer Ansel Adams. Beside tourism and recreation, lumbering is the primary economic activity in the sparsely populated mountains; copper, gold, tungsten, aluminum, and other metals and minerals are still mined. Some grazing is done and crops are raised, esp. in the W foothills.

Sierra Vieja also, **Vieja Mountains** range largely paralleling the RIO GRANDE for c.30 mi/50 km in SW Texas. They rise to 6467 ft/1972 m at an elevation known as Vieja, 40 mi/64 km NW of Marfa, and are continued (NW) by the VAN HORN Mts.

Sierra Vista city, pop. 32,983, Cochise Co., SE Arizona, 58 mi/93 km SE of Tucson and 15 mi/24 km N of the Mexican border. Formerly a service town for FORT HUACHUCA (W), it has grown quickly (esp. during the 1970s) as a retirement community. It lies in a ranching area.

Signal Hill **1.** city, pop. 8371, Los Angeles Co., SW California, 19 mi/31 km SSE of downtown Los Angeles and completely surrounded by LONG BEACH. The site of a major 1921 oil strike, it is a residential community amid numerous oil wells. **2.** see under SAINT JOHN'S, Newfoundland.

Signal Mountain see under WALDEN RIDGE, Tennessee.

Signal Peak in Arizona: **a.** see under KOFA Mts. **b.** see under PINAL Mts.

Sikeston city, pop. 17,641, Scott and New Madrid counties, SE Missouri, 30 mi/48 km S of Cape Girardeau and 25 mi/40 km W of the Mississippi R. (the Kentucky border). Essentially a Southern city, Sikeston has an economy largely dependent on the processing and shipping of cotton. It also processes other agricultural products, including soybeans, corn, and wheat.

Silent Places, the see under the NORTH, in Canada.

Silicon Forest see under BEAVERTON, Oregon.

Silicon Prairie see under NORTH DALLAS, Texas.

Silicon Valley name, popularized in the 1970s, for the N

Santa Clara Valley and environs, an area extending some 25 mi/40 km from PALO ALTO (NW) to SAN JOSE (SE), mostly in SANTA CLARA Co., NC California, just S of San Francisco Bay. Once primarily a fruit producing region, it became from the 1940s a research and manufacturing center for the electronics and computer industries; Stanford University was its initial academic base. Rapid expansion in the area during the 1950s and 1960s was stimulated by military and other Federal spending. A second major boom occurred in the 1980s as personal and business computer use multiplied. Chief Silicon Valley cities include Palo Alto, San Jose, SANTA CLARA, MOUNTAIN VIEW, MILPITAS, CUPERTINO, and SUNNYVALE.

Silk City, the see under PATERSON, New Jersey.

Sillery city, pop. 12,519, QUÉBEC Urban Community, S Québec, 4 mi/6 km SW of downtown Québec City, on the St. Lawrence R. The site of a 1630s Jesuit mission, it became industrial in the 19th century, and in the mid 20th century became a residential and commercial suburb, with a mix of office buildings, religious institutions, and housing.

Siloam Springs city, pop. 8151, Benton Co., extreme NW Arkansas, just E of the Oklahoma border, and 22 mi/35 km NW of Fayetteville, on the Ozark Plateau. It was founded in 1880 as a health resort because of its mineral springs, and has long been noted as a CHAUTAUQUA center and religious retreat. The city is a shipping center for livestock, fruit, and poultry producers. John Brown University (1919) is here.

Silverado in California: **a. Silverado Mine** see under CALISTOGA, Napa Co. **b. Silverado Canyon** former silver mining area in Orange Co., in the Santa Ana Mts., 11 mi/18 km E of Santa Ana, in the Cleveland National Forest.

Silver City **1.** ghost town in Owyhee Co., SW Idaho, on Jordan Creek in the Owyhee Mts., 48 mi/77 km SW of Boise. After an 1863 silver strike, the settlement became a major producer of gold and silver. It was county seat from 1866 to 1935 and had a population of about 5000. British investments and advanced transportation helped Silver City survive the late-19th-century silver crash. Active mining continued until 1912 and was sporadic through the 1930s. Today the deserted town is a tourist attraction that retains 40 of its original buildings. **2.** hamlet in Lyon Co., W Nevada, 4 mi/6 km S of VIRGINIA CITY and just NE of Carson City, in the Virginia Range, one of the settlements that boomed briefly in the 1860s during the COMSTOCK LODE's heyday. **3.** city, pop. 10,683, seat of Grant Co., SW New Mexico, 86 mi/138 km WNW of Las Cruces and immediately E of the Continental Divide, in the foothills of the Piños Altos Range. From the 1870s gold and silver were mined here, and the town was a shipping center. It was the boyhood home of Billy the Kid. Today the area has irrigated farms and ranches. The Santa Rita open-pit copper mine still operates, and nearby Tyrone (S), a former ghost town, is a copper mining center. Silver City is headquarters for Gila National Forest; lumbering and tourism are important. Western New Mexico University (1893) is here.

Silverdome see under PONTIAC, Michigan.

Silver Hill see under SUITLAND, Maryland.

Silver Lake also, **Silverlake** residential section of LOS ANGELES, California, between Echo Park (SE) and Hollywood (W), 2 mi/3 km NNW of Downtown. Developed around Silver L. Reservoir, it has many early-20th-century houses that were once home to Hollywood figures, and a diverse pop. including working-class Hispanics, Asian immigrants, gays, and artists.

Silvermine see under NEW CANAAN, Connecticut.

Silver Peak Range trending NW–SE for 50 mi/80 km in Esmeralda Co., SW Nevada. Its highest elevations are at Piper Peak (9450 ft/2880 m), 15 mi/24 km SW of the town of Silverpeak, and Magruder Mt. (9050 ft/2758 m), 25 mi/40 km SW of Goldfield. The range was once extensively mined for silver.

Silver Spring unincorporated community, pop. 76,046, Montgomery Co., C Maryland, 7 mi/11 km N of Washington, D.C. The area developed as a residential and commercial suburb following World War II. It houses several scientific research centers, including the applied physics laboratory of Johns Hopkins University, and other offices, including Seventh-Day Adventist world headquarters.

Silverton town, pop. 716, seat of San Juan Co., SW Colorado, on the Animas R., in the San Juan Mts., 38 mi/61 km NNE of Durango. Former hub of the San Juan mining district and a silver boom town from 1871, it grew with the arrival of the Denver and Rio Grande Railroad in 1883. Silverton is now a tourist and trade center near various metal deposits.

Simcoe town, pop. 15,539, seat of Haldimand-Norfolk Regional Municipality, extreme S Ontario, on the Lynn R., 38 mi/61 km SW of Hamilton and 7 mi/11 km N of L. Erie. Settled in the 1790s, it was named in 1875 for the first (1790s) lieutenant-governor of UPPER CANADA, John Graves Simcoe. A trade and processing center in a region producing tobacco, fruits, and vegetables, it also manufactures machinery and textiles.

Simcoe, Lake in S Ontario, between Georgian Bay (NW) and L. Ontario (S), 40 mi/65 km N of downtown Toronto. Up to 30 mi/48 km N–S and 24 mi/39 km wide, it covers 280 sq mi/725 sq km. In the N, it joins L. Couchiching at ORILLIA, and drains NW via the Severn R. to Georgian Bay; it is part of the TRENT CANAL system. In the S is fertile marshland, the province's largest market gardening area. Champlain visited the lake in 1615, and it was central to the fur trading PORTAGE route linking Georgian Bay and L. Ontario. Late in the 19th century, the lake attracted vacationers from the Toronto area. It is now a center for boating, fishing, and ice fishing, and a growing EXURBAN residential hub. BARRIE (W) is the largest city on the lake.

Simi Valley city, pop. 100,217, Ventura Co., SW California, 30 mi/48 km NW of Los Angeles, in the Simi Valley, which is separated from the SAN FERNANDO VALLEY (SE) by the Simi Hills. It was laid out in 1887 in a ranching and citrus raising area, and boomed in the 1960s as freeways reached it from Los Angeles. Incorporated in 1969, it is essentially a planned bedroom community, but has a variety of light industries.

Simpsonville town, pop. 11,708, Greenville Co., NW South Carolina, 11 mi/18 km SE of Greenville, a textile manufacturing center.

Simsbury town, pop. 22,023, Hartford Co., NC Connecticut, on the Farmington R., 10 mi/16 km NW of Hartford. It is a growing residential suburb of Hartford; local manufactures include chemicals and explosives. The Westminster (boys) and Ethel Walker (girls) prep schools are here. Stratton Brook State Park is in the W part. Simsbury was settled in 1660; the first copper coins in the Colonies, called Higley coppers, were minted here in 1737.

Sinclair town, pop. 500, Carbon Co., SC Wyoming, on I-80, 8 mi/13 km E of Rawlins, site of a huge oil refinery complex, opened in the 1920s.

Sinepuxent Bay inlet of the Atlantic Ocean in Worcester Co., SE Maryland, enclosed by the N end of ASSATEAGUE I. It is connected with Chincoteague Bay (S) and ASSAWOMAN BAY (N). Naval hero Stephen Decatur was born (1799) in Sinepuxent village, just to the W.

Singing River, the see PASCAGOULA R., Mississippi.

Sing Sing see under OSSINING, New York.

sink an area of low-lying land with little or no external drainage, in which rainwater or runoff collects and evaporates or passes into the ground, often forming a salt lake or salt flats.

sinkhole surface hole created when a subterranean hollow, formed in a soft rock (esp. limestone or chalk) formation by the dissolving action of water, collapses. Sinkholes may also occur where mine shafts or other underground works collapse.

Sinnemahoning Creek 40 mi/64 km long, in NC Pennsylvania. It is formed by the confluence of several mountain streams in Cameron Co., and flows SE past Emporium as the Driftwood Branch, receiving the Bennett Branch from the W and the First Fork from the N, to join the West Branch of the Susquehanna R. 8 mi/13 km WSW of Renovo, in Clinton Co.

Sioux Center city, pop. 5074, Sioux Co., NW Iowa, 43 mi/69 km NE of Sioux City. Dordt College (1955) is here.

Sioux City city, pop. 80,505, seat of Woodbury Co., NW Iowa, on the Missouri R., at its confluence with the Big Sioux and Floyd rivers. It is situated at the head of navigation on the Missouri, across the Big Sioux from North Sioux City, South Dakota (W), and across the Missouri from South Sioux City, Nebraska (S). A major transportation hub, Sioux City is the distribution and industrial center for a multistate region. The city has large livestock and hog markets and meatpacking houses, as well as grain processing facilities and markets. Manufactures include trucks, tractors, auto parts, processed honey, popcorn, fertilizers, electric tools, and fabricated metals and machinery. The town emerged in the 1850s, flourishing with the steamboat trade and as a supply point for pioneers and miners headed W. With the arrival of the railroad in 1868 and the rise of the meatpacking industry a little later, the population exploded from 1000 to 19,000 in under 20 years. Sioux City is the seat of Morningside College (1894), Briar Cliff College (1930), and Western Iowa Tech Community College (1966).

Sioux Falls city, pop. 100,814, seat of Minnehaha Co. and also partially in Lincoln Co., SE South Dakota, on the Big Sioux R., 75 mi/121 km NNW of Sioux City, Iowa. The largest city in the state, it is 15 mi/24 km NW of the corner of three states: South Dakota, Minnesota, and Iowa. Sioux Falls is an important distribution point for farm machinery, automobiles, and trucks, and a trade and shipping center for the surrounding agricultural region. Meatpacking is the chief industry, but grain milling and dairy processing are also vital to the economy, and steel products are manufactured. It is also a banking and medical center. The North American Baptist Seminary and Augustana (1860), Sioux Falls (1883), and Nettleton colleges are here. The first white settlement was established in 1856, but abandoned after Indian attacks. The building of a military post in 1865 led to resettlement. The availability of waterpower to process stone from nearby quarries spurred growth, and the arrival of the railroad in the late 1800s added to its further development. The Eros Data Center, which collects, processes, and releases information on the earth's surface gathered from satellite and aerial sources, is 16 mi/26 km NE of the city.

Sir Douglas, Mount peak (11,174 ft/3408 m) of the Rocky Mts., 35 mi/56 km SE of Banff, in SW Alberta, near the British Columbia border.

Sir Sandford, Mount see under SELKIRK Mts., British Columbia.

Sir Wilfrid Laurier, Mount see under CARIBOO Mts., British Columbia.

Siskiyou Mountains NE–SW trending subrange of the KLAMATH Mts., extending from near the coast of NW California to the Rogue R. valley in SW Oregon. Rising to a high at Mt. Ashland (7533 ft/2296 m), SW of Ashland, Oregon, the range includes Preston Peak (7310 ft/2228 m), c.30 mi/50 km E of Crescent City, California. The steep granitic mountains, a link between the COAST and CASCADE ranges, boast an exceptionally diverse flora, esp. in the Red Buttes Wilderness Area, and are home to ancient forests. The mountains include sacred sites of the Yurok and Karok; Happy Camp, home to the Karok and an active gold and jade mining area; and the ghost mercury-mining camp, Cinnabar. Lumbering, hunting, fishing, hiking, and fruit growing, esp. along the Rogue R., are carried on. The Oregon Caves National Monument has unusual marble formations. The **Siskiyou National Forest,** headquartered at Grants Pass, Oregon, includes the Kalmiopsis Wilderness, with Pearsall Peak (5098 ft/1554 m) along its E border.

Sitka city, pop. 8588, coterminous with Sitka Borough (2938 sq mi/7609 sq km), SE Alaska, on the W shore of Baranof I., in the ALEXANDER ARCHIPELAGO, 90 mi/140 km SSW of Juneau. In 1799 Aleksandr Baranof and the Russian-American Company established the fur post Fort St. Michael here at Old Sitka, N of the modern center; it was destroyed by the Tlingit, but in 1804 they were subdued; the Sitka National Historical Park commemorates this struggle, and contains the 1842 Russian Bishop's House, the oldest in RUSSIAN AMERICA, of which Sitka, also called New Archangel, was the capital until the sale of Alaska to the US in 1867. The settlement was the capital of American Alaska until 1900. After Juneau replaced it, Sitka declined in importance. In World War II it was an important training center and link in the US defense system. Today commercial fishing and tourism are central to its economy. Reminders of its Russian period include the 1848 St. Michael's Cathedral (rebuilt in the 1960s). Sheldon Jackson College (Presbyterian; 1878), built to educate Indians, is the state's oldest higher learning institution.

Sitting Bull Burial Site see under MOBRIDGE, South Dakota; also, FORT YATES, North Dakota.

Siuslaw National Forest 625,000 ac/253,000 ha (977 sq mi/2529 sq km), in six units along the Pacific coast of W Oregon, from near TILLAMOOK (N) to near COOS BAY (S), on the W of the Coast Ranges. This conifer forest, the only US national forest with extensive accessible shoreline, has 46 mi/74 km of public beaches. The OREGON DUNES National Recreation Area is in the S.

Six Flags chain of amusement and THEME PARKS that began with the Texas history–based Six Flags Over Texas (1961), in Arlington. Later units include Six Flags Over Georgia (1967), in Atlanta; Six Flags Over Mid-America (1971), in

Allenton, 25 mi/40 km WSW of St. Louis, Missouri; Six Flags Magic Mountain (1971), in Valencia (SANTA CLARITA), California; Six Flags Great Adventure (1974), in Jackson township, New Jersey, 18 mi/29 km ESE of Trenton and 48 mi/77 km SSW of New York City; and Six Flags Great America (1976), in GURNEE, Illinois.

Six Rivers National Forest c.1 million ac/400,000 ha (1562 sq mi/4050 sq km), in extreme NW California, extending 135 mi/220 km S from the Oregon border along the W of the Coast Ranges. It is named for the Smith, Klamath, Mad, Trinity, Eel, and Van Duzen rivers, which run through it. The Klamath National Forest lies E, Redwood National Park W. The Hoopa Valley Indian Reservation (pop. 2143), on the Klamath R., extends along the SW.

Sixteenth Street **1.** commercial thoroughfare in downtown DENVER, Colorado, running between the W side of the South Platte R. (NW) and Broadway (SE). The city's central high-end retail street, it is now largely a pedestrian mall, and is a tourist attraction. **2.** thoroughfare in NW Washington, D.C., running N from the White House, between MOUNT PLEASANT (W) and COLUMBIA HEIGHTS (E), then along the E of Rock Creek Park, through an upper-middle-class black residential area known as the Gold Coast, to the Maryland line at SILVER SPRING. It is generally more affluent than neighboring (E) FOURTEENTH St.

Sixtieth Parallel line (60° N) separating the Northwest Territories and Yukon Territory (N) from Manitoba, Saskatchewan, Alberta, and British Columbia (S). "North of Sixty" is a popular name for the territories, a definer of the "True North."

Skagit River 155 mi/250 km long, rising in the N CASCADE RANGE in extreme S British Columbia and flowing SW into NW Washington. It drains much of Mt. Baker–Snoqualmie National Forest and flows W into Skagit Bay of Puget Sound, entering it through a delta SSW of MOUNT VERNON. The Skagit, noted for scenic gorges, was a major lumbering river in the late 19th century. The Skagit Power Project, begun in the 1920s, provides Seattle with electricity produced at Ross, Diablo, and Gorge dams. Ross Dam (1949) forms 24 mi/38 km–long Ross L., which backs up to the British Columbia border within a popular 118,000-ac/47,600-ha national recreation area.

Skagway city, pop. 692, SE Alaska, 85 mi/135 km NW of Juneau, in the PANHANDLE, at the head of Lynn Canal and the mouth of the Skagway R. on the Taiya Inlet. Fourteen mi/23 km SSW of WHITE PASS and 17 mi/27 km S of CHILKOOT PASS, it is a gateway to the Yukon Territory (by way of British Columbia), and famous as the gateway to the KLONDIKE in the gold rush of 1897–98. Thousands flocked here to begin the dangerous journey over the mountains of the Coast Range to the goldfields in the upper valley of the YUKON R. The city is the S terminus of the White Pass and Yukon Railroad, built (1898–1900) to serve the mining camps, now an excursion line. As the N terminus of the INSIDE PASSAGE, it is (in summer) a major cruise ship port and tourist center. The 13,200-ac/5340-ha Klondike Gold Rush National Historical Park (1976) incorporates sites in the city and on trails to the passes.

Skaneateles town, pop. 7526, Onondaga Co., C New York, in the FINGER LAKES, at the N end of Skaneateles L., 7 mi/11 km E of Auburn. On the site of an Indian village, it was settled in the late 18th century, and was an important station on the Underground Railroad. Situated in an agricultural area, it cans foods, has such other manufactures as chemicals and paper, and is a summer resort.

Skaneateles Lake one of the FINGER LAKES in NC New York, 17 mi/27 km SW of Syracuse. It is 15 mi/24 km NW–SE, covers 14 sq mi/36 sq km, and lies 863 ft/263 m above sea level. It resembles a fjord in structure, and supplies water to Syracuse. In 1841, a water cure sanitarium was established here.

Skeena River 360 mi/580 km long, in WC British Columbia. It rises in the Skeena Mts. (in the interior plateaus) and winds generally SSW into Channel Sound of the Pacific Ocean, just S of PRINCE RUPERT. Its main tributaries are the BABINE and the Bulkley, both from the E. TERRACE is the largest settlement along its course. HUDSON'S BAY COMPANY posts were established in the area as early as the 1820s, and the river's use in trade grew in the late 19th century, when salmon fishing also flourished. As a transportation corridor to the Pacific, the Skeena and its tributaries have been served by the Grand Trunk Pacific (Canadian National) Railway since 1914, by the YELLOWHEAD HIGHWAY since the 1950s.

skid road also, **skidway** a road along which logs are skidded (hauled, or slid with the aid of gravity), as toward a mill. In cities that developed around lumber camps, it sometimes became **Skid Road,** a district frequented by loggers, known for its saloons and rowdy atmosphere. The prototype was what is now Yesler Way, in downtown Seattle, Washington, created in the 1850s. By the 1930s, Skid Road had sometimes, where lumber's heyday had passed, become **Skid Row,** a rundown district known for its flophouses and derelicts—whose personal "skid" added a meaning to the name.

Skokie village, pop. 59,432, Cook Co., NE Illinois, on the North Shore Channel, immediately W of Evanston and 20 mi/32 km NNW of Chicago's Loop. It is mainly a bedroom community for workers in Chicago and the metropolitan area. Local industries manufacture aluminum and plastic products, electronic components, motion picture and sports equipment, maps, and pharmaceuticals. Skokie is also a major regional retail hub. The name of the village is a Potawatomi word for "swamp." The area was settled by a group of immigrants from Luxembourg, and was a trading center for local agricultural products, shipping greenhouse produce to Chicago. A development boom occurred in the 1920s with the extension of rail service. Light industries such as printing and publishing moved to Skokie during World War II. Today's village has many Jewish residents. Hebrew Theological College (1922) is here, as is the National Jewish Theater's base.

Skowhegan town, pop. 8725, seat of Somerset Co., SC Maine. It lies on an island and along both banks of the Kennebec R., 16 mi/24 km NNW of Waterville. It is known for its summer school of art and sculpture, summer theater, and state fair. On former Indian ground, the town is graced by a 65-ft/20-m sculpture of an Abnaki by Bernard Langley. In 1775, Benedict Arnold camped at Skowhegan en route to Québec. Senator Margaret Chase Smith was born (1897) and lived here.

Skunk River 265 mi/427 km long, in C and SE Iowa. Its main branch, the **South Skunk,** rises in Hamilton Co. and flows S past Ames, then SE across the state's SE corner. It is joined by the 100 mi/160 km–long **North Skunk** in Keokuk Co. The

Skunk then flows SE to join the Mississippi R., 7 mi/11 km S of Burlington.

Sky City see ÁCOMA, New Mexico.

Skydome multipurpose domed arena, adjacent (W) to the CN TOWER, just SW of downtown TORONTO, Ontario. Seating 56,000, it opened June 3, 1989, as the world's first stadium with a fully retractable roof. It is home to the Blue Jays (baseball) and Argonauts (football).

Skylight, Mount 4920 ft/1501 m, in the Adirondack Mts., in Essex Co., New York, just SW of Mt. MARCY and 13 mi/21 km S of Lake Placid Village.

Skyline Drive 1. see under MANTI–LA SAL NATIONAL FOREST, Utah. **2.** scenic road running along the BLUE RIDGE Mts. in Shenandoah National Park, W Virginia. It covers 105 mi/169 km between FRONT ROYAL (NE) and Rockfish Gap, near WAYNESBORO (SW), from which it continues SW as the BLUE RIDGE PARKWAY. For most of its route the APPALACHIAN TRAIL parallels it.

Skyway see BRYN MAWR-SKYWAY, Washington.

Skyway System pedestrian walkway network in Minneapolis, Minnesota, connecting downtown buildings at the second floor level. Begun in 1962, the system features glass-enclosed, climate-controlled corridors that will ultimately link 64 city blocks.

Slater city, pop. 2186, Saline Co., C Missouri, 38 mi/61 km NNE of Sedalia. It is a trade and processing center for grain, livestock, and dairy products and has some light manufacturing. It was the birthplace of actor Steve McQueen (1930–80).

Slater Mill see under PAWTUCKET, Rhode Island.

Slatersville see under NORTH SMITHFIELD, Rhode Island.

Slave Lake town, pop. 5607, NC Alberta, 1 mi/2 km from the S shore of LESSER SLAVE L. and 131 mi/211 km NW of Edmonton. It has built its economy on local timber and oil resources and has long been a transportation hub between the Arctic and Hudson Bay watersheds. Riverboats had to pass here to reach the PEACE R. country early in the 20th century, leading to the original settlement of Sawridge (1906). A flood (1935–36) resulted in the town being moved 1 mi/2 km to its present site. The construction of the ALASKA HIGHWAY stimulated further growth during World War II.

Slave River 260 mi/420 km long, in Alberta and the Northwest Territories. From the SW end of L. ATHABASCA, it flows NNW into the Northwest Territories, on the SW edge of the CANADIAN SHIELD, past FORT SMITH, to the Great Slave L., which it enters through a delta. It constitutes an upper part of a continuous waterway that follows the MACKENZIE R. lowlands. It receives the PEACE R. 20 mi/32 km after leaving L. Athabasca. Near Fort Smith the Pelican Rapids, an ancient PORTAGE site, have been the focus of a controversy over hydroelectric development. The river is named for the Slavey, a DENE group.

Sleeping Bear Dunes National Lakeshore 71,105-ac/28,798-ha stretch of beach and dunes on the NW shore of Michigan's Lower Peninsula. It lies at the base of the Leelanau Peninsula W of Traverse City, in Leelanau Co., and includes North and South Manitou islands in L. Michigan. The massive dunes, rising to 460 ft/140 m, and 2.5 mi/4 km wide in places, lie atop a huge glacial moraine, forming steep bluffs along the lakeshore. Vegetation includes cottonwoods, white birch, cedar swamp, beach grass, and juniper.

Sleeping Giant 1. basaltic ridge comprising five successive rolling hills resembling a huge, prostrate man, 2 mi/3 km N of HAMDEN, SC Connecticut. Now encompassed in Sleeping Giant State Park, the hills are named for various parts of the anatomy, with the highest elevation at the "Stomach" (737 ft/225 m). Indian myth says the giant is the spirit Habbamock, doomed to eternal sleep for diverting the waters of the Connecticut R. **2.** see under THUNDER BAY, Ontario.

Sleepy Hollow valley in Westchester Co., SE New York, just E of the Hudson R., the setting for Washington Irving's *The Legend of Sleepy Hollow.* It is roughly in TARRYTOWN, NORTH TARRYTOWN, and IRVINGTON.

Slidell city, pop. 24,124, St. Tammany Parish, SE Louisiana, on the Bayou Bonfouca, 2 mi/3 km N of L. PONTCHARTRAIN and 27 mi/43 km NE of New Orleans. It is a computer center for National Aeronautics and Space Administration operations in the region, and also houses many NASA workers. Its longer-established industries include meatpacking, boatbuilding, and the manufacture of brick, tile, and other construction materials. Fishery and tourism are also important.

Slide Mountain 4204 ft/1282 m, the highest point in the CATSKILL Mts., SE New York, 20 mi/32 km WNW of Kingston, in Ulster Co.

Slim Buttes mountain range in NW South Dakota. It extends N–S for 20 mi/32 km, bending slightly SE for 15 mi/24 km at its S tip. The name derives from the narrowness of the range, only 2–3 mi/3–5 km wide in most places. The west-facing cliffs and east-sloping ridges and valleys rise to 3672 ft/1120 m. The 1876 Battle of Slim Buttes, between US troops under George Crook and an Indian band aided by Crazy Horse, was fought in Reva Gap.

Slippery Rock borough, pop. 3008, Butler Co., NW Pennsylvania, 50 mi/80 km NNE of Pittsburgh, on Slippery Rock Creek. In a farm and coal area, it is home to Slippery Rock State Teachers' College (1889).

Sloan village, pop. 3830, Erie Co., W New York, adjoining (E) Buffalo. Most of the village is part of the township of CHEEKTOWAGA; there are large railyards.

Smackover city, pop. 2232, Union Co., S Arkansas, 12 mi/19 km NW of El Dorado. Since oil was discovered here in the early 1920s, extraction and refining have remained important. The name arose by folk etymology from either *chemin-couvert* (covered "road," or stream) or *sumac-couvert* (overhanging sumacs).

Smallwood Reservoir see under CHURCHILL R., Labrador.

Smithers town, pop. 5029, Bulkley-Nechako Regional District, WC British Columbia, on the Yellowhead Highway and the Bulkley R., 130 mi/210 km E of Prince Rupert. In Babine homelands, it developed with the arrival (1913) of the railway, and today is a silver and lead mining center and railroad division point. Lumbering, diverse agriculture, and tourism are also important.

Smithfield 1. town, pop. 19,163, Providence Co., N Rhode Island, 10 mi/16 km NW of Providence, on the Woonasquatucket R. Settled by Quakers in the early 18th century, it includes the villages of Esmond, Georgiaville (the governmental center), Greenville, Spragueville, and Stillwater. There is apple, dairy, and poultry farming. Factories manufacture blankets and yarns and finish textiles. Bryant College (1863) is in the N part. **2.** in Virginia: **a.** town, pop. 4686, Isle of Wight Co., in the TIDEWATER, on the James R., 13 mi/21 km W of Newport News. A tobacco port in the 1630s, it is now known especially for its hams. The area also produces peanuts and lumber. **b.** plantation in Montgomery Co.: see under BLACKSBURG.

Smith Island archipelago, a group of three large and various small low, marshy islands in S Chesapeake Bay, 10 mi/16 km W of Crisfield, Maryland, 8 mi/13 km N–S and up to 4 mi/6 km wide. Settled in the 1650s, it was named for Captain John Smith, who was in the area in 1607. The group contains several small, isolated fishing hamlets, noted also for their wildfowl. The S end is in Virginia, the bulk in Somerset Co., Maryland.

Smith Mountain Lake see under ROANOKE R., Virginia.

Smiths Falls town, pop. 9396, Lanark Co., SE Ontario, on the Rideau R., 40 mi/64 km SSW of Ottawa. Midway on the RIDEAU CANAL, it was a 19th-century trade center, and is now a recreational and rail hub. Local industries produce chocolate, tools, and electrical items.

Smithsonian Institution Federal cultural organization that operates 14 museums and related sites and a number of other facilities. Its headquarters, the "Castle," on the S side of the MALL, in Washington, D.C., was designed by James Renwick and completed in 1855 to house the bequest of James Smithson (d.1829), its British benefactor. Primarily a museum at first, the Smithsonian became known as "the Nation's Attic." Other well-known Smithsonian sites on the Mall include the National Air and Space Museum and National Gallery. Facilities elsewhere include Washington's National Zoo, museums in Anacostia and New York City (the Cooper-Hewitt), storage facilities in Suitland, Maryland, and the Astrophysical Observatory in Cambridge, Massachusetts.

Smithtown in New York: **a.** unincorporated village, pop. 25,638, in Suffolk Co., on the Nissequogue R., on Long Island's North Shore, 2 mi/3 km N of Hauppauge. It is a residential and commercial suburb. **b.** town, pop. 113,406, including the village and other North Shore communities including Hauppauge, Nesconset, and St. James.

Smokey Bear Historical State Park see under CAPITAN Mts., New Mexico.

Smoky Hill River 540 mi/870 km long, in Colorado and Kansas. Formed by headstreams near Cheyenne Wells, in E Colorado, it flows E into Kansas; across the High Plains and through the Cedar Bluff Reservoir (1951) in Trego Co.; through the **Smoky Hill Uplands;** past Ellsworth; and through the nearby (SE) Kanopolis Reservoir (1948). It turns N at LINDSBORG, then ENE at SALINA. Just E of Salina the SALINE R. joins it from the W. At Solomon, the Solomon R., whose eastward course parallels the Smoky Hill's across much of NW Kansas, joins it. Passing S of ABILENE, the Smoky Hill continues ENE to join the REPUBLICAN R. at JUNCTION CITY, forming the KANSAS R.

Smoky Hills region occupying most of NC Kansas, comprising three hill ranges with notable physical features including Coronado Heights, N of Lindsborg; PAWNEE ROCK, a Santa Fe Trail landmark; and ROCK CITY, near Minneapolis.

Smoky Mountains see GREAT SMOKY Mts.

Smuggler's Notch see under Mount MANSFIELD, Vermont.

Smyrna 1. town, pop. 5231, Kent Co., C Delaware, along the Smyrna R., 11 mi/18 km NNW of Dover. Originally a Quaker settlement known as Duck Creek Crossroads, it developed as a commercial and shipping center for local poultry, fruit, and grain, and has food canning and packing plants. BOMBAY HOOK is 10 mi/16 km SE. **2.** city, pop. 30,981, Cobb Co., NW Georgia, 9 mi/14 km NW of Atlanta. Incorporated in 1872, it is a growing residential suburb, with some light industry. **3.** town, pop. 13,647, Rutherford Co., C Tennessee, on Stewart Creek, midway between Murfreesboro (SE) and Nashville (NW). A 19th-century agricultural trade center with manufactures including cedar chests, it is now home to a Nissan auto plant. Its airport (NE) hosts a major annual air show. The home and grave of Confederate hero Sam Davis are here.

Snake Range trending NE–SW, for 60 mi/100 km, E of the Schell Creek Range and just W of the Utah border, in White Pine Co., EC Nevada. Much of it is in the HUMBOLDT NATIONAL FOREST. Wheeler Peak, 35 mi/56 km SE of ELY, is the state's second-highest elevation, at 13,063 ft/3982 m, and has its only permanent ice. The 82,000-ac/33,200-ha Mt. Moriah Wilderness Area, in the N, rises to 12,067 ft/3678 m at Mt. Moriah. A highway (US 50) crosses the range through Sacramento Pass (C), its lowest point, at 7155 ft/2181 m. Below the pass, much of the range lies within the Great Basin National Park, established in 1986. The park includes Wheeler Peak and the Lehman Caves, 5 mi/8 km W of Baker, a labyrinth of calcite formations. A wilderness area with 3000-year-old bristlecone pines is along one of the many hiking trails through the 77,000-ac/31,000-ha park.

Snake River 1038 mi/1671 km long, in Wyoming, Idaho, Oregon, and Washington. The largest tributary of the COLUMBIA R., it takes its name from a Shoshonean people who lived along it. It rises on the S boundary of Yellowstone National Park, and flows S into Grand Teton National Park, through Jackson L. and the valley of JACKSON HOLE, before turning WSW to the Idaho border at the Palisades Reservoir. It then swings NW through SE Idaho until the Henrys Fork R. joins it NE of Idaho Falls. From here it begins a huge arc across S Idaho, in which it passes through the lava flow–dominated **Snake River Plain,** an arid plateau now home to extensive potato, vegetable, and other farming thanks to irrigation projects. In this section it flows SW past Idaho Falls and the FORT HALL Indian Reservation, and through the American Falls Reservoir; then W, through L. Walcott (formed by the Minidoka Dam) and past Burley and Twin Falls; and WNW to the Oregon border, through Strike Reservoir, formed by the C.J. Strike Dam. It crosses briefly into Oregon, where the OWYHEE R. joins it from the SW, then winds N, forming the Idaho-Oregon and Idaho-Washington borders, until it reaches Lewiston, Idaho. In this northward stretch, it is joined by the BOISE and Payette rivers (from the E), and continues into HELLS CANYON (the "Grand Canyon of the Snake"), where the SALMON R. joins it, also from the E. At Lewiston it receives the CLEARWATER R., from C Idaho. In its course through Idaho, the Snake, with its tributaries, drains almost the entire state, and provides water and power for S Idaho's agriculture and cities; its plain separates the Northern Rocky Mts. from the Middle Rockies (S) and the Great Basin. From Lewiston the river turns NW into Washington, and winds generally W to the Columbia R. just below Pasco and Kennewick. A series of dams on this stretch allow small-boat navigation as far upstream (140 mi/225 km) as Lewiston. Tributaries in Washington, where the river flows through the PALOUSE country, are noted salmon streams. The Snake was seen by whites first during the Lewis and Clark expedition, in 1805, and was known for a time as the Lewis R. It became an important link in westward expansion; the OREGON TRAIL paralleled its course in S Idaho.

Snedens Landing residential community below the PALISADES of the Hudson R., part of Orangetown, Rockland Co., SE New York, across the river from DOBBS FERRY, just N of the New Jersey line and 12 mi/19 km N of the George Washington Bridge. It was the site of a well-known ferry, in operation from 1758 to the end of World War II, and a mid-19th-century commercial center. Consisting of fewer than 100 houses, it has been a fashionable retreat for artists, writers, musicians, actors, and other creative people since the turn of the 20th century.

Snellville city, pop. 12,084, Gwinnett Co., NE Georgia, a residential suburb 23 mi/37 km ENE of Atlanta.

Snohomish County 2098 sq mi/5434 sq km, pop. 465,642, in NW Washington. EVERETT is its seat. Parts of the Mt. Baker–Snoqualmie National Forest and the CASCADE RANGE are in the E; many N Seattle suburbs, unincorporated communities as well as cities like LYNNWOOD and EDMONDS, are in the SW, on Puget Sound. Lumbering, dairying, fruit and poultry raising, and varied mining are important, and the aircraft industry is a leading employer. The pop. grew 38% in the 1980s.

Snohomish River see under SNOQUALMIE R., Washington.

Snoqualmie River 45 mi/72 km long, in WC Washington. It is formed by headstreams near the city of **Snoqualmie** (pop. 1546, King Co.), 27 mi/43 km E of Seattle, in the E CASCADE RANGE, and flows W and NW to merge with the Skykomish R. near Monroe, forming the 25 mi/40 km–long Snohomish R., which flows NW through Everett to Puget Sound. **Snoqualmie Falls,** just NW of Snoqualmie, drops 270 ft/82 m, and has a pioneer (1898) underground power-generating facility. In the 1980s, the falls were a backdrop for the television series *Twin Peaks,* which was filmed largely in Snoqualmie and in North Bend (city, pop. 2578), 3 mi/5 km SE. The **Snoqualmie Pass** area, 20 mi/32 km ESE in the Mt. Baker–Snoqualmie National Forest, is one of Washington's most popular ski resorts.

Snowbelt see FROST BELT.

Snowbird resort: see under ALTA, Utah.

Snowbird Mountains E extension of the UNICOI Mts., along the Cherokee-Graham county line in SW North Carolina. The range reaches its highest elevation (4743 ft/1447 m) N of Andrews, is within the NANTAHALA National Forest, and is the site of the Joyce Kilmer Memorial Forest (3880 ac/1571 ha), named for the poet who wrote "Trees."

Snowmass Village town, pop. 1449, Pitkin Co., WC Colorado, 7 mi/11 km W of Aspen. The popular Snowmass ski area is just outside the town and has some 2000 ac/810 ha of skiing terrain. **Snowmass Mt.** (14,092 ft/4298 m) is 9 mi/14 km SW of the town.

Snows, the see LES CHENEAUX Is., Michigan.

Snowshoe Peak see under CABINET Mts., Montana.

Snowy Mountain 3903 ft/1190 m, in the Adirondack Mts. in Hamilton Co., NC New York, slightly W of Indian L. and 10 mi/16 km SSE of BLUE MOUNTAIN LAKE.

Snyder city, pop. 12,195, seat of Scurry Co., NC Texas, 79 mi/128 km SE of Lubbock, in the Osage Plains. Beginning as a trading post built by Pete Snyder in 1876, the community grew into a cattle town; sheep, hogs, cattle, and cotton are still raised in the area. The opening of the large Canyon Reef oilfield caused a boom after 1950. Snyder is home to Western Texas College (1969).

Socastee unincorporated community, pop. 10,426, Horry Co., NE South Carolina, 6 mi/10 km W of Myrtle Beach. On the older road and bridge leading onto the GRAND STRAND, and on the Atlantic Intracoastal Waterway, it is a resort gateway community, and grew quickly in the 1980s.

Society Hill residential neighborhood in C Philadelphia, Pennsylvania, named for the Free Society of Traders, a stock company formed by William Penn. The area was once one of Philadelphia's worst slums, but a major renewal effort in the 1950s transformed it into one of the city's most affluent residential areas, with rows of Colonial town houses and 18th-century churches mixed with high-rise apartment buildings.

Socorro **1.** city, pop. 8159, seat of Socorro Co., WC New Mexico, on the Rio Grande and Interstate 25, 75 mi/120 km SSW of Albuquerque. Built on the ruins of Piro Pueblo, around the 1628 San Miguel MISSION (successor to a 1598 attempt), it was an important post on the Spanish route between Mexico and SANTA FE. A railroad and mining town before 1900, it was for many years a shipping center for silver, cattle, and flour producers. The New Mexico Institute of Mining and Technology (1889) and related businesses currently provide its economic base. **2.** town, pop. 22,995, El Paso Co., W Texas, on the Rio Grande, 13 mi/21 km SE of downtown El Paso. One of the oldest communities in the state, it developed in the early 1680s as Concepción del Socorro, a Spanish mission. Its economy has been based on irrigated farming, but it has experienced rapid suburban growth since the 1970s.

Soddy-Daisy city, pop. 8240, Hamilton Co., SE Tennessee, 18 mi/29 km NNE of Chattanooga, on the W side of Chickamauga L., in the Tennessee Valley. Local manufactures have included brick, tile, and textiles. The city incorporates the former villages of Soddy and Daisy.

SoHo commercial and residential district, lower Manhattan, New York City. *So*uth of *Ho*uston Street (whence its name) and Greenwich Village, it is now a widely known artists' and boutique zone. In the mid 19th century, the area became the world's most notable cast-iron district as that building technology was applied in constructing industrial warehouses and lofts. The same buildings attracted artists in the 1950s and 1960s, leading to SoHo's designation as an area in which certified artists may inhabit otherwise nonresidential buildings. In warehouse days, the area was called Hell's Hundred Acres for the frequency of fires in the tightly packed buildings. Some blocks N of Houston St. have recently been called NoHo in an effort to capture some of SoHo's aura.

Solana Beach city, pop. 12,962, San Diego Co., SW California, on the Pacific Ocean, 20 mi/32 km NNW of downtown San Diego. It is a residential and resort community in an area formerly occupied by fruit, truck, and flower producers.

Solano County 834 sq mi/2160 sq km, pop. 340,421, in NC California. It is bordered by the Carquinez Strait (SW), Suisun Bay (S), and the Sacramento R. (SE), and extends into low foothills in the W. FAIRFIELD is its seat; Vallejo, Benicia, Dixon, and Vacaville are other important cities. Most of the county is rich Sacramento Valley agricultural land, producing a wide variety of crops and livestock; industry is concentrated in the S ports.

Soldier Field sports stadium in Burnham Park, on L. Michigan, SE of the LOOP in Chicago, Illinois. Built in 1924, it has been the home field of the Chicago Bears (football) since 1971. It has also been the site of many different kinds of events, from boxing matches to a civil rights rally led by Martin Luther King, Jr. (1966).

Soledad city, pop. 7146, Monterey Co., WC California, in the SALINAS Valley, 33 mi/53 km SE of Monterey. Near the ruins of Mission Nuestra Señora de la Soledad (1791), it is the site (NW, along EL CAMINO REAL) of a state men's prison. Truck, dairy, and livestock farming and winemaking are major local occupations.

Solon city, pop. 18,548, Cuyahoga Co., NE Ohio, 15 mi/24 km ESE of Cleveland, of which it is a commuter suburb. It was founded c.1820 and named after the ancient Greek lawgiver. Frozen foods, mining equipment, sporting goods, and clothing are among local products.

Solvay see under GEDDES, New York.

SoMa see SOUTH OF MARKET, San Francisco, California.

Somers town, pop. 16,216, Westchester Co., SE New York, 21 mi/34 km N of White Plains. Hilly and largely rural, it is becoming increasingly suburban. IBM and Pepsico have corporate office parks here. The New Croton Reservoir lies S and E, and the Amawalk Reservoir is entirely within the town.

Somerset **1.** city, pop. 10,733, seat of Pulaski Co., S Kentucky, 60 mi/97 km S of Lexington. Agriculture (especially tobacco and livestock), timber, and stone have been the backbone of its economy. Furniture, auto parts, plumbing fixtures, feed, and glass are manufactured. DANIEL BOONE NATIONAL FOREST, just E, and L. Cumberland, just SW, draw visitors to the area. MILL SPRINGS is 15 mi/24 km SW. **2.** town, pop. 17,655, Bristol Co., SE Massachusetts, on the Taunton R. across (W) from Fall River. Settled in 1677 as part of Swansea (W), it separated in 1790. Somerset was famous for its clipper ships in the early 19th century. Industries include the manufacture of shellac, varnish, and paper products. **3.** unincorporated village, pop. 22,070, in Franklin township, Middlesex Co., E New Jersey, adjacent (NW) to New Brunswick. It is largely residential. Numerous events are held in its Garden State Exhibit and Convention Center. The Colonial Park Arboretum and Rose Gardens and a nature trail along the old Delaware and Raritan Canal are here.

Somerset County 305 sq mi/790 sq km, pop. 240,279, in NC New Jersey, bounded (NE) by the Passaic R. Its seat is SOMERVILLE. Its N section has affluent residential communities such as Bernardsville, Far Hills, and Basking Ridge, and is home to numerous corporate complexes. The county has been largely agricultural in character, producing vegetables, grain, and poultry, but is experiencing rapid suburbanization, particularly along Interstates 287 and 78, which cross in the NW.

Somers Point city, pop. 11,216, Atlantic Co., SE New Jersey, on Great Egg Harbor Bay, 10 mi/16 km SW of Atlantic City. Founded c.1695, it was called Egg Harbor at the time of the Revolution. A resort center on the Garden State Parkway, it is connected by causeway to Ocean City and the Atlantic coast, 2 mi/3 km E.

Somersworth city, pop. 11,249, Strafford Co., SE New Hampshire. It is on the Salmon Falls R., opposite Berwick, Maine, 5 mi/8 km N of Dover. The first cotton mill was established in 1822. The city was the town of Great Falls until 1893. Industries include dairy farming and the manufacture of woolens, footwear, yarn, and electrical machinery.

Somerville **1.** city, pop. 76,210, Middlesex Co., E Massachusetts. It is built on seven hills, along the Mystic R., surrounded by Boston, Cambridge, Arlington, and Medford. Somerville was part of Charlestown from 1630 to 1842. Brickmaking was established after the Revolutionary War. The Middlesex Canal (1802) and a railway in the 1830s encouraged industrial growth. After 1900, slaughtering and meat packing were major industries. Somerville now manufactures paper boxes, metal products, and foodstuffs. The city is a major bedroom community for Boston and Cambridge. Its residents are a mix of working-class European ethnics, young professionals, and students. **2.** borough, pop. 11,632, seat of Somerset Co., NC New Jersey, on the Raritan R., 10 mi/16 km NW of New Brunswick. Settled by Dutch traders in 1683, it was a Revolutionary War center. Somerville developed with the arrival of the railroad in the mid 19th century. While largely residential, it has important commercial, farm trade, and industrial sectors; manufactures include pharmaceuticals and electronic components. Among notable sites are the Wallace House, Washington's headquarters in 1778–79, and Duke Gardens. It is the seat of Somerset County College (1968).

Somes Sound see under MOUNT DESERT ISLAND, Maine.

Sonoma County 1604 sq mi/4154 sq km, pop. 388,222, in NW California. SANTA ROSA is its seat. On the Pacific Ocean (W), in the Coast Ranges, it is bordered S by MARIN Co. and San Pablo Bay, and drained by the Russian R. With its neighbor (E) NAPA Co., it forms the best-known US winemaking region; major wineries and vineyards are along the Sonoma Creek, in the Sonoma Valley (Valley of the Moon), from Sonoma (S) to GLEN ELLEN (N), as well as farther N, near HEALDSBURG. Long primarily rural and agricultural, with mineral and hot springs; dairy farms; a poultry industry center at PETALUMA; and famed apple orchards at SEBASTOPOL, it is increasingly urban and suburban, with industrial centers at Santa Rosa, Petaluma, and Healdsburg. **Sonoma** (city, pop. 8121), 16 mi/26 km SE of Santa Rosa, is a trade center in a wine, dairy goods, and fruit producing region. Founded in 1835 on the site of the 1823 Mission San Francisco Solano de Sonoma, it was the seat of the short-lived Bear Flag (California) Republic (June–July 1846), and its Buena Vista Vineyards have been well known since the 1850s. Tourism is central to its economy.

Sonora city, pop. 4153, seat of Tuolumne Co., EC California, just NE of New Melones L. (the STANISLAUS R.) and 50 mi/80 km E of Stockton, in the W foothills of the Sierra Nevada. On the MOTHER LODE, it became in the 1850s the "Queen of the Southern Mines," booming along with nearby (N) Columbia. Named by Mexican miners who retreated here from American hostility farther N, it was in turn taken over by American miners by 1852. Later an important lumber center, it is today a tourist magnet and EXURB.

Sonoran Desert largest North American desert, largely in the Mexican states of Sonora and Baja California, and covering some 30,000 sq mi/78,000 sq km in SW Arizona. California's MOJAVE and COLORADO deserts, on the W, are extensions. The Sonoran is known locally by several names. The GILA R. flows through its center, and it is sometimes called the Gila Desert. It is also called the Yuma Desert in the vicinity of YUMA. It is generally the hottest desert of North America, but has a wide range of terrains; it is noted for its native saguaro and organ pipe cactus, and for animals adapted to extremely harsh living conditions, but there is also irrigated agriculture along the lower Gila and Colorado rivers. The BABOQUIVARI, HARCUVAR, Maricopa, and other mountain ranges are here, along with the CABEZA PRIETA National Wildlife Refuge and BARRY M. GOLDWATER military range. Phoenix is on the NE, Tucson on the E.

Sonora Pass at 9628 ft/2935 m, through the SIERRA NEVADA, 24 mi/39 km WNW of Bridgeport, in EC California, where Alpine, Mono, and Tuolumne counties join. Widely used by explorers, emigrants, and gold seekers in the mid 1800s, it is today on Route 108. **Sonora Peak** (11,460 ft/3493 m) is just N.

Soo, the from the French *sault* (rapid), the region around SAULT SAINTE MARIE, the falls of the Saint Mary's R., in SC Ontario and Michigan's E Upper Peninsula. French explorers, the first Etienne Brulé in 1618, began European contact with the area. French and British outposts were maintained through the 18th and 19th centuries. From 1799 until it was destroyed in the War of 1812, there was a lock and canal here; in 1853 the US began to develop the first of the modern **Soo Canals.** Operative beginning in 1855, the two canals on the Michigan side are 1.6 mi/2.6 km long. On the Ontario side, a single canal opened 1895 is 1.4 mi/2 km long. The Soo Canals, among the world's busiest, brought L. Superior's ore and grain to the East, and eventually, with the opening of the SAINT LAWRENCE SEAWAY, to the world.

Sorel city, pop. 18,786, Bas-Richelieu Co., S Québec, 44 mi/72 km NE of Montréal, on the S bank of the St. Lawrence R. and the mouth of the R. Richelieu. Founded in 1672, it is the commercial hub for a farming region, and an industrial center. Manufactures include steel, furniture, clothing, synthetic fibers, plastics, and concrete. Shipbuilding (esp. important during World War II) and titanium smelting are also key. Grain is shipped from the port.

Soulard redeveloped historic district and commercial zone on the South Side of SAINT LOUIS, Missouri, 1 mi/1.6 km S of Downtown, near the I-44/I-55 junction, around the old Soulard Market. To the W of large railyards, it is one of the city's livelier entertainment areas.

Soul City black-created community projected by civil rights movement leader Floyd McKissick and others in the 1970s. Set along US 1 in Warren Co., N North Carolina, 9 mi/14 km NE of Henderson, it was to house 45,000 by the year 2000, but quickly ran into financial problems, and remains today a rural hamlet.

Souris town, pop. 1333, NE Prince Edward Island, at the head of Colville Bay, 45 mi/72 km NE of Charlottetown. Settled (1748) by Acadians, it was overrun (1750) by mice, giving it its name. The town is still a center of Acadian culture, as well as a fishing and lobstering port and commercial center for NE Kings Co. A ferry connects it with the Îles de la Madeleine, Québec.

Souris River also, **Mouse River** 435 mi/700 km long, in Saskatchewan, North Dakota, and Manitoba. It rises in SE Saskatchewan and flows SE into North Dakota, passing through L. Darling and by Minot. North of VELVA it turns N, and flows through the Salyer National Wildlife Refuge and into W Manitoba just NE of Westhope. In Manitoba it continues NE and enters the Assiniboine R. SE of Brandon.

South, the in the US, term with various historical and geographical meanings. Before the Civil War, it meant the **Slave States** S of the MASON-DIXON LINE. When the war began, it became synonymous with the **Confederacy** (Confederate States of America): Alabama, Arkansas, Florida, Georgia, Louisiana, Mississippi, North Carolina, South Carolina, Tennessee, Texas, and Virginia (minus what became West Virginia). Former slave states that remained with the Union (Missouri, Kentucky, Maryland, and Delaware) are known as **Border States** or **the Border South,** although that term is also taken to include Virginia, which before the war bordered on Free (Northern) territory, and sometimes also Tennessee (which like Virginia was divided in sympathies). The Civil War brought the end of the **Old South,** the slavery- and plantation-based economy and culture of much of the Confederacy; in its place a **New South** was said to be rising, with more diversified agriculture, a growth of industry, and different social arrangements. There have been several subsequent appearances of a "New South," as during 1920s industrialization and the more recent boom in the SUNBELT. From the post–Civil War era through the 1960s, the **Solid South** was those parts of the South considered absolutely loyal to the Democratic Party, in some areas the only functional political party for close to a century. The **Deep South** is the region thought of as most typically Southern in its economy and conservative politics, esp. Louisiana, Mississippi, Alabama, Georgia, South Carolina, and perhaps N Florida. The **Upper South** either is simply "up" in a map sense (e.g., Tennessee, North Carolina, and Virginia), or represents a combination of that idea with the concept of the **Upland South** (APPALACHIAN and PIEDMONT areas). The **Mid-South** is a loosely defined area extending roughly from Memphis, Tennessee, to Charlotte, North Carolina. **Down South** refers to map position; **Up South** is a term used, sometimes ironically, by 20th-century black migrants, for Northern cities in which they resettled. The **Southeast** is simply a quadrant of the US, the states S of the Mason-Dixon Line and Ohio R. and E of the Mississippi R. See also the SOUTHWEST.

South Amboy city, pop. 7863, Middlesex Co., EC New Jersey, across the Raritan R. (S) from Perth Amboy. Settled in 1651, it has rich clay beds, which have provided an industrial base. In 1832 the Camden and Amboy Railroad made South Amboy a major shipping point. Local munitions handling has led to two devastating explosions, in World War I and again in 1950.

Southampton in New York: **a.** village, pop. 3980, in Suffolk Co., on Long Island's SOUTH FORK, 33 mi/53 km SW of Montauk Point and 100 mi/160 km E of New York City. It is a well-known, affluent summer resort, attracting among others celebrities in the arts, with large estates along the beaches. Southampton was settled in 1640 by colonists from Lynn, Massachusetts; many Colonial buildings survive. Southampton College of Long Island University (1963) is here. **b.** town, pop. 44,976, including the village and other resort communities such as QUOGUE and Westhampton.

Southampton County 603 sq mi/1562 sq km, pop. 17,550, in SE Virginia. Its seat is Courtland. Bounded S by North Carolina, W by the Meherrin R., and E by the Blackwater R., and drained by the NOTTOWAY R., it has diverse agriculture, raising peanuts, cotton, and other products. The slave leader Nat Turner was born (1800) in Southampton Co., and led an 1831 rebellion that attempted to take Jerusalem (now Courtland). Turner and his approximately 70 fellow rebels were all executed.

South Anna River see under NORTH ANNA R., Virginia.

South Augusta unincorporated community, pop. 55,998, Richmond Co., E Georgia, a residential suburb adjacent (S) to Augusta.

Southaven city, pop. 17,949, De Soto Co., NW Mississippi, along the Tennessee line and 10 mi/16 km S of downtown Memphis. It is a primarily white residential suburb, in some ways an extension of Memphis's WHITEHAVEN district.

South Baltimore areas of BALTIMORE, Maryland, and adjacent Baltimore Co. along the PATAPSCO R., SE of Downtown. Although everything in the city S of Baltimore St. is "South," the term is used esp. of in-city (e.g., FELLS POINT) and noncity (e.g., the industrial zone of SPARROWS POINT) districts, whose residents have traditionally been working-class, although GENTRIFICATION has occurred in some neighborhoods.

South Bay in California: **a.** collection of waterfront communities in LOS ANGELES Co., on Santa Monica and San Pedro bays, from S of Venice to Long Beach, including Marina del Rey, Playa del Rey, Westchester, El Segundo, Manhattan Beach, Hermosa Beach, Redondo Beach, Torrance, Palos Verdes Estates, Rancho Palos Verdes, and the San Pedro section of Los Angeles. Although in parts heavily industrial and commercial, it is thought of as the center of the Los Angeles area's sun-and-surf popular culture. **b.** group of communities in SAN DIEGO Co., along the S half of San Diego Bay, including National City, Chula Vista, Palm City, San Ysidro, Imperial Beach, and Coronado. **c.** communities at the S end of SAN FRANCISCO BAY, chiefly in Santa Clara Co., but also (as Palo Alto) in San Mateo Co. Now dominated by San Jose, the area is more often thought of as SILICON VALLEY.

South Beach 1. also, **Art Deco District** see under MIAMI BEACH, Florida. **2.** coastal section, NE Staten Island, New York, on Lower New York Bay, between the site of the VERRAZANO-NARROWS BRIDGE (N) and Great Kills (S). In the late 19th century it was a fashionable resort, and after the 1928 opening of the Goethals Bridge and Outerbridge Crossing, became popular with New Jerseyans. The area was heavily developed after the 1964 opening of the Verrazano Bridge. The beaches are now little used because of pollution; the shoreline is a unit of the GATEWAY NATIONAL RECREATION AREA.

South Belmar see under BELMAR, New Jersey.

South Bend city, pop. 105,511, seat of St. Joseph Co., N Indiana, on the great bend of the St. Joseph R., 75 mi/121 km SE of Chicago and adjoining (W) MISHAWAKA. The French explorer La Salle camped here (1679) and signed a treaty with local Indians (1681). A Miami village, then a French mission, it became a fur trading post in the early 1820s. The Studebaker company, founded here in 1852, manufactured wagons, then automobiles, and played an important role in the economy until its closing (1963). Today South Bend has a variety of manufactures, including auto parts, missiles, farming, construction, and electrical machinery, medical instruments, pharmaceuticals, tools and dies, paints, and plastics. A railroad center set amid rich farmland, it is also a trading and shipping hub. The University of Notre Dame and St. Mary's College are just N, in NOTRE DAME.

South Berwick town, pop. 5877, York Co., extreme SW Maine. It is on the Salmon Falls R., opposite Dover, New Hampshire, and includes the Powder House and Spring Hill ski areas. Textile and shoe manufacture are the main industries. South Berwick is the 1849 birthplace of author Sarah Orne Jewett. The author Gladys Hasty Carroll also lived here. Jonathan Hamilton House (1788) and Berwick Academy are here.

Southborough town, pop. 6628, Worcester Co., EC Massachusetts, 14 mi/22 km E of Worcester and 24 mi/39 km WSW of Boston. Adjoining (S) Marlborough, and on Route 495, it is a largely residential suburb. Saint Mark's School (1865), a prep school, is here.

South Boston 1. familiarly, **Southie** section of EC Boston, Massachusetts, across Fort Point Channel from downtown Boston. It became part of Boston in 1804, having been part of Dorchester. Its older section is a residential community, heavily Irish. City Point and CASTLE I. extend to the E. The N part of South Boston, built on landfill, includes much of Boston's industrial dockland. **2.** independent city, pop. 6997, in, but administratively separate from, Halifax Co., S Virginia, 28 mi/45 km ENE of Danville, on the Dan R. In an agricultural area, it processes tobacco, flour, and lumber, and is a rail junction.

South Bradenton unincorporated community, pop. 20,398, Manatee Co., W Florida, a residential suburb S of Bradenton.

South Braintree see under BRAINTREE, Massachusetts.

Southbridge town, pop. 17,816, Worcester Co., S Massachusetts, on the Quinebaug R. and the Connecticut border, 21 mi/33 km SW of Worcester. Optical goods, tools, cutlery, and textiles have been products of this heavily French-Canadian mill town. It was settled in 1730, almost a century after abortive lead-mining efforts first brought whites into the area.

South Bronx popular name for S districts of the Bronx, New York, particularly as they were considered in the 1970s–90s to embody the worst of urban decay. Presidents Carter and Reagan made highly publicized visits, promising government action. Most of the area was the historic estate of MORRISANIA. MOTT HAVEN is the area observers most often focus on. Other parts of the South Bronx include Port Morris, Melrose, and Hunt's Point. The area was once heavily industrial; today it is a region of decayed housing and extreme unemployment, with attendant social problems.

South Brooklyn historic section, NW Brooklyn, New York, so called because it was the S part of the old city of Brooklyn. It was bounded N by Brooklyn Heights, E by the Gowanus Canal, S and W by Upper New York Bay, and included much of Brooklyn's waterfront, including RED HOOK. CARROLL GARDENS, COBBLE HILL, and BOERUM HILL are modern neighborhoods in parts of old South Brooklyn.

South Brunswick township, pop. 25,792, Middlesex Co., C New Jersey, on US 1 and the New Jersey Turnpike, 12 mi/19 km SW of New Brunswick. An expanding residential, commercial, and industrial suburb, it includes the unincorporated communities of Kendall Park (pop. 7127), Monmouth Junction (pop. 1583), and Dayton (pop. 4392). Princeton township is SW.

South Burlington town, pop. 12,809, Chittenden Co., NW Vermont. It is immediately E and S of Burlington, on the Winooski R., Potash Brook, and Shelburne Bay of L. Champlain. A commercial and residential suburb of Burlington, it is also the site of Burlington International Airport.

South Cape or **South Point** see KA LAE, Hawaii.

South Carolina state of the SE US, usually considered part of the Deep SOUTH (and classified by the Census Bureau as part of the South Atlantic region); 1990 pop. 3,486,703 (111.7% of 1980; rank: 25th); area 32,007 sq mi/82,898 sq km (rank: 40th); ratified Constitution 1788 (8th). Capital and most populous city: COLUMBIA. Other leading cities: CHARLESTON,

NORTH CHARLESTON, GREENVILLE, SPARTANBURG. South Carolina is bordered N and E by North Carolina, and W and S by Georgia (across the SAVANNAH R.). Its Atlantic Coast (SE), along which the ATLANTIC INTRACOASTAL WATERWAY runs, is fringed with BARRIER islands and beaches, including the GRAND STRAND (NE, the site of intensive development around MYRTLE BEACH) and part of the SEA ISLANDS (SW). Most of the state, the Low Country, is in the Atlantic COASTAL PLAIN. Here the PEE DEE, SANTEE, and Edisto rivers and their tributaries, as well as many smaller streams, empty through marshy estuaries or pass through a maze of islands. The ASHLEY and COOPER rivers meet to form the harbor of Charleston, one of the South's historic capitals and the center of the state's largest METROPOLITAN AREA. On the NW is the Federal Savannah River Plant, largely in BARNWELL Co., a center of nuclear processing and waste storage. Above the SANDHILLS and the FALL LINE lies the PIEDMONT region, covering almost all the rest of South Carolina. Columbia, in the state's C at the Fall Line, is one of South Carolina's industrial centers (as well as the seat of the University of South Carolina); others include ANDERSON (NW), ROCK HILL (NE), and Greenville and Spartanburg and their suburbs, in the far NW along Interstate 85, now a major development corridor. Above Greenville, in the extreme NW, is the BLUE RIDGE front, in which SASSAFRAS Mt. (3560 ft/1086 m) is the state's high point. English and West Indian planters settled in the Charleston area in 1670, and built the archetypal plantation economy, using slave labor to grow rice, indigo, and other crops, while enjoying a lavish lifestyle. In the mid 18th century Scotch-Irish farmers moved from the N into the Piedmont, establishing the contrasting UP COUNTRY economy and culture. During the Revolutionary War, South Carolina saw action at EUTAW SPRINGS, COWPENS, KINGS MOUNTAIN, the original Fort Moultrie (on SULLIVAN'S ISLAND, where a rough log fortification was the source of the nickname Palmetto State), and elsewhere. Low Country planters, their wealth augmented by the cotton boom of the early 19th century, were leaders in challenging Federal prerogatives, and in the eventual creation of the Confederacy; the 1861 attack on Charleston's FORT SUMTER began the Civil War. Although Charleston was spared, Columbia and other parts of the state were devastated at war's end, and South Carolina entered a long period of eclipse. The textile industry grew in the Piedmont through the late 19th century, but the Low Country remained in decline until World War II, when military spending and related development brought change. In the postwar period, influential South Carolina politicians negotiated massive military investment in the Charleston area and elsewhere (as at the PARRIS I. Marine base, SW). Since the 1960s, the state has experienced two other forms of rapid growth. Diversified industry has poured into the Greenville–Spartanburg area, attracted by low labor and other costs. Meanwhile, the South Carolina coast has become an important part of the SUNBELT; at Myrtle Beach, HILTON HEAD I. (SW), and numerous islands and communities in the Charleston area, retirement homes, vacation condominiums, golf clubs, and other forms of leisure development have multiplied quickly. Tourist, recreation, and convention trade is drawn by the climate, coastal scenery, the history and architecture of Charleston and vicinity, and beaches. Although modern industry, Northern vacationers, and Federal spending are key to its economy today, South Carolina remains a conservative and historically self-conscious state; this is due in part to the majority of its pop. comprising the same groups, white and black, who peopled it in the 18th and 19th centuries.

South-Central residential and commercial section of LOS ANGELES, California, 7 mi/11 km S of Downtown, along CENTRAL Ave. One of the poorest sections of the city, it suffered heavy damage in 1992 rioting. Long a black community, along with WATTS and COMPTON (SE), it has recently become home to increasing numbers of Hispanic immigrants.

South Charleston city, pop. 13,645, Kanawha Co., WC West Virginia, on the Kanawha R. opposite Charleston. An Indian mound 175 ft/53 m in circumference and 30 ft/9 m tall is in Staunton Park. South Charleston developed after a naval ordnance plant and several chemical companies were established here at the time of World War I, and remains a major chemical producing center.

South Dakota state of the NC US, considered part of the Upper MIDDLE WEST and a GREAT PLAINS state; 1990 pop. 696,004 (100.8% of 1980; rank: 45th); area 77,121 sq mi/199,743 sq km (rank: 17th); admitted to Union 1889 (40th). Capital: PIERRE. Most populous cities: SIOUX FALLS, RAPID CITY, ABERDEEN. South Dakota is bordered N by North Dakota; W by Montana (N) and Wyoming (S); S by Nebraska, with the MISSOURI R. forming the SE third of the boundary; and E by Minnesota (N, with the Bois de Sioux R. forming the N part of the boundary) and Iowa (S, across the BIG SIOUX R.). South Dakota and North Dakota constituted the Dakota Territory (1861) until admitted as separate states. Like its N neighbor, South Dakota has an E (less than half its area) that is part of the drift- and till-covered (see MORAINE) C lowland of the US; this is a rich PRAIRIE area in which wheat, corn, and other feed crops are grown, much for the state's sheep and cattle. The Missouri COTEAU (EC) flanks the Missouri R., which runs NNW–SSE through the middle of the state before forming the SE boundary. The river lies on the E edge of the unglaciated Missouri Plateau, a rougher, drier Great Plains area used for cattle and sheep ranching and some irrigated farming. In the SW are the famous BADLANDS, and to their W the BLACK HILLS, an isolated E outlier of the Rocky Mts., rising to 7242 ft/2209 m at HARNEY PEAK, the highest US elevation between the Appalachians (E) and the Rockies and their S extensions. The state rises generally from about 1000 ft/300 m in the E to over 4000 ft/1220 m in the W. In the E, the JAMES and Big Sioux rivers are N–S flowing E tributaries to the Missouri; in the W, the BELLE FOURCHE–CHEYENNE system and the Moreau, WHITE, and several other rivers are W–E flowing tributaries. The OAHE Dam, just NW of Pierre (C), backs the huge L. Oahe N into North Dakota and W along the Cheyenne R. South Dakota's intensive agriculture is symbolized by the Corn Palace in MITCHELL (SE), but livestock and wheat are typical products of most of the state. Gold (the HOMESTAKE MINE is the leading US producer), silver, and uranium are mined in the Black Hills. Aberdeen (NE) and Rapid City (SW) have agriculturally-related and other light industries, and Rapid City is the gateway to the Badlands and Black Hills. Sioux Falls is also industrial, and has benefited from state laws attracting plants and business offices from neighboring Minnesota and as far as New York. The Dakotas (named for the Western Sioux, also called Lakota) were seen by French travelers in the mid 18th century. Village-dwelling groups like the Arikara and Mandan were then in the area, along with some Sioux, who had already become horse-using plains hunters. The LOUISIANA PURCHASE (1803) brought the region under US control. There was little white presence, though, and the region had been promised (in 1868) to the Indians, before gold was found in the Black Hills (and publicized by George A. Custer) in 1874. In the ensuing rush, the Sioux were forced W and resisted, in an intermittent war that lasted until the 1890 massacre at WOUNDED KNEE. Thousands of Sioux remain in South Dakota, many living (with some other peoples) on the STANDING ROCK and Cheyenne River (NW), PINE RIDGE and ROSEBUD (SW), and other smaller INDIAN RESERVATIONS. Rapid settlement of the territory, from the 1870s, brought Easterners, Germans, Scandinavians, and other Europeans, who remain the dominant groups today. In the 20th century, the number of farms has gradually dwindled, while average farm size has grown, and many rural people have moved to the cities. The University of South Dakota is based at VERMILLION. Tourism is important esp. in the Black Hills, at Mt. RUSHMORE, at WIND CAVE National Park and JEWEL CAVE National Monument, and in the Wild WEST city of DEADWOOD; the CRAZY HORSE MEMORIAL is a noted work-in-progress.

South Dallas residential and commercial section of Dallas, Texas, S of Interstate 30 and N and E of the Trinity R. A collection of working- and middle-class neighborhoods extending SE from Downtown, it is home to most of Dallas's black residents. FAIR PARK lies on the N edge.

South Daytona city, pop. 12,482, Volusia Co., NE Florida, on the Halifax R. lagoon, just S of Daytona Beach, of which it is a residential suburb.

Southeast **1.** one of the quadrants of Washington, D.C., lying S and E of the Capitol. Largely residential, it includes much of CAPITOL HILL as well as ANACOSTIA and other neighborhoods across the Anacostia R. Parts of the Southeast closer to the Capitol are upscale, but the quadrant is generally the District's least affluent and most crowded. **2.** also, **East Bank** area of Minneapolis, Minnesota, SE of Downtown and E of the Mississippi R. Dominated by the University of Minnesota, it includes the neighborhoods of DINKYTOWN and PROSPECT PARK. There is a renovated waterfront development at the Falls of St. Anthony, site of the city's first European settlement. **3.** one of the five sections of PORTLAND, Oregon, a collection of residential and commercial neighborhoods E of the Willamette R. and S of Burnside St. It is a mixture of various ethnic communities, as well as a student bohemia near Reed College (S) and wealthy homes near LAURELHURST Park (N).

Southeast, the see under the SOUTH.

South El Monte city, pop. 20,850, Los Angeles Co., SW California, on the San Gabriel R. (E), 10 mi/16 km E of downtown Los Angeles. It is a predominantly Hispanic residential and industrial suburb, with varied light manufactures.

South End neighborhood in C Boston, Massachusetts, between the downtown and Back Bay (N and NW) and Fort Point Channel and the expressways that divide South Boston from the rest of the city (SE). Its large, well-preserved townhouses, built on landfill in mid 19th century, have become home to professionals who work in downtown Boston. It is a mixed area known for its art galleries, chic restaurants, and trendy shops.

Southern California inexact term reflecting the historical development of California. It is generally taken to include everything S of the TEHACHAPI Mts., in the TRANSVERSE RANGES near Santa Barbara. Although the earliest ALTA CALIFORNIA settlements (1760s) were in the San Diego area, and although Los Angeles was the largest one in the early 19th century, NORTHERN CALIFORNIA developed first, from the 1840s, while it was not until the 1860s, and esp. after the 1885 arrival of the railroad at Los Angeles, that the South began to grow. Oil discoveries, the movie and aircraft industries, World War II, and SUNBELT development, however, have now made it dominant. Los Angeles and San Diego are California's largest cities.

Southern Indian Lake see under CHURCHILL R., Manitoba.

Southern Pacific Railroad first organized in California in 1865, and by the 1870s controlling the development of the CENTRAL PACIFIC RAILROAD (which ceased to exist independently in 1884). Connecting Southern California with the transcontinental (Central Pacific) line by way of the CENTRAL (San Joaquin) VALLEY, the Southern Pacific then built E to Yuma, Arizona, and by 1883 had a line from Los Angeles via El Paso, Texas (near which in 1881 it connected with the SANTA FE RAILROAD, creating a second transcontinental route), to New Orleans, Louisiana; its best-known train, the *Sunset Limited,* travels this route, and in 1993 extended its schedule to Jacksonville, Florida, becoming the first US train to run coast to coast. The SP has also controlled bus, truck, steamship, and ferry lines, along with pipelines and PUBLIC LANDS granted during initial construction, and was attacked in 19th-century California as an "octopus" reaching into all aspects of the state's life. It remains one of the largest US railroads.

Southern Pines town, pop. 9129, Moore Co., SC North Carolina, in the SANDHILLS, 28 mi/45 km WNW of Fayetteville and just W of FORT BRAGG. In a fruit and truck gardening and timber area, it became a popular health resort in the 1880s, and was further developed in the 1920s to capitalize on the national golf craze. Surrounded by golf courses and other recreational facilities, it is today an increasingly popular retirement area, especially with former military officers.

Southern Tier region of W New York comprising the counties along the Pennsylvania border and well S of the ERIE CANAL. Until railroads arrived in the 1850s, it was economically isolated from SE New York; its main rivers, the Susquehanna and Allegheny, drain S through Pennsylvania. Binghamton and Elmira are the major cities; most of the area is agricultural.

South Euclid city, pop. 23,866, Cuyahoga Co., NE Ohio, 10 mi/16 km E of Cleveland, of which it is a commuter suburb. It is the seat of Notre Dame College of Ohio (1922).

South Fallsburg unincorporated village, pop. 2115, in Fallsburg township, Sullivan Co., SE New York, 5 mi/8 km NE of Monticello, in the BORSCHT BELT.

South Farmingdale unincorporated village, pop. 15,377, in Oyster Bay town, Nassau Co., SE New York, on Long Island's South Shore, just W of the Suffolk Co. line and Republic Airport. It is primarily residential.

Southfield city, pop. 75,728, Oakland Co., SE Michigan, 15 mi/24 km NW of Detroit. An affluent suburb, this major office and commercial center has a large sports arena and civic center. It also manufactures auto parts, precision tools, and sporting goods. Southfield is the seat of the Lawrence

Institute of Technology (1932) and the home of Duns Scotus College.

South Fork southern peninsula of the EAST END of Long Island, New York, terminating at MONTAUK POINT. It is still partly agricultural, producing corn and potatoes, but the economy is heavily dependent upon tourism. SOUTHAMPTON, EAST HAMPTON, Bridgehampton, AMAGANSETT, and SAG HARBOR are popular vacation spots and attract affluent summer and part-time residents. The popularity of the area has made it both expensive and crowded, with only one road, for the most part, connecting the different communities.

Southfork Ranch tourist attraction in Collin Co., NE Texas, 22 mi/35 km NE of Dallas, near Parker. The site was used for exterior shots for the long-running *Dallas* TV series. Once a working ranch, it is now a *Dallas* museum, exhibiting memorabilia of the show and its cast.

South Gate **1.** city, pop. 86,284, Los Angeles Co., SW California, 7 mi/11 km SE of downtown Los Angeles and immediately E of Watts. Incorporated 1923, it grew quickly after World War II as part of the industrial district that includes neighboring HUNTINGTON PARK, BELL, and MAYWOOD. Among its manufactures have been automobiles and auto and aircraft parts, a range of industrial and other machinery, paint, tile, furniture, chemicals, clothing, glass products, and electronic equipment. The city is predominantly Hispanic. **2.** unincorporated residential suburb, pop. 27,564, Anne Arundel Co., C Maryland, 12 mi/19 km S of downtown Baltimore, and just SE of Baltimore-Washington International Airport. The area is developing rapidly.

Southgate city, pop. 30,771, Wayne Co., SE Michigan, 12 mi/19 km SSW of Detroit. It manufactures auto parts and electronic and construction equipment, but is primarily a residential suburb of Detroit.

Southglenn unincorporated community, pop. 43,087, Arapahoe Co., NC Colorado, an affluent residential suburb 10 mi/16 km S of downtown Denver and adjacent (E) to Littleton.

South Hadley town, pop. 16,685, Hampshire Co., W Massachusetts, 12 mi/19 km N of Springfield, on the Connecticut R., with the Holyoke Range (including Mt. HOLYOKE) to the N. Founded in the late 17th century, South Hadley developed slowly. By the 19th century, it had several types of milling operations and a tannery; papermaking and farming are still principal industries. South Hadley is the seat of Mount Holyoke College (1837).

South Haven city, pop. 5563, Van Buren Co., SW Michigan, on L. Michigan at the mouth of the Black R., 37 mi/60 km WNW of Kalamazoo. This lakefront port and resort also has commercial fishing, processes and ships blueberries and fruit, and manufactures pianos and baskets. It is the birthplace (1858) of botanist, horticulturist, and educator Liberty Hyde Bailey. Michigan State College has a horticultural experiment station here. The Lake Michigan Maritime Museum has a 600 ft/183 m–long boardwalk displaying historic craft.

South Hero see under HERO ISLANDS, Vermont.

South Hills group of S suburbs of Pittsburgh, Pennsylvania, in Allegheny Co., including the communities of Brentwood, Whitehall, Castle Shannon, Dormont, Mt. Lebanon, West Mifflin, Pleasant Hills, Bethel Park, and Upper St. Clair.

South Holland village, pop. 22,105, Cook Co., NE Illinois, at the junction of Thorn Creek and the Little Calumet R., 17 mi/27 km S of Chicago. This mainly residential suburb also manufactures furniture, boxes, and concrete products. First settled by Dutch immigrants in 1846, South Holland boomed with the arrival of the Illinois Central Railroad in 1853. Truck farming eventually became the economic mainstay of the village. South Holland is the setting of Edna Ferber's novel *So Big*. It was here that the Federal government brought action to implement school desegregation for the first time outside the South under the 1964 Civil Rights Act.

South Holston Lake see under HOLSTON R., Virginia and Tennessee.

South Houston city, pop. 14,207, Harris Co., SE Texas, 10 mi/16 km SW of downtown Houston. Established in 1890, it was surrounded in 1948 by Houston (N,W,S) and Pasadena. Largely residential, it has also been an oil producer.

South Huntington unincorporated village, pop. 9624, in Huntington town, Suffolk Co., SE New York, in WC Long Island, 4 mi/6 km E of the Nassau Co. line and 3 mi/5 km SE of Huntington. It is a residential suburb.

Southington town, pop. 38,518, Hartford Co., C Connecticut, on the Quinnipiac R., 8 mi/13 km E of Waterbury. Since the early 19th century, its economy has been both agricultural and industrial; situated in a fruit growing region, it also produces hardware, airplane and radio parts, tools, pipe fittings, and paper boxes.

South Jamaica see under JAMAICA, New York.

South Jordan city, pop. 12,220, Salt Lake Co., NC Utah, on the Jordan R., a residential suburb 14 mi/23 km SSW of Salt Lake City. The Jordan River (Mormon) Temple is in the city. Salt Lake Co. Equestrian Park features summer horse racing.

South Kingstown town, pop. 24,631, Washington Co., S Rhode Island, 34 mi/55 km S of Providence and W of Pt. Judith, on Block Island Sound. The Narraganset Indians suffered their critical defeat here against Colonists in the Narraganset Fort Fight of Dec. 1675, at the Great Swamp. In 1723, the district, called Kings Towne or Kings Province, was divided into North Kingstown and South Kingstown. Today South Kingstown contains a number of villages, including Kingston, West Kingston (the county seat), Peacedale, and Wakefield. The economy centers around the University of Rhode Island (1892) at Kingston; there is also summer tourism along the shore, and some diversified light manufacturing.

South Lake Tahoe city, pop. 21,586, El Dorado Co., NE California, at the S end of L. TAHOE, at the Nevada border, 95 mi/153 km ENE of Sacramento. The largest community on the lake, it is a year-round resort. Heavenly Valley, just E, claims to be the largest US ski area. Lake Tahoe Community College (1975) is in the city.

South Lawndale see LITTLE VILLAGE, Chicago, Illinois.

South Miami city, pop. 10,404, Dade Co., SE Florida, 7 mi/11 km SW of downtown Miami, a residential suburb of the larger city. It has fruit and vegetable packing and baking industries.

South Miami Heights unincorporated community, pop. 30,030, Dade Co., SE Florida, 17 mi/27 km SW of downtown Miami, a growing residential suburb adjacent (W) to Cutler Ridge.

South Milwaukee city, pop. 20,958, Milwaukee Co., SE Wisconsin, on L. Michigan, 9 mi/14 km S of Milwaukee. Industrialized since 1891, it produces malleable castings, electrical appliances, and excavating and garden machinery. Factories also manufacture tile, wood, metal, plastic, and leather articles. Settled in 1835 as Oak Creek, the city is known for the Wisconsin Spectacle of Music, held here every July in Grant Park.

South Minneapolis group of neighborhoods in Minneapolis, Minnesota, S of Downtown. Developed mostly after World War II, it is a solid middle-class area of low-density, single-family, owner-occupied homes. The wealthier MINNEHAHA PARK area features older houses.

South Moresby National Park Reserve see under QUEEN CHARLOTTE Is., British Columbia.

South Mountain ridge extending about 65 mi/105 km from an area SE of Carlisle, Pennsylvania, across Maryland, into N Virginia. It is the NW prong, and CATOCTIN Mt. is the NE prong, paralleling it, of the BLUE RIDGE. At gaps in South Mt. E of SHARPSBURG, Union forces under George McClellan repelled Robert E. Lee's army (Sept. 14, 1862) in its first invasion of the North. The Confederates retreated toward Sharpsburg, and the battle of ANTIETAM took place.

South Mountains range rising to 2720 ft/829 m, within Phoenix South Mountain Park, 7 mi/11 km S of downtown PHOENIX, Arizona. The 15,728-ac/6370-ha municipal park includes Hidden Valley, strewn with granite boulders and adorned with saguaro cactus.

South Norfolk see under CHESAPEAKE, Virginia.

South Nyack village, pop. 3352, in Orangetown, Rockland Co., SE New York, immediately S of Nyack, on the W bank of the Hudson R., 24 mi/39 km N of New York City. It is situated at the W end of the TAPPAN ZEE Bridge.

South of Market also, **SoMa** commercial and residential section of SAN FRANCISCO, California, lying S of Market St. It was formerly called South of the Slot, in reference to cable car tracks on Market St. The Embarcadero is on the E, the China Basin, on the waterfront, S. The N part of the MISSION DISTRICT, SoMa had factories by the 1850s. Its last industrial prosperity came in World War II, after which it declined; Hispanic immigrants, artists, and others attracted to low rents moved in. From the 1970s massive renewal projects spurred redevelopment; the Moscone Convention Center, Yerba Buena Center (business and residential), and mixed-use Mission Bay Project (S) are among these. Today SoMa is a lively avant-garde, small business, and entertainment district.

South of the Border roadside service area and amusement park in Dillon Co., NE South Carolina, 7 mi/11 km NE of Dillon and just S of the North Carolina line. Opened in 1949 and just off Interstate 95, it is well known for its huge "sombrero" sign and its seemingly ubiquitous billboard and bumper-sticker advertising.

South Ogden city, pop. 12,105, Weber Co., N Utah, a residential suburb immediately S of Ogden.

South Orange officially, **South Orange Village** township, pop. 16,390, Essex Co., NE New Jersey, 4 mi/6 km W of Newark. It was separated from Orange in 1861. South Orange is essentially a suburb of Newark and New York City, and has some light industry. It is the seat of Seton Hall University (1856). South Mountain Reservation lies just W.

South Ozone Park see under OZONE PARK, New York.

South Park cultural and educational district in Southwest PORTLAND, Oregon. A 12-block corridor near the Portland State University campus, it is home to the Oregon Art Institute and the Oregon Historical Center.

South Pasadena city, pop. 23,936, Los Angeles Co., SW California, adjoining (S) Pasadena and 6 mi/10 km NE of downtown Los Angeles. HIGHLAND PARK is W. Mostly an affluent residential suburb, it has some scientific, electronic, and pharmaceutical manufactures.

South Pass 25 mi/40 km wide and 7550 ft/2303 m high, at the S end of the WIND RIVER Mts., on the Continental Divide in Fremont Co., SW Wyoming. It is a long, treeless valley, resembling a plain, with sagebrush hills and sand dunes. Discovered in 1812, it provided a convenient route over the forbidding Rocky Mts. An important unit in the OREGON TRAIL, South Pass was used by trappers in the 1820s, by Captain Bonneville's exploratory expedition in 1832, and later by pioneers and the military. From 1840 to 1860 an estimated 300,000 settlers traveled through the pass on their way W. In the late 1800s it was on the Pony Express route. **South Pass City,** 12 mi/19 km N of the pass, was a goldmining boom town in the 1860s and 1870s.

South Philadelphia residential and commercial district of Philadelphia, Pennsylvania, the oldest section of the city, near the junction of the Schuylkill and Delaware rivers. It was settled by Swedes in the 17th century, before William Penn's arrival. In the 19th century it was home to a small, segregated community of blacks and a large number of Irish immigrants. By the 1880s, East European Jews and Italians had taken over the housing abandoned by earlier residents; today the area is largely Italian. Naval and port facilities, Franklin Delano Roosevelt Park, the sports complex including VETERANS STADIUM, John F. Kennedy Stadium, the SPECTRUM, and the Food Distribution Center are all in South Philadelphia.

South Plainfield borough, pop. 20,489, Middlesex Co., NE New Jersey, adjacent (S) to Plainfield, and 7 mi/11 km NE of New Brunswick. It has research facilities, corporate headquarters, and manufactures including chemicals, pharmaceuticals, electrical supplies, and gypsum products.

South Plains see under LLANO ESTACADO, Texas.

South Platte River 424 mi/683 km long, in Colorado and SW Nebraska. It is formed by the confluence of headstreams near Hartsel, 30 mi/48 km ESE of Leadville, and winds SE, then NE, through the Rocky Mt. FRONT RANGE, and through DENVER, where it receives CHERRY CREEK. Continuing NNE to GREELEY, it receives Rocky Mt. streams including the Big and Little Thompson and Cache la Poudre rivers. From Greeley it turns E, then ENE, across NE Colorado, past Fort Morgan, Sterling, and Julesburg, into Nebraska, where it joins the NORTH PLATTE R. to form the PLATTE R. E of the city of North Platte. LODGEPOLE CREEK joins it near Julesburg. The South Platte and many, chiefly short, tributaries are extensively dammed to prevent flooding, irrigate dry High Plains land, and generate electric power.

Southport **1.** see under FAIRFIELD, Connecticut. **2.** town, pop. 11,571, Chemung Co., New York, adjacent (SW) to Elmira, between the Chemung R. (N) and the Pennsylvania border. Its Pine City section is the site of the Southport Correctional Facility, a maximum security state prison. **3.** city, pop. 2369, Brunswick Co., extreme S North Carolina, on the W side of the Cape Fear R. near its mouth, 16 mi/26 km SSW of Wilmington. On the Atlantic Intracoastal Waterway, it is an important yachting port, and a beach and fishing resort center. Cape FEAR is 6 mi/10 km SSE, and FORT FISHER is 5 mi/8 km NE across the river. The Sunny Point Military Ocean Terminal is 5 mi/8 km NNE, and the Brunswick nuclear power plant, operative since 1975, is 2 mi/3 km N.

South Portland city, pop. 23,163, Cumberland Co., SW Maine. It is on Casco Bay at the mouth of the Fore R., opposite Portland, of which it is a residential and commercial suburb. A shipbuilding center since the 17th century, South Portland now has an oil terminal, copperworks, rolling mills, lumberyards, and factories producing nylon, wire, and pipes. Fort Preble (1808–11), Southern Maine Vocational and Technical Inst., the Portland International Jetport, and much of the Maine Mall, the state's largest shopping complex, are in the city.

South River **1.** in the period of Dutch settlement (1631–1660s), the Delaware R., as distinguished from the Hudson, or North, R. **2.** borough, pop. 13,692, Middlesex Co., E New Jersey, on the South R., a tributary of the Raritan R., 5 mi/8 km SE of New Brunswick. It was settled in 1720. Its chief industry is clothing manufacture; lying in an area rich in clay and sand, South River also produces bricks, tiles, and other building materials.

South Sacramento see PARKWAY–SOUTH SACRAMENTO, California.

South Saint Paul city, pop. 20,197, Dakota Co., SE Minnesota, on the Mississippi R., 4 mi/6 km SE of St. Paul. Settled in the 1850s on the site of a Sioux village, it emerged as an important transportation hub for barge, overland, and, later, rail traffic. Stockyards were founded here in the 1880s, eventually developing into one of the world's largest public livestock markets. Related industries include meatpacking, tanning, and rail repair shops; construction materials are also produced. The Farmers Union Control Exchange is an important farm-supply cooperative. There has been recent commercial development along Highway 3, at the W edge of the city, along the border with WEST SAINT PAUL.

South Salt Lake city, pop. 10,129, Salt Lake Co., NC Utah, immediately S of Salt Lake City, of which it is a residential suburb.

South San Francisco city, pop. 54,312, San Mateo Co., NC California, on San Francisco Bay, at the S base of San Bruno Mt., which separates it from San Francisco, and immediately N of San Francisco International Airport. Heavily industrial since its days as a late-19th-century meatpacking center, it has lumberyards, smelters, foundries, and plants manufacturing metal products, chemicals, paints, machinery, aircraft parts, and medical and biotechnological products.

South Saskatchewan River see under SASKATCHEWAN R.

South Shore **1.** residential neighborhood, S of Jackson Park, on L. Michigan, on the SOUTH SIDE of Chicago, Illinois. A middle- and upper-middle-class neighborhood of apartment buildings and single-family homes, it has been primarily black since the 1960s. After a period of decline, the community stabilized itself residentially and commercially largely through the efforts of the South Shore Commission and the South Shore National Bank. **2.** in Massachusetts, region SE of Boston along the Atlantic Coast. It is an area of small residential towns and seaside resorts, never as commercially or industrially important as parts of the NORTH SHORE. In the late 20th century suburban development advanced through the area. **3.** of Long Island, New York, extending from New York City E along the Atlantic shore. It is a flat, sandy area, with barrier island beaches and inlets popular for boating. Generally more crowded than the NORTH SHORE, and generally less affluent, South Shore communities grew rapidly in the years after World War II. FIRE I. and JONES BEACH are among the best-known South Shore resorts. **4.** in Nova Scotia, the Atlantic coast from the area of Halifax SW to the Yarmouth area.

South Side **1.** collection of neighborhoods S of the LOOP in Chicago, Illinois. Although there have been pockets of affluence here (for example, PRAIRIE AVENUE, PILL HILL, KENWOOD, and SOUTH SHORE), the South Side has generally been poorer than the NORTH SIDE. Irish and black residents have predominated, and since the period after World War I, the South Side has been noted as a point of arrival for Southern blacks, the black cultural center of the Midwest, and, according to generally accepted calculations, the largest US black community. **2.** also, **South Saint Louis** sections of SAINT LOUIS, Missouri, S of Forest Park (on the W) and Downtown (on the E). The old **South End** was S of TOWER GROVE PARK. The area has been home for over a century to Germans and other European immigrant groups (like the Italians on the HILL), and this part of the city, along with adjacent suburbs in St. Louis Co., remains largely white. The huge Anheuser-Busch brewery is in the E, on the Mississippi R. CARONDELET is at the city's S extreme. **3.** collection of neighborhoods in Milwaukee, Wisconsin, S of Downtown. Originally a center for Irish and German immigrants, the South Side was dominated by Poles by the late 19th century. The communities of WALKER'S POINT and BAY VIEW are here, and ethnic diversity characterizes most neighborhoods.

Southside region: see under Commonwealth of VIRGINIA.

Southside Place see under WEST UNIVERSITY PLACE, Texas.

South Sioux City city, pop. 9677, Dakota Co., NE Nebraska, on the Missouri R. opposite Sioux City, Iowa. Founded in 1887, it is a trading and processing hub for grain, vegetable, fruit, and dairy producers. It also manufactures agricultural equipment.

South Station railroad terminal in Boston, Massachusetts, opened in 1900 to unify lines approaching the city from the S. It is along Fort Point Channel, across from SOUTH BOSTON and S from downtown. In the 1900s construction began to further unify bus, subway, and rail lines at the station. Renovations aimed at spurring business growth around the station and in the Fort Point area had been under way since the 1970s. The site of the Boston Tea Party (1773) is just N, along the channel.

South Street commercial and residential street in Philadelphia, Pennsylvania, running 3 mi/5 km between Society Hill (E) and University City (W). It is a popular retail and entertainment strip.

South Texas nuclear power plant: see under BAY CITY, Texas.

South Village see under GREENWICH VILLAGE, New York.

Southwark residential neighborhood in Philadelphia, Pennsylvania, between Queen Village (N) and South Philadelphia (S). Originally a district including all of what is now South Philadelphia below South St. and E of Broad St., it was a poor immigrant section from the 17th century. Dutch and Swedes settled in Queen Village, while English artisans and seamen built simple homes amid riverside warehouses. Germans, Italians, blacks, and Jews later occupied the area. Today, Southwark is a mix of artists, young professionals, and older working-class residents.

Southwest **1.** smallest of the quadrants of Washington, D.C., lying S and W of the Capitol. Once containing densely populated neighborhoods near the Potomac R., it was changed utterly by urban renewal in the 1950s and 1960s, becoming an area of scattered high-rise developments and massive freeways. The government complex around L'ENFANT PLAZA is here, as is the commercial waterfront along Maine Ave. Many of the Southwest's poorer pre-renewal inhabitants were forced into cheap housing in the SOUTHEAST, particularly in ANACOSTIA. **2.** one of five sections of PORTLAND, Oregon, W of the Willamette R. and S of Burnside St. Embracing Downtown, this historic commercial area includes the original core of the city and its present-day administrative center. OLD TOWN straddles the border with NORTHWEST, along the river; WEST HILLS is on the border farther W. Southwest neighborhoods include SOUTH PARK, LAIR HILL, PORTLAND HEIGHTS, and TERWILLIGER.

Southwest, the variously defined US region. Today, it may generally refer to the nation's SW quadrant, from Texas to S California. Historically and culturally, however, it has had other meanings. In the late 18th–early 19th centuries it was the **Old Southwest,** lands S of the NORTHWEST TERRITORY, including Alabama, Mississippi, Louisiana, Arkansas, Tennessee, and Kentucky, into which American pioneers were moving. The Southwest expanded to include Texas and what is now Oklahoma, New Mexico, and Arizona, at the same time that the Old Southwest was becoming culturally and politically part of the SOUTH. Since the Civil War, questions of definition have centered on where in Texas the line between South and Southwest (the latter both more "Western" in economy and more Spanish- and Mexican-influenced in culture) should be drawn; the BALCONES ESCARPMENT has been suggested as a convenient divider.

South Weymouth Naval Air Station see under WEYMOUTH, Massachusetts.

South Whittier unincorporated community, pop. 49,514, Los Angeles Co., SW California, a residential suburb adjacent (S) to Whittier and 14 mi/23 km ESE of downtown Los Angeles.

South Windsor town, pop. 22,090, Hartford Co., NC Connecticut, on the E bank of the Connecticut R. Separated from Windsor in 1845, it is primarily residential.

Spadina Avenue N–S thoroughfare in WC TORONTO, Ontario, running some 5 mi/8 km from L. Ontario (S) to near the North York city line. Named for an 1866 mansion that stands along it next to CASA LOMA, it passes W of QUEEN'S PARK and the University of Toronto. Spadina, Toronto's broadest avenue, has long been noted as an immigrant residential and commercial ("the Strip") center. Once largely Jewish, it is now also Chinese, Portuguese, and home to many other groups. At the Dundas St. intersection is the Kensington Market, famed for its diversity.

Spanaway unincorporated community, pop. 15,001, Pierce Co., WC Washington, 10 mi/16 km S of Tacoma, on Spanaway L. An 1840s agricultural settlement, it is now a growing residential suburb with a popular stock car racetrack.

Spanish Fork city, pop. 11,272, Utah Co., NC Utah, at the foot of the WASATCH RANGE, 8 mi/13 km S of Provo. It was settled by Mormons from Iceland in 1850. Surrounded by irrigated farms and ranches, the city produces flour and other agricultural items and canned goods, and manufactures clothing and explosives.

Spanish Fort former fortification and amusement park in NW New Orleans, Louisiana, 1.5 mi/2 km E of the WEST END and just S of L. Pontchartrain, on the Bayou St. John. A fort built early in the 18th century was garrisoned against British attack in 1814–15. Later in the 19th century the area became a prominent lakeside resort, and in the early 20th century a popular amusement park was here. Today it is in a lakefront residential district.

Spanish Harlem see under EAST HARLEM, New York.

Spanish Lake unincorporated community, pop. 20,322, St. Louis Co., EC Missouri, near the Missouri (N) and Mississippi (E) rivers and the Illinois border (E), 12 mi/19 km NNW of downtown St. Louis. Mainly a residential suburb, it also has several industries, including stone quarrying and the processing of wastepaper.

Spanish Trail also, **Old Spanish Trail** route developed in the 1830s, on the basis of 1770s Spanish explorations, to connect Santa Fe, New Mexico, with California. The 1776 Escalante expedition, hoping to reach Monterey, California, traveled NW from Santa Fe past Abiquiu, to the site of Durango, Colorado, down (N along) the Dolores R., into modern Utah, where it crossed the Colorado R. near Moab and the Green R. near Green River and proceeded W to the Sevier R. before turning back. A misconception grew that either the Green R. or the Sevier R. was the "San Buenaventura," a river that flowed to the Pacific coast. In the 1830s, American and Mexican traders pushed onward, to SW Utah, past modern Cedar City, across extreme NW Arizona, and found a rest stop at Las Vegas ("the meadows"), Nevada. From there the trail continued W across California's Mojave Desert, to the sites of Barstow and Victorville, through the Cajon Pass, and into the Los Angeles area. The Spanish Trail became an extension of the SANTA FE TRAIL, and in the 1840s also an extension of the MORMON TRAIL, as church settlement expanded into California.

Sparkill hamlet in Orangetown, Rockland Co., SE New York, 4 mi/6 km S of Nyack and immediately E of TAPPAN, on the PALISADES of the Hudson R.

Sparks **1.** locality in Baltimore Co., N Maryland, along Interstate 83, 18 mi/29 km N of central Baltimore. It is an area of developing office parks, just NW of Loch Raven Reservoir. **2.** city, pop. 53,367, Washoe Co., W Nevada, on the Truckee R., 3 mi/5 km ENE of downtown Reno. Incorporated in 1905, it is a railroad division point with repair shops. Tourism is now an important industry; there is also some light manufacturing. Sparks was founded as the W Nevada base of the Southern Pacific Railroad. It grew and prospered as a shipping point for nearby gold and silver mines. Favorable tax structures have aided in the city's development as a warehousing center and encouraged national corporations to build facilities here. Another economic asset is the area's irrigated agriculture, principally producing hay, potatoes, and onions. Part of the Reno metropolitan area, Sparks has grown rapidly, doubling in pop. since 1970.

Sparrows Point unincorporated industrial district in Baltimore Co., C Maryland, on the Patapsco R., 9 mi/14 km SE of Baltimore. One of the world's largest steel plants was founded here by the Bethlehem company in 1887; large shipyards date from 1890. There are extensive ship and rail terminals. The Francis Scott Key Bridge and Interstate 695 pass just N, and EDGEMERE is NE.

Spartanburg city, pop. 43,467, seat of Spartanburg Co. (pop. 226,800), NW South Carolina, 30 mi/48 km ENE of Greenville, in the foothills of the Blue Ridge Mts. Established as a courthouse village in 1785, it took its name from the Spartan Rifles, a local Revolutionary regiment. The area became noted for its cotton mills and ironworks, and after 1865 growth was spurred by the intersection of three major rail lines. Spartanburg is now the heart of a booming industrial complex that produces rubber and paper products, tires, footwear, electronics, clothing, chemicals, machinery, ceramics, and furniture. Interstate 85, the Greenville-Spartanburg Airport (about halfway between the cities), low labor costs, and other factors combined in the 1990s to continue to attract industry to the area. The city is home to Wofford College (1854), Converse College (1889), and several other schools.

Sparwood district municipality, pop. 4211, East Kootenay Regional District, extreme SE British Columbia, in the Rocky Mts., 6 mi/10 km NW of CROWSNEST PASS, Alberta, and 48 mi/77 km N of the Montana border, site of the largest soft coal mining operation in Canada.

Spavinaw town, pop. 432, Mayes Co., NE Oklahoma, just NW of Spavinaw L., and 54 mi/87 km ENE of Tulsa. It is the birthplace (1931) of baseball great Mickey Mantle.

Spear, Cape headland on the E side of the AVALON PENINSULA, in E Newfoundland, 5 mi/8 km SE of St. John's. The most easterly point in North America, at 52° 37′ W, it has a National Historic Park and the oldest extant lighthouse (1835) in the province, on a 245-ft/75-m cliff.

Spearfish city, pop. 6966, Lawrence Co., W South Dakota, on Spearfish Creek, 42 mi/68 km NW of Rapid City and 10 mi/16 km E of the Wyoming border. In a valley in the N BLACK HILLS, at the mouth of Spearfish Canyon, it is known for its scenery and is popular with tourists. Spearfish is a trade center for the surrounding region, which produces truck crops, grain, timber, and sugar beets. The High Plains Heritage Museum is located in the city, as is Black Hills State University (1883). Each summer area residents perform the Black Hills Passion Play here.

Spectrum, the indoor arena, part of the sports complex located in SOUTH PHILADELPHIA, Pennsylvania. Built in 1967, it is home to the Philadelphia 76ers (basketball) and Flyers (hockey), and seats 18,000.

Speedway town, pop. 13,092, Marion Co., C Indiana, within the city limits of INDIANAPOLIS, and 5 mi/8 km W of Downtown. It has been home to the Indianapolis Motor Speedway since it was built in 1901; the "Brickyard," now almost completely tarred over, is the site of many races, most prominently the annual (since 1911) Indianapolis 500, the NASCAR 200, and the US Nationals drag race. The 433-ac/175-ha speedway incorporates the famous pit row, "Gasoline Alley," the Indy Hall of Fame Museum, and a large golf course. Local manufactures include transmissions, railroad parts, electrical equipment, and steel castings.

Spenard largely commercial section of ANCHORAGE, Alaska, immediately WSW of Downtown, on the road to Anchorage International Airport. Developed in the 1920s along the route to L. Spenard, a resort, the area is now a mix of retailing and service strip, entertainment center, and red-light district.

Spence Bay see under BOOTHIA PENINSULA, Northwest Territories.

Spencer **1.** city, pop. 11,066, seat of Clay Co., NW Iowa, at the confluence of the Little Sioux and Ocheyedan rivers, 78 mi/126 km NE of Sioux City. An important railroad junction, it produces wood and food products. Fabricated metals, apparel, and chemical products are also manufactured. Grain and livestock from the area are shipped from the city. The Spirit L. resort area is 20 mi/32 km N. **2.** town, pop. 11,645, Worcester Co., C Massachusetts, 10 mi/16 km W of Worcester. It has been a manufacturing center since Josiah and Nathaniel Green began making shoes here in 1811. It also produces chemicals and plastics, and there are dairy farms.

Spencer County 400 sq mi/1036 sq km, pop. 19,490, in SW Indiana. Its seat is Rockport. The Ohio R. forms its S border, the boundary with Kentucky. Most of the county is agricultural, producing grain, livestock, and poultry. Oil wells and natural gas deposits are found in the S part, near Rockport, pop. 2315, which is the chief manufacturing center. Lincoln City, in the N, is the site of the 200-ac/81-ha Lincoln Boyhood National Memorial, the farm on which Nancy Hanks Lincoln is buried.

Spiegel Grove see under FREMONT, Ohio.

Spillville city, pop. 387, Winneshiek Co., NE Iowa, on the Turkey R., 10 mi/16 km SW of Decorah. A Czech settlement, it was home to composer Antonín Dvořák during the summer of 1893, when he completed his *New World Symphony.* The Northeast Iowa Area Vocational-Technical School is here.

Spindletop see under BEAUMONT, Texas.

Spiral Tunnels see under KICKING HORSE PASS, British Columbia; CANADIAN PACIFIC RAILWAY.

Spirit Lake see under IOWA GREAT LAKES.

Spiro city, pop. 2146, Le Flore Co., EC Oklahoma, 55 mi/89 km SE of Muskogee and 10 mi/16 km W of the Arkansas line, near the Arkansas R. It was founded in the mid 1890s close to the military post Fort Coffee (1834). It gins cotton and is a processing center for potatoes, corn, and other crops. Just E is an archaeological park containing nine mounds built (c.1200–1350) during the Mississippian culture.

Split Mountain peak (14,058 ft/4285 m) of the SIERRA NEVADA, on the E edge of Kings Canyon National Park, just S of the PALISADES PEAKS, in EC California. Mather Pass, through which the Pacific Crest Trail runs, is slightly NW; Taboose Pass (11,400 ft/3475 m) is S.

Spokane city, pop. 177,196, seat of Spokane Co., E Washington, at the falls of the Spokane R., 15 mi/24 km W of the Idaho border. The largest city between Seattle and Minneapolis, it is a trade and processing center for the region's lumber, mining, and agriculture. The North West Company established a fur trading post 12 mi/19 km NW in 1810, building the first non-Indian structure in the Northwest. The Northern Pacific Railroad brought growth, as Spokane became the primary trading and shipping point for the INLAND EMPIRE. Lumbering, agricultural development, and gold and silver strikes in the region stimulated related industries in the late 19th and early 20th centuries, many of which continue today. With the opening of the GRAND COULEE Dam (1941) and wartime government investment, aluminum reduction and rolling mills were added as important factors in the economy. Spokane underwent an economic boom in the early 1990s. Today its manufactures also include high-tech goods, paper, electrical equipment, and clay and cement products. Among the city's schools are Gonzaga University (1887), Fort Wright College (1907), and Whitworth College (1890). Downtown Riverfront Park was the setting of Expo '74, a world's fair. Fairchild Air Force Base is 9 mi/14 km SW of Downtown. The city is gateway to Trumbull National Wildlife Refuge, Mt. Spokane State Park, Colville and

Kaniksu national forests, and a variety of other nearby resort and recreational areas.

Spokane Indian Reservation see under COLVILLE INDIAN RESERVATION, Washington.

Spoon River 160 mi/258 km long, in Illinois. It rises in Stark Co., NW Illinois, then flows S and SW through farmland and past Wyoming and London Mills before joining the Illinois R. at Havana, in the WC portion of the state. The river gave its name to the fictional town whose residents' verse epitaphs make up Illinois-born Edgar Lee Masters's *Spoon River Anthology* (1915). The town was based in part on PETERSBURG, Illinois.

Spotsylvania County 404 sq mi/1046 sq km, pop. 57,403, in NE Virginia, bounded by the RAPIDAN and RAPPAHANNOCK rivers (N) and the NORTH ANNA R. (SW). Its seat is Spotsylvania (Spotsylvania Court House). The county is partly suburban and partly rural, with some agriculture and livestock raising. The site of a number of major Civil War battles, it attracts many tourists, especially to the historic independent city of FREDERICKSBURG (NE) and to the Fredericksburg and Spotsylvania National Military Park, whose various units commemorate such battles as CHANCELLORSVILLE, the WILDERNESS, and **Spotsylvania Court House.** At the latter, May 8–21, 1864, after the Wilderness, the advancing Union forces and the Confederates fought inconclusively. On May 12, the height of the battle, hand-to-hand combat at a bend in the trench lines called the Bloody Angle caused many of the day's 12,000 casualties.

Spring unincorporated community, pop. 33,111, Harris Co., SE Texas, 25 mi/40 km NNW of downtown Houston and just NW of Houston International Airport, on Interstate 45. It is primarily residential.

Spring Arbor unincorporated village, pop. 2010, in Spring Arbor township, Jackson Co., SC Michigan, 8 mi/13 km SW of Jackson. It is the seat of Spring Arbor College (1873).

Springdale 1. city, pop. 29,941, Washington and Benton counties, NW Arkansas, 9 mi/14 km NNE of Fayetteville, on the Ozark Plateau. Settled in 1850, it developed as an agricultural shipping center after the arrival of the railroad in 1881. The surrounding area produces grapes, peaches, apples, strawberries, wine, vinegar, eggs, and poultry. Trucking, light manufacturing, and tourism augment the city's economy, and the headquarters of the poultry company Tyson Foods is here. The Albert E. Brumley gospel music festival is held here. **2.** city, pop. 10,621, Hamilton Co., SW Ohio, a residential suburb 7 mi/11 km N of downtown Cincinnati. There is some light industry here; cosmetics are among its products. **3.** borough, pop. 3992, Allegheny Co., SW Pennsylvania, on the Allegheny R., 14 mi/22 km NE of Pittsburgh. It is largely residential. The environmental pioneer Rachel Carson (1907–64) was born here.

Springer Mountain peak (3782 ft/1154 m) in N Georgia, 14 mi/23 km NW of Dahlonega. Near the S end of the BLUE RIDGE, it replaced Mt. OGLETHORPE after 1958 as the S terminus of the APPALACHIAN TRAIL.

Springfield 1. city, pop. 105,227, state capital and seat of Sangamon Co., C Illinois, on the Sangamon R., immediately N of L. Springfield. In addition to its political importance, it is an agricultural, wholesale, industrial, and tourist center. Corn, wheat, soybeans, and livestock are raised in the region and traded, processed, and distributed here. Local manufactures include farm machinery, tractors, road machines, flour, feed, electronic and automotive equipment, boilers, and mattresses. Many insurance companies are headquartered here. Settled in 1818, Springfield became the third capital of Illinois in 1837. It was also a shipping and coal mining center until manufacturing burgeoned with the arrival of the Illinois Watch Company (1870). The city was the site of a devastating antiblack riot in 1908. Educational institutions include Springfield College in Illinois (1929), Lincoln Land Community College (1967), and Sangamon State University (1969). Springfield hosts the Illinois State Fair every August. Sites associated with Abraham Lincoln, such as the Lincoln Home and Lincoln Tomb and Monument, both National Historic Sites, draw visitors, as do the Old State Capitol and the Illinois State Museum, Illinois State Historical Library, and Vachel Lindsay Museum. **2.** city, pop. 156,983, seat of Hampden Co., SW Massachusetts, on the Connecticut R., 5 mi/8 km N of the Connecticut border and 80 mi/129 km W of Boston. It is a major industrial center, with an economy that includes manufacturing, insurance, and publishing (Merriam-Webster dictionaries are published here). Springfield was settled in 1636, burned during King Philip's War, and rebuilt. A US arsenal was established in 1777, and the town was a major supplier of arms during the Revolution, the Civil War (the Springfield rifle), World War I, and World War II. Firearms are still manufactured. In 1895 Charles and J. Frank Duryea founded the first American automobile company here, and in the same period major companies began to produce electrical equipment and appliances, toys and games, motorcycles, and a variety of other products. The city is the seat of American International College (1885), Springfield College (1885), and Western New England College (1919). Springfield is the birthplace of basketball, developed (1891) by James Naismith while teaching at Springfield College; the National Basketball Hall of Fame is in the city. **3.** city, pop. 140,494, seat of Greene Co., SW Missouri, in the foothills of the Ozark Plateau, 145 mi/232 km SSE of Kansas City. It was settled in 1829, but white settlement and city growth did not begin in earnest until 1850, after Indians had been moved from the region. Lying at the junction of major westward trails, it soon became a significant settlement. During the Civil War, it was held by both Union and Confederate forces. Situated in an agricultural area producing grain, fruit, livestock, poultry, and dairy goods, the city trades, processes, and ships these and other products. It has railroad shops, flour mills, stockyards, and steel mills, and diverse industries produce furniture, clothing, office equipment, auto trailers and truck beds, concrete, boats, lumber, and paper goods. Tourism is also important to Springfield, which serves as gateway to the Ozark–White R. region. A medical and educational center, it is the seat of Drury College (1873), Southwest Missouri State University (1906), Central Bible College (1922), and Evangel College (1955). Also here is a national cemetery (1867), with many Civil War graves, and nearby (SW) is WILSON'S CREEK National Battlefield. Units of the Mark Twain National Forest are S and E and Stockton L. is NE. **4.** township, pop. 13,420, Union Co., NE New Jersey, 8 mi/13 km SW of Newark. Settled c.1717, it was partially burned in the course of a Revolutionary War battle (1780). Today it is a commuter suburb and retail center, and has a few light industries. Springfield is adjacent (E) to the WATCHUNG Reservation. **5.** city, pop. 70,487, seat of Clark Co., WC Ohio, on Buck Creek, 25 mi/40 km NE of Dayton. Pioneers from Kentucky began arriving in 1799, and white settlement started in earnest in 1801, after a battle in which the Shawnee were defeated. An 1807 meeting of settlers and Indian chiefs, including Tecumseh, at a Springfield tavern established peace. The city is highly and diversely industrialized; automobile equipment, aircraft and missile parts, turbines and engines, chemicals, textiles, leather goods, plastics, glass, and electrical apparatus are among items manufactured. Springfield is the seat of Wittenberg University (1845). The Four-H Clubs were founded here in 1902. The Clarence J. Brown Reservoir is just NE of the city, and the Cedar Bog Nature Preserve is 6 mi/10 km N. **6.** city, pop. 44,683, Lane Co., NW Oregon, 4 mi/6 km E of downtown Eugene, between the Willamette and McKenzie rivers. Founded in 1849, it is a major center for Oregon's forest products industry, with a large Weyerhaeuser pulp and paper mill and plywood and hardboard plant. Its other manufactures include metal products, chemicals, trailers, fabricated steel, and animal feeds. The city is also a center for a fertile agricultural region and has facilities for the research and development of industrial glues and adhesives. It serves as a gateway to the McKenzie River Valley recreation area. **7.** in Pennsylvania: **a.** township, pop. 24,160, Delaware Co., 7 mi/11 km WSW of C Philadelphia, containing a number of suburban residential communities. **b.** township, pop. 19,612, Montgomery Co., 9 mi/14 km N of C Philadelphia. Just N of CHESTNUT HILL, it contains affluent residential suburbs. **8.** city, pop. 11,127, seat of Robertson Co., N Tennessee, 23 mi/37 km NNW of Nashville. Known for its tobacco auction, it also makes and ships tobacco products, electrical appliances, furniture, snack foods, flour, and stoves. **9.** town, pop. 9579, Windsor Co., SE Vermont. It is on the Black and Connecticut rivers, 30 mi/48 km NNE of Brattleboro. The town includes Springfield, Goulds Mill, and North Springfield villages. Waterpowered 18th-century industries included a sawmill, cotton, oil, and woolen mills, and a carding shop. The town's best-known industry, established in the mid 19th century, is the manufacture of precision machinery and tools. **10.** unincorporated community, pop. 23,706, Fairfax Co., NE Virginia, on the BELTWAY and I-95, just SW of Alexandria and 12 mi/19 km SW of Washington, D.C. A largely residential suburb, it also has manufactures including asphalt and fabricated steel. Adjacent **North Springfield** (unincorporated, pop. 8996) is similar.

Springfield Plateau see under OZARK PLATEAU, Missouri.

Spring Green town, pop. 1343, Sauk Co., S Wisconsin, on the Wisconsin R., 35 mi/56 km NW of Madison. In a timber, dairying, and livestock region, it produces cheese, lumber, flour, and feed. Frank Lloyd Wright's home and studio, at his Taliesin school, now headquarters of the Wright Foundation, is 3 mi/5 km S. There are several buildings designed by Wright at the site, as well as his furniture and much of his art collection. Another architectural landmark, the House on the Rock complex, designed by Alex Jordan, is 9 mi/14 km SW of Spring Green.

Spring Hill **1.** unincorporated community, pop. 31,117, Hernando Co., WC Florida, 34 mi/55 km NNW of Tampa, in a lake-filled and wooded area just E of the Gulf of Mexico. A booming residential and retirement community, it almost quintupled in population in the 1980s. **2.** residential neighborhood on the North Side of Pittsburgh, Pennsylvania, 2.5 mi/4 km N of the GOLDEN TRIANGLE. It is a largely German community of 19th-century brick and frame houses. **3.** town, pop. 1464, Maury and Williamson counties, C Tennessee, 28 mi/45 km SSW of Nashville. On the Nashville Highway, just W of Interstate 65, it became in 1991 the site of a much publicized new (General Motors) Saturn auto plant.

Springhill town, pop. 4373, Cumberland Co., NC Nova Scotia, in the Chignecto isthmus, 15 mi/24 km SE of Amherst. It has natural springs, and a penitentiary is today the largest employer, but the town is best known for its long and tragic mining history. Once the site of the deepest mine in Canada, it was a coal center from the 1830s through the 1950s, when the mines closed after the last (1958) of a series of fires and explosions; the Miners' Museum details the story. The Anne Murray Centre honors the career of the singer, who was born (1945) here.

Spring Lake village, pop. 2537, Ottawa Co., WC Michigan, on Spring L. and the Grand R., just E of L. Michigan and opposite Grand Haven (SW). It is a resort, has commercial fishing, is a shipping point for farm and orchard products, and has some light industry. Pioneer cartoonist and animated filmmaker Winsor McCay was born here (1867).

Spring Mountains NW–SE trending range, 40 mi/64 km long, in Clark Co., extreme S Nevada, paralleling the California border (SW). The mountains are rich in gold, silver, and platinum; valleys support farms and ranches. Charleston Peak, 35 mi/56 km WNW of Las Vegas, rises to 11,918 ft/3633 m. Lee Canyon, in the N, is a popular skiing area. The mountains, partly in TOIYABE NATIONAL FOREST, are covered with piñon and juniper at lower elevations, pine forest above.

Spring Park see under L. MINNETONKA, Minnesota.

Spring Valley **1.** unincorporated community, pop. 55,331, San Diego Co., SW California, 8 mi/13 km E of downtown San Diego. In a citrus producing area, it is a largely residential suburb developed since the 1960s. **2.** affluent residential section of NW Washington, D.C., in the extreme W corner of the District, along the Potomac R. and the Maryland line. It is one of Washington's most conservative white neighborhoods. American University (1893) is in the E. The area just S, along the river and MacArthur Blvd., known as the Palisades, has a higher proportion of apartment houses and commercial establishments. To the E, between the river and GEORGETOWN, is Foxhall, a residential neighborhood along Foxhall Rd., where some of the District's largest estates are situated. **3.** unincorporated community, pop. 51,726, Clark Co., S Nevada, one of the booming residential suburbs of LAS VEGAS. **4.** village, pop. 21,802, in Ramapo township, Rockland Co., SE New York, 7 mi/11 km W of Nyack and 35 mi/56 km NW of New York City. Just N of the New York State Thruway, it is one of Rockland County's larger suburban residential communities. **5.** see under HUNTERS CREEK VILLAGE, Texas.

Springville **1.** village, pop. 4310, in Concord township, Erie Co., W New York, 30 mi/48 km SSE of Buffalo. Settled in 1807, it was an early-19th-century popular music hub originally known as Fiddlers' Green. Situated in a dairy and poultry farming area, it is today a center for light manufacturing, stone quarrying, and lumbering. Springville was the birthplace of football coach Glenn S. "Pop" Warner (1871–1954). **2.** city, pop. 13,950, Utah Co., NC Utah, on Utah L. (W) and at the foot of the WASATCH RANGE (E), 5 mi/8 km SE of Provo. In an irrigated agricultural area producing fruit and sugar beets, it has canning factories and flour mills, and is a shipping center. The city's steel mills are also important to its economy. The Springville World Folk Festival is held annually.

Sprout Brook rural hamlet in CANAJOHARIE township, Montgomery Co., E New York, 20 mi/32 km SW of Johnstown. It was the birthplace (1882) of industrialist Henry J. Kaiser.

Spruce Grove city, pop. 12,884, C Alberta, 18 mi/29 km W of downtown Edmonton. A stop on the Grand Trunk Pacific (now Canadian National) Railway, it serves an agricultural area and is now also a bedroom suburb.

Spruce Knob peak, 4862 ft/1483 m, in Pendleton Co., NE West Virginia. The highest point in the state, it is in the Alleghenies, at the edge of the Eastern PANHANDLE, in the Spruce Knob-Seneca Rocks National Recreation Area and the MONONGAHELA NATIONAL FOREST.

Spurr, Mount see under ALASKA RANGE, Alaska.

Spuyten Duyvil (pronounced "spite'n dy-vil") section of the Bronx, New York, N of where the Harlem R. enters the Hudson. It gains its name from the old Spuyten Duyvil ("spouting devil," in Dutch, for its treacherous currents) Creek, now incorporated, by channeling, into the Harlem R. King's Bridge (1693) crossed the old creek.

Squamish district municipality, pop. 11,709, Squamish-Lillooet Regional District, SW British Columbia, at the head of Howe Sound and the mouth of the Squamish R., 30 mi/48 km N of Vancouver. Settled (1888) as a hop-farming and logging town, this seaport and railway terminus is in a diversified mining region. Industries include hydroelectric production and pulp and lumber milling. **Squamish** (or Stawamus) **Chief,** a granite monolith (2500 ft/762 m), attracts rock climbers. GARIBALDI PROVINCIAL PARK, the WHISTLER ski resorts, and other recreational attractions are nearby.

Squam Lake resort lake in C New Hampshire, on the boundary between Grafton, Belknap, and Carroll counties. It covers 6268 ac/2538 ha, and is 150 mi/242 km N of Boston. The movie *On Golden Pond* was filmed here. Concern about overdevelopment of lakeside property arose as owners sold parts of their property to compensate for a sharp increase in property taxes after 1988. There are about 1200 homes on the shores of the lake.

Squantum see under QUINCY, Massachusetts.

Squaw Mountain see under MOOSEHEAD LAKE, Maine.

Squaw Valley resort in Placer Co., NE California, in the Tahoe National Forest, in the Sierra Nevada, 5 mi/8 km NW of Tahoe City, on L. TAHOE. It was the site of the 1960 Olympic Winter Games. Squaw Peak reaches 9050 ft/2760 m. The area is also a summer resort.

Squirrel Hill residential neighborhood in the East End of Pittsburgh, Pennsylvania, 4 mi/6 km E of the GOLDEN TRIANGLE. Pittsburgh's largest and most populous area, Squirrel Hill has both mansions and row houses. An 18th-century farming community, it remained an isolated enclave of a few large estates until trolley and road connections set off rapid real estate development between 1900 and 1930. The Pittsburgh Center for the Arts is here.

St. see SAINT.

Stadacona former Iroquoian settlement on the site of the LOWER TOWN of QUÉBEC CITY, Québec, at the foot of Cap-Diamant. Visited by Jacques Cartier in 1534–35, it had by 1608, when Samuel de Champlain established his settlement here, become occupied by Algonquian speakers. An Indian trade center for perhaps thousands of years, it rapidly became the thriving French post of Québec.

Stafford Springs borough, pop. 4100, in the town of Stafford (pop. 11,091), Tolland Co., NE Connecticut, on the Willimantic R., 22 mi/35 km NE of Hartford. A noted 19th-century health resort, known for its sulfurous water, it now produces tools and dies, textiles, and chemicals.

Stagg Field former sports stadium in HYDE PARK, on the South Side of Chicago, Illinois. A squash court under the stands of the University of Chicago stadium was the site, on Dec. 2, 1942, of the first sustained nuclear chain reaction, created by a team of scientists led by Enrico Fermi.

Staked Plain see LLANO ESTACADO, Texas and New Mexico.

Stamford city and coterminous township, pop. 108,056, Fairfield Co., extreme SW Connecticut, at the mouth of the Rippowam R. on Long Island Sound, 21 mi/33 km SW of Bridgeport. Settled in 1641 by pioneers from Wethersfield, it was a farming community until the railroad reached it in the 1840s, then began to acquire industry. In the 20th century it was primarily a suburb of New York City, with some light manufacturing and industrial research, until the 1970s, when major corporations began to move offices here from New York. The city razed its deteriorating downtown and replaced it with skyscrapers, hotels, and an upscale shopping mall; today it has one of the largest concentrations of corporate headquarters in the United States. Since the late 1980s, however, its growth has slowed dramatically. Stamford's neighborhoods range from long-exclusive Shippan Point, which extends S into the Sound, to hilly, wooded Long Ridge and High Ridge, N of the Merritt Parkway.

Stamps city, pop. 2478, Lafayette Co., SW Arkansas, 33 mi/53 km ESE of Texarkana, in the RED R. bottomlands. In a cotton, lumber, and oil producing region, it is noted as the childhood home of writer Maya Angelou (1928–).

Standing Indian Mountain see under NANTAHALA Mts., North Carolina.

Standing Peachtree see under PEACHTREE CREEK, Atlanta, Georgia.

Standing Rock Indian Reservation 1,343,000 ac/543,915 ha, pop. 7956, in Sioux Co., SC North Dakota, and Corson Co., NC South Dakota, bounded by Cedar Creek (NW), the Cannonball R. (NE), and L. OAHE on the Missouri R. (E). Organized in 1868 with 4 million ac/1.62 million ha, it was reduced (1910) to its present size in order to open land for white settlement. The Upper and Lower Yanktonai Sioux live in the North Dakota section of the reservation; on the South Dakota side are the Hunkpapa and Blackfoot Sioux. Most of the land is made up of rugged hills, buttes, and grassland, punctuated by semiarid areas, and much of the farm or grazing land is rented to whites. Standing Rock College (1971) is on the reservation, in FORT YATES, North Dakota.

Stanford see under PALO ALTO, California.

Stanhope borough, pop. 3393, Sussex Co., N New Jersey, 8 mi/13 km NW of Dover. Settled in 1714, it became a major ironworking town on the old Morris Canal. The first anthracite furnace in the US was built here (1821). A few ironworkers' cottages are preserved. Stanhope is best known today as the site of Waterloo Village. Originally an independent village, established c.1760 as Andover Forge, it was renamed after Napoleon's defeat (1815). This ironworking settlement has been reconstructed and restored, together with a recreated Lenni Lenape (Delaware) village. A summer music festival is held here.

Stanislaus River 95 mi/153 km long, in NC California. It flows in three forks from the Sierra Nevada into the Central Valley, through New Melones L., formed by the 625 ft/190 m–high New Melones Dam (1979, replacing a 1926 structure) and through the smaller Tullock Reservoir; passes N of Oakdale; and enters the SAN JOAQUIN R. 12 mi/19 km WNW of Modesto.

Stanley city, pop. 1371, seat of Mountrail Co., NW North Dakota, 50 mi/80 km W of Minot. It is a trading center in a farming (flax, wheat, corn, dairy products) and coal mining area.

Stanley Park 1000-ac/405-ha municipal park in N VANCOUVER, British Columbia, at the tip of the peninsula in BURRARD INLET that forms its First Narrows; Coal Harbour, an early industrial zone, is on its E; English Bay is W. Established at the new city's request by Lord Stanley, governor-general in the late 1880s, it had earlier been used by the military and partly logged. Today it is Vancouver's best-known amenity, with paths and roads, a seawall promenade, Canada's largest aquarium, and other assets. The WEST END is immediately S, and the Lions Gate Bridge (1938) crosses from the park to WEST VANCOUVER.

Stanton city, pop. 30,491, Orange Co., SW California, 20 mi/32 km SE of downtown Los Angeles and adjacent (NW) to Garden Grove. It is a residential suburb with some light industry.

Staples city, pop. 2754, Todd and Wadena counties, C Minnesota, 28 mi/45 km W of Brainerd. A dairy processing city, it claims to occupy the geographical center of the state.

Stapleton industrial and commercial section, N Staten Island, New York. Many of Staten Island's docks are here; the district was designated the first US free trade zone in 1936. Stapleton has been industrial since the mid 19th century, when breweries and various light manufactures were established. Giuseppe Garibaldi lived here in the 1850s. Stapleton Heights, rising behind the industrial district, affords views of New York City and the harbor.

Stapleton International Airport opened 1929 on the NE boundary of DENVER, Colorado, 5 mi/8 km from Downtown. The ROCKY MOUNTAIN ARSENAL adjoins (N). Stapleton was replaced in 1995 by the 53–sq mi/137–sq km Denver International Airport, built 23 mi/37 NE of Downtown in the prairieland of Adams Co.

Starett City see under EAST NEW YORK, New York.

Star Island see under ISLES OF SHOALS, Maine and New Hampshire.

Stark County 574 sq mi/1487 sq km, pop. 367,585, in NE Ohio, intersected by the Tuscarawas R. Its seat is CANTON, which, along with its suburbs, makes up much of the county. There is dairy, fruit, grain, and livestock farming, as well as manufacturing at Alliance, Canton, and Massillon. Natural resources include coal, sand, gravel, and limestone.

Starkville city, pop. 18,458, Oktibbeha Co., NE Mississippi, 24 mi/39 km W of Columbus. It is the trade center for an area of dairy and cotton farms, and has various light manufactures. Mississippi State University (1878), the largest of the state's campuses, is just SE.

Starved Rock 2630-ac/1065-ha state park in La Salle Co., NC Illinois, on the Illinois R., 2 mi/3 km SE of La Salle. The oldest state park in Illinois, its wooded bluffs and canyons were the site of the French Fort St. Louis du Rocher (1682). The name derives from a legend in which the Illini were besieged here by their Potawatomi enemies and starved into submission.

state one of 50 self-governing constituent elements of the United States of America. The states created (1787–89) the Federal union, and under the constitution by which they established it, they retain all powers not specifically delegated to the national government (or remaining with the people themselves). From the 1780s, however, the creation of the NORTHWEST TERRITORY, the LOUISIANA PURCHASE, and other land accessions have defined the land on which the nation grew as (Federal) PUBLIC LANDS. Thus, much of the United States has never belonged to the states themselves. From the mid 19th century, the Federal government has granted lands directly to railroads, to the states, to various institutions (see LAND-GRANT), and, through the HOMESTEAD program, directly to settlers. It has also reserved land, for INDIAN RESERVATIONS (held by it in trust for Indian tribes), military establishments, NATIONAL PARKS, NATIONAL FORESTS, and a variety of other purposes. In an extreme example, the land of Nevada is over 80% Federal.

State College borough, pop. 38,923, Centre Co., C Pennsylvania, 70 mi/112 km NW of Harrisburg, in the Nittany Valley, near the geographic center of the state. In the late 18th century, it was at the core of a charcoal and iron industry, but today it is primarily the commercial center for the main campus (1855) of Pennsylvania State University, which is in the University Park section (N). State College also serves as a shipping point for the products of surrounding farmlands, especially oats and hogs. The Boal Mansion (1789) and Pennsylvania Military Museum are in Boalsburg (pop. 2206), 3 mi/5 km ESE. Nittany Mt., an Allegheny Mt. ridge, extends 20 mi/32 km NE, from just NE of State College to the Clinton Co. line.

State Fair Park see FAIR PARK, Dallas, Texas.

Staten Island third-largest (59 sq mi/152 sq km) and least populous (378,977) of New York City's five boroughs. Coextensive with **Richmond Co.,** the borough was itself called Richmond until 1975. Comprising a NE–SW oriented island 14 mi/23 km in length and up to 7 mi/11 km wide, with several neighboring small islands, it is bounded by the KILL VAN KULL, facing Bayonne, New Jersey (N); Upper NEW YORK BAY and the Narrows (NE); Lower New York Bay and Raritan Bay (SE and S); and the ARTHUR KILL, on the W, facing (from S to N) Perth Amboy, Woodbridge, Carteret, Linden, and Elizabeth, New Jersey. Named by Henry Hudson (1609) for the Dutch States General, it is dominated by a ridge of hills rising to 409 ft/125 m at TODT HILL, highest point on the US Eastern Seaboard S of Maine. It was part of the PATROONSHIP of PAVONIA in 1630. The British took control in 1664, and designated it Richmond Co. in 1683; jurisdiction was briefly disputed between New York and New Jersey. In the American Revolution, the island was a major British base. In the 19th century its farming and fishing villages were joined by seaside resorts, and eventually by the homes of wealthy New Yorkers, set in the hills. Ferry service from Manhattan (5 mi/8 km NE) had been initiated in 1829 by the island's Cornelius Vanderbilt. After the Civil War, industry developed on the N and NE shores. In 1898 Richmond, with a pop. of c.67,000, became part of New York City. In the early 20th century farming largely died out, and fishing and oystering, important in the SW, were stopped because of water pollution. The island continued to grow as a residential haven, reached by the famous Staten Island Ferry, later also by the OUTERBRIDGE CROSSING bridge (1928) to Perth Amboy and by the BAYONNE BRIDGE (1931). In 1950 it had a pop. of 191,555. In 1964, the VERRAZANO-NARROWS BRIDGE was opened, crossing the Narrows and connecting Long Island (E) with New Jersey, by way of new highways. Staten Island has subsequently boomed with tract and individual housing and commercial strips. It has housing and shipyards along the N and NE shores, and beaches along the SE; its older commercial center is Saint George (N), the county seat. Wagner College (1883, here since 1918) and the city's College of Staten Island (1955) are leading educational institutions. See also: FRESH KILLS; GREAT KILLS; GREENBELT; MARINER'S HARBOR; NEW BRIGHTON; NEW DROP; RICHMONDTOWN; SAILOR'S SNUG HARBOR; SAINT GEORGE; SOUTH BEACH; STAPLETON; TODT HILL; TOMPKINSVILLE; TOTTENVILLE.

Statesboro city, pop. 15,854, seat of Bulloch Co., E Georgia. The seat of Georgia Southern University (1906), it also processes lumber, peanuts, poultry, and cotton.

State Street N–S commercial thoroughfare, 14 mi/23 km long, in Chicago, Illinois. It runs from the GOLD COAST across the SOUTH SIDE to the Riverdale line. State Street serves as the main avenue in the LOOP and is lined with major department stores and hotels.

Statesville city, pop. 17,567, seat of Iredell Co., WC North Carolina, in the Piedmont, 40 mi/64 km N of Charlotte. It was settled in 1750 as Fourth Creek, by Scotch-Irish and Germans from Maryland and Pennsylvania, and established as Statesville in 1789. An industrial center in a dairying and tobacco producing region, it manufactures tobacco products, textiles, furniture, metal products, machinery, processed foods, and flour. Mitchell Community College (1852) is here.

Stateville see under JOLIET, Illinois.

Station Square commercial development, 40 ac/16 ha, in the MOUNT WASHINGTON section of Pittsburgh, Pennsylvania, on the Monongahela R. opposite Downtown, between the Smithfield and Fort Pitt bridges. An old freight yard and rail terminal has been converted into a retail and entertainment complex, extending activity of the GOLDEN TRIANGLE over to the SOUTH SIDE.

Statue of Liberty see under LIBERTY I., New York City.

Staunton independent city, pop. 24,461, seat of but administratively separate from Augusta Co., NC Virginia, 35 mi/56 km WNW of Charlottesville, between the Blue Ridge (E) and the Allegheny (W) mountains, in the S SHENANDOAH VALLEY. It produces flour, clothing, furniture, and air conditioners, and is a shipping center for livestock and fruit. Settled in 1732, Staunton served briefly as the capital of Virginia in 1781, and was occupied twice by Union forces during the Civil War. It is the seat of Mary Baldwin College (1842). The birthplace (1856) of Woodrow Wilson is now a museum.

Staunton River see under ROANOKE R.

Ste. see SAINTE.

Steamboat Springs city, pop. 6695, seat of Routte Co., NW Colorado, on the Yampa R., 92 mi/148 km WSW of Fort Collins. Settled in 1874, it became popular largely for its over 150 mineral springs. In 1913 skiing and ski jumping were introduced, and Steamboat Springs soon became a noted winter resort. It holds a winter carnival and summer music festival, is headquarters of the nearby Routt National Forest, and is known for its mountain scenery.

Steamtown National Historic Site see under SCRANTON, Pennsylvania.

Steele Narrows see under MEADOW LAKE, Saskatchewan.

Steel Pier see under ATLANTIC CITY, New Jersey.

Steelton borough, pop. 5152, Dauphin Co., SC Pennsylvania, 4 mi/6 km SE of Harrisburg, on the Susquehanna R. It has been a steel manufacturing center since its founding in 1865; the first practical production of Bessemer steel took place here in 1867.

Steens Mountain fault-block mass (rising to 9773 ft/2979 m) extending NNE–SSW for more than 30 mi/50 km in SE Oregon, 60 mi/100 km SSE of BURNS. Lava-capped and noted for its bowl-shaped glacial CIRQUES, it rises abruptly from the Alvord Desert (E) and slopes gently to the W.

Steepletop see under AUSTERLITZ, New York.

Steilacoom town, pop. 5728, Pierce Co., WC Washington, on Puget Sound, 8 mi/13 km SW of Tacoma. Settled in 1850, it became in 1854 the first incorporated community in Washington. An important 19th-century port, it is now largely residential, with a large state hospital. Tourists are drawn to historic buildings, including many state "firsts."

Steinbach town, pop. 8213, SE Manitoba, 30 mi/48 km SE of Winnipeg, in the Red R. basin. The site was settled in the 1870s by German Mennonites who had emigrated from Russia. The Mennonite Village Museum, a reconstruction of the original settlement, is just N. Steinbach continues to grow as a rural supply center, with diversified agriculture and woodworking as chief industries.

Steinway industrial neighborhood in N Queens, New York, on Steinway Creek and Bowery Bay (the East R.). It is sometimes considered part of ASTORIA, which lies SW. Steinway derives its name from William Steinway, who established his piano factory, still operating, in 1872. Steinway also developed a company town here, as well as North Beach, a resort on the site of nearby LaGuardia Airport. The district was an early center of the movie industry, active locally again since the 1970s.

Stellarton town, pop. 5237, Pictou Co., NC Nova Scotia, 3 mi/5 km SSW of New Glasgow. From 1798, when coal was discovered, until the 1950s, it was a mine center, at first (1820s–70s) called Albion Mines, then renamed for the local (stellar) coal. Pioneering mine and rail machinery was developed here in the 1820s. The town now has several manufacturing operations and a community college.

Stephenville **1.** town, pop. 7621, SW Newfoundland, on the N shore of SAINT GEORGE'S BAY, near its head, 40 mi/64 km SW of Corner Brook. Settled in the 1840s as a fishing and farming community, it was the site (1941–66) of Harmon Air Force Base, a US facility long the major employer. Today the town produces newsprint. An annual drama festival draws visitors. **2.** city, pop. 13,502, seat of Erath Co., NC Texas, on the Bosque R., 78 mi/126 km NW of Waco. Settled by the Stephens brothers in the 1850s, it is a noted nursery center, and the hub for an area producing cotton, pecans, peanuts, grain, dairy goods, and poultry. Tarleton State University (1899) is here, along with a Texas A & M research center.

Sterling **1.** city, pop. 10,362, seat of Logan Co., NE Colorado, on the South Platte R., 80 mi/129 km NE of Greeley and 26 mi/42 km S of the Nebraska border. It markets and ships cattle and agricultural products, refines beet sugar, and has been a gas and oil center since 1950. It has meat processing plants, railroad shops, and grain elevators, and manufactures steel and concrete products. Northeastern Junior College of Colorado (1941) and the Overland Trail Museum are here. Pawnee National Grassland is 20 mi/32 km NW. **2.** city, pop. 15,132, Whiteside Co., NW Illinois, across the Rock R. from Rock Falls, 13 mi/21 km SW of Dixon. Its most important product is builders' hardware; other manufactures include steel and steel products, nuts and bolts, mobile homes, and barber supplies. The city dates to 1839. **3.** city, pop. 2115, Rice Co., SC Kansas, 17 mi/27 km NW of Hutchinson. Founded in 1872, it is a processing center for wheat and salt, and the seat of Sterling College (1887). **4.** unincorporated community, pop. 20,512, Loudoun Co., N Virginia, 16 mi/26 km NW of Arlington Co., and just NE of Washington Dulles International Airport. It is a largely residential suburb, with business and industrial parks on the airport's perimeter.

Sterling Heights city, pop. 117,810, Macomb Co., SE Michigan, 20 mi/32 km N of Detroit. A residential and industrial suburb, it manufactures auto bodies and chassis, machinery, missile components, fabricated steel, and mechanical hoists.

Steuben County 1396 sq mi/3616 sq km, pop. 99,088, in SW New York, in the SW section of the FINGER LAKES, along the Pennsylvania border (S). Its seat is Bath. There is varied agriculture; the county is best known for its grape growing and wineries. Dairying is important, and there are large tracts of state forest. Manufactures include glass and other products at CORNING, the county's largest city. The Keuka L. region in the NE corner, which includes the winemaking village of HAMMONDSPORT, is a popular resort area.

Steubenville city, pop. 22,125, seat of Jefferson Co., E Ohio, on the Ohio R. at the West Virginia border, 50 mi/80 km S of Youngstown. Abundant coal and clay deposits in the area fostered its industrial growth. Steubenville is a major producer of steel and steel products. Other important manufactures include ferroalloys, fabricated metals, and paper and clay products. One of Ohio's oldest settlements, it was established (1797) on the site of Fort Steuben, built (1786–87) to protect government land agents from Indian attacks, and was the seat of the first land office in the NORTHWEST TERRITORY. In the Civil War, Steubenville was an important post of the Underground Railroad. It is the seat of the College of Steubenville.

Stevenson locality in Baltimore Co., NC Maryland, 8 mi/13 km NW of central Baltimore. Villa Julie College (1947) is here.

Stevens Point city, pop. 23,006, seat of Portage Co., C Wisconsin, on the Wisconsin R., 20 mi/32 km NE of Wisconsin Rapids. The center of an area rich in dairy cattle and potatoes, it manufactures paper products, furniture, fishing equipment, plastics, beer, and food products. Sentry Insurance Company, a publishing house, and a large needlecraft center are headquartered in the city. George Stevens founded a trading post here c.1839 to service the area's lumberjacks. The railroad stimulated growth in the 1870s. Polish immigrants settled in large numbers in the late 19th century. The University of Wisconsin at Stevens Point (1894) was originally a teachers' college.

Stikine River 335 mi/539 km long, in NW British Columbia and SE Alaska. It rises in the Stikine Ranges (see CASSIAR Mts.), and flows N and W, then S through the COAST Mts., reaching the Pacific Ocean just N of WRANGELL, Alaska. Its upper reaches are a Tahltan homeland, its lower section a Tlingit fishing area; the two peoples traditionally traded along the river. The Hudson's Bay Company was active here from the 1840s, and there was a gold rush on Telegraph Creek, a tributary, in 1861. In the 1890s steamboats carried adventurers some distance inland toward the KLONDIKE. Today, salmon fishing and wilderness recreation are important.

Stillman Valley see under BYRON, Illinois.

Still River in Connecticut: **a.** 30 mi/50 km long, rising in W Danbury, and flowing generally NE through Danbury and Brookfield to the Housatonic R., in New Milford. **b.** 15 mi/24 km long, rising in N Torrington, and flowing generally N through Winsted to the West Branch of the Farmington R. at the village of Riverton.

Stillwater 1. city, pop. 13,882, seat of Washington Co., SE Minnesota, on the St. Croix R. where it widens into L. St. Croix, across from Houlton, Wisconsin, 18 mi/29 km NE of St. Paul. Founded as a logging camp in 1839, it was the first town in the state, and hosted the 1848 convention to organize the Minnesota Territory. Local industries include dairy processing and the manufacture of shoes, plastics, and ventilating fans. Tourism and yachting also contribute to the economy. **2.** city, pop. 36,676, seat of Payne Co., NC Oklahoma, 50 mi/80 km NNE of Oklahoma City and 61 mi/101 km W of Tulsa. Founded a year after the city's settlement in 1889, Oklahoma State University has accounted for much of its growth. An agribusiness hub, Stillwater is surrounded by experimental farms, and trades and processes grain, cotton, livestock, poultry, and dairy goods. Among its manufactures are electronic components, hoses, and data forms. Oil and gas wells are nearby. The National Wrestling Hall of Fame is here.

Stingaree, the see under GASLAMP QUARTER, San Diego, California.

Stinking Water Mountains see under GLASS BUTTES, Oregon.

Stockbridge town, pop. 2408, Berkshire Co., W Massachusetts, 12 mi/19 km S of Pittsfield on the Housatonic R., in the Berkshire Hills. A summer resort, it has many large private homes and popular attractions, including the Norman Rockwell Museum; Chesterwood, the summer home of sculptor Daniel Chester French; Naumkeag, the summer "cottage" designed by Stanford White for diplomat Joseph Choate; the Berkshire Garden Center; and the 1739 Mission House, built by the Rev. John Sergeant, the first missionary to the Stockbridge Indians, and later the home of revivalist Jonathan Edwards. Part of TANGLEWOOD is in Stockbridge. Alice's Restaurant, celebrated in 1960s song by Arlo Guthrie, was in neighboring West Stockbridge, and is closed.

Stockton city, pop. 210,943, seat of San Joaquin Co., NC California, at the confluence of the San Joaquin and Calvaras rivers, 72 mi/116 km ENE of San Francisco and 40 mi/64 km SSE of Sacramento. A major inland seaport, it is connected to San Francisco Bay by a 60 mi/100 km–long deepwater channel through the San Joaquin Delta. A supply center during the 1840s gold rush in the Sierra Nevada, it was by the 1850s a trade and shipping center for grains and other produce of the CENTRAL VALLEY. It now ships large amounts of ore and grain. The city became industrialized after World War II. It processes tomato products, asparagus, other vegetables, fruits, nuts, and wine. Other industries include shipbuilding and a wide range of manufactures. The Sharpe Army Depot, naval facilities, Delta College, the University of the Pacific (1851), and several other colleges are here. The city, which has doubled in pop. since 1970, has a mix of new residential and old inner-city neighborhoods, and has since the 1850s had a broad mix of ethnic groups.

Stockton Plateau see under EDWARDS PLATEAU, Texas.

Stone City see under ANAMOSA, Iowa.

Stoneham town, pop. 22,203, Middlesex Co., NE Massachusetts. It is essentially a residential suburb, 12 mi/19 km N of Boston. The Stone Zoo, once an important tourist attraction, closed in 1990.

Stone Mountain massive monadnock (1686 ft/514 m) 14 mi/23 km ENE of Atlanta, Georgia. The largest exposed granite dome in North America, it rises 650 ft/198 m above the surrounding Piedmont Plateau. Its gray stone was once quarried for use in bridges, buildings, and roadways. The Confederate Memorial Monument, with equestrian reliefs of Jefferson Davis, Robert E. Lee, and Stonewall Jackson, designed by Gutzon Borglum, was carved (1917–67) into the mountain's NE wall. It is within 3200-ac/1300-ha Stone Mountain Park. The suburban city of **Stone Mountain** (pop. 6494) is just W.

Stone Mountains subrange of the W Appalachian chain, sometimes also considered part of the UNAKA RANGE, along the North Carolina–Tennessee border. It extends NE from near L. Watauga for c.30 mi/48 km into S Virginia, roughly paralleling the IRON Mts. (NW).

Stones River also, **Stone's River** battle site: see under MURFREESBORO, Tennessee.

Stonewall **1.** bar, on Christopher St. near Sheridan Square, GREENWICH VILLAGE, Manhattan, New York City. The militant reaction of its patrons to a police raid in July 1969 is regarded as the beginning of the gay liberation movement. A portion of Christopher St. has been redesignated Stonewall Place. **2.** see under PEDERNALES R., Texas.

Stoney Creek city, pop. 49,968, Hamilton-Wentworth Regional Municipality, S Ontario, at the W end of L. Ontario, adjacent (E) to Hamilton. Settled by LOYALISTS in the 1780s, it served an agricultural region with mills and later with canneries and a winery. Today this residential suburb has some light industry. It is the site of a bloody battle fought June 6, 1813, in which outnumbered British troops caused the retreat of invading American forces. The Women's Institutes, a worldwide organization, began here in 1897 in the Erland Lee Home, now a museum.

Stonington **1.** town, pop 16,919, New London Co., extreme SE Connecticut, on the Mystic and Pawcatuck rivers and Long Island Sound, at the Rhode Island border, 10 mi/16 km E of New London. Settled in 1649, it was an important early port and whaling center. In addition to fishing, tourist trade, and boatbuilding, it now has some manufacturing, including the production of tools and fabrics. Stonington includes the villages of MYSTIC and Pawcatuck and the borough of Stonington (pop. 1100). **2.** see under DEER ISLE, Maine.

Stono River tidal passage SW of Charleston, South Carolina. It runs SW–NE behind (N of) JOHNS and Wadmalaw islands and S between Johns and James islands to reach the sea between Folly and Kiawah islands. At its W end it joins the estuarial North Edisto R.; at its E end it joins Charleston Harbor. In 1739 the Stono was the site of an abortive slave rebellion centered around Rantowles, on its N side.

Stony Brook unincorporated village, pop. 13,726, in Brookhaven town, Suffolk Co., SE New York, on Stony Brook Harbor and Smithtown Bay, 5 mi/8 km WSW of Port Jefferson. Settled by colonists from Boston in 1655, it is an educational and tourist center for the North Shore of Long Island. Parts of the village have been restored to their 18th-century appearance. The State University of New York at Stony Brook (1957) is located here.

Stony Mountain community, SE Manitoba, 14 mi/23 km N of Winnipeg. Along with Grosse Isle, Argyle, Balmoral, Bunton, and Komarno, it forms the Rockwood rural municipality (pop. 6990). The Manitoba Penitentiary (1874) is here.

Stony Plain town, pop. 7226, C Alberta, 25 mi/40 km W of downtown Edmonton. Settled in the 1880s as an agricultural center, it is now a growing residential suburb.

Stony Point town, pop. 12,814, Rockland Co., on the W bank of the Hudson R., 5 mi/8 km SW of Peekskill. It was the site of an American blockhouse that was taken by the British (May 31, 1779) and made into a fort. This garrison was, in turn, successfully stormed by Patriot forces under Gen. Anthony Wayne (July 15–16, 1779), and soon abandoned. The town is largely residential. BEAR Mt. is in the N.

Storm King mountain, 1355 ft/413 m, in the HUDSON HIGHLANDS, overlooking the Hudson R. just NW of WEST POINT, Orange Co., New York. It is part of Palisades Interstate Park.

Storm Lake city, pop. 8769, seat of Buena Vista Co., NW Iowa, on Storm L., 35 mi/56 km S of Spencer. There are plastics manufacturing and food processing, and the city is also a summer lake resort. Buena Vista College (1891) is here.

Storrs unincorporated community, pop. 12,198, in the town of MANSFIELD, Tolland Co., NE Connecticut, 20 mi/32 km E of Hartford. It is the site of the principal campus of the University of Connecticut, formed from an agricultural college here since 1881.

Storyville former red-light district in DOWNTOWN New Orleans, Louisiana, just NW of the VIEUX CARRÉ. It was established in 1897 on the suggestion of Alderman Sidney Story, who proposed an ordinance to outlaw prostitution in all but a four-blocks-square district. The result was a boom in the trade in the designated area. Before the Navy had Storyville closed in Nov. 1917 as a danger to morale, it had become famous as an entertainment center, and it was the training ground of many early jazz greats.

Stouffville see under WHITCHURCH-STOUFFVILLE, Ontario.

Stoughton **1.** town, pop. 26,777, Norfolk Co., E Massachusetts, along the Neponset R., 20 mi/32 km S of Boston and adjoining (NW) BROCKTON. It furnished powder and cannon, cast by Paul Revere, to Revolutionary forces. Textile and shoe manufacture dates to the 1800s; the Reebok athletic footwear company is based here. Other industries make rubber goods, plastics, and tools. **2.** city, pop. 8786, Dane Co., S Wisconsin, on the Yahara R., 12 mi/19 km SE of Madison. In a dairying and farming area, it produces dairy items, canned food, foundry items, auto bodies, trailers, clothing, and electrical appliances.

Stow city, pop. 27,702, Summit Co., NE Ohio, 10 mi/16 km NE of Akron. While primarily a commuter suburb, it also produces stamping products, plastic pipe, adhesive-coated papers, foils, printed material, and film, among other manufactures. Stow's Adell Durbin Park is known for its arboretum.

Stowe town, pop. 3433, including Stowe village, Lower Village, and Moscow, in Lamoille Co., NC Vermont. It is SE of

Mt. Mansfield, 25 mi/40 km E of Burlington. Local ski areas, among the nation's oldest and largest, have been joined by other year-round sports and tourist facilities to create one of New England's major resort districts.

Strafford town, pop. 894, including Strafford and South Strafford villages, in Orange Co., EC Vermont. It is on the West Branch of the Ompompanoosuc R., 15 mi/24 km NW of White River Junction. A World War II copper-mining community, it is the site of the Justin Smith Morrill Homestead. Born here in 1810, Congressman and Senator Morrill gave his name to the 1862 Morrill Act, which led to the land-grant college system.

Strafford County 370 sq mi/958 sq km, pop. 104,233, in SE New Hampshire, bordering Maine. Dover is its seat. The county is drained by Salmon Falls and Cocheco rivers, the latter providing waterpower. Dover and Rochester are manufacturing centers. The University of New Hampshire is at Durham.

Strasburg city, pop. 553, Emmons Co., S North Dakota, 20 mi/32 km E of L. OAHE and 10 mi/16 km N of the South Dakota line. Settled and named by German farmers from Russia's Volga basin late in the 19th century, it lies in a wheat producing area. The home of bandleader Lawrence Welk (b.1903) has been turned into a museum of Russian-German life on the plains.

Stratford **1.** town, pop. 49,389, Fairfield Co., SW Connecticut, at the mouth of the Housatonic R., on Long Island Sound, adjacent (E) to Bridgeport. Founded in 1639, it is known as the home of the now defunct American Shakespeare Festival (1955–82). Local industries produce helicopters (Sikorsky), aircraft engines, roofing, plastics, industrial machinery, and brake linings; early activities included shipbuilding and oystering. The Bridgeport Municipal Airport is near the village of Lordship, on a peninsula to the SE. **2.** city, pop. 27,666, seat of Perth Co., S Ontario, on the Avon R., 85 mi/137 km WSW of Toronto. It was settled in the early 1830s as the center for colonizing the HURON TRACT. Initially Little Thames, it took its present name in 1835. An important rail center, it also manufactures wood products, auto supplies, and textiles. Tourism is important, centered on the Stratford Festival, held each summer since 1953, featuring Shakespeare's plays and a range of other drama and music.

Stratford Hall historic site in Westmoreland Co., SE Virginia, on the Potomac R., 35 mi/56 km ESE of Fredericksburg. Built in the 1730s, it is the birthplace (1807) of Robert E. Lee, and the ancestral home of the Lee family. WAKEFIELD, George Washington's birthplace, is 5 mi/8 km NW.

Strathcona **1.** also, **Old Strathcona** see under EDMONTON, Alberta. **2.** see under EAST END, Vancouver, British Columbia.

Strathcona Provincial Park 891 sq mi/2308 sq km, in C Vancouver I., SW British Columbia, 115 mi/185 km NW of Victoria. The province's oldest park (1911), it encloses a mountain wilderness; GOLDEN HINDE is the high point (7218 ft/2200 m). The Della Falls, three falls totaling 1444 ft/440 m, are in a remote S section.

Strathroy town, pop. 10,566, Middlesex Co., S Ontario, on the Sydenham R., 20 mi/32 km W of London. Its economy revolves around the poultry (turkey) industry, fruit and potato farming, and some light industry.

Stratton Mountain 3936 ft/1200 m, in Green Mountain National Forest, 25 mi/40 km NW of Brattleboro, SC Vermont. A popular skiing and hiking area, it is said to have provided inspiration for the development of the Appalachian and Long trails.

Strawberry Mountains see under BLUE Mts., Oregon.

Streamwood village, pop. 30,987, Cook Co., NE Illinois, 30 mi/48 km NW of Chicago. It is a residential community, a postwar subdivision development that was incorporated in 1957.

Streator city, pop. 14,121, La Salle and Livingston counties, C Illinois, on the Vermilion R., 16 mi/26 km S of Ottawa. Local industries produce building materials and canned goods, and there are railroad shops. Settled as Hardscrabble, the community was renamed Unionville after the Civil War. Streator grew as a junction on the Atchison, Topeka and Santa Fe Railroad.

streetcar suburb suburb or outlying city district that was developed along a streetcar line or lines, especially in the period from the late 1880s to the 1920s when street railways flourished, before the private automobile caused their decline.

Streetsboro city, pop. 9932, Portage Co., NE Ohio, on the Ohio Turnpike, 7 mi/11 km N of KENT. It is primarily commercial and residential.

Strip, the **1.** local name for a thoroughfare, sometimes outside a city center or between towns, characterized by a wide variety of commercial establishments, typically with a flashy, less than elegant atmosphere. **2.** also, **Las Vegas Boulevard** or **the Vegas Strip** in LAS VEGAS, Nevada, and its S suburbs. Along it are most of the city's and area's principal resort hotels and casinos. Touted by locals as the brightest street in the world, it is also known as "Glitter Gulch." **3.** see under SPADINA Ave., Toronto, Ontario. **4.** industrial area of Pittsburgh, Pennsylvania, along the Allegheny R., immediately NE of the GOLDEN TRIANGLE. Iron foundries and mills here have given way to produce markets in recent decades. There is an emerging trend of services and retail businesses moving into the old warehouses and factories.

Striver's Row popular name for two blocks of architecturally distinguished housing in Harlem, New York City. Now designated the St. Nicholas Historic District, the King Model Houses (1891), between 137th and 139th streets W of Adam Clayton Powell, Jr., Blvd. (Seventh Ave.) became in the 1920s and 1930s known as the home of preference for prominent, ambitious members of Harlem's black community, among them W. C. Handy, Eubie Blake, and Father Divine.

Strongsville city, pop. 35,308, Cuyahoga Co., NE Ohio, 15 mi/24 km SW of Cleveland, of which it is a commuter suburb. Local industries include textbook publishing and some light manufacturing.

Struthers city, pop. 12,284, Mahoning Co., NE Ohio, on the Mahoning R., adjacent to Youngstown (NW). It is an iron and steel manufacturing center.

Stuart city, pop. 11,936, seat of Martin Co., SE Florida, on the St. Lucie R. near the E end of the St. Lucie Canal (the E terminus of the Okeechobee Waterway) and just off the Atlantic Intracoastal Waterway, 35 mi/56 km NNW of West Palm Beach. Commercial and sport fishing, notably for shark and sailfish, are economically important, as is the processing of seafood, and the city is a yachting and resort center.

Studio City SE SAN FERNANDO VALLEY section of LOS ANGELES,

California, immediately SW of North Hollywood and 10 mi/16 km NW of Downtown. An affluent residential area, it has recently emerged as a center of the television industry.

Sturbridge town, pop. 7775, Worcester Co., SC Massachusetts, 18 mi/29 km SW of Worcester, on the Quinebaug R. It is the site of Old Sturbridge Village, a 200-ac/81-ha re-creation of a 19th-century farming village that is a tourist attraction and also sponsors research into 19th-century life in the area. There is also commercial development at the Massachusetts Turnpike/Interstate 84 junction in this otherwise rural, hilly town.

Sturgeon Bay city, pop. 9176, seat of Door Co., SW Wisconsin, on the DOOR PENINSULA, at the head of Sturgeon Bay (an inlet of Green Bay) and at the head of the Sturgeon Ship Canal, connecting Green Bay with L. Michigan, 38 mi/61 km NE of the city of Green Bay. The city has a flourishing tourism industry. It is a cherry growing center, with fruit packing plants, and has shipyards and processes dairy products. Potawotomi State Park is 2 mi/3 km W, and there are limestone quarries nearby.

Sturgis **1.** city, pop. 10,130, St. Joseph Co., S Michigan, 42 mi/68 km E of Niles and 2 mi/3 km N of the Indiana border. A resort founded in 1827, it manufactures furniture and other products. There are several Amish communities nearby. **2.** city, pop. 5330, seat of Meade Co., W South Dakota, 20 mi/32 km NW of Rapid City. A gold rush town founded in the 1870s, it is now a trade center for a mining and farming area and has some light industry. Also a tourist hub, it features a motorcyclists' gathering, a steam and gas threshing bee, and a balloon rally, each held annually. Numerous frontier buildings are preserved. Nearby are Bear Butte State Park, the Black Hills National Cemetery, and Old Fort Meade Museum on the grounds of the 1878 cavalry post.

Sturtevant village, pop. 3803, Racine Co., SE Wisconsin, 5 mi/8 km W of Racine. This suburban residential community also serves the surrounding truck farming area as a shipping center.

Stuttgart city, pop. 10,420, co-seat (with DeWitt) of Arkansas Co., EC Arkansas, 42 mi/68 km SE of Little Rock, in the Mississippi Alluvial Plain. Settled in 1878, it has been an agricultural processing and marketing center for rice, cotton, soybean, and timber producers. Irrigation and farm equipment and fertilizer are manufactured here, and the city has large rice silos. It hosts the annual World Championship Duck Calling Contest.

Stuyvesant Heights see under BEDFORD-STUYVESANT, New York.

subbarrio see under BARRIO, in Puerto Rico.

suburb a district or community outside the limits of a city, traditionally residential, less densely settled, and middle- or upper-class; a ring or zone of these communities is called **the suburbs.** The US Census Bureau does not use the classification, but subtracting residents of "central cities" from its METROPOLITAN AREA figures, it arrived at a 1990 estimate of 115 million residents of suburbs (or 46% of all Americans, up from 14% in 1930). Problems raised by suburbanization have been addressed by experiments in METROPOLITAN GOVERNMENT, more in Canada than in the US. The nature of the suburbs is changing; many are now industrial and commercial as well as residential. Some are growing EDGE CITIES; some have become poor residential communities. In this book, the term *suburban* is used in places to characterize (as residential and relatively less dense) communities that are actually within the limits of cities. See also EXURB.

Succasunna unincorporated village in Roxbury township, Morris Co., N New Jersey, 4 mi/6 km SW of Dover. Situated just S of Interstate 80 and L. HOPATCONG, it is residential. With neighboring Kenvil (N), it has a population of 11,781. The area is noted for its gravel pits.

Sudbury **1.** town, pop. 14,358, Middlesex Co., NE Massachusetts, 18 mi/29 km W of Boston, and adjoining (SW) Concord. It was an important town at the time of the Revolution; today it is an affluent suburb with some agriculture. Henry Wadsworth Longfellow's *Tales of a Wayside Inn* (1862) was set in Sudbury's Wayside Inn, built as Howe's Tavern in 1686 and later known as the Red Horse Tavern. **2.** city, pop. 92,884, seat of Sudbury Regional Municipality (pop. 161,210), C Ontario, on Ramsey L., 38 mi/61 km N of Georgian Bay and 210 mi/340 km NNW of Toronto. Nickel and copper ore were discovered here in 1883 during construction of the Canadian Pacific Railway. The city is now the center of a region that produces much of the world's nickel. Copper, gold, silver, lead, zinc, platinum, cobalt, sulfur, and iron ore are also mined from the **Sudbury Basin,** a 600–sq mi/1550–sq km depression in the CANADIAN SHIELD that is thought to have been created by meteorite impact. The city houses refineries and smelters, above which, at Copper Cliff, on the W side, rises the 1246-ft/380-m Super Stack, one of the world's tallest smokestacks, as well as machine shops, lumber mills, and brickworks. Laurentian University (1960), Cambrian College (1966), and the noted Science North museum are here. Surrounding lakes are popular for fishing. The REGIONAL MUNICIPALITY includes the adjacent towns of NICKEL CENTRE (E), Rayside-Balfour (NW, pop. 15,039), Valley East (N, pop. 21,939), and Walden (W, pop. 9805).

Sudlersville town, pop. 428, Queen Anne's Co., E Maryland, 18 mi/29 km W of Dover, Delaware, on the EASTERN SHORE. The agricultural town is known as the 1907 birthplace of baseball great Jimmie Foxx.

Suffern village, pop. 11,055, in Ramapo township, Rockland Co., SE New York, on the Ramapo R., at the New Jersey line, 28 mi/45 km NNW of New York City. Primarily residential, it is home to Rockland Community College (1959).

Suffield locality in SE Alberta, 24 mi/39 km NW of Medicine Hat. It gives its name to a huge Canadian Forces Base that lies NE, within which classified research is conducted at Ralston (just N), and at which US planes trained during the Vietnam War. The Suffield natural gas field is also here.

Suffolk independent city, pop. 52,141, including the former Nansemond Co., SE Virginia, 24 mi/38 km SW of Norfolk, on the Nansemond R., HAMPTON ROADS (N), and the DISMAL SWAMP (SE). It is a major market for peanuts and processor of peanut products; among its other industries are meatpacking, tea and coffee processing, and lumber. Suffolk was burned by the British in 1779 and was occupied by Union troops during the Civil War. At 409 sq mi/1059 sq km, it is (since 1974) the largest city in Virginia.

Suffolk County **1.** 57 sq mi/148 sq km, pop. 663,906, in E Massachusetts. Its seat is Boston; the county's other municipalities are the cities of CHELSEA and REVERE and the town of WINTHROP. Only Nantucket Co., among Massachusetts counties, is smaller in area. **2.** 911 sq mi/2359 sq km, pop. 1,321,864, in SE New York, in E Long Island. Its seat is RIVERHEAD. In the W it is typically suburban, with tracts of postwar homes and small villages; in some areas there has been significant commercial development, with many defense contractors, electronics companies, and financial institutions. Farther E there is still some agriculture, and on the NORTH FORK, at the E end, there is a thriving wine industry. The SOUTH FORK is a well-developed, affluent resort area.

Sugar Creek 85 mi/137 km long, in WC Indiana. It rises in SW Tipton Co., and flows SW past CRAWFORDSVILLE to the Wabash R. 6 mi/10 km N of Montezuma, in Parke Co.

Sugar Ditch see under TUNICA Co., Mississippi.

Sugar Hill popular name for a section of upper HARLEM, New York City, the area along Edgecombe, St. Nicholas, and Convent avenues above about 138th St. It lies along Coogan's Bluff, an escarpment that looks down on flat land to the E toward the Harlem R. Affluent Harlemites, many in the arts and politics, were felt in the 1920s–50s to favor Sugar Hill or STRIVER'S ROW for their residences.

Sugar Land city, pop. 24,529, Fort Bend Co., SE Texas, 18 mi/29 km SW of downtown Houston, near the Brazos R. It developed around sugar cane fields from about 1824, and still refines imported cane. Its economy also depends on oil, chemicals, figs, and food processing, and there is a state prison.

Sugarloaf Mountain **1.** 4237 ft/1292 m, in Franklin Co., W Maine, center of a popular ski area in Carrabassett Valley Township, 26 mi/42 km NW of Farmington. It is one of four Maine mountains that are first in the nation to receive the light of the rising sun. Since the 1970s Sugarloaf USA, a resort condominium community, has been developed. **2.** elevation (1282 ft/391 m) in NC Maryland, 10 mi/16 km S of FREDERICK. Composed predominantly of brown sandstone, it is E of the MONOCACY R. and SE of Lilypons, a community long known for production of pond lilies and ornamental fish.

Suisun Bay NE arm of SAN FRANCISCO BAY, connected to SAN PABLO BAY on the W by Carquinez Strait. Ten mi/16 km E–W, it receives the combined mouths of the Sacramento and San Joaquin rivers at PITTSBURG, on its E side. The Suisun Indians inhabited the area, including the saltmarshes N of the bay, until the mid 19th century. The S side is now largely industrial and military.

Suisun City city, pop. 22,686, Solano Co., NC California, on the Suisun Slough, a navigable connection with Suisun Bay, adjoining (S) FAIRFIELD, and 34 mi/56 km SW of Sacramento. It is a food processing and boatbuilding center. Solano Community College (1945) is here.

Suitland–Silver Hill unincorporated suburb, pop. 35,111, Prince George's Co., C Maryland, just E of Washington, D.C. It is composed of residential neighborhoods bisected by the Suitland Federal Center, which houses the Bureau of the Census, military, oceanography, hydrography, and map services, and the National Weather Service. The Smithsonian Institution maintains warehouses in Suitland, which developed following World War II.

Sullivan city, pop. 4663, seat of Sullivan Co., SW Indiana, 25 mi/40 km S of Terre Haute, in a dairy, poultry, grain, and timber producing area. Bituminous coal mines and oil and gas deposits are nearby.

Sullivan's Island island town, pop. 1623, c.4 mi/6 km long, in Charleston Co., SC South Carolina, at the E side of the entrance to Charleston Harbor, 5 mi/8 km SE of Charleston's BATTERY and across a channel 1 mi/1.6 km from FORT SUMTER (W). It was named for the captain of the *Carolina,* the first English ship to carry settlers to the area (1670). It is a beach resort with some residences. Fort Moultrie, originally called Fort Sullivan, was constructed at the island's W tip by Colonel William Moultrie. Under Moultrie's command an outnumbered Colonial garrison held out against a furious British bombardment (June 28, 1776); the fort was renamed in Moultrie's honor. At the beginning of the Civil War, a more recent (1807–11) structure was headquarters for the Confederate bombardment of Fort Sumter. Fort Moultrie is now a part of the Fort Sumter National Monument.

Sulphur city, pop. 20,125, Calcasieu Parish, SW Louisiana, 10 mi/16 km W of LAKE CHARLES, in an oil and livestock producing area. Oil was discovered nearby in 1924. A large sulfur dome, worked from 1905 to 1926, is in the city.

Sulphur Springs city, pop. 14,062, seat of Hopkins Co., NE Texas, 72 mi/116 km ENE of Dallas, in the BLACKLANDS. It acquired its name in the 1870s from the area's many mineral springs. Hopkins Co. is one of the largest US dairy producers, and the city has dairy and food processing and meatpacking plants. Its varied manufactures include clothing, plastics, valves, weather balloons, and fertilizer.

Summer nuclear power plant: see under BROAD R., South Carolina.

Summerside town, pop. 7474, SW Prince Edward Island, the province's second-largest community, in Bedeque Bay, on Northumberland Strait, 35 mi/56 km W of Charlottetown. It is a seaport, resort, and fox fur farming center, and exports seed potatoes and dairy products.

Summersville town, pop. 2906, seat of Nicholas Co., SC West Virginia, in an agricultural and coal mining area. In July 1861, Confederate spy Nancy Hart led an attack that briefly captured the town. On August 26, Union forces were beaten in a skirmish at Cross Lanes, 3 mi/5 km SW. On Sept. 10, an indecisive battle was fought at Carnifex Ferry, 10 mi/16 km SW.

Summerville town, pop. 22,519, Dorchester Co. (also in Berkeley and Charleston counties), SE South Carolina, 22 mi/35 km NW of Charleston. In the 18th and 19th centuries it was a summer (to escape coastal malaria) and then winter resort; many homes and estates of the period are preserved. Still a resort, it also produces lumber, fabric, and aluminum.

Summit **1.** village, pop. 9971, Cook Co., NE Illinois, immediately adjacent to SW Chicago and 10 mi/16 km SW of the Loop. Mainly a residential suburb, it also has one of the largest corn product plants in the world in which Argo manufactures cornstarch and many other items. It is located on (and named for) the ridge between the watersheds of the Mississippi and the Great Lakes. The portage here was long used by migrating Indians and, later, fur traders; before the advent of railroad and canal systems, it played a crucial role in the early growth of Chicago. Midway Airport is 2 mi/3 km E. **2.** city, pop. 19,757, Union Co., NE New Jersey, 10 mi/16 km W of Newark. Part of the Elizabethtown area purchased from the Lenni Lenape (1664), it was settled about 1720. Situated atop First WATCHUNG Mountain, it served as an important lookout during the Revolution. The community grew with the railroad's coming (1837), and Summit was separated from Springfield and New Providence in 1869. It is now an affluent suburb, with elegant homes and condominiums, and offices of pharmaceutical and financial companies. **3.** arena, opened 1975 on US Route 59, 5 mi/8 km SW of downtown Houston, Texas, next to Greenway Plaza. Seating

16,000, it is home to the Houston Rockets (basketball) and to various events.

Summit Avenue historic residential street in St. Paul, Minnesota, SW of Downtown, in MACALESTER-GROVELAND. Situated on a bluff overlooking the center of the city and the Mississippi R., it is the street along which lumber and railroad barons built their grand homes.

Summit County 412 sq mi/1067 sq km, pop. 514,990, in NE Ohio, bordered (NW) by the Cuyahoga R., by which, along with the Tuscarawas R., it is intersected. It contains a number of lakes, including the Portage Lakes. Its seat is AKRON, whose metropolitan area and economy dominate the county. The NE part of the county adjoins Cleveland's SE suburbs. Agriculture includes clover, corn, dairy, livestock, and poultry farming. There is manufacturing at Akron, Barberton, Cuyahoga Falls, and other cities. Limestone, sandstone, sand, gravel, salt, and clay are natural resources.

Sumner town, pop. 140, Chariton Co., NC Missouri, 18 mi/29 km SE of Chillicothe. It lies in an area that produces grain and livestock. Arkansas senator J.W. Fulbright was born here (1905).

Sumpter city, pop. 119, Baker Co., EC Oregon, 18 mi/29 km W of Baker, surrounded by the Wallowa-Whitman National Forest. Settled by North Carolinian farmers in 1862, it became a gold mining boom town in the 1890s with a population that reached 3000. When the ore ran out in 1916, it fell into steep decline.

Sumter city, pop. 41,943, seat of Sumter Co. (pop. 102,637), EC South Carolina, 42 mi/68 km ESE of Columbia. A trucking and commercial center, it was founded in 1785 as Sumterville, in honor of General Thomas Sumter, "the Gamecock of the Revolution." Its varied manufactures have included batteries, processed food, furniture, lumber, chemicals, veneer, and printed and dyed textiles. Cotton, tobacco, and soybeans are grown in the area. Shaw Air Force Base, 7 mi/11 km NW, is a training facility for reconnaissance fliers. Morris College (Baptist; 1908) and a branch of the University of South Carolina are in Sumter. The city grew rapidly in the 1980s.

Sumter National Forest 310,000 ac/125,550 ha, in three units in NW South Carolina. The Andrew Pickens Division (80,000 ac/32,400 ha) is in the BLUE RIDGE in the extreme NW, bordered by North Carolina and Georgia and the Chattooga R. The Enoree Division (110,000 ac/44,550 ha) lies along the Broad R., midway between Columbia (SE) and Greenville-Spartanburg (NW), in the PIEDMONT. The Long Cane Division (110,000 ac/44,550 ha) lies along the Savannah R. just NW of North Augusta.

Sun, Valley of the see VALLEY OF THE SUN, Arizona.

Sunapee, Lake in SW New Hampshire, on the boundary between Sullivan and Merrimack counties. This 9 mi/14 km–long, 3 mi/5 km–wide resort lake is the largest natural body of water in the Connecticut R. drainage basin. It lies at an altitude of 1100 ft/335 m; Mt. KEARSARGE rises to the E, and Mt. Sunapee (2683 ft/818 m) is S of the lake. Mt. Sunapee State Park is a year-round resort area. Lake Sunapee is noted for game fishing and its wooded shoreline. The Penacook name means "rocky pond."

Sunbelt also, **Sun Belt** term in use since the 1950s for areas of the US South and Southwest favored by vacationers and retirees for their climate. Their attraction to business, and their rapid growth, owe as much to low overhead (e.g., heat) expenses, to state laws favorable to industry (and inimical to organized labor), and to the proximity of Mexico (as a source of cheap labor or site of MAQUILADORA plants), as to weather. The term is broadly used, but most pointedly of Florida, Arizona, and Southern California.

Sun Bowl see under EL PASO, Texas.

Sunbury city, pop. 11,591, seat of Northumberland Co., EC Pennsylvania, on the Susquehanna R., 50 mi/80 km N of Harrisburg. It stands on the site of Shamokin, an Indian village, situated where the Shamokin Creek enters the Susquehanna, just below the latter's junction with its West Branch. Fort Augusta (1756) was established here during the French and Indian Wars. In July 1883, Thomas Edison began the world's first three-wire central electric lighting station here. Today Sunbury is a shipping center for the region's coal and agricultural products; it also manufactures textiles, metal products, and construction materials. The 3000-ac/1214-ha Augusta L. was created by the Shamokin Dam across the Susquehanna; this dam is said to be the world's largest "fabridam"—a dam that can be inflated and deflated.

Sun City 1. unincorporated community, pop. 38,126, Maricopa Co., SC Arizona, 14 mi/23 km NW of downtown Phoenix, of which it is a suburb. Founded in 1960, it is a planned retirement community. **2.** unincorporated community, pop. 14,930, Riverside Co., S California, 22 mi/35 km SE of Riverside and 8 mi/13 km ENE of Lake Elsinore. It is a growing residential and retirement community in the Perris Valley.

Sundance 1. resort on the SE side of Mt. TIMPANOGOS, 10 mi/16 km NE of Provo, in Utah Co., NC Utah. Bought by film star Robert Redford in 1969, it is home to the Sundance Institute, which trains movie directors here and sponsors a Jan. film festival in PARK CITY. **2.** town, pop. 1139, seat of Crook Co., extreme NE Wyoming, on I-90 and Sundance Creek, 16 mi/26 km W of the South Dakota line. Just S of the Bearlodge Mts. and NW of the BLACK HILLS, it was the site, at Sundance Mt. (5829 ft/1777 m), of Sioux ceremonies. A trading post from the 1870s, it had an airbase and nuclear reactor in the 1950s–60s. The area produces oil, coal, and livestock. Harry Longabaugh apparently acquired the nickname "the Sundance Kid" after an 1887–89 stay in the jail here.

Sunflower, Mount hill (4039 ft/1232 m) in NW Kansas, 29 mi/47 km SW of Goodland, near the Colorado boundary. It is the highest point in the state.

Sunflower Landing see under CLARKSDALE, Mississippi.

Sunflower River also, **Big Sunflower River** 240 mi/390 km long, in W Mississippi. One of the major rivers of the DELTA, it rises in Coahoma Co., just SE of Friars Point, and winds S past Clarksdale and near Cleveland and Indianola. It joins the YAZOO R. at the SE corner of the Delta National Forest.

Sunken Road, the see under CHANCELLORSVILLE, Virginia.

Sunny Point Military Ocean Terminal: see under SOUTHPORT, North Carolina.

Sunnyside 1. in New York: **a.** residential section, W Queens. Part of Long Island City, it became the site, in 1924–28, of Sunnyside Gardens, an influential housing development. Located just N of Newtown Creek, between Hunters Point and Woodside, Sunnyside is almost surrounded by cemeteries and Long Island Rail Road yards. **b.** see under TARRYTOWN. **2.** city, pop. 11,238, Yakima Co., SC Washington, in the lower Yakima Valley, 30 mi/48 km

SE of Yakima. Settled by the Christian Cooperative Colony in 1898, it developed as a livestock center after the railroad arrived in 1906. The Sunnyside irrigation project was one of the first in the state. The city is now an agricultural and commercial center, trading and shipping asparagus, tomatoes, grapes, wine, fruit, and cheese and other dairy products. Other industries include poultry and vegetable packing and sugar beet warehousing. The huge YAKIMA INDIAN RESERVATION is 10 mi/16 km SW.

Sunnyvale city, pop. 117,229, Santa Clara Co., NC California, at the S end of San Francisco Bay, adjacent (NW) to Santa Clara and 36 mi/58 km SSE of San Francisco. Settled in 1849, it was a ranching and fruit processing center until World War II, then boomed, growing tenfold in pop. between 1950 and 1970, as SILICON VALLEY burgeoned. It is a major manufacturer of computers and computer-related machinery, medical and optical devices, and other high-tech equipment, with aerospace and other research laboratories and a variety of other light manufactures. Salt flats on the bay lie N.

Sun Prairie city, pop. 15,333, Dane Co., SC Wisconsin, a suburb 11 mi/18 km NE of Madison. Traditionally a dairying center, it has undergone much recent residential development.

Sunrise city, pop. 64,407, Broward Co., SE Florida, 7 mi/11 km W of Fort Lauderdale. One of many suburban cities around Fort Lauderdale, it boomed during the 1970s as a home for retirees and other transplants to the Sunbelt. Also a commercial hub, it is home to Sawgrass Mills, a huge outlet mall.

Sunrise Highway major commercial strip in Nassau and Suffolk counties, Long Island, SE New York. It runs 60 mi/96 km from Valley Stream, on the New York City border, E to Center Moriches, along the South Shore. The road varies in width from 4 to 6 lanes and is bordered by shopping centers, restaurants, retail outlets, and other commercial enterprises.

Sunrise Manor unincorporated residential community, pop. 95,362, Clark Co., S Nevada, 4 mi/6 km NE of downtown LAS VEGAS, E of North Las Vegas and SW of Nellis Air Force Base. Is is one of the fastest-growing parts of the Las Vegas area, having increased almost tenfold in pop. since 1970.

Sunset Boulevard thoroughfare, 20 mi/32 km long, in LOS ANGELES and BEVERLY HILLS, California, between SILVER LAKE (E) and PACIFIC PALISADES (W). Passing through HOLLYWOOD, WEST HOLLYWOOD, BEL AIR, and BRENTWOOD, it is the scene of mansions, dilapidated businesses, night-life districts, and beachfront homes. **Sunset Strip,** the stretch in West Hollywood between Crescent Heights Blvd. and Doheny Drive, was from the 1940s a busy entertainment area.

Sunset Crater see under SAN FRANCISCO PEAKS, Arizona.

Sunset District also, **the Sunset** predominantly residential section of SW SAN FRANCISCO, California, lying S of Golden Gate Park, and extending to the Pacific (W). Haight-Ashbury lies NE and Twin Peaks E. An area of single-family homes built chiefly between the World Wars, long a stronghold of the native white middle class, the Sunset has recently acquired an international component; it also has many elderly residents. To the S, around L. Merced, is the Parkside district.

Sunset Limited see under SOUTHERN PACIFIC RAILROAD.

Sunset Park residential and commercial section, WC Brooklyn, New York. It lies S of PARK SLOPE and N of BAY RIDGE, along Upper New York Bay; much of the Brooklyn waterfront is here. The area takes its name, first used widely in the 1960s, from a 24-ac/10-ha park that, along with nearby GREEN-WOOD CEMETERY, was a popular 19th-century recreation area. From the 1840s Irish, German, and Polish immigrants came to live in what was then considered part of South Brooklyn or of Bay Ridge. Late in the 19th century Scandinavians moved into Sunset Park and Bay Ridge. The first cooperative housing in the US was established here by Finns in 1916. Along the waterfront, the huge Bush Terminal complex was built in the 1890s. The Brooklyn Army Terminal (1918) was the embarkation point for 80% of Europe-bound US troops in World War II; the facility closed in the 1970s. The elevated Gowanus Expressway runs between Sunset Park and its docks. The district is now about 50% Hispanic, and the large Jewish community in neighboring BOROUGH PARK has spread E into Sunset Park.

Sun Valley city, pop. 938, Blaine Co., SC Idaho, between the Sawtooth Range and the Pioneer Mts., at 6000 ft/1830 m, 3 mi/5 km NE of Ketchum. Built by the Union Pacific Railroad in 1936, Sun Valley Lodge launched the area as a winter resort. Now internationally known, the city has many sports facilities and is especially noted for its skiing, with slopes on Dollar and Bald mountains. The world's first chairlift was installed here. The resort also offers a variety of warm-weather sports and cultural events.

Superconducting Supercollider see under WAXAHACHIE, Texas.

Superdome see LOUISIANA SUPERDOME, New Orleans.

Superfund site any of some 1200 US sites on the National Priorities List, designated pursuant to 1980 and 1986 Federal laws as requiring cleanup, funded by a special "superfund," of various (e.g., military, industrial) hazardous wastes. The Environmental Protection Agency has responsibility for managing the cleanup. Superfund sites, some on Federal land, exist in all states, Guam, and Puerto Rico; almost 40%, however, are in five states: New Jersey, Pennsylvania, California, New York, and Michigan.

Superior city, pop. 27,134, seat of Douglas Co., extreme NW Wisconsin, at the W end of L. Superior, across the St. Louis R. estuary from Duluth, Minnesota (N). A port of entry and transportation hub, the Duluth-Superior complex has huge docks. Coal, iron ore, copper, taconite, limestone, coal, and grain are the most important of the many products brought here by rail and transshipped onto vessels bound for Chicago and the St. Lawrence Seaway. A pipeline delivers Canadian crude oil to refineries here. Superior also has shipyards, grain elevators, flour mills, and a number of heavy industries. Jesuit Father Claude Allouez founded a mission here in 1655, after which the area was visited regularly by trappers and traders. Permanent settlement dates to 1853, and the discovery of iron ore in the nearby GOGEBIC Range 30 years later caused a boom. The University of Wisconsin at Superior (1896) is here.

Superior, Lake largest and deepest of the GREAT LAKES, at the NW end of the chain, bordering Ontario (N and E), Minnesota (W), and Michigan's Upper Peninsula and Wisconsin (S). Some 350 mi/560 km E–W and up to 160 mi/265 km wide, it is the largest lake in the Western Hemisphere, covering 31,750 sq mi/82,235 sq km and reaching a depth of 1330 ft/405 m. Its surface is 600 ft/183 m above sea level, and it drains E into L. Huron via the St. Marys R., on which the canals and locks at SAULT STE. MARIE raise or lower ships 23 ft/7 m. The KEWEENAW

PENINSULA in Michigan, a major copper producing region, extends 65 mi/105 km into the S of the lake; 25 mi/40 km–wide Whitefish Bay is a SE arm, near Sault Ste. Marie. PUKASKWA National Park, in Ontario, is on the NE shore, and Michigan's PICTURED ROCKS National Lakeshore on the SE, while ISLE ROYALE National Park, in Michigan, the APOSTLE ISLANDS National Lakeshore, in Wisconsin, and Minnesota's historic GRAND PORTAGE all lie in the W. Superior is bordered by the CANADIAN SHIELD, by the Vermilion, Mesabi, Gogebic, and Ishpeming iron ranges, and by numerous coal deposits. Minnesota's Saint Louis R., on the W, is the headwater of the entire Great Lakes–St. Lawrence system. Ore boats and oceangoing freighters carry products from Thunder Bay, Ontario; Silver Bay, Two Harbors, and Duluth, Minnesota; Superior and Ashland, Wisconsin; and Houghton and Marquette, Michigan, through the GREAT LAKES–SAINT LAWRENCE WATERWAY. Most of the lake is navigable only about seven months of the year. Commercial as well as sports fishing is important in the lake's relatively unpolluted waters. The French explorer Étienne Brulé was probably the first European to view the lake, before 1620.

Superior Highlands also, **Superior Upland** extension of the CANADIAN SHIELD into NE Minnesota, where the area it covers, W of L. Superior, has come to be known as the ARROWHEAD REGION, site of the MESABI, VERMILION, and other iron ranges and mining districts. The NW portion of Michigan's UPPER PENINSULA and NW and N Wisconsin are a continuation E (across L. Superior), and also contain important mining areas.

Superior National Forest see under ARROWHEAD REGION, Minnesota.

Superstition Mountains range in C Arizona, E of Mesa, rising to 5057 ft/1541 m at Superstition Mt. It is the site of the legendary Lost Dutchman Mine, whose discoverer, Jacob Waltz, died in 1891, apparently taking its secret with him. Many deaths in the mountains have led to the belief that they are cursed. Weaver's Needle, a black basalt finger sticking up from the desert, is a landmark for those searching for the mine.

Sur, Point rocky promontory on the Pacific Ocean in Monterey Co., WC California, 20 mi/32 km S of Monterey. Pervasive dense fog in the area caused many shipwrecks until a lighthouse was built in 1889. Big Sur is the name of a hamlet 5 mi/8 km SE, along the Big Sur R., which flows from the SANTA LUCIA RANGE. The river's valley and surrounding area are famous for their scenery, their seclusion (now threatened by tourism and residential growth), and their association with writers Robinson Jeffers (late 19th century), Henry Miller (1940s), and the Beat poets (1950s). The local Esselen (or Esalen) people left their name to the Esalen Institute, the best-known of 1960s New Age retreats.

Surfside see under MIAMI BEACH, Florida.

Surrey district municipality, pop. 245,173, Greater Vancouver Regional District, SW British Columbia, between the Fraser R. (N) and Washington State, 15 mi/24 km SE of downtown Vancouver. It developed from the 1900s with the construction of bridges to New Westminster and Vancouver and the arrival of the railway. Agriculture and sawmilling have been important in an area that has boomed recently (35% pop. growth in 1986–91) as a residential and commerical suburb, becoming the province's second most populous municipality. DELTA lies W, LANGLEY E.

Surry County 281 sq mi/728 sq km, pop. 6145, in SE Virginia. Its seat is Surry (pop. 192). In the TIDEWATER, the county is bounded N and NE by the James R. and S by the Blackwater R. It is largely agricultural, with dairying and lumbering. BACON'S CASTLE is in the SE. The Surry nuclear power plant (1972) is on Gravel Neck, along the James in the extreme SE.

Susanville city, pop. 7279, seat of Lassen Co. (pop. 27,598), NE California, at the E base of the Sierra Nevada and the head (NW) of Honey Lake Valley, on the Susan R., 75 mi/120 km NNW of Reno, Nevada. Peter Lassen struck gold here in 1854, bringing on a brief boom. The city now has lumber mills, makes wood products, and is a cattle and sheep–area trade center. A state prison, just E, is a major employer. In addition, Lassen College (1925) is here, and Susanville is a gateway to Lassen Volcanic National Park, 40 mi/64 km W, and other lake and mountain areas.

Susitna River 300 mi/500 km long, in S Alaska. It originates in the Susitna Glacier on the S of the Alaska Range, and winds S, W, and SW, passing through the Talkeetna Mts., to Talkeetna, where it receives the Chulitna and Talkeetna rivers, widens, and flows S to COOK INLET, 25 mi/40 km W of Anchorage. Its valley and the MATANUSKA VALLEY (SE) are Alaska's agricultural center.

Susquehanna nuclear power plant: see under BERWICK, Pennsylvania.

Susquehanna River 444 mi/715 km long, the longest river on the US eastern seaboard. It rises in C New York, in OTSEGO L., and flows SW past ONEONTA and Sidney, then crosses into Susquehanna Co., NE Pennsylvania. Turning generally NW, it reenters New York and turns W past BINGHAMTON, where the CHENANGO R. joins from the N, and OWEGO, where the Owego Creek joins it. It then turns S into Bradford Co., NE Pennsylvania, and continues generally SE through the Allegheny Plateau to Exeter and PITTSTON, just NE of Wilkes-Barre, where the Lackawanna R. joins it. It then flows SW past Berwick, Bloomsburg, and Danville. At SUNBURY, it meets the 160-mi/260-km **West Branch,** which rises in SW Clearfield Co., C Pennsylvania, and flows NE, E, and SE past Lock Haven, Williamsport, and Lewisburg, to Sunbury. The West Branch's major tributaries are SINNEMAHONING and Bald Eagle creeks. Following its confluence with the West Branch, the Susquehanna flows S and SE, crossing Allegheny ridges and forming water gaps, past HARRISBURG and across the Piedmont Plateau, to empty into Chesapeake Bay at Havre de Grace, Maryland. On its lower course the JUNIATA R. is its major tributary. The Susquehanna is only locally navigable because of many obstructions and its shallowness; it has not been canalized, but some flood control projects have been undertaken. In June 1972, severe flooding occurred along its NE reaches, especially at Binghamton and other SOUTHERN TIER cities. There are hydroelectric dams at Safe Harbor, Pennsylvania, and Conowingo, Maryland, and nuclear plants in Pennsylvania near BERWICK and at THREE MILE ISLAND and PEACH BOTTOM.

Sussex **1.** town, pop. 4132, Kings Co., S New Brunswick, on the Kennebecasis R., 41 mi/65 km NE of Saint John. Home to Acadians, then LOYALISTS, from the late 18th century, it is an agricultural and light industrial center in the midst of an area of potash, gypsum, and salt mines. **2.** village, pop. 5039, Waukesha Co., SE Wisconsin, a suburb 15 mi/24 km NW of Milwaukee.

Sussex County 526 sq mi/1362 sq km, pop. 130,943, in

extreme N New Jersey, bounded by the Delaware R. (W) and New York (N). Its seat is Newton; other municipalities include Franklin, Hamburg, Ogdensburg, and Sparta. The county is mountainous and lake-filled, with Stokes State Forest and HIGH POINT State Park in its NW. It is largely agricultural, with farms that produce fruit, vegetables, and livestock, some light manufacturing, resorts, and an increasing suburban component.

Sussex Drive thoroughfare along the Ottawa R., from Wellington St. to Rideau Falls (the mouth of the Rideau R.), in NE OTTAWA, Ontario. Passing around LOWER TOWN, it was one of the city's early (mid-19th-century) commercial arteries, before UPPER TOWN became dominant. It is now lined on the water side by parkland, the site of the National Gallery of Canada and National Research Council. At its NE end, across the Rideau, in what was until the 1880s New Edinburgh, is **24 Sussex Drive,** the Prime Minister's residence, and, nearby at 1 Sussex Drive, Rideau Hall (or Government House), official residence of Canada's governor general.

Sutter Buttes roughly circular volcanic group, covering some 75 sq mi/194 sq km, NW of YUBA CITY and 45 mi/72 km NNW of Sacramento, in NE California. Rising to c.2000 ft/610 m above its surroundings, "the world's smallest mountain range," sacred to the Maidu and Wintu, was part of New Helvetia (see SACRAMENTO), and is now largely privately owned, grazed, and quarried. It is noted for its wildlife.

Sutter's Fort see under SACRAMENTO, California.

Sutter's Mill see under COLOMA, California.

Sutton **1.** town, pop. 6824, Worcester Co., C Massachusetts, 8 mi/13 km SSE of Worcester. It had a number of factories in the 19th century but, after the railroads passed it by, its industry declined, and it returned to farming, and remains essentially rural. **2.** town, pop. 1457, Merrimack Co., SC New Hampshire. It is 23 mi/37 km NW of Concord, and 4 mi/6 km E of L. SUNAPEE. The town is in an agricultural and resort area, with a number of lakes and ski slopes. **3.** also, **Sutton West** see under GEORGINA, Ontario.

Sutton Mountains see under NOTRE DAME Mts., Québec.

Suwannee River 240 mi/386 km long, in Georgia and Florida. It rises in the OKEFENOKEE SWAMP, and flows SW into Florida, winding W, S, and SE in a large bend before resuming a generally S course and emptying into the Gulf of Mexico. Surrounding cedar forests were cut down by the early 20th century. There are no major cities along the river, which is best known via Stephen Foster's 1851 song "Old Folks at Home" ("Swanee River").

Sverdrup Islands subgroup of the QUEEN ELIZABETH Is., in the ARCTIC ARCHIPELAGO, N Northwest Territories. A roughly circular group c.250 mi/400 km in diameter, they lie W of ELLESMERE I., and include Axel Heiberg (the largest), Ellef Ringnes, Amund Ringnes, Meighen, and several smaller islands. A Norwegian expedition led by Otto Sverdrup explored them in 1898–1902, and Canadian sovereignty was not firmly established until 1931. Remote and ice-covered, the Sverdrups are made up of uplifted sedimentary rocks newer than the Canadian Shield. The PARRY Is. lie SW.

Swains Island also, **Quiros** 1 sq mi/2.6 sq km, pop. 16, part (since 1925) of AMERICAN SAMOA. Some 225 mi/360 km NNW of PAGO PAGO, Tutuila, it is not part of the Samoa Is. chain. Privately owned and long under the jurisdiction of Britain's Gilbert and Ellice Islands colony, it came under US jurisdiction in 1925.

Swampscott town, pop. 13,650, Essex Co., NE Massachusetts. It is a NORTH SHORE suburb of Boston and Lynn, between Lynn and Marblehead on Massachusetts Bay. Tourism and commercial fishing are the main industries.

Swanee River see SUWANEE R.

Swanendael also, **Zwaanendael** see under LEWES, Delaware.

Swannanoa unincorporated community, pop. 3538, Buncombe Co., W North Carolina, in the Blue Ridge Mts., on the Swannanoa R., 9 mi/14 km E of Asheville. It is a resort and home to Warren Wilson College (1894).

Swan Peak see under FLATHEAD RANGE, Montana.

Swan Range in the N Rocky Mts., in Lake, Powell, and Flathead counties, NW Montana. These NW–SE mountains lie between the Mission (W) and Flathead (E) ranges. They include the Swan River State Forest and Swan River National Wildlife Refuge.

Swan River town, pop. 3917, W Manitoba, on the Swan R., 40 mi/64 km SW of Swan L., near the Saskatchewan border and 158 mi/255 km NNW of Brandon. A fur trading area in the 1800s, it was the subject of a rivalry between the Hudson's Bay and North West companies. Eventually it became a headquarters for missionary work by the Church of England. A farming and lumbering center, it lies in the Swan R. valley between the PORCUPINE and DUCK mountains. The Swan Valley Harvest Festival is held every Aug.

Swansea town, pop. 15,411, Bristol Co., SE Massachusetts, 3 mi/5 km NW of Fall River, on Mount Hope Bay and the Rhode Island border. It was the site of the first bloodshed of King Philip's War (1675). Formerly a shipbuilding and textile-producing town, it is now agricultural and suburban.

Swans Island island township, pop. 349, at the mouth of Blue Hill Bay, 8 mi/13 km SW of Mt. Desert I., Hancock Co., SE Maine. The main island, Swans, 6 mi/10 km long and up to 4 mi/6 km wide, is one of the Burncoat Islands, visited (1604) by Champlain, and noted for fishing and boating. Minturn is the chief settlement.

Swarthmore borough, pop. 6157, Delaware Co., SE Pennsylvania, 11 mi/18 km WSW of Philadelphia. A residential suburb, it is home to Swarthmore College (1864).

Swartz Bay see under SAANICH, British Columbia.

Sweet Auburn see AUBURN Ave., Atlanta, Georgia.

Sweet Briar hamlet in Amherst Co., C Virginia, 11 mi/18 km NNE of Lynchburg, in the SE foothills of the Blue Ridge Mts. It is the seat of Sweet Briar College for women (1901), and of the Virginia Center for the Creative Arts (1971), an artists' colony.

Sweetwater **1.** city, pop. 13,909, Dade Co., SE Florida, on the Tamiami Trail, 10 mi/16 km W of Miami, of which it is a residential suburb. **2.** city, pop. 11,967, seat of Nolan Co., WC Texas, 37 mi/60 km W of Abilene, on Interstate 20. Settled in 1877 around a dugout trading post, it moved to the present site when the Texas & Pacific Railroad arrived in 1881. Despite blizzard and drought in the 1880s, it survived as a trading center for wool, cattle, and cotton producers. Oil (discovered in the 1920s), sand, gypsum, and clay deposits have been exploited. The city ships grain, feed, wool, mohair, and livestock, and has various light manufactures. Sweetwater is noted as the World War II home (at Avenger Field) of the Women's Airforce Service Pilots (WASP) program, in which women pilots ferried bombers and flew other noncombat missions.

Sweetwater County 10,352 sq mi/26,812 sq km, pop. 38,823, in SW Wyoming. GREEN RIVER is its seat. Created by gold miners as Carter Co., it is Wyoming's largest county. It is watered by the Green R. (W) and Big Sandy R. (NW) and includes the GREAT DIVIDE BASIN and RED DESERT in the NE and Ashley National Forest and the FLAMING GORGE National Recreation Area in the SW. It is a mining and sheep raising area, also producing coal and oil. Tourism is important.

Swift Current city, pop. 14,815, SW Saskatchewan, 144 mi/232 km W of Regina, on Swift Current Creek. The city evolved from a Canadian Pacific Railway depot, and became a service center for a substantial wheat farming and livestock raising region. One of Canada's largest experimental farms is here. Local industries include dairying, meatpacking, the manufacture of animal feed and agricultural equipment, and some lumbering. Natural resources developed in the area include oil, helium, natural gas, and sodium sulfate.

Swift River also, **Quabbin River** 17 mi/27 km long, in WC Massachusetts. It rises in E Franklin Co. Most of its upper reaches have been inundated by the QUABBIN RESERVOIR, which provides water for the Greater Boston area. Boating is allowed on the lower section of the Swift R., below Winsor Dam (1939), which is 280 ft/85 m high and 2640 ft/805 m long. The river continues S to Three Rivers, where it is joined by the Quaboag R. to form the Chicopee R.

Swing Street popular name for 52nd St., Manhattan, New York City. Especially in the blocks W of Fifth Ave., it was in the 1930s regarded as the center of the jazz world. Its numerous clubs and bars have given place to office buildings.

Swissvale borough, pop. 10,637, Allegheny Co., SW Pennsylvania, on the Monongahela R., 6 mi/10 km ESE of Pittsburgh. Founded in 1760, it is a producer of railway communications and control equipment, industrial safety equipment, heat-resistant materials, and glassware.

Swope Park 1772-ac/718-ha city park, 7 mi/11 km SE of downtown KANSAS CITY, Missouri, one of the largest US municipal parks. With a wide variety of facilities, it is best known for its outdoor Starlight Theater. The BIG BLUE R. winds NNE through the park.

Sycamore city, pop. 9708, seat of De Kalb Co., N Illinois, 5 mi/8 km NE of DE KALB, on the South Branch of the Kishwaukee R. Founded in the 1840s, it is a trade center with metal and machine industries.

Sycamore Shoals see under ELIZABETHTON, Tennessee.

Sydenham River 100 mi/160 km long, in S Ontario. It rises NW of London and flows generally SW past Strathroy, Dresden, and Wallaceburg, to L. St. Clair.

Sydney city, pop. 26,063, seat of Cape Breton Co., on the South Arm of Sydney Harbour and E shore of CAPE BRETON I., extreme E Nova Scotia. It is the center of the mining/industrial cluster that includes Sydney Mines, GLACE BAY, NORTH SYDNEY, and NEW WATERFORD. In E Canada's major coalfield, it was a producer by the 18th century but more importantly a service town for the industry. From 1784 to 1820 it was the capital of the LOYALIST colony of Cape Breton Island. With the opening of its big steel plant in 1900, the city began to consume much of the region's coal, as well as Newfoundland iron ore, and developed ancillary industries. Gradual obsolescence of the mill, and decline in the coal industry, have left Sydney somewhat depressed, although it remains the area's commercial center.

Sydney Mines town, pop. 7551, Cape Breton Co., extreme E Nova Scotia, on the N side of Sydney Harbour, 8 mi/13 km NNW of Sydney, Cape Breton I. Coal was mined here from the early 18th century, some of the workings eventually extending up to 4 mi/6.4 km under the sea. The industry collapsed by the 1970s, leaving Sydney Mines depressed. NORTH SYDNEY is adjacent (SW).

Sylacauga city, pop. 12,520, Talladega Co., EC Alabama, 40 mi/64 km SE of Birmingham, in the Coosa Valley. Built on a large bed of translucent cream-white marble, it developed as a quarrying and processing center after 1840. It is also a market for local farm and timber products, and has textile and other light industries. The Supreme Court building in Washington is built of Sylacauga marble.

Sylmar N SAN FERNANDO VALLEY section of Los Angeles, California, N of San Fernando and 21 mi/34 km NW of Downtown, on the SE of the San Fernando Pass to Santa Clarita. Just SW of the San Gabriel Mts., it has been a rail shipping center for local olives. In Feb. 1971 it was at the epicenter of a destructive earthquake.

Sylvania city, pop. 17,301, Lucas Co., NW Ohio, on the Michigan border 10 mi/16 km NW of Toledo, of which it is a commuter suburb. Building materials, fertilizer, and tools are manufactured here. Large fossil beds have been discovered nearby. It is the seat of Lourdes College (1958).

Syosset unincorporated village, pop. 18,967, in Oyster Bay town, Nassau Co., SE New York, in WC Long Island, 9 mi/14 km NE of Mineola. It is a residential and commercial suburb.

Syracuse city, pop. 163,860, seat of Onondaga Co., C New York, at the S end of Onondaga L., midway between Albany and Buffalo. Originally the home of the Onondaga and the headquarters of the IROQUOIS CONFEDERACY, the site was fortified by the French in 1655. European settlement began in 1786, when a trading post was established at the mouth of Onondaga Creek. Saw and grist mills were built, and in 1797, local saltlands were leased for exploitation. Saltworks flourished until the Civil War, sustaining the three villages of Webster's Landing, Geddes, and Salina, which by 1886 had united to form Syracuse. Industrialization followed. Syracuse now manufactures jet engines, machinery, pharmaceuticals, chinaware, and electronic equipment. Its institutions include Syracuse University (1870) and several other colleges and professional schools. The city lies at the SE end of 5 mi/8 km–long Onondaga L., which has been severely polluted by local industry. Its metropolitan area includes CICERO, DE WITT, MANLIUS, SALINA, and GEDDES. The Onondaga Indian Reservation (pop. 771) is 6 mi/10 km S.

T

Taber town, pop. 6660, S Alberta, 115 mi/185 km SE of Calgary and 30 mi/48 km ENE of Lethbridge. A trade and processing center for an agricultural and ranching region, it has industries including beet sugar refining and vegetable canning. There are also oil and gas wells. The town was settled by Mormons in the early 20th century.

tableland see PLATEAU.

Table Rock peak (3157 ft/963 m) of the Blue Ridge Mts., in 3070-ac/1243-ha Table Rock State Park, NW South Carolina, 21 mi/34 km NW of Greenville, and near SASSAFRAS Mt. With vertical cliffs of gneiss and a flat top, it resembles a table, and, along with a nearby mountain called the Stool (2500 ft/763 m), is said to be where an Indian chief once sat to dine.

Tabor **1.** city, pop. 957, Fremont and Mills counties, SW Iowa, 25 mi/40 km SSE of Council Bluffs. An agricultural community, it was an abolitionist center before the Civil War, containing a station on the Underground Railroad and an arsenal and hospital for antislavery fighters in nearby Kansas. **2.** town, pop. 403, Bon Homme Co., SE South Dakota, 13 mi/21 km NW of Yankton. In a livestock and grain producing area, it was founded by the Hutterites, a Christian group believing in complete social equality and the sharing of property.

Tacoma city, pop. 176,664, seat of Pierce Co., WC Washington, on Commencement Bay, an inlet of Puget Sound, at the mouth of the Puyallup R., 25 mi/40 km S of Seattle. A major container port and railroad center, the city exports timber, fruit, flower bulbs, and many other products. Local industries include construction of agricultural machinery, boatbuilding, food processing, fishing, metalwork, and the manufacture of chemicals and wood and paper products. There is also a growing high-tech sector producing computer and electronic components. The University of Puget Sound (1888) and Pacific Lutheran University (1890) are here. The Hudson's Bay Company established Fort Nisqually here in the early 1830s, and the first sawmill opened in 1852. Settled in the 1860s, Tacoma boomed as a lumber processing and industrial center with the coming of the Northern Pacific Railroad in 1873. McChord Air Force Base is 5 mi/8 km S, and Fort Lewis is 10 mi/16 km SW. The city is a gateway to Mount Rainier National Park, 30 mi/48 km SE, and to Olympic National Park, 45 mi/72 km W.

Tacoma-Narrows Bridge also, **Narrows Bridge** 6000 ft/1830 m–long suspension bridge over Puget Sound, in WC Washington, connecting Tacoma with the Olympic Peninsula (NW). It is the successor to "Galloping Gertie," which swayed in the wind and collapsed in a storm in 1940, four months after completion.

Taconic Mountains also, **Taconic Range** or **Taconics** part of the APPALACHIAN Mt. system, running N–S for 150 mi/240 km roughly along the New York–New England boundary from N Connecticut to C Vermont, paralleling the BERKSHIRE HILLS (E). Geologically complex, the range has an angular look, with steep-sided peaks and valleys, because of shale and slate, abundant on the surface. It includes Mt. EQUINOX (3816 ft/1163 m) in Vermont, its highest point, and Mt. FRISSELL (2380 ft/726 m), whose S slope is the highest point in Connecticut.

Taconic State Parkway in SE New York, running 105 mi/169 km from just NW of WHITE PLAINS (S) to the New York State Thruway near Chatham Center in Columbia Co., some 20 mi/32 km SE of Albany (N). Constructed 1929–63, it curves its way from densely settled Westchester Co. into exurban and farming areas W of the Taconic Mts.

Tadoussac village, pop. 832, La-Haute-Côte-Nord census division, SE Québec, 113 mi/182 km NE of Québec City, in hilly country on the SAGUENAY R., near its mouth on the St. Lawrence R. One of the oldest European settlements in North America, on the site of a Montagnais trading village visited by Jacques Cartier in 1535, was the first (1599) fur and fish trading post in Canada, established on this strategic spot. Through the 17th and 18th centuries, Tadoussac was an important trade and treaty site. Today it is primarily a summer resort; the area is noted for its hunting and fishing, and forest industries are important.

Tahlequah city, pop. 10,398, seat of Cherokee Co., E Oklahoma, in the foothills of the Ozark Mts., 25 mi/40 km NE of Muskogee. It was the capital (1839–1906) of the Cherokee Nation, where the tribe established its own government and schools, and is still home to many Cherokee. Besides being a tourist site (the Cherokee Heritage Center is here), it is now a commercial hub for fruit, livestock, and other agricultural producers. Manufactures include lumber and machinery. Northeastern State University (1846) is here.

Tahoe, Lake on the border of NE California and W Nevada, 80 mi/130 km ENE of Sacramento and 4 mi/6 km W of Carson City. The largest US mountain lake, covering 200 sq mi/518 sq km, it is 21 mi/34 km long, up to 12 mi/19 km wide, and up to 1645 ft/501 m deep. It lies at an altitude of 6228 ft/1899 m, and is a year-round resort. One-third lies in Nevada, where there are gambling resorts along the shore. The California side, where SOUTH LAKE TAHOE is the largest city, is the site of ski and water resort and condominium development. The lake's human history goes back 10,000 years before John C. Frémont and Kit Carson were the first whites to see it (1844); the Washoe lived here in the 19th century and gave the lake its name ("big water" or "lake"). The area was heavily lumbered during the COMSTOCK LODE period (1860s–70s).

Tahoe National Forest c.830,000 ac/336,000 ha (1300 sq mi/3360 sq km), in NE California, N and W of L. TAHOE, largely in the Yuba R. watershed. In the Northern Mines area of the MOTHER LODE, where hydraulic mining in the 1860s–70s altered much landscape, it contains old mines, glacial lakes, and dense woods. The DONNER PASS and SQUAW VALLEY are here.

Takkakaw Falls see under YOHO NATIONAL PARK, British Columbia.

Takoma Park city, pop. 16,700, in Montgomery and Prince George's counties, C Maryland, on Sligo Brook Creek and the extreme NE boundary of Washington, D.C. It was founded along the Baltimore & Ohio Railroad in 1883. Early in the 20th century, Seventh-Day Adventists made the city their headquarters, establishing several institutions, including Washington Missionary College (1904), now Columbia Union College. Adventist headquarters are now in adjoining (NW) SILVER SPRING. Takoma Park is primarily a residential suburb. A campus of Montgomery College is here.

Talcottville hamlet in Leyden township, Lewis Co., C New York, 23 mi/37 km NNE of Rome. It was the ancestral home of writer Edmund Wilson (1895–1972), and the setting for his memoir *Upstate*.

Taliesin see under SPRING GREEN, Wisconsin.

Taliesin West see under SCOTTSDALE, Arizona.

Talkeetna Mountains range extending NE–SW for c.150 mi/240 km N of Anchorage, in S Alaska, N of the MATANUSKA VALLEY. The Talkeetna, Chulitna, and Susitna rivers converge near the community of **Talkeetna** ("where the rivers meet"; unincorporated, pop. 250), on the E. The range reaches its highest elevation at Sovereign Mt. (8846 ft/2696 m). The search for silver, coal, and furs brought settlers to the Talkeetnas. Devils Canyon, on the Susitna, is a kayaking mecca.

Talladega city, pop. 18,175, seat of Talladega Co., EC Alabama, 40 mi/64 km ESE of Birmingham, in the foothills of the Appalachian Mts. Scene of a Nov. 9, 1813 victory by Andrew Jackson's Tennessee Volunteers, opening the Creek War, it had been a Creek village. Local agriculture and marble, iron, and limestone deposits form the basis for local industry. The city is home to Talladega College (1867). The **Talladega Superspeedway** (Alabama International Motor Speedway) is 8 mi/13 km NNE, near Interstate 20; the 2.66 mi/4.3 km track claims to be the world's largest and fastest auto racetrack.

Talladega Mountains also, **Talladega Mountain** low range in EC Alabama, at the S end of the Appalachian chain, tapering down to hills S of Sylacauga. **Talladega National Forest** (371,000 ac/150,000 ha in two units) here includes CHEAHA Mt. (2407 ft/734 m), the highest point in the state, and Horn Mt. (1912 ft/583 m). Its smaller Oakmulgee section lies some 50 mi/80 km SW of Birmingham, along the N of the BLACK BELT.

Tallahassee city, pop. 124,773, state capital and seat of Leon Co., N Florida, 15 mi/24 km S of the Georgia border, in the PANHANDLE. In a hilly region dotted with live oak forests, lakes, rivers, and springs, it was an Apalachee village when De Soto arrived (1539); Spanish settlement began in the 1630s. The Indian village and a Spanish mission are part of the San Luis Archaeological and Historic Site. Tallahassee was made capital of the Florida territory in 1824 and became state capital in 1845. Florida adopted an ordinance of secession here (1861), and the city was successfully defended against Union attack at Natural Bridge, 13 mi/21 km SE, on March 6, 1865. State government is a prime employer in modern Tallahassee. In addition, the city is a market and processing center for tobacco, lumber, wood products, pecans, and other foods, and has some light industry. It has retained some antebellum atmosphere, with many 19th-century buildings and noted gardens. It is the seat of Florida State University (1851), Florida Agricultural and Mechanical University (1887), and Tallahassee Community College (1965).

Tallahatchie River 230 mi/370 km long, in N Mississippi. It rises NE of New Albany, along the Tippah-Union county line, and flows generally W and SW into the DELTA, then S to Greenwood, just N of which it joins the YALOBUSHA R. to form the YAZOO R. Just SE of Sardis, on its upper reaches, is the Sardis Dam (1940), which impounds Sardis L.

Tallapoosa River 268 mi/431 km long, in NW Georgia and E Alabama. It rises in Paulding Co., about 30 mi/48 km WNW of Atlanta, and flows W and SW into Alabama, turns S near Heflin, and flows past HORSESHOE BEND into L. Martin, formed by the Martin Dam near Red Hill. From the dam it flows generally S and then W to join the COOSA R. NE of Montgomery, forming the ALABAMA R.

Tallmadge city, pop. 14,986, Summit Co., NE Ohio, a residential and industrial suburb 5 mi/8 km NE of Akron.

Tallulah city, pop. 8526, seat of Madison Parish, NE Louisiana, 20 mi/32 km WNW of Vicksburg, Mississippi. In a rich lowland agricultural region, it produces cotton and cotton products, soybeans, lumber, and poultry. Nearby lakes and bayous are noted for fishing. US Department of Agriculture scientists here made important advances in cropdusting techniques at mid-century.

Tallulah River 40 mi/64 km long, in the Chattahoochee National Forest, in NE Georgia. It rises just below the North Carolina line and flows S and E through 1100 ft/336 m–deep **Tallulah Gorge** to join the Chattooga R. 3 mi/5 km SE of Tallulah Falls, forming the Tugaloo R. The river has a series of dam-created lakes, the largest L. Burton, and is a popular recreational area.

Tamalpais, Mount mountain with three crests, the highest East Peak (2604 ft/794 m), in Marin Co., NW California, across the Golden Gate (NW) from San Francisco. Both Mt. Tamalpais State Park and Muir Woods National Monument (553 ac/224 ha) are on its slopes, within the GOLDEN GATE NATIONAL RECREATION AREA. The Monument is known for stands of coast redwoods.

Tamarac city, pop. 44,822, Broward Co., SE Florida, 8 mi/13 km NW of Fort Lauderdale. A retirement suburb that has boomed since the 1960s, it has planned neighborhoods and a noted golf course.

Tamiami Trail roadway (US Route 41), c.105 mi/170 km long, crossing S Florida between Miami (E) and Naples (W), traversing the Everglades and the Big Cypress National Preserve. It is a favorite of tourists. From Naples, US 41 continues N to Tampa; the Trail's name contracts *Ta*mpa–*Mia*mi, and is often applied to the entire route.

Tammany Hall fraternal political organization in New York City, conceived of as residing within a headquarters lodge or "wigwam," along with various branches. Named for a 17th-century Delaware leader (Tamenend, or Tammany) who was friendly with William Penn and was consequently "canonized" (see also SAINT TAMMANY PARISH, Louisiana), it was founded in 1786 as one of several such organizations in eastern cities. At first essentially antiaristocratic, it became largely Irish in the early 19th century. With direct election of New York mayors (1834), Tammany became the classic Democratic urban political machine, and continued to function, with some periods of lesser influence, until the 1960s. The "hall" occupied a number of sites on Manhattan's LOWER EAST SIDE. In the 20th century headquarters were near UNION SQUARE.

Tampa city, pop. 280,015, seat of Hillsborough Co., WC Florida, on the Interbay Peninsula, on Old Tampa Bay (W), TAMPA BAY (S), and Hillsborough Bay (E and S), at the mouth of the Hillsborough R. Downtown Tampa is some 20 mi/32 km NE of St. Petersburg. It is linked with Clearwater by a causeway, with St. Petersburg by two bridges (across Old Tampa Bay), and with the Bradenton area by the Sunshine Skyway (across Tampa Bay). The area around modern Tampa was visited by the Spanish explorer Pánfilo de Narváez in 1528; in 1539 De Soto rescued the expedition's sole survivor. The hostility of local tribes prevented settlement until 1823, when Americans arrived and Fort Brooke (1824) was established. A civilian community grew up around it, and a town was incorporated in 1855. Union forces occupied Tampa and its fort in (1864). Significant economic growth came with the development of fishing and shipbuilding, the discovery of phosphates in the area (1883), the coming of the railroad (1884), and the introduction of a cigarmaking industry centered in YBOR CITY (1886). Tourism also developed rapidly in the late 19th century. During the Spanish-American War, US troops used Tampa as an embarkation point for Cuba. The city's growth continued during the Florida land boom of the 1920s, when many subdivisions were built, including the artificial Davis I., where many elegant homes are still located. The city and its population were greatly enlarged in 1953, when Tampa merged with several suburbs. Today Tampa is a major port, and has an international airport. The phosphate industry continues to be important; the city processes and ships the product. It also maintains a large shrimp fleet. It packs and distributes citrus fruit, brews beer, manufactures plastics and food products, and produces handmade cigars. The military is a factor in the economy, largely because of adjoining (S) MacDill Air Force Base. Busch Gardens, an Africa-centered theme park with tropical gardens and zoo; Tampa's Convention Center; and several museums and theaters draw tourists. The Tampa Bay Buccaneers (football), and Lightning (hockey), and horse and dog racing and jai alai facilities also attract visitors. The annual Gasparilla Festival celebrates a pirate legend. Railroad magnate Henry B. Plant's sumptuous Moorish-style Tampa Bay Hotel (1891) is today the administration building for the University of Tampa (1931). Also here are Tampa College (1890), the University of South Florida (1960), and Hillsborough Community College (1968).

Tampa Bay mitten-shaped inlet of the Gulf of Mexico S of Tampa and E of St. Petersburg, in Hillsborough and Pinellas counties, WC Florida. Fifteen mi/24 km wide at its mouth, it extends 23 mi/37 km NE to the Interbay Peninsula, where it divides into Hillsborough Bay, 8 mi/13 km N–S (on the E) and **Old Tampa Bay,** 15 mi/24 km N–S (on the W). The Pinellas Peninsula separates the bay from the Gulf of Mexico on the W. Numerous islands and the Pinellas and Egmont Key national wildlife refuges lie in the bay's mouth. The bay receives the Hillsborough R., and dredged shipping channels make it the major port of Florida's W coast. The Spanish explorer Pánfilo de Narváez landed at the bay in 1528, and De Soto explored it in 1539. In 1898, during the Spanish-American War, it was a point of embarkation for troops bound for Cuba.

Tampico village, pop. 833, Whiteside Co., NW Illinois, 11 mi/18 km SSW of Rock Falls. Ronald Reagan was born here (1911).

Tamuning unincorporated community, pop. 9534, W GUAM, just off Agana Bay (the Philippine Sea), 3 mi/5 km E of AGANA. It is a residential and industrial suburb of the capital. Won Pat International Airport is here. Tuma Bay (just N) is a center for Japanese tourism.

Tanana River c.600 mi/1000 km long, in W Yukon Territory and C Alaska. It is the YUKON River's main tributary. Rising N of the Alaska Range, it flows WNW to FAIRBANKS, then generally W to the Yukon at Tanana. Russian traders discovered its mouth around 1860, and it was long an important route to goldfields around Fairbanks and in the interior.

Tangier island town, pop. 659, Accomack Co., E Virginia, in the middle of CHESAPEAKE BAY. Covering approximately 9 sq mi/23 sq km, it was discovered in 1608 by John Smith, and settled in the 1680s. A remote place, accessible by boat only part of the year, Tangier is noted for its residents' distinctive speech and folkways. Long a major producer of crabs and other seafood, the island is now a popular tour boat destination.

Tangipahoa Parish 783 sq mi/2028 sq km, pop. 85,709, in SE Louisiana, bounded S by Lakes MAUREPAS and PONTCHARTRAIN, and N by the Mississippi line, and partly bounded by the Tchefuncte R. in the E. Its seat is Amite City (pop. 4236). The **Tangipahoa R.,** which rises NW of McComb, Mississippi, flows N–S through this parish to L. Pontchartrain, covering some 110 mi/180 km, and is a popular recreational resource. HAMMOND and PONCHATOULA are the largest cities. The parish is agricultural and forested, with resorts in the S.

Tanglewood **1.** summer music festival site in LENOX, Massachusetts, on the former estate of Mrs. Gorham Brooks. The Berkshire Music Festival began here in 1934. In 1938 a "shed" designed by Eero Saarinen to hold 6000 people was constructed; concertgoers also fill the surrounding lawns. It was on the Tanglewood estate that Nathaniel Hawthorne wrote *Tanglewood Tales* in 1853. Part of the estate lies in the town of STOCKBRIDGE. **2.** affluent residential section of Houston, Texas, 9 mi/14 km SW of Downtown. Development of the GALLERIA, just NE, in the 1960s, spurred growth here.

Taos town, pop. 4065, seat of Taos Co., N New Mexico, in the Sangre de Cristo Mts., on a branch of the Rio Grande, 55 mi/89 km NNE of Santa Fe. The town, formally Don Fernando de Taos, is one of the oldest (1600s) white settlements in the US. **Taos Pueblo** (also known as San Gerónimo de Taos; pop. 4681) just NE, is home to a Tiwa-speaking people. **Ranchos**

de Taos (unincorporated, pop. 1779) is S. Since the late 19th century, the Taos area has been home to many artists and writers, including D.H. Lawrence, whose ranch is preserved. Today, wealth and celebrity are also represented. Art, tourism, and farming and ranching contribute to the area's economy. **Taos Ski Valley** (N), near WHEELER PEAK, is the best-known of a number of nearby mountain resorts.

Tappan unincorporated village, pop. 6867, in Orangetown, Rockland Co., SE New York, on the New Jersey border, 7 mi/11 km NW of Yonkers. George Washington's headquarters here, at the De Wint Mansion (1700), and a number of other 18th-century buildings are preserved. Tappan is now a largely affluent suburb.

Tappan, Lake see under HACKENSACK R.

Tappan Zee widening of the Hudson R. between Irvington (S) and Croton (N), in SE New York. Its name is a combination of a local tribal term (for "cold springs") and the Dutch *Zee* ("sea"); once an important fishing area, it is today a recreational asset. It is 10 mi/16 km N–S, and up to 3 mi/5 km wide. The Tappan Zee Bridge (1955), between Tarrytown (E) and South Nyack (W), is some 2.6 mi/4.2 km over water, with a 1212-ft/370-m cantilevered main span.

Tara the plantation central to the novel (1936) and movie (1939) *Gone With the Wind.* A retreat from the 1864 siege and burning of Atlanta, it is set somewhere in CLAYTON Co., near JONESBORO.

Tarboro town, pop. 11,037, seat of Edgecombe Co., E North Carolina, on the Tar R., 15 mi/24 km ESE of Rocky Mount. It was founded in 1760. A marketing center for peanuts, cotton, and tobacco, it also manufactures machinery, textiles, fertilizer, cottonseed oil, and veneer.

Targhee National Forest 1.8 million ac/730,000 ha (2815 sq mi/7285 sq km), in SE Idaho and NW Wyoming, S of the Continental Divide and W of Yellowstone and Grand Teton national parks. The Henrys Fork of the Snake R., which rises here, is noted for its falls. The forest has a wide range of high peaks (to over 11,000 ft/3355 m), desert, and canyons.

Tarkio city, pop. 2243, Atchison Co., extreme NW Missouri, 56 mi/90 km NW of St. Joseph, 10 mi/16 km S of the Iowa border, and 15 mi/24 km E of the Missouri R. (the Nebraska border). It is a trading, processing, and distribution center for locally raised grain and livestock. The city is also the seat of Tarkio College (1883).

Tarpon Springs city, pop. 17,906, Pinellas Co., SW Florida, on the Anclote R. near its mouth on the Gulf of Mexico, 28 mi/45 km NNW of St. Petersburg. Its well-known natural sponge industry was founded in 1905, when Greek sponge divers arrived. The city retains a marked Hellenic flavor, and holds a variety of annual Greek festivals. Tourism and other light industries are also important.

Tarrant city, pop. 8046, Jefferson Co., C Alabama, 5 mi/8 km NNE of downtown Birmingham. Birmingham Municipal Airport is 2 mi/3 km S of this residential suburb.

Tarrant County 864 sq mi/2238 sq km, pop. 1,170,103, in NE Texas. Its seat is FORT WORTH. Drained by the West and Clear forks of the Trinity R., it has dairying and livestock raising, and crops include grains, pecans, cotton, and vegetables, but the county is increasingly occupied by the industry, commerce, and residential sections and suburbs of Fort Worth and ARLINGTON.

Tar River 217 mi/350 km long, in E North Carolina. It rises E of Roxboro, and flows generally SE and E to Rocky Mount and Tarboro, then to Greenville, its head of navigation. At Washington it becomes estuarial, and is known as the Pamlico R. Its 38 mi/61 km–long estuary enters PAMLICO SOUND from the NW.

Tarrytown village, pop. 10,739, in Greenburgh town, Westchester Co., SE New York, on the Hudson R., 24 mi/38 km N of New York City. Founded in 1645, it was developed by merchant Frederick Philipse, who acquired the land in 1680. Tarrytown is part of SLEEPY HOLLOW, made famous by Washington Irving, who lived here; his eccentric home, Sunnyside, is on the border (S) with Irvington. In the 19th century, Tarrytown was home to industrial magnates, among them Jay Gould, whose Gothic mansion, Lyndhurst, is now a museum. Tarrytown is both residential and industrial. Marymount College (1907) is here.

Tarzana SW SAN FERNANDO VALLEY section of LOS ANGELES, California, 20 mi/32 km WNW of Downtown. Largely residential, it was laid out in the 1910s on the estate of Edgar Rice Burroughs, creator of the *Tarzan* books.

Taughannock Falls see under L. CAYUGA, New York.

Taum Sauk Mountain peak (1772 ft/540 m) of the Saint Francois Mts., SE Missouri, W of Ironton. The highest point in the state, it was named for Taum Sauk, chief of the Piankishaws.

Taunton city, pop. 49,832, seat of Bristol Co., SE Massachusetts, on the Taunton R., 34 mi/55 km S of Boston. Colonial Taunton had a gristmill, ironworks (1652), and sawmill. It made bricks, produced textiles, built ships, and cast stoves in the 1800s. Iron, copper, and silver industries flourished from the 1820s. Heavy manufactures have included locomotives and printing presses. Electronics, leather, plastics, and kitchen ranges are also manufactured. A base of operations during King Philip's War (1675–76), Taunton was in the 1770s an early hotbed of Revolutionary sentiment. The largest Massachusetts city in area (50 sq mi/130 sq km), it has wooded rural parts as well as its industrial core.

Tavaputs Plateau see EAST TAVAPUTS PLATEAU, Utah.

Tawakoni, Lake see under SABINE R., Texas.

Taylor **1.** see under FORT SAINT JOHN, British Columbia. **2.** city, pop. 70,811, Wayne Co., SE Michigan, 20 mi/32 km SW of Detroit. Mainly a residential suburb, it also produces sand and gravel, wood and concrete products, glass, and machinery. The Detroit Metropolitan Wayne Co. Airport is 2 mi/3 km W. **3.** city, pop. 11,472, Williamson Co., SC Texas, 23 mi/37 km NE of Austin. Laid out in 1876, it is a commercial center for sheep, goat, cattle, cotton, poultry, nuts, and grain producers in the area. It also has publishing and a variety of other light industries.

Taylor, Mount high point (11,301 ft/3445 m) of the San Mateo Mts., 15 mi/24 km NE of GRANTS, in NW New Mexico. This extinct volcanic cone, called "Turquoise Mt." by the Navajo, and sacred to both the Navajo and the Pueblo, is within a section of Cibola National Forest.

Taylors unincorporated community, pop. 19,619, Greenville Co., NW South Carolina, on the Enoree R., 8 mi/13 km NE of Greenville. On the site of Chick Springs, a former summer resort, it is now just W of Greenville-Spartanburg Airport and GREER, in a thriving industrial/commercial/residential area.

Taylorsville-Bennion unincorporated community, pop. 52,351, Salt Lake Co., NC Utah, a rapidly growing residential suburb 9 mi/14 km S of Salt Lake City.

Taylorville city, pop. 11,133, seat of Christian Co., C Illinois, on the South Fork of the Sangamon R., 25 mi/40 km SE of Springfield. It processes the abundant local soybeans and manufactures paper, garments, and animal feed. Coal is mined in the vicinity. The city was settled in 1839. L. Taylor is just SE.

Tazewell County 650 sq mi/1683 sq km, pop. 123,692, in C Illinois, bordered by the Illinois R. (W). The Mackinaw R. flows across the county. The population is concentrated in the N, centered around the industrial cities of Pekin (the county seat), Morton, Creve Coeur, East Peoria, and Washington, some of which are also suburbs of Peoria, across the Illinois R. The C and S parts of the county contain coal mines and farmland.

Teach's Hole see under OCRACOKE I., North Carolina.

Teaneck township, pop. 37,825, Bergen Co., NE New Jersey, 2 mi/3 km E of Hackensack, between the Hackensack R. (W) and the PALISADES of the Hudson R. (E). It was settled by the Dutch in the mid 17th century. Major development came after the construction of the George Washington Bridge (1931), some 4 mi/6 km SE. Teaneck is primarily a New York–area bedroom community. It also manufactures such products as porcelain, spices, and fuses, and houses numerous office buildings. A campus of Fairleigh Dickinson University is here.

Teapot Dome oilfield in Natrona Co., SE Wyoming, 30 mi/48 km N of Casper. It gave its name to a notorious Harding administration scandal. Set aside as a naval oil reserve by President Wilson, the field was leased in 1922 by Albert E. Fall, Secretary of the Interior, to Harry F. Sinclair of Mammoth Oil Co., in return for gifts and loans. The scandal ended with prison terms for Fall and Sinclair, and Teapot Dome entered the American political vocabulary as a symbol of government corruption. Another reserve in California's ELK HILLS was also involved.

Tear of the Clouds, Lake see under HUDSON R.

Teche, the see BAYOU TECHE, Louisiana.

Technology Triangle see CANADIAN TECHNOLOGY TRIANGLE, Ontario.

Techwood residential and commercial district of NW Atlanta, Georgia, just S of the campus of the Georgia Institute of Technology (1888), 1 mi/1.6 km N of FIVE POINTS. In 1936 Techwood Homes, the first entirely Federally financed slum-clearance low-income housing project, was opened here. The Coca-Cola laboratories are just W. Facilities for the 1996 Olympics are in the area.

Tecumseh town, pop. 10,495, Essex Co., extreme S Ontario, adjacent (E) to WINDSOR and 8 mi/13 km E of its Downtown, on L. St. Clair. It is primarily residential.

Tehachapi Mountains range running transversely (E–W) in SC California for c.50 mi/80 km. Tejon Pass, at 4144 ft/1263 m, now on I-5, runs between the Tehachapis (E) and the San Emigdio Mts. (W). Often considered the dividing line between NORTHERN and SOUTHERN CALIFORNIA, the Tehachapis connect the Coast Ranges (W) with the S end of the Sierra Nevada (E). The range, sometimes considered one of the COAST RANGES, forms the S end of the San Joaquin Valley; Tehachapi Pass (3793 ft/1156 m) allows passage between the valley and the Mojave Desert to the SE. Double Mountain is the highest elevation, at 7988 ft/2435 m. The city of **Tehachapi** (pop. 5791, Kern Co.), just NW of the pass and 36 mi/58 km SE of Bakersfield, is a road and rail trade center; fruit and cement are produced, and a state prison is to the W.

Tejon Pass see under TEHACHAPI Mts., California.

Telegraph Hill residential neighborhood in NE SAN FRANCISCO, California, to the E of RUSSIAN HILL and NE of NORTH BEACH. Its 284-ft/87-m summit had an 1840s semaphore station that announced incoming ships; in 1853 the first telegraph station in the West began operations. The Coit Tower (1934), commemorating volunteer firemen, now crowns the summit. Once goatherding grounds, the hill was by the 1890s an artists' colony, and now has a variety of studios and affluent homes.

Telescope Peak high point (11,049 ft/3368 m) of the PANAMINT RANGE, in EC California. It rises dramatically (W) above Death Valley.

Tell City city, pop. 8088, Perry Co., S Indiana, 45 mi/72 km E of Evansville, on the Ohio R. It is a trade center in an agricultural and bituminous coal mining area. Furniture, electronic equipment, and boats are among the manufactures. It was settled in 1857 by Swiss immigrants.

Tellico Dam and Lake see under LITTLE TENNESSEE R.

Telluride town, pop. 1309, seat of San Miguel Co., SW Colorado, in the San Juan Mts., at 8500 ft/2592 m, 90 mi/145 km SSE of Grand Junction. Gold and silver mining began in the mountains here in 1875 and the settlement was named for tellurium, the matrix that held the precious metals. A boom town, it had many luxurious Victorian buildings, some now preserved. Skiing became popular in the 20th century and the construction of resorts (1971; 1993) made the town a popular site, because of its relative isolation without the traffic of such spots as ASPEN.

Temagami, Lake in NE Ontario, 50 mi/80 km NW of North Bay. Extending into long bays in all directions, it has a 370-mi/600-km shoreline, and is popular with canoeists and fishermen. The future of the heavily-logged surrounding area is the subject of controversy among locals, the Ojibwa, and environmentalists. Hundreds of islands dot the lake, and campsites dating back 6000 years have been found. The Bear Island Band, based in the lake's center, claim control of the land. The resort of **Temagami** (township, pop. 939), is on the NE. Canada's first boys' camp was established on the lake in 1900. Archie Belaney ("Grey Owl") began his career as a guide and conservationist here in the 1920s.

Temblor Range one of S California's COAST RANGES, extending NW–SE for c.50 mi/80 km from the S end of the DIABLO RANGE in the vicinity of Cholame to the San Emigdio Mts. It is near the S end of the San Joaquin Valley (E). The Caliente Range lies W, across the CARRIZO PLAIN. Early Spanish explorers were said to have felt earth tremors (*temblores*) here. The Temblors reach a high point at McKittrick Summit (4331 ft/1320 m). There are oilfields to the E, esp. in the vicinity of Taft and Maricopa.

Temecula city, pop. 27,099, Riverside Co., S California, 33 mi/53 km SE of Riverside, on I-15. Founded in 1882 on Murrietta Creek and the railroad through the Temecula Valley, it is a farming and grazing community rapidly becoming a residential EXURB.

Tempe city, pop. 141,865, Maricopa Co., SC Arizona, on the Salt R., a suburb 9 mi/14 km ESE of downtown Phoenix. Named for the Vale of Tempe in Greece, the settlement was founded in 1872 and grew up around a trading post, flour mill, and ferry. It developed as a residential center with light industry after World War II. The climate attracts health seekers and retirees. Agriculture, irrigated by the Salt R. Project, remains important in the area. Arizona State University (1885) has been central to Tempe's life; Frank Lloyd Wright's Grady Gammage Auditorium (1964) and noted art and geology museums are on campus, and 72,000-seat Sun Devil Stadium is home to the university football team and the National Football League's Phoenix Cardinals.

Temperanceville industrial area in the West End section, on the S side of Pittsburgh, Pennsylvania, on the Ohio R., 2 mi/3 km SW of the GOLDEN TRIANGLE. It was founded in 1837 as an alcohol-free community that ultimately fell short of its goals.

Temple city, pop. 46,109, Bell Co., C Texas, on the Little R., 35 mi/56 km SSW of Waco. Established by the Gulf, Colorado and Santa Fe Railroad in 1880, it grew as a division point with repair shops. Its dry, warm climate allowed it to become a leading medical center, with several hospitals and the Texas A&M University School of Medicine. It has a variety of manufactures, and nearby (W) FORT HOOD also affects the economy. Temple is the site of various state and Federal agricultural offices. Temple Junior College was founded in 1926.

Temple City city, pop. 31,100, Los Angeles Co., SW California, 10 mi/16 km ENE of downtown Los Angeles. Incorporated in 1960, it is a largely residential suburb with some light industry.

Temple Terrace city, pop. 16,444, Hillsborough Co., WC Florida, 7 mi/11 km NE of downtown Tampa. It is a residential suburb, and home to Florida College (1944).

Tenafly borough, pop. 13,326, Bergen Co., NE New Jersey, 5 mi/8 km NE of Hackensack. Settled by the Dutch in 1640, on the PALISADES of the Hudson R., it is a chiefly residential suburb, with office buildings and some light industry.

Tenderloin **1.** popular term for an urban district rife with vice. The name is attributed to a 19th-century New York police officer who, being transferred into the area that is now the GARMENT CENTER, on Manhattan's West Side, and seeing increased opportunities for graft, said that while he had been living on chuck steak, he would now be able to have some of the tenderloin. **2.** see under CIVIC CENTER, San Francisco, California.

Tennessee state of the SE US, variously considered part of the Upper SOUTH or Mid-South; 1990 pop. 4,877,185 (106.2% of 1980; rank: 17th); area 42,146 sq mi/109,158 sq km (rank: 36th); admitted to Union 1796 (16th). Capital: NASHVILLE. Most populous cities: MEMPHIS, Nashville, KNOXVILLE, CHATTANOOGA. Tennessee is bordered E by North Carolina; S by (E–W) Georgia, Alabama, and Mississippi; and W by the Mississippi R., across which are (S–N) Arkansas and the BOOTHEEL region of Missouri. Like its neighbor Kentucky, which borders it along the N except in the NE (where Tennessee adjoins the SW corner of Virginia), the state is some 400 mi/640 km E–W, and comprises three main sections (similar in many characteristics to Kentucky's). **East Tennessee** is Appalachian. On the E border are the GREAT SMOKY Mts., part of the UNAKA Mts. range of the BLUE RIDGE; here CLINGMANS DOME (6643 ft/2026 m) is the state's high point. To the W of the Smokies is part of the Great APPALACHIAN Valley, which extends from Pennsylvania SW to Alabama. The industrial Tri-Cities of BRISTOL, JOHNSON CITY, and KINGSPORT, in the extreme NE; Knoxville, in the C; and the industrial city of Chattanooga, in the SW, are within the valley, through which the TENNESSEE R. runs SW. The CUMBERLAND PLATEAU section of the Appalachian Plateau lies W of the valley. MIDDLE TENNESSEE is largely the NASHVILLE BASIN, a tobacco producing extension of Kentucky's BLUEGRASS and an industrially developing region centered on the capital, and lying between the E and W Highland Rim. The CUMBERLAND and DUCK rivers flow W across the basin. The northward loop of the lower Tennessee R., toward its junction with the Ohio R., separates **West Tennessee** from the rest of the state. This area, part of the JACKSON PURCHASE, is a lowland N extension of the Gulf COASTAL PLAIN, and is Tennessee's most Southern area, a grower of cotton and other former plantation crops, now producing largely wheat and soybeans. At the extreme SW is Memphis, commercial capital not only of West Tennessee but of Mississippi's and Arkansas's DELTA regions and of nearby SE Missouri. At the extreme NW is REELFOOT L., formed during the massive NEW MADRID earthquake of 1811. Tennessee has MOUND BUILDER sites, and was home to the Chickasaw (W), Cherokee (E), and other peoples when white settlement began in the mid 18th century. A W frontier territory of North Carolina, it became in part the short-lived (1784–88) state of FRANKLIN, before gaining acceptance as the state of Tennessee (taking its name from the river, in turn named for a Cherokee village on its upper reaches near the E border). In the 1820s–30s Tennessee was regarded as the center of Jacksonian (after Andrew Jackson, whose home near Nashville, the HERMITAGE, is today much-visited) democracy, the movement broadening the social base of American government. Like Kentucky, it developed along regional lines (independent farmers in the E hills, a slaveholding PLANTATION economy in the W), which led at the beginning of the Civil War to serious division, although Tennessee, unlike its N neighbor, joined the Confederacy. Many of the war's major actions were fought here, from SHILOH and FORT DONELSON to MURFREESBORO to CHICKAMAUGA and LOOKOUT MOUNTAIN. After the war, Memphis remained the center of a cotton economy, while coal and manufacturing began to assume dominant roles in Chattanooga, Knoxville, and Nashville. Much of rural Tennessee stagnated until the 1930s, when the TENNESSEE VALLEY AUTHORITY's works on the area's rivers brought electrification, flood control, and increased jobs. The secret World War II nuclear development at OAK RIDGE, near Knoxville, was revealed and expanded in the postwar period. Tennessee today has a range of types of industry, including new automobile manufacturing plants at SMYRNA and SPRING HILL, numerous power generation sites, chemical and synthetics manufacturing in the Kingsport area, and commerce and service industry hubs esp. in the Nashville and Memphis areas. Its agriculture is also diverse, with stock raising, dairy production, and soybean growing having balanced the older tobacco-and-cotton base. Coal mining and aluminum processing (as at Alcoa, near MARYSVILLE) are also important. Tourism draws on the popularity of both (largely white) country music (at Nashville's OPRYLAND) and black music (in Memphis); on recreational sites along the state's rivers (esp. at the LAND BETWEEN THE LAKES, NW) and in the E mountains; and on Appalachian folkways and Civil War history. Tennessee's people remain largely a mix of the groups that settled here in the late 18th and early 19th centuries—English, Scotch-Irish, German, French, and Dutch; the state is a center of Protestant religious organization. There is a large black minority, esp. in the SW. The University of Tennessee is at Knoxville. Nashville (Vanderbilt and Fisk universities) and SEWANEE (University of the South) are also noted academic centers.

Tennessee River 652 mi/1050 km long, in Tennessee, Alabama, Mississippi, and Kentucky. It is formed just E of Knoxville, Tennessee, by the junction of the FRENCH BROAD and HOLSTON rivers, and winds SW (as Fort Loudon L.) to LENOIR CITY, site of the Fort Loudon and Tellico dams, where the LITTLE TENNESSEE R. joins it from the SE. It continues W and then SW through the Great Appalachian Valley, with WALDEN RIDGE on the NW, into dam-created WATTS BAR L., in which the CLINCH R. joins it from the N, then into CHICKAMAUGA L., formed by a dam at Chattanooga. The Hiwassee R. joins it from the SE at the upper end of Chickamauga L. From Chattanooga it winds W and WSW through dam-created Nickajack L. and into N Alabama. Here it continues SW through Guntersville L., formed by the dam at GUNTERSVILLE, where it turns NW to Huntsville's S edge, and flows WNW to Decatur and to the WHEELER DAM. To the W is the WILSON DAM at MUSCLE SHOALS, beyond which the river swings NW into Pickwick L., becoming briefly the NE boundary of Mississippi; the Tennessee-Tombigbee Waterway here connects it with the Gulf of Mexico by way of Mississippi's TOMBIGBEE R. Pickwick L. extends over the border into W Tennessee, to Pickwick Landing Dam, S of SAVANNAH. The river winds NNE from the dam past SHILOH (Pittsburg Landing) and Savannah, and flows N into Kentucky L., which extends 184 mi/296 km N through Tennessee into W Kentucky, to the KENTUCKY DAM; in the lake the Tennessee is joined by the Duck R. (from the NE) and the Big Sandy R. (from the SW). Near the Tennessee-Kentucky border, the lake becomes the W boundary of the LAND BETWEEN THE LAKES (bounded on the E by the CUMBERLAND R.). From the Kentucky Dam, the Tennessee turns WNW to enter the OHIO R. on the E side of Paducah, Kentucky. The Tennessee's dams are projects of the TENNESSEE VALLEY AUTHORITY, part of a scheme that has controlled flooding on the river and its tributaries and created a 9-ft/2.7-m channel navigable by way of locks all the way to Knoxville. Steamboats have used the river since the 1820s, but navigational hazards and less accessible headwaters made it less useful than the Ohio as a gateway to the Midwest.

Tennessee-Tombigbee Waterway see under TOMBIGBEE R., Mississippi and Alabama.

Tennessee Valley Authority Federal body, established in 1933 to create an integrated system of dams, locks, channels, and other works on the Tennessee R. and its tributaries, which extend into seven states (Mississippi, Kentucky, Tennessee, Georgia, Alabama, North Carolina, and Virginia). Its mandate was to render a difficult river more easily navigable, control flooding, generate hydroelectric power for rural development, and foster environmental improvements through forestry, erosion control, etc. The TVA took over the WILSON DAM, built in World War I at MUSCLE SHOALS, Alabama, to manufacture nitrates and generate power, and has since built eight mainstream dams on the Tennessee (the Fort Loudon Dam, at LENOIR CITY, Tennessee; the WATTS BAR DAM; the CHICKAMAUGA Dam at Chattanooga; the 1968 Nickajack Dam just W of Chattanooga; Alabama's GUNTERSVILLE and WHEELER dams; the Pickwick Landing Dam, near SAVANNAH, Tennessee; and the KENTUCKY DAM, E of Paducah, Kentucky) and dozens on rivers in the Tennessee system (which include the Hiwasee, Toccoa, Holston, French Broad, Little Tennessee, Caney Fork, Clinch, Ocoee, Elk, and Watauga). Some of these dams are owned by the Aluminum Company of America and operated by the TVA. The Authority maintains a 630 mi/1014 km–long navigable channel from the Tennessee's mouth to KNOXVILLE, and has built and operated numerous coal-fired (since the 1940s) and nuclear-powered (since the 1970s) generating stations. It also administers the LAND BETWEEN THE LAKES area between the Tennessee and the Cumberland R. (E).

Tensaw River see under MOBILE R., Alabama.

Ten Thousand Islands group of numerous small islands in the Gulf of Mexico, in Collier and Monroe counties, SW Florida, c.20 mi/32 km SE of Naples. MARCO I., at the group's NW edge, is the largest of these mangrove-covered islands. Much of the group is within the Cape Romano–Ten Thousand Islands Aquatic Preserve.

Ten Thousand Smokes, Valley of see under KATMAI NATIONAL PARK AND PRESERVE, Alaska.

Terminal Island see under SAN PEDRO, California.

Terminal Tower office building in Cleveland, Ohio, 708 ft/216 m high. The city's tallest building and its most dramatic architectural landmark, the 52-story structure dates from the 1920s.

Terrace city, pop. 11,433, Kitimat-Stikine Regional District, WC British Columbia, on alluvial terraces (former banks) of the Skeena R., in the wilderness near the Hazelton Mts., 70 mi/113 km ENE of Prince Rupert. In a mining and fishing region, the city is on the YELLOWHEAD HIGHWAY and is linked by rail to KITIMAT (SW). Founded (1910) by the Grand Trunk Pacific Railway, it grew into a sawmill town. Today industries include lumbering and furniture manufacture; the city is a commercial and transportation center, the gateway to a variety of river, lake, and mountain recreation areas.

Terra Nova National Park 155 sq mi/400 sq km of forests and fjords on Bonavista Bay, 80 mi/130 km NW of St. John's, in E Newfoundland. Established in 1957, the park is noted for rocky headlands, glacial topography, and peat bogs with orchids and carnivorous plants. Evidence of prehistoric and Beothuk habitation has been found.

Terrebonne city, pop. 39,768, Les Moulins census division, S Québec, 13 mi/21 km N of Montréal, on the R. des Mille Îles, across (N) from LAVAL. Mills here on the Île des Moulins were important in the 18th and 19th centuries, and this was once a leading industrial center. Today it is a growing residential suburb.

Terre Haute city, pop. 57,483, seat of Vigo Co., W Indiana, on the E bank of the Wabash R., 70 mi/113 km WSW of Indianapolis. On a high plateau overlooking the river, it was named by the French for its "high land." Founded in 1811, it grew with the coming of the NATIONAL ROAD (1838), Wabash and Erie Canal (1849), and Richmond Railroad (1852), and with the discovery of coal nearby (1875), which spurred industrial development. It became a center of union activity, and was the birthplace (1855) and home of socialist leader Eugene V. Debs, whose 1890 house is preserved. Terre Haute remains a commercial and manufacturing center, also processing and shipping local agricultural products. Manufactures include bricks, aluminum and steel goods, glass containers, pharmaceuticals, plastics, chemicals, and clothing. There are several parks, including Fairbanks, site of songwriter ("On the Banks of the Wabash") Paul Dresser's 1858 birthplace. The city is the seat of Indiana State University (1865); the Rose-Hulman Institute of Technology (1874) is 5 mi/8 km E of Downtown.

Terrell city, pop. 12,490, Kaufman Co., NE Texas, 30 mi/48 km E of Dallas. It was laid out in 1872 when the railroad came through, although the BLACKLANDS farming area had been settled two decades earlier. Southwestern Christian College (1949; Church of Christ) and the Trinity Valley Community College health sciences center are here. The city is a banking and agricultural market center, and has various light manufactures. Terrell State Hospital is a large employer.

Terrell Hills see under SAN ANTONIO, Texas.

Terre-Neuve also, **Terra Nova** see under NEWFOUNDLAND AND LABRADOR.

territory **1.** region or district of a country that does not yet have status equal to that of the country's chief constituents or divisions (e.g., is not yet a US STATE or Canadian PROVINCE). Generally it has some self-government, including a legislature, and some combination of elected and (nationally) appointed administrative officials (that is, in US terms, it is an **organized territory,** preparing for eventual statehood). All states admitted to the US since the nation was formed by the original thirteen COLONIES have been organized first as territories, with a few exceptions (Kentucky, Maine, Texas, California, and West Virginia). In Canada, the Yukon Territory, as well as Manitoba, Saskatchewan, and Alberta, were carved from the Northwest Territories. **The Territory** or **The Territories** are terms variously used in the US and Canada to refer to areas (otherwise, sometimes, the FRONTIER) outside settled or metropolitan areas. See also INDIAN TERRITORY. **2.** land or lands separate from but belonging to a nation. The US territories of the Virgin Is., Guam, and American Samoa have limited local self-government and representation in national government; the Department of the Interior administers most of their affairs. See also Trust Territory of the PACIFIC ISLANDS; Commonwealth of PUERTO RICO.

Terry Peak mountain (7064 ft/2155 m) in the BLACK HILLS, 4 mi/6 km W of Lead, in WC South Dakota, near the Wyoming border.

Terwilliger industrial and residential district in Southwest PORTLAND, Oregon, on the Willamette R., S of Downtown. Having been rezoned for industry in the 1930s, Terwilliger lost a great deal of its 1890s–1900s housing stock after World War II. In the 1960s, residents formed the Terwilliger Community League, one of Portland's earliest neighborhood activist groups, and reversed the zoning change. Today, the area is increasingly residential in character.

Teslin River 120 mi/190 km long, in the S Yukon Territory. It flows out of 80 mi/130 km–long **L. Teslin,** which lies NW–SE across the Yukon–British Columbia border, ESE of Whitehorse, and flows NW to join the Yukon R. SE of Carmacks. Part of the "back door" route for 1890s gold seekers heading for the KLONDIKE, the lake and river now attract canoeists. **Teslin** (village, pop. 181) on the Alaska Highway on the lake's NE side, is a largely Teslin (Na-Dene) community.

Tesuque unincorporated community, pop. 1490, Santa Fe Co., NC New Mexico, in the Sangre de Cristo Mts., 7 mi/11 km N of Santa Fe, of which it is an affluent residential suburb. The **Tesuque Pueblo** (pop. 697) is just N. Today the Tewa-speaking pueblo produces pottery, painting, and sculpture; it was active in the 1680 Pueblo Revolt.

Teterboro borough, pop. 22, Bergen Co., NE New Jersey, 2 mi/3 km S of Hackensack. Teterboro Airport was important in early aviation and is now an air freight center. At the airport is the Aviation Hall of Fame and Museum.

Teton National Forest see under BRIDGER-TETON NATIONAL FOREST, Wyoming.

Teton Range see under GRAND TETON NATIONAL PARK, Wyoming.

Teton River 145 mi/233 km long, in NW Montana. It rises in several branches in the mountains of Lewis and Clark National Forest in NW Teton Co., near the Continental Divide. It flows generally E across Teton Co. and Chouteau Co., where it meets the Marias R., just before the Marias joins the Missouri R., 8 mi/13 km NE of Fort Benton.

Tewksbury town, pop. 27,266, Middlesex Co., NE Massachusetts, immediately SE of Lowell, 20 mi/32 km NNW of Boston. Originally (1637) part of BILLERICA, it is engaged in commercial flower growing, printing, woodworking, and the manufacture of electronic and missile components. On Route 495 and Interstate 93, Tewksbury is a growing industrial and residential suburb.

Texada Island in the Strait of GEORGIA, SW British Columbia, between Vancouver I. and the mainland, 50 mi/80 km NW of Vancouver. Thirty mi/48 km NW–SE and 4 mi/6 km wide, the mountainous island reaches 2892 ft/881 m. Ferries connect Vananda, on the N end, with the mainland, across the Malaspina Strait, and with Vancouver I. Iron and copper mining, fishing, and limestone quarrying are important.

Texarkana **1.** city, pop. 22,631, seat of Miller Co., SW Arkansas, adjacent (E) to Texarkana, Texas. Settled in 1874 at the junction of the Cairo and Fulton and Texas and Pacific railways, the twin cities are a market and shipping center for the surrounding area. Industries include the production of pine lumber, railroad cars, missile components, tires, brick, furniture, and mobile homes. The two cities are divided by State Line Ave. Their name is a combination of *Tex*as, *Ark*ansas, and nearby Louisi*ana*. **2.** city, pop. 31,656, Bowie Co., extreme NE Texas, 165 mi/267 km NE of Dallas. Texarkana College (1927) and a branch of East Texas State University (1971) are here, as are the 50–sq mi/130–sq km Red River Army Depot (1941), a major ordnance center, and a Federal prison.

Texas state of the SC US, variously considered part of the SOUTH, the SOUTHWEST, and (in its N) the GREAT PLAINS; 1990 pop. 16,986,510 (119.4% of 1980; rank: 3rd, but in 1994 the Census Bureau estimated that it had surpassed New York and ranked 2nd); area 268,601 sq mi/695,677 sq km (rank: 2nd); admitted to Union 1845 (28th). Capital: AUSTIN. Cities with over 100,000 pop.: HOUSTON, DALLAS, SAN ANTONIO, EL PASO, Austin, FORT WORTH, ARLINGTON, CORPUS CHRISTI, LUBBOCK, GARLAND, AMARILLO, IRVING, PLANO, LAREDO, PASADENA, ABILENE, WACO, MESQUITE. Texas is bordered E by Louisiana, with the SABINE R. and TOLEDO BEND RESERVOIR forming much of the boundary; NE by Arkansas, with the RED R. forming part of the boundary; N by Oklahoma, with the Red R. forming much of the boundary; and W by New Mexico. Along the SW the RIO GRANDE separates it from the Mexican states of (W–E) Chihuahua, Coahuila, Nuevo León, and Tamaulipas. On the SE, it has a 370-mi/600-km coast on the Gulf of MEXICO, much of it lined by PADRE, MATAGORDA, and other barrier islands. The largest state in the Lower 48, Texas lies in several topographical regions. In the E and SE is a portion of the Gulf COASTAL PLAIN, extending up to 200 mi/320 km inland from the coast, and comprising a series of rich black-earth prairies, along with swampy or wooded areas near the coast. In the NE of this region is the BIG THICKET, an area of dense wood, now much reduced, home to a unique mix of subtropical and temperate flora and fauna. In the extreme S is the WINTER GARDEN area, producer of much of the US winter vegetable crop, near the Rio Grande. The prairies have been major cotton and cattle producers; today, oil and gas are central to their economy. Houston is the chief city in the SE. The Coastal Plain ends at the BALCONES ESCARPMENT, which runs SW–NE and then N through the state, and is generally regarded as the dividing line between East and West Texas. Along it are San Antonio, Austin, and Waco; in the N, where the Escarpment disappears into the earth, Dallas (regarded as quite "Eastern" in its economy and culture) lies on the E, neighboring Fort Worth (regarded as quintessentially "Western") on the W, as though symbolizing the divide. To the NW of the Escarpment, in C Texas, are S extensions of the vast C lowlands of the US, from the HILL COUNTRY above Austin through a section of the OSAGE PLAINS closer to the Oklahoma line, where WICHITA FALLS is a leading city. On the S and W are the beginnings of the Great Plains; these include, in the S, extending to the Rio Grande, the EDWARDS and Stockton plateaus, noted stock raising areas. To their N and W, running up through the PANHANDLE, is part of the High Plains, the well-known LLANO ESTACADO or "Staked Plain." In extreme SW Texas is a region comprising the southeasternmost extension of the BASIN AND RANGE PROVINCE of the INTERMONTANE West; this harsh, dry zone is generally regarded as meeting the Great Plains here, on the W of the PECOS R.; the GUADALUPE Mts., however, which rise to 8751 ft/2667 m, the state's high point, are sometimes considered a S extension of the ROCKY Mts. The major rivers of Texas all run W–E toward the Mississippi R. Basin or NW–SE directly into the Gulf of Mexico. Among the former are the CANADIAN and Red, which cross the Panhandle. Among the latter are (W–E) the Rio Grande, with its tributary the Pecos; and the NUECES, SAN ANTONIO, GUADALUPE, COLORADO, BRAZOS, TRINITY, and Sabine. Owing to seasonal changes in level, none of these rivers have been important for transportation, but they has provided irrigation and, in places, where dammed, important recreational assets. The vast territory that is now Texas was inhabited by numerous small Indian groups, including Apache, Caddo, and Karankawa, when first seen by Spanish and French explorers in the 16th and 17th centuries. Later, other tribes were forced into and through Texas as white settlement expanded westward. Today, only the Alabama-Coushatta (in the depths of the Big Thicket) and the Tigua (in the far W, near El Paso) remain. The Spanish began settlement in Texas at Ysleta, near El Paso, after the 1680 New Mexico PUEBLO revolt. Through the 18th century their MISSIONS and trade posts expanded into S and E Texas, to San Antonio and as far E as NACOGDOCHES. The territory acquired its name from a term (also spelled *Tejas*) supposed to have referred to a confederacy of tribes or a "kingdom" somewhere in the E, and to mean "friends." Spanish development of Texas was, however, limited. The LOUISIANA PURCHASE (1803) extended US control over much of N Texas (including the Red R. valley and the Panhandle). In 1821, Mexico threw off Spanish rule, and in one of their first acts Mexican authorities authorized Americans led by Stephen F. Austin to establish a colony on the Brazos (see SAN FELIPE). By the late 1820s friction between the rapidly growing American community and Mexican authorities led to moves for Texan independence, and in 1835–36 this was achieved, in a conflict that included the massacres at the ALAMO and GOLIAD and ended with American victory at SAN JACINTO. In 1836–45, Texas was an independent republic. In 1845 the US annexed the rest of the modern state, along with parts of New Mexico, touching off the Mexican War, in which American control over the rest of the Southwest (except the Gadsden Purchase) was achieved. Having been settled largely by Southerners, the new state was slave territory, and joined the Confederacy. Military action in the Civil War was limited here to the 1863 battle at SABINE PASS and a rearguard action by fleeing Confederates at BROWNSVILLE, shortly before the June 19, 1865 GALVESTON declaration freeing the slaves (celebrated in annual "Juneteenth" festivities). After the war, the cattle industry expanded, the CHISHOLM TRAIL leading N to Kansas as railheads developed there. In 1901, at Spindletop, near BEAUMONT, the first big Texas oil strike occurred. When the EAST TEXAS OILFIELD was discovered in 1930, the state became the center of the OIL PATCH. The industry has subsequently spread to different parts of the state, including the PERMIAN BASIN around MIDLAND-ODESSA (SW), and the Houston area is now the center of what is popularly called the "Spaghetti Bowl" for its maze of pipelines and other facilities. Oil-related manufacturing, including the production of petrochemicals, became a major factor in the Texas economy by the mid 20th century. World War II military operations and the postwar arrival of Northern businesses seeking cheap labor and other lowered costs have made modern Texas the industrial heart of the SUNBELT. While diversified agriculture, stock raising, and oil extraction remain essential to its economy, the state has become a maker of automobiles, aerospace equipment, refined and fabricated metals, computer and other high-tech machinery, and a wide range of other goods. Financial and service enterprises and research and educational institutions have relocated here or grown with the accumulation of money created by, and the influx of workers attracted by, the primary industries. The MAQUILADORA plants along the Rio Grande, taking advantage of even lower labor costs in Mexico, have added another level to Texas's manufacturing structure in recent decades. Major state institutions, like the University of Texas, at Austin, and Texas Agricultural and Mechanical University, at COLLEGE STATION, are heavily funded and prestigious. Houston's TEXAS MEDICAL CENTER and NASA Manned Spacecraft Center are world-famous. At the end of the 20th century, Texas is a diverse society; its people are almost 26% Hispanic and 12% black, and have arrived here from all over North America and beyond. The "Lone Star State" takes its nickname from its flag, whose design recalls the independent Texas Republic.

Texas Alps see under ALPINE, Texas.

Texas City city, pop. 40,822, Galveston Co., SE Texas, 35 mi/56 km SE of Houston. This deepwater port on Galveston Bay ships petroleum products, metals, cotton, grain, sulfur, and other chemicals. Developed in the 1890s, it was rebuilt after a 1915 hurricane, and underwent expansion after World War II, with oil refineries, smelters, and chemical plants. A ship explosion and subsequent fires on April 16, 1947, killed

600 and destroyed much of the city, which was rebuilt and is today both industrial and residential. The College of the Mainland (1966) is here.

Texas Medical Center complex of several dozen medical and research institutions in Houston, Texas, 4 mi/6 km SW of Downtown, across Main St. from Rice University, and adjacent (S) to HERMANN PARK. Begun in 1944, it has grown to cover some 600 ac/240 ha, and includes University of Texas and Baylor University branches, as well as Methodist Hospital. Doctors Michael DeBakey and Denton Cooley began pioneering heart transplant work here in the 1960s. The center is a magnet for students and researchers from around the world.

Texas Stadium see under IRVING, Texas.

Texoma, Lake 89,000 ac/36,000 ha, in NE Texas, on the Red R., between Texas and Oklahoma, 75 mi/121 km N of Dallas. Impounded by the rolled-earth Denison Dam, built 1939–43, it is one of the largest US reservoirs, with a 550-mi/890-km shoreline in Texas and Oklahoma; its parks and resorts attract 9 million visitors annually. Hagerman National Wildlife Refuge borders the lake (S), and the Eisenhower State Recreation Area is on cliffs above it. The lake also impounds the WASHITA R., flowing S from Oklahoma.

T. F. Green Airport see under WARWICK, Rhode Island.

Thacher Island 0.5 mi/0.8 km long, just off Rockport, Cape ANN, Essex Co., NE Massachusetts. The Cape Ann lighthouse is on the island, which is a National Wildlife Refuge.

Thames River **1.** (pronounced "thaymz") 15 mi/24 km long, in SE Connecticut. An estuary, it extends from the confluence of the Shetucket and Yantic rivers at Norwich S to Long Island Sound between Groton (E) and New London (W). Lined with shipyards and military sites, it has been the site of Yale-Harvard boat races since 1878. **2.** 160 mi/260 km long, in extreme S Ontario. It rises NNW of Woodstock, and flows past Woodstock to LONDON, where the North Thames joins it, then SW to CHATHAM, before entering L. St. Clair, 15 mi/24 km WSW of Chatham. The Thames was imagined, in the 1790s, as the chief river of an UPPER CANADA whose capital would be London; but historical developments including the rise of York (Toronto) diverted growth from the area. In Oct. 1813 the battle of the Thames was fought at Moraviantown (Thamesville), 16 mi/26 km NE of Chatham, where Americans defeated British-Indian forces, including the Shawnee leader Tecumseh, who was killed here; having established superiority, however, the Americans withdrew.

The Colony city, pop. 22,113, Denton Co., NE Texas, 23 mi/37 km NNW of Dallas, on the E side of Lewisville L. A residential and recreational community, it doubled in population in the 1980s. Tourism and sailing are important. IBM has a facility here.

The Dalles officially, **City of the Dalles** city, pop. 11,060, seat of Wasco Co., NC Oregon, on the Columbia R., 70 mi/113 km E of Portland. The Dalles Dam (3 mi/5 km NE), completed in 1957, made the inland port city a terminal for oceangoing barges carrying local agricultural products, especially grain and fruit. Lewis and Clark camped at the site of the city in 1805, when it was still an Indian trading place. River rapids here, later submerged by the dam's backwaters, reminded early French explorers of drainage troughs (*dalles*), and thus the city was named. The Dalles was the last stop on the overland OREGON TRAIL; pioneers boarded boats here for Portland. Its contemporary industries include aluminum production, lumber and flour milling, salmon canning, and fruit processing.

Thelon River 550 mi/900 km long, in the Northwest Territories. Rising E of the GREAT SLAVE L., it winds generally N, then E across the TUNDRA of the CANADIAN SHIELD, widening into a series of lakes, including Aberdeen, Schultz, and BAKER, then entering CHESTERFIELD INLET of Hudson Bay. The Dubawnt R., its longest tributary, flows generally NE, over 525 mi/840 km, from near the NW Saskatchewan line through Dubawnt and other smaller lakes to join the Thelon and L. Aberdeen on the E boundary of the 15,000–sq mi/39,000–sq km **Thelon Game Sanctuary,** created in 1927 to protect muskoxen. The Keewatin (Caribou) Inuit for centuries based their lives on the Thelon area's caribou; many were relocated in the 20th century. BAKER LAKE is the river's chief settlement.

theme park type of amusement park, introduced in the 1950s, organized and designed around a unifying theme, such as an historic period, wildlife, or a fictional setting. SEA WORLD is a prominent example.

Theodore Roosevelt Lake also, **Roosevelt Lake** in the Tonto National Forest, C Arizona, 45 mi/72 km ENE of Phoenix. Fed by Tonto Creek from the N and the SALT R. from the E, it stretches some 23 mi/37 km NE–SW, is up to 2 mi/3 km wide, and is a popular recreational site. It was created by the **Theodore Roosevelt Dam,** built 1905–11, at 280 ft/85 m high considered the world's highest masonry dam.

Theodore Roosevelt National Park 70,416 ac/28,518 ha, in three units in the BADLANDS along the LITTLE MISSOURI R. in W North Dakota. First established in 1947, the park preserves Roosevelt's 1880s Elkhorn Ranch and two expanses of rugged land characterized by gullies and buttes, with surface lignite beds and large prairie dog and bison populations.

The Pas town, pop. 6166, W Manitoba, at the junction of the Saskatchewan and Pasquia rivers, 320 mi/515 km NW of Winnipeg. It developed around Fort-Paskoyac, a fur trading post established (1750) by the sons of the French-Canadian explorer La Vérendrye. The name may come from the Cree *opasquaow,* "narrows between wooded banks." The modern town's development has been spurred by the opening (1929) of the grain-transporting railroad to CHURCHILL (500 mi/800 km NE) and the 1960s creation of a huge wood and pulp producing complex. Today it is a distribution center for lumber, furs, fish, and minerals, with some local farming and a community college. A Trappers Festival is held every winter. Several Indian reserves are nearby, and the Clearwater L. Provincial Park is just N.

Thermopolis town, pop. 3247, seat of Hot Springs Co., WC Wyoming, on the BIGHORN R. just N of the Wind River Canyon, 112 mi/180 km NW of Casper. On land purchased from the Shoshone and Arapaho of the WIND RIVER INDIAN RESERVATION (SW), it was established in 1897 around "the world's largest hot springs," and is a resort and commercial center. Oil and ranching have also been important in the area.

Thetford town, pop. 2438, Orange Co., EC Vermont, on the Connecticut and Ompompanoosuc rivers, 14 mi/22 km NNE of White River Junction.

Thetford Mines city, pop. 17,273, L'Amiante census division, S Québec, 50 mi/80 km S of Québec City, on the R. Bécancour, in the Notre Dame Mts. Following the discovery of asbestos in the region in 1876, this became one of the major world producing centers, with both underground and open-face mines in operation. Chromium and feldspar are also exploited. Dairying, sawmilling, and diverse manufactures also contribute to the economy, and Thetford Mines is a regional service center.

The Village **1.** see GREENWICH VILLAGE, New York City. **2.** city, pop. 10,353, Oklahoma Co., C Oklahoma, a residential community 6 mi/10 km N of downtown Oklahoma City, and within its limits. L. Hefner is just W, NICHOLS HILLS just S.

The Woodlands unincorporated community, pop. 29,205, Montgomery Co., SE Texas, 29 mi/47 km NNW of downtown Houston, on Interstate 45. It is a residential suburb and home to corporate headquarters and oil companies.

Thibodaux city, pop. 14,035, seat of Lafourche Parish, SE Louisiana, on the Bayou Lafourche, 45 mi/72 km WSW of New Orleans. Settled around 1750 as a river port, it was incorporated as a town in 1838. St. John's Episcopal Church was established in 1841 by Leonidas Polk, the "Fighting Bishop" of the Confederate army. Thibodaux is now the market center of a region that produces sugar cane, corn, vegetables, and cotton. It has sugar refineries, foundries, and seafood canneries. The regional oil and gas industry is also important. The city is home to Nicholls State University (1948).

Thief River Falls city, pop. 8010, Pennington Co., NW Minnesota, at the junction of the Thief and Red Lake rivers, 44 mi/71 km ENE of Grand Forks, North Dakota. It is an agricultural trade center, and home to Northland Community College (1965).

Thielsen, Mount peak (9182 ft/2799 m) of the S CASCADE RANGE, 10 mi/16 km N of CRATER L. and just E of Diamond L., in the UMPQUA NATIONAL FOREST in SW Oregon. An extinct volcano, it is topped by a needlelike spire. The highest elevations of the Oregon section of the PACIFIC CREST TRAIL are in the Mt. Thielsen Wilderness, whose lands are in the Umpqua, Winema, and Deschutes national forests.

Third Ward **1.** one of the four quadrants of Houston, Texas, established by the city's 1839–40 charter and extending SE from Downtown. Today a conglomeration of inner-city neighborhoods, it is the business and educational center of Houston's black community, and also has a substantial Mexican population. Texas Southern University (1947), on the S, and the University of Houston (1927), on the SE, dominate the ward's more suburban outer edge. **2.** arts district in downtown Milwaukee, Wisconsin, E of the Milwaukee R. and S of the East–West Freeway. An area of neglected warehouses for a few decades, it has recently emerged as a mecca for artists and gallery owners. Many structures have been converted to upscale residential lofts. There is also a large gay community here.

Thirteen Colonies later, **Thirteen Original States** see under COLONY.

Thirty Thousand Islands see under GEORGIAN BAY, Ontario.

Thistletown see under ETOBICOKE, Ontario.

Thomaston **1.** town, pop. 6947, Litchfield Co., NW Connecticut, on the Naugatuck R., 8 mi/13 km N of Waterbury. It is best known as the home and workplace of Seth Thomas, who established his clockmaking business here in 1812. Other industries in the area include the manufacture of brass, glass, and machinery and truck farming. **2.** city, pop. 9127, seat of Upson Co., WC Georgia, 37 mi/60 km W of Macon. It manufactures textiles and processes lumber; the area produces fruit. **3.** town, pop. 3306, Knox Co., SC Maine. It is on the St. George R., an inlet of the Atlantic Ocean, just SW of and adjoining Rockland. A trading post around 1630, a fort in 1719, and a former shipbuilding center, Thomaston is today a popular yachting port, and home to Thomaston State Prison and a large cement works. Other industries include food canning and the manufacture of fabric and steel products. Montpelier, a reproduction of Revolutionary general Henry Knox's 1793 home, is in the town.

Thomasville **1.** city, pop. 17,457, seat of Thomas Co., SW Georgia, 30 mi/48 km NE of Tallahassee, Florida. A winter resort for the elite in the late 1800s, it is still known for quail hunting. Local products include cigars, fertilizer, lumber, vegetables, and roses. **2.** city, pop. 15,915, Davidson Co., C North Carolina, 5 mi/8 km SW of High Point. In an area that produces wheat, tobacco, and corn, it manufactures plastics, textiles, clothing, and construction materials, and has been noted for its furniture, especially chairs, since the 1870s.

Thompson city, pop. 14,977, NC Manitoba, 130 mi/210 km N of L. Winnipeg, on the Burntwood R. and the CANADIAN SHIELD. It was founded around a major nickel deposit discovered in the 1950s, around which a city was built by the provincial government and Inco. The economy remains dependent upon the export demand for nickel, although Thompson turns out copper, cobalt, and precious metal byproducts as well. Its integrated nickel mining plant was the first of its kind in the Western Hemisphere. The city has an airport and rail connections to the Churchill–The Pas line. The Mystery L. ski area is just N.

Thompson River see under FRASER R., British Columbia.

Thompsonville see under ENFIELD, Connecticut.

Thornhill see under VAUGHAN, Ontario.

Thornton city, pop. 55,031, Adams Co., NC Colorado, on the South Platte R., a residential suburb 7 mi/11 km S of downtown Denver.

Thorold city, pop. 17,542, Niagara Regional Municipality, S Ontario, on the WELLAND CANAL, adjacent to St. Catharines (N) and 8 mi/13 km W of Niagara Falls. It was founded in 1788. The War of 1812 Battle of Beaver Dams took place here on June 24, 1813; Iroquois warriors allied with the British surprised invading American troops, who had planned an attack on the British in the area. The British had been warned of the American advance by Laura Secord, who had walked 18 mi/30 km from QUEENSTON. The Americans were then persuaded to retreat toward the Niagara R. Following the construction of the canal, which began in 1829, Thorold developed as an industrial and shipping center; it manufactures paper, pulp, lumber, and abrasives.

Thousand Islands group of more than 1500 islands extending 50 mi/80 km into the St. Lawrence R. below (NE of) L. Ontario, in SE Ontario and N New York. The largest islands include 50–sq mi/130–sq km Wolfe, Amherst, and Howe, in Ontario; and Carleton, Grindstone, and Wellesley, in New York. Many of the scenic, wooded islands are privately owned, and most are resorts, summer homes, or fishing camps. The 7 mi/11 km–long **Thousand Islands International Bridge** spans Hill I., connecting the Ontario and New York mainlands. Twenty-three Canadian islands, most purchased in 1914 from the Mississauga tribe, are included in 260-ac/105-ha St. Lawrence Islands National Park, with headquarters at Mallorytown Landing. The islands are a glaciated extension of the CANADIAN SHIELD S toward the ADIRONDACK

Mts., and were populated by the Iroquois before the 17th-century arrival of French and English explorers, fur traders, missionaries, and soldiers. Tourism and resort trade have been important since the early 19th century; KINGSTON and GANANOQUE, Ontario, and WATERTOWN, New York, are major gateways.

Thousand Oaks city, pop. 104,352, Ventura Co., SW California, 35 mi/56 km WNW of downtown Los Angeles and just NW of the Santa Monica Mts. A high-tech research and manufacturing center, it developed rapidly in the 1960s from a rural village into an industrial and residential city, and has continued to grow. Electronics, aircraft parts, plastics, and precision instruments are among its manufactures. Some citrus groves remain. California Lutheran University (1959) is here.

Thread City, the see under WILLIMANTIC, Connecticut.

Three Forks town, pop. 1203, Gallatin Co., SW Montana, on the Jefferson R., 30 mi/48 km NW of Bozeman. The town is named for the place 4 mi/6 km to the NE where the Jefferson, Madison, and Gallatin rivers meet to form the Missouri. Located at this site is Missouri Headwaters State Park. Missouri Fur Company trappers built several trading posts here beginning in 1810, but were evicted by the Blackfeet. The settlement was reestablished (1908) by the railroad as a division point. Madison Buffalo Jump State Historic Site, which memorializes the ancient Indian hunting technique of stampeding bison over a cliff, is 7 mi/11 km N.

Three Mile Island 3.5 mi/5.6 km long, in the Susquehanna R. just S of MIDDLETOWN, Dauphin Co., SE Pennsylvania, and 10 mi/16 km SE of Harrisburg. The nuclear power plant opened here in 1974 suffered a partial uranium core meltdown on Mar. 28, 1979, in what is considered the worst US nuclear accident.

Three Rivers see TROIS-RIVIÈRES, Québec.

Three Rivers Stadium in Pittsburgh, Pennsylvania, on the Allegheny R. across from the GOLDEN TRIANGLE. Built in 1970, it is home to the Pittsburgh Steelers (football) and Pirates (baseball), and seats 59,000.

Three Saints Bay see under KODIAK I., Alaska.

Three Sisters three peaks in the CASCADE RANGE of WC Oregon, including the South Sister (10,358 ft/3157 m), 22 mi/35 km W of BEND; Middle Sister (10,047 ft/3062 m); and North Sister (10,085 ft/3074 m). All three volcanic cones are covered with glaciers, with Collier Glacier between the North and Middle sisters being the largest in Oregon. The **Three Sisters Wilderness** (285,202 ac/115,507 ha), in both Willamette and Deschutes national forests, contains important ecological sites, notably ancient forests in the French Pete Creek area that were the focus of conservation battles in the 1960s and 1970s.

Throgs Neck low-lying peninsula, extreme SE Bronx, New York, between the East R. and Long Island Sound, separated from the rest of the Bronx by Westchester Creek. It takes its name from John Throgmorton (or Throckmorton), a 17th-century settler. Until the 20th century, it was the site of coastal estates; today it is a middle-class residential community. The BRONX-WHITESTONE BRIDGE crosses to Queens from the W end of the peninsula. The Throgs Neck Bridge (1961), with an 1800-ft/550-m central span, crosses between the E end and Little Neck, Queens.

Thunder Basin National Grassland 1.8 million ac/729,000 ha plains area in the Powder River Basin of NE Wyoming. A sheep and cattle grazing area in the mid 19th century, it was ecologically devastated by homesteaders, and by the 1930s had become a dust bowl. A Federal reclamation project for cooperative grazing was established here in the late 1930s, and remains in operation today. The area also has a large antelope herd, many golden eagles, and much other wildlife. Today there are private ranches as well as government-owned land. There are substantial oil, gas, coal, and bentonite reserves here, many being tapped, notably by the Black Thunder Mine, one of the nation's largest coal producers.

Thunder Bay city, pop. 113,946, seat of Thunder Bay District, W Ontario, on the NW shore of L. Superior, at the W terminus of the SAINT LAWRENCE SEAWAY and the mouth of the Kaministikwia R. The city was created in 1970 with the consolidation of Ft. William and Port Arthur and adjacent townships, and named for the inlet of the lake where the river empties. Ft. William, on the site of an abandoned 1670s French fur post, grew around a fort built at the river's mouth by the NORTH WEST COMPANY in 1802, and was central to NWC fur operations until the 1820s. Port Arthur developed in the 1850s as a silver mining town just N. In the 1870s the railroad arrived, and the two communities became competing grain and ore ports; in 1906, they unified their harbor. Thunder Bay is now Canada's largest port in tonnage handled. Its facilities include one of the world's largest grain storage and transshipment depots, whose elevators dominate the cityscape. It is also the industrial center of an extensive CANADIAN SHIELD metal mining region. Leading manufactures include paper, pulp, transportation equipment, wood products, and flour. Fur farming, fishing, and tourism are also important. Lakehead University (1946) and Confederation College are here. Sibley Provincial Park, 20 mi/32 km E across the bay, is the site of the 7 mi/11 km–long Sleeping Giant, a rock formation prominent in Ojibwa legend.

Thunder Butte peak (2755 ft/840 m) in the unglaciated W section of the Missouri Plateau, NC South Dakota, SW of Glad Valley.

Tiburon town, pop. 7532, Marin Co., NW California, a residential suburb at the tip of the Tiburon Peninsula, on San Francisco Bay, facing ANGEL I. and 5 mi/8 km N of downtown San Francisco. Richardson Bay (W) separates it from SAUSALITO.

Ticonderoga village, pop. 2770, in Ticonderoga township, Essex Co., NE New York, in the Adirondack Mts., on low land between L. GEORGE and L. CHAMPLAIN, 40 mi/64 km NNE of Glens Falls. It was settled in the 17th century, and several French and Indian War battles took place at nearby FORT TICONDEROGA. The village has papermaking and wood industries, powered by the falls at the outlet of L. George. It is also a tourist center.

Tidal Basin inlet of the Potomac R., adjacent (SW) to the MALL, in SW Washington, D.C. Known for its spring cherry blossoms, it is also the site of the Jefferson Memorial (1943), a circular, domed structure on its SE side that, with its 19-ft/5.8-m statue of Thomas Jefferson, is a major tourist attraction. Potomac Park extends W, S, and SE of the Tidal Basin along the Potomac.

tidal bore see BORE.

Tidewater low-lying coastal region of E Virginia, extending from the FALL LINE (W) to sea level. The Tidewater comprises four peninsulas. Three are separated from one another by rivers. The NORTHERN NECK lies between the Potomac (N) and Rappahannock (S) rivers; the others lie between the Rappahannock and the York, and between the York and the James. The fourth part of the Tidewater is the EASTERN SHORE area at the S end of the DELMARVA PENINSULA, to the E across Chesapeake Bay. The homeland of the Powhatan Confederacy and the site of many early Virginia settlements and plantations, including JAMESTOWN and WILLIAMSBURG, the Tidewater has remained essentially rural and agricultural; sections, particularly the area around NEWPORT NEWS and HAMPTON, have become highly developed.

Tiffin city, pop. 18,604, seat of Seneca Co., NW Ohio, on the Sandusky R., 25 mi/40 km NE of Findlay. Settlement was begun in the area near Fort Ball, used as a depot by the army in the War of 1812. The city was named for Edward Tiffin (1766–1829), Ohio's first governor. Tiffin became an industrial center after the discovery of nearby natural gas in 1888. Today, it manufactures heavy machinery, pipe fittings, grinding wheels, wire/electrical products, glass, and pottery. It is the seat of Heidelberg College (1850) and Tiffin University (1888).

Tiffin River 75 mi/121 km long, in Michigan and Ohio. As Bean Creek, it rises in SE Michigan, and flows S past Hudson and Morenci and into NW Ohio, becoming the Tiffin in W Fulton Co. It continues S past Stryker and Evansport, joining the Maumee R. at Defiance.

Tifton city, pop. 14,215, seat of Tift Co., SC Georgia, 37 mi/60 km ESE of Albany. It is an agricultural center, handling local tobacco, pecans, tomatoes, and peanuts. Textiles and plastics are manufactured. Abraham Baldwin Agricultural College (1924) is here.

Tigard city, pop. 29,344, Washington Co., NW Oregon, a residential suburb 7 mi/11 km SW of Portland. It has experienced a commercial boom in recent years, and doubled its population in the 1980s. Food processing and the manufacture of sawmill equipment are important industries.

Tiger Stadium in Detroit, Michigan, 1.2 mi/2 km from the Detroit R. Situated in the middle of downtown Detroit, it is the home of the Detroit Tigers, and, with the demolition of Chicago's original Comiskey Park, the oldest (1912) major league baseball stadium.

Tikchik and Wood River Lakes series of 12 E–W oriented parallel glacial lakes N of BRISTOL BAY and E of the Kilbuck and Ahklun mountains, in SW Alaska. In an undeveloped wilderness accessible only by air, they are within 1.6 million-ac/650,000-ha Wood-Tikchik State Park, Alaska's largest. DILLINGHAM (S) is the gateway to an area noted for sport fishing.

Tilbury Town see under GARDINER, Maine.

Tilghman Island 3.5 mi/6 km long and 1.5 mi/2 km wide, in Talbot Co., E Maryland. It is a low, sandy island in Chesapeake Bay, on the N side of the CHOPTANK R. mouth, separated from the mainland by a narrow channel. Fairbank and Tilghman villages are the chief centers. Crabbing, oystering, fishing, seafood packing, and, increasingly, tourism are the main industries.

till see under MORAINE.

Tillamook city, pop. 3001, seat of **Tillamook Co.** (1101 sq mi/2852 sq km, pop. 21,570), NW Oregon, 63 mi/101 km W of Portland. It sits at the S end of 6 mi/10 km–long **Tillamook Bay,** a Pacific inlet with extensive mudflats, noted for clamming, crabbing, and oystering. British sailors found the bay by 1792, and it later became a resort center, with the cities of Garibaldi and Bay City on the NE, and the resort of Bay Ocean on the protective sandspit (W), which had to be abandoned in the 1950s because of erosion. Tillamook Co. is Oregon's dairy capital, noted esp. for cheddar cheese. Huge antisubmarine blimp hangars were built S of the city in World War II. Tillamook Head and Light are 28 mi/45 km N, near SEASIDE.

Tillmans Corner unincorporated community, pop. 17,988, Mobile Co., SW Alabama, a largely white residential suburb immediately SW of Mobile.

Tillsonburg town, pop. 12,019, Oxford Co., S Ontario, 27 mi/43 km ESE of London, on Big Otter Creek. It services an agricultural (esp. tobacco producing) region, and has varied light industry.

Times Beach former residential city in St. Louis Co., EC Missouri, on the Meramec R., just E of Eureka, and 24 mi/38 km SW of downtown St. Louis. Late in 1982 the Centers for Disease Control called for the complete and immediate evacuation of the city's approximately 2200 residents after soil samples showed high levels of toxic dioxin in the soil. The chemical had been deposited there when it was mixed with waste oil and sprayed on the streets for dust control in the 1970s. In 1983 the Federal government purchased Times Beach, the few remaining residents were moved, and the city was closed down and voted out of existence. Controversy over this action has continued.

Times Square area around the intersection of 42nd St. and Broadway, Manhattan, New York City. The Times Tower (completed 1904), which housed the *New York Times* offices, and New York theater activity made it, in the first decade of the 20th century, the "Crossroads of the World" and the Great White Way (see BROADWAY). The newspaper's offices subsequently moved, and legitimate theater gave way to burlesque and movie houses. Today Times Square has a few remaining theaters and many seedy emporiums and cinemas. Redevelopment plans are debated. The ALGONQUIN HOTEL and Port Authority Bus Terminal are in the area.

Timmins city, pop. 47,461, Cochrane District, EC Ontario, on the Mattagami R., 137 mi/220 km N of Sudbury. Settled following the discovery of gold in the area in 1909, it quickly became the commercial center of Canada's richest gold mining region. Most of the Porcupine region's gold mines are now closed, but mining for zinc, copper, and other base metals has expanded since the 1960s. Silver mining and the production of lumber, paper, and pulp, as well as tourism, are also important. At 1240 sq mi/3212 sq km, Timmins is the largest Canadian city in area.

Timms Hill 1952 ft/595 m, in Price Co., NC Wisconsin. In an area of resort lakes, 56 mi/90 km NW of Wausau, it is the highest point in the state.

Timonium see under LUTHERVILLE, Maryland.

Timpanogos Cave National Monument on the N slope of 11,750-ft/3581-m Mt. Timpanogos, in the WASATCH RANGE, 12 mi/19 km NE of Provo, in Utah Co., C Utah. Three interconnected limestone caverns here have stalactites, stalagmites, and helictites (which grow in all directions) in shades of green, yellow, and red.

Tinian limestone island, 39 sq mi/102 sq km, pop. 2118, in the Commonwealth of the NORTHERN MARIANA Is. in the W Pacific Ocean, 3 mi/5 km SW of SAIPAN. Before World War II this was a thriving Japanese community, producing sugarcane. US forces took the island in July 1944, and created North Field, at the time the world's largest airbase, for missions against Japan, some 1600 mi/2600 km NNW; among these were the atomic attacks on Hiroshima and Nagasaki. American, Japanese, and Korean memorials of the war period remain. The island's pop. is today predominantly Chamorro (see GUAM). Tourism and ranching are important.

Tinicum Island in the Delaware R., SW of S Philadelphia, Pennsylvania. It is separated (incompletely) from the Pennsylvania "mainland" by marshes and creeks including Darby Creek and Bow Creek. About 7 mi/11 km long, the "island" was the site of the first permanent white settlement in Pennsylvania, when it became (1643–55) the capital of NEW SWEDEN; remains from this period are in Governor Printz Park. Tinicum I. today is home to the Philadelphia International Airport and to chemical, paper, and power plants. **Tinicum** township (pop. 4440) includes Essington, site of a major Boeing aircraft plant.

Tinker Air Force Base see under OKLAHOMA CITY, Oklahoma.

Tinker Creek c.20 mi/32 km long, in Botetourt Co., SW Virginia, just W of the Blue Ridge. It rises along the NE foot of Tinker Mt., and flows S around the mountain's base, then SSW through HOLLINS. Carvin Creek joins it at the border of the city of Roanoke, and it then joins the Roanoke (Staunton) R. Annie Dillard's *Pilgrim at Tinker Creek* (1974) draws on her life in the area.

Tinley Park village, pop. 37,121, Cook and Will counties, NE Illinois, 26 mi/42 km SW of Chicago. Primarily a residential suburb, it emerged as a major center of commercial development during the 1980s. New office buildings are clustered along I-80 on the S perimeter of the village.

Tin Pan Alley less-than-complimentary term for the American popular music industry. There was apparently no original alley by the name, but the industry can be said to have been centered in Downtown Manhattan, New York City, at the end of the 19th century, in Midtown by the 1930s, and in Hollywood since then. One writer has described Tin Pan Alley as "the hinterland of song."

Tinseltown see under HOLLYWOOD, Los Angeles, California.

Tinton Falls borough, pop. 12,361, Monmouth Co., EC New Jersey, 2 mi/3 km SW of Eatontown, on the Garden State Parkway. Largely residential, it was formerly known as New Shrewsbury.

Tioga town, pop. 625, Grayson Co., N Texas, 50 mi/80 km N of Dallas, and just E of L. Ray Roberts (the TRINITY R.). In an oil and cattle producing area, it is known as the birthplace (1907) of Orvon Gene Autry, singing cowboy and baseball executive.

Tioga County 519 sq mi/1344 sq km, pop. 52,377, SC New York, in the SE portion of the FINGER LAKES, bounded by Pennsylvania (S). Its seat is OWEGO, on the Susquehanna R., which runs E–W in the S part. Tioga Co. is overwhelmingly agricultural; dairying is primary.

Tioga Pass at 9945 ft/3031 m, through the SIERRA NEVADA, along Highway 120, W of Mono L., in EC California. It provides E access to YOSEMITE NATIONAL PARK.

Tioga River 55 mi/89 km long, in Pennsylvania and New York. It rises in W Bradford Co., NE Pennsylvania, and flows N past Mansfield and Tioga, where it is dammed to form Hammond L., then into New York, where it joins the COHOCTON R. at PAINTED POST to form the CHEMUNG R.

Tionesta Creek 60 mi/100 km long, in NW Pennsylvania. It rises in several branches in the Allegheny National Forest, and flows generally SW to join the Allegheny R. at Tionesta, 12 mi/19 km ENE of Oil City. It has several flood control dams, one near Tionesta.

Tioughnioga River see under CHENANGO R.

Tippecanoe County 502 sq mi/1300 sq km, pop. 130,598, in WC Indiana. Its seat is LAFAYETTE. Traversed by the Wabash and Tippecanoe rivers, it is largely made up of rich farmland; grain and livestock are prominent among items produced. There are diversified manufacturing and packing plants in the Lafayette–WEST LAFAYETTE area.

Tippecanoe River 170 mi/275 km long, in Indiana. It rises in N Whitley Co., and flows W and NW through Tippecanoe L., in Kosciusko Co., then generally SW, passing through Marshall, Fulton, Pulaski, and White counties. Above MONTICELLO, it flows through L. Shafer, and below the city through L. Freeman, then winds S to join the Wabash R. Just SW of the confluence is BATTLE GROUND, where the Battle of Tippecanoe was fought Nov. 7, 1811. The river's name derives from a Potawatomi word for the buffalo, a fish.

Tipton city, pop. 2026, Moniteau Co., C Missouri, 30 mi/48 km SW of Columbia. It was laid out in 1858, the year it became the terminus of the Pacific Railroad and the place at which the Overland mail route to San Francisco began. During the Civil War, it was occupied at various times by Union and Confederate armies. Today there is some light manufacturing.

Tisbury town, pop. 3120, Dukes Co., SE Massachusetts, on N MARTHA'S VINEYARD. Tisbury, which includes the village of VINEYARD HAVEN, is one of the island's commercial centers, and the gateway to Martha's Vineyard for most visitors arriving by ferry.

Tisdale town, pop. 3045, EC Saskatchewan, 123 mi/198 km NE of Saskatoon. It is the retail and service center for a region of diversified agriculture. Related industries include flour milling, dairy and honey processing, and the manufacture of farming equipment.

Tishomingo County 434 sq mi/1124 sq km, pop. 17,683, in extreme NE Mississippi. IUKA is its seat. On Pickwick L. (the Tennessee R., NE) and the Tennessee (N) and Alabama (E) lines, it is passed through by the NATCHEZ TRACE and (since 1985) by canals connecting the Tennessee with the TOMBIGBEE R. (part of the Tennessee-Tombigbee Waterway). WOODALL Mt., Mississippi's highest point, and the N end of PONTOTOC RIDGE are in this agricultural, lumbering, and clay and stone producing county.

Titicut see under BRIDGEWATER, Massachusetts.

Titusville **1.** city, pop. 39,394, seat of Brevard Co., SE Florida, on the Indian R. lagoon, 35 mi/56 km ENE of Orlando. Connected by causeway to Cape CANAVERAL, some 15 mi/24 km to the E, the city grew quickly with the construction of space program facilities in the 1950s and 1960s. A popular winter resort, it offers access to the Cape's visitors' programs as well as to swimming, boating, and sport fishing. The city is also a center for the packing and shipping of citrus fruits and for commercial fishing. **2.** city, pop. 6434, Crawford Co., NW Pennsylvania, on Oil Creek, 41 mi/66 km SE of Erie. It is an industrial center, producing steel, oil well equipment, wood products, and electronic components. Founded in 1796 as a lumbering center, it was the site of the world's first successful oil well, drilled by Edwin L. Drake on Aug. 27, 1859; Drake Memorial State Park is near the spot. The city became a center of the 19th-century struggle between Standard Oil and the independent oil companies.

Tiverton town, pop. 14,312, Newport Co., SE Rhode Island, 8 mi/13 km NE of Newport and 18 mi/29 km SE of Providence, on the Sakonnet R. and the Massachusetts border. It includes the villages of North Tiverton and Tiverton Four Corners. Originally part of the Plymouth Colony, this area was the site of the Battle of Almy's Pea Field (1675) in King Philip's War. Tiverton was annexed to Rhode Island in 1746. Today it is a growing suburb with tourism, agriculture, and fishing.

Tobacco Road red clay road that, in the late 18th century, ran SE along ridges from N Georgia to the Savannah R. just SE of the site of AUGUSTA. Early upland tobacco producers had their product rolled in barrels along the road, then floated downriver to Savannah.

Tobacco Valley name for region along the Connecticut R. in N Connecticut, once a world center for shade (wrapper) tobacco culture. East Windsor, South Windsor, and East Hartford have all been important, but urban sprawl and changing economics have largely ended the business there, and it is now centered in the town of Granby (pop. 9369), just NW, along the Massachusetts border and away from the river. The valley's fields were also known for other crops, especially potatoes, grown in rotation with tobacco.

Tobermory see under BRUCE PENINSULA, Ontario.

Toccoa city, pop. 8266, seat of Stephens Co., NE Georgia, 84 mi/135 km NE of Atlanta. **Toccoa Falls,** just N, has a 186-ft/57-m drop on Toccoa Creek; Toccoa Falls College (1907) is here. The city has been an industrial center since the 1870s, producing furniture, tools, machinery, and textiles.

Todt Hill highest of a series of hills (the others are Fort, Ward, Grymes, Emerson, and Lighthouse hills) constituting the N–S "spine" of Staten I., New York. A serpentine outcrop, Todt Hill rises to 409 ft/125 m, the highest point on the US eastern seaboard S of Maine. Neighborhoods along Todt Hill, including some in Dongan Hills and New Dorp, are among Staten Island's most affluent.

Tohono O'odham Indian Reservation see PAPAGO INDIAN RESERVATION, Arizona.

Toiyabe Mountains NNE–SSW trending range, over 50 mi/80 km long, in Lander and Nye counties, C Nevada. Arc Dome is its highest peak, at 11,775 ft/3589 m. The SHOSHONE Mts. lie parallel (W).

Toiyabe National Forest over 3.8 million ac/1.54 million ha (5940 sq mi/15,400 sq km), in S, C, and W Nevada and in E California's SIERRA NEVADA. The largest Lower 48 national forest, it has scattered units in three areas: in the S, in the SPRING Mts., near Las Vegas; in C Nevada, in a series of NNE–SSW units enclosing (from W to E) the Paradise, SHOSHONE, Toiyabe, Toquima, and Monitor ranges; and on the Nevada-California border, in units adjacent (N) to Yosemite National Park and (E and N) to L. Tahoe.

Toledo city, pop. 332,943, Lucas Co., NW Ohio, at the SW end of L. Erie on Maumee Bay, at the mouth of the MAUMEE R. The first settlement arose around Fort Industry (1794), and the influx of pioneers accelerated after American troops defeated a coalition of British and Indians in 1813. Established in 1817, the villages of Port Lawrence and Vistula were united to form Toledo in 1833. The area was for a time claimed by both Michigan and Ohio. The bloodless Toledo War of 1835, settled by the Federal government, ended in the awarding of the TOLEDO STRIP to Ohio and the UPPER PENINSULA to Michigan. In the 1830s and 1840s Toledo's industrialization was fostered by the construction of the Wabash and Erie and Miami and Erie canals, the arrival of the Erie and Kalamazoo and other railroads, and the discovery of natural gas and oil in the area. Many oil and gas pipelines end here, and the city has major refining facilities. Its natural harbor helped make Toledo a leading port. It is a vital shipping point for coal, iron ore, and grain. The jeep is produced here, and Toledo is a major manufacturer of parts for the US auto industry. Grain milling, and the production of glass, tools, jet engines, iron bars, railroad ties, chemicals, and cosmetics are among Toledo's many other industries. Educational and cultural centers include the University of Toledo (1872), the Medical College of Ohio, the Toledo Museum of Art, and the Toledo Zoological Park.

Toledo Bend Reservoir 181,600 ac/73,550 ha, on the SABINE R., on the border between Texas and Louisiana. The two states joined in impounding it to provide municipal, industrial, and agricultural water supply, power, and recreational areas. Numerous parks and the Sabine National Forest lie along its wooded shores. It is Texas's largest lake.

Toledo Strip historic tract in NW Ohio. After Ohio's admission as a state (1803), its boundary with the Michigan Territory remained unclear. Until 1817 Federal surveys showed the land between the S end of L. Michigan and L. Erie to be in Michigan. After 1817 until 1835, Michigan continued to exercise jurisdiction over what the government now said was part of Ohio. In 1835 Ohio proclaimed the area to be Lucas Co., with Toledo its seat. The "Toledo War" of 1835–37, which involved militia maneuvers, was resolved when the government gave the Strip to Ohio, and in compensation gave Michigan the UPPER PENINSULA.

Tolland County 412 sq mi/1067 sq km, pop. 128,699, in NE Connecticut, on the Massachusetts border. Its seat is Tolland. Largely rural, it has no major cities. The economy is based on a mix of agriculture and manufacturing, and on commerce around the university community at STORRS and along Interstate 84.

Toll House, the see under WHITMAN, Massachusetts.

Tom, Mount highest point (1202 ft/367 m) in the Mt. Tom Range of W Massachusetts, near Easthampton. The basaltic range, believed to be the remnants of a lava flow, lies mostly in Mt. Tom State Reservation (1800 ac/729 ha), where dinosaur tracks, hiking and ski trails, and camping facilities can be found.

Tomah city, pop. 7570, Monroe Co., WC Wisconsin, 40 mi/64 km NE of La Crosse. It is a processing center in an agricultural region in which cranberries are a major crop; dairy products, lumber, and livestock are also handled.

Tomales Bay long, narrow inlet of the Pacific Ocean in Marin Co., NW California, separating the Point REYES peninsula from the mainland. Thirteen mi/21 km NW-SE and up to 1 mi/2 km wide, it lies directly over a segment of the SAN ANDREAS FAULT.

Tombigbee River 400 mi/640 km long, in Mississippi and Alabama, formed by the confluence of its East and West forks near Amory, Monroe Co., NE Mississippi. It runs S through the Columbus area before entering Alabama, where it winds SSE to DEMOPOLIS, and is joined by the BLACK WARRIOR R. Continuing S, it joins the ALABAMA R. N of the Mobile area. The Tombigbee was formerly a cotton shipping river in its lower course, S of Demopolis. The idea of using the river and its East Fork, which rose near IUKA, in extreme NE Mississippi, to connect the TENNESSEE R. with the Gulf of Mexico, discussed for a century, was realized in 1985 with the opening of the **Tennessee-Tombigbee Waterway.** The most expensive such project in US history, the waterway, 234 mi/377 km long, involves canalization from the Tennessee's Pickwick L. past Iuka to the East Fork, and extensive canalization of the East Fork and of the main river itself (S of Amory).

Tombstone city, pop. 1220, Cochise Co., SE Arizona, 65 mi/105 km SE of Tucson. Instead of his predicted tombstone, prospector Ed Schieffelin discovered silver here in 1877. By 1881, the rush had brought many more prospectors, adventurers, and outlaws, a population that included "Doc" Holliday, Wyatt Earp, and Johnny Ringo. Lawlessness prevailed, most famously in the 1881 gunfight at the O.K. Corral. Floods, strikes, and declining prices closed the mines by the late 19th century. A National Historic Site, the city is now a tourist center and health resort with a restored cemetery ("Boot Hill"), theater, newspaper office, and O.K. Corral. Many residents work at FORT HUACHUCA, 10 mi/16 km SW.

Tom Mix Wash see under FLORENCE, Arizona.

Tompkins County 477 sq mi/1235 sq km, pop. 94,097, in SC New York, in the FINGER LAKES and containing the S part of CAYUGA L. Its seat and only large city is ITHACA, which influences much of the economy of this small rural county. Agricultural products include dairy goods, grain, poultry, and fruit. There are resorts around the lake.

Tompkinsville waterfront section, NE Staten I., New York, SE of St. George and NW of Stapleton. From a village (1815) named for the governor of New York, it became one of Staten Island's most industrial ports and manufacturing districts. Bay Ridge, Brooklyn, is SE across the Narrows.

Toms River unincorporated village, pop. 7524, seat of Ocean Co., E New Jersey, on Toms R. (an inlet of Barnegat Bay), 22 mi/35 km SW of Asbury Park. It was settled in the early 18th century. During the Revolution, its harbor sheltered American privateers. The town was burned during a Tory attempt to seize its saltworks and warehouses (1782). The early economy was dependent on whaling, shipping, and fishing; with excellent sport fishing and boating facilities, it is now primarily supported by tourism, although there are also boatyards and shellfishing operations. Toms River is the seat of Ocean County College (1964). The borough of South Toms River (pop. 3869) is SW, across the inlet.

Tonawanda in New York: **a.** city, pop. 17,284, Erie Co., on the Niagara R. and the New York State Barge Canal, 10 mi/16 km N of Buffalo. Its industries manufacture chemicals, plastics, chains, hoists, paper products, and office supplies. **b.** town, pop. 82,464, S and E of the city, and including the Buffalo suburbs of Brighton and KENMORE.

Tongass National Forest c.17 million ac/6.9 million ha (26,560 sq mi/68,800 sq km), in SE Alaska, on the mainland Panhandle and the islands of the ALEXANDER ARCHIPELAGO. Established in 1902, and the largest US national forest, it has been largely protected from logging. Rain forest, glaciers, fjords, and waterfalls characterize the forest, which surrounds Ketchikan, Petersburg, Juneau, and Sitka.

Tongue River 265 mi/427 km long, in N Wyoming and SE Montana. It rises in the Bighorn Mts. W of Sheridan, Wyoming, and flows NE into Montana and through the Tongue R. Reservoir and the Northern Cheyenne Indian Reservation, to the Yellowstone R. at MILES CITY.

Tonka Bay see under L. MINNETONKA, Minnesota.

Tonopah unincorporated community, pop. 3616, seat of Nye Co., SW Nevada, at the S of the San Antonio Mts., 170 mi/274 km SE of Reno. It was a silver boom town after 1900; in 13 years its mines yielded nearly $10 million. Some gold is mined now, and livestock and grain are raised in the area. It is the site of the Central Nevada Museum.

Tonto National Forest c.2.9 million ac/1.17 million ha (4530 sq mi/11,740 sq km), in C Arizona, NE of Phoenix and bordered (N) by the MOGOLLON RIM. It contains numerous mountain ranges and wilderness areas, a number of dam-created lakes on the Salt and Verde rivers, and a wide range of plant life, from desert flora to coniferous woods. The **Tonto National Monument,** in the S, 45 mi/72 km E of Phoenix, overlooks THEODORE ROOSEVELT L. on the Salt R.; it protects 14th-century Salado cliff dwellings.

Tooele city, pop. 13,887, seat of Tooele Co., NW Utah, 28 mi/45 km SW of Salt Lake City. It was settled by Mormons in 1849. After the late-19th-century discovery of gold and silver in the nearby Oquirrh Mts., it became a smelting center. Today it remains a copper and lead smelting hub. Its main source of income, however, is the large nearby Army ordnance depot, which includes a number of weapons testing sites.

Topanga Canyon in the Santa Monica Mts. in Los Angeles Co., SW California, between WOODLAND HILLS (N) and Topanga Beach (S). Linking Santa Monica Bay to the SAN FERNANDO VALLEY, the canyon includes the communities of Fernwood, Topanga, Sylvia Park, and Glenview. Topanga Canyon Blvd. continues N across the Valley to CANOGA PARK and CHATSWORTH.

Topaz see under DELTA, Utah.

Topeka city, pop. 119,883, state capital and seat of Shawnee Co., NE Kansas, on both banks of the Kansas R. The site of an OREGON TRAIL ferry (1842), it was established (1854) by antislavery settlers led by Charles Robinson and Cyrus Halliday. Halliday chose it as a center for his Atchison, Topeka & Santa Fe Railroad. It was named state capital upon the admission of Kansas to the Union (1861). Topeka is a major processing center for livestock and grain, with many meatpacking plants and flour and feed mills. It is also an important shipping city with active railroad shops, and a commercial hub. Other significant businesses include insurance companies, tire, film, and pharmaceutical manufacturers, and publishing and printing houses. The city is the site of several mental facilities including the Menninger Foundation, founded as the Menninger Clinic in 1920. Forbes Air Force Base is just S. Topeka is the seat of Washburn University of Topeka (1865). The city's school board was the lead defendant in the *Brown* case, decided in 1954, in which the Supreme Court held public school segregation unconstitutional.

Toppenish city, pop. 7419, Yakima Co., SC Washington, in the Yakima Valley, 19 mi/31 km SE of Yakima. After the Northern Pacific Railroad arrived, the community developed as a cattle and horse shipping point. Beet sugar processing was important until 1980. Situated at the NE edge of the enormous YAKIMA INDIAN RESERVATION, and its commercial center, the city is the headquarters of the Yakima Nation. The Toppenish Creek Encampment, an annual powwow, is held here. In an agricultural area, the city produces dairy items and potatoes. The Toppenish National Wildlife Refuge is 5 mi/8 km S, and Fort Simcoe State Park is 27 mi/43 km W.

Topsfield town, pop. 5754, Essex Co., NE Massachusetts, 20 mi/32 km NE of Boston. Topsfield, which has chalk, sand, and gravel deposits, is known for the Parson Capen House (1683), an example of the style of English architecture popular in the Colonies in the 17th century. After early iron-producing attempts were unfruitful, the town remained agricultural, and today is a residential suburb on US 1 and Interstate 95.

Topsham town, including the villages of Topsham and Pejepscot, pop. 8746, in Sagadahoc Co., SW Maine. It is on the Androscoggin R. opposite Brunswick, 6 mi/10 km upstream from Merrymeeting Bay. Its mills took hydroelectric power from the Androscoggin. Topsham's history and industrial development have been closely associated with those of Brunswick.

Tornado Mountain peak (10,167 ft/3099 m) of the Rocky Mts., in SW Alberta, along the British Columbia border, 75 mi/121 km SW of Calgary.

Torngat Mountains raised and dissected portion of the E edge of the CANADIAN SHIELD, extending SSE–NNW for 125 mi/200 km between Hebron Fjord (S) and Cape Chidley (N), in N Labrador. The "mountains," partly in Québec, rise to 5420 ft/1652 m at the peak known as Mt. Caubvick in Newfoundland and Mont d'Iberville in Québec, the highest point in both provinces. Gneissic rocks from the Precambrian Era—at 3.6 billon years among the oldest dated rocks in North America—are found at Saglek Bay. Evidence of human activity 6000 years ago is found in the area. INUIT from farther S fish in the FJORDS of the region, and offshore oil and gas exploration is conducted from an airstrip in Saglek.

Toronto city and provincial capital, pop. 635,395, in S Ontario, on the N shore of L. Ontario, 310 mi/500 km WSW of Montréal, Québec. It is the third most populous Canadian city (after Montréal and Calgary); the center of the **Toronto Metropolitan Municipality,** Canada's most populous (2,275,771, including residents of SCARBOROUGH, YORK, NORTH YORK, EAST YORK, and ETOBICOKE); center of Canada's largest Census METROPOLITAN AREA (CMA), pop. 3,893,046; and the hub of the GOLDEN HORSESHOE, the country's most industrialized and heavily populated region. Known to Europeans (Étienne Brulé) by 1615, Toronto ("place of meeting") lay at the S end of Indian river-and-portage routes between L. Ontario and L. Huron, near the mouth of the HUMBER R. The French built forts here between 1720 and 1759, when the British took control of Canada. In 1793 a settlement was laid out as the capital of UPPER CANADA, and named York. It developed slowly, survived an American attack and occupation in April 1813, and grew after 1815 as European immigration accelerated. In 1834 it was incorporated as the city of Toronto. Commercial and industrial importance came in the 1850s with the arrival of the Grand Trunk and Great Western railroads, and the city grew along the lakefront and up the Humber and Don R. valleys. From the 1880s through the 1920s annexations multiplied Toronto's size. Financial and administrative strains exacerbated by the 1930s Depression brought pressure for metropolitan government, and in 1953 **Metropolitan Toronto** (popularly, "Metro") combined the city and eleven surrounding communities; in 1967 the twelve were reorganized into the present six. Metropolitan government oversees matters of regional concern, such as transportation, urban development, and social services. Perceived until the mid 20th century as the bastion of conservative, business-dominated British Canadian culture ("Toronto the Good" to those who found it moralistic; it also acquired the nickname "Hogtown," in reference to its supposed monopolization of all that was good in Canada), the city after World War II became home to large European (esp. Italian and Slavic), West Indian, and Asian populations, and is today a diverse and dynamic cultural, as well as commercial, industrial, and financial, center. Its port, rail, and trucking facilities and LESTER B. PEARSON (Toronto) INTERNATIONAL AIRPORT (in MISSISSAUGA, just W) are key to its economy. Local industries engage in printing and publishing, meatpacking, and the manufacture of chemicals, metal and rubber goods, agricultural machinery and implements, foods, and various other goods. In the 1970s institutions relocating from Montréal established Toronto as Canada's banking and financial hub; the Toronto Stock Exchange is the country's largest. Government is a major employer. Redevelopment of the waterfront has been among forces making the city a tourist magnet since the 1980s. The city's best-known educational institution is the University of Toronto (1827). York University (1959; now based in North York), and Ryerson Polytechnic Institute (1948) are among many others. The Royal Ontario Museum and Massey and Roy Thomson halls (music) are esp. well-known. See also: the ANNEX; BAY St.; the BEACH (and Woodbine); BLOOR St. (and the Danforth and High Park); CABBAGETOWN (and Regent Park); CASA LOMA; CHINATOWN; CN TOWER; DON R.; DUNDAS St.; EATON CENTRE; EXHIBITION PARK (and Fort York); FOREST HILL; HARBOURFRONT; HUMBER R.; ONTARIO PLACE; QUEEN'S PARK; QUEEN St.; ROSEDALE; SKYDOME; SPADINA Ave. (and Kensington Market); TORONTO Is.; YONGE St.; YORKVILLE.

Toronto Islands popularly, **the Island** archipelago in L. Ontario, 2 mi/3 km S of downtown TORONTO, Ontario. Centre, Olympic, Ward's, Muggs, South, and Algonquin islands were formed by material eroded from the Scarborough Bluffs (E) by the DON R., and formed a peninsula surrounding early Toronto's harbor. They were isolated in the 1850s when storms opened the Eastern Gap between Ward's I. and the mainland. Now reached by ferry, they are primarily parkland. Ward's (E) has most of the group's c.250 residences. There are beaches, yacht clubs, and the small-plane Island Airport (next to Hanlan's, or Gibraltar, Point, on the W) but no automobiles, restaurants, or stores.

Toro Peak see under SANTA ROSA Mts., California.

Torrance city, pop. 133,107, Los Angeles Co., SW California, 17 mi/27 km SSW of downtown Los Angeles center. Founded in 1911 as a planned industrial and residential community, it is now the commercial and financial center of the SOUTH BAY area, home to large malls and office complexes, but also a blue-collar, heavily industrial city. The drilling of oil and production of oil products and equipment are important. Manufactures have included aircraft and missile parts, plastics, iron and steel, chemicals, and a wide variety of metal and other materials. El Camino College (1947) is here. Torrance grew most quickly in the 1950s and 1960s.

Torrey Pines State Reserve and State Beach, 5 mi/8 km N of LA JOLLA in San Diego Co., SW California. Natural habitat of the rare Torrey pine, the 2000-ac/800-ha reserve is on bluffs overlooking the Pacific Ocean. The area is a center for hang gliding. DEL MAR is just N.

Torrington city and coterminous township, pop. 33,687, Litchfield Co., NW Connecticut, on the Naugatuck R. 30 mi/48 km W of Hartford. It is the commercial hub of NW Connecticut. The first machined brass products in the US were made here in 1834, and the city was long known for its metal manufactures. In 1850 Gail Bordon made the world's first condensed milk here. Torrington has a branch of the University of Connecticut.

Tortugas see DRY TORTUGAS, Florida.

Totowa borough, pop. 10,177, Passaic Co., NE New Jersey, adjacent (W) to Paterson. The area was a camping ground for Washington's army. Totowa produces steel and metal products, tools, furniture, plastics, processed foods, spices, cosmetics, and perfume.

Tottenville residential, industrial, and commercial section, extreme S Staten I., New York. The area was once a collection of fishing villages, with pottery an important local manufacture. The Billopp House (1680s) is known as the Conference House after an unsuccessful 1770s peace conference. Tottenville is across the Arthur Kill from Perth Amboy, New Jersey, with which it was connected by ferry until 1963. The Outerbridge Crossing bridge, just N, was opened in 1928.

Tougaloo locality in Hinds Co., WC Mississippi, 5 mi/8 km N of downtown JACKSON and just within the city limits, the seat of historically black Tougaloo College (1867).

Touro **1.** Touro Infirmary in New Orleans, Louisiana, facility established in the 1840s by Judah Touro (1775–1854), philanthropist who also founded New Orleans's first (1847) synagogue. It was celebrated by the jazz cornetist Muggsy Spanier, who survived a severe illness in its care, in the composition "Relaxin' at the Touro." **2.** Touro Synagogue in Newport, Rhode Island, second (now oldest surviving) US synagogue, designed by Peter Harrison, dedicated 1763 for the Sephardic congregation (established 1658) then headed by Isaac Touro, father of Judah.

Tower Grove Park 279-ac/113-ha municipal park on the South Side of Saint Louis, Missouri, 3 mi/5 km SW of Downtown. It was created after 1866 on the estate of Henry Shaw, an Englishman who had earlier (1859) established here (on the N) the Missouri Botanical Gardens (Shaw's Gardens). The latter, modeled on London's Kew Gardens, are the oldest major facility of the type in the US. They are noted for their Climatron (1969), a geodesic dome enclosing four separate environments, and for the tropical research carried on by staff members. Tower Hill Park is a noted example of Victorian-era park design. The Italian HILL neighborhood is just W.

Tower of the Americas see under HEMISFAIR PLAZA, San Antonio, Texas.

town **1.** in New England, the basic unit of local government, its affairs conducted primarily through regular town meetings. **2.** in US Census Bureau usage, followed in this book, a minor civil division, incorporated or unincorporated; the functional equivalent of a TOWNSHIP. **3.** in Canada, an urban municipality, larger than a village and smaller than a city (definitional lines vary from province to province). All provinces except Québec (which has VILLES) contain towns.

Town and Country city, pop. 9519, St. Louis Co., EC Missouri, 16 mi/26 km W of downtown St. Louis, an affluent suburb.

Town 'n' Country unincorporated residential community, pop. 60,946, Hillsborough Co., WC Florida, just NW of Tampa, on Old Tampa Bay. It boomed in the 1970s and 1980s.

township **1.** in US Census Bureau usage, followed in this book, a minor civil division (a primary subdivision of a COUNTY), providing local government in the New England states and in Michigan, Minnesota, New Jersey, New York, Pennsylvania, and Wisconsin. In some cases it is called a town (see TOWN 2.). **2.** in Canada, the designation of 475 local government entities (census subdivisions) in Ontario; another 68 in Prince Edward Island are designated **township and royalty. 3.** in the language of US land surveys (see PUBLIC LANDS; HOMESTEAD), a land division (part of a county) comprising 36 *sections* of 1 sq mi/2.59 sq km each; the *quarter section* of 160 ac/65 ha was the usual size of a settler's lot.

Towson unincorporated community, pop. 49,445, seat of Baltimore Co., N Maryland, 7 mi/11 km N of downtown Baltimore. Settled in 1750 by Ezekiel Towson, it became county seat in 1854, and in the 20th century developed as a residential, commercial, and industrial suburb, now on Baltimore's beltway (I-695). It is home to Goucher College (1885), Towson State University (1866), and other institutions and corporate headquarters.

Tracy **1.** city, pop. 33,558, San Joaquin Co., NC California, in the N San Joaquin Valley, 60 mi/96 km E of San Francisco and 16 mi/26 km SSW of Stockton, on the S of the San Joaquin Delta. Founded in the 1870s on the Southern Pacific Railroad, it is a trade and shipping center for producers of fruits and vegetables, esp. asparagus. It also has a military distribution depot and produces sugar, dairy goods, glass, and other products. ALTAMONT Pass, 13 mi/21 km W, was long a major gateway to the San Francisco Bay area. **2.** city, pop. 13,181, Bas-Richelieu census division, S Québec, 42 mi/68 km NE of Montréal, on the S bank of the St. Lawrence R. near the mouth of the R. Richelieu. A new (1954) city in a long-established industrial area, it processes iron, steel, and titanium, and is economically tied to the shipbuilding and other industry of neighboring (NE) Sorel.

Tradewater River 110 mi/177 km long, in W Kentucky. It rises in N Christian Co., near Hopkinsville, and flows generally NNW to the Ohio R., near Caseyville. It was an important early trade route.

trade winds prevailing winds in the zone from 10° to 30° from the equator. They blow toward the equator, replacing heated air there that rises and passes over them. In the Northern Hemisphere, this pattern and the earth's rotation cause them to blow from the NE. They bring heavy rainfall in some places in Hawaii, and were a challenge to 19th-century sailing vessels approaching California from the S.

Trail city, pop. 7919, Kootenay Boundary Regional District, SE British Columbia, on the Columbia R., at the mouth of Trail Creek in the Selkirk Mts., 240 mi/390 km ESE of Vancouver and 6 mi/10 km N of the Washington border. Founded (1895) as a mining and smelting town, it processes silver, zinc, lead, and other metals. Other industries include food processing, sawmilling, and hardware manufacture.

Trail of Death see under PLYMOUTH, Indiana.

Trail of Tears general term for routes over which the Cherokee and other southeastern peoples were forced westward into

Indian Territory (E Oklahoma) in the 1830s and 1840s. Despite treaties guaranteeing them parts of their homelands, and despite their adaptation to white settlement around them (suggested by their coming to be called the "Five Civilized Tribes"), the Choctaw, Chickasaw, Creek, Seminole, and Cherokee were evicted, following the Federal Indian Removal Act of 1830, through a series of maneuvers that included the spurious Choctaw treaty of DANCING RABBIT CREEK, and forced overland through the Southeast or to ports on the Mississippi or Ohio rivers. Florida's Seminole resisted (the Seminole War, 1835–42), and some escaped into the state's wildernesses, while others were shipped across the Gulf of Mexico. The Cherokee, based around New Echota (see CALHOUN), Georgia, were dispossessed of their lands in the S Appalachians after gold was discovered in the area. Some escaped into the mountains, where they remain as the Eastern Cherokee of North Carolina. The majority, however, over 15,000, were forced W in 1838–39, across Tennessee or Alabama, then S Kentucky and Illinois, and finally by several routes across Missouri and Arkansas. Some 25% died en route. In 1987 the Cherokee march to exile was recognized by establishment of the Trail of Tears National Historic Trail.

Trans-Alaska Pipeline 800 mi/1300 km–long oil carrier from PRUDHOE BAY on Alaska's Arctic NORTH SLOPE to the ice-free port of VALDEZ on PRINCE WILLIAM SOUND (S). Completed in 1977 against objections by environmentalists, the 48 in/122 cm–diameter pipeline carries an average of 2.1 million barrels of oil a day. The RICHARDSON (S) and DALTON (N) highways parallel it.

Transamerica Pyramid see under FINANCIAL DISTRICT, San Francisco, California.

Trans-Canada Highway built 1950–70 (in use throughout its length from 1962), between Victoria, British Columbia (where Mile 0 is at Beacon Hill Park), and St. John's, Newfoundland. Extending 4858 mi/7821 km, it is called the world's longest national highway and longest paved highway. In British Columbia, it follows the route of the CANADIAN PACIFIC RAILWAY from Vancouver E through the Fraser R. and Thompson R. canyons, through ROGERS PASS (where it was officially opened on July 30, 1962), to Kicking Horse Pass. It then continues (as Highway 1) through Calgary and Medicine Hat, Alberta; Moose Jaw and Regina, Saskatchewan; and Brandon and Winnipeg, Manitoba. To the W of Winnipeg, near PORTAGE LA PRAIRIE, the YELLOWHEAD Highway joins it, having roughly followed the CANADIAN NATIONAL RAILWAY's course from Prince Rupert, British Columbia, through the Yellowhead Pass to Edmonton, Alberta, and thence across the prairies. Continuing E into Ontario, the Trans-Canada divides E of Kenora; its northern route (Highway 17) passes through Dryden, while Highway 11 runs closer to the Minnesota border, through Fort Frances and Atikokan. The roads rejoin W of Thunder Bay. At Nipigon they diverge again, Highway 11 this time taking the northern route, through Kapuskasing and mining areas E of Timmins (largely along the CNR route, this is also part of the extension of Toronto's famous YONGE St.). The southern route, Highway 17, follows the L. Superior shoreline to Sault Ste. Marie, then proceeds E to Sudbury and North Bay, where the roads rejoin again and proceed E to Ottawa. At Sudbury, another alternate (designated Highway 69 and by other numbers) dips S from Highway 17 into C Ontario, pasing N of L. Simcoe, E through Peterborough, and ENE to rejoin the main road SW of Ottawa. From Ottawa the Trans-Canada continues E into Québec, where it passes through Montréal and then proceeds along the S of the St. Lawrence R., to Drummondville, Lévis-Lauzon, and Rivière-du-Loup, where it turns SE into New Brunswick, to Edmundston, Fredericton, and (turning E) Moncton. From Moncton the main highway proceeds SE into Nova Scotia, while a spur turns NE to Cape Tormentine, where ferries (being replaced by a bridge) take drivers to Prince Edward I. In Nova Scotia, the Trans-Canada passes through New Glasgow and across the Gut of Canso, to North Sydney, where ferries carry drivers to Channel–Port aux Basques, Newfoundland. On Newfoundland, the highway winds through Corner Brook, Grand Falls, and Gander, before ending at St. John's.

Trans-Pecos region of extreme W Texas, W of the PECOS R. and N of the Rio Grande. In the BASIN AND RANGE PROVINCE, it has valleys and basins (some undrained) at 3500–5000 ft/1100–1500 m, and its mountains, Texas's highest, are topped by GUADALUPE Peak (8749 ft/2668 m). A barrier to 19th-century travel, the Trans-Pecos is largely uninhabited and was long largely "wild" and lawless (see LANGTRY). In the 1850s the Army experimented with the use of camels to cross it. Its communities today include FORT DAVIS, ALPINE, and PECOS. The BIG BEND is in its S.

Transverse Ranges any of a number of mountain ranges generally trending in an E–W direction in S California. The spine of these ranges comprises the SAN BERNARDINO Mts. (E), the SAN GABRIEL Mts., and the SANTA YNEZ Mts. (W), but they also include the SANTA MONICAS and the SANTA SUSANAS. The Transverse Ranges, sometimes considered a part of the LOS ANGELES RANGES, are regarded, with the TEHACHAPI Mts. (just N), the dividing line between NORTHERN and SOUTHERN CALIFORNIA.

Transylvania colony organized by Richard Henderson and others (the Transylvania Company) in 1774 in what is now C Kentucky and N Tennessee. Based on grants by the Cherokees, it included lands between the Ohio (N) and the Kentucky (E) and Cumberland (W and S) rivers, embracing most of Kentucky and parts of Tennessee's NASHVILLE BASIN. Daniel Boone's WILDERNESS ROAD led to its first settlement, HARRODSBURG. Lying within the chartered westward territories of Virginia and North Carolina, Transylvania could not obtain recognition as a 14th colony, and during the course of the Revolution the two new states voided their agreements with the organizers.

Trappe town, pop. 974, Talbot Co., E Maryland, on an inlet of the EASTERN SHORE of Chesapeake Bay, 6 mi/10 km NNE of Cambridge. It is primarily agricultural. Crosiadore, the 1732 birthplace of John Dickinson, author of *Letters from a Pennsylvania Farmer,* is just S.

Trappers Alley market in Detroit, Michigan. Located in five buildings in GREEKTOWN once used in the fur processing industry, it now features fashionable stores, international gift shops, and ethnic restaurants.

Trashmore, Mount name applied locally to some of the growing sanitary landfills or rubbish dumps in or near American cities. In the early 1990s, notable examples were in Bridgeport, Connecticut, and Virginia Beach, Virginia. In other places the "Mount" was applied to the vicinity name, as in Mount Edgemere, in the ROCKAWAYS, Queens, New York.

Traverse City city, pop. 15,155, seat of Grand Traverse Co., also in Leelanau Co., at the head of Grand Traverse Bay, in the NW portion of the Lower Peninsula of Michigan. This year-round resort, which features boating, fishing, swimming, and skiing, is the center of a popular vacation region. Settled in 1847, it was a 19th-century lumbering center. The region is now famous for its cherries, which, along with other fruits, are canned, frozen, and shipped from the city. Manufactures include metal and wood products, machine tools and dies, hydrants, and clothing. Traverse City is host to the National Cherry Festival and the Northwestern Michigan Fair, and is the home of the Northwestern Michigan Symphony. It is the seat of Northwestern Michigan College (1951).

Travis Air Force Base see under FAIRFIELD, California.

Travis County 989 sq mi/2562 sq km, pop. 576,407, in SC Texas. Crossed (NE–SW) by the BALCONES ESCARPMENT, it is drained by the Colorado R., whose flood control dams provide power. An expanding educational, research, industrial, governmental, and commercial complex is centered around the state capital and the University of Texas, in the county seat, AUSTIN. Poultry, sheep, goats, and dairy and beef cattle are raised largely in the HILL COUNTRY (W and NW). The county produces fruit, pecans, grain, cotton, potatoes, limestone, and clay, and has many lake and hill recreational areas.

Treasure Island 400 ac/162 ha, in San Francisco Bay, California, between San Francisco (of which it is part) and Oakland, connected to YERBA BUENA I. (S) by causeway. Built with landfill on rocky shoals for the Golden Gate International Exposition of 1939–40, it became an air terminal, then a World War II naval training center and embarkation point. Its military function was ordered ended in 1993.

Tremblant, Mont one of the highest peaks (3175 ft/968 m) of the Laurentians in S Québec, 70 mi/115 km NW of Montréal. Its 2135-ft/650-m vertical drop lures skiers; the mountain is also the focal point of a 482–sq mi/1248–sq km provincial park. The resort of Mont-Tremblant (pop. 707) and a lake of the same name are nearby. Abenaki legend claims that the mountain will tremble when crossed by man.

Tremé residential and commercial district of New Orleans, Louisiana, just W of the VIEUX CARRÉ, above BEAUREGARD SQUARE. The old Faubourg Tremé (c.1800) developed between the Vieux Carré and the Bayou St. John (NNW); the urban neighborhood, one of the city's oldest black residential areas, developed by the 1830s.

Tremont largely residential section, C Bronx, New York. It lies S of Fordham and N of Crotona Park, with Bronx Park to the NE. The area was the focus of extensive urban renewal projects in the late 1960s, but a failing local economy led to continued depression. East Tremont is to the E, between Bronx and Crotona parks; both districts are heavily Hispanic in the 1990s.

Trent Canal also, **Trent-Severn Waterway** or **Severn Waterway** navigational system in S Ontario connecting L. Ontario at TRENTON with Port Severn on GEORGIAN BAY (L. Huron), constructed in stages between 1833 and 1920. From L. Ontario it proceeds generally WNW, following the Murray Canal to the Bay of Quinte at Trenton; the Trent R. to Rice L.; the Ontonabee R. through PETERBOROUGH, its major port en route, and several of the KAWARTHA Ls.; artificial channels to L. SIMCOE and L. Couchiching; and the Severn R. to the S shore of Georgian Bay. Covering 240 mi/390 km, it has 40-odd locks, including a huge hydraulic lift at Peterborough. Following early lumbering routes, it is today primarily recreational, and provides water for communities and hydroelectric projects in the area.

Trenton **1.** city, pop. 20,586, Wayne Co., SE Michigan, on the Detroit R. opposite GROSSE ILE, 18 mi/29 km SW of Detroit. The War of 1812 battle of Monguagon was fought in what is now an industrial and residential suburb of Detroit. The early economy was based on fishing and steamboat trade, and Trenton was (1860–80) one of the most important shipbuilding areas on the Detroit R. It now provides electrical power and manufactures steel, plastic, automobile and marine engines, and chemicals. **2.** city, pop. 88,675, state capital and seat of Mercer Co., WC New Jersey, at the head of navigation on the Delaware R., 25 mi/40 km NE of Philadelphia, Pennsylvania. It was settled c.1679 with the building of a mill on the Delaware's falls by English Quakers, and was then known as The Falls. It was renamed (1721) for William Trent, who laid out the town. A Revolutionary War center, it was the scene of two American victories (1776, 1777). Trenton became state capital in 1790, and twice (1784, 1799) served as temporary US capital. Its industrial development was spurred by the building of the Delaware and Raritan Canal and the coming of the railroad in the 1830s, and it was soon an important center for the manufacture of pottery, rubber, and steel cable. It still makes those products, and is a major river port and transportation center. Among its other manufactures are plastics, steel, plumbing fixtures, textiles, paper and metal products, automobile parts, tools and dies, flooring materials, and steam turbines. The New Jersey State Museum, Old Barracks (1758), and F.L. Olmsted's Cadwallader Park (1891) are here, along with the gold-domed Capitol (1792). After World War II, Trenton lost many of its residents and much business to neighboring EWING and HAMILTON townships, and declined through the early 1970s. Extensive redevelopment has since taken place in its downtown. **3.** city, pop. 6189, Butler Co., SW Ohio, 20 mi/32 km N of Cincinnati. A Miller beer brewery is situated here. Metal stamping is another local industry. **4.** city, pop. 16,908, Hastings Co., SE Ontario, on the W end of the narrow, 50 mi/80 km–long Bay of Quinte, an arm of L. Ontario, at the mouth of the Trent R. (the SE end of the TRENT CANAL), 94 mi/152 km ENE of Toronto. Settled by LOYALISTS from 1792, it developed as a lumbering and shipping, later as a manufacturing, center in an agricultural region. In World War I it was a munitions center. Modern industries include canning and the manufacture of textiles, machinery, and paper and steel products. The city is also a gateway to the Kawartha Ls., L. Simcoe, and Georgian Bay by way of the canal. Its airfield, a major Royal Canadian Air Force base before and during World War II, is 1 mi/2 km E.

tribal jurisdiction statistical area in Oklahoma, area designated by the US Census as "delineated by Federally recognized tribes . . . without a reservation." Until the 1980s called "Historic Areas," these are parts of the former INDIAN TERRITORY inhabited by tribes that were persuaded, in the years just before Oklahoma statehood (1907), to give up collective ownership of their land; the individual ownership that followed (the allotment system) led to the purchase of much of the land by non-Indians. The Osage reservation (see OSAGE Co.) is the only remaining INDIAN RESERVATION in Oklahoma. The TJSAs, totaling 48,779 sq mi/126,390 sq km, or 71% of the state, have a pop. (2,082,377) that is now only 9.6% (200,789) Indian; one or more tribal governments have forms of jurisdiction within them. The 17 TJSAs are: Absentee Shawnee–Citizens Band of Potawatomi; Caddo-Wichita-Delaware; Cherokee; CheyenneArapaho; Chickasaw; Choctaw; Creek; Iowa; Kaw; Kiowa-Comanche-Apache–Fort Sill Apache; Otoe-Missouria; Pawnee; Sac and Fox; Seminole; Tonkawa; Creek-Seminole Joint Area; and Iowa–Sac and Fox Joint Area.

TriBeCa residential and commercial section, lower W Manhattan, New York City. Its name refers to a *Tri*angle *Be*low *Ca*nal Street; the other sides of the triangle are Broadway and West St. A 19th-century cast-iron district like neighboring SOHO, it became trendy in the 1970s as home to artists of all sorts, and is now, like SoHo, heavily gentrified and touristed.

Triborough Bridge complex of bridges and viaducts connecting the Bronx, Manhattan, and Queens, New York, by way of Randall's and Ward's islands, over the Harlem and East rivers and the Hell Gate. Opened in 1936, it has a total elevated length of 17,710 ft/5402 m; its East R. suspension bridge is the longest unit, with a 1380-ft/421-m main span. Randall's I. is headquarters for the Triborough Bridge and Tunnel Authority, which was the power base of master planner Robert Moses.

Tri-Cities **1.** in Alabama: see QUAD CITIES. **2.** also, **Triple Cities** the industrial complex of BINGHAMTON, ENDICOTT, and JOHNSON CITY, SC New York, on the Susquehanna R. in New York's Southern Tier, famous as a shoemaking center. **3.** the industrial complex of JOHNSON CITY, KINGSPORT, and BRISTOL, Tennessee. **4.** the industrial and agricultural complex of KENNEWICK, PASCO, and RICHLAND, Washington, SE of the Hanford nuclear reservation.

Trimountain see under SHAWMUT PENINSULA, Massachusetts.

Trinidad city, pop. 8580, seat of Las Animas Co., S Colorado, on the Purgatoire R., 75 mi/121 km S of Pueblo and 13 mi/21 km N of the New Mexico border. Settled by the Spanish, whose influence can still be seen in its downtown architecture and brick streets, it was a stop on the SANTA FE TRAIL. The arrival of the railroad in the 1870s spurred its growth as a cattle center. Today Trinidad is a rail, shipping, and industrial center for a coal mining, dairy, and livestock region. It is the seat of Trinidad State Junior College (1925).

Trinity Bay **1.** Atlantic Ocean inlet, over 60 mi/100 km NE–SW and up to 25 mi/40 km wide, in SE Newfoundland, between the NW AVALON PENINSULA (SE) and the BONAVISTA PENINSULA (NW), 40 mi/65 km WNW of St. John's. Heavily indented, it is ringed with small OUTPORTS, including Heart's Delight, Heart's Desire, and HEART'S CONTENT, and has a maritime, fish-based history. **2.** NE arm of Galveston Bay, at the mouth of the Trinity R., in SE Texas. Two–12 mi/3–19 km wide, it is bordered by lowlands that are one of the major rice producing areas in the state. Anahuac (city, pop. 1993), a former Mexican military post and now a market center and the seat of Chambers Co., is at the bay's N end. The Houston Ship Channel passes SW.

Trinity Lake see under WHISKEYTOWN-SHASTA-TRINITY NATIONAL RECREATION AREA, California.

Trinity Mountains subrange of the KLAMATH Mts. in NW California, SW of Redding. The **Trinity Alps Wilderness** (500,000 ac/202,500 ha), formerly known as the Salmon–Trinity Alps Primitive Area, has peaks that have been likened to the Swiss Alps because of their glaciers and year-round snow cover. The Salmon and Trinity rivers rise in the mountains, and wolverine and the rare Brewer spruce are found here. Thompson Peak is the high point, at 9002 ft/2744 m. Hiking and logging are important.

Trinity River **1.** 130 mi/210 km long, in NW California. Its North Fork, the mainstream, rises in the Trinity Mts. section of the KLAMATH Mts. and passes S through Clair Engle L. (see WHISKEYTOWN-SHASTA-TRINITY NATIONAL RECREATION AREA). The 50 mi/80 km–long South Fork, which rises on the W edge of the YOLLA BOLLY–Middle Eel Wilderness, joins it near Salyer. The Trinity then flows NW, through the Hoopa Valley Indian Reservation, to the KLAMATH R., NE of Eureka. The river was hydraulically mined for gold in the 1870s. **2.** 550 mi/890 km long, in Texas. Its **West Fork,** 150 mi/240 km long, rises in Archer Co., S of Witchita Falls, and flows SE to Fort Worth, passing through the 9200-ac/3730-ha Eagle Mountain L., just NW of the city. The **Clear Fork,** 60 mi/100 km long, rises in Parker Co., flows SE, then swings NE through Benbrook L. to join the West Fork in downtown Fort Worth. The combined stream continues E to Dallas. On the city's W boundary it is joined by the **Elm Fork,** 100 mi/160 km long, which rises in Montague Co., near the Oklahoma line. The Elm Fork flows SE past Gainesville, then S to Dallas, passing through 29,400-ac/11,900-ha L. Ray Roberts, NE of Denton, then through LEWISVILLE L. After flowing SE through the heart of Dallas, the Trinity is joined 30 mi/48 km SE by the **East Fork,** 110 mi/180 km long, which flows S from Grayson Co., passing through L. Lavon and through 22,750-ac/9210-ha L. Ray Hubbard, E of Garland. The Trinity then flows generally SSE across the Coastal Plain, passing through L. LIVINGSTON, to TRINITY BAY, N of Galveston Bay and 36 mi/58 km E of Houston. The river is navigable only a short distance upstream from its mouth, but, with its dams and reservoirs, is a major irrigation and hydroelectric power source and recreational resource.

Trinity Site see under WHITE SANDS, New Mexico.

Triple Cities see TRI-CITIES, New York.

Tripyramid, Mount see under SANDWICH RANGE, New Hampshire.

Tri-State Expressway toll highway (I-294), 68 mi/109 km long, between South Holland, Illinois (near the Indiana line), and Rosecrans, Illinois (near the Wisconsin line). The expressway speeds traffic around the edges of Chicago, and passes near O'Hare International Airport.

Tri-Taylor historical residential neighborhood on the NEAR WEST SIDE of Chicago, Illinois, just SW of the Loop and W of CHICAGO CIRCLE. Its late-19th-century buildings house remnants of the Italian community that lived here before heavy redevelopment came to the area in the 1960s, along with a smattering of young professionals.

Trois-Rivières English, **Three Rivers** city, pop. 49,426, center of the Mauricie region, midway between Montréal (SW) and Québec City (NE) in S Québec, on the N bank of the St. Lawrence R., at the mouth of the R. SAINT-MAURICE, whose three channels formed by delta islands give the city its name. Settled in 1634, Trois-Rivières is one of the oldest communities in Canada, and a longtime regional center. In the 1850s, nearby timberland and ample hydroelectric power gave rise to lumber operations that eventually developed into the city's largest industry—the manufacture of pulp and paper, esp. newsprint. Other manufactures include electrical equipment, textiles, clothing, rubber, and iron products. Lumber, asbestos, and grain are shipped from the port. Trois-Rivières is a transportation hub and a cultural and tourist center; local attractions include the Forges of Saint-Maurice, a national historic site. Educational institutions include a branch (1969) of the Université du Québec. Much of the city was rebuilt after a 1908 fire. **Trois-Rivières-Ouest** (city, pop. 20,076) is a fast-growing, largely residential suburb.

Trojan nuclear power facility in Columbia Co., extreme NW Oregon, on US 30 and the Columbia R., 43 mi/69 km NNW of Portland and 5 mi/8 km SSE of Longview, Washington, operational since 1975, slated to close in 1996.

Trona Pinnacles see under RIDGECREST, California.

Trout Dale see under MARION, Virginia.

Troy **1.** city, pop. 13,051, seat of Pike Co., SE Alabama, 50 mi/80 km SSE of Montgomery, near the Conecuh R. Settled in 1824, it has an agricultural economy, including the processing of cotton, peanuts, and corn and the raising of livestock, and manufactures wood products, fertilizers, textiles, and truck bodies. It is home to Troy State University (1887). **2.** city, pop. 72,884, Oakland Co., SE Michigan, 10 mi/16 km SE of Pontiac. This largely residential and affluent community has, since the 1970s, developed as an area of corporate headquarters, office buildings, and other commercial facilities. It also makes hardware, auto parts, tractors, and electronic products. Walsh College of Accountancy and Business Administration (1968) is situated here. The Troy-Oakland Airport, N of the city, is often used by corporate jets and other private aircraft. **3.** city, pop. 54,269, seat of Rensselaer Co., E New York, on the E bank of the Hudson R., at the junction of the Mohawk and Hudson rivers, 8 mi/13 km NE of Albany. Initially part of Rensselaerswyck (see RENSSELAER), it was organized as Vanderheyden's Ferry in 1786, taking its present name three years later. The city's early development was fostered by the iron and steel industry. River trade was important during the 19th century, especially following the opening of the ERIE CANAL in 1825. The clothing industry also developed during this time, initiated by the invention of the detachable collar by a "Trojan" woman, and the introduction, in 1852, of the sewing machine. Apparel manufacture remains important. Troy also houses electrical, auto, and aircraft engineering industries, and produces textiles, metals, and processed foods. It is home to Rensselaer Polytechnic Institute (1824), Russell Sage College (1916), Hudson Valley Community College (1953), and the Emma Willard School for Girls (1821). **4.** city, pop. 19,478, seat of Miami Co., WC Ohio, on the Great Miami R., 18 mi/29 km N of Dayton. It was founded in 1807, and its industrialization was aided by the completion of the Miami and Erie Canal (1845). Today, paper and paper goods, aviation products, and farm equipment are among the items manufactured here. Troy is also a tobacco market. In 1913, it suffered a disastrous flood, which resulted in its becoming the first flood protection district in the US.

Troy Grove village, pop. 259, La Salle Co., NC Illinois, 8 mi/13 km N of La Salle. The Wild Bill Hickok State Memorial honors the soldier and frontiersman born here in 1837.

Troy Hill residential neighborhood on the NORTH SIDE of Pittsburgh, Pennsylvania, 2 mi/3 km N of the GOLDEN TRIANGLE. A working-class, mostly German community, it houses employees of nearby factories.

Troy Hills see PARSIPPANY, New Jersey.

Truchas Peaks group of three peaks, all over 13,000 ft/3962 m, some 25 mi/40 km NE of Santa Fe, in the SANGRE DE CRISTO Mts. in N New Mexico. It contains the second-highest point in the state (13,102 ft/3993 m), after WHEELER PEAK.

Truckee River 120 mi/190 km long, in NE California and NW Nevada. From the W shore of L. Tahoe (at Tahoe City), it flows generally N, then NE, past Truckee, California, and Reno, Nevada, into the S ends of PYRAMID and Winnemucca (just E; a PLAYA) lakes. With the Carson R. (S), the Truckee is part of the Newlands Irrigation Project, key to local agriculture.

True North see under the NORTH, in Canada.

Trujillo Alto unincorporated community (ZONA URBANA), pop. 44,336, Trujillo Alto Municipio (pop. 61,120), NE Puerto Rico, 7 mi/11 km SE of San Juan. Settled in the early 19th century by Canary Islanders, it is today a residential and commercial suburb of San Juan.

Trumbull town, pop. 32,016, Fairfield Co., SW Connecticut. It is an affluent residential suburb adjacent (NE) to BRIDGEPORT. Many of its residents commute to jobs in Stamford and Greenwich. There is some commercial and industrial activity along the town's S edge.

Trumbull County **1.** see under WESTERN RESERVE (Ohio). **2.** 612 sq mi/1585 sq km, pop. 227,813, in NE Ohio, bounded by Pennsylvania (E); intersected by the Grand and Mahoning rivers; and containing Mosquito L. Its seat is WARREN. The county contains cities that are essentially industrial suburbs of YOUNGSTOWN, such as Girard, Niles, and Warren, where steel milling is particularly important. Diversified agriculture here includes clover, dairy, grain, and livestock farming.

trunk line in railroading, by analogy with the structure of a tree, a main line off which branches diverge, and along which long-distance (through) trains travel. The ERIE RAILROAD was the first US line built (1830s–40s) following this concept. The main lines of some other major carriers, like the NEW YORK CENTRAL RAILROAD, were at first consolidations of series of short lines traveling in the same direction. DIVISION POINTS represent either the sites of such consolidation or the separation of individually managed parts of a line.

Truro **1.** town, pop. 1573, Barnstable Co., SE Massachusetts, near the N tip of Cape Cod, adjacent (SSE) to Provincetown. Formerly a port and a fishing center, it is now a summer resort and artists' colony; Edward Hopper lived and painted here in the 1930s, using the surrounding moors and dunes as subject matter. Truro's harbor is on Cape Cod Bay (W); its E coast is part of the Cape Cod National Seashore. **2.** town, pop. 11,683, seat of Colchester Co., C Nova Scotia, on the Salmon R., near the head of Cobequid Bay (Minas Basin), 52 mi/84 km NNE of Halifax. Settled by Acadians, then New Englanders, it is a rail hub and a commercial and industrial center in an agricultural and lumbering area. Industries include printing, food and beverage processing, metalworking, textile milling, and the manufacture of carpets, clothing, and building materials. Nova Scotia Agricultural College and teachers' and business colleges are here.

Truth or Consequences city, pop. 6221, seat of Sierra Co., SW New Mexico, on the Rio Grande and Interstate 25, 60 mi/100 km NNW of Las Cruces. Formerly Springs of Palomas, then (1916) Hot Springs, it changed its name in 1950 to that of Ralph Edwards's radio show, as a condition for being chosen as the site of a live broadcast. Ralph

Edwards Park and museum are here, A former health resort with mineral springs, the city is a trade center for livestock and agricultural producers. Elephant Butte (N) and Caballo (S) reservoirs are nearby.

Truxton rural town, pop. 1064, Cortland Co., C New York, on the East Branch of the Tioughnioga R., 11 mi/17 km NE of Cortland. Baseball manager John J. McGraw (1873–1934) was born here.

Tsaile see under NAVAJO INDIAN RESERVATION, Arizona.

Tsawwassen see under DELTA, British Columbia.

Tualatin city, pop. 15,013, Washington and Clackamas counties, NW Oregon, on the Tualatin R., a residential suburb 10 mi/16 km SW of Portland. The city has witnessed a spurt of commercial development in recent years, and doubled in population in the 1980s.

Tubac historic community in Santa Cruz Co., S Arizona, 18 mi/29 km N of Nogales and the Mexican border, on the Santa Cruz R. A Spanish PRESIDIO and MISSION established here in 1752, following a 1751 Pima revolt, formed the first European settlement in Arizona. After the 1854 GADSDEN PURCHASE, American prospectors moved into the area, making Tubac briefly a boom town. In the 1940s it began a third life as an arts colony, and is now much visited.

Tuba City see under NAVAJO INDIAN RESERVATION, Arizona.

Tuckahoe **1.** village, pop. 6302, in Eastchester town, Westchester Co., SE New York, 18 mi/29 km NNE of New York City. Primarily residential, it was a farming area until the early 19th century, when marble deposits were discovered E of the Bronx R.; Tuckahoe marble was used in the construction of the Capitol and the Washington Monument in Washington, D.C. **2.** unincorporated community, pop. 42,629, Henrico Co., E Virginia, just NW of Richmond. Along the James R. (S) and Tuckahoe Creek (W), it is a largely residential suburb.

Tucker unincorporated community, pop. 25,781, De Kalb Co., NW Georgia, 13 mi/21 km NE of downtown Atlanta, a heavily white residential suburb with a large commercial/industrial park, on Atlanta's beltway (Route 285).

Tuckerman Ravine glacial cirque in the SE side of Mt. WASHINGTON, in the Presidential Range of the White Mts. A catchbasin for snow blowing off the Presidential Range, it is noted for late spring skiing, with an 800-ft/244-m headwall, and was named for Dr. Edward Tuckerman, a lichenologist.

Tucson city, pop. 405,390, seat of PIMA Co., SE Arizona, on the Santa Cruz R., on a high desert plateau at the SW edge of the Santa Catalina Mts., 110 mi/177 km SE of Phoenix. Founded by Eusebio Kino in 1700 as a Jesuit MISSION on the site of a Hohokam PUEBLO, it was used as a walled fort by the Spanish in 1776 and ceded to Mexico in 1821. It became part of the US in the GADSDEN PURCHASE of 1854, and was occupied briefly by Confederate troops in 1862. Tucson served as territorial capital from 1867 to 1877. The arrival of the Southern Pacific Railroad in 1880, the development of irrigated farming, and the discovery of silver in TOMBSTONE and copper in BISBEE (both SE) stimulated growth. World War II brought industrialization and the 1950s pop. increase. Today Tucson's primary industries are the processing and transportation of local copper, cotton, and livestock; manufacturing; tourism; and retailing. Retirees are drawn to its dry, sunny climate and mixture of mountains and desert. Its manufactures include aircraft, optical equipment, and electronics. Davis-Monthan Air Force Base, on its SE border, is another large employer. The University of Arizona (1885), KITT PEAK Observatory, MISSION SAN XAVIER DEL BAC, the Tucson Museum of Art, and the Arizona–Sonora Desert Museum are among noted local institutions. The Saguaro National Monument is just E and W.

Tucumcari city, pop. 6831, seat of Quay Co., NE New Mexico, on Interstate 40 between Albuquerque (153 mi/246 km W) and Amarillo, Texas. At a former cattle trail watering point, it was founded in 1901 on the Rock Island Railroad. Today it is a tourist and truck stop and a trade center for cattle and grain producers. Conchas L. (NW) and Ute L. (NE), two important reservoirs on the CANADIAN R., are nearby.

Tudor City see under TURTLE BAY, New York.

Tug Fork see under BIG SANDY R., West Virginia, Virginia, and Kentucky.

Tug Hill see under ADIRONDACK Mts.

Tujunga residential section of LOS ANGELES, California, N of the VERDUGO HILLS and NW of La Crescenta, on the E of the San Fernando Valley. It was annexed to the city in 1932. It takes its name from **Tujunga** (or Big Tujunga) **Creek,** which flows from the San Gabriel Mts. (N) through Tujunga Canyon, and is dammed near Pacoima to form Hansen L. As the **Tujunga Wash,** it then flows across the Valley to join the Los Angeles R. at Studio City.

Tuktoyaktuk see under INUVIK, Northwest Territories.

Tukwila city, pop. 11,874, King Co., WC Washington, on the Green R., 8 mi/13 km SSE of downtown Seattle and just E of Seattle-Tacoma International Airport. It has residences, businesses related to the airport, and corporate offices.

Tulalip Indian Reservation see under MARYSVILLE, Washington.

Tulare city, pop. 33,249, Tulare Co., SC California, in the San Joaquin Valley, 40 mi/64 km SE of Fresno. A processing, shipping, and trade center for a cotton, fruit, and dairy goods producing area, it has a variety of creameries, cotton gins, and food packing plants. Founded in 1872 on the Southern Pacific Railroad, it lost its role as a regional hub to Fresno, but is still a junction for the SP and the Santa Fe. The county fairground and hospital are here. The city takes its name from the former TULARE L. (SW).

Tulare County 4808 sq mi/12,453 sq km, pop. 311,921, in SC California. Bordered (E) by the crest of the S Sierra Nevada, it lies largely (S and W) in the San Joaquin Valley. VISALIA is its seat; Tulare, Dinuba, and Porterville are other important communities. The Kaweah, Tule, and Kern rivers drain it from E to W. Parts of Kings Canyon and Sequoia national parks are in the N, while the rest of the county is heavily agricultural, producing cattle and varied crops.

Tulare Lake dry lake basin in the San Joaquin Valley, in SC California, E of the KETTLEMAN HILLS and just SW of CORCORAN. Once a lake 50 mi/80 km long and 35 mi/56 km wide, fed by the Kings, Kaweah, and Kern rivers, it became farmland when the rivers were channelized and diverted for irrigation. The name is from *los Tulares* (the place of rushes).

Tularosa Basin see under WHITE SANDS, New Mexico.

Tule Lake in Siskiyou and Modoc counties, N California, on the MODOC PLATEAU, near the Oregon border. Covering 13,000 ac/5265 ha, a small fraction of its postglacial size, it has been much reduced in the 20th century to create cropland. With Lower KLAMATH L. (W) and CLEAR L. (E), it is a magnet for waterfowl on the PACIFIC FLYWAY, and is within a National Wildlife Refuge. **Tulelake** (city, pop.

1010) is just N, 25 mi/40 km SE of Klamath Falls, Oregon. Just S is the LAVA BEDS NATIONAL MONUMENT. The area was central in the Modoc War (1872–73). In 1942–46 nearly 19,000 Japanese-Americans were interned at two sites in the Tule L. vicinity.

Tullahoma city, pop. 16,761, Coffee and Franklin counties, SC Tennessee, 63 mi/101 km SE of Nashville. Originally a Cherokee village, the settlement grew from a railroad construction camp in 1850. It was a Confederate base in Jan.–July 1863, after MURFREESBORO. Its economy has been based on grain, tobacco, cotton, lumber, and dairy products; today, baseballs are a major manufacture. The Air Force maintains the Arnold Engineering Development Center, an aircraft and missile testing facility, SE of the city; the University of Tennessee Space Institute was opened in 1964 along Woods Reservoir. Motlow State Community College (1969) is in the city.

Tulsa city, pop. 367,302, seat of Tulsa Co. (pop. 503,341), NE Oklahoma, on the Arkansas R., 96 mi/155 km NE of Oklahoma City. The second most populous city in the state, it is the center of a five-county (OSAGE, Rogers, Creek, Tulsa, and Wagoner) metropolitan area with a pop. of 708,954. Creek removed from Alabama (see TRAIL OF TEARS) settled here in the 1830s; the Osage and Cherokee were also in the area. By the 1880s rail shipping of cattle was important, and white settlement had begun; the city was incorporated in 1898. In 1901, the huge oil deposits in the Osage Hills (N) and elsewhere in the area were discovered, and a boom began. The city has grown steadily since then, the rate of decennial pop. increase dropping to close to zero only with the oil slump of the 1980s. The area also produces gas, coal, and sand, and cattle, grains, some fruits, and forage crops are raised, so that Tulsa has long been a commercial, financial, and transportation center. Manufacturing is now important, with aerospace machinery, oilfield equipment, electronic and communications devices, foods, and building materials and prefabricated houses esp. prominent. The University of Tulsa (1894) and Oral Roberts University (1965) are here. Oil refining is centered in the West Tulsa section, on the river. In 1971 the McClellan-Kerr Arkansas Navigation System, 446 mi/718 km long, connected Tulsa's NE suburb of Catoosa (city, pop. 2954, Rogers Co.), on the VERDIGRIS R., with the Mississippi, via the ARKANSAS R. Tulsa has large areas of upscale housing built during the boom years and spread over rolling, grassy terrain, largely S and E of Downtown. Just NE of Downtown is the Greenwood district, epicenter of a major race riot in the summer of 1921, later regarded as one of the black cultural hubs of the Southwest, largely demolished by 1950s URBAN RENEWAL (esp. highway) projects, but today rejuvenated to a degree.

Tumacacori historic locality in Santa Cruz Co., S Arizona, 4 mi/6 km S of TUBAC and 14 mi/23 km N of Nogales and the Mexican border. On the site of a Pima village, a Spanish MISSION church was begun in 1800; although used 1822–28, it was never completed, and was abandoned in 1848. The site is now a National Historic Park.

Tumwater city, pop. 9976, Thurston Co., WC Washington, on the Deschutes R., 2 mi/3 km SSW of Olympia. Washington's first permanent settlement (1845) N of Fort VANCOUVER, it was a mill town whose prosperity was powered by water. In the early 19th century it included gristmills, sawmills, breweries, a tannery, and furniture and box factories. The site of the original town is now part of Tumwater Historical Park. The Olympia Brewery is in the city, which is also known for its annual bluegrass festival.

tundra land zone beyond (in the Northern Hemisphere, N of) the limits (the tree line) of forests, up to the edge of permanent polar ice. In the US and Canada, it consists of level plain. PERMAFROST underlies most of it, so that during the brief growing season water from melted ice remains on or near the surface, and root systems are not deep. Characteristic vegetation is thus mosses, lichens, and dwarfed shrubs adapted to waterlogged, shallow soils. Animal life consists largely of insects, although species as large as caribou and polar bears move across tundra.

Tungsten see under LOGAN Mts., Northwest Territories.

Tunica County 460 sq mi/1191 sq km, pop. 8164, in NW Mississippi, in the N DELTA, on the Mississippi R. (W, NW). Its seat is the town of **Tunica** (pop. 1175). Overwhelmingly agricultural, producing cotton, rice, soybeans, corn, and timber, it is also extremely poor. According to the 1980 census, it was the poorest US county, with more than half of its residents (75% of whom are black) living below the poverty line; during the 1980s such localities as Sugar Ditch (in Tunica) attracted national attention as exemplars of problems of rural poverty and segregation. In the 1990s it was hoped that gambling casinos on the river (opened in 1992) would provide some economic improvement.

Tunkhannock Creek 30 mi/50 km long, a tributary of the Susquehanna R., in NE Pennsylvania. It rises in several branches in NE Susquehanna Co., and flows generally SW to join the Susquehanna at Tunkhannock. Martins Creek joins it from the N at Nicholson. The Tunkhannock or Nicholson Viaduct across the Tunkhannock is one of the largest concrete railroad bridges in the world, 240 ft/73 m high, and 2375 ft/724 m long.

Tuolumne Meadows see under YOSEMITE NATIONAL PARK, California.

Tuolumne River 155 mi/250 km long, in C California. It rises E of the Cathedral Range, near Mt. Lyell, in the SE of YOSEMITE NATIONAL PARK, and flows across the park, N of the Merced R., past Tuolumne Meadows and into the HETCH HETCHY Reservoir, which after 1908 inundated much of the famed Grand Canyon of the Tuolumne in order to supply San Francisco with water. Continuing WSW from the park into the Central Valley, it enters the Don Pedro Reservoir, impounded by the 585 ft/178 m–high New Don Pedro Dam (1971, replacing a 1923 structure), then flows to the SAN JOAQUIN R., 10 mi/16 km W of Modesto.

Tupelo city, pop. 30,685, seat of Lee Co., NE Mississippi, on the NATCHEZ TRACE Parkway, 47 mi/76 km ESE of Oxford. It is the shipping and processing center for a cotton growing and dairying region. The 1736 battle of Ackia (or Chickasaw Village), in which the Chickasaw defeated the French and prevented settlement in the area, took place somewhere just to the W. In 1859 the original settlement of Harrisburg was moved two miles E to the Mobile and Ohio railroad line; the new community, Gum Pond, was renamed Tupelo for the local tupelo (black gum) trees that supplied timber. During the Civil War a Union force led by A.J. Smith arrived here on July 14, 1864, aiming to prevent the Confederate forces of Stephen D. Lee and Nathan Bedford Forrest from harassing Sherman's march on Atlanta. Victorious in a bloody two-day battle, the Northerners were forced to retreat two days later because of low supplies. The Tupelo National Battlefield commemorates this battle. In the 20th century Tupelo took advantage of TENNESSEE VALLEY AUTHORITY power to industrialize and modernize, acquiring a variety of textile and other plants. The city is widely known as the birthplace (Jan. 8, 1935) of rock and roll legend Elvis Presley.

Turkey Point promontory in Dade Co., SE Florida, on BISCAYNE BAY, 9 mi/14 km ESE of Homestead, site of a nuclear power plant in operation since 1972.

Turkey River 135 mi/217 km long, in NE Iowa. It rises in Howard Co., and flows SE to the Mississippi R. 6 mi/10 km SSE of Guttenberg. It receives the Volga R. at Elkport.

Turlock city, pop. 42,198, Stanislaus Co., NC California, in the San Joaquin Valley, 13 mi/21 km SE of Modesto. Settled on the Central Pacific Railroad in the 1870s, it became an agricultural hub after the Turlock Irrigation District (begun 1877) drew on the waters of the Tuolumne R. (N), and is now a cattle, poultry, melon, other fruit, grain and hay, and vegetable producer. A California State University campus (1957) is here. **Turlock L.,** 17 mi/27 km NE, is a 3500-ac/1420-ha reservoir fed by the Tuolumne R. The Turlock L. State Recreation Area is on its N.

Turner Valley town, pop. 1352, SW Alberta, on the Sheep R., across from Black Diamond (town, pop. 1623), and 28 mi/45 km SSW of Calgary. Settled around 1900, it was the site of the discovery (1914) of the first major gas and oil field in Alberta, which led to a 30-year boom. By World War II, however, the fields had been depleted; the economy now depends on remaining petroleum services and tourism. The Kananaskis Country recreational area lies to the W.

turnpike **1.** historically (from 14th-century England) a road used only after paying a fee (toll), upon which a pike (barrier) was turned, allowing access. This system was employed from the 1780s through the mid 19th century to fund some US and Canadian roads. **2.** any of various 20th-century highways also collecting user fees (tolls) to defray costs of construction and maintenance. The building of the tax-supported US INTERSTATE HIGHWAY SYSTEM and other modern *freeways* has greatly reduced the role of toll highways in North America.

Turquoise Trail see under SANDIA Mts., New Mexico.

Turtle Bay residential and governmental section, Midtown East Side Manhattan, New York City. Lying N of KIPS BAY, the area was farmland in the 18th century, industrial by the mid 19th century. Its sheltered access on the East R. led to location of breweries, slaughterhouses, other manufactures, and eventually power plants here. The fashionable Tudor City apartment complex (1925–28) was built with almost no windows on the river side because of industrial odors. In 1946, however, industry was removed and Turtle Bay became home to the UNITED NATIONS, whose garden now extends over the cove that gave the area its name. Nathan Hale was executed in the vicinity on Sept. 22, 1776.

Turtle Creek small tributary of the Trinity R. in Dallas, Texas, running generally SSW from NORTH DALLAS, through HIGHLAND PARK, to Reverchon Park, 1.5 mi/2.5 km NNW of Downtown, thence into the Trinity. Forming a greenbelt on the W side of the city, Turtle Creek was the avenue of expansion of expensive housing as Dallas grew from the 1900s. Oak Lawn Blvd., which parallels (W) its lower course, and Turtle Creek Blvd. are noted for their apartment complexes.

Turtle Mountains plateau in Bottineau and Rolette counties, N North Dakota and S Manitoba. Rising 300–400 ft/91–122 m above the surrounding countryside, the formation runs 20 mi/32 km N–S and 40 mi/68 km E–W, and contains L. Metigoshe State Park and the INTERNATIONAL PEACE GARDEN. The Turtles have timber, small deposits of manganese, and numerous lakes, which accommodate year-round tourism. On the SE border of the plateau is the **Turtle Mountain Indian Reservation** (Ojibwa; pop. 4987).

Tuscaloosa city, pop. 77,759, seat of Tuscaloosa Co. (pop. 150,522), WC Alabama, 48 mi/77 km SW of Birmingham, on the Black Warrior R. at the Fall Line. The city is named for the Choctaw leader (Black Warrior) who defended S Alabama against Hernando de Soto in 1540. Established as a town by Creeks in 1809, it was burned four years later and the population forced to move west. The site was settled again in 1816, following the Creek War. Tuscaloosa served as the state capital in 1826–46, was occupied by Union troops in 1865, and was partially burned at the end of the Civil War. Agricultural until the 20th century, it now has diversified industries, based on agriculture and on nearby coal and mineral deposits. Manufactures include iron pipe, paper, tires, fertilizer, and lumber and cottonseed products. The other major factor in its life is the University of Alabama, founded in 1831, with some 20,000 students and numerous facilities. Stillman College (1876) is also here.

Tuscarawas County 570 sq mi/1476 sq km, pop. 84,090, in EC Ohio, intersected by the Tuscarawas R. Its seat is New Philadelphia. This largely rural county depends on agriculture (dairy, grain, and livestock) as well as manufacturing at Dover, New Philadelphia, and Newcomerstown. There are coal and clay deposits.

Tuscarawas River 125 mi/201 km long, rising in Summit Co., NE Ohio. It flows generally S through Stark and Tuscarawas counties past New Philadelphia, Midvale, Tuscarawas, and Newcomerstown, before crossing into Coshocton Co. It then flows W, joining the WALHONDING R. to form the MUSKINGUM R. at Coshocton. Several flood control dams are on the Tuscarawas and tributaries. Moravian missionaries led by David Zeisberger founded six Indian missions on the river in 1772–81.

Tuscarora Mountain ridge in SC Pennsylvania, part of the Appalachian system, extending some 75 mi/120 km between the Maryland border (SW) and the Juniata R. (NE).

Tuscarora Mountains N–S trending range, 40 mi/64 km long, between Tuscarora (N) and Carlin (S), in Elko and Eureka counties, NE Nevada. The mountains yielded the Young America silver vein in 1871 and the Grand Prize Bonanza vein in 1874, starting a gold and silver boom that lasted into the 1880s in the town of Tuscarora. In the mid 1980s, several gold mines reopened, bolstering the economy of communities such as ELKO (E). Recent activity has centered around Carlin, in the Humboldt R. valley.

Tusculum city, pop. 1918, Greene Co., E Tennessee, 4 mi/6 km E of Greeneville. It is the seat of Tusculum College (1794).

Tuscumbia city, pop. 8413, seat of Colbert Co., NW Alabama, one of the MUSCLE SHOALS area Quad Cities, on the Tennessee R., 6 mi/10 km SSW of Florence. The site of a Chickasaw town burned by American and Cherokee raiders in 1787, it has lumber mills and fertilizer factories. The birthplace (1880) and home of blind and deaf writer and lecturer Helen Keller is here. In the 1830s, the first railway W of the Allegheny Mts. ran from the center of town to the Tennessee, part of a design to bypass the Muscle Shoals that made Tuscumbia an important river port.

Tushar Mountains NW–SE trending range, 25 mi/40 km long, on the W edge of the Colorado Plateau, in Fishlake National Forest, SC Utah. The highest range in C Utah, they reach 12,173 ft/3710 m at Delano Peak, 17 mi/27 km NE of Beaver. Other peaks include Mt. Belknap (12,139 ft/3700 m) and Mt. Baldy (12,082 ft/3683 m). The mountains were heavily mined for gold in the late 19th and early 20th centuries.

Tuskegee city, pop. 12,257, seat of Macon Co., EC Alabama, 40 mi/64 km E of Montgomery. The site of an 18th-century French fort, it has a long agriculture-based history; industries include planing and grist mills and fertilizer and cottonseed oil plants. It is the seat of Tuskegee University, established in 1881 as Tuskegee Institute, an elementary and secondary school for black children. Founder Booker T. Washington served as principal from 1881 to his death in 1915. Botanist George Washington Carver worked at the institute as well (1896–1943), pursuing his famous experiments with such regional food plants as peanuts and sweet potatoes. During World War II, the Tuskegee Airmen, black fighter pilots, trained here. The **Tuskegee National Forest** (11,500 ac/4660 ha) lies NE of the city.

Tussey Mountain Appalachian ridge in SC Pennsylvania, rising 2225 ft/679 m and extending some 80 mi/130 km from the Maryland border (SW) to a point just E of State College (NE).

Tustin city, pop. 50,689, Orange Co., SW California, on the Santa Ana and Costa Mesa freeways, adjacent (E) to Santa Ana and 30 mi/48 km SE of Los Angeles. A small town, producing citrus products, into the 1960s, it is now a growing suburb with a variety of light industries. The Santa Ana Marine helicopter base is to the S. **Tustin Foothills** (unincorporated, pop. 24,358) is adjacent (E).

Tutuila see under AMERICAN SAMOA; PAGO PAGO.

Tuxedo Junction former streetcar crossing on the W side of Birmingham, Alabama, in a black residential and commercial section known in the 1920s–30s as Tuxedo Park. Composer Erskine Hawkins gave its name to his band's theme, which became a national hit just before World War II.

Tuxedo Park village, pop. 706, in Tuxedo township, Orange Co., SE New York, on the Ramapo R. and Tuxedo L., 15 mi/24 km NW of Nyack, just W of the New York State Thruway. Developed in 1886 by Pierre Lorillard, it began as a private residential community for the rich; its name became synonymous with wealth and power, and the dinner jackets worn here soon became known as *tuxedos*. Opened to somewhat more modest housing in 1941, it remains an affluent suburban community.

Tweedsmuir Provincial Park 3785 sq mi/9800 sq km, in WC British Columbia, 220 mi/350 km NNE of Vancouver. A vast, remote wilderness in the Coast Mts. (W) and Rainbow Range (E), it varies from dry prairie to ice-covered mountains. Headwaters of the E-flowing NECHAKO R. are in the N part, and the Bella Coola and Dean rivers flow W in the S. The largest British Columbia park is crossed in the S by Highway 20, between Bella Coola (W) and Williams Lake (E).

Twentieth-Century Limited see under NEW YORK CENTRAL RAILROAD.

Twentynine Palms city, pop. 11,821, San Bernardino Co., S California, at the edge of the COLORADO (S) and MOJAVE (N) deserts, 125 mi/200 km E of Los Angeles. It is bordered (N) by the huge Marine Corps Air Ground Combat Center, a "war games" facility that embraces the Bullion Mts. The Twentynine Palms (Luiseño) Indian Reservation is here. The city, an oasis and health resort on California Route 62, is also headquarters for the JOSHUA TREE NATIONAL PARK, just S.

Twillingate see under NOTRE DAME BAY, Newfoundland.

Twin Buttes Reservoir 9080 ac/3680 ha, in W Texas, 8 mi/13 km SW of SAN ANGELO. One of the largest earthfill dams built by the US Bureau of Reclamation here impounds the Middle and South Concho rivers; it is 8.1 mi/13 km long and reaches a height of 131 ft/40 m.

Twin Cities nickname for the adjacent cities of St. Paul and Minneapolis, in Ramsey and Hennepin counties, SE Minnesota.

Twin Falls city, pop. 27,591, seat of Twin Falls Co., SC Idaho, 135 mi/217 km SE of Boise. It is named for the Snake River's Twin Falls (200 ft/61 m), Shoshone and Auger, situated 4 mi/6 km NE of the city. Its population mushroomed in the early 20th century after the arrival of irrigation and the Union Pacific Railroad. The city is a trade, supply, and agricultural center for a fertile river valley that yields dairy products, fruits, and beet sugar. Manufactures include plastics and farm machinery. The College of Southern Idaho (1964) is here.

Twin Peaks **1.** prominences just over 900 ft/275 m high in C SAN FRANCISCO, California, at the SW end of Market St. After Mt. DAVIDSON (SW) the highest of the city's hills, they remain undeveloped and wooded. They were known to the Costanoans as an arguing married couple separated by the Great Spirit; Spanish settlers called them los Pechos de la Chola (the Indian Maiden's Breasts). Affluent residential neighborhoods like Forest Hill lie at their feet. The Sunset District is W, Noe Valley SE, the Castro NE. **2.** see under SNOQUALMIE R., Washington.

Twins, the two peaks of the Rocky Mts., in SW Alberta, North Twin (12,085 ft/3686 m) and South Twin (11,675 ft/3561 m), 50 mi/80 km SSE of Jasper, along the British Columbia border.

Twinsburg city, pop. 9606, Summit Co., NE Ohio, 18 mi/29 km NNE of Akron. The 6-ac/2-ha village square was donated by the Wilcox twins, Moses and Aaron, who settled the site in 1818. The Revco drugstore chain has its headquarters here.

Two-Hearted River 8 mi/13 km long, in Michigan's NE Upper Peninsula, formed by the confluence of several streams in Lake Superior State Forest, and flowing NE into L. Superior. It is a popular canoeing, fishing, and camping area, immortalized by Ernest Hemingway as "Big Two-Hearted River," although the trip his story described is thought to have involved another stream.

Two Rivers city, pop. 13,030, Manitowoc Co., EC Wisconsin, on L. Michigan, at the mouth of the East Twin and West Twin rivers, 5 mi/8 km NE of Manitowoc. It is a commercial fishing and cargo port and an industrial city, producing aluminum and electrical machinery. Fishermen settled here in 1836, and the economy was heavily dependent on sawmills and lumbering for most of the 19th century. A nuclear power facility at POINT BEACH is 8 mi/13 km to the N.

Tybee Island one of the SEA ISLANDS, in the Atlantic Ocean at the mouth of the Savannah R., 15 mi/24 km E of Savannah, in Chatham Co., E Georgia. Five mi/8 km long and 3 mi/5 km wide, and connected to the mainland by a causeway, it has beach resorts.

Tygart River also, **Tygarts Valley** or **Tygart Valley** 130 mi/210 km long, in C West Virginia. It rises in Randolph Co., in the MONONGAHELA NATIONAL FOREST, and flows generally N through Elkins, Philippi, and Grafton, where the Tygart R. Dam, built (1938) for flood control, impounds Tygart L. It then joins the West Fork at FAIRMONT, forming the Monongahela R. In the July 1861 Tygart Valley Campaign, Union forces drove Confederates S up the valley, winning battles at Laurel Hill (or Laurel Ridge) and Rich Mt., two sections of the same Allegheny ridge, on the W side of the river, on the same day.

Tyler city, pop. 75,450, seat of Smith Co., E Texas, midway between Dallas (W) and Shreveport, Louisiana. Settled in 1840, Tyler provided munitions to the Confederacy during the Civil War, and Camp Ford held up to 6000 Union prisoners. An agricultural and rail center when the EAST TEXAS OILFIELD was discovered in 1930, it became headquarters to many oil companies. Today it ships vegetables and fruit, and manufactures clothing, furniture, plastics, heating and cooling equipment, prefabricated houses, and ceramics. Tyler is famed for its flower industry. It is one of the world's largest rose producers; municipal gardens show many varieties, and the city hosts an annual Rose Festival and the East Texas Agricultural Fair. It is the seat of Texas College (1894), Tyler Junior College (1926), and the University of Texas at Tyler (1971).

Tyndall Air Force Base see under PANAMA CITY, Florida.

Tysons Corner unincorporated community, pop. 13,124, Fairfax Co., NE Virginia, 10 mi/16 km WNW of Washington, D.C. Situated on the BELTWAY and the Washington Dulles Access Road, this former farmland crossroads locality has become a commercial boom town, with shopping malls, office buildings, and a wide variety of service establishments.

U

Uharie see UWHARRIE.

Uinkaret Plateau tableland, c.6000 ft/1850 m high, extending N for about 50 mi/80 km from the GRAND CANYON, in N Arizona. In the ARIZONA STRIP, it lies between the Kanab (E) and Shivwits (W) plateaus. The **Uinkaret Mts.,** rising to 8028 ft/2447 m at Mt. Trumbull, are on the plateau. The Hurricane Cliffs separate the Uinkaret and Shivwits plateaus.

Uinta Mountains range of the Middle ROCKY Mts., extending 150 mi/240 km E–W, through the Wasatch-Cache and Ashley national forests, near the Wyoming (N) and Colorado (E) borders, in NE Utah. It is one of the few large E–W ranges in North America. The snow-covered, glaciated mountains are the most rugged in Utah, rising to 13,528 ft/4123 m at Kings Peak, the highest point in the state, 80 mi/130 km E of Salt Lake City. Other high peaks include Gilbert Peak (13,422 ft/4091 m), Mt. Emmons (13,428 ft/4093 m), Mt. Lovenia (13,220 ft/4029 m), and Tokewanna Peak (13,173 ft/4015 m). The 381–sq mi/987–sq km **High Uintas Wilderness Area,** in the C of the range, contains alpine meadows, coniferous forests, and hundreds of small lakes. The Bear, Weber, Provo, Uinta, and Duchesne rivers rise in the mountains, and the GREEN R. has cut a 3000 ft/915 m–deep red sandstone canyon through their NE portion, now in the FLAMING GORGE National Recreation Area. The 6768–sq mi/17,530–sq km **Uintah and Ouray Indian Reservation** (pop. 17,224; 15% Indian) lies along the S and to the SE, on the EAST TAVAPUTS PLATEAU, along the Green R. The 980,000-ac/400,000-ha (1530–sq mi/3966–sq km) **Uinta National Forest** is W and SW of the range, and is in fact largely in the WASATCH RANGE. The **Uinta Basin** is the section of the COLORADO Plateau S of the range.

Ukiah city, pop. 14,599, seat of Mendocino Co., NW California, in the Ukiah or Yokayo ("deep") Valley, on the Russian R., 100 mi/160 km NNW of San Francisco. The Latitude Observatory here is one of five established around 1900 by the International Geodetic Association at 39°08′ N. Mendocino College (1973) and a state hospital are also here. Winemaking, fruit packing, livestock raising, redwood lumbering, and the manufacture of masonite and plywood have all been important in this community founded in the 1850s on the road between San Francisco and Humboldt Bay (N). The Pomo, who lived in the area, were the subject of the paintings of Grace Hudson, whose home (1911) is now a noted museum.

Ulster County 1131 sq mi/2929 sq km, pop. 165,304, in SE New York, bounded by the Hudson R. (E). Most of the county is in the Catskill Mts., the E section is in the Hudson Highlands, and the SHAWANGUNK Mts. run diagonally N–S in its EC portion. Its seat, industrial hub, and largest city is KINGSTON. It is an exurban and agricultural county, growing apples, grapes, corn, and truck crops and raising dairy cattle and poultry. There are also popular resorts, including E parts of the BORSCHT BELT, in the SW.

Umatilla River 85 mi/140 km long, in NE Oregon. It rises in the Blue Mts. in Umatilla Co., in the N unit of the 1.4 million-ac/567,000-ha (2190–sq mi/5666–sq km) **Umatilla National Forest,** and flows W through the **Umatilla Indian Reservation** (271 sq mi/702 sq km; pop. 2502), then past Pendleton and NW to the Columbia R. at **Umatilla** (city, pop. 3046, Umatilla Co.), an 1860s gold rush supply center.

Umpqua River 110 mi/180 km long, in W Oregon, formed near ROSEBURG by the North Umpqua (100 mi/160 km long) and South Umpqua (95 mi/153 km long). Both headstreams rise on the W of the S CASCADE RANGE, in 985,000-ac/400,000-ha (1540–sq mi/3990–sq km) **Umpqua National Forest.** From Roseburg the Umpqua winds NW to the Pacific Ocean near Reedsport. Esp. in its upper branches, the Umpqua is a popular recreational river, and a noted trout and salmon spawning ground.

Unaka Range also, **Unaka Mountains** range of the W Appalachian chain, running NE–SW along the North Carolina–Tennessee border. It is sometimes described as comprising a series of ridges 2–15 mi/3–24 km wide, extending N into Virginia and S into Georgia and including the Iron, Holston, STONE, BALD, Chilhowee, GREAT SMOKY, and UNICOI ranges. These mountains are located largely within the Cherokee, Pisgah, and Nantahala national forests. The name is sometimes limited to the mountains in the vicinity of the Nolichucky R., rising to a high point of 5258 ft/1604 m at **Unaka Mt.,** 5 mi/8 km E of Erwin, Tennessee.

Unalaska Island one of the FOX Is., in the E ALEUTIAN Is., in SW Alaska. Some 75 mi/120 km E–W and 5–30 mi/8–48 km N–S, the windy, treeless island is a center for fishing, fish processing, and trapping by its Aleut pop. Settled by Russians in the 1760s, it was the center of fur trading activities in the Aleutians until the end of the 18th century. Dutch Harbor, on Amaknak I. in Unalaska Bay, on the NE side, is the site of a Naval base. The city of **Unalaska** (pop. 3089), immediately S, the oldest European settlement in the Aleutians, has a large Russian Orthodox church.

Uncle Tom's Cabin Historic Site see under DRESDEN, Ontario.

Uncompahgre National Forest 1.1 million ac/445,000 ha

(1720 sq mi/4450 sq km), on the Uncompahgre Plateau and the N slopes of the SAN JUAN Mts., in SW Colorado.

Uncompahgre Plateau NW–SE oriented tableland, 60 mi/100 km long, in SW Colorado, in the Canyon Lands section of the Colorado Plateau. The **Uncompahgre R.**, a 75 mi/120 km–long S tributary of the GUNNISON R., is to its E. **Uncompahgre Peak** (14,309 ft/4361 m) is E of the river, in the San Juan Mts.

Underground in Seattle, Washington: see under PIONEER SQUARE.

Underground Atlanta commercial district and tourist magnet in downtown Atlanta, Georgia, immediately S of FIVE POINTS. The city's 19th-century commercial center was covered by viaducts over rail lines in the 1890s–1940s, leaving an area regarded askance as "Under the Viaduct." Renovated in 1969, it was closed again in 1980, redeveloped by the city and the Rouse Corporation, and reopened in 1989. Housing three levels of shops, restaurants, and night clubs, it now receives an estimated 10 million visitors yearly.

Underground City French, **Ville souterraine** growing complex of underground, or protected aboveground, passageways, arcades, halls, and other spaces in downtown MONTRÉAL, Québec, connecting commercial, cultural, entertainment, and convention centers with each other and with the city's Métro (subway) system and train and bus stations. Now covering some 19 mi/30 km, it began in the early 1960s with the success of the Place Ville-Marie, an office and commercial complex (next to the Square DORCHESTER) that occupied a long-vacant construction site.

Underground Railroad metaphor used from the 1840s for the loose network of routes by which fugitive slaves left the SOUTH and escaped to hospitable places in the Free States (the North) or to Canada, esp. Upper Canada (Ontario). While the routes (and modes) of escape were varied, and aid along the way was most likely to be given on the spur of the moment, the "railroad" was highly publicized, in the language of a then new technology, as having "conductors" who took or directed "passengers" from "station" to "station." Escapees were mostly from the Upper South, and crossed into free territory esp. in Ohio and Indiana, but there were also important (and highly organized) routes through the Philadelphia area—where Quakers and others maintained centers in such communities as Germantown, Pennsylvania, and Lawnside, New Jersey—as well as farther to the W, where Nebraska City, Nebraska, and Janesville, Wisconsin, were among "stations." Major "conductors" included Harriet Tubman, originally from Cambridge, Maryland, who led many to her home in Auburn, New York; and Levi Coffin, of Newport (now FOUNTAIN CITY), Indiana, who made that community known as the "Grand Central Station" of the Railroad. Among settlements at the "end of the line" in Ontario were AMHERSTBURG, CHATHAM, and DRESDEN. Estimates of the number of "passengers" go as high as 75,000.

Ungava also, **Labrador-Ungava** major peninsular region of E Canada, now roughly 80% forming the Québec district of NOUVEAU-QUÉBEC, the remainder forming LABRADOR. Covering some 550,000 sq mi/1.42 million sq km on the Canadian Shield, it was HUDSON'S BAY COMPANY land, then (1869–1912) part of the Northwest Territories. In 1912 it became part of Québec, and in 1927 the E portion was adjudicated part of Labrador. Ungava is bounded by Hudson Bay (W), the Hudson Strait (N), and the Atlantic Ocean (E). Its northernmost extension, some 400 mi/640 km N–S and 350 mi/560 km wide, is known as the **Ungava Peninsula;** on its E is **Ungava Bay,** a 180 mi/290 km–wide inlet of the Hudson Strait. A region of tundra in the N, northern forest in the S, Ungava is sparsely populated, with Inuit and some Cree (S) communities and a handful of mining and governmental settlements.

Unicity see under WINNIPEG, Manitoba.

Unicoi Mountains subrange of the W Appalachian chain, sometimes considered part of the UNAKA RANGE, along the North Carolina–Tennessee border, between the Little Tennessee (N) and Hiwassee (S) rivers. In Cherokee and Nantahala national forests, the range includes Haw Knob (5472 ft/1668 m) and the SNOWBIRD Mts., an E extension.

unincorporated community in this book designates what the US Census Bureau now calls a *census designated place* (CDP), and formerly called an *unincorporated place.* It is the "statistical counterpart" of an incorporated place such as a city, borough, town, or village. Primarily suburban, unincorporated communities also include such urban entities as Honolulu, Hawaii.

Union **1.** township, pop. 50,024, Union Co., NE New Jersey, 4 mi/6 km SW of Newark. It was settled by colonists from Connecticut (1749), and originally called Connecticut Farms. The site of a 1780 battle, it was separated from Elizabethtown in 1808. Today such goods as steel, metal products, paint, lacquer, pharmaceuticals, and chemicals are manufactured. Union is the seat of Kean College of New Jersey (1855). **2.** city, pop. 9836, seat of Union Co., NW South Carolina, 26 mi/42 km SE of Spartanburg. It was settled late in the 18th century around the log cabin Union Church, which welcomed both Presbyterians and Episcopalians. On the Southern Railway, it has cotton, hosiery, and lumber mills, and also produces peaches, fertilizer, and bakery products.

Union City **1.** city, pop. 53,762, Alameda Co., NC California, on Alameda Creek and E San Francisco Bay, 15 mi/24 km SSE of Oakland, between Fremont (S) and Hayward (N). Incorporated in 1959, it is a residential and industrial suburb with nurseries, salt evaporators, a sugar refinery, and iron, steel, and aluminum plants. **2.** city, pop. 8375, Fulton Co., NW Georgia, 14 mi/23 km SW of Atlanta, a growing residential suburb. **3.** city, pop. 58,102, Hudson Co., NE New Jersey, on the Hudson R. across from Manhattan, 3 mi/5 km NE of Jersey City. It was created in 1925 from the consolidation of West Hoboken and Union Hill. It has long been known for the manufacture of embroidery and silk; also produced are soaps, perfume, corrugated paper, and light bulbs. The city has a large population of Latin American immigrants, and is a Hispanic hub, with particularly strong ties to the Cuban community in Miami, Florida. **4.** city, pop. 10,513, seat of Obion Co., extreme NW Tennessee, 5 mi/8 km S of the Kentucky border. It is a transportation hub for an agricultural area producing corn, cotton, soybeans, dairy goods, and livestock. Industries include meatpacking and the manufacture of textiles, auto parts, and clothing. REELFOOT L., 15 mi/24 km W, is one of a number of nearby recreational assets.

Union County **1.** 103 sq mi/268 sq km, pop. 493,819, in NE New Jersey, bounded by the Passaic R. (NW) and by Newark Bay and the ARTHUR KILL (E). Its seat is ELIZABETH, an important port and transportation hub. Part of the New York metropolitan area, the county is highly industrialized; products include chemicals, steel, foodstuffs, machinery, pharmaceuticals, tools, electronic and automotive parts, and automobiles. Industrial centers include LINDEN, PLAINFIELD, and RAHWAY. Among primarily residential communities are CRANFORD, ROSELLE, SCOTCH PLAINS, and SUMMIT. **2.** 437 sq mi/1132 sq km, pop. 31,969, in WC Ohio. Its seat is MARYSVILLE, which has some manufacturing. The county is largely rural, depending on agriculture (dairy, grain, livestock, and poultry). Natural resources include sand, gravel, and limestone.

Uniondale unincorporated village, pop. 20,328, in Hempstead town, Nassau Co., SE New York, in WC Long Island, immediately E of Hempstead. It is primarily residential. The Nassau Veterans Memorial Coliseum (1972; hockey, etc.) is here.

Union Lake locality in Oakland Co., SE Michigan, 8 mi/13 km WSW of Pontiac. It is a residential community on Union L., one of the many small lakes surrounding Pontiac. The Highland Lakes campus of Oakland Community College is here; across the lake (SW) is Proud L. State Recreation Area.

Union Pacific Railroad organized in 1862 as one of two lines (the other was the CENTRAL PACIFIC) to build the "Pacific Railroad," connecting the Atlantic and Pacific oceans. For its part in crossing the West, the UP was awarded sections of PUBLIC LANDS as well as loans based on mileage completed. When it met the Central Pacific (on May 10, 1869) at PROMONTORY, Utah, it had passed through Fremont and North Platte, Nebraska; Julesburg, Colorado; Sidney, Nebraska; Cheyenne, Laramie, Green River, and Evanston, Wyoming; and Ogden, Utah. The UP subsequently built NW from Granger, Wyoming, to Portland, Oregon, via Pocatello and Boise, Idaho, and acquired a number of smaller western lines. In 1900–13, before the government broke up the combination, it was merged with the SOUTHERN PACIFIC; during this period the Lucin Cutoff, built across the Great Salt L. past Promontory Point, shortened the main line significantly. Today the UP remains one of the largest US railroads; its system extends from Chicago and New Orleans W across Texas and via the original main line to both California and the Pacific Northwest.

Union Square **1.** 2.5 ac/1 ha, in the heart of downtown SAN FRANCISCO, California, just N of Market St. Nob Hill is NW, Chinatown N, the Financial District NE. Given to the city in 1850 and named during the Civil War, it is a center of varied activities including shopping and street entertainment. The St. Francis Hotel, on the W side, has been central to the city's social life. **2.** historic area in downtown Baltimore, Maryland, 15 blocks W of the INNER HARBOR. It comprises primarily three-story brick row houses. The H.L. Mencken House, where the writer spent most of his life, is here. Hollins Market is just E. **3.** urban park, lower Manhattan, New York City. Named for the junction of the BOWERY and BROADWAY, it was laid out in 1811. The area was fashionable, then in the 1850s became New York's theater district. After the theaters moved up Broadway, beginning in the 1870s, Union Square became a working-class shopping center and a scene of radical political activity. It has undergone renovation in the 1930s and again in the 1980s.

Union Station name in various US cities for a rail station or terminal serving a number of passenger lines, either separately owned or merged into one system. Among the best-known is Union Station in Washington, D.C., just NNE of CAPITOL HILL, designed in the 1890s Beaux-Arts style by Daniel Burnham. Serving the Baltimore & Ohio, Pennsylvania, and various Southern railroads, it fell into decline into the 1970s, and has since been extensively redeveloped, reopening in 1988 as a combination terminal/mall, now a popular tourist attraction. Chicago's 1925 Union Station, just W of the LOOP and the Chicago R., served the Pennsylvania, the Milwaukee Road, and other lines. In Los Angeles, the 1939 Spanish Colonial–Art Deco Union Station, immediately E of EL PUEBLO DE LOS ANGELES, was built on land near the Old Plaza that had been at the center of the city's BARRIO. All of these stations are now served by AMTRAK. The first urban station serving several railroads was Boston's SOUTH STATION; New York's 1910 Pennsylvania Station is another prominent example.

Union Stockyards historical industrial site in Chicago, Illinois, opened in 1865 along the South Branch of the Chicago R. (since 1900 the Chicago Sanitary and Ship Canal), 2 mi/3 km SW of the Loop. Constituting a square mile (2.6 sq km) of holding pens and the packing plants of such companies as Swift and Armour, the complex processed some 12 million animals yearly. Its businesses brought waves of immigrants into Chicago, particularly from Eastern Europe. Settling at first in adjoining BACK OF THE YARDS (S), BRIGHTON PARK and BRIDGEPORT (W), and other nearby neighborhoods, they spread out across the city. After a long decline, the yards ceased operation entirely in 1971, and the area entered a period of redevelopment.

Uniontown city, pop. 12,034, seat of Fayette Co., SW Pennsylvania, 45 mi/72 km SSE of Pittsburgh, on Redstone Creek just W of Chestnut Ridge, in the foothills of the Allegheny Mts., on Route 40 (the former NATIONAL ROAD). An early battle in the French and Indian War was fought July 3, 1754, at Fort Necessity, built by George Washington; the location is now part of Fort Necessity National Battlefield, 9 mi/14 km SE. Formerly a coal producing center, Uniontown now provides trade and marketing services and has diversified manufacturing, including aircraft parts, steel scaffolding, and clothing. It also produces lumber, coke, and water and gas meters. The Fayette campus of Pennsylvania State University (1934) is here.

United Empire Loyalists see LOYALISTS.

United Nations international organization that occupies land on the East Side of Manhattan, New York City, along the East River from 42nd to 48th streets in TURTLE BAY. On its 18-acre/7.3-ha site, a gift of John D. Rockefeller, Jr., facilities including the Secretariat Building and the General Assembly Hall were built 1947–53. Other New York sites occupied by the UN before the Turtle Bay facilities opened include the old New York City Building at FLUSHING MEADOWS-CORONA PARK (1946–49) and the village of LAKE SUCCESS, in Nassau Co. (1949–51).

United Province of Canada see PROVINCE OF CANADA.

United States of America federal republic, chiefly in North America; land area 3,536,342 sq mi/9,159,126 sq km (total area: 3,787,425 sq mi/9,809,431 sq km); 1990 pop. 248,709,873 (109.8% of 1980). Federal capital: WASHINGTON, in the District of Columbia. The US comprises 50 states—ALABAMA, ALASKA, ARIZONA, ARKANSAS, CALIFORNIA, COLORADO, CONNECTICUT, DELAWARE, FLORIDA, GEORGIA, HAWAII, IDAHO, ILLINOIS, INDIANA, IOWA, KANSAS, KENTUCKY, LOUISIANA, MAINE, MARYLAND, MASSACHUSETTS, MICHIGAN, MINNESOTA, MISSISSIPPI, MISSOURI, MONTANA, NEBRASKA, NEVADA, NEW HAMPSHIRE, NEW JERSEY, NEW MEXICO, NEW YORK,

NORTH CAROLINA, NORTH DAKOTA, OHIO, OKLAHOMA, OREGON, PENNSYLVANIA, RHODE ISLAND, SOUTH CAROLINA, SOUTH DAKOTA, TENNESSEE, TEXAS, UTAH, VERMONT, VIRGINIA, WASHINGTON, WEST VIRGINIA, WISCONSIN, and WYOMING—and the DISTRICT OF COLUMBIA. Residents of its overseas territories—the Commonwealth of PUERTO RICO, the United States VIRGIN ISLANDS, GUAM, AMERICAN SAMOA, the various PACIFIC ISLANDS, and NAVASSA I. (in the Caribbean)—as well as residents of the District of Columbia, enjoy varying degrees of self-government and political representation. The US has an elected bicameral (House of Representatives and Senate) Congress, with an elected president as the administrative head of state. In governmental theory, the states created the nation, by ratifying the 1787 Constitution; in practice, the Federal government has continually increased its supremacy over the states. The US shares land borders with Mexico (S) and Canada (N, largely along the FORTY-NINTH PARALLEL); its other nearest neighbors include Russia (across the BERING STRAIT, NW), the Bahamas and Bermuda (off the SE coast), and Cuba (S of Florida). Hawaii is the only US state not part of North America. The name *America* derives from that of Italian navigator Amerigo Vespucci (1454–1512), and has been used for the continent since the 16th century.

Unity town, pop. 1817, Waldo Co., SC Maine. It is on Unity Pond, 16 mi/26 km NE of Waterville. Unity College (1965) is here. Industries include agriculture, lumbering, food processing, and the manufacture of wood products.

Universal City **1.** SE SAN FERNANDO VALLEY section of LOS ANGELES, California, 9 mi/14 km NW of Downtown and just N of the CAHUENGA PASS. With the arrival of the 420-ac/170-ha **Universal Studios** from Hollywood in the 1960s, it quickly became a center of the US entertainment industry. **2.** city, pop. 13,057, Bexar Co., SC Texas, 14 mi/23 km NE of downtown San Antonio, just off Interstate 35. One of a cluster of largely residential suburbs, it is adjacent (NW) to RANDOLPH AIR FORCE BASE.

University see under OXFORD, Mississippi.

University Center **1.** noncensus, nonpostal designation for the vicinity of two SC Michigan colleges, between BAY CITY (NE) and SAGINAW (SW). Delta College (1957) is in Bay Co., 5 mi/8 km SW of Bay City. Saginaw Valley College (1963) is about 2 mi/3 km SSE, in Saginaw Co. **2.** institutional, residential, and commercial district of NE SEATTLE, Washington, 4 mi/6 km NNE of Downtown, N of the L. Washington Ship Canal (with Union Bay on the E, PORTAGE BAY on the W). It is home to the 33,500-student University of Washington (1861), whose campus was the site of the 1909 Alaska-Yukon-Pacific Exposition. The area around the university has a diverse pop. and many popular stores.

University Circle cultural and educational complex in Cleveland, Ohio, 5 mi/8 km E of PUBLIC SQUARE. Laid out in 1895 according to a 20-year master plan, it has many of the city's leading cultural institutions. These include the Cleveland Museum of Art, the Natural Science Museum, the Western Reserve Historical Society, and the Cleveland Orchestra's Severance Hall.

University City **1.** residential section of SAN DIEGO, California, 9 mi/14 km NNW of Downtown and immediately E of La Jolla, developed along the S of the University of California: San Diego campus (1960). **2.** city, pop. 40,087, St. Louis Co., EC Missouri, 8 mi/13 km WNW of downtown St. Louis. On the city line, it is a residential suburb. Washington University (1853) is here. **3.** neighborhood in W Philadelphia, Pennsylvania, home to educational institutions including the University of Pennsylvania and Drexel University, as well as the Civic Center, several hospitals, and the University City Science Center.

University Heights **1.** academic and residential section of SAN DIEGO, California, 6 mi/10 km NE of Downtown, E of Mission Valley and N of East San Diego. San Diego State University was established (1897) in this STREETCAR SUBURB, and fostered residential growth in the area. **2.** city, pop. 14,790, in Cuyahoga Co., NE Ohio, a residential suburb 8 mi/13 km E of Cleveland. John Carroll University (1886) is here.

University Park **1.** residential and institutional section of SE DENVER, Colorado, near the city line, 6 mi/10 km SSE of Downtown, home since 1891 to the University of Denver (1864). **University Hills,** just SE, is similar. **2.** village, pop. 6204, Cook and Will counties, NE Illinois, on Thorn Creek, 30 mi/48 km SW of Chicago and 8 mi/13 km W of the Indiana border. The seat of Governors' State University (1969), it is at the outer edge of the Chicago metropolitan area. **3.** town, pop. 604, Mahaska Co., SC Iowa, a suburb immediately SE of OSKALOOSA. It is the seat of Vennard College (1910). **4.** see under COLLEGE PARK, Maryland. **5.** see under STATE COLLEGE, Pennsylvania. **6.** city, pop. 22,259, Dallas Co., NE Texas, surrounded by N Dallas (5 mi/8 km N of Downtown), with HIGHLAND PARK adjacent (S). After Southern Methodist University was founded in 1911, the community grew around it, developing into a residential suburb.

University Place unincorporated community, pop. 27,701, Pierce Co., WC Washington, on Puget Sound, a residential suburb 4 mi/6 km WSW of downtown Tacoma. Around the turn of the 20th century, the community was selected to be the home of the University of Puget Sound. The project was never realized (the university is in Tacoma), but the name remained.

U.P. familiar abbreviation for Michigan's UPPER PENINSULA.

Up Country upland NW South Carolina, comprising part of the PIEDMONT but also including a small section of the Blue Ridge Mts., as distinguished from the Low Country, the SE portion of the state, which is part of the ATLANTIC COASTAL PLAIN. Distinct physical attributes of the two areas led to the development of distinct cultures. The rolling terrain, swift rivers, harder rocks, red clay, and sandy loams of the Up Country, settled largely in the mid 18th century from the north, encouraged the development of smaller farms and of industry. In contrast, the level alluvial regions of the Low Country, settled from the late 17th century by large proprietors, many from the West Indies, allowed the development of extensive rice, indigo, and later cotton, plantations.

Upland **1.** city, pop. 63,374, San Bernardino Co., SW California, at the S foot of the San Gabriel Mts., adjacent (N) to Ontario and 35 mi/56 km E of Los Angeles. Incorporated in 1906 in a citrus growing area, it has a variety of light manufactures and has grown steadily since the 1950s as a residential suburb. **2.** town, pop. 3295, Grant Co., EC Indiana, 11 mi/18 km SE of Marion. In an agricultural and lumber milling region, it is the seat of Taylor University (1846).

Upper Arlington city, pop. 34,128, Franklin Co., C Ohio, on the Scioto R., 5 mi/8 km SW of Columbus, of which it is a commuter suburb.

Upper Canada historic province, created from the W half of the Province of Quebec in 1791; the predecessor of modern Ontario, including lands W of the Ottawa R. and S of RUPERT'S LAND. Lightly populated before the American Revolution, the area quickly became home to many LOYALISTS, fostered by policies of the British government. Administration under the 1774 Quebec Act was unacceptable to the new residents, who wanted more American-style local democracy; SEIGNEURIES were abolished and free TOWNSHIPS established. Clergy Reserves (some also in Lower Canada) were established to support the Anglican church, Crown Reserves to pay government costs, both through rents. York (Toronto) gradually became dominant. In 1840, following rebellions both in Upper Canada (against oligarchy) and in LOWER CANADA (by the PATRIOTES against anglophone hegemony), Upper Canada became Canada West, part of the United PROVINCE OF CANADA (1841–67).

Upper Canada Village see under MORRISBURG, Ontario.

Upper Darby township, pop. 81,177, Delaware Co., S Pennsylvania, adjacent (SW) to Philadelphia, on Darby Creek. Its development has been closely linked with that of Philadelphia. While primarily residential, it has some light industry, producing aircraft parts, plastic, wood, and rubber products, and communications equipment. DREXEL HILL, Stonehurst, and Highland Park are among the township's communities.

Upper East Side see under EAST SIDE, New York City.

Upper Hill residential neighborhood in Pittsburgh, Pennsylvania, 1 mi/1.6 km E of the GOLDEN TRIANGLE. It is a middle-class black community of mostly small homes dating to the early 20th century.

Upper Iowa River 160 mi/258 km long, in Minnesota and Iowa. It rises in Mower Co., SE Minnesota, and flows ESE into Iowa at Chester, then generally E, past Decorah and through limestone cliffs to the Mississippi R., NW of Lansing. The Upper Iowa is one of the state's best-known scenic and recreational rivers. Its cedar-covered ledges are in places as high as 400 ft/122 m.

Upper Mississippi River National Wildlife and Fish Refuge about 200,000 ac/81,000 ha along both sides of, and on islands in, the Mississippi R., for 260 mi/420 km between the area of Wabasha, Minnesota, where the Chippewa R. joins the Mississippi (N) and the confluence of the Wapsipinicon R. and the Mississippi, 16 mi/26 km NE of Davenport, Iowa (S). Its headquarters are at Winona, Minnesota.

Upper Montclair residential section of MONTCLAIR, Essex Co., NE New Jersey, about 2 mi/3 km N of the town center. It is an upper-middle-class suburb. Montclair State College (1908) and Mountainside Park, with noted iris gardens, are here.

Upper Peninsula the broad N section of Michigan, with shores on lakes Superior (N), Michigan (S), and Huron (SE). It is also bordered by Wisconsin (W) and the St. Mary's R. (E). To the N and E lies Ontario, to the S, Michigan's LOWER PENINSULA. It was awarded to Michigan with statehood in 1837, ending conflicts with Ohio over the TOLEDO STRIP. The building of the MACKINAC BRIDGE (1957) made the area easily accessible from the Lower Peninsula. The Upper Peninsula is characterized by vast stretches of wilderness with world-renowned hunting and fishing. This region also has prodigious wood and mineral resources, particularly iron and copper, and has supplied both US and Canadian industry with ore for more than a century. Much of the area is covered by national and state forests. The PICTURED ROCKS NATIONAL LAKESHORE is on its NE coast, and the Seney National Wildlife Refuge is in the NE interior. The Upper Peninsula is sparsely populated, with only 3% (about 314,000 residents) of Michigan's population on close to 30% of the state's land.

Upper Saddle River borough, pop. 7198, Bergen Co., NE New Jersey, 11 mi/18 km NE of Paterson, and 2 mi/3 km S of the New York borders, on the SADDLE R. Primarily a residential suburb, it is also the site of several corporate headquarters.

Upper Sandusky city, pop. 5906, Wyandot Co., NW Ohio, on the Sandusky R., 19 mi/31 km NNW of Marion. Founded in 1843, it was laid out on the site of a Wyandot tribal center; a mission had been in the area since the 1820s. A mill town in a productive agricultural area that also had limestone quarries, it developed various industries. The Wyandot were moved to Kansas in the 1840s, but their museum remains here.

Upper South, the see under the SOUTH.

Upper Town **1.** section of OTTAWA, Ontario, W of the Rideau Canal, on high limestone cliffs on the S bank of the Ottawa R. The site before 1859 of a British military installation, it became home to the capital's government buildings, on PARLIAMENT HILL and in surrounding neighborhoods, and to the English-speaking, Protestant city that developed W of the older LOWER TOWN. **2.** French, **Haute-Ville** parts of QUÉBEC CITY, Québec, atop 320-ft/98-m Cap-Diamant. The Upper Town was settled after the LOWER TOWN, and long had chiefly military and religious (including the 1639 Ursuline Convent) establishments, while commerce and residences crowded below along the river. It was this high ground, fortified first by the French in the 17th century, and after 1759 by the British, that made Québec City the "Gibraltar of North America." On the SW, the French walls were replaced, in 1820–31, by the Citadel, still a military establishment, originally positioned to prevent attack across the PLAINS OF ABRAHAM or from the river below. In the 19th century businesses and residences located in the Upper Town, now the city's center. The Grande Allée, its major street, leads from the walls into the city's W suburbs, passing much of Québec's governmental and cultural establishment. The CHÂTEAU FRONTENAC dominates the Upper Town's E end.

Upper West Side see under WEST SIDE, New York City.

Upstate in New York, imprecisely defined region N of, and presumably not under the controlling influence of, New York City. While it almost always includes any area from Putnam Co. N, whether it includes Westchester Co. seems to depend on the speaker's intentions. Its opposite, Downstate, is a much less encountered term, used to distinguish something, such as an institution in New York City, from its counterpart Upstate.

Uptown **1.** in many, particularly older, cities, residential or residential/commercial districts as distinguished from DOWNTOWN. More desirable areas of cities tended to be on higher ground, away from industrial and commercial waterfronts, at times also upwind from mill smoke and odors. **2.** in SAN DIEGO, California, sections S of Mission Valley, SE of Old Town, N and W of Balboa Park, and W of University Heights and East San Diego. A collection of districts settled as suburbs from the late 19th century, it includes HILLCREST, MISSION HILLS, BANKERS' HILL, and MIDDLETOWN. **3.** in Chicago, Illinois, residential and commercial district on the North Side, 6 mi/10 km NNW of the Loop, flanked on the E by LINCOLN PARK, on L. Michigan. EDGEWATER is N, LAKE VIEW S. **4.** in New Orleans, Louisiana, section upriver of CANAL St., or W and SW of DOWNTOWN. Settled in the 19th century by Americans, it includes the GARDEN DISTRICT, IRISH CHANNEL, and CARROLLTON, and the Tulane, Newcomb, Loyola, and Xavier campuses. **5.** commercial area in Minneapolis, Minnesota, S of Downtown. It emerged in the 1980s as a trendy shopping and entertainment locale for young professionals and artists. **6.** in Manhattan, New York City, those sections above 59th St. (or the base of CENTRAL PARK, or 57th St.). Uptown includes the Upper West Side and Upper East Side, but perhaps most importantly HARLEM. **7.** in CHARLOTTE, North Carolina, the central business district. **8.** neighborhood of Pittsburgh, Pennsylvania, immediately E of the GOLDEN TRIANGLE, between the HILL and the BLUFF. Centered on FIFTH AVENUE, it has 19th-century row houses and commercial buildings chiefly serving wholesalers. Some recent gentrification of the decayed housing stock has occurred.

Uranium City see under L. ATHABASCA, Saskatchewan.

urban **1.** traditionally, of or relating to towns or cities, which were perceived as being densely populated and having a life based on commercial and other nonagricultural pursuits; the opposite of RURAL. **2.** in US Census terminology, of or relating to urbanized areas, defined as complexes with one or more central places and "densely settled surrounding territory," combining to include a pop. of at least 50,000. The surrounding territory (**urban fringe**) has a pop. density of at least 1000/sq mi (386/sq km). The Census enumerates as "urban" all residents in urbanized areas *and* in other incorporated or unincorporated places (cities, boroughs, villages, towns, unincorporated communities) with a pop. of at least 2500; all other persons live in rural areas. See also SUBURB; METROPOLITAN AREA. **3.** in Canadian Census terminology, of or relating to pop. centers of "dense concentration," defined as places with a pop. of at least 1000 at a density of at least 400/sq km (1036/sq mi).

Urbana **1.** city, pop. 36,344, seat of Champaign Co., Illinois, immediately E of Champaign. The University of Illinois has dominated both Urbana and Champaign since it was established in 1867. The huge school includes the Krannert Art Museum, Krannert Center for the Performing Arts, Museum of Natural History, and World Heritage Museum. Assembly Hall, one of the world's largest edge-supported domes, is also on the campus. Agricultural trading and processing and the manufacture of electronic components and metal castings are also important to the city's economy. Urbana was settled in the 1820s. **2.** city, pop. 11,353, seat of Champaign Co., WC Ohio, 13 mi/21 km NNE of Springfield. It is situated in a rich farming and livestock area. Among its principal manufactures are plastics, dies, machine tools, and automobile parts. It is the seat of Urbana Junior College (1850).

Urbandale city, pop. 23,500, Polk Co., C Iowa, immediately NW of Des Moines. Mostly a residential suburb, it also has some light industry and warehousing.

urban homesteading see under HOMESTEAD.

urban renewal name given in the 1950s to comprehensively planned attacks on the problems of the INNER CITY. Essentially processes of slum clearance, urban renewal programs concentrated on removing deteriorating housing, which was replaced with new housing or with roadways, public buildings, parks, etc. Where new housing was not the result, inhabitants of the affected area were dispersed; over time, protests by civil rights and community groups led toward more emphasis being placed on rehabilitation of existing housing stock.

Ursuline Convent see under VIEUX CARRÉ, New Orleans, Louisiana.

US 1 popularly, **Route 1** designated 1925 as the first numbered element of the INTERSTATE HIGHWAY SYSTEM, running some 2225 mi/3580 km between Calais, Maine, and Key West, Florida, and later extended another 207 mi/333 km N to Fort Kent, Maine. In the Northeast, it follows the routes of POST ROADS, including the BOSTON POST ROAD, in coastal areas of the older states. South of Baltimore, Maryland, it passes farther inland, through FALL LINE and other newer cities like Washington, D.C.; Richmond, Virginia; Raleigh, North Carolina; Columbia, South Carolina; and Augusta, Georgia, before returning to the coast at Jacksonville, Florida. It then proceeds down Florida's Atlantic coast to Miami, thence to Key West. The route adopted was in places the King's Highway of the Colonial period.

Utah state of W US, one of the MOUNTAIN STATES; 1990 pop. 1,722,850 (117.9% of 1980; rank: 35th); area 84,904 sq mi/ 219,901 sq km (rank: 13th); admitted to Union 1896 (45th). Capital and most populous city: SALT LAKE CITY. Other leading cities: WEST VALLEY CITY, PROVO, SANDY, OREM, OGDEN. Utah is bordered E by Colorado; N by Wyoming, which indents it in the NE; W by Nevada; and S by Arizona. In the SE, at the FOUR CORNERS, it also touches New Mexico. Almost two-thirds of the state, in the SE, lies on the COLORADO PLATEAU. Within this region are the Uinta Basin (NE, at the foot of the Uinta Mts.) and the Canyonlands, through which the COLORADO R. and its tributaries, including the GREEN and San Juan rivers, drain to the SW. On the W, Utah comprises part of the GREAT BASIN, including, in the NW, the GREAT SALT L. and its desert, with the BONNEVILLE SALT FLATS, parts of the bed of the glacial L. Bonneville. In the SC, the NNE–SSW trending PAHVANT RANGE, around which the SEVIER R. flows (into a SINK), separates the Great Basin from the Colorado Plateau. In the NE are segments of the Middle ROCKY Mts., including the N–S WASATCH RANGE, which extends into the state's C, and the E–W (unusual in this orientation) UINTA Mts., which in the NE include KINGS PEAK, at 13,528 ft/4126 m the state's high point. The vast majority of Utah's pop., and almost all its urban development, are in a strip along the W base of the Wasatches, on Great Salt and UTAH lakes, called the Wasatch Front. Salt Lake City, the first (1847) city in the area, now lies at the center of an agricultural, industrial, residential, and institutional complex established by the state's Mormon settlers. Throughout the rest of Utah, there are few cities of size. Home to the Ute (from which it takes its name), Paiute, and Goshiute, with seminomadic Navajos in the SE, the region was part of the large Southwestern territory claimed by Spain and after 1821 by Mexico. The 1776 Escalante expedition, striking NW from Santa Fe, New Mexico, in search of a route to California, wound through the SC along part of what became known as the SPANISH TRAIL. In the early 19th century, fur trappers worked in the mountains. From the 1840s, American explorers traveled in Utah, and California-bound parties crossed the Great Salt Lake Desert, but it was in July 1847, when Mormons under Brigham Young arrived in the Salt Lake Valley at the end of their trek from Nauvoo, Illinois, that settlement began. By 1848, the year that Mexico relinquished its claims on the territory, the Mormons had proclaimed Salt Lake City the capital of DESERET (a Mormon word meaning "beehive," which gives modern Utah its nickname), a state extending as far as California. The US government, however, in 1850 established the much smaller Utah Territory. With the 1860s discovery of gold in the NE, "Gentiles" (non-Mormons) poured in; the extension of the UNION PACIFIC RAILROAD to meet the CENTRAL PACIFIC at PROMONTORY, in 1869, further opened Utah to the outside world, and decades of conflict between the Mormons and Federal authorities followed. Many differences fueled the sometimes violent relationship, but it was the Mormon practice of polygamy that formed the obstacle whose abolition in 1890 opened the way to statehood. The theocratic agricultural community along the Wasatch Front grew in coexistence with the Utah of mines and smelters through the early 20th century, and the state has now developed a thriving mixed economy. Military expenditures have been important esp. since World War II, with facilities at TOOELE, DUGWAY, WENDOVER, and CLEARFIELD (Hill Air Force Base) among those operating on the over 60% of Utah land still owned by the Federal government. Aerospace and other military-dependent industries have now become important to Utah's cities, which are also producers of refined oil and metals and have diverse other manufactures. Cattle and dairy goods are the leading agricultural products, as irrigation is required for almost all crop growing. In addition to oil, coal, potash, and salt, Utah's mines are the source of a wide range of metals, including gold, silver, copper (see BINGHAM CANYON), iron, lead, vanadium, uranium, and zinc. Some early mining towns are now among resorts in the Wasatches and Uintas, which include PARK CITY, SNOWBIRD, ALTA, and SUNDANCE. In the late 20th century, tourism has come to be esp. important to Utah. Salt Lake City is a magnet as a religious capital, and the state also attracts visitors to an array of national parks in the S, including CANYONLANDS, ARCHES, CAPITOL REEF, BRYCE CANYON, and ZION, as well as national monuments including DINOSAUR, CEDAR BREAKS, NATURAL BRIDGES, RAINBOW BRIDGE, and TIMPANOGOS CAVE (the last in the N). The Glen Canyon National Recreation Area, with L. POWELL, is a mecca for boaters. While most of Utah remains unpopulated because of its harsh terrain and climate, the same qualities have thus become central to its appeal to visitors. Today, Utah is about two-thirds Mormon. Brigham Young University, in Provo, is the church's leading educational institution. The University of Utah is in Salt Lake City, Utah State University in LOGAN.

Utah County 1998 sq mi/5175 sq km, pop. 263,590, in NC Utah. PROVO is its seat. It is an area of irrigated farming, mining, and resorts. The large Utah L. lies within the county's borders. In the E is part of the WASATCH RANGE, including Mt. Timpanogos and the Timpanogos Cave National Monument, and part of the Uinta National Forest. In the W is part of the Oquirrh Mts. The county contains much of the **Utah Valley,** a fruit growing region noted for its cherries. Livestock, hay, sugar beets, and truck farm crops are also raised. Also in Utah Co. are iron, copper, silver, lead, and zinc mines, and several ski resorts.

Utah Lake largest freshwater lake in Utah, 32 mi/52 SE of GREAT SALT L. Some 23 mi/37 km N–S and up to 12 mi/19 km wide, the roughly triangular lake is fed by the Spanish Fork and Provo rivers, and is drained by the Jordan R., which then flows N into the Great Salt L. PROVO (E) is the largest lakeside city. A remnant of glacial L. Bonneville, it is used for the irrigation of Great Salt L. Valley agriculture; in recent years it has become seriously polluted.

Ute Mountain Indian Reservation 901 sq mi/2332 sq km, pop. 1320 (96% Indian), in extreme SW Colorado, S of Cortez and Mesa Verde, extending to the FOUR CORNERS. Towaoc is its headquarters; a park in the reservation preserves ANASAZI ruins. The adjacent (E) **Southern Ute Indian Reservation** (1059 sq mi/2742 sq km), has a pop. of 7804 (13% Indian); horseracing and a casino attract visitors.

Utica **1.** city, pop. 5081, Macomb Co., SE Michigan, on the Clinton R., 20 mi/32 km N of Detroit. It trades and ships local rhubarb, mushrooms, and dairy products, and manufactures auto parts. Along the river just to the NW is the Rochester-Utica State Recreation Area. **2.** city, pop. 68,637, seat of Oneida Co., C New York, on the Mohawk R. and New York State Barge Canal, 45 mi/72 km E of Syracuse. The first European settlers were Palatinate Germans and Dutch. Following the completion of the Erie Canal in 1825, Utica developed as a textile center; following World War II, diverse industries developed. The city now manufactures machinery, electronic and aerospace equipment, light metal products, refrigerators, pneumatic tools, cutlery, and beer, as well as textiles. Utica is home to Mohawk Valley Community College (1946), Utica College of Syracuse University (1946), the State University of New York College of Technology (1973), and the Munson-Williams-Proctor Institute (1919).

Utopia failed "communistic" housing scheme (1905–11) to establish LOWER EAST SIDE residents on a tract in the NW part of Fresh Meadows, Queens, New York, SE of Flushing. The name survives in the neighborhood and in the Utopia Parkway, a N–S highway through this part of Queens.

Uvalde city, pop. 14,729, seat of Uvalde Co., SC Texas, 79 mi/128 km WSW of San Antonio, on the Leona R., at the S edge of the EDWARDS PLATEAU. In a ranching area, the city exploits sand, lime, basalt, and asphalt deposits, and processes wool, mohair, honey, feed, and vegetables. Settled in 1853 next to Fort Inge (1849), it was a rough outpost through most of the 19th century. Southwest Texas Junior College (1946) and a Texas A&M research center are here. The former home of US vice-president John Nance "Cactus Jack" Garner (1868–1967) is a museum.

Uwharrie Mountains also, **Uharie Range** hilly remnants (1000 ft/300 m high), locally referred to as mountains, of a much older range in SC North Carolina, extending S of HIGH POINT and SW of ASHEBORO, to the vicinity of ALBEMARLE. The **Uwharrie R.** flows S from the High Point area for c.60 mi/100 km through **Uwharrie National Forest** (47,000 ac/19,000 ha), headquartered in Troy, to join the YADKIN R., forming the PEE DEE R.

V

Vacaville city, pop. 71,479, Solano Co., WC California, at the E base of the Vaca Mts., 30 mi/48 km SW of Sacramento. Founded in 1850 on cattle rangeland, it is a processing center for plums, cherries, tomatoes, corn, and citrus fruits raised in the surrounding valley. The California Medical Facility, a state prison, is just S. Travis Air Force Base, 7 mi/11 km SE, near FAIRFIELD, also provides employment. Vacaville has more than tripled in pop. since 1970.

Vadnais Heights city, pop. 11,041, Ramsey Co., SE Minnesota, a residential suburb 7 mi/11 km N of St. Paul. Primarily a bedroom community, it has experienced some commercial development in the 1980s along I-35E.

Vail town, pop. 3659, Eagle Co., N Colorado, on Gore Creek, in the White River National Forest, at 8150 ft/2486 m, 26 mi/42 km N of Leadville. One of North America's top ski resorts, it developed after World War II. Among its features are a ski school, bobsled course, and the Colorado Ski Museum and Ski Hall of Fame.

Val-Bélair city, pop. 17,181, QUÉBEC Urban Community, S Québec, 10 mi/16 km WNW of downtown Québec City, a residential suburb W of LORETTEVILLE, on the R. Nelson. VALCARTIER is on its NW.

Valcartier locality 14 mi/23 km NW of Québec City, S Québec, on the R. Jacques-Cartier, site of a military training camp established just before World War I, in which it was the major Canadian mobilization point. VAL-BÉLAIR is immediately SE.

Valcour Island see under PLATTSBURGH, New York.

Valcourt city, pop. 2284, Val-Saint-François census division, in the EASTERN TOWNSHIPS, S Québec, 21 mi/34 km WNW of Sherbrooke. Historically agricultural, it is noted as the birthplace of J. Armand Bombardier (1907–64), inventor of a system allowing vehicles to be driven over snow (best known in the Snowmobile), and founder (1942) of Bombardier, a major transport-equipment concern.

Valdese town, pop. 3914, Burke Co., W North Carolina, 7 mi/11 km E of Morganton, in the Piedmont and the E foothills of the Blue Ridge Mts. It was established in 1893 by a community of Provençal-speaking Waldensians, a Protestant group fleeing religious persecution in N Italy. Over time inhabitants affiliated with American (Presbyterian) churches, and their farms and vineyards gave way to textile plants; knitwear is now an economic mainstay.

Valdez city, pop. 4068, in SE Alaska, 125 mi/200 km E of Anchorage, on the Valdez Arm of PRINCE WILLIAM SOUND. It has been since 1977 the S terminus of the TRANS-ALASKA PIPELINE; oil from PRUDHOE BAY is stored in Valdez and shipped from its ice-free port. The Spanish explored the area and gave the name to the harbor in 1790; the city was founded in 1898 as a goldfield supply center, and survived as a fishing community. After its destruction by the March 1964 earthquake, Valdez was rebuilt 4 mi/6.5 km to the W of its original site.

Val-d'Or city, pop. 23,842, in the E Abitibi region, 48 mi/78 km ESE of Rouyn-Noranda, in SW Québec, at the headwaters of the R. Harricana. Developed during a 1930s gold rush, it still has some of the richest mines in the province. Local lumbering and farming as well as some diversified industry are also important in this regional service center. The Bourlamaque Miners' Village, a former COMPANY TOWN, is now a historic site.

Valdosta city, pop. 39,806, seat of Lowndes Co., S Georgia, 14 mi/23 km from the Florida line. Founded as Troupville, it was relocated in 1859 to its site near the area's first (Savannah–Mobile) railway, and renamed. It is an important center for the tobacco, timber, and cattle industries, and a naval stores (especially turpentine) market. Manufactures include textiles and metal goods. Small fishing lakes to the S bring tourists. Moody Air Force Base is 12 mi/19 km NNE. Valdosta State College dates to 1906.

Valencia see under SANTA CLARITA, California.

Valinda unincorporated community, pop. 18,735, Los Angeles Co., SW California, a largely residential suburb 15 mi/24 km E of downtown Los Angeles.

Valle Grande see under JEMEZ Mts., New Mexico.

Vallejo city, pop. 109,199, Solano Co., NC California, on Carquinez Strait, just E of San Pablo Bay, and the mouth of the Napa R., 25 mi/40 km NE of San Francisco. BENICIA is immediately SE. The city was named for, and is built on land donated by, General Mariano Vallejo, Mexican governor of ALTA CALIFORNIA, and served intermittently as California's state capital in 1852–53. The Naval Shipyard (1854) on Mare I., across the Napa (W), slated to close in the 1990s, has long been an economic anchor; the oldest in California, it is home to the California Maritime Academy (1929) and was central to a World War II boom here. Port business and agricultural processing and shipping are also important to the economy. Other industries include the manufacture of beverages, textiles, and paper containers.

Valley city, pop. 8173, Chambers Co., EC Alabama, W of L. Harding (the Chattahoochee R.). It is just SW of WEST POINT, Georgia, and is part of its industrial (textile) complex.

Valley, the **1.** see SAN FERNANDO VALLEY, California. **2.** see WILLAMETTE Valley, Oregon.

Valley and Ridge Province see under APPALACHIAN Mts.

Valley City city, pop. 7163, seat of Barnes Co., E North Dakota, on the Sheyenne R., 55 mi/89 km W of Fargo. After the arrival of the Northern Pacific Railroad (1872), it developed as an agricultural trading center. It now has a flour mill and deals in grain, livestock, and dairy products. Valley City State University (1889) trains teachers here. Bald Hill Dam, a flood control project on the Sheyenne R., created the 27 mi/43 km–long L. Ashtabula, a popular recreational site 11 mi/18 km NW of the city.

Valley East see under SUDBURY, Ontario.

Valley Falls industrial village, pop. 11,175, in Cumberland town, Providence Co., N Rhode Island, 5 mi/8 km N of Providence and just N of Pawtucket and Central Falls, on the Blackstone R. Manufactures include textiles, curtains, upholstery materials, yarn, and metal and wire products.

Valleyfield see SALABERRY-DE-VALLEYFIELD, Québec.

Valley Forge historic site in Montgomery Co., SE Pennsylvania, on the Schuylkill R., 3 mi/5 km SE of Phoenixville. It was the winter headquarters (1777–78) of Washington's army; by the spring, death and desertion had reduced their number from 9000 to 6000, but they emerged more disciplined and better trained, thanks to drilling by the German general von Steuben. The site of the encampment is now the 3500-ac/1400-ha Valley Forge National Historic Park. The village of Valley Forge, just W in Schuylkill township, Chester Co., has corporate and research facilities.

Valley of Fire 35,000-ac/14,130-ha state park containing dramatic polychrome sandstone formations, with many PETROGLYPHS and pictographs of the ancient ANASAZI and the Paiute, 40 mi/64 km NE of Las Vegas, and just NW of L. MEAD, in Clark Co., SE Nevada. The rocks and canyons have been sculpted by erosion since the Jurassic Period, 140 million years ago. Valley of Fire, the largest and oldest state park in Nevada, has headquarters at Overton (NE).

Valley of Ten Thousand Smokes see KATMAI NATIONAL PARK AND PRESERVE, Alaska.

Valley of the Moon see under GLEN ELLEN and SONOMA Co., California.

Valley of the Sun popular name for the valley in which PHOENIX, Arizona, and most of its suburbs, including Mesa, Scottsdale, Paradise Valley, Peoria, and Sun City, are situated. Some 75 mi/120 km E–W and up to 30 mi/50 km wide, this extension of the SONORAN DESERT, drained by the Gila (S), Salt (C), and Agua Fria (NW) rivers, and ringed by the Sierra Estrella (SW), White Tank (W), Mazatzal (NE), and Superstition (E) mountains, is one of the fastest-developing parts of the SUNBELT.

Valley Station unincorporated community, pop. 22,840, Jefferson Co., NC Kentucky, 10 mi/16 km SW of Louisville. It is a largely residential suburb.

Valley Stream village, pop. 33,946, in Hempstead town, Nassau Co., SE New York, just E of the QUEENS border. It is predominately residential, with various small businesses. The site was acquired from the Rockaway Indians by the Dutch in the late 1640s. Its rapid growth after World War II was spurred by housing developments built for returning veterans.

Valparaiso city, pop. 24,414, seat of Porter Co., NW Indiana, 18 mi/29 km SE of Gary and 12 mi/19 km S of L. Michigan. The trading and distribution center of a farming, poultry raising, and dairy area, it has manufactures including auto parts, steel, magnets, ball and roller bearings, food processing machines, and processed food. It is the seat of Valparaiso University (1859) and Valparaiso Technical Institute (1934).

Van Buren city, pop. 14,979, seat of Crawford Co., NW Arkansas, on the Arkansas R., 5 mi/8 km NE of Fort Smith. Settled in 1818, it was a trading post and outfitting point for westbound settlers. In 1873 it became a junction for railroad and river traffic. The discovery of natural gas in the 1900s attracted glass manufacturers and smelters. The local economy is now focused primarily on shipping and processing farm produce, including spinach, peaches, and strawberries. The city was noted as the home of the 1930s radio humorist Bob Burns.

Vance Air Force Base see under ENID, Oklahoma.

Van Cortlandt Park third-largest New York City park, 1146 ac/464 ha, in the NW Bronx, on the Westchester line. Woodlawn is E, Riverdale along a ridge to the W, and Kingsbridge Heights S. The Van Cortlandt mansion (1748) is in the park, as is Vault Hill, where diversionary fires were lit while Washington's troops marched to the battle of Yorktown (1781). Three major highways, the Henry Hudson and Mosholu parkways and Major Deegan Expressway, interchange in the park. Van Cortlandt Park is today the refuge largely of working-class residents of other Bronx neighborhoods, and is known as the scene of sporting events unusual in New York City: cricket matches, cross-country championships, and skiing.

Vancouver **1.** city, pop. 471,844, Greater Vancouver Regional District (pop. 1,542,744), SW British Columbia, on a peninsula between one mouth of the Fraser R. (S), the Strait of Georgia (W), and Burrard Inlet (N); Burnaby adjoins (E). Vancouver's metropolitan area, almost the same as the regional district, has a pop. of 1,602,502. Just N of the Washington border, the city is 125 mi/200 km NNW of Seattle. Set amid COAST Mts. scenery, it has a sheltered ice-free port, its climate affected by the warm Japan Current. The site of Squamish villages, it was seen by Europeans in the late 18th century, but first settled in the 1860s, when Gastown sprang up on Burrard Inlet. The small lumbering community became important as the terminus of Canada's transcontinental railroad in 1887, the year after it had been both incorporated as Vancouver and almost destroyed by fire. Rebuilt, it flourished with harbor activity, and has gradually become the leading North American Pacific port. Wood products, fish, Prairie Provinces grain, and mineral goods are leading exports; Asian manufactures lead imports. Cruise ship and ferry traffic has also long been important. The city is now the commercial and financial center of Pacific Canada. Shipbuilding, lumber and food processing, and varied manufactures are important, much of the activity now occurring in nearby suburbs. In addition, Vancouver's reputation for good living has made it a residential magnet. Until the mid 20th century its people were largely of British background, but its long-established Asian communities have grown in recent decades, making it a major E component of the so-called Pacific Rim. It now has some of America's largest Chinese and (Asian) Indian, as well as sizable Italian, Greek, Japanese, and other communities. The University of British Columbia (1908), with its campus at Point Grey, including a famous anthropological museum, is the best-known local institution. The 1986 world's fair (Expo) spurred tourism, already a major industry. The Canucks (hockey) play at the Pacific Coliseum, the Lions (football) at BC Place Stadium. The Vancouver International Airport is on Sea I. (SW), part of Richmond. See also: BURRARD INLET (and English Bay); CHINATOWN; DUNBAR HEIGHTS; EAST END (and Strathcona); FAIRVIEW; FALSE CREEK (and Granville I.); GASTOWN (and Granville); KERRISDALE; KITSILANO; LITTLE INDIA; LITTLE ITALY; NORTH SHORE; POINT GREY; SHAUGHNESSY; STANLEY PARK; WEST END. **2.** city, pop. 46,380, seat of Clark Co., SW Washington, on the Columbia R., 8 mi/13 km N of Portland, Oregon. Situated at the head of deepwater navigation on the Columbia, it is a major shipping center. Its natural advantages were apparent in 1824 when the Hudson's Bay Company founded Fort Vancouver as its NW headquarters. In 1846 boundary disputes with England were settled, and Vancouver, the oldest continuously inhabited white community in the state, passed to the US. Today, important manufactures include lumber, plywood and paper products, clothing, and aluminum products. Vancouver is also a distribution center for Columbia Basin hydroelectric power. The Fort Vancouver National Historic Site and the Pearson Airpark Museum, housed at the oldest operating American airfield, are here. The city is also gateway to the Columbia River Gorge National Scenic Area and headquarters for the Gifford Pinchot National Forest.

Vancouver Island largest Pacific coastal island in North America (12,408 sq mi/32,137 sq km), in SW British Columbia, separated from the mainland by (N–S) the Queen Charlotte, Johnstone, and GEORGIA straits, and from Washington State by the Haro and JUAN DE FUCA straits. Some 285 mi/458 km NNW–SSE and 30–80 mi/48–128 km wide, it has thick woods, mountains rising to 7218 ft/2200 m at GOLDEN HINDE, and numerous inlets, including FJORDS. A Salishan homeland, it became (1849) a British crown colony, and later joined (1866) British Columbia. Population centers, chiefly in the S and SW, include VICTORIA, SAANICH, ESQUIMALT, OAK BAY, NANAIMO, PORT ALBERNI, COURTENAY, NORTH COWICHAN, and CAMPBELL RIVER. With smaller adjacent islands, the total pop. is c.600,000. Industries include lumbering, sawmilling, pulp and plywood manufacture, fishing, tourism and outdoor recreation, diverse agriculture, and mining. Strathcona and Cape Scott provincial parks and Pacific Rim National Park are here. The island's backbone is part of the COAST RANGES.

Vandalia **1.** city, pop. 6114, seat of Fayette Co., SC Illinois, on the Kaskaskia R., 30 mi/48 km SW of Effingham. An agricultural distribution center, Vandalia served as the second state capital, 1820–39. Abraham Lincoln began his legislative career here (1834). The W end of the NATIONAL ROAD, Vandalia was also a station on the UNDERGROUND RAILROAD. **2.** city, pop. 13,882, Montgomery Co., SW Ohio, a residential suburb 8 mi/13 km N of Dayton. Its economy centers around truck farms and the manufacture of automobile parts. It is the site of the Trapshooting Hall of Fame.

Vandenberg Air Force Base along 50 mi/80 km of Pacific coastline in Santa Barbara Co., SW California, 50 mi/80 km NW of Santa Barbara. It is the major US West Coast missile and satellite launching facility. The economies of SANTA MARIA (just NE) and LOMPOC (just E) are heavily dependent on the base.

Vanderburgh County 236 sq mi/611 sq km, pop. 165,058, in SW Indiana. Its seat is the industrial city of EVANSVILLE. Its S boundary is the Ohio R., which forms the Kentucky border. Most of the county is agricultural, producing winter wheat, hogs, soybeans, and corn. There are also bituminous coal mines.

Van Horn Mountains range extending S for c.25 mi/40 km from near Van Horn, in far W Texas. They rise to 5786 ft/1765 m. Mica and silver have been mined in the range. The Wylie Mts., rising to 5031 ft/1534 m, lie to the E.

Vanier **1.** city, pop. 18,150, Ottawa-Carleton Regional Municipality, SE Ontario, on the Rideau R. near its mouth on the Ottawa R., surrounded by the city of OTTAWA, with the village of ROCKCLIFFE PARK on the N. Formerly the town of Eastview, it became a city in 1969, and is a largely residential suburb 2 mi/3 km NE of downtown Ottawa, with some government and other offices. **2.** city, pop. 10,833, QUÉBEC Urban Community, S Québec, across the R. Saint-Charles from downtown Québec City, a residential and commercial community entirely surrounded by the capital.

Van Meter city, pop. 751, Dallas Co., C Iowa, on the Raccoon R., 24 mi/38 km SW of Des Moines. This farming community is known as the birthplace (1918) of baseball great Bob Feller.

Van Nuys C SAN FERNANDO VALLEY section of Los Angeles, California, 15 mi/24 km NW of Downtown, and NW of Studio City and Sherman Oaks, in the Valley's "flats." It is the municipal government center for the Valley, has a large airport, and has been since the 1950s a center of aerospace, automobile, and defense manufacturing; its high-tech industries have recently slumped. Van Nuys is also an extensive residential and commercial suburb, noted for its malls.

Van Wert city, pop. 10,891, seat of Van Wert Co., NW Ohio, 26 mi/42 km WNW of Lima and 10 mi/16 km E of the Indiana border. It is situated in a fertile grain farming region. Clothing, dairy products, canned goods, fabricated metal products, and electronic equipment are among the goods manufactured here.

Varennes city, pop. 14,758, Lajemmerais census division, S Québec, 14 mi/23 km NNE of Montréal, on the S (E) bank of the St. Lawrence R., across from the N end of the I. de Montréal. A longtime farming community, it has become since the 1970s a center of the chemical and nuclear industries, with a national research facility and advanced hydrogen plant. Hospital pioneer Marie-Marguerite d'Youville, the first (1959) Canadian to be beatified, was born here in 1701.

Vashon Island residential and agricultural island, 13 mi/21 km N–S, in Puget Sound, WC Washington, in King Co., between Seattle (NE) and Tacoma (S). Named in 1792 by George Vancouver for a friend, it was settled in the 1870s. A sandbar connects Maury I. (E). Cattle, horses, berries, and orchids are raised, and there is an annual strawberry festival. Many residents commute to Seattle or Tacoma.

Vaudreuil city, pop. 11,187, Vaudreuil-Soulanges census division, S Québec, on the Trans-Canada Highway across the L. des Deux Montagnes (the Ottawa R.) from the SW end of the I. de Montréal, and 25 mi/40 km WSW of Montréal. A longtime agricultural community, it is now a growing residential suburb.

Vaughan **1.** hamlet in Yazoo Co., WC Mississippi, 35 mi/56 km NNE of Jackson. On the old Illinois Central Railroad line, it was the site of the crash of the *Cannon Ball* express, running between Memphis, Tennessee, and CANTON (14 mi/

23 km S), in which engineer Casey Jones was killed on April 30, 1900. The Casey Jones Museum State Park, just NE of Vaughan and near the crash site, is devoted to the accident and to the history of railroading. **2.** city, pop. 111,359, York Regional Municipality, S Ontario, 15 mi/24 km NW of downtown Toronto, on the Humber R. An explosively growing suburb (70% pop. gain in 1986–91), it includes the former agricultural communities of Kleinburg, site of the McMichael Canadian (art) Collection and Toronto International Film Studios; Maple, home to Canada's Wonderland, a well-known amusement park; and Woodbridge. North York (S), Richmond Hill (E), and Markham (SE) are adjacent. Thornhill, a residential suburb noted for several religious centers, is in the SE.

Vega Baja unincorporated community (ZONA URBANA), pop. 27,753, Vega Baja Municipio (pop. 55,997), NC Puerto Rico, 18 mi/29 km W of San Juan. About 4 mi/6 km S of the Atlantic Coast, it is near a number of popular beaches known for their unusual rock formations. The town is a trade hub in an area producing citrus, pineapples, and sugarcane, and there is some light manufacturing.

Velasco former town in Brazoria Co., SE Texas, at the mouth of the Brazos R. across (E) from FREEPORT, of which it became part in 1957. Settled in the early 1820s, it is the site of an 1832 battle between Texan and Mexican forces, and of the May 14, 1836 treaty ending the Texas Revolution. A 1909 hurricane destroyed much of the old town.

Velva city, pop. 968, McHenry Co., C North Dakota, on the Souris (Mouse) R., 20 mi/32 km SE of Minot. Laid out in 1891, it has lignite mines and trades in poultry, livestock, and grain. It is the birthplace (1912) of broadcast journalist Eric Sevareid, who wrote of his boyhood here.

Veniaminof, Mount active volcano (8825 ft/2690 m) of the ALEUTIAN RANGE, on the Alaska Peninsula, 40 mi/64 km SW of Chignik and 460 mi/740 km SW of Anchorage, in SW Alaska. It was named for Ivan Veniaminof of Siberia, who wrote a dictionary and grammar for the Aleut and Kodiak languages and was named the first (Orthodox) bishop of Alaska in 1841.

Venice 1. oceanfront section of LOS ANGELES, California, on Santa Monica Bay, immediately S of Santa Monica and 15 mi/24 km WSW of Downtown. Planned and initiated in the 1900s by tobacco magnate Abbott Kinney (d.1920) as an elegant, canal-crossed community, it failed to become the cultural center he had envisioned. Oil strikes in the 1920s contributed to its decline from middle-class beach resort to drab industrial suburb. In the 1950s, it was a beatnik center, and since the 1960s it has been a mecca for the young, the artistic, the elderly, and the gay, noted for its beach and boardwalk, its music and murals. Marina del Rey (unincorporated, pop. 7431), immediately S, continues the famed Venice Beach, a section of which was once known as the Muscle Beach of body worshipers. **2.** city, pop. 16,922, Sarasota Co., SW Florida, on the Gulf of Mexico, 18 mi/29 km SSE of Sarasota. A beachfront resort crossed by canals, it is a popular vacation locale noted for its tarpon fishing. Tourism, shipping of local vegetables, and light manufacturing are vital to its economy. Venice is the winter home (since 1960, replacing SARASOTA) of the Ringling Brothers Barnum & Bailey Circus, and houses the country's only training school for clowns.

Ventnor City city, pop. 11,005, Atlantic Co., SE New Jersey, on the Atlantic Ocean, adjoining (SW) Atlantic City. Situated on Absecon Beach, it is a primarily residential part of the Atlantic City resort complex.

Ventura officially, **San Buenaventura** city, pop. 92,575, seat of Ventura Co., S California, on EL CAMINO REAL (US 101) and the Santa Barbara Channel of the Pacific Ocean, 65 mi/105 km WNW of Los Angeles, N of the mouth of the Santa Clara R. It grew up, in an area inhabited by the Chumash, around Mission San Buenaventura (1782), the last founded by Junípero Serra. Incorporated in 1866, the city developed as a leading lemon growing center. Oil was discovered in nearby foothills in the early 1920s, and spurred growth; the region is a major California producer. Ventura has a large refinery and manufactures oilfield equipment. Citrus, avocado, and walnut groves, lima bean fields, tourism, and diverse manufacturing contribute to the economy; beaches, a large marina, and excursion boats to the Santa Barbara (Channel) Is. draw visitors. Ventura College (1925) is in the city.

Ventura Boulevard E–W commercial thoroughfare, 16 mi/26 km long, in the SAN FERNANDO VALLEY, Los Angeles, California. The Valley's main shopping strip runs through STUDIO CITY, SHERMAN OAKS, ENCINO, TARZANA, and WOODLAND HILLS. It parallels the VENTURA FREEWAY.

Ventura County 1862 sq mi/4823 sq km, pop. 669,016, in SW California, immediately NW of Los Angeles, in the TRANSVERSE RANGES, on the Pacific Ocean. Important cities include VENTURA (San Buenaventura), the county seat, and OXNARD, CAMARILLO, THOUSAND OAKS, SIMI VALLEY, MOORPARK, and SANTA PAULA. The N half of the county lies in the Los Padres National Forest. In the S, citrus orchards, oilfields, and military installations compete with the demand for residential development overflowing from Los Angeles and the San Fernando Valley to the SE, esp. along the Ventura Freeway (US 101).

Ventura Freeway limited-access highway (US 101), 75 mi/120 km long, between PASADENA (E) and VENTURA (W), in S California. It is the busiest link in the Los Angeles freeway network, residential development having saturated the SAN FERNANDO VALLEY and overflowed into Ventura Co. It parallels Ventura Blvd. across the Valley, and serves Glendale, Thousands Oaks, Camarillo, and Oxnard.

Verdigris River 351 mi/565 km long, in SE Kansas and NE Oklahoma. It rises SW of Emporia, and flows SE through dam-created Toronto L., then SSE past Neodesha, where it is joined from the W by the Fall R., to Coffeyville. Entering Oklahoma, it flows S through OOLOGAH L., and continues on the E of the TULSA area, passing through Tulsa's port of Catoosa, on the Arkansas R. (McClellan-Kerr) Navigation System, before joining the ARKANSAS R. 5 mi/8 km NE of Muskogee, just upstream from the mouth of the NEOSHO R. Its name refers to the color of certain copper ores.

Verdugo Hills also, **Verdugo Mountains** foothill section of the SAN GABRIEL Mts., on the E of the SAN FERNANDO VALLEY, in SW California, immediately N of Burbank and Glendale. They separate TUJUNGA, part of Los Angeles, from the rest of the Valley. **Verdugo City,** also on their N, is part of Glendale. The area was part of the first California RANCHO, Rancho San Rafael (1784).

Verdun city, pop. 61,307, MONTRÉAL URBAN COMMUNITY, S Québec, 4 mi/6 km S of downtown Montréal, on the Bassin de Laprairie (the St. Lawrence R.). Primarily residential, it has some industry. The Collège Jean-Jacques Olier (1951) is here.

Veregin see under KAMSACK, Saskatchewan.

Vergennes city, pop. 2578, on Otter Creek near L. Champlain, 20 mi/32 km S of Burlington, in Addison Co., WC Vermont. Prior to the Revolution, it was part of territory claimed by both New York and New Hampshire. During the War of 1812, a fleet was built at Vergennes, which under Commodore Thomas Macdonough waged the Battle of Plattsurgh in 1814, giving the US control of L. Champlain. Vergennes is today a dairying and commercial center.

Vermilion **1.** town, pop. 3891, EC Alberta, on the Vermilion R., 114 mi/184 km E of Edmonton. The center of a mixed farming area, it was first settled by squatters in the late 1890s. Homesteaders later replaced them and named the community Breage. They moved (1905) the town westward with the arrival of the Canadian National Railway, which stimulated rapid population growth. Lakeland College is here. **2.** city, pop. 11,127, Erie and Lorain counties, NC Ohio, on L. Erie at the mouth of the Vermilion R., 10 mi/16 km SW of Lorain. Its boating and fishing facilities are an attraction for summer tourists. Founded in 1808, it took its name from its red clay river banks, the source for paint used by the Ottawa Indians. Vermilion has substantial commercial fishing and some light industry. There are many stone quarries and dairy and wheat farms in the area.

Vermilion Bay inlet of the Gulf of Mexico, 32 mi/52 km S of Lafayette in St. Mary Parish, S Louisiana, at the mouth of the Vermilion R. Twenty mi/32 km NE–SW and 10 mi/16 km wide, it is separated from the Gulf by Marsh I. on the S, and joins Côte Blanche Bay on the E. The area is noted for its wildlife refuges, shellfishing, oil production, and SALT DOMES.

Vermilion County 900 sq mi/2331 sq km, pop. 88,257, in EC Illinois, bordered by Indiana (E). It is cut by the Vermilion R., formed by three streams at DANVILLE, the county seat. Outside the urban and commercial Danville area in the EC part of the county, it is agricultural, with many farms growing corn and soybeans.

Vermilion Iron Range area in St. Louis Co., NE Minnesota, extending NE from a region S of Vermilion L. to Ely, noted for its deposits of a hard type of iron ore obtained from underground mines. With production beginning in 1884, this was the first section of the state's Iron Ranges to be developed. Its importance diminished after the opening of the MESABI RANGE. Ely, Tower, and Soudan were important mining communities. Tower-Soudan State Park, on the S shore of 35 mi/56 km–long Vermilion L., contains the state's oldest and deepest mine, which extends nearly 2400 ft/732 m below the earth's surface.

Vermilion River **1.** 75 mi/121 km long, in E Illinois. It is formed by the North and South branches in Livingston Co., then flows generally NW, past Pontiac and Streator, to the Illinois R. at STARVED ROCK, opposite La Salle. **2.** 42 mi/68 km long, in NE Minnesota. It rises in Vermilion L. and flows NNW and ENE through the Superior National Forest to Crane L., near the Ontario border. **Vermilion Lake,** in St. Louis Co., is situated W of the VERMILION IRON RANGE and W of Ely, and is 35 mi/56 km long and 8 mi/13 km wide. There are numerous summer resorts along its irregular shoreline. A Chippewa reservation, Tower-Soudan State Park, and iron mines are located on its S shore.

Vermillion city, pop. 10,034, seat of Clay Co., SE South Dakota, on the Vermillion R., 23 mi/37 km E of Yankton. It is a processing center in a farming area that produces dairy items, cantaloupes, tomatoes, and grain. The city was founded in 1859, near the site of Fort Vermillion (1835), an American Fur Company trading post. It is the seat of the University of South Dakota, founded in 1862 and opened 20 years later, and an important local employer.

Vermillion River 150 mi/241 km long, in South Dakota. It rises in Lake Co., in the EC part, and flows S through L. Vermillion to the Missouri R. just S of the city of Vermillion.

Vermont northeastern US state, in N New England; 1990 pop. 562,758 (110% of 1980; rank: 48th); area 9615 sq mi/24,903 sq km (rank: 45th); admitted to Union 1791 (14th). Capital: MONTPELIER. Most populous cities: BURLINGTON, RUTLAND. Vermont is bordered N by Québec, with Lakes CHAMPLAIN and MEMPHRÉMAGOG lying across the boundary; E by New Hampshire, across the CONNECTICUT R.; S by Massachusetts; and W by New York, for more than half the boundary (N) facing it across L. Champlain. The state is dominated by the N–S GREEN Mts., an Appalachian range that gives it its name and that rises to 4393 ft/1340 m at Mt. MANSFIELD. On the W is the Champlain lowland, a glacial lakebed that provided an early corridor between Montréal and the St. Lawrence R. (N, via the R. Richelieu and land routes) and New York and the Hudson R. (S, via New York's L. George and short PORTAGES); this first brought whites (Samuel de Champlain, 1609) into what is now Vermont. Along the SW border is part of the TACONIC Mts., a slate and granite quarrying area where BENNINGTON is the largest community. Marble is quarried in the Green Mts., esp. at BARRE (NC). The Connecticut R. valley (E) has a number of small mill towns, among them WHITE RIVER JUNCTION, BELLOWS FALLS, and BRATTLEBORO; but most of the state's industry and almost half its pop. is in the Burlington area (NW), where since the 1950s computer, other high-tech, and a variety of light manufacturing industries and financial and commercial operations have expanded an economy based in part on older paper and textile mills (esp. in WINOOSKI) and the presence of the University of Vermont. The NORTHEAST KINGDOM, the state's remote and long economically marginal NE corner, has recently received some impetus from trade with (and home buying and recreational visiting by) Quebecers. Agriculture in Vermont centers on the Champlain valley, with scattered farms elsewhere throughout the state; dairying, orcharding, and the production of maple syrup are prominent, and ice cream, cheese, and maple products are made locally. Tourism and outdoor recreation are economically vital to Vermont. Champlain, BOMOSEEN, and other lakes are important, and the state's many noted ski resorts include KILLINGTON, PICO, STRATTON, and JAY peaks. The LONG TRAIL passes through the Green Mts. Academic centers including MIDDLEBURY, Bennington, WOODSTOCK, and MARLBORO draw thousands to summer schools and arts festivals, and dozens of small, typically "New England" villages draw visitors at all seasons. Inhabited by Abnaki (some of whom remain in the far N, in the MISSISQUOI R. area), the region was little settled by whites before the mid 18th century, when both New Hampshire and New York pressed claims on it; locals, led by Ethan Allen (born in Connecticut) and his Green Mountain Boys, advocated independence, and from the American Revolution until 1791, Vermont lived as a republic. Its pop. remains overwhelmingly Yankee, with French-Canadians (esp. in industrial towns, as in the Burlington area), Italians (in the Barre area), Irish, Welsh, and other sizable minorities. Its S has long been home to EXURBAN New Yorkers and some Bostonians; in the late 20th century, with increased highway access, much of the state has increasingly become home or a second home to urbanites and suburbanites who appreciate its scenery, quiet, and "traditional" lifestyle.

Vermont Yankee only Vermont nuclear power plant, opened 1972 in Vernon, Windham Co., extreme SE Vermont, 3 mi/5 km upstream from the Massachusetts line and just E of Interstate 91.

Vernon **1.** city, pop. 23,514, North Okanagan Regional District, S British Columbia, near the N end of OKANAGAN L., 32 mi/50 km NNE of Kelowna and 190 mi/310 km ENE of Vancouver. A missionary settlement (1840s) and ranch community (1860s), and a military camp during World War I, it is now a service and shipping center for the ranching and fruit growing N Okanagan Valley. Industries include fruit, vegetable, and dairy processing; tanning; and sawmilling. Nearby lakes and ski resorts attract visitors. **2.** town, pop. 29,841, Tolland Co., NC Connecticut, 12 mi/19 km NE of Hartford. Part of the town lies in Connecticut's central lowland, with gently rolling hills, part in the more rugged eastern highlands. In an agricultural area along Interstate 84, it produces potatoes along with paper products, television equipment, and plastics. Vernon includes urban Rockville as well as Vernon Center and Talcottville. **3.** see under NORTH VERNON, Indiana. **4.** township, pop. 21,211, Sussex Co., N New Jersey, 40 mi/64 km NW of New York City, along the New York border. In a wooded mountainous area, it is the site of a popular 1200-ac/486-ha amusement park; during the winter, the park is the location of the Vernon Valley/Great Gorge ski resort. Hidden Valley ski resort is also in Vernon. **5.** city, pop. 12,001, seat of Wilbarger Co., NC Texas, 46 mi/74 km WNW of Wichita Falls, on the Pease R., 11 mi/18 km SW of the Red R. (the Oklahoma line). A commercial center for a region producing oil, wheat, cotton, and cattle, it was established in 1880 on a Texas–Kansas cattle trail. It is headquarters for the vast W.T. Waggoner ranch, where the Electra oilfield was discovered in 1911. The city has various light manufactures. Vernon Regional Junior College (1970) is here.

Vernon Hills village, pop. 15,319, Lake Co., NE Illinois, a residential suburb 20 mi/32 km NW of Chicago.

Vero Beach city, pop. 17,350, seat of Indian River Co., EC Florida, on the INDIAN R. lagoon, 15 mi/24 km NNW of Fort Pierce. On the mainland and on Orchid I. (the Atlantic coast), it has 20 mi/32 km of beaches and noted sport fishing. It is also a shipping point for local citrus fruits, vegetables, and beef. Airplanes are manufactured, and there is a variety of light industry. Vero Beach is home to the spring training complex of the Los Angeles Dodgers (baseball), and to a Dodger farm team.

Verona borough, pop. 13,597, Essex Co., NE New Jersey, 6 mi/10 km SW of Passaic. Essentially a residential suburb, it is also a shopping hub, and has a variety of light industries.

Verrazano-Narrows Bridge double-decked automobile suspension bridge, opened 1964 between Staten I. and Brooklyn, New York. It crosses the NARROWS, between Upper and Lower New York Bay, and, with a central span of 4260 ft/1298 m, is the longest US suspension bridge. Its opening accelerated the development of Staten I.

Versailles city, pop. 7269, seat of Woodford Co., NC Kentucky, in the Bluegrass, 8 mi/13 km W of downtown Lexington. Founded in 1792, and historically a horse and whiskey producing center, it is now an affluent suburb.

Very Large Array radiotelescope facility on the Plains of San Agustin, WC New Mexico, at 7000 ft/2140 m, some 50 mi/80 km W of Socorro. Built 1974–81 as part of the National Radio Astronomy Observatory (other units are at GREEN BANK, West Virginia, and KITT PEAK, Arizona), it comprises 27 dish antennas 82 ft/25 m across, mounted on rail cars that move along tracks laid out in a Y, each arm up to 13 mi/21 km long. The Array photographs light waves from deep space.

Vestal town, pop. 26,733, Broome Co., SC New York, adjacent (SW) to Binghamton, along the Pennsylvania border. Suburban in the N, along the Susquehanna R., it produces building materials and is a recycling technology center. The S is rural.

Vestavia Hills city, pop. 19,749, Jefferson Co., C Alabama, 5 mi/8 km S of downtown Birmingham, on Shades Mt. Incorporated in 1955 and named for its landmark building, Vestavia Temple (1924, based on a Roman temple of Vesta), it is a residential suburb.

Veterans Stadium built in 1971 as part of the sports complex in South Philadelphia, Pennsylvania. It is home to the Philadelphia Eagles (football) and Phillies (baseball), and seats 65,000.

Vevay town, pop. 1393, seat of Switzerland Co., extreme SE Indiana, 15 mi/24 km E of Madison, on the Ohio R. In an area in which grain, livestock, tobacco, truck crops, dairy items, and flowers are produced, it was settled in 1796 by French Swiss, who established a noted winemaking industry. Edward Eggleston, author of *The Hoosier Schoolmaster* and other works depicting life in the region, was born here in 1837.

VIA formally, **VIA Rail Canada** government body that since 1978 has managed passenger rail service throughout Canada, taking over from both the CANADIAN NATIONAL and CANADIAN PACIFIC systems. Like AMTRAK in the US, it has expanded its role, from service management to provision and ownership of stations and equipment.

Vicksburg city, pop. 20,908, seat of Warren Co., W Mississippi, situated on bluffs above the Mississippi R. where it is joined by the Yazoo R., at the S extreme of the DELTA. The city rises on a series of terraces, and is noted for its precipitous streets. A Spanish outpost in 1790 and a mission established by Newitt Vick in 1814, it became by the 1820s a major river port. It is best known as the objective of the 1862–63 Vicksburg Campaign, which ended with the surrender of the strategically important city to Union forces led by U.S. Grant on July 4th, 1863. The Union victory, ending a 47-day siege, isolated Confederate states W of the Mississippi from those to the E and gave the Union complete control of the Mississippi. Today Vicksburg is a tourist center, attention focusing on the 1700-ac/690-ha Vicksburg National Military Park. It also ships cotton, livestock, lumber, and paper products. Refined oil, foundry products, lumber, chemicals, clothing, cottonseed oil, electrical equipment, and cement are among its manufactures.

Victoria **1.** city and provincial capital, pop. 71,228, Capital Regional District (pop. 299,500), SW British Columbia, at the SW tip of VANCOUVER I., overlooking the Juan de Fuca

Strait. It was founded (1843) as a HUDSON'S BAY COMPANY post, and prospered during the 1858 Fraser R. gold rush. It was the administrative center of Vancouver I. from 1843, and became capital of British Columbia in 1868. Its metropolitan area includes ESQUIMALT, OAK BAY, and SAANICH. A seaport and a commercial and distribution center, it is engaged in shipbuilding, lumber processing, fishing, food processing, and varied manufacturing, but is primarily a government and tourist center, noted for its gardens and British atmosphere. The University of Victoria (1963) and Victoria College (1903) are here. The city's well-known Beacon Hill Park is at the W terminus (Mile 0) of the TRANS-CANADA HIGHWAY. **2.** city, pop. 55,076, seat of Victoria Co., S Texas, 72 mi/116 km NE of Corpus Christi, on the Guadalupe R. It was established by Spanish settlers in 1824 and incorporated by the Republic of Texas in 1839. Many Germans settled here in the 1840s. Railroads brought economic growth to the cattle center later in the 19th century, and there has been petrochemical and natural gas production since the 1940s. The completion in 1963 of the 35 mi/56 km–long Victoria Barge Canal to the Gulf Intracoastal Waterway spurred industrial expansion, and the city has varied manufactures. The Victoria *Advocate,* published daily since 1846, is the state's second-oldest newspaper. Victoria College (1925), and the University of Houston: Victoria, are here.

Victoria Bridge French, **Pont Victoria** opened in Dec. 1859, the first bridge across the Saint Lawrence R. at MONTRÉAL, Québec. Built to carry Grand Trunk Railway trains, it established connections between the Atlantic coast and the Midwest (Windsor, Ontario). A noted engineering achievement of its day, it had a tubular, wrought-iron structure that was replaced with steel trusses at the end of the 19th century. Today it carries trains and road traffic between Montréal and Saint-Lambert, and has been joined by other bridges and tunnels including the Pont Jacques-Cartier or Harbor Bridge (cantilever, 1930), downstream, crossing the Île SAINTE-HÉLÈNE; and the Pont Champlain (continuous truss, 1962), upstream.

Victoria Island Canada's second-largest (and the world's ninth-largest) island, 83,896 sq mi/217,290 sq km, in the ARCTIC ARCHIPELAGO of the Northwest Territories. Separated from the mainland (S) by (W–E) Dolphin and Union Strait, Coronation Gulf, Dease Strait, and Queen Maud Gulf, and from BANKS I. (NW) by the Prince of Wales Strait, it is a largely flat CANADIAN SHIELD lowland, heavily glaciated and with a deeply indented coast that includes several long peninsulas. It rises to 2150 ft/655 m in the Shaler Mts. (N). A homeland of the Copper Inuit (see COPPERMINE), it has a small community at Holman (W); CAMBRIDGE BAY (SE) is its largest settlement.

Victoriaville city, pop. 21,495, Arthabaska census division, S Québec, 85 mi/137 km ENE of Montréal and 27 mi/43 km ENE of Drummondville, on the R. Nicolet, in the NOTRE DAME Mts. Agricultural machinery, furniture, sporting goods, clothing, and foundry products are among local manufactures; the city is also the service and processing center for a mixed farming region. The bilingual Collège de Victoriaville (1872) is here.

Victorville city, pop. 40,674, San Bernardino Co., S California, on the Mojave R., in the Apple Valley, at the S edge of the Mojave Desert, 50 mi/80 km NE of Los Angeles. A mining center from the 1870s to around 1900, it has produced granite, limestone, and gold, and is now the site of a number of cement plants. Poultry and cattle are raised locally. The city and area were used from about 1914 by movie studios filming westerns; tourists are now drawn esp. to the Roy Rogers–Dale Evans Museum. George Air Force Base, just NW in ADELANTO, is an economic asset, and Victor Valley College (1960) is here. Victorville grew rapidly in the 1980s as a residential community.

Vidalia city, pop. 11,078, Toombs and Montgomery counties, SE Georgia, 75 mi/120 km WNW of Savannah. Famous for the sweet onions grown in the region, the city is also home to fertilizer, cottonseed oil, and turpentine industries.

Vidor city, pop. 10,935, Orange Co., E Texas, 7 mi/11 km NE of Beaumont. A residential and industrial (steel) suburb in the PINEY WOODS, it was in the national spotlight in the early 1990s as the Federal government attempted to integrate its housing; it has a history of Ku Klux Klan activity.

Vieja Mountains see SIERRA VIEJA, Texas.

Vienna **1.** town, pop. 14,852, Fairfax Co., NE Virginia, 12 mi/19 km W of Washington, D.C., just outside the BELTWAY. A primarily residential suburb, it has a technology park. Vienna has grown dramatically since World War II. TYSONS CORNER is just NE, and WOLF TRAP FARM PARK is 2 mi/3 km N. **2.** city, pop. 10,862, Wood Co., NW West Virginia, on the Ohio R., 4 mi/6 km N of Parkersburg. The area was settled in the 1790s. Its industries have included truck farming and the manufacture of silk thread, vitrolite, and glass.

Vieques also, **Crab Island** island MUNICIPIO, pop. (with smaller nearby islands) 8602, 8 mi/13 km off the E coast of Puerto Rico. The fertile main island, 21 mi/34 km E–W and up to 4 mi/6 km wide, was annexed by Puerto Rico in 1854; it has sugarcane and pineapple plantations and pastures where cattle and hogs graze and a few wild horses roam, and produces refined sugar, charcoal, and dairy goods. The hilly island has a warm, dry climate and has become a popular beach resort locale. Its chief settlement is Vieques (pop. 2359), founded in 1843 and also called Isabela Segunda (or Isabela II), in the center. Two-thirds of the island, at either end, has been used by the US Navy since World War II for exercises and as a firing range. **Vieques Sound** (N) separates the island from CULEBRA, 10 mi/16 km away.

Vieux Carré also, **French Quarter** historic residential and commercial district in DOWNTOWN New Orleans, Louisiana. Centered around JACKSON SQUARE, it is the oldest (1718) part of the city. It is bounded by the Mississippi R. (SE), Iberville St. (SW), Esplanade Ave. (NE), and Rampart St. (NW). Its characteristic structures are French and Spanish colonial adaptations, mostly built by Spaniards and Americans following the Louisiana Purchase. Only one authentic French building remains, the Ursuline Convent (1750), thought to be the oldest building in the Mississippi Valley. All other 18th-century structures were destroyed by fires in 1788 and 1794. The term French Quarter is now commonly applied to an area larger than that of the Vieux Carré.

Vieux-Montréal English, **Old Montreal** original center of MONTRÉAL, Québec, on the waterfront on the N (W) shore of the St. Lawrence R., fronting Montréal's harbor, site of the first permanent settlement of the city, Ville-Marie, established in May 1642 and enclosed by a wall during the 18th century. Today it is an historic area, centered around the Place Jacques-Cartier, which slopes downhill from the Hôtel de Ville (City Hall). Nearby is the Place d'Armes, on the site where the Sieur de Maisonneuve defeated an Iroquois force in 1644. Significant sites include the Seminary of Saint-Sulpice (1685), Montréal's oldest building; the Basilique Nôtre Dame (1824–70); the Château Ramezay (1705), long the governor's mansion; and the Pointe-à-Callière, cleared in 1611 and used by the first settlers in 1642. In commercial decline after the mid 19th century, Vieux-Montréal has been substantially redeveloped since the 1960s, and is now an office, government, and visitor center. SAINT JAMES St. (Rue Saint-Jacques) passes along its W.

Vieux-Québec the older parts of QUÉBEC CITY, Québec, both in the LOWER TOWN and within the walls of the UPPER TOWN. Expansion of the city since the mid 20th century has occurred chiefly W and N of the Upper Town. Vieux-Québec is residential and commercial, and a major tourist attraction.

village **1.** in the US, an incorporated municipality, usually but not necessarily smaller than a town, borough, or city; the village of SKOKIE, Illinois, has a pop. of 59,432. For Alaska Native Villages, see under INDIAN RESERVATION. **2.** in Canadian census terminology, a census subdivision, found in all provinces except Newfoundland, Prince Edward Island, and Nova Scotia. Variants include **resort villages** (Saskatchewan) and **summer villages** (Alberta). Cree, Naskapi, and Northern Villages are types of INDIAN RESERVE. **3.** historically, a small settlement in an agricultural area, larger than a HAMLET; also, a small, cohesive community in an urban setting.

Village, the **1.** see GREENWICH VILLAGE, New York. **2.** see THE VILLAGE, Oklahoma.

Villanova locality in RADNOR township, Delaware Co., SE Pennsylvania, 12 mi/19 km NW of Philadelphia, the seat of Villanova University (1842) and Northeast Christian Junior College (1956).

Villa Park village, pop. 22,253, Du Page Co., NE Illinois, on Salt Creek, 20 mi/32 km W of Chicago. Originally a railroad suburb dating back to the early 20th century, it is a residential community that also has beverage and fertilizer plants.

ville in Québec, a census subdivision (municipality) designated in other provinces as either a TOWN or a CITY.

Ville Marie see under VIEUX-MONTRÉAL, Montréal, Québec.

Ville Platte town, pop. 9037, seat of Evangeline Parish, SC Louisiana, 35 mi/56 km NNW of Lafayette, in a rice, timber, and cotton producing region where there is also oil drilling.

Vinalhaven Island in the Atlantic Ocean at the mouth of Penobscot Bay, in Knox Co., SC Maine. Seven mi/11 km long N–S and 5 mi/8 km wide, the hilly island has a heavily indented coastline and is bordered by Isle au Haut Bay on the E. At the S end, in an area once quarried for granite, is the Armbrust Hill Wildlife Reservation. A ferry from the village of Vinalhaven connects it to ROCKLAND. Just N of the island is **North Haven Island,** 8 mi/13 km NE–SW, and 0.5–3 mi/1–5 km wide, with the village of North Haven on its S end. The Fox Islands Thorofare, which separates North Haven and Vinalhaven, is well known to sailors.

Vincennes city, pop. 19,859, seat of Knox Co., SW Indiana, on the Wabash R. (the Illinois border), 55 mi/89 km S of Terre Haute. The oldest town in Indiana, it was a French mission (1702), was settled by French fur traders, and was fortified by the Sieur de Vincennes (1732) and named for him (1736). The settlement grew up around the fort, was ceded to Great Britain (1763), and was captured (1779) by Americans under George Rogers Clark. It was capital of the Indiana Territory in 1800–13. Today it is a trade center for a wheat and fruit farming region that also produces oil, coal, gas, and gravel. Its industries make fabricated steel, glass, batteries, wood and paper products, plastics, glass, and other goods. The city has numerous historic sites, including the George Rogers Clark memorial (1932) in Clark Historical Park, the William Henry Harrison Mansion (1804), and the territorial capitol (c.1800). It is the seat of Vincennes University (1801).

Vine City residential and commercial district of downtown Atlanta, Georgia, 1 mi/1.5 km WNW of FIVE POINTS and just W of the GEORGIA DOME. Economically depressed, it is expected to be significantly affected by the staging of the 1996 Olympic Games.

Vineland city, pop. 54,780, Cumberland Co., S New Jersey, on the Maurice R., 31 mi/50 km SE of Camden. It was a planned agricultural community, developed in 1861. The wine grape industry that gave the city its name was destroyed by disease in the late 19th century. In 1951 Vineland merged with Landis township, growing to an area of 69 sq mi/179 sq km. Situated in a rich vegetable growing and poultry raising region, the city has many cooperative markets and is the agricultural trade, processing, and distribution center of S New Jersey. Also a manufacturing hub, it produces glassware, clothing, chemicals, cement blocks, foundry products, paper boxes, and machinery. The city is the seat of Cumberland County College (1964).

Vineyard, the see MARTHA'S VINEYARD, Massachusetts.

Vineyard Haven village in the town of TISBURY, Dukes Co., SE Massachusetts, on Martha's Vineyard. Vineyard Haven has ferry connections to Cape Cod, and is a busy summer resort, with boutiques, shops, and inns. Its harbor was an important refuge for British warships during the Revolution.

Vinings unincorporated community, pop. 7414, Cobb Co., N Georgia, 9 mi/14 km NW of downtown Atlanta, across the Chattahoochee R. (formerly via Paces Ferry) from the city. On high ground where W. T. Sherman viewed Atlanta at the beginning of this 1864 siege of the city, Vinings is now a commercial and residential suburb, with many new office towers.

Vinland unidentified land described in early-11th-century Norse literature, somewhere on the NE coast of North America. Following the accidental landfall, in c.986, of Bjarni Herjolfsson somewhere to the SW of Greenland, Leif Ericsson in c.1000 sailed W from Greenland and turned S when he encountered land. His first landfall he named Helluland ("land of stones"); it has been identified as mountainous S BAFFIN I. and perhaps the N Labrador coast. Farther S, Leif came to what he called Markland ("land of forests"), thought to be the S LABRADOR coast. He then spent the winter in a protected harbor in a place where his crew found timber, salmon, and grazing land for their animals. This he called Vinland. Arguments over its location hinge on the meaning of the name. If Leif meant "vine," it could not be as far N as N Newfoundland, where vines do not grow; if, however, he was following usage of his day and meant "grazing ground," the leading candidate has long been the N end of Newfoundland's GREAT NORTHERN PENINSULA. There, in 1960, the Norwegian Helge Ingstad found L'ANSE AUX MEADOWS, which many think is Vinland. Earlier candidates, based on the meaning "vine," have ranged from Virginia through Nova Scotia, with the mouth of Massachusetts's CHARLES R. and the area of Newport, Rhode Island, prominent among them. No fully accepted evidence of Norse settlement has, however, been found anywhere in North America except at L'Anse aux Meadows.

Violet unincorporated community, pop. 8574, St. Bernard Parish, SE Louisiana, on the E (N) bank of the Mississippi R., 10 mi/16 km ESE of New Orleans, at the W terminus of the Lake Borgne or Violet Canal, which connects the Mississippi with L. BORGNE. Its economy is largely maritime (fishing, seafood packing).

Virden town, pop. 2894, SW Manitoba, 40 mi/64 km W of Brandon and 172 mi/277 km W of Winnipeg, near the Assiniboine R. This former agricultural and grain shipping center in the prairie grew to prosperity in the 1950s with the discovery of rich oil resources, the first in the province to be commercially productive. Farming, potash mining, retail services, and manufacturing also contribute to the economy.

Virginia officially, **Commonwealth of Virginia** southeastern US state, the northeasternmost of the Confederacy, variously considered a Border State or part of the Upland SOUTH; 1990 pop. 6,187,358 (115.7% of 1980; rank: 12th); area 42,769 sq mi/110,772 sq km (rank: 35th); ratified Constitution 1788 (10th). Capital: RICHMOND. Most populous cities: VIRGINIA BEACH, NORFOLK, Richmond, NEWPORT NEWS, CHESAPEAKE, HAMPTON, ALEXANDRIA, PORTSMOUTH. Virginia is bordered N by Maryland and the District of Columbia (in the E, across the POTOMAC R.); by West Virginia (in the C and W); and by Kentucky (in the extreme W). On the S it is bordered by North Carolina (E) and Tennessee (extreme W). In the E, across CHESAPEAKE BAY, Accomack and Northampton counties occupy the S tip of the DELMARVA PENINSULA. The TIDEWATER, part of the Atlantic COASTAL PLAIN along Chesapeake Bay, is drained NW–SE and divided into "necks" (see NORTHERN NECK) by (N–S) the Potomac, RAPPAHANNOCK, YORK, and JAMES rivers; at the mouth of the last, in the extreme SE, is HAMPTON ROADS, an historic port and naval/industrial complex. Above (W of) the FALL LINE is the PIEDMONT, a rich agricultural region with Richmond on its SE, CHARLOTTESVILLE in the NC, and LYNCHBURG in the SW. The BLUE RIDGE runs SW–NE on the W of the Piedmont; on its W are ridges including the Iron Mts., rising to 5729 ft/1746 m (the state's high point) at Mt. ROGERS, near the North Carolina line. Also beyond the Blue Ridge lies the Great APPALACHIAN Valley, here known as the **Valley of Virginia;** its most famous section is the SHENANDOAH Valley (N). To the W of the valley are ridges of the ALLEGHENY Mts. and (SW) part of the CUMBERLAND PLATEAU, along the West Virginia and Kentucky borders. The NEW, CLINCH, and some other rivers in the valley flow SW or NW into the Mississippi R. watershed. At Virginia's SW tip is the CUMBERLAND GAP, through which 18th- and 19th-century pioneers traveled W toward the Ohio Valley and NORTHWEST TERRITORY. Home to various Algonquian peoples, including the tribes of the eastern Powhatan Confederacy, Virginia was the site of the first (1607) permanent English settlement in America, at JAMESTOWN. A plantation economy quickly developed in the Tidewater, with indentured European servants and (from 1619) African servants or slaves tending tobacco, indigo, and other crops; exports and other trade with the West Indies and Europe were important. By the 1620s a House of Burgesses elected by the planters was governing the colony, which was named for Queen Elizabeth I ("the Virgin Queen"). Agricultural prosperity, the ample space available, and relatively inactive Colonial government bred power and habits of independence among the planters, and by the 18th century Virginia was providing many of the men who took the Thirteen COLONIES toward separation from Britain, then filled early national leadership roles. In the Revolutionary War, Virginia provided a large proportion of the manpower of the Continental Army, with money and other resources; the last battle of the war was fought (1781) at YORKTOWN. After independence, Virginians were prominent in establishing Kentucky as a state, settling the Northwest Territory, exploring the LOUISIANA PURCHASE, and in other ways expanding the United States. The commonwealth itself began to lose prominence, however, its ties to the PLANTATION economy of the South attenuating to the point that it almost abolished slavery decades before the Civil War. Nevertheless, although it hesitated to join the Confederacy in 1861 (and the antislavery counties that now form West Virginia left it in 1863), it soon became the industrial and military leader (and Richmond the capital) of the Southern states. Much of the most serious action of the Civil War took place in Virginia, from BULL RUN (MANASSAS) to Lee's surrender at APPOMATTOX. War sites here are well known, including the WILDERNESS, FREDERICKSBURG, CHANCELLORSVILLE, SPOTSYLVANIA, Yorktown, COLD HARBOR, the Crater at PETERSBURG, Hampton Roads (where the *Monitor* and the *Merrimack* dueled), and the Shenandoah Valley, scene of many engagements. At war's end the commonwealth was devastated; it was not readmitted to the Union until 1870, and for the next three-quarters of a century recovered slowly. The development of a coal-and-railroad economy in the Appalachians, esp. around ROANOKE, brought some new wealth, and manufacturing gradually became central to Richmond (tobacco products, chemicals), Danville (textiles), Lynchburg, and other cities. World War II and expansion of the Federal government initiated a period of real change. Military expenditures have been central to the prosperity of Newport News, Norfolk, and the other cities of the Hampton Roads area, and the environs of Washington (esp. Alexandria and ARLINGTON Co., which were retroceded to Virginia in 1846, having been part of the DISTRICT OF COLUMBIA from 1791), within and outside the BELTWAY, have become home to many Federal installations (including the PENTAGON, the Central Intelligence Agency at Langley, and a number of military bases) and to thousands of Federal workers, in such communities as RESTON and FALLS CHURCH. TYSONS CORNER and ROSSLYN are representative of explosively growing new office-commercial-residential complexes near the national capital. This part of Virginia is diverse, its people largely non-Southerners, including many Asians and other recent immigrants. Away from the Washington and Richmond metropolitan areas, however, large parts of the commonwealth remain closer to their longtime Southern character, esp. the area known as Southside, along the North Carolina border to the W of the Hampton Roads, where peanuts, tobacco, hogs, and other crops continue to be raised on large farms and the pop. remains a "traditional" mix of long-established whites and blacks. Similarly, the Tidewater remains largely rural and agricultural, and the Appalachian towns of the N, NW, and SW are little touched by the growth of MEGALOPOLIS. Tourism and recreation are important esp. at such historic sites as George Washington's MOUNT VERNON, Thomas Jefferson's MONTICELLO, Civil War battlefields, and the old capital and THEME PARK of WILLIAMSBURG, and in the

Appalachian region (e.g., the Blue Ridge's SKYLINE DRIVE, the NATURAL BRIDGE, forests, and health resorts). The University of Virginia, founded by Jefferson, is at Charlottesville; the University of William and Mary, at Williamsburg, is the nation's second-oldest (1693).

Virginia city, pop. 9410, St. Louis Co., NE Minnesota, in the MESABI RANGE, 20 mi/32 km NE of Hibbing. Founded as a lumbering town, it has been a mining center since the discovery of taconite deposits in 1870. Vast mines surround the city, which processes ore into taconite pellets. Clothing and foundry products are also manufactured. Also a resort center, Virginia is a a gateway to Lookout Mt. Ski Area to the N, Superior National Forest and the Vermilion Iron Range to the NE, and many lakes throughout the area. It is the seat of Mesabi Community College (1918).

Virginia Beach independent city, pop. 393,069, in SE Virginia, adjacent to NORFOLK and CHESAPEAKE (W), and on CHESAPEAKE BAY (N) and the Atlantic Ocean (E). Formed by the merger of the town of Virginia Beach and Queen Anne Co. in 1963, it is now Virginia's most populous city. Long primarily a beach resort, it continues to rely on tourism; other sources of revenue are agriculture (grains, dairy products) and four large military installations (the Little Creek Naval Amphibious Base, Oceana Naval Air Station, Fleet Combat Direction Systems Warfare Training Center at Dam Neck, and Fort Story, an Army transportation command), with their residential and commercial communities. Areas of Virginia Beach outside its urban section (N) engage in horse raising and dairy farming, and the city's beaches and bays host a wide range of water sports. The Cape HENRY Memorial, at the entrance to Chesapeake Bay, commemorates the first landing (1607) by the Jamestown settlers. Virginia Wesleyan College (1961) straddles the line between Virginia Beach and Norfolk. The CHESAPEAKE BAY BRIDGE-TUNNEL connects Virginia Beach with the DELMARVA PENINSULA.

Virginia City **1.** town, pop. 142, seat of Madison Co., SW Montana, 34 mi/55 km NE of Dillon. One of Montana's oldest towns, it grew up after gold was discovered in nearby Alder Gulch in 1863. Eventually, local mines yielded $300 million before the ore was depleted. Virginia City served as the territorial capital from 1865 to 1876. Livestock and tourism are now economic mainstays, and much of the town has been reconstructed. **2.** hamlet, seat of Storey Co., W Nevada, in the E foothills of the SIERRA NEVADA, 15 mi/24 km SSE of Reno. It was settled in 1859 after two miners on Mt. Davidson found gold caked in blue-black dirt that proved to be incredibly rich silver ore; this was the discovery of the COMSTOCK LODE. During the 1860s Virginia City had a pop. of 30,000 and was a world-famous mining town; it produced over $1 billion in gold and silver in its boom years. During this time both Mark Twain and Bret Harte were residents, reporting for the *Territorial Enterprise.* It is known for the many sumptuous Victorian homes built by the suddenly wealthy. Tourism flourishes today partly because of the frontier architecture, much of which has been restored. Visitors are also drawn to the operating Virginia and Truckee Railroad, between Virginia City and Gold Hill (S), Piper's Opera House, and museums.

Virginia-Highland residential and commercial neighborhood of Atlanta, Georgia, 2.8 mi/4.5 km NE of FIVE POINTS, just W of DRUID HILLS. Having undergone revitalization by young urbanites in recent years, it is a popular entertainment zone.

Virginia Key resort island, c.2 mi/3 km long, in Dade Co., SE Florida, bordered by Biscayne Bay (S and W) and the Atlantic Ocean (E), c.1 mi/1.5 km S of Miami Beach. Part of Greater Miami, it is connected with the city (W) and Key Biscayne (S) by the Rickenbacker Causeway. A popular tourist destination, it is the site of the Miami Seaquarium and Marine Stadium.

Virginia Military District lands in modern Ohio reserved by the Commonwealth of Virginia in 1784, when the rest of its claims in the NORTHWEST TERRITORY were relinquished to the new national government, for homes for Virginia soldiers who had fought the British in the area during the Revolutionary War. Lying between the Miami (W) and Scioto (E) rivers, N of the Ohio R., in Scioto, Adams, Brown, Clermont, and adjacent counties, it became part of the new state in 1803.

Virginia Mountains roughly triangular NNW–SSE range in NW Nevada, between Reno (W), PYRAMID L. (NE), and the Carson R. valley (S). While its high point is Virginia Peak (8366 ft/2550 m), in the N or Pyramid Range section, its most famous is Mt. Davidson (7870 ft/2399 m), just W of Virginia City in the S section (called the Virginia or Washoe Range), site of the COMSTOCK LODE. The range has yielded vast mineral wealth, esp. in silver.

Virgin Islands, United States group of three major and some 40 smaller islands, totaling 133 sq mi/344 sq km (pop. 101,809), between the Atlantic Ocean (N) and the Caribbean Sea (S), some 40 mi/64 km E of Puerto Rico, across the Virgin Passage, some 1100 mi/1770 km ESE of Miami, Florida, and 1625 mi/2615 km SSE of New York City. Generally considered the northwesternmost of the Lesser Antilles, they are geologically the easternmost of the Greater Antilles (akin to Puerto Rico, Hispaniola, Cuba, and Jamaica), volcanic in origin and limestone-covered. Immediately NE are the smaller and less populous British Virgin Islands. The three main islands in the US group are SAINT CROIX, SAINT THOMAS, and SAINT JOHN. Mountainous, and with good sheltered harbors, they benefit from cool NE TRADE WINDS, but are occasionally subject to devastating hurricanes (like Hugo, in 1988). CHARLOTTE AMALIE, on St. Thomas, is the capital and largest community in this unincorporated US territory; other major settlements are CHRISTIANSTED and FREDERIKSTED, on St. Croix. Columbus landed at St. Croix on his second voyage (1493), and the group, whose number could not be counted, was named for the 5th-century St. Ursula and her Eleven Thousand Virgins. Native Caribs and Arawaks were soon exterminated. For most of two centuries the islands were chiefly a haven for pirates and privateers. After an abortive mid-17th-century Dutch attempt, the Danish West India & Guinea Company established a colony on St. Thomas in 1672. The Danes claimed St. John in 1683 and purchased St. Croix from France in 1733. The islands became the site of sugarcane plantations worked by slave labor. With the development of the European sugar beet industry and the end of slavery in 1848, they fell into economic decline. Late-19th-century treaties between the US and Denmark foreshadowed the 1917 US purchase of the Danish West Indies, in part to help protect the Panama Canal against anticipated German attack. Development of the islands has occurred largely since World War II. Their people, mostly descendants of slaves, are US citizens but without a vote in Federal elections. Livestock and sugarcane are raised, and sugar, rum, and bay rum are exported; in addition, African bauxite and Caribbean crude oil are processed. The islands' lifeblood, however, is tourism; beaches, surrounding waters, and vestiges of the colonial period all attract visitors.

Virgin Islands National Park 14,689 ac/5949 ha, including about 75% of the land area of SAINT JOHN, in the US Virgin Islands, as well as coastal waters; Hassel I., in SAINT THOMAS Harbor (off CHARLOTTE AMALIE) is also part. Established in 1956, the park preserves Carib and Danish (sugar plantation and mill) vestiges as well as beaches, coves, and hills. Its visitor center is at Cruz Bay.

Visalia city, pop. 75,636, seat of Tulare Co., SC California, in the San Joaquin Valley, on headwaters of the Kaweah R., 35 mi/56 km SE of Fresno. Founded in 1852 by Nathaniel Vise, and the oldest CENTRAL VALLEY city S of Stockton, it developed as an agricultural and cattle center. Citrus fruit, olives, grapes, cotton, and vegetables are grown locally, and there is some electronic and other light manufacturing. The city is a gateway to Sequoia and Kings Canyon national parks (E). The College of the Sequoias (1925) is here. Visalia has grown rapidly since the 1960s.

Vista city, pop. 71,872, San Diego Co., SW California, 7 mi/11 km E of Oceanside and 32 mi/51 km N of San Diego. In foothills along Buena Creek, this once primarily agricultural community, which has engaged in truck farming, poultry raising, and avocado, citrus, and flower growing, has expanded rapidly since the 1950s as a residential suburb.

Vizcaya also, **Viscaya** or **Villa Viscaya,** estate (1916) and gardens in the S part of Miami, Florida, on Biscayne Bay. Formerly the winter residence of industrialist James Deering, the 34-room Italian Renaissance–style villa is now the Dade County Art Museum. Outside is a 10-ac/4-ha complex of formal gardens, sculpture, pools, and fountains.

Vogtle nuclear power plant: see under WAYNESBORO, Georgia.

Volusia County 1113 sq mi/2883 sq km, pop. 370,712, in NE Florida, on the Atlantic Ocean (E). Its seat is DE LAND. It has a lively tourist industry, particularly in beachfront communities such as Daytona Beach, Ormond Beach, and New Smyrna Beach. Sprinkled with lakes and natural springs, the interior parts also rely on tourism; in addition, this section is filled with citrus groves.

Voorhees township, pop. 24,559, Camden Co., SW New Jersey, just S of Cherry Hill. It is primarily residential.

voyageurs see under COUREURS DE BOIS.

Voyageurs National Park 218,000 ac/88,300 ha, in N Minnesota, along the Ontario border. Some 80,000 ac/32,500 ha is water surface; the park memorializes the French commercial explorers who were in this area by the 17th century. Its headquarters are at International Falls. The Kabetogama Peninsula, the park's largest body of land, lies between Kabetogama L. (S) and Rainy L. (see RAINY R.). Namakan L., to the E, is an extension of Rainy L. SUPERIOR NATIONAL FOREST is adjacent to the SE.

W

Wabana see under BELL I., Newfoundland.

Wabash city, pop. 12,127, seat of Wabash Co., NC Indiana, on the Wabash R., 45 mi/72 km SW of Fort Wayne. Settled in 1827 following the 1826 Treaty of Paradise Springs, between the Miami and whites, it developed in the 1830s as a river and canal port, and flourished later in the century with the discovery of natural gas. It is a trade and processing center for a region producing corn, wheat, vegetables, fruit, and livestock. Among its manufactures are tires and other rubber goods, woodworking machinery, paperboard, furniture, and electrical products. Wabash claims to be the first city in the world to have had electrical illumination (March 31, 1880).

Wabash River 475 mi/765 km long, in Ohio, Indiana, and Illinois. It rises along the Darke-Mercer county line in W Ohio, and flows E, W, N, and then NW into Indiana, passing BLUFFTON, to HUNTINGTON. It then flows generally WSW through WABASH, LOGANSPORT, and LAFAYETTE. At Covington it turns and flows S to TERRE HAUTE. Ten mi/16 km SW of Terre Haute it forms the Illinois-Indiana border, continuing for some 200 mi/320 km SSW, past VINCENNES and NEW HARMONY, until it empties into the Ohio R. at the Indiana-Illinois-Kentucky junction. The river once acted as a spillway of glacial L. Maumee, of which L. Erie is now a remnant. It provided area tribes the easiest route between L. Erie and the Ohio Valley. Its Algonquian name means something like "water over a white bottom." During the 18th century the French used it as a transportation route between Louisiana and Québec. Early in the 19th century, American settlers moved up the Wabash Valley from the Ohio Valley. The river is navigable, and by 1853 the **Wabash and Erie Canal,** 460 mi/740 km long, followed it in part as it connected L. Erie with the Ohio R. at Evansville, but the development of railroads, also in the 1850s, left river and canal rarely used. The Wabash's chief tributaries are the White, Tippecanoe, Vermilion, Little Wabash, Eel, Salamonie, Mississinewa, and Embarrass rivers.

Wabush town, pop. 2331, SW Labrador, on Jean L., near the Québec border. It and neighboring (NW) LABRADOR CITY had their beginnings in the late 1950s as mining camps linked to the large iron-ore deposits in the nearby Wapussakatoo Mts.

W. A. C. Bennett Dam see under WILLISTON L., British Columbia.

Waccamaw River 140 mi/210 km long, in SE North Carolina and E South Carolina. It rises in 10,000-ac/4000-ha, roughly ovoid **L. Waccamaw,** 36 mi/58 km WNW of Wilmington, North Carolina, and flows SSW and SW to Winyah Bay near GEORGETOWN, South Carolina. Tidal in its lower reaches, as it flows behind the GRAND STRAND (once known as Waccamaw Neck), it is navigable to CONWAY, 44 mi/71 km above its mouth. The Atlantic Intracoastal Waterway follows it for 30 mi/48 km.

Wachovia see under WINSTON-SALEM, North Carolina.

Wachusett Mountain monadnock (2006 ft/612 m) in NC Massachusetts, 8 mi/13 km SW of Fitchburg. The highest mountain in the center of the state, it offers panoramic views of the peneplain. Mt. Wachusett State Reservation, between Princeton and Westminster, is a popular recreation area.

Wachusett Reservoir in Worcester Co., C Massachusetts, 5 mi/8 km NE of Worcester. Created by construction of the Wachusett Dam in 1906 on the South Branch of the Nashua R., it is 8.5 mi/14 km long, and supplies the Boston metropolitan area with water, some of which it receives through the Quabbin Aqueduct from QUABBIN RESERVOIR.

Waco city, pop. 103,590, seat of McLennan Co. (pop. 189,123), EC Texas, 85 mi/137 km SSW of Dallas, on the Brazos R. It was established in 1849 in a farming area near a Texas Ranger fort (1837) on the site of a Waco (Hueco) village burned by Cherokees in 1830. A CHISHOLM TRAIL river crossing after the Civil War, it had a cattle- and cotton-based economy before growth was stimulated by the railroad's arrival in 1881. Waco is now a commercial hub for the grain and cotton producing BLACKLANDS. Its varied manufactures include tires and dry-cleaning equipment. Baylor University was founded here in 1845, and among several other institutions is Paul Quinn College (1872), Texas's first black college. The city also has a number of large medical institutions, is known for its large 1870 suspension bridge, and draws substantial tourist and convention trade. The government siege and the fiery destruction of an armed religious (Branch Davidian) compound E of the city drew world attention to Waco in early 1993.

Waddington, Mount peak, 13,104 ft/3994 m, highest point in the COAST Mts., in SW British Columbia, 175 mi/280 km NNW of Vancouver. The Franklin and other smaller glaciers flow from it. Waddington is the highest mountain entirely within British Columbia.

Wade Hampton unincorporated community, pop. 20,014, Greenville Co., NW South Carolina, a predominantly white residential suburb on the NE side of GREENVILLE.

Wadmalaw Island see under JOHNS I., South Carolina.

Wadsworth city, pop. 15,718, Medina Co., NE Ohio, 12 mi/19 km W of Akron. Founded c.1815 by Vermonters, it was named for Elijah Wadsworth, a Revolutionary War general. The economy of the area was based on farming and trade until after the Civil War, when coal mining became the dominant industry. Matches, valves, cardboard containers, salt, processed foods, and rubber products have been among the city's subsequent manufactures. Approximately half of Wadsworth's residents commute to jobs in Akron or Cleveland.

Wagon Box battle site: see under BOZEMAN TRAIL, Wyoming.

Wahiawa unincorporated community, pop. 17,386, Honolulu Co., Hawaii, in C Oahu, on the Leilehua Plateau, 17 mi/27 km NW of Honolulu. A longtime pineapple growing and shipping center, it is also a commercial hub for local plantations and for SCHOFIELD BARRACKS and nearby Wheeler Air Force Base.

Wahoo city, pop. 3681, seat of Saunders Co., EC Nebraska, 34 mi/54 km W of Omaha. Founded in 1865, it is a trading and processing center for a grain and dairy farming region. Its light industries include the manufacture of building products. The city was the birthplace of baseball player "Wahoo Sam" Crawford (1880–1968), composer Howard Hanson (1896–1981), and movie industry titan Darryl F. Zanuck (1902–79).

Wahpeton city, pop. 8751, seat of Richland Co., extreme SE North Dakota, on the Minnesota border at the place where the Bois de Sioux and Otter Tail rivers join the Red R. of the North, 40 mi/64 km SSE of Fargo. Founded in 1869, it has printing and dairy plants and flour mills and is a processing and marketing center for cattle, poultry, and grain. Its manufactures include pottery and sheet iron. It is the seat of the North Dakota State College of Science (1889) and the Wahpeton Indian School, which serves Ojibwa and Sioux from Minnesota and the Dakotas.

Waialeale mountain in C KAUAI, Hawaii, rising to 5080 ft/1548 m. To the W it slopes down to the WAIMEA CANYON. Waialeale's NE slope, facing the TRADE WINDS, with annual rainfall sometimes over 480 in/1229 cm, and up to 350 rainy days a year, is sometimes considered the wettest spot on earth.

Waianae Mountains also, **Waianae Range** NW–SE volcanic range paralleling the W coast of OAHU, Hawaii, for 22 mi/35 km. Kaala, in the N, is the highest point on the island at 4039 ft/1231 m. The mountains demonstrate severe erosion, especially on the W side, which has dramatic valleys, and at the N end, which ends in steep sea cliffs.

Waikiki resort area on Mamala Bay, in SE HONOLULU, Hawaii. About 2 mi/4 km long, bordered by the Ala Wai Canal (N) and extending to Sans Souci Beach, near DIAMOND HEAD (SE), it was an early-19th-century resort of Hawaiian royalty, and by 1900 an exclusive urban district, which became widely known after World War II GIs were housed in the area. Behind its beaches stand high-rise hotels and residential buildings. Kapiolani Park is near Diamond Head.

Wailuku unincorporated community, pop. 10,688, seat of Maui Co., EC Hawaii, on the NE coast of MAUI I. An 1830s missionary and educational settlement, it is a port and service center, with a brewery and some other light industry, just E of the W Maui mountains. The nearby (W) Iao Valley, dominated by the 1200-ft/366-m Iao Needle, was the scene of a bloody 1790 battle between Maui warriors and the invading Hawaiian forces of Kamehameha I.

Waimalu unincorporated community, pop. 29,967, Honolulu Co., Hawaii, a residential and commercial suburb on the NE side of PEARL HARBOR, just E of Pearl City and just NW of Aiea.

Waimea Canyon also, the **Grand Canyon of the Pacific** extending N–S for some 15 mi/24 km through W KAUAI I., NW Hawaii, along the Waimea R. It reaches c.3600 ft/1100 m in depth. To the W is the Na Pali Coast, whose cliffs reach 4000 ft/1220 m. Captain James Cook made his first Hawaii landing (Jan. 20, 1778) at **Waimea** (unincorporated, pop. 1840, Kauai Co.), at the canyon's S end.

Wainwright town, pop. 4732, EC Alberta, 115 mi/185 km ESE of Edmonton. In farming and ranching country, it trades and ships wheat and cattle. Numerous oil and gas wells and an oil refinery are in the area. Founded (1905) as Denwood, the town was later moved 2 mi/4 km to a Grand Trunk Pacific Railway divisional point. Oil and gas were discovered in 1919. Nearby Camp Wainwright, a Canadian Forces Base, was a buffalo reserve until World War II.

Wainwright Building ten-story office building in downtown SAINT LOUIS, Missouri, just N of Busch Memorial Stadium. A pioneering steel-frame structure by Louis H. Sullivan, noted for its emphasis on the vertical, and influential on subsequent American design, it was completed in 1892.

Waipahu unincorporated community, pop. 31,435, Honolulu Co., Hawaii, on S Oahu, on the NW shore of PEARL HARBOR, 11 mi/18 km NW of Honolulu. The original settlement was surrounded by sugarcane fields, and developed around a sugar mill. It is now a residential suburb for Pearl Harbor and for workers at nearby industrial plants.

Waitsburg city, pop. 990, Walla Walla Co., SE Washington, on the Touchet R., 16 mi/26 km NNE of Walla Walla. Founded in 1859, it raised cattle, horses, and wheat, and had a gristmill. After the railroad arrived (1881), it prospered as a grain milling and shipping center. Situated in a fertile farm area, it trades and distributes wheat and apples. The poet Genevieve Taggard was born here (1894).

Wake County 854 sq mi/2212 sq km, pop. 423,380, in EC North Carolina, in the Piedmont, drained by the Neuse R. Its seat is the state capital, RALEIGH, which with its Federal and state offices, industry, and growing suburbs like CARY and GARNER, dominates the economy of a formerly essentially agricultural county.

Wakefield **1.** town, pop. 24,825, Middlesex Co., NE Massachusetts, on the Saugus R., 10 mi/16 km N of Boston. The villages of Greenwood, Wakefield Junction, and Montrose, as well as Crystal L. and L. Quannapowitt, are within its borders. The site of the first rattan factory in the world, Wakefield, now on ROUTE 128, manufactures leather products, electronic components, chemicals, and machinery, and is a residential suburb. **2.** middle-class residential section, extreme NC Bronx, New York. Lying along the Bronx R. (W), it juts into Westchester Co., adjoining MOUNT VERNON. Williamsbridge is S, Eastchester E. Woodlawn, to the SW, was once also called Wakefield. **3.** historic site in Westmoreland Co., SE Virginia, on the S bank of the Potomac R. near the mouth of Popes Creek; it is the birthplace (1732) of George Washington. The estate was acquired by his father, Augustine, in 1718. The original house is gone, but an eight-room house typical of construction in the area during the early 18th century is on the site. Wakefield is also known as Bridges Creek. STRATFORD HALL, the birthplace (1807) of Robert E. Lee, is 5 mi/8 km SE.

Wake Forest town, pop. 5769, Wake Co., NC North Carolina, 15 mi/24 km NNE of Raleigh, the first home of Wake Forest University, established here in 1834 as Wake Forest Institute, which moved in 1956 to Winston-Salem. The Piedmont mill town is now home to the Southeastern Baptist Theological Seminary.

Wake Island also, **Enenkio** coral ATOLL, in the WC Pacific Ocean, some 2300 mi/3700 km W of Honolulu and 480 mi/770 km N of the Marshall Islands. It includes three major islands—Wake, Peale, and Wilkins—and encloses a lagoon about 4 mi/6 km long and 2 mi/3 km wide. Landed on by British captain William Wake in 1796, it was annexed by the US in 1898. In 1935 it became a stopover for commercial flights between the US and Asia; Pan American Airways used it for its China clipper service and built a hotel. Developed by the US as a submarine and air base, Wake was attacked by the Japanese on Dec. 7, 1941, and after fierce resistance its garrison surrendered on Dec. 23. It was bombed continually by US forces 1942–45, and the Japanese surrendered it in Sept. 1945. Today the US Air Force uses it as a base. The Republic of the Marshall Is. has also claimed the atoll.

Walden see under SUDBURY, Ontario.

Walden Pond 64 ac/26 ha, in CONCORD, Middlesex Co., EC Massachusetts. Situated 1.5 mi/2.4 km SSE of Concord's center, along the Lincoln (SE) town line, it is the site of Henry David Thoreau's celebrated 1845–47 retreat, which led to *Walden* (1854). The pond, 0.35 mi/0.56 km E–W, now in the Walden State Reservation, is a tourist and recreational site. Tracks of the Massachusetts Bay Transit Authority (in Thoreau's day of the Boston and Fitchburg Railroad) pass along the SW shore.

Walden Ridge steep E edge of the CUMBERLAND PLATEAU in E Tennessee. A continuation of the ALLEGHENY FRONT, the NE–SW ridge, largely 1000–2000 ft/300–600 m high, lies between the SEQUATCHIE (W) and Tennessee (E) rivers. It extends NE from where the Tennessee cuts through it, just W of Chattanooga and N of the Georgia border (S), to the Crab Orchard Mts., then W of OAK RIDGE, up to Lake City, just S of Norris L. (N). Signal Mt., just NW of Chattanooga, is a S spur rising to 1400 ft/430 m, so named for its use for communications during the Civil War.

Waldorf town, pop. 15,058, Charles Co., S Maryland, 20 mi/32 km SSE of Washington, D.C. It is a tobacco market town, with large warehouses and processing plants, and a rapidly developing commercial district with a suburban shopping center.

Waldron city, pop. 3024, seat of Scott Co., W Arkansas, on the Poteau R., in the Ouachita Mts., 38 mi/61 km SSE of Fort Smith and 20 mi/32 km E of the Oklahoma border. Surrounded by the Ouachita National Forest, it is a processing and distribution hub for a poultry producing, lumbering, coal mining, farming, and dairying area.

Waldwick borough, pop. 9757; Bergen Co., NE New Jersey, in the foothills of the Ramapo Mts., on the SADDLE R., 7 mi/11 km N of Paterson. The area served as a camping ground for Washington's troops during the Revolution. Today it is an affluent New York–area residential suburb, with some light industry.

Walhonding River 20 mi/32 km long, in C Ohio. It is formed by the junction of the Mohican and Kokosing rivers, 16 mi/26 km NW of Coshocton, and flows E, joining the Tuscarawas and Coshocton rivers to form the Muskingum. Near Nellie on the newly formed Walhonding is the Mohawk Dam, which impounds Mohawk Reservoir; it is 2330 ft/711 m long by 111 ft/34 m high, and was completed in 1937.

Walker city, pop. 17,279, Kent Co., SW Michigan, on the Grand R., a residential suburb 5 mi/8 km NW of Grand Rapids.

Walker Mill unincorporated village, pop. 10,920, Prince George's Co., C Maryland, a residential suburb 8 mi/13 km E of Washington, D.C.

Walker Mountain ridge within the Valley and Ridge Province of the Appalachians, in Virginia, extending for nearly 110 mi/180 km, from the New R. NW of Radford (NE) to W of Bristol, along the Tennessee border (SW). It rises to 3953 ft/1206 m N of Marion, and is partially within Jefferson National Forest.

Walker Pass at 5245 ft/1599 m, in EC California, sometimes considered the S terminus of the SIERRA NEVADA. Route 178 goes through the pass, which is E of Isabella L. and Sequoia National Park, and 57 mi/92 km ENE of Bakersfield. It was named for Joseph Walker, frontiersman and guide, who first saw it in 1833.

Walker River 50 mi/80 km long, in W Nevada. Formed in Lyon Co., 35 mi/56 km SE of Carson City, by the confluence of the East and West Walker rivers, which rise on the California border in the SIERRA NEVADA, it flows N, then curves S around the WASSUK RANGE and enters the 534–sq mi/1384–sq km **Walker River Indian Reservation** (pop. 802, 77% Indian), a Paiute home. At the S of the reservation, it enters **Walker L.,** 24 mi/38 km long, 3–8 mi/5–13 km wide, and up to 1000 ft/300 m deep, a remnant of ancient L. Lahontan (see under CARSON R.).

Walker's Point residential neighborhood on the SOUTH SIDE of Milwaukee, Wisconsin, immediately S of Downtown. It is a working-class community of Mexican and Puerto Rican immigrants, and has the city's best intact collection of late Victorian architecture.

Walkerville see under WINDSOR, Ontario.

Walking Purchase lands obtained in E Pennsylvania by white settlers pursuant to an agreement with the Delaware, who had inhabited the area. William Penn agreed in 1682 to purchase as much land between the Delaware R. (E) and NESHAMINY CREEK (W) as could be walked northward in three days. Penn and companions then walked half that time, reaching the area of Wrightstown, near Newtown, Bucks Co., and declared that they had obtained enough land for present needs. In 1737, Penn's successors announced they would walk the remaining day and a half; but to do so they hired professional runners and woodsmen, who moved so quickly that they reached Broad Mt., some 28 mi/45 km NW of Allentown, in the allowed time. The Delaware protested, but were powerless to prevent occupation of the land "walked."

Wall town, pop. 834, Pennington Co., SW South Dakota, 45 mi/72 km E of Rapid City. Situated 10 mi/16 km N of Badlands National Park, it has a thriving tourist industry, and is the home of Wall Drug Store, widely known through its bumper sticker advertising.

Wallabout Bay former inlet of the East R., Brooklyn, New York, just N of the site of the Brooklyn Bridge. The name was originally *Waalen Boght,* Dutch for "Walloon's Bay," after an early resident. During the Revolution British prison ships were anchored here, and more than 11,000 captured Americans died from disease and lack of food. In 1801 the New York Naval Shipyard, later known as the Brooklyn Navy Yard, was established, and the natural shoreline has been much altered.

Wallace town, pop. 83, Codington Co., NE South Dakota, 25 mi/40 km NW of Watertown. Political leader Hubert Humphrey was born here (1911).

Wallaceburg town, pop. 11,846, Kent Co., extreme S Ontario, on the Sydenham R., 16 mi/26 km NW of Chatham and 38 mi/61 km ENE of Detroit, Michigan. Settled in the 1830s, it was a lumbering and shipbuilding center, and is today a deepwater port and manufacturer of glass, iron, brass, and wood products, sugar, auto parts, and plumbing supplies.

Walla Walla city, pop. 26,478, seat of Walla Walla Co., SE Washington, 105 mi/169 km SSW of Spokane and 4 mi/6 km N of the Oregon border. An agricultural processing center for its wheat and truck farming valley, it also has food processing plants, lumber mills, and a container factory. It is the seat of Whitman College (1859) and Walla Walla Community College (1967). The state penitentiary is on the city's NW outskirts. A fur trading post was established near here in 1818, and the missionary Marcus Whitman built the first European home in 1836. The restored Whitman Mission National Monument lies 7 mi/11 km W of the city. The US Army's Fort Walla Walla was founded here in 1856. It became the center of the pioneer settlement, and is now the site of a museum and park.

Walled Lake city, pop. 6278, Oakland Co., SE Michigan, on Walled L., 11 mi/18 km SW of Pontiac. A summer resort in a lake-filled recreation area, it has close access to canoeing and other activities at Proud L. State Recreation Area 5 mi/8 km to the NW.

Wallenpaupack, Lake in the Pocono Mts., NE Pennsylvania, on the boundary between Wayne and Pike counties. Measuring approximately 9 sq mi/23 sq km, it was formed by the damming of Wallenpaupack Creek.

Wallingford town, pop. 40,822, New Haven Co., SC Connecticut, 13 mi/21 km NNE of New Haven on the Quinnipiac R. Founded in 1667, it has a silver industry dating from about 1835; it also cultivates vegetables. Modern manufactures include instruments, electrical equipment, plastics, resins, and apparel. The exclusive prep school Choate Rosemary Hall is here.

Wallington borough, pop. 10,828, Bergen Co., NE New Jersey, on the Passaic R., 2 mi/3 km E of Passaic. It has a wide diversity of manufactures including paint, chemicals, steel tubing, electrical equipment, plastics, textile products, and cardboard boxes.

Walloon Lake unincorporated village in Charlevoix Co., on the E shore of Walloon L., in the N part of the Lower Peninsula of Michigan, 5 mi/8 km S of Petoskey. Focused on boating, fishing, and swimming, the community is the site of one of Ernest Hemingway's vacation homes.

Wallops Island in Accomack Co., E Virginia, on the E shore of the DELMARVA PENINSULA, NE of Assawoman Inlet and just SW of CHINCOTEAGUE and ASSATEAGUE islands. Covering about 6 sq mi/16 sq km, it is a NASA rocket and balloon launching base. Parts of the facility are 4 mi/6 km N, on the mainland.

Wallowa Mountains rugged marble and granitic range in the NE corner of Oregon, E of the BLUE Mts., including a number of the state's highest peaks. This alpine region, abounding with glacial lakes and meadows, and known popularly as "Little Switzerland," reaches its highest relief in the Eagle Cap Wilderness at Sacajawea Peak and Matterhorn, both c.10,000 ft/3050 m. Eagle Cap stands 9695 ft/2955 m. Mt. Howard (8256 ft/2516 m), at the S end of Wallowa L., is the site of an aerial tramway. The **Wallowa Valley,** along the Wallowa R. on the range's E, is the ancestral home of the Nez Perce, and there are a number of tributes to Chief Joseph, who is buried N of the lake, in the area. Gold has been mined in the mountains; timbering, farming, cattle ranching, and outdoor recreation are primary economic activities in the area today. The 2.3 million–ac/931,500-ha (3595–sq mi/9310–sq km) **Wallowa-Whitman National Forest,** with a separate division (W) in the Blue Mts., is headquartered in Baker.

Wall Street **1.** commercial street at the S end of Manhattan, New York City. It is on the site of a wall built 1653 to protect the colony of New Amsterdam from anticipated Indian attacks. Wall Street is home to the New York Stock Exchange and other financial buildings, and is proverbially the center of the US (and world) economy. **2. Wall Street of the West** see SEVENTEENTH STREET, Denver, Colorado. **3. Wall Street of Canada** before the 1970s, SAINT JAMES St., Montréal, Québec. Its role has now been taken over by BAY St., Toronto, Ontario.

Walnut **1.** city, pop. 29,105, Los Angeles Co., SW California, 20 mi/32 km E of downtown Los Angeles. Mount San Antonio College (1946) is in this growing residential suburb. **2.** village, pop. 1463, Bureau Co., NC Illinois, 23 mi/37 km N of Lincoln. Author Don Marquis was born here (1878).

Walnut Canyon National Monument 6 mi/10 km ESE of Flagstaff, NC Arizona, in the Coconino National Forest. It protects a cluster of more than 300 12th-century Sinagua cliff dwellings, on ledges in the gorge of Walnut Creek.

Walnut Creek city, pop. 60,569, Contra Costa Co., NC California, in the San Ramon Valley, 12 mi/19 km NE of Oakland. On Walnut Creek, among deep valleys and hills, NW of 3849-ft/1174-m Mt. Diablo, the city was founded during the 1849 gold rush. The arrival of the Central Pacific Railroad (1878) and a commuter line to Oakland (1914) stimulated growth. Fruits and walnuts are grown and processed in the vicinity. Other industries include food, chemical, and technological research and various light manufactures. The city grew most rapidly in the 1960s and 1970s, and has large suburban residential neighborhoods.

Walnut Park unincorporated community, pop. 14,722, Los Angeles Co., SW California, a largely Hispanic residential suburb 5 mi/8 km SE of downtown Los Angeles, adjacent (S) to Huntington Park.

Walnut Ridge city, pop. 4388, seat of Lawrence Co., NE Arkansas, 22 mi/35 km NW of Jonesboro. Williams Baptist College (1941) is here.

Walpole **1.** town, pop. 20,212, Norfolk Co., E Massachusetts, 18 mi/29 km SW of Boston, on the Neponset R., US 1, and Interstate 95. It is the site of the chief Massachusetts correctional institution, known as the Norfolk prison. The town produces floor coverings, paper, chemicals, and machinery, and has been industrial since its founding in 1659. **2.** town, pop. 3210, Cheshire Co., SW New Hampshire. It is on the Connecticut R., just SE of Bellows Falls, Vermont, and 13 mi/21 km NW of Keene. The manufacture of wood products has been important in this largely rural town.

Walt Disney World see under LAKE BUENA VISTA, Florida.

Waltham city, pop. 57,878, Middlesex Co., E Massachusetts, on the Charles R., 9 mi/14 km W of Boston. It was settled in 1634 and separated from WATERTOWN in 1738. The river furnished power for early gristmills and paper mills. In 1813, Waltham was the site of the first textile mill to complete the process of making cloth from raw cotton. The Waltham Watch Company (1854), one of the world's largest timepiece manufacturers, was based here for many years. In 1885 the first training school for nurses was established. Contemporary industries include electronic research and development, agricultural and pharmaceutical research, and the making of precision instruments, machinery, cameras, electronics, and fabricated metal products. Brandeis University (1948) and Bentley College (1917) are in Waltham.

Walt Whitman Bridge over the Delaware R., between Philadelphia, Pennsylvania, and Camden, New Jersey. Opened in 1957, it links SOUTH PHILADELPHIA and the Schuylkill and Delaware expressways with the North-South Freeway and the New Jersey Turnpike.

Wanaque borough, pop. 9711, Passaic Co., N New Jersey, on the Wanaque R., in the Ramapo Mts., 6 mi/10 km NW of Paterson. It includes the villages of Haskell and Midvale. Wanaque's plants produce knitted and printed items and metal powder. It is also residential. The **Wanaque Reservoir,** largest in the state (5 mi/8 km NNE–SSW), formed by a dam on the Wanaque R., lies just NW.

Wantagh unincorporated village, pop. 18,567, in Hempstead town, Nassau Co., SE New York, on Long Island's South Shore, 4 mi/6 km ENE of Freeport and 25 mi/40 km ESE of Manhattan. It is primarily residential. The **Wantagh State Parkway** connects the Northern State Parkway (N) with JONES BEACH, 6 mi/10 km S.

Wapakoneta city, pop. 9214, seat of Auglaize Co., on the Auglaize R., W Ohio, 12 mi/19 km SSW of Lima. Local manufactures include furnaces, furniture, mill products, plastics, and dairy products. There is mixed farming in the area as well. The Neil Armstrong Air and Space Museum in Wapakoneta was named for the astronaut, who was born here (1930). The Fort Amanda State Memorial, 9 mi/14 km W of the city, marks the site of a War of 1812 fortification.

Wappinger Creek 35 mi/56 km long, in SE New York. It rises in N Dutchess Co. and flows SSW past Poughkeepsie to WAPPINGERS FALLS, then into the Hudson R. at New Hamburg, 8 mi/13 km S of Poughkeepsie. It takes its name from the Algonquian Wappinger Confederation, who inhabited the area.

Wappingers Falls village, pop. 4605, in Wappinger town, Dutchess Co., SE New York, in the Hudson Highlands near the Hudson R., 7 mi/11 km S of Poughkeepsie. The 75-ft/23-m falls on Wappinger Creek here have produced waterpower since settlement in the early 18th century. The headquarters of Baron von Steuben were located in Wappingers Falls during the latter part of the Revolutionary War, and the Society of the Cincinnati was organized by military officers here in 1783. There are a number of light industries and business offices in the village.

Wapsipinicon River 225 mi/362 km long, in E Iowa. It rises NNW of McIntire, in Mitchell Co., almost on the Minnesota line, and flows SE through agricultural countryside, past Independence, Central City, Stone City, and Anamosa, before joining the Mississippi R. 15 mi/24 km NE of Davenport. Its chief tributaries are the Little Wapsipinicon R. and Buffalo Creek.

Ward's Island 255 ac/103 ha, between the East and Harlem rivers, New York City. It is part of the borough of Manhattan. Formerly separated from Randall's I. (N) by the Little Hell Gate, it is now joined by landfill. The Triborough Bridge roadway and Hell Gate railroad bridge pass over Ward's I. and cross from it to Astoria, Queens, over the Hell Gate. Previously used as a potter's field, immigration station, and military hospital site, Ward's I. today houses a large psychiatric hospital, the city's major sewage treatment plant, and much park space.

Wareham town, pop. 19,232, Plymouth Co., SE Massachusetts, at the head of Buzzards Bay, 16 mi/26 km NE of New Bedford. Located in a summer resort area, it has beaches and other tourist facilities. Industries include cranberry raising and canning, oyster fisheries, and some manufacturing. Wareham comprises the villages of Onset, Wareham, East Wareham, South Wareham, and West Wareham.

Warehouse District **1.** commercial and residential section of UPTOWN New Orleans, Louisiana, just S of CANAL St. and just N of the 1984 World's Fair site along the Mississippi R. After a period of decline, it has been gentrified and has become popular for its galleries and other attractions. **2.** see RIVERTOWN, Detroit, Michigan. **3.** commercial and entertainment area in Minneapolis, Minnesota, on the N side of Downtown. Many warehouses here had been abandoned by the 1950s and 1960s, when low property values attracted investors into what has become a popular and fashionable district. **4.** neighborhood in Cleveland, Ohio, along L. Erie, immediately W of Downtown. An upscale area of offices, loft apartments, and retail complexes, it has undergone a dramatic transformation in recent decades. Most of its 19th-century structures have been preserved and converted to residential and other uses.

Warminster township, pop. 32,832, Bucks Co., SE Pennsylvania, 19 mi/31 km NNE of Philadelphia. It is a largely residential suburb with a naval development facility connected with the WILLOW GROVE Naval Air Station, just SW.

Warm Springs **1.** resort city, pop. 407, Meriwether Co., W Georgia, 33 mi/53 km NNE of Columbus. The springs here were used by Indians before whites found them in the late 18th century. Franklin D. Roosevelt, who died here on April 12, 1945, had been treated here earlier for polio, and had established the Warm Springs Foundation in 1927. His "Little White House" is now a museum. **2.** unincorporated community, pop. 2287, Jefferson Co., NW Oregon, 90 mi/145 km SE of Portland. It is the trade center of the 1019–sq mi/2640–sq km **Warm Springs Indian Reservation,** home to various Sahaptin, Chinook, and Shoshonean groups since 1855. The reservation lies E of the Cascade Range, with the Deschutes R. forming its E boundary.

Warner Mountains N–S range (c.85 mi/137 km long) in the NE corner of California, to the E of GOOSE L., and extending into S Oregon. Largely flat-topped, the Warners rise to 9892 ft/3015 m at Eagle Peak, and are mostly within Modoc National Forest. The PIT R. rises here; Surprise Valley is E. The area is used for grazing, camping, hiking, and logging.

Warner Robins city, pop. 43,726, Houston Co., C Georgia, 17 mi/27 km SSE of Macon, on the Ocmulgee R. The agricultural hamlet of Wellston was renamed Warner Robins when Robins Air Force Base (home of the Flying Tigers) was established nearby in 1943. The city and base have been closely linked ever since; aircraft parts are manufactured, and the Museum of Aviation and headquarters for the Air Force Reserve are here.

Warr Acres city, pop. 9288, Oklahoma Co., C Oklahoma, a residential community 5 mi/8 km NW of downtown Oklahoma City, and within its limits. L. Hefner is just N, BETHANY just SW.

Warren **1.** city, pop. 144,864, Macomb Co., SE Michigan, adjacent (N) to Detroit. Industry developed and population grew from the 1920s. Both increased substantially after World War II, and this Detroit suburb became a major auto and truck manufacturing center. Also made here are tools and dies, electronic equipment, steel, and plastic. The General Motors Technical Center is in Warren, as is the US Army's Detroit Tank Arsenal. It is also the seat of Macomb County Community College (1954). **2.** city, pop. 50,793, seat of Trumbull Co., NE Ohio, on the Mahoning R., 13 mi/21 km NW of Youngstown. Settled c.1798 and capital of the WESTERN RESERVE, it developed as a major flax and agricultural center and an iron and coal producer. It is part of the Pittsburgh-Youngstown complex, and a major manufacturer and fabricator of steel. Manufactures also include steel mill machinery, electrical equipment, truck and automobile parts, blowers, tools, paints, and many other products. Native James Ward Packard manufactured the first Packard automobiles here. Local attractions include Phalanx Mill, a relic of a Fourierist colony of the 1840s. The city is home to a branch of Kent State University. **3.** city, pop. 11,122, seat of Warren Co., NW Pennsylvania, 54 mi/86 km SE of Erie, at the junction of Conewango Creek and the Allegheny R. Situated in a rich agricultural and timbering region, it was formerly an important lumbering center. With the discovery of oil in Pennsylvania in 1859, it developed an oil refining industry as well. Principal manufactures include metal products, oilfield equipment, furniture, electrical equipment, and plastics. The headquarters of the Allegheny National Forest are here, and the S end of the Allegheny Reservoir, at the KINZUA Dam, is 7 mi/11 km E. **4.** town, pop. 11,385, Bristol Co., E Rhode Island, on the Massachusetts border, the Kickemuit R., and Mt. Hope Bay, 9 mi/14 km SE of Providence. It was part of Swansea, Massachusetts, before 1746. Formerly a Wampanoag Indian center, it became an important shipbuilding community, and was active in the Revolution. Boatbuilding is still important, along with seafood canning and the manufacture of flooring, plastics, luggage, and automotive equipment.

Warren County 403 sq mi/1044 sq km, pop. 113,909, in SW Ohio, intersected by the Little Miami R. Its seat is Lebanon. The county lies between the suburbs of Dayton (N) and Cincinnati (SW). Its economy depends heavily on diversified agriculture, including fruit, grain, and livestock farming. Sand and gravel are exploited, and there is manufacturing at Franklin, Lebanon, and Waynesville.

Warrensburg city, pop. 15,244, seat of Johnson Co., WC Missouri, 50 mi/80 km SE of Kansas City. It is a trade and processing center for a livestock, dairy, agricultural, and coal mining region. Manufactures include clothing, electronic components, lawnmowers, and shoes. Warrensburg is the seat of Central Missouri State College (1871). Nearby are the Blackwater R. (N) and Whiteman Air Force Base (E).

Warrensville Heights city, pop. 15,745, Cuyahoga Co., NE Ohio, 10 mi/16 km SE of Cleveland, of which it is a commuter suburb. Some limited manufacturing takes place here.

Warrenton town, pop. 949, seat of Warren Co., N North Carolina, 14 mi/23 km NE of Henderson. A lumber milling and tobacco processing community, it was a social and political center in the first half of the 19th century, and has many noted old buildings.

Warrenville city, pop. 11,333, Du Page Co., NE Illinois, on the West Branch of the Du Page R., immediately N of Naperville and 25 mi/40 km W of Chicago. A residential suburb, it lies 4 mi/6 km E of the Fermi National Accelerator Laboratory.

Warsaw city, pop. 10,968, seat of Kosciusko Co., NC Indiana, on the Tippecanoe R., 36 mi/58 km WNW of Fort Wayne. In an agricultural region, it trades, processes, and ships local products, particularly dairy goods. Its manufactures include aircraft and auto parts, medical equipment, toys, furniture, and castings. In a lake-filled area, Warsaw is also a resort center.

Warwick city, pop. 85,427, Kent Co., EC Rhode Island, on the Pawtuxet R. and the W shore of Narragansett Bay, 10 mi/16 km S of Providence. It is composed of about 20 villages, many destroyed during King Philip's War (1675–76) and later rebuilt. The Pawtuxet powered early grist and fulling mills, and cotton became a major industry. Today Warwick has some light industry, producing jewelry, silverware, metals, and machinery, and there are two colleges. Landmarks include Revolutionary General Nathanael Green's homestead. Gaspee Day celebrates the 1772 burning of a British vessel at GASPEE POINT. Rocky Point, one of New England's oldest sea resorts, is one of several along Warwick's shoreline. T.F. Green Airport, serving the Providence area, is in Warwick.

Wasatch-Cache National Forest over 1.2 million ac/486,000 ha (1875 sq mi/4860 sq km), in NE and NC Utah. It incorporates much of the N UINTA Mts., including part of the High Uintas Wilderness Area; much of the Wasatch Range, including resorts near Salt Lake City; mountain areas N of Ogden, to (and just over) the Wyoming border; and, to the W, part of the Stansbury Mts., S of Great Salt L., including DESERET Peak.

Wasatch Range W spur of the Middle Rocky Mts., extending 250 mi/400 km N–S, from the BEAR R. in SE Idaho, past (E of) the Great Salt L., and into C Utah. Its highest peak is Mt. NEBO (11,877 ft/3620 m), 30 mi/48 km S of Provo. Mt. Timpanogos (11,750 ft/3581 m), 12 mi/19 km N of Provo, is the site of TIMPANOGOS CAVE NATIONAL MONUMENT. Much of the range is within the Wasatch-Cache and Uinta national forests, and the major cities of Utah, including Ogden, Salt Lake City, and Provo, lie on its fertile W side, at its feet, in an area called the **Wasatch Front.** The range is drained by the Ogden, Provo, and Weber rivers, and is mined for silver, gold, lead, and copper. Skiing is popular throughout, with major resorts at Alta, Snowbird, and Park City. At the S end of the range is the **Wasatch Plateau,** a raised tableland largely in the Manti–La Sal National Forest.

Wasco city, pop. 12,412, Kern Co., SC California, in the S San Joaquin Valley, 28 mi/45 km NW of Bakersfield. An agricultural center in an area also noted for oil production, it has various manufactures related to both industries.

Waseca city, pop. 8385, seat of Waseca Co., S Minnesota, 15 mi/24 km W of Owatonna, amid small lakes in a wheat growing area. Established in the 1860s, it processes local agricultural products, has a tourist industry, and is home to a University of Minnesota agricultural branch.

Washington state of the NW US, in the PACIFIC NORTHWEST; pop. 4,866,692 (117.8% of 1980; rank: 18th); area 71,303 sq mi/184,675 sq km (rank: 18th); admitted to Union 1889 (42nd). Capital: OLYMPIA. Most populous cities: SEATTLE, SPOKANE, TACOMA, BELLEVUE, EVERETT. Washington is bordered E by Idaho, with the SNAKE R. forming a small S part of the boundary; S by Oregon, with the COLUMBIA R. forming most of the boundary; and N by British Columbia. On the NW are the Strait of GEORGIA (N) and JUAN DE FUCA Strait (W), Pacific Ocean inlets that separate mainland Washington and its PUGET SOUND and SAN JUAN Is. from Vancouver I., British Columbia. On the W is the Pacific Ocean; GRAYS HARBOR and WILLAPA Bay are the major inlets on Washington's coast, and Cape ALAVA is the westernmost point in the Lower 48. The state is bisected (WC) by the N–S CASCADE RANGE, in which Mt. RAINIER (14,410 ft/4395 m) is its high point. Along the Pacific is a section of the COAST RANGES, including the rain-drenched OLYMPIC Mts. (on the Olympic Peninsula, N) and the WILLAPA HILLS. Between the Coast Ranges and the Cascades lies the Puget Trough, a lowland into which Puget Sound with its many arms reaches. Most of Washington's cities are along the E and S of Puget Sound, the major natural harbor on the West Coast N of San Francisco Bay. To the E of the Cascades the state is much higher and drier. The SE is part of the COLUMBIA PLATEAU, around which the Columbia R. circles, forming the BIG BEND region. On the NE are the Okanogan Highlands and SELKIRK Mts., W outliers of the Northern ROCKY Mts., separated from the Cascades by the valley of the OKANOGAN R., flowing S from British Columbia to meet the Columbia. In the SE corner is a section of Oregon's BLUE Mts., also part of the Northern Rockies. The heavily forested Cascades are drained W and S by the SKAGIT, COWLITZ, and other short rivers. In the E, the Columbia's tributaries include the YAKIMA and the CHELAN, flowing SE from the Cascades; the Snake, flowing W from Idaho and cutting across the Columbia Plateau; the SPOKANE, flowing W from Idaho on the plateau's N; and the PEND OREILLE, cutting across the NE corner. The Columbia Plateau, naturally semiarid and marked by canyons, COULEES, SCABLANDS, and LOESS hills, has been made a productive agricultural (esp. wheat, cattle, horses, and sugar beets) district by irrigation. The PALOUSE (SE) is famous as home to the Appaloosa horse. Spokane (E) is the metropolis of the INLAND EMPIRE, a vast region in which lumbering and dairy farming have been predominant; food processing and wood- and mineral-related industries are important here. WENATCHEE and YAKIMA, on the plateau's W, and WALLA WALLA, on its SE, are largely agricultural processing centers. Near the junction of the Snake with the Columbia (S) are the Tri-Cities, RICHLAND, PASCO, and KENNEWICK, since World War II intimately involved with the activities of the huge HANFORD nuclear reservation. On the plateau's N is the GRAND COULEE Dam, best-known of the many hydroelectric and irrigation projects on the Columbia, the most powerful US river. The Cascades are the scene of much lumbering, largely in the MOUNT BAKER–SNOQUALMIE, WENATCHEE, and GIFFORD PINCHOT national forests, and of the NORTH CASCADES and MOUNT RAINIER national parks. Also here, in the S, is Mt. SAINT HELENS, whose 1980 eruption awed the nation. On the Columbia R., facing Oregon, are the early settlement of VANCOUVER as well as KELSO and LONGVIEW, all lumbering and industrial port cities. On the coast, ABERDEEN and HOQUIAM (on Grays Harbor) are lumbering centers. On Puget Sound, Seattle and Tacoma and their suburbs are now a major manufacturing complex, turning out aircraft and aerospace equipment, ships, chemicals, fabricated metals, furniture and other wood products, foods, and computers and other high-tech equipment. BREMERTON and BANGOR are naval complexes. Seattle is a major Pacific port, carrying on much trade with Japan and the rest of East Asia. The Olympic Peninsula and Puget Sound's islands are largely residential and tourist areas; fishing and shellfishing are also important. The Chinook (SW, along the Columbia), Yakima, and Nez Perce (SE) were among peoples living here when whites arrived in the 1770s. George Vancouver sailed into Puget Sound in 1792, and the region soon became part of the OREGON country, in which British and American trappers and explorers coexisted uneasily until an 1846 treaty established the FORTY-NINTH PARALLEL as the N boundary of the Oregon Territory. In 1853 Oregon, approaching statehood conditions, was separated from what became the **Washington Territory** (including Idaho and part of Montana). Little of what is now Washington was settled before the 1880s, when the NORTHERN PACIFIC RAILROAD, followed by the GREAT NORTHERN RAILWAY, extended across the state, opening it to development and making the rapid growth of Seattle and Tacoma possible. Ports, shipbuilding, and aircraft manufacture (begun in Seattle at BOEING FIELD in 1916, but esp. after 1940) in both World Wars have been critical to Washington's industrial life. In the 1900s–20s, shipyard, lumber, coal mine, and other workers engaged in major radical labor actions in Seattle, Everett, and CENTRALIA, but post–World War I reaction brought them to an end. The state today has a balanced economy, with manufacturing, lumbering, wheat and other farming, coal and metal mining, fishing, military expenditures, and tourism all important. Its people are largely Yankees and North Europeans; the Hispanic and Asian minorities (each about 4%) are the largest. The huge YAKIMA and COLVILLE Indian reservations, E of the Cascades, are among the nation's biggest. The University of Washington is at Seattle, Washington State University at PULLMAN.

Washington **1.** see under HOPE, Arkansas. **2.** city, pop. 606,900, capital of the United States of America, coextensive with the District of Columbia, on the E bank of the Potomac R., 35 mi/56 km SW of Baltimore, Maryland. It is bounded by MONTGOMERY (NW, N, and NE) and PRINCE GEORGE'S (E and SE) counties, Maryland, and faces ARLINGTON Co. and ALEXANDRIA, Virginia, across the river. The city's center is just N of the confluence of the Anacostia R. with the Potomac, and 100 mi/160 km above the latter's mouth, at the head of navigation (the FALL LINE). Selected (1790) by George Washington as the site for the Federal capital, it was combined with GEORGETOWN, Maryland, and Alexandria to form the District of Columbia; since 1895 Georgetown has been part of Washington (Alexandria was returned to Virginia in 1846). Planned in the 1790s by Pierre L'Enfant, Washington grew slowly. In Aug. 1814 British forces took it, burning the White House, Capitol, and other buildings. It remained largely undeveloped through the Civil War, when it became in effect an armed camp, and narrowly escaped Confederate attack. Finally, at the beginning of the 20th century, elements of L'Enfant's plan were revived, and the city began to take its modern, monumental aspect. Divided into four quadrants (Northwest, Northeast, Southeast, and Southwest) centered on Capitol Hill, it has a grid street pattern combined with radiating major avenues, with many squares, circles, and parks. A city without heavy industry, it is primarily residential and institutional; the vast majority of its people and buildings are engaged in the work of the Federal government, or in work premised on proximity to the seat of government. The BELTWAY, circling the city in Maryland and Virginia, is proverbially a boundary inside which a distinctive (and self-regarding) governmental culture exists. But Washington also has a non-Federal life, with commercial and residential districts in which the activity of any large city goes on. Since the Civil War it has had a substantial black community, now a majority. The city is today the hub of a metropolitan area (MSA) including also five Maryland counties, six Virginia counties, and four independent cities in Virginia, with a pop. of 3,923,574; since the 1950s much government and government-related business, and many residents, have moved into the suburbs, both inside and outside the Beltway. In addition to government operations and installations, Washington is home to Georgetown (1789), George Washington (1821), Howard (1867), Catholic (1884), and American (1893) universities, along with a number of other schools; these and the Library of Congress, National Archives, Smithsonian Institution, National Gallery of Art, and numerous other institutions make it an educational and cultural center. Noted also for its parks, wide avenues, monuments, and other sites, it draws heavy tourist, as well as convention and other, traffic. For the city's political status, see DISTRICT OF COLUMBIA. See also: ADAMS-MORGAN; ANACOSTIA; BELTWAY; BROOKLAND; CAPITOL HILL; CATHEDRAL HEIGHTS; CHINATOWN; CLEVELAND PARK; COLUMBIA HEIGHTS; DUMBARTON OAKS; DUPONT CIRCLE; EMBASSY ROW; FEDERAL TRIANGLE; FOGGY BOTTOM; FORD'S THEATRE; FOURTEENTH St.; GEORGETOWN; GEORGIA Ave.; JOHN F. KENNEDY CENTER FOR THE PERFORMING ARTS; L'ENFANT PLAZA; LINCOLN MEMORIAL; the MALL (and Constitution Gardens); MOUNT PLEASANT; NORTHEAST; NORTHWEST; PENNSYLVANIA Ave.; RFK STADIUM; ROCK CREEK (and Park); SHAW; SIXTEENTH St.; SMITHSONIAN INSTITUTION; SOUTHEAST; SOUTHWEST; SPRING VALLEY; TIDAL BASIN; UNION STATION; WASHINGTON MONUMENT; WATERGATE; WEST OF THE PARK; WHITE HOUSE. **3.** city, pop. 10,099, Tazewell Co., C Illinois, a suburb 10 mi/16 km E of Peoria. Largely a residential community, it has a vegetable canning plant and other light industries. **4.** city, pop. 10,838, seat of Daviess Co., SW Indiana, 18 mi/29 km E of Vincennes. It is a trading, processing, and shipping hub in a grain and apple producing region. It has railroad shops as well as various manufactures. **5.** city, pop. 795, Mason Co., NE Kentucky, 3 mi/5 km SW of Maysville. Chartered in 1786, it was an important road and trading center in its first half-century. Confederate general Albert Sidney Johnston was born here in 1803. **6.** city, pop. 10,704, Franklin Co., EC Missouri, on the Missouri R., 45 mi/72 km WSW of St. Louis. An agricultural trade and shipping hub, it manufactures such goods as shoes, plastics, clothing, and dairy products. **7.** city, pop. 9075, seat of Beaufort Co., E North Carolina, at the mouth of the Tar R. (head of the Pamlico R. estuary), 19 mi/31 km ESE of Greenville. Founded in 1771, it was called Washington by 1776. In a grape, cotton, tobacco, and vegetable producing area, it has been a market center with textile mills. Beaufort Co. Community College (1967) is here. **8** see under WASHINGTON COURT HOUSE, Ohio. **9** city, pop. 15,864, seat of Washington Co., SW Pennsylvania, 24 mi/39 km SW of Pittsburgh, on the old NATIONAL ROAD. The area was the subject of a land dispute between Pennsylvania and Virginia before the Revolution. The city took an active role in the Whiskey Rebellion (1794). The city services regional agricultural, industrial, and coal mining interests, and manufactures glass, electronic products, and stainless steel. It is home to Washington and Jefferson College (1865). **10** see under COVENTRY, Rhode Island. **11** see WASHINGTON-ON-THE-BRAZOS, Texas.

Washington, Lake 25 mi/40 km N–S and 2–4 mi/3–6 km wide, in King Co., WC Washington. It forms the E boundary of Seattle, and is a major recreational center for residents, esp. sailing enthusiasts. BELLEVUE, RENTON, and KIRKLAND are on the E shore. MERCER I., at the S end, is connected by floating bridge to the rest of the city. The 8 mi/13 km–long **Lake Washington Ship Canal** and locks, built in 1917, give L. Washington access to PUGET SOUND, and are used extensively by both commercial and pleasure craft.

Washington, Mount **1.** highest peak (6288 ft/1918 m) in New Hampshire and in the NE US, apex of the PRESIDENTIAL RANGE of the White Mts., NC New Hampshire. Its bare summit, famous for rapid weather changes, is a great mass of talus blocks split off from bedrock. Just off the cone are relatively level areas, home to many alpine plants. TUCKERMAN and Huntington ravines (two glacial cirques on the SE slope) and the Great Gulf, the valley between Mt. Washington and the Northern Presidentials, are among notable natural areas. Trails, the Auto or Carriage Road (opened 1861), and the Cog Railway (completed 1869) ascend its slopes. The Mount Washington Observatory, radio and television transmitting facilities, a visitor center, and a museum dot the summit. The highest surface wind velocity ever detected—231 mi/372 km per hour—was recorded on its summit in 1934. The mountain, laced by an extensive network of trails, provides the focal point for a large summer and winter resort area. The Mount Washington Hotel, at BRETTON WOODS, hosted the International Monetary Conference of 1944. **2.** peak (7794 ft/2376 m) of the CASCADE RANGE, 30 mi/48 km NW of Bend, in WC Oregon. This volcanic elevation in the 52,516-ac/21,269-ha **Mt. Washington Wilderness** of Deschutes and Willamette national forests overlooks a large lava field.

Washington County **1.** 2586 sq mi/6698 sq km, pop. 35,308, in E Maine. The most easterly county in the United States, it is an agricultural, lumbering, fishing, and industrial area. It borders New Brunswick, and is drained by the St. Croix, Machias, East Machias, and Dennys rivers. Once the territory and hunting grounds of the Passamaquoddy, the county includes the 22,665-ac/9180-ha Moosehorn National Wildlife Refuge, and the Passamaquoddy reservation at Pleasant Point, NW of Eastport. Washington County, lightly populated and often economically distressed, is a major blueberry and pulp and paper producer. MACHIAS is the county seat. **2.** 455 sq mi/1178 sq km, pop. 121,393, in NW Maryland. HAGERSTOWN is its seat. The county is bounded N by Pennsylvania, and S and W by the Potomac R. It includes the ANTIETAM and

SOUTH MOUNTAIN battlefields, and popular hunting and fishing areas. The main industries are agriculture, limestone quarrying, sandpits, and food processing. **3.** 390 sq mi/1010 sq km, pop. 145,896, in EC Minnesota, bordered by the St. Croix R. and the Mississippi R. (S). One of the earliest areas of American settlement in Minnesota, it now partly consists of E suburbs of St. Paul, such as Woodbury, Oakdale, and Cottage Grove. STILLWATER, the county seat, is in a resort area along the St. Croix R. The lake-filled N part is also recreational. **4.** 836 sq mi/2165 sq km, pop. 59,330, in E New York, partially in the Adirondack Mts. (N), bounded by the Hudson R. (SW), L. George (NW), and Vermont (E). Its seat is Hudson Falls. Largely agricultural, the county relies on dairying and farming, timber, and limestone quarries. Containing the South Bay of L. Champlain and a number of small lakes, it is also a resort area. There is some manufacturing at Cambridge, Granville, Greenwich, Hudson Falls, and Whitehall. **5.** 727 sq mi/1883 sq km, pop. 311,554, in NW Oregon. HILLSBORO is its seat. Centered on the Tualatin River Valley, it extends from Portland suburbs such as BEAVERTON, TIGARD, and TUALATIN, in the E, to an agricultural region known for hazelnuts, apples, and wine from its C to its W. **6.** 958 sq mi/2481 sq km, pop. 204,584, in SW Pennsylvania, on the Monongahela R. (E) and the West Virginia border (W). Its seat is WASHINGTON. Its industrial centers include Donora, Canonsburg, and Charleroi. Coal mining and agriculture are important. **7.** 333 sq mi/862 sq km, pop. 110,006, in SW Rhode Island; bounded W by Connecticut and S by Block Island Sound. It is drained by the Hunt, Pawcatuck, Queen, and Wood rivers. The county contains lakes and state parks as well as resorts on Narragansett Bay and Block Island Sound. Its seat is West Kingston, in South Kingstown. Manufactures include textiles, thread, yarn, machinery, and wood and food products. Printing, granite quarrying, and farming are also important.

Washington Court House city, pop. 12,983, seat of Fayette Co., SW Ohio, on Paint Creek, 35 mi/56 km SSW of Columbus. Its name was changed from Washington in the 1820s to distinguish it from four other Washingtons then in the state; the name Washington is still sometimes used. It is a trading center for the surrounding agricultural area, in which livestock, poultry, and dairy farming predominate. The city also produces apparel, automobile and aircraft parts, fertilizer, and foodstuffs. Saddle horses, pacers, and trotters are raised locally.

Washington Crossing historic and recreational area comprising state parks in Pennsylvania (440 ac/178 ha) and New Jersey (292 ac/118 ha) on opposite sides of the Delaware R., 8 mi/13 km NW of Trenton, New Jersey, and 2 mi/3 km SE of New Hope, Pennsylvania. The parks commemorate the crossing by Washington's troops from Pennsylvania to New Jersey on Christmas night, 1776, for a surprise attack on Hessian forces at Trenton.

Washington Dulles International Airport 30 mi/48 km W of Washington, D.C., in Fairfax and Loudoun counties, NE Virginia. It serves both domestic and international airlines. Opened in the early 1960s, and served by the Washington Dulles Access Toll Road, it has led to rapid business, industrial, and residential development in such nearby communities as CHANTILLY, HERNDON, and STERLING.

Washington Heights residential and commercial section of upper Manhattan, New York City. It occupies the high ground from 193rd St. and Fort Tryon Park S to 155th St.; the area S to West 125th St. is sometimes included, but is otherwise known as HAMILTON HEIGHTS. Washington Heights was the site of many 18th-century mansions and farms. John James Audubon's home, Minniesland, was here, and he is buried in Trinity Cemetery. The Morris-Jumel Mansion (1765) was Washington's headquarters in 1776. Yeshiva Univ. and the Columbia Presbyterian Medical Center are here. The George Washington Bridge crosses to New Jersey from Washington Heights. The Audubon Ballroom, where Malcolm X was assassinated in 1965, occupied a building next to Columbia Presbyterian, and has been partially preserved. Washington Heights is a mixed neighborhood, once dominated by the Irish, in the 1930s home to many European Jewish refugees, now heavily Hispanic, especially Dominican. Broadway is its commercial spine; the Henry Hudson Parkway, in Riverside/Fort Washington Park, forms its W boundary.

Washington Island 20 sq mi/52 sq km, between L. Michigan and Green Bay, 5 mi/8 km off the tip of the DOOR PENINSULA, extreme E Wisconsin. It consists mainly of woods and rocky cliffs. Jackson Harbor on its NE shore is a fishing village, and the town of Washington is on its NW coast. Ferries land at Detroit Harbor on the S shore, and the island is a popular tourist destination. Once inhabited by Potawatomi Indians, it was explored by French traders on the 17th century and later settled by Icelanders.

Washington Monument 555-ft/169-m marble obelisk at the W end of the MALL, in Washington, D.C., just S of the White House. Begun in 1848 and completed, after many delays, in 1885, it is the world's tallest stone structure, and the second-highest structure in the District of Columbia, after the National Cathedral's tower.

Washington-on-the-Brazos also, **Washington** or **Old Washington** hamlet in Washington Co., SE Texas, 61 mi/98 km NW of Houston. Established in 1834 near a ferry on the Brazos R. in use since 1822, it was the site (1836) where the Texas Declaration of Independence and the new Republic of Texas constitution were created. In the mid 19th century it was a commercial center for the cotton producing Brazos Valley, and it was briefly (1842–46) the capital of the Republic. Today it has a 154-ac/64-ha State Historical Park.

Washington's Headquarters popular, sometimes official, name for a building or site occupied or thought to have been occupied by George Washington at some point during the Revolution. There is some overlap with the popular concept "George Washington Slept Here." The best-known headquarters is probably the one at VALLEY FORGE, Pennsylvania (winter 1777–78). The Craigie-Longfellow House in Cambridge, Massachusetts, is another (1775–76). The hamlet of Headquarters, N of Lambertville, New Jersey, was named because Washington was said to have spent three nights there before the battle of Trenton (Dec. 1776). After the battle of Princeton (Jan. 1777) he rested at Rocky Hill, 3 mi/5 km to the NE; in Aug.–Sept. 1783, while Congress met in Princeton, Washington again stayed there, in the Berrien House. In the winter of 1779–80, Washington's army was based at MORRISTOWN, New Jersey; he stayed nearby at the Ford House. In the final stages of the war Washington's headquarters included the Hasbrouck House in NEWBURGH, New York, and, at the battle of WHITE PLAINS, the Elijah Miller House in North White Plains.

Washington Square **1.** see under NORTH BEACH, San Francisco, California. **2.** urban park, Greenwich Village, Manhattan, New York City. Formerly a fashionable residential area, it is now chiefly home to New York University. The Washington Arch, built in 1892 by Stanford White, stands on the N side, at the foot of FIFTH AVENUE. The Triangle Shirtwaist Fire (1911) occurred in a building just E of the Square. **3.** municipal park in CENTER CITY, Philadelphia, Pennsylvania, NW of Society Hill and immediately SW of Independence National Historic Park. One of the original four open spaces laid out in William Penn's town plan, it was pasture, and later a burial ground. The Tomb of the Unknown Soldier of the American Revolution is here.

Washita River **1.** see OUACHITA R., Arkansas and Louisiana. **2.** 500 mi/800 km long, in Texas and Oklahoma. It rises near Miami, Roberts Co., in the N Texas PANHANDLE, and flows E into Oklahoma. Near Cheyenne (town, pop. 948, Roger Mills Co.), in the Black Kettle National Grassland, is the site of the Nov. 1868 Battle of the Washita, where George Custer's troops destroyed a Cheyenne force led by Black Kettle. The river winds SE across Oklahoma, through dam-created Foss L. and past Anadarko and Chickasha, into L. TEXOMA, where its waters join those of the RED R. Its name is sometimes spelled *Ouachita.*

Washoe County 6608 sq mi/17,115 sq km, pop. 254,667, in NW Nevada, bordered by the California (W) line and extending 170 mi/275 km N to the Oregon line. Its seat is RENO, which dominates the economy of the county's S section with its tourism, gambling, and manufacturing. PYRAMID L. lies within Washoe Co. Livestock is raised, and there is gold, silver, copper, and lead mining. Irrigated farming is practiced in the S.

Washtenaw County 710 sq mi/1839 sq km, pop. 282,937, in SE Michigan, drained by the Raisin, Huron, and Saline rivers. Its seat is ANN ARBOR. The county raises livestock, poultry, alfalfa, beans, corn, grain, and sugar beets, and makes dairy products. Ann Arbor and Ypsilanti have extensive manufacturing facilities. There has also been significant commercial development N of Ann Arbor. In the NW corner are many small lakes and resorts, the Pinckney and Waterloo state recreation areas, and the Gregory State Game Area.

Wasilla see under MATANUSKA VALLEY, Alaska.

Wassaic hamlet in AMENIA township, Dutchess Co., SE New York, 44 mi/71 km NE of Poughkeepsie, just W of the Connecticut border. Located in a dairy farming area, it was the 1856 site of the first production of condensed milk by Gail Borden (1801–74).

Wassaw Island one of the SEA ISLANDS, in the Atlantic Ocean 12 mi/19 km SE of Savannah, in Chatham Co., E Georgia. It is part of the Wassaw Island National Wildlife Refuge, and the site of a research project on the endangered giant loggerhead turtle.

Wassuk Range NW–SE trending mountains, 55 mi/90 km long, just W of WALKER L., in Mineral Co., W Nevada, reaching 11,245 ft/3427 m at Mt. Grant.

Waste Isolation Pilot Plant (WIPP) see under CARLSBAD CAVERNS, New Mexico.

Watauga city, pop. 20,009, Tarrant Co., NE Texas, a largely residential suburb of Fort Worth, 10 mi/16 km NNE of Downtown.

Watauga River 60 mi/100 km long, in North Carolina and Tennessee. It rises at Grandfather Mt., in North Carolina's Pisgah National Forest, and winds NW into Tennessee between Appalachian ranges. Seven mi/11 km E of Elizabethton, the 318 ft/97 m–high **Watauga Dam,** built in 1949, impounds **Watauga Lake,** which backs up almost to the North Carolina border, some 17 mi/27 km. The lake also receives waters of the Elk and other shorter rivers. Proceeding generally NW from the dam, the Watauga passes Elizabethton and enters the South Fork of the Holston R., 10 mi/16 km SE of Kingsport. The **Watauga Association** was a government established by settlers on the Watauga and on the Holston and Nolichucky rivers in 1772, on land leased from the Cherokees within the westward extension of North Carolina's charter. The Association went out of existence in 1775, and North Carolina reasserted control; the area was later (1784–88) part of the State of FRANKLIN, before Tennessee's admission to statehood.

Watch Hill village in Westerly township, Washington Co., extreme SW Rhode Island, 3 mi/5 km SE of Stonington, Connecticut, on a sandy peninsula on Block Island Sound. Watch Hill began its life as a beach resort in the latter half of the 19th century. A lighthouse and a Coast Guard station are in the area.

Watchung Mountains three basaltic ridges, First, Second, and Third Watchung Mountains, in an arc 40 mi/60 km long from S of Paterson to N of Somerville, N New Jersey. They rise to 500 ft/152 m. The Watchungs have been important strategically (to American Revolutionary forces) and economically (for quarries). Their slopes and heights provide forested breaks in New Jersey's heavy development, but several populous suburbs, such as the Oranges and SUMMIT (atop First Watchung Mountain) are here. The Watchung Reservation is largely in MOUNTAINSIDE.

Waterbury **1.** city and coterminous township, pop. 108,961, New Haven Co., W Connecticut, on the Mad and Naugatuck rivers, 23 mi/37 km SW of Hartford. In the 19th century, it was the nation's largest producer of brass products, and had a thriving clock industry; today its more diversified economy produces chemicals, computer components, television parts, lighting fixtures, clothing, and precision instruments. Mattatuck Community College (1967), Post College (1890), Waterbury State Technical College (1964), and an extension of the University of Connecticut are all located in the city, which is set on and between steep hills on both sides of the Naugatuck. **2.** town, pop. 4589, Washington Co., NC Vermont. It is on the Winooski R. where it is joined by the Little R., flowing S from Waterbury Reservoir, in the Green Mts., 11 mi/18 km NW of Montpelier. The NW section of the town is occupied by a unit of the Mt. Mansfield State Forest. The town's best-known industry is Ben & Jerry's ice cream factory, which has become a tourist attraction.

Wateree River see under CATAWBA R., South Carolina.

Waterford **1.** town, pop. 17,930, New London Co., SE Connecticut, on Long Island Sound adjacent (W) to New London. It is largely residential. Along the shore are Harkness Memorial State Park (SW) and Millstone, a former quarrying village now the site of the three-reactor Millstone nuclear plant (1970–86), at Millstone Point, 4.5 mi/7 km from downtown New London. Other villages include Quaker Hill and Graniteville. **2.** unincorporated community, pop. 66,692, Oakland Co., SE Michigan, 7 mi/11 km NW of Pontiac. The many lakes in this affluent residential suburb afford varied recreational facilities and provide settings for a number of summer camps. The Pontiac Lake State Recreation Area lies just to the SW.

Watergate apartment/office/commercial complex in NW Washington, D.C., just N of the John F. Kennedy Center, along the Potomac R., on the W edge of FOGGY BOTTOM. Situated near the confluence of ROCK CREEK with the Potomac, it was the scene, on June 17, 1972, of a break-in at Democratic Party offices that set in motion events leading to the 1974 resignation of President Richard Nixon.

Waterloo **1.** city, pop. 66,467, seat of Black Hawk Co., NE Iowa, on the Cedar R., just E of Cedar Falls and 46 mi/74 km NW of Cedar Rapids. Founded in 1846, it thrived as a center for saw and flour mills, a regional trade center, and, later, a railroad division point. Today, the city is an agricultural trade and industrial center; meatpacking is an important business. Its more than 150 manufactures include tractors (the largest industry), plastics, and heating and air-conditioning equipment. The Hawkeye Institute of Technology (1966) is here. The National Dairy Cattle Congress is held in Waterloo every September. **2.** town, pop. 7765, co-seat of Seneca Co., WC New York, in the FINGER LAKES between Seneca and Cayuga lakes, 7 mi/11 km ENE of Geneva. On the site of the Seneca village of Skoiyase, it was settled in the late 18th century. Waterloo's industries include the manufacture of automobile bodies and processed foods. It is also a summer resort. **3.** city, pop. 71,181, Waterloo Regional Municipality, S Ontario, 58 mi/93 km WSW of Toronto, adjoining (NW) KITCHENER. It was settled by Mennonites from the US before 1810; other German-speaking settlers followed, and a tight-knit commercial and agricultural community developed. Insurance was an early industry (1860s), and today the city is headquarters for five national insurance companies. The Seagram Company, which took over a distillery in the 1870s, has become one of Canada's largest liquor producers. The city's other industries include the manufacture of furniture, agricultural implements, bicycles, and cotton, paper, and metal products. The University of Waterloo (1959), with its affiliate Renison, Conrad Grebel, and St. Paul's United Colleges, and Wilfrid Laurier University (1973) are here. Building on the academic base, Waterloo has since the 1980s become part of the flourishing CANADIAN TECHNOLOGY TRIANGLE. With Kitchener, the city annually hosts the largest Bavarian festival in North America.

Waterloo Village see under STANHOPE, New Jersey.

Waterpocket Fold area of uplifted, folded rock extending some 100 mi/160 km NNW–SSE, from the CAPITOL REEF National Park (N) into the GLEN CANYON National Recreation Area (the Colorado R.), in S Utah. Elevations average 5000–7000 ft/1525–2135 m. Multicolored sandstone canyons and gorges formed by swift-flowing streams are found throughout the region. Shallow depressions that catch infrequent rainwater give the Fold its name.

Waterton Lakes National Park 203 sq mi/526 sq km, in extreme SW Alberta, bordering British Columbia and Montana. Within it are the Waterton Ls. and a section of the Waterton R. The land, once occupied by Blackfoot, was first explored by Europeans in 1858. Created in 1895, the park is adjacent to Montana's Glacier National Park, with which it forms the Waterton-Glacier International Peace Park, established (1932) by the Canadian Parliament and US Congress. The park is mountainous, with its highest point (9600 ft/2928 m) at Mt. Blakiston. A wide variety of plants and animals, including plains bison, are protected here.

Watertown **1.** town, pop. 20,456, Litchfield Co., NW Connecticut, adjacent (N) to Waterbury, on the Naugatuck R. Largely residential and formerly agricultural, it includes the industrial village of Oakville (pop. 8741). The Taft School, a prep school, is in the town. **2.** town, pop. 33,284, Middlesex Co., E Massachusetts, on the Charles R., adjoining (SW) Cambridge, and 8 mi/13 km W of Boston. The first New England town to elect a board of selectmen (1634), it was a center of political activity during the Revolution. In the 19th century, it was a center for Massachusetts Transcendentalists. Gristmills and cotton fulling were Colonial industries; the Watertown Arsenal manufactured heavy ordnance from 1816 to 1960. Modern industries produce electronics, machinery, medical equipment, and metal, rubber, and chemical products, and the town is also a bedroom community. The Perkins School for the Blind has been here since 1912. **3.** city, pop. 29,429, seat of Jefferson Co., NC New York, at the falls of the Black R., 10 mi/16 km E of L. Ontario. Organized in 1801, it developed as a lumber center. Once local timber sources were exhausted, industry developed, utilizing power from the 112-ft/34-m falls of the Black R. Manufactures now include hydraulic equipment, snowplows, ski lifts, thermometers, clothing, and electric motors. Watertown is also a gateway to the THOUSAND ISLANDS and N Adirondack resort areas. Jefferson Community College (1961) is here. SACKETS HARBOR is 11 mi/17 km WSW. **4.** city, pop. 17,592, seat of Codington Co., NE South Dakota, on the Big Sioux R., 90 mi/145 km NNW of Sioux Falls. It is a trading, railway distributing, and processing center for an extensive and diverse agricultural area. It has food processing and meatpacking industries and grain elevators. Manufactures include cement and rubber products, sashes, and doors. Lakes Kampeska and Pelican surround the city, and their recreational facilities make Watertown a popular resort. **5.** city, pop. 19,142, Dodge and Jefferson counties, SC Wisconsin, 35 mi/56 km NE of Madison. Local manufactures include machinery, furnaces, digital instruments, and wood and rubber products. Northwestern College (1865) is here. The city has been industrial since it was settled in 1836. A wave of German immigration followed the original New Englanders. Watertown is the site of what is widely considered the first American kindergarten, founded in 1856 by Margarethe Meyer Schurz on the grounds of Octagon House (1854).

Waterville city, pop. 17,173, Kennebec Co., SC Maine, on the W bank of the Kennebec R., opposite Winslow and 18 mi/29 km NNE of Augusta. It was a 17th-century trading post, and a military outpost (Fort Halifax, built 1754) during the French and Indian War. Today it is the seat of Colby (1813) and Thomas (1894) colleges, and a commercial hub.

Watervliet city, pop. 11,061, Albany Co., E New York, on the W bank of the Hudson R., across from Troy. The area was settled by the Dutch on land purchased from the Mohawks in 1630. In 1776, Mother Ann Lee founded the first informal Shaker community here. A US arsenal, established here in 1813, remains active. Industries manufacture steel products, abrasives, textiles, and brick.

Watkins Glen village, pop. 2207, seat of Schuyler Co., WC New York, in the FINGER LAKES, at the S tip of Seneca L., 21 mi/34 km WSW of Ithaca. It is situated amid spectacular scenery, including deep gorges, high waterfalls, and rocky cliffs, all of which attract many tourists. Its mineral springs have also made it a popular spa. Watkins Glen is a trading center for local farms, wineries, and saltworks. The well-known Watkins Glen International automobile racetrack is 3 mi/5 km SW.

Watson Lake town, pop. 912, extreme S Yukon Territory, on the LIARD R. and the ALASKA HIGHWAY, near the British Columbia border. Gateway to the Yukon from the SE, it is a trade and service center with an airport.

Watsonville city, pop. 31,099, Santa Cruz Co., WC California, on the Pajaro R., 3 mi/5 km E of Monterey Bay and 30 mi/48 km S of San Jose. Settled in the 1850s, it is a processing center for local strawberries, mushrooms, dairy goods, apples, vinegar, lettuce, and other agricultural products. Other industries include granite quarrying, brickmaking, and various light manufactures.

Watts residential and commercial section of S LOS ANGELES, California, adjacent to FLORENCE-GRAHAM (NE), WILLOWBROOK (SE), and SOUTH GATE and LYNWOOD (E), and 8 mi/13 km S of Downtown. Incorporated in 1907 and annexed by Los Angeles in 1926, it remained a racially mixed area until World War II, when an influx of black workers set off WHITE FLIGHT, followed later by middle-class black departure. The resulting GHETTO exploded in a destructive riot in Aug. 1965. Growth in the Hispanic and Asian populations of neighboring districts contributed to continuing tensions in Watts in the 1990s. Simon Rodia's **Watts Towers** (1921–54), built by hand and reaching up to 107 ft/33 m, are well-known reminders of an earlier day.

Watts Bar Dam on the Tennessee R. in Meigs and Rhea counties, E Tennessee, 50 mi/80 km NNE of Chattanooga, completed in 1942. A major TENNESSEE VALLEY AUTHORITY concrete dam with an earth-fill wing, it is 112 ft/34 m high and 2960 ft/903 m long. Providing flood control and power, it also has a lock allowing ships to pass upstream to KNOXVILLE. The Watts Bar nuclear power plant is just S of the dam. **Watts Bar Lake** backs up over 70 mi/110 km NE, and in several arms, from the dam. In addition to the Tennessee, it impounds waters of the CLINCH, Emory, and other, smaller rivers. Water from the LITTLE TENNESSEE R. enters it by way of the Tellico Dam at LENOIR CITY.

Watuppa Pond in Bristol Co., SE Massachusetts. FALL RIVER almost completely surrounds this 5 mi/8 km–long body of water, which has similarly sized Stafford Pond to its S, just across Interstate 95.

Waubesa, Lake in Dane Co., SC Wisconsin. Measuring 3 mi/5 km long and 1.5 mi/2.5 km wide, it is one of the FOUR LAKES chain near Madison, and is drained by the Yahara R.

Waucoba Mountain see under INYO Mts., California.

Waukegan city, pop. 69,392, seat of Lake Co., NE Illinois, between the Des Plaines R. (W) and L. Michigan (E), 47 mi/76 km N of Chicago and 9 mi/14 km S of the Wisconsin border. Situated on a high bluff overlooking L. Michigan, it is Illinois's first port of call along the SAINT LAWRENCE SEAWAY, with facilities for both lake and oceangoing ships. Local manufactures include outboard motors, wire and steel, gypsum and asbestos products, and pharmaceuticals. Originally the site of an Indian village, it was a French trading post and stockade until c.1760. American settlers arrived after 1820. Illinois Beach State Park is on L. Michigan immediately N. The city hosts an annual Coho Salmon Derby. Comedian Jack Benny was born here (1894).

Waukesha city, pop. 56,958, seat of Waukesha Co., SW Wisconsin, on the Fox R., 15 mi/24 km W of Milwaukee. It was founded on the site of a Potawatomi village in 1834. The city's name is a version of the Indian word for "fox," used to compare the animal's tail to the curving river. It was an important station on the Underground Railroad and a base for abolitionists. Natural springs made Waukesha a health resort after the Civil War, and it was a popular watering place until the early 1900s. Bottled waters are still an important product. Among the city's manufactures are motors, castings, and foundry and wood products. Three pre-Columbian mounds are preserved in Cutler Park. Waukesha is the seat of Carroll College (1846) and Mount St. Paul College (1962).

Waukesha County 554 sq mi/1435 sq km, pop. 304,715, in SE Wisconsin. Its seat is Waukesha. Drained by the Fox and Bark rivers, it is largely a dairying and farming area. Milwaukee suburbs occupy the E part and partially account for the county's large population. The processing of dairy products is a major industry, and there is manufacturing at Waukesha, Menomonee Falls, and Oconomowoc. The county has a number of resort lakes, particularly in its NW.

Waupun city, pop. 8207, Dodge and Fond du Lac counties, E Wisconsin, 17 mi/27 km SW of Fond du Lac. The area was settled in 1838. In a farming and dairying region, Waupun processes dairy products and produces beverages and canned vegetables. Its manufactures include shoes, vulcanizing machinery, brake linings, foundry products, and pumps and tanks. The city is known for the sculptures by such artists as Lorado Taft and James Earl Fraser that are displayed in its public areas.

Wausau city, pop. 37,060, seat of Marathon Co., C Wisconsin, on the Wisconsin R., 84 mi/135 km NW of the city of Green Bay. It was founded in 1839. The city's Algonquian name means "far away." In its early years lumber milling was its main industry. Wausau is now a trading center for the surrounding dairy farming area. Paper and paper pulp, wood and aluminum products, plastics, and industrial machinery are among the many items manufactured. Headquartered here, the Wausau Insurance Company is also important to the city's economy. A University of Wisconsin center (1933) is in Wausau. RIB MOUNTAIN State Park is 3 mi/5 km SW of the city.

Wauseon city, pop. 6322, seat of Fulton Co., NW Ohio, 32 mi/52 km WSW of Toledo. Local manufactures include aircraft and automobile parts, electrical equipment, and food products. There is farming and dairying in the area. Pioneer auto racer Barney Oldfield was born here (1878).

Wauwatosa city, pop. 51,308, Milwaukee Co., SE Wisconsin, immediately W of Milwaukee, of which it is a commuter suburb on the Menominee R. Its Algonquian name means "firefly," and refers to the numerous fireflies seen in thickets bordering the river. Steel scaffolding, metal parts, and electric motors are manufactured. The Annunciation Greek Orthodox church in the city was designed by Frank Lloyd Wright.

Wave Hill see under RIVERDALE, New York.

Waverly city, pop. 8539, seat of Bremer Co., NE Iowa, on the Cedar R., 14 mi/23 km NW of Waterloo. It is a trade center for the surrounding agricultural area. The main industries are food processing and the making of condensed milk, and excavating equipment is manufactured. Wartburg College (1852) is here.

Wawa mining community in the ALGOMA District, C Ontario, 100 mi/160 km NNW of Sault Ste. Marie, on the NE of L. Superior. The local L. Wawa is a stopover for migrating Canada geese (*wawa* is Ojibwa for "wild goose"). Founded in 1896 around the first of three gold rushes in a former (17th-century) fur trading area, it now has an economy based on iron ore and tourism, hunting, and sport fishing. Lake Superior Provincial Park lies just S.

Waxahachie city, pop. 18,168, seat of Ellis Co., NE Texas, 26 mi/42 km S of Dallas. Founded in the 1840s, it has been a cattle, cotton, and grain center in the BLACKLANDS, and has poultry, pecan, and honey processors. The city's manufactures include boats, fiberglass, refrigerators, and oilfield equipment. Southwestern Bible Institute (1927) is here, and there is an annual rodeo and livestock show. Waxahachie is an important moviemaking center, scene of the filming of *Bonnie and Clyde* (1967) and many subsequent films. The Superconducting Supercollider, an underground atomic particle accelerator being built in a ring around Waxahachie, was to have a 54-mi/87-km, roughly circular main tunnel. Federal funding cuts brought an apparent end to the project in 1993.

Waxhaw town, pop. 1294, Union Co., S North Carolina, 12 mi/19 km SW of Monroe, along the South Carolina border. Andrew Jackson was born (1767) in the Waxhaw Settlement, which lay in this area along the Catawba R.; the exact site is unknown, and both states have claimed him. Jackson himself felt that he had been born in South Carolina, and South Carolinians argue that the site may now be in North Carolina because of border changes, but was in South Carolina at the time. The Andrew Jackson State Park in South Carolina is 8 mi/13 km N of LANCASTER.

Wayah Bald see under NANTAHALA Mts., North Carolina.

Waycross city, pop. 16,410, seat of Ware Co., SE Georgia, 90 mi/145 km SW of Savannah. Founded in the 1820s, it gradually became a transportation hub, first of pioneer and stagecoach trails, then of railways. Today, sawmills, turpentine and honey production, and railyards characterize the economy, along with tourism. The city is a gateway to OKEFENOKEE SWAMP.

Wayland town, pop. 11,874, Middlesex Co., E Massachusetts, 15 mi/24 km W of Boston, on the Sudbury R. Truck gardening was long the economic mainstay of what is now an affluent suburb. Much of Wayland's W is part of the Great Meadows National Wildlife Refuge, along the Sudbury. L. COCHITUATE is SW, and the village of Cochituate is in Wayland.

Wayne **1.** city, pop. 19,899, Wayne Co., SE Michigan, on the Lower R. Rouge, an industrial and residential suburb 17 mi/27 km SW of Detroit. It was settled in the early 1820s. Its manufacturing capacity and its population grew markedly following World War II. The city produces aircraft and auto parts, oil and gas equipment, and foundry products. Several Ford Motor Company plants are situated here. **2.** city, pop. 5142, seat of Wayne Co., NE Nebraska, 23 mi/37 km NE of Norfolk. It is a trading hub for livestock, grain, dairy, and poultry producers. Wayne State College (1891) is here. The Winnebago (E) and Omaha (SE) Indian reservations are nearby. **3.** township, pop. 47,025, Passaic Co., NE New Jersey, 4 mi/6 km NW of Paterson. It was settled in the 18th century by Dutch, English, and French Huguenot farmers. The Dey Mansion (1740) was Washington's headquarters (1780). Mainly a New York–area residential suburb, Wayne has three lakes, a performing arts center, and a large retail shopping mall. Its industries produce rubber, chemicals, pharmaceuticals, electronic components, and machine tools. **4.** see under RADNOR, Pennsylvania.

Wayne County **1.** 615 sq mi/1593 sq km, pop. 2,111,687, in SE Michigan, drained by the Huron R. and the R. Rouge. Its seat is Detroit, and that city and its suburbs occupy nearly all but the S portion of the county. Its larger cities include DEARBORN and LIVONIA. Economically, it is one of the most important counties in the US. Known as the country's auto center, it has many major industrial installations. With declines in the American automobile industry from the 1970s, many Wayne Co. communities underwent severe economic stress. In the same period, there has been significant commercial expansion, with corporate office buildings springing up, particularly around Dearborn. Commercial fishing, salt mining, and shipbuilding are all practiced here. There are also nurseries and vegetable, dairy, and stock farms. **2.** 557 sq mi/1443 sq km, pop. 101,461, in NC Ohio. Its seat is WOOSTER. Diversified farming includes dairy, fruit, grain, livestock, and poultry. There is manufacturing at Orrville and Wooster. Natural resources include gas, oil, coal, sand, and gravel. Salt is produced, and there is a major fish hatchery S of Wooster. A number of Amish communities are scattered throughout the county.

Waynesboro **1.** city, pop. 5701, Burke Co., E Georgia, 30 mi/48 km SSW of Augusta. Settled in the 1780s in plantation country, it remains an agricultural center; it also produces fabricated metals, canned goods, and veneer, and is known as a bird dog training and testing center. The Vogtle nuclear power plant (1987) is nearby. **2.** borough, pop. 9578, Franklin Co., SC Pennsylvania, 50 mi/80 km SW of Harrisburg, just W of South Mt. Situated in a resort area, it manufactures machinery and metal products, clothing, and flour, and is a shipping center for regional fruit growers and dairy farmers. Waynesboro was occupied by the Confederate army in Oct. 1863. **3.** independent city, pop. 18,549, within Augusta Co., NC Virginia, in the SHENANDOAH VALLEY, just W of the Blue Ridge Mts., and 12 mi/19 km ESE of Staunton. It is an industrial and trade center in an agricultural area noted especially for its apples. The city produces stoves, plastics, flour, rayon, marine hardware, and pencils. A battle fought here on March 2, 1865, gave the Union army under Philip Sheridan a victory over the outnumbered Confederate troops of Jubal Early.

Waynesburg borough, pop. 4270, seat of Greene Co., extreme SW Pennsylvania, 38 mi/61 km S of Pittsburgh. Coal mining and dairy and livestock farming are important in the area. Waynesburg College (1849) is here.

Wayside Inn see under SUDBURY, Massachusetts.

Wayzata see under L. MINNETONKA, Minnesota.

Weatherford **1.** city, pop. 10,124, Custer Co., WC Oklahoma, 60 mi/96 km W of Oklahoma City. A commercial and processing center for wheat, cotton, and other agricultural producers, the city is also the seat of Southwestern Oklahoma State University (1901). **2.** city, pop. 14,804, seat of Parker Co., NC Texas, 30 mi/48 km W of Fort Worth. With an economy based on agriculture, it also makes electronic and oilfield equipment, silicone and plastic products, and fertilizer. Weatherford College (1869) is here, and the city has a number of medical facilities.

Weaverville see under WHISKEYTOWN-SHASTA-TRINITY NATIONAL RECREATION AREA, California.

Webster **1.** town, pop. 16,916, Worcester Co., C Massachusetts, on the French R., 18 mi/29 km S of Worcester, along the Connecticut border. Named for orator and statesman Daniel Webster, the town is on L. CHAUBUNAGUNGAMAUG, also called L. Webster. A textile producer since 1811, Webster has also manufactured shoes. **2.** town, pop. 31,639, Monroe Co., W New York, along L. Ontario and NE of Rochester across Irondequoit Bay. An industrial and residential suburb, it has corporate research facilities as well as plants producing metal products and canned goods. There is some summer tourism. **3.** see under CLEAR LAKE, Houston, Texas.

Webster, Mount see under PRESIDENTIAL RANGE, New Hampshire.

Webster City city, pop. 7894, seat of Hamilton Co., NC Iowa, on the Boone R., 18 mi/29 km E of Fort Dodge. The industrial and commercial center of an agricultural area, it produces boats and appliances.

Webster Groves city, pop. 22,987, St. Louis Co., EC Missouri, 9 mi/14 km SW of downtown St. Louis. Primarily a residential suburb, it also has some industry. The city is the seat of Webster University (1915) and Eden Theological Seminary.

Wedge, the **1.** in extreme NW Delaware, 800-ac/325-ha tract that was left unaccounted for when the MASON-DIXON LINE set (1760s) the Maryland-Pennsylvania boundary. The line did not clearly extend to touch the arc that had been created as the Delaware border in 1682 by drawing a circle 12 mi/19 km in radius around NEW CASTLE. Pennsylvania and Delaware disputed the Wedge until an 1893 joint commission awarded it to Delaware. Until resolution, the area was a frequent scene of duels and other illegal transactions. **2.** also, **Lowry Hill East** residential neighborhood in Minneapolis, Minnesota, SW of Downtown, immediately S of Loring Park. It is a diverse area, housing students, young professionals, and artists.

Weehawken township, pop. 12,385, Hudson Co., NE New Jersey, on the PALISADES of the Hudson R. opposite Midtown Manhattan, to which it is connected by the LINCOLN TUNNEL, and adjacent (N) to Hoboken. It has varied industries, office buildings, and railroad shops. Also available to New York City by ferry, Weehawken became a fashionable home for commuters in the 1980s and 1990s. It has older one-family homes as well as modern town houses and condominiums, many overlooking the Manhattan skyline. Weehawken's riverfront Highwood estate, later destroyed to make way for railroad tracks, was the scene of the Burr-Hamilton duel (1804).

Weeksville former black community, a village established in 1838 by James Weeks, a free worker, in what is now N CROWN HEIGHTS, Brooklyn, New York. One of the first free black communities in the Northeast, it survived until the 1870s. Remaining buildings were identified during a 1968 aerial survey of the area, and have been restored.

Weirton city, pop. 22,124, Brooke and Hancock counties, in the Northern PANHANDLE of West Virginia. It is on the Ohio R., 30 mi/48 km W of Pittsburgh, Pennsylvania, 25 mi/40 km N of Wheeling, and 4 mi/6 km NE of Steubenville, Ohio. The Weirton Steel Co. was established in 1910, and a booming company town grew around it, which incorporated as a city in 1947. Local industries include tin plating; tin can, chemical, cement block, and bottle manufacturing; and coal mining.

Weiser city, pop. 4571, seat of Washington Co., W Idaho, on the Snake R. at the mouth of the Weiser R., on the Oregon border, 60 mi/97 km NW of Boise. It is a trade, processing, and shipping center for a fruit, onion, corn, alfalfa, potato, sugar beet, and livestock producing region. The National Old-Time Fiddler's Contest is an annual event. A portion of HELLS CANYON is just W of the city.

Wekiva Springs unincorporated community, pop. 23,026, Seminole Co., EC Florida, 9 mi/14 km NW of downtown Orlando. It is a booming residential community amid lakes and golf courses, taking its name from Wekiva (or Wekiwa) Springs, one of Florida's largest and the source of the **Wekiva R.,** which flows 15 mi/24 km NE to join the Saint Johns R.

Welfare Island see under ROOSEVELT I., New York City.

Welland city, pop. 47,914, Niagara Regional Municipality, S Ontario, on the Welland River and Canal, 12 mi/19 km SW of Niagara Falls. Founded in 1830, with completion of the first Welland Canal, it developed as a market center for the Niagara fruit growing region, and more recently became an industrial center, making textiles, rubber goods, chemicals, and brass, iron, and steel items.

Welland Canal also, **Welland Ship Canal** waterway in extreme S Ontario, since 1959 a part of the SAINT LAWRENCE SEAWAY, designed to carry traffic between L. Ontario (N) and L. Erie (S), bypassing the NIAGARA R. and its falls. Four versions have been completed, in 1829, 1845, 1887, and 1932. Covering 28 mi/45 km of the Niagara Peninsula, the modern canal carries ships over the NIAGARA ESCARPMENT between Port Colborne on L. Erie and Port Weller on L. Ontario, which is 326 ft/99 m lower. Of its eight locks, numbers 4–6, in THOROLD, are "twin-flight," allowing one ship to be lifted as another is lowered. The Welland R. crosses under the canal at Welland. Parts of the earlier canals are popular recreationally.

Wellesley town, pop. 26,615, Norfolk Co., E Massachusetts, on the Charles R., 14 mi/23 km SW of Boston. It has some light industry and a shopping district, but is primarily an education center. Wellesley College (1870), on L. Waban, was originally a women's seminary. Babson College (1919), Massachusetts Bay Community College (1961), and a number of private schools are also in this affluent suburb. Wellesley Hills, Wellesley Fells, and Overbrook are included villages.

Wellfleet town, pop. 2493, Barnstable Co., SE Massachusetts, on N CAPE COD, 12 mi/19 km SSE of Provincetown. A summer resort and fishing village, it attracts artists and has chic boutiques, galleries, and restaurants. In the 19th century, it was a whaling and fishing center. Wellfleet includes South Wellfleet and Wellfleet villages. Its large harbor is on the Cape Cod Bay (W) side; its E coast is part of the Cape Cod National Seashore.

Wellington **1.** unincorporated community, pop. 20,670, Palm Beach Co., SE Florida, 13 mi/21 km SW of West Palm Beach and 8 mi/13 km W of Palm Springs, set amid lakes, wetlands, and golf courses, on the E edge of the Loxahatchee National Wildlife Refuge. It quadrupled in population in the 1980s. **2.** city, pop. 8411, seat of Sumner Co., S Kansas, 28 mi/45 km S of Wichita. It was established in 1871 and developed rapidly as a CHISHOLM TRAIL trading station. In the early 1930s the city grew with the exploration of nearby oilfields. Today it is a large wheat processing center and an important rail hub, and has some light manufactures.

Wellsville town, pop. 8116, Allegany Co., SW New York, 25 mi/40 km E of Olean, and 7 mi/11 km N of the Pennsylvania line, on the Genesee R. Indians used oil from the region and sold it to Europeans in the late 18th century; settled in 1795, Wellsville became a center of the early New York oil industry.

Wenatchee city, pop. 21,756, seat of Chelan Co., C Washington, on the Columbia R., just S of its junction with the Wenatchee R. It has been a major packing and shipping center for the area's apples and other fruit since the early 20th century, when the Columbia River Irrigation Project (1903) stimulated local agricultural development. Wenatchee also has lumber and flour mills and an aluminum smelting plant. Wenatchee Valley College (1939) is in the city, which is also the gateway to Wenatchee and Chelan national forests and the Cascade Mts. to the W.

Wenatchee River 65 mi/105 km long, rising on the E of the CASCADE RANGE in Washington, and flowing generally SE. It passes through the 2.1 million-ac/850,000-ha (3280-sq mi/8500-sq km) **Wenatchee National Forest** and joins the Columbia R. just above the city of Wenatchee, almost exactly in the center of the state. The river has many hydroelectric and irrigation dams, and the Wenatchee Valley, with its rich volcanic soil, is one of the world's chief apple-producing areas. The **Wenatchee Mts.,** an E spur of the Cascades, extend NW–SE for some 40 mi/64 km, paralleling (S of) the river, to the Columbia.

Wendake also, **Village-des-Hurons** see under LORETTEVILLE, Québec.

Wendover see under BONNEVILLE SALT FLATS, Utah.

Wentzville city, pop. 5088, St. Charles Co., EC Missouri, 40 mi/64 km WNW of downtown St. Louis. Founded in 1855, it was a major tobacco manufacturing center during the 1870s. On Interstate 70, it is home to a large General Motors assembly plant.

Werowocomoco also, **Powhatan Village** historic site, Gloucester Co., SE Virginia, on the N bank of the York R., nearly opposite the mouth of Queen Creek, in the TIDEWATER. It was in 1608 the center of the Powhatan Confederacy, a group of about 30 Algonquian-speaking tribes, under the leadership of Wahunsonacock (Chief Powhatan), whose daughter Matoaka (Pocahontas) later married the English colonist John Rolfe.

Weslaco city, pop. 21,877, Hidalgo Co., extreme S Texas, 35 mi/56 km WNW of Brownsville. It has several agricultural research and training centers; in the irrigated Lower Rio Grande Valley, the city cans and ships truck crops and citrus fruits. Its name is an acronym for the W.E. Stewart Land Company, which developed the site from 1917. Weslaco also has natural gas wells.

West, the **1.** in Canada, variously defined region, generally including everything W of the Great Lakes (but see NORTHWEST). **2.** in the US, variously defined region. Today it may generally be taken to include everything W of the Mississippi R., thus including such distinctive regions as the GREAT PLAINS, MOUNTAIN STATES, PACIFIC NORTHWEST, and SOUTHWEST. Historically, however, the meaning of "the West" has shifted. In the mid 18th century, it lay just W of the ALLEGHENY Mts., the great barrier separating older coastal settlements of the EAST from the (largely unexplored) interior. Eventually much of this territory became known as the MIDDLE WEST, with the West itself seen as lying beyond the next great mountain barrier, the Rockies. The term **Far West** (as distinguished from Middle West) has also been used for everything from the Rockies W; in some definitions, however, the four states in which the Rockies rise from the Great Plains (New Mexico, Colorado, Wyoming, and Montana) cannot be considered "Far West." Taking into account the expanse and changing characteristics of the Great Plains themselves, some observers set the E boundary of the West at either 98° W or 100° W (roughly from the E or C Dakotas through C Texas); land W of this line is generally higher and drier than that to the E, thus more suited to the traditionally "Western" pursuits of dry farming and stock raising. The **Wild West,** the proverbially lawless frontier (pre-statehood regions) of the 19th century, lay largely in Great Plains areas from W Kansas to E Wyoming.

West Adams residential section of LOS ANGELES, California, on the NW of SOUTH-CENTRAL, 4 mi/6 km WSW of Downtown, along the SANTA MONICA FREEWAY and Adams Blvd. It is a black community facing economic and related problems.

West Allis city, pop. 63,221, Milwaukee Co., SE Wisconsin, a residential and industrial suburb adjoining Milwaukee (SW). The headquarters of the Allis-Chalmers company, producers of industrial and farm machinery and trucks, is here. Among other manufactures are motors, electronic equipment, castings, and diverse iron and steel products.

West Augusta unincorporated community, pop. 27,637, Richmond Co., E Georgia, a suburb adjoining Augusta.

West Babylon unincorporated village, pop. 42,410, in Babylon town, Suffolk Co., SE New York, on Long Island's South Shore. It is primarily residential.

West Bank see CEDAR-RIVERSIDE, Minneapolis, Minnesota.

West Belmar see under BELMAR, New Jersey.

West Bend city, pop. 23,916, seat of Washington Co., SE Wisconsin, on the Milwaukee R., 28 mi/45 km NW of Milwaukee. Local manufactures include aluminum utensils, household appliances, outboard motors, farm machinery, and beverages. It was founded in 1845 as the site for a sawmill and gristmill. In 1911, the West Bend Aluminum Company was established, stimulating much industrial growth. A University of Wisconsin center (1968) is in the city. Lizard Mound County Park, 4 mi/6 km NE of here, has 30 Indian mounds in animal, bird, and geometric shapes.

Westborough town, pop. 14,133, Worcester Co., EC Massachusetts, 10 mi/16 km E of Worcester, at the junction of Route 495 and the Massachusetts Turnpike. Settled in the 1670s and industrial since the 1830s, it has manufactured electronics, tools, paper, machinery, leather, abrasives, and dyes. The birthplace (1765) of Eli Whitney is in the town, which also has a state hospital, school for boys, and state correctional school. Since the 1970s Westborough has become a location of choice for headquarters of computer and other corporations, a westward expansion of the ROUTE 128 complex.

West Branch city, pop. 1908, Cedar Co., EC Iowa, 10 mi/16 km E of Iowa City. This farming community is the birthplace (1874) of Herbert Hoover, and the site of the Herbert Hoover National Historic Site, which includes the Hoover Presidential Museum and Library.

Westbrook city, pop. 16,121, Cumberland Co., SW Maine, on the Presumpscot R., 6 mi/10 km W of Portland. Originally a section of Falmouth, it has a large paper mill, and produces wood products, machinery, shoes, textiles, crushed stone products, and jewelry. The home of Westbrook College

(1831), the city is part of the growing Portland suburban area.

Westbury village, pop. 13,060, in North Hempstead town, Nassau Co., SE New York, in WC Long Island, 23 mi/37 km E of Manhattan. Settled by English Quakers in 1665, it is primarily residential, although its S border is part of a heavily commercial strip that is a shopping mecca for much of Nassau Co. The Westbury Music Fair presents popular entertainment.

West Caldwell township, pop. 10,422, Essex Co., NE New Jersey, 9 mi/14 km W of Passaic. It houses commuters to New York City and its environs, a number of office buildings, and some light industry.

West Carrollton City also, **West Carrollton** city, pop. 14,403, Montgomery Co., SW Ohio, on the Great Miami R., 8 mi/13 km S of Dayton, of which it is a suburb. The river's excellent waterpower made it an industrial center. Paper mills here are among the largest in the state.

West Chester borough, pop. 18,041, seat of Chester Co., SE Pennsylvania, 25 mi/40 km W of Philadelphia. Although primarily residential, it also serves as an agricultural trade and banking center, has other business and research organizations, and is home to West Chester State College (1812).

Westchester **1.** unincorporated community, pop. 29,883, Dade Co., SE Florida, 6 mi/10 km WSW of downtown Miami, a residential suburb on the Tamiami Trail. **2.** village, pop. 17,301, Cook Co., NE Illinois, on Salt Creek, 14 mi/23 km W of Chicago. A densely populated inner suburb, it was founded by public utility magnate Samuel Insull in the 1920s as a quiet bedroom community at what was then the W edge of the Chicago area. Some 15,000 American elm trees were planted along the streets, and three forest preserve areas border the village. Today, Westchester has the less bucolic distinction of lying just SE of the intersection of three highways.

Westchester County 438 sq mi/1134 sq km, pop. 874,866, in SE New York, adjacent (N and NE) to New York City. Its seat is White Plains. Suburban Westchester contains extremes of great wealth, as in PURCHASE, SCARSDALE, and BRONXVILLE, and poverty, especially in parts of YONKERS and MOUNT VERNON. Since the 1960s, corporate giants, including IBM and Pepsico, have established headquarters in the county; however, high housing costs and taxes have discouraged others, and even the giants reduced their presence in the 1980s and 1990s. The county offers many amenities, including beaches, parks, boating facilities, and cultural centers.

West Chicago city, pop. 14,796, Du Page Co., NE Illinois, on the West Branch of the Du Page R., 30 mi/48 km W of Chicago. It manufactures movable buildings, building materials, rare-earth chemicals, gas mantles, and lighting implements. Railroad shops are also located here. The Fermi National Accelerator Laboratory is immediately SW.

West Columbia city, pop. 10,588, Lexington Co., C South Carolina, across the Congaree R. from Columbia. It is a primarily residential suburb, with some light manufactures. At the confluence of the Broad and Saluda rivers, where they form the Congaree, it was known until 1938 as New Brookland.

West Covina city, pop. 96,086, Los Angeles Co., SW California, at the E end of the San Gabriel Valley, 20 mi/32 km E of downtown Los Angeles. Rural and agricultural from its founding in the 1870s, it had citrus and walnut groves and, briefly, vineyards. After World War II, it grew rapidly with the Los Angeles metropolitan area, and is now a retail and service center and a bedroom community for Los Angeles and other nearby manufacturing and commercial cities.

West Dallas residential and commercial section of Dallas, Texas, just S of the Trinity R. and N of OAK CLIFF, and directly E of Downtown. The district is noted particularly for its huge public housing projects, built largely in the 1960s, and by the 1980s severely dilapidated.

West Des Moines city, pop. 31,702, Polk and Dallas counties, C Iowa, on the Raccoon R., immediately W of Des Moines. Originally known as Valley Junction, it grew up at the intersection of two major rail lines. Largely a residential suburb of the state capital, the city also manufactures cement and foundry products.

West Edmonton Mall commercial development in the W part of Edmonton, Alberta. The world's largest mall before the opening of BLOOMINGTON, Minnesota's Mall of America, West Edmonton covers almost 5.5 million sq ft/500,000 sq m, with some 800 establishments, 11 department stores, 10 aviaries, 7 amusement parks (including a 14-story roller coaster and a waterpark), 19 movie theaters, and a replica of Columbus's *Santa Maria.* Built in three phases, the last in 1985, it generated some 16,000 jobs, along with criticism that the boom occurred at the expense of downtown businesses.

West End **1.** residential and commercial section of N VANCOUVER, British Columbia, on a peninsula between STANLEY PARK (N), Downtown (SE), and FALSE CREEK (S). The most fashionable residential area of the city early in the 20th century, it became after the 1960s home to densely packed high-rise apartment and condominium blocks. Robson St., which passes through it, was formerly an ethnic STRIP ("Robsonstrasse"), and is now the city's most popular shopping and restaurant boulevard. **2.** residential and commercial district of SW Atlanta, Georgia, 2 mi/3 km WSW of FIVE POINTS. A historically black community with the ATLANTA UNIVERSITY CENTER in the NE and CASCADE HEIGHTS farther SW, it has undergone substantial renovation in recent years. The site of the battle of Ezra Church (July 28, 1864), a skirmish in W.T. Sherman's advance on Atlanta, lies in Mozley Park, just NW. The writer Joel Chandler Harris's home, Wren's Nest, is in the S. **3.** residential and resort section in the NW corner of New Orleans, Louisiana, on L. Pontchartrain at the METAIRIE boundary. At the turn of the 20th century the area, extending W into the Bucktown area of Metairie, was a center of lakeside amusements, including parks, restaurants, and boat and night clubs. SPANISH FORT was 1.5 mi/2 km E, MILNEBURG farther E. **4.** district of Boston, Massachusetts, lying N and W of Beacon Hill and downtown, along the Charles R. It is built partly on landfill. A fashionable garden area in the early 19th century, it became a tenement district by 1900. Beginning in 1958, urban renewal destroyed most of the old West End, replacing it with housing blocks, roadway, and parking lots. Surviving landmarks include the Massachusetts General Hospital (1811) and the house of Federalist leader Harrison Gray Otis (1796). **5.** section of SAINT LOUIS, Missouri, 4 mi/6 km WNW of Downtown. FOREST PARK dominates the area. Residential neighborhoods N and E of the park were fashionable before residents moved to W suburbs after 1950. Rehabilitation projects here have combined with an influx of young people and gays to resuscitate town house–lined streets, now a popular shopping area. Washington University is on the W. **6.** resort community in the city of LONG BRANCH, Monmouth Co., E New Jersey, on the Atlantic Ocean. It was a whaling center in the early 19th century. In the latter 19th through mid 20th century, West End was a summer retreat for wealthy urbanites. An area of beachfront estates, it was the birthplace of such notables as Dorothy Parker (1893) and Harry Frank Guggenheim (1890). **7.** neighborhood in Cincinnati, Ohio, immediately W of Downtown. Originally an area of single-family homes for first-generation German immigrants, it had deteriorated into a slum, according to municipal leaders, when in the 1960s, the first urban renewal project in Cincinnati was implemented here, with modern high-rise buildings replacing the old homes. **8.** renovated commercial and entertainment district immediately N of DEALEY PLAZA in downtown Dallas, Texas. In the early 20th century it was the site of Union Station (1916) and many warehouses; it is now a theater, tourist, and retailing district.

Westerly town, pop. 21,605, Washington Co., extreme SW Rhode Island, on the Pawcatuck R. and the Connecticut border. It includes nine villages, among them WATCH HILL and Misquamicut. A shipbuilding center in the 19th century, Westerly has also produced bleach and dyes and granite. It is now chiefly a resort area.

Western Addition residential and commercial section of C SAN FRANCISCO, California, W of Downtown and N of Haight-Ashbury, also called "the Fillmore" after its busiest commercial thoroughfare. In this fashionable late-19th-century suburban addition to the city, Victorian mansions became rooming and boarding houses in the early 20th century, and the area became international, populated esp. by European Jews. With the boom in city shipyards in World War II, black workers moved in. The Western Addition now has a mix of housing projects and rental buildings. Some GENTRIFICATION is occurring. The University of San Francisco (1855) is in the W. Japantown (Nihonmachi), with the commercial Japan Center (1968), is in the NE. The Fillmore Auditorium, the 1960s rock music mecca, is on Fillmore St. near Japantown.

Western Liberties see under WEST PHILADELPHIA, Pennsylvania.

Western Reserve lands in NE Ohio retained by Connecticut when it ceded (1786) its claims in the NORTHWEST TERRITORY. They today form ten entire counties and parts of four others, extending from the Pennsylvania border (NE) to the Sandusky area (NW). In 1792 Connecticut granted 500,000 ac/202,000 ha of these lands, the "Firelands," to citizens whose Connecticut homes had been burned by the British and Tories (see NORWALK). The remainder of the Reserve was sold to the commercial Connecticut Land Company. The entire area became Trumbull Co. of the Northwest Territory in 1800, then was subdivided as Ohio became (1803) a state. The Western Reserve's major settlements included Cleveland, Akron, Youngstown, Lorain, and Sandusky.

Western Shore see under EASTERN SHORE, Maryland.

Western Springs village, pop. 11,984, Cook Co., NE Illinois, 15 mi/24 km W of Chicago. A residential community, it was founded in 1871. It is named for local mineral springs where Potawatomi Indians and fur trappers once gathered, that are now in Spring Rock Park.

Western White House see under SAN CLEMENTE, California.

Westerville city, pop. 30,193, Delaware and Franklin counties, C Ohio, 10 mi/16 km NE of Columbus, of which it is a commuter suburb. Hanby House, once the home of Benjamin R. Hanby, who wrote the song "Darling Nellie Grey," is maintained as a state historical site. From 1909 to 1948, the national headquarters of the Anti-Saloon League was located in Westerville, which was known as "the Dry Capital of America." Otterbein College (1847) is here.

West Fargo city, pop. 12,287, Cass Co., E North Dakota, on the Sheyenne R., 5 mi/8 km W of Fargo. A suburb of the state's largest city, it has a meatpacking industry and is an agricultural distribution point. North Dakota State University (1890) is here.

Westfield **1.** city, pop. 38,372, Hampden Co., SW Massachusetts, 9 mi/15 km W of Springfield, on the Westfield R. Originally a trading post for the Massachusetts Bay Colony, Westfield is so named because when it was incorporated in 1669 it was the most western Massachusetts settlement. In the 19th century it manufactured nearly all of the nation's whips. More recent manufactures have included paper, furniture, machinery, firearms, bicycles, cigars, leather products, tools, and precision instruments. Westfield State College (1838), one of the state's first teachers' colleges, is in the city. **2.** town, pop. 28,870, Union Co., NE New Jersey, 8 mi/13 km W of Elizabeth. Settled in the late 1600s, it was part of Elizabethtown until 1794, and was a center of Revolutionary War activity. Today Westfield is mainly a residential suburb of New York City. Once a center of the American whip industry, it now produces such products as furniture and paper and leather goods.

West Florida historic jurisdiction now divided among four states on the Gulf Coast. When the British acquired Florida from Spain and parts of Louisiana from France in 1763, they created East Florida (all of modern Florida E of the APALACHICOLA R.) and West Florida. The latter included westernmost modern Florida and parts of modern Alabama, Mississippi, and Louisiana (excepting the city and area of New Orleans) W to the Mississippi R. In 1764 the British unilaterally expanded this area's N boundary from 31° N (the line of the current S Mississippi–Louisiana border) to a line drawn E from near Vicksburg. When they ceded West Florida to Spain in 1781, the Spanish claimed the northern line, but by a 1795 treaty the US retained the 31° N line. The 1803 LOUISIANA PURCHASE brought another controversy, over the (modern) Louisiana portion, and a revolt against the Spanish centered in Baton Rouge in 1810 declared a Republic of West Florida. An 1819 treaty finally brought all of both Floridas within US jurisdiction.

West Glacier hamlet in Flathead Co., NW Montana, on the Flathead R., 25 mi/40 km NE of Kalispell. It is the W entrance to Glacier National Park.

West Greenwich town, pop. 3492, Kent. Co., WC Rhode Island, 20 mi/32 km SW of Providence, extending to the Connecticut border. It includes the villages of Escoheag, Nooseneck (the governmental center), Nooseneck Hill, and West Greenwich Center. It is largely rural and forested. Along Interstate 95, the town is experiencing some high-tech office development.

West Hartford town, pop. 60,110, Hartford Co., C Connecticut, adjoining (W) Hartford. Primarily a residential suburb, it has some industry, including the manufacture of machine tools, chemicals, automobile parts, plastics, and electrical equipment. It is the site of St. Joseph College for Women (1932), the American School for the Deaf (founded 1817 by Thomas Gallaudet, the oldest such school in the nation), and the University of Hartford (1877).

West Haven city and coterminous township, pop. 54,021, New Haven Co., SW Connecticut, on New Haven Harbor across the West R. from New Haven. It separated from New Haven as part of the town of Orange, from which it seceded in 1921. It is a working-class suburb of New Haven, with some manufacturing, including pharmaceuticals, tires, textiles, and die castings. West Haven was sacked by the British in July 1779; a plaque in Savin Rock Amusement Park, a famous 19th- and 20th-century beach resort, marks the spot where the attackers landed. The University of New Haven (1920) is here.

West Haverstraw village, pop. 9183, in Haverstraw town, Rockland Co., SE New York, just W of the Hudson R., 8 mi/13 km NW of Nyack. At the building here popularly called the Treason House, Benedict Arnold and British Maj. John André plotted (1780) the betrayal of the garrison at WEST POINT. There are a number of light industries in West Haverstraw, which is also the site of the 200-ac/81-ha Marian shrine.

West Helena city, pop. 9695, Phillips Co., E Arkansas, 3 mi/5 km WNW of HELENA, of which it was originally a suburb, in the Alluvial Plain, near the Mississippi R. Lumber milling and the manufacture of wood products are its main industries.

West Hempstead unincorporated village, pop. 17,689, in Hempstead town, Nassau Co., SE New York, in WC Long Island, immediately W of Hempstead and 3 mi/5 km N of Rockville Centre. It is primarily residential.

West Hills **1.** see under HUNTINGTON, New York. **2.** residential and recreational district in the Northwest and Southwest sections of PORTLAND, Oregon, 2 mi/3.2 km W of Downtown, in the SE foothills of the Tualatin Mts. One of the city's wealthiest areas, West Hills contains Washington Park, with its noted zoo and rose test and Japanese gardens, and affluent residential neighborhoods SW to Council Crest Park.

West Hollywood city, pop. 36,118, Los Angeles Co., SW California, in the S foothills of the Santa Monica Mts., across Fairfax Blvd. (W) from HOLLYWOOD and NE of Beverly Hills. An early-20th-century bungalow district, it now contains the Los Angeles area's best-known gay community.

West Island loose term for areas in the W (officially; actually the SW) of the I. de MONTRÉAL, Québec, which are traditionally, or have become through 20th-century suburbanization, predominantly anglophone. These include a dozen municipalities W of LACHINE, some of which have been retreats for wealthy English-speakers from the city since the early 19th century. Their position reflects the city's basic division into an anglophone West End (and near suburbs like WESTMOUNT) and a francophone East End (with francophone suburbs to the E).

West Islip unincorporated village, pop. 28,419, in Islip town, Suffolk Co., SE New York, adjacent (E) to Babylon, on Great South Bay. It is residential. The Robert Moses Causeway on its E boundary connects Long Island with Captree State Park and FIRE I.

West Jersey see under EAST JERSEY.

West Jordan city, pop. 42,892, Salt Lake Co., NC Utah, on the Jordan R., a residential suburb 12 mi/18 km SSW of Salt Lake City. Settled in 1849, it still has a sawmill built (1850) by early settlers. There is some light industry.

West Kingston see under SOUTH KINGSTOWN, Rhode Island.

West Lafayette city, pop. 25,907, Tippecanoe Co., WC Indiana, on the Wabash R., adjacent to LAFAYETTE. On the site of Fort Ouiatenon, the first (c.1719) military post in the state, the city was formed (1888) from the consolidation of the communities of Kingston and Chauncey. It is essentially a residential suburb of Lafayette, with some industry. Purdue University (1869), one of America's oldest and largest land-grant institutions, is based on the city's W side.

Westlake city, pop. 27,018, Cuyahoga Co., N Ohio, 12 mi/19 km W of Cleveland. It is essentially a commuter suburb, but some light manufacturing is carried out. Among the items produced are construction components, cosmetics, ink, and plastics. On surrounding farmland, potatoes, corn, grapes, and wheat are grown.

Westlake Park see under MACARTHUR PARK, Los Angeles, California.

Westland city, pop. 84,724, Wayne Co., SE Michigan, a residential suburb 20 mi/32 km W of Detroit.

West Liberty town, pop. 1434, Ohio Co., NW West Virginia, in the Northern PANHANDLE, 9 mi/14 km NE of Wheeling. West Liberty State College (1837) is here.

West Linn city, pop. 16,367, Clackamas Co., NW Oregon, on the Willamette R., across (N) from OREGON CITY, and 10 mi/16 km S of Portland, of which it is a residential suburb.

West Little River unincorporated community, pop. 33,575, Dade Co., SE Florida, on the Little River Canal just N of the city line and E of Hialeah. It is a predominantly black residential suburb.

West Long Branch borough, pop. 7690, Monmouth Co., EC New Jersey, adjacent (W) to Long Branch. It was settled in 1711. The borough is now a residential, resort, commercial, and educational community, the seat of Monmouth College (1933).

West Los Angeles see under WESTSIDE, Los Angeles, California.

West Memphis city, pop. 28,259, Crittenden Co., NE Arkansas, across from MEMPHIS, Tennessee, on the W bank of the Mississippi R. Originally a logging camp, it remains a milling center. It also serves as a market, processing, and shipping center for DELTA corn, grain, rice, soybean, alfalfa, and cotton producers. Liquid fertilizers are among its manufactures.

West Mifflin borough, pop. 23,644, Allegheny Co., SW Pennsylvania, on the S bank of the Monongahela R., 7 mi/11 km SE of Pittsburgh. It is an industrial center producing coal and steel products, auto bodies, appliances, and cans. The Kennywood Amusement Park is here.

West Milwaukee village, pop. 3973, Milwaukee Co., SE Wisconsin, adjacent (W) to Milwaukee, of which it is a suburb. Steel castings are among the products manufactured here.

Westminster **1.** city, pop. 78,118, Orange Co., SW California, adjacent (NW) to Santa Ana and 25 mi/40 km SE of Los Angeles. Founded in 1870 as a Presbyterian temperance colony, it has industrial parks producing various light manufactures, as well as large commercial malls. It is noted as home to a sizable Vietnamese community, known locally as Little Saigon. **2.** city, pop. 74,625, Adams and Jefferson counties, NC Colorado, a mainly residential suburb 9 mi/14 km NW of downtown Denver. This rapidly growing city also has a number of industries, including the manufacture of telephone equipment and electrical products. **3.** city, pop. 13,068, seat of Carroll Co., N Maryland, 30 mi/48 km NW of Baltimore. Founded in 1764, it developed various manufactures and handled local agricultural products, and was a Union supply base during the Civil War. Today it is agricultural and houses some Baltimore commuters. Western Maryland College (1867) is here.

West Monroe city, pop. 14,096, Ouachita Parish, NC Louisiana, on the W bank of the Ouachita R., across from MONROE. It is primarily a residential suburb, set in rolling pine hills in a rich agricultural and forest region. Local farms produce cotton, sugar cane, truck crops, and soybeans. The city has a history as a pulp and paper producer, and there are oil wells in the vicinity.

Westmont village, pop. 21,228, Du Page Co., NE Illinois, a suburb 20 mi/32 km W of Chicago. It is a bedroom community.

Westmoreland historic township: see under WYOMING VALLEY, Pennsylvania.

Westmoreland County **1.** 1033 sq mi/2675 sq km, pop. 370,321, in SW Pennsylvania, SE of Pittsburgh and bounded by the Conemaugh R. (NE) and LAUREL HILL (SE). Its seat is GREENSBURG. The county is a coal producer, with industrial centers at JEANETTE, Ligonier, LATROBE, and MONESSEN. **2.** 227 sq mi/588 sq km, pop. 15,480, in E Virginia. Its seat is Montross. On the NORTHERN NECK, it is historically agricultural, today relying on truck farming, fishing, and tourism. In the county are WAKEFIELD, George Washington's birthplace, and STRATFORD HALL, the Lee family seat.

Westmount city, pop. 20,239, MONTRÉAL URBAN COMMUNITY, S Québec, on the W slope of Mt. Royal, immediately SW of downtown Montréal. It is traditionally the home, in elegant surroundings, of the wealthiest and most powerful of Montréal's English-speakers.

West New York town, pop. 38,125, Hudson Co., NE New Jersey, atop the PALISADES of the Hudson R., across from Manhattan, and 5 mi/8 km NE of Jersey City. Dutch settlement of the area dates from 1661. It was founded in 1790, and became a separate town in 1898. West New York has long been the major embroidery producing municipality in the US. Its other manufactures include textiles, clothing, radio parts, rubber and leather products, and toys. Its waterfront accommodates oceangoing vessels, and there are facilities of the New York Central Railroad. From the 1960s on, West New York and its neighbor, Union City, have become commercial centers for Cuban refugees, later joined by immigrants from the Caribbean and South America; 60% of residents are foreign-born.

West Norriton township, pop. 15,209, Montgomery Co., SE Pennsylvania, on the Schuylkill R., 14 mi/23 km NW of Philadelphia and adjacent (W) to NORRISTOWN. It is a largely residential suburb.

West Nyack unincorporated village, pop. 3437, in Clarkstown, Rockland Co., SE New York, 3 mi/5 km W of Nyack, and just S of DeForest L. It is primarily residential.

West of the Park in NW Washington, D.C., term for areas W of Rock Creek Park, which are largely more affluent than the rest of the District, including GEORGETOWN, SPRING VALLEY, and CLEVELAND PARK. While the District is 70% black, West of the Park remains 90% white.

Weston **1.** town, pop. 8648, Fairfield Co., SW Connecticut, on the Saugatuck R. adjacent (E) to Wilton. It is an affluent exurb and suburb set in rough, hilly country. **2.** town, pop. 10,200, Middlesex Co., NE Massachusetts. Situated 12 mi/19 km W of Boston, it is home to Regis College (1927). Lying W of Route 128, it is one of Boston's most affluent suburbs, with many large estates and much open land. **3.** see under YORK, Ontario.

West Orange township, pop. 39,103, Essex Co., NE New Jersey, 5 mi/8 km NW of Newark, in the WATCHUNG Mts. Originally called Fairmont, it was separated from Orange in 1862. Today it is part of a large suburban complex housing New York–area commuters. There are also office buildings and such manufactures as pharmaceuticals, clothing, and office equipment. Thomas Edison's home (1876–1931), "Glenmont," in the early "garden city" development of Llewellyn Park, and his laboratory complex (1887) are included in the Edison National Historic Site. Eagle Rock Reservation, with views of New Jersey and the Manhattan skyline, is NE.

Westover historic site in Charles City Co., SE Virginia, on the N bank of the James R. just E of BERKELEY and 8 mi/13 km E of HOPEWELL. The Georgian mansion was the seat (built 1730) of William Byrd II, one of Virginia's most powerful planters. An expedition from JAMESTOWN had built a tower, called West Tower, in the area in 1610. Westover is noted for its gardens.

Westover Air Force Base see under CHICOPEE, Massachusetts.

West Palm Beach city, pop. 67,643, seat of Palm Beach Co., SE Florida, on L. Worth (a lagoon) and the Atlantic Intracoastal Waterway, connected by bridges to PALM BEACH, just E, and by canal to L. Okeechobee to the W. Like Palm Beach, it was developed by railroad tycoon Henry M. Flagler in the early 1890s, in its case as a commercial center for the resort. Flagler's home here is now a museum. Manufactures include aircraft engines and parts, transistors, computers, aluminum and concrete building materials, and foods and beverages. It is a trade and shipping center for local citrus, vegetables, and cattle. Tourism is also important. The Atlanta Braves and Montreal Expos play spring training baseball in the city. Palm Beach Atlantic College (1968) and several smaller institutions are here. An international airport is on the SW outskirts.

West Park **1.** hamlet in ESOPUS township, Ulster Co., E New York, on the W bank of the Hudson R., 6 mi/10 km NNW of Poughkeepsie. It was the home (1873–1921) of naturalist John Burroughs. Father Divine (George Baker), cult leader of the 1930s, established one of his "heavens" here. **2.** municipal park in the ALLEGHENY section of Pittsburgh, Pennsylvania. It borders Allegheny Center, Allegheny West, and the Mexican War Streets. Originally laid out as a common grazing area for town residents, the park later was home to a prison. Today, the Pittsburgh Aviary is here.

West Paterson borough, pop. 10,982, Passaic Co., NE New Jersey, adjacent (SW) to Paterson. On the Passaic R., it was formerly a part of Little Falls. Essentially a suburb of Paterson, it has such manufactures as electronic, electrical, and photographic goods. Most of the large Garret Mt. Reservation is in the borough.

West Pensacola unincorporated community, pop. 22,107, Escambia Co., NW Florida, a residential suburb 3 mi/5 km from downtown Pensacola and just NE of Myrtle Grove.

West Philadelphia educational center and residential section of Philadelphia, Pennsylvania, W of the Schuylkill R., between CENTER CITY and UPPER DARBY township. An area of country estates originally known as the Western Liberties, West Philadelphia grew out of 19th-century working-class settlements on the river and post–Civil War subdivisions for the upwardly mobile. Today, the Protestant elite and its Irish and Jewish successors have been replaced by blacks and students in many neighborhoods. West Philadelphia includes the areas of UNIVERSITY CITY, POWELTON VILLAGE, Wynnefield, and OVERBROOK.

West Plains city, pop. 8913, seat of Howell Co., S Missouri, on the Ozark Plateau, 85 mi/136 km SE of Springfield and 16 mi/26 km N of the Arkansas border. It was laid out in 1858 and was subject to Confederate raids during the Civil War. The only sizable city in its region, West Plains has served as a livestock market and distribution point and also produces dairy products, flour, and lumber. Units of the Mark Twain National Forest are NE and NW.

West Point **1.** city, pop. 3571, Troup and Harris counties, W Georgia, 33 mi/53 km NNW of Columbus, on the Chattahoochee R. Settled in the 1820s, it became a cotton market when reached (1850s) by railroads. In 1866 what is now the West Point–Pepperell textile company was founded here, and the city continues to be a textile manufacturer. On April 16, 1865, one of the last skirmishes of the Civil War was fought here. **2.** city, pop. 8489, seat of Clay Co., NE Mississippi, 15 mi/24 km NW of Columbus. The site was purchased from Indians in 1844. Once the center of one of the South's largest grain growing and storage areas, it was the site of several skirmishes during the Civil War. It is now a processing center for cotton, dairy products, poultry, and livestock, with various light manufactures. The city is the seat of the black Mary Holmes College (1892). **3.** military community, pop. 8024, Orange Co., SE New York, on the W bank of the Hudson R. just SE of STORM KING and Crow's Nest mountains, about 50 mi/80 km N of New York City. West Point has been a US military post since 1778; it was at the center of Benedict Arnold's treasonous plot in 1780. The US Military Academy (1800) is here. **4.** town, pop. 2938, King William Co., E Virginia, at the confluence of the Mattaponi and Pamunkey rivers where they form the York R., 37 mi/60 km E of Richmond. In 1607 it was the seat of the Pamunkey tribe. A Colonial port by 1691, it gained importance after it was connected with Richmond by rail in 1861, and has been a major wood pulp producer.

West Point Dam and Lake see under CHATTAHOOCHEE R., Georgia.

Westport **1.** town, pop. 24,410, Fairfield Co., SW Connecticut, at the mouth of the Saugatuck R., 9 mi/14 km WSW of Bridgeport. An affluent residential town known for its artists' and writers' colony, it has some light industry, including the manufacture of toys, hardware, plastics, and soap. Westport, which includes the old fishing port of Saugatuck and Greens Farms, was a smugglers' haven during the Revolution and was invaded twice by the British. Sherwood I. State Park is on the coast. **2.** former town, now a residential, commercial, and institutional district of KANSAS CITY, Missouri. Platted in 1833, 4 mi/6 km S of the Missouri R., Westport competed with INDEPENDENCE (E) as the main supply point for westbound travelers on the SANTA FE TRAIL. To the N, on the river, was **Westport Landing,** a fur trade post established in the 1820s; this became the town of Kansas in 1838, and a city in 1853. Westport remained independent of Kansas City until 1897. Its center was the area now occupied by the **Westport Square** redevelopment zone, a popular shop, restaurant, and entertainment area just N of COUNTRY CLUB PLAZA. The Battle of Westport (Oct. 22–23, 1864) was fought 3 mi/5 km to the SSW, near modern 63rd St. and the PASEO, where Confederate troops under Sterling Price, despite taking hilltop positions, were forced into a retreat toward Arkansas by much larger Union forces under Alfred Pleasonton. **3.** town, pop. 1446, Essex Co., NE New York, on the W shore of L. Champlain, 24 mi/39 km N of Ticonderoga. It lies in a lumber producing region on the E edge of the Adirondack Mts.

Westport Plaza see under MARYLAND HEIGHTS, Missouri.

West Quoddy Head headland in Lubec, Maine. West Quoddy Head, the most easterly US point (66° 57′ W), has rock ledges 50–100 ft/15–30 m above the Bay of Fundy's tides, the greatest in the nation. It offers views of GRAND MANAN and CAMPOBELLO islands, and has a noted lighthouse.

West Reading see under READING, Pennsylvania.

West Roxbury southwesternmost district of Boston, Massachusetts, extending to the Charles R. at the Dedham line. It became part of Boston in 1874. Earlier, it was the site of Brook Farm (1841–47), a communal living experiment involving Margaret Fuller and other leading Transcendentalists and writers. West Roxbury today is among the most suburban in feeling of Boston's sections, with residential blocks surrounded by parkways. There are several large cemeteries and a Veterans Administration hospital.

West-Running Brook see under DERRY, New Hampshire.

West Sacramento city, pop. 28,898, Yolo Co., NC California, on the Sacramento R. opposite Sacramento, of which it is a residential and industrial suburb.

West Saint Paul city, pop. 19,248, Dakota Co., Minnesota, on the Minnesota R., a residential suburb immediately S of St. Paul. Founded in the 1850s, it has boomed as a bedroom community since World War II. Most recent commercial development has been along the Highway 52 corridor.

West Salem village, pop. 3611, La Crosse Co., W Wisconsin, 10 mi/16 km NE of La Crosse. It grew with the coming of the railroad (1858). In an agricultural area, it produces lumber and canned peas. Hamlin Garland was born here (1860), and his house has been preserved; his *Middle Border* books are set in this region.

West Seattle largely residential section of SEATTLE, Washington, 4 mi/6 km SW of Downtown, across ELLIOTT BAY. Alki Point, on the W, is the site of the original (1851) settlement of the city, moved the following year across Elliott Bay. Its beaches and Coast Guard light station draw visitors.

West Seneca town, pop. 47,830, Erie Co., W New York, adjacent (SE) to Buffalo, on Buffalo and Cazenovia creeks. Initially part of a Seneca reservation, the site was purchased and settled in 1842 by the Ebenezer Society, a German religious group who later moved to Iowa. The town was laid out as Seneca in 1851, taking its present name to avoid confusion with a town farther E the following year. West Seneca developed as an agricultural community, now specializing in nursery, greenhouse, and truck farming; it is also one of Buffalo's larger residential suburbs.

West Side **1.** in Chicago, Illinois, areas between the North and South branches of the Chicago R., including many neighborhoods that developed through the 19th and early

20th centuries, some annexed to the city, to house the swelling immigrant population. The term Northwest Side is given to parts of the West Side N of North Ave., including such neighborhoods as BELMONT-CRAGIN and ALBANY PARK, and, in the far NW, Edison Park and Norwood Park. These areas have tended to remain white, while the old BLACK BELT on the South Side has dispersed in part into such more southerly West Side neighborhoods as AUSTIN. There are also large Mexican, Puerto Rican, and Asian communities on the West Side, in areas like LAWNDALE and HUMBOLDT PARK. Outer sections of the West Side include parts of the BUNGALOW BELT, while inner sections contain some of the city's older housing. **2.** neighborhood in St. Paul, Minnesota, across the Mississippi R. from Downtown. Originally housing employees of nearby stockyards and factories, it emerged as a Mexican immigrant community following World War II. More recently, Hmong refugees from Indochina have clustered here. **3.** of Manhattan, New York City, generally, any part W of FIFTH AVENUE, particularly above 14th St., below which is the WEST VILLAGE. The West Side traditionally included many of Manhattan's less wealthy, often rougher, neighborhoods, including the TENDERLOIN, TIMES SQUARE, HELL'S KITCHEN, and SAN JUAN HILL. Except in the CHELSEA neighborhood, in the West 20s, the West Side is today largely commercial through Midtown. Above 59th St., where Central Park divides the island, is the Upper West Side, largely residential except for the Broadway corridor. MORNINGSIDE HEIGHTS, above 110th St., marks the N limit of what is usually considered the Upper West Side. **4.** in CLEVELAND, Ohio, areas W of Ontario Ave. and Downtown, traditionally made up of a series of European ethnic neighborhoods, characterized by rows of frame houses. **5.** popularly, **El Westside** in San Antonio, Texas, residential, commercial, and industrial areas W of Downtown, especially those W of San Pedro, Apache, and other creeks that feed into the San Antonio R. This is the historic heart of the city's Mexican community, somewhat isolated from the rest of the city not only by the waterways but by railroads and highways. Major area industries have included meatpacking, pecan shelling, and other food production. Government programs since the 1960s have addressed housing and related problems here, but parts of the BARRIO remain distressed. Our Lady of the Lake University is here, on Elmendorf L. **6.** collection of neighborhoods in Milwaukee, Wisconsin, W of the Milwaukee R. and N of the Menominee R. The West Side consists mainly of ethnically diverse working-class communities. RIVER WEST, SHERMAN PARK, and MERRILL PARK are here.

Westside collection of communities and neighborhoods in and adjacent (W) to LOS ANGELES, California. BRENTWOOD, BEL AIR, WESTWOOD VILLAGE, and PACIFIC PALISADES are here, along with the cities of WEST HOLLYWOOD, BEVERLY HILLS, and SANTA MONICA. Affluent and in sections extremely trendy, the area has been at the heart of Los Angeles's glamorous appeal since the 1950s. The name **West Los Angeles,** originally applied to the area adjoining (E) Santa Monica, has come to mean much the same thing.

West Springfield **1.** town, pop. 27,537, Hampden Co., SW Massachusetts, on the Westfield and Connecticut rivers, opposite Springfield. The town common was a campground for Revolutionary armies, and a drillground for farmers in Shays's Rebellion (1786–87). The Eastern States Exposition is held annually in Storrowtown Village. Industries have included railroad car and automobile repair and parts manufacturing, bookbinding, and the making of machines, tools, chemicals, and paper. **2.** unincorporated community, pop. 28,126, Fairfax Co., NE Virginia, just SW of SPRINGFIELD and 12 mi/19 km SW of Washington, D.C., just outside the BELTWAY and Interstate 95. It is a residential suburb.

West Tavaputs Plateau see under EAST TAVAPUTS PLATEAU, Utah.

West Tennessee see under JACKSON PURCHASE.

West Tisbury town, pop. 1704, Dukes Co., SE Massachusetts, in WC MARTHA'S VINEYARD. It is a popular summer resort with some agriculture, including a winery. The Martha's Vineyard airport is E, on the EDGARTOWN line.

West Town residential and commercial section of the NEAR WEST SIDE of Chicago, Illinois, along Milwaukee Ave., E of HUMBOLDT PARK and W of the Chicago River's North Branch. Formerly one of the city's Polish/East European districts, it has been since the 1960s a center of the Puerto Rican community.

West University Place city, pop. 12,920, Harris Co., SE Texas. Named for its proximity to Rice University, this affluent residential community, now completely surrounded by SW Houston, was developed beginning in 1917. It has some light industry. Southside Place (city, pop. 1392, S) and BELLAIRE (W) are adjacent.

West Valley City city, pop. 86,976, Salt Lake Co., NC Utah, a residential suburb immediately S of the W part of Salt Lake City. Settled by Mormons in 1848, it was incorporated as a city in 1980, merging the communities of Brighton, Granger, Hunter, and Pleasant Green.

West Vancouver district municipality, pop. 38,783, Greater Vancouver Regional District, SW British Columbia, on the N entrance to Burrard Inlet, across (NW) from downtown Vancouver. Separated (1912) from NORTH VANCOUVER, it is an affluent residential suburb, also noted for the recreational use of its mountainsides and streams.

West Village see under GREENWICH VILLAGE, New York.

Westville town, pop. 5255, La Porte Co., NW Indiana, 12 mi/19 km S of Michigan City. A state maximum-security prison is located here.

West Virginia northeastern US state, variously classified as a Border State or state of the Upper SOUTH (by the Census Bureau), as a South Atlantic state, or as an Appalachian state; 1990 pop. 1,793,477 (91.2% of 1980; rank: 34th); area 24,231 sq mi/62,758 sq km (rank: 41st); admitted to Union 1863 (35th). Capital and most populous city: CHARLESTON. Other leading cities: HUNTINGTON, WHEELING, PARKERSBURG. West Virginia is bordered SE and S by Virginia. Its East PANHANDLE extends between Virginia (S) and the POTOMAC R. and its North Fork, which separate it from Maryland (N). Its NC boundary is part of the old MASON-DIXON LINE separating it from Pennsylvania. The narrow North Panhandle extends between Pennsylvania (E) and the OHIO R. (N and W), across which is Ohio. The river then continues SW, forming the entire West Virginia–Ohio boundary, to the state's SW corner, where the Tug Fork of the BIG SANDY R. joins it from the SE, forming the border with Kentucky (SW). The state is composed essentially of those Virginia counties that, unsympathetic to the plantation South, refused to join Virginia in its 1861 secession from the Union. The line between Virginia and West Virginia runs along the ALLEGHENY FRONT, where SPRUCE KNOB rises to 4863 ft/1483 m, West Virginia's high point. Except for the Eastern Panhandle, which is in the Great APPALACHIAN Valley, the entire state is on the Allegheny Plateau section of the Appalachian Plateau. It is for the most part hilly, rugged, and heavily forested, allowing only small-scale farming, mostly dairying, poultry raising, and orcharding. Its huge deposits of coal, natural gas, and silica, on the other hand, and its position on the Ohio R., make it a major producer of metals (esp. steel), chemicals, and glass. These industries are most important in the KANAWHA R. valley (SW), where Charleston is situated; along the Ohio, esp. at Huntington (SW); and in the Northern Panhandle, esp. at Wheeling and WEIRTON. There are MOUND BUILDER sites in West Virginia, but the area was little occupied when Virginian fur traders and pioneers began to enter it at the end of the 17th century. German farmers from Pennsylvania arrived early in the 18th century, and gradually came into conflict with the French and their trans-Allegheny Indian allies; the French and Indian War (1754–63) was fought largely in the region. Settlement thereafter proceeded slowly, and the combination of independent farmers and early industrial communities along the Ohio (fostered in part by development of the NATIONAL ROAD and the BALTIMORE AND OHIO RAILROAD) made this part of Virginia unsympathetic to E Virginia, and in the Civil War the vast majority of West Virginians fought with the Union. The coal regions in the SW began to boom after the Civil War, as railroads made them accessible; COMPANY TOWNS developed, and labor conditions eventually led to strife, culminating in conflict in the Kanawha Valley and in the far SW, at BLAIR Mt. and in MINGO Co., in the 1910s–20s. West Virginia's continuous industrial growth lasted well into the 20th century, but fluctuations in the demand for coal now cause serious problems for the state's economy. Tourists are drawn by the state's Appalachian folkways, and the famous health spa at WHITE SULPHUR SPRINGS is one of a number of popular mountain resorts. The Eastern Panhandle, which is only 60 mi/100 km from Washington, D.C., has in recent decades become an EXURB and even a SUBURB of the capital; historic HARPERS FERRY and another old health resort, BERKELEY SPRINGS, are among communities here experiencing residential growth. West Virginia University is at MORGANTOWN (NC). A noted research center is the National Radio Astronomy Observatory facility at GREEN BANK (EC).

West Warwick town, pop. 29,268, Kent Co., EC Rhode Island, on the Pawtuxet R., 12 mi/19 km SW of Providence and adjoining (W) Warwick. It has been a textile center since 1794, and has other industries including biotechnology. Its administrative center is River Point; other villages include Arctic, Centreville, Crompton, and Natick.

Westwego city, pop. 11,218, Jefferson Parish, SE Louisiana, on the W (S) bank of the Mississippi R., opposite uptown New Orleans. A seafood processing and shipping center, it also manufactures ships, steel products, preservatives, chemicals, and commercial alcohol.

Westwood **1.** section of the WESTSIDE of LOS ANGELES, California, immediately W of Beverly Hills and 11 mi/18 km W of Downtown. Centered around the 1920s **Westwood Village** shopping center and the campus of the University of California at Los Angeles (1929), it is a trendy, youth-oriented area with affluent residential neighborhoods and some high-rise office development, esp. toward CENTURY CITY (SE). **2.** borough, pop. 10,446, Bergen Co., NE New Jersey, 7 mi/11 km N of Hackensack. It is primarily a New York–area bedroom community, with some light industry.

Westwood Lakes unincorporated community, pop. 11,522, Dade Co., SE Florida, 9 mi/14 km WSW of downtown Miami, a residential suburb just W of Olympia Heights.

West Yellowstone town, pop. 913, Gallatin Co., SW Montana, 70 mi/113 km S of Bozeman and near the Idaho and Wyoming lines. The W entrance to Yellowstone National Park, it is dependent on tourism. It lies at the end of the park that was destroyed by forest fires in 1988. The area was known to local Indians as the Land of Evil Spirits, and was shunned by most tribes. The ancient Sheepeaters once hunted here; their pictographs can be found on canyon walls near the town.

Wetaskiwin city, pop. 10,634, C Alberta, 37 mi/59 km S of Edmonton. The supply center for a mixed farming area, it has grain elevators, stockyards, creameries, a flour mill, a canned-milk plant, and a mobile-home factory. Natural gas and oil wells and coal mines are in the vicinity. Named "place of peace," it was originally a siding (1891) on the Calgary-Edmonton Railway. With the arrival of the Canadian Pacific Railway (1906), it grew as a division point, shipping wheat and cattle. The headquarters for the Battle River Regional Planning Commission are here.

Wethersfield town, pop. 25,651, Hartford Co., C Connecticut, on the W bank of the Connecticut R., immediately S of Hartford. It is primarily residential, but has some light industry, including the production of seeds and the manufacture of tools and dies, hydraulic valves, and electrical components. Founded in 1634 by settlers from Watertown, Massachusetts, it was one of the first permanent settlements in the state and one of the first inland settlements in New England. Wethersfield has more than 100 18th-century houses, including the Webb House (1752), where George Washington met the Count de Rochambeau to plan French and American troop movements during the Revolution.

wetlands lands covered all or most of the time by usually shallow waters, with ecosystems developed in these conditions; examples are bogs, mud flats, and swamps. In late-20th-century America, the protection of wetlands is an important scientific and political issue. The US government develops regulations and policy on wetlands through the Environmental Protection Agency; the ARMY CORPS OF ENGINEERS is charged with administering wetlands regulations and undertaking protective measures. Defined according to a complex formula involving such factors as soil and vegetation types and the proportion of time under water, wetlands in the US are estimated to cover some 100 million ac/40 million ha (15,625 sq mi/40,500 sq km).

Wet Mountains S extension of the FRONT RANGE of SC Colorado's Rocky Mts., partly in the SAN ISABEL National Forest, and extending SSE from the Arkansas R. to the Huerfano R., rising to Greenhorn Mt. (12,347 ft/3736 m) in the Greenhorn Range (S). Eroded and rolling, they are among the geologically oldest in the state. Mormon immigrants named them on seeing their green slopes after long travel over dry prairie.

Wetumpka city, pop. 4670, seat of Elmore Co., EC Alabama, on the Coosa R., 10 mi/16 km NE of Montgomery. On the Fall Line, it was a cotton shipping center until railroads through Montgomery took the business away. Fort Toulouse (1714), a French outpost, was here. The city now has light industries and is home to the Tutwiler prison, Alabama's women's facility.

Weyburn city, pop. 9673, SE Saskatchewan, 63 mi/101 km SE of Regina and 46 mi/74 km N of the North Dakota line, on the Souris R. and the Missouri Coteau. Much of its economy centers around an oilfield opened in the 1950s. Settled around 1900, Weyburn also serves as the distribution point for a grain and mixed farming region; has diverse light manufactures; and is an institutional center, with regional colleges and hospitals. The writer W. O. Mitchell, born here 1914, drew on Weyburn as the model for his fictional Crocus, Saskatchewan.

Weymouth town, pop. 54,063, Norfolk Co., E Massachusetts, on Hingham Bay and the estuarial Weymouth Fore and Back rivers, 12 mi/19 km SE of Boston. An early (1630s) farming and fishing community, it established an ironworks in 1771. Shoe manufacture dates to 1853; other industries have included the manufacture of fertilizer, lacquer, electronics, chemicals, and paper products. South Weymouth, one of several villages, is the site of a Naval Air Station, constructed in an area of piney woods, that extends into adjoining (S) Rockland.

Wharton city, pop. 9011, seat of Wharton Co., SE Texas, 50 mi/80 km SW of Houston, on the Colorado R. In a rice, cotton, oil, and sulfur producing area, it is a trade center with a variety of light industries, and home to Wharton Co. Junior College (1946) and the Gulf Coast Medical Center.

Wharton State Forest see under PINE BARRENS, New Jersey.

Wheat Belt general term for areas of the US and Canada in which wheat is the most important crop. While areas as widespread as the COLUMBIA PLATEAU of E Washington and Oregon, California's CENTRAL VALLEY, and parts of the Ohio R. valley have been important producers, the heart of the Wheat Belt lies W of the CORN BELT, on the higher, drier land of the Great Plains. Winter (autumn-sown) wheat predominates from Texas and Oklahoma through Kansas, Nebraska, and Wyoming; to the N it gives way to spring-sown varieties. The belt extends as far NW as Alberta's PEACE R. valley.

Wheatland see under LANCASTER, Pennsylvania.

Wheaton **1.** city, pop. 51,464, seat of Du Page Co., NE Illinois, 25 mi/40 km W of Chicago. It is a suburban residential community in a region producing corn, oats, and barley. The city has some light manufacturing, and there are nurseries here. However, it is best known as a center of religious education. The National Association of Evangelicals and the Theosophical Society of America are headquartered here, along with many other smaller groups. It is also the seat of Wheaton College, founded as a Wesleyan Methodist institution (1860), and *Christianity Today* is published here. Settled around 1837, Wheaton grew with the arrival of the railroad in 1849. The Robert R. McCormick Museum and Gardens and Billy Graham Center Museum are here. **2.** unincorporated suburb in Montgomery Co., C Maryland, 10 mi/16 km N of Washington, D.C. It is an affluent, largely residential community. With similar Glenmont, just N, it has a pop. of 53,720.

Wheat Ridge city, pop. 29,419, Jefferson Co., NC Colorado, adjacent to and NW of Denver, of which it is a residential suburb.

Wheeler Dam TENNESSEE VALLEY AUTHORITY dam, built 1936 on the Tennessee R., 17 mi/27 km E of Florence, NW Alabama. It is 15 mi/24 km upstream from the WILSON DAM. A concrete structure 72 ft/22 m high and over 6340 ft/1934 m long, it impounds **Wheeler L.** (or Reservoir), which backs 74 mi/119 km upstream to the GUNTERSVILLE Dam. The upper part of the former MUSCLE SHOALS lies under the dam and lake.

Wheeler Peak **1.** see under SNAKE RANGE, Nevada. **2.** highest elevation (13,161 ft/4011 m) in New Mexico, 13 mi/21 km NE of Taos in the SANGRE DE CRISTO Mts. Within Carson National Forest, it has alpine vegetation, unusual in the SW, and is noted for skiing. The TRUCHAS PEAKS were formerly thought to be higher.

Wheeling **1.** village, pop. 29,911, Cook and Lake counties, NE Illinois, on the Des Plaines R., 23 mi/37 km NW of Chicago. It is an affluent bedroom community. **2.** city, pop. 34,882, seat of Ohio Co., in the Northern PANHANDLE of West Virginia, on Wheeling Creek and the Ohio R., 48 mi/77 km SW of Pittsburgh, Pennsylvania. Founded in 1769 by Ebenezer Zane and his brothers, it was a pre-Revolutionary outpost around Fort Henry (1774), later (Sept. 1782) the site of one of the last Revolutionary skirmishes. The NATIONAL ROAD passed through, and the Wheeling Suspension Bridge, with a 900-ft/275-m central span, crossed the Ohio in 1849. Pro-Union during the Civil War, Wheeling was the state capital 1863–70. Iron and steel have been its main manufactures; other industries have turned out glass, coal and gas, metal products, tobacco, pottery, textiles, and chemicals based on local rock crystal. Wheeling Jesuit College (1954) and West Virginia Northern Community College (1972) are here. Wheeling is a center for country and gospel music; broadcasts from radio station WWVA are widely known.

Whidbey Island 36 mi/58 km NNW–SSE, in NW Washington, between Puget Sound (S), Skagit Bay (E), and Juan de Fuca Strait (NW), across Admiralty Inlet from the Olympic Peninsula (SW) and linked by bridge to Anacortes, on Fidalgo I. (N). OAK HARBOR is the largest island community. Whidbey has forests, open field, and farmland. A 19th-century lumbering and agricultural community, it now has a large loganberry farm, restored Victorian and modern homes, and Whidbey Naval Air Station, a major employer. The largest island in the Lower 48 after New York's LONG I., Whidbey is a popular tourist destination.

Whippany unincorporated village in Hanover township (pop. 11,538), Morris Co., NE New Jersey, 4 mi/6 km NE of Morristown. Lying near Interstates 287 and 80, it is, like neighboring (N) Parsippany-Troy Hills, a center for office buildings, research facilities, corporate headquarters, and shopping. Light manufactures include medical products and vending machines. In addition, Whippany is a New York–area residential suburb.

Whiskeytown-Shasta-Trinity National Recreation Area 254,000 ac/103,000 ha, in three units in N California, W and N of REDDING, at the head of the Sacramento Valley. Each unit encloses a major reservoir. The Trinity unit lies around Clair Engle, or Trinity, L., which inundated several small farming towns. Weaverville (unincorporated, pop. 3370, Trinity Co.), just SW, is an old gold rush town, now a trade and tourist center famous for its Joss House, the oldest Chinese temple in California. Many-armed Shasta L., in the Shasta unit, formed by a 600 ft/183 m–high 1945 Central Valley Project dam on the SACRAMENTO R., is California's largest artificial lake, with 370 mi/600 km of shoreline. It is very popular with boaters. The Whiskeytown unit, closest to Redding, lies around **Whis-**

keytown L., formed by a dam completed in 1963. It inundated the gold rush town of Whiskeytown.

Whistler district municipality, pop. 4459, Squamish-Lillooet Regional District, SW British Columbia, 54 mi/87 km NNE of Vancouver. It is one of Canada's best-known ski resorts, with almost 200 runs (including one with a 6900-ft/2100-m vertical drop) on Whistler and Blackcomb mountains. GARIBALDI PROVINCIAL PARK is immediately SE. Whistler is a year-round resort, also noted for its golf courses and music and arts festivals.

Whitby town, pop. 61,281, Durham Regional Municipality, SE Ontario, 27 mi/43 km ENE of Toronto, on L. Ontario. OSHAWA is adjacent (E). Settled in the 1840s, Whitby became a grain handling center because of its fine harbor and rail connections, then lost much of its business to Oshawa. Industries here have made clocks and steel. The town is now a fast-growing (34% pop. increase in 1986–91) residential and horticultural (marigolds) center. During World War II the noted "Camp X" here trained Allied spies and special-operations personnel.

Whitchurch-Stouffville town, pop. 18,357, York Regional Municipality, S Ontario, 22 mi/35 km N of Toronto. The village of Stouffville, founded in 1804, and the township of Whitchurch were consolidated in 1971; the town includes the communities of Ballantrae, Wesley Corners, and Pleasantville. In a fertile agricultural area, it is now experiencing suburban growth.

White Bear Lake city, pop. 24,704, Ramsey and Washington counties, SE Minnesota, on White Bear and Goose lakes, a suburb 10 mi/16 km NE of St. Paul. Settled in 1851, it was long a summer resort area for wealthy St. Paul families. Local industries today include sailboat building and truck farming. There has been a great deal of commercial development recently along the I-694 corridor in the S, along the border with MAPLEWOOD.

White Bird city, pop. 108, Idaho Co., NW Idaho, on White Bird Creek, in the Clearwater Mts., 50 mi/80 km SE of Lewiston. The first battle of the Nez Perce Indian War was fought here on June 17, 1877.

White Butte 3506 ft/1069 m, in Slope Co., SW North Dakota, 48 mi/77 km SW of Dickinson. Overlooking the Little Missouri National Grasslands, it is the highest point in the state.

White Center–Shorewood unincorporated community, pop. 20,581, King Co., WC Washington, a residential suburb 6 mi/10 km S of Seattle.

White City, the see under JACKSON PARK, Chicago, Illinois.

Whiteface, Mount see under SANDWICH RANGE, New Hampshire.

Whiteface Mountain 4867 ft/1484 m, in the Adirondack Mts., NE New York, 6 mi/10 km NE of LAKE PLACID. It is a popular skiing and recreational site.

Whitefish city, pop. 4368, Flathead Co., NW Montana, on Whitefish L., 15 mi/24 km N of Kalispell. A lake and ski resort just S of the Whitefish Range and surrounded by Flathead National Forest, it was originally a Great Northern Railroad repair and division point. It also has sawmills.

Whitefish Bay **1.** see under L. SUPERIOR. **2.** village, pop. 14,272, Milwaukee Co., SE Wisconsin, on L. Michigan, 5 mi/8 km N of Milwaukee. One of the largest villages in the state, it is a residential community set on bluffs overlooking the lake. American settlement dates from 1842.

Whitefish River 45 mi/72 km long, in the S part of the Upper Peninsula of Michigan. It rises in the SW corner of Alger Co., and flows SE into Delta Co., then SW to the N end of Little Bay De Noc. The river flows through an edge of the Hiawatha National Forest.

white flight movement of whites from urban or suburban communities when blacks or members of other minorities buy or rent housing or when school systems are integrated, usually resulting also in withdrawal of capital, services, etc. While observed as primarily racial, such movement is also clearly economically motivated, and may at times be considered "middle-class flight."

White Hall historic site: see under RICHMOND, Kentucky.

Whitehall **1.** town, pop. 4409, Washington Co., E New York, at the South Bay of L. Champlain, and the N end of the Champlain Canal, 22 mi/35 km NE of Glens Falls, on the Vermont border. It was settled in 1759. This traditional mill town and railroad center has a number of industries and is an Amtrak stop. **2.** city, pop. 20,572, Franklin Co., C Ohio, 7 mi/11 km E of Columbus, of which it is a commuter suburb. Manufactures include water coolers and packaged meats. US military reservations lie directly N of the city. **3.** borough, pop. 14,451, Allegheny Co., SW Pennsylvania, 5 mi/8 km S of Pittsburgh. It is a primarily residential suburb.

Whitehaven largely residential section of Memphis, Tennessee, S of Nonconnah Creek and W of the Memphis International Airport, along the Mississippi line. Once essentially white, it is now a more mixed area that includes Elvis Presley's GRACELAND. SOUTHAVEN, Mississippi, is immediately S.

White Hill see under CAPE BRETON HIGHLANDS NATIONAL PARK, Nova Scotia.

White Horse **1.** see under HAMILTON, New Jersey.

Whitehorse city and territorial capital, pop. 17,925, SW Yukon Territory, on the Yukon R. and the ALASKA HIGHWAY, 90 mi/140 km N of Skagway, Alaska. Just below Miles Canyon and the Whitehorse Rapids, at the Yukon's head of navigation, it became a staging point (1898) for the KLONDIKE gold rushes, and later the N terminus of the White Pass and Yukon Railway, from Skagway. It was a highway construction and air transport base and oil refining center, terminus of the Canol pipeline from Norman Wells, Northwest Territories, during World War II. It is now the Yukon's administrative center, a distribution and transportation hub for mining operations to the N, and an outfitting base for wilderness recreation. The Yukon's only city, it is home to 64% of its pop.

White House US executive mansion, situated at the center (technically in the NW) of Washington, D.C., at 1600 Pennsylvania Ave., just N of the MALL, with which it is connected by the Ellipse, a part of its 18-ac/7-ha grounds used for public events. Built 1792–1800 to plans by James Hoban, it was burned by British troops in 1814, and since then has been rebuilt and often modified; it contains 132 rooms. Among these the East Room and Blue Room, used for receptions and other events, are at times open to the public. The Oval Office has come to be regarded as symbolic of the presidency. The Rose Garden, on the grounds, has since the 1970s been the site of presidential announcements, bill signings, and "photo opportunities." Nearby sites closely associated with the White House include Lafayette Square, across the avenue (N), a common site for demonstrators against or supporters of presidential policy; and Blair House, just W of the square, now used as a guest house for foreign leaders, and in which Harry Truman resided while the White House underwent renovation (1949–52).

Whiteman Air Force Base see under SEDALIA, Missouri.

White Marsh unincorporated suburb of Baltimore, Maryland, pop. 8183, in Baltimore Co., 12 mi/19 km NE of Downtown, on US 1, Interstate 95, and White Marsh Run. There are several large sand and gravel quarries here. White Marsh recently acquired a large shopping mall, and plans for development include the construction of industrial and recreational parks, as well as housing.

Whitemarsh township, pop. 14,863, Montgomery Co., SE Pennsylvania, on Wissahickon Creek and the Schuylkill R., 14 mi/22 km NNW of Philadelphia. It was the site of Washington's encampment (1777) during the battle of GERMANTOWN and before he took his troops to VALLEY FORGE. Whitemarsh is today a largely residential suburb on the Pennsylvania Turnpike. It contains units of Fort Washington State Park.

White Mountains **1.** range in E Arizona, S of the Mogollon Rim and SW of Springerville. It rises to 11,420 ft/3481 m at Baldy Peak (or Mt. Baldy), known as White Mt. and sacred to the Apache. The summit, within the 1.7 million-ac/675,000-ha (2600–sq mi/6740–sq km) **White Mountain** (officially, Fort Apache) **Indian Reservation** (pop. 10,394), is closed to non-Indians in respect for the traditional Apache who make pilgrimages here. The range extends into the APACHE-SITGREAVES NATIONAL FOREST (E). The Apache, with headquarters at **Whiteriver** (unincorporated, pop. 3775, Navajo Co.), engage in ski resort operation, aerospace manufacturing, and catering to hunters and gamblers. Adjacent (SW) is the SAN CARLOS (Apache) reservation. Fort Apache, operational 1870–1922, just S of Whiteriver, was used by the government in subduing various Apache uprisings. **2.** range mostly in EC California, extending SE for c.55 mi/90 km from near Montgomery Pass (7167 ft/2185 m) in SW Nevada to the N part of the INYO Mts., NE of the OWENS Valley. The range reaches its greatest elevation at White Mountain Peak (14,246 ft/4342 m) and includes BOUNDARY PEAK (13,143 ft/4006 m), the highest point in Nevada, and Black Mt. (9081 ft/2768 m), near the S end. Mostly within Inyo National Forest, it also contains the Ancient Bristlecone Pine Forest (28,000 ac/11,340 ha), home to the shrublike pines that are the oldest known living trees, some over 4600 years old. **3.** glaciated mountain mass, a northern segment of the Appalachian Mts., occupying a large part of NC New Hampshire, from the Connecticut R. E into Maine. A scattered grouping of peaks composed of granite, gneiss, schist, and other rocks, they are thought to be the deeply glaciated and eroded remnants of a much higher range. Except for the summit of Mt. WASHINGTON (6288 ft/1918 m), which is in Mt. Washington State Park, most of the peaks are in the **White Mountain National Forest** (769,000 ac/311,500 ha), a preserve established in 1911 to protect the forests from devastation by logging companies. The White Mts. form the basis of one of the leading summer and winter resort areas in the northeastern US, and include the Old Man of the Mountain and the Flume in FRANCONIA NOTCH. Important passes include CRAWFORD, DIXVILLE, and PINKHAM notches. The PRESIDENTIAL RANGE, a subrange of the Whites, includes many of the tallest peaks. Other major subgroupings include the Franconia, Carter-Moriah, and Sandwich ranges. The KANCAMAGUS HIGHWAY connects Conway (E) with Lincoln (W). In Maine, the NE extension of the Whites is called the LONGFELLOW Mountains.

White Oak **1.** unincorporated suburb, pop. 18,671, Montgomery Co., C Maryland, 11 mi/18 km NNE of Washington, D.C., just outside the BELTWAY and W of Interstate 95. The Naval Surface Weapons Center is here. **2.** unincorporated residential suburb, pop. 12,430, Hamilton Co., SW Ohio, 9 mi/14 km NNW of Cincinnati and just W of North College Hill, on the fringe of the most heavily developed part of the Cincinnati area. The Census Bureau distinguishes neighboring **White Oak East** (pop. 3544) and **White Oak West** (pop. 2879).

White Oak Swamp see under FRAYSER'S FARM, Virginia.

White Pass at 2890 ft/881 m, 14 mi/23 km NNE of SKAGWAY, Alaska, on the border with NW British Columbia. It provided easier passage to the 1890s KLONDIKE gold rush territory (N) than did nearby (NW) CHILKOOT PASS. Its importance increased with the opening in 1900 of the White Pass and Yukon Railway between Skagway and WHITEHORSE, in the Yukon, which is today used for tourist excursions. The Klondike Highway, a spur (1978) of the ALASKA HIGHWAY, also goes through the pass.

White Plains city, pop. 48,718, seat of Westchester Co., SE New York, midway between the Hudson R. (NW) and Long Island Sound (SE). It is the commercial, retail, and financial center of Westchester, and has offices of a number of major corporations. Settled in 1683, it became an important post station for 18th-century stagecoaches. George Washington retreated to White Plains after evacuating New York City in 1776, and fought a battle here against Sir William Howe; Washington's headquarters are open to the public. The College of White Plains, a branch of Pace University, is here.

White River **1.** 720 mi/1160 km long, in Arkansas and Missouri. It rises on the N of the BOSTON Mts., in NW Arkansas, and flows NW to the E of Fayetteville and NNE through dam-created (1965) Beaver L. to the Missouri border, where it passes through Table Rock L., created by a dam (1959) SW of Branson. It then winds generally ESE through L. Taneycomo and Bull Shoals L. (1957), back across the Arkansas border, and continues SE. The BUFFALO R. joins it (from the W) at Buffalo City, and the North Fork (from the N) at Norfork. The White passes Batesville (the head of shallow-draft navigation) on its way to Newport, where the BLACK R. joins it (from the N). From Newport it flows S across the Mississippi alluvial plain, past Clarendon, through the White R. National Wildlife Refuge, and empties into the Mississippi R. just NW of (across from) Rosedale, Mississippi. A cutoff channel just above its mouth joins it with the ARKANSAS R. (W). The White is the major river of the Ozark Plateau, its lakes today popular recreational areas. **2.** in Indiana, created by the confluence of two branches: the **West Fork** rises near Bartonia, in Randolph Co., almost at the Ohio line, and flows 255 mi/411 km W and SW past Muncie, Anderson, Indianapolis, and Martinsville, to join the East Fork near Petersburg. The **East Fork,** 282 mi/454 km long, is formed by headstreams S of COLUMBUS, and winds through seven counties and the HOOSIER NATIONAL FOREST to the junction. The main stream then flows 52 mi/84 km SW to the Wabash R., opposite Mt. Carmel, Illinois. The West Fork is often designated simply the White R. **3.** 500 mi/805 km long, in Nebraska and South Dakota. It rises along Pine Ridge in Sioux Co., in NW Nebraska, and flows NE, passing the old frontier towns of Crawford and Chadron and entering Shannon Co., in SW South Dakota. The river provides irrigation for potato, alfalfa, and grain fields in the surrounding areas. It flows NE through the grassy hills of the PINE RIDGE Indian Reservation and along the S edge of the BADLANDS. It crosses much of SC South Dakota before joining the Missouri R. 10 mi/16 km SW of Chamberlain. **4.** 50 mi/80 km long, in EC Vermont. It rises in Granville, Addison Co., and flows S, E, and SE into the Connecticut R. at White River Junction. Its main tributaries are the First, Second, and Third branches.

White River Junction village, pop. 2521, Hartford town, Windsor Co., EC Vermont, on both sides of the White R., where it joins the Connecticut R., across from Lebanon, New Hampshire. It is a business center and railroad junction, the depot for Dartmouth College, in Hanover, New Hampshire, with which it is closely linked. Interstates 89 and 91 intersect just S.

White River National Forest 2 million ac/810,000 ha (3125 sq mi/8094 sq km), in NC and NW Colorado. Its NW unit surrounds the headwaters of the White R., which flows W to meet the Green R. in Wyoming. The MOUNT OF THE HOLY CROSS, several major ski resorts, seven WILDERNESS AREAS, a major elk herd, and popular hunting and fishing areas are within the forest.

White Rock city, pop. 16,314, Greater Vancouver Regional District, SW British Columbia, on Boundary Bay, 22 mi/35 km SE of Vancouver, on the Washington border. Separated from SURREY in 1957, it had earlier developed as a beachfront resort community. It is primarily residential.

White Rock Creek tributary of the Trinity R., c.15 mi/24 km long, flowing S through the E side of DALLAS, Texas. Dam-created, park-lined **White Rock Lake,** in East Dallas, is an important recreational resource for the city; the Dallas Arboretum and Botanical Gardens are here, and a number of mansions along the creek attest to the area's residential prestige.

White Sands largest known gypsum dune system in the world, in the Tularosa Basin, between the SAN ANDRES (W) and SACRAMENTO (E) mountains, in S New Mexico. The white rippling dunes are created by a series of actions including water transport of gypsum from higher elevations, evaporation and formation of crystals, and wind transport of the crystals. The resultant dunes, up to 60 ft/18 m high, are practically devoid of plant or animal life. The area includes the 144,000-ac/58,000-ha **White Sands National Monument,** 15 mi/24 km WSW of Alamogordo. The **White Sands Missile Range,** the largest US military installation (3 million ac/1.2 million ha), a test site for rockets and weapons, incorporates not only the White Sands but also parts of the JORNADA DEL MUERTO (W). The Trinity Site, where the first atomic bomb was detonated on July 16, 1945, is in the N, on the Jornada del Muerto side of the Sierra Oscura, some 54 mi/86 km NNW of Alamogordo.

White Settlement city, pop. 15,472, Tarrant Co., NE Texas, 8 mi/13 km W of downtown Fort Worth, and entirely within the larger city. A residential, industrial, and commercial community, it is adjacent (SW) to Carswell Air Force Base.

Whiteshell Provincial Park 1088 sq mi/2735 sq km, in SE Manitoba, 72 mi/116 km E of Winnipeg, southernmost of a string of provincial parks on the Ontario border. Established in 1931, this reserve on the CANADIAN SHIELD shows the effects of glaciation in its numerous lakes and rivers and granitic topography. Petroglyphs at Bannock Point date as far back as 3000 B.C. West Hawk L., the deepest in the province, is believed to have been formed by a meteorite. The **Whiteshell Nuclear Research Establishment** (1963) is at Pinawa, on the Winnipeg R. at the park's W boundary.

Whiteside Mountain peak (4930 ft/1504 m) in far SW North Carolina, between Cashiers and Highlands, in the NANTAHALA National Forest. Its 1800-ft/549-m sheer precipice, one of the highest in the E US, and white cliffs on its S face (the Devil's Courthouse), are popular with rock climbers.

White Station residential section of extreme E Memphis, Tennessee, 9 mi/14 km ESE of Downtown, adjacent (W) to GERMANTOWN. It is on the site of White's Station, a popular mid-19th-century resort at the end of an early rail line.

Whitestone largely residential section, NE Queens, New York, on the East R. between Powell's Cove and Little Bay, NE of FLUSHING. Farmed by Dutch settlers in the 1640s, it took its name from a highly visible rock at the landing place. Its neighborhoods include Malba, originally a private development, on the W, and Beechhurst on the E. The Bronx-Whitestone (on the W) and Throgs Neck (on the E) bridges both come ashore in Whitestone.

Whitestone Bridge see BRONX-WHITESTONE BRIDGE, New York.

Whitestone Hill Battlefield in Dickey Co., SE North Dakota, 20 mi/32 km NW of Ellendale. It is the site of what was reputedly the fiercest battle ever fought in North Dakota, a confrontation between US troops under Alfred Sully and a band of Sioux that resulted in the death of 19 soldiers and some 150 Indians. A granite monument and a museum memorialize the battle.

White Sulphur Springs city, pop. 2779, Greenbrier Co., SE West Virginia, in the Allegheny Mts., 8 mi/13 km E of Lewisburg, near the Virginia line. Named for the springs now on the grounds of the 1913 Greenbrier Hotel, the settlement developed as a spa in the 1770s. An earlier hotel served as hospital and headquarters to both Union and Confederate forces during the Civil War, and Confederates won a skirmish nearby in Aug. 1863. Presidents from Andrew Jackson to Woodrow Wilson summered here, and the resort has been used by the government for various purposes, including the interning of enemy diplomats during World War II and the secret construction in the 1950s of a supposedly nuclear bomb–proof mountain bunker for Federal officials.

White Tank Mountains range in C Arizona, W of Phoenix, rising to 4083 ft/1244 m. White Tank Mountain Regional Park (26,337 ac/10,666 ha) is noted for its Hohokam artifacts and PETROGLYPHS.

White Top Mountain also, **Whitetop** peak (5520 ft/1684 m) in the Blue Ridge Mts. of SW Virginia, 15 mi/24 km SSW of MARION, along the S border of the state, near the convergence of the North Carolina and Tennessee borders.

Whitewater city, pop. 11,520, Walworth and Jefferson counties, SE Wisconsin, on Whitewater Creek, 18 mi/29 km NE of Janesville. It is the center of a region rich in dairy products, poultry, and grain and truck farms. Manufacturing and food processing figure in the local economy. The University of Wisconsin at Whitewater (1868) is here. American settlement dates from 1837.

Whitewater River 70 mi/113 km long, in Indiana and Ohio. Its **West Fork** or main branch rises in S Randolph Co., E

Indiana, NW of RICHMOND, and flows S to Connersville, then SE across the Ohio border, where it empties into the Great Miami R. just above its junction with the Ohio R., W of Cincinnati. The Whitewater's **East Fork,** 55 mi/89 km long, rises just S of Richmond and joins the main branch near Brookville, Franklin Co., Indiana, having passed through 15 mi/24 km–long Whitewater L., a dam-created recreational resource.

Whiting city, pop. 5155, Lake Co., extreme NW Indiana, adjacent (N) to HAMMOND (W) and EAST CHICAGO (E), on L. Michigan. In the highly industrialized CALUMET area, just SE of Chicago, it has large oil refineries, and manufactures chemicals and soap.

Whitingham town, pop. 1177, including Whitingham and Jacksonville villages, in Windham Co., S Vermont. It is on Harriman Reservoir, formed by the earthen Harriman Dam (completed 1924) and formerly called L. Whitingham, along the Massachusetts line. In a maple sugaring and woodcrafting area, it was once noted for mineral springs that attracted those seeking cures for skin diseases. Brigham Young, Mormon leader, was born in the township in 1801.

Whitman town, pop. 13,240, Plymouth Co., SE Massachusetts, adjoining (E) Brockton, 20 mi/32 km SSE of Boston. The main industry of Whitman has been shoemaking; other products have included shoe and textile machinery, shoe polish, tacks, plastics, foundry products, and burial vaults. The 1709 Toll House, in Westcrook village, a tourist restoration, gave its name to the toll house cookie.

Whitman Mission National Monument see under WALLA WALLA, Washington.

Whitney, Lake 23,560 ac/9540 ha, in C Texas, on the BRAZOS R. in Hill, Bosque, and Johnson counties, 58 mi/93 km S of Fort Worth. A Corps of Engineers impoundment, it stretches 45 mi/72 km up the Brazos Valley and is one of the most popular water recreation areas in the nation, drawing 4 million visitors annually.

Whitney, Mount culminating peak (14,495 ft/4418 m) of the SIERRA NEVADA, and the highest elevation in the coterminous US, on the E border of Sequoia National Park, in the Inyo National Forest, EC California. Other peaks above 14,000 ft/4267 m within 6 mi/10 km of Whitney are Mts. Barnard, Langley, Muir, Russell, Tyndall, and Williamson. The slopes of Mt. Whitney, like the Sierra itself, drop precipitously to the E and gently to the W, and are covered with granitic boulders. The mountain was named for Josiah D. Whitney, geologist and leader of an expedition that sighted it in 1864. The first documented ascent was in 1873. The Kern R. Canyon is W.

Whittier **1.** city, pop. 77,671, Los Angeles Co., SW California, at the S foot of the Puente Hills, 13 mi/21 km SE of downtown Los Angeles. Founded in 1887 by a colony of the Society of Friends from the Midwest, who named it for John Greenleaf Whittier, the Quaker poet, it was at first an avocado and citrus producing center, then grew as a Los Angeles suburb. Whittier College (1887), Richard M. Nixon's alma mater, and Rio Hondo College (1960) are here. Industries include oil production and the manufacture of auto parts, tools, electronic equipment, and other machinery. **2.** residential neighborhood in Minneapolis, Minnesota, SW of Downtown. Situated E of the WEDGE and W of PHILLIPS, it is home to a mixture of young professionals and poorer transients. The Whittier Alliance is one of the city's oldest and most successful community activist groups.

Wichita city, pop. 304,011, seat of Sedgwick Co., SC Kansas, on both sides of the Arkansas R. at its confluence with the Little Arkansas R. On the site of a Wichita village (1863–65) created by pro-Union Indians driven from their homes in Oklahoma and Texas, it became a trading post in 1864, and in the early 1870s served as a station for cattle drives along the CHISHOLM TRAIL. It grew with the coming of the Santa Fe Railroad in 1872, and flourished as a cattle shipper and trade and grain processing hub for a vast prairie area. Development was further stimulated by the discovery of oil nearby in 1915. Today the city remains the commercial center of a wheat farming and stock producing region, with active markets, grain elevators, stockyards, flour and feed mills, meatpacking plants, rail shipping facilities, and railroad shops. It is also (since the 1920s) one of the largest US manufacturers of commercial, military, and private aircraft, with factories of the Beech, Cessna, and Boeing companies. Other important industries include the production of precision tools and appliances, oil refining, and printing. The city is the site of the Wichita Omnisphere and Science Center, and the seat of Wichita State University (1892), Friends University (1898), and Kansas Newman College (1933). McConnell Air Force Base, a bomber facility, lies on the city's SE edge.

Wichita Falls city, pop. 96,259, seat of Wichita Co., also in Archer Co., NC Texas, on the Wichita R., in the Red R. Valley, 104 mi/167 km NW of Fort Worth and 16 mi/26 km S of the Oklahoma line. Settled in the 1870s, it was named for now-disappeared 5-ft/1.5-m river falls (an artificial, 54-ft/16-m falls was constructed in the 1980s), became a cattle shipping center when the railroad reached it in 1882, and soon also handled large amounts of wheat. An oil boom around World War I spurred the development of related industries, and made the city an industrial and commercial center for much of NC Texas and S Oklahoma. Today it has varied manufactures including electronic components, fiberglass, and leather goods. Sheppard Air Force Base (1941), a NATO training center, is just N. Midwestern State University was founded in 1922.

Wichita Mountains low, rugged, NW-trending granitic range rising out of the OSAGE PLAINS in SW Oklahoma, NW of Lawton. An area some 60 mi/96 km long by 25 mi/40 km wide, they rise to 2464 ft/751 m at Mt. Scott. One of the oldest US mountain groups, they were named for the plains tribe. The Wichita Mts. Wildlife Refuge (59,020 ac/23,903 ha), established 1905, is home to a sizable buffalo herd.

Wichita River 250 mi/400 km long, in N Texas. Its North Fork or main branch rises E of the CAPROCK ESCARPMENT, in King Co., and flows E and ENE past WICHITA FALLS to join the RED R. 20 mi/32 km NE of the city. In its upper reaches it is joined by Middle and South forks. Below their junction it passes through 16,500-ac/6700-ha L. Kemp and the smaller Diversion L. Named for the tribe that once lived along it, the Wichita was unusual in this plains area in having a falls (only 5 ft/1.5 m high), at which Wichita Falls was established.

Wickenburg town, pop. 4515, Maricopa Co., WC Arizona, on the Hassayampa R., 50 mi/80 km NW of Phoenix. A processing center during the 1863 Vulture Mine gold rush, the settlement grew rapidly, and by 1866 it was Arizona's third largest. Cattle raising eventually replaced mining, and

Wickenburg also became an early dude ranch center. It is now primarily a winter resort.

Wickford village in NORTH KINGSTOWN, Washington Co., SC Rhode Island, on an inlet of Narragansett Bay, 17 mi/27 km S of Providence and 8 mi/13 km NE of Kingston. It is famous for its restored Colonial buildings and St. Paul's Church (1707), the oldest Episcopal church in New England.

Wickliffe city, pop. 14,558, Lake Co., NE Ohio, 13 mi/21 km NE of Cleveland, and 2 mi/3 km S of L. Erie. White settlement began in 1817, but Indians continued to live here until 1840. Today the city is chiefly a residential suburb of Cleveland, though items such as pipe machinery, lubricants, tools, and cranes are manufactured. Wickliffe is the seat of Telshe Yeshiva College (1876, Rabbinical) and Borromeo Seminary (1953, Roman Catholic).

Wicomico River in Maryland: **a.** 33 mi/53 km long, on the EASTERN SHORE. It rises near the Delaware border, and flows SW through SALISBURY, the head of navigation. Becoming estuarial, it ends in Monie Bay, an inlet of Chesapeake Bay. **b.** 37 mi/60 km long, in Charles Co., flowing S to the Potomac R., with a 2 mi/3 km–wide estuary.

Widefield see SECURITY-WIDEFIELD, Colorado.

Wilberforce unincorporated village, pop. 2702, in Xenia township, Greene Co., SW Ohio, 3 mi/5 km NE of Xenia, in hilly, wooded country. Wilberforce University (1856), the oldest black-run institution of higher learning in the US, and Central State University (1887) are here. Wilberforce is the site of the National Afro-American Museum and Cultural Center.

Wilbur Cross Parkway see under MERRITT PARKWAY, Connecticut.

Wildcat Creek 80 mi/130 km long, in C Indiana. It rises in NE Tipton Co. and flows generally N, then W, passing Kokomo and Burlington, to the Wabash R., 4 mi/6 km N of LAFAYETTE. It receives the **South Fork,** 40 mi/64 km long, just E of Lafayette.

Wildcat Mountain **1.** peak (1757 ft/536 m) in SE Missouri, W of TAUM SAUK Mt. and connected to it by a saddle. **2.** also, **Mount Wildcat** peak (4397 ft/1341 m) in the Carter Range of the White Mts., NE New Hampshire, just E of PINKHAM NOTCH. Actually a ridge with a number of lesser summits, it is noted for skiing and summer recreational use.

Wilderness, the battle site in rural NW Spotsylvania Co., NE Virginia, 15 mi/24 km W of Fredericksburg. A bloody, indecisive battle was fought here on May 5–6, 1864, between Union troops under Ulysses S. Grant and Confederates under Robert E. Lee. Total casualties were 26,000 over two days' struggle in dense second-growth woods, after which the armies regrouped for the battle of SPOTSYLVANIA Court House (May 8–21). The area of the Wilderness had also been the scene of maneuvering during the May 1863 battle of CHANCELLORSVILLE, just ESE.

wilderness area **1.** in the US, any of the areas designated under the Wilderness Act of 1964 and subsequent enactments. It may also be part of a NATIONAL FOREST, a NATIONAL PARK, or lands administered by the Bureau of Land Management or US Fish and Wildlife Service. Wilderness Areas are to preserve their "primeval character and influence," and to have no human habitation, permanent roads, structures, or commercial enterprises. Hiking, primitive camping, horseback riding, and "similar pursuits" are allowed, but use of motor vehicles of any sort is prohibited. **2.** in the US, any of the areas designated under the Wilderness Act of 1964 and subsequent enactments. It may also be part of a NATIONAL FOREST, a NATIONAL PARK, or lands administered by the Bureau of Land Management or US Fish and Wildlife Service. Wilderness Areas are to preserve their "primeval character and influence," and to have no human habitation, permanent roads, structures, or commercial enterprises. Hiking, primitive camping, horseback riding, and "similar pursuits" are allowed, but use of motor vehicles of any sort is prohibited. Earlier forms of wilderness area protection have existed since 1924, when New Mexico's Gila Wilderness (within the GILA NATIONAL FOREST) was established.

Wilderness Road from the Revolution until the 1840s (when the NATIONAL ROAD became more traveled), the most important westward route through the Appalachians. It was established in 1775 for the TRANSYLVANIA Company by Daniel Boone and a party of woodsmen. Boone followed animal and Indian paths and his own (1769) route (Boone's Trace) through the CUMBERLAND GAP. The Wilderness Road began at Fort Chiswell, a staging point 7 mi/11 km E of modern WYTHEVILLE, Virginia, where routes bringing settlers from the Tidewater and down the Shenandoah Valley met. It followed the Holston R. valley SW to Fort Watauga, at Sycamore Shoals, just W of Elizabethton, Tennessee, then cut NW through the Gap into Kentucky, passing through what is now the Daniel Boone National Forest, and ended at the settlement of HARRODSBURG, in the Kentucky R. valley. In the 1790s it was widened to accommodate wagons, and became a toll road. Today US Route 25E follows it in places.

wildlife refuge in Canada, **wildlife preserve** tract of land, body of water, or combination of both, set aside for the preservation of wild animals. The purposes of the refuge system include maintenance of fish and game stocks, protection of endangered species, preservation of migration (e.g., FLYWAY) sites, and provision of managed sports fishing and hunting, along with opportunities for research related to all these goals. In the US, commercial fisheries are now within the purview of the Department of Commerce. The US Fish and Wildlife Service, a bureau of the Department of the Interior, maintains some 460 **National Wildlife Refuges** and 150 **Waterfowl Production Areas,** covering together over 140,000 sq mi/360,000 sq km, as well as over 130 research facilities and **National Fish Hatcheries.** The first National Wildlife Refuge was established in 1903 at Pelican I., Florida. In addition, there are state wildlife refuge systems, some dating back to the 1870s, and private systems such as that of the Nature Conservancy. In Canada, a bird sanctuary at Last Mt., Saskatchewan, was the first (1887) in North America. A plains bison preserve at Wainwright, Alberta (1907), preceded the establishment (1922) of WOOD BUFFALO NATIONAL PARK, which has been called the world's largest wildlife preserve. The Canadian Wildlife Service is now engaged in the establishment of a growing system of **National Wildlife Areas** (the first was established in 1986 at Polar Bear Pass, on Bathurst I. in the Northwest Territories). The North American Waterfowl Management Plan, established in 1986 by the US and Canada to foster duck breeding, represents a step in the direction of international wildlife refuge systems.

wild, scenic, and recreational rivers pursuant to a 1968 US law, rivers under the administration of the National Park Service (as part of the NATIONAL PARK system) or of the US Fish and Wildlife Service (as part of the national WILDLIFE REFUGE system), with the design of keeping them free-flowing and accessible for public use and enjoyment. A **wild river** has little evidence of human presence along it; it is generally inaccessible except by trail. A **scenic river** may be reached in places by road, and may have some development along it. A **recreational river** may have been dammed; it is accessible by road or rail, and has more development along it.

Wildwood city, pop. 4484, Cape May Co., S New Jersey, on a 9 mi/14 km–long barrier island on the Atlantic Ocean, 33 mi/53 km SW of Atlantic City, and 6 mi/10 km NE of CAPE MAY. Settled in 1882, it merged with Holly Beach City in 1911. It flourished during the 1950s, and is known for its many period motels. Wildwood and the neighboring communities of **Wildwood Crest** (borough, pop. 3631), West Wildwood (borough, pop. 457), and North Wildwood (city, pop. 5017) are popularly known as "The Wildwoods." There are 5 mi/8 km of wide public beaches, together with a 2.5 mi/4 km–long boardwalk. Four large piers house amusement centers. A summer music festival is held annually.

Wilkes-Barre city, pop. 47,523, seat of Luzerne Co., NE Pennsylvania, in the WYOMING VALLEY, on the Susquehanna R., 15 mi/24 km SW of Scranton. It is an industrial city located in the middle of the ANTHRACITE BELT, which spurred its growth. Its diversified economy now produces electronic components, rubber and metal products, aircraft parts, boilers, and footwear. Established in 1769, Wilkes-Barre was burned on July 3, 1778, by the British and Indians, and again during the Pennamite Wars, a struggle between Pennsylvania and Connecticut for control of the area, in 1784. The city is the seat of Wilkes University (1933), King's College (1946), and a campus of Pennsylvania State University.

Wilkesboro town, pop. 2573, seat of Wilkes Co., NW North Carolina, on the Yadkin R. in the foothills of the Blue Ridge Mts., 52 mi/84 km WNW of Winston-Salem. Founded in 1777, it has produced wood and food products, and is home to Wilkes Community College (1965). **North Wilkesboro** (town, pop. 3384), across the river, separated in 1891 and became more industrial, with furniture, textile, and leather factories. It is today a major poultry processing center, home to the Holly Farms company.

Wilkinsburg borough, pop. 21,080, Allegheny Co., SW Pennsylvania, adjacent (E) to Pittsburgh. Primarily residential, it has no major industries, and serves as a retailing hub for the area. Wilkinsburg is the original home of KDKA, which originated the first commercial radio broadcast in 1920.

Willamette National Forest 1.675 million ac/679,000 ha (2618 sq mi/6780 sq km) in W Oregon, from the crest down the W slope of the CASCADE RANGE, for some 110 mi/180 km between the Mt. Hood National Forest (N) and the Umpqua National Forest (S). It has a number of well-known wilderness areas, including those around Mt. JEFFERSON, Mt. WASHINGTON, and the THREE SISTERS, and is one of the top US timber (esp. Douglas fir) producers.

Willamette River 300 mi/480 km long, in W Oregon. Its headstreams, the Coast and Middle forks, flowing from the W side of the CASCADE RANGE, meet just SE of EUGENE, and the main river then flows N past CORVALLIS, ALBANY, and SALEM, into the PORTLAND area, where it swings NNW to the Columbia R. just below (NW of) the city. A DISTRIBUTARY, the Multnomah Channel, continues N for 15 mi/24 km, around SAUVIE I., to meet the Columbia at St. Helens. The Willamette's headstreams and tributaries, including the McKenzie and Santiam rivers, are dammed for power and flood control. The **Willamette Valley** was one of the first (1830s) regions to be settled in the Oregon Territory, and now contains most of the state's pop. It is noted for its dairy, fruit, and vegetable production.

Willapa Hills range in extreme SW Washington, between the Pacific coast (W), the Chehalis R. (N and E), and the Columbia R. (S). Part of the COAST RANGES, and rising to 3110 ft/948 m at Boistfort Peak, they are mostly under 3000 ft/915 m, with rich vegetation and streams including the Willapa R. draining into 25 mi/40 km–long **Willapa Bay,** an inlet of the Pacific Ocean, in Pacific Co. The bay, bordered (W) by the North Beach Peninsula, offers a sheltered home or harbor for many kinds of waterfowl, migrating birds, fish, and shellfish; it is esp. known for its oysters. The Willapa National Wildlife Refuge embraces 14,297 ac/5790 ha around the bay.

Will County 844 sq mi/2186 sq km, pop. 357,313, in NE Illinois, bordered by Indiana (SE). The Des Plaines R. and the Chicago Ship and Sanitary Canal flow across the NW corner, meeting the Kankakee R. from the SW, to form the Illinois R. just over the Grundy Co. line. Industrial centers such as JOLIET, the county seat, and Lockport lie along the Des Plaines R. in the W, while the SW is an old coal mining area centered around Braidwood and Wilmington. The county's E half consists primarily of farmland. Its N edge, which includes the community of UNIVERSITY PARK, marks the farthest S reach of Chicago's suburbs.

Willcox city, pop. 3122, Cochise Co., SE Arizona, 65 mi/105 km E of Tucson. A livestock center since the 1880s, it also distributes locally grown fruit, nuts, cotton, and grain, and is a tourist base on Interstate 10 for nearby desert and mountain sites.

William P. Hobby Airport also, **Hobby Field** in Houston, Texas, 10 mi/16 km SE of Downtown. Opened as Houston International Airport in 1954, it was renamed in 1967, by which time its facilities were inadequate to demand; its role passed to HOUSTON INTERCONTINENTAL AIRPORT (1969); Hobby now handles primarily business and general aviation.

Williams see under BILL WILLIAMS Mt., Arizona.

Williams Bay village, pop. 2108, Walworth Co., SE Wisconsin, on L. Geneva, 25 mi/40 km SE of Janesville. It is the site of the University of Chicago's Yerkes Observatory (1892, with a 40-in/1.02-m refracting telescope, the world's largest).

Williamsbridge residential section, NE Bronx, New York. It lies directly E of Woodlawn Cemetery and the Bronx R., W of Baychester. The area takes its name from a 1673 bridge across the Bronx R. on the BOSTON POST ROAD, at the site of the modern intersection of Gun Hill and White Plains roads, where a village developed. Remnants of the late-19th-century village can be seen.

Williamsburg **1.** city, pop. 5493, seat of Whitley Co., SE Kentucky, on the Cumberland R. 27 mi/43 km WNW of Middlesborough, on Interstate 75. In an area of gas and coal deposits on the E edge of the DANIEL BOONE NATIONAL FOREST, it has agricultural and extractive industries, and is the seat of Cumberland College (1889). **2.** residential, formerly heavily industrial, section, N Brooklyn, New York. It lies just S of Greenpoint, W of Bushwick, NE of the Brooklyn Navy Yard district in Wallabout Bay, and N of Bedford-Stuyvesant. Originally part of Bushwick, it was laid out around 1810 by Jonathan Williams, a nephew of Benjamin Franklin. Lying along the East R., it shared Greenpoint's and Bushwick's 19th-century development; distilleries, shipyards, potteries, and other establishments made Williamsburgh, as it was then spelled, one of New York's industrial centers. In 1855, when it became part of Brooklyn, the final *h* was dropped. A mixed community since the 19th century, Williamsburg was heavily Irish and German before 1903, when the Williamsburg Bridge, from Manhattan's Lower East Side, opened. This brought Jews in large numbers; by the 1920s Williamsburg was Brooklyn's most densely populated area. A pioneer public housing development, Williamsburg Houses, was built in the 1930s. After World War II, members of the Satmar sect, escaping Eastern Europe, established one of the world's largest Hasidic communities in the district. Today, the Satmar community has established a second base in BOROUGH PARK, and in Williamsburg shares space, often uneasily, with an older Italian population and a growing Hispanic community. Former industrial lofts have also attracted artists. Williamsburg was the setting for Betty Smith's 1943 *A Tree Grows in Brooklyn;* the tree, the ailanthus, was imported from China in the mid 19th century to support silkworms, and grew well in Williamsburg's swampy soil. The Williamsburg Bridge, with a 1600-ft/488-m central span, now carries subways, pedestrians, and automobiles. **3.** independent city, pop. 11,530, seat of but administratively separate from James City Co., SE Virginia, between the James and York rivers, 46 mi/74 km SE of Richmond, and 6 mi/10 km NE of JAMESTOWN. It is known as the site of Colonial Williamsburg, a large-scale restoration that seeks to re-create the city as it was in the 18th century, when it served as Virginia's capital (1699–1780). The restored area, incorporating nearly 100 18th-century buildings and more than 400 buildings reconstructed on their original sites, is a major tourist attraction and the basis of modern Williamsburg's economy. Williamsburg was founded as Middle Plantation in 1633, and became the colony's capital after Jamestown burned. Much history was made here in the 18th century; after the capital was moved to Richmond in 1780, however, the city declined, beginning to recover only when the restoration began in 1926 with funds provided by John D. Rockefeller, Jr. The College of William and Mary (1693) is the second-oldest in the US; also here are Eastern State Hospital (1773) and the Abby Aldrich Rockefeller Folk Art Museum. Other tourist attractions are clustered in the vicinity, and there is a brewery.

Williamsfield locality in Ashtabula Co., NE Ohio, 26 mi/43 km SE of Ashtabula, 2 mi/3 km W of the Pennsylvania border. Albion Tourgée, a novelist of the Reconstruction period, was born here.

Williams Lake city, pop. 10,385, Cariboo Regional District, SC British Columbia, between the Fraser R. (W) and the Cariboo Mts. (E), 207 mi/333 km NNE of Vancouver. It is the service center for the Cariboo and Chilcotin cattle raising regions; local industries include sawmilling, agriculture, logging, and mining. Tourists are drawn esp. to the annual Stampede (rodeo), one of Canada's largest.

Williamson, Mount peak (14,375 ft/4382 m) of the SIERRA NEVADA, 6 mi/10 km N of Mt. WHITNEY and on the E border of Sequoia National Park, in EC California.

Williamsport city, pop. 31,933, seat of Lycoming Co., NC Pennsylvania, on the Susquehanna R. and Lycoming Creek, in the foothills of the Allegheny Mts., 75 mi/121 km NNW of Harrisburg. It was a prosperous lumbering center in the 19th century. As the timber supply dwindled, the city's economy diversified; it now produces electronic equipment, clothing, and metal and leather products. Williamsport is the birthplace of Little League Baseball; the sport's international headquarters are here, and the Little League World Series takes place here annually. Lycoming College (1812) and Williamsport Area Community College (1920) are here. The Allenwood federal prison complex is in Brady township, 7 mi/11 km SE.

Williamstown town, pop. 8220, Berkshire Co., extreme NW Massachusetts, 19 mi/31 km N of Pittsfield, at the confluence of the Hoosic and Green rivers, on the Vermont and New York borders. It is the seat of Williams College (1793), whose campus dominates Williamstown village.

Williamsville residential village, pop. 5583, in Amherst town, Erie Co., W New York, 10 mi/16 km NE of Buffalo.

Willimantic city, pop. 14,746, in the township of Windham, Windham Co., EC Connecticut, at the junction of the Willimantic and Natchaug rivers, 25 mi/40 km E of Hartford. It became known as the Thread City because as early as 1822 thread was manufactured; the American Thread Co. was founded here in 1854. Other manufactures have included textiles, yarn, metal products, tools, and hardware. Eastern Connecticut State University (1889) is here.

Willingboro township, pop. 36,291, Burlington Co., WC New Jersey, 13 mi/21 km NE of Camden. On Rancocas Creek near the Delaware R., the area was originally inhabited by the Lenni Lenape (Delaware), and was settled by English Quakers in the late 1600s. Called Levittown (1959–63), after the large real-estate firm that developed it, the core of the largely residential township was planned as a community of one-family homes and town houses, a residential suburb of Camden and Philadelphia. Its industries produce plumbing and printing supplies and electronic components.

Willington town, pop. 5979, Tolland Co., NE Connecticut, on the Willimantic R. and Interstate 84, 23 mi/37 km ENE of Hartford. Situated in a farming area, it includes the manufacturing villages of South Willington and West Willington.

Williston city, pop. 13,131, seat of Williams Co., NW North Dakota, on the Missouri R., 18 mi/29 km E of the Montana border and 105 mi/169 km W of Minot. Originating in 1880 as a port for steamers servicing the W Montana goldfields, it also became a railroad center after 1887. Today it is a trade and distribution hub for local grain, dairy products, coal, and oil. Fort Buford State Historic Site is 2 mi/3 km W.

Williston Lake also, **W. A. C. Bennett Reservoir** in NE British Columbia, covering 640 sq mi/1660 sq km. Extending over 120 mi/190 km NW–SE in the Rocky Mt. Trench, and with a 75 mi/120 km–long E arm, it is the largest freshwater body in the province and the biggest reservoir in North America. Created in 1968 by completion of W.A.C. Bennett Dam, W of Hudson's Hope on the Peace R., it was named for a provincial minister who encouraged the development of the pulp industry in the British Columbia interior, and is used to transport timber to mills at Mackenzie, on its SE shore. The Bennett Dam, one of the largest earthfill dams in the world, is 600 ft/180 m high.

Willmar city, pop. 17,531, seat of Kandiyohi Co., EC Minnesota, on Foot and Willmar lakes, 50 mi/80 km SW of St. Cloud. An 1856 settlement here was abandoned during the 1862 Sioux uprising. Willmar was reestablished in 1869 as a railhead construction camp, eventually becoming a rail administrative center and shipping point for local grain and livestock. Today, it is a trading and processing center for the region's poultry (especially turkey), cattle, dairy products, and grain. Industries include foundries, machine shops, printing, and the manufacture of children's furniture, clothing, and farm machinery. It is the seat of Willmar Community College (1961) and Willmar Technical College. Tourists visit the area's numerous lakes.

Willoughby city, pop. 20,510, Lake Co., NE Ohio, on the Chagrin R., 17 mi/27 km NE of Cleveland and 3 mi/5 km E of L. Erie. It grew up around a gristmill and a sawmill, both established in 1787. In the 1950s it underwent rapid expansion as a residential community. Current manufactures include auto parts, rubber products, chemicals, and electronic components.

Willow unincorporated community, pop. 285, at the SW base of the Talkeetna Mts., just E of the Susitna R. and 40 mi/64 km NNW of Anchorage, in SC Alaska. Chosen as the site of a new, more central state capital in 1976, this small road and railroad settlement was to be completely rebuilt and expanded, but funding for the project was rejected in a 1982 referendum, and the capital remains at JUNEAU.

Willowbrook also, **Willow Brook** unincorporated community, pop. 32,772, Los Angeles Co., SW California, 7 mi/11 km S of downtown Los Angeles, a residential and manufacturing community immediately N of COMPTON.

Willowdale see under NORTH YORK, Ontario.

Willow Grove unincorporated village, pop. 16,325, in Horsham township, Montgomery Co., SE Pennsylvania, 13 mi/21 km N of Philadelphia. Its industries include agriculture and clothing manufacture; it has an amusement park and a naval air station.

Willowick city, pop. 15,269, Lake Co., NE Ohio, on L. Erie, 15 mi/24 km NE of Cleveland, of which it is a commuter suburb.

Willow Run see under YPSILANTI, Michigan.

Wilmette village, pop. 26,690, Cook Co., NE Illinois, on L. Michigan and the North Shore Channel, 15 mi/24 km N of Chicago. An affluent residential community, it was named for Archange Ouilmette, the Potawatomi wife of the area's first European settler. She was granted land known as the Ouilmette Fields by the Treaty of Prairie du Chien (1829), on which the village was laid out (1869). Wilmette is the home of the Baha'i House of Worship (1921), the center of the Baha'i faith in North America.

Wilmington **1.** industrial and commercial section of LOS ANGELES, California, on Los Angeles Harbor, adjacent to Harbor City (NW), SAN PEDRO (SW), and LONG BEACH (E), and 20 mi/32 km S of Downtown. Founded in 1858 at the mouth of the Los Angeles R., it developed with San Pedro as the port for Los Angeles, and was annexed by the city in 1909. Today, it has an ethnically diverse community. Los Angeles Harbor College (1949), oil industry facilities, and the Civil War Drum Barracks are here. **2.** city, pop. 71,529, seat of New Castle Co., NE Delaware, on the Christina R., BRANDYWINE CREEK, and the Delaware R., 25 mi/40 km SW of Philadelphia, Pennsylvania. Before becoming a Quaker agricultural community in the 1730s, it was held by the Swedes, the Dutch, and the British. Its port, waterpower, and fertile farmlands contributed to 18th-century growth. Sawmills, gristmills, and paper mills were established along the Brandywine after the Revolutionary War; a gunpowder mill established in 1802 was the cradle of the Du Pont industrial empire. Wilmington produces chemicals; iron, fiber, leather, and steel goods; processed foods; flooring; refined oil; boats; railroad cars; and copper. It has been home through much of the 20th century to numerous corporations, headquartered here to take advantage of favorable Delaware laws. The city has, however, been losing population and business base, partly to its suburbs, since mid-century. **3.** town, pop. 17,654, Middlesex Co., NE Massachusetts, 9 mi/14 km SE of Lowell. Long a quiet agricultural community, it is now a growing suburb situated on Interstate 93 just N of ROUTE 128, with commercial and industrial zones set apart from its residential areas. **4.** city, pop. 55,530, seat of New Hanover Co., SE North Carolina, on a peninsula between the Cape Fear R. (W) and the Atlantic Ocean, 20 mi/32 km N of the river's mouth. The area was settled from the West Indies in the 17th century, and Wilmington itself was established (as New Liverpool) in 1730. It became an important port and in the 1760s a center of resistance to British taxes (the Stamp Act). The Battle of Moores Creek Bridge, in which Revolutionary forces defeated Scottish Tories, was fought 18 mi/29 km NW on Feb. 27, 1776, and in June 1781 Cornwallis briefly occupied the town. A center for blockade running during the Civil War, protected by FORT FISHER and other emplacements, it was the last Confederate port to close, on Jan. 15, 1865. In World War I, Wilmington was again important; dredging restored its standing as a deepwater port, situated in an agricultural and industrial area. Local farms and forests produce bulbs, flowers, peanuts, corn, tobacco, naval stores, and wood for pulp. Industries manufacture textiles, clothing, furniture, paper, refined petroleum, asphalt, chemicals, cement, gas, and steel tanks and boilers. There is a flourishing moviemaking industry. The city is home to a branch of the University of North Carolina (1947) and to Cape Fear Community College (1959). Its larger immediate unincorporated suburbs include Masonboro (E; pop. 7010), Wrightsboro (N; pop. 4752), Windemere (NE; pop. 4604), and Myrtle Grove (S; pop. 4275). **5.** city, pop. 11,199, seat of Clinton Co., SW Ohio, 30 mi/48 km SE of Dayton. Corn, livestock, and horses are raised on surrounding farms, for which Wilmington is a trade center. Manufactures include wood-boring tools, air compressors, metal and electrical products, and auto parts. Wilmington College (1870) is here. Cowan Lake State Park is 6 mi/10 km to the SW, and Caesar Creek State Park 8 mi/13 km to the NW.

Wilmore city, pop. 4215, Jessamine Co., C Kentucky, 15 mi/24 km SSW of Lexington. In the middle of the BLUEGRASS REGION, it is an agricultural trade center, and home to Asbury College (1890).

Wilshire Boulevard commercial thoroughfare, 16 mi/26 km long, between downtown LOS ANGELES, California (E), and SANTA MONICA (W). A prestigious retailing street, it passes through HANCOCK PARK, BEVERLY HILLS, and WESTWOOD, and along MACARTHUR PARK. Outside of Downtown, most commercial high-rise buildings are concentrated along Wilshire; a 1920s realtor initiated this trend by constructing a shopping center in what is now the Miracle Mile, 6 mi/10 km W of Downtown, attracting affluent motorists and drawing trade away from the older central business district. Just W of the Miracle Mile is the Carthay Circle area, a middle-class residential neighborhood. The term **Mid-Wilshire** is used imprecisely of neighborhoods W of MacArthur Park and E of Beverly Hills.

Wilson city, pop. 36,930, seat of Wilson Co., EC North Carolina, 40 mi/64 km ESE of Raleigh. An important bright leaf tobacco market and processing center, it also manufactures textiles, concrete products, truck and bus bodies, electronic components, agricultural equipment, lumber and wood products, and cottonseed oil. Barton (formerly Atlantic Christian) College (1902) and Wilson Technical Community College (1958) are here.

Wilson, Mount **1.** peak (5710 ft/1740 m) in the SAN GABRIEL Mts., just NE of Pasadena, in SW California, site of the Mt. Wilson Observatory, with its 100-in/254-cm telescope, since 1948 operated jointly by the Carnegie Institution and California Institute of Technology. The Wilson and Mount Palomar observatories are together known as the Hale Observatories after astronomer George Ellery Hale. Benjamin Wilson, a local lumberman, built the first modern trail to the mountain's summit in 1864. **2.** see under SAN JUAN Mts., Colorado.

Wilson Dam oldest and most powerful TENNESSEE VALLEY AUTHORITY dam, 2.5 mi/4 km E of Florence, NW Alabama, on the Tennessee R. Begun in 1918 as part of the World War I MUSCLE SHOALS nitrate project, it was completed in 1925 (its locks in 1927), and came under TVA control in 1933. It is 137 ft/42 m high and almost 4900 ft/1500 m long, and impounds **L. Wilson,** which extends 15 mi/24 km back upstream to the WHEELER DAM. Its main lock can lift vessels 100 ft/30 m. The lower part of the Muscle Shoals is now under the dam and lake.

Wilson's Creek Ozark Plateau stream, in Greene Co., SW Missouri, 12 mi/19 km SW of Springfield. Here a Civil War battle (Aug. 10, 1861) was fought between Confederate forces under Sterling Price and Union troops led by Nathaniel Lyon, who was killed in the course of fighting. The victorious Confederates were, however, unable to control Missouri. The 1750-ac/709-ha **Wilson's Creek National Battlefield** was established in 1960.

Wilton town, pop. 15,989, Fairfield Co., SW Connecticut, on the Norwalk R. and the New York border. Formerly a quiet exurb, it has undergone dramatic growth in the last decades of the 20th century, with a boom in corporate office and commercial space and increasing suburbanization.

Wilton Manors city, pop. 11,804, Broward Co., SE Florida, a residential suburb adjacent (N) to Fort Lauderdale, on the Middle R. Originally the site of orange groves, it was developed in 1926 during the Florida land boom.

Winchester **1.** city, pop. 15,799, seat of Clark Co., EC Kentucky, 18 mi/29 km ESE of Lexington. This largely residential Bluegrass community, incorporated in 1793, is also a market and shipping center for burley tobacco, bluegrass seed, and horses, cattle, and sheep, and has some light manufactures. It is headquarters for the DANIEL BOONE NATIONAL FOREST. The writer Allen Tate was born here in 1899. **2.** town, pop. 20,267, Middlesex Co., NE Massachusetts. Situated 8 mi/13 km NW of Boston, on the Aberjona R. and Upper Mystic L., it made leather and glue in the 19th century, but is now a residential suburb with some light industry. The Middlesex Fells Reservation makes up most of the town's E border. **3.** unincorporated community, pop. 23,365, Clark Co., S Nevada, a largely residential suburb 3.5 mi/6 km SW of downtown LAS VEGAS, W of the STRIP. **4.** independent city, pop. 21,947, seat of but administratively separate from Frederick Co., NW Virginia, in the N Shenandoah Valley, 70 mi/113 km WNW of Washington, D.C. Settled in 1732, and the oldest Virginia city W of the Blue Ridge Mts., it served as headquarters for George Washington when he surveyed the area and again when he commanded Virginia's troops in the French and Indian War (1754–63). The city was much fought over in the Civil War, changing hands many times. It is famous for its apples, and stages a spring apple blossom festival. It is home to the Shenandoah College and Conservatory of Music (1875). The writer Willa Cather was born (1876) in the hamlet of Gore, 10 mi/16 km NW.

Wind Cave National Park 28,300 ac/11,460 ha, on the E side of South Dakota's BLACK HILLS. Established in 1903, it incorporates limestone caverns with calcite crystals in honeycomb patterns; air currents passing through are responsible for the name. Since 1935 the park has included a grassland surface area noted for its bison, prairie dogs, pronghorn antelope, and other wildlife.

Windemere see under WILMINGTON, North Carolina.

Windham **1.** town, pop. 22,039, Windham Co., NE Connecticut, including the industrial city of WILLIMANTIC; the two were merged in 1983. **2.** town, pop. 13,020, Cumberland Co., SW Maine. It is on the Presumpscot R. and SEBAGO L. North Windham, 15 mi/24 km NW of Portland, is retail center for the Sebago region, with several shopping malls. South Windham, an industrial village, lies in two townships, with a residential and business section in Gorham and factories in Windham. St. Joseph's College (1912) is in Windham.

Windmill, the battle site: see under PRESCOTT, Ontario.

Window Rock unincorporated community, pop. 3306, Apache Co., NE Arizona, on the New Mexico border, 20 mi/32 km NW of Gallup. It is the capital of the huge NAVAJO INDIAN RESERVATION. Established in 1936 as the central agency headquarters for the reservation, it was named for a huge opening in the surrounding sandstone cliffs. The Navajo Council House and Navajo Tribal Museum are here, and the Navajo Nation Fair, one of the largest Indian fairs, is held annually.

Wind River 120 mi/193 km long, in W and WC Wyoming. It rises in several branches at the N end of the Wind River Range in NW Fremont Co., and flows generally SE through the Wind River Indian Reservation. The Wind turns NE at Riverton, where it is joined by the Popo Agie R. It continues through the Boysen Reservoir and Wind River Canyon and becomes the Big Horn R. just S of Thermopolis.

Wind River Indian Reservation 525,000 ac/213,000 ha, pop. 21,851, Fremont and Hot Springs counties, WC Wyoming. It is in the Wind River valley and is bordered by the SHOSHONE NATIONAL FOREST (W and S). Traversed by the Wind R., it includes Bull L. Diversion Dam, and a large hot springs near Fort Washakie. Wyoming's only reservation, it is home to the Arapaho. The headquarters is at Ethete. Economic activities include hide tanning and agriculture.

Wind River Range NW–SE trending mountains in WC Wyoming, extending 120 mi/190 km from SE of Yellowstone National Park (N) to SOUTH PASS and the Sweetwater R. (S). A granitic component of the Middle ROCKY Mts., it contains all but one (GRAND TETON is the exception) of Wyoming's highest peaks, including GANNETT PEAK (13,804 ft/4207 m), the state's high point. Rugged and snowcapped, with over 150 glaciers, the Wind Rivers are popular with climbers and hikers. The Wind R. flows from their E side.

Windsor **1.** town, pop. 27,817, Hartford Co., NC Connecticut, 6 mi/10 km N of Hartford, on the Connecticut and Farmington rivers. It includes Windsor, Wilson, and Poquonock villages, and is primarily residential. Windsor was the site of the first English settlement in Connecticut; a trading post was established in 1633; a permanent settlement of Colonists from Massachusetts was established by 1635. Since the 1950s, the town has added light industry and commerce to its economy, once dominated by shade tobacco growing. The Loomis Chaffee prep school is here. WINDSOR LOCKS is N. **2.** see under GRAND FALLS–WINDSOR, Newfoundland. **3.** city, pop. 191,435, seat of Essex Co., extreme S Ontario, on the Detroit R., opposite (S of) Detroit, Michigan. At 42° 18′ N, it is the southernmost Canadian city. French settlement of the area, which had been visited by missionaries a century earlier, began in 1749. The British took control in 1760, and LOYALISTS settled following the American Revolution. Windsor, founded in 1836, developed from the 1850s as a rail center and Great Lakes port. Walkerville, a COMPANY TOWN just NE of Downtown, was developed in the 1890s by the distillers Hiram Walker. The establishment of the Ford Motor Company of Canada in 1904 initiated auto industry and related development. The AMBASSADOR BRIDGE (1929) and Detroit–Windsor Auto Tunnel (1930) linked the two industrial centers. During Prohibition (1919–33), Windsor was a noted rumrunning base. In 1935, Windsor and neighboring East Windsor, Sandwich, and Walkerville were consolidated. World War II brought a boom to heavy industry; attempts to diversify followed the war. The University of Windsor (1962) is the successor to Assumption College (1857). St. Clair College (1967) is a technological center. Windsor today is a commercial and industrial center in a fertile agricultural region. In addition to automobiles and auto parts, it makes pharmaceuticals, iron and steel, salt, machinery, foods, and beverages. It is also Canada's leading port of entry from the US.

Windsor County 972 sq mi/2517 sq km, pop. 54,055, in EC Vermont. Woodstock is the county seat. The largest county in the state, it is bounded E by the Connecticut R. and drained by the Ottauquechee, White, Black, and Williams rivers. Summer and winter resorts, including Mt. ASCUTNEY, are here; the main industries make machinery, tools, textiles, printed materials, sports equipment, and chemicals. Lumber, marble, poultry, and dairy, wood, and metal goods also are produced.

Windsor Locks town, pop. 12,358, Hartford Co., NC Connecticut, on the Connecticut R., 12 mi/19 km N of Hartford. Commercial development began with completion of navigational locks on the Connecticut R. in 1829; early industries included a gristmill and a sawmill. Today, the area is an important center of aircraft manufacturing and produces tinsel, metallic thread, paper goods, and electronic parts. Bradley Field, a former military airbase, is now an international airport.

Windy City nickname for Chicago, Illinois, now generally accepted as referring to bitter winter winds off L. Michigan, although the city has lower average wind speeds than many other US cities. Originally, however, the name was applied by New York writers in reference to Chicago boosters around the turn of the century.

Winema National Forest 1.039 million ac/420,800 ha (1623 sq mi/4205 sq km), in SW Oregon, E of the crest of the Cascade Range, E and S of Crater L., extending to the Klamath Basin. Mt. McLoughlin (9495 ft/2894 m) is here.

Winesburg see under CLYDE, Ohio.

Winfield city, pop. 11,931, seat of Cowley Co., SE Kansas, on the Walnut R., 35 mi/56 km SSE of Wichita. In an agricultural and oil and gas producing area, it produces flour, feed, dairy goods, and other agriculture-related products. It also has foundries and industries producing oilfield equipment, steel goods, gas burners, and barrels. Winfield is the seat of Southwestern College (1885) and Saint John's College (1893).

Wingate town, pop. 2821, Union Co., S North Carolina, 5 mi/8 km E of Monroe, the seat of Wingate College (1896).

Winkler town, pop. 6397, S Manitoba, 58 mi/93 km SW of Winnipeg, 8 mi/13 km E of Morden, and 12 mi/19 km N of the North Dakota border. Since its founding in the late 1800s, it has been the trade, processing, and service center of the fertile Pembina Valley region. Mennonites from Russia came here and to STEINBACH in the 1870s, creating a rich farming region. After World War II, local retail business and industry grew, including the manufacturing of recreational vehicles, mobile homes, prefabricated houses, agricultural machinery, and metal and plastic products.

Winnebago, Lake the largest lake in Wisconsin, in Calumet, Fond du Lac, and Winnebago counties. It is 30 mi/48 km long and 3–10 mi/5–16 km wide, with an area of 215 sq mi/557 sq km. The Fox R. enters the lake at Oshkosh and drains it at Neenah and Menasha. Winnebago is the center of a popular recreational area, and is surrounded by summer cottages.

Winnebago County **1.** 516 sq mi/1336 sq km, pop. 252,913, in NC Illinois, bordered by Wisconsin (N) and cut by the Pecatonica and Rock rivers. In the Rock R. valley, the county seat, ROCKFORD, and its suburbs (Machesney Park and Loves Park), account for much of the SE portion of the county and dominate its economy. Suburbs of Beloit, Wisconsin (including South Beloit), are in the NE corner. The rest of the county is rural, with numerous dairy and truck farms. **2.** 449 sq mi/1163 sq km, pop. 140,320, in EC Wisconsin. Its seat is OSHKOSH. Bounded on the E by L. Winnebago, it is traversed by the Wolf and Fox rivers. It is mainly a dairy and farming area. There is large-scale manufacturing, particularly of paper and wood products, at Oshkosh, Menasha, and Neenah.

Winnebago Indian Reservation see under OMAHA INDIAN RESERVATION, Nebraska.

Winnemucca city, pop. 6134, seat of Humboldt Co., NC Nevada, on the Humboldt R. and Interstate 80, 150 mi/240 km NE of Reno. It was founded in 1859 as a fur trappers' trading post. Several emigrant trails passed through here. So did the Butch Cassidy gang, which robbed the First National Bank in 1900. Today the city is a trade center that ships livestock, has a bottling plant, and smelts gold, silver, copper, and tungsten mined in the vicinity. The Buckaroo Hall of Fame celebrates the region's cowboy culture, and there are several annual rodeos. The area's significant Basque population also has an annual festival.

Winnetka village, pop. 12,174, Cook Co., NE Illinois, on L. Michigan, 18 mi/29 km N of Chicago. An affluent bedroom community, it was originally a stop on the pre-European Green Bay Trail, and was settled by Americans in the 1830s. The village was the home of the Winnetka Plan, an experimental method of public school teaching, developed in the 1920s.

Winnfield city, pop. 6138, seat of **Winn Parish** (953 sq mi/2468 sq km, pop. 16,269), NC Louisiana, 43 mi/70 km NNW of Alexandria. It is an agricultural trade center. Kisatchie National Forest lies nearby, and lumbering is important. Huey Long (1893) and his brother Earl (1895) were born in this upland community; the parish was the base of their political power.

Winnibigoshish Lake see under CHIPPEWA NATIONAL FOREST, Minnesota.

Winnipeg provincial capital and largest city, pop. 616,790, SE Manitoba, at the confluence ("The Forks") of the Assiniboine R. and the Red R. of the North, 40 mi/64 km SSW of L. Winnipeg and 60 mi/100 km N of the border with Minnesota and North Dakota. In the wheat belt, in the geographic center of Canada, at the transition between the forested CANADIAN SHIELD (N and E) and the open prairie (S and W), it is home to 56% of Manitoba's pop. La Vérendrye, traveling from Québec, established Fort-Rouge here as a trade post in 1738. Later, the NORTH WEST COMPANY established Fort Gibraltar (1804), and the HUDSON'S BAY COMPANY Fort Douglas (renamed Fort Garry in 1821). Lord Selkirk's RED RIVER Colony was centered here from 1812, and strife between the MÉTIS (with NWC backing) and the colony and HBC peaked with the 1816 SEVEN OAKS incident (within modern city limits). Winnipeg itself was established as an 1860s crossroads, and was incorporated in 1873. It boomed after 1885, when the Canadian Pacific Railway arrived, becoming quickly the chief city of the Prairie Provinces. By 1914 it was a major rail hub, grain market, immigration gateway to the West, and commercial center. Economic hard times then set in, punctuated by an acrimonious General Strike in 1919, in which tensions between the older, anglophone middle and upper classes and the largely immigrant, Eastern European working classes came to the fore. World War II brought recovery, and the city grew with manufacturing and service industries. A 1950 flood on the Red R. destroyed much of the older Downtown, leading to extensive rebuilding in a less centralized pattern. Suburbs grew quickly, until in 1972, in an unprecedented step, the Manitoba parliament established Unicity (or the City of Winnipeg), a single metropolitan government for the urban complex. Today, Winnipeg's metropolitan area (CMA) has a pop. of 652,354, including the city and only seven small rural municipalities, so that almost 95% of its people live under city government. The old French city of SAINT-BONIFACE (E) is now part of Winnipeg. The city's North End was, from the late 19th century, home to Jews, Ukrainians, and other immigrant groups, while areas to the W and S were more established, and inhabited by English-speaking Ontarians, Scots, etc. Modern Winnipeg is more cosmopolitan. A governmental and cultural center, it is home to the University of Manitoba (1877), the University of Winnipeg (1871), and several other institutions, and to a branch of the Canadian Mint, noted museums, symphonic, dance, and theater organizations, a folk festival, and other assets. The Blue Bombers (football) play at Winnipeg Stadium, the Jets (hockey) at the Winnipeg Arena.

Winnipeg, Lake sixth-largest lake in Canada, in SC Manitoba. It extends 258 mi/416 km NNW–SSE and drains some 380,000 sq mi/984,000 sq km in the Saskatchewan, Red-Assiniboine, and Winnipeg R. watersheds, discharging into the NELSON R., which flows NE to Hudson Bay. Lake Winnipeg covers 9420 sq mi/24,400 sq km; it reaches 70 mi/113 km wide in the N, and is shallow (no more than 60 ft/18 m deep). In 1690, the English explorer Henry Kelsey was perhaps the first European to see it. Its Cree name means "murky waters"; rumors of a large, bad-tasting "sea" long made westbound adventurers think they were approaching the Pacific. The lake, the largest remnant of glacial L. AGASSIZ, has summer resorts around its S end, and a number of Indian reserves ring it. HECLA, the largest island, was an 1870s Icelandic settlement. Grand Rapids (NW), where the Saskatchewan R. system enters it, is an important hydroelectric generating site. The lake is noted for its wind and wave effects.

Winnipegosis, Lake eleventh-largest lake in Canada, in SC Manitoba, W of L. Winnipeg. It covers 2100 sq mi/5440 sq km; some 120 mi/190 km NNW–SSE, it drains via the short Waterhen R. into L. MANITOBA, thence into L. Winnipeg.

Winnipeg River 200 mi/320 km long, in W Ontario and SE Manitoba. It was long part of an important fur trade route from L. Superior west, despite its many falls and rapids. It flows NW from the LAKE OF THE WOODS near Kenora, Ontario, through a series of lakes and WHITESHELL PROVINCIAL PARK, discharging into the SE end of L. Winnipeg; hydroelectric plants on its lower course provide power for Manitoba. The Winnipeg's main tributary, the 330 mi/530 km–long English R., joins it from the NE near the Manitoba-Ontario line. In draining the Lake of the Woods, the Winnipeg also drains the RAINY R. system, from just W of L. Superior.

Winnipesaukee, Lake in EC New Hampshire, 45 mi/72 km NNE of Manchester. The largest lake in New Hampshire, it is a popular summer resort. Irregularly shaped, Winnipesaukee is 25 mi/40 km long and 12 mi/19 km wide, and contains some 365 tree-clad islands; 274 of these are habitable; some rise 400 ft/122 m above the water. The meaning of Winnipesaukee's name is disputed; some say it is "the smile of the great spirit." Wolfeboro, the largest town on the lake, has been a resort center for two centuries. Other lakeside communities include LACONIA, Weirs Beach, Meredith, and Center Harbor. The first boat race between Harvard and Yale was held here in 1852.

Winnsboro town, pop. 3475, seat of Fairfield Co., NC South Carolina, 25 mi/40 km N of Columbia. Settled in the mid 18th century, it was briefly occupied (1780) by the British general Cornwallis. During the Civil War, it was looted and partially burned by Union troops (1865), but many older structures remain. With textile and granite works, Winnsboro and unincorporated **Winnsboro Mills** (pop. 2275) also process and distribute local corn and livestock. Operations of the Mack Truck Co. moved here in the late 1980s.

Winona **1.** city, pop. 25,399, seat of Winona Co., SE Minnesota, on the Mississippi R. and L. Winona, across from Centerville, Wisconsin, and 42 mi/68 km E of Rochester. Situated at the base of towering bluffs and founded in 1851 as a shipping center for wheat, it became a prosperous logging and sawmilling town. After 1900, manufacturing came to dominate the economy. Today, the city produces cattle feed, flour, dairy products, and beverages, while building stone is made from limestone quarried nearby. Other facilities include rail repair shops and factories producing pharmaceuticals and cosmetics. Winona State University (1858), the College of St. Theresa (1907), and St. Mary's College (1912) are here, as is the headquarters of the UPPER MISSISSIPPI RIVER

NATIONAL WILDLIFE AND FISH REFUGE. **2.** city, pop. 5705, seat of Montgomery Co., NC Mississippi, 25 mi/40 km E of Greenwood. It is a processing center in an area that raises cotton, dairy and beef cattle, and poultry; auto parts are also manufactured. Once a stop on the Illinois Central Railroad, it now has an Amtrak station and is on Interstate 55.

Winona Lake town, pop. 4053, Kosciusko Co., NC Indiana, 1 mi/2 km SE of Warsaw. On Winona L., in the heart of a lake-filled region, it is a popular resort. Preserved here is the home of baseball player/evangelist Billy Sunday (1863–1935). Winona Lake is home to Grace College (1948), affiliated with the Brethren Church.

Winooski city, pop. 6649, Chittenden Co., NW Vermont. It is on the Winooski R., N of and adjacent to Burlington. The community developed after a woolen mill was established on the falls in 1835, and became a textiles center. St. Michael's College (1904) is here. Furniture, window screens, and wood and metal products have been significant manufactures. The city includes a large French-Canadian population, descendants of millworkers, and is now largely commercial.

Winooski River 95 mi/153 km long, rising N of Marshfield in Washington Co., NC Vermont, and flowing SW through the Green Mts. to Montpelier, where it receives the North Branch. It then flows NW past Waterbury, Richmond, Essex Junction, and Winooski, providing power for industry, to enter L. Champlain just N of Burlington. Its name derives from an Abnaki word for the wild onion, which grows along the river's banks.

Winslow **1.** city, pop. 8190, Navajo Co., NE Arizona, 55 mi/89 km ESE of Flagstaff. Settled in 1882 on the Atlantic and Pacific Railroad, it developed as a livestock shipping point. It has railroad shops, produces lumber, and is a tourist base for the Navajo and Hopi Indian Reservations (N), Meteor Crater (W), and Petrified Forest (E). **2.** see under BAINBRIDGE I., Washington.

Winsted city, pop. 8254, Litchfield Co., NW Connecticut, on the Still R. in the town of Winchester. A lake resort, it also produces tape, felt, electrical appliances, and fishing tackle; its industrial history stretches back to early-19th-century clockmaking. There is some farming. Winsted is the birthplace (1934) of consumer advocate Ralph Nader.

Winston County 613 sq mi/1588 sq km, pop. 22,053, in NW Alabama. Double Springs, in the BANKHEAD NATIONAL FOREST, is its seat. This small-farming area in the Red Hills rejected Secession in 1861. Citizens of Haleyville and other towns joined a force to represent "Free Winston" or the proposed state of Nickajack, and many eventually fought with the Union.

Winston-Salem city, pop. 143,485, seat of Forsyth Co., NC North Carolina, the W corner of the PIEDMONT TRIAD, on headstreams of Muddy Creek, E of the Yadkin R. and 23 mi/37 km W of Greensboro. The city was created in 1913 by uniting the two towns of Winston and Salem. Salem had been established in 1766 on a tract originally called Wachau (or, Anglicized, Wachovia), settled in 1753 by a group of Pennsylvania Moravians. Winston was laid out as the county seat in 1849. The communities produced woolens, wagons, and various other products until 1875, when R.J. Reynolds chose this site for his tobacco company. Winston-Salem is now one of the largest tobacco market and processing centers in the world, and a growing financial center. Other industries manufacture textiles, carpets, hosiery, knitwear, electronic and aircraft equipment, metal products, furniture, and dairy goods. The city is home to Salem College (1772), Wake Forest University (1834; moved here 1956), Winston-Salem State University (1892), Piedmont Bible College (1945), the North Carolina School of the Arts (1963), and Forsyth Technical Community College (1964).

Winter Garden **1.** city, pop. 9745, Orange Co., C Florida, 12 mi/19 km W of Orlando. On the S shore of L. Apopka, it is a citrus and truck processing center, with recent tourist and residential growth. **2.** agricultural region of S Texas, in Maverick, Zavala, Dimmit, Frio, and Lasalle counties. Artesian well water in this area just NE of the Rio Grande transformed a ranching economy in the 1920s. The area now produces huge vegetable and fruit crops, and is also popular with winter vacationers. CRYSTAL CITY is a major center.

Winter Haven city, pop. 24,725, Polk Co., C Florida, 14 mi/23 km E of Lakeland. With nearly 100 lakes within a 5 mi/8 km radius, some of them connected by canals in a 30 mi/48 km–long waterway, fishing and water sports are popular local activities. Winter Haven is also the spring training home of the Boston Red Sox, drawing tourists, retirees, and baseball fans. It lies in one of Florida's richest citrus raising areas. Among the city's manufactures are alcohol, sheet metal, concrete products, cigars, and molasses. Polk Community College (1963) is here, and the botanical gardens and water-skiing center at Cypress Gardens are 5 mi/8 km SE.

Winter Park **1.** town, pop. 528, Grand Co., NC Colorado, in the Arapahoe National Forest, at 9000 ft/2745 m, 40 mi/64 km NW of Denver. Berthoud Pass is just S, the Continental Divide just E. Development of the town dates from 1927, when the 7 mi/11 km–long Moffatt Tunnel across the Divide linked Denver with the area. A rope tow at Berthoud Pass (1937) and the construction of the Winter Park Ski Area (1940) ultimately transformed the town into one of Colorado's major skiing centers and a hub for many other winter sports. **2.** city, pop. 22,242, Orange Co., EC Florida, 5 mi/8 km NE of Orlando. Founded in the 1850s and formally laid out in the 1880s, it has a chain of small lakes within its city limits, connected by navigable canals. Noted for its parks and gardens, the city lies in a citrus growing area (the Temple orange was developed here), and is a shipping center for the fruits. Rollins College (1885) is the site of many cultural institutions; it has held a major Bach festival since the 1930s.

Winter Quarters see under MORMON TRAIL.

Winterset city, pop. 4196, seat of Madison Co., SC Iowa. A trade center in a wheat and livestock producing region, it is the birthplace (1906) of actor John Wayne. It has an annual Covered Bridge Festival.

Winter Springs city, pop. 22,151, Seminole Co., EC Florida, 12 mi/19 km NNE of Orlando. Just off L. Jessup in a lake-filled region, it is a residential community.

Winterthur see under CENTERVILLE, Delaware.

Winthrop town, pop. 18,127, Suffolk Co., NE Massachusetts, on a peninsula enclosing part of Boston Harbor, across from Logan International Airport. A suburb and coastal resort, it has several yacht clubs, but little industry. The Deane Winthrop House (1637) is a landmark; the town is named for Winthrop, who was the son of Massachusetts Bay Colony Governor John Winthrop. Neighborhoods include Ocean Spray, Court Park, Cottage Park, and Point Shirley (S), from which Boston's DEER ISLAND extends.

Wiregrass agricultural region of EC–SE Alabama, part of the

Gulf Coastal Plain, named for its characteristic ground cover. A major cotton region until the boll weevil (1910s), it now is noted for its peanut production, also raising truck and forage crops and cattle. DOTHAN is the largest city.

Wiscasset town, pop. 3339, seat of Lincoln Co., SW Maine. It is on the Sheepscot R. and US 1, 10 mi/16 km NE of Bath. An important early-19th-century seaport, the town has many examples of period architecture. Significant old buildings include the Lincoln County Museum and Jailhouse and the old Custom House. The Maine Yankee atomic power plant, opened in 1972, is SW of the town center, along the river.

Wisconsin state of the NC US, considered in the Upper MIDDLE WEST and as a GREAT LAKES state; 1990 pop. 4,891,769 (104% of 1980; rank: 16th); area 65,503 sq mi/169,653 sq km (rank: 23rd); admitted to Union 1848 (30th). Capital: MADISON. Most populous cities: MILWAUKEE, Madison, GREEN BAY, RACINE. Wisconsin is bordered S by Illinois. On the W are (S–N) Iowa, across the MISSISSIPPI R.; and Minnesota, across the Mississippi and SAINT CROIX rivers and a short land boundary (N). On the N Wisconsin has a shore on L. SUPERIOR; the city of SUPERIOR, APOSTLE Is., and CHEQUAMEGON BAY are here. On the NE is the UPPER PENINSULA of Michigan, largely across the MENOMINEE–Brule river system. On the E is L. MICHIGAN; the Wisconsin shore is deeply indented by GREEN BAY, which lies within (W of) the DOOR PENINSULA. The state has three main topographic sections. In the N and NW is part of the SUPERIOR HIGHLANDS, an extension of the CANADIAN SHIELD that extends from NE Minnesota through this region and into NW Michigan. TIMMS HILL, at 1952 ft/595 m, in Price Co., is the state's high point. Heavily forested and dotted with thousands of small lakes, this is an area with few cities of size (Superior, in the extreme NW, across from Duluth, Minnesota, is the largest), in which logging, mining (esp. along the Michigan border), and outdoor recreation have all been important. Roughly equivalent with what is locally called the "North Woods," it has scattered farms and residents who feel some sense of isolation from the rest of the state. The CHIPPEWA, WISCONSIN, and other rivers rise in this region and flow generally SW across the state to the Mississippi R. On the SE, from the Menominee R. to the Illinois line and extending W to the Madison area, is part of the vast C lowlands of the US. The FOX and WOLF rivers here join to flow through L. WINNEBAGO and then NE into Green Bay. The Door Peninsula, E of Green Bay, is the SW end of the NIAGARA ESCARPMENT, and a popular vacation area. Most of Wisconsin's people, cities, and industry are found within the lowland region; access to the Great Lakes and proximity to Chicago made the SE corner of the state its most developed section. The SW third of Wisconsin is its DRIFTLESS AREA, where slightly higher land apparently diverted the smoothing action of glaciers, leaving a rougher topography with many small hills and valleys that also extends S into Illinois and SW and W into Iowa and Minnesota. EAU CLAIRE, LA CROSSE, and WAUSAU are the larger communities in the region; the SAND COUNTIES lie along the E edge. In the early 19th century lead mining was important in the Driftless Area. French explorers and VOYAGEURS ventured into Wisconsin by the 1630s, and eventually learned from local inhabitants that a short portage between the Fox and Wisconsin rivers offered a route from L. Michigan to a great river, which proved to be the Mississippi. The Winnebago, Kickapoo, and other groups were first encountered here; later, pressure from the Ojibwa to the N forced Ottawas and others into the region, whose name derives from that of the river (its meaning is unclear). Green Bay and PRAIRIE DU CHIEN, at the opposite end of the Fox–Wisconsin route, were among the earliest French trading and missionary posts. Such French control as had developed before 1763 was then ceded to the British, who in turn ceded it (1783) to the new American government. Wisconsin became part of the NORTHWEST TERRITORY, although the British did not remove control fully until the War of 1812 was concluded. In the early 19th century Eastern and Border States migrants moved into the S; lead mining was important for a few decades, and then gave way generally to farming. After the Civil War, Germans and Scandinavians came in waves, providing labor for mining and for the booming lumber (and gradually more important, paper) industry, which concentrated in the Fox and Wisconsin river valleys, causing such cities as Green Bay, APPLETON, Wausau, and STEVENS POINT to flourish. Wisconsin agriculture also grew, coming to be more centered on dairy production; food processing became another important industry. In the SE, water and by now thoroughly developed railroad transport systems made Milwaukee, Racine, SHEBOYGAN, KENOSHA, and other lakefront cities prosperous, and Milwaukee grew gradually into one of America's leading heavy industrial centers; its Germans also created here a beermaking and cultural capital. Madison (SC) grew as a government and educational center, the University of Wisconsin developing into one of the most prestigious state institutions in the US; in the 20th century it has become a noted research hub also. BELOIT, Appleton, RIPON, and other cities are home to well-known small colleges. Today, Wisconsin has a balanced economy, with strong industrial, farm, forest industries, research, and tourism and recreation sectors. Visitors are attracted esp. by the Door Peninsula, the highly eroded Wisconsin DELLS and the lakes and forests of the North Woods. Except in the Milwaukee area, which has large Polish, black, and other more recently arrived communities; in Madison, with its diverse university community; and in a few other centers, most residents of the Badger State are descendants of early- and mid-19th century American, German, and Scandinavian settlers.

Wisconsin Avenue main E–W thoroughfare, 7.5 mi/12 km long, in Milwaukee, Wisconsin, between JUNEAU PARK and the Milwaukee Co. Fairgrounds in WAUWATOSA. It is the main downtown commercial strip.

Wisconsin Dells see under DELLS OF THE WISCONSIN.

Wisconsin Rapids city, pop. 18,260, seat of Wood Co., C Wisconsin, on the Wisconsin R., 40 mi/64 km SW of Wausau. It is the trade and distribution center of a cranberry producing area. Local industries include paper milling and dairy processing. Factories also produce paint, plastics, and kitchen appliances. The first wood pulp and paper mills were built here in 1837.

Wisconsin River 430 mi/692 km long, in Wisconsin. It rises at the Lac Vieux Desert in Vilas Co., just S of the Michigan border. The river flows generally S through the center of the state, passing Wausau, Stevens Point, Wisconsin Rapids, Wisconsin Dells, and Portage, where it is linked to the Fox R. by the Portage Canal. From Portage, the Wisconsin flows SW to enter the Mississippi just S of PRAIRIE DU CHIEN. The river provides power for about 50 hydroelectric plants, and a dam at Prairie du Sac creates L. Wisconsin. The DELLS OF THE

WISCONSIN, a dramatic sandstone gorge, is a popular recreational area.

Wise town, pop. 3193, seat of Wise Co., extreme SW Virginia, in the Cumberland Mts. near the Kentucky line, 12 mi/19 km NE of Big Stone Gap. It is a trade center for a bituminous coal mining and agricultural region, and the seat of Clinch Valley College of the University of Virginia (1954).

Wishram hamlet in Klickitat Co., SC Washington, on the Columbia R., 55 mi/89 km SW of Sunnyside. It was for thousands of years the home of the Wyampam Indians. Their traditional fishing grounds at Celilo Falls, 1 mi/2 km E, were covered by the backwaters of the Dallas Dam (1957). A railroad division point, Wishram is noted for its Pioneer Memorial.

Wissota, Lake in Chippewa Co., WC Wisconsin. Measuring 4 mi/6 km long and 2 mi/3 km wide, it is the largest artificial lake in Wisconsin, formed by a dam on the Chippewa R. at CHIPPEWA FALLS.

Wixom city, pop. 8550, Oakland Co., SE Michigan, 14 mi/23 km SW of Pontiac. A Ford assembly plant is situated here. Spencer Landing Field is just W of Wixom.

Woburn city, pop. 35,943, Middlesex Co., NE Massachusetts, 10 mi/16 km NNW of Boston. The Middlesex Canal (1803) spurred the city's development. Leather tanning and shoemaking were 19th-century industries in Woburn, which now manufactures pharmaceutical chemicals, photographic supplies, leather goods, gelatin, and tools, and engages in electronics research and development. The Rumford House was the birthplace (1753) of physicist Sir Benjamin Thompson, Count Rumford. Charles Goodyear first vulcanized rubber in Woburn, in 1839.

Wolcott town, pop. 13,700, New Haven Co., EC Connecticut, adjacent (NE) to Waterbury, on the Mad R. A hilly, largely rural community with many small rivers and reservoirs, it has shared in the region's industrial history, chiefly as a toolmaker. The educational reformer Bronson Alcott (1799) and clockmaker Seth Thomas (1785) were born in the town.

Wolf Point city, pop. 2880, seat of Roosevelt Co., NE Montana, on the Missouri R., 48 mi/77 km ESE of Glasgow. Settled in 1878 as a cattle town, it was named for the high hill that was a landmark for steamboat pilots. It makes dairy products, flour, and honey, and has a number of light industries. Annual events include the Wild Horse Stampede, Montana's oldest rodeo, and a large powwow held by Sioux and Assiniboine Indians, many of whom live in the city and in the FORT PECK reservation to its N.

Wolf River **1.** 60 mi/100 km long, in Mississippi and Tennessee. It rises in Benton Co., NE of Holly Springs, Mississippi, and flows WNW across the Tennessee line and into the Memphis area. Its North Fork rises WSW of Bolivar, Tennessee. Most of Memphis lies S of the Wolf, but residential Raleigh and Frayser lie N. Wolf Harbor, on the Mississippi R., has been the scene of much of the city's industrial and commercial development. In the 1880s–1910s, the Wolf was a major lumbering river. **2.** 210 mi/338 km long, rising in NE Wisconsin and flowing generally S. It passes Shawano and New London, where it receives the Embarrass R. The Wolf widens into L. Poygan below Fremont, and joins the FOX R. just beyond, at L. Butte des Morts, to enter L. Winnebago at Oshkosh. The Wolf was an important lumbering river in the late 19th century, and is considered one of the best rivers in Wisconsin for pike, pickerel, and bass fishing.

Wolf Trap Farm Park performing arts center in a 130-ac/53-ha national park in Fairfax Co., NE Virginia, just N of VIENNA and 14 mi/23 km WNW of Washington, D.C. Situated along the Washington Dulles Access Road, its Filene Center is the first such Federal facility. The Census-designated Wolf Trap area has a pop. of 13,133.

Wolfville town, pop. 3475, Kings Co., WC Nova Scotia, at the mouth of the Cornwallis R. on Minas Basin, 47 mi/76 km NW of Halifax, and just W of GRAND PRÉ. In a rich fruit-growing and dairying region, the town is an agricultural center and the seat of Acadia University (1838).

Wollaston see under QUINCY, Massachusetts.

Women's Rights National Historical Park see under SENECA FALLS, New York.

Woodall Mountain peak (806 ft/246 m) in extreme NE Mississippi, just SW of IUKA, the highest point in the state.

Woodbine see under ETOBICOKE and the BEACH (Toronto), Ontario.

Woodbridge **1.** town, pop. 7924, New Haven Co., SC Connecticut, adjacent (NW) to New Haven. Settled by 1660, it has remained agricultural, and is an affluent New Haven suburb. West Rock Ridge State Park lies E. **2.** township, pop. 93,086, Middlesex Co., NE New Jersey, adjacent (N) to Perth Amboy. Settled in 1665 by colonists from Massachusetts, it was an early industrial center, with a sawmill by 1682 and a printing press (first in the state) by 1751. The township includes the unincorporated village of Woodbridge (pop. 17,434), COLONIA, FORDS, ISELIN, and several other villages. Situated on Interstate 95, the Garden State Parkway, and other arteries, Woodbridge is now a business center, with many corporate headquarters, other office buildings, and a major retail mall. There is also a large residential component. Products manufactured here include ceramics from local clay deposits, electronic equipment, chemicals, and soft drinks. **3.** see under VAUGHAN, Ontario. **4.** unincorporated community, pop. 26,401, Prince William Co., NE Virginia, 10 mi/16 km SW of Alexandria, on Interstate 95 and the Occoquan and Potomac rivers. It is a suburb of Washington, D.C.; the Harry Diamond Laboratories, a military installation, is on the river.

Wood Buffalo National Park 17,300 sq mi/44,807 sq km, in NE Alberta and S Northwest Territories, bounded on the E by the Athabasca and Slave rivers. Canada's largest national park, it includes the former Buffalo National Park (1908). This immense subarctic wilderness, established in 1922, contains a variety of geographic regions and many lakes, including 555–sq mi/1437–sq km L. Claire, in the SE. The park protects more than 6000 wood bison and is the only nesting place for whooping cranes. Other species include plains bison, bear, moose, caribou, beaver, eagles, and a wide variety of plant life. Members of the Cree and other tribes live in the park.

Woodburn city, pop. 13,404, Marion Co., NW Oregon, 17 mi/27 km NNE of Salem. It is a processing center for local agricultural products, notably fruits and nuts. The city cans vegetables, produces fertilizer, and makes sausage and other processed meats. An Old Believer colony of Russian immigrant farmers makes its home here.

Woodbury **1.** city, pop. 20,075, Washington Co., Minnesota, a residential suburb immediately SE of St. Paul.

2. city, pop. 10,904, seat of Gloucester Co., SW New Jersey, 8 mi/13 km SW of Camden. Near the Delaware R., it was settled by the Quaker Wood family in the 1680s. In spite of Quaker attempts to keep it neutral, it became an important center during the Revolution, headquarters for both the British (1777) and Americans (1779). Woodbury is now primarily a residential suburb of Camden and Philadelphia. Located in a truck and dairy farming area, the city is also an agricultural distribution center. Manufactures include cement blocks, clothing, and electrical parts. A cultural hub, Woodbury has a symphony orchestra and various arts groups. The borough of **Woodbury Heights** (pop. 3392) adjoins (S), on the New Jersey Turnpike.

Woodbury Common see under CENTRAL VALLEY, New York.

Woodbury County 873 sq mi/2261 sq km, pop. 98,276, in WC Iowa. The Missouri and Big Sioux rivers form its W border, separating the county from South Dakota and Nebraska. The Little Sioux R. crosses the E portion. SIOUX CITY, in the NW corner, is the county seat and only urban center. The rest of the county is a wheat growing area.

Wood County 619 sq mi/1603 sq km, pop. 113,269, in NW Ohio, bounded (NW) by the Maumee R. Its seat is BOWLING GREEN. Corn, fruit, livestock, oats, poultry, and wheat are farmed here. There is manufacturing at Bowling Green and North Baltimore, as well as in the Toledo suburbs of Perrysburg and Rossford, in the N of the county. Clay and limestone are among its natural resources.

Wood Dale village, pop. 12,425, Du Page Co., NE Illinois, on Salt Creek, 20 mi/32 km NW of Chicago. A residential community, it is 3 mi/5 km W of O'Hare International Airport.

Woodhaven **1.** city, pop. 11,631, Wayne Co., SE Michigan, a residential suburb 18 mi/29 km SSW of Detroit. **2.** residential section, SC Queens, New York. It lies between Ozone Park, to the S, and Forest Park and the Interborough Parkway, to the N, just E of East New York, Brooklyn. Suburban housing development began in the area in the 1840s. By the 1860s Woodhaven boomed along with RICHMOND HILL, its E neighbor, as light manufacturing plants grew along Atlantic Avenue E from Brooklyn.

Woodinville unincorporated community, pop. 23,654, King Co., WC Washington, a growing residential suburb 13 mi/21 km NE of Seattle, 4 mi/6 km NE of L. Washington, and immediately E of Bothell, on the Sammamish R. It has long been noted as a dairy, nursery, and winery center.

Woodland city, pop. 39,802, seat of Yolo Co., NC California, 18 mi/29 km NW of Sacramento. Settled in the 1850s, it is the trade and processing center of a Sacramento Valley region producing rice, tomatoes, olives, fruit, alfalfa, and sugar beets. Plastics and mobile homes are manufactured.

Woodland Hills SW SAN FERNANDO VALLEY section of LOS ANGELES, California, 21 mi/34 km WNW of Downtown, in the N foothills of the Santa Monica Mts. It is an affluent residential area.

Woodlawn **1.** residential neighborhood on the South Side of Chicago, Illinois, just S of HYDE PARK and SW of JACKSON PARK, and 7 mi/11 km SSE of the Loop. It houses a middle- and working-class black community. **2.** unincorporated suburb of Baltimore, Maryland, pop. 32,907, in Howard Co., 7 mi/11 km NW of Downtown, at the junction of Interstate 70 and the Baltimore Beltway (I-695). It was formerly known as Powhatan, for a company that owned a mill here, and took its present name after the Woodlawn Cemetery Company bought much property in the area following a 1902 fire that destroyed the mill. Woodlawn now houses the Social Security Complex, the fifth-largest US Federal building, the administrative and record-keeping center of the Social Security system. Residential developments are extensive, and there are industrial, corporate, and retail parks. **3.** residential section, extreme NC Bronx, New York. It lies between Van Cortlandt Park (W) and the Bronx R. and Wakefield (E). Yonkers, in Westchester Co., is N. The neighborhood takes its name from **Woodlawn Cemetery** (1863), a 400-ac/162-ha burial ground to the S that contains the graves, among others, of financiers Jay Gould and F.W. Woolworth; Herman Melville; Mayor Fiorello LaGuardia; and a number of prominent musicians, including Duke Ellington and Miles Davis. During the Revolution Colonial munitions were stored in the area, which was subsequently called Washingtonville, later Wakefield.

Woodmere unincorporated village, pop. 15,578, in Hempstead town, Nassau Co., SE New York, on Long Island's South Shore, just E of John F. Kennedy International Airport. It is an almost entirely residential commuter suburb, one of the FIVE TOWNS.

Wood Mountain elevation (3325 ft/1013 m) in SW Saskatchewan, 110 mi/180 km SW of Moose Jaw. Sioux led by Sitting Bull took refuge here in 1876–80, after the LITTLE BIGHORN battle. An historic park includes a reconstructed 1876–1918 Mounted Police post.

Woodridge village, pop. 26,256, Du Page and Will counties, NE Illinois, on the East Branch of the Chicago R., 20 mi/32 km SW of Chicago. It is a residential community, largely inhabited by commuters to Chicago and nearby industrial parks. The ARGONNE NATIONAL LABORATORY is 4 mi/6 km SE.

Wood River city, pop. 11,490, Madison Co., SW Illinois, on the Mississippi R. at the Missouri border, 16 mi/26 km NE of St. Louis, and immediately S of East Alton. Lewis and Clark set out toward the Northwest from this area in May 1804. Part of the Wood River–Alton industrial complex, it was founded in 1907, when Standard Oil built a refinery here. Local manufactures include tank cars and pipeline terminals, as well as stone, clay, and glass products.

Wood River Lakes and **Wood-Tikchik State Park** see under TIKCHIK AND WOOD RIVER LAKES, Alaska.

Woods Hole village in the town of FALMOUTH, Barnstable Co., SE Massachusetts, at the SW tip of Cape Cod, 16 mi/26 km SE of New Bedford. A summer resort, it is also the home of the US Marine Biological Laboratory and a branch of the US Bureau of Fisheries. The Woods Hole Oceanographic Institution (1930) is also here.

Woods Hollow Mountains see under SANTIAGO Mts., Texas.

Woodside **1.** town, pop. 5035, San Mateo Co., NC California, an affluent residential suburb 5 mi/8 km NW of Palo Alto. It developed around the Woodside Store (1854), in a lumbering region on the E of the Santa Cruz Mts. Filoli, a 654-ac/265-ha estate with a noted house and gardens, was established here in 1916–19. **2.** residential and industrial section, NW Queens, New York. It is just NE of Sunnyside, with which it shares some characteristics, and was largely undeveloped until the subway arrived in 1918. Woodside is an area much passed through, by travelers on the Brooklyn-Queens Expressway or Long Island Rail Road; it has been home to manufacturers including the Bulova watch company. **3.** National Historic Park: see under KITCHENER, Ontario.

Woodstock **1.** town, pop. 6008, Windham Co., NE Connecticut, on the Massachusetts line, 9 mi/15 km SSE of Southbridge, Massachusetts. Settled in the 1680s, it has been primarily agricultural, with some textile manufacturing. **2.** city, pop. 14,353, seat of McHenry Co., NE Illinois, 33 mi/53 km E of Rockford and 50 mi/80 km NW of Chicago. A commercial and industrial center, it is in a dairy and farming region. Typewriters, beds, and metal products are manufactured. Founded in 1844, the city has recently become an outer suburb of the Chicago metropolitan area. **3.** town, pop. 4631, seat of Carleton Co., W New Brunswick, on the St. John R., 46 mi/74 km WNW of Fredericton and 13 mi/21 km E of Houlton, Maine. Near the upstream limit of 1780s LOYALIST settlement of the St. John Valley, it is a gateway and market town in an area producing dairy goods, apples and other fruit, lumber, and furniture. **4.** town, pop. 6290, Ulster Co., SE New York, in the foothills of the Catskill Mts., 10 mi/16 km NW of Kingston. It has been an artists' colony and exurb since the early 20th century, and has many galleries and boutiques. It is probably best known for the July 1969 rock concert, planned for Woodstock, that actually took place some 45 mi/72 km SW, at BETHEL. **5.** city, pop. 30,075, seat of Oxford Co., S Ontario, on the Thames R., 27 mi/43 km ENE of London. Founded in 1834, in a dairying and livestock raising region, it has since the 1850s, when the railroad arrived, had diverse industries. Its manufactures include furniture, wood and wire products, textiles, pianos, organs, stoves, auto parts, and garden tools. **6.** town, pop. 3212, including Woodstock, South Woodstock, West Woodstock, and Taftsville villages, on the Ottauquechee R. in Windsor Co., EC Vermont, 23 mi/37 km E of Rutland. In a dairy area, the town is a year-round resort and sports center, with ski areas and a noted village common and period architecture. The Stephen Daye Press and a medical college were both here at one time. **7.** town, pop. 3182, seat of Shenandoah Co., NW Virginia, 30 mi/48 km SW of Winchester, near the North Fork of the Shenandoah R. A trade center for an agricultural and lumbering region, it also has some manufacturing. Settled in the 1750s by Germans from Pennsylvania, it was at first called Müllerstadt. MASSANUTTEN Mt. stands above the town (E).

Woodville town, pop. 1393, seat of Wilkinson Co., SW Mississippi, 50 mi/80 km WSW of McComb and 7 mi/11 km N of the Louisiana line, on Highway 61. Settled in the 18th century, it has a number of antebellum homes and churches. Composer William Grant Still (1895) and jazz giant Lester Young (1909) were both born here. One mi/2 km E is Rosemont Plantation (1810), the boyhood home of Jefferson Davis.

Woodward city, pop. 12,340, seat of Woodward Co., W Oklahoma, 85 mi/137 km W of Enid and just E of the PANHANDLE. It was settled in 1893 when the CHEROKEE STRIP was opened for homesteading. On a cattle trail from Texas to Kansas, it became a trade and banking center. The city now markets and processes livestock, grain, and sorghums and engages in light industry. One of the largest Federal agricultural experiment stations is here.

Woodward Avenue major commercial thoroughfare, 27 mi/43 km long, between Detroit and Pontiac, Michigan. Following a Saginaw trail, it was the main radial artery NW from downtown Detroit, and served as the spine for many of Detroit's early commuter suburbs, including Highland Park, Ferndale, Royal Oak, Birmingham, and Bloomfield Hills. Within Detroit, the street leads from Jefferson Ave. and the Civic Center through GRAND CIRCUS PARK, NEW CENTER, and PALMER PARK.

Woonsocket city, pop. 43,877, Providence Co., N Rhode Island, 13 mi/21 km NNW of Providence, on the Blackstone R. and the Massachusetts border. It had a 1666 sawmill, a 1720 foundry, and an 1810 cotton mill, and in 1840 began woolen manufacturing. It is still primarily a woolen and worsted center, with a large French-Canadian population. The city has various other manufactures.

Wooster city, pop. 22,191, Wayne Co., NC Ohio, 30 mi/48 km SW of Akron. Founded in 1808, it was named for the Revolutionary general David Wooster. Currently, it is a trading center for the surrounding agricultural and oil drilling region. Manufactures include rubber and plastic products, paints, truck bodies, food products, pumps, and tools. The College of Wooster (1866) is here. The large Agricultural Research and Development Center, which is run by Ohio State University and includes the Secrest Arboretum, is just S of the city.

Wopsononock Mountain see under ALTOONA, Pennsylvania.

Worcester city, pop. 169,759, seat of Worcester Co., C Massachusetts, situated on and among hills, on the Blackstone R., 40 mi/64 km W of Boston. L. QUINSIGAMOND forms much of its E boundary. It is the second-largest city in Massachusetts and in New England, a trade, service, retail, and educational center for the state's midsection. Worcester has a diversified economy; sectors include manufacturing, insurance, banking, education, and research. Its institutions include Clark University (1887), the College of the Holy Cross (1843), Worcester Polytechnic Institute (1865), Worcester State College (1874), Assumption College (1904), and the University of Massachusetts Medical School. The first permanent community was begun in 1713. Textile manufacture began before the end of the 18th century. The city prospered with the development of the Blackstone Canal (1828), and, shortly thereafter, with rail connections to other cities, and became a major manufacturing center. Wire and paper products, wheels, railway cars, machinery, and other manufactures boomed. In the 20th century Worcester's industrial and technological base diversified; in the 1990s, in response to the decline of the state's heavy manufacturing base, the city sought to expand its role in such businesses as biotechnology.

Worcester County 1513 sq mi/3919 sq km, pop. 709,705, in C Massachusetts. Its seat is Worcester. Running N to S through the center of the state, it is the largest Massachusetts county. In the N is open countryside; the QUABBIN RESERVOIR lies W. The city of Worcester is a manufacturing and commercial center. Much of the county is rural, hilly, and agricultural, with mill towns situated along small but powerful rivers. In the E, it lies in the orbit of Route 495, Boston's outer beltway; the industry and commerce attracted by the highway, opened from the 1960s, has begun to alter lifestyles.

World Financial Center see under BATTERY PARK CITY, New York.

World Trade Center building complex, lower Manhattan, New York City. Its boxlike 110-story twin towers dominate New York's skyline. On completion in 1973, the N tower, at 1368 ft/417 m, was the world's tallest occupied building, but was soon surpassed by Chicago's SEARS TOWER.

Worth village, pop. 11,208, Cook Co., NE Illinois, on the

Calumet Sag Channel, a residential suburb 14 mi/23 km SW of Chicago.

Worthington **1.** city, pop. 9977, seat of Nobles Co., SW Minnesota, on Okebena L., 9 mi/14 km N of the Iowa border. It is the economic hub for surrounding farms, processing poultry (especially turkeys) and producing farm sprayers, luggage carriers, ice cream, concrete products, and alfalfa meal. Situated in a lake region, the city is also a summer tourist center. It was founded as a temperance colony in 1871. **2.** city, pop. 14,882, Franklin Co., C Ohio, on the Olentangy R., 3 mi/5 km N of Columbus, of which it is a suburb. There is some industry on the fringes of the city, but most residents commute to jobs in Columbus. Worthington was founded (1803) by settlers from Connecticut, whose New England background can still be discerned in its village green, churches, and other buildings.

Wounded Knee unincorporated village, pop. 18, Shannon Co., SW South Dakota, on Wounded Knee Creek, in the PINE RIDGE Indian Reservation, 12 mi/19 km NE of the village of Pine Ridge. A National Historic Site, it was the scene of an 1890 massacre of Sioux by US troops, the last major engagement of the Indian Wars. On Dec. 15, 1890, Sitting Bull was killed at the STANDING ROCK INDIAN RESERVATION by soldiers attempting to take him into custody. Several hundred Sioux, adherents of the Ghost Dance religion, left the reservation seeking refuge in the BADLANDS. They surrendered to government troops and were held overnight in an encampment at Wounded Knee Creek. On Dec. 29, an attempt was made to disarm them and a scuffle broke out. At least 153 Indian men, women, and children and approximately 30 US soldiers died. In time, Wounded Knee became associated with injustices suffered by Indians at the hands of the US government. In 1973, 200 members of the American Indian Movement occupied the village of Wounded Knee for 73 days, demanding a government response to Indian grievances. Two Indians were killed and a government agent was severely injured in exchanges of gunfire. Almost demolished in the siege, the village was finally peacefully evacuated.

WPA Works Progress Administration, massive New Deal agency (1935–43) responsible, among other things, for the creation or redevelopment of numerous urban parks, landscapes, and public buildings, as well as the construction of bridges and other elements of the INFRASTRUCTURE. After 1939 its name was officially the Work Projects Administration.

Wrangell city, pop. 2479, on the N end of Wrangell I. in the ALEXANDER ARCHIPELAGO, 80 mi/130 km NNW of Ketchikan, in SE Alaska. At the center of Alaska's logging activity, it also has fishing and canning industries, and was a supply point for miners heading up the Stikine R. during the Yukon gold rush of the 1890s. It was established in 1835 by Russian fur traders as a fortification against the Hudson's Bay Company, which succeeded, however, in occupying it in 1840. The city and island were named for Baron F. P. Wrangel, explorer and the first governor (1829–35) of RUSSIAN AMERICA. Shakes I., in Wrangell Harbor, is noted for its Tlingit totem poles.

Wrangell, Cape see under ATTU I., Alaska.

Wrangell Mountains range extending for c.100 mi/160 km in S Alaska, from the Chitina R. (S) and St. Elias Mts. (SE) to the Copper R. (NW), reaching 16,390 ft/4996 m at Mt. Blackburn. It includes the volcanic cones of Mt. Sanford (16,237 ft/4949 m) and **Mt. Wrangell** (14,163 ft/4317 m). The range, with its C covered by snowfields, also contains copper deposits. It lies within the Wrangell–St. Elias National Park.

Wrangell–St. Elias National Park and Preserve 13.19 million ac/5.34 million ha (20,607 sq mi/53,372 sq km), in SE Alaska, where the WRANGELL, ST. ELIAS, and CHUGACH mountains meet, on the border with KLUANE NATIONAL PARK, in the Yukon Territory. The two parks together contain the largest collection of glaciers and high peaks on the continent. The Malaspina Glacier, covering 1500 sq mi/3885 sq km, is the largest in North America. The park, with headquarters in Glennallen, is the largest in the US national park system. The largely remote area has been mined for gold and copper.

Wright unincorporated community, pop. 18,945, Okaloosa Co., NW Florida, in the PANHANDLE, 2 mi/3 km N of Fort Walton Beach. It is essentially a residential suburb, housing many military families from neighboring Eglin Air Force Base.

Wright Brothers National Memorial see under KITTY HAWK, North Carolina.

Wright City commercial city, pop. 1250, Warren Co., EC Missouri, 48 mi/77 km WNW of downtown St. Louis. It was the birthplace of theologian Reinhold Niebuhr (1892–1971).

Wright-Patterson Air Force Base see under DAYTON and FAIRBORN, Ohio.

Wrightsboro see under WILMINGTON, North Carolina.

Wrightstown see under FORT DIX, New Jersey.

Wrigley Field baseball stadium on the North Side of Chicago, Illinois, at Clark and Addison streets, 5 mi/8 km N of the Loop. Built in 1914 and home of the Cubs, it is noted for its ivy-covered brick walls and because it did not have lights for night games until 1988.

Wupatki National Monument see under PAINTED DESERT, Arizona.

Wurlitzer Park Village see under NORTH TONAWANDA, New York.

Wurtsmith Air Force Base 2 mi/3 km NW of Oscoda, in Iosco Co., EC Michigan, 160 mi/260 km NNW of Detroit, and just W of L. Huron. During the Cold War it was an important base for B-52 bombers, and had a 1990 pop. of 5080. Oscoda, a service community and beach resort (unincorporated; pop. 1061), is within Oscoda township (pop. 11,958).

Wyandanch unincorporated village, pop. 8950, in Babylon town, Suffolk Co., SE New York, in C Long Island, just SE of Deer Park. It is almost entirely residential.

Wyandotte city, pop. 30,938, Wayne Co., SE Michigan, on the Detroit R., 11 mi/18 km S of Detroit. The area was ceded to a white settler by the Wyandot Indians in 1818. The land was purchased by an iron company in 1854, a community was formed, and smelting soon began. The first commercial Bessemer steel was produced from a blast furnace constructed here in 1864, and Wyandotte became an early steel center. From 1872 to 1920, it was a major Great Lakes shipbuilding hub. Possessing large underlying salt deposits, it also became known for its chemical products. Today, the city's manufactures include brass and iron goods, soda ash, chlorine gas, dry ice, plastic, paint, auto parts, dairy products, toys and novelties, and industrial diamonds.

Wyandotte Cave limestone complex in Crawford Co., extreme S Indiana, 25 mi/40 km W of New Albany and just N of the Ohio R. Used by prehistoric tribes, it was first seen by whites in 1798. It has at least 23 mi/37 km of passages on several levels, and encloses 135-ft/41-m Monumental Mt., perhaps the world's largest underground "mountain."

Wyandotte County 149 sq mi/386 sq km, pop. 161,993, in NE Kansas, bounded by the Missouri R. (N and E) and the Kansas R. (S). Its seat, KANSAS CITY, occupies about half the county, and all of its NE. The city's industries and activities dictate much of the economic, political, social, and cultural life of the county. The balance of the county is engaged in diversified farming and dairying, and there are some natural gas fields.

Wyckoff township, pop. 15,372, Bergen Co., NE New Jersey, 7 mi/11 km N of Paterson. On Lenni Lenape (Delaware) lands, it was settled by Dutch farmers (1720), and many Dutch structures remain. Today it is primarily a New York–area residential suburb.

Wylie, Lake see under CATAWBA R., North Carolina and South Carolina.

Wylie Mountains see under VAN HORN Mts., Texas.

Wyncote unincorporated village, pop. 2960, in CHELTENHAM township, Montgomery Co., SE Pennsylvania. An affluent residential suburb just N of Philadelphia, it has some light manufacturing.

Wynne city, pop. 8187, seat of Cross Co., NE Arkansas, on the W slope of CROWLEY'S RIDGE, 43 mi/69 km W of Memphis, Tennessee. Founded in 1863 in the only hilly area of Arkansas's fertile DELTA, it is an agricultural trade center, with cotton and food processing industries, and ships such products as peaches and cucumbers.

Wyodak unincorporated community, Campbell Co., NE Wyoming, 9 mi/14 km E of Gillette. Situated near Donkey Creek, it is the site of one of the world's largest coal strip mines, opened in 1924.

Wyoming state of the W US, one of the MOUNTAIN STATES; 1990 pop. 453,588 (96.6% of 1980; rank: 50th); area 97,818 sq mi/253,349 sq km (rank: 10th); admitted to Union 1890 (44th). Capital and most populous city: CHEYENNE. Other leading cities: CASPER, LARAMIE. Wyoming is bordered E by Nebraska (S) and South Dakota (N); N by Montana; W by (N–S) Montana, Idaho, and Utah; and S by Utah (W) and Colorado (E). In the E the state lies in the GREAT PLAINS, with part of the Missouri Plateau on the N, drained to the N by the POWDER R. and to the NE by the BELLE FOURCHE R., which enters the BLACK HILLS in the NE corner. In SE Wyoming, the Southern ROCKY Mt. system, in the form of the LARAMIE and MEDICINE BOW mountains, ends S of the NORTH PLATTE R., which loops around it and heads E toward Nebraska. In the NW of the state are the Middle Rocky Mts., including the BIGHORN Mts. (NC) and the ABSAROKA and WIND RIVER ranges, which extend NW–SE toward C Wyoming. GANNETT PEAK, in the Wind Rivers, is the highest (13,804 ft/4210 m) point in the state, and Grand Teton, in the nearby Teton Range, is only slightly less high. At the S tip of the Wind Rivers is historic SOUTH PASS, through which westward migrants breached the Rockies. South of South Pass and the SWEETWATER R. lie a collection of basins called collectively the Wyoming Basin. Among these is the GREAT DIVIDE Basin, the only area in North America enclosed by the CONTINENTAL DIVIDE, and known in its S part as the RED DESERT. In Wyoming's NW corner are the adjoining GRAND TETON and YELLOWSTONE national parks, containing some of America's most extreme terrain. The SNAKE R., a headwater of the Pacific-bound Columbia R. system, flows S from Yellowstone through Grand Teton, carving out the well-known valley of JACKSON HOLE. The Yellowstone and BIGHORN rivers both flow N from NW Wyoming into Montana, and into the Missouri-Mississippi river system. In SW Wyoming, the GREEN R. flows S from the Wyoming Basin, into the Gulf of California–bound Colorado R. system. Wyoming was home to plains and mountain peoples including the Crow, Cheyenne, Sioux, Arapaho, and Shoshone, and was almost unvisited by whites until fur trappers began to work here in the early 19th century. Knowledge of the area accrued through their travels and various exploratory expeditions, and the North Platte R.–Sweetwater R.–South Pass route gradually became the main corridor along which the OVERLAND, OREGON, MORMON, and subsidiary trails crossed through the Rockies. FORT LARAMIE, Independence Rock, and FORT BRIDGER are among the landmarks of the route. The BOZEMAN TRAIL later cut NW from near Fort Fetterman to the SHERIDAN area, taking gold seekers to Montana through Sioux territory and occasioning much conflict. In the late 1860s the UNION PACIFIC RAILROAD cut across the territory's S, through Casper, Laramie, and GREEN RIVER. Increasing familiarity with the area, the HOMESTEAD Act (1862), and promotion by the railroads encouraged settlement by ranchers in the N and E, and grazing became central to white expansion; in addition to conflict with the Sioux and other tribes, open-range ranchers and fencebuilding "nesters" faced each other in the 1890s Johnson Co. "War." The archetypal Wild WEST region, Wyoming was the scene of much cattle rustling and other outlaw activity, recalled today by the names of SUNDANCE and the HOLE-IN-THE-WALL. Oil was first drilled here in the 1880s, and has been critical to the economy. The TEAPOT DOME reserve was the crux of a 1920s government scandal. Casper, GILLETTE, SINCLAIR, ROCK SPRINGS, EVANSTON, and many other communities are deeply involved in the energy business, which in Wyoming now also includes large-scale coal mining and extraction of natural gas, uranium, sodium carbonates, and other minerals and irons. While Cheyenne, as a government center, and Laramie, seat of the University of Wyoming, have more stable economic bases, other Wyoming cities have gained and lost pop., built quickly and declined almost as quickly, depending on the energy market. Cattle and sheep ranching and limited dry and irrigated farming remain the primary activities across wide expanses of Wyoming, which remains largely "open space" (with now even fewer people than Alaska). Almost half the land area is Federally controlled, and local politicians participated in the 1980s SAGEBRUSH "Rebellion." The WIND RIVER INDIAN RESERVATION is all that remains of former tribal domains. Tourism, dude ranches, mountain recreation, and vacation and second homes (esp. in the Jackson Hole area) bring money into the state. Wyoming's name (Algonquian for "big flats") was bestowed on it in the 1860s, despite some objections that, borrowed from the valley in Pennsylvania, it was inappropriate here.

Wyoming **1.** city, pop. 63,891, Kent Co., SW Michigan, on the Grand R., adjacent (SW) to Grand Rapids. This residential and industrial suburb of Grand Rapids began with an 1835 land grant. Metals, auto bodies, and household appliances are made here. **2.** city, pop. 8128, Hamilton Co., extreme SW Ohio, just N of Cincinnati, of which it is a suburb.

Wyoming County 595 sq mi/1541 sq km, pop. 42,507, in W

New York. Its seat is Warsaw. This rural county engages in dairying and other farming, producing vegetables, fruit, and grain. Letchworth State Park is in the E.

Wyoming Valley region running some 20 mi/32 km NE–SW in Luzerne Co., NE Pennsylvania, along the Susquehanna R. Part of the Pennsylvania ANTHRACITE BELT, it became in the 1760s the crux of a dispute between the Connecticut-based Susquehanna Company and Pennsylvanians. Following the first "Pennamite War" in 1769–71, the Connecticut group established the township of Westmoreland (1774), which included WILKES-BARRE and 16 other small settlements. In 1778, during the Revolution, Tories and Indians massacred a number of settlers. In 1782, the Continental Congress ruled for Pennsylvania in the dispute, but Connecticut pioneers refused to leave, leading to the second (1784) Pennamite War. Final resolution did not occur until 1799. Besides Wilkes-Barre, Wyoming Valley settlements include Exeter, Pittston, Kingston, and Nanticoke, as well as the boroughs of **Wyoming** (pop. 3255) and **West Wyoming** (pop. 3117). The Algonquian name, meaning "big flats," was adopted in 1868 for the territory that became the state of Wyoming.

Wyomissing see under READING, Pennsylvania.

Wytheville town, pop. 8038, seat of Wythe Co., SW Virginia, in the Great Appalachian Valley, 33 mi/53 km SW of Radford. Founded in 1792, it had lead and salt mines fought over by Union and Confederate forces in July 1863. It is now a trade and vacation center for the area. The WILDERNESS ROAD passed through the town. Wytheville Community College (1962) is here.

XYZ

Xenia city, pop. 24,664, seat of Greene Co., SW Ohio, 15 mi/24 km SE of Dayton. It is a commercial center for the surrounding area, one of Ohio's foremost agricultural regions, where dairy cattle and other livestock, fruit, grains, and some tobacco are raised. Xenia's manufactures include rope and twine, furniture, metal castings, synthetic rubber goods, plastics, paints, and foodstuffs. Founded on the site of a large Shawnee settlement in 1803, the city took its name from the Greek word for hospitality. In the early 19th century, pioneer industries including flour- and sawmills flourished. The coming of the railroad (1843) accelerated the pace of industrialization. Much of Xenia's business district was rebuilt after a tornado destroyed about half of the city in 1974.

Yaddo see under SARATOGA SPRINGS, New York.

Yadkin River 200 mi/320 km long, in WC North Carolina. It is formed by headwaters in the Blue Ridge Mts., NNW of Lenoir, and flows SE, then NE. It is dammed 4 mi/6 km W of Wilkesboro to form the W. Kerr Scott Reservoir, then continues ENE through Elkin and swings SE to the W of Winston-Salem. Winding S, it is joined N of Salisbury by the **South Yadkin** R., which flows E from Iredell Co. On the E side of Salisbury, it flows through 15 mi/24 km–long High Rock L., formed by a dam at High Rock Mt. Ten mi/16 km farther SE, it enters dam-created Badin L., then (3 mi/5 km SE of the Badin Dam) joins the Uwharrie R. to form the PEE DEE R.

Yakima city, pop. 54,827, seat of Yakima Co., SC Washington, on the Yakima R., in the foothills of the Cascade Mts., 90 mi/145 km SE of Tacoma. Originally a rail depot and cattle shipping point, it emerged as an important processing center for the fruit, hops, and other products of the irrigated farms around it. The region is also noted for its wineries, and Yakima houses the oldest brewery in the Northwest. Also in the city is a large forest products manufacturing complex. Yakima Valley College was established here in 1928. The city hosts the annual Central Washington State Fair. The huge YAKIMA INDIAN RESERVATION lies 5 mi/8 km S, and Yakima serves as the E gateway to Mount Rainier National Park.

Yakima Indian Reservation 2104 sq mi/5450 sq km, pop. 27,668, in SC Washington, on the E of the Cascade Range, S of Yakima and the Yakima R. Sahaptin tribes were settled here in 1859, after disputes over an 1855 treaty had led to the three-year Yakima War. Fort Simcoe (1856) was established to restore US control in the area. TOPPENISH is the reservation's business center; forest products are important to the area economy.

Yakima River 210 mi/340 km long, in SC Washington, rising in the CASCADE RANGE near Snoqualmie Pass, and flowing generally SE. It passes through Cle Elum, ELLENSBURG, and Yakima, joining the Columbia R. just below the city of Richland. The Yakima and its tributaries supply water for a vast area of orchards and farmland, through 2000 mi/3200 km of irrigation canals. The Yakima Valley is a major producer of apples, hops, mint, and livestock.

Yale locality in S British Columbia, at the head of navigation on the FRASER R., 80 mi/130 km ENE of Vancouver. It was an 1840s fur trading post from which, in the 1850s–60s gold rush, the Cariboo Road, to the BARKERVILLE gold mines, began. HOPE is 17 mi/27 km S.

Yalobusha River 165 mi/266 km long, in NC Mississippi. It rises in Chickasaw Co., and flows generally W through Grenada L. (impounded by a dam in 1947) to GRENADA, then turns SE to join the TALLAHATCHIE R. to form the YAZOO R., just N of Greenwood.

Yamacraw also, **Yamekraw** district just NNW of downtown SAVANNAH, Georgia, noted in the late 19th and early 20th century for the life of its black community, celebrated by the composer James P. Johnson and others. It took its name from the local tribe who negotiated the 1730s settlement of Savannah with James Oglethorpe.

Yamhill Historic District historic commercial neighborhood in Southwest PORTLAND, Oregon, on the Willamette R., in Downtown. Centered around a rejuvenated marketplace, it adjoins Waterfront Park.

Yampa River 250 mi/400 km long, in NW Colorado. It rises S of STEAMBOAT SPRINGS, turns W at the city, and flows W across the Wyoming Basin to the DINOSAUR NATIONAL MONUMENT, where it joins the GREEN R. The Yampa is popular for fishing and rafting.

Yankee Rowe nuclear power plant: see under ROWE, Massachusetts.

Yankee Stadium on the Harlem R. at East 161st St., the Bronx, New York. It is the home of the New York Yankees (baseball). Completed in 1923, it was called the "House that Ruth Built" because of Babe Ruth's importance to the franchise. Yankee Stadium was remodeled in the 1970s, reducing its seating capacity from about 75,000 to about 55,000.

Yankton city, pop. 12,703, seat of Yankton Co., SE South Dakota, on the Missouri R. and the Nebraska line, 55 mi/89 km SW of Sioux Falls. A trading, food processing, and shipping center for an area where grain, livestock, and dairy items are produced, it has grain elevators, poultry hatcheries, and creameries. Its manufactures include cement products, trailers, elevators, aircraft and electronic components, crates, brick, and sheet metal products. Yankton was settled in 1858 as a fur trading post. After the announcement of plans to confine the Sioux on reservations, it was the site of an Indian uprising (1861) and of a government fort (1862). In 1861–83 Yankton was the Dakota territorial capital. The old capitol has been preserved. It is the seat of Yankton College (1881) and Mount Marty College (1922). Lewis and Clark L., 4 mi/6 km to the W, is a popular recreational area.

Yaohan Plaza see under EDGEWATER, New Jersey.

Yaphank unincorporated village, pop. 4637, in Brookhaven town, Suffolk Co., SE New York, 7 mi/11 km NE of Patchogue. It is primarily residential. Camp Upton was an army induction center in World Wars I and II; the community lent its name to the 1918 Irving Berlin army musical *Yip, Yip, Yaphank*.

Yardley borough, pop. 2288, Bucks Co., SE Pennsylvania, on the Delaware R., 5 mi/8 km NW of Trenton, New Jersey. It produces chemicals and textiles; there is truck farming in the area.

Yardville see under HAMILTON, New Jersey.

Yarmouth **1.** town, pop. 21,174, Barnstable Co., SE Massachusetts, on Cape Cod, 4 mi/7 km E of Barnstable. It is a summer resort community situated on Cape Cod Bay (N) and Nantucket Sound (S). Cranberries are cultivated. In the 19th century, Yarmouth was an important fishing and shipping port. **2.** town, pop. 7781, seat of Yarmouth Co. (pop. 27,891), extreme SW Nova Scotia, at the entrance to the Bay of FUNDY, 135 mi/217 km WSW of Halifax. A late-19th-century wooden ship building center, it developed in the 1760s, when New Englanders settled where Micmac and Acadians had lived earlier. Today it is a port and fishing and resort center, with ferries to Maine ports, and a number of agricultural processing and other light industries.

Yauco unincorporated community (ZONA URBANA), pop. 18,158, Yauco Municipio (pop. 42,058), SW Puerto Rico, 15 mi/24 km WNW of Ponce, on the Yauco R. A hilly tobacco and sugarcane producing community, with some light manufactures, it has been widely known since the 19th century for its coffee, which produced a number of local fortunes.

Yazoo City city, pop. 12,427, seat of Yazoo Co., WC Mississippi, on the Yazoo R., 38 mi/61 km NNW of Jackson. Founded in 1824, and the site of a Confederate navy yard during the Civil War, it saw several skirmishes, and was partially burned in 1864. Almost completely destroyed by fire in 1904, it was rebuilt. An oil refinery went into operation after the state's first oil well began production nearby in 1939. Yazoo City is a trade center for cattle, soybean, corn, and cotton producers. Its industries make chemicals, fertilizer, machinery, and textiles.

Yazoo River 188 mi/303 km long, in WC Mississippi. It is formed by the confluence of the TALLAHATCHIE and YALOBUSHA rivers, just N of Greenwood, and flows SSW through the Mississippi Alluvial Plain to join the Mississippi R. at Vicksburg. It is the E limit of Mississippi's DELTA, which extends from Memphis, Tennessee (N), to Vicksburg, and is also known as the **Yazoo Delta** or **Yazoo Basin.** The Yazoo's valley is a center of cotton production. During the Civil War control of the river was critical in the Vicksburg Campaign. Chief cities along it are Greenwood and Yazoo City. Its largest tributary is the SUNFLOWER R., which joins it 26 mi/42 km NNE of Vicksburg after flowing S through the Delta.

Ybor City residential and commercial neighborhood occupying about 2 sq mi/5 sq km in downtown TAMPA, Florida. It is the center of Tampa's large Cuban community, and has many Latin-style open-air markets and restaurants. Cigarmaking was introduced to Tampa in 1886 by Vincente M. Ybor, for whom the quarter is named. The art of creating handmade cigars is still practiced here in a number of factories. The Ybor City State Museum traces the industry's history. Preservation Park contains a restored "shotgun shack" (1895) typical of homes of early cigar workers. The area also has a substantial Italian population.

Yeadon borough, pop. 11,980, Delaware Co., SE Pennsylvania, a residential suburb 6 mi/10 km SW of Philadelphia.

Yellow Brick Road see under LIBERAL, Kansas.

Yellow Dog railroad: see under MOORHEAD, Mississippi.

Yellowhead Pass at 3760 ft/1146 m, on the Continental Divide, in the Rocky Mts., between Alberta's Jasper National Park (E) and British Columbia's Robson Provincial Park (W), near the headwaters of the FRASER R. Used by Hudson's Bay Company traders in the 1820s as Leather Pass, it was later named for a blond Iroquois trapper, Tête Jaune, who stored goods just W at Tête Jaune Cache, British Columbia. Although the CANADIAN PACIFIC RAILWAY chose (1881) KICKING HORSE PASS, farther S, the Grand Trunk Pacific and CANADIAN NATIONAL railways later came through here; today a highway does also. The name **Yellowhead Highway** has been given to two routes: one is Highway 5, approaching the pass from KAMLOOPS, to the SSW. The other is Highway 16, from W of Winnipeg, Manitoba, which crosses C Saskatchewan and C Alberta, by way of Edmonton, and after traversing the pass proceeds NW through Prince George, British Columbia, terminating on the Pacific at PRINCE RUPERT.

Yellowknife city and territorial capital, pop. 15,179, Fort Smith Region, SW Northwest Territories, on the N arm of GREAT SLAVE L., at the mouth of the Yellowknife R., 170 mi/275 km N of the Alberta border. The only city in the Territories, and home to 26% of their pop., it is a gold mining and government, trade, and tourist center. Although there was a NORTH WEST COMPANY fur post here by the 1790s, the community really began with a 1930s gold rush, and has two operating mines. It was named, however, for the copper implements carried by the local Yellowknife (a DENE group). It now has a range of facilities and events drawing summer visitors, and has been the territorial capital since 1967.

Yellow Springs village, pop. 3972, Greene Co., SW Ohio, 8 mi/13 km SSW of Springfield. Founded in 1804 and named for the neighboring iron springs, it is best known as the seat of Antioch College (1852). Horace Mann, the first president of this progressive institution, is buried on the grounds. There is diversified agriculture in the area, and some light industry in the village. John Bryan State Park is 2 mi/3 km SE, on the Little Miami R.

Yellowstone County 2624 sq mi/6796 sq km, pop. 113,419, in S Montana, drained by the Yellowstone R. Its seat is BILLINGS. It is a ranching and farming area, with manufacturing at Billings. The county includes part of the Crow Indian Reservation.

Yellowstone Lake 137 sq mi/355 sq km and 20 mi/32 km long, in Yellowstone National Park, Teton Co., NW Wyoming. At an elevation of 7731 ft/2358 m, it is the largest body of water in the US at such an altitude and the largest of the park's lakes. It is fed and drained by the Yellowstone R., which flows through it S to N. Noted for trout fishing, it is also a refuge for rare species of waterfowl including trumpeter swans.

Yellowstone National Park 2.22 million ac/900,000 ha (3468 sq mi/8983 sq km), in the NW corner of Wyoming, extending into Montana and Idaho. Occupying a series of high plateaus, it has the world's largest collection of thermal features, over 10,000 in all, including some 300 GEYSERS and numerous FUMAROLES, hot springs, and bubbling mud (or "paint") pots. The most famous feature is the Old Faithful geyser, which now discharges every 75–90 minutes. The Snake R. runs S from the park, into GRAND TETON NATIONAL PARK. The Yellowstone R. runs N, through Yellowstone L. and the Grand Canyon of the Yellowstone, into Montana. The oldest US national park, Yellowstone was established in 1872 (YOSEMITE NATIONAL PARK was established earlier, but as a state park); an 1871 photographic expedition and promotional efforts by the Northern Pacific Railroad were among forces leading to its creation. The area's Sheepeater (Shoshonean) inhabitants had departed a few years earlier. The park has boardwalks, horse trails, and roads, and draws 2.5 million visitors yearly; commercialization and the pressure of visitors and nearby residential growth are causes of concern today, as is the proper way of managing the park's famous wildlife, including grizzly bears, elk, and pronghorn antelope.

Yellowstone River 671 mi/1080 km long, in NW Wyoming, S Montana, and W North Dakota. It rises just SE of Yellowstone National Park, and flows NW into the park, through Yellowstone L. and over Yellowstone Falls. Leaving the park's NW, it flows NW into Montana, then NNE to LIVINGSTON, where it turns and begins a generally ENE course across S Montana. Southwest of BILLINGS, it is joined by its Clark's Fork, from the SW, and widens; POMPEY'S PILLAR, NE of Billings, was the head of 19th-century steamboat traffic up the Yellowstone. Continuing ENE, it is joined from the S by the BIGHORN and ROSEBUD rivers, then at MILES CITY by the Tongue R., and near Terry by the POWDER R., all from the S. After passing Glendive, it joins the Missouri R. at Fort Union, on the Montanta–North Dakota line. The Yellowstone is the longest undammed river in the Lower 48. In its upper reaches it is famed for its scenery, its currents, and its trout fishing. In its lower E half it passes through dry ranching country, and widens into a relatively placid prairie watercourse. In the 19th century it was used by explorers, trappers, prospectors, and military expeditions. Today it is a recreational magnet, and in the E an irrigation source for ranchers and farmers.

Yellowtail Dam and Reservoir see under BIGHORN R., Montana and Wyoming.

Yellow Tavern battle site in Henrico Co., SE Virginia, 6 mi/10 km N of the center of RICHMOND. On May 11, 1864, Confederate troops under J.E.B. Stuart here resisted an assault by the more numerous Union troops of Philip Sheridan. Stuart died the next day from a wound. The site is along US 1 just W of the suburb of Chamberlayne.

Yemassee resort and agricultural town, pop. 728, Hampton and Beaufort counties, SW South Carolina, 20 mi/32 km NW of Beaufort, named for the Yamasee, who lived in the area 1687–1715, during a period of strife with settlers, before returning to their Florida homeland.

Yerba Buena Island 300 ac/122 ha, in San Francisco Bay, California, between San Francisco (of which it is a part) and Oakland, connected by a causeway to TREASURE I. (N). A longtime Indian fishing base, later called Wood or Goat I., it has been used by the military or Coast Guard since the 1860s. In the 1930s it became the midpoint of the SAN FRANCISCO–OAKLAND BAY BRIDGE, which tunnels through it. The name ("good herb," for wild mint) was also given (in 1825) to William Richardson's **Yerba Buena,** the settlement (on Yerba Buena Cove) in today's FINANCIAL DISTRICT that grew into the modern city.

Yerkes Observatory see under WILLIAMS BAY, Wisconsin.

Yockanookany River 65 mi/105 km long, in C Mississippi. It rises near Ackerman, in Choctaw Co., and flows SW, closely paralleling the NATCHEZ TRACE, to the PEARL R., 10 mi/16 km WSW of Carthage.

Yoho National Park 507 sq mi/1313 sq km, in SE British Columbia, in the Rocky Mts., just W of the Continental Divide, adjacent to Kootenay National Park (SE) and Alberta's Banff National Park (E). Established in 1886, it is an area of towering peaks, including Mt. Gordon and Mt. Stephen; valleys and passes, such as KICKING HORSE and Vermilion; the Wapta Icefield; several lakes, including O'Hara and Emerald; and waterfalls, most notably Takakkaw (1260 ft/384 m). The Burgess Shale, one of the world's most important fossil sources, is here. The CANADIAN PACIFIC RAILWAY, with its Spiral Tunnels, and the TRANS-CANADA HIGHWAY traverse the park.

Yoknapatawpha County fictional locale in NC Mississippi, the setting for much of William Faulkner's writing. Faulkner's county seat, Jefferson, is identifiable in some ways with OXFORD, where the writer lived, and Yoknapatawpha with LAFAYETTE Co.

Yolla Bolly Mountains also, **Yallo Bally** S subrange of the KLAMATH Mts., WSW of RED BLUFF, in NW California. The rounded, heavily forested mountains take their name from a Wintu term meaning "high snow-covered peaks"; elevations range from 800 ft/244 m to over 8000 ft/2440 m. Lightly visited, the area contains much wildlife, including wolverines, mountain lions, and falcons; "Bigfoot" has been sighted. Logging, grazing, and hiking are important. The **Yolla Bolly–Middle Eel Wilderness** (162,824 ac/49,629 ha) is in Mendocino and Shasta-Trinity national forests.

Yolo County 1014 sq mi/2626 sq km, pop. 141,092, in NC California. WOODLAND is its seat. In the S Sacramento Valley, along the Sacramento R. (E), it is drained by Cache and Putah creeks and numerous irrigation canals. A rich agricultural area, with its largest city DAVIS, it produces sugar beets, tomatoes, asparagus, alfalfa and grains, rice, fruit, olives, beans, livestock, and dairy goods, along with sand, gravel, and natural gas.

Yonge Street thoroughfare beginning at the harbor of TORONTO, Ontario, and running N. Built by Upper Canada Governor John G. Simcoe in 1795 as a 40 mi/60 km–long military road to L. SIMCOE, it now, as the "world's longest street," runs some 1180 mi/1900 km N and W, to NORTH BAY, through the CLAY BELT, and across Ontario, through THUNDER BAY, to Rainy River, on the Minnesota border S of Lake of the Woods. Designated Route 11, it is in places part of the TRANS-CANADA HIGHWAY. Yonge St. divides Toronto's streets

E and W, and in Downtown is central to the commercial district.

Yonkers city, pop. 188,082, Westchester Co., SE New York, on the E bank of the Hudson R., adjacent (N) to the BRONX. Yonkers is the fourth-largest city in the state. The Otis Elevator Company was founded (1854) and is still headquartered here. Other manufactures include pharmaceuticals, apparel, chemicals, and liquid sugar; there is also a printing industry. Yonkers was part of a vast land purchase made by the Dutch West India Company from local tribes in 1639; title eventually passed to Frederick Philipse of PHILIPSE MANOR. Yonkers Raceway (harness racing), the Hudson River Museum, Elizabeth Seton College (1961), St. Joseph's Seminary (1886), and St. Andrew's Golf Club (1888) are here. In the 1980s and 1990s Yonkers engaged in a protracted struggle over residential integration.

Yorba Linda city, pop. 52,422, Orange Co., SW California, 30 mi/48 km SE of Los Angeles and 10 mi/16 km NNE of Santa Ana. Until the 1960s a lightly populated community with oil wells, truck farms, and citrus and avocado groves, it is now a growing residential suburb. The birthplace (1913) and presidential library of Richard M. Nixon draw visitors.

York **1.** town, pop. 9818, seat of York Co., extreme S Maine. It is on the Atlantic Ocean, 43 mi/69 km SW of Portland. Maine's second town and the first British city on the American continent, York was chartered as Gorgeana in 1641 by Sir Fernando Gorges. When the Massachusetts Bay Colony took over in 1652, the charter was revoked, Gorgeana's status was reduced to town, and the name was changed to York. A 1692 Abnaki raid nearly destroyed the settlement. In 1811, Maine's first cotton mill was established. The town has many examples of Colonial architecture, including the Old Gaol Museum (1653), one of the oldest public buildings in America. **2.** in Ontario: **a.** early name (1793–1834) for TORONTO, changed on its incorporation as a city. It was disparagingly called **Muddy York.** **b.** city, pop. 140,525, Toronto Metropolitan Municipality, S Ontario, bounded by Toronto (S and E); North York (N); and Etobicoke (W). Created with the consolidation of the township of York and the town of Weston (NW, on the Humber R.) in 1967, it contains many of Toronto's closer, older residential suburbs. **3.** city, pop. 42,192, seat of York Co., SE Pennsylvania, 25 mi/40 km SSE of Harrisburg, on Codorus Creek and Interstate 83. In the fertile Pennsylvania Dutch farming area, it is a commercial center for the region. It also manufactures air-conditioning and refrigeration engines, turbines, farm and construction machinery, and roofing materials. York served as the nation's capital from Sept. 30, 1777, to June 27, 1778, while the British occupied Philadelphia. Here the Continental Congress adopted the Articles of Confederation. The city was occupied by Confederate forces during the Civil War, the largest Northern city to be taken. It has a campus of Pennsylvania State University, and is the seat of York College of Pennsylvania (1941). **4.** city, pop. 6709, seat of York Co., N South Carolina, 13 mi/21 km WNW of Rock Hill and 10 mi/16 km S of the North Carolina border. It was settled in the 1750s by Scotch-Irish Pennsylvanians. A railroad and trade center, it has some light industry and a large historic district.

York County **1.** 1008 sq mi/2611 sq km, pop. 164,587, southernmost county in Maine, between the New Hampshire border and the Atlantic Ocean. Alfred is its seat. Maine's oldest county, York until 1670 included the areas that are now Cumberland and Lincoln counties. Drained by the Salmon Falls, Saco, Mousam, Ossipee, and Piscataqua rivers, the county has Portsmouth Naval Shipyard, in Kittery, and numerous lake and coastal resorts. Main industries include dairy and truck farming, food canning, retailing, and fishing. Residential growth has made York Maine's second-most populous county. **2.** 906 sq mi/2347 sq km, pop. 339,574, in S Pennsylvania, on the Maryland border. Its seat is YORK. The county comprises an agricultural (dairying, tobacco, livestock) region surrounding the industrial and historic city of York. **3.** 685 sq mi/1774 sq km, pop. 131,497, in N South Carolina, bounded by North Carolina (N), the Broad R. (W), and the Catawba R. and Sugar Creek (E). Wylie is in the NE part. Its seat is YORK. The county's largest city is industrial ROCK HILL. York Co. is a rich agricultural area, noted for its peaches, cotton, grain, and vegetables, as well as for its poultry and dairy products. Timber is also cut and milled. Growth in recent decades is due in part to the prosperity of nearby (NE) CHARLOTTE, North Carolina. **4.** 113 sq mi/293 sq km, pop. 42,422, in SE Virginia, along the York R. Its seat is YORKTOWN. In the TIDEWATER, it is largely rural. There are some truck farming and livestock raising. The county is of great historic importance; Yorktown was the site of the last major battle of the American Revolution, and was besieged during the Civil War.

York Factory historical site on the SW shore of Hudson Bay and the N bank of the HAYES R., just E of the mouth of the NELSON R., 135 mi/217 km SSE of Churchill, in NE Manitoba. The oldest permanent settlement in the province, it was established by the HUDSON'S BAY COMPANY in 1684. It was subject to French attack in the early and late 18th century. The most important HBC post, commanding the mouth of the entire Saskatchewan R.–L. Winnipeg system, it flourished into the mid 19th century. Closed in 1957, it was in 1968 designated a National Historic Site.

York Regional Municipality pop. 504,981, in S Ontario, embracing many of Toronto's N suburbs, including the city of VAUGHAN and the towns of AURORA, EAST GWILLIMBURY, GEORGINA, MARKHAM, NEWMARKET, and RICHMOND HILL. It does *not* include York, North York, East York, or Toronto (formerly York).

York River estuary, 40 mi/64 km long and 1–2.5 mi/1–4 km wide, in the TIDEWATER, E Virginia. The PAMUNKEY and MATTAPONI rivers flow into it at WEST POINT. The York then flows SE to empty into Chesapeake Bay, 17 mi/27 km N of Newport News. The river was central in Virginia's 17th- and 18th-century history; WEROWOCOMOCO, YORKTOWN, and other sites are on its banks.

Yorkton city, pop. 15,315, in the PARKLANDS of SE Saskatchewan, 105 mi/170 km ENE of Regina. Settled in the 1880s, it is the distribution and processing center for a farming region. It is home to a substantial Ukrainian community.

Yorktown **1.** town, pop. 33,467, Westchester Co., SE New York, on the New Croton Reservoir, 6 mi/10 km E of Peeksill. It is an agricultural (orcharding) community becoming a N suburb of New York City. **2.** residential neighborhood in North Philadelphia, Pennsylvania, 1.6 mi/2.6 km N of City Hall, SE of the Temple University campus and E of Broad St. Twenty-five blocks were razed here in the 1950s as part of one of the nation's first urban renewal efforts; row houses for middle-class blacks were constructed. **3.** historic locality on the PENINSULA, in York Co., SE Virginia, on the S bank of the

York R., near its mouth on Chesapeake Bay, 12 mi/19 km N of Newport News. Once a bustling port, it was at the center of the final major battle of the Revolution, Sept.–Oct. 1781; when George Washington trapped Lord Cornwallis's British troops on the Peninsula, and escape by sea was cut off by the French, the British commander surrendered. The battlefield is today the 9300-ac/3770-ha Colonial National Historical Park; associated sites include the Moore House, where the articles of surrender were drawn up. Yorktown played a role in the Civil War, as well; George McClellan began his ill-fated 1862 Peninsular Campaign by setting siege to the town. Confederate troops abandoned their lines, which were established atop the old Revolutionary earthworks, just before his attack, and McClellan occupied the town before moving up the Peninsula toward Richmond.

Yorkville **1.** residential and commercial section, upper East Side Manhattan, New York City. Although sometimes defined as extending from 59th St. to 96th St. E of Lexington Ave., it is more commonly thought of as having a S boundary somewhere in the 70s; its center is around 86th St. and 3rd Ave., where a village on the BOSTON POST ROAD existed by the late 18th century. In the 19th century mansions dotted the area, but after the New York & Harlem railroad arrived (1834), Yorkville developed quickly. Brownstones built from the 1880s were occupied around 1900 by Germans moving N from the Lower East Side. Other Europeans followed, and Yorkville has incorporated Czech, Slovak, Hungarian, and Irish neighborhoods. In the late 19th century Jacob Ruppert's large brewery was in the area. East Side Park, on the East R., was renamed Carl Schurz Park in 1911, in honor of the German-American leader. Gracie Mansion (1799), N of the park, has been the official residence of New York City's mayors since 1942. Yorkville today is a fashionable home for young professionals, with some signs of the German days lingering, especially in restaurants and other establishments on 86th St. **2.** fashionable commercial district, midtown TORONTO, Ontario, immediately N of QUEEN'S PARK, centered around Yorkville Ave. and Bloor St. between YONGE St. (E) and Avenue Rd. (W). A village annexed by Toronto in 1883, Yorkville became bohemian by mid 20th century, but has recently been transformed into a stylish shopping, gallery, restaurant, and entertainment district.

Yosemite National Park 761,000 ac/308,000 ha (1189 sq mi/3080 sq km), in the heart of the SIERRA NEVADA, in EC California. Established as the first US state park in 1864, it became (largely though the efforts of John Muir) a national park in 1890. First seen by whites in c.1849, it was entered by troops pursuing the Yosemite (grizzly bear) Indians in 1851. **Yosemite Valley,** on the Merced R., was the early focus of interest. It is the site of the three-level **Yosemite Falls** (2425 ft/739 m, with an Upper fall of 1430 ft/436 m), of the 620-ft/189-m Bridalveil Fall, and of EL CAPITAN, the HALF DOME, and other famed granite peaks. The valley is today heavily visited, causing concerns for the area's pristine survival. In the park's S is the Mariposa Grove of big trees (sequoias). In the N is the much less visited TUOLUMNE R. valley, including the Tuolumne Meadows, a huge subalpine area at 8600 ft/2620 m, and the Grand Canyon of the Tuolumne. Downstream (W), the Tuolumne's valley, once considered the equal in beauty of the Yosemite Valley, now lies under the Hetch Hetchy Reservoir (1913), which stores water for the city of San Francisco. Mt. Lyell (13,090 ft/3990 m), in the SE, is the park's highest peak and site of its largest glacier. Entry into the park is chiefly through El Portal (W); TIOGA PASS is the only E entry.

Youghiogheny River 135 mi/217 km long, in West Virginia, Maryland, and Pennsylvania. It rises in Preston Co., West Virginia, on the W side of BACKBONE Mt., and flows NNE along the West Virginia–Maryland line and into Pennsylvania, through Youghiogheny River L., a reservoir formed by a 1944 dam near Confluence, Pennsylvania, where the Casselman R. joins it from the NE. Now under the reservoir is an important ford where Nemacolin's Path, later the Cumberland Road section of the NATIONAL ROAD, crossed the river; today US 40 crosses the reservoir here at Somerfield, Pennsylvania. The river continues NW, through Laurel Hill and Chestnut Ridge, to join the MONONGAHELA R. at McKeesport, SE of Pittsburgh. The Youghiogheny (pronounced "Yockagaynee," and popularly called "the Yok"), whose Algonquian name signifies "contrary," flows away from the sea, into the Mississippi R. system; rising near the Potomac's headwaters, it provided a short early route from the Atlantic coast into the interior. In the 1870s the BALTIMORE AND OHIO RAILROAD built through its valley, in which Connellsville, Pennsylvania, became a major provider of coal.

Young America city, pop. 1354, Carver Co., S Minnesota, 35 mi/56 km SW of Minneapolis, in a lake-filled agricultural area. With the city of Norwood (pop. 1351), which adjoins it (S), it is a farm trade center. Settled in the 1850s, Young America took as its name a reference to the vigor of the then westward-expanding nation.

Youngstown city, pop. 95,732, seat of Mahoning Co., NE Ohio, on the Mahoning R., 60 mi/97 km SE of Cleveland. It has long been a leading steel producer and distributor. Pioneers began settling the site in 1797. The discovery of iron ore and the building of Ohio's first blast furnace (1803) in the area were followed by discoveries of coal and limestone, precipitating Youngstown's rise as a major iron producer. Conversion to steel began in 1892, and eventually miles of steel plants lined the banks of the Mahoning. The local economy has been shaken during periods of decline in the US steel industry. Currently, other manufactures include aluminum extrusions, automotive equipment, asphalt pavers, office equipment, cement and cement products, forgings, dies, and jigs. The Butler Institute of American Art and the 2500-ac/1012-ha Mill Creek Park are situated here, as is Youngstown State University (1908).

Ypsilanti city, pop. 24,846, Washtenaw Co., SE Michigan, on the Huron R., 5 mi/8 km SE of Ann Arbor. Its first settlement was an early 19th-century French fur trading post. It was permanently settled in 1823, and named for the Greek patriot Demetrios Ypsilanti in 1832. It has been best known for its large auto plants, especially General Motors' huge Willow Run installation, which became famous for producing B-24 bombers in World War II. The 1993 closure of this factory and the consequent loss of some 4000 jobs profoundly affects the economy. Ypsilanti also manufactures sheet-metal machinery, paper, plastic, and ladders. It is home to Eastern Michigan University (1849) and Cleary College (1883), and the University of Michigan operates an aeronautics research center at Willow Run Airport.

Yreka city, pop. 6948, seat of Siskiyou Co. (pop. 43,531), extreme N California, 101 mi/162 km NE of Eureka, between the Klamath Mts. (W) and the Cascade Range (E).

An 1851 gold town, it subsequently became a ranching, lumbering, and trade center, hub for an extensive forest and mountain area. In 1941 it was briefly proposed as the capital of the would-be "State of Jefferson," incorporating parts of N California and S Oregon. Today it is headquarters for the Klamath National Forest (W), and a tourist center noted for its restored buildings.

Ysleta del Sur see under EL PASO, Texas.

Yuba City city, pop. 27,437, seat of Sutter Co., NC California, across the Feather R. (W) from MARYSVILLE and 40 mi/64 km NNW of Sacramento. Founded in 1849, it is a trade, processing, and shipping center for a region producing peaches, prunes, vegetables, rice, dairy goods, and nuts. The city has a sizable Sikh (Punjabi) community. The SUTTER BUTTES are just NW.

Yuba River 35 mi/56 km long, in NC California. It rises in three forks in the Sierra Nevada foothills, in the Tahoe National Forest, NE of Marysville, and flows SW to the FEATHER R., just below (SW of) Marysville. Lake Spaulding Dam, a hydroelectric facility on the 55 mi/90 km–long South Yuba, was completed in 1919. On the 55 mi/90 km–long North Yuba is the New Bullards Bar Dam (1970, replacing a 1924 structure), at 636 ft/194 m one of the highest in the US. The Yuba, site of extensive 19th-century gold mining, including hydraulic operations in the 1870s, today provides hydroelectric power and recreational opportunities.

Yucaipa city, pop. 32,824, San Bernardino Co., S California, on Yucaipa Creek in the S foothills of the San Bernardino Mts., 15 mi/24 km ESE of San Bernardino. Truck and poultry farms and apple orchards were longtime mainstays of this growing (since the 1960s) residential suburb. Crafton Hills College (1972) is here.

Yucca Mountain 5064 ft/1544 m, in Nye Co., SW Nevada, 100 mi/160 km NW of Las Vegas. At the SW corner of NELLIS Air Force Range and on the W of the NEVADA TEST SITE, and E of the Amargosa Desert, the 6 mi/10 km–long ridge has since 1987 been tested and groomed for opening around 2010 as the nation's only permanent repository for high-level radioactive wastes. Its dry desert conditions have been thought ideal for retarding the inevitable corrosion of waste casks, which will hold materials hazardous for 10,000 years. But not completely understood local water conditions, proximity to potentially active volcanoes, and FAULT lines in the area have raised concern, and controversy over the project continues. **Yucca Flats,** long central to US nuclear testing, is some 20 mi/32 km E.

Yucca Valley unincorporated community, pop. 13,701, San Bernardino Co., S California, N of the Little San Bernardino Mts. and 22 mi/35 km W of Twentynine Palms, in the Yucca Valley. It is a growing residential community.

Yukon city, pop. 20,935, Canadian Co., C Oklahoma, 13 mi/21 km W of downtown Oklahoma City, and on its limits. A residential suburb, it is also a trade center for grain, cotton, livestock, and dairy producers.

Yukon River 1978 mi/3185 km long, in the Yukon Territory and Alaska. It is the fifth-longest North American river. It flows from Tagish L., on the British Columbia–Yukon border, NNW to WHITEHORSE and through L. Laberge, N of which it is joined by the Teslin R. from the SE. It continues N to Carmacks, parallels the Klondike Highway NNW to Minto, and swings NW to Fort Selkirk, where the Pelly R. joins from the E. Continuing WNW, then N, it is joined at Stewart by the Stewart R. (from the E). Near DAWSON it is joined by BONANZA CREEK and the KLONDIKE R. (from the E), and is 1 mi/1.5 km wide. From Dawson it flows NW across the Alaska line to Fort Yukon, where the PORCUPINE R., flowing from the N Yukon Territory, joins it from the E. It then flows WSW and SW across the middle of Alaska. Its major tributary here is the TANANA, from the SE. A final swing NW brings it through its delta into the Bering Sea, S of NORTON SOUND. The Yukon drains most of the Yukon Territory and a large part of C Alaska. Its generally gentle gradients mean that it has little hydroelectric potential, but it has been an important transportation route. Russian fur traders knew its mouth in the 1830s, and HUDSON'S BAY COMPANY operatives dealing with local Na-Dene groups ascended it in the 1840s. In the 1890s it became a main route to the KLONDIKE goldfields. During the summer it is navigable all the way to Whitehorse, near its head, and gold seekers approaching from the S rafted down it to Dawson; steamboat traffic flourished before railroad, highway, and air travel eliminated the need.

Yukon Territory northwesternmost governmental division of Canada; land area 205,345 sq mi/531,844 sq km (rank: 8th of 12); 1991 pop. 27,797 (118.3% of 1986; rank: 12th). Capital and only city: WHITEHORSE. The Yukon Territory is bordered E by the Northwest Territories, with the SELWYN Mts. running along much of the boundary; S by British Columbia, along the SIXTIETH PARALLEL; and SW and W by Alaska. On the N it has a coast of over 100 mi/160 km on the BEAUFORT SEA, on the W edge of the MACKENZIE R. delta. The Selwyn and RICHARDSON mountains, along the territory's E, are part of the Canadian ROCKY Mts. In the SW, the SAINT ELIAS Mts. are part of the COAST Mts.; Mt. LOGAN, on the Alaskan border in KLUANE NATIONAL PARK, is Canada's highest point at 19,524 ft/5951 m. Between the two mountain groups, the Yukon's C is part of the INTERMONTANE Region. The YUKON R., fed by the PELLY, TESLIN, White, Stewart, and other tributaries, drains this area to the NW, into Alaska. In the N, the PORCUPINE R. flows NW, also meeting the Yukon in Alaska. The Peel R. and its tributaries (NC) and the headwaters of the LIARD R. (SE) flow E to the Mackenzie, being on the E side of the CONTINENTAL DIVIDE, which zigzags across the Yukon. In the remote, unorganized "North Western Territory," the Yukon became part of the NORTHWEST TERRITORIES in 1870, and one of its districts in 1895. In 1896, PLACER gold was discovered on BONANZA CREEK, a short tributary of the KLONDIKE R. (WC), and a furious gold rush ensued. The town of DAWSON suddenly had a pop. of 25,000, as adventurers approached from all directions, but esp. from the SW (from Skagway, Alaska, via the CHILKOOT and WHITE passes), from the NW (also from Alaska, but up the Yukon R.), and from the SE (up the Liard R., via the "all Canadian" or "back door" route). In 1898, the Yukon became a separate territory. By 1905 the individualistic hand-mining phase of the rush was over, large-scale dredging operations succeeded it, and the pop. shrank; only in recent decades has it returned to the 1901 level. The Yukon in the early 20th century was home to small DENE groups who had been here before the rush (as at Old Crow, on the Porcupine R.), and to small groups of miners, trappers, and others who made their lives in the woods. In World War II, strategic concerns brought the building of the ALASKA HIGHWAY through the territory, along with the Canol Road (see under SELWYN

Mts.) to the oilfield at Norman Wells, in the Northwest Territories. The NORTHWEST STAGING ROUTE, along which aircraft bound for the Pacific war passed to Alaska airfields, had several bases in the S. After the war, roadbuilding continued, with the KLONDIKE, CAMPBELL, and DEMPSTER highways connecting the Yukon with the outside; riverboats on the Yukon R. and bush pilots had earlier been almost the only available travel modes. Roads enabled the expansion of mining, now concentrated in the MAYO and FARO areas. Copper, lead, zinc, asbestos, and silver have all been important; the economy is so dependent on these operations that the Yukon is very prone to cyclical distress. Since the 1960s tourism and recreation have offered a source of diversification. The Alaska Highway and reminders of Dawson's gold rush period draw visitors, and the territory has become well known for its hunting and fishing. Kluane (in the extreme SW) and Northern Yukon (in the extreme N; see under BRITISH Mts.) national parks are remote, but the railroad between Whitehorse and Skagway, via the White Pass, has been resurrected as a tourist attraction. Whitehorse, which succeeded Dawson as the territorial capital in 1953, houses almost all the commercial and institutional establishments in the Yukon, along with 65% of the pop. Residents elect an assembly and a representative to the Federal House of Commons; the central government appoints a territorial commissioner and a representative to the Senate.

Yuma city, pop. 54,923, seat of Yuma Co., extreme SW Arizona, in an irrigated valley on Interstate 8 and the Colorado R., at the mouth of the Gila R., just E of the California and Baja California (Mexico) lines. It is a trade center for lettuce, citrus, date, melon, and alfalfa producers. Stock feeding and shipping, tourism, and light manufacturing are also important. Spanish explorers came through this Quechan-occupied area as early as 1540, and in the 1770s the river crossing was on one route N from Mexico to California. Gold prospectors bound W for California came through in the 1840s, and Yuma was a major river port. The community was destroyed by flood in 1862, then reestablished on higher ground. Yuma Territorial Prison (1875; now a museum) and the Laguna Dam (1909) were important factors in its growth. The city is the seat of Arizona Western College (1963). A Marine Corps Air station is on its SE, and the Army's Yuma Proving Ground lies 15 mi/24 km NE.

Yuma Desert see under SONORAN DESERT.

Zabriskie Point see under DEATH VALLEY, California.

Zachary city, pop. 9036, East Baton Rouge Parish, SE Louisiana, 14 mi/23 km N of Baton Rouge. In an agricultural area, it has recently experienced some growth as a residential suburb.

Zanesville city, pop. 26,778, seat of Muskingum Co., NC Ohio, on the Muskingum R. at the mouth of the Licking R., 52 mi/84 km E of Columbus. It was named for Ebenezer Zane, owner of the military bounty land on which it was founded (1797). Nearby deposits of clay, oil, natural gas, sand, limestone, and iron ore spurred the city's growth, as did its location on waterways and the NATIONAL ROAD and its two years (1810–12) as state capital. It was once considered the pottery capital of the US. Current manufactures include ceramic tiles and pottery, glass, transformers, sheet steel, batteries, radiators, cement, and hydraulic and farm machinery. Packaged meats and dairy items are also produced. The city is the site of the National Road-Zane Grey museum; the author, grandson of Zanesville's founder, was born here (1875).

Zeeland city, pop. 5417, Ottawa Co., W Michigan, 21 mi/34 km SW of Grand Rapids. Like the city of HOLLAND, just to its SW, Zeeland was settled by the Dutch in the mid 19th century. The city has several light industries. The surrounding area raises poultry, livestock, vegetables, grain, corn, and dairy cattle. Bacteriologist and writer Paul de Kruif was born here (1890).

Zelienople see under HARMONY, Pennsylvania.

Zephyrhills city, pop. 8220, Pasco Co., WC Florida, 23 mi/37 km NE of Tampa. Settled around 1911, at first a home for Union Civil War veterans, it has produced naval stores, wood products, and citrus and other crops, and is now in the midst of a growing residential area.

Zero Mile Post see under FIVE POINTS, Atlanta, Georgia.

Zía Pueblo pop. 637, in Sandoval Co., NW New Mexico, 30 mi/48 km NNW of Albuquerque. This Keresan-speaking PUEBLO participated in the 1680 revolt, but after the Spanish retaliated by killing 600 Indians in 1687, joined in raids on other pueblos. Zía is known for its ancient sun symbol, the official state emblem, and for its pottery and painting. Mission Nuestra Señora de la Asunción (1692) is here.

Zion city, pop. 19,775, Lake Co., NE Illinois, on L. Michigan, 45 mi/72 km N of Chicago and 3 mi/5 km S of the border with Wisconsin. Mainly a residential community, it has some industrial development, most notably a nuclear power plant (1973). The city was founded in 1901 by John Alexander Dowie, who made it the headquarters of his Christian Catholic Church. His successor, Glenn Voliva, developed Zion into a manufacturing center, with the church controlling its businesses and schools, and it was run theocratically until 1935. Illinois State Beach Park is along L. Michigan.

Zion National Park 147,000 ac/59,600 ha of canyons, waterfalls, desert, and sedimentary rock formations, 20 mi/32 km S of CEDAR CITY, in SW Utah. Zion Canyon is a series of massive red sandstone cliffs cut by the Virgin R., a tributary of the Colorado R. The Narrows is a section of the canyon 20–50 ft/6–15 m wide and 2000 ft/610 m high, with hanging gardens of wildflowers on its moist walls and ledges. The Great White Throne is a large sandstone mesa in the S section of the park.

Zoar village and former religious settlement, pop. 170, Tuscarawas Co., E Ohio, on the Tuscarawas R., 13 mi/21 km S of Canton. The site was settled in 1817 by a group of German Protestant Separatists who formed a self-sustaining communal corporation. In 1898 the community disbanded, and the property was divided. The former home of Separatist leader Joseph Baumeler and other buildings of historic interest have been restored.

zona urbana in Puerto Rico, an unincorporated community that includes the governmental center of a MUNICIPIO. There is no minimum pop. threshold for a *zona urbana,* which has no legal status or legal boundaries. The other form of unincorporated community in Puerto Rico, the *comunidad,* has at least 1000 pop.

Zug Island see under RIVER ROUGE, Michigan.

Zumbro River 50 mi/80 km long, in SE Minnesota. It is formed by the confluence of the **North Branch** (50 mi/80 km long) and the **South Branch** (60 mi/97 km long) just W of Zumbro Falls. It flows E to the Mississippi R. at the Wisconsin border, SE of Wabasha. The river drains a fertile agricultural region; a dam near Zumbro Falls provides electric power to the area.

Zuñi Mountains NW–SE trending range extending for c.70 mi/115 km and reaching a high point at Lookout Mt. (9112 ft/2777 m), 34 mi/56 km SE of Gallup, in NW New Mexico, on the CONTINENTAL DIVIDE.

Zuñi Pueblo pop. 7405, in McKinley and Cibola counties, NW New Mexico, on the Zuñi R. and the Arizona border, 32 mi/52 km S of Gallup. In 1540, Coronado's expedition came here in search of the reputedly golden cities of CIBOLA. An agricultural community, the PUEBLO is noted for its jewelry, pottery, and ceremonial dances.

Zwaanendael see under LEWES, Delaware.

MAPS

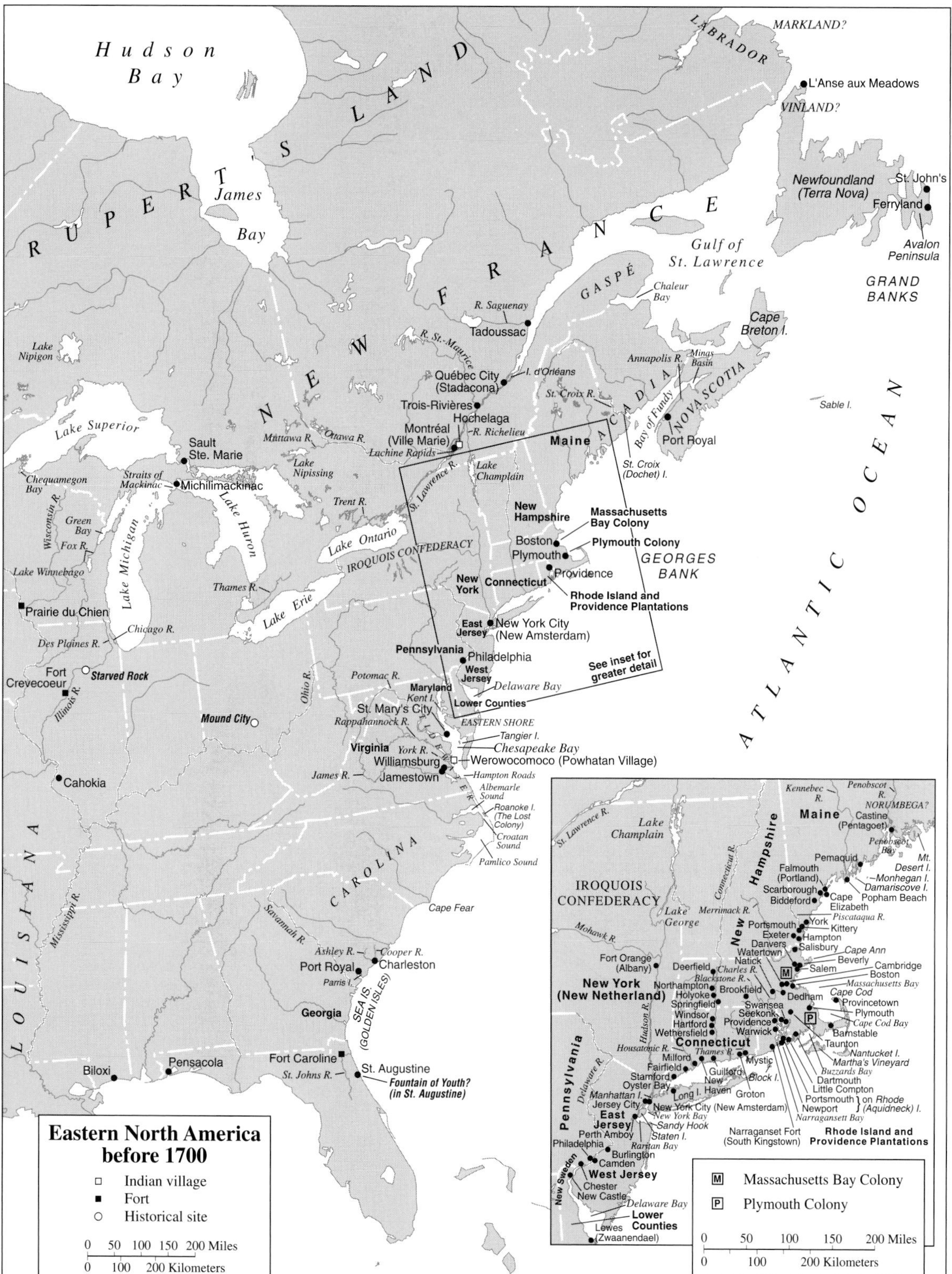

Hudson Bay
James Bay
RUPERT'S LAND
NEW FRANCE
LABRADOR
MARKLAND?
L'Anse aux Meadows
VINLAND?
Newfoundland (Terra Nova)
St. John's
Ferryland
Avalon Peninsula
GRAND BANKS
Gulf of St. Lawrence
GASPÉ
Chaleur Bay
Cape Breton I.
R. Saguenay
Tadoussac
R. St.-Maurice
Québec City (Stadacona)
I. d'Orléans
Trois-Rivières
Hochelaga
Montréal (Ville Marie)
R. Richelieu
Lachine Rapids
Annapolis R.
Minas Basin
St. Croix R.
ACADIA
NOVA SCOTIA
Bay of Fundy
Port Royal
St. Croix (Dochet) I.
Sable I.
Lake Nipigon
Lake Superior
Sault Ste. Marie
Mattawa R.
Ottawa R.
Lake Nipissing
Chequamegon Bay
Straits of Mackinac
Michilimackinac
Lake Huron
Trent R.
Wisconsin R.
Green Bay
Fox R.
Lake Michigan
Lake Winnebago
Lake Ontario
IROQUOIS CONFEDERACY
St. Lawrence R.
Lake Champlain
Maine
New Hampshire
Massachusetts Bay Colony
Boston
Plymouth
Plymouth Colony
GEORGES BANK
Providence
New York
Connecticut
Rhode Island and Providence Plantations
Thames R.
Lake Erie
Prairie du Chien
Chicago R.
Des Plaines R.
East Jersey
New York City (New Amsterdam)
Pennsylvania
Philadelphia
West Jersey
See inset for greater detail
Delaware Bay
Fort Crevecoeur
Starved Rock
Illinois R.
Ohio R.
Potomac R.
Maryland
Kent I.
Lower Counties
St. Mary's City
Mound City
Rappahannock R.
EASTERN SHORE
Tangier I.
Chesapeake Bay
Virginia
York R.
Williamsburg
Werowocomoco (Powhatan Village)
James R.
Jamestown
Hampton Roads
Cahokia
Albemarle Sound
Roanoke I. (The Lost Colony)
Croatan Sound
Pamlico Sound
ATLANTIC OCEAN
CAROLINA
LOUISIANA
Mississippi R.
Cape Fear
Savannah R.
Ashley R.
Cooper R.
Port Royal
Charleston
Parris I.
SEA IS. (GOLDEN ISLES)
Georgia
Fort Caroline
St. Augustine
St. Johns R.
Fountain of Youth? (in St. Augustine)
Biloxi
Pensacola
Eastern North America before 1700
Indian village
Fort
Historical site
0 50 100 150 200 Miles
0 100 200 Kilometers
Kennebec R.
Penobscot R.
NORUMBEGA?
St. Lawrence R.
Lake Champlain
Maine
Castine (Pentagoet)
Penobscot Bay
Mt. Desert I.
Pemaquid
Monhegan I.
Damariscove I.
Popham Beach
Falmouth (Portland)
Scarborough
Biddeford
Cape Elizabeth
IROQUOIS CONFEDERACY
Connecticut R.
New Hampshire
Lake George
Merrimack R.
Piscataqua R.
Mohawk R.
York
Portsmouth
Kittery
Exeter
Hampton
Danvers
Salisbury
Watertown
Cape Ann
Natick
Beverly
Fort Orange (Albany)
Deerfield
Charles R.
Salem
Cambridge
Boston
Blackstone R.
Massachusetts Bay
New York (New Netherland)
Northampton
Brookfield
Holyoke
Dedham
Cape Cod
Springfield
Swansea
Provincetown
Windsor
Seekonk
Plymouth
Hartford
Providence
Cape Cod Bay
Wethersfield
Warwick
Barnstable
Connecticut
Taunton
Hudson R.
Housatonic R.
Thames R.
Nantucket I.
Milford
Martha's Vineyard
Mystic
Buzzards Bay
Fairfield
Guilford
Block I.
Dartmouth
Stamford
New Haven
Little Compton
Pennsylvania
Delaware R.
Oyster Bay
Long I.
Groton
Portsmouth
Manhattan I.
on Rhode (Aquidneck) I.
Jersey City
New York City (New Amsterdam)
Newport
Narragansett Bay
East Jersey
New York Bay
Sandy Hook
Staten I.
Perth Amboy
Narraganset Fort (South Kingstown)
Rhode Island and Providence Plantations
Philadelphia
Raritan Bay
Burlington
Camden
New Sweden
West Jersey
Chester
New Castle
Delaware Bay
Lower Counties
Lewes (Zwaanendael)
Massachusetts Bay Colony
Plymouth Colony
0 50 100 150 200 Miles
0 100 200 Kilometers

Map 1

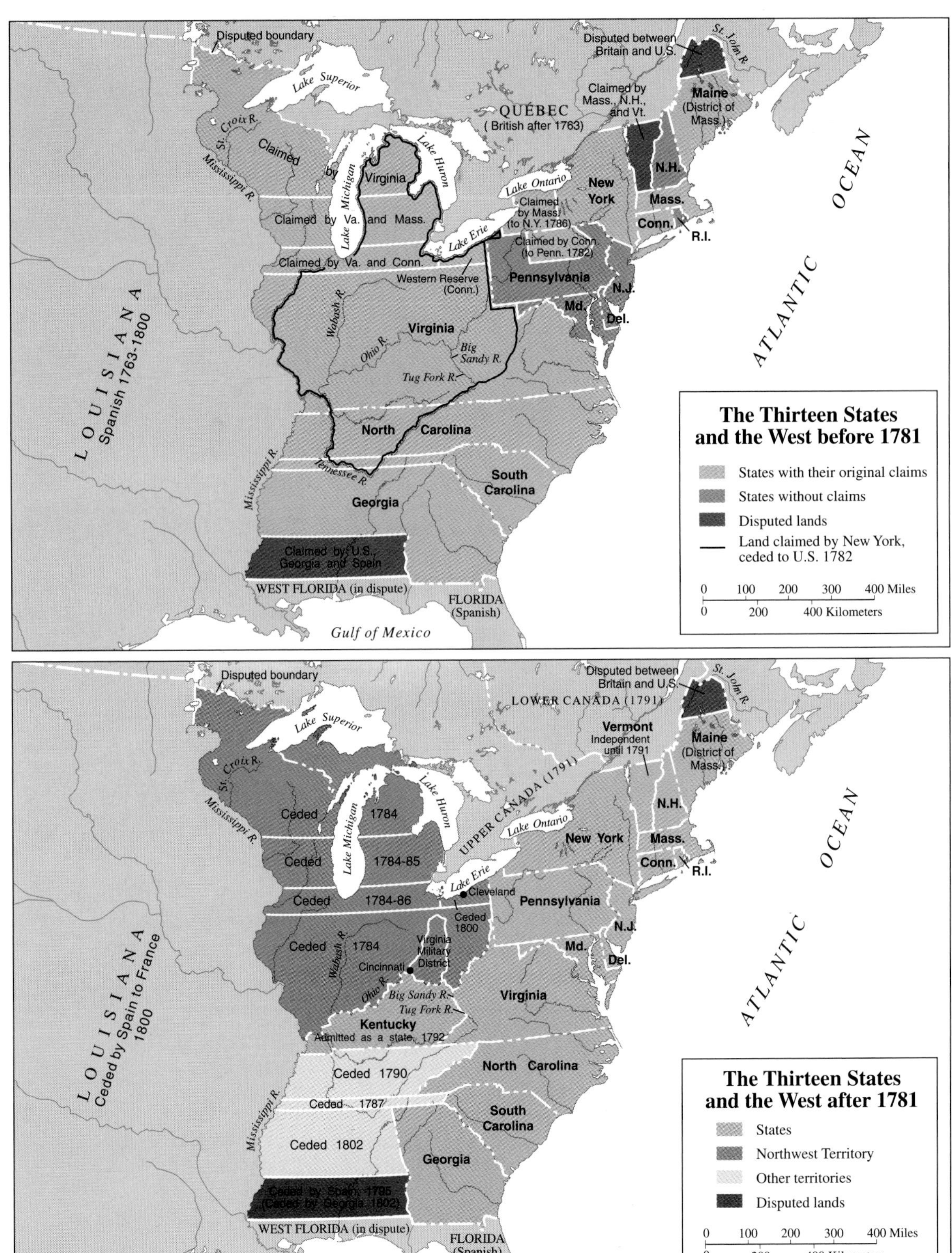

The Thirteen States and the West before 1781
States with their original claims
States without claims
Disputed lands
Land claimed by New York, ceded to U.S. 1782
0 100 200 300 400 Miles
0 200 400 Kilometers
Disputed boundary
Disputed between Britain and U.S.
St. John R.
Lake Superior
Claimed by Mass., N.H., and Vt.
Maine (District of Mass.)
QUÉBEC (British after 1763)
St. Croix R.
Claimed by Virginia
Mississippi R.
Lake Michigan
Lake Huron
Lake Ontario
N.H.
New York
Claimed by Mass. (to N.Y. 1786)
Mass.
Claimed by Va. and Mass.
Conn.
R.I.
Lake Erie
Claimed by Conn. (to Penn. 1782)
Claimed by Va. and Conn.
Western Reserve (Conn.)
Pennsylvania
N.J.
Md.
Del.
Wabash R.
Virginia
Ohio R.
Big Sandy R.
Tug Fork R.
LOUISIANA Spanish 1763-1800
North Carolina
Tennessee R.
South Carolina
Georgia
Claimed by U.S., Georgia and Spain
WEST FLORIDA (in dispute)
FLORIDA (Spanish)
Gulf of Mexico
ATLANTIC OCEAN
The Thirteen States and the West after 1781
States
Northwest Territory
Other territories
Disputed lands
0 100 200 300 400 Miles
0 200 400 Kilometers
LOWER CANADA (1791)
Vermont Independent until 1791
UPPER CANADA (1791)
Ceded 1784
Ceded 1784-85
Ceded 1784-86
Cleveland
Ceded 1800
Ceded 1784
Virginia Military District
Cincinnati
Kentucky Admitted as a state, 1792
LOUISIANA Ceded by Spain to France 1800
Ceded 1790
Ceded 1787
Ceded 1802
Ceded by Spain, 1795 (Ceded by Georgia 1802)

Map 2

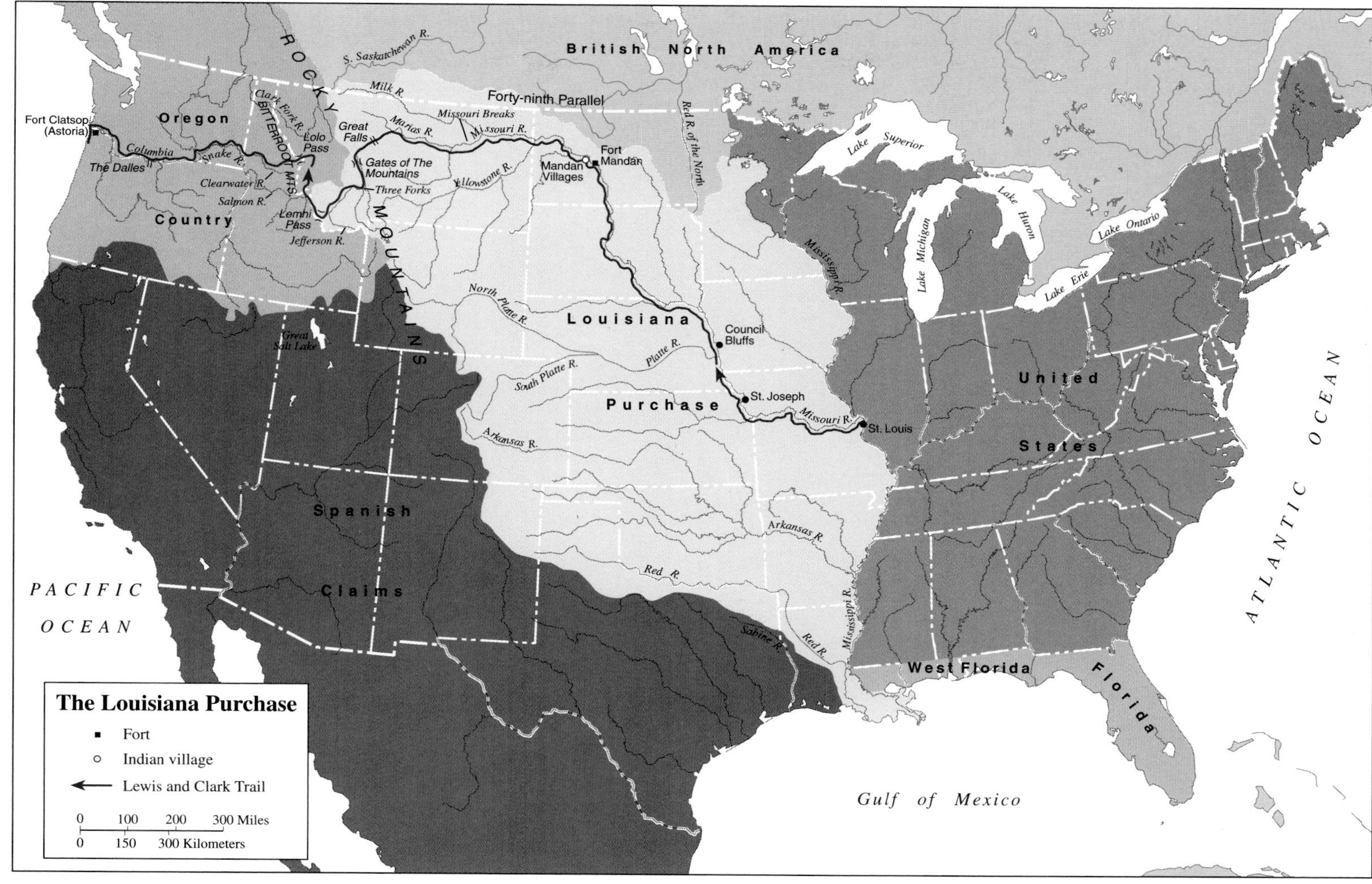

The Louisiana Purchase
Fort
Indian village
Lewis and Clark Trail
0 100 200 300 Miles
0 150 300 Kilometers
PACIFIC OCEAN
Gulf of Mexico
ATLANTIC OCEAN
Oregon Country
Spanish Claims
Louisiana Purchase
United States
British North America
West Florida
Florida
ROCKY MOUNTAINS
BITTERROOT MTS
Forty-ninth Parallel
Fort Clatsop (Astoria)
The Dalles
Columbia
Snake R.
Clearwater R.
Salmon R.
Clark Fork R.
Lolo Pass
Lemhi Pass
Jefferson R.
Great Falls
Gates of The Mountains
Three Forks
Marias R.
Milk R.
S. Saskatchewan R.
Missouri Breaks
Missouri R.
Yellowstone R.
Mandan Villages
Fort Mandan
Red R. of the North
North Platte R.
South Platte R.
Platte R.
Council Bluffs
St. Joseph
St. Louis
Arkansas R.
Red R.
Sabine R.
Mississippi R.
Great Salt Lake
Lake Superior
Lake Michigan
Lake Huron
Lake Erie
Lake Ontario

Map 3

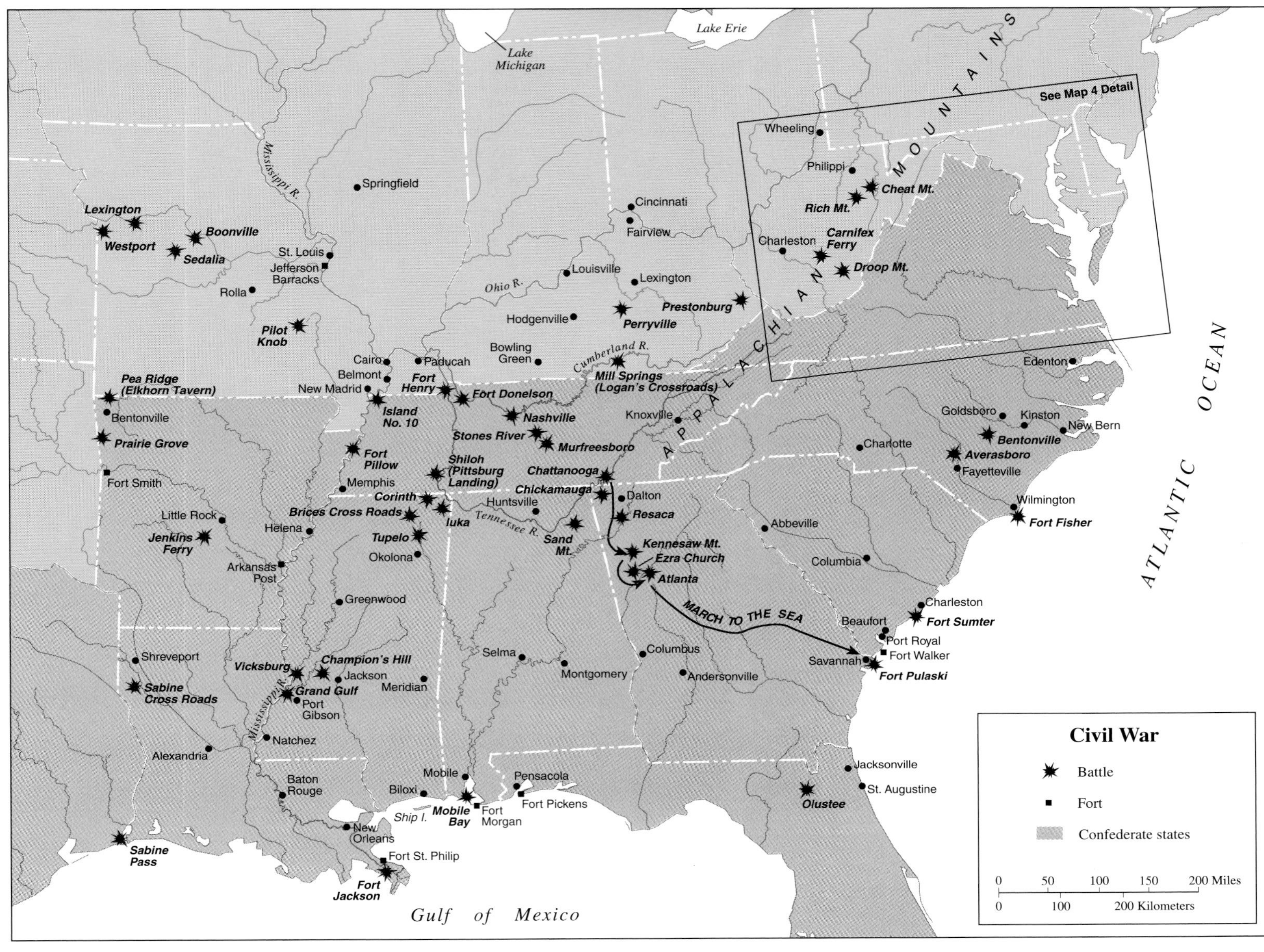

Civil War
Battle
Fort
Confederate states
0 50 100 150 200 Miles
0 100 200 Kilometers
See Map 4 Detail
Gulf of Mexico
ATLANTIC OCEAN
APPALACHIAN MOUNTAINS
Lake Michigan
Lake Erie
Mississippi R.
Ohio R.
Cumberland R.
Tennessee R.
Springfield
Lexington
Westport
Boonville
Sedalia
St. Louis
Jefferson Barracks
Rolla
Pilot Knob
Cincinnati
Fairview
Louisville
Lexington
Hodgenville
Perryville
Prestonburg
Wheeling
Philippi
Cheat Mt.
Rich Mt.
Charleston
Carnifex Ferry
Droop Mt.
Cairo
Paducah
Belmont
New Madrid
Fort Henry
Fort Donelson
Island No. 10
Bowling Green
Mill Springs (Logan's Crossroads)
Pea Ridge (Elkhorn Tavern)
Bentonville
Prairie Grove
Fort Smith
Nashville
Stones River
Murfreesboro
Knoxville
Edenton
Goldsboro
Kinston
New Bern
Bentonville
Averasboro
Fayetteville
Charlotte
Fort Pillow
Memphis
Shiloh (Pittsburg Landing)
Chattanooga
Chickamauga
Dalton
Corinth
Huntsville
Brices Cross Roads
Iuka
Resaca
Little Rock
Helena
Jenkins Ferry
Tupelo
Okolona
Sand Mt.
Kennesaw Mt.
Ezra Church
Atlanta
Wilmington
Fort Fisher
Abbeville
Columbia
Arkansas Post
Greenwood
MARCH TO THE SEA
Charleston
Fort Sumter
Beaufort
Port Royal
Fort Walker
Savannah
Fort Pulaski
Shreveport
Vicksburg
Champion's Hill
Jackson
Meridian
Selma
Montgomery
Columbus
Andersonville
Sabine Cross Roads
Grand Gulf
Port Gibson
Natchez
Alexandria
Baton Rouge
Mobile
Biloxi
Mobile Bay
Fort Morgan
Pensacola
Fort Pickens
Jacksonville
St. Augustine
Olustee
Ship I.
New Orleans
Fort St. Philip
Fort Jackson
Sabine Pass

Map 4

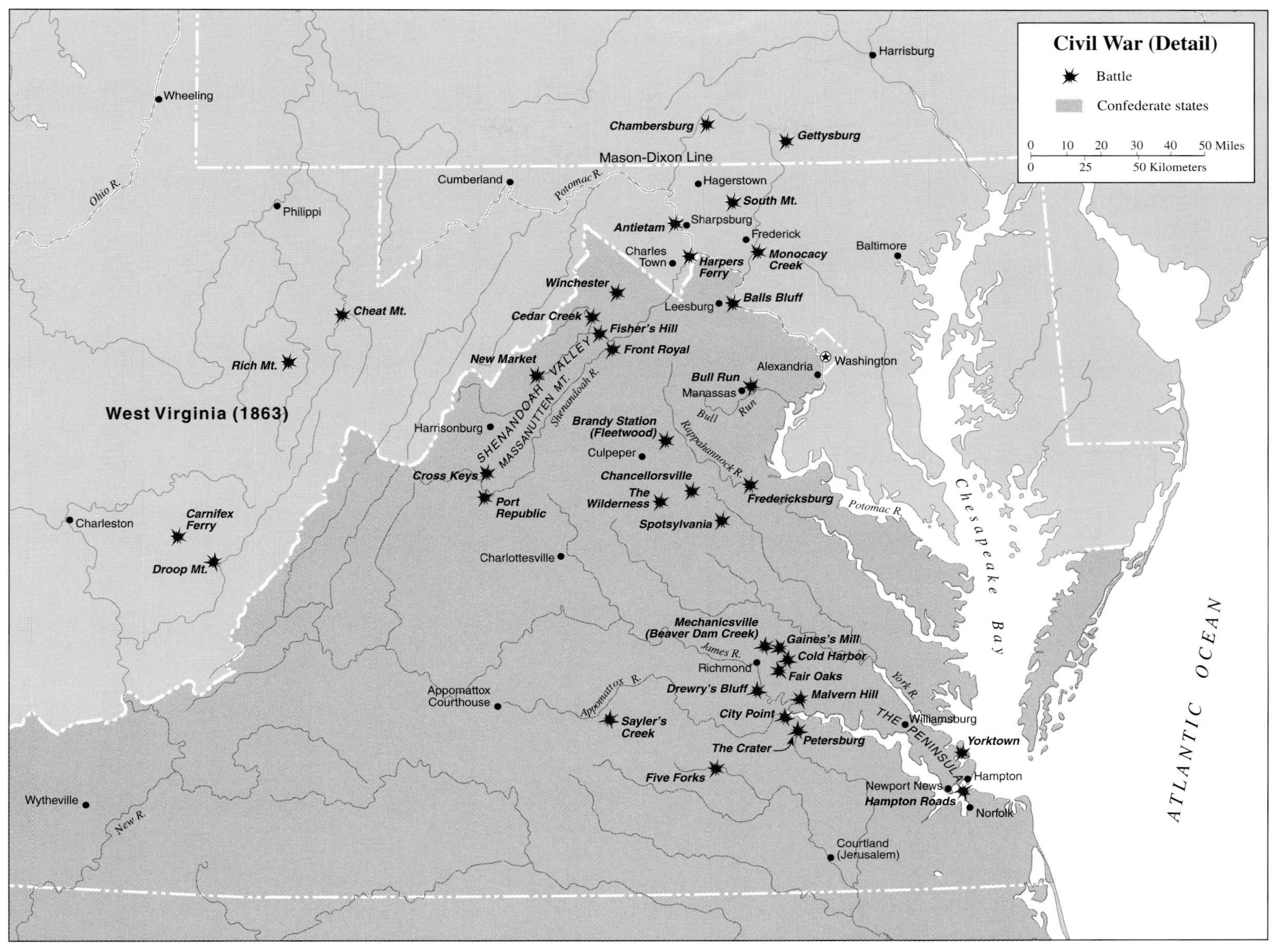

Civil War (Detail)
Battle
Confederate states
0 10 20 30 40 50 Miles
0 25 50 Kilometers
Harrisburg
Wheeling
Chambersburg
Gettysburg
Mason-Dixon Line
Ohio R.
Cumberland
Potomac R.
Hagerstown
Philippi
South Mt.
Antietam
Sharpsburg
Frederick
Charles Town
Harpers Ferry
Monocacy Creek
Baltimore
Winchester
Leesburg
Balls Bluff
Cheat Mt.
Cedar Creek
Fisher's Hill
Front Royal
New Market
Rich Mt.
Washington
Alexandria
Bull Run
Manassas
Bull Run
West Virginia (1863)
SHENANDOAH VALLEY
MASSANUTTEN MT.
Shenandoah R.
Harrisonburg
Brandy Station (Fleetwood)
Rappahannock R.
Culpeper
Cross Keys
Chancellorsville
The Wilderness
Fredericksburg
Port Republic
Potomac R.
Chesapeake Bay
Carnifex Ferry
Charleston
Spotsylvania
Droop Mt.
Charlottesville
ATLANTIC OCEAN
Mechanicsville (Beaver Dam Creek)
Gaines's Mill
James R.
Cold Harbor
Richmond
Fair Oaks
York R.
Appomattox R.
Drewry's Bluff
Malvern Hill
Appomattox Courthouse
City Point
THE PENINSULA
Williamsburg
Sayler's Creek
Petersburg
The Crater
Yorktown
Five Forks
Hampton
Newport News
Hampton Roads
Norfolk
Wytheville
New R.
Courtland (Jerusalem)

Map 4 (Detail)

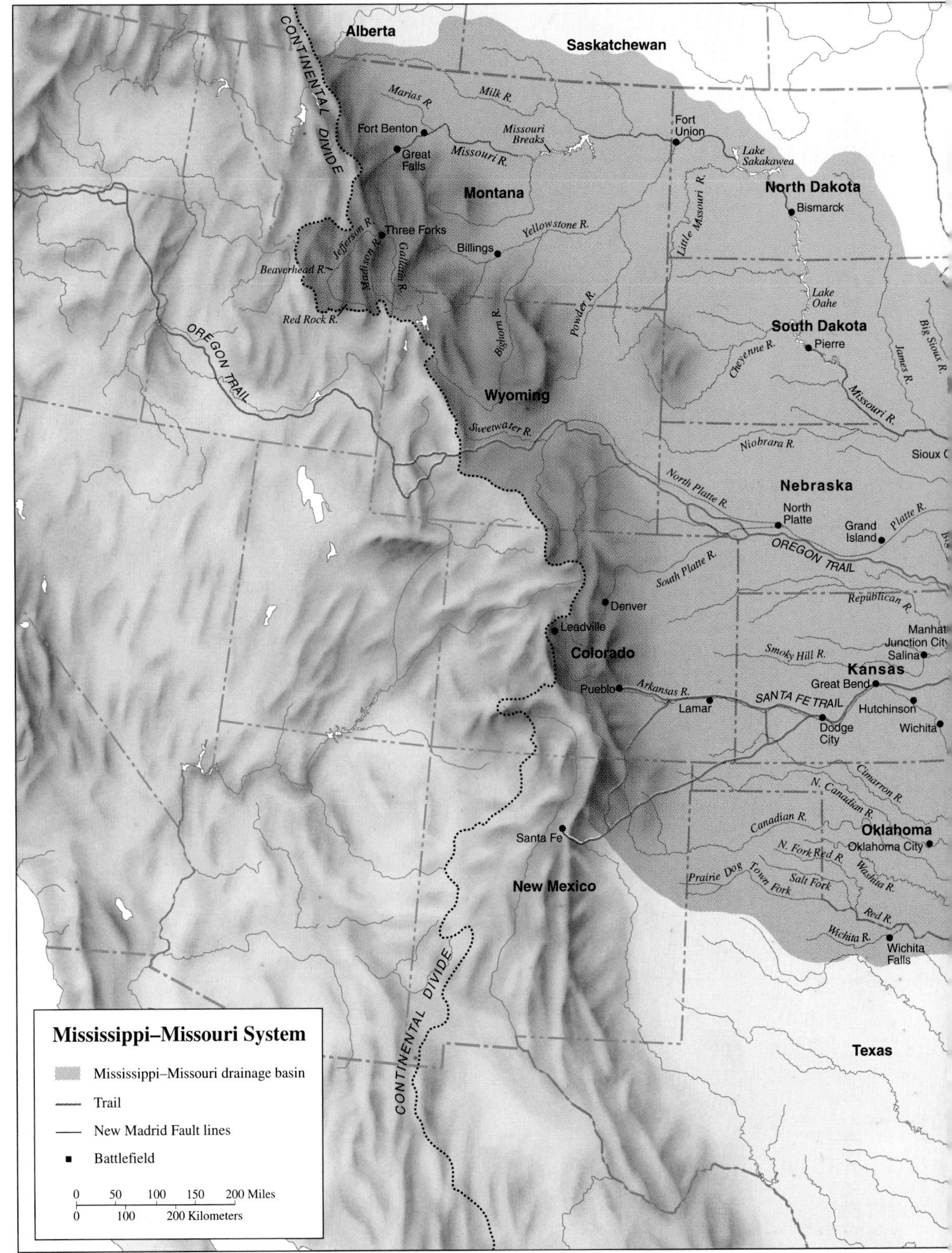

Alberta
Saskatchewan
CONTINENTAL DIVIDE
Marias R.
Milk R.
Fort Benton
Great Falls
Missouri Breaks
Missouri R.
Fort Union
Lake Sakakawea
Montana
North Dakota
Bismarck
Three Forks
Jefferson R.
Madison R.
Gallatin R.
Beaverhead R.
Red Rock R.
Billings
Yellowstone R.
Little Missouri R.
Lake Oahe
South Dakota
Pierre
Cheyenne R.
Bighorn R.
Powder R.
James R.
Big Sioux R.
Missouri R.
OREGON TRAIL
Wyoming
Sweetwater R.
Niobrara R.
Sioux C
North Platte R.
Nebraska
North Platte
Grand Island
Platte R.
OREGON TRAIL
South Platte R.
Republican R.
Denver
Leadville
Colorado
Smoky Hill R.
Manhat
Junction Cit
Salina
Kansas
Great Bend
Pueblo
Arkansas R.
Lamar
SANTA FE TRAIL
Hutchinson
Dodge City
Wichita
Cimarron R.
N. Canadian R.
Canadian R.
Oklahoma
Oklahoma City
Santa Fe
N. Fork Red R.
Washita R.
Prairie Dog Town Fork
Salt Fork
New Mexico
Red R.
Wichita R.
Wichita Falls
CONTINENTAL DIVIDE
Texas
Mississippi–Missouri System
Mississippi–Missouri drainage basin
Trail
New Madrid Fault lines
Battlefield
0 50 100 150 200 Miles
0 100 200 Kilometers

Map 5

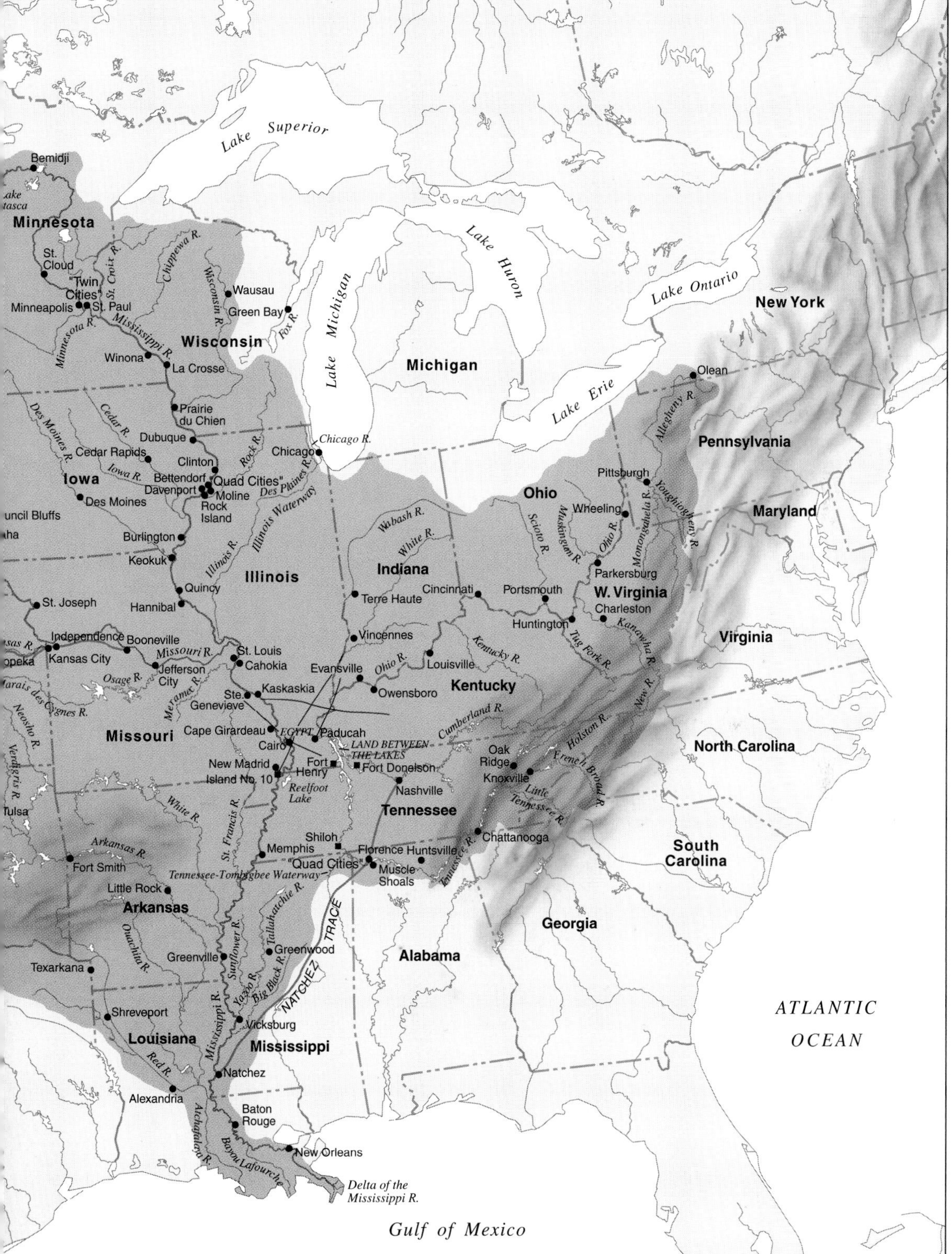

Lake Superior
Lake Michigan
Lake Huron
Lake Ontario
Lake Erie
Minnesota
Wisconsin
Michigan
New York
Pennsylvania
Iowa
Illinois
Indiana
Ohio
Maryland
W. Virginia
Virginia
Missouri
Kentucky
Tennessee
North Carolina
South Carolina
Arkansas
Georgia
Alabama
Mississippi
Louisiana
ATLANTIC OCEAN
Gulf of Mexico
Bemidji
St. Cloud
"Twin Cities"
Minneapolis
St. Paul
Wausau
Green Bay
Winona
La Crosse
Prairie du Chien
Dubuque
Cedar Rapids
Clinton
Chicago
Chicago R.
Bettendorf
Davenport
"Quad Cities"
Moline
Rock Island
Des Moines
Burlington
Keokuk
Quincy
Hannibal
St. Joseph
Independence
Booneville
Kansas City
Jefferson City
St. Louis
Cahokia
Kaskaskia
Ste. Genevieve
Cape Girardeau
EGYPT
Cairo
Paducah
LAND BETWEEN THE LAKES
Fort Henry
Fort Donelson
New Madrid
Island No. 10
Reelfoot Lake
Nashville
Terre Haute
Vincennes
Evansville
Owensboro
Louisville
Cincinnati
Portsmouth
Huntington
Charleston
Parkersburg
Wheeling
Pittsburgh
Olean
Oak Ridge
Knoxville
Chattanooga
Shiloh
Memphis
Florence
Huntsville
"Quad Cities"
Muscle Shoals
Fort Smith
Little Rock
Tennessee-Tombigbee Waterway
Greenville
Greenwood
Texarkana
Shreveport
Vicksburg
Natchez
Alexandria
Baton Rouge
New Orleans
Delta of the Mississippi R.
NATCHEZ TRACE
Mississippi R.
Minnesota R.
St. Croix R.
Chippewa R.
Wisconsin R.
Fox R.
Des Moines R.
Cedar R.
Iowa R.
Rock R.
Des Plaines R.
Illinois Waterway
Illinois R.
Missouri R.
Osage R.
Meramec R.
Marais des Cygnes R.
Neosho R.
Verdigris R.
Wabash R.
White R.
Ohio R.
Kentucky R.
Cumberland R.
Scioto R.
Muskingum R.
Monongahela R.
Youghiogheny R.
Allegheny R.
Tug Fork R.
Kanawha R.
New R.
Holston R.
French Broad R.
Little Tennessee R.
Tennessee R.
White R.
St. Francis R.
Arkansas R.
Ouachita R.
Sunflower R.
Tallahatchie R.
Yazoo R.
Big Black R.
Red R.
Atchafalaya R.
Bayou Lafourche
Tulsa

Map 5

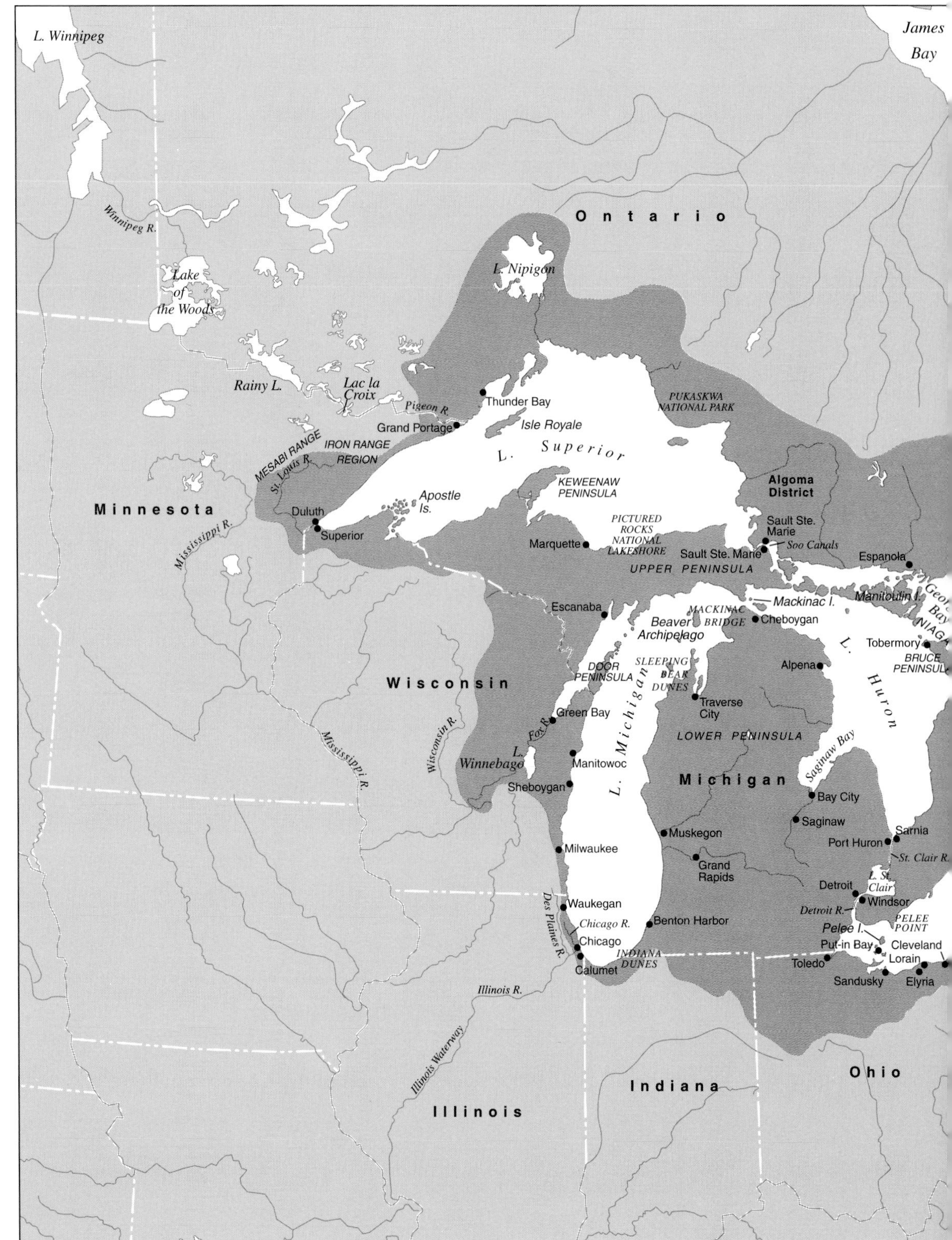

L. Winnipeg
James Bay
Ontario
L. Nipigon
Winnipeg R.
Lake of the Woods
Rainy L.
Lac la Croix
Pigeon R.
Thunder Bay
Grand Portage
Isle Royale
PUKASKWA NATIONAL PARK
L. Superior
MESABI RANGE
IRON RANGE REGION
St. Louis R.
KEWEENAW PENINSULA
Apostle Is.
Algoma District
Minnesota
Duluth
Superior
Mississippi R.
PICTURED ROCKS NATIONAL LAKESHORE
Marquette
Sault Ste. Marie
Soo Canals
Sault Ste. Marie
UPPER PENINSULA
Espanola
Manitoulin I.
Mackinac I.
Escanaba
Beaver Archipelago
MACKINAC BRIDGE
Cheboygan
Tobermory
L. Huron
BRUCE PENINSULA
Alpena
Wisconsin
DOOR PENINSULA
SLEEPING BEAR DUNES
Traverse City
Green Bay
Fox R.
L. Michigan
LOWER PENINSULA
Mississippi R.
Wisconsin R.
L. Winnebago
Manitowoc
Saginaw Bay
Michigan
Sheboygan
Bay City
Saginaw
Muskegon
Sarnia
Port Huron
Milwaukee
St. Clair R.
Grand Rapids
Detroit
L. St. Clair
Windsor
Des Plaines R.
Waukegan
Detroit R.
Chicago R.
Benton Harbor
Pelee I.
PELEE POINT
Chicago
Put-in Bay
Cleveland
INDIANA DUNES
Lorain
Toledo
Calumet
Sandusky
Elyria
Illinois R.
Illinois Waterway
Ohio
Indiana
Illinois

Map 6

Great Lakes–St. Lawrence System
Great Lakes–St. Lawrence watershed
0 50 100 150 200 Miles
0 100 200 Kilometers
Québec
R. Manicouagan
Anticosti I.
Baie-Comeau
GASPÉ PENINSULA
FORILLON NATIONAL PARK
Matane
Gulf of St. Lawrence
Rimouski
L. St.-Jean
R. Saguenay
Jonquière
Chicoutimi
Tadoussac
Riviére-du-Loup
R. St.-Maurice
Île d'Orléans
Québec City
Lévis-Lauzon
New Brunswick
Shawinigan
St. Lawrence R.
Trois-Rivières
Sorel
Maine
North Bay
Mattawa
Ottawa R.
L. Nipissing
Repentigny
St.-Jean-sur-Richelieu
Montréal
R. Richelieu
Lachine
Longueuil
St. Lawrence Seaway (Between Kingston and Montréal)
Ottawa
L. Champlain
Cornwall
Parry Sound
Morrisburg
St. Regis
Massena
Plattsburgh
Burlington
Gulf of Maine
Rideau R.
Prescott
Trent-Severn Waterway
St. Regis R.
Brockville
Ogdens-burg
Midland
L. Simcoe
Rideau L.
Gananoque
Kingston
Vermont
Orillia
Belleville
Peterborough
Trenton
THOUSAND IS.
Watertown
Cobourg
Sackets Harbor
Newcastle
Oshawa
Toronto
GOLDEN HORSESHOE
L. Ontario
Oswego
Niagara-on-the-Lake
Niagara Falls
Rochester
Niagara Falls
New York State Barge Canal (Erie Canal)
Mohawk R.
Welland
Buffalo
New York
Albany
Port Colborne
Lackawanna
Welland Canal
L. Erie
Genesee R.
Dunkirk
Erie
Hudson R.
ATLANTIC OCEAN
Pennsylvania

Map 6

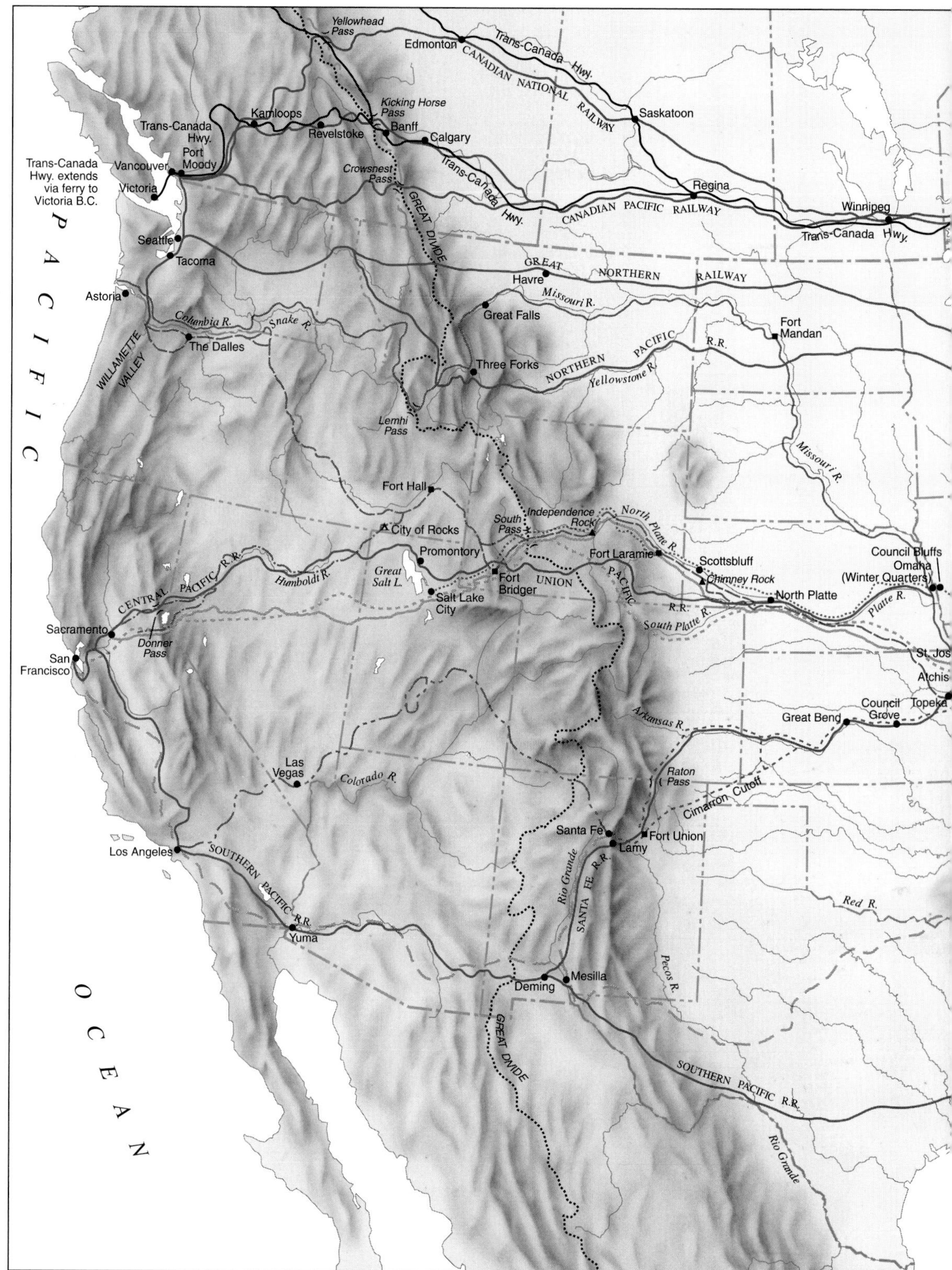

Yellowhead Pass
Edmonton
Trans-Canada Hwy.
CANADIAN NATIONAL RAILWAY
Saskatoon
Kamloops
Kicking Horse Pass
Trans-Canada Hwy.
Revelstoke
Banff
Calgary
Trans-Canada Hwy. extends via ferry to Victoria B.C.
Vancouver
Port Moody
Victoria
Crowsnest Pass
Trans-Canada Hwy.
Regina
CANADIAN PACIFIC RAILWAY
Winnipeg
Trans-Canada Hwy.
GREAT DIVIDE
Seattle
Tacoma
GREAT NORTHERN RAILWAY
Havre
Missouri R.
Astoria
Great Falls
Columbia R.
Snake R.
Fort Mandan
The Dalles
WILLAMETTE VALLEY
NORTHERN PACIFIC R.R.
Three Forks
Yellowstone R.
Lemhi Pass
Missouri R.
Fort Hall
Independence Rock
South Pass
North Platte R.
City of Rocks
Promontory
Fort Laramie
Scottsbluff
Council Bluffs
Omaha (Winter Quarters)
Chimney Rock
CENTRAL PACIFIC R.R.
Humboldt R.
Great Salt L.
Fort Bridger
UNION PACIFIC R.R.
Salt Lake City
North Platte
Platte R.
Sacramento
Donner Pass
South Platte R.
San Francisco
St. Jos
Atchis
Council Grove
Topeka
Arkansas R.
Great Bend
Las Vegas
Colorado R.
Raton Pass
Cimarron Cutoff
Santa Fe
Fort Union
Lamy
Los Angeles
SOUTHERN PACIFIC R.R.
Rio Grande
SANTA FE R.R.
Red R.
Yuma
Pecos R.
Deming
Mesilla
GREAT DIVIDE
SOUTHERN PACIFIC R.R.
Rio Grande
PACIFIC OCEAN

Map 7

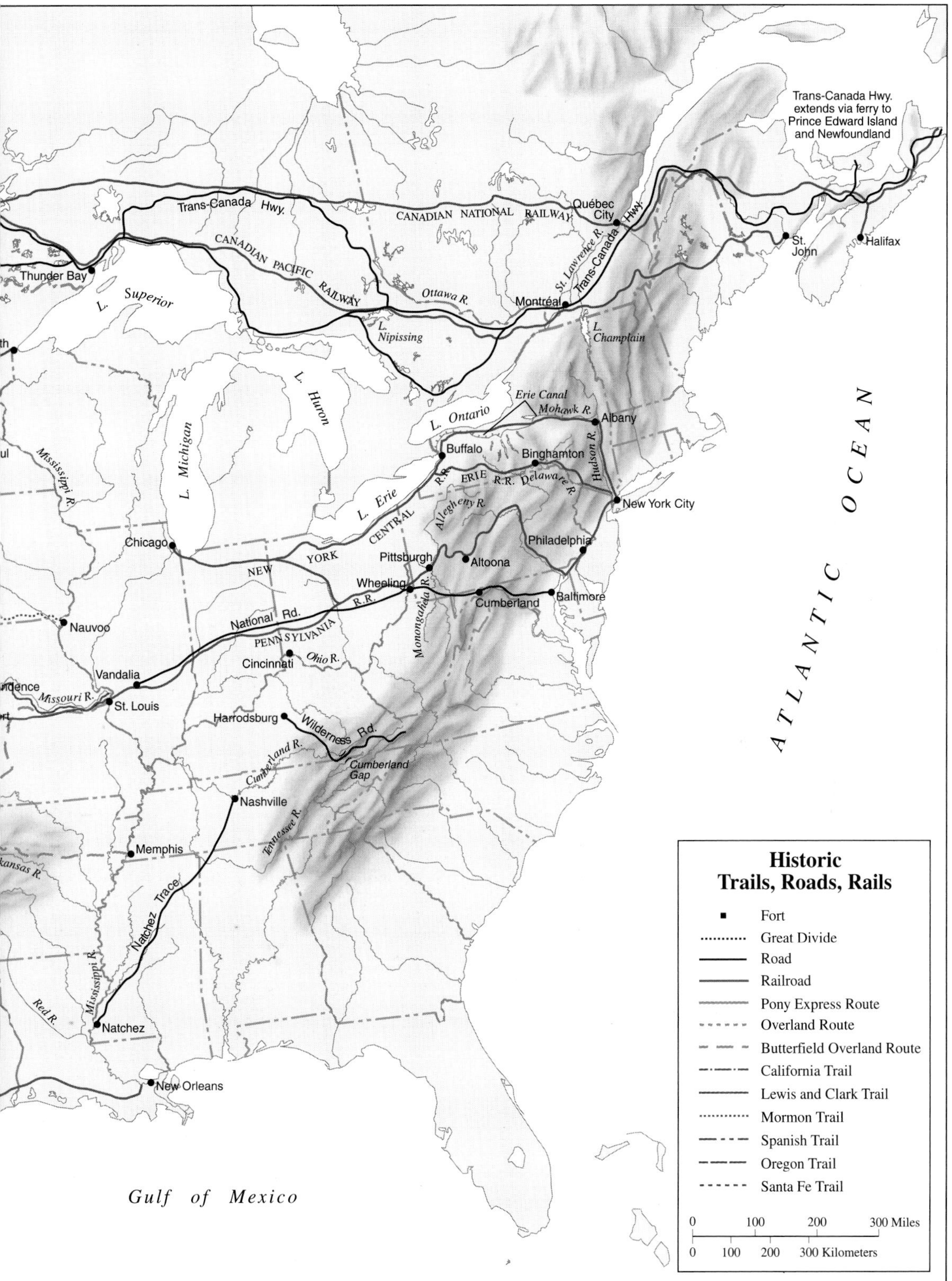

Trans-Canada Hwy. extends via ferry to Prince Edward Island and Newfoundland
Trans-Canada Hwy.
CANADIAN NATIONAL RAILWAY
Québec City
CANADIAN PACIFIC RAILWAY
Thunder Bay
L. Superior
Ottawa R.
St. Lawrence R.
Trans-Canada Hwy.
Montréal
St. John
Halifax
L. Nipissing
L. Champlain
L. Huron
L. Michigan
Erie Canal
Mohawk R.
Albany
L. Ontario
Buffalo
Binghamton
Hudson R.
ERIE R.R.
Delaware R.
New York City
L. Erie
Allegheny R.
NEW YORK CENTRAL R.R.
Mississippi R.
Chicago
Philadelphia
Pittsburgh
Altoona
Wheeling
Baltimore
Cumberland
Monongahela R.
National Rd.
PENNSYLVANIA R.R.
Nauvoo
Cincinnati
Ohio R.
Vandalia
Missouri R.
St. Louis
Harrodsburg
Wilderness Rd.
Cumberland Gap
Cumberland R.
Nashville
Tennessee R.
Memphis
Natchez Trace
Mississippi R.
Red R.
Natchez
New Orleans
Gulf of Mexico
ATLANTIC OCEAN
Historic Trails, Roads, Rails
Fort
Great Divide
Road
Railroad
Pony Express Route
Overland Route
Butterfield Overland Route
California Trail
Lewis and Clark Trail
Mormon Trail
Spanish Trail
Oregon Trail
Santa Fe Trail
0 100 200 300 Miles
0 100 200 300 Kilometers

Map 7

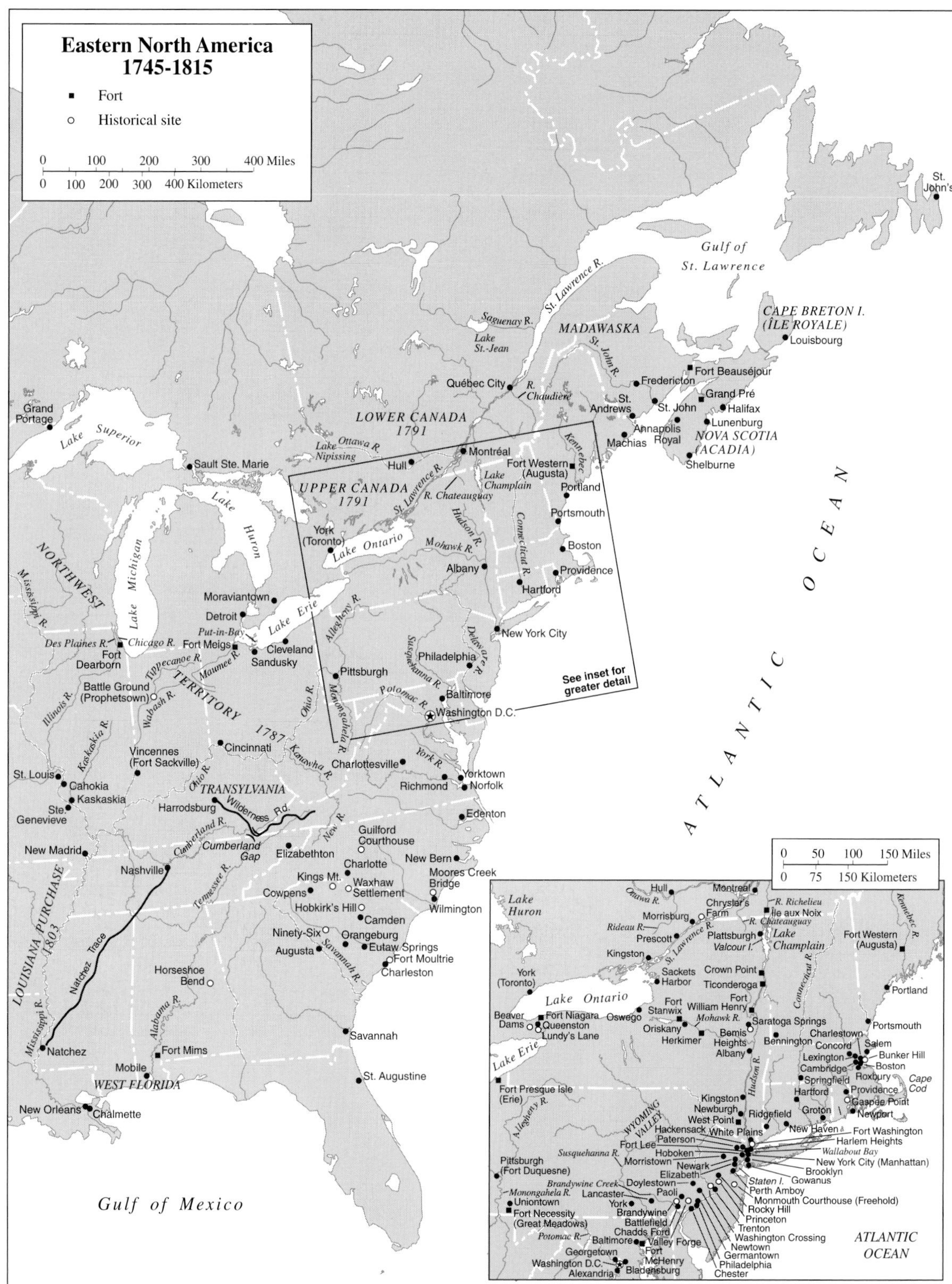
Eastern North America
1745-1815
Fort
Historical site
0 100 200 300 400 Miles
0 100 200 300 400 Kilometers
Gulf of St. Lawrence
ATLANTIC OCEAN
Gulf of Mexico
LOWER CANADA 1791
UPPER CANADA 1791
NORTHWEST TERRITORY 1787
LOUISIANA PURCHASE 1803
TRANSYLVANIA
WEST FLORIDA
MADAWASKA
NOVA SCOTIA (ACADIA)
CAPE BRETON I. (ÎLE ROYALE)
See inset for greater detail
Lake Superior
Lake Michigan
Lake Huron
Lake Erie
Lake Ontario
Lake Nipissing
Lake St.-Jean
Lake Champlain
St. Lawrence R.
Saguenay R.
St. John R.
Ottawa R.
Hudson R.
Mohawk R.
Connecticut R.
Kennebec R.
Delaware R.
Susquehanna R.
Potomac R.
Allegheny R.
Monongahela R.
Ohio R.
Kanawha R.
York R.
New R.
Cumberland R.
Tennessee R.
Savannah R.
Alabama R.
Mississippi R.
Illinois R.
Kaskaskia R.
Wabash R.
Tippecanoe R.
Maumee R.
Des Plaines R.
Chicago R.
R. Chaudière
R. Chateauguay
Wilderness Rd.
Natchez Trace
Cumberland Gap
St. John's
Louisbourg
Fort Beauséjour
Fredericton
St. Andrews
St. John
Grand Pré
Halifax
Lunenburg
Annapolis Royal
Machias
Shelburne
Québec City
Montréal
Hull
Fort Western (Augusta)
Portland
Portsmouth
Boston
Providence
Hartford
Albany
New York City
Philadelphia
Baltimore
Washington D.C.
York (Toronto)
Grand Portage
Sault Ste. Marie
Moraviantown
Detroit
Put-in-Bay
Fort Meigs
Cleveland
Sandusky
Fort Dearborn
Pittsburgh
Battle Ground (Prophetsown)
Vincennes (Fort Sackville)
Cincinnati
Charlottesville
Richmond
Yorktown
Norfolk
Edenton
St. Louis
Cahokia
Kaskaskia
Ste Genevieve
Harrodsburg
New Madrid
Nashville
Elizabethton
Guilford Courthouse
New Bern
Moores Creek Bridge
Wilmington
Charlotte
Kings Mt.
Waxhaw Settlement
Cowpens
Hobkirk's Hill
Camden
Ninety-Six
Orangeburg
Eutaw Springs
Augusta
Fort Moultrie
Charleston
Horseshoe Bend
Savannah
St. Augustine
Fort Mims
Mobile
Natchez
New Orleans
Chalmette
0 50 100 150 Miles
0 75 150 Kilometers
Lake Huron
Lake Ontario
Lake Erie
Lake Champlain
Ottawa R.
Rideau R.
St. Lawrence R.
R. Richelieu
R. Chateauguay
Valcour I.
Mohawk R.
Hudson R.
Connecticut R.
Kennebec R.
Allegheny R.
Susquehanna R.
Brandywine Creek
Monongahela R.
Potomac R.
WYOMING VALLEY
Wallabout Bay
Staten I.
Cape Cod
ATLANTIC OCEAN
Hull
Montreal
Morrisburg
Chrysler's Farm
Île aux Noix
Prescott
Plattsburgh
Kingston
York (Toronto)
Sackets Harbor
Crown Point
Ticonderoga
Fort Western (Augusta)
Portland
Portsmouth
Beaver Dams
Fort Niagara
Queenston
Lundy's Lane
Oswego
Fort Stanwix
Oriskany
Herkimer
Fort William Henry
Saratoga Springs
Bemis Heights
Albany
Bennington
Charlestown
Concord
Lexington
Salem
Bunker Hill
Cambridge
Boston
Roxbury
Springfield
Hartford
Providence
Gaspee Point
Groton
Newport
Fort Presque Isle (Erie)
Kingston
Newburgh
West Point
Ridgefield
New Haven
Hackensack
White Plains
Fort Washington
Harlem Heights
Fort Lee
Paterson
Hoboken
Morristown
Newark
New York City (Manhattan)
Brooklyn
Elizabeth
Gowanus
Pittsburgh (Fort Duquesne)
Doylestown
Perth Amboy
Lancaster
Paoli
Monmouth Courthouse (Freehold)
Uniontown
York
Brandywine Battlefield
Rocky Hill
Princeton
Fort Necessity (Great Meadows)
Chadds Ford
Trenton
Washington Crossing
Baltimore
Fort McHenry
Valley Forge
Newtown
Germantown
Georgetown
Washington D.C.
Bladensburg
Alexandria
Philadelphia
Chester

Map 8

Gulf of St. Lawrence
LONG RANGE MTS.
SHICKSHOCK MTS.
St. Lawrence R.
C A N A D I A N S H I E L D
NOTRE DAME MTS.
Québec City
Mt. Katahdin
LONGFELLOW MTS.
St. John
Halifax
Montréal
R. Richelieu
Ottawa
St. Lawrence R.
Lake Champlain
Mt. Washington
WHITE MTS.
Portland
ADIRONDACKS (extension of Canadian Shield)
Lake Huron
GREEN MTS.
Hudson R.
Connecticut R.
Toronto
Lake Ontario
Mohawk R.
Boston
Syracuse
CATSKILL MTS.
BERKSHIRE HILLS
TACONIC MTS.
Providence
Buffalo
Hartford
SHAWANGUNK MTS.
POCONO MTS.
KITTATINNY VALLEY
RAMAPO MTS.
Detroit
Lake Erie
Allegheny R.
New York City
Cleveland
BLUE MTN.
Lehigh R.
Delaware R.
Susquehanna R.
Philadelphia
Pittsburgh
CUMBERLAND VALLEY
Potomac R.
Baltimore
Columbus
Ohio R.
Youghiogheny R.
Monongahela R.
Harpers Ferry
Washington, D.C.
SHENANDOAH VALLEY
Cincinnati
ALLEGHENY FRONT MTS.
ALLEGHENY MTS.
SHENANDOAH MTS.
BLUE RIDGE
Kanawha R.
Big Sandy R.
Tug Fork R.
New R.
James R.
Richmond
Ohio R.
Lexington
Louisville
APPALACHIAN PLATEAU
Roanoke R.
ATLANTIC OCEAN
Cumberland R.
Cumberland Gap
Holston R.
UNAKA MTS.
Raleigh
CUMBERLAND
WALDEN RIDGE
Knoxville
French Broad R.
BLACK MTS.
Mt. Mitchell
GREAT SMOKY MTS.
Charlotte
Tennessee R.
Brasstown Bald
Springer Mt.
Tallulah R.
SAND MT
PIEDMONT
ATLANTIC COASTAL PLAIN
Columbia
Atlanta
Augusta
Savannah R.
Birmingham
Charleston
Macon
Montgomery
Appalachians
Appalachian Trail
Fall Line
0 50 100 150 200 Miles
0 100 200 Kilometers

Map 9

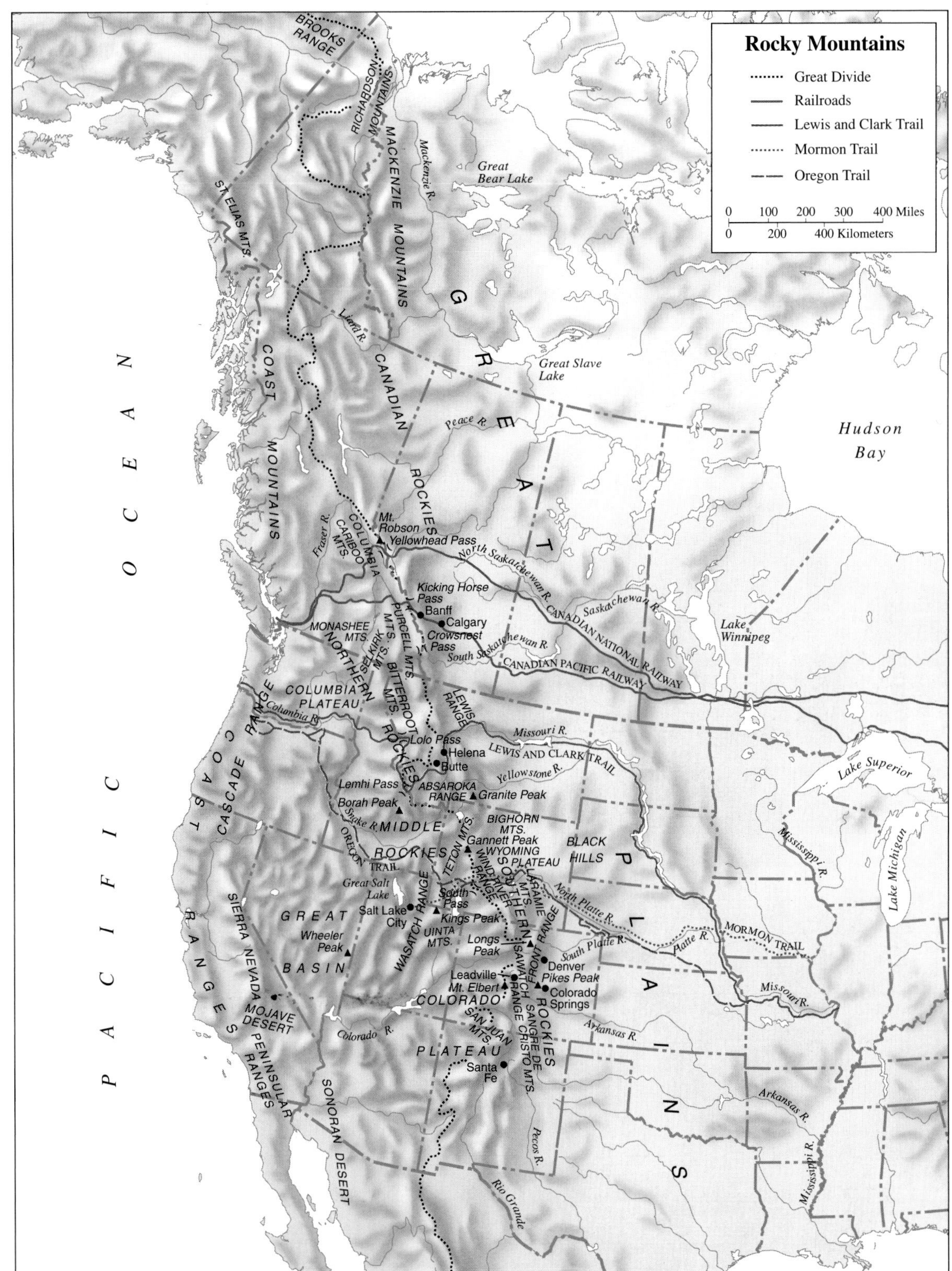
Rocky Mountains
Great Divide
Railroads
Lewis and Clark Trail
Mormon Trail
Oregon Trail
0 100 200 300 400 Miles
0 200 400 Kilometers
BROOKS RANGE
RICHARDSON MOUNTAINS
MACKENZIE MOUNTAINS
Mackenzie R.
Great Bear Lake
ST. ELIAS MTS.
GREAT PLAINS
Liard R.
Great Slave Lake
COAST MOUNTAINS
CANADIAN ROCKIES
Peace R.
Hudson Bay
PACIFIC OCEAN
Mt. Robson
Yellowhead Pass
Fraser R.
CARIBOO MTS.
COLUMBIA
North Saskatchewan R.
Kicking Horse Pass
Banff
Calgary
Crowsnest Pass
South Saskatchewan R.
Saskatchewan R.
CANADIAN NATIONAL RAILWAY
CANADIAN PACIFIC RAILWAY
Lake Winnipeg
MONASHEE MTS.
SELKIRK MTS.
PURCELL MTS.
NORTHERN
BITTERROOT MTS.
ROCKIES
COLUMBIA PLATEAU
Columbia R.
LEWIS RANGE
Missouri R.
Lolo Pass
Helena
Butte
LEWIS AND CLARK TRAIL
Lake Superior
Yellowstone R.
COAST RANGE
CASCADE RANGE
Lemhi Pass
ABSAROKA RANGE
Granite Peak
Borah Peak
BIGHORN MTS.
Snake R.
MIDDLE ROCKIES
OREGON TRAIL
TETON MTS.
Gannett Peak
WYOMING PLATEAU
BLACK HILLS
WIND RIVER RANGE
Mississippi R.
Lake Michigan
Great Salt Lake
LARAMIE MTS.
South Pass
Salt Lake City
WASATCH RANGE
Kings Peak
UINTA MTS.
SOUTHERN
FRONT RANGE
North Platte R.
Platte R.
MORMON TRAIL
South Platte R.
SIERRA NEVADA
GREAT BASIN
Wheeler Peak
Longs Peak
Denver
SAWATCH RANGE
Leadville
Mt. Elbert
Pikes Peak
Colorado Springs
Missouri R.
COAST RANGES
MOJAVE DESERT
COLORADO PLATEAU
SAN JUAN MTS.
SANGRE DE CRISTO MTS.
ROCKIES
Arkansas R.
Colorado R.
PENINSULAR RANGES
Santa Fe
SONORAN DESERT
Pecos R.
Rio Grande
Arkansas R.
Mississippi R.

Map 10

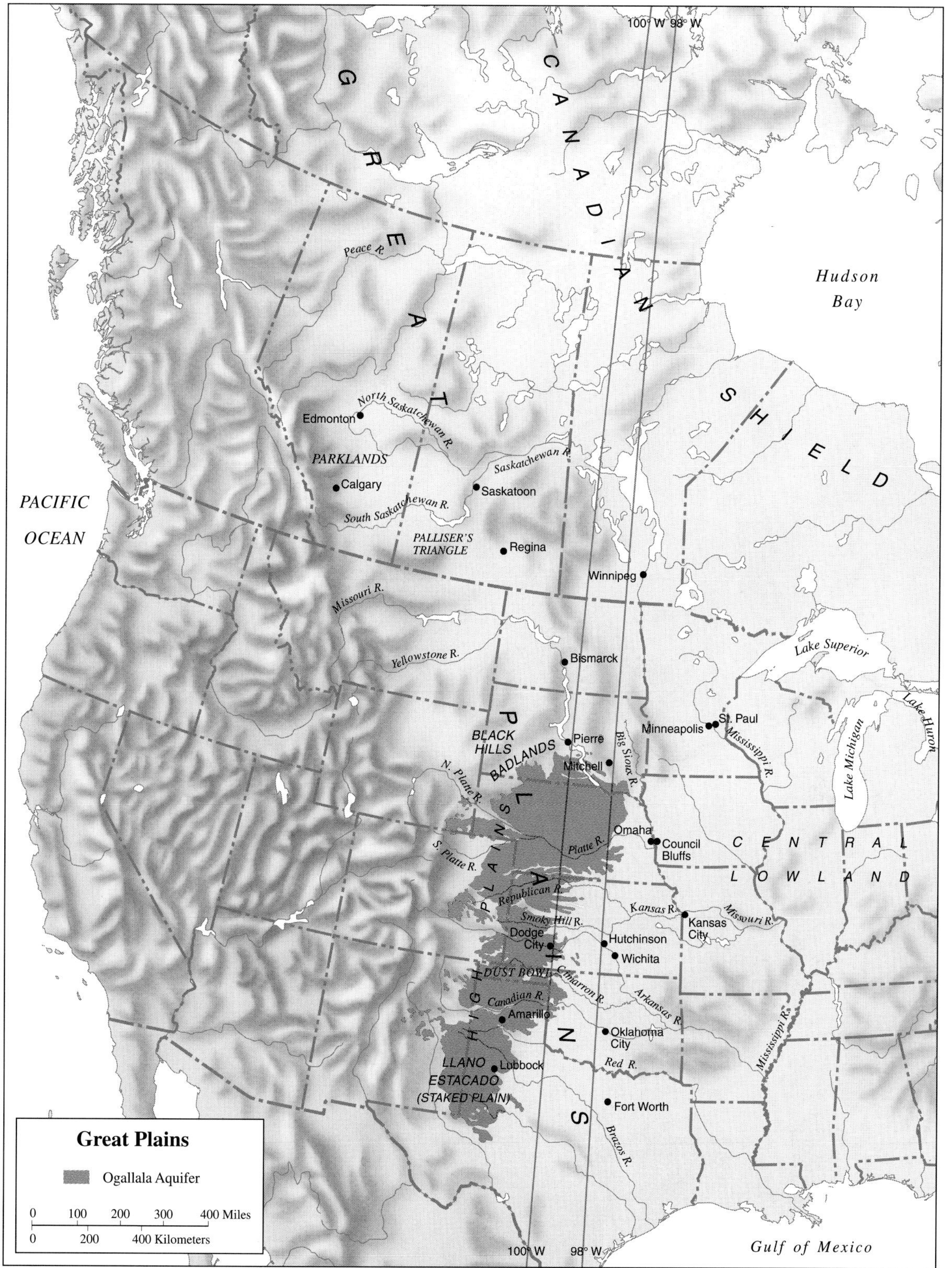

100° W
98° W
GREAT
CANADIAN SHIELD
Hudson Bay
Peace R.
North Saskatchewan R.
Edmonton
PARKLANDS
Saskatchewan R.
Calgary
Saskatoon
South Saskatchewan R.
PACIFIC OCEAN
PALLISER'S TRIANGLE
Regina
Winnipeg
Missouri R.
Yellowstone R.
Bismarck
Lake Superior
Lake Huron
Lake Michigan
BLACK HILLS
BADLANDS
Pierre
Mitchell
Big Sioux R.
Minneapolis
St. Paul
Mississippi R.
N. Platte R.
Omaha
Council Bluffs
PLAINS
CENTRAL LOWLAND
Platte R.
S. Platte R.
Republican R.
Kansas R.
Kansas City
Missouri R.
Smoky Hill R.
Dodge City
Hutchinson
Wichita
DUST BOWL
Cimarron R.
Arkansas R.
Canadian R.
Amarillo
Oklahoma City
HIGH PLAINS
Red R.
LLANO ESTACADO (STAKED PLAIN)
Lubbock
Fort Worth
Brazos R.
Gulf of Mexico
Great Plains
Ogallala Aquifer
0 100 200 300 400 Miles
0 200 400 Kilometers
100° W
98° W

Map 11

Canadian Shield
Canadian Shield
Grenville Province
0 100 200 300 400 Miles
0 200 400 Kilometers
ARCTIC OCEAN
Ellesmere I.
Queen Elizabeth Islands
Kalaallit Nunaat (Greenland) (DEN.)
Beaufort Sea
Melville I.
Banks I.
Devon I.
Baffin Bay
Somerset I.
Prince of Wales I.
Victoria I.
Davis Strait
Boothia Pen.
Cambridge Bay
Great Bear L.
Coppermine
Baffin I.
Mackenzie R.
Coppermine R.
Northwest Territories
Iqaluit
Labrador Sea
Great Slave L.
Yellowknife
Thelon R.
Baker Lake
Chesterfield Inlet
Southampton I.
Baker L.
Chesterfield Inlet
Slave R.
Peace R.
L. Athabasca
Ungava Bay
TORNGAT MTS.
Koksoak R.
Kuujjuaq
Athabasca R.
Churchill
Hudson Bay
Labrador
Reindeer L.
Churchill R.
Caniapiscau R.
Schefferville
Churchill R.
Smallwood Res.
Alberta
Manitoba
Belcher Is.
Grande R. de la Baleine
Saskatchewan
Nelson R.
Hayes R.
The Pas
Cedar L.
James Bay
La Grande R.
Québec
Manicouagan R.
Sept-Îles
Anticosti I.
Gulf of Saint Lawrence
Saskatchewan R.
L. Winnipegosis
L. Winnipeg
Moosonee
L. Mistassini
L. Manitoba
Ontario
Moose R.
L. St. Jean
Chicoutimi
Winnipeg
Kenora
L. Nipigon
Kapuskasing
Rouyn-Noranda
LAURENTIAN MOUNTAINS
St. Lawrence R.
Lake of the Woods
Rainy L.
Thunder Bay
Timmins
Québec
Shawinigan
Trois-Rivières
SUPERIOR HIGHLANDS
Wawa
Hibbing
Virginia
L. Superior
Sault Ste. Marie
Grenville
Montréal
Duluth
Sudbury
Ottawa R.
North Bay
Ottawa
Plattsburgh
L. Champlain
Minnesota
ADIRONDACK MOUNTAINS
L. Huron
ATLANTIC OCEAN
Wisconsin
L. Michigan
Michigan
Toronto
L. Ontario
Utica
New York
L. Erie

Map 12

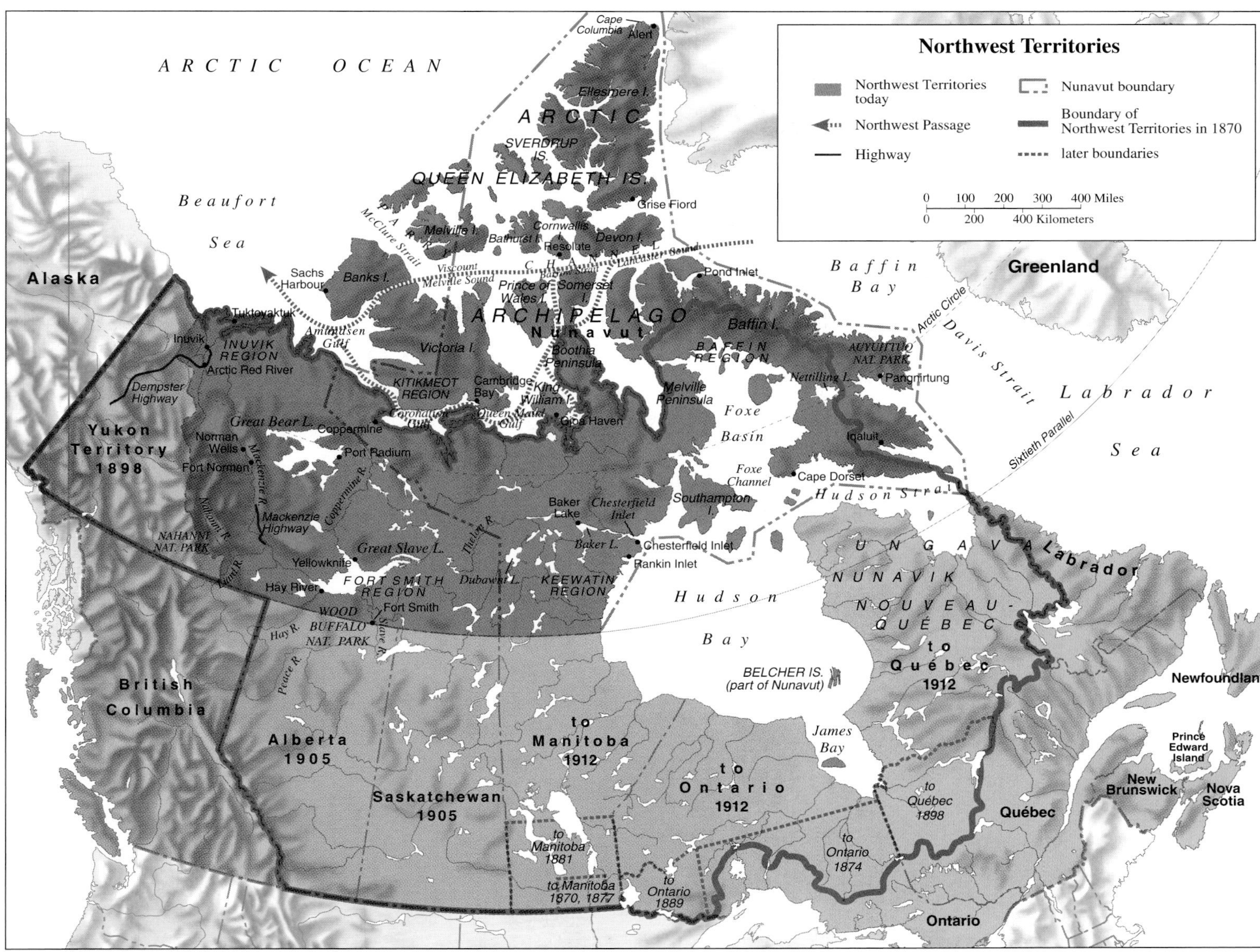
Northwest Territories
Northwest Territories today
Nunavut boundary
Northwest Passage
Boundary of Northwest Territories in 1870
Highway
later boundaries
0 100 200 300 400 Miles
0 200 400 Kilometers
ARCTIC OCEAN
Beaufort Sea
Alaska
Yukon Territory 1898
British Columbia
Alberta 1905
Saskatchewan 1905
to Manitoba 1912
to Manitoba 1881
to Manitoba 1870, 1877
to Ontario 1889
to Ontario 1912
to Ontario 1874
to Québec 1898
to Québec 1912
UNGAVA
NUNAVIK
NOUVEAU-QUÉBEC
Ontario
Québec
Labrador
New Brunswick
Prince Edward Island
Nova Scotia
Newfoundland
Greenland
Baffin Bay
Davis Strait
Labrador Sea
Arctic Circle
Sixtieth Parallel
Hudson Bay
James Bay
BELCHER IS. (part of Nunavut)
Hudson Strait
Foxe Basin
Foxe Channel
ARCTIC ARCHIPELAGO
QUEEN ELIZABETH IS.
SVERDRUP IS.
PARRY CHANNEL
Nunavut
INUVIK REGION
FORT SMITH REGION
KITIKMEOT REGION
KEEWATIN REGION
BAFFIN REGION
NAHANNI NAT. PARK
WOOD BUFFALO NAT. PARK
AUYUITTUQ NAT. PARK
Dempster Highway
Mackenzie Highway
Inuvik
Arctic Red River
Tuktoyaktuk
Norman Wells
Fort Norman
Great Bear L.
Coppermine
Port Radium
Yellowknife
Great Slave L.
Hay River
Fort Smith
Peace R.
Hay R.
Slave R.
Liard R.
Nahanni R.
Mackenzie R.
Coppermine R.
Thelon R.
Dubawnt L.
Baker Lake
Baker L.
Chesterfield Inlet
Rankin Inlet
Southampton I.
Cape Dorset
Iqaluit
Pangnirtung
Nettilling L.
Baffin I.
Pond Inlet
Melville Peninsula
Gjoa Haven
Boothia Peninsula
Prince of Wales I.
Somerset I.
King William I.
Cambridge Bay
Coronation Gulf
Queen Maud Gulf
Victoria I.
Banks I.
Sachs Harbour
Amundsen Gulf
McClure Strait
Viscount Melville Sound
Melville I.
Bathurst I.
Cornwallis I.
Resolute
Devon I.
Lancaster Sound
Grise Fiord
Ellesmere I.
Alert
Cape Columbia

Map 13

New York City and Environs
New York City
Bridge
Tunnel
0 1 2 3 4 Miles
0 2 4 Kilometers
NEW YORK
NEW JERSEY
Bergen Co.
Passaic Co.
Dobbs Ferry
White Plains
Hastings-on-Hudson
Scarsdale
Rye
Hudson R.
Yonkers
Mamaroneck
Bronx R.
Hutchinson R.
Passaic R.
Paterson
Fair Lawn
Tenafly
Westchester Co.
Bronx Co.
Mt. Vernon
New Rochelle
Long Island Sound
Paramus
Englewood
Riverdale
Woodlawn
Pelham Manor
Hackensack
Teaneck
Englewood Cliffs
Clifton
Glen I.
Garfield
GEORGE WASHINGTON BRIDGE
Inwood
BRONX
(Bronx Co.)
Co-op City
Passaic
Hasbrouck Heights
Teterboro
Ridgefield Park
Palisades Park
Fort Lee
Washington Heights
Tremont
City Island
Manhasset Bay
Port Washington
Passaic Co.
Essex Co.
East Rutherford
Teterboro Airport
Ridgefield
Eastchester Bay
Rutherford
Meadowlands
Edgewater
Harlem R.
Morrisania
Nutley
Cliffside Park
Montclair
Hunts Point
THROGS NECK BRIDGE
Kings Point
Great Neck
Manhasset
Lyndhurst
Passaic Co.
Hudson Co.
Morningside Heights
South Bronx
BRONX WHITESTONE BRIDGE
Verona
North Bergen
Guttenberg
Harlem
Rikers Island
Little Neck Bay
Belleville
North Arlington
West New York
Whitestone
Bloomfield
Hackensack R.
Weehawken
MANHATTAN
(New York Co.)
La Guardia Airport
Flushing Bay
Douglaston
West Orange
Astoria
Bayside
Lake Success
Union City
Elmhurst
East Orange
Orange
Kearny
LINCOLN TUNNEL
Long Island City
Jackson Heights
Flushing
North New Hyde Park
Woodside
Harrison
PULASKI SKYWAY
Hoboken
New Hyde Park
Bellerose
HOLLAND TUNNEL
Greenpoint
Long Island
Newark
Jersey City
Greenwich Village
Floral Park
Forest Hills
Kew Gardens
Essex Co.
Union Co.
The Battery
Bushwick
Hudson River
East River
Hollis
Elmont
Franklin Square
Ellis Island
Woodhaven
Newark International Airport
Brooklyn Heights
Bedford-Stuyvesant
Jamaica
Port Newark
Liberty Island
Governors I.
Ozone Park
St. Albans
Newark Bay
Park Slope
QUEENS
(Queens Co.)
Union
Gowanus
Crown Heights
East New York
Queens Co.
Nassau Co.
Red Hook
Valley Stream
Elizabeth
Upper New York Bay
Malverne
Brownsville
Bayonne
Sunset Park
Flatbush
John F. Kennedy International Airport
Howard Beach
NEW JERSEY
NEW YORK
BAYONNE BRIDGE
Kill Van Kull
BROOKLYN
(Kings Co.)
St. George
FIVE TOWNS
Hewlett
Linden
Mariners Harbor
The Narrows
Canarsie
Jamaica Bay
Woodmere
Tompkinsville
Midwood
Arthur Kill
Stapleton
Bay Ridge
Cedarhurst
Inwood
Gateway National Recreation Area
New Utrecht
Lawrence
Rahway
STATEN ISLAND
(Richmond Co.)
Union Co.
Bensonhurst
Middlesex Co.
VERRAZANO NARROWS BRIDGE
Gravesend
Floyd Bennett Field
Sheepshead Bay
Atlantic Beach
Carteret
Gravesend Bay
South Beach
Brighton Beach
Coney Island
Rockaway Inlet
Fresh Kills
New Dorp
The Rockaways
Woodbridge
Richmondtown
Lower New York Bay
Gateway National Recreation Area
OUTERBRIDGE CROSSING
Ambrose Channel
Perth Amboy
Tottenville
Raritan Bay
ATLANTIC OCEAN
Middlesex Co.
Monmouth Co.
Sandy Hook

Map 14

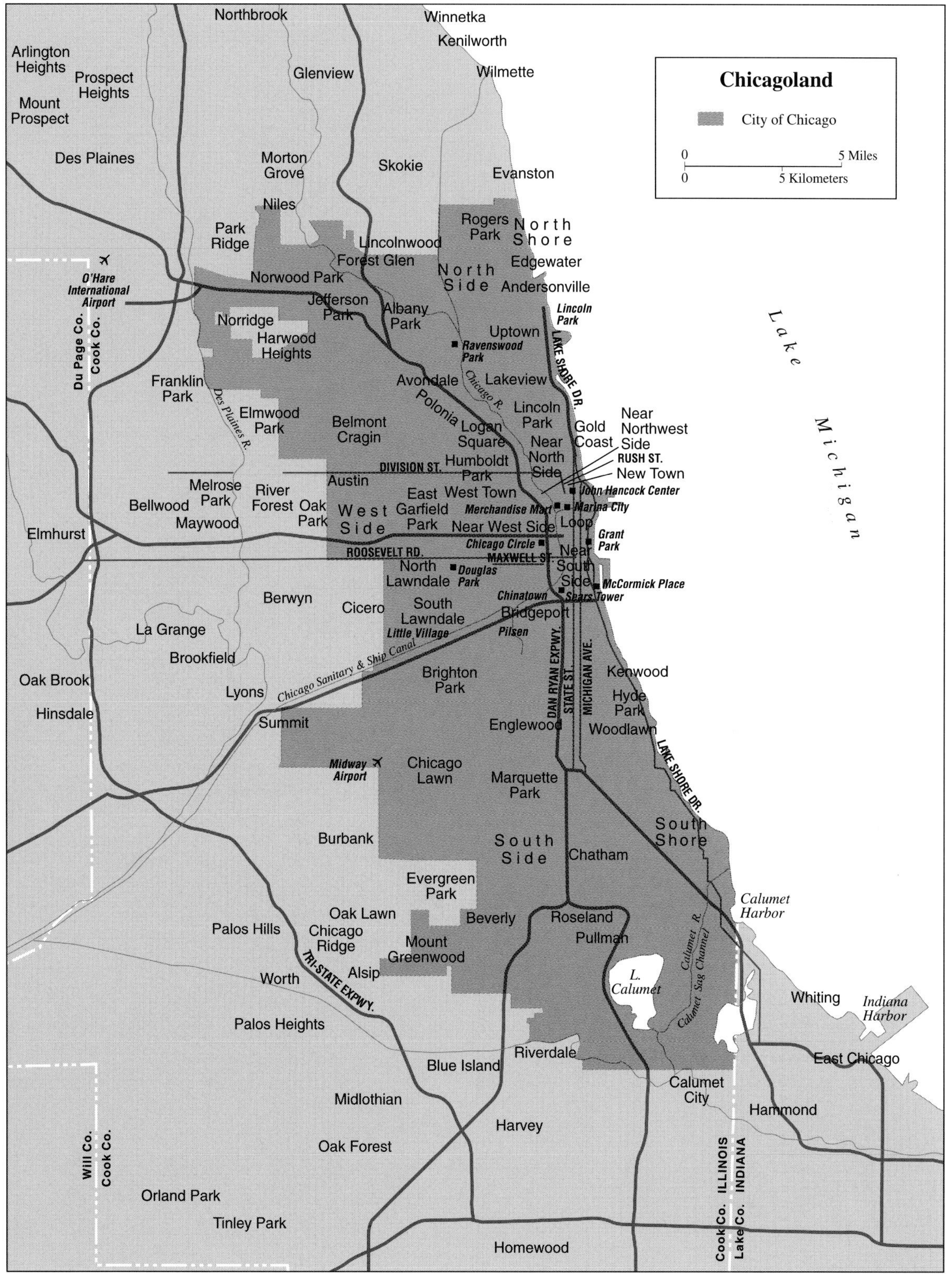
Chicagoland
City of Chicago
0
5 Miles
0
5 Kilometers
Northbrook
Winnetka
Kenilworth
Arlington Heights
Prospect Heights
Glenview
Wilmette
Mount Prospect
Des Plaines
Morton Grove
Skokie
Evanston
Niles
Park Ridge
Lincolnwood
Rogers Park
North Shore
Edgewater
Forest Glen
O'Hare International Airport
Norwood Park
North Side
Andersonville
Jefferson Park
Albany Park
Lincoln Park
Norridge
Harwood Heights
Uptown
Ravenswood Park
Du Page Co.
Cook Co.
LAKE SHORE DR.
Lake Michigan
Franklin Park
Avondale
Lakeview
Polonia
Chicago R.
Des Plaines R.
Elmwood Park
Belmont Cragin
Lincoln Park
Logan Square
Gold Coast
Near Northwest Side
Near North Side
RUSH ST.
Humboldt Park
DIVISION ST.
New Town
Melrose Park
River Forest
Austin
East Garfield Park
West Town
John Hancock Center
Bellwood
Oak Park
West Side
Merchandise Mart
Marina City
Maywood
Loop
Near West Side
Elmhurst
Chicago Circle
Grant Park
ROOSEVELT RD.
MAXWELL ST.
Near South Side
North Lawndale
Douglas Park
McCormick Place
Berwyn
Chinatown
Sears Tower
Cicero
South Lawndale
Bridgeport
La Grange
Little Village
Pilsen
Brookfield
Chicago Sanitary & Ship Canal
Brighton Park
DAN RYAN EXPWY.
STATE ST.
MICHIGAN AVE.
Kenwood
Oak Brook
Lyons
Hyde Park
Hinsdale
Summit
Englewood
Woodlawn
LAKE SHORE DR.
Midway Airport
Chicago Lawn
Marquette Park
South Shore
Burbank
South Side
Chatham
Evergreen Park
Calumet Harbor
Oak Lawn
Beverly
Roseland
Palos Hills
Chicago Ridge
Mount Greenwood
Pullman
Calumet R.
Calumet Sag Channel
TRI-STATE EXPWY.
Alsip
L. Calumet
Worth
Whiting
Indiana Harbor
Palos Heights
Riverdale
East Chicago
Blue Island
Calumet City
Midlothian
Hammond
Harvey
Will Co.
Cook Co.
Oak Forest
ILLINOIS
INDIANA
Orland Park
Tinley Park
Homewood
Cook Co.
Lake Co.

Map 15

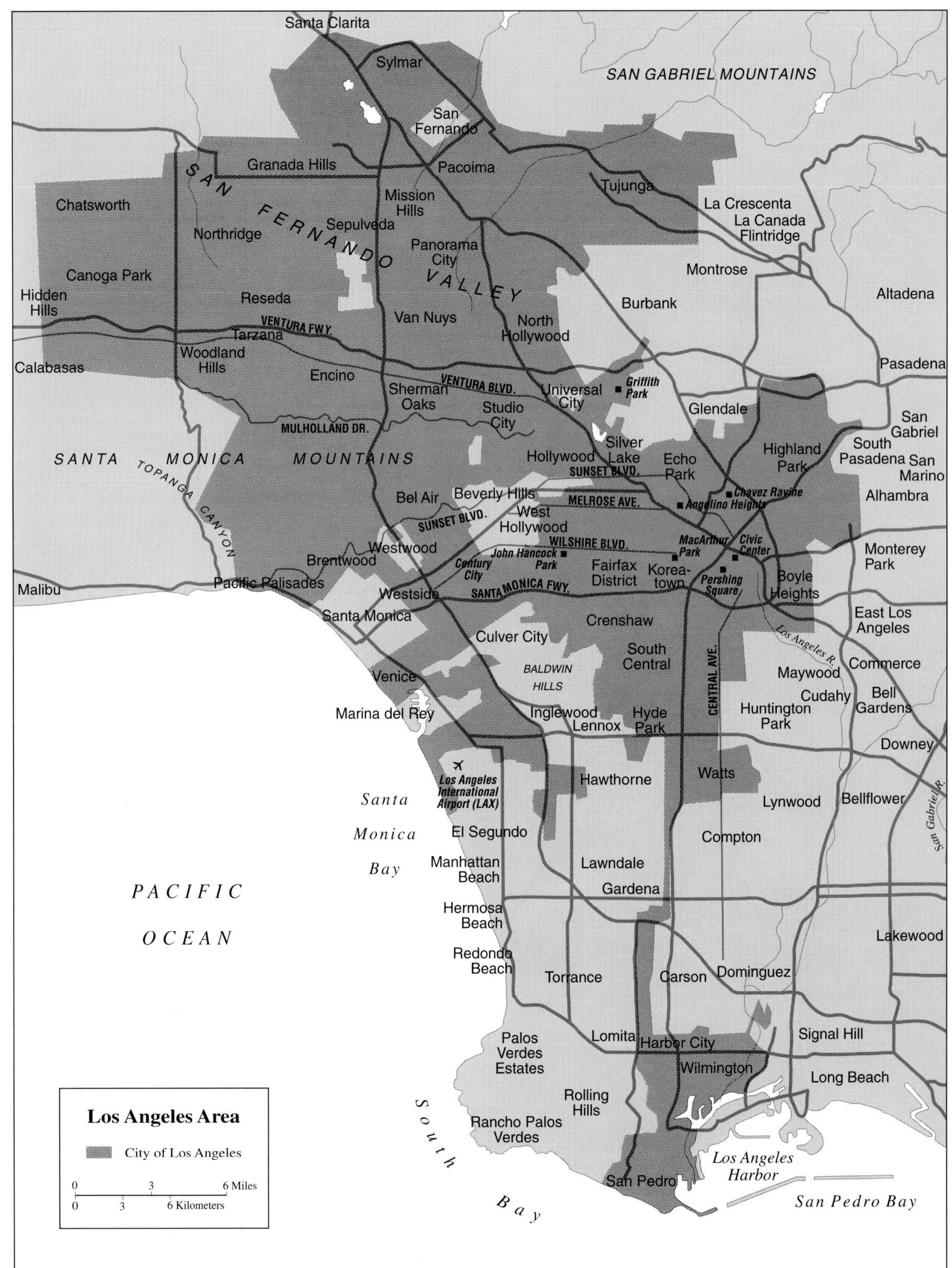
Santa Clarita
Sylmar
SAN GABRIEL MOUNTAINS
San Fernando
Granada Hills
Pacoima
Tujunga
La Crescenta
La Canada Flintridge
Chatsworth
Mission Hills
SAN FERNANDO VALLEY
Northridge
Sepulveda
Panorama City
Montrose
Canoga Park
Hidden Hills
Reseda
Burbank
Altadena
VENTURA FWY.
Van Nuys
North Hollywood
Tarzana
Woodland Hills
Calabasas
Encino
Pasadena
VENTURA BLVD.
Sherman Oaks
Universal City
Griffith Park
Glendale
Studio City
MULHOLLAND DR.
San Gabriel
Silver Lake
South Pasadena
SANTA MONICA MOUNTAINS
TOPANGA CANYON
Hollywood
Echo Park
Highland Park
San Marino
SUNSET BLVD.
Chavez Ravine
Alhambra
Bel Air
Beverly Hills
MELROSE AVE.
Angelino Heights
West Hollywood
SUNSET BLVD.
WILSHIRE BLVD.
MacArthur Park
Civic Center
Monterey Park
Westwood
John Hancock Park
Brentwood
Century City
Fairfax District
Korea-town
Pershing Square
Boyle Heights
Malibu
Pacific Palisades
SANTA MONICA FWY.
Westside
Santa Monica
Crenshaw
East Los Angeles
Culver City
Los Angeles R.
South Central
Commerce
BALDWIN HILLS
Maywood
Venice
Cudahy
Bell Gardens
Marina del Rey
Inglewood
Lennox
Hyde Park
CENTRAL AVE.
Huntington Park
Downey
Los Angeles International Airport (LAX)
Hawthorne
Watts
Santa Monica Bay
Lynwood
Bellflower
San Gabriel R.
El Segundo
Compton
Manhattan Beach
Lawndale
PACIFIC OCEAN
Gardena
Hermosa Beach
Lakewood
Redondo Beach
Torrance
Carson
Dominguez
Palos Verdes Estates
Lomita
Harbor City
Signal Hill
Wilmington
Long Beach
Rolling Hills
Rancho Palos Verdes
South Bay
Los Angeles Harbor
San Pedro
San Pedro Bay
Los Angeles Area
City of Los Angeles
0 3 6 Miles
0 3 6 Kilometers

Map 16

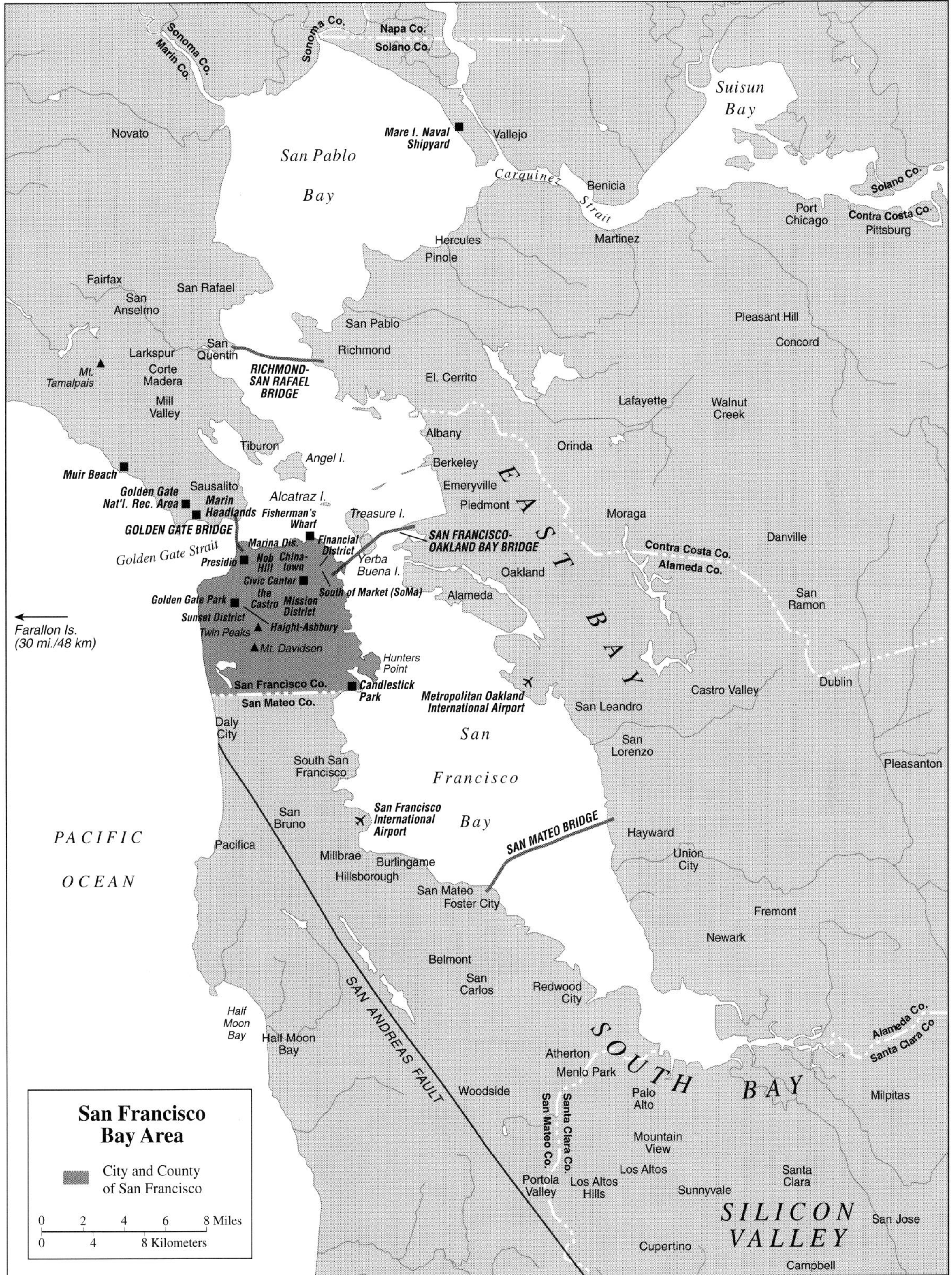
Sonoma Co.
Marin Co.
Sonoma Co.
Napa Co.
Solano Co.
Suisun Bay
Novato
Mare I. Naval Shipyard
Vallejo
San Pablo Bay
Carquinez Strait
Benicia
Solano Co.
Port Chicago
Contra Costa Co.
Pittsburg
Hercules
Pinole
Martinez
Fairfax
San Anselmo
San Rafael
San Pablo
Pleasant Hill
Concord
San Quentin
Richmond
Larkspur
Mt. Tamalpais
Corte Madera
Mill Valley
RICHMOND-SAN RAFAEL BRIDGE
El. Cerrito
Lafayette
Walnut Creek
Albany
Tiburon
Angel I.
Orinda
Berkeley
Muir Beach
Emeryville
Golden Gate Nat'l. Rec. Area
Sausalito
Marin Headlands
Alcatraz I.
Piedmont
EAST BAY
Moraga
GOLDEN GATE BRIDGE
Fisherman's Wharf
Treasure I.
SAN FRANCISCO-OAKLAND BAY BRIDGE
Danville
Golden Gate Strait
Marina Dis.
Financial District
Contra Costa Co.
Alameda Co.
Presidio
Nob Hill
China-town
Yerba Buena I.
Oakland
Civic Center
South of Market (SoMa)
Alameda
San Ramon
Golden Gate Park
the Castro
Mission District
Farallon Is. (30 mi./48 km)
Sunset District
Haight-Ashbury
Twin Peaks
Mt. Davidson
Hunters Point
San Francisco Co.
Candlestick Park
Metropolitan Oakland International Airport
Dublin
Castro Valley
San Mateo Co.
San Leandro
Daly City
San Francisco Bay
San Lorenzo
South San Francisco
Pleasanton
San Bruno
San Francisco International Airport
SAN MATEO BRIDGE
Hayward
PACIFIC OCEAN
Pacifica
Millbrae
Burlingame
Union City
Hillsborough
San Mateo
Foster City
Fremont
Newark
Belmont
SAN ANDREAS FAULT
San Carlos
Redwood City
Half Moon Bay
Half Moon Bay
SOUTH BAY
Alameda Co.
Santa Clara Co
Atherton
Menlo Park
Woodside
Palo Alto
Milpitas
Santa Clara Co.
San Mateo Co.
Mountain View
San Francisco Bay Area
City and County of San Francisco
Los Altos
Santa Clara
Portola Valley
Los Altos Hills
Sunnyvale
SILICON VALLEY
San Jose
0 2 4 6 8 Miles
0 4 8 Kilometers
Cupertino
Campbell

Map 17

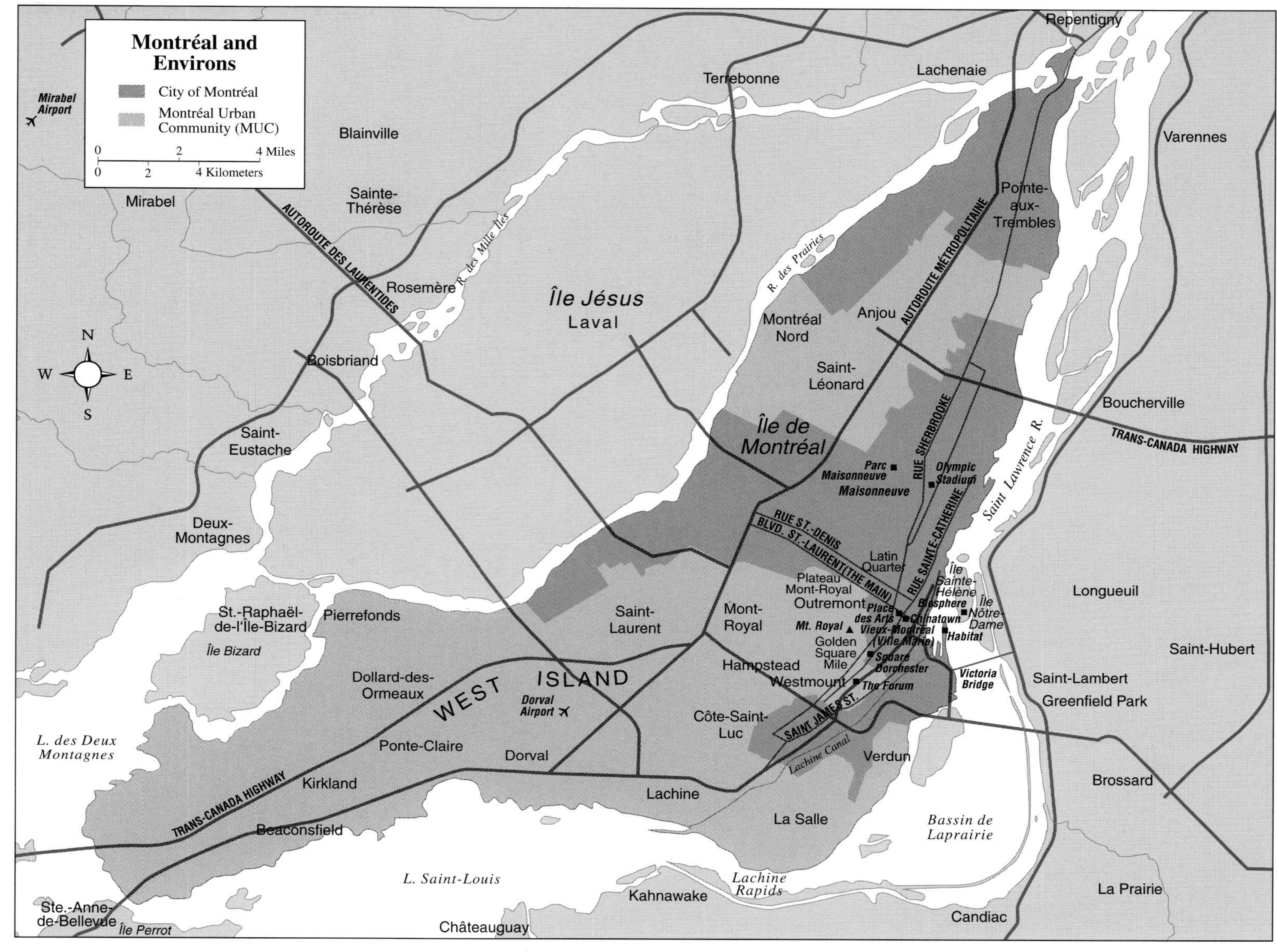

Montréal and Environs
City of Montréal
Montréal Urban Community (MUC)
0 2 4 Miles
0 2 4 Kilometers
N
W
E
S
Mirabel Airport
Mirabel
Blainville
Sainte-Thérèse
AUTOROUTE DES LAURENTIDES
Rosemère
R. des Mille Îles
Boisbriand
Saint-Eustache
Deux-Montagnes
Terrebonne
Lachenaie
Repentigny
Varennes
Île Jésus
Laval
R. des Prairies
Montréal Nord
Anjou
AUTOROUTE MÉTROPOLITAINE
Pointe-aux-Trembles
Saint-Léonard
Boucherville
TRANS-CANADA HIGHWAY
Île de Montréal
Parc Maisonneuve
Maisonneuve
RUE SHERBROOKE
Olympic Stadium
Saint Lawrence R.
RUE ST.-DENIS
BLVD. ST.-LAURENT (THE MAIN)
RUE SAINTE-CATHERINE
Latin Quarter
Plateau Mont-Royal
Outremont
Place des Arts
Chinatown
Mt. Royal
Vieux-Montréal (Ville-Marie)
Golden Square Mile
Square Dorchester
Westmount
The Forum
Île Sainte-Hélène
Biosphère
Île Nôtre-Dame
Habitat
Victoria Bridge
Longueuil
Saint-Hubert
Saint-Lambert
Greenfield Park
Brossard
La Prairie
Candiac
St.-Raphaël-de-l'Île-Bizard
Île Bizard
Pierrefonds
Saint-Laurent
Mont-Royal
Hampstead
Dollard-des-Ormeaux
WEST ISLAND
Dorval Airport
Côte-Saint-Luc
SAINT JAMES ST.
Lachine Canal
Verdun
L. des Deux Montagnes
Ponte-Claire
Dorval
Kirkland
TRANS-CANADA HIGHWAY
Lachine
La Salle
Bassin de Laprairie
Beaconsfield
L. Saint-Louis
Lachine Rapids
Kahnawake
Ste.-Anne-de-Bellevue
Île Perrot
Châteauguay

Map 18

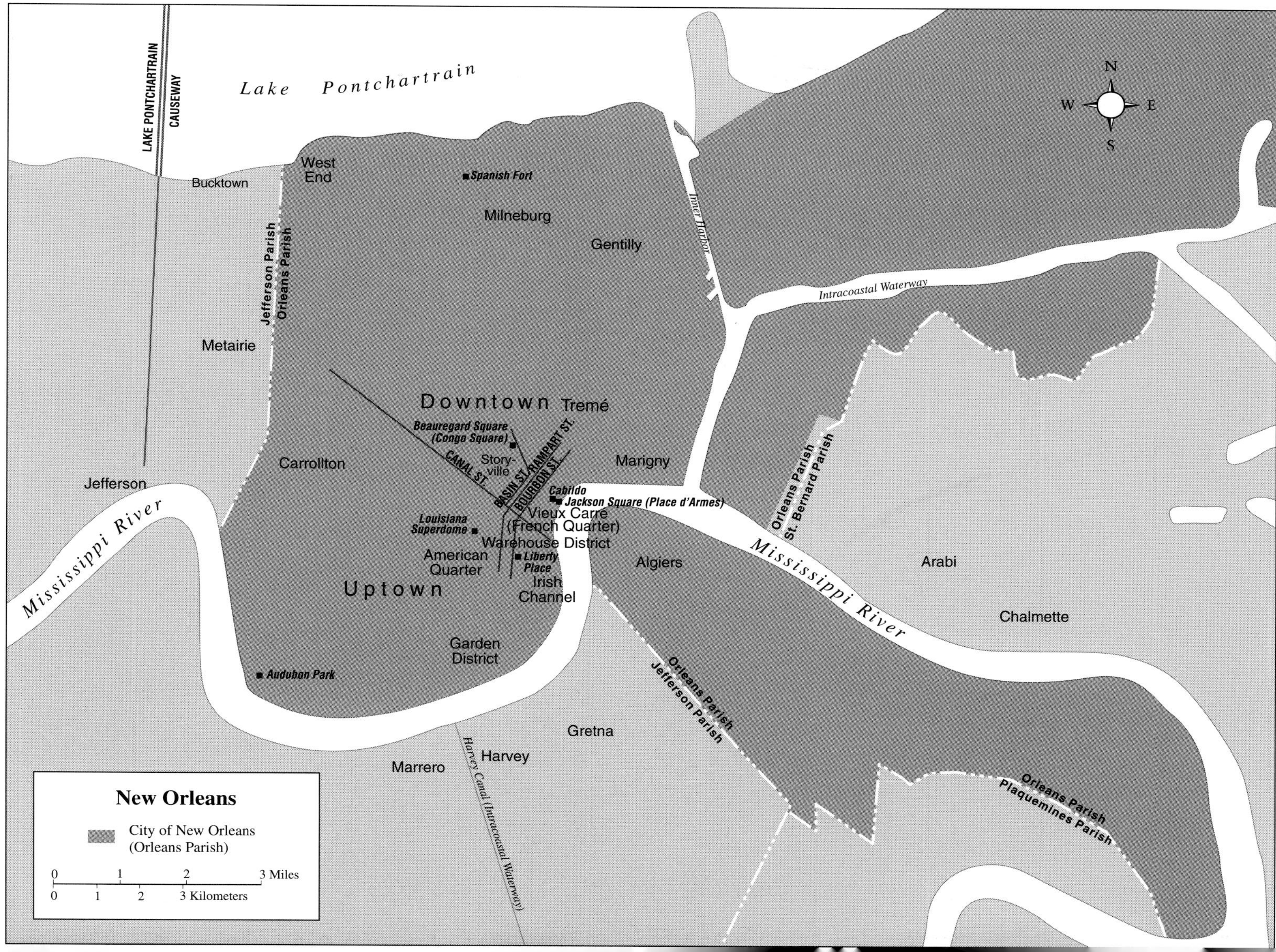
LAKE PONTCHARTRAIN
CAUSEWAY
Lake Pontchartrain
N
W
E
S
West End
Bucktown
Spanish Fort
Milneburg
Gentilly
Inner Harbor
Intracoastal Waterway
Jefferson Parish
Orleans Parish
Metairie
Downtown
Tremé
Beauregard Square (Congo Square)
CANAL ST.
Story-ville
BASIN ST.
RAMPART ST.
BOURBON ST.
Carrollton
Marigny
Jefferson
Cabildo
Jackson Square (Place d'Armes)
Vieux Carré (French Quarter)
Louisiana Superdome
Warehouse District
American Quarter
Liberty Place
Irish Channel
Uptown
Algiers
Orleans Parish
St. Bernard Parish
Mississippi River
Arabi
Chalmette
Garden District
Audubon Park
Orleans Parish
Jefferson Parish
Gretna
Harvey
Marrero
Harvey Canal (Intracoastal Waterway)
Orleans Parish
Plaquemines Parish
New Orleans
City of New Orleans
(Orleans Parish)
0 1 2 3 Miles
0 1 2 3 Kilometers

Map 19

Toronto and the Golden Horseshoe
City of Toronto
Toronto Metropolitan Municipality
R.M. Regional Municipality
0 5 10 15 Miles
0 5 10 15 Kilometers
Orangeville
Dufferin R.M.
Caledon
York R.M.
Richmond Hill
Markham
Durham R.M.
Whitby
Oshawa
Thornhill
Pickering
Ajax
Vaughan
Maple
Scarborough
Humber R.
North York
East York
Don Mills
Peel R.M.
Don R.
York
Brampton
Toronto
Wellington R.M.
Halton Hills
Acton
Etobicoke
Toronto Is.
CANADA
UNITED STATES
ONTARIO
Mississauga
Lake Ontario
GOLDEN HORSESHOE
Guelph
Milton
Halton R.M.
Oakville
CANADIAN TECHNOLOGY TRIANGLE
Waterloo R.M.
Kitchener
Waterloo
Cambridge
Burlington
Dundas
Ancaster
Hamilton
Niagara-on-the-Lake
N
W
E
S
Hamilton-Wentworth R.M.
Stoney Creek
Grimsby
Lincoln
St. Catherines
Thorold
Oxford R.M.
N.Y. State Barge Canal
Niagara Falls
Brantford
Brant R.M.
Pelham
Grand R.
Niagara Falls
Niagara R.M.
Welland Canal
Niagara R.
NEW YORK
Welland
Haldimand
Buffalo
Port Colborne
Haldimand-Norfolk R.M.
Lake Erie
ONTARIO
NEW YORK

Map 20